PENGUIN
The Pengu

Tony Russell was captivated by the blues as a teenager and their spell has held him ever since. After working for some years as press officer for an independent record label, he decided to go indie himself as a freelance music journalist, and he has written extensively about blues, jazz and early country music in both specialist and general magazines. He is the author of *Blacks, Whites and Blues* and *The Blues: From Robert Johnson to Robert Cray*, edited the partworks *The Blues Collection* and *Jazz Greats* and contributes a blues column to *Mojo*. He has also logged hundreds of hours as a blues and jazz radio presenter, served as a consultant on radio and TV programmes and compiled many reissues of blues, jazz and early country music. He lives with his partner and two children in Edwardian north London and in the hope that his record collection is not sinking their house into the subsoil.

Chris Smith worked for British Telecom in London until 1986, when he moved to Scotland to become a freelance writer while living off his wife's earnings. He now pursues these activities in Out Skerries, two of the Shetland Islands that Shetlanders call remote, and assiduously collects Air Miles in case there should be an unmissable blues gig in the deep south (Inverness). He is the author of *Hit the Right Lick* and *That's the Stuff*, respectively discographies of Big Bill Broonzy and Sonny Terry & Brownie McGhee, was a contributor to *The Guinness Encyclopedia of Popular Music* and translated Sebastian Danchin's *Blues Boy: The Life and Music of B. B. King* from the French. He has contributed many articles and reviews to specialist blues journals, and his work has featured in essay collections published by academic presses from Belgium to Mississippi. Chris is also a prolific author of LP and latterly CD notes.

Writer and discographer Neil Slaven has diligently avoided wealth and fame over several decades. In 1964 he started *R&B Monthly* and later the Blue Horizon label with his friend Mike Vernon. Joining Decca Records in 1966, he worked as a coordinator for the art department before donning the mantle of record producer. A long period of royalty-funded leisure and self-unemployment failed to prepare him for the delights of Social Security. He adds daily to the tally of sleevenotes he's logged in the last 30 years. In writing his contributions to *The Penguin Guide to Blues Recordings*, his deep interest in the Grateful Dead, Weather Report, Miles Davis, Jimi Hendrix, Terry Riley, John Adams, Edgar Varèse, Charles Koechlin and Toru Takemitsu stood him in no stead at all.

Ricky Russell is a freelance writer, musician and graduate in Popular Music from the University of Liverpool. His London roots have developed into twin branches of interest, in both blues and contemporary popular music in general. While working with artists at the Bishopstock Blues Festivals he discovered that, beyond the odd request for pear juice and less mud, blues musicians live to perform and share their energy.

Joe Faulkner studied at the Liverpool Institute of Performing Arts (LIPA) and graduated in Popular Music from the University of Liverpool. Alongside music journalism for a variety of publications, Joe has edited a guide to the music scene and nightlife in Liverpool, has acted as a musical director and theatrical composer, and privately teaches blues and rock guitar.

The Penguin Guide to **Blues** Recordings

Tony Russell
and
Chris Smith

with
Neil Slaven
Ricky Russell
Joe Faulkner

PENGUIN BOOKS

PENGUIN BOOKS

Published by the Penguin Group
Penguin Books Ltd, 80 Strand, London WC2R 0RL, England
Penguin Group (USA) Inc., 375 Hudson Street, New York, New York 10014, USA
Penguin Group (Canada), 90 Eglinton Avenue East, Suite 700, Toronto, Ontario, Canada M4P 3Y3
(a division of Pearson Penguin Canada Inc.)
Penguin Ireland, 25 St Stephen's Green, Dublin 2, Ireland (a division of Penguin Books Ltd)
Penguin Group (Australia), 250 Camberwell Road,Camberwell, Victoria 3124, Australia
(a division of Pearson Australia Group Pty Ltd)
Penguin Books India Pvt Ltd, 11 Community Centre, Panchsheel Park, New Delhi – 110 017, India
Penguin Group (NZ), cnr Airborne and Rosedale Roads, Albany, Auckland 1310, New Zealand
(a division of Pearson New Zealand Ltd)
Penguin Books (South Africa) (Pty) Ltd, 24 Sturdee Avenue, Rosebank, Johannesburg 2196, South Africa

Penguin Books Ltd, Registered Offices: 80 Strand, London WC2R 0RL, England

www.penguin.com

First published 2006
1

Copyright © Tony Russell and Chris Smith, 2006
All rights reserved

The moral right of the authors has been asserted

Set in Clarendon MT and Minion
Designed by Richard Marston
Typeset by Letterpart Ltd, Reigate, Surrey
Printed in Finland by WS Bookwell

Except in the United States of America, this book is sold subject
to the condition that it shall not, by way of trade or otherwise, be lent,
re-sold, hired out, or otherwise circulated without the publisher's
prior consent in any form of binding or cover other than that in
which it is published and without a similar condition including this
condition being imposed on the subsequent purchaser

ISBN-13: 978–0–140–51384–4
ISBN-10: 0–140–51384–1

Contents

Introduction vii
Acknowledgements xi
Distributors xii
Abbreviations xiii

Musicians A–Z 1

Compilations

Alabama 737
Basic Blues 737
Boogie Woogie 739
Chicago I (Prewar) 742
Chicago II (Postwar) 743
Concerts & Festivals 747
Detroit 751
Downhome 752
East Coast 754
Field Recordings 757
Guitar 767
Harmonica 768
Hillbilly Blues 772
Humour & Erotica 773
Jugbands 775
Label Histories & Showcases 776
Louisiana 790
Mandolin 792
Memphis 792
Miscellaneous I (Prewar) 793
Miscellaneous II (Postwar) 797
Mississippi 801
New Orleans 803
New York 806
Piano 807
Roots 810
Slide Guitar 812
St Louis 815
Stringbands 816
Texas 817
Topical & Documentary 820
Tributes & Songbooks 823
West Coast 826
Women 826
Zydeco 830

Index 835

Introduction

In a celebrated meeting of 1903, the bandleader and composer W. C. Handy, waiting for a connection at a small Mississippi railroad station, witnessed a fellow African-American singing, to his own guitar accompaniment, what seems to have been a blues. The event was commemorated in 2003 by a Year Of The Blues, but no one who knew their blues history would have regarded the gesture as signifying a genuine centenary. All the reliable evidence suggests that blues, or something very like it, has been sung and played in the southern United States since the 1890s. When we date its history from Handy's brief encounter, or from the supposedly first published composition with 'Blues' in its title, some nine years later, or from the first vocal record called a 'Blues' by an African-American artist in 1920, we are merely assigning historic status to incidents in the long journey of the blues from the obscurity of the rural South to the spotlights of today's world stage. No doubt they were significant incidents, but the roots of the blues lie deeper in time and wider in place.

Unfortunately for the historian, something like a generation, 25 or 30 years, elapsed before the phonograph record was used to document the sound of a black artist singing blues. Once that process got under way, African-American music was recorded vigorously, plentifully and in great variety, and almost immediately questions of definition began to take shape. The blues boom of the 1920s caused many records to be made that were not, by any standard musical definition, blues, and many artists to be recorded who were not, by any useful definition, blues singers – or, at least, not *only* blues singers. Consequently the subject-matter of this book, in its early stage, extends beyond the blues idiom, and heaping it all up and labelling it 'blues' is no more than a practical solution for dealing with it. We hope readers will find the strategy useful, perhaps even illuminating, but we are under no illusion that we are doing justice to the complexity of African-American vernacular music and its many decades of change and transformation.

That said, what the reader will find in these pages is descriptive and evaluative surveys of the recorded work of more than a thousand musicians who have worked primarily, if not always exclusively, in the blues idiom. For the most part, they are career blues artists – men and women who could write in the 'Occupation' box on their passport, 'blues musician'.

But – and we want to be very clear about this – the list of artists to whom we have devoted entries is not a rollcall of *all* the artists the reader might find in a catalogue or record store under the heading 'Blues'. Obviously we intended to include every artist who has what we consider a serious claim to a blues enthusiast's attention. But we couldn't expect every reader to agree with our conception of a serious claim, and we have doubtless omitted artists that at least some readers will think we ought to have included, and included others that they would have been content for us to omit.

For example, we have been selective in our coverage of blues-rock, especially when it seems more closely connected to rock than to blues. The artists in that genre whom we have included are predominantly those who record for blues labels. We have also been cautious about artists lately hailed in some quarters as purveyors of '21st-century blues', 'punk blues' or 'nu blues'. Some of them are making interesting music that's undoubtedly influenced by the blues, but there are hundreds of artists you can say that about, from Hank Williams to Bob Dylan to The White Stripes, and if we had added them all to our list this book would never have been finished. Anyway, we would argue that the core audiences for blues-rock and 'nu blues' are rather different from what we would identify as the mainstream blues audience. For what it's worth – and we think it is worth something – not many artists in either category are discussed in blues magazines or appear at blues festivals. We're aware that the dangers of a circular argument loom here, but, being bluntly practical, we decided that in both cases there was little point in trying to cover extensively a category in which the majority of our readers might take little interest.

For analogous reasons we have excluded artists whose work is predominantly in the soul idiom, though a few genre-straddling figures like Bobby 'Blue' Bland, Z. Z. Hill and Little Milton could not reasonably be overlooked and have been given at least selective entries. With rhythm & blues, in the older interpretation of that term, we have been a little more liberal, since, particularly in recent years, the tastes of blues enthusiasts have expanded to embrace many figures once considered peripheral, such as the honking saxophonists and sweet trios of the 1940s and '50s. Gospel music is beyond our remit but, if a blues artist has also recorded religious music, that fact may be mentioned, and in a few instances the records themselves have been admitted to the fold. Blind Willie Johnson and Reverend Gary Davis are special cases, and we have duly made exceptions of them.

The choice of recordings has been dictated by what is currently available on CD. We take no account of recordings that exist only in earlier formats (78 rpm singles, 45 rpm singles, EPs, LPs), nor of CDs that are no longer in print. (But see below, under 'Deletion', for more on the complicated matter of what constitutes 'in print'.) So far as CDs by individual artists or groups are concerned, we have tried to trace and write about everything that is presently available, but we shall undoubtedly have missed some. We also recognize with weary resignation that in a number of entries our attempt at comprehensiveness will have been scuppered by releases appearing between completion of the manuscript and publication. No doubt, too, some deserving new artists will have emerged during that period, too late for us to hear them.

While we have tried to be as comprehensive as possible in our coverage of US and European issues, we have been less assiduous in tracing labels in both territories that operate in a retail area of their own, producing cheap compilations for sale in remainder book stores, airport outlets, supermarkets and other locations beyond the orbit of the conventional record trade. Such issues can offer excellent value, and we frequently commend them when they do so, but very often the price of their cheapness is poor packaging and unreliable sound quality. We have excluded most Japanese releases, since they tend to be pressed in small quantities and, if you live outside Japan, are usually difficult to obtain. But in a few cases we have admitted them, where they offer the only, or much the best, access to certain albums or artists.

We have excluded from coverage – but readers should be aware of – custom-made CDs of blues LPs originally issued by the late Moses Asch on Folkways and its associated labels. Asch famously never deleted anything, and when the Smithsonian Institution took over his catalogue, it was on condition that everything from *The Country Blues* to *Sounds Of North American Frogs* should continue to be available. Smithsonian Folkways will accordingly burn to order copies of any LP on Folkways etc. The Smithsonian has since acquired other labels, among which Cook and Monitor issued a few blues albums. The complete holding can be browsed, and orders placed, at <www.folkways.si.edu>.

Compilations of recordings by many artists, such as CDs organized by locale, label of origin, period or subject-matter, are reviewed more selectively; there are thousands of such collections, and they are of unequal value. We have focused on those that seem most worthwhile. (This category is explained in more detail below, under 'Layout'.)

The reader may notice that some artists' entries are longer than those for similarly, or more, productive figures. This is often because the writer feels that the artist has been too cursorily treated in previous works of this kind and deserves better; indeed, not a few of the artists discussed in this book have never appeared in other guides. In any case, productivity is an unreliable index of an artist's worth. Then, too, each writer had some artists on his list about whom he just wanted to stretch out, even if it meant vexing the kind of reader (or, more likely, reviewer) who goes through such books bean-counting. So sue us. (A foolish consistency, says Emerson, is the hobgoblin of little minds.)

Layout

The main part of the book is arranged alphabetically by artist. Within each artist's entry, their currently available recordings are discussed in the order in which they were made. (Which is not necessarily the order in which the CDs containing them were issued.) This is a specimen CD entry:

***(*) **Texas Alexander: Vol. 1 (1927–28)**
Matchbox MBCD 2001 *Alexander; Eddie Heywood (p); Lonnie Johnson, Eddie Lang (g). 8/27–11/28.*

The star rating – see below for an explanation of this – is followed by the title and, on the next line, the label and catalogue number, then the participating musicians, with their instruments abbreviated, and the date, or date-span, of the recordings, in the form month/year.

If an album title appears on a CD in both a long and a short form, as regularly happens, for example, on the Document and Classics labels, we usually prefer the short form, as given on the spine. When two or more titles are cited for an album, separated by a double slash (//), the first is generally its original title and others are retitlings, usually by licensing companies. Similarly, when two or more catalogue numbers are given and separated by a double slash, the first is generally that of the US issue and the subsequent numbers apply to European co-issues or reissues – unless the European issue was the original, in which case the order is reversed. Where album titles are separated by a *single* slash (/), what you have is a twofer: normally, two original LPs reissued on a single CD but retaining their titles.

Where a CD has been issued by one company in several territories with different catalogue numbers, the latter may be territory-identified by the parenthesized abbreviations (A) (= American/US), (E) (= English/UK) and (Eu) (= continental Europe).

Albums issued under the umbrella of Original Blues Classics are so described even when, as sometimes occurs, they show the names of the original source labels, such as Prestige-Folklore, Contemporary or Riverside.

Inconsistencies in the style of a label's catalogue numbering are faithfully preserved, so that, for example, Bullseye Blues numbers will sometimes be shown as prefixed CDBB, sometimes CD BB and sometimes neither.

Final '2's or '-2' suffixes in catalogue numbers, which merely denote the CD format as opposed to any other, have been excluded throughout. So has 'CD' when it is a suffix, but not when it's a prefix, or part of a prefix. Some recent French releases have catalogue numbers with numerical suffixes that are *not* format identifiers, so these are given in full. Other inessential elements of catalogue numbers have sometimes been omitted, leaving a 'core' number which should be all that a reader needs to trace or order the CD. Albums that comprise more than one CD, whether packaged in adapted jewel-cases, longboxes or boxed sets, are so identified with abbreviations such as 2CD, which follow – but, please note, are not part of – the catalogue number.

When the label and catalogue number are bracketed – e.g. [Jericho CHO CD 601] – it means that the CD was deleted during the later stages of the book's preparation but may still be available. See 'Deletions' below.

The personnel shown for an album is collective; not every musician or instrument is heard on every track. If an album's personnel recurs without change, or with little change, on subsequent albums, that is signified by phrases such as 'As above', 'Similar to above' or 'As above, except …'. Producers are named when the writer judges the producer's contribution to be notable in some way. The abbreviations used for instruments and other musical elements are listed on page xiii.

Personnels and instrumentation are derived from album notes, standard discographies or both, but from time to time we have corrected errors in those sources, basing our corrections either on new evidence or on more careful listening. If a CD contains recordings by other artists as well as the one whose entry houses it, the cited personnel and date details apply only to the latter's tracks.

The cited dates are those of the original recording session(s). When that information is not available, we have quoted the year of the album's release. If precise (i.e. month/year) dates are given that are not derived from the notes or standard discographies, the reader can assume that they have been established either in consultation with the label or artist, or from contemporary printed sources such as *Living Blues* magazine.

Many blues CDs are not by a single artist but assemble tracks by several. Where more than three contributing artists are involved, we describe the CD as a 'various artists compilation' (VAC). Such compilations are mostly discussed, under regional or thematic category headings such as **Mississippi** or **Tributes & Songbooks**, in their own section (beginning on page 737). Many of them are also referred to in individual artists' entries, while some CDs that are technically VACs but include several items by one artist may appear both in that artist's entry and in a VAC category entry (or, in a few cases, only the former).

In the section dealing with VACs, full personnel data are not provided. Instead, the participating artists are listed in alphabetical order, and the number of tracks by each is specified in parentheses; if it isn't, it means that the artist has only one track on that VAC.

The authorship of an entry is signalled by the initials at the end. When an entry has mostly been written by one author but has been completed by another, all the text up to the first set of initials is by the original writer, and additional text with a second set of initials is by the updater. If the work of two writers is more interwoven, the entry is signed with both sets of initials (e.g. NS/TR), the primary writer's taking precedence. (In those cases, readers who like that sort of thing can amuse themselves by trying to determine which writer wrote which bits.) Some VAC category entries have been split between two writers, and in such instances each writer's contributions are individually credited.

As in the *Penguin Guide To Jazz Recordings*, artists' entries are preceded by short biographies. These are intended to be background sketches, briefly setting the scene in which the artist characteristically works or worked. They are not meant to supplant, or even, necessarily, to epitomize, the fuller biographies available in *Blues Who's Who* and similar reference works. The list of instruments assigned to an artist is collective: he or she does not necessarily play them all on every album.

Ratings

For better or worse, we have followed our colleagues on *The Penguin Guide To Jazz Recordings* in using star ratings as a form of critical shorthand. Like them, we urge readers to consult the accompanying text, in which these evaluations are often subjected to fine tuning. Readers should also be aware that the ratings are frequently relative. The *Guide To Jazz* offers the thought that 'a three-star record by one of the giants of the music is likely to be an inferior example of that musician … but for many lesser figures, it could be their signature session.' That's true, but so is the converse: an album by a prolific artist of the '30s, say, may be rated only **(*) because the music suffers from being heard (as it was never meant to be) at CD length, or in mediocre sound, but that isn't to say that the music as such is inferior to the product of any journeyman figure who ever achieved a three-star album. Again, context is all.

The ratings should be interpreted as follows:

****	excellent: the artist at, or very close to, his or her best
***(*)	very good indeed but with one or two minor faults
***	worthwhile; well up to the artist's average
**(*)	reasonably good, but in some respects disappointing
**	ordinary at best; for a normally well-regarded artist, a low spot
*(*)	thoroughly disappointing; barely worth notice
*	negligible

Sometimes the entire star rating is parenthesized. This often denotes some problem of presentation rather than of content. A typical case where such a rating might be applied would be an album, musically unexceptionable in itself, which has been marginalized or rendered irrelevant by other, superior productions. Another would be an album whose value is substantially diminished by the absence of notes or recording information, or by poor sound quality.

Parenthesized star ratings are also used, however, to signify that a CD is on the edge of relevance: for example, when a normally blues-centred artist makes music of a significantly different kind. So (***) may indicate an album that is worthwhile, up-to-the-mark, etc., but not exactly a *blues* album. In those cases it's particularly important for the reader to look at the accompanying text and see why the writer has arrived at such a judgement.

Occasionally a four-star rating is prefixed with a crown symbol (♛). These are CDs that we consider truly exceptional: cornerstones of a collection, the basic blues library, shoo-ins for any list of All-Time Best Blues Albums.

Terminology

'Prewar' and 'postwar' have special meanings for blues enthusiasts. What divides them is not so much World War II (as it affected the US, i.e. 1941–45) as a period from 1943 to 1944/45, commonly known as 'the Petrillo ban', when the American Federation of Musicians (president: James C. Petrillo), in dispute with the record and radio industries, forbade its members to do studio work in either domain, with the result that the record business more or less closed down. The end-date of that moratorium is imprecise because record companies came to individual agreements with the AFM at different times. But 'postwar' implies more than just 'after 1945' or thereabouts: the record industry that grew up after the AFM ban and World War II was not simply a return of the prewar system, in which popular music was largely controlled by three companies, but a multifarious business culture involving hundreds of new, independent labels in dozens of cities and providing access to the market for musicians and styles of music that had been ill served or ignored by the prewar industry. This altered state and the musical changes it instigated are often implied in the 'blues use' of 'postwar'.

'Piano trio' is used in this book as shorthand for a group of piano, bass and drums, and 'piano quartet' for that lineup plus guitar.

Recording Quality

There is not, on the whole, much wrong with the sonic quality of present-day blues recordings, unless they have been made with severe budgetary constraints, like the occasional issue on an artist's own label, though even there great improvements are being made. A substantial percentage of the music in this book, however, was recorded in earlier stages of technological development. Many of the performances discussed here were delivered into an acoustic horn rather than an electrical microphone, and the fidelity of those recordings to the original performances is highly variable. Almost all recordings up to the mid-1950s or thereabouts were first issued on 78 rpm (latterly 45 rpm) discs, and when reissued on CD have generally been derived from those discs, not all of which have survived in pristine condition. So in discussing music made in the pre-LP era we frequently comment on transfer quality, remastering, sound engineering or sonic restoration – all terms for the processes by which old discs are coaxed into revealing their musical content with a high degree of accuracy, while at the same time the effects of age, wear and damage are minimized. In recent years a good deal of new technology has been introduced into sound restoration, and some of it is highly effective, but it needs to be used with both technical skill and sensitivity to the original recorded sound; when it isn't, the results can be freakish.

Digital technology has also brought about a state of affairs where a record company can make an exact copy of another company's CD (where the material is no longer protected by copyright) and issue it on their own label without acknowledging, let alone paying for, the originating company's sound restoration, sourcing of original discs or other research, all of which may have been costly. That's how it comes about that Label A, after considerable trouble and expense, produce a boxed set of (say) an artist's complete recordings at a price reflecting their investment – only to see Label B, six months later, issue a very similar collection for a quarter of the price. Until someone is prepared to engage in legal action to make a test case, or the law itself changes, it is unlikely that this practice will cease. None of the writers of this book is a lawyer, but some of us know enough about the reissue business to recognize what might be considered sharp practice, and from time to time we comment on it.

Price

Unlike our colleagues on the *Guide To Jazz*, we often (but not invariably) identify issues as mid-price or budget-price, but it should be understood that these descriptions may apply only in their country of origin. Prices will in any case vary from retailer to retailer. Very roughly, 'mid-price' means a tag of about half to two thirds of the standard full price for a new album, and 'budget-price' one third or less.

Deletion

In the present retail market, availability is a highly variable state. CDs officially deleted from a company's catalogue may continue to be purchasable for months or years afterwards, either from specialist suppliers with unsold stock or from retailers who deal with distributors specializing in deletions and overstocks. Numerous CDs are included in this book which will not be found on their originating company's website but can be ordered from certain mail-order specialists. At the time the book was delivered to its publisher, the vast majority of the CDs discussed in it (aside from those actually reported as deleted) were in some sense available, though the reader might sometimes have to go to a little trouble to prove it. Whenever we discovered, either from a record company or from other reliable sources, that a CD was, for whatever reason, likely to be hard to find, we have tried to warn the reader by the use of a phrase like 'of uncertain availability'. If, by the time this book falls into your hands, 'uncertain availability' has turned into 'certain unavailability', there is always the secondhand (used) record market to investigate.

As noted above, brackets around an issue number mean that it has been officially deleted, but relatively recently, so, while its availability is necessarily uncertain, it may be findable without too much difficulty.

Tony Russell

Acknowledgements

First, thanks to Richard Cook for putting in many good words for us with Penguin Books, and, together with his co-author Brian Morton, for setting the bar in this field of endeavour so challengingly high with *The Penguin Guide To Jazz Recordings*. Thanks also to our patient editors and former editors at Penguin, Nigel Wilcockson, Georgina Laycock and Martin Toseland.

We have been greatly assisted by representatives of many record labels and distributors, who have provided us with product and information. We particularly appreciate the generosity of the following (in alphabetical order of company): Neil Scaplehorn (Ace), Bob De Pugh (Alligator), Richard Weize (Bear Family), Mike Gott (when at BGO), Gerrit Robs (Black Magic), Detlev Hoegen (Crosscut), Bill Trythall (Discovery), Johnny Parth and Gary Atkinson (respectively former and present owners of Document), Jean Buzelin (EPM Blues Collection), Jerry Gordon (Evidence) Richard Flohil, Holger Petersen and Chris Martin (Stony Plain), Lellie Capwell (Vanguard) and Hannes Folterbauer (Wolf).

We are also very grateful to (again, alphabetically by company): Bob Fisher (Acrobat), Guido van Rijn (Agram), Trish Wagner (Antone's/Texas Music Group), Tom Diamant, Annie J. and Erik Keilholtz (Arhoolie), Del Day (Ark PR), Tony Sweet (Armadillo), Andy Gray (BGO), Jan Mittendorp (Black & Tan), Ed Chmelewski (Blind Pig), Kate Moss (Blue Bella), Patrick Ford (Blue Rock'It), Greg Spencer (Blue Wave), Paul Reed (Bluetrack), Peter Moody (Boulevard), Josh Grimley (Burnside), Mike Siniscalchi and Kevin Johnson (Delmark), Michael Frank (Earwig), Andrew Galloway (Electro-Fi), Chris Millar (Fedora), Sue Williams (Frontier), Mike Gavin (Harmonia Mundi), Kevin Calabro (Hyena), Alan Robinson (Indiscreet PR), Eddie Dattel (Inside Sounds/Memphis Archives), John Stedman (JSP), Heiner Stadler (Labor), Mark Carpentieri (M.C.), Bob Merlis (Memphis International), Iain Murray and Graham Griffiths (New Note), Steve Saperstein (Night Train International), Pamela Brennan and Fred Litwin (NorthernBlues), Jerry Hall (Pacific Blues), John Adams (Powerhouse Productions), Peggy Sutton (PPR), Alan Price and Cliff White (Proper), Jim O'Neal (Rooster Blues), Dave Schlichting (Rounder and Bullseye Blues), Colleen Theis (Rykodisc), Dorothy Howe, Karen Pitchford and John Reed (Sanctuary), Sherwin Dunner (Shanachie), John Cronin (Sony/BMG Imports), Kajo Paukert (Telarc), Tyson Schuetze (Tomato), Pat Tynan (Pat Tynan Media) and Julie Allison (Universal).

We are indebted to many correspondents and fellow members of internet groups for valuable information, particularly Alan Balfour, Alasdair Blaazer, Scott Dirks, Bob Eagle, Fran Leslie (*Blues In Britain*), Robert Riesman, Howard Rye, Richard Spottswood, Jon Taylor and David Whiteis. Special thanks to Eric LeBlanc for assiduously compiling birth-and-death information, and to Mary Katherine Aldin for making it available as Eric's Blues Dates on the prewar blues website <http://launch.groups.yahoo.com/group/pre-war-blues/>. Also to Ken Smith at Red Lick Records <www.redlick.com>, and Frank Scott at Roots & Rhythm <www.rootsandrhythm.com>, both for answering innumerable queries and for saving themselves answering even more by publishing such informative catalogues and sales lists. We also express warm but necessarily unspecific gratitude to the many notewriters whose research and interview material we have absorbed.

Tony Russell is hugely grateful to Sally for her patience and support while he was working on the book. Also to Michael Gray, for listening and cheering-up services rendered under, and beyond, the Old Pals' Act. Further thanks to Mike Stephenson, Paul Swinton and Tony Watson for the loan of CDs, and to Mike Dodd at HMV Oxford Street.

Chris Smith wishes to thank Sheilagh Smith for discussion, encouragement and patiently enduring the creation of his share of this work.

Finally, TR, CS and NS especially acknowledge the interest and help of Keith Briggs, whose untimely death took a lot of the fun out of 2005 for many blues-lovers. We shall greatly miss the acute review of this book that he would assuredly have written for *Blues & Rhythm*.

Distributors

UK Distributors

Many of the recordings described in this book are distributed in the UK by these companies. Each distributor's contact details are followed by a selective list of labels handled.

Cadiz Music Ltd, 2 Greenwich Quay, Clarence Rd,
London SE3 0QL
(Tel.: 020 8692 3555; fax 020 8469 3300;
website: www.cadizmusic.com; email: info@cadizmusic.co.uk)
Armadillo, Blind Pig, Blue Blood, Manhaton, NorthernBlues, Nugene, Tradition & Moderne

Discovery Records Ltd, Nursteed Road, Devizes,
Wiltshire NN10 3DY
(Tel.: 01380 728000; fax: 01380 722244;
website: www. discovery-records.com;
email: info@discovery-records.com)
Acoustic Music, Arion, Best Of Jazz, Black & Blue, Black & Tan, Blue Moon, Buda, Classics, Definitive, Delmark, Dixiefrog, EPM Blues Collection, Frémeaux, Isabel, Powerhouse, Railway, Stunt

Forte Distribution, Unit 5G, Ramsden Rd, Rotherwas,
Hereford HR2 6LR
(Tel.: 08707 622864; fax: 08707 626015;
website: www.fortedistribution.co.uk;
email: info@fortedistribution.co.uk)
Old Hat

Harmonia Mundi UK Ltd, 45 Vyner St, London E2 9DQ
(Tel.: 020 8709 9509; fax: 020 8709 9501;
website: www.uk.hmboutique.com;
email: info.uk@harmoniamundi.com)
Evidence, Fedora

New Note Distribution, Pinnacle Building,
The Teardrop Centre, London Rd, Swanley, Kent BR8 8TS
(Tel.: 01322 616050; fax: 01322 615658;
website: www.newnote.com; email: info@newnote.com)
Basin Street, Chesky, Nagel Heyer, Telarc, Timeless

Proper Distribution, The New Powerhouse,
Gateway Business Centre, Kangley Bridge Road,
London SE26 5AN
(Tel.: 020 8676 5141; fax: 020 8676 5194;
website: www.properdistribution.com;
email: info@proper.uk.com)
ACT, Alligator, Antone's, Arhoolie, Black Magic, Blues Matters, Bullseye Blues, Candid, Classic Blues, Continental Blue Heaven, County, Crosscut, Daring, Delta Groove, Dialtone, Disky, Document, EasyDisc, El Toro, Essential, Fab14, Flying Fish, Greenhays, Hightone, HMG, Hyena, Hypertension, Indigo, Jasmine, JSP, Me & My Blues, Opus 3, Proper, Pussycat, Retrieval, Retro, Rooster Blues, Rounder, Ruf, Severn, Shanachie, Stony Plain, Storyville, Sugar Hill, Testament, Vanguard, Varrick, Waterlily Acoustics, Westside, Yazoo, Zed, Zoe

RSK Entertainment Ltd, Unit 4–5, Home Farm, Welford,
Newbury, Berks RG20 8HR
(Tel.: 01488 608900; fax: 01488 608901;
website: www.rskentertainment.co.uk;
email: info@rskentertainment.co.uk)
Collectables, Fat Possum, M.C., Red House, SPV, Wolf

Mail Order

Roots & Rhythm, P.O. Box 837, El Cerrito, CA 94530
(Tel.: (510) 526 8373; toll-free order line (US) 888-ROOTS-66; fax (510) 526 9001; website: www.rootsandrhythm.com;
email: roots@toast.net)

Red Lick Records, Porthmadog, Gwynedd, Wales LL49 9DJ
(Tel.: 01766 512151 [from overseas: +44 1766 512151];
answerphone: 01766 513010; fax: 01766 512851;
website: www.redlick.com; email: sales@redlick.com)

Both these companies carry many US, UK and other European blues labels for mail-order sale worldwide

Artists and companies are warmly invited to send their releases for consideration in a second edition. They should initially contact Tony Russell at: tonyrussell@bluetone.demon.co.uk.

Abbreviations

Instruments etc.

ac	accordion	euph	euphonium	sp	speech
ah	autoharp	fl	flute	ss	soprano saxophone
arr	arranger	flh	flugelhorn	syn	synthesizer
as	alto saxophone	frh	french horn	t	trumpet
b	bass	g	guitar	tamb	tambourine
bb	brass bass	h	harmonica	tb	trombone
bcl	bass clarinet	harm	harmonium	tbj	tenor banjo
bf	bass flute	hdu	hammered dulcimer	tg	tenor guitar
bgo	bongo(s)	imb	imitation bass	timb	timbales
bj	banjo	j	jug	tri	triangle
bs	baritone saxophone	k	kazoo	ts	tenor saxophone
bsn	bassoon	kb	keyboards	tu	tuba
bss	bass saxophone	ldr	leader	u	ukulele
btb	bass trombone	md	mandolin	v	vocal
c	cornet	o	organ	v eff	vocal effects
cel	celeste	p	piano	v grp	vocal group
cga	conga	pac	piano accordion	vb	vibraphone
cl	clarinet	perc	percussion	vc	violoncello
Cms	C-melody saxophone	prod	producer	vl	viola
cond	conductor	prog	programming	vn	violin
d	drums	psg	pedal steel guitar	vtb	valve trombone
Do	Dobro	rb	rubboard	wb	washboard
eff	effects	s	saxophone	wh	whistle/whistling
esg	electric steel guitar	sg	steel guitar	x	xylophone

Others

AFBF	American Folk Blues Festival
AFM	American Federation of Musicians
B&GR	*Blues and Gospel Records 1890–1943* (by Dixon, Godrich & Rye, 4th edition, Oxford, 1997)
BR	*Blues Records 1943–1970* (Volume One: A–K, by Leadbitter & Slaven, Record Information Services, 1987; Volume Two: L–Z, by Leadbitter, Fancourt & Pelletier, Record Information Services, 1994)
LA	Los Angeles
LC	Library of Congress
PD	public domain
R&B	rhythm & blues
VAC	various artists compilation

Marion Abernathy (1918–77)
VOCAL

Abernathy was popular in the '40s in the clubs of LA's Central Avenue. She recorded for several LA labels between 1945 and 1949, but little is known of her subsequent musical activities.

**(*) Marion Abernathy 1947–1949
Classics 5001 *Abernathy; Hot Lips Page, Joe Newman, unknown (t); Joe Britten, Henry Coker (tb); Marshall Royal (cl, as); Vincent Bair-Bey (as, bs); unknown (as); Paul Bascomb, Hal Singer, Tom Archia, Bumps Myers (ts); Maurice Simon (bs); Joe Knight, Gerald Wiggins, unknown (p); unknown (g); Carl 'Flat Top' Wilson, Charlie Drayton, unknown (b); Clarence Donaldson, Chico Hamilton, unknown (d); 'Hannah May', band (v). 8/47–3/49.*

Abernathy's voice has no great range but she handles blues efficiently, in a pungent style not unlike Lil Green's, and is very listenable when her material is good and her accompanists attentive. Both conditions are met on many of these tracks, especially the dozen with Hot Lips Page, which were recorded just before Christmas 1947 to stock King Records' catalogue before an AFM recording ban took effect. (Eight of those sides are also on the Page CD *Shoutin' The Blues* [Blue Boar CDBB 1010], together with recordings made at the same time by Wynonie Harris and Big Maybelle.) 'My Man Boogie' is a copy of the Gene Krupa hit 'Drumboogie', and 'Undecided' the Charlie Shavers composition, but most of the session is vigorous blues with sturdy solos by Page, Singer and Archia. The surrounding dates, also for King, are with other musicians but are broadly similar in character. Some of the transfers are noisy. TR

The Aces
GROUP

The trio of Louis Myers (q.v.), his brother Dave Myers (1926–2001) and Fred Below (1926–88) was formed in 1950 to back Junior Wells and accompanied him on some of his early recordings. They came to be regarded as the tightest backing group in Chicago, particularly when teamed with Little Walter.

*** Chicago Beat
Black & Blue BB 445 *Louis Myers (h, g, v); Willie Mabon (p); Eddie Taylor, Jimmy Rogers, Mickey Baker (g); Dave Myers (b, v); Fred Below (d). 12/70, 12/73.*
**(*) The Aces And Their Guests
Storyville STCD 8049 *Louis Myers (h, g, v); Bobby King, Joe Carter (g, v); Dave Myers (b, v); Fred Below (d); Johnny Drummer (v). 10/75.*

Chicago Beat shows a thoroughly professional crew sailing, for a change, under their own colours. They do so with some style, unhampered by what in other hands might be dead weight – 'Mojo Hand' (i.e. 'Got My Mojo Working'), 'Kansas City', 'Take A Little Walk With Me', etc. – and compacting time with 'Hoo-Doo Man', which the Myerses first recorded, with Junior Wells, 20 years before. Louis Myers plays precise harmonica on that, and elsewhere acidulous slide guitar. The group's sound is made denser by the addition of Chicago's two finest second guitarists, Eddie Taylor on the 1970 session and Jimmy Rogers in '73.

Louis Myers, having taken all but one of the vocals on *Chicago Beat* in his understated manner, moves aside for most of the Storyville session to make room for the guest vocalists. Carter, as both singer and guitarist, is an Elmore James acolyte, while Drummer has a young, flexible voice that's particularly attractive on a Big Maceo-styled 'Someday Baby'. King's only vocal is on 'Baby What You Want Me To Do', a selection typical of a programme overloaded with standards like 'Rock Me Baby', 'Sweet Home Chicago', 'Kansas City' (again) and 'Honky Tonk'. TR

Arthur Adams (born 1940)
VOCAL, GUITAR

Based in LA since 1964, the Tennessee-born Adams first made his reputation as a studio player and through his work on TV and movie soundtracks, but latterly has concentrated on the blues.

**** Back On Track
Blind Pig BPCD 5055 *Adams; Tom Poole, Lee Thornburg (t); Keith Crossan, Greg Smith (s); Hense Powell (kb, o); Neil Larsen, Mick Weaver (kb); B. B. King (g, v); Reggie McBride, Jim Garafalo, Lawrence Baulden, Ritt Henn (b); James Gadson, Alvino Bennett (d); Kevin Recard (perc); Reugenia Peoples, Voneta Thompson, Christy Brooks (v). 99?*

Adams's unostentatious guitar playing might lead an inattentive hearer to underestimate him. Anyone else will listen on a slow crescendo of admiration. His solos and fills, whether terse or copious, are unerringly appropriate to his material, a judicious mixture of blues and soul songs, and like his friend and model B. B. King, who guests on two tracks, he understands the power of pacing, of keeping something in reserve. He's also an excellent singer, somewhat in B. B.'s style as well. But what raises this album from estimable to outstanding is Adams's writing. Compositions like 'Who Does She Think She Is', 'Rehabilitation Song' and 'The Long Haul' are intelligent, adult themes, finely crafted, and although Adams sets a formidable standard in his own interpretations, that shouldn't deter other artists from investigating songs that can clearly take on lives of their own. TR

Jo-Jo Adams (c. 1918–88)
VOCAL

The Alabama-born Adams had found his way by the mid-'40s to Chicago, where he was quite well known for a decade or so as a singer, dancer and comedian. Though in appearance and sartorial style he was not unlike Cab Calloway, his work on record was chiefly in the jump-blues idiom.

**(*) Jo-Jo Adams 1946–1953
Classics 5083 *Adams; George Orendorff, Melvin Moore, unknowns (t); unknown (tb); Jewell Grant, Nat Jones (as); Maxwell Davis, Harold Ousley (ts); Francis Mikell, Dave Young (bs); unknowns (s); Garland Finney, Bill Huff, Eddie Baker, unknowns (p); Tiny Mitchell, Floyd Smith, unknown (g); Ralph Hamilton, Booker Collins, Sylvester Hickman, unknowns (b); Lee Gibson, Curtis Walker, Earl Phillips, unknowns (d). 1/46 or 2/46–53.*

Classics have gathered all Adams's recordings in his own name, mostly for Chicago labels but with an interlude in LA, where he recorded for Aladdin accompanied by a Maxwell

Davis lineup. One of those sides, 'When I'm In My Tea', is a Callowayesque dope song cut from the same roll as 'If You're A Viper', but elsewhere the smoke Adams blows is blue in one sense or the other – sometimes both, as in 'Around The Watch', a two-part recasting of 'Around The Clock'. Although much of his material is formulaic, and some of the recordings are gritty, Adams is a boisterous and personable vocalist. TR

Gaye Adegbalola (born 1944)
VOCAL, GUITAR, HARMONICA

Born Gaye Todd in Virginia, Adegbalola worked in education and theatre before joining Saffire – The Uppity Blues Women. She continues to teach blues vocal techniques and history, and has a long history of political activism, in the Civil Rights and Black Power movements and as a feminist.

**(*) Bitter Sweet Blues
Alligator ALCD 4870 Adegbalola; Jordan Valdina (kb, p); Warren Bernhardt (p); Rory Block (g, v); Mike DeMicco, Tom Principato (g); Carl Adami, Randy Mattson (b); Peter O'Brien, Clyde Connor (d); Jerry Marotta (perc); Resa Gibbs, Ysaye Barnwell, Juno Pitchford (v). 4/99.
*** Neo-Classic Blues
Hot Toddy Music HTMCD 1920 Adegbalola; Roddy Barnes (p). 6/03–3/04.

Bitter Sweet Blues is an uneven mix of originals and covers, with the most deeply felt songs being among the least satisfactory, as when producer Rory Block's tricksy arrangement dilutes the power of 'Nightmare' and its memories of incestuous abuse. 'Nothing's Changed' is about racism, but its silly-clever wordplay falls well short of an adequate response. Adegbalola and Block are fond of aggressive, hard rocking sounds, which suit the witty hymn to womanpower 'Big Ovaries, Baby', but the wit becomes coarse and facetious on 'The Dog Was Here First'. The results are usually better when the arrangements are less strident, as on an unaccompanied account of Waring Cuney's poem 'Images', or 'Front Door Blues', a sadly funny song about not quite coming out of the closet. A percussion-accompanied update of Bessie Smith's 'Jail House Blues' has considerable power, and Ma Rainey's lesbian strut 'Prove It On Me Blues' is also enjoyable – better, certainly, than 'Need A Little Sugar In My Bowl', where the lover is addressed as if s/he were a political rally. The disc's good moments make its patchiness the more apparent.

'Prove It On Me Blues' reappears on Neo-Classic Blues, which comprises well-known women's blues from the interwar years, Ellington's 'I Got It Bad And That Ain't Good', Speckled Red's 'The Dirty Dozens', three originals by Adegbalola and Barnes's affecting ballad 'Summer Sky'. In this context, 'classic blues' means blues which can be read as prefiguring contemporary feminist concerns. That's a long way from what Rudi Blesh meant when he coined the term in the '40s, but his model of blues history was also flawed and partisan. Adegbalola and Barnes's interpretations are straightforward and respectful of the originals, although a tendency to smooth out the contours of the original vocal lines is apparent, and notably disimproves Sippie Wallace's 'Up The Country Blues'. Ma Rainey, Bessie Smith, Alberta Hunter, Lucille Bogan and Mamie Smith are all successfully covered; a boogie treatment of Memphis Minnie's 'Pigmeat On The Line' works better than a similar arrangement of 'Nothing In Rambling', but Adegbalola's personalization of both lyrics is tactfully done. CS

Mozelle Alderson
VOCAL

Both Georgia Tom Dorsey and Big Bill Broonzy remembered her by name, but it was left to discographers to peel away the pseudonyms under which Mozelle Alderson did most of her recording work, such as Hannah May, Jane Lucas and Kansas City Kitty. Presumably a Chicago resident in her recording years, she disappeared from sight when they were over.

**(*) Blue Girls – Vol. 2 (1928–1930)
Document DOCD-5504 Alderson; Blind James Beck, Judson Brown (p, sp). c. 4/27–4/30.

Alderson's 'Mozelle Blues' is one of the earliest records to include the blues commonplace of a catfish swimming in the deep blue sea. It's difficult to evaluate her abilities on that and her other 1927 sides for the rare Black Patti label. The recordings were technically poor to start with, and as remastered here make hard listening. Not so 'Tight Whoopee': this exuberant, atmospheric – and audible – performance from 1930, when coupled with the slower 'Tight In Chicago', proved to be her finest record, and probably her pianist Judson Brown's too. As well as her seven sides, this compilation includes a sprightly piano solo, 'State Street Special', by her earlier accompanist, Blind James Beck, and recordings by Mary Dixon and others.

**(*) Kansas City Kitty & Georgia Tom (1930–1934)
RST Blues Documents BDCD-6023 Alderson; Georgia Tom Dorsey (p, v); poss. Eddie Morgan (p); Tampa Red (g); unknown (k). 5/30–11/34.

Most of these sides are more or less suggestive hokum songs, very similar to those on which Dorsey and Alderson collaborated in the guise of the Famous Hokum Boys. She is unfailingly chipper, in contrast to Dorsey's lugubrious humour, in the tenement dialogues and bedroom playlets of 'The Doctor's Blues' (similar in theme to the Famous Hokum Boys' 'Terrible Operation Blues'), 'Fish House Blues', 'Show Me What You Got' and 'Root Man Blues', the girls' school scenario of '"Gym's" Too Much For Me' and the abattoir rendezvous of 'Killing Floor Blues', where Dorsey courts Alderson with a 'nine-inch knife'. 'Knife Man Blues', which was unavailable for this CD but was included, with 'Do It Some More', on *"Too Late, Too Late Blues" – Vol. 1 (1926–1944)* (Document DOCD-5150), has a more unsettling ambiguity, the sexual metaphor wilting in a chill blast of random street violence. All the recordings are duets – in the sense that both artists sing, though not often at the same time – except for the last four sides, from 1934, which are solos by Alderson in a more up-to-date style, with a probably different pianist and an occasional and skilful kazoo player. TR

Herman Alexander (born 1925)
VOCAL, GUITAR, HARMONICA

Field recording trips proliferated between the '70s and '90s and, while a lot of interesting and accomplished musicians were discovered, eventually new talent became thin on the ground.

Regrettably, Memphis resident Herman Alexander is a typical example. Like Robert Cage and Scott Dunbar, he is a musical naif with very limited musical ability and an imperfect recall of the songs he has appropriated.

** Highway 61
Wolf 120.920 *Alexander.* 11/90.

The notes try to align Alexander with Fred McDowell and Ranie Burnette, noting that 'astonishingly' he hadn't been recorded before. Sadly, it's because better talents were available. Alexander's guitar playing works with individual strings rather than full chords, creating a simplistic rhythmic background for his faltering vocals. Versions of 'Poor Boy Blues' and 'You Got To Move' are brief, as are his three excursions on harmonica, the best being 'Baby Please Don't Go', on which he projects more confidence. Heard at greater length, as in 'Down Home Blues', in which he sings 'don't get out much all the time', his fundamental lack of talent becomes painfully obvious. The rest of this CD is by CeDell Davis. NS

Texas Alexander (1900–1954)
VOCAL

Born in rural Leon County, Texas, and a lifelong resident in the state, Alexander sang on city streets or in bars, usually accompanied by a guitarist. He lived in Dallas in the late '20s and recorded prolifically and quite influentially in the '20s and '30s. Among the musicians who played with him in later years were Lowell Fulson and Lightnin' Hopkins, and he was remembered by other Texan bluesmen like Frankie Lee Sims and Buster Pickens, yet little is known of his life.

***(*) Texas Alexander: Vol. 1 (1927–28)
Matchbox MBCD 2001 *Alexander; Eddie Heywood (p); Lonnie Johnson, Eddie Lang (g).* 8/27–11/28.

*** Texas Alexander: Vol. 2 (1928–1930)
Matchbox MBCD 2002 *Alexander; King Oliver (c); Clarence Williams (p); Bo Chatmon (vn); Lonnie Johnson, Eddie Lang, Little Hat Jones, Carl Davis, Sam Chatmon, unknown (g).* 11/28–6/30.

***(*) Texas Alexander: Vol. 3 (1930–1950)
Matchbox MBCD 2003 *Alexander; unknown (cl, as); Buster Pickens, unknown (p); prob. Bo Chatmon (vn); Sam Chatmon, poss. Willie Reed, Leon Benton, unknowns (g); unknown (b).* 6/30–50.

Though there are many echoes in Alexander's music of the field holler and the worksong, the long, slow trajectories of his singing seem more intimate than that, and their burdens more like stories, meditations or lover's cajolings. He has an eloquent moan – listen to the opening of 'No More Women Blues' – and a characteristic device of ending a line with a slide up to the tonic. He likes to sing about country matters, particularly farm animals ('Bantam Rooster Blues', 'Work Ox Blues'), and objects of daily life like cornbread, chewing tobacco and kitchen ranges. According to some reports he served time in jail. Certainly he was well acquainted with its musical culture, several of his recordings, such as 'Levee Camp Moan Blues' and 'Bell Cow Blues', drawing on traditional Texan prison-song motifs.

Most of those and the other tracks on *Vol. 1* are with Lonnie Johnson on guitar. What Johnson plays is often not much more elaborate than a single-string line approximating the contour of the vocal melody, as in, say, 'Section Gang Blues' and 'Levee Camp Moan Blues', but his timing, the swiftness of his musical imagination and the sumptuousness of his guitar sound are all so remarkable that he must be considered not Alexander's accompanist but his partner, a joint creator. Even richer are the settings of 'Work Ox Blues' and 'The Risin' Sun', where Johnson is joined by Eddie Lang; the guitarists may be black and white but the musical landscape is Technicolor. On four songs Johnson is replaced by the pianist Eddie Heywood, who grabs Alexander by the scruff of the neck and forces him to sing in tempo. Though less alluring than the sides with Johnson, these are by no means unsuccessful performances, and Heywood's solo on 'Sabine River Blues' has a fine air of Texan braggadocio.

With a couple of dozen sides by Alexander in the can, OKeh Records may have felt that it was time for a change in sound. At any rate, after two tracks of *Vol. 2*, Johnson disappears, never to return, and Eddie Lang steps in for four sides, two also featuring King Oliver on cornet. The following 15 tracks were recorded in Texas and have local guitarists, either Little Hat Jones or Carl Davis. Jones displays his trademark device of setting a fast tempo in his introduction and abruptly slowing down as soon as somebody starts singing; an extreme example is 'Johnny Behrens Blues', which is also intriguing because the lyrics offer no clue to who Johnny Behrens was. Davis, in sharp contrast to Jones's rhythmic, chordal approach, imitates Johnson's single-string manner but lacks both Johnson's imagination – he plays an identical intro to each of the six blues he accompanies – and his fine instrument. Meanwhile Alexander sails majestically through the songs, impervious to his surroundings.

Talk about impervious: Alexander's self-absorption finds its match on eight tracks, spread across *Vol. 2* and *Vol. 3*, by the Mississippi Sheiks, whose idea of accompaniment is playing just as if they were on their own. Several of these sedate blues are from noisy originals, a recurrent problem on both volumes, which were also remastered at a low level. The Sheiks having folded their tents, Alexander is next offered on *Vol. 3* the jaunty accompaniment of 'His Sax Black Tams', a trio playing reeds, piano and guitar. None of these six sides is musically distinguished, but the following eight, with two-guitar accompaniment by Willie Reed and another, are considerably better. These 1934 recordings include some of Alexander's most interesting lyrics, such as the autobiographical but enigmatic 'Normangee Blues', 'Polo Blues', which is not about polo, and 'Justice Blues', which is not about justice. The CD concludes with Alexander's last known recordings, 'Bottoms Blues'/'Cross Roads', from 1950, on which he was paired with pianist Buster Pickens and guitarist Leon Benton, an encounter rather than a meeting.

The deletion of *98° Blues* (Catfish KATCD 122) removed something that was needed: a single album that sampled Alexander's work in many settings and thus deflected the listener's attention from the consistency of his approach and his narrow range of tempos. TR

Bernard Allison (born 1965)
VOCAL, GUITAR

A teenaged Bernard Allison served two tours of duty with Koko Taylor's Blues Machine before moving to France and joining his father Luther's band. Since then, he's branched out on his own

with a series of albums that resist precise definition. He's inherited his father's eclectic approach to blues but whether the disparate elements he attempts to combine will coalesce into an identifiable personal style is yet to be established.

(*) Hang On!
Ruf 1061 *Allison; Thierry 'Juke' Menesclou (h); Michel Carras (kb); Don Torsch (o); Jay Golden (b); Vincent Daune (d); Luther Allison (v).* 6–7/92.

Allison is here attempting a synthesis of rock, funk and blues – in that order. An over-syncopated 'Cadillac Assembly Line' reveals the influence of Albert King but Jimi Hendrix and Stevie Ray Vaughan hold greater sway. An up-tempo 'Voodoo Thang' might be better titled 'Jimi B. Goode' but 'Missing Stevie' can't reproduce Vaughan's Texas shuffle. A ten-minute 'Voodoo Chile Medley' wallows in unflattering imitation, while 'Hang On' proclaims 'Jimi still lives on'. 'Looking Beyond' and 'Rockin' Robin' give the nod to Deep Purple, with a direct quote from 'Smoke On The Water' in the latter's coda. In his own 'Mai' and 'You're Hurtin Me', Allison affects the exaggerated vowel contortions his funk heroes practise, leaving the blues quotient of this album restricted to Bobby Rush's 'Action Speaks Louder Than Words' and 'Idols In Mind', in which he duets with his father.

* Funkifino
Ruf 7716 *Allison; Jerome 'Nils' Chaplet, Danny 'Boney' Fields (t, fl); Simon AnDrieux (tb); Cyril Guiraud (s); Stephen Le Navelan (kb, b, v); Joanna Connor, Mike Sene (g); Keem Yarbrough (b); Jeff Boudreaux, Frank Mantegari (d); Antonin Bastian, Ron Smith, Mike Robinson, The Allison Family (v).* 1–2/96.

Funkifyudu. This style of music was moribund long before Allison came to it and toiling in exhausted funk mines won't help him roll away the stone. More importantly, beyond a bluesy edge to the guitar solo in 'Looking For An Answer' and the slide guitar breaks in 'If', this record has no blues content whatsoever. An hour was wasted in listening to this album so that you don't have to.

*** Born With The Blues
Ruf 1017 *Allison; Matthew Skoller (h); Ron Levy (o, p); Will Crosby (g); Greg Rzab (b); Ray 'Killer' Allison (d); Ray C. Drain (v).* 97.

A failure of nerve or a consolidation? The results are eminently serviceable, although he persists in singing as though the backing band is Funkadelic. His guitar playing is by turns controlled or prone to the fret frenzy evident in his father's playing. Apart from 'Rocket 88', 'Garbage Man' and Freddie King's 'In The Open', the songs are his own, and in 'Baby Chile' he modestly admits, 'It's up to me to keep the blues alive', an aim he's subsequently failed to pursue.

**(*) Times Are Changing
Ruf 1027//(A) 1415 *Allison; Dan 'Boney' Fields, Steven Maylor (t); Prentice Wulff-Woesten (tb); Larry Weathersby (as, ts); Jeff Griffith (ts, bs); Andrew Love (ts); Bobby Rush (h, v); Andy Bailey, Tom Hunter (o, p); Keem Yarbrough (b); James Knowles (d); Jackie Reddick, Bertram Brown (v).* 98.

The prophetic nature of this album's title isn't borne out by its contents. Allison pays tribute to his father in two versions, one acoustic, the other electric, of 'Don't Be Confused', as well as well-made renditions of three of Luther's songs, including 'Bad Love' and 'Life Is A Bitch'. His own compositions, of which the best is 'I Can't Get You Out Of My Mind', are more amorphous, at times retaining a faint blue edge. He flirts with funk and soul and gets a lesson in the latter when Bobby Rush sings his own 'In The Morning'. Sly Stone's 'If You Want Me To Stay' and Johnny 'Guitar' Watson's 'Real Mother Fa' Ya'' are caricatures sunk by Allison's exaggerated vocals, so much at variance with his singing on the rest of the album. The abiding impression is of a talented musician dabbling in a number of genres without any sense of direction, without which change is pointless.

*** Kentucky Fried Blues
Ruf 1092 *Allison; Trevor Newman (t); Richard Martinez (tb); Mike Vlahakis (kb); Jeff Hayes (b); Craig Panosh (d).* 6/99.

Allison was probably promoting the previous album when he made this appearance at the W. C. Handy Festival in Henderson, Kentucky, which would explain the presence of 'Bad Love' and 'Life Is A Bitch' in his set, as well as 'Midnight Creeper'. The context is blues but the treatment is rock bombast, driven on by Panosh's stuttering drums. With audience participation, 'Bad Love' staggers to 14 minutes but the set's showpiece is a slow 18-minute saunter through Buddy Guy's 'Leave My Girl Alone'. Allison takes 12 choruses of guitar solo and the audience cheers when he steps on his wah-wah pedal. This is the blues as trophy-gathering and Allison is very good at it.

**(*) Across The Water
Tone-Cool TC CD 1178 *Allison; Joe Mulherin (t); Jim Spake (s); Bruce McCabe (kb, p); Mike Vlahakis (kb); Ernest Williamson (o); Paul Diethelm (Do, g); Kim Yarbrough, David Smith (b); James Knowles (d); William Brown, Jackie Johnson, Reba Russell (v) (d).* 00.

… and this is my rock album – undeniably well performed and recorded but once again retreading old ground that his contemporaries have long since abandoned. It's disconcerting to notice how easily his father's 'Love Is Free' fits in to the rock bombast. As it is, Luther's 'Change Your Way Of Living' and the closing 'I've Been Down' are the only overtly blues workouts here. Given that so many young blues musicians, black and white, are influenced as much by ZZ Top and Led Zeppelin as they are by more traditional bluesmen, perhaps young Allison is playing to his strength.

**(*) Storms Of Life
Tone-Cool TC CD 751135//Cooking Vinyl BLEUCD 001 *Allison; Larry McCabe (tb); David Eiland, Brian Simmonds (ts); Richard Rosenblatt (h); Ricky Peterson (o, p); Bruce McCabe (p); Paul Diethelm (g); David Smith, Jassen Wilber, Jim Kogl (b); Robb Stupka, Ron Sutton (d); Chico Perez (perc); J. D. Steele, Fred Steele, Kat Wilson (v).* 02.

To keep the blues alive, Allison enlists the services of Leon Russell, Johnny Winter, Dire Straits and ZZ Top to provide material, alongside songs by his father and Rico McFarland. The listener is promised 'infusions of funk, reggae, rock and a variety of blues styles'. The results are unquestionably entertaining but the menu reduces the blues to a flavouring rather than a staple diet. Winter's 'Mean Town Blues' and Allison's own Bo Diddley-inspired instrumental 'Speed Slide' most nearly fit the blues bill but otherwise commercial imperatives require a less rigorous observance of 12-bar etiquette. This may be the direction the blues must take in the future to remain viable and Allison may become one of its leaders. Whether this will sustain or revitalize the music remains very much open to question. NS

**(*) Higher Power
Ruf 1101 *Allison; Mike Vlahakis (kb, o, syn, clavinet); Bruce McCabe (p); Paul Diethelm (Do, g); Jellybean Johnson (g); Jassen Wilber (b); Ron Sutton (d); Brian Johnson (sugar bag shaker). 5–6/04.*

Like much of Allison's work, this is blues-rock, grandly gestural in pieces like the opening 'I've Learned My Lesson' or 'Next 2 U', but at least the emphasis is often on the first part of the term and, when Allison calms down for the dear-diary song 'New Life I'm In' or his father's 'Into My Life', he commands the sympathetic listener's attention. On the other hand, when he applies a blues-rock aesthetic to a simple blues like G. L. Crockett's 'It's A Man Down There', pumping up the song's natural, sly, Jimmy Reedish throb into an elephantine stomp, the result is rather ridiculous. The sheer insistence of Allison's attack will no doubt alienate some blues-lovers, but from time to time *Higher Power* suggests that he may be acquiring a more temperate manner. TR

Luther Allison (1939–97)
VOCAL, GUITAR, HARMONICA

Three years younger than Buddy Guy, the teenaged Luther Allison arrived in Chicago from Arkansas before Guy left Louisiana. Thereafter, though similar, their careers diverged as Guy became the popular face of young Chicago blues while Allison toiled unnoticed. After his 1969 debut for Delmark he became one of the few blues artists to join Motown, although the results failed to enhance his status. In the early '80s he moved to Europe, where he refined his style to accommodate a more rock-oriented audience. A decade later, with newfound but hard-won prestige, he was able to return in something like triumph to the US, where his popularity began to rival Guy's, but lung cancer cut short his enjoyment of his finest moment.

**(*) Love Me Mama
Delmark DE-625 *Allison; Jim Conley (ts); Jimmy Dawkins (g); Robert 'Big Mojo' Elem (b); Bobby Davis, Bob Richey (d). 6/69.*

A strong seller on its first release, this album now shows its age. In plain terms, Allison wasn't yet a good enough guitarist to work in a trio format and his frequent use of a wah-wah pedal hinders the flow of his invention. Unlike Magic Sam (whose 'Every Night About This Time' is an addition to the original LP's contents), he couldn't convincingly combine rhythm and lead guitar work, as the seven-minute instrumental 'Bloomington Closer' amply illustrates. He's further hampered by a programme overstuffed with the likes of 'Five Long Years', 'Help Me', 'Dust My Broom' and 'Little Red Rooster'. What isn't in dispute is that he already possesses a powerful and commanding voice that will improve further with age.

The Motown albums *Bad News Is Coming* (Motown 440 013 407) and *Luther's Blues* (440 013 409) are no longer in print, and a compilation from his three LPs for the label, *The Motown Years, 1972–76* (345 30612), is thought to have been deleted also.

*** Love Me Papa//Standing At The Crossroad
Evidence ECD 26015//Black & Blue BB 421 *Allison; Sid Wingfield (o, p); Dan Hoeflinger (g); Jim Campbell (b); Donald Robertson (d). 12/77.*

Recorded during his second visit to Europe, this finds Allison in blustering form, indulging both extremes of his talent. At his best, on the first take of 'Goin' Down', he winds his band into a taut machine; at his worst, dragging 11 minutes out of his own 'It's Too Late', he wastes several choruses on the same minimalist nonsense that regularly blights Buddy Guy's gigs. Nevertheless, in a programme that draws predominantly on evergreens such as 'Blues With A Feeling', 'Last Night', 'Key To The Highway' and 'Crossroad', he avoids clichés and imposes himself on songs that others fail to animate. Part of that effort requires him to take at least two 24-bar solos in each song, forcing the listener to combine appreciation with tolerance.

*** Live In Paris
Buda 82469//Ruf 161354 *Allison; Sid Wingfield (p); James Solberg (g); Kenny Berdoll [Bordeau?] (b); Danny Schmidt (d). 79.*

This finds Allison working hard to please a small and reticent Parisian audience. 'The Thrill Is Gone' is still in the setlist, as well as 'Sweet Little Angel', but an attempt to funk up 'My Babe' almost qualifies for a one-letter change in the verb. Despite its attribution to Leroy Carr, 'Early In The Morning' is an Elmore James-influenced slide feature, followed by an over-extended 'Tribute To Hound Dog' that ends with Allison thanking the audience and leaving the stage. This is the sixth song in a continuous sequence, leaving a question-mark over the sequencing of the four individual tracks that follow. Allison is in good voice and plays impressively at times but a harmonica feature, 'Luther's Shuffle', is an unnecessary exhibition of his versatility.

*(*) Serious//Life Is A Bitch
Blind Pig BP 72287//Encore! 493312 *Allison; Freddy Hovsepian, Tony Russo (t); Alain Hatot (ss, as); Jean-Louis Chautemps, Jean-Pierre Solves (s); Michel Carras (kb); Jacques Higelin (p); 'Fast Frank' Rabaste (g); Mario Satterfield (b); Jimi Schutte (d, v); J. Mattes (d); Sammy Ateba (perc). 1–2/84.*

Several of the albums Allison cut in Europe haven't made the transition to CD. Regrettably, this one did. In embracing the rock-blues he encountered on the Continent, Allison lost sight of his essential talent. 'Parking Lot', a headbanging anthem in light blue disguise, and the rock ballads 'Reaching Out' and 'Just Memories' are so contrived that a true blues like 'Show Me A Reason' sounds ponderous by comparison. The rock element is most obviously present in the guitar solos, which by definition take place at the top end of the fretboard. Meanwhile, Allison's vocals have undergone a virility bypass, as he intones deathless phrases like 'feel the vibrations'. This may not be bio-degradable but it is disposable.

*(*) Here I Come
Encore! 493332 *Allison; Michel Carras (kb); 'Fast Frank' Rabaste (g); Zox (b); J. Mattes (d). 7–9/85.*

With the possible exception of the opening title track and the closing 'Overseas Boogie', this album has no blues content.

(*) Hand Me Down My Moonshine
Ruf 1047//(A) 161413 *Allison; Thierry Menesclou (h); Bernard Allison (g, v); Patrick Verbeke (g); Zox (b).* 92.

An acoustic session that starts well but squanders its goodwill as Allison's initial restraint surrenders to self-indulgence. The opening 'Good Morning Love' uses its simple honesty to avoid the cloying sentiment that later undermines 'Castle'. 'Lightnin' Bolt' and 'Don't Burn My Bread' are effective slow blues but would have been improved by properly miked vocals. Eventually, Allison abandons any attempt to be succinct and mundanities such as 'I Need A Friend' and 'She's Fine' routinely exceed five minutes. The rhythmically confusing title track and the final 'Meet Me In My Own Hometown', with son Bernard on slide guitar, consume 15 minutes between them and try the patience. Better songs and concise arrangements would have improved what began as a promising project.

***(*) Where Have You Been?: Live In Montreux 1976–1994**
Ruf 1008//(A) 161342 *Allison; Wayne Jackson (t); Andrew Love, Fat Richard Drake (ts); Larry Byrne, Michel Carras (kb); Barry Beckett, Ernest Williamson (o); Jimmy Johnson, James Solberg (g); Jeff Aldrich, Mike Morrison, David Hood, Dave Smith (b); Jay Mattes, Roger Hawkins, Yvette Preyer (d).* 76–94.

Released months before his death, this compilation of appearances at the Montreux Festival documents his progress from a hardworking unknown to an artist approaching the pinnacle of his career. Apart from 'Sky Is Crying', the solitary inclusion from his 1983 set, the remaining songs form generous portions of his '76, '84 and '94 shows. Despite featuring Willie Dixon songs like 'The Same Thing' and 'Little Red Rooster', Allison is evidently still in thrall to B. B. King in matters of vocal and instrumental delivery, most obviously during 'Gamblers Blues'. A more individual voice is heard in the selections from '84, backed by the Muscle Shoals Rhythm Section, although 'Memories' and 'Spontaneous Improvisation' lack sufficient conviction. That's displayed ten years later on 'Put Your Money Where Your Mouth Is' and 'Bad Love' from his then new album. There are a couple of *longueurs* where onstage antics fail to translate to disc but in general this is a positive portrayal of Allison's artistic development.

***(*) Bad Love//Soul Fixin' Man**
Ruf 1021//Alligator ALCD 4820 *Allison; Wayne Jackson (t, tb); Andrew Love (ts); Ernest Williamson (kb); James Solberg (g); Dave Smith (b); James Robinson (d); Kpe Lee (perc); Jacquelyn Reddick, Jacqueline Johnson, Lee Bonner, Another Blessed Creation Choir (v).* 94.

Different album titles and running orders heavily underline the fact that a product has been devised, one that successfully packaged its artist for the blues marketplaces of America and Europe in the '90s. A mixture of Allison–Solberg originals, a couple of soul-blues from the Malaco team of Mosley and Johnson and an overtly gospel-tinged version of Guitar Slim's 'Things I Used To Do' display the artist's strengths, even if 'Soul Fixin' Man' was the only stone-cold 12-bar on offer. Nevertheless, this formula succeeded where earlier European experiments had failed. Allison's vocal and instrumental confidence stamps a definitive brand on these 12 tracks, although the altruistic anthem 'Freedom' strikes a false if earnest note. A product very much of its time, this became the template for the albums that followed.

**** Blue Streak**
Alligator ALCD 4834/Ruf 7712 *Allison; Wayne Jackson (t, tb); Andrew Love (ts); Ernest Williamson, Mike Vlahakis (kb); Bruce McCabe (p); James Solberg, Charlie Bingham (g); Dave Smith, Ken Faltinson (b); Steve Potts, Robb Stupka (d); Jacqueline Johnson, Jacquelyn Reddick (v).* 95.

As successful as the previous album had been for Allison, it won no awards, whereas this took five Handys in 1996. After an album with two titles, it was 'Cherry Red Wine', renamed 'Watching You' on the European issue, that took the award for best song. Like the rest of the set, it epitomized the blues of the '90s: brash, dynamic, commercial, more notable for its resources than for the sentiments expressed. Judicious amounts of slide guitar ticked the authenticity box and songs like 'Big City' and 'Move From The 'Hood' made mandatory social comments. 'Think With Your Heart' and 'Midnight Creeper' were gestures towards Southern soul, while 'What Have I Done Wrong' and 'You Don't Know' gave Allison ample scope for his finely honed but profligate guitar work. For all its accomplishments and its garland of awards, this album once again screams 'product!' from an artist who habitually referred to himself in the third person.

*** Pay It Forward**
Ruf 1060 *Allison; Serge Plume (t); Jel Jongen (tb); Allard Buwaldi, Sulaiman Hakim (ts); Jorgen Lang (h); Earnest Williams, Mike Vlahakis, Michel Carras (kb); Barry Beckett, Bruce Elsensohn, Kjelt Lauritsen (o); Kurt Clayton (p); Effendi Mumtaz (bouzouki); James Solberg, Bernard Allison, Joanna Connor (g, v); Charlie Bingham, Jimmy Johnson, Patrick Verbeke, Otis Grand, Kenn Lending, Anthony Palmer, 'Fast Franck' Rabaste, Thomas Fellow (g); Dave Smith, Ken Faltinson, David Hood, Steve Gomes, Jay Golden, Jens Elbol, Stan Mixon, Peter Giron (b); Steve Potts, Robb Stupka, Roger Hawkins, Lloyd Anderson, Neil Gouvin, Vincent Daune, Frank Larsen, Larry Ortega (d); Marla Glen, Constanze Friend (v).* 85–96.

The album title denotes Allison's generosity as a teacher and benefactor. Its contents are a series of vocal and instrumental duets from other Ruf albums, previously unissued tracks and alternative versions designed to illustrate the artist's ubiquity. Much of it is soul-oriented, including 'Dock Of The Bay', taken from the climax of a 1985 Montreux appearance, and 'I Wanna Be With You' from the *Blue Streak* sessions. Duets with Marla Glen, Constanze Friend and Joanna Connor are not quite what they're claimed to be, although 'Idols In Mind' with son Bernard, 'Still Called The Blues' with James Solberg and 'Perfume & Grime', a guitar duel with Otis Grand, bear repetition. Despite moments of notable musicianship, the composite nature of the chosen material and the fact that too often Allison isn't at his best prevent this from being the memorial his fans might wish to see.

*** Reckless**
Ruf 1012//Alligator ALCD 4849 *Allison; Wayne Jackson (t); Andrew Love (ts); Marla Glen (h, v); Mike Vlahakis, Rick Steff (o, p); Kurt Clayton (p); Bernard Allison (g, v); James Solberg (g); Dave Smith, Ken Faltinson (b); Steve Potts, Lloyd Anderson, Darin James, Willie Hayes (d).* 97.

Ruf and Alligator again opted for different running orders for these 14 tracks, with the boastful, slide-dominated 'I'm Back' opening one and closing the other. Also, 'Just As I Am' appears as a duet with Marla Glen on Ruf but as a solo vocal on Alligator. The mixture is much as before and, although Allison won three Handy awards, none was for this record. For all its ruthless efficiency, its rock-oriented arrangements and designer distress, its component parts fail to make a lasting impression. Allison works as hard as ever, straining vocals and high-treble fretboard workouts, but too often rock sensibility bludgeons material that requires more delicacy, such as O. V. Wright's 'You're Gonna Make Me Cry'. 'Pain In The Streets' and 'Will It Ever Change' wear prominent social badges. The only respite is 'Playin' A Losin' Game', an acoustic trio with son Bernard and Glen's harmonica. He may be 'Living In The House Of The Blues' but Allison wants to sing it in a stadium.

**** Live In Chicago
Ruf 1042//Alligator ALCD 4869 *Allison; Ken Anderson (t); Bobby Neely (ts); Willie Henderson (bs); Dave Rice, Mike Vlahakis (kb); Otis Rush (g, v); James Solberg, John Kattke, Eddie C. Campbell (g); Ken Faltinson (b); Robb Stupka, J. Mattes, Willie Hayes (d). 6/95–5/97.*

The requisite live extravaganza, recorded at three locations, including Allison's appearance at the 1995 Chicago Blues Festival and later the same year at Buddy Guy's Legends. He and the band are so well rehearsed that these versions of songs from the three previous Ruf/Alligator albums are easily the equal of the studio originals, apart from the *longueurs* of stage performance that don't translate to the living room. Rock-blues bombast is also present but for the most part kept in check. Most of the 18 titles are Allison–Solberg originals, the exceptions including the slide features 'Give Me Back My Wig' and 'It Hurts Me Too'. Also from the Blues Festival is a medley of 'Gambler's Blues' and 'Sweet Little Angel', on which Allison and Campbell appear with Otis Rush and his band. The remaining titles come from an appearance at the Zoo Bar in Lincoln, Nebraska, recorded just three months before the artist's death, underlining the fact that Allison died at the peak of his form. NS

Albert Ammons (1907–49)
VOCAL, PIANO, WHISTLING

Born in Chicago, Ammons learned from Hersal Thomas, the Yancey brothers and Doug Suggs, and worked as a cab driver with Meade Lux Lewis while building a local reputation. He became more widely known during the boogie craze of the '30s and '40s, which he, Lewis and Pete Johnson spearheaded; in the '40s Ammons and Johnson worked as a duo. Ammons performed at President Truman's inaugural in 1949, but illness sidelined him for most of his final year.

*** Albert Ammons 1936–1939
Classics 715 *Ammons; Guy Kelly, Harry James, Frankie Newton (t); J. C. Higginbotham (tb); Delbert Bright (cl, as); Ike Perkins, Teddy Bunn (g); Israel Crosby, Johnny Williams (b); Jimmy Hoskins, Eddie Dougherty, Sid Catlett (d). 1/36–4/39.*

*** Hey! Piano Man
JSP JSP 7747 4CD *As above. 1/36–4/39.*

With Ammons, the question is, 'Do you want the best of, the most of, or the whole of?' Members of the last group won't need our guidance, but for the 'most of' party, the three Classics CDs (above and below) collate the issued commercial recordings, in acceptable rather than outstanding sound. The first offers the sublime 'Shout For Joy' and the Blue Note solos, bracketed by jazz of variable quality; the Rhythm Kings' four tracks are pleasant, with 'Nagasaki' a lively opener. At the other end of the disc, Harry James has a good time on 'Woo Woo' and 'Jesse', but the Port Of Harlem Jazzmen are lacklustre, with Ammons under-recorded. The pertinent CD in JSP's box, which is shared with Meade Lux Lewis, Pete Johnson and Jimmy Yancey, covers the same ground in somewhat brighter sound. Unhelpfully, the booklet with the Ammons disc discusses Yancey and John Hammond.

♛ **** Ammons & Lewis – The First Day
Blue Note CDP 7 98450 *Ammons; Meade Lux Lewis (p). 1/39.*

Blue Note's first session, remastered about as well as it could be. The disc is shared with Meade Lux Lewis (see his entry for discussion), and includes the slightly gimmicky duets 'Twos And Fews' and 'Nagasaki'. Otherwise, though, this is the CD for listeners who want the best of, featuring Ammons in prime condition, revved up after the *From Spirituals To Swing* concert and eager to show what he can do. Blue Note's 12-inch masters give Ammons room to stretch out, and 'Boogie Woogie Stomp' and 'Bass Goin' Crazy' deserve their reputation as classics of the genre, but he also shows his paces as a considerable player of slow blues, above all with the meditative 'Chicago In Mind'.

*** Albert Ammons 1939–1946
Classics 927 *Ammons; Hot Lips Page (t); Vic Dickenson (tb); Artie Starks (as); Don Byas (ts); Lonnie Johnson (g); Israel Crosby, John Lindsay (b); Sid Catlett, Tom Taylor (d); Sippie Wallace, Mildred Anderson (v). 4/39–7/46.*

**(*) Albert Ammons 1946–1948
Classics 1100 *Ammons; Marvin Randolph, Orlando Randolph (t); Riley Hampton (as); Gene Ammons (ts); Ike Perkins (g); Israel Crosby (b); Jack Cooley (d, v); Alvin Burroughs, Jump Jackson, unknown (d). 11/46–1/48.*

Classics' second volume opens with the 1939 Solo Art solos, which rank with the Blue Notes for artistic and technical perfection; 'Mecca Flat Blues' features spectacular right-hand trills and tremolos which never become flashy. There's a six-year gap before the Commodore solos, where flashiness is a slight problem, perhaps the result of working in duo with Pete Johnson. Four sides for Commodore with a starry pickup band are disappointing; Page, Dickenson and Byas are all coarsely showy. Moving to Mercury, Ammons and a different set of Rhythm Kings accompanied an ebullient Sippie Wallace before settling in to a routine of boogies, blues and boogified pop. 'Swanee River Boogie' was a hit, and it's fun, but the formula was overused, and devalues the third Classics CD, where there's also too much of Ike Perkins's over-amplified guitar. A thoughtful 'Sweet Patootie Boogie' rings the changes, and a Rhythm Kings session with Albert's son Gene on tenor gets away from the novelties, if not very excitingly. Four late-1947 titles revert to 12-bar (and one 32-bar) boogie in grand style, and the final Rhythm Kings date includes a killer jazz reading of 'When You And I Were Young, Maggie'.

***(*) Albert Ammons – Boogie Woogie Man
Topaz TPZ 1067 *Similar to Classics CDs, except add Pete Johnson, Meade Lux Lewis (p). 1/36–2/44.*

***(*) **The Boogie Woogie Man**
Living Era CD AJA 5305 *As above, except add Joe Turner (v).*
1/36–7/46.
*** **Blues & Boogie Woogie King**
EPM Jazz Archives 15914 *As above.* 1/36–8/47.
***(*) **Albert Ammons**
Best Of Jazz 4057 *As above, except omit Lewis, Turner.* 1/36–late 47.

The best Ammons material is pretty much self-selecting, so there's heavy duplication and little to choose between these overviews. There's some coverage of the duos and trios with Johnson and Lewis, although only to the extent of one track on Best Of Jazz. Topaz include material by the Port Of Harlem Jazzmen, which could have been advantageously substituted, as could the Commodore band tracks on Living Era. EPM include too many of the late boogied-up pop tunes while omitting 'Shout For Joy' and anything from Solo Art. Despite occasionally suspect remastering, Best Of Jazz gets the casting vote.

(*) **Boogie Woogie Boys (1936–1941)
Document BDCD-6046 *Ammons; Guy Kelly, Harry James (t); Delbert Bright (as); Pete Johnson (p); Ike Perkins (g); Israel Crosby, Johnny Williams (b); J. C. Heard, Jimmy Hoskins, Eddie Dougherty (d); Alan Lomax, Lena Horne (sp).* 12/38–2/39.

All three of the big three are on this disc; Ammons features on two duets with Johnson from the soundtrack of the short film *Boogie Woogie Dream*, and on three alternative takes of commercial releases, of which 'Shout For Joy' is the most significant. More important – but sometimes very battered – are the recordings made for the Library of Congress the day after *From Spirituals To Swing*. Ammons contributes two fine but familiar boogies, 'Sweet Patootie Blues' and his best version of 'Suitcase Blues'. Accompanied by Johnson, he also sings a slow 'Dying Mother Blues' rather well.

*** **Boogie Woogie Stomp**
Delmark DD-705 *Ammons; Meade Lux Lewis (p, sp); Herbert Marshall (b).* 12/38–10/39.
(*) **The Boogie Woogie Trio Vol. 1 & 2
Storyville 103 8057 2CD *Ammons; Pete Johnson, Meade Lux Lewis (p).* 9–10/39.

These collections feature airshots from the Boogie Woogie Trio's residency at the Hotel Sherman, Chicago. Storyville's second disc presents this material complete, meaning that there's one more Ammons solo, and two versions of the six-handed 'Boogie Woogie Prayer'. There's little to choose for sound quality. By selecting the best of the airshots, Delmark make room for an informal four-title session which Lewis and Ammons cut in Chicago just before their Carnegie Hall triumph; it includes a fine Ammons version of 'Three Little Words'. The first disc of *The Boogie Woogie Trio Vol. 1 & 2* contains *inter alia* duets by Ammons and Johnson, as does *Boogie Woogie Boys* (Magpie PY CD 21); these duets are discussed in Johnson's entry.

(*) **Albert Ammons (1936–1946)
Document DOCD-1008 *Ammons; Guy Kelly, Ziggy Elman, Chris Griffin, Irving Goodman, unknown (t); Red Ballard, Vernon Brown, Vic Dickenson (tb); Delbert Bright (cl, as); Benny Goodman (cl, sp); Hymie Schertzer, Noni Bernardi, poss. Tab Smith (as); Art Rollini, Jerry Jerome, Don Byas, unknown (ts);* *Ike Perkins, Ben Heller (g); Israel Crosby, Harry Goodman, unknown (b); Jack Cooley (d, v); Jimmy Hoskins, Buddy Schutz, Sid Catlett, Red Saunders (d); Johnny Mercer, Joe Turner (v).* 1/36–10/46.

Six alternative takes from Decca, Mercury and Savoy (the last as part of the band accompanying Joe Turner) are non-revelatory, as are four airshots: three brief solos and a guest appearance with Benny Goodman, featuring Johnny Mercer singing an asinine lyric about Pine Top Smith. Four scuffed home recordings feature Ammons the singer – lively on 'I Had To Move That Thing', not as good on a two-part 'Dying Mother' as he was for the Library of Congress – and whistler (inferior to Meade Lux Lewis). Eight tracks from Commodore have superb sound, and although three are by that not very good band, the solos are spectacular. This one really is for completists, though. CS

Mike Andersen Band
GROUP

Andersen (born 1977), from Århus in Denmark, is a skilful singer of classic soul and R&B songs and a distinctive guitarist. He has appeared at many European blues festivals and has worked with numerous visiting acts. Drummer Mads Andersen (Mike's brother), bassist Dave Stevens, a founder member of Paul Lamb's Kingsnakes, and Mike Andersen have all toured with Otis Grand.

*** **My Love For The Blues**
Black & Tan CD B&T 014 *Thomas Caudery, Rasmus Bøgelund (t); Morten Elbek, Nils Mathiasen (ts); Lasse Lauridsen (bs); Claus Sand (kb, o, p); H. C. Nielsen (p); Mike Andersen (g, v); Dave Stevens (b); Mads 'Tiny' Andersen (d); Sisse Kold, Mette Ratzer (v).* 3–4/02.
(*) **Tomorrow
Black & Tan CD B&T 021 *Rasmus Bøgelund (t, flh); Nikolai Bøgelund (tb); Lasse Lauridsen (as, bs); Morten Elbek (ts); Claus Sand (kb, o, p); Mike Andersen (g, v); Dave Stevens, Kristian Kold, Ida Nielsen (b); Mads 'Tiny' Andersen (d, perc); Peter Bak (cga); Sisse Kold, Mette Ratzer (v); Al Agami (sp).* 4–6/04.

This is a tight and idiomatically knowing band, which gives it a good start, but the project on which it's engaged in *My Love For The Blues* is ambitious – making albums of bluesy soul songs in the idiom of Bobby Bland and Little Johnny Taylor. That it succeeds to a remarkable degree in bringing it off is due chiefly to Mike Andersen, who is both an elegant, unclichéd guitarist and an attractive and unclichéd singer. This is not impressive because the musicians are Danish; it's an album any young band could be proud of. *Tomorrow* delivers its payload of original songs with similar craft; all that's missing is some strong melodies, but in this kind of soul music that's quite a lot to miss. TR

Mildred Anderson
VOCAL

Anderson was from Brooklyn, and became a professional singer after graduating from high school in 1946. She was Bill Doggett's featured vocalist for three years, and their 1953

recording of 'No More In Life' was a hit. Anderson also recorded with Albert Ammons and Hot Lips Page, with whom she toured briefly.

** **Person To Person**
Original Blues Classics OBCCD-556 *Anderson; Eddie 'Lockjaw' Davis (ts); Shirley Scott (o); George Duvivier (b); Arthur Edgehill (d). 1/60.*

** **No More In Life**
Original Blues Classics OBCCD-579 *Anderson; Al Sears (ts); Robert Banks (o); Lord Westbrook (g); Leonard Gaskin (b); Bobby Donaldson (d). 9/60.*

Mildred Anderson's music lives where blues meets jazz-tinged ballads; she cited Ella Fitzgerald, Al Hibbler and Dinah Washington as influences, but is a lesser talent than any of them. On *Person To Person* her pitch is sometimes uncertain and her interpretations are anonymous, neither sweet enough for ballads nor salty enough for blues. The session seems to have been done quickly and without much rehearsal; the balance of the instruments is strange, with the musicians sounding as if they are playing behind closed doors, which are abruptly opened for solos. Shirley Scott is clearly unhappy, and does little more than comp, her tone sometimes recalling a roller-skating rink, sometimes a funeral home. Eddie 'Lockjaw' Davis does what he can, pulling a fine Coleman Hawkinsish solo out of thin air on 'I'm Free', but he too sounds ill at ease much of the time.

No More In Life is somewhat more successful; the programme is more blues-oriented, and both Anderson and her musicians sound much more comfortable, and better rehearsed. The album is nevertheless uneven; the title track is a version of the slow ballad that was Anderson's big hit, but her pitch and dynamics are erratic, as they are on Nat King Cole's 'I'm Lost'. Even the blues sometimes gives her trouble; an authoritative, sparky reading of 'I Ain't Mad At You' contrasts with a 'Roll 'Em Pete' where nobody has a clue how to make it jump. Oddly, given that Anderson can have problems even with harmonically straightforward material, 'That Ole Devil Called Love', an audacious attempt at Billie Holiday's style, is quite appealing, and provokes lively solos from Sears and Westbrook. Overall, however, *No More In Life*'s chief merit is that it's not as inessential as *Person To Person*. CS

Pink Anderson (1900–1974)
VOCAL, GUITAR

Spartanburg, South Carolina, was Pinkney Anderson's home, but he spent many years on the road with medicine shows. He learned most of his guitar skills from Simmie Dooley (1881–1961), and they recorded four titles together in 1928. In 1957, heart trouble curtailed Pink's travelling; instead he sang on the streets of Spartanburg, gambled, sold bootleg booze and rented his bedroom by the hour. He suffered a stroke in the '60s, but eventually recovered much of his playing ability, and in 1973 was briefly brought out of musical retirement by Roy Book Binder.

*** **Gospel, Blues And Street Songs**
Original Blues Classics OBCCD 524 *Anderson; Jumbo Lewis (wb). 5/50.*

The 1928 titles have been variously anthologized; they are conveniently together on *Sinners And Saints* (Document DOCD-5106). The ballads and 'coon songs' on *Gospel, Blues And Street Songs* were recorded in Charlottesville, Virginia, where Pink was performing with a fair, and valuably catch him when he was still an active medicine-show performer. His gritty, full-throated delivery is calculated to grab and hold the rubes' attention, and there's a welcome absence of subtlety, although Jumbo Lewis's washboard, added for one number, is all too appropriately lumbering. All seven songs on this disc were remade in 1961, but these earlier versions have more vigour and showmanship. The rest of the CD is by Rev. Gary Davis.

*** **Vol. 1 Carolina Blues Man**
Original Blues Classics OBCCD 504 *Anderson. 4/61.*

Pink Anderson thought of himself as an entertainer, rather than a blues singer, and learned most of his blues after meeting Baby Tate in 1954, but this is a session of quietly satisfying melancholy, with guitar work that is unobtrusively responsive to lyrics and mood. His voice is less forthright than it had been in 1950, but by the same token is well suited to the material. The sensation is of eavesdropping on a man singing for his own comfort and pleasure, with only the concluding 'Everyday In The Week' shifting into boastfulness – although, if reports of Pink's way with women are accurate, it doesn't exaggerate much.

*** **Vol. 2 Medicine Show Man**
Original Blues Classics OBCCD 587 *Anderson. 61.*

The best of Anderson's 1961 recordings, this album was made in New York, and he seems both energized by the trip north and relaxed by the familiarity of his street and medicine-show repertoire. Ray Charles's 'I Got A Woman', and 'South Forest Boogie', named after Pink's address in Spartanburg, were recent additions to the playlist, but they sit comfortably alongside the venerable likes of 'Chicken' and 'In The Jailhouse Now'. The racial self-satire in these and other songs is entirely neutralized by the gusto of their delivery. Pink was never a guitar virtuoso, and 'That's No Way To Do', his version of Willie Walker's masterpiece, 'South Carolina Rag', is not hiccup-free, but it is surprisingly successful.

** **The Blues Of Pink Anderson: Ballad And Folksinger Vol. 3**
Original Blues Classics OBCCD 577 *Anderson. 8/61.*

The notes report that 'Pink thought about it for several weeks' when asked if he would record a session of ballads, and the results are generally disappointing. 'Sugar Babe' and 'In The Evening' are blues, from records by Roosevelt Sykes and Leroy Carr respectively; without them, and a colourless account of the spiritual 'I Will Fly Away', LP length would not have been attained. 'Titanic' and 'Boweevil' are spirited enough, but it's all too obvious that Anderson hadn't played 'John Henry' or 'Betty And Dupree' for years. Pink is the only African-American known to have performed 'The Kaiser', presumably learned from one of several recordings by white country singers, but this track's documentary importance does not compensate for the general shortage of inspiration and energy. CS

Little Pink Anderson (born 1954)
VOCAL, GUITAR

By 1962, when Alvin Anderson sang 'Cottonfields' on the LP Blues/Music From The Film By Samuel Charters *(Asch 101), he'd appeared with his father, Pink Anderson, on Chief Thundercloud's medicine show and was carrying a pistol while working for Pink's bootlegging business. Anderson insists that his unorthodox childhood was not responsible for the addiction and criminality which are now firmly behind him. He played electric guitar as a teenager and in prison, but since leaving the penitentiary for the last time in 1996 he has become an exponent of his father's songs and style.*

*** Carolina Bluesman
Music Maker MMCD 24 *Anderson; Cool John Ferguson (g).* 02?

Most of Little Pink's blues and minstrel songs come from his father, some of them plainly via LPs made in the '60s. The guitar parts are played with fidelity and flair, Ferguson adding decoration that's always well thought-out, if occasionally superfluous. Some listeners may be disconcerted by a 21st-century African-American singing songs about chicken-stealing, crap-shooting and other stereotypes (some of them necessarily euphemized; voting is now 'them other folks' business', rather than 'them white folks' business'). In their day, these songs carried multiple and ironic meanings; it's no bad thing to be reminded of the history they embody, and few musicians are better equipped or more entitled to preserve them than Little Pink. He sometimes compromises with contemporary blues aesthetics by being arbitrarily dramatic on songs that were created as light-hearted entertainment, which is a pity; the more so since 'See That My Grave Is Kept Clean' and 'St. James Infirmary' indicate that when the lyrics do call for intensity, he can supply it with skill and sensitivity. CS

Little Willie Anderson (1920–91)
VOCAL, HARMONICA

Little Walter's friend, chauffeur, valet and occasional stand-in on club dates, but no mere copyist.

**** Swinging The Blues
Earwig CD 4930 *Anderson; Pete Haskin (as); Jimmie Lee Robinson (g, b); Robert Jr Lockwood, Sammy Lawhorn (g); Willie Black (b); Fred Below (d).* 7/79.

Anderson seizes his chance to record with gusto, and the stellar lineup of Chicago session veterans assembled to back him are equally enthused by what the booklet notes accurately call 'the nearest thing to a good [Little] Walter session since Walter's untimely decline'. It's obvious from the first bars that his late friend's playing is Anderson's wellspring, but he was an energetic and creative musician within his chosen style; the playlist includes only one Walter Jacobs composition, although 'Late Night' pastiches Walter's nocturnal mood music so effectively that it might as well be by him. Whether playing lead or rhythm, the guitarists share an exploratory, jazz-inflected approach to harmony and pulse, and are much encouraged in the latter aspect by Fred Below. It's thus paradoxical that 'Lester Leaps In' is more surprising in prospect than in execution, with Haskin (present only for this track) alone finding much opportunity for adventure. To say that this is the least successful of the four instrumentals is not to imply failure, however. Elsewhere, Anderson's appealingly raw voice is always effectively deployed, and is at its best on an in-the-alley reworking of 'West Side Baby'. CS

Ben Andrews (born 1961)
VOCAL, GUITAR

Born in the former Yugoslavia, Andrews was adopted by an American diplomatic family and grew up in the US. He ran away from school at 14 to play with Sonny Terry & Brownie McGhee, and he has also worked with other older musicians, especially Bo Diddley. Presently based in Maryland, he is building a following, through tours and festival appearances, in Holland, Belgium and Britain.

*** Stones In My Passway
Railway RR 002 *Andrews.* spring 99.
*** Journey
Powerhouse PR 9902 *Andrews; West Weston (h); Geoff Shaw (b).* 7/99.
**(*) Gallows Pole
Powerhouse PR 0104 *Andrews; West Weston (h, o); Roger Hubbard (md, g); Richard Studholme (md, b); Mike Thorne (d).* 00.
*** Preachin' The Blues
Mapleshade 56962 *Andrews; Mark Wenner (h); Larry Willis (p); Jeff Sarli (b).* 00.
*** The Blue Riders Ride Again
Railway RR 004 *As above.* 00.

Regular revisits to certain repertoires reveal Andrews's favourite artists: songs from Robert Johnson and Mississippi John Hurt appear on all of his CDs and Leadbelly, Blind Willie McTell and John Lee Hooker recur. It takes a musician of some skill to handle, as Andrews does on *Stones In My Passway*, the angularity of Johnson's title track, the fluidity of Hurt's 'Monday Morning Blues' or Pink Anderson's 'Travellin' Man', and the buck-dancing slide guitar melody of Oscar Woods's 'Don't Sell It, Don't Give It Away'. The different qualities of the original artists are commemorated rather than replicated in Andrews's arrangements, with their confident playing and appealingly husky singing. The same virtues are displayed on *Journey*, a largely solo set with three trio tracks. 'Phonograph Blues' is a neat segue of ideas from Robert Johnson via William Brown's 'Mississippi Blues' to Robert Lockwood.

Gallows Pole is a little different, five of its 12 tracks having four- or five-piece lineups that fetch Andrews from rural Mississippi or Georgia towards, say, Chicago. Hooker's 'Mad With You Baby', on which the aptly stuttering guitar is framed by Hammond organ, bass and drums, is the most successful of these; the group setting doesn't do a great deal for Johnson's 'Last Fair Deal Gone Down' or Gary Davis's 'Death Have No Mercy'. The solo tracks include strong versions of Hurt's 'Stagolee' and McTell's 'Broke Down Engine' and an 11-minute reading of the title song which owes little to Leadbelly but has some of the absorbed intensity of Kelly Joe Phelps.

Most of *Preachin' The Blues* is by the trio of Andrews, Wenner and Sarli, a strongly swinging skiffle ensemble that does well by raggy tunes like 'Salty Dog' and 'Diddy Wa Diddy' and improves on the *Gallows Pole* version of 'Last Fair Deal Gone Down', one of several songs this CD shares with that one. *The Blue Riders Ride Again* is essentially the same record in its UK issue. TR

Jake Andrews (born 1981)
VOCAL, GUITAR

Andrews made his name in Austin, Texas, coming up fast in the wake of guitarists like Stevie Ray and Jimmie Vaughan. The son of a rock guitarist (John 'Toad' Andrews of Mother Earth), he began playing young but quickly earned the approval of Albert Collins and others.

** Time To Burn
[Jericho CHO CD 601] Andrews; Darrell Leonard (t); Jon Blondell (tb, b); Joe Sublett (s); Tommy Eyre (kb); Doug Sahm, Jon Cleary (p); Mike Sconce (b, v); Tommy Taylor (d, v); John Porter (prod). 99.

* Jake Andrews
TMG/Antones TMG-ANT 0056 Andrews; Gary Slechta (t); John Mills (s); Riley Osbourn (o, p); Mike Sconce (b, v); David Robinson (d). 01.

The title song's flaming guitar line and boastful chorus, 'I've got time – time to burn', make a dramatic opening for Andrews's debut album, and the excitement is maintained on tracks like 'Just You And Me', 'Nobody's Fault But Mine' and 'Moment To Love' – not by his singing, which has little colour or blues character, but by incendiary playing. The mostly original material is mundane but allows Andrews to work in a variety of forms from the martial Bo Diddley rhythm of 'I Don't Wanna Go Home' to the swamp pop of 'I'm Glad For Your Sake' and the laidback jazz groove of 'Lover To Cry'.

Time To Burn undeniably showed promise, but of what? Anyone hoping that Andrews would lean in more of a blues direction on his next record would have found the Antones disc a great disappointment. It consists almost entirely of songs by Andrews which no one would give time to except their composer: melodically unmemorable and incoherent even when they are intelligible, they make one yearn for the firmer producer's hand that was laid on *Time To Burn*. But since, apart from Rudy Toombs's 'Takin' Care Of Business', the material has almost no point of contact with the central theme of this book, the view from Bluesville is of a musician moving rapidly out of town. TR

Fernest Arceneaux (born 1940)
VOCAL, ACCORDION

From Carencro, near Lafayette, Louisiana, Arceneaux learned accordion as a boy. He played in rock 'n' roll and R&B bands before focusing on zydeco. His band Fernest & The Thunders visited Europe several times in the '70s and '80s.

Arceneaux recorded albums for Blues Unlimited and Ornament in the '70s. Some of this material was reissued on *Rockin' Pneumonia* (Chrisly CD 30009) and *Gumbo Special* (Chrisly CD 40006), which appear to be unavailable.

** Zydeco Stomp
JSP JSPCD 258 Arceneaux; Victor Walker (p, b, v); Chester Chevalier (g); Clarence 'Jockey' Etienne (d). 7/81.

Cookie & The Cupcakes' swamp-pop 'Got You On My Mind', the accordion two-step 'Bernadette', the doleful blues 'I Can't Live Happy' … after five tracks the listener has a fair idea of the band's range, and will not be surprised by any of the remaining 13. The zydeco content is increased with a waltz-time 'Back To Louisiana' and a couple of other pieces, but the second half of the album is largely composed of R&B songs and blues. Chevalier, who plays in the manner of Lightnin' Slim on 'I Can't Live Happy', shifts into B. B. King gear for 'Sweet Little Angel' and 'Mean Woman'. Walker's bass guitar is hugely over-recorded throughout.

*** Zydeco Blues Party
Mardi Gras MG 1019 Arceneaux; John Hart (s); Paul 'Lil' Buck' Senegal [Sinegal] (g); Alonzo Johnson Jr (b); Joseph Edwards (d); Dalton 'Del' Arceneaux, Rockin' Dopsie Jr (rb). 94.

**(*) Old School Zydeco
Mardi Gras MG 1051 Arceneaux; Jerry Jumonville (s); Paul 'Lil' Buck' Senegal [Sinegal] (g); Alonzo Johnson (b); Joseph Edwards (d, rb). 6/00.

Whatever you expect from a zydeco band, Arceneaux is ready to serve it, from blues and New Orleans R&B to zydeco jump-up tunes and Cajun waltzes, but it's variety as you find it in a Shoney's salad bar: plenteous, eye-catching, rather bland. Both these albums are about one-third blues/R&B and two thirds zydeco/Cajun. *Zydeco Blues Party* is the livelier, drawing energy from the fusion of zydeco and – could it be? – King Sunny Adé in 'Zydeco Boogaloo', and from the use, in 'Bernadette', of a rhythmic figure so well known that they could have retitled the song 'Eh, Beau Diddlé'. *Old School Zydeco* similarly and rather deceptively opens with a long slow blues featuring Sinegal, and later produces another, 'So Long (I Hate To See You Go)', daringly credited to Arceneaux: it is, of course, Lowell Fulson's 'Reconsider Baby'. The zydecajun tunes are old-school enough, being drawn from Clifton Chenier, John Delafose and tradition, and the band is utterly solid, but Arceneaux fails to match his models in either the invention or the character of his playing. TR

Alphonse 'Bois Sec' Ardoin (born 1916)
VOCAL, ACCORDION

Alphonse Ardoin got his start in music playing 'tit fer (triangle) at dances for his cousin Amédé Ardoin. He worked with Canray Fontenot for many years until Fontenot's death in 1995. Bois Sec ('dry wood', from a childhood talent for getting out of the rain!) is the patriarch of a musical family: several of his sons are keeping the older styles alive, although sadly Gustav was killed in a road accident in 1974, and his grandsons Chris and Sean lead their own nouveau zydeco bands.

**** La Musique Creole
Arhoolie CD 445 Ardoin; Gustav Ardoin (ac, b, v); Canray Fontenot (vn, v); Morris Ardoin (g, v); Lawrence Ardoin (d); Isom Fontenot, Revon Reed (tri). 7/66, 5/71, 4/73.

Bois Sec Ardoin plays the 'French music' that predated zydeco, but was an important component of it. Race relations in francophone Louisiana have historically been as uneasy as in the rest of the USA, but if Cajuns and Creoles seldom socialized as equals, their music had many elements – language, instruments, repertoire, dance tempos and aesthetics – in common. Nevertheless, the swirling bluesiness of Ardoin's singing and playing are unmistakably African-American, even on waltzes, and even on *La Musique Creole*'s two versions of the last number played at French dances, 'Va-T-En', a.k.a. 'Home Sweet Home'.

In 1948, Bois Sec and Canray's first band, the Duralde Ramblers, included rhythm guitar and drums, but on the evidence of this CD's first 16 tracks, recorded on the way home from the Newport Folk Festival, that was quite unnecessary. With the modest but essential help of the triangle, and their own stomping feet, the duo function perfectly well as their own rhythm section. Ardoin's accordion is a single-action instrument, on which press and draw strokes produce a different note from the same button; this encourages rhythmic, riff-based playing, admirably complemented by Fontenot's keening fiddle lines.

The remaining nine titles were recorded in the early '70s, with three of Bois Sec's sons supplying accompaniment. The ambience is slightly more modern, but the younger generation are usually restrained, which makes the drumming on 'Ardoin Two-Step' – a paradoxical blend of strict tempo with zydeco energy – the more surprising. The numbers that diverge most from the old ways have vocals by Morris Ardoin. 'Le Boss', an improvised talking blues with a rockabilly tinge, was inspired by his failure to get a pay rise the same day. 'Jupe Courte' leans towards the sweetness of swamp pop, but Canray Fontenot's raspy fiddle puts the roughness back in. Bois Sec appears on neither of these excellent tracks; it may be relevant that he vetoed Gustav's attempts to sing like Cajun pop star Belton Richard.

The life of black farmhands and sharecroppers in rural Louisiana was not easy, as Bois Sec and Canray both knew at first hand. Especially before the advent of the mass media, social and dance music were a vital respite from the daily grind, and important elements in the efforts of individuals, families and communities to define and sustain themselves. These recordings catch two of Creole music's finest at their fiercely joyful peak.

(*) Allons Danser
Rounder CD 6081 *Ardoin; Dirk Powell (vn, b, tri, v); Kevin Wimmer (vn); Christine Balfa (g, tri, v); Steve Riley (d); Mitchell Reed (tri). 7/94, 6/97.*

In his ninth decade, Bois Sec Ardoin's voice wavers a little, and he sometimes has to strain for the high notes, but his singing is still authoritative, and his accordion playing as vigorous as ever. Except on the final track, a brief live recording, he's accompanied by Balfa Toujours, led by the daughter of one of Cajun music's greatest fiddlers, the late Dewey Balfa. Unfortunately, the marketing advantage conferred by the Balfa name is not matched by musical talent; the bass and guitar playing are stodgy, and when Dirk Powell switches to fiddle, he doesn't rise above generic. Kevin Wimmer is a better fiddler than Powell but not a front-rank player, and as singers Balfa and Powell are nothing out of the ordinary. 'Duralde Ramble' and 'Le Fond De Culottes' work up a considerable head of steam, thanks largely to Steve Riley, moonlighting from both the Mamou Playboys and his usual accordion, but too much of *Allons Danser* is second-rate Cajun music on which Bois Sec Ardoin happens to be present. CS

Amédé Ardoin (1898–1941?)
VOCAL, ACCORDION

Although not quite the first musician to record it, Ardoin was the leading exponent of African-American Louisiana French music in the '20s and '30s, and hugely influential upon other musicians of the region, both black and white. A popular player at house dances, while returning home from an evening's work he was the victim of a racist attack from which he never fully recovered, and his last years were spent in an asylum. His musical legacy has been shared by, among others, the white singer and accordionist Iry LeJeune and his own cousin Alphonse 'Bois Sec' Ardoin.

**** Prends Donc Courage: Early Black & White Cajun (Swamp Music Vol. VI)
Trikont US-0202 *Ardoin; Dennis McGee (vn). 12/29–12/34.*

**** I'm Never Comin' Back: The Roots Of Zydeco
Arhoolie/Folklyric 7007 *Ardoin; Dennis McGee (vn). 11/30–12/34.*

The deepest impression left by Ardoin's music is of a spirit near the end of its tether. In broken phrases he gasps out stories of rejection and recrimination, of love inhibited by hostile parents, of a world of trouble in which the singer wanders, orphaned, disenfranchised and, in a phrase that recurs in virtually every song, '*tout seul*' – all alone. Most of his tunes are in the typical South Louisiana dance forms of the waltz, one-step and two-step; only a few are called blues, and none, formally speaking, is one, yet all are suffused with blues feeling, which the insistent rhythms of his accordion, with a strange ambiguity, both accentuate and parry.

Ardoin recorded on four occasions, on all but the last accompanied by the fiddler Dennis McGee. It's only at the first (1929) session that McGee takes a joint melodic role, and these six tunes, heard both on the Trikont CD and on the VAC *Cajun Dance Party: Fais Do-Do* (Columbia CK 46784), are superb examples of the Cajun fiddle–accordion duet at its most tempestuous. The other sessions with McGee find the fiddling reduced to an almost purely rhythmic function, and Ardoin's last studio date was on his own. All 26 of these 1930–34 recordings are on the Arhoolie-Folklyric CD, which is enhanced by a thick booklet of biography and song transcriptions; the Trikont selects eight of them, its 14 tracks of Ardoin complementing 11 by the contemporary Cajun singer Cleoma Falcon. TR

Chris Ardoin (born 1981)
VOCAL, ACCORDION, ORGAN, GUITAR, BASS, DRUMS, RUBBOARD

Son of Lawrence 'Black' Ardoin and grandson of Bois Sec, Chris Ardoin first played accordion in public aged four; at nine he appeared at Carnegie Hall with his grandfather, and a year later recorded with his father's band.

*** That's Da Lick!
Maison de Soul MdS 1051 *Ardoin; Herman Guidry (g); Sean Ardoin (d, rb, v); Erica Ardoin, Quincy Alex (rb, v). 94?*

On *That's Da Lick!* Chris Ardoin and Double Clutchin' strike a happy balance between *nouveau zydeco* and the family's roots. Tributes to the late Gustav 'Bud' Ardoin and Clifton Chenier are sung in French, as is 'Good Man (Bon Homme)', which adapts the venerable "Tit Mom". The closing 'Load 'Em Up' combines double-kick drumming and earthy bass licks with a mellow accordion line that could have been recorded 40 years earlier. Both bass and accordion are played by 13-year-old Chris, and older brother Sean takes all the lead vocals; he's notably soulful on 'Don't Shake That Tree', which also features an intricate solo by Guidry. *Lick It Up!* (Maison de Soul MdS 1058) appeared a year later, but is only available on cassette.

*** Gon' Be Jus' Fine
Rounder CD 2127 *Ardoin; Derek 'Dee' Greenwood (g, b, v); Gabriel 'Pandy' Perrodin Jr (g, v); Sean Ardoin (d, v); Tammy Ledet (rb). 97?*

*** Turn The Page
Rounder CD 2157 *Ardoin; Bobby Broussard, Nathaniel Fontenot (g); Derek 'Dee' Greenwood (b); Sean Ardoin (d, v); Tammy Ledet (rb). 98?*

***(*) Best Kept Secret
Rounder CD 2162 *Ardoin; Nat Fontenot (g); Curley Chapman (b, rb, v); Dexter Ardoin (d); Charles Elam III (v). 1/00.*

Between the second and third Rounder CDs, Sean Ardoin split to form his own band (see his entry). The brothers are adamant that 'musical differences' is not a euphemism for sibling strife, but those differences may explain why the only development on the first two Rounder discs is towards loudness. 'We Are The Boys (Special Bad Boys Dance Remix)' on *Gon' Be Jus' Fine* is the zenith of that process, with wah-wah everything and a guitar solo whose tone seems modelled on Hendrix's 'Star Spangled Banner'. Listeners who don't hate this will agree that it's the best thing on the CD. The best thing on *Turn The Page* is a heartfelt version of the traditional 'Barres De La Prison'; between those extremes the band is an efficient dance machine, and its leader a masterly accordionist, but the sense of personal expression and adventure is missing.

Best Kept Secret remedies those deficits handsomely. In an almost completely reconstituted Double Clutchin', Chapman's subterranean bass stands out – as it's meant to; Ardoin's enthusiasm for low-frequency throb extends to playing second bass on 'Papa Was A Rollin' Stone'. (He also plays lead and rhythm guitars, and most of the rubboard.) Ardoin has matured into a strong songwriter, a powerful singer and an imaginative arranger; seismic bass and double-kick percussion transform John Delafose's 'I Don't Want Nobody Here But You' into a very surprising *nouveau* landmark. It seems impossible to confer distinction on Sheryl Crow's 'If It Makes You Happy', though.

*** Life
J&S JS 6106 *Ardoin; Nat Fontenot, Jay Doucet (g); Wayne Singleton (b); Eric Minix (d, v); Harold Guillory (rb, v). 02.*

*** Save The Last Dance
J&S JS 6110 *As above, except add Keith Clement (kb), Curley Chapman (b), John Belton (rb); omit Singleton, Minix (v), Guillory (v). 03.*

On *Life*, Nat Fontenot is again the only survivor from the previous CD, but Wayne Singleton is as inventive as his predecessor, and Eric Minix gives the double-kick beat a clipped friskiness by distributing it among bass drum, cowbell and side drum. Ardoin's accordion playing continues to be varied and imaginative – hear, for instance, the Tex-Mex ornaments and sonorities on 'Pass Me By' – and 'Call Me' features confident use, rather than the customary overuse, of a phase shifter on the vocals. The obligatory oldie (this time it's the waltz 'La Robe Barrée') begins to seem like tokenism, and in general *Life* isn't as compelling as *Best Kept Secret*; but for a 21-year old it's pretty remarkable.

Save The Last Dance keeps up the good work, although Minix's drumming is less adventurous, and Chapman's return doesn't often result in the expected earth tremors. The CD is a mostly likeable set of dance tunes, from two-steps to the do-your-own-thing of *nouveau zydeco*; on the downside are the unattractive quacking tone that Ardoin uses to mark the downbeat on 'Lonely Waltz', and the constipated funk rhythms of 'Master Key'. The most striking aspect of this CD, though, is the singing: Ardoin overdubs all the backing vocals, and the results are soulful, robust and remarkably spontaneous-sounding. A revival of Sam Cooke's 'Change Gone Come' [*sic*] doesn't match the original, but it comes very close.

**(*) Sweat
[unnumbered] *Ardoin; Nat Fontenot, Wayne Singleton (g); Curley Chapman (b); Brad Chambers (d); Will Scypion, Greg Guidry (rb, v); Harold Guillory (v). 04.*

Sweat, issued through <www.chrisardoin.com>, Ardoin's website, is fairly easily procurable. Ardoin wrote everything except a snippet of R. Kelly's 'Down Low', and is also arranger, engineer and producer. The band is now 'Chris Ardoin and NuStep', and their music is often more like contemporary R&B with an accordion than zydeco, old or *nouveau*, as commonly understood. There's nothing new about outside and mainstream sounds influencing zydeco, but the riffs Ardoin supplies for NuStep, and the lyrics he writes for himself, are often jejune; there's also too much phase shifting of the guitar, and it's fortunate that Ardoin's cheesy organ playing is only heard once. The old-school accordion and guitar on 'No Love Waltz', and the accordion-only blues 'Bury Me', are simply beautiful, though, and at 23 Ardoin has time to make the occasional comparative clunker. CS

Lawrence 'Black' Ardoin (born 1946)
VOCAL, ACCORDION

One of the sons of Alphonse 'Bois Sec' Ardoin, Lawrence initially played drums in the family band. When Bois Sec retired from dance playing in 1975 and his older son Gustav, who would have taken over his role, was killed in an accident, Lawrence took up the accordion and fronted the band for a decade or so. Since making Tradition Creole *he has been chiefly occupied in managing the career of his son Chris.*

*** Tradition Creole
Arhoolie CD 9012 *Ardoin; Sean Ardoin (s); Edward Poullard (vn); Dallas DeVille, Clarence Le Day (g); Joseph Landry (b); Donald Ray Ceasar (d); Alfred Pete (rb). 5/84.*

This is a thoroughly enjoyable album of Louisiana Creole dance music. The material, well chosen and sequenced, embraces old tunes such as 'I've Been There' – a version of the Creole standard 'Les Flammes D'Enfer' – and Amédé Ardoin's 'Midland Two Step', more recent numbers like the swamp-pop hit 'Matilda' or Clifton Chenier's 'Ay, Ai, Ai', and a sprinkling of waltzes and blues. Ardoin's voice tends to waver a little but his accordion playing is solid, and the ensembles are constantly energized by the interplay of drums and rubboard, by DeVille's decorative lead guitar lines, and, best of all, by Poullard's fiddling, indefatigably lithe and bluesy throughout. TR

Sean Ardoin (born 1969)
VOCAL, ACCORDION, DRUMS, RUBBOARD

Sean Ardoin was drumming at five, and playing accordion at 11; he was a member of his brother Chris's band until going out on his own in 1999.

*** Sean Ardoin And Zydekool
Zydekool ZK 1911–1 *Ardoin; Chris Ardoin (ac, g); Mark Whitfield*

(g, rhythm tracks); Tony Ardoin (g); Derek Greenwood (b, v); Scooby Worthy (d); Harold Guillory (rb); Sean Ardoin II (sp). 99.
*** **Pullin'**
Tomorrow TMR 70005 *Ardoin; Chuck Bush, Henry 'Trip' Wamsley (g, b, v); Raymond Williams (g, v); Drew Donaldson (g); Walter 'Bully' Judge (rb); Vanessa Ardoin (v). 01?*
***(*) **Home Brew**
Tomorrow TMR 70007 *Ardoin; Chuck Bush (g, b); Poppee Donatto (rb). 2/03.*
*** **Strictly For The Dancers**
Zydekool ZK 91102 *Ardoin; Chris Ardoin (g, b, rb, d); Trey Ardoin (g, v); 'Alex' (v). 04.*

Pullin' was issued to a good deal of acclaim, but its relentless high energy becomes wearing. The eponymous debut CD is a better vehicle for Ardoin's soulful singing and although the treacly acoustic guitar ballad 'You Complete Me' is a horrible mistake, it's the exception in a more varied set of songs, executed with a lighter touch and more humour. *Home Brew* is equally varied, and its stripped-down lineup makes the excellence of Ardoin's drumming very apparent. 'Fumba Laka Chumba' peddles some very odd stereotypes of West Indians, and 'Down In Louisiana' is trivial, but they're outweighed by the startling zydeco gospel song 'I'm Still Here', Bush's flawless guitar on the title track and the joyfully back-to-1920 accordion solo 'Back Porch'. Throw in a couple of fine soul ballads, the vivacious two-step 'Around The World', and the successful exploitation of rap and rock guitar on 'Kemo Sabe', and this is one of *nouveau zydeco*'s more interesting CDs.

If *Pullin'* has too much voom for its own good, *Strictly For The Dancers* goes the other way; after a noisy postmodern come-all-ye, the emphasis is on surprisingly mellow lovesongs, occasionally interrupted by barked commands to 'Get your hands up!' or just 'Bounce!' Chris Ardoin's bass is snakily inventive, but it serves a series of mostly unmemorable, auto-extruding tunes. The twinkling, quasi-Zairean lead guitar on 'In Your Eyes' is terrific, and 'Don't Leave Me' is a happy blend of old and *nouveau*, but a zydeco version of Outkast's 'Hey Ya' doesn't work at all. CS

Howard Armstrong (1909–2003)
VOCAL, VIOLIN, MANDOLIN, GUITAR

Armstrong grew up in east Tennessee, where there were few African-Americans, and from childhood his music always crossed otherwise rigid colour lines. With Ted Bogan and Carl Martin he formed a stringband in the early '30s, by which time Armstrong had been nicknamed 'Louie Bluie' by a drunken partygoer. The stringband migrated to Chicago, but its members had gone their separate ways by the end of the decade. Reunited in the '70s, Martin, Bogan & Armstrong (see Carl Martin's entry) were as good and eclectic as ever. Armstrong, the last surviving member, was still performing occasionally in his tenth decade. His multi-instrumental skill was but one facet of an extraordinary man who was also a polyglot, a gifted painter, a jeweller and an urbane raconteur.

Armstrong's two 1930 recordings on fiddle with the Tennessee Chocolate Drops can be heard on *Carl Martin/Willie '61* Blackwell (Document DOCD-5229); on the same CD he also plays violin and mandolin on either side of a 1934 disc, with Ted Bogan on guitar.

(***) **Louie Bluie**
Arhoolie CD 470 *Armstrong; Willie Sievers, Mary Shepard (p); Yank Rachell (md, v); Banjo Ikey Robinson (bj, v); Ted Bogan (g, v); Roland Martin, Bob Coxe (g); Carl Martin, Tom Armstrong (b); Elsie Loweroy (v). 4/30–84.*
**** **Louie Bluie**
Blue Suit BS-106D *Armstrong; John Rockwood (h); Ray Kamalay (g, v); Ralph Armstrong (b). 95.*

Arhoolie's *Louie Bluie* is the soundtrack of Terry Zwigoff's eponymous documentary, arbitrarily expanded to CD length with three vintage recordings by Sleepy John Estes and Yank Rachell, on which Armstrong does not appear. There are many delights here, including three of the '30s titles and Ikey Robinson's gleeful, pornographic rewrite of 'Darktown Strutters' Ball'. Armstrong and his associates' eclecticism is well portrayed; they range from white country music to sentimental pop to instrumental display, and Ted Bogan sings two songs which Howard taught him, in German and 'cottonfield Polish'. As with many soundtrack albums, however, the music's continuity suffers by being divorced from the visuals.

Arhoolie catch up with a bunch of senior citizens on a lads' night out, but Blue Suit's is a more cultivated exercise altogether. The programme is a similar mix of blues, ragtime, '20s pop and gospel, but this time it's played with a suave, jazzy sensibility. Armstrong shows off his masterful mandolin phrasing and an even more impressive fiddle technique, with much double and triple stopping and extended pizzicato passages. He skitters through some blues and pop hits, serenely observes that 'When He Calls Me I Will Answer', tells a few stories, and displays his linguistic skills with a chorus of 'Chinatown' in the appropriate language. Armstrong was 86 when this disc was recorded, but his inventiveness and energy would do credit to a man of 36. 'You can go too slow, but you can not go too fast,' he instructs his sidemen, before slamming into 'John Henry' like a downhome Paganini. CS

James Armstrong (born 1957)
VOCAL, GUITAR

The son of musicians, Armstrong grew up in southern California. As a young guitarist he was influenced by Jimi Hendrix, and later he gained experience by backing blues artists visiting LA, such as Albert Collins and Big Joe Turner. He developed his songwriting during a residency at Mr B's, a club in Santa Monica.

*** **Sleeping With A Stranger**
Hightone HCD 8068 *Armstrong; Jimi Stewart (o, p); Leroy Ball (b); Quentin Dennard (d); Bruce Bromberg (prod). 10/95.*
*** **Dark Night**
Hightone HCD 8096 *Armstrong; Kenny Baker (ts); Parris Bertolucci (o, p); Michael Ross, Joe Louis Walker, Doug MacLeod (g); Eric Hayslett (b, perc, v); Ian Hoffman (d, perc); Bruce Bromberg (co-prod). 10/98.*
*** **Got It Goin' On**
Hightone HCD 8126 *Armstrong; Mike Emerson (o, p); Jimmy Pugh (p); Michael Ross (g); Robert Watson, Endre Tarczy (b); Stanley Hale, David Tucker (d); Bruce Bromberg (prod). 9/00.*

Like Robert Cray, also originally a Hightone artist, Armstrong began his recording career as a man with no history: his blues start here, with not even a drifting echo of his forerunners. The world of *Sleeping With A Stranger* is one of shadows and night thoughts, a landscape of defeat ('Hard, Hard Blues') and insomnia ('Midnight Again') that he delineates in a weary, dried-out voice. He occasionally prompts comparisons with Joe Louis Walker, particularly in 'The Devil's Livin' There', a portrait of LA that shares the dystopian vision of Walker's 'City Of Angels'.

Walker makes a couple of guest appearances on *Dark Night*, as does Doug MacLeod, their relatively loquacious guitars valuably breaking up Armstrong's smooth but perhaps too even-tempered monologue. The making of this album was delayed by Armstrong's recovery from a shocking incident, when an intruder in his house knifed him in the left shoulder and threw one of his sons out of a window. Both recovered from their injuries, but on *Dark Night* Armstrong had to compensate for his left-hand stiffness by playing slide guitar.

Although he is fond of using blues and near-blues structures, Armstrong is not afraid of formal experiments or unusual subjects. 'Lil' James' on *Dark Night* is a tender song to his injured son, while 'Pennies And Picks' on *Got It Goin' On* is an ingenious musician-on-the-road number. The best track on *Got It Goin' On* is 'Shut My Eyes', its verses linked with an arresting guitar figure and bisected by a snarling slide solo, but elsewhere in this third album the listener may feel, and perhaps not for the first time, that Armstrong's music could use more decoration. He is an intelligent and subtle artist, but not always an emphatic one, and he might benefit if there were a little more going on in the production. As things stand, he always makes a worthy record, but can he be helped to make a great one? TR

Billy Boy Arnold (born 1935)
VOCAL, HARMONICA

No longer a youth but sounding ageless, William Arnold has had a fitful career since making his first records in the mid-'50s. Several of the songs he recorded for Vee-Jay, such as 'I Wish You Would', helped to ignite the British blues boom a decade later but subsequent sessions have been few. Visits to Europe during the '70s and '80s added to a small list that hasn't greatly expanded since. His early devotion to Sonny Boy Williamson I flavoured his harmonica skills but an equivalent stardom, even in the blues world, has eluded him. He remains a pleasant and dependable performer whose greatest achievements are most likely behind him.

Arnold's early sides 'I Wish You Would', 'I Was Fooled', 'I Ain't Got You' and 'Don't Stay Out All Night' are anthologized on *Vee-Jay Blues Volume 1* (Collectables COL-CD-7269) and *Volume 2* (COL-CD-7270). Others are on *Chicago Blues: The Vee-Jay Era* (Charly CDGR 145). All these CDs are of uncertain availability.

(*) Johnny Jones With Billy Boy Arnold
Alligator ALCD 4717 *Arnold; [Little] Johnny Jones (p, v). 6/63.*

Jones had been booked to appear at Chicago's Fickle Pickle coffeehouse and Arnold was an unscheduled guest, so the absence of rehearsal required each man to fall back on tried and tested repertoire. Arnold sings just five of the 13 tracks, relying upon Sonny Boy Williamson I's repertoire, as well as Mercy Dee Walton's 'One Room Country Shack'. Arnold is a less forceful performer than Jones, and his efforts are not helped by the poor quality of the original tapes, which had deteriorated during the 18 years before their release on LP. The mono sound was mixed in the headphones of recordist Norman Dayron, rendering Arnold's harmonica inaudible on Jones's tracks, but a better balance ensures that Arnold's 'Sloppy Drunk' and 'Early In The Morning' are the best performances here. By no means essential, this record's historical importance outweighs its technical shortcomings.

* Going To Chicago
Testament TCD 5018 *Arnold; Mickey Boss (ts); Mighty Joe Young, Jody Williams, Johnny Turner (g); Jerome Arnold, Robert Wilson (b); Clifton James, Mickey Conway (d). 6/66–8/77.*

Consisting of two 1966 sessions and one live performance from 1977, this is one of the few substandard releases on an otherwise reliable label. Arnold produced the first session, with Young, Williams, Jerome Arnold and James, but failed to capitalize on the talent at his disposal. After three nondescript songs, the session ends with transparent imitations of Chuck Berry and Lloyd Price. But these are better than the seven tracks recorded three months later without a drummer. Guitar and bass are lacklustre and Boss's tenor sounds like a drunken tugboat negotiating the Chicago river in thick fog. The final track, recorded at a Californian club, is equally desultory, with a catatonic band lending minimal support to Arnold as he strings together verses from 'Five Long Years', 'Stormy Monday' and 'Night Time Is The Right Time'. One to avoid.

**(*) Blowin' The Blues Away
[Blue Boar CDBB 1004] *Arnold; Tony McPhee (g); Alan Fish (b); Wilgur Campbell (d). 77.*

This material from the Red Lightnin' label has been reissued frequently (and this version may by now be unavailable). McPhee can be a thoughtful guitarist but too often he and his accomplices opt for a brisk canter through the signature riffs of Arnold's repertoire. Nor does his foot stray far from an effects pedal that distorts and confuses what he plays. Fish and Campbell abet his every move but have the merit of efficiency. Despite their evocation of lesser days gone by, these tracks are now old enough to warrant a certain regard. They may just be one of the better collaborations of their sort but posterity would have to be charitable to elevate them beyond their station.

**(*) Ten Million Dollars
Evidence ECD 26061 *Arnold; St James Bryant (p); Jimmy Johnson, John 'Mad Dog' Watkins (g); Larry Exum (b); Fred Grady (d). 12/84.*

This is one of the better French productions from this time but even so Arnold and the Jimmy Johnson band labour long to mine a nugget of no more than moderate value. The leader's voice, never strong, is rarely strained and his harmonica playing remains basic and functional. Johnson and Watkins alternate rhythm and lead, while Bryant steps up for the occasional solo. All play within themselves, counting the bars until Arnold's vocal returns. The title song is the best and longest track here, along with Sonny Boy Williamson II's 'Trust My Baby' and 'Last Night'. Other songs from Willie Dixon, Rosco Gordon and Guitar Slim were too familiar even then, as was yet another 'I Wish You Would'. A cut above remainder-bin fodder (just) but no forgotten masterpiece. NS

*** Consolidated Mojo
Electro-Fi 3392 *Arnold; Tom Mahon (p); Rusty Zinn (g); Ronnie James Weber (b); Mark Bohn (d); Mark Hummel (prod). 10/92.*

At the end of a tour with Mark Hummel's Blues Survivors, Arnold went into a studio with the band and briskly created a 14-track album which, for reasons the producer doesn't explain, remained unissued until 2005. It's less textured than the Alligator recording he made soon afterwards and even more rooted in his past, in that he remakes six of his ten Vee-Jay sides as well as Bo Diddley's 'I'm A Man', his first recording as a sideman. Sonny Boy Williamson I also receives his customary tribute in two tracks. Hummel describes Arnold's voice as 'just slightly tattered from the tour', which is a nice way of saying that he should have taken a few days' rest before the session, but his harp-blowing is undiminished. The band self-effacingly dedicates itself to reproducing the spirit, and often the letter, of Arnold's '50s recordings. TR

***(*) Back Where I Belong
Alligator ALCD 4815 *Arnold; Lester Butler, Hook Herrera, Randy Chortkoff (h); Andy Kaulkin, Rob Rio (p); Zach Zunis, Rick Holmstrom, Chris Faulk, Mike Flanagan (g); Tom Leavey, Willie Brinlee, Pete Cosey (b); Lee Smith, Jimi Bott (d). 93.*

His first new release for almost a decade found Arnold in California, backed by some of the state's leading Chicago-oriented musicians. Eight originals by him and the participating players fit seamlessly with rerecordings of three of his Vee-Jay songs plus Slim Harpo's 'Shake Your Hips', Sonny Boy Williamson I's 'Shake The Boogie' and Big Maceo's 'Worried Life Blues'. Arnold justifies the album title with sterling performances, allowing generous solo space for a trio of harmonica players. Zunis plays lead guitar throughout, exhibiting more taste and control than on his sessions with William Clarke. Both pianists put in strong idiomatic performances, soloing well when called upon to do so. The rhythm section's various combinations work well together, providing the sort of relaxed propulsion that Chicago-style blues requires. Without setting the world alight, this is perhaps Arnold's finest hour in the recording studio.

*** Eldorado Cadillac
Alligator ALCD 4836 *Arnold; David Zielinski (ts); Tony Zamagni (o); Carl 'Sonny' Leyland (p); Steady Rollin' Bob Margolin, James Wheeler (g); Steve 'Slash' Hunt (b); Chuck Cotton (d). 95.*

A return to Chicago consolidates the promise of Arnold's previous record without building upon it. An invigorating assault on 'I Ain't Got You' opens the album and promises much but, as entertaining as the following dozen tracks are, they fail to be as engaging as this. Apart from some profligate slide on 'Sunday Morning Blues', Margolin keeps himself severely in check and Wheeler is a competent but unexciting substitute. Leyland performs well throughout and is particularly impressive on Roosevelt Sykes's 'Sunny Road'. Zielinski appears on three tracks, failing to solo only on 'Man Of Considerable Taste' (to the tune of 'Hoochie Coochie Man'). Arnold's harmonica work is solid but uninspired and his vocals sound curiously restrained. Not so much an opportunity missed as one not fully realized.

*** Boogie 'N' Shuffle
Stony Plain SPCD 1266 *Arnold; Doug James, [Sax] Gordon Beadle (s); Matt McCabe (p); Duke Robillard (g); John Packer (b); Jeffery McAllister (d). 01.*

Arnold overcomes another inexplicable hiatus in his recording career with this relaxed and confident session produced by Robillard, who solos discreetly throughout. His band are seasoned professionals whose unforced musicianship makes a virtue of sparse arrangements. Arnold is in good voice and playing well if unspectacularly, in context with his accompanists. Half of the 12 tracks are his, the best of which are 'Greenville', describing an encounter with a determined woman on Nelson Street, and the opening 'Bad Luck Blues'. Six covers include Ray Charles's 'Blackjack', the best performance here, while 'Just Got To Know' and 'Every Night, Every Day' display Arnold's respect for the writing of Jimmy McCracklin. Less successful are Otis Blackwell's 'Home In Your Heart' and Leon Haywood's 'Just Your Fool', neither band nor singer adequately coping with such soul-oriented material. The album closes with a 17-minute interview sequence in which the artist talks about Sonny Boy Williamson I and his early days with Bo Diddley. A litle more music and a lot less chat might have been preferable. NS

Kokomo Arnold (1901–68)
VOCAL, GUITAR

Originally from rural north Georgia, James Arnold worked in various northern cities in his teens and early 20s, spent some time in the late '20s in Mississippi and cut his first recordings in 1930 in Memphis. He made his name as a Chicago-based recording artist between 1934 and '38. Never dependent on music for his living (he was said to be a bootlegger), he stopped recording after a dispute with his label and by the '50s had quit live performance too. When contacted by researchers in 1959 he was working as a janitor and had put music behind him.

*** Kokomo Arnold – Vol. 1 (1930–1935)
Document DOCD-5037 *Arnold. 5/30–3/35.*
*** Kokomo Arnold – Vol. 2 (1935–1936)
Document DOCD-5038 *Arnold; Roosevelt Sykes (p, v); unknown (p). 4/35–2/36.*
*** Kokomo Arnold – Vol. 3 (1936–1937)
Document DOCD-5039 *Arnold; Odell Rand (cl); Peetie Wheatstraw, Roosevelt Sykes, Albert Ammons, unknown (p); unknown (g); unknown (d); Alice Moore, Mary Johnson, Sam Theard (v). 5/36–3/37.*
*** Kokomo Arnold – Vol. 4 (1937–1938)
Document DOCD-5040 *Arnold; Peetie Wheatstraw, unknown (p); unknown (b). 3/37–5/38.*
***(*) Old Original Kokomo Blues
Wolf Blues Classics BC 001 *Arnold; Peetie Wheatstraw, unknowns (p); unknowns (b). 5/30–5/38.*
**** The Essential
Classic Blues CBL 200023 2CD *Arnold; Odell Rand (cl); Peetie Wheatstraw, Roosevelt Sykes (p, v); unknowns (p); unknown (g); unknown (d); Alice Moore, Mary Johnson, Sam Theard (v). 10/34–5/38.*
***(*) Original Kokomo Blues 1934–1938
EPM Blues Collection 15930 *Arnold; Peetie Wheatstraw (p, v); Alice Moore (v). 34–38.*

*** Bottleneck Guitar Trendsetters Of The 1930s
Yazoo 1049 *Arnold. 9/34–1/37.*

Embracing his 1930 Victor coupling and his first six sessions for Decca in 1934–35, Document's *Vol. 1* is the only album that presents Arnold purely as a solo artist, and it contains several of his most striking recordings. He played exclusively with a slide and in open tunings and could outdo most players of his time in the speed of both his fingerpicking and his slide handling, as may be heard on 'Paddlin' Madeline Blues', a bizarre reconstruction of the pop song 'Paddlin' Madeline Home', or 'The Twelves', a version of 'The Dirty Dozens'. Much of his work, however, was at the tempos, slow and medium respectively, of his doubly successful debut single for Decca, 'Milk Cow Blues' and 'Old Original Kokomo Blues', both of which became blues standards. Yet even at these cooler tempos he is always likely to throw in unexpected figures, double-time passages and other proofs of his disinclination to think like other guitarists. He has an unusual trick of singing the last phrase in a verse more loudly, perhaps by leaning in closer to the microphone. He also gives vent to impromptu-sounding comments or cries of self-encouragement, and frequently hums along with his guitar's responses. The total effect is thickly textured, eventful and highly idiosyncratic.

Vol. 2 is mostly in the same vein as its predecessor, but introduces a couple of exciting sides with an unknown pianist, 'Stop, Look And Listen' and 'Doin' The Doopidy', and two accompaniments to Roosevelt Sykes. The remaining volumes are largely split between solo recordings and duets with pianist Peetie Wheatstraw. Although Arnold often eased the burden of a busy recording schedule by redeploying tunes and guitar patterns he had already used, he offers some compensation to the modern listener, hearing him at CD length, in his language and the variety of his subject-matter, which, as well as narrative blues like 'Wild Water Blues' (*Vol. 3*) and 'Mean Old Twister' (*Vol. 4*), encompasses dance songs like 'Busy Bootin'' (*Vol. 2*), two pieces associated with Papa Charlie Jackson, 'Shake That Thing' and 'Salty Dog' (*Vol. 3*), or the stomp 'Set Down Gal' (*Vol. 4*).

All the Documents suffer from somewhat low volume and include several sides derived from poor originals. The selective compilations on Wolf and EPM sound somewhat better. Each has five of the above-mentioned songs, and there is as little to choose between them as the similarity of their titles may suggest. The Yazoo, split 50/50 with the contemporary but quite different slide stylist Casey Bill Weldon, would be excellent if all you wanted was seven well-picked songs by each artist. But the inexpensive 2CD on Classic Blues, which has decent sound, most of the namechecked titles and several examples of Arnold accompanying other singers, must be considered the best buy. TR

The Rocky Athas Group
GROUP

Guitarist Rocky Athas (born 1954) has been a notable runner in the Texan blues stable for many years. Growing up in the same neighbourhood as Stevie Ray Vaughan, he often played with him, and was also a close friend of Eric Johnson. During the '70s and '80s he was a driving force in the Texas-based nightclub band Lightning before moving on to join Black Oak Arkansas. The Rocky Athas Group was formed when the producer Jim Gaines advised Athas to put together a band as a vehicle for his playing. Vocalist Larry Samford (born 1949), also previously of Black Oak Arkansas, was drafted in to front the five-piece act.

***(*) Miracle
Armadillo ARMD 00017 *Willie Kelly (ts); Tommy Palmer (kb, v); Clark Findley, Riley Osbourn (kb); Rocky Athas (g); Robert Ware, Guthrie Kennard (b); Johnny Bolin, Jimmy Pendleton (d); Larry Samford, Tom Burns (v). 03.*

***(*) Voodoo Moon
Armadillo ARMD 00022 *Tommy Palmer, Ruf Rufner (kb); Rocky Athas (g, b, v); Guthrie Kennard (b, v); Bobby Baranowski (d, perc); Walter Watson (perc); Tracy Burns, Morris Price (v). 05.*

The group's collective musical experience is apparent on *Miracle* from the outset. The title track is a smooth slow number with a wonderfully Hendrixian clean guitar intro and a strong dynamic that confirms the group as one made up of consummate professionals. Jim Gaines's production is no doubt a considerable factor behind the high standards, and, combined with the musical talent, ensures that the results are strong. Athas's guitar work is individual, tasteful and surprisingly versatile, heard best on 'That Magic', where licks are built from subtle beginnings to an explosive peak. Samford's voice is smooth and clear, with a pleasing depth that enhances the thoughtful lyrics, showcased on the contemplative 'Bluesville', while the rest of the group supports the two focal points with aplomb. Though the overall sound is a little too generic to be truly exciting, the expertise of the performances and production raises the album to a high level.

Voodoo Moon is another high-calibre recording but stands apart from *Miracle* in its stronger sense of immediacy and movement. Athas's playing is pushed to new levels of fieriness; 'Muddy Water Blues' shares all the hallmarks that made Stevie Ray Vaughan's best work so riveting. Gaines's production is again superb and the band remains strong throughout the 12 songs, which occasionally depart from the stereotypes of the previous release, particularly in the moody title track and the acoustic numbers 'Sleep' and 'Preacher'. The record does seem to lack the energy that pushes a good album to greater heights, and it could be suggested that the act's competence breeds an over-relaxed approach. Nonetheless, this is a fine release by excellent musicians and strongly recommended. JF

B. B. & The Blues Shacks
GROUP

Founded in 1989, this band from Hildesheim, Germany, has appeared in clubs and festivals all over Europe. The group has also worked with visiting American blues artists R. J. Mischo, Erskine Oglesby, Kid Ramos, Tad Robinson and Smokey Wilson, and has received several awards from the German Blues News magazine.

**(*) Midnite Diner
Crosscut CCD 11070 *Michael Arlt (h, v); Chris Rannenberg (p); Andreas Arlt (g); Henning Hauerken (b); Andreas Bock (d); Marc Thijs (perc). 7/01.*

**(*) Blue Avenue
Crosscut CCD 11079 *Michael Arlt (h, v); Jürgen Magiera (o); Dennis Koeckstadt (p); Andreas Arlt, Alex Schultz (g); Henning Hauerken (b, v); Andreas Bock (d, v); Peter Behne, Helmut Meyer, Achim Mennecke (clapping). 4/03.*

Midnite Diner is retro from the intro, and unashamed of it. The track notes, part of a pastiche diner menu from the '50s, describe the music with phrases like 'Rockin' with the king, the plate royale' (B. B. King's 'Whole Lotta Love') or 'our T-bone steak' (the Walkerish title track). Dedicated to reproducing, often in ostensibly original compositions, the sounds of rhythm & blues half a century ago, the musicians apply themselves with affection and accuracy. But, like other bands working on this archaeological site, they tend to be more successful with lightweight or laidback material; a dramatic piece like 'Five To Twelve Blues', modelled on Otis Rush, demands a more mature voice. For its trip down *Blue Avenue* the band invited Alex Schultz to provide a second lead guitar voice on about half the tracks, but the thrust of the music, though heftier, is still backwards into the '50s. As before, the most successful performances are up-tempo pieces with a bluesy rockabilly air like 'Beauty Parlor Gossip' and relaxed shuffles like 'Can't Hide Love'. TR

Back Porch Blues
GROUP

Back Porch Blues – Jeffrey Dawkins, Whit Draper, Jon Wei and Sheila Wilcoxson – were active in the Pacific Northwest between 1988 and 1996 and won several awards from the Cascade Blues Association. Wilcoxson has since recorded in her own name.

*** Back To Basics
Burnside BCD 0008 *Jeffrey Dawkins (h, perc); Whit Draper (g); Mark French, Phil Baker, Jon Wei (b); Ken Ward (d); Jeannine Edelblut (perc); Sheila Wilcoxson (v).* 92.

This acoustic group combines an ability to play attractive and sometimes original music with the wit to make a record interesting enough to appeal to listeners beyond their own circle of fans. Draper is a versatile guitarist, clean but not clinical when playing with a slide, and Dawkins a decent harmonica player; each has an instrumental feature, Dawkins a brief 'NW Line' and Draper a medley of Charlie Patton licks. The rest of the album is a mixture of originals and older blues – Draper's 'Dark Of Night Blues' and Memphis Minnie's 'Black Cat Blues' are good examples of each – sung by Wilcoxson, whose range, spirit and almost tangible presence give the record much, but not all, of its character. TR

Backbone Slip
GROUP

Led by Mark Doyle and Joe Whiting, who have played together off and on since 1968, this group is sporadically active in the Central New York area. Its members have also recorded on, and Doyle has produced, some of Kim Lembo's albums.

** Avenue Breakdown
Blue Wave CD 122 *Mark Doyle (kb, g, perc); Paul Laronde, Mike Doyle (b); Mark Tiffault, Cathy Lamanna (d); Joe Whiting (v).* 1/93–3/94.

A repertoire derived in part from J. B. Lenoir, Percy Mayfield and Country Jim Bledsoe suggests a band with enquiring tastes, while a radical revision of Jimmy Reed's 'Bright Lights, Big City' and a version of Terry & McGhee's 'Walk On' without a harmonica imply a refreshing touch of contrariness. But the sheer disparity of the material and the settings – now acoustic slide guitars, now electric, now lounge-y keyboards – leaves the listener feeling that this is a band with an identity problem. An earlier CD, *Swamp Water* (Blue Wave CD 155), is currently out of print. TR

Backwards Sam Firk (born 1943)
VOCAL, GUITAR

It was under this nom de disque *that the musician and record-collector Mike Stewart made his (so far) only album, but the mask was worn as a joke rather than for concealment, and the CD reissue blows any cover it might have afforded. Stewart's other recordings, mostly on Adelphi albums, have been with veteran blues players, to whom he offers skilful, unobtrusive support.*

**(*) The True Blues And Gospel
Prospect 1103//Stella STCD 0002 *Firk; Delta X [Stephan Michelson] (g, wb, spoons); 'Fang' [Tom Hoskins] (g, v).* 68–69.

Skip James, Furry Lewis, Mississippi John Hurt, Bo Carter, Muddy Waters: a selection of the masters under whom he's studied gives some idea of the range of Stewart's interests. The blues ambience with which he has most affinity is that of easy-rocking, raggy guitarists like Hurt and Carter, or William Moore, whom he replays in 'Old Reliable One Way Gal', a duet with Hoskins, and 'Old Country Dump'. His singing is unassuming and several of the 19 tracks are instrumentals, among them 'Saturday Night Friction', based on Big Bill Broonzy's 'Saturday Night Rub', and a pretty duet version, with Michelson, of the parlour guitar piece 'Spanish Flangdang' (i.e. 'Spanish Fandango'). Weightier blues like 'Fixin' To Die' call for a more urgent delivery, and, wisely, he chooses few of them. TR

DeFord Bailey (1899–1982)
VOCAL, HARMONICA, BANJO, GUITAR

Bailey took up the harmonica while bedridden by a childhood attack of polio, which left him small and frail. For 15 years from 1926, he was both a star of WSM's famous country music show The Grand Ole Opry *and its only black member, demeaningly captioned 'mascot' in cast photographs. In 1941 he was fired, an innocent bystander in a turf war between the copyright agencies ASCAP, which administered many of his songs, and BMI, which WSM had joined. Bailey became embittered towards the music business, and steadfastly refused to make more records, but he did allow a friend, David Morton, to tape him privately.*

***(*) Harp Blowers (1925–1936)
Document DOCD-5164 *Bailey.* 4/27–10/28.

The young DeFord Bailey's 11 issued harmonica solos were aimed at the audience which tuned in to the Opry every week. Display pieces like 'The Fox Chase' and 'Old Hen Cackle' (transferred note for note from the fiddle) crossed racial boundaries, but it's surprising how many of these recordings – tunes like 'Up Country Blues' or 'Evening Prayer Blues', a musical impression of a celebrated Nashville preacher – sound uncompromisingly black. Whatever the racial complexities, there is no denying or withstanding Bailey's complete technical mastery, his rhythmic vitality and the subtle beauty and variety of his tone, from organ-like to oboe-like. It's a fact that there is only one harmonica playing on, for instance, 'Muscle Shoals Blues', but it's almost impossible to believe it. This is an utterly remarkable body of music. Via WSM, it reached the likes of Bert Bilbro, whose three instrumentals, included here, are transparently indebted to Bailey. 'Chester Blues' was issued as the reverse of a Bailey record, and it was long speculated that Bilbro was African-American, but two much less impressive vocal sides immediately identify him as white. That both are 'coon songs' is an irony that speaks for itself. The rest of the CD is makeweight; John Henry Howard is pallid in both senses, and George Clarke's strong playing recalls Noah Lewis, but is let down by listless guitar accompaniment.

**** The Legendary DeFord Bailey
Tennessee Folklore Society TFS-122 *Bailey*. 10/74–10/76.

Predictably, Bailey at 75 and older had slightly less wind, and most of the harmonica pieces here are comparatively brief. What had not changed were the beauty and variety of his tone and the precision of his rhythm; these are outstanding performances, which naturally include versions of most of his early recordings but also considerably expand his known repertoire. A mighty bonus is the inclusion of two banjo pieces and four with guitar, which incidentally demonstrate that Bailey was a more than adequate singer. The banjo playing on 'Lost John' (not the familiar song) seems to come from well before the days of recording, and is historically valuable as well as technically impressive. Also important is a relentlessly swinging version of 'Kansas City Blues', compiled from Jim Jackson's multiple versions, but exploring guitar complexities undreamt of by him. 'Evening Prayer', which appropriately ends the disc, has considerable ambient noise, but this is a minor consideration, set against the quality of DeFord Bailey's music and the good fortune of its preservation on tape. CS

Etta Baker (born 1913)
VOCAL, GUITAR, BANJO

A fingerpicking guitarist in the line of Rev. Gary Davis and Elizabeth Cotten, Baker has been playing guitar and banjo since early childhood, learning chiefly from her father, Boone Reid. A resident of Morganton, North Carolina, she first recorded in 1956 for the Tradition anthology Instrumental Music Of The Southern Appalachians, *after which many young guitarists tried to master her version of 'One Dime Blues'. Since the mid-'70s she has appeared often at festivals.*

Instrumental Music Of The Southern Appalachians *is not currently in print, but three of Baker's five tunes – 'Bully Of The Town', 'John Henry' and 'Railroad Bill' – are included in the VAC* Easy Pickins *(Tradition TCD 1090).*

**** One Dime Blues
Rounder CD 2112 *Baker; Cora Phillips (g).* 10/88–8/90.

Any lover of American vernacular guitar music will be delighted with this recording. Her limber fingers belying her years, Baker turns the pages of a fat folio of tunes that range from the 19th-century parlour guitar idiom ('Dew Drop', 'Spanish Fandango') through common-stock melodies like 'Lost John', 'Bully Of The Town', 'John Henry' (played delicately with a slide) and 'Railroad Bill' to blues ('Crow Jane', Blind Blake's 'Police Dog Blues') and a Ray Charles song. There are also less common pieces like 'Carolina Breakdown' or the minor-key 'Alabama Wagonwheel'. The two banjo tunes, 'Marching Jaybird' and 'Going Down The Road Feeling Bad', are entirely charming, and one yearns for more. Unfortunately the promising-looking *Black Banjo Songsters Of North Carolina And Virginia* (Smithsonian Folkways SF CD 40079) includes only one performance by Baker, and it is another version of 'Jaybird'.

*** Railroad Bill
Music Maker 91006 *Baker; Tim Duffy (g).* 5/95–6/98.

To be playing guitar at all at 85 is admirable; to be playing with Baker's ease and fluency is not far short of incredible. Only half a dozen of this album's selections duplicate the Rounder's, but the remaining 13 take a similar tour of the beauty spots of American guitar, adding visits to 'Candyman', 'Nobody's Business' and 'Chilly Winds', a faintly Merle Travis-like 'Mint Julep' and her own compositions 'Sunny Tennessee' and 'Miss A Little Miss'. The banjo complement is reduced to a single tune, 'Cripple Creek'. These intimate recordings were made in her living room, and during 'Carolina Breakdown' a finch flies in, cocks an ear to the lilting guitar and trills a second part. TR

Mickey Baker (born 1925)
VOCAL, GUITAR

McHouston Baker was born in Louisville, Kentucky. By the time he was 16 he was living in New York, where he became a leading session guitarist on blues and R&B recordings for labels such as Savoy and Atlantic. He formed a duet, Mickey & Sylvia, with the singer Sylvia Vanderpool and they had a hit in 1957 with 'Love Is Strange'. Moving in 1961 to France, he worked with Memphis Slim and as an all-purpose arranger and wrote several guitar tutors. He still lives in France but has not been active in blues for some time.

**(*) Mississippi Delta Dues
Universal/Maison De Blues 982 243–3 *Baker; The London Strings Orchestra (strings); Stefan Grossman (g); Les Sampson (b); Alan Roberts (d); Ray Cooper (wb, cga, maracas, tamb, perc).* 4/73.

During the '70s Baker occasionally played unplugged gigs, surprising listeners who knew him only as an electric guitarist with his decorous readings of old blues by Robert Johnson and Son House. This is the aspect of his music presented by *Mississippi Delta Dues*, on which he plays old blues repertoire, much of it from House, Johnson and Charley Patton, with acoustic guitar, assisted by Stefan Grossman and percussionist Ray Cooper. For some tracks, too, he arranged string parts, generally providing conventional orchestral colouring but on J. B. Lenoir's 'Alabama March' painting a more impressionistic backdrop, inspired, he reveals, by the work of the composers Penderecki and Xenakis. On its first issue the album was not greeted with much enthusiasm, no doubt because, in Baker's words, 'it went against the grain of the sentiments of blues purists … [and] we deliberately chose to ignore that mentality'. Thirty-odd years later, listeners will be more accustomed to textural experiment and Baker's strings are unlikely to frighten the horses. Their potency is uneven, though: Leroy Carr's 'Blues Before Sunrise' is pleasantly tinted (and delicately sung), but it's hard to discern any enhancement of the material in the setting of Son House's 'My Black Woman'. The original album is expanded by three previously unreissued pieces.

**(*) The Blues And Me
Black & Blue BB 456 *Baker; Louis Myers (h, g); Lloyd Glenn (p); Jimmy Rogers, Tiny Grimes (g); Dave Myers, Roland Lobligeois*

(b); Fred Below, Panama Francis (d). 12/73–5/74.

Baker's currently scanty CD catalogue gives little impression of the quick, clever guitar player who was so in demand in the New York studios of the '50s and '60s, but *The Blues And Me* is a little more revealing than *Mississippi Delta Dues*, in that Baker plays in a more up-to-date idiom and on at least some of the tracks uses electric guitar. His playing is livelier and his vocals more projected than on the earlier album, but *The Blues And Me* suffers, like so many Black & Blue projects, from an evident belief that putting an assortment of musicians who don't work together regularly into a studio and giving them a day's recording time is a reliable way of producing a worthwhile album. It's much more likely, of course, to encourage generic performances of standard repertoire. At least here the material is fresh, being mostly Baker–Memphis Slim compositions; the ensemble playing of Baker, Rogers and The Aces, who account for most of the tracks (those with Grimes come from *his* one-day session), is urbane, unadventurous and rather dull. TR

Willie Baker
VOCAL, GUITAR

'Exceptionally little is known of Willie Baker,' a notewriter commented more than a decade ago, and it remains true. The singer and 12-string guitarist was presumably a Georgian contemporary of Barbecue Bob and Curley Weaver, whom he greatly resembles.

*** Charlie Lincoln & Willie Baker (1927–1930)
RST Blues Documents BDCD-6027 Baker. 1–3/29.

Baker performs so like Barbecue Bob that one wonders if he was obeying his record company's instructions to copy a successful artist on a rival label. Of the nine tracks on this CD (the remainder is by Charlie Lincoln) 'Weak-Minded Blues', the nearly identical 'Weak-Minded Woman' and 'Crooked Woman Blues' are practically interchangeable with Barbecue Bob numbers, while 'No No Blues' and 'Sweet Patunia Blues' are themes popularized by Curley Weaver, who shared a good deal with Bob. Only in 'Ain't It A Good Thing' and 'Rag Baby' does Baker follow different promptings: the former is a theme also developed by Frank Stokes, 'Rag Baby' an archaic rag song whose guitar accompaniment is strongly banjoistic. TR

Long John Baldry (1945–2005)
VOCAL, GUITAR

In London in the '50s and '60s Baldry was involved with folk music, skiffle and blues. He sang in the first lineup of Alexis Korner's Blues Incorporated, then formed his own bands, The Hoochie Coochie Men and later Steampacket, employing a young Rod 'The Mod' Stewart as second-string vocalist. Elton John, Charlie Watts and Jimmy Page are just a few of the musicians who worked under his leadership. In 1980 he emigrated to Canada, where he worked as a studio singer, voice-over artist and actor as well as on the blues circuit, while continuing to visit Europe regularly.

(**(*)) It Still Ain't Easy
Stony Plain SPCD 1163//Hypertension HYCD 200122 Baldry; Bill Runge (ss, s, b); Pat Caird (s); Butch Coulter (h); Teddy Borowiecki (kb, p); Mike Kalanj (o); Willie MacCalder (p); Tom Lavin (g, tamb, v); David Raven, Amos Garrett, John King, Gaye Delorme, Lucky Peterson, Colin James, Al Walker, Laurie Coyle, Pat Coleman (g); Russell Jackson, Rene Worst (b); Daryl Bennett, Tony Coleman (d); Neil Shilkin, Charles Bell (prog); Kathi McDonald, Bobby King, Terry Evans, Corrine Hawkes, Kevin O'Brien (v). 91.

**(*) Right To Sing The Blues
Stony Plain SPCD 1232//Hypertension HYCD 297 167 Baldry; Bob Tildesley, Dean McNeill (t); Johnny Ferreira, David Babcock (s, v); Rusty Reed (h); Eric Webster (o, p); Papa John King (g, v); Colin James (g); Norm Fisher (b, v); Mike Lent (b); Al Webster (d, perc, v); Bohdan Hluszko (d); Kathi McDonald, Holger Petersen (v). 8/95–8/96.

**(*) Long John Baldry Trio Live//Evening Conversation
Stony Plain SPCD 1268//Hypertension 0191 HYP Baldry; Butch Coulter (h, g); Matt Taylor (g, v); Christina Lux (v). 9/99–00.

**(*) Remembering Leadbelly
Stony Plain SPCD 1275 Baldry; Hans Stamer (t, h, g, jh, v); Tom Colclough (cl); Butch Coulter (h); John Lee Sanders (kb, o, p, v); Jesse Zubot (vn, md); Andreas Schuld (g, u, zither, perc, v, prod); Norm Fisher (b); Chris Norquist (d, finger cymbals); Kathi McDonald, Sybel Thrasher, Tyee Montessori Elementary School Choir (v). 00/01.

On *It Still Ain't Easy* (the title alludes to his Warner Bros. album of 20 years earlier, *It Ain't Easy*), blues take a backseat to bluesy pop numbers. On *Right To Sing The Blues* the song selection is slightly more favourable to the blues, including Leroy Carr's 'Midnight Hour Blues' and Hot Lips Page's 'They Raided The Joint'. That ratio is maintained on the trio album (retitled in its European issue), which intersperses 'Back Water Blues' and 'Walk On' with songs by Tom Waits and Randy Newman. The choice of 'Whoa Back Buck' (which was also on *Right To Sing The Blues*) and 'Black Gal', and Baldry's fondness for the 12-string guitar, proved to be signals to his next project, an album of Leadbelly songs. It was recorded, according to the producer, with almost as little artifice as the originals, 'in John's bedroom [with] one cheap mike', but, as can be seen from the details above, the project was a little more elaborately realized than that. Both *Right To Sing The Blues* and *Remembering Leadbelly* are extended with interviews, the latter CD also including a few minutes of Alan Lomax talking about its subject.

Like the seasoned dramatic performer he is, Baldry delivers his large, mixed repertoire with immense panache and in a variety of interpretative styles, his favourite a stagey growl which at its ripest sounds a little too much like an actor of the 'laddie' school impersonating Howlin' Wolf. For readers already affectionately disposed to him this will not be a problem, but anyone who is made uncomfortable by obviously assumed accents may find they have to give Long John short shrift. TR

Marcia Ball (born 1949)
VOCAL, KEYBOARDS, ACCORDION

Raised in Vinton, Louisiana, Ball broke into the music scene around Austin, Texas, as the singer with a country band, Freda & The Firedogs, but soon switched to a mixed repertoire of R&B, soul and zydeco, with which she has toured the Southwest indefatigably since the mid-'70s.

**(*) Soulful Dress
Rounder CD 3078 Ball; Keith Winking (t); Kent Winking, Pat Mackrell (unspecified brass/reeds); Mark Kazanoff (as, ts); Nick

Connolly (o); Kenny Ray, David Murray, Stevie Ray Vaughan (g); Don Bennett (b); Wes Starr (d). 83.

**(*) Hot Tamale Baby
Rounder CD 3095 *Ball; Terry Tullos (t); Ernie Gautreau (vtb); Bill 'Foots' Samuel (as, ts, bs); Alvin 'Red' Tyler (ts); Craig Wroten (o, p); David Murray (g); Don Bennett (b); Doyle Bramhall (d, v); Elaine Foster, Lisa Foster, Sharon Foster (v).* 4/85.

** Gatorhythms
Rounder CD 3101 *Ball; Keith Winking (t); Jon Blondell (tb); Mark Kazanoff (ts, bs); Stephen Bruton, Derek O'Brien, James Hinkle, Jesse Taylor (g); Don Bennett (b); Rodney Craig (d, cowbell, tri); Angela Strehli, Lou Ann Barton (v).* 89.

*** Blue House
Rounder CD 3131 *Ball; Keith Winking (t); Randy Zimmerman (tb); Mark Kazanoff (ts, arr); Red Rails (bs); Paul Klemperer (s); David Webb (o); Rich Brotherton (md, g); Steve Williams (g); Don Bennett (b, v); Rodney Craig (d, v); 'Mambo' John Tranor (d, wb, cga); Jill Napoletan (v).* 94.

*** Let Me Play With Your Poodle
Rounder CD 3151 *Ball; Gary Slechta (t); Randy Zimmerman (tb); Mark Kazanoff (ts, bs, arr); Paul Klemperer (ts, v); Red Rails, Les Izmore (bs); Riley Osbourn (o); Steve Williams, Derek O'Brien (g, v); Clarence Hollimon (g); Don Bennett (b, v); David Carroll, Larry Fulcher (b); Fran Christina (d, v); Rodney Craig, George Rains (d); B. E. 'Frosty' Smith (perc); 'Mambo' John Treanor (wb, rb); Kristin Dewitt, Sarah Campbell, Doyle Bramhall, Alicia Jones, Mike Cross, Christina Mars, Beth Tomlinson (v).* 97.

** Presumed Innocent
Alligator ALCD 4879 *Ball; Wayne Jackson, Gary Slechta (t); Pat Breaux (ts, ac); Dan Torosian, Brad Andrew, Paul Klemperer (ts); Mark Kazanoff (bs); Gary Primich (h); Riley Osbourn (o); Pat Boyack, Casper Rawls, Derek O'Brien, C. C. Adcock, Sonny Landreth (g); Don Bennett (b, v); Roscoe Beck (b); Keith Robinson, Doyle Bramhall (d, v); Chris Hunter (d); Van Mouton (rb); Delbert McClinton, Susanne Abbott, Bonnie Bishop, Kristin Dewitt, Debbie Gardner (v).* 01.

**(*) So Many Rivers
Alligator ALCD 4891 *Ball; Lee Thornburg, Gary Slechta (t); Nick Lane (tb); Lon Price (as, ts); Greg Smith (ts, bs); Kaz Kazanoff (ts); John Mills (bs); Johnny Nicholas (h, v); Wayne Toups (ac, v); Red Young (o); James Pennebaker (vn, sg, g); Stephen Bruton (md, g, v); Pat Boyack (g); Don Bennett, Yoggie Musgrove, Chris Maresh (b); Tom Fillman, Keith Robinson (d); Deborah [Debra] Dobkin (perc); Lisa Tingle, Malford Milligan, Randy Jacobs, Alicia Jones, Kai Tolbert (v).* 03?

*** Live! Down The Road
Alligator ALCD 4903 *Ball; Al Gomez (t); Brad Andrew (ts); Mark Kazanoff (bs); Red Young (o); Pat Boyack (g); Don Bennett (b); Corey Keller (d); Angela Strehli (v).* 04?

For the opening track of her first Rounder album Ball sashayed in wearing the 'Soulful Dress' that once garbed Sugar Pie DeSanto. As an indication of the music to come, it wasn't a bad signpost: while there are no particular resemblances between the two singers, Ball's predilection for varieties of R&B does locate her on the vocal map closer to DeSanto than to, say, Koko Taylor. The touch of Professor Longhair in her piano playing on 'A Thousand Times' struck a New Orleans note that has resounded throughout her work; indeed, *Hot Tamale Baby*, her somewhat more elaborately produced next album, was out-and-out New Orleans R&B, an idiom she celebrated with namechecks in her composition 'That's Enough Of That Stuff'. Both these CDs and their slightly less gripping successor, *Gatorhythms*, are unexpanded transfers of LPs whose playing time was not lavish; Rounder might serve her better by putting most of the tracks on to one full-length CD.

Gatorhythms and subsequent albums had a higher percentage of her own songs. These are generally more vivacious than memorable, but *Blue House* has an arresting piece in the dead-slow 'St. Gabriel', about a wife convicted of murdering an abusive husband; here Ball's raw, yearning delivery and Steve Williams's chilling guitar catch exactly the intended mood of the song. 'I'm Just A Prisoner' and 'The Story Of My Life' on *Let Me Play With Your Poodle* are hurting songs with a comparably powerful effect. The title piece, Tampa Red's old nudge-nudge number, is frankly a dog, but people will keep trotting it out.

Ball always performs with plenty of spirit, and her piano playing is not so much an invitation to the dancefloor as a summons, but her voice hasn't a great deal of body, and her up-tempo tunes, despite a frequent tang of Creole spice, tend sometimes to evaporate on the tongue. Her singing on her later albums – but not on the disappointingly unfocused *Presumed Innocent* – is a little deeper and huskier and she appears to be pacing herself more thoughtfully. These are improvements that make the albums more enjoyable, but at this stage it seems unlikely that recordings will ever portray Ball in the round. Or perhaps one should say *studio* recordings, since *Live! Down The Road* is both more accessible and, indeed, livelier than several of its predecessors, with a nicely calculated balance of feisty up-tempo pieces like 'Big Shot' or 'The Right Tool For The Job' and affecting slower numbers such as 'Just Kiss Me' or Randy Newman's 'Louisiana 1927'. 'Poodle' gets another walk, and a long one, giving Boyack time to play a sequence of solos meticulously memorized from *Chuck Berry For Dummies*.

Ball has also participated in two trio albums with other women singers: *Dreams Come True* (Antone's ANTCD 0014), made in the late '80s with Lou Ann Barton and Angela Strehli, friends from the Texas blues network, and *Sing It!* (Rounder CD 2152), a 1997 meeting with Tracy Nelson and Irma Thomas. Each album mixes trio, duet and solo vocals on a repertoire that's wholly R&B rather than blues. TR

Tom Ball & Kenny Sultan
DUET

From Santa Barbara, California, Tom Ball (born 1950) and Kenny Sultan (born 1955) began working together in 1979. Twenty years on, they had covered (they estimated) more than a million miles in 12 countries, used up five vehicles and put in seven and a half thousand hours on stage performing 84,500 songs. (More statistics can be found in the booklet with 20th Anniversary LIVE!) Both have written instrumental tutors.

*** Bloodshot Eyes
Flying Fish FF 70386 *Ball (h, g, v); Sultan (g); Byron Berline (vn); Steve Fishell (g); Leroy Vinnegar (b).* summer 85.

*** Too Much Fun
Flying Fish FF 70532 *Ball (h, g, v); Sultan (g, v); Byron Berline (vn, v); Tom Lee (b, v); Jack Kennedy (b); Jody Eulitz (cardboard box, Samsonite cosmetic case, v).* 89.

*** **Filthy Rich**
Flying Fish FF-70619 *Ball (h, g, v); Sultan (g); Byron Berline (vn); Tom Lee, Randy Tico (b); Dean Dods (tu); Jody Eulitz (d, cardboard box).* 92.

*** **Double Vision**
Flying Fish CD FF 656 *Ball (h, g, v); Sultan (g, perc, v); Bill Flores (s); Joe Craven (vn, md, perc); Tom Lee (b); Jody Eulitz (d, cardboard box, v); Shanon Ward, Chris Uldricks (v).* 95.

Transforming Wynonie Harris's 'Bloodshot Eyes' from bellowing rhythm & blues to jaunty skiffle 'n' bluegrass sounds a trifle outré, until you remember that the song wasn't originally Harris's, or R&B, at all, but a Western Swing novelty number. So Ball and Sultan – and, on this track, fiddler Byron Berline – are simply putting the song in its place, or somewhere near it, and very entertainingly at that. Smile-on-your-face entertainment is what this duo does best, whether reshaping 'Your Red Wagon' or 'Don't Burn The Candle At Both Ends' or telling their own rueful comic story in 'Indiscretion Stomp'. When he first heard Ball & Sultan, George Thorogood remarks, 'I thought these guys were the second coming of Sonny and Brownie', and almost anyone is likely to say the same – at first hearing. 'But,' he goes on, 'I've come to realize they are, in fact, the first coming of themselves', and this is fair comment too, as becomes clearer on their next album, where a more capacious songbag bulges with pieces from Commander Cody, Dan Hicks and Cousin Joe, and everyone seems to be having, if not actually too much fun, at least his share of it. *Filthy Rich* boasts an even more eclectic repertoire, with songs derived from Ikey Robinson, Bo Carter, Rev. Gary Davis and Muddy Waters, and a pair from the Hank Williamses: Senior's 'Mind Your Own Business' and Junior's 'Whiskey Bent And Hell Bound'.

By the time they made *Double Vision*, Ball & Sultan were pleased enough with their songwriting to fill more than half the album with it. That their confidence was not misplaced is evident from 'Perfect Woman', which is funny, or 'Your Shoes Don't Fit My Feet', which is sharp as well, or from 'Roll Of The Tumblin' Dice', which has since been recorded by Lonnie Brooks. This last they perform with the cramped acoustic of an early Muddy Waters–Little Walter duet, but mostly they follow earlier models: on 'Automobile Mechanic', for example, they sound like a light-hearted Johnny Shines and Walter Horton.

*** **20th Anniversary LIVE!**
No Guru NG 2000 *Ball (h, g, v); Sultan (g).* 6/99.

Ball and Sultan celebrated, and why not, by doing some of the things they particularly like doing, such as resurrecting ancient common-stock songs like 'He's In The Jailhouse Now' and 'Fishin' Blues', trying for a Muddy–Walter effect in 'Honey Bee' and punctuating the programe with a guitar solo, here a 'Berceuse' by Ball and a ragtime medley by Sultan. A few numbers will be familiar to those who have bought the albums above, but the original songs include several that are fresh. TR

Tommy Bankhead (1931–2000)
VOCAL, GUITAR

Bankhead was born in Lake Cormorant, Mississippi, played his first gig at the age of 16, hung out with Howlin' Wolf's band in Memphis and worked with Sonny Boy Williamson II. Booked for a six-week gig in East St Louis in 1949, he remained there for the rest of his life. He backed Henry Townsend on his 1961 Bluesville album, but his own recordings were only locally distributed until he cut a couple of CDs not long before his death.

** **Message To St. Louis**
Fedora FCD 5017 *Bankhead; Erskine Oglesby (ts); Bob Lohr (p); Charles 'Nephew' Davis (b); Kenny Laurence (d).* 7/99.

** **Please Accept My Love**
Fedora FCD 5024 *Bankhead; Bob Lohr (p); Frank Goldwasser (g); Frank Dunbar (b); Keith Robinson (d).* 9/00.

St Louis blues enthusiasts praised Bankhead lavishly in his last years; one of them describes him in the notes to *Message To St. Louis* as a 'precious blues resource'. Listeners outside the partisanship zone may find it difficult to be so generous. Bankhead is a conversational singer with a small, wry voice and a guitarist with a clipped manner and sour tone. 'Goin' Back' runs in an apt John Lee Hooker groove but generally both material and performance on *Message To St. Louis* are unmemorable, and although Oglesby (who plays on six tracks rather than four as stated) usefully thickens the texture of the group, the bassist and drummer are colourless. The accompanists are more lively on *Please Accept My Love*, where Bankhead spends a good deal of time mining a Lowell Fulson vein. The title track and a few others are arranged for two guitars. TR

Chico Banks (born 1962)
VOCAL, GUITAR

Coming from a musical family (his father Jesse was a member of the Mighty Clouds Of Joy), Vernon Banks played his first professional gig at 14. Later he joined his brother Stanley in Little Johnny Christian's Chicago Playboys and in 1997 graduated to Mavis Staples's backing band. A devotee of the Isley Brothers, Parliament/Funkadelic and Earth, Wind & Fire, he also favours Jimi Hendrix and Albert King. With the release of his debut album, he was greeted as 'the blues' next big star'. The rest is silence.

** **Candy Lickin' Man**
Evidence ECD 26090 *Banks; 'Big James' Montgomery (tb, v); Charles Kimble (ts); Ronnie Hicks (kb); Ken Hampton (b); Lester Holmes (d); Mavis Staples (v).* 5/97.

Take the smooth falsetto vocals of Philip Bailey, the pedal paraphernalia of Jimi Hendrix, a tranche of Albert King's repertoire and a will to impress and you have an album like this. Unfortunately someone, hopefully not the artist, equates talent with self-indulgence, a plague of which engulfs most of these 70 minutes. Too often, an excellent backing band is consigned to comping behind choruses of needlessly complex guitar work. Banks also favours a harsh-sounding wah-wah pedal that dumps oleaginous cowflops over 'Red Dress', 'The Sky Is Crying' and 'All Your Love', the last sung by trombonist Montgomery. The album's one quiet spot, King Curtis's 'Soul Serenade', and Albert King's 'Got To Be Some Changes Made' show that Banks does indeed have the taste he neglects to engage elsewhere. 'It Must Be Love', sung by Mavis Staples, and 'Careless Things We Do' also reveal a nascent talent for songwriting that would serve him better than being this week's guitar star. NS

L. V. Banks (born 1932)
VOCAL, GUITAR

Banks was born and grew up in Mississippi. In the late '50s he began singing and playing around Leland and Greenville. In 1965 he moved to Chicago, where he has become a seasoned club performer. His son Tré (q.v.) has followed him into the blues business.

*** Let Me Be Your Teddy Bear (Chicago Blues Session Vol. 41)
Wolf 120.887 Banks; 'Big James' Montgomery (tb); Charles Kimble (s); Allen Batts (o, p); John Primer, Michael Thomas (g); Ike Anderson (b); Jerome Price (d). 10/95.

**(*) Ruby (Chicago Blues Session Volume 52)
Wolf 120.898 Banks; Allen Batts (p); Michael Thomas (g); Dave Kay (b); Jerry Price (d). 2/99.

Banks admires B. B. King, Bobby Bland and Z. Z. Hill, and from remarks quoted in the notes to *Let Me Be Your Teddy Bear* it appears that he does so not just because they are great artists but because they have a versatility to which he himself aspires. Perhaps he displays it at his club dates, but the album is solid blues, performed with little originality but irreproachable competence and vigour. All the tracks are Banks's compositions except 'I'm A Man' (Muddy Waters's 'Manish Boy') and a 'Tail Dragger' sung in the manner of Howlin' Wolf. It isn't clear if Banks is the chief guitar player; the solo on 'Born In The City' and some other passages might be by Primer. *Ruby* was made with a smaller group and recorded at a lower level, but these are not the only reasons for its different sound: Banks seems to be working towards a lighter, airier texture, though still with a familiar blues design. The process is epitomized by 'I Made A Mistake', which uses the springy line of 'Hi Heel Sneakers'. Again the songs are mostly Banks's and blues; the one soul number, 'Love Light' (Bobby Bland's 'Turn On Your Love Light'), is diminished by the small-group setting. Batts plays sturdily on both albums. TR

Barbecue Bob (1902–31)
VOCAL, GUITAR

Robert Hicks, from Walnut Grove, Georgia, learned guitar, as did his older brother Charlie and their friend Curley Weaver, from the latter's mother, Savannah Weaver. All of them played the 12-string instrument, but Bob's was the most dramatic style and for the brief period of his recording career he was by far the most popular on disc, thanks in part to the huge sales of his second release, the topical 'Mississippi Heavy Water Blues'. Because his day job was as a chef in a barbecue restaurant, Columbia Records gave him the nickname Barbecue Bob and photographed him for their publicity material in his work apron.

**** Barbecue Bob – Vol. 1 (1927–1928)
Document DOCD-5046 Barbecue Bob; Charlie Lincoln (g, v, sp). 3/27–4/28.

***(*) Barbecue Bob – Vol. 2 (1928–1929)
Document DOCD-5047 Barbecue Bob; Nellie Florence (v); Charlie Lincoln (laughing). 4/28–11/29.

***(*) Barbecue Bob – Vol. 3 (1929–1930)
Document DOCD-5048 Barbecue Bob; Buddy Moss (h); Curley Weaver (g, v); Charlie Lincoln, Dan Hornsby (sp). 11/29–12/30.

**** Chocolate To The Bone
Yazoo 2005 Barbecue Bob; Nellie Florence (v); Charlie Lincoln (laughing). 3/27–12/30.

***(*) The Essential
Classic Blues CBL 200026 2CD Barbecue Bob; Buddy Moss (h); Charlie Lincoln (g, v, sp, laughing); Curley Weaver (g, v); Nellie Florence (v). 3/27–12/30.

The big sound of the 12-string guitar made its full impact only on electrical recordings and if Barbecue Bob was not the first player to profit from that innovation he was certainly the first to do so on a national, or at least South-wide, scale. The thunder of his bass notes and strummed lower strings was pierced by darts of lightning as he touched the high strings, often with a slide. Accurate recording also brought out the warmth and friendliness of his singing, which suggest a man of sunny self-confidence – a character borne out by a two-part duet with his equally cheerful brother Charlie, 'It Won't Be Long Now', which consists mostly of comic exchanges about their girlfriends.

Recording relatively early, Bob was able to include in his repertoire several traditional songs which the record companies would soon regard as too oldfashioned to bother with, such as 'Easy Rider Don't You Deny My Name', 'Poor Boy A Long Ways From Home' and 'Corrine Corrina', a version of which he recorded as 'How Long Pretty Mama'. But he was a young man, not anchored in the past, and he embraced the new medium. 'Just wait till the next verse, I'll tell you what she said,' he teases the listener in 'Mamma You Don't Suit Me!', while in 'Chocolate To The Bone' he alludes to a recent recording (probably not coincidentally, for the same company): 'I'm just like Miss Lillian, like Miss Lillian, I mean Miss Glinn, you see – she said a brownskin man is just all right with me.'

The above songs, all on Document's *Vol. 1*, give a representative picture of his repertoire and the remaining volumes contain only a few surprises, though it's no chore at all to wait for them, carried along by Bob's effervescent guitar playing and his enjoyment of his own stories. On *Vol. 2* 'California Blues' is set to a racing rhythm appropriate for a song that begins with a train ride; there is a train in 'Yo Yo Blues', too, but the bouncing guitar figure had already been devised for this number by Curley Weaver, who called it 'No No Blues'. Two songs are delivered by Nellie Florence, an abrasively voiced friend of the brothers, with guitar by Bob and roars of laughter by Charlie. 'It Just Won't Hay', 'Honey Your [sic] Going Too Fast' and 'It's A Funny Little Thing' are obvious capitulations to the charms of 'It's Tight Like That'.

That intrusion of hokum continues in *Vol. 3* in 'She Moves It Just Right', 'She Shook Her Gin' and 'Twistin' Your Stuff' – the origin of which Bob makes explicit, beginning 'You all heard the song "Tight Like That" ...' Brother Charlie joins him for another two-part sketch, 'Darktown Gamblin'', in which they play craps and skin with appropriate sound effects and Charlie jives like Eddie Murphy's Southern grandfather. 'Atlanta Moan' relocates Tampa Red's slide blues 'Chicago Moan', but the outstanding blues on this volume is a vivid commentary on the gathering storm of the Depression, 'We Sure Got Hard Times'. The last surprise in store for the listener lies in the four tracks that conclude the album, issued under the name of the Georgia Cotton Pickers: Bob singing with himself and Curley Weaver on guitars and their teenaged friend Buddy Moss on harmonica. Had he lived, this swaggering ensemble music might have been Bob's passport through the Depression and into the changed musical world of the mid-'30s.

The Yazoo CD selects very evenhandedly from the three stages of Bob's career as represented by the Documents, omitting few of his best performances, and since its sound quality is consistently good this is the album for the selective buyer. The intrinsically good value of the Classic Blues 2CD – 36 well-chosen pieces, including the four by the Georgia Cotton Pickers – is slightly compromised by variable sound restoration. TR

John Henry Barbee (1905–64)
VOCAL, GUITAR

Barbee was a native of Tennessee who recorded for Vocalion in 1938; he told researchers that his real name was William George Tucker, and that shortly after the recording session he had shot his wife's white lover and gone into hiding. However, in 1937 he applied for Social Security as John Henry Barbee, giving his father's name as Beecher Barbee. It's certain that at some point he moved to Chicago, where he worked with the guitarist Willie B. James, and on Maxwell Street as a member of Moody Jones's band. While in Europe with the 1964 AFBF Barbee was diagnosed with cancer and left the tour early. Back home, he bought a car with his earnings from the trip, was involved in a fatal accident and died in jail awaiting trial.

**** Blues Masters Vol. 3
Storyville STCD 8003 *Barbee.* 10/64.

Barbee's early recordings are on *Memphis Blues 1927–1938* (Document DOCD-5159). Despite the retrospectively poignant circumstances of its recording, illness had no audible effect on the quality of *Blues Masters Vol. 3*; Barbee was still a skilful guitarist, and the passing years had attractively sandpapered his voice. 'Miss Nelly Grey' is a pleasant original, but Barbee was not a prolific composer, relying largely on standards like 'John Henry', 'That's All Right' and 'Worried Life Blues'. His energy and commitment enliven even the most familiar items, however; 'Dust My Broom' and 'I Heard My Baby' (a mistitling of 'I Held My Baby Last Night') both derive from Elmore James, and even in an acoustic setting they retain much of James's strangulated passion. 'Backwater Blues', which lasts for over six minutes, is dramatic rather than self-dramatizing, and a valuable corrective to versions served up by Big Bill Broonzy and Josh White in their later years.

**(*) Blues Live!
Storyville STCD 8051 *Barbee.* 10/64.

The eight songs on *Blues Live!*, which is shared with Sleepy John Estes, do not add much to the portrait of the artist, since versions of most of them appear on the studio-recorded CD. 'Somebody Done Change [sic] The Lock On My Door', which does not, confirms Barbee's assured handling of slow tempos, and 'Backwater Blues' is just as compelling in concert performance, but he seems tired on inferior renditions of 'John Henry' and 'Dust My Broom'. 'Boll Weavil', which appears to recycle Burl Ives's reworking for folkniks, is unusual, but hardly essential. CS

Blue Lu Barker (1913–98)
VOCAL

Louisa Dupont was born in New Orleans, and was a singer and dancer by the time she married guitarist Danny Barker (1909–94) in 1930. They moved to New York, and in 1938 Danny got Blue Lu on to records. Despite her dislike of public performance, she appeared with his band and others through the '40s. Postwar, she made more records, but retired from 1949 to 1964. The Barkers returned to New Orleans in 1965, and Blue Lu resumed performing until 1989, with another hiatus between 1967 and 1973.

** Blue Lu Barker 1938–1939
Classics 704 *Barker; Henry 'Red' Allen, Benny Carter, Charlie Shavers (t); Buster Bailey (cl); Chu Berry (ts); Sam Price, Lil Armstrong (p); Danny Barker, Ulysses Livingston (g); Wellman Braud, unknown (b); Paul Barbarin, O'Neill Spencer, unknowns (d); prob. band (v).* 8/38–12/39.

Blue Lu owes her 15 minutes of fame to Maria Muldaur's cover of 'Don't You Feel My Leg'. In 1938 Decca euphemized the title to 'Don't You Make Me High', but it's an anodyne effort. Blue Lu doesn't deserve her reputation for raunchiness, singing with faux-naif girlishness in a small, nasal voice, whether she's being hip or, less often, downhome. This technique is not without charm in small doses, and almost entirely without charm heard at length. Towards the end of her '30s recordings, Barker's delivery becomes a little more forthright, perhaps to compete with the flamboyant playing of Red Allen. Decca teamed her with some of the best session musicians in town, and their contributions are the most valuable aspect of this disc.

** Don't You Feel My Leg
Delmark DE-684 *Barker; Shad Collins, unknown (t); Teddy McRae, Jerry Jerome (ts); Norman Lester (p); Danny Barker (g); Ernest Williamson, unknown (b); Woodie Nichols, unknown (d).* 8–10/46.

This CD contains nine Apollo masters, including two songs not issued on 78 and an alternative take. Blue Lu is less annoyingly winsome; a couple of songs deal with difficult relationships, and she treats them with the seriousness they deserve. Also successful, because it suits her 'little girl' voice, is 'There Was A Li'l Mouse', a jazzy version of 'Froggy Went A-Courtin''. A remake of 'Don't You Feel My Leg' shows no advance on the '30s versions, however, and elsewhere she sings 'It's cold in the street, my shoe soles are beat, I'm a junkie with a habit, ain't had nothing to eat,' with complete indifference to meaning. The disc is completed by five songs from Wee Bea Booze (q.v.), and four by the obscure Baby Dee (Dolores Spriggs), fronting a lively band which includes a fiery trumpeter.

** Blue Lu Barker 1946–1949
Classics 1130 *Barker; Shad Collins, Ulysses Smith Jr, Earl Barnes, unknowns (t); Teddy McRae, Jerry Jerome, Dave Cavanaugh, James Jackson Jr, unknowns (ts); Norman Lester, Gerald Wiggins, Joe Pairs, unknown (p); Danny Barker, unknown (g); Ernest Williamson, Eddie Davis, Percy Gabriel, unknowns (b); Woodie Nichols, Peppy Prince, Paul Barbarin, unknowns (d); band (clapping, v).* 8/46–10/49.

The Apollo recordings, including the unissued titles but

minus the alternative take, are also on Classics, evidently dubbed from Delmark, who predictably offer better sound quality. The disc is completed by 17 titles recorded for Capitol in Los Angeles and New Orleans. Blue Lu now sings as forcefully as she knows how, and the results are her best recordings. There are some satisfying solos from the musicians, the pianists and tenorists being especially effective, but the Capitol sides are uneven; Blue Lu's territory is kittenish insinuation – blues for nightclubbers – but for every amusing *double entendre* number there's a weak novelty, a fussy arrangement or a beery male chorus.

*(*) Live At The New Orleans Jazz Festival
Orleans OR 2111 *Barker; Greg Stafford (t); Frank Naundorf (tb); David Grillier (cl); Walter Lewis (p); Danny Barker (g); Edmond Foucher (b); Shannon Powell (d). 89.*

Aged 75, Blue Lu had undergone a tracheotomy not long before this gig. She performs five songs, and one must admire her grit; unfortunately it's gone into her voice, which is a rasping monotone. On the other half of the disc, Danny Barker sings, and the band continues to be relentlessly ordinary. cs

Roosevelt 'Booba' Barnes (1936–96)
VOCAL, GUITAR, HARMONICA

Barnes spent seven years in Chicago from 1964, but otherwise Greenville, Mississippi, was his home. In 1982, he began operating the Playboy Club, on Greenville's violent, drug-ravaged Nelson Street, and both club and owner seemed to embody the town's blues history. Barnes's only album came late in his career, generating a wider reputation and some overseas engagements, but it was not long before cancer claimed him.

**** The Heartbroken Man
Rooster Blues R 2363 *Barnes; James 'T-Model' Ford (g); James Earl Franklin, Willie Miller (b); Terry Taylor (d). 88.*

Anyone who saw Booba Barnes in live performance will remember the high energy and the showmanship, even when his last illness was upon him. Some of that presence is inevitably lost in the transition to record, but *The Heartbroken Man* does about as well as it can in capturing Barnes and the Playboys' pared-down, cranked-up Delta blues funk, augmented on one track by T-Model Ford's guitar. Barnes took what he needed from the singing and guitar playing of Little Milton, a Nelson Streeter who made it to national status, but his biggest hero was Howlin' Wolf. His version of Wolf's earthquake growl was forced out of a lanky, rail-thin frame, and sounds as if it's had half the frequencies filtered out, but there's no denying the success of his assaults on the Wolf's repertoire, which sometimes fracture two or three songs into an almost new number. Even more startling is the way that Barnes scrapes the sophisticated, ladykilling veneer off songs associated with Milton and Bobby Bland, finding the raw pain of love and loss underneath. Playing harmonica, and accompanied by just bass and drums, he similarly reinvigorates 'Scratch My Back', converting Slim Harpo's novelty dance hit into a pounding summons to erotic action. Defiantly wild and unhomogenized, Booba Barnes's music was the real deal. cs

Barrelhouse Chuck (born 1958)
PIANO, ORGAN, VOCAL

Raised in Ohio, Chuck Goering moved with his family in 1972 to Florida, where he played in The Red Rooster Band. In 1979 he took himself off to Chicago to hang out with Little Brother Montgomery, Sunnyland Slim and Pinetop Perkins, becoming not only their pupil but their friend. He has worked extensively in the US and Europe and is an experienced session musician who has played on many dates for Delmark, Earwig, Black Magic and other labels.

*** Salute To Sunnyland Slim
Blue Loon 035 *Barrelhouse Chuck; The Blues Swingers (brass, reeds); Todd Levine (h, v); Johnny Tanner (h); Hash Brown, Billy Flynn, Rich Kirch (g); Betty Ducre, Calvin Jones, Rick Holmes, Frank Bandy, Michael Peters (b); S. P. Leary, John Carpender, Sam Lay, Willie Smith, Kenny Smith (d). 99?*

*** Prescription For The Blues
The Sirens SR-5004 *Barrelhouse Chuck; Erwin Helfer (p). 11/01–4/02.*

Barrelhouse Chuck is not a showy pianist. His few fast pieces are nearly all short – under two minutes – and the preponderance of slow, reflective blues suggests that these are what he prefers to play. On *Prescription For The Blues* the title track is recognizably in the spirit of its writer, Little Brother Montgomery, while 'Tin Pan Alley' evokes Curtis Jones and 'Johnson Machine Gun' Sunnyland Slim, but respect never slides into imitation, and in the Leroy Carr pieces 'Straight Alky Blues' and 'My Own Lonesome Blues' Chuck distances himself from the original treatments without diminishing their essence. As a singer, though no one would mistake him for one of his models, he has a firm grasp of the idiom, and when he adopts a husky, tremulous delivery in the manner of Little Brother Montgomery the effect is both poignant and personal. Helfer plays with characteristic sensitivity on three tracks, one a pretty duet for piano and farfisa organ on 'Ain't Nobody's Business'. Warm and accurate recording further enhances a quietly impressive album. Chuck also contributes to *8 Hands On 88 Keys: Chicago Blues Piano Masters* (The Sirens SR-5003).

The same general observations apply to the earlier *Salute To Sunnyland Slim*, where Chuck is heard mostly in band settings. (The impressive list of sidemen is an index of the respect musicians have for him.) There are only two of Slim's compositions, 'Depression Blues' and 'Going Back To Memphis', the point of the title presumably being that all Chuck's playing acknowledges the guidance of the man who called him 'my son'. This is a likeable album, but the message comes across more powerfully on its successor. TR

Dave Bartholomew (born 1920)
VOCAL, TRUMPET, ARRANGER

Bartholomew was born in Edgard, Louisiana, and raised in New Orleans, where he was taught music in high school. In the '30s he worked in various Louisiana bands and with Fats Pichon on Mississippi riverboats. After military service he led bands in Houston and New Orleans, where he hooked up with Lew Chudd of Imperial Records and began his long working relationship with Fats Domino. He was also closely associated as songwriter, accompanist and producer with Smiley Lewis.

Although not very active in the recording studio since the '60s, he has continued to play with his own jazz bands and occasionally with Domino.

**(*) Dave Bartholomew 1947–1950
Classics 5002 *Bartholomew; Joe Harris (as); Clarence Hall, Herb Hardesty, Lee Allen, Alvin 'Red' Tyler (ts); Fred Lands, Salvador Doucette (p); Meyer Kennedy, Ernest McLean, unknown (g); Frank Fields, Peter 'Chuck' Badie (b); Earl Palmer, Thomas Moore (d). 9/47–50.*

*** In The Alley
King KCD 6026 *Bartholomew; Willie Wells (t); Joe Harris, Holley Dismukes (as); Clarence Hall, Charles Edwards, Herb Hardesty (ts); Ted Buckner (bs); Fred Lands, Todd Rhodes, Salvador Doucette (p); Willie Gaddy, John Faire, Ernest McLean (g); Frank Fields, Joe Williams (b); Earl Palmer, Bill Benjamin (d); Tommy Ridgley (v). 4/49–1/52.*

*** The Very Best Of Dave Bartholomew
Bayou BCD-1003 *Bartholomew; Willie Wells (t); Joe Harris, Holley Dismukes, Wendell Duconge, unknown (as); Clarence Hall, Herb Hardesty, Charles Edwards, Lee Allen, unknown (ts); Ted Buckner (bs); Fred Lands, Salvador Doucette, Todd Rhodes, Fats Domino, Edward Frank, unknown (p); Ernest McLean, Willie Gaddy, Edgar Blanchard, poss. Pee Wee Crayton, Walter Nelson, Justin Adams (g); Frank Fields, Peter 'Chuck' Badie, Joe Williams, unknown (b); Earl Palmer, Thomas Moore, Bill Benjamin, Cornelius Coleman, Charles Williams, unknown (d); Tommy Ridgley (v). 4/49–11/57.*

*** Dave Bartholomew 1950–1952
Classics 5055 *Similar to* In The Alley. *50–11/52.*

The diversity of the music on these CDs, a natural consequence of Bartholomew's training, is also a signal that his orchestra should be judged primarily as a showband, given to broad gestures, such as the leader's trumpet slides that sound like ricocheting gunshots. On the first Classics, mostly derived from DeLuxe and Imperial, 'Stardust' is peppered with that effect, while 'High Society Blues' is Dixieland corn. 'Country Boy' and other tracks, between showy trumpet choruses, display Bartholomew as a singer with a swagger reminiscent of Louis Jordan, particularly so in 'That's How You Got Killed Before'. The second and more interesting of the Classics sets opens with four bustling tracks for DeLuxe, surprisingly not issued at the time, including a song about the then current craze of pyramid selling and a 'Basin Street Breakdown' in which the unidentified guitarist plays a trill on one note for 54 seconds. These sides are also among the nine by Bartholomew, mostly from DeLuxe, on *Gettin' Funky: The Birth Of New Orleans R&B* (Proper PROPERBOX 28 4CD).

After that Bartholomew signed with King. His first two sessions had good original blues material like 'In The Alley', 'Sweet Home Blues', 'High Flying Woman', but the backings by Todd Rhodes's band inevitably lacked the New Orleans spice of his previous work. On his first reunion with his homies, however, Bartholomew could do no better than produce a raucous and seemingly under-rehearsed two-part blues, 'Lawdy Lawdy Lord', and the singalong novelty 'My Ding-A-Ling', which rang no cash-register bells at the time but would have them pealing merrily a generation later when rehung by Chuck Berry. The King CD shares two of its numbers with the first Classics and the rest, apart from a couple of alternative takes, with the second.

Most of Bayou's 32 tracks, however, are on none of the other CDs, half of them coming from later King sessions. This is a very entertaining collection, ranging from sober blues like 'No More Black Nights' to 'Shrimp And Gumbo', a street cry set to a mambo beat, and 'The Monkey', a byblow of the 'Signifying Money' family of toasts. Bartholomew reportedly cedes the piano stool to Fats Domino on several tracks, among them 'Cat Music' (based on 'Hit That Jive Jack') and the jolly boogie 'Good News'. The presentation is poor (no notes or recording data), but against that must be set the excellent selection, sound and playing time.

*** The Big Beat Of Dave Bartholomew
Capitol 37599 *Similar to above. 50–57.*

This VAC includes eight of Bartholomew's band's recordings but is primarily concerned with illustrating his career as a producer for Imperial. He knew better than almost anyone how to dress up a simple theme and make it distinctive, and here his designer's hand can be discerned in recordings that he supervised, and sometimes co-wrote, for New Orleans stars both major and minor, among them Fats Domino, Smiley Lewis, singer/pianist Archibald, Tommy Ridgley, Chris Kenner and Jewel King. EMI's more extensive 2CD survey of Bartholomew as a producer, *Spirit Of New Orleans: The Genius Of Dave Bartholomew*, appears to be deleted. His subsequent recordings have mostly been in the Dixieland idiom. TR

Lou Ann Barton (born 1954)
VOCAL

From Fort Worth, Texas, Barton worked in the '70s with Stevie Ray Vaughan, Jimmie Vaughan and Roomful Of Blues. Despite a well-received first album in 1980 for Asylum, co-produced by Jerry Wexler, her regional reputation did not develop into a national one, and her career has mostly been spent in the Southwest.

** Read My Lips
Antone's ANT 0009 *Barton; David 'Fathead' Newman, Joe Sublett (ts); Mark Kazanoff, Rocky Morales (s); Kim Wilson (h, v); Reese Wynans (o, p); Mel Brown, Mike Kindred (p); Jimmie Vaughan, Derek O'Brien, Denny Freeman, David Grissom (g); Jon Blondell, Tommy Shannon (b); George Rains (d); Fran Christina, Diana Ray, Paul Ray (v). 89.*

'There are few visions more incendiary,' writes John T. Davis, 'than the sight of "Miss Lou Ann", trailing smoke, stalking out on to a stage in a miniskirt you could stick in a highball glass.' While that isn't a sight that can readily be translated into sound, Barton does come across on record as a woman who gives a song a good seeing-to. Growling, she drags Slim Harpo's 'Shake Your Hips' and Wanda Jackson's blues 'Mean Mean Man' over the rough stones of Derek O'Brien's and Denny Freeman's guitars, pausing now and then to stretch into a soul ballad like 'You'll Lose A Good Thing' or 'It's Raining'. At heart, though, her métier is rock rather than blues, as she demonstrated on her debut album *Old Enough*, reissued by Antone's (ANTCD 0021) in 1992 but currently out of print, and on the early (1969–78) recordings, some live and all ill-produced, that surfaced much later on *Sugar Coated Love* (Multimedia MIL 3043) or the identical *The Thunderbroad* (Blues Factory BFY 47005). TR

Johnnie Bassett (born 1935)
VOCAL, GUITAR

Born in Florida, Bassett moved with his family to Detroit in 1944. He played saxophone and clarinet in his high-school band, and guitar with older blues artists. As a member of Joe Weaver's Bluenotes he recorded with many of Detroit's R&B artists. Later he worked with Little Sonny, and in organ combos. In the '90s he formed the Blues Insurgents.

**(*) I Gave My Life To The Blues
Black Magic BMCD 9034 *Bassett; Dwight Adams (t); Scott Petersen, Keith Kaminski (as, ts); Chris Codish (o, p); R. J. Spangler (d). 5/96.*

**(*) Bassett Hound
Fedora FCD 5004 *Bassett; Bill Heid (p); Dwayne Dolphin (b); R. J. Spangler (d). 10/96.*

Bassett's days with organ groups probably helped to refine his undramatic style. There is no flamboyance, and little surprise, in his guitar playing: just the easy-rocking mellifluousness of a skilled club musician. He sings, too, in the amiable, unexcited manner of a man who has an axe to play but none to grind. *I Gave My Life To The Blues* might seem a little bland, if it were not for the horns sprinkling pepper on the dish now and then.

With only a piano trio for backup, the ambience of a quiet night-spot is even more marked on *Bassett Hound*. Pianist Bill Heid, a sideman with Bassett since 1991, didn't play on *I Gave My Life To The Blues* but contributed four of the tunes; here he wrote all 11. Mostly conventional blues, they average around five minutes each; a producer who wasn't also a band member might not have let the tape run so long on most of them. Bassett's albums for Cannonball, *Cadillac Blues* (CBD 29103) and *Party My Blues Away* (CBD 29109), are deleted. TR

Chris Beard (born 1957)
VOCAL, GUITAR

Beard grew up in a blues household – his father is Joe Beard – and around musicians like Buddy Guy and Matt Murphy. He began playing in the Rochester, New York, area in his teens, and put in more than two decades' apprenticeship in blues and R&B bands before making his first album in 1997; the following year it won him a Handy Award nomination for Best New Blues Artist.

**(*) Barwalkin'
JSP JSPCD 288 *Beard; Jim Hunt (t); Bruce Feiner (ts); Robert Feiner (bs); Brian Charette (o, p); Johnny Rawls (g, prod); Randy Lippincott (b); Barry Harrison (d). 97?*

**(*) Born To Play The Blues
JSP JSPCD 2148 *Beard; Eric Little (t); Alan Murphy (tb); Dominic Calabrese (as); Quinn Lawrence, Marvin Williams (ts); J. J. Moscato (kb); Paul Baldwin (g); Dave Daansen (b); Robert Garcia (d); Mary Ellen Hadgen, Toni Kirkland (v). 00?*

Beard's allegiance to the playing of Albert King is obvious on both albums but particularly in the thickly drawn guitar lines of the slow numbers 'Somebody's Sleeping' and 'It's Over' on *Born To Play The Blues*. The material, all Beard's except for Jimmy Morello's 'Silver Spoon' on the second CD, is written to familiar blues formulas, sung without much gusto and arranged and played with little dynamic variety. *Born To Play The Blues* is the more vigorous performance, with a busier, at times hyperactive, rhythm section and lusty interjections by the horns, but the unremitting pressure of the music becomes exhausting, and the listener may long for the relief of a more relaxed rendition like *Barwalkin*'s 'All Night Long' or 'Delivery Man'.

**(*) Live Wire
NorthernBlues NBM 0028 *Beard; Quinn Lawrence (brass, reeds); Alan Murphy, George Snell (kb); Brother Wilson, Steve Grills (g); Marvin Parker, Tony Jackson, Darren Robinson (b); Buddy Honeycutt (d). 04.*

Having opened with the grand guitar gestures of 'Born To Play The Blues', this long album maintains that fervid blues-rock temperature for half an hour or so with a two-part tribute to Luther Allison and a general subordination of words to music. But listeners who find that sort of thing exhausting should not wearily conclude that they have the measure of the album, which moves on to a sequence of cool-down pieces like Dennis Walker's 'Never Felt No Blues' and 'Can't Walk Away', sandwiching Allison's 'A Change Must Come': all impressively done with no recourse to overstatement. TR

Joe Beard (born 1938)
VOCAL, GUITAR

Born in Ashland, Mississippi, where he knew Matt Murphy and his brothers and the older bluesman Nathan Beauregard, Beard moved to Rochester, New York, at the age of 16 and soon began playing in public, first on bass, later on guitar, which he would practise on the porch of his neighbour, Son House. Becoming a seasoned club player, he opened shows by many visiting artists and toured in Europe in 1983.

*** Blues Union
AudioQuest AQ-CD 1039 *Beard; David 'Fathead' Newman (ts); Joe Dubuc (h); Bruce Katz (o, p); Ronnie Earl (g); Rod Carey (b); Per Hanson (d). 8/95.*

Beard's first album, *No More Cherry Rose* (Kingsnake), is no longer in print, leaving *Blues Union* as his earliest available work. He displays an impressive range of blues impersonations: 'Just To Be With You' sounds like Magic Slim, 'Think' like Jimmy McCracklin and 'Please Don't Light The Flame' like Jimmy Reed, while 'Sally Mae' and 'Late In The Evening' are stunningly accurate imitations of early John Lee Hooker and Lightnin' Hopkins respectively. Despite the puppetry, this is an entertaining set, enhanced by the ever-reliable Broadcasters. Not for the first – or, probably, the fiftieth – time, Earl gives a prodigal display of creativity, particularly when stretching out in duet with Katz during the Beard originals 'Feets Out In The Hall' and 'Telling It Like Is'. The album is mastered at rather a low level, and Beard's voice, which naturally sounds weary and older than his years, seems even more so by being submerged in the mix.

*** For Real
AudioQuest AQ-CD 1049 *Beard; Jerry Portnoy (h); Bruce Katz (o, p); Duke Robillard (g); Rod Carey (b); Per Hanson (d). 11/97.*

*** **Dealin'**
AudioQuest AQ-CD 1055 *As above.* 4/00.

Beard opens *For Real*, like its forerunner, with a brisk original number, 'Drinking Old Taylor'. It's immediately apparent that Duke Robillard is going to impress himself on the music as profitably as Ronnie Earl did last time out. It also becomes evident, as the CD spins, that Beard is not to be distracted from his favourite imitations: John Lee Hooker is remembered in 'Dirty Groundhog' and Lightnin' Hopkins in 'Airplane Blues', while 'Don't Start Me Talking' echoes Sonny Boy Williamson II's original. When not engaged in those appreciative exercises Beard often slips into a generic, but well-played and hearty, Chicago band idiom such as Muddy Waters would have approved. A thread of such performances also runs through *Dealin'*, interspersed with the usual bows to the masters – 'Holding A Losing Hand' in the manner of Hooker, 'If I Get Lucky' after Hopkins – and a more original, slow, meditative piece, 'That "So-Called" Friend Of Mine'. Excellent playing by Portnoy and Katz and well-chosen material distinguish both albums. If you esteem the artists and styles that Beard values, you will almost certainly be gratified by his knowing but unslavish representations of them.

Beau Jocque (1952–99)
VOCAL, ACCORDION

Andrus Espre's father, Sandrus, was an accordionist, but Andrus didn't take up the instrument until 1987, when he was laid up after falling 20 feet on to concrete at work and breaking his back. He also willed himself to walk again, despite the doctors' prognosis, and within a few years had turned professional, using his nickname, Beau Jocque ('big handsome guy' – he was 6' 6"). He and the Zydeco Hi-Rollers were the music's dominant force in the '90s, revolutionizing it with funk grooves, double-kick drumming and 'live sampling' of rock and rap: at the peak of his fame, there would be a mile of cars parked outside Richard's Club. Beau Jocque didn't let a 1996 heart attack slow him down, and was consolidating his reputation outside Louisiana and overseas when he suffered a second, fatal attack.

*** **This Is Beau Jocque!**
Mardi Gras MG 1057 *Beau Jocque; Kevin Navy (g); Retell Chavis (b); Joseph Carrier (d, v); Wilfred Pierre (rb).* 91.

This is simultaneously Beau Jocque's first and last CD; originally issued as *My Name Is Beau Jocque* (Paula PCD-1031), the material was reordered and rereleased after his death. The Zydeco Hi-Rollers heard here are actually Retell Chavis's Night Rockers, taken over and renamed; despite the inclusion of 2 Live Crew's 'Pop That Coochie', this is a largely traditional set, heavy on the two-steps and much influenced by Retell's Uncle Boozoo. Very different things were to follow, but this CD should not be overlooked.

*** **Beau Jocque Boogie**
Rounder CD 2120 *Beau Jocque; Ray Johnson (g, v); Chuck Bush (b, v); Steve Charlot (d, v); Wilfred Pierre (rb, v).* 2/93.
***(*) **Give Him Cornbread, Live!**
Rounder CD 2160 *As above.* 9/93.

(*) **Pick Up On This!
Rounder CD 2129 *As above, except add Gabriel Perrodin (g, v); Scott Billington (perc), DJ Batman (turntable).* 10–11/93.

Beau Jocque had put together the definitive version of the *nouveau* zydeco Hi-Rollers by the time he signed his initial two-album deal with Rounder. (*Give Him Cornbread, Live!* was issued posthumously.) As it would continue to be, the most compelling aspect of the Hi-Rollers' music on these three discs is the throbbing engine-room of drums, rubboard and, above all, Chuck Bush's counter-melodies on six-string bass. Ray Johnson's guitar is not without rock influences, but not overwhelmed by them, and his unfailing swing is both integrated with and a contrast to the funk undertow. There are some astonishing moments where past and future are seamlessly combined, as when (on both *Beau Jocque Boogie* and the live album) Bush plays the tune of 'I Went To The Dance Last Night' on bass. On the other hand, the waltzes, with the drums sledgehammering TWO! THREE! every bar, feel like uneasy, token salutes to tradition; they disappear altogether on later releases.

The chief drawback to Beau Jocque's music is Beau Jocque's voice, which is a narrow growl, occasionally varied with a falsetto wail. Every song is delivered full blast, and although the call-and-response vocal interplay with Charlot adds some variety, one or two CDs will be enough for most listeners. *Give Him Cornbread, Live!* is the best of these early recordings; a sizeable chunk of the setlist promotes, and therefore duplicates, *Beau Jocque Boogie*, but the adrenalin rush of a battle of the bands with Boozoo Chavis gives the live versions the edge, even if a draw was doubtless agreed in advance.

** **I'm Coming Home**
Mardi Gras MG 1046 *Beau Jocque; Michael Lockett (kb); Russell Dorion (g, voicebox); Joseph Chavis (g); Chuck Bush (b); Steve Charlot (d); Wilfred Pierre (rb).* 94.

Between contracts for Rounder, Beau Jocque released *Beau Jocque's Nursery Rhyme* on his own label; its four tracks and two unissued titles comprise half of this further posthumous release. Acting as his own producer, Beau Jocque is short of musical ideas, and Dorion overdoes the voicebox, which, albeit unintentionally, devalues the elegiac associations of the title track. The balance of the disc was recorded by the Hi-Rollers shortly after their leader's death, with guest accordionists Jo Jo Reed and Jeffrey Broussard; understandably, it was a somewhat subdued session.

♛ **** **Git It, Beau Jocque!**
Rounder CD 2134 *Beau Jocque; Ray Johnson (g, v); Joseph Chavis (g); Chuck Bush (b, v); Steve Charlot (d, v); Wilfred Pierre (rb, v).* 9/94.

Another live album, and Beau Jocque's best; he and the band were in inspired form, and this is one of those rare live discs that genuinely conveys the excitement and atmosphere of the night, down to a musical announcement of the winning raffle ticket. Chavis's Hendrix-influenced lead lines are in fiery contrast to Johnson's relatively more relaxed style, and the marvels of Chuck Bush's bass work are given due prominence in the mix. Even a 12-minute 'Shaggy Dog Two Step' is not a bit too long. This is the CD that explains why Beau Jocque was all-conquering in his time and place.

** **Gonna Take You Downtown**
Rounder CD 2150 *Beau Jocque; Michael Lockett (o, kb, perc, v); Russell Dorion (g, voicebox); Chuck Bush (b, v); Steve Charlot (d, v); Eric Minix (d); Wilfred Pierre (rb). 4/96.*
*** **Check It Out, Lock It In, Crank It Up!**
Rounder CD 2158 *Similar to above. 3/98.*

Gonna Take You Downtown's combination of a keyboard player with Beau Jocque finding jazzier chord voicings often makes for fussy, cluttered music, at its worst when Lockett plays a 'flute' solo on 'Knockin' On Heaven's Door'. (Bob Dylan and a flute: just what zydeco needs.) 'Kinder 2 Step' is old-style fun, and 'Make It Stank', with drum samples and tape loops, is new style technofun, but they close a disc that's usually disappointing, whether the band are covering War or D. L. Menard. *Check It Out, Lock It In, Crank It Up!* is less ambitious and more successful (and the keyboard usually complements rather than intruding), but there's a sense that the Hi-Rollers can do it in their sleep. 'Tequila' was not a good idea, but otherwise the song list is well chosen, with a splendid 'Keep A Knockin'' standing out.

(*) The Best Of Beau Jocque And The Zydeco Hi-Rollers
Rounder Heritage Series 11603 *As for relevant CDs above, except add Scott Ardoin (g). 2/93–3/98.*
*** **Classics**
Rounder 2178 *As above, except omit Ardoin. 2/93–3/98.*

On *The Best Of* Ardoin appears on two previously unissued live tracks, but there is nothing from the two live CDs which are Beau Jocque's best for Rounder. This is an ill-judged selection, heavy on riffing like a pneumatic drill and rock covers, light on traditionally based zydeco and hardcore blues. *Classics* is four tracks shorter and also has nothing live, but it's bluesier, rootsier and in every way preferable.

***(*) **Zydeco Giant**
Mardi Gras MG 1043 *Beau Jocque; Michael Lockett (kb); Ray Mouton, Kent Pierre Augustine (g); Chuck Bush (b, v); Eddie Bodin (d); Wilfred Pierre (rb, v). 99.*

Beau Jocque's first and, as it turned out, only new recording for Mardi Gras finds him turning down the volume at the bass end and exploring an eclectic range of material in a soundworld that's often close to *vieux zydeco*. The explorations are within blues and Louisiana music – no rock covers this time, although one song gets an effective house remix – and versions of 'Worried Life Blues' and 'Rock Me Baby' are Beau Jocque's best blues efforts. If the French of 'Pine Point Trail Ride' seems token, its relaxed subtlety (vocals included!) is not. 'That's My Car' is a fabulously bouncy two-step, the new guitarists sparkle on the jazzy 'Breezin'', and the whole CD is a promise sadly unfulfilled. CS

Robert Belfour (born 1940)
VOCAL, GUITAR

A late-flowering exponent of the north Mississippi riff-based style also heard in the work of his mentor Junior Kimbrough, R. L. Burnside and Jessie Mae Hemphill, Holly Springs native Belfour provides convincing proof of the tenacity of the area's musical traditions. More importantly, his refusal to emulate Kimbrough and Burnside's willingness to bend to contemporary pressures keeps the original folk art intact.

***(*) **The Spirit Lives On**
Hot Fox HF-CD-005 *Belfour. 1/94.*

Although there are obvious similarities between Belfour, Kimbrough and Burnside, his feels like the purer musical source. Each of the eight songs here, though all are riff-based, is given its own distinctive melodic signature. 'Boogie Chillen', 'Smokestack Lightning' and 'Catfish Blues' may be rather too familiar but they're moulded to Belfour's technique alongside his own 'Down The Road Of Love' and 'Holding My Pillow Crying'. He sings 'Smokestack' and 'Poor Boy Long Way From Home' in a Wolf-like tone, whereas his natural voice has a choked, nasal quality that complements the drone of his guitar figures. It would be too much to call his discovery a major event but his existence proves the durability of the music he plays. (The remainder of this VAC is by Big Lucky Carter, Mose Vinson, Glen Faulkner and David Evans.)

♛ **** **What's Wrong With You**
Fat Possum 80336 *Belfour; Bryan Barry (d). 00.*

Belfour shows an unwavering respect for the rhythmic pulse throughout this short but intriguing set. Most of the nine songs rely upon a combination of surging riffs and dominant chords that create the trance-like absorption peculiar to musicians from the Holly Springs area. Belfour's songs, including 'Walking The Floor', 'Holding My Pillow' and 'Bad Luck', mine a rich but concentrated seam of infidelity and loss, their subject-matter emphasized by the agitation implied in his constrained vocals. The legacies of John Lee Hooker (another local man made good) and Lightnin' Hopkins can be detected from time to time, the latter's archetypal solo figures cropping up in 'What's Wrong With You'. Producer Matthew Johnson apparently recognized the power in Belfour's music and resisted the temptation to import remixers and scratchers. In time he may realize the excellence of his decision.

***(*) **Pushin' My Luck**
Fat Possum 0369 *Belfour; Ted Gainey (d). 02.*

There's nothing new here but this is very much a consolidation of the skills Belfour displayed in *What's Wrong With You*. Gigs and some woodshedding have improved his guitar technique and eliminated the minor glitches present on the previous set. Moreover, his fragmented melodies have become more intricate without slowing the basic impetus of his music. If these ten songs have a fault, it's a lack of rhythmic variation, with no overtly slow songs apart from the final 'I'm Gonna Leave'. 'Sweet Brown Sugar' adopts Hooker's propulsive strumming and is one of the album's highlights, along with the title track, 'You Got Me Crying', 'I Got My Eyes On You' and 'Crazy Ways'. The drums that are present on five tracks are welcome but by no means necessary. NS

Carey Bell (born 1936)
VOCAL, HARMONICA, BASS

The scion of a large musical family, Carey Bell Harrington went through a long apprenticeship, taking instruction from the two Walters, Jacobs and Horton. He later worked and recorded with Muddy Waters, Willie Dixon, Earl Hooker and

Horton before leading his own band, often featuring his son Lurrie and one or more of his brothers. Bell's harmonica style draws largely on the two Walters and Junior Wells, without quite matching their originality. More often entertaining than inspiring, he's experienced fluctuating fortunes in what has become a long, sometimes turbulent career.

** Carey Bell's Blues Harp
Delmark DE-622 *Bell; Pinetop Perkins (p); Jimmy 'Fast Fingers' Dawkins, Eddie Taylor, Royal Johnson (g); Joe Harper (b); W. Williams, Sidney Thomas (d).* 2–5/69.

Listening to this album is like touring the ruins of a past civilization, marvelling at what it achieved and regretting its present dereliction. Despite the reputations of some of the musicians present, they manage only pale imitations of others' greater moments. The album was made at two sessions, one of which featured a lacklustre Perkins, and neither band does more than run through the changes with indifferent precision. Dawkins and Johnson strive for flashes of technical brilliance, trying without success to evoke Robert Lockwood and Luther Tucker. Bell is an intermittently effective vocalist but his harmonica playing lacks adventure and inspiration. His wielding of the chromatic instrument is ponderous and timid. The material chosen relies heavily on Little Walter and Junior Wells but these flaccid, overlong performances lack the tension and invention of the originals.

**(*) Heartaches And Pain
Delmark DD-666 *Bell; Bob Riedy (p); Lurrie Bell, Alabama Jr Pettis, Dave Specter (g); Aron Burton (b); Sam Lay (d).* 3/77.

In 1977 veteran producer Ralph Bass made ten 'quickie' albums, of which this was the last to be issued, 17 years later. Artists were required to come up with just eight songs, each to last approximately four minutes, with first takes a priority. Given the conditions, it's hardly surprising the musicians went for proficiency rather than inspiration. This one benefited from Bell being a member of Riedy's band at the time; it also represented his son Lurrie's recording debut, which he handles well under the circumstances. 'Carey Bell Rocks' is the first of three instrumentals, the only one to reveal a coherent structure. Songs weren't a problem either, since Bell had an ability to string unrelated verses together, a dubious talent he also applies to songs by Doctor Clayton and Little Walter. One can't blame the musicians for the exploitative nature of the session but the results are inevitably no more than pleasant.

*** Living Chicago Blues – Vol. I
Alligator ALCD 7701 *Bell; Bob Riedy (p); Lurrie Bell (g); Aron Burton (b); Odie Payne Jr (d).* 8/78 or 9/78.

This brief session, occupying a quarter of a VAC, is the antithesis of Bell's debut album. Riedy's band, including a subdued Lurrie Bell, is tightly organized, economic and precise. Bell responds with controlled and aggressive harmonica playing and sings with more authority than he previously evinced. His chromatic harmonica on 'Laundromat Blues' is particularly inventive. Two original songs, 'One Day' and 'Woman In Trouble', are derivative but confidently performed and leave the listener wishing the session had been extended.

*** Goin' On Main Street
Evidence ECD 26055 *Bell; Billy Branch (h); Tom Zydron (o); Lurrie Bell (g, v); Elisha 'Eli' Murray, Hubert Sumlin (g); Carey Bell Jr, Bob Stroger (b); Theodore 'Dino' Davies, Odie Payne (d).* 3/81–6/82.

A largely successful Chicago session first released in Germany, this finds Bell and son Lurrie in mildly impressive form. The latter sings the nine-minute 'I Am Worried', with frequent guitar solos that bring Buddy Guy to mind, as well as two live recordings from a 1981 European tour. Father Carey blots his copybook by claiming authorship of the title track but performs it and his other songs well enough. His harmonica playing stops short of being authoritative, relying too often on repetition to be compared with his mentors. His nascent trademark 'whinny', first heard on *Heartaches And Pain*, occurs twice. Branch appears on 'Tribute To Big Walter', an entertaining but under-achieving duet that emphasizes the loss of the deceased Horton. Like most of the other tracks, it outstays its welcome, challenging the musicians' inventiveness and the listener's patience.

**(*) Harpslinger
JSP JSP 5102 *Bell; Richard Studholme (g); Andy Pyle (b); Geoff Nichols (d).* 88.

Tracks 1–9 are from a studio session that continued a collaboration with Studholme begun on *Harpmaster* (JSP JSPCD 250, deleted); his band accompanies precisely and well. Bell responds with more first-rate harmonica work, showing invention at both ends of the unwieldy chromatic harmonica on the instrumental '85%'. The one drawback – and it's a significant one – is his increasing habit of whinnying through the harmonica mike. It happens at the end of the first two tracks and then erupts during an otherwise satisfying version of 'Blues With A Feeling'. The listener is left cowering in fear of its return, which happens all too frequently, although 'It's So Easy To Love You' escapes unscathed. This SACD release (replacing JSPCD 264) is augmented with four performances by Lurrie Bell, with Carey, from *Young Man's Blues* (JSPCD 2134).

*** Dynasty
JSP JSPCD 276 *Bell; Steve Bell (h); Jerry Soto (o); Lurrie Bell, Pete Allen (g, v); Tyson Bell (b); James Bell (d).* 88.
*** Brought Up The Hard Way
JSP JSPCD 802 *Bell; Jerry Soto (o); Louisiana Red, Lefty Dizz (g, v); Richard Studholme, Lurrie Bell, Pete Allen (g); Andy Pyle, Tyson Bell (b); Geoff Nichols, James Bell (d).* 88–90.

Two best-of compilations that juggle with the contents of previous LP and CD releases. One title from the original *Dynasty* is omitted and replaced by three tracks from Lurrie Bell's *Everybody Wants To Win*. Carey Bell leads five of *Dynasty*'s 12 tracks, indulging his whinny when so moved. 'The Gladys Shuffle' is a chromatic harmonica feature with no real theme, as is Steve Bell's 'New Harp In Town'. The set ends with a dragging slow blues sung by Pete Allen, taking more than eight minutes to run its course. *Brought Up The Hard Way* draws from all of the above releases and includes vocal features by Louisiana Red and Lefty Dizz with Bell's harmonica accompaniment. Of particular note is 'I'm Going Upstairs' from the Bell family sessions, which finds both father and guitar-playing son in stirring form, playing off one another in the course of several solo choruses. This is part of a 'Retrospectives' series and as such offers a very flattering sequence of music.

***(*) Mellow Down Easy
Blind Pig BP 74291 *Bell; Mark 'Lips Lackowitz' Hurwitz (h); Kevin McKendree (o); Steve Jacobs (g); Brian McGregor (b); Buddy Grandell (d).* 91.

An unexpectedly successful sequence of 13 songs finds Bell at the top of his game, singing confidently and blowing adept and often stirring harmonica solos. The band are restrained but supportive, with Jacobs restricting his virtuosity to 'For The Love Of A Woman'. Bell wrote four songs and collaborated on two of the three instrumentals, 'Delta Time' and 'Big Walter Strut'; the third is a particularly imaginative rendition of 'St Louis Blues'. Covers such as 'Five Long Years', 'Walkin' Thru The Park' and 'Walkin' By Myself' may be over-familiar but the originals 'Just Like You' and 'One Day', despite a dearth of sung verses, more than compensate. Overall, Bell achieves a level of excellence here that regrettably is yet to resurface.

***(*) Deep Down
Alligator ALCD 4828 *Bell; Lucky Peterson (p); Carl Weathersby, Lurrie Bell (g); Johnny B. Gayden (b); Ray 'Killer' Allison (d).* 94.

Bell benefits greatly from a high-quality backing band and a tight production team that curbs his habitual excesses. The programme includes the expected nods to Little Walter and Muddy Waters but Bell's own compositions are better than usual, particularly the slow blues 'When I Get Drunk', 'Lonesome Stranger' and a stark rearrangement of 'Shake 'Em On Down' ('Must I Holler'). Bell gets a passing grade for his singing, which is more about personality than technique. His harmonica solos, too, are confidently projected, although as a whole they constitute sequences of riffs rather than linear progressions. 'Jawbreaker', the expected chromatic feature, is all the better for being short, as are most of the other tracks. It tends to suggest that Bell might inherit the Chicago harmonica crown on merit rather than by default.

*** Good Luck Man
Alligator ALCD 4854 *Bell; Johnny 'Fingers' Iguana (p); Steve Jacobs, Will Crosby (g); T. A. James, Johnny B. Gayden (b); Tom Parker, Willie Hayes (d).* 97.

With four producers (one more than on *Deep Down*), the stolid air of the committee pervades this record. Bell continues to sing and play well enough – in 'Bell Hop' (an update of Little Walter's 'Evans Shuffle') he sounds like the true inheritor of his mentor's crown – but the spark is intermittent. This may be the result of using two backing groups, one his regular accompanists, the other composed of Crosby, Gayden and Hayes. The presence of lead guitarist Jacobs is a definite drawback, his crashingly inappropriate solos destroying the others' good work. The committee's proposal to use songs associated with employers and pals like Muddy, Johnny Young and Big and Little Walter might have succeeded if they'd avoided 'I'm A Business Man' and Jimmy Reed's 'Good Lover'. As it is the album's highlight is Bell's extended slow blues 'Teardrops', an example of restraint that Jacobs would have done well to mark. NS

*** Second Nature
Alligator ALCD 4898 *Bell; Lurrie Bell (g, v).* 04.

Credited to Carey & Lurrie Bell, *Second Nature* is an acoustic collaboration between father and son, who share the vocal duties. Carey's 'Short Dress Woman' is as exiguous as its subject, and Lurrie's concluding ballad, 'Here I Go Again', is mercifully short, but the son's stinging guitar and emotional singing give tunes as familiar as 'Rock Me' and 'Key To The Highway' an unexpected charge. Lurrie usually performs with more originality and commitment than his father, who sometimes traps himself in meandering solos, perhaps because he's unused to playing without a rhythm section. CS

Ed Bell (1905–66)
VOCAL, GUITAR

Bell grew up in Greenville, Alabama, where he learned from an older cousin, Joe Pat Dean. As well as the sides he made in his own name, it is practically certain that he made the recordings credited to Barefoot Bill and Sluefoot Joe. Reportedly tiring of the blues, he became a Baptist minister in Montgomery, Alabama.

**** Ed Bell (1927–1930)
Document DOCD-5090 *Bell; Clifford Gibson (p, g); Pillie Bolling (g, v).* c. 9/27–4/30.

The foggy acoustics of Bell's first recordings, for Paramount, cannot dim the vitality of his musical ideas, such as the insistently repetitive picking patterns of 'Mean Conductor Blues' and 'Frisco Whistle Blues'. The QRS session that followed some 18 months later was a less satisfactory affair inasmuch as Bell played guitar on only a couple of numbers; the others were accompanied, in his typically deliberate manner, by Clifford Gibson, and 'House Top Blues' and 'Rocky Road Blues' have much of the measured sobriety of Gibson's own recordings. By contrast, 'Grab It And Run' and 'Leaving Train Blues' are imitations, not unskilful ones, of Texas Alexander and Lonnie Johnson. Bell's subsequent sides for Columbia, such as 'My Crime Blues', 'Squabblin' Blues' and 'Barefoot Bill's Hard Luck Blues', are far better recorded, allowing the listener to appreciate the detail of the guitar accompaniments and the twisting contours of his vocal melodies, which at times have the lonesome ring of a field holler. The slower tempos of these later sides prohibit the rhythmic excitement of the Paramount recordings, a quality which in any case Bell seems to have exchanged for a more Gibsonesque approach to phrasing. The attractive picking on ragtime chord progressions in 'Carry It Right Back Home' and the similar 'She's A Fool Gal' makes a pleasant change. His two duets with Pillie Bolling, a Greenville associate, are trite variants of 'It's Tight Like That'; Bolling's own 'Brown Skin Woman' and 'Shake Me Like A Dog', his only, and undistinguished, solo record, complete the album. TR

Lurrie Bell (born 1958)
VOCAL, GUITAR

As a co-founder of the Sons Of Blues (see Billy Branch) and a member of Koko Taylor's backing band at 19, Carey Bell's eldest son seemed to be on the threshold of a notable career. The wild edge to his inventive guitar playing brought comparisons with a young Buddy Guy. But then something happened and a bright future toppled over into a nightmare present. Since his initial protracted lost weekend, Bell has made efforts to put the pieces back together but so far he's been unable to revive the promise of his early years.

*** Living Chicago Blues – Vol. III
Alligator ALCD 7703 *Bell; Billy Branch (h, v); Freddie Dixon (b); Jeff Ruffin (d).* 78.

Recorded as part of a survey of Chicago's blues bands, this features the original incarnation of the Sons Of Blues. Bell sings on just one of the three tracks included, a well-executed rendition of Freddie King's 'Have You Ever Loved A Woman'. His vocal sounds young and confident and his guitar playing combines sure-footed rhythm and imaginative solos with an acute sense of dynamics. Bell also appears with his father on the Lovie Lee session in this compilation.

*** Young Man's Blues
JSP JSPCD 2134 *Bell; Carey Bell (h, v); Steve Bell (h); Dave Bainbridge (o, p); Jack Hills (p); Lucky Lopez Evans (g, v); Pete Allen, Richard Studholme, Norman Beaker (g); Tyson Bell, Julian Taylor, Chip O'Connor (b); James Bell, Geoff Nichols, Tim Franks (d).* 89–4/90.

Everybody Wants To Win (JSP JSPCD 227), Bell's debut solo album, was recorded in Chicago with his father and brothers around him. Lurrie sang adequately and played well enough but seemed constrained by his siblings, as if not wanting to show off in their presence. Most of the songs were too long, Carey Bell's 'Second Hand Man' stretching to almost eight minutes. Perhaps realizing the album's shortcomings, JSP refurbished it as *Young Man's Blues*, surrounding a core selection of the original cuts with different recordings of many of the same numbers taken from a variety of live and studio settings, some of which first appeared on his father's now deleted JSP album *Harpmaster*. Two versions of 'Everybody Wants To Win' top and tail the collection, with Bell particularly impressive on the first. Five of the 13 tracks feature British musicians, who stand up well against the Bell family. NS

**(*) Phil Guy & Lurrie Bell (Chicago Blues Session – Volume 25)
Wolf 120.871 *Bell; Billy Branch (h); John Primer (g); Willie Kent (b); Tim Taylor, Earl Howell (d).* 10/89, 6/93.

The opening 'What Can A Poor Man Do' promises a gripping session, but 'Sweet Home Chicago' is ordinary and 'Everybody Wants to Win', retitled 'Nobody Wants To Loose [sic]', thrown away. Two numbers derived from Muddy Waters are given acoustic settings; thanks to Branch, who does good work throughout, 'Walkin' Thru The Park' is unexceptionable, but Bell delivers 'Goin' To Louisiana' as if on a bad trip. TR

***(*) Mercurial Son
Delmark DE-679 *Bell; Willie Black, Sho Komiya (b); Steve Cushing (d); Big Time Sarah, Scott Dirks (v).* 12/94–3/95.

Bell is the personification of this album's title, exhibiting vast potential at moments during a sequence of 12 songs, three of which are also present in alternate versions, that gradually diminish the initial promise. He plays with constant intensity, much of it seemingly random although nothing is thrown away. His solos feel exploratory in a way few of his contemporaries could evince but he becomes obsessive, hung up on nagging little phrases that negate his inspiration elsewhere. Most songs are written by drummer Cushing, including 'Your Daddy Done Tripped The Trigger' and 'Your Wild Thing Ain't Wild Enough', the latter's scurrilous lyrics intoned by Big Time Sarah. 'Just One Hour Behind The Sun' is sung a cappella, although Bell isn't a born vocalist and tries unsuccessfully to turn this weakness into a strength. Nevertheless, this is a perversely impressive achievement that he has so far failed to equal.

**(*) 700 Blues
Delmark DE-700 *Bell; Ken Saydak (o, p); W. Chamberlain (g); Harlan Terson (b); Kenny Smith (d).* 10–12/96.

No album better illustrates the fragility of Bell's disposition. The opener, 'I've Got Papers On You Baby', is confidently performed, with fluent and frequent guitar solos and a characterful vocal. Thereafter, Bell's performance gradually disintegrates, his solos (of which there are many) repetitive, his singing by turns lucid and deliberately vague. It's as if he's standing on the threshold of his own Stargate, serenading the monkey on his back, being drawn back to reality by the patient support of his backing band. There are tantalizing glimpses of a real musical brain, vaulting with originality, battling through the interference of its faulty connections. The results are morbidly fascinating but require stamina from the listener.

**(*) Blues Had A Baby
Delmark DE-736 *Bell; Arthur Scott (h); Joe Campagna, Joe Moss (g); Harlan Terson (b); Kenny Smith (d).* 4/95–11/97.

More in the same vein but also a retreat into tried and at times over-tested repertoire. The spotlight falls directly on Bell, and for the most part he does well, although 'Five Long Years' and 'Mean Black Spider' require a stronger voice than he possesses. As on the previous album, all the band songs follow identical arrangements, with many meandering guitar solos that fill their allotted space without leaving any memorable residue. Bell's autobiographical 'Raised On Blues' is the one notable exception, arriving too late to counterbalance the familiarity of what's preceded it. The last four titles are solo recordings from the *Mercurial Son* sessions, starting with an effective 'I'll Be Your 44' but descending via an overlong 'If I Had A Hammer' to mumbled versions of 'Mary Had A Little Lamb' and 'Rollin' And Tumblin''.

**(*) Kiss Of Sweet Blues
Delmark DE-724 *Bell; Ken Saydak (o, p); Rob Waters (o); Dave Specter (g); Harlan Terson (b); Mike Schlick (d).* 98.

Bell is more stable on this outing but it's at the expense of any real engagement with the material. With the exception of his two instrumentals and a final 'After Hours', all the songs have been written by members of his backing band, Dave Specter & The Bluebirds. Some, like 'Hiding In The Spotlight' and 'Somebody Help Me', seem to comment on his situation. Others, including the title track, feel over-literate and contrived and Bell sounds uncomfortable singing them. He and Specter solo frequently, often consecutively, but neither is tested or inspired to make a definitive statement. Bell's vocals remain coherent throughout but his lack of commitment seems like the result of medication. Unlike a surprisingly effective 'After Hours', 'Lurrie's Guitar Boogie' and 'Lurrie's Funky Groove Thang' are themeless expositions of a technique marking time, which might also describe the album.

*** Cuttin' Heads
Vypyr VP-1001 Bell; Kenny Anderson (t); Jerry Winston (as); Hank Ford (ts); Willie Henderson (bs); Carey Bell (h); Dave Rice, Roosevelt Purifoy (o, p); Michael Coleman (g); Willie 'Vamp' Samuels (b); Reggie Wright (d). 00.

Finally, a glimmer of hope. Bell holds himself together for most of this session, cutting the best version so far of 'I'll Be Your 44' and two near-ten-minute slow blues, 'Man And The Blues' and 'Leaning Tree', that include his most sustained and controlled singing and playing, despite amplification that makes his guitar sound like a distorted elastic band. He's abetted by organist Rice on 'Man' and Winston's alto sax on 'Tree', building effective climaxes during both songs. Elsewhere, 'I'll Play The Blues For You' acknowledges his debt to Albert King and 'I've Got A Watch On You' is a reworking of John Lee Hooker's 'Dimples'. His father plays on 'Call Me On The Phone' and a truncated 'Smokestack Lightning'. Bell's control slips towards the end and Little Milton's 'It's 4:59 In The Morning' finds him once again mangling the vocal line beyond coherence.

Second Nature (Alligator ALCD 4898), an acoustic duet album with his father, is discussed in Carey Bell's entry. NS

T. D. Bell & Erbie Bowser
DUET

Singer/guitarist Bell (born 1922) played banjo as a child, took up guitar in the Army and formed his first band in 1950. T. D. Bell & The Cadillacs held down a long residency at the Victory Grill in Austin, and toured extensively in west and central Texas, with forays to Arizona and New Mexico. Singer/pianist Erbie Bowser (1918–95) was a member of the band from the early '50s; previously he had been with the Sunset Royal Entertainers, and even during high-school vacations was a member of the North Carolina Cotton Pickers. Both men also worked extensively backing visiting blues artists. In the mid-'80s they came out of semi-retirement to form the Blues Specialists, resuming a busy, and now further-flung, touring schedule until Bowser's death.

*** It's About Time
Spindletop SPT-1001//Black Magic CD 9019 Bell; Bowser; Mark Kazanoff, Jon Smith, Charlie Jacobs (s); Mel Davis (h, v); Len Nichols, W. C. Clark (b); George Rains (d). 91.

The vigour of the Texas blues scene in Bell and Bowser's heyday meant that they could make a living by touring the clubs on their home turf, with no need of the publicity conferred by records; until the release of this disc, therefore, they were local heroes, virtually unknown outside afield. (In 1988, Bowser recorded solo for researcher Tary Owens, but his four instrumentals on *Texas Piano Professors* [Catfish CTF 1002] have not been transferred to CD.) *It's About Time* is an apposite title, both because wider exposure was overdue and because the disc's high quality is the fruit of long years playing together. The Blues Specialists were augmented with saxophonists for the recording session, and their terse, springy responses are an important factor in the CD's success; so much so, indeed, that they rather expose the emotional and tonal limitations of Mel Davis's chromatic harmonica. By way of compensation, Davis produces a cool, cool vocal on 'Cold Cold Feeling'. T-Bone Walker, who introduced that song, was T. D. Bell's avowed main influence, and he delivers brisk,

hard-edged versions of 'T-Bone Shuffle' and 'Bobby Sox Baby'. The tracklist is strong on numbers that Bell and Bowser's audiences wanted to hear and includes effective, unslavish covers of hits by Charles Brown, Ricky Allen, Bobby Bland and Little Willie John. 'I've Got Bad News Baby (Erbie's Blow Top Blues)' is another cover, being (despite the subtitle) the song Leonard Feather wrote for Dinah Washington. Ethical issues apart, it's a good showcase for Bowser's reedy singing and his gospelly, Ray Charles-influenced piano playing, which is excellent throughout, and particularly so on a lengthy exploration of 'After Hours'. CS

Buster Bennett (1914–80)
SOPRANO, ALTO AND TENOR SAXOPHONES, VOCAL

Joseph Buster Bennett was born in Pensacola, Florida, and is thought to have begun playing professionally in his teens in Texas. By 1938 he was based in Chicago, where through the fixer Lester Melrose he became a busy session musician, playing alto and soprano saxophones on dates by Washboard Sam, Big Bill Broonzy, Monkey Joe Coleman and other artists. In the '40s he made a number of vocal recordings in his own name, but after 1947 he disappeared from the studios. He died in obscurity in Houston.

**(*) Buster Bennett 1945–1947
Classics 5037 Bennett; Charles Gray, Harry 'Pee Wee' Jackson, Fortunatus Paul 'Fip' Ricard (t); Andrew 'Goon' Gardner (as); poss. Jimmy Coe (ts); Wild Bill Davis, poss. Boogie Woogie Allen, Willie Jones, unknown(s) (p); poss. Duke Groner, Israel Crosby (b); unknown(s) (d); unknowns (v). 2/45–12/47.

Like Peetie Wheatstraw, Bennett is often recognizable from his intros, which on his earlier sides tend to be phrased in much the same way whichever saxophone he's using. His intonation on the horn is matched by a similarly bristly vocal manner, with sometimes a Vinsonesque squeak at the end of the line. The majority of his recordings are slow or medium-paced blues, and there are stretches when the only factors holding tedium at bay are flashes of humour in the lyrics and the gusto that Bennett seldom fails to bring to his job. But the final session, with Gardner and Ricard, is insouciant small-group jazz, and likely to leave the listener wearing a smile that isn't merely tolerant. TR

Duster Bennett (1946–76)
VOCAL, HARMONICA, PIANO, GUITAR, DRUMS, PERCUSSION

Tony 'Duster' Bennett is the great lost icon of British blues. A one-man-band, a prolific composer and an evangelical Christian, he's remembered as much for his warmth and sincerity as he is for the extremes of stamina and sensitivity that he brought to his music. Through his friendship with Peter Green he was introduced to Blue Horizon, for whom he recorded several singles and three albums. Though subsequently out of the public eye, he continued to record until his death in a road accident.

***(*) The Complete Blue Horizon Sessions
Columbia/Blue Horizon 518517 2CD Bennett; Johnny Almond (ts, o); unknowns (strings); Peter Green (g, b); Anthony 'Top' Topham (g); John McVie, Andy Silvester, Tony Mills, Gerry Jemmott, Ray Babbington (b); John Cloury (d, v); Mick

Fleetwood, Dave Bidwell, Herbie Lovelle, Kenny Lamb, Phil Wainman (d); Mike Vernon (claves, prod); Stella Sutton, Viola Billups, Ernestine Pearce (v). 4 or 5/68–9/70.

Duster Bennett has been dead for 30 years but he is not forgotten by devotees of British blues. This impeccable collection of his albums and singles for Blue Horizon reveals why. Although he worked according to the one-man-band rules of Dr Ross and Juke Boy Bonner, Bennett had a poignancy all his own, particularly on thoughtful original compositions such as 'Things Are Changing', 'Trying To Paint It In The Sky' and 'Jumping At Shadows'. But he was no less persuasive on lighter, happier numbers, and his harmonica playing on rocketing tunes like 'Country Jam' takes the listener's breath away as surely as it never did his. Over the two and a half years of his association with Blue Horizon Bennett made a few shifts away from his one-man-band setup; few were unrewarding and some attractive, but it's the solo performances that give the clearest picture of what kind of artist and man he was. Bennett left many other recordings, but these are his most substantial legacy.

*** **Bright Lights Big City**
Castle CMDDD 579 2CD *Bennett; Peter Green, Keith Randall (g, v); Top Topham (g); Tony Mills, John Mostin, unknowns (b); unknown (k); unknown (j); unknown (d); unknown (wb); Stella Sutton Bennett, Richard Ford, unknown (v). 65–75.*

Much of this material was not intended to be issued, and it's of varying sound quality. Caught at a raucous gig in Surrey, Bennett plays 'It's A Man Down There' and the instrumental 'Fresh Country Jam' with astonishing strength, the latter apparently using circular breathing for its non-stop harmonica line. For once, the crowd's reaction is justified. Another live sequence, including 'Just Like A Fish' and 'I Choose To Sing The Blues', further illustrates the inventiveness of his harmonica playing. 'Georgina' and 'Glendora' are reminders of the jugband and skiffle traditions from which he came. Also notable are the reflective 'Back In The Same Old Bag', slide guitar treatments of 'Rock Of Ages' and, intriguingly, 'Blues With A Feeling', a couple of collaborations with Peter Green, including a run-through of 'Trying So Hard To Forget' (later featured on Fleetwood Mac's *Mr Wonderful*), and 'Can't Nobody Hide From God', which Duster and his wife Stella sing with quiet conviction, evoking the Blind Willie Johnson original. This efficient 41-track selection was made from the deleted Indigo albums *Jumping At Shadows, Out In The Blue, Blue Inside, I Choose To Sing The Blues, Comin' Home* and *Shady Little Baby*.

(*) Fingertips
Castle CMRCD 711 *Bennett; Billy Graham, Howie Casey, Dick Parry, Reg Brooks, Cecil Moss, Johnny Huckbridge, Mike Davis, John Donnelly (brass, reeds); Pete Wingfield (clavinet); Nicky Hopkins (p); unknowns (strings); Pip Williams (g, vb); Peter Frampton, Hughie Burns (g); Rick Wills, Rob Roberts, Boz Burrell (b); John Siomos, Terry Stannard, Phil Wainman, Ian Wallace (d); Morris Pert (perc); Sue & Sunny, Liza Strike, Barrie St John, Linda Kendrick, Ann Simmonds (v). 73–75.*

Towards the end of his time on Blue Horizon Bennett showed signs of musical restlessness, retiring the Jimmy Reed and Slim Harpo repertoire and advancing his own songs, which were not always in blues-related forms. *Fingertips*, which gathers some of his last studio recordings, finds him pursuing that policy, assisted by open-minded producers, and several tracks are quite elaborate studio confections in a soul idiom. They are interesting now more for who conceived them than for any special quality of their own. But those experiments didn't sideline the blues: there are pleasing versions of songs by Juke Boy Bonner and Sonny Boy Williamson II, lots of harmonica passages and a version of Harpo's 'I've Got To Be With You Tonight' sung with endearing plaintiveness. TR/NS

Tab Benoit (born 1967)
VOCAL, GUITAR, HARMONICA

Born in Baton Rouge and raised in Houma, Louisiana, where he still lives, Benoit was schooled in the local blues scene by men like Tabby Thomas and Raful Neal. Temperamentally an old-school musician, he has a taste for uncomplicated recording situations which create the same effect as live performance.

(*) What I Live For
Vanguard VMD 79543 *Benoit; Reese Wynans (o, p); Derek O'Brien (g); Steve Bailey (b); Kenny Aronoff (d). 10/93.*

*** **Standing On The Bank**
Vanguard VMD 79544 *Benoit; Paul English (o, p); Willie Nelson (g, v); Greg Rzab, Doug Therrien (b); Ray Allison, Allyn Robinson (d). 5/95.*

These are Benoit's second and third albums, originally made for the Houston-based Justice label. (The first, 1992's *Nice And Warm*, has not been reissued.) Each quickly demonstrates Benoit's strengths: fast, muscular guitar playing which even at its boldest avoids blues-rock overstatement, and material evenly divided between competent original songs, such as the title tracks, and received repertoire like Howlin' Wolf's 'Who's Been Talkin'' and Willie Love's 'Too Many Drivers At The Wheel' on *What I Live For*, or Albert King's 'Laundromat Blues' and Don Nix's 'Going Down' on *Standing On The Bank*. The latter CD's 'Match Box Blues' is also based on the version by Albert King, who is evidently one of Benoit's models. The sound of the earlier album is rather clotted, but *Standing On The Bank* achieves a splendid clarity. 'Rainy Day Blues', a quiet duet with Willie Nelson, and the solo 'Still Going Down The Road' have a pleasing old-time composure.

*** **Live: Swampland Jam**
Vanguard VMD 79545 *Benoit; Jumpin' Johnny Sansone (h, ac); Raful Neal (h); Chubby Carrier (ac); Henry Gray (p); Tabby Thomas (g, v); Doug Therrien (b); Allyn Robinson (d). 2–3/97.*

This was recorded at venues in New Orleans and Lafayette, Louisiana, with guest appearances by Sansone (twice), Gray (twice), Neal, Carrier and Thomas. Benoit's own songs, cast in blues forms and blues language, blend seamlessly with repertoire pieces like John Lee Hooker's 'Crawling King Snake' and Clifton Chenier's 'Hot Tamale Baby'.

(*) Homesick For The Road
Telarc CD-83454 *Benoit; Kenny Neal (h, g, v); Raful Neal (h, v); Bruce Katz (o); Debbie Davies (g, v); Rod Carey (b); Per Hanson (d). 9/98.*

A six-hander with Kenny Neal and Debbie Davies, backed by Ronnie Earl's Broadcasters: Benoit plays on nine of the dozen tracks, taking the leading role on 'Down In The Swamp', 'I Put A Spell On You' and 'Night Life', all songs he had recorded before.

*** **These Blues Are All Mine**
Vanguard VD 79546 *Benoit; Marc Adams (o, p); David Lee Watson (b); Allyn Robinson (d).* 99.

Despite the album's title, more than half of the songs are from other artists. Three that are associated with Albert Collins, 'Lights Are On, But Nobody's Home', 'Don't Lose Your Cool' and 'Travelin' South', bear witness to another of Benoit's exemplars. His singing, which up to this point has never been less than workmanlike but only occasionally more, finds a new expressiveness on Memphis Slim's 'Mother Earth' and the very fine title track.

*** **Wetlands**
Telarc CD-83530 *Benoit; Anders Osborne, Brian Stoltz (g, v); Carl Dufrene (b); Darryl White (d).* 9/01.

Essentially a trio album – Osborne and Stoltz appear only on the closing 'Georgia' – *Wetlands* reveals fresh aspects of Benoit's musical character, as he tackles the heartache of Otis Redding's 'These Arms Of Mine', the clumping zydeco of Boozoo Chavis's 'Dog Hill' and the happy dance number 'Stackolina'. If he also plays the uncredited harmonica on the last of these, it's his first recording on the instrument since his debut album.

(*) **Whiskey Store
Telarc CD-83559 *Benoit; Charlie Musselwhite (h); Reese Wynans (o, p); Jimmy Thackery (g, v); Tommy Shannon (b); Chris Layton (d); Rani (v).* 2/02.

Benoit and Jimmy Thackery, who receive joint billing, divide the vocals but combine their guitars in a powerful set, trenchantly accompanied by Wynans, Shannon and Layton. A chiefly blues programme embraces Mike Henderson's 'Whiskey Store', Guitar Slim's 'Bad Luck Blues' and Bob Dylan's 'Leopard-Skin Pill-Box Hat', and Benoit takes the chance to restore to the catalogue two more of the songs on his first album, 'Nice And Warm' and 'Bone Pickin''. But, as on *Homesick For The Road*, the presence of other strong musical personalities tends to obscure the individuality of his work.

*** **The Sea Saint Sessions**
Telarc CD-83573 *Benoit; George Porter (g, b); Brian Stoltz (g, v); Carl Dufrene (b); Darryl White (d); Monk Boudreaux (tamb, v); Cyril Neville (perc, v).* 2/03.

Fizzing New Orleans rhythms had enlivened some of the tracks on *Wetlands*, much of which was recorded at the city's celebrated Sea Saint Studios. Working there again, and again with Dufrene and White, Benoit continues his journey away from the Albert King effect of a decade before, towards a more individual, yet in some ways more typically South Louisiana sound. The long lines of his early playing have been fractured, the dense textures of his backing groups unravelled; altogether Benoit has engineered a rhythmic transformation of his music that has few parallels among his contemporaries.

*** **Whiskey Store Live**
Telarc CD-83584 *Benoit; Jimmy Carpenter (s); Ken Faltinson (o); Jimmy Thackery (g, v); Carl Dufrene (b); Darryl White, Mark Stutso (d).* 3/03.

Supported by musicians from both their bands, Benoit and Thackery rock a Maine arts centre with a vehement but controlled performance. Though four of the nine tracks run beyond eight minutes and the shortest of the others to six, there are no dips in the energy level; the slow blues retain their intensity and the up-tempo tunes their verve. It's also a model live recording, giving a sense of the occasion without sacrificing studio-quality balance. TR

Gladys Bentley (1907–60)
VOCAL

Bentley was well known as a male impersonator on the New York cabaret scene in the '20s and '30s, and from the '40s onwards in Los Angeles.

*** **Maggie Jones – Vol. 2/Gladys Bentley (1925–1929)**
Document DOCD-5349 *Bentley; unknown (p); Eddie Lang (g).* 8/28–3/29.

Bentley's earliest recordings, gathered here, are squarely in the blues idiom, with strong, low-pitched singing; the economical piano playing on these eight sides is thought not to be hers. Her muscular treatment of 'How Long – How Long Blues' amusingly confronts Frankie 'Half-Pint' Jaxon's version, coming, in terms of gender representation, from the opposite direction. She frequently employs a wordless growl with the effect of a kazoo or muted trumpet. Her '40s recordings of some of these titles and other songs, including a number of probably custom-made 'party records', await reissue. TR

Buster Benton (1932–96)
VOCAL, GUITAR

Born in Texarkana, Arkansas, Arley Benton worked in Chicago from the late '50s onwards, becoming known to the international blues community through his 1974 hit 'Spider In My Stew', produced by Willie Dixon, with whom he worked for four years. He visited Europe in 1983 and again, despite having lost a leg in a car accident, in 1985.

** **That's The Reason**
Ronn RCD-8005 *Benton; unknowns (s); Carey Bell, unknown (h); unknown (o); Lafayette Leake, unknown (p); unknowns (strings); Mighty Joe Young, unknowns (g); Willie Dixon or James Green, unknowns (b); Billy Davenport, unknowns (d); unknowns (v).* 66–70s?

*** **Spider In My Stew**
Ronn RCD-8002 *Benton; Ron Scott (ts); Carey Bell, Walter Horton, unknown (h); unknown (o); Lafayette Leake (p); Mighty Joe Young, Jimmy Johnson, unknowns (g); Willie Dixon or James Green, Freddie Dixon, Nolan Struck, unknown (b); Billy Davenport, Clifton James, Ray Allison, unknown (d).* 74–6/78.

At his best, as in the ominous 'Spider In My Stew' or the uplifting 'Sweet 94', Benton is a rugged, rough-dried figure cut from the same cloth as Byther Smith or Magic Slim. Unfortunately that side of him is not well lit by *That's The Reason*, where most of the material is second-rate (and the best tracks, 'Going Fishin'' and 'Spider In My Stew', are also on the other CD), and almost all of it is afflicted with terrible distortion. *Spider In My Stew* sounds somewhat better and also has the evenness of a record mostly derived from a single session, at which Carey Bell in particular was on top form.

** **Blues At The Top**

Evidence ECD 26030 *Benton; Billy Branch (h); François Rilhac, Lafayette Leake (p); Carl Weathersby, Johnny Littlejohn, Joe Beard (g); J. W. Williams, Bob Stroger (b); Moses Rutues, Odie Payne (d).* 11/83, 5/85.

** **Blues And Trouble**

Black & Blue BB 446 *As above.* 11/83, 5/85.

The Benton of *Spider In My Stew* is barely recognizable on *Blues At The Top*, drawn from two sessions originally held for the French Blue Phoenix label. The five cuts from '83, with Littlejohn or Beard as supporting guitarist, are mostly long, slow blues, uneventful but likeable; the best, 'Money Is The Name Of The Game', echoes the theme and, distantly, the shape of Otis Rush's 'Double Trouble'. The remaining ten songs, from '85, suffer from a weedy ensemble sound. Benton and Weathersby are generally under-recorded, and the pianist, for all the impression he makes on the proceedings, might as well have been on an extended Gauloise break. Benton's occasional attempts to funk it up ('My Lady', 'From Missouri', 'In The Guetto [sic]') are particularly weakened by this lack of resources. Branch manfully tries to fill the gaps with virtually continuous chromatic harp, and it is the producer's fault, not his, that the effect becomes wearisome. *Blues And Trouble* is much the same album – despite Black & Blue's claim, 'Cold Man' and 'Money Is The Name Of The Game' from the '83 session are not new to CD – but omits 'In The Guetto' and replaces 'The Hawk Is Coming' with a reading of Roy Brown's 'Hard Luck Blues'. Benton's three albums for Ichiban, made between 1988 and 1991, are currently unavailable. TR

Eric Bibb (born 1951)
VOCAL, GUITAR

With folksinger Leon Bibb his father, Modern Jazz Quartet leader John Lewis his uncle and Paul Robeson his godfather, Eric Bibb had no excuse for not entering music. Essentially self-taught but with some classical training, he presents in his writing an alliance between spirituality, realism and whimsy, less overtly religious than the prevailing tone of his initial release. He fashions his songs into minutely observed vignettes that habitually exclude unnecessary embellishment. More blues-oriented than suffused with the blues, Bibb's music dallies with blues figures and phrasing while aspiring to encompass a more populist vision.

(**(*)) **Spirit & The Blues**

Opus 3 19401//Earth Beat! R2 75686 *Bibb; Jenny Bohman, Derrick Walker (h); Janne Petersson (ac); Christer Lyssarides (md); Goran Wennerbrandt (g); Olle Eriksson (b); Bjorn Gideonsson (d, perc); The Deacons (Nevada Cato, Derek Huntsman, Bob Manning, Joe Watts) (v).* 1–6/94.

(**(*)) **Good Stuff**

Opus 3 19603//Earth Beat! R2 75265 *Bibb; Derrick Walker, Jenny Bohman (h); Janne Petersson (ac, o, p); Christer Lyssarides (md); Goran Wennerbrandt, Nick Malmestrom (g); Olle Eriksson (b); Bjorn Gideonsson (d); Hassan Bah (kalimba); The Deacons (Nevada Cato, Derek Huntsman, Bob Manning, Joe Watts) (v).* 96.

Bibb and his men are immaculately rehearsed, for Opus 3 was founded on the premise that nothing, from equalization to overdubs to editing, should impinge upon a performance. The pristine nature of the result, no matter how well played, insulates it from the tension inherent in blues playing. But then, *Spirit & The Blues* is dominated by spirituals, both original and traditional, while the remaining songs are rooted in Josh White territory. Bibb's voice has an attractive natural vibrato and he and his band perform empathetically and well. Trouble is, the demands of the recording process render most songs laidback to the point of insouciance. After seven minutes of 'Satisfied Mind', the accumulated religiosity of Bibb's moral homilies has become rather smug and sanctimonious. What begins as striking becomes ponderous.

The load is lightened for *Good Stuff*, the tone more secular. Though a devotional view is still apparent in 'New World Comin' Through' and 'Don't Ever Let Nobody Drag Your Spirit Down', it no longer dominates the set. Even so, Bibb's approach remains more cerebral than physical, his songs observational, their arrangements studied if not at times contrived. That doesn't apply to the simple intimacy of 'Saucer 'N' Cup', the second-line drive of 'Happy Home Recipe' and the clever adaptation of Tommy Johnson's bass-string runs in 'Too Much Whisky'. Still, engagement is the issue and there's little indication Bibb has dirt under his fingernails.

(***) **Home To Me**

Manhaton HATMAN 2001 *Bibb; David Wilczewski (ss); Nick Pentelow (ts); Derrick 'Big' Walker (h); Janne Petersson (ac, o, p); Roger Cotton (o); Levi B. Saunders (bj); Brian Kramer, Christer Lyssarides (g); Dave Bronze (b, perc); Bjorn Gideonsson (d, perc); Rene Martinez (cga); Corrina Hewat (harp, v); Bob Manning, Nevada Cato, André De Lange, Kofi Bentsi-Enchill, Cyndee Peters, Sara Finer, Marianne, Matilda, Katri, Emma, Falima, Annie, Sarah James, Wendy Roberts, Kate Bronze (v).* 99.

In much the same vein as its predecessor, *Me To You* (Code Blue, deleted), this set finds Bibb's earnestness unabated in a sequence of songs ('Livin' Lovin' An' Doin', 'Walk The Walk', 'Put Your Foot Down') that manage to combine positive action, moral improvement and 'new man' sensitivity. Luckily, other fare is on offer, including a long-out-of-date celebration of Nelson Mandela's release. Two blues themes, 'No More Cane On The Brazos' and 'Come Back Baby', are subtly undermined by their consciously dramatic performance. Only in 'For You' does unfettered sincerity reveal itself. Another huge cast is less oppressive than its size might suggest, displaying Bibb as an expert in marshalling his forces while he continues to fashion his own musical niche.

***(*) **Roadworks**

Manhaton HATMAN 2003 *Bibb; Janne Petersson (ac, p); Stan Keen (p); Steve Simpson (vn, md, g); Levi B. Saunders (bj); Dave Bronze (b, perc).* 00.

As the title implies, much of this set was recorded onstage with Simpson and Bronze in Europe and America, with sundry studio tracks cut along the way and one recorded in producer Bronze's bathroom. This latter, 'Shavin' Talk', is one of several tracks (including 'Panama Hat') that give the album a whimsical cast, tempering the prevailing seriousness of the blues and gospel numbers. Most impressive are 'For You' and 'Saucer 'N' Cup', two of Bibb's best songs, here projecting the human dimension that is often lost in the calculated precision of a lot of his work. Bibb's power is in his ability to create atmosphere, apparent here in the pauses before the applause begins.

(***(*)) Just Like Love
Opus 3˜20002 *Bibb; Derrick 'Big' Walker (h); Janne Petersson (ac, p, melodica, kalimba); Christer Lyssarides (md, g, zither); Olle Eriksson (b); Bo Juhlin (sousaphone). 1–5/00.*

By his own admission, Bibb wished to return to the spontaneous atmosphere of Opus 3's recording methods for a group of songs as yet untried in public. A dozen compositions, by turns confessional and whimsical, are interspersed with five instrumental fragments. Lovesongs to his wife and tales of remembered relatives, old friendships and past lives make this album a forgivable indulgence. Inevitably, religion is present ('Home In That Rock') but the set ends with a pair of odes to self-belief, 'That's Why I'm Here' and 'Prayin''. Where previously such didacticism was jarring and rather earnest, Bibb here adds a personal dimension that lends instruction through experience. A lack of fine-tuning makes these songs fresher and more inclusive than the calculation that hides behind some of his work. There's little blues content after 'Wrapped In Her Arms' begins the set but its tendrils weave their way through what follows.

(***) Painting Signs
Manhaton HATMAN 2005//Earth Beat! R2 74382 *Bibb; Janne Petersson (ac, o, p); Steve Simpson, Hans Theesink (md); Chuck Anthony, Colin Linden, Richard Studholme, Robbie McIntosh, Christer Lyssarides (g); Dave Bronze (b); Jon Saas (tu); Bjorn Gideonsson (d, perc); Henry Spinetti, David Rokeach (d); Rafael Sida (perc); Wilson Pickett, Linda Tillery, Emma Jean Foster, Cultural Heritage Choir (v). 01.*

Despite the inclusion of Jimmy Reed's 'Honest I Do', this album has little to do with blues. It's an eclectic set dedicated to Pops Staples, whose 'Hope In A Hopeless World' sets the tone for what Bibb refers to as 'spiritualized songs' such as 'I Heard The Angels Singin'', 'Got To Do Better' and a rerun of 'Don't Ever Let Nobody Drag Your Spirit Down' with an over-emotive Wilson Pickett in attendance. Too many songs have extended codas where little happens and Jimi Hendrix's 'Angel' is far too ethereal and cosmic alongside Bibb's go-getting gospel. Two tracks shine, one the title song, best described as 'Repulsion for the ears', the other 'Five Miles Above', its mild paranoia preparing the ground for the psychotic 'Painting Signs'. This is an ambitious record, essaying a broad spectrum of music that ultimately fails to gell. It may well be his best record to date but its presence in this book is questionable. His 2002 album *A Family Affair* (Manhaton HATMAN 2007//Tradition & Moderne T&M 023), shared with his father Leon, has no blues content.

(***(*)) Natural Light
Manhaton HATMAN 2011 *Bibb; Simon Clarke, Roddy Lorimer, Tim Sanders ('kick horns'); Janne Petersson (ac, o, p); Hubert Sumlin, Steve Donnelly, Robbie McIntosh, Kjell Segebrant (g); Dave Bronze (b); Martin Ditcham, Bjorn Gideonsson (d, perc); Henry Spinetti (d); Michele John-Douglas, Marion Powell (v). 03.*

This comes close to being the perfect blend of Bibb's musical aspirations, encompassing folksong, blues, religion and confessional balladry, with more wit than whimsy. Typical of this latter is 'Tell Riley', in which Bibb becomes Booker White leaving a message for his nephew as he travels to Chicago to record with the prediction that 'he'll B. B. King some day'. There are blues connections in 'Water Works Fine', with its mention of Sonny Terry, while 'Lucky Man Rag' finds him ending up with Leadbelly's Irene. Where previously Bibb's songs jumped between categories, here the blend is more subtle and effective. There are lovesongs, louche near-jazz, stomps and rags, topped off with a surprisingly successful revival of Jackie Wilson's 'Higher And Higher'. It's not blues but there's much to savour. NS

(***) Friends
Manhaton HATMAN 2015 *Bibb; Guy Davis (h, g); Charlie Musselwhite (h); Janne Petersson (ac, p); Rob Hewes (kb); Jerry Yester (p); Kristina Olsen (concertina, v); Michael Jerome Browne (vn, mandola, g, v); Byron Myhre (vn, md); Mamadou Diabate (kora); Harry Manx (mohan veena); Taj Mahal (gourd bj, g, v); Levi B. Saunders (bj, d loops, perc loops); Martin Simpson, Thomas Slaymaker, Djelimady Tounkara (g); Led Ka'apana (u); Leon C. (b, d, perc, prog, co-prod); Bill Lee (b); Pete Thompson (d); Kuljit (tablas); Cyd Cassone (brushes on gig box); Ruthie Foster, Odetta (v). 00s?*

At various festivals and other occasions, spread over several years, Bibb rendezvoused with artists he admired and wanted to make music with, and this is the scrapbook of those meetings. As is natural to his music, the range of idioms is very wide, encompassing gospel ('99½ Won't Do' with Guy Davis), contemporary folk (Guy Clark's 'The Cape', Kristina Olsen's 'If I Stayed') and his own multifarious compositions, some, like 'For You', previously recorded in different settings. Despite the sometimes impromptu circumstances in which they were taped, the performances have the crystalline clarity of Bibb's more planned recordings.

(***) A Ship Called Love
Telarc CD-83629 *Bibb; Memphis Horns (brass, reeds); Jonas Sjoblom (fl, tabla, windchimes, bells); Gary Compton (h); Glen Scott (kb, o, p, celeste, melodica, g, sampled b, d, cga, tamb, perc, vb, v); Desmond Foster (kb, g, b, perc, prog, v); Jim Pugh (kb, o); Janne Petersson (kb); Gordon Cyrus (programmed syn, b, perc); Corrina Hewat (electric Celtic harp); Levi B. Saunders (bj); B. J. Cole (psg); Paul Waller (Do); Figge Bostrom (g, prog, v); Amar Sundy, Chuck Anthony, Danny Flowers (g); Joacim Backman (b, handclaps); Kim [Keem] Yarbrough, Brian Shiels (b); Larry Crockett (d, cga); Brady Blade (d, tamb, handclaps); Cyd Cassone (perc); The Dixie Hummingbirds, Ruthie Foster, Nevada Cato, Psalm 4 (Paris Gilbert, André De Lange, Glen Scott), Alex Yeoman, Matilda Mandolina Bibb (v). 05.*

'Everywhere I go', Bibb sings in 'Troubadour', 'people ask me, "What kind of music do you play?" and I just say: "Gon' hear some blues, like a freight train rollin' through … gospel, soul and some good old rock 'n' roll … they call me a troubadour."' Hard to spot the rock 'n' roll, but, as anyone who has read or listened this far would expect, the rest of the menu is duly served, in lilting, tripping arrangements with many decorative instrumental effects, including (for the first and last time in this book) Celtic harp. 'Like Aretha Loves To Sing' and 'More O' That' are strung on a blues frame but most of the programme is lovesongs, now and then a little wet ('Faded Jeans'), but always set to pretty tunes. TR

Big Bad Smitty (1941–2002)
VOCAL, GUITAR

John Henry Smith was born in Jackson, Mississippi, was playing round Greenville by his late teens and made his first

recordings for his hometown's Ace label in 1970. He settled in St Louis in 1975, working as a truck-driver and playing at weekends, first in the black clubs of St Louis and East St Louis, but gradually also for white audiences. After the release of Mean Disposition he worked more widely in the US and toured Europe and Australia.

Five 1977 Ace recordings, three previously unissued, were on *Genuine Mississippi Blues ... Plus (The Ace (MS.) Blues Masters Volume 4)* (Westside WESM 579, deleted). On 'Smokestack Lightning' and 'How Many More Years' Smitty covers Howlin' Wolf, not as fiercely as the original but in a gritty downhome style.

* St. Louis Blues Today – Volume 2
Wolf 120.942 *Big Bad Smitty; Jimmy Bernard (h); James Cotton (o, g, d); Bill Doll Jr (g, b); Robert Doll (g); Marshall Dunn (b); D. Dixon (d). 88.*

*** Mean Disposition
Black Magic CD-9018//Aim 1037 *Big Bad Smitty; Arthur Williams (h); Bennie Smith (g); Durious Montgomery (b); Ray Hayes (d). 8/91.*

*** Cold Blood
HMG 1003 *As above, except Charles Rodgers (d) replaces Hayes; add Hubert Sumlin (g). 10/93.*

Despite the abysmal sound quality, it's just possible to gather from the eight sides on *St. Louis Blues Today – Volume 2* that, 11 years on from his Ace session, Smitty still has a voice as rough as a ripsaw. There's another version of 'How Many More Years', and there might be interesting echoes of Charley Patton in 'St. Louis On A High Hill', if one could decipher the vocal. The remaining six tracks are by Eugene Fluker (born 1935), a singer and guitarist originally from Mississippi who moved to St Louis at 18. 'Play My Guitar' sounds like a ventriloquist's dummy imitating Chuck Berry from inside a suitcase. He's slightly more convincing on B. B. King's 'Woke Up This Morning', but he too is kneecapped by the engineering.

When a recording is as incompetent as that, it's hard to tell whether the artist has anything going for him. Fortunately, thanks in part to producer Joel Slotnikoff, Smitty was able to prove his worth on two properly made albums. *Mean Disposition* has three Muddy Waters numbers and others by Wolf, Lil' Son Jackson (an early model) and Little Milton, whereas *Cold Blood* presses the Wolf button harder (four songs, all with Wolf's man Hubert Sumlin playing the lead parts) while acknowledging Lightnin' Slim, Junior Parker, Little Walter and, again, Muddy. Despite his years in St Louis, Smitty still sounds like an old pro from the Southern juke-joint circuit, a spiritual fellow-traveller of Frank Frost or 'Booba' Barnes, and Williams's harmonica and Bennie Smith's efficient second guitar only strengthen that impression. Smitty's guitar playing is brusque and calculatedly dissonant, and tends to be most effective on tunes with explicit patterns like 'Still A Fool' and 'Smitty's Boogie' on *Mean Disposition*, though he also works a Lightnin' Hopkins vein profitably in the solo 'Big Brazos' on *Cold Blood*. TR

Big Joe Louis (born 1961)
VOCAL, GUITAR, MANDOLIN

Offstage, Big Joe Louis is Alasdair Blaazer, a blues and gospel specialist at the Mechanical Copyright Protection Society in London and a knowledgeable blues record-collector. Born in Jamaica, he came to England in the '70s and formed the Blues Kings in the mid-'80s. The band has backed many American blues artists visting Britain, among them Lazy Lester, Carey Bell, Kenny Neal and Larry McCray.

*** Big Joe Louis & His Blues Kings
Ace CDCHD 833 2CD *Big Joe Louis; Tony Hilton (h, b); Little George Sueref (h, v); Little Paul [Besterman] (h); Jamie Rowan, Frank 'Smokey' Doubleday (p); Lloyd Gordon (b); Martin Deegan (d); Mike Vernon (prod). 12/88, 1/91.*

*** Big Sixteen
Ace CDCH 622 *Big Joe Louis; Little George Sueref (h, g, b, v); Carl Sonny Leyland (p); John Primer, David Purdy (g); Matt Radford (b); Brian Nevill (d). 5–11/95.*

Listeners who know the landscape of postwar blues will recognize Big Joe Louis as an experienced traveller there, with a special regard for Chicago and Southern blues of the '40s and '50s. *Big Joe Louis & His Blues Kings* couples his first two albums, the eponymous Blue Horizon of 1989 (and some outtakes from that session) and *The Stars In The Sky* (originally Tramp TRCD 9910) from 1992. Drop a needle anywhere on either album – the expression may not fit the format, but it's entirely appropriate to the spirit of the music – and you'll swiftly deduce that Louis has a close acquaintance with an enviable record collection. On *The Stars In The Sky*, for instance, you may notice the Muddy Waters-like slide playing on 'Baby Child', the shoebox acoustics of Snooky Pryor's 'Boogie Twist' or the Elmore James setting of the title song; on the earlier set, the guitar intro to 'You Can't Live Long' (Floyd Jones's 'Drink On Little Girl'), the Baby Face Leroy references in 'I Cried Last Night' or the mere inclusion of a *recherché* item like Houston Boines's 'Monkey Motion'. But these are no cold-blooded exercises in reanimation. Louis's vocals may be idiomatically correct but they are also strong and enthusiastic, and so is the ensemble playing. *Big Sixteen* has a somewhat higher percentage of original material, though the originality resides more in the words than in the tunes and musical arrangements, which again are full of allusions to rarities on Louis's shelves. The prodding guitar on 'Leaving On My Mind' might have come off a tape from the Sun studio *circa* 1953. Sueref plays harmonica with the same scrupulous sense of period as his leader and takes the vocal on several tracks, among them '3–6–9', 'Catfish' and 'Treat Your Daddy Right', all of which he would rerecord some five years later on his debut album away from the Blues Kings (for which see his entry). Both these CDs are enjoyable on any terms, but a more refined pleasure awaits the listener whose ears are as seasoned as Louis's. TR

Big Maceo (1905–53)
VOCAL, PIANO

Major 'Big Maceo' Merriweather was from Georgia; he was playing at parties and clubs in Detroit when a girlfriend encouraged him to try for a recording contract. Maceo formed a popular and successful duo with Tampa Red, but in 1946 a stroke paralysed his right arm. He struggled to keep working, with other pianists providing one or both hands at the keyboard, but died in poverty.

**** Chicago Piano Vol. 1
Fabulous FABCD 171 *Big Maceo; Tampa Red (g); Ransom*

Knowling, Alfred Elkins (b); Clifford 'Snags' Jones (d). 6/41–7/42.
**** Chicago Piano Vol. 2
Fabulous FABCD 172 Big Maceo; Eddie Boyd (p); Tampa Red (g, sp); Big Crawford (b); Melvin Draper, Charles Saunders, Tyrell 'Little T' Dixon (d). 2/45–2/47.
👑 ****** Big Maceo Vol. 1 (1941–1945)**
Document DOCD-5673 Big Maceo; Tampa Red (g); Ransom Knowling, Alfred Elkins (b); Clifford Jones, Tyrell Dixon, Melvin Draper (d). 6/41–2/45.
👑 ****** Big Maceo Vol. 2 (1945–1950)**
Document DOCD-5674 Big Maceo; Grace Brim (h); Eddie Boyd, Little Johnny Jones, James Watkins (p); Tampa Red (g, sp); John Brim (g); Big Crawford, Ransom Knowling (b); Tyrell Dixon, Charles Saunders, Odie Payne, Alonzo Tucker (d). 7/45–50.
***(*) Chicago Breakdown
[Blue Boar CDBB 1026] As for Fabulous CDs. 6/41–2/47.
**(*) The Best of Big Maceo With Tampa Red
Blues Forever CD 68013 As above. 6/41–2/47.
***(*) The King Of Chicago Blues Piano
Arhoolie Folklyric CD 7009 As above, except omit Boyd, Crawford. 6/41–10/45.
*** Tampa Red & Big Maceo 1941/1946 [sic]
EPM Blues Collection 15907 As above, except Tampa Red also plays k; omit Elkins. 6/41–10/45.

When God lured Georgia Tom away from the blues, He waited a few years before providing Tampa Red with a regular replacement, but made handsome amends for the delay. On both slow blues and boogies, Big Maceo played powerful, sometimes challengingly chromatic bass figures and anvil-sparking right-hand flourishes and solos. He could be a jovial singer, but more typical were husky, plaintively fatalistic accounts of trouble with women and the law. Maceo's revision of Sleepy John Estes's 'Worried Life Blues' entered the canon, his melancholy interpretation influencing almost every subsequent version; more generally, his playing and Tampa Red's amplified guitar foreshadow the sound of postwar Chicago.

The budget-priced Fabulous CDs contain the complete Victor and Bluebird recordings in outstanding sound, courtesy of out-of-print RCA CDs, and with brief notes. Vol. 2 includes four dispiriting titles recorded after the stroke; Eddie Boyd is a no more than adequate stand-in on piano, but these tracks don't detract from Maceo's own playing, which is equally splendid on slow blues and on the three up-tempo masterpieces, 'Texas Stomp', 'Detroit Jump' and 'Chicago Breakdown'.

However, the Fabulous discs are eclipsed by Document's two volumes, whose extensive notes include new information from surviving relatives and some striking family photographs. The sound of the RCA sides is predictably good, but material from other labels has also been carefully transferred. Vol. 1 includes a test pressing of the well-named 'Flying Boogie', made for Columbia, and Vol. 2 takes Maceo's story to its conclusion. Four titles recorded for Specialty, with Johnny Jones playing a close and beautiful imitation of his teacher, who sings nearly as well as ever, are the best of the post-stroke sides; the final recordings for Fortune, with James Watkins playing a right-hand piano part, are chaotic, but testify to Maceo's determination to keep making music.

Blue Boar, Blues Forever and Arhoolie draw on the RCA recordings. Blue Boar's 25 tracks are serviceably annotated, but include the complete Eddie Boyd session at the expense of better material. Arhoolie's 25-tracker is carefully remastered from clean 78s, and was issued by agreement with Maceo's surviving relatives. It omits all the sides with Boyd, but one of the earlier Victors is also missing, for no discernible reason. With only 18 tracks (including two with Boyd) and telegraphic, inaccurate notes, Blues Forever fall by the wayside.

The EPM CD, credited to Tampa Red & Big Maceo, usefully offers a different way to consider Maceo's music by mingling sides issued under his own name with accompaniments to 'Mister Tampa'. Only eight of 22 tracks feature Maceo as leader, but he generates many magnificent solos on the latter tracks, sometimes during most unpromising songs; the hokum throwback 'Let Me Play With Your Poodle' is a prime example. CS

Big Maybelle (c. 1920–72)
VOCAL

Mabel Smith was discovered singing in church as a teenager. She already had an imposing physical presence and a voice to match, and even then her secular repertoire included pop songs and jazz alongside the blues. By the time of her recording debut Smith was already addicted to heroin, and when she moved to OKeh and became Big Maybelle much of her energy was going into raising money to feed her habit. She remained a dynamic performer, as a memorable appearance in the film Jazz On A Summer's Day *confirms, and her voice stood up to the ravages of drugs remarkably well, but her material became less compelling, reaching its nadir when Rojac had her covering Top 40 hits. By 1970 her health was failing, and she was semi-retired; in 1972 she fell into a diabetic coma and died.*

**(*) Big Maybelle 1944–1953
Classics 5089 Big Maybelle; Reginald Adams, Ralph Bowden, Hot Lips Page (t); Joe Britton, Alfred Cobbs, Eli Robinson (tb); Vincent Bair-Bey (as); Bill Moore, Hal Singer, Tom Archia, Sam 'The Man' Taylor (ts); Dave McRae (bs); Christine Chatman, Joe Knight, Fletcher Smith (p); prob. Lonnie Johnson, James Cannady, Brownie McGhee (g); Roger Jones, Carl Wilson, Grachan Moncur, Al Hall (b); Horace Washington, Clarence Donaldson, Charlie Smith, Marty Wilson (d); Rose Marie McCoy (sp). 4/44–6/53.
**(*) Shoutin' The Blues
[Blue Boar CDBB 1010] Big Maybelle; Hot Lips Page (t); Joe Britton (tb); Vincent Bair-Bey (as); Hal Singer, Tom Archia (ts); Joe Knight (p); prob. Lonnie Johnson (g); Carl Wilson (b); Clarence Donaldson (d). 12/47.

Classics assemble a 1944 vocal with Christine Chatman's Orchestra, eight King sides and the first ten OKehs. The first four King tracks had been thought to feature Tiny Bradshaw's Orchestra, and hence only the second four are on *Shoutin' The Blues*, which is credited to Hot Lips Page, but aural evidence and Hal Singer's memories confirm that Page's band is heard throughout. Pre-OKeh, Maybelle sometimes reined her voice back, trying to conform with a preference for female band vocalists to sound refined and girlish. The gutbucket 'Too Tight Mama' and 'Bad Dream Blues', with Lonnie Johnson's dandified but ballsy electric guitar, stand out among the ballads and blues-ballads, but it was only when licensed to belt by OKeh that she developed a distinctive style. Both these CDs are aimed at specialists; unless Page is the specialism, Classics offer better value, but the OKeh sessions are best heard complete.

***(*) The Complete OKeh Sessions 1952–'55
Epic/OKeh/Legacy EK 53417 *Big Maybelle; Joe Wilder, Taft Jordan (t): Alfred Cobbs, Eli Robinson, Billy Byers (tb); Paul Ricci, Jerome Richardson (as); Sam 'The Man' Taylor, Maurice Simon, Budd Johnson (ts); Dave McRae, Leslie Johnakins, Heywood Henry (bs); Fletcher Smith, Lee Anderson, Al Williams, Ernie Hayes (p); James Cannady, Brownie McGhee, Mickey Baker (g); Grachan Moncur, Al Hall, Lloyd Trotman, Norman Keenan (b); Charlie Smith, Marty Wilson, Jimmy Crawford, Panama Francis, Herbie Lovelle (d); Rose Marie McCoy (sp). 10/52–3/55.*

These are Big Maybelle's most consistently bluesy recordings, and clearly OKeh wanted it that way; the cavernous tenor of Sam Taylor and Mickey Baker's stabbing guitar runs are prominently featured, and Maybelle herself is usually encouraged to sing as big and raspy as she knows how. (Sometimes she indulges in a mildly annoying squeak at the end of lines, but never does it automatically.) Highlights include 'Gabbin' Blues', made into a hit by Rose Marie McCoy's impeccably timed signifying, 'Maybelle's Blues' ('Ain't you sorry your woman ain't got great big legs like mine?') and 'Hair Dressin' Women', a mordantly funny attack on gossips. From time to time, ballads offer a welcome contrast; her Sarah Vaughan soundalike on 'Ain't No Use' can't be faulted. The disc declines towards its end; 'New Kind Of Mambo' makes one wonder what was wrong with the old kind, and the last four titles, arranged by Quincy Jones, are remarkably routine – none more so than the first and worst recording of 'Whole Lot Of Shakin' Goin' On'. Most of the time, however, Maybelle and her musicians offer an admirable blend of gospel ferocity, jazz timing and the salty honesty of the blues.

***(*) Candy!
Savoy SVY 17101 2CD *Big Maybelle; Sidney DeParis, unknown (t); Frank Rehak, Henderson Chambers, unknown (tb); Omer Simeon (cl); Dave McRae, Gigi Gryce, Sahib Shihab, unknowns (as); Warren Lucky, Buddy Lucas, Ernie Wilkins, Jerome Richardson, Jesse Powell, unknowns (ts); Leslie Johnakins, George Barrow, unknowns (bs); Robert Banks (o); Kelly Owens, Don Abney, Hank Jones, Danny Smalls, Eddie Wilcox, unknowns (p); Paul Winter, Julius M. Held, Seymour Miroff, Felix Orlewitz (vn); Mickey Baker, Kenny Burrell, Charles Macey, unknowns (g); Leonard Gaskin, Ed Sneed, Al Lucas, Abie Baker, unknowns (b); Sol Hall, Bobby Donaldson, Shep Shepherd, unknowns (d); prob. Rose Marie McCoy (v); unknown (sp). 5/56–8/59.*

***(*) Blues, Candy & Big Maybelle
Savoy SV 0264 *As above, except omit DeParis, Chambers, Simeon, Powell, Smalls. 5/56–3/59.*

When Big Maybelle moved to Savoy, she had an immediate hit with 'Candy', her gospel inflections transforming its pop sentimentality. Thereafter, she spent a lot of time cutting bluesy versions of the great pop standards. The obvious comparison, and one that obviously occurred to Savoy's Herman Lubinsky, is with Dinah Washington, but Dinah never featured Maybelle's abrupt, exciting transitions from seductive purr to fractured roar. Songs like 'All Of Me', 'Say It Isn't So' and especially 'So Long' prove that few singers were better at infusing pop tunes with bluesiness, and even 'Silent Night' and 'White Christmas' are more than respectable. She's ably assisted by her musicians, usually playing economically gorgeous charts by Basie arranger Ernie Wilkins. Maybelle also recorded a number of excellent hardcore blues for Savoy, among them her introspective two-part composition 'Blues Early Early', and 'Ramblin' Blues', a revision of 'Key To The Highway'.

Candy! presents the complete Savoys, including two previously unissued titles, on two CDs. It also includes an extra-contractual album of W. C. Handy songs recorded for Cub, who delivered the tapes to Savoy after legal action. This is an inoffensive but unremarkable set, with neither Maybelle nor the musicians looking for adventure. (Maybelle's motive was heroin; she insisted on cash down.) *Blues, Candy & Big Maybelle* omits this material, drawing its 28 tracks (of a possible 34) from all her Savoy sessions. There's the odd clunker, but it's less than half the price of *Candy!* and should satisfy most listeners.

** The Very Best Of Big Maybelle 'That's All'
Collectables COL-CD-5902 *Big Maybelle; unknowns (t); unknowns (tb); unknowns (s); unknown (h); unknown (p); unknowns (strings); unknown (g); unknown (b); unknown (d); unknowns (v). 5/64.*

This reissued Scepter LP weighs in at just over 30 minutes; most of it is pop, but not of the standard reached on Savoy. Maybelle's voice, although deeper and rougher, is still mighty, but most of the arrangements are either routine or fussy, and the backing vocalists veer from bombastic to cutesy. A brooding, trombone-heavy 'Don't Let The Sun Catch You Crying' stands out from its humdrum surroundings.

** Half Heaven, Half Heartache
[Westside WESM 589] *Big Maybelle; unknowns (t); unknowns (s); unknown (p); unknown (vn); unknown (g); unknown (b); unknown (d); unknown (vb); unknowns (orch); unknowns (v). 2/62, 63, 8/68.*

Half gospel, half ballads, in other words, reissuing two Brunswick LPs and some extra tracks. She's in awesome voice on the ballads, but the arrangements, though not bad, lack the jazzy edge that Ernie Wilkins supplied. 'The Price You Have To Pay', hitherto unissued, is classic deep soul; Brunswick preferred 'Cold Cold Heart', the worst Hank Williams cover ever made. The gospel segment thriftily reuses backing tracks from an LP by Linda Hopkins and Jackie Wilson. Five years later, the music is still blandly busy, and the chorus sounds like the Munchkins trying to be the Mormon Tabernacle Choir. Maybelle does her best, but only 'Do Lord', with prominent guitar, has a little distinction. Happily, *The Last Of Big Maybelle* (Muse MCD 5439), drawn from Rojac and Paramount, is deleted. CS

Big Rhythm Combo
GROUP

Big Rhythm Combo was a brief stopover on the career routes of its front men Lynwood Slim and Kid Ramos.

*** Too Small To Dance
Pacific Blues PBRC 9902 *Tom Dennison (tb); Jeff 'Big Dad' Turmes (bs); Spyder Mittleman (s); Lynwood Slim (h, v); Fred Kaplan (o, p, g); Kid Ramos (g); Tyler Pederson (b); Richard Innes (d, v); Jerry Hall, Willem van Dullemen (v). 11/93.*

Lynwood Slim and Ramos apart, the other members of BRC were Kaplan, Pedersen and Innes, all of whom had played with Lynwood Slim before and would do so again, as well as with

Ramos on his own-name debut in 1995. So there was nothing impromptu or speculative about this album – which isn't to imply that it's anything but lively. The nicely varied programme ranges from West Coast blues in the early T-Bone Walker idiom ('I Have Nothing Left', 'I Can't Denie [sic] It') and horn-led jump-blues ('Now Or Never', 'Big Fat Mamas') to almost Haleyesque rock 'n' roll ('Let It Go', 'Too Small To Dance'), with a brief shot of '60s Blue Note jazz in 'Song For Mr. Tiny'. Ramos is impressive whatever the style he's reproducing. The album was originally on Black Magic BMCD 9025 (now deleted) and was remixed when issued by Pacific Blues. TR

Big Three Trio
GROUP

Leonard Caston (1917–87) bragged that the Big Three Trio 'was the only trio singing blues in harmony. We were the very first to do this type of singing.' Not quite: Caston and Willie Dixon had been members of the Five Breezes, who recorded in 1940, and Dixon had been with the Four Jumps of Jive, but the Big Three were the first harmony group to be widely popular on the basis of a repertoire that featured blues prominently, if far from exclusively. Named in honour of Roosevelt, Churchill and Stalin, the trio made their last recordings in 1952, and were rather passé by the time they broke up in 1956, but they had paved a way for groups like The Clovers and The Midnighters.

*** The Big Three Trio
Columbia CK 46216 *Leonard Caston [sometimes as Baby Doo or Baby Duke] (p, v); Bernardo Dennis, Ollie Crawford (g, v); Willie Dixon (b, v); Charles Saunders, Hillard Brown, Buddy Smith (d). 3/47–6/52.*
** Poet Of The Blues
Columbia/Legacy CK 65593 *As above. 3/47–6/52.*

These CDs are credited to Willie Dixon, but that's misleading; the Big Three Trio were musical equals, and for much of the group's existence Leonard Caston was their musical director and chief songwriter. Leading or harmonizing, Dixon's growl is nevertheless immediately recognizable, and never more sinuously attractive than on 'Signifying Monkey', his cleaned-up version of an old toast. Caston and Crawford are less distinctive singers, but always entertaining, and their ringing piano and jazzy guitar lines are confident and inventive. (Bernardo Dennis, the guitarist on some early sides, left because he fell out with Dixon, not because of musical deficiencies.) The assorted studio drummers are also consistently good. Previously unissued tracks on the eponymous disc include 'O.C. Bounce' and Duke Ellington's 'Etiquette', respectively showcases for Crawford and Caston. Also previously unissued is 'What Am I To Do?' on which earthy, aggressive guitar work presages later developments in Chicago blues, a genre which always consisted of more than the transplanted and amplified sound of the Delta.

Poet Of The Blues selects ten songs from the The Big Three Trio and superglues them to an electric blues session whose merits are considered under Dixon's entry. The stylistic mismatch is extreme, and this is not a good way to meet the group. Despite heavy duplication with Columbia, it's worth looking for *Big Three Boogie* (Catfish KATCD 189, deleted), which included the namedropping cleverness of 1947's 'No More Sweet Potatoes' and Leonard Caston's stylish ode to partying, 'I Feel Like Steppin' Out'. CS

Big Time Sarah (born 1953)
VOCAL

Sarah Streeter from Coldwater, Mississippi, grew up in Chicago and first sang in clubs in her teens – 'more soul music,' she says, 'than blues'. In 1976 she met Sunnyland Slim and began singing with him and recording for his Airway label. She also worked on European tours with Erwin Helfer. Since the '80s she has been a regular on Chicago's North Side club scene. She claims Big Mama Thornton as an important model.

**(*) Blues With The Girls
EPM Blues Collection 15758 *Big Time Sarah; Stéphane Guerault (ts); Michel Carras (o, p); Larry Martin, Paul Pechenaert, Hubert Sumlin (g); Zox (b); Vincent Daune (d). 2/82.*

Big Time Sarah's voice is gruff and tough; few singers would be more convincing as a Howlin' She-Wolf. Although her five numbers on this French-recorded triple-hander with Bonnie Lee and Zora Young are mostly overdone pieces like 'Hound Dog', 'Fever' and 'Hoochie Coochie Man', she tackles them with brio, and the band responds in the same spirit and the outcome is surprisingly individual.

***(*) Lay It On 'Em Girls
Delmark DD-659 *Big Time Sarah; Bill McFarland (tb, v); Rodney Brown (ss, ts, v); Tony Llorens (o, p); Rico McFarland (g); Bill Hargrave (b); Michael Llorens (d); China Berry (v). 9/92.*
*** Blues In The Year One-D-One
Delmark DE-692 *Big Time Sarah; Rodney Brown (s, v); Tony Llorens (p); Emery Williams (g); Bill Hargrave (b); Ricky Nelson (d, v); Kevin Bibbs (v). 9/96.*
*** A Million Of You
Delmark DE-750 *Big Time Sarah; Kenny Anderson (t); Bill McFarland (tb); Hank Ford (ts); Matthew Skoller (h); Roosevelt Purifoy (o, p); Rico McFarland, John Hill, Richie Davis (g); Bill Hargrave (b); 'Curfew' Scott (d); Roberta Thomas (v). 2/00.*

Except for versions of 'Summertime' and 'Ain't No Sunshine', *Lay It On 'Em Girls* is a thoughtfully varied programme of blues, delivered with panache. Thoughtfully chosen, too, ranging from 'The Thrill Is Gone' and 'Evil Gal Blues' to Willie Dixon's recomposition 'Hoochie Coochie Woman'. What gives the album extra distinction is Rico McFarland's inventive settings – even the warhorses canter like young stallions – and the band's lively playing of them. McFarland isn't present on *Blues In The Year One-D-One* but otherwise the musicians are much the same and radiate the same confidence that they know Sarah's ways. As previous albums have shown, when she goes shopping for songs Sarah isn't afraid to pick familiar material, trusting to her design sense to make it her own, and she succeeds in giving a personal touch to 'Ain't Nobody's Business' and 'Down Home Blues'. She's less successful with 'Woke Up This Morning' and 'You Don't Love Me', but who wouldn't be?

It's good to hear McFarland again on *A Million Of You*, not only as a tart guitarist (splitting the lead parts with John Hill) but as the co-writer and arranger of the title track, 'Daydreaming', 'Stop Your Killing Me' and 'Jump!' These and some other selections are less generic songs than Sarah has tended to do in the past, and the charts are more modern, but she is quite flexible enough to do them justice. Apart from a long and characterless rendition of Earl Hooker's 'Blue Guitar' featuring McFarland and organist Purifoy, this is another entertaining album, further proof that Big Time Sarah has earned her nickname.

A video of her singing at Blue Chicago in June 2000, accompanied by Michael Coleman and others, is included in the enhanced-CD VAC *Mojo Mamas* (Blue Chicago BC 5005). TR

Big Twist (1937–90)
VOCAL, HARMONICA

In the '60s Larry Nolan worked as a drummer and singer on the bar-band circuit in southern Illinois, where he formed what would be the nucleus of the Mellow Fellows with Terry Ogolini and Pete Special. 'We're basically a from-the-gut rhythm and blues band,' Special once said, 'and our roots are in that golden era of R&B.' After Twist's death the band carried on as The Mellow Fellows and then the Chicago Rhythm & Blues Kings.

(**) **Big Twist & The Mellow Fellows**
Flying Fish FF 70229 *Big Twist; Ron Friedman (t); Mike Halpin (tb); Terry Ogolini (ts); Corky Siegel (h); Bob Pina (kb); Pete Special (g); Tim Caron (b); Melvin Crisp (d); Rubin Alvarez (perc); Jesse Dixon Singers (v); Willie Dixon (sp).* 80?
(*) **Playing For Keeps
Alligator ALCD 4732 *Big Twist; Don Tenuto, Paul Howard, Mark Ohlsen (t); Jim Exum, Mike Halpin (tb); Terry Ogolini (ts); Steve Eisen (bs); Sid Wingfield (kb, v); Chris Cameron (kb); Pete Special (g, v); Tango West, Tony Brown (b); Willie Hayes, Wayne Stewart (d); Gene Barge (v, prod); Robin Robinson, Nanette Frank (v).* summer 83.
*** **Live From Chicago! – Bigger Than Life!!**
Alligator ALCD 4755 *Big Twist; Don Tenuto (t); Terry Ogolini, Gene Barge (ts); Steve Eisen (bs); Sid Wingfield (kb); Pete Special, Marvin Jackson (g); Bob Halaj (b); Steve Cobb, Eric Jensen (d).* 1–2/87.

It has a couple of Willie Dixon songs, one introduced by the composer, but *Big Twist & The Mellow Fellows* is a soul rather than blues album, and not a very gripping one. With Alligator Records and veteran Chess producer Gene Barge behind them, however, the band mounts a different and punchier show on *Playing For Keeps*. Having songs like '300 Pounds Of Heavenly Joy' (another Dixon composition), 'We're Gonna Make It' and 'Polk Salad Annie' certainly helps. Big Twist has a strong, rumbling voice, more a trombone than a trumpet, which occasionally slides into a Howlin' Wolfish snarl; 'I Brought The Blues On Myself' is a good example, and a good song too. *Live From Chicago!*, taped over three nights at Biddy Mulligan's, offers a thicker slice of blues ('Built For Comfort', 'I Live The Life I Love', 'Steamroller Blues', etc.) and a vividly noisy club ambience. Later albums by the band are discussed in the entries for The Mellow Fellows and Chicago Rhythm & Blues Kings. TR

Esther Bigeou (c. 1895–c. 1936)
VOCAL

New Orleans born, Esther Bigeou toured the black theatre circuits from 1917 onwards, and the sessions which comprise her brief recording career seem to have been fitted in when she was not on the road. She retired from show business in 1930.

(*) **Esther Bigeou (1921–1923)/Lillyn, Ada & Alberta Brown (1921–1928)
Document DOCD-5489 *Bigeou; Peter Bocage, unknowns (c); John Lindsay, unknowns (tb); Lorenzo Tio Jr, unknowns (cl); Louis Warnick, unknowns (as); unknown (ts); Bob Ricketts, Clarence Williams, Steve Lewis, unknowns (p); Armand J. Piron, unknown (vn); Charles Bocage, unknown (bj); Charles Ysaguirre, unknowns (bb); Louis Cottrell, unknowns (d).* 10/21–12/23.

Esther Bigeou's recordings were made while the process was still acoustic, and the first half-dozen or so have orchestral backings which are both murky and, regardless of recording quality, undistinguished. Bigeou has plenty of vocal power but little in the way of subtlety or shading, and like the musicians she concentrates on reproducing the written notes rather than blueing or swinging them. Her other titles are accompanied only by the piano of Clarence Williams, which suits her voice better. Williams is in good form, and 'Beale Street Blues' is a likeable reading on the part of both artists, but Bigeou was a vaudevillian rather than a natural blues singer. She seems to be adopting the newly fashionable style to keep up with public and record-company demand, rather than being compelled by artistic necessity.

Of the trio of Browns who complete the CD, Lillyn claimed to have sung blues on stage as early as 1908. Longer familiarity with the form may explain why she handles it more successfully than Esther Bigeou, although the quality of her Jazz-Bo Syncopaters is also relevant to the success of her four numbers. Ada Brown's two songs complete the reissue of her output by Document; her powerful delivery is well supported by a lineup of distinguished New Orleanians in Chicago exile. Alberta Brown's strong and sultry voice recalls that of her fellow Dallasite, and Columbia label-mate, Lillian Glinn. This may explain why she only made one record; lack of talent certainly cannot account for it. CS

Birmingham Jug Band
GROUP

An unidentified band from, or at any rate recorded in, Birmingham, Alabama.

*** **Jaybird Coleman & The Birmingham Jug Band (1927–1930)**
Document DOCD-5140 *unknown (h, v); poss. Ben Covington (bj-md); unknown (g); unknown (j).* 12/30.

The recordings of the Birmingham Jug Band were added to those of Jaybird Coleman on this CD because it was once thought that the latter was a member of the group. There was never much weight in the proposition: Coleman was not primarily a team-player, and one of the strengths of the BJB is their tightness as an ensemble, even at the hectic tempos they often adopted. Compared with the carefully planned music of the Memphis Jug Band or Cannon's Jug Stompers, the BJB's is almost comically rough-and-ready. The songs are sketchy at best, the singer regularly deserting his post around the fifth or sixth bar and completing the verse on harmonica, and the band's eight recordings employ only three or four tunes. 'Birmingham Blues', for instance, is an instrumental take of the song that follows, 'Gettin' Ready For Trial'. But the blend of squalling harmonica, effervescent banjo-mandolin and thumping guitar makes for exhilarating and distinctive music. TR

Duffy Bishop Band
GROUP

Headed by singer Bishop and her husband, guitarist and songwriter Chris Carlson, this band has been popular in the Northwest US since the mid-'90s and has opened for many visiting acts. Bishop, who is also an actor, was voted Best Female Vocalist by the Cascade Blues Association each year from 1995 to 1999.

** Bottled Oddities
Burnside BCD 0018 *Henry Cooper (h, g); Chris Carlson (g, v); Keith Lowe (b); Dave Jette (d); Duffy Bishop, Paulette 'Diva' Davis, Luscious Lili Wilde (v).* 94.

** Back To The Bone
Burnside BCD 0023 *As above, except add Rudy 'Root Doctor' Draco (ss, ts, bs), Bob 'House Wine' Roden (ts), Norm Bellas (o).* 'Mardi Gras week' 96.

** Fly The Rocket
Burnside BCD-0032 *Greg Garrett, Gavin Bondy (t); Bryan Dickerson (cl, ts, bs); John Goforth (as, ts, fl, bf); Dover Weinberg (o, v); Janice Scroggins (p); Chris Carlson (g, v); Willy Barber (b); Carlton Jackson (d, v); Michael Partlow (d); Bobby Torres (perc); Duffy Bishop, Tom McGriff (v).* 99.

The opening tracks of *Bottled Oddities* are Howlin' Wolf's 'Evil' and Bessie Smith's 'Reckless Blues', both well done, but these prove to be the only standard blues repertoire on the album, the remaining songs being largely written by Bishop and Carlson, in a variety of idioms from the rockabilly of 'Come On Out' to the message-rock of 'Bath Of Love'. The material on *Back To The Bone*, apart from Johnny Winter's 'Ease My Pain' and an Otis Redding number, is a similar motley of original compositions, blues like 'Get Back To The Bone' or the Muddy Watersish 'Growing Old' being interwoven with songs whose affiliations are rather with rock, folk or swing. On these albums Bishop comes across as a vehement and versatile singer, ably seconded by Cooper on slide guitar, but somewhat in need of more diverse accompaniments, and of songs that are catchy as well as clever. *Fly The Rocket* at least answers the first call, the horn arrangements adding new textures, but Bishop has cultivated her ability to sing in different idiomatic costumes, and the matter-of-fact narrative of Ida Cox's 'Wild Women' is at odds with the style and subject-matter of most of the rest of the album. One suspects this is a band that delivers more from the stage than from the hi-fi. TR

Elvin Bishop (born 1942)
VOCAL, GUITAR

Bishop used a National Merit Scholarship to move from Tulsa, Oklahoma, to the University of Chicago. Rather than study physics, he investigated the South Side blues scene, studying guitar with Hound Dog Taylor and Little Smokey Smothers. There and on campus he met Paul Butterfield and they formed what became the Butterfield Blues Band. Bishop eventually lost out to Michael Bloomfield's flashier talents and after a move to California at the end of the '60s carved himself a solo career that included several albums and a Top Ten pop hit. His take on the blues is informed and affectionate without scaling the heights to which some of his contemporaries aspired.

*** Big Fun
Alligator ALCD 4767 *Bishop; Reynaldo 'Daddy Ray' Arvizu Jr (as); Terry Hanck, Nancy Wright (ts); Stevie Gurr (h, g, v); Norton Buffalo (h); Phil Aaberg, Dr John [Mac Rebennack] (kb); Michael 'Fly' Brooks (b); Gary Silva (d, v); Kathy Kennedy, Katie Guthorn (v); Whit Lehnberg & The Carptones ('mayhem').* 88.

***(*) Don't Let The Bossman Get You Down!
Alligator ALCD 4791 *Bishop; Ed Earley (tb); Reynaldo 'Daddy Ray' Arvizu (as, ts, cga); Johnny Bamont (ts); Stevie Gurr (h, g); Randy Forrester (kb); Luther Tucker (g); Karl Sevareid (b); Gary Silva (d); The Carptones [Bill Thompson, Jack Howe, 'Daddy Ray' Arvizu, Gary Silva, Ed Earley, Guitar Gypsey, Cal Valentine] (v).* 90.

These albums have a quality rarely encountered in records of their type – personality. Much of that is down to the garrulity of Bishop's singing and his quirky, angular guitar solos. Other factors are the wit embodied in the horn arrangements and the band's willingness to convey their enjoyment of what they're doing. Standouts on *Big Fun* are the inventive setting of Memphis Slim's 'Beer Drinking Woman', with a humorous gangster-movie spoken intro, and unhackneyed arrangements of Jimmy Reed's 'Honest I Do', with slide guitar and antiphonal saxes, and Leroy Carr's 'Midnight Hour Blues'. *Bossman* has a rousing opener in 'Fannie Mae', echoed by the closing 'Just Your Fool'; in between, there are songs from St Louis Jimmy, Memphis Minnie, Jimmy McCracklin and Junior Wells. If the albums have a fault, it's Bishop's inclination to indulge in his own form of blues rap, as in 'Fishin' Again' (*Big Fun*), 'My Whiskey Head Buddies', 'Soul Food' and 'Rollin' With My Blues' (*Bossman*). It's pleasant enough but it's an easy way out, taking just a little of the gilt off a prime piece of gingerbread. NS/TR

*** Ace In The Hole
Alligator ALCD 4833 *Bishop; Ed Earley (tb, v); 'Daddy Ray' Arvizu (as, v); Charlie Musselwhite (h); Randy Forrester (kb, v); Carl Lockett (g); Evan Palmerston (b); Larry Vann (d, v); Willie Jordan (cga, v); Joyce Garcia, Camille, The Carp-Tones [Ed Earley, 'Daddy Ray' Arvizu, Bill Thompson, Rick Meyers] (v).* 95.

An unchallenging set of good-time blues (mostly original) is typified by its opener, 'Another Mule Kicking In Your Stall', with Bishop chatting over its centre section, something he does throughout the whole of 'Home Of The Blues', a tribute to the musicians and clubs of Chicago, and most of an entirely too long 'Fishin''. The band is well-rehearsed and adept, with its unusual blend of trombone and alto sax working surprisingly well. 'Driving Wheel', 'Blue Flame' and a revisit to his pop hit 'Fooled Around And Fell In Love' are instrumentals largely devoted to Bishop's slide guitar. All of which is enjoyable but ultimately it's music with personality (again) but little purpose beyond its capacity to entertain. And that was probably the intention.

*** The Skin I'm In
Alligator ALCD 4859 *Bishop; Ed Earley (tb, v); Terry Hanck (ts); Charlie Musselwhite (h, v); Norton Buffalo (h); Randy Forrester*

(kb, v); William Schuler (g, v); Joe Louis Walker (g); Evan Palmerston (b); Larry Vann (d, v); Joe Thomas (v). 98.

A better record than its predecessor, with harder-edged guitar sounds and a more trenchant commitment in the backing tracks. There's an aggression in Bishop's playing that'll probably give this record more staying-power. He uses most of his solo space to wield a bottleneck in a taut if unadventurous fashion. He wrote ten of the 12 songs, the exceptions being Allen Toussaint's 'I'm Gone' and Mercy Dee's 'Shady Lane'. 'The Skin They're In' is about racial attitudes but can only declare 'it's a shame and a sin' and his other songs are similarly unchallenging. He still can't resist talking his way through an acoustic 'Radio Boogie' and an odd chorus in 'Slow Down' and 'Right Now Is The Hour'. Guests Buffalo, Musselwhite and Walker make small but telling contributions.

*** That's My Partner
Alligator ALCD 4874 *Bishop; Ed Earley (tb, perc, v); Terry Hanck (ts); Steve Gurr (h); S. E. Willis (ac, o, p, v); Albert 'Little Smokey' Smothers (g, v); Ian Lamson (g); Evan Palmerston (b); Bobby Cochran (d, v).* 1/00.

Recorded live at San Francisco's Biscuits & Blues, this joint album with Little Smokey Smothers is Bishop's acknowledgement of the help and friendship accorded him by Smothers soon after his arrival in Chicago. They share the vocals on the opening title track and equally thereafter, apart from 'Stomp', a Bo Diddley-influenced instrumental. The clean lines of Smothers's conventional guitar style contrast with Bishop's deliberately dirty tone. Bishop plunders his previous albums for adequate versions of 'Slow Down', 'Middle Aged Man' and 'The Skin They're In'. The band plays up to its trademark casual precision but someone forgot to build the set to the climax that 'Travelin' Shoes' doesn't provide. NS

**** Gettin' My Groove Back
Blind Pig BPCD 5100 *Bishop; John Middleton (t); Ed Earley (tb, perc, v); Carl Green, Terry Hanck (ts); Norton Buffalo (h, wb); Steve Willis (ac, p, v); Henry Butler (kb, o, p); Steve Lucky (p); Ian Lamson, Roy Rogers (g); Jerome Hammond, Sam Page, Steve Evans (b); Bobby Cochran, Larry Vann (d, v).* 05.

As observed above, Bishop has his own way of doing things. Who else would mix guitars, accordion and trombone into the stew of 'I'll Be Glad' ('when I get my groove back again') or concoct an almost electro-Hawaiian arrangement of Patsy Cline's 'Sweet Dreams'? The insistent stomp of the introduction to 'What The Hell Is Going On', the opening track, is replicated repeatedly throughout the album ('That's My Thing', 'He's A Dog', 'Got To Be New Orleans', etc.), vitalizing and differentiating melodies that might otherwise seem somewhat routine, and offsetting pieces like 'Come On Blues', a slow creeper on the pattern of Howlin' Wolf's 'Back Door Man', with Bishop's guitar reverb spinning like helicopter blades. TR

Sonny Black (born 1946)
VOCAL, GUITAR

'Black' (his real name is Bob Boazman) began playing guitar about the age of 19. In 1970 he teamed up with guitarist Mike Cooper. He has led a band of his own for over 20 years, and has played with numerous blues musicians visiting Britain.

*** Heart And Soul
Bluetrack BRCD 004 *Black; Mark Ramsden (ss); Andy Hamilton (ts); Bob Haddrell (o, p, v); George Pearson, Pete Stroud (b); Dino Coccia (d, perc).* 00.

*** Blues Of A Kind
Free Spirit FSCD 002 *Black; Lee Badau (s); Bob Haddrell (o, p); George Pearson (b); Damon Sawyer (d).* 2/02.

With its sleek arrangements and airy guitar sound, the mostly instrumental *Heart And Soul* seems to have been conceived for a broad canvas and the contrasting colours of blues and smooth jazz. Not at all typical British blues guitar work, then: more along the lines of Ronnie Earl or Robben Ford, and very suavely done. All the pieces are Black's compositions and most are played by the core quartet of himself, Haddrell, Pearson and Coccia, the saxes being added on just three of the 11 tracks. But for contrast there are a couple of solos, the acoustic 'Raggin' The Strings' and the limpid slide guitar piece 'Kelly's Blues'. *Blues Of A Kind*, which is entirely instrumental, is also a long way from a conventional blues guitar album, but in a slightly different direction. 'Paris After Dark', 'Café Cuba', 'Miles Away' and 'Night Drive' reaffirm Black's tastes in jazz, but now in the idiom of guitarists like Kenny Burrell and Grant Green. 'Strollin' Home' is a Blind Blakeish line that plays hide-and-seek with the piano accompaniment – Haddrell, incidentally, is admirable throughout – and Black again takes out his slide for 'Delta Swing' and a peaceful rendition of Charlie Patton's 'Some Of These Days' that deserved to be extended beyond a couple of minutes. Few tracks, in fact, go much further than the four-minute mark: Black evidently doesn't regard versatility as an excuse for overstatement. TR

Black Ace (1905–72)
VOCAL, GUITAR

Babe Karo Lemon Turner grew up on a farm in Hughes Springs, Texas. He took up the guitar seriously when he moved to Shreveport in the mid-'30s, and met Oscar Woods, from whom he learned the local slide guitar style, with the instrument held flat across the knees. Ace played initially at parties, but as his reputation grew he toured, broadcast, and made a few recordings. War service disrupted his musical career, and thereafter he worked at a variety of day jobs. Recorded again in 1960, he had no wish to resume the uncertain life of a professional musician.

**** Black Ace
Arhoolie CD-374 *Black Ace; Smokey Hogg (g).* 2/37, 8–9/60.

Paul Oliver writes that Black Ace's steel-bodied National 'was gathering dust in the attic' in the summer of 1960, but he seems to have needed virtually no practice to restore his skills to the level of 1937. His playing is often complex, ranging freely over the guitar neck, mixing warm, rich chords with dramatic glissandi and single-note runs, and pushing the songs forward with rumbling licks and slides on the bass strings. He never indulges technique at the expense of swing, however; the instrumental 'Bad Times Stomp' is an exemplary display of both. Ace's firm, authoritative singing carries a heavy vibrato, which is well suited to the seriousness of many of his lyrics. If there is a criticism to be made, indeed, it is that he always sounds rather preoccupied; even the automotive double meanings of 'Hitchhiking Woman' are delivered as if his life depended on it. The CD ends with Ace's six Decca recordings from 1937, which show that his younger self had a stronger voice, but that it had weakened remarkably little in 23 years. The original Arhoolie LP included a stately and moving 'Farther Along', which has been omitted, perhaps to save publishing royalties. (The issue is certainly not lack of playing time, and surely not inferior performance.) This is regrettable, but the CD is still a remarkable portrait of probably the last, and certainly the best, of the Shreveport slide guitarists.

*** Oscar 'Buddy' Woods & Black Ace (1930–1938) 'Texas Slide Guitars'
Document DOCD-5143 *As above.* 2/37.

The Decca recordings are also used to complete this disc, which is otherwise devoted to Oscar Woods (q.v.). Document's remastering is inferior to Arhoolie's, but the compilation usefully puts the young Ace in context, and confirms that he owed a great deal to his teacher. cs

Black Boy Shine
VOCAL, PIANO

Black Boy Shine (Harold Holiday) was active in and around Houston, to which he refers often in his songs. Robert Shaw remembered him as a smooth underworld figure and rated him the best of the Texas pianists.

*** Black Boy Shine & Black Ivory King (1936–1937)
Document DOCD-5278 *Black Boy Shine.* 11/36–6/37.
**(*) Leroy Carr & Black Boy Shine – Unissued Test Pressings and Alternate Takes (1934–1937)
Document DOCD-5465 *As above.* 6/37.

Few blues voices convey as plainly as Black Boy Shine's the 'quiet desperation' of Thoreau's famous dictum. His songs, most of them delivered at a dogged slow-medium tempo, are steeped in regret. 'If I had o' listened to what my first woman said, I wouldn't have been hoboin' all in this world today' ('Advice Blues'); 'When you fall in love with a woman, she tries to keep you down' ('Crazy Woman Blues'); 'Woke up this mornin', blues all on my mind – lookin' for my woman, gee, she was hard to find' ('Lonesome Home Blues'): such opening lines are typical of him, and the mood they set is seldom lightened as the songs proceed. The piano accompaniments are conceived as muted backdrops to the stories, and the shifts from major to minor in 'Married Man Blues' are a rare departure from habit. The only time the sun breaks through the cloud cover is when he plays the jaunty 'Brown House Blues', with a piano part reminiscent of Robert Cooper.

The first CD is rounded off with the recordings of Black Ivory King. One of at least three singer-pianists who were born David Alexander, this artist is thought to have been from Shreveport, Louisiana, and played around Louisiana and east Texas. At his sole recording session, in Dallas in February 1937, he delivered an exquisitely melancholic reading of the Texas train song 'Flying Crow', the topical 'Working For The PWA' and two other vocal blues, all enlivened by crisp right-hand playing.

The CD shared with Leroy Carr contains nine songs that Black Boy Shine recorded at his second session but which were never issued; seven of them are presented in two takes. In subject-matter and treatment they are all of a piece with the issued recordings, and only the dedicated fan of his music (or of Carr's) need feel pressed to investigate the album. TR

The Blackjacks
GROUP

The Blackjacks are a five-piece band based in Brighton, Sussex. Most of them have been playing since the '70s in blues, rock or country bands. Since coming together a few years ago they have played at several major English blues festivals.

**(*) High Roller
Blackjack BJ 002 *Wanderin' Wilf Taylor (h, v); Tom Arnold (o); Alan Chaplin (p); Mighty Mick Taylor, Rory Coolhand Cameron (g, v); Simon Tex Sparrow (b, v); King Louis Borenius (d, v); Phil Overhead (perc).* 02.

Making no attempt to hide their origins behind assumed accents, this lively band, augmented for the sessions by a couple of guest keyboards players and a percussionist, produces crisp music, all original, chiefly in the blues idiom but with occasional diversions into rockabilly like 'Blackjack Boogie'. Wilf Taylor's harmonica is particularly vivacious, and Mick Taylor is a versatile lead guitarist and primary vocalist, but the band carries no passengers. Well engineered and produced, the album is likely to give great satisfaction to The Blackjacks' followers, who for the time being probably constitute most of its market. The band's earlier CD, *What's The Deal?* (BJ 001), is no longer available. TR

Scrapper Blackwell (1904–62)
VOCAL, GUITAR, PIANO

Francis Blackwell, nicknamed for his hot temper, was working as a bootlegger in Indianapolis when a talent scout teamed him with Leroy Carr and brought the duo to Vocalion, where they wrote the book on piano–guitar duets. Carr's death in 1935, and the fierce argument that preceded it, seem to have upset Blackwell deeply, and he soon stopped recording; when found by Duncan Schiedt in 1955, he was living in poverty. He resumed playing, and was recorded again, but got into a fight in a Naptown alley and was fatally shot by his 75-year-old opponent.

**(*) Scrapper Blackwell – Vol. 1 (1928–1932)
Document BDCD-6029 *Blackwell; Bob Robinson, unknown (cl); Leroy Carr, Jimmy Blythe (p); unknown (k); Bertha 'Chippie' Hill, Teddy Moss, Black Bottom McPhail (v).* 6/28–3/32.
**(*) Scrapper Blackwell – Vol. 2 (1934–1958)
Document BDCD-6030 *Blackwell; Leroy Carr, Dot Rice (p); Josh White, Bumble Bee Slim (v).* 8/34–7/35, 6/58.
**(*) The Virtuoso Guitar Of Scrapper Blackwell
Yazoo 1019 *Blackwell; Leroy Carr (p, v); Tommie Bradley (g, v); poss. Eddie Dimmitt or Walter Cole (g); Black Bottom McPhail (v).* 6/28–12/34.
*** Hard Time Blues
Acrobat ACRCD 161 *Blackwell; Leroy Carr (p, v); Josh White (g).* 6/28–2/35.

Scrapper Blackwell's reputation has sometimes suffered from the impression that his first name was 'Leroy Carr and'. With but one exception, Carr was the singer on their duets, and Scrapper has been typecast as the junior partner, but, in truth, Carr would often have sounded rather bland without Blackwell's astringent guitar work. Whether as an accompanist – most famously to Carr, but also with great élan on Black Bottom McPhail's four sides – or as a solo act, Blackwell was a master of the guitar, producing rich, rhythmic chordal runs, and single-string treble flights that were simultaneously lyrical and percussive. At times, his display pieces approach the realm of absolute music, with instrumentals identified only by their key ('A Blues', 'D Blues', etc.). He was also a fine singer, and an acerbic songwriter. ('After a light shower, maybe we change our clothes,' he deadpans in 'Penal Farm Blues'.)

For Blackwell's early career, the Document CDs have the virtue of completeness, with *Vol. 2* also reissuing a rare EP from his second flowering, but completeness is also their downside. The first volume's small-group sides, variously with Teddy Moss, Chippie Hill plus an irritating kazooist, and 'Robinson's Knights Of Rest', do not have much to recommend them, nor do the second's four accompaniments to a lacklustre Bumble Bee Slim. More fundamentally, Document's sound quality is serviceable at best. *The Virtuoso Guitar*, originally an LP, was the first release to cherrypick Scrapper's early output, and it retains its virtues – clean originals, well remastered, and judicious selection for quality and variety – but 14 tracks is short weight for the CD era. (Tommy Bradley's track almost certainly features a capable Blackwell imitator, incidentally.)

Acrobat have satisfactory sound and plenty of splendid music, but subscribe to the junior partner theory; only eight tracks are by Blackwell solo, the remaining ten being Carr–Blackwell collaborations. Classics of blues performance and blues history though these are, a point is being missed here. Regrettably, *Bad Liquor Blues* (Catfish KATCD 152), the best selection of Blackwell's early work, is deleted.

(*) Scrapper Blackwell (1959/60)
Document DOCD-5275 Blackwell; Brooks Berry (g, v); 'Bud White' [Duncan Schiedt] (wh). 9/59–4/60.

♛ ****** Mr. Scrapper's Blues**
Original Blues Classics OBCCD-594 Blackwell. 7/61.

Blackwell's latterday singing always sounded older than his years, but his guitar and occasional piano were as impressive as ever. The 1959 material was recorded in concert; Blackwell is in good form, and the use of tape means that he is heard for the first time in performances that last more than four minutes, and occasionally more than five. The prevailing mood is elegiac; Scrapper was not unaware of the irony of a former record star singing 'Once I lived the life of a millionaire.' Brooks Berry, whom he accompanies on four numbers, is unfortunately both nervous and slightly distant. (Berry was no longer nervous when, again accompanied by Blackwell, she made the LP *My Heart Struck Sorrow* [Prestige/Bluesville BVLP 1074], which includes some of Blackwell's very finest playing. Two songs from it are on *The Bluesville Years Vol. 10: Country Roads, Country Days* [Prestige PRCD 9918].) The concert tapes had deteriorated slightly during 30 years in storage, but not to deterrent levels. More problematic are the first five 1960 tracks, once half an LP on the British 77 label; on these, the guitar is too closely miked, and has a string out of tune. Both faults are remedied on the remainder of the CD, and there is some marvellous music to be heard, but this is not the place to meet Blackwell for the first time.

Mr. Scrapper's Blues, on the other hand, is the ideal place to meet him for the last time. Blackwell again turns in extended performances, extracts maximum emotional depth from his songs, and applies his playing technique to the full. The added advantage is that he was recorded under optimum conditions, and with his skills honed by several years of renewed performance. He reprises some of his hits, both as a soloist and with Leroy Carr, but the version of 'Penal Farm' which ends his recording career is considerably different from the one which started it. Like the whole album, it has a much stronger sense of felt experience, of a life expressed in song. The Scrapper Blackwell heard on this session is a pebble on the shores of life – battered by the waves, but also sculpted and polished by them. The result is a moving and magnificent valediction. cs

Willie '61' Blackwell (1905–72)
VOCAL, GUITAR

The Tennessee-born Blackwell first played piano but after being injured in a fight took up guitar, learning from Jack Warren, brother of Robert 'Baby Boy' Warren, and, allegedly, from Robert Johnson, whom he met through knowing his stepson Robert Lockwood. After recording for Bluebird and the Library of Congress in the early '40s he settled in Detroit in 1944, working at the Chevrolet factory. He made a few public appearances between 1967 and 1971.

*** Carl Martin (1930–1936)/Willie "61" Blackwell (1941)
Document DOCD-5229 Blackwell; Alfred Elkins (imb). 7/41.

Blackwell's guitar playing is simple and all his songs have much the same tune, but he was a gifted composer whose blues are full of fresh-minted images. '[If you] don't believe I'm leaving, just meet me the first sunshiny day,' he sings in 'Bald Eagle Blues'; 'at the Statue of Liberty you will see your eagle rooster sail away.' And in 'Rampaw Street Blues': 'If I belonged to some organization and was way up in degree, I know some vehicle driver, boys, would have some mercy on me.' Contemporaries recognized his talent: Jazz Gillum recorded at least two of his numbers, 'Noiseless Motor Blues' and 'Machine Gun Blues', under different titles, and the latter song is also the original of Sunnyland Slim's 'Johnson Machine Gun'. He was fond of adopting an admonitory tone – 'Don't misuse me, baby, because I'm young and wild. You ought to remember, once you was a child,' he sings in 'Don't Misuse Me, Baby' – and of reflections like 'I'm not jealous but I'm superstitious – the most working men's that way' or 'I will admit I've been misused, by being a country boy'. These carefully wrought texts are read rather than sung, in a light, conversational voice.

His eight-song Bluebird session behind him, Blackwell returned to Memphis, where almost a year later he crossed paths with Alan Lomax, collecting for the Library of Congress's Archive of Folk Song. 'Four O'Clock Flower Blues', a rerecording of one of his Bluebird songs, with a floral metaphor most unusual in blues writing, is on *Negro Blues And Hollers* (Rounder CD 1501) and *The Land Where The Blues Began* (Rounder CD 1861), while *Mississippi Blues: Library Of Congress Recordings 1940–42* (Travelin' Man TM CD 07, deleted) houses 'Junior's A Jap Girl's Christmas For His Santa Claus', a war song with fantastical ideas: 'When Junior starts to teethin', baby, please write to me. Well, well, I'm gonna send him a Jap's tooth, so that he can cut his with ease.'

Both those recordings have bold lead guitar parts by Blackwell's buddy William Brown; in fact about half of 'Junior's …' is a lengthy guitar duet. Lomax took the opportunity of recording Brown on his own. 'Ragged And Dirty' was a good long variant of the piece Sleepy John Estes recorded as 'Broken Hearted, Ragged And Dirty Too', and there was a version of the old 'East St. Louis Blues', but in the six minutes of 'Mississippi Blues', with its limpidly beautiful guitar arrangement, Brown gave his visitor one of the jewels of the Archive's collection. All three recordings (and Blackwell's 'Four O'Clock Flower Blues' again) are on *Mississippi Blues & Gospel (1934–1942)* (Document DOCD-5320). TR

Big Al Blake (born 1945)
VOCAL, HARMONICA, GUITAR

Blake was born in Oregon, grew up in Oklahoma, became a blues fan in his teens and learned harmonica. In the '60s he moved to Chicago and from there to southern California, where he made friends with the guitarist Hollywood Fats and played in his band for almost 15 years. In the '90s he furthered his interest in playing earlier forms of blues.

*** Mr. Blake's Blues
Blue Collar Music BCM 7108 Blake; Fred Kaplan (p); Junior Watson, Kid Ramos (g); Larry Taylor (b); Richard Innes (d). 3/96–3/97.

On the harmonica tunes 'Old Time Boogie', 'The Honeydripper' and 'Easy (Very Greazy)' Blake conjures up the ghosts of Little and Big Walter, but when he switches to guitar he can evoke even earlier models, as in 'Leavin' California', 'Shelby Ford Blues' and 'Hoppin' Toad Blues', period-perfect duets with pianist Kaplan, played with economy and sung with muscle rather than mannerism. Such scrupulous empathy with old blues sounds will not commend Blake to the neophiliac, but conservative enthusiasts ought to approve of him. Watson joins the core group of Kaplan, Taylor and Innes on five tracks, while Ramos is on three, contributing Nighthawklike slide guitar to 'A Rambler And A Rollin' Stone'. TR

Bobby 'Blue' Bland (born 1930)
VOCAL

Born in Rosemark, Tennessee, Bland as a young man found music in nearby Memphis, where he fell in with Rosco Gordon, Johnny Ace and B. B. King in a loose aggregation known as 'The Beale Streeters'. After a few recordings for Chess and Modern he signed with the new Duke label and spent much of the '50s touring with its other star, Junior Parker, in the revue Blues Consolidated. *In 1957 'Farther Up The Road' was an R&B #1, the first of more than 20 R&B Top Ten placings. Like B. B. King (for whom he once worked as a driver) Bland toured the Southern chittlin circuit indefatigably for many years, playing to his core audience: mature, African-American, predominantly female. In the '70s ABC tried to reposition him as a mainstream soul singer, but his joining Malaco, one of the leading labels for Southern soul, brought him back to the people who care for him most.*

*** The "3B" Blues Boy
Ace CDCHD 302 Bland; Joe Scott, Melvin Jackson, Floyd Arceneaux (t); Pluma Davis, unknown (tb); Johnny Board, Jimmy Beck (as, ts); Bill Harvey, Robert Skinner, L. A. Hill, Bobby Forte, unknowns (ts); Rayfield Devers, unknown(s) (bs); Teddy Reynolds (o, p); Connie Mack Booker, Skippy Brooks, unknowns (p); Roy Gaines, Clarence Hollimon, Pat Hare, Wayne Bennett, unknowns (g); Hamp Simmons, unknowns (b); Sonny Freeman, John 'Jabo' Parks, unknowns (d); unknown (vb). 52–59.

*** Greatest Hits Vol. One – The Duke Recordings
MCA MCAD-11783 Bland; Joe Scott, Melvin Jackson (t); Pluma Davis (tb); Johnny Board, Jimmy Beck (as, ts); Bill Harvey, Robert Skinner, L. A. Hill, Bobby Forte (ts); Rayfield Davers (bs); Teddy Reynolds (o, p); Skippy Brooks, Johnny Young, unknown (p); Pat Hare, Wayne Bennett, Gerald Sims (g); Hamp Simmons, Phil Upchurch, unknown (b); Sonny Freeman, John 'Jabo' Parks, Harrell Porter (d); unknown musicians. 57–2/69.

*** Two Steps From The Blues
MCA 088 112 516//BGO BGOCD 163 Similar to above. 57–60.

***(*) The Voice
Ace CDCHD 323 Similar to above. 59–69.

(***) The Millennium Collection
MCA 088 112 158 Similar to above. 60–73.

**** The Anthology
MCA 088 112 596 2CD Bland; various accompaniments. 52–83.

At his best – or rather at his material's best: as a singer he seldom had a bad day – Bobby Bland in the '50s and '60s was among the great storytellers. 'Who Will The Next Fool Be', 'I Pity The Fool', 'Cry, Cry, Cry' – when he crooned or cantillated these arias of love and betrayal and resignation the listener was swept up in their emotional turbulence, borne on the swell of their heaving orchestrations, to be left at last, when the record finished, edified but exhausted.

It took him a few years to develop that skill. His husky voice was always lovely, but at the beginning of his career he modelled his style on B. B. King's, and it became distinctive only when he began listening carefully to the sermons of the Detroit preacher Rev. C. L. Franklin: 'that's where I got my squall from.' His early sides like 'Drifting From Town To Town' on *The Modern Downhome Blues Sessions Vol. 3: Memphis On Down* (Ace CDCHD 1003) were made with small groups, but once he was teamed with the bandleader Bill Harvey and arranger Joe Scott his recordings were transformed from low-budget B-movies to wide-screen epics, noisy with brass. It didn't work every time. The disconcertingly upbeat 'Blue Moon' or the Nashville-produced 'Share Your Love With Me', unlovably shared with the Anita Kerr Singers, are schlockwork. There, as quite often elsewhere, Bland drifts more than the 'two steps from the blues' of his most famous album. But when that happens you don't feel that he's losing his way, just straying, and before long he'll reassure you with the ferocious homily of 'Yield Not To Temptation' or a luscious slow blues like his reading of 'Stormy Monday', with Wayne Bennett's justly celebrated guitar line. Bennett was one of a string of first-class guitarists who put sinew into Bland's records, others including Clarence Hollimon, Pat Hare (briefly, but he's on 'Farther Up The Road'), Roy Gaines and, later, Mel Brown.

All the titles approved above are on *Greatest Hits* and (except for 'Farther Up The Road') *The Voice*. The latter offers much better value with 26 tracks as against 16, but is trumped by *The Anthology*, a superbly chosen and presented 49-track 2CD that ranges from Bland's first Duke single, 'Lovin' Blues', to the MCA albums of the early '80s (see below) but wisely concentrates on the Joe Scott years. *The Millennium Collection* is okay, but what can you do in a dozen tracks? One thing you can do is produce a *Two Steps From The Blues*, Bland's second Duke album, a certified tearjerker for more than 40 years, still available and still the only CD with his Duke version of 'St. James Infirmary'. Curiously, though, one of Bland's, and Scott's, most finely wrought jewels, 'How Does A Cheatin' Woman Feel' from 1960, the B-side of 'Yield Not To Temptation', has yet to find a place on any CD reissue.

(***) His California Album
BGO BGOCD 64 Bland; Chuck Findley, Paul Hubinon, Dick Hyde, Ernie Watts, Jack Kelson Jr (brass, reeds); Michael Omartian (o, p, arr, cond); unknowns (strings); Ben Benay, David Cohen, Larry Carlton, Mel Brown, Dean Parks (g); Wilton Felder, Max Bennett (b); Ed Greene (d); Ginger Blake, Julia Tillman, Maxine Willard (v); Sid Sharp (strings arr); Steve Barri (prod). 73.

(***) Dreamer
MCA MCAD 10415//BGO BGOCD 63 Similar to above. 74.

(**(*)) Get On Down/Reflections In Blue
BGO BGOCD 449 Similar to above (Reflections In Blue) or with unknown musicians (Get On Down). 75, 77.

(***) Greatest Hits Volume Two
MCA MCAD 11809 Bland; various accompaniments. 73–83.

The sumptuous production of *His California Album*, *Dreamer* and *Reflections In Blue* cossets Bland's voice as he strolls into the Technicolor soul sunsets of '(If Loving You Is Wrong) I Don't Want To Be Right', 'Ain't No Love In The Heart Of The City' and 'I Intend To Take Your Place'. It's all expertly done, but it's a rich mixture, high in sugars, and the flavour of the blues can be detected only intermittently. *Get On Down* is a country album, not a surprising move from a man who used to listen to the Grand Ole Opry on the radio, and by no means unsuccessful, but unlike Ray Charles, who had gone down that highway a decade earlier, Bland didn't equip himself with classic country songs, just typical ones. *Greatest Hits Volume Two* is a useful digest of this period, with 11 tracks from the four albums mentioned, a 'Let The Good Times Roll' from one of his collaborations with B. B. King, and four cuts from early-'80s albums, produced by Al Bell and arranged by Monk Higgins, that aren't on CD.

(***) Not Ashamed To Sing The Blues
Music Club MCCD 368 Bland; various accompaniments. 85–95.

Since 1985 Bland has recorded ten albums for Malaco, typically nine- or ten-track sets of soul and pop songs, and an occasional shot of the blues, with orchestral accompaniments, both the material and the music supplied by Malaco regulars like writers George Jackson, Larry Addison and Johnson–Mosley, arranger Harrison Calloway, and producers Tommy Couch and Wolf Stephenson. Bland's themes, as ever, carry him from heartbreak to exultation and it's an emotionally bumpy ride, though efficiently cushioned by the strings and background singers. If you're uncertain how far you want to follow Bobby Bland round this Southern-soul nightclub circuit, look for Music Club's handy selection from seven of the albums. TR

Blind Blake (c. 1890s–c. 1933)
VOCAL, GUITAR, PIANO, HARMONICA

Other than Blind Lemon Jefferson, no man was more popular than Blind Blake in the early years of blues recording, yet even less is known about him. He may have been from Florida; his name may have been Arthur Blake; the rest of his biography is even more speculative.

***(*) Blind Blake – Vol. 1 (1926–1927)
Document DOCD-5024 Blind Blake; poss. Jimmy Blythe (p); poss. Dad Nelson (k); prob. Cliff Moore (bones); Leola B. Wilson (v). c. 7/26–c. 10/27.

***(*) Blind Blake – Vol. 2 (1927–1928)
Document DOCD-5025 Blind Blake; Johnny Dodds (cl); prob. Blind Blake (h); Tiny Parham (p); Gus Cannon (bj); Jimmy Bertrand (slide-wh, woodblocks, x); unknown (wb); Elzadie Robinson, Bertha Henderson, Daniel Brown, unknown (v); poss. J. Mayo Williams (sp). c. 10/27–c. 5/28.

***(*) Blind Blake – Vol. 3 (1928–1929)
Document DOCD-5026 Blind Blake; unknown (c); Johnny Dodds (cl); Alex (?) Robinson, Charlie Spand, poss. Aletha Dickerson, unknown (p); Jimmy Bertrand (x); Elzadie Robinson (v). c. 5/28–c. 8/29.

**(*) Blind Blake – Vol. 4 (1929–1932)
Document DOCD-5027 Blind Blake; poss. Tiny Parham or Aletha Dickerson (p); Papa Charlie Jackson (bj, v, sp); Irene Scruggs, Laura Rucker (v). c. 8/29–c. 6/32.

***(*) All The Published Sides
JSP JSP 7714 5CD As for all above CDs. c. 7/26–c. 6/32.

**(**) The Essential
Classic Blues CBL 200035 2CD Blind Blake; Johnny Dodds (cl); prob. Blind Blake (h); Charlie Spand, Alex (?) Robinson, poss. Aletha Dickerson (p); Gus Cannon (bj); Jimmy Bertrand (slide-wh, woodblocks, x, sp); Elzadie Robinson, Bertha Henderson (v). c. 8/26–c. 6/32.

***(*) The Best Of Blind Blake
Wolf WBJ 017 Blind Blake; Johnny Dodds (cl); Alex (?) Robinson, poss. Tiny Parham or Aletha Dickerson (p); Jimmy Bertrand (x); poss. J. Mayo Williams (sp). c. 8/26–12/30.

**** The Best Of Blind Blake
Yazoo 2058 Blind Blake; prob. Blind Blake (h); Gus Cannon (bj); prob. Cliff Moore (bones); Jimmy Bertrand (x); poss. J. Mayo Williams (sp). c. 10/26–c. 6/32.

**** Ragtime Guitar's Foremost Fingerpicker
Yazoo 1068 Blind Blake; unknown (c); Johnny Dodds (cl); Charlie Spand, unknown (p); Jimmy Bertrand (slide-wh); unknown (x). c. 10/26–c. 10/31.

Blind Blake's most remarkable achievement as a recording artist was that in a career lasting almost six years, in which he made about 80 sides, he was never reduced, whether by slipping skill, waning inspiration or the single-mindedness of record-company executives, from a multifaceted musician to a formulaic blues player. One side of his first record, delusively titled 'West Coast Blues', was a sparkling guitar rag; one side of his last was a buck-dance tune distantly related to a Victorian music-hall song, 'Champagne Charlie Is My Name'. Between those covers lies a portfolio of African-American guitar tunes and songs unequalled for variety, vivacity and virtuosity.

Even in his instrumental show-off pieces Blake often didn't just play but chatted to the listener, or even spun a story: the back-country scenes of 'Southern Rag', described in the Geechie accent of the Georgia Sea Islands, lend it an air of the travelogue, while 'Sea Board Stomp', with its imitations of cornet, trombone and saxophone, is almost a playlet. If the point of the talking was to touch up the supposedly dull canvas of a mere guitar tune, it was unnecessary: pieces like those and 'Dry Bone Shuffle' and the exceptionally variegated 'Blind Arthur's Breakdown' are dance music of of rich texture and enormous brio. Even his hokum songs are brighter than the average, and the best of them, 'Diddie Wa Diddie', is still played.

The number of blues titles in Blake's discography is deceptive, since several of them, such as 'Buck-Town Blues' and 'Skeedle Loo Doo Blues', are rags in blues clothing. But genuine blues are numerous, and as well as being inventively played are often melodically unusual, like 'You Gonna Quit Me' and 'Walkin' Across The Country', or the evocative 'Georgia Bound' with its homesick lines 'potatoes in the ashes, possum on the stove … chicken on the roost, watermelon on the vine – I'll be glad to get back to that Georgia gal of mine'. Some, like 'Back Door Slam', are dramatized by stop-time guitar, while others are given settings that are complex or beautiful, like 'Chump Man Blues', with its fluent picking reminiscent of William Moore, or 'Police Dog Blues', a pattern decorated with harmonics and a rising bass-string figure that recalls Tommy Johnson.

Like his contemporary Eddie Lang, Blake could elide his brilliance as a soloist into less showy but no less expert playing as an accompanist. 'Hot Potatoes' with clarinettist Johnny Dodds and percussionist Jimmy Bertrand is excellent, the quartet side 'Sweet Papa Low Down' terrific, and the four-hander with pianist Charlie Spand, 'Hastings St.', deservedly famous, not least for Blake's teasing rap: 'You always tellin' me about Brady Street … wonder what is on Brady … must be something there very marvellous, mm, mm, mm …'

Document's four volumes tell their customary chronological story efficiently, but are marred by the unavailability of clean copies of some of Blake's later and rarer discs; listening is painful on a couple of tracks of *Vol. 3* and for longer stretches of *Vol. 4*. JSP's box sounds about the same but adds a number of alternative takes from Document's *"Too Late, Too Late"* series. Classic Blues' *Essential*, though an admirable selection, is spoiled by poor sound restoration. Yazoo sets the highest standard of sound but presents the buyer with an irritating dilemma. *Ragtime Guitar's Foremost Fingerpicker* contains many of the pieces singled out above; *The Best Of Blind Blake* has even more, but it duplicates ten tracks of the earlier issue, replaces 'Diddie Wa Diddie' with its inferior follow-up and omits excellent choices like 'Sweet Jivin' Mama' and 'Police Dog Blues'. It remains the album easiest to recommend, but the Wolf CD with the same title and *The Master Of Ragtime Guitar* (Indigo IGOCD 2046, deleted) are also valuable tickets to the Blind Blake Show. TR

Blind Mississippi Morris (born 1957)
VOCAL, HARMONICA, SAXOPHONE, GUITAR

Taught the harmonica by his cousin Robert Diggs, Morris Cummings spent his formative years in an institution for the blind before becoming an habitué of Beale Street. Despite an engaging personality on record, his partnership with Brad Webb has so far failed to achieve broader acceptance.

*** You Know I Like That
[Icehouse P2 53553] *Blind Mississippi Morris; Scott Thompson (t); Jim Spake (s); Greg Redding (o); Brad Webb, David Daniels (g); Dan Cochran (b); Tony Adams (d, perc, v). 95.*

This is roustabout blues-with-a-dash-a-rock, spearheaded by the leader's over-amplified harmonica and staunchly supported by the well-rehearsed Pocket Rockets. Guitarist Webb has a hand in writing most of the songs and consistently devises riff-based arrangements that avoid cliché and are tautly performed by musicians who value interaction above personal aggrandizement. Morris's hoarse vocals and ebullient harmonica playing are refreshingly confident and devoid of obvious influence. The shadow of Howlin' Wolf inhabits 'Nobody Ever Gives Me What I Want' and 'Mean St.' and Muddy's 'Still A Fool' is the only cover in a programme of originals. Of these, 'Going Back To Louisiana' and 'Junkyard Dog' are the best examples of the group's ability to vary sound textures to excite the listener's interest.

**(*) Bad To Worse
Boogie Barbecue 98 *As above, except Russell Wheeler (o) replaces Redding; add Larry Devo (vn), Pete Mendillo (d); omit Daniels. 98.*

The same spirit inhabits *Bad To Worse* (credited to The Pocket Rockets Featuring Blind Mississippi Morris) but this time cliché seems closer at hand even if it's not definitively present. Less effort has gone into sound schemes and arrangements and there's a sameness that counterbalances an improved fidelity. 'Built For Comfort' is this set's Wolf moment among a dozen originals, of which 'Hurry Sundown', 'Last Goodbye' and 'Hwy 17' are the most notable.

**(*) Back Porch Blues
Boogie Barbecue 99 *Blind Mississippi Morris; 'Robert Nighthawk' Tooms (p); Brad Webb (g, d); David Fowler (d). 99.*

The context of *Back Porch Blues* (credited to Blind Mississippi Morris & Brad Webb), a series of occasionally augmented duets, has been signposted by tracks from previous collections. Morris and Webb share an intuitive partnership enhanced here by the increased expectations the format places upon them. Fowler's drums lift the opening 'Juke', a long dissertation on Morris's juke-joint baptism and its consequences. The piano's presence on 'This Morning Before Sunrise' provokes an overt imitation of the Mayall/Clapton ambience on 'Lonely Years'. Thereafter, the mixture is as before, with both musicians performing well but rarely with any particular distinction.

**(*) Country Days
Boogie Barbecue [unnumbered] *Blind Mississippi Morris; Robert 'Nighthawk' Tooms (h, p); Russell Wheeler (o, p); Brad Webb (g, b); Daren Dortin (g); Spencer Thorne, Dan Cochran (b); Tony Adams (d). 01.*

Credited, like the foregoing CD, to Morris and Webb, this latest homemade product illustrates how rare it is to find artists doing what they want rather than pandering to what they think the audience wants. Nevertheless, this lacks the fruity abandon of their earlier albums. There's even a hint of pretentiousness to 'Falling Down Drunk Again', a repetitive minor piece more comfortable in a coffeehouse than a club, indicating the artists haven't entirely recovered from going acoustic. Band efforts like 'Hound Dog' (an original composition) and 'Greasey' (*sic*) have atmosphere applied with a trowel, whereas 'Country Days' and 'In The UK' lack a beating heart. Tooms plays harmonica chords behind Morris's lead on the instrumental 'Rocking Baby At Midnight' but is less effective at the piano on 'Just A Woman'. 'Rosie Mae' ends the album, a 14-minute soliloquy on the lady named that Morris performs solo on guitar. Pleasant but indulgent, as is the album. NS

*** Along The Blues Highway
Animated Music 302 066 491 *Blind Mississippi Morris; Russell Wheeler (o); Brad Webb (g); Dan Cochran (b); Tony Adams (d). 8/01.*

Morris's half of this CD was recorded at the Sunflower Blues Festival (for the other half see Chris Thomas King); as before, the band resolutely do their own tightly rehearsed and loosely played thing, but here the need to keep a festival audience gripped obstructs any temptation to artiness. The instrumental 'Night Roads' heads repetitively up a cul-de-sac, but even the nakedly touristic 'Beale Street Tonight' succeeds, thanks to getting the lyrics out of the way and concentrating on instrumental workouts. Wheeler's swirling B-3 is the most striking feature of the band's playing, closely followed by Webb's rock-tinged guitar. ('Dust My Broom' owes more to George Thorogood than Elmore James, and is none the worse for it.) Morris is usually one of the band – front man rather than star – but he's very much in charge when selling Muddy Waters's soul to Screamin' Jay Hawkins on the closing 'Going Back To Louisiana'. CS

Blisterstring
GROUP

A (possibly) one-off union of Frank Goldwasser (q.v.), Chris Millar and Kevin Hill.

*** The Highway Is Like A Woman
UnderSiege USCD 001 *Frank Goldwasser (h, g, v); Kevin Hill (b, tu); Chris Millar (d). 3/02.*

This is allusive music by players with a wide range of references and the skills to manipulate them. Sometimes the source material is imaginatively adapted, as in 'Chips Flying Everywhere', put together from 'Down The Dirt Road Blues' and other Charley Patton songs in a framework of slide guitar, tuba and percussion, or Percy Mayfield's 'The Highway Is Like A Woman', remapped to Chicago. The readings of Lowell Fulson's 'Black Night' and Junior Parker's 'Feelin' Good' are more by-the-book. Goldwasser's dexterity with blues guitar styles is impressive, and his singing is tougher than on his own-name album *Bluju*, recorded only a few months before. Admirers of small-group downhome blues could find this very much to their taste. TR

Rory Block (born 1949)
VOCAL, GUITAR, PIANO, SYNTHESIZER

The daughter of sandal-maker and old-time musician Allan Block, Aurora Block grew up in New York's Little Italy, took up the guitar at 14, promptly fell in love with the blues and began joining sessions in Washington Square or at her father's shop. Soon afterwards she accompanied Stefan Grossman on the album How To Play Blues Guitar, *then quit music for most of a decade while raising a family. After a brief flirtation with disco, she embarked on a recording and performing career in which she has constantly balanced traditional blues and her own compositions in a wide range of styles.*

**(*) The Early Tapes 1975/1976
Munich MRMCD 1 *Block; Alan Seidler (p); Ken Kosek (vn); Artie Traum (g); Roly Salley (b); Eric Valdina (d); Pat Murray (cga). 75–76.*

'Canned Heat', the opening track, declares an affection for the music of Tommy Johnson which will be displayed repeatedly on later albums. What follows – Bessie Smith's 'Nobody Knows You When You're Down And Out', Jimmie Rodgers's waltz song 'Why Should I Be Lonely', William Brown's 'Mississippi Blues', a guitar rag and a handful of originals – forecasts fairly accurately the make-up of many of her subsequent recordings. An unusual item among her own songs is 'Three Is A Crowd', a blues that Ken Kosek's fiddling imbues with the character of the Mississippi Sheiks. Whatever the piece, Block sings it without affectation, relying on a voice of considerable range and grace. This was quite an impressive debut (it first appeared, in a slightly different form, as a Blue Goose LP), but Block would soon improve on it.

*** High Heeled Blues
Rounder CD 3061 *Block; John Sebastian (h, g); Warren Bernhardt (p, harm); Robb Goldstein (hdu). 81.*

(***) Blue Horizon
Rounder CD 3073 *Block; John Sebastian (h); Larry Hoppen (p); John Kirk (vn); Larry Campbell (psg); Edgar Raspovic (g); Brian Allsop (b); Brian Brake (d). 82.*

*** Rhinestones And Steel Strings
Rounder CD 3085 *Block; Warren Bernhardt (p); Stephen Foote (syn); Gordon Titcomb (psg); Rob Wasserman (b); Robb Goldstein (hdu); The Persuasions (v). 83.*

(***) I've Got A Rock In My Sock
Rounder CD 3097 *Block; Taj Mahal, Stevie Wonder (h); Warren Bernhardt (p, syn); Vinnie Martucci, Arthur Stead, Stephen Foote (syn); David Bromberg (vn, g); Bud Rizzo (g); Scott Petito, Huey McDonald (b); Howard Johnson (tu); Gary Burke (d, perc); Donnell Spencer (d); Melody McCully, Pamela Vincent, Joyce Wilson (v). 86.*

*** Best Blues & Originals
Rounder CD 11525//Munich MRCD 137 *As for above CDs. 81–86.*

*** Best Blues & Originals – Volume 2
Munich NETCD 0043 *As for above CDs, except add Lee Berg (v). 77–86?*

*** Women In (E)motion
Tradition & Moderne T&M 107 *Block. 3–9/88.*

More explicitly than its predecessor, *High Heeled Blues* signalled one of the two directions that most of Block's albums would take over the next 20 years, with its mixture of challenging guitar blues learned from Robert Johnson ('Walkin' Blues', 'Crossroad Blues') and Skip James ('Devil Got My Man'), the gospel song 'Uncloudy Day', Bessie Smith's 'Down In The Dumps', the traditional folksong 'The Water Is Wide', a guitar rag and attractive original compositions like 'Since You Been Gone'. *Rhinestones & Steel Strings* takes a similar path with Willie Brown's 'Future Blues' and Robert Wilkins's 'That's No Way To Get Along', 'Sit Down On The Banks' from Rev. Gary Davis and 'The Golden Vanity' from the folk tradition. By contrast, *Blue Horizon*, though it checks the gospel and ragtime boxes and adds a couple of non-blues songs associated with Charley Patton, is mostly original, as is *I've Got A Rock In My Sock*, where the accompaniments are more varied and sometimes elaborate. With the next album, 1987's *House Of Hearts* (Rounder CD 3104//Munich MRCD 139), and its successor *Turning Point* (Special Delivery// Munich, deleted) Block achieved her goal of wholly original work, the material and its settings rooted to varying depths in the extensive garden of American and British folkmusic but nurtured by clever hands to distinctive flowerings.

Listeners whose capacity for appreciating well-made music is not confined to the blues will find much to enjoy in most if not all of these albums, since Block is not only an inventive writer but an affecting as well as a versatile singer. Those with stricter blues tastes will find more satisfaction in the CDs with unparenthesized ratings, especially in her scrupulously articulate guitar playing. Listeners unsure which party they belong to might begin with either *Best Blues & Originals* or *Best Blues & Originals – Volume 2*, each a selection from the four albums and so a handy linking road between Block's two directions. *Volume 2* adds 'Long Journey', an earlier recording from a Rounder VAC. Block's contribution to the *Women In (E)motion* series, taped at two concerts in Bremen, includes a lot of songs she had already recorded ('Future Blues', 'That's No Way For Me To Get Along', 'Walking Blues', 'Canned Heat', 'Mississippi Blues', etc.) but she delivers them ebulliently (perhaps, at times, a shade too ebulliently) and those who value the immediacy of a concert recording may prefer to hear them this way.

*** Mama's Blues
Rounder CD 3117//Munich NETCD 0022 *Block; Peter 'Madcat' Ruth (h); Richard Bell (p, syn); Warren Bernhardt, Vinnie Martucci (p); Jorma Kaukonen, Michael Mugrage, Paul Gabriel (g); Scott Petito, Rob Leon (b); Jerry Marotta (d); Sarah Brooks, The Payne AME Choir (v).* 91.

*** Ain't I A Woman
Rounder CD 3120//Munich NETCD 0038 *Block; John Sebastian (h); Alan Clark (o); Vinnie Martucci (p, syn); Warren Bernhardt (p); Brian Keane, Mark Knopfler, Brendan Croker, Shari Kane, John Hall (g); Scott Petito, Rob Leon, Anthony Jackson (b); Neil Wilkinson, Jerry Marotta (d); Jordan Block Valdina, The Payne AME Choir (v).* 92.

***(*) When A Woman Gets The Blues
Rounder CD 3139 *Block; Little Annie Raines (h); Warren Bernhardt (p); Jordan Block Valdina (v).* 95.

**** Gone Woman Blues: The Country Blues Collection
Rounder CD 11575 *As above, except add Brendan Croker (g).* 81–96.

On these CDs the ratio of Block's songs to other people's, which had previously seesawed, steadied around the 50/50 mark. *Mama's Blues* has fine readings of Tommy Johnson's 'Bye Bye Blues' and 'Big Road Blues' and songs by Robert Johnson, Bessie Smith and Buddy Boy Hawkins. On *Ain't I A Woman* Block completes the set of Tommy Johnson's key numbers, adding 'Maggie Campbell' and 'Cool Drink Of Water'; she also plays Robert Johnson's 'Come On In My Kitchen' and with Brendan Croker re-creates the lilting two-guitar theme of Lottie Kimbrough's 'Rolling Log'. Her singing, at least on the blues, is deeper and less crystalline than on earlier recordings.

Angel Of Mercy (Rounder CD 3126//Munich NETCD 47) (1994) was an all-original set with no blues content, and 1996's *Tornado* (Rounder CD 3140) virtually so, but the intervening year's *When A Woman Gets The Blues* provided what many of Block's fans must have been hoping for, an all-blues set. Well, almost: one track is hers, and another is the old-timey song 'Sweet Sunny South', but the other dozen are drawn from Son House, Charley Patton, Skip James, Blind Willie McTell – and, because it is important to her to acknowledge female forerunners, Mattie Delaney, Louise Johnson and Hattie Hart, whose 'I Let My Daddy Do That' she puts across with gusto.

Curiously, almost the entire contents of *When A Woman Gets The Blues* (everything except 'Sweet Sunny South') were rewrapped a couple of years later in *Gone Woman Blues*, together with virtually all the blues on *Mama's Blues* and *Ain't I A Woman* and a couple from elsewhere. Obviously this 24-track anthology is where blues enthusiasts unfamiliar with her work should begin their investigation.

*** Confessions Of A Blues Singer
Rounder CD 3154 *Block; Jordan Block Valdina (p, v); Bonnie Raitt, Mike Demicco (g); Scott Petito (b); Jerry Marotta (d).* 98.

To the list of her known favourites (Robert Johnson, Robert Wilkins, Patton, McTell) Block adds Booker White and Furry Lewis. The latter's 'Kassie Jones' is played not with slide but as a fingerpicking duet; Block plays both parts, as she does on several other numbers, very effectively on 'Titanic (When That Great Ship Went Down)', but the slide part on 'Ramblin' On My Mind' is taken by Bonnie Raitt. Block completes the album with two long originals, one, 'Life Song', a candid résumé of her musical and personal career. Vocally she continues to grow into her songs, exchanging the limpid clarity of her youth for a more weathered and subtler voice.

(**) I'm Every Woman
Rounder CD 3174 *Block; Annie Raines (h); Clifford Carter (kb, syn); Richard Bell (kb); Kelly Joe Phelps (g, v); Paul Rishell (g, prob. v); Jeff Mironov (g); Mark Egan, Neal Jason (b); Shawn Pelton (d); Gaye Adegbalola, Jordan Block Valdina, Keb' Mo', Rev. Herb Sheldon (v).* 02.

In her most ambitious album yet, Block takes on classic soul material like 'I Feel Like Breaking Up Somebody's Home' and pieces by Curtis Mayfield and Al Green, interspersing them with traditional songs like 'Rock Island Line', 'Ain't No Grave Can Hold My Body Down' and 'Pretty Polly', a duet with Kelly Joe Phelps. Some listeners may find the stark contrasts between tracks unsettling, and even a devotee may decide that, accomplished singer though she is, Block does not succeed in making all these disparate songs her own.

**(*) Last Fair Deal
Telarc CD-83593 *Block; Rob Davis (v).* 03.
**(*) From The Dust
Telarc CD-83614 *Block.* 05.

For admirers of Block's blues side, *Last Fair Deal* offers Robert Johnson's 'Last Fair Deal Gone Down' and 'Traveling Riverside Blues' and Son House's 'County Farm Blues', and *From The Dust* Johnson's 'Stones In My Passway', House's 'Dry Spell Blues' and Patton's 'High Water Everywhere'. The remaining pieces are original compositions and a couple of traditional gospel songs. *From The Dust* is dedicated, and the notes devoted, to Block's dogs, a subject that may not have the same vital interest for her listeners as it does for her. Both recordings have room, rather than studio, ambience and may

Michael Bloomfield (1943–81)

VOCAL, GUITAR, ORGAN, PIANO, SYNTHESIZER, BANJO, BASS, DRUMS

Michael Bloomfield grew up in a middle-class Jewish family in Chicago, and was turned on to blues by night-time radio. At 13 he procured his first guitar from his grandfather's pawnshop and after a few years' heavy practice was playing wherever he could, stopping only to absorb live music by Muddy Waters, Elmore James and other local players. As booker for the Fickle Pickle and Big John's he introduced Chicago's student audience to older blues artists like Big Joe Williams. In 1965 he joined Paul Butterfield to record the first Butterfield Blues Band album. They also played that year at the Newport Folk Festival, and accompanied Bob Dylan in his notorious first public performance with an electric band. Bloomfield subsequently played on Dylan's Highway 61 Revisited and extended the range of the Butterfield band with his work on East–West. Soon afterwards he left the group to found The Electric Flag, but when that fell apart so did Bloomfield, a victim of heroin. In the '70s he worked sporadically and recorded several eclectic alums for Takoma. He died of a possibly accidental drug overdose.

*** Don't Say That I Ain't Your Man!: Essential Blues: 1964–1969

Columbia/Legacy CK 57631//(E) 476721 *Bloomfield; Marcus Doubleday, John Wilmeth (t); Noel Jewkis (ss, ts); Gerald Oshita (ts, bs); Herbie Rich (ts, kb); Peter Strazza, Ron Stallings (ts); Snooky Flowers, Mark Teel (bs); Paul Butterfield (h, v); Charlie Musselwhite (h); Richard Santi (ac); Barry Goldberg, Mike Fonfara (kb); Mark Naftalin, Al Kooper, Ira Kamin (o, p); Ron Ruby (o); Brian Friedman (p); Orville Rhodes (sg); Sivuca (g, perc); Mike Johnson, Elvin Bishop, Fred Olsen, Michael Melford (g); Sid Warner, Jerome Arnold, Harvey Brooks, John Kahn (b); Norman Mayell, Billy Davenport, Buddy Miles, Eddie Hoh, Skip Prokop, Bob Jones (d); Dino Andino (cga); Nick Gravenites (perc, v); The Ace Of Cups, Diane Tribuno (v).* 12/64–5/69.

For a long time after his death Bloomfield seemed to have been forgotten by most of the blues world. There was a monument to his early prowess in his two albums with the Butterfield band and *Highway 61 Revisited*, but his own LPs went out of print and were not transferred to CD, and his contribution to electric blues guitar was acknowledged chiefly by other musicians. Recovering his legacy began with *Essential Blues*, snapshots of his playing with Butterfield, The Electric Flag (a stomping 'Killing Floor') and Al Kooper, prefaced by five surprisingly assured songs from audition sessions and rounded off with a couple of big-band tracks live from the Fillmore West. Despite a decent 11-minute reading of Albert King's 'Don't Throw Your Love On Me So Strong', long jams on familiar blues progressions aren't generally the best way to hear Bloomfield, unless you're a lover of extended guitar solos *per se*; if you are, try the reissued Bloomfield–Kooper *Super Session* (Columbia/Legacy 508071) and *The Lost Concert Tapes* (Columbia/Legacy 506034//510728). For listeners who have heard enough of that sort of thing, the passages that retain the power to impress are likely to be pithier; his two-minute solo in Butterfield's 'Work Song', wild as a snake-charmer's pipe, twisty as the snake, is still hair-raising.

*** If You Love These Blues, Play 'Em As You Please
Kicking Mule KMCD 9801 *Bloomfield; Ron Stallings (ts); Hart McNee (bs); Ira Kamin (o, p); Eric Kriss (p); Nick Gravenites (g, v); Woody Harris (g); Roger Troy, Doug Kilmer (b); Dave Neditch, Tom Donlinger (d).* 76–7/79.

**(*) Blues, Gospel And Ragtime Guitar Instrumentals
Shanachie 99007 *Bloomfield; unknown (o); unknown (p); Woody Harris (g); unknown (b); unknown (d).* late 70s.

* RX For The Blues
Music Trax 9131 *Bloomfield; unknown musicians.* late 70s?

*** Knockin' Myself Out
Fuel 2000 302 061 256 *Bloomfield; The Scabs (t, tb, cl, s); Kraig Kilby (tb); The Originals [Hart McNee, unknowns] (ts, bs); Mark Adams (h); Ira Kamin, Barry Goldberg (o, p); Mark Naftalin (p); David Shorey, Roger Troy (b, v); Douglas Kilmer, Henry Oden (b); Bob Jones (d, v); Tom Rizzo (d); Anna Rizzo, Marcia Ann Taylor (v).* 77–80.

*** The Best Of Michael Bloomfield
Takoma CDTAK 8905 *Similar to above.* 77–80.

In the last few years of his life Bloomfield recorded quite prolifically and very diversely for Norman Dayron, a friend since their time at the University of Chicago. Dayron produced four LPs for Takoma but evidently had a good deal left over, which has been dispersed on several albums, though sorting it out is a headache: some of them are scrupulously documented, but Shanachie's all-instrumental set has no recording information whatever. *Knockin' Myself Out* And *The Best Of* are primarily drawn from the Takoma LPs and have four items in common ('Mr. Johnson And Mr. Dunn', 'Your Friends', 'Orphan's Blues' and 'The Gospel Truth'). Three of the hymn tunes on Shanachie also appear on *If You Love These Blues, Play 'Em As You Please*, which is actually a twofer combining that 1976 album with the later Kicking Mule LP *Bloomfield/Harris*, a guitar duet set with Woody Harris.

If You Love These Blues, originally made as a tutorial disc for readers of *Guitar Player*, finds Bloomfield sauntering through blues history, playing original tunes and songs in the styles of Jimmie Rodgers, B. B. King, T-Bone Walker, Blind Blake and other guitarists, introducing them with a few words about his models and the key he's playing in. If you only know him from his electric work, you may be surprised at the versatility he brings to this amiable exercise. *Bloomfield/Harris* is an all-instrumental set of hymns and gospel songs. *Knockin' Myself Out*, by contrast, has upbeat numbers like Lil Green's title song, where he sounds like Leon Redbone, and 'Sloppy Drunk', often with cheerful intrusions by brass and reeds. On 'Mr. Johnson And Mr. Dunn', an *hommage* to Lonnie Johnson and Eddie Lang, Bloomfield plays both guitar parts, but that's small beer compared with some of his multitracking; on 'Peepin' An A-Moanin' Blues' he plays guitar, piano, banjo, bass and drums. *Knockin' Myself Out* and *The Best Of* sound as if they were made by a man who, though not without troubles, had found some place of contentment from which he could send happy, playful despatches in his music.

RX For The Blues is a shoddily packaged collection of poor-quality recordings, some live, several with prominent piano accompaniments which are probably his own. It seems unlikely to have been sanctioned by Bloomfield's estate, and should be avoided by his admirers. TR

Blue Junction
GROUP

From Århus in Denmark, these four musicians were variously in The Trouble Cats, the Frimer Band and Shades Of Blue before forming the Århus All Stars in 1994; they renamed themselves Blue Junction while recording their album.

*** 22:17
Intermusic INTCD 066 *Ole Frimer (g, v); Uffe Steen (g); Morten Brauner (b); Esben Bach (d).* 5/98.

It can only be their location that prevents Frimer and Steen from being widely recognized as first-rate blues guitarists. Frimer acknowledges models like Albert Collins and Johnny Winter, but his big, dirty tone on 'Get Out Of My Life Woman' is as much from Albert King; Steen, reportedly more of a Chicago-style player, nevertheless uncoils a fleet Gatemouth Brownish line on 'Junction Shuffle'. While the guitarists hold their busy – but never merely wordy – conversations, Brauner and Bach lay down invigorating, unclichéd rhythm patterns. Frimer's singing is serviceable at best, but it hardly matters: it's what the guitars are saying that one wants to listen to.

Steen has also made a trio album, *Play*, with Lennart Ginman (bass) and Adam Nussbaum (drums) (Stunt STUCD 01072). There is some blues content, including a version of 'Spoonful', but by and large this is a jazz record, somewhat in the style of John Scofield, and rather impressive. TR

The Blues Band
GROUP

All the members of this band have long pedigrees in British blues and rock. Paul Jones (born 1942) and Tom McGuinness (born 1941) were members of Manfred Mann, which had several pop hits in the '60s; McGuinness later formed McGuinness Flint with Hughie Flint, who had previously played with John Mayall. Early in 1979 Jones, McGuinness and Flint, needing two more musicians to fulfil a couple of London bookings, contacted Dave Kelly (born 1948), who brought Gary Fletcher to their first rehearsal. A band was born which, with only one change (Rob Townsend [born 1947] replaced Hughie Flint in the drum chair in 1982) and one hiatus, when they retired from the road in 1982–85, has lasted more than 25 years, though all its members continue to work in other contexts; Jones, for instance, is an experienced actor, while Kelly has written music for TV. The band is firmly plugged into the concert-hall and festival circuits in Britain and on the Continent.

**(*) The Bootleg Album/Ready
BGO BGOCD 497 2CD *Paul Jones (h, v); Rockin' Dopsie (ac); Bob Hall, Ian Stewart, Geraint Watkins (p); Tom McGuinness (md, g, v); Dave Kelly (g, v); Gary Fletcher (b); Hughie Flint (d); Chester Zeno (wb); The Paulettes (v).* 79–7/80.

**(*) Itchy Feet/Brand Loyalty
BGO BGOCD 498 2CD *Paul Jones (h, v); Bob Hall (p); Tom McGuinness, Dave Kelly (g, v); Gary Fletcher (b, v); Hughie Flint (d, perc); Rob Townsend (d).* 81–82.

**(*) Live
BGO BGOCD 496 *Paul Jones (h, v); Tom McGuinness, Dave Kelly (g, v); Gary Fletcher (b, v); Rob Townsend (d).* late 82.

**(*) Back For More
BGO BGOCD 506 *Wayne Jackson (t, tb); Simon Gardner (t); Peter Thoms (tb); Gary Barnacle (ts, bs); Andrew Love, Plas Johnson, Martin Dobson (ts); Paul Jones (h, perc, v); Peter Filleul (kb, o, syn); Katie Webster (kb); Micky Sanchez, Bob Hall, Big Joe Duskin (p); Dave Kelly (g, perc, v); Tom McGuinness (g, v); Gary Fletcher (b); Rob Townsend (d); Liz Kitchen (vb, perc); The Kokomo Singers (Frank Collins, Dyan Birch, Paddy McHugh) (v).* 89.

**(*) Fat City
BGO BGOCD 507 *Nat Adderley (c); Wayne Jackson (t, tb); Dick Hanson (t); Chris Gower (tb); Andrew Love, Ray Beavis (ts); Damian O'Malley, John 'Irish' Earle (bs); Paul Jones (h, v); Geraint Watkins (ac, p); Peter Filleul, Benny Gallagher (kb); Bob Hall (p); Dave Kelly, Tom McGuinness (g, v); Gary Fletcher (b); Rob Townsend (d, perc); Liz Kitchen (vb, perc); The Kokomo Singers (Frank Collins, Dyan Birch, Paddie McHugh) (v).* 9/90–6/91.

*** Homage
BGO BGOCD 583 *Mike Paice (s); Paul Jones (h, v); Lou Stonebridge (ac, o); Jools Holland, Peter Filleul (o, p); Jona Lewie, Bob Hall (p); Dave Kelly, Tom McGuinness (g, v); Gary Fletcher (b, v); Rob Townsend (d, perc); Liz Kitchen (perc); Fiona Hendley, The Kokomo Singers (Frank Collins, Dyan Birch, Paddy McHugh), Lan Myakicheff (v).* 8/92–7/93.

**(*) Wire Less
BGO BGOCD 494 *Paul Jones (h, v); Tom McGuinness (md, g, v); Dave Kelly (g, v); Gary Fletcher (b, v); Rob Townsend (d, wb, perc).* 8/94.

**(*) Live In Poland
BGO BGOCD 535 *Paul Jones (h, v); Dave Kelly, Tom McGuinness (g, v); Gary Fletcher (b, v); Rob Townsend (d).* 9/96.

**(*) Brassed Up
Cobalt CD 991 *Guy Barker, Tony Fisher, Martin Shaw, Derek Watkins, Raul D'Oliveira (t); Gordon Campbell, Richard Edwards, J. B. Higginbotham, Andy Wood, Mike Innes (tb); Nigel Hitchcock, Ray Warleigh, Peter King (as); Dave Bishop, Alan Skidmore, Pee Wee Ellis (ts); Jay Craig (bs); Paul Jones (h, v); Georgie Fame (o); Geraint Watkins (p); Gary Fletcher (g, b, v); Tom McGuinness, Dave Kelly (g, v); Rob Townsend (d, perc); Sam Kelly (perc).* 1/99.

*** Scratchin' On My Screen
Hypertension 1205 HYP *Paul Jones (h, v); Bob Hall (p); Tom McGuinness (md, g, v); Gary Fletcher (g, b, v); Dave Kelly (g, v); Martin Wild (d); Rob Townsend (perc).* 2–5/00.

**(*) Stepping Out
Hypertension 2213 HYP *Chris Barber (tb); Paul Jones (h, v); Ian 'Mac' McLagan (o); Tom McGuinness (md, g, v); Gary Fletcher (g, b, v); Dave Kelly (g, v); Rob Townsend (d, perc).* 2/01.

One of the reasons for The Blues Band's long career in the European blues milieu is their wide range of skills. Jones, Kelly and McGuinness are personable singers, each with a distinct character, and instrumentally Jones's harmonica and Kelly's snarling slide guitar are tools any band would be glad to be equipped with. It's a versatility most blues bands cannot emulate. Admittedly, some of them wouldn't wish to: they aim to work in particular styles, like Chicago or jump blues. The Blues Band have no such agenda. The best description for them, perhaps, is 'blues showband'. Hence another reason for their success: as a generic blues act they fit the requirements of the concert-hall and arts-centre audience more closely than a stylistically specific band would. If your enthusiasm for the blues is satisfied by going to a couple of shows a year and one of them is by The Blues Band, naturally you want an entertaining mixture of old and new blues, a few R&B classics, a touch of soul, slide guitar showpieces, harmonica features and so forth. In that arena The Blues Band have few rivals.

For a band working to such a blueprint, making records isn't necessarily a priority. If they do make them, it may be chiefly to sell them at gigs, which doesn't always encourage experiment. Quite a few of The Blues Band's albums are, indeed, documents of typical repertoire played as they typically play it, without cameos by other artists. (Pianist Bob Hall, who does often show up, is a friend from way back and practically an honorary sixth member.) Thus *The Bootleg Album/Ready*, *Itchy Feet/Brand Loyalty*, *Live* and *Live In Poland*. *Back For More*, *Fat City* and *Stepping Out*, on the other hand, are somewhat more elaborate productions framing programmes of entirely (*Fat City*) or almost entirely (*Back For More*, *Stepping Out*) original compositions, and they too may have most appeal to the band's core constituency. A curious diversion is *Brassed Out*, where the band is joined by various aggregations of British jazz and session musicians. The big-band chart written for 'Baby Please Don't Go' by saxophonist Peter King is very ingenious, and the core quintet also produce a clever arrangement of Duke Ellington's 'Creole Love Call', but the high percentage of original non-blues compositions and soul standbys like 'People Get Ready' won't be to everyone's taste.

Between those segments of their ouput, however, are three albums that could appeal to the listener who has no history of attending the band's shows, so long as he or she enjoys a wide range of blues and has no objection to hearing them sung in undisguised English accents. The unplugged sets *Wire Less* and *Scratchin' On My Screen* elicit oldfashioned blues like Memphis Minnie's 'Frankie Jean' (*Wire Less*), Muddy Waters's 'Can't Be Satisfied' and Robert Wilkins's 'New Stockyard Blues' (*Screen*), repertoire that encourages the team to sound like a jugband or skiffle group. Both are live recordings, the latter with much less room ambience and beefier sound. *Homage* is the band's only album of wholly received material, from Muddy Waters, Little Walter, Bo Diddley, Robert Johnson and the like. A point that should stressed, not just about *Homage* but about the band's use of standard blues material on all their albums, is that, although they obviously know the canonical recordings (this is a band that is seriously informed about the blues), they seldom copy them. Here, for example, 'That Same Thing', 'I Can Tell' and 'Wang Dang Doodle' are adroitly cut loose from the original readings by Muddy Waters, Bo Diddley and Howlin' Wolf (or Koko Taylor). Of all The Blues Band's likeable recordings, this may have the strongest appeal to readers of this book.

(*) Be My Guest
BGO BGOCD 600 *As for all above CDs.* 79–2/01.
*** The Blues Band Box
BGO BGOBBCD 1 4CD *As above.* 79–2/01.

The Blues Band and its devotees celebrated the group's 25th anniversary with a pair of complementary releases. *Be My Guest* is drawn from most of the band's back catalogue but takes only a couple from *Homage* and bypasses the acoustic sets *Wire Less* and *Scratchin' On My Screen* entirely, which, as the reader will gather, would not have been our approach to the job. The boxed set, carefully compiled to minimize duplication with *Be My Guest* (there's just one track on both, the *Back For More* cut of 'Bad Boy' with Plas Johnson and Big Joe Duskin), accords much better with our estimation of where the band's strengths lie. As well as large chunks of early work, from *The Bootleg Album* to *Brand Loyalty*, and adequate samples of several other albums, the box embraces about half of *Wire Less*, five tracks from *Scratchin' On My Screen* and four from *Homage*. There are also five previously unreissued tracks (three from the *Back For More* sessions) and an illustrated booklet with a careful history of the band, its members and its recordings by Roy Bainton. TR

The Blues Busters
GROUP

The core Blues Busters – Earl Banks (born 1936), Leroy Martin (born 1939), George Walker (1937–77), Thomas Cornes (born 1948) and James Price (born 1949) – were together as a group for little more than half a year; by the time their album was issued, the members had disappeared down other alleys of the Memphis music scene. Several of them still turn up in blues contexts from time to time.

**(*) Busted!
High Water HMG 6512 Thomas 'Blue' Cornes (o, p, syn); William 'Boogie Man' Hubbard (o, p); Earl 'The Pearl' Banks, Lee Roy Martin (g, v); James Price, 'Funky' John Cole (b); 'Chicken' George Walker (d, v). 7/83–1/84.

The thick sound of two guitars, alternating lead and rhythm, and a busy organ places the Blues Busters in a similar stylistic compartment to two other Memphis bands that also recorded for High Water, The Fieldstones and the Hollywood All Stars. There are, in fact, several personnel connections among the three groups. The Blues Busters frame their mostly slow or medium-paced blues in arrangements that are not particularly subtle but sometimes neat: the recurrent four-bar figure in 'Let Your Loss Be Your Lesson', for instance, freshens what might otherwise have been a routine performance. The ambience is that of '60s or early-'70s B. B., or sometimes Albert, King without a commanding vocal or instrumental presence, but the band's unflamboyant discipline may be an acceptable substitute for virtuosity. TR

Bo Diddley (born 1928)
VOCAL, GUITAR, VIOLIN

Otha Ellas Bates was never going to make it on a theatre hoarding but Bo Diddley ... there's a name to build a myth upon. And that's what he duly did, right from his self-proclaiming debut single. Thereafter, Bo was a 'Diddley Daddy', he met 'The Monster', he was 'A Gunslinger', 'A Lover' and 'A Lumberjack' as he spun variations on his 'shave-and-a-haircut-six-bits' beat. He may have appropriated that but the rest was original, along with strange-shaped guitars and eldritch amplification. Blues was an essential but not integral part of his musical mix and he strayed further from it as time went by. Inspiration ran dry after the first decade and recycling began but still the fascination remains.

***(*) His Best
MCA/Chess CHD-9373 Bo Diddley; Billy Boy Arnold, Little Walter Jacobs, Lester Davenport, Little Willie Smith (h); Otis

Spann, Lafayette Leake (p); Jody Williams, Billy Johnson (g); James Bradford, Willie Dixon, Jesse James Johnson, Chester Lindsey (b); Clifton James, Frank Kirkland, Billy Downing (d); Jerome Green (maracas); Cookie Vee (perc, v); The Moonglows, Bo-Ettes (v). 3/55–9/66.

*** The Essential Bo Diddley
Spectrum 544 348 *As above.* 3/55–9/66.
** The Millennium Collection
MCA 088 112 163 *As above.* 3/55–9/66.

The *Best* and *Essential* compilations, each of 20 tracks, are almost identical, the first preferring 'Crackin' Up' and 'Oooh Baby' for which the second substitutes 'Cadillac' and 'Cops And Robbers'. *The Millennium Collection*, with a mere dozen tracks (all found on the other sets), is a sales department's shoddy piece of calendrical exploitation. The trademark beat is present only on 'Bo Diddley' and 'Pretty Thing' and in a slower variation on 'Diddley Daddy' and 'Mona (I Need You Baby)'. Otherwise, tempos are satisfyingly varied, from the staccato stop-time bravura of 'I'm A Man' to the glorious onrush of 'Hey Bo Diddley' and 'Who Do You Love'. On the latter and 'I'm Looking For A Woman', Jody Williams's industrial guitar tone adds an extra, and welcome, energy. The open tuning of Bo's own guitar militates against the 12-bar conventions of 'Before You Accuse Me', a rarity in a repertoire for which chord-changes are superfluous. He's greatly helped by an array of first-rate musicians, both Leake and Spann at the piano stool and James and Kirkland at the drumkit, whether beating out jungle rock on their tom-toms or providing a piledriving snare and bass drum for the faster numbers.

Any Bo Diddley performance from this era has two striking assets: the first is the unique amplification he contrived for his increasingly bizarre guitars, the other is a strong and nuanced voice capable of many shades of expression, from the boastful swagger of 'Road Runner' to the loquacious jive of 'Cops And Robbers' and the off-centre doo-wop of 'Crackin' Up'. The only thing missing is an exhibition of his unique (in both style and sound) guitar technique. 'Mumblin' Guitar' would have fitted the bill admirably.

***(*) Bo's Blues
Ace CDCH 396 *As above, except omit Cookie Vee.* 3/55–9/65.

A broader, less commercially oriented and more personal choice of material, but even so it features eight titles common to the *Best* and *Essential* sets. Compiler Ray Topping had no other choice than to include 'Before You Accuse Me', 'You Don't Love Me (You Don't Care)', 'I'm A Man' and 'I'm Looking For A Woman'. Less immediately pertinent when set beside 'Blues, Blues', '500% More Man' and 'I'm Bad' are the disappointing 'Down Home Special', the curiously bland 'Heart-O-Matic Love', the manic 'Run Diddley Daddy' and the trivial 'Two Flies'. On the other hand, the alley-fiddle instrumental 'The Clock Strikes Twelve', 'Bo's Blues' (with a curious sound, neither harmonica nor violin, weaving through his vocal) and the overlooked 'Live My Life' illustrate how Bo's blues credentials persist alongside lighter fare. Nevertheless, it can't be said that this set proves its point, for Bo Diddley's music refuses to be definitively placed in any one music genre. One can only underline the amount of pleasure (guilty or otherwise) to be gained from immersing oneself in this particular hitchhiker's galaxy. NS

Richard Boals
VOCAL, GUITAR

Based in Ohio, Boals began playing professionally in the early '70s. He has released several CDs on his own label, Growlin' Bare. He currently lives in Albuquerque, New Mexico.

*(*) That's The Truth
JSP JSPCD 2140 *Boals; Jonny Viau (ts, didgeridoo); Troy Jennings (bs); Tom Mahon (p); John Marx (g); Rick Reed (b); Paul Fasulo (d); Jimmy Morello (prod).* 2/00.

The hand of Jimmy Morello lies heavily on this album: he produced it, provided the band and wrote most of the material. But while the musicians, particularly the horns and the pianist, keep things moving briskly, the songs are formulaic blues and Boals sounds like a thousand other journeyman rock singers. TR

Lucille Bogan (1897–1948)
VOCAL

Born in Mississippi, Bogan moved in her youth to Birmingham, Alabama. She made her debut recording during OKeh's session in Atlanta in June 1923, the first time blues was recorded on location in the South, and continued to record quite regularly, for several labels, over the next dozen years. It's uncertain whether she remained in the business after the mid-'30s.

**(*) Lucille Bogan (Bessie Jackson) – Vol. 1 (1923–1930)
Document BDCD-6036 *Bogan; Eddie Heywood, Henry Callens, Alex Channey, Will Ezell, prob. Cow Cow Davenport, Charles Avery (p); Papa Charlie Jackson (bj, sp); Tampa Red (g).* 6/23–3/30.
*** Lucille Bogan (Bessie Jackson) – Vol. 2 (1930–1933)
Document BDCD-6037 *Bogan; Walter Roland (p, sp); Charles Avery, unknown (p).* 3/30–7/33.
*** Lucille Bogan (Bessie Jackson) – Vol. 3 (1934–1935)
Document BDCD-6038 *Bogan; Walter Roland (p, g, sp); prob. Bob Campbell, prob. Josh White (g).* 7/34–3/35.
*** Reckless Woman 1927–1935
EPM Blues Collection 15985 *Bogan; Walter Roland (p, g); Will Ezell, Cow Cow Davenport, Charles Avery (p); Charlie Jackson (bj); Tampa Red, Bob Campbell, Josh White (g).* 27–35.
*** Lucille Bogan & Walter Roland
Yazoo 1017 *Bogan; Alex Channey, Charles Avery, Walter Roland (p); Papa Charlie Jackson (bj, sp); prob. Josh White (g).* c. 3/27–3/35.
**(*) Lucille Bogan & Walter Roland: The Essential
Classic Blues CBL 200032 2CD *Bogan; Walter Roland (p, g); Cow Cow Davenport, Charles Avery (p); Tampa Red, Bob Campbell (g).* 10/28–3/35.
*** Shave 'Em Dry: The Best Of Lucille Bogan
Columbia/Legacy CK 65705 *Bogan; Walter Roland (p, sp); Bob Campbell, Josh White (g).* 7/33–3/35.

The stiff, stagey performer of 'Pawn Shop Blues', Bogan's first recording, is unrecognizable as the feisty singer she would become. Her other 1923 sides are slightly more revealing, but the combination of unadventurous material, dull accompaniment and hard-worn discs is likely to deter any but the dedicated investigator. In 1927 recordings such as 'Sweet Patunia' and 'Jim Tampa Blues', however, the latter enthusiastically accompanied on banjo by Papa Charlie Jackson, Bogan is able to give a much better display of her powerful voice and boisterous manner. Over the next few years she constructed a persona of a tough-talking narrator – 'They call me Pig Iron Sally, 'cause I live in Slag Iron Alley, and I'm evil and mean as I can be,' she sings in 'Pig Iron Sally' – who knew the worlds of the lesbian and the prostitute. She reports from the former in 'Women Won't Need No Men' and 'B.D. Woman's Blues', and the latter in 'Tricks Ain't Walking No More' – best heard in the affectingly sombre version titled 'They Ain't Walking No More' that opens Document's *Vol. 2* – and 'Barbecue Bess'. Other notable recordings are 'Coffee Grindin' Blues', a piece she shared with a fellow Birmingham musician, Jaybird Coleman, and the first recording of 'Black Angel Blues', which after a gender change became a blues standard. Her piano accompanists range from the workmanlike Ezell to the exquisite Channey and Avery.

Thanks to generally better sound quality and the ever sympathetic accompaniment of Walter Roland, her mid-'30s recordings, which were inexplicably credited to 'Bessie Jackson', are the most approachable of her work. Typically they open with a declarative right-hand flurry by Roland and proceed at a slow tempo with a strong, rhythmic left-hand pulse, though sometimes they are peppier, as in 'Baking Powder Blues' or 'Shave 'Em Dry', a song that exists in two versions, one bowdlerized and the other extremely explicit. (The alleged alternative version of the latter on Document's *Vol. 3* is actually a slightly edited duplicate.) A couple of sides from this period, 'Tired As I Can Be' and 'I Hate That Train Called The M. And O.', vary the pattern by having attractive accompaniments on two guitars. Otherwise Bogan's themes remained much the same and she often redeployed melodies she had used before.

Listeners approaching her for the first time might try the Yazoo, which mingles seven of her most accomplished recordings with a similar measure of Roland's, but a better introduction is the EPM, a discriminating and inexpensive selection including most of the tracks singled out above. The Classic Blues 2CD, divided between Bogan and Roland in a ratio of approximately 2:1, looks like excellent value but the well-chosen programme is too often underscored with twittering and distortion caused by faulty sound treatment. The Columbia/Legacy collection confines itself to the mid-'30s sides and rarely intersperses Bogan's recordings with Roland's. The transfers aren't always as clean as might be expected, but the album does culminate in a long stretch of sexual straight-talking as Bogan sings both versions of 'Shave 'Em Dry', Roland ripostes with his version of the theme and Bogan has the last word with the previously unknown 'Till The Cows Come Home'. TR

Son Bonds (1909–47)
VOCAL, GUITAR

From Brownsville, Tennessee, Bonds was closely associated with that town's best-known musician, Sleepy John Estes, and accompanied him at a couple of sessions.

*** Son Bonds – Charlie Pickett (1934–1941)
Wolf WBCD-003 *Bonds; Hammie Nixon (h, j, v); Sleepy John Estes (g, v); Raymond Thomas (tub b, v). 9/34–9/41.*

Bonds's first batch of recordings, in 1934, were collaborations with Hammie Nixon, who played harmonica on the blues sides, such as the moving 'Trouble Trouble Blues', and blew jug on the sacred songs. His later sides were with Estes, whom he somewhat resembled in his wavering voice and choppy guitar style. At a 1941 session he and Estes set up interlocking guitar patterns behind '80 Highway Blues' and 'Come Back Home, Little Girl', as well as on three of Estes's titles. They and Raymond Thomas (tub bass) also made three recordings in something of a jive vein as The Delta Boys; 'Every Time My Heart Beats' was an urbane blues, while 'Black Gal Swing' modernized the traditional song 'Charmin' Betsy'. (Other Delta Boys recordings had lead singing by Estes and are mentioned in his entry.) Bonds's work is never mundane; perhaps Estes's restless imagination inspired him to look constantly for new topics. TR

Juke Boy Bonner (1932–78)
VOCAL, HARMONICA, GUITAR

Weldon Bonner grew up in Bellville, Texas, began playing guitar in his early teens and at 15 moved to Houston, where he won a talent contest. In the '60s, recovering from an operation, he began to write poetry, which was frequently published by a Houston newspaper, the Forward Times. *This led to him composing many original blues, displayed on two Arhoolie albums which attracted interest from the international blues community, but although he found work and further recording opportunities in Europe he was never able to make a steady living from his music, and died in poverty and obscurity.*

*** Goin' Down To Louisiana: The Goldband Downhome Blues Anthology
Ace CDCHD 821 *Bonner; Katie Webster (p); Guitar Joe (g); Sherman Webster, unknown (b); Little Brother Griffin, Lightnin' Mitchell (d). 1–12/60.*

One of Bonner's models was Jimmy Reed, and there is no mistaking the origin of the drawled vocals in his first (c. 1957) single, 'Rock With Me Baby'/'Well Baby', included in *Rural Blues – Vol. 2* (Document DOCD-5619) or *1950's Oakland Blues: Irma Records* (Wolf 120.613). The influence of Reed and his other idol, Lightnin' Hopkins, is present but less prominent in the striking recordings he made for Goldband in 1960, mostly unissued at the time but gathered on *Goin' Down To Louisiana*. Bonner's vision of the world about him was never rosy, and in 'Blue River Rising', 'My Time To Go' and 'Life Is A Dirty Deal' he translated his dissatisfaction into words and tunes that etch their grim message on the listener's consciousness and are unforgettable.

Bonner's ten tracks occupy exactly a third of the compilation; the other participants are Ashton Savoy, Al Smith, Tal Miller, Hop Wilson and Big Chenier. Most of these were artists who never made it out of their local scene but produced a few distinctive recordings, such as Chenier's rough-hewn 'The Dog And His Puppies' and Savoy's 'Need Shorter Hours', a drawling complaint about the rigours of the working week.

♛ **** Life Gave Me A Dirty Deal
Arhoolie CD-375 *Bonner; Alvin J. Simon (d). 67–69.*
***(*) Ghetto Poet
Arhoolie CD 9040 *As above. 12/67–5/74.*
*** The Sonet Blues Story: Juke Boy Bonner
Universal 98692516 *Bonner. 71/72.*

'Life is a nightmare, least that's the way it seems,' Bonner sings. 'Seems it's full of ups and downs, with a valley of shattered dreams.' The discontent that had been a feature of his earlier recordings was extended on his Arhoolie albums – which are reconstituted in almost their entirety on *Life Gave Me A Dirty Deal* – into a long catalogue of frustration, whose tone is evident from titles like 'Hard Luck', 'Watch Your Buddies', 'It Don't Take Too Much' ('[to] make you think you was born to lose') and the bitter sequence of songs about life in the city he made his home, 'Struggle Here In Houston', 'Going Back To The Country' ('… where there ain't nobody burning the buildings down'), 'I'm In The Big City' ('and I'm about to starve to death') and 'Stay Off Lyons Avenue' ('you go there green … last time you be seen'). The last of these is a talking blues, as is 'Being Black And I'm Proud', a rallying call for a self-respect that transcends colour. These pungent texts are driven home – nailed, as it were, to wayside tree or fence – by strong guitar rhythms and melancholic harmonica choruses. Few blues artists have used their music to send such direct social messages.

Ghetto Poet contains previously unissued material, from the same sessions and a couple of later ones, which, while not quite as riveting as the best of *Life Gave Me A Dirty Deal*, shares its expressiveness and candour: 'If I sound lowdown, people it's just the way I feel: I've had so much hard luck in my lifetime till it's hard to believe it's real.' Bonner's contribution to the *Sonet Blues Story* – which, it may be worth noting, since the reader will come across it again, was a 12-volume series produced by Sam Charters and issued in 1972 as *The Legacy Of The Blues* – was another set of autobiographical blues, but now the dominant strain is resignation, as if his bitterness and mordant humour have been eroded into a bleak acceptance of things as they are. TR

Bonnie Lee (born 1931)
VOCAL

Jessie Lee Frealls was raised in Beaumont, Texas, where she played piano in church and sang in local clubs. At 19 she briefly joined the Famous Georgia Minstrels Show, then headed for Chicago in 1958. She sat in around town and recorded singles for Mayo Williams as Bonnie 'Bombshell' Lee, but her career only blossomed after she met Sunnyland Slim in 1967. Health problems intervened for a while in the '70s, but Willie Kent encouraged a comeback. This too was derailed by illness in the shape of two heart attacks, but Kent again persuaded her to resume performing.

*** Blues With The Girls
EPM Blues Collection 15758 *Bonnie Lee; Michel Carras (p); Hubert Sumlin (g, v); Larry Martin, Paul Pechenaert (g); Zox (b); Vincent Daune (d); Zora Young, Big Time Sarah (v). 2/82.*

***(*) I'm Good
Wolf 120.853 *Bonnie Lee; Fred Laster (ts); Ken Barker (p); Johnny B. Moore, John Primer, Magic Slim, Luther Adams, Willie Davis (g); Willie Kent (b); Tim Taylor, Cleo Williams (d). 8/87–4/91.*

**** Sweetheart Of The Blues
Delmark DE-676 *Bonnie Lee; Kenny Anderson (t); John Meggs (as); Hank Ford (ts); Willie Henderson (bs); Billy Branch (h); Ken Saydak (o, p); Ken Barker, Vince Willis (p); Willie Davis, Johnny B. Moore, Steve Freund, Richie Davis (g); Willie Kent, Harlan Terson (b); Jon Hiller (d, tamb); Cleo Williams (d); Pete Nathan (maracas); Vince Varco (claves, guiro); Kay C. Reed, Theresa Davis (v). 8/94–3/95.*

Bonnie Lee's heroines are Ruth Brown and Dinah Washington, and she has said, 'I'm on a jazzy-bluesy kick,' but her recordings are not free of the in-your-face raunch that has lately been imposed and self-imposed on women blues singers. Still, her five tracks on *Blues With The Girls*, recorded in France, are the work of an individualist who copes easily with Hubert Sumlin's galloping tempos, and puts some swing into 'Baby What You Want Me To Do'. A concluding 'Well, I Love Ya', with the women as backing vocalists, proves again that Sumlin must never be allowed to sing.

I'm Good is named after Bonnie Lee's signature song, of which there's another version on Willie Kent's *Ain't It Nice* (Delmark DD-653). The material comes from four sessions, on all of which the musicians, recruited from Willie Kent's Gents and Magic Slim's Teardrops, give aggressive, imaginative and never obtrusive support. The drawback is an overuse of the growling rasp that's been ubiquitous since women's blues became pigeonholed as flag-waving for empowerment. On *I'm Good* the device is often applied mechanically, and its superfluity is apparent when it's left out and the hackneyed 'Bye, Bye, Baby' becomes fresh and charming. Similarly appealing, and from the same sessions, is 'What's The Matter' on the VAC *Chicago's Finest Blues Ladies* (Wolf 120.874), but the same disc's 'Let It Roll', from a 1992 concert with The Teardrops, panders to the mob.

For engineering, production and delivery (by singer and musicians alike), Bonnie Lee's best CD is *Sweetheart Of The Blues*. This is easily confirmed by comparing 'Baby What You Want Me To Do' with the EPM and Wolf versions, or 'I Need Your Love So Bad' with the rendition (retitled 'I Need Someone') on Wolf. The rasp is still there, but it's applied with far more discretion and artistry, and when it disappears, as on a lovely reading of Ella Johnson's ballad 'Since I Fell For You', the results are again admirable. Most songs are covers but, from Chicago standards to Big Mama Thornton and Ann Peebles, they're imaginatively selected, arranged and sequenced. On 'If You Be My Baby', Steve Freund sings and Bonnie Lee is absent; the track is unobjectionable, but it disrupts the flow. CS

Roy Book Binder (born 1941)
VOCAL, GUITAR

Inspired to take up guitar by Dave Van Ronk, Roy Bookbinder (who subsequently unbound his surname) became a pupil of Rev. Gary Davis in 1968, and brought Pink Anderson back to public performance in the early '70s. He has maintained a busy performing schedule for many years.

**(*) Travelin' Man
Genes GCD 1017 *Book Binder. 71.*

The playing on this set of cover versions is fine, and often outstanding, but listeners, especially those who know the originals, are likely to be disturbed by the singing. It's flat on Bo Carter's 'Biscuits', but timing is the more general problem; Bookbinder (the CD is so credited) doesn't have the relaxed, rhythmic looseness of the artists he's borrowing from, and too often this leads to false emphasis, and disjunctions between voice and guitar.

** **The Tampa Sessions '79**
PegLeg PL 7001 *Book Binder; Dave Jones (t, tb, euph); Tony Zaitz (cl); Knocky Parker (p); Sam Notto (tu); Billy Artlip (d); Danny Di Pietra (tamb); John McEwen, Libby McEwen, Ronny Elliot, Sammy Miller, Leslie Schaugaard, Bill Ziehl (v). 3/79.*

'Biscuits' turns up again, on pitch; so does 'Travelin' Man', with Book Binder blithely singing 'folks, let me tell you 'bout a man named Coon,' which is a bit much from a white man, even one who learned the song from Pink Anderson. The additional musicians on some tracks may be an attempt to muscle in on Leon Redbone's territory, but they sound uncomfortable with the material, and are either too reticent or aimlessly rococo. Book Binder's picking is again the best thing about the disc, most notably on 'Davis Travis Rag'.

*** **Bookeroo!**
Rounder CD 3107 *Book Binder; Phil Gazell (h); Stuart Duncan (vn, md); Jerry Douglas (Do); Russ Barenberg (g); Mark Hembree, Edgar Meyer (b); Kenny Malone (perc). 2/88.*

*** **The Hillbilly Blues Cats**
Rounder CD 3121 *Book Binder; David 'Rock Bottom' York (h, broom); Billy Ochoa (b). 12/91–2/92.*

** **Live Book … Don't Start Me Talkin' …**
Rounder CD 3130 *Book Binder; Jorma Kaukonen (g). 5/93.*

The singing on *Bookeroo!* is a vast improvement; patterned more after white country singers, it's relaxed, rhythmically comfortable and better matched to Book Binder's guitar playing. Jerry Douglas and Stuart Duncan are prominent and brilliant among the accompanists, with even hardcore blues numbers like Charlie Spand's 'Good Gal' and William Brown's 'Mississippi Blues' getting well-conceived hillbilly-cum-rockabilly makeovers. The result is an entertaining and unpretentious musical synthesis. Less varied instrumentally, *The Hillbilly Blues Cats* is just as likeable, although 'I Got Mine' lacks the irony it held for African-Americans of Pink Anderson's generation, and 'One Meat Ball' is as tediously facetious as usual. A comparison of 'Statesboro Blues' with the version on Genes is very instructive, showing how far Book Binder had come as an artist in 20 years. On these two discs, he's finally developed his own approach to the blues, making tradition-based music that's neither slavishly imitative nor self-indulgently experimental.

Unfortunately, self-indulgence predominates on *Live Book*, where Book Binder sings in a mannered and immensely irritating growl, which empties most of the songs of meaning. 'Statesboro Blues' is yet again instructive; this time, it's dreadful, disfigured by those nasty vocals and Jorma Kaukonen's empty flashiness. For what it's worth, Book Binder's affectionate reminiscences of Rev. Davis and Pink Anderson are amusingly related.

(*) **Polk City Ramble
Rounder CD 3153 *Book Binder; David 'Rock Bottom' York (h); J. P. Coley (b); Glenn Evans (perc). 4/96–3/97.*

Book Binder broadens out somewhat here, writing more, and more personal, blues which are mostly rather good. He also does Jimmy Murphy's Christian rockabilly classic 'Electricity' (very low voltage by comparison with the original), and songs by Billy Joe Shavers and Jason Wilber, who won a songwriting prize at the Merle Watson Memorial Festival in what must have been a thin year. The guitar work is uniformly excellent; it's a pity that Glenn Evans's intermittent percussion is as subtle as a smack in the mouth.

*** **The Radio Show**
PegLeg PL 7002 *Book Binder; Dave Carter (interviewer). 7/99.*

As advertised, this is a broadcast from public radio in Johnson City, Tennessee. There's musical content, of course, but little of it is new, and this is mainly a chance to meet Book Binder the raconteur. He's as amusing as he was on *Live Book*, with the added advantage of singing in his normal voice; he also has some perceptive things to say about the marketing of blues, both in the past and now. Some of his historical analysis is dubious, but at least the travelin' man is now named Boone.

(*) **Singer-Songwriter Bluesman
PegLeg PL 7003 *Book Binder. 2–3/01.*
*** **Live At The Fur Peace Station**
PegLeg PL 7005 *Book Binder. 02–04.*

One of the insights expressed on the previous CD is that the market favours singer/songwriters; hence this baldly self-proclaiming album. A good many of the songs are recycled from earlier discs ('Anywhere You Go' makes its third appearance), so this album of originals is not as original as it looks. The guitar playing is as expert as ever, but Book Binder seems content to make a living by doing the old routines one more time. Which is more or less what happens on *Live At The Fur Peace Station*, compiled from WOUB radio broadcasts from Jorma Kaukonen's guitar school. This is a better CD, though, for it catches Book Binder doing what he's best at: telling stories and playing his personal favourites, some new to record, some relearned from his early albums. 'Electricity' is still drab, and the attempt to replicate John Hurt's inflections on 'Mermaids Flirt With Me' grates, but Book Binder's reminiscences are, as ever, amusing and affectionate, and a first recording of 'Another Friend Like Me' is a winning tribute to Jesse Thomas. CS

James Booker (1939–83)
VOCAL, PIANO, ORGAN

Booker spent much of his life either contending with or revelling in drug addiction, which he attributed to morphine administered after a traffic accident in childhood. He was in and out of prisons across America in the '60s, culminating in a spell in Angola, after which he returned to his native New Orleans and played at bars in the French Quarter. As well as drug and alcohol problems, Booker had a wildly mutable personality with well-developed paranoid tendencies. With all these hellhounds on his trail, the surprise is not that this prodigiously talented musician died young; it's that he lived as long as he did.

** **Gonzo: More Than All The 45s**
Night Train NTI CD 7084 *Booker; unknown (t); Joe Harris, Clarence Hall, Herb Hardesty, Lee Allen, Robert Parker, Red Tyler, unknowns (s); unknown (fl); unknowns (g); Frank Fields, unknowns (b); Earl Palmer, Charles Williams, unknowns (d); Arthur Booker (v). 54–62.*

Fourteen-year-old Booker's vocal on 'Doing The Hambone' is dire; only the piano breaks hint at promise. Two doo-wop duets with the unrelated Arthur Booker are equally dispensable, then it's organ instrumentals all the way, including four credited on issue to Memphis drummer Earl Forest. Night Train claim that they feature Booker; 'not proven' seems the fairest verdict, but either way they're the disc's best tracks. More typical is 'Gonzo' (#10 R&B, #43 pop), with bright, splashy B-3 chords and a flute. The flip, 'Cool Turkey' (Booker delighted in slipping heroin references past producer Don Robey), has some bluesy guitar, but most of this stuff is little more than easy listening.

*** The Lost Paramount Tapes
DJM DJM-CD 10010 *Booker; David Lastie (ts); Alvin 'Shine' Robinson (g, v); David Johnson (b); John Boudreaux (d); Jessie Hills (tambs, v); Richard 'Didimus' Washington (perc). early 73.*

The master tapes disappeared, and this mix over-emphasizes the percussion, but it's valuable as Booker's only full album with a band. A Latinate 'Feel So Bad' is a misjudgement, and a sprightly 'Stormy Monday' a contradiction in terms. Booker was a piano professor (this disc includes the first of several spectacular versions of 'Tico Tico') and, as with many Crescent City musicians, blues for him was sometimes more a form than a medium for emotional expression. That said, his only vocal version of 'So Swell When You're Well' is rhythmically relentless, soulfully sung and a tour de force of right-hand elaboration.

**** Junco Partner
Hannibal HNCD 1359 *Booker. 2/76.*

The best of Booker's three studio albums is *Junco Partner*; it's very well recorded, and the notes include thorough but accessible musical analysis. Booker runs through his favourites, including 'Irene', 'On The Sunny Side Of The Street' and 'Make A Better World', and makes his habitual substitution of 'heroin' for 'Heaven' on the title track. 'Pixie' is an astounding exhibition of technique, with Booker simulating three hands at the keyboard. The CD is bookended by Chopin ('Black Minute Waltz') and Liberace ('I'll Be Seeing You'), both transformed into black music, and both reminders that seeing Booker as just a blues pianist is to stuff a wildly flapping pigeon into an ill-fitting hole.

**(*) United Our Thing Will Stand
Night Train NTI CD 2005 2CD *Booker; Reggie Scanlan (b); Jim Shurik (d). c. 74–76.*

**(*) A Taste Of Honey
Night Train NTI CD 2006 2CD *Booker. 77.*

Booker often approaches them very differently, but there still are too many multiple versions of various tunes on *A Taste Of Honey*, whose title gives fair warning of some dubious repertoire. Even so, Booker finds more than most musicians would in that song, 'The Godfather Theme' (on *United Our Thing Will Stand*) and 'Something', and his rendition of 'That's Life' is utterly convincing. The latter is part of a long medley on *United Our Thing Will Stand*, which is the more important of these sets because most of its first CD is devoted to Booker's mature organ jazz, including a version of 'Make A Better World' with exemplary bass and drums. On both releases the recording quality, veering from excellent to unacceptable, is a serious drawback, and both are simply too long; one excellent CD would have been preferable to four very mixed ones.

*** King Of The New Orleans Keyboard
JSP JSPCD 815 *Booker. 77.*

Recorded live in Hamburg, Booker confines himself almost entirely to blues and R&B (although 'Blues Rhapsody' is one of several examples of his outstanding stride playing), perhaps in line with his or his management's perception of European preferences. The piano has a clanking, ungrateful bass register, but Booker is in lively form; his interpretations of Ray Charles and Huey Smith (he once toured posing as Smith, who didn't want to travel) are joyful, and his singing of 'Please Send Me Someone To Love' poignant.

*** New Orleans Piano Wizard: Live!
Rounder CD 2027 *Booker. 11/77.*

Recorded in Switzerland, this concert finds Booker playing his more usual blend of jazz, pop and blues, and on a much better instrument. An enthusiastic audience goads him into overacting on the vocal numbers, and 'Come Rain Or Come Shine' stays resolutely pop, but his gleeful adventures in modulation make 'Something Stupid', of all things, pure pleasure.

***(*) Resurrection Of The Bayou Maharajah
Rounder CD 2118 *Booker. 77–82.*
***(*) Spiders On The Keys
Rounder CD 2119 *Booker. 77–82.*

These CDs draw on 60 hours of well-recorded tapes of Booker at the Maple Leaf Bar. Scott Billington notes that 'his inconsistency during these years could weed out all but the most patient fans', which makes it hard to understand Billington's enthusiasm for the tediously histrionic soul medley that opens *Resurrection Of The Bayou Maharajah*. Matters improve considerably thereafter and, if most of the tunes are more expected than Gottschalk's 'Gitanarias', their rendition usually isn't. The disc once more verifies Booker's ability to make the most hackneyed material into something new and surprising; highlights include his best version of 'Junco Partner' and, that rare thing, an introspective 'St. James Infirmary'.

Spiders On The Keys is a collection of instrumentals, beginning with the definitive version of 'Papa Was A Rascal', and ending up 'Over The Rainbow' by way of 'So Swell When You're Well', 'Eleanor Rigby' and 'Little Coquette'. Booker plays in all his many styles, from stomping R&B to semi-classical to jazz and stride. 'Piano Salad', five minutes extracted from a 30-minute ramble, goes nowhere gracefully, and more surprisingly 'He's Got The Whole World In His Hands' is also directionless virtuosity, but 'Besame Mucho' and that Beatles song are jazz of the very highest order, and 'Gonzo's Blue Dream' is a perfectly judged slow blues. This CD is the best available exposition of Booker's musical genius but, as can be inferred from some of the titles cited, its appeal to those primarily interested in blues may be limited.

*** Classified
Rounder CD 2036 *Booker; Red Tyler (ts); James Singleton (b); John Vidacovich (d). 10/82.*

A week before the *Classified* sessions Booker was hospitalized following a seizure, and for the first two days of studio time his demons stopped him playing anything coherent. On the last day, however, normality struck, and the CD was made in four hours. His very reliable working band of the time appears on four tracks, and Singleton and Vidacovich are on another. Given the difficult circumstances of its making, *Classified* is remarkably good, but the repertoire and its interpretation are both unadventurous compared to Booker's best work. CS

Wee Bea Booze (1920–75)
VOCAL, GUITAR

Muriel Nicholls was born in Baltimore and began to make her name in Harlem and on record in the early '40s. She toured extensively in the '40s, often billed as 'The See See Rider Blues Girl' after her success with that song. She had left the business by the mid-'50s.

**(*) Sammy Price & The Blues Singers – Vol. 2 (1939–1949)
Document DOCD-5668 *Booze; Sam Price (p); Abe Bolar, unknown (b); Hal West, unknown (d). 3/42–3/44.*

Initially employed by Decca to cover the songs and style of Lil Green, who was then making a good deal of money for Bluebird, Booze came into her own with a couple of revivals of blues first recorded in the '20s, 'See See Rider Blues', first cut by Ma Rainey (and subsequently re-covered even more profitably by Chuck Willis), and 'Mr Freddie Blues'. A plain, straightforward singer with no hip mannerisms, she also played guitar and is presumed to do so on most of her recordings, the evidence is almost inaudible. Her ten tracks on this CD have a postscript on *Female Blues: The Remaining Titles Vol. 2 (1938–1949)* (RST Jazz Perspectives JPCD-1528). Of her three titles 'These Young Men Blues' and 'So Good' are with a Price-led trio, while a 1946 remake of 'See See Rider' is with a quintet featuring electric guitarist Jimmy Shirley. Taking the song more briskly than she did in '42, Booze turns in an excellent swing vocal.

** Don't You Feel My Leg
Delmark DE-684 *Booze; George Kelly (ts); Larry Johnson (o, p); Chris Power (b); Panama Francis (d). 5/50.*

Booze has five tracks on this CD of blueswomen who recorded for Apollo. (The others are by Blu Lu Barker and Baby Dee.) She has moved away from her Lil Green style a little, but finds no opportunity to match the perkiness of her '46 'See See Rider' in these slow tunes with their sludgy organ playing. TR

Memphis Willie Borum (1911–93)
VOCAL, HARMONICA, GUITAR

Born and raised in Memphis, Borum learned to play harmonica, then guitar, in a milieu that included Noah Lewis, Frank Stokes and Sonny Boy Williamson I. Returning home after army service in World War II, he worked for a soybean oil company, but continued to make music occasionally at weekends.

*** Introducing Memphis Willie Borum
Original Blues Classics OBCCD-573 *Borum. 8/61.*
*** Hard Working Man Blues
Original Blues Classics OBCCD-578 *Borum. 8/61.*

A singer and songwriter who worked in the pensive manner favoured by fellow Memphis artists like Little Buddy Doyle and Will Shade, Borum was faintly heard in 1934 as second guitarist on Allen Shaw's 'Moanin' The Blues' (*Memphis Blues (1928–1935)* [Document DOCD-5014]). He also cut some records in his own name that were not issued. The OBC (originally Bluesville) albums, prompted by Sam Charters and studio-recorded in Memphis with rather too much echo, reveal an observant blues-writer, satisfied with the expressive forms he learned as a young man but by no means stuck in the past. The personal quality of his music struck Charters forcibly, but other listeners may find some of his performances merely workmanlike. 'Uncle Sam Blues' on *Hard Working Man Blues* is a tightly constructed memoir, matched on the other album by 'Overseas Blues', and it is apparent that his blues were an important part of Borum's life, irrespective of their possible commercial value. A seven-track selection is available on *The Bluesville Years Vol. 3: Beale Street Get-Down* (Prestige PRCD 9907). TR

Lisa Bourne
VOCAL

Originally from New Orleans, where as a child she learned to play clarinet and flute, Bourne went to college in Washington, DC, and sang in local clubs before moving to LA in 1996. She counts Billie Holiday, Betty Carter and Abbey Lincoln among her singing models.

**(*) Bluehipnotik
JSP JSPCD 3702 *Bourne; Jonny Viau (ts); Troy Jennings (bs); Kirk Fletcher, John Marx (g); Rick Reed (b); Paul Fasulo (d); Jimmy Morello (prod). 00?*

Bourne is a competent singer who has no irritating mannerisms. But she has no identifying ones, either, and although this is a relatively short album (ten songs, 37 minutes), listeners may find their attention sometimes being deflected from vocalist to band, especially when the hugely talented Kirk Fletcher takes a solo, as in 'I'm Looking', 'Tell Me Lies', 'Just Leave' and 'Louisiana Woman', each a different exercise from the others. John Marx, the other guitarist on the session, has his moments, too, taking the first solo in 'He's Trouble' and pulling all the stops out in the long slow blues 'Worry Mind'. The songs, all written for Bourne by her producer Jimmy Morello, are mostly blues – 'Soul Searching' is an ingenious exception – and unremarkable, but reasonably varied in subject-matter, tempo and arrangement. TR

Andy Boy
VOCAL, PIANO

Boy (this is supposed to have been his real surname) was based in Galveston, Texas, and was remembered by pianist Robert Shaw as 'a top kicker' there.

*** Joe Pullum – Vol. 2 (1935–1951)
Document DOCD-5394 *Boy; unknown (h); Joe Pullum, Walter 'Cowboy' Washington (v). 8/35–2/37.*

The great virtue of the Texan pianists was their contempt for the ordinary. The best of Andy Boy's eight sides in his own name, all found here, are full of novel progressions and odd decorative flourishes, grounded on easy-rocking left-hand patterns. His husky singing is to be heard best, perhaps, in

'Church Street Blues', which also has an attractive piano solo, but equally winning is 'House Raid Blues', a version – like fellow Texan Little Hat Jones's 'Kentucky Blues' – of the minstrel-era piece 'Traveling Man'. His accompaniments to the singer Joe Pullum show that he was able to cope with several kinds of material; 'Ice Man Blues', one of the two included here (the others are on the preceding volume), has buoyant playing unlike any on his own records. The CD also contains Boy's four strutting accompaniments to the stentorian singer Walter 'Cowboy' Washington. The remaining 11 tracks are by Pullum with other musicians. TR

Pat Boyack (born 1967)
GUITAR

Boyack grew up in a coal-mining family in Utah and began playing guitar at 15. Graduating from Utah State University with a degree in music, he moved to the Dallas–Ft Worth area in 1991, joined the blues scene and, in 1993, formed The Prowlers with John Garza and Doug Swancy, adding Jimmy Morello the following year as vocalist. For the last few years he has played with Marcia Ball.

**(*) Breakin' In
Bullseye Blues CD BB 9557 Pat Boyack (g); John Garza (b, v); Doug Swancy (d); 'Mr Percussion' (perc); Jimmy Morello (v). 5/94.

**(*) On The Prowl
Bullseye Blues CD BB 9577 As above, except add Scott Thompson (t), Jim Spake (ts, bs), Ron Levy (o); omit 'Mr Percussion'. 96.

How The Prowlers came to make *Breakin' In*, as the Dallas DJ and journalist Don O. recounts in the notes, was by making a demo tape and sending it to Rounder, who swiftly signed them and packed them off to Memphis to cut an album. You might be forgiven for wondering whether Rounder then sent the manufacturer the wrong tapes, because the production of *Breakin' In* is basic. Morello bawls the lyrics, Boyack plays all he knows, and the results, though about as subtle as *Police Academy 7*, are rather likeable. Boyack commands a lot of guitar styles: Chicago, West Coast, Texas – even, on 'Lover's Rhumba', a wide Dick Dale tremolo. Memphis, too, if you count the pastiche of early Howlin' Wolf in 'Happy At Home'. There's another Wolfish track, 'Mean Jealous Woman', on *On The Prowl*, a relatively smoother production but generally similar in character to its predecessor. All but one of the 25 tracks on these CDs are original songs by the band, predominantly by Morello, and written in familiar blues forms.

*** Super Blue & Funky
Bullseye Blues CD BB 9587 Gary Slechta (t); Randy Zimmerman (tb); Mark 'Kaz' Kazanoff (ts, bs, h); Les Izmore (bs); Riley Osbourn (o, p); W. C. Clark (g, v); Pat Boyack (g); Kevin Smith, Gil 'T' [Isais], Ted Sweeney (b); B. E. 'Frosty' Smith (d, perc); Fran Christina (d); Spencer Thomas (v). 97.

Not long after the release of *On The Prowl*, The Prowlers broke up. The band heard on *Super Blue & Funky* was drawn by producer Kaz Kazanoff from the pool of musicians he habitually uses, and inevitably there's an air of the Austin assembly line about the session, but Boyack is not abashed. His playing has developed continuously since *Breakin' In*, as he shows in the Western Swing-flavoured instrumental 'Ol' Blondie Swings Again' and the slow blues 'Righteous Love'. The latter is one of two numbers sung (very well) by W. C. Clark; the other vocals – including, in 'Think (Before You Do)', another addition to the Howlin' Wolf thread – are by Spencer Thomas, who proves to be a slightly more versatile singer than Jimmy Morello. TR

Eddie Boyd (1914–94)
VOCAL, PIANO, ORGAN

From Clarksdale, Mississippi, Boyd played in and around Memphis in the '30s. Moving to Chicago, he worked with Sonny Boy Williamson I and others before beginning his own recording career and enjoying a hit with his composition 'Five Long Years' in 1952. He recorded for Chess, with some success, and numerous other labels, but in the '60s left the US for Europe, settling finally in Finland.

*** Complete Recordings 1947–1950
EPM Blues Collection 16000 Boyd; unknowns (t); Oett 'Sax' Mallard (cl, as); Howard Dixon (as); J. T. Brown, Bill Casimir, unknown (ts); unknown (bs); James Clark (p); Lonnie Graham, Willie Lacey, Sam Casimir, unknown (g); Willie Dixon, E. L. Liggett, Ransom Knowling, Alfred Elkins, unknown (b); Booker T. Washington, Judge Riley, unknown (d). 4/47–50.

Boyd's debut recording, 'I Had To Let Her Go'/'Kilroy Won't Be Back', was a pair of up-tempo verse-and-refrain numbers, and most of the rest of his 1947 Victor output is in a similar vein, the exuberant singing interspersed with sax solos in the manner of contemporary recordings by Roosevelt Sykes; in fact 'Unfair Lovers' is an amusingly accurate imitation of Sykes, down to the cries of 'Mercy!' The 1948–49 Victors dispense with the saxophones but Boyd maintains a buoyant delivery on sides like 'Chicago Is Just That Way' and a positive attitude in 'Something Good Will Come To Me'. The CD was intended to be completed with couplings from Regal and Herald, but what is listed as 'I Gotta Find My Baby' from Regal is a duplicate of the next item on the programme, 'Lonesome For My Baby' from Herald, running about 15 seconds slower.

In 1952 Boyd recorded for J.O.B. what would prove to be his most enduring song, 'Five Long Years', a slow woman-trouble blues set against the background of the Chicago area's steel mills. It and its original coupling, 'Blue Coat Man', are on *Rough Treatment – The J.O.B. Records Story* (Westside WESD 223).

*** Chess Blues Piano Greats
MCA/Chess CHD2-9385 2CD Boyd; unknown (as); Little Sax Crowder, Purcell Brockenborough, unknown (ts); Lee Cooper, Robert Jr Lockwood, Ellis Hunter, unknowns (g); Alfred Elkins, Willie Dixon, unknown (b); Percy Walker, unknowns (d). c. 10/51–11/59.

The chart success of 'Five Long Years' nudged Chess to pay more attention to an artist whom they had already recorded but done nothing with, and soon Boyd came up with a couple of songs that resembled it in mood and tempo, '24 Hours' and 'Third Degree', which were almost as profitable. In these very slow, contemplative numbers and the similar 'Blues For Baby', 'Rattin' And Runnin' Round' and 'Picture In The Frame', Boyd wades through a swamp of despondency with lugubrious relish while tenor sax and guitar play gloomy descants. His 20 tracks, about a third of his Chess work, almost fill one disc of

Chess Blues Piano Greats, leaving room for four sides by Otis Spann. (The other disc is by Willie Mabon and Lafayette Leake.)

After leaving Chess, Boyd recorded four singles for Bea & Baby and Keyhole, all included in the VAC *Meat & Gravy From Bea & Baby* (Castle CMDDD 610 2CD). Assured performances are enhanced, if rather crudely, by studio echo that foregrounds his voice and Robert Jr Lockwood's guitar solos. He also made excellent recordings of five songs for a visitor from the Swedish Radio Corporation in 1964, accompanied by an unplugged Mike Bloomfield (*I Blueskvarter: Chicago 1964, Volume One* [Jefferson SBACD 12653/4 2CD]).

**(*) Five Long Years
Evidence ECD 26051 *Boyd; Jimmie Lee Robinson (g, b, v); Buddy Guy (g, b); Fred Below (d); Big Mama Thornton (v). 10/65.*

**(*) Eddie Boyd And His Blues Band Featuring Peter Green
Gottdiscs GOTTCD 008 *Boyd; Albert Hall (t); Rex Morris, Bob Efford (ts); Harry Klein (bs); John Mayall (h, v); Peter Green (g, v); Tony McPhee (g); John McVie (b); Aynsley Dunbar (d). 3/67.*

**(*) 7936 South Rhodes
BGO BGOCD 195 *Boyd; Peter Green (g); John McVie (b); Mick Fleetwood (d). 1/68.*

Five Long Years was the first of three albums Boyd cut in England in the second half of the '60s. Accompanied by fellow members of the 1965 AFBF and playing both piano and organ, he ran through numerous items from his back catalogue, such as the title song, 'The Big Question' and 'Blue Monday Blues'. The Evidence CD adds four tracks recorded a couple of weeks earlier in Hamburg, Boyd yielding the vocal mike to Robinson on 'Rosa Lee' and Thornton on 'Hound Dog'. He subsequently made two albums with local accompanists, *Eddie Boyd And His Blues Band Featuring Peter Green* with John Mayall's Blues Breakers (the horns are present on only one track) and *7936 South Rhodes* with some of the same players, though by then they were a partial lineup of Fleetwood Mac. In later interviews Boyd was less than appreciative of English musicians and producers, and in the case of *7936 South Rhodes* with some cause: Green's guitar could have stood being turned up a little, and McVie's bass guitar turned down a lot. Consequently the most satisfactory tracks are the Boyd–Green duets 'Be Careful' and 'She's Gone'. Green also plays well on … *And His Blues Band*, but he had not yet found the confidence he would display later on Otis Spann's *The Biggest Thing Since Colossus*. On all these albums Boyd gives a good performance of mostly slow blues in a typically contemplative vein. But there is not now much differentiation of mood or melody in his work, and recording a dozen tracks at a time with a single small and unvarying group, as on *Five Long Years* and *7936 South Rhodes*, only underlines it.

*** The Blues Of Eddie Boyd: Live In Switzerland 1968 [sic]
Storyville STCD 8022 *Boyd. 4/67.*

*** A Sad Day
EPM Blues Collection 15781 *Boyd. 3/80.*

From the late '60s onwards, Boyd recorded perhaps ten or a dozen albums in various European countries, of which these, from Switzerland and France respectively, appear to be the only ones available on CD. In the solo setting he is revealed to be a solid, unflashy pianist, not outstandingly inventive in instrumentals like *A Sad Day*'s 'My Mood' or 'The Charm' but admirable when accompanying his singing. The Storyville CD (which, despite its title, was recorded in 1967, in Lausanne), has no instrumentals but versions of several of his major songs, 'Five Long Years', 'Third Degree' and '24 Hours', the last as 'I'm Sitting Here Waiting'. The recording has plenty of presence but readers resistant to repetition are warned that about half the 17 tracks are at much the same slow tempo, often in the same key or with the same piano introduction. TR

Ishmon Bracey (1901–70)
VOCAL, GUITAR

A part-time blues singer from close to Jackson, Mississippi, Bracey was described by the historian Gayle Dean Wardlow as 'a rare combination of braggart, entertainer, musician, showman and eventually an ordained minister'.

***(*) Ishman Bracey & Charley Taylor (1928–1929)
Document DOCD-5049 *Bracey; 'Kid' Ernest Moliere (cl); Charley Taylor (p, sp); Charlie McCoy (md, g). 4/28–c. 1/30.*

Bracey's handsome, vibrato-laden voice generates a deeply melancholic effect on 'The Four Day Blues', 'Brown Mamma Blues' and, outstandingly, 'Trouble Hearted Blues', a blues cast in an early form not unlike Robert Wilkins's 'Rollin' Stone'. The fourth piece from this session, 'Leavin' Town Blues', is slightly more upbeat, a mood furthered by Charlie McCoy's sparkling mandolin. These four songs are included, excellently remastered from original Victor pressings and with an alternative take of 'Trouble Hearted Blues', on the VAC *Memphis Blues Singers Volume 2* (Frog DGF 22), whose companion volume *Memphis Blues Singers Volume 1* (DGF 21) has the earlier but equally absorbing Victor coupling of 'Saturday Blues' and 'Left Alone Blues'. The sonically more variable Document includes all the above titles and Bracey's later sides. The solo 'Woman Woman Blues' and 'Suitcase Full Of Blues' share the character of their forerunners, but the others' often interesting themes, such as 'Jake Liquor Blues', tend to be clouded by the poor condition of the originals. Some of these Paramount recordings are in a trio setting, where the irritant of Moliere's clarinet is fortunately soothed by Taylor's glorious piano playing. Taylor's own-name records, which complete the Document, are a curious mélange of mournful blues vocals, superb piano and comic dialogue. TR

Tiny Bradshaw (1905–58)
VOCAL

Myron Bradshaw entered the music business in the '20s as a drummer and singer, formed his first band in 1933 and first recorded the following year. Chiefly known in the '30s as a Harlem danceband leader, when he signed with King Records in 1949 he turned himself into a jump-blues leader and vocalist and became one of the label's most successful acts, having an R&B Top Ten hit in 1952–53 with 'Soft'. After a stroke in 1954 he cut back his recording and touring.

(***) Tiny Bradshaw 1934–1947
Classics 5011 *Bradshaw; Lincoln Mills, Shad Collins, Lawrence 'Max' Maddox, Billy Ford, Talib Daawud, Sammy Yates, Henry Glover, unknowns (t); George Matthews, Eugene Green, Leon Comegys, Andrew Penn, Alfonso King, John 'Shorty' Haughton,*

unknown (tb); Edgar 'Spider' Courance, Happy Caldwell (cl, ts); Bobby Holmes, Russell Procope, Sonny Stitt, Don Hill (as); Lowell 'Count' Hastings, George 'Big Nick' Nicholas, Pritchard Cheseman (ts); Charlie Fowlkes (bs); unknowns (s); Clarence Johnson, Duke Anderson, Wild Bill Davis, unknowns (p); Bob Lessey, James Manilus (g); Ernest Williamson, Leonard Swain, Curley Russell, unknowns (b); Arnold Boling, Earl Walker, Les Erskine, unknowns (d); unknown (vb); Jack Fine (v). 9/34–3/47.

*** **Breaking Up The House**
Proper PVCD 101 2CD *As above, except add Leslie Ayres (t), Orrington Hall (as, bs); Rufus Gore, Red Prysock (ts); Jimmy Robinson (o, p), Leroy Harris, Willie Gaddy (g), Clarence Mack, Eddie Smith (b), Calvin Shields (d), Dorena Deane, unknown (v). 9/34–7/51.*

The repertoire and presentation of the eight 1934 sides that open the Classics CD make it transparently clear that Bradshaw and his men were being used as Decca's answer to the then popular Cab Calloway orchestra. The remainder of the album, derived from '40s recordings for Regis, Manor and Savoy, portrays a swing band with the wide-screen sound of the era; on an up-tempo piece like 'Bradshaw Bounce' they occupy similar stylistic territory to, say, the Lucky Millinder orchestra. 'Take The Hands Off The Clock' with trenchant piano by Wild Bill Davis is a no-messing blues number, but apart from that and a couple of other tracks the music on this CD comes from the house next door to the blues. Its contents reappear, with some difference in equalization, as the first disc of the Proper set; the second similarly duplicates almost all of Classics' *1949–1951* (see below).

*** **Tiny Bradshaw 1949–1951**
Classics 5031 *Bradshaw; Leslie Ayres (t); Andrew Penn (tb); Orrington Hall (as, bs); Rufus Gore, Red Prysock (ts); Jimmy Robinson (o, p); Leroy Harris, Willie Gaddy (g); Clarence Mack, Eddie Smith (b); Calvin Shields (d); Mary Lou Greene, Dorena Deane, band (v). 11/49–7/51.*

*** **The EP Collection Plus**
See For Miles SEECD 703 *Bradshaw; Leslie Ayres, Lester Bass, Bill Hardman (t); Andrew Penn (tb); Orrington Hall, Ted 'Snooky' Hulbert (as, bs); Jimmy Cole (as); Rufus Gore, Red Prysock, Curtis Rose, Sil Austin, Noble Watts (ts); Alexander Nelson (bs); Leon Burns, Lovejoy Coverson (s); Jimmy Robinson (p); Leroy Harris, Willie Gaddy, Clarence Kenner, Clifford Bush (g); Clarence Mack, Eddie Smith, Sam Jones (b); Calvin Shields, Philip Paul (d); Tiny Kennedy, Mary Lou Greene, band (v). 11/49–1/55.*

*** **The Great Composer**
King KCD 653 *As above, except Burns also plays fl; add Ray Felder (ts), Osborne Whitford (fl), Jon Thomas (p); omit Nelson, Smith, Greene. 2/50–1/58.*

Much of Bradshaw's repertoire during his first few years at King was in the comic narrative idiom popularized by Louis Jordan and developed by his own label-mates Wynonie Harris and Roy Brown – songs like 'I'm Going To Have Myself A Ball', 'Two Dry Bones On The Pantry Shelf' and 'Snaggle Tooth Ruth', all written in collaboration with the King producer Henry Glover. Bradshaw's singing style was less boisterous than Harris's but more growling than Jordan's; sometimes, as in 'Walk That Mess', he indulged in a little Callowayesque scatting. This was the era when the honking tenor saxophonist ruled ballroom and jukebox alike. The tenorman Bradshaw used on many recordings, Rufus Gore, specialized in a hoarse squealing effect like an outraged Gloucester Old Spot, but others who spent time in his ranks were a little more conventional, such as Red Prysock, heard on 'Heavy Juice' and, very come-hitherishly, on 'Soft', or Sil Austin on 'Later'.

Classics' *1949–1951* and the King CD are a good fit. The former includes several of the abovementioned numbers in a selection largely devoted to songs, while *The Great Composer* is an almost entirely instrumental set, adding 'Soft', 'Heavy Juice', 'Later' and a couple of vocal tracks. Between them the two CDs contain 40 of Bradshaw's 50-odd King recordings. Further tenorists are heard on *The Great Composer*, Noble Watts on 'Cat Fruit' and Ray Felder on 'Bushes', while Prysock's 'Free For All' recycles the high-speed blues that Arnett Cobb recorded six years earlier as 'Go Red Go'. *The EP Collection Plus*, despite its collectorish title, is excellent value, its 29 tracks embracing all but one ('Bushes') of *The Great Composer* and a chunk of *1949–1951* and adding some that are on neither. Here too the emphasis is on succinct instrumentals. (*Walk That Mess! – The Best Of The King Years* [Westside WESA 824], an admirable collection, has been deleted, but much of its material is on *1949–1951*.) TR

Billy Branch (born 1951)
VOCAL, HARMONICA

Branch was born near Chicago but brought up in California, where he learned the basics of his instrument; he returned in 1969 to attend college, and got involved with the blues after attending a concert in Grant Park. He built a reputation around town, and took over from Carey Bell in Willie Dixon's Chicago Blues All Stars in 1979, at the same time working with the fledgling Sons Of Blues, who had been formed after a 1977 appearance by 'The New Generation of Chicago Blues' at the Berlin Jazz Festival. Numerous musicians have passed through the band, and the name has sometimes been mothballed, but Branch continues to lead a version of the Sons Of Blues – now perhaps more like hip uncles of the blues. He has also taught blues history and harmonica skills in Chicago schools.

In the early years, the Sons Of Blues were a partnership of equals, but Branch has become increasingly identified as the band's driving force and leader. The CDs discussed here are variously credited, but are most conveniently consolidated under Branch's name.

**** **Chicago's Young Blues Generation**
Evidence ECD 26114 *Branch; Lurrie Bell (g, v); Elisha 'Eli' Murray (g); J. W. Williams (b); Moses Rutues Jr (d). 6/82.*

This CD is credited to 'Billy Branch & Lurrie Bell and the Sons Of Blues', and Bell takes the vocals on five of its seven long numbers. All are covers of well-known songs, with 'Breaking Up Somebody's Home' as modern as it gets, but youthful enthusiasm and assertiveness, captured by excellent engineering, make everything sound newly minted. Bell's guitar is edgily inventive, and sometimes disturbingly violent; the transition from swooning lyricism to agitated fragmentation on 'Sweet Little Angel' is extraordinary. Murray also does good work, and Williams and Rutues are – as they continue to be on subsequent discs – an exemplary rhythm section. Branch's singing is a little stiff on two Sonny Boy Williamson II covers, but his big-toned harp serves stylish notice of a determination to go back to the future.

(***) Live '82
Evidence ECD 26049 *As above, except Williams and Rutues also sing; add Carey Bell (h, v). 11/82.*

Live '82 is also 100 per cent covers. ('My Kind Of Woman', claimed for tradition, is Sir Mack Rice's 'Cold Women With Warm Hearts'.) Their execution during an AFBF tour is adequate but hardly incendiary, although both guitarists reach unexpected places when soloing on 'Reconsider Baby'. The major drawback, though, is that the recordings sound as if they were made on a portable cassette player in row J. The credit is to 'Billy Branch and the S.O.B.s'; Branch, Rutues and Williams sing a song apiece, Carey Bell guests on another, and Lurrie Bell takes four.

***(*) Where's My Money?
Evidence ECD 26069 *Branch; Rufus Foreman (ts); Kurt Berg (bs); Jimmy Walker (p, v); Carlos Johnson, Pete Crawford (g); J. W. Williams (b, v); Moses Rutues Jr (d, v). 8–9/83.*

Originally an LP on Pete Crawford's Red Beans label, Where's My Money? is credited to 'Billy Branch and the Sons Of Blues'. Carlos Johnson's cool, lean stylings replace Lurrie Bell, but otherwise the mix is much as before, with some original compositions included for the first time. The veteran Jimmy Walker, with whom Branch worked in a trio in the '70s, leads on two tracks, one a fine reworking of 'Third Degree'. 'Son Of Juke' (i.e. 'Juke' with modulations) and Rutues's rendition of James Brown's 'Sex Machine' are showstoppers. 'Sons Of Blues', which is not, confirms that the customary obscurity of Sterling Plumpp's poetry is a cloak for banality.

**** As The Years Go Passing By
Black & Blue BB 461 *Branch; François Rilhac (p); Carl Weathersby, Buster Benton (g, v); J. W. Williams (b, v); Moses Rutues Jr (d, v). 5/85.*

As The Years Go Passing By is credited to the Sons Of Blues *tout court*. It was recorded in France, where the band were backing Buster Benton, who guests on 'In The Ghetto'. Weathersby plays beautifully logical and elegant guitar, but only gets to sing J. W. Williams's likeably lugubrious composition 'It Haven't Been Too Long'. Williams is the numerically dominant vocalist, but this is still a band of equals, as is most obvious on the high-spirited concluding instrumental, 'Fours'. None of them can find anything new in 'Rock Me Baby', but otherwise this is a thoroughly commendable session; even the several tracks which stretch out beyond seven minutes justify their length. The tasteful, idiomatic playing of local pianist Rilhac deserves a special mention.

**** Hubert Sumlin & Billy Branch
Wolf 120.868 *Branch; Ken Barker (p); Luther Adams, John Primer, Carl Weathersby, Johnny B. Moore (g); Willie Kent (b); Tim Taylor (d). 8/90–8/92.*

Branch's five tracks, all but one backed by Willie Kent & The Gents, are the meat in a Sumlin sandwich. The programme starts with 'Baby What You Want Me To Do' and the other songs are almost as familiar, but Branch and the band pounce on them gleefully, delivering renditions whose pulsating, dynamic cohesion transports listeners straight back to the early '50s. 'Just Your Fool', with only Weathersby and Moore in support, is a particular miracle of retrospection.

Branch has decidedly not been inactive since, but a CD on the Japanese GBW label disappeared with the company, and two made for Verve are deleted; so is *Sweet Home Chicago* (Charly CDDGR 274), which included six tracks recorded live at Buddy Guy's Legends. A 1998 collaboration with Kenny Neal is discussed in the latter's entry, and in 2003 *Billy Branch And The Sons Of Blues* (Blue Sun CD BS 1035) appeared on Branch's own label, which seems to be unprocurable outside Chicago. The following year saw the issue in Japan of *Don't Mess With The Bluesmen* (P-Vine PCD-25020), credited to Billy Branch & Carlos Johnson. CS

Paul Brasch (born 1975)
VOCAL, GUITAR

Active around Spokane, Washington, as a musician and boxer, Brasch was drawn to the blues by the music of Jimi Hendrix, though his subsequent models were earlier figures in blues and country music.

**(*) Find My Way
Burnside BCD-0033 *Brasch; Damian Coen (h); John Cage (perc). 99.*

Brasch's declared admiration for Son House is borne out not only by his choice of 'Empire State Blues' but by his slide playing on songs like 'Heel And Toe', 'Sittin' In My Kitchen' and 'Sweet Tooth'. He shows that he draws on other sources with the more legato playing on 'Goin' To Texas' and with the minstrel-like title tune, and he chooses a couple of country standards, 'Six Days On The Road' and 'I Heard That Lonesome Whistle Blow', though neither is improved by its rearrangement. But the first thought that will occur to most listeners is that Brasch must be a *big* fan of Kelly Joe Phelps. TR

Clarence Brewer (born 1949)
VOCAL, GUITAR

From Springfield, Missouri, Brewer is also a graphic artist and sculptor.

** King Clarentz
HMG HMG 1007 *Brewer; Joe Terry (kb); D. Clinton Thompson (g); Lou Whitney (b); Bobby Lloyd Hicks (d, perc). 99.*

King Clarentz is a blend of rock – the backing musicians are Springfield rock band The Skeletons – and learned-from-the-records Mississippi blues, with John Lee Hooker, R. L. Burnside, Elmore James and Robert Johnson all audible in the mixture. Instrumentally, it's an energetic thrash, enjoyable in a mindless sort of way, but Brewer's attempts at vocal dramatics are unattractive and arbitrary, and his attempts at social and political commentary have all the sophistication of a supermarket tabloid. Jessie Mae Hemphill's 'Spyin' and Talkin'' gets a successful reading. So does Procol Harum's 'Whiskey Train', which is not as surprising as it may seem, for, like most of Brewer's music, it's pastiche blues. CS

Blind James Brewer (1920–88)
VOCAL, GUITAR

Born in Brookhaven, Mississippi, James Brewer moved with his parents to Chicago in 1940. Partially blind from childhood, he became a street musician, and was often to be heard on Maxwell Street, singing both blues and sacred songs, the latter

with his wife Fannie, who was also blind. In the '60s and '70s he also played at clubs, particularly the No Exit, and at festivals.

Brewer's LPs *Jim Brewer* (Philo, 1974) and *Tough Luck* (Earwig, 1983) have yet to be issued on CD, but contrasting recordings from 1964 have surfaced on two compilations. The documentary set *… And This Is Maxwell Street* (Rooster Blues R 2641 3CD) contains long, stirring versions of the gospel standards 'When The Saints Go Marching In' and 'I'll Fly Away'; he also accompanies his wife Fannie on 'I Shall Overcome' and Carrie Robinson on 'Power To Live Right'. On these atmospheric tapes Brewer played electric guitar, as he normally did outdoors, but the five blues performances on *I Blueskvarter: Chicago 1964, Volume One* (Jefferson SBACD 12653/4 2CD) are with acoustic guitar. 'I Know A Woman, She Lives Up On The Hill' and 'Poor Kelly Blues' are in the spirit of Big Bill Broonzy, whom Brewer admired, while 'I Don't Want No Woman, She Got Hair Like Drops Of Rain' is based on an older picking pattern. TR

Curley Bridges (born 1934)
VOCAL, PIANO

Bridges began playing piano at 19 after hearing Albert Ammons, Pete Johnson and Piano Red. He settled in Washington, DC, after leaving the army, and was the singer and pianist with trumpeter Frank Motley's band for 13 years. The Motley Crew moved to Toronto in 1966; Bridges left the band in the same year, but has been based in Canada ever since, working as a solo act and in trios and larger bands.

**(*) Keys To The Blues
Electro-Fi 3358 Bridges; Chris Whitely (t, h, g); John Deehan (ts); Dan Whitely (g); Victor Bateman (b); Bucky Berger (d). 4/98.

Eight of Curley Bridges' vocals with Frank Motley are on the very enjoyable *Frank Motley And His Motley Crew And They're 'Honkin' At Midnight'* (DC 0400). His powerful baritone and forceful piano playing belie his 64 years on Electro-Fi's anthology of familiar blues and R&B standards of the '50s. Unfortunately, his voice is an inflexible instrument, and the delivery of the songs is consequently too similar. Bridges' piano work is more interesting, but it is usually submerged by the band, who go at every song hammer and tongs, seldom leaving him much space to solo. Chris Whitely's lead guitar, heard on three tracks, is distressingly coarse.

**(*) Mr. Rock 'N' Soul
Electro-Fi 3369 As above, except Pat Carey (ts) replaces Deehan. 4/01.

Despite the presence of material as familiar as 'Little Red Rooster', 'Caldonia' and 'I'm Gonna Move To The Outskirts Of Town', this is a more stylistically varied disc than *Keys To The Blues*, and overall a better one. It's better not least because the band usually stands back a little, although 'Rock 'N' Soul', a rare Bridges composition, and 'Ya Ya' are let down by mechanistic drumming; there are also several excessive guitar solos, that on 'Mo-Jo Re:Worked' (*sic*) being unrelievedly dreadful. 'Ya Ya' includes a fine solo by Bridges, however, and in general he has more scope to show what he can do on *Mr. Rock 'N' Soul*, and is more audible when doing so. As a result, it's possible to hear that he's one of the best blues pianists currently working, but his talent is not properly showcased by either of these CDs. CS

Eugene 'Hideaway' Bridges (born 1963)
VOCAL, GUITAR

Bridges grew up in New Orleans and was taught guitar by his father, who played professionally as Hideaway Slim before becoming a minister, whereupon he created a family gospel group in which Eugene played guitar. After service in the US Air Force, Eugene worked in Houston, where he formed his first band. In 1995 he moved to France, joined bass player Big Joe Turner's Memphis Blues Caravan, then touring, and returned with it to England, where he has worked since.

***(*) Man Without A Home …
Armadillo ARMD 00009 Bridges; Steve Trigg (t); Andy Gilliams (tb); Patsy Gamble (s); Andrew Butler (kb, o); Peter Zivkovic (p); Robin Clayton (b); Alan Savage (d); Mike Vernon (perc, prod); George Chandler (v). 12/99–2/00.

The polished production of 1998's *Born To Be Blue* (Blueside WESF 105, deleted) showcased a respectable talent, but it could hardly disguise the deeply familiar directions in which Bridges pointed it. Tracks like 'Achin' Heart' and the title song were ardent tributes to the influence of B. B. King as both singer and guitarist, while Sam Cooke was the moving spirit behind 'If You Don't Wanna Love Me', 'Good Times' and 'A Change Is Gonna Come'. Nevertheless, it was clear that Bridges had a good enough voice to measure himself against such models with dignity, and the supporters who helped to bring about another recording opportunity were rewarded, in *Man Without A Home …*, with a stylish album of greater individuality. The rich velvet texture of his voice can be felt in the soul ballads 'I'm Falling In Love', 'Always' (a composition Bridges' publisher might have done well to pitch to Whitney Houston) and the superb 'Man Without A Country, Man Without A Home', which also boasts a fine, long guitar solo. Other tracks are closer to conventional blues, while a guitar instrumental, 'Hideaway Slim', commemorates Bridges' father. The horn arrangements are exactly right on the four tracks where the horns appear. In fact, everyone sounds good on this admirable recording.

*** Jump The Joint
Armadillo ARMD 00015 Bridges; David Erickson (t); Jerry O'Sullivan (tb); Seth Kibel (ts); Randy Small (bs); Mats Qwarfordt (h); Paddy Milner, Richard Simmons (o, p); Daryl Davis (p); Guthrie Kennard, Otto Williams (b); Jimmy Pendleton (d). 02.

*** Coming Home
Armadillo ARMD 00021 Bridges; Shane Pitsch (t); Mark 'Speedy' Gonzales (tb); Seth Kibel (ts, bs, fl); Mats Qwarfordt (h); David Webb (o, p, syn); Ruf Rufner (o, p); Rocky Athas (g); Guthrie Kennard, Robin Clayton (b); Bobby Baranowski (d, cymbals); Pat Manske (bgo, tamb, shaker). 04/05.

Bridges' voice continues to be a living, breathing homage to the singers he admires, but it's unlikely that B. B. King would begrudge 'I Got The Blues' (*Jump The Joint*), 'I Wish Somebody Would Have Told Me' or 'Love Me Right' (*Coming Home*), or the shade of Sam Cooke object to 'She Want To Dance With Me' (*Jump The Joint*) or 'You're The One' (*Coming Home*), since Bridges' respect is matched by an ability to write songs in their spirit and bring them to life on record. *Jump The Joint* and *Coming Home* have nothing quite as arresting as the title song of the previous album, though a masterful performance of 'Walk The Back Streets', *Jump The Joint*'s only non-original number, comes close. 'I'm Going Back' on *Coming Home* fills a tiny gap on the shelf of topographical blues, being an affectionate tip of the hat to North Myrtle Beach, South Carolina. Bridges and his team maintain a high level of performance throughout, and careful production buffs both albums to a gloss. TR

John Brim (1922–2003)
VOCAL, GUITAR

Kentucky-born Brim, along with his harmonica- and drum-playing wife Grace, was a minor but worthy contributor to the postwar Chicago blues renaissance. Taking the precaution of running a dry-cleaning business throughout his fitful musical career, he cut a handful of records for small Detroit and Chicago labels before gaining an unsatisfactory contract with Chess that saw several sides unreleased or cancelled. His reputation with his peers ensured that his accompanists were always among the finest of the day. After a long hiatus, he made a couple of modestly successful albums in the '90s that brought him similarly modest acclaim.

*** John Brim 1950–1953
Classics 5086 Brim; Ernest Cotton (ts); Grace Brim (h, d, v); Little Walter, Jimmy Reed (h); James Watkins, Big Maceo, Roosevelt Sykes, Sunnyland Slim (p); Eddie Taylor, Pete Franklin, Louis Myers, David Myers (g); Moody Jones, Ernest 'Big' Crawford, unknown (b); Alfred Wallace, Fred Below, Elgin Edmonds (d). 50–12/53.

*** Authorized Blues
Anna Bea ABCD 451 As above, except Grace Brim does not play h; add John Brim Jr (g); omit Reed, Watkins, Big Maceo, Louis Myers, David Myers, Below, Edmonds. 51–52, 71.

Authorized Blues is in effect an artist-sanctioned bootleg containing almost all the sides Brim recorded before joining Chess in 1953. 'Dark Clouds' begins as a confrontation between his over-amplified guitar and Sykes's strident piano but on this and 'Lonesome Man Blues' Brim plays Elisha Cook Jr to Sykes's Sydney Greenstreet. Grace fares better in 'Going Down The Line', but the other side is omitted. The remaining titles come from J.O.B. sessions with Sunnyland Slim at the piano (and are also included in the VAC *Rough Treatment – The J.O.B. Records Story* [Westside WESD 233]). Five, including 'Hard Pill To Swallow' and 'Moonlight Blues', remained unissued at the time despite being uniformly excellent compositions. Brim's confidence as a vocalist increases to match the quality of his songwriting. A rather short compilation is completed with a pair of roughly recorded 1971 sides, matching the indifferent sound of some of the earlier material.

The Classics set sandwiches the same material, without the 1971 recordings but adding Grace's missing flipside, 'Leaving Daddy Blues', between an earlier coupling by Grace and half a dozen sides for Chess and Parrot, including the fine 'Rattlesnake', 'Lifetime Baby' and 'Ice Cream Man' with Little Walter. Superior contents and wider availability make this the best entrée to the Brims' early work.

**** Chicago Blues Session Vol. 12
Wolf 120.858 Brim; Billy Branch (h); John Brim Jr, John Primer (g); Willie Kent (b); Grace Brim, Timothy Taylor (d). 71, 89.

The aforementioned 1971 sides, 'You Put The Hurt On Me' and 'Movin' Out', were added to the CD version of this release, which otherwise comprises an exceptionally successful 1989 re-creation of the sound Brim achieved with his Gary Kings 35 years before. Branch and Primer fill the roles then taken by Little Walter and Eddie Taylor with ease and gusto, ably supported by Kent and Taylor. Sadly, there are just four tracks, 'Easy Papa Blues' and 'I'm Gonna Let You Go' being of particular note, leaving the listener to regret that a whole album was never contemplated. The remainder is by Pinetop Perkins.

*** The Ice Cream Man
Tone-Cool CD TC 1150 Brim; T. David Cunningham, 'Sax' Gordon Beadle (ts); Tino Barker (bs); Tom 'Mookie' Brill (h, b); Jerry Portnoy (h); Anthony Geraci (p); Bob Margolin (g); Michael 'Mudcat' Ward (b); Wes Johnson (d). 94.

Warmly received when first issued, this session re-creates everything from Brim's heyday except the strength of his vocals. Margolin wields a frenzied bottleneck on three numbers, including Muddy's 'Standing Around Crying'; otherwise he locks into rhythmic interplay with Brim. Portnoy and Brill evoke the two Walters, Jacobs and Horton, in their solos without matching the inventiveness of either. Horns are present on 'Lonesome Man Blues', one of three re-creations, the others being the title track and 'Tough Times'. The spirit of the latter invests 'Wake Up America', although here the talk is of 'our jobs' being taken by foreigners. A benevolent mix tends to smother Brim's faltering guitar work, particularly on a pair of instrumental workouts. His voice is at its best on an acoustic version of 'Going Down Slow'; elsewhere shortness of breath inhibits a fuller appreciation of its limited gifts.

***(*) Jake's Blues
Anna Bea ABCD 499 Brim; Rick Gerek (h); Billy Flynn, Jan Arenas (g); P. T. Pederson (b); Matt Liban (d); Grace Brim (v). 99.

A fresh set of musicians of lesser pedigree attempt the same feat as those on *The Ice Cream Man* and on the whole succeed better than their predecessors. Brim's vocals have become little more than conversational but sympathetic production makes a virtue of his limitations rather than hiding them. Gerek plays a number of excellent harmonica solos and Flynn contributes a reasonable facsimile of Robert Nighthawk's slide technique on 'What May Be Your Name' and 'Hey Baby'. The rest of the musicians fill their roles with commendable modesty, although this does lead to an uneventful instrumental, 'Walkin' With Grace', and a stolid 'I Just Got To Know'. Two takes of 'Dedicated To Grace' are an opportunity for Brim to commemorate his recently deceased wife and the set ends with a poorly recorded tape of her singing 'Me And My Chauffeur'. NS/TR

Big George Brock (born 1932)
VOCAL, HARMONICA

Brock was born in Grenada, Mississippi, and spent part of his early life in the Clarksdale area. In his teens he moved to St

Louis, where he owned several blues clubs in the '60s and '70s. He and his Houserockers were subsequently the house band at Climmie's Western Inn for 12 years. In recent years he has returned to Clarksdale to appear at blues festivals and record his first album.

(*) Clubcaravan
Cat Head [unnumbered] *Brock; Latasha Coatie (kb); Riley Coatie Sr (g); Tekora Coatie (b); Riley Coatie Jr (d). 5/05.*

Simply but appropriately accompanied by Arkansawyer Riley Coatie's family band, Brock delivers Chicago standards, such as 'Honest I Do', Sonny Boy Williamson II's 'Nine Below Zero' and Muddy Waters's 'Louisiana Blues', and original songs and harmonica tunes cast in the same mould. The studio sound is basic, the keyboard playing often murky, and Brock's voice, though strong on some numbers, is mixed a little too low on others. It's still an unmistakably oldfashioned Southern blues voice, and for many listeners that, and the unpretentiousness of the music, will outweigh any small imperfections. TR

Big Leon Brooks (1933–82)
VOCAL, HARMONICA

Brooks was playing by the age of six, when his family left Mississippi for Chicago. He worked with many big names in the '50s, and led his own band. Failing to break into the big time and dogged by health problems, Brooks abandoned professional music in 1957. He made a comeback in 1976, but soon became seriously ill, and died shortly before an LP was released.

(*) Let's Go To Town
Earwig CD 4931 *Brooks; Pinetop Perkins, Moose Walker (p); Louis Myers, Junior Pettis, Luther 'Guitar Junior' Johnson, Eddie Taylor (g); Bob Stroger, Freddie Dixon (b); Odie Payne Jr (d). 6–9/80.*

Brooks neatly summarized his harmonica playing and its limitations: 'I was playing mostly on Sonny Boy [Williamson I's] style, but I got my technique from listenin' at [Little] Walter play ... I got a more gross tone than Walter. His thinking ability is more faster but my tone is more grosser.' *Let's Go To Town* is an expanded version of the 1982 LP and, given the sad circumstances of its initial release, one longs for promise unfulfilled and genius cut off before recognition. The sober reality is that Brooks's playing was energetic and big-toned, but short on versatility and subtlety; he sang in a forced growl which restricted his expressive range without achieving the intended excitement and aggression. Despite backing from a starry array of veterans, there's a shortage of surprise and originality; four tracks on *Living Chicago Blues – Vol. IV* (Alligator ALCD 7704) don't alter the verdict. CS

Lonnie Brooks (born 1933)
VOCAL, GUITAR

Born Lee Baker Jr in Louisiana, Brooks began performing in the '50s as Guitar Jr, a professional name he abandoned in 1960 when he moved to Chicago, where Luther 'Guitar Jr' Johnson was already established. For most of two decades he worked on the club scene without attracting much attention, recording only a few singles (and an album in Europe), but after signing with Alligator he turned himself into one of the leading acts on the concert circuit. Many people came to know him – though they weren't aware of it, since his name wasn't mentioned – from a series of internationally screened TV ads for Heineken lager, in which he played a backporch bluesman whose wife walks out on him, only for a talent scout to walk in with a contract and change his life. Beer really can do that.

*** Live At Peppers 1968
Black Magic CD 9008 *Brooks; poss. A. C. Reed (ts); poss. Nolan Antoine (b); poss. Robert Titwell (d). 12/68.*

When the Belgian blues enthusiast George Adins recorded him at Pepper's Lounge in Chicago in 1968, Brooks had about ten years' record making behind him, including a couple of modest regional hits on Goldband while he was in Louisiana, but was not regarded as much more than a journeyman club artist. But journeyman status on the Chicago scene was not a rating to be sniffed at, if the performance this CD preserves is typical of what one could hear in a blues club in 1968. In such a context it's natural that Brooks should rely on familiar material like 'Hideaway', 'Sweet Little Angel' and 'You Don't Have To Go', or play his Chuck Berry riffs in 'Shakin' Little Mama', but the performances are full of energy. Black Magic apologize for the limitations of Adins's 'simple tape recorder' but it was good enough to catch the ambience of Pepper's Lounge as few other recordings have, and the album is a scarce and valuable document of everyday live blues.

** Sweet Home Chicago
Black & Blue BB 444 *Brooks; Little Mac Simmons (h); Willie Mabon (p); Hubert Sumlin (g); Dave Myers (b); Fred Below (d). 12/75.*

** Sweet Home Chicago
Evidence ECD 26001 *As above. 12/75.*

A lifeless French recording, in which Brooks does his best with standards of the order of 'Reconsider Baby' and 'Things I Used To Do' and the musicians accompany him like zombies. Evidence reissue the contents of the original LP, but Black & Blue add three alternative takes.

**(*) Let's Talk It Over
Delmark DD 660 *Brooks; Rob Waters (p); Bob Levis (g); Harlan Terson (b); Robert Taylor Layton (d). 3/77.*

*** Living Chicago Blues – Vol. II
Alligator ALCD 7702 *Brooks; Rob Waters (kb); Bob Levis (g); Harlan Terson (b); Casey Jones (d). 78.*

*** Bayou Lightning
Alligator ALCD 4714 *As above, except add Billy Branch (h). 79.*

*** Turn On The Night
Alligator ALCD 4721 *Brooks; Paul Howard (t); Bill McFarland (tb); Henri Ford (as, bs); Jerry Wilson (ts); Jimmy Jewell (s); Ken Sajdak (kb); Bob Levis (g); Harlan Terson (b); Billy Jackson, Merle Perkins (d). 80.*

Let's Talk It Over comes from the series of 1977 sessions produced by Ralph Bass and, like most of the other albums from that project (several of which have wound up as Delmark CDs), is businesslike and rather dull. Brooks's guitar sound is generic, and there's no attempt to instil variation through arrangement or surprising repertoire choices. A year later, however, Brooks contributed four strong performances to Alligator's *Living Chicago Blues* series, and within a year was making his debut on the label. Working with a seasoned band and having the luxury to think about an album before going into the studio to make it, he immediately produced first-rate work. From the wiggle-walk rhythm of the opening 'Voodoo Daddy' to the soul preaching of 'Watch What You Got', *Bayou Lightning* catches aspects of Brooks's music that had never been heard on record before. *Turn On The Night* was equally flattering, with its heartfelt reading of 'I'll Take Care Of You' and a lively set-closing 'Zydeco' on which Brooks gets his guitar to sound surprisingly like an accordion.

*** Hot Shot
Alligator ALCD 4731 Brooks; Abb Locke (ts); Ken Sajdak (kb); Dion Payton (g); Lafayette Lyle Jr (b); Perdis Wilson (d). 83.

Hot Shot achieves, at times, the sort of rock-blues synthesis that has eluded many more (and less) distinguished figures. 'Mr Somebody' is a very fine slow, minor-key blues with a gorgeous guitar solo, but most of the other numbers are fast and vigorous, some with unusually strong melodic character.

*** Wound Up Tight
Alligator ALCD 4751 Brooks; Jim Liban (h); Tom Giblin (kb); Osee Anderson, Larry Clyman, Johnny Winter (g); Noel Neal (b); Jimi Schutte (d). 86.

*** Live From Chicago: Bayou Lightnin' Strikes
Alligator ALCD 4759 Brooks; Tom Giblin (o, p); Osee Anderson, Ronnie Baker Brooks (g); Lafayette Lyle Jr (b); Jimi Schutte (d). 11/87.

*** Satisfaction Guaranteed
Alligator ALCD 4799 Brooks; Tom Giblin (kb); Ronnie Baker Brooks (g, v); Augustus Taylor (b); Kevin Mitchell (d); Koko Taylor (v). 91.

Hot Shot found Brooks with a new band, but by the time he came to make *Wound Up Tight* he had another. The album opens with a fleet Chuck Berry-styled 'Got Lucky Last Night', one of two tracks with guitar cameos by Johnny Winter, and continues to live up to its title until the penultimate track, 'Skid Row', when Brooks suddenly relaxes into a wry Lowell Fulson manner. Relaxation isn't a big feature of *Live From Chicago*, which mainly recycles songs from earlier Alligator albums, including two, 'Cold Lonely Nights' and the excellent 'Two Headed Man', from *Living Chicago Blues – Vol. II*. Brooks's mock sermonette before 'Born With The Blues' indicates that if he ever crossed the separating line he would be well qualified as a preacher. On this album, as on the previous couple, the listener may occasionally spot the Koko Taylor Effect, where a naturally rasping voice is made rougher by overuse. Taylor herself appears on *Satisfaction Guaranteed*, skirmishing amiably with Brooks on the closing track, 'The Price Is Right'. Before that, the listener is bounced along on a Big Dipper ride through, in the words of one of the songs, 'a little rock 'n' roll and some country blues', with many shifts of tempo and texture and a welcome dash of self-mockery in the macho stance of 'A Man's Got To Do What A Man's Got To Do' and 'Wife For Tonight'.

*** Roadhouse Rules
Alligator ALCD 4843 Brooks; Wayne Jackson, Scott Thompson (t); Andrew Love, Lonnie McMillan Jr (ts); Sugar Blue (h); Ernest Williamson (kb); Ronnie Baker Brooks (g); David Smith (b); Steve Potts (d); Jim Gaines (prod). 96.

By this point a faint whiff of formula had begun to hang about Brooks's albums. There would be a slow soul number, a strutting macho number, a don't-forget-I'm-from-Louisiana number ... and here are 'Too Little, Too Late', 'Rockin' Red Rooster' and 'Hoodoo She Do' to fill those slots. But as formulas go it's a roomy one, and it hasn't prevented the admission of unexpected items like 'Roll Of The Tumbling Dice', played on acoustic guitar with Sugar Blue on harmonica, a delightfully pastoral interlude between the rock-heavy 'Evil Twin' and 'One Track Train'.

*** DeLuxe Edition
Alligator ALCD 5602 As for previous seven Alligator CDs. 79–96.

A selection from Brooks's Alligator catalogue. It can't be faulted for balance, since there are two tracks from each album and a third from *Hot Shot*, but from the point of view of this survey it's thoroughly perverse, because it ignores virtually every track that has been commended here.

*** Lone Star Shootout
Alligator ALCD 4866 Brooks; Gary Slechta, Frank Vert (t); Randy Zimmerman (tb); Mark 'Kaz' Kazanoff (as, ts, bs, h, arr); Les Izmore (ts); Red Rails, John Mills, Dr Ernest Youngblood Jr (bs); Riley Osbourn (o, p); Marcia Ball (p); Long John Hunter, Phillip Walker (g, v); Derek O'Brien (g); Larry Fulcher (b); Frosty Smith (d, perc); John 'Mambo' Tranor (rb). 99.

Brooks's share of this eight-hander with Ervin Charles, Long John Hunter and Phillip Walker is to take some or all of the vocal on four tracks and play lead or rhythm on those and four others. Most of his vocal numbers are throwbacks to '50s south Louisiana, 'Feel Good Doin' Bad' an exercise in the manner of Lightnin' Slim, 'You're Playing Hooky' a Lonesome Sundown composition, and 'This Should Go On Forever' a prototypical swamp-pop ballad. His performances are okay, but a full album is overdue. TR

Big Bill Broonzy (1893–1958)
VOCAL, GUITAR, VIOLIN

An alternative birthdate of 1898 seems unlikely in the light of recent research by Robert Riesman; Scott, Mississippi, was the place. William Broonzy grew up in Arkansas, and his first instrument was the violin, but after migrating to Chicago around 1920 he learned guitar; by the time he recorded, his polished, swinging and resonant accompaniments were as unmistakable as his flexible, hollering vocals. Besides making many records, Big Bill was a busy session guitarist, a prolific songwriter and a talent scout. His 'race' records embody the blues' transition from South to North, and from folk music to mass entertainment, but when African-American tastes changed after World War II Broonzy successfully switched his focus to the growing white audience at home and in Europe, where he was much admired. His latterday concerts and recordings were a significant influence on white folk and blues guitarists, but after Broonzy's death his reputation suffered a temporary decline, as his place was filled by artists perceived to be more authentic.

(**(*)) Big Bill Broonzy Vol. 1 (1927–1932)
Document DOCD-5050 Broonzy; Georgia Tom Dorsey (p, sp); Steele Smith (bj, v, sp); Frank Brasswell (g, v, sp); John Thomas (g, sp); prob. Arthur Petties (g); poss. J. Mayo Williams (sp). c. 11/27–2/32.

**(*) Big Bill Broonzy Vol. 1 1927–1930
Masters Of Jazz MJCD 51 As above, except Dorsey also sings; omit Smith, Petties. 11/27–4/30.

BIG BILL BROONZY

**(*) Big Bill Broonzy Vol. 2 1930
Masters Of Jazz MJCD 56 *As above, except add 'Bill Williams' [Arthur Petties] (g, v), 'Hannah May' [Mozelle Alderson] (v).* 4/30–9/30.

**(*) Big Bill Broonzy Vol. 3 1930
Masters Of Jazz MJCD 66 *As above, except Petties also plays perc; Alderson also as 'Jane Lucas'.* 9–11/30.

**(*) Big Bill Broonzy Vol. 4 1930–1932
Masters Of Jazz MJCD 96 *As above, except add Steele Smith (bj, v, sp); omit Petties.* 11/30–3/32.

**(*) Big Bill Broonzy Vol. 2 (1932–1934)
Document DOCD-5051 *Broonzy; unknown (t); prob. Black Bob, unknown (p); Steele Smith (bj, v); poss. Teddy Edwards (bj); unknown (b); Jimmy Bertrand (wb); unknown (k); unknown (j).* 2/32–10/34.

**(*) Big Bill Broonzy Vol. 5 1932–1934
Masters Of Jazz MJCD 109 *As above, except add Roy Palmer (tb), Darnell Howard (cl), Ed Hudson (bj, v), Buddy Burton (wb); omit Smith.* 3/32–10/34.

*** Big Bill Broonzy Vol. 3 (1934–1935)
Document DOCD-5052 *Broonzy; Jazz Gillum (h, v); Black Bob (p, prob. sp); unknown (p); Zeb Wright (vn); Carl Martin (g, v); poss. Teddy Edwards, Louis Lasky (g); poss. Bill Settles (b); unknown (train wh); unknown (v).* 10/34–7/35.

**(*) Big Bill Broonzy Vol. 6 1934–1935
Masters Of Jazz MJCD 132 *As above, except add Teddy Edwards (bj, v), Irene Sanders (v), unknown (k); omit Black Bob (sp), Wright, Lasky, train wh.* 10/34–1/35.

*** Big Bill Broonzy Vol. 7 1935 [sic]
Masters Of Jazz MJCD 172 *Broonzy; Jazz Gillum (h, v); Cripple Clarence Lofton (p, v); Black Bob (p, prob. sp); unknown (p); Zeb Wright (vn); Carl Martin (g, v); Louis Lasky (g); poss. Bill Settles (b); Washboard Sam (wb, v); Bumble Bee Slim, unknowns (v); unknown (train wh).* 6/34–7/35.

*** Big Bill Broonzy Vol. 4 (1935–1936)
Document DOCD-5126 *Broonzy; Black Bob (p); Louis Lasky, Casey Bill Weldon (g, v); Bill Settles (b); Washboard Sam (wb, v); unknown (v).* 7/35–4/36.

**(*) Big Bill Broonzy Vol. 5 (1936–1937)
Document DOCD-5127 *Broonzy; 'Mr Sheiks', unknown (t); Arnett Nelson (cl); Black Bob (p); Charlie McCoy (md); Casey Bill Weldon (g, v); George Barnes, unknowns (g); Bill Settles, unknowns (b); poss. Fred Williams (d); unknowns (perc); Washboard Sam (v).* 5/36–1/37.

**(*) Big Bill Broonzy Vol. 6 (1937)
Document DOCD-5128 *Broonzy; 'Mr Sheiks', Alfred Bell, poss. Punch Miller (t); Black Bob, Aletha Robinson, Blind John Davis (p); unknowns (g); Bill Settles, unknowns (b); Fred Williams (d); unknown (perc); Washboard Sam (wb, v).* 1–10/37.

*** Big Bill Broonzy Vol. 7 (1937–1938)
Document DOCD-5129 *Broonzy; Punch Miller, prob. 'Mr Sheiks' (t); prob. Bill Owsley (cl, ts); prob. Buster Bennett (as); prob. Bill Osborn or Bill Austin (ts); Blind John Davis, Joshua Altheimer (p); George Barnes, unknown (g); Bill Settles, Oliver Hudson or Oliver Nelson, prob. Wilbur Ware, unknowns (b); Fred Williams (d).* 10/37–9/38.

**(*) Big Bill Broonzy Vol. 8 (1938–1939)
Document DOCD-5130 *Broonzy; prob. 'Mr Sheiks', unknown (t); Buster Bennett (as); Blind John Davis, Joshua Altheimer, Albert Ammons (p); unknowns (g); prob. Wilbur Ware, Ransom Knowling, unknowns (b); Fred Williams (d).* 9/38–12/39.

*** Big Bill Broonzy Vol. 9 (1939)
Document DOCD-5131 *Broonzy; Odell Rand (cl); Joshua Altheimer (p); Ransom Knowling (b); Fred Williams (d).* 5/39–12/39.

*** Big Bill Broonzy Vol. 10 (1940)
Document DOCD-5132 *Broonzy; Joshua Altheimer, Blind John Davis, Memphis Slim (p); Ransom Knowling (b); Fred Williams (d); Washboard Sam (wb).* 1–12/40.

*** Big Bill Broonzy Vol. 11 (1940–1942)
Document DOCD-5133 *Broonzy; Punch Miller (t); Buster Bennett (as); Jazz Gillum (h); Memphis Slim (p, sp); Horace Malcolm, Blind John Davis (p); Ransom Knowling, unknown (b); Judge Riley (d); Washboard Sam (wb, sp).* 12/40–3/42.

***(*) Big Bill Broonzy Vol. 12 (1945–1947)
Document BDCD-6047 *Broonzy; Johnny Morton (t); Buster Bennett, Sax Mallard (as); Don Byas, Bill Casimir (ts); Kenny Watts, Big Maceo, Charles Belcher, Memphis Slim, Bob Call (p); John Levy, Ransom Knowling, unknown (b); Slick Jones, Tyrell Dixon, Judge Riley (d).* 2/45–12/47.

(***(*)) Play Your Hand
Arpeggio ARB 009 *As above.* 2/45–12/47.

Twelve-bar blues came to dominate Big Bill's 'race' recordings, but his early sessions included numerous fast, ragtimey stomps and shuffles, especially when he played as a member of the Famous Hokum Boys. This group has its own entry, but its members also infiltrate this discussion via the first four Masters Of Jazz CDs. This series aims to reissue all sides on which Broonzy played, whether as name artist or accompanist, and the seven discs so far issued only make it as far as 1935. Especially on earlier volumes, the rarity of some source discs makes for wildly variable sound quality. These CDs are valuable study aids, but self-evidently they're aimed at completists; for example, *Vol. 7* – which is in effect a pleasant VAC, and at present the only place to find Washboard Sam's first 78 – dodges back to 1934 to pick up two Jazz Gillum sides not available when *Vol. 5* was compiled.

Document's 12 volumes of Broonzy the name artist are also marketed to dedicated collectors, and again the first three include some very battered originals; *Vol. 1* seems additionally to be the victim of incompetent remastering. There is some wonderfully lively music among these early tracks, though: notable on *Vol. 1* are 'House Rent Stomp' and 'Brown Skin Shuffle', and on *Vol. 2*, the bravura flatpicking displays 'Mistreatin' Mama Blues' and 'How You Want It Done?' *Vol. 2* marks various transitions: its first track is a farewell to hokum, and it includes Broonzy's last solo recordings until 1951; as blues becomes dominant in his music, so for several years does the piano–guitar combination. *Vol. 3* is interestingly varied, however, including the storming 'C & A Blues', with Louis Lasky, and two takes of 'C.C. Rider', featuring Bill's vigorous, countrified fiddling; he also saws away on three of eight tracks by the State Street Boys, a studio-created stringband.

Vol. 4 begins with two spirituals from the Chicago Sanctified Singers, but by this time Broonzy has settled into being a blues singer with a busy recording schedule. Particularly at slower tempos, he often recycles melodies and guitar figures, but his creativity as a musician and lyricist is such that his reworkings are more listenable than those of many artists similarly cursed with popularity. It helps, too, that most tracks on *Vol. 4* feature Black Bob's sparkling amalgam of blues and stride. 'Mountain Blues' puts new words to the tune of 'C & A Blues', for instance, but guitar and piano intertwine like copulating snakes. Midway through the CD, Bill leaves Bluebird for ARC, who seem to have preferred medium tempos, perhaps in the interest of product recognition. These first ARC recordings are consistently professional, though, and 'Big Bill Blues' is a gem of a signature piece; its rewriting as 'Pneumonia Blues', eight tracks and two months later, is a good example of Bill's ingenious reprocessing.

The sound on *Vol. 5* is frequently lifeless, and not helped by the use of some worn 78s, but it includes an introspective 'Lowland Blues' with Charlie McCoy's mandolin, a breezy 'Detroit Special' and an altogether magnificent 'Southern Flood Blues'. Alas, on the next track the inaccurate, unassertive 'Mr. Sheiks' (believed, but not proven, to be Alfred Bell) debuts on trumpet, signalling the start of a period during which Broonzy's producers made sporadic and variably successful attempts to hitch his wagon to the Harlem Hamfats' star. Bell is a bit better on *Vol. 6*, and seems to have taken his medication before two takes of the romping 'You Do Me Any Old Way'. About half of *Vol. 6* consists of alternative takes, among them four versions of 'Come Home Early', cut at two sessions; this makes it hard going for listeners who just want to be entertained. Black Bob bows out in the course of this disc; his deps are proficient, but have markedly less flair.

Even before Joshua Altheimer adds his sturdy, rolling pianistics to the mix, there's a sense on *Vol. 7* that Broonzy's work is coming out of a trough. This may be an artefact of fewer alternative takes and better sound, but Bill's bass-string runs on 'I Need You By My Side', and the way they stimulate John Davis, suggest otherwise. At sessions in March and May 1938 Broonzy only sang, and George Barnes plays ornately progressive electric guitar on six tracks. Add four titles featuring a showy Punch Miller and a lively session (concluded on *Vol. 8*) with a Hamfats-like 'Memphis Five', and this is one of Document's better self-compilers. The rest of the songs on *Vol. 8* are turned out with production-line efficiency, but despite varied personnels and plenty of witty lyrics – 'Baby I Done Got Wise' and 'Just A Dream' stand out – the disc lacks focus.

It's hard to understand why Odell Rand's work on the first nine tracks of *Vol. 9* has had a poor press; he's much less self-indulgent than usual, is obviously listening to what Bill and Josh are doing, and like them is chivvied along by Ransom Knowling. Otherwise, this disc and the first half of *Vol. 10* are showcases for the Broonzy–Altheimer partnership. The combination of Bill's (occasionally amplified) guitar with Josh's melodic resourcefulness and command of dynamics is a winning one, albeit not much helped by Fred Williams's unsubtle thumping. There's some wonderful singing on *Vol. 10*, too; Bill is out of his skin on 'Make My Getaway', and 'Midnight Steppers', with washboard, is party music incarnate. It's also part of Altheimer's last session before his early death, and although Blind John Davis is an adequate stand-in, the loss is a severe one. Memphis Slim, who turns up at the end of *Vol. 10*, has more to do on *Vol. 11*, which takes matters up to the 1943 recording ban. Slim's ringing treble and rumbling left hand are a fine match for Broonzy on 11 tracks; elsewhere Horace Malcolm and Davis do good work. Bill's singing continues to be inspired at times: 'When I Been Drinking' (with Malcolm), 'All By Myself' (with Slim) and 'I Feel So Good' (with Davis) are the essence of *joie de vivre*, and the gentle 'Key To The Highway', a one-off with harmonica and no piano, is deservedly famous.

Document's last volume (of which *Play Your Hand* is a copy) picks up when recording resumed after World War II. Four titles with the Don Byas Quartet make for an uneasy start, but thereafter Broonzy engages very successfully with the polished but hard-hitting brass- and reed-led jump blues that held sway in Chicago before guitar bands became dominant. His singing, songwriting and playing are as vibrant as ever, but a two-year layoff after these sessions suggests that they didn't find favour with the public.

**(*) Big Bill Broonzy 1949–1951
Classics 5078 *Broonzy; Antonio Casey (as); Carl Sharp (p); Ransom Knowling (b); Alfred Wallace (d). 1/49–9/51.*

(***) Big Bill Broonzy 1951 [sic]
Classics 5101 *As above, except add Sax Mallard (as), Bill Casimir (ts), prob. Memphis Slim (p), Ransom Knowling, poss. Big Crawford (b), Judge Riley (d). 1/49–12/51.*

*** Big Bill Broonzy 1951–1952
Classics 5124 *Broonzy; Blind John Davis (p); prob. Big Crawford (b). 12/51–3/52.*

*** The Complete Vogue Recordings
Sony/BMG 43512 3CD *Broonzy; Blind John Davis (p). 9/51–3/52.*

Classics seize the baton of chronology from Document, but omit alternative takes; a 1949 title first issued on CD was omitted from Classics' first disc, and appears as a footnote to the second. These discs mark the point where Broonzy began switching his attention from black record-buyers to white. On 1949–1951, eight sides for Mercury are followed by 12 recorded in France during his first European visit. The Mercury songs are performed with his habitual verve; on Vogue, Broonzy attempts to meet the perceived requirements of his new audience, and the pleasure of lively numbers like 'House Rent Stomp' and 'What I Used To Do' is counteracted by others where he slows down, applies excessive vocal melisma and plays elaborate guitar flourishes.

1951 is also transitional; it mops up that year's Vogue sessions and segues into tracks cut for Mercury via four sides recorded in London for Melodisc. A fine 'John Henry' apart, the Paris recordings are short of sparkle, in part because of the original engineering; the Melodiscs are more consistently lively, but surface noise sometimes obtrudes. The sound improves mightily when Classics reach the Mercury sessions, copied from digitally remastered sources. Ten sides with acoustic guitar get a lift from the bassists, and four with Sax Mallard's rocking little band are as fine an R&B session as Broonzy ever cut. Frustratingly, though, space limitations mean that the final six Mercury songs are held over to the next volume.

On the other hand, they're all in Bill's acoustic 'folk-blues' vein, and consort comfortably with the Paris recordings which supply the rest of 1951–1952: a 2/52 concert, with John Davis playing on three numbers, and a studio session the following month. Vogue's sound is much better than it was the year before, but at the Salle Pleyel poor microphone placement does the musicians no favours. Broonzy overdoes the portentousness on the concert's slower numbers, but elsewhere strikes a better balance between being a dignified representative of his race and a wisecracking charmer. 'Kind Hearted Blues' appears to be new to Bill's recorded repertoire, and is a quality piece of writing by a still creative composer and wordsmith.

Sony's recension of the Paris Vogue recordings includes nine alternative takes omitted by Classics; they are not revelatory and their consignment to a separate third CD is a sensible move. The aesthetic and musical advantages and drawbacks of these sessions have been discussed above; it remains only to add that the remastered sound of the 1951 material is significantly better than on Classics, and indeed than on previous legitimate releases. The Salle Pleyel concert still suffers from the original poor engineering and room echo, though, and an American compère's announcements fail to add period charm to the occasion.

*** **All The Classic Sides 1928–1937** [sic]
JSP JSP 7718 5CD *Similar to relevant CDs above.* c. 11/27–1/37.
*** **Big Bill Broonzy Part 2 1937–1940**
JSP JSP 7750 4CD *Similar to relevant CDs above.* 1/37–4/40.

JSP's box sets, with 127 and 101 tracks respectively, are a sort of Document-lite survey of Broonzy's early career as a name artist (mostly; some sides by the Famous Hokum Boys, the State Street Boys and other studio groups are also included). Both volumes are nicely presented, with discographical data and good notes, which admit that not all the sides are classics, and they're inexpensive. The sound on the first set is as variable as Document's, though, and seldom much better. For JSP, as for Document, this is in part a consequence of the unavoidable use of rare and worn 78s for the earlier tracks, but it's hard to know to whom this set can be commended without caveats: fanatical collectors will still have to go to Document, and more casual listeners may feel that *All The Classic Sides* proffers both a surfeit of tracks and a deficiency of good sound. Credit where it's due, however; Disc B includes by far the least worst reissue of the Big Bill & His Jug Busters coupling.

The sound on *Big Bill Broonzy Part 2*, though not brilliant, achieves a livelier ambience than Document's, and is more consistent, thanks in large part to the more general availability of source discs. Most readers will find that this collection offers adequate coverage of a time when Broonzy was feeding ARC's remorseless demand for product. Even his flair and inventiveness can't overcome an intermittent sense that he was being over-recorded, though, and some of his accompanists are journeymen. The numerous alternative takes – 26 tracks, but only 15 songs – on Disc A of this box may intimidate some listeners.

*** **Big Bill Blues**
Wolf BC 006 *Similar to relevant CDs above.* c. 11/27–3/42.
** **Big Bill Blues**
Fabulous FABCD 101 *Similar to relevant CDs above.*
c. 11/27–3/45.
***(*) **The Young Big Bill Broonzy**
Yazoo 1011 *Similar to relevant CDs above.* c. 10/28–10/35.
***(*) **Do That Guitar Rag**
Yazoo 1035 *Similar to relevant CDs above.* c. 10/28–6/35.
***(*) **Can't Be Satisfied**
Snapper Complete Blues SBLUECD 006 *Similar to relevant CDs above.* c. 10/28–5/41.
***(*) **I Can't Be Satisfied**
Collectors Edition CBCD 005 *Similar to relevant CDs above.* 4/30–9/38.
***(*) **Big Bill Blues**
Aim 0027 *Similar to relevant CDs above.* 4/30–9/38.

*** **Good Time Tonight**
Columbia CK 46219 *Similar to relevant CDs above.* 4/30–4/40.
**** **Warm, Witty & Wise**
Columbia/Legacy CK 65517 *Similar to relevant CDs above.* 4/30–5/41.
(***) **The Essential**
Classic Blues CBL 200002 2CD *Similar to relevant CDs above, except add Roosevelt Sykes, prob. Myrtle Jenkins (p), Alfred Elkins (b), Lil Johnson, St Louis Jimmy [Oden] (v).* 4/30–1/47.
(**(*)) **Where The Blues Began**
Snapper Recall SMDCD 248 2CD *Similar to relevant CDs above.* 4/30–1/49.
***(*) **Mississippi River Blues**
Past Perfect 204388 *Similar to relevant CDs above.* 3/32–9/38.
**** **Big Bill Broonzy**
Topaz TPZ 1038 *Similar to relevant CDs above.* 3/32–3/42.
(****) **Kings Of The Blues: Big Bill Broonzy**
Pulse PLSCD 684 *Similar to relevant CDs above.* 3/32–3/42.
***(*) **The Godfather Of Chicago Blues**
Saga Blues 982 117–0 *Similar to relevant CDs above.* 3/32–11/51.
(*) **Chicago Calling
[Blue Boar CDBB 1015] *Similar to relevant CDs above.* 2/35–7/41.
***(*) **Chicago 1937–1945**
Frémeaux FA 252 2CD *Similar to relevant CDs above.* 10/37–2/45.
***(*) **The Post War Years 1945/1949**
EPM Blues Collection 15967 *Similar to relevant CDs above.* 2/45–2/49.

The so-called 'blues revival' which began soon after Broonzy's death coincided with, and to some degree caused, an outbreak of indifference to his later music. This generated an assumption that his early records were not worth investigating, and it was some time before they were reissued in any quantity. That was an over-reaction; so, perhaps, is the plethora of selective surveys encouraged by reassessment, the expiry of copyrights and easy digital copying.

The Young Big Bill Broonzy, which started the critical tide turning, still has much to commend it; like *Do That Guitar Rag*, it concentrates on the early years, stressing Broonzy's prowess as a player of rags, hokum and fast blues. The Yazoo CDs remain very enjoyable, despite short playing time and remastering that was once state of the art and is now merely good.

Of three CDs imaginatively titled *Big Bill Blues*, that on Fabulous is ruled out by mastering that ranges from barely adequate to dreadful; 'Just A Dream', said to be from 1939, is a listless 1945 version with Don Byas. Aim's selection is shorter but better listening; the material probably derives from Collectors Edition (see below), and has been subjected to Aim's habitual bass-boosting, for once advantageously. The CD is devalued by some errors in the notes, and the absence of discographical details. These flaws also affect the Wolf collection (not surprisingly, since much of the booklet is recycled from Aim). Wolf's claim to reissue 'his 23 greatest songs' is a marketing ploy; many substitutions could be suggested (no 'C & A Blues', no ' Southern Flood', no 'All By Myself'?), but this is an entertaining set, although the problem of getting consistent sound out of variably clean originals has not been entirely solved.

This is not an issue for Columbia, working from metal parts. *Good Time Tonight* was supposedly replaced by *Warm, Witty & Wise* (with which it shares seven titles), but appears to be still available. Though shorter, the latter compilation is superior because it contains most of the greatest hits that once comprised a long-ago, near-platonic LP. *Good Time Tonight* may have been conceived as an unacknowledged sequel to that album, but some of its tracks come from sessions where Bill was feeding the machine. *The Godfather Of Chicago Blues* is split into Saga's customary two chapters: *Bronzeville Poet* and *Blues News*. 'Cotton Choppin' Blues' is sexual rather than topical, and 'Just A Dream' is the desultory 1945 remake, but otherwise this is a very good selection from Bill's post-Depression recordings for his African-American audience, with commendable variety in the instrumental lineups. Happily, the 'poetic' sides also feature a generous helping of jumping dance rhythms.

Of the three 2CDs, Snapper's is well selected and annotated but for the most part poorly remastered. Classic Blues have better but not brilliant sound, and include a few tracks that give an impression of Broonzy's work as an accompanist, but the notes are telegraphic and abandoning chronological order produces no fresh insights; rather the reverse, if anything. Frémeaux focus more narrowly. The sound quality of *Chicago 1937–1945* is acceptable rather than outstanding, but the programming is judicious and the notes thoughtful; it adds up to an enjoyable portrait of Broonzy in his heyday as the kingpin of Chicago blues.

EPM's postwar collection has useful notes and decent sound. A companion volume, *In Chicago 1932/1937* (EPM 15742), is deleted. The content of *1945/1949* is jump blues, from the period covered by Document's last volume and the first part of its successor on Classics.

I Can't Be Satisfied is sonically better than many Magnum Group productions. Its 18 tracks may supply Aim's 17 (see above); they clearly do supply the 16 on *Mississippi River Blues*, where the artwork copies Collectors Edition's mistitling of 'Big Billy Blues' and its misdating to 1946. Topaz's eponymous disc is superior to either of these, however, thanks to longer playing time, livelier sound and more extensive notes. *Can't Be Satisfied*, not to be confused with the similarly titled Collectors Edition, has generally good if sometimes rather bright sound, and its 20 tracks are sensibly chosen and adeptly programmed for contrast. The transfers on Pulse are notably good, thanks to copying from the deleted *I Feel So Good* (Indigo IGOCD 2006); the notes' brevity goes with a bargain price. The sound on Blue Boar is more variable, 'How You Want It Done?' is misidentified as 'C & A Blues' and there's too much Odell Rand.

**(*) In Concert With Graeme Bell & His Australian Jazz Band

Jasmine JASMCD 3007 *Broonzy; Roger Bell (t, v); Pixie Roberts (cl); Adrian Monsbourgh (as, v); Graeme Bell (p); Bud Baker (bj, g); Lou Silbereisen (tu, b); Johnny Sangster (d). 9/51.*

The concert happened in Düsseldorf, and five of the 23 tracks are announcements in German; Broonzy performs alone on four of the balance, is accompanied by the Antipodean Dixielanders on three, and has a walk-on part in the closing 'Saints'. The solo numbers are pretty good, but plenty of equally good versions are available. Monsbourgh's aimless alto undercuts 'I Feel So Good' and 'Who's Sorry Now', and 'Mama Don't Allow' was already tiresome by 1951.

**(*) Treat Me Right
Tradition TCD 1005 *Broonzy. 9/51–6/56.*

**(*) Baby Please Don't Go
Drive Archive DE2-41041 *Broonzy. 9/51–6/56.*

*** Absolutely The Best
Fuel 2000 302 061 090 *Broonzy. 9/51–6/56.*

*** Blues Is My Business
Fuel 2000 302 061 362 *Broonzy. 9/51–6/56.*

**(*) Big Bill Broonzy
Members Edition UAE 30262 *Broonzy. 9/51–57.*

**(*) St-Louis Blues
Collectors Edition CBCD 009 *Broonzy; Pete Seeger (bj). 9/51–57.*

The basis of all these discs is an LP which combined tracks recorded in Paris and Milan. Tradition and Drive Archive reissue the LP unaugmented, the latter company having markedly better remastering skills. The running time is only 35 minutes, but the programming offers attractive contrasts of mood and tempo. The mix of well-known blues, instrumental display pieces and pop songs is typical of Broonzy's latterday playlist; the absence of blues-ballads and protest songs is not. An overlong, over-dramatized 'Backwater Blues' (a.k.a. 'I Got Up One Mornin' Blues' on some issues) will try some listeners' patience. *Absolutely The Best* reorders the LP tracks, without making much difference to their impact, but the remastering is superior. The playing time is boosted by five up-tempo numbers from Storyville (see below), with the spoken introductions and audience applause savagely edited out. *Blues Is My Business* is *Absolutely The Best* with two extra tracks.

Members Edition tack on seven tracks from *Sings Folk Songs* (see below), among them a second 'Backwater Blues'. Sound quality is okay, but the notes are scattershot and unreliable. *St-Louis Blues* mixes seven tracks from the European sessions with most of *Sings Folk Songs*. Musically it's not a bad combination, but the notes are inaccurate about both broader trends and specific details.

(***) Remembering Big Bill Broonzy
BGO BGOCD 91 *Broonzy; Sax Mallard (as); Bill Casimir (ts); prob. Memphis Slim (p); Ransom Knowling, poss. Big Crawford (b); Judge Riley (d). 11–12/51.*

BGO reissue an 11-track Mercury LP; ten numbers are accompanied by acoustic guitar and bass, plus piano on 'Hollerin' The Blues', and one features Sax Mallard's band. The material is lively, but the playing time is very short. Between them Classics' *Big Bill Broonzy 1951* and *1951–1952*, discussed above, contain the complete 1951 sessions, but if it can be found the deleted *Black Brown & White* (Mercury 842 743) has them on one disc, and generously adds a track by Mallard's band without Broonzy.

**(*) Great Bluesmen In Britain
Avid AMSC 736 *Broonzy. spring 52.*

The six tracks on *Great Bluesmen* (which is shared with Josh White and Sonny Terry & Brownie McGhee) were recorded at a party, probably post-concert. Broonzy's voice certainly sounds tired and cigarette-roughened, and his intermittent cough is distracting. An instrumental version of 'Careless Love' generates a mighty swing, but there are better versions of all the other numbers available elsewhere.

**(*) On Tour In Britain, 1952
Jasmine JASMCD 3011/2 2CD *Broonzy; Dicky Hawdon (t); Keith Christie (tb); Ian Christie (cl); Pat Hawes (p); Nevil Skrimshire*

(g); Denny Coffey (b); Peter Appleby (d); Derrick Stewart-Baxter (interviewer). 2–12/52.

One of the defining qualities of Broonzy's late period is repetition; he was concertizing and recording before television became ubiquitous, and when the few blues LPs that existed were made expensive (in Europe, at least) by import duties. The value of Broonzy's recordings is therefore often dependent on the context in which he does the same thing over and over. This double CD contains concerts from opposite ends of both 1952 and Britain. There was a lot of whisky consumed backstage in Edinburgh, and although this doesn't affect Bill's playing and singing, it does lead him to over-emphasize slow numbers at the start of the gig, and throughout to supply long, rambling, disjointed commentaries. He's much more focused and alert in Hove, the concert is better programmed and the band accompanies two numbers enthusiastically; but weak and/or duplicated numbers, and the extensive non-musical content, make this a set for completists.

*** Black Brown & White
Evidence ECD 26062 *Broonzy; Blind John Davis (p).* 3/52–11/55.

Seven tracks from a concert in Antwerp, with Davis playing on four, are followed by six recorded at the Brussels home of Yannick Bruynoghe, who edited Broonzy's letters into his autobiography *Big Bill Blues*. Davis cajoles an inferior piano into expressiveness, adding new life to some familiar numbers; his meditative contributions to 'Lowland Blues' are notable. The home recordings (in fine sound) include a lively 'Nobody's Business', a powerful 'Texas Tornado' and a brief, charming 'Pretty Little Baby'.

*** Pye Blues Legends In London
Castle CMETD 562//Sanctuary CAS 36167 3CD *Broonzy; Leslie Hutchinson (t); Bruce Turner (as); 'Fred Hartz' [Kenny Graham] (ts); Benny Green (bs); Dill Jones (p): Jack Fallon (b); Phil Seamen (d); unknown (wh).* 10/55.

Two relaxed collaborations with British modernists are fairly successful; the fun continues when the band and friends constitute a 'live in studio' audience for another two songs, but the off-mike, off-key whistling by a band member towards the end of 'In The Evening' is irritating. 'Glory Of Love' and 'St. Louis Blues' get their usual swinging treatments, and 'Joe Turner Blues' features his party piece: using the guitar's tuning pegs to play the instrumental break. More surprisingly, Broonzy successfully transfers three numbers from his postwar R&B days to an acoustic solo format. Other CDs in this box are by Josh White and Terry & McGhee.

***(*) An Evening With Big Bill Broonzy Vol. 1
Storyville STCD 8016 *Broonzy.* 5/56.
***(*) An Evening With Big Bill Broonzy Vol. 2
Storyville STCD 8017 *Broonzy.* 5/56.

The recording quality is variable, and the flatpicking on 'John Henry' less spectacular than usual, but these two discs, recorded in a Copenhagen club over three nights, paint a thorough portrait of Broonzy's folk-blues repertoire, and of his ability to amuse, charm and instruct an audience. 'Big Bill Talks' (mainly about other active blues singers) is a handy corrective to the notion that he promoted himself as the last of the breed.

*** Big Bill Broonzy Sings Folk Songs
Smithsonian Folkways SF 40023 *Broonzy; Pete Seeger (bj, v).* 10/56–57.
**** Trouble In Mind
Smithsonian Folkways SFW CD 40131 *As above, except add Studs Terkel (interviewer).* 10/56–5/57.

Trouble In Mind is selected from Broonzy's Folkways recordings. Excellently engineered and adroitly sequenced, it's the best collection of his late-period music. There's plenty of passion and zest here: the surprising and very fine jazz singing on 'When Will I Get To Be Called A Man' is not the only instance of a deeper than usual involvement with the material. A live 'This Train', with Seeger, is the only item from *Sings Folk Songs* included on *Trouble In Mind*; *Sings Folk Songs*' tracks are individually acceptable, but collectively sound like the outcome of scratching around for material to fill an LP.

** Trouble In Mind
Spotlite SPJ-CD 900 *Broonzy; Norman Barnicle (g, prob. v).* 3/57.
** The Historic Concert Recordings
Southland SCD-20 *As above.* 3/57.

These CDs draw on tapes of a concert and party in Nottingham, England. Their tracklistings are slightly different, but mediocre recording quality and Broonzy's tiredness render them both superfluous. A local musician sits in on a concluding 'Goodnight, Irene', to no positive effect. CS

Angela Brown (born 1953)
VOCAL

Brown sang in church in her native Chicago, studied drama in college and took up blues singing after portraying both Bessie Smith and Ma Rainey on stage. She commands a loyal European audience.

**(*) The Voice Of Blues
Chrisly CR 60001 *Brown; Katie Webster (o, v); Erwin Helfer (p).* 11/87.

Brown makes an uneven debut with a set of older songs, many of them associated with Bessie Smith, plus a sprinkling of R&B. Helfer's restrained elegance is appropriate to the vintage material, but he doesn't bring enough energy to the likes of 'Stagger Lee'. Brown has a battery of blues techniques but applies them arbitrarily, veering abruptly from kittenish camp to a growl that's supposed to be raunchy and isn't. Katie Webster is added on the closing gospel song.

** Rod Mason's Hot Five Featuring Angela Brown
Timeless CDTTD 563 *Brown; Rod Mason (c, as, v); Joe Wulf (tb, v); Paul Harrison (cl); Jörg Kuhfuss (bss, tu); Ralf-Michael Peyer (p); Udo Jägers (bj, g).* 8/90.

Mason's band plays what might be called cruise-ship trad: pleasant, deliberately uncreative homage to the greats. Brown's five guest vocals fit in, but don't make this CD necessary.

*** Wild Turkey
Acoustic Music AMC 1017 *Brown; Christian Christl (p).* 1/91.
**(*) Live
Acoustic Music 319.1038 *Brown; Gary Wiggins (ts); Reggie Moore (p); Earl Bostic (b).* 6/93.

** If I Hadn't'a Been High
Slow Motion 3391212 *Brown; Thomas Feldmann (h); Wolfgang Roggenkamp (o, d); Christian Rannenberg (p); Todor Todorovic (g, v); Josef Kappl (b); Harriet Lewis, Gina Dunn, Lee Brown (v). 7–8/95.*

Things come right on *Wild Turkey*; Brown's singing is consistently powerful without being mannered, and well matched by Christl's muscular piano. The programme is varied and interesting, ranging from 'St. Louis Blues' (a long, remarkably engaged interpretation) to 'Miss Celie's Blues' from *The Color Purple*. 'I'm A Fool' is gospel singing in the majestic mould of Mahalia Jackson, and 'Million Dollar Secret' is over eight minutes long, but not self-indulgent; rather, it's just as long as is needed for Brown to give it the works. Brown has come a long way artistically since *The Voice Of Blues*.

Unfortunately she takes a step back on *Live*, and several more on *If I Hadn't'a Been High*. *Live* opens with another lengthy but much less appealing 'St Louis Blues', a too vulgar to be funny 'Black Drawers' and a detached account of Sippie Wallace's 'Woman Be Wise'. The concluding 'Back Water Blues' is also very long, but tastefully done and never imitative of Bessie Smith; it's preceded by an amusingly vampy 'Rock Around The Clock'. Most of the intervening tracks are jazz treatments of standards ('All Of Me', 'Stormy Weather' and the like); two of them are instrumentals by Wiggins. Their much higher quality is probably an indicator of what Brown and her musicians would rather be doing.

The accompanists on the Slow Motion CD are limited and largely predictable, the consistently coarse, too loud drumming being particularly easy to dislike. Brown works her voice too hard trying to make the performances interesting, and reverts to imposing arbitrary effects on the songs. 'Sunday Kind Of Love' gets a fine, restrained reading, and 'Back Door Hit'cha', accompanied only by Rannenberg, is a successful up-tempo excursion, but there's too much rabble-rousing.

***(*) Thinking Out Loud
Manhaton HATMAN 2002 *Brown; Nick Tidbury (t); Alan Tidbury (tb); James Evans (as, ts, bs, v); Carey Bell (h); Simon Callow (o, p, v); Nigel Bagge (g, v); Michael Coleman, Johnny B. Moore, unknown (g); Russell Brown (b, v); Roger Jones (d); Mike Vernon (perc, v); Willie Dixon (handclaps, v). 9–10/98.*

Thinking Out Loud steers firmly away from vaudeville and over-familiar songs and towards modern soul-blues. British backing band The Mighty 45s know what they're doing as both performers and arrangers, and their fat, horn-laden sound is not outclassed by the Chicago musicians overdubbed here and there. (The late Willie Dixon's duet with Brown is worked up from a demo cassette which he gave her.) *Thinking Out Loud* would have benefited from more textural variety, or from being a couple of tracks shorter; not until the gospel closer does the sound thin out a little, and Dixon's other composition, 'If That's The Way You Like It', proves again that he would have written better songs if they'd come less easily. Nevertheless, this is by some distance Angela Brown's best CD to date. cs

Buster Brown (1914–76)
VOCAL, HARMONICA

Born in Georgia (some sources give a 1911 birthdate), Buster Brown was recorded by the Library of Congress in 1943. He moved to New Jersey not long before recording 'Fannie Mae' for Fire Records. The song spent 25 weeks on the R&B charts, peaking at #1, and 17 weeks in the Pop Top 40. 'Sugar Babe' made #19 in 1962, but further success eluded Brown, and after leaving Fire he drifted from label to label.

**(*) The New King Of The Blues
Collectables COL-5110 *Brown; unknowns (s); Jimmy Spruill, Riff Ruffin, unknown (g); Jimmy Lewis (b); unknown (d); unknowns (v grp). 6/59–61.*

**(*) The Very Best Of Buster Brown
Collectables COL-6445 As above. 6/59–61.

Even in 1959 Buster Brown's downhome harp, falsetto whoops and raucous vocals were oldfashioned; to combine them with saxes and electric guitars was an eccentric gamble, but it paid off handsomely as 'Fannie Mae' and her compulsive, bouncing riff became a runaway hit. Fire attempted to repeat the trick, and the crossover, with bright and breezy updates of numbers from tradition ('John Henry', 'Raise A Ruckus Tonight') and pop ('Blues When It Rains', 'Is You Is Or Is You Ain't My Baby'). In a time of dance crazes there was inevitably a 'Madison Shuffle', and there was even the occasional hardcore blues like 'When Things Go Wrong', but Brown was a limited singer and instrumentalist, further constrained by Bobby Robinson's constant, often inappropriate application of springy rhythms like those which had propelled 'Fannie Mae' to success. The Moonglows' 'Sincerely' taps an unexpected talent for ballads, but it's an island in a sea of relentless, superficial cheeriness. Many readers will find the 22 tracks on *The Very Best Of* too many, and the 16 on *The New King Of The Blues* (which remains in catalogue for the time being) more than enough. A better bet may be to acquire 'Fannie Mae' on *The Collectables Blues Collection Vol. 1* (Collectables COL-5127), and the two intricately played, thoughtfully sung solos that Brown recorded for the Library of Congress; they're on *Deep River Of Song: Georgia* (Rounder CD 1828). cs

Charles Brown (1922–99)
VOCAL, PIANO, CELESTE

Brown was raised in Texas City, Texas, by his grandparents and introduced to the piano by his grandmother. As well as the light classical pieces she approved of, he absorbed blues from local honkytonk players, but his first paid gig was playing supper-club music at the Chicken Shack in LA. He then joined guitarist Johnny Moore's Three Blazers as pianist and vocalist. His intimate singing and the yearning lyric of the group's 1945 disc 'Driftin' Blues' made it a gigantic jukebox hit, guaranteeing him a prolific recording career, first with the Blazers, then in his own name, for several LA labels over the next 15 years. Despite several hits, including the seasonal songs 'Merry Christmas Baby' and 'Please Come Home For Christmas', in the '60s and '70s he could barely make a living from music, but in the last two decades of his life he was feted as an R&B pioneer and enjoyed another long spell in the spotlight.

*** Charles Brown 1944–1945
Classics 894 *Brown; Johnny Moore, Oscar Moore (g); Eddie Williams (b); Johnny Otis (d); Frankie Laine, Johnny McNeil, band (v). 44–9/45.*

**(*) Charles Brown 1946
Classics 971 *Brown; Johnny Moore (g); Eddie Williams (b). 46.*
**(*) Drifting & Dreaming
Ace CDCHD 589 *As above. 46.*
**(*) Charles Brown 1946–1947
Classics 1088 *As above, except add Oscar Moore (g). 46–late 47.*
**(*) Bobby Sox Blues
Collectors Edition CBCD 019 *As above. 46–late 47.*
*** Charles Brown 1947–1948
Classics 1147 *As above. late 47–48.*
*** Snuff Dippin' Mama
Night Train NTICD 7017 *As above. 45–48.*
*** Walkin' In Circles
Night Train NTICD 7024 *As above. 45–48.*
**(*) Charles Brown 1948–1949
Classics 1210 *As above, except add Herman 'Tiny' Mitchell (g), unknown (d); omit Oscar Moore. 11/48–3/49.*
**(*) Charles Brown 1949–1951
Classics 1272 *Brown; Jack McVea (cl); Freddie Simon, prob. Maxwell Davis (ts); Charles Waller (bs); Victor Arno, George Kast, Harry Bluestone, Marshall Sosson, Samuel Cytron, Henri Hill (vn); Herman 'Tiny' Mitchell, Chuck Norris, Jesse Ervin (g); Eddie Williams, Wesley Prince, poss. David Bryant (b); Walter Murden, Lee Young (d). 3/49–2/51.*
*** The Best Of Charles Brown: West Coast Blues
Blues Forever CD 68028 *Brown; Maxwell Davis (ts); Johnny Moore, Oscar Moore, Chuck Norris, Herman 'Tiny' Mitchell, poss. Jesse Ervin (g); Eddie Williams, Wesley Prince, unknown (b); unknowns (d). 45–9/51.*
*** Driftin' Blues, The Best Of Charles Brown
Collectables COL-5631 *Brown; unknown (t); unknown (tb); Freddie Simon, Maxwell Davis, prob. Lee Allen, unknown (ts); Red Tyler (bs); unknowns (s); Ernie Freeman (o); Johnny Moore, Chuck Norris, Jesse Ervin, Justin Adams (g); Eddie Williams, Wesley Prince, poss. David Bryant, Frank Fields (b); Johnny Otis, Walter Murden, prob. Jesse Sailes, Earl Palmer, unknowns (d); unknowns (v). 9/45, 11/48–10/56.*
***(*) The Classic Earliest Recordings
JSP JSP 7707 5CD *Brown; Maxwell Davis (ts); Johnny Moore, Oscar Moore (g); Eddie Williams (b); Johnny Otis, unknowns (d); Frankie Laine, Johnny McNeil, band (v). 44–1/50.*

In the late summer of 1945 Charles Brown recorded 'Driftin' Blues', a moonlight sonata of rootlessness and uncertainty. It was perhaps the first blues hit of the postwar period, and it expanded the language of the blues as dramatically as Leroy Carr's 'How Long – How Long Blues' 17 years earlier. The effect on the artist, however, was quite different. Unlike Carr, Brown was not committed to the blues. When 'Driftin' Blues' arrives on the first Classics CD, almost at the end, it is the first blues we have heard him sing. Despite its success, he did not allow it to direct his career: in his heyday, from the mid-'40s to the mid-'50s, blues was merely one aspect of his work, and not the dominant one. Sometimes he played boogies, or jazzy tunes like 'Be Sharp You'll See', 'Nutmeg' or 'Scratch Sheet', but mostly he sang popular songs, both standards and new pieces. He handled them like a crooner, somewhat in the manner of Nat 'King' Cole or the then popular Cecil Gant, but in a husky whisper redolent of low lights and rumpled sheets.

The instrumental setting, which hardly changed for a decade, was piano, bass and one or two guitars, one of them invariably played by Johnny Moore, the other, when present, almost always by his brother Oscar, who had earlier played with Nat Cole. Polished, even-tempered yet wiry, this combination recalled the piano–guitar sound of Leroy Carr and Scrapper Blackwell only to revise and relax it. To hear how deeply this new orchestration of voice and instruments impressed Brown's contemporaries, we need only turn to contemporary work by Ivory Joe Hunter, Floyd Dixon or, more strikingly still, the young Ray Charles – and, farther afield, Eddie Boyd or Willie Mabon.

Classics take the listener through Brown's first seven years with their customary care. The first two CDs cover sessions for Atlas, Exclusive, Philo and Modern Music. Ace's *Drifting & Dreaming* is devoted to the Modern Music recordings, thus overlapping much of the second Classics CD, and includes two items unissued at the time, 'You Are My First Love' and 'Copyright On Your Love'. It opens on 'Travelin' Blues' but this is no guide to the direction the CD subsequently takes, as Brown essays standards like 'It Had To Be You' or 'How Deep Is The Ocean' and the two-part 'Warsaw Concerto', then popular as the main theme of the war film *Dangerous Moonlight*.

Charles Brown 1946–1947 and *1947–1948* are drawn exclusively from Exclusive. There's a slightly larger proportion of blues, such as 'Snuff Dippin' Mama' and 'Groovy Movie Blues' on *1947–1948*, but they occupy no more than a third of his time, though one of them, 'Merry Christmas Baby' (*1946–1947*), is both his best-known composition and the blues' outstanding seasonal record. *Bobby Sox Blues* is almost the same as *1946–1947* but omits its last three tracks. The Night Train CDs are non-chronological selections from Exclusive, introducing two previously unissued alternative takes, and are admirable samplings for non-completists, so long as they find copies that don't suffer from faulty mastering.

Charles Brown 1948–1949 and *1949–1951* follow him to Aladdin, where a tenor saxophone occasionally thickens the ensemble but the blues quotient dips again, despite the popularity of the minor-key 'Trouble Blues' and Brown's third signature piece, 'Black Night'. Both of these are also on Collectables' *Driftin' Blues, The Best Of Charles Brown*, together with later Aladdin sides like 'Seven Long Days', 'Hard Times', 'Lonesome Feeling' and 'Fool's Paradise', as well as the original 'Driftin' Blues'. Unlike the carefully inclusive compilations described above, this is a blues-focused selection and therefore a good starting-point for readers unsure of their appetite for pop ballads. The Blues Forever CD does much the same job, concentrating on Brown's blues; the omission of some of his better-known numbers is offset by its budget price.

JSP's slipcased set is exhaustive and inexpensive, but not quite complete. Absent are 'It Ain't Gonna Be Like That' and 'With My Heart In My Hand', which are on *Walkin' In Circles*, and the two previously unissued tracks on *Drifting & Dreaming*. 'Homesick Blues' is missing from Disc D, the item playing at track 24 being the later 'I Stumbled Over You', which recurs in its proper place on Disc E. The set reveals the extent of Brown's relationship with the blues in a very clear light: of the 120 tracks, perhaps a fifth are blues or boogies.

** Sings Christmas Songs
King KCD-775 *Brown; unknown (o); unknowns (g); unknowns (b); unknowns (d); unknown (bells). 47, 9/60–8/61.*

Oozing with organs, tinkling with chimes, this sack of Christmas bonbons should be kept, if at all, for the holiday season. Cloying even then, at any other time it makes one's teeth ache. There's nothing wrong with the notion of a Christmas blues, and the original 'Merry Christmas Baby', included here, is a minor classic. There are a couple not unlike it, 'Please Come Home For Christmas' and 'Christmas Blues'. Otherwise the album is a series of Hallmark greetings cards. For collectors of kitsch, the blues offers no plumper turkey.

*** **Sunshine In My Life**
Collectors Edition CBCD 014 *Brown; Johnny Otis (p, d, vb); Leonard Feather (p); Shuggie Otis (g, b).* 74.

*** **The Very Best Of Charles Brown**
Stardust 881 *Similar to above.* 74.

Brown's activity in the '60s and '70s was sporadic. He made a few singles, and albums for Mainstream, ABC-Bluesway and Jewel, none of them currently available. *Sunshine In My Life* was recorded for Johnny Otis's Blues Spectrum label and, like other albums that Otis produced by veteran bluesmen at that time, was a pleasant low-budget affair with a quota of the artist's hits, here 'Driftin' Blues', 'Merry Christmas Baby' and 'Black Night'. Shuggie Otis slips easily into the Johnny Moore role. The Stardust CD is the same album expanded by two Christmas songs from a different session.

*** **One More For The Road**
Alligator ALCD 4771 *Brown; Harold Ousley (ts); Billy Butler (g); Earl May (b); Kenny Washington (d).* 8/86.

If any artist wearing a blue team shirt was going to tackle Sinatra and attempt to take possession of 'One For My Baby (And One More For The Road)', it was Charles Brown, and although he doesn't act out the barfly's world-weary monologue with quite Sinatra's subtlety, the nightclub-near-closing-time set is low-lit with great precision. That ambience, in fact, is perfectly realized throughout the album, as Brown dreams his way through some blues ('I Stepped In Quicksand', 'Travelin' Blues'), some standards, some originals and 'Route 66', with accompaniment as precisely tailored to his style as that of the Three Blazers.

(*) **Alone At The Piano
Savoy Jazz SVY 17326 *Brown.* 6/89–3/94.

**** **A Life In The Blues**
Rounder 11661-2074 *Brown; Danny Caron (g); Earl May (b); Keith Copeland (d).* 5/90.

*** **All My Life**
Bullseye Blues CD BB 9501 *Brown; Clifford Solomon (as, ts); Heywood Henry, David Sholl (bs); Dr John [Mack Rebennack] (o, p, v); Ron Levy (o); Danny Caron (g); Earl May (b); Keith Copeland, Kenny Blevins (d); Ruth Brown (v).* 5/90.

(*) **Blues And Other Love Songs
Savoy Jazz SVY 17295 *Brown; Houston Person (ts); Danny Caron (g); Ruth Davies (b); Gaylord Birch (d).* 1/92.

(*) **Someone To Love
Bullseye Blues CD BB 9514 *Brown; Clifford Solomon, Bobby Forte (ts); Bonnie Raitt (g, v); Danny Caron (g); Tommy McKenzie (b); Gaylord Birch (d).* 92.

*** **In A Grand Style**
Bullseye Blues & Jazz 9551 *Brown.* 92.

*** **Just A Lucky So And So**
Bullseye Blues CD BB 9521 *Brown; Stacy Cole, Brian Murry, Glen McArthur (t); Bruce Hammond, Maynard Chatters, Alonzo (tb); Warren Bell, Joe Salisbury (as); Clifford Solomon, Clarence Ford,* Fred Kemp (ts); Carl Blovin (bs); New Orleans Strings (vn, vl, vc); Danny Caron (g); Ruth Davies, Tommy McKenzie (b); Gaylord Birch (d); Big Chief Bo Dollis, Geechie (perc); Chuck Carbo, band (v); Wardell Quezergue (arr, cond).* 93.

*** **Cool Christmas Blues**
Bullseye Blues CD BB 9561 *Brown; Clifford Solomon, Bobby Forte (ts); Danny Caron (g); Ruth Davies (b); Gaylord Birch (d); Johnny Otis (vb).* 94.

Though he had been out of the public eye for some time and had every excuse for rustiness, Brown entered the '90s, and soon afterwards his 70s, looking and sounding like a man half his age. During his years on Bullseye Blues, his producer Ron Levy and guitarist Danny Caron ensured that, like a marshmallow robed in chocolate, his singing was carefully wrapped by sympathetic musicians such as the saxophonist Clifford Solomon, drummer Gaylord Birch and Caron himself, a stylist Johnny Moore would have appreciated. The albums are very consistent, blending blues and ballads, old material and new. The best track on *All My Life* is 'A Virus Called The Blues', a title with obvious resonance in 1990, delivered as a honey-and-vinegar duet with Dr John. Notable on *Someone To Love* are the title-song duet with his friend Bonnie Raitt and a remake of a jazz instrumental he first recorded nearly 50 years earlier, 'Be Sharp You'll See'. Otherwise it's a rather sleepy set.

Just A Lucky So And So is livelier, and the production more elaborate, with a horn section on 'Driftin' Blues' and sumptuous string arrangements on 'Black Night' and 'Gloomy Sunday' (which, when it first came out, was billed as 'the Hungarian suicide song'). Caron is in particularly good form. 'A Song For Christmas' may have prompted the next move, a new collection of yuletide songs. Actually only partly new: Brown has another go at 'A Song For Christmas' and remakes five songs from the King Christmas album, naturally including 'Merry Christmas Baby' and 'Please Come Home For Christmas'. The musicians treat the material straightforwardly, feeling no compulsion to deck it with holly, and on its own terms this is a successful album, though even in an admirer's house it will probably stay on the shelf for 11 months of the year.

In A Grand Style, issued after Brown's death, consists of solo blues and ballads recorded during previous Bullseye Blues sessions. The quiet gentility of the performances reveals a man satisfied that he has created a unique musical design and unprompted to tinker with it. Also issued posthumously, *A Life In The Blues* preserves a gig at New York's Lone Star Roadhouse, recorded with crystalline clarity. The programme is stuffed with Brown's standards like 'Driftin' Blues', 'Black Night', 'I Stepped In Quicksand' and the Christmas hits; that, and the high quality of the performances, makes the CD very easy to recommend, but it's further enhanced by an admirable biographical essay by Chip Deffaa and a DVD of the gig and other material.

During this period Brown also recorded *Blues And Other Love Songs* for Muse, with his trio of the time and the label's house producer, Houston Person, on tenor. The division between blues and other material is roughly even, but nothing else about the album is rough: Brown sidles with his customary grace down the melodic paths of ''Round Midnight', 'I've Got A Right To Cry' and several original compositions. The CD has been reissued by Savoy Jazz, who have also assembled tapes from various broadcasts to construct *Alone At The Piano*, a recital of standards ('Cottage

For Sale', 'I Got It Bad (And That Ain't Good)'), lesser-known popular songs and pieces from his own back catalogue. The ambience is warm and intimate, but the blues-light repertoire makes it an album for lovers of Brown in the round.

Brown's last studio albums were for Verve: *These Blues* (523 022) (1994), *Honey Dripper* (529 848) (1996) and *So Goes Love* (539 967) (1998). Caron, Solomon and bassist Ruth Davies were on hand throughout, and Birch on the first two, so the music followed its familar course. At the time of writing, these CDs had been deleted in most or all territories. TR

Clarence 'Gatemouth' Brown
(1924–2005)
VOCAL, GUITAR, HARMONICA, VIOLIN, VIOLA, MANDOLA, PIANO, DRUMS

Growing up in Orange, Texas, Brown acquired guitar and violin skills from his father, but the first instrument he played professionally, in the '40s, was drums. Soon, however, he fell under the spell of T-Bone Walker, whose influence, both instrumental and vocal, is manifest in his '50s recordings. In the '60s he led the house orchestra for the TV show The Beat! *Later, finding a new audience in Europe, he played at the Montreux Jazz Festival and gigged and recorded in France. By then the palette of his repertoire included the colours of country music, Cajun and jazz, which continued to tint his work. As he himself said, 'I refuse to be labeled as a blues player, jazz player, country player … I'm an American musician.'*

*** **'Gatemouth' Brown 1947–1951**
Classics 5030 *Brown; George Alexander, Nathan Irvine, unknown (t); Wilmer Shakesnider, Jack McVea (as); Maxwell Davis, Bill Harvey, unknown (ts); Fred Ford, unknown (bs); unknowns (s); Clarence Green, unknowns (p); Johnny Parker, unknowns (b); Harold Easton, unknowns (d); band (v). 8/47–51.*

*** **His First Recordings 1947–1951**
EPM Blues Collection 16020 *Similar to above. 8/47–52.*

* **Just Got Lucky**
Snapper Complete Blues SBLUECD 031 *As above, except omit Irvine, Harvey, Ford, Parker. 8/47–late 49.*

*** **'Gatemouth' Brown 1952–1954**
Classics 5127 *Brown; Nathan Irvine, Joe Scott, unknown (t); Al Grey, Pluma Davis (tb); unknowns (as); Bill Harvey, Johnny Board, unknowns (ts); Fred Ford, Bob Little, unknowns (bs); Paul Monday (o, p); Jimmy McCracklin, unknowns (p); Johnny Parker, poss. Joe Toussaint, Ray Johnson, unknowns (b); poss. San Francisco Jeff, Ellis Bartee, Jules Curtis, Duke Barker, unknowns (d); band (v). 52–54.*

*** **Peacock Recordings**
Rounder CD 2039 *As above, except add Henry Boozier (t), Allen Clark (bs), Carl Owens, Edward Frank (p), Nat Douglas (g), Carl Lott (b), Emile Russell (d); omit Irvine. 52–9/59.*

Brown started out as an unabashed T-Bone Walker stylist – see, for one example of many, 'Guitar In My Hand' on the first two CDs – but his assertion that Walker 'didn't have the speed like me, and couldn't stretch out' was at that stage mere bragging: for one thing, he hadn't Walker's skill in accenting away from the beat. But he was a good singer, more vehement than the suave Walker and with wider musical interests than Peacock permitted him to realize. He launched that label in 1949 (his own debut having been 18 months earlier for Aladdin) with sides like the Walkeresque 'Didn't Reach My Goal' and 'My Time Is Expensive', or 'Mary Is Fine', a boogie-blues recasting of an old smutty song. By 1951 he had moved farther from the Walker model, and the four tracks from that year are thoroughly assured blues with arrangements that make the band sound larger than it is. The EPM is identical in content (though slightly different in running order and equalization) to the first Classics, but to its 20 tracks adds four more – actually five, since one is the two-part 'Pale Dry Boogie', a beer ad. These duly open Classics' second set, which includes Brown's best-known early recording, 'Okie Dokie Stomp', as well as the ominous slow blues 'Dirty Work At The Crossroad' and the lively guitar–tenor exchanges of 'Gate Walks To Board'. *Just Got Lucky*'s 16 tracks are all on other CDs, and the remastering is so faulty that the CD is largely unlistenable.

The Rounder CD shares nine of its dozen sides with Classics' *1952–1954*, adding two items from 1956 and one from 1959. The clockwork alternation of slow blues and boogie is relentless, and some of the numbers promise more than they deliver, but selections like 'Gate's Salty Blues', a feature for his harmonica, and 'Just Before Dawn', ditto violin, and the lush 'September Song' nudge the listener into expectations which Brown's subsequent career would eventually fulfil.

** **Okie Dokie**
Aim 1304 *Brown; unknowns (brass, reeds, p, g, b, d, perc). 60s.*

The majority of these 13 sides, at least six of which were issued as singles around 1964–65, are guitar-led instrumentals, and may have been made in the wake of Albert Collins's success with broadly similar material. Lacking Collins's distinctive sound, they come over more like demos or backing tracks that were never fitted up with vocals. Apart, possibly, from the last track, a long live recording of 'River's Invitation', this album is of no interest to anyone but a completist.

*** **The Blues Ain't Nothing**
Black & Blue BB 428 *Brown; Mickey Baker, Jimmy Dawkins (g); Mac Thompson (b); Michel Denis (d). 12/71.*

*** **Gate's On The Heat**
Universal/Maison de Blues 982 246–7 *Brown; Wayne Jackson (t); Andrew Love, Ed Logan (ts); James Mitchell (bs); Ed Beyer (kb); Andre Herve (o, p); The London Strings Orchestra (strings); Joe Wright, Henry Vestine, James Shane, prob. Jerome Hayes (g); Michel Herve, Richard Hite, Joe Turner (b); Christian Devaux, Adolfo 'Fito' De La Parra, Calep Emphrey Jr (d); Philippe Rault (prod). 2/72–7/73.*

*** **Pressure Cooker**
Alligator ALCD 4745 *Brown; Xavier Chambon (t); Al Grey, Claude Gousset (tb); Michel Attenoux (as); Hal Singer, Arnett Cobb (ts); Milt Buckner, Stan Hunter (o); Jay McShann (p); Roland Lobligeois (b); Michael Silva, Paul Gunther, Chris Columbo (d). 3–8/73.*

*** **Sings Louis Jordan**
Black & Blue BB 936 *Brown; Arnett Cobb (ts); Milt Buckner (o); Jay McShann (p); Michael Silva (d). 7–8/73.*

*** **Just Got Lucky**
Evidence ECD 26019 *Brown; Al Grey (tb); Arnett Cobb, Hal Singer (ts); Milt Buckner (o); Jay McShann, Lloyd Glenn (p); Roland Lobligeois, Milt Hinton (b); Michael Silva, Paul Gunther, J. C. Heard (d). 7/73–7/77.*

Brown spent quite a bit of time in France in the '70s,

recording at least half a dozen albums. *Gate's On The Heat*, made for Barclay, looks at first glance as if it might belong to a gaggle of elaborate productions by that label, such as Mickey Baker's *Mississippi Delta Dues* or various Memphis Slim projects, which were often imaginative but sometimes fatally pretentious. Not so: thanks, no doubt, to the force of Brown's musical personality, the album is coherent and entertaining, and, if the country song 'Never Ending Love For You' is a bit of a stiff, the eco-blues 'Man And His Environment' and the pre-Watergate 'Please Mr. Nixon' stand up well enough 30 years later. The Black & Blue sets are, by comparison, straightforward. *The Blues Ain't Nothing* is a solid blues set, Brown breaking up the sequence of guitar numbers with one harmonica feature and a couple for violin. His reading of 'If I Get Lucky' follows the vocal contour of 'Big Boy' Crudup's recording with great fidelity. *Sings Louis Jordan*, a vigorous *hommage*, is enhanced by the presence of Arnett Cobb but might have been even better with a second horn. *Just Got Lucky* is a useful distillation of *Sings Louis Jordan*, tracks from another '73 date and about half of 1977's *Heat Wave*, made with the Glenn–Hinton–Heard trio and on its original release jointly credited to Glenn, who plays wonderfully throughout and nudges Brown to raise his game too. *Pressure Cooker* calls itself a selection from Brown's five Black & Blue albums but its sources are confined to three, five of the nine tracks coming from the LP *Cold Strange*, among them the tune 'Cold Strings', which is presumably what the LP should have been called (though Black & Blue's own CD reissue [59.096, deleted] offered another title, *Cold Storage*). *Cold* whatever was a good album, Brown playing lissom jazzy lines on cuts like 'Pressure Cooker', so much of *Pressure Cooker* is too, if somewhat chilled by the antiseptic studio ambience. None of its tracks are shared with *Just Got Lucky*.

*** Blackjack
Sugar Hill SHCD-3891 *Brown; Bobby Campo (t, flh, fl); Rod Roddy (p); Don Buzard (psg, Do); Jeff Pollard, Freddy Wahl (g); Leon Medica (b); David Peters (d).* 76.

This was the first of Brown's 'Panamerican' CDs. Five numbers wear the 12-bar brand, and four of them are instrumentals: the fleet guitar-led 'Pressure Cooker', 'Honey Boy', the moody dark-streets title tune and 'Song For Reneé (Gate's Tune)', featuring Brown's lush violin and a pastoral flute solo by Campo. 'When My Blue Moon Turns To Gold Again', 'Take Me Back To Tulsa' and 'Up Jumped The Devil' are Western Swing instrumentals, well done in the modern style, and 'Dark End Of The Hallway' a country song.

*** Alright Again!
Rounder CD 2028 *Brown; Stanton Davis Jr (t); Jim McMillen (tb); Bill 'Foots' Samuel (as, ts); Alvin 'Red' Tyler (ts); Joe 'Champagnski' Sunseri (bs); David 'Fingers' Fender (o, p); Larry Sieberth (p); Red Lane (g); Myron Dove (b); Lloyd Herrman (d).* 6/81.

*** One More Mile
Rounder CD 2034 *Brown; Bobby Campo (t, fl); Ernie Gautreau (tb); Bill 'Foots' Samuel (as, ts, bs, fl); Homer Brown (ts); Craig Wroten (p); Tommy Moran (psg, g); Miles Kevin Wright (b); Robert Shipley (d).* 10/82.

*** Texas Swing
Rounder CD 11527 *As for* Alright Again! *and* One More Mile. 6/81–10/82.

**(*) Real Life
Rounder CD 2054 *Brown; Mark Wells, Terry Tullos (t); Ernie Gautreau (vtb); Bill Samuel (ts, bs); Dennis Taylor (ts); Dan Matrazzo (kb); Luther Wamble (g); Harold Floyd (b); Lloyd Herrman (d).* 9/85.

*** Okie Dokie Stomp
Bullseye Blues & Jazz BBB 9622 *As for* Alright Again!, One More Mile *and* Real Life, *except add Louis Stephens (p).* 6/81–9/85.

Alright Again! is Brown the Peacock bluesman in state-of-the-art sound; he plays guitar almost throughout, urged by a shouting band. Bill Samuel takes the Johnny Board tenor sax role in 'Gate Walks To Board'. On *One More Mile* Brown drives an eight-man party through a Southwestern panorama of blues, jazz, cajun and country, taking a pedal steel guitarist on board for a couple of numbers. The mildly boppish 'Big Yard' and the straightforward but fast 'Flippin' Out' do most for his guitar playing, while of the vocals the most blues-connected are Roy Milton's 'Information Blues' and Cecil Gant's 'I Wonder'. The sensible way to acquaint yourself with these albums is to get *Texas Swing*, which embraces all but three of their 20 tracks. The shorter but cheaper *Okie Dokie Stomp* has nine tracks from them (all but one of which are also on *Texas Swing*), the title number and 'Okie Dokie Stomp' from *Real Life* and 'The Drifter' from the deleted Justice VAC *Blues For The Homeless*. *Real Life* is a club recording, from the Caravan Of Dreams in Fort Worth, but maybe not the hot chilli pepper you're hoping it'll be. Brown's voice shows signs of age – he can't quite do justice to a song like 'Please Send Me Someone To Love' any more – and the rather short programme (under 40 minutes) doesn't allow him to show his full hand; it's basically blues with a couple of dashes of jazz, and his country side is revealed only obliquely in a funky instrumental version of 'Frankie And Johnny'.

**(*) Standing My Ground
Alligator ALCD 4779 *Brown; Bobby Campo (t); Ernie Gautreau (tb); Bill Samuel (as, bs); Dennis Taylor (ts); Terrance Simien (ac); Larry Marshall (o); Garfield Verdine, Lawrence Sieberth (p); Tommy Moran, Rob Fleming (g); Harold Floyd (b); Lloyd Herrman, Kenny Brown (d); Earl Sally (rb); David Craig, Frank Smith, Mike Pace, Bobby Brown (v).* 89.

**(*) No Looking Back
Alligator ALCD 4804 *Brown; Bobby Campo (t, flh, fl); Terry Townson (t); John Touchy (tb); Bill Samuel (as, bs); Dennis Taylor (ts); Michael Holmes (o, p); Tommy Moran (sg, g); Ron Harris (g); Harold Floyd (b); Waldo LaTowsky (d); Michelle Shocked (v); Hound Dog Samuel [Bill Samuel?] (barking).* 91.

Brown didn't do a great deal of recording in the late '80s and early '90s, and, if these albums are any guide, the reason may have been that he was suffering from the musician's equivalent of writer's block. *Standing My Ground*, which could have been better titled *Marking My Time*, is a stodgy menu of blues with meagre and untempting side-orders of zydeco and country music. *No Looking Back* is another insipid set, with scarcely any country or Cajun flavouring. Brown and the band grill their jazz chops in 'C-Jam Blues', but throughout the two albums the energy that should have been imparted to the proceedings by the horn section is sapped by the inert studio sound. The only rogue note is struck by 'I Will Be Your Friend', a soppy duet with Michelle Shocked.

*** Back To Bogalusa
Blue Thumb 549 785 *Brown; Barney Floyd (t); Brian O'Neill (tb); Eric Demmer (as, ts, bs); Brent Rose (ts); Zachary Richard (ac);*

Joe Krown (kb, o, p); Sonny Landreth, Mike Loudermilk (g); Harold Floyd, David Hyde (b); David Peters (d, cga, perc); Pat Bickham, Reneé [sic] Brown, Gene Gunulfsen, Mike Pace (v). 01.

Brown joined the Universal family of labels in 1994, but most of his albums under that contract – *The Man* (Verve 523 761) (1994), *Long Way Home* (Verve 529 465) (1996), *Gate Swings* (Verve 537 617) (1997) and *American Music, Texas Style* (Blue Thumb 547 536) (1999) – have been deleted, as has *The Best Of Clarence 'Gatemouth' Brown/A Blues Legend* (Verve 527 435) (1995), which was drawn chiefly from French Barclay albums of the early '70s.

Brown has always been fond of songs that breathe the air of his native Southwest, and in *Back To Bogalusa* he puts together an entire album of them, drawing on the work of songwriters like Bobby Charles ('It All Comes Back', 'Why Are People Like That'), Delbert McClinton ('Lie No Better') and Hoyt Garrick ('Folks Back Home', 'Louisian'). Cajun echoes drift across the album's landscape – Zachary Richard's accordion, Brown's fiddling in 'Breaux Bridge Rag' – and Sonny Landreth puts the raccoons to flight with howling slide guitar on Lowell George's 'Dixie Chicken' and a couple of other numbers. Some of the songs are either too sentimental or too oblique to suit Brown's plain approach and grandfatherly voice, but his old blues heart beats strongly in Don Nix's 'Same Old Blues' and he struts his stuff like a Dixie chicken in the defiantly boastful 'Bogalusa Boogie Man'.

**(*) Timeless
Hightone HCD 8174 *Brown; Bobby Campo (t, fl); Mark Wells (t); Chris Belleau, Ernie Gautreau (tb); Jerry Jumonville (ts, bs); Dennis Taylor (ts); Bill Samuel (bs); Larry Marshall (o); Garfield Verdine, Dan Matrazzo (p); Tommy Moran (sg, g); Luther Wamble (g); Harold Floyd (b); Lloyd Herrman (d); Frank Willis Smith Jr (v).* 04.

There are several jazz subjects here, such as Ellington's 'Satin Doll', Joe Zawinul's 'Mercy, Mercy, Mercy' and 'Soft Winds' from the Benny Goodman book, and to some of them Brown characteristically applies the colours of Western Swing, a treatment he also affords 'Dark End Of The Hallway' in his broad-brush fiddle intro. But as other exponents of latterday Western Swing have found, there can be a thin line between polished small-string-group jazz and lounge music, and 'Unchained Melody' certainly drifts across it. The oddest gift in this very mixed party bag is 'The Drifter' – not the nine-minute blues but its four-minute introduction, where Brown raps about the Big Bang like some cosmological Lord Buckley. TR

Gabriel Brown (1910–60s?)
VOCAL, GUITAR

Though evidently a popular blues artist in Harlem in the last years of World War II and for a little afterwards, and recalled by Brownie McGhee as a competing club attraction, Brown had earlier moved in a wider circle that included the folklorist and writer Zora Neale Hurston, in some of whose plays he took acting roles.

**(*) Mean Old Blues 1943–1949
Flyright FLY CD 59 *Brown.* mid-43–8/49.

Brown's first recordings were for the Library of Congress, made in Eatonville, Florida, in 1935; the slide-guitar-accompanied 'Talking In Sebastopol' is on *Red River Blues* (Travelin' Man TM CD 08). Moving to New York City, he made a series of records for the Joe Davis label. The idiosyncratic guitar style and sour tuning of his first release, 'I Get Evil When My Love Comes Down' and 'You Ain't No Good', would change little through his more than two dozen recordings. Apart from some resemblance in his singing and playing to Blind Boy Fuller, he appears to have drawn little from known contemporaries or predecessors. The attraction of strong performances like the gambling song 'Black Jack Blues' is somewhat dimmed by a number of more or less formulaic recordings which have survived only on noisy discs. TR

J. T. Brown (1918–69)
TENOR SAXOPHONE, VOCAL

According to Little Brother Montgomery, John T. Brown served his apprenticeship in music by playing with the Rabbit Foot Minstrels. By the mid-'40s he was in Chicago, working with the drummer Jump Jackson. In the early '50s he made several singles and was well enough known to be able to tour with a band, but thereafter he worked chiefly as an accompanist, most famously for Elmore James but also on records by J. B. Lenoir, Muddy Waters and many others.

*** J. T. Brown 1950–1954
Classics 5157 *Brown; poss. John Oscar, unknowns (t); unknown (as); unknown (ts); Bob Call, Little Brother Montgomery, unknowns (p); unknown (g); Ransom Knowling, Big Crawford, unknowns (b); prob. Jump Jackson, unknowns (d); Grant Jones, Eddie Dark & The Eagleaires (v); Roosevelt Sykes, Anna Lee (sp).* 50–54.

*** Windy City Boogie
Delmark DE-714 *Brown; poss. John Oscar, unknown (t); unknown (as); Lafayette Leake (o, p); Little Brother Montgomery, Bob Call, Sunnyland Slim (p); Jody Williams, Matt Murphy, poss. Lee Cooper, unknown (g); Ransom Knowling, Big Crawford, Willie Dixon, unknowns (b); Fred Below, S. P. Leary, prob. Jump Jackson, unknowns (d); Eddie Dark & The Eagleaires (v); Roosevelt Sykes (sp).* 7/51–60.

Brown was no wizard of the tenor saxophone, but he evidently suited the many Chicago musicians he worked with. His tone is rough, with a wide vibrato – he was nicknamed 'the nanny goat horn' – and, at up tempos, a brazen excitability. *Windy City Boogie* gathers the fruit of sessions for United, J.O.B. and Atomic H. On the first United date, which produced the local hit 'Windy City Boogie', Brown's hearty blaring, both saxophonic and vocal, is supported by Little Brother Montgomery on piano and Roosevelt Sykes, confusingly, not on piano but providing cheery exhortations. A trumpeter plays elegant muted obbligati on the vocal numbers 'Blackjack Blues' and 'When I Was A Lad'. The next session swings from the boisterous party atmosphere of 'Walking Home' to the after-hours blues of 'House Party Groove', a feature for the not often recorded but excellent Bob Call. The later material is less finished, but altogether this is an enjoyable record of what sounds like a good-humoured man. Classics repeat a dozen of Delmark's tracks, adding an earlier four-tune date for Harlem including Brown's first recording of 'Black Jack Blues'; 'Nature Boy Blows It', a rerun of the up-tempo instrumental titled 'Rock-Em' on United; and three well-recorded sides made for Blue Lake but not issued at the time, of which the slow blues 'I'm Wise' is among his best vocals. TR

Kenny Brown
VOCAL, GUITAR

Brown grew up in Nesbit, Mississippi, the hometown of Joe Callicott, and by the time he was ten was playing guitar with the older man. Later he played with Johnny Woods and Fred McDowell, but his longest musical association was with R. L. Burnside, whom he accompanied for 20 years.

*** Stingray
Fat Possum 0344 *Brown; Jeff —— (s); unknown (h); Jimmy Can (o, d); John Wilson (g, b); Leo Schwann (g); Takeeshi Imura, Terrance Bishop (b); Cedric Burnside, John Convertino, Jamie Peters (d). 03.*

Brown recalls his after-school sessions with Joe Callicott in pleasant solo acoustic performances of the older man's 'You Don't Know My Mind' and 'Fare Thee Well Blues'. There's a further nod to Callicott in the lilting guitar part of 'All I Want', while the years of standing next to R. L. Burnside are implicit in the insistently repeated figures of 'France Chance' as well as the Burnside staples 'Goin' Down South' and 'Shake 'Em On Down'. But the listener will quickly deduce from the spitting guitar lines that Brown has more to do than conscientiously memorialize his teachers. Tracks like 'Shake 'Em On Down' and 'Brought You To The City' have been put through a post-production blender to yield the hill-country-electro-punk effect that has become Fat Possum's trademark, but the process is compatible with Brown's way of making music and the result is beneficial. TR

Lee Brown
VOCAL, PIANO

A member of the group of Tennessee musicians around Sleepy John Estes, alongside Hammie Nixon, Son Bonds and Charlie Pickett, Brown was subsequently more prolific than his modest talent perhaps merited. 'Little Girl, Little Girl' in 1937 was his one success and he returned to it at a further six sessions, including his last in 1946. By that time his association with guitarist Leroy Foster had brought him into contact with a young Muddy Waters.

**(*) Lee Brown (1937–1940)
Document DOCD-5344 *Brown; Charlie Shavers, Henry 'Red' Allen (t); Buster Bailey (cl); Rhythm Willie [Hood] (h); Sammy Price, poss. Lil Armstrong (p); unknown (g); unknown (b); unknown or poss. Sid Catlett (d). 8/37–4/40.*

Brown's first and only hit came from two days of New York sessions at which he also backed Estes and Pickett. His capering right-hand invention was indifferently supported by abbreviated bass patterns and that may have encouraged his record company to use the dependable Sammy Price on his next session and possibly Lil Armstrong later. An adequate lyricist, Brown rarely had an insight or waxed poetic; he was probably the only artist to use a 'bo weavil' as a sexual metaphor. His 9/39 session is notable for the presence of harmonica virtuoso Rhythm Willie, whose hyperactive and distinctly unbluesy profligacy is impressive if distracting on 'Little Brown Skin Girl' ('Little Girl, Little Girl' in disguise) and 'My Driving Wheel'. Two 1940 sessions with Henry 'Red' Allen's compact obbligatos stultify the senses with a procession of funeral tempos, one for 'Another Little Girl'. There's a sense of unfulfilled promise in Brown's music that reduces his involvement with artists of the calibre of Estes and Waters to coincidence rather than destiny.

**(*) Jazzin' The Blues
RST Jazz Perspectives JPCD-1515 *Brown; Red Allen (t); Fess Williams (cl); Oliver Alcorn (as); unknown (ts); Leroy Foster (g); Wellman Braud, Ernest 'Big' Crawford, unknown (b); unknown (d); Walter Martin (wb). 40–46.*

Brown's nine tracks on this VAC comprise his remaining 1940 session with Allen and a washboard player and two singles from 1946 for the Chicago and King labels, each with versions of 'Little Girl'. Both are more energetic than was previously the case, with Alcorn's vaulting alto sax having the edge on the unknown tenor soloist on the Chicago session. Listed as an alternative take, a second version of 'Bobbie Town Boogie', issued on 20th Century, is actually from a different date. Brown's King sessions, one previously unissued, with further unissued (and unauthorized) material by Jimmie Gordon and Johnnie Temple from the same source, form the final record in *Broke, Black & Blue* (Proper PROPERBOX 7 4CD). NS

Mel Brown (born 1939)
VOCAL, GUITAR, ORGAN, PIANO

A versatile guitarist who has accompanied B. B. King, Bobby Bland and many other artists, Brown is the son of the Jackson, Mississippi, blues singer and guitarist John Henry 'Bubba' Brown. He began learning guitar at 14 while recovering from meningitis, and at 19 moved to LA to make his living as a session musician. He played on numerous ABC-Bluesway albums in the late '60s and '70s and cut six of his own for ABC's Impulse! label (all deleted). From 1982 to 1989 he was in the house band at Antone's in Austin, Texas; he now lives in Canada.

** Homewreckin' Done Live
Electro-Fi 3370 *Brown; David Wiffin (s); John Lee (kb, v); Al Richardson (b); Jim Boudreau, Randy Coryell (d). spring 98.*

*** Neck Bones & Caviar
Electro-Fi 3363 *Brown; Al Lerman (h); John Lee (kb); Al Richardson (b); Jim Boudreau (d); Miss Angel, Alec Fraser (v). 6–9/99.*

Brown seldom steps out front, and is not as highly regarded as he should be in blues circles. *Neck Bones & Caviar* offers a couple of clues why. He prefers long, slow burners to the fast and flashy – even opening with one, Muddy Waters's 'Woman Wanted' – and he refuses to be stuck in the hard-blues mud, though he's excellent when he is, as on 'Lord, Have Mercy', where he switches to soulful piano. The sheer variety of his licks is hugely impressive: Brown has chops to make other guitarists drool.

Homewreckin' Done Live was taped at Wally's Pub in Guelph, Ontario, a setting that encouraged him to take his time over some songs: 'Turn On Your Love Light' and 'Spoonful' run over seven minutes, 'Hey Joe' to 12.10. He would be similarly expansive in the studio a year later, but there he would be playing most of the time, whereas here Lee and Wiffin are generously indulged with solo passages, which the latter spends in abrasive jabbering. Brown, however, is almost always worth listening to. Elmore James's 'The Sky Is Crying' (another long one at 8.27) is restyled *à la* T-Bone Walker, while Albert King's 'I'll Play The Blues For You' is filled with air and sent on a balloon flight, though Lee's keyboard solo nearly brings it down in Smoothjazz Woods. TR

Nappy Brown (born 1929)
VOCAL

Napoleon Brown Culp started singing with gospel quartets in North Carolina, but switched to blues for money and without qualms. After disappearing in the early '60s, beset by personal demons, Brown recorded a blues LP in 1969. In 1972 he had a gospel hit with the Bell Jubilee Singers, and in the '80s found a new blues audience in Europe and at home.

***(*) Night Time Is The Right Time
Savoy SVY 17074 2CD Brown; Reunald Jones, John Rains, Dud Bascomb (t); Jimmy Cleveland, Billy Verplanck, Buster Cooper, John Huston (tb); unknown (fl); Hilton Jefferson, Earl Warren (as); Sam Taylor, Al Sears, Budd Johnson, Warren Luckey, Henry Durant, Count Hastings, Jonathan Willingham, King Curtis, Phil Bodner, unknown (ts); George Berg, Maurice Simon, Dave McRae, Heywood Henry (bs); Robert Banks (o, p); unknowns (o); Howard Biggs, Fred Johnson, Sam Price, Ernie Hayes, Kelly Owens, Charlie Manz, unknowns (p); Mickey Baker, Everett Barksdale, Sal Salvador, Skeeter Best, Charlie Macey, Wally Richardson, Carl Lynch, unknowns (g); Abie Baker, Milt Hinton, Lloyd Trotman, Jimmy Schenk, Leonard Gaskin, Aaron Bell, unknowns (b); Jimmy Crawford, Dave Bailey, Connie Kay, Panama Francis, Red Alcott, Bobby Donaldson, Gene Brooks, Joe Marshall, Shep Shepherd, unknowns (d); Ray Barretto (cga); The Zippers, The Bad Boys, The Gibralters [sic], unknowns (v). 3/54–12/62.

Anyone who thinks that Ray Charles invented the gospelization of R&B should listen to Nappy Brown. From the outset, his stentorian voice is that of a larynx-mangling hard quartet lead; on 'That Man', his first hit, he sings a bass part as well. Brother Ray picked up Brown's revival of '(Night Time Is) The Right Time' and had the hit; Nappy's follow-up, 'Any Time Is The Right Time', is a blatant secularization of Pentecostal preaching. It's sometimes obvious that Savoy are trying to piggyback on Joe Turner's success with the teen audience; pop-blues like 'Just A Little Love' are pleasant, but not to be compared with 'Down In The Alley' or 'I've Had My Fun', an astounding gospel transformation of 'Going Down Slow'.

Savoy backed Brown with some of New York's finest studio musicians, putting heavy emphasis on muscular tenor solos; alongside them, Mickey Baker's guitar fills are especially worth hearing, but the other guitarists are not outshone. The downside is that even this careful selection cannot avoid what A&R man Ozzie Cadena called 'that diddly, diddly, diddly shit', the novelty songs that Herman Lubinsky saw as the road to fame (for Brown) and fortune (for Lubinsky). Titles like 'Piddily Patter Patter', 'Skidy Woe' and 'Goody Goody Gum Drop' speak for themselves; these excrescences are kept to a minimum, and some of them feature good solos, but they downgrade the collection as a whole.

**(*) Don't Be Angry
Savoy Jazz SV-0259 Brown; Reunald Jones (t); Jimmy Cleveland (tb); Sam Taylor, Al Sears, Budd Johnson, Henry Durant (ts); George Berg, Maurice Simon (bs); Robert Banks (o); Howard Biggs, Fred Johnson, Sam Price (p); Mickey Baker, Everett Barksdale, unknown (g); Abie Baker, Milt Hinton, Jimmy Schenk, Leonard Gaskin, unknown (b); Jimmy Crawford, Dave Bailey, Connie Kay, Panama Francis, Red Alcott, unknown (d); The Zippers (v). 3/54–10/56.

Don't Be Angry's 16 tracks come from an analogue master tape compiled for LP release, and the sound is inferior to the 2 CDs'. The music is mostly fine, of course, and the tortured emoting of 'I Want To Live', which is not on *Night Time Is The Right Time*, is rather more than that. On the other hand, it's all too easy to understand why the clammily patriotic 'Land I Love' was left off the later compilation; it's the only real carbuncle on *Don't Be Angry*, but shorter playing time means that there are also fewer beauty spots.

**(*) Tore Up
Alligator ALCD 4792 Brown; Andy Hagan, George Rollins (t); Billy McPherson (ts); Skip Lane (bs); Albey Scholl (h); Oliver Wells (o); Scott Alexander (p); Tinsley Ellis (g); Wayne Burdette (b); Michael McCauley (d); Yonrico Scott (cga). 8/84.

**(*) Just For Me
JSP JSPCD 274 Brown; Big Jay McNeely (ts); John Altman (s); Richard Studholme (h, g); Andy Pyle (b); Geoff Nichols (d). 88.

***(*) Deep Sea Diver
Grammercy 0113 Brown; Wayne King, Adrian Cox (t); Joseph Jennings (as, bs); Roderick A. Smith (ts); Haran Griffin (kb); Charlie Brown (g); Darryl Henley (b); St Anthony, Jimmy Jackson (d); Kim Brown, 'Karen' (v). 89.

*** I'm A Wild Man
New Moon NMC 9405 Brown; Rusty Smith (t); Dillard Moss (tb); Wally West (ts); Scott Adair (bs); Bill Newton (s); Randy Friel (o, p, clavinet, v); Skeeter Brandon (o, p); Phil Mazerick (p); Bob Margolin (g, v); Max Drake, Armand Lenchek (g); Calvin Johnson (b, v); Ed Butler (d, v); Shelly Flynt, Allison King, Annie Woods, Kirsten O'Rourke, Prince Taylor, Michelle Belanger (v). 94?

***(*) Who's Been Fooling You
New Moon NMC 9714 Brown; Rusty Smith (t); Dillard Moss (tb); Wally West (ts); Scott Adair (bs); Patrick Purnell (kb, v); Kym McKinnon (g, v); Barry Cronin (b, v); Jay Mahlstedt (d, v). 95?

The accompaniments on Alligator and JSP are generic versions of the Chicago guitar-band sound with added horns. Brown's voice is still powerful, but he seems disengaged from the material on *Tore Up*, not bothered about deploying his battery of vocal effects; songs like 'Losing Hand' and 'Hard Luck Blues' don't get the (melo)dramatic delivery they need. *Just For Me*, with fewer tracks, has a more varied and interesting playlist, including a couple of well-executed ballads and a revisited 'Night Time' where Brown and McNeely generate quite a head of steam. *Deep Sea Diver* is shorter yet (eight tracks, 37 minutes), but it's by no means negligible. The songs range from supper-club suavity to the gutbucket title track, and Brown gives them intelligently varied readings. He's backed by calmly competent session musicians who relish the classy charts they've been handed; the arrangements and their execution call to mind the glory days of B. B. King's '50s road bands. It's a pity, therefore, that the backing vocals are thin at times. Grammercy's cheapskate presentation is irritating, too.

New Moon's electric guitarists take their cue from the jazzier styles of Texas and the southwest (usually; 'Don't Hurt No More' was a semi-operatic workout on *Deep Sea Diver*, but here, accompanied by solo acoustic guitar in the manner of Muddy Waters, it's radically and successfully reinvented). The musicians on both CDs offer Brown confident, swinging settings, and he responds with commitment and playfulness. 'Shake, Rattle And Roll' is a dully obvious choice on the first of them, and it's no kindness to bring back 'Piddly Patter' on the second. Skeeter Brandon's gospelly playing is a big element in the success of *I'm A Wild Man*, but *Who's Been Fooling You* is preferable, with a more consistent sound, a band who know how to do backing vocals and, in 'I'm Too Cool', an anti-drug song that lives up to its title, getting the message across without nerdiness or finger-wagging.

(*) Best Of Both Worlds
Ripete 2242//[Westside WESF 104] *Brown; Richard Jones (t); Bernie Kenerson (as, ts, bs); Richard Crocker (s); Gary Bass (h); Patrick Purnell (kb, v); Randy Gilkey (kb); Kym McKinnon (g, v); Ronnie Waters (g); Barry Cronin (b, v); Dave Mann, Matt Robinson (b); Jay Mahlstedt (d, v); Fred Shaw (d); Kip Anderson, Mario Cartelli, Erin Kelley, Jim Kelley (v).* c. 95.

This CD is credited to Nappy Brown and Kip Anderson. Born in South Carolina in 1944, Anderson released singles on various small labels from 1959, licensing some to Vee-Jay and Checker; he recorded for Excello in the '60s, and made a CD for the defunct Ichiban in 1992. *Best Of Both Worlds*' initial market was the South Carolina Beach Music scene (white kids getting off on black dance music, as with Northern Soul in Britain), and it's predictably party-hearty. Anderson's voice is softer and more ingratiating than Brown's and they complement one another well enough. Two tracks, one an excellent remake of 'Don't Be Angry', derive from the *Who's Been Fooling You* sessions; elsewhere, the Blues Imperials' accompaniments are derivative, and often sabotaged by a loud, lumbering bass guitarist. There's seldom much interpretive effort by the vocalists, either, as is most obvious on 'It Should've Been Me' and 'Hit The Road Jack', which need, but don't get, some version of Ray Charles's ironic intensity. *Best Of Both Worlds* works as the soundtrack to a beer 'n' barbecue weekend, but can't stand up to more concentrated attention. CS

Piney Brown (born 1922)
VOCAL

Brown grew up in Birmingham, Alabama, where he sang in church with his sisters as The Young Blue Jays, named after one of the city's famous gospel quartets. At 18 he moved to Baltimore and began performing in clubs. In the late '40s and '50s he toured with Lynn Hope, Illinois Jacquet and Johnny Otis, in a group he formed with tenor saxophonist Ed Wiley, and with fellow singer Billy Brooks, meanwhile recording for various New York labels. In the '60s he settled in Dayton, Ohio, where he still lives and, occasionally, performs.

(*) Hoot & Holler Saturday Night!
Delmark DE-754 *Brown; unknowns (t, as, ts, p, g, b, d); band (v).* 48–50.

Like other singers at the end of the '40s, Brown was under the spell of Wynonie Harris, and Apollo probably commissioned these recordings partly out of pique at having lost Harris a few years before and seen him become hugely successful on King. The eight sides come from two sessions with different bands, the first a quintet headed by quite a good tenorist, the second a sextet with three horns. Brown sings heartily but without Harris's rasping tone – or his tendency to go over the top – and by the second date he is producing assured performances like 'Why Do I Cry Over You' and 'How About Rocking With Me'. The remainder of the CD is by the contemporary blues-shouter Eddie Mack. TR

Richard 'Rabbit' Brown (c. 1880–1937)
VOCAL, GUITAR

Brown spent much of his life in New Orleans, where he is reported to have worked as a street singer and as an occasional singing boatman on Lake Ponchartrain.

**** The Greatest Songsters (1927–1929)**
Document DOCD-5003 *Brown.* 3/27.

Brown's splendidly craggy voice and distinctive accent may be absorbed at length in 'Mystery Of The Dunbar's Child' and 'Sinking Of The Titanic', extended narratives that originally appeared on a 12-inch 78. Their detailed texts are enhanced by vivacious guitar playing with vigorous snapped bass-string runs, characteristics also of 'I'm Not Jealous' and 'Never Let The Same Bee Sting You Twice', beguiling vaudeville or minstrel-show pieces, and the deeply moving 'James Alley Blues'. The remainder of the CD is given over to Mississippi John Hurt and Hambone Willie Newbern. TR

Roy Brown (1925–81)
VOCAL

The New Orleans-born Brown was one of the most influential of the big-voiced singers of his era, but the role of blues singer was not one he initially coveted: he intended to be a pop crooner, until the response to 'Good Rockin' Tonight' (1947) rerouted his career path. After a decade of popularity he was driven into retirement by rock 'n' roll. A return to the business in 1970 under the aegis of Johnny Otis proved to be brief, and another in the late '70s, when he began to perform in public and make records again, was curtailed by his early death.

***(*) Good Rockin' Brown**
Ace CDCHD 1072 *Brown; Tony Moret, Wallace Davenport (t); Clement Tervalone (tb); O'Neil Jerome (as); Earl Barnes, Johnny Fontenette, unknown (ts); Walter Daniels, unknown (p); Bill Jones (g); Robert Ogden, Percy Gabriel (b); unknown (d).* 7–12/47.

***(*) Roy Brown 1947–1949**
Classics 5021 *Brown; Tony Moret, Wallace Davenport, Teddy Riley, unknowns (t); Clement Tervalone, unknown (tb); O'Neil Jerome (as); Earl Barnes, Johnny Fontenette, unknowns (ts); Leroy 'Batman' Rankins (bs, p); unknown (bs); Walter Daniels, Edward Santineo, unknowns (p); Bill Jones, Louis Sargent, unknowns (g); Robert Ogden, Percy Gabriel, Tommy Shelvin, unknowns (b); Frank Parker, unknowns (d).* 47–11/49.

***(*) Hard Luck And Good Rocking 1947–1950**
EPM Blues Collection 16017 *Similar to above.* 7/47–6/50.

**** Roy Brown 1950–1951**
Classics 5036 *Brown; Wilbur Harden, Leslie Ayres, Teddy Riley (t); Jimmy Griffin, Johnny Fontenette, Red Prysock (ts);*

Orrington Hall (ts, bs); Harry Porter, Leroy Rankins, Alexander Nelson (bs); Buddy Griffin, Edward Santineo, James Robinson, Charlie Nelson (p); Willie Gaddy, Edgar Blanchard (g); Ike Isaacs, Clarence Mack, Chuck Badie (b); Calvin Shields, George Jenkins, Wilbert Smith (d). 4/50–9/51.

**** Blues DeLuxe
King KCD 6019 *As above.* 4/50–9/51.

Brown's rich baritone introduced an almost operatic floridity to the art of blues singing. His melodramatic presentation turned the dilemmas of 'Long 'Bout Midnight' or 'End Of My Journey' into emotional Big Dippers: stepping on board disconsolate, he disembarked in despair. He righted the balance by recording many exuberant shout numbers and boogies. The hit 'Good Rockin' Tonight' spawned a brood of young uns like 'Rockin' At Midnight' and 'Boogie At Midnight', and then there was a bodacious notches-on-my-bedpost song, 'I Feel That Young Man's Rhythm' ('they call me the rock, 'cause I've got a mighty rock'), and the unfolding saga of Miss Fanny Brown. All this ground is covered on the first Classics CD. The second continues the chronological march through Brown's output on DeLuxe. 'Hard Luck Blues', his most nakedly emotional performance, is enhanced by the contrast with its scrupulously restrained band arrangement, and by its extraordinary coda of a final chord swelling and fading and a single curling figure on guitar. Less remarkable but carefully wrought slow blues readings such as 'Dreaming Blues', 'Long About Sundown' and 'Wrong Woman Blues' are interspersed, as before, with happy (and sometimes clappy) numbers like 'Cadillac Baby', 'Love Don't Love Nobody' and 'Good Rockin' Man', everything accompanied with gusto by a series of six- or seven-piece bands. The EPM CD bridges the two Classics sets, having 13 tracks from the first and eight from the second; many of the titles mentioned above are among them. The King CD is identical to the second Classics. *Good Rockin' Brown*, the debut release in 'The King & DeLuxe Acetate Series', is a more narrowly focused collection, covering Brown's DeLuxe sides over a six-month period in 1947 – not just the ones we knew but 13 hitherto unissued, all very good and with a clarity never found on DeLuxe's often villainous pressings.

*** Roy Brown 1951–1953
Classics 5090 Brown; Teddy Riley, Joe Bridgewater (t); Johnny Fontenette, Victor Thomas, Sammy Parker (ts); Alexander Nelson, Frank Campbell, Jim Wynn (bs); Charlie Nelson, Jimmy Williams, Jimmy C. Harris (p); Jimmy Davis, Bill Jennings (g); Chuck Badie, Tommy Shelvin, Lloyd Lambert, Clarence Jones (b); Wilbert Smith, Ray Miller, James Harris, Robert Sims, Albert 'June' Gardner (d). 9/51–12/53.

*** Mighty Mighty Man!
Ace CDCHD 459 Brown; Teddy Riley, Joe Bridgewater, Melvin Lastie, John Fernandez (t); Earl Battiste (as); Vic Thomas, Sammy Parker, Philip Scott, John Fontenette, Nat Perrilliat, Osborne Whitfield, Ray Felder, Johnny Griffin (ts); Walter Hiles, Julius Schedemayer (bs); Jimmy Williams, James C. Harris, James H. Thomas, Salvador Doucette, Frank McClure, John Thomas (p); Bill Jennings, Edgar Blanchard, Jimmy Davis, Charles Grayson, John Faire, Fred Jordan (g); Tommy Shelvin, Clarence Jones, Leonard Jefferson, Curtis Mitchell, Ed Conley (b); James Harris, Albert 'June' Gardner, Frank Parker, Placide Adams, Harry Nance, Edison Gore, ——McRudy (d). 3/53–5/59.

The first four tracks on *1951–1953* are from DeLuxe; the remainder, and all of *Mighty Mighty Man!*, are from King, which Brown joined in 1952. (At the same time King acquired the DeLuxe masters.) His new label was careful not to rock the boat in which Brown had sailed to success in the preceding years: 'Trouble At Midnight' all but duplicates the arrangement of 'Hard Luck Blues', and other numbers use a similar template, while 'Ain't No Rocking No More' is a sequel to 'Good Rockin' Tonight'. 'Mr. Hound Dog's In Town', untypically accompanied by a trio, is an excuse to cover 'Hound Dog' itself, and 'Bootleggin' Baby' alludes repeatedly to Eddie Vinson's 'Kidney Stew'. Most of those tracks are on both CDs, but *Mighty Mighty Man!*, unlimited by the complete-and-chronological principle of the Classics CD, follows the singer to the end of his King contract. By 1959 the tidal wave of rock 'n' roll was coming; Brown tried to ride it with 'Rinky Dinky Doo' and 'School Bell Rock', but it drowned him just the same.

(***) Greatest Hits
King Blues KSCD 1404 *As for relevant CDs above.* 7/47–12/52.
*** The Very Best Of Roy Brown: Rockin' At Midnight
Collectables COL-CD-2882 *Similar to above.* 7/47–53.
*** Good Rocking Tonight: The Best Of Roy Brown
Rhino R2 71545 *Similar to above.* 7/47–1/57.

The Rhino CD is a typically well-made and good-looking production which will appeal to buyers who prefer Brown's up-tempo numbers to his slow ones. It shares about two thirds of its contents with the EPM. All the tracks are from DeLuxe and King except the last, 'Let The Four Winds Blow', from Imperial. (*The Complete Imperial Recordings* [Capitol 31743] is deleted, no great loss.) Collectables' *Very Best* is drawn from a shorter and earlier period of Brown's work but stuffs in 25 tracks to prove that the title isn't over-bold. *Greatest Hits* includes numbers like 'Good Rockin' Tonight', 'Hard Luck Blues' and 'Miss Fanny Brown', but even a budget price is steep for only eight tracks. TR

Ruth Brown (born 1928)
VOCAL

Born in Portsmouth, Virginia, Ruth Weston left home to sing with a band and married its leader, trumpeter Jimmy Brown. After brief spells with the orchestras of Lucky Millinder and Blanche Calloway, she began recording for Atlantic in 1949 and had R&B chart hits with 'Teardrops From My Eyes' (1950), '5–10–15 Hours' (1952) and '(Mama) He Treats Your Daughter Mean' (1953), among others. Having quit the business in the '60s to raise her family, she returned in the mid-'70s and has been working steadily ever since, both recording and appearing in stage, movie and TV roles. She was active in the creation of the Rhythm & Blues Foundation.

(**) Ruth Brown 1949–1950
Classics 5003 Brown; Bobby Hackett, Harold Baker, unknowns (t); Will Bradley, Tyree Glenn (tb); Peanuts Hucko (cl, ts); Vincent Bair-Bey, unknown (as); Budd Johnson, Willie Jackson (ts); Ernie Caceres, prob. Heywood Henry (bs); Dick Cary (alto horn); Joe Bushkin, Earl Washington, Billy Taylor, Ernie Hayes, unknown (p); unknowns (strings); Eddie Condon, John Collins, unknowns (g); Jack Lesberg, Leonard Gaskin, unknowns (b); Sid Catlett, Roy Haynes, unknowns (d); unknown (chimes); The Delta Rhythm Boys, unknowns (v). 5/49–12/50.
(**) R. B. Blues
Arpeggio ARG 001 *As above.* 5/49–12/50.

(*) Ruth Brown 1951–1953
Classics 5084 *Brown; Taft Jordan (t); Jimmy Nottingham (tb); Burnie Peacock (as); Willis Jackson, Freddie Mitchell, Sam Taylor (ts); Heywood Henry, Pinky Williams, Paul Williams (bs); unknowns (brass, reeds); Billy Taylor, Harry Van Walls, Hank Jones, Kelly Owens, John Lewis, unknowns (p); unknown (cel); Mickey Baker, Rector Bailey, unknowns (g); George Duvivier, Lloyd Trotman, unknowns (b); Connie Kay, Joe Marshall, unknown (d); Joe M. Ricci (tamb); Budd Johnson Orchestra; The James Quintet (v). 2/51–12/53.*

(*) Mama, He Treats Your Daughter Mean
Indigo IGOCD 2550 *As for Classics CDs. 5/49–7/53.*

(*) A Proper Introduction To Ruth Brown: Teardrops From My Eyes
Proper INTRO CD 2067 *As above. 5/49–12/53.*

Although on her early records Brown sometimes sounds a little like Dinah Washington, she gradually achieved a distinct style, sassier and more streetwise, which made her one of the more influential singers of her era. But it *was* gradually: for over a year she was repeatedly recorded with bland lineups and moribund repertoire like 'Happiness Is A Thing Called Joe' or 'Dear Little Boy Of Mine', for which Atlantic's producers resorted to the aesthetics of Mitch Miller. The jaunty 'Teardrops From My Eyes', in an arrangement that foregrounded tenor sax and rhythm, broke the mould and was succeeded by more Rudy Toombs compositions such as '5–10–15 Hours' and 'Daddy Daddy', inconsequential bluesy numbers that Brown put over with vivacity. Yet selections like the pop ballad 'Good-For Nothin' Joe' and the frantic rock 'n' roll number 'Hello Little Boy' suggest that Atlantic were still uncertain how to present her. The story will slowly unfold on further Classics CDs, but readers unfamiliar with Brown's work are cautioned that the blues, or even blues-ish, content on *1949–1950* is scanty. Arpeggio merely duplicate the first Classics; Indigo and Proper select evenly and similarly from the two, eliminating many of the more outlandish performances.

(*) R+B=Ruth Brown
Bullseye Blues CD BB 9583 *Brown; Barney Floyd, Charlie Miller (t); Delfeayo Marsalis (tb); Wessell Anderson (as); Ed Petersen (ts); Victor Goines (bs); Bobby Forrester (o, p); Bonnie Raitt (g, v); Duke Robillard, Clarence 'Gatemouth' Brown, Rodney Jones (g); James Singleton, Rufus Reid (b); Herlin Riley, Akira Tana (d); Johnny Adams (v). 1–2/97.*

(*) A Good Day For The Blues
Bullseye Blues & Jazz 9613 *Brown; Charlie Miller, Abram Wilson (t); John Touchy (tb); Victor Goines (cl, bs); Ray Moore (as); Bill Easley (ts, f); Bobby Forrester, Davell Crawford (o, p); Duke Robillard (g); James Singleton (b); Akira Tana (d). 7–8/98.*

Brown does not sing with the power and clarity of her 20s, but on many of the songs chosen for these albums that's no shortcoming – indeed, the resignation of 'Too Little Too Late' (*R+B=Ruth Brown*) or the fine title track of *A Good Day For The Blues* demands that kind of voice. Blues as such are in short supply, and the only standard one is 'I'm Gonna Move To The Outskirts Of Town' (*R+B*), where she swaps humorous man-talk with Bonnie Raitt. Her own extended raps, as in 'That Train Don't Stop Here' on *R+B* and 'Can't Stand A Broke Man' and 'Cabbage Head' on *Good Day*, are amusing on first hearing but neither they nor the even more over-extended 'H. B.'s Funky Fable' (*Good Day*), a tall tale from the animal world, are likely to please any but a devotee the second time around. These are admirably arranged albums with sleek solos, but the artist they present is a cabaret diva rather than a straightforward blues singer. TR

Walter Brown (1917–56)
VOCAL

In 1941, 'Confessin' The Blues' conferred stardom on Jay McShann's band and its vocalist alike. Brown may already have been a heroin addict, and his newfound fame did nothing to discourage wild and unpredictable behaviour. He was in and out of the McShann band until 1944, when he went solo. Record companies kept trying until 1951, hoping for another 'Confessin' The Blues', but Brown was running a nightclub when drink and drugs finished him off.

*** **Jay McShann 1941–1943**
Classics 740 *Brown; Harold Bruce, Bernard Anderson, Orville Minor, Bob Merrill, Dave Mitchell, Jesse Jones, Willie Cook (t); Joe Baird, Lawrence Anderson, Alonzo Pettiford, Alfonso Fook, Rudy Morrison (tb); John Jackson, Charlie Parker, Rudolph Dennis (as); Bob Mabane, Harry Ferguson, Freddy Culliver, Paul Quinichette, Bill Goodson (ts); James Coe, Rae Brodely (bs); Jay McShann (p); Lucky Enois (g); Gene Ramey (b); Gus Johnson, Dan Graves (d). 4/41–12/43.*

(*) Blues Everywhere
[Westside WESF 110] *Brown; Tom Grider, Archie Johnson, Isaac Larkin, Bill Arter, Earl Shepherd (t); John McConnell, Joe Baird, Nat Clayton, Tommy Smith (tb); Edward Lee, Livingstone McConnell (as); Benny Miller, Cliff Jenkins, Charlie White, Jimmy Benner (ts); George Hall (bs); Skip Hall, Jimmy Green (p); Rudy Mason, Nick Buonadonna (g); Vic McMillen, Lawrence Burgan (b); Fred Riley, Charles Lee (d); unknowns (v). 12/45–7/46.*

(*) Walter Brown 1945–1947
Classics 5010 *As above, except add prob. Russell Royster (t), John Hardee (ts), Sammy Benskin (p), Tiny Grimes (g), Alvin Raglin (b), Eddie Nicholson (d). 12/45–47.*

(*) Walter Brown 1947–1951
Classics 5038 *Brown; unknown (t); John Jackson (as); Freddy Culliver, Harold Ashby, Ben Webster (ts); Bob Williams (bs); unknowns (s); Jay McShann, Willie Rice (p); Jimmy Walker, Herman Bell, unknown (g); Percy Gabriel, John Witt, Lloyd Anderson, unknown (b); Jesse Price, John Mosley, unknown (d); band (v). 6/47–51.*

*** **Forget Your Troubles And Jump Your Blues Away!**
Jasmine JASCD 376 *Similar to above CDs, except add William Hickman (t), Al Morgan (tb), Johnny Sparrow (ts), Bradbury Taylor (bs), James Skinner (d). 4/41–11/49.*

Walter Brown's singing is in the Kansas City tradition, but his voice is smaller and more nasal than the city's usual high-powered style; at times, it's almost wistful. It's also rather unvaried, which is a problem when Brown is heard at length. His lyrics are often very clever, but on *Jay McShann* it helps that they're mixed in with cutting-edge KC instrumentals. The downside is that it becomes obvious that the McShann band's swingmatism was greater than Brown's.

Westside issue all Brown's recordings for Queen, and one title on which someone else takes the vocal; eight tracks by Crown Prince Waterford complete the disc. Inevitably Brown remakes 'Confessin' The Blues', but he's trying to move with the times; he cranks up the vocal power as far as he can, probably in emulation of Wynonie Harris, but the needle never gets very far round the dial. The accompaniments, evenly split between a big band and an octet, reflect changes in the economics of swing. All the musicians do a good job, but never approach the class of McShann's lineups. *1945–1947* clones the Westside CD, replacing Waterford's tracks with four unspectacular songs recorded for Signature.

1947–1951 presents 16 Capitol sides, bookending them with four on Mercury and two on Peacock. Peacock's big-band arrangements are as dull as they are lush, but on Mercury McShann, Gabriel and Price are a collective miracle of rhythmic subtlety, carrying Brown to a level of relaxed, jazzy authority that he seldom attained. The Capitol sessions feature some stellar musicians; on four tracks Ben Webster's seductive gruffness is a high point, and Jimmy Walker contributes some sinewy guitar solos, but Brown refuses to be challenged, singing with determined detachment and minimal interpretation.

For casual listeners, Jasmine offer the best introduction to Walter Brown: all the McShann band vocals from the early '40s (including an airshot of 'Lonely Boy Blues' not on Classics), the complete Mercury session and six Capitol sides, including all those with Webster. cs

Cora Mae Bryant (born 1926)
VOCAL, SHAKER

Bryant is Curley Weaver's daughter. She runs a blues museum at her home in Oxford, Georgia, and promotes Atlanta's Giving It Back *festival, which celebrates the blues heritage.*

** Born With The Blues
Music Maker MMCD 22 *Bryant; Joshua Jacobson (g, v).* 99.
** Born In Newton County
Music Maker MMCD 39 *As above.* 03?

Jacobson has cloned his playing from Curley Weaver's. Six tracks on *Born With The Blues* are learned from Weaver's records, and another two are tributes to him; one of these also recollects his friends Blind Willie McTell and Buddy Moss. Bryant can't be faulted for either filial piety or historical awareness, but her singing makes for unrewarding listening, being grinding, inexpressive and monotonous. *Born In Newton County* is a bit better, but not much; Bryant is perceptibly trying to sing with more expression and subtlety, but seldom succeeds. An attempt at Barbecue Bob's 'Motherless Child', in its original version a bravura vocal display, is particularly ill-advised. cs

Danny Bryant (born 1980)
VOCAL, GUITAR

Raised in southern England, Bryant started playing the guitar at the age of 15 and immediately turned towards the blues, inspired largely by his mentor Walter Trout – the two often perform together – and gaining a high degree of parental support. Within a couple of years, Bryant had founded the RedEyeBand, with his father on bass and his mother acting as manager. By 2000 the act was Bryant's profession.

** Watching You
Blues Matters BMRCD 2002/2 *Bryant; Ben Keys (o, kb); Dominic Boucher (o); Ken Bryant (b); Andy Burt (d).* 02.
**(*) Shadows Passed
Blues Matters BMRCD 20039 *Bryant; Ben Keys, Richard Hammerton (kb); Ken Bryant (b); Andy Burt (d).* 03.
**(*) Covering Their Tracks
Blues Matters BMRCD 20046 *Bryant; Chris Cooper (kb); Ken Bryant (b); Andy Burt (d).* 04.

Bryant's debut is perfectly sound, showcasing a natural flair for the guitar and a rich, although by no means perfect, voice. Trout's influence shines like a beacon in Bryant's writing and instrumental identity, particularly in the tonal nature of the fluid Stratocaster licks. At times the band sounds a little aimless (a problem compounded by sloppy production) and could use tightening all round, but generally the performances are happily competent. Perhaps the chief flaw of *Watching You* is a reliance on tried and tested formulas in the songwriting, both harmonically and lyrically, seen particularly in the irritatingly melodramatic 'Living In The Lion's Den'.

Watching You signalled a need for general development from Bryant and his band, especially in harnessing some form of individuality. The follow-up goes some distance towards addressing this issue, although it doesn't check all the boxes hoped for. *Shadows Passed* presents a band seemingly more at ease, and sounding increasingly polished as a result. The Trout factor remains strong, although less overpowering than previously, and a handful of heartfelt ballads – notably 'One Love' and the Claptonesque 'Where The River Ends' – complements the harder moments. There are still cases of songs acting as slaves to (even more blistering) solos, but *Shadows Passed* is undoubtedly a more advanced recording than its predecessor.

Covering Their Tracks is divided into four new tracks and half a dozen familiar numbers. In the homegrown songs, the lyrics thankfully display both originality and substance, immediately evidenced by the opening 'This Is The Blues', an attack on critical judgements about Bryant's authenticity and depth. Musically, again, the writing is often uncomfortably bland, while the production is inconsistent. The cross-section of covers is of varying quality, from a butchering of Hendrix's 'Voodoo Chile' (not the ubiquitous 'Slight Return') to a tasteful take on Bob Dylan's 'Girl From The North Country', via an excellent rendition of Eddie Boyd's 'Five Long Years'. Given the shortcomings in Bryant's songwriting, the attention given to these covers, in spite of some flaws, is generally welcome, and hints at the act's potential. JF

Precious Bryant (born 1942)
VOCAL, GUITAR

Born Precious Bussey to a musical family in southwest Georgia, Bryant began playing guitar at six, and grew up performing in church and at parties. She was first recorded in 1969, but it was over ten years before she consented to appear outside her community.

*** Fool Me Good
Terminus 0201 *Bryant.* 01.
*** The Truth
Terminus 0407 *Bryant; Jake Fussell (g); Tony Bryant, Amos Harvey (b); J. D. Mark (d).* 04.

Precious Bryant uses an amplified guitar on *Fool Me Good*, but she balances her singing against it with ease, and, if anything, her voice is both stronger and more subtle than in

1984, when six live tracks on *National Downhome Blues Festival* (Southland SCD-21) were recorded. For the most part, she plays chordal accompaniments with a relaxed but clearly defined rhythm, and ranges surprisingly widely, touching base with soul on 'Don't Mess Up A Good Thing', and offering a confident 'Fever' that owes nothing to Peggy Lee. Bryant's blues range from the husky, reflective 'Broke And Ain't Got A Dime' to jumping dance music. She does a fine version of 'Black Rat Swing', but well-turned originals predominate; the absence of obvious covers (Jimmy Reed and Muddy Waters mop up half the tracks on Southland) is, albeit negatively, an index of her growth as an artist. There's some hesitancy when she fingerpicks on 'Georgia Buck', and 'Ups And Downs' is a dull gospel song, but fervent accounts of 'Don't Let The Devil Ride' and 'The Saints' more than redress that balance.

The additional musicians on *The Truth* do good work, especially Bryant's son, whose electric bass lines often have a chromatic, slithering jazziness. The old-time fingerpicking of 'Sugar Hill Blues' is very successfully energized by electric guitar, bass and drums, while yet remaining graceful. Bryant's repertoire continues to be eclectic: she covers Denise LaSalle and Irma Thomas as well as Little Walter ('My Babe', a lot more rocking and less dull than usual) and Memphis Minnie. This reflects her acquisition of songs from the radio; the mass media also inspire the original 'Dark Angel', a tribute to the superheroine of a TV series. The most captivating tracks here, thanks to the conviction that underpins them and infuses their delivery, are several well-known spirituals revived from Bryant's time as a member of a gospel quartet with her sisters. CS

Willie Bryant (1908–64)
VOCAL

Born in New Orleans, Bryant entered show business as a juvenile tap dancer, led his first band in 1934 at New York's Connie's Inn, acted on Broadway, was master of ceremonies at the Apollo Theater and a disc jockey, and occasionally sang with the band he led in the late '40s. He was known as 'The Mayor of New York'.

*** Blues Around The Clock
Delmark DE-685 *Bryant; Taft Jordan (t, v); Frank Galbreath, Archie Johnson, Henry Glover, Sammy Lowe (t); Steve Pulliam, Bob Range (tb, v); Ed Moran, Dan Minor (tb); unknown (ss); Tab Smith, Michael Hedley, Jimmy Powell, Bobby Smith (as); Johnny Hicks, Harold Stein, Eddie Leaves (ts); Haywood Henry (bs); Leonard Feather, Bill Doggett, Reggie Ashby, Larry Johnson, Duke Anderson, unknown (p); Chuck Wayne, Leroy Harris, Ralph Williams, Leroy Kirkland (g); Ben Brown, Billy Taylor, John Levy, Lee Stanfield, unknown (b); Walter Johnson, Panama Francis, Joe Murphy, unknown (d); Doc Pomus, Laurel Watson, poss. Ben Smith (v). 10/45–9/49.*

Ten of the 21 tracks feature Bryant's smooth, confidential singing. Some, like the two-part 'Blues Around The Clock', are backed by Tab Smith's Septette, and the altoist's wheedling tone leads you towards the cushioned comfort of the music like a maître d' suavely escorting you to the best table. A different but similar-sized group, drawn from Erskine Hawkins's orchestra, accompanies Bryant's urbanities on another two-parter, 'Blues Around The Country', and his amusing exchanges with trombonist/singer Bob Range in 'Algiers Blues'. Of the other numbers four are by Range, four by Doc Pomus and two by Laurel Watson; Pomus's are discussed further in his entry. TR

Buckwheat Zydeco
GROUP

Stanley 'Buckwheat' Dural (born 1947) has been a prominent figure in zydeco since the '80s. Born in Lafayette, he learned to play accordion from his father, 'a real Frenchman', but his was a generation that was stripped of its linguistic heritage by Louisiana educational policy, and Buckwheat's musical taste was reshaped by rock 'n' roll and R&B. He formed his first band in 1971. While playing keyboards with Clifton Chenier he rediscovered French music, and in 1978 he bought a new accordion and created his Ils Sont Partis Band, with which he developed an eclectic modern style of zydeco.

**(*) One For The Road
Paula PCD-21 *John Bell (ts); Stanley 'Buckwheat' Dural (ac, o, p, v); Russell Gordon (g); Ted Zerby (b); Jimmy Papillion (d); Elijah Cudges (rb). 79.*

The oldest album in Buckwheat's current catalogue will be chiefly appealing to conservative zydeco fans, with its plain but satisfying programme of blues, swamp-pop ballads and zydeco standbys. Except for occasional forays on organ, and piano on 'Zydeco Boogie Woogie', there isn't much here that Clifton Chenier wouldn't have done, and with more panache; on the other hand, there are few signs of the zydeco-for-tourists agenda that Dural would pursue in later years.

**(*) Turning Point
Rounder CD 2045 *Calvin Landry (t); Stanley 'Buckwheat' Dural (ac, o, p, v); Selwyn Cooper (g); Lee Allen Zeno (b); Nathan Jolivette (d); Elijah Cudges (rb). 4/83.*

*** Waitin' For My Ya Ya
Rounder CD 2051 *As above, except Zeno also plays g; Jimmy Reed (g) replaces Cooper. 4/85.*

*** Buckwheat's Zydeco Party
Rounder CD 11528 *As above CDs. 4/83, 4/85.*

*** Buckwheat's Zydeco Party, DeLuxe Edition
Rounder Heritage Series RRCD 11602 *As above. 4/83, 4/85.*

(***) Classics
Rounder CD 2177 *As above. 4/83, 4/85.*

Turning Point uncovers the sources of Buckwheat's music by embracing rock 'n' roll and soul as well as zydeco tunes, but only a rabid traditionalist is likely to be alarmed by the programme. *Waitin' For My Ya Ya* is another matter. Opening with the Dirty Dozen Brass Band's 'My Feet Can't Fail Me Now', it spends most of its time with soul hits like 'Someone Else Is Steppin' In' and 'Warm And Tender Love' or in New Orleans, and, apart from 'Buck's Step-Up', oldfashioned zydeco doesn't get much of a look-in. But the zydecorated versions of 'Ya Ya' and 'Tee Nah Nah' are fresh and fun, and Lee Allen Zeno's bass playing, always stimulating, steps up to frenetic in the closing 'Hot Tamale Baby'.

Rounder must think a lot of those two albums: they've revisited them repeatedly. *Buckwheat's Zydeco Party* contains most of them, the tracks it drops being mostly quite droppable, and the *DeLuxe Edition* is the same, with the addition of a flamboyant 'Let The Good Times Roll' from the *Ya Ya* sessions. Since both those well-filled compilations are available, it isn't clear why Rounder then issued *Classics*, which has eight tracks in common with them and only ten in all.

** **On A Night Like This**
Island 422–842 739 *Gregory Davis, Efrem Townes (t); Kevin Harris (ts); Roger Lewis (bs); Stanley 'Buckwheat' Dural (ac, o, p, v); Melvin Veazie, Paul Senegal [Sinegal] (g); Lee Allen Zeno (b); Nathan Jolivette (d); Elijah Cudges (rb, cowbell).* 87.
** **Taking It Home**
Island 422–842 603 *Calvin Landry (t); Anthony Butler (as); Dennis Taylor (ts, bs); Stanley 'Buckwheat' Dural (ac, o, p, v); Melvin Veazie, Robert James Ahern, Eric Clapton (g); Lee Allen Zeno (b); Herman 'Rat' Brown (d); Patrick Landry (rb); Lisa Mednick, Allison Young (v).* 88.
** **Where There's Smoke There's Fire**
Island 422–842 925 *Lee Thornburg (t); Dennis Taylor (ts); Steve Berlin (bs); Stanley 'Buckwheat' Dural (ac, o, p, v); David Hidalgo (g, d, v, prod); Melvin Veazie (g); Lee Allen Zeno (b); Kevin Menard (d); Wilbert Willis (rb); Mark Linett (tamb); Dwight Yoakam (v).* 90.
** **Menagerie: The Essential Zydeco Collection**
Mango 162–539 929 *As for* On A Night Like This, Taking It Home *and* Where There's Smoke There's Fire. 87–90.
(*) **The Ultimate Collection
Hip-O 314–542 346 *As for* One For The Road, Turning Point, Waitin' For My Ya Ya *and all Island CDs.* 79–94.

The SS *Buckwheat Zydeco*'s Island voyage begins with a couple of vivacious 12-bars at the start of *On A Night Like This*, but soon afterwards skipper Dural quits his anchorage in Blues Bayou and heads for the temperate but shallow waters of cajun–country crossover. The gazetteer song 'Creole Country' on *Taking It Home*, the bland 'Hey, Good Lookin'' on *Where There's Smoke There's Fire* and the outright schlock of 'Space Zydeco' on *Night Like This* suggest that Dural has decided not to mediate Creole culture but to mass-market it; if his artistic talent were with a brush, you feel, he'd be selling pictures of crawfish painted on driftwood. Hyperactive percussion and accordion give the occasional old-school zydeco tune like 'Drivin' Old Grey' (*Taking It Home*) or 'Buck's Hot Rod' (*Where There's Smoke*) some dancefloor zest, but each of the albums has too many tracks that take their time going nowhere in particular.

Menagerie is an abbreviated account of Buckwheat's Island time, containing two tracks from *On A Night Like This*, three from *Taking It Home* and six from *Where There's Smoke There's Fire*. *The Ultimate Collection* selects a similar tranche of 11 cuts from those albums, adding two from the probably deleted *Five Card Stud* (Island 314–524 018) and prefacing the Island chapter with half a dozen items from Paula, Rounder and the deleted Black Top album *100% Fortified Zydeco*.

(*) **Trouble
Tomorrow TMR 70001 *Curtis Watson, Andre Carter (t); Vince Williams (ts); Stanley 'Buckwheat' Dural (ac, o, v); Gerald Dural (kb); Joseph Chavis, Mike Melchione (g); Lee Allen Zeno (b); Kevin Menard (d); Patrick Landry (rb).* 97.
(*) **The Buckwheat Zydeco Story: A 20-Year Party
Tomorrow TMR 70002 *As for all above CDs, except add William Terry (ts), Wilbert Miller (h, perc), Ray Mouton (g), George Recile, Mike Burch (d), Sir Reginald M. Dural (rb, perc), Angie B. Stone, Debbe L. Cole (v).* 4/83–8/98.
** **Jackpot!**
Tomorrow TMR 70008 *Curtis Watson (t); Stanley 'Buckwheat' Dural (ac, kb, o, v); Paul 'Lil' Buck' Sinegal, Olivier Scoazec (g); Lee Allen Zeno (b, v); Gerard St Julien (g); Sir Reginald Master Dural (rb, v); Catherine Russell (v).* 05.

Trouble's generic but fast-moving zydeco dance tunes like 'Hard Chargin'' and 'Allons A Boucherie', invigorated by the rhythm section of Zeno, Menard and Landry, again hint that this is an exciting band in a club setting. The fabric of the music is also toughened by several blues, 'Crossroads' scoring rarity points as a zydeco interpretation of a Robert Johnson song. *The Buckwheat Zydeco Story* gathers one or two tracks from each of the Rounder and Island albums and *Trouble*, three from out-of-print albums and a closing 'Hey Baby' (the Bruce Channel song) from the 1998 Edmonton Folk Festival. *Jackpot!* is nine tracks of zydeco lite followed by three organ-led instrumentals – a slow blues, a faster blues and a whiff of reggae – brewed with a Booker T-bag. TR

Mojo Buford (born 1929)
VOCAL, HARMONICA

George Buford took the well-worn path from Mississippi via Memphis to Chicago. He was a member of the Muddy Waters band intermittently from the late '50s to the '80s, and now lives in Memphis, but was resident in Minneapolis for many years, working there with Lazy Bill Lucas and Jo Jo Williams.

(*) **State Of The Blues Harp
JSP JSPCD 2018 *Buford; Jack Hills (p); Richard Studholme (g); Bernice Cartwright (b); Geoff Nichols (d).* 89.
** **Champagne & Reefer**
Fedora FCD 5015 *Buford; Bob Margolin, Johnny Rapp (g); Paul Thomas (b); Chico Chism (d).* 9/98.

Beginning with his nickname, Buford has capitalized on his association with Muddy Waters, but JSP asked him not to do Muddy's songs. This avoids the double whammy of limited technique applied to an over-familiar playlist, but is not enough to save the session. As both singer and instrumentalist, Buford is sturdily energetic, but inflexible and unsubtle. At first, the aggressive ensemble sound grabs one's attention, and Studholme's confident, Earl Hookerish guitar has a welcome freshness, but Buford's limitations are soon monotonously apparent.

In the subsequent decade, Buford made three CDs, now out of print, for Blue Loon, and by the time of *Champagne & Reefer* he was just as energetic, and just as free from nuance. Most of this live set consists of dull versions of songs associated with Muddy Waters, on which Buford and his accompanists are coarsely predictable, and just close enough to the great man's sound to emphasize their distance from his genius. CS

Built For Comfort Blues Band
GROUP

This Central New York band was formed from members of two other groups, The Kingsnakes and The Corvairs. Fronted by the cousins Matt and Morris Tarbell, it gigs regularly on the East Coast.

** **Keep Cool**
Blue Wave CD 118 *Matt Tarbell (h, v); Jerry Neely (kb); Paul Laronde (g, b, v); Morris Tarbell (g); Mark Tiffault (d).* 6–11/92.
(*) **High Ballin'
Blue Wave CD 129 *Matt Tarbell (h, v); Mark Doyle (o, perc); Morris Tarbell (g); Larry Stringer (b); Dave Sisson (b); Kim Lembo (v).* 10–11/95.

The Tarbells are thoroughly idiomatic on their instruments,

and Matt is a passable vocalist, but the ensemble playing on *Keep Cool* is formulaic and at times, thanks to a repressive studio ambience, rather bloodless. The programme is evenly divided between received material and originals. *High Ballin'* has a larger proportion of the band's own songs such as 'You Burned Me', a slow blues with a scorching guitar solo. 'Easy Ride' is played by Morris Tarbell alone, on an acoustic National. This recording has more verve and intensity than *Keep Cool*. TR

Bull City Red
VOCAL, GUITAR, WASHBOARD

George Washington was Blind Boy Fuller's washboard player in Durham, North Carolina, and took the town's nickname as his own. Red's guitar features only on his own records, but his washboard is heard on many of Fuller's (where he was sometimes billed as Oh Red), and he also played behind Brownie McGhee, Sonny Terry and Buddy Moss. Red moved to coastal Virginia during World War II, to work in the shipyards; thereafter he disappears from view.

*** Blues & Gospel From The Eastern States (1935–1944)
Document DOCD-5644 Bull City Red; Gary Davis (g); poss. Sonny Jones (g, v); Sonny Terry (v). 7/35–7/39.

As a singer and guitarist, Red took Blind Boy Fuller as his exemplar; he wasn't Fuller's equal as a picker, but a bouncy 'Richmond Blues' and a truculent 'Pick And Shovel Blues' are the work of an artist who can make a song his own. (Fuller's 'Big House Bound' is a variant of 'Pick and Shovel Blues'; that it was recorded three years later suggests that the traffic was not all one way.) Gary Davis, who didn't have much time for other guitarists as a rule, seconds on three of Red's six issued blues, and plays a brilliant accompaniment to 'I Saw The Light', which was issued as by Blind Gary, but is logically included here. That song is the best of Red's spirituals; he plays washboard on six more where he, Terry and Jones collaborate as Brother George And His Sanctified Singers, but the lack of polish on these performances is calculated, and before long predictable. The CD is completed by eight tracks from Sam Montgomery, and two apiece from Poor Bill and Boy Green. Sometimes joined by a second guitarist, Montgomery is better as himself than when imitating Kokomo Arnold. Green's 'Play My Jukebox' is one of the finest recordings inspired by Blind Boy Fuller, and Poor Bill's flurrying guitar and smoky singing are worth hearing. CS

Bumble Bee Slim (1905–68)
VOCAL, GUITAR

Amos Easton was born in the seaport town of Brunswick in southern Georgia. He left home in his teens and found work wherever he could, sometimes singing and playing guitar. By 1928 he had reached Indianapolis, where he was clearly much influenced by Leroy Carr, whose style he would sedulously copy on many of his records. Between March 1934 and June 1937 he cut over 150 issued sides for Vocalion, Decca and, less often, Bluebird, then, tiring of the monotony of his work, abruptly left both Chicago and the record business. He made a couple of comebacks on the West Coast, in 1951 on Specialty and in 1962 with an album for Pacific Jazz.

**(*) Bumble Bee Slim – Vol. 1
Document DOCD-5261 Bumble Bee Slim; unknown (cl); Myrtle Jenkins, prob. Georgia Tom Dorsey, unknowns (p); prob. Charlie McCoy (md, poss. g); Willie Bee James, prob. Howard Armstrong, prob. Ted Bogan, unknown (g); unknown (v). c. 10/31–3/34.

Though he had evidently already met Leroy Carr, Slim didn't start copying him as soon as he secured a recording date: his first sides, for Paramount in 1931, were solo recordings with slide guitar in the vein of Tampa Red, and his 1932 Vocalions, backed by guitar and piano, owe their sound to records by Tampa and Georgia Tom, or Walter Davis. But when he next recorded, in 1934, his doleful manner and song titles like 'Baby So Long' made it obvious whose row he had decided to hoe, even though Carr was currently recording for the same label. This view of Bumble Bee Slim on his first flights would be more engaging if the transfers weren't mostly poor ones. Fortunately the sound improves on the last three tracks, where he is accompanied by a couple of decorative guitarists, probably Armstrong and Bogan.

**(*) Bumble Bee Slim – Vol. 2
Document DOCD-5262 Bumble Bee Slim; Jimmie Gordon, unknowns (p); prob. Howard Armstrong (vn, g); prob. Ted Bogan, prob. Charlie McCoy, prob. Willie Bee James, prob. Big Bill Broonzy, prob. Carl Martin (g). 3–10/34.

**(*) Bumble Bee Slim – Vol. 3
Document DOCD-5263 Bumble Bee Slim; Myrtle Jenkins, prob. Charlie Segar or Horace Malcolm (p); Ted Bogan (g, v); Big Bill Broonzy, prob. Carl Martin, prob. Charlie McCoy (g). 11/34–4/35.

*** Bumble Bee Slim – Vol. 4
Document DOCD-5264 Bumble Bee Slim; Myrtle Jenkins, Black Bob, Dorothy Rice, unknowns (p); Charlie McCoy, Big Bill Broonzy, Scrapper Blackwell, unknowns (g); prob. Washboard Sam (wb). 4–7/35.

*** Bumble Bee Slim – Vol. 5
Document DOCD-5265 Bumble Bee Slim; unknown (t); unknown (as, ts); unknown (ts); Myrtle Jenkins (p, sp); Black Bob, unknowns (p); Memphis Minnie (g, v); Casey Bill Weldon, unknowns (g); unknowns (b); unknown (perc); Jimmie Gordon (v). 7/35–2/36.

**(*) Bumble Bee Slim – Vol. 6
Document DOCD-5266 Bumble Bee Slim; Roy Palmer (tb); Arnett Nelson (cl); Peetie Wheatstraw (p, v); Myrtle Jenkins, Honey Hill (p); Bill Gaither, unknowns (g); unknown (sp). 2–8/36.

**(*) Bumble Bee Slim – Vol. 7
Document DOCD-5267 Bumble Bee Slim; unknown (cl); Honey Hill, Black Bob, prob. Myrtle Jenkins, prob. Albert Ammons (p); Bill Gaither, prob. Big Bill Broonzy, unknown (g); unknown(s) (b); unknown (k); unknown (wb). 8/36–1/37.

**(*) Bumble Bee Slim – Vol. 8
Document DOCD-5268 Bumble Bee Slim; unknown (t); unknown (cl, ts); Maurice Simon (as); Maxwell Davis (ts); Jewell Grant (bs); Willard McDaniel, prob. Albert Ammons, poss. Blind John Davis, unknown (p); Herman 'Tiny' Mitchell, unknown (g); Billy Hadnott (b); Oscar Lee Bradley, prob. Fred Williams (d). 1–6/37, 8–11/51.

**(*) Bumble Bee Slim – Vol. 9
Document DOCD-5570 Bumble Bee Slim; unknown (t); Roy Palmer (tb); unknown (cl, ts); Arnett Nelson, unknown (cl); Maurice Simon (as); Maxwell Davis (ts); Jewell Grant (bs); Black Bob, Myrtle Jenkins, Willard McDaniel, prob. Albert Ammons, poss. Blind John Davis, unknowns (p); Big Bill Broonzy, Herman 'Tiny' Mitchell, prob. Willie Bee James, prob.

Carl Martin, unknowns (g); Billy Hadnott, unknowns (b); Oscar Lee Bradley, poss. Fred Williams (d). 10/34–11/51.

Titles like 'Dead And Gone Mother' and 'Sad And Lonesome' on *Vol. 2* and 'Bleeding Heart Blues' on *Vol. 3* are accurate pointers to the preoccupations of Slim's material at this stage. His mode of presentation swings between outright Carrism ('Mean Mistreatin' Woman', 'Good Evening Blues', etc.) and a generic style, not unlike Jimmie Gordon's, that was probably a composite of several contemporary singers'. *Vol. 2*'s 'Rough Road Blues' is derived from Tommy Johnson, possibly by way of the McCoy brothers, while 'Bad Gal' is partly inspired by Joe Pullum's 'Black Gal What Makes Your Head So Hard?', of which Slim later (*Vol. 3*) made a close cover version. Little interrupts the sequence of slow and medium-paced blues but a cheerful piano solo, 'Deep Bass Boogie', with comments by Slim and the unidentified player, on *Vol. 2* and the brisk 'Tell Me What It's All About' and 'Everybody's Fishing' on *Vol. 3*. The quality of the transfers continues to be indifferent, though it will improve on the next two volumes.

The session straddling *Vol. 3* and *Vol. 4* is distinguished by the emphatic piano of Myrtle Jenkins, which seems to kick Slim into singing with a little more vim. By this point a pattern seemed to be emerging, wherein his Vocalion recordings had quite varied repertoire and treatment but his Deccas kept him firmly in the Carr seat, but Carr's death in mid-1935 plunged him into a round of tributes and memorial recordings on both labels that extends from 'The Death Of Leroy Carr' on *Vol. 4* to well into *Vol. 5*. Slim had been at this job for a while and these performances are about as good as copies and *hommages* get, but it must have been a spiritually unrewarding task, and one can imagine him giving a wry smile when offered a song called 'Sick And Tired Of Singing The Blues'. Fortunately he was soon to enjoy an invigorating encounter, in February 1936, with Myrtle Jenkins, Black Bob, Memphis Minnie and Casey Bill Weldon, which produced one of his finest blues interpretations, 'Ramblin' With That Woman', and the effervescent dance tune 'New Orleans Stop Time'.

The bulk of *Vol. 6* is two sessions with estimable pianists. At the first, with Jenkins, Slim reprised some of his hits so that they could be issued as 'New Big 80 Blues', etc., but also found an access to poignancy, and not one provided by Leroy Carr, in 'Fast Life Blues' and 'Rock Hearted Woman'. The next date was with Honey Hill and Bill Gaither, who was just beginning to challenge Slim as a Carr stylist. Slim responds by delivering 'Ease Me Down' in the manner of Peetie Wheatstraw, with whom he had had a mock argument, earlier on this CD, in 'No Good Woman'.

The first half of *Vol. 7* is also with Hill and Gaither, and Slim, suggestible as ever, sometimes edges close to Gaither's weary plaintiveness. Although formulaic in their presentation, his songs in this period are strewn with pithy lines like 'Every goodbye ain't gone – every shut-eye sure ain't sleep'. 'Slave Man Blues', from a later session, is an alluring minor-key number with snake-charmer clarinet. The 1/37 date split between *Vol. 7* and *Vol. 8* is notable for an incisive pianist, currently believed to be Albert Ammons. Slim's last recordings of the '30s, the majority of which weren't issued at the time, variously involve an enthusiastic trumpeter and a dull reeds player, but are spoiled by pallid piano playing. The four sides from 1951 show that he was at home with a larger group and a more modern sound, and that he could slip easily into the laidback Charles Brown manner ('Lonesome Old Feeling'), but

what possessed him to sing, and Specialty to record, a rewrite of the old square dance 'Ida Red'? These last three volumes suffer from the variable quality of the source material.

Vol. 9, a sort of postscript to Document's BBS story, consists of unissued sides from Vocalion. If it weren't that seven of them are heard in two takes, this would be rather a good selection of his work, varied in both repertoire and musical settings and, thanks to clean test pressings, generally easy on the ear. 'Sometimes' and the instrumental 'Tiny's Boogie' are unissued items from Specialty.

*** **The Essential**
Classic Blues CBL 200031 2CD *As for relevant Document CDs.* c. 10/31–11/51.
*** **The Blues: From Georgia To Chicago 1931–1937**
Frémeaux FA 261 2CD *As above.* c. 10/31–6/37.
* **Baby So Long**
Acrobat ACRCD 138 *As above.* c. 10/31–1/37.
(*) **Bumble Bee Slim 1934–37
Best Of Blues BOB 6 *As above.* 10/34–6/37.

The Classic Blues and Frémeaux issues are 36-track 2CDs, both soundly chosen. Each of them nods briefly to the Paramount session (but the Classic Blues set less briefly than it appears, since where it lists 'Baby So Long' it plays the Paramount 'Honey Bee Blues'), then plunges into the mid-'30s, the Classic Blues adding a couple of the later Specialty sides. Both collections include several of the songs singled out above; the Classic Blues scores rather higher in that respect, but the Frémeaux picks some interesting material not on the other, like '12 O'Clock Southern Train', where Slim acts the part of a railroad employee calling out route-stops in a kind of modified field holler, and 'The Jive Of Mine', which is based on Blind Blake's 'Too Tight'. Both have generally good sound, and either would make an excellent BBS starter pack. The Best Of Blues CD is also a sensible selection, and if the sound quality were a little better it would merit a similar rating. *Baby So Long* is a drab assortment made duller by the inclusion of three two-part numbers and then rendered unlistenable by misused sound-restoration tools. TR

Teddy Bunn (1909–78)
VOCAL, GUITAR

Bunn was an accomplished guitarist, and much in demand for session work in the '30s and '40s, but is best known for his membership of the Spirits Of Rhythm.

(*) **Teddy Bunn
RST Jazz Perspectives JPCD-1509 Bunn; Tommy Ladnier, Sidney De Paris (t); Mezz Mezzrow (cl); unknown (as); Walter Pichon (p, v); Clarence Profit, James P. Johnson, Sam Price, unknown (p); unknown (bj); Elmer James, Pops Foster, unknown (b); Zutty Singleton, Manzie Johnson (d); Bruce Johnson, unknown (wb); Spencer Williams, Buck Franklin, Fat Hayden (v). 9/29–3/40.

Teddy Bunn makes a number of appearances in *The Penguin Guide To Jazz On CD*, but this disc is chiefly concerned with the bluesier end of his activities. Six jazz titles under Mezz Mezzrow's leadership are wildly variable alternative takes of tracks on Classics 694; among them, 'If You See Me Comin'' is a pleasant feature for Bunn's guitar and his understated singing. Eight vocal duets with Spencer Williams are among the least appealing hokum releases; only on 'Tampa Twirl' does decent playing, by both Bunn and James P. Johnson, outweigh the juvenile lyrics. Buck Franklin's solitary title is another where one listens only for the guitar solo; Walter Pichon is an even duller singer, and Bunn is subdued on this 1929 coupling, although Henry 'Red' Allen is as vivacious as usual. Fat Hayden's two songs for Decca receive polished assembly-line accompaniment from Sam Price plus guitar and bass, but 'Voodoo Blues' has an interesting lyric, moving from hoodoo to cheerleading for Father Divine. The most consistently interesting tracks are five 1940 sides for Blue Note. 'King Porter Stomp' and 'Guitar In High' are able swing improvisations, while 'Bachelor Blues' and two takes of 'Blues Without Words' (which has words!) may take note of Josh White's success with a smooth blues makeover for the supper-club audience. CS

Michael Burks (born 1957)
VOCAL, GUITAR

Growing up in Camden, Arkansas, Burks learned from his father's playing and his record collection. As a young man he played locally for visiting artists, but he then took a break from music, and it was not until 1994 that he began working on the club and festival circuit in earnest. An appearance at the Chicago Blues Festival in 2000 won him a contract with Alligator Records.

**(*) From The Inside Out
Michael Burks MBCD 1000/Vent VR-30014 Burks; Stuart Baer (o, p); Vernon Allgood (b); Lance Womack (d). 97.

*** Make It Rain
Alligator ALCD 4878 Burks; Scott Thompson (t, flh); Jim Spake (ts, bs); Ernest Williamson (kb); Vasti Jackson (g); David Smith (b); Steve Potts (d). 00.

*** I Smell Smoke
Alligator ALCD 4892 As above, except add Billy Gibson (h); omit Thompson, Spake. 02?

Burks's playing on his debut album *From The Inside Out* is assured, with much of the torrential power of Albert King, an obvious model, but his material, though nominally original, tends to be conventional both in outline and in detail. His gruff singing, which strengthens the King connection, would have benefited from being more prominent in a mix that's somewhat clogged by the organ playing. *Make It Rain* and *I Smell Smoke* are greatly superior productions. Burks's compositional input is reduced to three numbers on each, making room for strong songs like 'Got A Way With Women' on the former, 'Willing To Crawl' on the latter and the title numbers on both. His guitar becomes a broad-tipped marking pencil, its lines thick and weighty, but the verve and skill of the backing musicians prevent it from obliterating what's distinctive in the material. *I Smell Smoke* has more dynamic variation, and a rare quiet piece in 'Lie To Me', but for the most part Burks's music is intense, with few dips in the level of sound or energy, and not for the faint-hearted. TR

Dan Burley (1907–62)
VOCAL, PIANO

At 15, Dan Burley was playing for Chicago rent parties and in barrelhouses, and learning from the best, but at the same time he was studying journalism in high school. He was employed by the Chicago Defender, *and from 1938 by the New York-based* Amsterdam News, *where he covered sports and entertainment, wrote socially aware music criticism and rapidly rose to be managing editor. He also wrote a column, and two books, in and about the jive language of Harlem hepcats. In the '50s, Burley returned to Chicago, where he was an associate editor of* Ebony *and* Jet. *Through all these activities he continued to make music, and to write songs.*

*** South Side Shake
Wolf WBJCD-008 Burley; Hot Lips Page (t); Jimmy Archey, Tyree Glenn (tb); Albert Nicholas (cl); John Hardee, Paul Quinichette (ts); Johnny Taylor (o); Leonard Feather (p); Tiny Grimes, Billy Mackel, Brownie McGhee, Sticks McGhee, Danny Barker, Tiny Mitchell, unknown (g); Jack Lesberg, Charles Harris, Pops Foster, Walter Page, unknown (b); Morey Feld, George Jenkins, Baby Dodds, Sonny Greer (d); Lionel Hampton (vb, v); Vanita Smythe (v); Freddie Carter, Dizzy Gillespie (sp). 1/45–2/51.

*** Circle Blues Session
Southland SCD-9 Burley; Brownie McGhee, Sticks McGhee (g); Pops Foster (b). 6/46.

Dan Burley's career as a recording artist was a fairly short interlude in a busy life, but he was no Sunday pianist. Wolf's CD compiles all the performances then known, either by or including him, embellishing them with an exhaustively researched booklet which is the definitive account of his life and music. Indeed, it's arguable that at times the annotation is more than the music deserves, most obviously when Burley is teamed with Johnny Taylor's fairground organ. In contrast, his collaboration with Leonard Feather, 'A Suite in Four Comfortable Quarters' ('Bedroom Blues', 'Living Room Romp', 'Kitchen Conniption', 'Bathroom Boogie'), is far better than its arch titles, and certainly the best set of piano blues by two music critics. Six sides, issued as an album of 78s by Circle, famously credit 'Dan And His Skiffle Boys', who were the McGhee brothers and Pops Foster; the music variously recalls the loose and lively sound of Cripple Clarence Lofton, with the two guitars generating a bouncy swing, and the more thoughtful, measured approach of Jimmy Yancey. Tempos are usually slow to medium, and the time signature 4/4, rather than the 8/8 of boogie.

Elsewhere, Burley collaborates with jazz musicians. Lionel Hampton, a friend from Chicago days, is said to have been encouraged to play boogie by Burley, who seldom played it himself; 'Ridin' On The L & N' is a successful exception. A radio broadcast with the Albert Nicholas band successfully blends Chicago blues piano with New Orleans jazz. Four titles for Arkay are more notable for solos by Jimmy Archey and John Hardee than for Burley's contributions; still more is this true of two long numbers, part of a jam session set up by Rudi Blesh, where the jazz is splendid, and Burley's contribution minimal.

Five of the six issued Circle numbers are on Southland, since both versions of 'Big Cat, Little Cat' on the CD are alternative takes. The six previously unissued sides (and an airshot of 'Dusty Bottom') are also on *Jazz & Blues Piano* (Document DOCD-5656), but the session is much better heard complete. The sound quality is naturally superior to that on Wolf, and it's usually obvious that economics, rather than musical quality, caused the unissued material to be held back. ('Landlady's Night', afflicted with wrong notes, is the exception.) The best of the new material is a warm, gently rocking tribute to the child prodigy Hersal Thomas, who died young, and is said to have taught Burley his first blues in elementary school. The remainder of the Southland CD is by Brownie and Sticks McGhee, and is discussed under the former's entry.

Both discs have their merits. The Wolf is invaluable to scholars, and has some memorable contributions from the jazz musicians, but the Circle session, although shorter, is more consistent and cohesive, and as such is probably to be preferred by anyone seeking an introduction to Dan Burley. CS

Adrian Byron Burns (born 1951)
VOCAL, GUITAR

Originally from Washington, DC, Burns has lived in Europe since the early '70s and has been involved in many kinds of music. He currently lives in Britain and is active on the international blues festival circuit.

**(*) Back To The Wood
Bluetrack BRCD 002 *Burns; Roger Inniss (b); Alan Hardman (d). 2–3/98.*

Burns plays with a fluency that occasionally recalls Brownie McGhee, but applies it, and a strong, distinctive blues voice, to a setlist that embraces Robert Johnson's 'Come On In My Kitchen' and 'Crossroads', Muddy Waters's 'She's 19 Years Old', Albert King's 'Born Under A Bad Sign' and Bill Withers's 'Ain't No Sunshine'. As if this eclectic mixture were not enough to make you remember him, he throws in some compositions of his own like a witty 'PC Blues' – not about political correctness but on the theme 'check out my CD-ROMs and play with my mouse'. An unexpected and different record. TR

Eddie Burns (born 1928)
VOCAL, HARMONICA, GUITAR

Growing up around Dublin, Mississippi, Burns heard many of the blues artists of the '30s and '40s on records that were played in his grandfather's juke-joint. He left home at 16, moving to Clarksdale, then Waterloo, Iowa, then, in 1948, Detroit, where he settled, made his first recording and did some work with John Lee Hooker. Since then he has played music part-time while holding down a day job and raising a family.

Burns's numerous, varied and often interesting singles, made at irregular intervals during five decades, are not easily found on CD. 'Hello Miss Jessie Lee' on *Stompin' Vol. 19* (Stompin' 319) is a 1952 reworking of Sonny Boy Williamson I's 'Good Morning Little School Girl'. It's also on *Detroit Blues* (JSP JSP 7736 4CD) with its flipside, 'Dealing With The Devil', and the earlier 'Papa's Boogie' and 'Notoriety Woman'. Burns's sides for Chess and Checker occasionally surface on MCA/Chess VACs; 'Treat Me Like I Treat You', for instance, is on *Chess Blues Guitar 1949–1969* (MCA/Chess CHD2–9393//[E] MCD 09393). Some 1951 recordings, made for the Detroit entrepreneur Joe Von Battle but never issued at the time, are included in the John Lee Hooker CD *Detroit Blues 1950–51* (Collectables COL-CD-5316).

**(*) Chicago Blues Festival 86
Black & Blue BB 733 *Burns; Billy Branch (h); Melvin Taylor (g); Nick Charles (b); Julian Vaughan (d). 11/86.*

**(*) Lonesome Feeling
Black & Blue BB 455 *As above.* 11/86.

Burns shares *Chicago Blues Festival 86*, and his sidemen, with his touring colleague, Little Joe Blue. 'In The State [*sic* Interstate] Highway' finds him sounding a little like Sonny Boy Williamson I; he also plays harmonica on 'This Old House' (not the Eartha Kitt number) and – duetting with Branch while the other musicians sit it out – on 'Wee Baby Blues'. On his other four tracks, where he plays guitar, he sings at the stately pace and with some of the vocal tone of Lowell Fulson. Since Burns is not an expressive guitarist and Taylor plays throughout as if he'd left his mind at O'Hare Airport, Branch is left to fill most of the canvas on his own. *Lonesome Feeling* reissued Burns's share of the Dutch-recorded session, extending it to a respectable album length with five more songs from the date, none of them exceptional.

*** Detroit
Evidence ECD 26024 *Burns; Joe Hunter (p); Frank Bryant (b); Bobby Smith (d).* 89.

Detroit, originally issued on Blue Suit, was Burns's first full album release since two recorded in Britain in 1972. (Nothing presently survives of these except two tracks on the VAC *Don't Worry 'Bout The Bear* [Indigo IGOXDCD 2503].) He took the opportunity to rerecord his regional hit of 1961, 'Orange Driver', whose opening phrase 'I can hear my name ringing', alluding to Sonny Boy Williamson I's 'My Black Name Blues', is just one of several echoes of the records he learned from as a teenager. Others are 'Bottle Up And Go' and 'New Highway 61', played solo on acoustic guitar in the cheerful manner of their originator, Tommy McClennan. The other acoustic solo track, 'Boom Boom', nods amiably to his old friend John Lee Hooker. The harmonica that was Burns's chief selling point for early blues collectors is brought out only for 'Kidman', the instrumental 'Time Out' and 'Blue Jay', a slightly rewritten version of Sonny Boy Williamson I's 'Blue Bird Blues'. On the remaining tracks he plays electric guitar with fair fluency. Joe Hunter, a partner from way back, plays apt piano, usually with economy bordering on the miserly, but more generously on 'Blue Jay'. Not a record to make the blood race, but estimable and likeable.

**(*) Snake Eyes
Delmark DG-758 *Burns; Roosevelt Purifoy (p); Jimmy Burns (g, v); Nick Charles (b); Larry Taylor (d).* 9/01.

There are more remakes of early recordings here, such as 'Hello Miss Jessie Lee', 'Papa Likes To Boogie' and 'Treat Me Like I Treat You', but they are outnumbered by new Burns compositions, albeit ones sometimes built up from recognizable foundations. Burns plays both electric and acoustic, and his unplugged duetting with his brother on 'Lend Me Your Love' and a few other tracks creates a pleasing domestic ambience. The main harmonica event is the instrumental 'Hastings Street Special'. Burns is a dependable performer, but in this context of mostly slow numbers and familiar tunes he is scarcely an exciting one. TR

Jimmy Burns (born 1943)
VOCAL, HARMONICA, GUITAR

A much younger brother of Eddie Burns, Jimmy was born in Dublin, Mississippi, and began playing guitar about the age of

ten. In 1955 he moved to Chicago, where he sang with vocal groups, notably The Medallionaires, and later worked in the soul field. In the '70s he returned to the blues he had enjoyed as a youth and became a part-time club artist. Joining Rockin' Johnny Burgin's band in the mid-'90s led to his debut album.

*** **Leaving Here Walking**
Delmark DE-694 *Burns; Chuck Desormeaux, John Brumbach (s); Martin Lang (h); Rockin' Johnny Burgin (g); Sho Komiya (b); Kelly Littleton (d). 4/96.*

This was a most unconventional first album. The blues Burns chose were not club standards of the '50s and '60s but older ones like 'Whiskey Headed Woman', 'Mean Mistreating Mama' and 'Catfish Blues', or – not quite so old, but obscure enough – his brother Eddie's 'Notoriety Woman'. Some of the album was not blues at all but a delightfully oldfashioned kind of soul that elicited a happy lyricism reminiscent of Sam Cooke, as in the gently guitar-accompanied 'Gypsy Woman' or 'Talk To Me'. A similar warmth suffuses the blues 'Miss Annie Lou', beautifully arranged for two guitars. Almost as impressive as Burns's range is the music around him: Burgin plays with imagination and Komiya with vitality.

Six months later, Burns and virtually the same band appeared at a benefit for Chicago DJ Steve Cushing's radio show. Two tracks were included on a CD commemorating the event, *Blues Before Sunrise Live – Volume One* (Delmark DE-699): another version of 'Leaving Here Walking' and Jimmy Rogers's 'You're The One'.

*** **Night Time Again**
Delmark DE-730 *Burns; Michael Jackson (ts); Allen Batts (p); Michael Dotson (g); Sho Komiya (b); Kenny Smith (d). 12/98–1/99.*

The reception given to *Leaving Here Walking* – an important trade organization voted it Blues Album Of The Year – may have encouraged Burns to make an even more imaginative second album; at any rate, he flexes some muscles not brought into play on the earlier set. Ten of the 14 titles are his own compositions, and they range in type from the blues of 'Hard Road' to 'Spend Some Time With Me' and 'Here It Is Night Time Again', with their fluid grace reminiscent of Robert Cray (which is hardly surprising, since Burns acknowledges similar models), and the more angular 'No Consideration' and 'Why You Wanna Start A Fight?', where Dotson's distorted guitar phrases are like the muttered comments of a sympathetically angry bystander. The most unusual track is '1959 Revisited: A Tribute', a tender evocation of the school-is-out doo-wop era. That this should end an album which also includes the Howlin' Wolf song 'Shake For Me', and do so without seeming odd, says something about the breadth of Burns's interests and the skill with which he balances them in his music.

*** **Back To The Delta**
Delmark DG-770 *Burns; Roosevelt Purifoy (p); Kevin Shanahan (g); Ron Lasken, Nick Charles (b); Greg Haar, Larry Taylor (d). 10/02.*

Even more than on his previous albums, Burns repeatedly brings off the trick of writing blues that sound older than he is yet owe nothing to specific antecedents. The meaty two-guitar riffs that open 'Stop The Train', 'Red Hot Mama' or 'Stranded In Clarksdale' have been mined from an inexhaustible seam of Mississippi blues; one could imagine men like Eddie Taylor or Magic Slim playing this line or that; but, except for the three songs expressly taken from other artists, the music bears no signature but that of the man who has conceived, sung and played it. There is more of this new-minted antiquarianism in the first nine tracks, with the Lasken–Haar backline, than in the six with Charles and Taylor and no second guitar. The latter, you might say, are not so much back to the Delta as up from it, and they could be heard as nudging the album forward through blues history – but not by much. TR

R. L. Burnside (1926–2005)
VOCAL, GUITAR

With Junior Kimbrough and Robert Belfour, Burnside was a prime exponent of the droning, intensely rhythmic guitar style indigenous to the hill country of north Mississippi. Adept at both finger-style and slide playing (learned from mentors Ranie Burnette and Fred McDowell), Burnside was initially perceived as an acoustic musician but became more at home with the amplified instrument he thrashed when on stage. Grasping the opportunity to market him to the hip-hop and rock crowd, his record company used some of his albums to experiment with remix engineers and scratch DJs.

***(*) **First Recordings**
Fat Possum 0365 *Burnside. 8/67.*

Field researcher George Mitchell's 1967 discovery of Burnside was roughly equivalent to Alan Lomax's location of Fred McDowell in the same area eight years previously but there comparison ends. Though a product of the same traditions, Burnside is a more eclectic performer, equally comfortable playing amplified or acoustic. This collection (an amplification of his segment of *Mississippi Delta Blues Vol. 2* [Arhoolie CD 402, deleted]) includes a significant part of his core repertoire – 'Long Haired Doney', 'Goin' Down South', 'Jumper On The Line', 'Poor Black Mattie' and 'Rollin' And Tumblin'' – as well as a 'Walkin' Blues' adopted from Muddy Waters, on which he uses a bottleneck in a style approximating the originals. Other songs are played finger-style in a combination of strummed and picked riffs that shadow and underline the vocal. Most achieve a trance-like continuity enhanced by a subtly increasing tempo. 'Skinny Woman' integrates a syncopated rhythm tapped on the guitar body as Burnside sings. These assured performances failed to emulate the impact of McDowell's initial efforts when first released but have since achieved an authority of their own.

***(*) **My Black Name A-Ringin'**
Genes GCD 9917 *Burnside; Red Ramsey, unknown (h); Jesse Vortis (g). 10/69.*

These tapes remained unissued and unknown for three decades. Five core songs are repeated, including 'Rollin' And Tumblin'' masquerading as 'Nine Days In Jail'. On 'Long Haired Doney' Burnside is joined by harmonica and guitar and on 'Catfish Blues' by two harmonicas, the second off-mike and intermittent. Vortis integrates confidently on 'Doney' but fares less well on a version of John Lee Hooker's 'Hobo Blues'. Ramsey's harmonica closely follows the vocal line on 'Two Trains Runnin'', while adopting a more rhythmic role on 'Tom Wilson's Place' (Yank Rachell's '38 Pistol'). 'Sat Down On My Bed And Cried' reveals the influence of Lightnin' Hopkins, being an adaptation of 'Bad Luck And Trouble'. 'My Black

Name A-Ringin" is performed rubato and on this and 'Peach Tree Blues' Burnside's vocal tone is reminiscent of Dr Ross, who shared his fascination with the songs of Sonny Boy Williamson I. Though less striking than the Mitchell tapes, this collection gives a better idea of Burnside's eclecticism and benefits from the occasional accompaniment.

**(*) Sound Machine Groove
High Water HMG 6501 *Burnside; Joseph Burnside, Daniel Burnside (g, b); Calvin Jackson (d). 10/79–7/80.*

Sound Machine was the family band Burnside used when performing locally. Sons Joseph and Daniel interchange between instruments while son-in-law Jackson provides the pulse. Jackson had trained in the area's fife-and-drum tradition and 'Jumper Hanging Out On The Line', 'Goin' Away, Baby' and 'Sitting On Top Of The World' are guitar and drum duets that reflect the style's cyclical simplicity. 'Going Down South' and 'Begged For A Nickel' (actually 'Bad Luck Blues') are performed solo. Thereafter, except for 'Rolling And Tumbling', Burnside dispenses with his guitar. His sons show a working understanding of soul and pop techniques but Jackson's rudimentary drumming undermines the sophistication to which they aspire. The starkness of the music is reflected in the lack of technical sweetening from the engineering staff.

**(*) Raw Electric 1979–1980
Inside Sounds ISC-0513 *Burnside; Robert Avant (g, v); Joseph Burnside, Daniel Burnside (g); Calvin Jackson, Dwayne Burnside (d). 8/79–8/80.*

If the preceding record was a silk purse, this is the sow's ear from which it was fashioned. The first dozen tracks were recorded at Burnside's home two months prior to the studio session that makes up most of *Sound Machine Groove*. The remaining five songs are taken from public performances. Despite the assertion that all this material is previously unissued, 'Sitting On Top Of The World' and 'Going Away, Baby' are common to both, and five other songs are present in different versions. The 'Raw' of the title is apposite, for children and adults make their presence felt and some songs end with applause and random comments. Everyone's playing is loose, sometimes fragmentary, and at times Jackson's odd snare and bass-drum syncopation functions more like a Bofors gun than a rhythmic pulse. Neither this nor the last album is essential to an understanding of Burnside's music but this is a more comprehensive example of the family band's potential.

**(*) Mississippi Blues
Arion ARN 60397 *Burnside. 10/79, 7/80, 83.*

These 11 numbers with acoustic guitar combine Burnside's usual repertoire with a trio of Hopkins pieces, including 'Nightmare Blues' and 'Death Bells', and an eerily exact interpretation of Hooker's 'When My First Wife Left Me'. Two bottleneck pieces, 'Sweet Little Angel' and 'Dust My Broom', are performed well enough, although the latter is overlong. Both feel imposed upon the artist rather than natural choices for the occasion. Nine of the tracks were recorded in France in 1983; 'Long Haired Doney' and 'Rolling And Tumbling' are earlier High Water recordings. Burnside is most effective on these, 'Poor Black Mattie' and 'Catfish Blues', singing in a higher register than usual and adding a 'crying' motif to some verse ends. But the album's shortness and its limited availability make it one for dedicated collectors only.

**** Mississippi Hill Country Blues
Swingmaster CD 2201 *Burnside; Red Ramsey (h). 67–11/84.*
**(*) Going Down South
Swingmaster CD 2203 *Burnside; Curtis Salgado (h). 2/86.*

Mississippi Hill Country Blues is probably the best and certainly the most enjoyable of Burnside's initial acoustic albums. With the exception of three tracks drawn from Mitchell's 1967 recordings, the album consists of sessions recorded in 1980–84. Core songs are present but they're merely part of a comprehensive 19-song repertoire that includes Ranie Burnette's 'Miss Maybelle' and other more or less original material. The 1967 songs, 'Mellow Peaches', 'I Believe' and 'Rolling And Tumbling' (the last with Ramsey's harmonica added), integrate surprisingly well. The warmth and intimacy of the recordings accord with Burnside's relaxed but concentrated approach, making this thoroughly recommendable. Five songs recorded in New Orleans are included in *Going Down South*, alongside material from LPs by mentor Ranie Burnette and harmonica player Johnny Woods, whom Burnside accompanies on two songs. Salgado plays florid harmonica on 'Going Down South' and an amusing if foul-mouthed pitch at 'Stack O'Lee And Billy Lyons'. A lacklustre 'Going Down South' and further takes on 'Can't Be Satisfied' and 'Walking Blues' are competent rather than impressive. Fortunately, the other artists' contributions make this an interesting collection.

**(*) Acoustic Stories
M.C. MC 0034 *Burnside; Jon Morris Nerenberg (h). 2/88.*

Artistic presentation and a W. C. Handy nomination can't mask or compensate for the brevity of this collection (under 35 minutes), recorded in New York during an East Coast tour. Despite the title, booming bass frequencies and a lack of treble clarity suggest that Burnside's guitar is lightly amplified. This allows for an eerie re-creation of Hooker's strumming technique on 'When My First Wife Left Me' and 'Hobo Blues'. Nerenberg's contributions, distant and echo-laden, are impressionistic rather than fully integrated and he lays out on the percussive 'Skinny Woman' and a final trio of songs taken from Howlin' Wolf, Lightnin' Hopkins and Robert Johnson. Burnside plays slide on 'Bottom', 'Walking Blues' and 'Death Bell Blues', a lightly disguised 'Rollin And Tumblin''. 'Monkey In The Pool Room' is a sanitized Dozens routine for the benefit of Nerenberg and the engineers. With just two core songs, the programme's diversity ought to make it attractive but its self-conscious artistry dilutes the brusque individuality normally associated with the artist.

**(*) Bad Luck City
Fat Possum FP 1001 *Burnside; Dwayne Burnside (g, b, v); Joseph Burnside (b); Calvin Jackson (d). 91.*

A curious record but a fitting one for the label's debut. Another Burnside son, Dwayne, steps into the limelight and proves to be the most adventurous of the brothers, adding flurries of single notes to his often frenetic rhythm playing. Jackson's drumming has improved but occasional failures of nerve interrupt the flow. Another broad spectrum of music, including Donnie Hathaway's 'The Ghetto', Willie Cobbs's 'You Don't Love Me' and three Howlin' Wolf songs, reflects the younger band members' taste. The biggest surprise is their father's success as an upfront shouting band singer on 'My

Eyes Keep Me In Trouble' and 'Shake For Me'. Nevertheless, what he refers to as 'Burnside style' is more enthusiastic than competent. Songs peter out or segue casually into the next, their rhythms turbid rather than tight. There's a stark division between uncertain versions of core songs like 'Jumper On The Line', 'Long Haired Doney' and 'Skinny Woman' (recast as 'All She Do'), the only ones to feature Burnside's guitar, and the covers that entertain customers at places like Syd's, the club in which this was recorded 'live' even though no audience can be heard. Much was made of this rough-hewn music being the 'real sound' of the blues live but hindsight might be less tolerant.

*** Well ... Well ... Well
M.C. MC 0042 *Burnside; Jon Morris Nerenberg (h); Calvin Jackson (d); Curtis Salgado (v). 5/86–4/93.*

Culled from tapes made on American and European tours, this set presents Burnside both on stage and in less formal surroundings. Opening with a brief radio interview, eight of the 18 tracks are taken from stage performances, including a 'Grazing Grass Rap' that puts the sword to a nervously amused audience. A further 'Bad Luck Monkey Rap' with Nerenberg and Salgado is less funny and overlong. Another tilt at 'Staggolee' in the same company is marked 'not suitable for airplay' for its uncompromising but entertaining language. After the two leave him alone with a tape recorder, Burnside performs 'Mojo Hand', 'Boogie Chillen', 'Can't Be Satisfied' and a strikingly sensitive version of Little Walter's 'Last Night' with slide guitar. 'Mellow Peaches' and 'Goin' Down South', with Jackson's thundering drums, were recorded in a shed. This time the broad spectrum of music is helped by the variety of settings, making this the preferred choice from the M.C. catalogue.

***(*) Too Bad Jim
Fat Possum 0307 *Burnside; Kenny Brown (g); Dwayne Burnside (b); Calvin Jackson (d). 93.*

This album more than any other brought about a sea-change in how Burnside would be recorded and in his status as a leading exponent of the hill country style. Producer Robert Palmer revealed this music's inherent power by accurately portraying the natural ambient sound of the rooms in which it was played. Various combinations of musicians are tried, following three solo performances of Hopkins songs, 'Short-Haired Woman', 'Miss Glory B' and 'Death Bell Blues'. Though the framework conforms to Hopkins's single-string riffs and turnarounds, some chordal emphases derive from Burnside's absorption of Hooker's staccato technique. The latter's 'When My First Wife Left Me' is one of a pair of duets with Jackson's drums, Brown's slide guitar thickens the sound of 'Fireman Ring The Bell' ('Rollin' And Tumblin'' without the identifying verse) and the full band rocks through '.44 Pistol' and a chiming 'Goin' Down South'. Coordination isn't always a priority but the powerful result always makes curious sense. This was the moment when artist and label established a successful formula. NS

** Heritage Of The Blues: No Monkeys On This Train
Hightone HCD 8152 *Burnside; Bob Corritore (h); Joseph Burnside, Daniel Burnside (g, b); Bruce Lopez (b); Calvin Jackson, Chico Chism (d). 10/79–3/94.*

To furnish their mid-price Heritage series with a Burnside album, Hightone coupled five tracks from *Sound Machine Groove* and five taped by Bob Corritore in the '90s, breaking up the programme – but not, after the first time or two, the listener – with four of his funny stories. All but one of the later tracks are solos with electric guitar, but Burnside had recorded most of them before when his voice was less coarse and his guitar playing more intricate. This is a poor introduction to its subject. TR

***(*)/* A Ass Pocket Of Whiskey
Matador OLE 214//Fat Possum FP 1026 *Burnside; Judah Bauer (h, kb, g); Jon Spencer (theremin, g); Kenny Brown; Russell Simins (d). 2/96.*

– and then we all dropped acid and fondled our flesh guitars ... To his credit, the leader of the Jon Spencer Blues Explosion had featured Burnside as his opening act on tour before the idea of a recording session was mooted. But what sounds like fun in a disused Mississippi farmhouse doesn't necessarily translate into a viable recording. The Blues Explosion is a post-punk, nursery-grunge band with more energy than expertise, which here is a perverse recommendation. Burnside enters enthusiastically into the fray, recorded during the course of one afternoon. Most of the repertoire is over-familiar but these highly charged and over-amped versions survive owing to Simins's bedrock timekeeping and the circularity of the guitar riffs. On the debit side, Bauer and Spencer's electronic idiocy fatally holes 'Walkin' Blues' below the water-line, and three of Burnside's motherfuckin' folktales quickly pall. The final 'Have You Ever Been Lonely', five minutes of free-form nonsense, all but scuppers the better things that have gone before. The choice of ratings reflects the strength of reaction this set inspires.

***(*) Mr. Wizard
Fat Possum 0301 *As above, except add Cedric Burnside (d). 9/94–11/96.*

Viable or not, the previous album provided the sonic template for every subsequent release. Here, seven group performances are sandwiched between a pair of solo slide guitar outings recorded in Burnside's home with amplification that makes the instrument sound as if it has been strung with slack baling wire. Two further songs from the session with the Blues Explosion, 'Alice Mae' and 'Highway 7', illustrate the best and worst of such impromptu affairs, the latter struggling too long to achieve coherence. The remaining songs feature Burnside, Brown and grandson Cedric stomping enthusiastically through 'Georgia Women', 'Snake Drive' and 'Rollin' And Tumblin'', before going slightly off the boil with 'Out On The Road' and 'Tribute To Fred', an instrumental whose title would have been more aptly applied to the solo version of McDowell's 'You Gotta Move' that ends the set with unexpected but proper respect.

*(*) Come On In
Fat Possum 0317 *Burnside; Lester Butler (h); Beal Dabbs (o, clavinet, b); Alejandro Rosso (o); Kenny Brown (g); Cedric Burnside, Joe Rameri, Joey Waronker (d); John Oreshnick (maracas). 98.*

Fat Possum's Matthew Johnson evidently hoped to capitalize on his artist's newfound popularity with younger audiences by engaging engineers/remixers Tom Rothrock and Beal Dabbs. Both prove to be devoid of imagination and construct superficial slabs of perversely punctuated monotony. That these travesties should then enable them to claim a share of the publishing rights seems iniquitous. The title track appears three times, once as a live solo performance and then 'treated' twice more by Rothrock. Dabbs demeans 'Don't Stop Honey' ('Shake 'Em On Down') and contrives an incomprehensible and tedious 'Shuck Dub'. 'Let My Baby Ride' is a lightly disguised 'Snake Drive', making its third consecutive appearance on a Burnside release, and 'Rollin' Tumblin'' makes its second. 'Just Like A Woman' is a relatively trick-free duet between the older and younger Burnsides, while the final 'Heat' is an explosive drum-dominated stampede. 'Let My Baby Ride' was also issued as a CD single (Fat Possum 1013) with previously unissued versions of 'Poor Boy A Long Way From Home' and 'Walkin' Blues', the latter a solo slide-accompanied performance and 'Poor Boy' featuring the trio and an unidentified bass player.

*(*) Wish I Was In Heaven Sitting Down
Fat Possum 0332 *Burnside; Johnny Dyer, Lynwood Slim (h); Andy Kaulkin (kb); Tommy Eyre (o); John Porter (md); Smokey Hormel, Rick Holmstrom, Kenny Brown, John Porter (g); Antony Genn, Jeff Turmes, John Porter (b); Steve Mugalian (d); Johnny Dyer (v); Iki Levy, Brad Cook (loops); DJ Swamp, DJ Pete B (scratching); Bill Smith, Sally Browder (Protools editing).* 00.

Undoubtedly the most expensive Burnside project to date, this takes no fewer than seven producers and a nondescript cast of sonic bandits to dissipate the essence of his music. Some elements work, such as the opening 'Hard Time Killing Floor' and its partial reprise, 'R. L.'s Story'. Using the chorus of the Skip James original, Burnside recites the tale of how two uncles, two brothers and his father were all killed in Chicago in the course of one year as slide guitars skirl and a DJ scratches. Even when called upon to sing, Burnside is obviously doing so to backing tracks, thus negating any possibility of interaction between artist and accompanists. The title track, sung to the sole accompaniment of Brown's slide guitar, is the only unembellished performance here. As the collection proceeds, there's a noticeable diminution in sonic interference, making 'Nothin' Man', 'See What My Buddy Done' and 'Chain Of Fools' seem almost conventional – but nothing more. While the intrusion of irrelevancies like looped tapes and banal disjointed noise is thus defeated, so too is the unique character of the artist they team up to traduce.

♛ **** Burnside On Burnside
Fat Possum 0343 *Burnside; Kenny Brown (g); Cedric Burnside (d).* 1/01.

Having tried everything else, the only logical option is to make a live album and this is it. Eight of its 11 songs were recorded at the Crystal Ballroom on Portland's Burnside Street, hence the album title, the remainder at the Great American Music Hall in San Francisco. Dispensing with formalities, the set jumps in with wild applause from which a strutting 'Shake 'Em On Down' emerges and sets the pace for what follows. Two solo performances, 'Walkin' Blues' and 'Bad Luck And Trouble', are separated by 'He Ain't Your Daddy', one of Burnside's folksy jokes, rewarded with gales of teenage laughter. Thereafter it's a race to the conclusion of 'Snake Drive' and further protracted applause. Each member of the trio knows his place and function, they've just never bothered to work out how to end a number together. Despite his age and infirmities, Burnside matches the energy of his younger partners and they hunt as a pack very effectively. Stripped of all contrivance, this set best displays the quintessential vigour of the Mississippi hill-country style. NS

Harold Burrage (1931–66)
VOCAL, PIANO

A native Chicagoan, Burrage prowled the periphery of jump blues for a number of years, making a handful of records before dipping his toe in the New Orleans rock 'n 'roll of Little Richard and Larry Williams. Long a favourite in West Side clubs, in the early '60s he became a pioneer of the city's burgeoning soul movement. Although he achieved nationwide success only a year before his death with 'Got To Find A Way', he was by then regarded as a mentor by younger singers Tyrone Davis and Otis Clay.

*** Messed Up!: The Cobra Recordings 1956–58
[Westside WESM 634] *Burrage; Harold Ashby, Lucius Washington, Abb Locke (ts); Henry Gray (p); Wayne Bennett, Magic Sam Maghett, Jody Williams, Mac Thompson, Otis Rush (g); Willie Dixon (b); Al Duncan, Billie Stepney, Odie Payne (d).* 56–58.

Though of peripheral blues interest, Burrage was an engaging singer with a characterful vocal style. Like many signed to Eli Toscano's Cobra label, he was somewhat at the mercy of A&R man Willie Dixon's compositional whims. When he wasn't writing for the likes of Muddy Waters and Howlin' Wolf, Dixon had a bookful of formulaic 'list' songs of which 'Wang Dang Doodle' is probably the best-known example. Burrage was presented with such industrial gems as 'One More Dance', 'I Don't Care Who Knows' and 'Stop For The Red Light'. 'You Eat Too Much' shows that he too was a reasonable practitioner of the genre, displaying more humour than his producer. Both were helped immeasurably by the quality of the backing musicians, notably in the guitar and drum departments. Jody Williams's ringing guitar phrases brighten both takes of 'Satisfied' and 'I Don't Care Who Knows', while Magic Sam solos on the demo of 'Hot Dog And A Bottle Of Pop'. Most songs also feature strong saxophone breaks by Harold Ashby. Unfortunately for Burrage, Little Richard was the *plat du jour* at the time and it was perhaps inevitable that his label would try to cook up their own recipe. But as good as they were, the Chicago musicians couldn't rock like their New Orleans counterparts and the listener senses the lack of commitment in Burrage's vocals on 'Betty Jean' and 'She Knocks Me Out'. Only 'A Heart (Filled With Pain)' hints at his subsequent career but the influence is more doo-wop than soul as Burrage imitates the clipped diction of the Platters' Tony Edwards. Eleven songs and six alternative performances don't make for a balanced programme but solid musicianship and the set's completeness are positive strengths. NS

J. C. Burris (1928–88)
VOCAL, HARMONICA, BONES, BODY PERCUSSION, PUPPETRY

Born in North Carolina, J. C. Burris was Sonny Terry's nephew. Moving to New York in 1949, Burris played on sessions for Terry and the McGhee brothers, but left for San Francisco around 1960, working there chiefly as a street musician until felled by a stroke in 1966. It was 1973 before he could perform

**** **Blues Professor**
Arhoolie 497 *Burris*. 6/75–76.
***(*) **Long Way By Myself**
Oosik 29757 7640 *Burris*. 10/79.

As a child, J. C. Burris learned the rudiments of blues harmonica from his 'Uncle Son', who gave him more tuition in New York; Burris owes much to his more famous relative, including playing 'upside down', with the bass notes on the right, but he doesn't try to emulate Terry's virtuosity. That quality shows up, rather, in his command of rhythm, whether playing bones and mouth harp together, body slapping in a style that goes back to slavery and beyond, making 'Mr Jack' (a wooden doll) dance or simply stomping out a swinging beat.

Burris's years of inactivity after his stroke made him into a thoughtful and introspective songwriter, and the 20 songs on *Blues Professor* are almost entirely original, with only 'Christmas Time Once Again' delving into common-stock verses. He wrote 'about poor J. C.'s life,' as he says when introducing 'Loneliness', and isolation, wandering and hardship are prominent themes. Nevertheless, his observation of how people behave towards each other generated a consistent and optimistic view of how they ought to behave, both personally and to achieve political and social justice. Burris's consciously leftist songs diagnose the sickness and prescribe the medicine, and preach without being preachy. He's also, let it be hastily added, a mighty entertaining performer, and the ten titles recorded in concert have huge energy and enthusiasm. The rest were recorded by Burris on a demo cassette, but are of surprisingly good sound quality.

Long Way By Myself consists of studio recordings made at the University of Santa Cruz. It supplies more evidence that Burris was an unacknowledged great among blues singer/songwriters, and includes a couple of rare covers. Lightnin' Slim's 'Rock Tonight Baby' is a real surprise, but the mood is mainly much more serious; even 'She Sold Her Thing' is a bitter tale of betrayal, not the hokum that might be expected. On the spoken 'Blues Is A Feeling' Burris draws a distinction between playing what you hear and what you feel, seeing the latter as the mark of a real blues singer. He makes his case on *Long Way By Myself*, but he also makes few concessions to fun; there's no percussion or puppetry here. The story about Sonny Terry inadvertently calling some hunters' dogs to him with his harmonica is charming, but Burris's cumulative seriousness is slightly daunting, and makes this CD easy to admire but slightly difficult to warm to. cs

Aron Burton (born 1938)
VOCAL, BASS

Burton has worked for Freddy King, Junior Wells and Fenton Robinson, and has been a busy session musician; his own band, including his guitarist brother Larry, was hired by Albert Collins to be the Icebreakers. In the '80s, Burton lived in Europe for several years, and at the time of writing is back, living in Berlin.

(*) **Past, Present, And Future
Earwig 4927 *Burton; Jorgen Lang (h); Pat Hall (kb, p, v); Kjeld Lauitsen (o, p); Champion Jack Dupree (p, v); Kenn Lending, Benno Rupp, Norman Marogg, Larry Burton (g); Svenni Svafnisson, Rene Mehrmann (b); Frank Larsen, Christian Willison, Ordy Somchai Sihaampai, Tino Cortez (d); Liska L. Swanstrom, Michael Frank (v)*. 3/86–1/93.

Burton's self-produced debut disc, *Usual Dangerous Guy*, which was recorded in Denmark, is here expanded with a track cut in Switzerland and a 1993 Chicago session. Burton establishes his credentials as both bassist and singer (although he has problems negotiating the tricky intervals of 'Rainy Night In Georgia'), but the European material lacks coherence; the musicians are all competent, but too many changes are rung, and the resultant sound is cluttered and underpowered. The Chicago band is far more forceful and consistent (although the barfly vocal chorus on 'Live Like A Beggar' is dreadful), but this only serves to emphasize the shortcomings of the earlier recordings.

***(*) **Live**
Earwig 4935 *Burton; Lester Davenport (h, v); Allen Batts (p, v); Michael Dotson (g, v); Kenny Smith (d, v); Liz Mandville Greeson (v)*. 3–12/95.

*** **Good Blues To You**
Delmark DE-727 *Burton; Kenny Anderson (t); Bill McFarland (tb); Hank Ford (ts); Lester Davenport, Billy Branch (h); Allen Batts (p); Larry Burton, Dave Specter, Lurrie Bell (g); Tino Cortez, Vern Rodgers (d)*. 8/98.

Live (which includes two studio tracks) catches Burton with his working band of the time; it functioned as a blues revue, with everyone getting a turn in the spotlight, rather than as leader plus backing musicians. A comparison of 'The Blues Is To Me' with its Danish predecessor is enough to show that *Live* is musically superior, but as important is that it strikes the elusive balance between innovation and continuity; Burton's four compositions are interspersed among material as familiar as 'Little Red Rooster' and 'Hound Dog'. Mandville-Greeson is dangerously camp on the latter song, and Smith's vocal on 'Hoochie Coochie Man' is feeble, but the musicians all play and (save as noted) sing with energy and imagination, never settling for dutiful reincarnation of their predecessors.

Most of *Good Blues To You* was written by one or other of the Burton brothers. Although the disc starts in grand style ('What a groove!' exclaims Aron at the end of 'No More Doggin'') and finishes well, it sags in the middle, with a sequence of long and not very strong songs, and an undernourished cover of Albert King's 'I'll Play The Blues For You'. However, it's proper to note that bracketing the run-of-the-mill majority are two of the finest recorded blues of the past 20 years, 'You've Been Gone Too Long' and 'The Woman I Met Out In The Rain'.

(*) **The Cologne Sessions
Schubert SCH-203 *Burton; B. Plant (h); Christian Rannenberg (p); Larry Burton, Freimuth Fischkal (g); Tommie Harris (d)*. 8/00.

Back in Europe, Burton reverts mainly to doing covers; only four songs are claimed as his own, among which 'River's Invitation' is a lawsuit waiting to happen. The musicians range from excellent (Larry Burton, Rannenberg) to awful (Plant, just weak enough to be annoying when he appears, which is fortunately not often). There's often a hint of strain in Aron

Burton's voice, perhaps the natural result of time passing; more of a problem is that the producers seem to have been reluctant to impose themselves on the musicians, with the result that most of the numbers go on too long (seven minutes of 'Walking The Dog' is about four too many) and their energy and focus are dissipated. CS

George 'Wild Child' Butler (1936–2005)
VOCAL, HARMONICA

Butler began playing harmonica as a child in rural Alabama – 'upside down because no one showed me how to hold it the right way'. In the late '60s he worked with Lightnin' Hopkins and recorded for Jewel, produced by Willie Dixon, who was impressed enough to tell him: 'Keep this work up and you gonna help keep the blues alive.' From the early '80s onwards he was based in Windsor, Ontario.

*** Lickin' Gravy
M.C. MC 0036 Butler; Pinetop Perkins (p); Sammy Lawhorn, Joe Kelly, Joe Zaklan, Wild Boar Moore, Jimmy Rogers (g); Earnest Johnson, Aron Burton (b); Nate Applewhite, Sam Lay (d). 6/76, 2/86.

With his Jewel sides and his 1969 album *Keep On Doin' What You're Doin'* (originally on Mercury; last available as Black Magic BMCD 9015) out of print, Butler's earliest accessible work is this set, first issued as *Funky Butt Lover* (TK-Roots) in 1976. 'I wanted to sound like other people I heard,' Butler said of his early efforts; '[Willie] Dixon had to teach me who I was.' Perhaps so, but a decade later he still finds it difficult to do someone else's song without sounding like him: 'Built For Comfort' and 'Spoonful' have a very recognizable Howlin' Wolf growl, and 'Rooster Blues' a perceptible whiff of Lightnin' Slim's record. Even 'None Of Nothing', which is his own song, is presented in a confiding narrative style that will remind many listeners of Sonny Boy Williamson II. But on the other original numbers he sounds more of a composite of his acknowledged vocal models – Wolf, Muddy Waters, Lightnin' Hopkins – and at every point he manifests both energy and an unswerving devotion to the Chicago idiom of the '50s and '60s. Perkins's and Rogers's contributions were added ten years later, Perkins slotting into the ensemble on eight tracks and Rogers on three.

*** These Mean Old Blues
Bullseye Blues CD BB 9518 Butler; Martyn C. Winning (ts); Richard Simmons, John Baggott (kb); Pete 'Guitar' Boss (g); Jon Southgate (b); Les Morgan (d); Mike Vernon (prod). 4–5/91.

*** Stranger
Bullseye Blues CD BB 9539 Butler; Matt Little (kb); Pete 'Guitar' Boss, Steve Harris (g); Mark Brown (b); Al Savage (d); band (v); Mike Vernon (prod). 12/93.

Fifteen years on, the Butler of *These Mean Old Blues* (originally issued on Blue Horizon as *The Devil Made Me Do It*) is still immovably immersed in his favourite sounds, and supported by band playing that's idiomatic and solid, whether rocking through the changes of the Muddyish 'No One Woman's Man' or conjuring a more reflective setting for 'It's A Pity', whose references to an American–Iraqi confrontation found a fresh resonance a dozen years later. What elevates Butler's records above many by players of his age, besides his obvious enthusiasm for making music, is his determination to tell his own stories rather than fall back on standard repertoire.

Stranger is cut from similar cloth, but by now Butler has lost the need to signal his stylistic preferences with overt allusions to Wolf or Muddy and he sounds like nobody but himself. The band is more assertive but always on the same track as the leader. Speaking of tracks, the sequence is entirely different from the printed one, and probably an improvement.

**(*) Sho' Nuff
APO APO 2015 Butler; Jimmy D. Lane, Jimmie Lee Robinson (g); Bob Stroger (b); Sam Lay (d). 1/00.

After the dense ensemble of the two preceding albums, *Sho' Nuff* has the more open-weave sound of a trio (Robinson plays only on 'You Had Quit Me'), and while this has no detectable effect on Butler's vivacity, the accompaniments often fall rather flat. A pianist would have made a significant and desirable difference. On the other hand, the album provides an uncluttered view of Butler's old-school harmonica playing, unaccompanied in 'Funky Things'. TR

Henry Butler (born 1949)
VOCAL, KEYBOARDS, ORGAN, PIANO, PROGRAMMING

Blind from birth, Butler is a classically trained pianist and singer. In the early '80s he worked with blues musicians and New Orleans jazz bands, then as a jazz soloist and bandleader; he also collaborated with the soul-jazz saxophonist Grover Washington and the avant-garde bassist Charlie Haden. Butler taught at Eastern Illinois University from 1990; since returning to his native New Orleans in about 1997, he has concentrated on the blues.

** The Game Has Just Begun
Basin Street BSR 0801 Butler; June Yamagishi, Shane Theriot (g); Raymond Weber (d, perc). 02.

***(*) Homeland
Basin Street BSR 0802 Butler; Vasti Jackson (g, v); Nick Daniels III (b, v); Raymond Weber (d, tamb, v). 03.

Of Butler's blues-oriented CDs, *Blues & More Vol. 1* (Windham Hill 10138) and *Blues After Sunset* (Black Top CDBT 1144) are deleted; Butler describes *The Game Has Just Begun* as 'a mostly blues conception', adding that 'a couple of pieces … may fit in to the so-called new age genre.' Yamagishi plays inventive blues-rock solos on most tracks, but the disc is dominated by Butler, programming most of the sounds, playing piano and singing in a booming growl leavened with occasional falsettos. Alongside blues, there's rock 'n' roll ('Great Balls Of Fire'), country soul (a slowed-down 'You Are My Sunshine') and rock ('Riders On The Storm'), all essayed with limited success. The 'new age' tracks make extensive use of synthesized bells; evaluation is just a vowel shift away. 'This Is Where I Live' has a strong lyric about adultery, but much of the rest is pretentious, portentous or (unless the title track's spoken passages are meant to recall Bobby 'Boris' Pickett's 'Monster Mash') unintentionally funny. *Vü-Dü Menz*, Butler's collaboration with Corey Harris (q.v.), is immeasurably more rewarding.

So is *Homeland*. Its patriotic title track is musically banal, and a closing 'Ode To Fess' is admirably played but verbally gauche; however, neither song is typical of a well-put-together set of blues, soul (a fabulous reading of 'I Stand Accused') and New Orleans R&B that ranges from Fats to funk. In his notes, Butler rightly draws attention to his percussive pianism on 'Henry's Boogie' and 'Some Iko', and throughout he plays and sings with far more directness and far less artiness. Some of the synthesized instruments (horns, saxes, strings) sound a mite thin, but this is because they're up against the real musicians' full-blooded playing. Jackson's composition 'Casino' (sung by Butler) is one of the few to consider current social issues in the Mississippi Delta, rather than presenting it as a blues theme park. CS

The Butler Twins
DUET

Clarence Butler (1942–2003), who sang and played harmonica, and Curtis Butler (1942–2004), guitar, were born near Florence, Alabama, and inherited blues musicianship from their guitar-playing father, Willie 'Butch' Butler, and his harmonica-playing friend Raymond Edwards. They moved to Detroit in 1962 to work in automobile factories and began playing music professionally in the early '70s.

**(*) Not Gonna Worry About Tomorrow
JSP JSPCD 257 Butlers; Eddie Harsch (o, p); Kenny Parker, Jeff Grand (g); Buster Wylie Tatterson (b); Martin Gross (d). 95.
*** Pursue Your Dreams
JSP JSPCD 268 As above, except add David Mathis (o, p), Chris Rummel (b), Bullet Bob (d). 95–96.

The Butlers give long service. Of the two dozen tracks on their pair of albums, only two are shorter than 5.20. Since this is not restlessly inventive music, most of the numbers could have been shortened without much being lost. This is more noticeable on *Not Gonna Worry About Tomorrow*, where the performances and the material, which are both reasonably good, are darkened to no useful purpose by the ominous studio sound. The recording of the drumkit makes Gross sound like a bored kid kicking over trashcans. *Pursue Your Dreams* is a better recording (except on 'Inner City Blues', a leftover from the earlier session), and although the band moves rather ponderously at times, this is a powerful set with some striking material. In 'Cold Winter Nights' the Butlers capture much of the molasses-thick intensity of vintage Muddy Waters, while the faultlessly archaic 'Jack Daniels And Me' could almost be an outtake from a '50s session by, say, Jimmy Rogers. 'How Long', on the other hand, has a sharp tang of middle-period B. B. King, accentuated by Kenny Parker's lead guitar line. Not long after *Pursue Your Dreams* the Butlers contributed four tracks to *Blues Across America – The Detroit Scene* (Cannonball CBD 29201, deleted) but they were not heard on record again. TR

Butterbeans & Susie
VOCAL DUET

Jodie Edwards (1895–1967) and Susie Hawthorne (1896–1963) sang and danced in vaudeville from childhood. They went through a stage marriage at 15 and 14, soon converting it into a real one. Happily married to the end, they made a comic career of pretending otherwise, as Butter, in his trademark too-tight suit, nightly rolled his eyes at the Junoesque Susie's raised fist. They were still in the business in 1959, and on the bill when James Brown made his debut at the Apollo Theater. In 1960, after a 30-year recording hiatus, they bowed out with an LP.

**(*) Butterbeans And Susie – Vol. 1 (1924–1925)
Document DOCD-5544 Butterbeans; Susie; King Oliver (t); Clarence Williams, Eddie Heywood (p). c. 5/24–c. 6/25.
**(*) Butterbeans And Susie – Vol. 2 (1926–1927)
Document DOCD-5545 Butterbeans; Susie; Louis Armstrong, Louis Metcalf (c); Robert Cheek (t); Kid Ory (tb); Johnny Dodds (cl); unknown (as); Eddie Heywood, Lovie Austin, Lil Armstrong (p); Tosh Hammond (one-string fiddle); Johnny St Cyr (bj); 'Grasshopper' (prob. Eddie Heywood) (v). c. 3/26–9/27.
*** The Vocal Duet Vol. 1
Clifford CARCD 1501 Butterbeans; Susie; Louis Armstrong (c); King Oliver, poss. Arthur Williams, poss. Henry 'Red' Allen (t); Kid Ory, Robert Freeman (tb); Johnny Dodds (cl); poss. Leon Spruell (as); Clarence Williams, Eddie Heywood, Lil Armstrong (p); Tosh Hammond (one-string fiddle); Johnny St Cyr (bj). c. 5/24–8/30.

Elevator Papa, Switchboard Mama (JSP JSPCD 329), which completed the reissuing of Butterbeans & Susie's early recordings with material from 1928–1930, is deleted, although nine of its titles are on the Clifford CD. That said, it's hard to imagine a present-day listener wanting the complete works for any purpose but historical enquiry. More than most, these artists suffer from being compiled into packages of two dozen sides, rather than two; the consistency – of tone, delivery and subject-matter – which made them favourites with their original audience is the very thing that works against enjoyment at CD length. Changing notions of what's funny are also a problem; marital squabbling may be a perennial comic standby, but some of the references to razors, bricks and fists are delivered with disturbing enthusiasm, and an irony that's barely detectable. On Document, a number of tracks are mastered from originals whose severely worn state is both an index of popularity and an obstacle to appreciation. Finally, Sue and Butter's usual pianist, Eddie Heywood, though accomplished, is rather sedate, and collectors have not been altogether wrong in reserving their enthusiasm for the occasional numbers where the accompaniment is supplied by some of the giants of jazz.

Noting, therefore, that Document's unswerving dedication to making the material available is as praiseworthy as ever, the recommendation has to go to Clifford, whose engineering, though nothing exceptional, has been done from relatively unbattered 78s. Equally important, the disc is a good selection of the team's strongest performances, in terms of both the verve of their sparring and the quality of the musicians; it includes the two titles with King Oliver, 'He Likes It Slow', with majestic backing from Armstrong's Hot Five, and three numbers accompanied by Eddie Heywood's Sons of Harmony, with whom Armstrong is plausibly reckoned to be sitting in. The only cause for regret is that of the two recordings featuring Tosh Hammond, Clifford elect to use 'Oh Yeah!', rather than the lubricious, and understandably unissued until much later, 'I Wanna Hot Dog For My Roll.' CS

Paul Butterfield Blues Band
GROUP

Paul Butterfield (1942–87) grew up in the Hyde Park section of Chicago, close to the South Side clubland. He began playing guitar and harmonica in his teens, learning the art of blues harp from Little Walter and Sonny Boy Williamson II, and more directly from Junior Wells and James Cotton. He put together the Paul Butterfield Blues Band in 1963 with his friend Elvin Bishop (q.v.) and former Howlin' Wolf sidemen Jerome Arnold and Sam Lay (q.v.), adding Michael Bloomfield (q.v.) and Mark Naftalin in 1964 to make an album for Elektra. The Paul Butterfield Blues Band and its successor East–West electrified the growing community of young white blues musicians working in current blues idioms. The band began to break up in 1967, and in his later work Butterfield moved away from a hardline blues repertoire. He did play on Muddy Waters's Woodstock Album and The Band's The Last Waltz, but drug and alcohol abuse and resulting health problems hastened his death.

*** **The Original Lost Elektra Sessions**
Rhino/Elektra 73505 Paul Butterfield (h, v); Mike Bloomfield (o, p, g); Mark Naftalin (o); Elvin Bishop (g); Jerome Arnold (b); Sam Lay (d). 12/64.

**** **The Paul Butterfield Blues Band**
Elektra 60647 Paul Butterfield (h, v); Mark Naftalin (o); Mike Bloomfield, Elvin Bishop (g); Jerome Arnold (b); Sam Lay (d, v). 65.

**** **East–West**
Elektra 60751 As above, except Mark Naftalin also plays p and Bishop also sings; Billy Davenport (d) replaces Lay. 66.

**** **Paul Butterfield Blues Band & East West**
Elektra 73517 2CD As for above two CDs. 65–66.

Listening to albums that have been called influential, or just great, it's sometimes hard to sniff the air of excitement that surrounded their making, or to detect the outlines of greatness through the accumulated haze of decades. No such problem with the Butterfield Blues Band's first, eponymous album. From the opening phrases of 'Born In Chicago', slammed down like a winning hand on a card table, this sextet of 20-year-olds fixes its listeners with a hard stare and buffets them with the sound of Chicago blues played loud, hard and from the inside. Bands from other places might have to conjure their blues from guesswork or fantasy; the Butterfield crew had the inestimable advantage of a team playing on its home ground, with local knowledge, and if their music now seems more grounded than most of their contemporaries', that's because it was. But although collective experience was crucial to the authenticity and confidence of the music, the band could not have achieved its swagger without its leader. At a time when many white musicians approached the blues vocal either gingerly or galumphingly, Butterfield sang it straight, without affectation, hesitation or embarrassment. He reserved eloquence for his harmonica, which he played with a penetrating tone all of his own making, far more aggressive than Cotton or Wells.

Bloomfield and Bishop are a tight guitar team but neither has a great deal of room to cut loose. The next album would provide it. *East–West* drove home the point of its predecessor in Chicago-styled pieces like 'Walkin' Blues' and 'All These Blues', but 'Two Trains Running' galvanized Muddy Waters's song. The band then made wholly individual statements in a dynamic translation of Nat Adderley's soul-jazz tune 'Work Song' and the 13-minute title track, a blues exploration into modal territory, with long, investigative solos by all three of the Bs.

And that was it. By the time the band came to make *The Resurrection Of Pigboy Crabshaw* (1967) Bloomfield had left, and the drift away from the style of the first two albums, begun here, continued on *In My Own Dream* and *Keep On Moving*. (*The Resurrection Of Pigboy Crabshaw* and *In My Own Dream* are currently together on Elektra 76500 2CD.) In 1971 Butterfield moved to Woodstock, New York, and founded a new band, Better Days, with guitarists Amos Garrett and Geoff Muldaur, which cut *Better Days* (Rhino/Elektra 70877) and *It All Comes Back* (Rhino/Elektra 70878). Butterfield was by then firmly set on a course towards a mixed music with reference points in soul and rock as well as blues, and these albums were quite successful on their own terms, but for many listeners they could never renew the raw excitement of the Butterfield–Bloomfield–Bishop partnership.

Further evidence of that phenomenon emerged in 1995, when the tapes of the first, rejected sessions for the band's debut album were brought to light after 30 years' seclusion in a vault. Interestingly, only two of the 19 numbers, the Bishop–Butterfield slow blues 'Our Love Is Driftin'' and the Little Walter tune 'Mellow Down Easy', would wind up on the album. The rest are mostly Chicago standbys like 'It Hurts Me Too' and 'That's All Right', done with typical economy but lacking the raw, skinned effect of the final product. TR

Robert Cage (born 1937)
VOCAL, GUITAR

Cage learned what skills he possesses from another Woodville, Mississippi, native, Scott Dunbar, a largely self-taught musical primitive comprehensively recorded in 1970. His mentor's scat vocals and simple propulsive guitar are clumsily reproduced in a style that is at once naive and surreal.

*(*) **Can See What You're Doing**
Fat Possum 0316 Cage; unknown (d); unknown (perc). 98.

It's rare that 30 minutes can feel simultaneously brief and endless. Sufficient time to consider whether this album should have been released at all. Cage has the most rudimentary abilities, made infuriating by a doggedness like that of a young child asking its parent the same question with the same inflection until it gets attention. Thus 'Little Eddie Blues', which strings two brief sequences of unison scat and guitar together for almost four minutes. 'Liza Jane' and 'Goodnight Irene' (the latter dispensing with its usual melody) consist of a verse and chorus repeated until the performer tires. 'Easy Rider' and 'Bundle Up And Go' fare little better. 'How Do You Get Your Rolling Done', with several two-line verses, is luxurious by comparison. A harshly distorted electric guitar adds random overtones to 'Get Outta Here' and 'Instrumental #5', both augmented by an unknown drummer and an arhythmic tambourine. If blues was nuclear fuel, this would be Chernobyl. NS

Chris Cain (born 1955)
VOCAL, GUITAR, KEYBOARDS

Born into an African-American and Greek family in San Jose, California, Cain began playing guitar about the age of nine or

ten. He has led bands since the '80s, frequently opening for Robben Ford and gradually breaking out of the California club circuit to wider recognition.

**(*) Late Night City Blues
Blue Rock'It BRCD 105 *Cain; Jon Ruff (t); Dave Eshelman (tb); Kevin Deibert (ts); Noel Catura (s); Lizz Fischer (kb); Ron Torbenson (b); Robert Higgins (d).* 87.

*** Cuttin' Loose
Blind Pig BP 74090 *Cain; Dave Eshelman (ts, bs); Noel Catura (ts); Dave Rampley (g); Ron Torbenson (b); Robert Higgins (d).* 8/90.

**(*) Can't Buy A Break
Blind Pig BPCD 5000 *As above, except add Danny Beconcini (kb); omit Rampley.* 92.

Cain works in the well-tried format of the six- or seven-piece band with two horns, as exemplified by the '50s B. B. King. As it happens he phrases a good deal like King, both on guitar and with his deep voice. He writes virtually all his material, not straying far beyond recognizable blues structures. The only flaw in these otherwise well-made albums is that their texture can be rather unvarying from track to track, but Cain appears to be working on the problem: in *Cuttin' Loose* he accompanies himself on piano on 'Never Knew I Could Be This Blue' and plays unplugged, oldfashioned guitar in 'I'm Going Through A Love Detox', while in *Can't Buy A Break*, as well as two more piano outings, he explores fusion and jazz coloration in 'Deep Freeze' and 'Gin 'N' Soda', the latter also giving unaccustomed space to the saxes.

*** Somewhere Along The Way
Blind Pig BPCD 5024 *Cain; Modesto Briseno (t); Bill Esparza (s); David Kirk Mathews (kb); Ron Johnson, Myron Dove (b); Ron E. Beck (d, v); Ms Rita (v).* 95.

*** Unscheduled Flight
Blue Rock'It BRCD 128//Crosscut CCD 11056 *Cain; John R. Burr, Tony Lufrano (kb); David Mathews (o); Garth Webber (g); Ron Johnson, Myron Dove, Dewayne Pate (b); Randy Hayes, Patrick Ford, Gabriel Ford, Ron E. Beck (d).* 97?

*** Cain Does King
Blue Rock'It BRCD 133 *Cain; Mic Gillette (t, tb); Skip Mesquite, John Lee Sanders (s); David K. Mathews (kb); Dewayne Pate (b); Patrick Ford (d); Mz Dee [Dejuana Logwood] (v).* 01?

**(*) Hall Of Shame
Blue Rock'It BRCD 137 *Cain; Tony Lufrano (kb); John R. Burr (o); Garth Webber (g); Dewayne Pate (b); Patrick Ford (d); Mz Dee [Dejuana Logwood] (v).* 03?

Even Cain's keenest fans may have been surprised by 'Trouble Makin' Woman', a very fine slow blues with a veiled guitar sound and nuanced singing. It's not in fact typical of *Somewhere Along The Way*. The Mathews–Johnson–Beck rhythm section gives the music a funkier sound, and Cain responds by playing long curving lines in the manner of Albert King, while Briseno and Esparza act the part of the Memphis Horns. Ray Charles's seducer's routine 'At The Club' gives Cain the chance to take the piano stool. *Unscheduled Flight* rings some changes in the rhythm section without significantly altering the overall effect, though from time to time, as in 'Good Old Days', Cain exchanges his customary guitar sound for something closer to Robben Ford's, and 'Blues For Curtis J' is fleet jazz playing. The dead-slow reading of Louis Jordan's 'Do You Call That A Buddy' is ingenious.

Cain Does King is, of course, a tribute album, and a particularly good one, since Cain's natural vitality is not in the least muted by his obviously deep respect for his subject. The dozen tunes, imaginatively selected from three decades of B. B.'s recordings, range from early work like 'I'm Gonna Quit My Baby' and 'Gamblers' Blues' to 'Hummingbird' and 'Take It Home'. Cain dresses his vocals *à la* King but inoffensively so, and the instrumental settings follow the spirit rather than the letter of the originals. 'World Got The Blues Before Sunrise' on *Hall Of Shame* is also a tribute, but to Albert King, and the Albertian effect that permeated *Somewhere Along The Way* and *Unscheduled Flight* is maintained through much of the album. Cain also makes a significant contribution to the Ford Blues Band's *In Memory Of Michael Bloomfield*. He has released two CDs on his own label, *Live At The Rep* in 1998 and *Christmas Cain* in 1990. TR

Charles Caldwell (1943–2003)
VOCAL, GUITAR

Caldwell worked in farming and as a tree planter before finding steady work making industrial fans, but through it all he kept the Gibson ES125 he'd bought when he was 14. He entertained at parties in exchange for free drinks, which no doubt aggravated the pancreatic cancer that killed him shortly after he recorded his only CD.

**** Remember Me
Fat Possum FP 1011 *Caldwell; 'Spam' [Tommy Lee Miles], Tino Gross, Ted Gainey (d).* 02–03.

Caldwell's music is in the modal north-Mississippi style familiar from Junior Kimbrough and R. L. Burnside, and his brooding singing and amplified guitar have a slamming rhythmic power commensurate with his 6' 8" frame; the drumming on seven tracks adds to the music's forcefulness, especially when provided by Spam, but is certainly not essential to it. It's not clear whether *Remember Me* is a sample of a large repertoire or most of a small one, and thanks to the sad circumstances of the CD's release, we'll never know. CS

Big Al Calhoun (born 1930)
VOCAL, HARMONICA

Alvin Calhoun was born in Leland, Mississippi, and was playing harmonica by the age of six – 'Grand Ole Opry stuff' until he heard Sonny Boy Williamson II on the radio. Tired of plantation life, he moved to Memphis in 1950, and to St Louis three years later. When not making music, Calhoun worked in electronics until his retirement.

**** Harmonica Blues
Arcola A CD 1003 *Calhoun; Henry Townsend (g).* 8/79.

Al Calhoun takes the vocal duties on half this CD, and accompanies Henry and Vernell Townsend on the balance. Calhoun's music is in no sense original; almost all his songs and most of his playing techniques pay homage to John Lee Williamson, and the songs that come from other sources are as familiar as 'My Babe' and 'That's All Right'. That's not the point, however; what matters is that Calhoun is an assured and commanding exponent of his material and his instrument. Henry Townsend's fierce amplified guitar is so intuitive and appropriate that to call it merely responsive seriously misrepresents the intimate commingling of instruments and voice, and the cumulative intensity that results; for once, it's worth wheeling out the clichéd 'telepathic'. If these tracks were on obscure 78s, they would sell for very large sums. CS

Joe Callicott (1899–1969)
VOCAL, GUITAR

A lifelong resident of Nesbit, Mississippi, Callicott (also spelled Calicott) made just one commercial record, in 1930; he also played second guitar on his friend Garfield Akers's two-part 'Cottonfield Blues', an acknowledged classic. Both men played in the rhythmic fingerpicking style still to be heard in the work of north Mississippi artists such as Robert Belfour and R. L. Burnside. Callicott was rediscovered and recorded in 1967 by musicologist George Mitchell and cut an album for Blue Horizon the following year.

**** North Mississippi Blues
Southland SCD-35 *Callicott.* 2/30–8/67.
**** Ain't A Gonna Lie To You
Fat Possum 0360 *Callicott.* 8/67.

Callicott quickly draws the listener into his world with the simple beauty of his songs and the timbre of his voice. His guitar playing is functional but dependable, a steady bass pulse with the thumb and simple melodies on the treble strings. There's an affinity with Mississippi John Hurt but Callicott is a lustier singer with an occasional falsetto lilt in his voice. These CDs both contain 12 tracks. *North Mississippi Blues* concludes with Callicott's two 1930 recordings, 'Traveling Mama Blues,' and 'Fare Thee Well Blues'; there's a remake of the latter on *Ain't A Gonna Lie To You*. Like others of his songs, notably a version of 'Frankie And Albert', it's literate and detailed; Callicot's compositions often run to eight verses. Unfortunately, these two CDs have six tracks in common, and they both overlap extensively with the deleted *Mississippi Delta Blues – Vol. 2* (Arhoolie CD 402). Although regarded as a minor figure, Callicott provides an accurate and characteristic microcosm of the blues of the '30s. NS/CS

Eddie C. Campbell (born 1939)
VOCAL, GUITAR, HARMONICA, BASS

Campbell made the trip from Mississippi to the West Side as a child, and took an early interest in the guitar, later adding motorcycles, women and martial arts. He worked as a sideman with various big names, and did some rejected sessions for Cobra and King, but a steady gig in Waukegan while white attention was focused on Chicago meant that he came to wider notice comparatively late. In 1984, Campbell left for Europe in a hurry following 'some heavy personal changes', returning eight years later.

**** King Of The Jungle
Rooster R 2602 *Campbell; Carey Bell (h); Lafayette Leake (p); Bob Stroger, Lurrie Bell (b); Clifton James (d).* 6/77.
**(*) Let's Pick It!
Evidence ECD 26037 *Campbell; Carlo Reys (h); Ruud van Ingen (p); Willem van Dullemen (g); Lex Nijsen (b); Harry Visscher (d).* 10/84.

**(*) Gonna Be Alright
Icehouse IHR 9423 *Campbell; Saskia Laroo, Angelo Verploegen (t); Jan Voeten (tb); Tom 'Mad' Jones, Rinus Groenveld (ts); Johnny Mars (h); Al Copley, Han van Dam (p); Elisha Blue (g, v); Bas van Velzen, Jose Luis (b); Olaf Keus, John McColgan (d).* 6–7/86.
***(*) That's When I Know
Blind Pig BPCD 5014 *Campbell; Tom Elferdink (as, ts, bs); Karl Outten, Ron Scott (o); John Pazdan, Bill Watkins (b); Keith Hudson, Robert 'Huckleberry Hound' Wright (d); Barbara Mayson Campbell, Jeff Taylor (v).* early 90s.
***(*) Hopes & Dreams
Rooster RBLU 2638 *Campbell; Lester 'Duck' Warner (t, tb, shaker); Tim Perryman (tb); Kenny Glover (as, ts); Billy Boy Arnold (h, sp); Ernest Lane (o, p); Jeff Jones (o); Loui Villeri (b); Robert 'Huckleberry Hound' Wright (d).* 12/99–1/00.

King Of The Jungle was evidence both of life in the West Side blues scene and of Campbell's considerable talent. It's easy to suggest influences on his playing, notably Magic Sam, and his admiration for Muddy Waters's singing is obvious, but even though two thirds of the tracks are covers (and 'Santa's Messin' With The Kid' is amusingly derivative), he impresses as very much his own man, and never as lazily imitative. Campbell is assisted by some of the most reliable session musicians then working in Chicago, and by Carey Bell in top form.

The two albums from Campbell's European exile that remain in catalogue suffer from the use of musicians who tackle every number at full throttle, seldom leaving space for each other or for Campbell; the hyperactive drummers are particularly wearing and unsympathetic. Campbell has to yell to make his singing heard above the tumult, and there's little of the vocal versatility and subtlety evident on CDs recorded before and after this interlude. There are good guitar solos here and there, and on *Gonna Be Alright* there are some inventive passages from Rinus Groenveld, but these are disappointing discs.

Fortunately, Blind Pig and Rooster are on hand to prove that they are also aberrations. The musicians on *That's When I Know* and *Hopes & Dreams* play with taste and intelligence, providing platforms from which Campbell can present himself. All compositions on both discs are original. ('Geese In The Ninny Bow (Hey!)' on *Hopes & Dreams* borrows from Stevie Wonder, but it's very creative borrowing.) Campbell impresses as a clever, thoughtful songwriter, although he occasionally drifts into self-absorption, and 'I'm Your Santa' on *Hopes & Dreams* is a jejune attempt to reprise the success of 'Santa's Messin' With The Kid'. Huckleberry Hound's drumming, with dynamics and tone colours artfully varied according to the mood of each number, is almost enough in itself to recommend these CDs. CS

Gene Campbell
VOCAL, GUITAR

An obscure musician, probably from east Texas but remembered by no contemporaries.

*** Gene Campbell (1929–1931)
Document DOCD-5151 *Campbell.* 11/29–1/31.

(*) Texas Blues (1927–1937)
Wolf WSE 112 *Campbell.* 11/29–1/31.

Many echoes in his vocal and instrumental phrasing and tone reveal Campbell as a student of the work of Lonnie Johnson – not only Johnson's own records but also his accompaniments to Texas Alexander: witness the Alexandrian moaned lines in 'Western Plain Blues'. There are also fleeting similarities in Campbell's guitar playing to that of Little Hat Jones and, in 'Robbin' And Stealin' Blues', Carl Davis. Like Davis with Alexander, Campbell is not shy of playing near-identical openings to several songs in a row, for example at his second session. He rounded off that date with a two-part 'Freight Train Yodeling Blues' – a Jimmie Rodgers imitation, of course, but exceptional among black *hommages* to America's Blue Yodeller in having a thoroughly idiomatic yodel.

The guitar playing at Campbell's third session has a much blunter edge. Perhaps the recording ambience was different, or the instrument – or perhaps another musician was playing for him, which would also explain the liberal use of sock chords, a technique Campbell employs nowhere else. At any rate, when he next recorded, only two months later, he had reverted to his original sound.

Although there may not be enough variety in the tunes and settings of Campbell's blues to hold every listener's interest throughout a CD, there is something striking about his work – and in this respect it is impossible not to be reminded of J. T. Smith, a contemporary and fellow Texan who recorded for the same company – namely, his literacy and his ability to stay focused on the subject of a song and not fall back on formulaic verses. Listen, for instance, to 'Wedding Day Blues', 'Levee Camp Man' or 'Toby Woman Blues'. The last of these and its original coupling, the very Johnson-and-Alexanderish 'Turned Out Blues', were unavailable when the Document album was compiled and arrived on *"Too Late, Too Late" – Vol. 2* (Document DOCD-5216). The Wolf CD puts a dozen of Campbell's recordings (none from the untypical third session) at the head of a VAC of Texas bluesmen. TR

Blind James Campbell (born 1906)
VOCAL, GUITAR

Leader of The Friendly Five, at the time of recording one of the last surviving African-American street bands.

***(*) Blind James Campbell And His Nashville Street Band
Arhoolie CD-438 *Campbell; George Bell (t); Beauford Clay (vn, bj); Bell Ray (vn, g, v); Ralph Robinson (tu).* 10/62, 4/63.

The Dixie Doodlers, an earlier version of James Campbell's band, recorded two sides in 1953, and even then sounded as if they had timewarped in from the '30s. These titles are available on *No Jive: Authentic Southern Country Blues* (Ace CDCHD 652) or in the boxed set *A Shot In The Dark: Nashville Jumps* (Bear Family BCD 15864 8CD). Another decade only increased the Friendly Five's anachronicity, although paradoxically there was by then a new audience for their recordings. The unusual conjunction of fiddles and brass, and the multi-instrumental skills of two band members, enabled the recording of a variety of lineups, from Campbell solo to the full squad, although balancing the instruments through one omnidirectional microphone was sometimes a challenge. Tunings are often approximate, and some numbers start raggedly, but there's always plenty of time for everyone to clamber aboard the departing train. In any case, a quest for the perfect take would have been alien to the spirit of their rough-and-tumble music.

In its heyday, Campbell's band had been in (mostly white) demand for square dances, fraternity parties and road houses. Their repertoire extended well beyond the blues, which nevertheless dominates this CD, since they knew that the producer's tastes tended that way. The resulting picture is inevitably partial, and the CD's increased length over the original LP confirms that they fitted their blues lyrics to a limited number of tunes. On the sacred side, they usually stick to the better known gospel songs, although a guitar and tuba version of 'Gambling Man' intriguingly breaks the grip of familiarity.

Musicologists may wish for more pieces like 'I Get So Blue When It Rains', or the raucous country breakdown 'Buffalo Gal', but as compensation, the band's blues performances are often committed and deep. Trumpeter George Bell was a formidable blues player, with a lyrical tone, and on 'Jimmy's Blues' he seems to be inside Campbell's head, playing the lowdown feelings that the latter expresses in song. Other performances to note include – despite their ubiquity on disc – 'John Henry' (a valuable version with banjo) and 'Baby Please Don't Go', surely the only recorded example of percussion by clattering a fiddle bow against a tuba. Valuable as documentary, this CD is also a considerable artistic success, and great fun. CS

John Campbell (1952–93)
VOCAL, GUITAR

The promise of John Campbell's commercial career became 'what if …' after his fatal heart attack. Extensive injuries sustained in a teenage drag-racing crash gave him time to concentrate on blues and, once recovered, he took to an itinerant life which eventually brought him to New York. His final albums saw him developing a dramatic new performance style that built upon the lessons of his blues apprenticeship.

*** Tyler, Texas Session
Sphere Sound CD 102 *Campbell.* 86?

Towards the end there was a deliberate attempt to portray Campbell's stage persona as a more threatening variation of Dr John's voodoo priest, but this undated solo demo session from his days as Johnny 'Slim' Campbell finds him playing his blues straight, on a 1952 Gibson SJ and a '30s National Resophonic. A dozen selections are predominantly shared between Robert Johnson, Muddy Waters, Elmore James and John Lee Hooker originals and a handful of semi-improvised instrumentals. Although there is only one Lightnin' Hopkins piece, 'Mojo Hand', his imprint is stamped all over Campbell's treble phrasing, except on 'Medley In C/Chump Man Blues', whose fingerpicking brings a pinch of Blind Blake to the mix. He uses the National for his slide pieces, including 'I Can't Be Satisfied' and K. C. Douglas's 'Watch Dog Blues', flaunting a confident and imaginative technique. Its limited-edition status may make this set hard but worthwhile to find.

*** A Man And His Blues
Blue Rock'It BRCD 120//Crosscut CCD 11019 *Campbell; Jerry Portnoy (h); Ronnie Earl (g); Per Hanson (d); Darrell Nulisch (v). 4/88.*

A less varied programme with an absence of slide features underlines Campbell's adherence to the delineations of Hopkins's verse schemes, not least in his re-creations of 'Going To Dallas' and 'Bluebird', two of four solo performances here. 'Deep River Rag' is intricately picked but can't mask its status as a party piece. The balance of the album consists of duets and trios with Portnoy, Earl and Hanson, while Nulisch takes over the vocal mike for a rousing stomp through Snooky Pryor's 'Judgment Day'. Dark and brooding imagery in 'Bad Night Blues', a Campbell original, lays the groundwork for the new direction he would soon take. A move away from an overtly traditional performance style, allied to a burgeoning confidence and distinctive delivery, led to a radical transformation in his stage image.

*** One Believer
Elektra 61086 *Campbell; Jimmy Pugh (kb); Gary Nicholson (g); Richard Cousins, Jimmy Pettit, Antoine Salley (b); Davis McLarty, Lee Spath (d). 3–5/91.*

Which came first, the image or the songs? Shoulder-length hair, bone jewellery and a tendency to glower took care of the former. More importantly, Campbell wrote nine of these ten songs with producer Dennis Walker, an important contributor to Robert Cray's popular rise. Perhaps they also devised the manner in which the singer performs them. Slower songs, like 'Devil In My Closet', 'Voodoo Edge' and 'One Believer', utilize a growling *Sprechstimme*, an imperfect echo of Johnny Cash's imperfect pitch, performed over minimal backing. Each thus becomes a drama, although in 'Edge' and 'Tiny Coffin' the lyrics become too literate for Campbell's overcharged delivery. Elmore James's 'Person To Person' is one of two opportunities to wield his slide, better employed when 'Take Me Down' doubles its tempo and becomes the template for his next and final album. All the material is blues-based but the form is subordinated to the task of enhancing Campbell's talismanic presence.

***(*) Howlin' Mercy
Elektra 61440 *Campbell; Zonder Kennedy (g); Jimmy Pettit (b); Davis McLarty (d); Elvin Diablo (perc). 8/92.*

By now, Campbell was forcefully inhabiting his new character, reflected in song titles like 'Ain't Afraid Of Midnight' and 'Firin' Line', the latter containing the line 'two rabid dogs fightin' in the street and they're as mean as the woman I've come to meet'. Bidding farewell to finesse, the album is awash with dumbed-down OTT slide solos and pounding rhythms. But it works. 'Saddle Up My Pony' (derived from but not derivative of Charlie Patton) and 'Wolf Among The Lambs' begin quietly, awash with reverb, before each mutates into a roaring dragstrip racer. Other brief respites include Tom Waits's 'Down In The Hole' and 'Love's Name' ('love is a wicked woman's tool'), one of seven compositions shared between Campbell, Dennis Walker and Zonder Kennedy. 'Look What Love Can Do' and 'Written In Stone' also throttle back from the general phlegm and furore. Kansas Joe's 'When The Levee Breaks' gets the Led Zeppelin treatment, thus accounting for the group members' names being added to the composer credits. Despite its populist approach, this was a consolidation

of Campbell's increasing reputation as a live performer. It now represents a not entirely satisfactory memorial. NS

Canned Heat
GROUP

Canned Heat was created by heavy-duty blues enthusiasts. Singer Bob 'The Bear' Hite (1945–81) and guitarist Henry Vestine (1944–97) were serious record-collectors, and Alan 'Blind Owl' Wilson (1943–70) a close student of the music who had met and played with several older blues artists. The band that achieved pop chart success in 1968 with 'On The Road Again' and 'Going Up The Country', both based on old blues recordings, had coalesced that year with Larry Taylor (bass) and Adolfo (Fito) de la Parra (drums) but the lineup did not endure, and by the time they scored their biggest hit, 'Let's Work Together', in 1970 Vestine had been replaced by Harvey Mandel. Over the next 35 years there would be many other personnel changes, involving such players as Walter Trout, Junior Watson and Robert Lucas (qq.v.).

** Don't Forget To Boogie
Varèse Sarabande 302 066 345 *Al Wilson (h, g, v); Henry Vestine (g); Stuart Brotman (b); unknown (d); Bob Hite (v). 66.*

** Straight Ahead
Thunderbolt CDTB 130 *Al Wilson (h, g, v); Henry Vestine (g); Stuart Brotman, Larry Taylor (b); Fito de la Parra, unknown (d); Bob Hite (v). 66, 69.*

Don't Forget To Boogie holds, and *Straight Ahead* draws from, a 1966 session by an early lineup, produced by Johnny Otis. At this stage Canned Heat were predominantly a covers band, deploying blues and R&B repertoire by Muddy Waters, John Lee Hooker, Bo Diddley and so on. Their relaxed delivery is in sharp contrast to their manner three years later, exemplified by five sonically villainous tracks on *Straight Ahead* that come from the LP titled *Live At Topanga Corral*, actually recorded at the Kaleidoscope. These CDs are only for dedicated Heat-seekers.

*** Boogie With Canned Heat
EMI 576095 *unknowns (horns); Al Wilson (h, g, v); Dr John [Mack Rebennack] (p); Henry Vestine (g); Larry Taylor (b); Fito de la Parra (d); Bob Hite (v). 67.*

*** Living The Blues
BGO BGOCD 591 2CD *Similar to above, except add Joe Sample (p); Wilson also plays fl. 68.*

***(*) Uncanned!: The Best Of Canned Heat
EMI 29165//CDEM 1543 2CD *Al Wilson (fl, h, g, v); Dr John [Mack Rebennack] (p, v); James Shane, John Lee Hooker (g, v); Henry Vestine, Harvey Mandel, Joel Scott Hill (g); Larry Taylor, Antonio de la Barreda, Richard Hite (b); Frank Cook, Fito de la Parra (d); Bob Hite, Little Richard (v). 4/67–11/72.*

*** Let's Work Together (The Best Of Canned Heat)
EMI/Liberty 93114 *As above, except add The Chipmunks (v); omit Hooker, Dr John. 4/67–10/71.*

*** The Very Best Of
EMI 526778 *Similar to above. 67–72.*

Boogie With Canned Heat and *Living The Blues* capture the band that resolutely put blues on the rock agenda in the late '60s. The former contains 'On The Road Again', a jaunty recasting of a Floyd Jones recording, which was an unexpected hit in both the US and Britain, while *Living The Blues* has the bucolic 'Going Up The Country', adapted from Henry Thomas, with Wilson playing the panpipes part on flute. Much else on *Living The Blues*, however, is more characteristic of the band's aggressive performance style, notably the vastly extended 'Refried Boogie'. Readers coming fresh to Canned Heat may do better to defer a visit to the original albums until they've taken in the wider view provided by one or another of the compilations. *Uncanned!* offers the most luxurious tour, with its long, meticulous notes and a thoughtful selection that embraces both the familiar ('Going Up The Country', 'Let's Work Together', etc.) and the unheard: 13 tracks are previously unissued. The single-CD *Best Of*s contain a lot of the same material but plenty of other stuff besides; not much more than half of *Let's Work Together* is duplicated on *Uncanned!*. The boogie-till-you-drop side of the band is illustrated by 'Gotta Boogie (The World Boogie)' on *Uncanned!* and the 11-minute 'Fried Hockey Boogie' on *Let's Work Together*; both are essentially expansions of John Lee Hooker's 'Boogie Chillen'. Canned Heat's 1970 collaboration with Hooker, *Hooker 'N Heat*, is discussed in his entry.

**(*) Historical Figures And Ancient Heads/The New Age
BGO BGOCD 672 *Clifford Solomon (ts); Charles Lloyd (fl); Fito de la Parra (p, d); Little Richard (p, v); Ernest Lane, Ed Beyer (p); Joel Scott Hill, James Shane (g, v); Henry Vestine, Harvey Mandel (g); Richard Hite (b, v); Tony de la Barreda (b); Bob Hite, Clara Ward Singers (v).* 71–72.

** Live At The Turku Rock Festival
Bear Tracks BTCD 979 409 *Bob Hite (h, v); Joel Scott Hill (g, v); Henry Vestine (g); Antonie de la Barreda (b); Fito de la Parra (d).* 8/71.

**(*) Canned Heat 1967–1976: The Boogie House Tapes
Ruf 1050 2CD *Al Wilson (h, g, v); Bob Hite (h, v); Magic Dick (h); Ed Beyer (p); Joel Scott Hill (g, v); Henry Vestine, Harvey Mandel, James Shane, Chris Morgan (g); Larry Taylor, Tony de la Barreda, Richard Hite (b); Fito de la Parra (d).* 67–76.

**(*) Human Condition
Aim 1071 *Bob Hite (h, v); Mark Skyer (g); Chris Morgan (g); Richard Hite (b); Fito de la Parra (d); Chambers Brothers (v).* 77.

** Boogie Assault//Live In Oz
Aim CD 1003//Mystic MYSCD 148 *Ricky Kellogg (h, v); Walter Trout, Mike Halby (g, v); Ernie Rodriguez (b, v); Fito de la Parra (d).* 82.

**(*) Reheated
Varèse Sarabande 302 061 092//SPV 858805 *James Thornbury (h, g, v); Junior Watson (g); Larry Taylor (b); Fito de la Parra (d).* 7/88.

**(*) Burnin'
Aim CD 1033 *As above.* 4/90.

**(*) Internal Combustion
[Connoisseur Collection FPCC 001]//Aim 1044 *James Thornbury (h, g, v); Ronnie Barron (p); Junior Watson, Henry Vestine, Harvey Mandel, Ira Ingber (g); Ron Shumake, Larry Taylor (b); Fito de la Parra (d); John Lee Hooker (sp).* 91–92.

Canned Heat had never had a settled lineup, and after 1970, when Mandel and Taylor left and Wilson died, shockingly young, of a drug overdose, a succession of musicians occupied a guitar chair. *Historical Figures And Ancient Heads* reflects this fluidity by featuring three of them and is altogether a rather directionless set, blues lying uncomfortably next to self-indulgent guitar jams, its most memorable track a collaboration with Little Richard, 'Rockin' With The King' (also to be found on the *Best Of* collections discussed above). The BGO issue couples it with *The New Age*, a not specially distinguished album that concluded their contract with Liberty. The next two decades would be assiduously documented by fans with tape recorders, and the legacy of those electronic Boswells is a stack of CDs, sometimes on obscure labels and often unauthorized, like the '71 Finland gig commemorated on *Live At The Turku Rock Festival* (possibly no longer in print: if so, no loss) or the '82 Australian tour album *Boogie Assault* on Aim (though the retitled Mystic release has the band's approval). *The Boogie House Tapes* is a superior example of the breed, assembled (with the band's imprimatur) from miscellaneous studio recordings, radio and TV appearances, and an international assortment of festival and club gigs. The sound quality is variable, but the material is a satisfactory mixture of the band's standbys and some uncommoner songs, with not too much boogie excess. *Human Condition* is a reissue of a Takoma album with the short-lived Morgan–Skyer guitar team, while *Reheated*, the Australian-recorded *Burnin'* and *Internal Combustion* are drawn from the period when the chief singer was James Thornbury and the guitar role shared by himself and Junior Watson – a less brutish formation than some of its forerunners. Whether out of sentiment or because it's what audiences expect, the band is often to be heard revisiting its past, as in *Internal Combustion*'s segue from a 'John Lee Hooker Boogie' to de la Parra's Wilsonesque vocal on 'Remember Woodstock'. Thanks to their international fanbase, there may well be other CDs from this period to be dug up by the assiduous record-hunter.

**(*) Blues Band
Ruf 1040//Mystic MYS CD 120 *Robert Lucas (h, g, v); Henry Vestine, Junior Watson (g); Larry Taylor, Greg Kage (b); Fito de la Parra (d).* 10–11/96.

**(*) Boogie 2000
Ruf 1041//1453 *David Woodward, Mike Forbes (s, fl); Robert Lucas (h, g, v); Michael Finnigan (o); Rob Rio (p); Larry Taylor (g, v); Javier Batiz (g); Greg Kage (b, v); Fito de la Parra (d, perc); Mike Pacheco (cga, perc); Cannibal & The Headhunters (Robert 'Rabbit' Jaramillo, Richard 'Scar' Lopez, Charlie 'Chaz' Munoz, Greg 'Lucky' Esparza) (v).* 3–5/99.

**(*) Friends In The Can
Ruf 1066 *Stanley Behrens (s, fl, h, cga, v); Mike Finnigan (o); Dallas Hodge, Corey Stevens, Robert Lucas, Walter Trout (g, v); John Paulus, Roy Rogers, Harvey Mandel, Henry Vestine (g); Greg Kage (b, v); Larry Taylor (b); Fito de la Parra (d, timbales, perc); John Lee Hooker, Taj Mahal (v).* 87/88, 3/01–12/02.

The late-'90s Canned Heat, with Robert Lucas filling the Bob Hite role, was faithful enough to the band's traditions when left alone to do its thing, as on *Blues Band*, but the more diversified *Boogie 2000* has a few items that sit oddly on a Canned Heat album, such as Kage's white-bread vocal on 'World Of Make Believe'. *Friends In The Can* is a neat idea: an album by Canned Heat – in a can. It's actually a flat metal box of the kind that might hold ten cigarillos, and the contents duly smoke, though perhaps not like Cubans. Old Can hands who enjoy the band's staple of the where-I-step-a-flower-dies boogie will find much to help them roll back the years, like the Doc Martens stomp of 'Let's Work Together' – presented in two versions, one fronted by Robert Lucas – or the Al Wilsonish singing of Stanley Behrens, who also plays a harmonica that can strip paint. For listeners outside the campfire circle there may be more interest in Taj Mahal singing 'Never Get Out Of These Blues Alive' as a tribute to the bluesman Canned Heat were closest to, followed by The Boogie Man himself in an outtake from the *Healer* sessions, a sprightly 'Little Wheel'. TR

Gus Cannon (1883–1979)
VOCAL, BANJO, JUG

In the early years of the last century the Mississippi-born Cannon travelled the South with medicine shows. In the late '20s, based in Memphis, he formed a jugband which rivalled the city's other such group, the Memphis Jug Band, but evidently sold, and so made, fewer records. For some 30 years Cannon lived in obscurity, until his composition 'Walk Right In', rerecorded by the folk group The Rooftop Singers, was 1963's most left-field hit. After that he did some further playing in public and on record, and accepted the status of a grand old man of Memphis music.

***(*) **Gus Cannon – Vol. 1 (1927–1928)**
Document DOCD-5032 *Cannon; Noah Lewis (h, v); Elijah Avery (bj, g); prob. Hosea Woods (k); Ashley Thompson (g, v); Blind Blake (g).* c. 11/27–9/28.

(**) **Memphis Blues
Wolf WSE 108 *Cannon; Blind Blake (g).* c. 11/27.

***(*) **Gus Cannon & Noah Lewis – Vol. 2 (1929–1930)**
Document DOCD-5033 *Cannon; Noah Lewis (h, v); Hosea Woods (g, k, v); unknown (j).* 9/29–11/30.

**** **Sleepy John Estes/Gus Cannon**
[JSP JSPCD 3406] 2CD *Cannon; Noah Lewis (h, v); Elijah Avery (bj, g); Hosea Woods (g, k, v); Ashley Thompson (g, v); unknown (j).* 1/28–11/30.

**** **The Complete Works 1927–1930**
Yazoo 1082/3 *As above.* 1/28–11/30.

**** **The Best Of Cannon's Jug Stompers**
Yazoo 2060 *As above.* 1/28–11/30.

When jugband music enjoyed a brief revival in the '60s, it was generally its comic aspect – the barnyard noises of jug and kazoo, and nonsense songs like 'Boodle Am Shake' – that was exploited rather than its capacity to deliver lilting dance music in what could be ravishing instrumental settings. No records exemplify that gentler side of jugband performance more gracefully than those of the small groups led by Gus Cannon. When playing in the streets and parks of Memphis, or in outlying west Tennessee towns like Brownsville and Ripley, Cannon's Jug Stompers may have made looser, funkier music, but their Victor recordings of 1928–30 are miracles of discipline and economy. The lead role is generally filled by Noah Lewis, a harmonica player with an exquisite sound and a penchant for elegant melody, Cannon contributing a countermelody on banjo and a sporadic bass part on jug. On the 1928 sessions they are supported by the propulsive guitar of Ashley Thompson or Elijah Avery, and these sides, a mixture of ragtime tunes, blues and standard pieces like 'Bugle Call Rag', are both their finest work and some of the most perfectly balanced ensemble recordings in African-American music. The group's later sides tend to be rowdier and more raucous,

thanks in part to the guitarist, singer and entertainer Hosea Woods, who knew old common-stock or vaudeville numbers like 'Mule Get Up In The Alley' and 'Bring It With You When You Come', to which Cannon added his own delightfully jaunty composition 'Walk Right In'. Yet amidst this merriment can be found 'Going To Germany', a blues soberly sung by Lewis to match his earlier rendition, brusque but haunting, of 'Viola Lee Blues'.

JSP's 2CD (which regrettably may no longer be available) contains all 26 of the Victor recordings in superb transfers. As if that were not enough, the companion Estes disc also contains Noah Lewis's seven recordings away from the Jug Stompers: three harmonica solos and four songs with a jugband lineup that lacks the Stompers' free-and-easy swing. The two Yazoos are close contenders, but *The Complete Works*, despite its title, lacks 'Springdale Blues' and 'Riley's Wagon', and *The Best Of*, though restoring those songs, omits three of the rag tunes. The Documents between them round up all the Jug Stompers sides, the seven Lewises and – what the other sets all lack – Cannon and Woods's 1929 duet on Brunswick, 'Last Chance Blues'/'Fourth And Beale', but the transfer quality is somewhat inferior.

Document's *Vol. 1* also has the half-dozen banjo songs Cannon cut earlier for Paramount, mostly with Blind Blake seconding on guitar. On 'Poor Boy, Long Ways From Home' he plays slide banjo, the only example of this technique on African-American recordings of the period. Another remarkable survival, 'Can You Blame The Colored Man', is a comic song about the black leader Booker T. Washington being invited to dinner at the White House. By comparison 'Jonestown Blues', 'Madison Street Rag' and 'My Money Never Runs Out', which would all be redone by the Jug Stompers, are less arresting, but the session as a whole has great historical resonance. It is also included on Wolf's *Memphis Blues* alongside the complete '20s/'30s output of Robert Wilkins.

*** **Walk Right In**
Stax SCD-8603 *Cannon; Will Shade (j); Milton Roby (wb).* 6/63.

It is 1963, and a catchy, folksy little song called 'Walk Right In' has walked right into the US pop charts and on up to #1. Its writer proves to be a septuagenarian banjo player and one-time jugband leader in Memphis, and a local record company promptly trundles the old man and some friends into their studios to make an album. What could be more natural? Quite a lot, because that local label was Stax, the hit factory of Southern soul, and Gus Cannon's bewhiskered blues and old-time songs like 'Salty Dog', 'Make Me A Pallet On Your Floor' and 'Gonna Raise A Ruckus Tonight' came from a past that really was another country. The album disappeared almost immediately and became a collector's item of fabulous rarity. Now available on CD, there's not much more than half an hour of it, and a good deal of that is Cannon reminiscing about the old days, but it provides an exuberant, fascinating and unique encounter with the prehistory of the blues.

Seven years later Cannon contributed two banjo songs, 'Lela' and 'Goin' Back (To Memphis, TN)', to *On The Road Again* (Genes GCD 9918), an album shared with Bukka White and Furry Lewis. They are a little rough, but, as always, full of personality. TR

Carolina Slim (1923–53)
VOCAL, GUITAR

Born in Leasburg, North Carolina, Edward P. Harris joined the migration to the northeastern cities. He died in Newark, New Jersey, while undergoing an operation.

**(*) Carolina Slim (1950–1952)
Document BDCD-6043 *Carolina Slim; unknowns (g); unknowns (d); unknowns (wb); unknown (v).* 7/50–6/52.

**(*) Carolina Blues 1950/1952
EPM Blues Collection 16053 *As above.* 7/50–6/52.

A short life and, until recently, the lack of a photograph do not a Robert Johnson make. Nor does an array of colourful pseudonyms. (Carolina Slim also had records issued as Jammin' Jim, Country Paul and Lazy Slim Jim.) When taking inspiration from Blind Boy Fuller's ragtime blues, Slim is relaxed, confident and good-humoured, producing a jumping version of Fuller's 'Rag Mama Rag', and a two-guitar 'Mama's Boogie' with shimmering slide. 'Sidewalk Boogie', with overdubbed traffic noise, manages to sound like spontaneous commentary on the passing parade, as does the dialogue about girls on 'Carolina Boogie', too long for release on 78, but happily retained until the LP format arrived. Unfortunately, Harris spent much of his studio time imitating Lightnin' Hopkins, sometimes very accurately, sometimes rather tentatively, but almost always without the fire and creativity of his model. Two versions of Walter Davis's 'Your Picture Done Faded', done in the Hopkins manner, capture something of their composer's graceful resignation, but their success is not typical.

There is nothing to choose between the sound quality of these two releases. Slim is not the most essential blues artist, but Document, with the complete recordings (27 tracks), do a more thorough job than EPM, who omit five, among them 'Black Chariot', one of Slim's best Hopkins covers. CS

Leroy Carr (c. 1899–1935)
VOCAL, PIANO

Born in Nashville, Tennessee, Carr settled in Indianapolis in his 20s. He was introduced to the guitarist Scrapper Blackwell and shortly afterwards, in 1928, they made their first record together. Its instant success gave them the basis of a career as a duet, but it was always in danger of being undermined by Carr's heavy drinking and Blackwell's volatility and was prematurely ended by Carr's death in 1935. One sign of their influence is the queue of imitators who followed them, headed by, but by no means confined to, Bill Gaither, Bumble Bee Slim and Frank 'Springback' James; another, the substantial folio of blues standards they originated.

***(*) Leroy Carr – Vol. 1 (1928–1929)
Document DOCD-5134 *Carr; Scrapper Blackwell (g); unknown (k).* 6/28–3/29.

***(*) Leroy Carr – Vol. 2 (1929–1930)
Document DOCD-5135 *Carr; Scrapper Blackwell (g, v).* 6/29–1/30.

***(*) Leroy Carr – Vol. 3 (1930–1932)
Document DOCD-5136 *As above.* 9/30–3/32.

**** Leroy Carr – Vol. 4 (1932–1934)
Document DOCD-5137 *Carr; Scrapper Blackwell (g, sp).* 3/32–8/34.

**** Leroy Carr – Vol. 5 (1934)
Document DOCD-5138 *Carr; Scrapper Blackwell, Josh White (g, sp).* 8–12/34.

**** Leroy Carr – Vol. 6 (1934–1935)
Document DOCD-5139 *As above.* 12/34–2/35.

**(*) Leroy Carr & Black Boy Shine – Unissued Test Pressings and Alternate Takes (1934–1937)
Document DOCD-5465 *Carr; Scrapper Blackwell, Josh White (g); Bobby Phillips (v).* 8–12/34.

Carr's first record, 'My Own Lonesome Blues'/'How Long – How Long Blues', added a new dialect to the language of the blues. His husky singing and unaggressive conversational manner set a new emotional pitch for the delivery of blues lyrics, while the combination of piano and guitar, Carr playing chiefly in the middle range at sedate tempos, Blackwell inscribing resonant single-string lines, initiated a form of accompaniment that would dominate blues recording for a quarter of a century. It's also more than likely that the characteristic ambience of Carr's work and its many imitations helped to create the common perception of the blues as a music of melancholy, ruefulness and regret.

That ambience was steadily built up throughout Carr's short but productive career. Probably two thirds of his recordings are slow or slow-medium blues on subjects like a lover's desertion or misbehaviour (e.g. 'Mean Mistreater Mama', which has become a standard), loneliness, imprisonment or alcoholism. Outstanding among them are a handful of songs he recorded between 1932 and 1935 such as 'Midnight Hour Blues', 'Hurry Down Sunshine', 'Blues Before Sunrise' and 'When The Sun Goes Down', which distil the raw liquor of grief into a spirit of complex and lingering flavour. The poetic skill that reaches its peak in these night thoughts is fleetingly displayed in numerous other pieces, and even a routine subject can elicit ingenious responses, like the couplet in 'Jail Cell Blues': 'I done told you, baby, the jailhouse is a lonesome place, But I ain't so bad, mama, I just done fell from grace.' Or the punning last line of 'I Believe I'll Make A Change': 'Gonna turn off this gas stove, I'm bound for a brand new range.'

Amidst these conventionally structured blues Carr regularly inserted songs of different weight, style and tempo, such as 'Naptown Blues', with its scat chorus and stop-time accompaniment, an unexplicit but jolly version of 'The Dirty Dozen', and a somewhat similar hokum piece, 'Papa Wants To Knock A Jug'. The cheerful 'Gettin' All Wet', 'That's Tellin' 'Em', 'Papa Wants A Cookie', 'Carried Water For The Elephant' and 'Papa's On The House Top' have the bouncing simplicity of children's playground chants. All these are on the second and third Documents, but later volumes have similarly buoyant numbers like 'Don't Start No Stuff' and 'Bo Bo Stomp' on *Vol. 5* and 'It's Too Short' on *Vol. 6* – a CD which ends with Carr's magnificent last session, culminating in the almost unbearable poignancy of his final recording, 'Six Cold Feet In The Ground'.

Carr also recorded a few songs written in conventional popular styles of the time, such as 'How About Me?' (by Irving Berlin) and 'Think Of Me Thinking Of You' on the first Document, 'Let's Make Up And Be Friends Again' and 'Let's Disagree' on the third and 'Arlena' on the sixth. His wistful, intimate delivery of those numbers anticipates '40s blues crooners like Cecil Gant (an obvious admirer), Charles Brown and, obliquely, Nat King Cole.

The unissued-and-alternate set, shared with Black Boy

Shine, has seven tracks by Carr; four are alternative takes of songs heard on other Documents, leaving two takes of 'Lonesome Man Blues' and one of 'The Stuff Is Here (And It's Mellow)', a duet with the female singer Bobby Phillips.

***(*) **Whiskey Is My Habit, Good Women Is All I Crave: The Best Of Leroy Carr**
Columbia/Legacy C2K 86929 2CD *Carr; Scrapper Blackwell (g, v); Josh White (g).* 6/28–2/35.
*** **Prison Bound Blues**
Snapper Complete Blues SBLUECD 012 *As above.* 6/28–2/35.
** **The Essential**
Classic Blues CBL 200039 2CD *As above.* 6/28–2/35.
** **Leroy Carr & Scrapper Blackwell 1929–1935**
Best Of Blues BOB 10 *Carr; Scrapper Blackwell (g, v).* 2/29–2/35.

Although a prolonged study of the Documents will yield many rewards, some listeners will probably be content with a selective compilation. Columbia's 40 tracks carefully skirt his non-blues repertoire but include most of the other titles singled out above, generally well remastered but with a few surprisingly foggy transfers. *Prison Bound Blues* does a good job at half the length and a budget price. Random programming and faulty remastering relegate *The Essential* to a poor third. Best Of Blues offer 16 cuts by Carr and seven by Blackwell; the Carr items are oddly chosen and the remastering primitive.

Hurry Down Sunshine (Indigo IGOCD 2016, deleted), should the reader come across it, is a sound selection, but the one to look for in the used-record racks is the 2CD *Sloppy Drunk* (Catfish KATCD 108, deleted), which was not only carefully remastered but contained in its 44 tracks (about a third of Carr's output) nearly all his best work. TR

Chubby Carrier (born 1967)
VOCAL, ACCORDION

Roy Carrier Jr played drums for his father and Terrance Simien before forming his own Bayou Swamp Band.

(*) **Boogie Woogie Zydeco
Flying Fish FF 70575 *Carrier; David LeJeune (g); Rodney Dural (b); Troy Carrier (d); Kevin Carrier (rb).* 91?
(*) **Dance All Night
Blind Pig BPCD 5007 *Carrier; Michael Peavy (as); David LeJeune (g, v); Brandon J. Henry (b); Clint 'The Chief' Redwing (d, v); Mike Chaisson (rb).* 93?
(*) **Who Stole The Hot Sauce?
Blind Pig BPCD 5032 *Carrier; Michael Peavy (s); Billy Branch (h); Ronnie Boudreaux (g, v); Corey Duplechin (b, v); Sammy Neal (d); Mike Chaisson (rb, perc); Theresa Davis, Byron Woods (v).* 96?
(*) **Too Hot To Handle
Louisiana Red Hot LRHR 1106 *Carrier; Mike Broussard, Lance Ellis (as, ts, v); John Garr (g, v); Corey Duplechin (b, v); Trey Landry (d); Mike Chaisson (rb, cga, perc).* 2/98.
*** **Take Me To The Zydeco**
Swampadelic [unnumbered] *Carrier; Calvin Owens Blues Orchestra (brass, reeds, other instruments); Alcedrik Rodd (t); Carl Landry (as, ts, bs); Phil Chandler (o); Cookie Chavis (g); Corey Duplechin (b, v); Lupe Valdiviez (d); Earl 'The Pearl Slicker' Salley (rb).* 01?

(*) **Ain't No Party Like A Chubby Party
Swampadelic [unnumbered] *Carrier; Chuck Bagby (t); Josh Keen (tb); Leroy Marshall (as, ts); Dikki Du Carrier, Roy Carrier (ac, v); Rick Lagneaux (kb, v); D'Jalma Garnier (vn, box g); Dave Malone (g, v); Dwayne Dugas (g); Corey Duplechin (b, v); Lupe Valdiviez (d); Earl Sally (rb); Misty Carrier (v).* 03?

Flying Fish's title track reworks 'Zydeco Et Pas Salé', and the disc also features a 'Creole Two Step' and songs by Clifton Chenier and Rockin' Sidney. Later CDs acknowledge the past – *Dance All Night* includes 'Rock Me Baby' and a surprising version of Bob Wills's 'Stay A Little Longer' – but more characteristic are music for culturally non-specific thrash dancing and laundry lists of Louisiana clichés like gumbo, 'gators and zydeco itself. *Who Stole The Hot Sauce?* is particularly prone to these: 'Rockin' In The Cradle Of The South' is virtually a tourist brochure set to music.

Boogie Woogie Zydeco features exceptionally crisp, articulate and well-recorded percussion, but it also introduces a recurrent feature: loud and hackneyed blues-rock guitar solos, at their most obnoxious on *Who Stole The Hot Sauce?* On *Too Hot To Handle*, John Garr turns the volume down a bit, and plays more inventively. The saxes are also a positive aspect of this disc – they make 'Turn On Your Love Light' far better than the version on *Dance All Night*, for instance – but the interaction between band and audience is even more irritating than usual.

Carrier's most successful CD to date is *Take Me To The Zydeco*; he and the band continue to pursue relentlessly fast tempos, but with such self-belief as to compel surrender. The blues-rock guitar and the bayou banalities are still there, but infrequently enough to be bearable, and the brass and reeds add fire and textural variety. It's a pity that the Calvin Owens Blues Orchestra only appears on the title track; this synthesis of zydeco with big-band blues hints at rich creative possibilities. The tastefully titled *Ain't No Party Like A Chubby Party* begins and ends with clichés, but it takes a turn for the better midway, with dance grooves that enjoyably combine Chenier-ish accordion with funky bass licks, a fabulous revival of Bébé Carrière's fiddle breakdown 'Blue Runner' and a jolly 'Family Jam' with Roy and Dikki Du. These tracks almost make the triteness around them bearable. CS

Roy Carrier (born 1947)
VOCAL, ACCORDION

Carrier played washboard and guitar in family bands from childhood, taking up the accordion as a teenager after losing part of his right index finger. Before becoming a fulltime musician in 1987, he spent 16 years working as an oil driller, alternating seven days on the rigs with seven on land playing music. In 1980 Carrier opened the Offshore Lounge in Lawtell.

*** **Soulful Side Of Zydeco**
Zane ZNCD 1003 *Carrier; George Attle (g); Paul Newman (b); Troy Carrier (d); Deran Carrier (rb).* late 80s.
(*) **Zydeco Strokin'
Paula PCD-1044 *Carrier; Raymond Randle (g, v); Kevin Carrier (b); Troy Carrier (d); Kevin Broussard (rb).* 94?
***(*) **At His Best**
Zane ZCD 1010 *As above, except add Paul Newman (b), Gerard St Julien Jr (d), Jimmy Searlie, Mike Chaisson (rb).* late 80s–mid 90s.

Carrier's digital deficit has stopped him playing piano accordion, but his main man is unmistakably Clifton Chenier. *Zydeco Strokin'* was originally issued by Lanor on cassette, and Zane's selective surveys are also drawn from that label's catalogue. Carrier's seven tracks on *Soulful Side Of Zydeco* marry euphonious, retro accordion to slick, pulsating bass lines. Unfortunately the programming, which alternates tracks between Carrier and Joe Walker, makes for disruptive listening.

At His Best uses seven tracks from *Zydeco Strokin'*, and apart from a version of 'Tequila' with 'The Flintstones' as coda, they are indeed the Paula CD's best items; it's otherwise dominated (though not entirely; 'Marie' is one more disguise for 'Jolie Blonde') by monotonous riffing and underdeveloped lyrics. *Zydeco Strokin'* is also lifelessly engineered, whereas *At His Best* has been masterfully tweaked by Bob Jones; there is no contest for sound quality. Musically, *At His Best* is mostly a superior selection of slamming, funky dance music. The exceptions to superiority are 'Tequila' (see above) and 'Roy's In Town', a disruptive attempt at *tendresse*; the exception to funkiness is 'My Baby Wants To Leave Me', an excellent B. B. King medley sung (and supposedly written!) by Randle.

**** **Offshore Blues & Zydeco**
Chubby Dragon CD 1003//Right On Rhythm ROR 008 *Carrier; Raymond Randle (g); Ronald Carrier (b); Troy Carrier (d); Kevin Carrier (rb, v).* 96?

*** **Nasty Girls**
Right On Rhythm ROR 002 *As above, except add Kevin Broussard (rb).* 6–9/96.

The bass playing here is both less upfront and less inventive; Ronald Carrier is usually content to run the standard changes. The upside is that Randle's consistently bluesy guitar gets more of a look-in. *Nasty Girls* was recorded in various clubs, and catches much of the energy of zydeco live, but also some of its intermittent monotony: the lyrics and music of 'Watch That Dog' and 'Jump That Rope' are desperately insubstantial. As the notes frankly admit, the recordings were made on fairly basic equipment, and the sound is adequate but variable.

Much better, both sonically and artistically, is *Offshore Blues & Zydeco*. This is Carrier's most explicit homage to Clifton Chenier, but although his admiration for the great man is obvious, Carrier never descends into robotic imitation; rather, he works creatively within the soundscape that his hero and distant cousin created. The result is one of the finest 'old-time zydeco' CDs of recent years.

*** **Twist & Shout**
Right On Rhythm ROR 004 *Carrier; Pandy 'Guitar Gable Jr' Perrodin (g, v); Tony Bush (b); Calvin Sam (d); Phillip Carrier (rb, v).* 2/98.

***(*) **Whiskey-Drinkin' Man**
Right On Rhythm ROR 009 *Carrier; Russell Gordon (g); Kevin Carrier (b, v); Troy Carrier (d, v); Wayne Kahn, Robert Lavern (rb).* 01?

Both these discs mix some live tracks with the studio majority. *Twist & Shout* was recorded in Maryland with a Night Rockers lineup that doesn't seem to have lasted. This is no bad thing, since the rhythms are often, and the vocal responses invariably, automatic; equally regrettable is that Perrodin gets just one solo. *Twist & Shout* runs – well, not out of steam; this is zydeco, after all – but out of ideas some time before its last track. That said, it's worth noting fine, archaic readings of 'Bye Bye Black Girl' (learned from Carrier's father) and 'My Little Woman (Wanted To Fight)'. Far less necessary is 'Jambalaya'; presumably requested by a punter, and sketchily recalled, it's a pastiche of a pastiche.

The return of Kevin Carrier's bass invigorates the Night Rockers on *Whiskey-Drinkin' Man*; he plays at both the artistic and the decibel levels of the best Lanor sides, but superior engineering ensures that he doesn't overbalance the economical, punchy sound of the band as a whole. One can only regret that the producer persuaded Carrier to cut 'My Toot Toot', and 'Ti Garçon' proves that 'Jolie Blonde' is the only waltz he knows, but helter-skelter versions of 'Bugga Bear', John Delafose's 'Co-Fet?' and the impromptu instrumental 'Time To Start' make up for these shortcomings in style.

*** **Living Legend**
Severn CD-0031 *Carrier; Raymond Randle (g); Kevin Carrier (b, v); Steve 'Skeeter' Charlot (d, v); Phillip Carrieré [Carrier], Wayne Kahn (rb).* 04.

With *Living Legend*, Carrier moves to a label with wider distribution; a pity, then, that it's not a better release. The notes make much of Carrier's status as a link to the Chenier–Dopsie–Chavis generation, and three la-la tracks (accordion and percussion only) are a fun history lesson; but there are too many compromises with *nouveau zydeco*'s hammering rhythms, and the attempts to revive Beau Jocque's backchat with Steve Charlot lack spontaneity. That said, Charlot's rap on 'Got Something For You Baby' is as unexpected as it's successful, and Carrier's buzzing accordion is always a pleasure, never more so than on the blues medley 'You Told Me That You Loved Me'. CS

The Carrière Brothers
DUET

Joseph 'Bébé' Carrière (1908–2001), fiddle, and Eraste 'Dolan' Carrière (1900–1983), one-row accordion, lived near Lawtell, Louisiana, making their living as farmers. They played together for house dances, to both black and white audiences, and in later years, with family members, in the Lawtell Playboys.

*** **The Carrière Brothers**
Arhoolie CD 512 *Eraste Carrière (ac, v); Joseph 'Bébé' Carrière (vn, v); Linton Broussard (d).* 4/74.

The Carrières' years of playing at local functions gave them a repertoire that stretched from old dance tunes like the mazurka 'La Robe À Parasol' and 'Carrière Polka' to more modern zydeco pieces, taking in Cajun standards and blues. More often than not, Eraste plays the melody and Bébé responds with a wailing harmony, and on repertoire like 'Chère Catin Blues', 'Colinda', 'Jolie Catin', 'Hey Mom!' and 'Home Sweet Home' they are barely distinguishable from Cajun musicians of their generation. Sometimes, however, Bébé leads on fiddle while Eraste plays, in effect, a rhythm guitar part on accordion, as in 'Lake Arthur Stomp' or Bébé's songs 'Madame Faielle' and 'Planté Dans La Porte De Ma Maison'. This is highly acculturated music, less revealing than, say, Canray Fontenot's about the old Creole repertoire, but enjoyable on its own terms. TR

Karen Carroll (born 1958)
VOCAL

A native Chicagoan, Carroll comes from an extremely musical extended family: her mother is the jazz and blues singer Jeanne Carroll, and her godparents the jazz guitarist George Freeman and the blues singer Bonnie Lee. She began singing in 1988, worked with Eddie Lusk in his 'Professor's Blues Revue', and in 1990 made the first of many trips to Europe, where she is also known as a gospel singer.

***(*) Had My Fun
Delmark DE-680 Carroll; Ken Saydak (o, p); Johnny B. Moore, Bob Levis (g); Johnny B. Gayden (b); 'Baldhead Pete' [Cleo Williams] (d); band (v). 7/95.
** Talk To The Hand
Delmark DE-707 Carroll; Kenny Anderson (t); Hank Ford, Sonny Seals (ts); Willie Henderson (bs); Roosevelt Purifoy (o, p); Vince Varco (string syn); Walter Scott, Johnny B. Moore (g); Willie 'Vamp' Samuels Jr, Mike Riley (b); Jon Hiller, 'Baldhead Pete' (d); Roberta Thomas (tamb, v); Kay Reed, Theresa Davis, Mae Koen, Diane Christiansen (v); Jeanana Fordjour (sp). 3/96, 1/97.

The first four songs on *Had My Fun* were taped in performance at Blue Chicago, the club (though not the location) where Carroll first sang seven years earlier; she shows off the stagecraft she has mastered in that time with her 'dirty girl' rap before 'Love Her With A Feeling'. The rest of the album, though studio-recorded, has the same vivacity – which is saying something, given a programme that includes songsheets as well-thumbed as 'Help Me', 'Spoonful' and 'Confessin' The Blues'. The reason is partly that Carroll uses her deep, growling, gravelly voice both subtly and to powerfully emotive effect, and partly the playing of Saydak and Moore, who shadow her every move. The three combine devastatingly in 'Goin' Down Slow', which Delmark understandably recycled on their VAC *Women Of Blue Chicago* (DD-690).

The notes on *Talk To The Hand* begin with the observation 'The best musicians transcend styles and techniques', notewriter's code for 'This isn't what you're expecting and you may not like it.' Blues-lovers will have no trouble with Lefty Dizz's 'Ain't That Nice' and a B. B. King-styled 'How Blue Can You Get', nor with the blues-monologue 'Neked J Blues', but they may not enjoy being jerked from numbers like that to 'Misty Blue' or Carroll's pop-soul compositions 'Don't Make Me Wait' and 'I Need A Friend'. Such material may help to establish her versatility but it contrasts uneasily with the honest plainness of the blues pieces – and, as *Had My Fun* proved, it's within the constraints of genre that Carroll does her best work.

A few months after most of *Talk To The Hand* was made, Carroll cut a couple of numbers at Blue Chicago that were used to bookend the VAC *Red Hot Mamas* (Blue Chicago BC 5001). 'Sweet Home Chicago' opens with her singing to John Duich's acoustic slide guitar, then shifts gear into a noisy band performance; 'Blue Chicago Blues' reunites her with Johnny B. Moore. TR

Bo Carter (c. 1893–1964)
VOCAL, GUITAR

Armenter Chatmon, from near Bolton, Mississippi, first played bass or banjo in stringband aggregations with other members of his family. About the end of the '20s he began to specialize in guitar. He disliked playing at dances, preferring to serenade white listeners, and so far as the African-American audience was concerned his chief arena was the recording studio, in which he cut over a hundred sides, mostly under the name of Bo Carter, between 1928 and 1940. He lost his sight in the '30s and is believed to have been musically inactive after World War II.

*** Bo Carter – Vol. 1 (1928–1931)
Document DOCD-5078 Carter; Lonnie Chatmon (vn); Charlie McCoy (md, v); Walter Vincson (poss. g, v); Mary Butler (v); unknown (sp). c. 11/28–6/31.
*** Bo Carter – Vol. 2 (1931–1934)
Document DOCD-5079 Carter; Lonnie Chatmon (vn). 6/31–3/34.
*** Bo Carter – Vol. 3 (1934–1936)
Document DOCD-5080 Carter; prob. Harry Chatmon (p). 3/34–2/36.
*** Bo Carter – Vol. 4 (1936–1938)
Document DOCD-5081 Carter. 2/36–10/38.
*** Bo Carter – Vol. 5 (1938–1940)
Document DOCD-5082 Carter. 10/38–2/40.
**(*) The Essential
Classic Blues CBL 200028 2CD Carter; Lonnie Chatmon (vn, sp); Charlie McCoy (md, v); Walter Vincson (g, v, sp); Sam Chatmon (g, v); Dan Hornsby, unknown (sp). c. 11/28–2/40.
*** Twist It Babe (1931–1940)
Yazoo 1034 Carter; unknown (sp). 6/31–2/40.
***(*) Banana In Your Fruit Basket
Yazoo 1064 Carter. 6/31–10/36.

Carter's first recordings, in 1928, were in a trio with his brother Lonnie on fiddle and Charlie McCoy on mandolin, and their spirited performances of the minstrel song 'Good Old Turnip Greens' and 'Corrine Corrina' (of which this is the first recording) give some impression of the stringband ensembles in which these musicians served their apprenticeship. Resuming his recording career after a two-year gap, Carter took a quite different tack, playing on his own and concentrating on blues, novelty songs and novelty blues. From then on, a large part of his repertoire consisted of teasing songs on sexual themes – see any of the above CDs, but particularly *Banana In Your Fruit Basket*, which includes, in addition to the title song, 'Pin In Your Cushion', 'Ram Rod Daddy', 'My Pencil Won't Write No More', etc., etc. – and because of the nature of that material some commentators have belittled it as trite and repetitive. Others side with the guitarist John Miller, who in his notes to *Twist It Babe* calls Carter 'one of the bona-fide geniuses of country blues ... probably the most sophisticated of all country bluesmen from a harmonic viewpoint, playing with perfect facility in five tunings ... [with] consistent originality in his melodic and rhythmic concepts.' The two views are not so much opposed as moving on parallel lines, since the trite-and-repetitive party pays little attention to Carter's guitar playing, while Miller is attentive to little else.

One would guess that for many present-day listeners Carter's metaphors tend to exhaust quite quickly whatever ingenuity and wit they had, not only because they are repetitive but because his unemotional delivery appears to lend them no shading of humour or playfulness. That shortfall in verbal satisfaction is often compensated for by the musical entertainment of the gracefully twirling guitar accompaniments, especially in 'Cigarette Blues', 'All Around Man' and the irresistible 'Twist It, Baby', a tune impossible to listen to without a tap of the foot and a twitch of the lips. The melody of 'Twist It, Baby' predates the blues, and there are other recordings, such as 'Who's Been Here' or 'Old Devil', in which Carter sounds as if he is reaching back to music of earlier times. But he was by no means in thrall to the past: in 'Howling Tom Cat Blues', one of several themes he recorded first for OKeh and then a few years later for Bluebird, he covers a contemporary hit by J. T. Smith, while in his first recording for the latter label, 'Bo Carter Special', he introduces himself as a radio star: 'Bo Carter is a man, broadcasts all over this land.' Others of his songs replicate themes or melodies used by Lonnie Chatmon and Walter Vincson as the Mississippi Sheiks, a duet to which he may occasionally have added himself.

Given the comments above, the extended view of his work offered by the five Document volumes might be judged rather too much of a good thing. This is least true of *Vol. 5*, in which his boredom with devising phallic symbols pricked him to compose blues on a variety of other subjects; unfortunately, by then he was seldom applying the same imagination to his accompaniments. Of the selective compilations the Yazoos combine well-chosen programmes – most of the tracks singled out above are on one or the other – with superior transfer quality and informative notes, but are short-measured at 14 tracks each. The Classic Blues 2CD, marrying length and good track-selection, appears to offer excellent value, but about half of its 36 tracks are blighted by defective sound-treatment. TR

Goree Carter (1930–90)
VOCAL, GUITAR

Although he was one of the more prominent T-Bone Walker disciples, what fame Carter enjoyed was brief and largely confined to his home state of Texas. From the evidence of his earliest records, he was capable of more originality than many of his subsequent records required. Army service curtailed his recording career, to which he never returned, living out his life in the same Houston house in which he'd been born.

*** The Complete Recordings Volume 1 (1949–1951)
Blue Moon BMCD 6025 *Carter; Nelson Mills, unknown (t); Conrad Johnson, Henry Hayes (as); Sam Williams, Ed Wiley (ts); Little Willie Littlefield, Lonnie Lyons, Willie Johnson (p); Nunu Pitts, Donald Cooks (b); Allison Tucker, Ben Turner (d); Edward Carter (wh).* 49–51.

**(*) Unsung Hero
Collectables COL-CD-5264 *As above.* 49–50.

**(*) The Complete Recordings Volume 2 (1950–1954)/The Remaining Lester Williams (1949–1956)
Blue Moon BMCD 6036 *Carter; Henry Hayes (as); Ed Wiley, unknowns (ts); unknowns (bs); Willie Johnson, unknowns (p); Donald Cooks, unknowns (b); Ben Turner, unknowns (d).* 51–54.

Eighteen years old when he first recorded, Carter was a surprisingly adept guitarist whose first inspirations were Johnny Moore and Barney Kessel. His debut track, 'Sweet Old Woman's Blues', 'Rock Awhile' and 'Back Home Blues' have fluent and original guitar solos with little hint of Walker's influence. Thereafter, he adopts a T-Bone tone and technique of varying accuracy and consciously imitates Walker's vocal timbre. Songs like 'I'll Send You', 'Workin' With My Baby' and 'What A Friend Will Do' are well arranged and performed but remain imitative and mechanical. The odd forays into balladry ('Serenade') and exotic rhythm ('Drunk Or Sober') were ill-advised, as was a Charles Brown caricature ('Every Dog Has His Day'). All those titles are on Blue Moon's *Volume 1*, whose later tracks, and those on *Volume 2*, convey a sense of evaporating will, which may explain the subsequent direction of Carter's life.

The Collectables set has just 14 tracks, with adequate dubbing of records that occasionally exhibit groove distortion and surface noise. Blue Moon add a further dozen tracks, which, with the nine on *Volume 2*, make up a complete survey of Carter's recording career. NS

The Carter Brothers
GROUP

Albert (born 1935), Jerry (born 1936) and Roman (born 1938) Carter started life in Garland, Alabama, but the family moved to California in 1949. Soon afterwards the brothers began playing together – Jerry on piano, Al on guitar and Roman handing most of the singing – and in 1958 they made their first recordings. Resuming their musical career in the mid-'60s after military service, they had hits in the Southern market with 'Southern Country Boy' and 'Booze In The Bottle' and were active on the club circuit, but after a few years they quit the business. A comeback album in 1997 was well received but not widely circulated.

** Blues On Tour: The Jewel Recordings 1965–69
[Westside WESD 235] 2CD *unknowns (brass, reeds); unknown (o); Jerry Carter (p, v); Roman Carter (g, v); Al Carter (g); unknowns (b); unknowns (d); unknowns (v).* 65–69.

'Booze In The Bottle' is quite an elegant exercise in the manner of B. B. King, and there are a few other slow blues in a similar idiom, such as 'I've Been Mistreated (For Five Long Years)', 'I Woke Up Smilin'' or 'Wrong Number', that well-disposed listeners will probably enjoy for Roman Carter's anguished singing. But far too much space on this 36-track 2CD is occupied by unimaginative novelty numbers, lethargic instrumentals and tracks that were understandably left on the shelf by their original producers. A large parcel for a small gift.

Coming Back Singing The Blues, with which the Carters reported back for blues duty in 1997, was issued only in Japan (P-Vine PCD 5292). TR

Tommy Castro (born 1955)
VOCAL, GUITAR

Born and raised in San Jose, California, Castro started playing guitar at ten, initially inspired by Mike Bloomfield, Eric Clapton and Elvin Bishop. He was soon trailing the footsteps of great figures from the worlds of both blues and classic soul. He started his own group in San Francisco in 1993. They toured relentlessly and would later become the house band on NBC's Saturday Night Live Comedy Showcase, which boosted

Castro's profile. He's won streams of awards, toured with countless top-billed acts and earned the praise of, in particular, B. B. King, a longtime hero.

(*) Exception To The Rule
Blind Pig BPCD 5029 *Castro; Tom Poole (t); Terry Russell (tb); Keith Crossan (ts, bs, v); Austin DeLone [Audie deLone] (o, p); Jimmy Pugh, Stu Blank (o); Randy McDonald (b, v); Shad Harris (d, v).* 95.

(*) Can't Keep A Good Man Down
Blind Pig BPCD 5041 *Castro; Keith Crossan (s, v); Jim Pugh (o, p); Commander Cody (p); Randy McDonald (b, v); Shad Harris (d, v).* 97.

*** Right As Rain**
Blind Pig BPCD 5051 *Castro; Tom Poole (t); Keith Crossan (s, v); Jimmy Pugh (kb, o); Dr John [Mack Rebennack] (o, p); John Turk (p, v); Randy McDonald (b, v); Billy Lee Lewis (d, v); Delbert McClinton, Ron E. Beck, Roosevelt Winchester, Charles Jones, L. Z. Love, Cheryl Serame, Jeanie Tracy, Annie Stocking (v).* 98?

***(*) Live At The Fillmore**
Blind Pig BPCD 5059 *Castro; Tom Poole (t); Keith Crossan (s); Jimmy Pugh (kb); Randy McDonald (b); Billy Lee Lewis (d).* 3/99.

*** The Essential Tommy Castro**
Blind Pig BPCD 8004 *As for above four CDs.* 95–99.

*(*) Guilty Of Love**
33rd Street 3305//Dixiefrog DFGCD 8524 *Castro; Jimmy Pugh (o, p); Stu Blank (p, v); Jeff Tamaleir (g); John Lee Hooker, Karen Goodman, L. Z. Love, Pamela Rose (v).* 01.

** Gratitude**
Dixiefrog DFGCD 8553 *Castro; Tom Poole (t); Keith Crossan (s); Curtis Salgado (h, v); John Turk (o, p, v); Randy McDonald (b); Billy Lee Lewis (d); Michael Peliquin, Sista Monica Parker (v).* 03.

** Triple Trouble**
Telarc CD-83585 *Castro; Jimmy Hall (ts, h, v); Reese Wynans (o); Lloyd Jones (g, v); Tommy Shannon (b); Chris Layton (d).* 03.

*** Soul Shaker**
Blind Pig BPCD 5094 *Castro; Tom Poole (t, flh); Keith Crossan (s, fl); Jim Pugh (o, p); Kevin Bowe (o, g, b, d prog, v); Roy Rogers, Steve Spirn (g); Randy McDonald (b, v); Chris Sandoval (d, perc); Armando Morales (cga); Bryan Hanna (perc, d prog); The New Directions, Roy Tyler, Marcus Walker, Curtis Fullard, Russell Branch, Reneé Austin (v).* 05.

Castro's consistency alone is praiseworthy: seven studio albums in a decade, with a core sound, largely gained from the Blind Pig debut, that he's stood by faithfully for most of his career. This style crosses familiar 12-bar progressions and funk grooves with a ubiquitous lacing of soul sensibility, achieved by regular spaces for a saxophonist and trumpeter in a lineup which has changed little over the years, and above all through Castro's vocals, which are faultlessly controlled and sound better and better through his first three albums. A newcomer should look into the helpful *Essential* compilation for Castro's best early work. He and his band tend to write most of the songs, solo or in collaboration, the material unfolding coherently without breaking new ground or indicating interesting differences between the writers. Guitarwise, Castro serves well-measured blues scales (his tight technique clearly honed by seven-days-a-week gigging), presented in a bed of standard Stratocaster tones with drizzles of Albert Collins, Buddy Guy and Stevie Ray Vaughan. As he admits, 'There's no genius going on here', but what you're unlikely to find as much of elsewhere is the exemplary full-on collision of traditional soul and blues. Though somewhat deflated by lyrical banality, Castro goes one step further with his voice, sounding at times uncannily like Wilson Pickett, then giving off faint whiffs of James Brown and Ray Charles in 'huh' refrains, and the sweet scent of Otis Redding's free-for-all codas of yaps and wails. It's pulled off best in the fiery *Live At The Fillmore*, where an understandably exuberant crowd rocks to Castro's blitzy lead playing in 'My Time After Awhile' and a howling version of James Brown's 'Sex Machine'. In 2001 Castro and Blind Pig parted for a time, and the albums that followed seemed to suck out the vibrancy that Castro built his reputation on, but in 2005 he returned to Blind Pig for an improved, invigorated release. RR

Catfish Keith (born 1962)
VOCAL, GUITAR

Keith Kozacik is a Midwesterner who determined to become a blues musician at the age of 15 after hearing Son House.

(*) Pepper In My Shoe
Fish Tail FTRCD 001//Orchard 800916 *Catfish Keith; Peter 'Madcat' Ruth (h); Randy Sabien (vn).* 90.

(*) Jitterbug Swing
Fish Tail FTRCD 002//Orchard 800915 *As above, except omit Ruth.* 4/92.

(*) Cherry Ball
Fish Tail FTRCD 003//Orchard 800920 *Catfish Keith.* 5/93.

(*) Fresh Catfish
Fish Tail FTRCD 004//Orchard 800921 *As above.* 1/95.

(*) Twist It, Babe!
Fish Tail FTRCD 005//Orchard 800917 *As above, except add Marty Christensen (b).* 4–6/97.

(*) Pony Run
Fishtail FTRCD 006//Orchard 800918 *Catfish Keith; Radoslav Lorkovic (p).* 99.

*** A Fist Full Of Riffs**
Solid Air SACD 2011 *Catfish Keith.* 01.

Catfish Keith is an intensely energetic guitarist with a formidable technical arsenal. His admiration for and knowledge of his sources (which extend somewhat beyond blues, to jazz, the Bahamas and Hawaii) is self-evident. There's evidently a sizeable audience for his reinterpretations of African-American music; what's puzzling is that anyone having more than a nodding acquaintance with the originals should have much time for the reinterpretations. One cannot be other than impressed by Catfish's playing skills (predictably, the all-instrumental *A Fist Full Of Riffs* is their best showcase), but his singing features all the worst temptations of white revivalism: arbitrary changes of tone and dynamics, attempts to sound black that range from unconvincing to embarrassing, and pervasive overacting as an alternative to cultural roots. CS

Jimmy Cavallo (born 1927)
VOCAL, TENOR SAXOPHONE

After navy service in World War II Cavallo led an R&B band at North Carolina beach resorts and in his hometown of Syracuse, New York. In the '50s he worked on Alan Freed's rock 'n' roll

shows and appeared in the movie Rock, Rock, Rock. In December 1956 Cavallo's Houserockers were the first white rock 'n' roll band to play the Apollo Theater. Forty-odd years later Cavallo still plays the resort circuit in Florida.

** Rock The Joint!: The Jimmy Cavallo Collection 1951–1973
Blue Wave 146 *Cavallo; unknown musicians.* 51–73.
*** The Houserocker!
Blue Wave 143 *Cavallo; Chris Sawyer (ts); Rodney Zajac (bs); Andy Rudy (p); Ron Spencer (g); Pat DeSalvo (b); Ross Moe (d).* 10/01.

In the '50s Cavallo was a kind of regional Bill Haley for the Italian community of central New York state. His 1951 coupling 'Rock The Joint'/'Leave Married Women Alone' suggests that he was considerably more hip than Haley to the black music that seeded both men's repertoire, but a good deal of the other material carefully collected on *Rock The Joint!* is rock 'n' roll of a routinely chuckleheaded kind. Fortunately it's the hipness that's reaffirmed on *The Houserocker!*. In particular, Cavallo has a very nice way with a slow blues like 'I've Got News For You' or 'I'm Gonna Move To The Outskirts Of Town'. Most of the programme, though, is shout numbers like Wynonie Harris's 'Lovin' Machine' and 'Bloodshot Eyes' and Roy Brown's 'Fanny Brown', or easier-rocking tunes from the Fats Domino book, all of which Cavallo takes on with a verve that belies his age, singing like a man who has listened with equal attention to, say, Jimmy Witherspoon and Louis Prima. The dozen tracks are followed by half an hour of entertaining reminiscence. TR

John Cephas & Phil Wiggins
DUET

Born in Washington, DC, in 1930, singer/guitarist 'Bowling Green' John Cephas was raised in the Virginia town after which he's nicknamed. He played for house parties with his cousin, the formidable, unrecorded David Talliaferro, until the '60s, when he became a civil service carpenter. In the mid-'70s, Cephas re-emerged, working with pianist Big Chief Ellis. They were joined by singer and harmonica player Phil Wiggins in 1976, and when Ellis died in 1977, Cephas and Wiggins became a duo, since when they have toured the world, de facto successors to Sonny Terry and Brownie McGhee. Wiggins, also born in DC (in 1954), is a self-taught player, who developed his style working with street singer Flora Molton. Acutely conscious of the need to keep tradition and heritage alive, the two men have worked with prisoners and addicts, and in educational programmes. Cephas serves on the board of the National Council for the Traditional Arts.

**(*) Goin' Down The Road Feelin' Bad
Evidence ECD 26093 *Cephas; Wiggins.* 10–11/80.
*** Sweet Bitter Blues
Evidence ECD 26050 *Cephas; Wiggins; Margie Evans (v).* 3/81–4/83.

Most of *Goin' Down The Road Feelin' Bad* was recorded at Cephas's home, but the recording quality is first-class, and both men are keen to display their instrumental accomplishment and a broad, largely traditional repertoire. Cephas immediately establishes himself as a terrific guitarist; occasionally he stumbles, but this is a mark of adventurousness, rather than a problem. Critics on autopilot describe Wiggins's playing as call-and-response; in fact he plays a busy, arpeggiated version of the melody line both behind and between Cephas's vocals. On this disc he's hyperactive, and although his ability is evident, it's a relief when the treadmill occasionally slows down.

Sweet Bitter Blues combines a studio session with European concert recordings. There's more emphasis on original and semi-original songs, including a first version of the striking 'Dog Days Of August'. Cephas's singing is more dramatic, and on 'St. James Infirmary' and 'Bye Bye Baby' he's way over the top, but these are exceptions; a second version of the latter song, with amplified guitar and Margie Evans, is excellent. Wiggins sings lead on 'Last Fair Deal', which earns bonus points for being not just a Robert Johnson song before they became compulsory, but a non-obvious one, successfully transmuted into the Piedmont style.

***(*) Dog Days Of August
Flying Fish FF 70394 *Cephas; Wiggins.* 84.

All the right balances are struck here; Cephas is dramatic without being portentous, Wiggins is busy without being hyper, and the eight lengthy tracks are an assured blend of tradition and originality. Most striking is 'Cherryball', faithful to Skip James's eerie vision, but subtly personalized. 'Hard Time Killing Floor Blues' is less successful; the harmony humming, also featured on 'Roberta', is stiffly reminiscent of the Carolinians behind Josh White.

**(*) Guitar Man
Flying Fish FF 70470 *Cephas; Wiggins; Chris Rounds (d).* 89.
***(*) Flip, Flop, And Fly
Flying Fish FF 70580 *Cephas; Wiggins; Norvus Miller Sr, Norvus G. Miller, Larry Porter, Rurcell Miller (tb); Don Rouse (cl); Daryl Davis (p); Tal Farlow, John Stewart (g); Joseph Summers (tu); Jeff Hopper, Rob Thomas (b); Steve Williams, Calvin Harris (d); Gil Carter (rumba box); Julia Olin (v).* 92.

On *Guitar Man* Cephas and Wiggins seem to be marking time, picking tunes like 'Careless Love' and 'Corinne' that will fill a disc with the minimum of rehearsal. There's also a frequent reversion to histrionic singing and fussy harmonica. *Flip, Flop, And Fly*, on the other hand, goes for experiment and genre-busting from its rock 'n' roll outset, one of four tracks with clarinet, piano, bass and rumba box. Of the others, an up-tempo 'One Kind Favor' is predictably peculiar, but the pop tunes 'When I Grow Too Old To Dream' and 'Today I Started Loving You Again' are very winning. Even more likeable is 'Darkness On The Delta', where Cephas croons like a country Herb Jeffries before Tal Farlow takes a bop solo. 'Banks Of The River', with a trombone shout band, makes a rousing conclusion, and if the rest of the disc is more orthodox, it's also notable for some strong originals, and a respectable attempt at Skip James's 'Devil Got My Woman'.

*** From Richmond To Atlanta
Bullseye Blues Basics 9633 *Cephas; Wiggins; Chris Rounds (d).* 84–92.
**** Bluesmen
Chesky JD 89 *Cephas; Wiggins.* 10/92.

Bullseye pick four tracks from each of the three Flying Fish albums, and anyone made nervous by the more radical aspects of *Flip, Flop, and Fly* can rest assured that they have been rigorously excluded. This is a good, medium-priced introduction, but you might as well pay a little more and get *Dog Days Of August*. Or there's *Bluesmen*, unimaginatively titled, consisting almost entirely of cover versions, and their best CD to date. The material ranges from Blind Boy Fuller and Skip James (two more splendid *hommages*) to rhythm and blues tunes as well-known as 'Big Boss Man', 'Little Red Rooster' and 'The Things I Used To Do', but everything is confidently assimilated and reworked, with just enough flavour of the originals remaining to season the stew. On 'Blake's Rag', Wiggins's taste for the frantic pays dividends as he conjures up a harmonica analogue of Blind Blake's guitar acrobatics.

**(*) Cool Down
Alligator ALCD 4838 *Cephas; Wiggins; Don Rouse (cl); Daryl Davis (p); Eddie Pennington (g); Skip Wiggins (b, v); Gil Carter (perc); Djimo Kouyate (kora).* 95.

**** Homemade
Alligator ALCD 4863 *Cephas; Wiggins; Daryl Davis (p).* 98.

*** Somebody Told The Truth
Alligator ALCD 4888 *Cephas; Wiggins; Tal Farlow, John Stewart (g); Rob Thomas (b); Steve Williams (d).* 92–02.

Cool Down is excellently recorded, but at times rather dispassionate and calculated; 'The Blues Will Do Your Heart Good' recalls the portentous philosophizing that Brownie McGhee sometimes went in for. The additional musicians are not used very effectively; the kora on 'Special Rider Blues' doesn't blend as well as back-to-Africa romanticism wants it to, and Travis-picker Eddie Pennington only shines on 'Nine Pound Hammer'. 'Caroline In The Morning' is a beautiful instrumental meditation on coming home to Caroline County, Virginia, and the concluding 'Twelve Gates To The City' is splendid, but too often *Cool Down* is self-conscious and self-dramatizing. *Homemade* is much better, because Cephas and Wiggins are usually content to take their inspiration from tradition, without trying to make statements about history and their place in it. (The namechecking 'I Was Determined' is an exception.) The result is an unpretentious, well-balanced blend of old favourites and new, but old-sounding, compositions.

'Darkness On The Delta' from 1992 turns up again on *Somebody Told The Truth*. The CD is otherwise a newly recorded set of duo material, but some tracks are repertoire staples: 'Burn Your Bridges', 'Railroad Bill' and 'Last Fair Deal Gone Down' (not as good as the live version on Evidence) are not new to disc. This is another well-programmed set, however. Listeners who don't have the earlier versions won't mind the retreads; for those who do there's compensation in the shape of an edgy reading of Skip James's 'Sick Bed Blues' and the witty patter and jugband harp of 'The Pimp In The Pink Suit'. 'Darling Cora' is disappointing, though; learned from a 1927 recording by the white Kentucky banjoist B. F. Shelton, it needs at least a touch of his chilly fatalism to work. CS

Sean Chambers (born 1969)
VOCAL, GUITAR

Chambers emerged on the blues scene in Florida in the early '90s. 'My heroes,' he says, 'range from Hendrix, Clapton, Billy Gibbons, Robin Trower and Stevie Ray to Lightning Hopkins, Muddy Waters, Freddie, BB and Albert King.' Since the release of Strong Temptation he has led his trio on tour in the US and overseas, as well as working as bandleader for Hubert Sumlin.

**(*) Strong Temptation
Vestige VSTG 0815 *Chambers; Scott Smalley (b); Rich Russo (d).* 98.

Heated to the point of being feverish, this is the kind of album that a young guitarist needs to get out of his system. That done, he can cool off and decide whether to settle for a round of applause from *Total Guitar* magazine ('arguably the most impressive, sure-footed dynamic blues debut since SRV's *Texas Flood*') or work at being a postgraduate blues musician. Chambers brings plenty of skill and energy to a mostly original set – the exceptions include Johnny Winter's 'Mean Town Blues' and Freddie King's anthem for the terminally adolescent, 'Me And My Guitar' – and when he finally essays a slow blues, the closing 'You Was Wrong', he settles into its Albert Collins/SRV groove and plays with bravado and taste. TR

Grady Champion (born 1969)
VOCAL, HARMONICA

Born in Canton, Mississippi, Champion began singing as a child in his church choir. He emerged as a blues artist in the late '90s, based in Florida.

**** Payin' For My Sins
Shanachie 9020 *Champion; Mike Turner (t, g); Habenero Horns (horns); Mike Thomson (kb, o, p); Alan Mirikitani (g, tamb); Ben Peeler (g); Richard Cousins, James Intveld (b); Lee Spath (d); Antoine Salley, Nikki Mirikitani (perc); Thomisene Anderson (v); Dennis Walker (prod).* 2/99.

Following a privately made debut album, *Goin' Back Home* (Grady Shady GSCD 1003), Champion produced in *Payin' For My Sins* one of the outstanding records of its year. Not until track 6, an intense version of 'Goin' Down Slow', do you encounter an honest-to-goodness blues, yet this is unarguably, impressively and at times coruscatingly a blues album. Champion sings with passion and his occasional harmonica choruses are oldfashioned blues blowing down to the bone. The material often employs other structures than 12-bar blues, but Champion plunges everything he handles, from 'Ain't No Love In The Heart Of The City' to the saucy 'My Rooster Is King', into a deep blue dye. The listener who is sometimes reminded of Joe Louis Walker or the young Robert Cray is not offbeam: Dennis Walker, Champion's producer and co-writer, has worked closely with both. The superb band, which includes Cray's former bassist Richard Cousins, is headed by a very fine guitarist in Mirikitani.

*** 2 Days Short Of A Week
Shanachie 9029 *Champion; Habenero Horns (horns); Alan Mirikitani (s, g, b, v); Arlen Schierbaum (kb); Mike Turner, Duke Robillard (g); James Intveld (b); Lee Spath; Antoine Salley (perc); Thomisene Anderson (v); Dennis Walker (prod).* 7/00.

This is a well-made record, but no match for its predecessor. It starts promisingly with Champion chanting the lyric of 'Wine And Women' to a chorus of genial barflies, but most of the other nine songs, almost all written by Champion, alone or jointly with Dennis Walker, are blues with nothing particularly distinctive about their lyrics or, except for Mirikitani's rolling guitars on 'Brother, Brother' and Robillard's hot solo on 'Nothing I Can Do', their settings. Choosing R. Kelly's 'When A Woman's Fed Up' shows that Champion has a good enough voice for R&B (in the current sense of the term), but we knew that already, and the song sits as comfortably on the album's menu as a raspberry on a porkchop. TR

Ray Charles (1930–2004)
VOCAL, PIANO, ORGAN, KEYBOARDS, CELESTE, ALTO SAXOPHONE

Ray Charles Robinson was born in Albany, Georgia, but spent his childhood in Greenville, Florida. At the age of five or six he he lost his sight, possibly through congenital glaucoma, and went to the Florida School for the Deaf and Blind, where he learned to read music in Braille. While still in his teens he made his way to Seattle and then to LA, where he played piano for Lowell Fulson and led his own trio. After recording for Down Beat (1949–52) he signed with Atlantic in 1952 and over the next seven years created an extraordinarily diverse body of music, both drawing on and blending blues, gospel and jazz, and culminating in the R&B #1 (and Pop #6) 'What'd I Say', whose opening 12 bars, played on the then novel Fender Rhodes electric piano, are among the most famous introductions in popular music. He then moved to ABC-Paramount, a mainstream label with the potential to expand his audience, where he had pop hits with 'Hit The Road Jack', 'Unchain My Heart' and others, and scored in the album charts with **Modern Sounds In Country And Western Music** *(1962). Thereafter Charles was a man for all musical seasons, who could hold on to one age-group with his renditions of standards and show tunes while capturing another with his cameo as a music-store owner in the movie* The Blues Brothers. *In the '90s he received a Grammy Lifetime Achievement Award and similar honours from the Rock 'n' Roll Hall of Fame and the Songwriters Hall of Fame. The 2004 biopic* Ray, *with a remarkable central performance by Jamie Foxx, reminded the world what it had recently lost.*

*** **Ray Charles 1949–1950**
Classics 5000 *Charles; G. D. McKee, Tiny Webb (g); Milton Garred, Ralph Hamilton (b); unknown (d). 49–50.*
(*) **Alone In The City
Collectors Edition CBCD 016 *Charles; Teddy Buckner, Billy Brooks, Fleming Askew (t); Marshall Royal, Earl Brown (as); Jack McVea, Stanley Turrentine, Maurice Simon (ts); Charlie Waller (bs); G. D. McKee, Tiny Webb, Louis Speiginer, Oscar Moore (g); Milton Garred, Ralph Hamilton, Billy Hadnott, Johnny Miller, Frank McClure (b); Rudy Pitts, Eddie Piper (d); band (v). 49–11/51.*
(*) **Rocking Chair Blues
Pulse PLSCD 536 *Similar to above. 49–51.*
(*) **The Best Of Ray Charles
Blues Forever CD 68016 *Similar to above. 49–51.*
(*) **The Early Years
King KCD 5011 *Similar to above. 49–51.*
(*) **The Soul Of A Genius
Ocium OCM 3017 *Similar to above. 49–51.*
*** **Blues Before Sunrise**
Pazzazz 2004 *Similar to above. 49–51.*

*** **The Complete Swing Time & Down Beat Recordings 1949–1952**
Night Train NTICD 2001 2CD *Similar to above, except add unknowns (g, b, d). 2/49–51/52.*
(*) **Legend: The Best Of The Early Years
Music Club MCCD 581 2CD *Similar to above. 49–51/52.*
*** **Mess Around**
Proper PVCD 137 2CD *As above, except add Freddie Mitchell, Pinky Williams (ts); Dave McRae (bs); Mickey Baker (g), Lloyd Trotman (b); Connie Kay (d). 2/49–6/53.*
*** **Ray Charles 1950–1952**
Classics 5050 *Similar to Alone In The City, except add unknowns (t, s, b, d). 50–9/52.*

It's curious, given the originality of his later work, that Charles spent the best part of three years, at the start of his recording career, imitating Charles Brown and Nat 'King' Cole. Perhaps, as a young man fresh on the scene, he was doing what was asked of him by his record company. The present-day listener, who knows what's going to happen next, can occasionally hear Charles getting himself ready for it: the vocal on 'She's On The Ball' is a little more assertive than Brown's would have been. By 'Misery In My Heart' and 'The Snow Is Falling', recorded in 11/51, he is singing with full gospel fervour and wholly recognizable. But collections chiefly drawn from before that point, like most of the single CDs above, are in effect album-length tributes to the domination of the Brown–Cole party on the West Coast of that era.

After Charles became famous, these early recordings were repeatedly licensed, relicensed or pirated, becoming long-stay residents in the retirement home of the 99-cent bin. The listed items are the better ones from a stack of CDs that have been drawn from these juvenilia. Discographically this period of Charles's work is a nightmare, since many songs have been reissued under two, three or more titles. Our recommendation goes to the inexpensive Proper 2CD, since it gathers most of them (and at the end of Disc 2 tiptoes into the Atlantic output) and the booklet attempts a coherent discography. Night Train's 2CD is almost identical in content and running order, except that it substitutes five alternative takes for the six Atlantic cuts.

(*) **The Genius Sings The Blues
Atlantic 73524 *Charles; Wallace Davenport, Frank Mitchell, Joe Bridgewater, Riley Webb, Marcus Belgrave, John Hunt, unknowns (t); David 'Fathead' Newman (as, ts, bs); Bennie Crawford (as, bs); Auguste 'Dimes' Dupont, O'Neil Gerald (as); Joe Tillman, Don Wilkerson (ts); Warren Bell, unknown (bs); unknowns (s); unknown (sg); Edgar Blanchard (g); Frank Fields, Lloyd Lambert, Roosevelt Sheffield, Edgar Willis, unknown (b); Elandro Smart, Oscar Moore, William Peeples, Teagle Fleming, unknowns (d); unknown (cga); The Raelettes (v). 9/52–6/59.*
*** **The Atlantic Story 1952–54**
Avid AMSC 798 *Charles; poss. Jesse Drakes, Wallace Davenport, Frank Mitchell, Joe Bridgewater, Charles Whitley, unknowns (t); August[e] 'Dimes' Dupont, O'Neil Gerald, unknown (as); Freddie Mitchell, Pinky Williams, Warren Hebrew, Joe Tillman, Don Wilkerson, unknown (ts); Dave McRae, Warren Bell, Dave Newman (bs); Mickey Baker, Edgar Blanchard, Wesley Jackson (g); Lloyd Trotman, Frank Fields, Jimmy Bell (b); Connie Kay, Alonzo Stewart, Oscar Moore, Glenn Brooks (d); Candido Camero (cga); band, unknown (v). 9/52–11/54.*

*** **Ray Charles 1953–1954**
Classics 5134. *Similar to above.* 5/53–11/54.

***(*) **Ray Charles Live**
Atlantic 81732 *Charles; Marcus Belgrave, Lee Harper, John Hunt (t); David 'Fathead' Newman (as, ts); Bennie Crawford (bs); Edgar Willis (b); Richie Goldberg, Teagle Fleming (d); The Raelettes (v).* 7/58, 5/59.

(***) **The Genius Of Ray Charles**
Atlantic 81338 *Charles; Marcus Belgrave, John Hunt, Clark Terry, Ernie Royal, Joe Newman, Snooky Young (t); Melba Liston, Al Grey, Quentin Jackson, Tom Mitchell (tb); Bob Brookmeyer (vtb); Marshall Royal, Frank Wess (as); Billy Mitchell, David 'Fathead' Newman, Paul Gonsalves, Zoot Sims (ts); Bennie Crawford, Charlie Fowlkes (bs); unknowns (woodwinds, strings); Allen Hanlon, Freddie Green (g); Wendell Marshall, Edgar Willis, Eddie Jones (b); Ted Sommer, Charles Persip (d); Ralph Burns, Quincy Jones (arr, dir).* 5–6/59.

**** **The Best Of Ray Charles: The Atlantic Years**
Rhino/Atlantic 71722 *Charles; Wallace Davenport, Frank Mitchell, Joe Bridgewater, Charles Whitley, Riley Webb, Joshua Willis, John Hunt, Ricky Harper, Marcus Belgrave, unknowns (t); Bob Brookmeyer (vtb); David 'Fathead' Newman (as, ts, bs); O'Neil Gerald (as); Freddie Mitchell, Pinky Williams, Joe Tillman, Don Wilkerson (ts); Dave McRae, Warren Bell, Cecil Payne, Emmett Dennis, Hank Crawford (bs); unknowns (woodwinds, strings); Mickey Baker, Wesley Jackson, Allen Hanlon (g); Lloyd Trotman, Lloyd Lambert, Jimmy Bell, Roosevelt Sheffield, Paul West, Edgar Willis, Wendell Marshall (b); Connie Kay, Oscar Moore, Glenn Brooks, William Peeples, Panama Francis, Milton Turner, Teagle Fleming, Ted Sommer (d); Mongo Santamaria (cga); The Cookies, The Raelettes (v).* 5/53–5/59.

Charles's seven years at Atlantic were a period of extraordinary ferment and experiment. He was attempting, at the same time, to establish himself in the existing field of R&B, to stake a claim in the more recent one of soul-jazz and to create an entirely new form that rewrote the themes of the blues in the language of gospel music. The first thoroughgoing example of that audacious synthesis was 'I've Got A Woman' in 1954; listening to it half a century later gives you the feeling that you have been let into the secret machine-room of popular music to see the wheels go round. In the year that followed, 'This Little Girl Of Mine' and 'Hallelujah I Love Her So' used the same gospel setting of dramatic piano intro, reiteration and call-and-response to frame the erotic celebration of their lyrics. Charles was boldly going where no one had so blatantly gone before; he could hardly have made his intention clearer if he'd erected a sign saying 'Soul Music – This Way'.

Even that considerable project was not enough to absorb all his energy and ingenuity. He made an instrumental jazz album, playing piano in a trio or with a small horn band (*The Great Ray Charles*), and then two more with the vibraharpist Milt Jackson, *Soul Brothers* and *Soul Meeting*, where he also played alto sax on a few tracks. (These should be covered in the 2006 edition of *The Penguin Guide To Jazz Recordings*.) Then, in the final year of his contract, he suggested further and even more surprising possibilities. *The Genius Of Ray Charles*, which employed Quincy Jones's and Ralph Burns's orchestras on repertoire like 'Alexander's Ragtime Band' and 'Come Rain Or Come Shine', insinuated that he could become an all-round entertainer like Nat 'King' Cole, while the single 'I'm Movin' On' – the Hank Snow song, with added pedal steel guitar – pointed to an even more improbable future in country music. Both straws, as it turned out, showed exactly how the winds were blowing. Within a few years Charles had made two hugely successful country albums *and* taken on a role like Cole's as a black singer deeply embedded in mainstream popular music.

Meanwhile, back with the blues ... in moving to Atlantic Charles had not left the blues behind him, and for a year or two he would occasionally revert to his earlier, Charles Brown-styled manner, as in some of the tracks on *The Genius Sings The Blues*. This is a short, odd collection that goes beyond its remit in including 'I'm Movin' On' yet overlooks blues sides like Walter Davis's 'Come Back Baby' or 'Blackjack', which appropriates the tune of Jimmy Wilson's 'Tin Pan Alley'. But it's obvious that neither Charles nor his producers Jerry Wexler and Nesuhi Ertegun saw him as a long-term bluesman, and from his second session onwards he diversified into rueful comic pieces, half song, half recitation, such as 'It Should've Been Me' and 'Greenbacks', and blues-based pop songs like Doc Pomus's 'Lonely Avenue'. An excellent window on these and other crucial Atlantic sides, which takes in virtually all the songs mentioned in this and the first paragraph, is *The Atlantic Years*. Some, but not all, of those recordings are also on the chronological Classics and almost chronological Avid CDs, which are near-identical. In the wake of the movie *Ray* the reader may expect to be offered further selections from this *oeuvre*.

Its predictive importance aside, the appeal of *The Genius Of Ray Charles* will be chiefly to those who care more about what Charles was turning into than what he had been. *Ray Charles Live* is simply a wonderfully vivid live album, regardless of genre. The first ten tracks were recorded at the 1958 Newport Jazz Festival, and Charles doesn't open his mouth until about 20 minutes in, when he sings the blues 'The Right Time'; the remaining six are from a concert at the Herndon Stadium in Atlanta, almost a year later, and are a mixture of jazzy instrumentals and vocal numbers, including what was about to become the biggest hit of his life, 'What'd I Say'. The interaction of Charles, The Raelettes and the band, and the audience's response, is particularly electric at the Atlanta gig.

The Birth Of Soul (Rhino/Atlantic 82310 3CD) contained all the studio recordings Charles made for Atlantic except for the three jazz albums and *The Genius Of Ray Charles*, but is reportedly deleted.

**** **Genius & Soul: The 50th Anniversary Collection**
Rhino 72859 5CD *Charles; various accompaniments.* 2/49–90s.

**** **The Definitive**
Atlantic/Rhino 73556 2CD *As above.* 5/53–97.

***(*) **Ultimate Hits Collection**
Rhino 75644 2CD *As above.* 5/53–97.

*** **The Very Best Of Ray Charles**
Rhino 79822 *As above.* 50s–90s.

*** **The Very Best Of Ray Charles Volume II**
Rhino 79967 *As above.* 50s–90s.

*** **Anthology**
Rhino 75759 *As above.* 60–90s.

After leaving Atlantic Charles was never the same musician again. That, of course, was part of the point: he craved a nationwide, and ultimately international, audience that Atlantic, which was perceived as a black-oriented label, could not win for him. If that meant extending his musical range, no problem: he had been doing that for some time, and he had a long way farther to go. He was, after all, one of the most expansively talented musicians of his time, gifted with a voice veined with passion and pain and fingers that knotted the emotional ambiguities of the blues with the incessant beat of gospel music. No less importantly, he was an arranger with a rare talent for shaping his material. But after Atlantic that material was increasingly sourced from other musical reservoirs than the blues. Only the compositions of Percy Mayfield, who was retained by Charles's organization as a house writer and supplied him with 'Hit The Road Jack', 'Hide Nor Hair', 'At The Club' and other well-wrought pieces, kept a line open from the early days.

So it's not the job of a book with our title to comment at length on most of Ray Charles's work after 1960. It should be unnecessary to stress that this is no reflection on the quality of the work, which includes such well-loved and, in their different ways, unique recordings as 'Hit The Road Jack', 'I Can't Stop Loving You', 'In The Heat Of The Night' and the devastating 'Georgia On My Mind'. We simply acknowledge that blue is now only one colour on Charles's palette, and often not a primary one. But in fairness to the reader who wants to investigate all of Charlesville, not just the blues quarter, we offer a selection of guidebooks.

Genius & Soul is the most exhaustive, with 102 tracks: after three from Down Beat and a couple of dozen from Atlantic, the listener is taken on a lengthy tour of Charles's assignments over the next four decades, from the two volumes of *Modern Sounds In Country And Western Music* to collaborations with Willie Nelson and Chet Atkins, by way of 'Let's Go Get Stoned', The Beatles' 'Yesterday' and 'Eleanor Rigby', 'Rainy Night In Georgia' and 'America The Beautiful'. *The Definitive* ventures to epitomize almost as long a period in 46 tracks, a tough assignment that it brings off with great success. *Ultimate Hits Collection* has 36 tracks, 26 of which are also on *The Definitive*. The *Very Best Of* sets each contain 16 cuts; all of the first's and nine of the second's are on *The Definitive*. *Anthology* differs from all the preceding collections by being drawn exclusively from ABC but, once more, most of its 20 tracks are to be found on *The Definitive*.

*** Berlin, 1962
Pablo PACD 5301 *Charles; Marcus Belgrave, Wallace Davenport, Phillip Guilbeau, John Hunt (t); Henderson Chambers, James Harbert, Keg Johnson, Dickie Wells (tb); David 'Fathead' Newman (as, ts, fl); Hank Crawford, Rudy Powell (as); Don Wilkerson (ts); Leroy Cooper (bs); Sonny Forrest (g); Edgar Willis (b); Bruno Carr (d); The Raelettes (v). 3/62.*

This concert recording is a snapshot of the Ray Charles band a little before *Modern Sounds In Country And Western Music*, and finds him working with a relatively bluesy repertoire that includes some of the Atlantic-period hits like 'I Got A Woman' and 'The Right Time', as well as the Percy Mayfield songs 'Hide Nor Hair' and 'The Danger Zone'. The mixing desk isn't always alert to the featured instrumentalists, but most of the numbers are done at the length of singles anyway, so there isn't a great deal of soloing. One of the few exceptions is 'Georgia On My Mind', virtually a duet by Charles and 'Fathead' Newman, whose flute, recalling the fife music of older times, gives the performance a colour strikingly different from the string arrangement of the studio recording. TR

Sam Chatmon (1897–1983)
VOCAL, GUITAR

One of Henderson Chatmon's many musical children, Sam was an occasional recording member of the Mississippi Sheiks, and in 1936 he and his brother Lonnie cut a session as the Chatman [sic] Brothers. When located by researchers in 1960, Sam had only recently resumed playing after a long layoff but was, if anything, more vigorous than in his youth. Active until not long before his death, he recorded a number of LPs, told tall stories ('I helped raise up those King boys ... All brothers') and grew the most magnificent beard in blues history.

**** Sam Chatmon 1970–1974
Flyright FLY CD 63 *Chatmon; Will Scarlet (h, j); Sue Draheim (vn); Kenny Hall (md); Ed Littleton (Do); Joe Gwaltney (g). 7/70–9/74.*

Most of this disc was recorded in San Diego, where Lou Curtiss presented Chatmon in concert from the mid-'60s onwards. Kenny Hall appears on two tracks, on one of which, a lengthy and splendid jam session, the other musicians join in. Sam's singing is extraordinarily vigorous, and his ability to invent dirty metaphors apparently inexhaustible. As a guitarist, he was usually a steady timekeeper rather than a virtuoso, but regular concerts sharpened his skills, and there is a good deal of lively and inventive fingerpicking here. Playing for essentially the same audience each time also prompted Chatmon to recall a number of songs that he hadn't played for many years, and the CD contains both the best, and the most varied, of his latterday recordings. It is the more valuable because none of his latterday LPs has so far made it to CD, although the Chatman Brothers session is on *Mississippi Sheiks – Vol. 4* (Document DOCD-5086), and the VAC *I Have To Paint My Face* (Arhoolie CD 432) includes titles from 1960. CS

Boozoo Chavis (1930–2001)
VOCAL, ACCORDION

Wilson Chavis had what was probably the first zydeco hit recording with 'Paper In My Shoe' in 1954, but for most of the next 30 years he was little heard on record, preferring to remain in Lake Charles, Louisiana, and concentrate on training quarter-horses. He returned to music in the mid-'80s as a kind of throwback, playing the diatonic button accordion rather than the piano accordion favoured by Clifton Chenier and his followers, and preferring oldfashioned Creole dance music to their more eclectic and blues-influenced repertoire.

** The Lake Charles Atomic Bomb
Rounder CD 2097 *Chavis; unknowns (g); unknowns (b); Little Brother Griffin (d, v); unknowns (d). c. 55–c. 64?*

Though this CD is subtitled '(Original Goldband Recordings)', the 'Paper In My Shoe' that opens it is, as the notes admit, not the original. (For that, and its flipside 'Boozoo Stomp', look on the VAC *Rural Blues – Volumes One & Two* [BGO BGOCD 384].) Although Eddie Shuler of Goldband, who produced both versions, echoed the crudity of the original by ensuring that guitar and bass were out of tune, he evidently found it impossible to recapture its blithe randomness. Chavis, for his part, seems to be in the process of yielding to the song's mistitling: on the original he plainly sang about a pebble in his shoe – as Ella Fitzgerald had when she originated the number with Chick Webb's band in 1938 – but on the remake he lands somewhere between 'paple' and 'paper'. A few boxily recorded and probably early tracks like 'Forty One Days', 'Bye Bye Catin' and 'Telephone Won't Ring' have a pleasant simplicity. Most of the rest, however, is ungainly. The bass may be better tuned than it was on 'Paper' but the playing is often as tangential, and the guitar solo on 'Comma Lemma Chapo Sha' is as absurd as the spelling.

***(*) **Zydeco Trail Ride**
Maison de Soul MDS-1034 *Chavis; prob. Carlton Thomas (g); Classie Ballou Jr (b, v); prob. Rellis Chavis (d); prob. Wilson Chavis Jr (rb); band (v). 86–90.*

Accompanied by family and friends rather than players who don't understand, or scorn, what he's doing, Boozoo sounds like another musican altogether, an impetuously rhythmic accordionist spurred by an equally peppy band. The programme is heavy with one-step and two-step tunes ('Zydeco Coteau', 'Boozoo's Trail Ride Breakdown', 'Motor Dude Special', etc.), interspersed with a few blues and the first recording of 'Paper In My Shoe' where everyone's in tune. Classie Ballou Jr takes over the vocal mike for a boisterous version of 'Harlem Shuffle' decorated with Seinfeldesque bass figures. The drumming and rubboard playing are terrific. The contents of the LP *Zydeco Trail Ride* have been augmented with tracks from Boozoo's previous (and probably unavailable) Maison de Soul albums: six from *Louisiana Zydeco* (MDS-1017) and three from *Boozoo Zydeco* (MDS-1021).

** **Zydeco Live!**
Rounder CD 2069 *Chavis; Carlton Thomas (g); Shelton Jackson (b); Rellis Chavis (d); Wilson Chavis Jr (rb, v). 3/88.*

Though playing to an audience (at Richard's Club in Lawtell, Louisiana), Boozoo and his men are not noticeably more animated than they are in the studio. Thomas, in fact, is rather subdued. Apart from a version of 'Drifting Blues', a number that doesn't suit Boozoo very well, the programme is insistent dance music, appropriate for the setting but too unvarying for a record. The album is shared with Nathan Williams & The Zydeco Cha-Chas, playing at the same venue.

*** **Zydeco Homebrew**
Maison de Soul MdS-1028 *Chavis; Nathan Fontenot (g); Classie Ballou Jr (b); Rellis Chavis (d); Anthony Chavis (rb). 89.*

Aptly titled, this is a strong draught of zydeco tunes, including two waltzes, with a couple of blues chasers in 'Keep Your Dress Tail Down' and 'Sugar Bee'. 'Pray For Me' is a version of the Creole standard 'Flammes D'Enfer'. Fontenot, replacing the usually lively Carlton Thomas, is either a very reticent guitarist or ill served by the recording balance, leaving Boozoo's accordion as the only frontline instrument. The loss of textural variety is no great price to pay for the opportunity to hear clearly how proficient he is on the older repertoire like 'Jolie Catan' and 'Jealous Man Two-Step'.

(*) **Boozoo, That's Who!
Rounder CD 2126 *Chavis; Poncho Chavis (ac, v); [Carlton] Guitar Thomas, Nathaniel Fontenot (g); Classie Ballou Jr (b); Rellis Chavis (d); Charles Chavis (rb, v). 5/93.*

** **Live! At the Habibi Temple**
Rounder CD 2130 *As above, except omit Poncho Chavis. 9/93.*

(*) **Who Stole My Monkey?
Rounder CD 2156 *As above, except omit Fontenot. 9/98.*

(*) **Johnnie Billy Goat
Rounder Heritage Series RRCD 11594 *As above Rounder CDs. 5/93, 9/93, 9/98.*

The best things on the studio-recorded *Boozoo, That's Who!* are the older zydeco numbers such as 'Grand Mary's Two Step' or 'Oh Bye Mon Neg', which set the listener walking across a bridge into the past, or 'Billy Goat Number Three' and 'Oh Bye Bye', where the band skips like a spring lamb. Beside those, original pieces like the title song and 'Little Lula Don't You Go To Bingo' are rather shapeless. Unfortunately both came up again, together with 'Grand Mary', 'Billy Goat' and other familiar repertoire, at the Habibi gig, which has the workmanlike but unglittering character of the earlier live set and almost no audible sign of the response Boozoo got from a crowd of, allegedly, 1500 dancers.

Who Stole My Monkey? is one of the few records in this book that carry a 'Parental Advisory/Explicit Content' notice, for uninhibited versions of 'Uncle Bud' and 'Deacon Jones'. This is the most traditional of Boozoo's Rounder albums, with versions of old Cajun and Creole repertoire like 'Allons À Lafayette' and 'I Went To The Dance' and an amiable solo reading of 'Baby Please Don't Go'. *Johnnie Billy Goat* is a balanced selection from the preceding three albums, with three previously unissued numbers from the Habibi Temple recording and interesting notes by Boozoo's Rounder producer, Scott Billington.

*** **Down Home On Dog Hill**
Rounder 2166 *Chavis; Scott Billington (h, prod); David Greely (vn); Sonny Landreth (g); Classie Ballou Jr (b); Rellis Chavis (d); Charles Chavis (rb, v). 4/01.*

The astute pairing of Chavis and Landreth makes this perhaps the older man's most accessible record. Landreth's sweet-and-sour slide guitar adds a rich tang to the meat-and-potatoes menu of Creole dance tunes and blues, and with Greely's fiddle also spicing the dish on nine of the 13 tracks, the flavours are intriguingly layered. 'Negre Est Pas Là' is Chavis's way with 'Diggy Liggy Lo'. TR

C. J. Chenier (born 1957)
VOCAL, ACCORDION, SAXOPHONE, KEYBOARDS, FLUTE

C. J. grew up seeing little of his father Clifton Chenier, and as a boy had no interest in either the accordion or zydeco music; instead he took up piano and saxophone and played soul and funk. In 1978 his father enlisted him in his band to replace tenorist John Hart, and a few years later began training him on the accordion. After Clifton's death in 1987 C. J. took over some of his bookings and launched his own recording career. Since then he has grown steadily as a musician and leader.

*** **My Baby Don't Wear No Shoes**
Arhoolie CD 1098 *Chenier; Harry Hypolite (g, v); Selwyn Cooper (g); Wayne Burns (b); Joseph Edwards (d); Cleveland Chenier (rb). 3/88.*

Clifton Chenier may have been an absentee father, but you can almost sense his presence on his son's debut album. Some of the tunes are Clifton's – 'I'm Coming Home', 'My Baby Don't Wear No Shoes', 'Banana Man' – but even on his own material (when it is his: the composer credits are a little generous in that respect) C. J. is obviously exuding what he soaked up from his years alongside his father on the bandstand. The dominant flavour is the blues, with a dash of old-school zydeco in 'My Baby Don't Wear No Shoes' and a spritz of *nouveau* in 'Check Out The Zydeco'.

*** Too Much Fun
Alligator ALCD 4830 *Chenier; Wayne Jackson (t); Andrew Love (ts); Floyd Newman (bs); Harry Hypolite (g, tri, v); Jamie Kelly (g, perc, v); Mark Major (g, perc); Vasti Jackson (g); John Frederick (b, perc, v); Greg Gordon (d, perc); Clifford Alexander Jr (rb, perc); Steve Eisen (cga).* 95.

**(*) The Big Squeeze
Alligator ALCD 4844 *Chenier; Steve Howard (t); Jon Smith (ts); Jerry Jumonville (bs); Vasti Jackson (g, b, perc); Harry Hypolite (g, tri, v); Michael Great Bear Clair (g, perc, v); Mark Major (g, perc); Glenn Griffin (b, perc); Greg Gordon (d, perc); Clifford Alexander (rb, perc); Sam Fishkin, Brian Jensen (perc).* 96.

**(*) Step It Up!
Alligator ALCD 4882 *Chenier; Marshall Cyr (t); Pat Breaux (ts); Tim Betts, Wayne Dalcourt (g, perc); Glenn Griffin (b, perc); Nick Daniels III (b); Brian Brignac (d, perc); Randy Carpenter, Ernie Haynes (d); Lynn Boudreaux (cga, perc); James Joseph Alfred (rb); Tony Daigle (tri).* 01.

In the notes to *Too Much Fun* C. J. describes his repertoire: 'Fast songs … some slow sentimental ones like "Got You On My Mind" … some old-time zydeco like "Louisiana Two Step" and a couple of my dad's songs with new arrangements. But one thing we don't have is this new type of zydeco that's big in Louisiana now, where they just play one riff over and over and shout out some words and don't even ever change chords. What we're playing here are real songs.' If that was a policy statement, there was no departing from it on *Too Much Fun* and *The Big Squeeze*. *Too Much Fun*, along with the titles mentioned above, dips into the rock repertoire for 'Man Smart, Woman Smarter' and borrows the Z. Z. Hill hit 'Down Home Blues' in order to translate it into French, while *The Big Squeeze* rediscovers Arthur Alexander's 'Every Day I Have To Cry Some' and Smokey Smothers's 'I Can't Judge Nobody' (and, less profitably, 'Teddy Bear'), but both albums acknowledge paternal and regional traditions, and when C. J. reaches back for an old-as-the-swamps two-step like 'No Shoes Zydeco' it's almost as if Clifton were on the stand again. *Step It Up!*, however, has less both of Clifton's legacy (just one tune, 'Johnny Can't Dance') and of the slow blues that C. J. does rather well, upping the quota of hard-rocking dance music and blues stomps like 'Eat More Crawfish' and 'Road Dog'. TR

Clifton Chenier (1925–87)
VOCAL, ACCORDION, HARMONICA

The international popularity of zydeco music is largely due to Chenier, an artist as significant in the development of the genre as Bill Monroe was to bluegrass or Bob Wills to Western Swing. Whereas most of his predecessors had played the diatonic button accordion, Chenier favoured the chromatic piano accordion, on which he developed fresh approaches both to traditional French songs and to blues. Initially known only in his native south Louisiana and in black French communities in Texas and California, he ultimately became a world traveller with his Red Hot Louisiana Band, which almost always included his brother Cleveland (1921–91) playing rubboard.

Chenier's first recordings were made in Lake Charles in 1954 and issued on small West Coast labels; four are on *Elko Blues Vol. 1* (Wolf 120.614) and two on *Elko Blues Vol. 2* (Wolf 120.615). 'Rockin' The Bop' and 'Louisiana Stomp' (*Vol. 1*) and 'Rockin' Hop' (*Vol. 2*) have the hectic excitement, and the documentary sound, of live recordings from a dancehall.

*** Zodico Blues & Boogie
Specialty SPCD-7039//Ace CDCHD 389 *Chenier; Lionel Prevost (ts); James K. Jones (p); Phillip Walker, Lonesome Sundown (g); Louis Candy (b); Wilton Siemen (d); Cleveland Chenier (rb).* 4–9/55.

*** Bayou Blues
Specialty SPCD 2139 *As above.* 4–9/55.

When these recordings were made, the currency of zydeco was accepted only in Louisiana, West Texas and a few enclaves on the West Coast, and it's not surprising that a label like Specialty should have tried to put Chenier across primarily as a bluesman. The one French title, 'Ay-Te Te Fee' (i.e. 'Eh, Petite Fille'), is a brisk blues, and he also sings Guitar Slim's 'The Things I Did For You', performances that have some of the air of Fats Domino, if Fats had swapped his piano for a piano accordion. Several of the 12 tunes found on both CDs (*Zodico Blues & Boogie* adds one more and six alternative takes) are accordion-led instrumentals at tempi from fast boogie to the dead-slow 'The Cat's Dreamin''. These were soulful and, at the time, startling, recordings, and any of them might have been a novelty R&B hit. But Chenier's star was not quite due to rise.

*** Bon Ton Roulet
Arhoolie CD-345 *Chenier; John Hart (ts); Elmore Nixon (p); Morris Chenier (vn); Felix James Benoit, unknown (g); Joe Morris [Brouchet], unknown (b); Robert St Judy [St Julian] (d); Cleveland Chenier (rb) (d).* 2/64–9/73.

**** Louisiana Blues And Zydeco
Arhoolie CD 9053 *Chenier; Elmore Nixon (p); Cleveland Keyes (g); Fulton Antoine (b); Madison Guidry, Robert St Judy [St Julian] (d); Cleveland Chenier (rb).* 5/65.

These CDs contain most of the contents of Chenier's first three LPs for Arhoolie, which probably did more than any other records to rekindle zydeco fervour in its own lands and ignite it abroad. *Louisiana Blues And Zydeco*, his first album, is reissued in its entirety with eight unissued numbers from the same session. Its repertoire is strong in old-time French tunes such as 'Zydeco Sont Pas Sale', 'Eh, 'Tite Fille' and a couple of waltzes, but also contains very fine blues performances like 'Louisiana Blues' and 'I Can Look Down At Your Woman', which Chenier sang with enormous feeling. (This CD replaces the somewhat different *Louisiana Blues And Zydeco* on Arhoolie CD 329.) *Bon Ton Roulet* is heavier with blues material ('If I Ever Get Lucky', 'Black Gal', 'Baby, Please Don't Go', 'Black Snake Blues', etc.) but does include Chenier's versions of the regional standards 'Jole Blonde' and 'Cher Catin', two of several tracks involving his uncle on fiddle, possibly Chenier's only recordings with that instrument. Three previously unissued tracks from 1964, a couple of instrumental boogies and a dramatic slow blues, 'I'm On The Wonder', are by a trio with pianist Elmore Nixon and a drummer.

*** Live! At The 1966 Berkeley Blues Festival
Arhoolie CD 484 *Chenier; Francis Clay (d).* 4/66.

This was Chenier's first appearance before a mainly white

audience and he is a little diffident about music that he imagines will seem strange, but his performance is dynamic and absorbing. He plays nine numbers, a mixed bag of blues, zydeco tunes and R&B hits, accompanied only by Francis Clay, the drummer with the Muddy Waters Band, which was also on the festival bill. 'This was the stripped-down Chenier sound which I heard when I first met him at a beer joint in Houston's French town,' explains Arhoolie's Chris Strachwitz. The album's other contributors are Lightnin' Hopkins and Mance Lipscomb.

*** Sings The Blues
Arhoolie CD 9041 *Chenier; prob. Cleveland Keyes (g); prob. Joe Morris [Brouchet] (b); Robert Peter (St Julian) (d); Cleveland Chenier (rb). 4/69.*

*** Zydeco Blues
Fuel 2000 302 061 411 *As above, except add prob. John Hart (ts), unknown (g). 4/69, 77.*

*** King Of The Bayous "I'm Coming Home"
Arhoolie CD-339 *Chenier; Elmore Nixon (p); Raymond Monett, Antoine Victor, Cleveland Keyes (g); Joe Morris [Brouchet] (b); Robert St Judy [St Julian] (d); Cleveland Chenier (rb). 11/69, 5/70.*

***(*) Out West
Arhoolie CD-350 *Chenier; John Hart (ts); Steve Miller (p); Paul Senegal [Sinegal], Elvin Bishop (g); Joe Morris [Brouchet] (b); Robert Peter [St Julian] (d); Cleveland Chenier (rb). 71, 5/73.*

All of *Sings The Blues* and most of *Zydeco Blues* come from a 1969 Houston session produced by Roy Ames that was well recorded, well executed and, of course, heavy on the blues. *Sings The Blues* (replacing the similarly titled but deleted Arhoolie CD 351, which also contained later recordings) has one more track from the session ('Rosemary'), but *Zydeco Blues* adds three from a 1977 gig in Santa Cruz.

The 1969 part of *King Of The Bayous* is much enhanced by the presence of pianist Elmore Nixon, and the performances, even when they're of such well-worn material as 'Release Me', are heartfelt. The sound of the '70s recordings, another blues-heavy set, is brighter but almost all you can hear between the accordion and the percussionists is the bass: the guitar seems to have been lost in the mix.

Out West, made in 1973, was Chenier's first album with tenor saxophonist John Hart and guitarist Paul Senegal added to the core trio of Morris/Brouchet, Peter/St Julian and Cleveland Chenier. Subsequent recordings with that quintet reveal it to be the best band Clifton Chenier ever led, but on this occasion, untypically, it was augmented with Elvin Bishop and Steve Miller, who contribute usefully to a big, exciting ensemble and a mesmerizing performance of one of Chenier's blues staples, 'I'm On The Wonder'. The original album is extended by four previously unissued tracks from the session and three more from a 1971 radio appearance.

*** Live At St. Mark's
Arhoolie CD-313 *Chenier; Felix James Benoit (g); Joe Morris [Brouchet] (b); Robert St Judy [St Julian] (d); Cleveland Chenier (rb). 11/71.*

**(*) The King Of Zydeco Live At Montreux
Arhoolie CD-355 *Chenier; Paul Senegal [Sinegal] (g); Joe Morris [Brouchet] (b); Robert St Julian (d); Cleveland Chenier (rb). 7/75.*

(**) Cajun Swamp Music
Charly CPCD 8237 *As above. 7/75.*

There are enclaves of Louisiana-born Creoles outside Louisiana; one is in Richmond, in the San Francisco Bay Area, and *Live At St. Mark's* was recorded at a church hall there, apparently at a dance; you don't get much impression of the several-hundred-strong crowd up on their feet, but the performance derives atmosphere from exchanges between artist and audience. The repertoire is largely familiar, in fact if not in title. It's a loose, freewheeling show where, in the absence of a horn player or an aggressive guitarist, the spotlight falls on Clifton and Cleveland.

At the 1975 Montreux Jazz Festival the Chenier brothers, at least, gave lively performances. That much the recording makes clear, but a lot of the time the playing of the rest of the band suggests either a bad case of jetlag or a good case of whisky the night before. Senegal eventually shakes off his torpor to play with a bit of pep on 'Money'. The setlist is a revolving prism showing every facet of Chenier's music, from 'Jambalaya' to 'Cher Catin', 'Release Me' to 'I'm On The Wonder'. Arhoolie's notes state that *Live At Montreux* is 'the only legal and authorized release' of the festival tapes, the point being that the Charly CD – which contains almost all the same songs, in a different order – was licensed from Tomato, who issued the material first but were successfully sued by the artist for non-payment of royalties.

**** Bogalusa Boogie
Arhoolie CD-347 *As above, except add John Hart (ts). 10/75.*

'This was probably the most perfect recording session I ever had with Clifton Chenier,' Chris Strachwitz remarks in his notes, 'and … the best version of the Red Hot Louisiana Band during Clifton's long career.' True. Chenier and his men march through the varied programme with gusto, the recording is full of presence and John Hart seizes the opportunity to write the rulebook for zydeco saxophone. If you could own only one Clifton Chenier CD, this would be it.

**** Zydeco Legend!
Maison de Soul MDS-CD-105 *Chenier; prob. Warren Ceasar (t); prob. C. J. Chenier (as); John Hart, prob. Gabriel King (ts); Glen Himel (p); Paul Senegal [Sinegal], Sherman Robertson (g); Sherman Thomas, poss. Alonzo Johnson Jr (b); Robert Peter [St Julian] (d); Cleveland Chenier (rb). 11/75, 83/84.*

With *Bogalusa Boogie* less than a month behind them, it's not surprising that the Red Hots here play as if they're on a roll – a rockin' roll on 'You Can't Sit Down', 'Road Runner' and 'Choo Choo Ch-Boogie'. But along with stuff for the younger set come waltzes ('Nonc Helaire', 'You Used To Call Me') and zydeco favourites like 'Johnny Can't Dance'. All those are in the first ten tracks, which formerly made up the LP *Boogie 'N' Zydeco*. The remaining eight come from the album currently available as *King Of Zydeco* (see below), and the difference in the two bands and their repertoires makes for a potent combination.

**(*) Frenchin' The Boogie
Universal/Maison de Blues 982 246-9 *Chenier; Lon Price (ts); Stanley 'Buckwheat' Dural (o, p); Paul Senegal [Sinegal], Jeff Pollard (g); Leon Medica (b); Robert Peter St Julian (d); Cleveland Chenier (rb, v). 2/76.*

Recorded in Louisiana for the French album series *House Of*

The Blues, this is almost entirely devoted to R&B and blues standards like 'Keep A Knockin'', 'I Got A Woman', 'I Just Want To Make Love To You' and 'Don't You Lie To Me'. Chenier brings what fizz he can to this unimaginative setlist but in the dead air of the studio even some of that goes flat. One track has been added to previous releases.

*** Clifton Chenier And His Red Hot Louisiana Band In New Orleans
GNP-Crescendo GNPD 2119 *As for* Bogalusa Boogie, *except add* Benny Grunch (b). mid-70s?

This is one of Chenier's lesser-known albums, but it's not to be scorned. The band doesn't work up a sweat as on *Bogalusa Boogie* or the relevant part of *Zydeco Legend*, but plays as if for a chilling-out audience, with the gently rocking 'Mon Vieux "Buggy"' and 'Pousse Cafe Waltz', the swamp-pop ballad 'Jusque Parce Que Je T'Aime' and several slow blues like 'Cotton-Picker Blues' and 'Tous Les Jours (Everyday)'. John Hart's tenor is extensively featured, mostly in rhythmic figures or doubling the accordion melody, and Senegal takes some good blues solos.

**(*) Squeezebox Boogie
Just A Memory JAM 9141 *As for* Bogalusa Boogie. 8/78.

The band don't seem to have looked forward to this Montreal club gig. The sluggishness of the opening 'Rock Me Baby' (far too long at 6.02) isn't fully dispelled until past the halfway mark, with 'Zydeco Cha Cha' and 'Whole Lotta Lovin''. By that time Senegal can actually be heard; the preceding cuts sound like duets for accordion and tenor sax.

***(*) Live! At Grant Street
Arhoolie CD 487 Chenier; C. J. Chenier (as); unknown (g); unknown (b); Robert Peter [St Julian] (d); Cleveland Chenier (rb). 4/81.

**** Live! At The Long Beach And San Francisco Blues Festivals
Arhoolie CD 404 Chenier; Warren Ceasar (t); C. J. Chenier (as); Sherman Robertson (g); Alonzo Johnson Jr (b); Robert St Judy [St Julian] (d); Cleveland Chenier (rb); band (v). 82–83.

These are excellently recorded souvenirs of three high-energy shows. On *Grant Street*, taped at a Lafayette dancehall, Clifton is playing a new electronic accordion, but the 'effects' mentioned in the notes are barely noticeable. The festival sets have none of the same material. The 11-minute sequence of 'What'd I Say?' and 'Party Down' from Long Beach is some of the most exhilarating playing ever recorded by a Red Hot lineup, and the audience responds in the same spirit.

*** I'm Here!
Alligator ALCD 4729 Chenier; Warren Ceasar (t); C. J. Chenier (as); Gabriel King (ts); Danny Caron (g); Wayne Burns (b); Robert St Julian (d); Cleveland Chenier (rb). 81/82.

*** King Of Zydeco
Ace CDCH 234 *Similar to above, except* Sherman Robertson (g), prob. Alonzo Johnson [Jr] (b) replace Caron, Burns; band (v). 83/84.

In the late '70s Chenier was hampered by a blood condition and *I'm Here!* was his first studio recording in four or five years. The strain of playing while on thrice-weekly dialysis led him to invest in a more technically sophisticated (and so labour-saving) instrument and a larger band, in which the horn parts could provide the arrangements with some of the colour formerly inked in by the accordion. (Ceasar's trumpet overdoes the purple passages, though.) It's a solid set, with a good deal of perennial blues repertoire, but 'Zydeco Disco' and 'The New Zydeco' tempt the listener with more modern dance rhythms.

What's now *King Of Zydeco* was also recorded for Alligator but after a disagreement with the company Chenier bought the tapes and had them issued on the local Caillier label as *Country Boy Wins A Grammy*. Unusually for Ace, there are no personnel data, but the band is probably much the same as on *Live! At The Long Beach And San Francisco Blues Festivals*. Robertson is definitely the guitarist, since Chenier calls him on to solo in 'Love Me Or Leave Me', which he does very well. The track is not the standard but a blues, as are several others, like 'Mama Told Papa', a brisk run round the changes of Junior Parker's 'Feelin' Good'; 'Zydeco Jazz' is simply an instrumental blues with a squealy alto solo. As much the band's album as the leader's, and none the worse for that.

*** 60 Minutes With The King
Arhoolie CD-301 *As for source CDs*. 64–82.
*** The Best Of Clifton Chenier
Arhoolie CD 474 *As for source CDs*. 64–83.
*** Zydeco Sont Pas Salé
Arhoolie CD 9001 *As for source CDs*. 65–82.

These are introductory compilations drawn from Arhoolie's remarkable back catalogue, and all good. *60 Minutes* and *The Best Of* have a few repertoire duplications, but on the whole the three sets stay out of each other's way. *Zydeco Sont Pas Salé*, which is mid-priced, is devoted to songs in Creole French – traditional Louisiana tunes, five blues and the swamp-pop 'Je Marche Le Plancher'. *The Best Of* concludes with a 15-minute radio interview by Chris Strachwitz. TR

Roscoe Chenier (born 1941)
VOCAL, GUITAR

Chenier worked with various Louisiana bands from 1958, including those of Lonesome Sundown and Leroy Washington, and made a fine single with C. D. Gradnier's Blue Runners in 1961. He formed his own band in 1980.

*** Roscoe Style
Black & Tan CD BT 001 Chenier; Arend Bouwmeester (ts); Tom Schepp (h); Roel Spanjers (o, p); Jan Mittendorp (g); Ellio Martina (b); Frank Bolder (d). 97.

Roscoe Chenier (Avenue Jazz R2 71805) is deleted, and *Roscoe Rocks* (Bayou BR-1004) very poorly distributed, which on the evidence of this disc is a pity. Chenier may be keeping a moribund sound alive almost single-handed, but he does so with some flair. There are a few original compositions included, but most tracks are covers, either of the greats of swamp blues or in their manner. Chenier's imitation of Lightnin' Slim is too careful, and still manages to be shaky at times, but elsewhere he signals his respect for the originals while still sounding like himself, and plays guitar that's both warm and piercing. His Dutch accompanists are all very effective; Bolder and Spanjers are outstanding. CS

Chicago All Stars
GROUP

Willie Dixon formed and led successive versions of this touring band from 1969 onwards.

** Chicago All Stars
Wolf 120.291 *Walter Horton (h, v); Sunnyland Slim (p, v); Johnny Shines (g, v); Willie Dixon (b, v); Clifton James (d).* prob. early 70.

All the singers run through their favourite numbers. Shines sings with his usual 200 per cent commitment and plays fiery guitar throughout, Horton and Slim are in good but not top form, and James and Dixon are reliable, although one of the things Dixon can be relied on for is an irritating high-register solo, here inflicted on 'Sunnyland Boogie'. The big drawbacks are the recording quality, which has the muddiness that says 'airshot', and the mixing, which is eccentric. The drums are too far forward, and everyone else's singing and playing keep switching from relatively clear to muffled and distant; Sunnyland Slim, of all people, sounds as if he's singing in the next room. There's better material available by all concerned, and it renders this CD redundant.

**(*) Good Advice
Wolf 120.700 *Carey Bell (h, v); Butch Dixon (p); John Watkins (g, v); Willie Dixon (b, v); Freddie Dixon (b, sp); Greg Jackson (d).* 91.

That high-register solo turns up in the closing instrumental; this time it incorporates 'Jingle Bells'. *Good Advice*, which presents another, much better recorded concert, is credited to Willie Dixon & The Chicago Allstars. The focus is firmly on Dixon, with Bell and Watkins getting one song apiece, respectively an original 'So Hard To Leave You Alone' and Jimmy Reed's 'You Don't Have To Go'. Watkins's slide guitar is as unimaginative as his choice of material, but Bell plays commandingly throughout. Butch Dixon is a gifted pianist, but his chromatic colorations and jazzy meanderings sometimes clash with the more direct approach of the other musicians. Dixon Sr pontificates about the universality of the blues, but confines himself to his (admittedly vast) back catalogue. Everyone works hard, but too often the numbers continue well past the point where everything has been said. CS

Chicago Blues Reunion
GROUP

What it says: a get-together of veterans of the '60s North Side scene, such as Nick Gravenites, Barry Goldberg, Harvey Mandel and Corky Siegel.

**(*) Buried Alive In The Blues
Out Of The Box 3016 CD+DVD *Corky Siegel (h, v); Barry Goldberg (kb, o, p, v); Nick Gravenites, R. Zach Wagner (g, v); Harvey Mandel (g); Rick Reed (b); Gary Mallaber (d, perc); Sam Lay (d, v); Tracy Nelson (v).* 10/04.

This triumphal gig at Fitzgerald's in Berwyn, Illinois, begins with the now anthemic 'Born In Chicago' – the opening track, almost 40 years ago, of the debut LP by the Paul Butterfield Blues Band, sung here by its composer, and Butterfield's friend, Nick Gravenites. This is the only outright commemoration of the band that sparked so many others, not a few of them featuring Goldberg, Mandel or Siegel. The rest of the programme, though played fairly Chicago-style, is not drawn from the standard Chicago folio; apart from one Willie Dixon song and a couple by Slim Harpo, most of the material comes from within the band, Gravenites contributing (among others) a long 'Death Of Muddy Waters' and Mandel going for blues-rock overkill with the instrumentals 'Snake' and 'GM Boogie'. Gravenites is the chief vocalist and brings a gravelly authority to the role, but Sam Lay's medley of 'Hound Dog' and 'Roll Over Beethoven' is as run-of-the-mill as you might expect. That sort of generic obviousness permeates the set, giving it something of the character of a Blues Brothers routine. The DVD contains the concert and interviews. TR

Chicago Rhythm & Blues Kings
GROUP

Until 1993 the Chicago Rhythm & Blues Kings were The Mellow Fellows, backing the singer Big Twist on several albums and making one of their own soon afterwards.

*** Chicago Rhythm & Blues Kings
Blind Pig BPCD 5058 *Don Tenuto (t); Gene Barge (ts, v, prod); Terry Ogolini (ts); Michael Logan, Sid Wingfield, Matt Rose (kb); David Mick (g, v); Bob Halaj (b, v); Willie Hayes, Wayne Stewart (d); Ernie Peniston (v).* 99?

Though their lineup might seem to locate them on the same square of the stylistic map as Roomful Of Blues, the Kings differ in foregrounding the horns and keyboard players and pushing the guitar down in the mix. That, at least, is the balance on this album, perhaps tilted by the several guest players, who include in Barge a highly experienced veteran of Chicago blues and R&B sessions; as well as producing, blowing tenor and occasionally singing, he wrote four of the 11 numbers. The ensemble plays with punch and gusto throughout a well-mixed programme of blues, jazz and soul numbers, including a 'Wallflower Boogie' that's much less predictable than it sounds and an attractive theme by Ogolini and Tenuto, 'Mo Too-Do-Loo', with echoes of South African township jazz. Excellent party music. TR

The Chicago String Band
GROUP

An attempt to re-create bygone black stringband music, using musicians who grew up in the South but were all longtime Chicago residents.

**(*) The Chicago String Band
Testament TCD 5006 *John Wrencher (h, v); Carl Martin (vn, g, v); Johnny Young (md, v); John Lee Granderson (g, v); Bill Foster (g).* 6/66.

In 1966, neither the reissuing of black stringbands recorded on commercial 78s nor the issuing of non-commercial field recordings were as extensive as they have since become, and this session was a bright research idea, which also seemed likely to be fun. The musicians were asked to develop a playlist and rehearse without input or suggestions from producer Pete Welding, but in the event they didn't fulfil his 'express purpose of re-creating for recording the raucous, exuberant sound of the stringband.' What they mostly did was to retrofit Chicago blues styles with conscientious versions of the stringband sound; only 'John Henry' has the authentic tang of older days and ways. The CD is always pleasant entertainment, but it would never have happened without, and doesn't always transcend, the academic impulse behind it. CS

Eric Clapton (born 1945)
VOCAL, GUITAR

It's not just that Eric Clapton espoused the blues but that he reinvented the vocabulary of blues guitar playing to a degree that echoed, though faintly, the innovations of T-Bone Walker a quarter-century before. Throughout a 35-year career that has encompassed peaks and troughs of equal magnitude, Clapton has often returned to the blues wellspring. Blues songs form a part of most of his albums but the essence of his craft is contained in those discussed below.

*** Unplugged
Reprise 45024 *Clapton; Chuck Leavell (kb); Andy Fairweather Low (g); Nathan East (b, v); Steve Ferrone (d); Ray Cooper (perc); Katie Kissoon, Tessa Niles (v).* 92.

Reborn classics 'Layla', 'Tears In Heaven' and 'Running On Faith', their tunefulness enhanced by Clapton at a vocal high point, include smatterings of bluesy acoustic lead guitar. Such songs serve a not necessarily blues-bent Clapton audience, and ensure a smooth course for an assortment of covers: Big Bill Broonzy, Muddy Waters, Leadbelly and Robert Johnson are all recast in the bluesier half of *Unplugged*. Clapton eschews a guitar god's tendency to prophetic over-indulgence, opting for a balanced roots sound that delivers blues, with carefully placed solos, as well as it supports the steering chord movements of his commercial songwriting. The styles are blended expertly in 'Old Love', which Clapton wrote with his compatible peer Robert Cray. Intimacy and informality defined the concerts in this popular MTV series of acoustic strip-downs, and Clapton's became a seminal appearance. In Johnson's 'Malted Milk' he seems to be fulfilling an intense personal destiny with sublime guitar sauntering, while the slide groove of Waters's 'Rollin' And Tumblin'' invites audience handclaps and affirms the warmth of this most approachable of acoustic (semi-)blues albums. RR

***(*) From The Cradle
Reprise 45735 *Clapton; Roddy Lorimer (t); Tim Sanders (ts); Simon Clarke (bs); Jerry Portnoy (h); Chris Stainton (kb); Andy Fairweather Low (g); Dave Bronze (b); Jim Keltner (d).* 94.

Bolstered by the exceptional success of the *Unplugged* album and video (Reprise 38311), Clapton elected to go the whole hog and prepare a record of uncompromised blues. Cut almost completely live, these 16 tracks are an eclectic mix of predominantly Chicago blues, with flavours of Texas and California and a timeframe that stretches from the '30s to the '60s. After decades of laudable reinterpretation, Clapton chose to reproduce the arrangements of the original records, including (of necessity) 'Hoochie Coochie Man', 'It Hurts Me Too' and 'Blues Before Sunrise', the latter pair in their Elmore James guise. Likewise Lowell Fulson's 'Reconsider Baby', although the same writer's 'Sinner's Prayer' inclines towards its Ray Charles incarnation. Clapton is on exceptional playing form, many times approaching an ecstatic delivery without invoking frenzy on tunes like mentor Freddie King's 'I'm Tore Down' and 'Someday After A While'. He's not quite so successful vocally, forcing 'Blues Before Sunrise' and yielding to all-too-sincere imitation of Muddy Waters in 'Hoochie Coochie Man', although he cannot reproduce Muddy's deep blues roar on 'Standing Around Crying'. NS

**(*) Me And Mr Johnson
Reprise 48730 *Clapton; Jerry Portnoy (h); Billy Preston (o, p); Andy Fairweather Low, Doyle Bramhall II (g); Nathan East, Pino Palladino (b); Steve Gadd, Jim Keltner (d).* 04.

'At first it scared me in its intensity,' remarks Clapton of his early encounters with Robert Johnson's music. So it's undoubtedly a personal, committed tribute when he and his band perform 14 Johnson songs, among them his best-known. What's hard to accept about this record is that it either disregards or misinterprets what set Johnson apart – indeed, what wowed teenagers like Clapton (or Keith Richards, or Peter Green, or …). Johnson's howling, untamed confessions keep you guessing what's coming next, whether spellbinding guitar passages or his impossible singing range. The character of these 12-bar shuffles contradicts that: they're repressed, steady, even complacent. Clapton attempts Johnson's falsetto breaks in 'Me And The Devil Blues' and 'Stop Breakin' Down Blues', but lacks Johnson's incisive raw edge and prompts you to return to his version (though that was surely part of Clapton's intention anyway). The studio sound is dry, uncomplicated, presumably so as to foreground the performances, yet these unfold with little gain in intensity or purpose, leaving only an assured and solid recounting of a great artist's vision, the guitars and harmonicas a little less banal than Clapton's withered vocals. RR

Cortelia Clark (1907–69)
VOCAL, GUITAR

A blind Nashville street singer and vendor of shopping bags, Clark was brought to RCA by a local talent scout. Chet Atkins signed him, apparently to please Bob Ferguson, who was writing country hits for the label and signing stars like Dolly Parton. The resulting LP generated considerable media buzz: so much so that in 1967 Clark beat Peter, Paul & Mary, Ravi Shankar, Richard & Mimi Farina, and Pete Seeger to a Grammy. (By then the record had sold 670 copies.) Clark continued to live in poverty (with no electricity, he couldn't even play his album) and died from burns after a kerosene heater exploded.

** Blues In The Street
Collectors' Choice Music CCM-487 *Clark.* 12/65.

Clark was a songster, playing country, gospel, pop and familiar blues like 'Every Day I Have The Blues' and 'Trouble In Mind'. Most of his songs seem to have been learned from the radio – it's a safe bet that 'Walk Right In' came from the Rooftop Singers rather than Gus Cannon – and set to basic boom-chang chords. He makes changes to the lyrics, partly at least because of reliance on memory: his version of the Everley Brothers' 'Bye Bye Love' is unusual, to say the least, and there are some interesting added verses on his version of 'Careless Love'. Clark was a secure musician within his limits, but they were narrow, and the LP's reappearance on CD is almost as surprising as its Grammy. The recordings were indeed made in the street, but extra honking and tyre squeals were added, supposedly in the interest but actually to the detriment of authenticity. This nonsense is all in the left channel, and can be muted, but only completists and scholars will want the opportunity. CS

W. C. Clark (born 1940)
VOCAL, GUITAR

Wesley Curley Clark has been playing around Austin, his hometown, since his teens, first on bass, then guitar. He was in bands led by T. D. Bell and Blues Boy Hubbard, worked for a couple of years with Joe Tex, and in the '80s joined Stevie Ray Vaughan and Lou Ann Barton in the Triple Threat Revue. In the '90s he led his own band and made three critically well-received albums for Black Top.

*** From Austin With Soul
Alligator ALCD 4884 Clark; Gary Slechta (t); Randy Zimmerman (tb); Mark 'Kaz' Kazanoff (as, ts, prod); Les Izmore (s); Riley Osbourn, Gray Gregson (kb); Marcia Ball (p, v); Derek O'Brien, Pat Boyack (g); Larry Fulcher (b); Barry 'Frosty' Smith (d, perc); Mike Cross (v). 01.

*** Deep In The Heart
Alligator ALCD 4897 Clark; Gary Slechta (t); Randy Zimmerman (tb); Mark Kazanoff (s, h, perc, v, arr, prod); John Mills (s); Riley Osbourn, Nick Connolly (kb); Marcia Ball (p, v); Derek O'Brien, Pat Boyack (g); Larry Fulcher, Kevin Smith (b); Barry 'Frosty' Smith (d, perc); Tony Braunagel (d); Paul Mills (perc); Ruthie Foster (v). 03/04.

Alligator adds new artists to its roster comparatively seldom, but one suspects that the company pricked up its corporate ears when Clark became available. As he proved on his albums for Black Top (all unfortunately deleted), he is a happy long-term resident in the border country between Texas blues and Memphis soul, a spiritual kinsman of Bobby Bland. His Alligator debut, produced like its predecessors by Kaz Kazanoff and featuring many of the Austin scene's usual suspects, breaks no new ground, nor would one want it to: songs like 'How Long Is A Heartache Supposed To Last?' or 'Real Live Livin' Hurtin' Man' are the work of an artist who has little to learn about telling a story. Virtually the same team worked on *Deep In The Heart*, an equally attractive set in which Clark ranges athletically and expertly from John Hiatt's 'Tip Of My Tongue' to the timeless blues of 'My Texas Home'. TR

William Clarke (1951–96)
VOCAL, HARMONICA, GUITAR

Self-taught until his six-year friendship with George 'Harmonica' Smith, Clarke became a leading purveyor of the Californian tradition of transposed Chicago blues. A series of self-produced albums for small independent labels led to a contract with Alligator Records that brought him nationwide recognition. A constant touring schedule and a heavy drinking habit brought about his collapse in March 1996. Treated for congestive heart failure, he remained sober until his death eight months later following emergency surgery for a stomach ulcer.

*** Now That You're Gone
Watchdog WD-1006 Clarke; Mitch Kashmar, George Smith, Joe Lodovici (h); Fred Kaplan (p); Hollywood Fats, Ronnie Earl, Junior Watson (g); Bill Stuve (b); unknown(s) (d). 80s.

*** Tip Of The Top
KingAce KACD 1063 Clarke; George 'Harmonica' Smith, Charlie Musselwhite (h); Fred Kaplan (p, g); Rob Rio (p); Ronnie Earl, Junior Watson, Joel Foy, Hollywood Fats, Steve Killman, Bruce Thorpe (g); Willie Brinlee, Bill Stuve (b); Jerry Monte (d). 85–86.

These were posthumous releases, *Now That You're Gone* a selection of old tapes that Clarke compiled shortly before he died, *Tip Of The Top* a reissue of an album first released in Europe in 1987, with four previously unissued tracks and a tribute note written by Charlie Musselwhite, who also appears on one track. Clarke's biggest debt is paid in full on *Top* with 'Tribute To George Smith', a seven-minute-plus chromatic harmonica instrumental performed with unflagging invention. Elsewhere, Little Walter and Junior Wells are evoked in Clarke's comprehensive technique. Apart from original material, he draws upon the work of Jimmy Witherspoon, Big Bill Broonzy, Robert Lockwood and Jerry McCain. He's very well served by an array of tough and effective guitarists, of whom Watson, Foy and Hollywood Fats are most notable. The merit of these collections is their unremitting focus on blues, untrammelled by Clarke's later, not wholly successful experiments with swing jazz, making them fitting memorials.

***(*) Blowin' Like Hell
Alligator ALCD 4788 Clarke; John Marotti (t, tb); Jon Viau (ts, bs); Fred Kaplan, Steve F'dor (p); Alex Schultz, Zach Zunis, Rick Holmstrom, John Marx (g); Willie Brinlee (b); Eddie Clark (d). 90.

It's plain from the opening bars of Roy Brown's 'Lollipop Mama' that Clarke is a very inventive harmonica player. Little Walter's tone and technique in this, 'Lonesome Bedroom Blues' and his own 'Looking To The Future' are evident but so too is an originality that transcends its inspiration. Three instrumentals, including the title track, are further chances to impress, even if the latter's reliance upon repetitive staccato riffs renders it formulaic. Clarke's an engaging but lightweight singer who only finds true engagement in 'Must Be Jelly', one of several songs present that take on a jazzier ambience. He's aided on this and others by Schultz, a thinking guitarist whose solos build on an internal logic and avoid cliché. Zunis is a plank-spanker by comparison, too willing to indulge in fashionable treble frenzy. The Handy Awards gave the album its imprimatur by judging 'Must Be Jelly' its 'Blues Song Of The Year' for 1991.

***(*) Serious Intentions
Alligator ALCD 4806 Clarke; John Marotti (t, tb); Jon Viau (ts); Troy Jennings (bs); Fred Kaplan (p); Alex Schultz, Zach Zunis, Al Blake (g); Flaco 'Slim' Medina, Willie Brinlee, Tyler Pederson (b); Lee Campbell, Eddie Clark, Jimi Bott (d). 92.

Influences are more polarized in this collection. On the one hand, Muddy Waters, Jimmy Rogers and the Aces are evoked in 'Soon Forgotten', 'Driving My Life Away' and the instrumental 'Chasin' The Gator'; on the other, a perfectly adequate, perfectly dull run-through of Nat Adderley's 'Work Song'. Clarke's vocals are stronger and more characterful, his harmonica playing, both diatonic and chromatic, more forceful and discrete, its integration with a well-recorded horn section well conceived. Zunis's relegation to rhythm guitar allows Schultz to better display his taste and discretion, adding a taste of T-Bone to the album's magnum opus, 'It's Been A

***(*) Groove Time
Alligator ALCD 4827 Clarke; John Marotti (t); Jon Viau (ts); Troy Jennings (bs); Fred Kaplan, Steve F'dor, John 'Juke' Logan, Andy Kaulkin (o, p); Alex Schultz, Kid Ramos, Little Henry, Greg Verginio, Barry Levenson, Al Blake (g); Tyler Pederson (b); Bob Newham, Jimi Bott, John Moore, Eddie Clark (d). 94.

Consistency has become a watchword by now but to attempt it over the course of 15 tracks is the plucky side of foolhardy. *Groove Time* is Clarke's flawed masterpiece, hampered by over-arrangement and self-indulgence. On both chromatic and diatonic harmonica, Clarke forgoes his mentor George Smith's recommendation of brevity, taking solos five and six choruses long. A sequence of ideas that previously flashed through a 12-bar sequence now has a whole chorus devoted to each of them. A posse of guitarists is favoured likewise, with only Schultz and Ramos repaying with interest. This set's jazz interlude, 'A Good Girl Is Hard To Find', is hobbled by a clodhopping drummer and a too-strident pianist. Nevertheless, Clarke and his minions punch out a glorious racket whose exuberance is infectious and ultimately forgivable.

**(*) The Hard Way
Alligator ALCD 4842 Clarke; Jon Viau (ts); Troy Jennings (bs); Steve F'dor, Fred Kaplan (p); Jeff Ross, Greg Verginio, Alex Schultz (g); Rick Reed, Tyler Pederson (b); Eddie Clark, Bob Newham (d). 96.

In his booklet note, Clarke refers to this as 'my bluesiest and at the same time my jazziest' release. Unfortunately, he's not even half right. What jazz he attempts with 'Moten Swing', 'Walkin'' and his own 'The Boss' is self-indulgent, blustering and pedestrian. Despite the inclusion of songs by Muddy Waters, Mercy Dee Walton and Leroy Foster, the blues his band plays feels stilted and subtly off-centre. The one exception is Roy Brown's 'Letter From Home', which features Schultz, Kaplan, Pederson and Newham from *Groove Time*. Clarke himself sings over-theatrically and the breathing and gargling mannerisms he previously indulged sparingly now pepper every harmonica solo. His reliance upon the chromatic instrument blunts the angry genius of his diatonic play. This was the last recording before his death and perhaps deteriorating health had something to do with the album's incremental failures.

*** DeLuxe Edition
Alligator ALCD 5607 As for Alligator CDs above. 86–96.

A cunning ruse to disguise what is in fact a 'Best Of' compilation, this draws tracks from all four of Clarke's Alligator releases and adds three previously unissued performances. All such albums are subjective and this one is no exception. Two tracks, 'Trying So Hard' and 'Must Be Jelly', are taken from *Blowin' Like Hell*, which is probably more worthy of inclusion than *The Hard Way*, from which three are featured including the sprawling instrumental 'The Boss', and four from *Groove Time*. His attempts at marrying blues and jazz swing were never fully realized but have their place in any collection of his work. What this album lacks is an example of Clarke and his band vividly re-creating the Chicago blues of Little Walter and Jimmy Rogers, as in 'Chasin' The Gator' from *Serious Intentions* and *Groove Time*'s 'The War Is Over'. NS

Dr Clayton (1898–1947)
VOCAL

Peter Clayton grew up in St Louis but did all his recording in Chicago. If a publicity photograph is to be believed, when performing he wore large round 'bop spectacles' and went barefoot. His wife and family died in a fire in 1937, precipitating a decline into alcoholism.

***(*) Doctor Clayton (1935–1942)
Document DOCD-5179 Clayton; Beatrice 'Toots' Willis, Blind John Davis (p); Robert Lockwood (g); unknown (b); Alfred Elkins (imb); Ransom Knowling (bb). 7/35–3/42.

Clayton first recorded, as Jesse Clayton, in 1930: 'Station House Blues' and 'Neckbone Blues' are on *Piano Blues – Vol. 2 (1927–1956)* (Document DOCD-5220). He next recorded in 1935 – the two songs open his own Document CD – but his career on disc really starts with his 1941 recording of 'Roaming Gambler'. Singing in a drawl punctuated by falsetto whoops and cries of 'knock yourself out, man!', Clayton lurches through his songs giving a virtuoso impersonation of a literate drunk subject to intermittent bouts of euphoria. In ''41 Blues' he offers a solution to the international situation: 'This whole war would soon be over, if Uncle Sam would use my plan: let me sneak in Hitler's bedroom with my razor in my hand.' 'Black Snake Blues', which owes nothing to earlier songs of that title, has some sparkling passages by Davis. Lockwood, on the other hand, is under-recorded for much of this session, but asserts himself a little in 'Back Door Man Blues' and gets a solo in 'Jitterbug Swing'.

After recording what would prove to be his best remembered song, 'Confessin' The Blues', Clayton moved from Vocalion to Bluebird. His voice was thereafter more controlled, though still an instrument of considerable flexibility; at times he sounds a little like a rowdy Joe Pullum. His lyrics maintain their individuality, what with references to Sen-Sen cachous and Superman and hip expressions like 'solid mellow'. The vividly topical 'Pearl Harbor Blues' culminates in a startling verse: 'We sold the Japanese brass and scrap-iron, and it makes my blood boil in the veins – 'cause they made bombs and shells out of it, and they dropped them on Pearl Harbor just like rain.' Davis's accompaniments are neat and, except for the opening chorus of 'Pearl Harbor Blues', undemonstrative, and the most striking musical passages are Ransom Knowling's brass bass solos on the last six titles. But in terms of storytelling this is a most unusual and fascinating record. Clayton's half-dozen 1946 recordings, which are equally interesting, were on *Doctor Clayton And His Buddies (1946–1947)* (Old Tramp OTCD-05, deleted). TR

Eddy Clearwater (born 1935)
VOCAL, GUITAR, KEYBOARDS, HARMONICA

'Clear Waters – that's Muddy Waters' son,' said Big Bill Broonzy in 1956. No doubt Jump Jackson (then his booking agent) wanted people to think so, but left-handed guitarist Edward Harrington is Carey Bell's cousin, and a nephew of Rev. H. H. Harrington, for whose Atomic-H label he made his

first records in the '50s. He later turned his nickname into a surname, dubbed himself 'The Chief' and donned a war bonnet for his stage act. A tireless touring artist since the mid-'70s, Clearwater mixes West Side blues with soul, C&W and homages to Chuck Berry.

**(*) Hillbilly Blues
Redita CD-145 *Clearwater; 'Pasquale', 'Richard' (t); Chuck Smith, Jesse Anderson, Gene Redd (ts); 'H. B.', Bobby Little (bs); Lazy Bill Lucas, Rayburn Williams, Sonny Thompson, Allen Batts (p); John Hudson, Jesse Pariles, Bobby King, Mark Wydra (g); Jimmie Lee Robinson, 'Amando', Emmett Sutton, Mac Thompson, Scott Meyer (b); Richard Rogers, Pete Perez, Louis Batista, Jon Hiller, unknown (d); unknown (gong); Eddy Bell, The Clearaires, unknowns (v). 58–79.*

On many of *Hillbilly Blues*' 29 tracks Clearwater plays guitar in Eddy Bell's rockabilly band, whose other members he once memorably described as 'three Mexicans, a hillbilly and a Polock'. (Bell eventually became a polka star under his real name, Eddie Blazonczyk.) These tracks are mostly good examples of their genre, which is outside our remit; outside almost any genre is 'The Great Great Pumpkin', which answers the important question, 'What would Sun Ra have sounded like if he'd been white?' Whether as leader or band member, Clearwater spends much of his time duckwalking in Chuck Berry's wake, with excursions towards Ray Charles and – on 'A Minor Cha Cha' – Jody Williams. Marginality, derivativeness and the inherently poor sound of some of the original 45s cumulatively make this a CD for the specialist.

**(*) Black Night
Storyville STCD 8036 *Clearwater; Jimmy Dawkins (g); Sylvester Boines (b); Fred Below (d). 11/76.*

**(*) Chicago Blues Nights Vol. 2
Storyville STCD 8043 *As above. 11/76.*

*** Boogie My Blues Away
Delmark DD-678 *Clearwater; Mack Simmons (h); Bob Riedy (p); Thomas Eckert (g); Aron Burton (b); Sam Lay (d). 3/77.*

***(*) Chicago Daily Blues
Wolf 120.897 *Clearwater; Abb Locke (ts); Dimestore Fred [Stoop] (h); Allen Batts (o, p); Jimmy Johnson, Thomas Eckert, Mark Wydra (g); Marvin Jackson, Scott Meyer (b); Casey Jones, Jon Hiller (d); Leroy Brown (v). 77–10/79.*

Most of the songs on *Black Night*, recorded live for MCM, are too long and too familiar; only the topical but not very political 'Chicago Dailey [sic] Blues' is an exception. Fred Below gives his usual 200 per cent, which helps keep Dawkins and Clearwater together, but they don't bring much insight to a hackneyed playlist. Four more songs from this session bulk out *Chicago Blues Nights Vol. 2*, which is otherwise an Eddie Taylor CD. 'I Came Up The Hard Way' is a strong original, and 'Three Ways To Skin A Cat' a weak one; 'Let's Jam' is a paint-by-numbers instrumental, and 'Let's Boogie' one of Clearwater's trademark Chuck Berry imitations. It reappears on Delmark, as do 'Mayor Daley's Blues' and 'Came Up The Hard Way'. The latter is one of two songs with nugatory harmonica, but already this CD is an improvement. Veteran producer Ralph Bass ensures that a one-day session doesn't sound rushed, and keeps meandering at bay. Riedy is at ease pastiching Johnnie Johnson or decorating a slow blues, Eckert plays tactful rhythm guitar rather than jostling for space as Dawkins did, and Clearwater's solos have a crackling clarity.

The weak points are a muffled ambience and adequate but everyday vocals.

Wolf find another way to misspell Hizonner, whose song appears in two more (and, it should be said, better) versions. Eight well-recorded studio tracks are notable for Batts's keyboard obbligatos and for Jimmy Johnson, making the most of a generous allocation of solo space on four numbers. There are some strong originals (and yet another 'Came Up The Hard Way') alongside the mayoral mantra, and the Chuck Berry soundalike '2 x 9' has freshness and flair. A 1977 club set is there to fill the disc, and is surfeited with standards. Abb Locke is occasionally out of step, but 'The Things I Used To Do' is the only outright disappointment, and even 'Johnny B. Goode' rings a bell for most of his 7.40.

***(*) The Chief
Rooster Blues R 2615 *Clearwater; Abb Locke (ts); Chuck Smith (bs); Carey Bell (h); Lafayette Leake (p); Lurrie Bell (g); Joe Harrington (b); Casey Jones (d); Leroy Brown (maracas, v). 11/79.*

**(*) Eddy Clearwater & Carey Bell
Wolf 120.869 *Clearwater; Chuck Smith (ts); Carey Bell (h, v); Allen Batts (p); Bob Stroger (b); Casey Jones (d). 80.*

***(*) Flimdoozie
Rooster Blues RBLU 2622 *Clearwater; Abb Locke (ts, bs); Sugar Blue (h); Leo Davis (o, p); Otis Rush, Will Crosby (g); Herman Applewhite (b); Tim Austin (d); Leroy Brown (v). 9/85–4/86.*

**(*) Blues Hang Out
Black & Blue BB 460 *Clearwater; Will Crosby (g); Herman Applewhite (b); Tim Austin (d); Big Time Sarah (v). 12/89.*

**(*) Blues Hang Out
Evidence ECD 26008 *As above. 12/89.*

**(*) Help Yourself
Blind Pig BP 74792 *Clearwater; Carey Bell, Little Mike (h); Will Crosby (g); Bob Stroger, Kurt Krahnke (b); Brian 'B. J.' Jones (d); Jeff Taylor (v). 92?*

Clearwater made three albums for Rooster, but though formally in catalogue, *A Real Good Time – Live!* (Rooster Blues R 2625) has proven elusive. Previous CDs track his progress from imitator to creator: *The Chief* arrives at maturity. The influences are still obvious, but Clearwater has absorbed them and synthesized his own version of the West Side sound. Its delivery is enhanced by a cohort of skilful, enthusiastic veterans and three family members; then 20 years old, Lurrie Bell supplies at least one of the polished guitar solos. All tracks except 'I'm Tore Up' are originals and – with the exception of 'One Day At A Time', which is eco-blah, set to an irritating tune – attractive ones.

The Wolf CD starts well, with a breezy revival of 'I'm Gonna Move (To The Outskirts Of Town)', but soon falls into the common traps of live recording: stale songs spun out with pointless solos, musical facetiousness (even 'I'm Gonna Move' includes a 'what was he thinking?' Satchmo imitation) and obsequious announcements. Allen Batts plays wonderful piano throughout, and Casey Jones is a rock, but this band is otherwise less than the sum of its parts.

As was surely intended, Otis Rush's presence on five of *Flimdoozie*'s eight tracks is its major selling point. His gilded lines dart through the vocals, and some memorable solos goad Clearwater to his instrumental best. With all that going on, the solid contributions of the other musicians are in danger of being overlooked, especially Will Crosby, whose outro on the otherwise trivial title track is a little gem. On this CD as elsewhere, Clearwater the singer sometimes tries to simulate the West Side's trademark emotional bravura by unattractive bawling. Its other drawback is the sense that a checklist is being ticked off: fast blues, minor-key blues, rock 'n' roll, oops! nearly forgot the topical number.

The band on *Blues Hang Out* is that on *Flimdoozie*, minus the guest musicians. Recorded in Black & Blue's usual haste, it probably features the band's setlist (because playable without much rehearsal), plus three poor Big Mama Thornton imitations. This is a mostly lacklustre CD, with numerous familiar songs recurring. Among them are an unexpectedly fine version of 'I Came Up The Hard Way', featuring a note-perfect rendition of Otis Rush's solo from 'All Your Love (I Miss Loving)', and a more tedious than ever 'Chicago Daley Blues', revived thanks to the working of heredity in Chicago politics.

On *Help Yourself*, Clearwater seems to have had to: this is another under-produced disc, which starts off-puttingly, with a Jimmy Reed song sandwiched between two trivial novelties. There's some improvement thereafter: the minor-key 'Messed Up World' is one of Clearwater's best topical efforts, and 'Chicago Weather Woman' and 'Big Time Gambler' arouse regret that he hasn't done more singing in their mellow, T-Bone Walkerish manner. Crosby and Bell do some good work, but have to battle a stodgy, over-loud rhythm section.

*** Mean Case Of The Blues
Bullseye Blues CD BB 9584//Cleartone CR 9601 *Clearwater; Steven Frost (t); Mike Peavy (s); Billy Branch (h); Allen Batts, Jerry Soto (kb); Mark Wydra (g); Dave Knopf (b); Jerry Porter, Brian Jones (d); Alyssa Jaquelyn (v).* 96?

**(*) Cool Blues Walk
Bullseye Blues & Jazz 9614 *Clearwater; Al Basile (c); Doug James (bcl, bs); Dennis Taylor (ts); Jerry Portnoy (h); Tom West (o, p); Marilynn Mair (md, mandola); Mark Davis (md, mandocello); Duke Robillard (g); John Packer (b); Marty Richards (d, maracas).* 98.

**** Reservation Blues
Bullseye Blues & Jazz 9636 *Clearwater; Dennis Taylor (ts); Doug James (bs); Carey Bell (h); Matt McCabe (p); Duke Robillard (g); John Packer, Patrick McKeever (b); Jeff McAllister (d, perc).* 00.

**(*) Rock 'N' Roll City
Bullseye Blues 9640 *Clearwater; Dennis Taylor (ts, bs); Steve Conn (o, p); George Bradfute (bj, g, b); Eddie Angel, Danny Amis (g); Pete Curry (b); Jimmy Lester (d).* 03?

At 60-plus, Clearwater can no longer strain after vocal intensity, and his singing on Bullseye is the better for it, ranging from a hoarsely soulful bark to relaxed smoothness. *Mean Case Of The Blues* elicits good performances from the musicians, with Branch and (as ever) Batts leading the pack, but some of the material arouses qualms: covers of Nat 'King' Cole's 'Send For Me' and Gene Allison's platitudinous 'You Can Make It If You Try' are unsuccessful, and there's an overdose of blues about singing the blues. The next two releases were co-produced by Duke Robillard, and feature his band. *Cool Blues Walk* mixes deftly arranged soul and rockabilly with the blues, which include a defiantly retro, utterly convincing Willie Dixon impersonation on 'I Just Want To Make Love To You'. The entire CD is devalued, however, by the abysmal 'I Love You', with its bathetic lyrics and clichéd melody. *Reservation Blues* is, finally, an almost unqualified success; 'Easy Is My Style', though not disastrous, is one more confirmation that Eddy shouldn't cover Magic Sam. 'I Wouldn't Lay My Guitar Down' (one of three fine rock 'n' roll numbers) gets a terrific revival, the title track and the blues-gospel hybrid 'Walls Of Hate' are mature and nuanced topical commentary, and Carey Bell plays a tremendous harp obbligato on 'Find Yourself'.

Rock 'N' Roll City is a collaboration with surf guitar revivalists Los Straitjackets; it starts out as a jolly set of up-tempo blues and rock 'n' roll, including a romping revival of 'Hillbilly Blues' from 1958, but there's a serious loss of focus midway. The Rubicon is crossed at 'Before This Song Is Over', another soppy Clearwater ballad, whose innate unattractiveness is compounded by a rickety vocal. 'Let The Four Winds Blow', which also has pitch problems, is sung with surprising apathy, and a banal Christmas ditty makes an anticlimactic closer. CS

Willie Cobbs (born 1932)
VOCAL, HARMONICA

Born in Arkansas, Cobbs headed for Chicago in 1947, and was in the Army during the '50s, but for many years he's been back in the South, operating clubs and recording for small local labels. Several of these were set up by Cobbs himself, using the royalties from his much-covered hit 'You Don't Love Me'.

**(*) Down To Earth
Rooster Blues R 2628 *Cobbs; Winston Stewart (o, p); L. C. Luckett (syn, p, g, tamb); Johnny Rawls (g, b, v); John Mohead (g); Leonard Washington (d); Vera Cobbs (v).* 94?

**(*) Jukin'
Bullseye Blues & Jazz 9629 *Cobbs; Scott Thompson (t); Jim Spake, Lannie McMillan (ts); James Mitchell (bs); John Weston (h); Charlie Hodges (o); Fred Hodges (p); Mabon 'Teenie' Hodges, Earl The Pearl [Banks], Thomas Bingham (g); Leroy Hodges (b); Howard Grimes (d); Bertram Brown, Mashaa, William Brown (v).* 00?

Since these CDs appeared, Cobbs has issued *Pay Or Do 11 Months & 29 Days* (Wilco WCD 1004) on the latest of his own labels, which appears to have ceased operations. *Down To Earth* and *Jukin'* are uneasy blends of downhome blues and retro soul. On the former Rawls and Luckett, formerly of the O. V. Wright band, collaborate with Cobbs on the arrangements, and are co-composers of four tracks. Cobbs composed the rest, among them a revival of 'You Don't Love Me'. He comes up with some imaginative lyrics, but for the most part they get insipid, cluttered production. Much of *Jukin'* consists of familiar standards. The Hi house band, some sturdy brass arrangements and Willie Mitchell's co-production save the material from staleness, but some tracks are over-extended, and the occasional rock-influenced slide guitar is a mistake. The main drawback of both discs, however, is Cobbs himself; his harmonica playing is often thin and shrill, and as a singer he's a ham actor who tries to impose excitement and urgency by haphazard, unmotivated changes of vocal tone. CS

James Cole
VOCAL, VIOLIN, GUITAR

This mysterious figure led a Depression-era band of great versatility.

*** Tommie Bradley–James Cole Groups (1928–1932)
Document DOCD-5189 *Cole; unknown (as); poss. Sam Soward*

(p); Eddie Dimmitt (md); Tommie Bradley (g, v); Buster Johnson (poss. g, v); unknown (b); unknown (k); Roosevelt Pursley (j); unknown (wb); unknown(s) (v). 6/28–1/32.

At five sessions held over three and a half years, various permutations of the above musicians wove the 15 pieces of a quilt that historians of African-American music still finger with fascination. Lining up now as a stringband, now a washboard band, now a jugband, the Cole men deliver vaudeville songs ('Adam And Eve'), standard popular songs ('Runnin' Wild', 'Sweet Sue'), old-time breakdowns ('Bill Cheatum', 'I Got A Gal') and blues whose melodies and violin playing recall the early work of Lonnie Johnson. Yet members of the crew could turn from that kind of repertoire to an *au courant* blues like 'Pack Up Her Trunk Blues' or 'Please Don't Act That Way', which are both done in a style surely derived from Leroy Carr and Scrapper Blackwell.

Confusion with the Coles and Colemans of Cincinnati (exacerbated by the inclusion of some of their work in this collection) has led some commentators to locate this group of musicians in that city. No one there has ever remembered them. The Carr/Blackwell association and Cole's involvement as guitar accompanist with Alura Mack and other singers make at least as good a case for a provenance in or around Indianapolis – where their first release, 'Bill Cheatum'/'I Got A Gal', was actually recorded. Whatever the band's origin, its recordings encode valuable information about ill-documented musical practices. TR

Deborah Coleman (born 1956)
VOCAL, GUITAR

Coleman was born in Portsmouth, Virginia, grew up in a musical family, was playing guitar by the age of eight, and at 15 was in her first band. She took some years off to raise her daughter Misao and work as an electrician, but returned to the business in 1994, forming the first lineup of the Thrillseekers. She presently lives in Chesapeake, Virginia.

**(*) Takin' A Stand
New Moon NMC 9406 Coleman; Randy Friel (o, p, syn); Skeeter Brandon (o, v); Ann Rabson (p); Armand Lenchek, Max Drake (g); Ben Palmer, Calvin Johnson (b); Ed Butler, Russ Wilson (d); Shelly Flynt, Allison King (v). 94?

**(*) I Can't Lose
Blind Pig BPCD 5038 Coleman; Paryss, Joanna Connor (g); Chuck Webb (b); Slam (d). 97?

**(*) Where Blue Begins
Blind Pig BPCD 5048 Coleman; Mike Vlahakis (kb); James Solberg, Joanna Connor (g); John Lundberg (b); Robb Stupka (d); Ollie Bolds (v). 98?

Coleman's guitar playing on these early albums – economical, pithy, unostentatious – is more impressive than her singing, which has plenty of attitude but doesn't reveal a voice with a great deal of range or texture. *Where Blue Begins* is the better of the Blind Pigs inasmuch as she's playing with more sophisticated musicians, the James Solberg Band, but the unvaryingness of the settings has a similar effect to the drab studio sound of its predecessor, in that it leaches some of the colour and character out of Coleman's music. Both are more evident in *Takin' A Stand*, especially in the forceful title number, but all three sets find a talented artist searching unsuccessfully for an ideal conjunction of musicians, material and something more.

**(*) Soft Place To Fall
Blind Pig BPCD 5061/Ruf 1049 Coleman; Billy Gibson (h); Ernest Williamson Jr (kb, o); Jack Holder, Billy Crawford (g); Dave Smith (b); Steve Potts, Marty Binder (d). 00?

**(*) Livin' On Love
Blind Pig BPCD 5070 Coleman; Al Gamble (p); Billy Crawford, Jimmy Thackery (g); Debra 'Nardi' Salyer (b); Marty Binder (d); Reba Russell (v). 01?

Coleman may have expected to find new doors opening to her with Jim Gaines's sleek production of *Soft Place To Fall* for her calling-card. Certainly radio stations not in the habit of playlisting blues artists could well have felt comfortable with sassy AOR numbers like 'Look What You Do To Me', 'So Damn Easy' or the title cut with its springy Dire Straitsish guitar line – let alone the punchier 'Nothin' To Do With Love', a song one could easily imagine done, not very differently, by Tina Turner. Listeners who insist on blues content can take refuge in the grooves of 'Another Hoping Fool', 'What Goes Around' or 'I'm A Woman', as well as in Coleman's consistently incisive guitar playing.

Only three songs on *Soft Place To Fall* are Coleman's; *Livin' On Love* doubles the quota, which from the perspective of this survey is not necessarily an improvement, though 'Don't Talk In My Sleep' is quite ingenious. Compositions by Lowell Fulson ('Bending Like A Willow Tree') and Mighty Mo Rodgers ('Heaven's Got The Blues') offer a partial blues counterweight.

*** Soul Be It!
Blind Pig BPCD 5079 Coleman; Billy Crawford (g); Debra 'Nardi' Salyer (b, v); Jason Paul (d). 02?

Coleman had recorded all eight of these songs on her studio albums, but implies that she enjoyed the opportunity of remaking them in a concert setting (the Sierra Nevada Brewery in Chico, California). 'The "live" performance for me,' she says, 'is nothing short of mesmerizing,' and listeners who aren't made restive by such things may likewise be captivated by the extended guitar solos in 'I'm A Woman' or 'Goodbye Misery' (the latter by Crawford). Stretched though the music may be, it is seldom thin. Coleman sounds more relaxed, and there's a little more colour in her singing. This is the easiest of her albums to recommend.

** What About Love?
Telarc CD-83595 Coleman; Ken Clark (o); Hiromasa Suzuki (g); Noel Neal (b); Per Hanson (d). 11/03.

Moving to Telarc, Coleman equips herself with new musicians and material but reveals no new aspect of her music. Her mission statement for the album was to 'keep it real ... live and spontaneous'; it isn't, in fact, a live recording, but an unpretentious studio production with uncomplicated arrangements. Consequently one's attention is focused on the songs and Coleman's handling of them. As a singer with style rather than power, she requires strong songs if she is to do herself justice, and here fails to come up with any. Only the opening track, 'Bad Boy', has a conventional blues form, and neither that nor the other numbers are likely to impress themselves on the listener's imagination or memory. TR

George Coleman (1923–99)
VOCAL, WHISTLING, OIL DRUMS, MARACAS, PIANO

Born in Florida, Coleman learned to play the standard drumkit aged 12, and wandered in Texas, working as a labourer and street entertainer. He started hitting 55-gallon oil drums with padded hammer handles in the late '40s, and played for tourists in Galveston between 1954 and 1968, when he moved the act to San Antonio. He was ill, and consequently inactive, from the early '90s.

*** Bongo Joe
Arhoolie CD-1040 *Coleman.* 7/68.

George 'Bongo Joe' Coleman's serio-comic spoken philosophies are in a tradition that goes back to Bert Williams and forward to rap. Improvised instruments have also been a persistent feature of music in the African diaspora, although Coleman's steel drums, unlike those of the Trinidadian pan orchestras, were not pitched. He did modify them to achieve the sound he wanted, however – with an axe and a hammer. (Coleman was also a self-taught piano player, good enough to jam with Dizzy Gillespie at the New Orleans Jazz & Heritage Festival one year; 'After Hours', his only issued recording on piano, is one of two tracks on *Field Recordings Vol. 6: Texas (1933–1958)* [Document DOCD-5580].) His street performances mainly featured drum-accompanied whistling of jazz and pop tunes, but Arhoolie understandably encouraged him to monologize, and to sing, just once, on the ironic, all too accurately titled, 'I Wish I Could Sing'.

All this is perhaps no more than appealingly eccentric; what makes Bongo Joe unique is the sour, satirical surrealism of his commentaries. He took a jaundiced view of men, women, preachers, police forces and governments, and the results – even if occasional blues formulas do find their way into his stream of consciousness – are like nothing else in black music. ('You don't do it according to Hoyle, you don't do it according to Nietzsche or Socrates; you have to do it according to yourself.') Not easy on the ears, George Coleman is a treat for the mind; this is not a CD one wants to play very often, but when one does, there's no substitute. CS

Jaybird Coleman (1896–1950)
VOCAL, HARMONICA

Born in Gainesville, Georgia, Burl C. Coleman spent much of his life in Alabama, where he reportedly worked on minstrel shows.

***(*) Jaybird Coleman & The Birmingham Jug Band (1927–1930)
Document DOCD-5140 *Coleman; poss. Ollis Martin (h); Vance Patterson, unknown (p); Bertha Ross (v); unknown (wh).* 7/27–4/30.
*** Alabama Blues
Wolf WSE 113 *As above.* 7/27–4/30.

Most of Coleman's 15 recordings, gathered on the Document, are solos, but it is difficult not to think of them as dialogues with his harmonica, which does not merely alternate with the sung lines but responds equally or even, at times, more expressively. The power of these performances depends greatly on Coleman's ability to set his own rhythmic agenda; on the few recordings in which other instruments are involved he sounds constrained. If his recorded work gives us a true picture, Coleman, unlike most of his contemporaries, had no interest in using the harmonica for sound effects, such as imitating trains or fox chases; his art, you might say, is abstract rather than representational. As such it is austere, with none of the winsomeness of tune players like Noah Lewis or Will Shade, but the listener willing to decipher it through the storm of surface noise will be rewarded with music of compelling emotional force. All but two of these recordings are also on *Alabama Blues*, a VAC completed by the work of harmonica players 'Bullet' Williams and Ollis Martin and a few cuts by Clifford Gibson. TR

Jesse 'Monkey Joe' Coleman
VOCAL, PIANO

Coleman was born in New Orleans, perhaps in the first decade of the 20th century, and raised in Jackson, Mississippi. His half-brother was the pianist Coot Davis. Around the mid-'30s he was using the name Monkey Joe and working in both cities. Later he moved to Chicago, where he made numerous records in 1938–39. Then and later he frequently worked with Walter Vinson, and recorded with him for Riverside in 1961. He is believed to have died in 1966.

**(*) Monkey Joe – Vol. 1 (1935–1939)
Document DOCD-5412 *Coleman; unknown (cl); Buster Bennett (as); Blind John Davis (p); Charlie McCoy (md, g); Walter Vincson, Willie B. James (g); Ransom Knowling, unknown (b); Fred Williams (d); Lulu Scott (v).* 8/35–3/39.
**(*) Monkey Joe – Vol. 2/Roosevelt Scott (1939–1940)
Document DOCD-5413 *Coleman; Buster Bennett (as); Blind John Davis (p); Willie B. James, Big Bill Broonzy (g); Alfred Elkins (vocal b); Fred Williams (d); Roosevelt Scott (v).* 3–9/39.

Coleman was one of numerous recording artists in the '30s who, lacking the distinction to stand out from their surroundings, melted into them to create moderately satisfying but essentially anonymous music. With his high, plaintive voice and matter-of-fact piano playing he somewhat resembles Curtis Jones, particularly when accompanied by the same musicians (McCoy, James, Williams). His first recordings, with guitarist Walter Vinson, are by some way his best, the piano playing marked by imagination and a firm touch. The imagination, at least, is much diminished on his later sides, with an occasional exception like 'New York Central', which uses the melody of 'Vicksburg Blues' and which Coleman executes with the skill to be expected of a sometime acquaintance of Little Brother Montgomery.

The 3/39 session spread across the two volumes is among the dullest of a dull period, guitar and drums combining in a monotonous thump while the singer plods through eight blues sharing two melodies. Buster Bennett blows alto manfully, but doesn't succeed in putting any wind beneath Coleman's wings. The following session, Coleman's last in his name, replaces the drummer with Alfred Elkins vocalizing the bass part, a small improvement. Coleman was also the pianist on the dozen recordings, made at two sessions in 1939 and '40, by Roosevelt Scott, a singing acquaintance from Jackson, Mississippi. The playing is formulaic but Scott delivers his well-written blues briskly in a style pitched between Peetie Wheatstraw and Johnnie Temple.

Coleman's last recordings, with Vinson in 1961, are on

Chicago: The Living Legends – South Side Blues (Original Blues Classics OBCCD 508). TR

Michael Coleman (born 1956)
VOCAL, GUITAR

Coleman was born and raised in Chicago, a son of the drummer Cleo Williams, alias Baldhead Pete. He first learned bass guitar, then guitar. In his teens he was in a Top 40 band but also worked with Johnny Dollar, Johnny Christian and, for much of the '80s, James Cotton, playing on his Alligator albums High Compression and Live From Chicago.

(*) **Back Breaking Blues (Chicago Blues Session Vol. 18)
Wolf 120.865 Coleman; Johnny Cotton (tb); James Lockett (s); Professor Eddie Lusk, Joachim Palden (p); Frank Collier (b, v); Donald Coleman (d). 10/90.

*** **Shake Your Booty**
Wolf 120.880 Coleman; Mike Joung (s); John Choeny (o, p); Mike Sterling (b); Merle Perkins, Donald Coleman (d). 3/94.

***(*) **Do Your Thing!**
Delmark DE-747 Coleman; Kenny Anderson (t); Bill McFarland (tb); Hank Ford (ts); Matthew Skoller, Todd Bartelstein (h); Marty Sammon (kb); Vince Varco (syn); Willie 'Vamp' Samuels, Sam Green (b); Merle Perkins (d). 7/00.

'You can't change the blues,' Coleman says, 'the only thing you can do is just make it funky', and his staccato guitar playing is a perfect expression of that philosophy. But although the rhythms and accents of his music reflect the listening and playing experiences of his youth in the '70s, they have also been shaped by two decades of solid blues work. Consequently he can move from a slow, melancholic blues to a funky party number, as he does on Shake Your Booty when he follows 'Lost My Job In The City' with 'Shake Your Booty', and by sheer force of musical personality make the abrupt gear-change feel smooth and well-judged.

Coleman was first heard on record in his own right on Alligator's showcase album The New Bluebloods (ALCD 7707); the song he used there, 'Woman Love [A] Woman', is redone on Back Breaking Blues and is one of the best performances on a confident but somewhat unrelaxed album. Shake Your Booty, though it has a few warhorses on board ('Got My Mojo Working', 'Kansas City', 'Tore Down'), is the better CD, Coleman adeptly making his rhythmic point by playing both lead and rhythm guitar parts. But Do Your Thing! is his application to front-rank status, and as such very persuasive indeed. It's a valuable gift that he always sounds as if he's not only absorbed in his music but enjoying it. Whether sending a funky 'Message Of Love' or skilfully handling his middleweight voice so that it can bear the load of serious blues like 'Cold, Cold Feeling' and 'Tin Pan Alley', he exudes an infectious pleasure in being able to do what he does so well. TR

Albert Collins (1932–93)
VOCAL, GUITAR, HARMONICA

Collins grew up in Houston, learning guitar from his cousin Lightnin' Hopkins, and was leading a band before he was out of his teens. 'Freeze' (1958) was a regional hit, and he had others in the early '60s, but he didn't find a larger stage for his dramatic performances until he moved to LA in 1968 and began recording for Imperial. Even so, he found it impossible to make a living from music, and spent most of the '70s working in construction. The turnaround in his fortunes came in 1978, when he began to be managed by Bruce Iglauer and record for Alligator. In 1985 he was the only black blues artist to appear at the Live Aid concerts, and then only in a guest spot with George Thorogood, but in the same year he shared a Grammy with Johnny Copeland and Robert Cray for Showdown!

*** **Truckin' With Albert Collins**
MCA MCAD 10423 Collins; Frank Mitchell (t); Henry Hayes (as); Big Tiny (ts); Walter McNeill (o); Bill Johnson (b); Herbert Henderson (d). 62/63.

Collins serves treats like 'Frosty', 'Kool Aide' and 'Sno-Cone Part II' (what happened to Part I?) from his Telecaster deep-freeze. All the tracks are instrumentals except for the slow blues 'Dyin' Flu'. A short album, and terribly of-its-time, but with undeniable charm.

(*) **Love Can Be Found Anywhere (Even In A Guitar)/Trash Talkin'
BGO BGOCD 364 Collins; unknowns (brass, reeds, o, b, d). 68–69.

(*) **The Complete Imperial Recordings
EMI CDP-7-96740 2CD As above, except add unknowns (p, g). 68–70.

Collins's Imperial albums had a patchouli waft of the hippie era, but more in the way they looked than in their contents. That said, they stand up to inspection less sturdily than the Alligators that followed them, partly because Collins does little singing – the majority of the tracks are instrumentals or talking blues – and partly because the proceedings are conducted at a brisk tempo di jukebox. But anyone who likes Texas guitar shuffles, especially when played with superior accompanists, imaginatively produced and well engineered, will enjoy a lot of what's on these albums. BGO simply reissue the first and second LPs, while The Complete adds the third, The Compleat [sic] Albert Collins.

** **Thaw Out At The Fillmore**
Snapper Complete Blues SBLUECD 032 Collins; unknowns (o, b, d). 69.

This set, taped – not too badly – at the Fillmore West in San Francisco, has been round the block a few times, for instance as Live At The Fillmore West (Catfish KATCD 156) and part of Rockin' With The Ice Man (Blue Boar CDBB 1001) and In Concert (Castle CLACD 427) (all deleted). The hollow acoustic of the hall emphasizes the chill factor of Collins's playing on tunes like 'Thaw Out' and 'Deep Freeze', but his singing is rather tentative, a couple of the tracks are inconsequential and on the whole the concert setting doesn't tell us anything we didn't know, or couldn't have guessed, about his music.

♛ **** **Ice Pickin'**
Alligator ALCD 4713 Collins; A. C. Reed (ts); Chuck Smith (bs); Alan [Allen] Batts (kb); Larry Burton (g); Aron Burton (b); Casey Jones (d). summer 78.

*** **Frostbite**
Alligator ALCD 4719 Collins; Paul Howard (t); Bill McFarland (tb); Jerry Wilson (ts); Henri Ford (bs); A. C. Reed (s); Allen

Batts (kb); Marvin Jackson (g); Johnny Gayden (b); Casey Jones (d). 79.
*** Frozen Alive
Alligator ALCD 4725 *Collins; A. C. Reed (ts); Allen Batts (o); Johnny B. Gayden (b); Casey Jones (d). 3/81.*
**(*) Don't Lose Your Cool
Alligator ALCD 4730 *Collins; Abb Locke, Dino Spells (as, ts); A. C. Reed (ts); Chris Foreman (kb); Larry Burton (g); Johnny B. Gayden (b); Casey Jones (d, v). 81.*
**(*) Live In Japan
Alligator ALCD 4733 *Collins; A. C. Reed (ts, v); Larry Burton (g); Johnny B. Gayden (b); Casey Jones (d, v). 12/82.*

It was easy to say at the time that *Ice Pickin'* was Collins's finest record, since its predecessors had always had a strong whiff of their time, and by the late '70s it was beginning to smell a little stale. His Alligator debut was an astute blend of instrumentals from his personal freezer ('Frosty', 'Sno-Cone'), dryly humorous pieces like Lowell Fulson's 'Honey, Hush!' and Johnny 'Guitar' Watson's 'Too Tired', and wholly serious numbers like Freddie King's 'When The Welfare Turns Its Back On You' and T-Bone Walker's 'Cold, Cold Feeling'. Though little of the material is his own, he gives everything an entirely personal treatment, boldly coloured by jabbing, expressive guitar lines.

Frostbite isn't quite so exciting but has some striking things like 'Don't Go Reaching', the sort of crazy-going-on-surreal song you might expect to find Willie Dixon's name on, and 'Snowed In', a nine-minute narration with effects. *Frozen Alive* was recorded at a bar in Minneapolis, which explains crowd-pleasers like 'Caldonia' and 'Things I Used To Do'; the deepest performance here is a fervent eight-minute version of 'Angel Of Mercy'. *Don't Lose Your Cool* continues the chilly wordplay with the title track and Oscar Brown Jr's 'But I Was Cool!', a piece that probably came across better live. It also follows its predecessors' implied rules in including a couple of long, slow numbers, the better of which is Percy Mayfield's 'My Mind Is Trying To Leave Me'. But somehow the most gripping moments of previous albums are never quite revisited, and for once Collins seems to be merely huffing and puffing rather than genuinely blowing hot (or cold). *Live In Japan* boasts a vigorous performance and good concert ambience, but doesn't seem to have worn quite as well as the other Alligator albums. 'Stormy Monday' starts strongly but the mood is dissipated, and the best track is the eight-minute 'If Trouble Was Money'.

**** Showdown!
Alligator ALCD 4743 *Collins; Allen Batts (o); Johnny Copeland, Robert Cray (g, v); Johnny B. Gayden (b); Casey Jones (d). 85.*
*** Cold Snap
Alligator ALCD 4752 *Collins; Hollywood Paul Litteral (t); Bob Funk (tb); Crispin Cioe (as, bs); Arno Hecht (ts); Jimmy McGriff, Allen Batts (kb); Mel Brown (g); Johnny B. Gayden (b); Morris Jennings (d, perc). 86.*

Showdown! is a six-hander with Johnny Copeland and Robert Cray; Collins, as senior partner, receives first billing, is the sole singer on 'The Moon Is Full' and 'Blackjack' and contributes vocally or instrumentally (or both) to all the other tracks, taking one of his infrequent harmonica outings on 'Bring Your Fine Self Home' and reminiscing amiably with Copeland about the old days in Houston on 'Black Cat Bone'. His long solo in the middle of Cray's feature 'The Dream' is one of the most incendiary passages in his entire output.

Cold Snap is an unusually lively studio album; no doubt Collins, who was already on a roll careerwise, was also excited to be working with musicians like Mel Brown and Jimmy McGriff. 'Lights Are On But Nobody's Home' and the cheating blues 'Too Many Dirty Dishes' are the longest tracks and maybe the strongest, but 'A Good Fool Is Hard To Find' and the playful 'I Ain't Drunk' aren't far behind.

*** DeLuxe Edition
Alligator ALCD 5601 *As for all previous Alligator CDs.* summer 78–86.

A pretty good, often excellent selection from Collins's Alligator back catalogue, including 'Master Charge' and 'When The Welfare Turns Its Back On You' from *Ice Pickin'*, 'If Trouble Was Money' (*Live In Japan*) and 'I Ain't Drunk' (*Cold Snap*), as well as *Frozen Alive*'s 'Cold Cuts', a feature for Gayden's hyperactive bass playing.

**(*) Iceman
Pointblank VPBCD 3 *Collins; Hollywood Paul Litteral (t); Bob Funk (tb); Crispin Cioe (as, bs); Arno Hecht (ts); Eddie Harsch (kb); Charles Hodges (o); Debbie Davies, Mabon 'Teenie' Hodges, Jack Holder (g); Johnny B. Gayden (b); Soko Richardson (d, perc); Debbie Jamison, Vicki Loveland (v); Jim Gaines (prod). 91.*
**(*) Collins Mix
Charisma 39097//Pointblank VPBCD 17 *Collins; Steve Howard, Wayne Jackson (t); Jon Smith, Jeff Robbins, Branford Marsalis, Andrew Love (s); Kim Wilson (h); Ernest Williamson (kb, o); Coco Montoya, Nico Lyras, Gary Moore, B. B. King, Michael Toles (g); Johnny B. Gayden (b); Marty Binder (d); Jim Gaines (co-prod). 92/93.*
*** Live '92–'93
Pointblank (A) 40658//(E) VPBCD 27 *Collins; Steve Howard (t); Jon Smith, Jeff Robbins (ts); Bobby Alexis (o); Pete Thoennes (g); Johnny B. Gayden (b); Marty Binder (d). 7/92–9/93.*

Iceman, Collins's first album for Virgin's new blues label, accentuated the funk elements in his music, a strategy to which bassist Gayden was very well equipped to contribute. What with purely instrumental tracks ('Blues For Gabe') and ones with low vocal content ('Mister Collins, Mister Collins', 'Put The Shoe On The Other Foot', 'Head Rag'), this seems at times like a regression to Collins's Imperial days, but there's a long slow blues of high quality, 'Don't Mistake Kindness For Weakness'.

Collins Mix, his last studio recording, could have been titled *Collins Remix*, since virtually all the tracks are remakes of numbers on other albums, such as 'Mastercharge', 'Don't Lose Your Cool' and 'The Moon Is Full'. Neither the horn arrangements nor the guest appearances – by Branford Marsalis on 'Honey Hush', Gary Moore on 'If Trouble Was Money', B. B. King on 'Frosty' and Kim Wilson on 'Tired Man' – go very far towards transforming the material, which makes the album rather superfluous. You might jump to a similar conclusion about the contents of *Live '92–'93*, which are all previously recorded pieces too, but that would be doing the album an injustice. The nearly 11-minute version of 'Lights Are On But Nobody's Home', with a squalling tenor solo by Smith and some characteristically playful guitar, is a vivid example of Collins in person as many will fondly remember him, and the whole album has loads of atmosphere. TR

Sam Collins (1887–1949)
VOCAL, GUITAR

Collins's stamping ground was the Mississippi–Louisiana border region, and his music has stylistic affinities with King Solomon Hill and Ramblin' Thomas, also from those parts. At some time after his recording career ended, Collins migrated to Chicago.

**** Sam Collins (1927–1931)
Document DOCD-5034 *Collins; John D. Fox (v). 4/27–10/31.*
***(*) Jailhouse Blues
Yazoo 1079 *Collins. 4/27–10/31.*

Black Patti advertised 'Crying Sam Collins and His Git-Fiddle', and it's his falsetto singing that is immediately striking. Although often described as eerie, it lacks the banshee weirdness of King Solomon Hill, but neither does Collins seek the refined elegance of a Joe Pullum. What he offers, rather, is rough but controlled power; his voice seems to have an in-built echo chamber, surging, fading, and riding the waves of its own melisma like a surfer, perfectly poised but always aware of the roiling energy underneath. Collins's guitar playing makes no claim to virtuosity, and it has often been pointed out that he is sometimes out of tune by the standards of concert music. In practice, this is not a problem, for the guitar fits perfectly with his singing, functioning, especially when he plays slide, as a responding and commenting second voice. Perhaps more likely to distract listeners is Collins's grasp of blues chord sequence, which is imperfect, especially on his earlier recordings; the harmonies sometimes change in unexpected places, and verses have to be extended beyond the intended 12 bars before they can be resolved. However, any listener who knows that creation precedes codification will recognize in Collins an artist who is working within a conscious, consistent aesthetic. As might be expected from his date of birth, his playlist bridges the gap between blues and the earlier African-American repertoire of minstrel and medicine-show songs; conscious of the need to cover hits like 'Yellow Dog Blues', 'Hesitation Blues' and 'Salty Dog', Collins also made the first recording of 'The Midnight Special', and elsewhere produces such striking and original images as 'Yonder come the Devil, for to set this town on fire.'

Yazoo's 16-title selection has that company's usual merits, of quality remastering and thoughtful programming, but Document's completeness is to be preferred. Of six titles not on *Jailhouse Blues*, two where Collins accompanies John D. Fox are mainly interesting for the obvious influence of Ramblin' Thomas, but another two are quite simply Collins's masterpieces. 'Lonesome Road Blues', sung in the tenor register, and the originally unissued 'My Road Is Rough And Rocky' are respectively versions of 'In The Pines' and the prison song 'Long Gone'. On both of them, the imperiousness of Collins's singing and the otherworldly strangeness of his lyrics generate performances that haunt the memory. These songs are absent from *Jailhouse Blues* only because Yazoo had already issued them, on *Lonesome Road Blues: 15 Years In The Mississippi Delta 1926–1941* (Yazoo 1038), but they are much better heard in context. CS

Joanna Connor (born 1962)
VOCAL, GUITAR

Connor grew up in Worcester, Massachusetts. She took up music as a career in 1981 and three years later moved to Chicago, where she played with Johnny Littlejohn and Dion Payton's 43rd Street Blues Band before forming her own band in 1987.

*** Believe It!
Blind Pig BP 73289 *Connor; Garrick Patton (as); Phil Baron (kb); Anthony Palmer (g); Stan Mixon (b); B. J. Jones (d); John Zdon (tamb); Matt Snyder (cga); Jacqueline Parker, Denise Parker (v). 89.*
**(*) Fight
Blind Pig BPCD 5002 *Connor; Scott Thompson (t); Jim Spake (s); Greg Redding (kb); Anthony Palmer (g); Stan Mixon (b); Tim Austin, Brian 'BJ' Jones (d); Jackie Reddick, Jackie Johnson (v); Jim Gaines (prod). 92.*

Connor stands out among blues-rock guitarists. Although she can play a barnstorming solo with the best of them, she is as eloquent in the concise language of the blues as she is in the prolixity of rock. *Believe It!* was a very confident debut, on which she tackled songs by or associated with Freddie King, Robert Cray, Billy The Kid Emerson and Aretha Franklin, as well as a couple of her own. *Fight*, after Robert Johnson's 'Walkin' Blues', is mostly original songs, which are likeable but undistinguished, though the busy rhythmic figures created by Palmer and Mixon do a good deal to make them sound better than that. Connor's singing is feisty but one-dimensional.

*** Big Girl Blues
Ruf 1010//Blind Pig BPCD 5037 *Connor; Larry Ortega (o, d, perc, v); Anthony Palmer, Karl Ratzer (g); Stan Mixon (b, v); John Sass (tu). 96.*
**(*) Slidetime
Blind Pig BPCD 5047 *Connor; Anthony Palmer, Ron Johnson (g); Vic Jackson (b); Boyd Martin (d); Jovaughn Mixon, Darnell Wilcher, Andrea Variames (v). 98.*

Connor is popular in Germany, thanks in part to the support of Thomas Ruf, who has produced recordings by her for Inakustik and his own Ruf label. *Joanna Connor* (Inakustik 9012), *Living On The Road* (Inakustik 9022), *Nothing But The Blues* (Inakustik 9060) and *Rock & Roll Gypsy* (Ruf RRCD 9.01315) are of uncertain availability; not so *Big Girl Blues*, a studio session from Munich. Texturally this is her richest playing on record so far, as she overlays the basic tracks with further guitar parts, sometimes slide figures with a fuzzy, droning sound not unlike Sonny Landreth's. Her singing is stronger and more flexible, too.

Slidetime, recorded in Chicago, brings out more of Connor's versatility on slide guitar, though it's kept quite strictly in an accompanying rather than dominant role, and there are no instrumentals. As with *Big Girl Blues*, conventional blues don't get much of a look-in, though the album ends gently in a 'Pea Vine Blues' (not Charley Patton's) done as an acoustic duet with Ron Johnson.

*(*) The Joanna Connor Band
M.C. MC-0046 *Connor; Ted Reynolds (h); Roosevelt Purifoy (o); Mike Wheeler (g, v); Anthony Palmer (g); Stan Mixon (b); Bryant T. (d, perc, v); Andrew Variames (v). 12/01–01/02.*

Connor speaks in the notes of the 'relief' she feels at being 'finally given the ... gift of being able to make the music I wanted and needed to make' – an implicit slight on her previous labels which will prompt curious listeners to find out what this freedom has achieved. Most obviously, it seems to have released a gush of original songs like 'No Black Or White', 'Lunar Love', 'Six Child' and 'Morning Praise' that are as mawkish and platitudinous as they are melodically dull. TR

Al Cook (born 1945)
VOCAL, PIANO, GUITAR, BASS, JUG, WASHBOARD

As he recounts in his candid autobiographical notes to The White King Of Black Blues, *Cook (born Alois Koch) grew up in a working-class family in Vienna and was drawn to American music at the age of 15 by seeing an Elvis Presley movie. He later discovered blues and has been playing it ever since, either solo or with small groups of like-thinking friends.*

** Victrola Blues
Wolf 120.952 Cook; Chris Sandera (h); Dana Gillespie (p, v); Charlie Lloyd (p); Harry Hudson (g, d, wb, spoons); Mike Jerry (b). 3–4/93.

**(*) The White King Of Black Blues
Wolf 120.959 Cook; Erik Trauner (h, g); Charlie Lloyd, Martin Pyrker, Axel Zwingenberger (p); Chris Peterka (vn); Hans Theesink (md); Robert Shumy (g); Manfred Chromy, Dani Gugolz (b); F. G. Hacker, Harry Hudson (d); Dana Gillespie (v). 7–10/95.

**(*) Down In Boogie Alley
Wolf 120.969 Cook; Charlie Lloyd (p); Robert Shumy (b); Harry Hudson (d, wb, v). 12/97–1/98.

**(*) The Country Blues
Wolf 120.972 Cook; Stephan Rausch (h); Charlie Lloyd (p); Katie Kern, Karin Daym (g, v); Rev. Frank TT (v). 11/00–3/01.

**(*) The Birmingham Jam
Wolf 120.973 As above, except add Chris Peterka (vn), Siggi Fassl (g, v), Harry Hudson (wb, perc, v), Sabine Pyrker (wb). 11/03–6/04.

Cook loves the blues of the '20s and '30s, and idiosyncratically shows it by catching the music in a distorting mirror. The *hommages* which pack *Victrola Blues* are close imitations of the guitarists and pianists he admires, but the lyrics are his own, though they bristle with allusions to the work of his models. This can produce disconcerting effects, when fairly plausible Big Bill or Tampa Red guitar lines or a typical St Louis piano piece are fitted out with unfamiliar verses; the more so when they are delivered in a variety of generic impersonations of black singing. These are sometimes jarring, as in the opening track, 'Bad Boy Blues', where Cook seems to be aiming for the vocal manner of a 'Bullet' Williams or Jaybird Coleman. But what strikes one listener as a crude masquerade may be another's sensitive impression, and perhaps Cook's obvious devotion to the music that inspires him will be sufficient evidence that his intentions are honourable.

His subsequent albums, following the example of *Victrola Blues*, have tracklistings full of familiar-sounding titles that are not what they appear to be, such as 'Heavy Suitcase Blues', 'Ramblin' Man Blues' or 'Old Southland Blues'. These are on *The White King Of Black Blues*, for which he gathered Austrian and other friends to celebrate his 50th birthday. *Down In Boogie Alley* consists of a dozen trio and quartet performances, then five solo numbers with guitar. Cook's singing is still problematic: having achieved in 'Rollin' Man Blues' a polished variation on Robert Johnson's 'Steady Rollin' Man', he spoils its finish with a raw vocal.

The Country Blues, like its forerunners, juggles learned and invented elements to a degree that generally sustains the claim 'All titles by Al Cook', though the experienced listener will not need Cook's detailed notes to identify the input of Tommy Johnson, Bo Weavil Jackson and Blind Lemon Jefferson. The concluding 'Bobo's Boogie' is a piano solo. Cook more than once refers to his 'unfortunate love' of playing blues piano; perhaps this is an oblique apology for not having mastered it, but comparison with his playing on *Victrola Blues* proves that he is coming along nicely.

In *The Birmingham Jam* Cook invents radio station ACBK ('Al Cook's Blues Kitchen') and puts on a programme by himself and his friends, which he links with avuncular comments in an Austro-Afro-American accent which perhaps only his admirers will not find a shade embarrassing. As usual, his command of a variety of blues guitar styles is impressive, his singing inconsistently convincing. Of the rest of the gang the most striking player is Katie Kern, who contributes a couple of lissom lead guitar parts. TR

Henry Cooper
VOCAL, GUITAR, HARMONICA

Cooper began playing blues harmonica as a teenager in Eugene, Oregon, after hearing a record of the Paul Butterfield Band. He took up guitar a few years later and played in several bands in Eugene and Portland. Moving in the early '90s to Seattle, he played with Duffy Bishop's band for five years before going solo.

**(*) Slide Man
Burnside BCD-0036 Cooper; Andrew Larsen (o); Eric Bryson (b); Andrew Cloutier (d). 99?

Cooper is more versatile than the title allows: as well as playing slide guitar, in a variety of styles from Hawaiian ('Wicked Wacky Blues') to early Muddy Waters ('No Fears') to Elmore James ('Find My Kinda Woman'), he blows harmonica on several tracks, notably 'Love The Life You're Livin'', where, having re-created on guitar the insistent rhythm of the young John Lee Hooker, he doubles the facsimile effect by adding a harmonica part exactly in the style of Hooker's occasional accompanist Eddie Burns. With all that going on, listeners who don't care about vocals won't mind that Cooper is not much, indeed very little, of a singer. What remains to be done the band does in a businesslike manner, with a feature spot for Larsen in 'King Me', a pastiche (surely) of those dumb but infectious organ-led instrumentals that occasionally showed up on the pop charts in the '60s. Cooper preceded this album with a personal release, *Baby Please* (High Action 7001), and has since issued another. TR

Little Cooper (born 1928)
VOCAL, HARMONICA

The Arkansas-born Timothy Cooper began playing in 1950 in St Louis, where his first appearance in public was with the veteran guitarist Clifford Gibson. He founded his own band,

The Drifters, in 1955 and played at numerous clubs in St Louis and East St Louis in the '50s and '60s, recording briefly and obscurely in 1959. He reappeared on the St Louis scene at the city's 1993 blues festival.

*** Baby I'm Back
Black Magic CD 9033 *Cooper; Gene Cooper (p); Glen Cooper (g, v); Randy Rhodes (g); John Smith (b); Ricky Tucker, Kenny Rice (d). 95.*

Judging from these 11 tracks, all original compositions, Cooper likes a slow blues groove and has a band very well equipped to accompany him in it. He is the least excitable harmonica player you are ever likely to hear, and by no means a thrustful singer, but thanks to the tightness of the band, elegant playing by his brothers Gene and Glenn, and small but meaningful touches of individuality in the songwriting and arrangements, the music is seldom torpid. TR

Trenton Cooper (born 1923)
VOCAL, PIANO

Born (like Bill Clinton) in Hope, Arkansas, Cooper took up piano at 12, taught by his mother. As a youth he played blues, but in his 20s he switched to jazz, learning from records of Erroll Garner and Earl Hines. In his 30s he became a high-school teacher and eventually rose to the post of Director of Cooperative Education at the University of Arkansas in Pine Bluff. For many years he has played only for friends.

**(*) The Piano Styles Of Trenton Cooper
Wolf 120.919 *Cooper. 10/81, 11/90.*

In the 1990 recordings, which come first on the CD, it's presumably Cooper's leaning towards jazz that inspires the curious harmonic substitutions and melodic alterations he applies to blues standards like 'How Long Blues'. Sometimes, though, as in 'Baby What You Do For Me', such oddities may be due to faulty technique. When he sings, which he does on fewer than half of the CD's tracks, it's in a small, quavery voice, sometimes slightly off-pitch but by no means harsh. On the two takes of 'Everyday I Have The Blues' he indulges in scat singing. The 1981 tapes, though technically inferior, reveal a musician of fewer peculiarities, in somewhat better form and more in touch with his inner bluesman, notably in a thoughtful four-minute study based on 'After Hours'. Most of the 15 tracks are about 20 seconds longer than stated. TR

Johnny Copeland (1937–97)
VOCAL, GUITAR

Born in Louisiana, Copeland was raised first in Arkansas and then in Houston, Texas, where he began playing guitar in his teens in a group with Joe Hughes. After having some success with 'Rock And Roll Lilly' (Mercury, 1958) he cut singles for various Houston labels, and others, throughout the '60s. In 1975 he moved to New York, where his career was galvanized six years later by his Rounder album Copeland Special*, and for the next decade or so he was a first-class traveller on the international blues circuit.*

** Ghetto Child
Sanctuary CAS 36017 *Copeland; Curtis Mitchell, unknowns (t); unknown(s) (tb); Johnny Manning, L. A. Hill, Harold Bennett,*
unknowns (ts); unknowns (bs); Ronnie Baron, unknowns (o); Connie Mack Booker, unknowns (p); unknowns (g); unknowns (b); Johnny Prejean, unknowns (d); unknowns (v). 8/60–90.

** At His Best
M.I.L. Multimedia 3040 *Similar to above. 8/60–90?*

** Working Man's Blues
Aim 1303//Fuel 2000 302 061 260 *Similar to above. 8/60–90?*

** The Crazy Cajun Recordings
[Edsel EDCD 581] *Copeland; Curtis Mitchell, unknowns (t); unknown (as); Johnny Manning, L. A. Hill, unknowns (ts); prob. Augie Meyers, unknown (o); unknowns (p); Joey Long, unknowns (g); unknowns (b); prob. Johnny Prejean, unknowns (d). 9/63–73/74.*

Copeland's immediate success, when he was launched on the international blues scene in the early '80s, made it all the more puzzling that he had eluded most blues enthusiasts' notice for more than 20 years. These collections go a long way to solving the mystery. Anyone trawling the R&B singles market in the '60s and early '70s for promising blues artists might have approved of Copeland's gritty singing but shrugged at the mixture of uncompelling soul numbers and R&B ballads on which it was generally employed. *Ghetto Child*, *At His Best* and *Working Man's Blues* are selections of singles and unissued recordings from three decades, with a good deal of duplication and triplication, while *The Crazy Cajun Recordings*, produced by Huey Meaux, are mostly from the early to mid-'60s. Collectively the four CDs show that the blues seldom got a look-in and, when they did, were subject to wildly variable standards of production.

**** Texas Twister
Rounder CD 11504 *Copeland; John Pratt, Yusef Yancey, Ben Bierman (t); Garrett List, Bill Ohashi, George Lewis, Emmet King (tb); George Adams (ss, ts); Joe Rigby (as, ts, bs); Byard Lancaster (as, ts); Sam Furnace (as, bs); Arthur Blythe, Kotti Asalé (as); Greg Alper, Bert McGowan (ts); Brooklyn Slim [Paul Oscher] (h); Anthony Browns (o); Ken Vangel (p); John Leibman, Ken Pino, Richie Fliegler, Joel Perry, Stevie Ray Vaughan, Jimmy Hyacinthe, Malina (g); Don Whitcomb, Michael Merritt, Brian Miller (b); Candy McDonald, Mansfield Hitchman, Julian Vaughan, Jimmy Wormworth (d); Michael Finlayson, Halial, John Claude Kungnon, Souliman Moamed (perc). 81–85.*

**** When The Rain Starts Fallin'
Rounder CD 11515 *As above, except add Archie Shepp (ts); omit Brooklyn Slim. 81–85.*

*** Honky Tonkin'
Bullseye Blues BBB 9621 *Similar to* Texas Twister. *81–89.*

Like anyone apprenticed in the clubs of Texas, Copeland can deliver an up-tempo shuffle that goes straight to the feet. 'Claim Jumper', 'Natural Born Believer', 'Don't Stop By The Creek, Son' and 'Houston' on *Texas Twister* and the title track and 'Midnight Fantasy' on *When The Rain Starts Fallin'* lack nothing in danceability, and 'Don't Stop' is further vitalized by a guest appearance by Stevie Ray Vaughan. Copeland also follows local custom by slipping in an occasional R&B ballad like 'It's My Own Tears' or 'Jessanne'. But the armchair listener will not feel left out. Copeland's hoarse, emotional singing is highly potent on slow blues, and each album has at least two or three outstanding performances such as 'I De Go Now', with its writhing two-minute guitar solo, and 'Honky Tonkin'' on *Twister* and, on *Rain Starts Fallin'*, 'Make My Home Where

I Hang My Hat' and 'North Carolina', the latter decorated by Archie Shepp with a rustic tenor sax solo.

The Rounder compilations are drawn from Copeland's first four Rounder albums, *Copeland Special*, *Make My Home Where I Hang My Hat*, *Texas Twister* and *Bringing It All Back Home*, and drawn generously: only six of the source albums' 37 tracks are omitted. While the first three albums were fairly conventional, *Bringing It All Back Home* was a collaboration with musicians from the Ivory Coast. The material was not always as exotic as song titles like 'Kasavubu', 'Abidjan' and 'Bozalimamalu' implied, and, despite some notewriter's flim-flam about roots, neither African nor African-American participants are likely to have discovered any ancestral connections. Nonetheless, the textures of the music were unusual and pleasing. Each of the Rounder compilations has three examples. *Honky Tonkin'* is a shorter, cheaper trip through the same catalogue, with three tracks from the later album *Boom, Boom* (see below).

**** Showdown!
Alligator ALCD 4743 *Copeland; Albert Collins (h, g, v); Allen Batts (o); Robert Cray (g, v); Johnny B. Gayden (b); Casey Jones (d). 85.*

Copeland's features on this six-hander with Albert Collins and Robert Cray are 'Lion's Den', a fast-moving number in the vein of 'Claim Jumper', and 'Bring Your Fine Self Home', a loitering Jimmy Reed groove with Collins blowing harmonica. He also splits vocal and guitar roles with Collins on 'Black Cat Bone', a memorial to Hop Wilson, and with both partners on 'T-Bone Shuffle', and plays solos on Collins's 'Albert's Alley' and 'Blackjack'. Some of Copeland's most inflammatory guitar playing is to be found on this album, but just as much of an asset is the jovial interplay between him and Collins.

*** Ain't Nothin' But A Party
Rounder CD 2055 *Copeland; Bert McGowan (ts); Ken Vangel (kb); Ken Pino (g); Michael Merritt (b); Dwayne Broadnax (d). 7/87.*

**(*) Boom, Boom
Rounder CD 2060 *As above, except add Joel Perry (g); omit McGowan. 89.*

Copeland's earlier Rounder albums would prove to be the acme of his recording career; these are no more than postscripts. *Ain't Nothin' But A Party* was recorded at Houston's Juneteenth Festival. The title track does little more than announce itself for six minutes, but the unusual slow treatment of 'Baby Please Don't Go' makes up for it, and the live atmosphere is well caught. *Boom, Boom* is a studio recording with a few potentially strong songs but the chilly ambience represses much of Copeland's vocal energy.

*** Further On Up The Road
Aim 1032 *Copeland; Teo Leyasmeyer (p); Ken Pino (g); Randy Lippincott (b); Dwayne Broadnax (d). 6–7/90.*

Another live set, cut on tour in Australia (and also issued as *Live In Australia* on Black Top CD BT-1139, now deleted), but a more substantial one than *Ain't Nothin' But A Party*. As usual, the performances that linger are the slow blues, an impassioned 'Cut Off My Right Arm' and thoroughly personalized versions of 'That's All Right' and 'Love Her With A Feeling'. The settings may be a little monotonous at times (a horn or two would have been beneficial) but Copeland is in good spirits and fine, raucous voice.

Regrettably, his three '90s albums for Universal labels, *Flyin' High* (EmArcy 517 512), *Catch Up With The Blues* (Verve 521 239) and *Jungle Swing* (Verve 527 466), have been deleted in most if not all territories. The first reunited him with Houston colleagues like Joe Hughes and Joel Perry, *Jungle Swing* restated the message of *Bringing It All Back Home*, and all three contained performances of similar intensity to the best moments on the earlier Rounder albums, as well as likeable diversions into country music ('Jambalaya', 'Pedal To The Metal') and guest spots by Dr John on *Flyin' High* and Lonnie Brooks and Gatemouth Brown on *Catch Up With The Blues*. TR

Martha Copeland
VOCAL

Billed by Columbia as 'everybody's mammy', Copeland was popular in her day, but attempts to research her life have drawn a blank.

** Martha Copeland – Vol. 1 (1923–1927)
Document DOCD-5372 *Copeland; Louis Metcalf (c); Bubber Miley (t); Ernest Elliott, Bob Fuller (cl); Eddie Heywood, Cliff Jackson, Phil Worde, Louis Hooper, Porter Grainger (p); Bert Howell (vn); Buddy Christian (bj); Sidney Easton (v). 9/23–8/27.*

** Martha Copeland – Vol. 2 (1927–1928)/Irene Scruggs (1926–1930)
Document DOCD-5373 *Copeland; Irving Peskin, Bubber Miley (c); Bob Fuller, Clarence Adams (cl); Andrew Mead (as); Porter Grainger, Rube Bloom, James P. Johnson, J. C. Johnson (p); Ralph Jones (vn). 10/27–8/28.*

Copeland's singing is euphonious and her diction clear, but her delivery is rather unvaried. 'Bank Failure Blues', with its threats of violence if her money isn't secure, makes an intriguing riposte to those who would see blues singers as a revolutionary vanguard, and 'Wylie Avenue Blues' is a surprising plug for Pittsburgh. The lyrics of these songs are more interesting than Copeland's performance of them, however, and this is the norm. She seldom digs very far below the surface, and even manages to defuse the potent sexual symbolism of 'Black Snake Blues'. Some of the accompaniment is by top-flight jazz musicians, but Copeland doesn't give them much to respond to, and they sound dutiful rather than enthused. Eleven songs by Irene Scruggs round out *Vol. 2*'s dozen by Copeland. CS

Shemekia Copeland (born 1979)
VOCAL

The daughter of Johnny Copeland, Shemekia first sang in public with her father at the age of eight, and later opened for him at gigs. Since her debut album in 1998 she has been in great demand at blues festivals, where her fiery performances reveal a stagecraft remarkable for her age.

*** Turn The Heat Up
Alligator ALCD 4857 *Copeland; Larry Etkin (t); Robert Funk (tb); Crispin Cioe (as, bs); Arno Hecht (ts); Brian Mitchell (kb); Joe Louis Walker (g, v); Jimmy Vivino, Michael Hill, 'Monster' Mike*

Welch (g); Michael Merritt (b); James Wormworth, Barry Harrison (d). 98.

Turn The Heat Up was the most attention-grabbing debut by a Chicago blueswoman since Valerie Wellington's Million Dollar Secret 15 years earlier. But whereas Wellington seemed to have studied almost exclusively at the feet of Koko Taylor, Copeland was a subtler blend of Taylor, Etta James, and most of all, herself. Though the enthusiasm of 'My Turn Baby' (with a guest appearance by Joe Louis Walker), 'Big Lovin' Woman' and the title number was infectious, she was even more impressive on slow, moody pieces like 'Married To The Blues', 'Salt In My Wounds' and her father's 'Ghetto Child'.

**** Wicked
Alligator ALCD 4875 *As above, except add Sugar Blue (h), Doña Oxford (p), Arthur Neilson (g), Eric King (b), Fred Walcott (perc), Ruth Brown (v); omit Walker, Hill, Welch (g). 00.*

The promise of Turn The Heat Up was emphatically ratified by its successor. Like the earlier album, Wicked is stuffed with songs by Jon & Sally Tiven, Joe Hudson, and co-producers Jimmy Vivino and John Hahn, but here they are even more arresting. Any artist, let alone a young woman near the beginning of her career, would be gratified to be handed material like the neon-night soul of 'Up On 1-2-5' or the wistful 'The Fool You're Looking For'. Better still is 'Love Scene' (by Hahn, Jon Tiven and Copeland herself), a clever conceit – 'I'm ready for my love scene, looking for a leading man' – set to a timeless soul melody. Vivino lays his guitarist's cards on the table with a flourish, whether playing the lowdown acoustic slide of 'Beat Up Guitar' or rocking out on the opening 'It's 2 A.M'.

*** Talking To Strangers
Alligator ALCD 4887 *Copeland; Dr John [Mack Rebennack] (o, p, v, prod); Jason Ladayne (o, p); Arthur Neilson, Hugh McCracken (g); David Barard (b, perc, v); Jason Langley (b); Herman Ernest (d, perc, v); Larry McDonald, Fingers Hahn (perc). 02.*

If not quite as startlingly good as Wicked, Talking To Strangers finds Copeland on high form, with another handful of imaginative new songs (several from Hahn, Jon Tiven and Hudson) and the backing of a New Orleans crew under the baton of Dr John. Cheating and sexual double-dealing are her targets in 'Two's A Crowd' and 'Too Much Traffic', and there's a neat recomposition of Charles Brown's 'Merry Christmas Baby' as 'Happy Valentine's Day', but the emotional temperature warms on 'Livin' On Love', and 'Sholanda's' is a witty song about a beauty salon where a girl can get her hair seen to and, while she's about it, her life. Neilson grabs the guitar parts with gusto.

**** The Soul Truth
Alligator ALCD 4905 *Copeland; Steve Patric (t); Charles Rose (tb); Jim Horn (as, ts, bs, bss); Harvey Thompson (ts); Chuck Leavell (kb); Eddie Gore (o, p); Carl Marsh (o, syn); Felix Cavaliere (o); Steve Cropper (g, v, prod); Bob Britt, Reggie Wooten (g); David Santos, Shake Anderson, John Billings (b); Steve Potts, Chester Thompson (d); Tom Roady (perc, shakers); Mark Williams, N-Nandi Bryant, Lisa Cochran, Tom Hambridge, Dobie Gray (v). 05.*

The title warns that this will not be a conventional blues album, but the reader would have guessed as much anyway: Copeland's range has always extended beyond genre, and The Soul Truth is a logical successor to Talking To Strangers, the only significant difference being that both the material and the playing are even better. Again, many of the songs come from the workshop of John Hahn, collaborating with Steve Cropper, Joe Hudson and others, and the opening sequence of 'Breakin' Out', with its snaky guitar riff, 'Who Stole My Radio?' and 'Poor, Poor Excuse' revs the album up to a level from which it never drops, even in quieter numbers like 'Used'. As for Copeland, she has abandoned her early (though slight) tendency to throw a dash of Koko into a song whether it needed it or not, and has matured into a singer both subtle and feisty. TR

Al Copley (born 1952)
PIANO, VOCAL

Almon Copley grew up on Rhode Island, forming his first blues band in 1967, and was a founder member of Roomful Of Blues. He left the band in 1984 to go solo, based in Europe, where he has played with saxophonists Hal Singer and Sil Austin and made many festival appearances.

**(*) Good Understanding
Bullseye Blues CD 9596 *Copley; Kim Wilson (h); Duke Robillard (g); Preston Hubbard, Vinzenz Kummer (b); Fran Christina (d); José Avilla (bgo). 3–6/92.*

**(*) Live At Montreux
One Mind OMCD 1201 *Copley. 7/93.*

Although the core session for Good Understanding was an accident of coinciding schedules – both Copley and the Fabulous Thunderbirds were on tour in the Netherlands, and happened to be in Amsterdam on the same night – the association between them went back many years: Robillard had also been a charter member of Roomful Of Blues, and Christina one of their first drummers. Not surprisingly, the music is a genial collaboration from first to last. The New Orleans flavoured 'Doin' It' and 'What Do I Do?' move sinuously, but Copley's casual singing is best suited to slow, ruminative numbers like Amos Milburn's 'Bad Bad Whiskey' and his own 'Sunshine Moonlight', and these are also the tunes he plays with the most imagination. Robillard and Wilson take their parts with courteous restraint.

Copley keeps the Montreux set interesting with a mixed programme of boogies and blues at several tempos; set against that the slightly colourless singing and the leaden clapping with which the audience greets 'Goin' Back To The Country' and 'Everything's Gonna Be Alright'. He also recorded two albums for Black Top, Automatic Overdrive and, jointly with Hal Singer, Royal Blue, both deleted. TR

Bob Corritore (born 1956)
HARMONICA

Corritore grew up in Chicago, where he began playing harmonica in his teens. After producing albums by Little Willie Anderson and Big Leon Brooks for his Blues Over Blues label, he moved in 1981 to Arizona, where he works in Phoenix as a record producer, talent booker and radio presenter.

*** All-Star Blues Sessions
HMG HMG 1009 *Corritore; Eddie Hollis (o); Henry Gray (p, v); S. E. Willis, Pinetop Perkins, Tom Mahon (p); Lil' Ed Williams,*

Jimmy Rogers, Clarence Edwards, R. L. Burnside, Bo Diddley, Jimmy Dotson, Dino Spells (g, v); Johnny Rapp, Buddy Reed, Robert Jr Lockwood, Bob Margolin, Rusty Zinn, Paul 'Texas Red' Halperin, Kid Ramos (g); Paul Thomas, John 'Pops' McFarlane, Scott Meyer, Bruce Lopez (b); Chico Chism (d, v); Elmer Scott, Greg Zark, Richard Innes, Brian Fahey (d); King Karl, Nappy Brown (v). 4/86–3/98.

The only constant on these 16 tracks is Corritore himself, playing harmonica with a series of front men whom he corralled while they were visiting Phoenix. Although not a major-league player on the level of Kim Wilson or James Harman, he is versatile enough to fit into Chicago-style lineups with Jimmy Rogers, Henry Gray or Dino Spells, play dirty like Lazy Lester with Clarence Edwards and jam on Wes Montgomery's 'Naptown Blues' with Robert Jr Lockwood. Buyers less interested in the host than in his guests will find Edwards (who has two cuts) and Gray (three) on particularly good form, likewise Nappy Brown, stretching out with Kid Ramos in a long 'Driftin' Blues', and, if Bo Diddley's 'Little Girl' is sadly ordinary, it may be some recompense to hear the little-recorded King Karl deliver a lithely rocking 'Cool Calm Collected'. TR

Ike Cosse (born 1955)
VOCAL, GUITAR, HARMONICA

Isaac Cosse (pronounced 'cosy') is one of the many beneficiaries of his record label's policy of searching out untried blues talent. A semi-pro with aspirations beyond his present status, Cosse has a way with words not entirely matched by his abilities as a performer. In the current climate, it's hard to see how he'll make the impression he so obviously desires, and it may be as a songwriter that his ambition will be realized.

** The Lowdown Throwdown
JSP JSPCD 283 Cosse; A. J. Johnson (t); 'Sha-Ba-Ka' (as); Charles McNeil (ts); Patrick 'Big Bones' Norris (h); Earl Slack (o); Sid Morris (p); Myron Dove (b); Cecil A. Daniels (d); Dennis Dove, Pat A. Ross (v). 97.

Cosse's better songs are those, like the opening 'Bang Bang Girls', that follow an often humorous narrative to an ironic end. Thus 'I Just Wanna Rent', 'She's Expensive' and 'My Baby's So Cynical'. 'Doggy Style', while wanting to be salacious, is just plain naive. 'When I Get Home' would like to be a downhome blues but ends up as just another pastel shade in Cosse's palette of watercolours. Most of his vocals are talked/sung but when he tackles a soul ballad, 'Let It Happen', his timbre is thin and querulously pitched. His musicians function adequately as a unit but only McNeel and Slack show any command of their instruments. Overall, Cosse hasn't the performance skills to carry off the self-conscious cleverness in his writing, thus making a disadvantage of his principal asset.

**(*) Cold Blooded World
JSP JSPCD 2147 Cosse. 00.

It took bravery on Cosse's part to make a solo album so soon in his recording career but there's little commercial value in courage. With just an amplified acoustic guitar and harmonica, the emphasis is upon the quality of his songwriting, which is here somewhat improved. 'That's The Blues', about guns in schools, and the self-explanatory 'The Blues Is The Blues Is The Blues' are among his better efforts but these are counterbalanced by the tweeness of 'Have A Good Time' and 'The Truth'. The verses and chorus of 'Bad Decision' manage to encompass both these extremes. Elsewhere, there's a formlessness to his writing that fails to mature into full-blown whimsy. The instrumental 'Ike's Blues' displays both the weakness of his harmonica playing and the strength of his guitar work, the latter too infrequently used in the project as a whole. Nevertheless, this is a notable improvement on his debut release. NS

Sean Costello (born 1980)
VOCAL, GUITAR

Costello won a talent contest organized by the Beale Street Blues Society in 1994. He made an acclaimed debut album in 1996, played guitar in Susan Tedeschi's band around 1997–99, and subsequently led his own Jivebombers.

***(*) Call The Cops
Blue Wave CD 136 Costello; Paul Linden (h, p); Carl Shankle (b); Terrence Prather (d); Jay Sheffield (v). 96.

Costello's retro playing, flawlessly re-creating sounds from the '50s, allies him with guitarchivists like Kirk Fletcher or JW-Jones, but his range is even wider than theirs, encompassing not only T-Bone Walker but the measured slide playing of Robert Nighthawk in 'Anna Lee' and a Muddy Waters/Jimmy Rogers amalgam in 'My Favorite Things'. Although his up-tempo shuffles are style-perfect, he's perhaps at his best in slow blues like 'Blues Para Mi Angelita', where he reveals not only expertise but imagination. Linden is a splendid foil on both instruments. Costello sings like a kid, but then he was.

*** Cuttin' In
Landslide LDCD 1025 Costello; Paul Linden (h, p, v); Neal Wauchope (o); Matt Wauchope (p); Melvin Zachary, Dave Roth (b); Tim Gunther, Bill Edwards (d); Chris Uhler (perc). 10/99.

Three years on, Cuttin' In finds Costello singing with more confidence, though in a generic young-white-guy manner that lacks the distinction of his playing and makes one impatient for him to finish and get to the guitar solo. Unfortunately this sometimes takes a while and the solo space is then shared with other musicians, so there's rather less of Costello's playing than on Call The Cops. A noteworthy exception to these strictures is the long reading of Otis Rush's 'Double Trouble', a challenging number that Costello plays with bravado and sings pretty well too. With selections like Little Walter's 'Ah'w Baby', compositions by Willie Dixon and Sonny Boy Williamson I, and an original 'Who's Been Cheatin' Who' that seems to be rooted in Jazz Gillum's 'Tell Me Mama', the album has something of a classic Chicago bias, but Costello touches other bases in 'I Got Loaded', 'Those Lonely Lonely Nights' and a Gatemouth Brownish instrumental, 'Jumpin' Salty'.

***(*) Moanin' For Molasses
Landslide LDCD 1027 Costello; Ken Gregory (t); Adam Mewherter (tb); John Longo (ts); Paul Linden (h, p, v); Matt Wauchope (o, p, v); Melvin Zachary (b, v); Terrence Prather (d); Chris Uhler (cga); Clarence Cameron, Cheryl Grier, Virgil Williams, Jon Liedman (v). 1/01.

Another exceptional album, rich in variety, good songs, singing that's now a few degrees above tolerable, and guitar playing that has little left to prove. No one, on the evidence of his records, could call Costello a self-centred musician: he makes room for other players, he doesn't indulge his own writing (though it's not at all bad) and he doesn't go in for extended powerplay. It's a rare number that runs beyond five minutes, and the longest one here is 4.09, a very strong treatment of the Buddy Guy song 'No Lie'. Consequently his performances are packed with condensed energy and creativity, as if each of them had been made as a single. This is so uncommon nowadays that one would like Costello for it even if he were only an average player. In fact, as these records make clear, he is one of the outstanding blues musicians of his generation.

*** **Sean Costello**
Tone Cool/Artemis/Rykodisc RCD 17301 *Costello; Mark Pender (t); Jerry Vivino (s); Paul Linden (h, kb); Matt Wauchope, Glenn Patascha (kb, o, p); Jimi Zhivago (g); Melvin Zachary, Willie Weeks, Byron Isaacs (b); Tony Leone (d, perc); Terrence Prather, Steve Jordan, Levon Helm (d); Amy Helm, Fiona McBain (v).* 05.

This must have rocked a few of Costello's admirers back on their heels. After three albums of impeccable retro-blues, he used his Tone Cool debut to serve notice that he wasn't going to be stuck in that groove, thanks very much. What you get instead is songs by Tommy Johnson, Robert Ward, Bob Dylan and Johnny 'Guitar' Watson and a sheaf of bluesy originals arranged in classic soul style and delivered with a ravaged intensity. TR

Elizabeth Cotten (1893–1987)
VOCAL, GUITAR, BANJO

Cotten was born in Chapel Hill, North Carolina. (The date given here is from her Social Security application. Other sources give 1892 and 1895, and Cotten implies 1898 on her Arhoolie CD.) She took up the banjo and guitar in childhood, playing them left-handed and upside-down. Cotten was in domestic service from the age of 12, married at 15 and shortly thereafter joined the church, virtually giving up the guitar for 25 years. In the '40s she moved to Washington, DC, where she worked for Charles and Ruth Seeger, who were composers, musicologists and the parents of Mike and Peggy Seeger. It was a few years before the family discovered that Cotten was a fellow musician and Mike Seeger began recording her. Her first LP included 'Freight Train', which became a standard of the folk revival. On the strength of the album's popularity, Cotten played some concerts and made more recordings, but she only began touring regularly after retiring from domestic work in the late '70s and her mid-80s.

*** **Freight Train And Other North Carolina Folk Songs And Tunes**
Smithsonian Folkways CD SF 40009 *Cotten.* 57–58.

***(*) **Shake Sugaree**
Smithsonian Folkways SFW CD 40147 *Cotten; Brenda Evans (v).* 2/65–1/66.

In 1972 Libba Cotten received the Burl Ives Award for her 'unique contribution to folk music', but her repertoire and sound are typical of the pre-blues music of the Carolinas: rags, reels, spirituals and (from later on) the occasional blues, played skilfully and euphoniously – usually: there is a nasty discord at the end of 'I Don't Love Nobody' on *Freight Train*. That CD reissues the first of her three Folkways LPs; it was recorded informally, and the sound quality is acceptable rather than hi-fi. *Freight Train*'s playing time is short but Cotten's fingerpicking is charming; she sings on half the tracks, however, and her small, scratchy and tuneless voice is by no means as beguiling as her playing, except on a set of three dance tunes where her singing functions as a drone accompaniment to the banjo.

Shake Sugaree is an expanded version of Cotten's second LP, and has much better sound, longer playing time and extensive, affectionate annotation. Some tracks are brief (26 of them fill an hour), and Cotten's singing remains the drawback that must not be spoken of, but her playing continues to be delightful and accomplished; several banjo tunes transferred to the guitar are especially fascinating. Most tunes are recalled from childhood and youth, but there are also some intricate, newly composed ragtime instrumentals. To her great-grandmother's accompaniment, 12-year-old Brenda Evans sings the title track enchantingly.

*** **Live!**
Arhoolie CD 477 *Cotten.* 12/83.

Arhoolie's recording quality is very good, but while this makes Cotten's singing louder, it's no more attractive; *Live!*'s most valuable tracks are the instrumentals 'Washington Blues' and 'Jumping Jack'. The latter is a banjo tune on guitar; it develops considerable momentum thanks to Cotten's use of her thumb to play melody. By 1983 she had professionalized herself, developing a stage presentation which involved telling stories of her life, playing some instrumentals and encouraging her audiences to join in the singing of her best-known songs. After many years of dealing with small children there was nothing Cotten didn't know about manipulating an audience, and their readiness to applaud and/or laugh at virtually anything she says becomes cloying; the singalongalibba aspect is not especially enticing, either. As a raconteur, Cotten has verve and sly timing, and her instrumental skills are completely intact; they overcome the CD's drawbacks, the biggest of which is her collusion with the sentimentality of her listeners. CS

James Cotton (born 1935)
VOCAL, HARMONICA

Cotton left Tunica, Mississippi, in his teens to meet and learn from Sonny Boy Williamson II. In the early '50s he played with Howlin' Wolf and recorded a few sides for Sun before moving to Chicago, where he played with Muddy Waters for 12 years. From the mid-'60s onwards he led his own band, touring and recording prolifically. Since the late '80s the texture of his voice has been progressively coarsened by throat cancer, but he continues to blow harmonica with energy and determination.

Three of the four sides Cotton recorded for Sun in 1953–54 are on *Mystery Train* (Rounder CD SS 28), a CD mostly devoted to Junior Parker, whose recording of the title track is plainly the inspiration for Cotton's 'Hold Me In Your Arms'. 'Cotton Crop Blues' is little more original, having been first recorded by Tampa Red more than 20 years earlier, but Cotton sings it as if it were a breaking news story, accompanied with irritable brilliance by the guitarist Pat Hare.

*** The Blues Never Die!
Original Blues Classics OBCCD 530 *Cotton; Otis Spann (p); James Madison, 'Dirty Rivers' [Muddy Waters] (g); Milton Rector (b); S. P. Leary (d); band (v). 10/64.*

Cotton was still with Muddy Waters when he made this pleasant, unspectacular album, issued under the name of Otis Spann though the two men share the vocal role evenly. Cotton sings and plays well on mostly familiar numbers; his best performance is the slow blues 'One More Mile To Go', which he sings like a man nearly exhausted but still determined to reach his goal, while the band croons the title in the background. Cotton had first recorded the song the previous year (see the VAC *Meat & Gravy From Bea & Baby* [Castle CMDDD 610 2CD]). Most of this CD is also on the VAC *The Bluesville Years Volume Two: Feelin' Down On The South Side* (Prestige PRCD 9906).

**** Chicago/The Blues/Today! Vol. 2
Vanguard VMD 79217 *As above, except omit 'Dirty Rivers', Rector. 12/65.*

Cotton's tracks on this CD were one of the strongest sets of the entire *Chicago/The Blues/Today!* project. Between pugnacious readings of 'Cotton Crop Blues' and 'West Helena Blues' and less striking but very competent performances of 'Love Me Or Leave' and 'Rocket 88', he and Spann collaborate in an exquisite version of 'Black Night', disguised under the title 'The Blues Keep Falling'. The rest of the CD is by Homesick James and Otis Rush; the album's contents are also on *Chicago/The Blues/Today!* (Vanguard 172/74 3CD) and Cotton's set is included in his *Best Of The Vanguard Years* (see below).

**(*) Feelin' Good
Acrobat ACMCD 4009 *Cotton; Paul Serrano (t); John Watson, Louis Satterfield (tb); James [Gene?] Barge (ts); Delbert Hill, McKinley Easton (bs); Paul Butterfield, Billy Boy Arnold (h); Albert Gianquinto (p); Elvin Bishop, Luther Tucker (g); Bob Anderson (b); Sam Lay, Francis Clay (d). 62/63, 3/67–2/68.*

Most of this CD started life as *The James Cotton Blues Band*, the first of three albums for Verve in which Cotton tried to mix a blues-soul amalgam, somewhat in the style of Junior Parker. The music indeed has plenty of verve, and some variety, but it is not enhanced by sounding as if it had been recorded in an aircraft hangar; on the instrumental 'Blues In My Sleep' the echo turns the music into aural minestrone. Anyone who manages to hear past it will find these to be enthusiastic performances, with a good deal of intense soloing by Gianquinto and Tucker. The first five tracks, from 1962 or '63, are informal recordings with Butterfield, Arnold and Bishop. Although Cotton claims Sonny Boy Williamson II as his chief model, it's clear from these sides how much he owes to the first Sonny Boy.

Much of *The James Cotton Blues Band*, and a few tracks from its two successors, was gathered on *Best Of The Verve Years* (Verve 527 371, deleted).

** Midnight Creeper
Just A Memory JAM 9145/6 2CD *Cotton; Albert Gianquinto (p); Luther Tucker (g); Bobby Anderson (b); Francis Clay (d). 9/67.*

These 30-odd songs were taped at a gig in a Montreal café a few months after the first Verve LP session (see *Feelin' Good*). Several of the numbers from that session reappear here, but the smaller group cannot do justice to orchestrally conceived pieces like 'Good Time Charlie' or 'Turn On Your Lovelight', and the recording is consistently lifeless. The more intimate setting does reveal how closely Cotton follows other people's recordings: 'I Don't Know' is virtually a line-by-line imitation of Willie Mabon's version, while in 'Black Night' and 'Tramp' Cotton not only duplicates the arrangements of Lowell Fulson's recordings but mimics his timbre. The 2CD set absorbs the contents of the earlier single-CD releases *Seems Like Yesterday* (JAM 9138), *Late Night Blues* (JAM 9140) and *It Was A Very Good Year* (JAM 9144).

*** Cut You Loose!
Vanguard VMD 79283 *Cotton; Mike Fender (bst); Martin Fierro (ts, bs); Wayne Talbert (o, p); 'Jeremiah Jenkins' (o); Michael Tschudin (p); James Cook, Guitar 'Junior', Peter Malick (g); Eddie Adams (b); Joe Rodriguez (d). 4/68.*

The variety of the settings, from the nudging horns on 'River's Invitation' to the stripped-down group on 'Honest I Do', makes this one of the most approachable and uncomplicatedly enjoyable of Cotton's albums. Like its predecessors, it calls on Cotton for almost no compositional input, and instead he canters through standards, but with a little less respect for their originals. The concluding 'Negative 10–4' is a jazz instrumental featuring Talbert (its composer) and Fierro, incongruous in itself and doubly so since Cotton makes no contribution to it.

***(*) Best Of The Vanguard Years
Vanguard VCD 79536 *As for* Chicago/The Blues/Today! Vol. 2 *and* Cut You Loose!. *12/65, 4/68.*

This handily gathers up the album discussed immediately above, with an alternative take of 'Next Time You See Me', and Cotton's five tracks from *Chicago/The Blues/Today! Vol. 2*.

In the '70s Cotton recorded *Taking Care of Business* (Capitol), last available on *Chicago Blues Masters Vol. 3* (Capitol 36288 2CD, deleted), and *100% Cotton*, *High Energy* and *Live And On The Move*, all for Buddah, which have been reissued at least twice on CD but are not currently in print.

**(*) Take Me Back
Blind Pig BP 72587 *Cotton; Pinetop Perkins (p); Sam Lawhorn, John Primer (g); Bob Anderson (b); Sam Lay (d). 8/80.*

Cotton is in reminiscent mood, remembering Muddy Waters ('Clouds In My Heart'), Howlin' Wolf ('Killing Floor') and Little Walter ('My Babe', 'Take Me Back') and giving a sensitive reading of Otis Spann's 'Hungry Country Girl', but his singing is a little constricted and the band plays as if supplying background music for a senior citizens' bridge evening.

**(*) High Compression
Alligator ALCD 4737 *Cotton; Danny Fields (t); Johnny Cotton (tb); Douglas Fagan (ts); Eddie Harsch (kb); Pinetop Perkins (p); Magic Slim, Michael Coleman (g); Aron Burton, Noel Neal (b); Robert Covington, Ray Allison (d). 84.*

*** Live From Chicago
Alligator ALCD 4746 *As above, except omit Perkins, Magic Slim, Burton, Covington. 2/86.*

High Compression presents Cotton as both traditionalist, playing 'Diggin' My Potatoes' and four other tracks with the

Perkins–Magic Slim–Burton–Covington lineup, and progressive, on five cuts with the other musicians, a blues-funk setting for which Cotton now sounds a little too old. *Live From Chicago*, a boisterous set from Biddy Mulligan's, has that same larger band, but since the horns are mixed back the effect is of a conventional Chicago-style band with occasional flourishes. By now Cotton's singing has become rather indistinct, but he blows with his customary authority.

*** Mighty Long Time
Antone's 74208 *Cotton; Mark Kazanoff, Red Rails (ts); Choo Bari (bs); Mike Kindred, Pinetop Perkins, Denny Freeman, Mel Brown, Reese Wynans (p); Jimmie Vaughan, Derek O'Brien, Matt Murphy, Luther Tucker, Hubert Sumlin, Wayne Bennett (g); Sarah Brown, Calvin Jones, Larry Eisenberg (b); George Rains, Willie Smith (d). 91.*

After all his years with Muddy, Cotton could produce, especially when backed by sympathetic musicians, near-replica performances of numbers like 'Sugar Sweet' or 'Blow Wind Blow'. He could also essay a more than passable Howlin' Wolf impression on 'Moanin' At Midnight' and 'Three Hundred Pounds Of Joy', a fair one of Bobby Bland on 'Call It Stormy Monday', assisted by Wayne Bennett (who played on the original), and an echo of Sonny Boy Williamson II's harmonica on 'Mighty Long Time'. Such exercises in re-creation, often supported by old friends like Murphy, Tucker and Sumlin, take up most of this album, interspersed with his own 'Hold Me In Your Arms' and 'Northside Cadillac'.

**** Deep In The Blues
Verve 529 849 *Cotton; Dave Maxwell (p); Joe Louis Walker (g); Charlie Haden (b). 8/95.*

*** Fire Down Under The Hill
Telarc CD-83497 *Cotton; David Maxwell (p); Rico McFarland (g); Darrell Nulisch (v). 9/99.*

By the '90s there wasn't much left of Cotton's voice, but what there was he used to moving effect; his harp playing remained both strong and, when it needed to be, subtle. Both of these albums are acoustic. Perhaps that direction was taken out of respect for his diminished vocal powers, but it proves to be artistically just the right way to go. Cushioned by sympathetic musicians, unpressed by a drummer, Cotton delivers each piece at the speed and length that suit him and produces some of the most eloquent music of his career. *Deep In The Blues* is the better of the two albums, thanks in part to the excellence of his accompanists, not least Haden, a bassist incapable of sounding ordinary. It also releases several of those rare birds, compositions with Cotton's own name on them (though 'Everybody's Fishin'' is older than him, and 'Country Boy' is surely Pee Wee Hughes's song), and has cameos by Walker and Haden. *Fire Down Under The Hill* replaces Walker with Rico McFarland, a fine musician but perhaps not best heard in an all-acoustic setting, where he is discreet sometimes to the point of invisibility, leaving Maxwell with the major share of the accompaniment. 'Something To Remember You By' makes an affecting closing track and altogether it's a rewarding record, but it shows us nothing that the previous album hadn't revealed in a more dramatic light.

*** 35th Anniversary Jam
Telarc CD-83550 *Cotton; Kim Wilson (h, v); David Maxwell (p); Lucky Peterson (g, v); Mike Williams, G. E. Smith, Jimmie Vaughan (g); Noel Neal (b); Per Hanson (d); Shemekia Copeland, Ronnie Hawkins, Syl Johnson, Maria Muldaur, Kenny Neal, Bobby Rush, Koko Taylor (v). 6/01.*

All Cotton does on this anniversary get-together is play, leaving the vocals to a strong team of guest singers. Some of the selections are from the era when he was coming up, like 'Rocket 88', sung by Syl Johnson, 'Don't Start Me Talking' (Kenny Neal) or 'River's Invitation' (Kim Wilson), while others are drawn from the well of his own back catalogue, Ronnie Hawkins getting hold of 'Hold Me Baby' and Lucky Peterson picking 'Cotton Crop Blues'. But this is not one of those birthday photographs where you can't see the subject for the crowd of well-wishers. Cotton's blowing is as downright and deep-dyed blue as ever – witness the instrumentals 'The Creeper' and 'Blues For The Hook' – and there's never any doubt whose record it is.

**(*) Baby, Don't You Tear My Clothes
Telarc CD-83596 *Cotton; C. J. Chenier (ac, v); Marcia Ball (p, v); David Maxwell (p); Dave Alvin, Peter Rowan, Doc Watson, Merle Watson, Rory Block (g, v); Derek O'Brien (g); Noel Neal (b); Per Hanson (d); Chris Gaffney (tamb, v); Bobby Rush, Odetta, Jim Lauderdale (v). 10/03.*

35th Anniversary Jam won a W. C. Handy Award, which may explain why its successor was conceived along similar lines: the basic tracks by a core group, with overdubs by singers, since Cotton again takes no vocals. But it's a rather different guestlist, drawing in figures from country music like Jim Lauderdale, Peter Rowan, who does Bill Monroe's 'Muleskinner Blues', and the Watsons, obviously on an old recording (of 'How Long Blues') into which Cotton has intricated his harp part. Cotton plays as well as ever on most of these and his four instrumentals, but the core band is somnolent and the programme is poorly sequenced, with four longish slow numbers in a row. TR

Sylvester Cotton
VOCAL, GUITAR

Other than that he was in Detroit in 1948, nothing is known about Cotton; Chris Smith in the notes to his only CD describes him as 'an enigma with a music-shaped hole where his life story ought to be', but speculates that he might have been from Mississippi.

**(*) Blues Sensation – Detroit Downhome Recordings 1948–49
Ace CDCHD 869 *Cotton. 9–10/48.*

This is blues archaeology at its keenest: of the 19 tracks exhumed from the vaults of Bernie Besman's Sensation label, only three were issued at the time they were made, and one of those was miscredited to John Lee Hooker. Numbers like 'Stranger In Your Town Blues' suggest that Cotton had listened attentively but not slavishly to Lightnin' Hopkins, while others like 'Single Man's Blues' have a more trenchant beat somewhat reminiscent of Tommy McClennan. These possible sources are mentioned only to give the reader a vague notion of how he sounds; essentially he is an artist with his own peculiar way of doing things. This sometimes takes the form of improvised autobiographical anecdote, as when he and his companion go out for a meal: 'We went to the restaurant, said, "A table for two" – said I told that waitress, "Bring me and my wife some food.'" Even more striking is 'I Tried', a sort of epitaph to his recording career: 'Every baby have to crawl before he walk ... I want you to excuse all the mistakes in this song, Lord, 'cause this is the last one I'll ever play – maybe ...' Six tracks, also previously unissued Sensation recordings, are tacked on at the end by another intriguing Detroit-based obscurity, the singer/guitarist Andrew Dunham. TR

Cousin Joe (1907–89)
VOCAL, PIANO

His improbable real name was Pleasant Joseph; born in rural Louisiana, Cousin Joe learned ukulele and guitar before taking up the piano, worked as a singer and dancer in the streets and clubs of New Orleans and toured with jazz bands. Joe moved to New York in the '40s, and became popular on the Harlem circuit, but went back to the Crescent City in 1947 to get away from the New York drug scene. He made his first visit to Europe in 1964, and became a frequent visitor.

**(*) Vol. 1 1945–1946
Blue Moon BMCD 6001 *Cousin Joe; Hot Lips Page, Dick Vance, Leonard Hawkins, Lemon Boler (t); Mezz Mezzrow, Tony Scott (cl); Sidney Bechet (ss); Pete Brown, Earl Bostic (as); Al Sears, Ray Abrams, John Hardee (ts); Harry Carney (bs); Sam Price, Leonard Feather, Kenny Watts, Ernie Washington, George Parker (p); Danny Barker, Jimmy Shirley (g); Pops Foster, Lloyd Trotman, Leonard Gaskin, Jimmy Jones (b); Sid Catlett, J. C. Heard, Arthur Herbert, Eddie Nicholson (d). 3/45–c. 6/46.*

**(*) Vol. 2 1946–1947
Blue Moon BMCD 6002 *Cousin Joe; Shad Collins (t); Tyree Glenn, Dickie Wells (tb); Tony Scott (cl); Earl Bostic, Pete Brown, unknown (as); John Hardee (ts); Hank Jones, Paul Gayten, Steve 'Hoggie Beetle' Henderson, Billy Kyle, Sam Price (p); Jimmy Shirley, Edgar Blanchard, Al Casey, Danny Barker (g); Jimmy Jones, Warren Stanley, Al Matthews, Lloyd Trotman, Pops Foster (b); Eddie Nicholson, Robert Green, Arthur Herbert, Woodie Nichols, Kenny Clarke (d). c. 8/46–7/47.*

**(*) Vol. 3 1947–1955
Blue Moon BMCD 6013 *Cousin Joe; Dave Bartholomew, Thomas Jefferson (t); Wendell (or Homer) Eugene, unknown (tb); prob. Joe Harris (cl, as); Willie Humphrey, unknown (cl); prob. Joe Thomas (as); Lee Allen, Clarence Hall, Herb Hardesty, Sam Butera, unknown (ts); unknown (bs); Sam Price, Salvador Doucette, Dave 'Fatman' Williams, unknowns (p); Billy Butler, Ernest McLean, unknowns (g); Percy Joell, Frank Fields, Clement Tervalone, unknowns (b); Dorothea Smith, Earl Palmer, Freddie Kohlman, unknowns (d); Elsie Jones, band (v). 11/47–55.*

*** Complete Recordings 1945–1955
Night Train NTI CD 3001 3CD *As for above three CDs. 3/45–55.*

*** New York & New Orleans Blues 1945/1951
EPM Blues Collection 16031 *As above, except omit Jefferson, Eugene, unknown (tb); Humphrey, unknown (cl); Thomas, Butera, unknown (bs); Williams, Tervalon, Kohlman, Elsie Jones. 3/45–9/51.*

Probably because he wasn't a union member, Cousin Joe appears only as a vocalist on these discs, except on two tracks where he accompanies the insipid Elsie Jones. Joe's strongest talent was as a wordsmith, in which capacity he supplied himself with some of the blues' wittiest and most original lyrics. He was a pleasant but unexceptional singer and a limited melodist; hence his most successful records are those where clever words meet classy accompanists given room to solo.

Night Train's 3CD package contains the same tracks as Blue Moon's separate discs, and for those who want the complete works the choice is clear; both labels have had to work with some noisy originals, but Night Train's remastering has more presence, and the set is budget-priced. However, and notwithstanding some distinguished names on the early sides, it's not until about halfway through the second disc, and a session with marvellously intricate guitar by Al Casey, that either the accompaniments or Joe's vocals make much impact. His subsequent recordings for Signature and Decca feature some of his cleverest lyrics, slyly sung and boosted by some standout musicianship, notably from Kyle, Price, Butler and Kenny Clarke. Fifteen tracks on the third disc were recorded after Joe's return to New Orleans and are patchy; an ingenious, spirited two-part 'A.B.C.'s' contends with Elsie Jones, an unfortunate mambo arrangement of 'Dinah', and 'I Saw Mommy Kissing Santa Claus'.

For listeners disinclined to use the skip button, EPM offer a good selection, mainly of New York recordings, in acceptable sound. It would have been improved by substituting – among many possibilities – 'Evolution Blues' and 'Chicken A La Blues' for two tedious spirituals.

**(*) Bad Luck Blues
Evidence ECD 26046 *Cousin Joe; Clarence 'Gatemouth' Brown, Jimmy Dawkins (g); Mac Thompson (b); Ted Harvey (d). 11/71.*
**(*) Bad Luck Blues
Black & Blue BB 436 *As above. 11/71.*

Bad Luck Blues was one of three LPs recorded in a single day, with Brown, Dawkins and Cousin Joe taking turns as leader. Here, Chicago, Texas and New Orleans collaborate with cautious professionalism but don't always avoid head-on style collisions: Joe surrenders gracefully to rhythms that have nothing to do with the Crescent City, and Brown's frequent use of a phase-shifter is irrevocably dated. Joe's piano playing is competent but inexpressive and, although his singing has verve, it lacks variety, and often conveys an unwarranted self-admiration. Black & Blue add three alternative takes to the material licensed by Evidence.

**(*) New Orleans Piano Blues
Jazz Crusade JCCD-3091 *Cousin Joe. 9/78.*
**(*) The Blues Of Henry Gray & Cousin Joe
Storyville STCD 16057 *Cousin Joe. 8/84.*

Recorded in London despite its title, *New Orleans Piano Blues* (which is shared with jazz veteran Alton Purnell, recorded in Australia) captures a typical Cousin Joe solo gig. Some of his lines are genuinely amusing, and alongside the old favourites are less-expected numbers like 'Hogwash Junction Function' and 'Mess Around' (which is 'Pine Top's Boogie Woogie', not the Ray Charles tune). The drawbacks are Joe's dully predictable piano playing, combining staccato chords with repetitive trills, and his complacent narcissism, which finds its most annoying expression in mechanical laughter at his own jokes. No audience could possibly find Joe as delightful as he finds himself.

Similar positives and similar strictures apply to the Storyville half-CD, which actually was recorded in New Orleans, again in concert. Joe tones down the self-admiration a little, and plays a fine instrument. 'Everything That's Made

Of Wood Once Was A Tree' and 'Come Down People' (boosting the World's Fair then going on in town) are lively, clever openers, but Joe soon settles for doing his greatest hits. Though not great, this is a better concert than the London one; perhaps Joe was fired up by the enthusiasm of a hometown audience – or perhaps he knew that they wouldn't be so willing to let him coast. CS

Cousin Leroy
VOCAL, GUITAR

Originally from the Carolinas, he recorded in New York, and his surname was Rozier; nothing else seems to be known about Cousin Leroy.

*** Froggy Went A Courtin'
Blue City BCCD-813 *Cousin Leroy; Sonny Terry (h); Champion Jack Dupree (p); Larry Dale (g); Sid Wallace (b); Gene Brooks (d). 7–8/57.*

Cousin Leroy has 15 tracks; the other 14 are by Sonny Terry, who plays on most of Leroy's numbers. Sonny's under strict orders not to deploy his trademark whoop, for Leroy and the band are modelling their sound on contemporary Chicago blues. The repertoire is largely derivative – Muddy, Eddie Vinson, Hooker, Bo Diddley and Blind Lemon all make their mark – but not tediously so; the musicians are professional but not detached, and Dale plays some stormy guitar. Leroy's fame among collectors has rested largely on 'Crossroads', a cover of 'Rollin' Stone' with an added opening verse about the Devil tuning his guitar; it's still striking now that the image has become the white world's favourite blues cliché. Blue City evidently have access to Ember's masters, since four unissued songs and three alternative takes are included. If there were any notes, they would doubtless be silent about this aspect of the release. CS

Ben Covington
VOCAL, HARMONICA, BANJO-MANDOLIN

According to Big Joe Williams, Covington was a street and medicine-show entertainer who pretended to be blind, hence his occasional sobriquet on records, 'Bogus Ben Covington'. He also recorded as Ben Curry. (This identification has not yet been accepted by B&GR but the evidence is compelling. Which was his true surname is uncertain.) Williams also remembered him, perhaps accurately, as a member of the Birmingham Jug Band. Reportedly born in Mississippi, possibly somewhere around Columbus, Covington is thought to have died in the mid-'30s.

*** Alabama: Black Country Dance Bands (1924–1949)
Document DOCD-5166 *Covington. c. 9/28–c. 1/32.*

Of the ten sides issued under variants of Covington's name, eight have been recovered and are included in this compilation. (For most of its other tracks see Daddy Stovepipe.) When he chants the comic songs 'Adam And Eve In The Garden' and 'I Heard The Voice Of A Pork Chop' his voice sounds small and pugnacious, but a year later, when he made 'Boodle-De-Bum Blues' and 'It's A Fight Like That', it was recorded with more warmth. A hokum artist rather than a blues singer, he performs with a brio that increases with the years, and his 1932 sides are positively boisterous. He accompanies himself on all these recordings with banjo-mandolin and shrill harmonica, a setting that does not prepare one at all for the astonishing 'Mule Skinner Moan' on the VAC *Times Ain't Like They Used To Be – Vol. 5* (Yazoo 2063). Surviving on a test pressing from a hitherto unknown Paramount session in 1929, the piece is a worksong with roots in the prison-song tradition, the vocal melody rising and falling like a field holler over a tentative piano: all the more entrancing for being so utterly unexpected. TR

Robert Covington (1941–96)
VOCAL, DRUMS

Mississippian by birth, Covington transferred to Chicago in 1965, where he put his drumming skills, first acquired in school, at the service of Little Walter, Fenton Robinson and other artists. Through the '80s and early '90s he was the drummer and second singer in Sunnyland Slim's band. Latterly he led his own band at Kingston Mines.

**(*) Blues In The Night
Evidence ECD 26074 *Covington; Steve Jensen (t); Billy McFarland (tb); Paul Haney (as); John Brumbach, Gary Wiggins (ts); Scott Bradbury (h); Sumito Ariyoshi (o, p); Chris Rannenberg (p); Carl Weathersby, Peter Crawford, Bob Levis, Jon McDonald (g); Harlan Terson, Bob Anderson (b); Marvin Jackson (d). 12/83, 11/87–3/88.*

During his years with Sunnyland Slim, Covington cut a single, 'I Want To Thank Ya' (included on this CD), and sang a couple of numbers on his leader's album *Chicago Jump*. He then made what proved to be his only album, an energetic performance, sympathetically recorded. He had a fine, flexible voice, not hugely distinctive, but not borrowed from any better-known stylist either. As well as being able to handle both a blues standard like 'I Just Want To Make Love To You' and an airier soul number like 'Trust In Me', he gave a skilful Joe Williams presentation to the title track, a song not every vocalist could make work in a blues context. TR

Ida Cox (1896–1967)
VOCAL

Ida Prather, from Toccoa, Georgia, ran away to join a minstrel show in 1910, and her career in tent shows, clubs and theatres lasted until 1945, when she suffered a stroke. She made a swansong LP in 1961. Cox took her stage name from her first marriage, to fellow performer Adler Cox; she later married Jesse Crump, who accompanied her on some of her records.

**** Ida Cox – Vol. 1 (1923)
Document DOCD-5322 *Cox; Tommy Ladnier (c); Jimmy O'Bryant (cl); Lovie Austin, Jesse Crump (p); unknown (vn). 6/23–12/23.*

**** Ida Cox – Vol. 2 (1924–1925)
Document DOCD-5323 *Cox; Tommy Ladnier, Elmer Chambers, Howard Scott, unknown (c); Charlie Green, unknown (tb); Don Redman (cl, ss); Jimmy O'Bryant, poss. Stump Evans, unknown (cl); Charles Harris (as); unknown (ts); Lovie Austin, Fletcher Henderson (p); Milas Pruitt, Charlie Dixon (bj); Miles Pruitt (g); unknown (perc); unknown (eff). c. 3/24–4/25.*

***(*) Ida Cox – Vol. 3 (1925–1927)
Document DOCD-5324 *Cox; Tommy Ladnier, Bob Shoffner, poss. Bernie Young, prob. Shirley Clay, unknown (c); poss. Charlie Green, poss. Kid Ory or Albert Wynn (tb); Jimmy O'Bryant, Johnny Dodds (cl); Jesse Crump (o, p); Lovie Austin (p); Papa Charlie Jackson (bj, v); Houston Woodfork (bj); W. E. Burton (d, poss. woodblocks); poss. Jasper Taylor (d).* 4/25–c. 7/27.

***(*) Ida Cox – Vol. 4 (1927–1938) [sic]
Document DOCD-5235 *Cox; poss. Dave Nelson, poss. B. T. Wingfield (c); Shad Collins (t); Roy Palmer, Dickie Wells (tb); unknown (cl, as); unknown (cl); Buddy Tate (ts); Jesse Crump, poss. Tiny Parham, James P. Johnson (p); unknown (bj); Walter Page (b); Jo Jones (d).* c. 7/27–12/39.

Paramount's billing of Ida Cox as 'The Uncrowned Queen of the Blues' was not simply marketing hype; Cox's commitment to her material makes her one of the finest vaudeville singers. She takes each song on its own terms, and is always concerned to phrase for meaning and emotional content, hardly ever falling into predetermined patterns. Her recordings were very popular, and very influential; there's a small thesis to be written on phrases, verses and songs of Cox's that passed into folk traditions. It's well worth getting past the deficiencies of Paramount's sound quality to find out why.

These four discs gather Cox's recordings for Paramount, and *Vol. 4* also includes (and misdates) two songs from the 1939 *From Spirituals To Swing* concert. The first two volumes include some alternative takes; there are 13 more on *Classic Blues & Vaudeville Singers (1921–1930) The Alternative Takes* (Document DOCD-5573), and nine on *Classic Blues, Jazz & Vaudeville Singers – Vol. 3 (1922–1927)* (Document DOCD-5626).

Her own talent aside, Ida Cox was usually well served by her musicians. Ladnier, O'Bryant and Austin, who are heavily featured on Document's first two volumes, were first-rate blues players, offering alert, emotive commentary rather than mere accompaniment; the interplay between Cox and Ladnier, whose vocalized tone and phrasing take their cue from King Oliver, is particularly outstanding. There's a slight decline in quality on *Vol. 3*; Ladnier disappears after the first two tracks, heading for Europe, and Paramount replaced him with a parade of generally less effective cornettists. Three collaborations with Papa Charlie Jackson are let down by his perfunctory singing and playing, and other tracks are devalued by clippety-clopping percussion. Nevertheless, there is still much to enjoy, not least six accompaniments by Jesse Crump. He plays reed-organ on two of them, and its funereal funkiness on 'Coffin Blues' is very winning.

Crump's percussive yet lyrical piano features on two thirds of *Vol. 4*'s 24 tracks; eight where he is the only accompanist are as good as anything in Cox's repertoire. The limited cornettist and four-square banjoist added on the other eight are regrettable, but the songs are superior, with 'Fogyism' an outstandingly interesting catalogue of superstitions. On Cox's last Paramount sessions, there's a sense of a career winding down, as African-American tastes changed and the Depression hit record sales; she still had what it took, though, as she confirmed ten years later at Carnegie Hall, overcoming an echo as intrusive as Paramount's surface noise.

***(*) Ida Cox – Vol. 5 (1939–1940)
Document DOCD-5651 *Cox; Hot Lips Page, Henry Allen (t); J. C. Higginbotham (tb); Edmond Hall (cl); James P. Johnson, Fletcher Henderson, Cliff Jackson (p); Charlie Christian (g); Artie Bernstein, Billy Taylor (b); Lionel Hampton, Jimmy Hoskins (d).* 10/39–12/40.

These Vocalion sessions were set up by John Hammond, and it was probably his money that assembled the accompanying 'All-Star Band'. Ida Cox's pitch had dropped and her range narrowed, but she retained all her ability to read a song. The accompaniments are as superb as might be expected; Christian's advanced playing and Johnson's piano are only the most outstanding elements. The music is sophisticated swing rather than gutbucket blues, whether Ida is essaying the risqué with 'One Hour Mama', re-creating old favourites like 'Death Letter Blues' or coming up to date with a song about being laid off from the WPA. The 19 tracks include eight alternative takes (one of them a 13-second false start), and one is sometimes being educated rather than entertained, but the quality is far too high to make it of interest only to completists.

**** The Uncrowned Queen Of The Blues
Black Swan BSCD-7 *Cox; Tommy Ladnier, unknown (c); unknown (tb); Jimmy O'Bryant, poss. Stump Evans, unknown (cl); Charles Harris (as); unknown (ts); Lovie Austin, Jesse Crump (p); unknown (vn).* 6/23–c. 8/24.

(****) The Essential
Classic Blues CBL 200017 2CD *As for relevant CDs above.* 6/23–12/40.

These are handy compilations for the listener who doesn't want the complete works. Black Swan's 20 tracks draw on Cox's earlier recordings, mainly those with Austin, Ladnier and O'Bryant. The selection could have been improved by being made either more varied or less; there's only one track with Jesse Crump, and 'Blues Ain't Nothin' Else But!', with a New York band, makes for a lurching stylistic change. Substituting 'Chicago Bound Blues' or 'Chattanooga Blues' would have made a very good selection even better.

With 36 tracks spanning her early career, at budget price and in acceptable sound, *The Essential* looks like a clear winner, but there are some presentational problems. The tracks are ordered by the compiler's whim rather than chronologically; that's not necessarily a bad thing, but it is a disadvantage here, particularly in the absence of discographical details. The listener doesn't get much sense of how Cox's art developed and changed in the long term, or of how she responded to the demands of each session in the short term. The 1939–40 material is interspersed among the '20s recordings, and the contrast is jarring. None of that detracts from the music itself, which is generally splendid, although again the selection is not unimprovable.

**(*) Blues For Rampart Street
Riverside OJCCD-1758 *Cox; Roy Eldridge (t); Coleman Hawkins (ts); Sammy Price (p); Milt Hinton (b); Jo Jones (d).* 4/61.

Ida Cox was reluctant to record this session, on the grounds of religion and rustiness, and she was right. Her range had become very narrow and flat at the bottom, and her phrasing is sometimes uncertain. The accompaniment is by a band of greats, rather than a great band; Eldridge and Hawkins are reluctant to be venturesome, seemingly for fear of throwing Cox off course. Most tracks are re-creations of old favourites, and occasionally she makes her vocal limitations irrelevant ('Wild Women Don't Have The Blues' is actually wilder than the original), but the session was essentially a vanity project for John Hammond and Orrin Keepnews. cs

Kurt Crandall
VOCAL, HARMONICA

Though he has played in other parts of the US, Crandall is currently based in Kansas City.

**(*) True Story
Relevant RR 099 *Crandall; Mike Sedovic (p); Karl Angerer (g, b); Pete Kanaras (g); Ralph Ybarra (b); Jaisson Taylor (d, v); Tom Baker (perc, v).* 04.

Crandall seems to have the talent, as harmonica player, singer and songwriter, to make an impressive album. This isn't quite it, chiefly because he hasn't fully absorbed, and sublimated, the influence of his models, and on most of the tracks they can still be detected, like faint background voices. It's okay that there should be something of Little Walter in the harmonica playing, but the casually hip lyrics, the delivery and even sometimes the melodies of songs like 'Self-Servin' Ah Ah' and 'Bed Has One Pillow' n-letter to Rick Estrin. Recordingwise ntiquarian, and he found friends of e studio was full of vintage guitars, neral effect is in roughly the same cises by Junior Watson, Kid Ramos lie & The Nightcats. TR

n 1953)

Robert Cray's musical grounding was in the church-based soul and R&B of Sam Cooke and Ray Charles, until a 1969 meeting with Albert Collins opened him up to the blues. His first band was formed five years later and his first album made in 1978, although it wasn't released until 1980. Looking and sounding like a revived Magic Sam, Cray placed himself at the forefront of the blues revival of the '80s with a series of albums that won handfuls of awards. By the following decade, the traditional blues elements had been expunged from his repertoire, as his records reflected his respect for soul heroes like Z. Z. Hill and O. V. Wright. In the '90s, his gigs and records became rather too stylized and obsessive but recent efforts indicate a softening of the image and a new maturity in his writing.

*** Who's Been Talkin'
Mercury 546 700 *Cray; Nolan Smith (t); David Ii (ts); Curtis Salgado (h, v); David Stewart, Nat Dove (p); Richard Cousins, Dennis Walker (b); Tom Murphy, Buster Jones (d).* 78.

A quietly competent if rather short debut album combines Cray's nascent songwriting talent with a series of covers from the pens of Willie Dixon, Sonny Thompson, Howlin' Wolf, Sam Myers and O. V. Wright. There's a surfeit of good musicianship but primarily it's impressive in hindsight. Cray's band and Nat Dove's session musicians tend too readily to politeness and this blunts the trenchancy of 'Who's Been Talkin'' and 'Sleeping In The Ground'. With just two sax solos, the spotlight is thrown on Cray's often pointillistic guitar work, which is by turns fluent and mannered. 'If You're Thinkin' What I'm Thinkin'' and 'Nice As A Fool Can Be' are firm pointers towards the direction his songwriting would take, while his singing hasn't yet developed the nasal quality that would become such a feature of his later work.

*** Bad Influence
Mercury 830 245 *Cray; Warren Rand (as); Mike Vannice (ts, o, p); Richard Cousins (b); David Olson (d); David Ii (perc); Phillip Walker, Tony Mathews, Night Train Clemens (v).* 83.

Still delivering short measure (even with two bonus tracks, the album lasts only 42 minutes), this nevertheless charts the beginning of the Cray phenomenon. 'Phone Booth' was a gig opener for the next decade and the title track enjoyed similar longevity. Cray has a hand in most of the originals, although 'March On' and 'No Big Deal' are slight in comparison to 'Where Do I Go From Here' and 'Waiting For The Tide To Turn'. Johnny 'Guitar' Watson's 'Don't Touch Me' is recast in the Cray band's increasingly familiar mould, while Eddie Floyd's 'Got To Make A Comeback' is a model of simplicity. Vannice takes a handful of well-constructed sax solos and the band as a whole is a model of efficiency. The ingredients for success are here assembled; all that's needed is a touch of magic.

***(*) False Accusations
Hightone HCD 8005//Mercury 530 244 *Cray; Nolan Smith (t); David Ii (ts); Peter Boe (kb); Dale Wilson (g); Richard Cousins, Dennis Walker (b); David Olson (d).* 85.

Not quite magical, this is the first Cray concept album, if a relentless focus on adultery and failed relationships can be called such. Melancholy predominates. The protagonist in these songs is rarely angry, rather resigned to his fate, whether put upon or racked with guilt. The latter emotion inhabits the album's bookends, 'Porch Light' and the extraordinary 'Sonny'; other adulterers are found 'Playin' In The Dirt' or declaring it's 'The Last Time (I Get Burned Like This)'. Cray's voice has taken on a nasal whine appropriate to the songs' complaining texts, while his guitar solos are even more pointillistic, adding a dimension of inarticulate torture to the prevailing gloom. Given the waves of negativity that wash across the listener, this is a surprisingly satisfying album, the template for several years to come.

In 1985 Cray was also a junior partner in the triumvirate that made *Showdown!* (Alligator ALCD 4743), for which see the entries for Albert Collins and Johnny Copeland.

**** Strong Persuader
Mercury 830 568 *Cray; Wayne Jackson (t, tb); Andrew Love (ts); Peter Boe (kb); Richard Cousins (b); David Olson (d); Lee Spath (perc).* 86.

Occupying the same emotional territory as *False Accusations*, this is the one that persuaded the public, helped by significant airtime on MTV. 'Smoking Gun', about how love can lead to murder, became an American Top 40 hit, while the album reached #13 in the album chart. 'Right Next Door (Because Of Me)' was an even better song, from which the album's title was taken, closely followed by 'More Than I Can Stand'. The final trilogy of 'I Wonder', 'Fantasized' and 'New Blood' concentrate on the protagonist's inability to forget a lost love, diametrically opposed to the pyrrhic victory described in 'I Guess I Showed Her'. Cray sings and plays with utter confidence, abetted by a band that relishes precision. Hindsight identifies the merest hint of a formulaic straitjacket but this wasn't the time for restraint.

***(*) Don't Be Afraid Of The Dark
Mercury 834 923 *As above, except add David Sanborn (as); omit Spath.* 88.

With slightly less emphasis on ruined relationships, this is a subtly themed album, with several of its vignettes taking place after dark. The title track stresses the comfort of company, while 'Night Patrol' is about the plight of the homeless. In 'Your Secret's Safe With Me', Bob observes the nocturnal adventures of a cheating woman – not his, for a change. Elsewhere, in 'Don't You Even Care' and the excellent 'Across The Line', he's the put-upon party, as usual. But the album ends on a surprisingly optimistic note with 'Laugh Out Loud', which is what he does having found the ideal relationship after all the failures charted in previous albums. Once again, the musicianship is immaculate; David Sanborn's alto enlivens 'Acting This Way', providing a welcome respite from Cray's guitar solos, good as they habitually are. The return of the Memphis Horns continues the drift towards the classic sounds of the Hi and Stax labels.

***(*) Midnight Stroll
Mercury 846 652 *Cray; Wayne Jackson (t, tb); Andrew Love (ts); Jimmy Pugh (o, p); Tim Kaihatsu (g); Richard Cousins (b); Kevin Hayes (d, perc); Antoine Salley, O. Washington, Night Train Clemens, Madison Cooper (perc).* 90.

A change of personnel injects more active keyboards and a stronger rhythmic pulse. The subject-matter remains the same but there's definitely more imagination in the arrangements. The title track ends the album, chained to a repetitive riff that dulls the ear, but what precedes it is very much up to form. Songs like 'The Forecast (Calls For Pain)', 'These Things' and 'Bouncin' Back' see more commitment from Cray, including full-throated screams in the latter pair. Contrastingly, 'The Things You Do To Me' is a poised and quiet lovesong that avoids the funereal qualities of 'My Problem'. There's a note of over-confidence about 'Walk Around Time', a man's plea for his own 'space' that could lead to rueful 'Consequences'. With a successful formula in place, there's perhaps a slackening of artistic tension now the hunger for success has been assuaged but this is still fine music-making.

*** I Was Warned
Mercury 512 721 *Cray; Wayne Jackson (t, tb); Andrew Love (ts); Jim Pugh (kb); Tim Kaihatsu (g); Karl Sevareid (b); Kevin Hayes (d).* 92.

With the departure of Richard Cousins, the makeover of the Cray band is complete. But there's no longer a blues connection and as good as Cray's new music is, it now operates in a stylistic vacuum recognizably his own but detached from any explicit mooring. The songs, with collaborators like Steve Cropper and Boz Scaggs, have become less specific, apart from 'He Don't Live Here Anymore', about the death of a parent. Best here are two ballads, 'The Price I Pay' and 'A Whole Lotta Pride', sensitively sung and immaculately played, as are all the backing tracks. The rhumba-based title track is the only one to outstay its welcome, with five choruses of guitar solo unwinding towards the fade. Otherwise, succinctness is the keyword for an entertaining album that doesn't quite live in the memory once it's over.

*** Shame And A Sin
Mercury 518 517 *Cray; Mark Pender (t); Edward Manion (ts, bs); unknown (h); Jim Pugh (o, p, x); Albert Collins (g); Karl Sevareid (b); Kevin Hayes (d).* 93.

The next logical step was for Cray to produce himself and he makes a fairly good job of it. There's an open, ambient sound to the band tracks but this sometimes makes the drumkit too intrusive and some of the quirky arrangements might have been smoothed over with the guiding presence of a producer. A blues dimension returns with '1040 Blues', 'You're Gonna Need Me' (with Albert Collins's clattering guitar breaks), 'I'm Just Lucky That Way' and 'Well I Lied', the latter's short sharp shock being particularly effective. On the other hand, 'Passing By' and 'Up And Down' are dirge-like and obsessive, with Cray turning inwards and failing to project. Most serious of all is the disappearance of the positive attitude that made *False Accusations* and *Strong Persuader* such entertaining catalogues of disharmony and failed relationships.

**(*) Some Rainy Morning
Mercury 526 928 *Cray; Jim Pugh (kb); Karl Sevareid (b); Kevin Hayes (d).* 95.

An appropriately moist title (from 'Tell The Landlord', the album's only blues) for what is probably Cray's creative nadir – not that the record is badly made or lacking in expertise, just that the material on which so much effort has been expended isn't worthy of it. Spiritless and self-indulgent, song after song lumbers by, each hampered with an unnecessarily fussy arrangement. Cray's guitar provides the only respite and even that seems trapped in its own introspective dance. The rest of the band are metronomically precise, not quite automata but willing androids. Ten years on from his greatest achievements, Cray badly needed to re-establish contact with his younger self and his inspiration.

*** Sweet Potato Pie
Mercury 534 483//(E) 534 698 *As above, except add Wayne Jackson (t), Andrew Love (ts).* 97.

Something of a return to form, this set contrasts revivals of O. V. Wright's 'Save It' and Otis Redding's 'Trick Or Treat' with Cray's own more angular compositions. That said, 'Jealous Minds' (by Pugh and Hayes) and 'I Can't Quit' pay their respects to the Memphis soul tradition. Nevertheless, several of his other songs, including 'Back Home', the insipid 'Little Birds' and 'Simple Things', are dangerously close to being turgid and too long for no good reason. Self-production has become synonymous with self-indulgence and good musicianship is wasted on unmemorable material. Pugh's 'The One In The Middle' and Cray's 'Not Bad For Love' save the day, the latter doubling its tempo for an extended guitar solo.

***(*) Take Your Shoes Off
Rykodisc RCD 10479 *Cray; Scott Thompson, Wayne Jackson (t); Jack Hale (tb); Jim Horn, Jim Spake, Andrew Love, Doug Moffat, Bobby Keys (ts); James Mitchell (bs); Jo-El Sonnier (ac); Steve Jordan (kb, g, perc, v, prod); Jim Pugh (kb); Karl Sevareid (b); Kevin Hayes (d); Nashelles (v).* 99.

A new label and producer Steve Jordan provide much-needed stimuli for Cray's reinvention. Willie Mitchell wrote the opening 'Love Gone To Waste' and its Hi rhythm sound dominates these 12 tracks, particularly Mack Rice's '24-7 Man' and 'It's All Gone'. The warmer sound qualities draw more natural and approachable performances from Cray, who dispenses with the anguished whine that had become such a part of his vocal arsenal. 'All The Way' (written with his wife Susan) and 'Let Me Know' benefit from this new maturity, while the strutting 'What About Me' and Jimmy Pugh's 'Living

Proof' provide Cray with ample solo space. An eerily accurate version of Willie Dixon's 'Tolling Bells' completes an album that marks a determined return to form.

**** Shoulda Been Home
Rykodisc RCD 10611 *Cray; Ben Cauley (t); Jack Hale (tb); Andrew Love (ts); Jim Pugh (kb); Steve Jordan (g, d, perc, v); Karl Sevareid, Willie Weeks (b); Kevin Hayes (d). 01.*

The promise of *Take Your Shoes Off* is here fulfilled, as a new sensitivity invests Cray's vocal in 'Already Gone', his best composition for some time, played with exceptional restraint by all concerned. On the same level of achievement are 'Anytime', 'Out Of Eden', Jim Pugh's nine-minute opus that forms the centrepiece of the album, and 'Far Away', which Cray co-wrote with his wife. Mack Rice's 'Love Sickness' and Elmore James's 'Cry For Me Baby' and 'The 12 Year Old Boy' sound almost anachronistic by comparison, as if, like the fragmentary 'Renew Blues', they come from a part of Cray's past that he might now confidently put behind him. His stock-in-trade remains the vicissitudes of relationships but now acceptance tempers the frustration, indicating that artistic maturity has arrived. NS

**(*) Time Will Tell
Sanctuary 84613//(E) SANCD 194 *Cray; Cynthia Robinson (t); Jerry Martin (ts, tamb); Jim Pugh (kb); Turtle Island String Quartet (David Balakrishnan, Evan Price [vn]; Danny Seidenberg [vl]; Mark Summer [vc]); Karl Sevareid (b); Kevin Hayes (d); Luis Conte (perc). 03.*

'Good musicianship wasted on unmemorable material' was the verdict on a couple of earlier albums, and *Time Will Tell* prompts a similar judgement, although the polish of any performance by this experienced band tends to conceal weaknesses in the woodwork. All the songs were written by members of the band, Pugh's fuzzy meditations on war ('Distant Shore') and death ('Up In The Sky') fortunately balanced by Cray's somewhat more focused compositions 'Survivor' and 'Times Makes Two'. The latter closes the album memorably with Cray's guitar obsessively repeating itself, like a rotating beam from a lighthouse piercing the massing clouds of strings. TR

Pee Wee Crayton (1914–85)
VOCAL, GUITAR

The most prominent of the guitarists to bask in the shadow of T-Bone Walker's innovative playing, Connie Curtis Crayton did well for a late starter. He was already 30 when, as a result of watching Walker's act and with his subsequent help, he took up the guitar. Careful to foster mannerisms of his own but developing little over the years, his reputation rested on a series of hard-edged guitar features and frequent 'Battles Of The Blues' with Walker and others. In a long career that saw him fourth best-selling 'race' artist of 1949 before entering a slow decline in public interest, Crayton missed out on the blues revivals of the '60s and '70s, remaining essentially in thrall to his mentor.

*** Blues After Hours: The Essential Pee Wee Crayton
[Indigo IGOCD 2526] *Crayton; Ernie Royal, Harry Edison (t); unknown (as); Buddy Floyd, Ben Webster, unknowns (ts); unknowns (s); David Lee Johnson, Jay McShann, Jack LaRue, Willard McDaniel, unknowns (p); Bill Davis, Joe Comfort, unknowns (b); Al 'Cake' Wichard, Alvin Stoller, unknown (d). 47–51.*

*** The Modern Legacy Volume 1
Ace CDCHD 632 *Similar to above. 48–51.*
*** Blues Guitar Magic: The Modern Legacy Volume 2
Ace CDCHD 767 *Similar to above. 49–52.*

Crayton made his recording debut with Ivory Joe Hunter in 1946 and had a couple of his own records issued before being signed to Modern in 1948 to cover T-Bone Walker's 'I'm Still In Love With You'. But it was the record's B-side, a cover of Avery Parrish's 'Blues After Hours', that became a hit, the first time a guitar instrumental had done so. Thereafter his sessions were divided between up-tempo instrumentals ('Bounce Pee Wee', 'Rockin' The Blues'), blues ('Central Avenue Blues', 'Louella Brown') and blues-ballads ('When Darkness Falls', 'Tired Of Travelin''). Almost all of these are on *The Modern Legacy Volume 1*. Sadly, Crayton was limited as an improviser, the keynote phrase of 'Texas Hop' cropping up too often in subsequent solos. Nor was he a naturally talented singer, and at slower tempos his indifferent pitching and enunciation were particularly noticeable. Even so, his records were well made, with several notable soloists in the various personnels, making this an entertaining if slightly underwhelming experience.

Blues Guitar Magic is another random trawl through Crayton's Modern sessions, made more coherent by being less reliant upon alternative takes than its predecessor. On occasions, in 'Phone Call From My Baby' and 'Tired Of Travelin'', his vocals sound more assured, although the hit ballad 'I Love You So' and several others suffer from suspect intonation. Ten instrumental features, though innocuous and entertaining, draw attention to the paucity of his ideas and their repetition. Crayton's weak flame flourishes best when supported by the larger orchestral forces heard on 'Louella Brown' and 'Huckle Boogie'. At slower tempos and with less augmentation, his lack of confidence, both vocal and instrumental, becomes glaringly obvious.

Blues After Hours has the pre-Modern single 'Don't Ever Fall In Love'/'Pee Wee Special' but otherwise draws virtually all its material, including most of the tracks singled out above, from the two Ace CDs, and is perhaps the most attractive of the three sets; unfortunately it is likely to be hard to find.

**(*) Things I Used To Do
Vanguard VMD 6566 *Crayton; Larry Nash (p); Lloyd Rowe (g); Ben Brown (b); Robert Lee Dupree (d). 8/70.*
*** The Essential Recordings
Purple Pyramid CLP 0960 *Crayton; Little Willie Jackson (as); Jackie Kelso, Clifford Solomon (ts); Big Jim Wynn (bs); unknown (h); Johnny Otis (p, d, vb); Shuggie Otis (g, b). 74.*

The defects of *Things I Used To Do*, among them an over-recorded bass, lightweight material like 'Peace Of Mind', 'You Were Wrong' and 'Little Bitty Things', and guitar solos that are more gesture than substance, outweigh its better passages such as the slow blues 'My Kind Of Woman' and a long, genial reading of 'S. K. Blues'. *The Essential Recordings*, originally cut for Johnny Otis's Blues Spectrum label, may bear a fallacious title but it's certainly superior to the Vanguard session and possibly Crayton's best from this period. A principal reason for its success is the quality of his backing musicians, not least the multi-instrumental abilities of Otis Sr and Jr. 'Texas Hop' and 'Blues After Hours' are to be expected and these versions are by no means shabby. 'Don't Forget To Close The Door' and 'My Baby's On The Line' are effective reworkings of 'I Got News For You' and 'The Telephone Is Ringing' respectively, as is 'If I Ever Get Lucky'. But it's not all good news. Little Richard's 'Lucille' is inappropriate in this company and Crayton hasn't the voice to bring off 'Need Your Love So Bad'. Worse, 'Louella Brown', though listed, isn't present. Though it may be hard to find, this is a set with some pleasant surprises.

*** Early Hour Blues
Blind Pig BPCD 5052 *Crayton; Claude Williams (t); Fred Clark (as, ts, bs); Marshall Crayton Jr, Bill Clark (ts); Fernando Harkles (s); Rod Piazza (h); Honey Piazza, Llew Matthews (p); Doug MacLeod (g); Eric Ajaye, Dan Fredman (b); Soko Richardson, Lee Spath (d). 8/83–12/84.*

A conflation of two albums made during his last years, this set finds Crayton coping well with modernity, though the first session suffers from over-arrangement. His guitar playing is more considered and his voice has deepened appreciably. Five of the 11 tracks are instrumentals, including an inevitable 'Blues After Hours' and its clone 'Early Hours'. Crayton's vocal is overwhelmed on the funk-fussy opener, 'Blues At Daybreak', but B. B. King's 'When I'm Wrong' finds him singing and playing with authority. Piazza takes a harmonica solo on this but is otherwise content to blend with the brass section. Indifferent production values hamper appreciation at times but overall this is a surprisingly successful set that misses being the 'affirmation of greatness' its traycard proclaims. NS/TR

Enrico Crivellaro
GUITAR

From Padua in Italy, Crivellaro has played with James Harman and in the Royal Crown Revue.

*** Key To My Kingdom
Electro-Fi 3379 *Crivellaro; Scott Steen (t); Jeff Turmes (ts); Bruce Katz (o, p); Alex Schultz (g); Rick Reed (b); Steve Mugalian (d); Finis Tasby, James Harman (v). 1/03.*

That this is so attractive a debut is owing in part to the astute choice, as guest vocalists, of Finis Tasby on six numbers and James Harman on two – but only in part, for Crivellaro is a skilful guitarist who doesn't merely command several blues styles but applies them inventively to a well-chosen programme that ranges from Percy Mayfield's 'You're In For A Big Surprise' and Ruth Brown's 'Rain Is A Bringdown', both well sung by Tasby, to lithely executed instrumentals, such as Ramsey Lewis's 'The "In" Crowd', Donald Byrd's 'Black Jack' and the original 'Train To Venice', in which Crivellaro sounds somewhat – but not obtrusively so – like Ronnie Earl. Contributions by Steen and Katz add to the album's appeal. TR

G. L. Crockett (c. 1929–67)
VOCAL

The Mississippi-born George L. Crockett was active on the Chicago music scene from the early '50s. His first single – billed as by G. 'Davy' Crockett since the movie about 'the hero of the Alamo' was popular at the time – was the rockabilly 'Look Out Mabel'. It made little impression and he didn't record again for seven or eight years, when he had the hit of his career, such as it was, with 'It's A Man Down There'.

**(*) Rockin' With The Blues: G. L. Crockett Meets Big Walter Price
Official OF-CD 5679 *Crockett; Lorenzo Smith (ts); unknowns (s); Henry Gray, unknowns (p); Louis Myers, unknown (g); Reggie Boyd, unknown (b); unknowns (d); unknowns (v grp). 57–65.*

Crockett recorded only eight sides, which, with two alternative takes, make up his portion of this CD. His meagre output is no index of his talent. He had a light, wheedling voice that suited the pop-blues he was sometimes allowed to record, and his last single, 'Think Twice Before You Go'/'Gonna Make You Mine', was very attractive. But it was also somewhat derivative, a recurrent problem: of the sides for which he's chiefly remembered, 'Look Out Mabel' was firmly rooted in Junior Parker's 'Mystery Train' and 'It's A Man Down There' was a pert imitation of Jimmy Reed. A few tracks suffer from severe distortion. The rest of the CD is by Big Walter Price. TR

Arthur 'Big Boy' Crudup (1905–74)
VOCAL, GUITAR

Arthur Crudup was over 30 before he began playing guitar, but soon became a popular recording artist, commuting from Mississippi to Chicago for sessions every few months. With tastes changing, Victor ended his contract in 1954; Crudup moved to Virginia, becoming a labour contractor. Towards the end of his life, he found a new audience, to whom he was extravagantly mis-sold as 'the father of rock and roll' on the strength of three songs recorded by Elvis Presley. At least the Presley connection got Crudup some gigs; he was dead before publishing royalties were extracted from Hill & Range.

**(*) Big Boy Crudup – Vol. 1 (1941–1946)
Document DOCD-5201 *Crudup; Joe McCoy, Ransom Knowling (b); Melvin Draper, Charles Saunders, Jump Jackson, Judge Riley (d). 9/41–9/46.*
**(*) Big Boy Crudup – Vol. 2 (1946–1949)
Document DOCD-5202 *Crudup; Ransom Knowling (b); Judge Riley (d). 9/46–3/49.*
**(*) Big Boy Crudup – Vol. 3 (1949–1952)
Document DOCD-5203 *As above, except add J. Sheffield (b), N. Butler (d). 3/49–1/52.*
**(*) Big Boy Crudup – Vol. 4 (1952–1954) [sic]
Document DOCD-5204 *Crudup; J. J. Jones (ts); Sonny Boy Williamson II (h, sp); Robert Dees, Percy Lee Crudup, unknown (h); Edward Lumpkin, Thomas Patten, unknown (p); Joe Willie Wilkins, Robert Fulton, unknown (g); 'Sam', Charles Holloway, Joe Thomas, unknowns (b); Lafayette Lawson, Willie Willis, unknowns (d). 1/52–62.*
*** Dirt Road Blues
Past Perfect 204399 *Similar to above CDs. 9/41–4/51.*
***(*) The Very Best Songs
Wolf Blues Classics BC 005 *Similar to above CDs. 9/41–8/52.*
***(*) The Essential
Classic Blues CBL 200025 2CD *Similar to above CDs. 9/41–4/54.*
*** That's All Right Mama
Bluebird 61043 *Similar to above CDs. 9/41–4/54.*

*** Rock Me Mamma [sic]
Bluebird 55155 *Similar to above CDs.* 9/41–4/54.

(***) Everything's Alright
Our World 3303 *Crudup; Ransom Knowling (b); Jump Jackson, Judge Riley (d).* 2/46–10/47.

Arthur Crudup had a clear, ringing voice, and was a capable lyricist and an astute snapper-up of songs from other artists; 'Mean Old 'Frisco' was his composition, and while his version of 'Rock Me Mama' was not the first, it was an important step in the song's journey to canonical status. Crudup's music also spurred the rise to popularity of the electric ensemble. He only played in E, and his guitar technique and melodic invention were both limited. It's not quite a case of 'the slow tune and the other one', and the sameness didn't matter to the people who bought his 78s; they were attracted by the words, the singing and the bouncy drum and bass rhythms. It's a problem when the songs are collected on CD, though.

There are some gems tucked away on Document's middle two volumes, but the first and last are the most rewarding. *Vol. 1* starts with ten beautiful tracks where a string bass is the only support; the first four, which are Crudup's only recordings with acoustic guitar, include the piercingly hollered 'If I Get Lucky' and the desolate 'Death Valley Blues'. *Vol. 4* wraps up the Victor trio sides, then presents rough, tough juke-joint music, recorded in Mississippi with harmonica players and other friends; 'Make A Little Love', with Sonny Boy Williamson II and Joe Willie Wilkins, is outstanding. On the final Victor sides the trio format was abandoned, but the Atlanta R&B musicians used were uninventive. Document tack on two tracks recorded by Fire which are not on the Collectables CD discussed below.

Most listeners will prefer a selection. *Dirt Road Blues*' 16 tracks have adequate sound, but stop short of the Mississippi recordings. Our World trumpet their audio processing, which creates a fuzzy ambience in which the drums seem louder. On 'Ethel Mae', something called 'pseudo stereo' has been mishandled, and Crudup duets with his own echo. Classic Blues' 36 tracks include all the important songs, at bargain price and in superior sound. Programming for variety of tempo and style mitigates the problem of sameness, but the switches into and out of the customary trio format are sometimes abrupt, a drawback compounded by the lack of discographical data. Wolf's remastering is warmer, but preserves more of the (generally slight) surface noise. The title invites disputation, but these 22 chronologically ordered tracks are a better selection than the 22 on *That's All Right Mama*. Perhaps thanks to the Presley association, *That's All Right Mama* seems to have stayed in catalogue despite sharing ten tracks (again of 22) with Bluebird's more recent *Rock Me Mamma*, which is better programmed and features extensive and knowledgeable notes.

***(*) Mean Ole Frisco
Collectables COL-CD-5130 *Crudup; unknown (g); unknown (b); unknown (d).* 62.

***(*) Rock Me Mama
Tomato TOM-2003 *As above.* 62.

(***) That's Alright Mama
Laserlight 17 246 *As above, except omit unknown (g).* 62.

In 1960, Lightnin' Hopkins's 'Mojo Hand' had been a surprise hit for Fire, and Bobby Robinson was looking to repeat its guitar-bass-drums formula. Arthur Crudup was happy to oblige, mainly with reprises of his old hits. The resulting LP sold poorly, but this was one of Crudup's most successful sessions, thanks to the springy momentum imparted by the rhythm section and an occasional, unobtrusive second guitarist. Collectables' 18 tracks and Tomato's 14 both include material not issued by Fire. *That's Alright Mama* is mid-price; so it should be, at ten tracks and 25 minutes.

*** After Hours
Camden 523802 *Similar to above CDs.* 9/41–62.

After Hours draws on the Victor and Fire catalogues; its 25 tracks are an unexceptional selection in adequate sound, but notes and programming alike are not very coherent, and the CD amounts to less than the sum of its parts.

** Look On Yonder's Wall
Delmark DE-614 *Crudup; Edward El (g); Dave Myers, Ransom Knowling (b); Judge Riley (d).* 5–6/67.

** Arthur 'Big Boy' Crudup Meets The Master Blues Bassists
Delmark DD-621 *Crudup; Willie Dixon, Ransom Knowling (b).* 6/68–11/69.

Crudup had retained most of his vocal strength in old age, and could still project a song with conviction, but he seldom went faster than slow; the music on these sessions wears slippers and dozes in its armchair. Eddie El was as basic a guitarist as Crudup, and Dave Myers sounds bored to distraction. Not even Crudup's old associates Ransom Knowling and Judge Riley (who appears on the tracks with El and Myers) can gee him up. CS

James Crutchfield (1912–2001)
VOCAL, PIANO

Crutchfield was already a veteran of the Louisiana lumber camps and Mississippi jukes when he settled in St Louis in 1948. He continued to perform until not long before his death.

**(*) St. Louis Blues Piano
Swingmaster CD 2205 *Crutchfield.* 10/83.

Crutchfield first recorded in 1957, cutting six titles which were not issued until 2000, on *Biddle Street Barrelhousin'* (Delmark DE-739). He was a forceful singer and pianist, tending towards the hollering of Roosevelt Sykes on the St Louis repertoire, but the strongest influence on his music remained the Louisiana tradition; he learned from Little Brother Montgomery in Bogalusa, and plays Brother's 'Forty Four Blues', although not without some radical simplification. On most tracks there is a generous helping of wrong notes – too many to be construable as either exotic spicing-up of the harmonies or eccentric individualism. Despite this, Crutchfield's performances are authoritative and interesting, and the CD is an important piece of documentation. There's certainly enjoyment to be had from listening to it, and probably enough to outweigh the intermittent wincing as his fingers make another emergency landing. CS

Albert Cummings
VOCAL, GUITAR

Cummings worked in the construction trade in his hometown in western Massachusetts, not taking up music professionally

until his late 20s. He had long been an admirer of Stevie Ray Vaughan and, after he played support for Double Trouble, Chris Layton and Tommy Shannon took him under their wing, producing and playing on his first record. Since then he has filled high-profile support slots with everyone from Sheryl Crow to B. B. King.

** From The Heart
AJC 1101//Under The Radar UTR 2709 *Cummings; Reese Williams, Riley Osbourn (kb); Tommy Shannon (g, b, prod); Johnny Moeller (g); Chris Layton (d, prod).* 03.

**(*) True To Yourself
Blind Pig BPCD 5092 *Cummings; Riley Osbourn (kb, p); Tommy Shannon (b); B. E. Frosty Smith (d); Jim Gaines (prod).* 04.

From The Heart is archetypal blues-rock cliché, though Layton and Shannon's playing and production roles lend clarity and shape. If he sang the way he wrote, Cummings could be the preacher you quickly ignore as you pass him on the street, thanklessly advising you to 'live life your own way' and never 'judge a book by its cover 'cause there's so much more than you'll discover.' Imagine Stevie Ray minus the slamming sweeps or chunky tone, and an earnest voice but of limited blues scope. There's a brief respite when he wrenches out the moody 'Barrel House Blues', with a rousing solo and mean whammy-bar judders, and later on he features funky Stratocaster snatches of Robert Cray.

The follow-up is rife with snappy funk and wah-wah solos. As before, Cummings wrote most of the tracks and the lyrics offer more ingenuous wisdom, but his voice wraps around the songs with more assurance. 'Come Up For Air' is a brand of Walter Trout-spawned white-boy riff-rock that modern blues axemen have adopted as surely as the band website forum (hear Aynsley Lister's *Everything I Need* for a British approximation). Since it's mostly strict blues it permits Cummings to expand his style with wails and thrusts, best displayed in the outro of 'Your Sweet Love'. It nicely sets up lush, spacious acoustic soloing in 'Sleep' and the penultimate track 'Lonely Bed', a slow blues which provides the album with an atmospheric climax. (Although, again, listen to Lister make this style arguably more gripping; even better, check out Shemekia Copeland's 'Married To The Blues' on *Turn The Heat Up* for the real thing.) RR

Nick Curran
VOCAL, GUITAR

Curran grew up in Portland, Maine. His father Mike encouraged his guitar playing by giving him records of Duke Robillard and Jimmie Vaughan, and by the time he was 15 he was playing in Mike's band. He had spells with the rockabilly singers Ronnie Dawson and Kim Lenz and moved to Dallas, where he worked with Hash Brown and recorded for Texas Jamboree. He later settled in Austin. He won a W. C. Handy Award in 2004 for 'Best New Artist Debut' and currently plays with the Fabulous Thunderbirds.

*** Doctor Velvet
Blind Pig BPCD 5081 *Curran; Rev. Murph Motycka (ts, bs); Joe Morales (ts); Gary Primich (h); Matt Farrell (p); Jimmie Vaughan (g); Eric Mathew Przygocki (b); Damien Llanes (d); Mike Barfield, Rachel Fenton, Caroline Gnagey, Bobby Horton (v).* 03.

*** Player!
Blind Pig BPCD 5091 *Curran; John Abrahamsen (t); Carl Querfurth (b); Paul Klemperer (ts, bs); John Doyle, Gordon Beadle (ts); Doug James (bs); Kim Wilson (h); Riley Osbourn (p); Eamon McLoughlin (strings); David Leroy Biller (g); Preston Hubbard (b, v); Damien Llanes (d, v).* 04.

Curran and his combo, the Nitelifes, are a fresh, young and accomplished retro band who dispense blues in jump and Chicago styles, rockabilly, doo-wop and honkytonk in impeccable '50s dress. On *Doctor Velvet* Curran's genial, unmannered singing has the range to encompass a Louis Prima-ish 'Don't Be Angry', the doomy pop blues 'She's Gone' and Hank Williams's 'Cold Cold Heart', while his period-perfect guitar rides the border country between West Coast blues and rockabilly with blithe skill. *Player!* is a similar serving of originals with a side-order of received repertoire like Wynonie Harris's 'Down Boy Down' and T-Bone Walker's 'Evenin'', garnished as before with stinging guitar and seasoned on a few tracks by Kim Wilson or the Roomful Of Blues horns. Both albums are enjoyable but one suspects that these cool cats are best witnessed prowling a stage rather than a studio. TR

Eddie Cusic (born 1926)
VOCAL, GUITAR, HARMONICA

War service apart, Eddie Cusic has spent his life in Mississippi. He combined music with part-time work, but gave up performing in the '60s, the better to support his family, and re-emerged as a musician only after retiring in 1989.

*** I Want To Boogie
HMG HMG 1005 *Cusic.* 12/97.

Eddie Cusic composed only two of the 15 songs on his CD, which otherwise consists of cover versions of familiar blues standards, learned partly by oral transmission and partly from hit records of the '50s. Many of the usual suspects are present – 'Big Boss Man', 'Hoochie Coochie Man', 'Reconsider Baby' and more – but this doesn't mean that Cusic is a dully predictable, uncreative musician. He plies the same honourable trade as did James 'Son' Thomas, his partner in the jukes for many years: that of recycling and reshaping the material of nationally known record stars into live and local entertainment. As with many a Mississippian, his chords change slowly under the vocal line, when they change at all, and the resulting harmonic disjunctions are often agreeably peppery. There is much laidback pleasure to be had from Cusic's flurrying acoustic guitar and relaxed, grainy singing. CS

Daddy Stovepipe (1867–1963)
VOCAL, HARMONICA, GUITAR

Johnny Watson, from Mobile, Alabama, was a travelling musician who recorded in the '20s and '30s as 'Daddy Stovepipe', sometimes with his wife 'Mississippi Sarah', and ended his life playing on Chicago's Maxwell Street.

*** Alabama: Black Country Dance Bands (1924–1949)
Document DOCD-5166 *Daddy Stovepipe; 'Mississippi Sarah' Watson (j, v); unknown (poss. j, humming); Whistlin' Pete (wh).* 5/24–2/35.

If we accept Watson's report of his birthdate, he was 57 when he made his first recordings, which were among the earliest blues recorded by a male artist, preceding Papa Charlie Jackson's by some three months. As such they are of great interest, not least for their relative modernity: at this point in history a middle-aged musician might be expected to have delivered something cast in a more antique mould than Watson's 'Sundown Blues' and 'Stove Pipe Blues'. He stayed close to the blues throughout his recording career, often creating with his wife Sarah what amounted to a two-person jugband. Apart from the sacred coupling of 'Read Your A.B.C.s' and 'Do You Love Him?', and a roguish duet rendition of 'You Rascal You' mysteriously titled 'The Spasm', their recordings were all blues, with sprightly harmonica solos. The CD is completed by recordings of Ben Covington (q.v.) and the Mobile Strugglers, a stringband. The recordings Donald Hill made of Watson in Chicago in 1960, issued on the Heritage LP *Blues From Maxwell Street*, have not been transferred to CD. TR

Julius Daniels (1902–47)
VOCAL, GUITAR

From Charlotte, North Carolina, Julius Daniels was the first Carolina blues singer to record. He worked at various menial jobs, and was a fireman at the time of his death from heart failure.

**** Georgia Blues & Gospel (1927–1931)
Document DOCD-5160 *Daniels; Bubba Lee Torrence, Wilbert Andrews (g). 2–10/27.*

Annoyingly titled – recording in Atlanta doesn't make Daniels, or his music, Georgian – this is still a historically and musically significant collection. Daniels's powerfully projected baritone suggests a street singer; so does the variety of his repertoire, which traverses blues, gospel and songster material in a mere seven songs. The blues range from *double entendre* to tough reflections on arrest and imprisonment, and include the first recording of 'Crow Jane Blues'. Unusually, the guitars on that song take a while to agree the key, but it does have the finest of Daniels's invariably fine vocals. Alternative takes of four songs exist, and it's a index of the skill of Daniels, and of his second guitarists, that these are gripping listening, not mere grist to the scholarly mill. The two gospel songs feature glowing slide guitar, and some enigmatic lyrics ('Mother and father remember well, your daughter Elizabeth ringin' in Hell'). Covering the distance from there to the appropriately galloping rhythms of 'Can't Put The Bridle On That Mule This Morning' is no problem at all to this authoritative artist.

Of the other artists on the CD, George Carter and Lil McClintock are also resonant singers, probably from the streets. Carter, who recorded in Chicago, is presumed to be from Atlanta on stylistic grounds, although nobody there remembered him. He sounds older than the circle who learned guitar from Curley Weaver's mother. Male artist Lil (i.e. 'Little') McClintock, who recorded in Atlanta, was from South Carolina! He mixes songster material and gospel, accompanying himself on the secular sides with chugging chords, and on the religious ones with slide. Lillie Mae, accompanied by piano and guitar for two of her songs, and by piano and two guitars for the other two, manages a creditable imitation of Ma Rainey on 'Buggy Jail House Blues', but is otherwise a purveyor of light-hearted dance music and sexual metaphors. The tracks by Daniels, McClintock and Lillie Mae are also on *Atlanta Blues* (JSP JSP 7754 4CD). CS

Blind Teddy Darby (1906–75)
VOCAL, GUITAR

Darby was a Kentuckian who grew up in St Louis. He lost his sight in 1926. An affray landed him in the city workhouse, where he learned to play guitar, and on his release he began to play in public. Through the local talent scout Jesse Johnson he joined parties of St Louis bluesmen who recorded for Paramount in 1929 and Victor in 1931. Later he worked with pianists Tom Webb and Peetie Wheatstraw; it was Webb's murder in the '50s that finally disenchanted him with the music business. His 1960 recordings for Pete Welding have never been issued.

*** Blind Teddy Darby (1929–1937)
Document BDCD-6042 *Darby; prob. Baby Jay (c); Ike Rodgers (tb); Henry Brown, Tom Webb, Peetie Wheatstraw, poss. Jimmie Gordon (p); Casey Bill Weldon (g); unknown (b). 9/29–4/37.*

As a guitarist Darby is interesting but not, in a city that could boast Henry Townsend and Charley Jordan, outstanding. As a singer, however, he is quite extraordinarily mercurial. One can see why discographers once doubted that all the Darbys were one man. It is as if he spent his peak recording years in a state of high receptivity, retuning himself, from song to song, to the stylistic signals given off by his contemporaries.

'My Laona Blues' from his first session owes something to Townsend or Henry Spaulding, though the rhythm of the guitar and the evenly accented piano frame the vocal more sedately. The same date's 'Lawdy Lawdy Worried Blues' seems to be a unique blues melody, a kind of eight-bar cousin of the 'Going To Brownsville'/'Minglewood Blues' tune, while 'Built Right On The Ground' from 1931 has a melodic connection with a tune used by Cincinnati's Kid Cole. A 1933 session with Webb was issued under the borrowed name Blind Squire Turner. 'Squire was a good old friend of mine,' Darby recalled. 'He wanted to be popular with the girls and so he said, "Darby, make a record and name it after me."' The relaxed mood of 'Low Mellow' may for some listeners recall the Sparks Brothers. Darby's individual turns of phrase are complemented by their delivery: whereas many singers elide words to convey typical blues postures of crying, moaning or wailing, Darby enunciates them deliberately, like a man patiently arguing with someone slightly deaf. In the same session's 'Bought A Bottle Of Gin' and 'Pitty-Pat Blues' he is plainly trying on Leroy Carr's hat, and it is no bad fit, but by 1937, when he made his last pre-World War II recordings, he has doffed that headgear and seems undecided whose to borrow next. In 'The Girl I Left Behind' it is Bill Gaither's; the song concerns his trip to Chicago to record it. 'Bootleggin' Ain't Good No More' is drawn from his experiences in the liquor business. Like much blues of the late '30s this session has an air of the purpose-built. Darby's career thus ends not with the individuality of his earliest sides nor with the mask-swapping of his middle period but on a quiet note of stylistic anonymity. TR

Cow Cow Davenport (1894–1955)
VOCAL, PIANO

Charles Davenport was born in Alabama, and said that he became an entertainer after being expelled from a seminary for playing the piano too friskily. He went on the TOBA circuit in a double act with Dora Carr before teaming up with Ivy (or Iva) Smith, and eventually joining Vocalion as a recording artist, staff pianist and songwriter. Davenport and Smith put together a touring revue but it didn't prosper, and he was jailed for repeatedly using the tour bus as security for loans. By the time he was free, arthritis had deprived Cow Cow of the use of his right arm. He gradually recovered some of his abilities, and early white interest in jazz led to occasional gigs and recordings. His young fans got him elected to ASCAP, but Davenport's last years were impoverished.

**** Cow Cow Davenport – Vol. 1 (1925–1929)
Document DOCD-5141 *Davenport; Shelton T. Reamey, B. T. Wingfield (c); Eddie Heywood (p); Leroy Pickett (vn); Buster Johnson, Tampa Red (g); Dora Carr, Sam Theard (v); Ivy Smith (sp). 10/25–5/29.*

**(*) Cow Cow Davenport – Vol. 2 (1929–1945)
Document DOCD-5142 *Davenport; Joe Bishop (flh); Sam Price (p); Teddy Bunn (g, v); Richard Fullbright (b); Sam Tarpley, Ivy Smith (v). 5/29–45.*

It's appropriate that *Vol. 1* opens with Dora Carr belting out Davenport's best-known number, 'Cow Cow Blues'. Davenport's lyric (often called 'Railroad Blues') is a good one, but he didn't bother to sing it on record until 1938, and even his celebrated piano solo didn't appear until 1928. Document claim to offer takes A and B of Cow Cow's 'Cow Cow', but have used take A twice; the error is corrected on *"Too Late, Too Late" – Vol. 5* (Document DOCD-5411). Often mislabelled a boogie classic, 'Cow Cow Blues', with its characteristic heavy bass figures and sprightly right hand, is more of a blues-ragtime hybrid, like other themes in his instrumental repertoire. There was more to Davenport than instrumentals, though, and *Vol. 1* is a compendium of versatility, including vaudeville duets, comedy routines, soberly wistful blues ('Jim Crow Blues' has a remarkable protest lyric) and display pieces like 'Chimin' The Blues' and 'State Street Jive', one of several items featuring Davenport's trademark chromatic basses.

Vol. 2 opens with more fine piano solos, but they're succeeded by five undistinguished hokum sides from 1930 with vocal assistance from Sam Tarpley and Ivy Smith. It would be eight years before Cow Cow recorded again; his right arm was still in bad shape, and Sam Price played piano. Joe Bishop's mellow flugelhorn, Teddy Bunn's precise picking and Cow Cow's growl all have their appeal, but they don't coalesce into satisfactory performances. Even more disappointing are eight sides recorded for Comet in 1945. Davenport's right hand is much weaker, and he's either short of left-hand ideas or no longer able to play complex chromatic bass runs. 'Jump Little Jitterbug' is affected by speed fluctuations.

*** Ivy Smith & Cow Cow Davenport (1927–1930)
Document BDCD-6039 *Davenport; B. T. Wingfield (c); Leroy Pickett (vn); prob. Walter Fennell (g); unknown (eff); Ivy Smith, unknown (v). c. 1/27–6/30.*

Ivy Smith's clear, light-voiced singing seldom has the extroversion of her spoken patter on 'State Street Jive' (on *Vol. 1*), although this disc's 'Barrelhouse Mojo', which is a forerunner of 'State Street Jive', is an exception. Davenport usually provides economical and supportive accompaniments; he is especially good on 'Shadow Blues', about death paying a visit, and makes effective use of his trademark heavy basses on the train number 'Cincinnati Southern Blues', and the flood theme 'Southern High Waters Blues'. There is distracting but bearable vocal pre-echo on a number of tracks.

**(*) Cow Cow Davenport – The Accompanist (1924–1929)
Document BDCD-6040 *Davenport; Shelton T. Reamey, poss. Cicero Thomas (c); Clarence Williams, Eddie Heywood (p); Dora Carr, Hound Head Henry, Jim Towel, Memphis Joe [Byrd], Southern Blues Singers, Sam Theard (v). c. 1/24–7/29.*

Carr and Davenport made more use of the 12-bar AAB form than most vaudeville duos, and their half-dozen tracks are more serious than the usual run of such things. Hound Head Henry's vocal gimmicks (laughing, crying, imitations of trains, steamboats, dogs and roosters) are a barrier to enjoyment. Jim Towel's songs, about hoodoo and buckwheat cakes, are throwbacks to minstrelsy, and interesting culturally, but not musically. Memphis Joe is pretty good on 'Plenty Gals Blues', but the harmonizing on the Southern Blues Singers' three songs is undistinguished. Sam Theard does the familiar 'You Rascal You' and 'The Lover And The Beggar', not a medieval morality tale but a plain man's guide to pimping. In short, these variably talented singers are linked only by Davenport's presence.

** Cow Cow Davenport 1926–38
Best Of Blues BOB 5 *Similar to above CDs.* 3/26–5/38.

The sound quality varies from acceptable to lacklustre, and there is no discernible basis of compilation, other than the availability of the source 78s; it's certainly not a 'best of'. About half the tracks feature Ivy Smith, solo or in duet, and four are by Hound Head Henry. There is a smattering of classics, 'Goin' Home Blues', 'Cow Cow Blues' and 'Struttin' The Blues' (from a scuffed disc) among them, but its randomness makes this CD superfluous.

*(*) Cow Cow Davenport – Vol. 3 (Unissued 1940s Acetate Recordings)
Document DOCD-5586 *Davenport; Peggy Taylor (v); unknown male (sp). c. 43.*

These private recordings were acquired from Davenport's widow, Peggy Taylor, who sings on three numbers. Cow Cow's right hand is very weak, the piano is out of tune and the surface noise varies from heavy to hurricane force. The CD is completed by two 1951 acetates of Mama and Jimmy Yancey, recorded in their apartment by Dick Mushlitz, who plays inoffensive but redundant banjo.

**(*) The Essential
Classic Blues CBL 200033 2CD *Similar to above CDs.* 10/25–45.

The Essential is carefully remastered and includes all the best material, but not all of it is essential by any means. The need to fill two CDs leads to the inclusion of Jim Towel, Hound Head Henry and the Southern Blues Singers, and of material from the sad 1943 and 1945 recordings. CS

Jed Davenport
HARMONICA

Believed to be a medicine-show entertainer, Davenport seems to have been active in Memphis in the '20s and '30s, though his known recording work was crammed into little more than a year. The question of who played in his Beale Street Jug Band, long an object of controversy, was largely resolved by the discovery of a contemporary photograph.

***(*) Memphis Harp & Jug Blowers (1927–1939)
RST Blues Documents BDCD-6028 *Davenport (h, prob. k, sp);*

unknown (p); poss. Charlie Pierce (vn); prob. Charlie McCoy (md, g, poss. v); Joe McCoy (g, v); Henry L. Castle (g, poss. v); unknown (j); unknowns (v, sp). 9/29–10/30.

Davenport's 1929 sides, four duets with guitarist Joe McCoy (recording as Joe Williams), introduce his highly vocalized style but hardly prepare one for the six exuberant recordings he made the following year with his Beale Street Jug Band. There is no more exciting jugband music on record than 'Beale Street Breakdown', with its dense weave of alley fiddling and virtuoso harmonica playing. The calmer 'You Ought To Move Out Of Town' and 'Save Me Some' are verse-and-refrain numbers similar to the contemporary work of Memphis Minnie and Kansas Joe McCoy, and the latter is probably one of the singers. Unlike their contemporaries the Memphis Jug Band and Cannon's Jug Stompers, Davenport's crew recorded only blues, but the small changes in instrumentation or arrangement from one number to the next keep the music constantly refreshed. Unfortunately the show-off 'Piccolo Blues', which Davenport packs with effects, is a poor transfer; it may be heard properly on *Ruckus Juice & Chittlins, Vol. 2* (Yazoo 2033). That CD's companion *Vol. 1* (Yazoo 2032), which selects 'You Ought To Move Out Of Town', shows the band's photograph, with a clearly identifiable Joe McCoy and the 12-string guitarist Henry L. Castle, alias 'Too Tight Henry'. Later in 1930 Davenport accompanied Castle in a group called the Beale Street Rounders, and their two sides are also on the RST Blues Documents CD, a compilation made all the more valuable by the remarkable music of Little Buddy Doyle (q.v.). TR

Lester Davenport (born 1931)
VOCAL, HARMONICA

Davenport left Mississippi for Chicago at 14. He hung around blues clubs, where older players like Big Boy Spires noticed him and gave him opportunities to play. In 1955 he accompanied Bo Diddley on a few recordings. Over the next couple of decades he concentrated on his job as a spray painter and on raising his family, but in the '70s, now known as 'Mad Dog', he was a regular player at West Side taverns and in the '80s he worked with Big Daddy Kinsey & The Kinsey Report. He has recorded with Willie Kent (Ain't That Nice [Delmark, 1991]).

**(*) When The Blues Hit You
Earwig CD 4923 *Davenport; Sunnyland Slim (p); John Primer, Willie Davis (g, v); Robert Stroger (b); Robert Covington (d, v).* 8/91.

All but one of the dozen songs on *When The Blues Hit You* are shown as Davenport originals, but as commonplace titles like 'I'm Gonna Move', 'All My Life' and 'My Baby's Gone' suggest, there's little that's unfamiliar in the music. 'My Baby's Gone', for instance, reworks the tune of 'Since I Met My Baby', while 'All My Life' draws from Little Walter's 'Last Night'. Davenport admits he was inspired by Walter and, although his singing is less subtle, he does a good job of playing in approximately Walter's manner on both chromatic and diatonic harps. Sunnyland Slim is his reliable self, but the musician who gets the session's, and the listener's, blood flowing is John Primer.

*** I Smell A Rat
Delmark DG-763 *Davenport; Detroit Jr, Allen Batts (p); Jimmy Dawkins, Billy Flynn (g); Bob Stroger, Sho Komiya (b); Jimi Schutte (d). 7/01.*

In some ways this is the Earwig all over again: a decidedly retro set of songs with heard-it-before titles like 'Bad Treatment', 'So Long' and 'Goin' Away', played by an ensemble with strong guitar and piano. But the recording is much brighter and more favourable to Davenport's singing, and the two guitarists, heard together throughout, are sufficiently different in style to give the recording an interestingly variegated texture, thickened by Detroit Jr and Stroger on the first seven tracks and Batts and Komiya on the remaining six. TR

Debbie Davies (born 1952)
VOCAL, GUITAR

Born in LA into a family of musicians, Davies began playing guitar while at college. In the '80s she worked with Maggie Mayall & The Cadillacs and with Albert Collins, playing in his band and opening his shows. Since 1992 she has led her own band.

** Picture This
Blind Pig BPCD 5004 *Davies; Mark Pender (t); Ed Manion (ts, bs); Kevin Zuffi (o, p); Albert Collins (g); Karl Sevareid (b); Kevin Hayes (d.). 93.*

**(*) Loose Tonight
Blind Pig BPCD 5015 *Davies; Mark Pender (t); Ed Manion (ts, bs); Greg 'Fingers' Taylor (h); Jeff Levine (o); Teo Leyasmeyer (p); Paul Opalach (g, b); Danny Klein (d). 94.*

**(*) I Got That Feeling
Blind Pig BPCD 5039 *Davies; Ernest Williamson (o, p); Lenny McDaniel (p, v); Coco Montoya, Tab Benoit (g, v); Dave Smith, Billy Ottinger (b); Steve Potts, Don Castagno (d); Jim Gaines (prod). 97.*

**(*) Round Every Corner
Shanachie 9010 *Davies; Frank London (t); Jim McElwaine (s); Jeremy Baum (o, p); Bob Hoffnar (psg); Jonathan Sanborn (b); Stuart Stahr (d); Lauren Stauber. 98.*

Davies proves on her debut that she can punch hard both with her own material, as when she disses a former lover in '24 Hour Fool', and with songs like 'Better Off With The Blues' and 'Don't Take Advantage Of Me', but there's not much variation in the settings. In that respect *Loose Tonight* is more complimentary, the arrangements framing feisty vocals like 'This Man Is Killin' Me' and the assured guitar playing which she learned in part from Albert Collins (who guested on *Picture This*) but has adapted to her own less extrovert style. The material, however, is mundane, a problem that she and producer Jim Gaines address on *I Got That Feeling* with a more wide-ranging selection of songs. 'Tired Angels', 'Let The Heartaches Begin' and 'I Could Get Used To This' show her to be quite an accomplished soul singer, but such material doesn't sit altogether compatibly alongside blues-inflected performances like 'Rockin' You Baby' or sexy ones like 'Homework', where she threatens her man with dismissal if he doesn't do his; evidently it's not washing-up that's the issue here. Davies extended her range with this set, but whether it was in directions that would prove valuable was uncertain.

Curiously, *Round Every Corner* offers a song called 'Homework' too, but it's the one recorded by Otis Rush. Davies's sly treatment brings it to a lower emotional temperature than Rush's, and it's generally true of the album, apart from a yearning guitar solo in 'Blue & Lonesome', that intensity of performance is to be found less in the blues tracks than in pieces like John Fogerty's 'Who'll Stop The Rain', which hints that Davies could switch, if she ever wanted to, to the tough-gal country style of a K. C. Dalton or Lucinda Williams.

(*) Homesick For The Road
Telarc CD-83454 *Davies; Kenny Neal (h, g, v); Raful Neal (h, v); Tab Benoit (g, v); Bruce Katz (o); Rod Carey (b); Per Hanson (d). 9/98.*

In this six-hander with Kenny Neal and Tab Benoit, Davies has a leading role on five songs. Four were written by or with her frequent collaborator Don Costagno, but with the exception of the fetchingly vulnerable 'So Cold', where Davies plays acoustic with Benoit, they are not his best work, and 'Money' never recovers from the pratfall of its opening line, 'Money … makes the world go round.'

(*) Tales From The Austin Motel
Shanachie 9019 *Davies; Dave Brown (t); Jim McElwaine (ts); Jeremy Baum (o); Anthony Geraci (p); Tommy Shannon, Joe Ferry (b); Chris Layton (d). 99?*

Davies's smouldering fire, stoked here by the engine-room of Stevie Ray Vaughan's Double Trouble, licks around three Willie Dixon songs and a bunch of her own like 'Just Stepped In The Blues'. Much the best of the former is 'Walking By Myself', which she does with just acoustic guitar and bass, her feline vocal giving the song an entirely new cast. The soul-blues classic 'As The Years Go Passing By' is less suited to her voice, but she plays it commandingly.

*** Love The Game**
Shanachie 9030 *Davies; Doug James (ts, bs); 'Sax' Gordon Beadle (ts); Bruce Katz (o, p); Duke Robillard (g, v, prod); Coco Montoya (g, v); Jay Geils (g); Alan J. Hager (b); Don Castagno (d). 01?*

Perhaps all she needed to fully realize her talent on record was a fellow guitarist as producer. At any rate, this is Davies's most focused album, with her best blues guitar work and plenty of it. The help helps: the mix of lead and rhythm parts by Davies, Robillard and Montoya on 'Can't Live Like This No More' is exhilarating, and the compositional input of Jon and Sally Tiven on three songs extends the stylistic range of the album without shifting its centre of gravity. The energy seems to seep away a little towards the end, but this is much the easiest of Davies's albums to recommend.

*** Key To Love**
Shanachie 9034 *Davies; Peter Green (h, g); James Cotton (h); Bruce Katz (o, p); Paul Opalach, Mick Taylor (g); Alan 'A. J.' Hager (b); Don Castagno (d); The Frigidaires (v). 02.*

This is an explicit celebration of the music of John Mayall, a major influence on the teenaged Davies when she began playing blues guitar. Since Davies is a superior singer, and on particularly good form on this album, her readings of 'Hard Road', 'Dream About The Blues' and other songs may touch listeners unmoved by Mayall's own versions. The guest appearances are brief but striking, Green doubling harmonica and guitar on 'Nature's Disappearing' and Taylor playing gorgeously throughout 'Hard Road', but Davies's own guitar lines on 'Dream About The Blues' or 'Steppin' Out' demonstrate that she has earned her place in such company.

**** All I Found**
Telarc CD-83626 *Davies; Bruce Katz (o, p); Arthur Neilson (g); Noel Neal (b); Per Hanson (d). 12/04.*

'There were some great vibes in the studio for this session,' says Davies, 'and I hope ya'all [sic] can feel 'em!' Absolutely not. She is a reliable player and her sidemen are all admirable, but the music they produce evinces nothing so much as a politely (but incompletely) masked boredom. The listener's expectations are immediately deflated by the clichéd guitar line of 'Made Right In The USA', and none of the remaining ten tracks has the means to refloat them. Davies's singing, though not her primary skill, is nowhere near as colourless as it's been made to sound, but the chief problem here is the relentless ordinariness of the material, epitomized by the four minutes of instrumental cage-pacing that are despairingly (but aptly) titled 'So What'. TR

Boo Boo Davis (born 1943)
VOCAL, HARMONICA, DRUMS

In Drew, Mississippi, the young James Davis played makeshift percussion in his family's Lard Can Band. Moving to St Louis, he worked with Doc Terry and Little Aaron before forming the Davis Brothers Band. After his brothers died, Davis played drums for Arthur Williams (one of whose CDs has several Davis vocals) before switching to harmonica.

(*) East St. Louis
Black & Tan CD B&T 005 *Davis; Arthur Williams (h); Roel Spanjers (o); Bob Lohr (p); Larry Griffin (g); Greg Edick (b); Frank Bolder (d). 99.*

*** Can Man**
Black & Tan CD B&T 012 *Davis; Wybren Feenstra (p); Jan Mittendorp (g); Greg Edick (b); Erik Spanjers (d); Dirk Vermeij (perc). 12/01.*

(*) The Snake
Black & Tan CD B&T 018 *Davis; Tommy Schneller (ts); Roel Spanjers (o); Wybren Feenstra (p); Jan Mittendorp (g); Jasper Mortier (b); J. J. Goossens (d); 'Cortez' (perc). 9/03.*

Davis plays drums on *East St. Louis*, except when Bolder deps. When not using his natural voice, Davis usually imitates Howlin' Wolf, but on one track he ventures a strangulated B. B. King. In all these guises his singing lacks nuance. Highly repetitive dance music draws much of its power from the use of small but significant variation, a skill that Davis doesn't have; most of the songs here are overlong, underdeveloped and on the wrong side of the line between hypnotic and narcotic. Davis is poorly served by some of his musicians, too; Griffin is versatile but too tasteful, Williams is disengaged and often distantly recorded, and Lohr's chromatic elaborations don't suit transplanted Delta blues.

On subsequent CDs, Davis plays harmonica; his skills are basic, but without the responsibility of timekeeping, his singing, though no more subtle, is looser and livelier. The backing musicians on *Can Man* are louder and much more aggressive, with a blues-rock tinge; this is not the authentic sound of East St Louis (although Feenstra's piano is very idiomatic), but the energy surge makes for music that holds one's attention more successfully. Even so, Davis's limitations are still apparent – perhaps even to himself; he has a curious habit of saying, 'Thank you, Davis!' as if worried that nobody else will.

The notes to *The Snake* make much of its allegedly combining 'Boo Boo's rough sound with that of contemporary R&B', but in practice this amounts to no more than the inclusion of two soul-blues, and perhaps of 'Crown Royal', an Amos Milburn-like shuffle which, however, carries a most un-Milburnian anti-drink message. Otherwise, the blues-rock accompaniments are again powerful, swinging and competent, and Davis's harmonica and singing remain four-square, unembellished and not terribly interesting. CS

CeDell Davis (born 1927)
VOCAL, GUITAR, HARMONICA

His hands crippled by polio before his tenth birthday, Ellis Davis was forced to devise his own method of guitar playing, tuning strings to accommodate the oscillations of the butter knife clenched in his right hand. The sometimes dissonant result, combining true and transient notes that obey their own logic, makes it hard for accompanists to do more than keep time, although Davis spent a decade working with Robert Nighthawk. It comes as no surprise to learn that Ornette Coleman has been a successful jamming partner.

*** Highway 61
Wolf 120.920 *Davis.* 11/90.

As bizarre as Davis's guitar playing may sound, prolonged exposure to its fractured harmonies imposes a sort of structure upon its skirls and curlicues. His voice is almost an instrument in itself, a powerful sound ejected via his adenoids and nasal passages. All this would be difficult to take if it wasn't for the quality of his songs, their humour and their often twisted logic. The eight gathered here, including 'Chicken And A Hawk' and ''74 Is A Freight Train', illustrate why Robert Nighthawk took him as a travelling companion. Two, 'When I Woke Up This Morning' and 'Sugar Mama', are the only examples of Davis playing harmonica, which he does in the conventional manner. The CD is shared with Herman Alexander.

*** Feel Like Doin' Something Wrong
Fat Possum 0322 *Davis; R. L. Burnside, Louis X. Erlanger (g); Ron Miller (b); Walter Perkins (d).* 94.

Producer Robert Palmer was obviously hearing ancient harmonies when he signed Davis but by then he'd already shared a stage with him. It's Davis's unique alternative tuning that sets him apart; in all other respects his blues obey the conventions. The three band tracks, including the opening 'I Don't Know Why', were recorded in New York with a trio of jazz and punk rock musicians who tuned themselves to his guitar. 'Boogie Chillen No. 2' is sung to the backing of Burnside's accurate Hooker pastiche. The remaining tracks are performed solo. Davis contrives to play both rhythm and lead and can pick his notes with precision even if they're not the expected ones. His songs are conventional by comparison, often shot through with shafts of humour as in 'If You Like Fat Women' and 'She Got The Devil In Her'. A brief but bizarre stab at 'Green Onions' closes a demanding but rewarding experience.

** The Best Of
Fat Possum/Capricorn 42083 *Davis; Derek Trucks (g); Col. Bruce Hampton ('lhazoid'); unknown (b); unknown (d).* 95.

Interviewed by *Guitar Player* in January 1997, Davis expressed his dissatisfaction with his first album – and was even less complimentary about this. Released during the combative association between Fat Possum and Capricorn, *The Best Of* was poorly distributed and remains hard to find. Backed by a group of young hopefuls, including teenage slide guitar prodigy Derek Trucks, Davis toils in vain during 'Rock' and 'CeDell's Boogie', sometimes audibly, to encourage their engagement. But all save Trucks merely bump and clatter with sulky competence in his wake. Hampton's rare and randomly plucked intrusions on guitar are wholly gratuitous. Davis's material once again combines wry humour ('My Dog Won't Stay Home'), belligerence ('Broke And Hungry') and sentiment ('Laura Mae') in equal measure but the woeful lack of support undercuts all the effort he applies.

*** The Horror Of It All
Fat Possum 0315 *Davis; Kenny Brown (g); Dale Beavers (b); Calvin Jackson, Sam Carr (d).* 98.

Despite its brevity this is probably the most representative of Davis's albums, finding him at ease with himself, fully indulging his instrumental and lyrical quirks. It confirms his status as the Harry Partch of the blues, and the garage ambience of label owner Matthew Johnson's production, most evident on 'Keep On Snatchin' It Back' and 'Mistreatin' Me', underlines it. Nevertheless, the self-conscious album title and 'The Horror' that inspires it feel imposed, as do the photos of Davis's wheelchair on both disc and sleeve. The song itself is rubato and holler-like, containing passages of discordant slide and finger-style phrases and a solitary melancholic verse. Calvin Jackson plays ambient drums on the boogie 'Chicken Hawk' and the other musicians accompany a revisit to 'If You Like Fat Women'. Davis ends with the rather confused 'Tojo Told Hitler', after which he states, 'That's it. I ain't gonna do no more.'

***(*) When Lightnin' Struck The Pine
Fast Horse FH 003 *Davis; Jeffrey Barnes (ts, h); Alex Veley (o, p); Scott McCaughey (psg, g, b); Peter Buck (g, surdo, b); Thomas Houston Jones (g); Danny Balls (b); Joe Cripps, Barrett Martin (d, perc).* 02.

The album title denotes when a new star is born but in this case it's one revitalized. The large castlist, including R.E.M.'s Peter Buck, are all subservient to Davis's fluid bar schemes. The discordant whine of his slide guitar is often lost within the welter of amplification but the drummers keep a solid rhythm, pleasantly muddied by the imprecision of distorted guitars. Davis's vocals emerge in an accent like clotted cream; at times his voice is like another instrument. B. B. King's 'Woke Up This Morning' has never sounded so countrified, nor Fulson's 'Reconsider Baby', here masquerading as 'So Long, I Hate To See You Go'. Originals like 'Pay To Play', 'Give Me That Look' and 'Rub Me Baby' are shot through with Davis's laconic humour, at its height in the toast 'Propaganda'. A marvellous antidote to the anodyne session fodder that's sucking the life out of the blues. NS

Reverend Gary Davis (1896–1972)
VOCAL, GUITAR, BANJO, HARMONICA, PIANO

Born in Laurens, South Carolina, Gary Davis was blind from infancy. By the age of eight he was proficient on guitar, harmonica and banjo, and at 15 was a member of Willie Walker's stringband. Moving to Durham, North Carolina, he played in the streets and met Blind Boy Fuller, whose guitar playing owes a great deal to Davis. Ordained in 1937, Rev. Davis remarried in 1943, and soon moved to New York. He was well placed to come to the attention of the folk revival, and although it was some time before he began to be recorded in depth, from the late '50s he made a steady living from concert and coffeehouse appearances, and as tutor to a series of students. Davis was increasingly prepared to accommodate his new audience by playing secular music, which made it easier for them to concentrate on his guitar skills, and often to pigeonhole his sacred music as an oxymoronic 'holy blues'. This is a wrongheaded notion, but even if he had stuck exclusively to gospel, this guide would be incomplete without Gary Davis, who developed African-American guitar music into a personal style of unparalleled complexity and brilliance which had a profound influence on more than one generation of musicians.

Until nearly the end of his life, Rev. Davis's guitar playing (thumb-and-forefinger plus very active and sophisticated chording) was almost invariably magnificent, and it would be otiose to repeat this when discussing each CD. Many songs recur from disc to disc (although of course their performances differ in detail), and a painstaking comparison of tracklistings would also make wearisome reading. This entry looks at difference rather than similarity, focusing on presentation, on repertoire and performances of particular interest or brilliance, and occasionally on grounds for disappointment.

**** **The Complete Early Recordings Of Rev. Gary Davis**
Yazoo 2011 *Davis; Brownie McGhee (g); Bull City Red (v). 7/35–45.*

♔ **** **The Vintage Recordings (1935–1949)** [sic]
Document DOCD-5060 *As above. 7/35–45.*

By 1935, Gary Davis was already a master guitarist, fusing melody, rhythm and harmony into a complex, contrapuntal style that was far beyond the imagination, let alone the technique, of most blues guitarists, then or since. He began his recording career with two reluctant blues performances, and there may be guilt, as well as religious fervour, behind the ferocity with which he then attacks his gospel songs. Equally, he may simply be doing what he did to compete with traffic noise in the streets of Durham; the steel-bodied guitar used on the 1935 recordings, which blurs his bass runs somewhat, was probably also a weapon for aggressive *al fresco* evangelism.

Yazoo's compilation is not complete, despite its title, for 'Lord, I Wish I Could See', unissued on 78, was not available at the time of compilation. Document dub it from a now deleted Columbia anthology. Both CDs include two titles cut for Lenox in 1945 (not 1949, as has been generally stated), which are Davis's first on a wooden-bodied instrument; on one of them Brownie McGhee plays tentative second guitar. Document add the 'Civil War March' recorded for Folkways and legitimately reissued on *If I Had My Way* (below).

Document's *Vintage Recordings*, distinguishable by its two-colour cover, is a remastered version of *Rev. Blind Gary Davis (1935–1949)*, which had black-and-white artwork and the same issue number. The notes to *The Complete Early Recordings* include useful technical discussion of Davis's playing, but only Document can genuinely claim complete coverage of this period, and the improved sound on *The Vintage Recordings* aces out Yazoo.

***(*) **If I Had My Way: Early Home Recordings**
Smithsonian Folkways SFW CD 40123 *Davis; Sister Annie Davis, Kinny Peebles (v). 45–early 53.*

'Civil War Parade' and 'Marine Band' are programmatic marches, but otherwise *If I Had My Way* is all gospel. Many of the songs were not recorded again, and the duet vocals with Rev. McKinley Peebles (who also has a track to himself, on which he plays guitar) are unique on record. The disc is important documentation of Rev. Davis's contemporary Christian repertoire, but for the same reason its appeal to the non-specialist may be limited.

***(*) **Sonny Terry & His Mouth Harp/Blind Gary Davis The Singing Reverend**
Collectables COL-CD-5607 *Davis; Sonny Terry (h). 4/54.*

This CD is dubbed from two ten-inch LPs, the other being by Sonny Terry. Terry and Davis had known each other since Durham in the '30s, and their eight titles are thrilling, although 'Motherless Children' is scarcely rehearsed, and nearly falls apart during the instrumental break. The source LP was not in pristine shape, and surface noise is sometimes distracting.

***(*) **The Sun Of Our Life**
World Arbiter 2005 *Davis; unknown (p, v); Tiny Robinson, congregation (v). 55–57.*

Not issued until 2002, *The Sun Of Our Life* uniquely includes material from a church service, including an apocalyptic 20-minute excerpt from an hour-long sermon. This may deter some listeners, but there's much valuable music on the rest of the disc, including several guitar improvisations that didn't become fixed in Davis's repertoire, a beguiling duet version of 'Candy Man' with Tiny Robinson, and perhaps his finest version of 'Coco Blues'.

**** **Gospel, Blues And Street Songs**
Original Blues Classics OBCCD 524 *Davis. 1/56.*
**** **Pure Religion And Bad Company**
Smithsonian Folkways SF 40035 *Davis. 6/57.*

Gospel, Blues And Street Songs reissues an LP shared with Pink Anderson. (See the latter's entry for the blues and street songs.) Davis's session is one of his best, catching him in particularly ferocious voice, but the husky hoarseness that he sometimes deploys on *Pure Religion And Bad Company* is equally appealing. The latter disc's version of 'Candy Man' is among the most delightful. Its other blues and ragtime pieces – bad company to the pure religion – are all instrumental; 'I Didn't Want To Join The Band', which transfers blues piano playing to the guitar, is especially outstanding.

***(*) **Demons And Angels: The Ultimate Collection**
Shanachie 6117 3CD *Davis; prob. Pete Seeger (bj, v); 'Suzie', unknowns (v); Barry Kornfeld (sp). 58–66.*

'Ultimate' is a selling ploy, but it's worth taking it seriously enough to note that, despite some attractive photos, there are no tracks featuring Rev. Davis on banjo or harmonica. Nor is *Demons And Angels* ultimate in the sense of being a greatest hits package; there's no 'Candy Man' and no 'Samson And Delilah'. Rather, this painstakingly annotated boxed set is a thorough exploration of the range of Davis's guitar playing and songbook, including many songs and tunes not available elsewhere on record, and many exceptional performances of well-known items. The 1958 recordings on the set's first disc even include remakes of the blues he first recorded in 1935. There are also some *longueurs*, notably 'Soon My Work Will All Be Done' with Seeger (aurally) and a lowing chorale. The sound is always acceptable, but the acoustics vary from session to session on the second and third discs' home and concert recordings, and on a couple of the live tracks Davis bumps the microphone with his guitar. Often musically splendid, *Demons And Angels* is not an entry-level package.

**** **Harlem Street Singer**
Original Blues Classics OBCCD 547 *Davis*. 8/60.
**** **Say No To The Devil**
Original Blues Classics OBCCD 519 *Davis*. c. 61.
**** **A Little More Faith**
Original Blues Classics OBCCD 588 *Davis*. 8/61.
**** **The Guitar And Banjo Of Reverend Gary Davis**
Original Blues Classics OBCCD 592 *Davis*. 3/64.

These former LPs come from sessions supervised by the folklorist Kenneth S. Goldstein, and they were not happy occasions, thanks to Goldstein's insistence on stopping at the least mistake. It was five years before Davis made studio recordings again, and even then he refused to do second takes. It's curious, therefore, that these four medium-priced discs should be some of Davis's finest work, and collectively make an ideal introduction to him. *Say No To The Devil* introduces the lustrous sound of his 12-string guitar, and his simple but very expressive harmonica. Despite its title, there's also a harp piece on the all-instrumental (and all-secular) *Guitar And Banjo*. There are no tunes on this disc that Davis didn't record elsewhere at some stage, but these versions are all excellently recorded and played with his habitual virtuosity. 'Devil's Dream' and 'Please Baby' become very different when played on a clattering six-string banjo.

*** **Blues & Ragtime**
Shanachie 97024 *Davis*. 62–66.

A steady flow of concert and teaching work meant that Davis was probably at his technical peak when these recordings were made, but he was not always at his artistic best. 'Children Of Zion' apart, *Blues & Ragtime*'s content is secular, and occasionally even mildly risqué, as on 'Hesitation Blues'; this number lasts 12 very repetitive minutes, and even Rev. Davis can't sustain its interest that long. Guitarists will find *Blues & Ragtime* valuable for the notation and tablature of five numbers, but they will need to condone tape hiss on some tracks and a loud, cackling audience on others.

*** **Live At Newport**
Vanguard VCD 79588 *Davis; Barry Kornfeld (g, v)*. 7/65.
*** **Live & Kickin'**
Just A Memory JAM 9133 *Davis*. 1/67.

In concert, Rev. Davis often simplified his playing (which doesn't mean that it became simple) and stuck to his greatest hits; that's the case on both these CDs. On *Live At Newport* his habitual sniff is more intrusive than usual, and in a couple of places he garbles the lyrics, but he's fired up by a large and enthusiastic audience, whether warning that 'Death Don't Have No Mercy' or cutting up on 'She Wouldn't Say Quit'. Unfortunately the original LP has been sloppily extended, with 'Soldier's Drill' (which is musically fine, but jarring after the elegiac 'I'll Do My Last Singing In This Land Somewhere') and Kornfeld's smirking, narcissistic lead vocal on 'Cindy'. *Live & Kickin'*, recorded in Montreal, is a routine night by the standard that Davis could reach; it includes what seems to be the only recording of a recently composed 'Mind How You're Living', but otherwise holds no surprises.

(*) **O, Glory: The Apostolic Studio Sessions
Genes GCD 9908 *Davis; Larry Johnson (h); The Apostolic Family Chorus (John Townley, Monica Boscia, Jerry Novac, Bobby Brooks), Sister Annie Davis (v); Stefan Grossman (sp)*. 64–3/69.

This disc (now probably hard to find) includes a sample of Davis's basic, four-square piano; it's one of three tracks where the Apostolic Family Chorus's vanilla harmonies suck the life out of Rev. and Mrs Davis. More important are the only recording of Davis playing five-string banjo and three tracks on which he and Larry Johnson drive each other to give of their best.

** **Good Morning Blues**
Biograph BCD 113 *Davis; Larry Breezer (g)*. 3/71.
(*) **From Blues To Gospel
Biograph BCD 123 //High Coin SABRECD 2008 *Davis*. 3/71.

Signs of age and infirmity are apparent; Davis's playing is slower, there are occasional picking mistakes, and his voice is sometimes tired. All this is relative; even in decline Davis was a fierce singer, and a better guitarist than most guitarists at their peak. 'You Better Get Right' approaches the fire of his best performances, but *From Blues To Gospel* is not the way to encounter Davis for the first time. The session originally appeared on two LPs, and *Good Morning Blues*, which is shared with Leadbelly and the harmonica-playing evangelist Dan Smith, has the five remaining, and weakest, titles. The out-of-tune playing on 'Whistling Blues' and the wrong notes on 'How Happy I Am' are depressing.

(*) **Heroes Of The Blues: The Very Best Of Rev. Gary Davis
Shout Factory DK 30257 *Davis; The Apostolic Family Chorus, Sister Annie Davis (v)*. 7/35–3/71.

Sony mine their own catalogue for this retrospective, but only for three titles from Davis's ARC sessions and three from Biograph; unhappily both 'Whistlin' Blues' and 'How Happy I Am' (see above) are among the latter. Six tracks come from the Prestige/Bluesville sessions reissued on Original Blues Classics and two, including 'Candy Man', are from Smithsonian Folkways. These are all predictably admirable, as is 'Out On The Ocean Sailing', which is the five-string banjo piece from *O, Glory*. Thanks to the Apostolic Family Chorus, the same can't be said of the other title from that disc. The inclusion of weak tracks when better ones were available necessarily means that this CD doesn't live up to its subtitle. cs

Guy Davis (born 1952)
VOCAL, GUITAR, HARMONICA, BANJO, MANDOLIN, BASS, STRING PROGRAMMING, KEYBOARD, WASHBOARD, TAMBOURINE, PERCUSSION, STOMPS, CLAPS, DIDGERIDOO

The son of actors Ossie Davis and Ruby Dee, Davis is himself an actor, writer and director as well as a musician.

(*) **Stomp Down Rider
Red House RHR CD 80 *Davis*. 11/93.

Stomp Down Rider is a rather distant concert recording, presenting an accomplished guitarist, in both East Coast and Delta styles. Davis is equally good on harmonica, although his rack playing is less enticing than the solo showpiece 'Miller And The Pigs'. Davis had been performing off-Broadway as Robert Johnson, and three Johnson songs are included, but he doesn't do much with them beyond replication; Blind Willie McTell's 'Georgia Rag' and an adaptation of 'Candy Man' are much better. Four Davis compositions on themes of wandering, rejection and shelter are carefully crafted but rather callow, the work of a man still finding a blues-based voice for his art.

**** Call Down The Thunder
Red House RHR CD 89 *Davis; Jimmy Recchionne (h, stomps, claps); Genovis Albright (kb); Pete Seeger (bj); Abdul Wali Muhammad (g); Harvie Swartz, Joe Ferry (b); Richie Morales (d); Gerard Buckley, Mike Mirtsopoulos, Thom Wolke, Peter Beckerman, Al Hemberger, Ted Hemberger (stomps, claps).* 4–5/96.

Studio-recorded, *Call Down The Thunder* is a great improvement in every direction, not least sound quality. Most tracks are Davis compositions, and although he's not immune from soppiness, his lyrics and delivery are generally much more assured and subtle; 'See Me When You Can', a tribute to his grandmother, is particularly strong. The one Robert Johnson number is vigorously, rather than reverentially, handled, and songs by Mance Lipscomb and Noah Lewis are similarly used as confident vehicles for Davis's self-expression; 'Run Sinner Run' is an especially successful deployment of his growling voice.

**** You Don't Know My Mind
Red House RHR CD 113 *Davis; Rob Robinson (kb); Paul Geremia (g); Barry Sonjohn Johnson (b, claps); Ivan Ramirez (d, perc, claps); Olu Dara, Tiye Giraud, Cheryl Williams (v).* 98.

**** Butt Naked Free
Red House RHR CD 142 *Davis; T-Bone Wolk (ac, o, md, b); Levon Helm (md, d); John Platania (g, tamb); Mark Murphy (b); Gary Burke (perc).* 00.

These releases show Davis growing in confidence, working in a variety of musical settings, and exploring further aspects of the past by composing and re-composing it. *You Don't Know My Mind* opens with a hectoring protest song, and the sentimental 'Everything Is Gonna Be Alright' is a disappointing closer, but everything between is splendid. Respectful but not time-bound adaptations of 'Po' Boy' and the title track are notably successful, and 'Dorothy Is Harlem Bound' is an outstanding guitar display piece. 'Georgia Flood' is a pastiche of old-style topical gospel songs, but an uncommonly good one.

Butt Naked Free also ranges from vocal with guitar to full band; Blind Willie McTell's 'Writing Paper Blues' is too rocked-up, but an even more thunderous arrangement works well on 'Waiting For The Cards To Fall'. The CD is a well-balanced blend of *double entendre* fun and serious meditations on life and death. The concluding 'Raining In My Soul' is the most serious and heartfelt of these, but it disappoints as both writing and performance. More successful are 'Sometimes I Wish', based on Gary Davis's 'Death Don't Have No Mercy', and 'Sugarbelle Blue', with pretty John Hurt-style fingerpicking and a wry, intelligent lyric about growing up too fast in a small town. Davis does not always achieve his goals, but his skill and creativity command respect, and the successes outweigh the occasional failures.

**** Give In Kind
Red House RHR CD 161 *Davis; Zoe B. Zak (ac, v); Keith Slattery (o, p); Ken Whitely (md, bj); W'ali Muhammad (g); Mark Murphy (b); Gary Burke (d); David Helper (v).* 01.

**** Chocolate To The Bone
Red House RHR CD 164 *Davis; T-Bone Wolk (o, ac, md); Nerak Roth Patterson (g); Mark Murphy (b); Howard Johnson (tu); Gary Burke (d); David Helper (claps, v).* 03.

**** Legacy
Red House RHR CD 175 *Davis; T-Bone Wolk (ac, md); Zoe B. Zak (ac, v); John Platania (g, v); Mark Murphy (b); Gary Burke (d, perc); David Helper (v); Martial Davis (rap).* 04.

On *Give In Kind*, sentimentality still breaks through at times in Davis's own lyrics, but it's usually tempered by tough melodies and arrangements. He's at his most successful when combining respect for the past with inventive new arrangements, on songs by Big Bill Broonzy, Fred McDowell, Leroy Carr, Henry Thomas and Sleepy John Estes. The same process is applied in the opposite direction, and with equal success, when Estes and Rachell's guitar and mandolin sound is used on Davis's composition 'Lay Down By My Side'. On previous discs, there's occasionally a sense that Davis is pursuing sonic experiments for their own sake, rather than for what they bring to the songs. That's almost entirely absent here; the exception is 'Layla, Layla', which proves that just because you can play a didgeridoo, it doesn't mean that you should.

Chocolate To The Bone and *Legacy* continue the good work along much the same lines as *Give In Kind* (though thankfully without the didgeridoo). On both discs, but more noticeably on *Legacy*, Davis sometimes imposes a wide vocal vibrato, perhaps feeling that he should start sounding like an elder statesman. This really isn't necessary; it's always obvious that he's been doing a lot of hard thinking about both the content and the context of his music. What's especially pleasing is that this never emerges as portentousness or preachiness; see, for instance, 'Uncle Tom's Dead' on *Legacy*, where Davis and his son rap wittily, but with serious intent, about young blacks' indifference to the blues. CS

Maxwell Street Jimmy Davis (1925–95)
VOCAL, GUITAR

It's not certain when Clarksdale-born Charles Thompson changed his name; he sometimes said that he did it in World War II to avoid the draft, but he was logged as Charles Thomas when he made unissued recordings for Sun in 1952. In his teens, Davis learned guitar from John Lee Hooker, and performed in travelling minstrel shows, buck dancing and walking barefoot on broken glass. He spent the '50s oscillating between South and North, and worked with Hooker in Detroit for a while before settling in Chicago. Davis became a living landmark on Maxwell Street; for a while, he operated the Knotty Pine Grill there, playing outside to attract customers. His '60s recordings didn't translate into wider performing opportunities, and when festival bookers finally woke up in the late '80s, his revived career was sadly abbreviated.

*** Chicago Blues Session Vol. 11
Wolf 120.857 *Davis; Lester Davenport (h); Kansas City Red, Timothy Taylor (d).* 11/88–2/89.

Like John Lee Hooker, his one-time neighbour and teacher, Jimmy Davis played modal, one-chord blues, and even though he was a *genius loci* of the famous Chicago flea market, his '60s solo recordings are essentially unmodified Delta blues. His eponymous LP for Elektra is regrettably absent from CD, but tracks recorded around that time appear on *Modern Chicago Blues* (Testament TCD 5008) and *Takoma Blues* (Takoma CDTAK 8907), and are well worth hearing.

More than two decades on, Davis was still an energetic performer, whether alone or with intermittent assistance from harp and drums. His singing had become more extrovert and less brooding, and his acoustic guitar work, though always rhythmically secure, is sometimes very turbulent; 'That's All Right' is frenzied by comparison with Jimmy Rogers's wistful progenitor, and the concluding 'Dust My Broom' is delightfully cavalier with phrase and verse length. Davis could still do haunted lonesomeness very well, as on 'Two Trains Running' and 'In Your Bedroom', and there's also a vein of mordant humour in his make-up ('Take your false teeth out, baby, please let me scratch your gums'). Less alluring is his tic of randomly dropping into a scratchy approximation of Howlin' Wolf's vocal style, but he doesn't overdo it, and 'Going Upstairs', a more extended outing for the gimmick, is oddly enjoyable, albeit a mere shadow of the mighty Wolf. *Chicago Blues Session Vol. 11* is not at the level of Davis's earlier work, but its unpretentious enthusiasm is very winning. CS

Blind John Davis (1913–85)
VOCAL, PIANO

Davis's personal preference was for jazz, but in the '30s and '40s he was a prolific blues session pianist, his rolling right hand recognizable on hundreds of records. In 1952, he was an early visitor to Europe with Big Bill Broonzy, but dropped out of sight in the '60s. In 1973 he was persuaded to make a comeback, and toured frequently in Europe and at home.

**(*) Blind John Davis – Vol. 1 (1938–1952)
Document DOCD-5647 *Davis; George Barnes, unknown (g); Alfred Elkins, Ransom Knowling, unknown (b); unknown (v).* 4/38–2/52.

Six recordings from the '30s (one with an unknown vocalist) find Davis the singer hankering none too successfully after the jivey extroversion of Waller and Armstrong; 'Booze Drinking Benny' is amusing, but George Barnes's electric guitar is the most exciting aspect of these sides. Eight 1948 titles are heavy on ballads and ballad-like blues, probably in hopeful emulation of Cecil Gant. They are attractively sung, but only the wistful 'No Mail Today' lingers in the memory. A concluding set of instrumental blues and boogies, recorded in Paris, showcases Davis's technique and is the best of the disc; the boogies are especially satisfying.

*** My Own Boogie
Pastels CD 20.1621//Past Perfect 204396 *Davis*. 4/73.
*** The Incomparable
Oldie Blues OLCD 7003 *Davis; Rob Langereis (b); Louis Debij (d).* 6/74.

These European recordings offer well-balanced programmes of mostly familiar blues and boogies. Vocal heartache and instrumental display are both done with such proficiency that one almost doesn't notice Davis's disengagement from the material. *My Own Boogie*, recorded live, is the better performance, although a slight but pervasive tape hiss may annoy some listeners; on *The Incomparable*, aloofness occasionally descends into flippancy, and the bass and drums are coldly predictable.

** Blind John Davis
Evidence ECD 26056//Bellaphon CDLR 72002 *Davis; Jeanne Carroll (v).* 4/83.

This might have been an interesting session, with Davis recalling songs by friends and contemporaries like Big Bill, Tampa Red and Doctor Clayton, but there's clear evidence of declining powers. The mind writes cheques that the fingers can't cash, resulting in wrong notes, stumbles and trips down blind alleys. Davis also seems to have trouble remembering some of the lyrics; perhaps in an attempt to distract from these problems of execution, he sings them in a nervously jovial bellow that soon ceases to appeal. Jeanne Carroll makes a mannered appearance on the final track. CS

Larry Davis (1936–94)
VOCAL, GUITAR

Born in Kansas City, Missouri, but raised around Little Rock, Arkansas, Davis first played drums with local dancebands, then bass, then began singing. In the mid-to-late '50s he worked with Fenton Robinson, first in St Louis, then in Little Rock, and they recorded for Duke, Davis having a regional hit with 'Texas Flood', a song made more famous 25 years later by Stevie Ray Vaughan. Around 1970 Davis began playing guitar, but in 1972 he was seriously injured in a motorcycle accident and for much of the decade he was only fitfully active. Encouragement from Albert King (a former employer) and the St Louis producer Oliver Sain rekindled his career, leading to the critically acclaimed album Funny Stuff, *European tours and further recording.*

'Texas Flood' is on *Blues Masters, Volume 6: Blues Originals* (Rhino R2 71127) and other VACs. Davis's late-'60s work for the Virgo and Kent labels, which includes a delectable reading of 'As The Years Go Passing By', is currently available only on a Japanese release, *Sweet Little Angel* (P-Vine PCD 5402).

**** Funny Stuff
Rooster Blues RBLU 2616 *Davis; Oliver Sain (as, ts, bs, o, p, prod); Johnnie Johnson (p); Phil Westmoreland (g); Jimmy Hinds (b, d); Eugene Johnson (b); Billy Gayles, Don Smith (d).* 81.

Like his old running buddy Fenton Robinson, Davis is a wonderful singer, yearningly melismatic on slow blues like his own 'Teardrops', B. B. King's 'Worried Dream', Albert King's 'Got To Be Some Changes Made' and the wistful 'Walk Out Like A Lady'. He's also a piercing guitarist, prolific in long, humming sustained notes. (After his accident, he said, 'I couldn't ring the note like the average guitar player. It was kind of distorted and I liked it.') Sain's production departs from standard blues practice by foregrounding the vivacious rhythm section, giving the music some of the colour of contemporary Southern soul.

**(*) I Ain't Beggin' Nobody
Evidence ECD 26016 *Davis; Oliver Sain (as, ts, o, p, prod); Phil Westmoreland (g, b); Ronnie Guyton (b); Keith Robinson (d).* 85/86.

Sain's hands were busy on this production, since as well as his other duties he wrote five ninths of the repertoire. Unfortunately he doesn't seem to have applied them with much sensitivity to the mixing. The sound is cloudy, the bassist and drummer (who aren't a patch on the players on *Funny Stuff*) are conventionally positioned and Davis's guitar is seldom allowed to be as penetrating as it was on the previous album. Chuck Willis's 'Please Don't Go' is sung and played with great concentration, but the album as a whole betrays the talent that was so astutely presented on *Funny Stuff*.

**(*) Blues Knights
Evidence ECD 26042 *Davis; A. C. Reed (ts); Maurice John Vaughn (g); Douglas Watson (b); Julian Vaughn (d). 11/85.*

Recorded during a French tour, *Blues Knights* is shared with Byther Smith, the two men using the same musicians. Davis's four songs are numbed by a lifeless studio and a band that hasn't either the size or the skill to frame his music appropriately. Nevertheless, 'Giving Up On Love' and a remake of 'Teardrops' are handsome performances that Davis's admirers ought not to miss.

*** Sooner Or Later
Bullseye Blues CDBB 9511 *Davis; Wayne Jackson (t, tb); Andrew Love (ts); Ron Levy (o, prod); James Rudy (p); Thomas Bingham (g); George Journigan (b); Curtis Steele (d). 92.*

Aided by well-chosen musicians, an attentive producer and the experienced engineers of Ardent Studios in Memphis, Davis gives his most detailed performance since *Funny Stuff*. Eleven years have eroded his skills somewhat: his voice is a little coarser, and the guitar solos come less often. That said, 'Letter From My Darling' is delivered with magnificent tenderness, and the deliberate guitar choruses of 'Goin' Out West', 'Little Bluebird' or the instrumental '102nd St. Blues' could have been played by no one else. TR

Martha Davis (1917–60)
VOCAL, PIANO

Born in Kansas, Davis grew up in Chicago and attended Du Sable High School, where she was a contemporary of the pianist Dorothy Donegan. By her early 20s, having come under the influence of Fats Waller, she was playing in Chicago's jazz clubs. After World War II she moved to LA, where she began recording, both in her own name and in duets with Louis Jordan; the success of the latter won her a contract with Decca. With her husband, the bass player Calvin Ponder, she had a successful nightclub act in the '50s as 'Martha Davis & Spouse', appearing on radio and TV and in several telescriptions, made for an early version of the video jukebox.

**(*) Martha Davis 1946–1951
Classics 5123 *Davis; unknown (ts); poss. Ulysses Livingston, Leo Blevins, Ralph Williams, John Collins, unknowns (g); poss. Chas. Gray, Calvin Ponder, unknowns (b); poss. Buzz Johnson, Lee Young, Art Blakey, unknowns (d). 8/46–12/51.*

In a taxonomy of black artists Martha Davis would be in a subspecies of female cabaret singers who are also deft pianists – alongside, say, Nellie Lutcher, though her voice is somewhat lower and she doesn't subscribe to Lutcher's little-girl manner. Though competent with blues and boogie woogie, she seems happier with a wider range of material. Writing little of her own, she hangs out with a lot of professional songwriters and occasionally brings home something rather good like 'The Same Old Boogie', a gentle putdown of Ella Mae Morse's 'Cow Cow Boogie', or the unusual lyric of 'Why Am I', in which a young woman nervously contemplates her first sexual experience. Davis's music may contain too many pop songs of the 'Marshmallow Moon' type for some readers' taste, but it is at least leavened with wit and a gentle come-hitherishness. TR

Little Sammy Davis (born 1928)
VOCAL, HARMONICA

Davis was born in Winona, Mississippi. In the '50s he lived and worked in Florida, and later in Poughkeepsie, New York, where, after a spell out of music, he began playing again in 1988.

**(*) I Ain't Lyin'
Delmark DE-682 *Davis; Tom Hunter (p); Fred Scribner (g); Brad Lee Sexton (b); Brad Scribner (d). 5/93, 11/94.*

Before this album, Davis's recorded output consisted of a couple of singles made for Rockin' in 1953 with Earl Hooker on guitar, reissued on *Rockin' The Blues* (Rockin' HTCD 5502), and a session with Eddie Kirkland for one of his Trix albums. *I Ain't Lyin'* thus arrived out of left field, so far as many blues enthusiasts were concerned, but was immediately recognized as the work of a man who had learned his trade from Little Walter and his contemporaries and saw no need for a refresher course. A few selections ('When I Leave', 'Shorty') take Davis out of his range, but on the straightforward blues numbers 'That's My Girl', 'Someday', 'California Blues' and 'Play Me For A Fool', and the instrumental 'Devil's Trail', played on chromatic harp, he is entirely at home with the music, and his band's support is both appropriate and stylish. TR

Walter Davis (1912–64?)
VOCAL, PIANO

Davis was a teenager with a flair for words when he arrived in St Louis in 1925. He made his first recordings five years later as a protégé of Roosevelt Sykes, who played on his first six sessions. Thereafter, Davis supplied his own often halting accompaniment, assisted by an assortment of guitarists who struggled to complement his wayward phrasing. It's safe to say Davis's records weren't bought for their musicality but for the stories he told in his songs, his lyrics always literate and clearly enunciated. Both his singing and playing styles were fixed early and never changed. Despite their narrow confines, he was a prolific recorder, making him an important artist to listen to but one to be sampled cautiously.

***(*) First Recordings 1930–1932
Document DOCD-5681 *Davis; Willie Kelly [Roosevelt Sykes] (p); Henry Townsend (g). 6/30–2/32.*
*** Walter Davis – Vol. 1 (1933–1935)
Document DOCD-5281 *As above, except add Big Joe Williams (g). 8/33–7/35.*
*** Walter Davis – Vol. 2 (1935–1937)
Document DOCD-5282 *Davis; Henry Townsend, Robert Lee McCoy (g). 7/35–5/37.*

*** **Walter Davis – Vol. 3 (1937–1938)**
Document DOCD-5283 *As above, except McCoy also sings; add Yank Rachell (md, g).* 5/37–6/38.
(*) **Walter Davis – Vol. 4 (1938–1939)
Document DOCD-5284 *Davis; Yank Rachell (md); Henry Townsend (g).* 6/38–7/39.
** **Walter Davis – Vol. 5 (1939–1940)**
Document DOCD-5285 *Davis; Booker T. Washington (v).* 7/39–7/40.
** **Walter Davis – Vol. 6 (1940–1946)**
Document DOCD-5286 *Davis; Jump Jackson (d).* 7/40–2/46.

Roosevelt Sykes's sturdy accompaniments to *First Recordings* and the first half of *Walter Davis – Vol. 1* make these the most instructive exhibitions of Davis's talent as a songwriter. His 'M & O Blues' was popular enough to run to two further outings, while 'Railroad Man Blues' and 'Howling Wind Blues' typify the sometimes specific nature of his songs' settings. 'That Stuff You Sell Ain't No Good' is an early indication of his talent with suggestive material, later revealed in 'You Don't Smell Right', 'Dentist Blues', 'Guiding Rod' and, most famously, 'Think You Need A Shot'. The presence of guitarists Williams and Townsend on eight tracks, including 'Sloppy Drunk Again' and 'Sweet Sixteen', makes this his most exciting early session. Thereafter, while his compositional skills remain high, the skeletal nature of his piano playing taxes both musician and listener. 'Moonlight Is My Spread', 'When Nights Are Lonesome', 'I Like The Way You Spread Your Wings' and a handful of others stand out from their session-mates but a sort of nadir is reached in 1939 with an 18-track solo session, luckily spread over *Vol. 4* and *Vol. 5*. The latter also contains the relief of eight tracks by singer Booker T. Washington, whose energy prompts a lively response from his accompanist. Davis continued to record until America's entry into World War II and his final session included 'Frisco Blues' and 'Biddle Street Blues', two curious instrumentals, the former lively and offering itself as an inspiration for Thelonious Monk, the latter representing what today would be called a backing track.

*** **Walter Davis – Vol. 7 (1946–1952)**
Document DOCD-5287 *Davis; John Moore, unknown (ts); Leonard Caston, Henry Townsend, unknown (g); unknown (b); Jump Jackson, Charles Saunders, unknown (d).* 2/46–7/52.

The hardening of the beat in postwar blues was applied to Davis's material with little audible effect beyond the occasional baffled accent. Davis responded to drumkits and amplified guitars with noticeable energy although his songs remained virtually homophonic, leaving little for his accompanists to do but provide aural decoration. 'Santa Claus Blues' goes to a chaotic extreme, where two guitarists, one of them Townsend, engage in a war of attrition, oblivious to their supposed roles. Davis's songs remained as literate as ever, largely devoted, like 'I Would Hate To Hate You (Like I Love You)', to sexual politics. But 'Things Ain't What They Used To Be' addressed the problem of black soldiers returning from the war to find prejudices unchanged at home. Even so, by his final session Davis had become an anachronism, his music too gentle and amorphous for the public taste. NS

*** **Please Remember Me**
EPM Blues Collection 15949 *As for relevant CDs above.* 6/30–2/47.

*** **The Essential**
Classic Blues CBL 200016 2CD *As above.* 6/30–7/52.
**** **Don't You Want To Go?**
Fabulous FABCD 204 *As above.* 6/30–7/52.

As an epitome of Document's seven volumes *The Essential* is expansive, picking its 36 tracks from almost all Davis's sessions and making room for many of the songs singled out above, as well as his most recycled composition, 'Come Back Baby'. His questioning, tentative approach to themes of erotic tension sets a mood reminiscent of Leroy Carr, and he disrupts it only rarely with light-hearted motifs like 'Stop That Train In Harlem'. 'Come Back Baby' is also on *Please Remember Me*, an independent-minded selection that largely avoids Davis's better-known pieces. Both collections, however, are trumped by *Don't You Want To Go?*, whose 17 tracks show Davis in the best possible light, whether leading Williams and Townsend through the romping ribaldry of 'Sweet Sixteen' or quietly spelling out grief in the haunting 'Tears Came Rollin' Down', one of his last recordings and arguably his finest. This astute collection also has clean sound and a crazily generous price-tag. TR

Jimmy Dawkins (born 1936)
VOCAL, GUITAR

Dawkins began playing the blues as a teenager in Mississippi. He moved to Chicago at 19 and had his apprenticeship in West Side clubs through the '60s, recording as a sideman with Wild Child Butler and Johnny Young and on several albums for Delmark, which gave him his own album debut in 1969. During the '70s his reputation spread beyond Chicago, especially in France, where he toured and recorded repeatedly, but the '80s were leaner times and he had some health problems. Anxious to promote artists he felt were being neglected, he wrote about them for the British magazine Blues Unlimited. *Today, through his company Leric, he works for them as musician, producer, promoter or publisher, but occasionally he comes out from behind the scenes to cut an album of his own.*

*** **Fast Fingers**
Delmark DD-623 *Dawkins; Eddie Shaw (ts); Lafayette Leake (o, p); Mighty Joe Young (g); Ernest Gatewood, Joe Harper (b); Lester Dorsie (d).* 11/68, 1/69.
*** **All For Business**
Delmark DE-634 *Dawkins; Jim Conley (ts); Sonny Thompson (o, p); Otis Rush (g); Ernest Gatewood (b); Robert Crowder, Charles Hicks (d); Andrew 'Big Voice' Odom (v).* 10–11/71.

From the first track of *Fast Fingers*, the big tremolo on the guitar, the chuntering tenor sax and a studio sound that is both resonant and murky announce a proponent of the West Side style, a man who has listened attentively to Otis Rush and Magic Sam. He is undeniably quick in the digital domain, playing agitated flurries of guitar between every vocal phrase. Despite titles like 'It Serves Me Right To Suffer' or 'I Wonder Why', which have been at least once round the blues block, all the dozen songs are ostensibly his own, a claim one would want to dispute over 'I Don't Know What Love Is', which has a strong resemblance to Albert King's 'Don't Throw Your Love On Me So Strong'. But one suspects from the long guitar intros and longer solos that Dawkins enjoys playing more than singing, a notion upheld by the next album, on which most of the vocals are by 'Big Voice' Odom. The West Side flavour is enhanced by the presence of Sonny Thompson, joint architect of the Freddie King sound, and of Otis Rush himself, who contributes at length to 'Cotton Country', 'Sweet Home Chicago' and a previously unissued 'Jammin' With Otis'. Like its predecessor, *All For Business* is above all a guitarist's record, but Dawkins is some guitarist.

(*) Born In Poverty
Black & Blue BB 429 *Dawkins; Jerome Van Jones (o); Cousin Joe (p); Clarence 'Gatemouth' Brown, Otis Rush (g); Mac Thompson, James Green (b); Ted Harvey, Bob Plunkett (d).* 11/71, 11/74.

(*) Tribute To Orange
Evidence ECD 26031 *As above.* 11/71, 11/74.

In November 1971 *Fast Fingers* was awarded the Grand Prix du Disque de Jazz by the Hot Club of France. Three days later Dawkins was in a Toulouse studio to cut an album for Black & Blue, reissued here together with half of a later album for the same label, the rest of which was by Odom. For the '71 session he had Gatemouth Brown and Cousin Joe, because they were in the same touring package; providing Dawkins with the kind of accompaniment he was used to was not their natural game, and he is forced to play a Coltrane role and drench the music in sheets of sound. The '74 tracks have a denser ensemble, thanks to the presence of Rush and an organist. Dawkins is the only vocalist throughout; if he really had an aversion to the task, he conquers it well. *Born In Poverty* differs from *Tribute To Orange* only by adding an extra take of 'Off Business' (i.e. 'All For Business') and an 'Instrumental Shuffle'.

*** Blisterstring**
Delmark DE-641 *Dawkins; Sonny Thompson (p); Jimmy Johnson (g); Sylvester Boines (b); Tyrone Centuray (d).* 5/75 or 6?/75.

Blisterstring was the last blues session at the famous Ter-Mar studio where innumerable Chess records were made, many of them engineered, as this was, by Malcolm Chisholm. Dawkins's guitar sounds huge and utterly dominates the band, fortunately so on the tracks where Johnson plays wah-wah rhythm guitar, a touch that dates the music as surely as if Dawkins had come to the session in a kaftan. In songs like 'Welfare Line' and 'Peeple [sic] Will Talk' the album marks the leader's transition as a singer from tentative to assured. He has also pared down his guitar playing, exchanging the frantic space-filling of his first two albums for a more economical and deliberate style.

*(*) Vol. 2 "I Want To Know"**
Storyville STCD 8048 *Dawkins; Jimmy Johnson (g); Sylvester Boines (b); Tyrone Centuray (d); Andrew 'Big Voice' Odom (v).* 10/75.

** Come Back Baby**
Storyville STCD 8035 *Dawkins; Richard Kirch (g); Sylvester Boines (b); Tyrone Centuray (d).* 11/76.

These were among several albums taped on two visits by the French producer Michelle Morgantini with the intention of presenting contemporary Chicago blues 'the way it is played every night in dozens of clubs and lounges'. But, as *Living Blues* reported of the '75 sessions, 'the recording was done on weekday afternoons to keep crowd noise to a minimum; most of the few spectators at Ma Bea's were other musicians hoping to get in on the sessions.' So neither *"I Want To Know"* nor *Come Back Baby*, recorded at an equally empty Big Duke's, has any genuine club ambience. The former is also marred by a defective vocal mike and a setlist with too many standards like 'Rock Me Baby' and 'Driving Wheel'. Odom sings only on 'Are You Ready'. (He did an entire album with the same lineup a year later.) Unless you are interested in Dawkins solely as a guitarist, *"I Want To Know"* is practically unlistenable. *Come Back Baby* gets closer to the sound Dawkins achieved on *Blisterstring*, but the programming is stupid, opening with two long, slow blues and relegating all the up-tempo numbers to the end, Kirch is mixed too low and 'Ode To Billy Joe' – appearing for the third time in Dawkins's discography – isn't worth 7.46.

(*) Hot Wire 81
Evidence ECD 26043 *As above, except James Schutte (d) replaces Centuray.* 3/81.

The seven long tracks of this Paris recording give Dawkins room to tell unhurried stories about hard times ('Welfare Line') and troubled relationships ('Kold Actions') – and, in 'Peepers Music' (i.e. presumably, 'People's Music'), the blues itself. This is seriously meant music that one wants to listen to closely, but since the guitar playing subscribes to the careful minimalism of *Blisterstring* and most of the tempos are slow, staying alert is sometimes hard work.

** Feel The Blues**
JSP JSPCD 282 *Dawkins; J. T. Burks (h); Professor Eddie Lusk (kb, p); Rick Kurch [Richard Kirch] (g); Fred Barnes (b); Michael Scott (d); Nora Jean Wallace (v).* 85.

There's good original material here, like 'Last Days' and 'Have A Little Mercy', but to keep your attention fixed on it you have to try to block out Lusk's ghastly keyboards and occasional outbreaks of effects on the rhythm guitar. The recording sounds as if it was done in a tunnel and although JSP remixed the tapes for the CD issue, there isn't much edge to Dawkins's vocals.

** Blues From Iceland**
Evidence ECD 26064 *Dawkins; 'Blue Ice' Bragason, Gudmundur Pétursson (g); Haraldur Porrsteinsson (b); Ásgeir Óskarsson, Jóhann Hjörleifsson (d).* 4/91.

*** Kant Sheck Dees Bluze**
Earwig 4920 *Dawkins; 'Professor' Eddie Lusk (o, p); Billy Flynn (g); Johnny B. Gayden (b); Ray Scott (d); Nora Jean Wallace (v).* 6/91.

Dawkins's appearance at a club in Reykjavik was effected by the singer and writer Chicago Beau, who takes his place on four of the ten tracks on *Blues From Iceland*. Pétursson is evidently at home with this sort of music but the bassist sometimes drags, and the guest's guitar is under-recorded. Two months later, Dawkins was back on home ground, and not just literally: the fat rhythm of Flynn, Gayden and Scott was precisely what the last few albums had lacked. Dawkins rediscovers the sustained, rasping guitar of *Blisterstring* and applies it like a chainsaw. Meanwhile Lusk makes up for the JSP gig by playing with restraint, mainly on piano. The point of the street spelling – 'Beetin Nockin Ringin', 'Gittar Rapp', the title number, etc. – isn't clear: it doesn't signal any raids on the musical vocabulary of hip-hop or rap. This is straight-ahead West Side or, as Dawkins now spells it, Wes Cide blues, from the neighbourhood where he started out.

*** **West Side Guitar Hero**
Fedora FCD 5022 *Dawkins; John Suhr (o); Frank Goldwasser (g); Henry Oden (b); Chris Millar (d).* 10/01.

(*) **Tell Me Baby
Fedora FCD 5032 *As above, except Danny Camarena (b) replaces Oden; add Roger Perry (kb, g, b), Rich Kirch (g).* 7/03.

Dawkins recorded several times in the '90s, but albums like *B Phur Real* (Wild Dog) and *Me, My Gitar And The Blues* (Ichiban) have vanished. *West Side Guitar Hero* is a bare-bones production that gives a sharp, clear image of Dawkins at 65: a guitarist whose fingers are still fast but don't have to keep proving it, and a singer whose voice, though somewhat attenuated, has suffered no loss in feeling. There's more offbeat orthography ('Wess Cide Rock', 'She Leff Me', 'So Wurrid'), which, he now explains, serves to distinguish his songs from others with similar but conventionally spelled titles. *Tell Me Baby* has a fuller, guitar-packed sound, which sometimes masks the clarity of the vocals, and several of the tracks, like 'Rumping 'N' Stomping', seem to have been prolonged merely for the sake of jamming. TR

Geno Delafose (born 1972)
VOCAL, ACCORDION, KEYBOARDS, ORGAN, PIANO, DRUMS

Geno Delafose was a member of his father John's Eunice Playboys at the age of eight, playing rubboard; by the age of ten, when he made his recording debut with the band, he was one of zydeco's finest drummers. Delafose later mastered the accordion, and is featured as singer and accordionist on his father's last two CDs. He took over the leadership of the Eunice Playboys after his father's heart attack, and now leads French Rockin' Boogie. Geno Delafose plays old-time zydeco, rather than the funk grooves and English lyrics of nouveau zydeco; *if he's spotted a market niche, he's filling it with style, grace and turbocharged energy.*

*** **French Rockin' Boogie**
Rounder CD 2131 *Delafose; Steve Howard (t); Joe Cabral, Derek Huston, Jon Smith (ts); Shelton Broussard, Bobby Broussard, Charles Prudhomme (g); Tony Delafose (b); Germaine Jack (d); Steve Nash, Paul Delafose (rb); Scott Billington (perc).* 2/94.

**** **That's What I'm Talkin' About!**
Rounder CD 2141 *Delafose; Bobby Broussard (g); Stanislas Chambers (b, v); Germaine Jack (d, perc); Steve Nash (rb).* 1/96.

**** **La Chanson Perdue**
Rounder CD 2151 *Delafose; Dirk Powell (vn, b); Steve Riley (vn); Christine Balfa (g, tri); Joseph 'Cookie' Chavis (g); John 'Popp' Esprite (b, v); Germaine Jack (d, rb); Steve Nash (rb); Scott Billington (v).* 1/98.

When *French Rockin' Boogie* is measured against Geno Delafose's work with his father (see the next entry), there's an unaccustomed sense of effort. (It was recorded when John Delafose's heart attack and marital problems were stressing both the family and the Eunice Playboys, who had recently undergone personnel changes.) From any other 22-year-old this would be a remarkable debut CD, and by any standard it's a good one, but it's overproduced: the title track doesn't improve Shirley and Alphée Bergeron's classic Cajun rocker by transferring it to piano accordion, and elsewhere the brass and reeds create textures that are no more than interesting. It's only towards the end of the disc that the band play at their pounding best.

On the other hand, Delafose and French Rockin' Boogie play at their best throughout *That's What I'm Talkin' About!* The ethos is unashamedly retrospective; John Delafose, Amédé Ardoin ('One Step Des Chameaux', with ferocious drumming from Germaine Jack), Iry Lejeune and Clifton Chenier are among its sources, and always its presiding spirits, even when the songs are Delafose originals. Stanislas Chambers does a decent job of filling Tony Delafose's shoes, and Cajun guitarist Bobby Broussard's inventive blues playing has a likeable country twang at times. This is the Delafose express back on the right track, and going full steam ahead.

La Chanson Perdue is even more traditionally based. Dance tunes dominate the playlist; Germaine Jack's exuberance and John Esprite's thunder-thumb give them a relentlessness unavailable to their originators, who include Bois Sec Ardoin, Canray Fontenot, the Balfa Brothers and Lawrence Walker. On this disc Delafose celebrates the connections between Cajun and Creole music, which, unlike many contemporary zydeco artists, he has no problem acknowledging and exploring; on three tracks he's assisted by Christine Balfa and Dirk Powell of Balfa Toujours (much better here than with Bois Sec Ardoin) and on two by Steve Riley, with whom he once played in a high-school band.

***(*) **Everybody's Dancin'**
Times Square TSQ-CD-9034 *Delafose; Michael Doucet (vn); Lee Tedrow (g, v); John Esprite (b, v); Jude 'Curley' Taylor (d, v); Wilfred 'Caveman' Pierre (rb); Tony Daigle (tri).* 02.

Everybody's Dancin' appears on Delafose's own label and is self-produced, although not much production seems to have been needed; French Rockin' Boogie, joined on three numbers by the great Cajun fiddler Michael Doucet, came off the road after four years and laid down most of the CD in first or second takes. The blend is as before: old tunes from Nathan Abshire, Boozoo Chavis and Adam Hebert among others, new tunes by Delafose that sound old, and a few pop covers. It's the last that prompt a slightly cooler recommendation. Sam Cooke's 'What A Wonderful World' is imperfectly recalled and perfunctorily sung, and the country ballad 'What Do You Want With His Love' is weak material, initially sung out of tune. We also take a dim view of attributing Bébé Carrière's 'Le Bluerunner' to 'traditional, arranged by Geno Delafose'. CS

John Delafose (1939–94)
VOCAL, ACCORDION, VIOLIN, RUBBOARD

A homemade fiddle was Delafose's first instrument, and as a teenager he played harmonica at dances. He took time out to marry and raise a family, but bought an accordion in his early 30s and formed the Eunice Playboys, recruiting mainly from his sons and nephews. In the early '80s, a version of 'Joe Pitre A Deux Femmes' established Delafose's reputation locally, and he travelled more widely as his fame increased; the Playboys were on the way to a festival in Rhode Island in 1993 when he suffered a major heart attack. Delafose recovered following surgery, but in the aftermath his marriage broke up and he left the family band. He made a comeback with other musicians and was working at a dance when he died.

***(*) **Joe Pete Got Two Women**
Arhoolie CD-335 *Delafose; Charles Prudhomme (g); Joseph*

Prudhomme (b); Geno Delafose (d); Tony Delafose (d, rb); John Delafose Jr (rb). 5/81–5/82.

John Delafose was determined to keep in touch with the roots of zydeco; the song that kick-started his career came from Bois Sec Ardoin, he played more waltzes, and sang more songs in French, than most of his contemporaries, and he was readier than some of them to acknowledge the links between Creole and Cajun music. *Joe Pete Got Two Women* naturally features his hit (and a rather dull follow-up, 'Joe Pete Lost His Two Women'), but for the most part it's gloriously unconcerned with fashion and trends. Particularly when he plays button accordion, Delafose's music has the unrelenting drive of zydeco at its best. Just listening to 'Prudhomme Stomp', 'Co-Fe' and 'You Took My Heartache' one after another is exhilarating and exhausting, never mind dancing to them.

When Delafose switches to piano accordion, he sometimes sounds too much like Clifton Chenier in his swirly, 'poor man's zydeco Ray Charles' mode; 'Rag Around Your Head' is the most blatant example of straightforward Chenier imitation, and 'Crying In The Streets' comes close behind, but is saved by Charles Prudhomme's astringent guitar obbligato. A piano accordion version of the venerable 'Mardi Gras Song' succeeds remarkably well, however, and 'Mother's Day Blues' has an aching sincerity.

Throughout, the Eunice Playboys are admirably tight and unstoppably energetic, especially when Geno Delafose (then ten years old!) takes over on drums for the disc's second half, playing accents and fills all over the kit, and all over the tunes, in places that are sometimes most unlikely, and always spot-on. The last four tracks, recorded live at a festival, make for a riotous climax, with even 'La Valse A Creole' (mistitled 'Las Valse De Freole') settling into a manic groove.

**** Zydeco Live!
Rounder CD 2070 *Delafose; Gene Chambler, Charles Prudhomme (g); Tony Delafose (b); Geno Delafose (d); Germaine Jack (rb). 3/88.*

***(*) Heartaches And Hot Steps
Maison de Soul MdS-1035 *As above.* 89?

Zydeco Live!, recorded at Richard's Club in Lawtell, is shared with Willis Prudhomme's band. This half-disc is John Delafose's finest hour on record, for he seems to be galvanized by playing for dancers, and by support from the definitive Eunice Playboys rhythm section: Tony Delafose, abandoning the drums to play light-fingered but rock-steady bass, brother Geno on drums, and their cousin Germaine Jack on rubboard. Throughout, Geno and Germaine play percussion duets, rather than just keeping time, although they do that impeccably as well. The playlist is mainly R&B-oriented, but 'Poor Man Two Step' is as retro as anyone could wish for. The R&B emphasis is all to the good, in any case, for it showcases the astonishing lead guitar solos of Gene Chambler, who deploys exquisite tone, complex, jazzy licks, and the precise, hair-raising timing of a trapeze artist; at times, he sounds like a Kenyan *benga* guitarist playing blues – or perhaps like a blues guitarist playing *benga*.

Heartaches And Hot Steps continues the good work, but it's a notch below *Zydeco Live*: the recording is less vivid, and the musicians don't have an audience to whip up and be whipped up by. Nevertheless, Chambler continues to play wonderful licks, the rhythm section can't be faulted and John Delafose leads from the front, singing with verve aplenty and, on 'Hungry Man Blues', a surprising, snarling edginess. The set is a well-chosen mélange of waltzes, two-steps, blues and pop: highlights include a version of Sam Cooke's 'Wonderful World' that's stripped down, funked up, half-remembered and wholly terrific, and 'Broken Hearted', which confidently combines mellow, retrospective accordion with hammering *nouveau* rhythms.

***(*) Père Et Garçon Zydeco
Rounder CD 2116 *Delafose; Geno Delafose (ac, d, v); Charles Prudhomme (g); Tony Delafose (b); Germaine Jack (d, rb, v). 12/91.*

***(*) Blues Stay Away From Me
Rounder CD 2121 *As above, except Tony Delafose also sings; add Scott Billington (p), Paul Delafose (rb). 4/93.*

Both these CDs are credited to 'John Delafose and the Eunice Playboys featuring Geno Delafose'; *le garçon* plays accordion and sings on five of *Père Et Garçon's* 14 tracks, and on eight of *Blues Stay Away From Me's* 15. When he does so, Germaine Jack takes over the drumkit, and the rubboard is played by John or Paul Delafose respectively.

Only 19 on *Père Et Garçon*, Geno fronts the band with as much authority as his father, and often with more vocal energy. John Delafose's health was failing for some time before his heart attack, but he should not be pictured as a semi-invalid, carried by the band; 'Down In Texas', based on Dewey Balfa's 'Quand J'Etais Pauvre', is a consummate piece of songmaking, yearning and forceful at the same time, and the title track, on which Delafose *père* sings and plays rubboard, with only Geno's accordion and Germaine Jack's drums for company, is a very high-octane variant of Clifton Chenier's 'Zydeco Et Pas Salé'. Geno's 'Watch That Dog' taps into the then current craze, sparked by Boozoo Chavis's 'Dog Hill', for zydeco dog songs and sound effects, and it falls into the musical coarseness that Chavis was prone to; on the opposite flank, John's version of 'I Can't Stop Loving You' is relatively effete, and too obviously semi-improvised. These lapses are exceptions, however; 'Two Step Farouche' is aptly named, Amédé Ardoin's 'Midland Two Step' is not far behind it for wildness, and the waltzes, 'Friday Night' and the old favourite 'Grand Mamou' (which has extraordinary drumming by Jack), swing like mad.

On *Blues Stay Away From Me*, Delafose and the Eunice Playboys look both backwards and forwards. Probably in recognition of the rising popularity of Beau Jocque's *nouveau zydeco* in the early '90s, the drumming, though still supple, is heavier on the bass pedal, and Tony Delafose's bass guitar is much more prominent in the mix. This is all to the good, since his playing is fabulously rich, dark and elegant, and the high energy rhythm section seems to have reinvigorated John Delafose. Some of the looking back is less successful. The title track is a disorganized account of the old Delmore Brothers' hit, and when John Delafose plays violin, he does little more than add texture and colour to two accordion-led numbers; his intonation on 'Joe Simien Special' is scratchily unpleasant. In all other respects, however, the last John Delafose CD is another splendid mix of traditional Creole numbers and up-to-date zydeco, with 'Scott Playboy Special', learned by listening to *Le Rendezvous Des Cajuns* on the radio, thrown in for *lagniappe*. 'I Can't Forget You (Je Ne Peux Pas T'Oublier)' makes up for the shortcomings of 'I Can't Stop Loving You' on *Père Et Garçon Zydeco*; played first as a waltz, then as a two-step, it is none other than 'I Can't Stop Loving You', given new lyrics and credited to 'trad. arr. Geno Delafose'. Let's call it the folk process in action. cs

The Delta Jukes
GROUP

The Delta Jukes were formed after Frank Frost's death in 1999 to perpetuate the sound and spirit of the Jelly Roll Kings, for whom Sam Carr had been the drummer and sheet-anchor.

*** Working For The Blues
Black Magic 9044 *John Weston (h, v); Fred James (p, g, b); Dave Riley (g, v); Sam Carr (d).* 7/00.

**(*) Down In The Delta
R.O.A.D. RDBL-42 *Andrew 'Shine' Turner (g, v); Fred James (g); Dave Riley (b, v); Sam Carr (d).* 03?

Playing mainly at festivals, the Delta Jukes are prolonging the life of a music that's dying out in its original habitat, as producer Fred James readily acknowledges. Still, Riley is an effective, no-frills lead guitarist and singer, Weston's gloomy voice and sinuous chromatic harp are better on Black Magic than on some of his own CDs, and any projects that keep Sam Carr drumming must be worthwhile. Weston and Riley share most of the songwriting on *Working For The Blues*; a couple of Riley's songs are assembled from the Big Box of Blues Clichés, but Weston continues to be a witty, original pessimist. *Down In The Delta* is credited to Sam Carr's Delta Jukes and of course his drumming is immaculate, if rather low in the mix. The cliché-mongering continues, although surprisingly Turner's 'Blues With A Feeling' is a strong, original lyric counselling against violence. His 'Shine', about growing up black with red hair, bucks the trend amusingly, too, and the Jukes get points for snatching 'You Need Love' back from Led Zeppelin; but there are too many blues about the blues and, on songs like 'Juke Joint Saturday Night' and 'Down In The Delta', too much pandering to tourists' fantasies. cs

Detroit Junior (1931–2005)
VOCAL, PIANO

Despite the nickname, Emery Williams Jr was an Arkansas-born Chicago resident with a fondness for New Orleans rhythms; his previous residence in the Motor City inspired the nom de disque, *conferred by his first record label. 'Money Tree' was a local hit on Bea & Baby, and Williams was stuck with a moniker he didn't like. He recorded singles for various labels, scoring again on USA with 'Call My Job', and was in Howlin' Wolf's band from 1969 to 1975.*

**(*) Turn Up The Heat
Blue Suit BS 105D *Detroit Junior; B. J. Emery (tb); Maurice John Vaughn (g, v); Freddie Dixon (b); Michael McGee (d).* 94.

*** Take Out The Time
Blue Suit BS 109D *Detroit Junior; B. J. Emery (tb, v); Maurice John Vaughn (ts, g, v); Eddie Burns (h, v); Kenny Pickens (b); Mike McGee (d); Singing Angels, Julia Rockwood, Kevin Rockwood, Kevin Burns, Lonesome Bob, Johnny Porkchop, Joe 'Mojo' Buehler (v).* 97.

** Live At The Toledo Museum Of Art
Blue Suit BS 118D *Detroit Junior.* 6/01.

*** Blues On The Internet
Delmark DE-777 *Detroit Junior; Sonny Cohn (t); Eric Schneider (as, ts); Lurrie Bell, Maurice John Vaughn, Jimmy Dawkins, Willie Davis (g); Bob Stroger (b); Kenny Smith (d); Zora Young (sp).* 8/04.

Detroit Jr's early hits marked him out as a perceptive and funny songwriter; 'Call My Job' is on *The USA Records Blues Story* (Fuel 2000 302 061 209), and 'Money Tree' on *Meat & Gravy From Bea & Baby* (Castle CMDDD 610 2CD). There are more witty tales of ghetto life, and some lively dance tunes, on *Turn Up The Heat*, but muffled recording and the jangle of an electric piano subvert the positive qualities, and setting 'Killing Floor' to a second-line strut was a really bad idea. *Take Out The Time* is much better recorded, but Detroit concentrates more on party specials, and on paying tributes to his inspirations, notably Ray Charles, Fats Domino and Amos Milburn. He makes a good fist of 'Chicken Shack Boogie' (where Vaughn's tenor sax is a real bonus), and even of 'What'd I Say', but can't find anything new in 'Trouble In Mind', and makes a dog's breakfast of 'Blueberry Hill'. These lapses are redeemed, though, by 'Take Out The Time' and 'Slow Dancing', clever lyrics sung and accompanied with great subtlety and soulfulness.

Detroit plays a superb concert grand on *Live At The Toledo Museum Of Art*, and selects some unusual songs, including compositions by Percy Mayfield and Brook Benton; but they keep company with chestnuts like 'Honest I Do', 'Key To The Highway' and 'Every Day I Have The Blues'. Detroit had been unwell, and his voice is somewhat diminished, but his many rhythmic and harmonic errors are more fundamental flaws.

He's back on track for *Blues On The Internet*, much more in command and assisted by reliable musicians, surprisingly including Basie alumnus Sonny Cohn. (The need for their assistance is illuminated by a video clip of 'Hot Pants Baby', performed solo. Some of its many wrong notes are on the band version, too, but they're artfully camouflaged.) Zora Young enhances an effective revival of 'Call My Job', but Detroit's voice is no longer flexible enough to be 'Messin' With The Kid'. Most songs are originals: the topical commentary 'Less Violence, More Love' is trite in the extreme, but elsewhere Detroit proves that he's still a clever writer; the title track amusingly updates the woman who stays out all night long to one who stays on-line all night long. This is an inessential but pleasant CD. cs

Floyd Dixon (born 1928)
VOCAL, PIANO

Dixon left his birthplace in Marshall, Texas, in his teens to settle in LA, where he won talent contests and a recording contract with Modern. He also recorded for Supreme with bassist Eddie Williams's group, and later for Aladdin, Specialty and other labels. Among his charting sides were 'Broken Hearted' and 'Call Operator 210', but not his best-known number, 'Hey Bartender'. He moved to the San Francisco Bay Area in 1974. He virtually quit the music business in the '80s but was encouraged to return.

*** Cow Town Blues
Ace CDCHD 740 *Dixon; Buddy Floyd, Maxwell Davis (ts); Tiny Webb, Chuck Norris (g); Eddie Williams, Bill Davis, unknown (b); Ellis 'Slow' Walsh, Al 'Cake' Wichard (d).* 48–50.

The delivery immediately recalls Charles Brown, likewise the mixture of slow blues and pop compositions. The musical settings also replicate Brown's, exactly in the case of bassist Eddie Williams, but substituting Tiny Webb or, later, Chuck Norris for guitarist Johnny Moore. A tenor is occasionally added to beef up the ensemble, but essentially the strategy is plain: Dixon was to provide Modern with what Brown (himself a former Modern artist) was currently serving up on Aladdin – husky, confiding vocals and slow-trickling piano – and he does his job skilfully on tracks like 'Mississippi Blues', 'Drafting Blues', 'Dallas Blues' and 'It's Getting Foggy'. That said, he was not wholly in thrall to his forerunner, as animated performances like 'That'll Get It' and 'Houston Jump' attest, though here there is more than a hint of Amos Milburn. Seven tracks are previously unissued.

*** **Marshall Texas Is My Home**
Specialty SPCD-7011//Ace CDCHD 361 *Dixon; Carlos Bermudez, Joe Howard, prob. Plas Johnson, unknown(s) (ts); unknown (bs); Chuck Norris, Jimmy Lewis, unknowns (g); Walter Cole, Billy Hadnott, unknowns (b); Minor Robinson, Rudolph Pitts, Earl Palmer, unknowns (d). 53–57.*

Cow Town Blues was drawn from the Modern archives; these are from Specialty and various smaller labels. Dixon continues to operate in the two gears typified by the Brown study 'Old Memories' and the boisterous party numbers 'Hole In The Wall' and 'Hey Bartender', but there are exceptions like 'Carlos', a tenor sax-led instrumental in the Tiny Bradshaw vein, and the gospel rave-up 'Judgement Day'. By 1957 Dixon is making valiant attempts to play the rock 'n' roll game with 'Rita' and the Little Richardish 'Oooh Little Girl'. Half the 22 tracks are previously unissued, including a solo demo of 'Call Operator 210'.

Four sides from 1962 with Johnny Guitar Watson are on the VAC *Rockin' This Joint Tonite* (JSP CD 2146), but since two are instrumentals, 'Late Freight Twist' featuring Watson and 'Tell Me, Tell Me' an unidentified tenor, and one of the vocal numbers is 'Me Quieres', a piece of mock-Chicano fluff, only avid Dixonians need seek it out.

*** **Wake Up And Live!**
Alligator ALCD 4841 *Dixon; Joe Campbell (t); Danny 'Bone' Weinstein (tb); Eddie Synigal (ts, bs); Charlie Owens (bs); Port Barlow (g, prod); Leslie Baker, Mark Goldberg, Rick Reed (b); Eddie Clark, James Arvans, Jimi Bott (d). 96.*

Coming after some rather iffy homemade jobs, this album arrived with a sheen of craft and care that was very welcome. Producer Port Barlow, as well as getting that right, plays the apt guitar. Dixon's voice is rougher, which has the advantage of erasing his likeness to Charles Brown, and if the piano cadences of 'You're The Only One For Me' are a throwback to his first model, other slow blues like 'Livin' A Lie' are fully individual creations. The title track and 'My Song Is Don't Worry', adapted from a poem he used as his answering-machine message, are vehicles for his buoyant philosophy of life. TR

Mary Dixon
VOCAL

Apparently a Texan, Dixon made some excellent recordings in New York in 1928–29 and appeared in the revue Hot From Harlem *in 1933.*

*** **Blue Girls – Vol. 2 (1928–1930)**
Document DOCD-5504 *Dixon; Louis Metcalf, Ed Allen (c); prob. Ernest Elliott, poss. Albert Socarras (cl); J. C. Johnson (p); unknown (g). 7/28–10/29.*

Oddly, in view of her subsequent work, Dixon's first recordings were of the popular songs 'Dusky Stevedore' and 'I Can't Give You Anything But Love'. (Also to be found on *Tight Women And Loose Bands 1921–1931* [Timeless CBC 1–068].) After a break of some months and a change of label, she embarked on a series of blues recordings notable for pungent lyrics and a defiant manner, such as 'You Can't Sleep In My Bed', 'All Around Mama' and 'Daddy, You're A Low-Down Man'. Metcalf or Allen respond with forceful muted cornet phrases, while Dixon occasionally inserts a chorus of growled vocalese.

Among the other singers presented on this compilation are Mozelle Alderson (q.v.) and Issie Ringgold, whose way with recitative is reminiscent of Sophie Tucker and who is backed by a swaggering cornettist. TR

Willie Dixon (1915–92)
BASS, GUITAR, VOCAL

Such was his skill and reputation as a songwriter that it's hard to assess Willie Dixon the performer. A towering, corpulent figure who could wield a bass fiddle like a tennis racket, the essential benevolence of his character was evident in his rumbling bass voice. By stating 'I am the blues' (the title of his autobiography), he ensured he was wholly identified with the music, but as a wordsmith his abilities were spread over a wider canvas. The man who wrote 'Little Red Rooster' and 'Hoochie Coochie Man' also penned 'Violent Love' and 'Don't Let That Music Die' but he seemed happiest when compiling 'list' songs like 'Wang Dang Doodle'. A master of his craft, he tailored songs for Muddy Waters, Howlin' Wolf, Little Walter, Lowell Fulson, Koko Taylor and Bo Diddley, among many others, and had a hand in their production. On his own (relatively few) singles and albums he settled for competence rather than the creativity he demanded as a producer.

**** **The Chess Box**
MCA/Chess CH3–16500 3CD *Dixon; Harold Ashby (ts); Leonard 'Baby Doo' Caston, Lafayette Leake (p); Ollie Crawford (g); Fred Below, Al Duncan (d). 11/55–64.*

Dixon's recordings with the Big Three Trio are covered in that entry. *The Chess Box*, with just six tracks (of 36) performed by Dixon himself, is more of a sampler of the Chess and Checker labels and of Chicago blues in general, but it commemorates the wealth of fine music for which Dixon was responsible, in whole or in part. Muddy Waters, Howlin' Wolf, Little Walter, Bo Diddley, Lowell Fulson, Eddie Boyd, Willie Mabon, Koko Taylor, Sonny Boy Williamson II, Jimmy Witherspoon and Little Milton are all represented by the hugely successful songs that Dixon wrote, arranged and produced for them. In that company, his own contributions pale in significance, which may be as he preferred it.

(*) **The Original Wang Dang Doodle – The Chess Recordings And More
[MCA/Chess CHD 9353] *Dixon; Harold Ashby, J. T. Brown (ts); Billy Branch, Stanley Behrens (h); Lafayette Leake, Leonard 'Baby Doo' Caston, Johnnie Jones, Arthur 'Butch' Dixon (p); Ollie Crawford, Jody Williams, Hubert Sumlin, John Watkins, Johnny B. Moore, Cash McCall (g); Jerome Arnold, Freddie*

Dixon, Rob Wasserman (b); Fred Below, Al Duncan, Junior Blackman, Clifton James, Jimmy Tillman, Chuckie Burke (d). 2/54–90.

These 14 tracks are merely snapshots from a long and prolific career. Dixon's voice can carry a tune but the bag it's in is Wal-Mart rather than Gucci. The original 'Wang Dang Doodle' was cut in 1954, presumably intended as a single but never released. There were three singles in all and the record company are cheapskates for not including the B sides of two of them. 'Crazy For My Baby' and '29 Ways' enjoyed a brief half-life but his version of 'Walking The Blues' lacks the humour and atmosphere of Jack Dupree's original. Most of the remainder do him no favours apart from a dramatic rendition of 'Tail Dragger', cut as a guide for Howlin' Wolf. 'I Just Want To Make Love To You' from 1989 and a bass duet with Rob Wasserman a year later close a collection that fails to give even a vague outline of Dixon's achievements.

**(*) Willie's Blues
Original Blues Classics OBCCD 501 Dixon; Harold Ashby (ts); Memphis Slim (p); Wally Richardson (b); Gus Johnson (d). 12/59.

Prestige, for whose Bluesville label this album was originally recorded, chose Dixon as one of their earliest signings, based no doubt on his track record for Chess and other Chicago labels. Trouble is, Dixon chose to record a batch of his lesser compositions, 'Nervous', 'Good Understanding' and 'Youth To You' among them. His accompanists fulfil their roles adequately but the recording ambience hardly invites audience participation. The brevity of the project is emphasized by the addition of nine tracks from Bluesville sessions by Memphis Slim (who receives joint credit on the CD), which complement the mundanity of the Dixon tracks.

**(*) Baby Please Come Home!
Original Blues Classics OBCCD 582 Dixon; Memphis Slim (p, v); Philippe Combelle (d). 11/62.

Dixon and Memphis Slim (again jointly credited) had just finished the first AFBF tour of Europe when this live set was recorded at the Trois Mailletz in Paris. They'd already recorded a number of albums and toured together, and their performance often lapses into a rather mechanical competence. There are three duets and Slim sings another three songs, leaving Dixon a sequence of six that includes 'The Way She Loves A Man', 'African Hunch With A Boogie Beat' and 'Cold Blooded', the latter a lightly disguised 'Five Long Years'. He'd begun to adopt the patriarchal stance later expressed in *I Am The Blues* but the audience is at least as interested in itself as it is in the performers. They supply the requisite applause but no more than the performance deserves.

**(*) I Am The Blues
Columbia CK 53627//Mobile Fidelity MFCD 872 Dixon; Walter Horton (h); Lafayette Leake (p); Johnny Shines, Mighty Joe Young (g); Sylvester Boines (b); Clifton James (d). 69.
*** Poet Of The Blues
Columbia/Legacy CK 65593 As above. 12/47–69.

For a man prepared to associate himself so closely with the music, *I Am The Blues* is a distinct disappointment. All nine songs are classics of their kind, including 'Hoochie Coochie Man', 'Spoonful', 'Little Red Rooster' and 'I Can't Quit You Baby'. Dixon certainly exerts himself on occasions, as do Horton and Leake, but there's plainly been no preparation for the session. Solo choruses too often begin in confusion and meander to a conclusion and endings are as indecisive as what has preceded them. Twice as many tracks remain unissued as those issued here. One can only speculate on their quality. *Poet Of The Blues* is a mid-price compilation that combines *I Am The Blues* with ten sides by the Big Three Trio.

*(*) Willie Dixon & Johnny Winter With The Chicago All Stars
Thunderbolt CDTB 166 Dixon; Walter Horton (h); Lafayette Leake (p); Lee Jackson (g); Clifton James (d). 5/71.

Recorded from 'an audience perspective', this Houston gig makes a nonsense of the CD format. The sound, never good, degenerates as the recorder gets pushed further from the stage. The Chicago All Stars perform the first four numbers before Winter takes over at the microphone. Dixon puts a lot of energy into a dire reading of 'Sitting And Crying The Blues', 'Spoonful' and 'I Just Want To Make Love To You', while Horton raises the musical standard significantly in the instrumental 'Chicago Here I Come'. NS

Lefty Dizz (1937–93)
VOCAL, GUITAR, HARMONICA

Described in his heyday as a 'Clown Prince of the blues' for his 'one-handed guitar gymnastics, comical expressions, and strolls through the audience' (Jim O'Neal in Living Blues), Dizz, born in Arkansas but raised in Chicago, was active on the South Side blues scene from the mid-'60s, when he played with Junior Wells under his given name of Walter Williams. He later joined Hound Dog Taylor's Houserockers, toured Europe with the Chicago Blues Festival in 1979 and recorded several albums in France and England.

**(*) Shake For Me
Black & Blue BB 453 Dizz; Big Moose Walker (p, v); Willie James Lyons (g); Mojo Elem (b); Odie Payne (d). 6/79.
**(*) Ain't It Nice To Be Loved
JSP JSPCD 259 Dizz; Carey Bell (h); Jerry Soto (p); Lurrie Bell (g); Tyson Bell (b); James Bell (d). 89.

Inevitably these recordings convey nothing of Dizz's wild stage act. But enough is left on the JSP album, at least, to hold the attention even of listeners who have no memorial video to play in their head. Although the backing of the Bell family band is more dutiful than inspiring, Dizz sings and plays energetically, happy with a selection of songs that includes Hound Dog Taylor's 'Sadie', his own 'Bad Avenue' and 'I Feel Like Jumping' – which should be 'I Feel Like Chopping', since it's based in part on Charley Patton's 'Down The Dirt Road Blues' – and a 'Look On Yonder's Wall' on which he sounds, not for the only time, like a country cousin of Magic Sam, though not in the out-of-tune harmonica solo, fortunately the only one he put on record. *Shake For Me* portrays him as a generic performer of road-tested club material like 'Take Out Some Insurance' and 'Things That I Used To Do'. He is good at this, and his reading of 'Cummins Prison Farm' is as convincing as any, but the album barely hints that he was capable of more individual work. For a 1975 duet recording with Louisiana Red see the latter's entry. TR

Johnny Dollar (born 1941)
VOCAL, GUITAR

Dollar, whose given name is John L. Sibley, is a younger brother of Lefty Dizz. He was born in Greenville, Mississippi, grew up in California and served 12 years in the US Marines. He began playing in Chicago clubs in the '70s, initially as a singer, later also playing guitar. A 'Chicago Blues 1980' tour of France led to his debut album, My Soul Is Blue *(Isabel), and he made a second album in the US in 1986, but in recent years he has not worked much.*

**(*) My Baby Loves Me
Wolf 120.803 Dollar; Steve Hawkins (t); Darrell Creasy (tb); Ozzie Stamford (s); Leo Davis (kb, p); Herb Walker (g, g syn); Robert Fetzer, Kelvin 'Bo' Holmon (g); Johnny B. Gayden (b); Willie Hayes (d, v); Vivian Williams (v). late 90s or early 00s.

Dollar waited a long time to make this, his third album: just how long is unclear, since no recording date is given, and the notes merely refer to it as his 'first recording in over a decade'. The music offers no clues; there's a slight datedness to the ensemble sound on some of the numbers, but that may be deceptive. It's a well-made record, with vivacious bass playing by Johnny B. Gayden, but it may not be the one to reclaim the audience Dollar found with its predecessors. Though it opens with Detroit Jr's 'Call My Job', and later there is an unhackneyed reading of 'The Things I Used To Do', the emphasis is firmly on soul material like 'That's The Way Love Is' and 'If Loving You Is Wrong (I Don't Want To Be Right)', which Dollar delivers in a velvety wrapping. TR

Fats Domino (born 1928)
VOCAL, PIANO

A native of New Orleans, Antoine Domino was becoming a name in local clubs when he was spotted by the bandleader Dave Bartholomew and Lew Chudd of Imperial Records. Signed to Imperial, he caused a stir with his first record, went on to rack up many R&B hits and in time penetrated the pop charts as well. During the '50s he not only sold more records than any forerunner in black music but was hugely popular on R&B and rock 'n' roll package tours. The influence of his triplet-rich piano playing spread far and wide into popular music, and his recordings made their mark upon contemporary Jamaican idioms. Since the '60s he has toured intermittently but recorded seldom.

*** The Early Imperial Singles 1950–1952
Ace CDCHD 597 Domino; Dave Bartholomew (t); Joe Harris, Wendell Ducongé (as); Herb Hardesty, Clarence Hall, Robert 'Buddy' Hagans (ts); Alvin 'Red' Tyler (bs); Ernest McLean, Walter Nelson, Harrison Verrett (g); Frank Fields, Billy Diamond (b); Earl Palmer, Cornelius Coleman (d). 12/49–10/52.

*** The Imperial Singles Volume 2 1953–1956
Ace CDCHD 649 Domino; Dave Bartholomew (t); Wendell Ducongé, Clarence Ford (as); Herb Hardesty, Buddy Hagans, Lee Allen (ts); Walter Nelson, Ernest McLean (g); Frank Fields (b); Cornelius Coleman (d). 10/52–11/55.

*** The Imperial Singles Volume 3, 1956–1958
Ace CDCHD 689 As above, except Ford also plays ts, bs; add Warren Bell, unknowns (s), Allen Toussaint (p), Justin Adams, Willie Jones, unknown (g), Jimmie Davis, unknown (b), Charles Williams, Earl Palmer, unknown (d), unknowns (v). 2/55–11/58.

The Fats Domino most people know is the man who, in the second half of the '50s, added to his solid reputation as an R&B artist a wide following in the pop arena, with a slew of releases that regularly placed high in the charts in both categories. This is the period covered by *The Imperial Singles Volume 3*, when releases like 'I'm In Love Again', 'Blueberry Hill', 'Blue Monday', 'I'm Walkin'' and 'Whole Lotta Loving' achieved Top Ten status in both lists and almost every other track, whether 'A' or 'B' side, registered on the charts, several even doing so in the UK. Domino appeared to have discovered a magic recipe, adding calculated pinches of exotic New Orleans accent and rhythm to blues-based pop, ballads and country songs.

It's fascinating, knowing what's to come, to rewind the videotape of history back to Domino's first recordings. His early sessions find him shuffling through a wardrobe of styles, trying on Professor Longhair, Amos Milburn, maybe Roy Brown; when he does find the makings of what became his own manner, as in 'The Fat Man' or 'Goin' Home', he doesn't seem to realize quite what he's got, and falls back on more impersonal material like 'Trust In Me'. For all that, *Volume 1* is an absorbing study of a style in the making. Much of *Volume 2* is spent at the drawing-board, too, and for a while Domino seems to lose the blueprints, as he wanders through 1954 with barely a hit to his name, but with 'Ain't That A Shame' he triumphantly solves his problems, and the rest is pop music history.

Since these CDs contain every single that Imperial issued (and a few rejected sides that were exhumed later), there are dandelions among the dahlias, such as 'Korea Blues' (*Volume 1*), ruined by Bartholomew blowing shrill fanfares over the vocal, or dull songs like 'I Lived My Life' (*Volume 2*). On *Volume 3* it becomes apparent that Domino's expanding appeal was not gained without compromise, more often in the quality of the material than of his or the band's performance, though the really trifling numbers usually prove to be the ones that made only a faint impression on the charts or none at all, such as 'Yes My Darling', 'Don't You Know I Love You' or 'The Prisoner's Song'. Appearances can be deceptive, though: 'When My Dreamboat Comes Home' is a pop song without much promise, but Domino boards it with a swashbuckling horn section that sounds as if it might have been taken on in Jamaica. The sheer *joie de vivre* of a performance like this is a key to Domino's success: even in the gloomiest song he sounds as if jollity is just around the corner, and it's impossible to listen to him for long without a smile.

*** Fats Domino 1949–1951
Classics 5025 As for The Early Imperial Singles 1950–1952, except omit Verrett. 12/49–4/51.

*** The Fat Man: The Essential Early Fats Domino
[Indigo IGOCD 2513] As above. 12/49–6/51.

*** The Fat Man
Ocium OCM 3020 As above. 12/49–6/51.

*** Rockin' On Rampart
Proper PVCD 120 2CD As for The Early Imperial Singles 1950–1952, except add unknown musicians. 12/49–10/52, unknown dates.

*** Fats Domino 1951–1952
Classics 5060 Domino; Dave Bartholomew (t); Wendell Ducongé (as); Herb Hardesty, Robert 'Buddy' Hagans (ts); Walter Nelson,

Harrison Verrett (g); Frank Fields, Billy Diamond (b); Cornelius Coleman (d). 6/51–12/52.

*** **Fats Domino 1953**

Classics 5095 *As above, except add Lee Allen (ts); omit Verrett, Diamond.* 2–12/53.

The first two volumes of Classics' complete-and-chronological sequence cover approximately the same period as *The Imperial Singles 1950–1952* but add a few tracks that weren't issued as singles. The third volume has a larger proportion of recordings that Imperial didn't risk as singles but slid on to the market on EPs and LPs, including the bravura boogies 'Swanee River Hop', 'Domino Stomp' and 'Fats' Frenzy'. The Indigo and Ocium sets are identical in content (i.e. much the same as the first Classics) as well as in title, both adding half a dozen sides by Joe Turner and Smiley Lewis on which Domino plays piano. The first disc of the Proper 2CD also dogs the tracks of the first two Classics sets, while the second contains recordings described as 'recorded at various unknown locations on various unknown dates'. Since Domino rarely fiddles with a winning formula, these are acceptable versions of many of his signature pieces like 'Blueberry Hill', 'I'm Walkin', 'Jambalaya (On The Bayou)' and 'Let The Four Winds Blow'. The dozen tracks by Domino on *Gettin' Funky: The Birth Of New Orleans R&B* (Proper PROPERBOX 28 4CD) are from 1949–50 and are all to be found on the first Classics set.

*** **Legends Of The 20th Century**

EMI 521714 *As for The Imperial Singles Volumes 1–3, except add unknowns (strings), Roy Montrell (g).* 12/49–5/61.

*** **The Fats Domino Jukebox**

EMI Capitol 37600 *As above.* 12/49–11/61.

*** **Blues Kingpins**

Virgin 82742 *As above.* 12/49–55.

These are hits collections, containing 25, 20 and 18 tracks respectively, and consequently are more or less interchangeable. *Legends* is not only the longest but the most winningly presented, in a book-like format with good notes, and the reader who expects to be content with one Domino album need look no further.

***(*) **Out Of New Orleans**

Bear Family BCD 15541 8CD *Similar to all above CDs.* 12/49–4/62.

Compiled with this label's customary care, this massive boxed set gathers all the 200-odd recordings Domino made for Imperial, together with a few alternative and undubbed takes, and documents them in a substantial and prodigally illustrated book. Readers unacquainted with the later recordings are warned that they took Domino a long way from the kind of material with which he began his career.

After leaving Imperial in 1962 Domino spent the rest of the decade recording for other labels, generally with his familiar gang of musicians, usually led by Dave Bartholomew, whose influence may be detected in the frequent swings towards a Las Vegas Dixieland idiom. New material was added to the band's book, but without displacing the hits. Most of these albums are currently unavailable, and in any case they are beyond our remit, but it may be worth noting, if only because of the label it appears on, that *Fats Is Back* (Bullseye Blues & Jazz 9616) is a reissue of a 1968 LP that differed from its forerunners by giving Domino a sheaf of new (to him) songs like Barbara George's 'I Know' and the Beatles' 'Lady Madonna' (which was inspired by Domino) and 'Lovely Rita'. TR

Georgia Tom Dorsey (1899–1993)
VOCAL, PIANO

The Georgia-born Dorsey arrived in 1916 in Chicago, where he attended music college and worked as a band pianist for, among others, Ma Rainey. In 1928 he began arranging and writing for Chicago Music, a publishing company owned by J. Mayo Williams, and recording both as an accompanist and in his own name for the Brunswick and Vocalion labels, whose black music catalogues were overseen by Williams. His duet recording with guitarist Tampa Red of 'It's Tight Like That' was an enormous hit and gave the two men several years of profitable recording work in the hokum and novelty blues field. In 1930 he founded his own gospel music publishing company, and in 1932 left the blues business to become choral director of the Pilgrim Baptist Church and devote himself exclusively to writing, publishing and promoting gospel songs, which he continued to do for almost half a century.

(*) **Georgia Tom – Vol. 1 (1928–1930)

RST Blues Documents BDCD-6021 *Dorsey; poss. Bob Call (p); Tampa Red, Bob Robinson, Scrapper Blackwell, prob. Ikey Robinson, unknown (g, v); Foster & Harris (v).* c. 9/28–2/30.

(*) **Georgia Tom – Vol. 2 (1930–1934)

RST Blues Documents BDCD-6022 *Dorsey; Scrapper Blackwell (g, poss. v); Big Bill Broonzy, Tampa Red (g); unknown group (v); poss. Frankie Jaxon (sp).* 2/30–3/34, late 50s.

*** **Come On Mama Do That Dance**

Yazoo 1041 *Dorsey; Mozelle Alderson (poss. p, v); Tampa Red (g, v); Scrapper Blackwell (g, poss. v); unknown (perc); Frankie Jaxon, Foster & Harris, Bertha 'Chippie' Hill, Stovepipe Johnson (v).* 28–32.

Dorsey was very prolific, but much of his work was done jointly with Tampa Red or in groups like the Hokum Boys and Famous Hokum Boys. The RST Blues Documents CDs are, as usual with this label, based on his discography in *B&GR*, which for technical reasons is virtually restricted to recordings for which he received the sole or primary credit on the original issues. His many duets with Tampa Red are mostly to be found on CDs by the latter, especially his first five Document volumes, while the work of the Famous Hokum Boys, rounded up on two Wolf CDs, is discussed in their entry. The investigative reader will also need to consult the entry on Mozelle Alderson.

About a third of the tracks on *Vol. 1* are hokum duets with Tampa Red or another singer/guitarist. (Six were actually issued as by the Hokum Boys, but other recordings with this credit generally do not involve Dorsey.) He brings to this material a quizzical vocal manner and a bouncy but unassertive touch on piano. On slow blues, however, such as 'Grievin' Me Blues' or 'Broke Man's Blues', he employs an attractively wistful delivery, which in 'All Alone Blues' becomes positively doleful as he reflects, 'I was king for the season, when my girl was in this town. Now she's gone and left me, I feel my castle tumblin' down,' and asks, 'What are we but mortals, moulded from the pot of clay? At noonday we crumble, when evening comes we fade away.' The CD ends with a track, and *Vol. 2* begins with seven more, from a session at which he was accompanied with verve by Scrapper

Blackwell; 'Maybe It's The Blues' gives a good idea of Dorsey's pianistic abilities at a romping tempo. Slower pieces from this date and from subsequent sessions with Big Bill on guitar have some of the resigned manner of Leroy Carr, while the two-part 'M & O Blues' acknowledges the earlier recording by Walter Davis. In abrupt contrast, 'Then My Gal's In Town' is a peppy Charleston number. The sound quality on both albums is very variable.

The first sign of Dorsey's musical activities taking a new direction was his recording in 1932 a couple of tuneful compositions in the gospel idiom that he had a large part in creating. 'How About You' and 'If You See My Saviour' are also found on *Come On Mama Do That Dance*, a lively tour of his early career with examples of hokum, blues, duets with Mozelle Alderson and miscellaneous accompaniments. Well remastered and, considering its brevity (14 tracks), quite wide-ranging, this compilation gives a more accurate account than the Blues Documents CDs of Dorsey's versatility. TR

Double Trouble
DUET

The long chapter of their working relationship with Stevie Ray Vaughan closed, bassist Tommy Shannon (born 1947) and drummer Chris Layton have recorded with other Texan contemporaries like Debbie Davies.

** Been A Long Time
Tone-Cool TC 1180 *Layton (p, d, perc); Shannon (g, b); Mark Kazanoff (s); Charlie Sexton (o, p, mando-g, g, b, perc); Reese Wynans (o, p); Denny Freeman (o, g); Bill Willis, Riley Osburn (o); Dr John [Mack Rebennack] (p, v); Aimes Asbell, Lara Hick, Leigh Mahoney, Sara Nelson (strings); Doyle Bramhall II, Jimmie Vaughan, Susan Tedeschi (g, v); Kenny Wayne Shepherd, Van Wilks, Gordie Johnson, Eric Johnson, Willie Nelson, Derek O'Brien (g); Malford Milligan, Tommy Taylor, Lou Ann Barton, Jonny Lang, Ravon Fuster, Greg Sain, Karen Kohler, Martha Merriel, Yashika Vaughn (v); Glover Gill (strings arr).* 01?

Double Trouble put out the word that they were making an album, and guests came piling in to the party. Not everyone brought great food – there's a run of songs with all the bite and zing of supermarket jello – but the hungry listener will eventually find the meaty pies of 'Groundhog Day', strongly sung by Jonny Lang with blistering slide guitar by the song's composer, Gordie Johnson, and the trio rendition of Muddy Waters's 'She's All Right' led by Doyle Bramhall II, and the spicy combination platters of Susan Tedeschi and Kenny Wayne Shepherd in 'Rock And Roll' and Jimmie Vaughan and Lou Ann Barton on Johnny 'Guitar' Watson's 'In The Middle Of The Night'. Willie Nelson's contribution is an acoustic guitar part in Dr John's ballad 'Baby, There's No One Like You'. TR

K. C. Douglas (1913–75)
VOCAL, GUITAR

Unlike most Mississippians, when K. C. Douglas hit the road he moved west to California rather than north. He recorded a couple of 78s in the late '40s, and had a small hit with 'Mercury Boogie'. In 1956, some recordings Douglas had made for a folklorist were released on one of the first blues LPs, and from 1959 onwards he recorded intermittently for Chris Strachwitz. He led an electric band around the East Bay bar and dance circuit at weekends, and was planning to become a fulltime musician on retirement from his day job, but he didn't make it to 65.

*** K. C.'s Blues
Original Blues Classics OBCCD-533 *Douglas.* 2–3/61.
**** Big Road Blues
Original Blues Classics OBCCD-569 *Douglas.* 2/61.

In general, 'country blues' is a term of limited usefulness, when it's not actively misleading, but in K. C. Douglas's case there's a certain validity. To the end of his life, he referred to himself as 'just a country boy', and *K. C.'s Blues* is replete with images of rural life – roosters, dogs, gravel roads, even a track called 'Born In The Country'. In 1961, Douglas was being encouraged to recall the music he'd grown up with, for he had associated with Tommy Johnson, then no more than a name on exceedingly rare 78s, and former membership of the circle around Johnson made K. C. a valuable informant, almost irrespective of his musical merits.

Fortunately, those merits were considerable. As an acoustic guitarist, Douglas was less percussive, and more melodic, than many of the Drew school, combining a steady bass with fingerpicked runs whose easy grace sometimes recalls Mississippi John Hurt. The influence of Johnson and his associates is apparent; as well as the title track (with an interpolation from 'Maggie Campbell Blues'), *Big Road Blues* includes a version of 'Canned Heat'. Douglas several times fitted new words to Ishmon Bracey's 'Saturday Blues' as with 'Meanest Woman', on *K. C.'s Blues*, and 'Little Green House', recorded for Galaxy in 1967 and included, with its flipside, on *All Night Long They Play The Blues* (Specialty SPCD-7029//Ace CDCHD 440). His inspirations range more widely, however. The first of these CDs is a pleasant set of mostly original compositions, but surprisingly, *Big Road Blues*, which consists mostly of cover versions, and themes as well known as 'Catfish Blues' and 'Bottle Up And Go', has more commitment and musical adventurousness. The CD probably draws on the repertoire that Douglas was playing for the (then still sizeable) African-American audience for the older blues; as such, it has the vitality of music that's integral to its listeners' lives, and the security conferred by regular practice. A musician who can find something new to say in 'Move To Kansas City' and 'Key To The Highway' is a force to be reckoned with, and not just to be listened to for what he conveys about the music of others.

**(*) Mercury Blues
Arhoolie 475 *Douglas; unknown (ts); Richard Riggins (h); George Hurst (p); Ron Thompson (g); unknown (b); Jimmy Ramey, Jim Marshall (d).* 60, 8/63, 73–74.

The original version of 'Mercury Boogie' (a.k.a. 'Mercury Blues') is available on *Rock N' Roll Vol. 4: 1948* (Frémeaux FA 354), and a 1959 rerecording is one of three titles on *I Have To Paint My Face* (Arhoolie CD 432). Chris Strachwitz obviously, and rightly, thought that it was important to document Douglas's music, but it's difficult not to feel that *Mercury Blues*, the CD, is also a thanks offering for 'Mercury Blues', the nice little earner. Publishing royalties from covers by Steve Miller, David Lindley and Alan Jackson (#1 on the country charts in 1992) have made valuable contributions to the

Arhoolie exchequer over the years, and it's no surprise that a further version should be this CD's title track.

Eleven of its songs once made up a very enjoyable LP, containing a side of band recordings, and a side with just guitar and harp. Unfortunately, the expansion to 22 tracks makes it obvious that the LP used all the best material. The acoustic songs are as captivating as ever, particularly when decorated by Riggins's harmonica, and a solitary track with tenor sax and a rhythm section, once on an Arhoolie 45, is a valuable glimpse of another facet of Douglas's music; but the first 12 titles are from the '70s band session, and there is just too much of it. Douglas was anxious to make his mark, and had written a lot of new material, but quantity, and similarity of arrangement, overwhelms quality. Riggins and Marshall were members of the working band, but Bob Smith's bass was replaced by Ron Thompson on lead guitar. The results are unsatisfactory, for Thompson, though very competent, is scarcely ever inspired. His licks and tone are polished, polite and predictable, the underripe fruit of painstaking, wannabe study. This is the more regrettable because Riggins and Marshall have the sweaty, unbuttoned energy of a dancehall Saturday night, and on 'Catfish Blues', and the manic 'Richard's Ride' they give a tantalizing sample of what the session could have been. CS

Shy Guy Douglas (1917–84)
VOCAL, HARMONICA

Based in Nashville, Tom Douglas attracted some attention in 1949 after appearing at a talent show, and over the next couple of decades recorded a number of singles for local labels.

**(*) Stone Doin' Alright
Black Magic BM 9205 *Douglas; unknown (t); unknowns (s); unknown (o); Richard Armstrong, unknowns (p); Al Gunter, Arthur Gunter, unknowns (g); Big Jim, unknowns (b); Clarence Bailey, Earl Gaines, unknowns (d); Ted Jarrett (v). 49–69.*

Bizarrely versatile, Douglas switched during his recording career from the Nat 'King' Cole styling of his debut disc 'I Should Have Known' to the Jimmy Reed-like 'What's This I Hear?', stopping en route to commit the rock 'n' roll foolishness of 'Yankee Doodle' ('I lost my noodle ...'). It's in the downhome settings that he's most convincing, the more so when he begins to play harmonica, but only readers with a lot of curiosity about mildly interesting obscurities should expect to get much from this album. An efficient roundup of his (often not very well produced) singles, it omits only his four 1954 sides for Excello, which are on *No Jive: Authentic Southern Country Blues* (Ace CDCHD 652). The best of them, the brooding 'No Place Like Home' with a menacing guitarist, is also his best recording. TR

Nat Dove (born 1939)
PIANO, VOCAL

Born in Bryan, Texas, Dove has worked extensively on the West Coast. His playing is to be heard on several Hightone albums produced by Bruce Bromberg and Dennis Walker, for instance by Robert Cray, Lonesome Sundown and Phillip Walker, and he has also recorded with Big Mama Thornton, Bee Houston and other artists. He is the author of instructional books on blues and gospel piano, and latterly has been a frequent visitor to Japan.

**(*) Deep Blues Experience
Tri-Clef Music TCM 351 *Dove; Nagasaki Slim, Natsuko Miura (h); Tad Miura, Kunitsugu Soejima (g); Koichi Somei (b); Yuji Takagi (d). late 90s?*

A set of blues standards is not the ideal showcase for Dove's talents. His work with other artists is distinguished by moments of acute responsiveness, details that quietly enhance a performance. Here, preoccupied with the roles of singer, bandleader and chief soloist, he is too busy to concentrate on such specific playing and is constrained to give a performance that seldom rises above a steady competence. His task is not made easier by a programme of stock material like 'Got My Mojo Working', 'Reconsider Baby' and the like, and although he is billed as 'The Texas Boogie King' there is no boogie woogie to be heard. TR

Down Home Super Trio
GROUP

The DHST consists of R. J. Mischo, Frank Goldwasser and Richard Innes, who have frequently worked together on each other's and other people's albums.

*** In The House
Crosscut CCD 11081 *R. J. Mischo (h, bass d, v); Frank Goldwasser (g, v); Alex Schultz, Billy Flynn (g); Richard Innes (d). 11/03.*

It isn't clear from the notes if this 'supergroup' was formed just for the 2003 Lucerne Blues Festival, where this recording was made, or has a more substantial existence. It's not important: with all their shared experience, the core members effortlessly form a cohesive trio. (Schultz sits in on two numbers and Flynn on one.) Mischo is at his best, whether in the fat, rhythmic playing of 'Keep On Running' or the finer tracery of 'Grand Casino'; his vocals are okay too, especially Willie Nix's rueful rap 'Just Can't Stay Here'. Goldwasser's singing is more mannered, but on guitar he gets all sorts of lowdown and dirty effects which, when combined with the bass-heavy drumming, create a very plausible '50s juke-joint template for songs that sound as if they belong to that period anyway, like Mischo's 'Keep On Running' and 'They Try To Kill Me' or Goldwasser's 'Homesick Blues'. TR

Downchild Blues Band
GROUP

Downchild started life in a Toronto bar in 1969, became the leading Canadian blues band of the '70s and entered their fourth decade still very much active, in the US as well as Canada, and with founder Donnie Walsh still at the helm. They have worked with many leading blues acts, played thousands of gigs in their own right and recorded more than a dozen albums.

**(*) It's Been So Long/Ready To Go
Stony Plain SPCD 1242 *Bob Heslin (t); David Woodward (ts); Pat Carey (s); Donnie Walsh (h, g, v); Mike Fonfara (o); Jane Vasey, Ray Harrison, Gene Taylor (p); Mike McKenna (g); Dennis Pinhorn (b, v); Jim Milne (b); Paul Nixon, Sonny Bernardi (d,*

v); Bill Bryans (d); Tony Flaim (v). summer 75, 87.

This CD combines two albums made a dozen years apart. When Walsh wields his slide, the music on 1975's *Ready To Go* is a little like that of a contemporary US group, George Thorogood & The Destroyers, but his harmonica playing, Jane Vasey's piano and Tony Flaim's singing layer the sound somewhat differently. After Vasey's death in 1982 the band took a break from recording before returning with *It's Been So Long*. Now there was sometimes a flavour of Roomful Of Blues in the Downchild mix, though harmonica-led pieces like 'Off The Cuff' connected the band to an older downhome idiom. Most of the songwriting on both albums, as on virtually all of the band's recordings, is by Walsh, and while he can create a serviceable fit of lyric and melody – given that most of the tunes are blues or near-blues – it would be hard to identify a really memorable union. But this is likeable party music.

**(*) Gone Fishing
Stony Plain SPCD 1139 *Peter Jeffrey (t); Pat Carey (s); Donnie Walsh (h, g); Michael Fonfara (o); Gene Taylor (p); Pat Rush (g); Dennis Pinhorn (b); Marty Vickers (d); Richard 'Hock' Walsh (v). 89.*

**(*) Good Times Guaranteed
Blue Wave CD 126 *Peter Jeffrey (t); Pat Carey (s); Donnie Walsh (h, g, v); Chuck Jackson (h, v); Michael Fonfara (kb); Gary Latimer (b, v); Tyler Burgess (d, v); Steve Ambrose, Jerry Stiff, Joe Reynolds, Mark Green, Ben Steel (v). 93.*

**(*) Lucky 13
Blue Wave CD 134 *As above, except Gary Kendall (b, v), Jim Casson (d, tamb, v) replace Latimer, Burgess; add Dave Woodward (ts); Jeffrey also flh, Carey, Fonfara also v. 96.*

Gone Fishing was the last Downchild album featuring the chesty vocals of 'Hock' Walsh, who also shared the songwriting more or less evenly with his brother, the one non-original track being a lumbering version of Howlin' Wolf's 'Howlin' For My Darling'. *Good Times Guaranteed* introduced Chuck Jackson as the band's singer. He is aptly restrained on 'Big Hill' but sometimes affects a Wolfman Jack growl that becomes tiresome. Donnie Walsh, as 'I Am Mister Downchild' reveals, is no singer, but he reaffirms his power as a harmonica player, and does so again, even more trenchantly, on *Lucky 13* in instrumentals like the title track and 'Soaring'. These are honest but unstartling albums, and the urge to visit them may be confined to the band's followers.

*** A Matter Of Time: The Downchild Collection
Blue Wave CD 141 *Bob Heslin, Wayne Jackson, Peter Jeffrey (t); James Warburton (as); Ron Jacobs, Larry Bodner (ts, bs); Dave Woodward, Nat Abraham (ts); Vic Wilson (bs); Pat Carey, Rich House, Tony Rondolone (s); Donnie Walsh (h, g, v); Michael Fonfara (kb, p, v); Gene Taylor, Jane Vasey, Richard Whitehouse (p); Mike McKenna (g); Gary Latimer (b, v); Dennis Pinhorn, Gary Kendall, Jim Milne (b); Tyler Burgess, Jim Casson (d, v); Sonny Bernardi, Craig Kaleal, Paul Nixon, Cash Wall, Bill Bryans, Marty Vickers, Frank Russell (d); Tony Flaim, Richard 'Hock' Walsh, Chuck Jackson, John Witmer, Steve Ambrose, Jerry Stiff, Joe Reynolds, Mark Green, Ben Steel (v). 71–96.*

**(*) Body Of Work: The Downchild Collection Vol. 2
Blue Wave CD 144 *Similar to above. 74–96.*

A Matter Of Time, however, has more to offer the uncommitted listener. Blue Wave selected 20 tracks from a dozen albums, spanning Downchild's first quarter-century of record-making. The product is an attractive introduction to a band that likes to reshape itself from time to time. Eight of the vocals are by Tony Flaim, who seems from this distance to have been their best singer, though it's interesting to hear a younger 'Hock' Walsh sounding very Witherspoonish on 'Shotgun Blues'. (Both men died in 2000.) John Witmer makes a good job of 'Tramp', one of half a dozen blues standards that interrupt the sequence of originals and thereby add to the album's accessibility. *Body Of Work*, drawn from many of the same albums, concentrates on Donnie Walsh's songwriting. TR

Little Buddy Doyle
VOCAL, GUITAR

Memphis musicians remember Doyle as a diminutive blues singer who played on the city's streets in the '30s.

**** Memphis Harp & Jug Blowers (1927–1939)
RST Blues Documents DOCD-6028 *Doyle; prob. Walter Horton (h); prob. Jack Kelly (g). 7/39.*

Doyle's recordings show a flair for striking language that may remind some listeners of Baby Boy Warren or Willie '61' Blackwell. Indeed, Warren's 'Let's Renew Our Love' may be a deliberate echo of Doyle's 'Renewed Love Blues'. Certainly 'Sweet Man Blues' as recorded by Frank Edwards and Leroy Dallas and 'Grief Will Kill You' by Memphis Willie Borum were derived from Doyle's originals – borrowings that give due credit to a fascinating blues-writer. These thoughtful songs are enhanced in Doyle's recordings by superb harmonica, now thought, after much dispute, to have been played by the young Walter Horton, and by succinct guitar playing. To this CD's eight tracks (the remainder are by Jed Davenport) Document later added a ninth, the unissued-on-78 'Slick Capers Blues', on *"Too Late, Too Late Blues"* (DOCD-5150). TR

Ray Drew (born 1935)
VOCAL, GUITAR

Ray Drew started out in gospel music, but was a blues and soul guitarist by 1960. He's led a restless life, chasing audiences in his native Missouri, New Mexico, Illinois, Texas and Oklahoma; currently, he operates a restaurant in Oklahoma City. Drew played guitar in Bobby Bland's band intermittently for 11 years, and also worked briefly for Bo Diddley.

*** Too Much Lovin'
Midnight Creeper 1001 *Drew; Fred Nicholson (kb, p); David Kimbrough Jr (g, v); Artemus Le-Sueur (b); Kinney Kimbrough (d, v). 96.*

Ray Drew seems to be an admirer of '60s vocal group The Falcons and their accompanists, The Ohio Untouchables; his gospelly singing owes a lot to Wilson Pickett, and his guitar work incorporates a pretty good approximation of Robert Ward's shimmering vibrato. For *Too Much Lovin'*, Drew is teamed with a band whose Mississippi juke-joint music occasionally combines uneasily with his brand of soul-blues; Kinney Kimbrough is adrift in a world of his own on the concluding 'Set Me Free', for example. Drew can't match Percy Sledge's yearning authority on 'Warm And Tender Love' (and the Kimbroughs' shaky harmonies are no help), but there's warmth and tenderness aplenty in his molasses-slow reading of the wicked Pickett's hit '634-5789'. Most of the other tracks are Drew's own compositions, and while they are seldom memorable in themselves – in particular, the instrumental 'Oklahoma Shuffle' never escapes predictability – Drew's enthusiasm, his vocal power and his glowing guitar tone make them pleasant listening. CS

Driftin' Slim (1919–77)
VOCAL, HARMONICA, GUITAR, DRUMS

Elmon Mickle grew up in a small town near Little Rock, Arkansas. In his teens he met and learned from Sonny Boy Williamson I, and by the late '40s he was playing on Arkansas radio stations. He recorded in 1952 as Driftin' Slim (or Smith), in 1959–60 in his own name and later in the '60s as Model 'T' Slim. All but his earliest sides were cut in LA, where he spent the last 20 years of his life. Primarily a singer and harmonica player, he also worked as a one-man-band, a format highlighted on his only album.

Two sides recorded for Modern in 1952 are included in *The Travelling Record Man: Historic Down South Recording Trips Of Joe Bihari & Ike Turner* (Ace CDCHD 813) and *The Modern Downhome Blues Sessions Volume 1: Arkansas & Mississippi 1951–1952* (Ace CDCHD 876). 'My Little Machine' and 'My Sweet Woman' are ragged but hearty Southern juke-joint music with brash harmonica and hyperactive guitar by Baby Face Turner. 'I Got To Get Some Money' on *Elko Blues Vol. 1* (Wolf 120.614) has some of the same rough-cut individuality, but the remaining four sides from these 1959–60 sessions are ruined by poor accompaniments and worse sound.

*(*) Somebody Hoo-Doo'd The Hoo-Doo Man
Original Blues Classics OBCCD-590 *Driftin' Slim; Jack Wall (g); Ike Parker (b); Guy Jones (d).* 12/66–6/67.

Slim's one album was recorded by Pete Welding for his Milestone label. These names are not normally harbingers of trouble, but on this occasion somebody, or something, manifestly did put a hoodoo on the proceedings. On five tracks the blame can fairly be shifted on to a backing trio who are simply not up to the job; on 'Give An Account' they take so little account of what Slim's doing that at the halfway mark they are eight bars ahead of him. But the solo tracks, a mixture of one-man-band performances, harmonica pieces and a tale, are nearly all equally, if differently, disappointing. As a one-man-band Slim is a distant also-ran behind Dr Ross, his versions of other people's songs like 'How Many More Years?' and 'Standing Around Crying' are sluggish, and when he revisits his own 'My Little Machine' the listener feels like handing him an oilcan. TR

Johnny Drummer (born 1938)
VOCAL, HARMONICA, KEYBOARDS

Thessex Johns has been on the Chicago scene, as band member and bandleader, since leaving the Army in 1959, initially as a drummer (hence the pseudonym) and latterly as a singer.

**(*) It's So Nice
Earwig CD 4944 *Drummer; Jim Simms (kb prog, g); Willie Townes (kb prog); Jimmy Johnson, Rick Hall (g); Mae Coen, Diane Madison, Theresa Davis, Nanette Frank (v).* 1/94, 12/97–1/98.

*** Unleaded Blues
Earwig CD 4948 *Drummer; Allen Batts (p); Luther 'Slim' Adams, Chuck Kramer, Anthony Palmer (g); Felton Crews (b); Dave Jefferson (d); Calvin 'Kadakie' Tucker (cga); Liz Mandville Greeson, Bruce Thompson, Michelle Thompson (v).* 00.

More than 20 years before the soul-blues that dominates on Earwig, Drummer contributed three pleasant renditions of Chicago standards to *The Aces And Their Guests* (Storyville STCD 8049). *It's So Nice* is very different, not only stylistically, but also in its extensive use of synthesized 'instruments'; the first half of the CD (recorded last) is acceptable, thanks to springy drum programming and Simms's taut, economical guitar lines, replaced on two tracks by the richly inventive Jimmy Johnson. Even here, though, the virtual brass and strings sound thin at times, and the 1994 tracks offer 'drumming' that would be hamfisted if fists were involved, twittery arrangements and amateurish backing vocals. Drummer composed most of the songs, and on this showing is a fluent but not very interesting lyricist and a predictable melodist; as a singer, he manages seductive and aggressive, but not distinctive.

Unleaded Blues is better, mainly because the instrumentalists are chaps, not chips. Allen Batts gets on with it in his usual no-nonsense fashion, the rest of the rhythm section follow suit, and the guitarists are all good – in the case of Luther Adams, very good. The songs are stronger, too, 'Stop Cheating' (a dire C&W-style duet) and 'I Feel So Good' (trivial rock 'n' roll) apart. None of the others is a classic-in-waiting, and both lyrics and delivery sometimes pastiche Johnny Taylor and his like; but 'Born In The Delta' is a gracious tribute to the grandmother who raised Drummer in Mississippi, and 'I'm Gonna Sell My Cadillac, Buy Myself A Mule' is not the only instance of an offbeat wit at work. CS

Scott Dunbar (1904–94)
VOCAL, GUITAR

Dunbar was born on a plantation near Woodville in southwestern Mississippi and began playing guitar at ten. He spent virtually his entire life in Woodville and around nearby Lake Mary, where he made a living as a fisherman and tourist guide. He recorded a few songs for Frederick Ramsey in 1954, which were issued on Folkways, and a couple of long sessions in 1970 from which a selection was issued on Ahura Mazda.

*** From Lake Mary
Fat Possum 80338 *Dunbar.* 2–4/70.

Living in near-isolation from the currents of blues activity, Dunbar created a performing style of extraordinary singularity. On guitar, in a variety of tunings, he would 'line out' the melody of a song and continue to play it in unison with his voice, keeping a strong rhythm which he emphasized by stamping his foot. Vocal and instrumental passages were then interspersed with interludes of wordless chanting, a kind of serendipitous blues echo of Irish diddling or mouth music. His repertoire was partly original and partly learned from records, and once he acquired a song he evidently cherished it: four of the five tunes he recorded in 1954, 'Memphis Mail', 'Vicksburg Blues', 'Forty-Four Blues' and 'Easy Rider', reappeared, scarcely changed, 16 years later. From the discography of the 1970 sessions in *BR* it transpires that he knew many common-stock reels and country songs, but Ahura Mazda, understandably angling their selection towards the only market they could hope to reach, chose mostly blues material, though they let the record end with a 'Blue Yodel', inspired by rather than copied from Jimmie Rodgers, and 'Goodnight Irene'. Thirty years later Fat Possum simply reissued this remarkable album on CD, allowing a new generation to enter the private but utterly genial soundworld of Scott Dunbar. TR

Little Arthur Duncan (born 1934)
VOCAL, HARMONICA

At 16 Duncan left Indianola, Mississippi, for Chicago, where he met Little Walter and began playing harmonica. A construction worker by day, in his time off he played with John Brim, Floyd Jones, Eddie Taylor and others. He also ran a West Side bar, Artesia's, later renamed the Backscratcher's Social Club. Until the '90s he was unknown outside Chicago, but in recent years he has performed elsewhere and begun to build a modest catalogue of recordings.

*** Singin' With The Sun
Delmark DE-733 Duncan; Martin Lang (h); Rockin' Johnny Burgin, Billy Flynn, Eddie Taylor Jr (g); Sho Komiya (b); Kenny Smith (d). 2/99.

**(*) Live In Chicago!
Random Chance RCD 3 Duncan; Rockin' Johnny Burgin (g); Karl A. Meyer (b); Ashward Gates, Twist Turner (d). 7–9/99.

After a few minutes of *Singin' With The Sun*, listeners unfamiliar with Duncan will probably be wondering why they haven't heard about him before. The title track, a recast 'Smokestack Lightnin'', and 'Bad Reputation', based on 'Killing Floor', declare Howlin' Wolf as an inspiration, and Jimmy Reed's squealing high-register harp and slurred singing are another style that Duncan can copy just so. He has his own songs, too, but the feel of the music, thanks in great part to the perfectly attuned band, is thoroughly retro. There are enthusiasts who believe that Chicago blues was at its best in the '50s and '60s: this album might have been custom-made for them. So might *Live In Chicago!*, though the recording has less punch than the studio set, and one misses a second guitarist. Bassist Meyer's assertion in the notes that 'you will never catch Little Arthur singing a slow blues' is refuted by laidback readings of 'Asked Her For Water' (Wolf again) and 'I'm A King Bee', but most of the remaining seven tracks are uppish. TR

Big Al Dupree (1923–2003)
VOCAL, PIANO, SAXOPHONES

Dupree played alto and tenor in the bands of Doug Finnell and Buster Smith respectively, and toured with Smith, backing T-Bone Walker and Pee Wee Crayton. He later pursued a steady and successful career as a pianist in Dallas lounges, playing jazz, ballads, standards and the occasional blues.

*** Big Al Dupree Swings The Blues
Dallas Blues Society DBS 8902 Dupree; Teddy Morgan, Hash Brown (g); Eric Mathew (b); Esten Cooke (d). 95.

Swings The Blues is the work of a seasoned entertainer, ready and able to supply whatever's asked of him. On this set, Dupree runs through a folio of largely familiar jazz-blues standards, culled from the repertoires of Joe Turner, Eddie Vinson, Jimmy Rushing, Louis Jordan and T-Bone Walker. He also shows off his range with 'Sheik Of Araby' and the witty 'Nosey Woman', the CD's only Dupree composition. His piano playing, influenced by the likes of Teddy Wilson, Oscar Peterson and Nat Cole, deploys a quirky, melodic right hand and powerful but elegant chordal basses; his singing is as smokily relaxed as his overdubbed alto and tenor saxes. The band only met Dupree just before the session, but their playing is usually assured, and tactful without being reticent. Once or twice Teddy Morgan is briefly carried away by speed and volume, pitfalls which Hash Brown, substituted on 'T-Bone Blues' and 'Juice Head Baby', avoids with aplomb.

***(*) Positive Thinking
Fedora FCD 5007 Dupree; Hash Brown (g); Charles Nugent (b); T. J. Johnson (d). 4/98.

The increased confidence hinted at by the CD's title is manifest in both playlist – seven of the 12 titles are Dupree compositions – and performance: vocals, piano and alto saxophone overdubs are all more extrovert and energetic here, and if *Swings The Blues* is good, *Positive Thinking* is better. It's possible to do a direct comparison: versions of Felix Gross's 'Early This Morning' appear on both discs, and *Positive Thinking* is a clear winner for swing, energy and venturesomeness by all the musicians. Nugent and Johnson (who is remarkably good on 'Early This Morning') have regularly backed Dupree, and this no doubt accounts for some of the improvement, but equally important is Hash Brown, playing without rehearsal, but infallibly idiomatic and inventive. Dupree confirms that he is a witty, creative lyricist and composer (and doubtless the only one ever to slant-rhyme 'ear to ear' with 'antipathy', or 'Testarossa' with 'caviar'.) Only Nugent's bass guitar, which is sometimes sullen-toned, and usually reluctant to venture beyond the harmonic basics, lets the side down just a little. CS

Champion Jack Dupree (c. 1909–92)
VOCAL, PIANO, DRUMS

William Dupree was orphaned in infancy by a fire, which at different times he blamed on the Ku Klux Klan and an accident. Dupree emerged from the New Orleans Colored Waifs' Home with some piano skills, and took up the boxing which earned him his nickname. He hoboed for a time before settling in Indianapolis, and relocated to New York after wartime service as a cook in the Navy and a spell as a prisoner of war. In 1959 Dupree visited Britain, liked the more relaxed racial atmosphere and decided to stay. His music and comedy were much loved by European audiences, and for the rest of his life he moved from country to country, spending his last 15 years in Germany.

***(*) New Orleans Barrelhouse Boogie
Columbia CK 52834 Dupree; Bill Gaither, Jesse Ellery (g); Wilson Swain, Ransom Knowling (b). 6/40–11/41.

Jack Dupree was a rough-and-tumble pianist, but on these OKeh recordings energy, enthusiasm and a rich, Creole-accented voice overcome his technical limitations and a good few wrong notes. A southpaw boxer, he pummels the basses as if they were an opponent while his right hand unfurls emphatic trills. The craftily ambiguous drug song 'Junker Blues' features the rolling, eight-bar *ostinato* that Fats

Domino's 'The Fat Man' later popularized. Other songs also have socially aware lyrics, about TB, prison and Depression-era relief programmes, and the erotic poetry of 'Morning Tea Blues' is striking. Always, though, Dupree aims to entertain; he's at his most enjoyable when urging his girlfriend to do the 'Dupree Shake Dance' or romping through 'New Low Down Dog' and 'Black Woman Swing'. Alternative takes from these sessions, and some indifferently recorded sides made for Folkways in the mid-'40s, appear on the VAC *Chicago Blues Vol. 2 (1939–1944)* (Document DOCD-5444).

**** Dupree Shake Dance
Blues Forever CD 68022 *As above, except Brownie McGhee (g) replaces Gaither; add Count Edmondson (b). 6/40–45.*

***(*) The Gamblin' Man 1940/1947
[EPM Blues Collection 15919] *Dupree; Jesse Powell (ts); Brownie McGhee (g, v); Bill Gaither, Jesse Ellery (g); Wilson Swain, Ransom Knowling, Count Edmondson (b); Daddy Merritt, Baby Dodds (d). 6/40–5/47.*

** Champion Jack Dupree (1940–1950)
Best Of Blues BOB 9 *Dupree; Sonny Terry (h); Jesse Ellery, Brownie McGhee (g); Wilson Swain, Ransom Knowling, Count Edmondson, unknown (b); Daddy Merritt (d). 6/40–50.*

These CDs combine selected OKehs with early postwar recordings. (Missing since the demise of the LP is a well-reasoned selection of Dupree's recordings for small New York labels.) Blues Forever's 14 OKehs in good sound are prefaced by four later sides from Continental, with Brownie McGhee playing his nuts off on electric guitar. *The Gamblin' Man* is less cohesive; alongside nine OKehs and six tracks from Joe Davis (see below) are a fifth item from Continental, both sides of an Alert 78 and two Brownie McGhee titles where Dupree pays scant attention to either Brownie or Baby Dodds. Some originals are slightly hissy. The Best Of Blues disc is an ex-LP with six tracks apiece from OKeh and Continental, a ragged pair from an Apex 78 and four Folkways titles. The sound is mediocre and the rationale, which was to fill gaps in early '80s LP collections, is unpersuasive.

***(*) The Joe Davis Sessions
Flyright FLY CD 22 *Dupree. 4/45–3/46.*

***(*) Walkin' By Myself
[Zircon Bleu 504] *As above, except add Brownie McGhee (g), Count Edmondson (b). 4/45–3/46.*

(***) Rum Cola Blues
Arpeggio ARB 003 *Dupree. 4/45–3/46.*

The 20 songs on Joe Davis's eponymous label were Dupree's only solo recordings for the African-American market. By 1945 his basses were more polished, though not invariably; 'Johnson Street Boogie Woogie' is a bitonal fumble. Leroy Carr's input can still be heard, but he nods more often to Peetie Wheatstraw. The songwriting continues to be original, encompassing the pornographic 'Wet Deck Mama', the witty 'Love Strike Blues', the moving memorial 'FDR Blues' and its more obviously opportunistic flipside, 'God Bless Our New President'.

Flyright's release, licensed from Davis's heirs, is presumably the source for the other two. For those unconcerned with legal niceties, Zircon Bleu add six of the Continental recordings, once more arousing regret that no disc includes all eight. *Rum Cola Blues* rules itself out; the notes, reprinted from *Me And My Mule* (see below), are irrelevant to the CD's content.

**(*) Me And My Mule
Collectors Edition CBCD 010 *Dupree; Mickey Spider (t); Jesse Powell, Sidney Grant, Willis Jackson (ts); George Smith (h); Brownie McGhee, Mickey Baker, Jerome Darr (g); Cedric Wallace, Barney Richmond, Joe Williams, Lloyd Trotman, Ivan Rolle (b); Gene Moore, Alfred Dreares, George DeHart, Cliff Leeman, Cornelius Thomas, Calvin Shields (d); 'Mr Bear' [Teddy McRae] (foot tapping); Little Willie John (v). 49–11/55.*

*** Blues For Everybody
King KCD 6014 *As above, except add Milton Batiste (t), Nat Perilliat (ts), Papa Lightfoot (h), Edwin Moire (g), Earl Johnson, John Taylor, Charles Connor (d), 'Mr Bear' [Teddy McRae], Babs Gonzales (v); omit Spider, Powell, Smith, Richmond, Moore, Dreares, Little Willie John. 7/51–9/55.*

*** Walkin' The Blues
Collectables COL-CD-2874 *As above, except add George Smith (h), Barney Richmond (b), Alfred Dreares (d). 7/51–11/55.*

**(*) Champion Jack Dupree Sings The Blues
King KCD-735 *As above, except omit McGhee, Darr, Williams, Thomas, DeHart, 'Mr Bear' [Teddy McRae], Gonzales. 4/53–11/55.*

**(*) Two Shades Of Blues
Ember CJSCD 800 *Dupree; Sidney Grant (ts); George Smith (h); Jerome Darr, Mickey Baker (g); Cedric Wallace, Joe Williams, Lloyd Trotman, Barney Richmond (b); Cornelius Thomas, George DeHart, Cliff Leeman, Alfred Dreares (d); 'Mr Bear' [Teddy McRae] (foot tapping). 2/55–11/55.*

Dupree had his only R&B hit at King when 'Walking The Blues' reached #6. Like many of his King sides, it was a comic monologue with music; unlike many of them, it didn't add to the hilarity with a fake speech impediment. There are some amusing gags in these routines, but in changed times 'Harelip Blues' and its ilk don't tickle the ribs very hard. There's some fine guitar from McGhee and Baker, who departs from his usual sophistication to play gutbucket slide on one session. George Smith's harmonica is a surprising success, but Papa Lightfoot is tentative and under-recorded.

Two Shades Of Blues reissues an LP shared with Jimmy Rushing. The sound is excellent, but the odd couple only have five tracks each. All Dupree's five are among seven tracks on *Me And My Mule*, issued by the same parent company. It was a smart idea to include three Little Willie John sides where Dupree plays piano, and a dumb one to pad the CD with four Muddy Waters songs and one by Sonny Boy Williamson II. *Blues For Everybody*, carefully programmed for variety, is a good 20-track selection, but includes none of the four titles featuring George Smith; *Sings The Blues* has two of them among its 16 tracks, but no notes and too much of the harelip stuff. *Walkin' The Blues* lists 28 tracks, omitting only an alternative take and two songs with vocals by Brownie McGhee. Superior sound quality makes this the one to get, but readers should make sure that all 28 tracks are present; copies of the initial pressing, which omitted three titles, may still be around.

(***) Shake Baby, Shake
Rondolette 10645 *Dupree; Pete Brown (ts); Larry Dale (g, sp); Stick McGhee (g); Al Lucas (b); Gene Moore, Willie Jones (d); band (v); 'Mr Bear' [Teddy McRae] (sp). 9/56–10/57.*

RCA were chasing Atlantic's crossover success with black music; Dupree and his musicians play along, boisterously updating 'Pine Top's Boogie Woogie' into 'Old Time Rock And Roll'. Reworkings of 'Walking The Blues' hedge the bet, and there are several fine, straightforward blues included, but 'Lollipop Baby' is an ill-advised venture into C&W. The LP bootlegged by Rondolette includes numerous significantly different alternative takes and remakes; without notes or session data these multiple versions will bewilder most listeners.

♛ **** Blues From The Gutter
Atlantic 82434 *Dupree; Pete Brown (as); Larry Dale (g); Wendell Marshall (b); Willie Jones (d).* 2/58.

A breezy remake of 'Walking The Blues' throws the listener off guard before the music plunges into drugs, disease and death. Brown and Dale supply alert commentary, the rhythm section is crisp, and Dupree's singing, powerful throughout, is hair-raising on 'Evil Woman'. *Blues From The Gutter* should be depressing but isn't; the urban underbelly isn't glamorized and consequently isn't trivialized by these songs, which are about confronting and surviving the dark side of life. It's the one essential Jack Dupree CD.

**(*) Natural & Soulful Blues/Champion Of The Blues
Atlantic 92530//Collectables COL-CD-6818 *Dupree; Alexis Korner (g); Jack Fallon (b).* 59.

This disc combines two Atlantic LPs recorded in London and Copenhagen. On *Natural And Soulful Blues* Fallon is helpful, although his bass slides are a touch precious, and Korner is starchily academic on four tracks; *Champion Of The Blues* is solo. Dupree is usually adequate, but 'Johnson Street Boogie Woogie' (different from the one on Joe Davis) is at the limit of his technique, and 'New Vicksburg Blues' parsecs beyond it. He's already retooling for the new audience with ingratiating songs like 'Snaps Drinking Woman' (sic), sentimentality that sometimes becomes mawkish self-pity, and accounts of racism that can seem overblown unless it's understood that Dupree is using the first person to recount both his own and the collective experience.

*** New Orleans Barrelhouse
Magpie PYCD 53 *Dupree.* 9/60.

These recordings were made at the home of Francis Wilford-Smith, and the sound is adequate but not studio quality. That's an acceptable trade for hearing Dupree at ease and eager to recall his music from the New Orleans days onward. In a very varied programme, standouts include a storming 'Mean Old Frisco' and 'London Special', which compares his polite reception by Heathrow officials with what he was used to back home; truly, the past is a foreign country.

**(*) The Blues Of Champion Jack Dupree Vol. 1
Storyville STCD 8019 *Dupree; Finn Otto Hansen (t); Mogens Seidelin, Ole Christiansen (b); Ib Lindschouw, Alex Riel (d).* 7/60–2/64.

**(*) Trouble, Trouble
Storyville STCD 8013 *Dupree; Stuff Lange (g).* 12/60–10/61.

*** Blues Masters Vol. 6
Storyville STCD 8006 *As above, except add Mogens Seidelin (b).* 12/60–6/62.

*** Champion Jack Dupree Of New Orleans
Storyville STCD 8015 *As above.* 12/60–6/62.

**(*) The Blues Of Champion Jack Dupree Vol. 2
Storyville STCD 8020 *As above, except omit Lange.* 12/60–6/62.

***(*) Truckin' On Down
Storyville STCD 8029 *Dupree; Stuff Lange (g); Mogens Seidelin, Ole Christiansen (b); Ib Lindschouw, Alex Riel (d).* 12/60–2/64.

**(*) The Blues Of Champion Jack Dupree
Storyville STCD 8031 *As above.* 10/61–2/64.

There's remarkably little repetition of material among these CDs; Dupree knew an enormous number of songs and composed new ones easily – sometimes too easily. He got a great deal of studio time in Copenhagen but not much quality control, either at the time of recording or when material was selected for release.

The Blues Of Champion Jack Dupree Vol. 1 is an expansion of a well-made 12-track LP, which includes a tremendous revival of 'Gin Mill Sal' and an improbably good version of the burlesque standby 'Anyone Here Want To Buy (My) Cabbage'. Unfortunately, five of the added tracks feature a flashy, intermittently relevant trumpeter.

Most of *Trouble Trouble* was recorded in 10/61, and it's obvious that Dupree was feeling melancholy and isolated. These emotions are part of the blues, of course, but this is not the only Storyville CD where the mumping and grumping are excessive. There's also too much of Lange's cautious guitar. 'Free And Equal', quietly bitter but guardedly optimistic, is one of Dupree's better homilies on race, and a long, solo 'Blues Before Sunrise' is gripping.

Blues Masters Vol. 6 has some of Dupree's best singing; he essays blues-ballads like 'In The Dark' and 'Tomorrow Night' with great success, but both his memory and his interpretation of 'Please Send Me Someone To Love' are poor. As it is throughout the Storyville recordings, Seidelin's bass is firm and steady, with occasional outbreaks of frisky string-snapping.

Champion Jack Dupree Of New Orleans is another varied and interesting selection. 'Shake Baby, Shake' is splendid; so is the liberation of 'Fine And Mellow' from Billie Holiday's knowingness. The desperately sad 'Christina, Christina Blues' turns Brownie McGhee's rocking lovesong into a lament about access to a child.

On *The Blues Of Champion Jack Dupree Vol. 2*, a medium-paced opener is followed by ten slow, mostly gloomy blues before the mood lightens and the tempos increase. There are some effective tracks – 'I'm A Gamblin' Man' is an exceptional piece of writing about self-destructiveness – but they're drowned in a sea of Eeyorishness.

Truckin' On Down emphasizes older songs from Dupree's own recordings and those of others, and is the best of the Storyville CDs, with self-indulgent grumbling kept firmly in check. Leroy Carr's influence is very strong; an alternative take of 'Blues Before Sunrise' is even better than the version on *Trouble Trouble*.

The Blues Of Champion Jack Dupree sans volume number is another gallery of gloom, with 'Self-Pity', 'Suicide Blues' and 'Have You Ever Been Alone' appearing successively! Like *Truckin' On Down*, it has banal and blimpish notes by Derrick Stewart-Baxter.

*** From New Orleans To Chicago/Champion Jack Dupree And His Blues Band
BGO BGOCD 649 2CD *Dupree; Albert Hall (t); Rex Morris, Bob Efford (ts); Harry Klein (bs); John Mayall (h); Mickey Baker (g, tamb, v); Tony McPhee (g, foot tapping, sp); Eric Clapton (g); Malcolm Pool, John Baldwin (b); Keef Hartley, Ronnie Verrell*

(d); Bill Shortt (wb); Mike Vernon (wh). 11/65–4/67.

Two UK Decca LPs are reissued here. The presence of Mayall, McPhee, Clapton and Hartley on *From New Orleans To Chicago* once made it a collector's item but, that aside, they, Pool and Shortt do good work, respectful without being stilted or awed. McPhee makes a dreadful stooge on the crosstalk routine '(Going Down To) Big Leg Emma's', and his acoustic guitar has moments of disconnection, but he and Clapton are confident and idiomatic. Producer Mike Vernon went for variety in moods, subjects, tempos and textures, and *From New Orleans To Chicago* is a rounded, well-sequenced portrait of the artist: comedy, dance music and pathos are carefully balanced, as are originals and covers.

His Blues Band are a loud and lively squad of session musicians, plus Mickey Baker, who'd moved to Europe in 1961. Harelippery makes a final appearance on 'Troubles', and the whistling on 'Barrelhouse Woman' is otiose but, while less well-known, this is the stronger disc, thanks to Baker's fierce, ingenious guitar work, which often drives the rhythm section rather than being driven by it. Jack grumbles unconvincingly about the Board of Trade (!) on 'Cut Down On My Overheads', but the CD is dominated by hits from the '30s and '40s like 'Louise', 'Caldonia' and 'Come Back Baby'; from the same era comes an unexpected, enjoyable 'Garbage Man'. Baker is remarkable on a rocked-up revival of 'Baby Let Me Lay It On You', and 'Georgiana', an ode to Dupree's recently born daughter, is movingly sincere.

** Jivin' With Jack
Jasmine JASMCD 3008/9 2CD *Dupree.* 5/66.

Dupree was off form the night of this Manchester concert: some of the jokes are mistimed, the serious blues have little emotional depth and there are too many wrong notes. The recording quality is adequate at best; at times the vocal level fluctuates, reaching inaudibility when Dupree interacts with an equally inaudible audience member.

**(*) Dupree 'N' McPhee: The 1967 Blue Horizon Session
Ace CDCHM 1063 *Dupree; Tony 'TS' McPhee (g).* 5/67.

Most of this session was unissued until 2005. McPhee's guitar, played in a variety of Mississippi-inspired styles, is the only accompaniment; Jack mixes songs recalled from his New York days with retitled standards and semi-improvised numbers like 'Down In Clarksdale' (*sic*; he sings 'Clarksville'), and 'My Baby Told Me'. The CD is a pleasant, well-recorded 40 minutes, but to say that it's unique in Dupree's output is to describe, not to evaluate. The sparks seldom fly; McPhee's playing is accomplished but mildly academic, and Dupree seems reluctant to invest much emotion in the songs. 'My Home In Mississippi' is an exception that makes the rule more apparent.

**(*) The Complete Blue Horizon Sessions
Columbia/Blue Horizon 518516 2CD *Dupree; Bud Parks (t, flh); Terry Noonan (t); Johnny Almond (ts, bs); Alan Skidmore, Les Wigfield (ts); Jim Chester (bs); Christopher Turner, Duster Bennett (h); Richard Studt, Reg Cole, Barry Wilde, Peter Oxer (vn); Mick Taylor (sg, g); Chris Anderson, Stan Webb, Paul Kossoff, unknown (g); Stuart Brooks, 'Wallace Tring' [Gary Thain], 'Eduardo Givenzano' [Alex Dmochowski], unknown (b); 'Big Chief Drumstick' [Keef Hartley] (d, perc); Simon Kirke,* 'Harris Dundee' [Aynsley Dunbar], unknown (d); Mike Vernon (perc). 4/68–6/69.

This 2CD contains the sessions that produced the LPs *When You Feel The Feeling You Was Feeling* and *Scoobydoobydoo*, plus the salvageable elements of a hitherto unissued live recording. In the late '60s Dupree was ubiquitous on the British blues scene, where he was both stamp of authenticity and court jester (a role that the original cover of *Scoobydoobydoo* made explicit). Signs of the times: the audience at the Angel Hotel, Godalming, gives Jack three hearty hip, hip, hurrahs, and he responds with a joke about a bride disconcerted that her amputee groom 'don't have but one foot'. The crowd is more fired up than the music objectively warrants, but these tracks do convey the affection in which Dupree was held, and his ability to get an audience eating out of his hand.

The sessions for the first album produced a number of items held back until this release; they range from valuable ('Whiskey, Look What You Done To Me', as fine a serious blues as Dupree ever cut) to trivial ('Juke Box Jump'). All the Blue Horizon material features rhythm sections that are competent or better, but these first sessions are superior; Christopher Turner's fussy harmonica on two tracks is a drawback, but the guitar work of Paul Kossoff and, on two tracks, Stan Webb is a considerable bonus. Kossoff occasionally prophesies the blues-rock of Free, but he does so creatively and tastefully, and Webb's swing playing on 'How Am I Doing It' is simply delightful.

Unfortunately, it's completeness that drags down *The Complete Blue Horizon Sessions*' rating. *Scoobydoobydoo* (from sessions which generated no unissued material) has been criticized for excessive post-production tinkering. The over-dubbed horns are indeed rather dense, and the seasick violinists on 'Old And Grey' and 'I Want To Be A Hippy' (a better lyric than it sounds) were a serious misjudgement; but nearly 40 years on it's apparent that the biggest blemish on an uneven record is Mick Taylor's coarse and reductive playing, especially on lap steel.

** St. Claude And Dumaine
Fuel 2000 302 061 229 *Dupree; Victor Brox (pocket c, h, o); Nick Evans (tb); Ray Warleigh (as, ts); John Moorshead (g); Mogens Seidelin, Alex Dmochowski (b); Aynsley Dunbar (d).* 12/60–8/69.

Five Storyville tracks bring *St. Claude And Dumaine* to CD length; on the balance – an unaccompanied vocal and six tracks with the Aynsley Dunbar Retaliation plus horns – Chicago blues, modern jazz, traditional jazz and rock tussle for accompanimental supremacy as Jack placidly does his thing. Only Brox's moaning cornet on 'Blues From 1921' and Moorshead's fierce guitar emerge victorious from the brawling confusion. The original LP's 'Japanese Special' has wisely been omitted; its post-Coltrane antics can be found – but there's no reason to look – on the deleted but still around *Home* (Charly CDBM 40).

** Oh Lord, What Have I Done?
Chrisly CM 30007 *Dupree.* 5/71–10/72.
***(*) Blues At Montreux
Collectables COL-CD-6331 *Dupree; King Curtis (as, ts); Cornell Dupree (g); Gerry Jemmott (b); Oliver Jackson (d).* 6/71.

Chrisly offer six long tracks from two German concerts. Dupree could work an audience like few others, but the magic seldom translates to disc without the visuals. The anti-racist title track sustains its forcefulness through 12 sometimes hyperbolic minutes, but elsewhere wrong notes, both facetious and inadvertent, are once again a problem.

Credited to King Curtis & Champion Jack Dupree, *Blues At Montreux* was originally an Atlantic LP. It also has six long tracks, but what a difference a band makes, especially one with musicianship so complete and intuitive that for once playing without rehearsal comes off. When not performing heroic acrobatics as Jack adds bars, drops bars and changes the metre, the stuttering sax, fiery guitar, chthonic bass and apple-crisp percussion have a roaring good time playing blues changes while the nominal co-leader tags along.

** Le Poids Lourd Du Blues
Warner Blues 36956 *Dupree; King Curtis (as, ts); Pete Brown (as); Larry Dale, Alexis Korner, Cornell Dupree (g); Wendell Marshall, Jack Fallon, Gerry Jemmott (b); Willie Jones, Oliver Jackson (d). 2/58–6/71.*

Tracks from Dupree's four Atlantic LPs, reassembled into a pointless mishmash.

**(*) The Legacy Of The Blues Vol. 3
GNP-Crescendo GNPD 0013 *Dupree; Paul Rowan (h); Peter Curtley (g); Bernie Gallagher (b); Hughie Flint (d). 72.*
**(*) The Sonet Blues Story: Champion Jack Dupree
Universal 986 924-9 *As above. 72.*

The comedy routine 'Drunk Again' includes a good joke about a barfly preacher, and 'Roamin' Special' unexpectedly sets James Oden's 'Monkey Faced Woman' to a rough version of the '44 Blues'; as it fades Dupree seems to be playing the basses with his elbow. The rest is the usual blend of entertainment, self-pity and topicality, accompanied by a dutiful British version of the Chicago sound. Universal's reissue has improved sound and five additional tracks. A second version of 'Vietnam Blues', with different key, structure and lyrics, affords an insight into Dupree's creative processes; so does his blowing the chord changes in the solo by jumping from an 8-bar to a 12-bar structure.

** Bad Luck Blues
Blue Nose BN 074 *Dupree; Oskar Klein (t); Stix Steiger (h); Dinu Logoz, Bernie Wenger, Chris Lange (g); Andy Casagrande (b); Philipp Winiger (d); Goofy Egloff (v). 5/74.*

Swiss band Freeway 75 accompany on six over-extended live tracks, which include two versions of 'It Hurts Me Too', and appear as themselves on another six. They cope fairly well with Dupree's eccentricities, but the accompaniment is usually routine. It rises a little way above that on three numbers where Klein sits in, but his New Orleanian trumpet is often incompatible with the band's Chicago-derived style. Jack seems to have been in more than usually capricious mood during this tour, and some of his keyboard clowning is very tiresome.

*** Axel Zwingenberger And The Friends Of Boogie Woogie Vol. 5: Champ's Housewarming
Vagabond VRCD 8.88014 *Dupree; Christian Dozzler (h, ac); Axel Zwingenberger (p); Erik Trauner, Markus Toyfl (g); Daniel Gugolz (b); Michael Strasser, Torsten Zwingenberger (d). 2/88.*

**** Axel Zwingenberger And The Friends Of Boogie Woogie Vol. 6: On Stage With Champion Jack Dupree
Vagabond VRCD 8.90016 *Dupree; Axel Zwingenberger (p); Torsten Zwingenberger (d). 2/88.*

Dupree is a non-playing vocalist on these collaborations with the Zwingenberger brothers; on the first of them, members of Vienna's Mojo Blues Band join in. These musicians are some of European blues' most polished and idiomatic, and *Champ's Housewarming* was obviously fun for all concerned. Jack's singing is sometimes a little strained, but the steady tempos give him no room for aimlessness. Still more is this true of *On Stage*. Recorded live after the studio sessions, it largely avoids the usual setlist, and features Dupree's best singing since leaving the USA; at nearly 80, 'Do You Think Of Me?' is among the best performances of his career. He's committed to the material in a way that he often wasn't, and the Zwingenbergers don't stop pushing for a second. It's a pity their attention to musical detail didn't transfer to post-production, and lead to the excision of some poorly told jokes and a long patch of laughter at a sight gag.

**(*) Live – With The Big Town Playboys
JSP JSPCD 807 *Dupree; Alan Nicholls (ts); Andy Silvester (g); Ian Jennings (b); Clive Deamer (d); band (v). 4/89.*

Most of the songs Dupree performed at the Burnley Blues Festival had been standard concert fare for many years, but the presence of his daughters by an English ex-wife inspired a moving rendition of 'Bring Me Flowers While I'm Living'. The Playboys don't always suppress Dupree's propensity for meandering and whimsy, and Nicholls's tenor is underemployed, but the rhythm section are vigorous and Silvester's jazzy playing is a welcome change from the usual Chicago sound.

**(*) Axel Zwingenberger And The Friends Of Boogie Woogie Vol. 7: Champion Jack Dupree Sings Blues Classics
Vagabond VRCD 8.92018 *Dupree; Axel Zwingenberger (p); Mogens Seidelin (b); Michael Strasser (d). 9/90.*

Made between the final New Orleans sessions, this CD features a number of songs not on record anywhere else. It's therefore of some documentary importance, but Dupree's singing has lost some of its force and flexibility, perhaps because of surgery for cancer earlier in 1990.

**(*) Back Home In New Orleans
Bullseye Blues NET CD 9502 *Dupree; Teddy Riley (t); Alvin 'Red' Tyler, Fred Kemp (ts); 'Sax Gordon' Beadle (bs); Kenn Lending, Wayne Bennett (g); Walter Payton Jr (b); Stanley Stephens (d). 5/90.*
**(*) Forever And Ever
Bullseye Blues CD BB 9512 *Dupree; Lynwood 'Cookie' Cook, 'Tino' Barker (ts); 'Sax Gordon' Beadle (bs); Kenn Lending, John Mooney (g); Walter Payton Jr (b); Kerry Brown (d); Bo Dollis (tamb, v). 5/91.*
***(*) One Last Time
Bullseye Blues CD BB 9522 *As above, except add Earl Turbinton (as), 'Lil Crip' Adams (cowbell); omit Barker, Mooney. 5/91.*
**(*) A Portrait Of Champion Jack Dupree
Rounder Heritage Series RRCD 11586 *As for Bullseye Blues CDs. 5/90–5/91.*

A Portrait is compiled, not very deftly, from the three

Bullseye CDs. Made when Dupree was in town for the New Orleans Jazz & Heritage Festival, they were his first American recordings since 1958; he'd revisited New York in 1982, but hadn't seen his hometown for very many years. The hero's welcome he got seems to have enabled Dupree to forget his frail health, and the enthusiasm he and the musicians put into these last recordings is very apparent.

That's not to say they're all outstanding CDs, much as one might like the narrative to end that way. The argument that most of the songs are familiar can be disregarded, since it applies with equal justice to most of the other records in this entry, but equally the presence of New Orleans musicians doesn't automatically work magic. On *Back Home In New Orleans* the horn players and Wayne Bennett find Jack's eccentric timing and cavalier harmonies hard to deal with. Walter Payton is an imperturbable buttress on all three discs, though; so is Kerry Brown on the 1991 sessions.

Kenn Lending is also unfailingly good. He'd been Dupree's regular guitarist since 1979, and was thoroughly at home with his music, keeping him on track and playing inventive fills and solos. They made many albums together, but much of Dupree's European work has not been transferred to CD; a paradoxical selling point of these New Orleans recordings is the chance to hear a Danish musician. Lending makes 'Third Degree' the highlight of *Forever And Ever*, but elsewhere the guest-star syndrome does its evil work; John Mooney's slide guitar on three tracks is quite inappropriate.

Best of the bunch is *One Last Time*, which was only recorded because *Forever And Ever* was completed in a day, leaving two days of studio time free. Cook and Beadle seem to be overdubbed on the few tracks where they appear, and the weight of responding to Dupree falls on Lending and Turbinton. They both do a great job, playing with intuitive, improvisatory passion. A further advantage is that Jack, having run low on songs he could crank out on autopilot, excavated several that he'd hadn't done for years: a lascivious 'Bad Blood', a jovial 'Jail Bait', and a rollicking 'Hey Mary' are all resurrected from the mid-'40s. All in all, *One Last Time* makes a pretty good leave-taking. CS

Big Joe Duskin (born 1921)
VOCAL, PIANO

A preacher's son from Birmingham, Alabama, Duskin moved in his teens to Cincinnati and played blues and boogie-woogie piano at clubs in the city and in neighbouring Newport, Kentucky. After army service in World War II he took a day job and, in deference to his father's wishes, gave up music; he would not resume playing until his father died, more than 20 years later. In the '80s he frequently toured, and occasionally recorded, in Europe.

*** Cincinnati Stomp
Arhoolie CD 422 Duskin; Steve Tracy (h); Jimmy Johnson, Bob Margolin (g); Truck Parham (b); S. P. Leary, Ben Sandmel (d). 77–78.

*** Down The Road A Piece
Wolf 120.713 Duskin; Michael Strasser (d). 5/82.

A more than competent boogie practitioner with a powerful left hand, Duskin ranges in his repertoire from boogie standards to blues favourites. *Cincinnati Stomp* exemplifies the former with 'Honky Tonk Train' and 'Yancey Special', the latter with 'Mean Old Frisco' and 'Little Red Rooster', which he sings with the blaring strength of Sunnyland Slim or Champion Jack Dupree. Two thirds of the 18 tracks are solos. The hour-long recital that constitutes *Down The Road A Piece* was recorded, well, at a Vienna club. Duskin sings and plays with huge appetite and Strasser is very discreet. Listeners who prefer their piano music unadorned will probably find this the most satisfying of Duskin's albums. However, anyone planning to make a collection of them should be aware that seven of the tunes are also on *Cincinnati Stomp*, and two more recur on the next album.

*** Don't Mess With The Boogie Man
Sanctuary CAS 36040 Duskin; Paul Clarke (as, bs); Alan Nicholls (ts); Dave Peabody (g); Ian Jennings (b); Mickey Waller (d). 3/88.

Ten years on from his debut, Duskin cut this album during a visit to England. As on *Down The Road A Piece*, the boogie/blues balance is tilted towards vocal blues, with a Sunnyland Slim/Roosevelt Sykes flavour evident in numbers like 'Down On My Bended Knees', 'Ida B' and 'Mean And Evil', the last of which in particular has excellent oldfashioned blues piano playing. The boogie-woogie features are the title song, Freddie Slack's 'Cuban Sugar Mill', the Pete Johnson/Joe Turner 'Low Down Dog', Earl Hines's 'Boogie Woogie On St. Louis Blues' and another trenchant version of 'Yancey Special'.

*** Live At Quai Du Blues
Viper 597803 Duskin; Amar Sundy (g); Eddie Jones (b); Butch Miles (d). 03.

The setting of a French club seems to have prompted Duskin to summon a ghost many of his listeners would recognize: both the explanatory introductions and the powerful vocals on numbers like 'Ida Bea' and 'Call My Job' recall Memphis Slim. The programme is typical Duskin, the blues songs interspersed with unspectacular but firmly executed instrumentals like 'Boogie Woogie On St-Louis Blues', 'Yancey Special', 'Cow Cow Boogie' and Albert Ammons's '6th Avenue Express'. Sundy joins in on a few pieces at the end. It's a respectable performance, marred only by very rough singing on the slight 'Oodle Adle', which Viper unflatteringly place first. TR

Johnny Dyer (born 1938)
VOCAL, HARMONICA

Dyer grew up, like Muddy Waters, on the Stovall plantation in Rolling Fork, Mississippi. At 19 he moved out to the West Coast, where he met and learned from George 'Harmonica' Smith and played alongside Shakey Jake, Harmonica Fats and Rod Piazza.

**(*) Jukin'
Blind Pig BPCD 5028 Dyer; George 'Harmonica' Smith, Rod Piazza (h); Honey Piazza (p); Steve Killman, Mike [Junior] Watson (g); 'Wild' William Brimlee (b); Bob 'The Pacemaker' Newham (d). 83.

On his debut album, originally issued on the Murray Brothers label, Dyer was supported by Rod Piazza's Mighty Flyers, Piazza himself and George Smith each making a cameo appearance. Smith's is on 'Everybody Talking' – actually Sonny Boy Williamson II's 'Eyesight To The Blind', and one of four tracks not on the original LP – and Dyer is left to concentrate on what proves to be the album's strongest vocal performance, propelled by jets of piano from Honey Piazza. As a singer he has the mumbling manner of Williamson or Jimmy Reed, but on harmonica he is more forthright than either, and gives the chromatic instrument a good workout in 'Slippin' And Slidin'. Apart from Bill Haley's 'Two Hound Dogs', an odd choice, and 'Okie Dokie Stomp', a feature for the band, most of the tracks sound like generic Chicago harp-and-guitar-band material, lightly coloured by Dyer's hand.

His work in the '90s, consisting of two CDs for Black Top, *Listen Up* and *Shake It!*, and tracks for the Cannonball compilation *Blues Across America – The Los Angeles Scene*, is currently out of print. TR

Snooks Eaglin (born 1936)
VOCAL, GUITAR, WASHBOARD, TOM-TOMS

Blind from babyhood after an operation for the removal of a brain tumour, Fird Eaglin voraciously played everything he heard on records and the radio, be it jazz, blues, pop or country; he was a consummate guitarist long before he accompanied Sugar Boy Crawford on Chess, aged 17. When not playing R&B in New Orleans clubs, Eaglin busked with an acoustic guitar, which is how folklorist Harry Oster recorded him. At first lionized by white fans, happy that Big Bill Broonzy wasn't the last of the line, he was later shunned as just an eclectic copyist. Neither misapprehension made much difference to Eaglin, who'd seen little money from the LPs that were released. He went on to cut some R&B sessions, but had virtually retired by 1971, when he was sought out for the New Orleans Jazz & Heritage Festival. Since then he's kept busy playing and recording his technically brilliant, infallibly swinging electric guitar music.

(***) **New Orleans Street Singer**
Storyville STCD 8023 *Eaglin; Lucius Bridges (g, v); Percy Randolph (wb). c. 2/58–59.*

♛ **** **Country Boy Down In New Orleans**
Arhoolie CD 348 *Eaglin; Percy Randolph (h, wb, v); Fird Eaglin Sr (h); Lucius Bridges (g, wb, v). 58–59.*

***(*) **That's All Right**
Original Blues Classics OBCCD 568 *Eaglin. 59.*

(***) **Rural Blues**
Fantasy 24716//Ace CDCHD 705 2CD *Eaglin. 59.*

Before considering Snooks Eaglin the acoustic blues singer, we must consider Harry Oster, the folklorist hustler. Besides issuing an LP, which forms the core of Arhoolie's CD, on his Folk-Lyric label, Oster licensed material to other companies on a deliriously non-exclusive basis; songs are duplicated, and occasionally triplicated, on Storyville, Arhoolie and OBC.

On top of that, the LP reissued on OBC appears (minus one track) as part of *Rural Blues*. This disc is shared with Robert Pete Williams, a pairing which probably seemed less odd as a double LP. Williams enthusiasts wishing to investigate Eaglin may find it useful, but the mid-priced OBC disc is a better-value introduction to the punchy rhythms of his acoustic blues.

That's All Right is also the best remastered of these discs; *New Orleans Street Singer* is muffled and lifeless by comparison. It's also too long, with an overdose of slow and medium tempo blues; the one track with Bridges and Randolph only emphasizes the problem. Snooks's husky voice, with its paradoxically velvet roughness, is well suited to soulfully emotional blues, but it begins to seem mannered after 75 minutes.

The best of these discs is *Country Boy Down In New Orleans*, which combines generous playing time with varied material. The title track is utterly beguiling, and alongside the blues standards are country music, pre-blues like 'Possum Up A Simmon Tree', gospel and the second-line strut of 'Mardi Gras Mambo'. The disc sets Snooks's street music in context; with Randolph and Bridges frequently present, and taking some lead vocals, it's as much a presentation of harmonica and washboard band music as of Eaglin's guitar (and occasional percussion) skills. *Country Boy Down In New Orleans* is both exemplary documentation and splendid entertainment.

In mid-2005, a Smithsonian Folkways CD of Oster's recordings was in preparation; we understand that every effort was being made to avoid duplications.

(*) **The Complete Imperial Recordings
Capitol 33918 *Eaglin; unknowns (t); prob. Meyer Kennedy (as); Clarence Hall, Warren Payne (ts); Clarence Ford (bs); James Booker, unknown (p); Frank Fields, unknown (b); Robert French, Smokey Johnson, unknown (d); unknowns (v). 4/60–4/63.*

Eaglin's R&B singing is often dark and jagged, and it's easy to hear why he sometimes billed himself as 'Li'l Ray Charles'. Dave Bartholomew oversaw seven sessions, and supplied most of the songs, but no hits resulted. There are some very intense performances here, including an outstanding 'C.C. Rider', and in lighter vein there's an inspired remake of James Waynes's lilting 'Travelin' Mood'. Even on the weaker songs, Eaglin can take off into solos that are amazingly logical, fluent and daring, racing away from the melody into a world of his own. Unfortunately, he's too often handed impossibly mawkish or trivial lyrics, and several songs are burdened with unnecessary vocal groups. A 'best of' would have been preferable to a 'complete'.

***(*) **I Blueskvarter 1964, Volume Three**
Jefferson SBACD 12658/9 2CD *Eaglin. 6/64.*

Eaglin the 'folk-blues' artist had a last renaissance in 1964, when Olle Helander of the Swedish Broadcasting Corporation came by. Eaglin was very reluctant to record, but the ten tracks on this VAC are highly enjoyable. Probably in line with Helander's expectations, Snooks revisits the sound and repertoire of the Oster recordings. The exception is an off-the-cuff 'Hello Dolly'; played to pacify a crying child, it's an unlikely fusion of jazz, pop and flamenco.

**** **The Sonet Blues Story: Snooks Eaglin**
Universal 986-926-15 *Eaglin. 6/71.*

(****) **Best Of Snooks Eaglin**
Grammercy 0182 *Eaglin; Clarence Ford (ts); Ellis Marsalis (p); George French (b); Bob French (d). 6/71–11/77.*

The 1971 Sonet recordings marked Eaglin's solo comeback, with a set of flamboyantly played and sung numbers that bridge the gap between Oster and Imperial. Universal's reissue adds three bonus tracks and has excellently remastered sound. Eaglin's second album for Sonet was made with a small band; its reappearance on Universal was impending as we went to press. Meanwhile, Grammercy have 17 of the two LPs' 24 tracks. The albums could have been fitted on to a CD complete; further irritants are the lack of notes and no more than adequate sound. Both sessions stress blues and R&B, although the jazzy 'San José' and the flamenco showpiece 'Funky Malaguena' serve notice that Snooks can't be labelled that easily, and even a chestnut like 'Boogie Children' [sic] gets a unique treatment. The musicians on the band sides had worked with Eaglin on live dates around town, and knew his style inside out. Our recommendation must nevertheless be to wait for Universal to do it right.

*** The Blues Of Snooks Eaglin & Boogie Bill Webb
Storyville STCD 8054 *Eaglin; George Porter Jr (b, v); Kenny Blevins (d, v). 10/85.*

These 12 live tracks derive from a video made at Storyville Hall. Not even Eaglin can make 'Mustang Sally' other than tourist fodder, and a half-remembered 'Johnny B. Goode', though musically more interesting, is probably out of the same box. Otherwise, the setlist is typically genre-dissolving, ranging from blues by artists as various as Ray Charles, J. B. Lenoir and Freddie King to Motown to go-go (Trouble Funk's 'Drop The Bomb', with Porter monstrously clever on bass) and rock 'n' roll. Eaglin even revives 'Country Boy Down In New Orleans'; the words are loosely recalled, but it's just as charming when amplified and set to a second-line strut. The Boogie Bill Webb tracks used as filler have their own merits, but they don't sit comfortably alongside Eaglin's far more sophisticated conceptions.

***(*) The Crescent City Collection
Fuel 2000 302 061 122 *Eaglin; Keith Winking, Steve Howard, Rick Trolsen (t); Mark Kazanoff, Ward Smith (ts, bs); Grady Gaines, David Lastie, Mr Excello, Saxy Boy, Fred Kemp (ts); John Autin (kb); Ron Levy, Sammy Berfect (o, p); Matt McCabe (p); Ronnie Earl, Anson Funderburgh (g); George Porter Jr, Erving Charles Jr, Rhandy Simmons, Lloyd Lambert, Little Snooks Jr (b); Herman V. Ernest III, Smokey Johnson, Marc Wilson, David Lee, Jeffrey Alexander (d). 2/88–12/95.*
♛ **** The Way It Is
Money Pit 1111 *Eaglin; Tony Dagradi (ts); Jon Cleary (kb, o, p, v); Derwin 'Big D' Perkins (g, v); Erving Charles Jr, Cornell Williams (b, v); Raymond Weber, Jeffrey 'Jellybean' Alexander (d, perc, v). 6–7/00.*

In the '80s, Eaglin signed with Hammond and Nauman Scott's Black Top, making five CDs with bands convened from the top New Orleans session musicians, and guest appearances by younger guitar heroes. These discs' deletion was one of the sadder consequences of Black Top's demise, but they should not be impossible to find. Fuel 2000's selection from them includes plenty of astonishing guitar solos, but it's unsatisfactory because the material is entirely New Orleans R&B, which means omitting jazz, flamenco, gospel, rock 'n' roll and blues acquired from T-Bone Walker, Guitar Slim, Charles Brown and others. *The Crescent City Collection* is very good as far as it goes, but it over-emphasizes the frantic, and doesn't do justice to Eaglin's ability to make anything from 'I'll See You In My Dreams' to 'Drop The Bomb' his own.

The Way It Is, produced by the Scott brothers, reinforces the point with its mixture of blues, jazz, funk and 'Cubano Mambo'. It also uses smaller forces than are the norm on *The Crescent City Collection*, ensuring that the energy is channelled and the focus firmly on Eaglin's playing. The opening track is a Meters-style strut, with wah-wah guitar and a quote from Grandmaster Flash's 'The Message'; it's followed by a Gatemouth Brown guitar boogie, a modern blues by James Harman and a gorgeous chamber jazz reading of 'Trees'. The disc continues in similar vein, proving once again that 'eclectic' is an inadequate word for Eaglin's tastes, and that 'masterful' doesn't begin to describe his guitar skills. These truths were self-evident when he was a 22-year-old prodigy; they still are now that he's a 70-something prodigy. CS

Ronnie Earl (born 1953)
GUITAR

Born Ronald Earl Horvath in New York, Earl began playing guitar in his 20s, after seeing Muddy Waters. Among his models he cites Buddy Guy, Otis Rush, B. B. King and Robert Jr Lockwood. After a long spell with Roomful Of Blues (1980–88) he formed his own band, The Broadcasters, which, besides its own work, has accompanied Jimmy Rogers and Joe Beard on record. Earl himself has made innumerable guest appearances on other artists' albums.

**** Blues And Forgiveness
Crosscut CCD 11042 *Earl; Bruce Katz (o, p); Rod Carey (b); Per Hanson (d). 93.*
**** Blues Guitar Virtuoso Live in Europe
Bullseye Blues CD BB 9552 *As above. 93.*

A few years ago Earl had a catalogue of a dozen or more albums, but deletion has cut a swathe through that list, felling five CDs on Black Top (and a sixth selected from them) and one on Antone's. So his earliest available work in his own name is three albums from 1993, the studio-recorded *Still River* (see below) and the German concert recording issued by Crosscut as *Blues And Forgiveness* and by Bullseye Blues as *Blues Guitar Virtuoso Live In Europe*. So far as the concert sets are concerned, the reader unfortunate enough never to have heard Earl will find no better introduction to his blues playing. 'San-Ho-Zay', 'The Stumble' and 'Blues For The West Side' are eloquent declarations of love for the work of Freddie King and Magic Sam, while 'Thank You Mr. T-Bone' blows kisses to another avatar of modern blues guitar. Playing in these styles, Earl combines expert knowledge and superb technique without letting his obvious respect for his sources subdue his own musical initiatives. These are explicit in the original tunes, especially Katz's 'Contrition' and Earl's 'Rego Park Blues', slow pieces that Earl plays like a lacemaker.

The two issues of the concert are not identical, and the Crosscut is to be preferred, since it plays the tracks in the listed order (the Bullseye goes awry after track 7) and adds another, Albert Collins's 'Backstroke'. The track timings are way out on both.

*** Still River
AudioQuest AQ-CD 1018 *Earl; Larry Etkin (t); Anders Gaardmand (s); Bruce Katz (o, p); Rod Carey (b); Per Hanson (d). 2/93.*
*** Language Of The Soul
Bullseye Blues CD BB 9554 *Earl; Paul Ahlstrand, Kevin Watson (ts); Bruce Katz (o, p); Adrienne Hayes, Eddie O'Brien (g); Rod Carey (b); Per Hanson (d); The Gospel Mets, Edith Langston, Rosetta Smith, Lisa Hale (v). 94?*

The jazz sense that motivated 'Moanin'' on the previous

CDs has free play on *Still River* in tracks like 'Soul Serenade' and 'Eyes That Smile', and on *Language Of The Soul* in 'Indigo Burrell' and 'Eddie's Gospel Groove', but there is blues playing aplenty on pieces as varied as 'Blues For The West Side' and 'Chili Ba Hugh' (*Still River*) and a slow 'Blues For Martin Luther King', 'Harvard Square Stomp' and 'Green Light' (*Language Of The Soul*). The latter album's 'Blue Guitar', done in the manner of its creator, Earl Hooker, and 'Bill's Blues', in that of Big Bill Broonzy, incidentally make a point about Earl's talent: there are guitarists who might match him on the former or the latter, or conceivably on both, but few if any who could have made the rest of the album too.

**** Eye To Eye
AudioQuest AQ-CD 1043 *Earl; John Sebastian (h); Bruce Katz (o); Pinetop Perkins (p, v); José Alvarez, Tony Levis (g); Calvin Jones (b, v); Willie 'Big Eyes' Smith (d).* 3/96.

A few guest spots aside, this is a quartet album by Earl, Perkins, Jones and Smith, and could as well have been discussed in Perkins's entry, since he takes all but two of the vocals and his piano playing is prominent throughout, the CD ending with a solo reading of 'Forty Four Blues'. Earl, presented with an opportunity to play at being Muddy Waters, deliberately ignores it and simply plays a variety of beautifully apt guitar lines. Perkins, understandably pleased at finding a collaborator so empathetic yet so unassuming, snaps out of his coasting mode and gives one of his best recorded performances.

*** Grateful Heart: Blues & Ballads
Bullseye Blues CDBB 9565 *Earl; David 'Fathead' Newman (ts); Bruce Katz (o, p); Rod Carey (b); Per Hanson (d).* 6/95.
*** Healing Time
Telarc CD-83490 *Earl; Anthony Geraci (kb); Jimmy McGriff (o); Michael 'Mudcat' Ward (b); Mark Greenberg, Don Williams (d, perc).* 7–8/99.

If few contemporary guitarists could have made themselves so at home with such a varied programme as *Language Of The Soul*, assuredly none could have gone on to conceive and execute *Grateful Heart*, dedicated to three musicians Earl counts as 'early inspirations [who] continue to be sources of great light and joy', John Coltrane, Roland Kirk and Duane Allman. (There is also a track inscribed to Carlos Santana.) Six of the 12 pieces are colloquies with Newman, whose fleecy tone on 'Drown In My Own Tears' is gorgeously compatible with Earl's buffed line.

Having shown earlier that he enjoys bluesy jamming with a Hammond organ, Earl devoted two of the longest tracks of *Healing Time* to duets with one of the masters of that timeless idiom, Jimmy McGriff. Seconds after one of these urbane grooves has faded, Earl is off on a visit to the clangorous soundworlds of early John Lee Hooker and Muddy Waters in 'Catfish Blues', but that's uncharacteristic of the album as a whole, which, like *Grateful Heart*, is rich in meditations and satiny ballads.

***(*) Ronnie Earl And Friends
Telarc CD-83537 *Earl; Kim Wilson (h, v); James Cotton (h); David Maxwell (p); Luther 'Guitar Jr' Johnson (g, v); Paul Marrochello, Tim 'Juice' O'Connor (g); Jimmy Mouradian, Michael 'Mudcat' Ward (b); Levon Helm (d); Irma Thomas (v).* 10–11/00.

It would be offensive to describe albums like *Grateful Heart* and *Healing Time* as smooth jazz, but they may be a little too smooth or jazzy for admirers who discovered Earl in his Roomful days. That constituency may be happier with … *And Friends*, where oldfashioned blues rules and Earl gets to jam with buddies like Luther 'Guitar Jr' Johnson ('All Your Love', 'Bad Boy') and Irma Thomas, who is riveting in 'New Vietnam Blues'. Kim Wilson, who sings and plays on six tracks – on two of them twin-harping with James Cotton – does enough, and well enough, to have earned a joint billing.

*** I Feel Like Goin' On
Stony Plain SPCD 1289 *Earl; Dave Limina (o, p); José Alvarez (g); Jimmy Mouradian (b); Lorne Entress (d); Silver Leaf Gospel Singers (v).* 03?
***(*) Now My Soul
Stony Plain SPCD 1298 *As above, except add Greg Piccolo (ts, v), Kim Wilson (h, v), Rod Carey (b).* 04?

Acknowledgement is the main business of *I Feel Like Goin' On*, with selections like 'Blues For Otis Rush', 'Little Johnny Lee' for Hooker, 'Big Walter' for Horton and 'Wolf Dance' and 'Howlin' For My Darlin'' for Howlin' Wolf and Hubert Sumlin. A secondary theme is compassion for the homeless, expressed in 'Alone With The Blues', played solo, and a long, slow 'Blues For The Homeless' shared with Limina, playing both organ and piano. Limina is also featured on 'Travelin' Heavy', another affectionately retro Hammond-and-guitar groove. Earl is never boring, but this virtually all-instrumental set, where the majority of the tracks stretch beyond six minutes, will probably best please his most ardent admirers. *Now My Soul* is not all that different, with its further bows to Horton and Rush and a similar gesture of respect to Magic Sam, and more organ–guitar pieces like Jimmy Smith's 'Blues For J', but having guest vocalists on half the tracks widens its appeal. The outstanding cuts are 'Kay My Dear', a slow blues obituary to a deceased friend, and a long and suspenseful reading of Rush's 'Double Trouble', sung by Kim Wilson. For *The Duke Meets The Earl* (Stony Plain//Dixiefrog), Earl's duet album with Duke Robillard, see the latter. TR

Easy Baby (born 1934)
VOCAL, HARMONICA

Alex Randle went north in 1956, with musical experience in Mississippi, Memphis and West Memphis under his belt. Years of playing in Chicago taverns preceded his recording debut, which did not lead to fame and fortune. He still makes occasional live appearances.

**** Sweet Home Chicago Blues
P-Vine PCD-5206 *Easy Baby; Eddie Taylor (g); Mac Thompson (b); Kansas City Red (d).* 3/77.

Sweet Home Chicago Blues originally appeared on Barrelhouse, and is a triumph for that label's 'forward to 1950' ethos. Easy Baby's main harmonica influence is Little Walter Jacobs, but Randle is a much stronger singer than Walter (which is not, admittedly, a difficult thing to be). Most of the songs are Chicago favourites, but Easy Baby usually makes them his own; the mambo intro and coda to 'Walking Thru The Park' lack the authority that Little Walter brought to the Muddy Waters original, but this is an uncharacteristic falling off. Much of the disc's success is attributable to the quality of the backing band. Eddie Taylor's fleet-fingered playing is unflaggingly inventive, even on the likes of 'Rock Me Baby' and 'Sweet Home Chicago', which in 1977 was not the cliché it has become; the occasional distortions as Mac Thompson goes into the red zone add to the 'live in studio' feeling; and Kansas City Red's drumming, crisp, uncluttered and briskly alert, is so good that the CD is worth hearing just for him.

***(*) If It Ain't One Thing, It's Another
Wolf 120.805 *Easy Baby; Allen Batts (p); Johnny B. Moore, Eddie Taylor Jr (g); Sho Komiya, Karl Meyer (b); Timothy Taylor, Sam Lay, Ashward Gates (d). 6–9/00.*

Nearly a quarter of a century later, Easy Baby was taking it – what else? – easy, living quietly, going to church and somewhat restricted by arthritis. Fortunately, he had kept up his playing skills, and not let religion, age or the indifference of record companies diminish his enthusiasm. *If It Ain't One Thing, It's Another* was recorded at a more leisurely pace than its distant predecessor, and with more varied, if not always superior, accompaniment. The outstanding session contributes four tracks with backing by Johnny B. Moore on acoustic guitar, Sho Komiya's upright bass and Ashward Gates, playing with brushes; 'Good Morning Little Schoolgirl' and Rice Miller's 'Let Me Explain' are triumphs for restraint in general, and for Moore's guitar skills in particular.

Elsewhere, Moore plays electric guitar with his habitual taste and skill. Of the other accompanists, Eddie Taylor Jr, present alongside Moore on seven titles, is occasionally a bit too busy, but in this he is better than Sam Lay, whose four appearances are usually much too busy. Tim Taylor and producer Karl Meyer are efficiently supportive, taking their cue from Allen Batts, who provides self-effacing textural and harmonic enrichment, only stretching out on the Spirit Of Memphis Quartet song which makes an unusual but splendid final (and title) track.

Easy Baby himself is generally in fine form, playing powerful riffs and solos, and is particularly striking when he switches to chromatic harmonica. His voice has developed what can usually be called a strong vibrato, but must occasionally be described as a quaver. As may be inferred, he sometimes doesn't have the energy the songs need, and 'All Pretty Women' is the disc's least successful track for this reason. 'Lovey Dovey' also disappoints, lacking both the fire and the cockiness of the Junior Wells original. On the other hand, 'Howlin' For My Darlin'' with the damper down, and cheery affection substituted for Howlin' Wolf's sexual ferocity, is a surprising success. Minor gripes apart, the disc as a whole is a welcome and long overdue comeback. CS

Archie Edwards (1918–98)
VOCAL, GUITAR, UKULELE

Archie Edwards was born in rural Virginia; his father was a musician as well as a farmer and moonshiner, and Archie took up the guitar aged eight, first playing in public in 1933. After military service, he moved to Washington, DC, in 1946, and virtually abandoned music until he was spurred to resume by meeting and working with Mississippi John Hurt in the '60s. There was a two-year hiatus following Hurt's death, but Edwards became an important figure on the DC blues scene, both as a performer and because of the weekend jam sessions which he hosted at his Alpha Tonsorial Palace. In 1981, Edwards retired from government service, and was able to devote more time to performing at festivals and clubs in North America and Europe.

*** The Toronto Sessions
NorthernBlues NBM 0006 *Edwards. 6/86.*
*** Blues 'N Bones
Mapleshade 5629 *Edwards; Mark Wenner (h); Richard 'Mr Bones' Thomas (bones). 4–10/89.*

'I play what they call the old Piedmont style, but I call it East Virginia blues.' Archie Edwards was strongly aware of the history of the blues, and of his role as both preserver and developer of the music; his playing is recognizably descended from tradition, and he learned many songs from records, but more than many a Piedmont guitarist, he developed his own sound. His association with Mississippi John Hurt was an important element in this, but Edwards is chiefly recognizable by an idiosyncratic approach to harmony and structure. His chords sometimes contain unorthodox intervals, and there are unexpected disjunctions in his playing, as he switches, adroitly but abruptly, between ideas. This is especially obvious on the Mapleshade disc, where Mr Bones has to perform some very nimble acrobatics to keep in sync, even on a song as well known as 'John Henry'. That should not be taken to mean that Edwards is hard on the ears, or an incompetent musician; rather, he asks listeners to share his respect for the music of past days, but to be ready to take a risk when exploring its possibilities.

The Toronto Sessions is a well-programmed selection of Edwards's blues guitar playing at its most polished. *Blues 'N Bones* ranges wider and digs deeper, including the stringband number 'Payday', the fine ragtime instrumental 'Saturday Night Hop' and a version of Jimmie Rodgers's 'T For Texas' with baritone ukulele. Six songs appear on both discs, but the addition of bones and harmonica on Mapleshade makes for a very different sound. Both CDs are well recorded, and despite their overlapping content they offer complementary, rather than competing, portraits of the artist. CS

Moanin' Bernice Edwards (born c. 1906)
VOCAL, PIANO

Bernice Edwards was a close friend of the Thomas family, whose recorded members were the siblings George, Hersal and Sippie, and their niece Hociel. The Thomases left for Chicago, but Edwards stayed behind in Houston. She married and joined the church shortly after her last recording session.

*** Texas Piano – Vol. 1 (1923–1935)
Document DOCD-5224 *Edwards; Black Boy Shine (p); poss. Ramblin' Thomas, Howling Smith [J. T. 'Funny Paper' Smith] (g). c. 2/28–4/35.*

Bernice Edwards was in her late teens or early 20s in 1928, when she made 12 of her 16 issued recordings, but if her lyrics are the least bit autobiographical, she had seen plenty of life's underside. She emphasizes the strategies that a woman must adopt to survive in an unforgiving world: 'When you see me comin', with my dirty, dirty duckins on, You know my man's in trouble, there's got to be some hustlin' done' portrays a woman who works as a fieldhand by day and walks the streets at night. Even without the sketchy biographical details supplied by Sippie Wallace, Edwards's fluttering, melodic right hand and harmonically busy bass figures would locate her in Houston, and identify her as one of the few female members of the 'Santa Fe' group, and one of the earliest to record. The 'Santa Fe' pianists rode the freight trains from job to job, when they weren't hanging out, drinking and gambling; if Edwards participated in that life, she must have been a tough cookie. Her first two songs are an ill-judged attempt at vaudevillian chirping, but thereafter her slate-dark voice and slow tempos are highly effective vehicles for the songs of a self-proclaimed 'High Powered Mama' and 'Jack Of All Trades'. In 1935, she recorded again, with commandingly increased vocal power; on two lively instrumental stomps, she and 'Funny Paper' Smith are joined by Black Boy Shine, hammering out tremolo figures at the top end of the piano.

The CD is completed by members of the Thomas family, of whom Hociel has her own entry. George W. (1883–1937) is represented by three numbers. His composition 'The Rocks', a disjointed hybrid of blues and ragtime, with boogie bass figures in some strains, is played by Clay Custer, often assumed, but not proven, to be George W. under a pseudonym. 'Fast Stuff Blues' and 'Don't Kill Him In Here', with Papa Charlie Hill on guitar, are more successful in building a bridge between ragtime's formality and the looser sound of the Houston piano blues. Similarly transitional is 'Hersal Blues', by George's much younger brother. Hersal Thomas (1906–26) was a prodigy, whose early death from food poisoning robbed the blues world of a major talent; 'Suitcase Blues', with its ominously swinging bass figures, ascending breaks and elegant tremolos, was justly admired and highly influential, in particular on Albert Ammons. CS

Clarence Edwards (1933–93)
VOCAL, GUITAR

Born near Baton Rouge, Louisiana, Edwards began playing blues in the area in his teens. He was taped by the local folklorist Harry Oster in 1959–62 and by Chris Strachwitz in 1970, but little came of these and other small exposures, and he quit music for more than a decade. His 1990 album Swamp's The Word *was enthusiastically greeted by the blues community and led to festival appearances in the US and Europe, but illness brought his career, and his life, to a close soon afterwards.*

Four of Edwards's recordings for Oster, with his brother Cornelius on guitar and Butch Cage on fiddle, are on *Country Negro Jam Session* (Arhoolie CD 372). In 1970 he recorded both for Strachwitz – two tracks are on *Louisiana Blues* (Arhoolie CD 9004) – and for Blue Horizon; four numbers from the latter session are on *Swamp Blues* (Ace CDCHD 661).

*** Swamp's The Word
Blues Factory BFY 47008 Edwards; Harmonica Red (h); Bill Guess (p, perc); Henry Gray (p); Michael Ward (vn); A. G. Hardesty (b); Pick Delmore (d); Ronnie Houston (cardboard box); Bruce Lamb, Mike Shepherd, Steve Coleridge (perc). 2/90.

Edwards's previous recordings had mostly been versions of stock blues songs, and *Swamp's The Word*, with repertoire like 'Hi Heel Sneakers', 'Things I Used To Do', 'Hoochie Coochie Man' and 'Walking The Dog', confirmed that his talent was for interpretation rather than invention. Since the interpretations were often in the style of '50s Excello recordings by local contemporaries like Lightnin' Slim, and were deliberately produced to sound so (note, for instance, the percussive effects on 'Lonesome Bedroom Blues'), Edwards was playing to the tastes of knowledgeable blues fans, and the warmth of the response to the original release of the album may have been kindled by a feeling that more records ought to be made on such oldfashioned principles. Present-day listeners without that agenda may react a little differently. Edwards has an impeccable old-Southern blues voice, and it's a pleasure to hear him trace the contours of Muddy Waters's 'Still A Fool', but he can't be said, here or elsewhere, to be doing much mapmaking of his own. This album was previously available on Red Lightnin' RLCD 0090 (deleted), but the Blues Factory, which may be difficult to find, appears to be its only currently available issue.

**(*) Louisiana Swamp Blues – Vol. 4
Wolf 120.925 Edwards; Harmonica Red (h); Michael Ward, Scott Shipman (vn); S. Shipman (md); Harold Washington, Roosevelt Boudreaux (g); A. G. Hardesty, David Hill, Steve Coleridge (b); Pick Delmore, Jess Kenchin, Ronnie Houston (d). 90–91.

At least some of these recordings were made around the time of *Swamp's The Word*, and the 'Hi Heel Sneakers' here is merely another mix, clarifying Michael Ward's violin line, but 'Driving Wheel', 'Don't Got Over' (i.e. 'Done Got Over It') and 'Cold [*sic* Coal] Black Mare' are different versions. The album is likeable for much the same reasons as its predecessor, the ensemble playing on 'Free Will' and 'Awful Blues' again recalling Lightnin' Slim singles of 30-odd years earlier. The album concludes with laidback performances of two Jimmy Reed numbers by the singer and harmonica player Oscar 'Harp' Davis.

**(*) I Looked Down That Railroad (Till My Eyes Got Red And Sore)
Last Call 7422508 Edwards; Oscar Davis (h, v); Harmonica Red, unknown (h); Henry Gray (p); Gina Forsyth (vn); Andrea Curbelo, Pat Morrison (g); Steve Coleridge (b, perc); A. G. Hardesty, John E. Bidgood (b); Pick Delmore, Ronnie Houston, unknown (d); Battlerack Scatter, Harold Washington (perc). early 90s.

Edwards looks farther afield for his material, drawing from Earl Gaines, Denise LaSalle and Bo Diddley (though the track listed as Bo's 'She's Fine She's Mine' is actually Willie Cobbs's 'You Don't Love Me'), but preserves his manner of sounding like a younger, more flexibly voiced brother of Lightnin' Slim, especially on 'I'm Your Slave'. Nine of the 16 tracks are from club dates and one from a broadcast overseen by a tongue-tied DJ: 'What was the same of that song again?' Edwards: ' "Ups And Downs".' DJ: 'Uh … how've your ups and downs been goin', okay?' TR

David 'Honeyboy' Edwards (born 1915)
VOCAL, GUITAR, HARMONICA

Given the astonishing feats of memory in his autobiography The World Don't Owe Me Nothing, *there's a case for supposing Edwards to be a better raconteur than musician.*

Like his early mentor Big Joe Williams, Edwards has always had a healthy disregard for metre, expanding and contracting the bar lengths of his songs at will, songs whose lyrics in the main tend to be fragmentary and repetitive. The results can be endearing or mildly annoying, as circumstance dictates. With the passing of John Lee Hooker, however, Edwards has become the doyen of Mississippi country blues, even if longevity hasn't necessarily improved his skill.

***(*) Delta Bluesman
Earwig CD 4922 *Edwards; Carey Bell (h); Sunnyland Slim (p); Floyd Jones (g); Aron Burton (b); Kansas City Red, Robert Plunkett (d). 7/42–12/91.*

As a precursor to Edwards's autobiography, *Delta Bluesman*'s historical importance would have been better served without the four band tracks with Bell, Sunnyland, Burton and Plunkett, none of which achieves coherence. Jones and Red fare better with 'Bad Whiskey And Cocaine' through lacking the temerity to interrupt Edwards's erratic flow. The majority of the album consists of his 1942 recordings for the Library of Congress, introduced by Alan Lomax. The 27-year-old was a more dextrous guitarist but over the course of a dozen songs his control progressively slips as he indulges bass runs and treble figures learned from Joe Williams. He plays rack harmonica on 'Wind Howlin' Blues' and 'The Army Blues' in a manner reminiscent of J. D. Short, another Williams associate. Four further solo tracks cut in London in 1991 are mildly eccentric (e.g. his frenzied slide guitar in 'Number 12 At The Station') but satisfying.

The LC recordings can also be found in full on *Big Joe Williams And The Stars Of Mississippi Blues* (JSP JSP 7719 5CD) and in part (five tracks) on the VAC *Mississippi River Blues: Library of Congress Recordings 1940–1942* (Travelin' Man TM CD 07, deleted).

*** Crawling Kingsnake
Testament TCD 6002 *Edwards; John Lee Henley (h, v). 3/64, 7/67.*

Edwards's idiosyncrasies are perfectly captured in these two sessions, the first with Henley on harmonica, who also sings 'Blue And Lonesome' and 'Ida Lou Blues', the latter adapted from his 1958 single 'Knockin' On Lula Mae's Door'. Henley's presence restrains Edwards for the most part, although his slide playing on 'My Baby's Gone' threatens to carry him away. Eight solo performances from 1967 typify his curious combination of loose rhythms and frantic clusters of notes in the frequent guitar solos. Apart from homages to Robert Johnson and Tony Hollins, there are echoes of Tommy Johnson in his accompaniments to 'Blues Like Showers Of Rain' and 'Bull Cow Blues'. Short playing time is made up with an 18-minute interview segment in which a relentless Pete Welding interrogates Edwards at length about Robert Johnson.

**(*) Don't Mistreat A Fool
Genes GCD 9914 *Edwards; Big Walter Horton (h); Johnny Shines, Big Joe Williams, Michael Stewart (g). 69–71.*

More 30-year-old recordings that, apart from 'Hot Springs Blues' and 'Howlin' Wind', see the first light of day without unduly enhancing Edwards's reputation. Those titles, along with '61 Highway #2' and 'Little Boy Blue', are his most consistent efforts here, least troubled by explosively inept guitar work. None of the guests apart from Stewart contributes much, although Horton gets in a few choruses during 'You're The One'. 'Myrtle Mae' lifts Nighthawk's 'Anna Lee', with Edwards attempting to emulate the latter's slide style. 'Bull Cow Blues #2' and '(Meet The) Mornin' Train' once again make wobbly use of Tommy Johnson's snapping bass-string runs, while 'B & O Blues' (which he claims to have written) falters from his obsession with a poorly played incidental riff. Such wayward habits prevent this from being the record it might have been.

***(*) I've Been Around
Savoy Jazz 17297 *Edwards; Walter Horton (h); Eddie El (g). 5/74–5/77.*

By recording Edwards over the course of three years in a variety of settings, producer Pete Lowry compiled the most consistent examples of the artist's compact but vital talent thus far. Horton appears on four songs, reticently on all but 'Take Me In Your Arms' (better known as 'Love Me Over Slow'), while El's amplified guitar keeps Edwards on the rails in three, including 'Things Have Changed', one of only three songs to feature slide guitar. The seven solo selections include homages to Patton, Tommy Johnson and Rube Lacey, although Edwards quickly inserts verses of his own into each. Most feature an acoustic guitar save 'You're Gonna Miss Me', on which Edwards also plays a rack harmonica. Diligent editing ensures that the eccentricities evident on other albums aren't allowed to proliferate.

***(*) Mississippi Delta Bluesman
Smithsonian Folkways SFW CD 40132 *Edwards. 79.*

Consistency apparently became a watchword, for this is the most satisfying single session Edwards has produced, encompassing influences from his young manhood and postwar blues talents such as Magic Sam, Bobby Bland and Junior Parker. 'Big Fat Mama' and 'Pony Blues' turn up again, as does a medley of 'Sweet Home Chicago' and 'Dust My Broom', but this time alongside Robert Petway's 'Catfish Blues'. 'Blues Worry Me All The Time' becomes an impressive exhibition of rack harmonica. The only detrimental factor is his habit of drawing out every song by alternating repeated verses with instrumental choruses. This and the half-remembered lyrics of Magic Sam's '(Every)Things Gonna Be Alright', 'Further On Up The Road' and others require the exercise of a degree of tolerance.

**(*) White Windows
Evidence ECD 26039 *Edwards. 9/88.*

This collection has the merit of revisiting some of Edwards's previous achievements and featuring material a little different from the favourites regularly trotted out. However, the presence of 'Take A (Little) Walk With Me', 'Going Down Slow' and 'Roll & Tumble Blues' is a reminder of his annoying habit of only half learning a song. These might be called 'personal interpretations' but they're fundamentally sloppy and half-realized. This, combined with his perennially clumsy slide playing in 'Drop Down Mama', 'Build Myself A Cave' and others, changes what might otherwise be endearing to a matter of endurance, only ameliorated by acceptable versions of '61 Highway' and 'Shake 'Em On Down'.

*** The World Don't Owe Me Nothing
Earwig CD 4940 *Edwards; Rick 'Cookin'' Sherry (h, wb); Carey Bell (h). 2/96–8/97.*

Released to coincide with his autobiography, this finds Edwards negotiating his ninth decade with a series of live and studio recordings that are both valiant and vague. His vocals emerge in shouted gobbets of sometimes incoherent syllables while his guitar pursues a course of its own. At these times, Bell shows commendable alertness and dexterity in suggesting that logic persists where none is evident. Despite the booklet information, there are five live recordings, including two originals, 'Every Now And Then' and 'My Mama Told Me', and a final, chaotic 'Hide Away', the latter pair propelled by Sherry's washboard. In four interview segments Edwards talks of Robert Johnson's death, meeting Robert Nighthawk, his own arrival in Chicago and how he came to know Carey Bell, who sings 'So Hard To Leave You'. There are many surreal moments here but given Edwards's iconic status, the listener must of necessity forgive and enjoy in roughly equal measure.

**(*) Shake 'Em On Down
APO APO 2010 *Edwards; Madison Slim (h); Jimmy D. Lane (g). 2/99.*

Listening to these 14 songs is like watching a guttering flame. Edwards's attempts to perform 'High Water Everywhere' and 'Pony Blues' make uncomfortable listening; in his effort to snap his bass strings his singing approaches incoherence. The harmonica player, present on ten tracks, does well to follow the vagaries of Edwards's wayward metre. Lane is added on four of these, modestly shoring up the rhythm. As well as Patton, the programme draws on St Louis Jimmy, Booker White, Lightnin' Hopkins, Roosevelt Sykes and Johnnie Temple – and Edwards's 'Standing On The Corner' leans heavily on Jimmy Rogers's 'You're The One'. Rogers is mentioned during a 13-minute interview section that otherwise strings together some of the usual stories. The fact that Edwards is still performing in his late 80s doesn't necessarily need this documentation. NS

Frank Edwards (1909–2002)
VOCAL, HARMONICA, GUITAR

Georgia-born, Edwards grew up in Florida, where Tampa Red encouraged his guitar playing. He added rack harp around 1934 and settled in Atlanta, where he was a member of a stringband when not on the road. An encounter with Tommy McClennan resulted in his 1941 recording session; Edwards stayed on in Chicago for a time, working with Muddy Waters (who knew him as 'Black Frank') and others. Back in Atlanta, Edwards recorded two songs in 1949, but they were not issued until the LP era, by which time he had quit music. Located in 1971, he began playing at festivals and locally; he had been recording on the day of his fatal heart attack.

*** Country Blues Collector's Items (1930–1941)
Document DOCD-5426 *Edwards; unknown (b); Washboard Sam (wb, sp). 5/41.*

Despite his experience as a band musician, Edwards was *sui generis*; even Washboard Sam seems subdued by his blasting harmonica, clanking steel guitar and powerful, pinched vocals. 'Sweet Man Blues' is based on a Little Buddy Doyle recording, but the other three songs here are originals, sometimes made difficult to understand by Edwards's strong accent and personal grammar. The hit of the session is the stomping 'We Got To Get Together', which Edwards liked well enough to remake in 1949, long after its call for wartime solidarity was redundant. This version is not on CD, but its flipside, 'Love My Baby', with Curley Weaver seconding, is on *Harmonica Blues Vol. 2* (Frémeaux FA 5059 2CD). The balance of *Country Blues Collector's Items* is by Tommy Griffin (q.v.) and One Arm Slim, a minor Peetie Wheatstraw imitator.

(***) Georgia Country Blues
Wolf 120.913 *As above, except add Steve Carson (g), 'Popcorn' [Arthur Clover] (wb). 5/41–12/72.*

In 1972, Edwards cut *Done Some Travelin'* (Trix 3303) for Peter B. Lowry. In the early '90s, Edwards sent a tape of the album to Wolf, misrepresenting it as new recordings. Wolf were presumably acting in good faith when they issued an LP on Best Of Blues, but no such excuse applies to this release, which makes no mention of Lowry and gives Edwards a false credit as producer. Two spirituals (one an intriguing minor-key makeover of 'The Saints') are replaced by the 1941 recordings.

Edwards had a reputation in Atlanta for 'funny time', but in fact it was very steady, meaning that he could play unusual rhythms. Some musicians may have found him hard to accompany, but Carson and Popcorn do good work when they appear (separately). Even when amplified, Edwards's guitar is gentler and more subtle than it was the '40s; so is his singing, but the harp is still aggressive. It's also fairly simple, as befits a rack player, but there's a clear debt to Sonny Boy Williamson I. Most of Edwards's songs are self-composed, but he takes the ones that aren't down unexpected musical byways. His singing remains hard to understand, but enough of the lyrics come through, on the anti-clerical 'Chicken Raid' and others, to prove that Frank Edwards was a true original. He sometimes sounds like a bemused visitor from another dimension, but it's worth getting used to his idiosyncrasies. Ethical readers may prefer, however, to look for the deleted *I've Been Around* (32 Jazz 32185), which was both a legitimate and a complete reissue of the Trix LP.

(**(*)) Chicken Raid
Music Maker MMCD 47 *Edwards; Danny 'Mudcat' Dudeck (g); unknown (b); Janet Daniel, Cool John Ferguson (d); Washboard Sam (wb, sp). 5/41–3/02.*

The 1941 recordings turn up again at the end of *Chicken Raid*, with erroneous and incomplete recording details. The idea may be to insinuate that 'We Got To Get Together' is the postwar version; if not, then Music Maker are guilty only of being too lazy to check Edwards's recollections against *B&GR*.

The rest of *Chicken Raid*, cut between the ages of 87 and 93, is naturally more subdued: Edwards plays his guitar and rack harp solo, in a trio and with Cool John Ferguson on drums. The four tracks with Ferguson, cut on the day Edwards died, are physically the strongest of these late performances, but they are all pretty extraordinary for a man of his age. It's difficult to recommend them on their own merits, though; as a musician and songwriter, Edwards has come down to a limited stock of melodic ideas, and as a singer he spends most of the time communing quietly and almost incomprehensibly with himself. CS

Teddy Edwards
VOCAL, TIPLE, GUITAR

'Big Boy' Edwards, as he was often called on his records, was around Chicago in the '30s and perhaps earlier. Big Bill Broonzy recalled working with him and Papa Charlie Jackson.

**(*) Big Boy Teddy Edwards (1930–1936)
Document DOCD-5440 Edwards; Black Bob (p); Papa Charlie Jackson (bj); Big Bill Broonzy, unknown (g); prob. John Lindsay (b). 7/30–5/36.

Edwards's last recording was a cameo on a Hokum Boys session, an appropriate *envoi* for an artist who was never more than a bit-player on the Chicago blues scene. His earliest sides, accompanied only by his rudimentary tiple playing, are monotonous, but with the addition of other musicians his sessions become merrier affairs and he takes more vocal liberties, occasionally interspersing his strangled delivery with passages of scat singing. The two-part 'Who Did You Give My Barbecue To?' and the non-blues 'Louise', both of which he recorded twice, were probably his chief calling-cards. Most of his other recordings are conventional blues of their period, conventionally backed by piano and guitar, such as 'It Was No Dream' and 'Hoodoo Blues'. The best performed (and recorded) is 'W-P-A Blues', a cover of Casey Bill Weldon's song. TR

Big Mojo Elem (1928–97)
VOCAL, BASS

Robert Elem left Mississippi for Chicago in 1951. He played guitar with 'Big Boy' Spires, Otis Rush and Freddie King, but during his long stay in King's band switched to electric bass, which not many Chicago blues musicians played at that time. In the '60s he worked with West Side musicians such as Jimmy Dawkins. A popular figure on the city's blues scene, he was respected for his commitment and his fine voice.

Elem recorded little in his own name before the '70s. A couple of 1967 tracks with a band featuring Luther Allison, 'Move On Out Of Town' and 'Slow Down Baby', are on *Sweet Home Chicago* (Delmark DD-618).

** Mojo Boogie
Storyville STCD 8041 Elem; Willie James Lyons, Wayne Bennett (g); Fred Below (d). 10/77.
*** Mojo Boogie
St George STG 7703 Elem; Tuxedo Ron De War (ts); Studebaker John (h, g, b); Rokko Jans, Mark Brumback (p); Jr Kreher (g); Dave 'Thick Soul' Trumfio, Chris Lopes (b); Twist Turner (d, perc); Jo Armstead (v). 94.

Elem liked the songs of J. B. Lenoir, particularly 'Mojo Boogie', hence his nickname and the title used for both his albums. The Storyville was originally issued on MCM and, like several others on that French label, portrays the artist in a dim light: the ensemble sound is monotonous, there are too many slow numbers and the programming is insensitive. Elem puts his heart into his singing and Below is his usual reliable self, but the recording gives neither Lyons nor Bennett the chance to sound really good.

The St George album shows how the job should have been done. Elem and producer George Paulus came up with a programme that allowed the singer to display his range, including songs that took him back to his early days in Chicago like 'Big Boy' Spires's 'Murmur Low' (as 'Big Fat Mamma Blues') and Leroy Foster's 'Boll Weevil'. Elmore James's 'Fine Little Mama' and Elem's own 'Too Much Trouble' and 'New Year's Resolution' elicit powerfully abrasive vocals. Tempos, arrangements and song types are thoughtfully varied to create a thoroughly enjoyable album. TR

Tinsley Ellis (born 1957)
VOCAL, GUITAR

Ellis was born in Atlanta but raised in Florida. B. B. King's gift of a broken string after a gig set him on the path to becoming a blues musician. Returning to Atlanta, he joined the Alley Cats before forming the Heartfixers with Chicago Bob Nelson; he became the band's lead singer when Nelson left. Ellis disbanded the Heartfixers in 1988 to pursue a solo career that continues to flourish quietly to this day.

**(*) Cool On It
Alligator ALCD 3905 Ellis; Dave Cotton (ts, bs, v); Scott Alexander (p); Wayne Burdette (b, v); Michael McCauley (d, v); Jerome Radway (maracas); Christie Vaughn, Jeni Michelson (v). 86.

Ellis is the star of the show here, although the Heartfixers function well as an ensemble. Half of the ten songs are originals but only the nine-minute slow blues 'Time To Quit' makes any solid impression. The rest of his songs and versions of Bo Diddley's 'Hong Kong Mississippi', Chuck Berry's 'Tulane' and Marty Robbins's 'Sugaree' are more entertaining than edifying. Ellis solos often and well, Cotton's tenor sax gets space in 'Sugaree' and 'Second Thoughts' and the album ends with a respectable thrust at 'Wild Weekend', a 1962 instrumental first perpetrated by the Rockin' Rebels. A straight transfer of the LP, this would have benefited from added material.

** Georgia Blue
Alligator ALCD 4765 Ellis; Bob Enos (t); Greg Piccolo (ts); Doug James (bs); Oliver Wells (o); Ricky Keller (kb, b, perc); Wayne Burdette (b); Yonrico Scott (d, perc); Terry Simpson, Pat Buchanan, Jerome Olds (v). 88.

Although competently performed, this is a failure of nerve on Ellis's part. Cast in the mould of *Cool On It*, the choice of covers is over-ambitiously diverse, encompassing Tampa Red, the Meters, and Albert and Freddie King, and the playing too tentative to suggest that Ellis is in command of the proceedings. His own songs are competent, with 'You Picked A Good Time' and 'Crime Of Passion' the most notable, but his singing fluctuates from naive to characterless, lacking the confidence he'd shown on the previous album. Four instrumentals draw attention to the lack of bite in arrangements and execution.

**(*) Fanning The Flames
Alligator ALCD 4778 Ellis; Oliver Wells (t, o, p); Stutz Wimmer (ts); Ricky Keller (kb, b); Ralph Mattarochia (kb); Wayne Burdette (b); Yonrico Scott (d, perc); Guy Locke (d); Pat Buchanan, Terry Simpson (v). 89.

Ellis takes a further step in the direction of blues-rock while the gap between his instrumental and vocal talents widens. Arrangements are beginning to become formulaic, too often fading out on hyperactive guitar solos. With 'So Many Tears' and 'Dangling By A Thread' he tries a quieter approach but his self-conscious singing undermines his intentions. 'Leavin' Here' contains his best vocal performance but strong backing tracks like those of 'Must Be The Devil' and 'Pawnbroker' are short-changed by Ellis's lack of natural ability, making the comparison with Stevie Ray Vaughan that some writers were beginning to formulate seem exaggerated.

(*) Trouble Time
Alligator ALCD 4805 *Ellis; Mike Haynes, Michael Holton (t); Chris McDonald (tb); Sam Levine (ts); Oliver Wells (kb, o); Mike Boyette (o, p); Chuck Leavell (p); Peter Buck (g); Ricky Keller, James Ferguson (b); Scott Meeder, David Sims (d).* 91.

Ellis continues to mark time, subduing some of the rock aspects in his playing but still not creating a sufficiently distinct style. In 'Sign Of The Blues' he sings about 'some other guitar man … making front page news', as if that might be the criterion by which he wishes to be judged. Most of the 12 songs are self-written, and it begins to look as if his powers of composition are as proscribed as his vocal ability. The album is certainly entertaining but it's hard to see it as anything other than the product of an average talent with something of an identity crisis.

*** **Storm Warning**
Alligator ALCD 4823 *Ellis; Albey Scholl (h); Chuck Leavell (o, p); Oliver Wood (g, v); Derek Trucks (g); James Ferguson (b); Stuart Grimes (d, v); Count M'Butu (perc).* 94.

A reunion with Eddy Offord, engineer/producer of *Cool On It*, brings forth the best album of his solo career thus far. For once, there's a sense of real thought having gone into the arrangements and a grown-up use of dynamics. Several tracks, 'Cut You Loose', 'Early In The Morning' and 'The Sun Is Shining' among them, begin quietly before surrendering to Ellis's need to show off, at its worst towards the end of a previously restrained version of 'Mercy, Mercy, Mercy', when he slaps on rock insensitivity with a trowel. His singing has improved but his songs continue to sound contrived, with the exception of 'A Quitter Never Wins', later taken up by Jonny Lang. Trucks's Duane Allman-inspired slide is heard on two tracks, easily outshone by an on-form Ellis, who manages to control himself through a confident rerun of Freddie King's 'Side Tracked'.

(*) Fire It Up
Alligator ALCD 4852 *Ellis; Kevin McKendree (p); Rob McNeely (g); Scott Koziol, Donald 'Duck' Dunn (b); Tad Parker, Scott Meeder, Kennard Johnson (d).* 97.

The incendiary title signals an album of predominantly blues-rock that despite being produced by Tom Dowd fails to set Ellis above his contemporaries. His newfound understanding of contrast is put to further scrutiny but once again it's a study of extremes rather than nuances. 'Change Your Mind' is commendable for its restraint but in general an extended guitar solo like the one in 'Are You Sorry' can't avoid tipping over into excess for its own sake. Magic Sam's 'Look What You Done' is a rare blues in a programme that includes songs by Fred James, Danny Kirwan and David Hidalgo alongside five of Ellis's own. The results are well-recorded and listenable but not memorable.

* **Hell Or High Water**
Telarc CD 83531 *Ellis; Kevin McKendree (o, p); Kenny Kilgore (g); Phillip 'Philzone' Skipper (b); Scott Callison (d); Donna Hopkins (v).* 02.

Ellis and producer Offord finally expunge the last vestige of blues from his repertoire. With the exception of the acoustic 'Set Love Free', these 12 self-penned songs are springboards for Ellis's guitar work, and once again too many march grandiosely into a fadeout. Nor have his vocals improved; he now sounds like a winded Jim Morrison without a hint of a dangerous edge. Instrumental competence remains high but it's wedded to a set of songs whose lyrics are uniformly weak and trite. From a halfway decent blues singer/guitarist Ellis has become a nondescript pop singer with a halfway decent guitar technique. His ambition may be satisfied but his fan base might think otherwise. NS

** **The Hard Way**
Telarc CD-83608 *Ellis; Adam Mewherter (tb); Marcus James (s, tamb); Sean Costello (h); Kevin McKendree (kb, o); Oliver Wood (g); The Evil One (b); Richie Hayward, Wes Johnson (d); Count M'butu (cga, bgo, shaker); Donna Hopkins, Lola Gulley, Vicki Salz (v).* 10–12/03.

'And It Hurts', with a line faintly reminiscent of 'What'd I Say', the Jimmy Reed-styled 'Fountain Of Youth', the acoustic 'Her Other Man' and the snarling '12 Pack Poet' give this set more blues content than several of its predecessors, but Ellis sings as if someone's pointing a gun at him and the songwriting rarely rises above run-of-the-mill. A big improvement over *Hell Or High Water*, though.

(*) Live – Highwayman
Alligator ALCD 4904 *Ellis; Todd Hamric (kb, v); The Evil One (b, v); Jeff Burch (d).* 05.

Back with Alligator after an artistically so-so spell on Telarc, Ellis celebrates with a full-on live recording from Chord On Blues, 'premier blues club and steakhouse' of St Charles, Illinois. As you'll gather from lines like 'Seems like nowadays ain't nothin' made to last' ('A Quitter Never Wins') or 'They say the world must be round, and so I sailed the seven seas' ('To The Devil For A Dime'), Ellis is not taking the hard road of originality this time out, and his flaming solos are drawn from a well-used shelf of the guitar library. But if you enjoy blues-rock pomp and circumstance – paraded, it should be said, with considerable skill – you'll be delighted to know that *Live – Highwayman* holds almost 80 minutes of it. TR

Queen Sylvia Embry (1941–92)
VOCAL, BASS

Born in Arkansas, Embry moved to Memphis and then Chicago, where she met her second husband, guitarist John Embry, and began playing bass with him. She worked with Lefty Dizz at The Checkerboard and Kingston Mines, and recorded an album with John Embry for Razor. She later left blues for her first love, gospel music.

*** **Living Chicago Blues Vol. IV**
Alligator ALCD 7704 *Embry; Ralph Lapetina (kb); Buddy Scott, Sam Good (g); Dino Alvarez (d).* 80.

*** **Midnight Baby**
Evidence ECD 26057 *Embry; Carey Bell (h); Lovie Lee (p); Jimmy Dawkins (g, v); Philip Meeks, Jimmy Rogers, Louisiana Red (g); Tyrone Centuray, Charles 'Honeyboy' Otis (d); band (v).* 4–11/83.

Embry's voice is rasping, with a wide vibrato, and not in the least ingratiating, and when she has a story of her own to tell, as in 'Going Upstairs', one of four tracks on the Alligator VAC, or 'Life And Troubles' on Evidence, she holds the listener firmly in her grasp. Other people's numbers, such as 'The Things That I Used To Do', which she does on Evidence as 'Can't Get Along', are a little less effective, but the combined vitality of singer and band on both CDs keeps ordinariness at bay. The bulk of *Midnight Baby* (credited to 'Blues Queen Sylvia') was recorded in Chicago with Dawkins, Meeks and Centuray, who work hard and make lively music, Dawkins getting down and dirty on tracks like 'Baby, What Do I Do' and 'Midnight Baby', where he sings a duet with Embry. The last two tracks were recorded, later in the year, at a concert in Germany. Nothing much happens on the overlong 'I Love You', but on a second reading of 'Baby, What Do I Do' Louisiana Red and Jimmy Rogers re-create the twin-guitar thrust of the early Muddy Waters band, and Embry responds with one of those unaccompanied codas that Muddy enjoyed. TR

Sleepy John Estes (1904–77)
VOCAL, GUITAR

Estes was born near Ripley in Lauderdale County in eastern Tennessee, and lost the sight in his right eye in a boyhood accident. In his teens his family moved to Brownsville, Tennessee, where he met the younger Yank Rachell and began playing music with him in the vicinity and in Memphis, where they were talent-spotted by Victor and recorded in 1929 and '30. After a five-year break Estes returned to the studio for Decca and continued to record until 1941. He lived for some years in Memphis, where he recorded without outcome for Sun in 1952, but on becoming completely blind returned to Brownsville. It was there that the documentary film-maker David Blumenthal, following a tip-off from Big Joe Williams, traced him in 1961. The word was passed to Bob Koester of Delmark Records and Estes soon afterwards embarked on a second voyage in music that would take him to festivals all over the US and to Europe and the Far East.

(*) **Sleepy John Estes – Vol. 1 (1929–1937)
Document DOCD-5015 *Estes; Hammie Nixon (h, sp); 'Tee' (h); Jab Jones, poss. Johnny Hardge (p); Yank Rachell (md, v); Charlie Pickett (g); Lee Brown (k).* 9/29–8/37.

*** **Sleepy John Estes – Vol. 2 (1937–1941)**
Document DOCD-5016 *Estes; Robert Lee McCoy (h, g); Hammie Nixon (h); Son Bonds (g, k, v, sp); Charlie Pickett (g); Raymond Thomas (b); unknown (wb).* 8/37–9/41.

**** **The Essential**
Classic Blues CBL 200009 2CD *Estes; Robert Lee McCoy (h, g); Hammie Nixon (h, sp); Jab Jones, poss. Johnny Hardge (p); Yank Rachell (md); Son Bonds (g, k, v, sp); Charlie Pickett (g); Raymond Thomas (b); Lee Brown (k).* 9/29–9/41.

*** **The Blues/From Memphis To Chicago 1929–1941**
Frémeaux FA 258 2CD *Similar to above.* 9/29–9/41.

♛ **** **I Ain't Gonna Be Worried No More 1929–1941**
Yazoo 2004 *Similar to above.* 9/29–9/41.

*** **Brownsville Blues**
Wolf Blues Classics BC 003 *Similar to above.* 9/29–9/41.
*** **The Man Who Cried The Blues 1929–1941**
EPM Blues Collection 15940 *Similar to above.* 9/29–9/41.
(*) **Working Man Blues
Fabulous FABCD 112 *Similar to above.* 9/29–9/41.
(*) **Tennessee Blues
Wolf Blues Jewels WBJ 015 *Similar to above.* 9/29–9/41.
*** **Someday Baby Blues**
Snapper Complete Blues SBLUECD 028 *Similar to above.* 9/29–48.
**** **Sleepy John Estes/Gus Cannon**
[JSP JSPCD 3406] 2CD *Estes; 'Tee' (h); Jab Jones, poss. Johnny Hardge (p); Yank Rachell (md).* 9/29–5/30.

The 25-year-old man who sat down to record 'The Girl I Love, She Got Long Curly Hair' for a travelling Victor unit in Memphis would prove to be one of the company's most striking finds in a city full of distinctive blues artists. High, blurred, plaintive, his voice sounded like that of a man on the verge of tears; sometimes it would even break, momentarily, as if overwhelmed by emotion. Yet, oddly for an artist who would become known for his composition, his first sides were mostly impersonal: local standards ('The Girl I Love' is 'Goin' To Brownsville') or common themes like 'Divin' Duck Blues' ('if the river was whiskey and I was a …'). It was only gradually that he revealed, or was encouraged to reveal, his own storytelling in pieces like 'Street Car Blues'. Here and elsewhere, especially in 'Milk Cow Blues' and 'Whatcha Doin'?', the trio of Estes, Yank Rachell and Jab Jones imparts an infectious bounce, Rachell trickling rivulets of mandolin notes on to the stolid piano–guitar rhythm.

But while the Victor sides are remarkable, it is on his Decca recordings that Estes tells his most gripping stories and, particularly when partnered by Hammie Nixon, makes his most affecting music. Nixon is the nightingale of blues harmonica and his parallel melodies echoing Estes's singing on 'Someday Baby Blues' and 'Drop Down Mama', to mention just the most famous of their duets, are beautiful in their understated melancholy. The contrast of curt guitar chording and fine-tooled harmonica lines produces music that swings even at the slowest tempos, and on high-speed stomps like 'Stop That Thing' races to the finishing-line with thoroughbred zest.

In these recordings from the second half of the '30s, notably in 'Down South Blues' and 'Hobo Jungle Blues', Estes is one of the blues' most explicit documentarians of the Depression. But he was not inspired only by the extraordinary events of his time. It was his particular skill to depict in his blues the necessary daily negotiations of black life in a white-owned South. 'I play for the colored, I play for the whole, All you got to do, act kinda nice,' he explains in 'Clean Up At Home'. His hometown stories about Martha Hardin, whose house burns down in 'Fire Department Blues', or the new public school he welcomes in 'Working Man Blues' ('I think that's very nice: the children can go in the day, old folks have it at night'), are balanced by what it doesn't seem inappropriate to call, by analogy with the practice of West African *griots*, praise-songs, typically about local white men like the subject of 'Lawyer Clark Blues': 'He said if I just stay out of the grave, he'd see that I won't go to the pen.'

The Documents, as usual, claim to be complete: well, yes and no. Vol. 1 includes four of the Estes–Rachell Victors on which Rachell is the only singer, yet *Vol. 2* excludes the three tracks by The Delta Boys (Estes, Son Bonds and Raymond Thomas) on which Bonds sings the lead. *Vol. 1* suffers from poor transfers and low-level mastering. The Classic Blues 2CD, a Document production, shows a considerable improvement in sound quality and with 36 tracks and a low price offers excellent value. The Frémeaux also has 36 tracks, 24 in common with the Classic Blues set. Better than either is the Yazoo, which is well chosen, including all but one of the songs singled out above and avoiding the unsatisfactory 1940 session with Robert Lee McCoy, and typically well remastered.

The Wolf Blues Classics, EPM Blues Collection and Snapper Complete Blues sets, each on its own a deserving collection, duplicate each other very extensively. The Fabulous CD is also a good selection, and inexpensive, but poorly presented and with some bad transfers. *Tennessee Blues* is a pointless double-hander of 12 tracks by Estes and ten by Bukka White, who spent the most creative part of his life in Mississippi anyway. The JSP confines itself to the Victor recordings, together with four contemporaneous sides by Rachell and seven by Noah Lewis, but the transfers are outstandingly good. Readers who are not seduced by that consideration may yield to the charms of this inexpensive 2CD anyway, since the other disc contains the complete Victor output of Gus Cannon's Jug Stompers.

*** The Legend Of Sleepy John Estes
Delmark DD-603 *Estes; Hammie Nixon (h); John 'Knocky' Parker(p); Ed Wilkinson (b).* 3–6/62.
*** Brownsville Blues
Delmark DD-613 *As above, except add Yank Rachell (g), Ransom Knowling (b); omit Parker.* 3/62–2/65.
**(*) Goin' To Brownsville
Testament TCD 6008 *Estes.* 4/62.

Learning of Estes's unsuspected survival, Bob Koester was quick to get him into a studio, and after a couple of sessions was in a position to surprise and delight blues enthusiasts with *The Legend Of Sleepy John Estes*. As he would prove to do on all his latterday albums, Estes drew extensively on the portfolio of his earlier recordings, though this was not always recognized at the time: he had cut 'I'd Been Well Warned' in 1948 (as 'Stone Blind') and 'Rats In My Kitchen' in 1952, but neither recording had yet come to discographers' notice. Though age had coarsened his voice a little, he was able to recapture the momentum of 'Milk Cow Blues' playing on his own, and of 'Drop Down Mama' with Nixon at his elbow, before leading the quartet at a romping tempo through 'Stop That Thing'.

The four solo tracks on *The Legend* were only part of a larger session, as was revealed by *Brownsville Blues*, in particular in its expanded form on CD. But solo performance is not the point of this second album: its focus is on Estes as an oral historian. Brownsville lies at the heart of his work like Yoknapatawpha County in Faulkner's or Lubbock, Texas, in Terry Allen's, and the album is a scrapbook of its characters, some, like auto repairman Vassie Williams, familiar from earlier sightings, others newly added like the lawyer Pat Mann or the policeman 'Mr Buddy' and 'Mr Hunter' in 'City Hall Blues'. The bareness and simplicity of Estes's performance only serve to draw the listener closer to these small stories of small-town life.

The Testament CD, recorded a month after Estes's first session for Delmark and then archived for 36 years, contains a few songs he seldom or never recorded elsewhere, such as 'Sweet Sugar Mama' and Big Bill Broonzy's 'Just A Dream' (as 'It Was A Dream'), and three gospel songs, including 'I'm Goin' Home', which he had recorded on *Brownsville Blues* as 'God Can Use Me'. It is a long (73.26) and diffuse album whose accessibility is somewhat diminished by the absence of any accompaniment but Estes's guitar.

*** Broke And Hungry
Delmark DD-608 *Estes; Hammie Nixon (h); Yank Rachell (md, g); Mike Bloomfield (g).* 3/64.
*** Newport Blues
Delmark DE-639 *Estes; Hammie Nixon (h, j, v); Yank Rachell (p, md, g, v).* 7/64.
*** Blues Live!
Storyville STCD 8051 *Estes; Hammie Nixon (h, j).* 10/64.
**(*) In Europe
Delmark DD-611 *As above.* 10/64.

The Estes of these albums is the artist who captivated European audiences in the '60s. *Broke And Hungry* was his first studio reunion with Yank Rachell, whose mandolin and spoken asides on the opening title track immediately establish a mood of good humour and fellowship. Fattened by Nixon's harmonica and, on four tracks, second guitar by Mike Bloomfield, the ensemble playing is the busiest to be heard on Estes's later recordings, and it would have been even better had Rachell kept his mandolin in tune. 'Olie Blues', which features bravura guitar playing by Rachell, is a fresh entry in Estes's songlist, as are 'Electric Chair' and Arthur Crudup's 'So Glad I'm Livin". 'Sleepy John's Twist' is a lyric for the present set to a tune from the past, 'Liquor Store Blues'.

Newport Blues was recorded on the way home from the 1964 Newport Folk Festival but not issued until 2002. Even at that stage a couple of pieces could be noted as additions to Estes's known repertoire ('Newport Blues' and a 'BK Blues' for Bob Koester), and besides there were features for his companions, Nixon singing 'NYC Breakdown', 'Worried Mind Blues' and 'Poor Mother's Child' and Rachell 'New Doorbell Ring'. Even more unexpectedly, Rachell plays piano on the latter two tracks. Koester comments: 'John's mood was so buoyant we were dealing with a different personality.'

In Europe was studio-recorded in Copenhagen and London during Estes's first trip overseas, with the 1964 AFBF. He gestures politely to new friends, rewriting 'Liquor Store Blues' as 'Denmark Blues' for Karl Knudsen of Storyville Records, which issued *In Europe* in Europe, and referring in 'I Stayed Away Too Long' to Paul and Valerie Oliver. The long and previously unissued 'Blues For JFK', Estes's post-assassination rewrite of 'I Stayed Away Too Long', was added to the CD reissue. The seven tracks on *Blues Live!* were recorded in a Copenhagen folk club the day before the studio session and some of the performances are more vigorous. 'Mountain Cat Blues' is a retitled 'Rats In My Kitchen'. The remainder of the CD is by the singer/guitarist John Henry Barbee, taped on the same occasion.

**(*) Electric Sleep
Delmark DD-619 *Estes; Carey Bell (h, b); Sunnyland Slim (p); Jimmy Dawkins (g); Earl Hooker, Joe Harper (b); Odie Payne Jr (d).* 12/68.

The title was Delmark's little joke. Muddy Waters had

recently made a gesture to the youth market with his supposedly psychedelic album *Electric Mud*, and now here was the venerable John Estes treading the same flower-strewn path. In fact part of the joke was that his collaborators, unlike those of Waters, simply played in the prevailing Chicago blues-band idiom. So, no turn-on, but a tune-in would have been a good idea – Dawkins is off-key, sometimes blatantly, for much of the two-day session – and as for dropouts, Bell's harmonica is absent on seven of the 13 tracks, thus removing the responsorial voice that in Estes's music is almost always an enhancement. 'Sweet Little Flower' appears to be a new entry in his portfolio, but the puzzlingly titled 'Newport Blues' (not the same as the title song of *Newport Blues* above) is the same commemorative piece as 'Blues For JFK' on *In Europe*.

*** Mississippi Delta Blues Jam In Memphis, Vol. 2
Arhoolie CD 386 *Estes; Tommy Garry (h); Mike Stewart (g). 6/69.*

Estes's segment of an album recorded at the Memphis Blues Festival and shared with Nathan Beauregard and Booker White is succinct performances of 'Need More Blues', 'Little Laura', 'Rats' (i.e. 'Rats In My Kitchen') and 'President Kennedy Stayed Away Too Long' (i.e. 'Blues For JFK') – all songs he had recorded several times before, but vigorously propelled by Stewart's guitar and Garry's very Nixon-like harmonica. They were not his last sides – he continued to record into the '70s – but as the latest currently available on CD they are a worthy chapter-ending to the career of a profoundly singular creative artist. TR

David Evans (born 1944)
VOCAL, GUITAR, KAZOO

Raised in Massachusetts, Evans graduated in Classics from Harvard before doing fieldwork in the South between 1965 and 1973, and earning postgraduate degrees in Folklore at UCLA. He has directed the Ethnomusicology programme at the University of Memphis since 1978. Evans's field recordings and writings on blues constitute a very significant body of research and interpretation. As a musician, he has worked solo and with African-American artists, and has led the Last Chance Jug Band since 1989.

*** Shake That Thing!
Inside Memphis ISC-0501 *Evans; Jobie Kilzer (h, j); Dick Raichelson (p); Richard Graham (b, wb, perc, j); Tom Janzen (d). 97.*

Shake That Thing! is by the Last Chance Jug Band, who maintain the good-time ethos of the old Memphis groups, but play through amplifiers and feature a prominent drummer. This 'power jugband' lineup brings new perspectives to songs as well known as 'Kansas City Blues' and 'Mister Crump', rescuing them from fossilized familiarity. The revisionism isn't always successful; Evans sometimes has to bellow to be heard, and replacing Charlie Pickett's erotic intimacy with bluster on 'Let Me Squeeze Your Lemon' was a serious mistake. Nevertheless, there is much to enjoy, from the rowdy 'Who Pumped The Wind In My Doughnut?' to the spiritual 'Time Is Winding Up', which gets a makeover of Pentecostal power.

**** Match Box Blues
Inside Memphis ISC-0514 *Evans; Jobie Kilzer (h); Dick Raichelson (p); Amy Adcock (b, tamb); Jack Adcock (wb, perc, j). 5/01.*

Members of the jugband assist here, but the lineups vary from solo to the full ensemble, and the acoustic, drumless format is a better setting for Evans's hollering vocals and versatile playing. Evans creates his songs in the same way as the folk-blues singers discussed in his book *Big Road Blues*: by combining musical and lyrical elements, both original and acquired from others, to make something new. 'Match Box Blues', for example, is not a painstaking copy of the original, but a medley of Jeffersonian verses and licks, incorporating ideas learned from Roosevelt Holts during fieldwork. Evans has the advantage of having learned many songs, and much of his guitar technique, from traditional blues singers at first hand. His understanding of the rhythms and dynamics of their music was no doubt hard-won, but its expression is intuitive and personal, and he is a subtle, idiomatic performer. CS

Joe Evans & Arthur McClain
DUET

These versatile musicians were from east Tennessee and may have formed part of a circle of players in the Knoxville area that included Carl Martin and Howard Armstrong (and later Lesley Riddle and Brownie McGhee).

***(*) Two Poor Boys (1927–1931)
Document DOCD-5044 *Evans, McClain (g, v); one or the other (p, vn, md, k). 7/27–5/31.*

The interrelationship of black and white musics in the South is sharply illuminated by the work of The Two Poor Boys, as Evans and McClain were billed on some of their discs. They recorded a single issued piece in 1927, the pop song 'Little Son Of A Gun'. All their other recordings were made at a two-day session in 1931. The common-stock pieces 'John Henry Blues', 'Old Hen Cackle' and 'Sourwood Mountain' are accompanied on mandolin and guitar, the former played with great vivacity; these performances might be regarded as African-American previews of bluegrass. Amidst these and other pieces in the same vein are a sheaf of blues with piano-and-guitar or two-guitar accompaniment. Who played what on these – and their other – recordings is a matter for speculation, but it seems likely that the blues singer here is Evans. 'Mill Man Blues' and 'My Baby Got A Yo-Yo' have melodic and textual links with songs recorded by Carl Martin and the obscure singer/guitarist Billy Bird, suggesting that Bird, like the others, was from east Tennessee. (Some would say that Bird *was* Evans or McClain; readers interested in testing that theory can find his recordings on *Rare Country Blues – Vol. 3* [Document DOCD-5642].) 'Down In Black Bottom', by contrast, sounds as if it was brewed in Alabama by someone like Jabo Williams.

As if all this flexibility were not enough, the duo return to the guitar-and-kazoo sound of their first record with 'Take A Look At That Baby' (a flapper-era pop song, published as 'What Do I Care What Somebody Said?'), carbon-copy the Mississippi Sheiks' 'Sitting On Top Of The World', resuscitate a 'coon' song of the Bert Williams era ('Georgia Rose') and deliver, in the funereal 'New Huntsville Jail', what must be a parody of the contemporary hillbilly hit 'Birmingham Jail'. For 'effortless eclecticism', as Chris Smith calls it in his notes, The Two Poor Boys are unmatched in the recording logs of their time. TR

Leo (Lucky Lopez) Evans (born 1937)
VOCAL, GUITAR

Evans was born in a small town near Hattiesburg, Mississippi, spent part of his youth in Milwaukee, and in the '60s moved to Chicago, where he played with Howlin' Wolf and other artists. He has also worked in California and Madison, Wisconsin. He was last reported, some years ago, back in Milwaukee.

Evans has hardly been lucky in his recording career. Other than the album described below, his only available track is 'Coming Down With The Blues', recorded about 1966/67 and included in the VAC *Sweet Home Chicago* (Delmark DD-618).

**(*) Southside Saturday Night
JSP JSPCD 2142 *Evans; Jack Hills (kb, o, p); Richard Studholme (g); Henry Thomas, Mark Clements (b); John Webster, Luce Langrider (d). 11/89–4/90.*

Evans's biting guitar and an echo-filled studio ambience give this recording the sort of raw power one associates with artists like Byther Smith or Magic Slim. His voice, too, though it's sometimes too far down in the mix, has a gripping earnestness. Altogether it's an album that can cast quite a spell – the more so if you simply absorb its mood rather than pay close attention to the songs, which tend to to be inchoate and repetitive. 'Good Lovings' has a strong punchline – 'If you walk out of my life, I hope you fall and break your neck' – but in the course of nearly eight minutes Evans wears it out with overuse, and other numbers like 'Extra Extra', a remake of 'Coming Down With The Blues' (see above), similarly work their good lines too hard. The best song, not Evans's, is 'Pay Check', which is presented in both studio and live versions. TR

Will Ezell (1892–1963)
VOCAL, PIANO

Texas-born, Ezell played in jukes around Shreveport before moving north to Detroit and Chicago. He was a frequent accompanist for Paramount, and took Blind Lemon Jefferson's body back to Texas for burial. Ezell disappeared from view after his last recording session, but over 30 years later his death certificate listed his occupation as 'musician'.

**(*) Will Ezell (1927–1931)
RST Blues Documents BDCD-6033 *Ezell; Dave Nelson, Baby Jay (c); Blind Roosevelt Graves (g); Uaroy Graves (tamb); Marie Bradley, Ora Brown, Bertha Henderson, Sam 'Slim' Tarpley (v). c. 2/27–c. 1/31.*

Will Ezell was mainly an instrumentalist, singing (perfectly respectably) on only five of the 16 sides issued under his name. His pianism traces an interesting course from ragtime, through early use of walking basses, to confident handling of boogie woogie. Ezell took to newer idioms with ease: the boogie of 'Playing The Dozen' was recorded at the same session as his ragtime masterpiece, the wonderfully titled 'Bucket Of Blood'. The CD's highlight is a four-title session with the Graves brothers and Baby Jay, including the marvellously springy 'Pitchin' Boogie' and a 'Hot Spot Stuff' that jumps on the black bottom bandwagon. (Other titles by this team are on *Blind Roosevelt Graves* [Document DOCD-5105].) In the end, though, Ezell is easier to admire than to like. It's not his fault, but it doesn't help, that he recorded exclusively for famously lo-fi Paramount, and that the CD starts with a batch of accompaniments to undistinguished chanteuses and ends with two dull comic songs by Tarpley. CS

Fabulous Thunderbirds
GROUP

Texas's best-known blues band was founded by guitarist Jimmie Vaughan and harmonica player Kim Wilson in 1974 with bassist Keith Ferguson, drummer Mike Buck and, briefly, singer Lou Ann Barton. Based in Austin, they were the house band at the city's prime blues club, Antone's. After four albums for Chrysalis they signed with Epic and charted in 1986 with 'Tuff Enuff' and 'Wrap It Up', and subsequently with the album Tuff Enuff. *Vaughan left the band in 1989 and was replaced by Duke Robillard. After a quiet period in the early '90s, Wilson reassembled the group in late 1994 with Gene Taylor and Kid Ramos. The current lineup includes guitarists Kirk Fletcher and Nick Curran.*

*** Girls Go Wild
Benchmark 8002 *Kim Wilson (h, v); Jimmie Vaughan (g, v); Keith Ferguson (b); Mike Buck (d). 79.*
*** What's The Word?
Benchmark 8003 *As above. 80.*
**(*) Butt Rockin'
Benchmark 8004 *As above, except add Greg Piccolo (ts), Doug James (bs), Al Copley (p). 81.*
*** T-Bird Rhythm
Benchmark 8005 *Kim Wilson (h, v); Jimmie Vaughan (g, v); Keith Ferguson (b); Fran Christina (d). 82.*
*** Tacos Deluxe
Benchmark 8001 *As for above four CDs. 79–82.*
*** Collection
Disky DC 886092 *As above. 79–82.*

The Fab Ts' first album – originally issued on Takoma and titled *The Fabulous Thunderbirds*, later acquired by Chrysalis and renamed *Girls Go Wild* – announced the arrival of a tight, club-seasoned blues band with roots deep in Southern blues styles of the '60s, as witnessed by cuts like Jerry McCain's 'She's Tuff' and Slim Harpo's 'Baby Scratch My Back'. They maintained their exciting twin thrust of drive and economy (it was a rare number that went beyond four minutes) on the three albums that followed. *What's The Word?* gave more exposure to Kim Wilson's songwriting, which would later be one of the band's chief strengths but at this point was fairly conventional, not to say derivative: 'Learn To Treat Me Right', for instance, runs smoothly on the wheels of a Jimmy Reed-type melody, while 'I Believe I'm In Love' (*Butt Rockin'*) and 'Can't Tear It Up Enuff' (*T-Bird Rhythm*) are set in well-worn rockabilly grooves. But as a makeover of the 'swamp blues' of Slim Harpo, Lightnin' Slim and Lazy Lester, touched up with dabs of rock 'n' roll, the music of the Fab Ts was a winsome styling of the blues for the early '80s.

The first four Benchmarks are reissues of the Chrysalis albums; *Girls Go Wild* and *Butt Rockin'* each have three bonus tracks and *What's The Word?* four, three of them live. Readers who don't need a complete account of the period could be very happy with Disky's packed but inexpensive *Collection*, which crams in six tracks from *Girls Go Wild*, nine from *What's The Word?*, six from *Butt Rockin'* and four from *T-Bird Rhythm*. *Tacos Deluxe* is a slighter compilation, containing 11 tracks from the four original albums (of which all but two are also on Disky) and two live bonus tracks.

*** Tuff Enuff
Epic ZK 40304 *Kim Wilson (h, v); Geraint Watkins (ac, p); Al Copley (kb); Chuck Leavell (p); Jimmie Vaughan (sg, g, b, v); Preston Hubbard (b, v); Fran Christina (d, v); Cesar Rosas, David Hidalgo (v).* 86.

**(*) Hot Number
Epic ZK 40818//(E) 450949 *Wayne Jackson (t); Jack Hale (tb); Andrew Love (ts); Jim Horn (bs); Kim Wilson (h, v); Chuck Leavell (kb); Jimmie Vaughan (g, b, v); Dave Edmunds (g, v); Preston Hubbard (b, v); Fran Christina (d, v).* 87.

** Powerful Stuff
Epic 45094//(E) 463382 *Similar to above.* 89.

*** Walk That Walk, Talk That Talk
Epic 47878//(E) 468524 *Kim Wilson (h, v); Duke Robillard, Kid Bangham (g); Preston Hubbard (b); Fran Christina (d).* 91.

*** Hot Stuff – The Greatest Hits
Epic 53007//(E) 472226 *As for above four CDs.* 85/86–12/91.

A common judgement of the Fab Ts' Epic period is that it began well with *Tuff Enuff* – can't argue with success, right? – but *Hot Number* and *Powerful Stuff* were disappointingly submissive to the aesthetic of mainstream rock. Hindsight nudges us to reconsider that reading. *Powerful Stuff* certainly has too much rock pomp-and-circumstance for its own good, but even in *Tuff Enuff* there were signs of the music being, if not actually dumbed down, at least written in big letters with hyphens in the dif-fic-ult words: melodramatic soundscaping, crashing drums. According to this interpretation, *Hot Number* is a better album than was thought at the time, notably in the contribution of Kim Wilson, who wrote most of its material and sings pieces like 'Stand Back', with its neat arrangement for the Memphis Horns, and 'How Do You Spell Love' with huge vigour. *Walk That Walk* is a separate case, since it was the band's first album after the departure of Jimmie Vaughan; the claim that it took two men to fill his place makes glib copy but fails to acknowledge that Duke Robillard and Kid Bangham created a quite different and very effective sound with their fat two-guitar lines, for instance in Bo Diddley's 'You Can't Judge A Book By Its Cover'. *Hot Stuff* is a somewhat skimpy 'best of', drawing five of its 11 tracks from *Tuff Enuff* and a couple from each of the others.

**(*) Roll Of The Dice
Private Music 82130 *Kim Wilson (h, v); Gene Taylor (kb); Leon Pendarvis, Ron Russell (o); David Grissom, Kid Ramos, Danny Kortchmar (g); Steve Jordan (b, d, perc); Harvey Brooks (b); Fran Christina (d); Babi Floyd (v).* 95.

***(*) High Water
High Street 10357 *Kim Wilson (h, g, v); Daniel Kortchmar (kb, o, p, g, v); Steve Jordan (o, g, b, d, perc, v).* 97.

There are memorable passages on *Roll Of The Dice*, like 'Takin' It Too Easy', deftly pinned to the frame of 'Catfish Blues', and the swamp stomper 'Do As I Say', where harmonica and keyboards interact to create the effect of a Cajun accordion, but several tracks are weighed down by the blustering overstatement that marred some of the Epic work.

How invigorating, then, to move to *High Water*, where a spartan mix of harmonica, guitar and drums recalls the Memphis sound of the late '40s that blueprinted the next decade's developments in Chicago. Yet without archival rummaging, and using entirely new material, Wilson, Kortchmar and Jordan conjure in tracks like 'Hand To Mouth' and 'That's All I Need To Know' the lean, terse music of the young Howlin' Wolf or Junior Parker. The title cut shifts the timeline a few years further on, having a delicious flavour of the young Otis Redding.

*** Live
Sanctuary SANCD 116 *Lee Thornburg (t); Jeff Turmes, Steven Marsh (s); Kim Wilson (h, v); Gene Taylor (kb); Dave Mathews (o); Kid Ramos (g); Willie Campbell (b); Steve Hodges (d); Mindy Stein, Valerie Pinkston (v).* 2/00.

The Fab Ts' only currently available live album is a typically forthright performance (also captured on DVD) with an untypically self-effacing choice of material: just three Kim Wilson compositions, all from way back, and 11 from the blues library. Readers who enjoy relentlessly full-on blues action will find this very much to their taste; others may wish that the variety of the band's sources, among them Magic Sam, T-Bone Walker, Bo Diddley and Smiley Lewis, was matched by more shifts in approach and dynamic level and not so often obscured by pervasively high-energy playing. Wilson has a bravura solo harmonica passage in B. B. King's 'Early Every Morning'.

*** Painted On
Artemis/Tone-Cool 51633//Artemis-Tone–Cool/Rykodisc RCD 17311 *Brian Swartz (t); Lon Price (ts); Terry Landry (bs); Steve Berlin (s, kb, perc, prod); Kim Wilson (h, v); Gene Taylor (p); Nick Curran (g, v); Kirk Eli Fletcher (g); Ronnie James Weber (b); Jimi Bott (d); Rachel Nagy (v).* 11–12/04.

With guitarists Fletcher and Curran out in front, the latest lineup of the Fab Ts has a fatter sound than any of its forerunners, but it's the fatness of solid muscle, which they show off with the pride of bodybuilders in romp 'n' stomp numbers like 'Get To Get Out', 'Two-Time Fool', 'Only Daddy That'll Walk The Line' and 'You Torture Me'. After 30 years' trading, this looks like a brand that will go on selling as long as Kim Wilson cares to market it. TR

Famous Hokum Boys
GROUP

Once it was realized that there was an African-American market for records, it was rapidly subjected to market research, and the Famous Hokum Boys were one result. Not to be confused with the Hokum Boys, the group only existed in the recording studios.

(***) Famous Hokum Boys – Vol. 1 (1930)
Wolf WBCD-011 *Georgia Tom [Dorsey] (p, v); Big Bill Broonzy (vn, g, v); Frank Brasswell, Bill Williams [Arthur Petties] (g, v); Hannah May [Mozelle Alderson] (v).* 4–9/30.

*** Famous Hokum Boys – Vol. 2 (1930–1931)
Wolf WBCD-012 *Similar to above.* 9/30–1/31.

Vol. 1 is characterized by varyingly worn copies, and remastering that is no more than dutiful. As ever with hokum, the songs treat largely of 'it', 'that thing' and 'that stuff', and their nudging humour inevitably palls when heard at a length that was never intended. Against these negatives must be weighed the driving, skintight exuberance of guitar duets like 'Black Cat Rag' and 'Saturday Night Rub'; nor should Georgia Tom's sprightly piano playing be overlooked.

Originals and transfers on *Vol. 2* are generally better, although 'Alabama Scratch' is inadvertently well named. Mozelle Alderson, who debuts towards the end of the first disc, is heard on most tracks, now as Jane Lucas, and her breezy chirping adds an enlivening sexual frisson; she can also do a very convincing drunken partygoer. *Vol. 2* opens an entertaining window on vanished ghetto worlds: the bad gin, chittlins and dance crazes of the rent party, the bad puns and bewhiskered crosstalk routines of burlesque. Occasionally, the humour is interrupted by the sober realism of 'Rent Man Blues' and 'Double Trouble Blues', but the CD is most memorable for Georgia Tom, lasciviously prospecting in Lucas's anatomy on 'Terrible Operation Blues', and for the consistent brilliance of the guitar players. On balance, the talent deployed makes the repetitive innuendo which it serves endurable. CS

Johnny Farmer (born 1932)
VOCAL, GUITAR

Fat Possum's crusade to counteract the insidious progress of showbiz blues continues with bulldozer-driver Farmer, who is quoted as saying, 'I don't want to make no record; that's not what I do.'

*(*) Wrong Doers Respect Me
Fat Possum 0321 *Farmer*. 98.

Farmer taught himself to play guitar by listening to his favourite records, and his grasp of slide technique is what you'd expect from a 'dozer driver. Most of these records seem to have been made by Muddy Waters, for the opening three tracks are approximations of 'Burying Ground', 'Rolling Stone' and 'Feel Like Goin' Home'. 'I Can't Be Satisfied', 'Deep Down In Florida' and 'Screamin' And Cryin'' turn up later, along with an 'It Hurts Me' which usually has 'Too' appended. A serious lack of teeth adds character to Farmer's vocals and it's possible – just – to indulge the vagaries of his piratical slide wielding. 'Lonely Road', played finger-style, bears some hallmarks of originality but it's a lonely distinction. His lack of a desire to record is honest and there's cause to doubt the record company's intentions in making him do so. NS

Deitra Farr (born 1957)
VOCAL

Farr took up music seriously after graduating from college, sitting in with Chicago veterans on club appearances. She was a member of Mississippi Heat from 1993 to 1996.

**(*) The Search Is Over
JSP CD 284 Farr; Peter Bartels (t); Will Redding (tb, v); Rodney 'Hot Rod' Brown (ts); Roosevelt 'Mad Hatter' Purifoy (kb); Johnny Rawls (g, v); Harlan Terson (b); Allen Kirk (d, v). 97.
***(*) Let It Go!
JSP JSP 5105 Farr; Peter Bartels (t); Johnny 'Showtime' Janowiak (tb); Rodney 'Hot Rod' Brown (ts); Matthew Skoller (h); Roosevelt 'Mad Hatter' Purifoy (kb); Billy Flynn (g); Willie 'Vamp' Samuels (b, v); James E. Knowles (d); Ardella Williams (v). 05.

Farr's husky contralto makes a welcome change from the in-your-face assertiveness that Koko Taylor's dominance has made normative among women blues singers; on *The Search Is Over* she's tastefully complemented by Johnny Rawls's crisp guitar lines, and by horn arrangements that owe much to Stax circa 1967. A pedant would point out (and the notes are extensively pre-emptive about it) that the content is mostly soul with a blue tinge. Most listeners will not find this a problem, but they may feel that the songs, all by Farr or Rawls, are rather similar, and that some of them are too long. 'Waiting For The Blues', in particular, leads one to ask, in the title of another track, 'How Much Longer'? Music with gospel roots, and gospel's use of repetition, needs to make more assiduous use of variation and climax.

The long interval between *The Search Is Over* and *Let It Go!* seems to have been profitably used. Farr composed all the songs, which feature intelligent, original lyrics that don't shy away from the messy, complex nature of real-world relationships, and get thoughtful, individualized readings; 'In A Dark Place', about depression, is an especially striking match of words, voice and a very tight band. The jazz singing on 'A Week From Today' feels imposed rather than intuitive, and Flynn's guitar could have done with a bit less polish, but this is far better than the assembly-line raunch churned out by most female blues singers. Audiophiles get not only the SACD option, but also ten of the 12 songs remixed in Surround Sound on a separate layer. CS

H-Bomb Ferguson (born 1929)
VOCAL, PIANO

Robert Ferguson says that he began playing piano as a child in his father's storefront church in Charleston, South Carolina. At 18 he went on the road with Joe Liggins & The Honeydrippers. In the '50s he recorded raucous singles for Savoy and other New York labels and toured with Wynonie Harris, whom he idolized. In the rock 'n' roll era he moved to Cincinnati and worked locally. He more or less retired in the early '70s but returned to the business a decade or so later with some new songs (a couple of which won Handy Awards) and a bunch of improbable wigs.

There's little in catalogue from Ferguson's glory days. Two unissued sides from a 1953 session were exhumed on *Shouting The Blues* (Specialty SPCD-7028//Ace CDCHD 439), and proved to have been cut from a roll of Wynonie Harris Tweed.

**(*) Wiggin' Out
Earwig 4926 Ferguson; Eric Neuhausser (s); Matthew Skoller (h); Marty Charters (g); John Smith (b); Keenath Malachi Williams (d, v). 2/93.

Exposed to Ferguson for the first time on this album, a listener might well be puzzled about where he hails from: if 'My Brown Frame Baby' signals a devotee of the Wynonie Harris approach, the chattering rhythms of 'Shake Your Apple Tree', 'Meatloaf' or 'Ha Ha Ha, I Don't Want You No More' are signposts to New Orleans. Ferguson's voice is grainy with age and his piano playing rather clumping, but a robust, enthusiastic band steers him knowingly through an amiable programme of original numbers and, no longer able to

Thomas 'Big Hat' Fields (born 1950)
VOCAL, ACCORDION

Fields played rubboard as a child, but only took up the diatonic accordion in 1993, learning from an older, retired player, Paul Harris. His motivation was to exploit the out-of-state market for live dance music, but he soon became well-liked at home too.

*** Louisiana Zydeco Man
Maison de Soul MdS-1073 Fields; Andrew Donaldson (g, v); Geneva Fields (b, v); Martin Guilbeu (d); Paulo Edwards (rb). 98.

*** Big Hat Zydeco Mix
Maison de Soul MDS-1081 Fields; Curnis Andrus (ts); Jean Pierre Audel (h, rb); Marty Christian (g, v); Geneva Mouton (b, v); Joseph Edwards (d); Rodney Bernard (rb, v). 1/04.

The spirit of Boozoo Chavis presides closely over *Louisiana Zydeco Man*, generally in the no-frills delivery and specifically in a not very successful 'Took The Paper From His Shoe'. *Louisiana Zydeco Man* takes more note than *Big Hat Zydeco Mix* of *nouveau zydeco*'s power-chord approach, but both are enjoyably retro in manner and content, with a significantly higher French quotient than is usual these days. Both also feature splendid rhythm sections in which Geneva (Mrs Thomas) Fields's chuckling bass guitar is a constant. Her soulful tenor voice is another welcome feature, especially on *Louisiana Zydeco Man*, where her husband too often chooses keys that take his voice into its lowest register, limiting it to a near-monotone: think Tex Ritter with an accordion. Fields does this less often and with more control on *Big Hat Zydeco Mix*, which is also improved by the richer textures made possible by the inclusion of a tenor sax. Additionally, Fields's accordion playing is less derivative and the engineering more vibrant. Marty 'White Boy' Christian (so billed in the notes!) closes the CD with an engaging zydebilly take on J. B. Lenoir's 'Talk To Your Daughter'. CS

The Fieldstones
GROUP

The Fieldstones were formed in 1974 by musicians who had played in bands led by keyboard player Leroy Hodges, who died in that year. Health problems led to a break-up in the early '90s, and some members have since died, but after *Memphis Blues Today!* was reissued as a CD in 1997, Carnes revived the band with the survivors; they continue to perform around Memphis.

**(*) Memphis Blues Today!
High Water HMG 6505 Bobby Carnes (o, p); Willie Roy Sanders (g, v); Wordie Perkins (g); Lois Brown (b); Joe Hicks (d, v). 3/81–7/82.

***(*) Mud Island Blues
High Water HMG 6519 As above, except add Wordie Perkins (p), Clarence Nelson (g), Little Applewhite (v). 3/81–8/83.

The Fieldstones' performances at Green's Lounge and the J & J are the stuff of legend, but they often sound bland on *Memphis Blues Today!* Joe Hicks is a propulsive drummer, and the fat and funky bass of Lois Brown is admirable, but the suggestion that the guitarists are heirs of the Memphis twin-guitar sound of Stokes and Sane or Kansas Joe and Memphis Minnie is excessive: Perkins and Sanders play conventional lead and rhythm, occasionally switching roles. Bobby Carnes plays chordal fills which are generally discreet to the point of inaudibility. As might be expected of a bar band, the material mixes covers of recently popular songs with dance tunes, and a leavening of older pieces like 'Short Haired Woman' and 'Saddle My Pony'. Hicks is the better of the two vocalists, relaxed, expressive and, as befits a singing drummer, swinging; Sanders is enthused by the power of gospel-influenced vocalists like B. B. King and Roy Brown, but too often he arbitrarily imposes that sound on the lyrics. See his entry for a CD released under his name in 1999.

Not released until 2005, *Mud Island Blues* is altogether better, once turned up far enough to overcome the low recording level. Sanders revives 'Cross Cut Saw' from his days with the Binghampton Blues Boys and Hicks covers Albert King effectively, but tradition-based songs and strong originals predominate. Carnes is more audible here, but most of the improvement stems from the presence of the late Clarence Nelson on most tracks, and of Little Applewhite on four. Nelson was a busy gigging and studio guitarist, and his ideas and technique are of a more sophisticated order than the rest of the band's. He plays lines that are sleek and jazzy but imbued with lowdown blues feeling, and even when there are three guitars present their interplay is purposeful and uncluttered. The controlled but passionate soulfulness of Applewhite's singing is perhaps what Sanders is aiming at; it's a target he hits to great effect on 'Old Woman From Downhome' and 'Old Black Mattie'. CS

Fillmore Slim (born 1935)
VOCAL, GUITAR

Clarence Sims moved from his native New Orleans to the West Coast in 1955; there he recorded a few singles, and claims to have opened for or worked with many big names when not pimping women. Slim concentrated on his musical skills while doing a five-year prison sentence, and after his release in 1985 became a regular at Troyce Key's Eli's Mile High Club in Oakland. Slim is probably still better known for his appearance in the documentary *American Pimp* (he no longer is one) than for his music.

*** Born To Sing The Blues
Mountain Top MTP-9803 Fillmore Slim; Carl Green (as); Bobby Spencer, Bobbie Webb (ts); Bernard Anderson (bs); Dave Wellhausen (h); Jim Pugh (o, p); Mark Naftalin (p); Frank Goldwasser (g, b); Carl Robinson, Troyce Key (g); Ted Butler, Charles Banks (b); Chris Daniels (d). 2/87.

Fillmore Slim claims that some hip-hop fans buy his CDs 'to have me autograph them. They don't play 'em; they put 'em on their walls so that can say they got O[riginal] G[angsta] Fillmore Slim ... They buy my music because of who I am.' It's hard to say whether their pride or his is more depressing, but the hip-hoppers are missing out on a rough-edged but competent singer and guitarist, who writes some interesting songs.

Born To Sing The Blues is an expanded remix of an LP recorded at Eli's Mile High Club (without an audience) and issued on an eponymous label. It's credited to Clarence

'Guitar' Sims, which may not help its marketing but has a certain appropriateness; the session took place not long after Slim's release from prison, and he does seem to have been trying to make it as a musician without trading much on his past as a pimp. The major influence, as may be inferred from the artist credit, is Johnny 'Guitar' Watson, and Slim's playing is tight, inventive and considerably more focused than on some later recordings. Troyce Key contributes a fine lead on two tracks, but apart from Slim's own determination, the main driver of the CD's success is the swinging drumming.

*** **Other Side Of The Road**
Fedora FCD 5016 *Fillmore Slim; Les Nunes (tb); Ron Catalano (ts); Hannsjoerg Scheid (kb, b); J. J. Malone (p); Frank Goldwasser (g); Jeff Henry (b); Chris Millar (d). 8/99.*
(*) **Funky Mama's House
Fedora FCD 5030 *Fillmore Slim; Tim Bird (ts); Terry McDonald (bs); Roger Perry (kb, g, b); Frank Goldwasser (g); Leonard Robinson (b); Chris Millar (d). 4/03.*

On *Other Side Of The Road*, Slim gets consistent support from the Fedora house band. Given his self-projection as an urban superfly, it's not surprising that 'Down On The Farm' looks disdainfully back at sharecropping; unfortunately Goldwasser's solo accompaniment to this song sounds like the pastiche it is, and lets down the evocative lyrics. This is not typical, however, and *Other Side Of The Road*, though no masterpiece, is worth hearing.

Funky Mama's House rather obviously packages Slim's outsider status for white consumption: it starts with four weak, underwritten songs, among them a 'Street Walker' that can only be characterized as hypocritical. Thereafter the standard improves, but there are too many calculated tribute songs, whether to clubs ('Tabby Thomas' Place', 'Down At Eli's') or musicians. 'Earl King' seems to be from the heart, though, and is far better sung than 'I Cross My Heart', dedicated to Buddy and Johnny Ace. 'Stagger Lee' gets a respectable reading, and the long 'Saturday Night' is a pungent one-chord recollection of country juke-joint carousal.

** **The Game**
Mountain Top MTP 69 *Fillmore Slim; Bobbie Webb (as, ts, bs); Gary Smith (h); Richard Younger (o, p); Frank Goldwasser, Leonard Gil (g, b); Steve Gannon (g, v); Rusty Zinn (g); John Haines (d); 'Frank Stick-Em' [Terrance Sims] (rap). 04.*

This CD relies even more heavily on the supposed glamour of 'The Game', a song which bookends the disc in rap and blues versions. The rhythmic trade-offs between Slim and his son on the rap version are whippy, but to enjoy it requires overlooking the vicious vacuity of lines like 'Mackin' ain't easy but someone's got to do it.' 'Playboy' and 'Mackin' are variants of 'The Game', and symptomatic of a general shortage of ideas. The rock 'n' roll of 'Big Brass Monkey', revived from a Dootone 45, bucks the trend engagingly, as does 'Texas Woman', one of the few tracks where Slim escapes narcissism, but elsewhere there's a parade of unimaginative guitar solos, and a heavy-handed drummer keeps the music earthbound. CS

Kirk 'Eli' Fletcher (born 1977)
GUITAR

From Compton, California, Fletcher first played guitar in his father's church, but was converted to blues by his brother playing him B. B. King's Live At The Regal. *His musical education was furthered by friends like Al Blake and Junior Watson, on whose tube amp sound he has modelled his own. He works regularly with Lynwood Slim and Kim Wilson, has recorded with Slim, Lisa Bourne and Frank Goldwasser, and visited Europe in 2000. He currently plays with the Fabulous Thunderbirds.*

*** **I'm Here And I'm Gone**
JSP JSPCD 2119 *Fletcher; Jonny Viau (ts, arr); Troy Jennings (bs, arr); Tom Mahon (p); Alex Schultz (g); Rick Reed (b); Paul Fasulo (d); Jackie Payne, John Marx (v); Jimmy Morello (arr, prod). 99?*

Whether working out with a brisk 'Church Street Boogie' or bench-pressing a heavyweight blues like 'I'm Not Your Fool', Fletcher is as fit and muscular a blues guitarist as may be heard anywhere. His measured, Otis Rush-like playing in 'Silver Spoon' is remarkably mature. Yet he comes out of nowhere – or Compton, which in blues terms is much the same thing. Guitar is all he offers: lacking either the confidence or the chops to sing too, he is assisted by a couple of more seasoned hands.

*** **Shades Of Blue**
Crosscut CCD 11076 *Fletcher; Kim Wilson (h, v); Red Young (o, p); Jeff Turmes (g, b); Ronnie James Weber (b); Kenny Sara, Richard Innes (d); Janiva Magness, Finis Tasby (v). 1–2/02.*
*** **Shades Of Blue**
Delta Groove DGPCD 101 *As above. 1–2/02.*

It's difficult for a non-singing guitarist to imprint individual character on a recording, and versatility can work against that end, giving an impression of skilful adaptability rather than singleness of artistic purpose. Fletcher leaves the listener in no doubt about his capability, doing a South Side stomp on 'Club Zanzibar' and a West Side flight on Magic Sam's 'That's Why I'm Cryin'', recalling the booming guitar of Lonesome Sundown's 'My Home Is A Prison' and weaving slinkily with Red Young's organ in 'The River's Invitation' and 'Blues For Boo Boo'. Wilson, as ever, is a good man to have riding pillion, and Tasby too is excellent. The US Delta Groove issue has two extra tracks and an alternative take of 'Club Zanzibar'. *Shades Of Blue* is a creditable album, but it's going to take more than this to thrust Fletcher into the spotlight. TR

Sue Foley (born 1968)
VOCAL, GUITAR

After some experience in bands in Ottawa (her birthplace) and Vancouver, Foley moved in the early '90s to Austin, Texas, and quickly established herself on the blues scene there.

*** **Young Girl Blues**
Antone's TMG-ANT 0019 *Foley; Kim Wilson (h); Denny Freeman, Reese Wynans (p); Derek O'Brien (g); Jon Penner, Sarah Brown (b); Robert Grant, George Rains (d). 92.*
*** **Without A Warning**
Antone's TMG-ANT 0025 *Foley; Riley Osbourn (o); Gene Taylor (p); Jon Penner (b); Freddie 'Pharaoh' Walden (d); Angela Strehli (v). 93.*
*** **Secret Weapon**
Antone's TMG-ANT 0050 *Foley; Kim Wilson (h); Jon Penner (b); Robert Grant, Freddie 'Pharaoh' Walden (d). 90–93.*

Much of her debut album consisted of genial versions of songs learned from Memphis Minnie, Tampa Red, Lightnin' Slim, Earl Hooker and others, but 'Gone Blind' and 'Time To Travel', original lyrics set to guitar parts that John Lee Hooker might have played 40 years earlier, served notice that Foley was more than a likeable interpreter with a decent record collection. *Without A Warning*, despite a higher percentage of nominally original material, is an almost equally blues-centred set, with quite a lot of fast guitar playing in the Magic Sam manner. *Secret Weapon* is a collection of outtakes from those albums: songs by Memphis Minnie and Bob Dylan, a pair of rocking Earl Hooker guitar numbers, 'The Leading Brand' and 'Guitar Rumba', and Joe Liggins's vaguely Latin, vaguely Hawaiian blues tune 'Tanya'. Less to be expected was a solo rendition of the venerable rag song 'Make Me A Pallet On Your Floor' and, from a session in 1990, 'Born Blind', a gutsy duet with Kim Wilson that summons up the ghosts of Muddy Waters and Little Walter.

(*) Big City Blues
Antone's TMG-ANT 0037 *Foley; Teddy Roddy (h); Craig Simicheck (o, p); Riley Osbourn (p); T. S. Bruton (md, g, v); Jon Penner, Chris Maresh (b); Freddie 'Pharaoh' Walden (d); Toni Price, Donna Pearl, Carla Campos, Amber July Morton, Della Luiese Price (v).* 94/95?

As a singer Foley makes no attempt to match the authenticity of accent she achieves in her guitar playing. If her feisty manner reminds the listener of anyone, it might well be Chrissie Hynde. It isn't a big voice, and in fast, noisy numbers like 'Howlin' For My Darlin'' or the less than successful Dylan cover 'If You Gotta Go' it risks being submerged. Fortunately she balances them with slow, caressing treatments of Willie Dixon's 'As Long As I Have You' and 'My Baby's Sweeter'. The closing 'Girl's Night Out' feels like a tribute to dumb-but-memorable guitar tunes of the '60s as played by, say, The Ventures.

(***) **Walk In The Sun**
Antone's TMG-ANT 0306 *Foley; Debra Peters (ac); Riley Osbourn (kb); Stephen Bruton (md, g); Jon Penner (b); Freddie Walden (d); Sarah Elizabeth Campbell, Larry Fulcher, Malford Milligan (v).* 96.

(***) **Ten Days In November**
Shanachie 8031 *Foley; Jeremy Baum (o, p); Jonathan Sanborn (b); Stuart Stahr (d); Joe Ferry (perc, handclaps).* 98.

It may have been coincidence that from time to time on *Walk In The Sun* Foley sounded like the then very much in-vogue Sheryl Crow. On the other hand, the broad range of the material, and the confidence she brought to it, encouraged one to think, yes, she might be being just that canny. Then again, the sneering inflection of 'Love Sick Child' and parts of 'Try To Understand' (the bits without the John Lee Hooker guitar riff) suggested a youthful infatuation, not yet quite shaken off, with Bob Dylan round about the time of *Blonde On Blonde*, and what could have been more unfashionable than that?

There were similar Dylanish touches, in both the style of the writing and the musical settings, on several tracks of *Ten Days In November*, such as 'Highwayside', 'Through The Night' or 'The Forest'. This was another all-original set ('Promised Land' is hers, not the Chuck Berry song), well done but not, except for the raggy guitar on 'New Roads', very blues-oriented.

*** **Love Comin' Down**
Shanachie 8036 *Foley; Mark Mullins (tb); Joe Cabral (s); Richard Bell, Ken Pearson (o, p); Colin Linden (Do, g, prod); Terry Wilkins, Richard Price (b); Miche Pouliot (d, perc); Bryan Owings (d); Anders Osborne, Sara Lenz, T. J. Littlefield (handclaps); Lucinda Williams (v).* 00.

(*) Where The Action Is
Shanachie SH 8038 *Foley; Richard Bell (kb, o, p); Colin Linden (Do, g, v, prod); Dave Roe, Mike Turenne, Brad Jones (b); Bryan Owings (d, perc); Tom Bona, Ken Coomer (d); Doug Ashby (v).* 02.

The sensual gaze that Foley levels at the prospective buyer from the box of *Love Comin' Down* is gently parodied by the faux-leopardskin rug she is stretched out on. The same ambivalence – is this body heat or a Madeline Kahn parody of it? – flickers like a loosely connected torchbeam across the landscape of this artfully lit album, falling now on the licking flames of 'Let Me Drive', now the glowing embers of 'Same Thing', now the cooling ashes of 'Empty Cup'. Foley exchanges the uncompromising blues outfits of her early albums for a larger wardrobe, Linden skilfully dressing the sets to match her subtler ensembles. But in the background one can still discern the dark-suited figures of John Lee Hooker and Lightnin' Hopkins, watchful and, one suspects, approving.

Where The Action Is shows that Foley has not only profited from a decade's experience of recording and songwriting, but has put in some work on her singing, which is now equal both to the varied demands of her material and to the sometimes strident ensemble sound, for instance on the Jagger–Richards 'Stupid Girl'. For listeners who require the regular sustenance of the blues, however, versions of Etta James's 'Roll With Me Henry' and Mattie Delaney's 'Down The Big Road Blues' may be too short commons.

*** **Change**
Ruf 1096 *Foley; Graham Guest (kb); Mike Turenne (b); Tom Bona (d).* 12/03.

This Toronto club gig is something of a throwback to Foley's early-'90s albums, with a repertoire strong in standard and original blues, all played on acoustic guitar, a few with no other accompaniment. Working without the safety net of studio improvement or retakes, she wobbles on the wire a few times, but the candour of her performance is very appealing. TR

Canray Fontenot (1922–95)
VOCAL, VIOLIN

Canray Fontenot's father, Nonc Adam, was a celebrated accordionist in his area of Louisiana. Canray made his first fiddle at the age of nine, and was playing in dancebands at 14, when both his parents died. He led a stringband in the late '30s, and shortly thereafter teamed up with accordionist Bois Sec Ardoin. In the early '60s, they came to the attention of folklorists, and Fontenot was acclaimed as the greatest living exponent of French Creole fiddle music; he made numerous festival appearances, but still had to work fulltime to support his family.

*** **Louisiana Hot Sauce, Creole Style**
Arhoolie CD 381 *Fontenot; Bois Sec Ardoin, Edward Poullard (ac); Michael Doucet (vn, md); Tommy Comeaux (md, g); Morris Ardoin, Danny Poullard, David Doucet, Sonny Landreth*

(g); Gustav Ardoin, Tina Pilione (b); Lawrence Ardoin, Tommy Alesi (d); Billy Ware (perc). 5/71–6/91.

The first eight tracks on *Louisiana Hot Sauce* come from sessions held in 1971 and 1973, with accompaniment by Bois Sec Ardoin and members of his family. 'Les Barres De La Prison' is a superbly soulful blues waltz and, like the other three titles issued on LP in the '70s, is markedly superior to the previously unissued items from these sessions; 'Lorita's Blues', for instance, is under-rehearsed, badly balanced and in an uncomfortable key for Canray's vocal.

The next 13 tracks were recorded at home in 5/81, with Michael Doucet variously playing second fiddle and mandolin. 'La Valse De Mom Et Pop' and 'Two-Step De Grand Mallet', both fiddle duets, are lively examples of the dance rhythms shared by the white and black French-speaking communities, but when Doucet plays mandolin, it's generally less well integrated; he's obviously not expecting some of the deliberate dissonances on 'Hey, Hey Blues', which turns into a rather aimless jam. This session, made in a single day, is too rushed to be entirely successful; Doucet seems to be trying to elicit as many items from Fontenot as he can, and many of them are rather brief. 'Le Slow Drag A Nonc Adam' is a fine piece but, at just over a minute, it's a demonstration of how the number goes rather than a real dance tune. Nevertheless, there are some fine performances here: 'La Robe Barrée' and 'La Jog Au Plombeau' are splendid blues waltzes, and the twin fiddles play perfectly integrated lead and rhythm on 'Old Carpenter's Waltz'. 'Malinda' is an adventurous attempt to combine the Creole music of Louisiana with that of the Caribbean, and a lot more successful than 'Jig Cajin', 55 seconds of Scots-Irish pastiche, imperfectly understood by both musicians.

A laboured 'Fi-Do', recorded in 1991 with Danny and Edouard Poullard, and a closing solo version of 'Bernadette' bracket four 1985 titles, one an unaccompanied vocal, the rest backed by Michael Doucet's band Beausoleil. Three of these performances are also on Beausoleil's *Allons A Lafayette & More* (Arhoolie CD 308) – which also includes a better version of 'Shoo, Black' than the one on *Louisiana Hot Sauce*, where the band are clearly still learning the number, and play some nasty dissonances at the start. 'Canray's Breakdown', with Sonny Landreth's Dobro strongly featured, harks back to the Western Swing that Fontenot played in the '30s, and the unaccompanied drinking song 'La Table Ronde' is also important documentation. 'Les Blues A Canray' is a second version of 'Lorita's Blues'; the arrangement, with prominent but ill-assorted Dobro, is very different from the version with the Ardoins, but not much better.

The unevenness of these final tracks is a microcosm of *Louisiana Hot Sauce* as a whole. Canray Fontenot's determination to preserve the older black fiddle music of Louisiana, and to create new material within it, made him a national treasure, and the disc includes many valuable and enjoyable tracks. Taken as a whole, however, it is somewhat disappointing, having been bulked out to CD length by the inclusion of inferior material. CS

The Charles Ford Band
GROUP

Brothers Mark, Robben and Patrick Ford, from Ukiah, California, formed the Charles Ford Band, named after their father, in 1970, and have occasionally reconstituted it. See also the entries for Mark Ford, Robben Ford and The Ford Blues Band.

*** The Charles Ford Band
Arhoolie CD 353 *Mark Ford (h); Robben Ford (g, v); Michael Osborn (g); Stanley Poplin (b); Patrick Ford (d). 1–3/72.*

The Fords got part of their early training in blues playing from Paul Butterfield, and this set has some of the flavour of the Butterfield Blues Band: less firmness, perhaps, in the fast pieces but showing considerable individuality in the laidback 'Blue And Lonesome' and 'Reconsider Baby'. Both Mark and Robben display precocious talent on this impressive album.

***(*) A Reunion – Live
Blue Rock'It BRCD 101//Crosscut CCD 11043 *Ken Baker (s); Mark Ford (h, v); Steve Czarnecki (kb); Robben Ford (g, v); Stan Poplin (b); Patrick Ford (d). 9/82.*

*** As Real As It Gets
Blue Rock'It BRCD 124//Crosscut CCD 11048 *Mark Ford (h, v); Russell Ferrante (kb); Robben Ford (g, v); Michael Osborn (g); Stan Poplin (b); Patrick Ford (d). 83.*

Commemorating ten years since their debut, and the recent death of their father, the Ford brothers got together to play some gigs and record *A Reunion – Live*. As Patrick acknowledges in the notes, there were a few technical problems. Mark's blistering harmonica on the opening 'The Cotton Creeper' is somewhat down in the mix, and stays there for some time, which reduces the effect of his stirring playing in the long, slow reading of 'Forty Days And Forty Nights', but by the penultimate track, his own 'Lookin' For A Woman', he is better balanced. Robben's guitar is always to the fore, and his bravura playing is some of his best blues work on disc. *As Real As It Gets*, also recorded in concert, offers second readings of '40 Days' and 'That Will Never Do'; the former and a very long 'Driftin' Blues' are aerated by Russell Ferrante's piano passages, and Robben's guitar playing has more of the character of his later work with The Blue Line. TR

Mark Ford (born 1953)
VOCAL, HARMONICA

Ford has played with his brothers Robben and Patrick on and off since the late '60s and is on many albums made by Robben, The Ford Blues Band and Garth Webber.

** With The Robben Ford Band
Blue Rock'It BRCD 110//Crosscut CCD 11031 *Ford; Robben Ford (g); Roscoe Beck (b); Tom Brechtlein (d). 11/90.*

**(*) Mark Ford & The Blue Line
Blue Rock'It BRCD 129//Crosscut CCD 11061 *As above, except add Tony Lufrano (kb), Garth Webber (g). 2/98.*

The open weave of the quartet setting gives Mark Ford a lot of space to fill, and it's a challenge to which, on his first album, he isn't always equal. His harmonica expertly negotiates the twists of the instrumental 'Up And Out' and the more level contours of 'On The Road Again' (the Canned Heat number, oddly credited to 'J. Oden') or 'Fool For Love', but his singing, nasal and unnuanced, hasn't enough weight to balance his brother's assured and, at times, peppery guitar playing, and one feels that the album credit should have been reversed to *The Robben Ford Band With Mark Ford*. His singing was somewhat more seasoned by the time he made his second album, which was also more sympathetically engineered, putting voice and harmonica squarely on top of the ensemble; the result is a performance signally more confident than its predecessor. Robben Ford, Beck and Brechtlein – The Blue Line – play with the composure acquired from several years of working together. The material, all original, is not often in standard blues forms, but is arguably most effective when it is. *On The Edge* (Blue Rock'It BRCD 119//Crosscut CCD 11045) is jointly credited to Ford and Garth Webber and is discussed in the latter's entry. TR

Robben Ford (born 1951)
VOCAL, GUITAR, SAXOPHONE, PIANO

Robben Ford's first instrument was saxophone, but he was converted to the guitar in high school after hearing Mike Bloomfield with the Butterfield Blues Band. With his brothers Patrick and Mark he formed The Charles Ford Band (q.v.). After a period with Jimmy Witherspoon, he joined Tom Scott's LA Express in 1976; later he co-founded The Yellowjackets. He rejoined his brothers in 1982 for a reunion album and further recordings and tours. During the '90s he worked chiefly with his trio The Blue Line. Ford has also worked with major pop and jazz names, including Joni Mitchell, David Sanborn and Miles Davis.

*** Discovering The Blues – Live
Avenue Jazz R2 72727 *Ford; Paul Nagle (kb); Stan Poplin (b); Jim Baum (d). 72.*
(***) Sunrise
Avenue Jazz R2 75630 *As above. 72.*
(***) Schizophonic
Avenue Jazz R2 71624 *As above. 76.*
*** Anthology: The Early Years
Avenue Jazz R2 72760 2CD *As above, except add Jimmy Witherspoon (v). 72, 76.*

Discovering The Blues was a startling debut. Even this early in his career Ford was a hugely gifted player, capable of filling the large canvases of 'Sweet Sixteen' (12.32), 'It's My Own Fault' (10.27) and 'Raining In My Heart' (10.31) with colour and detail. His debts to older masters like B. B. King are often clear, but from a musician in his early 20s it would be unreasonable to expect anything else. What's particularly impressive is how restrained he is: even his fastest and deftest playing is achieved without overstatement or bluster. *Sunrise* – recorded, like *Discovering The Blues*, in performance at the Ash Grove and the Golden Bear – and *Schizophonic*, a studio recording, have some blues tracks but are predominantly jazz sets and signals of his direction in the late '70s and '80s.

While the individual albums appear to be still available, anyone but a devotee will do very well with the 2CD *Anthology*, containing as it does most of the contents of the three albums, as well as two tracks from 1976's *Live* with Jimmy Witherspoon. Readers excited by the prospect of two hours' youthfully athletic guitar playing will probably not mind too much that it comes with youthfully bland singing.

The Inside Story (Elektra 61021) (1978) is from Ford's Yellowjackets period and thus consists of impeccably played fusion music.

** Talk To Your Daughter
Warner Bros. 25647 *Ford; Vince Denham, Brandon Fields (s); Mark Ford (h); Russell Ferrante (kb, p, syn); Brian Mann, Bill Payne (syn); Roscoe Beck (b, v); Vinnie Colaiuta, Jeff Porcaro (d). 88.*

On paper this is quite a blues-heavy programme, with songs by J. B. Lenoir, B. B. King and Albert King, but several tracks are wormholed by dweedling synthesizers, and the entire programme fights for breath in a scrupulously antiseptic studio. Nearly two decades have done little to add weight or texture to Ford's voice.

***(*) The Blues Collection
Blue Rock'It BRCD 127//Crosscut CCD 11054 *Ford; Mark Ford, Charlie Musselwhite (h); Russell Ferrante (kb); Espen Fjelle (o); Skip Rose, Clay Cotton (p); Stan Poplin, Gerald Pedersen, Steve Ehrman[m], Roscoe Beck (b); Patrick Ford, Vinnie Colaiuta, Tom Brechtlein (d); Jimmy Witherspoon (v). 71–91.*

Blue Rock'It assembled this two-decade survey from their own and their German partner Crosscut's catalogues, adding three tracks licensed from Arhoolie. There are cuts by the 1971–72 Charles Ford Band, including a previously unissued and stridently accomplished guitar workout on 'Excuse My Blues', collaborations with Charlie Musselwhite, Mark Ford and Jimmy Witherspoon, and three other previously unreleased tracks, two with the Ferrante–Beck–Colaiuta lineup from 1984. If you're curious about Ford but would prefer to hear him in blues contexts, this is the album you should listen to first, and will probably keep.

**(*) Robben Ford & The Blue Line
Stretch GRS 11022 *Ford; Dan Fornero (t); Bob Malach (s); Mark Ford (h); Bill Boublitz, William 'Smitty' Smith, Russell Ferrante (kb); Roscoe Beck (b); Tom Brechtlein (d). 92.*
**(*) Mystic Mile
Blue Thumb 050 008//STD-1107 *Ford; Dan Fornero (t, flh); Bob Malach (s); David Grissom (g); Roscoe Beck (b, v); Tom Brechtlein (d, v); Chick Corea (eff). 93.*
*** Handful Of Blues
Blue Thumb 057 004//BTD-7004 *Ford; Mark Ford (h); Russell Ferrante (kb, p); Ricky Peterson (o); Henry Butler (p); Danny Kortchmar (g); Roscoe Beck (b, v); Tom Brechtlein (d, v). 95.*

Apart from good versions of Otis Rush's 'My Love Will Never Die' on the first, and 'Chevrolet' and 'I Just Want To Make Love To You' on the last, there isn't much received blues repertoire on these albums, and the original compositions, with the exception of 'Prison Of Love' on *Robben Ford & The Blue Line*, are not particularly striking. *Handful Of Blues* maintains a bluesy feel throughout and is the most appealing of the three.

**(*) The Authorized Bootleg
Blue Thumb 057 013//BTD-7013 *Ford; Bill Boublitz (p); Roscoe Beck (b, v); Tom Brechtlein (d, v). 12/95.*

For this acoustic set, recorded at Yoshi's in Oakland, Ford recalled songs from *Talk To Your Daughter*, *Robben Ford & The Blue Line* (one each) and *Handful Of Blues* (four). He hadn't previously recorded 'Don't Let The Sun Catch You Crying' or 'Lovin' Cup', but the latter, a Paul Butterfield tune, would show up on *Supernatural*. Some admirers of Ford's playing may welcome the opportunity to hear it unplugged; others may judge the results too lightweight.

T-MODEL FORD

(***) Tiger Walk
Blue Thumb 057 012//BTD-7012 *Ford; Bob Malach (ts); Ronnie Cuber (bs); Bernie Worrell (o, clavinet); Benmont Tench (o); Russell Ferrante (p); Charlie Drayton (b); Steve Jordan (d, perc); Lenny Castro (perc).* 97.

(**) Supernatural
Blue Thumb 547 596//BTD-7596 *Ford; Lee Thornburg (t); David Woodford (s); Ricky Peterson (o); Michael McDonald (p, v); Russell Ferrante (p); Greg Kurstin (syn); Jimmy Earl (b); Vinnie Colaiuta (d); Luis Conte (perc); Sweet Pea Atkinson, Kevin Sandbloom, Anne Kerry Ford, Julie Christensen, Perla Batalla, David Batteau (v).* 99.

Tiger Walk is a blues-funk set, all instrumental and all original except for a sultry reading of Ann Peebles's 'I Can't Stand The Rain'. The more elaborately produced *Supernatural* shows a different side of Ford, characterized by lovesongs like 'Don't Lose Your Faith In Me'. With the exception of the already mentioned 'Lovin' Cup' on *Supernatural*, there is little for the blues fan on either album, and still less on 2001's *Jing Chi* (Tone Center TC 40212), a jazz set by a trio of Ford, Vinnie Colaiuta and bassist Jimmy Haslip.

*** A Tribute To Paul Butterfield
Blue Rock'It BRCD 134 *Ford; Mic Gillette (t, tb); John Lee Sanders (fl, s, v); Andy Just, Mark Ford (h, v); Gabriel Ford, John R. Burr, Mark Naftalin (kb); Volker Strifler (g, v); Dewayne Pate (b); Patrick Ford (d, v); Garth Webber (v).* 01?

In which the Fords and some friends join to acknowledge the influence – which in the case of the Ford brothers was profound – of the Paul Butterfield Band. Andy Just and Mark Ford divide the harmonica role, each playing on six tracks, and both play as well as they have anywhere; the vocals are fairly evenly split between them, Robben and Strifler. Robben plays apocalyptic guitar on 'Last Hopes Gone' and 'In My Own Dream'. As usual with tribute albums, the performances are more respectful than innovative.

**(*) Blue Moon
Concord CCD-2112 *Ford; Lee Thornburg (t); David Woodford (ts, bs); Charlie Musselwhite (h); Neil Larsen (o, p); Russell Ferrante (p, syn); Roscoe Beck, Jimmy Earl (b); Tom Brechtlein, Vinnie Colaiuta (d); Louis Pardini, Julie Christiansen (v).* 10/01.

Anyone coming to *Blue Moon* after the last two somewhat discouraging Blue Thumb sets would have taken heart from the spitting guitar of the opening track, Little Walter's 'Up The Line'. Ford plays with similar attack on a few more numbers, returning to the Little Walter songbook for the closing 'The Toddle', and offers a transformational reading of Big Maceo's 'The Way You Treated Me (You're Gonna Be Sorry)', but original songs like 'Don't Deny Your Love' restore the atmosphere of earlier and less hard-edged albums like *Supernatural*.

** Keep On Running
Concord CCD-2212 *Ford; Dan Fornero (t); Edgar Winter (as, ts, bs); Bob Malach (ts); John Mayall (h); Ivan Neville (kb, o, v); Jeff Babko (kb); Jimmy Earl (b); Toss Panos, Steve Potts (d); Siedah Garrett, Mavis Staples, Ray Williams, Terry Evans (v).* 03.

It's remarkable how Ford continues to sing with the scrubbed clarity of a surfer-rocker; you wonder if, like some Californian Dorian Gray, he has a hidden tape-recording of his real fiftysomething voice, cracked and hoarse. Such a youthful style serves him well enough in pop songs like 'Badge' or 'Peace Love And Understanding', less well in 'Homework' or 'My Time After Awhile'. Wherever he went to find the darker guitar sound of parts of *Blue Moon*, he evidently didn't want to go there again. TR

T-Model Ford (born c. 1924)
VOCAL, GUITAR

Ford fits his record company's profile exactly, a juke-joint entertainer with little ostensible interest in music's formal structures who took up guitar in his 50s. With his partner Spam he plays in the few remaining clubs on Nelson Street in Greenville, Mississippi, once the haunt of Willie Love and Roosevelt 'Booba' Barnes. A long and at one point murderous life is reflected in the brute force of his sonic barrage and the crude discursiveness of his songs. As producer Matthew Johnson might assert, T-Model Ford would be inept – if he knew where it was.

**(*) Pee Wee Get My Gun
Fat Possum 0303 *Ford; Frank Frost (o); Sam Carr, Spam [Tommy Lee Miles] (d).* 97.

Listeners may convince themselves what they're hearing is the 'real' unsophisticated blues as played in establishments they are unlikely ever to visit. What they're getting is an untutored musician caught in the headlights of a recording studio, not frozen but consciously performing. This is a long-standing team; one member sets an unvarying rhythm over which the other freely ranges. When Frost and Carr come on board for 'Been A Long Time' and 'Feel So Bad', the universal discomfort is palpable. Ford plagiarizes at will and these ill-disguised songs are mixed with his own Beckettian dialogues, strings of often belligerent non sequiturs that in 'I'm Insane' include the mantra 'I'm gonna put my foot in your ass'. The fact that his accent often becomes impenetrable merely seasons the pot. As an antidote to the assembly-line production fodder found elsewhere, it works. But an ability to relish the bizarre is required.

** You Better Keep Still
Fat Possum 0318 *Ford; Spam [Tommy Lee Miles] (d).* 98.

Despite a stated aversion to the recording methods of more conventional blues labels, Fat Possum's Matthew Johnson is pig-headed when it comes to letting remixers loose on his own product. A matched pair of the breed overwhelm 'Pop Pop Pop', an inconsequential song made more illegible by their interference. A kind person would call this album experimental, the less forgiving would prefer unfinished, maybe even scrappy. 'The Old Number' is Muddy's 'Still A Fool' (itself an adaptation of 'Catfish Blues'); 'Come Back Home' is Wolf's 'Smokestack Lightning' to the life. Buddy Guy covered 'Look What All You Got' but this and 'To The Left, To The Right' are less than fragments. Two parts of 'If I Had Wings' bookend the set, the first a perverted cowboy song reiterating Ford's mantra (see above), the second vague, repetitive and overlong. A quote from Jim Thompson's *The Nothing Man* adds pretentiousness to the album's list of woes.

*** She Ain't None Of Your'n
Fat Possum 80335 *Ford; Frank Frost (o); Sam Carr, 'Spam' [Tommy Lee Miles], Bryan Barry (d). 00.*

In a less singular artist this would be a return to form. Instead of imposing versatility of one sort or another, Ford is allowed to cut loose in his accustomed fashion. The ingredients remain as before: 'Sail On' is the alternative title for Muddy's 'Honey Bee', 'How Many More Years' is another outrageous lift from Howlin' Wolf. 'Wood Cuttin' Man' is his take on 'Crosscut Saw', while 'Leave My Heart Alone' uses the framework of Hooker's 'Boom Boom'. 'When Are You Coming Back Home' from the session with Frost and Carr is an earlier version of the previous album's 'Come Back Home'. The lyric to the opening 'She Asked Me So I Told Her' consists of little more than its title. 'Chicken Head Man' manages to encompass love for his woman and his consumption of chicken heads. The appearance of a fresh drummer on three titles makes no overt difference to Ford's singleminded assault on his equipment and fails to inhibit the continuity that makes this the most attractive of his albums.

**(*) Bad Man
Fat Possum 0363 *Ford; Robert Chaffe (o); Jojo Hermann (p); Jim Mize (g); 'Spam' [Tommy Lee Miles] (d); Tate County Singers (v). 02.*

T-Model returns for his 10,000-mile service, his trusty Spam at his side. His newfound fame seems to have improved his guitar playing but only in so far as to regularize his riff and chord playing. The voice remains raddled and phlegmy, the songwriting plagiaristic, this time homing in on Howlin' Wolf ('Ask Her For Water') and Willie Dixon ('Backdoor Man'). Unintelligibility remains a problem, although there's no lack of energy. Spam's ambient drumkit is as metronomic as ever and the guests enhance the mayhem, Mize on 'Bad Man', Chaffe and Hermann on 'The Duke', an uneventful instrumental. A handful of girls add their voices and clapping hands to 'Let The Church Roll On'. Much of this is rollicking stuff but it's all been heard before. NS

The Ford Blues Band
GROUP

Patrick and Mark Ford played with their brother Robben in The Charles Ford Band (q.v.). They formed The Ford Blues Band in the late '80s and began recording a series of albums for Patrick's Blue Rock'It label. Mark left after a couple of albums, his place being taken by Andy Just. Based in northern California, the band has also built a reputation in Germany through regular concerts and a licensing deal with Crosscut.

**(*) The Ford Blues Band
Blue Rock'It BRCD 108//Crosscut CCD 11024 *Mark Ford (h, v); Garth Webber (g, v); Ron Gurewitz (b); Patrick Ford (d, v). 89.*

*** Here We Go!
Crosscut CCD 11029 *Mark Ford, Andy Just (h, v); Jeff Stratton (g); Stan Poplin (b); Patrick Ford (d). 4/90.*

**(*) Breminale '92
Blue Rock'It BRCD 114//Crosscut CCD 11038 *Andy Just (h, v); John Wedemeyer (g); Stan Poplin (b); Patrick Ford (d, v). 6/92.*

**(*) Hotshots
Blue Rock'It BRCD 121//Crosscut CCD 11041 *Andy Just (h, v); John R. Burr (p); Scotty Johnson (g, v); John Wedemeyer (g); Dewayne Pate, Stan Poplin (b); Patrick Ford (d, v); Steve Siacotos (v). 93, 8/94.*

With its selection of songs from J. B. Lenoir, Little Walter, Jimmy Reed, and others, *The Ford Blues Band* is the group's album most rooted in received repertoire. Mark Ford blows vigorous harmonica and shares the vocals with Webber. *Here We Go!* and *Breminale '92* were recorded in concert in Germany. *Here We Go!* marks the arrival of Andy Just, not only an excellent harmonica player but a rather tougher singer than the other vocalists in the band, one of whom, in any case, has left since the first album – guitarist Webber, replaced by Jeff Stratton. Just plays tour de force solos on Little Walter's 'Blue And Lonesome' and the original 'Fool For Love', and he and Mark Ford engage in an intricate and exciting chase sequence in 'Fannie Mae'. The departure of Mark Ford left Just as the front man on *Breminale '92*, which introduced guitarist John Wedemeyer; two years on, it was his turn to be replaced, by Scotty Johnson, who also sings four numbers on *Hotshots*. Again, it's Just's harmonica playing that commands attention on these two albums. *Breminale '92* suffers from the twin common faults of live recordings, overplaying and overacting.

*** Fords And Friends
Blue Rock'It BRCD 126//Crosscut CCD 11052 *Andy Just, Mark Ford (h, v); Tony Lufrano (kb); Scotty Johnson, Chris Cain, Charlie Musselwhite (g, v); John Wedemeyer, Robben Ford, Luther Tucker (g); Dewayne Pate (b, v); Stan Poplin (b); Patrick Ford (d, v); Gabriel Ford (perc); Lowell Fulson, Fenton Robinson (v). 93–96?*

Unwrapping this collection yields several treats: vocals by Lowell Fulson ('Happy Anniversary Baby') and Fenton Robinson ('Hey Sister'), Charlie Musselwhite playing slide guitar ('Tell Old Bill'), a recording made shortly before his death by Luther Tucker ('Luther's Lament') and a couple of tracks reuniting the Fords with brother Robben, 'Sahara Moon' and 'The Sign'. But this isn't to say that the album is only as good as its guests: Patrick Ford's songs are likeable and the core band's playing is tight and varied.

*** 1999
Blue Rock'It BRCD 130//Crosscut CCD 11063 *Andy Just (h, v); David Mathews (kb); Volker Strifler, Robben Ford (g, v); Dewayne Pate (b); Patrick Ford (d). 99?*

*** In Memory Of Michael Bloomfield
Blue Rock'It BRCD 136 *Mic Gillette (t, tb); Brad Catania (t); John Lee Sanders (s, v); Andy Just (h, v); John R. Burr (kb); Tony Lufrano (o, p); Volker Strifler, Chris Cain, Robben Ford (g, v); Dewayne Pate (b); Patrick Ford (d); Mz Dee [Dejuana Logwood], Regina Espinoza (v). 02?*

**(*) Another Fine Day
Blue Rock'It BRCD 138 *Tom Poole (t); Kevin Porter (tb); John Lee Sanders (s); Andy Just (h, v); Mark Ford (h); John R. Burr (kb); Volker Strifler (g, v); Garth Webber (g); Dewayne Pate (b); Patrick Ford (d, v); Gabriel Ford (v). 03?*

The main variable in this band's history has been the position of guitarist/joint vocalist. Its latest holder, Volker Strifler, is a versatile guitarist and an okay singer with a less assertive style than Just, whose singing and playing on *1999* are his most assured work on record: check 'I Have My Doubts' for the one and 'Zip It Up' for the other. Robben Ford sings and plays on the closing 'Daydreamin'', an easy, summery groove that acts as a cool-down after the muscle-flexing of the previous tracks.

The band's first recordings of the new millennium were tributes to two of the Ford family's first models, Paul Butterfield and Michael Bloomfield. The Butterfield album is credited to Robben Ford and is discussed in his entry. He is also a major player at the Bloomfield memorial, singing and playing lead on four numbers; the other is Chris Cain, who sings on two and plays lead on eight. Each has moments of sounding uncannily like his hero – Ford in 'I Got A Mind To Give Up Living' and the outro of '59th Street Bridge Song', Cain in 'Stop' – but each, too, draws on his own considerable resources, and Strifler makes his mark on the proceedings with burning-rubber solos in the closing moments of 'Groovin' Is Easy' and 'Peter's Trip'. The album is interspersed with fragments of an interview with Bloomfield – curiously chosen, inasmuch as he talks mostly about Butterfield.

The addition of brass and reeds to the tribute albums seemed a good enough idea to be redeployed on *Another Fine Day*. While the horns add considerable drive, they leave much less room for a harmonica, though Just gets an outing in 'Jelly Jam' and Mark Ford plays soulfully on 'Reap What You Sow', the album's longest and most memorable performance. TR

Guy Forsyth (born 1968?)
VOCAL, GUITAR, HARMONICA, UKULELE

Forsyth grew up in Kansas City, Missouri, where he was inspired by a John Hammond concert to make a career as a blues musician. Moving to Austin, Texas, he joined the Sixth Street club scene and formed a band. He was also a founder member of the Asylum Street Spankers, an old-time showband.

*** High Temperature
Lizard LDCD 80001 *Forsyth; Keith Bradley (g); Rob Douglass (b); Rich Chilleri (d).* 6/93.

Forsyth is gifted with a strong, snarling voice and considerable versatility on guitar and harmonica, and when he applies himself to a set of blues, as he does in *High Temperature*, he is a match for any of his contemporaries. There are good renditions of received repertoire here: a version of Elmore James's 'Done Somebody Wrong' with slide playing almost indistinguishable from James's, a long '19 Years' (Muddy Waters's 'She's Nineteen Years Old') and a Jimmy Reed number with a perfect replica of his piping harmonica sound. Much of the rest is original, though tracks like 'Answering Machine', 'Hard Pushin' Papa' and the menacing 'Evil Man' are rife with echoes of past masters.

*** Needle Gun
Antone's ANT 0039 *Forsyth; Stan Smith (cl); Keith Bradley (g); Gil 'T' Isais (b, v); Rich Chilleri (d); Wammo (wb, bgo, perc, v); Stuart Sullivan (perc); Abra Moore (v).* 95.

The combination of poetry and shimmering slide guitar on the opening 'Don't Stand Still (Snakeboy's Lament)' is reminiscent of Tom Waits, and the verse in the title number and one or two other songs falls into Waits measures. Forsyth easily transfers their louche swagger and *film noir* ambience into his more conventional blues selections like 'This Is Hip' or Little Walter's 'Temperature' and a couple of remakes of original songs first heard on *High Temperature*, 'Taxi' and 'Don't Turn Me In'. 'I'm A Hog For You' gets a suitably raucous reading, or rather shouting. Forsyth again shows an enviable command of all his resources, while hinting a little more pointedly that next time he may choose to deploy them on different material. Sure enough, 1999's *Can You Live Without* (Antone's 0043) was the work of a singer/songwriter who had flogged the blues river and now had other fish to fry …

**(*) Steak
Antone's TMG-ANT 0048 *Forsyth; Stan Smith (cl); Don Leady (ac, vn); Gil 'T' [Isais] (p, b); Steve James (md, 6-string bj, g); George Rarey (g); Frosty [B. E. Smith], George Rains, Johnny Benoit (d); Wammo (wb, perc, found objects); Dave McNair (shaker).* oo.

… but *Steak* put a blues-flavoured dish back on the table, though the spices sprinkled on it – distorted guitars, toolshed percussion – may be too tangy for lovers of plain cooking. The programme is almost seamless, songs sometimes merging into each other, original blues compositions wrapping a few received pieces like Muddy Waters's 'Louisiana Blues' and Otis Rush's 'My Love Will Never Die' and the dark Waitsian narrative 'Thibodaux Furlough'. Not a lot of harmonica but sheets of steel slide guitar. TR

Jesse Fortune (born 1930)
VOCAL

Fortune grew up in Hattiesburg, Mississippi, moved to Chicago in 1952 and sang in clubs with artists like Otis Rush and Buddy Guy. Spotted by Willie Dixon, he cut two remarkable singles in 1963 for USA but 'didn't get anything out of that session, not a quarter.' Since the late '60s he has worked as a barber on Chicago's West Side.

Fortune's first recordings, made with a formidable lineup including Walter Horton, Lafayette Leake and Buddy Guy, were three songs by Willie Dixon, 'Too Many Cooks', 'Good Things' and the much inferior 'God's Gift To Man', and Leake's composition 'Heavy Heart Beat'. His high voice and fervent delivery recall Guy's early recordings. The rhumba rhythm of 'Too Many Cooks' is a characteristic touch by Dixon, who produced the session. The issued takes of the four titles are on *Call Back Lost Time* (Westside WESA 843), a compilation chiefly concerned with recordings by Ike Turner's Kings Of Rhythm.

*** Fortune Tellin' Man
Delmark DD-658 *Fortune; Dez Desormeaux (ts, bs); John Brumbach (ts); Ken Saydak (o, p); Bob Dogan (p); Dave Specter (g); Mike McCurdy (b); Mark Fornek (d).* 7/92.

Three decades later, an artist most enthusiasts had little expected to hear again made a return, backed by Dave Specter & The Bluebirds, with whom he had been singing for a year or so. A forceful singer with a wide Jimmy Rushing vibrato, he had lost hardly any of his vocal range and he generates a lot of energy on his album's title track and a remake of 'Too Many Cooks'. 'Gambler's Blues' and 'Be Careful With A Fool' reflect his regard for B. B. King. 'Get Mad At My Money', a slow blues which he wrote himself, elicits not only impassioned singing but pungent solos from Specter and Saydak. Specter's guitar playing is typically varied, lithely darting in 'Too Many Cooks', jazzier in 'Dark Is The Night' and the instrumentals 'Sandu' (a blues composed by the jazz trumpeter Clifford Brown) and the *film noir*ish 'Specter's Walk'. A third instrumental, 'Ain't About

Money', features Saydak's boogie piano playing. As much the band's record as the singer's, *Fortune Tellin' Man* ought to satisfy admirers of either. TR

Baby Face Leroy Foster (1923–58)
VOCAL, GUITAR, DRUMS

Surprisingly little is known about a musician fondly remembered by his peers. He grew up in Mississippi but by the mid-'40s had reached Chicago, where he played in a group with Sunnyland Slim and Sonny Boy Williamson I, then teamed with Muddy Waters and Little Walter.

♛ **** Leroy Foster 1948–1952
Classics 5137 *Foster; Little Walter (h, g, v); Snooky Pryor (h); Sunnyland Slim (p); Muddy Waters (g, v); poss. Jimmy Rogers, Robert Jr Lockwood (g); Big Crawford, Alfred Elkins, unknown (b); unknown (d). 11/48–52.*

The handful of sides Foster cut between 1948 and 1952 are among the most memorable performances in the Southern blues idiom then reshaping itself in Chicago. His delivery, always less assertive than that of his friend Muddy Waters, is at its most intimate and sexy in 'Take A Little Walk With Me'; the coupling of this song and 'My Head Can't Rest Anymore', both with calm, affecting harmonica by Snooky Pryor, originated on J.O.B. but was understandably purchased for rerelease by Chess. A 1950 trio date with Waters and Little Walter, Foster playing the basic drum part, produced the fine 'Boll Weevil' and 'Red Headed Woman' and a two-part 'Rollin' And Tumblin''; the first half has wordless humming and moaning by all three musicians, while Foster sings the verses on the second. The drumbeat throughout has the urgency of tom-toms. No blues recording comes closer to the entranced intensity of the ring shout. Foster's only other sides were cut for J.O.B. in 1951–52. Although his singing on the slow blues 'Pet Rabbit', 'Louella', 'Late Hours At Midnight' and 'Blues Is Killin' Me' is almost dreamy, it holds its own against Sunnyland Slim's sometimes tumultuous piano playing. Untimely death robbed the blues of a most distinctive musician. TR

Willie Foster (1921–2001)
VOCAL, HARMONICA

Born near Leland, Mississippi, Foster was a boyhood acquaintance of Jimmy Reed. After military service in World War II he settled in St Louis and later Chicago, where he played with Muddy Waters in the '50s. In 1963 he returned to Mississippi and spent the rest of his life there, playing occasionally and enjoying a few years of wider celebrity in the '90s.

**(*) I Found Joy
Palindrome PRD 21459 *Foster; Mark Goodwin (o, p); Bobby Mack (g); Bret Coats (b); Dan Frezek, Jimmy Pate (d). 96?*

**(*) Live At Airport Grocery
Mempho [unnumbered] *Foster; unknown (o); Charlie Ricker, Skeeter Provis (g); Donnie Brown (b); Frank Vic, Larry Wright (d). 99?*

Emerging from the shadows with *I Found Joy*, Foster offers an affable collection of old man's memories. In particular he recalls his childhood friend Jimmy Reed, reproducing his upper-register harmonica playing in 'Where Can She Be' and taking 'Big Boss Man' at a fast enough clip to prompt his liveliest blowing of the session. In 'I Found Joy', however, he departs from Reed's template to create an optimistic slow blues about his new and upward-heading career. 'Ready For The Blues' is loosely based on Muddy Waters's 'I'm Ready', something he felt entitled to do because, he claimed, he gave Waters and Willie Dixon the hook phrase. His singing is rather congested – not surprisingly, given his age – and isn't too well recorded, but his harmonica playing is energetic.

Live At Airport Grocery was recorded at a barbecue joint in Cleveland, Mississippi, where Foster used to play in the '60s. His gentle, confiding vocals have their charm, but most of the nine numbers are longer than they need to be, and the band doesn't play assertively enough to make the extensions worthwhile. The CD had only limited circulation and may be hard to find. The same is true of the other album he cut about that time, *At Home With The Blues* (RMD Music [unnumbered]).

Another singer and harmonica player with the same name was active in Chicago in the '50s, Little Willie Foster (born 1922). His 'Falling Rain Blues'/'Four Day Jump' (Parrot, 1953) is on *Down Home Blues Classics: Chicago 1946–1954* (Boulevard Vintage BVBCD 1014 4CD), and 'Crying The Blues'/'Little Girl' (Cobra, 1957) on *Goin' Down To Eli's: The Cobra & Abco Rhythm & Blues Anthology 1956–1958* (Westside WESA 868). TR

T. J. Fowler (1910–82)
PIANO

Fowler grew up around Detroit and studied piano, composition and arranging at the Detroit Conservatory of Music. He began playing for dances at a hall owned by his father. After spells with other leaders he formed his own band in 1947 and over the next five years recorded for Sensation and Savoy. Having numerous other business interests, he confined his musical activities to the Detroit area, where he was well known into the '60s.

**(*) T. J. Fowler 1948–1953
Classics 5103 *Fowler; John Lawton, Dezie McCullers (t); Frank Taylor (as, v); Lee Gross (as); Walter Cox (ts); Calvin Frazier (g, v); Henry Ivory, Gene Taylor (b); Clarence Stamps, Floyd 'Bubbles' McVay (d); Freddie Johnson, Alberta Adams, unknown, band (v). 48–11/53.*

For Detroit audiences in the late '40s Fowler filled the role of a Roy Milton or Joe Liggins, leading a small horn-and-rhythm band through blues, boogies and occasionally pop numbers. A few years on, tracks like 'Night Crawler' or 'Camel Walk', with prominent trumpet and tenor, suggest a regional variant of the Tiny Bradshaw sound. The addition of blues guitarist Calvin Frazier on the second Savoy session in 7/52 sharpens the band's attack; the blues instrumentals 'Back Biter' and 'Wine Cooler' are good jukebox material, and Frazier's vocal numbers 'Got Nobody To Tell My Troubles To' and 'Little Baby Child' have much more than their obscurity to recommend them. TR

Carol Fran & Clarence Hollimon
DUET

Hollimon (1937–2000) was playing guitar professionally before he graduated from high school in 1957. He played on many

sessions at Duke/Peacock, then moved to New York to become house guitarist at Scepter/Wand. By the early '80s he was back in Houston, and not getting much work. Marriage to Carol Fran (born 1933), who was then working in New Orleans clubs, stopped him drinking too much and revived both their musical careers. In the '50s Fran had toured with Guitar Slim and recorded for Excello – 'Emmitt Lee' was a regional soul hit – and in a pop vein for New York labels. The couple worked in Houston with a band or as a duo, eventually gaining wider recognition.

***(*) It's About Time
JSP JSPCD 2139 *Fran; Hollimon; Jonny Viau (ts); Troy Jennings (bs); Tom Mahon (p); John Marx (g, v); Rick Reed (b); Paul Fasulo (d). 1/00.*

Two early-'90s CDs on Black Top are deleted; this one was recorded a few months before Hollimon's death. Despite the billing to 'Carol Fran & Clarence Hollimon' she sings, in a robust soul-blues vein, on only four tracks; John Marx sings a lively rock 'n' roll/blues cross on three, one features Hollimon's only recorded vocal (Jimmy Reedish, and no more than adequate), and the balance are instrumentals. The real star of this CD, again despite the billing, is Hollimon's guitar. He plays with very clean articulation, even at fast tempos, varies his tone tastefully from hard and shiny to smoothly mellow, and has an enviable command of dynamics, with every note getting its own weight, accenting and volume. The record is slightly let down by the homogeneity of its arrangements, notwithstanding some effective and dextrously integrated baritone sax solos. cs

Keith Frank (born 1972)
VOCAL, ACCORDION, KEYBOARDS, GUITAR, BASS, RUBBOARD, PERCUSSION

Son of the great Preston Frank, Keith Frank was his father's drummer aged nine; he led his own band in high school, and inherited the Soileau Zydeco Band in 1990 when Preston went into semi-retirement. Like Beau Jocque, with whom he had a far from friendly rivalry, Keith Frank has been a key player in the conversion of zydeco to a high-volume, high-energy music, influenced by rock, reggae, funk and hip-hop.

*** Get On Boy!
Zydeco Hound ZH-1001 *Frank; prob. George Attle (g); Jennifer Frank (b, v); Brad Frank (d); prob. James 'Chocolate' Ned (rb). 93.*

Originally a cassette for bandstand sale, *Get On Boy!* was issued on CD in 1999. Brad Frank was 11 years old in 1993 and Jennifer, chirruping 'My Name Is Jen', sounds not much older, but their musicianship is entirely mature; so is that of the older James Ned and George Attle (a.k.a. George Lee on some CDs), who almost certainly complete the lineup. 'Murdock' is Boozoo Chavis's 'Zydeco Heehaw' and 'Huh' reworks D. L. Menard's 'Back Door', but most of the material is self-penned, and much of it is innovatively played at the lower end of the accordion. The band's music is mercilessly danceable, but short-winded lyrics are a drawback; too often, Frank is content to write a clever verse and repeat it, rather than developing his ideas. Sometimes banality trumps cleverness: 'Going To McDonalds' must be heard to be believed.

*** What's His Name?
Maison de Soul MdS 1053 *Frank; George Attle, Nathaniel Fontenot (g); Jennifer Frank (b, v); Brad Frank (d); James 'Chocolate' Ned (rb, v). 94?*

**** Movin' On Up!
Maison de Soul MdS 1055 *As above, except omit Fontenot. 95?*

**(*) Only The Strong Survive
Maison de Soul MdS 1062 *Frank; Jennifer Frank (kb, v); George Attle (g); Robby 'Mann' Robinson (b); Brad Frank (d); Eric 'Ice' Cole (rb). 96?*

***(*) You'd Be Surprised!
Maison de Soul MdS 1063 *Frank; George Attle (g); Jennifer Frank (b, v); Brad Frank (d); Curley Chapman (rb); Francis Gradney (v). 96?*

**(*) On A Mission
Maison de Soul MdS 1069 *As above, except add James 'Chocolate' Ned, Aaron Laws, Joe 'Chopper' Chavis (rb); omit Gradney. 98?*

What's His Name? made Keith Frank a star, and subsequent releases made him Maison de Soul's biggest-selling artist. They're all dominated by the riptide rhythms of *nouveau zydeco* and by Keith Frank originals, leavened with oldies from sources as varied as Bob Marley, Little Milton, The Rolling Stones and Arthur Conley. *Movin' On Up!*'s title song is the theme from the '70s sitcom *The Jeffersons*; its aspirational content chimes with Frank's own ambition and determination, which are frequent motifs of his songwriting (and of his CD titles). Their unattractive flipside is a chippy aggression towards his musical rivals and emulators, which mutates under criticism into an equally dislikeable self-pity.

The best of these CDs is *Movin' On Up!*, where a transparent recording balance gives due weight to hyperactive drumming and highly inventive six-string bass. The accordionless 'Pieces To My Heart' is a feature for Frank's soulful singing, and for Attle's scintillating guitar, whose excellence can be missed when the full band is on a power trip. *Only The Strong Survive* sounds cluttered by comparison as it tries to find a role for Jennifer Frank while flaunting the short-lived poaching of Zydeco Force's bassist. The second guitar on *What's His Name?* similarly muddies the texture, if to a lesser degree.

On *You'd Be Surprised* Keith Frank's singing and playing are exceptionally fierce, and the nicely varied playlist includes a witty, parodic 'Fred The Rasta Man' and a jolly revival of 'Hello Josephine'. By the time of *On A Mission*, the interjection of 'Yeah, you right!' and 'Eh, toi!' is mechanical, and the band's creativity seems constricted by *nouveau zydeco*'s ceaseless, sometimes mind-numbing energy. They cast around for new roads to self-expression, but 'Satisfaction' is horrible, 'Zydeco Et Pas Salé' is a poor tribute to Clifton Chenier and the allusion to NWA's 'Straight Outta Compton' on 'Coming Straight From Soileau' is feeble.

**(*) Live At Slim's Y-Ki-Ki
Shanachie 9018 *As above, except add Scott Ardoin (g); omit Laws. 9/98.*

**(*) Ready Or Not
Shanachie 9023 *Frank; George Attle (g, v); Kent August (g); Jennifer Frank (b, v); Brad Frank (d, v); James 'Chocolate' Ned (rb, v); Raoul Ceaser (v). 00.*

The Soileau Band hasn't toured as extensively as some zydeco outfits; Keith Frank seems largely content to be world-famous in Louisiana. Nevertheless, these two self-produced CDs appear on an out-of-state label. Both are disappointing. Much of *Live* lacks both atmosphere and excitement, and 'Hey Pretty Baby (With Your Teeth So White)' is another case of a good idea (building a song around toothpaste brands) wrecked by underdevelopment; but John Delafose's 'Ço Fa' (*sic* 'Quoi Faire?') and Preston Frank's 'Why You Wanna Make Me Cry?' and 'Maymel' are harbingers of an imminent engagement with tradition. *Ready Or Not*'s mixture of *nouveau zydeco*, blues, R&B, reggae and '50s rock 'n' roll seems constructed as a primer of Frank's musical tastes for the wider audience; unfortunately, most of its execution is equally calculated.

**** The Masked Band
Louisiana Red Hot LRHR 1135 *As above, except add Carlton Frank (vn), Curley Chapman (rb, v); omit August, Ceaser*. 00.

It's no secret that this CD is by Keith Frank and the Soileau Zydeco Band, billed as the Creole Connection. It could be filed under C, F or M, but it's worth seeking out under any of them. The aim of the 'masked band' project is to experiment with sounds both new and – more often – traditional, without alienating the core *nouveau zydeco* audience; hence the presence of Keith's great-uncle Carlton on fiddle, and the inclusion of 'La Valse De Mon Grande Père' (*sic*), 'Chère Ici, Chère La-Bas' and 'Jolie Bassette' alongside 'Games People Play' and 'She Is Shaking Her Big Butt'. Keith Frank considerably overuses cowbell overdubs, but that's excusable when everyone is on such form and having such fun. This CD gets a higher rating than most of the others, not because of a reactionary 'Picasso could draw properly when he wanted to' critical perspective, but because it foregrounds Keith Frank the musician and bandleader, whose talents outshine those of Keith Frank the songwriter.

*** Keith Frank And The Soileau Zydeco Band
Maison de Soul ValueDisc VMS 7003 *As above, except omit Carlton Frank, Chapman*. 01?

A six-tracker and priced accordingly, this disc is a useful introduction to Keith Frank. The synthesized wah-wah riff on 'We Got The Power' soon wears out its welcome, but the other two originals are fine, as are tribute covers of Rockin' Sydney and Boozoo Chavis. 'Hold That Tiger' is surely the only song in this book to quote the Kinks' 'You Really Got Me'.

***(*) The Zydeco Icon
SoulWood SWR-5800 *Frank; Joe Sample (p): George Lee (g, v); Kent August (g), Jennifer Frank (b, v); Brad Frank (d, perc, v); Demetric Thomas (rb, perc, v); Jason Simien (perc, v); Corey Ledet (v); Ronald Wayne (rap)*. 02.

A jokey title and a picture of the band in gorgeously tacky disco threads set the tone. The first release on Frank's own label presents a band having fun in a light, relaxed, open style that takes *nouveau zydeco* in some interestingly *vieux* directions. Alongside more expected sounds, the CD explores reggae ('The Lion In The Jungle') and rock 'n' roll ('Mardi Gras 2nd Line', on which the Crusaders' Joe Sample guests). A *nouveau* take on 'Jambalaya' works well, as does the venerable 'Petite Au La Grosse' (*sic*). On the downside, the tuneless child singing on 'Hit The Road [Jack]' is a touch too whimsical for comfort, and 'Party Down' only adds a new cliché to the heap. Continuing the unlikely use of British pop, 'It's Alright' quotes extensively from Mungo Jerry's 'In The Summertime'!

*** Going To See Keith Frank
Soulwood SWR 005 *Frank; Lawmax Williams (tb); Ricky Julien Sr (as); unknown (h); George Attle (g); Jennifer Frank (b, v); Brad Frank (d, v); Curley Chapman (rb, v); Demetric Thomas (rb)*. 04?

Going To See Keith Frank features the numbers most requested by audiences at gigs. Most of them are new to CD, but bootleg recordings of some have found their way to the local airwaves, and the logic of this release is obvious. The music continues eclectic: 'Hungry For Your Love' is country meets rock meets zydeco meets Howlin' Wolf, and 'Flamenco Flatpickin Medley' is just that. Dan Penn's 'Nine Pound Steel' gets a quality interpretation, unlike a lumpy attempt at the Meters' 'Shake Down', and 'Do You Wanna Dance?' is joyfully interpolated into 'Got To Get The Feeling'. The energy level is surprisingly moderate for a set of bandstand favourites, though, and 'Keith Frank Will Make You Sweat' is not the only self-regarding lyric; it's also not the only one that could have done with more work. CS

Preston Frank (born 1947)
VOCAL, ACCORDION

Nowadays best known as Keith Frank's father, Preston Frank was popular on the zydeco circuit in the '70s and '80s, leading the Swallow/Soileau Family Band and playing in an oldfashioned style based on his family's traditions and the recordings of Cajun accordionist Aldus Roger. Keith took over the band in the '90s, but Preston has continued to perform at festivals.

**** Born In The Country
SoulWood SWR-5801 *Frank; Brad Frank (kb, d, v); Carlton Frank (vn); Keith Frank (g, rb); Jennifer Frank (b, v); Demetric Thomas (rb)*. 02.

Preston Frank made half an LP for Arhoolie in 1981, and tracks from it can be heard on various Arhoolie VACs, but *Born In The Country* is his long overdue debut CD under his own name. Uncle Carlton Frank's appealingly scratchy fiddling is from back in the day, but the other members of the family band effortlessly switch from their customary *nouveau* sound to a delightful and thoroughly traditional style; the exception is Jennifer, whose pulsating, modernistic six-string bass meshes perfectly with the CD's old and oldfashioned songs, waltzes and two-steps. One could wish that Preston's voice were further forward in the mix, but *Born In The Country* is a splendid portrait of a musical patriarch whose creative juices are still flowing. CS

Guitar Pete Franklin (1927–75)
VOCAL, GUITAR, PIANO

Despite his nickname, Indianapolis-born Edward Lamonte Franklin played piano and guitar with equal facility, taking his inspiration respectively from Leroy Carr (who lodged at his mother's house for a time) and Carr's partner, Scrapper Blackwell.

*** The Blues Of Pete Franklin: Guitar Pete's Blues
Original Blues Classics OBCCD 560 *Franklin*. 7/61.

Three of the four titles cut at Guitar Pete Franklin's 1949 recording session are available on Tampa Red's *Vol. 14*

(Document DOCD-5214). His 1961 session consisted mainly of cover versions, perhaps because it was recorded in a single day. Pete's guitar playing always marches in the footsteps of Scrapper Blackwell, but the four tracks with piano range somewhat beyond Carr's influence, most successfully on Curtis Jones's 'Lonesome Bedroom Blues'. Less impressive is 'Six White Horses', an attempt at Walter Davis's tonal elusiveness, on which Franklin hits too many wrong notes. The recording quality is adequate, although occasionally Franklin seems to sway away from the vocal microphone. The two-track stereo, with voice in one channel and instrument in the other, does realism no favours, but it does both explain and justify Guitar Pete's nickname, showcasing his mastery of Blackwell's blend of fast single-string runs and ringing chords. As a singer, Franklin emulates Leroy Carr's introspective huskiness effectively, but one senses that the aggression of 'I Got To Find My Baby' and 'Black Gal' is a more accurate reflection of his own personality. A long, intense 'Guitar Pete's Blues' is the final and most valuable track, hinting at a potential for self-expression that was never properly explored by a too slender recorded legacy. CS

Calvin Frazier (1915–72)
VOCAL, GUITAR

Robert Johnson looms over Frazier's small entry in B&GR. Through his cousin Johnny Shines, Frazier met Johnson in Arkansas and had enough time to witness and absorb aspects of his playing and singing. In 1937 the Frazier family, all musicians, left Memphis for Detroit, and the following year, only three months after Johnson's death, Alan Lomax recorded Frazier and his partner Sampson Pittman there for the Library of Congress – recordings that are the only contemporaneous evidence of Johnson's influence. Frazier made a handful of records for Detroit labels in the '50s, leaving scant evidence of the reputation he then enjoyed.

**(*) This Old World's In A Tangle
Laurie LCD 7001 Frazier; Sampson Pittman (g). 10–11/38.

The title song, in one whole performance and a fragment, 'I'm In The Highway, Man' and 'She's A Double-Crossin' Woman' are indelibly stamped with Johnson's touch. Two versions of 'Lilly Mae' are likewise imbued with Johnson's vocal mannerisms. Throughout ten duets, the interplay between the two guitars (Pittman playing slide) is all but flawless, best shown in an instrumental 'Blues' and their version of 'Pinetop's Boogie Woogie'. Regrettably, however, there are detrimental factors in this presentation, the first unavoidable. Owing to the deterioration of the original acetates, sound quality veers from acceptably bad to virtually unlistenable. The second has to do with the accompanying 40-page booklet, which attempts to place these recordings in their historical context but does so with heavy-handed doses of error and supposition, and a set of woefully inaccurate lyric transcripts that at times border on the nonsensical and undermine the intrinsic merit of the music. The contents of this CD have also been absorbed into the VAC *Detroit Blues* (JSP JSP 7736 4CD).

By the '50s Frazier was using an electric guitar and working in a number of musical settings. He plays on some recordings by pianist T. J. Fowler (q.v.) but is encountered most often with the flamboyant Washboard Willie. A single recorded with the latter for JVB, 'Rock House' and 'We'll Meet Again', is on *Detroit Blues Rarities 1: Blues Guitar Killers!* (P-Vine PCD-5416). NS

Steve Freund (born 1952)
VOCAL, GUITAR

Brooklyn-born, Freund settled in Chicago in the mid-'70s and worked with, among others, Walter Horton, Floyd Jones and Koko Taylor, but for the longest time – 18 years – with Sunnyland Slim. In the mid-'90s he moved to San Francisco, where he played and recorded with Boz Scaggs.

**(*) "C" For Chicago
Delmark DE-734 Freund; Terry Hanck, Sam Burckhardt (ts); Willie Henderson (bs); Kim Wilson (h); Rob Waters, Austin de Lone (o); David Maxwell, Wendy DeWitt (p); Boz Scaggs, Dave Specter, Pete Crawford (g); Harlan Terson, Tim Wagar, Justin O'Brien (b); Bob Carter, Mark Fornek, Kevin Coggins, Mot Dutko (d); Mark Hannon, Paula Burns (v). 2/97, 6/99.

*** I'll Be Your Mule
Delmark DE-752 Freund; Brian Schwab (t); Steve Horne (tb); Clark Dean (ss); Van Kelly (as); Dave Clark (ts); Ed Enright (bs); Steve Guyger (h); Mark 'Mr B' Braun (p); Dave Specter (g, prod); Pete Crawford (g); Bob Stroger, Harlan Terson (b); Kenny Smith (d). 9/00.

Perhaps his years with Sunnyland Slim impressed on Freund how valuable is the presence of an assertive pianist, whether inside the standard blues-band ensemble or in duet with a guitarist. At any rate, both his albums have such a player. David Maxwell is a strong thread in the fabric of *"C" For Chicago*, notably on the duet 'Pallet On The Floor', '38th Street Blues' and 'Everytime I Get To Drinking', a Sunnyland Slim number which elicits fine playing alike from him, Freund and Kim Wilson. Half the album's material is original, and reasonably good of its kind, but the track that lingers when the album is over is a touching version of Duster Bennett's 'Jumping At Shadows'.

The balance of original and found material is almost the same on *I'll Be Your Mule*, with another echo of Sunnyland Slim in 'When I Was Young', but this is an altogether more confident and varied album. Here the partner at the piano stool is Mark 'Mr B' Braun, a very fine player for this sort of context, outstanding in the duet 'Something To Remember You By' and scarcely less formidable on many other tracks. Occasionally the instrumentation evokes older models: 'Big Blue Mama' and 'A Dollar A Mile', with Steve Guyger on harmonica, come in a '60s wrapping, while 'Fine Lookin' Woman' is an up-tempo B. B. King styling and the bustling horn riffs of 'Fittin' To Go' are fleetingly reminiscent of certain Elmore James arrangements. But these are not fall-back settings for an artist without ideas of his own: throughout, Freund sets himself higher standards of technique and invention than on his previous album, and meets them. On guitar, that is: his singing is merely okay. But that won't matter very much, so long as he continues to collaborate with musicians as good as these and a producer as attuned as Dave Specter.

Freund's joint album with Specter, *Is What It Is* (Delmark DE-779), is discussed in Specter's entry. TR

Frank Frost (1936–99)
VOCAL, HARMONICA, ORGAN, GUITAR

Frost's 1962 recording debut for Sam Phillips defined him as an exemplar of downhome blues, unfettered music purveyed in the juke-joints of Mississippi, a reputation later enhanced by a small part in the film Crossroads. A protégé of harmonicists Willie Foster and Rice Miller, Frost was adept at recycling others' material with an energy and directness that redefined its worth. With bandmates Jack Johnson and Sam Carr, as the Jelly Roll Kings, he acquired a reputation that elevated the group to the international festival circuit. However, internal squabbles, an indifference to celebrity irrigated by too much alcohol and a tendency to go fishing limited the band's potential as its records (and Frost's own) became fewer and farther between. Still revered for his past achievements, Frost became a cherished regular at the King Biscuit Blues Festivals held in Helena, Arkansas.

***(*) Big Boss Man: The Very Best Of Frank Frost
Collectables COL-CD-5921 *Frost; Jack Johnson (g); unknown (b); Sam Carr (d). 4/62.*

The Sun studio took some of the earthiness out of the then Nighthawks' sound but the essence of their rough-and-ready relish was caught admirably, as was their concision, with only 'Lucky To Be Living' and 'So Tired Living By Myself' breaking the three-minute barrier. Rhythms are kept simple, solos are at a premium and the emphasis is on Frost's functional harmonica breaks, whereas Johnson's guitar spends most of its time providing bread-and-butter riffs. The title track and 'Baby You're So Kind' reveal a kinship with the Jimmy Reed songbook, and there are occasional nods to Bo Diddley and Howlin' Wolf. 'Crawlback', 'Now Twist' and 'Jack's Jump' are simple instrumental workouts. The rating would have been higher but for the inexplicable omission of 'Everything's Alright' and 'Just Come On Home', a mere four and a half minutes of music that would have completed the original album. The presence of the previously unavailable 'You're So Kind' is insufficient recompense.

***(*) Harpin' On It (The Complete Jewel Recordings)
[Westside WESM 633] *Frost; Arthur Lee Williams (h); Chip Young (b); Sam Carr (d). 3/66.*

Four years on, little has changed in what might be termed Frost's signature sound. Produced by Scotty Moore, these sides impress by their succinctness, trimmed of all excess, with a dedication to rhythm illustrated by Carr's total avoidance of percussive decoration. Most solos are taken by Williams, another stranger to exhibitionism (except on his 'Harpin' On It'), although Rice Miller flourishes creep in at times. Frost, who mainly plays guitar, moves to harmonica for the instrumental 'Harp And Soul', the only time competition rears its head. Songs by Eddie Boyd and Howlin' Wolf and a brief 'Got My Mojo Working' sit comfortably alongside Frost's own efforts, although these, such as 'My Back Scratcher', barely conceal their origins. His lazy diction and a pleasing catch in his voice make this a short but enticing album.

*** Midnight Prowler
Earwig CD 4914 *Frost; Jack Johnson (g, b, v); Ernest Roy (g); Sam Carr (d, v); Walter Roy (d). 6/86–2/88.*

Eight tracks by the original Jelly Roll Kings and six where Frost and Johnson are backed by the Roy Brothers make for an entertaining mixture of styles and energies. Alongside songs by Little Walter, Muddy Waters, Sonny Boy Williamson II and a ramshackle 'Mustang Sally' are five Frost originals that can't quite hide their origins. He's on excellent form, with enough stamina and invention to make his frequent harmonica solos, including Walter's 'Quarter To Twelve', fresh and convincing. Odd, though, that Slim Harpo's 'Scratch My Back' and 'My Back Scratcher', Frost's near-identical rewrite, should be cut at the same session. Both Roy brothers play well but *les vrais* Jelly Roll Kings finish a moderately rewarding set with three stompers to which each contributes some vocal assistance.

** Deep Blues
Appaloosa AP 086//Evidence ECD 26094 *Frost; Fred James (g); Bob Kommersmith (b); Waldo LaTowsky (d, p). 12/91.*

Frost's economical style had by now been compromised by a debilitating drink habit. His poor diction and constricted throat make his vocals hard to discern, while his short-winded harmonica playing seldom rises above the perfunctory. Nevertheless, James's band work hard to encourage their leader to greater effort, best portrayed on 'Repo Man' and a revisit to 'Pocket Full Of Money'. Most of the songs, several taken from the above compilation, fail to escape from formulaic arrangements, only 'Somebody Tell Me' breaking the mould to notable effect. The final (and title) track is an instrumental reading of 'I Almost Lost My Mind'. The effort expended by the backing band to melt the permafrost saves this from being a complete disaster – but only just.

*** Keep Yourself Together
Evidence ECD 26077 *Frost; Fred James (o, g); Bob Kommersmith (b); Sam Carr (d). 12/93.*

The opening title track flatters to deceive for Frost sounds strong and engaging. But as the following ten tracks play out, the alertness and combative spirit are dissipated in formulaic arrangements and over-indulgent inconclusive solo sequences. By the time Frost gets to Little Walter's 'Just A Feeling', neither his coarsened vocal tone nor the faltering harmonica solos do the justice to the tune that was previously within his scope. Sam Carr's drumming is characteristically dependable throughout, the bass playing likewise and James makes frequent efforts to enliven the proceedings with both finger and slide. Because of their collective Trojan will, this is a better record than otherwise might have been the case.

**(*) The Jelly Roll Kings
HMG HMG 1006 *Frost; Fred James (g, b); Sam Carr (d, v). 99.*

A better physical condition reinjects some strength into Frost's vocals and harmonica playing but still the result, particularly a revamped 'Jelly Roll King', is a pale reflection of his younger self. James and Carr work hard to ameliorate his shortcomings and initially they enliven his performance. But the instrumentals 'Helena Hop' and 'Mess Around' are non-events, what few ideas Frost has being spoiled by poor execution. Carr sings/talks his splendidly titled 'Owl Head Woman' from the drumstool and it's not always easy to discern what he's on about. James is selfless in his attempts to bolster Frost's fragile energies, and his solos are succinct and faultlessly played. In fact, if it wasn't for Frost's fairly glorious past, this would be an enjoyable listening experience, though it's too pristine to evoke a juke-joint and stops short of being impressive. NS

Blind Boy Fuller (1907–41)
VOCAL, GUITAR, KAZOO

Fulton Allen began playing guitar in 1927, shortly before losing his sight. Dependent on music for a living, he worked with Sonny Terry, Gary Davis and Bull City Red in the streets of Durham, North Carolina. Local businessman and talent scout J. B. Long brought Fuller to ARC's attention in 1935, and he became a popular and influential recording artist, cutting no fewer than 129 songs in the six years before his death.

***(*) **Blind Boy Fuller – Vol. 1 (1935–1936)**
Document DOCD-5091 *Fuller; Gary Davis (g); Bull City Red (wb). 7/35–4/36.*
***(*) **Blind Boy Fuller – Vol. 2 (1936–1937)**
Document DOCD-5092 *As above, except add Dipper Boy Council (g); omit Davis. 4/36–7/37.*
***(*) **Blind Boy Fuller – Vol. 3 (1937)**
Document DOCD-5093 *Fuller; Sonny Terry (h). 7/37–12/37.*
***(*) **Blind Boy Fuller – Vol. 4 (1937–1938 [sic])**
Document DOCD-5094 *As above, except add Charlie Austin (h), Dipper Boy Council (g), Bull City Red (wb). 7/37–12/37.*
***(*) **Blind Boy Fuller – Vol. 5 (1938–1940)**
Document DOCD-5095 *As above, except add poss. Sonny Jones (g); omit Austin, Council. 10/38–3/40.*
**** **Blind Boy Fuller 1935–1938**
JSP JSP 7735 4CD *As for above CDs, except omit Jones. 7/35–10/38.*
*** **Blind Boy Fuller – Vol. 6 (1940)**
Document DOCD-5096 *Fuller; Sonny Terry (h, v); Jordan Webb (h); Bull City Red (wb, v); Brownie McGhee (v). 3/40–6/40.*
(*) **The Essential
Classic Blues CBL 200012 2CD *Fuller; Sonny Terry (h, v); Gary Davis, poss. Sonny Jones (g); Bull City Red (wb, v). 7/35–6/40.*
***(*) **East Coast Piedmont Style**
Columbia CK 46777 *As above except Terry and Red do not sing. 7/35–7/39.*
*** **Screamin' And Cryin' Blues**
Aim 0022 *As above. 7/35–7/39.*
***(*) **Truckin' My Blues Away**
Yazoo 1060 *Fuller; Bull City Red (wb). 7/35–7/39.*
(*) **Blind Boy Fuller 1935–1940
Best Of Blues BOB 4 *As above, except add Sonny Terry (h), Gary Davis (g). 7/35–3/40.*

Received wisdom and an old LP title used to interpret the Carolina blues as *Blind Boy Fuller On Down*, but it's now recognized that Fuller blended his own ideas with those of numerous forerunners and contemporaries, among them Buddy Moss, Josh White, Gary Davis, Blind Blake and Blind Lemon Jefferson. The resulting synthesis had an enormous influence in the Piedmont states and beyond, and in that sense Fuller did indeed father a style. Revisionism has sometimes gone too far, though, tacitly accepting Davis's curmudgeonly assessment: 'He would have been all right if I had kept him under me long enough.' In fact, Fuller was an exceptional guitarist, brimming with original melodic and rhythmic ideas, which both complement his vocal lines and are strikingly independent of them. As a songwriter, he was imaginative and poetic on slow blues, and often ingenious on up-tempo rags

and bawdy numbers. Nor should it be forgotten that in Bull City Red and Sonny Terry he had two ideal accompanists; Gary Davis and Floyd Council were also very successful collaborators, albeit less frequently.

In a recording career as intensive and compressed as Fuller's, there's inevitably some repetition; most of those bawdy numbers are variants of Tampa Red's 'What's That Tastes Like Gravy'. There's some loss of musical quality, too, on Fuller's final session, when serious illness was hampering his blues singing and prompting him to participate in some uninspired spirituals. Most of the time, however, his ringing, bouncy steel guitar, his attractively sandpapered voice and his dynamic delivery stand up well to being heard at length, even in Document's variable and never outstanding sound. JSP's box has the first 100 tracks of a possible 138 (the 100th is conveniently the last of a session); it's competitively priced, attractively packaged and much better remastered.

Even so, the complete or near-complete works will be too much for most listeners. The Best Of Blues disc, which expands an LP that brought together 'the remaining titles' (i.e. those not on LP by the mid-'80s), has indifferent sound, lacks coherence and is short on top-quality performances. *Truckin' My Blues Away* is well mastered and has very useful notes, but with only 14 tracks, which stress Fuller's guitar prowess at the expense of his street band music, it paints an incomplete picture. *East Coast Piedmont Style*, with 20 tracks in even better sound, is similarly tunnel-visioned; Sonny Terry only appears once. Aim's 18-tracker is short on Terry, rags and greatest hits. Classic Blues' mid-priced double CD offers the most comprehensive coverage of these selective surveys, but the notes are sketchy, the sound is indifferent and an alternative take of 'Rag Mama Rag' plays where 'Black And Tan' is listed. CS

Jesse Fuller (1896–1976)
VOCAL, HARMONICA, KAZOO, GUITAR, FOTDELLA, WASHBOARD, HI-HAT CYMBAL, BUCK DANCING

Born in Georgia in 1896, Fuller was given away by his mother to a family who overworked and abused him. He ran away as soon as possible, and became a self-reliant adult, whose billing as 'The Lone Cat' mirrored his offstage reserve. Leaving Georgia with a circus in 1920, Fuller hoboed across the country, ending up in California, where he worked at a variety of jobs, including appearances as a silent-movie extra. In 1950, he took up music again, deciding that a one man band was less likely to include troublemakers. He soon obtained steady work on the folk circuit, and was an early visitor to Britain. Ill health rendered him largely inactive during the '70s.

**** **Frisco Bound**
Arhoolie CD-360 *Fuller. 4/55, 11/62.*
**** **Jazz, Folk Songs, Spirituals, & Blues**
Original Blues Classics OBCCD 564 *Fuller. 1–4/58.*
**** **The Lone Cat**
Original Blues Classics OBCCD 526 *Fuller. 9/58.*
♛ **** **San Francisco Bay Blues**
Original Blues Classics OBCCD 537 *Fuller. 63.*
**** **Jesse Fuller's Favorites**
Original Blues Classics OBCCD 528 *Fuller. 5/63.*

To quote the sleeve of one release, 'Jesse Fuller sings and

accompanies himself in actual live performance on twelve-string guitar, harmonica, kazoo, cymbals and fotdella. No overdubbing, multiple recording, tape editing or other electronic techniques have been used to create any of his sounds.' The hi-hat replaced a foot-operated washboard, which can be heard on some earlier recordings; the buck dancing, accompanied by simultaneous guitar playing, was his set-closer in live performance. Fuller's unique selling proposition was the mellow boom of the fotdella ('I play it with my fot, and it goes "della, della, della" '), a home-made six-string double bass, strung with piano wire and played with his big toe.

All this makes Fuller sound like a novelty act, which, of course, he was; what he was not, however, was a mere novelty act. His instruments were at the service of his talent, not the other way about; his harmonica playing pushes the limits of what can be done with a rack-held instrument, and as a guitarist he could be exceptional, both technically and emotionally, as shown by the spirituals 'Amazing Grace' and 'Hark From The Tomb', on Arhoolie, or the breathtaking 'John Henry', also played with a slide, on *San Francisco Bay Blues*. Even the rasp of his kazoo is the perfect complement to his powerful, gritty vocals.

Although the blues was naturally part of his repertoire, Fuller was a songster rather than a blues singer. (On an unissued concert tape, he remarks, 'I'm gonna sing an old country blues. I don't care about country blues too much, but this is Tampa Red.') If the one-man-band rig was a musical hippogriff, a fabulous, hybrid monster, its operator was a musical coelacanth, a surviving example of a species thought to be extinct. He played many venerable pop songs – even his theme song, 'San Francisco Bay Blues', is one such – and was equally adept at jazz, waltzes, children's songs, spirituals, hillbilly numbers, worksongs, instrumental display pieces like 'Fingerbuster', and extraordinary survivals from the medicine-show and vaudeville stages, such as 'Fables Aren't Nothing But Doggone Lies', and 'Preacher Lowdown', which is traceable to a recording by Bert Williams.

Within this large songbook, there are pieces that recur again and again, above all 'San Francisco Bay Blues', of which there are versions on *Elko Blues Vol. 1* (Wolf 120.614), the *Arhoolie Records 40th Anniversary Collection* (Arhoolie CD 491), *Newport Folk Festival: Best Of The Blues 1959–68* (Vanguard 3VCD 193/95 3CD) and two of the CDs considered here. The large repertoire and the multiple recording of certain songs recall Leadbelly, but so do the consistent high quality of Fuller's performances, his command of his instruments and his ability to charm an audience. Any Jesse Fuller CD is rewarding listening, and they are all about as good as each other, be it for variety, historical interest or entertainment value. *San Francisco Bay Blues* gets a crown because it is exceptionally well programmed, and an infallible cure for low spirits. With due warning that his music is dangerously addictive, it's the CD for anyone who just wants one Jesse Fuller record. CS

Johnny Fuller (1929–85)
VOCAL, GUITAR

Fuller was born in Mississippi but grew up in Vallejo, California, where he sang in a gospel group in his teens. His first recordings were in the gospel idiom, but in the '50s he began recording blues. He had some success with 'Johnny Ace's Last Letter' and the rock 'n' roll novelty 'The Haunted House', and on the strength of the latter did some work in rock 'n' roll package shows. He continued to be active in Oakland clubs in the '70s and early '80s.

*** West Coast R&B And Blues Legend Vol. 1
Official OF-CD 3278 *Fuller; unknowns (s); Walter Robinson (h); unknowns (o); George Hurst, unknown (p); Eugene Keel, R. Dixon, unknown(s) (b); Tommy Ramerson, unknown(s) (d); unknown (vb); unknown (v).* c. 3/54–3/55.

**(*) West Coast R&B And Blues Legend Vol. 2
Official OF-CD 3279 *Fuller; Que Martyn, Lee Allen, unknown (ts); Red Tyler (bs); unknowns (s); unknowns (o); George Hurst, Salvador Doucette, Al Reed, unknowns (p); unknowns (strings); Justin Adams, unknowns (g); R. Dixon, Frank Fields, unknowns (b); Tommy Ramerson, Earl Palmer, unknowns (d); unknown (vb); unknowns (v).* 8/55–62.

Fuller's earliest sides are reflective slow blues, delivered with an air of quiet, slightly ominous drama reminiscent of his contemporary Jimmy Wilson; 'Roughest Place In Town' is based on Wilson's 'Tin Pan Alley'. Fuller himself claimed Charles Brown as a model, a connection confirmed by selections like 'Sunny Road' and 'Fool's Paradise', but his deep, resonant voice removes him from the ranks of fulltime Brown imitators, and on some recordings his pacing and mordant guitar phrasing anticipate the sound of Lonesome Sundown a few years later. After 'Johnny Ace's Last Letter' his repertoire became much more diverse, embracing pop ballads like 'My Heart Is Bleeding' and 'Whispering Wind', while a series of sides with New Orleans sidemen like 'Stop, Look And Listen' inevitably took on some of the colouring of Fats Domino's bluesy rock 'n' roll. 'First Stage Of The Blues' is a deliciously blatant ripoff of Sun-period Elvis Presley. Fuller had extraordinary vocal versatility, but the material on which it was deployed was often either derivative or simply second-rate, and the listener who follows his progress through these two collections may feel a vivid sense of waste. The CDs assemble most of his singles but lack notes or recording data. Four tracks on *Vol. 2* are also on *Oakland Blues: The Irma Recordings* (Wolf 120.613). His well-received 1973 album *Fullers Blues*, with Phillip Walker's band, which in his lifetime was issued only in Australia, has not been transferred to CD. TR

Preston Fulp (1915–93)
VOCAL, GUITAR

From near Winston-Salem in North Carolina, Fulp recorded for a folklorist as long ago as 1937, accompanying Wheeler Bailey, but he was not recorded again until a few months before his death.

** Sawmill Worker
Music Maker MMCD 20 *Fulp.* 93.

Fulp's falsetto voice is striking, and he starts with a confident 'Careless Love' which includes some interesting lyrical variations. Much of his performing career was spent playing for white dances and with white stringbands, and this is reflected in his style and repertoire, which includes songs like 'Wedding Bells', 'Banks of the Ohio' and 'Renfro Valley'. The recordings on this disc are of some historical importance, but after the opening track it's obvious that Fulp was a long way past his best. He has trouble remembering lyrics and makes frequent mistakes on guitar; even a piece as simple as 'Farther Along' becomes an anagram of itself. Regrettably, *Sawmill Worker* can't be recommended except for study purposes. CS

Lowell Fulson (1921–99)
VOCAL, GUITAR

With T-Bone Walker, Fulson was the most important singer/guitarist on the West Coast in the first decade after World War II, elegantly synthesizing the leisurely acoustic blues of his Southwestern youth and the piano trio idiom of late-'40s LA. As a boy in Oklahoma he played in a family stringband, and in Texas he accompanied Texas Alexander, but after army service he settled in California, where he recorded prolifically and with steady sales for Swing Time and other labels. In the '60s and '70s, more adaptable than many of his contemporaries, he shifted into a soul-blues idiom, without losing his blues audience: his set at the 1978 San Francisco Blues Festival was described as 'the high point of the festival's entire six-year history'. In later years he was able to return to the style of his heyday, but he continued to refresh his music with new compositions.

***(*) Lowell Fulson 1946–1947
Classics 5044 *Fulson; Eldridge McCarty, Rufus J. Russell (p); Martin Fulson (g); Bob 'Big Dad' Johnson, Arthur Robinson (b); Dickie 'Little Man' Washington, Asal 'Count' Carson (d); band (v). 6/46–early 47.*

*** My First Recordings
Arhoolie CD 443 *As above, except add Earl Brown (as), unknown (ts), unknown (bs), unknown (o), Lloyd Glenn (p), Billy Hadnott, unknown (b), Bob Harvey, unknown (d). 6/46–53?*

*** 3 O'Clock Blues
[Zircon Bleu 510] *As for* Lowell Fulson 1946–1947*, except add Quedellis Martyn (ts), King Solomon (p), unknowns (p, g, b, d), Mabel — (sp). 6/46–48.*

*** A Proper Introduction To Lowell Fulson: Juke Box Shuffle
Proper INTRO CD 2042 *As for* My First Recordings*, except add Vernon 'Geechie' Smith (t), Don Hill, unknown (as), Maxwell Davis, another unknown (ts), another unknown (bs), Jay McShann (p), Lloyd Lambert (b), Jesse Sailes, another unknown (d), Mabel — (sp); omit unknown (o), Washington. 6/46–10/53.*

* Trying To Find My Baby
Snapper Complete Blues SBLUECD 030 *Similar to above. 46–48.*

*** The Original West Coast Blues
Collectors Edition CBCD 025 *As for* 3 O'Clock Blues*, except omit King Solomon. late 46–early 48.*

***(*) Lowell Fulson 1947–1948
Classics 5071 *As for* 3 O'Clock Blues*. 47–early 48.*

***(*) Lowell Fulson 1948–1949
Classics 5122 *Fulson; Earl Brown (as); Rufus J. Russell, Jay McShann, Ellis 'King' Solomon, Lloyd Glenn (p); Arthur Robinson, Floyd Washington, Billy Hadnott, unknown (b); Asal 'Count' Carson, Bob Harvey, unknown (d). early 48–49.*

Fulson's earliest recordings were guitar duets with his brother Martin, melodically almost indistinguishable, at their busiest gently medium-paced, sometimes moving as slowly as molasses on a cold day. At times Fulson seems to be not just playing in the past but living there, especially in the two-part 'River Blues', a version of the ancient Texas prison song Smokey Hogg called 'Penitentiary Blues'. There in particular, but to some degree throughout all these albums, Fulson's use of melisma and his relaxed vocal timing irresistibly recall his model, Texas Alexander.

The duet performances were interspersed with recordings with small groups, usually a piano quartet, and after a year or so supplanted by them. This setting, too, produced music that might have been designed for night-owls and other birds in flight from the din of the everyday world: quiet, thoughtful blues about women and other worries, their meandering guitar lines shaded by trickling piano and maybe a discreet drummer's hushed brushes.

My First Recordings shares 22 tracks with *1946–1947* and adds four later combo sides. *The Original West Coast Blues*' 18 tracks are also on one or the other of the first two Classics CDs; so are most of *3 O'Clock Blues*' 25, but three come from the period covered by Classics' third volume. All these albums and the Proper are good value – unlike *Trying To Find My Baby*, an astute selection ruined by distortion on more than half the tracks – but the orderly presentation and the sorted-out chronology of the Classics CDs give them the edge for serious collectors.

*** San Francisco Blues
Black Lion BLCD 760176 *Similar to* Lowell Fulson 1948–1949*. early 48–51/52.*

*** Mean Old Lonesome Blues
Night Train NTI CD 7110 *Similar to above. 6/46, 48/49–53.*

*** Volume 2: I'm A Nightowl
Acrobat ACRCD 291 *Similar to above, except add David 'Fathead' Newman (ts), unknowns (s, p, b, d), band (v). 48–9/54.*

These albums, derived from Swing Time (*I'm A Nightowl* adding a few from Aladdin and Checker), present Fulson in band settings. (The only exceptions are 'Good-bye, Good-bye' on *Mean Old Lonesome Blues*, which is the 1946 duet piece 'My Baby Left Me' retitled, and 'Three O'Clock Blues' on *I'm A Nightowl*.) The piano-led lineup was in time augmented with Earl Brown's alto saxophone, though most of *San Francisco Blues* was recorded before that development. On the later sides Fulson's guitar playing is not only clarified by more amplification but tends to be less discursive. For a vivid lesson in how his music changed during this period, put on *San Francisco Blues* or *I'm A Nightowl* and skip from the pensive reading of Walter Davis's 'Come Back Baby' to the punchy 'Let Me Ride In Your Little Automobile'. Similarly, on *Mean Old Lonesome Blues*, Fulson swings between the meditative style of 'Blues With A Feeling' and the jump-blues energy of 'Guitar Shuffle'.

At the time of writing *San Francisco Blues* was of uncertain availability, while *Mean Old Lonesome Blues* was the only one of Night Train's four Fulson CDs currently in print, though it was likely that any or all of the others – *Back Home Blues* (NTI CD 7001), *Everyday I Have The Blues* (NTI CD 7007) and *Sinner's Prayer* (NTI CD 7011) – might be reinstated. Like them, it's a random assortment of Swing Time sides, including several previously unissued numbers and takes, but almost no information on participating musicians or recording dates. But little of it is available elsewhere (none on *San Francisco Blues*), and its haphazard mixture of recordings from numerous sessions is both informative and entertaining. *I'm A Nightowl* is those things too, but also sequenced in a more orderly fashion, equipped with notes and recording data, and with very good sound – altogether the pick of these three.

**** Lowell Fulson 1946 To 1953
JSP JSP 7728 4CD *Fulson; Vernon Smith (t); Don Hill, Earl Brown (as); Que Martyn, Maxwell Davis, unknown (ts); unknown (bs); unknown (o); Lloyd Glenn (p, cel); Eldridge McCarty, Rufus J. Russell, King Solomon, Jay McShann, unknown (p); Martin Fulson, Tiny Webb (g); Bob 'Big Dad' Johnson, Arthur Robinson, Ralph Hamilton, Billy Hadnott, unknowns (b); Dickie 'Little Man' Washington, Asal 'Count' Carson, Jesse Sailes, Bob Harvey, unknowns (d); band (v); unknown (sp).* 46–53.

This 113-track programme more or less follows the order of Fulson's discography in *BR*, which experts are in the process of revising. If you require your listening to be chronologically shipshape, collect the Classics CDs (see above). If you don't care whether the Big Towns came before the Down Towns, this slipcased set, just a few tracks short of complete for the period it covers, would appear to be your best bet – so long as you really, really like Lowell Fulson.

*** The Complete Chess Masters
MCA/Chess CHD2–9394//[(E) MCD 09394] 2CD *Fulson; unknowns (t); unknowns (tb); Earl Brown, Charles Williams, unknown (as); David Newman, Eddie Chamblee, John Johnson, Milt Thomas, Choker Campbell, Louis Williams, Big Jay McNeely, unknowns (ts); Leroy Cooper, Big Jim Wynn, unknowns (bs); unknown (o); Lloyd Glenn, Jimmy Smith, unknowns (p); Irving Ashby, unknown (g); Willie Dixon, Billy Hadnott, Sylvester Morton, unknown (b); Fred Below, Saul Samuels, Robert Sims, unknowns (d); unknown (vb); unknowns (v).* 9/54–11/63.

It's a pity this set may no longer be in print, since it not only covers a decade of Fulson's career that's otherwise inaccessible on CD but provides a detailed account of an artist trying every trick in the book to replicate an early success. Fulson's first Chess single, 'Reconsider Baby', was a substantial hit and has become a standard. Over the next nine years he cut 40-odd tracks for the label, in a variety of styles from blues to ballad to rock 'n' roll. Several, like 'Tollin' Bells' and 'Hung Down Head', were more than usually interesting, but nothing recaptured the sales of 'Reconsider', and by the early '60s novelty numbers like 'Can She (Do It)', a twist song, were showing the gap between Chess's strategy and Fulson's natural game.

*** Black Nights: The Early Kent Sessions
Ace CDCHD 804 *Fulson; Melvin Moore, Bob Harman (t); unknowns (brass, reeds); Maxwell Davis, Lloyd Glenn (p); Larry Green, Arthur Wright, Arthur K. Adams, Rene Hall (g); Curtis Tillman, Ronnie Brown (b); Chuck Thomas, unknown (d).* 5/64–2/67.

(***) Tramp/Soul
Ace CDCHD 339 *As above, except add 'Pete' (g).* 5/64–12/66.

*** The Tramp Years
Ace CDCHD 755 *As above, except add George Smith (h), unknown (o), unknown (g), unknown (b), Jimmy McCracklin (v), unknowns (v grp).* 65–68.

*** The Final Kent Years
Ace CDCHD 831 *As above, except add unknowns (h, p, g, b, d); omit 'Pete', Tillman, Thomas, McCracklin.* early 67–2/78.

In 1964 Fulson's manager Fats Washington brought him to Kent Records, which had lately lost its best-selling blues artist, B. B. King. Over the next four years Fulson produced 20-odd singles and three albums, recorded with small-group backings but often with horn parts superimposed by the arranger, Maxwell Davis. The material was predominantly in conventional blues forms, many of the songs written by or in collaboration with Washington, such as 'Black Nights', but with occasional diversions like the half-narrated, half-sung 'Tramp'. Those two numbers were hits, and 'Black Nights' dictated the form of many subsequent recordings. Like the contemporary work of Albert King, these economical, emphatic performances proved that blues could still find a market if given a little contemporary gloss. But their success is not due only to savvy arrangements: at this point in his career Fulson's voice was a wonderfully subtle, sexy instrument.

The contents of *Tramp/Soul*, which couples two of the Kent LPs, have been entirely subsumed into *Black Nights* and *The Tramp Years*. *The Final Kent Years*, which rounds up what's left (and, like the other two CDs, includes previously unissued material), shows in its more busily arranged pieces like 'Let's Go Get Stoned' and 'The Letter' how Fulson was moving into a blues-funk style, though there are suggestions that he was also aware of contemporary work by B. B. King. The CD is completed by an eight-song set from 1978 (*Lovemaker*, originally issued on Big Town), which returns Fulson to a small-band setting, but one with the same rhythmic vitality as the later Kent sides and, thanks to one of the uncredited guitarists, something of a rock edge.

**(*) I've Got The Blues (... And Then Some!): The Jewel Recordings 1969–71
[Westside WESD 234] 2CD *Fulson; Melvin Moore, Bob Harman (t); Big Jay McNeely (ts); Bob McNeely (bs); unknowns (brass, reeds); unknown (h); unknown (kb); Barry Beckett, unknown (o, p); Maxwell Davis (p, prod); Eddie Hinton, unknowns (g); Curtis Tillman, David Hood, Ronnie Brown, unknowns (b); Chuck Thomas, Roger Hawkins, Abraham Mills, unknowns (d); Fats Washington, Sonny Thompson (prod).* 1/69–71.

** I've Got The Blues
Fuel 2000 302 061 082 *Similar to above.* 10/69–71.

** Blue On Blues
Fuel 2000 302 061 192 *Similar to above.* 10/69–71.

**(*) I've Got The Blues
Jewel JCD-5009 *Fulson; unknowns (brass, reeds, kb, g, b, d); Fats Washington, Sonny Thompson (prod).* 70–71.

Fulson recorded two albums for Jewel, *In A Heavy Bag* and *I've Got The Blues*, and a couple of handfuls of singles, the whole lot collected on the Westside 2CD set. At the time, the Muscle Shoals funk settings of a few of the tracks on *In A Heavy Bag*, especially the Beatles' 'Why Don't We Do It In The Road', gave some of Fulson's longtime admirers fits of the vapours, but with hindsight it seems that Fulson settled in this groove more comfortably than some similarly placed contemporaries. In any case, the Muscle Shoals recordings are greatly outnumbered by material from other sessions, some of it in the contemplative slow blues idiom of the Kent period, some, like 'Trouble Everywhere' or 'Cheating Woman', aerated by rock guitar. Several producers went to a lot of trouble to find novel settings for this fundamentally generic blues material; it can't be said that their efforts often enhanced it, but indulgent listeners may decide that their volatility was harmless and even, at times, amusing.

The Fuel 2000 version of *I've Got The Blues* has 18 tracks

against Westside's 39 and omits many of the better, and the more peculiar, pieces. The original Jewel LP titled *I've Got The Blues* is also available separately. *Blue On Blues* couples six of the Jewel sides with six by T-Bone Walker.

** The Ol' Blues Singer
Sanctuary CAS 36067 *Fulson; Bud Brisbois, Dalton Smith, Thomas Shepard, Lew McCreary (brass); Jackie Kelso, Mike Henderson, Don Menza (s); Ben Benay (h, poss. g); Marvell Thomas (kb); Larry Muhoberac (o, arr, cond); James Getzoff, Leonard Malarsky, Harry Bluestone, Lou Klass, Murray Adler, Bonnie Douglas, Carl LaMagna, Gareth Nuttycombe, Samuel Boghossian, Raymond J. Kelley, Jan R. Kelley (strings); Steve Cropper, Michael Toles (g); Tommy Cathey, Reinie Press (b); Al Jackson Jr (d); Bobbie Hall (perc); Carolyn Willis, Julia Tillman, Maxine Willard (v). 70/71.*

The basic tracks were recorded in Memphis, then sent to Hollywood to be coated in orchestral icing by studio musicians, possibly following the recipe dictated by B. B. King's 'The Thrill Is Gone' and *Indianola Mississippi Seeds*. Actually 'smothered' would sometimes be nearer the mark than 'coated'. Tough though Fulson's music is, it needs room to breathe, and here it gasps like a beached whale. The songs, at least, are mostly Fulson's, though 'Kansas City Bound' is Jim Jackson's old number, in what must surely be its most grandiose version.

*** Blue Shadows
Stony Plain SPCD 1233 *Fulson; Mark Hasselbach (t); David Woodward (ts); Bill Runge (bs); Robin (h); Robbie King (o); Willie MacCalder (p); Tom Lavin (g, ldr); Jack Lavin, Jim Milne (b); Chris Norquist (d); Jim Byrnes (v). 81.*

Recorded in Vancouver with the Canadian band Powder Blues, this session wasn't issued until 16 years later. It's worth the exposure: although the songs are from a well-thumbed setlist, the spirited but never bumptious playing of Powder Blues provides comely and appropriate settings for 'Reconsider Baby', 'Blue Shadows', 'Sinner's Prayer' and 'Guitar Shuffle'. The ten-track programme is followed by a 17-minute interview in which Fulson reminisces about his early days and some of his musical associates.

***(*) One More Blues
Evidence ECD 26022//Black & Blue BB 430 *Fulson; Mike 'Iceman' Vannice (ts); Art Hillary (o, p); Phillip Walker (g); Dennis Walker (b); Johnny Tucker (d). 4/84.*

The band on this Paris date is Phillip Walker's, and Fulson could not have found a more sympathetic accompanying group: laidback, economical yet pithy, they embody the qualities intrinsic to his music. Much of the material is new and some of it, like 'Thanks A Lot For The Offer', 'Ten More Shows To Play' and 'One More Blues', all co-written with Dennis Walker, is excellent. The greater part of the guitar playing is by Phillip Walker.

**(*) Think Twice Before You Speak
JSP JSPCD 290 *Fulson; John Altman (s); Hammy Howell (p); Eddie C. Campbell (g); Wayne Elliott (b); John Dummer (d). 9/84.*
**(*) Think Twice Before You Speak
JSP JSP 5103 *As above.* 9/84.

Some of the tracks from this London session have a pleasant laidback feel to which Altman and Howell contribute idiomatically, but the mood proves difficult to sustain and other numbers are lackadaisical. The problem does not lie with Fulson, who sings admirably and uses a good deal of fresh material like 'Parachute Woman', but with the unimaginative rhythm guitar playing of Eddie C. Campbell, who can have been enlisted only because he was in England at the time; musically he has little in common with Fulson, and he lets no rhythmic light into 'Come Back Baby' and 'Sinner's Prayer', guitar duet pieces modelled on Fulson's earliest sides. The second issue is in Super Audio format and revises the running order.

*** It's A Good Day
Rounder CD 2088 *Fulson; Earl Turbinton (as); Alvin 'Red' Tyler (ts); Ron Levy (o, p, syn); Willie Tee (syn); Eugene 'High Rise' Ross (g); 'Luscious' Lloyd Lambert (b); David Lee Jr (d). 11/87.*
*** Hold On
Bullseye Blues CDBB 9525 *Fulson; Joe Campbell (t); Bernard Baisden (tb); Bobby Forte, William Zimmerman (ts); Eddie 'Saxman' Synigal (bs); Ron Levy (o, prod); Jimmy McCracklin (p); Terry 'Big T' DeRouen, 'Pee Wee' Thomas (g); Ray Cooksey (b); Craig Kimbrough (d); Margaret Love Carter, James 'Bull' Parks (v). 5/92.*
**(*) Them Update Blues
Bullseye Blues CDBB 9558 *Fulson; Wayne Jackson (t, tb); Andrew Love (ts); Ron Levy (o); Leon Haywood, Darby Hicks Jr [Ron Levy] (p); Terry 'Big T' DeRouen (g); James B. Wyatt (b); Craig Kimbrough (d). 95?*

Fulson's guitar sound is sometimes rather thin and angular, but otherwise these are carefully made recordings. *It's A Good Day* is enriched by a sustaining set of songs from his much-travelled briefcase, some previously recorded by himself or friends like Phillip Walker ('Blues And My Guitar'), but here rearranged for a four-piece band, occasionally augmented by horns. Fulson took the opportunity to rerecord the three songs co-written with Dennis Walker that he had premiered on *One More Blues*.

Hold On and *Them Update Blues* have more new material: notable pieces on the former include 'Working Man' and Jimmy McCracklin's 'Real Name Is Danger Zone' and 'Love Is The Bottom Line'. The songs on *Them Update Blues* are less striking and occasionally his singing is a little tired, but most artists in their 70s would be glad to close their recording account sounding so resilient. TR

Anson Funderburgh (born 1954)
GUITAR, VOCAL

Funderburgh formed his Rockets in Dallas in 1978, initially with Darrell Nulisch as singer and harmonica player. Sam Myers took over both roles in 1986. A hardworking band, popular on the blues club and festival circuit, the Rockets recorded regularly in the '80s and early '90s for Black Top.

** Which Way Is Texas?
Bullseye Blues BBCD 9619 *Funderburgh; Gary Slechta (t); Mark Kazanoff (as, ts); John Mills (bs); Sam Myers (h, v); Gentleman John Street (o, p); Eric Mathew Przygocki, Johnny Bradley (b); Wes Starr (d, perc). 03?*

The deletion of Funderburgh's seven albums for Black Top obliterated about a decade of his recorded career. He was also one of the three guitarists (the others were Debbie Davies and Otis Grand) who came together for *Grand Union* (Blueside WESF 107), but this too has been deleted. Of his two currently available albums, *Change In My Pocket* (Bullseye Blues & Jazz 9573) is billed as a collaboration with Sam Myers (and is discussed in his entry), but *Which Way Is Texas?*, though Myers sings on ten of the 13 tracks, is not. Go figure.

Newcomers meeting Funderburgh and the Rockets for the first time may find it hard to square what they've read or heard about the band with the clumping, by-the-numbers playing on *Which Way Is Texas?* (or *Change In My Pocket*). What's called for is a collection of the best tracks on their Black Top CDs, and someone should compile one. TR

Bob Gaddy (1924–97)
VOCAL, PIANO

Born in West Virginia, Gaddy took up with the blues while serving in the navy during World War II. On discharge, he moved to New York, and entered the performing and recording circle around Brownie McGhee. His musical career languished in the '60s, but underwent a modest revival after researchers found him working as a chef in 1986.

** Harlem Blues Operator
[Ace CDCHD 407] *Gaddy; Jimmy Wright, Matt Gray (ts); Jack Dupree (p); Brownie McGhee, Joe Ruffin, Jimmy Spruill, unknowns (g); poss. Al Hall, unknowns (b); Gene Moore, Gene Brooks, unknown (d). 55–60.*

Using material licensed from Old Town, the LP of which this CD is an expanded version was eagerly awaited, but proved a severe disappointment. More tracks do nothing to change that judgement. Some of the earlier sides have their moments, notably the rocking 'Out Of My Name' and its flipside 'Paper Lady', with Riff Ruffin's stinging guitar and Gaddy's delicate right-hand tracery. 'Come On Little Children', previously unissued, is lively, sax-led black rock 'n' roll. Most of the disc, however, consists of attempts to emulate hitmakers like Fats Domino, Johnny Ace and Guitar Slim, doomed by weak material, cursory, uninspired production, or both. Gaddy's earlier, and much better, recordings can be heard on *Best Of Harlem & Jax Records Vol. 2: Rockin' Blues & Boogie* (H&J 102) and *Vol. 3: More Rockin' Blues & Boogie* (H&J 103). CS

Roy Gaines (born 1934)
VOCAL, GUITAR

Brother of saxophonist Grady, Roy Gaines began his professional career aged 16 in the Roy Milton band. Five years later he was a session guitarist for Duke and Peacock before being recruited by Chuck Willis, who took him to New York. While working and recording with Willis, Gaines made his own records for Groove and later DeLuxe. As well as being a prolific session and road musician, he crossed over into jazz, accompanying Jimmy Rushing and Billie Holiday and working with The Crusaders. After years off the limelight, he re-emerged during the 1990s, cutting a number of albums (one, no longer available, on his own Black Gold label), and became a firm favourite on the festival circuit.

**(*) Superman
Black & Blue BB 451 *Gaines; Gene 'Mighty Flea' Connors (tb);* *Milt Buckner (o); David 'Panama' Francis (d). 2/75.*

A curious mixture of generations and musical disciplines, not to mention instrumentation, finds Gaines indecisive about whether to play blues or jazz. 'Stormy Monday Blues' and a marathon 'Once I Was A Gambler' take effective care of the former but two takes each of the title track and 'Happy Birthday Blues' are blowing vehicles for what emerges as a subtly mismatched band. Francis is too inflexible to badger soloists to greater effort and Buckner is no Jimmy Smith, so any hope of summoning Grant Green's ghost is lost. The Mighty Flea is impervious to his surroundings and acquits himself fairly well. Gaines has his moments but his playing doesn't stand up to close examination, as an overlong stab at Wes Montgomery's 'Bumpin' On Sunset' (here mistitled) confirms. It's a case of 'we know you can play, please don't try so hard'.

*** Bluesman For Life
JSP JSPCD 2110 *Gaines; Johnny Viau (ts); Troy Jennings (bs); Tom Mahon (p); John Marx (g); Rick Reed (b); Paul Fasulo (d). 4/98.*

An entertaining set that emphasizes Gaines's gifts as an interpreter, since most of these 11 tracks were written by producer Jimmy Morello. 'It's Midnight Baby' is Aaron Walker to a T, while 'You Went Back On Your Word' follows the tramlines of 'Things I Used To Do'. There's generous time for soloists, principally Viau and Mahon, but Jennings gets his chance on 'Lulu Mae'. 'Jump In My Cadillac' and more T-Bone with 'You're Gonna Wish I Had Stayed' complete the titles that impress, although what remains is more than serviceable. Gaines's voice is well recorded and his solos are fluid, although an occasional fluff is allowed to remain in an otherwise good take. On the traycard Gaines thanks every artist he's worked with, underlining a suspicion he's not entirely graduated from his previous subordinate role.

*** New Frontier Lover
Severn CD-0008 *Gaines; Chris Walker, Bill Moore (t); John Jensen (tb); Scott Young (ts); Scott Silbert, Steve Williams (bs); Steve Guyger (h); Benjie Porecki (o, p); David Maxwell (p); Steve Gomes (b); Robb Stupka, Joe Maher (d). 00.*

Gaines paid tribute to his earliest mentor with *I Got Those T-Bone Walker Blues* (Groove Note GRV 2002, currently unavailable) and the influence can be heard here in 'You Can't Make Nobody Love You' and 'Texas Millionaire'. These and the last four tracks, all featuring Maxwell's piano, are the most rewarding performances on an album that ultimately isn't as distinctive as it ought to be. A six-piece brass section is under-recorded, only fitfully realizing the power it should deliver. 'My Woman, My Blacksnake And Me' and 'Roll Your Own Biscuit' take on a hint of Chicago blues with Guyger's amplified harmonica. 'Roy's Theme' provides a compact display of Gaines's guitar technique, which elsewhere sputters when it ought to shout. The songs are all Gaines's own, with a handful of collaborators, but his lyrics misfire as often as his solos.

***(*) In The House
Crosscut CCD 11074 *Gaines; George Pandis (t); Johnny Viau (ts); Troy Jennings (bs); Neal Wauchope (o, p); Billy Haynes (b); Chad Wright (d). 11/01.*

On this evidence, taped at the Lucerne Blues Festival,

Gaines is at his best when forced to be spontaneous. He and his band work hard and well through a set that combines older material like 'Lucille Works For Me', his jibe at B. B. King, and the sanctimonious 'W. C. Handy Sang The Blues'. There's something false about 'Standing Up For Women's Rights' when later he sings 'Petrol For Your Tank' but lyric content is not what this set is about. It's sometimes hard for the instruments to be heard clearly but most are featured during 'Rag Blues', while Viau gets more chances elsewhere. Gaines performs well, his vocals are strong and his solos benefit from his need to entertain rather than preen. But finishing with 'Do You Know What It Means To Miss New Orleans' was a big mistake. NS

Bill Gaither (1910–70)
VOCAL, GUITAR

Gaither was born in Belmont, Kentucky, but spent his teens in Louisville, where an uncle who played mandolin in one of the city's jugbands may have encouraged him to learn guitar. In 1932 he moved to Indianapolis and joined the blues circle there. A few months after the death of Leroy Carr, the city's best-known bluesman, in 1935, he began recording, soon adopting the nom de disque Leroy's Buddy, and eventually cutting over a hundred sides. In 1940 he returned to Louisville, where he ran a radio repair shop. Army service overseas in 1942–45 left him with a nervous condition that prevented him making music; he went back to Indianapolis and spent his last years working in a café.

*** **Bill Gaither – Vol. 1 (1935–1936)**
Document DOCD-5251 *Gaither; Honey Hill (p, cel); unknown(s) (b); unknown (spoons).* 12/35–10/36.

*** **Bill Gaither – Vol. 2 (1936–1938)**
Document DOCD-5252 *As above, except add Frank Busby (v).* 10/36–6/38.

(*) **Bill Gaither – Vol. 3 (1938–1939)
Document DOCD-5253 *Gaither; prob. Edgar Saucier (as); Honey Hill, unknown (p); unknown (g); unknown (imb); unknown (d).* 6/38–6/39.

*** **Bill Gaither – Vol. 4 (1939)**
Document DOCD-5254 *Gaither; Honey Hill (p); unknown(s) (b).* 9–10/39.

(*) **Bill Gaither – Vol. 5 (1940–1941)
Document DOCD-5255 *Gaither; unknowns (p); prob. Jesse Ellery (g); unknowns (b); unknown (d).* 6/40–11/41.

*** **The Essential**
Classic Blues CBL 200018 2CD *Gaither; Honey Hill, unknowns (p); prob. Jesse Ellery, unknowns (g); unknowns (b); unknowns (d); unknown (spoons); Frank Busby (v).* 12/35–11/41.

Gaither's first three (1935) sides are untypically (as it would prove) upbeat, two stomps and the chipper 'Tired Of That Same Stuff All The Time', in which he pertly corrects himself: 'I'm tired of that same shi– … stuff all the time'. The song became one of his signature numbers, remade several times under similar titles like 'Tired Of Your Line Of Jive'. But then, beginning with 'Pains In My Heart', he settles into the role of a Leroy Carr memorialist, justifying himself in 'After The Sun's Gone Down': 'Once in the evening, we sat talkin' face to face, When Leroy Carr told me, "Some day you'll have to take my place."' His guitar phrases, which have the clang of a steel-bodied instrument, are often very similar in style to Scrapper Blackwell's with Carr, markedly so on the 1936 'Stoney Lonesome' and 'You Done Showed Your D.B.A.', but he does not have Blackwell's ability to ring out above the piano.

Occasionally he obeys the promptings of other styles that were in the '30s air: 'Bad Luck Child', for instance, follows the contours of Joe Pullum's 'Black Gal'. He may also have intentionally dogged the footsteps of his fellow Carr acolyte Bumble Bee Slim, for example in 'Gravel In My Bread', which not only alludes to Slim's 'Bricks In My Pillow' but is sung in his manner. Vol. 1, which embraces all the music discussed so far, ends with the out-of-character 'Who's Been Here Since I Been Gone', a tune like a children's game song, with slapped double bass, a percussive effect like tap dancing and Honey Hill doubling piano and celeste.

Gaither made the bulk of his recordings before he was 30, and his voice never lost the freshness of youth, so that when he sings reflective numbers in the Carr idiom he often sounds like Carr's sunnier younger brother. He spends a good deal of Vol. 2 doing just that, whether on plain remakes of Carr songs like 'You're A Mean Mistreater' and 'Sunrise Blues' ('Blues Before Sunrise') or on the slightly more distanced 'Just The Wrong Man' or 'Blake Street Blues'. The formularization of the material begins to be echoed in the accompaniments: the piano introductions to 'New Little Pretty Mama' and 'I'm Wise To Your Sweet Line Of Jive' are virtually identical, and the intro to the next side cut, 'I Just Keep On Worrying', uses some of the same melodic material. But at any time Gaither is capable of transcending his limitations and achieving an effect of reminiscence or melancholy that is not merely borrowed, as in 'Rocky Mountain Blues' or 'In The Wee Wee Hours', an adaptation of 'Midnight Hour Blues' that is as convincing as its original. ''Leven Light City' (an early recording of the standard 'Sweet Old Kokomo') and 'Prisoner Bound' are sung by the obscure but estimable Frank Busby, accompanied by Gaither and Hill.

The ingenious writing of the first track, 'Old Coals Will Kindle', encourages the listener to hope that Vol. 3 may be less Carr-oriented than its predecessor, and to a considerable extent it is. Though the feel of the music does not at first change greatly, Gaither sets aside Carr's book of words and produces compositions all his own like 'Old Coals', 'Babyfied Ways Girl' and 'Champ Joe Louis', about, and recorded the day after, the boxer's match with Max Schmeling. Honey Hill marks two and a half years' service as Leroy's Buddy's buddy with a couple of solos, 'Boogie Woogie' ('Pine Top's Boogie Woogie') and 'Set 'Em', a jaunty blues. The rest of Vol. 3 is with a trio of New York-based musicians. Like his fellow Decca artist Peetie Wheatstraw when put in the same boat, Gaither sounds different, but not very interestingly so. The accompanists, anonymous in both senses, break Gaither's connection with the Carr–Blackwell sound but do not rewire him to an equally charged source.

Hill returns for the sessions that fill Vol. 4 and, apart from an unidentified bassist, furnishes all the accompaniment on those 23 titles. Freed of the duty to play guitar, and perhaps stimulated by the bareness of the setting, Gaither does consistently fine work. The Carr inheritance is now receding to a noise-off and his cadences are mostly his own, though he borrows Johnnie Temple's in 'Another Big Leg Woman' and 'See Me Grieve Blues', Joe Pullum's in 'Evil Yalla Woman', and, rather surprisingly, Billie Holiday's in 'Fairy Tale Blues'. The best performances on this disc are among the most affecting blues of their era: listen, for example, to 'Stony Lonesome Graveyard', a calmly told tale of sorrow, especially its exquisitely sung final verse. Hill plays with unfailing grace on the slow blues and spins his boogie-woogie wheels enthusiastically beneath 'Bloody Eyed Woman'.

Why did Gaither record a 'Life Of Leroy Carr' in 1940, five years after its subject's death? Perhaps at the insistence of his new label, OKeh, which seems to have decided to haul him back to the Carr style of his early recordings. That's certainly the flavour of his 6/40 sides, accentuated by Gaither playing his guitar louder and more Blackwellishly than ever before, though he wanders over into Lonnie Johnson territory on 'Money Kills Love'. But the Carr influence fades again in the two 1941 sessions that make up the rest of Vol. 5, and Gaither's stylistic references, when he makes them, are to active contemporaries like Big Maceo ('Worried Life Blues') or Peetie Wheatstraw ('Moonshine By The Keg') – an amusingly accurate impression). There are some gritty transfers on this CD, but no signs of decline in Gaither's singing or writing.

The Classic Blues selection is quite well made, spanning Gaither's entire career and embracing several of the tracks mentioned above, including those by Frank Busby and Honey Hill, but a missing track on the second disc disorganizes the stated running order. TR

Cecil Gant (1913–51)
VOCAL, PIANO

'The G.I. Sing-sation' who caused such a stir in the closing year of World War II was an army private based in LA who allegedly got his first break while performing at a war-bond rally. After the runaway success of his composition 'I Wonder', which also charted in versions by Roosevelt Sykes and Louis Armstrong, he recorded prolifically for the LA labels Gilt-Edge and 4 Star, and in Nashville, which was probably his hometown, for Bullet, Dot and Decca, meanwhile playing in nightclubs throughout the country.

(*) The Complete Recordings Volume 1 – 1944
Blue Moon BMCD 6022 *Gant; unknown(s) (b). 6–?9/44.*

*** The Complete Recordings Volume 2 – 1945**
Blue Moon BMCD 6023 *Gant; unknown (as); unknown (p); unknown (g); unknown(s) (b); unknown (d). 45.*

*** The Complete Recordings Volume 3 – 1945–1946**
Blue Moon BMCD 6029 *Gant; unknown (as, ts); unknown (sg); Ted Swinney or Ernie Newton, unknown(s) (b); poss. Farris Coursey, unknown(s) (d); Numa Lee Davis, band (v). 45–46.*

*** The Complete Recordings Volume 4 – 1946–1949**
Blue Moon BMCD 6035 *Gant; poss. Charles Grant (ts); poss. Jack Charmella (g); Ted Swinney or Ernie Newton (b); poss. Farris Coursey (d); 'Dorothy', band (sp). 46–49.*

Cecil Gant occupies a unique place in the history of black music. His wartime record 'I Wonder', though the first release on a new label, not only created unprecedented demand among retailers and jukebox distributors but shook other entrepreneurs into starting record companies devoted to black music. This makes him interesting, but does it make him relevant? Someone who had heard only 'I Wonder' and certain other early recordings for Gilt-Edge might not think of him as a blues artist at all, but rather as a suburban cousin of Nat 'King' Cole or, in Arnold Shaw's phrase, a 'sepia Sinatra'. He could pitch a spirited boogie woogie, but that was practically *de rigueur* for a pianist in the '40s. Honest-to-God blues are indeed only occasional guests in his early repertoire. Probably, like his contemporary Charles Brown, Gant yearned to be an artist unconfined by genre, and perhaps it was his failure to reach that goal, to recapture the stardust moment of 'I Wonder', that drove him, again and again throughout his recording career, into the easier role of the boozing, boogying bluesman.

But to look so far ahead is to anticipate later episodes in a series that is planned to assemble Gant's complete work. In these volumes Gant is cresting a wave, dispensing boogies, ballads, boisterous Fats Wallerish songs and, occasionally, blues to an audience growing warm with the war-winning euphoria that suffuses 'The Grass Is Getting Greener'. This is on *Volume 2*, which offers a wider view of Gant's abilities. Tracks like 'Blues In L.A.' and 'I Gotta Gal' show him to be a blues singer of considerable individuality, now touching, now dry. The blues on *Volume 3* give us some idea of his models, 'Stella' being derived from Roosevelt Sykes and 'In The Evening When The Sun Goes Down' from Leroy Carr, though Carr's effect is more obvious in Gant's own blues 'Special Delivery'. This CD ends with the first four sides for Bullet, and *Volume 4* adds the rest. The Bullets are very relaxed recordings ('relaxed' sometimes being a euphemism for 'slightly squiffy'), typified by playlets like 'Ninth Street Jive' and 'Cecil's Jam Session', but Gant exercises his boogie-woogie muscles in 'Boozie Boogie' and 'Bullet Boogie'. Either *Volume 3* or *Volume 4* would be a good entry-point to this series. *Volume 1* is necessarily but, to anyone less than fanatic about the subject, perhaps rather tediously preoccupied with documenting the many variant recordings of 'I Wonder' and the tune usually coupled with it, 'Cecil Boogie' (five and four versions respectively), as well as three takes of 'Wake Up, Cecil, Wake Up'. Thanks largely to the research of Konrad Nowakowski, this series is disentangling Gant's complicated discography; it has already gathered and issued for the first time his debut recordings for Leroy Hurte's Bronze label. Some of the *Volume 1* tracks are a little hard on the ear, but generally Blue Moon has done very well indeed to extract so much from Gilt-Edge's often villainous shellac pressings, let alone the fragile material of their picture discs. Similar care has gone into the presentation. This promises to be a definitive survey of a fascinating artist.

*** We're Gonna Rock: The Essential Cecil Gant**
[Indigo IGODCD 2519] 2CD *Gant; Wingy Manone (t); unknown (ts); unknown (p); unknown (sg); unknowns (g); unknowns (b); unknowns (d); unknown (vb); unknowns (v). 6/44–1/51.*

*** Cecil Gant**
Flyright FLY CD 61 *As above, except omit Manone, unknown (vb). c. 8/44–46/47.*

(*) Cecil's Boogie
Jazz Colours 874749 *Gant; unknown (as); unknown (sg); unknown (g); unknowns (b); unknowns (d); unknown (vb). c. 8/44–47?*

(*) Cecil's Jam Session
[Zircon Bleu 502] *Gant; Wingy Manone (t); unknown (as); unknown (g); Ted Swinney or Ernie Newton, unknown (b); poss. Farris Coursey, unknown (d); unknown (vb). c. 8/44–49?*

The Flyright and Zircon sets hardly overlap at all (only two duplications in 46 tracks) and between them exemplify almost all of Gant's output, the first focusing on the Gilt-Edge period, the second moving on through the 4 Star and Bullet catalogues, picking up quite a bit of surface noise along the way. 'It's All Over Darling' on the Flyright is the nearest Gant ever came to Leroy Carr. The Indigo ravaged those predecessors, duplicating about three quarters of each, but added three sides from Gant's last sessions for Decca. It's a well-made selection, and at the price the best value (if it can be found). The Jazz Colours CD, an inexpensive German issue, has only a dozen tracks, mostly from Gilt-Edge, but two ('Time Will Tell' and 'Long Distance Call') are on no other CD. Curiously missing from all these albums is what was once the only Gant performance to command collectors' respect, 'Hogan's Alley', a trenchant medium-tempo boogie-woogie piano solo. Last spotted on *Uptown Boogie* (Catfish KATCD 132, deleted), it will doubtless reappear. TR

Clarence Garlow (1911–86)
VOCAL, GUITAR

Louisiana-born, Garlow was based for much of his career in Beaumont, Texas. His recording of 'Bon Ton Roula', which reached the R&B Top Ten in 1950, gave him a career, but he was unable to sustain it with further hits and retired at the end of the '50s. He re-emerged in 1984 at the San Francisco Blues Festival and made a few more festival appearances before his death.

**(*) Clarence Garlow
La Cienega LACGA 701 Garlow; Shelby Lackey, Jewel Grant (as); Wilmer Shakesnider, Curtis Babineaux, Maxwell Davis, Lionel Prevost (ts); unknown (bs); Lazy Lester, poss. Joseph Bob (h); Emma Dell Lee (p, v); Mildred Smith, Katie Webster, Willard McDaniel, unknown (p); unknown (g); Ice Water, Red Callender, unknowns (b); Johnny Marshall, Bill Parker, Little Brother Griffin, Peppy Prince, unknowns (d); band (v). 49–57/58.

Garlow made many of his records in the idiom of T-Bone Walker and Pee Wee Crayton. They were often disadvantaged by modest production, but a deeper problem was that Garlow could never quite raise himself to the level of his models. Consequently his West Coast-styled slow blues and guitar-led instrumentals, such as 'I'm Just A Cry Cry Baby' and 'Blues As You Like It' respectively, are rarely more than brave attempts to step up in class. Recording for Jay Miller in Louisiana he sounded more downhome, and when supported by a harmonica player rather than a saxophonist he slipped easily into a Lightnin' Slim/Lonesome Sundown idiom. It's all quite entertaining, but as you move through this efficient 24-track selection you realize that Garlow managed to spin out a fairly productive recording career – 30-odd issued tracks over 13 years – largely by recycling 'Bon Ton Roula' and a few other basic motifs. TR

Larry Garner (born 1952)
VOCAL, GUITAR

Quiet, articulate and thoughtful by nature, Garner writes songs addressing current issues, always clear-sighted and peppered with common sense and wry humour. A long apprenticeship with gospel groups, amateur club sessions and a 1991 recording debut culminated in a professional career a few years later. His no-nonsense image and unhistrionic guitar playing encourage the view that he is a rarity on the contemporary blues scene, an intelligent man with things to say.

***(*) Double Dues
[JSP JSPCD 273] Garner; Frank Mitchell (ts); Oscar Davis, Terry Dockery (h); Marc Adams (o, p); Pat Morrison (g); Spencer Williams, Joe Hunter (b); Ronnie Houston, Floyd Saizon (d); Steve 'Keyboy' Coleridge (perc). 91.

A cassette circulated in 1990 was the first indication that a major talent had emerged in Baton Rouge, Louisiana, and it set in train the circumstances from which this self-produced album emerged. (Three items from that cassette have since been issued on the VAC *Louisiana Swamp Blues – Vol. 5* [Wolf 120.926].) *Double Dues* was competently assembled, using two sets of largely unknown musicians, and the quality of its songwriting is immediately impressive. Two songs from the cassette, 'No Free Rides' and 'Shut It Down', are revisited in a ten-song programme that encompasses the IRS ('The Taxman'), gossips ('Tale Spreaders') and interracial marriage ('California Sister'), among several original takes on the conventional blues topic of failed or failing relationships. 'Broke Bluesman' is the first in an ongoing series of amusing vignettes of a touring musician's life: 'the women ain't lined up backstage screaming to take a bluesman home'. Throughout, the arrangements are plain and straightforward, the soloing precise and competent. Their only fault is a tendency to meander to a close; the deletion of extended codas could have accommodated at least two more songs. The exception is 'Shut It Down', nine minutes of song and recitative on the subject of self-determination that sustains interest to its end. The cited issue is deleted but at presstime the album was being considered for rerelease in SACD format.

*** Too Blues
JSP JSPCD 2111 Garner; Frank Mitchell (ts); Darryl Jefferson (kb); Joe Hunter (b); Floyd Saizon (d). 93.

The title, with an entirely apposite irony, derives from a comment made by a leading blues label owner while suffering a lapse in concentration. The observation gains credibility when seen in the context of 'wit won't sell records while exhibitionism will', and using 'Kleptomaniac' as a song title can induce incomprehension in a potential audience. This and other songs illustrate the pleasure Garner derives from his wordplay, at its most witty and engaging in 'Dog House Blues', where the 'broke bluesman' arrives home to suffer the consequences imposed by a wife pre-empted nightly by the blues club. Temporary residence in the family kennel is also withheld since there's a litter there already. 'It's a cold feeling when your dog puts you out.' (An earlier recording of the song is one of Garner's five tracks on *Louisiana Swamp Blues – Vol. 3* [Wolf 120.924].) 'Love Her With A Feeling' also contains a long and loving monologue on the (ultimately sexual) delights of bathing and massage. Taking solace from others' misfortunes is the subject of 'Thought I Had The Blues', better realized than the pedagogic 'Mr. & Mrs. Pain'. 'Somebody (Riding Song)' finishes the album weakly with a long dissertation on his audiences' perceptions of what constitutes blues. The hectoring tone would become more muted once Garner turned professional.

***(*) **Baton Rouge**
Evidence ECD 26106 *Garner; Steve Howard (t); Jon Smith (ts); Terry Dockery (h); David Torkanowsky (o, p); Larry McCray (g, v); Richard Comeaux (g); Willie Weeks (b); Steve Potts (d); Charlene Howard, Nick Daniels, Juanita Brooks, Charles Elam III, Rahsaana Ison, Kimberley Longstreth (v).* 5–7/95.

This is the album its predecessor, *You Need To Live A Little* (Verve 523 759, deleted), should have been. Several of the same musicians return but the presence of singer/guitarist Larry McCray acts as a catalyst on Garner's good humour. Their duet on 'Airline Blues' is the clearest indication of their camaraderie, also apparent on the imperative 'Blues Pay My Way', an acknowledgement of Garner's recent professional status. The opening 'Jook Joint Woman' delineates another character in the artist's burgeoning *comédie humaine*. 'The Road Of Life' and 'The Haves And The Have Nots' are country-music-friendly observations that wag an admonitory finger at a world that ought to be 'high on music' rather than on drugs. Garner's own 'New Bad Habit' appears to be a 'video poker machine', which he lays aside in order to recommend those seeking Louisiana blues to 'Go To Baton Rouge'.

The artist is well served by his studio band; their accompaniments are supple and responsive, abjuring the hint of pretension apparent in their previous outing. The only lapse occurs in the instrumental 'Street Doctor', which parades their musicianship without engaging the listener's interest. What Garner has stated was his best album thus far was only released in Europe at the time (as Verve 529 467, now deleted), necessitating its US reissue by Evidence five years later.

(*) **Standing Room Only
Ruf 1024 *Garner; Al Gamble (h); Ernest Williamson Jr (o, p); Dave Smith (b); Steve Potts (d); Jackie Johnson, Rebecca Russell (v).* 1/98.

A new label and a new producer, but this is the least personal of Garner's albums and the closest he has come to feeding the machine the blues industry has become. While the expected intelligence is on display, the songs and the manner of their recording lack the warmth of his previous efforts. This is particularly noticeable in 'Strangers Blues', a dark tale of incest, prostitution and ultimate redemption that remains coldly objective and lacks the writer's usual benevolence. Elsewhere, his accustomed perspective is evident in 'A Driving Woman', 'Out In The Country', 'Keep The Money' and 'PMS' (who else would write a song about pre-menstrual tension?). The inclusion of Gatemouth Brown's 'Drifter' and Henry Gray's 'Cold Chills', while tipping the nod to fellow Louisianians, makes this the first album to go beyond the artist's own resources. The quality of musicianship is high throughout but the noticeable increase in guitar solos suggests an attempt by his new label to fill the gap left by the then recent demise of Luther Allison. It's unlikely that guitar-god is one of Garner's ambitions and, for that reason if for no other, this album remains a false trail to the essence of his craft.

***(*) **Once Upon The Blues**
Ruf 1044 *Garner; Seiji 'Wabi' Yuguchi (h); Ernest Williamson Jr (o, p); Joe Hunter (b); Lester Delmore (d).* 00.

… And that essence is displayed here, delivered with the fraternal 'arm-around-the-shoulder' candour of his best work. That is, once 'Where Blues Turns Black' (co-written with Peggy Smith), a darkly portentous tale both allusive and obscure, is out of the way. This and 'The Muddy River' evoke John Hiatt both in the arrangements and in Garner's vocal tone. Humour invests 'Slower Traffic Keep Right', the singer's protests peaking when he spots a dog behind a steering wheel. 'I Ain't The One' is an extended addition to the ongoing 'broke bluesman' saga, in which he wearily rejects an offer of nightlong combative sex. Other telling portraits enliven 'A Real Gambling Woman', 'I Won't Tell Your Mama', 'If She Tells You No' and the autobiographical 'Edward Had A Shotgun', while 'Virus Blues' tackles cyberspace and the wholly exploitative hysteria that surrounded Y2K. Garner continues to impress with the breadth of his inspiration, even when tackling the subjects most frequently prone to cliché in other artists' work. The musicians respond to their leader's example and deliver performances that are at once proportionate and concise. Garner's guitar solos are similarly structured, their fluency tempered by the taste imposed by appropriate production. NS

Al Garrett (born 1934)
VOCAL, GUITAR

A native of Memphis, Garrett took up the guitar at ten, learning from his father. Moving to Los Angeles in 1957, he took up the bass while in the army, playing in a jazz trio. After his discharge, he sat in with West Coast blues bands and backed visiting stars. He was a member of Roy Brown's band for a time, and also worked and recorded with Smokey Wilson and C. C. Griffin. As a lead guitarist, Garrett led his own band, the Rhythm Rockers.

*** **Out Of Bad Luck**
Fedora FCD 5010 *Garrett; Bobby Logan (ts); Sal Navarro (p, g); Clarence Walker (g); Robert 'Bilbo' Walker (b); Chris Millar (d).* 4/98.

Garrett's long and steady career as a gigging musician and bandleader in small California clubs seems to have been an ideal preparation for recording this CD. He and his band play with no-nonsense professionalism, running briskly through a set of Chicago and West Coast favourites from the '50s and '60s in just over 40 minutes. They also do Calvin Leavy's 'Cummins Prison Farm', which is rather languidly sung; 30 years after the events that inspired it, this is perhaps not surprising. That performance is the exception, however, and elsewhere Garrett's singing is strong and soulful, reminiscent of B. B. King, Magic Sam and his old boss Roy Brown (all of whom are covered), but not lazily derivative of any of them. Bobby Logan's tenor sax is an admirably gritty pearl in the textural oyster; its value is illustrated, but not in a good way, when Sal Navarro's over-excited lead guitar substitutes on 'You Give Me Nothing But The Blues'. On the rest of the disc, Garrett's own lead, which recalls Wayne Bennett and (again) Magic Sam, is emotive but controlled, dramatic without being histrionic. He's heard at his best, as both singer and guitarist, on the concluding 'Sail On', where he manages (no small achievement) to make the listener forget that Muddy Waters ever recorded it. CS

Paul Geremia (born 1944)
VOCAL, GUITAR, HARMONICA, PIANO

A third-generation Italian-American, Geremia left agricultural college in 1966 to take to the road as a musician. He has

performed throughout the United States, Canada and Europe, and has opened for older bluesmen like Pink Anderson, Skip James and Yank Rachell. His first recordings were in 1968 for Folkways (*Just Enough*) and Sire (*Paul Geremia*).

**(*) I Really Don't Mind Livin'/My Kinda Place
Flying Fish FF 70395 *Geremia; Del Long (p); Tony Medeiros (g); Paul Del Nero (b); Mark Topp (d).* 82, 86.

The first of the two albums put together here consists of Geremia's own songs, which frequently draw on much older ideas, like the Blind Willie Johnson slide guitar melody of 'Somethin' Gotta Be Arranged', the Blind Blakeish ragtime blues picking of 'Diggin' Uncle Sam's Backyard' and the faint echo of Blind Willie McTell in 'Slidell Blues'. Alluding to these sources should not be read as belittling the recomposition Geremia has applied to them. *My Kinda Place* is mostly received repertoire, from McTell, Scrapper Blackwell, Blind Lemon Jefferson and others, though Geremia's claim 'I always try to improvise ... rather than be satisfied with duplicating the originals' is generally justified.

**(*) Live From Uncle Sam's Backyard
Red House RHR CD 101 *Geremia.* 6/91.
**(*) Gamblin' Woman Blues
Red House RHR CD 54 *Geremia; Del Long (p); Rory McLeod (b).* 93.
*** Self Portrait In Blues
Red House RHR CD 77 *Geremia; Howard Armstrong (vn, md, sp); Rory McLeod (b).* 9/94.
*** The Devil's Music
Red House RHR CD 127 *Geremia; Rory McLeod (b).* 9–12/98.
*** Love, Murder & Mosquitos
Red House RHR CD 172 *Geremia; Martin Grosswendt (vn, bj); Jim Bennett (md); Rory McLeod (b).* 04.

Live From Uncle Sam's Backyard, recorded in concert in Minneapolis, repeats six songs from the Flying Fish albums, but their echo of Blind Willie McTell is amplified with versions of his 'Dying Crapshooter's Blues' and 'Broke Down Engine', and Geremia adds songs from the repertoires of Bo Carter, Blind Boy Fuller and Robert Johnson. The performance was solo, whereas *Gamblin' Woman Blues* mixes solo and trio tracks. So far as the former are concerned, the listener may sometimes wish – and this is not the only album of which it's true – that Geremia or his producer had tried another take or two to eliminate slight picking errors. But his revision of Barbecue Bob's 'She Moves It Just Right' and romps through Big Bill's 'Good Liquor Gonna Carry Me Down' and Jelly Roll Morton's 'Dr Jazz' are fine.

Self Portrait In Blues is a well-judged collection of blues classics such as Leroy Carr's 'Midnight Hour Blues', Charley Patton's 'Shake It And Break It' and Skip James's 'Devil Got My Woman' and original compositions that are amusing or catchy and sometimes both, as in 'Kick It In The Country' or Geremia's rewriting of 'Johnny B. Goode' as 'Henry David Thoreau' ('He could transcendentalate just like ringin' a bell'). A good-humoured and enjoyable programme, further enhanced by the fiddling of the matchless Howard Armstrong on four tracks.

The artists who originally inspired Geremia are still much in his mind on *The Devil's Music*, where he sings pieces created by Jefferson, Fuller, McTell and Robert Johnson. McTell's 'Statesboro Blues' suits his husky voice best. As usual, much of what he has heard has been transformed into original compositions that resonate with sounds or phrases from the past, like the fluently played slide guitar songs 'If A Woman's Love Was Whiskey' and 'Still Think About You'.

The approving comments above can be applied with equal enthusiasm to *Love, Murder & Mosquitos*. There are further pieces from Patton, Jefferson and Broonzy and others from Tampa Red, Mississippi John Hurt and – unusual choices – Sam Collins and George Carter, whose 'Slow Mama Slow' and 'Rising River Blues' Geremia invests with a fetching languor. At this point there are few musicians in his line of work offering so attractive a synthesis of interpretation and creativity. TR

Clifford Gibson (1901–63)
VOCAL, GUITAR

Kentucky born, Gibson settled in St Louis, probably in his 20s, and remained there for the rest of his life. He recorded quite prolifically between 1929 and 1931, then disappeared from that arena for almost 30 years before making a couple of singles for the local Bobbin label. Latterly a street entertainer, he was locally famous for his performing dog, which did tricks on a box while he was playing.

***(*) Beat You Doing It
Yazoo 1027 *Gibson.* c. 6–12/29.
***(*) Clifford Gibson (1929–1931)
RST Blues Documents BDCD-6105 *Gibson; Roosevelt Sykes (p); R. T. Hanen (prob. J. D. Short), Jimmie Rodgers (poss. g, v).* c. 6/29–6/31.

The sharpness and brilliance of Gibson's guitar sound, which is unique in blues, depended on his using a capo placed as high as the fifth or even seventh fret. That and his preference for open tunings served to separate his style from that of his most obvious model, Lonnie Johnson. The limpid clarity of his playing is matched by his calm delivery, which in turn suits the resigned and reflective character of his addresses to the listener. Again like Johnson, he is prone to somewhat gloomy generalization: 'A hard-headed woman – just like a bulldog without a chain,' he comments in 'Hard-Headed Blues', and later, 'when a dumb man tries to gamble, he expect to lose – when you got a hard-headed woman, you're bound to have a blues.' In 'Society Blues' he embroiders the picture of the blues singer as a devil-may-care sportsman: 'Cigarettes is my pleasure, and whiskey I do crave, And some long, tall and slender to follow me to my grave.'

Beat You Doing It has good transfers and notes but only 14 tracks. (Four others had previously been reissued by Yazoo on *Alabama Blues* [1006], it being supposed at the time that Gibson might have been an Alabamian.) The Blues Documents CD runs to 23, and some of the extra tracks are unusually interesting. R. T. Hanen, who is very likely to be J. D. Short, sings the arresting 'She's Got Jordan River In Her Hips' ('... daddy's screamin' to be baptized') and may play the uncredited second guitar that entangles Gibson's lines in 'Railroad Man Blues'. Gibson accompanies the country singer Jimmie Rodgers on a rejected take of 'Let Me Be Your Sidetrack' (on the issued take Rodgers played the only guitar): a valuable recording, not only as a rare example of cross-racial collaboration but for the coruscating countermelody Gibson devises as he plays Lonnie Johnson to Rodgers's Texas Alexander.

Gibson's 1960 recordings, issued as by Grandpappy Gibson, are gathered on *Rural Blues – Vol. 2 (1951–1962)* (Document DOCD-5619). His guitar playing, still recognizable, fits awkwardly into the company of a modern guitar–bass–drums trio fronted by a T-Bone Walker-styled guitarist, and the novelty song 'The Monkey Likes To Boogie' simply makes him sound out of touch, but 'No Success Blues' and 'I Don't Want No Woman', blues with much of the character of his earlier work, have something timeless at their core. TR

Lacy Gibson (born 1936)
VOCAL, GUITAR

Gibson grew up in Salisbury, North Carolina, where he was taught guitar by his mother. In 1949 he moved to Chicago, where he was exposed to blues for the first time. Under the tuition of musicians like Lefty Bates, Matt Murphy and Wayne Bennett, he worked on becoming an all-round guitarist. He played in a lounge band with his friend Milton Rector, cut an album for his then brother-in-law Sun Ra's label, then spent a couple of years with Son Seals. There were also recordings with Willie Mabon, Buddy Guy, Willie Dixon and other bluesmen. Only intermittently active in music in the '80s and '90s, latterly because of ill health, he is rumoured to be contemplating a comeback.

*** Crying for My Baby
Delmark DE-689 *Gibson; Sunnyland Slim (p); Lee Jackson (g, v); Willie Black (b); Fred Below (d).* 3/77.

*** Living Chicago Blues Vol. III
Alligator ALCD 7703 *Gibson; King Solomon (kb); Sebastian Danchin (g); Snapper Mitchum (b); David Anderson (d).* 8/79.

**(*) Switchy Titchy
Black Magic CD BM 9002 *Gibson; Abb Locke (ts); Sunnyland Slim, Allen Batts (p); Snapper Mitchum (b); Robert Covington (d).* 11–12/82.

The best introduction to Gibson's regrettably small body of recordings is his share of the VAC *Living Chicago Blues Vol. III*, four well-chosen numbers sung and played with enormous energy. He is gifted with a strong, virile voice, rich in soul inflections, and the discrimination to vary his approach according to the needs of the material. The same thoughtfulness and versatility suffuse his guitar playing. *Crying For My Baby*, a session supervised by Ralph Bass that was not issued in the US until almost 20 years later, has more character than most of the other albums Bass produced around that time, but the recording of Gibson's guitar somewhat dulled its flavour. In that respect *Switchy Titchy* is an improvement, and instrumentals like 'Quaker City' and Jody Williams's tune 'Lucky Lou' are lively demonstrations of his range and imagination. The balance is less kind to his voice, perhaps deliberately, since it's coarser than on the earlier recordings. TR

Dana Gillespie (born 1949)
VOCAL, PIANO

Since the mid-'60s Dana Gillespie has sung in many styles and done all kinds of acting work, from appearances in Hammer horror films to parts in the London productions of the musicals *Catch My Soul* (a rock *Othello*) and *Jesus Christ Superstar*, in which she played Mary Magdalene. In the '80s she had successful records in the pop field but was also able to develop her long-running love of blues into regular work, particularly in Austria with the Mojo Blues Band and pianists Axel Zwingenberger and Joachim Palden, associations she still maintains.

*** Blues It Up
Ace CDCHD 950 *Gillespie; Pete Thomas (cl, s); John Altman (ss); Frank Mead (as); Bimbo Acock, Dave Bitelli, Angel, Mike Paice (s); Craig Mackie, Dave Rowberry, Bob Hall (p); Erik Trauner, Sam Mitchell, John Bruce (g); Pete Scott, Paul MacCallum, Charlie Hart (b); Kieran O'Connor, Chris Hunt (d); Mike Vernon (perc, prod); Rocky Sharpe, Eric Rondo, The Dewdrops (v).* c. 82–12/88.

Blues It Up is a selection from the deleted albums *Blue Job*, *Below The Belt* (both for Ace) and *Sweet Meat* (Blue Horizon). If the titles don't convey the slant of Gillespie's repertoire, perhaps some individual tracks will: 'My Man Stands Out', 'Big Ten Inch Record', 'Sixty Minute Man' ... In short (though the phrase is hardly appropriate), she likes a song with a point, and she serves the spicy menu with winks and wiggles that are almost audible. Connoisseurs of sustained metaphor are recommended to visit 'Joe's Joint'.

** Boogie Woogie Nights
Wolf 120.950 *Gillespie; Martin Wichtl, Christian Plattner (ts); Joachim Palden (p); Helmut Mejda (d).* 12/90.

*** Big Boy
Wolf 120.951 *Gillespie; Mel Collins (as, ts, bs); Martyn [sic] Winning (ts); Joachim Palden (p); Pete 'Guitar' Boss, Magic Slim, John Primer (g); Roger Sutton, Nick Holt (b); Les Morgan, Earl Howell (d); Mike Vernon (perc, v, prod); Ing. Neubauer (v).* 6–7/92.

These are credited jointly to Gillespie and Palden, a skilful boogie-woogie player. On *Boogie Woogie Nights*, recorded live at Vienna's Jazzland club, Gillespie essays a couple of Bessie Smith blues, for which her voice at this stage hadn't the weight; the skipping tempo of 'One Track Mind' suits it better. *Big Boy* has more numbers in that vein, as well as two tracks where she is accompanied by Magic Slim & The Teardrops, a surprising but not unsuccessful combination. Palden, movingly easily from the boogie woogie of 'Blow Crazy' to the New Orleans rhythm of 'Take Me To The Top' and the authoritative slow blues playing of 'Treat Me Tender Tonight', convincingly earns his joint billing. In view of Gillespie's track record, it should be pointed out that 'Fine And Fany Free' is a misprint.

*** Blue One
Wolf 120.956 *Gillespie; Mike Paice (s, h); Robert C. Brookes (h, v); Rolf Harris (ac, jh); Steve Lima (o, b, v); Dominic Brethes (o); David Malin (p, d, perc, v); Dave Rowberry, Joachim Palden (p); Todd Sharpville, Andy Winfield, Ed Deane (g); John Kaethner, Roger Sutton (b); Cris Hunt, Michael Strasser (d); Nick Hogarth (prog); Laura Sawyer, Nick James, Laura Pallas, Rikki P. Washington, Tina Grace, Gareth Marks (v).* 90s.

**(*) Have I Got Blues For You
Wolf 120.962 *Gillespie; Mike Paice (s, h); Pete Thomas (s); Rolf Harris (ac, jh, wobbleboard, v); Steve Lima (kb, b, v); Bob Ross (kb, b); David Malin (p, tamb, perc, v); Dave Rowberry, Tim Richards (p); Ed Deane (g, v); Gary Shaw, Todd Sharpville, Hans Thesink (g); Adrian Stout (b); Cris Hunt (d); Lisa Baron, Ani Frank (v).* 90s.

**(*) Back To The Blues
Wolf 120.967 *Gillespie; Mike Paice (s, h); Pete Thomas (s); Dino Baptiste (h, kb, o, p, v); Steve Lima (kb, v); Nick Hogarth (kb); Ed Deane, Andy Winfield (g, v); Dominic Miller, Todd Sharpville, Tim Renwick (g); Javier Garcia (b); Chris Hunt (d, wb); David Malin (tamb, v); Nathalie Corbin, Lizzie Gudgeon, Frankie Miller, Ani Frank (v).* 90s.

The conceit on these albums is that every song has 'Blue' or 'Blues' in its title – which you might think no great feat of song-collection, given Gillespie's interests, but all the material is her own. Some of it is bluesy rather than blues, but the songs are often cleverly conceived, her voice is harder and stronger than on her earlier recordings and many tracks are adorned with inventive guitar by Ed Deane or Todd Sharpville. Noteworthy straight blues performances on *Blue One* include 'Blue Papa' and 'Big Daddy Blues' with Joachim Palden, and on *Have I Got Blues For You* 'Paint The Town Blue' and 'Blue Blood', a gripping duet with slide guitarist Hans Theessink that shares some of its DNA with Blind Willie Johnson's 'God Don't Never Change'. These two albums also contain what no other records in this book can boast: sideman appearances by Rolf Harris. *Back To The Blues*, despite its title, has the same sort of mixed repertoire as its forerunners. The tracks with most appeal to the blues-centred listener will probably be the title number and 'The Sky Will Still Be Blue', with slide guitar by Deane. As noted above, Gillespie plays piano, but she does so only fleetingly on these and previous albums, and not at all on the next.

** Staying Power
Ace CDCHD 891 *Gillespie; Matt Holland (t, flh); Martin [sic] Winning (cl, s); Nick Payn (s, fl); Mike Paice (s, h); Dino Baptiste (kb, o, p, v); Matt Schofield (g, v); Fred P G, Todd Sharpville (g); Javier Garcia (b); Evan Jenkins (d, cga, perc); Corinna Greyson, David Malin, Steve Lima (v).* 02?.

The nudge-and-wink compartment of Gillespie's music is filled here by 'It's What He's Got', a leering performance in a perky jazz setting, the title song, 'Sweet Tooth' and the boogie 'All Loved Up'. 'I Sigh For You' belongs on the straight-ahead-blues shelf, but the remaining tracks are a mixture of bluesy rock numbers and more sultry pieces like 'Timeless' – all very professionally done, but less likely to catch the ear of the passing blues fan than most of her previous albums. TR

Jazz Gillum (1904–66)
VOCAL, HARMONICA

Born in Mississippi, William McKinley Gillum was raised by an uncle, from whose harsh regime he ran away at the age of seven. Reaching Chicago in 1923, Gillum joined the local music scene, made a 78 in 1934, and recorded again the following year as a member of a stringband. That might have been the end of it, had not British HMV heard his 1934 record and concluded that Gillum had potential playing hits from the musicals! He didn't, but RCA's Eli Oberstein retrieved some of the wasted time by cutting a session for the 'race' market, which relaunched Gillum's career. In the early '60s Memphis Slim got Gillum some folk-club and recording dates, but he was very rusty. In 1966 he was fatally shot during an argument.

*** Jazz Gillum – Vol. 1 (1936–1938)
Document DOCD-5197 *Gillum; prob. Black Bob, prob. Blind John Davis, Joshua Altheimer (p); Big Bill Broonzy, George Barnes (g); prob. Ransom Knowling, unknowns (b); unknown (d); prob. Washboard Sam (wb).* 6/36–12/38.

**(*) Jazz Gillum – Vol. 2 (1938–1941)
Document DOCD-5198 *Gillum; John Cameron (ts); Joshua Altheimer (p); Big Bill Broonzy (g, v); prob. Ransom Knowling, prob. Alfred Elkins, poss. Al Collins, unknown (b); Washboard Sam, 'Amanda Porter' (prob. Ann Sortier) (wb).* 12/38–7/41.

**(*) Jazz Gillum – Vol. 3 (1941–1946)
Document DOCD-5199 *Gillum; Horace Malcolm, Blind John Davis, Roosevelt Sykes, Big Maceo (p); Big Bill Broonzy, Leonard Caston (g); Alfred Elkins, Ransom Knowling, unknown (b); Amanda Porter (wb).* 7/41–2/46.

***(*) Key To The Highway 1935/1942
EPM Blues Collection 15840 *As above CDs, except Black Bob definitely present; Broonzy also plays vn; add Carl Martin (g), poss. Bill Settles (b); omit Sykes, Maceo, Caston.* 1/35–7/42.

*** Jazz Gillum – Vol. 4 (1946–1949)
Document DOCD-5200 *Gillum; Big Maceo, James Clark, Eddie Boyd, Bob Call (p); Leonard Caston, Willie Lacey, Pete Franklin (g); Alfred Elkins, Ransom Knowling (b); Judge Riley (d).* 2/46–1/49.

**(*) Jazz Gillum 1935–1946
Best Of Blues BOB 14 *Similar to above CDs.* 1/35–2/46.

***(*) Harmonica Chicago Blues 1934–1947
Frémeaux FA 260 2CD *Similar to Document CDs.* 6/34–11/47.

*** The Essential
Classic Blues CBL 200021 2CD *Similar to Document CDs, except add Curtis Jones (p, v).* 4/36–11/47.

***(*) Take One More Chance With Me
Acrobat ACMCD 4007 *Similar to Document CDs.* 4/36–1/49.

***(*) Roll Dem Bones
Wolf Blues Jewels WBJ 002 *Similar to Document CDs.* 3/38–1/49.

Gillum sang in a low-pitched, often mournful voice, and usually played in first position, with little use of note-bending and vocalized tones. He also played only before, between and after verses, never using the rapid alternation of voice and instrument that was the trademark of Sonny Boy Williamson I and others. But if Gillum's music isn't flashy, it's accomplished, reliable and mellow, and his lyrics are often clever. Migration is a frequent theme, in terms of sometimes ironic nostalgia for the South, or warnings of the dangers of urban life; fittingly, 'Key To The Highway' was his greatest hit. Gillum's earliest recordings are delightful, countrified dance music; after World War II he easily adapted to the developing electric band sound. There's plenty to admire in between, not least the guitar work of Bill Broonzy, but these early and late sessions are Gillum's most exciting material; on the postwar sides, he gets support from first-class pianists, and Willie Lacey and Pete Franklin play advanced, jazzy guitar.

Document fulfil their 'complete in chronological order' mission statement – almost: Gillum's 1934 debut, 'Early In The Morning'/'Harmonica Stomp', wasn't available for *Vol. 1*. It was first reissued on *Bluebird Recordings 1934–1938* (Bluebird 66717, deleted); failing that, 'Harmonica Stomp', important as Gillum's only instrumental, is on *Harmonica Chicago Blues*, and completists can find both sides on *"Too Late, Too Late" – Vol. 8* (Document DOCD-5574) or *Big Bill Broonzy – Vol. 7* (Masters of Jazz MJCD 172). As so often, Document's rationale entails stretches of similarity (but not, in this case, monotony), and inferior material is included willy-nilly; alongside 'Key To The Highway', for instance, *Vol. 2* also has eight titles with indifferent tenor sax.

There are a number of good selections from Gillum's output available, but the Best Of Blues CD, with its lifeless transfers and semi-random content, is not one of them. *Roll Dem Bones* is also a collector-oriented gap-filler, but a better one, concentrating on the postwar material, and *Key To The Highway* is a very good selection from the earlier sides. *Harmonica Chicago Blues* covers most of Gillum's career, in good sound and with annotation that's thorough and – apart from the remarkable mistranslation of 'guitare électrique' as 'acoustic guitar' – reliable. *The Essential* adds two far from essential sides where Gillum accompanies a somnolent Curtis Jones; they don't compensate for the absence of discographical data and variable sound quality. *Take One More Chance With Me* is well mastered, well annotated and has the discographical details; unlike *Harmonica Chicago Blues* and *The Essential*, it includes two of the last issued Victor sides, featuring Pete Franklin's exciting guitar work. It has the added attraction of a bargain price. CS

Lloyd Glenn (1909–1985)
PIANO

Texas-born, Glenn played in territory bands before moving to California in 1941. He became a busy session musician and A&R director, was largely responsible for Lowell Fulson's early hits and recorded a couple himself. In the '60s, Glenn was mainly active as a producer, but in the next decade he resumed touring; in this role he accompanied Gatemouth Brown and Joe Turner, and recorded again in France.

*** Lloyd Glenn 1947–1950
Classics 5016 Glenn; Jake Porter, unknown (t); Marshall Royal, unknown (as); Gene Porter, Maxwell Davis (ts); unknown (bs); Gene Phillips (g); Art Edwards, Billy Hadnott, Bill Davis (b); Bill Street, Bob Harvey, Al Wichard (d); Earl Burton (bgo); Geraldine Carter (v). 12/47–11/50.

**(*) Honky Tonk Train
Night Train NTI CD 7002 Glenn; Jesse Thomas (g, v); unknown (g); Billy Hadnott, unknown (b); Bob Harvey, unknown (d); Earl Burton (bgo); Joe Pullum (v). 11/50–51.

**(*) Lloyd Glenn 1951–1952 [sic]
Classics 5069 Glenn; Billy Douglas (t, v); Alvin Alcorn, Hiram Harding (t); James 'Geechy' Robinson, Frank Jacquet (tb); Herbert Hall (cl, as, bs); Louis Cottrell (cl, ts); Gus Patterson, Harold 'Dink' Taylor (as); James Peterson, Freddie Simon, Johnny Crawford (ts); Ferdinand Dejan, Lowell Fulson, Tiny Webb (g); James Johnson, Billy Hadnott, Winston Williams (b); Albert 'Fats' Martin, Bob Harvey, Jesse Sailes, Earl Hyde (d); Willis Threats (bgo, v); Earl Burton (bgo); unknown (sleighbells); Merle Turner, unknown (v). 1/36–52.

Glenn's later recordings remain largely unreissued; as ever, Classics' content is determined by what's out of copyright. On Swingtime, Glenn, Hadnott and Harvey, sometimes augmented by bongos, turned out a series of instrumentals. Glenn's steady left hand, indebted to the big three of boogie, and his rolling, Texan treble figures are very recognizable. Harvey's brushes and Hadnott's jogging bass are also trademarks, and these records are consistent, professional and – when heard in bulk – rather anonymous.

Classics' second volume deals mostly in this material, but travels back to 1936 for its final third, to reissue Glenn's debut sides as a member of Don Albert's jazz band. This outfit's music was usually more sweet than hot, and Merle Turner defines the word 'irritating'. There's more satisfaction to be had from Classics' first disc. About half of it is trio sides, which will suffice for most listeners; they include the big hits, 'Chica Boo' and 'Old Time Shuffle'. This material is preceded by some fiery jump blues, with tough but nuanced guitar by Gene Phillips, and, on 'New Flying Home' and 'Jumpin' With Lloyd', Maxwell Davis playing ferocious tenor. Only Geraldine Carter, blandly nasal on four tracks, is a letdown.

Night Train's CD is unsatisfactory. Three of its 15 numbers are by Edgar Hayes's Starduster, with elegant guitar by Teddy Bunn, but seemingly – since Hayes was a pianist – without Glenn. He accompanies Joe Pullum on two titles, and Jesse Thomas on four; these are all available, and better contextualized, on those artists' Document CDs. Of six tracks actually by Glenn as leader, a purported unissued take of 'Old Time Shuffle' is an alternative version of 'Blues Hangover', and an alternative take of 'Honky Tonk Train' is not noted as being one. CS

Lillian Glinn
VOCAL

Glinn (born c. 1902) was singing in her Dallas church when talent-spotted by Hattie Burleson, and briefly became a star on records and the TOBA circuit. She soon tired of life 'in the world', and returned to the church with no regrets. She had moved to California by 1970, when she gave Paul Oliver a single, reluctant, interview.

**** Lillian Glinn (1927–1929)
Document DOCD-5184 Glinn; unknown (c); Pete Underwood (t); unknown (cl); Willie Tyson, Taylor Flanagan, unknowns (p); unknown (bj); Perry Bechtel, unknown (g); Octave Gaspard, unknown (bb). 12/27–12/29.

Lillian Glinn was compared to Bessie Smith by the African-American press in Dallas, and if her warm contralto doesn't have Smith's brass-lunged power, she does share with the Empress a wide-awake, intelligent approach to lyrics, and the ability to phrase for maximum impact, bearing down on key words and notes in a way that must have had them standing and cheering at Atlanta's '81' and the Park Theater in Dallas. Notwithstanding the eagerness with which she re-embraced religion, on the evidence of her records Glinn was one of the sexiest singers on the circuit. Her masterpiece, 'Shake It Down', with an anonymous, effective cornettist, is among the finest of the numberless songs that nominally introduce a new dance. Its celebrity has overshadowed the gusto and directness of songs like 'Wobble It A Little Daddy' (one of the frankest lyrics to use the key/keyhole metaphor), 'I Love That Thing' and her swansong, 'Cravin' A Man Blues'. She's noteworthy also for her comments on the relative desirability of yellow, brown and black men, which come so frequently that the topic must have been her gimmick. In a short career, Glinn had the benefit of consistently good session musicians, among them Willie Tyson, with his distinctively chiming piano, Octave Gaspard, playing slow-dragging, asthmatically erotic brass bass, and the white guitarist Perry Bechtel, by far the most self-consciously jazzy of her accompanists. Her 22 songs are a consistently impressive, vibrantly alive body of work. CS

Mae Glover
VOCAL

At the time of her first recordings Glover may have been based in or near Huntington, West Virginia. Little else is known about her background or activities, but in later life she devoted herself to gospel music, a calling in which she was still engaged in 1960.

**(*) Mae Glover (1927–1931)
Document DOCD-5185 *Glover; James Parker (t, v); Charles O'Neil (p); John Byrd (g, v, sp). 7/29–2/31.*

Glover made four of her dozen extant recordings with guitar accompaniment and eight with trumpet and piano. Most listeners will wish it had been the other way round. Her collaborations with Byrd are exuberant and sexy, their dialogue in 'Gas Man Blues' following the venerable plot of the penniless householder settling her bills in the bedroom. 'Pig Meat Papa' is a spirited exercise in the blue yodel idiom of the country singer Jimmie Rodgers. Little of that brio survives in her other session's more conventional songs and dreary accompaniments; if it had, it would mostly have been lost in the transfers from what were often wretched copies.

Glover's recordings are preceded on this CD by six by May Armstrong and four by Side Wheel Sally Duffie, both of whom were thought at the time (1993) to be pseudonyms for Glover. There are similarities, but not enough to make a strong case for either identification. Armstrong is a good, vehement singer, accompanied by what sound like St Louis musicians on violin or mandolin and piano. Duffie is less expressive, but partnered by pianist Will Ezell in unusually inventive form. TR

Frank Goldwasser (born 1960)
VOCAL, GUITAR, HARMONICA

Paris-born, Goldwasser was led to the blues by Hound Dog Taylor's Natural Boogie. In 1982, at the prompting of Sonny Rhodes, with whom he'd worked the year before, he moved to the San Francisco Bay Area, where Troyce Key hired him for the house band at Eli's Mile High Club. He also toured with Jimmy McCracklin and worked with other area artists. More recently he has done session and touring work with several Fedora artists. He presently lives in Southern California.

**(*) Bluju
Crosscut CCD 11077 *Goldwasser; Lee Thornburg (vtb); Jim Calire (ts, bs, ac, o, p); Dave 'Woody' Woodrow (ts, bs); Red Young (o); J. J. Malone (p); Alex Schultz (g, b); Kirk Fletcher, Phillip Walker (g); Gerald Johnson, Rick Reed (b); John Hanes (d, cga, perc); Paul Fasulo (d); Lorenzo Martinez (cga, perc); Souhail Kaspar (tabla); Cynthia Manley, Jessica Williams (v). 10–11/01.*

This is Goldwasser's first album in his own name; he made two previous CDs, *Blues For Esther* and *Bleedin' Heart* (Globe), now deleted, as Paris Slim. He's an accomplished guitarist who knows his blues history well enough to drop allusions to numerous guitar players of the last 50 years. His own history is most closely touched by 'Playing In The Park' and 'Three Sisters', where he meets old Bay Area friends Phillip Walker and J. J. Malone, and by 'Back Door Key', written by a former employer, Lowell Fulson. For some listeners these unassuming, affectionate performances may be the album's high points, along with the bravura instrumental 'Bluju'. Other selections display imagination and colour, but those qualities are unfortunately less evident in the singing.

Goldwasser has also recorded with Blisterstring and the Down Home Super Trio (qq.v.). TR

Memo Gonzalez
VOCAL, HARMONICA

Growing up in a Mexican family in Dallas, Texas, Gonzalez was encouraged to develop his musical abilities on the cornet. He switched to harmonica while playing with the long-running Dallas collective The Weebads. On tour with the group in 1993 Gonzalez met Turkish bassist Erkan Özdemir, and completed the lineup of The Bluescasters with German musicians before relocating to Europe in 1997.

*** 10.000 Miles
Stumble ST 13 *Gonzalez; Thomas Feldmann (ts); Geraldo Giancarlo (bs); Roel Spanjers (o, p); Kai Strauss (g, v); Erkan Özdemir (b); Ralf Nackowitsch (d). 98.*

** Big Time In Big D
Continental Blue Heaven CBHCD 2008 *Gonzalez; Kai Strauss (g, v); Anson Funderburgh, Mike Morgan, Johnny Moeller (g); Erkan Özdemir (b); Klaus Schnirring (d). 03.*

Although Gonzalez and The Bluescasters will never win awards for musical or lyrical depth with *10.000 Miles*, the 16 tracks are offered with no pretence and demonstrate an act enjoying itself immensely. In spite of casting Gonzalez as the driving force, The Bluescasters frequently behave more as a vehicle for Strauss's inventively colourful licks. The overriding aesthetic of the music hangs on Özdemir's shuffled walking-bass excursions, but a wide range of musical and dynamic ideas keeps the interest sustained. Best of all is 'Let's Burn' with its alternation between a light, retro, surf-styled 12-bar and a stinging, mouth-harp-led Chicagoan romp.

Sadly, in the years between *10.000 Miles* and *Big Time In Big D*, the band's energy seems to have drained away. Although musical differences between the two releases are minimal, the later album sounds like a band going through its paces with a distinct lack of passion – dangerous for an outfit that depends on getting toes tapping. The rhythm section, under Schnirring's influence, has moments resembling the groove of a karaoke backing track, while evidence of progression elsewhere is sparse. The swinging 'Angel In High Heels', however, returns to the form of the earlier release. JF

Jimmie Gordon
VOCAL, PIANO

Almost nothing is known of Gordon's life. From his records it is possible to guess that he was born in the first decade of the 20th century, but suggestions that he may have been from, or spent time in, St Louis are not borne out by anything in his music. He led a combo at Chicago's Club Blue Flame in the '40s.

*** Jimmie Gordon – Vol. 1 (1934–1936)
Document DOCD-5648 *Gordon; unknown (t); unknowns (as, ts); Chuck Segar, prob. Horace Malcolm, poss. Dot Rice, unknowns (p); Charlie McCoy (md, g); Scrapper Blackwell, poss. Carl Martin, unknowns (g); prob. John Lindsay, unknown (b); unknown (v). 3/34–10/36.*

The photograph on the booklet, blown up from ancient

newsprint, is not so much a face as an arrangement of ink blots. This is appropriate, inasmuch as Gordon spent most of his recording life making anonymous music, much of it at the instigation of the producer Mayo Williams, whose nickname, as it happens, was 'Ink'. He joined the black roster of Decca Records soon after it started business in the US in the summer of 1934 and was promptly deployed to make cover versions of hit songs recorded by artists on other labels, such as 'Mean Mistreatin' Blues', originally done by Leroy Carr for Vocalion, and 'Black Gal Blues (What Makes Your Head So Hard)', recorded by Joe Pullum for Bluebird. The barefacedness of Decca's tactics is revealed by their issuing the latter as by 'Joe Bullum'. The setting for these and Gordon's other recordings was the then commonplace piano–guitar combination, the latter role generally taken by Charlie McCoy, the former at least sometimes by Gordon himself. His vocal manner, like his sometime associate Bumble Bee Slim's, was modelled on that of Leroy Carr, but, in his case even more than Slim's, with most of the character drained off.

For all that, he was capable of writing telling songs and giving performances with some emotional depth, like 'Graveyard Blues' ('what's the use of lovin' me, baby, after I'm dead and gone? If you didn't love my flesh, mama, how can you love my bones?') or 'Bed Springs No. 2' and 'Soon In The Morning', which are sensitively accompanied by Scrapper Blackwell and possibly Dot Rice. He also makes something very attractive out of Eddie Miller's song 'I'd Rather Drink Muddy Water'. There are curiosities, too, like 'I'll Take You Back', a swing number with an almost Caribbean gaiety, backed by Bumble Bee Slim's Rhythm Riffers. This may have suggested that like his label-mate Johnnie Temple he could usefully be teamed with the Harlem Hamfats, and some of that group, most audibly Charlie McCoy on mandolin, back him on 'She Sells Good Meat'.

**(*) Jimmie Gordon – Vol. 2 (1936–1938)
Document DOCD-5649 *Gordon; Joe Bishop (flh); Odell Rand (cl); Sammy Price, Horace Malcolm, poss. Peetie Wheatstraw, unknown (p); Charlie McCoy (md, g); Teddy Bunn, Lonnie Johnson, poss. Joe McCoy, unknown (g); Richard Fullbright, poss. John Lindsay (b); prob. Fred Flynn, unknown (d).* 11/36–10/38.

**(*) Jimmie Gordon – Vol. 3 (1939–1946)
Document DOCD-5650 *Gordon; Frankie Newton, unknown (t); Pete Brown, prob. Buster Bennett (as); unknown (ts); Sammy Price, unknown (p); poss. Ike Perkins, unknown (g); unknowns (b); Zutty Singleton, Sid Catlett, unknown (d); unknowns (v).* 4/39–46.

Vol. 2 opens with Gordon resuming his role as Decca's cover-jobbing bluesman, duplicating Walter Davis's 'Jacksonville' and 'Think You Need A Shot'. Then, following the previous year's experiment, a larger complement of Harlem Hamfats personnel joined him for some of his 1937–38 sessions, billed as his Vip Vop Band. The same band-credit was also used for other groupings of musicians: on one occasion, what sounds like Peetie Wheatstraw on piano and Lonnie Johnson on electric guitar, presences that prompt the ever-malleable singer to affect Wheatstraw's manner on 'Bleeding Heart Blues'.

Like Johnnie Temple, Gordon interspersed new compositions with occasional retrievals from earlier days. 'Alberta Alberta' on *Vol. 2* is a rewrite of 'Corrina Corrine', and *Vol. 3* offers the old murder tale 'Delhia', a secularization of the gospel song 'Nobody Knows The Trouble I See' and an apparently new 'bad man ballad', 'Trigger Slim', which seems to be loosely based on 'Stavin' Chain'. These and his other 1939–40 recordings are with Vip Vop Band lineups organized by the pianist Sammy Price, who imparts some boogie-woogie vigour to 'The Boogie Man' and '(Roll 'Em Dorothy) Let 'Em Jump For Joy'. A more cautious boogie-woogie player, quite likely Gordon himself, is heard on 'Boogie Woogie Blues' – alone, for this and his other 1941 sides were budget-cut to solo piano accompaniment. The result is not unpleasing, since Gordon's years of experience have given his voice some individuality at last, and he puts over numbers like 'Lookin' For The Blues' with a resigned melancholy. True to old form, he throws in one more cover, of Memphis Slim's 'Beer Drinking Woman'.

Vol. 3 concludes with four sides recorded in 1946 for King, with a small group now called his Bip Bop Band. A spelling mistake or an acknowledgement of recent developments in jazz? Probably the latter, to judge from the flamboyant gestures of the trumpeter and tenorist in 'Rock That Boogie'. Document's transfers are almost unlistenable, however, and the sensible place to hear these recordings, and four others made at the same time but not issued, is on the last disc of *Broke, Black & Blue* (Proper PROPERBOX 7 4CD). The tenor player's lazy elegance in 'Mistreated Blues' and 'It's Time To Go' and the trumpeter's varied playing throughout the session make it practically certain that jazz musicians of known standing are at work here. As for Gordon, he sings with such verve that one feels he has finally found his métier. Unfortunately it would be, so far as we know, his last recording opportunity. TR

Rosco Gordon (1934–2002)
VOCAL, PIANO, GUITAR

Gordon's principal claim to fame was the creation of 'Rosco's Rhythm', a lolloping shuffle beat that found favour in the West Indies in the late '50s and metamorphosed into ska (an onomatopoeic description of the guitar's role), the sprightlier forerunner of reggae. No virtuoso himself, Gordon led a happy band of incompetents into Sam Phillips's Memphis studio in 1951. Claiming inspiration from Charles Brown, Nat 'King' Cole and Ivory Joe Hunter, he was a looser cannon than any of them. Unaware of his status in the tropics, Gordon pursued a long, fitfully rewarding career that ultimately failed, with the notable exceptions of 'No More Doggin'' and 'Just A Little Bit', to surpass its early shambolic triumphs.

*** Bootin': The Best Of The RPM Years
Ace CDCHD 694 *Gordon; Raymond Thomas (as); Willie Sims, Willie Wilkes, unknown (ts); Richard Sanders (bs); unknown (g); unknown (b); John Murry Daley, Earl Forest (d).* 2/51–53.

(***) A Proper Introduction To Rosco Gordon: No More Doggin'
Proper INTRO CD 2065 *Gordon; Richard Saunders (as, bs); prob. Ray Jones (as); Willie Sims, Willie Wilkes, prob. Adolph Duncan (ts); Billy 'Red' Love (p); Pat Hare, unknown (g); Tuff Green, unknowns (b); John Murry Daley, unknown (d); Bobby Bland, band (v).* 2/51–53.

Many of these recordings, among them 'Roscoe's Boogie', 'Ouch! Pretty Baby' and 'Saddled The Cow (And Milked The Horse)', teeter on the brink of dissolution, with lurches in tempo and the congenital inability of those present to end as an ensemble. Soloists, encouraged to blow their brains out, stagger from arhythmic curlicues to rasping honks and howls. The leader's vocals are powerful, his diction often deliberately obscured in glutinous imitation of Charles Brown. And yet there were hits. 'Booted' was cut for both RPM and Chess and although the latter version proved more popular, both were credited when the song became an R&B #1. Later, 'No More Doggin'', the sinuous shuffle that established 'Rosco's Rhythm', became the template for 'New Orleans Wimmen', 'Lucille' and 'Throwin' My Money Away'. 'Doggin'' flattered to deceive by its relative coherence but in the main R&B's answer to Thelonious Monk made music that managed to be both unintentionally hilarious and masochistically entertaining. Proper take 18 tracks from Ace, including almost all those mentioned above, and add half a dozen items from other sources, one being the Chess version of 'Booted'.

*** I'm Gonna Shake It!: The Sun Recordings
Varèse Sarabande 302 066 385 *Gordon; Adolph (Billy) Duncan, Charles Taylor (as); Willie Sims, Willie Wilkes, Harvey Simmons, Lionel Prevost (ts); Richard Sanders (bs); James Jones (p); Pat Hare, Foree Wells, Phillip Walker, poss. Thomas Harwell, unknown (g); Tuff Green, Louis Willie Canty (b); John Murry Daley, Jeff Grayer, Joe W. Payne (d).* 12/51–7/57.

Despite early contractual confusion, Sun's owner Sam Phillips kept faith with Gordon and continued to record him prolifically. 'Decorate The Counter', a raucous follow-up to 'Booted', and 'I Wade Through Muddy Water' were mastered for a never-released 1952 single. A sequence of four singles, perhaps cut at Phillips's behest and released between 1955 and 1957, wandered into mainstream pop and rockabilly. 'Do The Chicken', 'Shoobie Oobie' and 'Cheese And Crackers' live up (or down) to their trivial nature but they represent gleanings from a crop of material that would emerge in the LP and CD eras.

Like those he aspired to emulate, Gordon had a certain facility as a songwriter but a limited vision for subject-matter. Retreads of 'No More Doggin'' were common, including 'That's What You Do To Me', 'Let's Get High' and 'Real Pretty Mama'. Ballads such as 'Tired Of Living' were mercifully few, though improved in execution. Fast tempos continued to confound him and his band, causing 'T-Model Boogie' and 'I'm Gonna Shake It' to flirt yet again with disaster.

***(*) Memphis Tennessee
Stony Plain SPCD 1267 *Gordon; 'Sax' Gordon Beadle (ts); Doug James (ts); Matt McCabe (p); Duke Robillard (g); John Packer (b); Jeffery McAllister (d).* 00.

Gordon pushes his deteriorating vocal cords to their extreme on 11 of his own songs and Billy Eckstine's 'Jelly Jelly', backed by the excellent Robillard band. 'Bad Dream', 'No More Doggin'', 'Just A Little Bit', 'Let's Get High' and the tiresome 'Cheese And Crackers' are put through their paces once more, decked out with solos from both saxmen and Robillard himself, while the opener, 'Memphis, Tennessee', is a relocation of 'New Orleans, La.'. When they're not soloing, the saxes form an inventive section, playing apposite arrangements that sound at once new and nostalgic. Only a melodramatic 'Now You're Gone' and 'You Don't Care About Nothing', the latter performed solo, impede the perfect progress of a satisfying programme which ends with a 17-minute interview in which Gordon reminisces with some humour about his early career. NS

**(*) No Dark In America
Dualtone 80302–01158 *Gordon; Jeff Coffin (cl, s, fl); Lij (o, b, ocarina, perc, v, co-prod); Brad Jones (o, b, vb); Nate Shaw (o); Chris Carmichael (vn, vl, vc); Jacob Lawson (vn); Joe Pisapia (g, v); Audley Freed, George Bradfute (g); Warren Pash (b, v); Sam Baker, Dave Jacques (b); Mickey Grimm (d, perc, marimba); Ken Coomer (d, v); Jennie Okon, Joe Esser, Lorraine Dobson (v).* 97?–02.

Memphis Tennessee seemed to be Gordon's swansong, but in his last years he laid down a number of tracks for his admirers Chris King and Lij, who painstakingly filled them out with other parts to produce this posthumous release. Pains needed to be taken not only because Gordon was, rhythmically speaking, a hard man to play with (they must have known that going in) but because some of the recordings, like 'You Look Bad When You're Naked', were done on a piano not so much distressed as grief-stricken. Then, too, his voice was untrustworthy: on form in the trenchant slow blues 'Love On Top Of Love', one of the album's high points, and appropriately wavering on the title track, a memorial to 9/11, but unequal to the slow pop songs 'Girl In My World' and 'You Don't Care About Nothing'. What may outweigh these imperfections for a sympathetic listener is the mood of the album as a whole and the vivid impression it leaves of the odd, errant but admirable man who made it. TR

Otis Grand (born 1950)
GUITAR

Grand's inspiration was triggered early on by early-'60s instrumental bands and particularly surf guitar stylist Dick Dale, whose influence lurks in the shadows of Grand's extensive, intimate relationship with the blues like a sporadic affair. Originally from Beirut, Lebanon (his real name is Fred Bishti), Grand settled in London in 1986 to build a premier rhythm & blues band and a reputation for bullish opinions and high expectations of his colleagues. He is repeatedly voted UK Blues Guitarist Of The Year, has been nominated for Handy awards and has deservedly won the respect of the world's finest bluesmen, many of whom have joined him on stage and in the studio.

*** Nothing Else Matters
Sanctuary CAS 36072 *Grand; Bob Enos (t); Rich Lataille (as); Dave Scholl (ts, as); Gordon Beadle (ts); Tom 'La Bumba' Mahfood (bs); Sugar Ray Norcia, Curtis Salgado (h, v); Anthony Geraci (o, p); Leroy Lewis (g); Michael 'Mudcat' Ward (b); Neil Gouvin (d); Kim Wilson (v).* 1/94.

*** Perfume & Grime
Sanctuary CAS 36073 *Grand; Stac(e)y Cole (t); Joe Saulsbury Jr (as); Gordon Beadle, Mike Hobart (ts, bs); Amadee Castenell (ts); Curtis Salgado (h, v); Al Rapone (ac); Steve Diamond (kb); Bruce Eisensohn (o, p); Afro Williams (p, cga); Chuck Chaplin, Eddie Bo, Bruce Katz (p); Effendi Mumtaz (bouzouki); Luther Allison, Joe Louis Walker, Dave 'Gangsta' Faulk (g); Steve Gomes, Rod Carey (b); Rob[b] Stupka (d, timbale); Neil Gouvin (d); Darrell Nulisch, Brother Roy Oakley, Toni Lynn Washington (v).* 2/96.

***(*) In Grand Style: The Otis Grand Collection
Castle CMDDD 578 2CD *As above, except Joe Louis Walker also sings; add Lorenzo Parry, Calvin Owens (t), Peter Acock (as, ts), Pee Wee Ellis (ts), Peter Bogart, Mick Weaver (o, p), Steve Clayton (p), Dan Quinton (b), Marc Wilson (d, perc), Earl Green, Jimmy Nelson (v). 90–96.*

**(*) Live Anthology
Mystic MYSCD 140 *Grand; Matt Winch, Johnny Adams (t); Bimbo Acock (as, ts); Barrie Martin (ts); Mike Hobart (bs); Steve Diamond, Jon Henderson, Peter Bogart (o, p); Constance Honey, Chico Lopez, Dave Stevens, Dan Quinton (b); Mads Andersen, Pascal Delmas, Steve Griffiths (d); Brother Roy Oakley, Curtis Salgado (v). 90s.*

Grand concocts an aggressive flavour that rarely pops up elsewhere on the British blues menu. Without distortion, the edge comes from his heavy picking technique and preference for uncompromising flourishes of gritty notes. Six albums and two compilations down the line, he's currently represented by four CDs. *Nothing Else Matters* finds him on good form, backed by a strong band. He mostly splits writing duties with lyricist Lori Basson, though her familiar couplets vanish beneath his in-your-face playing, to be rescued by the complementary vocalists Salgado, Wilson and Norcia. At times he evokes the cheeky presence of Freddie King, especially in the crisp '5 to 99 Blues', while 'Looking Good' calls up Grand's twisty mistress, surf rock, to complete the record with some super syncopation.

Perfume & Grime unfolds in a similar fashion but with a more impressive mob of guests. In the fiercer numbers Grand displays a natural dexterity few blues guitarists can match, but what's interesting is how he applies this approach to mellower soul-blues compositions, subtly embellishing them with a refreshing sharpness. The title song is a high point, curtly departing from the familiar: Effendi Mumtaz trades bouzouki licks with Grand's pleading, Stevie Rayish lead lines in the prelude, before the mood drops perfectly into a band-backed slow blues groove, which then greets Luther Allison for a classic final solo. 'Grime Time' also tries to deviate from its straight blues companions, but the blend of funk and tremolo guitars, sleazy sax, socially conscious lyrics and an uncomfortable pseudo-rap never sounds convincing.

For those already familiar with Grand, his *Live Anthology* is more of the same, punctuated, adept guitar work beside reliable vocals and accompaniments, and thus recommended listening. Meanwhile, for new fans, the Castle release, which includes the best of the albums above and the deleted *He Knew The Blues*, is essential. It unfolds on a cheery note with high-spirited blues and lots of instrumental room. Part of the pleasure of hearing this range of work is the opportunity to chart Grand's studious appreciation of blues guitarists old and new, from the jazz-tinged, biting tones of T-Bone Walker to the contemporary New England blues scene. In his tune 'SRV (My Mood Too)' the cruising lead passage sounds like B. B. King on heat, while 'Don't Talk About Me' resounds with a juicy guitar breakdown and fabulous heartfelt soloing. Vocally, there are standout appearances by Earl Green, especially in 'Your Love Pulls No Punches', but the best moment arrives when Joe Louis Walker performs his own excellent 'Leave That Girl'. In general, though the focus on instrumental indulgence over voices and songs may discourage some listeners, Grand's blues has both taste and conviction. *In Grand Style* is testimony that a British artist (as he proclaims himself to be) can stand in the first echelon of hardcore American players. RR

John Lee Granderson (1913–79)
VOCAL, GUITAR

Granderson left west Tennessee, where he was born, at the age of 15 and moved to Chicago, where he worked as a car mechanic until he was forced by an injury to retire in 1964. Though a part-time musician, he was a keen one, who played alongside figures like Big Joe Williams and Robert Nighthawk. During the '60s he recorded often for Pete Welding of Testament Records.

*** Hard Luck John
Testament TCD 5031 *Granderson; Prezs Thomas (h); Jimmy Walker (p); Carl Martin (vn); Johnny Young (md); Bill Foster, William Mack (g). 62–66.*

A many-sided display case for Granderson's talents, this album shows him performing solo, with fellow guitarist Bill Foster and in various trio and quartet lineups. 'Watch Out, Girl' with Martin and Young is from the Chicago String Band (q.v.) session. As a singer he is robust rather than winsome. Songs by Sonny Boy Williamson I ('Decoration Day'), Big Maceo ('Texas Blues') and Arthur Crudup ('Death Valley Blues') identify one musical period that was close to his heart, but he also gladly played blues of an earlier vintage, like 'Minglewood Blues', or style, like 'This Is Your Last Chance' or 'Got To Bend You Over, Baby'. This ability to walk out on to different stages of blues history and give performances appropriate to each, which was probably what made him so attractive to a historian like Welding, should have a similar appeal for listeners who know their way around that history, but may be too allusive for those who don't.

Further recordings from this period are with the Chicago String Band and on the VACs *Can't Keep From Crying* (Testament TCD 5007) and *Modern Chicago Blues* (Testament TCD 5008). He also contributed several songs to the VAC *I Blueskvarter – Chicago 1964, Volume Two* (Jefferson SBACD 12655/6 2CD). In 1975, when he had virtually retired from public performance, he recorded a couple of songs with slide guitar that turned up on now deleted JSP compilations, 'Lonesome Blues' on *Chicago Blues* (JSP CD 401) and 'Rollin' & Tumblin'' on *Chicago Blues 2* (JSP CD 405). TR

Coot Grant & Kid Wesley Wilson
DUET

Leola B. Pettigrew (born 1893) married Isaiah Grant in 1913, and appeared with him on stage as Coot Grant, retaining the name after her remarriage, to singer-pianist Wesley Wilson (1893–1958), following Isaiah's death in 1920. Alongside their theatrical and recording activities (the latter under numerous pseudonyms), the Wilsons were prolific songwriters; Bessie Smith insisted that they furnish the songs at her last session. They hit lean times in the '40s, and a comeback, prompted by the early jazz revival, stalled when Wesley suffered the first of a series of strokes. Their last years were spent in poverty.

**(*) Grant And Wilson – Vol. 1 (1925–1928)
Document DOCD-5563 *Grant; Wilson; Louis Armstrong, Joe Smith, poss. B. T. Wingfield, poss. Rex Stewart, unknown (c);*

Charlie Green, unknown (tb); Buster Bailey, unknown (cl); unknown (s); Fletcher Henderson, poss. Tiny Parham, poss. Jimmy Blythe, Porter Grainger, unknown (p); Charlie Dixon (bj); Blind Blake (g). c. 3/25–11/28.

**(*) Grant And Wilson – Vol. 2 (1928–1931)
Document DOCD-5564 *Grant; Wilson; poss Rex Stewart (c); Charlie Green (tb); Buster Bailey (cl); Fletcher Henderson (p); unknown (vn); prob. Eddie Lang, Lonnie Johnson, unknowns (g); Harry McDaniels, unknown (g, v). 11/28–8/31.*

**(*) Grant And Wilson – Vol. 3 (1931–1938)
Document DOCD-5565 *Grant; Wilson; Charlie Shavers (t); Sidney Bechet (cl); Sam Price (p); Teddy Bunn, unknown (g); Wellman Braud (b); O'Neill Spencer (d). 9/31–5/38.*

*** The Vocal Duet Vol. 2
Clifford CARCD 1502 *Grant; Wilson; Louis Armstrong, Joe Smith, unknown (c); Charlie Shavers (t); Charlie Green, unknown (tb); Buster Bailey, unknown (cl); Fletcher Henderson, Porter Grainger, Sam Price, unknown (p); Charlie Dixon (bj); Teddy Bunn, unknown (g); Wellman Braud (b); O'Neill Spencer (d). c. 10/25–5/38.*

The henpecked man and domineering woman are archetypes of entertainment in many cultures; among African-Americans, Grant and Wilson were stars of the genre, although the sparring on stage and records bore no relation to their long and loving real-life marriage. Coot also recorded solo, often credited as Leola B. Wilson, and Kid cut a number of duets with Harry McDaniels as Pigmeat Pete and Catjuice Charlie. Document's first volume finds the Wilsons backed by an assortment of jazz musicians on most tracks; Louis Armstrong is inevitably the most impressive, but he is in distinguished company. Coot appears solo on nine pensive, emotionally committed sides. On six of these (also available on *Blind Blake Vol. 1* [Document DOCD-5024]), she is accompanied by Blind Blake at his most dazzling. Most of the originals are Paramounts, and some are acoustically recorded, but transfers have been done carefully, and listeners prepared to make allowances will find this an enjoyable disc.

Vol. 2 begins with five sides whose battered state is bearable on the lively 'Uncle Joe', and regrettable on the porno classic 'Big Trunk Blues'. Thereafter, the Wilsons move to Columbia, and the sound improves radically. Unfortunately, nearly half the disc comprises not very funny hokum duets by Pigmeat Pete and Catjuice Charlie, given monotonous guitar accompaniments. Two self-accompanied titles by Wesley expose the limitations of his piano playing, even on his theme song, 'Dem Socks Dat My Pappy Wore', which generated one of his many pseudonyms, Socks Wilson. These drawbacks are the more unfortunate because, in 'Boop-Poop-A-Doop', the CD includes Leola Wilson's finest hour. Coot gives this tale of a singer who 'wanted to be a yodeler like Helen Kane' her comically erotic all, and Lonnie Johnson plays guitar with casual brilliance, as he also does on the early ladette's anthem 'You Need A Woman Like Me'.

On Document's final disc, the accompaniment is mostly by Wesley Wilson and an efficient, anonymous guitarist, suggesting that it was the wit of Kid and Coot's dialogues that chiefly appealed to the original purchasers of their records. Notions of what's funny in the war between men and women have changed, but perhaps not as much as is often supposed. With a little effort and empathy, there is still fun to be had from numbers like 'Keep Your Hands Off My Mojo' and the similarly themed 'Lollypop' ('Keep your nasty hands off it!'). More likely to appeal to modern mindsets, though, are Leola's proclamations of sexual independence and enthusiasm on songs like 'I Can't Get Enough' and 'Take Me For A Buggy Ride', the latter one of the songs supplied to Bessie Smith in 1933. The CD ends with a four-title session for Decca; 'Uncle Joe', taken far too fast for the singers, but not, of course, for Sidney Bechet, is the best of these. The band version of 'Toot It Brother Armstrong', with Charlie Shavers hitting the great man's high notes, is oddly less effective as homage than a test, made four years earlier for Columbia, with only guitar and piano.

Clifford's compilation goes most of the way towards dealing with the problem posed, here and elsewhere, by Document's 'complete recorded works in chronological order' policy: there can be no tests for quality, variety or how much of a good thing is too much. It includes all the sides with Armstrong (less one alternative take), the pair with Joe Smith, the rambunctious 'Scoop It', and all the Deccas with Bechet. Catjuice Charlie is firmly declared an unperson. Nine titles from the '30s with piano and guitar are a good, representative selection. On the negative side are the use of an alarmingly worn disc for the opening track, and a rash of annoying typos, but the disc's usefulness, as the only selective overview of Grant and Wilson, just saves it from a bracketed third star.

** Mezz Mezzrow, 1947
Classics 1095 *Grant; Wilson; Sidney Bechet (cl, ss); Mezz Mezzrow (cl); Wellman Braud (b); Baby Dodds (d). 9/47.*

Coot and Kid's last fling, half a dozen titles for Mezzrow's short-lived King Jazz label, is conveniently gathered here. The disc is directed at jazz rather than blues collectors, but is an economical way to acquire these songs, minus two alternative takes of 'Whoop This [*recte* Miss] Wolf Away From My Door'. (The session can also be had – but not cost-effectively, so we omit details – in a 3CD set on GHB, credited to Sidney Bechet, and spread across three separate anthologies of *The King Jazz Story* on Storyville.) Coot has a tougher edge to her voice than hitherto; Kid duets with her only on one track, otherwise confining himself to playing piano. All concerned are clearly having fun, but Mezzrow's limited stock of ideas is apparent, and it's not Bechet's finest hour, either. cs

Tibor Grasser (born 1970)
PIANO

Grasser was born in Vienna, and had lessons in classical piano from an early age. He discovered boogie woogie in the late '80s, and made his public debut in 1990.

*** Kansas City Bounce
Document DOCD-7005 *Grasser; Daniel Gugolz (b); Peter Müller (d). 5–6/98.*

Grasser's transfer of boogie from the Middle West to *Mitteleuropa* features unsurprising covers of Albert Ammons and Pete Johnson, but he is also impressed by the quirky rhythms and harmonies of Jay McShann, doing good work on covers of 'Hootie Blues' and 'My Chile'. On fast display numbers like 'Woo Woo' and 'Roll 'Em Pete', Grasser is too busy maintaining the original tempos to put much expression into his bass figurations, and the live 'Hello To Muenster' falls into crowd-pleasing flashiness. Fortunately, Grasser seems to prefer slow and medium tempos, in which he plays with great swing, especially when assisted by the rhythm section of the Mojo Blues Band. His own compositions, which make up half of *Kansas City Bounce*, are consistently tasteful and interesting; 'Dark Fantasies' is harmonically ingenious, with a curling chromatic bass line which avoids a perfect cadence for over four minutes, while the finger-tangling 'K. C. Bounce' showcases Grasser's command of polyrhythms, as composer and performer alike. 'Tokyo Boogie' and the lengthy, reflective 'My Own Thing', though more orthodox, are also evidence of a creative mind at work in an idiom sometimes inimical to creativity. Grasser also contributes five tracks to *Great Boogie Woogie News* (Document DOCD-7001). Both discs are of uncertain availability. CS

Blind Roosevelt Graves
VOCAL, GUITAR

Graves (born c. 1908) was from Mississippi and, according to Ishmon Bracey, was a street and juke-joint musician. His partly sighted brother Uaroy (born c. 1913) played the tambourine with him and sang harmony. Roosevelt Graves spent his last years in Gulfport, Mississippi, where he is believed to have died in the '60s.

***(*) Blind Roosevelt Graves (1929–1936)
Document DOCD-5105 *Graves; Baby Jay (c); Will Ezell, Cooney Vaughn (p); Uaroy Graves (tamb, v); unknown (k). 9/29, 7/36.*

Though the Graveses had probably never met Baby Jay and Will Ezell before their 1929 session for Paramount, and there might seem little common ground between a gospel duo from Mississippi, a cornettist from St Louis and a blues pianist, their collaborations are assured and spirited. The Graveses evidently had no objection to secular material – half the session is blues or hokum numbers like 'Bustin' The Jug' – but they rise to a higher level of performance in their duetting on sacred songs like 'Take Your Burdens To The Lord' and 'Telephone To Glory'. Whatever the song, it is expertly steered from the piano stool by Ezell, Baby Jay punctuating the vocals with short, stabbing phrases on muted cornet.

Interesting though that session is, it fades swiftly from the memory once the listener is caught in the embrace of the brothers' last six recordings, made in Hattiesburg, Mississippi, in 1936. 'Hittin' The Bottle Stomp', 'Skippy Whippy', 'Dangerous Woman' and 'Barbecue Bust', credited to the Mississippi Jook Band, are effervescent blues instrumentals with the very fine pianist Cooney Vaughn racing through the changes and Uaroy Graves extracting more rhythmic pep from a tambourine than one would have thought possible. Amid these dance tunes are two wonderful sacred duets with guitar and tambourine, 'Woke Up This Morning (With My Mind On Jesus)' and 'I'll Be Rested (When The Roll Is Called)'. It is hard to think of another session in the annals of recorded African-American music that so joyously evokes the spirit of both Saturday night and Sunday morning. TR

Blind Arvella Gray (1906–80)
VOCAL, GUITAR

Gray was born in Somerville, Texas. He lost his sight, and two fingers of his left hand, in a shooting, after which he made his home in Chicago and his living from singing and playing at various outdoor locations, including the Maxwell Street market, the Englewood shopping centre and the Jazz Record Mart. In 1960 he was taped by Paul Oliver, the recordings appearing on the Heritage LP Blues From Maxwell Street *and on the documentary album* Conversation With The Blues.

*** I Blueskvarter: Chicago 1964, Volume Two
Jefferson SBACD 12655/6 2CD *Gray; Olle Helander (interviewer). 5/64.*

**(*) The Singing Drifter
Conjuroo 001 *Gray. 9/72.*

Gray was a street singer, and equipped for that role with a powerful voice, but his facility on guitar was limited by his injuries; it's somewhere recorded that when he got on a streetcar and began singing and playing, the passengers would pay him to get off. In the '60s and '70s he was one of the Sunday regulars on Maxwell Street, visited by both Chicagoans and foreign blues-fanciers, but, whether because of his rugged style or his predilection for gospel songs, he failed to attract the attention of local blues labels. When he finally cut an album, it was for Birch, a tiny label primarily concerned with country music, which may explain why it opens with the country song 'There's More Pretty Girls Than One'. Gray's signature piece was the blues-ballad 'John Henry', sung with slide guitar accompaniment, which he typically spread over seven minutes or so; it's well suited to his declamatory style, which is otherwise displayed on sacred standards like 'Motherless Children Have A Hard Time'. Thanks to the addition of four previously unissued tracks, all gospel songs, Conjuroo's CD is even more devotionally weighted than its LP predecessor, and the only blues number is a string of floating verses looped over a firmly strummed guitar accompaniment and titled 'Those Old Fashioned Alley Blues'. The appeal of *The Singing Drifter* may be chiefly to admirers of guitar evangelists like Rev. Pearly Brown or Blind Connie Williams. Readers who prefer their music godless should check out the Jefferson VAC. Gray's four tracks, all secular, include another 'John Henry' and another long generic blues, 'Have Mercy, Mister Percy', but his voice is younger and less gravelled and his guitar playing livelier, and he gives the interviewer from Swedish Radio a fascinating account of his life. TR

Henry Gray (born 1925)
VOCAL, PIANO

Born and raised in Louisiana, Gray moved to Chicago after service in World War II. A pupil of Big Maceo, he began playing in clubs, first with Little Hudson, later with Morris Pejoe. He also accompanied Jimmy Rogers and other Chess artists, notably Howlin' Wolf, playing in his band from the mid-'50s to the late '60s. He then returned to Louisiana, where he has worked round the Baton Rouge area with local artists like Tabby Thomas and Silas Hogan.

In 1970 Gray recorded, among a bunch of fellow Louisiana artists, for both Arhoolie and, a few months later, Blue Horizon. Three tracks from the former session are on *Louisiana Blues* (Arhoolie CD 9004), and four from the latter on *Swamp Blues* (Ace CDCHD 661); see COMPILATIONS: LOUISIANA for both.

**(*) The Blues Of Henry Gray & Cousin Joe
Storyville STCD 8053 *Gray. 8/84.*
**(*) Louisiana Swamp Blues – Vol. 2
Wolf 120.923 *Gray; Jess Kenchin (d). 4/90.*

(*) Thibodeaux's Cafe
Sidetrack/Cambayo SCK 006-E *Gray; Ricky Cool (h); Chris Haigh (vn); Andy Silvester, Andrea Curbelo (g); Steve Coleridge (b); O. T. Otero (d); Salvador Douezy (perc).* 92.

(*) Don't Start That Stuff
Sidetrack/Last Call 7422468 *Gray; Paul Jones, Shakey Vick (h); Chris Haig (vn, md); Andrew Curbelo, Andres Mendez (g); Steve Coleridge (b); Keith 'The Baron' Webb (d); Barriemore Barlow (perc).* mid-90s?

*** Plays Chicago Blues**
Hightone HCD 8131 *Gray; Bob Corritore (h); Bob Margolin, Kid Ramos, Johnny Rapp (g); John 'Pops' McFarlane, Paul Thomas (b); Chico Chism (d).* 1/96–10/97.

On the Storyville, taped in performance in New Orleans, Gray observes local pieties by singing a couple of Fats Domino numbers, but he is better on material that connects with his Chicago days, such as 'Cold Chills' and 'Bright Lights, Big City'. His nine numbers are coupled with nine by Cousin Joe. The three 1988 tracks on the VAC *Blue Ivory* (Blind Pig BP 74591) are solo readings of Memphis Minnie & Kansas Joe's 'I'm Talkin' About You' and a 'Finger Snappin' Boogie' and 'Lucky, Lucky Man' with a band. Gray's five tracks on Wolf (the other six are by singer/guitarist Rudi Richard) include repeat readings of 'Cold Chills' and 'Talkin' About You'. By now it's clear what he does best – sing blues standards with hoarse geniality to a thumpingly rhythmic piano accompaniment – and the only factor likely to make a difference is the standard of his backing musicians. *Thibodeaux's Cafe* and *Don't Start That Stuff* were produced by Steve Coleridge, an admirer, and involve his band Short Fuse. Gray's six tracks on the former (which also has songs by Clarence Edwards and Short Fuse) and all of the latter were recorded in England, partly in the studio and partly at gigs.

Readers investigating Gray's work for the first time should take note that he has a fairly static repertoire. The tracklist for *Plays Chicago Blues* includes 'Talkin' 'Bout You', 'How Many More Years', 'It Hurts Me Too', 'How Could You Do It', 'Everybody's Fishin'', 'They Raided The Joint' and 'Ain't No Use', all of which appear somewhere on the previous albums, some more than once. But if you haven't got those albums, you can choose to regard *Plays Chicago Blues* as a useful roundup of what are obviously his favourite numbers. There's a nod, naturally, to the Wolf and a couple of songs from the Elmore James folio, while 'Talkin' 'Bout You' and 'Everybody's Fishin'' are memories of old Memphis. The band plays by the Chicago book, generically but with a good deal of oomph, helping Gray to make the best of what he's got. Subsequent albums for Lucky Cat have proved elusive and may no longer be available. TR

Lee Green
VOCAL, PIANO

Leothus Green, or 'Porkchops', was remembered by Little Brother Montgomery as a Vicksburg clothes-presser and occasional pianist. Roosevelt Sykes admired his playing and travelled with him for some years. He is thought to have died about 1945.

*** Lee Green – Vol. 1 (1929–1930)**
Document DOCD-5187 *Green; unknown (as); Nathaniel Dogan (p); unknown (g); unknown (wb); F. T. Thomas (v); unknown (sp).* 7/29–1/30.

*** The Way I Feel: The Best Of Roosevelt Sykes And Lee Green**
Yazoo 2066 *Green; unknown (g); Roosevelt Sykes (sp).* 8/29–11/30.

*** Lee Green – Vol. 2 (1930–1937)**
Document DOCD-5188 *Green; poss. Charlie Jordan, poss. Sleepy John Estes or Charlie Pickett, poss. Willie B. James (g); poss. Hammie Nixon (j); Roosevelt Sykes (sp).* 11/30–10/37.

Little Brother Montgomery claimed he taught Green the '44 Blues' in the early '20s – 'and later years he taught them to Roosevelt [Sykes] so they beat me to Chicago and put them out.' There can be little doubt that Green was impressed by Montgomery: his 8/29 recording 'Number Forty-Four Blues', a less showy version than the one Sykes cut two months earlier, is close to Montgomery's, while the shake in his singing of 'Running Drunk' and 'Death Bell Blues' is practically mimicry. But there is less of that influence in numbers like 'Gambling Man Blues' and 'Down On The Border', where Green's clear, nasal voice and lugubrious manner seem to connect him with certain contemporaries in St Louis. 'Little Eddie Jones' and 'Bad Man Napper', coupled on the original disc, are in effect a two-part blues about the same crime, possibly a *cause célèbre* of the period. 'I Don't Care If The Boat Don't Land' and 'Wash Day And No Soap', for which Green supposedly vacated the piano stool for one Nathaniel Dogan, a figure otherwise unknown in blues history, are novelty pieces whose humorous edge time has permanently blunted. Several of the tracks on *Vol. 1* are acoustically challenging, but first-rate performances like 'Dud-Low Joe' (his version of the tune Montgomery called 'Farish Street Jive') and 'Memphis Fives' fend off the brackets that would otherwise fall around the third star.

Vol. 2 begins with a clutch of songs that Green had recorded for Gennett or Paramount a year and a half earlier and was now economically recycling for Vocalion. 'Train Number 44', 'Death Alley Blues', 'Pork Chop Blues' and 'Maltese Cat Blues' are all worth hearing again, since they are better recorded and survive on less-damaged discs, and so give the listener more access to detail like the charnel-house setting of 'Death Alley Blues': 'Down in Death Alley, bloody skulls and bones – my sweet woman be crying, be crying, she found out where that I'm gone.' The Vocalion remake of 'Five Minute Blues', however, offers nothing new, since the recording on *Vol. 1* is identical; the 1929 Paramount version that should have appeared there can be found on *Piano Discoveries (1928–1943)* (Document BDCD-6045). 'Train Number 44', which is interspersed with dialogue between Green and Roosevelt Sykes, also opens a sequence of Green's recordings on *The Way I Feel*. The eight sides, all from Vocalion and excellently remastered, include 'Death Alley Blues', 'Memphis Fives' and 'Number Forty-Four Blues'.

Green then took a rest from recording for nearly four years, returning to join the Decca roster with some old pieces ('Memphis Fives', '44 Blues') and some new, generally sounding less like Montgomery and more like Sykes. Another three years passed before his next, and last, spell of recording. Now he sounds subdued, which suits very well the melancholy of 'The Way I Feel'; a version of the old song 'Nobody Knows The Way I Feel This Morning', it is his most affecting vocal performance. But most of his 1937 sides have a poignantly autumnal quality, sometimes, as in 'My Best Friend', reminiscent of Leroy Carr. His final recording, 'Lookin' Up To Down', ends with a defiant exit line: 'I just say goodbye to trouble, fare-you-well to blues. Now I'm going to a party, I've got on my dancing shoes.' Way to go, Lee. TR

Lil Green (1919–54)
VOCAL

Green was allegedly discovered by R. H. Harris of The Soul Stirrers, who heard her singing in church while she was serving a prison sentence. Released, she embarked on a singing career in the late '30s in Chicago, where she also began recording and had an immediate hit with 'Romance In The Dark', soon followed by the even more successful 'Why Don't You Do Right?', which was profitably covered by the young Peggy Lee. In her peak years she appeared at all the most celebrated black venues, replacing her original trio with a big band, but by the end of the '40s she was losing her popularity and, soon, her health.

*** **1940–1941**
Classics 5072 Green; Simeon Henry (p); Big Bill Broonzy (g); Ransom Knowling (b). 5/40–7/41.

*** **Why Don't You Do Right? 1940–1942**
[EPM Blues Collection 15821] As above. 5/40–1/42.

*** **Romance In The Dark**
Fabulous FABCD 124 As above. 5/40–1/42.

*** **Lil Green 1942–1946**
Classics 5099 Green; Howard Callender, Alonzo Fox, Frederick Neely, Julius Brooks, Ben Stroud (t); James Whitney, Henry Stratham, Stanford Grier (tb); Richard Fox, Richard Overton, Elmer Williams, Howard Robertson, Vince McCleary (s); Simeon Henry, Jimmy Nelson (p); Big Bill Broonzy, Sam Casimir (g); Robert Montgomery, Walter Johnson, unknown (b); Red Saunders, Morey Feld (d). 1/42–7/46.

Lil Green's voice on her earliest recordings was rather hard and shrill, but soon she displayed a loitering sensuality that half recalled Billie Holiday and half anticipated the young Dinah Washington, as in 'My Mellow Man', 'Why Don't You Do Right?' or 'Love Me', the latter two among several numbers written for her by Joe McCoy. Such songs gradually took over her repertoire, edging out feistier material like the drug song 'Knockin' Myself Out'. Whatever the material, she was most ably supported by Simeon Henry, a pianist incapable of playing a graceless phrase.

A piano trio accompanies Green throughout the first Classics CD, which includes the songs mentioned above, and about two thirds of the second. The highlight of the 1942 session is 'You Got Me To The Place', an intimate note to an illicit lover with a delicate electric guitar solo by Broonzy. The '45 recordings restore some of the bullishness of 'Knockin' Myself Out' in 'Mr. Jackson From Jacksonville' and the sexy 'Now What Do You Think'; the only regulation blues number is 'Boy Friend', based on Curtis Jones's 'Palace Blues'. The six orchestrally accompanied 1946 items are also on the Jazz Perspectives CD discussed below.

Romance In The Dark has 16 of its 18 tracks in common with *Why Don't You Do Right?*, but omits 'You Got Me To The Place' and 'My Mellow Man'; on the other hand, it's cheaper and a little better remastered.

*** **Lil Green (1946–1951)**
RST Jazz Perspectives JPCD-1527 Green; Howard Callender, Alonzo Fox, Frederick Neely, Julius Brooks, Ben Stroud (t); James Whitney, Henry Stratham, Stanford Grier (tb); David Young, prob. Maxwell Davis (ts); Richard Fox, Richard Overton, Elmer Williams, Howard Robertson, Vince McCleary, Steve Madrick, Russell Banzer, Chester Grimes, Lem Johnson, Budd Johnson, unknowns (s); Jimmy Nelson, Luther Henderson, Roy Parker, Simeon Henry, unknown (p); Dan Perri, Hurley Ramey, Willie Lacey, unknown (g); Walter Johnson, Al Hall, Bill Settles, Ransom Knowling, unknown (b); Red Saunders, Denzil Best, Curtis Walker, poss. Morey Feld, unknown (d). 7/46–9/51.

*** **Lil Green 1947–1951**
Classics 5127 Green; Howard Callender (t); David Young, unknown (ts); Steve Madrick, Russell Banzer, Chester Grimes, Lem Johnson, Budd Johnson, unknowns (s); Luther Henderson, Roy Parker, Simeon Henry, unknowns (p); Dan Perri, Hurley Ramey, unknowns (g); Al Hall, Bill Settles, unknowns (b); Denzil Best, Curtis Walker, unknowns (d). 4/47–9/51.

By the mid-'40s Green was among the most popular female artists on the black showbiz circuit, and her recordings reflected her concert work by framing her voice with a swing orchestra. The arrangement and overheated lyric of 'Blowtop Blues' made for an up-to-the-minute jukebox hit, but Green could also put over 'You've Been A Good Old Wagon' and 'Aggravatin' Papa' with a real feel for the style of the Bessie Smith generation. In contrast, the resigned cadences of 'Daddy Daddy Blues' irresistibly recall the Billie Holiday of 'Billie's Blues', and the altoist chimes in with an *hommage*, of sorts, to Lester Young. Not a lot of room is made for solos, but a breathy tenor sax man is heard on 'Last Go Round Blues', and 'No Good Man' has a good muted trumpet solo by Howard Callender, the reeds meanwhile threading the verses with the riff from 'Blues In The Night'. A 1947 session for Victor with a quintet elicited some of her most swaggering blues vocals ('I Gotta Have It', 'Walkin' And Talkin'), but it was her last for the company she had been with since 1940. All that was to come was a pair of singles for Aladdin and Atlantic, both well stocked with the brio and confidence that Green had steadily built up over the years. Classics omit the 1946 sessions, which were on their previous album, but duplicate tracks 7–22 of the RST. TR

Peter Green (born 1946)
VOCAL, GUITAR, HARMONICA, BASS

From the East End of London, Peter Greenbaum gravitated towards the guitar at the age of ten, showing an interest in Muddy Waters, B. B. King and the Shadows' Hank Marvin. In 1966, now Peter Green, he seized the vacancy left by Eric Clapton in John Mayall's Bluesbreakers. The following year he left, with John McVie and Mick Fleetwood, to form Fleetwood Mac, adding Jeremy Spencer and Danny Kirwan. Fleetwood Mac helped Green consolidate his reputation as one of the most important and respected figures on the British blues/rock scene, but the pressures of the group's success, coupled with the increasingly alarming effects of his experiments with LSD, caused him to leave the band in 1970. Over the next two decades he released solo albums and participated in various short-lived Fleetwood Mac reunions and other collaborations, between unlikely day jobs (hospital orderly, gravedigger) and spells in asylums. In 1996 he formed the Splinter Group, which has been a relatively stable project despite early personnel changes. In 1998 he was inducted into the Rock & Roll Hall of Fame.

***(*) **Jumping At Shadows: The Blues Years**
Sanctuary 81181 2CD Green; with various lineups of Fleetwood

Mac, Brunning Sunflower Blues Band, Nick Pickett, Duster Bennett. 67–70.
*** Man Of The World: The Anthology
Sanctuary 86359//(E) SMEDD 014 2CD *Green; with various lineups of Fleetwood Mac, Brunning Sunflower Blues Band.* 68–88.

These 2CD compilations explain much of the reverence attached to Green's name and his early recordings. Since the bulk of his studio work in this period is owned by Columbia, Sanctuary evade the problem by using alternative mixes, demos and live recordings. The quality is, for the most part, excellent, and the rarity value may make the selections of interest to hardened Green fans. These mixes chart the guitarist's technical prowess and his acclaimed dynamism and tone. The presence on both sets of favourites like 'Black Magic Woman' and 'Oh Well' is logical, but *Jumping At Shadows* offers a more attractive package by the lights of this book, showcasing Green's blues work, while *Man Of The World* collects slightly more of his less focused or genre-specific subsequent recordings. That said, both releases remain excellent cross-sections of the man's work, worthy of investigation.

* The Enemy Within: Post Modern Blues
Castle CMRCD 563 *Green; 'The Raven' (s, kalimba, g, v); Lawrence Garman (h); Gypie Mayo (g, b); Mick Green, Ed Deane, Gary Peters (g).* 86.

This was originally released in 1986 as *Two Greens Make A Blues* (previously *A Touch Of Sunburn*). Peter Green's contribution appears to be minimal. The collaboration was headed by 'The Raven' – a college lecturer named Laurie Gane – and assorted musicians from acts including The Pirates and the Dave Kelly Band. The result, postmodern or not, is dire: over-indulgent, poorly produced, devoid of musicality, unoriginal, third-rate nonsense.

***/*(*) Splinter Group/Destiny Road
Sanctuary SMDCD 466 2CD *Green; Derek Nash (ts, bs); Joe Green (ts); Roger Cotton (kb, o, p, g); Spike Edney (kb); Kate Short, Guy Theaker, Malcolm Allison, Naomi Fairhurst (strings); Nigel Watson (md, g, v); Dave Murray, Peter Stroud (b); Cozy Powell, Larry Tolfree (d, perc); Jennie Evans, Debbie Miller (v).* 97, 99.
** Reaching The Cold 100
Eagle EAGCD 224 *Green; Roger Cotton (kb, g, v); Nigel Watson (g, v); Peter Stroud (b, v); Larry Tolfree (d).* 03.

Aside from the two opening acoustic Robert Johnson songs, *Splinter Group* is a live album, recorded during the act's '96 European tour. The edge delivered by the live environment helps the performances to rank among the most driven and exciting of Green's later work. Though his playing is off at times, echoes of his former greatness can be heard. High points include a mature version of 'The Stumble' and hugely expressive harmonica playing on the live version of Johnson's 'Steady Rollin' Man'. Though ultimately the fare is temperate and uninspiring, there is still much worth listening to.

The same can't really be said of *Destiny Road* (currently available in a 2CD with *Splinter Group*) and *Reaching The Cold 100*, which lose whatever exhilaration could be heard in the live performances of *Splinter Group*. Of the two, the setlist on the later album is more focused and defined, but neither release is memorable. It is worth mentioning that Green's written contribution to both efforts, apart from instrumental passages on *Destiny Road*, is non-existent, while his share of the guitar limelight is also unclear. The best examples of the Splinter Group formula are certainly found on the later album, in the forms of the heartfelt 'Don't Walk Away From Me' and the Johnson-influenced 'Can You Tell Me Why (a.k.a. Legal Fee Blues)'.

Reaching The Cold 100 is bundled with a four-track bonus EP, where the Splinter Group revise three classic Green numbers – 'Black Magic Woman', 'Green Manalishi' and 'Albatross' – and Otis Rush's 'It Takes Time'. In the absence of the original energy and excitement, the result is predictably pale; the EP acts as a testament more to the strength of Green's former self than to his current ability. JF

'Diamond' Jim Greene (born 1951)
VOCAL, GUITAR

Greene was born in Chicago, where he remembers as a child hearing the street singer Blind Arvella Gray. He began playing guitar in his late teens. In his 30s he learned from John Cephas and the members of Saffire. He has appeared at festivals in continental Europe.

* Just A Dream
Black Magic CD 9032 *Greene; Keith Dunn (h); Willem van Dullemen (g).* 5/95.

Greene is a competent guitarist, the more so when playing with a slide, and only occasionally, as in a repeatedly fluffed 'Booger Rooger Blues', does his ambition outreach his skill, but he sings without control or discretion, swaying and wobbling through Peg Leg Howell's 'Skin Game Blues' or Tommy Johnson's 'Canned Heat Blues' like a trainee tightrope-walker. Attempting three of Skip James's most celebrated songs, 'Hard Time Killin' Floor Blues', 'Cypress Grove Blues' and 'Devil Got My Woman', was not so much indiscreet as a serious miscalculation of his resources. TR

Lil Greenwood (born 1924)
VOCAL

Lil Greenwood moved from Alabama to San Francisco in 1949, and was recruited by Roy Milton. She spent three years with Milton, then returned to the Bay Area club scene. Between 1958 and 1960 she sang with Duke Ellington's Orchestra; afterwards she made a few records and did some acting on TV. She continues to sing jazz, and recently issued a live vanity CD, From Lil With Love.

***(*) Walking And Singing The Blues
Ace CDCHD 874 *Greenwood; Charles Gillum (t); Jackie Kelso, Joe Lutcher (as); Eddie Taylor (ts); Camille Howard, Lee Jones (p); Johnny Rogers, Tiny Mitchell, Jesse Ervin (g); Lawrence Kato, Mario Delagarde (b); Roy Milton, Rudy Pitts, Al Wichard (d); The Four Jacks, Little Willie Littlefield, Thurston Harris & The Lamplighters (v).* 49–10/52.

Greenwood was a versatile vocalist, and on *Walking And Singing The Blues*, which collates her recordings for Modern and King, she prowls confidently through belting boogies, torchy ballads, collaborations with vocal groups and melodramatic, Roy Brownian wailing. At her toughest, Greenwood is very tough indeed, and she gets consistently enthusiastic support from top-class musicians, but some of the CD's content is completist, and it drags the overall quality down a little: 'My Last Hour' is impossibly hammy, and 'Once In A While' and 'It's Too Soon To Know' (two of four tracks with piano only, which seem to be demos or rehearsals) are vapidly adenoidal. However, these lapses are more than redressed by the roguish sexual exuberance of 'Dissatisfied Blues', the soulful interplay with The Lamplighters on 'Mercy Me', and the sheer power of dancefloor-fillers like 'Boogie All Night Long'. CS

Tommy Griffin (1907–78)
VOCAL

Griffin is believed to have been from Jackson, Mississippi, and may have got on record through his acquaintance with Jacksonites like Walter Vinson.

**(*) Country Blues Collector's Items (1930–1941)
Document DOCD-5426 Griffin; Eddie Hill, Ernest '44' Johnson (p); Walter Vincson (g). 2/30, 10/36.

A local reputation as a singer and a writer of original blues may have earned Griffin his two tickets to a wider celebrity. On both his sessions he was partnered by a stylish pianist – Hill in 1930, Johnson in 1936 – who may have been constrained by the formula-ridden repertoire; Johnson, at least, impressed Little Brother Montgomery and Pinetop Perkins as a player with more than just accompanying skills. The differences in form and presentation between the two sets of recordings are suggestive and would repay the attention of the historically minded listener, but to other ears Griffin's high-pitched, mournful voice and small bag of stylistic tricks may become wearisome before his 13 tracks are done. The album – which is correctly titled … *Items Vol. 2* in the Document catalogue (there being a predecessor on DOCD-5169) but nowhere else – is filled up with the four pre-World War II recordings of Frank Edwards and four by the singer One Arm Slim, a Peetie Wheatstraw imitator. TR

The Griffin Brothers
GROUP

James and Edward 'Buddy' Griffin were born in Norfolk, Virginia, and studied music at Juilliard, where Jimmy played trombone and Buddy piano. Settling in Washington, DC, in the late '40s, they assembled a band of local musicians to play the Eastern dancehall circuit, hiring as vocalists Margie Day (born 1926) and Tommy Brown (born 1931). Between 1950 and 1952 the band recorded for Dot, having good sellers with 'Little Red Rooster' and 'Tra La La', but it broke up towards the end of 1953 and the brothers pursued separate careers.

**(*) Blues With A Beat
Acrobat ACRCD 209 Jimmy Griffin (tb); Wilbur Dyer (as); Virgil Wilson, Noble Watts (ts); Buddy Griffin (p, v); Jimmy Reeves, Wilbur Little (b); Nab Shields, Belton Evans (d); Margie Day, Tommy Brown (v). 50–53.

As Dave Penny recounts in his notes, part of the reason why Margie Day had so short a spell with the band was that promoters and their record label irritated the Griffins by giving her top billing. One can hear why: her good-humoured singing on 'Little Red Rooster' (not the Howlin' Wolf number), 'Sadie Green' and 'Ace In The Hole' surfs the riffs with great self-assurance, giving character to a band that without her was a conventional jump-blues unit. A good one, certainly, as can be deduced from stomping tunes like 'Blues With A Beat', but probably not posing a substantial challenge to, say, Buddy Johnson. Tommy Brown, very much the second-string vocalist here, got most of his ideas from other singers, 'Tra La La' being a cover of Tommy Ridgely's record, 'Weepin' And Cryin'' a Roy Brown imitation and 'Double Faced Deacon' a leaf from Wynonie Harris's book. 'Double Faced Deacon' and 'House Near The Railroad Track' belong on this CD only by association, since Brown cut them (for Savoy in 1951) after he left the Griffins. TR

Felix Gross (?1915–85?)
VOCAL

This singer and bandleader recorded for four significant labels in the late '40s and early '50s but even the producers of The Complete Recordings *are unable to tell us much about him. He was probably a Texan, had moved to LA by the mid-'40s, and played drums, though evidently not on his own records. He is mentioned occasionally in the trade papers of the period.*

** The Complete Recordings 1947–1955
Blue Moon BMCD 6038 Gross; unknowns (t); Henry Coker (tb); Jewell Grant, unknowns (as); Buddy Floyd, Maxwell Davis, Joe Howard, unknowns (ts); Lee Wesley Jones, prob. Little Willie Littlefield, Bob Call, unknowns (p); Tiny Webb, unknowns (g); prob. Ralph Hamilton, Bill 'Bassy' Day, unknowns (b); prob. Jesse Sailes, Minor Robinson, unknowns (d). 47–55.

These are neatly executed small-group sides in the jump-blues idiom, but thousands of records were made in this period that could be similarly described, and many of them are better known and more highly rated by present-day listeners. Part of the reason for Gross's low standing may be that he is a rather nondescript singer, limited to a few melodies and cadences; another part may be his lyrics, which are contemporary in their language but not remarkably inventive, amusing or hip. Shopworn titles such as 'You Don't Love Me', 'Worried About You Baby' or 'You Done Me Wrong' are a fair index of the banality of his songwriting. As usual, Blue Moon has done its work with great care, but it is hard to work up much enthusiasm for the outcome. Four of the tracks also appear on *Swing Time Shouters* (Night Train NTI CD 7010) and six on *Swing Time Shouters Volume 2* (Night Train NTI CD 7014). TR

Myrick 'Freeze' Guillory (born 1954)
VOCAL, ACCORDION, RUBBOARD

Guillory is Queen Ida's son; he joined his mother's band in the '70s.

**(*) Nouveau Zydeco
GNP-Crescendo GNPD 2203 Guillory; Mike Galasatis (t); Mark Trozell (tb); Bernard Anderson (ts, bs); Greg Brown (ts); David Cowden (bs); Queen Ida (ac, tamb, v); Pat Rickey, Doug Dayson (kb); James Hurley (vn); Terry Buddingh (g, b); Denny Geyer (g, v); Richard L. Nelson, Gary Myrick (g); Willie Riser (b); Jimmy Sanchez, Ben Holmes III (d); Chilly Willie (rb, v); Chester 'Tin Man' Lelea, Terry Lewis (rb); Eddie Barrero (cga); Russell Branch, David Lige, Joe Chapel (v). 91?

Nouveau Zydeco isn't *nouveau zydeco* in the Beau Jocque/ Keith Frank sense; the title seems intended to signify dynastic succession. A horn section is overdubbed on some tracks, but the core band on these live recordings is *maman*'s musicians of the time; the percussionists pack a persistent punch, and Bernard Anderson plays a notable series of gutsy tenor solos. Queen Ida reclaims the leader's role for the middle third of the disc, and is much less bland than usual, except on 'Five Lonely Years And A Nite'. This greasily Oedipal duet encapsulates the CD's big drawback: Guillory is a hot and skilful accordionist, and the tradition-based tracks are pleasant enough, but he has a fatal penchant for writing kitsch ballads, and a plummily orotund voice with which to sing them. The enforced mating of Lake Charles and Las Vegas reaches a horribly compelling climax on 'Zydeco In D Minor', where both the tune and its delivery are unsettling echoes of Frankie Laine and 'Ghost Riders In The Sky'. It's no surprise that *Nouveau Zydeco* is Guillory's only recording as leader. CS

Guitar Curtis (1940–95)
VOCAL, GUITAR

Curtis Colter learned from his Crockett neighbour Frank Robinson but played in a more modern style; he cited Long John Hunter as his main influence, but was also indebted to Albert Collins, Guitar Slim and Freddie and Albert King. He gigged quite widely in the Southwest, and was a favourite in Navasota; he was killed in a car crash returning from there to Crockett.

** Deep East Texas Blues
Black Magic CD 9028 *Guitar Curtis; Mark 'Kaz' Kazanoff (ts); Derek O'Brien, Slim Richey (g); Tary Owens, Joe Kelley, Art Langston (b); Mike Buck, Ted Roddy (d).* 94–95.

Guitar Curtis's six tracks on *Deep East Texas Blues* (the balance are by Frank Robinson) are his total recorded legacy. Half of them are instrumentals, which are energetic but derivative and not immune to cliché; the best of them is the moody 'Crockett Blues', but 'My Thang' and 'Curtis Shuffle' are dully predictable. 'Navasota Part I' and 'Navasota Part II' feature an autobiographical monologue, but are also mainly instrumental; despite the titles, they are two versions of the same piece. 'Going To Navasota', Colter's only real attempt at songwriting, strings together commonplaces about his hopes for stardom. CS

Guitar Gabriel (1925–96)
VOCAL, GUITAR, BANJO

Robert Jones was born in Atlanta and grew up in North Carolina; his father, Sonny Jones, was a guitarist who made a few records. Robert learned to play in his teens and became an itinerant blues singer, sometimes working on medicine shows. During a stint with a fair he became Guitar Gabriel, but when he recorded in Pittsburgh in 1970, his producer dubbed him Nyles Jones. My South My Blues (Gemini S7101) was highly regarded by European collectors, and a single drawn from it was a local hit, but Jones saw no money, and went back to Winston-Salem, where he played in clubs, drink houses and the street. He was poor, sick and an alcoholic when Timothy Duffy found him in 1991, but the talent was still there. With Duffy as his manager and accompanist, Gabriel spent his last years appearing at clubs and festivals in North America and Europe to considerable acclaim.

(**) Toot Blues
Karibu Productions [unnumbered] *Guitar Gabriel; Timothy Duffy (g); Luther 'Captain Luke' Mayer (v).* 3/91.

*** Deep In The South
Cello 91001 *Guitar Gabriel; Michael Parrish (p); Timothy Duffy (g).* 8–12/91.

Issued by Music Maker, *Toot Blues* originally appeared on a cassette, whose inlay card is used as artwork for this CD-R incarnation. This looks shoddy, and there's some tape hiss, too. These aspects would matter less if the music were better. Gabriel's voice is strong, and it's obvious that he had been a good musician, and could be again, but at this point he often has to conceal his deficiencies behind combinations of clowning, random guitar chaos and Duffy's inappropriate slide accompaniment. Captain Luke sings a mannered 'Careless Love'.

Deep In The South was previously issued as Karibu CD 925. After a few months of practice Gabriel's singing is more disciplined and his playing markedly improved, but he continues to need support; fortunately, Duffy has developed a style that fits better. Gabriel's blend of Piedmont blues with Lightnin' Hopkins is usually gentle and reflective, but he can be outspoken, as when remembering the indignities of sharecropping in 'Southland Blues'. *Deep In The South* mixes self-composed and traditional songs with tunes learned from records by Slim Harpo, Mercy Dee Walton and others, but they all become Guitar Gabriel originals.

*** Volume 1
Music Maker MMCD 0494 *Guitar Gabriel; Mark Levinson (flh, b); Michael Parrish (p, g); Timothy Duffy (g); Ardie Dean (d).* 2–4/94.

Not many last recordings are called *Volume 1*, but the connotation of renewal is appropriate; Gabriel was continuing to improve, both technically and as a songmaker. There are some very original lyrics here, among them 'Here Comes The Devil', full of strange and striking images, 'Blues For Dorothy', which is a moving tribute to Gabriel's late girlfriend, and an outstandingly filthy 'You Gotta Watch Yourself'. The accompanists do a fine job, with none of the slight pushiness occasionally found on *Deep In The South*. It's a pity, therefore, that the disc fizzles out. The banjo on 'Hospital Blues' is played with an unsuitable guitar technique, 'Back In The Western Days' would be too long even if much of its ten minutes were not catastrophically under-recorded, and 'Two Brothers' is a dull story, not given authority by what seem to be overdubbed piano and flugelhorn. CS

Guitar Nubbit (born 1923)
VOCAL, GUITAR

Alvin Hankerson was born in Florida, grew up mostly in Georgia and in his early 20s moved to the Boston area. His barbershop in Roxbury, Massachusetts, was just down the street from a record store owned by Skippy White, and it was for White's Bluestown label that he recorded a few singles, under a recording name given him because he had lost part of his right thumb in an accident. One of the singles, 'Georgia Chain

Gang'/'Hard Road', aroused some interest when issued in the UK, but attempts to record him at album length were unsuccessful.

*** Bluestown Story Volume 1
Wolf WBJ 013 *Guitar Nubbit.* 62, 65.

'Georgia Chain Gang', a seemingly autobiographical narrative over an insistent guitar, was Guitar Nubbit's most striking piece, but his other songs, though in conventional blues forms, were written without much recourse to blues clichés. His freshness of approach, dry delivery and guitar playing that was sometimes reminiscent of Blind Boy Fuller, whom he admired as a young man, made him an exciting discovery in the mid-'60s. Forty years on, he seems not a great talent but a singular one. His ten tracks are preceded by 11 by Alabama Watson, a younger singer/guitarist whom White recorded in 1965; they are mostly derivative, usually of Junior Parker or Lightnin' Hopkins, and the erratic coordination of voice and guitar marks Watson as an amateur. TR

Guitar Shorty (born 1939)
VOCAL, GUITAR

David William Kearney was born in Houston and raised in Florida. While working with the Walter Johnson orchestra he was spotted by Willie Dixon, who produced his first record for Cobra in 1957. In the early '60s he settled in Seattle, where he had some influence on the young Jimi Hendrix; in the '70s he moved to LA. His first album, for the UK label JSP, won a W. C. Handy Award and nudged local labels into taking an interest in him. Since then he has taken his place among the leading live acts on the blues scene.

** Billie Jean Blues
Collectables COL-5724 *Guitar Shorty; unknowns (kb, g, b, d).* c. 87–89.

**(*) The Blues Is All Right
Collectables COL-5725 As above. c. 87–89.

These recordings were made by the producer Swamp Dogg (Jerry Williams Jr) at several studio and club sessions. Most of the club performances are over-extended, some self-defeatingly: Shorty is a firecracker of a guitarist, but he fizzles out long before the end of 'Shorty's Theme #2' (11.19) or 'We Don't Give A Shit & The Blues Is All Right' (16.14), both on *Billie Jean Blues*. *The Blues Is All Right* opens with another supersize helping of that tune, and three more numbers pass the ten-minute mark, but it's the superior album, with more vocal numbers for Shorty to put across in his brusque Texan-Muddy-Waters manner, and better and more varied material, including three B. B. King numbers from different stages in his career, 'The Thrill Is Gone', 'How Blue Can You Get' and 'Never Make Your Move Too Soon'. The backing musicians earn points for stamina rather than invention.

*** My Way Or The Highway
JSP JSP 5107 *Guitar Shorty; Lorenzo Parry (t); Peter Beck (as, ts); Mike Hobart (bs); Buzz Brown (h); Tony Ashton (o); Otis Grand (g, prod); Dan Quinton (b); Daniel Strittmatter (d).* c. 5/91.

Shorty plays less guitar on this set, leaving some of the solos for Grand (in the left channel). This is a virtue in itself and the album has others, like its diversity of material and its, for Shorty, brevity: only one number goes over six minutes. There are some strong songs, too, such as the title piece, 'No Educated Woman' and the confessional 'Down Thru' The Years'. This SACD release replaces the deleted JSPCD 2117.

My Way Or The Highway was followed by three '90s albums for Black Top, *Topsy Turvy*, *Get Wise To Yourself* and *Roll Over, Baby*, all deleted.

**(*) I Go Wild!
Evidence ECD 26119 *Guitar Shorty; Scott Matthews (s, kb, g, d); Alden Clark (kb); Jim Pugh (o); Chris Hayes, Terry DeRouen (g); Glenn Letsch, Howard Deere (b); Danny Gerass (d).* 4/01.

Shorty's prolixity as a guitarist is even more tightly reined here, with only two numbers exceeding five minutes, but the restriction has the adverse effect of making him play at full throttle almost all the time. Pugh, not to be outdone, constantly erupts with long, loquacious organ statements. 'Just Warming Up' and 'In The Morning' provide a couple of welcome dips in the dynamic level, the latter's floating soul melody establishing a peaceful mood very much at variance with the macho braggadocio of the title song, 'Lesson In Love' and others.

*** Watch Your Back
Alligator ALCD 4895 *Guitar Shorty; Jesse Harms (kb, perc, eff); Electric Viv Johnson (g); Sweet William Bouchard (b); Alvino Bennett (d, perc).* 04.

If you haven't come across Guitar Shorty, this is a good place to meet him. His guitar playing is hotter and more penetrating than ever, but it doesn't swamp the songs – which, for once, are all by other people, several, such as 'Story Of My Life', by his co-producer, Jesse Harms. That has two beneficial results for the listener: succinct, concentrated performances, and a lot less of Shorty riding his testosterone pony. TR

Guitar Slim (1926–59)
VOCAL, GUITAR

Born in Mississippi, Eddie Jones began as a dancer. By 1950 he was in New Orleans and poised to become Guitar Slim, famous for his brightly coloured suits, hair dyed to match and 350-foot guitar lead. After the national success of 'The Things That I Used To Do', Slim reverted to being a Southern favourite; Specialty dropped him in 1956 and Atco failed to revive his popularity. Although he'd given up drinking, alcohol and hard living contributed to Slim's early death.

***(*) Guitar Slim 1951–1954
Classics 5139 *Guitar Slim; Frank Mitchell, Roosevelt Brown (t); Gus Fontenette (as); Joe Tillman, Charles Burbank, Oett 'Sax' Mallard (ts); Calvin Cage, Herman Butler (s); Huey Smith, Ray Charles, John Gerard, Lawrence Cotton (p); Hugh Dickson, Lloyd Lambert, unknown (b); Willie Nettles, Oscar Moore (d); band (v).* 5/51–9/54.

Classics preface Slim's first three Specialty sessions (copied from one or other of the CDs discussed next) with his four debut sides on Imperial and a J-B 78. These tracks feature some tasty piano from Huey Smith, and there's clear evidence of the potential that was to be realized with 'The Things That I Used To Do', but Slim is still finding the confidence to transcend (though without escaping) Gatemouth Brown's influence.

**** The Things That I Used To Do
Ace CDCHD 318 *As above, except add Dalton Rousseau (t), Clarence Ford (as, bs), Luther Hill Jr (as); omit Cage, Butler, Smith, Dickson, unknown (b), Nettles. 10/53–12/55.*
**** Sufferin' Mind
Specialty SPCD 7007 *As above. 10/53–12/55.*

Slim's style owed a lot to T-Bone Walker and Gatemouth Brown, but he sang with gospel passion, and his playing combined aggression, high volume and a rounded, singing tone. His big hit, one of several numbers that are secularised gospel songs, presents the definitive version of Slim's sound, and variations of it feature on most of his Specialty recordings; some performances start raggedly and some have novelty lyrics, but Slim usually makes them exciting and involving; only 'I Wanna Love-A You' is beyond redemption. Art Rupe famously described 'The Things That I Used To Do' as 'the worst piece of shit I ever heard', and even after sales proved him wrong, he seemed unsure how to produce Slim; later releases often featured disastrous organ, bass and second-guitar overdubs. Happily, they have been expunged from these collections of Specialty material; *Sufferin' Mind* offers two more tracks and some alternative takes.

**(*) Atco Sessions
Atlantic 81760 *Guitar Slim; Dalton Rousseau, James Miller, Raymond Bryan, Joe Morris (t); Gus Fontenette (as); Joe Tillman, Miller Sam (ts); Red Tyler (bs); unknowns (s); Lawrence Cotton, unknown (p); Edgar Blanchard, Les Spann (g); Lloyd Lambert, unknown (b); Oscar Moore, unknown (d); band unknowns (v). 3/56–1/58.*

The guitar sound on Atco is thinner and more acid, closer to that of Gatemouth Brown; indeed, a cover of Brown's 'My Time Is Expensive' is one of the best tracks here. Slim could still sing and play with conviction, as 'Along About Midnight' and 'Guitar Slim Boogie' respectively prove, but the good material is interleaved with unsuccessful attempts to make him more pop-friendly, using sentimental songs that might have suited Fats Domino, saccharine horn charts and unidiomatic vocal groups. CS

Guitar Slim Jr (born 1951)
VOCAL, GUITAR

Rodney Armstrong is the son of Eddie 'Guitar Slim' Jones. He has worked in African-American clubs in New Orleans since his teens, but his attempts to become more widely known seem to have been stalled by personal problems.

**(*) The Story Of My Life
Orleans OR 4188//Sky Ranch SR 652311 *Guitar Slim Jr; Milton Batiste (t); Ernest Watson (ts); Keith Fazarde (kb, vb); Jon Cleary, A. J. Loria (p); Stanley Atkins, David B. Moorland (g); Rene Coman, Charles Moore (b); Shannon Powell, Kerry Brown (d); Diane Watson (claps); Sylvia Joseph, Oneida Joseph (v). 87.*
**(*) Nothing Nice
Warehouse Creek WCRC 1224 *Guitar Slim Jr; Wayne Jackson (t, tb); Andrew Love (ts); Art Wheeler (h, kb, g, tamb); George Wayne (g); Douglas T. Potter (b); Jack Burnette (d). 93.*

Seven of the ten songs on *The Story Of My Life* were written and recorded by Slim's famous father, and a quoted comment suggests that he is resigned to customer demand for this material. Comparison is unavoidable; it's impossible to go further than 'conscientious', but even if these numbers could be divorced from their history, the mark wouldn't improve much. This is the more regrettable because the rump of the disc suggests that Armstrong is a good soul singer, albeit derivative of Otis Redding, and a considerable guitarist, with a complex, rhythmically loose style that owes little to his father.

Only three tracks on *Nothing Nice* were written by the elder Slim, but perversely they're the best of the bunch; even 'The Things I Used To Do' is handled successfully. The rest of the CD is soul and soul-blues, but subtlety takes a hike as Slim's undoubted talent in this vein is impeded by cluttered, fussy arrangements and a four-armed drummer. CS

Buddy Guy (born 1936)
VOCAL, GUITAR

George 'Buddy' Guy is the uncrowned King of Chicago Blues, a role he characteristically disparages but eminently deserves. Arriving from Louisiana in 1957, he, along with Magic Sam, Otis Rush and Freddie King, changed the nature of Chicago blues while still revering heroes like Muddy Waters. Combining B. B. King's declamatory vocals with a guitar style that reflected the flamboyance of Guitar Slim, Guy built on his live reputation with a series of records that enjoyed critical rather than commercial success. A partnership with Junior Wells bore early fruit when in 1970 they toured with The Rolling Stones but in the ensuing years their act degenerated into self-indulgence and fell out of favour. (Some of their joint recordings are discussed here, some in Wells's entry.) For more than a decade, Guy's career was in the doldrums, even though his cause was espoused by Eric Clapton, who acclaimed him as the greatest living guitarist. His fortunes changed in 1991 when he made Damn Right, I've Got The Blues, *with guest appearances by Clapton, Jeff Beck and Mark Knopfler. Subsequent releases dispensed with celebrity names and the attempt to broaden his appeal outside a strict blues context foundered. Even so, these records helped to consolidate the reputation he continues to enjoy.*

*** Call Back Lost Time
[Westside WESA 843] *Guy; Harold Ashby, Bob Neely, Carlson Oliver, Eddie Jones (ts); McKinley Easton, Jackie Brenston (bs); Harold Burrage (p); Otis Rush, Ike Turner (g); Willie Dixon (b); Odie Payne (d). 58.*
*** Southern Blues
Paula PCD-26 *As above. 58.*

Within a year of his arrival in Chicago, Guy cut two singles for Artistic. The first, 'Try To Quit You Baby'/'Sit And Cry [The Blues]', was very much in the mould of 'I Can't Quit You Baby' by Otis Rush, present on rhythm guitar. The second, 'You Sure Can't Do', vocally and instrumentally plagiarized Guitar Slim's 'The Things I Used To Do', while 'This Is The End' (from which Westside's album title is taken) was the supercharged version of B. B. King's style that would characterize the next stage in Guy's recording career. Alternative takes of the latter songs are also included in a collection that shows Guy's attacking style was already fully formed. The other contributors to this VAC are Ike Turner, Betty Everett and Jesse Fortune. Fortune also has tracks on *Southern Blues*, which adds two songs from the demo tape Guy brought north with him in 1957.

*** The Complete Chess Studio Recordings
MCA/Chess CHD2-9337 2CD *Guy; Sonny Turner, Murray Watson (t); Jarrett Gibson (ts, bs); Bob Neely, Abb Locke, Gene Barge, A. C. Reed, Milton Bland (ts); Donald Hankins (bs); Junior Wells, Sonny Boy Williamson II (h); Lafayette Leake, Leonard Caston (o, p); Little Brother Montgomery, Otis Spann (p); Lacy Gibson, Robert Nighthawk, Matt Murphy (g); Jack Meyers, Reggie Boyd, Leroy Stewart, Phil Upchurch (b); Fred Below, Phil Thomas, Al Duncan, Clifton James, Charles Stepney (d).* 3/60–8/66.

***(*) Buddy's Blues
MCA/Chess CHD 9374 *As above.* 3/60–8/66.

***(*) The Buddy Guy Collection
Spectrum 544 355 *As above.* 3/60–8/66.

Right from the start, Guy's Chess sessions were a frustrating mixture of the inspired and the inept. For every 'First Time I Met The Blues' or 'Stone Crazy' there were trivialities like 'American Bandstand' or 'Baby Baby Baby', as the label experimented with ways to break their artist out of the blues mould. Since Guy wrote many of these shallow confections, he must have been a willing participant. This practice continued intermittently for the duration of his Chess contract. An occasional rough gem such as 'I Suffer With The Blues' would be succeeded by the execrable 'Lip Lap Louie' and much of this dross remained unissued for some years. *The Complete Chess Studio Recordings* was compiled to exploit Guy's raised profile with the release of *Damn Right, I've Got The Blues* and the chronological layout of these 43 tracks and four alternative takes or mixes does as much damage as justice to Guy's reputation. *Buddy's Blues* and *The Buddy Guy Collection* are near-identical compilations that filter out almost all of the second-rate material from these sessions to give a more flattering account of Guy's status as a blues musician.

*** This Is Buddy Guy!
Vanguard VMD 79290 *Guy; Norman Spiller, George Alexander (t); A. C. Reed, Bobby Fields (ts); Leslie Crawford (bs); Tim Kaihatsu (g); Jack Meyers (b); Glenway McTeer (d).* 7/65.

This live California session catches Guy at the peak of his first flowering, the voice strong (more often a scream), the guitar work frenetic. Its principal drawback is the dated nature of the repertoire, which mixes first-class blues ('I Had A Dream Last Night', 'You Were Wrong') with over-extended soul workouts – '(You Give Me) Fever', 'Knock On Wood' and an interminable closing 'I'm Not The Best'. For all the energy he expends, Guy just doesn't have the wit or the spontaneity to be a good soul singer. That doesn't worry the audience, who readily respond to the call-and-answer routines the singer demands of them. What may be electric at the venue is monotonous in the home but as a microcosm of the changing nature of the blues at the time, this will do.

***(*) A Man And The Blues
Vanguard VMD 79272 *Guy; A. C. Reed, Bobby Fields (ts); Donald Hankins (bs); Otis Spann (p); Wayne Bennett (g); Jack Meyers (b); Lonnie Taylor, Fred Below (d).* 9/67.

A similar mixture to the previous album, this set is slanted slightly more towards the blues, in particular the title track and 'Sweet Little Angel', both of which gain immeasurably from the presence of Otis Spann. His piano has little to contribute to 'Money (That's What I Want)' or 'Mary Had A Little Lamb', both given rather arbitrary workouts. Guy is in good voice and the quality of his backing band draws a meritorious performance from him. 'I Can't Quit The Blues', 'Just Playing My Axe' and 'Jam On A Monday Morning' are improvised in the studio, leading to a few indecisive moments, but overall this is Buddy Guy transcending the stasis of his later Chess career.

**(*) Hold That Plane
Vanguard VMD 79323 *Guy; Gary Bartz (as); A. C. Reed (ts); Junior Mance, Mark Jordan (p); Ernest Johnson, Bill Folwell, Freebo (b); Jesse Lewis, Barry Altschul, David 'Rip' Stock (d).* 11/69.

This is a tale of mismatched musicians poorly produced. Jazz pianist Junior Mance plays well throughout but pays little or no attention to what's going on around him. To start with 'Watermelon Man', hackneyed even then, was a poor decision and indifference in tempo and performance during 'I'm Ready' typifies much of what transpires. The only time Guy lets loose is 'Come See About Me', an eight-minute instrumental that survives the backing musicians' initial inability to come together. The lack of a proper balance in 'My Time After Awhile' undermines an otherwise successful effort, even though it lacks a guitar solo. Guy performs well enough but a sense of a duty being done suggests that he's as dissatisfied as the listener.

***(*) As Good As It Gets
Vanguard VCD 79509 *As for above Vanguard CDs.* 7/65–11/69.

*** My Time After Awhile
Vanguard VCD 141/142 *As for above Vanguard CDs.* 7/65–11/69.

*** The Complete Vanguard Recordings
Vanguard 3 VCD 178/80 3CD *As for above Vanguard CDs.* 7/65–11/69.

As Good As It Gets and *My Time After Awhile* shuffle tracks from the previous three albums. Five tracks are duplicated but the former set earns extra merit by containing four previously unreleased items: a 'Slow Blues' instrumental from the *This Is Buddy Guy!* concert and 'Poison Ivy', 'You Got A Hole In Your Soul' and 'The Dream' from the *A Man & The Blues* sessions. While all are welcome, not least for Otis Spann's presence on three, only 'The Dream' really impresses and why do both sets include Junior Wells's 'Stormy Monday', even if Guy is present in the backing band?

**(*) Buddy And The Juniors
MCA MCAD 10517//BGO BGOCD 399 *Guy; Junior Wells (h, v); Junior Mance (p).* 12/69.

Three weeks after recording *Hold That Plane*, Guy was back in the studio with Mance and his buddy Wells. What was apparently intended as an acoustic session was compromised by Wells's use of an amplified harmonica. Guy's guitar was thus threatened and ultimately overwhelmed by Mance's piano in the four numbers on which he plays. Six tracks are evenly divided between the two singers; the seventh, 'Riffin'', is an instrumental duet. Wells essays 'Hoochie Coochie Man', 'Rock Me Mama' and 'Ain't No Need', the last a minimally disguised 'My Babe'. Guy tries to emote during 'Five Long Years' but with no band behind him, the attempt is stillborn. Both men are at their most natural during the opening 'Talkin' About Women Obviously'. Not an album to pay more than a budget price for.

***(*) Stone Crazy
Isabel IS 647901//Alligator ALCD 4723 *Guy; Phil Guy (g); J. W. Williams (b); Ray 'Killer' Allison (d). 10/79.*

An extraordinary session cut in Toulouse, France, in which Guy plays some of the most aggressive, almost demented, guitar work of his career. Much of it is repetitive, played so fast and with such little regard for metre, Guy all the while grunting and snarling, that one can only guess at the frame of mind he was in at the time. With just six songs, the opening 'I Smell A Rat' the longest at over nine minutes, there's little release from the tension he creates, with the possible exception of 'She's Out There Somewhere', vaguely based on 'Dust My Broom'. Faced with such an overtly undisciplined leader, the backing band can do little more than cling to their patterns and hope to recognize their cues. This is not the place to find Guy at his best but it's certainly the most passionate.

*** Live At The Checkerboard Lounge, Chicago, 1979
JSP JSPCD 262 *Guy; Phil Guy, Little Phil Smith (g); J. W. Williams (b); Ray Allison (d); L. C. Thurston (v). 10/79.*

Guy endured the best part of a decade outside the spotlight but he didn't stop recording. This live set has historical as well as musical significance. It accurately portrays the atmosphere at a blues gig at a time when interest in the music was in decline. Even so, he enjoys a symbiotic relationship with his small audience, most in evidence during 'The Dollar Done Fell'. Inevitably, there are *longueurs* during the nine-minute 'I've Got A Right To Love My Baby', two versions of 'Tell Me What's Inside Of You' that notch up more than 16 minutes and two parts of 'Buddy's Blues' that encompass ten. The best audience reaction is inspired by 'The Things I Used To Do' but, otherwise, Guy works and plays hard on all but 'Don't Answer The Door', which is sung in similar fashion by Thurston. This isn't Buddy Guy at his best but at his most idiomatic and that makes it interesting.

*** Breaking Out
JSP JSPCD 272 *Guy; Maurice John Vaughn (ts); Jene Pickett, 'Professor' Eddie Lusk (kb); Phil Guy (g, v); William McDonald, Doug Williams (g); Nick Charles, J. W. Williams (b); Merle Perkins, Ray Allison (d). 80–81.*

Guy was perhaps rash to indulge in tone-dividers and fuzz pedals for an album on which he otherwise plays rather well. This is in fact a remixed version of the master tapes, designed to bring some clarity to what was originally a bit of a sonic dustbin. Even so, the guitar technology reduces the instrumental 'Me & My Guitar' to undifferentiated noise. Most of the trick boxes are absent from 'She Winked Her Eye' (actually a remake of 'She Suits Me To A Tee') but this is unaccountably faded after one chorus of Guy's guitar solo. Some of the other songs aren't up to much but his performance usually saves them. For this issue, the original final song, 'Feeling Sexy', is replaced by a pair of Phil Guy performances on which his brother plays, not necessarily a wise decision.

***(*) Alone & Acoustic
Alligator ALCD 4802 *Guy; Junior Wells (h, v). 5/81.*

This is a surprisingly successful session, given that the pair already had a reputation for under-performing. Both musicians had their serious caps on and the only thing trivial here is the occasional song choice such as 'Diggin' My Potatoes' or 'High Heel Sneakers'. Guy comes up with three original songs, including the opening 'Give Me My Coat And Shoes', one of two on which he plays 12-string guitar. He performs solo on four songs, two of them John Lee Hooker pastiches. More strikingly, Wells plays it straight throughout, though his habit of elaborating on half-remembered songs comes to the fore. Nevertheless, his singing is cliché-free and he plays effective if somewhat restricted harmonica.

***(*) D.J. Play My Blues
JSP JSPCD 256 *Guy; Phil Guy (g, v); Doug Williams (g); Mike Morrison (b); Ray Allison (d). 12/81.*

***(*) DJ Play My Blues
JSP JSP 5104 *As above. 12/81.*

***(*) Buddy's Blues 1979–1982
JSP JSPCD 801 *As for all above JSP CDs. 79–82.*

***(*) The Complete JSP Recordings 1979–82
JSP JSPCDBLUESBOX 102 3CD *As above. 79–82.*

*** Collected
Music Club 50163 *As above. 79–82.*

The informed opinion is that *D.J. Play My Blues* is the best of Guy's JSP albums and this is substantially true. Here his guitar tone is clean and, in 'Dedicated To The Late T-Bone Walker' (actually 'Cold, Cold Feeling') and the title song, muted and controlled. The other impressive track, 'Blues At My Baby's House', removes the boxing gloves and punches above its weight. The other five tracks aren't far behind this high standard, with the exception of a perfunctory version of Otis Rush's 'All Your Love', which just doesn't suit his vocal timbre. Once again, the album ends with two Phil Guy performances on which Buddy plays. The SACD edition (JSP 5104) adds the instrumental 'Comin' On' and an alternative take of 'Girl You're Nice & Clean' but the important bonus is the sound, which even on regular CD players is perceptibly fuller. *Buddy's Blues* is basically a best-of, taking three well-chosen tracks from each of the albums and yet again topping off with two from brother Phil. *The Complete JSP Recordings* is merely the three albums presented in a slipcase for something under £15, a bargain in any language. *Collected* gathers 13 tracks from the same source, with a handful of duplications with *Buddy's Blues*, resulting in superior playing time.

*** The Very Best Of Buddy Guy
Rhino R2 70280 *As for relevant CDs above. 57–81.*

Not exactly what it claims to be but a very reasonable sampling of Guy's career from 'The Way You Been Treating Me', one track from the demo tape he took with him to Chicago in 1957, to three tracks from *D.J. Play My Blues*. In between is a selection of tracks from Artistic, Chess, Vanguard and Blind Pig, and while one might not agree with all the choices, the mixture of live and studio material tries to give the broadest picture, musically and historically, of Guy's skills as a singer and guitarist. Rather than satisfying an appetite for the artist's work, though, this might just whet it.

***(*) Damn Right, I've Got The Blues
Silvertone 1462//(E) ORE CD 516 *Guy; Wayne Jackson, Sid Gauld (t); Neil Sidwell (tb); Andrew Love, Malcolm Duncan (ts); Mick Weaver (o); Pete Wingfield (p); Mark Knopfler, Neil Hubbard, John Porter, Jeff Beck, Eric Clapton (g); Greg Rzab (b); Richie Hayward (d); Tessa Niles, Katie Kissoon, Carol Kenyon (v). 91.*

Not so much a comeback, more a restatement of intent,

with a programme that combines several stalwarts from Guy's stage repertoire with a handful of new songs and a couple of eclectic crowd-pleasers. There are times in the opening title track and an extended 'Five Long Years' when he over-eggs the vocal and instrumental pudding but this is very much in the nature of the man. Elsewhere, in 'There Is Something On Your Mind' and 'Black Night', his backing band, a diverse mixture of American and British musicians, impose the sort of restraint that draws the best out of him. 'Mustang Sally' and 'Early In The Morning' are brash, brassy and rife with guest stars whose contributions flatter their leader. A Grammy Award winner, this is the album that helped to elevate Guy beyond being merely a bluesman.

*(*) Last Time Around – Live At Legends
Silvertone 41629//(E) 0591212 *Guy; Junior Wells (h, v).* 3/93.

Released after Wells's death in 1998 but recorded five years earlier, these acoustic duets are a deplorable travesty of what they'd done a decade earlier in *Alone & Acoustic*. Having started conventionally with a trio of Jimmy Reed songs, Guy makes every effort to keep things on an even keel but he's defeated by a partner in the throes of Tourette's Syndrome. Wells's battery of pops, squeaks, screams and stutters destroys 'What'd I Say' and 'Hoochie Coochie Man' and holes Guy's original 'I've Been There' below the water-line. Mercifully, he calms down for a closing medley of 'Oh Baby'/'You Better Watch Yourself' and an almost tic-free 'Hoodoo Man'. It must be said that the audience reacts to his pantomime with their own ecstatic dementia but this CD's use in the home should be confined to training budgerigars.

*** Feels Like Rain
Silvertone 41498//(E) ORECD 525 *Guy; Darrell Leonard (t); Joe Sublett (ts); Jimmie Powers (h); Marty Grebb (o, p, v); Mick Weaver, Tom Canning, John Philip Shenale (o); John Mayall (p, v); Bill Payne, Ian McLagan (p); Bonnie Raitt (g, v); Johnny Lee Schell, John Porter, David Grissom (g); Greg Rzab, Rick Cortes (b); Richie Hayward, Joe Yuele (d); Tony Braunagel (perc); Mike Finnegan, Rene Geyer, Paul Rodgers, Travis Tritt (v).* 93.

A rerun of the *Damn Right* formula brought another Grammy but both the guests and the repertoire fell short of further burnishing Guy's reputation. He does well enough with 'She's Nineteen Years Old', 'Sufferin' Mind' and his own 'She's A Superstar' but, in an attempt to show versatility, he proves to be out of his depth with Marvin Gaye's 'Trouble Man' and John Hiatt's title track. By comparison, 'Some Kind Of Wonderful' and James Brown's 'I Go Crazy' pass muster but no more. While Guy can scream a blues, his voice lacks the depth of timbre and subtlety to carry off more sophisticated material. His guitar work also lacks clarity as he employs various effects pedals that reduce his often frenzied playing to white noise.

*** Slippin' In
Silvertone 41542//(E) ORECD 533 *Guy; Reese Wynans (o, p); Johnnie Johnson (p); David Grissom, Scott Holt (g); Tommy Shannon, Greg Rzab (b); Chris Layton, Ray 'Killer' Allison (d).* 94.

Dispensing with guests, horn sections and popular song covers, this is Buddy Guy in his proper blues guise. That said, some of the song choices, such as 'Shame, Shame, Shame', and questionable production, like adding surface noise to Charles Brown's 'Trouble Blues', dent the otherwise firm control exhibited. Guy's vocals are sometimes tentative but he's strong in his own 'Little Dab-A-Doo', Fenton Robinson's '7–11' and 'I Smell Trouble'. Then again, the serious message in 'Cities Need Help' required a stronger vocal performance than he delivers. Two bands, his own and the surviving members of Double Trouble, provide accompaniment, with Johnnie Johnson's piano a constant. Everyone plays well but the mix favours each drummer; at times their contributions are louder than Guy's vocals, making this a good rather than a great record.

***(*) Live! The Real Deal
Silvertone 41543//(E) ORE CD 538 *Guy; Ron Tooley (t); Dennis Wilson (tb); George Young (as); Lenny Pickett (ts); Lew Del Gatto (bs); Leon Pendarvis (o); Johnnie Johnson (p); G. E. Smith (g); Paul Ossola (b); Shawn Pelton (d).* 96.

Even after his elevation to the world stage, Guy's live performances can still be irritatingly shallow and crowd-pleasing but this teaming with the band from *Saturday Night Live* isn't one of them. Guy is near the top of his form on a set drawn from gigs at his own Chicago club, Legends, and Irving Plaza in New York City. The repertoire favours his past successes, including 'Let Me Love You Baby', 'First Time I Met The Blues' and 'Damn Right, I've Got The Blues', and convincing portrayals of 'Sweet Black Angel' and Bobby Bland's 'Ain't That Lovin' You'. There are no medleys of half-completed numbers, no ultra-quiet meanderings, and the verbal tics are restrained to 'make it so funky they can smell it'. Fortunately, this album's success isn't to be judged by the olfactory nerves; the pleasure is entirely aural.

** Heavy Love
Silvertone 41629//(E) 0591182 *Guy; Reese Wynans (kb); Jonny Lang (g, v); Jack Holder, Steve Cropper (g); David M. Smith (b); Richie Hayward (d); David Z (perc); Jessica Boucher, Bekka Bramlett (v).* 98.

A catalogue of bad decisions hamstrings this record. With very few exceptions (the title track and Guy's own 'Had A Bad Night'), the song selections are either inappropriate for his voice, poorly arranged or both. Production values are shoddy: an over-loud snare drum sounds like an amplified dustbin, a consistently poor vocal sound amplifies the weaknesses of Guy's technique, when it can be heard, and a concentration on medium-paced funk arrangements saps his authority. A hectic and monotonous attempt at 'Saturday Night Fish Fry' is an emasculation of the song and its performer, the addition of Jonny Lang on 'Midnight Train' superfluous. Unlike the previous album, this smells.

*** Buddy's Baddest: The Best Of Buddy Guy
Silvertone 41677//(E) 0591232 *As for above Silvertone CDs, except add Chuck Domanico (b).* 91–98.

A glance at the composition of these 14 tracks from five albums indicates their individual worth; four are taken from *Damn Right, I've Got The Blues*, three from *Feels Like Rain*, two from *Slippin' In* and one each from *Live! The Real Deal* and *Heavy Love*. These are augmented by three previously unissued titles, 'Miss Ida B', 'I Need Your Love So Bad' and 'Innocent Man'. Of these, the first is good enough to have been on *Damn Right* or *Feels Like Rain*, the Little Willie John song reveals the essential weakness of Guy's voice and the third is an acknowledged adaptation of 'Mannish Boy'. As a summation of his work for the label thus far, it's good enough; as a stand-alone compilation it's probably a bit better.

♛ **** Sweet Tea
Silvertone 41751//(E) 9260182 *Guy; Bobby Whitlock (p); Jimbo Mathus (g); Davey Faragher (b); Spam [Tommy Lee Miles], Sam Carr, Pete Thomas (d); Craig Krampf (perc).* 01.

After a three-year hiatus, Guy returns with a monumental album that commandeers the music and the production style of Mississippi's Fat Possum label, in the process reviving the danger and abandon that had been eliminated from his recorded persona. The album takes its title from the Oxford, Mississippi, studio in which it was recorded. The production style is deliberately rough: count-ins and comments are left in, instruments are devoid of studio sweetening. Guy responds by singing and playing as though his life depends upon it. Most impressive is a monolithic reworking of Junior Kimbrough's 'Baby Please Don't Leave Me', one of four Kimbrough songs present; another is a 12-minute 'I Gotta Try You Girl'. Other Fat Possum artists drawn upon are CeDell Davis, T-Model Ford and Robert Cage, along with the Kimbrough arrangement of 'Tramp' and Guy's own 'It's A Jungle Out There'. That may well be true but it's certain Buddy Guy is the king of it. NS

**(*) Blues Singer
Silvertone 44259 *Guy; Jimbo Mathus, Eric Clapton, B. B. King (g); Tony Garnier (b); Jim Keltner (d); The Perrys (snaps, claps).* 03.

In 1963 Guy sat alongside his mentor, both of them unplugged, to make the album *Muddy Waters Folk Singer*. Forty years later he takes the same turn in his own road, reworking songs of past masters from Son House and Johnny Shines to Smokey Hogg and Frankie Lee Sims. In contrast with his full-bodied and often poignant singing, beautifully exemplified by 'Lonesome Home Blues', the Memphis Willie Borum song that closes the album, Guy's acoustic guitar playing is meagre, too insubstantial to give any individual flavour to pieces like John Lee Hooker's 'Sally Mae' or 'Black Cat Blues'. The group rendition of 'Crawlin' Kingsnake' with Clapton and King is better, and Skip James's 'Hard Time Killing Floor' is strikingly well suited to Guy's voice. Like its predecessor, this was recorded at the Sweet Tea studio, but it's a weaker brew. TR

Phil Guy (born 1940)
VOCAL, GUITAR

A younger brother of Buddy Guy, he played in Baton Rouge with Raful Neal and other local artists before moving to Chicago in 1969 to join his brother's band. He subsequently worked for Junior Wells. In the '80s he formed his own band and recorded albums for JSP, Isabel and Red Lightnin'.

**(*) Phil Guy & Lurrie Bell (Chicago Blues Session – Volume 25)
Wolf 120.871 *Guy; [Golden] Big Wheeler (h); Leo Davies [Davis] (p); John Primer (g); Willie Kent (b); Jody Young (d).* 1/92.
*** Say What You Mean
JSP JSPCD 2135 *Guy; Jamie Finegan (t, string syn); Bruce Feiner (ts); Robert Feiner (bs); Marty Sammon (o, p); Johnny Rawls (g); Mike Nunno (b); Reggie Barnes (d); Alvin Carter Sr (cga); Burt Teague (shaker).* 99.

Guy demonstrates on his five tracks of the Wolf CD that he is a fierce singer and an attacking, if conventional, guitarist; that he does so on largely standard blues and soul material like 'Part Time Love', '[Turn On Your] Love Light' and 'Sky Is Crying' may not have been by choice. *Say What You Mean* marked his return to JSP after a break of several years. (His earlier albums for the label are deleted.) The Johnny Rawls–Bruce Feiner production, more efficient than imaginative, places him at the centre of a swirl of sound, and he responds with a focused performance of emotional vocals and incendiary guitar. In the notes, referring to his earlier recordings, he says, 'I was too much into the slow blues. I'm ready to boogie to stay in the game,' but slow and medium-paced numbers predominate, some soul songs but more of them blues like 'Fixin' To Die', a rewrite of Booker White, and 'Last Time'. In the peppier 'Last Of The Blues Singers' he announces that that's what he is ('everybody else is gone'), which, apart from anything else, does no justice to his label's extensive catalogue of current blues singers. TR

Steve Guyger
VOCAL, HARMONICA

Guyger grew up around Philadelphia, where he began playing harmonica in 1971. Four years later he met Paul Oscher, with whom he has frequently collaborated. He played with Jimmy Rogers in his road band throughout the '80s and into the '90s, and acknowledges Rogers's influence on his songwriting. He has also recorded with Steve Freund and Roy Gaines.

**(*) Live At The Dinosaur
Horseplay HP 330033 *Guyger; David Maxwell (kb); Steve Freund (g); Steve Gomes (b); Steve Ramsay (d).* 96/97.
*** Past Life Blues
Severn CD-0002 *Guyger; Brian Bisesi, Rich Yescalis (g); Steve Gomes (b); Joe Maher (d).* 9/97.

Whether as harmonica player, singer or songwriter Guyger is a proud traditionalist, dedicated to the idiom of '50s/'60s Chicago. Though his harmonica technique is enviable, his playing is calm, without extravagant gestures, and what he seems to value most is getting a limpid, deep blue tone, as in instrumental tracks like 'Snake Oil' and 'Blue Mambo' on *Past Life Blues*. When singing he sometimes employs a quaver in the manner of Sonny Boy Williamson II, sometimes a slackmouthed delivery like Jimmy Reed's, but the results are never very satisfying. *Past Life Blues* is the better of the two CDs, not for the ensemble work, which is more reticent than Maxwell and Freund's playing on the live set, but because the performances are more concise – 17 numbers as against 12, in much the same playing time. For his shared album with Paul Oscher, *Living Legends – Deep In The Blues* (Blues Leaf), see Oscher's entry. TR

Bob Hall (born 1942)
PIANO, VOCAL

By day a patent attorney, by night and at weekends Bob Hall plays blues and boogie-woogie piano. In a career of more than 40 years he has played with Jo Ann Kelly, Alexis Korner, The Groundhogs, Savoy Brown, Rocket 88 and The Blues Band, besides accompanying scores of American blues musicians who

have visited Britain, both on tour and on record. He is also much in demand at blues and boogie-woogie festivals throughout Europe. Latterly he has worked in a duo with his partner, the singer Hilary Blythe.

****(*) At The Window**
Sanctuary 72392 *Hall; Top Topham, Dave Peabody (g); Robert Bond (d).* 90.
**** Don't Play Boogie**
Sanctuary 81277 *Hall; Steve Beighton (ts); Paul Lamb (h); Top Topham, Dave Kelly (g); Hilary Blythe (b, v); Dave Raeburn (d); Frank White (v).* 98–99.

Hall is a versatile pianist, equally at ease negotiating the intricacies of Montana Taylor's 'Detroit Rocks' or Harry Shayne's 'Mr Freddy Blues' and accompanying his singing of Leroy Carr's 'Blues Before Sunrise' (all on *At The Window*). Unlike some blues and boogie-woogie players, he enjoys collaborating with other musicians: half of *At The Window* is either with Peabody, playing acoustic guitar, or with Topham and Bond, while all the tracks on *Don't Play Boogie* involve several musicians. Hall also makes a point of writing much of his material, and of singing it, and one suspects that some of his admirers would be satisfied with a little less of the latter, since his voice is insubstantial. For them, the most rewarding parts of these albums will be Big Maceo's 'Chicago Breakdown' and Pete Johnson's 'Death Ray Boogie' on *Don't Play Boogie* and, in particular, the five tracks at the end of *At The Window*, recorded at a Swiss festival. The sound is barely passable, but Hall proves himself a master of the austere arts of unaccompanied blues and boogie piano. TR

Juanita Hall (1901–68)
VOCAL

Raised by her grandparents in New Jersey, Juanita Long Hall studied music at Juilliard and had a long and successful career as a singer and actress. She sang in the chorus of Show Boat *in 1928, had parts in the movies* Paradise In Harlem *(1940) and* Miracle In Harlem *(1944) and appeared in several Broadway musicals, her award-winning performance as Bloody Mary in* South Pacific *(1949) followed by roles in* House Of Flowers *(1954) and* Flower Drum Song *(1958). Earlier she sang with the Hall Johnson Choir and, in 1935, founded a choir of her own.*

***** Sings The Blues**
Original Jazz Classics OJCCD 1928 *Hall; Doc Cheatham (t); Buster Bailey (cl); Coleman Hawkins (ts); Claude Hopkins (p, arr); George Duvivier (b); Jimmy Crawford (d).* 58.

Hall encountered the blues by accident, one day in her childhood, when she overheard a record of Bessie Smith's 'Down Hearted Blues'. Years later she was able to commemorate the occasion in *Sings The Blues*, a dozen blues and vintage standards, several associated with Bessie, which she sings skilfully and idiomatically, enacting them with a swagger in keeping with their origins in vaudeville. Cheatham and Bailey respond to this elegizing of a bygone age by drawing on their first-hand memories of it, and play with carnival extravagance. Even Hawkins, normally reserved, has moments of broad humour. What all this produces is unusual but not incongruous: an album of blues and blues-related songs that is not steeped in the melancholy traditionally associated with the idiom. 'Nobody Knows You When You're Down And Out' is taken seriously, as it should be, but for the most part the mood is buoyant. While there is nothing singular about Hall's voice, she does what she can to make these venerable songs her own – sometimes, for example, tinkering gently with the lyrics – and the listener is only occasionally, and never obtrusively, reminded of earlier singers and older versions. The odd juxtaposition of 'I Don't Want It Second Hand' and 'Second Hand' calls for a note: the former is Hall's own, while the latter is Perry Bradford's composition 'I Ain't Goin' To Play No Second Fiddle'. Hall made other blues recordings, such as *A Tribute To Bessie Smith* (Aamco), which have not been issued on CD. TR

John Hammond (born 1942)
VOCAL, HARMONICA, GUITAR

Hammond's father was the jazz enthusiast and record producer of the same name but, since his parents separated when he was five, John Jr discovered the blues for himself, through radio and records. When he began playing music in the early '60s it was as a blues interpreter. Although he has frequently worked in collaboration with electric bands, he has never deserted the acoustic solo setting in which he began. In recent years he has begun to draw his material from other sources than the blues repertoire in which he once specialized, but the quality and commitment of his work are unimpaired.

****(*) John Hammond**
Vanguard VMD 2148 *Hammond.* 63.
**** Big City Blues**
Vanguard 79153 *Hammond; Billy Butler, James Spruill (g); Jimmy Lewis (b); Bobby Donaldson (d).* 64.
**** Country Blues**
Vanguard 79198 *Hammond.* 1/65.
***** So Many Roads**
Vanguard VMD 79178 *Hammond; Charlie Musselwhite (h); Garth Hudson (o); Michael Bloomfield (p); Robbie Robertson (g); Jimmy Lewis (b); Levon Helm (d).* 65.

It was obvious from the start that Hammond knew the blues library well and chose his repertoire from it with discrimination. It was partly for those reasons that his early albums were treated at the time with great respect. Forty years on, they may be judged less deferentially. *John Hammond*, consisting entirely of received repertoire, often unpredictably handled, is quite an impressive debut, its chief fault a melodramatic delivery. On *Big City Blues*, however, his singing leapfrogs over mannerism to land only a little short of parody. Amidst the histrionics the surprising lineup behind him often makes attractive music. *Country Blues* is somewhat more controlled, but Hammond has not yet found anything interesting to do, either vocally or on guitar, with songs like Robert Johnson's 'Traveling Riverside Blues', and his 'country blues' approach to later pieces like Jimmy Reed's 'Little Rain' is unilluminating.

Thanks to the presence of some of The Band, *So Many Roads* is probably the most widely known of Hammond's '60s albums. Gratifyingly, it is also the best. Robbie Robertson's mordant guitar lines give the music a much-needed toughness; Lil' Son Jackson's 'Gambling Blues' has real menace, and the chuntering version of Bo Diddley's 'Who Do You Love' is a huge improvement on the one on *Country Blues*. Hammond's voice has settled into what sounds like a fairly consistent pastiche of Muddy Waters, with an occasional bad-boy snarl reminiscent of Mick Jagger, but in this context it works.

**(*) Sooner Or Later
Water 105 *Hammond; Willie Bridges (ts, bs); Gordon Fleming, George Stubbs (p); Herman Pittman (b); Charles Otis (d). 71?*
** Southern Fried
Water 106 *Hammond; Gene 'Bo-Legs' Miller (t); Ed Logan (ts, bs); Joe Arnold, Lewis Collins (ts); James Mitchell (bs); Barry Beckett (kb); Eddie Hinton, Duane Allman, Jimmy Johnson (g); David Hood, Marlin Greene (b); Roger Hawkins (d). 72?*

These albums, originally on Atlantic, find Hammond restyling his music according to contemporary fashion in Memphis and Muscle Shoals, though his material is a swatch mostly from Chicago designers like Howlin' Wolf (six numbers on the two CDs), Sonny Boy Williamson II, Elmore James and Muddy Waters. The fusion of blues and Southern soul that worked for a heavyweight front man like Albert King is not so apt for a less imposing singer and guitarist. *Sooner Or Later* is merely uneventful, while *Southern Fried* goes seriously wrong with its plodding versions of Chuck Berry's 'Nadine', Junior Parker's 'Mystery Train' and Wolf's 'Riding In The Moonlight'.

**(*) You Can't Judge A Book By The Cover
Vanguard VCD-79472 *As for* Big City Blues *and* So Many Roads, *except add Barry Beckett (kb), Eddie Hinton (p, g), Spooner Oldham, Randall Bramlett (p), Duane Allman (g), David Hood, Tommy Cogbill (b), Roger Hawkins (d, perc), Kenny Buttrey (d). 64–73.*

Three or four tracks each from *Big City Blues, So Many Roads, Southern Fried* and *Can't Beat The Kid* (Capricorn 5361362, deleted) compose this sampler of Hammond in an electric context; its availability is uncertain.

*** Solo
Vanguard VMD 79380 *Hammond. 6/76.*
**(*) Hot Tracks
Vanguard 79424 *Hammond; Mark Wenner (h); Jimmy Thackery (g); Jan Zukowski (b); Pete Ragusa (d). 9/79.*

After more than a decade away, Hammond returned to Vanguard to make the live-in-studio *Solo*. The years had transformed him. His guitar playing was richer in texture, the vocal overacting had nearly all been eliminated; he was a man playing the blues, rather than a boy playing with them. Even in a song as resonant as 'Hellhound Blues' (Robert Johnson's 'Hellhound On My Trail') he discovered a quiet place where he could tell his story in his own way. On *Hot Tracks* he was accompanied by the Washington, DC-based band The Nighthawks. Unlike *So Many Roads*, it was not a collaboration that was likely to strike sparks out of the music, but it proved that Hammond could make a decent album in the Chicago bar-band style. It also gave his harmonica playing more prominence than on previous albums. Working through a programme of familiar material by Howlin' Wolf, Little Walter, Bo Diddley and the like, front man and band do their job with unostentatious efficiency.

**(*) At The Crossroads: The Blues Of Robert Johnson
Vanguard VMD 79751 *Hammond; Charlie Musselwhite, Mark Wenner (h); Garth Hudson (o); Michael Bloomfield (p); Billy Butler, James Spruill, Robbie Robertson, Jimmy Thackery (g);*
Jimmy Lewis, Jan Zukowski (b); Bobby Donaldson, Levon Helm, Pete Ragusa (d). 64–9/79.
**(*) Best Of The Vanguard Years
Vanguard VCD 79555 *Similar to above, except add unknowns (g, b, d). 64–79.*

Best Of is a so-so selection from the foregoing Vanguard albums, six items coming from *So Many Roads* and fewer from the others, plus a track each from *John Hammond* and the deleted *Mirrors* (1967) and two previously unissued songs 'from an unmarked tape': 'Ask Me Nice' with a band and a solo 'Hellhound Blues' that's different from the one on *Solo* but almost as engrossing. *At The Crossroads* was also achieved by a scour of the Vanguard catalogue, which drew on seven Hammond albums and the VAC *Blues At Newport*; given Hammond's predilection for Robert Johnson songs, it wasn't difficult to find 14 of them, though the quality of his interpretations varies according to how seasoned he was when he recorded them, and the majority are early rather than late. Whatever Hammond may feel about the recycling of these old tapes, he must surely be embarrassed by the notes, which claim that Johnson's 'legacy languished in complete obscurity for 50 years' and Hammond 'not only found Robert Johnson, he brought him back to life'.

**(*) John Hammond
Rounder CD 11532 *Hammond; Charles Brown (s); Bob Montalto, Robbie Kondor, Kyril Bromley (p); Sherman Holmes (b); Charles Otis (d); 'Washboard Chaz' Leary (wb). 80–81.*
**(*) Live
Rounder CD 3074 *Hammond. 83.*

John Hammond is drawn from *Mileage* (Rounder CD 3042) and *Frogs For Snakes* (CD 3060), which are of uncertain availability. Since only a few tracks have been omitted, the album should satisfy all but completists. Hammond dips into his favourite sources, choosing four numbers by Sonny Boy Williamson II, three by Muddy Waters and two each by Howlin' Wolf, Robert Johnson and Big Joe Williams, and performing most of them in small-group arrangements. There are also some solos, and a few duets with pianist Montalto, such as Leroy Carr's 'Big 45', and with washboardist Leary, but despite this care to vary the settings, and the addition, unusual in a Hammond context, of a saxophone to some of the *Frogs For Snakes* tracks, it's a rather grey and unexciting programme. *Live* is a solo set, recorded in performance at the California club McCabe's, with a typical programme of '20s/'30s 'country' blues by Blind Boy Fuller, Charley Patton and Robert Johnson and later pieces associated with Howlin' Wolf and Jimmy Reed. As noted above, the latter respond less well to being transformed into solo acoustic pieces. Never much given to note-for-note replicas, Hammond offers independently minded readings such as John Estes's 'Drop Down Mama' whipped by frenzied slide guitar, or a version of Fuller's 'Cat Man Blues' intercut with the guitar part of Johnson's 'Phonograph Blues'. Six songs have been added to the dozen on the original LP.

*** Nobody But You
Virgin 41772 *Hammond; Ken Whitely (p, md, tbj, g, b, perc, v, prod); Gene Taylor (p, v); Paul James (g, d, v); Terry Wilkins (b); Bucky Berger (d). 1/87.*

There had been signs earlier, but this is the recording (originally issued on Flying Fish FF 70502) that clearly foretold the Hammond of the '90s: a mature artist, confident enough in his skills to wander off the high street of imitation and *hommage* and investigate the alleys and sideroads of adaptation and reinvention. At this point his tinkerings with his source material are mostly tentative – Ken Whitely's Yank Rachellish mandolin added to Arthur Crudup's 'If I Get Lucky', a quiet bass gently rocking Blind Boy Fuller's 'Lost Lover Blues', that sort of thing – but the album as a whole feels like muscle-flexing for more robust activity.

*** **Trouble No More**
Pointblank 88257//(E) VPBCD 15 *Hammond; Rick Estrin (h); Mitch Woods, Charles Brown (p); Charlie Baty, Roy Rogers, Danny Caron (g); Brad Sexton, Tim Drummond, Larry Taylor (b); Dobie Strange, James Cruce (d); J. J. Cale (prod). 93.*

*** **Found True Love**
Pointblank 40655//(E) VPBCD 26 *Hammond; Charlie Musselwhite (h); Mr B (p); Duke Robillard (g, prod); Marty Ballou (b); Jeffery McAllister, Neil Gouvin (d); Soozie Tyrell (v). 95?*

*** **Long As I Have You**
Pointblank 45514//(E) VPBCD 44 *Hammond; Rick Estrin (h); Steve Lucky (p); Charlie Baty (g); Ronnie James Weber (b); June Core (d); Washboard Chaz Leary (wb). 98?*

Most of Hammond's '90s albums for Virgin's Pointblank label, beginning with 1992's *Got Love If You Want It* (last on Charisma 92146, now deleted), were archaeological digs through several strata of blues styles. *Found True Love*, for example, works backwards from the gumboot stomp of Howlin' Wolf's 'Howlin' For My Darling' to Leroy Carr's ''Fore Day Rider Blues' and Blind Willie McTell's 'Warm It Up To Me'. Charlie Musselwhite joins in to great effect on 'Someday Baby Blues'. On *Trouble No More* and *Long As I Have You* Hammond is accompanied almost throughout by Little Charlie & The Nightcats, whose assertive playing combines well with singing that is deeper and generally more relaxed than on previous recordings. Around the halfway mark on *Trouble No More* is an acoustic intermission consisting of Cliff Carlisle's suggestive 'That Nasty Swing' and a pretty version of Blind Willie McTell's 'Love Changin' Blues'. *Long As I Have You* finds Hammond heading for Chicago, following a route signposted by Sonny Boy Williamson II ('Don't Start Me Talkin''), Jimmy Rogers ('Goin' Away Blues'), Howlin' Wolf ('Crying At Daylight') and Otis Rush ('So Many Roads, So Many Trains' revisited). Here the acoustic part of the programme, three duets with Leary, comes at the end and seems an arbitrary postscript to an album that's preoccupied with capturing band styles of the '40s and '50s. As exercises in historical reconstruction, tracks like Baby Boy Warren's 'I Got Lucky' are almost as perfect as Colonial Williamsburg.

*** **Wicked Grin**
Pointblank 50764//(E) VPBCD 55 *Hammond; Charlie Musselwhite (h); Augie Meyers (ac, o, p); Tom Waits (p, g, prod); Larry Taylor (b); Stephen Hodges (d, perc). 00/01?*

***(*) **Ready For Love**
Back Porch 80599 *Hammond; Augie Meyers (ac, o, p); Soozie Tyrell (vn, v); David Hidalgo (md, g, v, prod); Frank Carillo (g); Marty Ballou (b); Stephen Hodges (d, perc). 03?*

Wicked Grin is a good collection of Tom Waits songs, but since Waits's originals are mostly in catalogue and Hammond handles the material with enormous respect, one may wonder what point is being made other than that Hammond is a big Waits fan. Evidently the reverse is also true: 'John,' says Waits, 'has a blacksmith's strength and rhythm', and he clearly intends the remark to be approving. The two are in fact old friends, having first shared a stage in the mid-'70s. Hammond recorded a Waits song on *Got Love If You Want It*, and played on Waits's *Mule Variations* (1999). The settings of *Wicked Grin* replicate the twilight ambience Waits has made his own – the more so because he plays on most of them – and the only element missing is Waits's serrated vocal attack. For all that, this is one of Hammond's most successful recordings, uncovering skills and interests seldom hinted at on earlier albums. The process continues, with even more striking results, on *Ready For Love*. There are only two Waits songs ('Gin Soaked Boy' and 'Low Side Of The Road'), but the skid row mood of *Wicked Grin* is re-created in 'Slick Crown Vic' (a rare Hammond original), 'No Chance' and a wonderfully sinister reading of 'The Same Thing', only to be lightened – if briefly – by the out-and-out honkytonk of George Jones's 'Color Of The Blues' and 'Just One More'. That its connections with the blues seem, on paper, to be skimpy hardly matters. *Ready For Love* reveals an irreducibly blues-rooted artist making adventurous, idiosyncratic music. TR

Hosea Hargrove (born 1929)
VOCAL, GUITAR

From the Austin area, Hargrove has been playing the small blues clubs of West and Central Texas since his teens; he gave some guitar lessons to Jimmie and Stevie Ray Vaughan.

(*) **I Love My Life
Fedora FCD 5011 *Hargrove; Charlie Prichard (g); Sal Navarro (b); Chris Millar (d). 5/98.*

Hosea Hargrove cites Lil' Son Jackson as a major influence, but seems most comfortable playing clangorous, loping dance music, in the footsteps of Frankie Lee Sims. The bassist only appears on two tracks; usually, the second guitar carries the bass line, resulting in a powerful but supple and open-textured sound. 'Things I Used To Do' and 'I'm A King Bee', on which Hargrove plays solo, are less successful, for he sounds aimless without a rhythm section, and 'Hoochie Coochie Man' is also rather listless. When the covers are less obvious choices, Hargrove does much better, borrowing successfully from the Carter Brothers and Lonesome Sundown. He also contributes some unpretentious, oldfashioned originals, among which the slow, threatening 'Big Gun' stands out. Also an attention grabber is the very different 'Hawaii', which is a blues surf instrumental. The CD's best tracks only serve to increase one's regret that Hargrove does not always reach the standard of which he is capable. CS

Harlem Hamfats
GROUP

The recording director J. Mayo Williams is credited with assembling the pieces of this band, putting together musicians of diverse backgrounds and playing histories. The group is believed to have existed solely in the recording studio, where it not only made several dozen sides of its own but accompanied the singers Rosetta Howard, Johnnie Temple, Jimmie Gordon and Frankie Jaxon. Despite several personnel changes – the singer Joe McCoy is the only constant – the band retained a distinct style.

*** Harlem Hamfats – Vol. 1 (1936)
Document DOCD-5271 *Herb Morand (t); Odell Rand (cl); Horace Malcolm (p); Charlie McCoy (md, v); Joe McCoy (g, v); Andrew Harris (b); Pearlis Williams (d). 4–11/36.*

*** Harlem Hamfats – Vol. 2 (1936–1937)
Document DOCD-5272 *Herb Morand (t, v); Chris Reggell (cl, ts); Odell Rand (cl); Horace Malcolm (p); Charlie McCoy (md); Joe McCoy (g, v); Andrew Harris, Ransom Knowling, John Lindsay (b); Pearlis Williams, Fred Flynn (d); Rosetta Howard (v). 12/36–10/37.*

*** Harlem Hamfats – Vol. 3 (1937–1938)
Document DOCD-5273 *Herb Morand (t, v); Odell Rand, Buster Bailey (cl); Horace Malcolm (p); Charlie McCoy (md); Joe McCoy (g, v); John Lindsay (b); Fred Flynn (d); Rosetta Howard (v). 10/37–4/38.*

**(*) Harlem Hamfats – Vol. 4 (1938–1939)
Document DOCD-5274 *Herb Morand (t, v); Ann Cooper (t); Odell Rand (cl); Chris Reggell (as); Horace Malcolm, prob. Black Bob (p); Charlie McCoy (md); Joe McCoy (g, v); John Lindsay, unknown (b); Fred Flynn (d); Lil Allen (v, sp); Rosetta Howard, Alberta Smith (v). 4/38–9/39.*

*** Let's Get Drunk And Truck
Fabulous FABCD 253 *As for relevant CDs above. 4/36–10/37.*

*** Hamfat Swing 1936–1938
EPM Blues Collection 15893 *As above. 4/36–4/38.*

Ham fat is not an ingredient you expect to find in Martha Stewart, nor was the music of the Harlem Hamfats designed to accompany gracious living. It was jukebox entertainment for blue-collar black Americans, cleverly conceived and executed with flair. The Hamfats can be described as the first group to promote a successful synthesis of jazz and urban blues – if 'jazz' is shorthand for the presence of trumpet and clarinet as lead voices, and 'urban blues' for the voice/piano/guitar blend pioneered by Leroy Carr and Scrapper Blackwell. Herb Morand's trumpet is the dominant horn, and the effect is of a youngish Louis Armstrong, flanked, in Odell Rand, by a vaudeville clarinettist of more than average ability, fronting a conventional Chicago blues band of the '30s. The main singer – for the first year of the band's life virtually the only singer – is the gravelly Joe McCoy.

The band was launched on to the 'race' records market in the late spring of 1936 with the coupling 'Oh! Red'/'Lake Providence Blues'. 'Oh! Red', a springy blues with solos by the horns and Charlie McCoy's twinkling mandolin, was an immediate hit. 'Move Your Hand', 'Sales Tax On It' and 'We Gonna Pitch A Boogie Woogie' generate the same drive, while 'Southern Blues' and the minor-key 'Weed Smoker's Dream' move more languorously. These, all on *Vol. 1*, are vocal numbers and more or less blues, but at the end of the CD a couple of instrumentals appear, one of which, 'Hamfat Swing', is a conventional 64-bar tune, and on *Vol. 2* the band's repertoire expands with more compositions that might have been played by any swing group of the period, such as 'Keep It Swinging Round And Round' and 'Jam Jamboree'. Morand also takes over some of the singing, this too in a very Armstrong-derived manner. Some of the sessions included in this and the remaining volumes are by the Hamfats accompanying Rosetta Howard, and are discussed in her entry.

Though the trumpet and Rand's broad but not unsubtle clarinet divide much of the solo space, they sometimes leave room for Horace Malcolm, an unobtrusive pianist who occasionally cuts loose to enjoyable effect, and for Charlie McCoy, almost always on mandolin rather than guitar, though he contributes characteristic guitar lines to 'Rampart And Gravier Blues' and the band's soulful arrangement of 'Black Gal You Better Use Your Head'. These are units of a 1937 session that occupies the first ten tracks of *Vol. 3*: embracing both blues numbers and swing features such as 'Tempo De Bucket', 'Root Hog Or Die' and 'Toodle Oo Blues', this is the Hamfats' most explicit statement of their eclectic musical policy, and their most vivacious session.

Three weeks later the band made the appropriate change in the percussion department and moonlighted, though for the same label, as the Palooka Washboard Band, chiefly to produce cover versions of the recent hits 'We Gonna Move [To The Outskirts Of Town]' and 'Back Door'. Their four sides are on *The McCoy Brothers – Vol. 2 (1936–1944)* (RST Blues Documents BDCD-6020).

In 1939 the Hamfats moved from Decca to Vocalion. At the same time they took on a second singer, Alberta Smith, and exchanged Morand for Ann Cooper. Smith was herself replaced at the year's second session by Lil Allen. Both new singers are less imposing than Rosetta Howard, Cooper is calm where Morand was vigorous, Charlie McCoy is inaudible on the first date and absent on the second, and altogether the music is Hamfat Lite (or Lean), a tepid coda to the performance that had begun three and a half years earlier with such brio.

Hamfat Swing, which confines itself to the band's best years, is an excellent summary of their work, embracing 'Oh! Red', 'Weed Smoker's Dream', 'Root Hog Or Die' and several collaborations with Rosetta Howard. *Let's Get Drunk And Truck* is derived from an LP whose echoey transfers made the music sound as if it had been carefully re-created decades later for a movie soundtrack – clean, sharp and implausible; but the 14 tracks were impeccably chosen, and the CD costs next to nothing. TR

James Harman (born 1946)
VOCAL, HARMONICA

An Alabamian, Harman learned harmonica from his father and formed his first band at 16. In the '70s he lived in Florida and New Orleans before settling in LA, where he joined a cadre of top-flight harmonica players including William Clarke, Rod Piazza, Kim Wilson and Rick Estrin. His bands have included a number of formidable guitarists, such as Hollywood Fats and Kid Ramos.

Harman's catalogue has been despoiled by deletion: four albums made for Black Top in the early '90s (*Do Not Disturb*, *Two Sides To Every Story*, *Cards On The Table*, *Black & White*) have disappeared, likewise two for Cannonball, including a reissue of his acclaimed Rivera set *Extra Napkins*, and earlier sets for Rivera and Rhino (*Thank You Baby*, *Those Dangerous Gentlemen*, *Strictly Live In '85*).

**(*) Blues Harp Summit
Charly CDGR 272 *Harman; Robbie Eason (g); Joe Leaon (b); Michael Cherry (d). c. 91.*

*** Icepick's Story
Me And My Blues MMBCD 702 *Harman; unknowns (s); Jeff Turmes (p, g, b); John 'Juke' Logan, Fred Kaplan (p); Joel Foy,*

Ted 'Kid' Morgan, Robbie Eason, Anson Funderburgh (g); Joe Leaon (b); Stephen Mugalian (d, perc); Esten Cooke, Michael Cherry, Lee Campbell (d). 91–95.

Icepick's Story was made by chipping pieces from Harman's Black Top albums – fortunately so, since they have melted away. All the songs were written or co-written by Harman; titles like 'Dirt Road' or 'Stranger Blues' simply provide familiar opening sentences for otherwise new stories, which he tells in a voice striated with pain and frustration. It's as much a singer's album as a harp player's: there are no instrumentals, and on some songs Harman is not the main soloist, leaving that role to one or another of the admirable guitarists. *Blues Harp Summit* is a club recording without much presence. (It was done at Buddy Guy's Legends for a TV music series.) Harman has 11 tracks; the others are by Rod Piazza and Studebaker John.

*** **Lonesome Moon Trance**
Pacific Blues PBCD-2304 Harman; Thomas A. Mahon, Carl Sonny Leyland, Steve F'dor, Gene Taylor (p); Jeff 'Big Dad' Turmes (g, b); Kid Ramos, Kirk 'Eli' Fletcher, Enrico Crivellaro, Dave Gonzales, Robert Charles (Robby) Eason, Elmo 'Buddy' Reed, 'Steady Rollin'' Bob Margolin, Junior Watson, Nathan James (g); 'Brother Miles' Reed, Buddy Clark, Joseph Leaon (b); Alan West (d, perc); Stephen T. Hodges, Paul V. Fasulo, Steve Mugalian (d); James Michael 'Bonedaddy' Tempo (perc); King Cotton, Donny Gerrard, Gregory 'Popeye' Alexander (v). 03.

Harman makes records carefully, planning a particular lineup for each track; hence the lengthy castlist for this set, and hence, too, the very different results, from the downhome 'Miss Bessie Mae Blues' (dedicated to a former dog), 'Time Will Tell' and 'Bad-Luck Life', where Margolin and Eason re-create Muddy Waters and Jimmy Rogers, to the impressionistic title number, with its voodoo-talking guitar by Nathan James, and the coolly satirical 'Piecework Politicians'. Like all Harman's work, this is both highly original and deeply rooted. TR

Harmonica Fats (1927–2000)
VOCAL, HARMONICA

Born Harvey Blackston in Louisiana, Harmonica Fats was an Angeleno by the time he began performing professionally in 1956. In the '60s and '70s he cut singles for small labels. From 1969 to 1975, Fats was a fulltime musician; thereafter, he took a day job while continuing to perform, but did not record again until after he began working with the Bernie Pearl band in the mid-'80s. He was Lonnie Brooks's foil in the Heineken lager TV ads.

*** **I Had To Get Nasty**
Bee Bump BB CD 02 Harmonica Fats; Hollis Gilmore (ts); Leon Blue (kb); Bernie Pearl (g, v); Big Terry DeRouen (g); Michael Barry (b); Albert Trepagnier Jr (d). 5/91.
(*) **Two Heads Are Better …
Bee Bump BBCD-04 Harmonica Fats; Bernie Pearl (g). 7/94.
(*) **Blow, Fat Daddy, Blow!
Bee Bump BB CD 05 As above. 12/95.

His growling voice and roly-poly, pop-eyed presence made Harmonica Fats an enjoyable live performer, but his playing was basic and his melodic ideas limited. These drawbacks are evident when he and Pearl perform as a duo; Pearl commands a variety of guitar styles, but there's an uncomfortable mismatch between his polished technique and Fats's uncomplicated chugging. Comparisons have sometimes been made with the rough-and-smooth mix of Sonny Terry and Brownie McGhee, but Sonny's technical mastery was as complete as Brownie's; that's not so here.

Most of *I Had To Get Nasty* is loud, lively and much better. Pearl and De Rouen play fierce electric guitar, Gilmore's tenor growls right back at Fats, and Trepagnier drums with extraordinary energy and swing. A duo version of 'Louisiana Blues' predicts the unsatisfactory future, and the marimba effects on 'Baby, You' are tacky; these tracks are further confirmation that a full-tilt electric band was the right setting for this limited but likeable artist. CS

Harmonica Slim (born 1921)
VOCAL, HARMONICA

Born in Tupelo, Mississippi, Richard Riggins claims to have worked with many famous names, and to have been Muddy Waters's brother-in-law for a time. He moved to California in 1949, eventually teaming up with fellow Mississippian K. C. Douglas. In the '70s, Riggins made two fine singles for Blues Connoisseur under his real name. He returned to the Fresno blues scene after Douglas died, but made no more recordings until the '90s; the first of them, Back Bottom Blues *(Trix 3323), is deleted. Riggins should not be confused with Travis Blaylock, also nicknamed Harmonica Slim.*

(*) **Give Me My Shotgun!
Fedora FCD 5001 Harmonica Slim; Jackie Turner (g); Jeff Henry (b); Chris Millar (d); Johnny 'Da-Doo' Wilson (v). 3/97.
(*) **Cold Tacos And Warm Beer
Fedora FCD 5023 As above, except add Sal Navarro (p), Hosea Leavy (g, b, v), Frank Goldwasser (g, b); omit Turner, Henry. 2/00.

Slim's seven songs on *Give Me My Shotgun* are spirited personalizations of traditional numbers. He plays down-to-earth, forceful harmonica, whether accompanying his own gnarly singing or backing Johnny Wilson's vigorous covers of Jimmy Reed and Bobby Bland. Wilson also does songs by Howlin' Wolf and Junior Parker; Slim is absent from these, and from a concluding instrumental which, like the rest of the CD, is diminished by the band (Blues West)'s fussy, texturally limited and rhythmically rigid playing.

There's more too-busy drumming on *Cold Tacos And Warm Beer*, but Goldwasser and Leavy are notably looser than their predecessors on guitar and bass. Leavy takes several strong vocals (the disc is jointly credited), but sometimes strays into unfocused bawling. Wilson does another Wolf cover, and on the title track he and Riggins have a laddish conversation, which amuses them almost as much as it irritates the listener. 'She Wants To Boogie' and 'The 'Frisco Railroad' showcase Slim's rhythm-driven playing and singing, but their downhome straightforwardness is not typical. Two mercifully brief numbers have pointless synthesized 'surface noise' added. CS

Richard 'Hacksaw' Harney (1902–73)
VOCAL, GUITAR

Prior to his 1969 rediscovery, Harney was known only for recording two pairs of accompaniments, to Walter Rhodes and

Pearl Dickson, with his brother Maylon (as 'Pet' and 'Can') in 1927. But his skills were celebrated by Robert Lockwood, Houston Stackhouse and Big Joe Williams, Lockwood stating that Harney was the only man able to compete with Robert Johnson. Asked how he coped when his brother was murdered soon after their sessions, Harney replied, 'Well, then I had to learn how to play both parts.'

***(*) **Sweet Man**
Genes GCD 9909 *Harney.* 2/72.

The startling complexity of what Harney attempts here is made all the more impressive by the knowledge that he'd suffered a mild stroke less than three months beforehand. That and a 20-year hiatus in his playing had removed the gloss from his technique but its ambition and incisive musicality were undiminished. Compositions like 'Ragtime Blues', 'Laughing Pallet' and 'Home Skeen Ball' are in a predominantly pre-blues idiom, each very precisely arranged to achieve specific effects. Often, as with the title track and 'Pallet', the melody is first presented on the bass strings, the latter utilizing choked notes to simulate laughter. On these and 'Five Foot Two', Harney also achieves percussive impetus from thumping the guitar with the heel of his hand while brushing the strings as he chords. '12 Pound Rag #2' is slow and meditative with pizzicato effects to suggest mandolin technique. If stylistic comparisons have to be made, Blind Blake and Mississippi John Hurt could be mentioned, but Harney's dexterity and singular harmonic enterprise deter any such attempts. Though flawed, this record is a reminder of the richness and diversity that rapidly disappeared from blues music as the recording era progressed. NS

Janice Harrington (born 1942)
VOCAL

Harrington began entertaining professionally in 1969 on a USO tour of Southeast Asia. She has been resident in Europe since 1980. An actress and an all-round entertainer, she is as at home on cruise ships and in Las Vegas as at jazz and blues festivals.

*** **Magic**
Nagel Heyer NH 1020 *Harrington; Steen Vig (s); Henning Verner (kb); Kenn Lending (g); Svenni Svafnisson (b); Frank Larsen (d); Mette Fanenskov (v).* 4/88.

Janice Harrington has recorded several gospel albums and a Dinah Washington tribute, but so far *Magic* is her only CD within this book's purview. It mixes originals with familiar tunes acquired from Jimmy Reed, Magic Slim ('I Ain't Doing Too Bad') and tradition ('C.C. Rider'). Harrington is a soulful singer, not especially big-voiced (which is no bad thing), but always accurate and animated; she gets very idiomatic backing from a Danish band whose forceful Chicago-style blues leave space for some jazzy excursions. Lending plays with great rhythmic freedom and tonal variety throughout, and there are some notable keyboard and bass solos, but some tracks descend into meandering, among them the concluding 'Seven Days A Week Man Blues'. This otherwise clever gender reassignment of 'Gang Of Brownskin Women' is further let down by a twee dialogue with Lending's guitar and a sub-Millie Jackson raunchy rap. Elsewhere, though, Harrington avoids most of the clichés that beset latterday women's blues. *Magic* is not so outstanding that its 15 years on the shelf are a tragedy, but it's good enough to make them a puzzle. CS

Corey Harris (born 1969)
VOCAL, GUITAR, STEEL GUITAR, KAZOO, WHISTLE, PERCUSSION

Born in Denver, Colorado, Corey Harris became a professional musician in New Orleans after attending college, conducting postgraduate anthropological research in West Africa and teaching French. The historical awareness of his debut CD has continued to inform his music, even as it has become increasingly original, and increasingly driven by a sense of the unity in diversity of black musics and cultures. Harris brings an acute intelligence to both words and music, and seems able to incorporate any influence that appeals to him, while never parading eclecticism or virtuosity for their own sake. If the blues needs someone to be the future of the blues, Corey Harris is probably the one.

*** **Between Midnight And Day**
Alligator ALCD 4837 *Harris.* 9/94.

Recorded in six hours, *Between Midnight And Day* consists mostly of songs from the 78-rpm era; Fred McDowell is as up to date as the covers get, and the three originals are pastiches of bygone Delta blues styles. Harris's powerful baritone commands immediate attention, and he had already acquired an impressive mastery of a range of guitar styles. For one so young, coming to this music as an outsider by geography, history and social class, *Between Midnight And Day* is remarkably successful, but it does present a musician finding his way into the idiom. Sometimes Harris doesn't know how to make the songs his own, and his attempts to do so by emotional *force majeure* seem imposed and arbitrary; two covers of Muddy Waters suffer particularly in this respect. For all its merits, *Between Midnight And Day* is valuable chiefly as a hint at future possibilities.

**** **Fish Ain't Bitin'**
Alligator ALCD 4850 *Harris; Keith 'Wolf' Anderson, Charles Johnson (tb); Chris Severin (b); Anthony 'Tuba Fats' Lacen (tu); Harry 'Point Man' M. Dennis Jr (perc).* 10–12/96.

💀 **** **Greens From The Garden**
Alligator ALCD 4864 *Harris; Tracy Griffin (t); Mark Mullins (tb); Harry 'Pointman' Dennis (fl, djun-djun, rainstick, perc, v); J. Plunky Branch (ss); Leonard Blair (s); Henry Butler (p); Michael Ward (vn); Jamal Milner (md, g, v); Victor Brown (b); Craig Klein (tu); John Gilmore (d); Darrell Rose (cga, djembe, perc); Hamza (tamb, perc); Mr Greenjeans (rainstick, v); Imhotep (djembe); Herlin Riley (wb); Bro. Munier, Culture Fruit, Sista Teedy, Billy Bragg (v).* (98).

It's obvious from the first track, an engaging blend of Delta blues and second-line rhythm, accompanied by grunting tuba and a pair of blatting, funky trombones, that *Fish Ain't Bitin'* benefits from more considered production, and from Harris's engagement with the music of New Orleans. By this stage, he has developed an individual songwriting voice, commenting with passion, humour and epigrammatic intelligence on chicken pox, police brutality and social deprivation, as well as more traditional topics. He is also better able to match his delivery to the material, and if the original 'Berry Owens Blues' fails (just) to reincarnate Charley Patton, a version of Son House's 'Preaching Blues' is startlingly successful. The CD could have been a couple of tracks shorter without disadvantage, but it's proof of Harris's growing ability to revitalize tradition, rather than merely re-create it.

Nothing that had gone before could have predicted *Greens From The Garden*, however. Self-produced, and phenomenally self-assured, it explores and combines multiple facets of black music, tying them together with talent, and snippets of interviews about the cooking and eating of greens. The interviews make a laborious metaphor for negritude; they don't become tedious with repetition, but it's what lies between them that matters. 'Basehead', raging against the effects of crack cocaine on the black community, launches the disc with a thundercloud of bass and percussion, within which flickers the lightning of Harris's lap steel. The steel guitar reappears on 'Eh La Bas' (New Orleans parade music, slowed down and funked up) and 'Just a Closer Walk with Thee' (ska). If that seems to cover a lot of ground, factor in, among other things, acoustic guitar blues in the styles of Blind Blake and Robert Nighthawk; a setting of a Woody Guthrie song; a waltz in French, with mandolin, soprano sax and African percussion; and a blues-reggae hybrid with I-Three style backing vocals. If *Greens From The Garden* were a movie, it would be show reel, travelogue and historical epic all in one, and all of them nominees for best picture.

**** **Vü-Dü Menz**
Alligator ALCD 4872 *Harris; Henry Butler (p, v); Clifford Alexander (wb)*. 00.

Credited to Corey Harris & Henry Butler, *Vü-Dü Menz* returns to acoustic blues – and indeed to just plain blues, plus a little gospel. Harris and Henry Butler may have wanted to explore the possibilities of the piano–guitar duet, long near-moribund in blues, but they seem also, and perhaps mostly, to have been out to have fun. There are serious moments, but the overriding mood is celebration: of women, of dance music and of 'Down Home Livin''. Two titles with washboard are the nearest thing on record for about 60 years to back-country barrelhouse music, and the unaccompanied closer, 'Why Don't You Live So God Can Use You?', confirms that successful explorers have always set out from, and returned to, a secure base camp.

Between Alligator and Rounder, Harris issued *Live At Starr Hill* (Njumba 0001 2CD), which is only available from www.coreyharrismusic.com.

*** **Downhome Sophisticate**
Rounder RRCD 3194 *Harris; Olu Dara (wood t): John D'Earth, Mark Maynard, Jeff Decker (s); Henry Butler (kb, o); Jamal Milner (md, g, v); Vic Brown, Houston Rose (b); John Gilmore (d); Darrell Rose (perc); Davina Jackson, Davita Jackson (v); Rob Jackson, Daniel Norman (rapping)*. 01.

***(*) **Mississippi To Mali**
Rounder 3198 *Harris; Sharde Thomas (fife, v); Bobby Rush (h); Ali Farka Touré (njarka, g, v); Ali Magassa (g, v); Aubrey Turner (lead d, bass d); Otha Andre Evans (bass d, v); R. L. Boyce (lead snare); Rodney Evans (bass snare); Sam Carr (d); Souleyman Kane (perc, v); Darrell Rose (djembe, sabar lam, bougrabou)*. 3/02–9/03.

On *Downhome Sophisticate* Harris attempts, even more explicitly than on *Greens From The Garden*, to create a pan-Africanist fusion music incorporating blues, reggae, rap, West African traditional music and Congolese *soukous*. The results are less successful, however. The CD is dominated by aggressive, amplified playing, which would not matter if it did not so often stray into cliché-spinning, while the use of African and Caribbean elements often seems naively admiring,

like holiday snaps taken by a musical tourist through a rose-tinted camera lens. Harris's commitment to exploration is admirable, but *Downhome Sophisticate* is not the route map to the lost city of gold.

Nor is *Mississippi To Mali*, but it is much more successful and accessible. It was made as Harris was working with Martin Scorsese on *Feel Like Going Home*, whose eponymous soundtrack CD (Columbia/Legacy 512568) is in many ways a set of footnotes to this one. *Mississippi To Mali* features collaborations with the Rising Star Fife and Drum Band, with Bobby Rush and Sam Carr, and with Malian traditional musicians, on both blues and African tunes. The affinity of Mali's modal, drone-based traditional music with some (far from all) kinds of blues has understandably been seized on as a Holy Grail by some boosters of the idea that 'blues came from Africa'. This theory is helped along by African musicians' awareness of what interviewers want to hear but, whatever the ins and outs, the collaborations on *Mississippi To Mali* are very enjoyable. The blues songs undergo considerable changes to fit with Malian modes, but there are intriguing similarities between Touré's lines on *njarka* (one-string fiddle) and Sharde Thomas's on fife. The unvaried clack of Kane's percussion is a minor drawback to an intriguing experiment.

(***) **Daily Bread**
Rounder 3219 *Harris; Olu Dara (t, g, v); Harry Dennis Jr (fl, djun-djun, shaker, djembe); Henry Butler (o, p); John Gros (o); Morwenna Lasko (vn); Houston Ross, Vic Brown (b); John Gilmore (d); Darrell Rose (perc, cga)*. 8–9/04.

Daily Bread is almost all in Jamaican and Cuban-based styles; even O. V. Wright's 'A Nickel And A Nail' gets a thorough makeover. It's all very tastefully done, and one shouldn't underestimate the percussionists' achievement in finding ways to swing in Latin and reggae rhythms, but, even stretching definitions as far as Harris would probably encourage, this CD is very low on blues. In this context 'The Peach' (Harris, Dara and their acoustic guitars, weaving a laidback conversation around a familiar blues metaphor) seems positively exotic. CS

Peppermint Harris (1925–99)
VOCAL, GUITAR

Harrison Nelson grew up in Texarkana, Texas, served in the US Navy during World War II and settled afterwards in Houston, where he learned guitar with the assistance of Lightnin' Hopkins. In 1950 he had a regional hit with 'Raining In My Heart' (Sittin' In With) and the following year a national one with 'I Got Loaded' (Aladdin). He continued to record, sporadically, through the '50s and '60s, also working as a writer for Modern, Specialty and Duke, but by the '70s he was working outside music and drinking problems prevented him resuming his career.

(*) **I Got Loaded
Blue City BCCD-815 *Harris; Jewell Grant (as, bs); Henry Hayes (as); Ed Wiley, Maxwell Davis, Brother Woodman, unknown (ts); poss. Jim Wynn, unknown (bs); unknown (s); Willie Johnson, Gerry Wiggins, Willard McDaniel, unknowns (p); Goree Carter or Nelson Carson, Tiny Webb, Chuck Norris, unknowns (g); Donald Cooks, Red Callender, unknowns (b); Ben Turner, Jesse Sailes, unknowns (d); unknowns (v)*. 11/50–c. 60.

It's cheaply presented (but not cheap), with no notes or

information, but one must reluctantly direct the curious reader to this collection of tracks from Sittin' In With, Aladdin and other labels, since it offers the most detailed picture of Harris's early work. On the slightly woozy drinkers' anthems like 'I Got Loaded' and 'Have Another Drink And Talk To Me' he sounds, naturally enough, like a less polished Amos Milburn, while softer material elicits crooning in the Charles Brown manner – early signs of an identity problem that would dog Harris throughout his career. He does sometimes individualize his work with nifty lyrics, and his voice is attractively youthful, but in terms of melody and arrangement there's a great deal of repetition, so the generous playing time (76.38, 30 tracks) is a mixed blessing.

(*) Penthouse In The Ghetto
M.I.L. Multimedia MIL 3033 *Harris; unknowns (brass, reeds, h, kb, string syn); Teddy Reynolds, Honeywoon Davis (p); Leo O'Neal (psg); Clarence Hollimon, Clarence Green, unknowns (g); George Brown, unknowns (b); Jeff Grails, unknowns (d); unknowns (v).* c. 58–3/75, later.

** **Texas On My Mind**
Aim 1301 *Similar to above.* c. 58–3/75, later.

These collections focus on Harris's recordings for the Houston producer Roy C. Ames; *Penthouse In The Ghetto* is the Home Cooking LP *Being Black Twice* with six tracks added. Either Ames or Harris himself put him through some novel hoops at these sessions, presenting him as a country singer on tracks like 'Fantasy' and 'I'll Learn To Love Again', settling into a jazzy late-period-Jimmy-Witherspoon groove for 'Here Come The Blues' and a Lowell Fulson one for 'Sinner's Prayer', and updating Big Bill's 'Just A Dream' post-Watergate for 'The President's Lawyer'. The notes are silent about the provenance of the added tracks, but the rather wrecked singing suggests that they were made in Harris's later years; one would like to know who the two busy guitarists are on 'Penthouse In The Ghetto', though. *Texas On My Mind* is a shorter version of the foregoing (12 tracks as against 20) that omits most of the cited songs.

*** **Lonesome As I Can Be (The Jewel Recordings 1965–72)**
[Westside WESA 909] *Harris; unknowns (brass, reeds, o, p, g, b, d, v).* 65–72.

The half-dozen singles that Harris recorded for Jewel in the late '60s were probably too oldfashioned for their own good, the vocal presentation and deliberate tempos pitched unmistakably in a Lowell Fulson key. For some readers this will be good news, and indeed for a blues-lover this is the least problematic of Harris's CDs, offering a bluesy programme with good sound, appropriate backings and several decent guitarists. It may not be easy to find but will repay the search. TR

William Harris
VOCAL, GUITAR

Harris is thought to have been born in Glendora, Mississippi. He made his first recordings in Birmingham, Alabama, and may have worked around that city. Little else has ever been discovered about him.

***(*) **William Harris & Buddy Boy Hawkins (1927–1929)**
Document DOCD-5035 *Harris; Joe Robinson (g, sp).* 7/27–11/28.

Harris's *modus operandi* of singing in a controlled shout over insistent guitar patterns is most effective on his faster songs, 'I'm Leavin' Town' and 'Bullfrog Blues', where he also adds to the songs' impetus by delaying expected resolutions: extending the texts of first lines, or repeating the second lines to create 16-bar verses. Except for 'Hot Time Blues', the song recorded by Frank Stokes around the same time as 'Take Me Back', his other pieces are slower blues, enhanced by his rich, powerful voice. The Document CD contains what at the time of its issue were his nine surviving recordings, including a very worn copy of 'Electric Chair Blues'. A tenth side, 'Bad Treated Blues', which is Harris's version of the commonplace 'Crow Jane' melody, and a cleaner copy of 'Electric Chair Blues' were later issued on *"Too Late, Too Late" Vol. 3* (Document DOCD-5276). Better transfers of 'Bullfrog Blues', 'Hot Time Blues' and 'Kansas City Blues' can be found on the VAC *Mississippi Masters* (Yazoo 2007). TR

Wynonie Harris (1915–69)
VOCAL

Harris started out, like his model Joe Turner, as an extrovert singer who projected a powerful voice from within horn-heavy jump-blues bands. Like Turner, too, his ability to deploy that skill on bluesy novelty songs gave him a cachet in the early rock 'n' roll years that sustained his career longer than many of his contemporaries'. Originally from Omaha, Nebraska, he entered show business as a dancer, took up singing and in 1944 joined Lucky Millinder's orchestra. Between 1947 and 1957 he recorded with considerable success for King, enjoying three R&B #1s and immense popularity on the club and theatre circuit, but changing tastes stole his audience and throat cancer his life.

*** **Wynonie Harris 1944–1945**
Classics 885 *Harris; Freddie Webster, Joe Jordan, Curtis Murphy, Elton Hill, Howard McGhee, Russell Jacquet, Teddy Buckner, Jimmy Moorman, unknown (t); Gene Simon, Alfred Cobbs, Joe Britton (tb); Jack McVea (as, ts); Preston Love, Bill Swindell, John Brown (as); Elmer Williams, Eddie 'Lockjaw' Davis, Teddy Edwards, Illinois Jacquet, Johnnie Alston, unknown (ts); Ernest Leavy, Arthur Dennis (bs); Ellis Larkins, Lee Wesley Jones, Bill Doggett, Bob Mosley, Walter 'King' Fleming, unknown (p); Lawrence Lucie, Stanley Morgan, Ulysses Livingston, Gene Phillips, Herman Mitchell, unknown (g); Al McKibbon, Bob Kesterson, Charles Mingus, Frank Clark, Oscar Pettiford, Clarence Jones (b); Panama Francis, Johnny Otis, Al Wichard, Rabon Tarrant, unknown (d).* 5/44–12/45.

*** **Everybody Boogie!**
Delmark DE-683 *Harris; Russell Jacquet, Teddy Buckner, Jimmy Moorman, unknown (t); Jack McVea (as, ts); John Brown (as); Illinois Jacquet, Johnnie Alston, unknown (ts); Arthur Dennis (bs); Bill Doggett, Bob Mosley, Walter 'King' Fleming, unknown (p); Ulysses Livingston, Gene Phillips, Herman Mitchell, unknown (g); Charles Mingus, Frank Clark, Oscar Pettiford, Clarence Jones (b); Al Wichard, Rabon Tarrant, unknown (d).* 8–12/45.

*** **Wynonie Harris 1945–1947**
Classics 1013 *Harris; Joe Morris, Wendell Culley, Jackie Allen, Joe Newman, Pat Jenkins, unknowns (t); Herbie Fields (cl, as, ts); Tab Smith, unknowns (as); Arnett Cobb, Allen Eager, unknowns (ts); Charlie Fowlkes, Larry Belton, unknown (bs); Bill Doggett (o); prob. Chester Slater (p, v); Milt Buckner, Herman 'Sonny'*

Blount, Leonard Feather, unknowns (p); Billy Butler (g, v); Billy Mackel, Mary Osborne, unknowns (g); Percy Joell (b, v); Charlie Harris, Al McKibbon, unknowns (b); Dorothea 'Dottie' Smith (d, v); George Jenkins, Walter Johnson, unknowns (d); Big Joe Turner, bands (v). c. 12/45–c. 7/47.

*** **Wynonie Harris 1947–1949**
Classics 1139 Harris; Jesse Drakes, Bob Merrill, Hot Lips Page, Cat Anderson, Joe Morris, Bill Martin (t); Clyde Bernhardt, Gerald Valentine, Joe Britton, Matthew Gee, Moses Gant (tb); Elwyn Fraser, Don Stovall, Vincent Bair-Bey, Frank 'Floorshow' Culley, Leroy Harris (as); Stafford Simon, Dexter Gordon, William Parker, Hal Singer, Tom Archia, Freddie Douglas, Johnny Griffin, Orrington Hall (ts); Elmer Alexander, William McLemore, Curtis Peagler (bs); Archie 'Skip' Hall, Joe Knight, Albert 'Birdie' Wallace, Elmo Hope, Simeon Hatch, unknown (p); Rene Hall (g); Edgar Brown, Carl Wilson, Jimmy Butts, Gene Ramey, Frank Skeete, unknown (b); Clarence H. Burt, Clarence Donaldson, Connie Kay, Kelly Martin, Calvin Shields, unknown (d); unknown, bands (v). 12/47–10/49.

*** **Wynonie Harris 1950–1952**
Classics 1289 Harris; Joe Wilder, Lammar Wright, Frank Galbraith, Andrew 'Fats' Ford, Howard Thompson, Willie Wells (t); Henderson Chambers, Tyree Glenn, Harry DeVito, Alfred Cobbs (tb); Bill Graham (as, bs); Curby Alexander, Rudy Powell, Alonzo Lucas, Ted Buckner, Howard 'Holley' Dismukes (as); Joe Allston, John Hartzfield, John Hardee, John Greer, Reuben Philips, Charles 'Lefty' Edwards, Louis Stephens (ts); Numa 'Pee Wee' Moore (bs); Milt Buckner, Sonny Thompson, Duke Parham, Todd Rhodes, Sarah McLawler (p); James Cannady, Jimmy Shirley, Alonzo Tucker (g); Bruce Lawrence, Carl Pruitt, Joe Williams (b); Sammie 'Sticks' Evans, Alfred Walker, James Crawford, Herman Bradley, Solomon Hall, William 'Benny' Benjamin, Les Erskine (d); The Royals (v). 5/50–1/52.

After a couple of curtain-raisers from 1944 with the Millinder band, the first Classics CD spends its time covering Harris's activities in the second half of 1945, recording for Philo (four tracks) and Apollo (16) with groups led by Illinois Jacquet and Jack McVea, among others. The Apollo sides, plus two rejected takes, are also on the Delmark CD, an attractive and well-remastered collection and their official reissue site. The influence of Joe Turner is heavy at first, but Harris quickly begins to emerge as a stylist in his own right, as on 'Here Comes The Blues', which has a lovely long introduction by Jacquet, or 'Time To Change Your Tune' (sic 'Town'), from a date with, possibly, Wardell Gray.

Wynonie Harris 1945–1947 tracks him through brief affiliations with Hamp-Tone, Bullet and Aladdin, ending neatly at the close of a 7/47 session and thus enabling the next volume to start at the beginning of his ten-year contract with King. By now he is slipping into a routine of slow and medium blues, often humorous or at least wry, interspersed with boogie tunes. The arrangements leave solo space for brass and reeds players which, since Harris was fortunate in his accompanists, is often profitably used, for example by Tab Smith on the first Aladdin date. The last Aladdin session juxtaposes Harris and Joe Turner in a two-part 'Battle Of The Blues'.

On *1947–1949*, from the set of romping tunes cut in the week around Christmas 1947, 'Blow Your Brains Out' is a feature for tenorists Tom Archia and 'Oklahoma' (Hal Singer), 'Crazy Love' spots a declarative Hot Lips Page, and all the tunes rock-steady bass playing by Carl 'Flat Top' Wilson. (Most of these are also on the Hot Lips Page CD *Shoutin' The Blues* [Blue Boar CDBB 1010].) Some of Harris's best-loved recordings occur in this album, like 'Good Rockin' Tonight', 'I Feel That Old Age Comin' On' and 'All She Wants To Do Is Rock', all urged on by handclapping that parodies the affirmation of a revival meeting. *1950–1952* presses on through Harris's King catalogue, adding such justly celebrated numbers as 'Good Morning Judge', 'Mr. Blues Is Comin' To Town' and a song from King's country list, the Western Swing bandleader Hank Penny's 'Bloodshot Eyes', which Harris delivers as if in amphetamine-driven frenzy.

***(*) **Rockin' The Blues**
Proper PROPERBOX 20 4CD As for Classics CDs. 5/44–10/50.
***(*) **Bloodshot Eyes: The Essential Wynonie Harris**
[Indigo IGODCD 2516 2CD] Similar to above. 7/45–7/51.

The Proper box embraces what's gone before: 81 tracks in all. The Indigo double reduces the total to 50, but since it does so by omitting tracks rather than whole sessions, it covers much the same ground as the larger set – actually a little more, because it extends into 1951. Both are admirable selections as far as they go, and very good value, but since they were restricted, when they were issued, to what was then out of copyright, they lack several key sides.

*** **Lovin' Machine**
Ace CDCHD 843 Harris; Frank Galbraith, Howard Thompson, Willie Wells, Lammar Wright, Jimmy Nottingham, John Hunt, Hal Mitchell, Frank Humphries (t); Alfred Cobbs, Henderson Chambers, Fred Zito, Cornelius Tate (tb); Alonzo Lucas, Ted Buckner, Howard 'Holley' Dismukes, Burnie Peacock, Jimmy Powell, Hilton Jefferson (as); Maxwell Lucas (ts, bs); John Greer, Charles Edwards, Louis Stephens, Count Hastings, Harold Clark, Rufus Gore, Robert Darby, David Van Dyke, Red Prysock, David Brooks, Ray Felder, Hal Singer (ts); Bill Graham, Walter Hiles, Tommy Parkson, Leslie Johnakins (bs); Herbert Parham, Todd Rhodes, Don Abney, Eddie Smith, Sir Charles Thompson, Kelly Owens (p); Clifton Best, Mickey Baker, Clarence Kenner, Kenny Burrell, Leo Spann (g); Carl Pruitt, Joe Williams, Aaron Bell, Clarence Mack, George Duvivier, James Royal (b); Solomon Hall, William Benjamin, James Crawford, Bill Warren, Specs Powell, Edison Gore, Steve Boswell, Shadow Wilson, Calvin Shields (d); The Royals (v). 2/51–7/57.

*** **Women, Whiskey And Fish Tails**
Ace CDCHD 457 Harris; Frank Humphries (t); Cornelius Tate (tb); Hilton Jefferson (as); Maxwell Lucas (ts, bs); Dave Brooks, Wesley Brooks, Rufus Gore, Robert Darby, David Van Dyke, Red Prysock, Fred Clark, Ray Felder, Count Hastings, Hal Singer (ts); Walter Hiles, Tommy Parkson, Leslie Johnakins (bs); Sonny Thompson, Eddie Smith, Sir Charles Thompson, Kelly Owens (p); Bill Johnson, Mickey Baker, Clarence Kenner, Kenny Burrell, Leo Spann (g); Oscar Crummie, Clarence Mack, George Duvivier, James Royal, Carl Pruitt (b); Isaac Cole, Bill Warren, Specs Powell, Philip Paul, Edison Gore, Steve Boswell, Shadow Wilson, Calvin Shields (d). 11/52–7/57.

Lovin' Machine starts up approximately where the Proper and Indigo sets stop (but overlaps part of Classics' *1950–1952*). Over the next few years Harris would record some of his most catchy songs, such as the title number, 'Bloodshot Eyes' and 'Quiet Whiskey'. Jazz enthusiasts of the time, for whom his previous work, indulgently viewed as 'jazz-blues shouting', had been a succession of mature but firm Camemberts, found these new songs a little too runny, but for the generation of

American teenagers who listened by night to Southern DJs like Hoss Allen and John Richbourg they were warm invitations into the secret raunchy world of R&B. *Women, Whiskey And Fish Tails* covers much the same period but was selected with a collector's eye for B-sides, album tracks and generally lesser-known numbers. Both CDs are excellently annotated by Harris's biographer, Tony Collins.

***(*) Bloodshot Eyes – The Best Of Wynonie Harris**
Rhino 71544 *As for relevant CDs above.* 7/47–11/54.
***(*) Good Rockin' Tonight**
King KCD 6002 *As above.* 12/47–9/53.

The reader who expects to be satisfied with just one CD of Wynonie Harris will do very well with either of these collections, though their emphasis on up-tempo songs means that he or she will get hardly a glimpse of Harris's skill with a slow blues. The Rhino has 18 tracks, the King 20. They share 11 cuts, including all the four-star songs like 'Good Rockin' Tonight', 'Bloodshot Eyes', 'Good Morning Judge' and 'Quiet Whiskey'. The King is all from King, whereas the Rhino ropes in one earlier recording. Both are well annotated. The Rhino looks better, but the King is considerably cheaper. TR

Alvin Youngblood Hart (born 1963)
VOCAL, GUITAR, BANJO, MANDOLIN, CONCERTINA

A virtuoso multi-instrumentalist who came to prominence during the black 'retro revival movement' of the '90s, Gregory Edward Hart has gone on to confound adherents and critics alike by revealing different sides of himself in successive albums. His mastery of prewar blues techniques is matched by an encyclopaedic interest in music both popular and arcane. His unwillingness to be typecast as a musician of one particular style may yet become career-threatening.

**** Big Mama's Door**
[OKeh BK 67593] *Hart; Chris Seibert (p); Taj Mahal (md, g, v); Bill MacBeath (b).* 96.

Few artists in the last decade have released such an impressive and accomplished debut album. Hart steps up to the plate as a confirmed but inventive traditionalist, combining works by Charley Patton, Blind Willie McTell and Leadbelly with songs that set original lyrics to tunes in the styles of Bukka White, Kokomo Arnold and others, and does it with no hint of parody or imitation. The spontaneity and clarity of his slide guitar playing on 'Joe Friday' and 'Rest Your Saddle' are complemented by the ebullience of his idiomatic vocals. 'Pony Blues' and Papa Harvey Hull's 'France Blues' are recast with complex but flowing guitar parts, while McTell's 'Hillbilly Willie's Blues' is performed on banjo. Taj Mahal's presence on three tracks and his glowing encomium in the booklet merely over-egg an already rich pudding.

**** Territory**
Hannibal HNCD 1431 *As above, except add Bill Ortiz (t), Marty Wehner (tb), Jules Broussard (as, ts), Pete Sears (ac), Brian Godchaux (vn), Barry Lowenthal (d), Josh Jones (cga, perc).* 98.

As its title implies, *Territory* covers a substantial swathe of musical ground, travelling from solo acoustic vignettes to full-on electric extravagance. Three songs associated with Leadbelly create the album's acoustic core: the outlaw ballad 'John Hardy', a sentimental pop song, 'Dancing With Tears In My Eyes', and 'Sallie, Queen Of The Pines (For Walter Boyd's Mama)', an imaginative original that places Leadbelly (under an alias) in prison, yearning to be home. A long atmospheric introduction to 'Countrycide (The Ballad Of Ed & Charlie Brown)' sets the stage for a true story of racial tensions in 1886. Forays into Western Swing and reggae lighten the mood but the most startling event here is an uncompromising tilt at 'Ice Rose', a complex Beefheart sound picture as energized as the electricity that feeds it.

***(*) Start With The Soul**
Hannibal HNCD 1449 *Hart; Scott Thompson (t); Jim Spake (ts); East Memphis Slim [Jim Dickinson] (kb); Bill MacBeath, Larry Fulcher (b); Daren Dortin, Frosty Smith (d); Susan Marshall, Jackie Johnson (v).* 00.

Territory's confident step into modernity forms the triumphal arch through which *Start With The Soul* loudly and belligerently strides. Here amplification is king. Even the staccato 'A Prophet's Mission', its historical context also rife with sardonic augury, is sung to a lone electric guitar. Blues as such is in short supply, confined to the final tracks, the instrumental 'Maxwell Street Jimmy', commemorating the Chicago street musician, and 'Will I Ever Get Back Home', attributed to Joe McCoy but in the style of Tommy Johnson. Tracks culled from Black Oak Arkansas, The Sonics and Chuck Berry lack the allusive depth of his own compositions. Despite moments of musical and textual inspiration, the reliance upon rock techniques flattens the landscape and blunts the angry force of Hart's intellect.

*** Down In The Alley**
Memphis International DOT 0203 *Hart.* 02.

The confusion Hart managed to implant in his audience seems to have found an echo in his own determination, for it's unclear whether this return to the 'authenticity' of *Big Mama's Door* is intended as a forward or retrograde step. These 12 monaural recordings are drawn from such sources as Furry Lewis, Bukka White, Leadbelly, Son House, Skip James, Charley Patton and Sleepy John Estes. Hart is particularly strong when he's reviving the spirit of a blues standard without imitating its original performance, as in 'Judge Bouche', 'How Long Before I Change My Clothes' and 'Alberta'. But 'Devil Got My Woman' and 'Jinx Blues' stray too close to their inspiration for the comfort of both artist and audience. Hart plays banjo and mandolin on several tracks but the overdubs on 'Bootlegger's Blues' and 'Broke And Hungry' fail to settle comfortably in the sound picture, producing an album reminiscent of his debut without reproducing its daring originality. NS

***(*) Motivational Speaker**
Artemis/Tone-Cool 51632//Tone-Cool/Artemis/Rykodisc RCD 17310 *Hart; Scott Thompson (t); Jim Spake (h); Richard Rosenblatt (h); Jim Dickinson (p); Richard Ford (psg); Audley Freed, Luther Dickinson (g); Gary Rasmussen (b, v); Robert P. Kearns (b); Edward R. Michaels (d, tamb, gong, cowbell, v); Susan Marshall (v).* 10/04.

Having 'Big Mama's Door' as the opening track may look promising to readers who enjoy Hart best unplugged, but the sly subtitle '(Might Return)' ought to prepare them for the thick small-group sound, somewhat reminiscent of *Start With The Soul* and manifestly inspired by Jimi Hendrix. Fortunately it isn't the full-on sonic assault that the earlier album was. The listener can escape from the high winds of the title track and 'Stomp Dance' into the long, free opening passage and measured tempo of 'In My Time Of Dying', and later into a pair of honkytonk songs, Doug Sahm's 'Lawd I'm Just A Country Boy In This Great Big Freaky City' and Johnny Paycheck's 'The Meanest Jukebox In Town', which Hart sings and plays with unerring idiomatic skill. If those hypothetical readers are now concluding that *Motivational Speaker* sounds like a bumpy ride, they should be alerted to Hart's powerfully bleak translation of Booker White's 'How Long Before I Change My Clothes'. This may be a hard album for some of Hart's admirers to take, especially after the apparent stylistic backpedalling of *Down In The Alley*, but it is well worth persevering with. TR

Little Hatch (born 1921)
VOCAL, HARMONICA

Provine Hatch Jr was born into a sharecropping family in Sledge, Mississippi, and grew up in Helena, Arkansas, where he began playing harmonica and guitar. After wartime service in the US Navy he settled in Kansas City, raising a family, working as a security guard for Hallmark Cards and playing in clubs at weekends. A 1972 album on a one-off German label earned him some work in Europe, but he did not record again for 20 years. He now lives on his farm in El Dorado Springs, Missouri.

** Goin' Back
APO APO 2007 *Hatch; Bill Dye (g). 2–5/98.*

Thanks to the fine recording quality, this album gives a vivid impression of two friends playing for each other, offstage and unplugged. Such music can be intimate, but it can also be uneventful, and so it proves here. Despite the combination of harmonica, slide guitar and songs from the Muddy Waters book, 'She's Nineteen Years Old' and 'Buzz On' (i.e. 'Honey Bee') do not generate the power of the early Muddy Waters–Little Walter duets they cannot help evoking. Other pieces drawn from Elmore James, Jimmy Reed and Slim Harpo similarly fail either to match the character of the originals or to replace it with something equally interesting. Part of the reason is that most of the performances are about two minutes longer than they needed to be, the extra space being filled with repeat verses or unsurprising instrumental choruses. Dye is a good accompanist who plainly knows his partner's ways, and Hatch's singing is pleasant in its confiding, unassertive way, but his harmonica playing is miserly. TR

Buddy Boy Hawkins
VOCAL, GUITAR

Walter Hawkins refers in his recordings to both Alabama and Mississippi, and either state may have been his home, but it was in Birmingham, Alabama, that he was recruited for recording by the talent scout Harry Charles.

**** William Harris & Buddy Boy Hawkins (1927–1929)
Document DOCD-5035 *Hawkins; unknown (sp). c. 4/27–6/29.*

Hawkins's slow blues, such as 'Workin' On The Railroad' or the potent 'Jailhouse Fire Blues', have distinctively lugubrious vocal melodies and guitar accompaniments notable for their sometimes unusual but always apt choices of notes and chords and for their haunting tone, especially as reproduced on his first, acoustic recordings. Another aspect of his music is revealed in pieces like 'How Come Mama Blues', 'Snatch It And Grab It' and 'Raggin' The Blues', where the vivacity of his singing is matched by superbly executed ragtime guitar playing. The most unusual work of this remarkable artist is 'Voice Throwin' Blues', a rendition of 'Hesitating Blues' in which he duets with his ventriloquial other. The dozen recordings on this CD are his entire work. TR

Roy Hawkins (1904–74)
VOCAL, PIANO

One of a rash of Californian singer/pianists to flourish at the end of the '40s, Hawkins never achieved the critical regard bestowed upon Charles Brown, Amos Milburn, Jimmy McCracklin and Little Willie Littlefield, despite penning two durable blues standards. An attempt to rewrite history is in progress.

*** The Thrill Is Gone
Ace CDCHD 754 *Hawkins; unknown (t); unknown (tb); Buddy Floyd, Maxwell Davis (ts); unknown (bs); Willard McDaniel, Lloyd Glenn (p); Ulysses James, Chuck Norris, Johnny Moore (g); unknown (b); Jesse Sailes (d). 11/49–54.*

Hawkins was in his mid-40s when he began his recording career with Down Town, later transferring to Modern. He sang with a harder-edged tone and a more pronounced vibrato than Charles Brown but his voice lacked sufficient distinction to elevate him above the crowd. Soon after his first Modern session he lost the use of an arm in a car crash; thereafter the piano chair was occupied by the likes of McDaniel and Glenn. The first of Hawkins's significant compositions, 'Why Do Things Happen To Me' (later changed to 'Why Do Everything Happen To Me'), spent four months in the R&B charts in the spring of 1950. His other though briefer success, 'The Thrill Is Gone', came a year later. B. B. King was responsible for the elevation of both songs; his 1969 recording of the latter was a #3 R&B hit and crossed over into the Pop Top 20. Half a century on, Hawkins's songs, though well-written, sound formulaic but the addition of the cream of LA session men keeps the recipe piquant. 'Wine Drinkin' Woman', 'On My Way', 'Just A Poor Boy' and 'I'm Never Satisfied' are among the better examples of the insouciant mastery of the musicians cited above. NS

Clifford Hayes (c. 1893–c. 1955)
VOCAL, VIOLIN, ALTO SAXOPHONE

Clifford Hayes took up the violin at an early age and joined Earl McDonald's Louisville Jug Band in 1914. The two men had a falling out in 1919 over Hayes's lifelong propensity for fiddling of the financial kind, and thereafter led separate bands. Hayes took up alto saxophone in the '20s, probably as a by-product of his ongoing attempts to combine stringband music with jazz. When McDonald's Ballard Chefs became radio stars in the '30s, Hayes returned to the jugband format which he had abandoned in 1927, and was still leading one when he died.

*** Clifford Hayes & The Louisville Jug Bands – Vol. 1 (1924–1926)
RST Jazz Perspectives JPCD-1501 *Hayes; Theodore Boone (c);*

Lockwood Lewis (as, v); Curtis Hayes, Cal Smith, Freddie Smith (bj); Earl McDonald (j, v); Rudolph Thompson, Henry Clifford (j); Sara Martin, Cora Gray (v). 9/24–12/26.

***(*) Clifford Hayes & The Louisville Jug Bands – Vol. 2 (1926–1927)

RST Jazz Perspectives JPCD-1502 *Hayes; Johnny Dodds (cl); Lockwood Lewis (as, v); Cal Smith, Freddie Smith, Curtis Hayes (bj); Earl McDonald (j, v); Henry Clifford (j). 12/26–4/27.*

Clifford Hayes was not the most accomplished musician in Louisville, and other musicians disliked his swindling ways, but he was the town's busiest organizer of bands and recording sessions. RST's four volumes are built around him, but they include bands in which he took no part (and whose members are accordingly not listed). Like their counterparts elsewhere, the Louisville bands played ragtime, pop music, minstrel and 'coon' songs as well as blues. They also leaned very strongly towards jazz, and in their hands the jug became more than a novelty instrument.

Eight of the first ten titles on *Vol. 1* are by Sara Martin, and are discussed in her entry; the remaining two are instrumentals, issued as by Sara Martin's Jug Band. Whistler & His Jug Band have no connection with Clifford Hayes. Buford 'Whistler' Threlkeld was a virtuoso of the nose whistle; his band's four tracks revive 1900s pop-ragtime, with only 'I'm A Jazz Baby' acknowledging more recent musical fashions. The Old Southern Jug Band and Clifford's Louisville Jug Band complete *Vol. 1*. Their instrumentation (fiddle, jug, cornet and two banjos) is Clifford Hayes's first attempt to combine jazz and stringband music; banjoists Cal Smith and Curtis Hayes dominate the music with sophisticated chordal progressions.

Vol. 1 closes – pointlessly, since it could have fitted on *Vol. 2* – with the first recording by the Dixieland Jug Blowers, who occupy the first 12 tracks of *Vol. 2*. The lineup was unique and eccentric: violin, alto sax, two or three banjos (tenor, six-string and plectrum), and two jugs. Victor added the great clarinettist Johnny Dodds to four titles (and two alternative takes), but he's absent from the sessions' tour de force, 'Banjoreno', where the three banjos achieve a remarkable contrast of tone colours. The tracks with Dodds have overshadowed the rest, but 'Louisville Stomp', with tenor and bass jugs blowing alternate beats and a fine solo by Cal Smith, should not be overlooked.

Clifford Hayes is absent from the second half of *Vol. 2*, which features Earl McDonald's Original Louisville Jug Band and Whistler's Jug Band. The McDonald band (Lucien Brown on alto sax, Ben Calvin's mandolin and Cal Smith on banjo) made perhaps the greatest blues and pop session by a Louisville band; everyone plays with tremendous energy and dash, and the vigour with which McDonald belts out jug and vocal choruses one after another is startling. Whistler's men are spurred on by the earthshaking jug blasts of Rudolph 'Jazz Lips' Thompson, an unbelievable 13 years old at the time of recording.

***(*) Clifford Hayes & The Louisville Jug Bands – Vol. 3 (1927–1929)

RST Jazz Perspectives JPCD-1503 *Hayes; Hense Grundy (tb); George Allen, Lockwood Lewis (ss, as); Dan Briscoe, Johnny Gatewood, Earl Hines (p); Cal Smith (bj, g); Earl McDonald (j); Elizabeth Washington, Prince LaVaughn (v). 6/27–2/29.*

Clifford's Louisville Stompers, who occupy *Vol. 3*'s last 14 tracks, present the jazz sound that Clifford Hayes had been trying to achieve for some time; fiddle, trombone, piano, four-string guitar and definitely no jug, thank you. The second version of the Dixieland Jug Blowers, heard on the opening ten tracks, is a first draft of the Stompers: fiddle, two saxes, guitar, trombone, piano, jug and occasional vocalists. These sessions are important mainly for the new textures created by ringing stride piano, Cal Smith's intricate single-string runs and the grunts, rasps and growls of Hense Grundy, who seems, at times, to be playing both jug and banjo lines on trombone.

The Stompers' music is unequivocally jazz rather than blues, but it provided Clifford Hayes with a setting where his limitations became a strength; his simple, bluesy wailing is an acidic counterpart to Cal Smith's daring tenor guitar adventures, with their strong influence from Lonnie Johnson. The sides which most excite jazz fans are those with Earl Hines, who was called in by Victor for the 2/29 sessions. Hines is very good, needless to say, but he's not stretched by the Louisvillians, and one can understand why a musician of his sophistication remembered them dismissively (and unfairly) as 'a hillbilly group'. The star of the show is Cal Smith, who charges into brilliantly unexpected solos track after track.

*** Clifford Hayes & The Louisville Jug Bands – Vol. 4 (1929–1931)

RST Jazz Perspectives JPCD-1503 *Hayes; Jimmy Strange (t); Hense Grundy (tb); George Allen (cl); Sippie Wallace (p, v); Kid Coley (prob. p, v); Earl Hines, Johnny Gatewood (p); Cal Smith, Freddie Smith (g); Earl McDonald (j); Jimmie Rodgers, Ben Ferguson, John Harris (v). 2/29–6/31.*

RST's final volume begins with three tracks which wrap up the Louisville Stompers sessions; the Kentucky Jazz Babies pairing, recorded eight months later, differs only in adding the splendid, King Oliverish Jimmy Strange. There follow eight titles by Phillips's Louisville Jug Band, another outfit with a passion for jazz and an unusual lineup (C-melody sax, guitar, jug, kazoo and 'walking-cane flute') which produces some very listenable music; the silvery purling of Charles Adams's flute and 'Hooks' Tilford's light, airy sax contrast piquantly with Carl Reid's hoarse jug work and the turkey gobbling of his 'jazzhorn'.

Kid Coley's four titles, with melodramatic delivery and doggerel lyrics, are included because Clifford Hayes plays violin. Whistler and his band (but not his nose whistle) turn up one last time, with manic renditions of 'Foldin' Bed' and 'Hold That Tiger'. On the final tracks George Allen and Cal Smith play as much jazz as they can get away with, but Clifford Hayes had been forced by public taste to revert to blues, and to restore a jug to the team that accompanies Ben Ferguson, John Harris and hillbilly superstar Jimmie Rodgers.

***(*) Louisville Stomp

Frog DGF 6 *Hayes; Hense Grundy (tb); Johnny Dodds (cl); Lockwood Lewis (ss, as, v); George Allen (ss, as); Dan Briscoe, Johnny Gatewood (p); Cal Smith, Freddie Smith, Curtis Hayes (bj); Earl McDonald (j, v); Henry Clifford (j); Elizabeth Washington, Prince LaVaughn (v). 12/26–6/27.*

***(*) Frog Hop

Frog DGF 10 *Hayes; Hense Grundy (tb); Sippie Wallace (p, v); Dan Briscoe, Johnny Gatewood, Earl Hines (p); Cal Smith (g). 6/27–2/29.*

***(*) Clifford Hayes And The Dixieland Jug Blowers

Yazoo 1054 *Hayes; Hense Grundy (tb); George Allen (cl, ss, as); Lockwood Lewis (ss, as); Dan Briscoe, Johnny Gatewood, Earl*

Hines (p); Cal Smith (bj, g); Freddie Smith (g); Earl McDonald (j); Elizabeth Washington, Prince LaVaughn, Ben Ferguson (v). 6/27–6/31.

Louisville Stomp brings together the complete recordings of the Dixieland Jug Blowers, and is credited accordingly. *Frog Hop* contains all the recordings of Clifford Hayes's Louisville Stompers, among them not only 'Tenor Guitar Fiend' and 'Tippin' Through', which are missing from RST, but also eight alternative takes from the sessions with Hines. Unfortunately, these are mostly weaker than the issued ones – in some cases embarrassingly so. On both CDs the remastering of mint originals is all that could be desired.

Despite short playing time Yazoo's 14 tracks are a carefully chosen and well-mastered selection. It focuses mainly on Clifford Hayes's experiments in chamber jazz, and the title is slightly misleading, since only four tracks are by the Dixieland Jug Blowers; two more are by Ben Ferguson, and the rest by the Louisville Stompers. The music is excellent, but the listener doesn't get much sense of the raucous context from which the Stompers' refined and considered music emerged. CS

Johnny Heartsman (1937–96)
GUITAR, FLUTE, ORGAN, BASS, VOCAL

Heartsman grew up in Oakland, California, and as a young guitarist studied the work of T-Bone Walker, Pee Wee Crayton and Lafayette Thomas. He did session work for the producer Bob Geddins in the early '50s before making his own mark with the two-part instrumental 'Johnny's House Party' in 1957. Most of his work for the next decade was in the background, as a session musician or producer, or accompanying artists when they visited the San Francisco Bay Area. In the late '60s and '70s he worked in other musical contexts, and settling in Sacramento in 1976 kept him somewhat out of the blues loop, but in the late '80s he returned to the blues, played widely in the US, toured Europe and Japan and cut several albums.

*** Bay Area Blues Blasters – Vol. 1
El Cerrito ECR 01004 Heartsman; Al Berry, Bobby Forte, Gino Landry, Lovejoy Coverson (s); General Chalmers (o); Bobby Reed, unknowns (b); Fred Casey, Bob Wells (d). 57–64.

The nine of these 26 tracks that were issued under Heartsman's name, all instrumentals, are an eloquent testimony to his skill as a guitarist. 'Besame Mucho', spread over both sides of a single, takes off into spacey invention, while his explorations of a riff in tunes like 'Sizzling' could have earned him a revival in the 'acid jazz' era. The remaining tracks are singles from the '60s by singers such as Jesse James, Ray Agee, Joe Simon and Rudy Lambert, many of which were arranged and produced by Heartsman and feature him on guitar or flute; there is a definitive example of his slashing guitar on Tiny Powell's superb version of 'My Time After While', later copied by Buddy Guy. At least two of Powell's other three numbers involve guitarist Eddie Foster, an admirer of Heartsman, and another such is Eugene Blacknell (or Blackwell), who zips through 'Jump Back'.

**** Sacramento
Crosscut CCD 11018 Heartsman; Gary Wiggins (ts); Rex Kline (d). 1/88.

***(*) The Touch
Alligator ALCD 4800 Heartsman; Scott Lindefeldt (tb); Joe Espinosa (as, ts); Ray 'Rainbow' Fields (bs); Rich Forman (g, v); Eric Tyrell (b, v); Artis Joyce (b); Tony Dey (d, v); Big John Evans (d); J'Neen (v); Dick Shurman (prod). 91.

*** Made In Germany
Inakustik INAK 9025 Heartsman; Mike Titré (h, g); Todor 'Toscho' Todorovic (g); Frizze Winnacker (b); Martin Schmachtenberg (d). 6/93.

Dick Shurman, in his notes to *Sacramento*, succinctly describes Heartsman's guitar chops. 'He has one of the most instantly recognizable styles on his axe, a dynamic blend of lightning double picking high on the neck, a trademark moan using the volume knob on his Fender Strat, and lowdown chording and rhythm patterns which spring in part from his early training as a bassist. Among blues stylists, he can play more notes without sounding too busy than any other guitarist.' *Sacramento* is a particularly clear demonstration of his powers, since he plays all the guitar, bass and organ parts, reveals a more than serviceable voice and wrote virtually all his material, in a variety of blues-related styles – an example of multiskilling that has few parallels in recorded blues.

The Touch has more participants but Heartsman again plays all the guitar solos and keyboard parts on a programme of largely original and very varied material. This combination of instrumental virtuosity and wry songwriting will remind many listeners of Jody Williams, and it's no accident that both artists have been encouraged and produced by Dick Shurman. *Made In Germany* was taped at a concert in Osnabrück and has all the usual characteristics of a gig recording: generous solo space for the sidemen, a safer repertoire (blues standards like 'Cold Cold Feeling' and a rather lounge-y reading of Bill Withers's 'Ain't No Sunshine') and extended performances: most of the numbers run to seven or eight minutes, and 'Flip, Flop & Fly' to 11.14. Heartsman naturally reaps more from this acreage than a less adept scytheman, but it's the other albums that really show what he could do. TR

Lucille Hegamin (1894–1970)
VOCAL

Lucille Nelson from Macon, Georgia was in the business at 15, and married Bill Hegamin about 1914. (They divorced in 1923 and she remarried, but kept the stage name.) She made her first records in the wake of Mamie Smith's success, and became an in-demand artist on disc and stage. Hegamin left show business in 1933, but made a few recordings in 1961 at the urging of her old friend Victoria Spivey.

(***) Lucille Hegamin – Vol. 1 (1920–1922)
Document DOCD-5419 Hegamin; Wesley Johnson (t); Jim Reevy, prob. Charlie Irvis (tb); unknowns (cl); Clarence Harris, prob. Harvey Boone (as); unknown (ac); Bill Hegamin, Wilton 'Peaches' Kyer (p); Ralph Escudero (bb); Kaiser Marshall, unknowns (d). c. 11/20–4/22.

*** Lucille Hegamin – Vol. 2 (1922–1923)
Document DOCD-5420 Hegamin; unknown (c); prob. Elmer Chambers, Demas Dean, unknowns (t); prob. Herb Flemming, 'Wilson', unknowns (tb); prob. Garvin Bushell, Harold Hatter, unknown (cl, as); unknowns (cl); unknown (as); prob. Rollen Smith (ts); Sam Wooding, Cyril J. Fullerton, J. Russel Robinson, unknowns (p); prob. Charlie Dixon, Sterling Conaway or Maceo

Jefferson, unknowns (bj); unknowns (bb); prob. Joe Young, George Barber, unknown (d). 4/22–c. 10/23.

*** **Lucille Hegamin – Vol. 3 (1923–1932)**
Document DOCD-5421 *Hegamin; unknowns (t); unknowns (tb); unknowns (cl); unknown (bcl); unknown (as); unknown (ts); unknowns (s); Clarence Williams, Irving Williams, unknowns (p); unknowns (vn); unknowns (vc); Buddy Christian, unknowns (bj); unknowns (bb).* c. 10/23–3/32.

Lucille Hegamin gets the nod from historians as an early trailblazer, but it's sometimes a dutiful acknowledgement. Her art, and that of other contemporary women singers, seems often to be regarded as the old covenant, superseded when Bessie Smith handed down the definitive version of female blues singing, and it's true that Hegamin never internalizes her material, or seems to be opening a window into her soul. Her version of Bessie's hit 'Down Hearted Blues' (on *Vol. 2*) isn't the least bit down-hearted; like most of her music, it's melodious, enthusiastic, extrovert and lively, and it's odd that these qualities seem so little valued. Hegamin was an entertainer who sang blues and other songs, rather than a blues singer, and she did so with panache; it's worth trying to hear her music on its own artistic and historical terms.

Among its consistently good performances, *Vol. 1* includes her big hits 'Arkansas Blues' and 'He May Be Your Man (But He Comes To See Me Sometimes)', the latter in two versions. It's let down, however, by the poor sound of some of the original discs, which results from both inherent technical limitations and wear and tear. The acoustic recording process also means that the backing musicians usually mutter amorphously to themselves, with only the clarinet coming through clearly. *Vol. 2* has better sound, a third version of 'He May Be Your Man' and a final track by the white singer Martha Pryor, miscredited on the original disc. The songs continue to be mostly verse-and-chorus, and to treat of new dances, two-timers and *nostalgie du Sud*. There's no great depth of feeling, but that's not what either Hegamin or the songs are offering; she invariably gives the material all she's got, which is admittedly sometimes more than it deserves. *Vol. 3* continues in the same vein, but with a higher proportion of out-and-out pop songs in the mix, ranging from the famous likes of 'Hard Hearted Hannah' and a splendid 'Dinah' to the long-forgotten, effervescent 'Here Comes Malinda'. Only the narrow-minded will find such excursions down Tin Pan Alley other than delightful.

(*) Lucille Hegamin – Vol. 4 (1920–1926) Alternative Takes & Remaining Titles
Document DOCD-1011 *Similar to above CDs.* c. 11/20–c. 2/26.

The alternative takes collected here are seldom very different from those on the previous three volumes; to say that *Vol. 4* is for completists is not adverse criticism, but a statement of fact. Four titles appear on CD for the first time, two of them from a 78 which, though credited to Lucille Hegamin, is plainly by someone else, as yet unidentified.

(*) Songs We Taught Your Mother
Original Blues Classics OBCCD-520 *Hegamin; Henry Goodwin (t); Cecil Scott (cl); Willie 'The Lion' Smith (p); Gene Brooks (d).* 8/61.

(*) The Bluesville Years Vol. 8: Roll Over, Ms. Beethoven
Prestige PRCD-9916 *As above.* 8/61.

Shared with Alberta Hunter and Victoria Spivey, the Prestige disc is *Songs We Taught Your Mother* with six additional tracks by Spivey. Hegamin had retained her charm, spot-on timing and clear enunciation, and sounds far younger than her 67 years. Her pitch is occasionally a bit wayward, but her four songs are pleasant souvenirs of a vanished era, adorned by the elegant wind-chimes of Willie 'The Lion' Smith's piano. CS

Bill Heid
VOCAL, PIANO

Heid was exposed to blues and R&B on radio when growing up in Pittsburgh, Pennsylvania. Travelling round the United States and picking up old records, he earned himself an entry in the Guinness Book of World Records for hitchhiking 400,000 miles. He began playing piano in 1963 and organ in 1967. As an organist he has accompanied many well-known jazz musicians and recorded several albums for Savant, while as a blues keyboardist he has played with Fenton Robinson and Son Seals. Based in Detroit, he works regularly with Johnnie Bassett.

** **We Play The Blues**
Black Magic CD 9042 *Heid; Dwight Adams (t, flh); Russ Miller (as, ts, fl); Keith Kaminski (ts, bs); Brian Miller (h); Johnnie Bassett (g, v); Rick Matle (g); Pat Prouty (b); R. J. Spangler (d).* 1/00.

Heid is a very competent player with a wide frame of reference and here he has excellent collaborators. Bassett is a smoothly accomplished guitar player, and the horn players occasionally produce a very plausible '60s Blue Note sound. When Bassett takes the vocals the music, all written by Heid, has a modicum of character, but when Heid is the singer his sub-sub-Mose Allison style only draws attention to the ordinariness, and occasionally the derivativeness, of his songwriting. The final track, described as 'a hip-hop blues song not suitable for blues purists!', is five minutes of etiolated lounge music. TR

Erwin Helfer (born 1936)
PIANO

Helfer learned from fellow Chicagoans of earlier generations such as Cripple Clarence Lofton, Sunnyland Slim and Jimmy Walker, with whom he made two albums. In the '50s, while at university in New Orleans, he played with Punch Miller and other senior jazz figures; he also worked for some years, and recorded, with Mama Yancey. In 2001 he revived his label The Sirens to issue CDs of many of his teachers and friends.

(*) Rough And Ready
Testament TCD 5011 *Helfer; Jimmy Walker (p, v); Willie Dixon (b); Lillian Walker (v).* 64.

This album is a collaboration with Walker. Half of the 20 tracks are piano duets, and Walker has four solos; these are covered in Walker's entry. The remainder, which are by Helfer with Willie Dixon on bass, are mostly original pieces like 'Give Me 5 Cents Worth Of Love', 'Sneaky Pete' and 'Fringe Benefit', each of which has individual touches, and a faithful reading of

Jimmy Yancey's 'Four O'Clock Blues', all somewhat dulled by the rudimentary recording.

**** I'm Not Hungry But I Like To Eat – BLUES!
The Sirens SR-5001 *Helfer; John Brumbach (ts). 9/01.*

At this point Helfer had been playing blues and boogie woogie for almost 50 years and the music holds no secrets for him. Whether engaging in an exuberant finger-dance on the keyboard in 'Homage To Pete Johnson' or creating the pensive mood of the title tune or 'Nobody Knows You When You're Down And Out', he examines every corner of a melody, discovering subtleties which lesser musicians either fail to notice or shrink from exploring. Technically gifted, he has no need to make a show of speed, and the majority of the 15 tunes are taken at modest tempos, though with abundant variation of type and atmosphere. Four pieces are duets with tenor saxophonist Brumbach, whose gentle lyricism has a gritty coating almost reminiscent of Albert Ayler – an extraordinary and affecting combination. The recording does full justice to a beautiful instrument and a comprehensively talented player.

(***) St. James Infirmary
The Sirens SR-5006 *Helfer; Skinny Williams (ts). 12/01.*

This is an album of duets with tenor saxophonist Skinny Williams and so billed. Williams's approach is essentially melodic and has an unhurried grace which Helfer complements with similarly relaxed but elegant playing. About half the programme is standards like 'These Foolish Things', 'Honeysuckle Rose' and 'Stormy Weather' (hence the bracketed rating); of the blues 'Trouble In Mind' is notable for an exquisite piano passage that is pure Jimmy Yancey. The two men handle their fine old fabrics with the appreciative care of master tailors, but if your preference is for less leisurely music you can probably give the album the go-by. TR

Jessie Mae Hemphill (born 1940)
VOCAL, GUITAR, DIDDLEY BOW, BASS DRUM, SNARE DRUM, TAMBOURINE, LEG BELLS, HAT BOX

Jessie Mae Hemphill from Como, Mississippi, is the granddaughter of singer and multi-instrumentalist Sid Hemphill, and the niece of singer and guitarist Rosa Lee Hill; her parents and two aunts were also musicians, but never recorded. Jessie Mae did a little performing at picnics and in church, but it was only in 1979 that she decided, as the last of the family still playing music, to make it her career. She toured widely, and won a Handy for Feelin' Good *in 1991, but was sidelined by a stroke in 1993.*

*** Get Right Blues
Inside Sounds ISC-0519 *Hemphill; David Evans (g); Lois Brown (b); Joe Hicks (d); Compton Jones (tamb, hat box, diddley bow, v); Bettye Mitchell (tamb); Glen Faulkner (diddley bow); Napoleon Strickland (v). 2/79–11/85.*

**(*) She-Wolf
High Water HMG 6508 *Hemphill; David Evans (g); Calvin Jackson, Joe Hicks (d); Compton Jones (tamb, hat box). 7/79–12/80.*

*** Feelin' Good
High Water HMG 6502 *Hemphill; David Evans (g); R. L. Boyce (d); Compton Jones (tamb). 1/84–1/88.*

*** Heritage Of The Blues
Hightone HCD 8156 *As for above two CDs, except add Lois Brown (b), Bettye Mitchell (tamb), Compton Jones (diddley bow). 7/79–1/88.*

*** Mississippi Blues Festival
Black & Blue BB 457 *Hemphill; David Evans (g); Hezekiah Early (d). 3/86.*

** Dare You To Do It Again
219 Records TNR1003A 2CD *Hemphill; Sharde Turner [Thomas] (fife); Davis Coen, Steve Gardner (h, g); Tramp Camp (vn, md, mandola); Greg Humphreys (sg); Robert Belfour, Ruthie Foster (g, v); Kenny Brown, Papa Mali, Jimbo Mathus (g); Garry Burnside, Chris Chew, Eric Deaton (b); R. L. Boyce, Kent Kimbrough, Cedric Burnside, Andre Evans, Rodney Evans (d); Cyd Cassone (perc, v); band (v); DJ Logic (remixing). spring 03.*

When David Evans met her in 1979, Jessie Mae Hemphill had only a small repertoire, including the diddley bow piece 'Take Me Home With You, Baby', included on *She-Wolf* and *Heritage Of The Blues*. (A second version appears on *Get Right Blues*.) Evans worked with her on developing her music, creating complementary second-guitar parts, and Hemphill expanded her repertoire and added percussion instruments.

She-Wolf captures this development in progress, but potential is more often apparent than its realization. None of the tracks is a failure, but Hemphill doesn't always manage to introduce variety into the north Mississippi hill-country sound, whose bedrock is the hypnotic, one-chord drone, mainly because she relies too heavily on repetition when constructing her lyrics. Nor does it help that the two excellent drummers are frequently low in the mix by comparison with the metronomic, texturally unvaried foot tambourine.

Feelin' Good begins with six 1988 recordings which are Hemphill's best. These songs are more dynamically recorded than those on *She-Wolf* and more dynamic altogether. Boyce's hailstorm drumming derives from the fife and drum tradition, Evans's bottleneck is more aggressive and, above all, Hemphill sings and plays as if she were battling the din at a juke-joint. The balance of the CD was recorded solo in 1984. Hemphill's own drumming is overdubbed on four tracks; unfortunately the foot tambourine also features extensively. 'Lord, Help The Poor And Needy', with hand tambourine as the only accompaniment, is a deep and successful closing number, and Choctaw leg bells (an insignia of her ancestry) make an intriguing sound on 'Rolling And Tumbling'.

Heritage Of The Blues is a couple of dollars cheaper than the two High Water CDs which are its main source but lacks their extensive annotation. Three unissued tracks include a further example of diddley bow playing (by Compton Jones, accompanying Hemphill on 'Baby, Please Don't Go'). Moderately and advantageously biased toward the later recordings, *Heritage Of The Blues* also selects the best items from *She-Wolf*.

Get Right Blues, the most recently released Hemphill CD, includes the earliest recordings. The content is drawn about equally from 1979 and the mid-'80s and, while it doesn't provoke any rethinking of Hemphill's status as an artist, the disc is carefully programmed. As a result, the foot tambourine on four tracks provides variety rather than monotony, and the exiguousness of some compositions is effectively disguised. Three tracks with diddley bow and some touching, archaic church songs contrast well with band blues like 'Streamline Train', where Hemphill overdubs thunderous drumming, and

'Jessie's Love Song' and 'Shake Your Booty', which feature Joe Hicks and Lois Brown of The Fieldstones.

The seven tracks – but only five songs – on *Mississippi Blues Festival*, which is shared with Hezekiah & The House Rockers, were recorded during a tour of France. Evans and Early make effective contributions on two tracks; the remainder are vocal/guitar solos. Two versions (one with band) of the prosaic autobiography 'My Daddy's Blues' is too many, but good recording, the absence of tambourines and Hemphill's commitment outweigh the familiarity of most of the material.

Dare You To Do It Again was recorded by the nonprofit Jessie Mae Hemphill Foundation; the star is confined by her stroke to singing and playing tambourine, and confines herself to church songs. (The Rising Star Fife & Drum Band play a dynamic 'Little Sally Walker', and Ruthie Foster sings a blues with power but little soul.) Despite the array of accompanying talent, this is a disappointing production – or rather non-production: many tracks are self-indulgently over-extended, there's a superfluity of inter- and intra-song chatter and laughter, and Hemphill is sometimes at harmonic and rhythmic odds with the musicians. A 12-minute 'God Is Good To Me', with Robert Belfour accompanying, is a focused, intense exception, but neither a good track nor a good cause excuse a mostly bad record. CS

Duke Henderson
VOCAL

Henderson led a life of two overlapping parts. In the LA of the '40s and early '50s he was a blues shouter and R&B disc jockey, but he gradually modulated into a gospel promoter, preacher and gospel DJ, compering back-to-back radio shows of gospel music and R&B and alternating the identities 'Brother Henderson' and 'Big Duke'. By the '60s, however, he had put the blues behind him and was reading ads on XERB for a local spiritualist. He died in 1972.

*** Get Your Kicks
Delmark DD-668 Henderson; Karl George, Teddy Buckner, prob. Jesse Perdue (t); George 'Happy' Johnson (tb); Marshall Royal (cl, as); Gene Porter (cl); Jewell Grant (as); Jack McVea (ts, bs); Lucky Thompson, Wild Bill Moore (ts); Wilbert Baranco, Bob Mosley (p); Gene Phillips, unknown (g); Shifty Henry, Frank Clarke, prob. Charles Mingus (b); Lee Young, Rabon Tarrant (d). 11–12/45.

Kirk Silsbee in his entertaining notes calls Henderson a second-string Wynonie Harris. True, Henderson's clothes are all cast-offs, but they fit him well and he wears them with style, and when he is surrounded by first-rate players the effect is very appealing. The six tracks from a session with Lucky Thompson's All-Stars, for instance, are full of ravishing passages by Thompson like the opening choruses of 'S.H. Blues' and 'Not Worth A Dime', the obbligati in 'S.H. Blues' and 'Fool Hearted Woman' and the penultimate chorus of 'Mama Bear Blues'. 'Oo Wee Baby, Oo Wee', which from its title one might take to be a romp in the manner of Joe Turner, is a laidback slow blues with an exquisite opening chorus by Jack McVea. Such sensitive readings are interspersed with up-tempo numbers with sketchy vocal parts like 'Let's Get Vootin' and 'Boogie Man Blues', well-oiled vehicles for muscular riffing and solos. The recordings, originally made for Apollo, have survived remarkably well. TR

Mike Henderson & The Bluebloods
GROUP

A Nashville-based quartet of session musicians take time out from their day jobs to gather at the city's Bluebird Café and play some blues. It's as simple as that. Henderson (born 1951) and bassist Glenn Worf were first partnered in The Snakes, a similarly practical band that blended blues and mainstream pop, while Reese Wynans graduated from Stevie Ray Vaughan's Double Trouble.

***(*) First Blood
Dead Reckoning DR 0006 Mike Henderson (h, g, v); Reese Wynans (p); Glenn Worf (b); John Gardner (d). 96.

This is a true bar band, their mission to entertain and enjoy themselves, both of which they achieve with ease. When live tapes proved unsuitable, a two-day recording session produced 27 titles from which ten were selected for this release. The accent is on sprightly tempos, typified by the 'traditional' opener 'When I Get Drunk'. This is streamlined, punchy music with each musician refining his role to its essence. Solos by Wynans and Henderson are succinct and propulsive, underpinned by Worf's strutting string bass and Gardner's piledriving snare. This formula is repeated in 'Hip Shakin' and 'Give Me Back My Wig', with subtle alterations in each arrangement. Unusually, Henderson's slide solos concentrate on bass and middle ranges, lending dark drama to their fluency. He also plays amplified harmonica on Otis Spann's 'Bloody Murder'. 'How Many More Years' is performed as a shuffle and Patton's 'Pony Blues' uses 'Vicksburg Blues' as its template. The Snakes recorded 'Pay Bo Diddley' with the Diddley Daddy joining in the choruses; this unfocused rerecording is the album's only dud. Songs by Elmore James, Freddie King and Sonny Boy Williamson II complete an energetic and genuinely entertaining set.

*** Thicker Than Water
Dead Reckoning DEAR 0012 As above, except John Jarvis (p) replaces Wynans. 98.

The recipe is as before but the cake sags a bit in the middle. Jarvis is a capable replacement for Wynans, slightly less percussive but with a broader palette. The imaginative slide playing that lifted the previous album is less in evidence; nevertheless Henderson combines finger and slide phrasing with aplomb and plays harmonica on the opening 'Keep What You Got', 'My Country Sugar Mama' and 'All My Money's Gone'. The last is one of five originals, 'Angel Of Mercy', 'Whiskey Store' and 'Tears Like A River' among them, that are blues-oriented rather than 12-bar-based. Covers include songs by Floyd Jones, Eddy Clearwater, Howlin' Wolf and Sonny Boy Williamson II, whose 'Too Young To Die' is mistitled 'Scared Of That Child'. All the elements that previously jelled so convincingly are still present but, in diversifying the content, the band has diluted its impact. Although it's three seconds shorter than its predecessor, this album feels longer. NS

Rosa Henderson (1896–1968)
VOCAL

Born in Kentucky, Rosa Deschamps started out in carnival and tent shows about 1913, then moved into vaudeville, in a double

act with her husband, Douglas 'Slim' Henderson. By 1923, Rosa Henderson had reached New York, where she appeared in a number of shows in the '20s and '30s; she was also in the London production of Showboat in 1928. Her husband's death that year hit her very hard. She made one more record, appeared in Yeah Man in 1932 and withdrew from show business.

(*) Rosa Henderson Vol. 1 (1923)
Document DOCD-5401 *Henderson; Elmer Chambers or Howard Scott, Henry Busse, Frank Siegrist, Tom Morris (c); Teddy Nixon, Sammy Lewis (tb); Edgar Campbell, Ross Gorman (cl); Don Redman, Hale Byers, Don Clark (as); Coleman Hawkins (ts, bss); Don Clark, Fletcher Henderson, Ferdie Grofe, Louis Hooper, unknown (p); Charlie Dixon, Mike Pingitore (bj); Jack Barsby (bb). 5/23–12/23.*

(*) Rosa Henderson Vol. 2 (1924)
Document DOCD-5402 *Henderson; Elmer Chambers, Joe Smith, Howard Scott, prob. Rex Stewart (c); Harry Smith (t); Teddy Nixon (tb); Don Redman (cl, as); Bob Fuller (cl); Coleman Hawkins (ts); Fletcher Henderson, poss. Porter Grainger, Edgar Dowell, Cliff Jackson (p); Charlie Dixon (bj); Lincoln M. Conaway (g); Ralph Escudero (bb); Kaiser Marshall (d); unknown (eff, perc). 2/24–c. 9/24.*

(*) Rosa Henderson Vol. 3 (1924–1926)
Document DOCD-5403 *Henderson; Rex Stewart, Louis Metcalf, unknowns (c); Jake Frazier (tb); Bob Fuller (cl); Cliff Jackson, Louis Hooper, Fats Waller (p); Elmer Snowden (bj); Joe Davis (train wh); unknown (bells). c. 9/24–5/26.*

(*) Rosa Henderson Vol. 4 (1926–1931)
Document DOCD-5404 *Henderson; Louis Metcalf, Demas Dean, unknowns (c); Jake Frazier (tb); Bob Fuller, unknown (cl); Louis Hooper, Cliff Jackson, poss. Edgar Dowell, Porter Grainger, James P. Johnson, unknowns (p). 5/26–8/31.*

(***) **The Essential**
Classic Blues CBL 200024 2CD *Similar to above CDs. 6/23–8/31.*

***(*) **Rosa Henderson 1923–1931**
Retrieval RTR 79016 *Similar to above CDs. 7/23–8/31.*

Rosa Henderson was a versatile singer with a relaxed command of rhythm, equally at home with lightweight, melodious pop and lowdown, note-bothering blues. Her hundred-odd sides were released on a dozen labels under as many artist credits, which may be why she remains obscure by comparison with the Smiths, Ma Rainey or Ida Cox; whatever the reason, she deserves to be better appreciated.

It can't be denied, however, that – thanks largely to their accompaniments – Henderson's recordings are variable. Add lacklustre sound restoration, and Document's four volumes are sometimes heavy going. On most of *Vol. 1*, Fletcher Henderson (no relation) self-effaces his way through piano lead sheets, although he plays with panache on 'Got The World In A Jug'. The accompaniments on *Vol. 2* are more varied and more exciting; Fletcher Henderson's small groups feature more heavily than his solo piano, but he pirouettes delightfully through 'My Papa Doesn't Two-Time No Time'. *Vol. 2* also includes 'Strut Yo' Puddy', a fine feature for Rex Stewart, and 'Back Woods Blues', an outspoken attack on Southern segregation. As on *Vol. 1*, some poor-quality originals are used; no fewer than three tracks, including 'Back Woods Blues', start abruptly because of damaged discs.

On Document's last two volumes, the quality of both material and delivery declines. There's a rambunctious 'Nobody Knows The Way I Feel Dis Mornin' on *Vol. 3*, and *Vol. 4*'s 'Chicago Policemen Blues' is acerbic, but both songs feature Bob Fuller at his most self-indulgent. The accompanists goose Ms Henderson into action on *Vol. 4*'s 'Rough House Blues' and 'Slow Up Papa', but the liveliness of these songs, and of one or two others, is not typical. She may have been trying to emulate Ethel Waters's more intimate, sophisticated style, but usually she only manages to sound uninvolved.

Retrieval's is the better of the two selective compilations. Remastered from clean 78s, its 20 tracks are a mostly judicious choice from her best performances; they include two test pressings not available to Document. Retrieval miss four-star status because the running order differs from the tracklisting, and for including 'Struttin' Blues', accompanied by an invincibly unidiomatic subset of Paul Whiteman's Orchestra. Classic Blues have trouble finding 36 tracks that can truly be called essential; careful programming can't conceal the dullness of Fletcher Henderson's piano, and several songs come from scuffed and scratchy 78s. CS

Big Boy Henry (1921–2004)
VOCAL, GUITAR, KAZOO

From coastal North Carolina, Richard Henry was a fisherman and preacher when not playing blues. He made some home recordings in the '40s and early '50s, released much later on LP, and in 1952 he cut an unissued session in New York with Sonny Terry & Brownie McGhee. Henry gave up blues for many years, resuming in the late '70s; in 1983, 'Mr. President', a musical complaint to Ronald Reagan, won a W. C. Handy Award. Henry was instrumental in bringing together a group of retired fishermen to sing net-hauling songs as the Menhaden Chantymen, who can be heard on Won't You Help Me To Raise 'Em? *(Global Village CD 220), but arthritis restricted his activities with them, and limited his guitar playing.*

*** **Carolina Blues Jam**
Erwin Music EM 9301 *Henry; Chicago Bob Nelson (h, v); Gary Erwin (p, wb, v); Dave Peabody (g, v); Ted Donlon (b, v); Jay Niver (d, v); Sandra Hall (v). 2/93.*

***(*) **Poor Man's Blues**
New Moon NMC 9508 *Henry; Mike Wesolowski (h); Lightnin' Wells (md, g); Max Drake (g); Calvin Johnson (b); Russ Wilson (d, wb). 1/94.*

*** **Beaufort Blues**
Music Maker MMCD 27 *Henry; Michael Parrish (p, g); Guitar Gabriel, Lightnin' Wells, Timothy Duffy (g). 90s.*

Henry plays simple but effective guitar on two tracks each of *Beaufort Blues* and *Poor Man's Blues* (which also has a song where he blows kazoo), but for the most part he depends on others to accompany his singing, which still has a preacher's power. *Carolina Blues Jam* is pleasant, and the musicians play proficiently, but the piano is an ill-assorted addition to the Piedmont guitar and harmonica blues, and Peabody's accent, lurching from side to side of the Atlantic, makes 'Talkin' With Mr. Henry #1' uncomfortable listening. The playing on *Poor Man's Blues* is more idiomatic and intuitive, and it's probably no coincidence that Henry is more humorous on the dance tunes, more thoughtful on the slow blues, and generally more energetic and committed. *Beaufort Blues* is a gentler, more laidback set, with nicely varied if sometimes predictable accompaniments, which provide a secure, encouraging backdrop to Henry's singing and story telling. On 'Tell Me What To Do', Lightnin' Wells accompanies a promisingly soulful vocal by Big Boy's son Luther. CS

Hezekiah & The House Rockers
GROUP

Hezekiah Early (born 1934) took up harmonica at 13 or so, and played fife, snare and bass drum at picnics until about 1970. He abandoned the harmonica in 1950, when he became a drummer, but resumed playing it, simultaneously with his drumkit, in 1979. The House Rockers were active in the Natchez area from 1959 onwards, and were joined by trombonist Peewee Whittaker in 1963. Born around 1900, Whittaker brought many years' experience in minstrel shows, jazz and R&B to the band. Guitarist James Baker (born 1948) joined in 1978, adding rock 'n' roll, soul, country music and disco to the mix. Whittaker retired in 1988, not long before his death, and Baker also left the band, which now features a more orthodox personnel of guitar and bass in addition to Early.

**** Hezekiah And The House Rockers
High Water HMG 6511 *Leon 'Peewee' Whittaker (tb, v); Hezekiah Early (h, d, v); James Baker (g). 8/83.*

*** Mississippi Blues Festival
Black & Blue BB 457 *As above. 3/86.*

It will be apparent that the House Rockers were not a standard blues lineup, and even James Baker does not play conventional lead guitar. Instead, he plays bass figures on a six-string instrument, through a bass amplifier, and producer David Evans rightly points out that the resultant soft, breathy sound can be compared to that of a tuba. In effect, The House Rockers were a wind and percussion band. They often played for white parties and receptions, and this, together with the musicians' varied performance histories, generated an eclectic repertoire: alongside a core of conventional blues numbers, their eponymous CD includes versions of 'Whole Lot Of Shakin' Goin' On', 'Disco Fever' and the originally black, but long since universal, 'When The Saints Go Marchin' In'.

'The Saints' is given a far from conventional treatment, though, with Early's playing clearly reflecting both his admiration for Natchez harp hero Papa Lightfoot and his experience in fife and drum bands. Elsewhere 'Alabama Bound' explicitly reinterprets the fife and drum sound on harmonica and snare drum, and is one of five titles played by Early alone. These are a wonderfully rough, archaic set of performances, which supply a salty contrast to tracks by the full band. On these, Early's drumming is infallibly swinging, and his harp and Whittaker's trombone share the lead lines, their contrasting timbres and registers twining around each other in time-honoured call and response. The textures and colours of the House Rockers' music are, or rather were, a refreshing alternative to the dominant guitar-band sound. Their mission was to supply good-time party music, and their philosophy, even on songs with titles like 'Worried Blues' and 'Low Down Dirty Shame', can be summed up in the title of another: 'I'm Gonna Jump My Blues Away'.

Mississippi Blues Festival, which is shared with Jessie Mae Hemphill, was recorded in France, and serves as an addendum to the High Water CD. The House Rockers' five songs are familiar and all taken at a medium-tempo lope, but there are no duplications with High Water, and only 'Don't Mess With My Toot Toot' fails to carry the listener along. For Early's 1997 collaboration with Elmo Williams, *Takes One To Know One* (Fat Possum 0313), see Williams's entry. CS

Edna Hicks (1895–1925)
VOCAL

Edna Landreaux, born in New Orleans, was in show business by 1916 and married John Hicks about 1920. She played piano, but not on any of her issued records, and was a half-sister to Lizzie Miles, who seems to have facilitated her recording career. In August 1925, Edna Hicks was in Chicago, appearing in Plantation Follies, *when she was involved in a domestic accident with gasoline, and died of her injuries.*

**(*) Edna Hicks – Vol. 1 (1923)
Document DOCD-5428 *Hicks; Elmer Chambers (c); Teddy Nixon (tb); Don Redman (cl); Coleman Hawkins (ts); Porter Grainger (o, p); Phil Ohman, Clarence Johnson, Fletcher Henderson, Lemuel Fowler, Charles A. Matson (p); Charlie Dixon (bj); Kaiser Marshall (d). 3–c. 11/23.*

**(*) Edna Hicks – Hazel Meyers – Laura Smith – Vol. 2 (1923–1927)
Document DOCD-5431 *Hicks; unknown, Joe Smith (c); prob. Don Redman (cl); unknown (ss, as); Porter Grainger, Fletcher Henderson (p). 12/23–1/24.*

Commentators seem to agree in describing Edna Hicks as 'light voiced,' but this can only be by comparison with the likes of Bessie Smith and Ma Rainey. Hicks is a penetrating singer but not a very nuanced one, and she makes few attempts to suit her delivery to a particular lyric. Her accompanists, on the other hand, are very variable, but this is not always an advantage. Clarence Johnson is first-rate but appears on only three titles, while Phil Ohman and Charles Matson are dispensable vaudevillians. Porter Grainger is wildly inconsistent, and Lem Fowler often too reticent, although he sparkles on his own composition 'Wicked Dirty Fives'. One title on *Vol. 1* is accompanied by Fletcher Henderson's Orchestra, and another by his Hot Four; these outfits include the young Coleman Hawkins, but his playing is still immature and cautious. Hicks's contribution to *Vol. 2* consists of half a dozen tracks; Joe Smith's cornet is notably good on three of them. For the record, there are two alternative takes on *Classic Blues, Jazz & Vaudeville Singers – Vol. 4 (1921–1928)* (Document DOCD-5627) and a further two on *Classic Blues & Vaudeville Singers – Vol. 5 (1922–1930)* (Document DOCD-5654). CS

George Higgs (born 1930)
VOCAL, HARMONICA, GUITAR

North Carolinian George Higgs took up the harmonica as a youngster, taught by his father and influenced by DeFord Bailey and Peg Leg Sam. He learned guitar as a teenager, and played for parties. He switched to gospel quartet music for a while, but decided that there was less hypocrisy among blues singers. Higgs recorded with Elester Anderson in the early '70s, but nothing was issued; he has since continued to play at festivals and in educational programmes.

*** Tarboro Blues
Music Maker MMCD 19 *Higgs; prob. Lightnin' Wells (g). 00?*

On harmonica, Higgs offers archaic tunes like 'Reuben' and 'Greasy Greens', played unaccompanied except on the final track, where there is a guitarist in support. Higgs's guitar songs are situated within the familiar soundscape of the Carolina blues, with an expected influence from Blind Boy Fuller. His playing is very competent and, like his dry, relatively unemotional singing, it recalls the sound of Baby Tate from Spartanburg, South Carolina. These comparisons do not mean that Higgs is a colourless soundalike; rather, he's a likeable keeper of the traditional flame. CS

Walter T. Higgs
VOCAL, HARMONICA

Originally from Port Arthur, Texas, Higgs is a member of long standing in the Austin blues society, playing in the house band at Antone's and on the Sixth Street strip.

** Just A Few Miles To Go
Doc Blues DB 6802 Higgs; Jimmy Shortell (t); Mark [Kaz] Kazanoff (ts); Les Izmore (bs); Riley Osbourn (o, p); Derek O'Brien, Johnny Moeller (g); Larry Fulcher (b); George Rains (d); James Fenner (cga); Bradley Williams (rb); Rob Richardson (v). 01?

Higgs is an accomplished harmonica player, forceful but not overbearing. It would have been interesting to hear him blow all the way through a number, but the dozen original tunes on this CD all have vocals, and he isn't striking either as a singer or as a composer. Still, it is his record, and he shouldn't so often have been mixed down into the ensemble where one can't hear him properly. TR

Bertha 'Chippie' Hill (1905–50)
VOCAL

Born in Charleston, South Carolina, Hill was singing in New York at the age of 16, and a few years later in Chicago. She gave up recording, and to some extent performing, in the '30s while raising her family. In 1946–48 she recorded for Rudi Blesh's Circle label, appeared in his radio series This Is Jazz, *and sang in clubs in New York and Chicago and at the 1948 Paris Jazz Festival. She was killed in a traffic accident.*

*** Bertha "Chippie" Hill (1925–1929)
Document DOCD-5330 Hill; Louis Armstrong, Shirley Clay (c); Preston Jackson (tb); Artie Starks (cl, as); Richard M. Jones (p, v, sp); Georgia Tom Dorsey, Leroy Carr, unknown (p); Johnny St Cyr, Ikey Robinson (bj); Scrapper Blackwell (g, v); Tampa Red (g); Bill Johnson (b); prob. Cliff Jones (d); unknown (k); The Two Roys (v); Frankie Jaxon (sp). 11/25–3/29.

On ten of the 15 OKeh sides she recorded between 1925 and '27 Hill was accompanied by Louis Armstrong – an Armstrong who was engaged at the time, with his Hot Five or Seven, in nothing less than inventing a new jazz language. Fragments from that creative fire sometimes land upon his recordings with Hill, such as 'Low Land Blues' and 'Lonesome Weary Blues', and flames leap in his every phrase in 'Pratt City Blues'. Almost any singer would find it enervating to work continuously at such a temperature, and in several of these collaborations Hill takes the role of junior partner, her voice somewhat small, somewhat hard, sometimes straining in an unsuitable key.

By the time of her Vocalion recordings (1928–29) she had found the means of giving more body to her voice, as in 'Hard Time Blues', where she is accompanied with great care by Tampa Red and Georgia Tom. These sessions elicited new versions of two of her OKeh sides, both very different in concept from the earlier recordings. 'Pratt City Blues', hijacked by Bill Johnson's bass playing and decorated with shouts of encouragement by Frankie Jaxon, is no match for its predecessor, but 'Trouble In Mind' is in almost all respects superior: the recast text is longer and more interestingly shaped, and Hill's reading is far more subtle. To lose Armstrong is, as always, to lose much, but the less dramatic cornet part, thought to be by Shirley Clay, responds to the singer's mood with great sensitivity.

Five of Hill's 1946 Circle recordings are on *Montana Taylor/"Freddie" Shayne (1929–1946)* (Document DOCD-5053). The years had not treated her voice unkindly, and she sounded at ease chanting 'Black Market Blues' and 'Mistreatin' Mr. Dupree' in the company of pianist Taylor. Two sides with pianist 'Freddie' Shayne and trumpeter Lee Collins recapture something of the ambience of her earliest recordings, though it's doubtful if OKeh's management would have been receptive to lines in 'Charleston Blues' like 'I'm goin' back to the fish house, baby, and get me some good shrimps – I've gotta feed, baby, two or three hungry old pimps.'

**(*) Jazzin' The Blues (1943–1952)
Document DOCD-1019 Hill; Wild Bill Davison (c); Jimmy Archey (tb); Albert Nicholas (cl); Ralph Sutton (p); Danny Barker (g); Pops Foster (b); Johnny Blowers, Baby Dodds (d). 7–8/47.

Hill's eight songs on this VAC were done for *This Is Jazz* broadcasts, hence the preponderance of well-known repertoire like 'Careless Love', 'Baby Won't You Please Come Home' and 'Some Of These Days'. She negotiates them well enough, but her voice is a little frayed at the edges and the accompaniments are conventional. The bulk of the rest of the CD is by Lizzie Miles (q.v.) and Ruby Smith, née Ruby Walker, a niece of Bessie Smith who finds her own style in the drawling sensuality of 'You Satisfy' and 'Port Wine Blues', cleverly accompanied by a Gene Sedric group. TR

Michael Hill (born 1952)
VOCAL, GUITAR

The best of Brooklyn-born Hill's songs reflect, with humour and positivity, the drama of black life on New York's city streets. Initially inspired by watching Jimi Hendrix, Hill took up the guitar in 1970. He learned his trade in Top 40 bands and as a session musician and developed a style of songwriting that mirrored the social awareness of men like Marvin Gaye and Curtis Mayfield. Soon after its inception in 1985, Hill became part of Vernon Reid's Black Rock Coalition, an aggregation of black performers across the arts. His own band, at first called Bluesland and later the Blues Mob, was very much a family affair until the pressures of touring caused some members to drop out. While placing himself in the broad blues tradition, Hill succeeds in giving the music some much-needed contemporaneity.

***(*) Bloodlines
Alligator ALCD 4821 Hill; Fred McFarlane (o, p); Vernon Reid (g); Kevin Hill (b); Tony Lewis (d); Wynette Hill, Kathy Hill (v). 94.

This is very much the shock of the new, especially in the context of Alligator's then-current artist roster. A rock sensibility infuses most of these 14 songs, including an adaptation of 'Signifyin' Monkey', here segued with Hill's own 'Watch What You Say', leavening political correctness with humour. More important, though, are the songs in which social awareness is a major ingredient, including 'Can't Recall A Time', 'Evil In The Air' and 'Hard Blues For Hard Times'. Vernon Reid's 'Soldier's Blues', the only non-original, puts it succinctly: 'the American Dream is just hopin' you get home alive'. Hill's achievement is to get his message across without being contentious, thus validating his music and the genre in which he chooses to work.

***(*) **Have Mercy!**
Alligator ALCD 4845 *Hill; Hector Colon (t); Roger Byam (as, ts); Randy Gilmore (ts); Vincent Velez Jr (bs); E. J. 'The Professor' Sharpe (o, p); Fred McFarlane (p); Peter Cummings, Kevin Hill (b); Tony Lewis (d); Wynette Hill, Kathy Hill (v). 96.*

It's a matter of 'have *déjà vu*', as well, for this is very much a rerun of *Bloodlines*, with a little more variety and a less persistent foot on the heavy pedal. Social commentary is still high on the agenda, with 'Falling Through The Cracks', 'Backyard In Brooklyn' and 'Bluestime In America'. The personnel changes have had little effect on the music, the most notable change being a cleaner, less rock-oriented tone to Hill's guitar. There's less grandstanding in his solos, the instrumental 'Rest In Peace' with its slide filigree a case in point. The only false note is struck in 'Women Make The World Go 'Round' but this is compensated for by the trenchant version of Hound Dog Taylor's 'She's Gone' that finishes the album.

*** **New York State Of Blues**
Alligator ALCD 4858 *Hill; E. J. 'The Professor' Sharpe (kb); Peter Cummings, Kevin Hill (b); Tony Lewis (d). 98.*

A blurring of focus takes the edge from this release. With the exception of 'Anytime, Anywhere' and 'This Is My Job', there's less evidence of a social conscience in Hill's writing and these songs are buttressed by the populism of 'Papa Was A Rollin' Stone' and Stevie Wonder's 'Living For The City'. On the other hand, 'Never Give Up On You' finishes the album on a note of intimacy and truth, as Hill plainly refers to his own relationship. The standard of musicianship remains high but there's not so much sense of purpose about it, even though 'A Case Of The Blues' and the title song concern themselves with the mechanics of blues-making. There's skill in the arranging of the cover songs but the effect is a dilution of Hill's pioneering acuity.

*** **Larger Than Life**
Dixiefrog DFGCD 8517 *As above, except William McCellan (d) replaces Lewis. 01.*

Something of a return to form re-establishes Hill's expertise at combining social issues with listenable music. Here he tackles police heavy-handedness ('41 Shots'), the correlation of welfare and ghetto violence ('Larger Than Life') and the echoes of slavery ('Monticello Nights'). Even so, there's an air of howling in the wilderness about much of it and maybe an awareness of futility has crept into his lyrics. Hill's softer side is on show in 'Blessings' but he and the band take evident pleasure in a storming reworking of George Clinton's 'Cosmic Slop'. As good as much of this album is, there's now an air of familiarity about the Blues Mob's music where once originality held sway.

(*) **Electric Storyland Live
Ruf 1088 2CD *Hill; Ana Popovic (g); Pete Cummings (b, v); Bill McClellan (d, v). 03?*

Here recording as a trio (Popovic appears on one track) at two different venues, Hill is hampered by a muffled vocal sound throughout both sets, whereas bass and drums have better definition at the second. As good a guitarist as Hill undoubtedly is, it was a mistake to dispense with a keyboard player, especially when in the first set he has some trouble with his continuity and soloing. Luckily, he has a full trick bag, which enables him to paper over the cracks and impress a willing if small audience. He's on better form at the second location but there's still a hole in the sound. The repertoire draws from all his previous albums but most heavily from *Bloodlines* and *Larger Than Life*. Hill's songs are often topical and interesting and his warm personality is easily transmitted to both audience and listener but he seems to be in something of a creative cul-de-sac. NS

*** **Black Gold & Goddesses Bold!**
JSP JSP 5109 *Hill; David Barnes (h); Colin John (g, v); Vernon Reid; Hubert Sumlin (g); Bill McClellan (d, v). 04.*

These are, in effect, two half-albums, intersecting. The songs defined by *Goddesses Bold!* include paeans to women of today like the 'New York Doll' – 'she's fearless and full of heart, she's been through a hell of a lot, and she demands full respect' – and the impeccably new-man testifying of 'Specialization': 'Let me specialize in your mind, specialize in your heart, make your satisfaction my science and my art – study your desires, major in your wants, focus on your back and zoom in on your front … ' This from the music that gave us 'What's That Smells Like Gravy?' and 'Banana In Your Fruit Basket'? We've come a long way, guys. *Black Gold* identifies a group of songs critical of George W. Bush and the war in Iraq. Their honesty and intelligence are sometimes a little diminished by their reliance on slogans, but the closing 'Home I Love' makes its points very forcefully. The two programmes are threaded together by the serpentine guitars of Hill and John, assisted on one track each by Reid and Sumlin. TR

Z. Z. Hill (1941–84)
VOCAL

Arzel Hill was born in Naples, Texas, grew up in Dallas and sang on the gospel circuit. About 1960 he gave himself the professional name of Z. Z. Hill, switched to secular music and soon afterwards made his first recordings. From the mid-'60s he was a popular name in what would later be called Southern soul, recording for Kent, Atlantic, United Artists and Columbia, though one of his most successful singles, 'Don't Make Me Pay For His Mistakes' (1971), was for his brother Matt's Hill label. In 1981 he revived his flagging career by signing with Malaco and, in the following year, scoring one of the biggest blues hits of the decade, 'Down Home Blues'.

Hill's output in the '60s and '70s is beyond the remit of this book, but it's worth noting that his 1971 blues hit 'Don't Make Me Pay For His Mistakes' is on *Turn Back The Hands Of Time* (Night Train NTI CD 7016).

(**(*)) Z. Z. Hill
Malaco MALCD 7402 Hill; Whit Sedener, Kenny Faulk, Chris Colclessor, Dana Teboe (brass, reeds); Carson Whitsett (kb); David Chappel, Melissa Ross, Marguerite Haldeman, Bogdan Chruszcz, Guy Weddle, Marjorie Lash, Stuart McDonald, Jorge Orbon, Gail Bauser (strings); Dino Zimmerman, Johnny Barranco (g); Don Barrett, George Allen (b); James Robertson (d); Fern Kinney, Jewell Bass, Thomisene Anderson, Valerie Williams, Tommy Tate (v). 81.

*** Down Home
Malaco MALCD 7406 Hill; The Muscle Shoals Horns (brass, reeds); Carson Whitsett (kb); The Jackson Strings (strings); Dino Zimmerman, Leroy Emmanuel (g); Ray Griffin (b); James Robertson (d); Thomisene Anderson, Jewell Bass, Charlotte Chenault (v). 81.

*** The Rhythm & The Blues
Malaco MALCD 7411 Hill; Harrison Calloway, Ben Cauley, Harvey Thompson, Charles Rose, Walter King (brass, reeds); Carson Whitsett, Haran Griffin (kb); Mickey Davis, Claudette Hampton, Bob McNally, Peggy Plucker, John Frantz, Anne Mason, Bennett Randman (strings); Dino Zimmerman, Jimmy Johnson (g); Ray Griffin (b); Owen Hale (d); Thomisene Anderson, Jewell Bass, Valerie Williams (v). 82.

**(*) I'm A Blues Man
Malaco MALCD 7415 Hill; Harrison Calloway, Ben Cauley, Harvey Thompson, Charles Rose, Jim Horn (brass, reeds); Carson Whitsett (kb); Carl Marsh (syn); Mickey Davis, Anne Mason, Claudette Hampton, Peggy Plucker, Kathy Robinson, Janet Dressler, Ben Randman, Brian Gum, Linda Geidel (strings); Dino Zimmerman, Jimmy Johnson, Vasti Jackson (g); Ray Griffin (b); James Robertson (d); Glen Holmes (perc); Thomisene Anderson, Jewell Bass, Valerie Williams (v). 84.

(**(*)) Bluesmaster
Malaco MALCD 7420 As above, except add Ronnie Eades, Walter King (brass/reeds), Bob McNally, John Frantz (strings), Leroy Emmanuel (g), Don Barrett (b), Owen Hale (d), Charlotte Chenault (v). 84.

Hill was a plausible blues singer when he was required to be by songs like 'Blue Monday' (*Z. Z. Hill*), 'Down Home Blues' and 'When It Rains It Pours' (*Down Home*), 'Wang Dang Doodle' and 'Get You Some Business' (*The Rhythm & The Blues*) and the title track of *I'm A Blues Man*, which namechecks Jimmy Reed and Muddy Waters. It would be just possible to select from these five albums a single CD that you could describe as Z. Z. Hill singing the blues and annoy nobody but a pedant. It would be less than fair to Hill, whose chief skill was as a commentator on the game of sexual and emotional oneupmanship played year-round in the arena of Southern soul, exemplified by 'Cheatin' In The Next Room', 'Everybody Knows About My Good Thing' and Denise LaSalle's 'Someone Else Is Steppin' In'. LaSalle also wrote the acute 'You're Ruining My Bad Reputation', a story of a man made good – or brought down? – by love: 'I'm walking round in overalls so you can wear Calvin Klein ... I'm walking the floor at midnight with Pampers in my hand ...' Most blues enthusiasts, and certainly those who enjoy Bobby Bland, should not find it difficult to appreciate these songs or Hill's enactment of them. What may be troublesome are the orchestral arrangements, which, especially on *Z. Z. Hill* and *Bluesmaster*, are often overscored with strings and background vocals that even a Nashville producer might consider excessive.

*** In Memorium 1935–1984
Malaco MALCD 7426 *As for above CDs.* 81–84.
**(*) Greatest Hits
Malaco MALCD 7437 *As above.* 81–84.

The blues enthusiast who's curious about Hill and prepared, repertory-wise, to meet him halfway could begin with these selections, which are culled from the preceding albums but emphasize the central three. *In Memorium* has ten tracks and *Greatest Hits* 11, only 'Down Home Blues' and 'Someone Else Is Steppin' In' appearing on both. *In Memorium* is the bluesier of the two. TR

Algia Mae Hinton (born 1929)
VOCAL, GUITAR, BANJO, BUCK DANCING

The youngest of 14 children of a musical family in North Carolina, Hinton learned to play from her mother, and entertained locally while raising her family and working the land. Wider recognition began to come her way in the '70s.

*** Honey Babe
Music Maker 91005 Hinton; Lightnin' Wells (h); Tim Duffy (g); Taj Mahal (b). late 90s.

Some of the wider attention Hinton attracted was as a woman in the Piedmont blues, to be added to the list alongside Libba Cotten and Etta Baker, but in her immediate and extended family anyone who did not make music, regardless of gender, was the exception. There's an inevitable Jimmy Reed tune, but Hinton's music mainly preserves the pre-blues and stringband repertoire of the region. She's an able guitarist, and a more euphonious singer than either Cotten or Baker, and, if her party piece, buck dancing while playing guitar behind her head, inevitably loses something without the visual aspect, the lively five-string banjo on the white country song '[I'm Just Here To Get My Baby] Out Of Jail' is compensation. It's regrettable that at times the string bass on four tracks overloads the microphone.

If it can be found, another *Honey Babe* (Hin-Tone HT 82929), recorded in 1996, is artistically superior, but its distribution was extremely limited. CS

Silas Hogan (1911–94)
VOCAL, GUITAR

Born and raised in Louisiana, Hogan learned guitar from his uncles and began playing at parties in the '30s. He moved to Baton Rouge in 1939, worked in oil refineries and became part of the lively local blues scene, switching to electric guitar when he formed the Rhythm Ramblers in 1951. Hogan cut a single for Reynaud records, but only began recording more extensively in 1962 at J. D. Miller's Crowley studio, for release on Excello. He was let go when Miller and Excello got into dispute, but he remained active, and recorded again in the early '70s for Blue

Horizon, Arhoolie and, ironically, Excello. He continued to perform into the '90s at festivals, and locally at Tabby Thomas's Blues Box.

**** **So Long Blues**
[Ace CDCHD 523] Hogan; Sylvester Buckley, Whispering Smith (h); Katie Webster (o, p); Isaiah Chatman, Al Foreman, Lazy Lester, 'Slim' (g); Rufus Thibodeaux, Bobby McBride (b); Sam Hogan, Burnell Hayney, Jeffrey Holden (d). 7/62–1/65.

Silas Hogan's recordings are among the finest to emerge from the Baton Rouge synthesis of local tradition with Jimmy Reed's rolling rhythm and Lightnin' Hopkins's moody arpeggios. Hogan was 51 when he connected with J. D. Miller, and his music is always conscientiously crafted, the work of a man who takes what he's doing seriously. That doesn't mean that he's habitually solemn; 'Trouble At Home Blues' is both realistic and cartoonishly witty about pest infestation: 'I've got roaches in my kitchen, mouses like a drove of coons ... These rats done got so brave round here, people, they shut the gas off on my stove.' Elsewhere, Hogan deftly conjures up the apprehensive tedium of waiting at the airport for a girlfriend, or the 'Dark Clouds Rolling' which reinforce a deserted lover's gloom. (He finds out at the end of the song that 'She's with your friend, she's well and doing fine'; Hogan's delivery conveys that this is desolating news with exemplary subtlety.) Hogan usually recorded with his working band, sometimes augmented from Miller's squad of studio musicians; their relaxed energy, Hogan's graceful singing and Miller's deft production were a reliably magical combination. *Trouble* (AVI/Excello CD 3005), which covered much the same ground as *So Long Blues*, is out of print, but North American readers may be able to find copies.

***(*) **The Godfather – Louisiana Swamp Blues Vol. 6**
Wolf 120.927 Hogan; Oscar 'Harpo' Davis (h); Sam Hogan (g, d); Bruce Lamb, Julian Piper (g); David Carroll, David Hill (b); Jess Kenchin (d). 4/88, 4/90.

Hogan's early '70s recordings were of high quality (those for Blue Horizon are on *Swamp Blues* [Ace CDCHD 661]), but they didn't send producers scurrying to Baton Rouge. The town mostly stayed off record-company radar until the late '80s, when Englishman Julian Piper became a participant observer in the local scene, interviewing, playing with and producing sessions by surviving musicians. Hogan is still in vigorous voice on *The Godfather*, although time has added a slight quaver; he only plays on six (of 11) tracks, but since guitar heroics were never part of his soundworld, it doesn't matter. The playlist mostly consists of remakes of the Excello recordings, plus Lightnin' Hopkins's 'Mr. Charlie' and a couple of Lightnin' Slim's hits; for the most part the musicians successfully re-create the sound of the '60s, a task made easier by the continued presence of Sam Hogan, son of Silas and a drummer of unsung greatness. Only Oscar Davis's contribution is problematic; described as 'the best harp player in town', he's usually short of both volume and ideas.

The Godfather is completed by four solo tracks from Hogan's longtime associate Arthur 'Guitar' Kelley (1924–2001), accompanying himself on electric guitar. Kelley (who is also on *Swamp Blues*) was one of the unheralded treasures of Baton Rouge, and his brooding songs come across well in this format. He's well nicknamed, too; tuning his three lower strings to a chord so that he can play unfretted bass lines, he often sounds like two guitarists. Kelley's heavy breathing is sometimes rather intrusive, but not to the point of spoiling the performances. CS

Smokey Hogg (1914–60)
VOCAL, GUITAR, PIANO

Andrew Hogg was born in Westconnie, Texas, and learned guitar from his father. In the '30s he and Black Ace played for dances in small East Texas towns, and in 1937 Hogg made a solitary 78. A decade later, after military service in World War II, he returned to recording, initially in Dallas, thereafter migrating between Texas and LA as recording and performing opportunities offered themselves. Hogg only scored two R&B chart entries, but he was a consistent seller, with an extensive output on numerous labels. Unfortunately, he drank to excess, and was being treated for stomach cancer when he died from a haemorrhaging ulcer.

*** **Deep Ellum Rambler**
Ace CDCHD 780 Hogg; unknown (tb); unknown (ts); Hadda Brooks, Dorothy Broyles, unknowns (p); unknown (g); Bill Davis, unknowns (b); Al Wichard, Edward 'Sharky' Hall, unknowns (d). 47–8/51.

(*) **Serve It To The Right
Ace CDCHD 866 As above, except add poss. Maxwell Davis (ts), poss. Al Wichard (cga). 47–52.

*** **Midnight Blues**
Ace CDCHD 1019 As for *Deep Ellum Rambler*, except add Austin McCoy (p), Wesley Prince (b), unknowns (v). 47–9/52.

*** **Good Morning Little School Girl 1947/1951** [sic]
EPM Blues Collection 16026 Hogg; unknown (tb); Joe Fritz (ts, v); Ed Wiley (ts); Hadda Brooks, Dorothy Broyles, Willie Johnson, Austin McCoy, unknowns (p); Goree Carter (g); Bill Davis, Donald Cooks, Wesley Prince, unknowns (b); Al Wichard, Sharky Hall, Ben Turner, unknowns (d). 47–52.

(*) **Angels In Harlem
Specialty SPCD-7020/[Ace CDCHD 419] Hogg; unknown (h); Lue Freddie Simon (ts); Austin McCoy, Henry McDade, Willard McDaniel, unknown (p); unknown (g); Bill Davis, unknown (b); Sharky Hall, Al Wichard, unknown (d). 2/49–12/57.

Smokey Hogg's two 1937 recordings, reissued on "*Too Late, Too Late*" – *Vol. 4* (Document DOCD-5321), show why he sometimes billed himself as 'Little Peetie Wheatstraw'. His admiration for Wheatstraw and Big Bill Broonzy persisted; he covered a number of their records, and borrowed elements of their vocal styles. Hogg covered many other records by '30s and '40s artists, but he also wrote original lyrics, and revived venerable pre-blues reels and play-party songs. In all these modes, his singing and playing, whether on guitar or occasional piano, are always instantly recognizable. Hogg's purported piano work is so independent of the vocal line that some have doubted he's playing it, but the harmonies and timing are so consistently strange over such a long period that the case seems pretty solid.

Here we approach the problem many listeners have with Smokey Hogg. Especially as a guitarist, he employed a unique vocabulary, forming unorthodox chords and using a drone bass. This made his music more modal than tonal, and a problem to accompany; still more problematic were his disregard for conventional phrase lengths and his tendency to break time. Some have dismissed Hogg as an untutored country musician who bewildered his more sophisticated accompaniments by ignoring them, and although this charge is not without foundation – some of Hogg's records are indeed anarchic – it has often been grossly exaggerated. It seems more useful to see his music as an attempt, creative but sometimes awkward, to fuse the city blues of Chicago, Dallas and LA with the dance tunes of deep East Texas and the worksongs of the Brazos River prison farms. Hogg's lyrics often deal with the stresses of life in the big city, and speak nostalgically of returning to the country, which no doubt commended him to listeners who had recently migrated to Texan and West Coast cities.

Ace's heroic attempt to rehabilitate Hogg draws on recordings for Modern and Combo. All three CDs are excellently mastered, include many previously unissued titles and present significant new discographical findings. It's only right to say that there are some strange interactions between Hogg and his musicians. 'Little School Girl' on *Deep Ellum Rambler* is sometimes in two keys at once, there are some abrupt rhythmic adjustments, and the drummer and pianist linger on after Hogg decides that the song is ended. 'Look In Your Eyes Pretty Mama' on the same disc is of great interest, with Hogg deploying a slide guitar technique which he undoubtedly acquired from Black Ace, but Dorothy Broyles has no idea where either of them is going next.

Ace's other two CDs include similar moments of organized chaos, and anyone who cannot live with musical unpredictability is not going to enjoy Smokey Hogg. However, if one makes an effort to enter his musical universe (which is not simply a euphemism for 'if one ignores the cock-ups'), the rewards include vigorous, confident cover versions, trenchant reworkings of traditional songs and witty original lyrics. *Serve It To The Right* is the least well compiled of the three, featuring too many medium-tempo songs with guitar, piano, bass and drums; its notes, however, are exceptionally good (and not just because they independently come to much the same assessment of Hogg's music as this discussion).

Angels In Harlem's first six titles are exercises in mutual wariness. Austin McCoy did better afterwards on Modern, but here he's unnerved by Hogg's wayward time and weird harmony; only the jump blues 'You Better Watch That Jive' succeeds, because Hogg, McCoy and Davis go at it bull-headed, and to hell with the body count. On subsequent sessions, Specialty's Art Rupe replaces McCoy with less timorous pianists and adds drummers with orders to keep the tempo steady at all costs. The results are livelier, with Hogg forced to pay some attention to what the band are doing; even so, there's a moment on the title track when Smokey and the sax player meet like two cars on a blind bend, slamming on the brakes and edging nervously past each other. The last two tracks, from 1952 and Ebb, are also Hogg's last recordings; he plays no instrument and is in poor shape. The Latin rhythm on 'Good Mornin' Baby' (a remake of his hit 'Little School Girl') is stunningly incongruous.

Smokey Hogg parlayed his popularity into sessions for many labels; a baker's dozen of titles made for Imperial, in similar style and with some of the same accompanists as on Modern and Specialty, is on *Texas Guitar Killers* (Capitol 33915 2CD). Hogg also recorded fairly extensively for Bob Shad in Houston, but *Sittin' In With Smokey Hogg* (Mainstream MDCD 906) is deleted. EPM commendably include five titles from those sessions, with smoky (what else?) tenor saxes, and Goree Carter's coolly modernistic guitar on three of them. (There's also a track without Hogg, sung by Joe Fritz.) Otherwise, EPM mainly rely on Modern, but from elsewhere there's the anguished spiritual 'He Knows How Much We Can Bear' and Hogg's one unquestionable masterpiece, the two-part 'Penitentiary Blues', an agonized account of the horrors of the Texas prison system, based on an old worksong. Made without access to company files, EPM's discographical speculations are confident, plausible and often wrong, but this is the CD for those who just want a taste of what Hogg could do when he was in form. cs

The Hokum Boys
GROUP

'The Hokum Boys' was a brand name, used by any record company which considered that it fitted the product. As well as the material considered here, there were Hokum Boys records by Georgia Tom & Tampa Red, one side by Blind Blake, and titles with Big Bill Broonzy as the featured artist. These are considered under the respective artist entries; the Famous Hokum Boys also have their own entry.

** The Hokum Boys (1929)
Document DOCD-5236 *Bob Robinson* (cl, bj, v); *Alex Hill, Jimmy Blythe* (p, v); *Alex Robinson, Dan Roberts, Banjo Ikey Robinson,* unknown (g, v); unknown (g); unknown (v). 6–12/29.

Hokum, which aimed to provide light-hearted entertainment to African-American record-buyers, is probably the blues genre found least entertaining by latterday white listeners, who put up with it, if at all, for the high-quality guitar playing. (Less often noticed is the harmonically and rhythmically interesting piano work of Alex Hill and Jimmy Blythe.) The lyrics deal extensively in innuendo, but also treat aspects of the urban North which recent migrants from the South found challenging, among them violence, gambling, gossip, noisy neighbours who fuelled their parties with bootleg liquor, the difficulty of forming stable relationships and the consequent prevalence of prostitution. It's no small achievement to make fun out of this material, but compilation into CD format does hokum a disservice by emphasizing its thematic and musical repetitiveness. This disc will interest social historians and emulous guitarists, but few others.

** The Hokum Boys & Bob Robinson (1935–1937)
Document DOCD-5237 *'Mr Sheiks'* (t); *Arnett Nelson* (cl); *Black Bob, Albert Ammons,* prob. *Aletha Dickerson Robinson,* unknown(s) (p); *Casey Bill Weldon, Big Bill Broonzy* (g, v); *Bill Settles,* unknown(s) (b); *Washboard Sam* (wb); *Teddy Edwards, Bob Robinson,* unknown (v). 12/35–3/37.

The Depression nearly killed the record industry but when sales revived so did the name, and some of the repertoire, of the Hokum Boys. (This CD includes similar material by various Bob Robinson groups.) The first seven titles feature Casey Bill Weldon, singing lead and playing precise, athletic steel guitar. Less effete than the general run of hokum, these performances are worth hearing. The rest of the disc is unfortunately dominated by the vocals of Bob Robinson and the clarinet of Arnett Nelson. Nelson had considerable feeling for the blues, but seems determined to submerge it in vaudevillean effects, while the absence of the preceding disc's flashy guitar work exposes the dullness of Robinson's vocals. cs

Dave Hole (born 1948)
VOCAL, GUITAR

Though born in Cheshire, England, Hole grew up in Perth, Australia. He began playing rock 'n' roll in his teens, later moving on to blues. After a football injury to his left hand he adopted an unconventional approach to the guitar, playing with his left hand over the neck and the slide on his index finger. He took up music professionally in the early '70s and played around Western Australia. His first album, Short Fuse Blues, received rave reviews, leading to recording deals with Provogue and Alligator and access to the European, and later American, club and festival circuits, where he is regarded as one of the blues' premier slide guitarists.

*** Short Fuse Blues
Provogue PRD 7036//Alligator ALCD 4807 *Hole; Bob Patient (kb); John 'Hambone' Wilson (b); Ronnie 'Greystoke' Parker (d, perc).* 90.

**(*) The Plumber
Provogue PRD 7046 *As above, except Wilson also plays kb; add Gary Ridge (perc).* 92/93.

*** Working Overtime
Provogue PRD 7056//Alligator ALCD 4814 *As for Short Fuse Blues, except Rudy Miranda (d, perc) replaces Parker.* 93.

*** Steel On Steel
Provogue PRD 7078//Alligator ALCD 4832 *As above.* 2/95.

*** Whole Lotta Blues
Provogue PRD 7093 *As for above CDs.* 90–95.

*** Ticket To Chicago
Provogue PRD 7102//Alligator ALCD 4847 *Hole; Ken Anderson (t); Steve Eisen (ts); Brian Ripp (bs); Billy Branch (h); Tony Z. (o, p); Johnny B. Gayden (b); Ray 'Killer' Allison (d); Gene Barge (arr); Bruce Iglauer (co-prod).* 10–11/96.

**(*) Under The Spell
Provogue PRD 7120//Alligator ALCD 4865 *Hole; Bob Patient (kb); Michael Vdelli (g); Roy Daniel (b); Ric Whittle (d); Cliff Blackburn (perc).* 99.

*** Outside Looking In
Provogue PRD 7131//Alligator ALCD 4881 *Hole; Bob Patient (kb); James Hewgill (p); Roy Daniel (b); J. Mattes (d).* 00/01.

*** The Live One
Provogue PRD 7141//Alligator ALCD 4890 *As above, except add Ric Eastman (d), Bruce Iglauer (co-prod); omit Hewgill.* 12/01–7/02.

Hole shares the aesthetic of Hound Dog Taylor and George Thorogood, generating intensity at a high dynamic level, typically backed by a rhythm section that does little more than urge him on. Climatically speaking, his music is stormy and tempestuous, pierced with the lightning of his slide playing, and mild days are infrequent. His albums are largely, *The Plumber* wholly, made up of original songs, generally in blues forms, which tend to be more successfully realized than blues standards like 'Travelling Riverside Blues' (*Whole Lotta Blues*) or 'I Can't Be Satisfied' (*Working Overtime*). *Whole Lotta Blues* was a mid-term report drawn fairly evenly from *Short Fuse Blues*, *Working Overtime* and *Steel On Steel* but with only one track from *The Plumber*; a limited-edition release, it may no longer be available.

For *Ticket To Chicago* Hole made just such a purchase and, galvanized by collaborating with a formidable band of local musicians, outdid his previous work in tracks like 'My Bird Won't Sing', where his slide playing is huge and magisterial. He then returned to working with Australian musicians. *Under The Spell* is, by his standards, low-key but he rediscovers his vigour on *Outside Looking In*, trenchantly redrafting the melody of 'It Hurts Me Too' in the title track and rattling the studio walls with a Bo Diddleyesque 'Insomniac'. For *The Live One*, recorded in venues in Australia and Chicago, he spends most of his time with tunes he had already recorded like 'Berwick Road', 'Demolition Man', 'Bullfrog Blues' and 'Jenny Lee', but the live setting elicits all the power familiar to owners of his other albums. TR

John Dee Holeman (born 1929)
VOCAL, GUITAR, BODY PERCUSSION

From North Carolina, Holeman took up the guitar aged 14. His music blends the Piedmont styles of Blind Boy Fuller and his heirs with the Texas sound of Lightnin' Hopkins. Holeman is also a storyteller, and until a recent back injury was an accomplished buck dancer.

** Country Girl
Mapleshade 01232 *Holeman; Fris Holloway (p).* 4/88.

**(*) Piedmont Blues De Caroline Du Nord
Inédit W 260043 *Holeman.* 2–3/92.

*** Bull Durham Blues
Music Maker 91004 *Holeman; Taj Mahal (p, g, b, body perc).* 3/98.

Holeman is a skilful guitarist on both acoustic and electric instruments, but a negligible composer; his 'Chapel Hill Boogie', which appears on both Inédit and Music Maker, is a generic boogie pattern, fitted with semi-traditional lyrics. As a consequence, all three discs consist almost entirely of well-known songs, from tradition or by other artists, given a confident but often rather anonymous delivery.

The Mapleshade and Inédit CDs are live recordings, made respectively in Washington, DC, and Paris, France. (The last track on Inédit, a demonstration of 'Patting Juba', was recorded in Dallas at an unspecified date.) The recording quality of both discs is acceptable rather than outstanding. *Country Girl*, on which the artist credit is to 'John Dee and Fris', is marred by the electric-piano playing of Fris Holloway; the two men have been associates since the '70s, but on this disc it sounds as if they met on the day of the recording. Holloway is tentative, and sometimes unsure of the key; he also appears to be entranced by his instrument's wah-wah, bass guitar, organ and other effects keys, using them extensively and with almost unerring lack of taste. This nullifies some otherwise good performances, among them an improbable downhome version of 'I Can't Quit You Baby', and a long, introspective 'I Hate To See That Evenin' Sun Go Down'.

Piedmont Blues De Caroline Du Nord is the better for Holloway's absence and, but for its recessed sound, would earn a stronger recommendation. For all the merits of Holeman's playing and singing, however, there's a surfeit of over-familiar material on this CD, and he seldom makes one hear songs by Lightnin' Hopkins, Arthur Crudup, Blind Boy Fuller and Memphis Minnie as if they were newly minted. 'You Better Believe What I Say', credited to Jimmy Reed, is a performance of considerable authority, however, done in an ominous, Hopkins-echoing style. Holeman also finds new facets to three more songs credited to Reed (but not many on 'Baby, You Don't Have To Go'), and he puts unexpected passion into 'I

Don't Care Where You Go', his version of Muddy Waters's reading of 'Worried Life Blues'.

Bull Durham Blues is the best of the bunch, although Taj Mahal's contribution is valuable only on 'Chapel Hill Boogie', where he plays guitar; his piano on 'Mistreated Blues' is good, but overwhelms the guitar, his bass on 'Sweet Home Chicago' is far too loud, and his contribution to 'Hambone' is inaudible. This is much the best recorded of the CDs under discussion, and Holeman sounds energized and enthusiastic. He demonstrates again that he is one of the few musicians to be inspired by Jimmy Reed's music, rather than merely impressed by its popularity; 'Big Boss Man' artfully combines Reed's four-in-a-bar lope with raggy Piedmont guitar figures. That song is one of several which are recycled favourites, making a second – or, in the case of 'Little Country Gal', a third – appearance on CD, but superior sound quality makes the *Bull Durham Blues* versions preferable in all cases. Holeman also explores some of the Piedmont standards which are surprisingly absent from the earlier discs, turning in good versions of 'Step It Up And Go' and 'Crow Jane', and he achieves a remarkable synthesis of bluegrass vocals and blues guitar on Lester Flatt's 'God Loves His Children'. CS

Hollywood All Stars
GROUP

From the late '70s to the mid-'90s the Hollywood All Stars were the premier bar band in and around the north Memphis suburb from which they took their name, and although the band no longer exists some of its members, such as 'Boogie Man' Hubbard (born 1931) and Donald Valentine (born 1964), continue to play in Memphis clubs.

**(*) Hard Hitting Blues From Memphis
High Water HMG 6518 *Charles Campbell (as, ts); Gilmore Daniel (as, v); William 'Boogie Man' Hubbard (o, p); Bobby Carnes (p); Ben Wilson (g, v); Clarence Nelson (g); Calvin Valentine (b); Donald Valentine (d). 9/83–12/86.*

This is about as hard hitting as a toddler throwing snowballs, but that isn't a fault. One would guess that the audience for a blues band in a Memphis suburb 20 years ago was, like the band itself, predominantly middle-aged, and that the mostly somnolent tempos and relaxed delivery of the music were entirely appropriate as a background to unhurried conversations and a setting for unstrenuous dancing. Ben Wilson (born 1938) is the main singer, good in an undemonstrative way on B. B. King's 'Gambler's Blues' and Freddy King's 'It's Too Bad' ('… things are going so tough'), a little more spirited on Muddy Waters's 'Mannish Boy'; he also contributes a couple of archaic solo pieces, 'Going 'Cross The Bottom' and 'That's My Woman'. This is an expanded reissue of the band's only LP, produced by local academic and blues promoter David Evans in 1987. TR

Hollywood Blue Flames
GROUP

Hollywood Fats's band, almost 20 years on, with Kirk Eli Fletcher stepping into the guitarist's shoes.

**(*) Soul Sanctuary
Delta Groove DGPCD 102 *Al Blake (h, g, v); Kim Wilson (h);* *Fred Kaplan (o, p); Kirk Eli Fletcher (g); Larry Taylor (b); Richard Innes (d). 05.*

Al Blake neatly updates Jimmy Oden's 'Soon Forgotten', changing 'Give me a pencil and paper' to 'Give me a calculator'. Most of the other 12 tracks are originals, some a little formulaic but others, such as 'Black Cat Bone' and 'My National Inquirer [*sic*] Baby', written with flashes of wit or ingenuity. Songs and performances alike are impeccably idiomatic, but there are quite a few bands around today who can bring off that trick, and a group with the pedigree of the Hollywood Blue Flames should go one step further, achieving individuality as well as authenticity. That said, this is an enjoyable session of determinedly retro music, culminating in a relaxed acoustic duet by Blake and Kim Wilson on 'You're Sweet'. TR

Hollywood Fats (1954–86)
GUITAR

As a teenaged blues fan in LA in the '60s the prodigiously talented Michael Mann worked his way up to playing with Jimmy Witherspoon and Muddy Waters. When not on the road, he played with Al Blake and Fred Kaplan, who became the core of the Hollywood Fats Band that cut its sole album, Rock This House, *in 1979. After a few years with James Harman and The Blasters, Fats succumbed to heroin. His band has reconvened as the Hollywood Blue Flames.*

*** Hollywood Fats Band
Crosscut CCD 21069 2CD *Hollywood Fats; Al Blake (h, v); Fred Kaplan (p); Larry Taylor (b); Richard Innes (d). 79.*

Present-day actors in the theatre of West Coast blues, such as Kid Ramos or Kirk Fletcher, are watched from the wings by the tubby, moustachio'd ghost of Hollywood Fats, a musician some of them are too young to have seen in person, though they know his work from *Rock This House*. The original album, which has been reissued several times and may still be available on Aim 1035, accounts for Disc 1 of the Crosscut set. Fats's playing is quite impressive, but the listener meeting him for the first time with 25 years' hindsight may reflect that there are at least half a dozen players working along similar lines today who have progressed further; Fats's reading of 'Okie Dokie Stomp', for instance, seems rhythmically very square. But the outtakes and such that make up Disc 2 broaden the picture of his skills, revealing more of a guitarist who confidently straddled the blues styles of California and Chicago and a band that rode pillion with equal assurance. TR

Rick 'L.A. Holmes' Holmstrom
(born 1965)
VOCAL, GUITAR

Holmstrom grew up in Alaska and moved to Redlands, California, at 18. He began playing music with friends in the mid-'80s, then joined William Clarke and, in 1991, Johnny Dyer. More recently he has put in several years with Rod Piazza's Mighty Flyers. He is a great admirer of Junior Watson and has recorded with him, as well as with Clarke, Dyer, Piazza, Smokey Wilson and others.

**(*) Gonna Get Wild
Tone-Cool 1176 *Holmstrom; Kad Kadison, Red Naugahyde, Steve*

Marsh (ts); Jeff 'Big Dad' Turmes (bs, b, v); Johnny Dyer (h, v); Rod Piazza (h); John 'Juke' Logan (o); Honey Piazza, Andy Kaulkin (p); Junior Watson (g, b); Marco Fiume, Henry Carvajal (g); Bill Stuve (b); Steve Mugalian (d, rb, v); Chris Hunter (tamb, handclaps, v); Teddy Morgan, Bobby Horton (handclaps, v); Poppy Atkins, Curtis Cunningham (v). 00?

**(*) Hydraulic Groove
Tone-Cool 51134//Cooking Vinyl BLEUCD 003 *Holmstrom; Ronald Dziubla (ts, bs); Jeff Turmes (bs, b); Genome (kb, o, p, cel, perc, remix); John Medeski (o); Dale Jennings (b); Steve Mugalian, Donny Gruendler (d, perc); Stephen Hodges, Iki Levy (perc); Donny Gerrard (v); Johnny Dyer (sp); Robert Ward, Rufus Thomas (sample); DJ Logic (remix). 02.*

Holmstrom is a guitarist with oldfashioned virtues. He doesn't care to play particularly loud, preferring to concentrate on tone. He admires succinctness: 'I like those old songs where there's just one solo, and it's 12 bars or maybe 24, … quick and out.' He works in an essentially West Coast tradition, acknowledging forerunners like T-Bone Walker, Pee Wee Crayton and Junior Watson, but he is not limited by it.

On his 1996 debut album, *Lookout!* (Black Top CD BT-1125, deleted), he was not confident enough in his voice to record any vocals. By the time he came to cut *Gonna Get Wild* he had got over that, and, while he won't win any awards with his singing, it does at least have an unpretentious casualness. An unlisted track 13 is a slow and easy tune along the lines of 'After Hours'. This is a likeable album but, if Holmstrom had looked more widely for material than in his own notebooks, it might have been something more.

Hydraulic Groove is something else. Holmstrom's evident aim was to give blues some textural variety by using compositional elements of modern dance music and hip-hop, most explicitly in 'These Roads', 'Knock Yourself Out' and the two versions of 'Shake It, Part 2', which are layered by the use of sampling, panning, dropouts and other techniques. Other pieces may have nothing more outré than a prominent percussion track or Martian keyboard effects. It's all quite cleverly done, but the album's flights of invention are thwarted by earthbound material. TR

Nick Holt (born 1940)
VOCAL, BASS

Holt is Magic Slim's brother, and has been a mainstay of The Teardrops since 1960.

**(*) You Better Watch Yourself
Wolf 120.883 *Holt; Eddie Shaw (ts); Chris Sandera (h); Magic Slim, John Primer (g, v); Earl Howell (d). 2/89–6/95.*

When The Teardrops play live, Nick Holt is an occasional singer; this CD puts him front and centre at greater length. Compiled from songs recorded over six years, *You Better Watch Yourself* lacks coherence, seeming to exist only because a CD's worth of material has accumulated. In some cases, an additional take would have been beneficial; in nearly all cases, the drummer is too prominent in the mix. On four tracks, Eddie Shaw's tenor is powerful but also supportive and tactful, unlike Chris Sandera's grandstanding harmonica work elsewhere. Holt's voice is as big as his physique, but he sometimes makes abrupt and arbitrary changes of level. By his own admission, Holt sometimes finds it difficult to coordinate his singing and his bass playing, and he can be heard coming adrift from the band on 'When You Got A Headache'. Between them, this track and its successor, a magnificent live version of 'As The Years Go Passing By', neatly encapsulate the disc's inconsistencies. CS

Scott Holt (born 1966)
VOCAL, GUITAR

Not long after he started playing guitar, the Tennessee-born Holt determined that his was a blues pathway. In 1987 he met and befriended Buddy Guy, who gave him lessons and soon invited him to sit in on jam sessions at his Chicago club Legends. In 1989 Holt joined Guy's band, where he remained for a decade until deciding to form his own group in 1999.

*** Chipped Front Tooth
Gracetone 54617 *Holt; Tab Benoit (ac, psg, v); Gene Haffner (kb); Richard Sanders (b); Marshal Weaver (d); Janet Kenyon (v). 03.*

Holt explains of this record's ethos, 'Sometimes it's the little imperfections that make something more beautiful,' which is why it was almost entirely recorded in one day in the middle of a tour. Even so, it maintains a standard of reliable, quality musicianship that barely reveals a hiccup unless you're listening doubly hard for one. Holt co-writes half the material with Richard Fleming, the other songs being borrowed from established blues artists like Howlin' Wolf and Willie Mabon, whose 'I Don't Know' is treated with Holt's heartfelt Southern-accented voice and spider-web knowledge of the fretboard. 'One Day Away' is pretty, romantic and gospel-tinged, country music seeps through 'If I Could', and in Sugar Pie DeSanto's 'Moanin' For You Girl' Holt's funky wah guitar practically makes the gurning goldfish-mouth expressions for you. All in all Holt sits comfortably in his blues-twigged nest, but as yet shows no promise of threatening life-forms on the upper branches of the genre. RR

Roosevelt Holts (1905–94)
VOCAL, GUITAR

Holts started playing guitar in 1930, and spent some time working with Tommy Johnson, who was married to his cousin. He was 60 before he recorded, sought out by researchers interested in the Johnson connection, but was still a vigorous musician with a broad repertoire.

*** The Franklinton Muscatel Society
Blue Moon CDBM 091 *Holts; Herlin Holts (h); L. V. Conerley (g). 8/65–3/69.*

This CD begins with songs from Holts's first recording session, and he sounds slightly tentative, but rapidly becomes much more forceful and authoritative. Holts went on to make superior versions of 'Big Road Blues' and 'Maggie Campbell Blues', but those included here are still worthwhile; 'Maggie Campbell' is one of three tracks featuring strong guitar interplay with L. V. Conerley, who also appears solo, singing two spirituals. Holts's association with Tommy Johnson has always loomed large in estimations of his importance, but this disc usefully shows him ranging further afield; the instrumentals 'Corina' and 'Burke Holmes' Piece' come from the days when black music was making the transition from reels to blues, and Holts also recalls a number of hits from the '30s and '40s, sometimes with effective support from his brother's harmonica. A number of LPs which contained better performances have yet to appear on CD, but *The Franklinton Muscatel Society* is a good portrait of a considerable musician. CS

Home Cookin' Featuring Brenda Boykin
GROUP

Based in the San Francisco/Oakland area, Home Cookin' is augmented for recording sessions, but the core lineup is Boykin plus guitar, bass and drums, performing an eclectic mix of R&B, blues, soul and country music.

*** Home Cookin'
Blue Dot BDR CD102 *Jim Pugh (p); Anthony Paule (g); Tim Wagar (b); Tyler Eng (d); Ellen Peters (tamb, v); Brenda Boykin; Christine Vitale (v).* 97.

Home Cookin's debut CD is mostly cover versions, but it begins with one of three compositions by Boykin. 'Ila Mae' is a splendid, raunchy number, reminiscent of Ruth Brown on Atlantic, until Paule's guitar solo, which seems determined to stress that the band's instrumentation is the same as Led Zeppelin's. This is followed by 'Lover Please', done in a chaotically fussy version of Professor Longhair's style. Happily, the disc improves enormously after this unpromising start, and establishes that Home Cookin' can pick good songs and give them original treatments. 'Don't You Lie To Me' and Jimmy Reed's 'Aw Shucks, Hush Your Mouth' are both cleverly rescued from predictability by the catchy stop-time shuffle of Rosco Gordon's 'Just A Little Bit', Jimmie Rodgers's 'T For Texas', done slow, black and yodel-free, and the Fats Domino hit 'What A Price', accompanied only by acoustic guitar, are even more radically reinvigorated. Equally, Home Cookin' know when to leave well alone; Mary Lou Williams's 'Little Joe From Chicago' and 'That's Alright Mama', in the Elvis, Scotty and Bill arrangement, are advertisements for the band's versatility and – in not trying to improve the unimprovable – their good taste. Also successfully covered are Ivory Joe Hunter, Ike Turner, Little Walter and Jim Reeves (!) on a distaff reworking of '(S)he'll Have To Go'. It's all great fun, provided one starts at track 3.

*** Afrobilly Soul Stew
Blue Dot BDR CD103 *Charles McNeal (ts); Jim Pugh (o, p); Anthony Paule (g, perc, v); Tim Wagar (b, perc); Tyler Eng (d, perc, v); Brenda Boykin; Calvin Tillery, Glen Walters (v).* 99.

Boykin's songwriting accounts for eight of the 14 tracks on *Afrobilly Soul Stew*, and despite her accurate enough description of the band's music as a blend of rock 'n' roll, blues, country, jazz and gospel, her own writing leans heavily towards straight-ahead blues. She's a good writer; the slinky 'Mary Anne (Just Plain Mary Anne)' is a classic tribute to a man-stealer, and 'Brick House In Memphis' showcases her authoritative way with a slow blues. Elsewhere, eclecticism continues to be the rule, with Presley, Buck Owens ('Crying Time') and Slim Harpo all raided successfully. 'My Babe' is, for once, not Willie Dixon's cliché-fest but the Righteous Brothers' soul rave-up, and 'Chains' gets a long, slow and intense workout that miraculously owes nothing to the Beatles' version. The closing 'Rivers Of Babylon' disappoints, for Home Cookin' can't find a way to make it new, and 'Zydeco Gumbo' has been put through the blender, to emerge as baby food for musical tourists. As with the previous disc, however, a couple of failures can be discounted against the success of the rest. CS

Homesick James (born 1910 or 1914?)
VOCAL, GUITAR

Though often given the proper name James Williamson, he was born John William Henderson in Somerville, Tennessee. His mother Mary was a slide guitarist. A mercurial guide to his own past – David Whiteis calls him a 'weaver of myths, self-creator par excellence' – he has claimed birthdates in 1910 and 1914, while the files of the Chicago Local 208 of the AFM give 1924. He is thought to have arrived in Chicago in the '30s or '40s, where he had a steel-mill job, but continued to go south for musical work, playing with Sleepy John Estes and Sonny Boy Williamson I. He claimed to have recorded with Little Buddy Doyle in Memphis in 1939, but his first certified recordings were in 1952 for Chance. He played with Elmore James, his cousin, on and off from 1954 until Elmore's death. Since the late '90s he has been a member of the Delta Blues Cartel.

**(*) Chicago Slide Guitar Legend
Official 5253 *Homesick James; Donald Hankins (bs); Snooky Pryor (h); Lazy Bill Lucas, Lafayette Leake, Sunnyland Slim, Willie Mabon (p); Johnny Shines, Evans Spencer (g); Alfred Elkins, Hound Dog Taylor, Milton Rector, Willie Dixon (b); Willie Knowling, Clifton James, unknown (d); Washboard Sam (wb).* 6/52–71.

Fifteen of these 26 tracks are Homesick's 1952–53 recordings for Chance. Most of them were not issued at the time, and one can guess why: they are often disorganized, the musicians' tuning is sometimes amiss, and Homesick shows a Hookeresque uninterest in structural convention and rhyme. The best of them are with Pryor and the impetuous Lazy Bill Lucas. The remainder of the CD is singles for USA, Colt and Bea & Baby (the last also available on *Meat & Gravy From Bea & Baby* [Castle CMDDD 610 2CD]) and odd tracks from compilations. The USA recording of 'Crossroads', which had a brave air of Elmore James about both the vocal and the slide playing, caused some interest at the time and remains one of his most coordinated performances.

** Blues On The South Side
Original Blues Classics OBCCD 529 *Homesick James; Lafayette Leake (p); Lee Jackson (b); Clifton James (d).* 1/64.

Elmore James's death in 1963 left his cousin with the opportunity to replicate his music for the new, international blues audience. No one was better placed to do it; whether no one was better equipped is another matter. Pete Welding in his notes to *Blues On The South Side* implies that Homesick's slide guitar playing closely resembles Elmore's, calling it 'impassioned, ululant'. In fact it is neither: his sound is curiously veiled, and he seldom ventures upon Elmore's darting forays up the fretboard. 'The Cloud Is Crying' is a sketched copy of Elmore's 'The Sky Is Crying' but with Leake sitting out it lacks the colour of the original's storm-filled canvas. His singing is somewhat closer to his cousin's, but is not shown to advantage in a stiff rendering of Robert Johnson's 'Stones In My Passway'. 'The Woman I'm Lovin'' disappears abruptly just past the two-minute mark, as does 'Crawlin'', played over the 'After Hours' riff on bass.

The following year Homesick contributed four songs to *Chicago/The Blues/Today! Vol. 2* (Vanguard VMD 79217), reissued on *Chicago/The Blues/Today!* (Vanguard 172/74 3CD).

*** The Big Bear Sessions
Castle CMDDD 712//Sanctuary CAS 36075 2CD *Homesick James; Snooky Pryor (h); Bob Hall (p); Martin Stone (g); Roger 'Trigger' Hill, Bob Brunning, Harvey Weston, Jimmie Lee Robinson (b); Uncle Tom Farnell, John Hunt, Pete York (d). 2/73–10/75.*

*** Sad And Lonesome
Wolf 120.409 *Homesick James; Snooky Pryor (h). 10/79.*

Homesick's British tours with Snooky Pryor in the '70s produced a number of recordings, both live and in the studio, for the Big Bear label, which are tidily collected on *The Big Bear Sessions* (together with Pryor's recordings of the time, which are not all with Homesick). Some of Homesick's best recorded work is here, ranging from powerful solos with acoustic slide guitar, such as 'Homesick's Original Dust My Broom', to driving band tracks with electric slide, the reliable Pryor and supportive piano by Bob Hall. *Sad And Lonesome*, recorded in Vienna during a later European tour, is an acoustic duet set by Homesick and Pryor, Homesick singing eight numbers and Pryor five. The bare setting cannot help exposing the untidiness of Homesick's music, but the two men work so well together that the album is very likeable.

*** Goin' Back In The Times
Earwig CD 4929 *Homesick James; David 'Honeyboy' Edwards (g). 8/92.*

Homesick's only solo album – or nearly solo: Edwards plays second guitar on four tracks (three identified plus 'Kissing In The Dark'). Casting his mind back, he recalls old running buddies like Yank Rachell and Big Joe Williams, and old songs like 'Kissing In The Dark' and the 'Rollin' And Tumblin'' riff he uses for 'Bitin' Me And Shakin' Me All Up And Down'. The Elmore connection, for once, is ignored: he plays slide on only one number, Lightnin' Hopkins's 'Rocky Mountain', and there he sounds more like the young Muddy Waters. Elsewhere he accompanies himself with quiet chords and modest single-string lines that perfectly match the ruminative mood of the occasion. Now and then the nostalgic references seem a little forced, the mantle of memorialist a little too self-consciously worn – 'I'm still alive today, carryin' these traditions all alone,' he boasts in the title track – but other reflections seem to stem from deeper or more private memories. 'When you run from town to town, better know just what you're runnin' from,' he sings. ''Cause you may be runnin' [from] the same thing your daddy just come from.'

** Sweet Home Tennessee
Appaloosa AP 073 *Homesick James; Billy C. Farlow, Rags Murtagh (h); Richard Flemming, Walter Ferguson (p); Casey Lutton, Fred James, Bleu Jackson (g); Doug Cook (b); Waldo LaTowsky, Doug James (d). 7/91.*

** Juanita
Evidence ECD 26085 *Homesick James; Fred James, David 'Guitar' Jones (g); Casey Lutton (b); Jim Karstein (d). 2/93.*

**(*) Got To Move
[32 Blues 32175] *Homesick James; Jeff Levine (p); Ron Thompson (g); Joe Rosato (b); Chris Millar (d). 2/94.*

**(*) The Last Of The Broomdusters
Fedora FCD 5006 *Homesick James; Ron Thompson (o, g); Jeff Henry (b); Chris Millar (d). 12/97.*

Whichever birthdate one trusts, these '90s albums are the work of an elderly man and might be expected to chart a decline in his powers, but if anything the reverse is true: *The Last Of The Broomdusters* has more vitality than *Sweet Home Tennessee* and *Juanita*, made four to six years earlier. *Tennessee* and *Juanita*, both produced by Fred James, give Homesick the opportunity to revisit his back catalogue, the former including remakes of 'Can't Afford To Do It' and 'Woman I Love' and the latter of 'Lonesome Ol' Train' (his debut single) and Elmore's 'I Can't Hold Out'. Both sets also have standards like 'Come Back Baby' (*Tennessee*), 'Someday Baby' and 'Careless Love' (*Juanita*), to which he adds nothing: dull albums and, in the case of *Juanita*, almost soporific. *Got To Move*'s Elmoresque gestures are 'Dust My Broom' and 'Hawaiian Boogie', while its standards include 'That's All Right', which uses the tune and opening figures (played, for him, fairly well) of Muddy's 'I Can't Be Satisfied', and 'Highway 51', enlivened by Millar's martial drumming. Unexpectedly, there are a couple of solo performances of Blind Boy Fuller songs, 'Three Ball Blues' and 'Lost Lover Blues', his singing of the latter fragile and private. Thompson stiffens the music's sinews on the band tracks, but the effect is marred by the album having been mastered at a low level.

Homesick's slide playing, unassertive and often awkward on those sets, has more attack and edge on *The Last Of The Broomdusters*, and there are moments, as in 'Shake Your Money Maker' or 'Truck Drivin' Woman' (an original, not the country song), when the spirit of Elmore is present as something more than a wraith. Again, Thompson's prodding guitar lines improve the muscle tone of the music, notably in 'Kissin' In The Dark' and 'Crutch And Cane'. Homesick's singing, as often elsewhere, drifts between indistinct and barely comprehensible.

** My Home Ain't Here
Fedora FCD 5053 *Homesick James; John Long (g); Chris Millar (d, prod). 4/04.*

Six and a half years after *The Last Of The Broomdusters* Homesick is still up to making a record, and indeed polished off these ten tracks in an evening. Producer Chris Millar draws the listener's attention to the backup guitarist, John Long, an old friend and accompanist of Homesick, commending his ability to play the 'Eddie Taylor style bass patterns' that Homesick likes for an underpinning. It was worth saying, because the listener might otherwise wonder why Long so rigorously restricts himself to a fuzzy marking of the beat and the chord changes. It isn't pretty but it does have the desired effect of eliciting a performance by the leader that is probably as controlled as can be expected at this point. Nevertheless there is no hiding the frailty of his voice or the cautiousness of his playing, and only 'Please Set A Date' and 'Crossroads' give much of an impression of his former powers. TR

The Hoodoo Kings
GROUP

Biographical details of Raful Neal and Tabby Thomas will be found in their own entries. Eddie Bo (Edwin J. Bocage, born

1930) *has recorded in a variety of styles since 1955, and has worked as a producer for New Orleans record companies.*

** The Hoodoo Kings
Telarc CD-83532 *Raful Neal (h, v); Eddie Bo (o, p, v); Rockin' Tabby Thomas (g, v); Greg Hoover, Denny Breau (g); Dan Corbett (b); Darren Thiboutot (d); Kelly Jones (v).* 10/00.

Eddie Bo's recording career under his own name has been extensive, but erratic in quality; readers may wish to investigate *Check Mr. Popeye* (Rounder 2077), drawn from his late '50s and early '60s singles for Ric, or 1995's *New Orleans Solo Piano* (Night Train NTI 7025). While neither CD is essential, they are certainly more worthwhile than this cynical marketing exercise, which blends elements of once vigorous local traditions into a musical lowest common denominator that can be peddled under a New Orleans brand name. Neal and Thomas are both past it as vocalists, and don't venture beyond the basics on their instruments; Bo is more vigorous and able in both departments, but sounds restrained and uncomfortable much of the time. The backing musicians are stodgily efficient. It's an achievement, if not an admirable one, to confer generic anonymity on material as strong as the Mardi Gras anthem 'Big Chief', Clifton Chenier's 'If I Get Lucky' and Neal's murder blues 'Luberta'. CS

Earl Hooker (1930–70)
GUITAR, VOCAL

A musician who inspired the highest esteem among his contemporaries, Hooker had a mercurial personality that informed his eclectic and technically superior guitar style. But his restless and self-absorbed character constantly contrived to thwart the development of a substantial career. Much of the repertoire on which his reputation rests was recorded for small independent labels whose poor distribution likewise prevented large-scale success. He suffered from tuberculosis from childhood, and the relentless progress of the disease during his final year was at fatal odds with the flurry of touring and recording activity in which he participated. Despite the excessive critical glow it sometimes acquires, Hooker's career remains a succès d'estime whose merit exceeds a large percentage of the available evidence.

***(*) Blue Guitar
Paula PCD-18 *Hooker; Julian Beasley (as); A. C. Reed (ts, v); Jarrett Gibson (ts); Donald Hankins, Jackie Brenston (bs); Junior Wells (h, v); Johnny 'Big Moose' Walker (o, p); Tall Paul Hankins (p); Lacy Gibson, Reggie Boyd (g); Earnest Johnson, Jack Meyers (b); Harold Tidwell (d, v); Fred Below, Billie Stepney, Bobby Little, Casey Jones (d); Lillian Offitt, The Earlettes (v).* 60–62.

Few producers seemed capable of directing Hooker in the studio but Mel London, owner of the Chief and Age labels from which these titles are drawn, was a notable exception. Like Hooker, London was an ideas man who worked the singles market and for a while Hooker and Junior Wells were his prime candidates. Their first collaboration, 'Calling All Blues', an atmospheric instrumental issued as by Elmore James, inspired further outings, including 'Galloping Horses A Lazy Mule', 'Blues In D Natural' and 'Universal Rock'. 'D Natural' recasts 'Everyday I Have The Blues' and highlights Hooker's smoothly integrated slide and finger-style playing, while 'Rock' is a lightly disguised 'Got My Mojo Working'.

There's more in this vein, including 'Rocking With The Kid', 'These Cotton Pickin' Blues' and, most striking of all, 'Blue Guitar', a memorable adaptation of 'Rock Me Baby'. 'Will My Man Be Home Tonight' and 'Oh Mama' from Hooker's first session for London are sung by Lillian Offitt, while female duo The Earlettes perform on 'Win The Dance' and 'That Man', and two instrumentals by organist Walker, 'Off The Hook' and 'The Bright Sound', are also included. With a few worthy but mundane exceptions, Hooker's work with London provides the solid basis for much of his subsequent reputation.

**(*) Smooth Sliding
[Blue Boar CDBB 1006] *As above, except add Bobby Fields, unknown (ts), unknown (o), Fred Roulette (esg), unknown (g), unknown (b), Muddy Waters Jr, Little Tommy, Frank 'Crying Shame' Clark (v).* 60–68.

With the demise of Mel London's operation, Hooker made an arrangement with Jim Kirchstein of Cuca Records in Sauk City, Wisconsin, whereby he could indulge his urge to play during a series of all-night sessions. Two albums from these dates have been released but the better one, *Play Your Guitar, Mr Hooker* (Black Top CDBT-1093), is no longer available. *Smooth Sliding* (which is substantially similar to the deleted *There's A Fungus Amung Us* [Catfish KATCD 134]) is less discriminating, consisting largely of instrumental excursions that often outlast their effectiveness. With the exception of 'Hold On (I'm Coming)', 'Dust My Broom' and 'Something You Got' (here shown as 'Something You Ate'), all are written by Hooker. Titles like 'Hooker Special', 'The Foxtrot' and 'End Of The Blues' are as arbitrary as the efforts of players who'd travelled over a hundred miles in the middle of the night for the privilege. Hooker is never short of invention but an absence of form and direction in his playing signals what the presence of a producer might have provided, making this a less attractive proposition than the previous compilation. The CD also includes six Mel London-produced titles from *Blue Guitar*.

***(*) Two Bugs And A Roach
Arhoolie CD 324 *Hooker; Carey Bell (h, v); Louis Myers, Little Sam Davis (h); Joe Willie Perkins (o, p); Steve Miller (p); Fred Roulette (esg); Geno Skaggs (b); Willie Nix, Willie Williams, Levi Warren, Bobby Johnson, 'Tony' (d); Andrew 'B. B. Jr' Odom (v).* 52–53, 7/69.

This is perhaps the best example of late-period Hooker, though not without its *longueurs*. For the most part cut in Chicago with then current band members, it finds Hooker at his most relaxed, largely devoid of the freneticism that could creep into his playing. He sings 'Anna Lee' and 'You Don't Want Me'. The former and an instrumental 'New Sweet Black Angel' contain his best exhibitions of the limpid slide technique he learned from Robert Nighthawk. Odom lives up to his nickname, forcing spurious emotion into 'You Don't Love Me', while a young Carey Bell lacks coherence as he delivers 'Love Ain't A Plaything'. The title track sports a 'Say Man' routine between Hooker and Odom, referring in part to the TB that had kept Hooker off the road the previous year. 'Wah Wah Blues' and 'Earl Hooker Blues' indulge the newly fashionable device he'd adopted during his incapacitation, although its use demonstrably inhibits rather than enhances his improvisations. Most telling of the instrumentals is 'Off

The Hook', which here becomes a jazz-inflected compendium of tasteful playing.

The concluding tracks come from the start of his recording career, 'Sweet Black Angel' deriving from a 1952 Florida session for Rockin', 'Guitar Rag', 'I'm Going Down The Line' and 'Earl's Boogie Woogie' from a 1953 session for Sun in Memphis. Despite cruder recording methods, it's obvious that Hooker's technique was already in place and that he progressed little in the intervening years. It also underlines, for all his ongoing interest in fresh material and technology, how much he relied upon a bedrock repertoire.

*** The Moon Is Rising
Arhoolie CD 468 *Hooker; Louis Myers, Carey Bell (h); Steve Miller (o, p); Pinetop Perkins (p); Freddie Roulette (esg); Eddie Taylor (g); Geno Skaggs (b, v); Dave Myers (b); Bobby Johnson, Levi Warren, Willie Williams, Arthur 'Dogman' Jackson (d); Andrew Odom (v). 11/68–9/69.*

Somewhat less than more of the same. Built around the original album *Hooker And Steve*, this collection gathers up the remaining fragments from previous sessions plus live recordings from Pepper's Lounge in Chicago. The nine tracks are largely vehicles for improvisation and neither Hooker nor Miller is short of inspiration, but each tune's lack of formal structure cripples any notion of solid achievement. Even so, this is superior to anything from the Bluesway sessions that surrounded it. Hooker sings the title track and 'Conversion Blues' (actually 'Swear To Tell The Truth' in light disguise). Skaggs sings 'I'm Your Main Man', which would have remained in the ether if Slim Harpo hadn't written 'I'm A King Bee'. 'Little Carey's Jump' allows Bell to recycle his favourite Little Walter riffs, while Odom's repetitive 'Take Me Back To East St. Louis' is the weakest song present. The final quartet of live recordings constitutes more than half an hour's playing time but once again the effortless parade of virtuosity, while superior to much of what could be heard in Chicago at the time, is enjoyable but curiously numbing. Great musicians are expected to come up with great moments but Hooker settles for a smooth transition from one riff to the next. What ought to resemble mountain climbing becomes a weightless float in the Dead Sea.

**(*) Sweet Black Angel
[One Way MCAD 22120] *Hooker; unknown (t); unknown (tb); unknown (ts); Little Mack Simmons (h, sp); Ike Turner (p); unknown (b); poss. Soko Richardson (d). 5/69.*

*** Simply The Best
MCA MCAD-11811 *Hooker; A. C. Reed, Otis Hale, Red Holloway (ts); Donald Hankins (bs); Sonny Terry (h, v); Jeff Caro (h); Johnny 'Big Moose' Walker (o, v); Ike Turner (p, g); Charles Brown (p, v); Lafayette Leake, Ray Johnson (p); John Lee Hooker (g, v); Brownie McGhee, Paul Asbell, Mel Brown (g); Earnest Johnson, Geno Skaggs, Jesse Knight, Jimmy Bond (b); Bobby Little, Frank Swan, Roosevelt Shaw, Soko Richardson, Panama Francis, Paul Humphrey, Ed Thigpen (d); Muddy Waters, Andrew Odom (v). 56–62, 5–9/69.*

The idea of *Simply The Best* is good but the realization falters somewhat short of the title's promise. All but six of the 19 tracks are drawn from sessions Hooker cut in LA for Bluesway during the summer of 1969. His own and his cousin John Lee's albums were cut the same day and others by Brownie McGhee & Sonny Terry, Johnny 'Big Moose' Walker,

Andrew 'Voice' Odom and Charles Brown were made under similar constraints. Three tracks, 'Drivin' Wheel', 'Sweet Home Chicago' (with a rare Hooker vocal) and 'Sweet Black Angel' come from the Blue Thumb album *Sweet Black Angel*, made with Ike Turner immediately prior to the Bluesway sessions. 'You Shook Me' is Hooker's 'Blue Guitar' used as a backing track for Muddy Waters's vocal, one of several leased or purchased from Mel London. A pleasant but inconsequential 'Frog Hop' is one side of a 1956 Argo single (its B side, 'Guitar Rumba', by some unfathomable logic appeared on *Chess Blues Guitar 1949–69* [MCA/Chess CHD2–9393//(E) MCD 09393]), while 'Tanya' comes from a 1962 Checker single. This latter has been remixed from the original four-track tape but the compilers ignored the chance to mix two further unissued tracks from the session.

The Blue Thumb titles succeed despite Hooker's ongoing wah-wah fetish and the producers' determination that none should last three minutes. Lack of preparation and insufficient studio time hamper all the Bluesway titles; professionalism carries the day – just. Hooker's own 'Don't Have To Worry' is one exception, an extended and meditative version of Charles Brown's 'Drifting Blues' another. Two tracks from John Lee Hooker's album are indecisive studio jams, while others by McGhee & Terry, Walker and Odom have moments of coherence without once implying that anyone has their eye on posterity. The packaging plays the 'legendary' card as if it was an ace but no collection can call itself 'the best' without containing the requisite evidence.

Sweet Black Angel has also been reissued in its 28-minute entirety. Despite the ease with which Hooker and Turner collaborate, titles such as 'Shuffle', 'Country And Western', 'The Mood' and 'Funky Blues' make plain the transitory nature of the session and the music made. Both CDs are of uncertain availability. NS

John Lee Hooker (1917?–2001)
VOCAL, GUITAR

Hooker was born in Clarksdale, Mississippi, where he learned something about the guitar from his stepfather Willie Moore. After spells in Memphis and Cincinnati he settled in the mid-'40s in Detroit. Between 1948 and 1952 he recorded hundreds of sides, issued on many labels, and was one of the most visible and influential figures of the period. Thereafter his discography was more straightforward, and in 1955 he settled into a nine-year association with Vee-Jay which yielded his best-selling songs, 'Boom Boom' and 'Dimples'. His response to the challenge of rock 'n' roll was first to remake himself as a 'folk blues' artist, playing acoustic guitar, then to plug in again and equip himself with backing bands, a strategy that enabled him to surf the waves of musical change until the mid-'70s, when he seemed to subside into near-retirement. His triumphant return to major-league blues in 1988 with The Healer *established him on the international stage for the rest of his life. As well as keeping up a regime of personal appearances and albums, he achieved a fame unprecedented in the blues through collaborations with rock personalities like Van Morrison, contributions to movie soundtracks and appearances in TV ads.*

Hooker's recordings in the late '40s and early '50s have been issued over and over, officially and unofficially, coherently and randomly. Since it's impossible to work through them in strict chronological order, they are discussed in groups according to their original labels, and the narrative necessarily jumps forwards and backwards in time.

**** **Graveyard Blues**
Specialty SPCD-7018//Ace CDCHD 421 *Hooker; Eddie Burns (h); Andrew Dunham (g).* 11/48–4/50.

(****) **Blues Brother**
Ace CDCHD 405 *Hooker; Eddie Burns (h); prob. James Taylor (g).* 11/48–4/51.

*** **Coast To Coast Blues Band/Anywhere–Anytime–Anyplace: His Original Recordings 1948/52**
BGO BGOCD 363 *Hooker; Eddie Burns (h); Eddie Kirkland (g).* 11/48–c. 9/51.

**** **The Collection 1948–52**
EMI 93741 *Hooker; James Watkins (p).* 11/48–52.

***(*) **Alternative Boogie: Early Studio Recordings, 1948–1952**
Capitol 33912 3CD *Hooker; Eddie Burns (h); James Watkins (p); Andrew Dunham, Eddie Kirkland, unknown (g).* 11/48–52.

♛ **** **The Legendary Modern Recordings**
Ace CDCHD 315//Flair 39658 *Hooker; James Watkins, Boogie Woogie Red (p); Eddie Kirkland (g); Tom Whitehead (d).* 11/48–54.

(****) **Original Folk Blues ... Plus**
Ace CDCHM 530 *Hooker; Johnny Hooks, Otis Finch (ts); Bernie Besman (o); James Watkins, Boogie Woogie Red, Bob Thurman (p); Eddie Kirkland (g, v); unknown(s) (b); Jimmy Turner, Tom Whitehead (d); unknown (x); unknown (v).* 11/48–54.

***(*) **House Rent Boogie**
Ace CDCHD 799 *As above, except add poss. Eddie Burns (h); omit Watkins.* 11/48–54.

***(*) **Everybody's Blues**
Specialty SPCD-7035//Ace CDCHD 474 *Hooker; Johnny Hooks (ts); Eddie Kirkland (g); John Griffith, Theophilus Roosevelt (unknown instruments, prob. p and b); Tom Whitehead (d).* 4/50–10/54.

Hooker's recordings for the producer Bernie Besman, who issued some on his own Sensation label and licensed many more to Modern, were chiefly solo exercises for voice, crudely amplified guitar and stamping foot: pieces like 'Hobo Blues', 'Half A Stranger', 'I'm In The Mood' and the still stunning 'Boogie Chillen'. Often melodically negligible, these performances make their effect by incessant rhythms, piquant dissonances and an air of primitive weirdness almost unique in the blues at that relatively advanced stage in its history. Hooker's handling of amplification owes nothing to T-Bone Walker or B. B. King: for him, as for Bo Diddley, it is an enhancement or a planned distortion of the original acoustic sound, not a starting-point for a new method. Haphazard experiment, perhaps even blind chance, gives these recordings their singularity.

As well as those solo pieces, and the duets with Eddie Kirkland that are usually just more elaborate versions of the same thing, Hooker occasionally recorded with small bands, perhaps bidding for the attention of jump-blues enthusiasts: thus 'Ride 'Til I Die', 'Hug And Squeeze You' and 'Shake, Holler And Run', the last a particularly coarse, roaring, pell-mell performance that almost nudges Joe Turner's version into the lounge. Hooker needs sidemen as brazen as this to stretch him, a fact illuminated by the later Vee-Jay sessions with house rhythm sections, which are restrained and restraining.

The Legendary Modern Recordings is packed with Hooker's landmark songs – 'Boogie Chillen', 'Sally Mae', 'Hobo Blues', 'Drifting From Door To Door', 'Crawling King Snake', 'I'm In The Mood' – and if you could buy only one of these albums, this would be it.

Graveyard Blues, *Blues Brother* and part of *Everybody's Blues* were assembled from recordings made by Besman and sold to Specialty. Although the material is of similar quality to the sides licensed to Modern, Specialty did little with it: of the 64 items on the three CDs only 16 were issued in the era in which they were made. The originals must have been well kept, because the sound quality is very good, and on *Everybody's Blues* often superb. As well as many typical solo performances there are three notable duets with Eddie Burns's querulous harmonica on *Graveyard Blues*, along with an interesting revision of 'Boogie Chillen', 'Henry's Swing Club'. Oddly, *Graveyard Blues* recycles, without comment, about three quarters of *Blues Brother*, and, since the rest of the latter is on *Everybody's Blues* (except for the original 'Boogie Chillen', which is everywhere), one wonders why *Blues Brother* remains in the Ace catalogue. The remainder of *Everybody's Blues* includes several rough-cut tracks from 5/54 with a small group.

Both *Original Folk Blues ... Plus* and *Coast To Coast Blues Band* reissue LPs, the former with a few titles added, the latter not. *Original Folk Blues* was something of a hits collection, and many of the tracks are on *The Legendary Modern Recordings*. *Coast To Coast* brought to light a batch of previously unissued Besman recordings, which are not to be found on Ace, except sometimes in alternative takes. The sound is splendidly clear, but with only 14 tracks the album can't be given more than a three-star rating. In any case, it's been swallowed up by the 3CD *Alternative Boogie*, a handsomely presented (but only fitfully available) set of mostly unissued items: just 12 of the 56 tracks made it on to 78s. Among them may be found, under the title 'The Great Disaster Of 1936', a song about the dancehall conflagration that later inspired Howlin' Wolf's 'The Natchez Burning', and, as 'How Long Can This Go On', a version of Leroy Carr's 'How Long – How Long Blues'.

With five CDs from this period already in catalogue, Ace used *House Rent Boogie* to present six previously unissued tracks and others that were making their first appearance on CD. Some that are described as 'small combo recordings' have nothing more than two guitars, Hooker's and Kirkland's, sometimes interlocking, sometimes floating apart, always excitingly unpredictable; listen to the cascading figures of 'How Can You Do It' or 'It's Stormin' And Rainin''. Occasionally overdubs give us two Hooker guitars at once, and it's suggested that the overdubbed harmonica on this version of 'I'm In The Mood' is his too, which would be a first, but Eddie Burns is a likelier bet.

The Collection contains retitled alternative takes of 'Boogie Chillen', 'Crawling King Snake', 'Hobo Blues' and two or three others, plus rejected sides; much of this material was unknown until it was issued on LP in the '70s. Readers uninterested in hunting down every Hooker recording can probably let it go, but keener collectors will hardly turn their noses up at 16 consistently gripping performances in very good sound quality and at an attractive price.

*** **Detroit 1948–1949**
Savoy SVY 17078//Atlantic/Savoy 92910 *Hooker; James Watkins (p); Curtis Foster (d).* 12/48–49.

*** **Early Years: The Classic Savoy Sessions**
Metro Doubles METRDCD 532 2CD *As above, except add Eddie Kirkland (g), unknown (b), unknown (d). 12/48–49, 61.*

As well as recording for Besman, Hooker did some after-hours sessions for an early manager, Elmer Barbee. The recordings were acquired by Savoy, who issued a few of them on 78s and more, 30-odd years later, on LP. They currently occupy all of *Detroit 1948–1949* and the first disc of *Early Years*. Unsurprisingly, they are very much in the style of the early Moderns, a mixture of deliberate blues and busy boogies, mostly solo but a few in trio format. The recording quality is often fuzzy, and on the trio sides something worse, but at this stage Hooker seldom put a foot wrong, and his admirers will be glad to have these elusive sides in their entirety. The other disc in the *Early Years* set is *Sittin' Here Thinkin'*, discussed below.

(****) **Don't You Remember Me?**
King KCD 6009 *Hooker. c. 12/48–c. 8/50.*
(****) **John Lee Hooker**
Pulse PLSCD 349 *As above. c. 12/48–c. 8/50.*
(***) **Sings Blues**
Ember EMBCD 3356 *Hooker. c. 8/49–c. 8/50.*
**** **I'm A Boogie Man: The Essential Masters (1948–1953)**
Varèse Sarabande 302 066 597 *As above, except add Eddie Kirkland (g). c. 12/48–c. 8/50, 7/53.*

Joe Von Battle sold several batches of Hooker recordings to King, who issued them as by Texas Slim. Hooker is often on top form and pieces like 'Moaning Blues' and 'The Numbers', with their intricate weave of wordless vocal and scattershot guitar notes, are colossal. Most of these CDs are derived from early LP reissues and the sound quality is compromised by echo, inconsistent level and surface noise, but old hands raised on those bad old LPs may be so used to the sound that the non-musical signal has become an intrinsic part of the performances, as if Hooker recorded them during an electrical storm. Varèse Sarabande seem to have let a little light into the murk, earning our primary recommendation. They have also added three tracks from the 7/53 DeLuxe session that are not on *Don't Turn Me From Your Door* (see below). Good transfers of the 16 King sides (of which Ember choose only 12) are also to be found on Body & Soul's *Complete* volumes (see below).

*** **Jack O'Diamonds**
Eagle EAGCD 279 *Hooker. summer 49.*

An extraordinary story lies behind the release of this material. One evening in 1949, Hooker played for a small gathering of Detroit jazz fans. Film animator Gene Deitch recorded it, only to emigrate with the tapes to Prague. Fifty years later, a blues fan who remembered Deitch's cartoons in a long-dead collectors' magazine looked him up. Deitch mentioned the tapes and, at the visitor's urging, went looking for them. One turned up in his basement; the other was retrieved from a New York acquaintance to whom he'd lent it 40-odd years before. The result: an hour of the young Hooker, less than a year into his recording career, not only live (and quite well recorded) but performing material he never touched again – 'Water Boy', 'Rabbit On The Log', gospel songs like 'Old Blind Barnabus' and 'Ezekiel Saw The Wheel', and an archaic blues, 'Six Little Puppies And Twelve Shaggy Hounds' – as well as blues standards like 'Trouble In Mind' and 'Catfish Blues'.

Both the singing and the relentlessly rhythmic guitar playing evoke the Hooker of the 'Boogie Chillen' days, yet there are intriguing differences.

**** **The Complete Vol. 1**
Body & Soul 305701 2CD *Hooker; James Watkins, unknown (p); prob. J. Scarber (g); Curtis Foster (d). 6/48–2/49.*
**** **The Complete Vol. 2**
Body & Soul 306314 2CD *Hooker; Eddie Burns (h); James Watkins (p); Andrew Dunham (g); Curtis Foster (d); unknown (v). 49.*
**** **The Complete Vol. 3**
Body & Soul 306787 2CD *Hooker; James Watkins (p); Curtis Foster (d). 49–11/50.*
**** **The Complete Vol. 4**
Body & Soul 307424 2CD *Hooker; Boogie Woogie Red (p); Eddie Kirkland (g); Curtis Foster (d). 50–8/51.*

This ongoing series of 2CDs is planned to reissue Hooker's entire early work in chronological order – which entails sorting out its chronology, or at any rate making some educated guesses about it. *Vol. 1* immediately establishes its value to the serious collector by including seven gritty test pressings of recordings made before his first Modern session, and nine more that were cut over the next three or four months. (Most but not all of these were previously on *Boogie Awhile*, discussed below.) *Vol. 2* opens with five more test pressings and an obscure Danceland 78 issued as by Little Pork Chops, and also has one of the King sessions described above. *Vol. 3* and *Vol. 4* are mostly composed of Besman sessions, but *Vol. 4* interrupts them first with a dozen or so surprisingly well-recorded sides that were issued on the small Detroit labels Staff and Gotham, including a potent 'Catfish', and later with the first Chess session (see below). (The Staff/Gotham material was previously on *Gotham Golden Classics* [Collectables COL-CD-5151, probably deleted].) These sets would recommend themselves on grounds of convenience alone (if you define convenience as 'everything, and in the right order'), but they are enhanced by careful presentation and Neil Slaven's watchful notes.

(***(*)) **Boogie Awhile**
Krazy Kat KKCD 05 *Hooker; Jimmy Miller (t); Johnny Hooks (ts); James Watkins, Joe Woods (p); Curtis Foster, Tom Whitehead (d); band (v); Joe Von Battle (sp). c. 9/48–early 53.*
*** **Hommage**
Trilogie 205941 3CD *Hooker; James Watkins, Bob Thurman (p); Eddie Kirkland (g, v); poss. unknown (d). c. 9/48–7/53.*
*** **Boogie Chillen**
[Zircon Bleu 513] *Hooker; Eddie Burns (h). 11/48–c. 9/49.*
*** **Boogie Chillen 1948–1949**
EPM Blues Collection 15988 *Hooker; Eddie Burns (h); James Watkins (p); Andrew Dunham (g); Curtis Foster (d). 11/48–9/49.*
*** **The Boogie Man**
[Blue Boar CDBB 1028] *Hooker; Eddie Burns (h); Andrew Dunham (g). 11/48–49.*
***(*) **The Blues/Young and Wild 1948–1949**
Frémeaux FA 265 2CD *As above. 11/48–49.*
**** **The Classic Early Years 1948–1951**
JSP JSPCD 7703 4CD *Hooker; Eddie Burns (h); James Watkins, Boogie Woogie Red (p); Andrew Dunham, Eddie Kirkland (g); Curtis Foster (d). 11/48–c. 9/51.*

*** **A Proper Introduction To John Lee Hooker: I'm In The Mood**
Proper INTRO CD 2038 *Hooker; Eddie Kirkland (g). 11/48–52.*

*** **Blues From The Motor City**
Saga Blues 982 077–2 *Hooker; Jimmy Miller (t); Johnny Hooks (ts); Eddie Burns (h); Bernie Besman, unknown (o); Boogie Woogie Red, Joe Woods (p); Eddie Kirkland (g, v); Andrew Dunham (g); Curtis Foster, Jimmy Turner, Tom Whitehead (d). 11/48–53.*

***(*) **Too Much Boogie**
Indigo IGODCD 2542 2CD *Hooker; Johnny Hooks (ts); Bernie Besman (o); Boogie Woogie Red (p); Eddie Kirkland (g, v); Curtis Foster, Jimmy Turner, Tom Whitehead (d). 4/50–53.*

The biggest first: the slipcased sets on JSP and Trilogie contain large selections taken chiefly from Modern but also sampling JVB, Chance, Staff/Gotham, etc. Trilogie add about a dozen cuts from Chess, while JSP pick all the Kings. Trilogie offer no notes but reasonable sound and a very low price; the JSP set costs more but does have notes (again by Neil Slaven) and offers 100 tracks to Trilogie's 60, scoring a victory on points.

Frémeaux's 2CD confines itself to 1948–49 and is a very good selection. Indigo's *Too Much Boogie* starts later, carrying on from *Boogie Chillen* (Indigo IGOCD 2122, deleted). Approximately similar, though shorter, selections are efficiently provided by EPM, Proper and Saga Blues, as well as by Zircon and Blue Boar, though these two are disappearing from view. Krazy Kat's *Boogie Awhile* is mostly given over to unissued material and rarities, most of which has by now been subsumed into the Body & Soul series. Given the quality of Hooker's work in this period, all of these collections, large or small, are musically deserving, and their ratings vary only to take account of factors like presentation and value for money.

*** **The Complete 50's Chess Recordings**
MCA/Chess MCD 09391 2CD *Hooker; Jimmy Miller (t); Johnny Hooks (ts); Bob Thurman (p); unknown (cel); Eddie Kirkland, unknown (g); unknown (b); Tom Whitehead (d). 50–53/54.*

These 31 sides were mainly recorded at two sessions in 1951 and '52 and surpass much of Hooker's contemporary Modern work in the clarity of the studio sound. Musically, too, they are very fine. At the '51 session Hooker gives a gripping performance, whether brooding over magic remedies in 'Ground Hog Blues' or threatening violence with agitated foot-stomping in 'Leave My Wife Alone'. The '52 date is rather different: once past 'Walkin' The Boogie', of which a treated version, with double-tracking and overdubs, was Hooker's only hit for Chess, he settles down to ruminate over old songs such as Sonny Boy Williamson I's 'Sugar Mama' and 'Bluebird', '[Baby] Please Don't Go' and 'Worried Life Blues', interspersed with sober pieces like 'Love Blues' and 'Apologize', all played solo: excellent in their way, but not the chart-threatening singles Chess probably hoped for. Dave Sax in his notes rightly praises the recording quality of these sessions, only to be traduced by remastering that riddles much of the first disc with distortion. The second half of the second disc is a miscellany of ill-documented and crudely recorded sides later acquired by Chess, some with a raucous small band. The set absorbs the contents of *Plays & Sings The Blues* (MCA/Chess CHD-9199) and *House Of The Blues* (MCA/Chess CHD-9258), which may no longer be available, like *His Best Chess Sides* (MCA/Chess CHD-9383), which also drew on the 1966 Chess album *The Real Folk Blues* (see below).

*** **Don't Turn Me From Your Door**
Atco 82365 *Hooker; Eddie Kirkland (g, v); unknown (b). 7/53, 61.*

The bulk of this album was recorded by the Miami producer Henry Stone in 1953. On 'Misbelieving Baby' and 'I Ain't Got Nobody' (both evidently mistitled) Hooker alternates a throbbing bass with clangorous chords, creating an effect not quite replicated elsewhere. Other numbers like 'My Baby Put Me Down' are more akin to what he had lately been doing on Modern. Scattered through that sequence are four 1961 sides, also produced by Stone, that reflect a change in Hooker's method, but the clarity of the recording throughout reduces the difference.

(*) **I'm John Lee Hooker
[Collectables COL-CD-7100]//Charly SNAP 130 *Hooker; Jimmy Reed (h); Frankie Bradford, Joe Hunter (p); Eddie Taylor (g); George Washington, Quinn Wilson, Everett McCrary (b); Tom Whitehead, Richard Johnson, Earl Phillips (d). 10/55–1/59.*

*** **Testament**
Charly SNAJ 705 3CD *Hooker; Otis Finch, Hank Cosby (ts); Andrew 'Mike' Terry (bs); unknowns (s); Jimmy Reed (h); Frankie Bradford, Joe Hunter, unknowns (p); Eddie Taylor, Lefty Bates, Larry Veeder, unknowns (g); George Washington, Quinn Wilson, Everett McCrary, Sylvester Hickman, Bill Lee, James Jamerson, unknowns (b); Tom Whitehead, Richard Johnson, Earl Phillips, Jimmy Turner, Benny Benjamin, unknowns (d). 10/55–64.*

*** **This Is Hip (The Best Of)**
Snapper SMDCD 187 2CD *As above, except omit Lee. 10/55–64.*

*** **The Best Of**
Prism Leisure PLATCD 535 *Similar to above. 10/55–61.*

(*) **Is He The World's Greatest Blues Singer?
[Collectables COL-CD-7107] *Similar to above. 10/55–7/63.*

*** **Don't Look Back**
Snapper Complete Blues SBLUECD 020 *Similar to above. 10/55–64.*

*** **The Masters**
Eagle EAB CD 065 *Similar to above. 10/55–64.*

*** **Dimples: The Best Of John Lee Hooker**
Charly SNAP 022 *Similar to above. 3/56–64.*

*** **Boom Boom**
Pulse PDSCD 578 2CD *Similar to above. 3/56–64.*

When Hooker's Vee-Jay sides first appeared, as singles, they were heartening indications that honest and ungimmicky blues were still being made; heard at intervals, as they were, they gave a hard-won pleasure that one might not stop to examine in detail. Taken at a draught, decades later, they are a little less compelling. Putting Hooker with an efficient band was presumably intended to relieve him of rhythmic chores and give him room to flex vocal or instrumental muscle, but he gains little from it: he is always his own most interesting rhythm provider, and neither his singing nor his guitar playing is particularly enhanced by having freer rein. Indeed, in most group contexts he is ill equipped to be a lead guitarist at all.

Still, there are many worthwhile performances to be found, especially in the first three or four years. (From about 1960 on, Hooker's commissions from Vee-Jay were less for singles than for albums, which are discussed individually below.) Anyone who wants to understand the development of Hooker's music will need to mine some way into the Vee-Jay lode. Very good introductions are provided by the 2CDs *This Is Hip*, with 36 tracks, and the ultra-cheap *Boom Boom*, with 28 – but don't think of buying both, since they have 18 tracks in common. *Don't Look Back* spans the same period but about half its tracks are not on *This Is Hip*. Eagle and Charly provide 20-track selections of the best-known sides, and Prism an 18-track ditto; inevitably they duplicate each other heavily. Collectables' *I'm John Lee Hooker* is the original 12-track Vee-Jay album; the Charly issue adds four numbers. *Is He The World's Greatest Blues Singer?* may be a reasonable question but the CD hardly helps you to answer it, since it contains only a dozen tracks, not exceptionally well chosen. The serious Hookerologist will have to look hard at *Testament*, whose 60 tracks give strong coverage of the more interesting early sessions and include many lesser-known pieces.

**(*) The Country Blues Of John Lee Hooker
Original Blues Classics OBCCD 542 *Hooker*. 4/59.
** Burning Hell
Original Blues Classics OBCCD 555 *Hooker*. 4/59.
*** That's My Story
Original Blues Classics OBCCD 538 *Hooker; Sam Jones (b); Louis Hayes (d)*. 2/60.

These albums, originally recorded by the jazz and folk label Riverside, required Hooker to play only acoustic guitar. What motivated this redirection, and in particular the 'classic blues' repertoire of the first album, was a view of blues – you might say a politics of blues – very much of its time. To Riverside Hooker was an artist 'firmly a part of the great blues tradition … an heir of such men as Blind Lemon [Jefferson]', who had been compelled to 'function largely in the strange, musically hybrid area known as "rhythm-and-blues"'. It was to the credit of both artist and idiom that 'the real blues spirit' was able 'to fight its way through souped-up rhythmic monotony and inane lyrics'. Hence *The Folk Blues Of John Lee Hooker* (as *The Country Blues Of John Lee Hooker* was alternatively titled on LP), with its songs associated with earlier figures like Jefferson, Charley Patton ('Pea Vine Special'), Leroy Carr ('How Long Blues', 'I'm Prison Bound') and Sonny Boy Williamson I ('Good Mornin', Lil' School Girl') – though, as always with Hooker, the result is not exact commemoration so much as highly personalized allusion.

That's My Story exchanges the format of a 'country blues' recital for a programme of more recent material, such as Charles Brown's 'Drifting Blues' (here called 'I'm Wanderin''), Rosco Gordon's 'No More Doggin', Bobo Jenkins's 'Democrat Man' and the R&B hit 'Money'. Hooker is backed on all but three tracks by Jones and Hayes 'to free [him]', as the sleevenotes phrase it, 'from the burden of carrying the full rhythm load'. The explanation reveals a serious misunderstanding of Hooker's way of working. The 'full rhythm load' is no 'burden' but an almost inescapable responsibility of the expressive style Hooker invented for himself. But even with that said, *That's My Story* is an album with many striking passages: the unexaggerated autobiography of the title track; the abrupt zigzagging in 'Democrat Man' from Jenkins's song to a memory of the much older 'Red Cross Store'; the way Jones echoes Hooker by playing an identical line an octave lower.

Burning Hell lies between the other albums, having a few 'country blues' items like 'Baby, Please Don't Go' and 'I Rolled And Turned And Cried The Whole Night Long' (i.e. 'Rollin' And Tumblin''), newer songs from other artists, such as Lightnin' Hopkins's 'Short-Haired Woman' and Howlin' Wolf's 'Smokestack Lightnin'', and items from his own back catalogue like 'Graveyard Blues' and 'How Can You Do It?' *The Country Blues Of John Lee Hooker* was not a gripping record but at least it had an agenda: *Burning Hell*, lacking any such objective, is merely a set of disparate songs weakened by the acoustic setting. Take away Lightnin' Hopkins's amplification and you simply change the character of his music. Take away Hooker's and you almost invariably diminish it. It isn't just that his impetuous rhythm and clanging chords are strikingly emphasized by electricity; they are positively energized by it.

**(*) Travelin'
[Collectables COL-CD-7101] *Hooker; Lefty Bates (g); Sylvester Hickman (b); Jimmy Turner (d)*. 3/60.
**(*) Travelin'
Charly SNAP 145 *As above, except add Everett McCrary (b), Richard Johnson (d)*. 58, 3/60.

Travelin' was the first of Hooker's Vee-Jay albums to be recorded at a single session. Cut from the same cloth, the performances have little variety in texture and not much in tempo. Collectables reissue the original album; Charly extend it by four 1958 tracks that were not issued at the time.

**(*) The Folk Lore Of John Lee Hooker
[Collectables COL-CD-7129] *Hooker; Jimmy Reed (h); Lefty Bates (g); Bill Lee, Quinn Wilson (b); Earl Phillips (d)*. 4/60–1/61.

Title, cover art and Pete Welding's notes indicate that Vee-Jay were reaching for Hooker's perceived new audience among folkniks, yet only 'Tupelo' and 'The Hobo' ('Hobo Blues'), from his set with acoustic guitar at the 1960 Newport Folk Festival, represent the 'folk blues' angle Hooker had begun to develop a year earlier; the rest is typical of his Vee-Jay work, especially the four tracks with a band. 'Five Long Years' is, for Hooker, an unusually faithful version of someone else's song, in that he preserves not only Eddie Boyd's storyline and melody but also his rhymes. 'Take Me As I Am' is a venture into the pop-ballad idiom and so a forerunner of recordings like 'I Cover The Waterfront'.

*** Sittin' Here Thinkin'
Savoy Jazz SVY 17228 *Hooker; Eddie Kirkland (g); unknown (b); unknown (d)*. 61?

Allegedly recorded in 1961 but not issued until long afterwards. The three or four items with Kirkland sound less like 1961 than, say, 1954, and it may be that two sessions are involved, but, whatever the chronology, it's hard-wearing medium-grade Hooker.

*** That's Where It's At!
Stax 4134//SCD24 4134 *Hooker; Steve Alaimo (g, v); unknown (b)*. 61.

These ten tracks are thought to have been recorded by Henry Stone at the same time as the four '61 items on *Don't Turn Me From Your Door* (see above). Hooker is in one of his brown studies, chanting thoughtfully over repetitive guitar figures and a steady bass. He takes the opportunity, in 'Teachin' The Blues', to sum up his philosophy: 'These fancy chords don't mean nothin' if you ain't got that beat. Throw the fancy chords away.' 'Feel So Bad' is a good-humoured musical conversation with Steve Alaimo. The stereo picture is annoying, with Hooker's voice all in the right speaker, the guitar either spread or mostly on the left.

*** Burnin'
[Collectables COL-CD-7106]//Charly SNAP 041 *Hooker; Hank Cosby (ts); Andrew 'Mike' Terry (bs); Joe Hunter (p); Larry Veeder (g); James Jamerson (b); Benny Benjamin (d). 61.*
**(*) The Big Soul Of John Lee Hooker
[Collectables COL-CD-7102] *Similar to above, except add 'The Vandellas' [actually Mary Wilson, Jackie Hicks, Marlene Barrow, Louvain Demps] (v). 62.*

Burnin' is another album cut at a single session but it has more texture and spirit than *Travelin'*. Hooker presides over 11 tracks of uncomplicated, danceable music, pushed by the saxes. 'What Do You Say', surprisingly, is an adaptation of Howlin' Wolf's 'Howlin' For My Darlin'. *The Big Soul* (done at two sessions) furnished Hooker with the largest instrumental cushion he had yet enjoyed, but the arrangements are uninventive and only odd tracks like 'Send Me Your Pillow' spark either artist or listener.

*** Live At Sugar Hill Volumes 1 & 2
Ace CDCHD 938 *Hooker. 11/62.*
*** Live At Sugar Hill Vol. 2
Fantasy FCD 7714 *Hooker. 11/62.*

Playing amplified guitar, Hooker draws on a repertoire quite closely related to his recent Vee-Jay work – 'I Like To See You Walk', for instance, is a variant of 'Dimples' – but also throws in numbers associated with others like 'My Babe' and 'Key To The Highway'. Despite its title, the Fantasy CD is not the same as the second half of the Ace, but contains 19 more tracks from the same source, all previously unissued.

*** On Campus
[Collectables COL-CD-7103] *Similar to The Big Soul Of John Lee Hooker. 63.*

Despite the title, which suggests an unplugged 'folk blues' set, this was a studio album, Hooker's last such for Vee-Jay. About half the tracks have a five-piece band and are quite spirited; the rest, which are mostly by Hooker with only a drummer behind him, find him revisiting songs from his early recording days like 'Half A Stranger', 'Bottle Up And Go' (a remembrance of Tommy McClennan, whose work he liked) and 'My Grinding Mill'. The enquiring reader would do well to check this out.

*(*) Concert At Newport
[Collectables COL-CD-7105] *Hooker; unknown (b). 7/63.*
*(*) Live At Newport
Vanguard VCD 79703 *As above, except add Bill Lee (b). 6/60, 7/63.*

Hooker's repertoire choices at the 1963 Newport Folk Festival were mostly stock pieces like 'Hobo Blues' and 'Boom Boom', his guitar playing is often skeletal and the recording quality is indifferent. Even Hooker's keenest admirers will find little of value here. Vanguard add a couple of songs from the 1960 event; with 17 tracks listed, it looks like more, but four are merely introductions.

**(*) In Person
[Collectables COL-CD-7104] *Hooker; Lefty Bates, poss. Roebuck 'Pop' Staples, unknown (g); Quinn Wilson, unknowns (b); Earl Phillips, unknown (d). 1/61–64.*

Most of this fairly dispensable CD is from 1964; one of the tracks that isn't, 'You're Gonna Need Another Favor', is live (from Newport in 1963) but it's the only one that makes sense of the title.

**(*) Hooker & The Hogs
Sanctuary CAS 36076 *Hooker; Tom Parker (o, p); T. S. McPhee (g); Pete Cruickshank (b); Dave Boorman (d). 48–49, 11/64.*
**(*) The Complete 1964 Recordings
RPM RPMSH 208 *As above, except add unknown (g), unknown (b), unknown (d). spring–11/64.*

The Groundhogs were reputedly Hooker's favourite British backing group, and they competently provide the sort of backing he had by that time become used to. (The horns that were dubbed on to some previous issues of this session have been removed.) The group's playing is somewhat anonymous but, compared with the inexorable boogieing of some of Hooker's later bands, such discretion is no bad thing. The reading of 'Waterfront' is distinctly pretty. Still, the sedateness of the music is ungenerously shown up by the addition of four bonus tracks from the late '40s, their provenance unspecified but actually from King and Regent, whose wretched sound quality fails to conceal the younger man's greater vigour.

The Complete 1964 Recordings is an interesting idea. Hooker attended only two sessions that year: one, as we know, in London, and an earlier date in Chicago for Vee-Jay. RPM put them together. The most notable side from the Vee-Jay session is Hooker's first recording of 'It Serves Me Right To Suffer', based on Percy Mayfield's 'Memory Pain'; in later years it would be one of his staples.

**(*) It Serve You Right To Suffer
MCA MCAD 12025//BGO BGOCD 335 *Hooker; Dickie Wells (tb); Barry Galbraith (g); Milt Hinton (b); Panama Francis (d). 11/65.*

One suspects that some of Hooker's '60s albums were made simply because a company wanted an example of this charismatic – and saleable – artist in its catalogue. Impulse!, the originating label in this case, had a distinguished jazz list, and there was nothing illogical about wanting to broaden it with some 'roots' music. But was this the way to go about it? Hooker plus a rhythm section plus a scoop of well-used repertoire like 'Sugar Mama', 'Decoration Day' and 'Bottle Up And Go' was a tested formula, and all too likely to produce formulaic music. And so it proves. The only tracks with an edge of surprise are 'Money', oomphed along by Dicky Wells's trombone (its only appearance on the album), and the contemplative reading of the title number.

**(*) The Real Folk Blues
[MCA/Chess CHD-9271] *Hooker; Lafayette Leake (o, p); Eddie Burns (g); unknown (b); Fred Below (d). 5/66.*
*** The Real Folk Blues/More Real Folk Blues
MCA/Chess 088 112 821 *As above. 5/66.*

The Real Folk Blues got its name because at the time Chess had a series of albums with that title. It would have made sense if Hooker had done one of his acoustic sets like the

Riversides, but in fact it's a band-accompanied session, not psyched-up enough to be an *Electric Hook* but busy and, by the standards of mid-'60s Chicago, moderately up to date. Eddie Burns takes much of the weight off the leader, while the other musicians maintain a pulse and don't get in the way. They all drop out for 'The Waterfront', leaving Hooker to take a meandering journey through a radical remapping of the pop song 'I Cover The Waterfront'.

The Real Folk Blues/More Real Folk Blues (previously *The Complete Chess Folk Blues Sessions* [MCA MCD-18335]) adds to the nine tracks on the original album nine more, previously unissued, from the same session. These provide several surprises, like an 'I Can't Quit You Baby' that carries a perceptible stamp of Otis Rush, a thrusting 'Mustang And GTO' and a lively 'Deep Blue Sea', rolling on a piano wave. 'This Land Is Nobody's Land' is a meditation on strife and equality, prefiguring pieces like 'The Motor City Is Burning' on *Urban Blues* (see below).

**(*) Live At Cafe Au-Go-Go
BGO BGOCD 39 *Hooker; Otis Spann (p); Muddy Waters, Sammy Lawhorn, Luther Johnson (g); Mac Arnold (b); Francis Clay (d).* 8/66.

**(*) Life At Cafe Au-Go-Go (And Soledad Prison)
MCA MCAD 11537 *As above, except add Luther Tucker, Charlie Grimes (g), Lex Silver (b), Ken Swank (d).* 8/66, 6/72.

On his first album for ABC's Bluesway marque, Hooker was backed at Café Au-Go-Go by the Muddy Waters band. Muddy himself does little with his guitar, soloing only on 'Heartaches And Misery', while George Smith, listed as playing harmonica, is inaudible. Spann, however, solos with his customary pungency on 'When My First Wife Left Me' and 'Never Get Out Of These Blues Alive'. The occasion also produced what appears to be the first recording of one of Hooker's later-life staples, 'I'm Bad Like Jesse James'. MCA's two-in-one contains all of *Cafe Au-Go-Go* and most of the otherwise unavailable *Live At Soledad Prison*, a 1972 concert where Hooker and his companions gave a vigorous performance, pleasing their audience with songs like 'Serve Me Right To Suffer' and 'Bang Bang Bang Bang', a souped-up 'Boom Boom'.

**(*) Urban Blues
MCA MCAD 10760//BGO BGOCD 122 *Hooker; Louis Myers (h); Eddie Taylor (g, b); Buddy Guy (g); Phil Upchurch (b); Al Duncan (d); Al Smith (prod).* 9–11/67.

**(*) Simply The Truth
BGO BGOCD 40 *Hooker; Hele Rosenthal (h); Ernie Hayes (o, p); Wally Richardson (g); William Folwell (b); Bernard 'Pretty' Purdie (d); Bob Thiele (prod).* 10/68.

One way for a producer to deal with Hooker's idiosyncratic timing and structure without using up a lot of expensive studio time was to get a groove going, and the nature of Hooker's music is such that one groove will often do for several songs. Except for tempo changes and an occasional sideman's break, little happens on these two albums to differentiate the music, and the listener's attention is fixed firmly on Hooker singing the words. Several of the songs on *Urban Blues* are recycled from his Vee-Jay days, like 'Boom Boom Boom', but there are also a couple by the veteran blues-writer Jimmy Oden.

It's hard to discern in these and some subsequent ABC sessions any of the virtues of Hooker's earlier recordings: the concentrated energy, the arresting unison of voice and guitar, above all the rhythmic variety and freedom that arose from Hooker's having to do so much of the work himself. Success relieved him of that task and assigned it to musicians like those on *Simply The Truth*, described in the notes as 'a fully contemporary rhythm section'. Doubtless they made his music contemporary and, in their terms, more rhythmic, but in the process they deprived it of something – you might call it self-absorption – that could not be subtracted without permanent loss.

**(*) If You Miss 'Im ... I Got 'Im
BGO BGOCD 392 *Hooker; Jeff Carp (h); Johnny 'Big Moose' Walker (o, p); Earl Hooker, Paul Asbell (g); Gino [Geno] Skaggs (b); Roosevelt Shaw (d); Ed Michel (prod).* 5/69.

Two bluesmen called Hooker – hey, we gotta get 'em in the studio together! According to producer Ed Michel, though, this was no put-up job: Earl and John Lee had already joined forces to play gigs before this session was conceived – 'it was a working band.' And at this point in John Lee's career it was a combination with possibilities: his long winding narratives left oodles of space for Earl to dart in with a flurry of notes or wah-wah phrases, as in 'If You Take Care Of Me, I'll Take Care Of You' or 'I Wanna Be Your Puppy, Baby'. What John Lee's music couldn't provide was a setting in which Earl might execute the shimmering slow blues lines of a 'Sweet Black Angel', but that probably wasn't what Earl wanted to be doing any more. Inasmuch as it answers a 'what if?', this was an album worth making, but it can't be judged a great success.

*(*) Nothing But The Blues
Blue Moon CDBM 070 *Hooker; Lowell Fulson (g); Carey Bell (b); S. P. Leary (d).* 11/69.

This seems to be the closest one can get to the LP *I Feel Good*, recorded in Paris and issued on Carson and Jewel, but it isn't very close. At least one track is missing, and three have been added ('Call It The Night', 'We Are Cooking' and 'Bottle Of Wine') that are plainly warm-ups, and just plain annoying. The running order and track timings are almost totally out of sync with Blue Moon's printed details. The music hidden behind this screen of confusion proves to be desultory. Fulson seems nonplussed (as well he might) at being asked to play with Hooker and, for all one hears of him, might as well have stayed in his hotel.

**(*) Get Back Home ...
Black & Blue BB 423//Evidence ECD 26004 *Hooker.* 11/69.

When this was made Hooker was not much given to performing on his own and, as it turned out, he would not make another solo album for over six years. Anyone hoping for a throwback will be disappointed: even when playing at up tempos, as on 'Big Boss Lady', he discovers neither the invention nor the strange sonorities of his early work. 'Boogie Chillen' and 'I Wanna Ramble' come closest, but here as elsewhere one wishes that the microphone had picked up more of his foot-tapping; attenuated as it is, it sounds less like feet than fingernails. 'Hi Heel Sneakers' is a cover, which is rare, and, rarer still, a faithful one.

**(*) Rock With Me
Acrobat ACRCG 701 *Hooker; unknown (p); Lowell Fulson, prob. Steve Miller, Jim Kahr, unknown (g); Carey Bell, Roger Brouse,*

unknowns (b); S. P. Leary, Ken Swank, unknowns (d). 11/69–6/76.

This was a mess to start with – its contents drawn from the Paris session above, from undocumented sessions in the early '70s, from a German club gig in 1976, and elsewhere – and its disorder has been aggravated by the appearance, in the track 4 position, of an unlisted 7.27 song with verse-swapping between Hooker and 'Steve' (probably Miller), which naturally throws out the running order for the rest of the CD. Five tracks, thought to date from 1973, were previously issued on *Hard Times* (Carlton Sounds 30360 00962, deleted), but 'I Hated The Day I Was Born' is extended from the earlier CD's 9.36 to 18.33. All these are very listenable, and 'Sally Mae', without the piano and drums, has some of the flavour of its older recordings.

*** **Hooker 'N Heat**
EMI 97896//Magic 393023 2CD *Hooker; Al Wilson (h, p, g); Henry Vestine (g); Antonio de la Barreda (b); Fito de la Parra (d). 5/70.*

Canned Heat were deep-dyed Hooker fans, and their collaboration was one of the few occasions when younger musicians partnered him to wholly beneficial effect. Actually the full group plays on only five tracks, chugging unintrusively and sometimes indefatigably – 'Boogie Chillen No. 2' goes to 11.35; the rest are either solos or duets with Al Wilson, a musician whom Hooker greatly admired. The Boogie Man sounds as if he enjoyed the date, and that pleasure continues to warm the listener today.

(*) **Endless Boogie**
MCA MCAD 10413//BGO BGOCD 70 *Hooker; Dave Berger (h); John Turk (o, p); Cliff Coulter (p, g, b); Mark Naftalin (p); Jesse Davis, Steve Miller, Mel Brown, Jerry Perez, Dan Alexander (g); Carl Radle, Gino [Geno] Skaggs (b); Jim Gordon, Billy Ingram, Ken Swank, Reno Lanzara (d); Bill Szymczyk, Ed Michel (prod). 11/70.*

'Pots On, Gas On High' and 'Endless Boogie, Parts 27 And 28', the latter based on a rhythmic figure rather like that of 'What'd I Say', are l-o-n-g jams, between them taking up more than 20 minutes. You need to remember that in 1970 a bunch of musicians unhurriedly exploring a riff would be greeted with benignly nodding heads; today's listeners may be more likely to respond with irritably drumming fingers. There's time-marking in some of the other five tracks, too, but the meditation 'Sittin' In My Dark Room' very effectively creates an atmosphere of shadows and black coffee, and the threnody 'Kick Hit 4 Hit Kix U (Blues For Jimi And Janis)' delivers a sober anti-drug message.

(*) **Free Beer And Chicken**
BGO BGOCD 123 *Hooker; Mic Gillette (t, tb); Greg Adams (t); Emilio Castillo, Lenny Pickett (ts); Steve Kupka (bs); Sam Rivers (fl); Robert Hooker (kb, o, p); Cliff Coulter (kb, p, syn, clavinet, b); Fatz Wess (syn, tom-tom); Sugarcane Harris, Michael White (vn); Peter Berg (coconut bj); Howard Roberts, Hollywood Fats, Jim Kahr, Wa Wa Watson [Melvin Ragin], Charlie Grimes, Jim Thorson, Luther Tucker, Boyd Albritton, Jim Caroompas (g); Skip Olson (b); Ron Beck, Ken Swank (d); Kenneth Nash (cga, kalimba, balafon, cymbals, bell, shaker, griot bells); Joe Cocker (tamb, v); Ed Michel (prod). 5/74.*

The album credits which Ed Michel compiled for the original ABC issue of *Free Beer And Chicken* (and which only owners of that LP will ever have seen) thank 'all the patient players who labored resiliently on the sessions, only dimly suspecting the true nature of the Gumbo being constructed'. A good deal of money and ingenuity went into giving Hooker a sharp contemporary wardrobe and although his longtime fans didn't much care for the new look he himself was delighted with it. Long afterwards, his biographer Charles Shaar Murray reveals, it was still his favourite album and often on his car tapedeck. This is some reason for the assiduous student of Hooker's work to pay attention to the album, but is there any more to it? Hard to say: it could scarcely betray its time more graphically if it came with a free spliff attached, but it is part of Hooker's allure that he could sail through such exotic seas with aplomb. And buried in the concluding medley 'Collage' is a version of 'Sittin' On Top Of The World' whose concatenation of coconut banjo, kalimba and serrated electric violin may be the weirdest music Hooker ever put his name to – which is saying something.

*** **The Best Of John Lee Hooker 1965–1974**
MCA MCAD 10539 *Hooker; Mic Gillette (t, tb); Greg Adams (t); Emilio Castillo, Lenny Pickett (ts); Steve Kupka (bs); Louis Myers, Jeff Carp, Dave Berger (h); Cliff Coulter (kb, syn, clavinet); Johnny 'Big Moose' Walker (o, p); Robert Hooker (o); Otis Spann, Mark Naftalin, unknown (p); Van Morrison (g, v); Barry Galbraith, Eddie Burns, Muddy Waters, Sammy Lawhorn, Luther Johnson, Wayne Bennett, Eddie Kirkland, Earl Hooker, Paul Asbell, Steve Miller, Dan Alexander, Elvin Bishop, Hollywood Fats, Jim Kahr (g); Milt Hinton, Mac Arnold, Phil Upchurch, Eddie Taylor, Gino [Geno] Skaggs, unknown (b); Panama Francis, Francis Clay, Al Duncan, Ken Swank, unknown (d). 11/65–5/74.*

With three tracks each from *It Serve You Right To Suffer* and *The Real Folk Blues*, 'I'm Bad Like Jesse James' from *Live At Cafe Au-Go-Go*, four numbers from *Urban Blues* and further sides from *Endless Boogie, Free Beer And Chicken*, etc., this is a well-conceived and useful epitome of Hooker's work across an important decade.

*** **Alone: The First Concert**
[The Blues Alliance TBA-13009] *Hooker.* 2/76.
*** **Alone: The Second Concert**
[The Blues Alliance TBA-13013] *Hooker.* 2/76.

Many blues enthusiasts seemed to give Hooker up for lost during the '70s, as his success with *Endless Boogie* and subsequent ABC albums diverted him from solo performance and into the orbit of people like Van Morrison. Perhaps some idealists reckoned that you had only to drag the man away from these fashionable friends and sit him down on stage at a small club and you'd get the Hooker of 25 years earlier, moanin' and stompin'. If so, they were deceiving themselves. Hooker had got away from that dark-night-of-the-boogie manner and was working with more rhythmic freedom, stretching his songs like gum, scattering bursts of chords and then falling back into a contemplative near-silence. That Pinteresque approach can be nerve-racking or simply boring, but on these records of an engagement at Hunter College in New York it is persuasive and engrossing. Rarely have Hooker's late-night, black-coffee, sick-with-the-blues soliloquies been so grippingly and intimately delivered – or, thanks to the experienced engineer Malcolm Addey, so beautifully recorded. Unfortunately, neither these nor an earlier issue, *Alone*

(Rhino/Tomato 70387), may be easy to find, but their reappearance on another label is likely.

John Lee Hooker & the Coast to Coast Blues Band Live in Concert Featuring Jim Kahr (Chrisly CD 30003), recorded in Cologne in 6/76, was Hooker's first recording outside the USA since 1969, and, discounting *Jealous*, which was mostly recorded in Vancouver, his last. Its current availability is uncertain, which is also true of *Rising Sun Collection* (Just A Memory RSCD 001), taped at a Canadian club gig in 1977.

**(*) The Cream
Fuel 2000 302 061 139 2CD *Hooker; Pete Karnes, Charlie Musselwhite (h); John Garcia Jr, Ron Thompson (g); Mike Milwood (b); Larry Martin, Ken Swank (d).* 9/77.

Hooker and his then band, recorded in performance at the Keystone in Palo Alto, California. All the numbers are longish, and the closing 'Boogie On' stretches to 13.45, giving Musselwhite plenty of blowing room. 'Tupelo' is dedicated to that city's most famous son ('a really good friend of mine'), who had died shortly before. Good in parts but insufficiently varied to keep a grasp on the listener for more than an hour and a half. (Previously on Rhino/Tomato 70388.)

**(*) The Real Blues: Live In Houston 1979 [sic]
JSP JSPCD 812 *Hooker; unknown (g); unknown (b); unknown (d).* prob. 8/78.

The seven songs in this set are mostly fixtures in Hooker's later repertoire like 'Jesse James Blues' and 'It Serves You Right To Suffer', though the latter is done more briskly than usual. The first four numbers are with the band, whose guitarist takes over a good deal of the lead work, but 'Never Get Out Of These Blues Alive', 'Boogie Chillun' and 'Dead Wagon Blues' (actually 'TB Sheets') are by Hooker alone, and quite compelling. The accuracy of the title – the latter part of it, at least – is questionable, since an authoritative discography places the occasion in Telluride, Colorado, a year earlier.

**(*) Jealous
Virgin/Pointblank 41763//(E) VPBCD 46 *Hooker; Ian Berry (horns); Robbie King (kb); Deacon Jones (o); John Sanders (p); Mike Osborn, Bruce Kaphan, Jamie Bowers (g); Larry Hamilton, Jim Guyett (b); Tim Richards, Bowen Brown (d); Alison Hogan (v).* 82.

When it first came out on LP, four years after it was recorded, *Jealous* broke an eight-year silence, but it was on a small label and few people heard it. *The Healer* was still a few years in the future, and Hooker's star was not high in the blues sky. Part of the effect of *The Healer* has been to pull records like this out of hiding, and *Jealous* proves to be worth a muted cheer. Osborn's guitar spins in some unexpected directions: out into space on 'Well Well', but on the refreshingly kick-ass 'Boogie Woman' more in the direction of Morocco. 'Ninety Days', heard twice, finds Hooker half-remembering Chuck Berry's 'Thirty Days'. The dullness that sometimes infected Hooker's '70s recordings is largely fought off, but *Jealous* probably won't quicken the heartbeat of any but the dedicated Hooker collector.

***(*) The Healer
Virgin/Pointblank 49318//(E) VPBCD 53 *Hooker; Steve Berlin (s); Charlie Musselwhite (h); David Hidalgo (ac, g); Chester Thompson (kb, syn); Bonnie Raitt (g, v); Roy Rogers (g, prod); Carlos Santana, Robert Cray, Henry Vestine, George Thorogood (g); Richard Cousins, Larry Taylor, Conrad Lozano, Steve Ehrmann (b); Ndugu Chancler, Scott Matthews, Fito de la Parra, Louie Perez (d); Armando Peraza (cga); Chepito Areas (timbales).* 1/87–4/88.

Hooker's first widely circulated album in almost a decade, *The Healer* caught the ear of the world and gave him a future that even his most ardent supporters could not have predicted. His erotic conversation with Bonnie Raitt in 'I'm In The Mood' goes far beyond the recycling of an old hit, and the hard-grained duet with George Thorogood similarly refreshes the 40-year-old 'Sally Mae'. On these, and often elsewhere, Hooker sings with the brooding sexuality of his best work, meanwhile stomping on guitar in a manner some listeners might have despaired of ever hearing again. Credit is due to his producer, Roy Rogers, for recapturing flavours from the past without merely rereading the recipes; the tracks with Canned Heat ('Cuttin' Out') and Los Lobos ('Think Twice Before You Go') recall but do not imitate the momentum of the '60s band sides on Vee-Jay. 'Baby Lee' with the Robert Cray Band is less potent, and the closing 'No Substitute', played on 12-string guitar, is so inward as to be uncommunicative, but there was quite enough here to make ridiculous any notion that Hooker might be a spent force.

*** Mr. Lucky
[Charisma 91724]//Virgin 86237//Silvertone ORE CD 519 *Hooker; Ken Baker (s); John Hammond (h, g); Chester Thompson (kb); Jimmy Pugh, Deacon Jones, Booker T. Jones (o); Johnnie Johnson (p); Robert Cray, Van Morrison (g, v); Michael Osborn, Tim Kaihatsu, Albert Collins, Ry Cooder, Carlos Santana, Johnny Winter, Keith Richards (g); Steve Ehrmann, Richard Cousins, Jim Guyett, Nick Lowe, Maurice Cridlin, Benny Rietveld, Jeffrey Ganz, Larry Taylor (b); Scott Matthews, Kevin Hayes, Bowen Brown, Jim Keltner, Gaylord Birch, Tim Compton (d); Raul Rekow (cga); Karl Perazzo (timbales); Bobby King, Terry Evans, Willie Greene (v); Roy Rogers (prod).* 4/90–5/91.

*** Boom Boom
Charisma 86553//Pointblank VPBCD 12 *Hooker; John Hammond (h, g); Charlie Musselwhite (h); Jimmy Pugh (kb); Deacon Jones (o); Mitch Woods (p); Jimmie Vaughan, Robert Cray, Tim Kaihatsu, Rich Kirch, Billy Johnson, Albert Collins, Mike Osborn (g); Richard Cousins, Jim Guyett, Steve Ehrmann (b); Kevin Hayes, Scott Matthews, Bowen Brown (d); Roy Rogers (prod).* 2/87–92.

**(*) Chill Out
Virgin/Pointblank 40107//(E) VPBCD 22 *Hooker; Chester Thompson (kb); Booker T. Jones, Deacon Jones (o); Charles Brown, John Sanders (p); Van Morrison (g, v); Roy Rogers (g, prod); Carlos Santana, Danny Caron, Rich Kirch, Billy Johnson, Bruce Kaphan (g); Benny Rietveld, Ruth Davies, Mac [Maurice] Cridlin, Jim Guyett (b); Gaylord Birch, Scott Matthews, Bowen Brown (d); Raul Rekow (cga); Karl Perazzo (timbales).* 2/87–93.

**(*) Don't Look Back
Pointblank 42771//(E) VPBCD 39 *Hooker; Gregory Davis (t); Roger Lewis (ts, bs); Steve Berlin (bs); John 'Juke' Logan (h); Charles Brown, Jim Pugh, John Allair (kb); Van Morrison (g, v, prod); David Hidalgo, Cesar Rosas, Danny Caron (g); Conrad Lozano, Ruth Davies, Richard Cousins (b); Victor Bisetti, Kevin Hayes (d).* 96.

After *The Healer* it looked as if collaborations with other musicians were the way to market Hooker – and (not to sound cynical about it) also the way to ensure interesting and perhaps even surprising performances, given that almost all the material Hooker wanted to play came from deep in his back catalogue. *Mr. Lucky*, for instance, has those very well-used titles 'This Is Hip' and 'Crawlin' Kingsnake'. Neither is transformed but both are enlivened, by Ry Cooder and Keith Richards respectively, and 'Backstabbers' is sharpened by Albert Collins's petulant guitar. The tracks with John Hammond, 'Father Was A Jockey' and 'Highway 13', are by comparison rather pallid. 'Stripped Me Naked' with Santana recalls the spacey mood of 'The Healer', but the most striking combination is that of Hooker and Van Morrison on the dream-like 'I Cover The Waterfront'.

Boom Boom recruited several previous helpers (Cray, Collins, Hammond, Musselwhite) but three tracks are with elements of Hooker's then regular band, three are solos and the album as a whole is more homogeneous than its predecessors. Repertoire like 'Sugar Mama', 'Bottle Up And Go' and the title track again indicates Hooker's preoccupation with re-examining past work, but 'Trick Bag (Shoppin' For My Tombstone)' and 'I Ain't Gonna Suffer No More' are new additions to his library of brooding, inward-looking narratives. In contrast, 'Hittin' The Bottle Again' sounds like country music as reimagined by Eugene Chadbourne.

Both *Boom Boom* and *Chill Out* contain tracks recorded for *The Healer* but held over, and some of *Chill Out*, such as the numbers with Santana and Morrison, may have been made at the *Mr. Lucky* sessions, but others were new, like two with Charles Brown and his group, one an unusually by-the-book reading of Brook Benton's pop hit 'Kiddio'. By now Hooker seems to have regained his taste for going it alone, and six tracks are solos or backed by a second guitarist. Several of them are new compositions, though 'composition' is too formal a word for 'If You've Never Been In Love' and 'Talkin' The Blues', in which Hooker soliloquizes about the meaning of his music.

In the light of what's been said about the sources of Hooker's material, *Don't Look Back* was an odd title to put on any new album of his, especially when it contained 'Dimples', 'Travellin' Blues', 'Frisco Blues' and other pieces of similar age. But the title song explicitly disowns nostalgia, though that's clearer from Morrison's contribution: Hooker, here and elsewhere, is not so much advancing a narrative as breaking it down into detached thoughts and phrases. This time there are no solos, but groupwork involving Los Lobos and the Charles Brown combo.

*** **The Best Of Friends**
Pointblank 46424//(E) VPBCD 49 *Similar to above five CDs, except add Gil Bernal (ts, v), Eric Barber (bss), Bill Payne (kb), Ike Turner (p), Ben Harper, Eric Clapton, Johnny Lee Schell (g), Juan Nelson, Samuel Taylor, Reggie McBride (b), Dean Butterworth, Joachim Cooder (d).* 10/87–9/96, 5–6/98.

Ten tracks from the five preceding albums, supplemented by three 1998 recordings with guests. 'Burnin' Hell' with Ben Harper and Charlie Musselwhite kicks ass more ingeniously than 'Boogie Chillen' with Clapton, while Ike Turner and a couple of saxes impose a thumping beat on 'Big Legs Tight Skirt'.

*** **Face To Face**
Eagle EAGCD 266 *Hooker; Dean Moore (s); Ron Thompson (o, g); Tony Saunders (o, b); Jim Pugh (o); Dan Zemelman, Johnny Johnson (p); Anthony Cook (syn, g); Warren Haynes, Roy Rogers, Robert Young, Elvin Bishop, Billy Johnson, Johnny Winter, Dickey Betts, George Thorogood (g); Jack Casady, Ruth Davies, Joe Thomas, Steve Ehrmann, Ollan Christopher Bell (b); Marlon Green, Kevin Hayes, Bowen Brown, Scott Mathews, Kevin Williams (d); Van Morrison, Terrance Kelly, Gail Benson, Tina Bryant, Zakiya Hooker (v).* 2/87–late 90s?

No clues are provided about how this farrago was put together, but the acknowledgement that all but two tracks come from 'original sessions produced by Roy Rogers' appears to tie them to the *Healer*–*Don't Look Back* period. Conveniently Hooker himself clarifies the matter by announcing, at the start of 'Turn Over A New Leaf', 'this is 1987 … things gonna change.' So they did, but most of the best tracks here are the throwbacks: 'Boogie Chillen' and 'Wednesday Evening Blues', done as duets with Thorogood, and 'Mad Man Blues', a splendid stomp by Hooker, Thorogood and Rogers. Of the other guests, the guitarists tend to decorate their numbers without enhancing them, while Van Morrison, singing along on 'Dimples', turns it into party music. Hooker's daughter Zakiya is the primary singer on 'Mean Mean World', a remix of the track on her deleted 1993 album *Another Generation Of The Blues*, whose producer Ollan Christopher Bell reworked some of the tracks on *Face To Face*. This is unlikely to feature in anyone's Top Ten of John Lee Hooker albums, but it's an amiable, upbeat last message from the grand old man.

*** **Trilogy**
Dressed To Kill DTKBOX 90 3CD *Hooker; various accompaniments.* 48–63.

**** **The Ultimate Collection: 1948–1990**
Rhino 70572 2CD *Hooker; various accompaniments.* summer 48–90.

*** **The Best Of John Lee Hooker**
Music Club MCCD 020 *Hooker; Hank Cosby (ts); unknown (s); Jimmy Reed (h); Joe Hunter, unknowns (p); Eddie Kirkland, Eddie Taylor, Eddie Burns, unknowns (g); George Washington, Quinn Wilson, Everett McCrary, unknowns (b); Tom Whitehead, Richard Johnson, Earl Phillips, unknowns (d).* c. 4/51–5/66.

*** **The Essential Collection**
Half Moon HMNCD 019 *Hooker; various accompaniments.* 4/51–9/71.

Finally, some surveys that are more extensive than those described earlier. *Trilogy* is not to be confused with the 3CD set on Trilogie (see above), though it's also a cheap slipcased affair: 64 tracks, about two thirds from Vee Jay, with average sound quality and no notes. Okay, but you can do better, even at these prices.

Can Music Club's *Best Of* still be in catalogue after 15 years? Apparently so – and why not, when for the price of a couple of drinks you get a sound choice from Chess (eight sides) and Vee-Jay (14), with all the usual hits. *The Essential Collection*, also inexpensive, is an ingeniously assembled compilation from Chess – both the early solo sessions and *Real Folk Blues* – and miscellaneous Bluesway and ABC albums of the '60s and '70s. Some surprises here.

Rhino's *Ultimate Collection* is on another level altogether. Spanning Hooker's entire career on record, from the bright dawn of 'Boogie Chillen' and 'Sally Mae' to the golden sunset of 'I'm In The Mood' with Bonnie Raitt (a previously unissued live recording), this well-produced set tells as much of its subject's story as it can in 31 tracks, which proves to be a good deal. Material has been derived from Modern, Vee-Jay, Chess, the folk-blues albums for Riverside, the more progressive sets for Bluesway, and further sources. Of course there are the personal standards like 'Boom Boom', 'Dimples', 'I Cover The Waterfront' and 'It Serves Me Right To Suffer', but other choices are less obvious and more canny, making it a thoroughly recommendable starter pack. TR

Lightnin' Hopkins (1912–82)
VOCAL, GUITAR, PIANO, ORGAN

Born near Centerville, Texas, Sam Hopkins was surrounded by siblings who played guitar. In his youth he associated with Blind Lemon Jefferson and Texas Alexander. Settling in Houston, he played in the bars of the Fifth Ward, and by 1946/47 his reputation was sufficient to get him noticed both by Aladdin Records in LA and by the Houston-based Gold Star Records. For a decade he recorded prolifically for both labels and for many others; then, after a short spell of obscurity in the rock 'n' roll years, he became one of the most successful – and, again, prolific – contributors to the 'folk blues' idiom, turning out innumerable albums and performing in coffeehouses and at folk festivals, though seldom travelling overseas because of his aversion to flying.

**** **His First Recordings Vol. 1 1946/1947** [sic]
EPM Blues Collection 15978 *Hopkins; Thunder Smith (p); Joel Hopkins (g); unknown(s) (d).* 11/46–2/48.

**** **Lightnin' Hopkins 1946–1948**
Classics 5014 *As above.* 11/46–2/48.

**** **His First Recordings Vol. 2 1948**
EPM Blues Collection 15994 *Hopkins.* 2/48.

**** **Lightnin' Hopkins 1948**
Classics 5023 *Hopkins.* 48.

**** **Lightnin' Hopkins 1948–1949**
Classics 5045 *Hopkins; unknown (s); unknown (p); Frankie Lee Sims, unknown (g); unknown (b); prob. L. C. Williams (tap dancing).* 48–49.

**** **Lightnin' Hopkins 1949–1950**
Classics 5079 *Hopkins.* 49–50.

♛ **** **The Gold Star Sessions Vol. 1**
Arhoolie CD 330 *Hopkins; unknown (s); unknown (p); Joel Hopkins, Frankie Lee Sims (g); unknown (b); prob. L. C. Williams (tap dancing).* 47–50?

♛ **** **The Gold Star Sessions Vol. 2**
Arhoolie CD 337 *As above, except omit Joel Hopkins, Williams.* 47–50?

Between November 1946 and some time in 1949 or '50 Lightnin' Hopkins made almost a hundred recordings, about half each for Aladdin and Gold Star. He was accompanied on a few of them, most creatively by the pianist Thunder Smith on the first ten for Aladdin, but chiefly what one hears on these remarkable discs is Lightnin' alone, singing and playing with an unremitting earnestness. The temptations of unrestricted playing time or performing to indulgent audiences lay in the future: at this point he was condensing his narratives for jukebox singles of two and a half or three minutes' duration, and there is scarcely a slack or superfluous passage to be heard. The sheer subtlety of his voice and guitar, and the interdependence of the two, places many of these performances in the top rank of recorded blues.

Although Lightnin's earliest sides provide glimpses of his Texan forebears – the wilful vocal and guitar lines, reminiscent of the recordings of Texas Alexander, in numbers like 'Thinkin' And Worryin''; the references to Blind Lemon Jefferson in 'Fast Mail Rambler' and to J. T. Smith in 'Howling Wolf'; the antique 16-bar theme 'Honey Babe' – it is obvious that a fresh and startlingly original artist has appeared, one whose voice moves unerringly through different emotional registers, compelling attention and belief. His guitar is hardly less arresting. Although he deals almost exclusively in familiar blues patterns and plays in only a few keys, he frequently surprises the listener with melodic and harmonic variations, and from time to time unlooses a flamboyant break or chorus, or an intricate line paralleling the vocal melody, that takes the breath away. His instrument tends to be recorded with more room echo on the Aladdins, more solidity on the Gold Stars. Strictly, one should say 'his main instrument', since he liked to sit down at a keyboard sometimes and knock out a tune. At one of the Gold Star dates he found an organ and produced the endearingly knobbly 'Organ Boogie' and 'Zolo Go'.

The EPM CDs began a complete-and-chronological survey which seems to have petered out after two volumes. Classics have begun the same project and stayed with it; the fourth, *1949–1950*, contains a final tranche of Gold Star sides and the first three for the next label with which Lightnin' would be associated, RPM (see below). The Arhoolies are the official releases of the Gold Star material. For the reader unfamiliar with Lightnin', any of these albums will be a revelation.

***(*) **King Of The Texas Blues**
[Zircon Bleu 508] *Hopkins; Thunder Smith (p); unknown(s) (d).* 11/46–2/48.

***(*) **Lightnin's Boogie**
Past Perfect 204390 *As above.* 11/46–2/48.

(**) **Nightmare Blues
Going For A Song GFS 247 *As above.* 11/46–2/48.

*** **Short Haired Woman**
Snapper Complete Blues SBLUECD 023 *As above.* 11/46–49.

**** **Jackstropper Blues**
Snapper Recall SMDCD 362 2CD *As above, except add Joel Hopkins, Frankie Lee Sims (g).* 11/46–49 or 50.

*** **Blues Kingpins**
Virgin 82740 *Hopkins; Thunder Smith (p); unknown(s) (d).* 46–50/51.

**** **The Blues/King Of Texas 1946–1952**
Frémeaux FA 271 2CD *Hopkins; Thunder Smith (p); Joel Hopkins, Frankie Lee Sims (g); Donald Cooks (b); L. C. Williams (tap dancing).* 11/46–10/52.

**** **All The Classics 46–51**
JSP JSP 7705 5CD *As above.* 11/46–51.

*** **Houston Town Blues**
Saga Blues 982 077–2 *Hopkins; Thunder Smith (p); Joel Hopkins (g); Donald Cooks (b); Ben Turner, unknown (d).* 11/46–54.

** **Moon Rise**
Arpeggio ARB 005 *Hopkins.* 11/47–2/48.

** **Lightnin' Hopkins (1947–1969)**
Best Of Blues BOB 3 *Hopkins; Jeff Carp (h); Johnny 'Big Moose' Walker (p); Joel Hopkins, Paul Asbell (g); Donald Cooks, Gino [Geno] Skaggs, unknown (b); Francis Clay, unknown (d).* 47–5/69.

Most of these compilations are mined from the same Aladdin–Gold Star lode as the preceding CDs. *King Of The Texas Blues* began a march through the Aladdin recordings that was not continued, and it may no longer be available. *Lightnin's Boogie* and *Nightmare Blues* have much the same material (*Lightnin's Boogie* pulling in two Thunder Smith vocals from the same sessions) but the latter doesn't follow recording order, allowing it to begin with the eight-bar theme 'Down Baby', one of Lightnin''s most affecting performances (also, of course, on various other CDs). It's extremely cheap but marred by poor use of CEDAR sound processing. *Moon Rise*, also restricted to Aladdin, is brief and horribly presented. The others, apart from *Blues Kingpins* and *The Blues/King Of Texas 1946–1952*, draw from both source labels, and while *Short Haired Woman* is rather oddly chosen and sequenced, the 40-track 2CD *Jackstropper Blues* is an excellent selection, containing key repertoire pieces like 'Short Haired Woman' and 'Fast Life Woman' and the stunning 'Tim Moore's Farm', and encapsulating Lightnin's genius both admirably and inexpensively. Should you come across *Feel So Bad* (Indigo IGOCD 2119, deleted), it too is a well-made collection.

Blues Kingpins is a discriminating 18-track selection from Aladdin, Gold Star and RPM. *Houston Town Blues*' 22 tracks also acknowledge the Aladdin–Gold Star period but bypass RPM and add some of the very fine material recorded by Bob Shad (see *Hello Central* below). *The Blues/King Of Texas 1946–1952* takes a similar line through Hopkins's early output but dwells longer on the Shad recordings, which account for 16 of the 36 tracks. This 2CD set is more expensive than *Jackstropper Blues* but does an even better job of introducing Lightnin' in the round. Better yet, because of its size (126 tracks), is the JSP boxed set, which virtually envelops the Aladdin–Gold Star work, touches on RPM and slices a good-sized piece of the Shad material. A few omissions and inadvertent duplications brush some of the gilt from the gingerbread, but *All The Classics* remains a very attractive bargain.

The LP that lies behind the Best Of Blues CD was compiled as a gap-filler, gathering sides, chiefly from Gold Star and RPM but also from other '40s and '50s labels, that had been omitted from previous collections. Since then Hopkins's work in that period has been redistributed on CD, and this selection has lost most of its point. The CD release is expanded by half a dozen numbers from the 1969 Poppy album sessions, more logically available on *Lightnin'!* (Arhoolie CD 390) (see below).

**** **Jake Head Boogie**
Ace CDCHD 697 *Hopkins*. 2/48–50/51.
**** **Lightnin' Hopkins 1950–1951** [sic]
Classics 5133 *Hopkins; unknown (b)*. 49/50–51.

More than most Hopkins albums, *Jake Head Boogie* may leave the listener feeling that a certain kind of creativity has disappeared from the blues scene – the restless imaginative impulse that spins songs out of air. 'You may turn your radio on soon in the morning,' Hopkins begins in 'War News Blues', rolling into an impromptu communiqué about the state of his world, borrowing phrases from other blues, whirling off in other directions as chance words prompt other thoughts. The material is Lightnin's entire output for RPM, including about ten alternative takes, and Ace have been to some trouble to find the recordings in their sonically most authentic form. The end product belongs to the company of essential Lightnin' Hopkins albums.

Classics gather all the issued RPMs – except for the first three, which are on their *1949–1950* (see above) – and some tracks that surfaced later on albums, adding three from Specialty and four from Sittin' In With (see below).

(***) **Ground Hog Blues**
Universe UV 115/2 2CD *Hopkins; Joel Hopkins (g); Donald Cooks (b)*. 48–49, 51–52.
***(*) **Hello Central: The Best Of Lightnin' Hopkins**
Columbia/Legacy 516493 *Hopkins; Donald Cooks (b); Connie Kroll (d)*. 50–51.

The recordings on *Hello Central* were made by Bob Shad for Sittin' In With and others of his labels (though 'Happy New Year', the only item with drums, appears to have crept in from another session). In quality of performance few of them fall far short of Lightnin''s earlier work, and several, such as 'Hello Central', 'Broken Hearted Blues' and 'Long Way From Texas', are outstanding. Some of Lightnin''s waywardness is curbed by the bassist, who may not play all the right notes but keeps up a throbbing pulse; and, although the studio echo is sometimes cavernous, the sound of the guitar is relatively natural and undistorted.

Ground Hog Blues has the same Shad recordings and a few more, randomly mixed with ten Gold Stars, most of which were at one point licensed to Shad. Buyers are hardly likely to complain at that, but they may be disappointed by the sketchy notes and inconsistent sound quality, and they'll certainly be surprised to discover that three of the Gold Stars are not by Lightnin' at all but Lil' Son Jackson.

*** **The Remaining Titles – Vol. 1: 1950–1961**
Document DOCD-5609 *Hopkins; Melvin 'Jack' Jackson (p, sp); Donald Cooks, unknown (b); unknowns (d); L. C. Williams (prob. perc, v)*. 50–12/61.

This was compiled in 1998 to fill what were, at the time, gaps in Lightnin's CD discography but, since some of the CDs then available have been deleted, its aim is compromised. It remains both a valuable collection of obscurer sides for the avid collector and an absorbing album in its own right. The bulk of the material is from '50s sessions for Specialty, Sittin' In With (including two beautiful collaborations with L. C. Williams and a Funny Paper Smithish 'I've Been A Bad Man'), Mercury, TNT and Chart; the TNT and Chart singles, from 1955/56, were the last he made for black record-buyers, though the TNT 'Moanin' The Blues' is raw enough to have been cut much earlier. 'The Slop' has Lightnin' and Jackson playing the same piano.

*** **Stayin' Home With The Blues**
[Spectrum 554 157] *Hopkins; Donald Cooks (b)*. 47, 52, 60.

Chronologically bookended by 'Shining Moon' from Gold Star and a 'Mojo Hand' from 1960 are seven eighths of Lightnin's Mercury session (the missing title is on *The Remaining Titles* above). Lightnin' plays acoustic guitar and sounds, at times, interestingly unlike himself. The remainder of the CD is by Memphis Slim.

***(*) **Remember Me**
Ember EMBCD 006 *Hopkins; Donald Cooks (b); Ben Turner (d); Ruth Ames (v)*. 4/54.
*** **Lightnin' And The Blues: The Herald Sessions**
Buddah 74465 99782 *As above, except omit Ames*. 4/54.
*** **The Herald Recordings 1954**
Collectables COL-CD-5121 *As above*. 4/54.

*** The Herald Recordings 1954 Vol. 2
Collectables COL-CD-5181 *As above, except add Ruth Ames (v).* 4/54.

At a couple of sessions in April 1954 Lightnin' recorded his last substantial body of work for what was then his primary audience, 26 sides for Herald, which yielded 13 singles and what subsequently became a highly collectable album, *Lightnin' And The Blues*. Though most of the material is of a familiar cast, performances like 'Sittin' Here Thinkin', 'Please Don't Go Baby' and 'Life I Used To Live' appear to catch Lightnin' in a profoundly reflective mood, and some of his guitar figures writhe like cobras. In contrast, the instrumental 'Early Mornin' Boogie' has a carefree rockabilly air reminiscent of Junior Parker's 'Feelin' Good'. Two numbers have vocals by Ruth Ames, a tough singer. The Buddah reissues the 12-track Herald LP, adding four numbers. The Collectables sets between them assemble the entire output, but the Ember does the same on one CD and therefore wins our recommendation, with the caveat that several tracks suffer from distortion, sometimes severe; those that are also on the Buddah tend to be less flawed on that CD.

*** Lightnin' Hopkins
Smithsonian Folkways CD SF 40019 *Hopkins.* 1/59.

Sam Charters, who recorded this album, writes on its CD reissue, 30 years later, that 'this is still, for me, his most exciting musical statement'. 'Exciting' might not be the word everyone would choose to describe this intimate, unplugged performance, but it was greeted on its original release with considerable enthusiasm, a response moulded by interpretations of the blues as folk music, suspicion of electric guitars, and other views current in the '50s and '60s among the sort of people who bought Folkways albums. It remains an estimable record, its slight pieces like 'Come Go Home With Me' or 'She's Mine' offset by an authoritative reading of the old Texas theme 'Penitentiary Blues'. A couple of minutes' 'Reminiscences Of Blind Lemon' are interesting but even if they weren't the tape wouldn't have been wasted, because Lightnin' talking is as captivating as Lightnin' singing.

*** Country Blues
Tradition TCD 1003 *Hopkins; Luke 'Long Gone' Miles (v).* 2/59.
*** Autobiography In Blues
Tradition TCD 1002 *Hopkins.* 2–7/59.
*** The Tradition Masters
Tradition TCD 1084 2CD *Hopkins; 'Long Gone' Miles (v).* 2–7/59.

The folklorist Mack McCormick, who supervised the Tradition sessions, divides the songs that they elicited into three groups: pre-existing blues that Lightnin' had appropriated ('Bottle Up And Go', 'Trouble In Mind'), original compositions that formed part of his settled repertoire ('Short Haired Woman'), and songs that he invented, recorded once and then let go, such as the touching 'Mama And Papa Hopkins'. All these pieces are on *Autobiography*, but songs illustrating the same categories can readily be found on *Country Blues*. Both albums are very satisfying examples of Lightnin' in a private setting, and the recording lends warmth to both voice and acoustic guitar. *The Tradition Masters* couples the two CDs.

(**(*)) Drinkin' In The Blues
Collectables COL-CD-5143 *Hopkins; John 'Streamline' Ewing (tb); Sonny Terry (h, v); Brownie McGhee, Big Joe Williams (g, v); Jimmy Bond (b); Earl Palmer (d).* c. 6/60–c. 10/65.
(**(*)) Prison Blues
Collectables COL-CD-5144 *Hopkins; John 'Streamline' Ewing (tb); Jimmy Bond (b); Earl Palmer (d); Luke 'Long Gone' Miles (v).* 2/59, c. 10/65.
(**(*)) Mama And Papa Hopkins
Collectables COL-CD-5145 *Hopkins; Earl Palmer (d).* 2–7/59, c. 10/65.
(**(*)) Nothin' But The Blues
Collectables COL-CD-5146 *Hopkins; John 'Streamline' Ewing (tb); Don Crawford (h); Jimmy Bond (b); Earl Palmer (d).* 2/59, 10/65.

These four albums were excavated 'from the vaults of Everest', a cheap LP label notorious for slovenly and ill-documented productions. Scattered through them on no discernible principle are the 27 Tradition sides also on Tradition TCD 1002 and 1003 (see above), which are nearly all on *Prison Blues* and *Mama And Papa Hopkins*; some performances from the c. 6/60 'summit meeting' (see below) and a few solo recordings made about the same time, nearly all on *Drinkin' In The Blues*; and material recorded in 10/65 for albums originally issued by Verve-Folkways and Polydor, mostly on *Drinkin' In The Blues* and *Nothin' But The Blues*. (For more on these 10/65 recordings see the discussions of *King Of The Texas Blues* [Acrobat] and *The Texas Bluesman* [Blues Encore] below.) There is three-star material on each of these four CDs, sometimes a good deal, but its haphazard arrangement and its availability on better organized albums make it impossible to recommend them.

**(*) Blues
Collectables COL-CD-6373 *Hopkins; Sonny Terry (h, v); Big Joe Williams, Brownie McGhee (g, v); Donald Cooks, Jimmy Bond (b); Ben Turner, Earl Palmer (d); Luke 'Long Gone' Miles (v).* 4/54–10/65.
**(*) The Very Best Of Lightnin' Hopkins
Tradition TCD 1071 *Similar to above, except omit Cooks, Turner.* 2/59–10/65.
**(*) Blowin' The Fuses: The Greatest Hits 1959–65
Empire 545 450 634 *Similar to above.* 2/59–10/65.
**(*) Chicken Minnie
TKO/Magnum TKCD 023 *As above.* 2/59–c. 6/60.

These draw on the same three sources as the quartet above: the 1959 Tradition sessions, the c. 6/60 'summit meeting' and the 10/65 album date. *Blues* also takes five tracks from the Herald sessions. *The Very Best* (which isn't) selects fairly evenly, whereas *Blowin' The Fuses* is about half-and-half from '59 and '65; the only '60 number, the title track, is one on which Hopkins didn't appear. *Chicken Minnie* avoids the '65 date but includes two tracks of uncertain provenance. For the serious Hopkins collector these are far too patchwork, but a casual buyer will find plenty of at least averagely good Hopkins on all of them.

*** Lightnin' Hopkins & The Blues Summit
Fuel 2000 302 061 101 *Hopkins; Sonny Terry (h, v, sp); Brownie McGhee, Big Joe Williams (g, v, sp); Jimmy Bond (b).* c. 6/60.

During the summer of 1960 Lightnin', Big Joe Williams, Sonny Terry and Brownie McGhee all happened to be in LA. World Pacific Records took advantage of this rare conjunction and recorded them together, both in the studio and in performance at the Ash Grove. An album of six long tracks was duly issued; other tracks, reportedly from the same sessions, appeared more obscurely on lesser labels. That whole group of songs, reshuffled, often retitled, and mixed in varying proportions with other recordings by the participants, has stocked numerous albums under all their names, such as Big Joe Williams's *Have Mercy!* (Tradition TCD 1014) and part of Terry & McGhee's *Rediscovered Blues* (Capitol 29376 2CD). But *Lightnin' Hopkins & The Blues Summit*, which reissues the original World Pacific LP and adds five tracks, four by the same quartet, is the most intelligible document of the occasion. (Or occasions: most of the album appears to be studio-recorded, but 'Blues For Gamblers' is live.)

Part of the motive for this 'summit meeting' was, reputedly, the settling of an old score: years before, Brownie McGhee had recorded a cheeky 'Letter To Lightnin' Hopkins', and Lightnin' wanted to respond. The atmosphere is charged with the electricity of several wily old blues magicians topping each other's tricks. Their occasionally, and perhaps not always entirely playfully, barbed asides add a whiff of brimstone. Altogether, the performance tells us things about the four men that their other records don't generally convey, and anyone with a special fondness for any of the artists really ought to hear it.

*** **Last Night Blues**
Original Blues Classics OBCCD 548 *Hopkins; Sonny Terry (h, v); poss. J. C. Burris (h); Leonard Gaskin (b); Belton Evans (d).* 10/60.

*** **Lightnin'**
Original Blues Classics OBCCD 532 *As above, except omit Terry, Burris.* 11/60.

***(*) **Lightnin' In New York**
Candid CCD 9010 *Hopkins.* 11/60.

(***(*)) **Take It Easy**
Past Perfect 220377 *Hopkins.* 11/60.

(***) **Mojo Hand**
Collectables COL-CD-5111 *Hopkins; unknown (b); Delmar Donnell (d).* 11/60.

*** **Houston Bound**
Relic 7058 *As above.* 11/60.

*** **Mojo Hand**
Universe UV 089 *As above.* 11/60, 7/65.

*** **The Essential Recordings**
Purple Pyramid CLP 0943 *As above.* 11/60.

In the '60s it often seemed that Hopkins, like John Lee Hooker, had been taken in hand by folklorists, issued with an unamplified guitar and politely requested to indulge the archaeological interests of his new listeners. That he managed this self-marketing strategy with such aplomb is a proof not only of his irreducibly independent spirit but also of the ways in which his music was intrinsically different from Hooker's. For one thing, it was never so urban. Though he spent most of his life in a city, Lightnin' seemed to look up at a country sky. His allusions to farm life or fishing are not nostalgic: he had his own sense of community and place and memory. What was in his head was largely unaffected by where he hung his hat.

All these albums originate in recordings made in New York within the space of about a month. *Last Night Blues* and *Lightnin'* were the first two of a long series of albums for Prestige, and well recorded by Rudy Van Gelder. Lightnin's performances are unfailingly fluent, perhaps because he doesn't challenge himself: almost all the songs on *Lightnin'* are well-tried pieces from his core repertoire like 'Automobile Blues', 'Katie Mae' and 'Back To New Orleans' (i.e. 'Baby Please Don't Go'), while Sonny Terry's contribution to *Last Night Blues* is entirely, and discreetly, responsive. (Some of the harmonica playing may in fact be by J. C. Burris, whom Lightnin' addresses on a couple of tracks.)

Thanks to the engineer, Bob d'Orleans, *Lightnin' In New York* sounds wonderful, and Lightnin' seems to feel specially at ease, essaying experiments that he seldom or never repeated. 'Mister Charlie' is mostly storytelling – a beguiling story, but Lightnin's voice would have made the Houston electoral register interesting – until he suddenly breaks into singing and guitar playing, with a dramatic effect that goes straight to the heart. 'Your Own Fault' and 'Lightnin's Piano Boogie' feature his delightfully lopsided piano playing, while 'Take It Easy' has him switching from guitar to piano continuously, except for a passage when he manages to play both at once. There is not much of the lighter, crowd-pleasing side of his latterday work: just 'Mighty Crazy', which he came to rely on a lot, but this is its longest and possibly best version. The other songs are laments and meditations from deep inside, the guitar playing perhaps a little gentler than usual. *Take It Easy* is the same programme.

The Collectables, Relic, Universe and Purple Pyramid CDs represent a session for Bobby Robinson's Fire label; Collectables offer the original nine-track LP, reissued without augmentation, while Relic add four unissued tracks, Universe five, plus a live 'Mojo Hand' from the 1965 Newport Folk Festival, and Purple Pyramid six, plus two strays. The Relic, derived from the original master tapes, is probably the one to get. Lightnin' is focused and businesslike and delivers a strong and varied sequence of songs; the bassist and drummer are unobtrusive but very much there. Lightnin' accompanies himself on piano in 'Have You Ever Loved A Woman?'.

*** **Blues In My Bottle**
Original Blues Classics OBCCD 506 *Hopkins.* 7/61.

***/**(*) **Blues In My Bottle/Walkin' This Road By Myself**
Ace CDCHD 930 *Hopkins; Billy Bizor (h, v); Buster Pickens (p); Donald Cooks (b); Spider Kilpatrick (d).* 7/61, 2/62.

(*) **Smokes Like Lightning
Original Blues Classics OBCCD 551 *As above.* 1–2/62.

(*) **How Many More Years I Got
Fantasy FCD-24725//Ace CDCH 409 *As above.* 2/62.

Lightnin' chanting the R&B hit 'Wine Spodee-o-dee' on *Blues In My Bottle* is no more than a couple of minutes of fun, but it neatly demonstrates his range of reference, coming straight after 'Buddy Brown's Blues', a reminiscence of Texas Alexander. Other songs too, like 'Sail On, Little Girl', 'Jailhouse Blues' and 'Catfish Blues', are probably or certainly modelled on earlier versions. The *echt* Lightnin' is expressed in 'DC-7', a song about his suspicion of flying, and 'Death Bells'. The latter is unfortunately dropped from the Ace twofer, which however offers the only access (other than the Prestige boxed set, for which see below) to *Walkin' This Road By Myself*. This album is notable for 'Happy Blues For John Glenn', inspired by media reports of the astronaut's successful return to Earth from his orbital flight in *Friendship 7*. The song is not outstanding by Lightnin's standards, but it reminds us of one of the reasons why he was an outstanding bluesman. The sessions that sourced *Walkin' This Road By Myself* also furnished the material for two further Bluesville albums, *Lightnin' And Co.* and *Smokes Like Lightning*. All three break away from the guitar-only format and on several tracks call in friends like Pickens (playing on what would prove to be his final session), but there is little to distinguish one album from another and the quality of Lightnin''s performances is variable. *How Many More Years I Got* consists of parts of *Walkin' This Road By Myself* and *Smokes Like Lightning* and all of *Lightnin' And Co.*, which is not available separately.

*** Lightnin' Strikes
[Collectables COL-CD-7128] Hopkins; Elmore Nixon (p); Ivory Semien (d). 61–62?
*** Lightnin' Strikes
Charly SNAP 136 As above. 60–62?

The two tracks with fellow Houstonians Nixon and Semien (and huge echo), 'Got Me A Louisiana Woman' and 'War Is Starting Again', are unpolished but packed with atmosphere. The remaining eight numbers, probably from a different session but with a similar studio sound, are solos, accompanied on an electric guitar that is both throbbing and piercing. Creatively speaking, this is Lightnin' on no more than good form, rising to very good indeed in 'Walking Round In Circles', but the sonic effects lend the music a strangeness that some listeners may find attractive. The Collectables CD reissues the ten tracks of the original Vee-Jay LP, whereas Charly add four bonus tracks from 1960, such as 'Big Car Blues' and 'Stool Pigeon Blues', that can be found on several other Hopkins collections.

*** Po' Lightnin'
Arhoolie CD 403 Hopkins; Geno Landry (b); Victor Leonard, Spider Kilpatrick (d). 11/61–12/69.

Po' Lightnin' contains further Arhoolie recordings, chiefly from 1961–62 and mostly previously issued on LP, that had not been selected for *Texas Blues* or *Lightnin'!* (both discussed below), but it's by no means a bag of leftovers. In 'Up On Telegraph Avenue' Lightnin' describes meeting a hippie chick and 'smoking hay', while in 'Gin Bottle Blues' he announces that he's trying abstinence. His ability to make a good blues out of the weather is reaffirmed by the long 'Ice Storm Blues' and 'Hurricanes Carla & Esther'. On three tracks he accompanies himself on piano and for two others he moves to the organ, his playing on 'My Baby's Gone' sounding like incidental music for an Ed Wood movie.

**(*) Hootin' The Blues
Original Blues Classics OBCCD 571 Hopkins. 5/62.

Recorded at the Second Fret in Philadelphia, this set gives an accurate idea of the repertoire Lightnin' tended to choose when playing for folkclub audiences, such as 'Ain't It Crazy', 'What'd I Say?' (here titled 'Me And Ray Charles'), 'In The Evening' and 'Meet Me In The Bottom'. The most gripping track is the opening 'Blues Is A Feeling', which begins with a couple of minutes of Lightnin' musing in rhymed couplets, a kind of archaic rap.

*** Goin' Away
Original Blues Classics OBCCD 552 Hopkins; Leonard Gaskin (b); Herbie Lovelle (d). 6/63.

The high points of this session are the title track, suffused with rural quiet, and 'Business You're Doin'', an old rag song similar to 'Take Me Back', which Lightnin' plays as if he's been listening to John Hurt. (He would remember it again in 'Get It Straight' on *Down Home Blues*, 'Take Me Back' on *My Life In The Blues* and *The Texas Bluesman* and 'Shaggy Dad' on *King Of The Texas Blues* [see below for all].) 'You Better Stop Her' ('from ticklin' me under the chin') may also tap a folk memory of a pre-blues piece. Gaskin and Lovelle show up some of the rhythm sections Lightnin' used in later years: though their touch is light, they are propulsive rather than merely responsive and never allow the music to drag.

*** The Hopkins Brothers
Arhoolie CD 340 Hopkins; Joel Hopkins (g, v); John Henry Hopkins (g, v). 2/64, 3/65.

'This remarkable recording,' writes Arhoolie's Chris Strachwitz, 'was the result of [Lightnin'] inviting me to join him, his mother and brother Joel, in visiting his long lost oldest brother John Henry ... whom [Lightnin'] considered to be the best "songster" in the family.' John Henry (born 1901) sings six pieces, Joel (born 1903) three, Lightnin' four, and there are a few duets. John Henry is revealed as a rougher-hewn version of Lightnin', while Joel's strongly rhythmic guitar style throws back to Blind Lemon Jefferson. Several of the songs are obviously improvised on the spot, like 'I Got A Brother In Waxahachie', and the ambience of a reunion is intensified by the brothers' backchat and the appreciative cries of other family members.

*** The Swarthmore Concert
Original Blues Classics OBCCD 563 Hopkins. 4/64.

The repertoire Lightnin' offers his audience at the Swarthmore College Folk Festival is standard-issue ('Mojo Hand', 'Trouble In Mind', 'My Babe', 'It's Crazy' [i.e. 'Ain't It Crazy'], etc., etc.) and the performances are unexceptional, but all the same this is an album worth considering. The track timings imply that the concert lasted little more than half an hour, but only because they take no account of Lightnin's introductions, which add another quarter-hour or so to the programme. These good-humoured and often playful spiels – 'We used to live in the country, way down in the fields. Y'all may not know what a field is' – give an accurate impression of Lightnin' as he was seen and heard on many a campus in the '60s, and so help to explain why it is not only blues specialists who remember him with affection.

**(*) Soul Blues
Original Blues Classics OBCCD 540 Hopkins; Leonard Gaskin (b); Herbie Lovelle (d). 5/64.
**(*) Double Blues
Fantasy FCD-24702//[Ace CDCH 354] As above. 5/64.

This session produced two Prestige albums, *Down Home Blues* and *Soul Blues*. Most of the former and all of the latter are on *Double Blues*, while *Soul Blues* is also available individually. Gaskin and Lovelle's parts were probably added at overdub sessions. On *Down Home Blues* only 'I Was Standing On 75 Highway' is Lightnin' at full strength, but *Soul Blues* has a few distinctive pieces like 'I'm Going To Build Me A Heaven Of My Own' – not out of atheistic contrariness but in order to give 'lovin'' women a happy home'. 'I'm A Crawling Black Snake', which has little in common with Blind Lemon

Jefferson's song, is framed by oddly impressionist guitar playing.

*** The Complete Prestige/Bluesville Recordings
Prestige 7PCD 4406 7CD *Hopkins; Sonny Terry, poss. Billy Bizor (h, v); Buster Pickens (p); Leonard Gaskin, Donald Cooks (b); Belton Evans, Spider Kilpatrick, Herbie Lovelle (d); Samuel Charters (interviewer).* 10/60–12/64.

Assembled in this boxed set are the 11 Prestige-Bluesville LPs described above, their contents shuffled, where necessary, to restore their original recording order; then, at the end, the Prestige double album *My Life In The Blues*, otherwise unavailable, which contains half a dozen unremarkable performances taped at what sounds like a noisy party, and eight far more interesting passages of reminiscence in which Lightnin' describes his family, learning to play guitar, meeting Texas Alexander, making records and other topics.

Bill Belmont claims in his producer's note that 'it is the material on the Bluesville LPs for which he is best remembered', but Sam Charters, who contributes the illuminating essay that follows, knows better, and goes no further than saying, 'everything that is [Lightnin'] is here somewhere'. This is true, but it is scattered unevenly over the 120 tracks, and some aspects of Lightnin', such as his piano playing, are never seen. From another point of view, however, the set gives an unusually detailed account of how a jazz record label advised by a folklorist dealt with the music of a highly individual blues artist.

*** The Best Of Lightnin' Hopkins
Prestige PRCD 5711 *Hopkins; Sonny Terry, Billy Bizor (h); Buster Pickens (p); Leonard Gaskin, Donald Cooks (b); Belton Evans, Spider Kilpatrick, Herbie Lovelle (d).* 10/60–12/64.
** Straight Blues
Original Blues Classics OBCCD 586 *Hopkins; Leonard Gaskin (b); Herbie Lovelle (d).* 7/61–12/64.

The reader will have gathered that it's best to be suspicious of *Best Of* in a Hopkins album title. Prestige's is derived from most of Lightnin's dates with the label and, as far as 16 tracks can represent so large and varied a body of work, it does its job well, presenting him solo, with old Houston friends and with session musicians. Oddly, Sonny Terry's presence on the two cuts from *Last Night Blues* is acknowledged neither on the box nor in the booklet. *Straight Blues* lines up a dozen tracks from *Walkin' This Road By Myself*, *Down Home Blues* and *My Life In The Blues* (see above) in an aimless and sonically indifferent selection.

**(*) Cadillac Man
Drive 41004 *Hopkins; Sonny Terry (h, v); Brownie McGhee, Big Joe Williams (g, v); Jimmy Bond (b).* c. 6/60–64.
**(*) Good Rockin' Tonight
Blue Moon CDBM 118 *As above.* 5/59–64.

Cadillac Man has five tracks from the 'summit meeting' period, followed by all (six tracks) of an unremarkable 1964 Guest Star LP taped before a quiet audience at Houston's Bird Lounge. *Good Rockin' Tonight* is much the same but in random order, swelled by four tracks from the Tradition sessions.

(***) The Little Darlin' Sound Of Lightnin' Hopkins: Lightnin' Strikes Twice
Koch KOC-CD-9850 2CD *Hopkins; Curley Lee [Billy Bizor] (h, v, v eff, sp).* 64.

This compilation returns to catalogue the contents of *The Lost Texas Tapes Vols 1–5* (Collectables COL-CD-5203 to 5207, deleted). They include the half-dozen tracks taped at the Bird Lounge (see the preceding review) and excerpts from another evening there when Lightnin' was joined by the harmonica player Billy Bizor. The rest is studio work, some of it very good; seasoned collectors may recognize cuts like 'Lightnin's Love', 'The Jet' and 'This Time We're Gonna Try' as elements of Lightnin's Blue Horizon LP *Let's Work Awhile*. The recordings are dated to 1967–68 but were definitely made earlier, as their producer Aubrey Mayhew's notes seem to confirm. So far, so not bad at all, but at track 12 on the second disc the collection goes haywire. That number, 'Back In Mothers [sic] Arms', is a repeat of the earlier-placed 'I Wish I Was A Baby', while the closing 'Chicken Minnie' seems to come from somewhere else in Lightnin's discography – but the six items between them are much older recordings by Leadbelly and Josh White (probably from Asch) or by an unidentified Irish (or mock-Irish) folksinger. From the fact that they are all listed as Hopkins compositions, it would appear that, incredibly, no one at Koch noticed.

**(*) Live At Newport
Vanguard 79715 *Hopkins; Francis Clay (d).* 65.

This amiable set from the Newport Folk Festival is largely stocked, as might be expected, with common pieces like 'Mojo Hand', 'Baby Please Don't Go' and 'Trouble In Mind', but includes a long, ostensibly autobiographical 'Cotton Patch Blues'. Although Lightnin' says several times that he needs to warm up his fingers, he pulls off some startling guitar runs.

*** Kings Of The Blues: Lightnin' Hopkins
Pulse PLSCD 682 *Hopkins; John 'Streamline' Ewing (tb); prob. Don Crawford (h); Jimmy Bond, John Howard (b); Earl Palmer, Bill Brown (d).* 50/51, 7/60, 64–5/69.
*** King Of The Texas Blues
Acrobat ACRCD 121 *As above.* 64–5/69.

The centrepiece of these collections is a rather weird album Lightnin' recorded in about 10/65 for Verve-Folkways, accompanied by bass, drums and jazz trombonist John 'Streamline' Ewing (on most of the tracks according to *BR* but actually audible on only two). Among some routine but perfectly acceptable blues and boogies Lightnin' remembers an old song his brother Joel also sang, 'Good Times' ('… here, better down the road') and the rag song 'Shaggy Dad'. On the Acrobat CD this unusual set is preceded by four sixths of the Guest Star album (see above) and followed by four very fine but ill-transferred cuts from *California Mudslide (And Earthquake)* (see below). The Pulse jumbles the same 17 titles and adds 'Big Car Blues' from 1960 and two RPM sides from a decade earlier, in awful sound. A third RPM side, 'Sittin' Down Thinkin'', is not by Lightnin' at all but the obscure Big Bill Dotson. These are not top-drawer Lightnin' albums, but they earn their third stars by rounding up some obscure material and by being very cheap.

*** Fishing Clothes: The Jewel Recordings 1965–69
[Westside WESD 228] 2CD *Hopkins; Wild Child Butler, unknown (h); Barry Beckett (kb); Elmore Nixon (p); Eddie Hinton (g); David Hood, unknown (b); Roger Hawkins, unknown (d). 65–69.*

At the time these sides were made, some leading bluesmen were making severely compromised recordings for a mainly white audience, but Lightnin's Jewels were scattered upon the Southern market and came, by and large, in natural settings, with bass and drums, sometimes piano, occasionally harmonica. Though his subject-matter is much the same as it was 20 years earlier, this is the mellower music of a man too experienced to be surprised by life but not too jaded to be moved by its jokes, ironies and puzzles. This set assembles the complete Jewel sessions, which include 15 previously unissued items; it's a pity that it may be difficult to find.

**(*) Live! At The 1966 Berkeley Blues Festival
Arhoolie CD 484 *Hopkins; Francey [Francis] Clay (d). 4/66.*

Lightnin''s seven numbers are largely standbys like 'Goin' To Louisiana (Mojo Hand)', 'Big Black Cadillac' and 'Short Haired Woman', but they and his introductions go down well with the crowd. The rest of the CD is by Clifton Chenier and Mance Lipscomb.

*** Texas Blues
Arhoolie CD 302 *Hopkins; Geno Landry, Geno Scaggs [Skaggs] (b); Victor Leonard, Spider Kilpatrick, Harold 'Frenchy' Joseph, Francis Clay (d). 11/61–12/69.*

**(*) The Texas Bluesman
[Blues Encore CD 52005] *Hopkins; Don Crawford (h); Jimmy Bond (b); Earl Palmer (d). 11/61–12/67.*

Both *Texas Blues* and *The Texas Bluesman* contain half a dozen songs (but not quite the same half-dozen) from 12/67, powerful performances with a resonant electric guitar filling the studio. *Texas Blues* surrounds them with pieces from five other sessions, ending with the brooding slow blues 'Black And Evil', while *The Texas Bluesman* adds a couple of 1961 Arhoolie items and the whole of a 10/65 Verve-Folkways album – confusingly, not the one previously alluded to but an entirely different set, with bass, drums and an occasionally overdubbed, rather poor, harmonica. It was no more than an average Hopkins album, but this inexpensive (and probably elusive) release appears to have been its only issue on CD.

**(*) The World Is In A Tangle
M.I.L. Multimedia MIL 3036 *Hopkins; Billy Bizor (h); Elmore Nixon, Cedric Hayward (p); Lawrence Evans (b); Ivory Lee Semien, Ben Turner (d). 55–4/68.*

** Houston Gold
TKO/Magnum TKCD 072//Blue Moon CDBM 111 *As above, except omit Bizor. 55–4/68.*

** Lonesome Life
Collectables COL-CD-5262//Blue Moon CDBM 093 *Similar to above. 61–69.*

**(*) Free Form Patterns
Collectables COL-CD-5542//[Fuel 2000 302 061 315] *Hopkins; Billy Bizor (h, v); prob. Wild Child Butler (h); unknown (p); Duke Davis (b); Danny Thomas (d). 2/68.*

The first three CDs focus on Houston sessions in 1968–69 and have numerous tracks in common; the first two are prefaced by a 1955 TNT single, and all three add one or more sides from 1961. All the '60s sessions were supervised by Roy Ames and, while they are less ramshackle than some of his productions, they aren't particularly well recorded and don't elicit from Lightnin' anything he hadn't done many times before. That said, 'Rainy Day In Houston', 'A Man Like Me Is Hard To Find', 'Born In The Bottoms' and 'Cryin' For Bread' have enough of the quintessential Lightnin' to reward a serious collector of his work. All of them are on *The World Is In A Tangle* (a reordered version of the deleted *Rainy Day In Houston* [Indigo IGOXCD 537]), which also has more tracks than the others.

Free Form Patterns opens with the story-song 'Mr. Charlie' (previously recorded on the 1960 Candid album); this is by Lightnin' on his own, but for the remainder of the CD he is accompanied by the bassist and drummer from the Texas band The 13th Floor Elevators, with harmonica playing by Bizor, who has features in 'Fox Chase' and 'Baby Child', or (probably) Wild Child Butler, and on two numbers an uncredited pianist. Despite these interpolations it's a rather lacklustre affair. This set may also be available as *Reflections* (Bellaire 1140).

***(*) California Mudslide (And Earthquake)/Los Angeles Blues
Ace CDCHM 546//Rhino 72173 *Hopkins; John Howard (b); Bill Brown (d). 5/69.*

In 'California Mudslide' Lightnin' adapts an old Texas flood blues to apply to recent heavy rains in the Golden State, but several other pieces have been dredged from deep in his repertoire and hardly altered, among them 'Rosie Mae', 'No Education' (formerly 'Another Fool In Town') and a very affecting 'New Santa Fe'. 'Los Angeles Blues' and 'Antoinette's Blues' (formerly 'Candy Kitchen') are played on piano, 'Jesus, Will You Come By Here' and 'Los Angeles Boogie' on organ.

**(*) Lightnin'!
Arhoolie CD 390 *Hopkins; Jeff Carp (h); Johnny 'Big Moose' Walker (p); Paul Asbell (g); Geno Scaggs [Skaggs] (b); Francis Clay (d). 12/67, 5/69.*

**(*) In The Key Of Lightnin'
Tomato TOM-2098 *As above. 5/69.*

Most of *Lightnin'!* comes from a 5/69 session for Poppy. Except for Francis Clay, who's on several tracks, the listed musicians play only on 'Rock Me Baby'. The programme contains a good deal of familiar stuff, not outstandingly well done. The last four tracks, from an earlier Arhoolie session, are solos and more engrossing. *In The Key Of Lightnin'* contains unissued material from the Poppy session, with the full band on 'What'd I Say' and 'Katie May'. Five tracks are snatches of inconsequential talking.

** Legacy Of The Blues Vol. 12
GNP-Crescendo GNP 10022 *Hopkins; Ira James (h); Rusty Myers, Ozell Roberts (b); Larry 'Bones' McCall (d). 74.*

**(*) Lightnin's Boogie
Just A Memory JAM 9151 *Hopkins; Phillip Bowler (b); Walter Perkins (d). 6/77.*

Lightnin''s '70s recordings are among his least known. *Blues Is My Business* (Edsel EDCD 353) and *You're Gonna Miss Me* (Edsel EDCD 357), from 1971, were somewhat over-egged puddings; even more so *It's A Sin To Be Rich* (EmArcy 517 514), an expensive 5/72 production with Mel Brown, Jesse Ed Davis, etc., etc., and a guest appearance by John Lee Hooker. Only

Hopkins completists should bother to hunt down these deleted items.

Legacy Of The Blues Vol. 12, with its soporific accompaniments and puny guitar sound, is one of Lightnin"s dullest records. *Lightnin's Boogie* was taped before a Montreal club audience, who tend to clap or hum along in the more predictable passages, which, given a setlist that includes 'Trouble In Mind', 'Goin' To Louisiana' (i.e. 'Mojo Hand') and 'Rock Me Baby', are not uncommon. But Lightnin' is in good voice and amiable mood and his guitar is beefy, and the CD, though far from essential, does his reputation no harm.

(*) Forever
EPM Blues Collection 15779 *Hopkins; Larry Martin (b); Andy McCobb (d). 7/81.*

Age could not wither him. At almost 70 Lightnin' Hopkins was barely distinguishable from himself 20 years earlier. The only thing wrong with this Houston club performance is its reliance on stock material ('Baby Please Don't Go', 'Mojo Hand', 'Rock Me Baby', two versions of 'Watch Yourself', etc.). 'Don't Let That Bad Sun Shines [*sic*] Down On Me' is 'Shining Moon' from half a lifetime before.

***(*) The Very Best Of Lightnin' Hopkins**
Rhino 79860 *Hopkins; Sonny Terry (h, v); Thunder Smith (p); Donald Cooks, Leonard Gaskin, unknowns (b); Belton Evans, unknowns (d). 11/46–7/61.*
**** Mojo Hand: The Lightnin' Hopkins Anthology
Rhino R2 71226 2CD *Hopkins; various accompaniments. 11/46–74.*

Taking on Lightnin' Hopkins's back catalogue and trying to epitomize it, and him, in 41 tracks is a challenge any devotee would welcome – and then quail at. Rhino's *Mojo Hand* fulfils the brief very skilfully, selecting from early, middle and late work, acoustic and electric, solo and accompanied. The presence of numbers as varied as 'Death Bells', 'Coffee Blues', 'Mr. Charlie', 'Needed Time' and 'Shaggy Dad' is a clear sign of knowledgeable and discriminating compilation. *The Very Best* has an even harder row to hoe, yet in 16 tracks it manages to choose very well from nine labels: an excellent primer.

***(*) The Best Of Lightning Hopkins**
Arhoolie CD 499 *Hopkins; Geno Scaggs [Skaggs], Geno Landry (b); Harold 'Frenchy' Joseph, Francis Clay, Victor Leonard (d). 47–50, 61–69.*

Again a *Best Of*, but this is on Arhoolie, a label whose long commitment to Lightnin"s music earns it respect. It has range – seven examples of early work from Gold Star, ten from Arhoolie sessions – and variety: there are examples of Lightnin' playing piano and organ, and a neat segue from the original 'Big Mama Jump' to Lightnin' listening to the record years later and talking about it. Imposing as early sides like 'Tim Moore's Farm' or 'Unsuccessful Blues' are, they do not cast the later performances into the shade. Well chosen, cleverly sequenced, wholly absorbing. TR

Walter Horton (1917–81)
HARMONICA, VOCAL

Less feted than Little Walter Jacobs or Rice 'Sonny Boy Williamson' Miller but in talent at least their equal, Walter Horton was at his best when working as an accompanist. Records by Muddy Waters, Jimmy Rogers and Johnny Shines, among many others, were immeasurably enhanced by his presence. Horton was one of very few musicians capable of elevating the slightest material into something approaching a masterpiece. His own records were relatively few and workmanlike, as if the burden of leadership restricted his creativity. Alcoholism and a delicate constitution (whence the nickname 'Shakey') hampered his last years but he remained capable of moments of fitful brilliance.

***(*) Mouth Harp Maestro**
Ace CDCH 252 *Horton; Phineas Newborn Jr, unknown (p); Joe Hill Louis (g, perc); Calvin Newborn (g); prob. Phineas Newborn (d). 51.*

Horton first recorded supporting Little Buddy Doyle in 1939 and 12 years later made his own debut under the pseudonym 'Mumbles'. His acoustic harmonica sounds anachronistic alongside the contemporary assurance of the Newborn family band on the first four tracks, and Calvin Newborn's over-busy jazz chords during 'Jumpin' Blues' and 'Hard Hearted Woman' hinder his otherwise fleet harp playing. His hoarse, unnuanced voice is better suited to the slower tempos of 'Black Gal' and 'So Long Woman', where the piano dominates the guitar's choppy rhythms. The collaboration with Joe Hill Louis, recorded months earlier, is thoroughly satisfying, each musician swapping the lead with deceptive ease during the instrumental 'Cotton Patch Hot Foot'. Three of the five remaining tracks have second takes with the occasional addition of an unknown pianist. Horton's vocals are relaxed and strong as he injects drama into Robert Lockwood's 'Little Boy Blue' and his own 'Walter's Blues'. (Other tracks on this CD are by Jim Lockhart and Alfred 'Blues King' Harris.)

*** Harmonica Blues Kings**
Delmark DD-712 *Horton; John Cameron, Red Holloway, Harold Ashby (ts); Lafayette Leake, Memphis Slim (p); Lee Cooper (g); Willie Dixon (b); Fred Below, unknown (d); Tommy Brown (v). 8–11/54.*

Despite top billing, Horton's eight tracks (the rest are by Alfred Harris) consist of two takes of 'Hard Hearted Woman' and 'Back Home To Mama' and four on which he accompanies singer Tommy Brown. His songs benefit from Dixon's arrangements but vary little in performance. Horton concentrates on the low and middle ranges of his amplified harmonica, producing long, saxophonic notes, with just one treble squeak in the first take of 'Hard Hearted Woman'. Rice Miller cut 'Back Home To Mama' as 'Bring It On Home To You' and probably did a better job of it. Tommy Brown is an enthusiastic but mundane singer whose 'Southern Woman' provides Horton with his only solo of the session. Otherwise his varied and persistent embellishments are too low in the mix to be fully appreciated, hampered as they are by Harold Ashby's equally active tenor sax.

*** I Blueskvarter: Chicago 1964, Volume One**
Jefferson SBACD 12653/4 2CD *Horton; Robert Nighthawk (g). 5/64.*

These six duets with Nighthawk, recorded by Olle Helander for Swedish radio, include an instrumental version of 'Trouble In Mind'. The guitarist provides the most basic rhythms over which Horton's harmonica leaps and dances, sounding more comfortable and inventive than on a formal session. His harmonica is amplified on all save Johnny Temple's 'Louise, Louise'.

Though given equal billing with Johnny Shines and Johnny Young on *Chicago/The Blues/Today! Vol. 3* (Vanguard VMD 79218, also reissued on *Chicago/The Blues/Today!* [Vanguard 172/74 3CD]), Horton in fact only contributes 'Rockin' My Boogie', a poorly recorded and performed instrumental. He does play on the other 12 tracks by Shines and Young, but these 1965 sessions are not the best place to experience his skill with the harmonica.

***(*) Big Walter Horton With Carey Bell
Alligator ALCD 4702 Horton; Carey Bell (h, b); Eddie Taylor (g); Joe Harper (b); Frank Swan (d). 72.

A short but perfectly formed session that reunites Horton with longtime partner Taylor and provides an early showcase for Bell, here referred to as Horton's protégé. Four of the 11 tracks are instrumentals, of which 'Lovin' My Baby' is probably the best. Bell gets few opportunities to solo but performs solidly in an accompanying role. He replaces Harper on bass for three songs, including 'Have A Good Time' and 'Christine', but both men are entirely too loud throughout, Harper particularly so on the last instrumental, 'Temptation Blues'. Horton begins in top form but begins to waver as the set goes on and is at his most reticent during 'Under The Sun'. Nevertheless, and despite its brevity, this is one of the best of Horton's sessions from this era.

**(*) They Call Me Big Walter
[Stony Plain SPCD 1208] Horton; Bob Derkash (p); Steve Boddington (g); unknown (b); unknown (d); Nancy Nash (v). 74.

It would be easy to dismiss this curious meeting of a young Canadian blues band with the venerable Horton were it not for the evident tolerance the harmonica player had for his eager new friends. That said, the most satisfying performances here, 'John Henry' and 'Turkey In The Straw', are both played solo. Otherwise, he puts on his usual show, with hoarse vocals on 'Hard Hearted Woman' and 'Sugar Mama' and occasional flights of improvisational genius on the other seven tracks. There's also an interview during which incomprehension and deliberately misleading humour vie for dominance.

*** Fine Cuts
Blind Pig BP 70678 Horton; Mark Kazanoff (ts); Ron Levy (p); John Nicholas (g); Larry Peduzzi (b); Terry Bingham, Martin Gross (d). 77.

*** Can't Keep Lovin' You
Blind Pig BP 71484 As above, except Nicholas also sings. 77.

Horton is on form for most of *Fine Cuts*, apart from rather perfunctory run-throughs of 'La Cucaracha' and 'Don't Get Around Much Anymore' and a very short solo train imitation, 'Hobo Blues'. He trots out a number of old favourites, including 'Need My Baby', 'Everybody's Fishin'' and '(Polly) Put The Kettle On', along with a very good 'Worried Life' and 'Stop Clownin''. With the exceptions previously cited, Horton's harmonica playing is close to his best, a stirring blend of tone and execution. He never was a good singer and his memory sometimes fails him when it comes to lyrics but this was very much the manner of the man, here recorded with his idiosyncrasies intact.

Can't Keep Lovin' You is more from the same session, topped off with a handful of tracks from John Nicholas's own album for the label. The former six tracks are by no means leftovers; there's a good 'Hard Hearted Woman', a surprisingly tough 'Tin Pan Alley' and three instrumentals, one of them Joe Liggins's 'Honeydripper'. Nicholas sings 'Careless Love', one of three duets that also include the instrumental 'Gettin' Outta Town', which turns out to closely resemble the earlier 'Walter's Boogie'. There's much to enjoy here but for the woefully short playing time. This and *Fine Cuts* would fit easily on to one value-for-money CD.

*** Walter 'Shakey' Horton Live
Pacific Blues CD 9801 Horton; Robert Bingham (g); James Smith (b); David Larson (d). 1/79.

Improvements in equipment mean that this Minneapolis club gig is very well recorded. With supportive but unobtrusive backing, Horton is encouraged to play long and well. Set regulars 'Mean Mistreater' and 'Little Boy Blue' are anything but perfunctory and along with 'All Because Of You' find Horton inspired to play cohesive solos that stretch over several choruses. There's even a loquacious reinterpretation of 'Shake Your Moneymaker' and the set ends with a reasonably faithful reading of 'Don't Get Around Much Anymore'. With eight songs in a 50-minute-plus set, Horton has ample time to display an inventiveness that rarely flags, making this one of his better showcases.

*** Live At The Knickerbocker
JSP JSPCD 2152 Horton; Little Anthony Geraci (p); Ronnie Earl (g); Michael 'Mudcat' Ward (b); Ola Dixon (d); Sugar Ray Norcia (v). 80.

This band is in effect an early incarnation of Ronnie Earl's Broadcasters and their overt musicianship draws a superior performance from Horton himself. The first three numbers are sung by Norcia, with the slow blues 'Lord Knows I Tried' evolving into a major guitar feature. Horton takes the stage for 'Walter's Shuffle' and quickly tunes himself into their level of competence. 'Little Boy Blue' and 'It's Not Easy', the latter a punning reference to 'Easy', his 1953 duet with Jimmy DeBerry, benefit from improving integration between harmonica and guitar, which reaches its peak in 'Two Old Maids', based on Sonny Boy Williamson I's 'Polly Put The Kettle On'. Earl plays Nighthawk-derived slide on 'What's On Your Worried Mind' and the set closes with 'Walter's Swing', an eight-minute jam that retains its energy throughout. NS

Son House (1902–88)
VOCAL, GUITAR

Despite his fame as the tutor of both Robert Johnson and Muddy Waters, Eddie House Jr didn't pick up a guitar or play blues until he was 25; until then he'd tried to live a Christian life, occasionally preaching in the Baptist church, and a tension between worldly and religious impulses is often reflected in his music. In 1943, House moved from Mississippi to Rochester, New York. When 'rediscovered' he was infirm and out of practice, but, managed and cared for by Dick Waterman, he regained much of his old power, and made music until 1975, by which time Alzheimer's and Parkinson's diseases were adding their weight to chronic alcoholism.

**** Masters Of The Delta Blues: The Friends Of Charlie Patton
Yazoo 2002 *House; Willie Brown (g).* c. 6/30.
**** Son House And The Great Delta Blues Singers (1928–1930)
Document DOCD-5002 *As above.* c. 6/30.
**** Screamin' And Hollerin' The Blues
Revenant 212 7CD *As above.* c. 6/30.

That Son House's Paramount 78s were commercial failures (one only surfaced in 2005) says nothing about their quality; more challenging is the suggestion that Delta blues and their high reputation are a construct of white enthusiasts from the '40s onwards. There's some truth in this argument, but more in its corollary: House's three two-part blues and one test pressing with second guitar, created in the infernal laboratory that was segregated, Depression-stricken Mississippi, embody the alienation and isolation of the modern condition, whatever the listener's cultural background. As House himself sang, 'These blues is worthwhile to be heard,' for their use of arresting, highly wrought language to confront love, sex, death, natural and economic disasters, race and religion. Musically, House's machete slide guitar and soulful preacher's bark are not, as sometimes asserted, the essence of the blues, but they are among its most visceral and gripping expressions.

These seven recordings cannot stand alone, of course: Yazoo and Document supplement them with tracks by Willie Brown, Kid Bailey and others (see COMPILATIONS: MISSISSIPPI). Revenant depict House as part of Charley Patton's circle, in better sound and extravagant packaging; for those who can't afford the concomitant high price, *Legends Of Country Blues* (JSP JSP 7715 5CD), also discussed under COMPILATIONS: MISSISSIPPI, doubtless sourced these tracks from Revenant.

***(*) A Proper Introduction To Son House
Proper INTRO CD 2016 *House; Leroy Williams (h); Fiddlin' Joe Martin (md, v); Willie Brown (g, v).* c. 6/30–7/42.
(***(*)) Delta Blues
Snapper Complete Blues SBLUECD 002 *As above.* c. 6/30–7/42.

Both these CDs combine the six then available Paramount sides with selected Library of Congress recordings. Neither includes the Paramount test pressing: Snapper claim to do so, but the 'Walkin' Blues' that plays is the stringband version from 1941. Proper's remastering of the Paramount sides is better (that is, it uses better source CDs). The Library of Congress tracks are musically miraculous (see below for discussion), but both CDs omit significant material. Proper's *Introduction* is the better disc, but it's preferable to acquire the Paramounts almost complete on Document and the Library of Congress sessions complete on Travelin' Man.

♛ ****** The Complete Library Of Congress Sessions 1941–1942**
Travelin' Man TM CD 02 *As above, except add Alan Lomax (sp).* 9/41–7/42.
***(*) Delta Blues
Arpeggio ARB 004 *As above, except omit Lomax.* 9/41–7/42.

***(*) The Field Recordings 1941/42
[Zircon Bleu 501] *As above, except Brown does not sing.* 9/41–7/42.
(***) Delta Blues
Biograph DK 30170 *As above.* 9/41–7/42.

Son House was probably at his creative and technical peak when he met Alan Lomax. Guitar-accompanied Delta blues (including some significant pieces played without a slide) are the heart and soul of these sessions, but there are also four band numbers of mighty cumulative power, some unaccompanied levee camp hollers, a rag song and the patriotic waltz (!) 'American Defense'. It's a measure of the rapport established that House also sang 'County Farm Blues', a stern indictment of the Southern prison system, by a man who'd served time for manslaughter.

Travelin' Man's 19 tracks are in about as good sound as can be got from the original discs. Biograph omit 'Fo' Clock Blues' (on which House only speaks), the unaccompanied 'Camp Hollers', a conversation about tunings, and a vehement 44-second burst of 'Special Rider Blues', played to check recording levels. Nearly half of 'Levee Camp Blues' is also missing, although this is not admitted. Add lamentable remastering, and Biograph are ruled out.

The other CDs, derived from Travelin' Man, are sonically acceptable. *The Field Recordings* is shared with Muddy Waters, recorded during the same field trips; this is a neat concept, but it limits House to 11 tracks. Arpeggio depart from chronology, which does no musical harm, but there's little point in acquiring 16 songs with superficial notes when the full complement and erudite commentary are available.

**(*) 'Live' At Gaslight Café, 1965
Document DOCD-5663 *House.* 1/65.
** Son House In Concert
Blue Moon CDBM 020//Magnum America TKCD 050 *House.* 4/65.
** New York Central Live!
Acrobat ACRCD 162 *House.* 4/65.
** Son House Revisited
Fuel 2000 302 061 249 2CD *House.* 1–4/65.

Two concerts from the early days of 'rediscovery' are involved here. Document's is a New York club date, dubbed from a distractingly hissy tape; *Son House In Concert* and *New York Central Live!* contain 38 minutes extracted from a set at Oberlin College. *Son House Revisited* is issued by agreement with House's estate. It includes the New York material, minus an incomplete song and just as hissy, and the whole of the Oberlin concert, in very poor sound indeed. Blue Moon and Acrobat have more presence, but House was in poor form that night, and plays a glut of wrong notes. He's more accurate in New York, if far from error-free, and there's more sense of the shamanic ferocity that could emerge during his latterday concerts.

*** Father Of The Delta Blues: The Complete 1965 Sessions
Columbia 471662 2CD *House; Alan Wilson (h, g).* 4/65.
***(*) The Original Delta Blues
Columbia/Legacy 489891 *As above.* 4/65.

Son House's comeback LP constitutes the first disc of *Father Of The Delta Blues*, and the first nine tracks (of 14) on *The Original Delta Blues*. That LP created a justified sensation in 1965, for although House's playing was simpler, it still possessed great emotional and physical force. So did his singing, whether on brief, unaccompanied spirituals or the more than nine minutes of 'Levee Camp Moan'. *Father Of The Delta Blues*' second disc contains five alternative takes and seven previously unissued songs, which clarify why it took three days to generate an LP's worth of material; House's execution on most tracks is less confident and 'Shake It And Break It' is not the only one that's simply embarrassing. *The Original Delta Blues* is preferable; it selects the best unissued songs, and omits the announcements and false starts that are an additional irritant on the double CD.

***(*) **Martin Scorsese Presents The Blues: Son House**
Columbia/Legacy (A) CK 90485//(E) COL 512574 *Similar to above CDs.* c. 6/30–4/65.

***(*) **Heroes Of The Blues: The Very Best Of Son House**
Shout Factory DK 30251 *Similar to above CDs.* c. 6/30–4/65.

It's arguable that the Paramount, Library of Congress and Columbia recordings are best heard separately, for each session has a different stylistic, acoustic and aesthetic unity, but subject to that caveat, these are excellent overviews, well annotated and splendidly remastered. Shout Factory draw the majority of their material from the '40s; Columbia predictably have more from 1965. The discs share eight tracks, and neither includes any of the two-part Paramount discs in full.

*** **At Home (1969)**
Document DOCD-5148 *House; Evie House (tamb, sp).* 9/69.

***(*) **Delta Blues And Spirituals**
Capitol Blues Collection D 108935 *House; Alan Wilson (h); Delta Dave [Kelly] (g).* 6–7/70.

By 1969 old age had stripped House's guitar playing down to its essentials, and he would sometimes fluff a line, but the blues retained their power to possess him, and through him the listener. 'Sundown Blues' from Document's informal sessions is a gripping example of House losing himself in the blues and entering a realm of altered consciousness more usual in gospel music. The disc includes some affecting unaccompanied spirituals and two mule-driving hollers, and House adds new – or more likely very old – verses to 'Preachin' The Blues'. There are better Son House recordings, but *At Home* is valuable for more than completist reasons.

Delta Blues And Spirituals contains material from two London club dates where House was galvanized by the enthusiasm of the audience, and by sensitive accompaniment on three tracks. In turn, the strength of his performance fired up the audience, creating an extraordinary feedback loop; on two concluding spirituals the mutual fervour approaches that of a religious revival. David Evans's important essay on House's music and the worldview it expressed enhances a remarkable farewell recording. CS

Bee Houston (1938–91)
VOCAL, GUITAR

Edward Wilson Houston was born and grew up in San Antonio. He began playing guitar in his teens, and his band backed artists touring the Southwest such as Junior Parker and Bobby Bland. In 1961 he moved to LA, where he played and recorded with Little Johnny Taylor and Big Mama Thornton. His work on Thornton's Arhoolie album Ball N' Chain *prompted Chris Strachwitz to record him in his own right. He was still playing with Thornton in 1975 and appeared with her that year at the Berkeley Blues Festival, but after that he virtually disappeared.*

(*) **The Hustler
Arhoolie CD 9008 *Houston; William Anthony (t); Jay Hodge (as, ts); Wilbert 'Jiggs' Hemsley, Alex Nelson, Sonny Campbell, Everett Minor (ts); Richard Brown (bs); Big Mama Thornton (h, v); Nat Dove (p); Terry DeRouen (g); Charles Givens, Frank 'Honeyboy' Patt, Curtis Tillman (b); Fred Cooper, Eddie Jones, Chuck Davenport, Gus Wright (d); Willie Molette (v).* 1/68–3/70.

Houston was an engaging guitarist, given to playing a lot on the lower strings and fond of tremolo picking. He was also, as Strachwitz notes, a man with his own views about intonation. One of his producers 'spent almost half the session trying to get Bee in tune' and, as the products of that date reveal, the effort went for naught. Listeners resistant to slightly off-pitch guitar had better avoid those eight tracks, though in doing so they'll miss a good deal of attacking and inventive playing – and urgent singing, for Houston and his occasional deputy Willie Molette were strong, distinctive vocalists. These tracks and ten from two other sessions are warmed by band arrangements whose busy rhythms are very much of their time: the pumping energy of the instrumental 'Freddy's Bag' is only an Afro's breadth away from blaxploitation movie music. 'Woke Up This Morning', sung by Big Mama Thornton, is a hitherto unissued track from the date when Houston accompanied her on *Ball N' Chain*.

Houston's only other available recording is an indifferent 1971 concert tape of 'Hi Heel Sneakers' on *Leavin' Chicago* (Blue Moon CDBM 141). He may also play, as a member of Thornton's Hound Dogs, on tracks on this VAC by her and other artists. TR

Frank Hovington (1919–82)
VOCAL, GUITAR, BANJO

Frank Hovington played for dances and parties in his native Delaware, and his recollections of a number of unrecorded musicians are evidence of a lively African-American musical scene, of which he is one of the few recorded representatives. Hovington also jammed with Philadelphian musicians on visits to that city, sang in gospel quartets and worked with jazz musicians when living in Washington, DC, between 1948 and 1967. Intelligent and articulate, he nevertheless remained a casual labourer all his life.

♛ **** **Gone With The Wind**
Flyright FLY CD 66 *Hovington.* 7/75.

Proud of his talent, Frank Hovington was nevertheless reluctant to perform in public, and seemed to have no professional ambitions as a musician. He played the Smithsonian Festival in 1971, thereafter retreating into rural obscurity, and became something of a legend among blues cognoscenti as a result. *Gone With The Wind* was recorded at his home, after Bruce Bastin and Dick Spottswood came by, hoping that he would be there and willing to record. The results are one of the treasures of field recording, and not just for their remarkable sound quality. Hovington's music was firmly within the blues traditions of the Southeastern states, but the man himself was almost never a copyist; 'Got No Lovin' Baby Now', recognizably derived from Blind Boy Fuller, is very much an exception. Few of his numbers were originals, although 'Sing Sing Blues' and the instrumentals '90 Going North' and 'C.C. Blues' (the latter a banjo solo) are superior compositions; in the main, Hovington took numbers that were widespread in tradition, or well known from recordings, and gave them authoritative and original arrangements. The blues-ballads 'John Henry' and 'Railroad Bill' are outstanding examples, both having unusual verses and unique guitar embellishments, while 'Trouble In Mind' and 'Nobody's Darling But Mine' show off the timing, and in the former case the advanced harmonies, which earned Hovington the nickname 'Be-Bop' when he played jazz in DC. Even songs as well known as 'Red River Blues' and 'Mean Old Frisco' take off in unexpected but always logical directions which reinvigorate and defamiliarize them. Frank Hovington's music insists that you pay attention to its originality and complexity, and doing so is always worthwhile. By 1980, he was in poor health and poverty, and recorded again as Guitar Frank, reluctantly and in fear of losing his Social Security checks. His talent was undiminished by adversity, as may be heard on *Living Country Blues* (Evidence ECD 26105 3CD). CS

Rosetta Howard (c. 1914–74)
VOCAL

Howard was born in Chicago and spent much of her professional life there, singing in clubs with bands led by Jimmie Noone, Sonny Thompson and others. She retired from the business about the end of the '40s and in the following decade sang for Tom Dorsey at the Pilgrim Baptist Church.

Howard's 1937–38 recordings with the Harlem Hamfats are collected on that band's *Vol. 2* (Document DOCD-5272) (seven tracks), *Vol. 3* (Document DOCD-5273) (seven) and *Vol. 4* (Document DOCD-5274) (five). Her most famous sides were among her first: 'Let Your Linen Hang Low', a salacious duet with Joe McCoy, and the marijuana anthem 'If You're A Viper'. David Evans claims in his notes that these early recordings 'must … have posed a serious challenge to those who were building a cult around the singing of Billie Holiday'. This is too well-disposed to Howard. Her voice has strength and character, and given a blues or a bluesy swing song at slow or medium tempo she reliably produces a sultry effect, but the interpretative power and rhythmic subtlety of Holiday's singing are beyond her. That said, the sturdy attitude expressed in 'Rosetta Blues' and 'Worried Mind Blues' on *Vol. 2* is most attractive, as is the positive message of practical fidelity delivered in 'Stay On It' (*Vol. 3*).

*** Rosetta Howard (1939–1947)
RST Jazz Perspectives JPCD-1514 Howard; Charlie Shavers, Henry 'Red' Allen, Johnny Morton (t); Buster Bailey, Barney Bigard (cl); Sax Mallard (as); Bill Casimir (ts); Leonard Caston (p, v); Lil Armstrong, Bob Call, unknown (p); Bernardo Dennis (g, v); Ulysses Livingston, Big Bill Broonzy, unknown (g); Willie Dixon (b, v); Wellman Braud, Ransom Knowling, unknown (b); O'Neill Spencer, Charles Saunders, Alphonse Walker, Judge Riley, poss. Sid Catlett (d). 6/39, 10–12/47.

This CD opens with two 6/39 sessions at which Howard was accompanied by sextets similar in lineup to the Hamfats, the first fronted by Shavers and Bailey, the second by Allen and Bigard. (The first session is also on *Charlie Shavers And The Blues Singers* [Timeless CBC 1–025].) The repertoire is almost exclusively blues, and all the horns find solo space. Eight years of recording silence intervened, then Howard returned in the company of the Big Three Trio (Caston, Dennis and Dixon), whose harmonized humming makes a fetching frame for her deep-voiced blues singing on 'I Keep On Worrying', 'When I Been Drinking', 'Help Me Baby', which opens with a piano figure from Big Maceo's 'Worried Life Blues', and 'Where Shall I Go'. Her final session was with a septet with three horns; Big Bill played guitar, and his vocal influence is evident in the two blues, 'You Made Me Love You' and 'Plough Hand Blues'. TR

Peg Leg Howell (1888–1966)
VOCAL, GUITAR

Joshua Howell grew up in rural Georgia and began playing guitar at about the age of 21. He lost his right leg in a shooting. About 1923 he moved to Atlanta, where he operated as a bootlegger before taking up music, in which he was often joined by the fiddler Eddie Anthony, guitarist Henry Williams and other musicians, though he also performed on his own, mostly on the city's streets. After Anthony's death in 1934 he quit music, and in 1952 he lost his other leg through diabetes. In 1963, frail and wheelchair-bound, he was interviewed and recorded for the last time; the performances were released on a Testament LP with the caveat that they were of strictly documentary value, and are unlikely to be reissued.

***(*) Peg Leg Howell & Eddie Anthony: Vol. 1 (1926–1928)
Matchbox MBCD-2004 Howell; Eddie Anthony (vn, v); Henry Williams (g, v); Waymon 'Sloppy' Henry (poss. g, v). 11/26–8/28.

Rugged and without artifice, Howell's early solo recordings like 'Coal Man Blues' do not lack appeal but they are rather overshadowed by his trio sides with Anthony and Williams, which give us a stringband music both less suave and more diverse than that of their near-contemporaries the Mississippi Sheiks. Anthony leads his colleagues through 'Beaver Slide Rag' (a fast blues), 'Too Tight Blues' (half blues, half rag) and 'Peg Leg Stomp' ('Bugle Call Rag') with scarcely a pause in his deft and very bluesy fiddling. 'Georgia Crawl' and 'Lonesome Blues' are delivered in much the same manner by Anthony and Williams alone.

The demands of a recording contract evidently encouraged Howell to polish his guitar playing, and within a year of his debut he was able to produce the delicate yet insistent accompaniment to 'Skin Game Blues', one of several archaic pre-blues songs in his repertoire. A few months later he used a slide prettily on 'Please Ma'am', a piece largely played on one chord, and 'Rock And Gravel Blues'. Whether the more trenchant slide playing on 'Sloppy' Henry's 'Canned Heat Blues' and the vaudeville song 'Say I Do It' is also Howell's is open to doubt.

*** Peg Leg Howell & Eddie Anthony: Vol. 2 (1928–1930)
Matchbox MBCD-2005 As above, except add poss. Ollie Griffin, unknown (vn), Jim Hill (md, v), 'Tampa Joe' (g, v); poss. omit Williams. 8/28–12/30.

Howell is definitely present on only ten of this CD's 21 tracks. 'Turkey Buzzard Blues' with Anthony is a rare African-American recording of 'Turkey In The Straw' which also contains an early appearance of the phrase 'hoochie coochie man'. 'Broke And Hungry Blues' and 'Rolling Mill Blues', a variant of the common-stock song '900 Miles', have a fiddler whose wavering, ghostly tone is not at all like Anthony's. A few days later Howell cut four sides with Jim Hill, who brings his mandolin to the fore on 'Chittlin' Supper', an instrumental blues with chitchat, and 'Away From Home'.

Eight sides, recorded for OKeh rather than Columbia (Howell's patron), are credited to 'Tampa Joe & Macon Ed'. The nominal echo of Tampa Red & Georgia Tom was deliberate: one side of the duo's first recording, 'Worrying Blues', is based on Tampa Red's 'It's Grieving Me', while the reverse, 'Wringing That Thing', is a 'Tight Like That' variant. Macon Ed is certainly Eddie Anthony, but the identity of Tampa Joe is elusive – indeed, the duo's two sessions may feature different Tampa Joes, for the second couples Anthony's fiddle with a slide guitar. The mystery deepens on 'Try That Thing', where the lead singer sounds not unlike Barbecue Bob. 'Warm Wipe Stomp' reprises the melody of 'Too Tight Blues'. A second fiddler is heard on 'Tantalizing Bootblack'; there are also two fiddles on the final track, 'I'll Play My Harp In Beulah Land', a sacred song (unissued on 78) performed by several voices and a stringband, but the participants are not obviously related to any of the combinations heard before. Both CDs were remastered at a low level but the transfer quality is acceptable. All Howell's recordings, as well as those by Williams & Anthony and Macon Ed & Tampa Joe and the 1928 'Sloppy' Henry sides, are also on *Atlanta Blues* (JSP JSP 7754 4CD). TR

Howlin' Wolf (1910–76)
VOCAL, HARMONICA, GUITAR

Chester Arthur Burnett was born in West Point, near Tupelo, Mississippi. As a teenager he went on the road with his guitar and harmonica, encountering Robert Johnson, Elmore James and Sonny Boy Williamson II. In Memphis he made a great impression on Sam Phillips of Sun Records, who recorded him at length for Chess, and when Wolf moved to Chicago in 1953 he became one of Chess's major acts. The blues revival of the '60s expanded his audience, previously limited to Chicago clubs like Sylvio's Lounge and the 708, to international proportions, and in 1970, like his rival Muddy Waters, he made an album in London with British admirers. Illness reduced his travelling in the '70s, but the determined fan could still find him holding court at West Side hangouts like the Blue Flame or the 1815 Club.

**** Memphis Days – The Definitive Edition, Vol. 1
Bear Family BCD 15460 *Howlin' Wolf; Walter 'Tang' Smith (tb); Charles Taylor, unknowns (ts); unknown (s); James Cotton (h); William Johnson, L. C. Hubert, poss. Albert Williams (p); Willie Johnson (g); unknown(s) (b); Willie Steele (d).* 5/51–10/52.
**** Memphis Days – The Definitive Edition, Vol. 2
Bear Family BCD 15500 *As above, except add Ike Turner (p).* 5/51–10/52.
**** Howlin' Wolf 1951–1952
Classics 5056 *Howlin' Wolf; unknowns (s); Ike Turner, poss. Albert Williams, L. C. Hubert (p); Willie Johnson, Calvin Newborn (g); poss. Tuff Green (b); Willie Steele (d).* 5/51–1/52.
(***) Wolf At Your Door
Arpeggio ARB 015 *As above, except omit Newborn.* 5/51–2/52.
*** Howlin' At The Sun
Charly CPCD 8235 *As for* Memphis Days – The Definitive Edition, Vol. 2. 5/51–10/52.
*** Come Back Home
Snapper Complete Blues SBLUECD 017 *As above.* 5/51–10/52.
*** A Proper Introduction To Howlin' Wolf: Memphis Days
Proper INTRO CD 2001 *As above.* 5/51–late 52 or 53.
*** The Wolf Is At Your Door
Indigo IGOCD 2543 *As above, except add Calvin Newborn (g).* 5/51–late 52 or 53.
**** Howling Wolf Sings The Blues
Ace CDCHM 1013 *As for* Howlin' Wolf 1951–1952, *except omit unknowns (s).* 9/51–2/52.
*** Moanin' At Midnight: The Memphis Recordings
Fuel 2000 302 061 220 *As for* Memphis Days – The Definitive Edition, Vol. 2. 9/51–52.
(***) Cadillac Daddy
Rounder CD SS 28 *As above.* 1/52–late 52 or 53.
*** Howlin' Wolf 1952–1953
Classics 5098 *As above, except add unknown (d).* 2/52–late 52 or 53.

Between 1951 and '52 (or possibly '53) Wolf recorded simultaneously for Chess and Modern. The Chess material was produced by Sam Phillips at the Sun studio in Memphis, Modern's by Ike Turner, more informally, in West Memphis, Arkansas. The Phillips/Chess material amounted to 30 distinct songs and ten alternative takes, the Modern material to about half as much. Most of the accompanying musicians are involved in both series of recordings, and there is some duplication of repertoire.

These pre-Chicago recordings are regarded by some of Wolf's admirers as his finest. They certainly have qualities that are not so apparent in his later work. Phillips recorded his voice with such care that one hears not only its obvious characteristics like power and abrasiveness but chuckling humour and even tenderness. Also, in Willie Johnson Wolf found not a sideman but a man to stand beside, an equal partner, whose guitar lines in pieces like 'Highway Man' or the magnificent 'My Troubles And Me' are as expressive as Wolf's singing and as intrinsic to the performance.

The enthusiastic and tidy-minded reader can round up all this material by buying just three CDs, Bear Family's *Memphis Days – The Definitive Edition, Vol. 1* and *Vol. 2* for the Phillips/Chess sides and *Howling Wolf Sings The Blues* (Ace) for Modern's. The recordings which they exhaustively document are also scattered, incompletely, across the other nine CDs listed above. *Howlin' At The Sun* and *Come Back Home* (which are virtually identical), the *Proper Introduction* (which isn't very different) and *Cadillac Daddy* (too short to be good value) confine themselves to Phillips's recordings, while the Arpeggio, Indigo, Fuel 2000 and Classics CDs mix them with Modern's. The best buys, for the reader content with just one CD from this period of Wolf's work, are the first Classics collection, the Indigo and the Ace. (The Arpeggio is almost the same as the Indigo but unattractively presented.) What gives Ace and Classics the edge is their inclusion of all the 1951 Modern sides, which are redolent with the smoking guitar playing – as Wolf himself describes it in 'House Rockin' Boogie' – of Willie Johnson. There's also a remarkable tearaway solo, possibly by a different guitarist, on 'Keep What You Got'. (Both these items are omitted by Indigo.) Tracks like those, which are in effect proto-rock 'n' roll, are balanced by 'Crying At Daybreak' and 'Moaning At Midnight', set to the riff Wolf and Johnson would later immortalize in 'Smokestack Lightnin''. Ace further score with their superb presentation.

**** His Best
MCA/Chess CHD 9375//(E) MCD 09375 *Howlin' Wolf; Adolph 'Billy' Duncan, Abb Locke, J. T. Brown, Arnold Rogers (ts); Donald Hankins (bs); Ike Turner, Otis Spann, Hosea Lee Kennard, [Little] Johnny Jones, Henry Gray, Lafayette Leake (p); Buddy Guy (g, b); Willie Johnson, Jody Williams, Hubert Sumlin, Smokey Smothers, Abe Smothers, Freddy King, Jimmy Rogers (g); Willie Dixon (b, sp); Alfred Elkins, Andrew McMahon (b); Willie Steele, Earl Phillips, S. P. Leary, Fred Below, Sam Lay (d). 5/51–8/64.*

♛ **** The Collection
Spectrum 112047 *As above, except add Jerome Arnold (b), Junior Blackman (d); omit Duncan, Locke, Abe Smothers, Elkins, Leary. 5/51–8/64.*

**** The Genuine Article – The Best Of Howlin' Wolf
MCA/Chess MCD 11073 *Howlin' Wolf; Adolph 'Billy' Duncan, Abb Locke, J. T. Brown, Arnold Rogers, Eddie Shaw (ts); Donald Hankins (bs); Jeffrey Carp (h); Stevie Winwood (o); Ike Turner, Otis Spann, Hosea Lee Kennard, [Little] Johnny Jones, Henry Gray, Lafayette Leake, unknown (p); Buddy Guy (g, b); Willie Johnson, Lee Cooper, Jody Williams, Hubert Sumlin, Smokey Smothers, Abe Smothers, Freddy King, Jimmy Rogers, Eric Clapton (g); Willie Dixon (b, sp); Alfred Elkins, Andrew McMahon, Bill Wyman, unknown (b); Willie Steele, Earl Phillips, S. P. Leary, Fred Below, Sam Lay, Cassell Burrows, Charlie Watts (d). 5/51–5/70.*

***(*) His Best, Vol. 2
MCA/Chess CHD-12026 *As above, except add unknowns (ts), Albert Williams, L. C. Hubert, Lee Eggleston (p); Jerome Arnold, unknown (b), Junior Blackman, unknown (d); omit Turner, King. 12/51–5/70.*

What Chicago, and in particular Willie Dixon, gave to Wolf's music was drama. Studio echo, carefully defined drum sound and other devices provided Wolf with an aural stage to stalk, and the result was definitive, unimprovable performances like 'Smokestack Lightnin'' and 'I Asked For Water (She Gave Me Gasoline)', songs evocative of the back-country South yet charged with urban electricity. Then, during 1959–64, he had an extraordinary run of terrific songs. *His Best* and the very similar but cheaper *The Collection* share many of them – 'Wang Dang Doodle', 'Back Door Man', 'I Ain't Superstitious', 'Spoonful', 'The Red Rooster', 'Goin' Down Slow', 'Built For Comfort', 'Killing Floor' – but *The Collection* goes a few better by adding 'Down In The Bottom', 'Tail Dragger' and the idiotic but lovable dance number 'Do The Do'. The sequence is a stunning object-lesson in how to take a handful of melodically generic blues and make each of them distinct and memorable. No doubt Dixon's hand was crucial in recasting these ancient texts, some of which harked back to figures of his and Wolf's youth like Charley Patton, but consider the help he had: pianists of the calibre of Spann, Jones and Gray, and the young Hubert Sumlin at his riotous, inventive best.

The Genuine Article has many of the same tracks as *His Best* but drops 'Shake For Me', 'Built For Comfort' and 'Hidden Charms' (whose charm is indeed well hidden), replacing them with six other Chicago recordings, an acoustic solo 'Ain't Goin' Down That Dirt Road' and the *London Howlin' Wolf Sessions* recording (see below) of 'The Red Rooster'. This last is also on *His Best, Vol. 2*, which of course dovetails neatly with *His Best*, adding a number of second-grade (but still very good) early and late sides as well as tracks from the glory years of the early '60s like 'Down In The Bottom', 'You'll Be Mine', 'Just Like I Treat You' and 'Tail Dragger'.

** Howlin' Wolf/Moanin' In The Moonlight
MCA/Chess CHD 5908 *Similar to* His Best. 5/51–12/61.

A twofer containing the two most important of Wolf's Chess albums ought to be a very satisfactory entry-point to his music. *Moanin' In The Moonlight*, drawn from singles made between 1951 and '58 ('Evil', 'Smokestack Lightnin'', 'I Asked For Water', etc.), is unexceptional, but *Howlin' Wolf* (often, thanks to its bizarre cover design, called 'the rocking chair album'), which contains many of the early-'60s classics listed above, has been transferred from a fake-stereo pressing and sounds dreadful.

*** The Real Folk Blues/More Real Folk Blues
MCA 112 820 *Howlin' Wolf; Adolph 'Billy' Duncan, J. T. Brown, Arnold Rogers, Eddie Shaw, unknown (ts); Donald Hankins (bs); Otis Spann, Hosea Lee Kennard, [Little] Johnny Jones, Lafayette Leake, Lee Eggleston, unknown (p); Buddy Guy (g, b); Willie Johnson, Lee Cooper, Jody Williams, Hubert Sumlin, Smokey Smothers (g); Willie Dixon, Alfred Elkins, Jerome Arnold, Andrew McMahon, unknowns (b); Fred Below, Earl Phillips, Junior Blackman, Sam Lay, unknown (d). late 52 or 53–4/65.*

The early '50s and early '60s are the twin peaks of Wolf's career, but the terrain between them is only metaphorically flat. Quite a lot of mid-'50s work is on view here, from early Chicago sides like 'I'm The Wolf' and 'Rockin' Daddy' to the unusual 'Nature'. Willie Johnson, who eventually followed Wolf to Chicago, is on a few sides before handing over to Sumlin. Wolf's post-'Killing Floor' world is briefly investigated in sides like 'My Country Sugar Mama', where Lafayette Leake's piano intro sounds so like Big Maceo that it's eerie. The CD puts together two old LPs; *The Real Folk Blues* was also available on its own (MCA/Chess CHD 9273) but may be deleted. A third of the tracks are also on *His Best, Vol. 2*.

**(*) Chicago Blue
Tomato TOM-2103 *Howlin' Wolf; Adolph 'Billy' Duncan, Arnold Rogers, Eddie Shaw, unknown (ts); Donald Hankins (bs); Hosea Lee Kennard, Henry Gray, Lafayette Leake, Lee Eggleston, unknown (p); Willie Johnson, Smokey Smothers, Hubert Sumlin, Jimmy Rogers, Buddy Guy, unknown (g); Willie Dixon (b, sp); Alfred Elkins, Andrew McMahon, unknowns (b); Earl Phillips, Sam Lay, Cassell Burrows, unknown (d). 52 or 53–4/66.*

This contains two Memphis recordings, 'Streamline Woman' and 'Hold On To Your Money', the latter featuring what may be the only drum solo on a Wolf record, and eight Chicago ones, mostly from the '60s, including 'Commit A Crime', which wasn't issued at the time. The album is short and unprepossessing-looking and the sound is sometimes mediocre but few of the tracks are currently available elsewhere.

**(*) Rockin' The Blues – Live In Germany 1964
Acrobat ACMCD 4010 *Howlin' Wolf; Sunnyland Slim (p); Hubert Sumlin (g); Willie Dixon (b); Clifton James (d). 11/64.*

**(*) Kings Of The Blues
Pulse PLSCD 595 *As above.* 11/64.

(*) Killing Floor
Blue Moon CDBM 121 *As above and for* The London Howlin' Wolf Sessions. 11/64–late 70.

At this Bremen concert, at least in the form in which it has been preserved on record, Sumlin is nowhere near loud enough to give the performances the bite of the original studio recordings, but Sunnyland Slim and a vigorous Dixon keep up the momentum and Wolf is in good voice. The Acrobat and Pulse issues are identical in content; *Smokestack Lightning – Live In Germany 1964* (Collectors Edition CBCD 026) is the same set but from an inferior source and barely listenable. The same is true of the seven tracks from the concert that are included in *Killing Floor*; the remaining nine cuts on this CD are from the London session (see below) and a later Chess date in Chicago, though the notes will not tell you that.

*** **The London Howlin' Wolf Sessions (DeLuxe Edition)**
MCA 112 985 2CD *Howlin' Wolf; Jordan Sandke (t); Dennis Lansing (ts); Joe Miller (bs); Jeffrey M. Carp (h); Steve Winwood (o, p); Ian Stewart, Lafayette Leake, John Simon (p); Eric Clapton, Hubert Sumlin (g); Bill Wyman (b, shaker, cowbell); Klaus Voorman, Phil Upchurch (b); Charlie Watts (d, cga, perc); Richie [Ringo Starr] (d). 5–6/70.*

Though Wolf was initially suspicious of working with British musicians, thinking that they wouldn't be able to execute his music as he wanted to hear it, he apparently came away from the week-long London session quite pleased, a verdict that many listeners over the years have echoed. The British musicians, for the most part, get it; Clapton is excellent, Ian Stewart reliable as ever on piano. Sometimes the arrangement clings a little too lovingly to that of the original recording, as in 'The Red Rooster' or 'Who's Been Talking?', but perhaps that was how Wolf, or the Brits, wanted it. But not always: 'Do The Do', for instance (and you wonder who suggested this delightful but not particularly well-known number), throws out Chess's burping saxes and rides on a guitar riff. The London tapes were taken back to Chicago and remixed, sometimes with extra or replacement parts, but Disc 2 of this set lets us hear seven of the songs in unvarnished London versions, as well as some alternative 1970 mixes. Disc 1 contains the original album as it was issued, an honest piece of work with no awkward period touches. Bill Dahl's notes draw on producer Norman Dayron's vivid memories of the session, the packaging is handsome and altogether this is an exemplary reissue.

(**(*)) The Legendary Masters Series
Aim 0003 *Similar to above, except add Eddie Shaw, unknown (ts), Lee Eggleston, Henry Gray (p), Buddy Guy, unknown (g), unknowns (b), Sam Lay, Cassell Burrows (d). 4/65–70.*

This negligible release holds two late Chess singles, 'I Walked From Dallas' and 'My Mind Is Ramblin'', and ten tracks from the London session.

*** **Live And Cookin' At Alice's Revisited**
MCA/Chess CHD-9339 *Howlin' Wolf; Eddie Shaw (ts); Sunnyland Slim (p); Hubert Sumlin, L. V. Williams (g); David Myers (b); Fred Below (d). 1/72.*

A gig at Alice's Revisited, a North Side Chicago coffeehouse, gives an accurate picture of Wolf and his band in public. It's a pleasure to hear Sumlin high in the mix, and it would have been even more of one if Wolf's vocal mike had been as fairly treated. By 'Call Me The Wolf' some of the bandsmen have slipped out of tune; Wolf, about to embark on a harmonica solo, plays a single chord, hears the problem and puts the harp down again. The difficulty surmounted, he proceeds with a programme in which his personal standards are remarkably thin on the ground, culminating in two long, magnificent tracks not included on the original LP, 'The Big House' and 'Mr Airplane Man'.

** **Live At Joe's Place 1973**
Wolf 120.100 *Howlin' Wolf; Eddie Shaw (ts, v); Detroit Jr (p, v); Hubert Sumlin (g); Andrew McMahon (b, v); S. P. Leary (d). 5/73.*

Wolf had not long been out of hospital, following a car accident, when he appeared at Joe's Place in Cambridge, Massachusetts, in the spring of 1973. He sings on only four of the 13 numbers and, although he tackles them like the great-hearted artist he was, he inspires a lively groove in 'Blind Love', this is not a performance to cherish. The rest of the programme is songs by his sidemen or instrumentals led by Shaw, not very sympathetically recorded and interspersed with too much presentational chatter.

*** **The Back Door Wolf**
MCA/Chess CHD-9358 *Howlin' Wolf; Eddie Shaw (ts); Detroit Jr (kb, p); Hubert Sumlin, Willie Harris (g); James Green or Andrew McMahon (b); S. P. Leary (d). 8/73.*

The Back Door Wolf was produced by Ralph Bass, who demanded a lot of echo, particularly on the title track, a slow blues jog led by Eddie Shaw; it's his only playing on the album, but he contributed four of the songs, including a 'Watergate Blues' and the arresting 'Coon On The Moon', which celebrates some little-known African-American scientific pioneers. Bass also had Detroit Jr switch on some tracks to an electric keyboard programmed to sound like a harpsichord, a period touch but not a particularly irritating one. Sumlin plays with the edge of his youth, and Wolf sings with imperturbable gravity. 'I'm still a back door man, but I ain't gonna tote my .44 no more,' he declares in the opening 'Moving'. 'I'm still built for comfort, and my name ring everywhere I go.' So this is no valediction; nor is the final track, 'Can't Stay Here', since its title is derived from a Charley Patton song, remembered from more than 40 years before.

**** **The Chess Box**
MCA/Chess CHD3-9332 3CD *Howlin' Wolf; various accompaniments. 5/51–8/73.*

This lavish boxed set spans Wolf's entire recording career on Chess, from his debut single 'Moanin' At Midnight'/'How Many More Years' to 'Moving' from *The Back Door Wolf*, a well-chosen *envoi*. In between are about a dozen more of the Phillips Memphis recordings, virtually all the great sides of the early '60s, the London 'Red Rooster' and a good deal more, accompanied by a profusely illustrated booklet with essays by Chris Morris and Dick Shurman. Thanks to MCA's attention to Wolf's back catalogue over the years, there is little here that isn't available somewhere else, but it's entirely right that they should also have constructed this handsome memorial. TR

Johnny Hoy & The Bluefish
GROUP

Hoy (born 1957) became a blues fan in his teens and began playing harmonica at 18. He founded The Bluefish in the '80s, then re-formed it, after a break, in the '90s. Based in Martha's Vineyard, the group plays all over the Northeast, and is reputed to have been President Clinton's favourite blues band.

**(*) Trolling The Hootchy
Tone-Cool CD TC 1151 *Johnny Hoy (h, v); Teo Leyasmeyer, Jeremy Berlin (p); Buck Shank (g, v); Danny Kortchmar (g); Barbara Hoy (b, v); Mickey Bones (d, rb, bones); Marco Jean Renaud, Mike Canfield (d).* 95.

**(*) You Gonna Lose Your Head
Tone-Cool CD TC 1157 *Johnny Hoy (h, v); Jeremy Berlin (ac, o, p); Buck Shank, Slim Bob Berosh, Danny Kortchmar (g); Barbara Puciul Hoy (b, tamb, v); Tauras Biskis (d, wb, perc); Winston Grennan (d).* 96?

**(*) Walk The Plank
Tone-Cool CD TC 1166 *David Sholl (ts, bs); Johnny Hoy (h, v); Jeremy Berlin (ac, o, p, perc, v); Claudia Mogel (vn); Bruce Millard (md); Don 'Psycho-Picker' Groover (bj, g); Geoff Pattison (psg); Slim Bob Berosh, Troy Gonyea, Buck Shank (g); Barbara Puciul Hoy (b, perc, v); Tony Garnier (b); Tauras Biskis (d); Charlie Esposito (v).* 98.

The USP of this band is Hoy's voice, barking or slurring the lyrics and occasionally percolating them through the harmonica, producing something of the effect of Tom Waits played backwards. There are at least a few blues standards on each album; some are enterprisingly unstandard, like the laidback 'No More Doggin' on *Trolling The Hootchy*, others satisfyingly retro, like 'Mellow Chick Swing' and 'Just To Be With You' on *You Gonna Lose Your Head*. Hoy's original numbers, cast in blues, rock 'n' roll, country and cajun moulds, are likeable rather than memorable; *Walk The Plank* is perhaps their most varied showcase. A more recent live album with a new lineup, *In Action*, has had limited distribution. TR

Joe 'Guitar' Hughes (1937–2003)
VOCAL, GUITAR

In his teens Hughes was a member of the Dukes of Rhythm with Johnny Copeland, whom he taught to play. After the group broke up in the '60s, Hughes worked as a sideman for Little Richard, Bobby Bland and others, but spent the next decade back in Houston, largely sidelined by disco. A 1985 festival appearance in the Netherlands brought him new audiences in Europe and at home.

*** Down & Depressed: Dangerous
Munich NETCD 0044 *Hughes; Sonny Boy Terry (h); Tanya F. Richardson (b); David 'Poochie' Lartigue (d).* 3/93.

**(*) Texas Guitar Slinger
Me & My Blues MMBCD 1 *Hughes; Nelson Mims III, Keith Anderson (t); Jeff Cooper, Bruce Melville (tb); Don Slocomb Jr (s); Charles Rhinehart (kb); Rickey L. Morris, Paul Chevalier, Mark May (g); Jerry Jenkins (b); Norvell Holmes (d).* 3–5/95.

***(*) Stuff Like That
Blues Express BEI-0002 *Hughes; Marvin McFadden (t); Mic Gillette (tb); George Brooks (s); Dave Matthews (kb); Tim Brockett (o); Bobby Murray (g); Leonard Gill (b); Tony Coleman (d).* 00.

Albert Collins was a neighbour in Houston, and he and Hughes drank from the same musical fountain; on the title track of *Texas Guitar Slinger*, Hughes acknowledges various other Houstonians, but his incisive, economical playing is deep-rooted rather than derivative. *Down & Depressed: Dangerous* was recorded in the Netherlands with Hughes's touring band; perhaps fortunately, it doesn't make good on the ominous promise of its title. It's a respectable set, notable for some idiosyncratic bass guitar, but Hughes and the band seldom rise higher than professional; exceptions are his elegant blues-ballad, 'I Wanna Know', and an authoritative revival of 'Don't Throw Your Love On Me So Strong'.

Texas Guitar Slinger disappoints, despite some strong songs and a sizeable horn section, which suits Texas electric guitar music better than the harmonica. Hughes performs with ardour, but is let down by engineering that makes the horns sound thin, distant and murky. This disc may still be findable as Bullseye Blues BB 9568, which is deleted, as are two CDs for Double Trouble and one on Black Top.

Five of the nine songs on *Stuff Like That* are revived from the two CDs already discussed, and the high quality of these later versions blows the earlier discs away. *Stuff Like That* features studio recordings with an audience present, made by engineers who know their business, and Hughes responds admirably to the audience's enthusiasm, the terse brass and reed charts played by big-lunged musicians, Brockett's sinuous, coiling organ riffs and a tight rhythm section. CS

Helen Humes (1913–81)
VOCAL

Born in Louisville, Kentucky, Humes first recorded in her early teens, under the patronage of the local guitarist Sylvester Weaver. Resuming her career in the '30s, she sang with the Harry James and Count Basie orchestras. In the mid-'40s she moved to LA, where she recorded prolifically for several of the city's new labels. Although mostly successful with blues numbers, she preferred to be thought of as a singer of standards, and in later years made several exquisite recordings in that idiom with first-rate jazz musicians. Though she periodically left the music business for other work, she never stayed away for long, and in the '60s and '70s she travelled widely.

*** Helen Humes 1927–1945
Classics 892 *Humes; Dizzy Gillespie, Bobby Stark, Ross Butler (t); Herbie Fields (cl, as); Jimmy Hamilton (cl); Pete Brown, John Brown (as); Prince Robinson, Wild Bill Moore (ts); Ernest Thompson (bs); poss. DeLoise Searcy, J. C. Johnson, Sammy Price, Leonard Feather, Bill Doggett (p); Lonnie Johnson, Sylvester Weaver, Walter Beasley, Chuck Wayne, Elmer Warner (g); Charlie Drayton, Oscar Pettiford, Alfred Moore (b); Ray Nathan, Denzil Best, Charles Harris (d).* 4/27–summer 45.

*** Complete 1927–1950 Studio Recordings
The Jazz Factory JFCD 22844 3CD *Humes; Harry James, Buck Clayton, Dizzy Gillespie, Bobby Stark, Ross Butler, Snooky Young, John Anderson, Pete Candoli, Jack Trainor, Vernon Smith, unknowns (t); Eddie Durham, Vernon Brown, Williams Woodman, George Matthews, Britt Woodman (tb); Herbie Fields (cl, as); Jimmy Hamilton, Scoville Brown (cl); Jack Washington (as, bs); Earl Warren, Pete Brown, John Brown, Willie Smith, Edmond*

Hall, Marshall Royal (as); Herschel Evans, Prince Robinson, Wild Bill Moore, Tom Archia, Corky Corcoran, Maxwell Davis, Lester Young, John Hardee, Rudy Williams, Henry Bridges, Dexter Gordon (ts); Ernest Thompson, Jack McVea, Maurice Simon (bs); poss. DeLoise Searcy, J. C. Johnson, Jess Stacy, Sammy Price, Leonard Feather, Bill Doggett, Arnold Ross, Jimmy Bunn, Meade Lux Lewis, Eddie Beal, Ram Ramirez, Teddy Wilson, Ernie Freeman, unknowns (p); Lonnie Johnson, Sylvester Weaver, Walter Beasley, Chuck Wayne, Elmer Warner, Allen Reuss, Dave Barbour, Irving Ashby, Mundell Lowe, unknowns (g); Walter Page, Charlie Drayton, Oscar Pettiford, Alfred Moore, Red Callender, Jimmy Rudd, Jimmy Butts, Leonard Bibb, unknowns (b); Jo Jones, Ray Nathan, Denzil Best, Charles Harris, Henry Tucker Green, Chico Hamilton, Oscar Bradley, J. C. Heard, unknowns (d). 4/27–11/50.

*** **Blue Prelude 1927–1947**
Topaz TPZ 1073 Humes; Dizzy Gillespie, Bobby Stark, Ross Butler, Snooky Young, Buck Clayton (t); George Matthews (tb); Herbie Fields (cl, as); Jimmy Hamilton (cl); Pete Brown, John Brown, Willie Smith (as); Prince Robinson, Wild Bill Moore, Tom Archia, Corky Corcoran, John Hardee (ts); Ernest Thompson (bs); J. C. Johnson, Sammy Price, Leonard Feather, Bill Doggett, Arnold Ross, Eddie Beal, Ram Ramirez (p); Sylvester Weaver, Walter Beasley, Chuck Wayne, Elmer Warner, Allen Reuss, Barney Kessel, Mundell Lowe (g); Charlie Drayton, Oscar Pettiford, Alfred Moore, Red Callender, Walter Page (b); Ray Nathan, Denzil Best, Charles Harris, Henry Tucker Green, Shadow Wilson, Jo Jones (d); Harry James & His Orchestra; Count Basie & His Orchestra. 11/27–6/47.

*** **Today I Sing the Blues 1927–1947**
EPM Blues Collection 15938 As above, except add Scoville Brown (cl), Lester Young, Maxwell Davis, Rudy Williams (ts), Jimmy Bunn, Teddy Wilson (p), Dave Barbour (g), Jimmy Rudd, Jimmy Butts (b); omit Beal, Kessel, Wilson, Harry James & His Orchestra. 11/27–12/47.

*** **Her Best Recordings 1927–1947**
Best Of Jazz 4058 As above, except add Harry James & His Orchestra; omit Stark, Fields, Robinson, Archia, Corcoran, Feather, Ross, Wayne, Reuss, Pettiford, Callender. 11/27–12/47.

*** **He May Be Your Man**
[Blue Boar CDBB 1019] Humes; Bobby Stark, Ross Butler, Snooky Young (t); Herbie Fields (cl, as); John Brown, Willie Smith (as); Prince Robinson, Wild Bill Moore, Tom Archia, Corky Corcoran, Lester Young, Maxwell Davis (ts); Ernest Thompson (bs); Leonard Feather, Bill Doggett, Arnold Ross, Jimmy Bunn (p); Chuck Wayne, Elmer Warner, Allen Reuss, Dave Barbour (g); Oscar Pettiford, Alfred Moore, Red Callender, Jimmy Rudd (b); Denzil Best, Charles Harris, Henry Tucker Green (d); Harry James & His Orchestra; Count Basie & His Orchestra. 12/37–12/45.

*** **Helen Humes 1945–1947**
Classics 1036 Humes; Snooky Young, Buck Clayton, unknown (t); George Matthews (tb); Scoville Brown (cl); Willie Smith, Edward Hale (as); Tom Archia, Corky Corcoran, Lester Young, Maxwell Davis, Wild Bill Moore, William Woodman, John Hardee, Rudy Williams (ts); Ernest Thompson (bs); Arnold Ross, Jimmy Bunn, Meade Lux Lewis, Eddie Beal, Ram Ramirez, Teddy Wilson, unknown (p); Allen Reuss, Dave Barbour, Irving Ashby, Mundell Lowe, unknown (g); Red Callender, Jimmy Rudd, Walter Page, Jimmy Butts, unknown (b); Henry Tucker Green, Chico Hamilton, Jo Jones, prob. Denzil Best, unknown (d). 45–12/47.

*** **In Her Own Words**
Ocium OCM 0012 Humes; Buck Clayton, unknowns (t); George Matthews (tb); Scoville Brown, unknown (cl); Willie Smith, Edward Hale (as); Wild Bill Moore, William Woodman, John Hardee, Rudy Williams (ts); Meade Lux Lewis, Eddie Beal, Ram Ramirez, Teddy Wilson, unknowns (p); unknown (cel); Irving Ashby, Mundell Lowe, unknowns (g); Red Callender, Walter Page, Jimmy Butts, unknowns (b); Chico Hamilton, Jo Jones, prob. Denzil Best, unknowns (d); The Contrastors (v). 46–12/48.

If you knew Helen Humes only from her later-life albums you would never suspect that she had once been a spirited interpreter of salty blues. Her early sides like 'Do What You Did Last Night' were rather hot stuff for a 13- or 14-year-old; by the '40s she was recording decidedly salacious material, and by 1950 the startling 'Airplane Blues' (regrettably only to be found on The Jazz Factory). Like Wynonie Harris, though with very different means, she could deliver smutty or celebratory blues with panache, as well as with sound musical instinct. The seven- or eight-piece bands typically heard behind her include many notables, several of whom claim their blues choruses with aplomb. Though her material became a little formulaic, the ingenious lyrics and the versatility of her approach keep monotony at bay.

The first Classics CD, after dealing with the teenage recordings, several of which have sedately pretty guitar duet accompaniments by Sylvester Weaver and Walter Beasley, leapfrogs a decade and rediscovers the singer in 1942, now grown up and vastly more skilled, in the company of Pete Brown and Dizzy Gillespie, the former very robust, the latter hardly audible. Sessions with groups led by Leonard Feather or Bill Doggett introduce the songs that defined her raunchy side, 'Fortune Tellin' Man', 'He May Be Your Man' and 'Be-Baba-Leba'. Helen Humes 1945–1947 continues the story in much the same vein ('Drive Me Daddy', 'Jet Propelled Papa') but also catches her on less rowdy material like 'Blue And Sentimental' and 'Today I Sing The Blues', both from a series of dates with Buck Clayton. The last 14 tracks are also the first 14 of In Her Own Words, which is somewhat better remastered.

What the Classics leave out is a few years at the end of the '30s when she recorded as vocalist with the Harry James and Count Basie bands, singing an occasional blues but concentrating on quality popular songs like 'If I Could Be With You One Hour Tonight' and 'Between The Devil And The Deep Blue Sea', which she phrases with delicate swing. This period is documented briefly by the EPM Blues Collection, in more depth by the Topaz, and quite thoroughly by the Best Of Jazz and Blue Boar sets. All four then proceed to her '40s work, thus overlapping the relevant portions of the Classics CDs. Readers in search of a single CD epitomizing Humes's first 20 years on record will do best with the EPM, a good selection, focused on her blues work but not confined to it. Those with a greater appetite should address themselves to The Jazz Factory's 3CD set, which contains everything mentioned so far except the vocals with Basie, and pushes on into 1950.

Humes often remarked that she was at heart a ballad singer; her career as a blues singer had been dictated by other people's tastes than her own. In three magnificent albums made for Contemporary between 1959 and 1961, 'Tain't Nobody's Biz-ness If I Do (Original Jazz Classics OJCCD-453), Songs I Like To Sing! (OJCCD-171) and Swingin' With Helen (OJCCD-608), she seized the opportunity to prove her case. Perhaps the best is Songs I Like To Sing!, where she sails majestically through the programme, expertly steered by the arranger and conductor Marty Paich, with Ben Webster and Art Pepper vying for the post of First Officer. But since all three sets are largely concerned with popular standards, interested parties are recommended to read about them, and her other late work, in the more appropriate pages of *The Penguin Guide To Jazz Recordings*. TR

Mark Hummel (born 1955)
VOCAL, HARMONICA

Hummel grew up in LA. During the '70s he played in Berkeley with Ron Thompson, Mississippi Johnny Waters and others. His first album was issued in 1985. He has toured extensively in the USA and Europe, building a name as one of the best harmonica players of his generation.

**(*) Feel Like Rockin'
Flying Fish FF 70634 *Hummel; Oscar Meyer (t); Gino Landry (s); Rick Estrin (h); Charles Brown (p, v); Jim Pugh, Jim Monroe (p); Brownie McGhee, Sue Foley (g, v); Rusty Zinn, Shorty Lenoir (g); Ronnie James, Marc Carino, Jon Penner (b); Jimi Bott, Mark Bohn, Bob Grant (d); band (v). 85–93.*

Most of these 16 tracks were recorded in 1991 or '93 with different rhythm sections but Zinn playing guitar on both dates. In this band setting Hummel reveals himself as an easygoing singer and agile harmonica player; for evidence of the latter, harpophiles should sample the instrumental 'Lost In The Shuffle' or his chromatic playing on 'Third Time Out' and 'Where You At'. Zinn plays a smart Magic Sam line on 'City Livin''. Three tracks are from the '80s. 'I'm Gonna Quit' with Foley from 1989 precedes her own debut album, but the recording is defective. The others are amiable collaborations with Brownie McGhee and Charles Brown.

*** Married To The Blues
Flying Fish FF 70647 *Hummel; John Firmin (ts); Rob Sudduth (bs); Charlie Musselwhite (h); Jim Pugh (kb); Steve Lucky (p); Rusty Zinn, Duke Robillard (g); Vince Elhers (b); Lance Dickerson, Jim Overton (d); band (v). 3/95.*

Naturally more focused than the eight-year survey that was *Feel Like Rockin'*, *Married To The Blues* gives Hummel the support of a stable lineup, occasionally augmented with the saxophones from The Johnny Nocturne Band, and elicits excellent harp playing in a variety of manners, from the New Orleans beat of 'No Buts, No Maybes' to the Chicago idiom of 'Can't Judge Nobody' and the very fine title track. 'High Steppin'' is a bravura duet with Charlie Musselwhite, while 'Bluesman' is a tribute to the Berkeley set of musicians Hummel worked with in the '70s.

*** Heart Of Chicago
Tone-Cool TC 1158 *Hummel; Barrelhouse Chuck (p); Steve Freund (g, v); Billy Flynn, Dave Myers (g); Bob Stroger (b); Willie 'Big Eyes' Smith (d). 96/97.*

Hummel had paid Chicago dues on previous albums, but evidently he needed to declare his affection for classic Chicago blues ways more explicitly; the result was this sturdy set accompanied by seasoned locals. Much of the repertoire comes from city fathers, such as Sonny Boy Williamson I's 'Step Back Baby' and Tampa Red's 'But I Forgive You', and the new compositions are firmly in the idiomatic mould, 'Peaches Tree' being grown from an Elmore James graft and 'Rollin' From Side To Side' blending harp and slide guitar in vintage Muddy style. Hummel's singing is much more convincing on this material.

*** Low Down To Uptown
Tone-Cool CD TC 1169 *Hummel; Bill Ortiz (t); Terry Hanck (ts); Rob Sudduth (bs); Steve Lucky, David Maxwell, Charles Brown (p); Junior Watson, Charles Wheal, Mike Welch (g); Ronnie James Weber, Mike McCurdy (b); June Core, Mark Bohn (d); Brenda Boykin (v). 1/97–2/98.*

**(*) Golden State Blues
Electro-Fi 3375 *Hummel; John Firmin (ts); Rob Sudduth (bs); Steve Lucky (kb); Charles Wheal, Rusty Zinn, Anson Funderburgh (g); Steve Wolf, Randy Bermudes (b); Marty Dodson, Paul Revelli (d). 1–4/02.*

**(*) Blowin' My Horn
Electro-Fi 3386 *Hummel; Mel Brown (kb); Charles Wheal (g); Steve Wolf (b); Marty Dodson (d). 9/03.*

His Chicago itch relieved – though it's to be hoped that he'll be afflicted by it again – Hummel returned to his home turf and friends like Zinn and the Nocturne crew, expanded on *Low Down To Uptown* to include Ortiz and Boykin. Junior Watson's guitar tone wraps the music on *Low Down* like fat round a joint of beef, and the sheer weight of pieces like 'Po' Man's Shoe Shine' makes Hummel's early work seem undernourished. The flavour of *Golden State Blues*, however, thanks to the choice of material and the somewhat sterilized studio sound, aligns it with the Flying Fish albums, which some listeners may judge a retrograde move. *Blowin' My Horn* avoids the sound problem, being a live recording, though not a very vibrant one, but Hummel's singing has too little colour or animation to carry the burden of half a dozen long numbers at slow or medium tempos. TR

Alberta Hunter (1895–1984)
VOCAL

Alberta Hunter left Memphis for Chicago at 16; by the time she made the first records issued in Paramount's 'race' series, she'd worked her way up from the seamy Dago Frank's to the classy Dreamland. Always an all-rounder, she first visited Europe in 1927, and the following year played opposite Paul Robeson in the London run of Showboat. During World War II and the Korean conflict Hunter entertained the troops with USO. In 1957 she retired from showbiz, knocked 12 years off her age and trained as a nurse; compelled to retire at 70 (so the hospital thought; she was 82!) she made a triumphant return, starring at the Cookery in Greenwich Village, recording again and appearing on talk shows and at the Carter White House.

**(*) Alberta Hunter – Vol. 1 (1921–1923)
Document DOCD-5422 *Hunter; unknown (c); prob. Elmer Chambers, Phil Napoleon, unknowns (t); poss. Chink Johnson, prob. George Brashear, Charlie Panelli, unknowns (tb); prob. Don Redman, Jimmy Lytell, unknowns (cl); prob. Ernest Elliott, unknown (as); unknowns (ts); Fletcher Henderson, Eubie Blake, Frank Signorelli, unknown (p); Charlie Dixon (bj); unknowns (bb); Jack Roth (d). c. 5/21–2/23.*

ALBERTA HUNTER

**(*) Alberta Hunter – Vol. 2 (1923–1924)
Document DOCD-5423 *Hunter; prob. Elmer Chambers, Joe Smith, Tommy Ladnier (c); prob. George Brashear, (tb); prob. Don Redman or Ernest Elliott, Jimmy O'Bryant (cl); Fletcher Henderson, Fats Waller, Lovie Austin, unknown (p); Charlie Dixon (bj); Elkins–Payne Jubilee Quartette (v).* 2/23–2/24.

**(*) Alberta Hunter – Vol. 5 (1921–1924) The Alternate Takes
Document DOCD-1006 *Similar to above CDs.* c. 5/21–2/24.

**(*) Alberta Hunter – Vol. 3 (1924–1927)
Document DOCD-5424 *Hunter; Louis Armstrong, unknowns (c); unknown (t); Aaron Thompson, Charlie Irvis, unknowns (tb); unknown (cl, as); unknown (cl); Buster Bailey, Sidney Bechet (ss); unknown (as); Lil Armstrong, Clarence Williams, Perry Bradford, Mike Jackson, unknown (p); Buddy Christian, unknown (bj); unknown (d).* 11/24–2/27.

**(*) Alberta Hunter – Vol. 4 (1927–1946)
Document DOCD-5425 *Hunter; Charlie Shavers (t); Buster Bailey, Leroy Jones (cl); Fats Waller (o); Lil Armstrong, Eddie Heywood Jr, Sam Clanton, unknowns (p); Al Casey, unknowns (g); Wellman Braud, Al Matthews (b).* 5/27–c. 46.

*** Young Alberta Hunter
Mojo CD-MOJO-310 *Similar to relevant CDs above.* c. 5/21–c. 46.

(***) Tell The Difference
Arpeggio ARB 007 *Similar to relevant CDs above.* 5/27–c. 46.

**(*) Beale Street Blues
Collectors Edition CBCD 006 *Similar to relevant CDs above, except add Jack Jackson's Orchestra.* c. 5/21–6/40.

In 1922 Alberta Hunter wrote 'Down Hearted Blues', Bessie Smith's first issued recording and a great lyric. Its arc from resignation to triumph ('I've got the world in a jug and the stopper in my hand') proves that her understanding of the blues was not shallow, but her early recordings are very variable in quality; often she seems more concerned to enunciate clearly than to convey emotion. Paramount recruited her as a cabaret star and made her a recording star, but her popularity seems to have waned with the advent of earthier singers governed by a more distinctively black aesthetic. Throughout her career, the quality of Hunter's performances was heavily dependent on chemistry with her accompanists. If they were lacklustre, so was she; conversely, if they had fire and jazz feeling, Hunter would give her best. More than usually, therefore, Document's self-imposed remit of presenting everything available regardless of quality makes for hard listening. Additionally, Document's first two volumes and the collection of alternative takes derive from Black Swan and Paramount, and some of the original discs are exceptionally rough even by those companies' standards.

Of the selective surveys, *Tell The Difference* can be ruled out: the sound is fairly vivid, but the gaps between tracks are often disconcertingly short, and at least on the copy used for evaluation, the final track is digitally defective. *Beale Street Blues*, from the same parent company, shares ten tracks with *Tell The Difference*; the remastering is less good but adequate. This disc is diminished, however, by three tracks with Jack Jackson's British danceband, recorded when Hunter was in cabaret at the Dorchester in 1934. These have a little camp charm, but are of no blues interest whatever; for what it's worth, they and more are on *The Legendary Alberta Hunter – The London Sessions* (DRG Disques Swing 5195).

Young Alberta Hunter is the preferred choice, alike for annotation, sound quality and selection, although like the other two it inexplicably ignores an excellent session with Ladnier and O'Bryant, which is on Document's second volume. From her early days there are two titles with Armstrong and Bechet (although neither song offers much opportunity to solo) and one – which is enough – featuring Fats Waller on pipe organ. A 1946 single is musically and sonically dull, but 'My Castle's Rockin'' and 'Boogie Woogie Swing' from 1940 have Eddie Heywood in uncharacteristically lively form. Hunter responds in kind, as she does on three tracks with fine, anonymous guitar and piano. These were not issued at the time of recording, but it's only clear why in the case of Maceo Pinkard's ode to miscegenation, 'You Can't Tell The Difference After Dark'. Most valuable is a six-track session with Shavers, Bailey, Lil Armstrong and Braud; it's the classic instance of Hunter responding to her accompanists and vice versa, and it peaks with a version of 'Fine And Mellow' that's far superior to Billie Holiday's. These six sides are also on *Charlie Shavers And The Blues Singers* (Timeless CBC 1–025).

**(*) Songs We Taught Your Mother
Original Blues Classics OBCCD-520 *Hunter; J. C. Higginbotham (tb); Buster Bailey (cl); Cliff Jackson (p); Sidney De Paris (tu); Zutty Singleton (d).* 8/61.

**(*) Alberta Hunter With Lovie Austin And Her Blues Serenaders
Original Blues Classics OBCCD 510 *Hunter; Jimmy Archey (tb); Darnell Howard (cl); Lovie Austin (p); Pops Foster (b); Jasper Taylor (d).* 9/61.

These former LPs were Hunter's only recordings while working as a nurse; her voice had deepened, but her pitch was secure and her enunciation still precise. The session with Lovie Austin *et al.* was recorded under severe time pressure (Hunter was between trains in Chicago) and, despite a band of veteran greats, it disappoints. Three tracks, and 14 out of 38 minutes, are instrumental jazz, and are the best of the disc, despite Austin being severely under-recorded; three of the vocal tracks are rather sanctimonious spirituals, and two are competently rendered popular songs which don't give the band much to chew on. Only a rowdy 'St. Louis Blues' and a warm revival of 'Downhearted [*sic*] Blues' hint at what might have been. Accompanied by another stellar band, Hunter does four of the *Songs We Taught Your Mother*. (Lucille Hegamin and Victoria Spivey share the balance of the disc.) For straightforwardness, honesty and emotional commitment these are Hunter's best recordings, slightly marred by Buster Bailey's intermittently over-elaborate responses.

*** Amtrak Blues
Columbia CK 36430 *Hunter; Doc Cheatham (t); Vic Dickenson (tb); Budd Johnson (ts); Gerald Cook (p); Billy Butler (g); Aaron Bell (b); Jackie Williams (d).* 78.

*** Downhearted Blues Live At The Cookery
Varèse Sarabande 302 066 247 *Hunter; Gerald Cook (p); Jimmy Lewis (b).* late 70s or early 80s.

In her last phase, Hunter recorded four LPs for Columbia, of which only *Amtrak Blues* is currently available. She still stressed popular song alongside the blues, but in line with the expectations of a new audience her delivery is more consistently salty and swinging; her jazzy reading of Irving Berlin's 'Always' is a highlight of this disc. Inevitably, 'marvellous for her age' was used as a selling point, but in sober truth Hunter's accuracy, timing and vigour were pretty astonishing. 'Amtrak Blues' and 'I've Got A Mind To Ramble' are two of her deepest blues interpretations, and she even convinces (just) when impersonating sexually voracious totty on 'My Handy Man Ain't Handy No More'.

Similar comments apply to the live CD. It too ranges from blues to pop and jazz, and Cook and Lewis are brilliantly inventive and effortlessly tasteful throughout. By all accounts, Hunter's impact on her audiences at the Cookery was extraordinary, and *Downhearted Blues* does much to explain this. Some of the audience reaction is in response to her age, regardless of musical quality, but much of it is a well-deserved response to charisma, energy and commitment. cs

Ivory Joe Hunter (1914–74)
VOCAL, PIANO, CELESTE

Some sources give a 1911 birthdate; east Texas was certainly the place. Hunter came from a musical family, and found work in carnivals and tent shows. By 1933, already going after better pay in white clubs, he was still rootsy enough to record 'Stackolee' for the Library of Congress; its surface noise, and not much else, can be heard on "Too Late, Too Late" – Vol. 10 (1926–1951) (Document DOCD-5601). Many of Hunter's commercial recordings feature lively horns and tough, boogie-inflected piano, but his music is often as polished as his horn rims, as warm as his pipe and as comfortable as his tweed jackets. In a long career, Hunter was at home with blues, ballads, country, rock 'n' roll, soul and pop; he was also a prolific, much-recorded songwriter.

*** Ivory Joe Hunter 1945–1947
Classics 5015 Hunter; Ernie Royal, unknowns (t); unknowns (tb); John Patterson, Eddie Taylor, Wardell Gray, Baker Millian (ts); unknown (bs); unknowns (s); Charles Brown (p); Johnny Moore, Pee Wee Crayton, unknown (g); Eddie Williams, Charlie Oden, Commodore Lark, unknown (b); Chuck Walker (d); 'Aurelia' (v). 45–47.

*** Ivory Joe Hunter 1947
Classics 5026 Hunter; Sonny Turner, Harold Baker, unknown (t); Tyree Glenn (tb); Andy Goodrich (cl, as); Russell Procope, unknown (as); John Patterson, Baker Millian, Sammy Ford, unknown (ts); Owen Bradley (g); Commodore Lark, Jimmy Lewis, Oscar Pettiford, unknown (b); Chuck Walker, Johnny Jarette, Sonny Greer, unknown (d). 47–12/47.

**(*) Ivory Joe Hunter 1947–1950
Classics 5049 Hunter; Harold Baker, poss. Henderson Williams, Taft Jordan, Ludwig Joe Jordan, Reunald Jones (t); Tyree Glenn (tb, vb); Leo Williams (tb); Russell Procope (cl, as, ts); Johnny Hodges, Pete Clarke, Joe Evans (as); Eddie ['Lockjaw'] Davis, Harry Porter, Budd Johnson, Elmer Williams (ts); Al Townsend (bs); Ray Nance (vn); Oscar Pettiford, Wendell Marshall, Frank Skeete, Bill Pemberton, Harold Holmes (b); Sonny Greer, Leon Abrams, Kelly Martin, Chuck Walker (d). 12/47–5/50.

**** Blues At Sunrise
[Indigo IGODCD 2515] 2CD *Similar to above CDs.* 45–5/50.

*** I Almost Lost My Mind 1945–1950
EPM Blues Collection 15999 *Similar to above CDs.* c. 45–late 50.

** Ivory Joe Hunter Sings 16 Of His Greatest Hits
King KCD-605 *Similar to relevant CDs above.* 9/47–8/49.

*** The King Sides Volume 1
Collectables COL-CD-2881 *Similar to relevant CDs above.* 9/47–7/49.

** Ivory Joe Hunter 1950–1951
Classics 5113 Hunter; Ludwig Joe Jordan, Reunald Jones, unknowns (t); Leo Williams (tb); Joe Evans, unknowns (as); Budd Johnson, Elmer Williams, unknowns (ts); unknown (bs); unknowns (strings); unknowns (g); Harold Holmes, unknowns (b); Chuck Walker, unknowns (d); band (v). 5/50–11/51.

Hunter's debut recording, 'Blues At Sunrise', accompanied by Johnny Moore's Three Blazers, offers a tougher version of Charles Brown's sophisticated sound; its ballad flipside parades Hunter's versatility, and comes from the side of his music that holds less appeal for many present-day listeners. Classics' sound quality is usually acceptable, but some early titles come from worn 78s. The label's dogged completism ('I Like It' on *1947* features Ellingtonians playing calypso!) is both admirable and a drawback; mixed with riff-based R&B, and some wonderful collaborations with Ellington's men, is material that defines the blandness of pre-Elvis pop. 'I Almost Lost My Mind', an R&B #1 for MGM in 1950, retains its caressing charm, and 'Guess Who', also on *1947–1950* and later revived by B. B. King, features expressive playing by Glenn and Nance; but many tracks, even – or perhaps especially – some of Hunter's other Top Ten hits, are mainly of historical interest. *1950–1951*, particularly, is packed with ballads that are as sickly as they're slick; in their company the swing instrumentals 'U Name It' and 'Music Before Dawn' sound even better than they are.

EPM and Indigo, selecting for bluesiness, are preferable. EPM are let down by some hissy originals and unexceptional remastering; *Blues At Sunrise*, with 50 mid-price tracks, offers the best selection, sound and value for money. Collectables' *Volume 1* contains 25 of Hunter's 32 King recordings, making the content of the putative *Volume 2* a puzzle. Collectables have mainly omitted the more gooey numbers, and those that remain are interspersed among tougher sides. This is consequently a more enjoyable CD than King's *16 Greatest Hits*, most of which are ballads or ballad-like blues; their cumulative lushness is cloying.

***(*) Since I Met You Baby: The Best Of Ivory Joe Hunter
Razor & Tie RE 2052 Hunter; Taft Jordan, Ludwig Joe Jordan, Reunald Jones (t); Leo Williams, Frank Saracco, Frank Rehak, Urbie Green (tb); Pete Clarke, Joe Evans, Romeo Penque, Leon Cohen, unknown (as); Budd Johnson (ts, bs); Elmer Williams, Jesse Powell, Seldon Powell, Sam Taylor, unknown (ts); Ernie Caceres, Dave McRae (bs); Wild Bill Davis, Dick Hyman (o); Moe Wechsler, Mike Stoller (p); Mickey Baker, Al Caiola, Billy Mure, Allen Hanlon, Everett Barksdale, Kenny Burrell, unknowns (g); Bill Pemberton, Harold Holmes, Hayward Cheeks, Lloyd Trotman, unknowns (b); Kelly Martin, Chuck Walker, Joe Marshall, unknowns (d); unknown (cga); Phil Kraus (perc); unknowns (orch); The Ivorytones [Cues], Myriam Workman, Marcia Neil, Elise Bretton, Robert Miller, Arthur Malvin, Ralph Nyland, Jimmy Leyden, Harold Anderson, John Anderson, Willie Williams, Gonzalo Mero (v). 10/49–3/58.

***(*) Blues, Ballads & Rock 'N' Roll
Ace CDCHD 747 *As above, except add unknown (bs), Rudy Williams, unknowns (v); omit Taft Jordan, Ludwig Joe Jordan, Jones, Leo Williams, Clarke, Evans, Elmer Williams, Caceres, Pemberton, Holmes, Martin, Walker, Malvin, Leyden.* 10/54–59.

Razor & Tie start with five MGM sides before moving on to the Atlantic years which are the sole focus on Ace. There's heavy duplication between these CDs, and neither is free from novelties, sentimentality and cynical attempts to separate teenagers from their allowances. Ivory Joe only gets close to lowdown on 'All About The Blues'; 'I'll Never Leave You Baby' and 'Yes I Want You' borrow their melodies from Blind Lemon Jefferson and Joe Pullum, but none of their manner.

Still, despite glossy production values and sometimes intrusive backing vocals, Hunter is often irresistible on Atlantic, above all on 'Since I Met You Baby' with its chiming piano and velvet alto sax. 'A Tear Fell', 'Empty Arms' and the Ted Daffan–Jimmie Davis composition 'Worried Mind' extend the exploration of country music that Hunter had pioneered on 1949's 'Jealous Heart', and which was about to pay off for Solomon Burke and Ray Charles. *Since I Met You Baby* wins on sound quality and consistency; the Ace CD has more tracks, but some of them are of doubtful merit.

** Ivory Joe Hunter/The Old And The New
Collectables COL-CD-6234 *As above, except add Arthur Malvin, Jimmy Leyden, Trudy Martin, Audrey Marsh, Glenn Cross, Carter Farriss, Bob Harter (v); omit Penque, Seldon Powell, Taylor, unknown (bs), Davis, Stoller, Barksdale, Burrell, Trotman, Kraus, Harold Anderson, John Anderson, Willie Williams, Mero, Rudy Williams, unknowns (v). 10/54–6/57.*

This CD combines two Atlantic LPs. The eponymous disc includes several fine tracks, which can be heard on Ace or Razor & Tie, and several that are less fine. 'Worried Mind' apart, *The Old And The New* is bland, fussily arranged pop, reaching its vapid nadir with 'I'll Take You Home Again Kathleen'.

** Blues At Midnight
M.I.L. Multimedia MIL 3038 *Similar to Classics 5015 and 5026, except add Aubrey Dunham (ts), Olivia Brown (o), Ted Hawley (g, v), Terry Mallett, Terrance Guidry (g), Earl Smith, George Brown (b), Chuck Campbell, Carl Lott (d), unknown (maracas), Sharon Smith (v). 45–47, 4–5/68.*

** Jumping At The Dew Drop
Aim 1305 *As above. 45–47, 4–5/68.*

After leaving Atlantic in 1958, Hunter spent two years with Dot, then label-hopped while living comfortably on his publishing royalties. These CDs have slightly different track-listings, but both are an uneasy blend of early material with newer recordings. Roy Ames's session musicians are competent but unimaginative and, in Guidry's case, loudly unsympathetic; Hunter's classic C&W composition 'The Cold Grey Light Of Dawn' is a diamond among the rhinestones. CS

Long John Hunter (born 1931)
VOCAL, GUITAR

Another transposed Louisianian, Hunter was inspired by a B. B. King gig in Beaumont, Texas, to take up music. Fired by an urge to entertain, he found his target audience in the border towns of El Paso, Texas, and Juarez, Mexico. Over succeeding decades, a sequence of singles he cut during the '60s took on sufficient importance for a full-scale resuscitation of a foundering career. Though tempered by age, Hunter still re-creates on record and stage the rowdy ambience of his earlier success.

*** Ooh Wee Pretty Baby
Norton CED 270 *Hunter; unknown (tb); unknown (ts); unknown (p); unknown (g); unknown (b); unknown (d); Dennis Roberts, Sonny Guitar (v). 61–71.*

It's easy to believe the reputation Hunter built for raucous entertainment in Juarez's Lobby Bar. By his own admission, he was backed by a ragged band of manically inspired Mexican musicians who couldn't speak English but knew how to rock. Cut for the Yucca label in Alamogordo, New Mexico, pumping instrumentals like 'El Paso Rock' and 'Slash' (sort of 'Tequila' with a worm) contrast with tough vocal workouts, 'Ride With Me' and 'Border Town Blues' among them. There's a refreshing crudity to both the sound quality and the musicianship, the latter exemplified by a hyperactive drummer who performs like Peck Curtis on speed. Both sides of singles by Roberts and Sonny Guitar are included but they fail to emulate the brusque energy of Hunter's own efforts. Hunter didn't have his eye on posterity then and this music succeeds because of that now.

***(*) Ride With Me
Alligator ALCD 4861 *Hunter; Gary Slechta (t); Mark Kazanoff (ts); Red Rails (bs); Ed Guinn (o); Erbie Bowser (p); T. D. Bell (g, v); Derek O'Brien (g); Sarah Brown (b); George Rains (d). 92.*

First released in 1992 and reissued six years later, this album was Hunter's stepping-stone on to the festival circuit and it continues to impress. It's tightly arranged and played and his backing band, including veteran pianist Bowser, manage to be supportive and unobtrusive, Kazanoff taking a number of apposite solos. Hunter's vocals are lighter than before but no less convincing and his guitar playing is a model of conciseness and quiet authority. The title track sets the tone for what follows, a mixture of taut rockers and plangent slow blues. Another veteran, Bell, gets to duel guitars in 'West Texas Homecoming', the album's one light-hearted indulgence. Released by Alligator after the following albums, this one sets a higher standard than they manage to achieve.

**(*) Border Town Legend
Alligator ALCD 4839 *Hunter; Keith Winking, Martin Banks (t); Mark Kazanoff, Art Lewis (ts); Red Rails (bs); D. B. Cooper (o); Johnny Nicholas (p, g); Joe Kelley, Derek O'Brien, Michael Henry Martin, 'Guitar' Jake Andrews (g); Dave Keown, Sarah Brown (b); Kevin Taylor (d); Hunter Harmonettes (v). 96.*

Hunter's first album for a major blues label begins well but succumbs to the dread miasma of studio competence in its final stages, thereby falling short of its title. No wrong notes are played by leader or band but too often what is played lacks the vital spark that animated *Ride With Me*. This doesn't apply to 'T-Bone Intentions', a fully committed 'Grits Ain't Groceries' and the instrumental 'Lone Star Shootout', the latter featuring five guitarists including Hunter himself. Elsewhere, the other major fault of contemporary blues sessions, over-indulgence, diminishes tracks such as 'Ole Red' and 'Arkansas', the latter moribund way before its conclusion. 'Marfa Lights' and 'Nasty Ways' would have been better served with a less casual approach by all concerned. The result isn't a bad album but it lacks anything that would distinguish it from the hundreds like it.

**(*) Swinging From The Rafters
Alligator ALCD 4853 *Hunter; Martin Banks, Gary Slechta (t); Kevin Brown (as, ts, bs); Mark Kazanoff (ts, h); Les Iz Moore*

[Izmore] (bs); Mark Hamm, James Polk (kb); Derek O'Brien (g); Dave Keown (b); Kevin Taylor (d, v). 97.

The title refers to one of the more outlandish exploits that Hunter got up to at the Lobby Bar, but sadly what swinging takes place here remains earthbound. Once again, the musicians are immaculately prepared, the horn arrangements fill out the sound and everyone locks into place. On the other hand, they forgot to bring their spontaneity with them and that includes Hunter, whose vocal and guitar contributions are plainly overdubbed rather than performed in the heat of creation. Apart from Willie Love's 'V-8 Ford' and a remake of 'I Don't Care', most of the songs are the product of a committee made up of Hunter and three of the various producers and executive producers. The pristine nature of the finished album effectively erases the raw energy that characterized Hunter's earlier work, energy that he still possesses. NS

(*) One Foot In Texas
Doc Blues DB 6805 *Hunter; Gary Slechta (t); Les Izmore (bs); Mark 'Kaz' Kazanoff, John Mills (s); Gary Primich (h); Nick Connolly (kb); Tom 'Blues Man' Hunter (g, v); Derek O'Brien (g); Tommy Shannon (b); Chris Layton (d). 03?*

Jointly billed to Long John and his younger brother Tom, this is an amiable, laidback set of Texas shuffles and slow blues. Long John is the stronger and more charcterful singer, and 'Roll Over & Cover My Head' and 'I Give You All My Money' are absorbing slow blues, but there is a tendency to rely on well-tried settings, 'In Love With A Stranger' being laid over the organ-and-rhythm pattern of 'Green Onions' and 'Talkin' Country' using the riff from 'Hoochie Coochie Man'. The long 'Riffing And Reminiscing' has the brothers sharing inconsequential childhood memories before swapping licks, probably more to their own satisfaction than to the listener's. TR

Mississippi John Hurt (1893–1966)
VOCAL, GUITAR, HARMONICA

Birthdates of 1892 and 1894 are also reported; by the time he was two, Hurt had moved from Teoc to the eyeblink settlement of Avalon, his home for most of his life. He kept in practice after his 1928 sessions, and tried to record again, but had to support himself at a variety of labouring jobs until 'Avalon Blues' led Tom Hoskins to him in 1963. Thanks to his amiable personality and accessible music, Hurt was the most successful of the 'rediscoveries' of the '60s, and seems to have taken easily to the very different career that opened up in the last four years of his life.

**** 1928 Sessions
Yazoo 1065 *Hurt. 2–12/28.*
**** Avalon Blues: The Complete 1928 OKeh Recordings
Columbia/Legacy CK 64986 *Hurt. 2–12/28.*
***(*) The Greatest Songsters (1927–1929)
Document DOCD-5003 *Hurt. 2–12/28.*
***(*) Candy Man Blues
Snapper Complete Blues SBLUECD 010 *Hurt. 2–12/28.*

In the days before recording, a style could be formed in comparative isolation, especially if a musician didn't have the itch to travel. John Hurt's ragtimey fingerpicking and soft singing don't sound like most black music from the Delta, but he wasn't detached from his world, where a gentle smile and an easygoing passivity were among the possible defences against racism. Hurt played for dances – but never in juke-joints, where he could hardly have made his voice heard – and his singing and playing often have a forceful rhythmic impetus. It's worth noting, too, that murder, domestic violence and the vexations of working for the man are recurrent topics.

Still, his 13 surviving early recordings define Hurt as the most charming of songsters, whether he's narrating tales of mayhem, sighing for Avalon and its women from a New York studio, peddling the mild salacities of 'Candy Man' or evangelizing (rather repetitiously, it must be said). Columbia, applying noise reduction more subtly than elsewhere, and Yazoo, working from clean 78s, both offer first-class sound. So do Snapper, but *Candy Man Blues* gets marked down for naively patronizing notes: 'he was happy to just be a farm hand in Avalon and play for the locals … Unlike many of the blues men of the twenties and beyond, Hurt was a hard working and good citizen who played music for the pure joy of it.' Document are several sonic notches down, but add the important recordings of Richard 'Rabbit' Brown and Hambone Willie Newbern.

**(*) Avalon Blues 1963
Rounder CD 1081 *Hurt. 4/63.*
*** Library of Congress Sessions July 1963
Flyright FLYCD 06 *Hurt. 7/63.*
***(*) D.C. Blues
Fuel 2000 302 061 407 2CD *Hurt. 7/63.*
*** Worried Blues 1963
Rounder CD 1082 *Hurt. 3/64.*

Having found Hurt alive and picking, his discoverers were keen to record him at once. *Avalon Blues* is a landmark recording, but not a very good one. Plucked from his home turf by white strangers, Hurt seems uneasy; dry-mouthed with nerves, he sometimes traps himself in an uncomfortable key, and on guitar he hesitates, stumbles and plays wrong notes. For all its importance in proving that Hurt was still a capable musician, who knew more songs than he'd recorded in 1928 (and who could play a little harmonica), *Avalon Blues* is eclipsed by later '60s recordings.

Two sessions for the Library of Congress just three months later secured almost 100 tunes, although some lyrics were sketchily remembered. At ease in his new milieu, and aware that he and his music are admired and respected, Hurt performs with assurance; a nasty fretting mistake on 'Frankie And Albert' is quite atypical. The 21 songs selected by Flyright are among the sessions' best, but several infrequently recorded items have been omitted in favour of more familiar material. All Flyright's tracks are among the 36 on *D.C. Blues*, which includes a fine sequence of eight spirituals, notable among them an exquisite arrangement of 'Oh Mary Don't You Weep'. Fuel 2000's remastering is excellent, and the notes, which draw on Dick Spottswood's memories of Hurt and these sessions, are a corrective to some of the sentimentality prevalent elsewhere.

By the time *Worried Blues* was cut before a small audience, Hurt had made a triumphant appearance at the Newport Folk Festival, and worried was the one thing he wasn't. On its own terms, the disc has considerable merits, but the playing time is short and most songs are available elsewhere in as good or better versions.

**** Today!
Vanguard VMD 79220 *Hurt. 7/64.*
*** The Immortal
Vanguard VMD 79248 *Hurt; Patrick Sky (g). 65–66.*

*** **Last Sessions**
Vanguard VMD 79327 *As above.* 2–7/66.
***(*) **The Complete Studio Recordings**
Vanguard 3 VCD 181/83 3CD *As above.* 7/64–7/66.

Vanguard's studio recordings show Hurt's voice and guitars off to advantage, and on *Today!*, where the songs are among those he performed most often, he plays and sings at the peak of his latterday powers. *The Immortal* and *Last Sessions* (on each of which producer Patrick Sky joins in twice) document a gradual decline from that peak. *Last Sessions*, in particular, conveys a sense of scratching around for material; new lyrics are fitted to old guitar parts, and some tracks are short because that's all Hurt can remember. There are signs of fatigue on 'Farther Along', and on 'Waiting For You' the second guitar seems necessary for the first time. This falling-off shouldn't be overstated, though; Hurt died on 2 November 1966, but a session held as late as the previous July has much to offer, and *The Immortal* includes first-class versions of 'Richland Women Blues' and 'Nearer My God To Thee'. *Today!* is clearly the best of the three, but it makes sense to get it as part of *The Complete Studio Recordings*, which supplies all three discs for less than the cost of any two bought separately.

*** **Memorial Anthology**
Genes GCD 9906/7 2CD *Hurt; Pete Seeger, Toshi Seeger (interviewers).* 11–12/64.

The interview consumes about half an hour, and about half the playing time of Disc 2; there's some useful information among a good deal of amiable chat, but who will play it twice? Most of the musical content comes from concerts at a Washington coffeehouse. The mix favours the lower frequencies, and this is not the best place to hear Hurt's slide tour de force, 'Talking Casey' (here called 'K. C. Jones Blues'). On the other hand, the bias to the bass both emphasizes the drive imparted by Hurt's thumb and darkens his vocal timbre, making a number of songs sound less serene than usual; by Hurt's usual standard, 'Stagolee' is ferocious.

(*) **Legend
Rounder CD 1100 *Hurt.* 65.

Apparently recorded informally, *Legend* has excellent sound, but since there are so many competing versions available of the songs it includes, it's necessary to be fairly severe about the verbal slip in 'Stack-O-Lee' and the wrong notes in 'Pera Lee' and 'Let The Mermaids Flirt With Me'.

👑 **** **The Best Of Mississippi John Hurt**
Vanguard VCD 19/20 *Hurt.* 4/65.
**** **Live**
Vanguard VCD 79072 *Hurt.* 4–7/65.
(**(*)) **Satisfying Blues**
Collectables COL-CD-5529 *Hurt.* 4/65?
(**(*)) **In Concert**
Blue Moon CDBM 083//Magnum America TKCD 021 *Hurt.* 4/65?
(**(*)) **Live**
Columbia River CRG 120007 *Hurt.* 4/65?
(*) **Ain't No Tellin'
Aim 0010 *Hurt.* 4/65?
(**(*)) **Revisited**
Fuel 2000 302 061 149 *Hurt.* 4/65?
(*) **Frankie & Albert
Tomato TOM-2070 *Hurt.* 4/65?
(**(*)) **Lonesome Blues**
Blitz HHMMCD 325 *Hurt.* 4/65?
(*) **Kings Of The Blues: Mississippi John Hurt
Pulse PLSCD 681 *Hurt.* 4/65?

These CDs derive from two concerts played at Oberlin College, Ohio, supposedly on the same day. One show appears on Vanguard (*Live* adds three songs from the 1965 Newport Folk Festival); the other CDs contain varying amounts of material from the other concert, in varying orders. *Live* is an accurate if rather bald description, but *The Best Of* might lead one to expect a greatest hits compilation. In fact, since that's more or less what Hurt's concerts were, and since *The Best Of* is a high-quality recording of an artist at the top of his game, it's not inaccurately titled. It's also the best example on disc of Hurt charming his audience into submission; even haters of audience participation will find the concluding 'You Are My Sunshine' hard to resist.

Hurt seems less focused on the non-Vanguard recordings, and on several songs a slipped bass string booms and rattles distractingly. *Satisfying Blues* adds LP surface clicks to the annoyance; that it has only 15 tracks of a possible 21 is almost a bonus. The very cheap *Lonesome Blues* is also dubbed from vinyl; its sound quality is distractingly variable, and 'Richland Women Blues' is omitted. Fuel 2000 offer 18 titles, dropping those worst affected by bass-string buzz, but their sound is inert, as it is on Columbia River, Blue Moon and Magnum America, three labels owned by the same parent company. Their 21 tracks also appear on Aim, Tomato and Pulse, on all of which they have much more presence; Tomato have virtually eliminated the string rattle. *Frankie & Albert* is the best version of an inessential gig. Completists should note the presence (except on Collectables) of Hurt's only (and quite risqué) recording of 'Shake That Thing'.

*** **Rediscovered**
Vanguard VCD 79519 *Hurt; Patrick Sky (g).* 7/64–2/66.

Rediscovered is a selection from the studio albums and the Oberlin concert. It's pleasant – how not? – but between them *Today!* and *The Best Of* have it beaten for both programming and consistent musical quality. CS

J. B. Hutto (1926–83)
VOCAL, GUITAR

Joseph Benjamin Hutto grew up in Augusta, Georgia, and at 21 moved to Chicago. He worked for a while as drummer and singer with Johnny Ferguson, then took up guitar, playing almost exclusively with a slide and in open tunings. In 1954 he formed his own band, the Hawks, and made some notable recordings for Chance. Over the next three decades he led a series of bands in Chicago, then in Seattle and Boston. His style is faithfully commemorated by his nephew, Lil' Ed Williams.

Hutto's Chance sides, whether up-tempo numbers like 'Combination Boogie' and 'Lovin' You' or the slower pieces 'Pet Cream Man' and 'Dim Lights', have the drive of the best Chicago music of their period. They are often reminiscent of contemporary work by Jimmy Rogers or Muddy Waters, particularly 'Things Are So Slow', whose echoes of 'Hoochie Coochie Man' are accentuated by George Mayweather's harmonica phrasing. All six of the Chances are on *Down Home Blues Classics: Chicago 1946–1954* (Boulevard Vintage BVBCD 1014 4CD).

(*) Chicago/The Blues/Today! Vol. 1
Vanguard VMD 79216 Hutto; Herman Hassell (b); Frank Kirkland (d). 12/65.

(*) Masters Of Modern Blues
Testament TCD 5020 Hutto; Big Walter Horton (h); Johnny Young (g); Lee Jackson (b); Fred Below (d). 6/66.

*** Hawk Squat**
Delmark DD-617 Hutto; Maurice McIntyre (ts); Sunnyland Slim (o, p); Lee Jackson (g); Junior Pettis, Dave Myers, Herman Hassell (b); Frank Kirkland (d). 8–12/66, 5/68.

(*) Stompin' At Mother Blues
Delmark DE-778 Hutto; Lee Jackson (g); Herman Hassell, Bombay Carter (b); Frank Kirkland, Elbert Buckner (d). 12/66, 12/72.

*** Slidewinder**
Delmark DD-636 Hutto; Lee Jackson (g); Bombay Carter (b); Elbert Buckner (d). 12/72.

Though almost 20 years separate Hutto's Chance singles from the latest of these albums, and he would continue to record for another decade, his music remained virtually unaltered throughout his working life. From the start it was rough, aggressive and exciting, and it never lost those qualities, but he also stayed true to his original inspiration, the early music of Elmore James.

He had five cuts on *Chicago/The Blues/Today! Vol. 1*. (The remainder were by Junior Wells and Otis Spann. This material has also been reissued on the 3CD *Chicago/The Blues/Today!* [Vanguard 172/74].) The sound, as usual in this series, is clear but thin, and Hutto's guitar is not always in tune. The ensemble on *Masters Of Modern Blues* is denser but the boxy recording subdues both voice and guitar, and although this was the most distinguished band Hutto ever recorded with, the results are disappointing. *Hawk Squat* was a better-made album altogether. By the standards of what had gone before, it was also a little different, Sunnyland Slim stomping stolidly on organ and McIntyre blowing uningratiating tenor on several tracks. The slow blues 'Too Late', 'The Same Mistake Twice' and 'Too Much Pride' are Hutto's best work on album thus far.

Lacking the sax and keyboards, *Slidewinder* returns the listener to the spare ensemble sound more typical of Hutto's work. The title track, 'Boogie Right-On' and, especially, 'Young Hawks' Crawl' are pepped up by busy rhythm guitar and bass playing, the latter by William 'Bombay' Carter, a well-known Chicago figure who didn't make many records. The slower numbers, on which Hutto doesn't play with a slide all the time, are sometimes calmer than usual – 'Blues Do Me A Favor', for instance, sounds less like Elmore James than like Jimmy Rogers. *Stompin' At Mother Blues* adds half a dozen unissued tracks from the *Slidewinder* session to a dozen taped two years earlier in the club Mother Blues. Playing again in a trio with Hassell and Kirkland, Hutto strips the blues machine down to its basic working parts. The resulting music has energy and purpose, but it isn't for people who get bored easily.

** Hip Shakin'**
Wolf 120.896 Hutto; Brewer Phillips, Small Blues Charlie (b); Ted Harvey, Fritz Ozmec (d). 76–77.

** Live 1977**
Wolf 120.289 Hutto; Mike Allen (p); Brewer Phillips (g, v); Mark Harris (b); Ted Harvey (d). 6/77.

After the death of Hound Dog Taylor, Hutto took over his band, The Houserockers – guitarist/bassist Brewer Phillips and drummer Ted Harvey – for a couple of years. These are the musicians heard on two tracks of *Hip Shakin'* and, augmented, throughout *Live 1977*. Despite the number of players, the ensemble sound on *Live 1977* is undernourished and Hutto's voice somewhat distant: another addition to the blues' large pile of attractive-looking but ultimately unsatisfactory live recordings. 'Hip Shakin'' and 'Milkman Blues' on the other CD are even less well recorded. The rest of *Hip Shakin'* is sonically slightly better and Hutto's guitar playing, at least, comes over clearly, but long, slow pieces like 'Garbage Man' or 'The Things I Used To Do' simply need to have more going on instrumentally than a terse guitar, drums and a barely audible bass.

** Keeper Of The Flame**
Wolf 120.292 Hutto; Steve Coveney (g); Norman McCloud, Bob Case (b); Leroy Pina (d). 7/79, 2/80.

*** Slidin' The Blues//Slideslinger**
Black & Blue BB 449//Evidence ECD 26009 Hutto; Steve Coveney (g); Kenny Krumbholz (b); Leroy Pina (d). 4/82.

**** Rock With Me Tonight**
Bullseye Blues & Jazz BBB 9620 Hutto; Rich Lataille (as); Greg Piccolo (ts); Doug James (bs); Ron Levy (p); Brian Bisesi (g); Kenny Krumbholz (b); Leroy Pina (d); Scott Billington (prod). 2–3/83.

The band with Steve Coveney and Leroy Pina that Hutto formed in 1979 and kept together for three years furnished the best setting his music had had for ages. That isn't yet apparent on either the four studio tracks or the seven live ones of *Keeper Of The Flame*, but *Slideslinger* (as it was called when it was first issued, and still is on Evidence) presents Hutto as he deserves to be heard. Coveney not only makes himself felt as rhythm guitarist but has the confidence to take some of the lead role, thus varying the texture of the music, while Hutto himself is in tune, eschews his more random improvisations and seldom goes on too long. Yet there remained admirers who felt that the fabric of his music would be even more attractive if it were more thickly woven, and they had the chance to hear their theory tested on what would prove to be his last recording. *Rock With Me Tonight* (formerly Varrick VRCD 006, with two previously unissued tracks added) augments the basic four-piece on several numbers with piano and the reedsmen from Roomful Of Blues, putting a fat, chewy roll round the hot dog of Hutto's voice and guitar. His slide playing is his sharpest and fullest on disc, his voice is in fine shape, the material is excellent – altogether a near-perfect album, and one's glad for his sake as well as ours that he was granted the time and resources to make it. TR

Harry 'Big Daddy' Hypolite (1937–2005)
VOCAL, GUITAR

Growing up in St Martinville, Louisiana, Hypolite worked at a local club where he saw and heard Guitar Slim, Gatemouth Brown and others. He played guitar with Clifton Chenier and his son, C. J.

** Louisiana Country Boy**
APO APO 2016 Hypolite; Big John Amaro (o); Jimmy D. Lane (g, Do); Loui Villeri (b); Bruce Cahoon (d). 2/00.

Hypolite's service with Clifton Chenier is reflected in his

gruff, phlegmy singing and in the presence of four of the accordionist's songs, some of which he sings partly in French. The other numbers, apart from 'Big Bad Girl', a mildly ingenious twist on Jimmy Reed's 'Big Boss Man', and the standards 'Just A Little Bit' and 'Wine Spodee-O-Dee', are Hypolite's – even 'The Sun Is Shining' and 'Milk Cow Blues', which prove to owe little, if anything, to well-known songs with those titles. 'The Sun Is Shining' consists of a single non-rhyming verse sung four times, making Hypolite a credible competitor to Tutu Jones in the songwriting category of the Unhandy Awards. 'For Better Or For Worse' and 'Louisiana Country Boy' don't rhyme either, but a generous person might argue that there it contributes to, or at least doesn't detract from, the effect of autobiographical storytelling. A more astringent listener may call it simply poor workmanship, add that Hypolite's guitar playing is cautious and inexpressive, and conclude that this is not much of an album. TR

Bill Jackson (1906–75)
VOCAL, GUITAR

Born in rural Maryland, Jackson began playing guitar in his teens. He moved in middle life to Philadelphia, where he worked as a building superintendent, janitor or chauffeur. In 1961–62, encouraged by the collector Pete Welding, he recalled, rehearsed and recorded the songs of his youth.

*** Long Steel Rail
Testament TCD 5014 *Jackson.* 1/62.

Unlike his fellow Philadelphians Doug Quattlebaum and the gospel singer Blind Connie Williams, Jackson was never a street singer, and his intimate performances shine with a polish acquired by years of homework. Accompanying himself on 12-string guitar, he delivers blues ('Last Go Round', 'Blues In The Morning') and rag songs and other non-blues pieces like the title track, 'Old Rounder Blues', 'Freight Train Runs So Slow', 'Don't Put Your Hands On Me' and a pretty guitar arrangement of 'Careless Love'. Although he modelled himself on no recorded predecessor, Jackson sometimes employs figures suggestive of other Eastern players. Welding asserted that he exemplified a once lively regional tradition. TR

Bo Weavil Jackson
VOCAL, GUITAR

Though early reissues assigned him a provenance either on the East Coast or somewhere near the Mississippi River, Jackson, whose first name may have been James, came from around Birmingham, Alabama, where he sang on the streets and was spotted by the local talent scout Harry Charles, who secured him two recording dates.

*** Backwoods Blues (1926–1935)
Document DOCD-5036 *Jackson.* 8–9/26.

Jackson sang in a high, piercing voice, accompanying himself on 'Some Scream High Yellow', 'Pistol Blues' and 'Why Do You Moan?' with complex guitar phrases. He was one of the first musicians to be recorded playing slide guitar, as in the stunning 'You Can't Keep No Brown' and some sacred songs. Having made these sides for Paramount under the billing of Bo Weavil Jackson, he recorded as Sam Butler for Vocalion, providing that label with its first issues by a male rural blues artist. Here too he accompanied himself sometimes with slide, sometimes fingerpicked guitar. None of these dozen recordings, however, made much impact on the newly discovered market for such music, and Jackson returned to obscurity. For the other recordings on this CD, by Bobby Grant, Lane Hardin and King Solomon Hill, see COMPILATIONS: MISCELLANEOUS 1 (PREWAR).

'Devil And My Brown Blues' and a version without slide of 'You Can't Keep No Brown', both unissued on 78 but surviving on a Vocalion test pressing, are on *Times Ain't Like They Used To Be Vol. 7* (Yazoo 2067) and *Vol. 8* (Yazoo 2068) respectively. TR

Bullmoose Jackson (1919–89)
VOCAL, TENOR SAXOPHONE

Colleagues in the Lucky Millinder band began calling Benjamin Clarence Jackson 'Bullmoose' after a comic-strip character he supposedly resembled. He was hired by Millinder in 1943, after several years of playing in bands around his hometown of Cleveland, Ohio. The connection with a popular leader won him a decade of recording dates with King and some notoriety for his song about a 'big ten inch ... record of the band that plays the blues', before rock 'n' roll edged him out of the spotlight. In the '60s and '70s he led a jazz group part-time, and in the '80s he worked with the Johnny Otis orchestra.

*** Bull Moose Jackson 1945–1947
Classics 5054 *Jackson; Harold 'Money' Johnson, Frank Galbraith, unknown (t); Al Cobbs, Gene Simon, Joe Britton (tb); Burnie Peacock, Sammy Hopkins (as); Sam 'The Man' Taylor, unknown (ts); Ernest Price (bs); unknowns (s); Sir Charles Thompson, unknowns (p); Bernie MacKey, unknown (g); Beverley Peer, unknowns (b); Panama Francis, unknowns (d); Annisteen Allen, band (v).* 8/45–8/47.

** Bull Moose Jackson 1947–1950
Classics 5105 *Jackson; Frank Galbraith, Harold 'Money' Johnson (t); Ted 'Snooky' Hulbert (as, bs); Eugene Adams (as); Frank Wess, Harold Clark, Sam Taylor (ts); unknowns (s); Billy Mann, Irving Greene, unknown (p); unknown (g); Carl Pruitt, Franklin Skeete, Johnny Allen, Eddie Smith, unknown (b); Les Erskine, Kelly Martin, unknown (d).* 9/47–9/50.

** Bull Moose Jackson 1950–1953
Classics 5156 *Jackson; Harold 'Money' Johnson, Frank Galbraith, Johnny Coles, Joe Wilder, Leslie Ayres, Lester Bass (t); Andrew Penn, Leon Comegys (tb); Snooky Hulbert (as, bs); Eugene Adams, Burnie Peacock, Joe Collier, Herb Geller (as); Sam Taylor, Benny Golson, Harry Porter, Big John Greer, Count Hastings, Red Prysock, Rufus Gore, Charlie Rouse (ts); unknown (o); Irving Greene, Bill Doggett, Tadd Dameron, Jimmy Robinson, Don Abney (p); unknowns (strings); John Faire (g); Eddie Smith, Carl Pruitt, Jymie Merritt, Lloyd Trotman, Clarence Mack (b); Kelly Martin, Jerry Potter, Jo Jones, Les Erskine, Philip Paul, Panama Francis (d); band (v).* 9/50–5/53.

*** Bad Man Jackson That's Me
King KCD 6016 *As for Bull Moose Jackson 1945–1947 and 1950–1953, except add Curtis Pigler, Ray Felder (ts), Walter Hiles (bs), Gene Kee (p), Clifford Bush (g), Edison Gore (d); omit Coles, Peacock, Collier, Golson, Porter, Mann, Dameron, unknowns (strings), Faire, Skeete, Allen, Merritt, Francis.* 8/45–1/55.

*** **A Proper Introduction To Bull Moose Jackson: Bad Man Jackson**
Proper INTRO CD 2035 *Similar to above CDs.* 8/45–5/53.

(**(*)) **Original Blues**
King KSCD 1409 *Similar to above.* 8/47–1/55.

Jackson was a respectable jazz tenorman, and on Johnny Hodges' 'Hodge Podge', his own 'Bearcat Blues' or the frenetic 'Jammin' And Jumpin'' and 'Hold Him Joe' he had the chance to prove it. But he was also a reasonably versatile singer, and like anyone of that description who spent long on the King roster he was put to work on whatever the management thought would sell, especially comic novelty songs in the Louis Jordan manner such as 'Oh John', 'Fare Thee Well, Deacon Jones, Fare Thee Well' and 'Big Fat Mamas Are Back In Style Again', with occasional dips into repertoire from the company's hillbilly catalogue like Moon Mullican's 'Cherokee Boogie' and Wayne Raney's 'Why Don't You Haul Off And Love Me'. He tackled all these jobs with unhysterical enthusiasm, like a muted Wynonie Harris, but he was also happy in the calmer waters of easy-rocking blues.

The first Classics CD stops before Jackson had recorded the titles cited above – most of which turn up on 1947–1950, with 'Bearcat Blues' and 'Hodge Podge' arriving on 1950–1953 – but numbers like 'I Know Who Threw The Whiskey In The Well' or 'Sneaky Pete' sketch the shape of things to come. The sequence of King sessions is briefly interrupted by four sides in the same vein for Super Disc. The second Classics, all from King, swamps the half-dozen Jordanesque pieces with three times as many pop ballads, all as bland as their titles ('Come Back To Me', 'Don't Ask Me Why', 'Sometimes I Wonder', etc.) and virtually indistinguishable. There's a further tranche of this woeful material on 1950–1953, some of it delivered in the manner of Nat 'King' Cole and tricked out with strings.

About half of Proper's *Bad Man Jackson* is drawn from the first Classics CD and half from King's *Bad Man Jackson That's Me*; both *Bad Man*s – unlike *Original Blues*, a footling eight-track sampler – are good and generous selections of his more durable material, including all the previously mentioned numbers. The latter is bookended by two takes of 'Big Ten Inch (Record)'; it probably wasn't the number he would have wished to be best known for, but it has poked its way irresistibly into the ho-ho folio. TR

Calvin Jackson (born 1961)
VOCAL, DRUMS

From Tate County, Mississippi, Jackson had experience in his teens of singing with a gospel choir and playing drums with his father-in-law, R. L. Burnside, as well as absorbing the local tradition of fife and drum music practised by Napoleon Strickland and Othar Turner. He has also worked with Junior Kimbrough, CeDell Davis and Jessie Mae Hemphill.

(*) **Goin' Down South
Me And My Blues MMBCD 6//Beatville BVB 6001 *Jackson; Lazy Lew Beckers (h, perc); Cass Ian (g, v); Carel De Neeve (b).* 11/98.

The album, which was recorded in the Netherlands, is credited to Calvin Jackson & Mississippi Bound, the party of the second part being Dutch musicians who create a colourful ensemble sound distantly related to the north Mississippi hill-country music Jackson plays with his associates at home. Guitarist Cass Ian does not attempt to mimic the fierce individuality of a Kimbrough or Burnside, settling sometimes for a lissome part-rockabilly style that would have been approved in '50s Memphis circles, as in 'Hard To Get Along' and 'All Night Boogie', or at other times, less interestingly, for a basic John Lee Hooker beat ('Thin Ice', 'When My First Wife Left Me'). Two gospel numbers are done with slide guitar, 'Grinnin' (Son House's 'Grinnin' In Your Face') and 'It's Gonna Rain', redolent of Roebuck Staples. Jackson's husky voice is well up to the challenge of a varied repertoire. An easy record to enjoy, equally easy to forget. TR

Papa Charlie Jackson (c. 1885–1938)
VOCAL, BANJO, GUITAR

Paramount publicity material identifies Jackson's birthplace as New Orleans, but he had moved to Chicago by 1924, when Paramount's J. Mayo Williams saw him singing in the street and recruited him for the label. Composer credits suggest that his real name was William Henry Jackson.

*** **Papa Charlie Jackson – Vol. 1 (1924–1926)**
Document DOCD-5087 *Jackson; unknown (bj); Ida Cox (v).* c. 8/24–c. 2/26.

*** **Papa Charlie Jackson – Vol. 2 (1926–1928)**
Document DOCD-5088 *Jackson; Freddie Keppard (c); Eddie Vincent (tb); Johnny Dodds (cl); Arthur Campbell (p); unknown (bj, sp); Jasper Taylor (woodblocks, sp).* c. 2/26–c. 9/28.

(*) **Papa Charlie Jackson – Vol. 3 (1928–1934)
Document DOCD-5089 *Jackson; poss. Lovie Austin (p); Blind Blake (g, v); Ma Rainey, Hattie McDaniel (v).* c. 9/28–11/34.

Papa Charlie Jackson was the first self-accompanied male blues singer to be a best-seller on record, and the first to cut songs as familiar as 'Salty Dog', 'I'm Alabama Bound' and 'All I Want Is A Spoonful', but all too often he's mentioned in passing, deemed important only as a trailblazer for the Southern blues guitarists. Jackson doesn't conform to latterday ideas of what a blues singer should be; he usually played the banjo, for one thing, and although he was far from being the blues' answer to George Formby, many of his songs are cheerful vaudevillian numbers, designed to amuse and/or supply dance rhythms, without much introspection or emotional depth. A 14-track LP, *Fat Mouth* (Yazoo L-1029), which concentrated on Jackson's more showy accompaniments, has not been transferred to CD, and Document's three discs, with 78 tracks between them, may seem a daunting prospect to the casually interested listener. (There are also four alternative takes on "Too Late, Too Late" – Vol. 4 [Document DOCD-5321], and eight on "Too Late, Too Late" – Vol. 11 [Document DOCD-5625].)

In fact, Papa Charlie's music is often very rewarding, distinguished as it is by structural variety, instrumental proficiency, magpie eclecticism and some unusual subject-matter; 'Jackson's Blues', on *Vol. 1*, for instance, is a tribute to a black Chicago politician, whose help Papa Charlie had evidently sought. His six-string banjo, tuned like a guitar, has a light, staccato sound, well suited to his comparatively small baritone voice. The variety of Jackson's chords and the speed and precision with which he deploys them outdo the average blues guitarist's, and, together with his regular rhythm, suggest that he had experience as a band member. It's surprising, therefore, that his collaborations with Ida Cox on *Vol. 1* are disappointingly limited.

There is much to like elsewhere on this disc, although allowances must be made for the quality of both the original recordings (all acoustic Paramounts) and the remastering. 'Shake That Thing', credited by Georgia Tom with starting the hokum craze, was Jackson's greatest hit, and is so well known that the hectic proficiency of its banjo playing is often overlooked. Other highlights include his occasional guitar playing; 'Jackson's Blues' seems to be the first recorded example of a piano walking bass transferred to guitar, and on 'Texas Blues' he achieves a pretty sound by replacing the guitar's third string with a banjo string. 'I'm Alabama Bound' and 'Drop That Sack' feature a second banjoist, whose fast and furious flatpicking often drowns out the nominal lead artist's playing. Jackson's songs cover a wide range of subjects, sometimes employing unusual structures, like the 12-bar verse and 16-bar chorus of 'I'm Going Where The Chilly Winds Don't Blow', about imprisonment. 'The Cats Got The Measles' and 'I'm Alabama Bound' draw on oral tradition, and the murder ballad 'Coffee Pot Blues' sounds as though it does too, although there are no other recordings of this theme. 'I Got What It Takes But It Breaks My Heart To Give It Away' seems to be a cover of a Lucille Hegamin recording, with no attempt to change the lyrics to suit a male singer; by contrast, the well-known 'Mama Don't Allow It (And She Ain't Gonna Have It Here)' is radically transformed into a tale of a country girl coming to town and being entrapped by a pimp. Urban life, with its bustle, glamour and stress, is a recurring subject; 'Maxwell Street Blues' is one of a number of songs which paint a vivid picture of the Chicago scene, with Jackson asking the desk sergeant to release his girlfriend, arrested for soliciting at the famous open-air market.

There are fewer famous songs on *Vol. 2*, although Papa Charlie's star status is confirmed by his vocal chorus on Freddie Keppard's Jazz Cardinals' less than stunning version of 'Salty Dog'. (This is take 2; take 1 is on *The Complete Johnny Dodds Vol. 1* [Classics 589].) Despite the lack of hits, *Vol. 2* is the most rewarding of the three, in part because its last 15 tracks are electrically recorded, so that the sound quality improves markedly. A second banjoist turns up again on the first two songs so recorded, but this time the balance is far better, and both musicians can be heard clearly. On 'She Belongs To Me Blues', they knock off a quadruple-time instrumental break of breathtakingly casual brilliance. Elsewhere, there is some delightfully euphonious guitar playing on two takes of 'Up The Way Bound'. Jackson continues to produce lively sketches of everyday life, gently satirizing young dandies ('The Sheik Of Desplaines Street'), describing what may have been his day job ('Coal Man Blues') and reporting from the racetrack on 'Lexington Kentucky Blues'. 'Long Gone Lost John' comes from deep in the folk repertoire, but it's an upstart beside 'No Need Of Knocking On The Blind', whose story of an old man deceived by a young wife can be found in Boccaccio's *Decameron*! Measured against that ancestry, 'Bright Eyes', a sentimental Great War song quoting 'Tipperary', and 'Look Out Papa Don't Tear Your Pants', a comic song introducing pseudo-Hawaiian singing and a quote from 'Spanish Flangdang', seem almost routine. The only predictable thing about this CD is that it's impossible to predict what Jackson is going to do next, and it's very stimulating listening.

Vol. 3 is less satisfactory, for a variety of reasons. As musical fashions changed, Papa Charlie seems to have lost some of his popularity, and to have reacted by singing more orthodox, but often less interesting, 12-bar blues. His voice had become deeper and less expressive, and sometimes he sounds decidedly lacklustre. He also seems to have decided to play more guitar, and to imitate Blind Blake when doing so. Jackson's admiration for Blake is understandable, but he doesn't achieve more than diligent emulation, losing his own pzazz without acquiring much of Blake's. They were paired by Paramount on a two-part disc of crosstalk with music; they obviously had fun and enjoyed each other's playing, but the original disc is very worn. Much better are a pair of sombre duets with Ma Rainey; much worse is the two-part 'Dentist Chair Blues', with Hattie McDaniel, long before *Gone With The Wind*, overacting dreadfully as the lady who needs a quick-filling dentist. *Vol. 3* is not without its moments: 'Jungle Man Blues' is an ingenious bad man's boast ('I wear a scorpion for my watch fob, a rattlesnake for my chain'), and 'Self Experience' is as fascinating as its simultaneously enigmatic and forthright title. An evidently true story of being arrested in a speakeasy, it's both Jackson's last recording for Paramount and the last of his tales of ghetto life. Four years later, there was a final session for OKeh, which began with a remake of 'Skoodle-Um-Skoo'. Its undiminished vigour is not typical, either of that session or the last years of Papa Charlie's recording career. Too often, the *joie de vivre* is much diminished, perhaps as he reflects on the loss of stardom and tries unsuccessfully to regain it, perhaps simply with the onset of middle age. CS

Fruteland Jackson (born 1953)
VOCAL, GUITAR

Born in Mississippi, Jackson moved to Chicago as a child. His music marries acoustic sounds with original lyrics.

** I Claim Nothing But The Blues
Electro-Fi 3364 Jackson; Michael Pickett (h, v); Ken Whitely (p, md, bj, g, j, wb, perc, v); Tyler Yarema (p, v); Alec Fraser (b, v). 9/99.
**(*) Blues 2.0
Electro-Fi 3380 Jackson; Chris Whitely (t, h, g); Mel Brown (p, g); Ken Whitely (md, bj, wb, v); Alec Fraser (b, bass d, v). 1/03.

Jackson is a forceful singer and an adventurous guitarist, but on his debut CD he's too often let down by his songwriting, which is boobytrapped with platitudes ('Life is good when you're happy, and it's bad if you're sad') and doggerel. It's no doubt true, in relation to Helena's King Biscuit Blues Festival, that 'People come from all over the world, to this Mississippi river town, They stay in hotels and motels, right on the levee camp ground,' but so what? The novelty 'Mango Bango', set to Latin rhythms, is simply unspeakable, and the busy production, using various instrumental combinations, too often seems to be an attempt to disguise weak material.

The instruments are deployed with less promiscuity and more thought on *Blues 2.0*, and 'When in doubt, wheel Mel Brown out' proves a good plan on three tracks. Jackson's writing shows signs of improvement, too: the Blind Blakean 'Moon Man Rag' is a clever riposte (perhaps) to Saffire's 'Ragtime Rag', and Bo Carter's pencil writes some more, thanks to new verses about Viagra. There are still too many banalities, though: a eulogy for Jimmie Lee Robinson and 'Blues On The Banjo' are among numerous tracks whose potential is punctured by prosaic texts. Many songs are repetitiously over-extended: only 'Sometimes Bad Man Blues', with Brown splendid on acoustic lead guitar, and a 'Big Road Blues' where Jackson woefully fails to impose himself come in under three minutes. CS

Big George Jackson (born 1949)
VOCAL, HARMONICA

A Minneapolis native, Jackson grew up listening to musicians like Mojo Buford and Milwaukee Slim. Learning harmonica, he was chiefly inspired by Paul Butterfield and Walter Horton.

** Beggin' Ain't For Me
Black & Tan CD B&T 003 *Jackson; Jeremy Johnson, Phil Schmid (g); John Schroder (b); Dwight Dario (d). 4/97.*
*** Big Shot
Black & Tan CD B&T 009 *As above. 00?*

'What moves me,' says Jackson, 'is that late '40s, early '50s and '60s style of blues,' and that response is evident from his harmonica playing, which he displays very creditably on *Beggin' Ain't For Me* in 'Fee Fi Fo Fam' ('– I smell the blood of a bluesman') or, using the chromatic instrument, 'Fat's Jump'. He mostly sings his own songs, which are unexceptional, in a voice that has size but not much depth or warmth. Nonetheless, a reasonably good album might have come of this session had the band, which sounds nervous as it is, not been mixed into the middle distance. They get a much better break in *Big Shot*, though they still need more assertive bass playing, and the two guitarists generate an insistent John Lee Hookerish pulse on tracks like the title song and 'What You Got'. Jackson, too, has profited from three years' further collaboration and blows with energy and enterprise on 'The Daddy', 'Friday Evening' and elsewhere. Apart from Jimmy Reed's 'Found True Love' and Walter Horton's 'Hard Hearted Woman', most of the songs are again Jackson's. The unlisted twelfth track is a slower reading of the opening 'St. Paul Woman' and convincingly re-creates the sound of Muddy Waters in the '50s; conservative listeners may find it to be their favourite.

*** Southern In My Soul
Black & Tan CD B&T 016 *As above, except Johnson also plays d and perc, and Schmid perc; add Billy Flynn (g, b). 2–5/03.*

After more than six years' working together, Jackson and his band are like the cast of a long-running sitcom: not merely polished ensemble players but so used to each other that they can predict the next line or expression. Johnson and Schmid are not showy guitarists – often their playing is quite conventional – but they listen to Jackson carefully, and respond to him with an ease that creates the impression not of a studio recording but of some old friends dropping by to play for a while.

Urban blues styles of the '50s and '60s, even the Chicago bar-blues idiom, make a shallower impression on this album than on its predecessors. It genuinely is Southern in its soul, and old Southern at that: the sound of tracks like 'Go For A Ride', with its repeated tight spirals of guitar and tremulous harmonica phrases, has not often been heard, perhaps not often made, for most of half a century. It's a calculated effect, of course. Jackson is not some mysterious holdout from another time; he simply likes visiting there. But as artifice goes, it sounds remarkably unartificial. TR

Jim Jackson (c. 1884–1937)
VOCAL, GUITAR

An experienced medicine-show performer and occasional Memphis street singer, the Mississippi-born Jackson had one of the biggest blues hits of the '20s with his 'Jim Jackson's Kansas City Blues'.

*** Jim Jackson – Vol. 1 (1927–1928)
Document DOCD-5114 *Jackson. 10/27–8/28.*
*** Jim Jackson – Vol. 2 (1928–1930)
Document DOCD-5115 *Jackson; Georgia Tom [Dorsey] (p, v, sp); Speckled Red (p, v); Tampa Red (g, v). 8/28–2/30.*

It may be difficult for modern listeners to appreciate 'Jim Jackson's Kansas City Blues' as its first hearers did. As the title implies, it was Jackson's version of an existing song, allegedly composed by Memphis singer Robert Wilkins and already recorded by the Memphis Jug Band, but perhaps only Memphians would have been aware of that. To others it may have been quite original: in its shape, in its textual patchwork of folk phrases ('It takes a rockin' chair to rock, rubber ball to roll'), topical and topographical allusions (boll weevils, Beale Street) and sexual braggadocio, and in Jackson's genial narrative manner. Perhaps even the plodding rhythm had a certain charm. At any rate, the record sold hugely, focusing the attention of its sponsors, first Vocalion and then Victor, on coming up with further episodes or soundalikes. Jackson duly furnished these, but also persuaded both labels to accept other material, with the happy result that his documented repertoire is one of the deepest lodes of non-blues songs current among African-American musicians in the first quarter of the 20th century.

Prominent among these are comic songs from around the turn of the century such as 'I'm A Bad Bad Man', which draws on a composition of 1894, and 'I'm Gonna Start Me A Graveyard Of My Own', based on 'I'm Goin' To Live Anyhow, 'Till I Die', published in 1901. These songs are rife with stereotypes of African-American low life (razors, crap games, etc.) which Jackson retails with a gusto only exceeded in his lip-smacking narrative 'I Heard The Voice Of A Pork Chop', a jovial parody of a hymn. The guitar accompaniments are simply conceived and unhandily played.

Vol. 1 includes all the abovementioned songs – some in several versions, since Jackson recorded them for both his labels and some also survive in alternative takes – and other entertaining pieces like 'I'm Wild About My Lovin'', which is related to Cannon's Jug Stompers' 'Bring It With You When You Come', and 'Old Dog Blue', sung over a strum that may have originated in banjo playing. *Vol. 2*, which has fewer duplications, is a similar stew of blues and comic songs. Among the latter are 'This Ain't No Place For Me', 'Traveling Man' and another stereotype-heavy piece, 'What A Time', as well as a couple that turn out to be medleys, 'Long Gone' and 'Bye, Bye, Policeman', which bizarrely prefaces the title song with an extract from Ernest Hogan's 1895 composition about dances of the day, 'Pas Ma La'. Of the blues, 'I'm Gonna Move To Louisiana' and 'Ain't You Sorry Mama?' are in the 'Kansas City' vein, while 'Hey Mama – It's Nice Like That' is Jackson's contribution to the folio of 'It's Tight Like That'-alikes. These are all two-parters, and so is the jolly musicians' party issued as 'Jim Jackson's Jamboree', hosted by Georgia Tom and featuring excellent cameos by Speckled Red and Tampa Red.

After a few sessions for Victor, Jackson had returned to Vocalion, which took less interest in his 'songster' repertoire, and the second half of *Vol. 2* is almost all blues, mostly at the turgid tempo of 'Kansas City', though the concluding renditions of 'Hesitation Blues' and 'St. Louis Blues' are quite vivacious. There are signs that Jackson is trying to individualize his blues performances – here a guitar intro, there a line or two of scatting – but there is little alteration in his basic approach, which is to treat a blues as a humorous or pointed story to be told rather than sung, and without the distraction of instrumental decoration. It is an aesthetic that was plainly not shared even by local contemporaries like Frank Stokes, let alone by men half a generation younger like Tommy Johnson or Charley Patton, yet one meets versions of it occasionally in later blues, for instance in the work of Willie Blackwell.

A pair of duets by 'Liza Brown' and 'Ann Johnson' (actually Ozie McPherson and, possibly, Coot Grant), recorded in New York, are included in *Vol. 2* because they have a Jim Jackson playing guitar and, on 'Let's Get It Straight', singing. It is not a context in which one would expect to find 'our' Jim Jackson, and sure enough, neither guitar nor voice resembles his in the least. Probably 'Jim Jackson' served as a nominal stereotype, a kind of black John Doe, which would also explain its appearance in a 'Negro Vaudeville Sketch' recorded in about 1908 and titled 'Jim Jackson's Affinity'. This was included in *"Too Late, Too Late" – Vol. 2 (1897–1935)* (Document DOCD-5216) as an authentic Jim Jackson item. It would be pretty to think so, but the recording is almost certainly by studio performers, and white ones at that. TR

John Jackson (1924–2002)
VOCAL, GUITAR, BANJO

Raised in the Blue Ridge Mountains, Jackson worked from childhood as a manual labourer. After moving to Fairfax, Virginia, in 1950 he became a combination cook, butler and chauffeur, and also the community's gravedigger. Jackson learned to play at an early age, acquiring songs from friends, family, radio and records; he performed for house parties, but virtually gave up music after a violent incident at one such event, just before he moved to Fairfax. By 1964, Jackson had resumed playing occasionally, and was fortunately carrying a guitar when folklorist Chuck Perdue encountered him. From then until not long before his death, he enchanted audiences worldwide with his musicianship, his insights into musical history and his modest, genial personality.

**** Don't Let Your Deal Go Down
Arhoolie CD-378 *Jackson; Mike Seeger (g).* 4/65–10/69.
**** Country Blues & Ditties
Arhoolie CD-471 *Jackson.* 4/65–10/69.

John Jackson always played music that appealed to him, whatever its source, although sadly he never recorded his version of 'Blue Suede Shoes'. His taste, magpie enthusiasm and good memory (the latter no doubt fostered by his illiteracy) made him a living almanac of blues, rags, spirituals and popular songs, acquired from both black and white sources; *Country Blues & Ditties* includes songs by Ernest Tubb, the Delmore Brothers and Roy Acuff, as well as the more expected Jimmie Rodgers. As a guitarist, Jackson was an exceptional talent; his favourite artists were Blind Boy Fuller and Blind Blake, and he was one of the few blues singers to have tackled Blake's technically daunting songbook both successfully and at length. He was also an adept knifestyle guitarist, and frailed the banjo in an archaic, energetic style. The warm Virginia twang of his singing is simply delightful. The Arhoolie CDs reshuffle the contents of three LPs, and there is little to choose between them as showcases for the brilliance of Jackson's playing and the breadth of his repertoire. *Don't Let Your Deal Go Down* would have been improved by the omission of the track with Mike Seeger, who sows harmonic and rhythmic confusion too often.

***(*) Front Porch Blues
Alligator ALCD 4867 *Jackson; James Jackson (g, v).* 99.

The apparent 30-year recording gap is illusory; two fine LPs, made for Rounder in 1972 and 1982, have not yet been transferred to CD. The Alligator set includes new versions of a couple of songs that are on the Arhoolie discs, but Jackson at 75 was resting on his porch, not his laurels. Noteworthy in a high-quality programme are a lively version of the Tin Pan Alley standard 'Just Because' and a deeply felt reading of Reverend Gary Davis's 'Death Don't Have No Mercy'. John Jackson had not mellowed with age – no surprise, since he was always about as mellow as a human being could be – and if his voice on this disc has taken on a certain creakiness, it's the comfortable creak of an old rocking chair; his guitar playing is of undiminished excellence. On the final track, Jackson plays backup behind his son, James, and while paternal pride is understandable, it's all too apparent that James had big shoes to fill. This makes for a deflationary end to an otherwise splendid record. CS

Lil' Son Jackson (1915/16–76)
VOCAL, GUITAR

Melvin Jackson's recording career was short but surprisingly prolific for such a small if perfectly formed talent. He benefited from a postwar appetite for country blues created by Lightnin' Hopkins and John Lee Hooker, although his music lacked the strength of character that theirs exhibited. A 1956 auto crash ended his professional career; his 'rediscovery' four years later and an unissued 1963 session merely punctuated a contented life away from music.

**** Texas Blues "The Gold Star Sessions"
Arhoolie CD 352 *Jackson.* 48–49.

What is so captivating in Jackson's work is the contrast between his soft-edged, plaintive singing and the sinewy thump of his guitar playing. The vocal line may drift like a cloud, wafting the listener into Jackson's world of self-questioning and uncertainty, but the guitar never quits its relentless heartbeat rhythm. This singular character would be somewhat compromised on later recordings with bands, but on 'Gambling Blues', 'Cairo Blues', 'Bad Whiskey, Bad Women' and the rest of the ten sides gathered here he is on his own, and they are his chief legacy. (For the remainder of this outstanding album see L. C. Williams and COMPILATIONS: TEXAS.)

The deleted *Complete Imperial Recordings* (Capitol 31744 2CD) collected 55 titles recorded at 11 sessions over a five-year period. Although Jackson is entirely convincing and entertaining in solo performances like 'Ticket Agent Blues' and his quasi-hit 'Rockin' And Rollin', once he is backed by a small band his music tends to become confused or disintegrated. His last Imperial sessions, where he plays solo again, regain much of the strength and confidence of his early work.

*** Blues Come To Texas
Arhoolie CD 409 *Jackson. 7/60.*

Jackson's contentment in his retirement can be seen in the photograph adorning the booklet to this session, recorded during his vacation by then schoolteacher Chris Strachwitz. The subject stands with hand on hip among the paraphernalia of the Dallas body shop to which he'd returned after recovering from his auto accident. Strachwitz overcame Jackson's initial reluctance to perform and was rewarded with a notably successful set of recordings that nevertheless confirmed in the producer's mind that the artist had 'a rather limited repertoire although he played the material he knew extraordinarily well.' Jackson conscientiously put in some practice and the results compare very favourably with the best of his Gold Star and Imperial recordings, several of which are revisited here, including 'Cairo Blues', 'Roberta Blues', 'Groundhog Blues', 'Ticket Agent' and 'Sugar Mama'. Three previously unreleased songs were added to this CD reissue, of which an ambitious but ill-conceived 'Buck Dance' is the least successful. 'I Walked From Dallas' is an alternative performance of the opening 'Blues Come To Texas', with distant echoes of Blind Lemon Jefferson. NS/TR

David Jacobs-Strain (born 1983)
VOCAL, GUITAR, DIDDLEY BOW

Raised in Oregon, Jacobs-Strain began playing guitar at nine, and at 15 was on the faculty at the Port Townsend Country Blues Festival.

** Skin And Bones
Hang-Dog Music HDM-9902 *Jacobs-Strain. 12/97–4/99.*
** Stuck On The Way Back
NorthernBlues NBM 0012 *Jacobs-Strain; Kenny Passarelli (o, b); Peter Joseph Burtt (kora, tamboura, mbira, cajon, djembe, handclaps, v). 10–11/01.*

Aware that he's a long way from the 'delta blues' (lower case 'd' *sic*) that inspired him to play, Jacobs-Strain says that he works 'in the tradition of the music' rather than trying to reproduce the old styles. Accepting, then, that he's trying to make his own artistic statements within a blues-based framework, one must assume that his unsystematic imitation of African-American vocal techniques and speech patterns is not intended to sound quite as mannered and masturbatory as it does. Jacobs-Strain's singing is often ham acting that bears little relation to the lyrics, but what else is likely to happen when a white teenager from the Pacific Northwest tries to channel the experiences embodied in 'Poor Black Mattie', 'Back Water Blues' and 'Linin' Track'? On *Stuck On The Way Back*, Jacobs-Strain moves further into the 'blues-based singer/songwriter' territory of his mentor Otis Taylor, purveying social and political opinions that radiate naive, adolescent self-importance. Jacobs-Strain's command of the guitar is impressive, needless to say, but as a white youth expressing himself through black music, there's a lot more to be said for Eminem.

** Ocean Or A Teardrop
NorthernBlues NBM 0024 *Jacobs-Strain; Joe Filisko (h); Kenny Passarelli (o, p, b, d loops, chains); Joe Craven (vn, md, oud); Peter Joseph Burtt (kora, 'wash tub d', shakers, 'trash can v', v); Danny Click (g); Kendrick Freeman (d, djembe, cga); Mark Clark (d); Tim Stroh (d loops); Anne Weiss (v). 2/04.*

Jacobs-Strain's voice has matured considerably, but it continues to be callow and unconvincing on a solo version of 'The Girl I Love'. This song is not typical of *Ocean Or A Teardrop*, which stresses energetic, rock-tinged treatments of traditional material ('Kokomo Blues' and Blind Willie Johnson's 'Soul Of A Man') and original compositions that marginalize blues in favour of arty obscurantism and blame-America-first politics. Musically, the CD is better than its predecessors – the combination of blues guitar with jazz fiddle on 'Yelapa Breakdown' is very winning – but it offers little to blues fans as the term is usually understood. CS

Elmore James (1918–63)
VOCAL, GUITAR

Elmore James's signature slide guitar riffs have become a blues cliché and yet few if any have been able to reproduce their potency. Although born Elmore Brooks, by his teens he had taken the surname of his stepfather, Joe Willie James. At some point he presumably met or heard Robert Johnson, from whom he learned 'Dust My Broom' and 'Standing At The Crossroads'. He certainly struck up a long association with Sonny Boy Williamson II, through whom he was able to make his first recording of 'Dust My Broom'. The tune with its iconic slide phrase became the backbone of a 12-year recording career, and, despite its frequent repetition, audiences and record-buyers never tired of its dramatic impact when combined with James's plangent vocals. He had as little time for recording contracts or union strictures as he did for healthy living. Heart disease finally took its toll just as the blues was beginning to make inroads into popular culture, and he was denied the benefits of the wider exposure that would undoubtedly have accrued.

**** The Classic Early Recordings
Ace ABOXCD 4//Flair 39631 3CD *James; James Parr (t); Boyd Atkins (as, ts); unknown (as); J. T. Brown, unknown, Raymond Hill, Maxwell Davis (ts); Jewel Grant, unknown (bs); Sonny Boy Williamson II (h); Ike Turner, [Little] Johnny Jones, Willard McDaniel, Edward Frank (p); Eddie Taylor (g); Leonard Ware, Ransom Knowling, Ralph 'Chuck' Hamilton, Frank Fields, unknown (b); Frock O'Dell, Odie Payne Jr, Jesse Sailes, Earl Palmer, unknown (d). 8/51–1/56.*
**** The Best Of Elmore James – The Early Years
Ace CDCHD 583 *Similar to above. 8/51–1/56.*
***(*) Elmore James 1951–1953
Classics 5082 *James; J. T. Brown (ts, v); unknown (ts); Sonny Boy Williamson II (h); Ike Turner, [Little] Johnny Jones (p); Leonard Ware, Ransom Knowling, unknown (b); poss. Frock O'Dell, Odie Payne, unknown (d). 8/51–4/53.*
***(*) Blues Kingpins
Virgin 82738 *James; James Parr (t); Boyd Atkins (as, ts); J. T. Brown, Maxwell Davis, unknown (ts); Jewel Grant (bs); Ike Turner, [Little] Johnny Jones, Willard McDaniel, unknown (p); prob. Ransom Knowling, Chuck Hamilton, unknowns (b); Odie Payne, Jesse Sailes, unknowns (d). 4/52–55.*

*** **Let's Cut It: The Very Best Of Elmore James**
Flair 86257 *Similar to above.* c. 10/52–1/56.
*** **Blues After Hours**
Ace CDCHM 1043 *Similar to above.* 4/53–1/56.

The original Trumpet version of 'Dust My Broom' gets the boxed set set off to a perfect start, followed by a couple of hairy sessions supervised by Ike Turner cut before that contract ran out. Retitled 'I Believe', the song was a hit again for Meteor when James cut it in Chicago a year later with what had been Tampa Red's band, who now became the Broomdusters. A transfer to Flair brought forth 'Can't Stop Lovin'', 'Make My Dream Come True' , 'Strange Kinda Feeling' and 'Sho' Nuff I Do', songs that showed he could do more with a guitar than just wield a bottleneck. A shrewd pairing with Maxwell Davis's Californian session men, including a horn section that threw his signature riff back at him, gave fresh perspective to 'Standing At The Crossroads', 'Sunny Land' and 'Late Hours At Midnight'. Almost exactly four years after his debut, James recorded 'Dust My Blues' in New Orleans before returning to Chicago for a final Modern session from which 'Wild About You Baby' and 'Long Tall Woman' were released. Though eclipsed by some of his later recordings, these songs merit their 'classic' distinction, if only to delineate James's increasing stature as an artist. The box set includes every song and take that survives from the original sessions. Where several takes are offered, the devotee won't necessarily receive further enlightenment from what are near-identical performances of formulaic songs. That doesn't diminish the value of a package that includes a lavishly illustrated and information-packed 40-page booklet as a complement to the important music it contains. Those who don't wish to examine these sessions in detail are more than amply provided for by *The Best Of Elmore James*, an 80-minute compilation that brings together 28 of the 39 recordings covered in greater detail in the box set. *Blues Kingpins, Let's Cut It* (formerly also on Ace CDCH 192) and *Blues After Hours* are slimmer (18-track) selections with much of the same material.

Classics take a slightly different tack, their complete-and-chronological policy dictating the inclusion of a J. T. Brown date for Meteor on which James plays guitar. *1951–1953* is also the only James CD currently available that ropes in his 1953 Checker session. Here 'Dust My Broom' becomes 'She Just Won't Do Right', while 'Country Boogie' gives solo space to Brown's querulous saxophone. Three further titles, interesting but undistinguished, remained unissued until the LP era.

**** **Rollin' And Tumblin'**
Snapper Recall SMDCD 231 2CD *James; Danny Moore (t); J. T. Brown, unknowns (ts); Paul Williams (bs); Sammy Myers (h); [Little] Johnny Jones, Johnny Acey, Johnny 'Big Moose' Walker (p); Eddie Taylor, prob. Wayne Bennett, prob. Jimmy Spruill, Riff Ruffin (g); Homesick James, Willie Dixon, unknowns (b); Odie Payne, Fred Below, Johnny Williams, King Mose [Taylor], unknowns (d).* 57, 11/59–2/63.
*** **Person To Person**
Snapper Complete Blues SBLUECD 019 *Similar to above, except add Sonny Boy Williamson II (h), Leonard Ware (b), Frock O'Dell (d).* 8/51, 57, 11/59–2/63.
***(*) **The Complete Fire And Enjoy Sessions Part 1**
Collectables COL-CD-5184 *James; J. T. Brown, unknown (s); [Little] Johnny Jones (p); prob. Jimmy Spruill (g); Homesick James (b); Odie Payne, unknown (d).* 11/59–60.

***(*) **The Complete Fire And Enjoy Sessions Part 2**
Collectables COL-CD-5185 *James; Danny Moore (t); unknowns (ts); Paul Williams (bs); Sam Myers (h); Johnny Acey, Johnny 'Big Moose' Walker (p); prob. Jimmy Spruill, Riff Ruffin (g); Homesick James, unknowns (b); Odie Payne Jr, Johnny Williams, King Mose [Taylor], unknown (d).* 60–61.
***(*) **The Complete Fire And Enjoy Sessions Part 3**
Collectables COL-CD-5186 *James; Sam Myers (h); Johnny 'Big Moose' Walker (p); unknowns (b); King Mose [Taylor], unknowns (d).* 61–2/63.
***(*) **The Complete Fire And Enjoy Sessions Part 4**
Collectables COL-CD-5187 *James; Johnny 'Big Moose' Walker (p); unknown (b); unknown (d).* 2/63.
***(*) **For Collectors Only – Complete Fire And Enjoy Recordings**
Collectables COL-CD-8829 4CD *As for above Collectables CDs.* 11/59–2/63.
**** **The Sky Is Crying**
BMG/Camden 52376 *As above.* 11/59–2/63.
***(*) **The Immortal Elmore James – King Of The Bottleneck Blues**
Music Club MCCD 083 *Similar to above.* 57, 11/59–2/63.
***(*) **Shake Your Moneymaker: The Best Of The Fire Sessions**
Buddah 99781 *Similar to above.* 11/59–61.
*** **Dust My Broom**
Tomato TOM-2097 *Similar to above.* 11/59–61.

Elmore's final contract was with the New York producer Bobby Robinson, proprietor of Fire, Fury, Enjoy and other labels, who recorded him in Chicago, New Orleans and New York during the course of four years. The six sessions were a mixture of tightly arranged band dates and less-regimented small-group recordings, the last an extended session during which James performed his typical club set. 'Dust My Broom' and its variants turned up with increasing frequency but there was a sequence of first-rate songs, including 'Done Somebody Wrong', 'Fine Little Mama', 'Something Inside Me', 'I'm Worried', 'Stranger Blues' and 'Bleeding Heart' (later adopted by Jimi Hendrix), that were among the best Elmore had ever recorded. Just as good were 'Shake Your Money Maker' and 'Look On Yonder Wall', cut in New Orleans with Sam Myers on harmonica. The last sessions were less closely supervised but there's a sort of doomed grandeur to these versions of 'Hand In Hand', 'Twelve Year Old Boy' and 'Make My Dreams Come True'.

Most of these titles can be found in the selections offered by Snapper Recall, Camden, Music Club and Buddah. Snapper's 2CD opens with James's seven excellent sides for Chief, which are not available *en bloc* anywhere else, and then picks its way discriminatingly through the Robinson sessions. The buyer who settles on this purchase will have nearly everything that's on Camden, Music Club and Buddah but, should *Rollin' And Tumblin'* be hard to find, the Camden set is a more than adequate substitute. The Tomato is shorter (15 tracks) and less well presented but does include four cuts that *Rollin' And Tumblin'* overlooks. The Snapper Complete Blues issue echoes its label-mate by choosing four of the Chief sides (prefaced by James's debut recording of 'Dust My Broom'), then, irritatingly for the tidy-minded shopper, mixes well-known Robinson recordings like 'The Sky Is Crying' and 'Standing At The Crossroads' with items from the final session such as 'Pickin' The Blues' and 'Up Jumped Elmore' which have been ignored by all the other selective CDs. If it's important to you to eliminate these problems of duplication and omission, and you're prepared for multiple takes and a good deal of studio chatter, you have the option to eavesdrop on the entire Robinson tapes through Collectables' four volumes, available separately or in a set. NS/TR

♛ **** The Sky Is Crying: The History Of Elmore James
Rhino R2 71190 *James; Danny Moore (t); unknown (as); J. T. Brown, unknowns (ts); Paul Williams, unknown (bs); Sonny Boy Williamson II, Sammy Myers (h); Ike Turner (p, g); [Little] Johnny Jones, Willard McDaniel, Johnny Acey, Johnny 'Big Moose' Walker (p); Homesick James, Eddie Taylor (g, b); prob. Willie Johnson, prob. Wayne Bennett, prob. Jimmy Spruill, Riff Ruffin (g); Leonard Ware, Chuck Hamilton, poss. Ransom Knowling, Willie Dixon, unknowns (b); Frock O'Dell, Jesse Sailes, Odie Payne, Henry 'Sneaky Joe' Harris, Fred Below, Johnny Williams, King Mose [Taylor], unknown (d). 8/51–61.*

If you don't care to investigate James in depth but simply want a best-of that represents all of his output, go placidly amid the noise and haste of the record store and pick out a copy of this Rhino CD. Core songs of James's repertoire like 'Dust My Broom', 'The Sky Is Crying', 'It Hurts Me Too', 'Shake Your Moneymaker' and 'Standing At The Crossroads' are judiciously selected from different stages of his life. There are also three cuts from the 1960 Chess session (which, since the deletion of *Whose Muddy Shoes* [MCA/Chess CHD 9114], you won't easily find elsewhere): colossal versions of 'The Sun Is Shining' and 'I Can't Hold Out', and 'Madison Blues', which gave such a foothold to the young George Thorogood. James didn't play accompanist to other artists very much, but there's one famous example here, where he backs Big Joe Turner on 'T.V. Mama'. Although he is chiefly thought of as a singer and guitarist of tightly wound intensity, it's worth remembering that James was capable of calmer performances, and the compilers duly acknowledge it with 'Sunny Land' and 'My Best Friend'. A track or two from the remarkable Meteor 1952 session would have made this better still, but even so it's essential. TR

Etta James (born 1938)
VOCAL

Jamesetta Hawkins grew up in LA and San Francisco, sang in a church choir and made a rowdy debut as a 16-year-old with 'Roll With Me Henry'. Moving from Modern to Chess in 1960, she recorded R&B, pop and soul and had several hits like 'All I Could Do Was Cry', but for part of the '80s her career was hindered by drug problems. Since then, however, she has reclaimed her position in the front rank of soul-blues singers. Her recording of 'I Just Want To Make Love To You' was a surprise hit in the UK in 1995.

(***) Hickory Dickory Dock
Ace CDCHM 680 *James; Don Johnson, Dave Bartholomew (t); Maxwell Davis, Lee Allen, Harold Battiste, unknowns (ts); Jim Wynn, unknown (bs); unknowns (s); Devonia Williams, unknowns (p); Chuck Norris, Justin Adams, unknowns (g); Chuck Hamilton, unknowns (b); Leard Bell, Earl Palmer, unknowns (d); Abbye Mitchell, Jean Mitchell, Richard Berry, Harvey Fuqua, The Dreamers, unknowns (v). 11/54–58.*

Like Esther Phillips, James probably profited early in her career from her not-quite-jailbait sexiness, on display in performances like 'Roll With Me Henry', 'W-O-M-A-N' (an answer to Bo Diddley's 'I'm A Man') and the frantic rock 'n' roll number 'Tough Lover'. These and her other Modern sides are accomplished exercises in several R&B idioms of the day (hence the parenthesized rating) and have enthusiastic backings directed by Maxwell Davis or Dave Bartholomew.

James's Chess recordings – at any rate, those that are currently available – fall outside our purview, but to the inquiring reader who enjoys soul and R&B of the period concerned we commend *Tell Mama: The Complete Muscle Shoals Sessions* (MCA 088 112 518) from 1967–68, which gathers fervent performances like 'Tell Mama' and the number most closely associated with her, 'I'd Rather Go Blind'. There is less unanimity about the merits of her late-'70s set *Deep In The Night* (Bullseye Blues CD BB 9579), produced by Jerry Wexler, which includes the popular 'Sugar On The Floor', or about *Stickin' To My Guns* (Island 842 926//CID 9955) from 1990, though her version of Tony Joe White's 'Out Of The Rain' is a show-stopper.

*** Life, Love & The Blues
Private Music 82162 *James; Lee Thornburg (t, tb); Tom Poole (t); Jimmy Z. [Zavala] (s, h); Dave [David K.] Mathews (kb); Mike Finnigan (o); Josh Sklair (Do, g); Bobby Murray, Leo Nocentelli (g); Sametto James (b); Donto James (d, perc). 98.*

*** Matriarch Of The Blues
Private Music 82205 *As above, except Mathews also plays p, Sklair also plays kb and Finnigan also sings; add Ross Locke (perc, v), Goldman Redding (v). 00.*

**(*) Burnin' Down The House
Private Music 11633 *James; Lee R. Thornburg (t, flh, tb); Ronnie Buttacavoli (t, flh); Tom Poole (t); Jimmy Z. Zavala (ts, h); David L. Woodford (bs); David K. Mathews (kb, clavinet, p); Mike Finnigan (o, v); Josh Sklair, Bobby Murray (g); Sametto James (b); Donto James (d); Luis Conte (perc). 12/01–1/02.*

*** Let's Roll
Private Music 11646 *James; Lee R. Thornburg (t, tb); Tom Poole (t); Jimmy Z. Zavala (ts, bs, h); David K. Mathews (kb, o, p); Josh Sklair (syn, bj, g); Bobby Murray (g); Sametto James (b); Donto James (d, perc, v). 03.*

**(*) Blues To The Bone
RCA Victor 60644 *James; John 'Juke' Logan (h); Mike Finnigan (p); Josh Sklair, Bobby Murray, Brian Ray (g); Sametto James (b); Donto James (d, perc); Steve Davis, Yoshann Rush (v). 04.*

James's mature style is fervent yet cool and unsentimental; she delivers the messages of her songs with toned muscularity rather than the bodybuilder's swagger of a Tina Turner. The toughness of her musical personality is partly scar tissue from wounds, some of her own inflicting, in what she can now wryly call 'this changeable music business'. These days she sails, professionally and personally, with a more even keel, and on *Matriarch Of The Blues* she comes into harbour like a stately galleon, her sails filled with the warm wind of support from friends and family. (Her sons Donto and Sametto not only play on the album but were its joint producers.) James approaches 'Hound Dog' with a saucy, skirt-twitching strut, and brings a tough-cookie snarl to O. V. Wright's 'Don't Let My Baby Ride'. 'Try A Little Tenderness', however, receives a genuinely tender treatment, and in 'You're Gonna Make Me Cry' – another O. V. Wright number, affectingly sung in duet with Mike Finnigan – and Little Milton's 'Walking The Back

Streets', the two songs a 13-minute sequence of slow-blues melancholy, she digs down deep.

Matriarch followed the direction of *Life, Love & The Blues*, which had been seen as a return to the mother country of blues and soul after some exotic, and not always rewarding, trips in other regions. Actually *Life, Love* is no more or less of a blues album than its successor. Though there is solid blues repertoire like 'Born Under A Bad Sign', 'Spoonful' and 'Hoochie Coochie Gal', the album is more the kind of soul-blues blend found in the later work of Little Milton, or in Z. Z. Hill. Naturally, James handles it with aplomb, though at times so phlegmatically as to sound a little disengaged.

Burnin' Down The House, recorded in performance at the House Of Blues in Hollywood, celebrates some of her fans' favourite songs, though the performances are rather uneven. The secular preaching of 'Come To Mama' and the slyly sensual 'You Can Leave Your Hat On' compensate for an unmomentous reading of 'My Funny Valentine' and a version of 'I'd Rather Go Blind' that replaces depth with gloss. The material on *Let's Roll* comes mostly from Gary Nicholson or Kevin Rowe, with only Billy Wright's 'Stacked Deck' drawn from the blues library, but the new songs have been written to James's strengths and the band has been playing with her long enough to place every note tellingly.

Blues To The Bone is just that: no horns, just settings of harmonica and guitars to frame a dozen standards, mostly from '50s/'60s Chicago, such as 'Lil' Red Rooster', 'You Shook Me' and 'The Sky Is Crying'. A pulsating 'Crawlin' King Snake' is very effective, but some of the arrangements are pedestrian and the readings dispassionate, leading the listener to question whether a programme of blues classics is the best way for James to use her unquestionable talent.

James's other Private Music albums include *Time After Time* (82128), *Love's Been Rough On Me* (82140), *Heart Of A Woman* (82180) and *Blue Gardenia* (11580); none of them are particularly blues-oriented, and the last is a collection of popular standards. TR

Frank 'Springback' James
VOCAL, PIANO

A few small clues might be interpreted as giving James an Alabama provenance, but otherwise little can be deduced from his music about this dedicated follower of Leroy Carr who recorded for several labels in the '30s.

**(*) Frank "Springback" James & George Curry (1934–1938)
Document DOCD-5289 James; Willie B. James (g); prob. Fred Williams (d). 8/34–6/37.

On almost all his recordings, both James's singing – 'laconic but resonant', as Chris Smith well describes it – and his playing seem calculated to put the listener in mind of Leroy Carr. The impression is deepened by his frequent recourse to subjects that Carr also treated, such as rejection and misfortune, exemplified by 'Mistreated Blues', 'Lonesome Love Blues' and 'I'm On My Way'. With the addition on some sides of a guitarist who approximates the role of Scrapper Blackwell, the impersonation is complete. True, he shifts out of the low gear characteristic of Carr's blues to play 'Springback Papa', which uses the tune of 'The Dirty Dozens', at a romping tempo. Other uppish numbers are 'Poor Coal Loader' – at least on its first appearance; the remake of a year or so later, 'Poor Coal Passer', is quieter – and 'Hellish Ways', his treatment of Carr's 'Tired Of Your Low Down Ways'. The CD also includes three sides (unissued on 78) by George Curry, another Carr devotee, accompanied by a pianist who knows his way round Carr's style and an under-recorded guitarist. TR

Nathan James (born 1978)
VOCAL, GUITAR, HARMONICA, FOOT PERCUSSION

James has played electric guitar in James Harman's band since the late '90s; Harman co-produced his acoustic debut album.

*** This Road Is Mine
Pacific Blues PRBC-2301 James; Ben Hernandez (h, b, k, v); James Harman (h, shaker, v). 8/02.

Nathan James has Lonnie Johnson's playing down pat on 'Woke Up With The Blues In My Fingers', and he also does good work when inspired by Tampa Red and Blind Boy Fuller; his rack harmonica on two tracks is very accomplished. His singing makes moderate, not unattractive use of John Lee Williamson's tongue-tied sound, but his imitation of Doctor Ross is disquietingly minstrelly, and 'Please Slow Down', an attempt to compose in a Delta blues style, is rhythmically gawky. Harman and Hernandez sing lead from time to time, the former with a veteran's growly authority. Hernandez is fun on 'Hip Shakin' Mama', which pastiches Blind Boy Fuller, but melodramatic on a self-composed spiritual. *This Road Is Mine* is derivative but, subject to the qualifications noted, it makes agreeable, light-hearted listening. CS

Skip James (1902–69)
VOCAL, PIANO, GUITAR

Nehemiah Curtis James was born in Yazoo City, Mississippi, and raised by his mother on a plantation near Bentonia, Mississippi. He began playing guitar at about 15, taught by Henry Stuckey, and later developed his piano playing, which would occasionally win him jobs in whorehouses. He recorded on both instruments for Paramount in 1931. Other than music, he made his living in part from bootlegging and gambling, until his father re-entered his life and directed him towards a career in the Baptist ministry. 'Rediscovered' by blues enthusiasts in 1964, he made a momentous appearance at the Newport Folk Festival which he followed with several recording sessions and sporadic engagements at colleges and coffeehouses. He spent his last years in Philadelphia, dying there of cancer.

♛ **** Complete Early Recordings
Yazoo 2009 James. 2/31.

***(*) Skip James (1931)
Document DOCD-5005 James. 2/31.

***(*) Cypress Grove Blues
Snapper Complete Blues SBLUECD 007 James. 2/31.

***(*) 50 Years Mississippi Blues in Bentonia: Skip James & Jack Owens 1931–1981
Wolf WBJCD 009 James. 2/31.

The sombre mood of 'Cypress Grove Blues', 'Hard Time Killin' Floor Blues' and, above all, 'Devil Got My Woman', his most famous composition, coupled with his eerily high voice, encourage us to think of Skip James's work in terms of introspection and melancholy. In fact he operated at several emotional temperatures: wheedling a romantic prospect in 'Cherry Ball Blues', playing for dancers in the piano stomps 'How Long "Buck"' and 'If You Haven't Any Hay Get On Down The Road', exulting in his own speed in the dashing 'I'm So Glad'. All these, together with a couple of gospel songs and several other blues on both his instruments, were made at a single session, and the resulting releases are among the rarest and most prized of blues 78s. It would be difficult to listen to them without some sense of awe, even if they were not quite as good as we might wish, but they are, in fact, awesome in their singularity and aching beauty.

Yazoo's is the only collection to consider. The others all have the same 18 tracks, but the Document and Wolf are much less well remastered and the Snapper, no doubt copied from Yazoo, lacks its valuable notes by James's biographer, Stephen Calt. The Wolf also has five pieces by Jack Owens (q.v.), a Bentonian who shared some of James's repertoire.

*** She Lyin'
Genes GCD 9901 *James; unknown (d).* 8/64, late 64.
**(*) Skip's Piano Blues
Genes GCD 9910 *James; unknown (g, v).* 10/64.

In the winter of 1964–65 James went into hospital for surgery, the effects of which appear to have been both physically and emotionally traumatic. Those who believe that something vital was lost from his music as well can summon these recordings as evidence, for they were made beforehand: *She Lyin'* at a studio session (intended for a Takoma LP that was never issued) and a coffeehouse date or dates, and *Skip's Piano Blues* also in a studio but more informally. Though there are clear traces of rust on James's performance, his guitar playing on *She Lyin'* is the strongest and most coherent of all his '60s work, and 'I'm So Glad', 'Devil Got My Woman' and 'Hard Time Killin' Floor Blues' are superior to any later versions. The piece that gives the album its name is mistitled: it's not 'She Lyin' but 'Sealion', a children's song on which James spends little more than a minute. Another curiosity is Amos Milburn's 'Bad [Bad] Whiskey'. An unidentified drummer, playing with brushes, is heard on 'Illinois Blues' and 'Look Down The Road'.

She Lyin' portrays James exclusively as a guitarist; *Skip's Piano Blues* shows his other talent. As a pianist he was hardly less striking, his rhythms diffuse but controlled. By 1964 he was rusty, but '22–20' has much of its old spirit and swing; 'Black Gal' is more effective as a piano piece than with guitar, and 'Special Rider', once it settles down, is interesting too. An unidentified guitarist (possibly more than one) can be faintly heard now and then. The album is worth the time of the committed enthusiast, but it is seldom more than a distant echo of his younger work.

** "Live" Vol. 1: Boston 1964 & Philadelphia 1966
Document DOCD-5149 *James; Lorenzo Meeks James (v).* 11/64, 66.

The 'Boston 1964' part is four songs (studio-recorded, not live) which the collector Bernie Klatzko issued on vinyl 78s, a pleasing idea at the time. The '66 Philadelphia concert is from an amateur tape and the guitar is recorded a little more strongly than the voice. Unfamiliar titles mask repertoire staples: 'Special Lover Blues' is 'Special Rider', and 'Someday You Gotta Die' is 'Crow Jane'. The CD was first issued in 1992; its 2004 rerelease can be identified by the full-colour cover.

**(*) Hardtime Killing Floor Blues//Hard Time Killing Floor Blues
Biograph BCD 122//Shout Factory 30169 *James.* 12/64.
**(*) Today!
Vanguard VMD 79219 *James; Russ Savakus (b).* 1/66.
** Rare And Unreleased
Vanguard VCD 79705 *James; Russ Savakus (b); Lorenzo Meeks James (v).* 1/66.
** Devil Got My Woman
Vanguard VMD 79273 *James.* 3/67.
**(*) Blues From The Delta
Vanguard VCD 79517 *James; Russ Savakus (b).* 1/66, 3/67.
** Hard Time: Best Of Skip James
Universe UV 094 *As above.* 1/66, 3/67.

At the time they were issued, James's '60s albums were momentous events and were received with more gratitude than scrutiny. Forty years on, with all dues to nostalgia long ago paid, the conscientious listener must judge them to be uneven and, when set against earlier versions, technically flawed. Much of the power of 'I'm So Glad' in 1931 lay in the excitement of James's virtuosity; take that away and you have a song with little more substance than a children's rhyme. The version on *Today!* is pretty but inconsequential, nothing in it suggesting the impact of the original or the qualities that might be adapted for a successful rock performance. 'Devil Got My Woman' (*Hard Time Killing Floor Blues, Devil Got My Woman*) and 'Special Rider' (*Today!*) are fragile in comparison with their wiry forerunners, yet even they do not convey a sense of waste like the overlong, over-deliberate versions of standards like 'Black Gal' ('My Gal' on *Today!*) and 'Careless Love' (*Devil*), or the perfunctory 'Look At The People Standing At The Judgement' (*Devil*), which is simply not up to James's standard at any stage in his recording career.

What's missing in these late recordings is the conciseness of his playing as a young man. His exceptional timing had slipped from him, and what he once executed with accuracy and flair he now fumbled or rushed. Accompaniments that formerly had a logic to them are dismembered into ill-fitting segments. From time to time he could still produce music that touched the edge of greatness, but in the end there could be no concealing the fact that it had once *been* great.

And yet even those who most value his past should not scorn the Skip James of *Today!* His playing is less at sea on the simpler pieces like 'Crow Jane' and 'Drunken Spree', and his voice has not lost its penetrating, ethereal clarity. Nor is *Hard Time Killing Floor Blues* to be overlooked. Although James's health was shaky, he warded off fatigue through a long day's recording, to make an album that at its best stands a pace or two ahead of *Today!* As with all James's recordings, there's considerable duplication of repertoire: it has about half a dozen titles in common with *Today!* and *She Lyin'*, but a different half-dozen in each case. The Biograph issue appears to have replaced an earlier version titled *Greatest Of The Delta Blues Singers*, with a different track order (which Shout Factory preserve) but the same catalogue number.

Devil Got My Woman, once past the opening and rather gripping 'Good Road Camp Blues', is a sadder affair. *Blues From The Delta* makes as good a job as possible of the 'best of' commission, dropping three tracks each from *Today!* and *Devil* (thereby losing 'My Gal' and 'Look At The People') and adding two previously unissued songs. Universe attempt a wider retrospective of the Vanguard recordings by selecting four tracks each, not all good ones, from *Today!* and *Devil* and a dozen from the tapeboxes that supplied *Rare And Unreleased*. As the reader will gather from the remarks that follow, that decision wasn't likely to produce a definitive 'best of', and didn't.

The performances on *Rare And Unreleased*, finally presented to the public 35 years after they were recorded, prove to be deeply disappointing. Close students of James's work may be glad to hear him attempting non-generic pieces like 'Lazy Bones' and 'Somebody Loves You', and there is a generous portion of his piano playing (seven tracks), but the gospel songs, which are numerous, are drably performed and only in 'One Dime Was All I Had' does James hint at the excitement of his best work. On the CD these recordings are assigned to 1967, implying that they are outtakes from the *Devil Got My Woman* date, but a Vanguard source recently stated that they were made at James's first (*Today!*) session.

**(*) Heroes Of The Blues: The Very Best Of Skip James
Shout Factory 30245 *James*. 2/31, 64–67.

A collection of two 1931 sides and 14 culled from Biograph, Adelphi and Vanguard can't justify being called the 'very best' of Skip James, but as a sampler of his later-life recordings it could be useful to buyers who aren't sure where to start.

**(*) "Live" Vol. 2: Bloomington, Indiana. March 30, 1968 – Part 1
Document DOCD-5633 *James*. 3/68.

**(*) "Live" Vol. 3: Bloomington, Indiana. March 30, 1968 – Part 2
Document DOCD-5634 *James*. 3/68.

Most of the interest of these CDs lies in their presenting an entire concert, lightly edited if at all, complete with introductions, retunings, applause and so forth. The repertoire holds no surprises for the listener who knows James's earlier '60s albums ('Hard Headed Woman Blues' is 'My Gal'), and he plays, at best, about as well as on the Vanguards, but the programme is not overburdened with gospel numbers, the recording is clear and James's prefaces to the songs give the listener an accurate impression of how he sometimes presented himself, diffident yet playful. These are 2004 reissues of CDs that first appeared five years earlier, with the same catalogue numbers but slightly different titles. TR

Steve James (born 1950)
VOCAL, GUITAR, MANDOLIN, GUITAR-BANJO

As a teacher, writer and performer, James carries his skills and knowledge lightly. Born in New York City, he arrived in Texas via Tennessee, adding hillbilly and country music to a grounding in blues and jazz. Whether fingerpicking or wielding a slide or combining the two, his precision is exemplary. From earnest beginnings his playing and singing have coalesced in an entertaining and relaxed maturity.

*** Two Track Mind
Antone's ANT 0024 *James; Bill Ginn (p); John Hanley (g)*. 93.

The self-consciousness hovering over the album title reflects the finesse with which James sets out his stall. Its 13 tracks draw upon a wide and diverse repertoire, sampling the work of Charlie Poole, Sam McGee, Mance Lipscomb, Sylvester Weaver and Big Bill Broonzy, with just one original, 'County Line Road', dedicated to Texas guitarist John Vandiver. The panache with which he tackles Weaver's 'Guitar Rag' and McGee's 'Amos Johnson Rag' signals the chutzpah of a man who finds the complex conventional and relishes the challenge of adding an extra flourish. That he succeeds is a measure of his talent but the less eager musicianship of Poole's 'Milwaukee Blues', 'Frankie And Albert' and the 'Spanish Fandango' that ends the set is equally impressive. The humour of 'Huggin' And Chalkin", where two men meet while circumnavigating the same plump woman, introduces a much-needed sense of fun that undercuts moments of over-achievement elsewhere.

*** American Primitive
Antone's ANT 0030 *James; Gary Primich (h); Danny Barnes (g, bj); Mark Rubin (b, bb)*. 94.

There's less of the peacock about this set, evenly divided between well-chosen covers and complementary originals. The latter bring James's laconic humour to the fore, although 'Banker's Blues' borders on the cynical. One can almost hear Woody Guthrie singing this bitter tale of how moneyed crooks escape justice while the poor man gets the slammer. Its parallel is Uncle Dave Macon's 'All In, Down And Out Blues', written as an ironic comment upon the Wall Street crash. Resonances abound, not least in the five band tracks, including Bumble Bee Slim's 'Greasy Greens' and Hank Penny's 'Hadacol Boogie', that jostle along in best jugband style. James's (a)musings on death inhabit 'My Last Good Car' and 'Will And Testament Blues', while his best humour is saved for 'Grain Alcohol' and the long, discursive 'The Change'. Tampa Red's 'Boogie Woogie Dance' and a final 'Guitar Medley' are the obligatory virtuoso features.

***(*) Art And Grit
Discovery/Antone's 74706 *As above, except add Ann Rabson (p), Bob Brozman, Cindy Cashdollar (g)*. 96.

The generosity of spirit present alongside James's usual expertise makes this his most satisfying album. Three slide guitars skirl and scamper through Jimmie Tarlton's 'Ooze It To Me Mama', setting the tone for what follows. Other band performances include Noah Lewis's 'Viola Lee Blues', Big Joe Williams's 'Juanita Stomp' and James's 'Lookit Th' Dog'. Best by far is a rip-snorting 'Downbound Train', a traditional song here using Chuck Berry's lyrics. 'Blues Widow' and 'Liberty' are duets, the first with Rabson stabbing bass notes behind James's mandolin, the other an instrumental with James and Barnes on guitars. 'Hot Time In The Old Town Tonight' is a slide feature, an adaptation of an arrangement learned from Sam McGee. Only a plaintive 'Farewell The Roses' briefly punctures the bonhomie. James's notes provide historical context for each song, leaving the musicians to entertain rather than instruct.

*** Boom Chang
Burnside BCD 0038 *James; Gary Primich (h); Alvin Youngblood Hart (md, g); Cindy Cashdollar (Do, g); Mark Rubin (b, tu, vc)*. 00.

A move to a new label doesn't disturb a sovereign recipe. The theme here is travel, even when the subject of 'Been All Around This World' is on Death Row. In contrast, 'Saturday Night In Jail' is a rollicking affair, as the band celebrate the consequences of a roister too many. 'Galway Station Blues' finds its protagonist 'five thousand miles from home' waiting for a bus to the next gig, longing for a chance encounter with a waitress like the one in 'Willie's Place'. Roosevelt (Grey Ghost) Williams's 'Way Out On The Desert' is propelled by Rubin's roundly slapped bass, while 'Squaw Teat Mountain Breakdown' has Primich's squawking harmonica for company. The standout here is 'Stack Lee's Blues', an ingenious reworking of the fatal encounter with Billy Lyons. Luke Faust's 'Seeds' closes the album, emphasizing that it's the journey rather than the goal that's important. James makes an engaging travelling companion. NS

*** Fast Texas
Burnside 48 *James; Cindy Cashdollar (Do, sg); Del Rey (g); Ruthie Foster, Cyd Cassone (v). 10/02.*

Though this is not a fully themed album, much of the material (fast or not) is associated with Texas, including a 'Jack O' Diamonds' from Mance Lipscomb, '4 Or 5 Times' from Milton Brown, blues by Texas Alexander and Little Hat Jones, Hop Wilson's 'Chicken Stuff', boiled down to a slide guitar solo, and Blind Willie Johnson's 'Rain Done Fell On Me'. James's own 'Freestone County Blues' also sticks a pin in the state map. Very pretty guitar parts by Cashdollar and Rey further enhance James's attractive, relaxed performances. TR

Frankie 'Half-Pint' Jaxon (1897–1953)
VOCAL, SCRAPER

Nicknamed for his 5'2" stature, Jaxon was a professional entertainer by 1910, and during 30 years in the business was at various times a dancer, comedian, bandleader, producer, songwriter and actor, as well as a singer. Like his fellow female impersonator Mae West, he knew that sex is such a serious matter that laughter is the only possible response; unlike her, he was all manic energy, with the bounce of a squash ball and the comic timing of a camp Fats Waller. Resident in Chicago when he first recorded, Jaxon later moved to New York. In 1941 he took a job at the Pentagon, transferring to Los Angeles in 1944; nothing is known of him thereafter.

(*) Frankie 'Half-Pint' Jaxon – Vol. 1 (1926–1929)
Document DOCD-5258 *Jaxon; prob. Freddie Keppard, Punch Miller (c); Lem Johnson, poss. Vance Dixon (cl); De Lloyd Barnes, Blanche Smith Walton, William Barbee, Jimmy Flowers, Georgia Tom Dorsey, unknowns (p); Robert Waugh (vn); Ikey Robinson (bj); unknown, Tampa Red (g); Bill Johnson (b); unknown (bb); unknown (k, j, v); Sid Catlett, poss. Jasper Taylor (d); unknowns (v). 5/26–7/29.*

*** Frankie 'Half-Pint' Jaxon – Vol. 2 (1929–1937)
Document DOCD-5259 *Jaxon; Punch Miller (c); Bob Shoffner, George Mitchell, Guy Kelly, Herb Morand, unknown (t); Preston Jackson, unknown (tb); Dalbert Bright, Odell Rand, Buster Bailey, unknown (cl); Kenneth Anderson (as); David Young (ts); prob. Charlie Johnson, Jerome Carrington, Horace Malcolm, unknowns (p); unknown (bj); Charles Ducastaign, Joe McCoy, Charlie McCoy, unknown (g); Johnny Frazier, Ransom Knowling, unknown (b); unknown (bb); Tubby Hall, Pearlis Williams, unknown (d); unknowns (v). 7/29–7/37.*

** Frankie 'Half-Pint' Jaxon – Vol. 3 (1937–1940)
Document DOCD-5260 *Jaxon; Herb Morand, Henry 'Red' Allen, Jonah Jones (t); Odell Rand, Barney Bigard, Rupert Cole (cl); Horace Malcolm, Lil Armstrong, unknown (p); Charlie McCoy*

(md, g); Joe McCoy, unknown (g); John Lindsay, Wellman Braud, unknown (b); Fred Flynn, Sid Catlett (d); Prince Budda (vb); Walter Martin (wb). 7/37–4/40.

Vol. 1 opens with two atypical chances to hear Jaxon's natural tenor at some length, but he's soon off into the seaside-postcard world that remained his preferred habitat, his falsetto gasps, shrieks, chuckles and moans conveying mock affront and real delight at the antics of women and men in polymorphous pursuit of each other. (More in this vein, as vocalist with Tampa Red's Hokum Jug Band, will be found on *Tampa Red Vols 1–4* [Document DOCD-5073/4/5/6]; see that artist for discussion.) The present disc begins with some noisy transfers but soon improves, and includes a number of outstanding items, among them the first versions of Jaxon's lubricious theme song, 'Fan It'; two songs with sublime cornet decoration, thought to be by Freddie Keppard; another pair where Bill Johnson's musclebound swing and a hot kazoo encourage Jaxon to caper even more energetically than usual; and Ikey Robinson's stringband, hurtling through 'My Four Reasons' at Formula 1 speed. Vol. 1 also includes (from a worn original) 'Operation Blues', a raunchy piece of medical malpractice recorded with Georgia Tom and issued on an under-the-counter party label.

However, listeners who just want a representative sample will find Vol. 2 more consistent, and of better sound quality. It documents Jaxon moving on from hokum to swing, but starts with him fronting the Cotton Top Mountain Sanctified Singers. This jazz-accompanied studio group performs three spirituals with great vigour, gorgeous cornet from Punch Miller and every appearance of sincerity. (The following day, Miller and Jaxon cut a song which begins, 'Now, Corinne Brown of Chicago town was a snakehip, shakin' queen.') The bulk of the CD consists of eight titles with the Hot Shots, a big band which Jaxon assembled for the 1933 Chicago World's Fair, and another eight with the Harlem Hamfats. The Hot Shots were a well-rehearsed ensemble, with a classy book of arrangements, and they take good advantage of their soloing opportunities. Only the two-part sketch 'The Mortgage Blues' has dated beyond redemption. The Hamfats obviously loved working with Frankie Jaxon, and vice versa; 'The Dirty Dozen' is surprisingly tame, but elsewhere the band, and Herb Morand in particular, enthusiastically follow Jaxon's injunction to 'Take it, you cats! Swing it!', working themselves into an ecstatic lather of boogie on 'Wet It'.

Vol. 3 has half a dozen more sides with the Hamfats, and Jaxon is otherwise accompanied by various combinations of distinguished New York jazz musicians, but the performance energy declines progressively, and his voice becomes increasingly hoarse and decreasingly supple. The spark reignites briefly on four titles propelled by Sid Catlett's shuffle rhythms and Barney Bigard's optimistic clarinet, but this is the least necessary disc of the three. Jaxon's penultimate recording, 'Gimme A Pig's Foot And A Bottle Of Beer', inevitably provokes comparison with Bessie Smith and, sadly, the gap is as large as that between her height and his. CS

Abner Jay
VOCAL, HARMONICA, BANJO-GUITAR, BANJO, DRUMS

Jay was from Fitzgerald, Georgia. As a young man he played banjo on Silas Green's Minstrel Show, while in later life he

toured the Southeast in a camper van, putting on a one-man minstrel show in shopping malls and at flea markets. He died in 1993.

(**) One Man Band
Subliminal Sounds SUBCD 7 *Jay. 70s?*

For the reader who approaches this album in the hope of learning something about archaic African-American music, only bemusement awaits. Although much of the *schtick* that makes up a large part of the programme is venerable – comic stories and jokes about elephants, honeymoons, Tom Dooley and Adam and Eve – almost all the songs sound as if they originate with Jay, and allusions to texts recorded by other artists in this book, such as 'Bring It With You When You Come' (Cannon's Jug Stompers), are few and fleeting. 'Woke Up This Morning' is the only blues. Except for one of two versions of a cocaine ditty, on which he plays acoustic banjo, all the pieces are accompanied on electric six-string banjo, drums and occasionally harmonica, and sung in an uningratiating bellow. The swish on some tracks betrays that they were taped from discs; the notes are silent about their provenance, but they appear to come from *Swaunee Water And Cocaine Blues* and perhaps others of his three or four LPs, which probably reflect the act he put on in the '60s and '70s. Fortunately, a performance taped at a folk festival shortly before his death and issued on *Blues Routes* (Smithsonian Folkways SFW CD 40118) proves that in another setting he could produce music of a different kind. In his orotund singing of 'Bluetail Fly', accompanied on banjo and harmonica, a dim outline of the minstrel stage does, finally, take form. TR

Doug Jay (born 1953)
VOCAL, HARMONICA

The Florida-born Jay began playing playing harmonica after hearing records of Little Walter. In the late '70s he was in The Allstars From Charlottesville, and later with Bob Margolin. He spent the first half of the '90s in California, where he made his first solo recording. In 1993 he toured in Europe with the Mojo Blues Band and he has revisited regularly ever since.

**(*) Jackpot!
Crosscut CCD 11083 *Jay; 'Sax' Gordon Beadle (ts); Thomas Feldmann (bs); Roel Spanjers (o, p); Chris Rannenberg (p); Christoph 'Jimmy' Reiter (g, v); Jasper Mortier (b); Andre Werkmeister (d, perc, v). 2–3/04.*

If you didn't know beforehand that Jay was drawn to blues harmonica by the work of Little Walter, you would guess it from 'Giddy-Up', a poised medium-tempo blues instrumental. The Otis Spann songs 'It Must Have Been The Devil' and 'Half Ain't Been Told' have a similar '50s-Chicago ambience, but Jay is equally at home in other musical locations: witness the tumbling boogie 'I Jump', the Louis Jordanesque setting of 'When I Get Lucky' and the contemporary styling of 'Ya Hoodoo Me'. The album is credited to Doug Jay & The Blue Jays, and the core band of Reiter, Mortier and Werkmeister is as versatile as its leader. Jay's singing, resonant but unnuanced, is no more than serviceable, but on harmonica he can hold his own with all but the best of his peers. TR

Blind Lemon Jefferson (1893–1929)
VOCAL, GUITAR

Reportedly blind from birth, Jefferson grew up in Wortham and Mexia, Texas, began playing in the streets of East Texas towns in the 1910s and later probably made his home in Dallas. Several musicians, notably Leadbelly, claimed that they had acted as his guide, but others who knew him vouched for his independence – according to Thomas Shaw, 'Lemon could go anywhere he want to go by himself' – and musicians both black and white claim to have seen him all over the South. Signed by Paramount, in 1926 he gave the African-American record industry its first-ever hit by a male singer/guitarist and laid a path for numberless successors. He died, less than four years later, in circumstances that remain obscure.

***(*) Blind Lemon Jefferson – Vol. 1 (1925–1926)
Document DOCD-5017 *Jefferson. c. 12/25–c. 12/26.*
*** Blind Lemon Jefferson – Vol. 2 (1927)
Document DOCD-5018 *Jefferson; George Perkins (p). 3–c. 10/27.*
*** Blind Lemon Jefferson – Vol. 3 (1928)
Document DOCD-5019 *Jefferson; unknown (p). c. 2–c. 8/28.*
**(*) Blind Lemon Jefferson – Vol. 4 (1929)
Document DOCD-5020 *Jefferson. c. 1–9/29.*
***(*) Blind Lemon Jefferson
JSP JSP 7706 4CD *As for Document CDs. c. 12/25–9/29.*
♛ ****** The Best Of Blind Lemon Jefferson**
Yazoo 2057 *Jefferson; unknown (p). c. 12/25–9/29.*
*** Long Lonesome Blues
World Arbiter 2006 *Jefferson. c. 3/26–9/29.*
**(*) The Best Of Blind Lemon Jefferson
Wolf WBJCD 016 *Jefferson; George Perkins (p). c. 3/26–9/29.*
**** King Of Country Blues
Yazoo 1069 *Jefferson. c. 4/26–3/29.*
*** Black Snake Moan
Snapper Complete Blues SBLUECD 013 *Jefferson. c. 5/26–9/29.*
(**) Cat Man Blues
Collectors Edition CBCD 021 *Jefferson; George Perkins, unknown (p). c. 11/26–9/29.*
(**) Moanin' All Over
Tradition TCD 1011 *Jefferson. c. 11/26–9/29.*

Jefferson's second release, 'Got The Blues'/'Long Lonesome Blues', had not long been on sale in the spring of 1926 when Paramount commissioned him to rerecord it. The company probably feared that the original masters would wear out before the demand had died down, something that had happened rarely in the six-year history of African-American vernacular recording, and never before for a male artist. Until then the 'race' record business had been built almost entirely on blues sung by women with pianists or bands. Jefferson offered instead blues sung by a man playing guitar – playing it, moreover, with a busyness and variety that showed up many of those pianists and bands as turgid and ordinary. The discovery that there was an audience for Jefferson's type of blues revolutionized the music business: within a few years female singers were out of favour and virtually all the trading in the 'race' market (jazz aside) was in men with guitars.

But Jefferson is a figure of more than historical stature. If he had few forerunners, he had just as few equals. 'Got The Blues' opens with the arresting line 'The blues come to Texas, loping like a mule'; the guitar mirrors the image, but Jefferson was prone to accelerate during a performance, and by the end of the song he is galloping. The tempo also increases in 'Long Lonesome Blues', so that Jefferson's clusters of riffs and pull-offs become more and more dextrous. Almost 80 years later this is still guitar playing of extraordinary and thrilling virtuosity; how must it have sounded to its first hearers?

Such capricious but exciting playing decorated other early records like 'Black Horse Blues', but often – and, as the recording dates became frequent, increasingly – the guitar part was subservient to the singing. Working on the streets, Jefferson had developed a voice that was piercing and distinct, and his lyrics, though sometimes wordy and often idiosyncratic, are usually intelligible even through the hail of surface noise from the average Paramount disc. Whether he was the creator of lines like 'I'm broke and hungry, ragged and dirty too – mama, if I clean up, can I go home with you?' ('Broke And Hungry') or merely the first person to record them is probably beyond research, but such thoughts and expressions, once he recorded them, ignited the imaginations of inventive musicians and supplied prefabricated ideas to dull ones.

Though in many ways an original, Jefferson does not stand outside tradition. His repertoire includes songs that preceded him, such as 'Corinna Blues', a version of 'Easy/C.C. Rider', the rag songs 'Beggin' Back' (i.e. 'Take Me Back') and 'One Dime Blues', the buck-dance tune 'Hot Dogs' and a sheaf of religious texts which he sets to pattern-picked guitar parts, including what has become his most famous piece, 'See That My Grave Is Kept Clean' (also known as 'One Kind Favor'). Another older piece, 'Jack O' Diamond Blues', he plays with a slide, sounding rather like his contemporary Ramblin' Thomas. That likeness may have been fortuitous, but it's more than probable that guitar parts such as the ones he devised for 'Big Night Blues' and 'Bed Spring Blues' served as blueprints for younger Southwestern players like J. T. Smith.

At his sessions in the summer of 1928 Jefferson began to preface songs with comments, greetings or spoken couplets or verses. Perhaps Paramount hoped to individualize recordings that they feared were becoming indistinguishable: for his guitar accompaniments Jefferson was relying almost continuously on parts and figures he had used before. His last session, in 9/29, makes for rather depressing listening. Songs like 'Bakershop Blues' or 'Fence Breakin' Yellin' Blues', most of them probably written by others, patently fail to inspire him, his guitar playing is somnolent and his voice shows signs of strain. Three months later he was dead.

For excellence of remastering – a matter of primary importance, since Jefferson recorded all but two of his nearly a hundred sides for the technically inferior Paramount label – the Yazoos are unquestionably the front-runners. *The Best Of* seems to be a mute revision of the earlier *King Of The Country Blues*, for it shares 14 of its tracks but substitutes important pieces like 'Got The Blues', 'Long Lonesome Blues', 'Jack O' Diamond Blues' and the remarkable ''Lectric Chair Blues'. Yet it omits the unusual 'Right Of Way Blues', while adding an ill-judged cover of Leroy Carr's 'How Long – How Long Blues' whose piano accompaniment is much too regular to consort with Jefferson's natural wilfulness as a guitarist. That said, one can hardly quibble with the album's title, since nearly all of Jefferson's core pieces are included, and Stephen Calt's notes are an illuminating commentary on Jefferson's work. Owners of *King Of The Country Blues* need not feel pressed to replace it, but the reader coming to Jefferson afresh will find no better introduction than Yazoo's *The Best Of*.

World Arbiter claim that their Sonic Depth Technology brings 'great clarity' to *Long Lonesome Blues*. The transfers do sound natural, with none of the distorting effects of ill-handled sound treatment, but surface noise is very high, so there are no grounds for preferring this to Yazoo's *The Best Of*, which in any case duplicates it extensively. Cockily subtitling their album *Lemon's Texts Revealed*, World Arbiter also provide lyric transcriptions, but these are not faultless either. The four Documents have everything, bar a few alternative takes, which can be found dotted through the label's *"Too Late, Too Late"* series of VACs. The transfers are variable but generally serviceable and the albums are attentively annotated by Bob Groom. JSP also give us Lemon unsqueezed – his complete work in an inexpensive boxed set – but the sound quality is not significantly better than Document's. The other second-tier reissues on Wolf and Snapper Complete Blues are riddled with duplications, both of the Yazoos (and necessarily the Documents) and of each other. The better is the Snapper, which was chosen with discrimination and includes, what the Yazoos both lack, Jefferson's only non-Paramount record, the OKeh disc of 'Black Snake Moan' and 'Match Box Blues'. (The version of the latter on the Yazoos is the second Paramount recording, Jefferson's liveliest take. The OKeh coupling was also on *Match Box Blues: The Essential Recordings Of Blind Lemon Jefferson* [Indigo IGOCD 2075, deleted].) The Wolf CD devotes a good deal of space to the lacklustre late work. Both *Cat Man Blues* and *Moanin' All Over* manage to avoid most of Jefferson's best recordings. The former's remastering and presentation are wretched, and the latter's complement of nine tracks is ludicrously poor value. TR

Jelly Roll Kings
GROUP

Their name inspired by Frank Frost's 1962 single, the band and its audience flourished a decade or so later under a halo of romantic nostalgia engendered by the words 'downhome blues' and 'juke-joint'. The evocation of ramshackle and raucous music-making with a frisson of imminent danger proved an irresistible draw. But as its members engaged in solo careers, the Kings became an occasional unit, its gigs infrequent and its commitment compromised.

** Rockin' The Juke Joint Down
Earwig 4901 *Frank Frost (h, o, p, v); Jack Johnson (g, v); Sam Carr (d). 79.*

Meant to represent a typical set in some mythical juke-joint, this album suffers from indifferent sound and playing, a failure of nerve on both sides of the studio control room window. Carr's engagingly busy drum style is woefully under-recorded and rarely makes its presence felt. Johnson's ampli-fier sounds like an irritated wasp and he displays an equally annoying penchant for keeping rhythm by striking his guitar strings without forming a note, producing a sound like squeaky springs. Frost is the most active participant but plays harmonica on just six of 15 tracks, a burbling Farfisa organ on a further six and piano on three. He sings five songs and Johnson three, while both men grunt a coprophiliac 'Slop Jar Blues'. Six instrumental features, among them 'Honeydrippin' Boogie', 'Cleo's Back' and 'Jelly Roll Stroll', display a lack of understanding that signposts inadequate preparation. Mis-takes and uncomfortable moments are frequent throughout the set, although its final sequence from the harmonica showcase 'Jelly Roll Stroll' to Chips Moman's 'Burnt Biscuits', including a hectic 'Have Mercy Baby' and Little Walter's 'Just A Feeling', signals a slight return to form. But it's too little too late.

*** Off Yonder Wall
Fat Possum 0310 *As above, except add Terry Jackson (g).* 97.

This was Robert Palmer's final production stint before his last illness and it vindicates both producer and band. The players sound confident and alert and the instruments are properly recorded: Carr's drumming is snappy and his kit is audible at all times, the guitar amplification is fuller and Johnson's rhythm and lead playing are better coordinated. The only disappointment is Frost's apparently willing confinement to electric piano and organ. His only vocal contribution is 'So Lonesome', a slow blues that benefits from a more mellow guitar tone. It's one of four group compositions, leading off with an arresting 'Frank Frost Blues', in which Johnson chastises his friend for his continued drinking. 'Fishing Musician' details one of the hobbies that kept the musicians out of the studio, while the uneventful instrumental 'Fat Back' is one of a couple of tracks that outstay their welcome. That's not the case with 'Baby Please Don't Go', a largely instrumental 'That's Alright Mama' and 'Sitting On Top Of The World' played as a slide feature. 'Have Mercy Baby' and its crying chorus are repeated and the set ends with a raucous version of Johnson's 'I'm A Big Boy Now', bringing an enjoyable album to a close with some idiosyncratic yodelling. NS

David Johansen & The Harry Smiths
GROUP

In the '70s Johansen (born 1950) sang with the New York Dolls, a glam-rock band that played a small part, through its brief managerial connection with the English entrepreneur Malcolm McLaren, in the genesis of punk. In the '80s he went solo and more mainstream, and subsequently developed an eclectic cabaret act.

*** David Johansen And The Harry Smiths
Chesky JD 196//Chesky Super Audio SACD 225 *David Johansen (h, g, v); Brian Koonin (md, g); Larry Saltzman (bj, g); Kermit Driscoll (b, didgeridoo); Joey Baron (perc).* 11–12/99.
**(*) Shaker
Chesky JD 236 *David Johansen (h, v); Brian Koonin (md, g); Larry Saltzman (Do, g); Kermit Driscoll (b); Keith Carlock (d, perc).* 11/01.

The group's name alludes to the producer of the epochal *Anthology Of American Folk Music*, which had been reissued on CD not long before they formed. Johansen had clearly been inspired by that collection, as well as supplied with some of his material, such as Rabbit Brown's 'James Alley Blues', though his mishearing of Brown's ''cause I was born in the country, she thinks I'm easy to rule' spoils one of its best verses. Given Johansen's background it may be worth stating that his ear for folk idiom is keen, though his approach varies from the conventional, as in John Hurt's 'Richland Woman' and Sonny Boy Williamson II's 'Don't Start Me Talking', to the decidedly renovative in Ramblin' Thomas's 'Poor Boy Blues' and Louise Johnson's 'On The Wall'. In such company Oscar Brown Jr's 'Somebody Buy Me A Drink' in its Tom Waits-like setting reads less oddly than one might expect.

A curious record, then, at times excessively mannered, at times likeably ingenious. That its oddball charm might be difficult to replicate was confirmed by *Shaker*, a set of blues that seem on paper to be well chosen for Johansen's style, like Robert Wilkins's 'I'll Go With Her' or Furry Lewis's 'Furry's Blues' and 'Kassie Jones', yet are unequal in performance. Johansen's superbly distressed voice, which on the first album was a prism refracting the music in unexpected directions, sometimes edges here towards the distorting-mirror effect of not quite parody, but too studied imitation. The most striking track is the one modern song, 'My Morphine', another performance steeped in the intellectual-wino manner of Tom Waits. TR

Alfred 'Snuff' Johnson (1913–2000)
VOCAL, GUITAR

Born to sharecropping parents, by the age of 15 Alfred Johnson was working as a ranch hand and playing guitar (and, of course, dipping snuff). He performed in church and at country suppers, sometimes as a member of a stringband. Settling in Austin in 1945 after war service, Johnson continued to play informally for parties and worship. He came to white attention in the mid-'70s, but turned professional only in the late '80s, appearing at venues in Austin.

**(*) Black Cowboy Blues And Church Songs
Documentary Arts CD-1001 *Johnson.* mid-'70s.
*** Will The Circle Be Unbroken
Black Magic CD 9026 *Johnson; 'Chester Fields' [Kim Wilson] (h); Leighton Hamilton (g); George Rains (d).* 4–5/89.

Snuff Johnson's steady thumb beat is that of a guitarist who learned his trade in Mance Lipscomb's part of Texas, but he is not in Lipscomb's musical league. The creosote darkness of Johnson's voice is initially arresting, but his guitar playing is no more than serviceable, and his repertoire limited.

Black Cowboy Blues And Church Songs is a misleading title, for its secular songs are in no sense peculiar to black cowboys. When not recombining verses from oral tradition, Johnson, like many another blues singer, drew extensively on recordings; Joe Pullum's 'Black Gal' and John Lee Hooker's 'Hobo Blues' are on both CDs. The Documentary Arts release is well annotated, and does a more thorough job of exploring Johnson's religious music, but in keeping with the label's name, it is documentation, minimally produced, and with hesitations and fluffed notes allowed free passage.

By the time of *Will The Circle Be Unbroken*, Johnson's command of his instrument had improved, and, whereas the earlier set is all acoustic, the Black Magic CD also features the amplified guitar which he usually played for African-American audiences. There is accompaniment on most tracks, either by second guitar or harmonica and drums, and the results are clearly superior, with Johnson sounding much more comfortable when other musicians supply a harmonic and rhythmic context. This CD confirms, with care and affection, that he was no more, but equally no less, than a good minor league musician. CS

Buddy Johnson (1915–77)
VOCAL, PIANO

Johnson's orchestra was loved by dancers for its easy-swinging (and easy to dance to) rhythm on numbers like 'Walk 'Em'. Regulars at the Savoy Ballroom in Harlem, the band played the entire black dancehall circuit; a 1950 tour took in 133 engagements in 23 states. Woodrow Wilson Johnson grew up in South Carolina, playing piano and writing music in his teens, moved to New York in 1938 and began recording for Decca the following year. His chief vocalist was his sister Ella (1923–2004), but he also introduced the popular crooner Arthur Prysock. In the '50s, now on Mercury, Johnson was successful for a time with a big-band sound that sometimes edged towards rock 'n' roll, but by the early '60s he had more or less left the business for the church.

*** **Buddy Johnson 1939–1942**
Classics 884 *Johnson; Chester Boone (t, v); Courtney Williams, Shad Collins (t); Dan Minor (tb); Don Stovall (cl, as); Joe Eldridge, Scoville Brown, Leslie Johnakins, Bill Bowen (as); Sonny Fredericks, Kenneth Hollon (ts); Leonard Ware, unknown (g); Frank Clarke, unknown (b); Kenny Clarke, Alfred Taylor, unknown (d); Ella Johnson, The Mack Sisters, Warren Evans (v).* 11/39–1/42.

*** **Buddy Johnson 1942–1947**
Classics 1079 *Johnson; Chester Boone (t, v); Courtney Williams, Prince Jones, Isaac Larkin, John Lawton, Willis Nelson, Gus Aiken, Dupree Bolton, Henry Glover, Bert Turner, Frank Brown, John Wilson, Frank Royal, Andrew Wood (t); Dan Minor, Bernard Archer, Leonard Briggs, Jonas Walker, Gordon Thomas, William Harrison, Clement Tervalone (tb); Leslie Johnakins, Bill Bowen, Joe O'Laughton, Maxwell Lucas, Al Robinson (as); Kenneth Hollon, Frank Henderson, Jimmy Stanford, David Van Dyke (ts); Teddy Conyers (bs); Leonard Ware, Arnold Adams, Jerome Darr, Bernie McKay (g); Frank Clarke, Leon Spann (b); Kenny Clarke, Alfred Taylor, Gus Young, George Jenkins, Teddy Stewart, Emmanuel Simms (d); Ella Johnson, Warren Evans, James Lewis, Arthur Prysock (v).* 1/42–1/47.

*** **Buddy Johnson 1947–1949**
Classics 1115 *Johnson; Frank Royal, Andrew Wood, Willis Nelson, Calvin Strickland (t); Steve Pulliam, Bernard Archer, William Harrison, Donald Cole, Julius Watson (tb); Harold 'Geezil' Minerve (as, v); Joe O'Laughton, Al Robinson (as); David Van Dyke, Purvis Henson (ts); Teddy Conyers (bs); Bernie McKay (g); Leon Spann (b); Emmanuel Simms (d); Ella Johnson, Arthur Prysock (v).* 10/47–12/49.

*** **The Band That Swings The Blues**
[Blue Boar CDBB 1027] *Similar to above CDs.* 10/40–12/49.

*** **Jukebox Hits 1940–1951**
Acrobat ACMCD 4028 *Similar to above.* 10/40–12/51.

*** **Walk 'Em**
Ace CDCHD 623 *Similar to above.* 10/40–1/52.

Johnson started off leading a septet and built it into a 17-piece band, but whatever the size of his unit it was always a versatile swing ensemble that played from a book containing not just blues but ballads, standards, dance tunes and novelties. Readers who enjoy the sound and the breadth of repertoire of the Louis Jordan groups will have little trouble with early Buddy Johnson as heard on Classics' *1939–1942*; there's less humour and a few more ballads, but the general approach is similar. 'Boogie Woogie's Mother-In-Law', from 1941, is unusual in featuring amplified steel guitar. The second Classics CD embraces 'That's The Stuff You Gotta Watch' and 'Since I Fell For You', two of Ella's best-known vocal numbers, and Buddy's cover of Nellie Lutcher's hit 'Fine Brown Frame', while *1947–1949* contains roaring big-band charts like 'Li'l Dog', 'Down Yonder' and 'Shake 'Em Up' and the topical 'Did You See Jackie Robinson Hit That Ball?', sung by Arthur Prysock.

Readers without much of a taste for big-band swing might do better to restrict themselves to the Ace, Acrobat and Blue Boar CDs – probably just one, since all three have many tracks in common. The Blue Boar (which may not now be easy to find) has all the items singled out above; Ace and Acrobat have only some of them, but are better annotated. The Acrobat is cheaper, but the Ace extends further into Johnson's Decca contract to include tracks like 'Root Man Blues', which is arranged and sung (by Harold 'Geezil' Minerve) to sound like an amiable parody of Roy Brown.

The boxed set *Buddy & Ella Johnson 1953–1964* (Bear Family BCD 15479 4CD), which gathered their Mercury and Roulette recordings, has, regrettably, been deleted. TR

Edith Johnson (1903–88)
VOCAL, PIANO

Edith Johnson was married to St Louis record shop owner and talent scout Jesse Johnson, and became a recording artist through his contacts. She later became an entrepreneur, turning the De Luxe Music shop into a restaurant after Jesse died; when recorded again in 1961, she was running a taxi company.

(*) **Honey Dripper Blues
Agram Blues AB 2016 *Johnson; Baby James (c); Ike Rodgers (tb); Clarence Williams, Roosevelt Sykes, Count Basie, Henry Brown (p); unknown (g); Charles O'Brien (interviewer).* 12/28–11/29, 5/61, 4/80.

Edith Johnson was a talented lyricist, drawn to the favourite St Louis themes of sexual betrayal and violence. She uses the nasal voice then characteristic of St Louis blueswomen, but with a warmer, less abrasively edgy tone than usual. Her occasional piano playing is basic, but better than her own estimate of it as 'plunkety-plunk'. *Honey Dripper Blues* presents the 14 sides (including three versions of the title song, her biggest seller) that she recorded in a 12-month career. These are somewhat arbitrarily padded out with three Roosevelt Sykes numbers (cut at sessions where he accompanied her), an ill-assorted title from 1961 and a lengthy interview, which has value as documentary but little as entertainment. The annotation is first-class, as always with Agram, and sound quality is decent, although one title comes from a much abused original. CS

Herman E. Johnson (1909–75)
VOCAL, GUITAR

Johnson spent much of his life going from town to town, chasing whatever employment opportunities existed in Louisiana for an uneducated labourer. When recorded, he was working as a school janitor in Scotlandville.

*** **Louisiana Country Blues**
Arhoolie CD 440 *Johnson.* 61.

The romantic image of the solitary blues musician, singing about his troubles with no audience but himself, is seldom encountered in practice; even at its most personal, the blues usually functions as a social music, with the 'I' of the lyric also the 'we' of its listeners. (A good example is Smoky Babe, also from Scotlandville, with whom *Louisiana Country Blues* is shared.) Herman E. Johnson appears to have been an exception, however. His guitar lines usually follow the vocal melody, rather than supplying a rhythmic pulse, which suggests that he was not a dance musician; while he must have had some interaction with other musicians – he mixes traditional songs with his own compositions, and his knifestyle playing is reminiscent of Ramblin' Thomas – there's no indication, in either Johnson's own account of his life or folklorist Harry Oster's gloss on it, that he made music other than privately. Most of his songs are gloomy accounts of his troubles with women and work; 'Depression Blues' combines the two, in a powerful account of the frustration of looking for work in a recession, and its effect on family life. Johnson's music is an instance of another seldom-encountered trope – the blues as songs of sorrow, presenting the raw data of misery. Not surprisingly, this makes for bleak and depressing listening; even the two gospel songs included offer no catharsis. CS

Big Jack Johnson (born 1940)
VOCAL, GUITAR, MANDOLIN

In the '60s, '70s and '80s Johnson was a member of Frank Frost's Jelly Roll Kings, but in the mid-'80s he began to work in his own name, and he has led a succession of bands called The Oilers, since his day job is delivering heating oil in the area around his home in Clarksdale, Mississippi. Seasoned by many years on the Southern juke-joint circuit, he is a live performer of enormous energy, which has only rarely been captured on record.

*** The Oil Man
Earwig 4910 *Johnson; Frank Frost (p); Walter Roy (b); Ernest Roy (d). 6/86.*

**** Daddy, When Is Mama Comin Home?
Earwig 4916 *Johnson; Elmer Brown (t); Bill McFarland (tb, arr); Hank Ford (ts); Vince Willis (kb, p); Frank Frost (syn); Larry Burton, John Primer (g); Aron Burton (b); Earl Howell, Sam Carr (d). 2/88–9/89.*

Johnson is quite a versatile singer, sometimes sweet like Junior Parker, sometimes genially snarling in the manner of Howlin' Wolf. A good vocal balance isn't one of the strong points of *The Oil Man*, however, and the best things on the album are 'Catfish Blues' and 'I'm Gonna Give Up Disco And Go Back To The Blues' (the latter based on Parker's 'Mystery Train'), up-tempo numbers that Johnson's guitar and the no-frills Roy brothers propel into exhilarating dance music. The slower numbers like 'Driving Wheel' (also modelled on Parker) and 'Part Time Love' would perhaps have been improved by a larger band, and for his next album Earwig duly provided one. Its slick Chicago sound and McFarland's extremely inventive horn charts helped to reveal Johnson as a more interesting performer than the downhome journeyman of *The Oil Man*. He also increased his compositional input from three numbers to a full album, and while some of the songs are unexceptional others are unusual, like 'Mr. U.S. A.I.D.S.', one of the first blues on the subject, or the title number. Johnson also likes to slip off his blues shoes and caper in different footwear, as in 'Steel Guitar Rag' on *The Oil Man* and the Latin-funk 'Doodley Squat' on *Daddy*.

***(*) Live In Chicago
Earwig CD 4939 *Johnson; Lester Davenport (h); Allen Batts (p); Michael Dotson (g); Aron Burton (b); Kenny Smith, Tino Cortez (d). 6/94–3/95.*

Johnson had shown his affection for country music on both his previous albums, so nobody should have been surprised when he opened *Live In Chicago* with 'Pistol Packin' Mama' – except that this isn't Al Dexter's song but an artful blues recomposition in the style of Albert King. As sequenced here, Johnson then proceeds to Ivory Joe Hunter's 'Since I Met You Baby' and B. B. King's 'Sweet Sixteen' by way of 'Night Train' and 'Twist', the sheer variety of the setlist compensating for the sometimes uneventful ensemble playing, though Johnson does a lot to mask that with a guitar sound as gritty as Magic Slim's. The recording may keep the audience in the distance but the feel of a band on stage is vividly realized.

**(*) We Got To Stop This Killin'
M.C. MC 0033 *Johnson; Rodger Montgomery (g, v); Maury 'Hooter' Saslaff (b); Chet Woodward (d). 2/96.*

**(*) All The Way Back
M.C. MC 0035 *Johnson; Bob Rushford (h); Little Anthony Geraci (o, p); Chris Dean (g, v); Maury 'Hooter' Saslaff (b); Chet Woodward (d). 3–9/97.*

**(*) Roots Stew
M.C. MC 0039 *Johnson; Wild Child Butler (h); Chris Dean (g); Maury 'Hooter' Saslaff (b); Dale Wise (d). 10/98–99.*

After the transformative exercise of the previous two Earwigs, these albums for his new label found Johnson – not relaxing: he is too robust a performer to be accused of that – but rediscovering the downhome straightforwardness of the Jelly Roll Kings. Hearing this by no means unsophisticated musician playing in a simpler, older style, one is sometimes reminded of certain recordings by Eddie Taylor or the Burns brothers.

But these are not altogether satisfactory records. Songs often go on too long. Johnson is not an uninventive guitarist, but to push a slow blues instrumental like 'Late Night With Jack' (*Roots Stew*) to 7.18 is to risk losing the listener's attention. One misses the rhythmic collaboration of guitar and keyboards, so well achieved when Johnson and Frost worked together; Geraci is animated on *All The Way Back*, but for all that it's an unexciting album. *Roots Stew* has Johnson's first recordings on mandolin, a stomping 'Cherry Tree' and, in 'Beale Street', a slow blues travelogue about Memphis.

**(*) The Memphis Barbecue Sessions
M.C. MC 0045 *Johnson; Kim Wilson (h, g, v); Pinetop Perkins (p); Mark Carpentieri (d). 10/00.*

Three tracks apart, this is a duet album by Johnson and Wilson, often unamplified, and it has the warmth of a couple of deeply experienced musicians playing for each other. But, partly because it was their first meeting and partly because label-head Carpentieri requested it, they chose a largely standard repertoire of pieces like 'My Babe', 'Smokestack Lightning' and 'Big Boss Man' that subdue Johnson's individuality; the only track that has that stamp is 'Get Along Little

Cindy', an ancient breakdown from Johnson's stock of country tunes, played on mandolin. TR

James 'Stump' Johnson (1902–69)
VOCAL, PIANO

Nicknamed 'Stump' because he was short and stocky, Johnson was born in Tennessee, and moved with his family to St Louis in 1909. His brother Jesse ran the DeLuxe Music shop, where a record-company scout heard Stump playing in 1928. He didn't make a living from blues piano, but it did bring him a string of girlfriends and enough money to finance his main interest, gambling. Johnson's recording career ended in the Depression, and he was drafted during World War II, but by 1944 was managing a hotel for Jesse. In 1960 he was working for the St Louis tax department and moonlighting as 'a policeman', perhaps meaning a security guard.

*** James 'Stump' Johnson (1929–1964)
Document DOCD-5250 Johnson; poss. Baby Jay (c); Alex Hill, Roosevelt Sykes, Aaron 'Pine Top' Sparks (p); Harry Johnson (vn, g); unknown (md); Tampa Red, poss. Dewey Jackson, 'Joe C. Stone' [prob. J. D. Short], unknown (g); Dorathea [Doretha] Trowbridge (v); Edith Johnson (sp). c. 12/28–8/33, 11/64.

'The Duck's Yas-Yas-Yas', Stump Johnson's first recording and his biggest hit, enabled him to market his talents to a succession of record companies over the next five years. His piano playing is uncomplicated, and usually relies on the chordal bass figures typical of St Louis, although 'Bound To Be A Monkey' proves that he could knock out an eight-to-the-bar walking bass. An unusual feature of Stump's style is his extensive use of the Scotch snap; especially on slower numbers, this short-long dotted rhythm gives his accompaniments a yearning quality that's well suited to songs like 'The Snitcher's Blues', about the fickleness of friends, or 'Baby B. Blues' and 'My Babe Blues', which sigh after lost love. As well as nurturing romantic longings, Johnson was a tough commentator on brothel and barrelhouse frolics, and understandably irked, on 'Jones Law Blues', by attempts to strengthen Prohibition. He can be startlingly forthright, requesting Dorathea Trowbridge to 'raise your left leg, my baby, and give me your tongue, that's the way to make me do the beedle-e-bum,' or recalling that 'I was listening to the tune of a saxiephone 'cross the way, where Gutbucket Kelly showed her drawers till day.'

Stump's seven sessions to 1933 were spread across six labels, and he took the opportunity – or was encouraged – to remake various numbers; mama kept buying a chicken and thinking it was a duck, 'The Snitcher's Blues' and 'My Babe Blues' both turn up twice, and 'Soaking Wet Blues' on Paramount became 'Heart Is Right Blues' for OKeh. Repetition doesn't entail tedium, however, for producers teamed Johnson with a variety of accompanists. 'You Buzzard You' on Paramount, accompanied only by a slide guitarist, is unusual in failing for lack of rehearsal; elsewhere, Paramount successfully employed various permutations of cornet, mandolin and guitar, while OKeh used Stump's brother Harry on guitar and violin. From time to time other pianists were drafted, among whom Roosevelt Sykes was especially effective, pushing Johnson to sing with unaccustomed force. On two titles for Brunswick, Stump is joined by Tampa Red, whose immaculate steel guitar licks only need amplification to become the sound of postwar Chicago.

The CD ends with four tracks recorded by Paul Affeldt in 1964: two versions of 'The Snitcher's Blues', 'Bound To Be A Monkey' and 'The Duck's Yas Yas Yas'. The longest lasts just over two minutes, there is no vocal microphone, and Johnson is in poor shape. It would have been preferable had these performances never been released, for, on Affeldt's own admission, 'Stump was trying to recover from two recent strokes, and was very distressed by playing here, mentioning several times that he'd really have to practise before he'd be ready to record again.' CS

Jimmy Johnson (born 1928)
VOCAL, GUITAR, HARMONICA, ORGAN, PIANO

An older brother of Syl Johnson and bassist Mack Thompson (Thompson is their real name), Jimmy Johnson began playing in his early 20s after moving from Mississippi to Chicago, where he worked as a welder. He first played gospel music, then in the '60s in various clubs' house bands. In the '70s he played behind Jimmy Dawkins and Otis Rush, and by the '80s was working steadily in his own name, but his progress was brutally interrupted by a car accident in 1988 in which two members of his band were killed. I'm A Jockey (Birdology) won a Handy award in 1996.

**(*) Ma Bea's Rock
Storyville STCD 8050 Johnson; Jimmy Dawkins (g); Sylvester Boines (b); Tyrone Centuray (d); Andrew 'Big Voice' Odom (v). 10/75.

**(*) Pepper's Hangout
Delmark DD-745 Johnson; Bob Riedy (p); David Matthews (b); Jon Hiller (d). 3/77.

**(*) Tobacco Road
Storyville STCD 8042 Johnson; David Matthews (g); Ike Anderson (b); Dino Neal (d). 10/77.

Johnson's singing, elegant yet passionate, is one of the wonders of the blues world, and his clean-cut, inventive guitar playing hardly less impressive. That too few people are aware of this may be due, in part, to his not always being presented in a setting that does him justice. Amateurish recording reduces his seven numbers on *Ma Bea's Rock* to the level of rehearsals, yet the fervent readings of Otis Rush's 'So Many Roads' and B. B. King's 'My Own Fault' are so good that one ignores the poor production. (The remainder of the CD is by Luther Johnson Jr.) In *Pepper's Hangout*, a session brusquely directed by Ralph Bass, Johnson strives against a dull repertoire ('High Heel Sneakers', 'The Things That I Used To Do') and an unfamiliar backing trio to produce an honest and moderately enjoyable evening's work that reveals about half of his capability. *Tobacco Road*, recorded at Chicago's Golden Slipper, allows him to extend himself and range from B. B. King's 'Sweet Little Angel' to 'Breaking Up Somebody's Home', but he is hampered by sludgy rhythm guitar playing, and again the production is rudimentary.

*** Living Chicago Blues – Vol. I
Alligator ALCD 7701 Johnson; Carl Snyder (kb); Larry Burton (g); Ike Anderson (b); Dino Alvarez (d). 2/78.

***(*) Johnson's Whacks
Delmark DD 644 Johnson; Jerry Wilson (ts); Carl Snyder (p); Rico McFarland (g); Ike Anderson (b); Dino Alvarez (d). 10/78, 2/79.

*** North/South
Delmark DD-647 *Johnson; Carl Snyder (o, p); Professor Eddie Lusk (o); Larry Burton, Criss Johnson (g); Larry Exum (b); Ike Davis (d); unknowns (v).* 8/81–2/82.

Johnson's four tracks on the VAC *Living Chicago Blues Vol. I* were more considerately produced and made an attractive showcase for his music, especially in 'Serves Me Right To Suffer' and a 'Feel Like Breaking Up Somebody's Home' far more stylish than the version on *Tobacco Road*. On *Johnson's Whacks*, however, he was given the opportunity to work with his own material rather than familiar covers, and revealed how little he was inclined to live in the past. Take the opening track, 'The Twelve Bar Blues': if there's anything the blues are not much given to it's punning, but Johnson cheerfully perverts traditional blues lines for plays like 'I drank a dozen Buds but I don't feel any wiser'. This flipness is only for effect; elsewhere it's with respect that he handles old ideas. But no more than respect: to the received patterns he brings wit and vivid expressions, and there is not one song that marks time on familiar ground. One might ask why numbers like 'Strange How I Miss You (When I Haven't Even Lost You Yet)' have not been taken up by other artists, but perhaps Johnson's interpretations are so individual that they deter reproduction.

The only significant flaw of *Johnson's Whacks* was that Johnson's voice was set back somewhat and sounded rather thin; in the warmer recording ambience of *North/South* both voice and ensemble are more substantial. This is another set of clever and often amusing compositions with hardly a formula of language or scene-setting to be detected. It places slightly less emphasis on conventional blues than its predecessor, occasionally reconnecting Johnson to the soul music to which he apprenticed himself in the '60s.

*** Heap See
Black & Blue BB 427 *Johnson; Jene Pickett (o, p); Larry Exum (b); Fred Grady (d).* 11/83.
*** Bar Room Preacher
Alligator ALCD 4744 *As above.* 11/83.

This Paris-recorded set ignores the artist who carved his own niche on *Johnson's Whacks* and *North/South* and re-creates the earlier, more orthodox Jimmy Johnson, playing numbers like 'Little By Little', 'You Don't Know What Love Is' and 'Same Old Blues'. By this time, however, he is a more confident performer, the album is rich in fast, fertile guitar playing, and the reading of T-Bone Walker's 'Cold, Cold Feeling' is gorgeous. *Heap See* adds four tracks by almost the same band fronted by singer/guitarist John 'Mad Dog' Watkins; the retitled Alligator confines itself to the nine tracks by Johnson but reorders them in a more artfully contoured programme.

**(*) Livin' The Life
Black & Blue BB 448 *Johnson; Jesse Lockridge III (o, p, v); James Cloyd (b, v); David Russell (d).* 11/90.

Like the previous album, *Livin' The Life* relies on standard material but, unlike it, pays little regard to its suitability. 'You Don't Have To Go', 'The Sky Is Crying' and 'Born Under A Bad Sign' simply do not bring out the particular qualities of the artist. Only Johnson's own 'I Used To Be A Millionaire' has the yearning ruefulness that is his authentic manner.

**(*) I'm A Jockey
Dreyfus Jazz/Birdology FDM 37021 *Johnson; Kenny Anderson (t); Edwin Williams (tb); Byron Bowie (ts, bs); Hank Ford (ts); Billy Branch (h); Lucky Peterson (kb, o, p, g); Jesse Lockridge (p); Calvin 'Vino' Louden (g); Anthony Morris (b); David Russell (d); Gregorio Guadaloupe (perc); Elen Samuels, Theresa Davis (v).* 6/93.

There are some commonplace numbers here. 'As The Years Go Passing By' was a song Johnson had to tackle eventually, and he does it as well as an admirer would expect, but he brings nothing much new to 'In The Midnight Hour', and the oldfashioned Chicago stomp of 'Highway 13' and 'Look On Yonder's Wall' is not his métier. Elsewhere he gets to do less hackneyed pieces like Percy Mayfield's 'The Highway Is Like A Woman' – very well – and several numbers of his own which don't have the spark of earlier compositions. Clearly some thought went into this album, but the result is uneven, impersonal and unappealing.

**(*) Every Road Ends Somewhere
Ruf 1046 *Johnson; Claude Egea (t, flh); Frank Lacy (tb); Paul Cerra (ts); Kenny Lee (kb, o, p); John Randolph, Luther Allison (g); Anthony Morris (b); William Ellis (d); Arnaud Frank (perc).* 3–4/97.

High-pitched and yearning, Johnson's voice is vulnerable to over-large or over-loud bands. Sometimes here it is swamped by the the bluster of the horns and keyboards, sometimes merely edged aside to make room for prolix solos, but the cumulative effect is to drain some of Johnson's individuality and even, at times, as on 'Ain't No Way', to reduce him to a competent generic artist. As often, the slowest numbers are the most successful, here 'Black Night' and 'My Baby By My Side'. Allison guests on 'End Of The Road'.

**(*) "Two Johnsons Are Better Than One!"
Evangeline GEL 4028//Evidence ECD 26122 *Johnson; Syl Johnson (h, g, v); Anthony Space (kb); Will Crosby, Ronnie Peterson, Jon Tiven (g); Frank Collier, Beenie Man, Sally Tiven (b); Darrell Peyton, Aaron Turner (d); Syleena Johnson (v).* 11/00–1/01.

The material Jimmy brought to this fraternal get-together was mostly songs he had recorded a decade or two earlier, such as 'I Used To Be A Millionaire' and 'Living The Life' from *Livin' The Life*, 'Ashes In The Ashtray' from *Johnson's Whacks* and 'I Can't Survive' from *North/South*, and none of them is improved. Syl seems to have approached the project more adventurously, cutting several new numbers written in collaboration with Jon and Sally Tiven as well as a new version of 'Is It Because I'm Black?' The performances are often joint efforts, the brothers divvying up vocals and guitar parts and Jimmy playing piano and organ on Syl's 'Dangerous'. The album is interesting as a map of two roads travelled, but it's not the place to strike up an acquaintance with Jimmy Johnson. TR

Johnnie Johnson (1924–2005)
(VOCAL,) PIANO

Johnson's personal taste was for big-band jazz, but his fame rests on his participation in Chuck Berry's hit records. Johnson was a vital part of the Berry sound, and in later life he claimed, with some plausibility, that he was owed a writer's credit on many songs. The courts decided otherwise, however.

*** Blue Hand Johnnie
Evidence ECD 26017 *Johnson; Oliver Sain (ts); Steve Waldman, Herb Sadler, David Pruitt, Tom Maloney (g); Dick Pruitt, Gus Thorton [Thornton] (b); Keith Robertson, Kent Hinds, Pat O'Connor, Kenny Rice (d); Barbara Carr, Stacy Johnson (v).* 88–90.

Johnson continued gigging around St Louis after leaving Chuck Berry, but only came to wider attention in the late '80s when he appeared in Taylor Hackford's Berry biopic. He recorded several CDs as a result, but *Blue Hand Johnnie*, originally released on Pulsar, seems to be the only one currently available. It has two advantages over the likes of *Johnnie B. Bad* (Elektra/Nonesuch 61149): there are no rock-star guests looking to pay tribute and/or gain cred, and Johnson's poor Johnnie-one-note singing is quarantined. The outcome is a pleasant anthology of St Louis blues and R&B, marketed as a Johnnie Johnson release. Some of the repertoire is rather obvious ('Johnnie B. Goode', 'See See Rider', 'Baby What You Want Me To Do'), but it's effectively done, and 'Black Nights' and 'Talkin' Woman', respectively sung by Carr and Stacy Johnson, are rather more than that. Outside the magical interplay of the Chuck Berry records, Johnnie Johnson was a lively, enjoyable and middleweight pianist; *Blue Hand Johnnie* gets it right, by presenting him as a hardworking local musician rather than a God of Rock. CS

Larry Johnson (born 1938)
VOCAL, GUITAR

Even as a teenager, Johnson was playing blues (initially on harmonica) that his Georgia contemporaries regarded as oldfashioned, and he has stuck devotedly to his last. Settling in New York in 1960 after service in the navy, he associated with Brownie McGhee and Alec Seward, but learned, above all, from Rev. Gary Davis; unlike most of Davis's students, he sought to acquire techniques and chords, rather than specific pieces. Personal problems limited Johnson's activities for many years, but he re-emerged in the '90s.

Johnson recorded LPs for Prestige and Blue Horizon in the mid-'60s. *The Prestige/ Folklore Years Vol. 2: The New City Blues* (Prestige PRCD 9902) and *The Bluesville Years Vol. 6: Blues Sweet Carolina Blues* (Prestige PRCD 9914) each include three tracks from the Prestige LP, *The Blues: A New Generation*. Johnson's dislike of this early effort, with second guitarist Hank Adkins, was far too self-lacerating.

***(*) Fast And Funky
Baltimore Blues Society BBS 100 *Johnson; Nick Perls (g).* 4/70.

Fast And Funky, originally released on Blue Goose, was recorded after Johnson had recast his style under the spell of Gary Davis, and is a showcase for his guitar technique. Johnson sings and plays with a hip young dude's confident swagger, but the results are more fast than funky. Blue Goose's owner, the late Nick Perls, who plays on one track, made no secret of valuing instrumental technique above all, and viewed blues lyrics with indifference bordering on contempt. *Fast And Funky* is consistent with this aesthetic; polished to a high gloss, it often dazzles, but seldom glows.

** Midnight Hour Blues
Biograph BCD 138 *Johnson; John Hammond Jr (h, g, v).* 2/71.

Midnight Hour Blues is a head-on collision between Hammond's Delta-derived slide style and Johnson's ragtime picking. Hammond's harmonica playing is seldom more than basic, and his attempt to sing black on 'Tell Me Mama' is an embarrassment. 'Red River Blues' lopes along pleasantly, but like the rest of the CD, it never rises above competence.

**** Blues For Harlem
Armadillo ARMD 00005 *Johnson; Ian Briggs (h); Bernie Marsden (o, interviewer); Michael Roach (interviewer).* 6/99.

LPs cut in the '80s for L+R and Spivey, with harmonica player Nat Riddles, haven't been transferred to CD, and 1990's *Railroad Man* (JSP JSPCD 237) is deleted. At the time of recording *Blues For Harlem*, Johnson had reached the age that Gary Davis was when they first met; he had recorded a couple of Davis's secular pieces before, but only now, it seems, did he feel able to perform gospel songs by the man who 'not only changed my life, but gave me life.' 'Banks Of The River' and 'Death Don't Have No Mercy' movingly convey a coming to terms with the approach of old age and mortality. There's no sense of weariness, though; even well-known songs like 'Mean Ol' Frisco' and 'Things I Used To Do' sound fresh and new, and 'Trouble In Mind' for once plumbs the emotional depths implied by its title. Johnson at 62 has a deeper, stronger voice, and is as fine a guitarist as he was at 31. Time and hard times have added insight and maturity to his performances, and *Blues For Harlem* is a deep, and very involving, personal statement.

** Two Gun Green
Armadillo ARMD 00013 *Johnson; Mats Qwarfordt (h, v); Brian Kramer (g, v); Pa Ulander (b, v); Jim O'Leary (d, perc, v).* 7/01.

Two Gun Green is a great disappointment after *Blues For Harlem*. Johnson plays electric guitar except on the final track, a revival of 'Charlie Stone', first recorded for Blue Goose. He's backed (again except on 'Charlie Stone') by 'Brian Kramer and the Couch Lizards', who are actually Kramer's Stockholm-based trio plus a British drummer. The CD begins with a series of songs on which droning riffs, propelled by crass and crashing drumming, are extended well beyond their welcome. This is not Junior Kimbrough-like trance-dance music, unfortunately; it's dull repetition, because the songs aren't based on strong musical or verbal ideas, and don't have anywhere interesting to go. Later, the disc shifts to a sort of postmodern skiffle, with 'Old Time Religion' and 'Goodnight Irene', vocal choruses that somehow manage to be both ragged and mechanistic, and mutually self-regarding backchat. ('Say, where you going tonight, Brian?' 'Oh, I don't know, guess I'll go down to the local pub and have an ale.' Oh, please.) 'Back To The Groove' combines riffing and skiffle (riffle?) in a five-minute climax of stupefying dullness. CS

Lil Johnson
VOCAL

'Lil Johnson was a big-voiced, exuberant singer of blues, hokum and vaudeville songs who in an eight-year career recorded more than 60 songs, and that is very nearly all that is known about her.' Thus Howard Rye 12 years ago, and little can be

added. After making a few discs in 1929 she disappeared from the record scene until 1935, when she returned to cut hokum numbers like 'Get 'Em From The Peanut Man (Hot Nuts)' and 'Press My Button (Ring My Bell)', which sustained a busy recording career for a couple of years. Although she must have been acquainted with several of Chicago's leading musicians, she has left almost no biographical footprint on the sands of history, and no photograph of her is known to exist.

*** **Lil Johnson – Vol. 1 (1929–1936)**
Document DOCD-5307 *Johnson; Montana Taylor, Charles Avery, Black Bob, unknown (p); Tampa Red, poss. Big Bill Broonzy (g); prob. Bill Settles, unknown(s) (b). 4/29–4/36.*

(*) **Lil Johnson – Vol. 2 (1936–1937)
Document DOCD-5308 *Johnson; Lee Collins, prob. 'Mr Sheiks', unknown(s) (t); Arnett Nelson, unknown(s) (cl); Black Bob, poss. J. H. Shayne, unknown (p); Big Bill Broonzy, unknown(s) (g); John Lindsay, prob. Bill Settles, unknowns (b). 4/36–3/37.*

(*) **Lil Johnson – Vol. 3/Barrel House Annie (1937)
Document DOCD-5309 *Johnson; prob. 'Mr Sheiks', unknown (t); unknown (cl); unknown (ts); Black Bob, poss. Horace Malcolm, unknowns (p); Big Bill Broonzy, unknown (g); unknowns (b); prob. Fred Williams, unknown (d); unknown (v). 3/37–40s.*

If Lil Johnson's five 1929 recordings were all she had left, she would probably be held in higher regard. Her acrid singing is superbly accompanied on one song by Montana Taylor and on four by Charles Avery; of the latter, 'House Rent Scuffle' rivals Mozelle Alderson's 'Tight Whoopee' for zest. The second stage of her career, in the '30s, was mostly dedicated to raunchy novelty songs. Howard Rye, in his appreciative notes, cites with approval Rosetta Reitz's view that Johnson 'wasn't a burdened by a European man's idea of women's sexual health', and certainly few women have spent so much recorded time extolling funky hedonism. But if for modern listeners her sagas of hot nuts, pressed buttons and meat balls sometimes pall a little, there are, scattered through her CDs, a good number of graver blues like *Vol. 1*'s 'Shake Man Blues' and 'Evil Man Blues', which have more than a touch of Lucille Bogan in their delivery, *Vol. 2*'s 'Black And Evil Blues', a cover of Alice Moore's song, and some of her last recordings on *Vol. 3* like 'You Can't Throw Me Down' and 'When Your Troubles Are Like Mine'. Her accompaniments are chiefly interesting for the versatile piano playing of Black Bob, occasional guitar solos by Big Bill Broonzy, and trumpet and clarinet work ranging from expert to barely competent.

Listeners unafflicted by the bug of completism should probably confine themselves to *Vol. 1*, since it includes most of her best and her best-known sides and the other volumes are weakened by mediocre transfers and some second-rate material. But anyone venturing to the next stage will be rewarded with the startlingly dirty 'My Baby (Squeeze Me Again)' and a wonderful vaudeville number, 'Was I?', that Johnson sings as if temporarily invaded by the spirit of the young Sophie Tucker. *Vol. 3*'s main attractions are that quite a lot of its tracks were never issued on 78s and that it concludes with four artfully smutty songs delivered in an attractively relaxed manner by the even more obscure Barrelhouse Annie. TR

Lonnie Johnson (1899–1970)
VOCAL, GUITAR, BANJO, VIOLIN, PIANO, HARMONIUM, KAZOO

Incorrect birthdates of 1889 (a misprint in The Country Blues*) and 1894 (given by Big Bill Broonzy) are often quoted. The place was New Orleans, where Alonzo Johnson was a member of his family's stringband from an early age. All except his mother and his brother James were wiped out by the Spanish flu after World War I, while Lonnie was in Europe with a revue. Moving to St Louis, in 1925 he married the singer Mary Johnson and signed for OKeh. Johnson recorded steadily as a blues singer and accompanist until 1952; he was also an important jazz guitarist, recording with Armstrong and Ellington and making a series of trailblazing duets with Eddie Lang. The '50s were a relatively slack period, but in 1960 Johnson was traced by white enthusiasts, and resumed recording and playing concerts until not long before his death.*

(*) **Lonnie Johnson – Vol. 1 (1925–1926)
Document DOCD-5063 *Johnson; James 'Steady Roll' Johnson (p, vn, bj); John Arnold, DeLoise Searcy (p). 11/25–8/26.*

(*) **Lonnie Johnson – Vol. 2 (1926–1927)
Document DOCD-5064 *Johnson; John Erby, DeLoise Searcy, Cozy Harris (p); James 'Steady Roll' Johnson (vn, g); Helen Humes, Joe Brown, Raymond Boyd (v). 8/26–8/27.*

Lonnie Johnson was a dreadful kazooist (only once on record, fortunately), a pioneering genius on guitar, and competent but limited on his other instruments; even on guitar, however, extensive recording meant that he often shuffled a pack of recognizable licks and flourishes. Also fully developed by the time he recorded were his bittersweet vocals, at once confident and confiding, and his capacity for writing closely argued, original lyrics, which often employ striking turns of phrase. He gave free rein to his moralistic, misogynistic, misanthropic and sentimental streaks, but his range was far from being defined by them; he was also, for instance, a notable composer of topical blues.

At the outset, Johnson seems to have been anxious to set out his stall; *Vol. 1* has more violin than guitar, and by track 1 of *Vol. 2* he's played all his instruments, often alongside his almost equally adept brother. Given the limitations of Lonnie's fiddling and the frequently indifferent sound quality, this is not a CD for casual listeners. The sound is not much better on *Vol. 2*, but once past the opening track's harmonium and fiddle, the music is more inviting. It includes the first of Johnson's astonishing guitar solos, whose title, 'To Do This, You Got To Know How', concisely sums up both his abilities and his attitude. Far less essential are a brace of accompaniments to each of the 13-year-old Helen Humes and the artless Joe Brown and Raymond Boyd; it's no surprise that the latter pair never recorded again.

*** **Lonnie Johnson – Vol. 3 (1927–1928)**
Document DOCD-5065 *Johnson; Porter Grainger, DeLoise Searcy, Jimmy Blythe, Thomas 'Jaybird' Jones (p); Matthew Prater (md); Nap Hayes (g); 'Keghouse' (v). 10/27–2/28.*

Some tracks sound as if they were recorded next to a frying pan, but the transfers have more life, and *Vol. 3* is an enjoyable blend of blues (the opening 'St. Louis Cyclone Blues', made just four days after the windstorm, is a classic, and he finds unsuspected depths in 'Kansas City Blues'), exploratory guitar solos and collaborations with others; Lonnie's violin playing with Hayes and Prater is his best on record. Improved sound enables a proper appreciation of Johnson's guitar playing for the first time. The talent is obvious; what's sometimes missed is his consistent use of superior instruments, which give his playing a resonance and richness that's missing from many blues guitar records of the time.

***(*) Lonnie Johnson – Vol. 4 (1928–1929)
Document DOCD-5066 *Johnson; King Oliver (c); Victoria Spivey, J. C. Johnson (p, v); Clarence Williams, unknown (p); Eddie Lang (g); Hoagy Carmichael (perc, v); Spencer Williams, Jimmy Foster (v). 3/28–5/29.*

*** Lonnie Johnson – Vol. 5 (1929–1930)
Document DOCD-5067 *Johnson; Victoria Spivey (prob. p, v); J. C. Johnson, James P. Johnson, unknown (p); Eddie Lang (g); Spencer Williams (prob. scraper, v); Clarence Williams (woodblocks, v). 5/29–1/30.*

**** Blue Guitars Volumes I & II
BGO BGOCD 327 2CD *Johnson; King Oliver (c); Louis Armstrong (t); Albert Nicholas, Charlie Holmes (as); Teddy Hill (ts); Luis Russell (p); Eddie Condon (bj); Eddie Lang (g); Pops Foster (b); Paul Barbarin (d); Hoagy Carmichael (perc, v); Texas Alexander (v). 2/28–11/29.*

The above CDs contain all Johnson's duets with Eddie Lang, and two sides by Blind Willie Dunn's Gin Bottle Four, who were Lang, Johnson, Oliver and Carmichael. The duets' technical brilliance, melodic and harmonic originality and sheer beauty defined the possibilities of the jazz guitar for some time to come. BGO's remastering is far superior to Document's, and the two LPs reissued are more logically conceived: the duets are augmented by some Johnson solos, rather more Lang solos, accompaniments to Texas Alexander and collaborations with Louis Armstrong.

Inferior sound apart, Document's chronologism is a problem, for it spreads the Lang–Johnson material over two volumes, and mingles them with blues, hokum and two-part duets with Victoria Spivey. The latter are very funny and timed to a nicety, and some of the blues are classics, among them 'Careless Love', the protest song 'Broken Levee Blues' (both on *Vol. 4*) and *Vol. 5*'s paranoiac 'She's Making Whoopee In Hell Tonight'; even some of the hokum is listenable, for Lonnie's guitar and James P. Johnson's piano. Nevertheless, the shifts of mood and style are disruptive.

*** Lonnie Johnson – Vol. 6 (1930–1931)
Document DOCD-5068 *Johnson; Clarence Williams (poss. p, prob. gourd, v); James P. Johnson, Alex Hill (p); Spencer Williams (prob. perc, v); Clara Smith (v). 1/30–2/31.*

*** Lonnie Johnson – Vol. 7 (1931–1932)
Document DOCD-5069 *Johnson; Fred Longshaw (p). 2/31–8/32.*

The remastering on these discs is bog-standard, and there's a certain similarity in delivery and accompaniment, but they're better than 'for completists only'. There are no instrumentals, and Johnson's occasional switching to piano is scant compensation (he was a one-idea man on that instrument), but his guitar accompaniments often contain flashes of exceptional virtuosity, and his lyrics continue to treat original topics originally, whether he's being witty, sentimental, morbid or sexist. On *Vol. 6* Johnson and Clara Smith spar amusingly across four duets, on which their rich voices are admirably matched.

**** Lonnie Johnson – Vol. 1 (1937–1940)
Document BDCD-6024 *Johnson; Roosevelt Sykes, Joshua Altheimer (p); unknown (g, sp); prob. Alfred Elkins, unknown (b); unknown (d); unknown (eff). 11/37–5/40.*

*** Lonnie Johnson – Vol. 2 (1940–1942)
Document BDCD-6025 *Johnson; Lil Armstrong, Blind John Davis (p); Dan Dixon (g, v); unknown (g, sp); prob. Alfred Elkins, Andrew Harris (b). 5/40–2/42.*

**(*) Lonnie Johnson – Vol. 3 (1944–1947)
RST Blues Documents BDCD-6026 *Johnson; Bob Shoffner (t); 'Clarence' (as); Blind John Davis, Richard M. Jones (p); Ransom Knowling, unknowns (b); 'Mr Bates' (d); Carl Jones, Red Nelson [Wilborn] (v). 12/44–6/47.*

The Depression nearly killed the American record industry. Lonnie Johnson was one of the few blues singers to record in 1932, but thereafter even he faced a five-year hiatus. These three volumes were originally issued on RST, but the first two have been remastered and transferred to Document (which means that there are two Vols 1 and 2 on Document; take care when ordering). Johnson had kept working on radio and the bandstand while away from the recording studios; his instrumental prowess, expressed on a superb 12-string guitar, was further refined and developed, and his singing remained full of emotional expressiveness.

Vol. 1 contains his finest prewar work; on the first 16 titles Johnson, sometimes sensitively assisted by Roosevelt Sykes, revisits his habitual preoccupations with his habitual ingenuity, and the instrumentals 'Swing Out Rhythm' and 'Blues For The West End' are heart-stopping highwire acts. The remastering on this batch is well above Document's normal run. It's adequate on the balance of the CD, where Johnson moves from Decca to Bluebird, and forms a partnership with Joshua Altheimer, though sadly only for eight songs.

Vol. 2 includes four acetates recorded in a Chicago club; only 'More [*recte* I Got] Rhythm' generates much excitement. The balance is from Bluebird, and although Johnson continues to pursue harmonic sophistication and rhythmic freedom, there's a sameness about both the guitar–piano–bass combination and the vocal delivery; remakes of 'Crowing Rooster Blues', 'He's A Jelly Roll Baker' and 'She's Making Whoopee In Hell Tonight' (as 'The Devil's Woman') are less weighty than their predecessors. In the other pan of the scale are three fine lyrics prompted by America's entry to World War II, and 'Chicago Blues', caustically dissing the city's inhabitants.

Apart from two sides where Johnson is a member of the band behind Carl Jones, *Vol. 3* consists of collaborations with Blind John Davis on Bluebird, Disc and Aladdin. (Davis's presence on the latter label is evident, albeit determined aurally.) The music is fine, but it holds few surprises and is let down by Disc's swishy pressings and RST's merely adequate mastering.

***(*) The Rhythm & Blues Years 1947/1952
EPM Blues Collection 16043 *Johnson; Hot Lips Page, Charlie Hooks (t); Holley Dismukes (as); Hal Singer, Tom Archia, Paul Renfro, Ray Felder, Eddie Smith, Red Prysock, Louis Stephens (ts); Ted Buckner (bs); James Clark, John Hughes, Joe Knight, Herman Smith, Frank Payne, Simeon Hatch, Willie Wilkins, Jimmy Robinson, Todd Rhodes (p); Jerry Lane, unknown (g); Roy Coulter, Carl Wilson, Monte Morrison, Edwyn Conley, Franklin Skeete, Paul Parks, Tommy Smith, Clarence Mack, Joe Williams, unknown (b); Clarence Donaldson, Leon Abramson, Nelson Burton, Calvin Shields, Bill Benjamin, unknown (d); Dirty Red [Nelson Wilborn] (v). 6/47–6/52.*

*** Me And My Crazy Self
King KCD 6027 *Johnson; Charlie Hooks (t); Holley Dismukes (as); Hal Singer, Tom Archia, Ray Felder, Eddie Smith, Red*

Prysock, Louis Stephens (ts); Ted Buckner (bs); John Hughes, Joe Knight, Herman Smith, Simeon Hatch, Willie Wilkins, Jimmy Robinson, Todd Rhodes (p); Roy Coulter, Carl Wilson, Monte Morrison, Paul Parks, Tommy Smith, Clarence Mack, Joe Williams (b); Bobby Donaldson, Nelson Burton, Calvin Shields, Bill Benjamin, unknown (d). 12/47–6/52.

Shortly after signing with King, Johnson had an enormous hit with 'Tomorrow Night', the apotheosis of his balladeering, but it's not on either of these discs; *Me And My Crazy Self* was compiled to complement a now-deleted CD that did include it, and EPM disdain this side of Johnson's work. Johnson continued to play the electric guitar that he'd introduced on Aladdin, and King often added brass and reeds to the usual piano, bass and drums. Johnson had plenty of experience as a band musician, amplification was an ideal medium for his single-string lines, sustained notes and finger vibrato, and he had no problem singing over larger forces. King draw on master tapes, but EPM's 78-derived sound is just as good. These discs have eight titles in common; EPM offer a slightly longer selection, including two successful covers of the Delmore Brothers' hillbilly blues and two Aladdin-derived accompaniments to Dirty Red.

(*) Lonnie Johnson 1949–1952
Classics 5153 *Johnson; Charlie Hooks (t); Holley Dismukes (as); Ray Felder, Eddie Smith, Red Prysock, Louis Stephens (ts); Ted Buckner (bs); Simeon Hatch, Willie Wilkins, Jimmy Robinson, Todd Rhodes (p); Franklin Skeete, Paul Parks, Tommy Smith, Clarence Mack, Joe Williams (b); Leon Abramson, Nelson Burton, Calvin Shields, Bill Benjamin, unknown (d). 11/49–6/52.*

Classics assemble Johnson's last six sessions for King. Lonnie sings with habitual conviction, and there's plenty of poised, elegant electric guitar, often in eloquent conversation with the saxophonists on the CD's second half. A final session with trumpet and three saxes incites some of Johnson's most lungbusting vocals. Nevertheless, chronological completism entails a certain saminess of tunes, tone and delivery; some transfers are from 78s in dodgy condition; and there's a heavy dose of ballads, which even those who enjoy this aspect of Johnson's work are likely to find trying. This is a rewarding disc for completists – but only for them.

(*) Hot Fingers
Arpeggio ARB 013 *As for relevant CDs above.* 11/25–11/30.
*** Steppin' On The Blues
Columbia CK 46221 *As above.* 11/25–8/32.
*(*) The Essential
Classic Blues CBL 200011 2CD *As above, except add whichever of 'Henry Moon' and 'George Thomas' is not Lonnie Johnson (g), prob. Henry Johnson (perc), Mooch Richardson (v).* 11/25–2/42.
**** The First Of The 'Guitar Heroes' 1925–1947
Frémeaux FA 262 2CD *As for relevant CDs above.* 11/25–12/47.
**** The Original Guitar Wizard
Proper PROPERBOX 81 4CD *As above, except add Bubber Miley, Freddie Jenkins, Artie Whetsol (t), Kid Ory, Tricky Sam Nanton (tb), Barney Bigard (cl, ts), Johnny Dodds (cl), Johnny Hodges (ss), Harry Carney (bs), Duke Ellington (p), Johnny St Cyr, Fred Guy (bj), Wellman Braud (b), Sonny Greer (d).* 11/25–6/52.
*** Playing With The Strings
Snapper Complete Blues SBLUECD 014 *As for relevant CDs above.* 1/26–2/41.

(*) Mr Johnson Blues
Aim 0025 *As above.* 4/27–3/32.
(*) Rambler's Blues
Our World 3306 *As above.* 8/27–12/47.
*** Blues Guitar Pioneers
Boulevard Vintage BVBCD 1010 4CD *As for relevant CDs above.* 1/28–9/50.
*** Blues In My Soul 1937/1946
EPM Blues Collection 15903 *As above, except add Peetie Wheatstraw (p, v).* 11/37–7/46.

These CDs are all selective surveys. Whatever its musical merits, *The Essential* can be ruled out; only 11 of its 36 tracks play where they're listed, and two are not listed at all. The sound on Arpeggio varies from acceptable to too bright to very noisy, depending on the source disc used, and there are inaccuracies in the discographical data and notes. Columbia spread the net a little wider, including a duet with Victoria Spivey and an accompaniment to Texas Alexander. The notes are excellent and the sound surprisingly recessive; on 'Toothache Blues', with Spivey, the level fluctuates alarmingly. Our World's aggressive audio processing adds echo and boosts the bass end; Aim also take a hands-on approach, but clarity is no compensation for bass frequencies turned up to 11. On both these discs, Johnson's music is reflected in a funhouse mirror.

Frémeaux's double CD is judiciously selected, well-enough mastered (once past a muffled opening track), chronologically programmed (which is advantageous with Johnson) and thoughtfully annotated. All these comments also apply to *The Original Guitar Wizard*, which includes as well Johnson's three guest spots with Louis Armstrong, and 'Misty Morning' with Duke Ellington. The final disc in the set has extensive duplication with the comparable King and EPM CDs, but it also includes 'Tomorrow Night'; so does *The Very Best Of Lonnie Johnson* (Collectables COL-2897), which contains 24 King sides, but was released too late to receive detailed consideration here.

Johnson's share of *Blues Guitar Pioneers* (the others are T-Bone Walker, Lowell Fulson and B. B. King) favours instrumentals, which comprise 16 of the first 18 tracks, ten of them being duets with Eddie Lang. The music is splendid, of course, but this weighting, and the absence of any vocal numbers earlier than 1937, makes for an unbalanced picture of Johnson's artistry, to which the notes usefully supply a corrective.

Blues In My Soul and *Playing With The Strings*, drawn from shorter time periods, are also good selections, but the sound quality of both is variable. Twelve of the latter's 20 tracks are instrumentals; EPM's 20 include two accompaniments to Peetie Wheatstraw. We should mention another *Playing With The Strings* (JSP JSPCD 335, deleted), about half of which features Johnson sitting in with Charles Creath's Jazz O-Maniacs, Armstrong, Ellington, the Chocolate Dandies and Clarence Williams's Jug Band. The Creath track is Johnson's debut recording, not available elsewhere, but more notable for Leonard Davis's mournful trumpet than for Johnson's alley fiddle. Clarence Williams's musical fart-jokes are superfluous, but the rest of the jazz is magnificent. The remastering is not always up to John R. T. Davies's usual standard.

(*) Blues By Lonnie Johnson
Original Blues Classics OBCCD 502 *Johnson; Hal Singer (ts); Claude Hopkins (p); Wendell Marshall (b); Bobby Donaldson (d).* 3/60.

*** **Blues & Ballads**
Original Blues Classics OBCCD-531 *Johnson; Elmer Snowden (g, v); Wendell Marshall (b)*. 4/60.

***(*) **Blues, Ballads And Jumpin' Jazz, Vol. 2**
Original Blues Classics OBCCD 570 *As above*. 4/60.

*** **Losing Game**
Original Blues Classics OBCCD-543 *Johnson*. 12/60.

*** **Idle Hours**
Original Blues Classics OBCCD-518 *Johnson; Cliff Jackson (p); Victoria Spivey (v)*. 7/61.

*** **Another Night To Cry**
Original Blues Classics OBCCD-550 *Johnson*. 4/62.

*** **Lonnie Johnson Est Un Maître**
Warner Blues 25573 *As for above six CDs, except Spivey also plays p*. 3/60–4/62.

Johnson's singing was as strong as ever in the '60s, but his songwriting was less various, focusing more on the toils of lost love, and his blues accompaniments were less adventurous and more predictable. He also sang more ballads; that he did so very well indeed (hear, for instance 'What A Difference A Day Makes' on *Losing Game*) will not quell the unease of many listeners.

Donaldson's pitter-patting percussion on *Blues By Lonnie Johnson* is largely incompatible with the ensemble sound, but all these CDs have their moments; with one exception, however, they seem to be the work of a man grateful for the chance to make a little money from his music, but not particularly stirred by the music itself. The exception is *Blues, Ballads And Jumpin' Jazz, Vol. 2*, which remained unissued until 1994. Much of the content is 'jumpin' jazz' ('Lester Leaps In', 'C-Jam Blues' and the like), and on much of it Snowden's *soigné* acoustic guitar is the lead instrument, supported by Lonnie's electric rhythm guitar. The talk between numbers manages to be both stagey and spontaneous, but the music is full of fireworks; that it has only one foot in the blues camp is no reason to ignore its worth.

Warner Blues' sensible selection includes a vocal duet and a guitar solo from *Woman Blues!* (Original Blues Classics OBCCD 566), credited to Victoria Spivey with Lonnie Johnson and discussed in her entry.

**** **Blues Masters, Vol. 4**
Storyville STCD 8004 *Johnson; Otis Spann (p)*. 10/63.

Had they not been booked for the 1963 AFBF, it seems unlikely that Otis Spann and Lonnie Johnson would have recorded together; chalk one up for Europe. It seems an improbable partnership, but even in the thunderous ensemble of the Muddy Waters band Spann was a lyrical, poetic pianist, with a finely tuned ear for harmony and turn-on-a-dime rhythmic awareness. His work with (decidedly not behind) Johnson spurs the latter into his most eager and inventive latterday performances, including a 'Tomorrow Night' that's a good substitute for the hit version, a profound six-minute 'Clementine Blues' and the thrilling instrumental 'Swingin' With Lonnie'.

(*) **The Unsung Blues Legend
Blues Magnet BLM-1001 *Johnson*. 65.

*** **The Complete Folkways Recordings**
Smithsonian Folkways CD SF 40067 *Johnson*. 67.

Those who cannot stomach Johnson the ballad singer should note that this appraisal assumes tolerance for 'My Mother's Eyes', 'Prisoner Of Love', 'Rockin' Chair' and 'Summertime' (all on both discs) and similar material. Johnson plainly loved songs like these, singing them with utter sincerity and often more than a passing jazz inflection. *The Unsung Blues Legend* was taped informally on non-professional equipment; the sound is quite good, but from time to time Johnson's voice overloads the microphone. That apart, it can't be gainsaid that a CD which starts with songs by Frank Sinatra and Kurt Weill, includes 'Danny Boy' and mixes pop with blues in an 11:7 ratio is not for most blues fans.

The Folkways material, which was put on a shelf by Moses Asch and forgotten for 15 years, has a higher proportion of blues, including a 'Mister Trouble' that shows Lonnie could still deliver inimitably original songs. His guitar playing is still assured and elegant, but the repetition of ideas and effects is troublesome. It could be argued that this is nothing new in Johnson's blues, but it's indubitably more noticeable on these last recordings.

Worth noting, but marginal for most, is *Stompin' At The Penny* (Columbia COL 476720); credited to Lonnie Johnson, it reissues a limited-edition Canadian LP recorded in 1965. The original credit to 'Jim McHarg's Metro Stompers featuring Lonnie Johnson' paints a more accurate picture of the division of labour. It includes a very fine 'Trouble In Mind', his most moving version of 'My Mother's Eyes', and a rip-roaring solo on 'China Boy', but along the way there's a lot of competent, enthusiastic and dispensable Dixieland revivalism. CS

Luther 'Georgia Boy'/'Snake' Johnson (1934–76)
VOCAL, GUITAR

Born in Georgia, Johnson learned guitar first from his father, then at reform school and in the army. Moving to Chicago in the early '60s, he worked with Elmore James, and led his own band before Muddy Waters recruited him at Otis Spann's suggestion. In the early '70s Johnson settled in Boston, and was a mainstay of the local scene until, like Spann, he died prematurely from cancer.

*** **Born In Georgia**
Black & Blue BB 462 *Johnson; Dusty Brown (h); Sonny Thompson (p); Johnny Shines (g); Emmett Sutton (b); Bill Warren (d)*. 11/72.

***(*) **On The Road Again**
Evidence ECD 26046 *Johnson; Johnny Shines (g)*. 11–12/72.

***(*) **On The Road Again**
Black & Blue BB 439 *As above*. 11–12/72.

*** **Lonesome In My Bedroom**
Evidence ECD 26005 *Johnson; Little Mac Simmons (h); Willie Mabon (p); Lonnie Brooks, Hubert Sumlin (g); Dave Myers (b); Fred Below (d)*. 12/75.

*** **They Call Me The Popcorn Man**
Black & Blue BB 431 *As above*. 12/75.

As 'Little Luther', Johnson had a single on Checker in the '60s; 'Twirl' is reissued on *House Rockin' Blues* (Ace CDCHD 610). He made some well-regarded recordings later in the decade, fronting the Muddy Waters band, but *Mud In Your Ear* (Muse MCD 6004) is deleted.

Born In Georgia mixes standards ('Every Day I Have The Blues', 'Hoochie Coochie Man', 'Bright Light [sic] Big City' and the like) with self-composed soul-blues that favour choppy, repetitive riffs. Johnson sets out his stall as an animated singer, and Bill Warren does excellent work in both milieus, but Sonny Thompson is uncomfortable, seldom going beyond mechanical block chording. The three tracks with Shines are the CD's best material, and prompted the recording of *On The Road Again*, where Johnson plays solo except on 'Little Red Rooster'.

Much of *On The Road Again* is as familiar as that song – 'Catfish Blues', 'Rock Me Baby' and 'Things I Used To Do' are all present – but Johnson is eminently successful performing alone, and this is no dully routine set. His singing combines the ebullient authority of his old boss with the brooding introversion of John Lee Hooker, and his guitar playing is also darkly powerful, with a strong tendency towards modal harmony. Johnson approaches the songs as if no one had ever recorded them before, his timing and command of rhythm are the equal of Hooker's, and *On The Road Again* is one of the triumphs of European recording. Black & Blue's latest version is reordered, and an alternative take of 'Impressions From France' and a previously unissued 'Boom Boom' are added to the original release licensed by Evidence. Readers will find whichever version is easier to obtain in their territory perfectly satisfactory.

Similarly, *They Call Me The Popcorn Man* is a revision of *Lonesome In My Bedroom*, although Black & Blue's extra tracks (an alternative take of the predictably dispensable title track, and a version of 'Got My Mojo Working') are of doubtful necessity. The session was recorded only three months before Johnson's death, but he shows no sign of failing powers. He's backed by a stellar band, and apart from Simmons, whose harmonica is generic and reclusive, they play enthusiastically. Familiar titles and songwriters recur, but Johnson's own compositions are more in evidence. Unfortunately, the songs and their delivery are uneven: 'Rock Me Slow And Easy' is a fine country shuffle, but 'Please Give Me That Love' is dull, repetitive boogaloo. The ensemble find bluesy depths in 'Little Queenie' that Chuck Berry can never have imagined, but the extended ending to 'Long Distance Call' is as irritating in Johnson's hands as it was in Muddy's. CS

Luther 'Guitar Jr' Johnson (born 1939)
VOCAL, GUITAR

Luther Johnson was born in Itta Bena, Mississippi; his musical mentor in Chicago was Magic Sam, and Johnson's playing and singing perpetuate the wired-up, emotional sound epitomized by Sam and Otis Rush, with a generous helping of soul stirred in. Johnson spent seven years with Muddy Waters from 1973; thereafter he settled in New England and formed the Magic Rockers, with whom he continues to tour busily.

(*) Ma Bea's Rock
Storyville STCD 8050 *Johnson; Willie James Lyons (g); Willie Kent (b); Tyrone Centuray (d).* 10/75.

Ma Bea's Rock, which is shared with Jimmy Johnson, was recorded live in Chicago; though far from brilliantly engineered, it has more atmosphere than many of Marcelle Morgantini's club sessions. A fervent 'All Your Love' is the best of several faithful Magic Sam impersonations, and the clever lyrics on 'Got A Mind To Travel' show that Johnson also has his own creative voice, but 'I Believe My Time Ain't Long' and 'You Gotta Have Soul' are too repetitious to please.

(***) **Luther's Blues**
Evidence ECD 26010 *Johnson; Jerry Portnoy (h); Pinetop Perkins (p); Bob Margolin (g); Calvin Jones (b); Willie Smith (d).* 11/76.
(***) **Luther's Blues**
Black & Blue BB 441 *As above.* 11/76.

The backing on *Luther's Blues*, which was recorded in Europe, is by the Muddy Waters band minus Muddy. The disc's midsection comprises hot-blooded covers of Luther Allison, Otis Rush and Albert King; these are well worth hearing, but they're surrounded by the over-familiar likes of 'Too Many Drivers', 'Sweet Home Chicago' and 'Boogie In The Dark', performed with a seasoned professionalism that excludes emotional investment or musical risk-taking. Black & Blue add two alternative takes.

*** **Doin' The Sugar Too**
Bullseye Blues CD BB 9563 *Johnson; Bob Enos (t); Porky Cohen (tb); Rich Lataille (as); Greg Piccolo (ts); Doug 'Mr Low' James (bs); Ron Levy (o, p); Walter Smith (b); Michael Avery (d).* 6/83.

***(*) **I Want To Groove With You**
Bullseye Blues CD BB 9506 *Johnson; 'Sax' Gordon (ts, bs); Ron Levy (o, p); Buster Paterson (b); Glenn Rogers, 'Spider' Webb (d).* 90?

**** **It's Good To Me**
Bullseye Blues CD BB 9516 *Johnson; 'Sax' Gordon (ts); Richard 'Rosie' Rosenblatt (h); Joe Krown (o, p); 'Buster' Wylie (b); 'Tuffy' Kimble (d).* 92?

**** **Country Sugar Papa**
Bullseye Blues CD BB 9546 *Johnson; John Abrahamsen (t); 'Sax' Gordon (ts, bs); 'Tino' Barker (bs); Richard Rosenblatt (h); Ron Levy (o); Eric 'Two Scoops' Moore (p): 'Buster' Wylie (b); Keith 'Smitty' Smith (d); Buck Taylor, Bird Taylor (v).* 93?

The Bullseye Blues CDs establish Johnson as Magic Slim's only rival for the extent of his songbag and the muscularity of his performance. *Doin' The Sugar Too*, an augmented reissue of an LP recorded for Rooster Blues, is Johnson's first really satisfactory release, not least in having more sonic presence than its predecessors. Johnson ranges comfortably from the title track's funky soul to lowdown covers of Fenton Robinson and Otis Spann and an imaginative arrangement of 'I'm Ready'. The Roomful Of Blues Horns play with brio on five tracks, but their standardized arrangements and Levy's intermittent grandstanding on organ devalue the disc a little.

Of the CDs actually recorded by Bullseye, *I Want To Groove With You* is let down by curiously muffled recording on the opening and closing tracks, and by 'Texas Cowboy', a cheesy venture into C&W. The violence of 'Graveyard Dogs' is disturbing, but it's not the only song to show off Johnson's talent as a songwriter. (The same can't be said of 'Call Me Guitar Junior', created by changing 'Slim' to 'Junior'.) On *It's Good To Me* and *Country Sugar Papa* the breadth of Johnson's repertoire and the vigour of his delivery (even on occasional tracks where he plays alone) continue to impress. Both CDs have superb sound, and the Magic Rockers and the guest musicians play with intuitive swing and collective empathy; Rosenblatt's occasional harp is remarkable. 'Walkin' With You

Baby' on *Country Sugar Papa* may be the finest Broomdusters-style recording since Elmore James's death; Johnson immediately trumps it with 'If The Blues Was Whiskey', which out-Rushes Otis Rush.

**(*) Slammin' On The West Side
Telarc CD-83389 Johnson; 'Sax' Gordon (ts, bs); David Torkanowsky (o, p); Eric Moore (p); Brian Bisesi (g); George Porter Jr (b); Herman Ernest (d, perc); Debbie Hambelton (v). 9/95.

***(*) Live At The Rynborn
M.C. MC 0037 Johnson; Lynwood 'Cookie' Cooke (ts); Otis 'Big Blues' Doncaster (h); Eric Moore (kb); Skip 'Mississippi Skippy' Philbrick (g); Andy Karlok (b); K. D. Bell (d). 9/95.

***(*) Got To Find A Way
Telarc CD-83445 Johnson; Lynwood Cooke (ts); Travis Colby (kb); Brian Bisesi (g); Randy Lippincott (b); Ola Dixon (d). 3/98.

***(*) Talkin' About Soul
Telarc CD-83476 Johnson; Tom 'Bones' Malone (t, tb); Crispin Cioe (as, ts, bs); Jerry Portnoy (h); David Maxwell (o, p); Brian Bisesi (g); Randy Lippincott (b); Kenny 'Beedy Eyes' Smith (d, perc); Catherine Russell (perc, v). 8/00.

Despite its title, *Slammin' On The West Side* teams Johnson with a New Orleans rhythm section. They are efficient and professional, sometimes too much so for the music's good. The problem is compounded by a mix that gives the instruments equal weight in the ensemble, and from which Johnson's vocals have to fight their way out. Sax Gordon's tenor is played with markedly less edginess than on Bullseye Blues, and gets an excessive amount of solo space. Two tracks where Johnson accompanies himself on admirably oldfashioned acoustic guitar are the best of the disc.

If nothing else, 'Hello Josephine' on *Live At The Rynborn* shows how the New Orleans–Chicago synthesis ought to be done, but the disc is also better generally. It's very much a collective effort, and although the harmonica often seems superfluous – there because it's what audiences expect to see in a blues band – the musicians are tight and together, yet loose and free-flowing too. Philbrick plays acolyte's guitar on two tracks, one a retread of 'If The Blues Was Whiskey' which concisely differentiates this (merely excellent) record from the masterly *Country Sugar Papa*.

Telarc had an attack of common sense for *Got To Find A Way*, and used the Magic Rockers, who play with the aggression necessary to support and inspire Johnson. Ola Dixon's uncomplicated swing is a particular treat throughout; as she has said elsewhere, 'I may not be anything fancy, but I can sure keep time.' Johnson's singing and playing are a touch less torrid than on Bullseye Blues, but this is a very satisfactory CD. An acoustic-guitar-accompanied 'Sometimes I Wonder' appears as a multimedia extra.

Talkin' About Soul is fairly heavy on the music named, including – *rara avis*! – a breathtakingly exciting, piano-led (and guitarless) cover of 'I Got A Woman'. It's the best of the soul numbers, although a medley of Joe Scott's 'You've Got Bad Intentions' and 'Crying Won't Help You' is a surprising success. As before, the band is a good one, with sturdy horn charts, creative keyboard work and classy drumming from Willie 'Big Eyes' Smith's son. In the light of his earlier work, though, Johnson sometimes seems to coast; only on the final third of the disc does he attain the sweat-popping emotiveness that was the virtual norm on his best Bullseye Blues CDs. CS

Margaret Johnson
VOCAL

Johnson's early recordings were with Clarence Williams groups, and she may have been one of his protégées. Appearances on the vaudeville circuit are logged from 1922 to 1932, but nothing is known of her subsequent life.

*** Margaret Johnson (1923–1927)
Document DOCD-5436 Johnson; Tom Morris, Bubber Miley, Louis Armstrong (c); Charlie Irvis, Aaron Thompson (tb); Bob Fuller (cl, as); unknown (cl); Sidney Bechet (ss); poss. Ernest Elliott (as); Robert Cooksey (h); unknown (conc); Clarence Williams, Henry Palmer, Bob Ricketts, Mike Jackson, poss. Phil Worde, Porter Grainger (p); Buddy Christian, unknown (bj); Bobby Leecan (g); unknown (b). 10/23–9/27.

Some of Margaret Johnson's records have been collectors' items practically since the dawn of record-collecting – chiefly, no doubt, because of the company she kept, but also because her strong middle-range voice was less weakened than many singers' by the acoustic recording process, and she rises resolutely above the ensembles of 'E Flat Blues' and 'Nobody Knows The Way I Feel This Mornin''. Bechet is not specially interesting on the tracks where he appears, but Armstrong, having played his part quietly in 'Papa, Mama's All Alone Blues', chose to decorate the double-time passages of 'Changeable Daddy Of Mine' with a crackling solo and a further break that anticipates his momentous solo two and a half years later in 'Potato Head Blues'. With Armstrong fresh in one's memory, Morris cannot help sounding rather quaint, but his muted solos are attractive in the well-recorded 'When A 'Gator Holler, Folks Say It's A Sign Of Rain'. The clarinettist Bob Fuller plays on this and 'Graysom Street Blues' with what, for him, was restraint, but on 'Stinging Bee Blues' looses his menagerie of effects. By that time Johnson may have become inured to odd noises in the studio: at an earlier session she had been cautiously led through the melody by a concertina player. 'When A 'Gator Holler' and Johnson's other late recordings are straightforward blues, and she shows herself to be as confident and competent in that idiom as several better-known contemporaries. Unfortunately she was given no further opportunity to prove it.

Another take of the buoyant 'Second-Handed Blues' and two other tracks from that session with the guitarist Bobby Leecan and harmonica player Robert Cooksey are on *Leecan & Cooksey – Vol. 1 (1924–1927)* (Document DOCD-5279). TR

Mary Johnson (1905–c. 70)
VOCAL

Born in Mississippi, Mary Smith moved to St Louis at an early age, and became an entertainer despite her mother's conviction that this was the road to Hell. She was married to Lonnie Johnson from 1925 to 1932, when they divorced. In 1936 she rejoined the church; a 1955 session, singing gospel with a Dixieland band, failed to produce issuable material.

***(*) Mary Johnson (1929–1936)
Document DOCD-5305 Johnson; Ike Rodgers (tb); Henry Brown, Judson Brown, Roosevelt Sykes, Peetie Wheatstraw (p); Artie Mosby (vn); Tampa Red, Kokomo Arnold (g). 5/29–5/36.

Mary Johnson was an artist with a consistently bleak view

of the world, expressed in songs which are almost entirely concerned with mistreatment by men. Blues is seldom a music of unrelieved sadness, but there are no cheerful songs at all in her recorded output. Nor is the blues often explicitly autobiographical, but 1932's 'Rattlesnake Blues' and 'Mary Johnson Blues' are clearly a response to the recent, acrimonious end of her marriage. Johnson's singing is raw, direct and without theatricality, driven by lyrics which combine unblinking realism with authentic and individual poetry: 'I once was a married woman, sorry the day that I ever was; I was a young girl at home, and I did not know the world.'

Mary Johnson is well served by her accompanists. Of particular note is the teamwork of Henry Brown and Ike Rodgers, achieving telling emotional commentary with great economy of means. Tampa Red's piercing slide guitar and Judson Brown's piano also combine well in support of Johnson's sorrowful delivery. Judson Brown was a magnificent, infrequently recorded pianist, and the two songs where he is the only accompanist are among the treasures of blues piano.

Not many blues singers have shared Mary Johnson's talent for transforming their raw material into finished and unique art. One who did was also named Johnson, but Robert fits contemporary notions of the blues singer (footloose, male, guitar playing) better than Mary, who made her remarkable music to support her widowed mother. The bracketed fourth star reflects lacklustre CD sound, not musical or artistic shortcomings. CS

Merline Johnson
VOCAL

For one of the most prolific female blues artists of the '30s, Merline Johnson remains a biographical black hole, despite recording almost a hundred songs, of which 70 were issued. Two photographs show her to have been a comfortably plump woman with a fetching smile but beyond the suggestion that she may have been born in Mississippi nothing is known about her. The bulk of her recordings were made between 1937 and 1941, with a last, unissued, session in March 1947, after which she vanished. Despite her nom de disque, 'The Yas Yas Girl', her records were only mildly suggestive. Though her plain voice was sweetened by an attractive vibrato, Johnson ultimately lacked the personality of her rivals Lil Johnson, Georgia White and Memphis Minnie.

*** **The Yas Yas Girl – Vol. 1 (1937–1938)**
Document DOCD-5292 Johnson; prob. Alfred Bell (t); Bill Owsley (cl, as); Eddie Miller, Black Bob, Aletha Robinson, Blind John Davis (p); prob. Charlie McCoy (md); George Barnes (sg, g); Big Bill Broonzy, Willie Bee James (g); Ransom Knowling (b); Fred Williams (d). 5/37–4/38.

*** **The Yas Yas Girl – Vol. 2 (1938–1939)**
Document DOCD-5293 Johnson; Punch Miller, Walter Williams, Lee Collins (t); Buster Bennett (ss, as); Bill Owsley (ts); Blind John Davis, poss. Joshua Altheimer (p); Casey Bill Weldon (sg); George Barnes (g); Bill Settles (b); Alfred Elkins (vocal b); Fred Williams (d). 5/38–8/39.

(*) **The Yas Yas Girl – Vol. 3 (1939–1940)
Document DOCD-5294 Johnson; Lee Collins (t); Buster Bennett (as); Joshua Altheimer, Blind John Davis (p): Big Bill Broonzy (g); Alfred Elkins (vocal b); Fred Williams (d). 8/39–10/40.

*** **Female Chicago Blues (1936–1947)**
Document DOCD-5295 Johnson; Blind John Davis (p); Big Bill Broonzy (g); Ransom Knowling, unknown (b); Judge Riley (d). 6/41–3/47.

The trenchancy of Johnson's singing underlines a hint of masculinity in her performances, more in the delivery than in the content. That impression is enhanced by her clear diction and confident projection. Although she did it sparingly, she's perhaps the only woman to directly imitate Peetie Wheatstraw, not just in 'Working On The Project' but also in 'See Saw Blues' from 1940. Echoes of Big Bill Broonzy and Jazz Gillum also resound, and Gillum recorded an answer to her 'Got A Man In The 'Bamma Mine'. She was obviously a cherished member of the Lester Melrose stable, which explains the presence of stalwarts such as Black Bob, Joshua Altheimer, Blind John Davis and Broonzy in her backing bands. She flirted with a more jazz-oriented style in the middle of her career, backed by Her Rhythm Rascals and Her Jazz Boys, and did a fair imitation (though nothing more) of Billie Holiday in 'Fine And Mellow'. A later tilt, singing 'Stop And Listen' to the tune of 'St. Louis Blues', was less successful. Her voice coarsened around 1939 and a tendency to sing slightly flat became noticeable rather than interesting. Her last sessions, on the VAC *Female Chicago Blues*, dispensed with larger ensembles and her singing regained its poise to the accompaniment of Blind John Davis's sometimes florid piano. Though never achieving the status of required listening, the Yas Yas Girl's records are of dependable quality and entertaining. NS

Pete Johnson (1904–67)
VOCAL, PIANO, DRUMS

Raised in a Kansas City orphanage, Johnson started out as a drummer. In the '30s he teamed up with singing bartender Joe Turner; their appearance with Albert Ammons and Meade Lux Lewis at the 1938 From Spirituals To Swing concert sparked the boogie-woogie craze, but when it faded Johnson became yesterday's man, and had to work outside music in the '50s. He later made a modest comeback, even visiting Europe in 1958, but a series of strokes kept him in virtual seclusion during the '60s.

(*) **Boogie Woogie Boys
Document BDCD-6046 Johnson; Harry James (t); Albert Ammons (p, v); Johnny Williams (b); J. C. Heard, Eddie Dougherty (d); Alan Lomax, Lena Horne (sp). 12/38–41.

***(*) **Pete Johnson 1938–1939**
Classics 656 Johnson; Harry James, Hot Lips Page (t); Buster Smith (as); Albert Ammons, Meade Lux Lewis (p); Lawrence Lucie, Ulysses Livingston (g); Johnny Williams, Abe Bolar (b); Eddie Dougherty (d); Joe Turner (v). 12/38–12/39.

*** **Hey! Piano Man**
JSP JSP 7747 4CD Johnson; Harry James (t); Ulysses Livingston (g); Johnny Williams, Abe Bolar (b); Eddie Dougherty (d); Albert Ammons (v). 12/38–12/39.

***(*) **Pete Johnson 1939–1941**
Classics 665 Johnson; Hot Lips Page (t); Eddie Barefield (cl, as); Don Stovall (as); Don Byas (ts); Albert Ammons (p); Ulysses Livingston, John Collins (g); Abe Bolar (b); A. G. Godley, James F. Hoskins (d); Joe Turner (v). 12/39–6/41.

Kansas City jazz often seems to be the foundation of Johnson's boogie playing; at times he sounds like the Count

Basie Orchestra turned into ten fingers. Johnson usually keeps his basses light and lean, overlaying right-hand parts conceived like brass and reed solos; swerving away from the ground rhythm and extending across the boundaries of choruses, they are played with exceptional strength and clarity, as if struck by chrome-plated hammers.

There are some all-time classics on *1938–1939*, including 'Boo Woo', with Harry James spectacular on trumpet, 'Roll 'Em, Pete' and 'Climbin' And Screamin'', which is essentially the same theme without Joe Turner's ebullient vocal. 'Buss Robinson Blues' is a fine medium-tempo effort, but Johnson's slow blues playing is sometimes unfocused, prowling elaborately round the melody rather than getting to grips with its emotional content. On the other hand, his blues playing as a band member was very fine; never more so than when accompanying Joe Turner in a lineup including Hot Lips Page and Buster Smith.

Nothing on *1939–1941* quite matches its opening, the 18 incomparably inventive choruses of 'Holler Stomp', but there are plenty of good things on offer. Among them are the reflective 'You Don't Know My Mind', where Johnson lets the blues speak with simple eloquence, and A. G. Godley's drumming, as precise and relentless on the wild 'Death Ray Boogie' as on the dreamy 'Just For You'. There are eight duets with Albert Ammons, with Jimmy Hoskins assisting; for obvious reasons, these had to be worked out in advance, if only in general terms, and although tracks like 'Sixth Avenue Express' are musically exciting and technically ingenious, after a while one feels that a crowd-pleasing formula is being applied one more time.

On *Boogie Woogie Boys*, which also includes tracks by Lewis and Ammons, Johnson participates in an alternative take of 'Boo Woo' and the piano duets with Ammons from the short film *Boogie Woogie Dream*. Three numbers credited to him were recorded for the Library of Congress the day after *From Spirituals To Swing*; on these, Johnson accompanies Ammons singing 'Dying Mother Blues', plays the already inevitable 'Roll 'Em', and inflicts his own indifferent vocals on a 'Fo' O'Clock Blues' that's almost submerged in surface noise.

The Library of Congress titles begin Johnson's share of the JSP box. 'Dying Mother Blues' is admirably remastered, but the other two titles are very rough. The rest of the CD – the Harry James coupling, the ten Solo Art sides, 'Boogie Woogie' from Columbia and the six Blue Note solos – is of much higher quality, but listeners must either endure or skip these uncompromising opening tracks.

***(*) **Boogie Woogie Boys**
Magpie PY CD 21 *Johnson; Albert Ammons, Meade Lux Lewis (p); James F. Hoskins (d); Joe Turner (v). 12/38–5/44.*

(*) **The Boogie Woogie Trio Vol. 1 & 2
Storyville 103 8057 2CD *Johnson; Albert Ammons, Meade Lux Lewis (p); Don Lamond (d). 9/39–12/47.*

Magpie's *Boogie Woogie Boys* begins with material from the 'Spirituals To Swing' concerts; Johnson accompanies Joe Turner and participates in a trio with Ammons and Lewis, who also appear solo, and in duet on 'Double-Up Blues'. The bulk of the disc consists of duets by Ammons and Johnson: the Victor items which appear on Classics' second volume (plus an alternative take), and ten titles from radio transcription discs. The merits and drawbacks of the Victor material are discussed above; by 1944, Ammons and Johnson had perfected their duet playing, and the radio transcriptions are artistically superior to the Victors, not least because their pulse is innate rather than tick-tocked by a drummer. The 1941 'Cuttin' The Boogie' is interesting, but the harmony and rhythm of 1944's version are extraordinarily daring. Johnson and Ammons cover a wider range of styles and material too, from boogie and blues to ragtime and pop tunes. Among the latter, 'Lady Be Good' is simply great jazz, with some stunning counterpoint, and even 'Pistol Packin' Mama' is soon transformed into superior boogie.

Storyville's first disc is another outing for the 1944 radio duets, plus four solos-with-drummer from a Just Jazz concert. The balance of the disc is by Meade Lux Lewis and discussed in his entry. Storyville's sound quality is inferior to Magpie's, and the solos are impaired by Gene Norman's encouragement of barnstorming, and by Johnson's use of flippant quotation, caught from Art Tatum, the boppers or both. Storyville's second disc contains airshots from the Hotel Sherman; Johnson plays six solos, and participates in two trios. The showy 'Jo Jo' and the shuffle 'Mama's Blues' have their merits, but this is not the place for casual listeners to hear Johnson, thanks to the muffled sound (which does not obscure an audience member tapping a glass out of rhythm on 'Boogie Woogie Jump').

**** **Pete Johnson 1944–1946**
Classics 933 *Johnson; Hot Lips Page (t); Clyde Bernhardt, J. C. Higginbotham (tb); Albert Nicholas (cl); Don Stovall (as); Budd Johnson, Ben Webster (ts); Jimmy Shirley (g); Abe Bolar, Al Hall (b); Jack Parker, J. C. Heard (d); Etta Jones (v). 2/44–1/46.*

(****) **Atomic Boogie**
Savoy 92909 2CD *As above, except omit Jones. 1/46.*

Classics' third volume begins with eight fine solos, recorded for radio and later issued by Brunswick; 'Lights Out Mood' and 'Mr. Freddy Blues' are among Johnson's best slower blues, and 'Dive Bomber' and 'Answer To The Boogie' are two of his most artistically and technically perfect boogies. Moving to National, Johnson worked with starry lineups of swing musicians. Classics' last eight tracks were originally an album of 78s called *Pete Johnson's Housewarmin'*; beginning with a piano solo, instruments are added as the musicians 'arrive'. This may sound gimmicky, but it generates some fabulous jazz. Classics omit the talking between numbers, which does no harm; these links are included on *Atomic Boogie*, which contains all Joe Turner's National recordings and most of Pete Johnson's. There is consequently no room for two enjoyable accompaniments to Etta Jones, and the sound is not noticeably better than on Classics.

*** **Central Avenue Boogie**
Delmark DD-656 *Johnson; Charles Norris, Carl Lynch (g); Bill Davis, Al McKibbon (b); Jesse Price, J. C. Heard (d). 4/47–11/47.*

This CD draws on two Apollo sessions; on both the amplified guitarist is an equal partner with Johnson. There's some empty flash ('66 Stomp') and gimmickry ('Minuet Boogie'), but the guitarists' boppish inventiveness challenges Johnson; 'Yancy Street Boogie' [*sic*] and 'Swanee River' travel a long way from their familiar starting-points, and four takes of 'Hollywood Boogie' are distinct and creative approaches to the 'Roll 'Em, Pete' theme. The CD is completed by three tracks by the singer and pianist Arnold Wiley (1989–1964), a versatile

Missouri-born entertainer who also recorded for the Detroit label Sensation, material carefully recovered and annotated on *The Doc Wiley Trio: Wild Cat Boogie (The Ace 10" Series Vol. 4)* (Ace CDCHM 899).

**** Roll 'Em Pete
Topaz TPZ 1075 *As for relevant CDs above.* 12/38–4/47.

From the title track to the Apollo sessions, this is a very well-selected overview – mostly; the Apollo items are 'Minuet Boogie' and '66 Stomp'. The occasional track is slightly hissy, but not to a bothersome degree.

**(*) Pete Johnson (1939–c. 1947)
Document DOCD-1009 *Johnson; Cy Baker, Ziggy Elman, Chris Griffin, Emmett Berry, Shorty Sherock, Frankie Newton, Hot Lips Page (t); Red Ballard, Vernon Brown, Jack Teagarden, Benny Morton, Clyde Bernhardt (tb); Benny Goodman, Jimmy Hamilton, Barney Bigard, Albert Nicholas (cl); Hymie Schertzer, Noni Bernardi, Les Robinson, Don Stovall (as); Arthur Rollini, Jerry Jerome, Eddie Miller, Don Byas, Budd Johnson, Ben Webster (ts); Teddy Wilson (p, cel); Jess Stacy, Albert Ammons (p); Ben Heller, Nappy Lamare, Ernest Ashley, Leonard Ware, Jimmy Shirley (g); Harry Goodman, Johnny Williams, Hank Wayland, Dallas Bartley, Al Hall, Abe Bolar, unknown (b); Buddy Schutz, Lionel Hampton, J. C. Heard, poss. Johnny Otis, Nick Fatool, Harold West, Jack Parker, unknowns (d); unknowns (orch); Joe Turner, Lena Horne, Etta Jones (v); Gino Hamilton, Milton Cross, Virginia Pine, Russell Morrison, Cab Calloway, Ernie 'Bubbles' Whitman, Fred MacMurray, Tom Shirley, unknowns (sp).* 1/39–c. 47.

Among these broadcasts, film soundtracks and alternative takes are some wartime transcriptions made for the armed forces. They are important in showing Johnson and Ammons developing their duets during the AFM ban on commercial recording, but they also include a crude, perfunctory 'Sixth Avenue Express' and a disjointed collaboration with Joe Turner. Turner and Johnson offer compensation, once an asinine announcer has stopped braying, with tremendous versions of 'Roll 'Em, Pete' and 'Goin' Away Blues' from a 1940 broadcast. The alternative takes have their merits, but the complete soundtrack of *Boogie Woogie Dream* is surplus to requirements for all but the most dedicated enthusiast.

**(*) The St. Louis Parties (1954)
Document DOCD-1017 *Johnson; Tom Harris (p, v); Charlie Castner, Donald 'J. J.' Stoll (p); Bill Atkinson (v).* 7–8/54.

Recorded at the homes of a white fan and an African-American friend of Johnson's, the material on this disc greatly extends his known repertoire; there are blues and boogie, of course, but the emphasis is on ballads and jazz. Johnson also switches to drums on one track in support of Tom Harris's lively boogie piano. The recordings were made on professional equipment, and the party atmosphere is well (and occasionally too well) captured. Inevitably there's intermittent confusion on two tracks where his three disciples share the keyboard with Johnson, but the fun outweighs it. A few tracks have regrettable vocals; Harris massacres a couple of Joe Turner songs, and Bill Atkinson, who hosted the second party, isn't much of a singer either. Musicologically, *The St. Louis Parties* is

of great interest, but as entertainment it's marginal for most blues and jazz fans. CS

Robert Johnson (1911–38)
VOCAL, GUITAR

Born in Hazlehurst, Mississippi, Johnson grew up with a succession of stepfathers and for a time took the surname of one of them, C. D. Spencer; he was also known by some as Robert Dusty. Eventually he claimed the name of his birth father, Noah Johnson. As a teenager living in the Delta town of Robinsonville he hung around older musicians such as Willie Brown, Charley Patton and Son House; House was quite impressed by his skill on harmonica, but at first thought little of his guitar playing, an estimate he revised when Johnson returned to town after a year or two of wandering and listening to other musicians. The wandering continued for the rest of Johnson's life: as well as traversing much of the Deep South, he is said to have reached New York and Canada, his path intersecting those of Sonny Boy Williamson II, Johnny Shines, Howlin' Wolf, Honeyboy Edwards and many others. At two sessions for ARC-Brunswick in Texas in 1936 and '37 he recorded 29 songs, not all of which had been released when he died in the summer of 1938 near Greenwood, Mississippi, poisoned, it's thought, by the partner of a woman with whom he had been having an affair. Although he was remembered by many of his contemporaries, and several of his songs entered the standard repertoire thanks to reworkings by his stepson Robert Jr Lockwood, Elmore James, Muddy Waters and others, it was only with the release of the LP King Of The Delta Blues Singers *in 1961 that Johnson began to be perceived as a blues artist far out of the ordinary. The romantic aura of a blossoming talent plucked too soon was intensified by conflicting testimonies about his life and death and the absence, for many years, of any photograph. Thanks to the accumulated tributes of rock musicians like Eric Clapton and Keith Richards, writers, film-makers and other cultural spokespersons, Johnson has come to be regarded as the one unqualified genius produced by the blues, though in recent years there have been some attempts by revisionist scholars to cool that fervour.*

**** The Complete Recordings
Columbia/Legacy (A) C2K 46222//(E) 467246 2CD *Johnson.* 11/36, 6/37.
♛ **** The Complete Recordings
Columbia/Legacy C2K 64916 2CD *Johnson.* 11/36, 6/37.
**** King Of The Delta Blues Singers
Columbia/Legacy (A) CK 65211//(E) 487844 *Johnson.* 11/36, 6/37.
♛ **** King Of The Delta Blues Singers
Columbia/Legacy (A) CK 65746//(E) 493006 *Johnson.* 11/36, 6/37.
♛ **** King Of The Delta Blues Singers (Vol. 2)
Columbia/Legacy COL 517457 *Johnson.* 11/36, 6/37.
(****) Contracted To The Devil
Columbia 509010 *Johnson.* 11/36, 6/37.
(***) Martin Scorsese Presents The Blues: Robert Johnson
Columbia/Legacy 512573 *Johnson.* 11/36, 6/37.

Millions of words have been written about Robert Johnson, expressing every opinion from the quasi-religious conviction of Eric Clapton – 'He is the most important blues musician who ever lived' – to the scepticism of certain blues historians who regard him as no more than an interesting transitional figure between Son House and Muddy Waters. To see Johnson clearly the reader needs to steer a steady course between fanatics and debunkers, understanding the context of his music – the undeniable influence of House and Lonnie Johnson, his many allusions to records that were around when he was learning his trade – but at the same time recognizing the skill with which he synthesized those elements, and the wholly individual character of much of the finished work. In particular, Johnson deserves to be acknowledged as a master of the complete blues: the song conceived as a dramatic whole rather than an arbitrary sequence of scenes, of verses casually pinned to a formulaic accompaniment. The emotional architecture of a performance like 'Come On In My Kitchen', its tender erotic plea echoed by tremulous slide guitar, or of 'Hellhound On My Trail', a distraught, fragmented reconsideration of Skip James's 'Devil Got My Woman'; the intricate interdependence of voice and guitar in 'Walkin' Blues' and 'Preachin' Blues' – all this attests to a concept of blues composition that was beyond the scope of many of Johnson's contemporaries. Except in a few performances when he fell back on conventional phrasing, like the Lonnie Johnson-influenced 'Malted Milk' and 'Drunken Hearted Man', the borrowed elements of Johnson's music are always reshaped, and the echoes of their originators all but lost in the bright, clear, totally unified sound of his voice and guitar. He seems, too, to have understood instinctively how to use a recording microphone, discovering its potential for warmth and intimacy, confiding his blues rather than reporting them.

The care with which Johnson composed his songs is revealed in his alternative takes, of which we fortuitously have many: the reason *The Complete Recordings* is a well-filled 2CD is that 12 of his 29 recorded pieces exist in two versions, and since that set was issued an alternative take has come to light of 'Traveling Riverside Blues', first released on the 1998 edition of *King Of The Delta Blues Singers* (Columbia/Legacy [A] CK 65746//[E] 493006). (Because so many CDs in this entry have identical titles, catalogue numbers will often be cited for the sake of clarity.) That item aside, *The Complete Recordings* is what it says it is, and therefore an indispensable foundation-stone of any blues collection. Although the 1990 US longbox release (Columbia C2K 46222) is the most attractively presented version, both it and its parallel UK issue in a conventional 2CD jewel-case (CBS 467246) are inferior in sound restoration to the 1995 rerelease on Columbia/Legacy C2K 64916, which evidently profited from some higher-quality source material and more refined remastering techniques. Even this later edition doesn't represent the best current sound restoration: to take a track at random, the first take of 'Cross Road Blues', though significantly improved on the 1995 *Complete Recordings*, sounds better still on the 1998 *King Of The Delta Blues Singers*, equally better, though slightly differently equalized, on the 'Mastersound' (gold disc) facsimile edition of that album (Columbia CK 52944, regrettably deleted), and equally better again on the 2003 *Martin Scorsese Presents* selection, though there it's mistakenly described as take 2.

Correct track-identification isn't usually a problem on these 'official' (i.e. Columbia) CDs but transfer quality, as the reader will be realizing, is a can of worms. If you have no particular audiophiliac cravings, the second edition of *The Complete Recordings* is plainly the best choice: as well as perfectly reasonable sound it has, like its forerunner, a fat booklet with a competent biography and all the lyrics. But if you insist on hearing Johnson with state-of-the-art accuracy, and for that are prepared to sacrifice some of the alternative takes, we recommend you buy the 1998 *King Of The Delta Blues Singers* and the 2004 *King Of The Delta Blues Singers (Vol. 2)*, which, as well as providing at least one well-brushed recording of each of Johnson's songs, bring them to you more or less as they were first disseminated on LP in 1961 and 1970 respectively, allowing you to relive Keith and Eric's experience of growing wonder as track after astonishing track burn themselves into your cerebral cortex.

By comparison, the other official CDs are pointless. The Scorsese set was prompted by his film series and the Year Of The Blues, but with only 14 tracks it can hardly compete, and the added interpretations of 'They're Red Hot' by Cassandra Wilson and 'Last Fair Deal Gone Down' by Keb' Mo' are no more than after-dinner mints. *Contracted To The Devil* is better value with 24 tracks, but it won't cost you much more to buy the full set. And with Johnson, more than almost anyone else, you really do need the full set.

***(*) **Steady Rollin' Man**
Snapper Recall SMDCD 234 2CD *Johnson*. 11/36, 6/37.
*** **Robert Johnson**
DejaVu Retro Gold R2CD 40–14 2CD *Johnson*. 11/36, 6/37.
***(*) **The Blues/San Antonio-Dallas 1936–1937**
Frémeaux FA 251 2CD *Johnson*. 11/36, 6/37.
*** **A Proper Introduction To Robert Johnson: Cross Road Blues**
Proper INTRO CD 2010 *Johnson*. 11/36, 6/37.
*** **His Recorded Legacy**
Jasmine JASMCD 3001 *Johnson*. 11/36, 6/37.
*** **Devil On My Trail/The Complete Songbook**
New Sound 2000 NFM 006 *Johnson*. 11/36, 6/37.
*** **The Complete Collection**
Prism PLATCD 278 *Johnson*. 11/36, 6/37.
(*) **Deal With The Devil Vol. 1
Arpeggio ARB 006 *Johnson*. 11/36.
** **Deal With The Devil Vol. 2**
Arpeggio ARB 010 *Johnson*. 6/37.

These CDs, and the others discussed later in this entry, are just some of the many 'unofficial' (non-Columbia) releases of Johnson's work. If we were considering nothing but his music, every one would have a four-star rating, but here, more than usually, the reader is likely to want to know about selection, sequencing, sound, annotation and packaging. Rather than comment on each of those aspects for every CD, we have passed judgement in the star ratings.

The three 2CD sets at the head of the list are complete or nearly so. Snapper offer the same contents as Columbia's *Complete Recordings*, plus the 'new' alternative take of 'Traveling Riverside Blues'. DejaVu omit that item and one of the takes of 'Stop Breakin' Down Blues'. Frémeaux drop a few more alternative takes. The remaining CDs are complete inasmuch as they provide at least one take of each of Johnson's 29 songs. Proper and New Sound arrange them in the order in which they were recorded, while Jasmine and Prism don't. Arpeggio opt for chronological order but spread them over two CDs; the second adds the alternative takes from the 6/37 session but not, although the notes imply otherwise, the 'new'

'Traveling Riverside Blues'. The sound quality is noticeably worse on *Vol. 2*, but the presentation is equally poor on both volumes.

** **The Last Of The Great Blues Singers**
Fabulous FABCD 102 *Johnson*. 11/36, 6/37.
*** **The R. L. Spencer Legacy**
[Zircon Bleu 515] *Johnson*. 11/36, 6/37.

Given that several single CDs have managed to include at least one take of all Johnson's songs, readers may wonder why these albums fall short, with only 24. The reason is that five of his recordings – 'When You Got A Good Friend', 'Phonograph Blues', 'If I Had Possession Over Judgement Day', 'Drunken Hearted Man' and 'Traveling Riverside Blues' – were not released at the time but made their first appearance on LPs issued decades later, and therefore still enjoy the protection of copyright. The Fabulous CD is very cheap but the sound is muddy and some tracks have been ruined by ill-applied restoration. It does throw in an alternative take of 'Ramblin' On My Mind', though. Zircon's is better produced and, enterprisingly, adds four recordings directly influenced by Johnson's, Robert Jr Lockwood's 'Take A Little Walk With Me' and 'Little Boy Blue', Johnny Shines's 'Evil Hearted Woman' and Muddy Waters's 'Kind Hearted Woman'. *Hellhound On My Trail* (Indigo IGOCD 2017, deleted) had 24 tracks, adequate sound and mediocre notes.

*** **Hellhound On My Trail**
Delta 47 012 *Johnson*. 11/36, 6/37.
(*) **The Masters
Eagle EAB 067 *Johnson*. 11/36, 6/37.
*** **From Four Till Late**
Snapper Complete Blues SBLUECD 001 *Johnson*. 11/36, 6/37.
(*) **The Devil's Blues
Metrodome METRO 406 *Johnson*. 11/36, 6/37.
(*) **Robert Johnson
MM 7243 8420272 *Johnson*. 11/36, 6/37.
(*) **Crossroad Blues
Reactive REMCD 504 *Johnson*. 11/36, 6/37.
*** **Crossroad Blues**
Going For A Song GFS 442 *Johnson*. 11/36, 6/37.

Most of these sets offer between 18 and 22 tracks (Delta are exceptional in running to 25) and are competitively priced, but almost always at the cost of attractive presentation or useful notes. If you were looking for an inexpensive Johnson CD to give as a present, Snapper and Going For A Song would fill the bill well enough. But if you really care about the recipient, do it right: spend a bit more and take the four-star route. TR

Shirley Johnson (born 1949)
VOCAL

Johnson sang soul and pop around her native Norfolk, Virginia, before moving to Chicago in 1983 and concentrating on blues.

** **Looking For Love**
Appaloosa AP 094 *Johnson; Maurice John Vaughn (ts, g, v); Allen Batts (kb); Michael Grady Sr (g, v); Charles Crane (g); 'Uncle Ben', Darryl Achols, J. R. Fuller (b); Jeff Taylor, Michael Grady Jr (d)*. early 90s.

*** **Killer Diller**
Delmark DG-757 *Johnson; Kenny Anderson (t); Hank Ford (ts); Willie Henderson (bs); Roosevelt Purifoy, Allen Batts (o, p); Robert Ward, John Primer, Maurice John Vaughn, Johnny B. Moore, Rockin' Johnny [Burgin] (g); Willie 'Vamp' Samuels, Mike 'Sleepy' Riley (b); Tim Austin, 'Baldhead Pete' [Cleo Williams] (d); Kelly Littleton (bass d); Roberta Thomas (v)*. 2/96–10/02.

Released in 1994, *Looking For Love* is 'prentice work; the setlist is mostly blue-rinsed soul, Johnson's singing is one-dimensional and the accompaniments are generic. Two Casey Jones compositions are the CD's strongest and bluesiest numbers, and they get Johnson's most effective delivery, but Jeff Taylor's plodding rhythm makes it a puzzling pity that Jones didn't play on these tracks as well as arranging. *Killer Diller* is a significant improvement; Johnson conveys a sense of power in reserve, and has acquired the skills to give each song its own interpretation. She rejuvenates 'As The Years Go Passing By' and 'It Hurts Me Too', and makes an unlikely success of 'Little Wing'. A crack squad of guitarists, deployed over five sessions, play integrated, organic solos rather than showing off. There are lesser moments: 'Somebody Have Mercy' plods, and fussy melodies obfuscate the lyrics on 'Not For The Love Of You' and 'Love Abuse'. For the most part, though, *Killer Diller* is a considered, intelligent and enjoyable album. CS

Tommy Johnson (c. 1896–1956)
VOCAL, GUITAR, KAZOO

Johnson grew up on the Miller Plantation near Jackson, Mississippi, and in nearby Crystal Springs. His brothers LeDell, Mager and Clarence were also musicians, and LeDell had taught a teenaged Tommy the rudiments of guitar by the time he eloped with a girlfriend to the Delta. There Johnson's music was greatly influenced by Charley Patton and his circle; subsequently, he spent some time wandering outside Mississippi before returning to Crystal Springs. Recording was a brief interlude in a career of entertaining at parties and enslavement to alcohol, but both first-hand in Mississippi and indirectly through his records and those of his admirers, Johnson was an immensely influential artist.

**** **Tommy Johnson (1928–1929)**
Document DOCD-5001 *Johnson; Kid Ernest Moliere (cl); Charley Taylor (p); Charlie McCoy (g); unknown (perc); prob. Ishmon Bracey (sp)*. 2/28–c. 12/29.
(****) **Tommy Johnson (1928–1930)** [sic]
Wolf WSECD 104 As above, except omit Bracey. 2/28–c. 12/29.

A curious but welcome recurrence in Johnson's posthumous career has been the discovery of lost and unknown material; between Wolf's 'complete works' and Document's, a copy of Paramount 12950 turned up, as did an unissued alternative take of 'Black Mare Blues' and two tests of a previously unknown song. Accordingly, and despite its acceptable sound and musical glories, Wolf's 12-tracker is redundant. Recently, yet another test pressing, of a sentimental ballad, complete with Jimmie Rodgers-style blue yodel, has emerged. 'I Want Someone To Love Me' is available on *Times Ain't Like They Used To Be Vol. 8* (Yazoo 2068).

Johnson's recording career began with Victor; of eight songs recorded, seven are on CD, one of them in two takes. On four numbers Charlie McCoy plays busy, mandolin-like guitar, ably complementing Johnson's playing, which is relatively simple, but powerfully rhythmic and perfectly matched to his lyrics. 'Canned Heat Blues' is about his alcoholism, and stares unblinking into the eye of death, but most of Johnson's songs were assembled from a fairly small complement of traditional verses. They often begin with a startling image, and the results are allusive, strange and enigmatic; Johnson's glowing tenor, rising at times to an effortless, airy falsetto, confers a fitting elegance and grace on them. 'Big Road Blues', mixing optimism and alienation over an obbligato ascending bass line, is one of the blues' finest and most widely imitated compositions.

The Paramount recordings present some problems; the label's notoriously poor sound is aggravated by extreme rarity: every one of nine songs (including two alternative takes) is from the only known 78 or test — and the tests, having lain unplayed, have the best intrinsic sound. Both takes of 'Black Mare Blues' are mutilated by Moliere, a New Orleans jazz musician whose tasteless laughing clarinet is utterly at odds with Johnson's mood and rhythms. However, the other Paramounts are a priceless extension of our knowledge of Johnson's music; some of them rework themes already recorded, but 'I Wonder To Myself' is a nifty ragtime piece (with two not exactly vital kazoo solos), and 'Untitled Song (Morning Prayer Blues)' (sic) is reckoned by Don Kent to be 'far and away Johnson's most inventive [guitar] piece'. His singing continues to be regal.

Legends Of Country Blues (JSP JSP 7715 5CD), which also contains all Johnson's available recordings except 'I Want Someone To Love Me', is discussed in COMPILATIONS: MISSISSIPPI. If a sustained encounter with Paramount's wall of static is too much, an alternative is to hear Johnson in the company of his Mississippi contemporaries on Masters Of The Delta Blues: The Friends Of Charlie Patton (Yazoo 2002). Four of Johnson's five excellently transferred tracks are from Victor; the exception is 'Button Up Shoes', which is Yazoo's title for the song exalted by Kent. This disc illuminates Johnson's musical and historical importance from a differerent angle, but even Kid Ernest can't much weaken the case for the (almost) complete works. CS

Blind Willie Johnson (1897–1945)
VOCAL, GUITAR

Based in Marlin, Texas, Blind Willie Johnson sang gospel songs in the streets and at church programmes and conventions. His common-law widow, Angeline, told Sam Charters that he was blinded as a child when his stepmother threw lye in his face after a quarrel with his father, but recent research by Michael Corcoran suggests that he was born blind. The assumption that the silvery second voice on some of Johnson's records is Angeline's seems to be refuted by Willie B. Richardson's circumstantial memories, recounted to Dan Williams, and it appears that Johnson consorted with both women for a time before settling down with Angeline.

(****) **The Complete Blind Willie Johnson**
Columbia/Legacy C2K 52835//(E) 472190 2CD *Johnson; Willie B. Richardson, unknown woman (v). 12/27–4/30.*

(****) **Dark Was The Night**
Columbia/Legacy CK 65516//(E) 489892 *As above. 12/27–4/30.*

♔ **** **Praise God I'm Satisfied**
Yazoo 1058 *As above. 12/27–4/30.*

♔ **** **Sweeter As The Years Go By**
Yazoo 1078 *As above. 12/27–4/30.*

(***(*)) **The Soul Of A Man**
Universe UV 096 *As above. 12/27–4/30.*

(***(*)) **The Soul Of A Man**
Snapper Complete Blues SBLUECD 008 *As above. 12/27–4/30.*

**** **King Of The Guitar Evangelists**
Saga Blues 982 077-9 *As above. 12/27–4/30.*

In 1928 Blind Texas Marlin recorded two songs at the end of a Blind Willie Johnson session; they were never issued, and not even their titles are known. They may be secular songs by a pseudonymous Johnson, but his 30 issued recordings are all gospel music. Why, then, is he in this book? Although the concept of 'holy blues' is a comfort to non-religious white listeners rather than a reality, there was considerable overlap of resources and techniques between blues singers and 'guitar evangelists'. Johnson's records sold well and were very influential; his songs entered the repertoires of musicians as distant and dissimilar as Mance Lipscomb, Fred McDowell and Gary Davis, and his prowess with the slide was widely admired and emulated. Ultimately, though, Johnson is here because a picture of black folk music in the '20s and '30s is incomplete without his driving rhythms, his beautiful slide playing and his ferocious, sandblasted *basso falsetto*.

Which is not to say that everything's perfect. Only the born-again are likely to have no problem with the triteness of 'If It Had Not Been For Jesus', and Johnson himself has trouble with its chords and its waltz rhythm; 'Go With Me To That Land' is also not much of a lyric, although some artful string-bending redeems it. Five duets with an unknown woman, apparently recruited in New Orleans for a session held there, suffer somewhat from her unfamiliarity with Johnson's material.

On the whole, though, the standard of Johnson's recordings is extraordinarily high, whether the accompaniment is slide guitar or the insistent, percussive rhythms that Johnson usually favoured when a human second voice was present. He played slide on most of the titles from his first session, and they're unimprovably good; paramount among them, and arguably in American vernacular music, is the virtually wordless 'Dark Was The Night – Cold Was The Ground', where voice and guitar become one. Of his work without slide, 'If I Had My Way I'd Tear The Building Down' is as fearsome as its subject, Samson, and 'Let Your Light Shine On Me' is a tour-de-force of accelerating descent through three vocal registers.

All the available CDs have advantages and drawbacks. *The Complete* is as advertised, and has lengthy, if oddly torpid, annotation by Sam Charters, but the music has been subjected to aural overcleaning, and emerges scrubbed but sonically lifeless. To a lesser degree the Legacy CD has a similar problem, and with only 16 tracks important songs are omitted. The two *Souls Of A Man* appeared in the wake of the Wim Wenders film. Both have respectable sound, but Snapper's front-cover claim to supply 'twenty haunting spiritual blues songs from the Mississippi slide-guitar player' inhibits a recommendation. With 25 tracks, Universe's *Soul Of A Man* omits fewer of Johnson's greatest songs, but neither disc takes account of recent biographical research, and there's a whiff of opportunism about both.

Short playing time is the biggest drawback to *Praise God I'm Satisfied*, whose 14 titles were selected in the LP era. Yazoo's second CD makes amends by reissuing the balance; automatically, it's weighted with slightly lesser material, but careful programming minimizes the effect of this. More important, on both discs Yazoo have obtained a full, warm and vivid sound from 78s, amply compensating for slight surface noise and the occasional distorted bass note. David Evans's annotation of *Sweeter As The Years Go By* is excellent, and Stephen Calt's on *Praise God I'm Satisfied* is also useful, although a reference to 'the aridity of his intellectual horizon' is the pot sneering at the kettle. The Yazoo CDs (plural, please note) get the vote.

King Of The Guitar Evangelists is the next best alternative, with 22 tracks, a budget price and excellent mastering. This release carries the first notes to take advantage of Michael Corcoran's discoveries; they also sneer gratuitously at Sam Charters's account, based on what have turned out to be the fantasies of Angeline Johnson. The tracks are split into chapters called *With His Wife* and *Alone With God*; four of the vocal duets actually feature the unknown woman from the New Orleans sessions.

Most of its content is outside our scope, but readers seeking to place Johnson in the broader context of African-American gospel music will be well served by *Blind Willie Johnson & The Guitar Evangelists* (JSP JSP 7737 4CD). CS

Albinia Jones (1914–89)
VOCAL

Born Albennie Jones in Gulfport, Mississippi, she was working in clubs in New York by the late '30s. Active for a decade or more, latterly in partnership with the comedian Nipsey Russell, she retired after a disabling fall from a stage.

**(*) Vocal Blues & Jazz – Vol. 4 (1938–1949)
Document DOCD-1020 *Jones; Frankie Newton, Dizzy Gillespie, unknown (t); Edmond Hall, Gene Sedric (cl); Don Byas, unknowns (ts); Cliff Jackson, Sam Price (p); Leonard Ware, Billy Butler, unknowns (g); Oscar Smith, Percy Joell, unknowns (b); Hal 'Doc' West, Dorothea Smith, unknowns (d)*. 12/44–2/49.

Jones had a strong, penetrating voice and a natural gift for singing the blues. When teamed with superior musicians, she could turn out first-rate records; 'What's The Matter With Me? (Don't You Wear No Black)' from her first session, with Frankie Newton and Edmond Hall, goes like a rocket. Her next date, with Don Byas, produced strong versions of 'Evil Gal Blues' and 'Salty Papa Blues' (recently introduced by Dinah Washington), but later sessions with groups organized by Sam Price suffered a little from unexciting material. She has 15 tracks here; the album is filled up with odd pieces by Helen Humes, Ethel Waters (with Duke Ellington), Rosetta Tharpe and Betty Roché. TR

Andrew 'Jr Boy' Jones (born 1948)
VOCAL, GUITAR

Jones grew up in a musical family in Dallas, and by the age of 16 was hanging out with Freddie King. Later he toured with him and with Johnny Taylor, Katie Webster (playing on her album Swamp Boogie Queen*) and Charlie Musselwhite, whose band he led for seven years. At home in Dallas he has played and recorded with R. L. Griffin.*

*** I Need Time
JSP JSPCD 278//Bullseye Blues CDBB 9588 *Jones; Marvin Washington (o); Oliver Mowat (p); Christole Jones (b); Tommy Hill, Charles 'Sugar Boy' Meyers (d)*. summer 96.

**(*) Watch What You Say
Bullseye Blues & Jazz CD BB 9602 *Jones; Steve Howard (t); Richard Martinez (tb); Bill Samuels (ts, bs); Tommy Young (o, p); Ronnie Bramhall (o); Tommy Tucker (b); Tommy Hill (d, v)*. 98.

***(*) Mr. Domestic
Galexc GLXC 7001 *Jones; Shawn Phares (kb, v); Tommy Tucker (b, v); Tommy Hill (d, v)*. 02.

Jones's long preparation for his first album in his own name ensured that it was technically irreproachable, with a warm and well-balanced sound. The songs, all originals, are a considered blend of serious ('I Need Time', 'These Bills') and light-hearted ('Big Leg, Heavy Bottom'), delivered in a voice that's serviceable rather than distinctive. The Bullseye Blues version changes the running order slightly, raising the excellent title song to opening position, but listeners to either issue who require track-to-track variation may want to reorder the programme a little more. That aside, *I Need Time* is an impressive debut.

No adjustments are needed to the programming of *Watch What You Say*, a smooth concoction of slow blues interspersed with shuffles and other brisker pieces, but the texture doesn't change very much from track to track and the horns could profitably have been brought in on more than three of them. That said, the quartet setting of *Mr. Domestic* might seem to have been an ill-advised move, but in fact it elicits a much more emphatic performance, with a welcome high score of lively tempos. His guitar tone less suave than on the previous albums, Jones breathes the spirit of Johnny Copeland into the title song, one of several pieces that comment wryly on the small dramas of home life. 'Blues Belly' amusingly prioritizes soul food over fitness programmes: 'I wanna lose some weight and I'm gonna try – after some barbecued ribs and sweet potato pie. I don't know how long this is gonna last – I had a big slice of cake with my glass of Slimfast.' This may be the hardest of Jones's albums to find but it's by some way the best. TR

Billy Jones (born 1953)
VOCAL, GUITAR

Jones grew up in North Little Rock, Arkansas, absorbed music in his family's blues café and began playing guitar. In the '70s he put together a band to play for clubs and military bases, and since then he has opened shows for many blues and soul acts.

** Tha' Blues
Black & Tan CD B&T 023 *Jones; Roel Spanjers (kb, o, p, syn); Gabriel Peeters (g, d, perc); Jan Mittendorp (g); Nico Heilijgers (b); Cortez (perc)*. 12/04.

Jones sets a good groove and, with well-judged support by his Dutch associates, gives several of these songs a laidback swing not unlike J. J. Cale's. His voice is soft-edged and unaggressive, and the Sam Cooke effect of 'Make Love Tonight' comes easily to him. Readers who are fond of Keb' Mo or Eric Bibb may be attracted by the surface of Jones's music, but will soon discover that surface is all it has. From the bromide of the opening track's 'Love is such a serious thing/We gotta try and work this out/And there's no reason we can't be together/Just you and me, baby, that's what it's all about' to the closing 'Da' Love Doctor' ('Well, they call me da' love doctor/Cause I got patients all over town'), Jones's songs are assembled from a Kiddiekraft Konstruction Kit of blues and soul clichés. TR

Curtis Jones (1906–71)
VOCAL, PIANO

Born in Naples, Texas, Jones began playing piano in his teens and worked around Dallas until 1929, when he lit out for Kansas City and the Midwest, then New Orleans, before arriving in Chicago in 1936. The success of his first release, 'Lonesome Bedroom Blues', assured him of a recording career for several years, but because of ill health and other factors he was not much employed in the '50s. In the early '60s, however, he was reactivated and moved to Europe, where he spent the rest of his life, travelling widely (France, Germany, Poland, Morocco), recording a couple of albums in England and joining the 1968 AFBF.

**(*) Curtis Jones – Vol. 1 (1937–1938)
Document DOCD-5296 Jones; prob. Punch Miller (t); George Gant (as); Charlie McCoy (md, g); Willie B. James, Hobson 'Hot Box' Johnson, poss. Big Bill Broonzy (g); unknown(s) (b); Fred Williams (d); Washboard Sam (wb). 9/37–5/38.

**(*) Curtis Jones – Vol. 2 (1938–1939)
Document DOCD-5297 Jones; Charlie McCoy (md); Hobson 'Hot Box' Johnson, prob. Joe McCoy or Willie B. James, unknown (g); Ransom Knowling, unknown(s) (b); prob. Fred Williams, unknown (d); Lillie Mae Kirkman (v). 6/38–6/39.

**(*) Curtis Jones – Vol. 3 (1939–1940)
Document DOCD-5298 Jones; Jazz Gillum (h); Hobson 'Hot Box' Johnson (g); unknown (b); Fred Williams, poss. Judge Riley (d); Lillie Mae Kirkman (v). 6/39–9/40.

**(*) Curtis Jones – Vol. 4 (1941–1953)
Document DOCD-5299 Jones; Lorenzo King (ts); L. C. McKinley (g); Ransom Knowling, Alfred Elkins (b); Judge Riley (d). 1–8/41, 5/53.

*** Lonesome Bedroom Blues 1937–1941
EPM Blues Collection 15831 Jones; George Gant (as); Jazz Gillum (h); Charlie McCoy (md, g); Willie B. James, Hobson 'Hot Box' Johnson, prob. Joe McCoy (g); Ransom Knowling, unknown(s) (b); Fred Williams, poss. Judge Riley (d); Washboard Sam (wb). 9/37–8/41.

'It's lonesome in my bedroom, just me myself alone – I have no one to love me, each night when I come home. A room without a woman is like a heart without a beat – seem like every woman I get always wants to mistreat me.' Jones's 'Lonesome Bedroom Blues' can be heard as a blues equivalent of the tears-in-your-beer honkytonk song that was emerging in country music in the late '30s: a sucker punch into the gut of the single man living in a rooming house and spending his evenings in a bar with a jukebox. It was an immediate hit, remaining in catalogue for much of the following decade, and over the next four years Jones turned out dozens of blues-and-trouble compositions, sung in the bleak Texas manner of men like Black Boy Shine to tidy, unexciting piano accompaniments.

He managed this workload by taking some care to come up with novel ideas for songs. 'Palace Blues', recorded in 3/38, alludes to the abdication of Edward VIII, the British king who wished to marry an American divorcée: 'Girlfriend, girlfriend, I done give up my palace for you – only trying to prove that my real love was true'. 'The season is almost here, babe, come let us rehearse our game,' he begins in 'Love Season Blues', though the promise of an extended baseball metaphor is not sustained. Occasionally he found reason to be lively, as in the reverse side of 'Lonesome Bedroom Blues', 'You Got Good Business' ('daddy want to trade with you'), or 'Let Me Be Your Playmate'.

If the unchangingness of Jones's tunes, tempos and settings tends to lull the listener into inattention, he or she may be jolted by the startling declaration at the beginning of 'Alley Bound Blues': 'I have been singing sentimental songs all over town, and I haven't made no headway, so you know I'm alley bound.' It seems that the blues singer we know from records was only one aspect of Curtis Jones – and since the next song he cut, 'Who You're Hunchin'', and two more from a session three months later, 'I'm With You Again' and 'I'm Losing My Mind Over You', were departures from the blues, he would appear to have fought off a complete transformation into a bluesman. Nevertheless, his recorded repertoire remained thick with blues. As he sang in 'Blues In The Alley', 'I love to play swing music, but the blues they will never die.' Few were as lurid as 'War Broke Out In Hell', a violent fantasy that seems to have been inspired by an actual or imagined prison revolt.

Vol. 2, which contains all the songs mentioned in the preceding paragraph, ends with three by Lillie Mae Kirkman, and *Vol. 3* opens with two more. These are likeable performances: she is a poised singer, and the piano playing is excellent, though not much like Jones's. His first recordings on *Vol. 3*, 'I'm In The Mood For You' and 'Who You Lovin'', are pop songs, and second-rate ones, but at least a break in the chain of his blues, which are becoming increasingly homogeneous. Another diversion is 'Solid Jive', a hipster strut that opens a session for Bluebird; the other three numbers are blues, but they sound unusually interesting because Bluebird's recordings were technically so much better, and throw a brighter light on his piano playing. Jones then returned to OKeh (formerly Vocalion), to be teamed on his next date with the harmonica player Jazz Gillum. There are characteristic touches in the lyrics, like 'My baby is a pilot, she's got that aviation love, and soon we'll be sailin' through the blue skies up above' ('Moonlight Lover Blues'), but not many. Gillum's solo passages are vague to the point of absent-mindedness.

The bulk of *Vol. 4* is the two 1941 sessions with which Jones concluded the first stage of his recording career. 'It's A Solid Sender' is a jive number that anticipates Cecil Gant, while among the blues the most distinctive is 'Tin Pan Alley', which, with elements of other Jones compositions, provided the template for the later hit by Jimmy Wilson. A dozen years later Jones recorded four sides for the Chicago label Parrot with a well-matched small group. Both his singing and his playing seem to fit the stylistic conventions of the '50s well, but these would be his only recordings during the decade.

All the Documents are diminished to some extent by the use of poor originals; indeed, anyone who wants to hear a decent copy of his most popular record must look elsewhere.

Fortunately one can be found on the EPM CD, along with 'Tin Pan Alley', 'Solid Jive' and 22 other tracks, making this the most recommendable album of his early work. Given the somewhat cool view of Jones's work expressed above, it is fair to quote the notewriter Jean Buzelin's enthusiastic response to it: 'His stylistic limitations, far from provoking the monotony engendered by so many of his contemporaries, arouse a desire to delve to the very core of his undemonstrative and harrowing art ... to comprehend the personal drama he is attempting to exorcize through his music.'

(*) Trouble Blues
Original Blues Classics OBCCD 515 *Jones; Robert Banks (o); Johnny 'Moose John' Walker (g); Leonard Gaskin (b); Belton Evans (d).* 11/60.

**** Lonesome Bedroom Blues**
Delmark DD-605 *Jones.* 1/62.

It was immediately apparent from the opening bars of 'Lonesome Bedroom Blues' on his Bluesville LP (reissued, misdated 1961, on the OBC CD) that neither Jones's voice nor his hands had suffered during his lean years in the '50s. Unfortunately his admirable selection of old and new blues was not furnished with admirable accompaniment. Banks's organ, present on every track except 'Please Say Yes', clogs the flow of the music like a hairball in a wastepipe, and his effects on the last verse of 'Love Season' sound as if they were borrowed from the soundtrack of *It Came From Outer Space.* Walker is more *à propos*, adding a neat T-Boneish line to 'Suicide Blues'.

The Delmark, however, is Jones's masterwork. Undistracted by unnecessary or unsympathetic accompanists, he is able to set his own rhythmic agenda for each performance. The slightly anaemic artist of the earlier recordings gives way to a performer who is both trenchant and profuse, and the album contains more and better piano playing, both on the vocal numbers and in the instrumental 'Rolling The Blues', than he had ever committed to record. (Another fine piano solo, 'Takin' Off', is on *Blues Piano Orgy* [Delmark DE-626].) The several new songs like 'Tour Blues' have been written with a recognizably quirky hand, and old favourites like the title track, 'Highway 51' and 'Tin Pan Alley' are reviewed with a new eye. The album is garlicky with character.

Jones's subsequent British recordings *In London* (Decca, 1963) and *Now Resident In Europe* (Blue Horizon, 1968) – on both of which he recorded some songs with guitar, his first instrument – are not currently available on CD. A track from the Decca sessions, 'Roll Me Over', is on the VAC *The Blues Scene* (Deram 844 801). TR

Eddie Lee Jones
VOCAL, GUITAR

'Mustright' (that is, Muskrat) Jones (born 1929) was recorded at his Lexington, Georgia, home after a chance meeting with folklorist Bill Koon. Jones made further, unissued recordings in 1977, and in 1980 played a concert in Athens, Georgia; he is believed to be dead.

**** Yonder Go That Old Black Dog**
Testament TCD 5023 *Jones; prob. Mrs Jones, another woman, unknown man (v).* 8/65.

Jones sings in a growling holler, and is a forceful, rhythmic guitarist in both regular and bottleneck styles. He takes some material from commercial recordings, including a fine version of 'Stop And Listen', but there are also several fervent spirituals, and a number of songs that predate the blues: 'John Henry' is well known, but Jones adds touches of his own, while 'I Got A Yellow Gal' and other dance tunes seem to be stripped-down versions of old fiddle pieces. The vigorous, enthusiastic music preserved by these front-porch recordings was made in a context of poverty, isolation and racial tension; its importance to the local African-American community is obvious on those tracks where neighbours turned the recording session into an impromptu party. CS

Eddie 'One-String' Jones
VOCAL, MONOCHORD

Recorded in Los Angeles, Jones was a skid row hobo, and reluctant to talk about his past life, but his instrument, singing style and repertoire identify him as probably from Mississippi, as does a reference to 'doing seven [years] in Natchez'.

*** One-String Blues**
Gazell Documents GDCD 6001//Takoma TAKCD 1023 *Jones; Frederick A. Usher (interviewer).* 60.

Research has revealed the 'one-string' (a.k.a. jitterbug and diddley bow) to be a descendant of the West African monochord zither, and to be a more common instrument, especially in Mississippi, than it seemed in 1960. Even so, Eddie Jones's recordings are still among the most gripping examples of what can be done with a 2 x 4, a broom wire, a paint-can resonator, a whittled stick and an empty half-pint bottle. Jones's repertoire consists of well-known songs like 'John Henry', 'Rolling And Tumbling' and 'I'll Be Your Chauffeur', given a gritty, tonally restricted delivery, and interspersed with asides to himself in the manner of Tommy McClennan. It's the accompaniment that compels attention, however; pitched percussion, as the string is tapped with a stick, supplies rhythmic momentum, and the bottle flickers along the string, producing keening, wraith-like harmonics which give even the most familiar numbers a dissonant, alien eeriness. Jones's unexpurgated version of 'The Dozens' (the first released on disc) still retains its power to startle.

The CD is completed by six tracks from another hobo. Edward Hazelton was a harmonica player, originally from Sumter, South Carolina, and was recorded in Los Angeles at the same time as Jones. Hazelton plausibly claimed to have known Sonny Terry and Blind Boy Fuller in Winston-Salem, and his playing is like a simplified version of Terry's. Hazelton's harmonica fills are often rather disconnected from his singing, but he is compelling listening, a man driven and possessed by music, which he describes as 'something like a eatin' cancer'. 'Poor Boy Travelling From Town To Town' has documentary realism: 'Yes, I knock on doors, beg them to give me a piece of bread.' CS

Floyd Jones (1917–89)
VOCAL, GUITAR

Born in Marianna, Arkansas, Jones spent his youth in Mississippi, where he began playing guitar in the '30s. Moving to Chicago in 1945, he played on Maxwell Street with his cousin Moody and Snooky Pryor and made singles for several small

labels, graduating to Chess and Vee-Jay. He took up bass to increase his work opportunities but was never able to make a living from music. Even recording opportunities came rarely in later life to this serious singer and songwriter.

***(*) Floyd Jones 1948–1953
Classics 5130 *Jones; Billy Howell (t); Snooky Pryor (h, sp); Little Walter (h); Sunnyland Slim (p); Moody Jones (g, b); Jimmy Rogers, Eddie Taylor (g); poss. Willie Coven, Elgin Edmonds, Alfred Wallace. unknowns (d). 11/48–2/53.*

Until quite recently, one could collect Floyd Jones's early work only by buying several VACs. Now it's all neatly arranged on one CD. His first recordings were 'Keep What You Got', a boogie tune similar to what Joe Williams and Sonny Boy Williamson I were doing about the same time, and 'Stockyard Blues', a focused song about the rising cost of living; both feature razor-sharp harmonica playing by Snooky Pryor. Jones would return to a topical theme – again partnered by Pryor – at a later session with 'Ain't Times Hard', but in the recordings that intervened he repeatedly harked back to music he must have heard in his youth, in particular that of Tommy Johnson, whose 'Big Road Blues' he remade as 'Dark Road' (twice, with different instrumentation) and as 'On The Road Again'; 'Early Morning' also has a Johnson ring. Elsewhere he makes music broadly similar to contemporary work by Muddy Waters and Jimmy Rogers, though he hasn't their polish. His most commercially savvy recordings were done at Vee-Jay, where studio echo made his singing, which was sometimes rather gentle and reflective, sound tougher. 'Schooldays (On My Mind)', 'Ain't Times Hard' and 'Any Old Lonesome Day' are also enhanced by the groupwork of Pryor, Sunnyland Slim and Eddie Taylor. On the initial pressing the first [J.O.B.] recording of 'Big World', with its bizarre trumpet part, was accidentally omitted and the Chess version appeared twice. This was subsequently corrected. Ten of these 18 sides are also gathered on *Down Home Blues Classics: Chicago 1946–1954* (Boulevard Vintage BVBCD 1014 4CD).

** Masters Of Modern Blues
Testament TCD 5001 *Jones; Big Walter Horton (h); Otis Spann (p); Eddie Taylor (g); Fred Below (d). 6/66.*

This session was designed to produce an album with the vocals evenly divided between Jones and Eddie Taylor. The band was well chosen and Jones's eight numbers included some of his best compositions like 'Dark Road', 'Hard Times' and 'Stockyard Blues', but this is a dull, monochrome recording. The sound is stodgy, the voice too low in the mix, and neither Horton nor Taylor plays with much energy. TR

Johnny Jones (born 1936)
VOCAL, GUITAR

Until researchers finally paid attention to the history of black music in Nashville, Johnny Jones belonged to the legion of underrated supporting players. Born in Edes, Tennessee, he spent his teens in Chicago, where he did a little playing in clubs. Returning to Tennessee, he hooked up with the producer Ted Jarrett and became one of black Nashville's leading studio guitarists. He also led a band at the New Era club which included the young Jimi Hendrix, played rhythm guitar in the house band on the '60s TV show *The Beat!* and cut a number of singles for local labels. By the late '70s he had left the music business, but he was coaxed out of retirement to play at the 1997 Blues Estafette in Holland, which led to further work and several recording dates.

*** I Was Raised On The Blues
Black Magic BM 9036 *Jones; Dennis Taylor (ts, bs); Phil Rugh (o); Fred James (p, g); Jeff Davis (b); Herb Sucher, Andy Arrow (d); Mary-Ann Brandon, Earl Gaines (v). 1/98.*

**(*) In The House
Crosscut CCD 11066 *Jones; Billy Earheart (o); Fred James (g, v); Jeff Davis (b); Andy Arrow (d); Charles Walker, Mary-Ann Brandon (v). 11/99.*

*** Blues Is In The House
NorthernBlues NBM 0007 *Jones; Dennis Taylor (ts, bs); Billy Earheart (kb, o); Fred James (g); Jeff Davis (b); Bryan Owings (d); Charles Walker, Mary-Ann Brandon (v). 1–12/00.*

Years of studio work obviously taught Jones the value of conciseness. Even when he has the space to stretch out, as in the versions of 'Can I Get An Amen' on *I Was Raised On The Blues* and *In The House*, or 'I Could Be Dangerous' on *Blues Is In The House*, his solos are characterized by continuity rather than reiteration. Whether singing or playing, he phrases cleanly and articulately, and if sometimes, particularly on long slow blues like the ones mentioned, he reflects the enveloping influence of B. B. King on musicians of his generation, it's never blatant. *In The House* was taped at the Lucerne Blues Festival and apart from 'Can I Get An Amen' is all different material from the earlier studio recording, well done but with less variation of texture. The lead vocalist on half of the dozen songs, acknowledged with a joint credit, is another Nashville-based artist and past associate, Charles Walker, whose acrobatic soul singing is often effectively distraught but occasionally rather forced. The confusingly titled *Blues Is In The House* puts Jones back in the studio and in command (Walker is on hand only for a duet on the title song and some backgrounding) and elicits his most finished performance. Two clever numbers, 'Love Recession' and 'Stacked In The Back', were written by another Nashville associate, Clifford Curry, with whom Jones played on the VAC *Blues Across America: The Nashville Scene* (Cannonball CBD 29206, deleted); there's also a neat 'Farm Boy', done in the style of '50s Chicago, a Robert Wardish instrumental, 'Really', and several serviceable numbers by Fred James, making this the most varied of Jones's CDs. These are not innovative albums but reaffirmations of blues principles by a mature and individual craftsman. TR

Johnny Yard Dog Jones (born 1941)
VOCAL, HARMONICA, GUITAR

This Johnny Jones grew up in East St Louis, singing gospel music with his mother's encouragement, and gaining his first exposure to blues by changing the records as his father played checkers with his friends. Jones began playing harmonica and guitar at the age of ten, and was soon hanging out in blues clubs. Moving to Chicago at 18, he played guitar with family gospel groups, but since 1971 he has been a resident of Detroit, where he began singing blues as a member of Bobo Jenkins's band. At the present time, Jones has given up public performance.

*** Ain't Gonna Worry
Earwig CD 4937 *Jones; Detroit Junior (p); Johnny B. Moore (g); Bernard Reed (b); Kenny Smith (d). 3/96.*

Yard Dog's long involvement with gospel music is very apparent in his singing; he refers to himself as a 'blues/soul vocalist', and cites Archie Brownlee of the Five Blind Boys Of Mississippi among his influences, alongside O. V. Wright and Johnnie Taylor. Nevertheless, *Ain't Gonna Worry* is usually pretty much hardcore blues; 'Your Used To Be', which is the CD's most undiluted soul music, is also its least successful track, coming in just behind 'Cry For Me Baby', an Elmore James song taken much too fast. These lapses are not typical, and *Ain't Gonna Worry* is an enjoyably oldfashioned, unpretentious collection of blues, owing more to Chicago than Detroit, despite Jones's long residence in the latter city. As a singer, he is sometimes reminiscent of Howlin' Wolf, most explicitly on 'Ain't Gonna Worry No More', one of three tracks where he demonstrates his considerable command of the guitar. On the minor-tinged 'Anything But Without You', his emotional singing strongly and successfully recalls Otis Rush. Like most of the CD, these songs are Jones compositions, and he is a useful songwriter, even if none of his compositions seems destined to become a classic. Jones's harmonica playing is basic but effective, and he sensibly allows the ever-reliable Johnny B. Moore to take most of the instrumental limelight. This was a very promising debut disc, and it's a great pity that Jones has since dropped out of music. CS

Lloyd Jones (born 1950)
VOCAL, GUITAR

In the '70s Jones led the blues band Brown Sugar in his hometown of Portland, Oregon. He was then playing both drums and guitar, but gave up drums about 1980. In 1985 he formed The Lloyd Jones Struggle – 'because I was 35, nobody knew me by my name and I was playing for 35 bucks a night'. *Guitar Player* has called his music 'dancable [sic] ham-fisted blues', maybe not quite the testimonial Jones is looking for, but Robert Cray rates him, which probably compensates.

** Small Potatoes
Burnside BCD-0042 *Jones; Rich Cooper (t); Warren Rand (as); Rudy Draco, Bob Roden (ts); Curtis Marquart, Michael Bard (bs); Glen Holstrom (kb); Dave Stewart (p); Jim Solberg, Don Campbell (b); Mike Klobas (d); Brian Davis (perc); Linda Hornbuckle, Lisa Hart, Myrtle Brown, Curtis Salgado (v).* 88.

**(*) Have Mercy – Live
Burnside BCD-0012 *Jones; Rudy Draco (ts, bs); Bob Roden, Terry Hanck (ts); Glen Holstrom (o, p); Jim Solberg (b, v); Mike Klobas (d).* 93.

**(*) Love Gotcha
Blind Pig BPCD 5057 *Jones; Steve Cannon (t); Rudy Draco, Renato Caranto (ts); Glen Holstrom (o, p); Ben Jones (b); Don Worth (d); Terry Evans (v).* 99.

Small Potatoes, credited to The Lloyd Jones Struggle, was Jones's second album. (His first, *The Lloyd Jones Struggle* [Criminal, 1987], has not been reissued on CD.) The all-original programme is rife with unmemorable songs and sprawling arrangements. *Mercy – Live* is an improvement inasmuch as it reduces the original material to two songs by Jones and one by saxophonist Terry Hanck, filling up with Jimmy Rogers's 'Going Away Baby', Muddy Waters's 'Gone To Main Street' and songs by Tampa Red, Ray Charles and Roosevelt Sykes. The band is no Roomful Of Blues; the saxes and organ give it breadth and depth, but not much

distinctiveness. *Love Gotcha*, like 1995's *Trouble Monkey* (AudioQuest AQ-CD 1037, probably unavailable – a pity, since it's his best album), is 75 per cent original songs, most of which effervesce and are gone, pfft. 'Old News', a slow blues, is okay, if conventional. Jones sings, as is his habit, with a vehemence that doesn't always seem to have much to do with the lyrics. TR

Maggie Jones
VOCAL

Maggie Jones was from Hillsboro, Texas, and used her real name, Faye (or Fae) Barnes, on some of her first records. She moved to New York in the early '20s and appeared in African-American theatres in the Northeast. Jones stayed in show business after she stopped recording, and had a small role in the famous Blackbirds Of 1928 revue, which took her to Europe. By 1934, she had returned to Texas and was performing in Fort Worth, but there is no trace of her after that date.

**(*) Maggie Jones – Vol. 1 (1923–1925)
Document DOCD-5348 *Jones; Louis Armstrong (c); Charlie Green (tb); Donald M. Redmond, Lemuel Fowler, Fletcher Henderson (p); Sam Clark (bj); 'Alabama Joe' [J. M. 'Doc' Miller] (g); unknown (eff).* c. 8/23–4/25.

**(*) Maggie Jones – Vol. 2/Gladys Bentley (1925–1929)
Document DOCD-5349 *Jones; Joe Smith, Harry Cooper, Louis Metcalf (c); Micky Bloom (t); Charlie Green, Pete Pellezzi, Jake Frazier (tb); Bob Fuller (cl, as); Buster Bailey, Louis Maesto (cl); Elmer Snowden (as, bj); Fletcher Henderson, Nick Moleri, Louis Hooper, Cliff Jackson, Clarence Williams (p); Charlie Dixon (bj); Christian Maesto (d); unknown (eff).* 5/25–6/26.

Maggie Jones kicked off her recording career with an undistinguished disc for each of Black Swan, Pathé and Paramount, but when she joined Columbia in October 1924 the acoustic and artistic quality of her recordings improved at once. Jones has been overshadowed by her label-mates Bessie and Clara Smith, but she had outstanding natural resources. A slow, rich vibrato adds emotion to her powerful contralto, and she usually sings within a narrow range, dramatizing the lyrics by bending and sustaining notes, effortlessly but never mechanically.

Despite these gifts, *Vol. 1* includes a disproportionate number of disappointing performances, for Jones is too often ill-served by her accompanists. The nadir is reached on two sides where the hillbilly guitarist 'Doc' Miller plays a zombie strum, but more startling is the inconsistency displayed by Charlie Green. His responses on 'Box Car Blues' and 'Western Union Blues' are lively and appropriate, but elsewhere he too often doodles aimlessly. More disconcerting still is Louis Armstrong, playing uninspired, generic responses on 'Poor House Blues' and 'If I Lose, Let Me Lose (Mama Don't Mind)'. These are moments of aberration, of course. Louis is far better on 'Screamin' The Blues', 'Good Time Flat Blues' and 'Anybody Here Want To Try My Cabbage'; his daring solos on the latter two songs make his affection for these recordings in later years easy to understand. Armstrong does pretty well on 'Thunderstorm Blues', too, but some idiot wreaks havoc with a thunder sheet and a wind machine.

Vol. 2 contains Maggie Jones's last 16 recordings. Unfortunately, most tracks either combine strong accompaniments with weak material or vice versa. The four opening titles are an attempt to move towards popular song; on two of them, Henderson's Hot Six are ill at ease and, if anything, less idiomatic than the white St Louis Rhythm Kings on their two. These songs are greatly preferable, however, to half a dozen blues featuring the instantly recognizable (and instantly dislikeable) laughing and sobbing reed work of Bob Fuller. When a second reed player is heard, it's Elmer Snowden, abandoning his usual banjo, and every bit as prone as Fuller to cheap and nasty effects. Louis Metcalf's precise, lyrical cornet features on four titles which are this disc's best performances, but not quite its saving grace. The CD's instrumental defects are the more regrettable because Jones is in great voice throughout. CS

Paul Jones (1946–2005)
VOCAL, GUITAR

Jones lived in Mississippi all his life; when not making music, he worked at a cotton gin, and from 1971 as a welder.

*** **Mule**
Fat Possum 0305 *Jones; Big Jack Johnson, Kenny Brown (g); Sam Carr (d).* 2/95.
*(*) **Pucker Up Buttercup**
Fat Possum 80328 *Jones; 'Pickle' (d).* 7/99.

Mule is credited to Paul 'Wine' Jones, a nickname which seems not to have lasted. Produced by the late Robert Palmer, it teams Jones with Frank Frost's band. The songs are set to hypnotic riffs, with minimal harmonic movement; their lyrics, even those with recognizable antecedents, like 'Diggin' Momma's Taters' or 'Coal Black Mare', are built from fragments, repeated with slight variation. Textural interest is created by the use of slide, and – less attractively – wah-wah. This is Mississippi juke-joint dance music, and on this showing Jones is one of its lesser lights, but *Mule* is still a worthwhile CD; the accompanists, and in particular the splendid Sam Carr, push Jones to the limit, and a beneficial inch beyond.

Pucker Up Buttercup was produced by Matthew Johnson after Fat Possum changed hands, and its heavy guitar distortion and ferocious drumming are typical of the label's switch to a 'new punk blues' aesthetic. Unfortunately, songs and production alike go well beyond minimal, and arrive at perfunctory. Jones himself seems uneasy with his makeover; the last track is called 'Guess I Done Fucked It All Up', but the lyric, in its entirety, is a repeated 'Guess you gonna fuck it all up'. This may not be a comment on the CD but, if it were, it would not be an unfair assessment. CS

Tutu Jones (born 1966)
VOCAL, GUITAR, DRUMS

Johnny Jones Jr was born in Dallas, the son and nephew of blues guitarists. He began playing drums as a child, and in his preteens and teens worked on the road with R. L. Griffin, Little Joe Blue and Z. Z. Hill. Blue encouraged him to work on his guitar playing, which he began to feature more in the early '80s. In the mid-'90s he received several nominations in the W. C. Handy Awards.

** **I'm For Real**
JSP JSPCD 2112 *Jones; Linny Nance (o, kb); Carl 'EG' Caldwell,* *Dan 'Preacher' Cooper (b); Anthony 'Ant' Henry, Ty Grimes (d).* 11/92, 3/94.
** **Blue Texas Soul**
Bullseye Blues CD BB 9571 *Jones; Wayne Jackson (t, tb); Andrew Love (ts); Linny Nance (kb); Ron Levy (o, p); Sammy Rayhoney (g); Carl Caldwell (b); Brent Nance (d).* 96.
** **Staying Power**
Bullseye Blues CD BB 9611 *As above, except add Marvin Washington (p), Sheila White Jones (v); omit Levy.* 98.

Jones produced *I'm For Real* himself, so there was no one to suggest that the title track might be redone without fingering errors, or that this and the opening track, 'Sweet Woman', could profit from more elaborate lyrics than a single verse repeated three or four times. Some of the other songs on the album (which are all mysteriously credited to 'Jonhny [sic] Livingstone') are a little better written, but seldom well enough to be interesting. That this poverty of imagination was not just first-album nerves is made clear by its successor, where polished arrangements fail to conceal the dullness of Jones's compositions like 'It's Been A Mistake' and 'I've Been Loving You'. *Blue Texas Soul* also deepens the impression left by its forerunner that Jones is a facile guitarist, approximately three parts Albert King to one of Albert Collins, with an undeveloped sense of dynamic variation.

For *Staying Power* Jones was again his own sole producer and wrote all the songs, but by then he had learned something about both roles and the album is reasonably successful on those and other fronts, though the TV-music arranger's clichés that spotted *Blue Texas Soul* have not all been rubbed away, and the instrumental 'Romance Avenue' is little more than smooth-jazz doodling. But whether singing, playing or writing, Jones has yet to speak in an original voice. TR

Charley Jordan (c. 1890–1954)
VOCAL, GUITAR

Jordan found his way from Arkansas to St Louis in the mid-'20s and remained there for the rest of his life. When not playing music he worked as a bootlegger and in the course of that business was shot in the spine and permanently disabled. As well as recording quite prolifically for several years, he is credited with composing numerous blues for his friend Peetie Wheatstraw and other artists, and occasionally served record companies as a talent scout or fixer.

*** **Charley Jordan – Vol. 1 (1930–1931)**
Document DOCD-5097 *Jordan; Peetie Wheatstraw (p); St Louis Bessie (Bessie Mae Smith) (v).* 6/30–3/31.
*** **Charley Jordan – Vol. 2 (1931–1934)**
Document DOCD-5098 *Jordan; unknown (cl, s); Peetie Wheatstraw (p); unknown (vn); 'Hi' Henry Brown (g, v); unknown (traps).* 9/31–8/34.
(*) **Charley Jordan – Vol. 3 (1935–1937)
Document DOCD-5099 *Jordan; Peetie Wheatstraw (p); unknown (b); Verdi Lee, Mary Harris (v).* 10/35–11/37.

Jordan's highish voice was best suited to jocular songs like 'Keep It Clean', of which he recorded four versions, or to the caustic humour of 'Starvation Blues': 'Now I almost had a square meal the other day, But the garbage man come, and he moved the can away.' The subject of hard times was common in his work, as titles like 'Hungry Blues', 'Tough Times Blues' and 'Tight Time Blues' attest, but his compositions on other themes are often equally focused

('Greyhound Blues', 'Workingman's Blues') and he appears to have taken unusual care to write unusual lyrics.

The skipping rhythms of his recordings with solo guitar such as 'Keep It Clean', 'Dollar Bill Blues', 'Hunkie Tunkie Blues' or 'Just A Spoonful', all found on *Vol. 1*, tended to become more military when he was joined by the pianist Peetie Wheatstraw. Jordan dominates the duet to great effect in the unusual tune of 'You Run And Tell Your Daddy', but generally the two men make measured and deliberate music, somewhat in the spirit of Leroy Carr and Scrapper Blackwell, which at times becomes too formulaic for its own good, as in the four tracks, barely distinguishable in melody and tempo, that open *Vol. 2*. What earns that CD an unbracketed third star is the remarkable sextet of blues by 'Hi' Henry Brown, a grumpy-sounding singer with some unusual preoccupations – a 'Hospital Blues' about graverobbing; a 'Titanic Blues' notable for its bleakly unmoralizing standpoint – which are dramatized by the intricate guitar duetting and Jordan's adventurous lead lines.

Vol. 3 first shifts the spotlight away from Jordan's singing by presenting five sides on which he accompanies the vocalists Verdi Lee or Mary Harris; the latter's 'No Christmas Blues' and 'Happy New Year Blues' make a particularly absorbing coupling. For almost half the CD Jordan is off the stage altogether: the four 1935 recordings by singer Leroy Henderson are accompanied by Wheatstraw and Casey Bill Weldon, with any further guitar playing probably by Teddy Darby, while the seven tracks credited to The Two Charlies, even though one of them is named Charlie Jordan, plainly originate from somewhere other than St Louis, possibly southwestern Virginia or east Tennessee. But they are well-executed blues with some very pretty guitar breaks, and form an agreeable intermission in the Jordan programme.

Readers more taken with Jordan's guitar playing than with his songs might be content with the eight carefully chosen and well remastered sides, plus the four by 'Hi' Henry Brown, that are evenly divided between *St. Louis Town 1929–1933* (Yazoo 1003) and *St. Louis Blues 1929–1935* (Yazoo 1030). A largely similar selection of seven tracks can be found on *St Louis Blues (1929–37)* (Wolf WSE 110) alongside work by Henry Townsend and Henry Spaulding. TR

Louis Jordan (1908–75)
VOCAL, CLARINET, ALTO AND BARITONE SAXOPHONES

Tutored by his father Jim, Louis Jordan played saxophone in his teens with the Rabbit Foot Minstrels. In his 20s, after working for local Arkansas bands, he moved to New York, recorded with Clarence Williams and joined Chick Webb's orchestra. In 1938 he created his Tympany Five and secured a residency at the Elks Rendezvous club in Harlem. Over the next few years, recording frequently for Decca and playing in theatres and nightclubs across the country, he became one of the biggest draws in black entertainment, and during the '40s he had many R&B chart hits, recorded duets with Louis Armstrong, Ella Fitzgerald and Bing Crosby, and appeared in numerous feature films and shorts. He continued to tour and record, though without the same success, through the '50s, and, although sidelined by rock in the '60s, saw a revival of interest in his music in his last years.

(*) Louis Jordan & His Tympany Five 1934–1940
Classics 636 *Jordan; Courtney Williams (t); Stafford Simon (cl, ts, fl); Lemuel Johnson, Kenneth Hollon (cl, ts); Clarence Johnson, Arnold Thomas (p); Charlie Drayton (b); Walter Martin (d); Rodney Sturgis, Yack Taylor, Daisy Winchester, Mabel Robinson (v). 34–3/40.*

*** **Louis Jordan & His Tympany Five 1940–1941**
Classics 663 *Jordan; Courtney Williams, Freddy Webster, poss. Kenneth Roane, Eddie Roane (t); Stafford Simon, Kenneth Hollon (cl, ts); Arnold Thomas (p); Charlie Drayton, Henry Turner, Dallas Bartley (b); Walter Martin (d). 4/40–11/41.*

*** **Louis Jordan & His Tympany Five 1941–1943**
Classics 741 *Jordan; Eddie Roane (t); Arnold Thomas (p); Dallas Bartley, Jesse 'Po' Simpkins (b); Walter Martin, Shadow Wilson (d); band (v). 11/41–10/43.*

*** **Louis Jordan & His Tympany Five 1943–1945**
Classics 866 *Jordan; Eddie Roane, Leonard Graham, Aaron Izenhall (t); Freddie Simon, Joshua Jackson (ts); Arnold Thomas, William Austin, Bill Davis (p); Carl Hogan (g); Jesse Simpkins, Al Morgan (b); Shadow Wilson, Slick Jones, Razz Mitchell, Eddie Byrd (d); Bing Crosby (v). 11/43–7/45.*

*** **Louis Jordan & His Tympany Five 1945–1946**
Classics 921 *Jordan; Aaron Izenhall (t); Joshua Jackson, James Wright (ts); Bill Davis (p); Carl Hogan (g); Jesse Simpkins (b); Eddie Byrd, Christopher Columbus [Joe Morris] (d); Harry Dial, Vic Lourie (perc); Ella Fitzgerald (v). 7/45–10/46.*

*** **Louis Jordan & His Tympany Five 1946–1947**
Classics 1010 *Jordan; Aaron Izenhall (t); James Wright, Eddie Johnson (ts); Bill Davis, Bill Doggett (p); Carl Hogan (g); Jesse Simpkins, Dallas Bartley (b); Christopher Columbus [Joe Morris] (d); The Calypso Boys (perc). 10/46–12/47.*

*** **Louis Jordan & His Tympany Five 1947–1949**
Classics 1134 *Jordan; Aaron Izenhall, Bob Mitchell, Harold Mitchell (t); Eddie Johnson, Josh Jackson (ts); Bill Davis, Bill Doggett (p); Carl Hogan, Ham Jackson (g); Dallas Bartley, Billy Hadnott (b); Christopher Columbus [Joe Morris] (d); unknown (perc); Martha Davis, Ella Fitzgerald (v). 12/47–8/49.*

*** **Louis Jordan & His Tympany Five 1950–1951**
Classics 1238 *Jordan; Louis Armstrong (t, v); Aaron Izenhall (t); Joshua Jackson (ts); unknown (bs); Wild Bill Davis (o); Bill Doggett, poss. Hank Jones (p); Bill Jennings (g, perc); John Collins (g); Bob Bushnell, Ray Brown (b); Christopher Columbus [Joe Morris], Charlie Smith (d); unknown (perc); Ella Fitzgerald (v). 6/50–3/51.*

*** **Complete 1950/52 Decca Recordings**
Definitive DRCD 11226 2CD *Similar to above. 6/50–2/53.*

**** **Louis Jordan and the Tympany Five**
JSP JSPCD 905 5CD *As for all Classics CDs. 12/38–12/50.*

***(*) **Jivin' With Jordan**
Proper PROPERBOX 47 4CD *As for all Classics CDs, except add Emmett Perry, Harold 'Money' Johnson (t), Leon Comegys, Bob Burgess, Alfred Cobbs (tb), Oliver Nelson (as), Reuben Phillips, Irving 'Skinny' Brown (ts), Marty Flax, Numa 'Pee Wee' Moore (bs), Jimmy Peterson, John Malachi (p). 12/38–11/51.*

♛ **** **Let The Good Times Roll**
Bear Family BCD 15557 8CD + LP *As above, except add Maxwell Davis, Lowell 'Count' Hastings (ts), Earl Warren (bs), Chester Lane (p), Bert Payne (g), Thurber Jay (b), Charlie Rice, Johnny Kirkwood (d), Nelson Riddle Orchestra, Valli Ford (v). 12/38–1/54.*

For many years Louis Jordan was an anomaly in the literature of African-American music. His work before 1943 is listed not in *B&GR* but in *Jazz Records*, yet he has no entry in *The Penguin Guide To Jazz Recordings*. He has been patronized by jazz critics as an agreeable entertainer, and left in the cold by blues enthusiasts searching for backstreet or downhome authenticity. Yet his music has persistently refused to fade away; on the contrary, it has been recharged by revivals of interest in jump blues and swing. In today's more liberal critical climate, he stands secure in his reputation as one of the incontestably great figures of the last century, a raunchy yet sophisticated MC at the endless party of African-American music.

If his genius is enshrined in the tiny, expertly written sitcoms of 'Saturday Night Fish Fry', 'Ain't Nobody Here But Us Chickens' and 'Beware', it is evident too in his incomparable versatility: with equal expertise and gusto he delivered ruminative blues like 'I'm Gonna Move To The Outskirts Of Town', the mock-Caribbean 'Stone Cold Dead In De Market', the wartime hip talk of 'G.I. Jive' (a wonderful Johnny Mercer lyric), even the cosmopolitan crooning of 'Azure-Te (Paris Blues)'.

It's absorbing to listen to Jordan's first four years of recording and see a conventional swing vocalist slowly transform himself into a jivemeister. 'At The Swing Cat's Ball' (1939) is not very different from later celebrations of good times, but Jordan has still to acquire the good-humoured authority that would elevate him to an arbiter of hip. 'You Ain't Nowhere' hints at his dexterity with the language of cool, but is delivered with the detachment of the incidental vocalist. In fact, in most of his 1938–39 sides Jordan is still anchored in '30s swing – but then, early in 1940, he cuts 'June Tenth [sic Juneteenth] Jamboree', a melodic draft of 'Five Guys Named Moe', and soon afterwards 'You Run Your Mouth And I'll Run My Business' and 'Chicken Ain't Nothing But A Bird', first in a long line of poultry patter-songs. He's on his way, though he can still wander off into Disneyland after 'Two Little Squirrels' or go all Cab Calloway in 'Do You Call That A Buddy?' It's perhaps in his last prewar session that it all comes together, in the mock melancholy of 'What's The Use Of Getting Sober (When You Gonna Get Drunk Again?)' and the inspired nonsense of 'Five Guys Named Moe'. Then come those fabulous years in the mid-'40s, the era of 'Caldonia', 'Choo Choo Ch'Boogie' and 'Barnyard Boogie' (more chickens), of 'Boogie Woogie Blue Plate', the best song ever to include the word 'spigot', and of 'Let The Good Times Roll', the national anthem of Euphoria.

Classics make their usual deliberate foray through this exhilarating landscape. *1934–1940* commences with four Jordan vocals for other leaders, then three by his band backing the singer Rodney Sturgis; subsequent CDs take in not only the Decca recordings but V-Discs and transcriptions (see below for more on these). The Definitive 2CD covers similar (but not identical) ground to Classics' *1950–1951*, then carries on (despite its title) to 2/53.

Of the boxed sets, Bear Family's is the best by a long distance. It contains Jordan's entire Decca output over 16 years, consisting of more than 200 songs, on eight CDs (with the seven duets with Ella Fitzgerald cordoned off, for legal reasons, on a bonus LP), the package enhanced by an excellent and copiously illustrated booklet. As so often with this label, it is hard to conceive how the job could have been done much better. Such comprehensiveness and rigorous quality control, however, do not come cheap, and inevitably this expensive set has generated budget-priced abridgements on Proper and JSP. The JSP, with 131 tracks, is virtually complete as far as it goes but stops three years short of the Bear Family; the Proper, with 109, is somewhat selective.

***(*) **Louis Jordan**
Masters Of Jazz R2CD 8025 2CD *As for relevant CDs above.* 12/38–12/47.

***(*) **The Anthology**
Universal MCAD 211907 2CD *Similar to above.* 12/38–5/53.

*** **Louis Jordan & His Tympany Five Vol. 1 1939/44**
EPM Jazz Archives 15837 *Similar to above.* 3/39–44.

***(*) **Man Alive – It's The Jumping Jive**
Avid AMSC 674 2CD *Similar to above.* 3/39–12/47.

***(*) **Let The Good Times Roll**
Pie PIESD 172 *Similar to above.* 3/39–8/49.

*** **Let The Good Times Roll!**
Coolnote PWKS 4251 *Similar to above.* 3/39–8/49.

*** **Louis Jordan 1938–1950**
Frémeaux FA 5017 2CD *Similar to above.* 3/39–8/50.

***(*) **Jumpin' And Jivin'**
Snapper Recall SMDCD 520 2CD *Similar to above.* 3/39–12/50.

*** **The Father Of Rhythm 'N Blues & Rock 'N Roll**
Saga Jazz 0664572 *Similar to above.* 39–52.

(***) **Swingsation**
GRP 059 951//GRD-9951 *Similar to above.* 3/39–5/53.

*** **At The Swing Cat's Ball**
MCA MCAD 12044 *Similar to above.* 3/39–1/54.

***(*) **Choo Choo Ch'Boogie**
Living Era CD AJA 5296 *Similar to above.* 11/41–4/47.

*** **Five Guys Named Moe**
Prism Leisure PLATCD 277 *Similar to above.* 11/41–11/47.

***(*) **Saturday Night Fish Fry**
Jasmine JASMCD 2561 *Similar to above.* 11/41–8/49.

*** **The Best Of Louis Jordan**
MCA 324079 *Similar to above.* 11/41–1/54.

***(*) **Five Guys Named Moe**
MCA MCLD 19048 *Similar to above.* 7/42–8/49.

(***) **The Essential Collection**
Spectrum 544 328 *Similar to above.* 7/42–5/53.

(***) **The Very Best Of Louis Jordan**
Music Club MCCD 085 *Similar to above.* 7/42–5/53.

(***) **The Best Of/20th Century Masters/The Millenium Collection**
MCA 088 112 065 *Similar to above.* 7/42–5/53.

*** **Louis Jordan & His Tympany Five Vol. 2 1945/51**
EPM Jazz Archives 16035 *Similar to above.* 1/45–11/51.

The enduring appeal of Jordan's music, latterly promoted to a general audience by the long-running stage show based on it, *Five Guys Named Moe*, has ensured widespread coverage, often on mid- and budget-priced CDs. There seems to be general agreement on ten or a dozen sides that are all but indispensable, and 'Ain't Nobody's Here But Us Chickens', 'Choo Choo Ch'Boogie', 'Five Guys Named Moe', 'Is You Is Or Is You Ain't (My Baby)', 'Let The Good Times Roll' and 'What's The Use Of Getting Sober', among others, will be found on most of the selective albums listed above. The reader who reckons to be satisfied with one representative set can choose without hesitation from the 2CDs on Masters Of Jazz, MCA (*The Anthology*), Avid and Snapper Recall, which all have 40 or more tracks, or the single CDs on Pie, Coolnote, Saga Jazz, Living Era, Prism, Jasmine and MCA (*Best Of*, *Five Guys Named Moe*), which have at least 20. Small differences in the ratings for these albums indicate the quality of presentation or notes. Albums rated (***) are fine as far as they go but, with fewer than 20 tracks, don't offer comparable value.

**(*) On Film
Krazy Kat KKCD 17 *Jordan; Eddie Roane, Aaron Izenhall (t); James Wright, Eddie Johnson, Paul Quinichette (ts); Arnold Thomas, William Austin, Bill Davis, Bill Doggett (p); Carl Hogan, James Jackson (g); Dallas Bartley, Jesse Simpkins, Al Morgan, Billy Hadnott (b); Walter Martin, Shadow Wilson, Slick Jones, Razz Mitchell, Christopher Columbus [Joe Morris] (d). 42–2/48.*

This carefully retrieves Jordan's music for the movies *Caldonia, Reet Petite & Gone* and *Look Out Sister* and some short features. Almost all the songs can be found among his disc recordings, but the soundtrack versions are sometimes extremely lively, and it's a pity the sound quality makes them arduous to listen to.

**(*) The V-Disc Recordings
Collectors Choice WSCCM 66612 *Jordan; Eddie Roane, Leonard Graham (t); Freddie Simon (ts); Arnold Thomas, William Austin (p); Jesse Simpkins, Al Morgan (b); Shadow Wilson, Razz Mitchell (d). 11/43–7/45.*

*** The 'V' Discs & More
[Zircon Bleu 514] *As above, except add Aaron Izenhall (t), Josh Jackson, James Wright, Eddie Johnson (ts); Bill Davis, Bill Doggett (p); Carl Hogan (g); Dallas Bartley (b); Eddie Byrd, Christopher Columbus [Joe Morris] (d). 11/43–12/47.*

In the last couple of years of World War II Jordan rerecorded some of his more popular numbers on V-Discs, for consumption by US troops overseas. He added a couple of spoken introductions addressed to listening service personnel, but didn't stray far from the arrangements he had already used. He did, however, throw in a few songs that he didn't record elsewhere, like 'Nobody But Me' and the blues 'The End Of My Worry', thereby commending these albums to completists. Collectors Choice gather the 14 V-Disc sides and leave it at that, while Zircon augment them with 11 Deccas from approximately the same period.

**(*) Jumpin' And Jivin' At Jubilee
Collectors Choice CCM 10352 *Jordan; Eddie Roane (t); Arnold Thomas (p); Jesse Simpkins, Al Morgan (b); Shadow Wilson, Slick Jones (d); band (v). c. 9/43–c. 5/44.*

**(*) Live Jive
A Touch Of Magic DATOM 4 *Jordan; Eddie Roane, Aaron Izenhall (t); James Wright, Josh Jackson (ts); Arnold Thomas, Bill Davis, Bill Doggett (p); Bill Jennings (g); Al Morgan, Jesse Simpkins, Bob Bushnell (b); Slick Jones, Christopher Columbus [Joe Morris] (d); Bixie Crawford (v). c. 44–c. 6/49.*

**(*) Louis Jordan & His Tympany Five
Storyville 2012080 *As above. c. 44–c. 6/49.*

These too document Jordan's contribution to maintaining military morale overseas, being derived from transcriptions made for the Armed Forces Radio Service. Proved repertoire naturally predominates, and the recording quality isn't up to Decca's, so these are essential only to serious collectors, who need to be aware that Collectors Choice offer only ten tracks (though at least a couple are medleys), while the other two CDs duplicate each other extensively. Storyville's, with 23 tracks to *Live Jive*'s 17, is the better buy.

*** 1944–1945
Circle 53 *As for The 'V' Discs & More, except add Slick Jones (d); omit Doggett, Bartley, Columbus. 1/44–7/45.*

Unlike the AFRS material and some of the V-Discs, these recordings from the World transcription company have survived in excellent condition. They also embrace a bunch of songs Jordan didn't put on any other records, such as the instrumentals 'Re-Bop' and 'Sweatin' On Swing Street', and the blues 'Paper Boy'.

** Rock & Roll Call
Bluebird 66145 *Jordan; Bob Mitchell (t); Reuben Phillips (as); Seldon Powell, Lowell 'Count' Hastings (ts); Haywood Henry (bs); John Kirkwood (s, d); Maurice Simon, Jerome Richardson, Dave McRae (s); Chester Lane (p); Olivette Miller (harp); Bert Payne (g); Thurber Jay, Lewis Albert Martin (b); Frank Grillo, Hindai Butts (d); Francisco Pozo, Rafael Miranda (perc); Debbie Smith (v). 3/55–4/56.*

The trajectory of Jordan's recording career sometimes wobbled after he left Decca. His spell with Aladdin, tidily documented by *The Complete Aladdin Sessions* (EMI CDP 96567, deleted), found him as funny and feisty as ever, albeit with a little less punch, since the recording engineers emphasized singer over band. His subsequent year with RCA's Vik label was largely spent on trivial pop-R&B provided by house writers. Sometimes, as in 'Whatever Lola Wants (Lola Gets)' the R&B element disappeared altogether. *Rock & Roll Call* is therefore for heavy-duty Jordanists only.

*** No Moe!: The Greatest Hits
Verve 512 523 *Jordan; Ernie Royal (t); Jimmy Cleveland (tb); Budd Johnson (ts, bs); Sam 'The Man' Taylor, Austin Powell (ts); Jackie Davis (o); Ernie Hayes (p); Mickey Baker, Irving Ashby (g); Wendell Marshall, Billy Hadnott (b); Charlie Persip, Marvin Oliver (d); Francisco Pozo (bgo). 10/56, 8/57.*

Jordan spent much of his time with Mercury re-creating his hits, but the quality of the accompanying musicians guarantees that the versions of 'Caldonia', 'Salt Pork West Virginia' and so forth are unfailingly bright. Standards like 'Sunday' and 'Sweet Lorraine' refresh the repertoire. The bulk of the 16 tracks come from the much better '56 session, produced by Quincy Jones.

**(*) Louis Jordan & Chris Barber
Black Lion BLCD 760156 *Jordan; Pat Halcox (t); Chris Barber (tb); Ian Wheeler (cl, as); Eddie Smith (bj); Dick Smith (b); Graham Burbidge (d). 9/62.*

The last thing you expect to hear on a Louis Jordan record is a banjo, and at times the trad-jazz setting created by the Barber band seems slightly at odds with the spirit of Jordan's music, but overall this is a personable collaboration that gives familiar pieces like 'Choo Choo Ch'Boogie' a new paint job without altering their general appearance, and allows Jordan to blow with a little more freedom than usual. There isn't much of it, though: Jordan's nine tracks occupy less than half an hour. The remaining five are roughly contemporary recordings by the Barber band.

*(*) One Sided Love Then Sakatumi
Connoisseur VSOP CD 324 *Jordan; Julius 'Billy' Brooks, Herbert Anderson, unknowns (t); unknowns (tb); Teddy Edwards, unknown (ts); unknown (bs); unknown (fl); John Houston (p); unknowns (strings); unknowns (g); Dallas Bartley, unknown (b);*

Billy Moore, unknown (d); unknown (tamb); unknown (v). 12/68–69.

This set was produced by veteran R&B bandleader Paul Gayten, who wasted what must have been a substantial budget on absurdly rococo arrangements pasted on to trifling material like 'Watch The World', 'New Orleans And A Rusty Old Horn' and the awful 'Sakatumi'. Teddy Edwards, normally a man of sound instinct, wrote and arranged five numbers which are not much better. Luckily this was not Jordan's farewell recording.

*** **The Essential Recordings**
Purple Pyramid CLP-0962 *Jordan; Bob Mitchell (t); Irv Cox (ts); Shuggie Otis (o, p, g, b); Johnny Otis (p, d).* 72.

*** **I Believe In Music**
Evidence ECD 26006 *Jordan; Irv Cox (ts); Duke Burrell (p); Louis Myers (g); John Duke, Dave Myers (b); Archie Taylor, Fred Below (d).* 11/73.

Produced by Johnny Otis for Blues Spectrum, the session now called *The Essential Recordings* had the producer's usual agenda of re-creating the artist's hits in the spirit of the original recordings. Jordan sounds in excellent shape, and the versions of 'Choo Choo', 'Good Times', 'Fish Fry' and other golden oldies have a great deal of the spirit of three decades earlier. *I Believe In Music*, recorded when Jordan and a late-model Tympany Five were appearing in France, has less instrumental zip but does boast a handful of relatively obscure Jordania like 'Three-Handed Woman' and 'Every Knock Is A Boost'. To the original 11-track LP have been added four previously unissued instrumentals with the Myers–Myers–Below rhythm section. Louis Jordan's musical life (as presently represented on CD) thus ends not with joviality or jive but with the often forgotten side of his music, the sinewy alto playing that was admired by Charlie Parker and Sonny Rollins. TR

The Jubirt Sisters
GROUP

Ann, Carol and Lynn Jubirt grew up in Memphis, always exposed to music thanks to their mother's record collection and get-togethers with family and friends. They began singing together at school and in church and in the '80s became quite well known in the Memphis area.

** **Sing! Sister! Sing!**
High Water HMG 6515 *The Jubirt Sisters; Tim Turner (t); John Lux (cl, ts); Alan Clayton (as, ts); Wes Walker, Glenn Cashman (ts); Sal Crocker, David Joyner (bs); Frisco Jack [John Stover] (h); Thomas 'Blue' Cornes (o, p, syn); Otto 'Bobby' Carnes (o); Oscar Smith, Napoleon Dodson III, Clarence Nelson, Willie Roy Sanders (g); Jasper Bernard Dodson, Lois Brown (b); Carlton DeWitt Dodson, Rick O'Neal, Joe Hicks (d).* 3/82–1/84.

The Jubirt Sisters present themselves in the cover photograph in electric-blue satin, befringed and sequinned, clearly modelling themselves on the Pointer Sisters and rather touchingly not quite succeeding. The connection doesn't extend to their music, which is mainly blues ('Wang Dang Doodle', 'School Girl Blues', 'You Got Me Running') with a sprinkling of bluesy rock numbers like 'Proud Mary' and 'Steamroller Blues'. Female vocal trios in this area are uncommon enough to make the album appear promising, but the Jubirts' harmonies sound untextured and sometimes, thanks to poor recording balance or mixing, insubstantial. The accompaniments are commonplace, 'School Days', done in the manner of the Andrews Sisters, is incongruous and 'When The Saints Go Marching In' is, as nearly always, a mistake. TR

Andy Just
VOCAL, HARMONICA, GUITAR

Just began playing harmonica in the '70s, originally influenced by Charlie Musselwhite and later by Mark Ford. In the late '70s and '80s he led several bands in the San Francisco area and recorded three albums, moving away from the blues but returning to it in the '90s, when he joined The Ford Blues Band and played on most of their albums.

(*) **Don't Cry
Blue Rock'It BRCD 117//Crosscut CCD 11044 *Just; Ken Baker (horns); Mark Whitney (ts, bs); Noel Catura (ts); Garth Webber (g, v); Dave Gonzales, Knut Reiersrud (g); Kirk Bryant, Jamie Brewer, Danny Danero (b); Patrick Ford (d).* 93–94.

Just is an agile and imaginative harmonica player, and anyone who enjoys good blues harp should approve of the instrumentals 'The Slam' and 'Struttin' At The Rooster', the latter with jazzy accompaniment by two acoustic guitars. The title song, a Bobby Bland number, gallops along with guitarist Garth Webber flicking his whip and at barely two minutes is disappointingly short. For some listeners these may be the album's best tracks. Just's singing is well-judged on 'Don't Cry' but more often he is melodramatic, bludgeoning the lyrics of his compositions 'She's Sweet' and 'Treat Me Right', and his attempt to sing Sonny Boy Williamson II's 'Mighty Long Time' in the manner of its originator was ill-advised. TR

The JW-Jones Blues Band
GROUP

Headed by guitarist Josh Wynne-Jones (born 1981) from Ottawa and featuring Southside Steve Marriner (born 1985) on harmonica, The JW-Jones Blues Band was formed in 1998 and issued its first album two years later. Both Wynne-Jones and Marriner have won awards from Canadian blues organizations.

*** **Defibrillatin'**
Crosscut CCD 11067 *Southside Steve Marriner (h, v eff); Pierre Chrétien (o, p); JW-Jones (g, v); Nathan Morris (b); Steve Hiscox (d).* 6/02.

*** **Bogart's Bounce**
NorthernBlues NBM 00010//Crosscut CCD 11073 *Southside Steve Marriner (h, wh, v); Kim Wilson (h, v); Tortoise Blue (o); Gene Taylor (p, v); JW-Jones (g, v); Nathan Morris (b, v); Mike Ktenas (b); Matt Sobb (d, v); Roxanne Potvin (v).* 1/02.

*** **My Kind Of Evil**
NorthernBlues NBM 00021//Crosscut CCD 11082 *Rick Rangno (t); Brian Asselin, Steve Trecarten (ts); Frank Scanga (bs); Kim Wilson (h, v); Geoff Daye (o, p); JW-Jones (g, v); Nathan Morris (b); Bill Brennan (d, box); Colin James, Roxanne Potvin (v).* 1/04.

JW-Jones has extraordinarily facility and unswervingly oldfashioned taste, and a few minutes in his company on *Defibrillatin'* will explain the admiring testimonials from fellow guitarists Rick Holmstrom, Otis Grand and Alex Schultz. His primary inspiration seems to be the West Coast guitarists of the '40s and '50s and their legatees, the line from T-Bone Walker to, say, Junior Watson, but tracks like 'Batyology' (presumably one for Little Charlie) and 'Dizzy Spell', with their jazzy guitar/organ exchanges, suggest that his listening has been wide-ranging and attentive. It would be pleasant to be able to add that he's a strong singer too, but that judgement must be reserved for later. Marriner is impressive on harmonica.

Bogart's Bounce opens with an up-tempo instrumental, 'Flatline', and closes with another, 'Goldtop Groove'. The brash rock 'n' roll of the former and the softer-toned jazz of the latter enclose another set of performances in which JW-J continuously teases the listener with his stylistic versatility. Note, for example, how he builds a fire on 'Understanding A Woman' and stokes it to a blaze in his solo. His singing is still unformed, and it was wise to bring in Kim Wilson to sing the attractive 'Time To Move On'. Marriner continues to play with brio and also takes a couple of vocals. This is not quite as thrilling as *Defibrillatin'*, but no less accomplished.

Two years on, Marriner has left the group but Wilson is again on hand to produce and occasionally play on *My Kind Of Evil*, and the sound is thickened on several tracks by a four-piece horn section. The Chicago-style 'Cheating Woman', with chromatic harp and Otis Rush-like guitar, and 'Aching Pain' are balanced by romping jump-blues instrumentals like 'Slow Down' and 'Code Blue', all of them testifying to JW-J's developing talent. TR

Candye Kane
VOCAL

A former stripper and porn star, Kane is fondly remembered as a uninhibited performer on the LA punk scene of the '80s. More recently she has appeared at the Notodden and San Francisco Blues Festivals.

**(*) The Toughest Girl Alive
Bullseye Blues & Jazz 9605 *Kane; Robbie Smith (t, v); April West (tb); Bob Mathes (ts); Troy Jennings (bs); Nina Goldin (p, vb); Marcia Ball (p, v); Lisa Otey (p); Jeff Ross (Do, g); Steve Wilcox, Dave Alvin, Marco Fiume (g); Greg Willis, Larry Taylor (b); Joey Vee (d, tamb, v); Andy Paley (marimba); Scott Billington (perc); Carole Propp, Wendy Fraser, Earl Thomas (v). 99.*

Kane's USP is that she can play the piano with her breasts, but she doesn't do so here, or indeed touch it with any part of herself. Instead she concentrates on songs, mostly her own, advancing her philosophy that 'you just gotta be who you were born to be', straight, gay, dominatrix, nun, whatever. It probably doesn't play too well in the heartlands, but liberals and other urban sophisticates should get a kick out of it. As for blues fans, while some of the material may be on the periphery of their interests, tracks like 'I'm The Toughest Girl Alive', 'Let's Commit Adultery' and Julia Lee's 'Scream In The Night' are well within bounds. Kane is a spirited singer and the album is replete with shouting little-big-band arrangements featuring rambunctious horn, piano and guitar solos.

**(*) Whole Lotta Love
Ruf 1091 *Kane; Chris Tedesco (t); Nick Lane (tb); Brandon Fields (s); Charlie Musselwhite (h, g, v); R. J. Mischo (h); Steve Utstein (o); Steve Goldstein, Rev. Billy C. Wirtz, Nic. ten Broek (p); Kyle Jester (g, v); Jeff Ross (g); Larry Taylor, Bryan Ugartechea (b); Richie Hayward, Paul Fasulo (d); Liz Hooper, Jenny Meltzer (v). 03.*

**(*) White Trash Girl
Ruf 1084 *Kane; Gary Slechta (t, v); Randy Zimmerman (tb, v); Mark 'Kaz' Kazanoff, John Mills (s, v); Gary Primich (h); Riley Osbourn (kb, o, p); Jeff Ross, Johnny Moeller, David Grissom (g); Preston Hubbard (b); Damien Llanes (d); Thomas Ruf, Andrew Halbreich, Adam Brauer (v). 11–12/04.*

Whole Lotta Love has less of Kane's own material, and gives a little less sense of her as an outré character, but it permits a broader display of her skill as a blues and near-blues singer, in a well-chosen programme that embraces Billy Valentine's Jordanesque 'Fit, Fat And Fine', Willie Dixon's 'Whola Lotta Love', Etta James's 'Something's Got A Hold On Me' (a storming opener) and Big Bill Broonzy's 'What's That I Smell?' – the last done as a duet with Charlie Musselwhite (acoustic guitar and responses) that amusingly echoes Memphis Minnie & Kansas Joe.

White Trash Girl restores the predominance of Kane's compositions, and in the title track and 'Misunderstood' she again states her case that people should be valued for what they are rather than devalued by stereotyping. 'Masturbation Blues' needed to be a better song to deserve the notice its title may earn it, but a strong reading of Bull Moose Jackson's 'Big Fat Mamas Are Back In Style' and other fervent performances confirm that Kane is not just a novelty act, and the bustling accompaniments push her to deliver a likeable set of party music.

Kane's previous CDs, which include *Home Cookin'* (1994), *Knock Out* (1995) and *Diva La Grande* (1996) for Antone's and *Swango* (1999) for Sire, may be available from <www.candyekane.com>. TR

Keb' Mo' (born 1951)
VOCAL, GUITAR, BANJO, MANDOLIN, BASS, HARMONICA

Kevin Moore served a long apprenticeship during several incarnations in LA bands, including Papa John Creach's, and vocal groups, all the while honing his songwriting skills. He was drawn towards blues and his stage name was coined for those times he played it onstage. He played bluesmen in the plays Rabbit Foot, Spunk *and* Lost Highway *and was seen as Robert Johnson in the film* Can't You Hear The Wind Howl. *Despite appearing at blues festivals with the likes of Robert Lockwood and Honeyboy Edwards, he remains a successful songwriter working within a blues context rather than a blues musician.*

***(*) Keb' Mo'
OKeh 478173 *Keb' Mo'; Tommy Eyre (o, p); James Hutchinson (b); Laval Belle, Quentin Dennard (d); Tony Braunagel (perc). 94.*

This album's austere artwork belies the attractiveness of its contents. Split between solo turns and sparse group accompaniments, these 11 originals and two Robert Johnson songs reveal a musician of taste and ingenuity. 'Love Blues', 'Angelina' and 'Dirty Low Down And Bad' are 12-bar blues but 'Every Morning' and 'She Just Loves To Dance' function well within the milieu. Mo's background in popular music is evident in 'Anybody Seen My Girl' and others, which can sound earnest by comparison. There's warmth and personality in his vocals and originality in his finger-style and slide guitar work. The backing musicians contribute as much colour as they do rhythm, lending a sculpted sound to each track on which they're present. This is blues as entertainment and Keb' Mo' disguises his love for the music with his thorough professionalism.

**(*) Just Like You
OKeh/Epic 67316//(E) 484117 *As above, except Munyungo Jackson (perc) replaces Braunagel; add Darrell Leonard (t), Jim Price (tb), Jim Gordon (cl), Larry Davis (h), Tommy Eyre (11-string g), John Porter (Do), Ricky Fataar (d), Jackie Ferris, Jean McClain, Bonnie Raitt, Jackson Browne (v). 96.*

Apart from an intriguing arrangement of Robert Johnson's 'Last Fair Deal Gone Down', there's little blues in evidence, despite 'Perpetual Blues Machine'. The presence of Raitt and Browne hints at the freeway fare – 'More Than One Way Home', 'Just Like You', 'The Action' – which this record dispenses. Homilies like 'Momma, Where's My Daddy' and 'Lullaby Baby Blues' stop just short of the cloyingly sentimental, and earnestness, leavened with a little humour, returns with 'I'm On Your Side' and 'You Can Love Yourself'. Despite comparable musicianship, this set lacks the firm character of the previous album. Instead of challenging his audience, the artist here backs off and massages their complacency.

** Slow Down
OKeh/Epic/550 Music 69376//(E) 491613 *Keb' Mo'; Reggie Young (tb); Gerald Albright (ts); Joellen Friedkin (ac, kb, syn); John Barnes, John Lewis Parker (kb); Colin Linden (md, g); Anders Osborne (g, v); Reggie McBride (b); Laval Belle (d); Munyungo Jackson (perc); Sir Harry Bowens, Sweet Pea Atkinson, Lisa Linson (v). 98.*

** The Door
OKeh/Epic/550 Music BK 61428//(E) 501000 *Keb' Mo'; Lewis Soloff (t); Michael Davis (tb); Lawrence Feldman (as, ts); David Mann (ts); Greg Phillinganes (kb); Scarlet Rivera (vn); Thomas Tally (vl); Gerri Sutyak (vc); Clayton Gibb (bj); Greg Leisz (sg); Reggie McBride, 'Ready' Freddie Washington (b); Steve Jordan, Sergio Gonzalez (d, perc); Jim Keltner (d); Leon Ware, Marva Kicks, James 'D-Train' Williams, Dennis Collins (v). 00.*

In the context of this book, *Slow Down* is the album in which Kevin Moore fingerpops his way further down the freeway towards anonymity. Keb' Mo' is fleetingly present in Robert Johnson's 'Love In Vain', the opening 'Muddy Water' and 'Everything I Need' but for the most part this is very ordinary music-making, designed for Californian FM radio. Unlike previous albums, all the original songs are collaborations, subject to the compromises that committees impose. Moore's voice remains expressive, even when delivering banal lyrics that too often embrace clichés like 'I can hear the Delta calling'. Unfortunately, it seems that Keb' Mo' is in full retreat from the unique persona of his initial success.

Like its predecessor, *The Door* has little to do with blues apart from an attempt to turn 'It Hurts Me Too' into a rock anthem. The mixture is very much as before: tastefully arranged songs, some like 'It's All Coming Back' and 'Gimme What You Got' with gentle humour, others ('Loola Loo', 'Don't You Know') too cutesy for their own good, and then the oleaginous 'Mommy Can I Come Home'. Each song has a warm, intimate sound and the backing musicians never exceed their remit. Mo's voice is in itself an attractive instrument but his appetite for whimsy defeats his previous musical stance. NS

*** Martin Scorsese Presents The Blues: Keb' Mo'
OKeh/Epic/Legacy EK 90496//(E) 512577 *Keb' Mo'; Tommy Eyre, Joellen Friedkin, Greg Phillinganes (kb); Colin Linden (g); James 'Hutch' Hutchinson, Reggie McBride, Nathan East (b); Steve Jordan (d, perc); Laval Belle, Jim Keltner, Ricky Lawson (d); Tony Braunagel, Munyungo Jackson (perc). 94–00.*

A handy summary of Keb' Mo' so fa', tallying six tracks from *Keb' Mo'*, three from *Just Like You*, four from *Slow Down* and one from *The Door*, plus 'Crapped Out Again' from the soundtrack of *Tin Cup* and 'Peace Of Mind', recorded for Scorsese's TV series *The Blues*.

**(*) Keep It Simple
OKeh/Epic EK 86408//(E) 515297 *Keb' Mo'; Jeff Paris (h, kb, o, p, md); Greg Phillinganes (kb, p); John Hobbs (kb); Andrea Zonn (vn, v); Sam Bush (md); Paul Franklin (Do); Robert Cray, Robben Ford, John Porter (g); Reggie McBride, Nathan East, Willie Weeks (b); Ricky Lawson, Steve Ferrone, Chad Cromwell (d); Munyungo Jackson (perc); Alex Brown, Bobette Jamison-Harrison, Phillip Ingram, Shannon Curfman, Vince Gill, Amy Grant (v). 04.*

… and simple it is, the songs gloved in suede arrangements for guitars, rhythm and tinkling keyboards, with now and then a hint of mandolin or banjo. If you were having a lingering lunch on your deck in Mendocino, looking out over the sunny Pacific, this featherlight music would be its perfect accompaniment. If you live in Akron or Accrington, creating that ambience may take a little imagination. In terms of the blues, Mo' still has them – this may be his bluesiest album since *Keb' Mo'* – but they are distinctly 21st-century blues, concerned with house-buying in California, holidays in France, cable TV, the menu at Starbucks. 'My bills are paid and my checks don't bounce,' he sings in 'Prosperity Blues'. 'I can't even crack a frown, since the blues slipped out of town.' But probably just for a weekend at the beach. TR

Jack Kelly (c. 1900–1960)
VOCAL, GUITAR

Kelly is believed to have been from north Mississippi but spent most of his adult life in Memphis, where he sang on the streets and associated with musicians such as Frank Stokes, Dan Sane and Will Batts and later Little Buddy Doyle and Walter Horton.

*** Jack Kelly & His South Memphis Jug Band (1933–1939)
RST Blues Documents BDCD-6005 *Kelly; Will Batts (vn, prob. g, v); Dan Sane, Little Son Joe (g); 'Doctor' D. M. Higgs (j, v). 8/33, 7/39.*

Of the 14 sides recorded by the South Memphis Jug Band in 1933, all included here, eight have Kelly as singer. All are blues cut from much the same pattern, in which the hoarse vocals are potently accompanied by Kelly's and Sane's guitars, Higgs's jug and Batts's fiddle. 'Policy Rag' and 'Doctor Medicine', also by that quartet, are brisker blues performances, primarily instrumental but scattered with remarks by Higgs and asides by some of the others. The remaining four sides are sung by

Batts with two guitars, one Kelly's and the other probably his own; again, there is not much melodic variation, but the guitar lines are skilfully interwoven and the mood of the performances is gripping. The rest of the album is the output of a 1939 session by Kelly with Batts and Little Son Joe. Little has changed in six years: Kelly's interest in food, expressed earlier in 'Red Ripe Tomatoes', is renewed in 'Neck Bone Blues' and the references to steak in 'Joe Louis Special', and only in the up-tempo 'You Done Done It' does he stray from his favourite slow blues tune. Batts continues to play with limited technical resources but impeccable blues phrasing.

Kelly's last known recordings were in 1952 with Walter Horton for the then new Sun label, but no complete copy of the disc credited to 'Jackie Boy & Little Walter' has yet been found. TR

Jo Ann Kelly (1944–90)
VOCAL, GUITAR

A blues fan from her teens, the London-born Kelly began singing and playing in clubs in the '60s, a career path she maintained for the rest of her life, though latterly more in continental Europe than in Britain. Originally a solo performer in the 'country blues' idiom, she later experimented with other genres and in various group settings.

*** Black Rat Swing: The Collectors' Jo Ann Kelly
Castle CMDDD 596 2CD *Kelly; Chris Trengrove, Dave Brooks, Andy McDonald (s); Steve Rye, Paul Rowan, Wolfie Witcher (h); Geraint Watkins (ac); John Stevens (kb); Bob Hall (p, md); Dick Wellstood (p); Dave Kelly, Tony McPhee, Simon Prager, Pete Emery, Adrian Pietryga, Danny Kirwan, Phil Taylor, Steve Donnelly (g); Iain Thompson, Bob Brunning, Lucas Lindholm, Tony Ellis, Dave Suttle (b); John Dummer, Pete Miles, Keef Hartley, Rolf Ahrens (d); The Kokomo Singers (v).* 66–88.

*** Blues & Gospel: Rare & Unreleased Recordings
Blues Matters BMRCD 20041 *Kelly; Andy McDonald, Laura Sanders (s); Steve Rye, Wolfie Witcher (h); Alan Dunn (kb); Gil Kodyline, Bob Hall (p); Stefan Grossman, Sammy Mitchell, Tom McGuinness, Phil Taylor (g); Tony Ellis (b); Mel Wright (d); The Morrison Singers (Jackie & Donna) (v).* late 67–3/84.

Kelly was a wonderful interpreter of acoustic guitar blues, especially the songs of her idol Memphis Minnie like 'Nothin' In Rambling', but the lovingly gathered tapes on *Black Rat Swing* also reveal her as a convincing singer of tough Chicago-style blues ('I Can't Quit You Baby'), Southern soul ('Feel Like Breaking Up Somebody's Home') and unaccompanied field hollers ('Rising Sun Shine On'). The home recordings and demo tapes, which span her entire professional career, are often lo-fi – it isn't only her remarkable performance of the unaccompanied 'Levee Camp Holler' but the wavering quality of the tape that makes it sound like a Library of Congress field recording – but Kelly's commitment to her music is often spellbinding. This set comprises most of the deleted Mooncrest CDs *Key To The Highway*, *Talkin' Low* and *Tramp 1974*.

Blues & Gospel earns the 'Rare' of its subtitle by starting with four songs from a limited-edition EP; the remaining dozen tracks include five from a London concert with Stefan Grossman, their only recorded meeting, and a couple with Mel Wright's Quaggy Delta Blues Band, the whole package lovingly annotated by Peter Moody. If you have enjoyed retracing Kelly's career on *Black Rat Swing*, this will give similar pleasure.

***(*) Jo-Ann Kelly
BGO BGOCD 429 *Kelly.* c. 68.

Kelly reportedly didn't care for this album, possibly because she had only bad memories of the brouhaha with which it was promoted in the United States on its original release. As a performance – or rather a series of them, for it was recorded piecemeal – it may be her best album; certainly it's the best document of her 'country blues' side, with its absolutely confident forays into the work of Memphis Minnie, Muddy Waters, John Lee Hooker, Robert Johnson, Charlie Patton and Son House. Her voice is a blend of echoes of blues singers she admired, not a thoroughgoing imitation but thoroughly plausible.

*** Women in (E)Motion
Traditional & Moderne T&M 110 *Kelly; prob. Pete Emery (g).* 9/88.

Singing at a concert in Bremen, Germany, Kelly predictably but, as always, soulfully recalls Memphis Minnie, in 'Where My Good Man At', 'Ain't Nothin' In Ramblin' and 'Black Rat Swing'. She also applies a Barbecue Bob guitar part to a very fine version of Marshall Owens' 'Try Me One More Time', and sings a cappella on 'Death Have Mercy', Vera Hall's version of the gospel song Ralph Stanley sang so eerily in the movie *O Brother, Where Art Thou?* Her voice is less dependable on her own 'Weekend Blues' and 'Come See About Me', but she more than makes up for these few lapses with a remarkable 'God Bless The Child'. TR

Vance Kelly (born 1954)
VOCAL, GUITAR

The Chicago-born Kelly began playing in clubs in his teens, encouraged by the singer Mary Lane. He played disco in the '70s but returned to the blues at the end of the decade. From 1987 to '90 he worked with the saxophonist A. C. Reed, then went out on his own. His debut CD, Call Me, *earned him major US awards.*

***(*) Call Me
Wolf 120.877 *Kelly; Eddie Shaw (s); David Honeyboy [Edwards] (h); Erskine Johnson (kb); John Primer (g); Johnny Reed, Nick Holt, Lee Johnson (b); Rick King (d); Joan Baby, Robert Kelly (v).* 1–2/94.

*** Joyriding In The Subway
Wolf 120.886 *Kelly; Michael Jackson (s); Erskine Johnson (kb); John Primer, Grown Man, Rick King (g); Johnny Reed (b); Mark Daffender (d); Vivian Kelly (v).* 2/95.

*** Hands Off
Wolf 120.891 *Kelly; James Montgomery (tb); Charles Kimble (s); Billy Branch (h); Benny Brown (kb, v); Carl 'CC' Copeland (b, v); Mark Diffenderfer, Patrick McGee (d); Vivian Kelly, Denice Pleasant, Delores Scott (v).* 1/97.

**(*) What Three Old Ladies Can Do
Wolf 120.801 *Kelly; John Walls, Johnnie Drummer (kb); J. Parker (g); Andre McCottry, Mark Miller (b); Patrick McGee (d); Dolores Cotton, Terry Vance (v).* 10/98.

** Nobody Has The Power
Wolf 120.815 *Kelly; Edward Williams (s); Melvin Robinson, John Walls (kb, v); Mark Miller (b, v); Charles Hancock (d, v); Vivian Vance Kelly (v).* 10/03.

Kelly's debut opens rather obliquely with two Johnny Taylor songs. He does them very well, and brings similar skill later to McKinley Mitchell's 'End Of The Rainbow', but it's his handling of a conventional blues that one wants to inspect. When one arrives, his own 'Hurt So Bad', its busy guitar intro and impassioned vocal signal that his is no run-of-the-mill talent, and the message is repeated by further originals like the title song and 'Dog On A Chain'. Enviably flexible, Kelly's voice extends to both soulful pleading and an impressive throat rasp.

In terms of repertoire, Kelly's next two albums were similar assortments of attractive original songs and strong material from elsewhere, very often from soul sources. *Joyriding In The Subway*, for instance, has Jimmy Hughes's 'Steal Away' and Little Milton's 'Foot Loose & Fancy Free', and *Hands Off* compositions by Luther Ingram and Benny Lattimore. In time Kelly acquires the knack of writing effective soul numbers himself, such as 'Stay With It' on *Hands Off*.

Joyriding is a spirited follow-up to *Call Me*, and if Kelly loses his way in the tangled bedsheets of the Barry Whiteish, 'From The Heart', he finds it again in 'I Got A Blues Attitude' and 'I Can't Win From Losing'. *Hands Off* starts a little indecisively with 'Mustang Sally' and 'Little Red Rooster', songs to which Kelly brings energy but no new thoughts, but settles into a good blues groove with Johnny Laws's 'Crying For You', his own 'Bad Taste In My Mouth' and Z. Z. Hill's 'Blues Man'. Unsupported by another guitarist, Kelly plays with speed and invention on blues and soul numbers alike, negotiating the shifting contours of Lattimore's 'Straighten It Out' with panache.

The momentum built up by three highly creditable albums is dissipated by the ones that have followed. On *What Three Old Ladies Can Do* Kelly gives his usual assured performance but his ability to find, or write, suitable material has temporarily deserted him, and the arrangements are overbearing and too clogged by treacly keyboard effects. *Nobody Has The Power* has a few blues and soul tracks, almost all hackneyed ('I'll Play The Blues For You', 'Steppin' In', 'Rock Me Baby'), but the title number, 'Sending You A Message' and 'Finally I Found You', all written by Kelly's wife and sung in duet with his daughter, are vapid pop songs that rewire the Barry White connection. TR

Willie Kent (1936–2006)
VOCAL, BASS

Kent was born in Sunflower and raised in Shelby, Mississippi, but lived in Chicago since his teens. He became a regular patron of the blues clubs and formed his first band in 1958, taking up bass when a sideman showed up drunk. For part of the '70s he headed Sugar Bear & The Beehives at Ma Bea's, and in the early '80s he assembled the first of several lineups of Willie Kent & His Gents. He also worked with other leaders, among them Eddie Taylor and Buster Benton, and played in Europe and Japan. After 1989, when he retired from his day job as a truckdriver, he played music fulltime, repeatedly earning Handy Awards as Bass Player Of The Year.

** Ghetto
Storyville STCD 8046 *Kent; Willie James Lyons, Big Guitar Red [Walter Smith], Luther Johnson Jr (g); Tyrone Centuray (d).* 10/75.

Kent's first album was recorded by Marcelle Morgantini for MCM and suffers, like many of her projects, from erratic engineering, the lifeless atmosphere of an empty club, and programming that puts a sequence of slow vocal blues at the start, though there are several livelier numbers later which could have been mingled with them. 'Chili Con Carne' (Kenny Burrell's 'Chitlins Con Carne') and 'Bobby's Rock' are instrumental features for the little-recorded but promising Willie James Lyons (1938–80), who plays throughout and receives joint credit. Kent sings with stolid competence, but the poor production makes it hard to appreciate him fully.

**(*) Willie Kent & His Gents (Chicago Blues Session Vol. 21)
Wolf 120.867 *Kent; Billy Branch (h); Ken Barker (p); Eddie Taylor, Johnny B. Moore, John Primer, Luther 'Slim' Adams, Jake Dawson (g); Tim Taylor (d).* 8/84–4/91.

***(*) Ain't It Nice
Delmark DD-653 *Kent; Lester 'Mad Dog' Davenport (h); Ken Barker (o, p); Luther 'Slim' Adams, Jacob [Jake] Dawson (g); Timothy Taylor (d); Bonnie Lee (v).* 3/91.

Willie Kent & His Gents snapshots three lineups. The earliest, with Eddie Taylor and Moore, plays relaxed, spacious music with filigree guitar work by Taylor, but some of the later sessions have a more explicit beat and fiercer guitar playing by Primer or Dawson, good on 'One More Moment' (correctly, 'One More Mile') and 'Me And My Baby' respectively. Better recorded and more rehearsed than *Ghetto*, this CD gives a fairer account of Kent's singing, which is direct, hearty and firmly rooted in the '50s. The last of the lineups, with Branch giving way to Lester Davenport, is heard throughout *Ain't It Nice*, where the continuity of the sound shows what this seasoned lineup can do with an hour-long blues programme. An improved version of 'One More Mile' captures the Muddy Waters sound of the '50s that is obviously one of Kent's models, but the insistent undertow of 'Ain't It Nice' and the spacey 'Feel So Good' prove that he is comfortable in more modern settings. Dawson and Adams complement each other's playing faultlessly.

*** Live At B.L.U.E.S. (Chicago Blues Sessions Vol. 30)
Wolf 120.876 *Kent; Eddie Shaw (ts, v); Ken Barker (o, p); Johnny B. Moore (g, v); Jake Dawson (g); Cleo Williams (d); Bonnie Lee (v).* 7/93.

*** Too Hurt To Cry
Delmark DE 667 *Kent; Malachi Thompson (t); Steve Berry (tb); Sonny Seals (ts); Billy Branch (h); Kenny Barker (o, p); Jacob [Jake] Dawson, Willie Davis, Johnny B. Moore (g); Tim Taylor (d).* 93/94.

Live At B.L.U.E.S. is a typical club show, in that most of the programme is standards like 'Mother In Law Blues', 'Black Night' and 'Tin Pan Alley', often extended to six or seven minutes, and there are guest spots for Moore, Shaw and Bonnie Lee (reprising 'I'm Good' from *Ain't It Nice*). The preponderance of slow numbers in a set lasting nearly 75 minutes may tax some listeners' endurance, but the animated ensemble playing on the closing 'If You Got To Love Somebody' will reward their patience. The outstanding track is Buddy Guy's 'A Man And His Blues', which elicits an intense vocal and matching guitar playing by Moore and Dawson. Understandably, Kent brought it to the table again for his next studio album, *Too Hurt To Cry*, where it receives a more reflective treatment, the guitars backing off to let Branch be the chief soloist. The rest of the material is mostly Kent's, admirably varied in weight and tempo and often attractively framed by the horns. Each of these albums has its virtues, but the planning that went into *Too Hurt To Cry* gives it more staying-power.

**(*) Everybody Needs Somebody
Wolf 120.889 *Kent*; Hank Ford (s); Ken Barker (o, p); Carlos Showers (g, v); Willie Davis, Jake Dawson (g); Cleo Williams (d). 95–96.

The first three tracks were recorded in Chicago with Dawson and Davis on guitars; Dawson, who hasn't been heard as much as he deserves to be on preceding albums, slithers like a viper in 'Don't Mess With My Baby'. The remaining nine numbers come from an engagement in Austria, for which Dawson was replaced by Showers, and include a couple that were already on disc, 'Too Hurt To Cry' and a third version of 'One More Mile'. The former apart, the songs are all received repertoire and, since the band approach them in their customary straightforward manner, the performance is rather run-of-the-mill.

**(*) Long Way To Ol' Miss
Delmark DE-696 *Kent*; Kenny Barker, Ken Saydak (o, p); Vernon 'Chico' Banks, Willie Davis, James Wheeler (g); 'Baldhead Pete' [Cleo Williams] (d); band (v). 8/96.

*** Make Room For The Blues
Delmark DE-723 *Kent*; Kenny Anderson (t); Hank Ford (ts); Willie Henderson (bs); Ken Saydak (kb); Kenny Barker (p); Vince Varco (syn); Billy Flynn, Jake Dawson, Willie Davis (g); James Carter (d). 2/98.

Back with Delmark again, Kent is prompted, as usual, to expand his repertoire from his own resources: eight of 13 songs on *Long Way To Ol' Miss* are his, and ten of 13 on *Make Room For The Blues*. On the former, Chico Banks, less than a year away from his own debut album, efficiently takes on the role of snarling lead guitarist formerly filled by Jake Dawson; the latter reclaims his place on about half of *Make Room* but his playing is now more circumspect and less individual. Still, *Make Room* is the better record, both for its slightly less generic songs and for showing – what the Wolf albums hardly reveal – that Kent can put aside his public manner and sing with restraint and even delicacy.

In 1998 he also recorded a duet album with Lil' Ed Williams, *Who's Been Talking* (Earwig CD 4941), discussed in Williams's entry, and sang a couple of numbers at an unplugged session with Johnny B. Moore, *Acoustic Blue Chicago* (Blue Chicago BC 5004).

*** Comin' Alive
Blue Chicago BC 5006 *Kent*; Kenny Anderson, Burgess Gardner (t); Larry B. J. Weathersby (ts); Willie Henderson (bs); Allen Batts (o, p); Twist Turner (o, tamb); Erskine Johnson (p); Haguy F. King, Jacob [Jake] Dawson (g); Dave Jefferson (d); The Gospel Supremez (Shirley Johnson, Diane Womack, Joi Fité) (v). 01.

What's never in doubt with Willie Kent is the conviction he puts into his songs. 'Born In The Delta' is his own story, told in commonplace language but made compelling by its authenticity. 'Bad Luck', another well-worn blues theme, similarly acquires a personal ring. With performances like these and the closing 'Someone You Should Know', a hymn in blues form, *Comin' Alive* maintains Kent's track record of well-made and rewarding albums. TR

Peter Kern (born 1973)
VOCAL, GUITAR

Kern is Austrian, and began playing guitar at seven; first exposed to the blues at 12, he was a fulltime performer by the age of 15.

***(*) Young And Restless
[Document DOCD-7006] *Kern*; Siggi Fassl (g, v). 9–12/98.

Considering that he's simultaneously working in two foreign languages – English and the blues – Peter Kern is remarkably assured and fluent. At 14, he was shown a few things by Iverson Minter, but fortunately 'When I Met Louisiana Red' is the only song on *Young And Restless* to adopt that artist's bombastic approach. Kern's fellow Viennese blues singers Erik Trauner and Siggi Fassl (who assists on three tracks) are acknowledged as influences, but inevitably most of the inspiration comes from records. As a consequence, Kern ranges more widely, both stylistically and historically, than do most African-American artists; John Hurt, Frank Stokes, Robert Lockwood, Jimmy Reed and Elmore James are just some of his sources, whether for complete songs or for settings of his own lyrics. The latter occasionally stray into the navel-gazing world of the singer/songwriter, but Kern usually manages to close the frontier between personal and narcissistic. As a guitarist, he is at his best on the ragtime-based sounds of Hurt and Stokes, but is admirably successful in the styles of almost all his inspirations; as a singer, he doesn't quite have the gravitas to handle Lightnin' Hopkins, even when it's the light-hearted Lightnin' of 'Shake That Thing', and 'You Better Help Yourself', inspired by the Robert Johnson of 'Hellhound On My Trail', is a gallant failure, on a disc that's otherwise very successful because Kern's technique is always at the service of his commitment to the blues as an expressive medium. At presstime this CD was still sporadically available. CS

Junior Kimbrough (1930–98)
VOCAL, GUITAR

Rockabilly icon Charlie Feathers, who learned from David Kimbrough when they grew up in the north Mississippi hill country, described him as 'the beginning and end of music'. That's a bit strong, but the sound that Kimbrough made, blending blues, soul and fife-and-drum rhythms into a droning, erotic dance/trance music, was powerful medicine for the troubles of his African-American neighbours, in jukes and at his Sunday house parties. Not until the '90s, after appearing in the documentary Deep Blues and signing with Fat Possum, did he achieve wider fame. From 1991, Kimbrough operated a juke-joint when he felt like it. (The only way to find out if Junior's Place was open was to go there on Sunday night.) Visiting rock stars sometimes sat in, but their reputations meant nothing in Chulahoma, and those who couldn't blend were swiftly encouraged to desist. Shortly after its owner's death, Junior's was torched by an arsonist.

***(*) Do The Rump!
High Water HMG 6503 *Kimbrough*; George Scales, Earl 'Little Joe' Ayers (b); Calvin Jackson, Allabu Juju (Winston Doxey) (d). 7/82, 8/88.

(*) All Night Long
Fat Possum 80308 *Kimbrough; Garry Burnside (b); Kenny Malone (d).* 92.

**** **Sad Days, Lonely Nights**
Fat Possum 80306 *Kimbrough; Kenny Brown (g); Garry Burnside (b); Cedric Jackson (d).* 4/93.

♛ **** **Most Things Haven't Worked Out**
Fat Possum 80309 *As above, except Kenny Malone (d) replaces Jackson.* 90s.

Recorded first, *Do The Rump!* was Kimbrough's third release, issued after his success on Fat Possum. Most of it was recorded at Rust College, an African-American institution in Holly Springs. The extensive notes will not be needed by those who agree with Fat Possum that musicologists are the Devil's spawn, and the only thing to do with a brain is fry it; but even those who don't hold that view will find that Kimbrough and his musicians sound inhibited, playing carefully rather than with the abandon of later recordings.

All Night Long was recorded at Junior's juke, but falls well short of capturing the sweaty, intoxicated sensuality of his music. The recording levels are low, and the music sounds distant, as if played behind a curtain. *Sad Days, Lonely Nights*, also recorded at Junior's Place, is louder, funkier and altogether better. The drummer is much further forward in the mix, Junior plays and sings with possessed intensity, and Brown's second guitar adds depth and richness to the texture; occasionally he steps forward with a snarling solo, bringing news of Jimi Hendrix to Chulahoma.

Most Things Haven't Worked Out is a further improvement, and Junior Kimbrough's best record. On the opening 'Lonesome Road', played solo, Kimbrough gets mighty confused towards the end, but his performance, like the rest of the disc, is so committed that it doesn't matter. The band match him all the way; Brown continues the good work, including some notably ominous slide on the title track, Burnside grinds like a truck in low gear, and Malone's tom-tom, ride cymbal and hi-hat are thunder, lightning and hail respectively.

(*) God Knows I Tried
Fat Possum 80320 *As above, except add Dale Beavers (b).* 7/92–1/97.

(*) Meet Me In The City
Fat Possum 80333 *Kimbrough; Charlie Feathers (g); Garry Burnside (b); Kenny Malone (d).* 76, 93–2/96.

These are posthumous releases, collated from diverse sessions. There are good things on both; *Meet Me In The City*'s title track (recorded in 1976 by the BBC's Anthony Wall, with Charlie Feathers quietly seconding) is the definitive manifestation of Kimbrough's floating trance music, and the erotic charge of 'How Do You Feel' on *God Knows I Tried* is ferocious. Some tracks come from fairly low in the barrel, though; 'Tramp' on *God Knows I Tried* remakes one side of Junior's 1968 Philwood single, but Kimbrough doesn't care that he doesn't remember it well, and the band comp listlessly. On *Meet Me In The City*, three home recordings of indeterminate date have been de-noised, but the amplifier still drones like a low-flying aircraft. Neither CD is the place to meet Junior Kimbrough for the first time.

(*) You Better Run: The Essential Junior Kimbrough
Fat Possum 80340 *As for Fat Possum CDs above, except Feathers also sings.* 69–2/96.

'Meet Me In The City' reappears, quite rightly, on this attempted 'best of;' so does 'Tramp', with less justification. Three songs from *All Night Long* are louder and clearer this time, but still not as good as the later recordings with Kenny Brown. Despite its shortcomings, it's worth noting that *You Better Run* opens with 'Release Me', recorded by Charlie Feathers in 1969, and not available elsewhere on Fat Possum. Feathers plays bopping rhythm guitar and sings an imperfectly recalled version of the country standard as Junior improvises a brooding blues around and through it. Chaos and collapse always threaten, but never quite arrive. The budget-priced VAC *Not The Same Old Blues Crap II* (Fat Possum 80342) includes the delightful (and considerably more coherent) 'Feel Good Again', recorded at the same time. CS

Lottie Kimbrough
VOCAL

Possibly born in Kansas City, certainly raised there, Kimbrough became known as a tavern entertainer in the '20s and recorded for several labels during the decade. She married a William Beaman and on some of her recordings used her married name.

**** **Kansas City Blues (1924–1929)**
Document DOCD-5152 *Kimbrough; unknown (t); Simon Hoe (cl); Clifton Banks (as); Jimmy Blythe, Paul Banks, unknown (p); prob. Milas Pruitt, prob. Papa Charlie Jackson (bj); Miles Pruitt (g); Sylvester Kimbrough (k, v); Winston Holmes (v, sp, wh, eff).* c. 3/24–c. 11/29.

If her half-dozen 1924 sides on Paramount had been all Lottie Kimbrough recorded, she would probably be considered a singer of the second or third rank, strong-voiced but without singularity. Fortunately she encountered the ingenious and ambitious Winston Holmes, a Kansas City promoter who helped her to get a hearing at Gennett Records: the result was 'Rolling Log Blues' and 'Goin' Away Blues', performances of haunting beauty. Kimbrough's rueful but resigned vocals, underpinned by Miles Pruitt's quirky guitar, make the most of the lovely melodies. The price paid for this opportunity was Holmes's decision to participate in the session by talking, singing, yodelling or, on 'Lost Lover Blues', doing bird-imitations, but so dominant is Kimbrough's personality that the listener soon hardly hears him. The following year she rerecorded her two best numbers for Brunswick, again with Pruitt and in very similar settings.

To Kimbrough's 14 sides and three by her higher-voiced brother Sylvester the Document CD adds six 1929 sides by Holmes and guitarist Charlie Turner (see the latter). Four of Kimbrough's Paramounts and one side of her Meritt coupling are on the revised (2004) version of *The Best Of Country Blues Women Vol. 1 (1923–1930)* (Wolf WSE 117), while alternative takes of all her Paramounts are on *Elzadie Robinson – Vol. 2 (1928–1929)* (Document DOCD-5249). TR

Albert King (1923–92)
VOCAL, GUITAR

Albert Nelson was born in Indianola, Mississippi, but grew up in Osceola, Arkansas. Based in the '50s and early '60s in St Louis, he recorded for the local Bobbin label, was taken up by King Records and had a hit in 1961 with 'Don't Throw Your

Love On Me So Strong'. But it was his signing with Stax Records that changed the course of his career, and in the late '60s and early '70s he was one of the two or three most influential figures in the blues. He was more successful than many of his contemporaries in gaining the attention of new audiences, and his engagements took him all over the United States and overseas, but after the mid-'80s his activity was limited by ill health.

**(*) Door To Door
MCA-Chess CHD-9322//[(E) MCD 09322] *King; Wilbur Thompson (t); Harold White (ts); Freddie Robinette (bs); [Little] Johnny Jones, Sam Wallace (p); John Brim (g); Lee Otis Wright, unknown (b); Theotis Morgan, unknown (d). 11/53, 3/61.*

King's portion of this CD includes his 1953 debut recordings, 'Bad Luck Blues' and 'Be On Your Merry Way', and the template of the artist he would become is already visible, the voice slightly phlegmy, the delivery unhurried, the playing deliberate. Most of the remaining six tracks are from a 1961 session in St Louis with a larger group, showing greater assurance in his singing and more facility in his playing. The remaining six cuts are by Otis Rush.

***(*) More Big Blues
Ace CDCHD 827 *King; Wilbur Thompson (t); Harold White (ts); Freddie Robinette (bs); unknown (o); Sam Wallace, Johnnie Johnson, James Vaughn, Ike Turner (p); Lee Otis Wright (b); Theotis Morgan, Kenny Birdell Rice (d). 59–62.*
*** Let's Have A Natural Ball
Modern Blues MBCD-723 *As above. 59–4/63.*
*** The Big Blues
King KCD-852 *As above, except add unknowns (v grp). 59–4/63.*
** Mean Mean Blues
King Blues KBCD 471 *Similar to above. 59–61.*

King's three years or so with Bobbin are the laboratory in which he developed his sound. Over half a dozen sessions his accompanists don't change very much – though there are some important transfers at the piano – but his material is quite diverse, from the jump jazz of 'Let's Have A Natural Ball' to the B. B. King styling of 'Don't Throw Your Love On Me So Strong'. His playing on slow numbers has acquired his trademark sound of massive effort, a guitarist's impression of a bulldozer. Now and then he adapts an older song, for example remaking Tampa Red's 'Don't You Lie To Me' as 'I Get Evil', but most of his material originates here, including numbers he would play for the rest of his life like the velvety 'Blues At Sunrise'.

More Big Blues, which assembles the Bobbin singles, the masters sold on to King and some previously unissued alternative takes, is the most comprehensive reissue of this material and recommended. *Let's Have A Natural Ball* and *The Big Blues*, which differ little from each other, are shorter selections from the Bobbins plus one or two later tracks from King. *Mean Mean Blues*, at eight tracks, is shorter still.

**** Born Under A Bad Sign
Stax SCD 723//SCD24 723 *King; Wayne Jackson (t); Joe Arnold (ts, bs, poss. fl); Andrew Love (ts); Booker T. Jones (p); Steve Cropper (g); Donald 'Duck' Dunn (b); Al Jackson Jr (d). 3/66–6/67.*

♛ **** King Of The Blues Guitar
Atlantic 82017 *As above, except Jones also plays o; add Donald Levi (p). 3/66–3/68.*

Almost 40 years after they were made, these performances are still extraordinarily impressive for how much is in them. *Born Under A Bad Sign* was first issued at a time when albums were collections of singles, and when singles, designed for radio and jukebox play, seldom ran for much more than three and a half minutes, often quite a bit less. In fact few tracks here exceed 3.00, and there is scarcely a metre of tape that is not packed with musical incident: the stabbing phrases of the Memphis Horns (Jackson, Arnold and Love), Dunn's earth-shaking bass, Jones's diamantine piano fills, the restless explorations of King's guitar. In songs like the title number, 'Crosscut Saw' and 'Laundromat Blues', a tale of hot whispers during the hot-wash cycle, King brought absolute blues credibility to the well-made commercial single. The SCD24 issue, like others below with that prefix, has been subjected to 24-bit remastering. *King Of The Blues Guitar* is the 11 tracks of *Born Under A Bad Sign* augmented with six others from the same period.

**(*) Years Gone By
Stax SCD-8522 *King; unknown (t); unknowns (s); Booker T. Jones (p); Steve Cropper (g); Donald 'Duck' Dunn (b); Al Jackson Jr (d). 68.*
**(*) Years Gone By – Plus!
Stax (E) CDSXD 045 *As above, except add other musicians (see below). 66/67–1/71.*

'Drowning On Dry Land', 'If The Washing Don't Get You, The Rinsing Will' and 'You Threw Your Love On Me Too Strong', the last a remake of the Bobbin, are good songs well suited to King's style, but too many of the surrounding tracks on *Years Gone By* are similarly paced, which reduces their impact and makes for a dull programme. *Plus!* is the original album plus three alternative takes, plus odd alternatives from dates in 1966–67 and 'Shake 'Em Down' from the *Lovejoy* session; most of these additional tracks are also on *Hard Bargain* (below). A further bonus is the 1969 single 'Cold Sweat'/'Can't You See What You're Doing To Me' (also on *Funky London*, below).

**(*) Live Wire/Blues Power
Stax SCD-4128//SCD24 4128//(E) CDSXE 022 *King; James Washington (o); Willie James Exon (g); Roosevelt Pointer (b); Theotis Morgan (d). 6/68.*
*** Wednesday Night In San Francisco
Stax SCD-8556//SCD24 8556 *As above. 6/68.*
*** Thursday Night In San Francisco
Stax SCD-8557//SCD24 8557//(E) CDSXE 032 *As above. 6/68.*

Live Wire/Blues Power, recorded during King's first headline gig at San Francisco's Fillmore Auditorium, enjoys the status of one of the blues' great live albums, but the rosette it was awarded by its first wave of listeners faded long ago. Of its six tracks three are instrumentals ('Watermelon Man' not much more than a warm-up) and 'Blues Power' an overlong self-promotional rap to the audience; the full-on assault of voice and guitar is confined to 'Please Love Me' and a long 'Blues At Sunrise'. This is King packaged for a guitar-obsessed generation (the musician credits read 'Albert King – guitar': nothing more), and King's playing was only a part of his artistry. The quality of the recording is fair, but the CD was mastered at much too low a level.

Years later, Stax went back to the tapes of the two-night engagement and found another two albums' worth of material. Many of the numbers had probably been passed over because King had recorded them before, such as 'I Get Evil', 'Personal Manager' and 'Born Under A Bad Sign' on *Wednesday* and 'Crosscut Saw' on *Thursday*, or because they were blues perennials like *Thursday*'s 'Call It Stormy Monday', 'Drifting Blues' and 'I'm Gonna Move To The Outskirts Of Town'. Nevertheless, these second and third helpings from the Fillmore fill more space than *Live Wire/Blues Power* (45.00 and 52.36 against 38.04), have more songs and are properly mastered, and listeners unswayed by received opinion should find them more worthwhile. At the same time, they may wonder what's supposed to be so historic about this merely very good gig.

**(*) Live '69
Tomato TOM-2068 King; unknowns (brass, reeds, o, b, d). 5/69.

Recorded less than a year after the Fillmore engagement discussed above, but not issued until 2003, this concert from Madison, Wisconsin, is intriguingly unlike it in several respects. The sound is not of recorded-for-issue quality and the ensemble is oddly balanced, the horns backgrounded and the drums, in quieter passages, virtually inaudible, so that at times King's singing and playing move with almost no discernible rhythmic pulse but their own. The effect, at first weird, soon becomes rather attractive, and the long, floating version of 'As The Years Go Passing By', with a vocal so soft you could curl up inside it, is hauntingly beautiful. 'Personal Manager' is also distinctively done, with distant, pretty horn harmonies behind the vocal, but 'Please Come Back To Me' loses one's attention long before its 17 minutes are up. The most striking difference, however, between this and either *Live Wire/Blues Power* or the later live albums from Montreux is that for their braggadocio and stuff-strutting *Live '69* substitutes an almost meditative calm.

** Blues For Elvis
Stax SCD24 8504//(E) CDSXE 073 King; unknowns (brass, reeds); Marvell Thomas (o, p); Michael Toles (g); Donald 'Duck' Dunn, James Alexander (b); Willie Hall (d); unknown (v grp). 69.

Despite Albert Goldman's ridiculously faux-funky notes ('Albert here is gonna play you Elvis the way he should be played – not just the tunes, mindja, but the whole hog', etc.), this is good oldfashioned exploitation. Some fine mind at Stax put 'King' (Elvis) together with King (Albert), and the result was this album, originally titled *King Does The King's Things*. Albert goes along with it in good humour, though a few moments of 'Jailhouse Rock' are enough to suggest that he is not having his natural ball, and 'Don't Be Cruel' is further evidence that he's working against his grain. But, successful or not, these are at least reinterpretations, not copies, with crisp playing by the uncredited brass and reeds and the unflappable rhythm section.

**(*) Jammed Together
Stax SCD-8544//(E) CDSXE 028 King; unknowns (brass, reeds); Booker T. Jones (o); Pop Staples, Steve Cropper (g, v); Donald 'Duck' Dunn (b); Al Jackson Jr (d). 69.

This is credited to Steve Cropper, Pop Staples and Albert King, in that order. Each has one vocal number, King's being 'What'd I Say'; all three play guitar on eight of the ten tracks, and two, 'Trashy Dog' and 'Knock On Wood', are King–Cropper duets. The weaving of the guitar lines – Staples's shimmering, Cropper's rock-and-rolling, King's plain and direct – yields attractive textures, the themes are varied and catchy and no one is disposed to upstage his colleagues: altogether a jam with long shelf-life.

***(*) Lovejoy
Stax SCD-8517 King; Wayne Jackson (t); Andrew Love (ts); John Gallie, Barry Beckett (kb); Jesse Ed Davis, Jimmy Johnson, Tippy Armstrong, Wayne Perkins (g); Donald 'Duck' Dunn, David Hood (b); Jim Keltner, Roger Hawkins (d); Sandy Konikoff (perc); Jeanne Greene, Mt Zion Singers (v); Don Nix (arr). ?70–1/71.

**** I'll Play The Blues For You
Stax SCD-8513 King; Wayne Jackson, Ben Cauley, Mickey Gregory (t); Jack Hale (tb); Lewis Collins (as); Andrew Love, Harvey Henderson (ts); James Mitchell (bs); Tommy L. Williams (s); Allen Jones (kb); Michael Toles (g); James Alexander (b); Willie Hall (d); unknown (perc); unknowns (v). 1–4/71.

**** I'll Play The Blues For You/Lovejoy
Stax (E) CDSXD 969 As for the above two CDs. ?70–4/71.

*** I Wanna Get Funky
Stax SCD-8536//SCD24 8536//(E) CDSXE 081 King; Wayne Jackson (t); Jack Hale (tb); Lewis Collins (as); Andrew Love (ts); James Mitchell (bs); Winston Stewart, Lester Snell, Marvell Thomas (kb); Memphis Symphony Orchestra (strings); Donald Kenzie [Kinsey], Bobby Manuel, Vernon Burch, Michael Toles (g); James Alexander, prob. Earl Thomas (b); Willie Hall (d); Henry Bush, Hot Buttered Soul (Pat Lewis, Rose Williams, Diana Lewis) (v). 7/72, 74.

For some listeners at the time, Stax's policy in the early '70s of seasoning King's salad greens with a contemporary sauce was like delivering a hapless village maiden into the hands of Baron Funkenstein. At this distance, it's far from clear that flirting with funk was dealing with the Devil. The arrangement of 'Crosscut Saw' on *I Wanna Get Funky*, for example, is not better or worse than the original, simply different – and it would be a loyal fan indeed who denied that King's music could stand a little adaptation from time to time. Certainly the meandering narratives of the same album's 'That's What The Blues Is All About' and ''Til My Back Ain't Got No Bone' are refreshed by their non-standard settings. The best thing on the album, though, is the not particularly funky but exquisite arrangement of 'Walking The Back Streets And Crying'.

Lovejoy and *I'll Play The Blues For You* have funky moments but were responsive to other vibrations then in the air. Listening now to *I'll Play The Blues For You*, one's struck less by the period detail than by the timeless concord of artist, material, musicians and producers. The arrangements don't call for King to play huge solos, and the choruses he does play are artfully stagelit by the other musicians. He probably never bettered these versions of 'I'll Play The Blues For You' and 'Breaking Up Somebody's Home'. *Lovejoy*, partly made in LA and partly in Muscle Shoals, wears the smell of its era like a cologne, but numbers like 'Corina, Corina', 'Going Back To Iuka' and 'She Caught The Katy And Left Me A Mule To Ride' have more than Brut strength. The English Stax CD combining the two albums is one of the best bargains around.

*** The Lost Session
Stax SCD-8534//SCD24 8534//(E) CDSXE 066 *King; Blue Mitchell (t); Clifford Solomon (as, ts); Ernie Watts (ts); John Mayall (h, o, p, g, prod); Kevin — (o, p); Lee King (g); Larry Taylor (b); Ron Selico (d). 8/71.*

The accompaniment provided by John Mayall's band is space-filled and uninsistent and King's guitar sound is thinner than usual – which produces the surprising result that this usually hard-hitting bluesman sometimes sounds almost gentle, particularly at the crawling tempo of 'Cold In Hand', 'All The Way Down' and 'Sun Gone Down'. That probably explains why the tapes were left on the shelf until an enquiring producer found them 15 years later. The album may not be a major addition to the King corpus, but admirers looking for something a little different should enjoy its fresh material and lightness of touch.

**(*) Blues At Sunset
Stax SCD-8581 *King; Norville Hodges, Wilbur Thompson (t); Rick Watson (ts); Winston Stewart, James Washington (o); Vernon Burch, Donald Kinsey (g); James Alexander, Bill Rennie (b); Donnell Hagan or Bruce McCormick, Sam King (d). 8/72, 7/73.*

*** Blues At Sunrise
Stax SCD-8546//(E) CDSXE 017 *As above, except omit Stewart, Burch, Alexander, Hagan/McCormick. 7/73.*

Blues At Sunrise was recorded at the Montreux Jazz Festival. *Blues At Sunset* has four more songs from the same event, preceded by King's set from the 'Wattstax' festival a year earlier in LA. The LA recordings are rather boxy, and the five numbers are well-tried repertoire like 'Match Box Blues', 'I'll Play The Blues For You' and 'Angel Of Mercy', but King was working to an audience that wasn't particularly receptive to the blues. The Montreux set is better recorded, particularly on *Sunrise*, and that CD also breaks new ground with numbers like 'For The Love Of A Woman' and a ten-minute 'Roadhouse Blues'.

** The Blues Don't Change
Stax SCD-8570//(E) CDSXE 085 *King; Memphis Horns [Wayne Jackson (t); Andrew Love (ts); prob. others (brass, reeds)]; Lester Snell, Marvell Thomas, Winston Stewart (kb); Michael Toles, Vernon Burch, Bobby Manuel (g); Donald 'Duck' Dunn, Earl Thomas (b); Al Jackson Jr, Willie Hall (d); William C. Brown III, Henry Bush, Hot Butter & Soul [i.e. Hot Buttered Soul] (v). 3/73–7/74.*

Well, *these* blues don't change – much. This was Stax's most blatant attempt to make King's music sound other than what it was, but, Stax being Stax and King being King, they didn't get very far. The arrangement of the instrumental 'King Of Kings' is not so much busy as hyperactive, and overfeeding swells some other tracks to an uncomfortable girth, but what one chiefly notices is that King doesn't seem very engaged with the material – none of which, as it happens, is his own.

**(*) Hard Bargain
Stax SCD-8594 *King; Wayne Jackson, poss. Ben Cauley (t); Andrew Love, Packy Axton, Tommy Williams, Joe Arnold, Fred Ford, Ed Logan (ts); Barry Beckett (kb); Booker T. Jones (o, p); Isaac Hayes (p); Steve Cropper, Michael Toles, Jimmy Johnson, Tippy Armstrong, Wayne Perkins (g); Donald 'Duck' Dunn, James Alexander, David Hood (b); Al Jackson Jr, Willie Hall, Roger Hawkins (d). 3/66–1/71.*

**(*) Funky London
Stax SCD-8586 *King; Ben Cauley, Mickey Gregory, prob. Wayne Jackson (t); Harvey Henderson, Tommy Williams, prob. Andrew Love. poss. unknown(s) (ts); unknowns (bs); unknowns (fl); Bobby Manuel (kb, g); Winston Stewart, Lester Snell (kb); unknown (o); Michael Toles (g); Donald 'Duck' Dunn, James Alexander, Erroll Thomas (b); Al Jackson Jr, Willie Hall (d); Sandy Kay [prob. Sandy Konikoff] (perc); Tommy Elrod, Louis McCall, Sidney Kirk (unknown instruments – two prob. flutes). 1/70–7/74.*

These are footnotes to the Stax chapter. *Hard Bargain* consists of B-sides, alternative takes and five previously unissued songs, nearly all from 1966–68. 'Shake 'Em Down' is a welcome extra from the *Lovejoy* session in Muscle Shoals. At least half of this album is also on the UK release *Years Gone By – Plus!* (above). *Funky London* is made up of leftovers from various dates; five come from *The Blues Don't Change* sessions. Six of the nine tracks were previously unissued. It's overloaded with meandering and overlong instrumentals like 'Sweet Fingers', but has one very attractive slow blues in 'Lonesome', which starts from Curtis Jones's 'Lonesome Bedroom Blues'.

**** Blues From The Road
Fuel 2000 302 061 318 2CD *King; Nate Fitzgerald, Steve Wilson, Wayne Preston (brass, reeds); James Washington (kb); Rory Gallagher, Louisiana Red (g); Lonnie Turner (b); Joe Turner (d); Lowell Fulson (v). 7/75.*

Back at Montreux, two years on from *Blues At Sunrise*, King made an album that not only outshone his '73 performance but left *Live Wire/Blues Power* in the shade. The two CDs contain more than 90 minutes of music and, since there are only a dozen numbers, several are very long, but never to their disadvantage, thanks to arrangements that are brightly coloured by the horns and vitalized by an energetic rhythm section. Even stock King pieces like 'I'll Play The Blues For You' and 'Matchbox Holds My Clothes' (i.e. 'Matchbox Blues') sound fresh, and the reading of 'As The Years Go Passing By', with an elegant solo by Rory Gallagher, is gorgeous. The set also includes – what a previous issue, *Albert Live* (Rhino/Tomato 71622//Tomato CD 269626), had omitted – the almost 16-minute 'Jam In A Flat' (more accurately, 'Don't Throw Your Love On Me So Strong And Variations'), with guitar cameos by Gallagher and Louisiana Red and a guest vocal by Lowell Fulson.

*(*) King Albert
Charly SNAP 048 *King; Fred Wesley (tb); The Horny Horns (brass, reeds); Rudy Robinson (kb, arr); Aaron Willis, Ray Tini Jr, James McCarthy, Dennis Robbins, Eddie Willis, Aaron Willis Jr, Glen Goins (g); Anthony Willis, John Fraga (b); Dwayne Lomax, John (The Bee) Badanjek, Ronald Wright (d); Barbara Huby, Larry Fratangelo (perc); Brandye (Pam Vincent, Cynthia Douglas, Donna Davis) (v). 5–6/77.*

King made this in Detroit, accompanied on the basic tracks by local bluesman Little Sonny Willis's band. Sonny himself didn't play but contributed two of the eight songs. None of the rest are King's, and, with the exception of 'Call My Job', he doesn't sound at ease in any of them – which is hardly surprising, beleaguered as he is by chittering guitars and a twittering vocal group. On its original release, blues wits retitled it *'King Awful*.

** Talkin' Blues
Thirsty Ear 57129 *King; unknowns (brass, reeds, kb, g, b, d). poss. 2/78.*

These seven tracks from a good but not great gig are mostly stock pieces like 'Blues At Sunrise', 'Born Under A Bad Sign' and 'I'll Play The Blues For You'. The addition of four segments from an undated interview, three of them brief and none packed with interest, does little to enhance an album that will be superfluous to any but completists. A larger selection from the same engagement was issued as *Chicago 1978* (Charly Blues Legends CBL 754, deleted), and a smaller one, dated 10/77, as half of *I'll Play The Blues For You* (Tomato CD 269614//Charly CPCD 8166, shared with John Lee Hooker, also deleted).

*** New Orleans Heat
Charly SNAP 122 *King; Allen Toussaint, Robert Dabon, Wardell Quezergue (kb); Leo Nocentelli (g); George Porter Jr (b); June Gardner, Leroy Breaux, Charles Williams (d); Kenneth Williams (perc); unknowns (v). 78.*

With its string-synths and its air of a pop-soul-blues statement, this CD (previously on Rhino/Tomato 70699) might be seen as King's rather laggardly attempt to echo the B. B. King of 'The Thrill Is Gone'. Indeed, 'The Feeling' is a rather similar piece of work, and the mood of 'I Got The Blues' – meandering lines against a background of satin – recalls the general effect of B. B.'s *Indianola Mississippi Seeds*. However, the New Orleans flavour stirred in by producer Toussaint and the Meters' Nocentelli and Porter distinguishes this set from a merely strategic move and lends a piquancy that's almost always pleasant and sometimes usefully masks deficiencies in King's performance. These are few and brief, lapses of attention rather than of imagination.

** Guitar Man: An Essential Collection
Varèse 061129 *As for* King Albert *and* New Orleans Heat, *except add Bob Bryant, John Roberts (t), George Bohanon, Donald Cooke (tb), unknowns (brass), Jerome Richardson, Ernie Fields, Herman Riley, Roland Cooke (reeds), Joe Sample, Bert de Coteaux, Jerry Peters, Marvin Jenkins (kb), unknowns (strings), Wa Wa Watson, Billy Fender, Greg Poree, Jay Graydon, Roy Gaines (g), Charles Rainey, Henry Davis, Scott Edwards, William Upchurch (b), James Gadson, Paul Humphrey, Harold Mason (d), King Errisson, Joe Clayton (cga), unknown (tamb), Bob Zimmitti (perc), Lani Groves, Maxine Willard, Denise Williams, Julia Tillman, Dee Ervin, Jeane Arnold, Alex Brown (v). 6/75–78.*

**(*) A Truckload Of Lovin': The Best Of Albert King
Snapper Recall SMDCD 186 2CD *As for* Blues From The Road, King Albert *and* New Orleans Heat, *except add unknowns (brass), Jerome Richardson, Ernie Fields (reeds), Joe Sample, Bert de Coteaux, Jerry Peters, unknown (kb), unknowns (strings), Wah Wah Watson, Billy Fender, Greg Poree, unknown (g), Charles Rainey, Henry Davis, unknown (b), James Gadson, unknown (d), King Errisson (cga), Lani Groves, Maxine Willard, Denise Williams, Julia Tillman, Dee Ervin, Jeane Arnold (v); omit Louisiana Red, Fulson. 6/75–78.*

**(*) The Feeling
Snapper Complete Blues SBLUECD 016 *Similar to above. 6/75–78.*

These compilations from King's Utopia albums of the late '70s have chunks (the Snapper 2CD more substantial ones) of *King Albert* and *New Orleans Heat* (see above). *Guitar Man* adds three from the critically disliked *Albert*, while the Snapper 2CD bites off several tracks from the '75 Montreux show (see *Blues From The Road*) and a couple from the questionably dated Chicago gig (see *Talkin' Blues*). Their chief interest at present, then, is their access (four or five tracks each) to the currently out-of-print original *Truckload Of Lovin'*, a richly produced album that doesn't stand high in King's work but did disseminate one good song, Mack Rice's 'Cadillac Assembly Line', which all three sets include.

*** Crosscut Saw: Albert King In San Francisco
Stax SCD-8571//[(E) CDSXE 076] *King; Tony Llorens (o, p); Larry Burton (g); Gus Thornton (b); Michael Llorens (d). 3/83.*

*** Rainin' In California
Wolf 120.500 *King; Oliver Jackson (t); Ed Hurley (tb); Tony Lorenz [Llorens] (o); Leon Blue (p); Gus Thornton (b); Michael Lorenz [Llorens] (d). 9/83.*

*** In Session
Stax SCD-7501 *King; Tony Llorens (o, p); Stevie Ray Vaughan (g, v); Gus Thornton (b); Michael Llorens (d). 12/83.*

*** I'm In A Phone Booth Baby
Stax SCD-8560//(E) CDSXE 083 *King; Cal Lewiston (t); Steve Douglas (ts, bs); Tony Llorens (o, p); Gus Thornton (b); Michael Llorens (d). 1/84.*

Crosscut Saw, King's first album in five or six years, was a reassuringly back-to-basics set: no fancy arrangements or backing singers, just his road band and a programme of mostly plain old blues like 'Honey Bee' and 'I'm Gonna Move To The Outskirts Of Town', gussied up with a song about a recent visit by Elizabeth R, 'They Made The Queen Welcome', with a verse to cherish: 'She went to this big dinner, up in this big hotel,/Tony Bennett was singing, but I could tell she wasn't feeling too well.' 'Floodin' In California', a rewrite of Larry Davis's 'Texas Flood', also turns up as 'Rainin' In California' on the Wolf album of that name, a well-recorded set from the Long Beach Blues Festival with potent versions of 'I Wonder Why', 'I'll Play The Blues For You' and 'The Sky Is Crying'. The last of these had a calmer reading on King's next studio album, *I'm In A Phone Booth Baby*, following another Elmore James number, 'Dust My Broom', but most of the other songs were new compositions like 'Brother, Go Ahead And Take Her' and the title number, written and co-written respectively by Dennis Walker, and Doug MacLeod's 'Your Bread Ain't Done'. Tony Llorens, though listed as playing acoustic piano, is more often heard at the organ, where his solos take up a lot of the space normally occupied by his leader's guitar.

In Session is taken from a Canadian TV series of that name, which paired musicians who seldom had the chance to play together. Stevie Ray Vaughan had been an admirer of King since he was a teenager, and as they jam together it becomes obvious how deeply his playing was rooted in the older man's. The interludes of conversation are brief, leaving room for seven long songs, including a 15-minute 'Blues At Sunrise'. Readers chiefly interested in King may balk at an album with so much familiar material ('Overall Junction', 'Match Box Blues', 'Don't Lie To Me', etc.), but for others it's a rare opportunity to eavesdrop on two great musicians showing unaffected respect for each other, both in their words and in their playing.

***(*) The Ultimate Collection
Rhino R2 71268 2CD *As for relevant CDs above. 11/53, 64–1/84.*

***(*) **Blues Masters: The Very Best Of Albert King**
Rhino R2 75703 *As above.* 60–6/75.

There's little to criticize in the tightly packed (39-track) *Ultimate Collection*: the absence of the Bobbin/King recordings is regrettable, and the Utopia/Tomato albums might have had more consideration, but there are good versions, often the best, of core repertoire like 'Angel Of Mercy', 'Crosscut Saw', 'I'll Play The Blues For You', 'Laundromat Blues' and so on. The set is well annotated and attractively packaged but, at the time of writing, of uncertain availability.

The single *Blues Masters* CD shares 13 of its 16 tracks with *The Ultimate Collection* and improves its coverage by including two Bobbin recordings, 'Let's Have A Natural Ball' and 'Don't Throw Your Love On Me So Strong'. Then there are a dozen from Stax (seven from *Born Under A Bad Sign* or nearby sessions) and 'Cadillac Assembly Line' from 1975: as far as it goes, a very fair summary.

***(*) **Blues For You: The Best Of Albert King**
Stax (E) CDSXD 120 *As above.* 5/67–1/84.
*** **The Best Of Albert King**
Stax (E) CDSXK 122 *As above.* 68–1/84.

Blues For You has 20 tracks, fewer than half of which are on the Rhino sets. It draws extensively from the *Years Gone By–Lovejoy–I'll Play The Blues For You* period, which is all to the good, and ends with two cuts from the '68 Fillmore engagement, 'Crosscut Saw' and an excerpt from 'Blues Power'. The version of 'Born Under A Bad Sign' that opens the CD, though dated 1979, is the 1967 original. The second Stax *Best Of* is mostly a reduced version of the first, its weight boosted at the end with a few live cuts drawn from the back catalogue. TR

B. B. King (born 1925)
VOCAL, GUITAR, PIANO

Riley B. King comes from a poor farming family in central Mississippi. As a teenager he sang in a gospel group, but then took up guitar. By his early 20s he was trying to make a living in the clubs around Memphis, where he eventually secured a job as a DJ, 'the Pepticon Blues Boy', on the new, black-staffed, local station WDIA. Now equipped with a professional name, B. B. (for 'Blues Boy') King recorded a couple of singles for Bullet before signing with Modern, whose RPM label he boosted repeatedly into the R&B charts of the '50s, beginning with 'Three O'Clock Blues'. Meanwhile he toured incessantly with a substantial band, playing almost every night for year after year. In 1962 he graduated to a mainstream label, ABC, where his work was only intermittently successful, but towards the end of the decade, judiciously promoted by his new manager, Sidney Seidenberg, he began to perform on the rock circuit, where his intense singing and playing and pleasant stage manner won him a new audience, young and white, that was enthusiastic about blues–rock interactions like the 1970 album Indianola Mississippi Seeds. *Since then King has taken on the role of a suave ambassador for the blues, playing all over the world and collaborating with musicians in many other fields.*

*** **The 1950–1951 Modern Recordings**
Ace CDCHM2 835 2CD *King; prob. Willie Mitchell (t); Hank Crawford (as); Solomon Hardy, Richard Sanders, Ben Branch (ts); Ford Nelson, Phineas Newborn Jr, Johnny Ace, Ike Turner (p); James Walker (b); E. A. Kamp, Phineas Newborn Sr, Ted Curry, unknown (d).* c. 9/50–51.

♛ **** **The RPM Hits 1951–1957**
Ace CDCHD 712 *King; prob. Willie Mitchell, Floyd Jones, Kenny Sands, unknowns (t); George Coleman (as, ts); Hank Crawford, Lawrence Burdine (as); Ben Branch, Bill Harvey, Maxwell Davis, Johnny Board (ts); Floyd Newman, unknown (bs); unknowns (s); Ike Turner, Connie Mack Booker, Millard Lee, unknowns (p); James Walker, Tuff Green, Jymie Merritt, unknowns (b); Ted Curry, unknowns (d); Charles Crosby, unknown (cga); The King's Men, unknowns (v).* 51–57.

***(*) **Do The Boogie**
Ace CDCH 916 *Similar to above.* 52–56.
*** **The Fabulous B. B. King**
Ace CDFAB 004 *Similar to above.* 52–57.
***(*) **My Sweet Little Angel**
[Flair 39103]//Ace CDCHD 300 *King; Kenny Sands, Henry Boozier, unknowns (t); Pluma Davis (tb); Lawrence Burdine (as); Maxwell Davis, Johnny Board, unknowns (ts); Floyd Newman, Barney Hubert (bs); unknowns (s); unknown (o); Millard Lee, unknowns (p); Jymie Merritt, Marshall York, unknowns (b); unknown (tu); Ted Curry, Sonny Freeman, unknowns (d).* 55–61/62.

**** **The Vintage Years**
Ace ABOXCD 8 4CD *Similar to above CDs.* c. 9/50–61/62.

Producing half a dozen or so singles a year, King had space to develop his ideas, and one can hear on the early sides his transformations of the West Coast styles of the day, pre-eminently T-Bone Walker's. If King's blend of long, singing notes with abrupt, chattering clusters was prompted by listening to Walker, the incessant bending of the long notes and the rhythmic capriciousness of the clusters are King's contribution, inspired by models as different as the slide guitar playing of his cousin Booker White and the rhythmic vitality of Django Reinhardt. Both Walker and King, in their playing, echo speech patterns, but whereas Walker's instrumental conversation is fluent and moderate, King's is irregular and excitable; the phrases sometimes rush out in a torrent, sometimes stutter as if log-jammed. Yet the record that defined King's early career came from another model, Lowell Fulson. 'Three O'Clock Blues', as recorded by Fulson three years earlier in a guitar duet with his brother, meandered like a country stream. King made something else out of it entirely. Against a funeral march of horns he wails like a mourner, and the guitar intro and solo scream out of near-silence.

The RPM Hits 1951–1957 is exactly what it says on the box, the songs that first made King famous: 'Three O'Clock Blues', 'Please Love Me', 'You Upset Me Baby' (all R&B chart-toppers), 'Every Day (I Have The Blues)', 'Ten Long Years', 'Sweet Little Angel' and 20 more, in state-of-the-art sound. Many of these are among the dozen tracks on the budget-price *The Fabulous B. B. King*. Some of them also occur on *My Sweet Little Angel* or *Do The Boogie*, interspersed on both with alternative versions and unissued pieces. With the obvious reservation about overlap, all these are generous and appetizing slices of the deep-dish pizza that is King's Modern music. *The 1950–1951 Modern Recordings* has another agenda. 'This is not a collection for the casual B. B. King fan,' the notes warn. Indeed not: it focuses on a few months at the very beginning of King's contract with RPM, and the majority of the items are presented in two or even three takes; there are 33 tracks but only 18 titles.

The Vintage Years, produced with the perfectionism that distinguishes Ace releases from unsanctioned knock-offs of the same material, is a four-basket shopping trip through King's Modern Market. The biggest eggs are all in the first, a mixture of hits on RPM (embracing all the titles cited above) and Kent plus versions of other important pieces in King's folio like 'How Blue Can You Get'. Disc 2 concentrates on 1951–52, Disc 3 on the mid-to-late '50s and Disc 4 on Kent singles and a few album tracks, yielding a total of over a hundred items: not the entirety of the King/Modern archive, but thoroughly representative and with no significant omissions. It's accompanied by an almost exhaustively informative booklet. Readers who value a minimalist domestic decor could hardly do better than buy this and MCA's *King Of The Blues*; in the neat confines of two 4CD longboxes they'll have about 180 recordings (with fewer than a dozen duplications) spanning more than 40 years.

(***) B. B. King 1949–1952
Classics 5053 *King; Nathan Woodward, prob. Willie Mitchell (t); Sammie Jett (tb); Hank Crawford (as); Ben Branch, Solomon Hardy, prob. Richard Saunders (ts); J. P. Louper (s); Phineas Newborn Jr, Ford Nelson, Johnny Ace, Ike Turner (p); Tuff Green, James Walker, unknown (b); Phineas Newborn Sr, E. A. Kamp, Ted Curry, unknown (d). 49–52.*

(**(*)) Three O'Clock Blues
Snapper Complete Blues SBLUECD 026 *As above, except omit unknown (b). 49–52.*

(***) A Proper Introduction To B. B. King: Woke Up This Morning
Proper INTRO CD 2022 *King; Nathan Woodward, prob. Willie Mitchell, Floyd Jones, unknown (t); Sammie Jett (tb); George Coleman (as, ts); Hank Crawford (as); Ben Branch, Solomon Hardy, prob. Richard Saunders (ts); Bill Harvey, unknown (ts); unknown (bs); J. P. Louper, unknowns (s); Phineas Newborn Jr, Ford Nelson, Johnny Ace, Ike Turner, Connie Mack Booker, unknown (p); Tuff Green, James Walker, unknowns (b); Phineas Newborn Sr, E. A. Kamp, Ted Curry, unknowns (d); Onzie Horne (vb); Charles Crosby (cga). 49–52/53.*

(***) The Very Best Of B. B. King
Disconforme CDX 7715 2CD *King; various accompaniments. 49–61.*

*** B. B. King 1952–1953
Classics 5148 *King; Floyd Jones (t); George Coleman (as, ts); Hank Crawford (as); Ben Branch, Bill Harvey, poss. Maxwell Davis, unknown (ts); poss. Fred Ford, unknown (bs); unknowns (s); Johnny Ace, Ike Turner, Connie Mack Booker, unknown (p); Tuff Green, James Walker, unknowns (b); Phineas Newborn Sr, Ted Curry, unknowns (d); Charles Crosby (cga); Onzie Horne (vb). 1/52–53.*

*** Blues Kingpins
Virgin 82712 *King; various accompaniments. 52–61/62.*

Snapper and Proper offer decent selections of King's early work, with 14 tracks in common, but there is no reason to prefer them to Ace's superior productions. Classics have set out on their customary chronological journey through King's catalogue but are taking their time about it. Disconforme gather three of the four Bullet sides and 37 from RPM and Kent, not very intelligibly chosen and randomly sequenced. The label might have used the space available to give some details of what one's listening to, rather than print the tracklisting three times. The pick of this bunch is *Blues Kingpins*, an efficient 18-track greatest-hits collection.

*** The Best Of The Kent Singles 1958–1971
Ace CDCHD 760 *King; Kenny Sands, Henry Boozier, unknowns (t); Pluma Davis (tb); Lawrence Burdine (as); Johnny Board, Bobby Forte (ts); Barney Hubert (bs); unknowns (s); unknown(s) (o); Millard Lee, Lloyd Glenn, Jimmy McCracklin, Duke Jethro, unknown(s) (p); unknowns (strings); unknown(s) (g); Marshall York, Ralph Hamilton, Leo Lauchie, unknowns (b); Ted Curry, Sonny Freeman, Jesse Sailes, unknowns (d); The Vocal Chords (v). 58–61/62.*

The date in the title is a little deceptive: by 1971 King hadn't recorded for Kent for almost a decade. Kent, however, had continued to pump out 45s from the stock of recordings he had made in the late '50s and early '60s. Some of these were then reissued, later in the '60s, with overdubs, to give them an air of up-to-dateness. Ace have largely ignored these treated recordings, on the fair grounds that they seldom improved on the originals, but do include the more artfully expanded 'Worry, Worry, Worry' to show that Kent at least occasionally knew what they were doing. Several of these singles reached the R&B charts, the two-part 'Sweet Sixteen' making it to #2, and, even after King had moved on to a larger label, Kent registered several minor hits like 'Blue Shadows' and 'The Jungle'. So this CD is a valuable sidebar to the ABC/Bluesway story of the '60s, as well as an entertaining collection of crisp, unfussy blues singles.

**(*) Spotlight On Lucille
Flair 86231//Ace CDCH 187 *King; unknowns (brass, reeds, o, p, b, d). 60/61.*

An all-instrumental album similar to *Easy Listening Blues* (see below) and sharing a couple of its tracks. As the leading soloist King is uneven and quite often dull. One's prompted to wonder if these were made not to be instrumentals but as backing tracks; at any rate, there's something hollow and unsatisfying about it all. The sound quality is excellent.

**** My Kind Of Blues
Ace CDCHM 881 *King; Lloyd Glenn, poss. Millard Lee (p); Ralph Hamilton, unknown (b); Jesse Sailes, Sonny Freeman (d). 3/60, unknown dates.*

**(*) Wails
Ace CDCHM 882 *King; Kenny Sands, Henry Boozier, unknown (t); Pluma Davis (tb); Lawrence Burdine (as); Johnny Board, unknown (ts); Barney Hubert (bs); Millard Lee (p); Marshall York, unknown (b); unknown (tu); Sonny Freeman (d); Count Basie Orchestra; Tommy Dorsey Orchestra. c. 59–c. 61.*

*** King Of The Blues
Ace CDCHM 897 *As above, except add unknown (ts), unknown (o), Lloyd Glenn, Jimmy McCracklin, unknown (p), unknown (b), unknown (d). 3/60, unknown dates.*

**(*) The Soul Of ... B. B. King
Ace CDCHM 986 *King; Floyd Jones, Kenny Sands, Henry Boozier, unknown (t); Pluma Davis (tb); unknown (ss); George Coleman (as, ts); Lawrence Burdine (as); Bill Harvey, Maxwell Davis, Johnny Board, unknown (ts); Barney Hubert, unknown (bs); unknowns (s); unknown (o); Connie Mack Booker, Millard Lee, unknowns (p); James Walker, Marshall York, unknowns (b); Ted Curry, Sonny Freeman, unknowns (d). 52–61.*

(*) Blues In My Heart
Ace CDCHM 996 King; unknowns (ts, o, p, b, d). poss. late 61, unknown dates.

(*) Easy Listening Blues
Ace CDCHM 1011 King; unknowns (brass, reeds); Maxwell Davis (ts); unknown(s) (o); Lloyd Glenn, unknowns (p); unknowns (b); unknowns (d). 55, c. 61.

(*) More B. B. King
Ace CDCHM 1034 King; Kenny Sands, unknowns (t); unknown (tb); Johnny Board, Bobby Forte, unknowns (ts); unknowns (s); unknown (o); Millard Lee, Duke Jethro, unknowns (p); unknowns (strings); Leo Lauchie, unknowns (b); Sonny Freeman, unknowns (d); band (v). 55–61.

**** Singin' The Blues**
Ace CDCHM 1041 King; prob. Willie Mitchell, Floyd Jones, Kenny Sands, unknown (t); George Coleman (as, ts); Hank Crawford, Lawrence Burdine (as); Ben Branch, Bill Harvey, Maxwell Davis, Johnny Board (ts); Floyd Newman, unknown (bs); unknowns (s); Ike Turner, Connie Mack Booker, Millard Lee, unknowns (p); James Walker, Tuff Green, Jymie Merritt, unknowns (b); Ted Curry, unknowns (d); Charles Crosby (cga). 52–56.

****/*** Singin' The Blues/The Blues**
Flair 86296 As above, except add Henry Boozier (t), Barney Hubert (bs), Marshall York (b). 52–58/59.

*** The Great B. B. King**
Ace CDCHM 1049 King; Kenny Sands, Henry Boozier, unknowns (t); Pluma Davis (tb); Lawrence Burdine (as); Maxwell Davis, Johnny Board, unknowns (ts); Barney Hubert, unknown (bs); unknowns (s); unknown (o); Millard Lee, unknowns (p); Marshall York, unknowns (b); Ted Curry, Sonny Freeman, unknowns (d); The King's Men, unknowns (v). 53–65.

King's albums on the budget label Crown, derived from his years of singles for RPM and Kent, are cumulatively a superb exposition of the power and breadth of his music in the '50s. Ace's release of *My Kind Of Blues* initiated a series of reissues of the Crown LPs with their original cover designs. Since most of the LPs ran to only ten tracks, each of the CDs adds at least eight bonus tracks from approximately the same period, some previously unissued.

My Kind Of Blues is one of the great B. B. King albums, and at one time – possibly still – one of his own favourites. The setting could not be simpler, just a piano trio headed by the vastly experienced Lloyd Glenn, and King digs back into his past for ageless blues like 'Someday Baby', 'Driving Wheel' and 'Fishin' After Me (Catfish Blues)'. The bonus tracks continue the theme with Casey Bill Weldon's 'Somebody Done Changed The Lock On My Door' and Memphis Minnie's 'Looking The World Over'.

Wails, in contrast, gives King a big-band setting, to which he responds by choosing some pop material like 'I Love You So' and 'My Silent Prayer'. Among the bonus tracks, maintaining the orchestral theme, are recordings with the Count Basie and Tommy Dorsey bands, and a 'Why I Sing The Blues' which the notes erroneously identify with his later hit (see *Live & Well* below). *King Of The Blues* has the same band as the bulk of *Wails* but the programme is mostly blues, as are the ten bonus tracks, which include re-creations of early-'50s sides like 'When My Heart Beats Like A Hammer' and '3 O'Clock Blues', the latter a shadow of its predecessor. In the notes to *The Soul Of …* John Broven candidly describes it as 'something of an incoherent collection from sessions past', which is true, but there were still interesting things to be found on those old tapes, such as versions of Walter Davis's 'Come Back Baby', Roy Brown's 'Hard Luck Blues' (as 'The Road I Travel') and, surprisingly, Tampa Red's 1951 recording 'Green And Lucky Blues'.

Both the original contents of *Blues In My Heart* and the added tracks have King working with a small group (one saxophone and rhythm); the consistency of sound and a preponderance of slow and medium-tempo blues make for dull listening, and the album's only recommendation, other than to completists, is that it contains King's first recording of 'Downhearted' (a.k.a. 'How Blue Can You Get'), which became a personal standard. From the same period comes *Easy Listening Blues*, which reissues a set of instrumentals and adds eight more, a couple, like the T-Boneish 'Boogie Rock', from as far back as 1955. This too is a less than riveting album, but it's rare that one hears King do nothing but play, and just occasionally he does something one might not have heard before. *More B. B. King*, other than retrieving a couple of overlooked tracks from 1955, belongs to 1960–61; three songs with strings are fairly dreadful, but several others are intriguing throwbacks, 'I Can Hear My Name' to Sonny Boy Williamson I's 'My Black Name' and 'Bad Luck Soul' to Blind Lemon Jefferson.

Singin' The Blues, the first of the Crown LPs, superbly epitomizes the whole series, acknowledging King's early models like T-Bone Walker in 'You Upset Me Baby' or Lonnie Johnson in 'Bad Luck', and perhaps Al Hibbler or one of his kind in the ballad 'You Know I Love You', and also embracing his original recordings of 'Three O'Clock Blues', 'Ten Long Years', 'Everyday (I Have The Blues)', 'Sweet Little Angel' and 'Crying Won't Help You': self-evidently a near-faultless album. *The Blues*, not yet incorporated into the Ace/Crown series but coupled with *Singin' The Blues* on a Flair twofer (or, if you can find it, the deleted Ace CDCHD 320), is merely a good one. So is *The Great B. B. King*, which leads off with the original two-part 'Sweet Sixteen' and 'Quit My Baby', derived from Dr Clayton's 'Cheating And Lying Blues', and, though it never scales those heights again, contains some interesting curiosities, as well as the ludicrous teenbeat number 'Bim Bam'.

Many of the recordings on these CDs are also available on differently conceived compilations (see earlier in this entry), and readers intending to build a collection of King's early work will need to do some careful comparison shopping. Two points should be made about the Crown-based CDs: they have a historical dimension, in that the original LPs, sold as they were in 99-cent bins in supermarkets, were how many people were first exposed to King in the '60s; and though Ace price them somewhat higher, they are still very inexpensive.

***(*)/**(*) Mr. Blues/Confessin' The Blues**
BGO BGOCD 665 King; Carl Adams, unknowns (t); John Watson (tb); William Green, Jewel Grant, Lawrence Burdine (as); Maxwell Davis, Vernon Slater, unknown (ts); Floyd Turnham, Johnny Board (bs); unknowns (s); Duke Jethro, unknown (o); Lloyd Glenn, unknown (p); Leo Blevins, unknown (g); Ralph Hamilton, Leo Lauchie, unknown (b); Jesse Sailes, Sonny Freeman (d); Belford Hendricks Orchestra, Teacho Wilshire Orchestra. 3/62–4/63, 9/64–6/65.

Mr. Blues, which compiles King's first batch of singles for ABC, appears to draw a line under the RPM and Kent recordings and open a new chapter in his work: the blues content has been radically reduced, in favour of pop ballads like Jesse Belvin's 'Guess Who' and Lonnie Johnson's 'Tomorrow Night', with orchestral accompaniments. Artistically and commercially unsuccessful, its policy was overturned first by *Live At The Regal* (see below) and then by *Confessin' The Blues*, a set of blues standards as defined in the work of predecessors like Big Joe Turner and Jimmy Rushing, such as 'How Long', 'Wee Baby' and 'Cherry Red', accompanied by King's regular band. He gives respectable accounts of this venerable material but the numbers are too brief to accomodate much guitar.

♛ **** Live At The Regal
MCA MCAD 11646//MCD 31106//BGO BGOCD 235 *King; Kenny Sands (t); Johnny Board, Bobby Forte (ts); Duke Jethro (o); Leo Lauchie (b); Sonny Freeman (d). 11/64.*

In-concert recordings that do full justice both to the performer and to the occasion are uncommon. *Live At The Regal* is certainly one, and, although King has since made numerous other live albums, none of them has surpassed the communal atmosphere of celebration that was created one winter evening in Chicago in 1964. The material is almost all chosen from King's favourites ('It's My Own Fault', 'How Blue Can You Get', 'You Upset Me Baby', etc.), but the point of the album is not what songs he sang but how he built them into a performance. This is a recording of iconic significance, which several musicians have declared brought them to an appreciation of the blues, and it only gains lustre with the passing years. Vinyl devotees can still obtain it as Ace CH 86.

***(*) Blues Is King
MCA MCAD-31368 *King; Kenneth Sands (t); Bobby Forte (ts); Duke Jethro (o); Louis Satterfield (b); Sonny Freeman (d). 11/66.*

The audience, though audibly enjoying themselves, don't play as prominent a part as on *Live At The Regal*, but otherwise this in-performance recording from an unnamed Chicago club has nearly all the strengths of the earlier album. The sound King gets on his guitar is as hard and penetrating as a diamond-point drill, but his songs are not so relentlessly macho: though he brusquely stands for no nonsense in 'Tired Of Your Jive' and declares himself the master of his own house in an intimidating 'Don't Answer The Door', he ends on a note of can't-help-myself affection in 'Gonna Keep On Loving You'. The balance isn't perfect and the editing is sometimes abrupt, but this is unquestionably King's second-best live album.

** Blues On Top Of Blues
BGO BGOCD 69 *King; Hobart Dotson, John Browning, Henry Boozier, unknowns (t); Pluma Davis, unknown (tb); Lawrence Burdine (as); Johnny Board (ts); Barney Hubert (bs); unknowns (s); Duke Jethro, unknown (o); unknown (p); Billy Butler (g); Leo Lauchie, unknown (b); Sonny Freeman, unknown (d); Johnny Pate (arr, cond). 67.*

There are straightforward blues here like 'Having My Say', 'Worried Dream' and 'Paying The Cost To Be The Boss', but they are oases of satisfaction in a desert of unmemorable songs and overbearing orchestral charts.

*** Great Moments With B. B. King
MCA MCAD 4124//(E) MCD 04124 *As for Confessin' The Blues, Blues Is King and Blues On Top Of Blues. 6/65–67.*

A sort of mid-term report on the ABC/Bluesway project, containing nine tracks from *Blues Is King*, eight from *Blues On Top Of Blues* and five from *Confessin' The Blues*.

**(*) Lucille
MCA MCAD 10518//BGO BGOCD 36 *King; Mel Moore (t); John Ewing (tb); Bobby Forte (ts); Cecil [Big Jay] McNeely, Bob McNeely (s); Maxwell Davis (o); Lloyd Glenn (p); Irving Ashby (g); David Allen (b); Jesse Sailes (d); unknown (v grp); Bob Thiele (prod). 12/67.*

Ten minutes of 'Lucille', B. B.'s celebrated narrative about his guitar, seem like an over-leisurely way to begin the proceedings, and the album as a whole, though seldom boring, is uneventful, the songs unstartling and the playing safe; without the credit, no one, surely, would have detected Big Jay McNeely in the well-behaved horn section.

*** His Best – The Electric B. B. King
MCA MCAD 11767//MCAD 27007//BGO BGOCD 37 *King; Carl Adams, Kenneth Sands, McKinley Johnson, Hobart Dotson, John Browning, Henry Boozier (t); Pluma Davis (tb); Lawrence Burdine (as); Vernon Slater, Bobby Forte, Johnny Board (ts); Barney Hubert (bs); Duke Jethro, Maxwell Davis (o); Lloyd Glenn (p); Irving Ashby, unknown (g); Leo Lauchie, Louis Satterfield, David Allen, unknown (b); Sonny Freeman, Jesse Sailes (d); Maya Angelou (v). 65–8/68.*

This is not a conventional 'best of' but a selection of sides previously issued as singles and a couple of session leftovers. The former include the admonishing 'Don't Answer The Door' and 'Sweet Sixteen', both two-part pieces, the latter a noisy live recording probably from the 11/66 concert that made *Blues Is King*; 'All Over Again', sometimes known as 'I Got A Mind To Give Up Living', a tremendous song; and a curiosity in 'The B. B. Jones', a lightweight dance number co-written, and with backing vocals, by the writer Maya Angelou. Although this looks like an issue compiled to fill a gap between more considered albums, it has good performances and a fair number of above-average songs to recommend it.

*** Live & Well
MCA MCAD 31191//BGO BGOCD 233 *King; Patrick Williams, unknown (t); unknown (as); Lee Gatling, unknown (ts); Paul Harris (o, p); Charles Bowles (o); Al Kooper (p); Hugh McCracken (g); Gerry Jemmott, Val Patillo (b); Herbie Lovelle, Sonny Freeman (d); Bill Szymczyk (prod). 1–3/69.*

**(*) Completely Well
MCA MCAD 11768//MCAD 31039 *King; unknown (t); unknowns (s); Paul Harris (kb, o, p); unknowns (strings); Hugh McCracken (g); Gerry Jemmott (b); Herbie Lovelle (d); Bill Szymczyk (prod). 6/69.*

The 'live' part of *Live & Well* was recorded at New York's Village Gate with members of King's road band, the rest in the studio with a group of musicians who were not blues specialists but gave King's music a freshness to which he plainly responded. The album also made an important addition to King's repertoire in 'Why I Sing The Blues', a song co-written by King and the veteran promoter Dave Clark which aspires to tell the history of the music. The success of the studio segment encouraged Bluesway to make King's next album entirely at The Hit Factory with the same core group, but the formula didn't work the second time, and the playing on most of the tracks seems fussy. Nonetheless, *Completely*

Well has a place of respect in King's discography, because it introduced the lovely 'The Thrill Is Gone'.

**** Indianola Mississippi Seeds
MCA MCAD 31343//BGO BGOCD 237 *King; unknowns (brass, reeds); Carole King (kb, p); Leon Russell, Paul Harris (p); unknowns (strings); Joe Walsh, Hugh McCracken (g); Bryan Garofalo, Gerry Jemmott (b); Russ Kunkel, Herbie Lovelle (d); Sherlie Matthews, Merry Clayton, Clydie King, Venetta Fields (v); Jimmie Haskell (arr); Bill Szymczyk (prod). 1/69, 5–6/70.*

At the time, King's collaboration with rock luminaries such as Carole King, Russell and Walsh semed to some of his admirers to be a step on a risky path. They should have trusted the instincts of artist and producer a little more. All these years later, *Seeds* still feels like a record of an unforced, enjoyable encounter. The programme, embracing three songs conceived with veteran writer Dave Clark (one of them, 'Go Underground', an outtake from the *Live & Well* studio session) and concluding with Russell's delicate 'Hummingbird', elicits some of King's most polished and heartfelt singing, Carole King's soulful piano figures steer the ensemble sound away from generic predictability, and the string coloration is unintrusive yet vital.

*** Live In Cook County Jail
MCA MCAD 11769//MCD 31080 *King; John Browning (t); Booker Walker (as); Louis Hubert (ts); Ron Levy (p); Wilbert Freeman (b); Sonny Freeman (d). 9/70.*
(*)/* Completely Well/Live In Cook County Jail
BGO BGOCD 602 *As for relevant CDs above. 6/69, 9/70.*

As for the Regal engagement almost six years earlier, King took to Cook County Jail a six-piece band and a book drawn almost exclusively from his back catalogue; indeed, the first three songs on the album, 'Every Day I Have The Blues', 'How Blue Can You Get' and 'Worry, Worry, Worry', had all featured in the Regal setlist. He was playing to a different sort of crowd, though; it wasn't merely that they were, in the sharpest sense, a captive audience, but they were mostly young black men, not King's primary constituency. It attests to his skill as a performer that he seems to get to them – in particular in 'Worry, Worry, Worry', which is King at his best and most fluid, now preacher, now standup comedian.

*** Live In Japan
MCA MCAD-11810 *King; John Browning (t); Joseph Burton (tb); Earl Turbinton (as); Louis Hubert (ts); Ron Levy (p); Wilton [Wilbert] Freeman (b); Sonny Freeman (d). 3/71.*

Much of the programme is from the front of the band book – 'Every Day I Have The Blues' and 'How Blue Can You Get?' again, 'Chains And Things' and 'Hummingbird' from *Indianola Mississippi Seeds*, 'Sweet Sixteen', 'The Thrill Is Gone' – but the performances (two shows in Tokyo a few days apart) brim with vitality and King lets loose some blistering solos, both on songs and on the instrumental workouts 'Jamming At Sankei Hall' and 'Hikari #88'. The balance doesn't always favour his voice.

** In London
MCA MCD 18223//BGO BGOCD 42 *King; Jim Price (t, tb, kb); Ollie Mitchell (t); Chuck Findley (tb); Bill Perkins (cl, bs); Bobby Keys (s); Duster Bennett, Steve Marriott (h); The Mystery Shadow (o); Gary Wright (kb, o, p); Rick Wright (kb); Jerry Ragovoy, Pete Wingfield (p); unknowns (strings); John Uribe, Mac Rebennack [Dr John], David Spinozza, Paul Butler, Alexis Korner (g); Klaus Voorman, John Best, Greg Ridley (b); Jim Keltner, Ringo Starr, Jim Gordon, Barry Ford, Jerry Shirley (d); Jos[h?]ie Armstead, Tasha Thomas, Carl Hall (v). 6–7/71.*

King recorded the basic tracks in London, hence the presence of locals like Bennett, Marriot, Wingfield, etc., but the tapes were taken back to the US and 'modified' – extensively – in LA and New York, leaving little flavour of a King abroad. 'Ghetto Woman' has the air of something from *Indianola Mississippi Seeds*, and 'Blue Shadows' and Wingfield's composition 'The Power Of The Blues' are pleasing enough, but much of what remains is half-hearted or insignificant.

*** Live In Kansas City
Blues Factory BFY 47017 *King; Edward Rowe (t); Joseph Burton (tb); Cato Walker (as); Bobby Forte (ts); Louis Hubert (bs); Ron Levy (p); Milton Hopkins (g); Wilbert Freeman (b); prob. Sonny Freeman (d). 72.*

A probably unsanctioned, crudely edited but vividly recorded document of a concert in Kansas City which caught King and his band on brave form, whether retailing old stories like 'Sweet Little Angel' and 'I've Got A Mind To Give Up Living' or newer repertoire like 'Ain't Nobody Home' and 'Guess Who'. Though only nine tracks are listed, King gets through more material, for example seguing from 'Nobody Loves Me But My Mother' to a fast instrumental; there are also passages of a kind not normally heard on official live albums, like the piano–guitar duet at the start of 'King's Shuffle'. (Formerly on Charly Blues Legends CD CBL 752.)

** Guess Who
MCA MCD 10351//BGO BGOCD 71 *King; Edward Rowe, Ernie Royal, Steve Madaio (t); Joseph Burton, Garnett Brown (tb); Dave Sanborn (as); Earl Turbinton, Bobby Forte, Gene Dinwiddie, Trevor Lawrence (ts); Louis Hubert, Howard Johnson (bs); Ron Levy, Frank Owens (p); Milton Hopkins, Cornell Dupree (g); Wilbert Freeman, Gerry Jemmott (b); V. S. [Sonny] Freeman, Bernard Purdie (d); unknowns (v); Joe Zagarino (prod). 72.*

*(*) To Know You Is To Love You
MCA MCD 10414 *King; Andrew Love, Wayne Jackson & Memphis Horns (brass, reeds); Dave Crawford (kb, v, prod); Charles Mann (kb, v); Stevie Wonder, Ron Kersey (kb); Norman Harris, Roland Chambers, Eli Tartarsky (g); Ronnie Baker (b); Earl Young (d); Larry Washington (cga); Vince Montana (vb). 73.*

*(*) Friends
BGO BGOCD 125 *As above, except add Will Boulware (kb), unknowns (strings), Deryll Inman (g); omit Mann, Wonder. 74.*

Guess Who, *To Know You Is To Love You* and *Friends* are early members of a group of albums that attempt to portray King as something other than a bluesman. The failure of such records to be more than intermittently worthwhile can be attributed to two basic facts: King is not really at home singing this sort of material, and can be at something of a loss when playing it. As he had remarked some years earlier, 'You know, if I could sing pop tunes like Frank Sinatra or Sammy Davis Jr, I don't think I still could do it, 'cause Lucille don't want to play nothin' but the blues. And I think I'm pretty glad about that.' *Guess Who* has a couple of Jerry Ragovoy songs after the style of 'Ain't Nobody Home' on *In London*; the title song is an old Jesse Belvin ballad. The orchestral settings are trite and lack interesting solo passages. The original cover showed King asleep on a beach, his guitar a good arm's length away, and the title written in sand. There's no need to labour the irony. Most of the eight songs on *To Know You Is To Love You* and the seven on *Friends* were written or co-written by their producer and give King nothing worthwhile to work with. On *Friends*, with its playing time of 28.35, at least the agony is not prolonged.

*** B. B. King & Bobby Bland – Together For The First Time ... Live
MCA MCD 04160//BGO BGOCD 161 *King; Melvin Jackson, Edward Rowe (t); Joseph Burton (tb); Cato Walker (as); Bobby Forte (ts); Louis Hubert (bs); Michael Omartian, Ron Levy, Theodore [Teddy] Reynolds (kb); Mel Brown, Ben Benay, Milton Hopkins (g); Wilbert Freeman (b); Sonny Freeman, Harold Potier Jr (d); Charles Polk, Tommy Punkson, Theodore Arthur, Leo Penn, Joseph Hardin Jr, Alfred Thomas (unknown instruments).* 74.

*** Bobby Bland & B. B. King – Together Again ... Live
BGO BGOCD 162 *King; Oscar Brashear, Albert Aarons, Snooky Young (t); Garnett Brown, Benny Powell (tb); Red Holloway (ts); Jerome Richardson (bs); James Toney (o); Robert Anderson (p); Milton Hopkins, Johnny Jones, Ray Parker (g); Rudy Aikels, Loui Villeri (b); Harold Potier, John Starks (d); Viola Jackson (v).* 3/76.

Twenty-five years after they first worked together, King and Bobby Bland met in Memphis for a 'live in the studio' recording before an invited audience, accompanied by musicians from their bands (and others), and engaged in a genial swap-meet of standards both generic and personal, interspersed with reminiscences and amiable joshing. Two years later they had a return match, this time at the Coconut Grove in LA with a locally hired big band; Bland, who had come off as the junior partner in Memphis, asserts himself more and gets first billing. The programme is broadly similar, but the band is obviously more rehearsed, cutting a fine dance groove for 'Feel So Bad'. The setup of two blues champions jousting for the audience's favours is appealing but, because of their chitchat and their long, meandering medleys, these albums are best visited occasionally rather than often.

** Midnight Believer/Take It Home
BGO BGOCD 604 *King; Steve Madaio, Dick Cary, Gary Grant (t); Charles B. Findley, George Bohanon, Bob Enevoldsen, Jack Redmond (tb); Abe Most (cl); Dennis Quitman, Kurt McGettrick, Gary Herbig, Eddie Miller, Larry Williams, Kim Hutchcroft (reeds); Wilton Felder (ts, b); Joe Sample (kb); unknowns (strings); Dean Parks, Ronald Bautista, Paul M. Jackson Jr (g); Robert 'Pops' Popwell (b); Nesbert 'Stix' Hooper, James Gadson (d, perc); Paulinho Da Costa (perc); Julia Waters Tillman, Maxine Waters Willard, Luther Waters, Oren Waters (v).* 78–79.

** Take It Home
MCA MCAD 11770 *As above, except omit Cary, Bohanon, Enevoldsen, Most, McGettrick, Herbig, Miller, Bautista, unknowns (strings), Popwell.* 79.

Midnight Believer and *Take It Home*, King's last studio albums of the '70s, were collaborations with The Crusaders, a fellow ABC act, and the trio's concepts gave King's music an entirely fresh gloss. Most of the songs on both were written by Joe Sample and Will Jennings, in a Crusaders idiom rather than one approximating to King's, and very few of them went on to be incorporated into his repertoire. Although the New Orleans parade-band setting of 'I Just Can't Leave Your Love Alone' on *Midnight Believer* is surprising and fun, in general the songs are not located in either the actual or the imaginative geography of King's musical background, but rather in the international show business world he had come to inhabit.

**(*) Lucille Talks Back
MCA Special Products MCAD 22023 *King; various accompaniments.* 11/66–78.

The 1975 ABC album *Lucille Talks Back* is currently unavailable, but three good tracks from it appear on this identically titled set that's in fact a compilation from several ABC albums, the earliest *Blues Is King*, the latest *Midnight Believer*. There are only ten tracks but it's budget-priced accordingly. Worth the notice of the serious King collector.

*(*) There Must Be A Better World Somewhere
BGO BGOCD 124 *King; Waymon Reed, Charlie Miller (t); Tom Malone (tb); Hank Crawford (as); David 'Fathead' Newman (ts); Ronald Cuber (bs); Dr John [Mack Rebennack] (kb, p); Hugh McCracken (g); Wilbur Bascomb (b); Bernard 'Pretty' Purdie (d); Donny Gerrard, Carmen Twillie, Vennette Gloud (v).* 81.

All but one of the six longish songs were composed by Dr John and Doc Pomus, who, unlike (say) Dave Crawford, had some idea of what King's strengths were, but the results will not satisfy his core constituency any more than they appear to have satisfied him: the only piece that has stayed in his repertoire is the title song, which he delivers with exactly the right air of resignation. *Love Me Tender* and the very good *Blues 'N' Jazz* (both 1982) appear to be currently out of print.

*** Sweet Little Angel
Blue Moon CDBM 142 *King; Calvin Owens (t, dir); unknowns (brass, reeds, p, g, b, d, perc); Chris Brubeck (tb, b); Neil [sic Bill] Smith (cl); Dave Brubeck (p).* 1/83.

*** The Great B. B. King
Pulse PLSCD 298 *As above, except omit Brubecks, Smith.* 1/83.

*** And His Orchestra Live
Fabulous FABCD 127 *As above.* 1/83.

Recorded in concert during MIDEM, the annual music-trade fair in Cannes, France, this set in all its manifestations has the look of a cheap and possibly unsanctioned release but turns out to be very listenable and even, in some respects, estimable. The extended introduction by the band, the delayed entrance of King's vocal on some tracks, the grandstanding 'yada-yada' trumpet solo on 'Guess Who' – these are characteristics of live performance that are often played down in planned live albums. A generation from now, listeners who want to know exactly what a typical B. B. King gig of this period sounded like may value this probably unscheduled, and more or less unedited, documentary recording. The setlist has no surprises, but King's reading of 'All Over Again' is stunning. Blue Moon and Pulse programme the tracks better than Fabulous; Blue Moon add another, a 'Jamming With Brubeck' that has King doing just that – actually with two Brubecks – and extends the running-time by 13 minutes. That CD's contents are also Disc 2 of *Luminescence* (TKO/Magnum/Meteor CDMT 503 2CD), Disc 1 being by Pat Metheny, the Heath Brothers and the Brubeck quartet on the same occasion.

*(*) Six Silver Strings
MCA MCAD-5616 *King; David Crawford (kb, prod); various musicians.* 85?

'B. B. King's 50th Album,' it proclaims. The occasion deserved better. Five songs were supervised, and mostly co-written, by David Crawford, a producer who unfailingly debases the coinage of King's music. The remaining three, 'In The Midnight Hour', 'My Lucille' and 'Into The Night', come from the soundtrack of John Landis's romcom *Into The Night* and were produced by Landis and Ira Newborn; in this context it doesn't mean much to say that the first number is the album's best track, but it's the only one a discriminating fan will play twice.

* King Of The Blues '89
MCA MCAD-42183//MCD 06038 *King; James Pugh (tb); Alan Rubin, Randy Brecker, The Muscle Shoals Horns (brass, reeds); Robert Magnuson (as, ts); Lou Marini (ts); Ronald Cuber (bs); Marty Grebb, Tom Scott (s); Al Kooper (kb, g, b, d, v); Jerry Williams (kb, g, d prog, v); Carson Whitsett, Clayton Ivey, Ernest Williamson (kb); various (strings); Steve Cropper, Michael Toles, Michael Spriggs (g); Ray Griffin (b); Mick Fleetwood, James Robinson (d); Trade Martin ('rhythm instruments', v); Rodney Kelly (prog); Stevie Nicks, Loralei Wehba, Bonnie Raitt, Chris Mancini, The Jim Gilstrap Singers, Alfa Anderson, Liliana Pumpido, Joe Amato, Luci Martin, Alfred Rios, Jewell Bass, Catherine Henderson, Tomisene Anderson (v).* 88.

A corporate effort. Nine of the 11 tracks were written by their producers (Jerry Williams, Trade Martin and Frederick Knight); the other two – Gamble–Huff's 'Drowning In A Sea Of Love' and Benny Latimore's 'Let's Straighten It Out' – were produced by Al Kooper, who plays all the instruments on them. King sings manfully and plays characteristic guitar on one or two tracks. The blues 'Take Off Your Shoes' is good enough to earn a rerun on a compilation but most of the other songs are inconsequential and the synthetic arrangements will make your brain hurt.

**(*) Live At San Quentin
MCA 088 112 517//(E) MCLD 19253 *King; James Bolden (t); Walter King, Edgar Synigal (s); Eugene Carrier (kb); Leon Warren (g); Michael Doster (b); Calep Emphrey (d).* 90.

Twenty years on from *Live In Cook County Jail*, another record of King playing for prisoners. Three numbers survive from the earlier engagement, 'Every Day I Have The Blues', 'Sweet Sixteen' and 'The Thrill Is Gone', together with songs of a similar vintage like 'Sweet Little Angel' and the newer 'Never Make A Move Too Soon' and 'Into The Night'. Actually the songs listed are only part of the story: well before the end of 'Never Make A Move''s 7.52 King has switched to (of all things) 'Catfish Blues'. His spiels are more repetitive, and less amusing, than usual, and the concluding 'Rock Me Baby', in which he bisects the audience to sing half-lines at each other, is blues pantomime. Johnny Cash put on a better show at this venue.

*** Live At The Apollo
GRP GRD-9637//MCA MCD 09637 *King; James Morrison, Joe Mossello, Glen Drews, Harry 'Sweets' Edison (t); George Bohanon, Urbie Green, Robin Eubanks, Paul Faulise (tb); Jeff Clayton, Jerry Dodgion (as); Plas Johnson, Ralph Moore, Glen Smulyan (ts); Gene Harris (kb, p); Kenny Burrell (g); Ray Brown (b); Harold Jones (d).* 11/90.

During 1990 King went on a world tour with the Philip Morris Superband, led by pianist Gene Harris. *Live At The Apollo* commemorates that collaboration. The ten songs are a mixture of tried classics such as 'Sweet Sixteen', which receives an ingenious new arrangement, and more recent acquisitions like 'When Love Comes To Town'. The orchestral playing is some of the best King has ever been treated to. A sleek album.

**(*) There Is Always One More Time
MCA MCAD 10295 *King; Neil Larsen (kb, o); Joe Sample (p); Michael Landau, Arthur Adams (g); Freddie Washington (b); Jim Keltner (d); Lennie Castro (perc); Paulette Brown, Valerie Pinkston-Mayo, Bunny Hull (v).* early 91.

With its shiny wide-screen studio sound, this album may be more impressive on first hearing than its material – mostly by Joe Sample and Will Jennings, the team from *Midnight Believer* and *Take It Home* – quite deserves. On closer attention, it may all seem a little too contrived, giving King a succession of roles but denying him the chance to play himself.

*** Blues Summit
MCA MCAD 10710 *King; James Bolden, Ben Cauley (t); Melvin Jackson, Walter King, Nancy Wright, Lee Allen (s); Memphis Horns, Jeff Lewis, Tim Devine (unspecified brass and reeds); Kim Wilson (h); James Toney, Jim Pugh, Mike Eppley (kb); Katie Webster (p, v); Randy Waldman (string syn); Lowell Fulson, Albert Collins, Buddy Guy, Robert Cray, Joe Louis Walker, John Lee Hooker (g, v); Leon Warren, Vasti Jackson, Mabon 'Teenie' Hodges, Robert Murray, Roy Rogers (g); Michael Doster, Richard Cousins, Henry Oden (b); Tony Coleman (d, perc); Calep Emphrey Jr, Kevin Hayes, Paul Revelli (d); Antoine Salley (perc); Koko Taylor, Maxine Waters, Julia Tillman Waters, Maxayne Lewis, Etta James, Irma Thomas, Ruth Brown (v).* 2–3/93.

The album opens on 'Playin' With My Friends', which is what *Blues Summit* is all about. It is indeed a friendly affair, with no grandstanding; certainly not by the host, who solves the inherent stylistic discrepancy between himself and John Lee Hooker by letting the guest have his way and amiably urging him on from the background. If he is elsewhere more assertive it's never at the expense of the other performer. Besides, he has his own way in a nine-minute two-song medley with his regular band, though it's a pity he hams up 'Nobody Loves Me But My Mother'. King has certainly made more considerable albums, but few as genial.

**(*) Lucille & Friends
MCA MCD 33008 *King; various accompaniments.* 70–94.

The sales of *Blues Summit* prompted MCA to compile this set of collaborations spanning 25 years, from 'Hummingbird' with Leon Russell off *Indianola Mississippi Seeds* to 'Spirit In The Dark' with Dianne Schuur from their MOR collaboration *Heart To Heart* (GRP 059 772). 'Playin' With My Friends' with Robert Cray and 'You Shook Me' with John Lee Hooker are from *Blues Summit* itself. Not all the tracks are from King's own back catalogue: 'Caught A Touch Of Your Love' with Grover Washington Jr and the excellent 'BB's Blues' with Branford Marsalis come from albums by the saxophonists, and 'Frosty' with Albert Collins from the latter's *Collins Mix*. 'All You Ever Give Me Is The Blues' with Vernon Reid is previously unissued. It may sound like a ragbag, and it is, but in showing

King working with artists as different as Stevie Wonder, Bobby Bland and U2 it reminds us that no other bluesman of his time could have done it.

**(*) Deuces Wild

MCA MCACD-11711//(E) MCD 11722 *King; Darrell Leonard, Brian Murray, Jamil Sharif (t); Joe Sublett, Joseph Saulsbury Jr (ts); Carl Blouin, Greg Smith (bs); Mick Jagger (h, v); Mickey Rafael (h); Tommy Eyre (kb, o, p); Paul Carrack (kb, o, v); Chris Stainton, Jon Cleary (kb, p); D'Angelo (kb, v); Billy Payne (kb); Leon Pendarvis, C. J. Vanston (o); Jools Holland (p); various (frh, strings); Eric Clapton, Bonnie Raitt, Marty Stuart, David Gilmour (g, v); Neil Hubbard, Johnny Lee Schell, Hugh McCracken, Randy Jacobs, Keith Richards, Ron Wood, Dean Parks, Michael Landau (g); Pino Palladino, Reggie McBride, James 'Hutch' Hutchinson, Daryll Jones (b); Tony Braunagel (d, perc); Andy Newmark, Steve Jordan, Jim Keltner, Charlie Watts, Kenny Aranoff (d); Lenny Castro, Paulinho Da Costa (perc); Simon Climie, Paul Waller (prog); Wardell Quezergue (arr, cond); Van Morrison, Tracy Chapman, Mick Hucknall, Sir Harry Bowens, Terence Forsythe, Vincent Bonham, Dr John [Mack Rebennack], Dionne Warwick, Zucchero, Joe Cocker, Heavy D, Willie Nelson (v); John Porter (prod). 97?*

With status come duties. Ensconced at the head of the boardroom table, CEO of Blues Inc., King makes nice to other music-business leaders. Not that all his fellow players hold court cards – The Rolling Stones, Van Morrison and Willie Nelson, yes, Mick Hucknall and Joe Cocker at a pinch, but Marty Stuart? Jools Holland? Tracy Chapman? Actually Chapman's bleakly feline reading of 'The Thrill Is Gone' is one of the more convincing rearrangements of a King song, much better than the overtired 'Three O'Clock Blues' with Jeff Beck or the merely retraced flightpath of 'Hummingbird' with Dionne Warwick. 'Ain't Nobody Home' with D'Angelo is pretty, Hucknall slips easily into the mood of 'Please Send Me Someone To Love' and Raitt plays notably dirty slide on 'Baby I Love You'. But a hardline blues fan might ask why the deuce B. B. bothered.

**(*) Blues On The Bayou

MCA MCD 11879 *King; James Bolden, Stanley Abernathy (t); Melvin Jackson (s); James Sells Toney (kb); unknowns (strings); Leon Warren (g); Michael Doster (b); Calep Emphrey Jr (d); Tony Coleman (perc); band (v). 98.*

B. B. tells us in the notes that he wanted this to be simple: his songs, his band, himself as producer. 'Working that way, the record was cut in four days. All live, all real. No overdubs, no high-tech tricks. Just basic blues.' Yes, well, B. B. can't have checked the production master, because 'I'll Survive', 'Darlin' What Happened' and 'If I Lost You' have had strings added (no great improvement), but in other respects the album sounds the way B. B. intended it. Most of the tracks are indeed blues, and 'Shake It Up And Go' certainly goes back to basics. The new numbers probably won't be keepers, his voice is sometimes a little worn, and the closing guitar choruses of 'Blues In "G"' sound like the playing of a man too weary to think, but 'I Got Some Outside Help I Don't Need' is B. B. not too far from his best.

*** Let The Good Times Roll

MCA 088 112 042 *King; Marcus Belgrave (t); Hank Crawford (as); David 'Fathead' Newman (ts); Neil Larsen (o, p); Dr John [Mack Rebennack] (p, v); Russell Malone (g); John Heard (b); Earl Palmer (d); Lenny Castro (perc). 99?*

'Louis Jordan was way ahead of his time,' King says, and the perky tunes and cool jive-talk of 'Ain't Nobody Here But Us Chickens' and 'Saturday Night Fish Fry' do indeed sound almost as hip as when they were introduced 50 years before. A longtime admirer, King affectionately reshapes 18 songs associated with Jordan, from sober blues ('I'm Gonna Move To The Outskirts Of Town') to secular sermons ('Beware, Brother, Beware') and cheerful party pieces such as 'Choo Choo Ch'Boogie'. He doesn't play a lot of guitar – which is faithful to the model, for Jordan didn't feature it much either – and his voice sounds a little frayed at the edges, but Belgrave, Crawford and Newman lovingly evoke the Tympany Five's exuberant small-group settings.

*** Makin' Love Is Good For You

MCA 088 112 299 *King; James Bolden, Stanley Abernathy, Darrell Leonard (t); Joe Sublett (ts); Walter R. King, Melvin Jackson (s); James Toney, Tommy Eyre (kb); Leon Warren, John Porter (g); Michael Doster (b); Calep Emphrey Jr (d); Tony Braunagel (perc). 00?*

With a title like this you might expect Chef from *South Park*, but it's King who cooks up the quiet storm on a not noticeably blues-lite album. This is no return to the MOR of '70s albums like *Friends* and *To Know You Is To Love You*. The contents are mostly straightforward blues, relieved by the individuality of A. C. Reed's 'I'm In The Wrong Business', Barbara George's soul classic 'I Know' and Buddy Johnson's pop-blues 'Since I Fell For You'. The hour-long programme is steered efficiently by what appears to be King's basic road unit, and the mood sways gently from reflective to unfrenetic. This is, after all, a man in his mid-70s.

*** Riding With The King

Reprise 47612 *King; Eric Clapton (g, v); Joe Sample (kb, p); Tim Carmon (o); Doyle Bramhall II (g, v); Andy Fairweather Low, Jimmie Vaughan (g); Nathan East (b); Steve Gadd (d); Paul Waller (d prog); Arif Mardin (string arr); Susannah Melvoin, Wendy Melvoin (v). 00?*

John Hiatt's opening title number is produced with a rock portentousness reminiscent of 'When Love Comes To Town', King's collaboration with U2, but thereafter the programme is almost unalloyed blues from King's back catalogue, like 'Ten Long Years', 'Three O'Clock Blues', 'Help The Poor' and 'When My Heart Beats Like A Hammer'. Clapton's playing is exceptionally sensitive throughout, his singing exudes back-porch relaxation, and King responds with equal warmth. Apart from the concluding 'Come Rain Or Come Shine', which finds our co-drivers stuck in the middle of the road, there's nothing here to perturb even King's strictest fans, and a good deal they should admire.

**(*) B. B. King & Friends – 80

Geffen/Chronicles B 0005263 *King; Jerry Hey, Gary Grant (t); William Frank Reichenbach (tb); Brandon Fields (s); Van Morrison (h, v); Robbie Buchanan (kb, o); Guy Babylon, Chris Stainton, Brian Mitchell (kb); Luke 'The Duke' Smith (o); Elton John (p, v); unknowns (strings); John Mayer, Glenn Frey, Billy F. Gibbons (g, v); Davey Johnstone, Clem Clemson, Eric Clapton, Mark Knopfler, Larry Campbell, Dean Parks (g); Bob Birch, Yolander Charles, T-Bone Wolk, Leland Sklar (b); Nigel Olsson,*

Ian Thomas, Billy Ward, Russell Kunkel (d); John Mahon (perc); Nathaniel Kunkel (shaker); Roger Daltrey, Gloria Estefan, Daryl Hall, Bobby Bland, Sheryl Crow (v). 2–6/05.
(*) B. B. King & Friends – 80
Geffen/Chronicles (Eu) 9885355 *As above*. 2–6/05.

As the castlist indicates, King gets a good deal of help in both vocal and guitar departments, but this is no cosmetic attempt to hide the marks of time: we should sound so good at 80. He celebrated his birthday, he writes, with 'some of my favorite tunes as well as songs that I love but have never recorded before', but the second category is small and the bulk of the album is personal standards like 'Ain't Nobody Home', 'There Must Be A Better World Somewhere' and 'Hummingbird'. Some of the celebs made their trips to London, New York or Burbank to no great purpose: Sheryl Crow is surprisingly insipid in 'Need Your Love So Bad', and Mayer and Gibbons fade from the memory the moment their tracks are over. But Clapton adds melancholy to 'The Thrill Is Gone' and Knopfler and King take their guitars for an elegant slow dance in 'All Over Again'. The warmest moment is King's duet with Bobby Bland on 'Funny How Time Slips Away', an amicable, unsentimental conversation between two old magicians. The European issue adds an alternative take of the duet with Van Morrison, 'Early In The Morning'.

**** King Of The Blues
MCA MCAD4–10677 4CD *King; various accompaniments*. 49–91.

This is not quite the in-depth career survey it may appear, since King's ground-breaking work in the '50s is epitomized in just ten tracks (out of 77), while the artistically variable '60s and '70s furnish several dozen. On the other hand, Ace has got the earlier period down cold with *The Vintage Years* (see above), so *King Of The Blues* is expansive where it needs to be. MCA took the opportunity to recirculate half a dozen singles tracks that had never been on albums, and to release seven performances that had never been issued at all. The really disappointing albums have been sampled briefly or ignored. An admirably handled production (Dave Booth, Colin Escott and Andy McKaie share credit), with a gorgeous booklet.

*** Martin Scorsese Presents The Blues: B. B. King
Universal B0000487–02 *King; various accompaniments*. c. 9/51–98.
***(*) Anthology 1962–1998
MCA 088 112 410 2CD *King; various accompaniments*. 62–98.
*** How Blue Can You Get? Classic Live Performances 1964–1994
MCA MCAD2–11443 2CD *King; various accompaniments*. 11/64–94.
*** The Very Best Of B. B. King
MCA MCBD 19505 *King; various accompaniments*. 66–92.

Except for two RPM tracks on the Scorsese compilation, the first two CDs are commendable selections from King's ABC/Bluesway and subsequent MCA output. *Anthology* offers versions of many of his most celebrated songs ('Sweet Sixteen', 'Sweet Little Angel', 'Don't Answer The Door', 'How Blue Can You Get', etc.), thereby filling a similar role in the American catalogue to the UK release *His Definitive Greatest Hits* (see below), with which it shares about two thirds of its contents. *Scorsese Presents* is a little less predictable, including, for instance, 'Inflation Blues' from the regrettably deleted *Blues 'N' Jazz*, but rather short. *Very Best* consists of 16 tracks from MCA holdings, mixing proved repertoire like 'The Thrill Is Gone', 'Hummingbird' and 'Ain't Nobody Home' with less obvious choices, some good, some not.

How Blue Can You Get? was a good idea: King is a consistent live performer and a compilation of his in-person recordings ought to be very satisfying, so long as it's carefully selected, which this is. A chunk of *Live At The Regal* and *Blues Is King* is followed by tracks from several other live albums. On the second disc the guestlist includes Bobby Bland, Ruth Brown and Joe Louis Walker, some of these collaborations being previously unissued.

**** His Definitive Greatest Hits
Universal 547340 2CD *King; various accompaniments*. 65–93.

King's inexorable expansion from the leading blues figure of the African-American community to a globetrotting superstar is charted almost step-by-step in this excellent 34-track set. All the milestones are checked: 'The Thrill Is Gone' and 'Hummingbird', the concerts at the Regal and San Quentin, the stage meetings with Bobby Bland, the collaborations with The Crusaders and Gary Moore, Robert Cray and U2. There's something of a trough in the first half of the '80s, and the autopilot version of 'In The Midnight Hour' might usefully have been dropped in favour of a cut from the neglected *Blues 'N' Jazz*, but generally this finds King riding the crest of the wave. 'Definitive' applies only as far back as 1965; for his previous two decades the reader will need an Ace compilation or two. TR

Bobby King (1941–83)
VOCAL, GUITAR

King learned guitar alongside his Arkansas contemporaries Fenton Robinson and Larry Davis, and is reckoned by sound judges to have been the best of the three. He moved to Chicago by the end of the '50s, and in the next decade recorded for Federal and other labels. In the late '70s King suffered a series of strokes. He regained his playing abilities for a time, but a further stroke forced him out of music and into obscurity until his early death.

**(*) Chaser
Storyville STCD 8047 *King; Leonard Gill (g); Snapper Mitchum (b); Bill Warren (d); Muddy Water [sic] Jr (v)*. 10/75.

People who saw King perform were awed by his technique and inventiveness, and the instrumental title track gives some idea of what he could do. It's not every musician who can construct a fresh, unpredictable intro to 'Stormy Monday Blues', or turn 'My Babe' into soul-blues, but those songs also epitomize this CD's defects: almost total reliance on overfamiliar material, and a tendency to spin songs out to excessive length. Recorded by an inexperienced producer in an almost empty Chicago club, the session is suffocated by an acute shortage of atmosphere and inspiration. King is better memorialized by four tracks on the VAC *Chicago Blues From Federal Records* (Ace CDCHD 717). CS

Chris Thomas King (born 1964)
VOCAL, HARMONICA, ORGAN, KEYBOARDS, PIANO, MANDOLIN, GUITAR, BASS, DRUMS, PERCUSSION, MIXING, DJ SCRATCHING

King is the son of Baton Rouge veteran Tabby Thomas, and gained early experience at his father's club. After cutting his

first LP, he moved to Los Angeles and Europe, then back to Baton Rouge before settling in New Orleans. His geographical restlessness has been paralleled by a series of musical mutations and experiments. King is also an actor, and made a considerable impression playing a blues singer in the film O Brother, Where Art Thou? and as Blind Willie Johnson in The Soul Of A Man.

(*) It's A Cold Ass World – The Beginning
Arhoolie CD 9020 *King; Joe Hunter (b); Tammy Hunter (d); Kevin Famous (v).* 86.

** **A Young Man's Blues**
Hightone HCD 8150 *King; Juan Magee (kb, v); Jim Cox (o); George Doering (g); Kevin White, Courtney Audain (b, v); Paul Mills (d, perc, v); Brannen Temple (d); Reagae Clark, Leon Haywood (v).* 89–91.

** **Simple**
Hightone HCD 8043 *As above, except Clark also plays perc; add Clive Ross (toasting).* 91.

Arhoolie's debut disc was retitled and reissued, with the credit changed from Chris Thomas, in the wake of *O Brother, Where Art Thou?* The young King, as he then wasn't, composed all the songs and plays all the instruments, except on one track. The search for his own voice, and the search for commercially and artistically viable ways to update the blues, have been leitmotifs of King's career. At this stage he was heavily indebted to older musicians, with Buddy Guy, Chuck Berry and Hendrix the chief creditors. There's plenty of tenebrous energy, but the overdubbing sometimes makes for inflexibility, the writing seldom transcends pastiche, and several tracks are too long.

Most of *Simple* (which remains credited to Chris Thomas) is blues-rock, usually sub-Hendrix, although 'Whatever Happened To The Revolution' may put some listeners in mind of Slade; on a couple of acoustic tracks, King comes over like a male Tracy Chapman. Most songs are again self-composed, and most of them are immature and undistinguished. Bob Marley's 'War', which is neither, gets a delivery that isn't supposed to be casual, but sounds it, the lively toasting apart.

Like the Arhoolie CD, *A Young Man's Blues* is after moviegoers' money; to seven tracks from *Simple* are added three pleasant soul-blues from the earlier, deleted *Cry Of The Prophets* (Sire 26186), and a pretentious, previously unissued 'Devil's Daughter' from the *Simple* sessions.

** **Chris Thomas King**
Scotti Bros. 75526 *King; Amos Singleton (syn); Sean Griffin (p, d prog).* 97.

*** **Me, My Guitar And The Blues**
Blind Pig BPCD 5064 *King.* 99?

***(*) **The Legend Of Tommy Johnson Act 1: Genesis 1900's–1990's**
Valley Entertainment VE 15156//Stony Plain SPCD 1279 *King; Sharon Foster, Lisa Foster, Charles Elam III, Earl Smith Jr (v).* 01.

These discs (and others now deleted) were recorded by King and issued under licence. *Chris Thomas King* is an album of songs about love lost and found, very quiet and restrained by comparison with its predecessors. Tenderness, sometimes shading into uxoriousness, is not an attitude commonly struck by blues singers, so it's regrettable that these songs and their performance can only be described as wet. It's difficult to imagine 'I'll Play The Blues For You', the only non-original, without Albert King's gruff paternalism, and certainly the other King fails to find a successful alternative. At best he comes over as an anorexic Barry White.

Despite an unpromising title, *Me, My Guitar And The Blues* is much better; the love ballads are limited to two, and the CD is a well-judged mix of songs and settings, from solo acoustic blues to multitracked 'band' items. There's some feeble writing ('Times was good, sometimes bad'), but the general level is much higher than hitherto; in particular, the anti-drug lament 'Cain', successfully blending blues and rap, proclaims the maturation of King's art since the debut album's 'Cocaine'. Also striking is the perfectly integrated rap interlude on 'Born Under A Bad Sign'. King had obviously been listening to Delta slide guitarists; 'Stones In My Passway' is a faithful but not slavish interpretation of Robert Johnson, and the semi-original 'Superstitious Blues' is equally convincing.

Better still is *The Legend Of Tommy Johnson*. 'Inspired in part by the movie *O Brother, Where Art Thou?*' and furnished with a jokily academic note purporting to tell the story of Tommy McDowell Johnson, it looks like a cynical attempt to piggyback on the success of the movie. If so, never mind; 'Johnson's odyssey from worksong to solo acoustic blues to electric band blues, to being the subject of fake tribute recordings by 'the Voodoo Dolls', is thoroughly entertaining, with the bone-rattling rocker 'Do Fries Go With That Shake?' a standout. It's not perfect: mistiming and misheard lyrics slightly mar 'Trouble Will Soon Be Over', wrong notes are a more serious handicap to 'Canned Heat Blues', and the closing track is tediously anthemic. Still, King is having great fun, and it's impossible not to join him.

**** **Along The Blues Highway**
Animated Music 302 066 491 *King.* 7/01.

Recorded live at the Kalamazoo Blues Festival, this half-CD (the balance is by Blind Mississippi Morris) finds King performing an impassioned solo set with amplified guitar accompaniment. 'Alive' is a fine rap-blues fusion, and the most radical item in a playlist that strikes an assured balance between traditional structures and original lyrics. The recording quality is outstanding.

***(*) **Dirty South Hip-Hop Blues**
21st Century Blues 21CB-CD-2106 *King; Tabby Thomas (v); Son House, Loafer, Nina Simone (samples).* 02.

***(*) **The Soul Of Chris Thomas King: The Roots**
21st Century Blues 21CB-CD-2107 *King; James Cotton (h); Darryl White (d); Sharon Foster, Lisa Foster, Charles Elam III, Earl Smith Jr (v).* 7/98–03.

Most listeners would take the unlisted closing track of *Dirty South Hip-Hop Blues* to be rap pure and simple, but King insists that 'This is the blues of the 21st century, and I don't give a damn if ya can't get wit' me,' adding, 'I don't give a damn what the purists say, they wouldn't know blues if it bit 'em anyway.' Attempts to pre-empt discussion usually indicate that there's something to be discussed, but self-evidently rap is the prevailing voice of today's black ghetto in the way that blues used to be.

On most of *Dirty South Hip-Hop Blues*, King attempts to fuse blues and rap as both music and worldviews. He often succeeds brilliantly, as on 'Da Thrill Is Gone From Here', where Tabby Thomas sings the chorus line of Roy Hawkins's song as his son raps about the impact of violence, drugs and urban decay. Also outstanding are 'Mississippi KKKrossroads', which transforms a cliché beloved of white romantics into a challenge to racism, and an entirely traditional 'Hard Time Killing Floor Blues', as featured in a certain movie. Less successful is 'Poetry Of Young Bill', a spoken 12-bar blues (not a talking blues in the usual sense) that revisits Tommy McDowell Johnson. Not successful at all is 'Gonna Take A Miracle', a thoroughly platitudinous response to 9/11. Unquestionably, though, this CD is challenging and rewarding, the work of an artist who continues to grow by being unafraid to experiment and explore.

The Soul Of Chris Thomas King: The Roots includes three songs cut for Black Top in the late '90s; 'Hellhound On My Trail' (with Cotton) was the title track of a Telarc tribute VAC; and 'John Law Burned Down The Liquor Sto" comes from Robert Mugge's film *Last Of The Mississippi Jukes*. Six tracks are recycled from *O Brother, Where Art Thou?* and *Dirty South Hip-Hop Blues*; the rest seem to have been newly recorded for release in 2003, the so-called 'Year of the Blues'. There's nothing wrong with King's commercial instincts; happily, there's not much wrong with his musical instincts either. The accompaniment is acoustic-guitar-dominated, and 11 of the 19 tracks are covers, of Son House, Skip James, Leadbelly and the Johnsons: Robert, Blind Willie and Tommy. As already noted, the latter two artists are not well served, and two of the four Leadbelly songs are cursory, but *The Roots* proves that the old songs retain their emotional and artistic power: and that, in its own way, is experiment and exploration too.

*** Why My Guitar Screams And Moans
21st Century Blues 21CB-CD-2110 King; Aubrey Dunham (as, ts). 04.

Whether the CD's title is a riposte to George Harrison or not, *Why My Guitar Screams And Moans* is by no means all loud guitar exhibitionism; 'A Song For Mama' is remarkably similar in sound and spirit to Paul McCartney's 'Let It Be'. King continues to combine blues, R&B (in its contemporary meaning) and rap, either by inserting blues guitar interludes and blues lines into rap numbers and soul ballads, or by bringing a rapper's sensibility to the creation of blues lyrics. The writing is generally undistinguished, though, with a sentimental streak even on the more macho numbers, and there's seldom much originality about the rockish guitar work. The jazzy clarity of King's guitar on 'Down' is admirable, though, and the hedonistic rap 'Louisiana Party' is fun; so is a bone-rattling cover of Prince's 'Kiss'. King has worked out how to bring blues and rap together without the marriage sounding forced, but *Why My Guitar Screams And Moans* is less attention-grabbing than *Dirty South Hip-Hop Blues*. cs

Earl King (born 1934)
VOCAL, GUITAR, PIANO

New Orleans-born, Earl Silas Johnson IV began playing guitar in his teens. A printing error on his first Specialty single, 'My Mother's Love', gave him his professional name. He subsequently recorded for Ace and had a regional hit with 'Those Lonely, Lonely Nights', which put him on the touring circuit. In 1960 Dave Bartholomew signed him to Imperial on the strength of his composition 'Come On (Let The Good Times Roll)'; it wasn't a hit, but King scored one later with 'Trick Bag'.

After leaving Imperial he made his living as a producer and writer, but he returned to recording in his own right in the '80s.

'Those Lonely, Lonely Nights' and the rest of King's Ace recordings are on *Earl's Pearls: The Very Best Of Earl King (1955–1960)* (Westside WESM 520, deleted).

**(*) Come On: The Complete Imperial Recordings
Okra-Tone OKR-CD-4970 King; Leroy Derbigny, Dave Bartholomew, Wardell Quezergue (t); Waldron 'Frog' Joseph (tb); Morris Bechamin, James Rivers (ts); Edward 'Kid' Jordan, Carl Blouin (bs); James Booker, Willie Tee (p); George Davis, George French, Irving 'Punchy' Williams (b); Robert French, Joe Butler (d); Gerri Hall, Benny Spellman, Bobby Lacour (v). 10/60–11/62.

People who worked with King, such as Dave Bartholomew and Ace's Johnny Vincent, thought highly of him as both a performer and a writer. Until we find that someone filmed those late-'50s dances in South Louisiana where, according to Vincent, 'the girls used to swoon right in the aisles', all we can do to test those producers' judgement is listen to the songs he wrote and recorded. They're a tricky bag. King's voice had youth and a plaintive appeal, and the records, thanks to Bartholomew and the musicians, are seldom less than well-made R&B, but in those days New Orleans studios made R&B records the way Philip Morris made cigarettes: efficiently, copiously and uniformly. King's compositions would have to be very good indeed to stand out, and only 'Come On' and 'Trick Bag' do.

*** King Of New Orleans
Fuel 2000 302 061 113 King; Bob Enos, Keith Winking (t); Porky Cohen, Rick Trolsen (tb); Rich Lataille (as); Mark 'Kaz' Kazanoff (ts, bs, fl); Greg Piccolo, Mr Excello, Saxy Boy, Ernest Youngblood Jr, I. B. Goode (ts); Doug James (bs); David Torkanowsky (kb, o, p); Ron Levy, Richard 'Dickie' Reed (o, p); Sammy Berfect (o); Ronnie Earl, Snooks Eaglin (g); George Porter Jr (b, v); Rory McLeod, Steve Gomes (b); Herman V. Ernest III (d, perc, v); John Rossi, Kenny Blevins, Per Hanson (d). 2/86–1/93.

Jeff Hannusch concludes his notes to *Come On* with the judgement that King's Black Top albums were 'excellent' but his Imperial work 'must certainly be touted as the pinnacle of his career'. That's not a view that will be given any shrift here. The Black Tops were *Glazed* (with Roomful Of Blues), *Sexual Telepathy* and *Hard River To Cross*; each supplies five items to *King Of New Orleans*, and the remaining track, 'Life's Ups And Downs', is from the *Sexual Telepathy* sessions. These records had qualities you may search for in vain in King's earlier work: inventive arrangements, spare but attractive guitar solos and, in the songwriting, a wealth of unusual subjects and angles, witnessed in songs like 'Sexual Telepathy', 'Medieval Days' and 'Iron Cupid' (and less winningly in 'Happy Little Nobody's Waggy Tail Dog'). The once boyish voice has been hickory-smoked by age but is no less subtle an instrument. Bill Dahl, who produced and annotated this collection, did an excellent job, but look what he had to work with. TR

Freddie King (1934–76)
VOCAL, GUITAR

This King adopted his mother's maiden name, having been born Fred Christian in Gilmer, Texas. It was fortuitous that B. B. King came along to lend the name kudos. Already

influenced by Lightnin' Hopkins and Big Boy Crudup, Freddie arrived in Chicago aged 16 and joined a number of young musicians, Magic Sam, Syl Johnson and Luther Allison among them, who were striking a new path away from the traditions of Muddy Waters and Howlin' Wolf. King may have recorded with the latter just prior to joining Federal in the summer of 1960, where he teamed up with pianist/A&R man Sonny Thompson. Beginning with 'You've Got To Love Her With A Feeling', their collaboration produced a string of notable songs and instrumentals that exerted influence upon the likes of Eric Clapton and Peter Green. Though feted by this younger generation, King in his own career earned more esteem than success. A string of live recordings, licit and otherwise, emerged after his death to lend further substance to his reputation.

**** **Blues Guitar Hero: The Influential Early Sessions**
Ace CDCHD 454 *King; Gene Redd, Clifford Scott (s); Sonny Thompson (p); Fred Jordan (g); Bill Willis (b); Philip Paul (d); unknowns (v). 8/60–11/62.*

***(*) **Blues Guitar Hero Volume 2**
Ace CDCHD 861 *As above, except add Bobby King, Lonnie Mack (g), Oscar Crummie, Benny Turner (b), Frank Charles (d). 7/61–9/66.*

***(*) **Texas Sensation**
King KCD 6007 *As above CDs. 8/60–9/66.*

***(*) **The Very Best Volume 1**
Collectables COL-CD-2824 *As above. 8/60–7/61.*

***(*) **The Very Best Volume 2**
Collectables COL-CD-2825 *As above. 1–11/62.*

***(*) **The Very Best Volume 3**
Collectables COL-CD-2826 *As above. 9/63–9/66.*

The brevity of King's commercial success is indicated by the first seven titles on *Blues Guitar Hero*, which represent the sum of his entries in the R&B and Hot 100 charts. They show that 'Hideaway' and 'San-Ho-Zay' fared better than 'Lonesome Whistle Blues' and 'See See Baby', with 'I'm Tore Down' his most successful vocal performance. The collaboration between King and Thompson was genuinely productive but the later sessions settled into a routine that valued competence over inspiration. Not that the latter quality was entirely absent, just fitfully resurrected over subsequent sessions. *Blues Guitar Hero Volume 2* covers the second half of his Federal contract and increases the ratio of instrumentals to vocals. The latter consist of more cover songs than before, reducing the impact of a notable King–Thompson composition like 'Someday After Awhile (You'll Be Sorry)'. Nothing original was cut at his final 1966 King session, the prelude to a two-year hiatus in recording. *Texas Sensation* distils into one 20-track compilation the essence of the previous volumes for those who require just one piquant bite of the King biscuit. The three volumes of *The Very Best* contain one take of each of the 77 songs Freddy (as he was denoted on labels) cut for the King labels but what's gained by conciseness is compromised by the packaging, whereas over the 48 titles of its two volumes *Blues Guitar Hero* adds a handful of alternative takes and a pair of informative essays. NS

(*) **Freddie King
Warner Blues 36955 *King; Joe Newman, Melvin Lastie, Martin Banks, Ernie Royal (t); King Curtis, David 'Fathead' Newman, Willie Bridges, Trevor Lawrence, George Coleman, Frank Wess (ts, bs); Hugh McCracken (h); James Booker, Gary Illingworth,*
George Stubbs (p); Billy Butler, Cornell Dupree (g); Gerry Jemmott (b); Norman Pride, Kenneth Rice (d). 7/68–7/69.

(*) **My Feeling For The Blues
Atlantic 90352//[Repertoire RR 4170] *As above, except Curtis also plays marimba; omit Joe Newman, Lastie, David Newman, Booker, Illingworth, Butler, Pride. 7/69.*

My Feeling For The Blues, King's second album for Cotillion, left much to be desired, and a CD reissue that neglects to augment the meagre playing time emphasizes the disappointment of a project that portrays the artist as a mainstream blues player, all hopes of the hit parade spent. Hoary blues standards 'Yonder Wall', 'Stormy Monday', 'Ain't Nobody's Business What We Do', a couple of stalwart B. B. King tunes, an uninspired instrumental workout on 'What'd I Say' – and what do you say? Much of the playing is lacklustre. Tempos are flaccid. There's no bite or aggression to reflect the energy King tries to insert in his vocals and guitar solos. Curtis takes a couple of choruses in 'Stumble' but they lack the nervous fire of his earlier work. He and King co-wrote the title instrumental but it's typical of the venture that King's best playing on the album is faded after a mere two minutes. Warner's entry in their series *Les Incontournables* is at least better value, containing all but one track of *My Feeling For The Blues* and eight of the dozen on the previous year's *Freddie King Is A Blues Master*, but the latter was as dreary an album as its successor, the tempos crawling like a wounded animal looking for somewhere to die. NS/TR

*** **King Of The Blues**
EMI/Shelter 34972 2CD *King; unknown (fl); Leon Russell (o, p, g); Rev. Patrick Henderson (o, p); Jon Gallie, Robert Griffin (o); unknowns (strings); Don Preston (g, v); Bobby Turner (g); Donald 'Duck' Dunn, Benny Turner, Carl Radle (b); Charles Blackwell, Charles Myers, Dean O'Neill, Jim Gordon, Al Jackson, Jim Keltner (d); Claudia Lennear, Kathi McDonald, Joey Cooper, O'Neill Twins (v). 10/70–11/72.*

*** **Best Of The Shelter Records Years**
The Right Stuff/Capitol 27245 *As above. 10/70–11/72.*

Despite the favours his Shelter albums did for King's career, the music they contain reflects the awkward phase blues was going through in the early '70s. Originally titled *Getting Ready …*, *Texas Cannonball* and *Woman Across The River*, all three were produced and arranged by Leon Russell, who created backing tracks of needless complexity, further hampered by the blurred pulse of two drummers, which at times resembles a wind-up toy repeatedly striking a chair-leg. Each album contrasts blues standards such as 'Five Long Years', 'That's All Right' and 'Hoochie Coochie Man' with original songs by Russell and Don Nix, including 'Same Old Blues', 'Living On The Highway' and 'Me And My Guitar'. Once in a while a number is performed straight, but too often what was then current musical fashion dictates otherwise. *King Of The Blues* presents near-complete versions of each album, supplemented by six previously unissued tracks from the final sessions. *Best Of The Shelter Records Years* brings together 18 of the issued sides programmed for listening rather than chronology; the merely inquisitive might find its succinctness more attractive.

*** **Burglar**
BGO BGOCD 137//Universal Special Products 831 815 *King; Ron Carthy (t); Steve Gregory (ss, ts); Chris Mercer, Mick Eves (ts); Bud Beadle (bs); Brian Auger, Dick Sims (o); Roy Davies, Pete*

Wingfield (p, clavinet); Bobby Tench, Eric Clapton, George Terry (g); DeLisle Harper, Carl Radle (b); Steve Ferrone, Jamie Oldaker (d); Mike Vernon (perc, prod); Pat Arnold, Vie, Misty Browning (v). 74.

This album shows that English musicians were as much in thrall to what was then being called funk as their American counterparts. In the haste to be intensely rhythmic, the obsessive concentration on playing riffs inevitably results in uninspiring and metronomic stasis. Nevertheless, King sings (sometimes over-forcefully) and plays well, even if his guitar solos rarely descend below the eighth fret. For all their angularity, the arrangements are properly voiced, although no space is left for a brass or keyboard soloist. The material is eclectic, with songs from J. J. Cale, Mel London, Earl King and Jerry Ragovoy, 'Sugar Sweet' with backing from the Clapton band, a couple of studio jams and 'Only Getting Second Best', co-written by Mike Vernon. The result makes pleasant rather than compulsive listening, primarily because it now sounds trapped very much in its time. NS

(*) Larger Than Life
BGO BGOCD 593 King; Ron Carthy, John Thomas, Darrell Leonard (t); Jerry Jumonville (as, ts); Chris Mercer, Mick Eves, Steve Gregory, David 'Fathead' Newman (ts); Bud Beadle, Joe Davis (bs); Jim Gordon (s, o); Sonny Burke (kb, clavinet); Alvin Hemphill (o); Pete Wingfield, K. O. Thomas, Louis Stephens (p); Roy Davies (clavinet); Bobby Tench, Mike O'Neill, Andrew Jones Jr, Melvin 'Wah Wah' Ragin (g); DeLisle Harper, Robert Wilson, Benny Turner, Henry Davis (b); Steve Ferrone, Big John E. Tomassie, Charles Meyers, James Gadson (d); Sam Clayton (cga); Mike Vernon (perc, prod); First Priority (v). 74–75.

A chunk of this was recorded at the Armadillo World Headquarters in Austin, Texas, in 4/75. They were the only concert recordings to be issued in King's lifetime, and, unlike some of the live material issued later, do him justice. 'You Can Run But You Can't Hide' is replete with typically snakelike guitar playing, while on Bob Dylan's blues 'Meet Me In The Morning' and 'The Things I Used To Do' he and 'Fathead' Newman swap phrases like a couple of dudes on the street shooting the breeze. 'Have You Ever Loved A Woman', with a different lineup and sound balance (so presumably from another set: the Armadillo recordings spanned three nights), may be the first sighting of guitarist Andrew 'Jr Boy' Jones (q.v.). The Austin tapes proving insufficient for an album, Mike Vernon produced further tracks in Hollywood (which King didn't think much of) and found 'It's Your Move' among the outtakes from Burglar – yielding an album that, though it has its moments, feels more contrived than organic. TR

*** **Stayin' Home With The Blues**
[Spectrum 552 887] As for Burglar and Larger Than Life. 74–76.

A generously timed compilation from his RSO albums (three tracks from Burglar, five from Larger Than Life and six from Freddie King 1934–1976), this sports a large proportion of live recordings, several with the participation of the Eric Clapton band. The longest tracks, 'Gambling Woman Blues' and 'The Things I Used To Do', are also the best. Elsewhere, repeatedly exhorting an audience to say 'yeah' makes for tedious armchair listening. Clapton and slide-wielding George Terry share the solo space; much gets played but little of consequence emerges. King is fully engaged, as usual, but for all the energy he expends his vocal and instrumental parameters are audibly constrained.

*** **Live At The Electric Ballroom, 1974**
Topcat TCD 2952 King; Alvin Hemphill (o); Lewis Stephens (p); Sam — (g); Benny Turner (b); Mike Kennedy (d). 74.

A number of live tapes of similar repertoire and questionable origin emerged during the '90s but this one, recorded by Lewis Stephens at the Atlanta venue, has the endorsement of the artist's family. By 1974 King had made several swings through Europe to significantly more acclaim than he received in his homeland. His energy onstage was impressive but despite the audible enthusiasm of the crowd, he still felt the need to bellow, 'This is the blues. Are you listening?' Sometimes the tempos are a touch frenetic but the band struggles through. Best here is an 11-minute 'Sweet Home Chicago' that spends its first half as a duet between King and Stephens. As a prelude to the gig, 'That's Alright' and 'Dust My Broom' are the only examples of King playing acoustic guitar, during an interview with Dallas DJ Jon 'Big D' Dillon. These, acceptable sound quality and 68 minutes' playing time make this a reasonable proposition.

***(*) **Key To The Highway**
Wolf 120.900 King; Alvin Hemphill (o); Nat Dove, Lewis Stephens (p); Bernard Pearl, Floyd Bonner, Mark Pollak (g); Curtis Tillman, Benny Turner (b); William Henderson, Mike Kennedy, Calep Emphrey Jr (d). 70–75.

*** **Let The Good Times Roll**
Wolf 120.800 King; Alvin Hemphill (o); Louis Stephens (p); Floyd Bonner, Mark Pollak (g); Benny Turner (b); Mike Kennedy, Calep Emphrey Jr(d). 74–75.

***(*) **Live In Germany**
King Biscuit KBR 001 As above, except add Edd Lively (g). 75.

The measure of King's status in Europe is evident from the audience reaction on these live tapes from France and Germany. (Four tracks on Key To The Highway were cut in California in 1970.) There was obviously a standard set, which means that several songs turn up on at least two albums, among them 'Have You Ever Loved A Woman' (twice on Highway), 'Big Legged Woman', 'Sweet Home Chicago', 'Key To The Highway', 'Woman Across The River' and 'It Ain't Nobody's Business'. Sound quality, often in full stereo, is excellent throughout, given the recording equipment available at the time. King sings with significant force and plays with more facility and lyricism than on Electric Ballroom. Drawbacks to Let The Good Times Roll include draconian editing, a preponderance of slow material and the fact that the band is introduced twice. There's little to choose between Key To The Highway and Live In Germany but if one has to be superior then the latter shades it.

** **The Essential Collection Vol. 1**
Blue Moon CDBM 128 King; unknown (o); Lewis Stephens (p); Bugs Henderson, unknown (g); unknown (b); unknown (d). 72–76.

** **The Essential Collection Vol. 2 – Boogie On Down**
Blue Moon CDBM 129 As above. 72–76.

** **Boogie On Down**
Blue Moon CDBM 503 2CD As above. 72–76.

** **Palace Of The King**
Blue Moon CDBM 089 As above. 74–76.

The variations in sound quality, atrocious editing and the

application of various sonic solutions like reverb to these tapes seriously impinge upon the musicianship on display. They were recorded at a number of locations in Texas and Oklahoma, including a gig at the Texas Opry House in Houston. King and his consort play long and loud, too often resorting to rave mode, an extreme that pleases a roaring audience but fails to translate to the listener's living room. *Boogie On Down* contains the same material as both volumes of *The Essential Collection* but the hyperbolic title is totally inappropriate. *I'm Tore Down* (Indigo IGOXCD 533, deleted) distilled the best titles from these tapes and added material from *Palace Of The King* without quite creating a silk purse.

**** **Hideaway: The Best Of Freddie King**
Rhino R2 71510 *King; Ernie Royal, Martin Banks (t); Trevor Lawrence, Willie Bridges (ts, bs); Gene Redd, Clifford Scott, George Coleman, Frank Wess (ts); Earl Payton (h); John Gallie (o); Leon Russell (p, g); Billy Emerson, Sonny Thompson, George Stubbs (p); Robert Lockwood, Fred Jordan, Cornell Dupree, Don Preston (g); Robert 'Mojo' Elem, Bill Willis, Oscar Crummie, Gerry Jemmott, Donald 'Duck' Dunn (b); Thomas McNulty, Philip Paul, Kenneth Rice, Charles Blackwell, Charles Myers (d). 57–10/70.*

For those who require just one Freddie King compilation in their collection, this 20-tracker is probably the one to get. It begins with 'Country Boy' and 'That's What You Think', both sides of his obscure debut single for El-Bee, and continues with a judicious selection from the best of his Federal recordings, including 'Have You Ever Loved A Woman', 'I'm Tore Down' and 'Someday After Awhile (You'll Be Sorry)'. 'My Feeling For The Blues' is the sole representative from his two Cotillion albums, while 'Palace Of The King' and 'Going Down' are taken from his 1971 Shelter album *Getting Ready* … These latter titles contributed to an upsurge of interest in King, a springboard from which he leapt gratefully into the punishing international schedule that probably shortened his life.

*** **Ultimate Collection**
Hip-O 314 520 909 *Similar to above. 8/60–75.*

Hyperbole spoils the impact of a collection with a wider chronology but no better ingredients than the previous album. Indeed, it covers much the same ground, minus his first single but with the addition of a couple of RSO tracks at the end. There's a more balanced selection of Federal and Shelter sides but that's at the expense of the superior quality of the earlier recordings. For those faced with the choice, the Rhino set remains the better deal. NS

Little Freddie King (born 1940)
VOCAL, GUITAR

Fread E. Martin [sic] learned to play blues from his father in McComb, Mississippi; he left for New Orleans in his teens, and made music when not repairing TVs, working on the docks or in prison. He became Little Freddie King in the '60s, and made an LP with Harmonica Williams in 1970. King has long been a mainstay of the Jazz & Heritage Festival, and has appeared in Europe.

(*) **Swamp Boogie
Orleans OR 1611 *King; Bobby Lewis DiTullio (h); Crazy Rick Allen (o, p); Earl Stanley (b, tamb, Indian yells); Robert Wilson,* *Jason Sypher (b); Kerry Brown, Bradley Wisham (d); Carlo Ditta (tamb, Indian yells). 94–95.*

*** **Sing Sang Sung**
Orleans OR 2511 *King; Bobby Lewis DiTullio (h); Anthony Anderson (b); Wacko Wade Wright (d). 3–8/99.*

***(*) **You Don't Know What I Know**
Fat Possum FP 1022 *As above except add Jimmy Bones (kb), Martin Tino Gross (g, d, scratching), Mo Hollis (b). 04.*

Much of King's music on Orleans borrows from artists who were popular locally and nationally in the '50s and '60s. Prominent inspirations on *Swamp Boogie* include Jimmy Reed, Lightnin' Slim, B. B. King and, of course, Freddie King, although 'San Ho Zay' is pared down to fit the limitations of his namesake's playing. That's not to denigrate King's abilities, which serve the music well enough; the boundaries of *Swamp Boogie*'s appeal are set by desultory accompanists and the inclusion of generic instrumentals and the overworked 'What'd I Say'. *Sing Sang Sung*, recorded live, is better, despite an often under-recorded harmonica. It has more punkish energy, and its smaller forces throw the spotlight on King, whose guitar work is more detailed and forceful as a result. The long catalogue of disasters 'If You Want To Know The Blues You Got To Walk In My Shoes' owes debts to both Lightnin' Slim and Lightnin' Hopkins, but it's a considerable composition. Among several covers, Hopkins's 'Rocky Mountain' and John Lee Hooker's 'Hobo Blues' get convincingly personalized treatment. 'Bad Chicken', another tiresomely predictable instrumental, invites use of the skip button, however.

Given King's history of drinking, violence and jail time, it's surprising that Fat Possum took so long to latch on to him, but the meeting is a happy one. The additional musicians only appear on two remixes, but King and the band from *Sing Sang Sung* are encouraged to play louder, using more distortion and fewer chord changes. There are borrowings from Hooker, Bo Diddley and Frankie Lee Sims, but only Hopkins's 'War News Blues' is a straight(ish) cover, and Fat Possum encourage the originality hinted at by 'If You Want To Know The Blues You Got To Walk In My Shoes'. The sampling, scratching and overdubbing on the remixes is effectively done, adding a dimension rather than being mere dilettantism. Notwithstanding doubts about Fat Possum's apparent mission to Chulahomogenize all living blues singers, this CD has a lot more going for it than its predecessors. CS

Little Jimmy King (1968–2002)
VOCAL, GUITAR

Little Jimmy King caused quite a stir in the blues world when he came to prominence in the '90s. Born Manuel Gales in Memphis, he honed his skills on Beale Street. He changed his name partly because his guitar playing had a strong resemblance to that of Jimi Hendrix and partly because of an endorsement by his mentor Albert King, with whom he was touring by 1988. Like both men, the left-handed King played his instrument upside-down. He died from an untimely heart attack.

***(*) **Little Jimmy King And The Memphis Soul Survivors**
Bullseye Blues CD BB 9509 *King; Andrew Love (ts); Archie Turner (o, p); Ron Levy (o); Teenie Hodges (g); Melvin Lee (b); Cedric 'Cowboy' McCory, Greg 'Foots' Morrow (d). 91.*

**** **Something Inside Of Me**
Bullseye Blues CD BB 9537 *King; Scott Thompson (t); Jim Spake (ts, bs); Ron Levy (o); Tommy Shannon (b); Chris Layton (d, perc).* 94.

**** **Soldier For The Blues**
Bullseye Blues CD BB 9582 *King; Lannie McMillan (ts); Lester Snell, Archie Turner (kb); Thomas Bingham (g); Leroy Hodges (b); Steve Potts (d); William Brown, Bertram Brown, Mashaa, Jackie Johnson (v).* 97.

***(*) **Live At Monterey**
Bullseye Blues & Jazz 9612 *King; Wayne Jackson (t, tb); Andrew Love (ts); Archie Turner (o); Michael Taylor (g); Victor Butler, Melvin Lee (b); Roy Cunningham, Cedric 'Cowboy' McCory (d).* 02.

And The Memphis Soul Survivors is a superb debut. King's key influences are both unmistakable from the opening instrumental 'King's Crosstown Shuffle', but licks are dealt out with maturity, confidence and a natural sense of timing that elevate him far above the rank of imitator. Each track radiates youth and exudes a lively energy, particularly in the funky treatment of Sly Stone's 'Sex Machine' and the Stevie Ray Vaughan-influenced 'Another Blues Stringer'. While there are opportunities for development in the original songs, which at times are slightly superficial, this is an unquestionably strong exposition.

Perhaps the most striking thing about *Something Inside Of Me* is the substantially increased refinement of King's musicianship and writing. 'Under Pressure' sends a firm nod in Hendrix's direction but King retains an identity of his own in the 16th-note funk backing to his guitar workouts, which are notably more structured here than on the previous album. A sharper focus in the songwriting is evident in the narrative of 'Win, Lose Or Draw', the dual personalities of guitar and voice alternating in their laments. Elsewhere, a storming cover of Cream's 'Strange Brew' shows a band performing with brilliant unity, while the solo guitar piece 'Resolution #1' is a fascinating sound painting, representing a wonderful affinity with – and continuing exploration of – the instrument.

Soldier For The Blues, arranged and produced by Willie Mitchell, who also penned two of the tracks, 'Living In The Danger Zone' and 'It Ain't The Same No Mo', has a considerably more relaxed feel. King's performances throughout are splendid, displaying new levels of openness; his increasingly distinctive instrumental identity is nowhere more apparent than in the guitar lines of the closing cut 'I Got Sick One Day'. Though the album lacks the unchecked rawness of *Something Inside Of Me*, the primary emphasis is merely diverted towards the Memphis soul sound for which Mitchell is renowned. The result is an insightful and equally successful variation on King's other works, with 'I'm Doing Fine' and 'We'll Be Together Again' proclaiming the new aesthetic.

Live At Monterey actually consists of seven numbers from the 1999 Monterey Bay Blues Festival and four studio tracks from '94. The live tracks perfectly demonstrate King's captivating guitar and vocal displays. Predictably, a Hendrixian air wafts through the performances, but the players interlock with a tightness usually lacking in Hendrix's live shows. The Albert King influence flows equally strongly, especially in Little Jimmy's vocals, which are consistently exceptional. The more ferocious live treatment of the two Willie Mitchell numbers from *Soldier For The Blues* strengthens the assumption that that album was a deviation from King's natural style, which is revealed in 'Don't Burn Down The Bridge' and 'Standing In The Rain'. The studio recordings are of the ilk and calibre of those on *Something Inside Of Me*, adding value, depth and, coupled with the live tracks, a welcome cross-section of the output of a regrettably short career. JF

Saunders King (1909–2000)
VOCAL, GUITAR

King's father was a minister in the Sanctified church in Oakland, California, and King began singing and playing at church functions in his teens. In the late '30s he sang with the Southern Harmony Four and with Les Hite's orchestra. Taking up electric guitar, he led his own group, which recorded for Rhythm in 1942, just before the AFM strike emptied the recording studios for a couple of years. He continued with club and recording work in the '40s and '50s but by the early '60s had more or less retired, though in 1979 he made a cameo appearance on an album by his son-in-law, the singer and guitarist Carlos Santana. B. B. King claims him as an early model.

*** **Saunders King 1942–1948**
Classics 5064 *King; Sammy Deane, Eddie Walker (t); poss. Bob Barfield (cl, as); Eddie Taylor (ts); Johnnie Cooper (p, cel); Travis Warren, Cedric Haywood (p); Joe Holder, Vernon Alley (b); Bernard 'Bunny' Peters, Bill Douglas, Douglas Kinnard (d); band (v).* 6/42–12/48.

*** **Cool Blues, Jumps & Shuffles**
Ace CDCHD 865 *King; Sammy Deane, Eddie Walker, unknowns (t); poss. Bob Barfield (cl, as); Curtis Lowe, unknown (as); Eddie Taylor, prob. Jerome Richardson, unknowns (ts); Johnnie Cooper, Travis Warren, Cedric Haywood, poss. Brad Curtis, unknowns (p); Joe Holder, Vernon Alley, Lawrence Cato, Addison Farmer unknowns (b); Bernard 'Bunny' Peters, Bill Douglas, Bobby Osiban, Earl Watkins, unknowns (d); band (v).* 6/42–2/54.

*** **Saunders King 1948–1954**
Classics 5149 *King; Eddie Walker, Allen Smith, unknown (t); Pony Poindexter, Curtis Lowe (as); Eddie Taylor, Kermit Scott, Jerome Richardson, unknowns (ts); Cedric Haywood, poss. Brad Curtis, unknown (p); Lawrence Cato, Vernon Alley, Addison Farmer, unknowns (b); Bobby Osiban, Bernard 'Bunny' Peters, Earl Watkins, unknowns (d).* c. 48/49–2/54.

That Saunders King's place in musical history should have been assured by a blues is purely accidental: he made 'S. K. Blues' in response to members of his band, who bet that he couldn't put across such a number. The listener impressed by King's assured, if decorous, delivery and puzzled by his employees' disbelief needs to absorb more of his work. Some of it is pop songs of the kind that his contemporaries T-Bone Walker and Cecil Gant might have chosen, such as 'Get Yourself Another Fool' or 'Quit Hangin' Around Me', but rather more of them are pieces without even that tinge of blue, like 'I'd Climb The Highest Mountain' and 'Imagination' ('I dreamed that I was rich and that I did receive/A cottage full of bliss in the land of make-believe'), or standards like 'Danny Boy' and 'Summertime', all of which he delivers with a devotional tenderness that will make testier listeners want to kick him in the pants.

Yet he made quite an attractive edifice out of the two-part

'S. K. Blues', and when he returned four years later to construct 'S. K. Jumps', also in two parts, to much the same design, he sounded quite at home in the idiom, even if he was buying all his groceries from Joe Turner ('Believe I will and, baby, sometimes I believe I won't … Yes, yes, putti putti, ee-baba-le-ba …'). At any rate, he convinced his original audience: as the discography included in Ace's excellent booklet shows, blues remained a significant part of his repertoire, and this is duly reflected in the programme of all three CDs. His deep-toned guitar playing is not always featured, perhaps because he took his time over developing an approach to playing slow blues, but he is lively in the boppish 'Swingin''. The accompaniments, usually by six- or seven-piece groups, are in the style of Roy Milton or Joe Liggins. Even by the standards of West Coast blues in the '40s this is polite music, but its elegance vividly evokes a nightclub era almost beyond recall.

Classics' first volume proceeds systematically through King's work for Rhythm, while the second carries the story on through affiliations with Aladdin, Modern and Flair. The more selective Ace CD has all the tracks mentioned above. Several of the items that are only on Classics are interesting – 'The Atom Leaps' (1942–1948) sounds like the Artie Shaw orchestra on a bender – but they are sometimes very lo-fi, and the second Classics CD has the further problem that 14 of its 24 tracks were pre-empted by Ace. King's 1961 remakes of his most celebrated numbers, 'S. K. Blues' and 'What's Your Story, Morning Glory?', are on *All Night Long They Play The Blues* (Specialty SPCD-7029//Ace CDCHD 440). TR

Willie King (born 1943)
VOCAL, GUITAR

King's teacher, Albert 'Brook' Duck (1908–2000), told him that in the old days blues about women were a coded way of attacking the bossman. Not exclusively, perhaps, since misogyny still flourishes in rap alongside 'Fuck Tha Police'. Poverty, racism and oppression are still live issues, however, and King divides his music into 'sweet' and 'struggling' blues. He appears with his band, the Liberators, in the Alabama–Mississippi borders and lately further afield, runs the Freedom Creek Blues Festival and leads the Rural Members Association, a community action group.

*** **I Am The Blues**
Rural Members Association RMA 2000 *King; Aaron 'Hard Head' Hodge (g); Mike McCracken (b); Willie James Williams (d). 99.*
(*) **Freedom Creek
Rooster Blues R 2642 *As above, except add Johnnie B. Smith, Al Kinnanam 'Kenny' Smith (b), Aaron 'Hard Head' Hodge, Willie Lee Halbert (v). 2/00.*
*** **Living In A New World**
Rooster Blues ROB-CD-2647 *As above, except add Kevin Hayes (as, tamb), Henry Smith (kb, o, p), Robin Corbett (b); omit McCracken, Johnnie B. Smith, Al Smith. 2/02.*
***(*) **Jookin' At Bettie's**
Freedom Creek Music FCM 2004 *King; Rick Asherson (h, kb); Debbie Bond (g, v); Aaron Hodge (g); Travis Hodge (b); Willie James Williams (d); Willie Lee Halbert (v). 5/04.*

The limited-edition *Walkin' The Walk Talkin' The Talk* (no label or number), an excellent collaboration with singer/guitarist Birmingham George Conner, may still be available from King by mail-order (Rural Members Association, 791 Old Memphis Road, Aliceville, AL 35442) or at gigs.

I Am The Blues concentrates on the cathartic Saturday-night side of King's music. There are rhythmic and harmonic clashes between King and the band on the opening 'Strolling With Willie', but things settle down thereafter. and the disc is a good showcase for King's nimble, bright-toned guitar playing, and for songwriting and singing that often owe a lot to Howlin' Wolf.

Recorded live at a Mississippi juke-joint, *Freedom Creek* is the first CD on which 'struggling blues' predominate. Willie Lee Halbert repeats the ends of King's lines in an aural representation of solidarity that's initially arresting; unfortunately, most of the time Halbert is as automatic and predictable as an echo, and the songs often turn into over-extended, rambling jams.

Studio-recorded, *Living In A New World* is more focused; the songs are not prolonged beyond their natural lives, Halbert offers responses rather than mere repetition and Hayes and Henry Smith add textural variety. Nevertheless, there's a shortage of ideas, alike in the music, where very similar vamps and licks recur, and in the lyrics; there's no gainsaying King's accounts of iniquities past and persistent, but the line 'I ploughed the mule, I picked the cotton' appears at least once too often. That said, 'The Stomper' is a joyful celebration of celebration, and there's cumulative power in the eight angry minutes of 'Terrorized', the more so because of King's matter-of-fact delivery. For all the strength of his diagnoses, however, King's prescriptions – roughly speaking, peace, love and understanding – are simplistic.

Jookin' At Bettie's returns to the venue where *Freedom Creek* was recorded, and King returns to self-publishing. Apart from *Walkin' The Walk Talkin' The Talk*, this is his best CD to date, and in the throbbing 'Troubles To The Wind' it includes his finest recorded performance. Only one of the eight tracks is under six minutes, but the tight, thrusting directness of *Living In A New World* continues. The music remains riff-based, but King overlays intuitive, conversational guitar lines that vary excitingly from lyrical to harsh. Asherson's keyboard is a mixed blessing, though; used as an organ, it fills out the sound with a sleazy sexiness, but the electric piano switch permits an icy, rinky-dink texture that's unnatural and alienating. CS

King Biscuit Boy (1944–2003)
VOCAL, HARMONICA, GUITAR

Richard Newell grew up in Hamilton, Ontario, discovered blues through the radio and began to build a record collection. Inspired by Little Walter, he took up harmonica, but his early experience in bands was chiefly as a singer. Between 1967 and 1970 he worked for Ronnie Hawkins, who gave him his stage name; when he left Hawkins it was with the rest of the band, who named themselves Crowbar and backed him on the albums Official Music and Gooduns before they broke up. After tours in the UK, Canada and the USA he recorded briefly for Epic, then rejoined Hawkins for the rest of the '70s. For the remainder of his career he was often out of the spotlight and sometimes out of action.

***(*) **Official Music**
Stony Plain SPCD 1220 *King Biscuit Boy; Moe Koffman, Steve*

Kennedy, Greg Mudry (brass, reeds); Doug Riley (o, p); Kelly Jay (p, perc); Rick Bell (p); John 'Greyhound' Gibbard, Rheal 'Ray' Lanthier (g); Roly Greenway (b); Larry Atamanuik (d); John R. (perc). 4–5/70.

*** **Gooduns**
Stony Plain SPCD 1222 *King Biscuit Boy;* 'Slide' Tallman (tb); Steve Kennedy (s); Kelly Jay (p, v); Rick Bell (p); The Daffodil String Ensemble (strings); Rheal Lanthier, The Ghetto (g, v); Roly Greenway (b, v); Sonnie Bernardi (d, v); Larry Atamanuik, Mr Sunshine (d). 6/70–8/71.

*** **Badly Bent**
Stony Plain SPCD 1228 *As for above two CDs, except add* Allen Toussaint (kb, prod), Mac Rebennack [Dr John], Leo Nocentelli (g), George Porter Jr (b), Mr Sunshine (d), unknowns (v). 4–5/70–75.

Readers old enough to remember – or inquisitive enough to want to hear – a rocking blues combo with something of the spirit of the early J. Geils Band and the young George Thorogood should (re)acquaint themselves with *Official Music*. In many hands 'Biscuit's Boogie', a version of Junior Parker's 'Feelin' Good', would become a tedious thrash long before nine and a half minutes were up, but Newell and company work it joyfully all the way. A 'Highway 61' with screaming slide guitar, a gleeful reading of Little Johnny Jones's 'Hoy Hoy Hoy' and a handful of Chicago-style barn-burners like 'Don't Go No Further' and the original 'Badly Bent' maintain both tempo and temperature at a high level. Newell is a forthright singer and blows harmonica with inventiveness and passion, but what comes across most forcefully on *Official Music* is what an ass-kicking band this was.

Newell and Crowbar parted company soon after that album was released, and its follow-up had to be put together from material in the can. Fortunately most of it was pretty good stuff and the resulting album lived up to its title with high-octane versions of 'Barefoot Rock', Little Walter's 'Boom Boom (Out Go The Lights)', Willie Dixon's 'Twenty Nine Ways' and the Professor Longhair tribute 'Bald-head Rhumba Boogie'. 'The Boogie Walk' features Newell on just about everything: vocals, harmonicas, guitars and, from the simplicity of the playing, probably 'Mr Sunshine''s drums as well. This is more than a makeweight, but an unplugged version of Blind Willie McTell's 'Georgia Rag' is slighter.

Badly Bent contains five well-chosen tracks from *Official Music*, including 'Biscuit's Boogie' and the Taj Mahalish version of 'Corinna, Corinna', two from *Gooduns* and three from Newell's short spell with Epic: 'I'm Gone' and 'Mean Old Lady' from the 1974 album *King Biscuit Boy*, which was produced by Allen Toussaint, not to Newell's satisfaction, and a punchy 1975 B-side, 'I'm Writing You A Letter'.

*** **Urban Blues Re:Newell**
Blue Wave CD 124 *King Biscuit Boy;* Jesse O'Brien (p); Johnny 'V' Mills (g, v); Paul 'Big Daddy' LaRonde (b, v); Shawn O'Halloran (b); Mark Tiffault, Paul Panchezak (d); Kim Lembo (v). 4/94.

With the disappearance of *Down The Line*, a 1982 session originally issued on Red Lightnin' and transferred to CD as Sequel NEB CD 849 (deleted), *Urban Blues Re:Newell* is the only readily available album from King Biscuit Boy's later years. Though he had had health problems, he sings and plays with most of his erstwhile vigour on a programme replete with unusual blues and R&B selections (Johnny Fuller, Big Al Downing, Geno Parks) and a few originals. The accompaniments are no better than generic, but Newell's musical personality is expansive enough to make that unimportant. TR

Big Daddy Kinsey (1927–2001)
VOCAL, GUITAR, HARMONICA

In 1944 Lester Kinsey moved from Mississippi to Gary, Indiana, where he worked at US Steel and with local groups. In the late '60s he led a family band comprising himself and sons Donald, Ralph and Kenneth, but after Donald and Ralph pursued independent careers, Big Daddy went into artist management, production and promotion. In 1978 Big Daddy's sons formed the Kinsey Report, and he made a belated recording debut with them.

***(*) **Bad Situation**
Rooster Blues R 2620 Kinsey; Paul Howard (t); Bill McFarland (tb); Henri 'Hank' Ford (ts); Nate Armstrong, Billy Branch (h); Floyd Johnson (o); Pinetop Perkins, Frankie Hill (p); Donald Kinsey (g, perc); Kenneth Kinsey (b, v); Ralph 'Woody' Kinsey (d, bgo); Janis Patton, Robin Robinson, Valerie Wellington (v). 84.

(*) **Can't Let Go
Blind Pig BP 73489 Kinsey; Matthew Skoller (h); Lucky Peterson (kb); Donald Kinsey, Ron Prince (g); Kenneth Kinsey (b); Ralph Kinsey (d); Vycki Z. Walls, Yvonne Jackson (v). c. 89.

Before the Jackson Five became Gary's claim to fame, the city was an eastern extension of the Chicago blues scene, and even without a heartfelt 'Tribute To Muddy' on *Bad Situation*, Big Daddy Kinsey's singing and occasional slide guitar make it obvious who his musical hero was. *Bad Situation* very successfully puts Big Daddy's old-line blues into rhythmically busy, percussion-heavy settings that owe a lot to Donald's time with Albert King, and to his and Ralph's encounters with rock music and Southern soul. Nate Armstrong and Pinetop Perkins are obviously having a ball fitting in with these newfangled noises, as is the younger but retro-minded Billy Branch. Forceful horn sections add to the fun on three tracks, and the mixing gives all the musicians a punchy presence, although the intermittent backing vocals, chirpy where soulfulness is needed, are regrettable.

Can't Let Go is disappointing, mainly because of engineering that makes the music sound thin, distant and bland; even Lucky Peterson seldom makes his presence felt. Big Daddy's singing on 'Do You Need Me Like I Need You?' manages to cut through the fog, and Donald responds with some incendiary, modernistic guitar. The rock-tinged 'I'm A Lover' and a concluding eight-minute cover of Muddy's 'Howlin' Wolf' also have their merits, but they don't outweigh the deficiencies elsewhere; 'Going To New York' may be the most dispensable of the blues' many dispensable Jimmy Reed covers. CS

The Kinsey Report
GROUP

Ralph (born 1952), Donald (born 1953) and Kenneth (born 1963) Kinsey grew up in Gary, Indiana. In their teens Ralph (drums) and Donald (guitar) played with their father, Big

Daddy Kinsey. Donald left in 1972 to join Albert King, then Peter Tosh and The Wailers. In 1978 Donald, Ralph, Kenneth (bass) and guitarist Ron Prince became The Kinsey Report to back Kinsey Sr again. In 1987 the band contributed to Alligator's The New Bluebloods, and in the same year made their debut album for the label.

**(*) Edge Of The City
Alligator ALCD 4758 *St James Bryant (o); Donald Kinsey (g, v); Ron Prince (g); Kenneth Kinsey (b); Ralph Kinsey (d); band (v). 87.*

**(*) Midnight Drive
Alligator ALCD 4775 *Donald Kinsey (g, v); Ron Prince (g); Kenneth Kinsey (b); Ralph Kinsey (d, perc); band (v). 89.*

*** Smoke And Steel
Alligator ALCD 4860 *'Mad Dog' Lester Davenport (h); Roosevelt Purifoy, Anthony Space (kb); Donald Kinsey (g, v); Dave Miller, Will Crosby (g); Kenneth Kinsey (b); Ralph Kinsey (d, perc, v); Nancy Shaffer, Lasandra Maloney, band (v). 98.*

The second generation of Kinseys come from an impeccable blues background. 'Everything we do has got a blues foundation,' Donald has said. 'We can't get around that. It's us.' But they are very far from being guardians of tradition. From the start it was obvious that they were not going to follow their father down a Muddy road. The resonances from *Edge Of The City* and *Midnight Drive* came from roughly the same direction as Robert Cray's, but less ringingly because the Kinseys' original material lacked the freshness or wit of Cray and his writing collaborators, and Donald, though an astringent guitarist, hadn't yet developed a voice of much weight or character. There followed two albums for Pointblank, *Powerhouse* (1990) and *Crossing Bridges* (1991), both deleted. A few years on, the band returned to Alligator, without Prince, to make *Smoke And Steel*, an album with much of the textural and dynamic diversity that had been lacking from its forerunners. Except for 'Code Of The Streets', an elegy for black youth imprisoned in gang culture, the original songs are still rather unmemorable, but thoughtful arrangements and Donald Kinsey's airborne guitar solos go a long way to hide the fact. TR

Eddie Kirkland (born 1928)
VOCAL, GUITAR, HARMONICA

Born in Jamaica (he's recently claimed that the year was 1923) and brought to Alabama aged two, Kirkland made his way north, initially with a medicine show, and reached Detroit at 15. He cut singles for King and various local labels, and became the best accompanist John Lee Hooker ever had. In the '60s, Kirkland returned to the South and shifted towards soul for a time, joining Otis Redding's band and having a regional hit with 'The Hawg'. Since the '70s he has played blues and soul-blues for white audiences.

**** It's The Blues Man!
Original Blues Classics OBCCD 513 *Kirkland; King Curtis, Oliver Nelson (ts); George Stubbs, Herman Foster (p); Billy Butler (g); Jimmy Lewis (b); Ray Lucas, Frank Shea (d); Elise Shoulder (v). 12/61–3/62.*

Prestige were bemused by *It's The Blues Man!*; the original notes desperately suggest that it's 'perfect for Twisting'. Well, yes, if you can twist to a synthesis of industrial-strength electric guitar contortions, the vocal passion of the Pentecostal churches ('Man Of Stone' has more fire than anything Ray Charles ever did in this line) and the rhythmic force of James Brown. King Curtis and his musicians are sometimes taken aback by Kirkland's dark rawness, but they're equal to the challenge of creating a Hastings Street Saturday night in the studio.

Despite 'The Hawg', things were pretty slow when Peter B. Lowry found Kirkland in Macon, Georgia. Their encounter restarted his touring career and resulted in two early-'70s LPs, *Front And Center* (mostly solo) and *The Devil And Other Blues Demons* (jangling, riff-based and heavily influenced by contemporary soul and funk). They were reissued as *The Complete Trix Recordings* (32 Blues 32166 2CD), which is deleted but very much worth looking for.

**(*) Have Mercy
Evidence ECD 26018 *Kirkland; prob. Oliver Sain (p); John Spector (g); William Troiani (b); Kent Hinds (d); The Iketts [sic] (v). 88.*

Whatever it does for the wallet, steady touring may not be the best thing for an artist's music; all the songs here are Kirkland compositions, but too often high energy is being used to camouflage weak, repetitious material. The Iketts know it, too, singing like bored answering machines while the electric piano clanks and jangles thinly rather than fleshing out the harmonies. The socially concerned 'Young Man Young Woman Blues' rises above its surroundings, but the cod-reggae of 'Golden Sun' is risible.

** All Around The World
Deluge DEL D 3001 *Kirkland; Mike St Peter, Eric Pricpakula, Sam Hall (s); Richard Bell (o, p); David Maxwell (o); John Lee Hooker (g, v); Colin Linden, Mark Emerick, Billy Boardman (g); Jim Guyet, Jon Dymond, Scott Miller, Timo Kielnecker (b); Bowen Brown, Gary Craig, Dirk Cordes, Ray Anthony (d); Lenjes Robinson (perc); band (v). 4/90–4/92.*

** Some Like It Raw
Deluge DEL D 3007 *Kirkland; Billy Boardman (g, v); Timo Shanko (b, v); Ray Anthony (d). 9/93.*

**(*) Where You Get Your Sugar From?
Deluge DEL D 3012 *Kirkland; Sam Hall (s); Peter Re (o, p); Mike Castellana (g, v); Jack Cannon (b, v); Andy Plaisted (d, perc, v); Jamo (perc); Christine Ohlman, Rob Robertson, Lynn-Anne Crisci (v). 3/95.*

The decline in songwriting and performing skills continues; on *All Around The World* Kirkland's voice is often strained, the songs are unmemorable and the sound is thin. Hooker burbles distractedly on two tracks, proving that you can get away with anything once the rock press has elected you God. The energy of Kirkland's live performances is celebrated, but it doesn't translate to *Some Like It Raw*. Eccentrically, the CD both starts and finishes with interminable, monotonous set-closers. In between are poor songs, thrashed to within an inch of their life, and over-familiar ones similarly abused. There's some improvement on *Where You Get Your Sugar From?*: the rhythms roll rather than jittering, and the lyrics have more chance to speak for themselves. (This is not always advantageous: 'Lover Bone' is a stinker.) Ultimately, though, the band's wall of blues-rock is numbing. On Trix, 'Pity On Me' was fierce, spare and full of meaning; here it's one more loud track.

*** Lonely Street
Telarc CD-83424 *Kirkland; Kenny Neal (h, g); Richard Bell (o, p); Christine Ohlman (g, v); Greg Hoover, Tab Benoit, Cub Koda, Sonny Landreth, G. E. Smith (g); Jim Thacker (b); Jaimoe [sic] (d, perc, v); Darren Thiboutot (d). 5/97.*

**(*) Democrat Blues
Blue Suit BS-119D 2CD *Kirkland; Emmanuel Young, Dave Ray (g); Leon Horner, Calvin 'Fuzzy' Samuels (b); Duke Dawson, Andre Wright (d). 7/98–10/02.*

***(*) Movin' On
JSP JSPCD 2131 *Kirkland; Jamie Finegan (t); Bruce Feiner (ts, o); Robert Feiner (bs); Greg Hoover (g, v); Jim Thacker (b, v); Darren Thiboutot (d, v). 99?*

Fitzgerald refuted: there are second acts in American lives. Initially, *Lonely Street* is too much in-your-face, as Landreth, Benoit and Koda take turns to rock things up, but then it shifts into well-recorded soul-blues, with a botched version of Barrett Strong's 'Money (That's What I Want)' the only major letdown. A revived 'Snake In The Grass' is inferior to the version Trix bought from Capricorn, but Kirkland unveils some strong new songs. Sadly, one of them is 'Gates Of Heaven', written for his mother's funeral. It makes a moving closer, and is included, without Bell's organ and piano overdubs, in a generous enhanced section of videos, photos and press cuttings.

Movin' On also suggests that Kirkland's flirtation with the substandard is over. The ambience of the recording is rather clinical, and the occasional, presumably overdubbed, horns materialize abruptly, as if playing behind a soundproof door that's suddenly opened, but it's heartening that a 71-year-old is writing no-nonsense slow blues as intense as 'Got To Find Me 'Nother Woman' and 'Swanee River', and funk as savage as 'Don't Monkey With Me'; still more pleasing is that his gigging band brings such commitment to the enterprise.

Democrat Blues is the least satisfactory of these recent releases. It mixes acoustic studio recordings with extracts from a concert where the under-rehearsed pickup band is Ray, Samuels and Wright (a jazz drummer who seems to find blues idioms very difficult). Since Kirkland mainly sings recent compositions of his own, the musicians are usually reduced to following what he's doing, once they've figured out what it is. The package includes a 23-minute bonus disc, titled *Hastings Street Grease Sessions*, where Detroit veterans Young, Horner and Dawson supply much more sympathetic backing on a deliberately retro set. This disc would get ***(*) on its own, but five of its six tracks can be heard, in better company, on the VACs *Hastings Street Grease Vol. 1* and *Vol. 2* (Blue Suit BS-110D and BS-111D). CS

Bob Kirkpatrick (born 1934)
VOCAL, GUITAR

Kirkpatrick was born and grew up in north Louisiana, where he began playing guitar as a boy. In 1958 he moved to Dallas, where, after jobs in other sectors, he eventually became an adviser to the federal food-stamp programme. In the late '60s he played in a local band. Following an appearance at the Newport Folk Festival he cut an album for Folkways in 1973, but he was unable to give much time to music until after he had retired from his day job, in the early '90s.

** Going Back To Texas
JSP JSPCD 269 *Kirkpatrick; Wilford C. Sims (s); Harry James Bright (o, p); Jerry DeCicco (b); Degge James (d). 1–2/96.*

**(*) Drive Across Texas
Topcat TC 02012 *Kirkpatrick; Steve Coleridge (h, g, b, perc); unknown (ac); Jon Dyke (kb, perc); Brendan Perkins (g, perc); Jose Hernandez, Kevin Thorpe (g); Floyd Pintado (d, perc); Peter Hague (d); Aurora Hernandez (perc). 99.*

Kirkpatrick's interest in blues was stimulated by B. B. King, and the imprint of the more famous man's style is evident on both these albums, both vocally and instrumentally, though Kirkpatrick's habit of playing firmly on the beat, in which he is faithfully supported by his accompanists, deprives the King manner of its fluidity. The songs on *Going Back To Texas* are the artist's; there isn't much more to say about them, and if this were his only album he would risk appearing to be little more than a celebrity soundalike. The more collaborative songwriting on *Drive Across Texas* paradoxically makes Kirkpatrick sound more individual, an effect that's heightened by the variety of the tempos and arrangements. Unfortunately the Topcat CD may not be much easier to find than its original issue on Red Lightnin' RLCD 0099, now deleted. TR

Cub Koda (1948–2000)
VOCAL, HARMONICA, GUITAR, BASS, DRUMS, PERCUSSION

Cub Koda grew up in Detroit and played drums and guitar in high-school bands. He founded the rock band Brownsville Station in 1969 and wrote their 1973 hit 'Smokin' In The Boys' Room'. When the band broke up in 1979 he began contributing a 'Vinyl Junkie' column to Goldmine *magazine, and subsequently compiled and annotated blues and other compilations. In the early '80s he worked with the Houserockers, formerly Hound Dog Taylor's band.*

(**(*)) Welcome To My Job – The Cub Koda Collection 1963–1993
Blue Wave CD 121 *Koda; Rusty Creech, Joey Gaydos, Brewer Phillips, Left Hand Frank [Craig], Mike Hayward (g); Paul 'Big Daddy' LaRonde (b, v); Pete Bankert, Michael 'Mudcat' Ward, Vic Javierre (b); Doug Hankes, Fred Schmidt, Ted Harvey, Per Hanson, Mark Tiffault (d). 9/63–5/93.*

**(*) Live At B.L.U.E.S. 1982
Wolf 120.290 *Koda; Eddie [Eddy] Clearwater (g, v); Brewer Phillips (g); Ted Harvey (d). 9/82.*

Welcome To My Job is drawn from ten albums, a couple of singles and unissued tapes spanning three decades. Blue Wave call it 'a multi-label comprehensive collection … 70+ minutes of roots rockin', guitar-driven, rock & roll, rockabilly, blues & all points in between'. The slightly scatty fervour of the description gives fair notice that this is an album directed at long-term admirers. Blues fans whose interest in Koda, however cordial, is not central to their lives will probably prefer the B.L.U.E.S. gig. Koda makes no attempt to bury his rock 'n' roll roots beneath a mulch of assumed blues accent, so what looks from the tracklist like a Hound Dog Taylor celebration – and, given the immutability of Phillips and Harvey, you would expect to be one, willy nilly – is that only obliquely, and has a different flavour, younger and brasher. Clearwater makes a guest appearance, singing his 'Chicago Daily Blues'. TR

Koerner, Ray & Glover
GROUP

John Koerner (born 1938), Dave Ray (1943–2002) and Tony Glover (born 1940) met in the early '60s in Minneapolis and began playing together in coffeehouses. In 1963, encouraged by Paul Nelson, editor of The Little Sandy Review, they made an album to sell at gigs; reissued later that year by Elektra, Blues, Rags & Hollers caught the wave of interest in 'folk blues' and was listened to attentively by many other musicians who were discovering the same music, among them Bob Dylan and John Lennon. All three maintained musical careers, though seldom working as a trio; Koerner has three albums on Red House, while Glover has written extensively about blues harmonica playing.

**(*) Blues, Rags & Hollers
Red House RHCD 76 *'Spider' John Koerner (h, g, v); Tony 'Little Sun' Glover (h, v); Dave 'Snaker' Ray (g, v).* 3/63.
**(*) [Lots More] Blues, Rags & Hollers
Red House RHRCD 130 *As above, except Koerner also plays k.* 9/63.
**(*) Blues, Rags And Hollers & Lots More Blues Rags And Hollers
Elektra 76506 2CD *As for above CDs.* 3–9/63.
**(*) The Return Of
Red House RHRCD 131 *As above.* 10/65.

To their Minneapolis friends, Koerner, Ray & Glover seemed pretty wonderful, and they duly boosted them in The Little Sandy Review and wrote sleevenotes saying things like ' "One Kind Favor" [on Blues, Rags & Hollers] has a somber and foreboding quality that reminds one of Buñuel or Bergman.' Reading this 40-odd years later, one must remind oneself that these writers probably had only a sketchy acquaintance, at best, with genuinely 'somber and foreboding' music like that of, say, Skip James. Purged of their supporters' exaggeration, Blues, Rags & Hollers and its successors are revealed as good-hearted collections of blues and old-time songs performed with reasonable competence and some independence of spirit. The singers adopt black vocal manners only occasionally and, when they derive their material from specific recordings, like Muddy Waters's 'Honey Bee' or Booker White's 'Fixin' To Die' on [Lots More] or the various Leadbelly songs which Ray contributes to all three CDs, they usually avoid direct imitation. Ray is the least mannered singer and the subtlest guitarist, Koerner the most ebullient performer. Despite the billing, nearly all the performances are duets or solos; there are just two trios on the first album and one each on the others. Glover plays on only a third of Blues, Rags & Hollers and less than a quarter of [Lots More]. One suspects that these were men whose musical differences, and perhaps ego clashes, would always stand in the way of their forming a cohesive group. TR

Alexis Korner (1928–84)
VOCAL, GUITAR, PIANO

Alexis Korner's Blues Incorporated was Britain's first serious blues band. Korner, who was of Greek and Austrian Jewish extraction, was one of the tiny group of British enthusiasts in the '50s who knew something about both jazz and blues, and by 1955 he was working regularly with the harmonica player Cyril Davies (1932–64). He formed Blues Incorporated in 1962, the first lineup including, as well as Davies, singer Long John Baldry and tenor saxophonist Dick Heckstall-Smith, future stalwarts of the local blues scene; later formations embraced both jazz musicians and members of R&B bands-in-the-making like The Rolling Stones. Korner's leanings towards jazz set him apart from many of the new generation of specialized blues enthusiasts, and in the '70s he increasingly played either outside Britain or on the fringe of the blues idiom, in bands like New Church, CCS and Snape, though Rocket 88 pulled him back towards the blues fold. For many years he delighted and informed radio listeners with his BBC programmes devoted to blues, soul, gospel and what had not yet come to be called world music.

***(*) R&B From The Marquee
Radioactive RRCD 036 *Korner; Dick Heckstall-Smith (ts); Cyril Davies (h, v); Keith Scott (p); Spike Heatley (b); Graham Burbidge (d); Long John Baldry (v); Jack Good (prod).* 62.
*** Red Hot From Alex
Castle CMRCD 293 *Korner; Dave Castle (as, fl); Art Themen, Dick Heckstall-Smith (ts); Ron Edgeworth (o, p); Danny Thompson (b); Barry Howten (d); Herbie Goins (tumbas, v).* 3/64.

It's curious that one of Britain's pioneer blues groups, probably the first to feature standards-to-be like 'I Got My Mojo Working', should have been so very much *not* a typical blues band of any period or style. Charles Fox, in his notes for the LP issue of Red Hot From Alex, described Blues Incorporated as 'standing halfway between Muddy Waters and Charlie Mingus'. The album did in fact end with a Mingus tune, 'Haitian Fight Song', and, if there were no Muddy numbers, there had been four on the earlier R&B From The Marquee. That set, which introduced many Britons to 'Mojo' and 'Hoochie Coochie Man', had an immediate influence on a generation of nascent blues fans and musicians; more than 40 years on, it is not only iconic but still good listening, thanks in large part to Davies's fiery harmonica playing. Having opened a new pathway, however, Korner himself quickly took another direction: 1963's Alexis Korner's Blues Incorporated (See For Miles SEECD 457, deleted) dropped Davies and Baldry and had largely original material, while the following year's Red Hot From Alex introduced a more urbane and jazzy vocalist, Herbie Goins, though the majority of the numbers were instrumental, fusing elements of the blues and modern jazz. That sort of blending was intrinsic to Korner's musical thinking. Unlike some of the musicians who learned from him and became a great deal more famous, he had no interest in playing within the stylistic conventions of Chicago blues or any other school. Such brave perversity may not have done much for his income, but it produced music that even now can be surprising.

**(*) Bootleg Him!
Essential ESMCD 806 *Korner; Victor Brox (c, p, v); Henry Lowther, Harold Beckett (t); Chris Pyne, Malcolm Griffiths (tb);*

unknowns (brass); Ray Warleigh (as); Dick Heckstall-Smith, poss. Art Themen, Lol Coxhill (ts); John Surman (bs); unknowns (reeds); Cyril Davies, Robert Plant (h, v); Steve Miller, poss. Johnny Parker, unknown(s) (p); Peter Thorup (g, v); unknown(s) (g); Andy Fraser, Jack Bruce, prob. Danny Thompson, Colin Hodgkinson (b); John Marshall, unknowns (d); Annette Brox (tamb, v); Herbie Goins, Paul Rodgers, unknowns (v); unknown others. 61–71.

(*) Musically Rich ... And Famous
Essential ESD CD 653 2CD *Korner; Victor Brox (c, p, v); Henry Lowther, Harold Beckett (t); Chris Pyne, Malcolm Griffiths, Nick Evans, Mike Zwerin (tb); Ron Aspery (ss); Ray Warleigh, Elton Dean (as); Lol Coxhill, Dick Morrissey (ts); John Surman (bs, p); Eddie Mordue (bs); Mel Collins (s); Robert Plant (h, v); Duster Bennett (h); Tim Hinkley (kb, o); Zoot Money (kb, p, v); Steve Miller (p, v); Nicky Hopkins, Tony O'Malley (p); Pete Sayers (Do, bj); Peter Thorup, Steve Marriott, Keith Richards (g, v); Peter Frampton, Danny McIntosh Jr, Eric Clapton (g); Boz Burrell (b, v); Andy Fraser, Rick Wills, Alan Spenner (b); Ian Wallace, Gaspar Lawal, Tony Carr (d, perc); John Marshall, Terry Stannard, Adrian Tilbrook, Kenn Gudman, Graham Broad, Stu Speer (d); Annette Brox (tamb, v); Paul Rodgers, Irene Chanter, Barry St John, Liza Strike, George Caldwell, Jim Diamond, Chris Farlowe (v). 11/67–6/82.*

These collections span various lineups of Blues Incorporated, New Church, CCS and Snape, as well as solo and duo recordings, some from concerts. As can be seen from the castlists, especially that of *Musically Rich ... And Famous*, many prominent blues, jazz and rock musicians worked with Korner. It may not be entirely clear to present-day listeners why this was so, since Korner's own talents were unremarkable: his singing was mannered and as a guitar player he was not a natural soloist. What attracted his collaborators was a restless imagination that made music-making in his company adventurous and testing. Besides his penchant for Mingus, illustrated on *Bootleg Him!* by 'Dee' and 'Oh Lord, Don't Let Them Drop That Atomic Bomb On Me', he drew material from sources as varied as Curtis Mayfield, Thomas Dorsey, Ray Charles, Mance Lipscomb and James Taylor. The expansive *Musically Rich* (32 tracks, five shared with *Bootleg Him!*) boards the listener for a longer and more diverse tour, taking in collaborations with various rock *éminences* before they were *grises*. Inevitably some of this has not worn well. Most listeners will not linger over the solo acoustic version of Jagger and Richards's 'Honky Tonk Woman', and Korner's readings of the country songs 'Blood On The Saddle' and 'Wreck Of The Old 97' are truly terrible. There's recompense in the slightly freakish combination, on 'Hey Pretty Mama', of Chris Farlowe, Eric Clapton and John Surman.

(*) Alexis Korner & Friends – The Party Album
Essential ESMCD 805 *Korner; Mike Zwerin (tb); unknowns (brass); Art Themen, John Surman, unknowns (reeds); Paul Jones (h, v); Zoot Money (kb, v); Eric Clapton (g); Colin Hodgkinson (b); Stu Speer (d); Chris Farlowe, others (v). 79.*

**** Me**
Essential ESMCD 807 *Korner. 79.*

The *Party Album* was recorded at a concert for Korner's 50th birthday. Old friends were at hand, and not just musicians: 'Finkle's Cafe' was a tune from *R&B From The Marquee*, 'Captain's Tiger' from *Alexis Korner's Blues Incorporated*, 'Skipping' and 'Stormy Monday Blues' from *Red Hot From Alex*. No matter: they're good tunes, and they elicit warm contributions from the substantial band that assembled for the occasion. This is slimmed down for a segment of small-group numbers featuring Jones, Money, Farlowe and others, but the band reassembles for the closing 'Stormy Monday'.

The notes to *Me*, Korner's only solo album, deal frankly with the issue of his skills, citing the judgement of a one-time pupil: 'a man of great taste who was struggling to play guitar'. In fact his playing here, better recorded than usual, has considerable muscle and rhythmic verve. What's more problematic is the songs – 'Honky Tonk Woman' again, and some unmemorable originals – and Korner's singing of them, which, as the notes admit, contains 'occasional wayward pitching and alarming vocal improvisations'. It is an honest warts-and-all performance, and for admirers that may be enough. TR

Smokin' Joe Kubek (born 1956)
VOCAL, GUITAR, KEYBOARDS

The Smokin' Joe Kubek Band, fronted by Texan guitarist Kubek and Louisiana-born vocalist and guitarist B'nois King (born 1943), was playing at Huey's in Memphis when people from Rounder Records happened to drop in; the result was an association that would last for almost a decade.

**** Steppin' Out Texas Style**
Bullseye Blues CDBB 9510 *Kubek; Sax Gordon (ts); 'Tino' Barker (bs); Ron Levy (o, p); B'nois King (g, v); Greg Wright (b); Phil Campbell (d, telephone). 91.*

**** Chain Smokin' Texas Style**
Bullseye Blues CDBB 9524 *Kubek; Jim Spake (s); Ron Levy (o); Bnois King (g, v); Greg Wright (b, v); Phil Campbell, Paul 'Big Foot' Lee (d); The Texas Tonies (v). 92.*

Texans like to think of themselves as hellraisers, and some Texan music comes with a strong whiff of fire and brimstone. This Texas-based band defies the stereotype. Kubek plays with infernal skill, but King sings in a smooth, unstrained manner, at the other end of the blues vocal range from a Johnny Copeland or a Long John Hunter. Junior Parker might be closer to the mark. The band's first couple of albums lived up to their 'Texas style' billing, being hearty but not unsubtle blends of original material, carefully chosen items from elsewhere, such as Jimmy McCracklin's 'Steppin' Out' (a.k.a. 'Steppin' Up In Class') on the first album or T-Bone Walker's 'Little Girl', with Kubek on lap steel, on the second, and occasional instrumentals highlighting Kubek's guitar, not only on Texas shuffles but on slow blues like *Steppin' Out*'s 'Square Bizness'. King's singing is sometimes a little too laidback for the good of the songs, but not on *Chain Smokin*''s 'Just For A Little While', a slow blues with lovely guitar.

**** Texas Cadillac**
Bullseye Blues CDBB 9543 *Kubek; Bnois King (g, v); Bobby Chitwood (b); Ralph Power (d). 94.*

(*) Cryin' For The Moon
Bullseye Blues CDBB 9560 *As above, except Kenneth Stern (d) replaces Power. 95.*

**** Got My Mind Back**
Bullseye Blues CDBB 9578 *Kubek; Bnois King (g, v); Paul Jenkins (b); Mark Hays (d). 96.*

Despite its title, *Texas Cadillac* carries a 'we went to Chicago and got the blues!' decal, its trunk loaded with material from Little Walter, Muddy Waters, Eddie Taylor, Jimmy Reed and Willie Dixon. The one King–Kubek composition, 'TV Light', a homily addressed to 'all you cats out there in CD Land', has a memorable chat-up line: 'Darlin', you ought to see how that TV light is bouncin' off your skin ... must be a commercial on now, darlin', 'cause you're lookin' *real* good.' *Cryin' For The Moon*, in contrast, is entirely original songs by members of the band or producer Ron Levy. Kubek frequently colours his guitar with studio effects, and while one can't reproach him for wanting to experiment, the process doesn't give the band anything it signally lacked.

Perhaps Kubek felt that way too, since there's less of it on *Got My Mind Back*. Another all-originals set, it opens with Hound Dog Taylorish slide on the title track. Unlike some contemporaries, Kubek has the taste and discretion to turn down the heat occasionally, as in 'Cryin' By Myself' or the instrumental 'All The Love There Is', where the guitar (effect-aided here) soars over the sea-spray of the cymbals, faintly reminiscent of 'Albatross' or Stevie Ray Vaughan's 'Lenny'.

(*) Take Your Best Shot
Bullseye Blues & Jazz CDBB 9600 *Kubek; Bnois King (g, maracas, v); Jimmy Thackery, Little Milton (g); Guthrie Kennard (b); Jimmy 'Blue Shoes' Pendleton (d); Jason Latshaw (cga, perc); Holly Bullamore, Jose Fumando (tamb); Brian Lacy, Shannon Ernst (clapping); Jackie Johnson, Susan Marshall (v).* 98?

(*) Bite Me!
Bullseye Blues & Jazz BB 9617 *Kubek; Gary Slechta (t); Mark 'Kaz' Kazanoff (ts, h); Les Izmore (bs); Bnois King (g, v); Jerry Hancock (b, perc); Jas Stephens (d, perc).* 00.

*** Served Up Texas Style! Best Of The Smokin' Joe Kubek Band Featuring Bnois King**
Bullseye Blues & Jazz BEYE 9642 *As for all Bullseye Blues CDs above.* 91–00.

The very different ensemble sound that's evident from the first bars of *Take Your Best Shot* may be due in part to the new rhythm section, but it probably reflects the new producer too. After five albums of Ron Levy's generally unobtrusive production, Jim Gaines's busier, punchier sound may have seemed to the band like a worthwhile change. Another contributing factor is King's guitar playing, here heard more, and more in a joint lead role, than before. *Bite Me!* puts a harmonica on a Kubek album for the first time but otherwise follows the template of its predecessor. *Served Up Texas Style!* sums up the Bullseye Blues decade with selections from each album: generally two but three from *Take Your Best Shot*, including Little Milton's guest appearance on 'One Night Affair'. With sound choices like 'TV Light' and 'Got My Mind Back', and two previously unissued numbers from the *Texas Cadillac* sessions, this serves its purpose as a showcase very well.

Listeners may feel that they can detect traces of metal fatigue ...

*** Roadhouse Research**
Blind Pig BPCD 5080 *Kubek; Bnois King (g, v); Paul Jenkins (b); Ralph Power (d).* 02.

*** Show Me The Money**
Blind Pig BPCD 5090 *As above, except add Anson Funderburgh (g).* 04.

... and, if so, will echo the words of Mel Brooks and offer a laurel and hearty handshake to Kubek and King for *Roadhouse Research*. Jointly credited for the first time, the pair celebrate a change of label by rehiring a bassist and drummer from the past, sandblasting the production gloss of the last two albums and going back to basics. King sings 'Healthy Mama' as if briefly possessed by the spirit of Howlin' Wolf, but thereafter reverts to his normal lower-key manner. Musical conservatives will enjoy 'Cryin' Shame': 'Well, you know, it's hiphop this and hiphop that – I'm kinda tired of hearing that crap. I've spent my life learnin' to play – now they're just talkin', gettin' all the pay. It's a cryin' shame ...' *Show Me The Money*, also jointly credited, is cut from the same plain but hard-wearing cloth. Atmospheric tracks like the opening 'I Saw It Coming', a tune memorable enough to etch itself instantly upon the memory, or 'Burnin' To The Ground' maintain the band's reputation for strong, satisfying albums. TR

Lady Bianca (born 1955)
VOCAL, PIANO

Bianca Thornton was born in Kansas City, grew up in the San Francisco Bay Area and has lived in Oakland since the '70s. She studied at the San Francisco Conservatory of Music and performed with numerous artists at its theatre. Since the late '80s she has worked on the club and festival circuit in northern California. Etta James and Koko Taylor are among the singers she particularly admires.

** **Best Kept Secret**
Telarc CD-83367 *Lady Bianca; Louis Easman (t); Wayne Wallace (tb); Melecio Magdaluyo (as, bs); Ron Stallings (ts); Dave Matthews (o, p); Mick Milo (syn); Joe Goldmark (esg); Carl Lockett (g); Tony Saunders (b); Dave Rokeach (d); Gibbie Ross (cga, timbales); Pauline Lozano (v).* 8–9/94.

(*) Rollin'
Rooster Blues RBLU 2644 *Lady Bianca; Louis Easman (t); Wayne Wallace (tb); Jim Norton (ts, bs); Melecio Magdaluyo (ts); Dave Mathews (o); Carl Lockett (g); Tony Saunders (b); Dave Rokesch [Rokeach] (d, perc); Gibby Ross (cga); Stanley Lippitt (v); Diane Cheng (sp).* 10/00–1/01.

Lady Bianca writes all her material, in collaboration with her partner Stanley Lippitt, and it has taken a little while for them to discover what songs work best for the artist she seems to be working towards becoming: the sassy blues diva of *Rollin'* rather than the acrobatically versatile wannabe of *Best Kept Secret*. The most successful tracks on the first album are the least adventurous – the title song and 'Ooh, His Love Is So Good', both slow blues – but she sings them with spirit, and her confidence in her powers is more justified there than in songs like 'How Do I Tell My Little Sister?', where her pitching is uncertain. Listeners who like a larger serving of blues will much prefer *Rollin'*, where she plays her more focused role with panache, sometimes strutting ('Lookin' At My Man'), sometimes slinking ('Easy Lovin'). TR

Paul Lamb (born 1952)
HARMONICA

Born in Blyth in Northumberland, England, Lamb became interested in the blues in his teens and in blues harmonica when he first heard the playing of Sonny Terry. Later, having absorbed the styles of Little and Big Walter, he joined the band Smokestack Lightnin', where he met his longtime musical partner, guitarist Johnny Whitehill. They subsequently formed the Blues Burglars and, in 1989, the King Snakes. Lamb, the band and their albums have all received numerous British blues awards. Lamb's harmonica has also been heard on TV ads, pop albums and the London stage.

***(*) **Harmonica Man**
Castle CMEDD 701//Sanctuary CAS 36105 2CD *Lamb; Steve Weston (o, p); Paul Riordan (kb, g, prog); Piano Willie (p); Johnny D. [Dickinson], Chad Strentz (g, v); Johnny Whitehill, Martin Febia (g); Rod Demick (b, v); P. J. White, Dave Stevens, Jim Mercer (b); Ed Bowman, Alan Savage, Daniel Strittmatter, Martin Deegan, Sonny Below (d); Bill Sharp, Earl Green, Geordie Nares, Tania Evans, Betty Anne Sempra (v). 86–5/02.*

*** **Live At The 100 Club 14th May 2002**
Sanctuary CAS 36083//Castle CMRCD 1280 *Lamb; Johnny Whitehill (g); Rod Demick (b, v); Sonny Below (d); Earl Green (v). 5/02.*

*** **I'm On A Roll**
United Producers UPRBCD 1001 *Lamb; Lee Badau (ts); Nick Lunt (bs); Chad Strentz (p, g, v); Raul de Pedro Marinero, Ryan Lamb (g, v); Rod Demick (b, v); Sonny Below (d, v). 05.*

For much of the '90s the King Snakes were undisturbed by personnel changes and the Indigo albums *Fine Condition*, *She's A Killer*, *John Henry Jumps In* and *The Blue Album* profited from that continuity. Johnny Whitehill, matching Lamb in versatility, steadily advanced to the top class of blues guitarists, while Chad Strentz, though not a singer to make one's blood race, handled a variety of songs very capably. The King Snakes' material and settings were almost always firmly rooted in blues ground, but the band seldom sounded merely generic. Those and four of the band's other five albums (four for Indigo, one for Blue Horizon) have been deleted, but *Harmonica Man* selects three dozen tracks fairly evenhandedly from that catalogue, adding the title number, which, billed as by Bravado, had some chart success in the UK in 1994. (The band's admirers should nevertheless scout the used-CD racks for *Take Your Time And Get It Right* [Indigo IGOXCD 531], their best studio album.) The 100 Club gig was an experiment in quick production, the album being edited, mastered, manufactured and released within a couple of weeks. Lamb's harmonica might sometimes be higher in the mix, but otherwise the CD rarely betrays the speed of its making, and the club atmosphere is palpable.

Raul de Pedro Marinero, the new lead guitarist on *I'm On A Roll*, has a hard act to follow, and may need some time to make a comparable impression on the band. Lamb blows with his customary power and invention and the mostly original programme is well sequenced. TR

Lamont Cranston Blues Band
GROUP

The Lamont Cranston Blues Band, led by Pat Hayes, have been playing in the Twin Cities area of Minneapolis–St Paul, Minnesota, since the mid-'70s. They have accompanied many visiting artists.

(*) **Tiger In Your Tank
Cold Wind CWR 8808 *Tony Moen (t); Pete Masters (tb); Joe Chandler, Paul Scher (s); Pat Hayes (h, g, v); Danny Rowles (kb); Bob Bingham (g); Bill Black (b); Jim Novak (d). 88.*

What the LCBB tend to do best is rock at speed on numbers like 'Hurry Hurry Baby', 'House Party' or 'Sittin' On It' (Wynonie Harris's 'Sittin' On It All The Time'), but thanks to Hayes's controlled singing and Bingham's guitar playing, 'As The Years Go Passing By' is just as creditable. Hayes also plays good slide on Elmore James's 'Quarter Past Nine' and harmonica on the instrumental 'Shadow's Groove'. Pity it's over so quickly. The rerelease of this set in 1999 – remastered, but the balance is still imperfect – somewhat compensated for the deletion of the LCBB's Atomic Theory albums *Lamont Cranston Blues Band* (ATM 1119) and *Roll With Me* (ATM 1134), recorded in the second half of the '90s with a different lineup but much the same approach. TR

Ernest Lane (born 1931)
VOCAL, PIANO

Lane's father was a pianist in Clarksdale, and he started on piano as a schoolboy, learning from Pinetop Perkins and alongside Ike Turner. After the army found out that he'd joined up at the age of 14 and discharged him, Lane teamed up with Robert Nighthawk, recording behind him in 1949. Moving between Chicago and Mississippi, Lane worked with Earl Hooker and Houston Stackhouse among others before forming his own band in Little Rock in 1952. Four years later he moved to California and became a weekend musician until recruited by Ike Turner in the early '60s. Low pay led him to quit after two years, followed by most of the band. They became the Goodtimers, and were hired to back up The Monkees (!) but broke up fairly swiftly. Lane became a truck driver; since retiring, he's been reunited with Turner on a few tours.

*** **The Blues Is Back!**
Acoustic Music 319.1331 *Lane; Mack Johnson (t); Lee Dombecki, Derrick B. Edmondson, Big Jay McNeely (ts); Wali Ali, Seth Blumbery, Steve Gannon, Willie J. Laws (g); Rick Jones (b); James Gadson (d). 2/04.*

Before *The Blues Is Back!* Lane's issued output under his own name totalled four singles between 1952 and 1983. He's an acceptable rather than a memorable singer, and a proficient, professional pianist, as evidenced by his session work over the years, and most obviously on this CD by the instrumentals 'Lane Shuffle' and 'Boogiein' At Leon's Place', which is Albert Ammons's 'Boogie Woogie Stomp'. The other musicians are equally professional; the core band is Ali, Jones and Gadson, and they supply an infallibly funky swing. Only McNeely, guesting on one track, plays at their level of inspiration, though, and the horn arrangements are usually predictable, distant and foggy. There's a preponderance of Lane originals among the songs, and on their evidence he's an unexciting writer, prone to marrying hackneyed lyrics with conventional blues and soul licks. Lane's piano and the rhythm section are decidedly worth hearing; if only they were working on stronger material. CS

Jimmy D. Lane (born 1966)
VOCAL, GUITAR

Lane is the son of Jimmy Rogers (James A. Lane) and grew up surrounded by Chicago blues legends. He began playing guitar at 21, learning from Jimi Hendrix on record and Stevie Ray Vaughan in person. During the '90s he worked either in his father's band or with his own trio Blue Earth.

** Long Gone
APO APO-2003 *Lane; John Koenig (g, tamb); Freddie Crawford (b); Jim Keltner (d, tamb).* 10/95–1/96.

*** Legacy
APO APO 2005 *Lane; Carey Bell (h); David Krull (o, p); Jimmy Rogers (g, v); Hubert Sumlin (g); Freddie Crawford (b); Per Hanson, Sam Lay (d).* 10/97.

'Jimi Hendrix was really the reason why I picked up a guitar,' Lane has said. 'I heard "Hey Joe" and that was it.' No one listening to *Long Gone* needs to be told this. From the opening number, Jimi's 'Hear My Train A Comin'', the influence of Hendrix flows through *Long Gone*, very nearly drowning whatever individuality Lane may possess. Even well-known vehicles like 'Rollin' Stone' and 'Boom Boom' are carnapped, taken to the chopshop and fitted with JIM 1 plates. The only respite from this power-trio assault is an attractive acoustic version of Jimmy Rogers's 'I'm In Love'. When he came to make *Legacy* two years later, Lane had evidently rethought his musical policy. There are still a few explosions of Jimiolatry, but they are separated by cuts like the long, slow 'In This Bed', nine minutes of finely controlled singing and playing with a wonderful chromatic solo by Carey Bell, or 'Going Downtown', which could have been made by his dad – and by 'Another Mule Kickin' In My Stall' and 'One Room Country Shack', which *are* fronted by Jimmy Rogers, and are his last recordings. This is an altogether more mature and personal statement. TR

Jonny Lang (born 1981)
VOCAL, GUITAR, GUITAR SYNTHESIZER, ELECTRIC SITAR, PERCUSSION

Aged just 13, Jon Gordon Langseth emerged from Fargo, North Dakota, gaining attention for his expressive guitar playing and promising showmanship. After taking guitar lessons with Ted Larsen, Lang graduated to become front man of Larsen's blues band. They soon moved to Minneapolis and became a local attraction, fuelling a major-label bidding war that resulted in a deal with A&M and one of the blues scene's most hyped arrivals of the '90s.

**(*) Smokin'
Eagle EAGCD 238 *Lang; Mike Bullock (s, harp); Dave Ferreira (kb); Ted Larsen (g, v); Jeff Hayes (d); Mike Larsen (d, v); Jenny Thom, Marcia Langseth (v).* 95.

At 14 Lang recorded an album of straight 12-bar blues to which he contributed some of the writing. *Smokin'* is the sound of a young talent still finding its niche, Lang's voice less broken and ranging than it would become. His guitar playing already situates him within a cluster of more recognized contemporary blues musicians, with clear influence especially from Stevie Ray Vaughan. The material is fairly standard but Lang's own compositions are as strong as much of the rest. Moreover his freshness gives the album some clout – '"E" Train' is a good example of his blistering soloing, while the slow blues 'Nice And Warm' demonstrates voice and guitar marrying with exceptional fluency. The album closes with a commendable solo acoustic version of Robert Johnson's 'Malted Milk'. For a fan, *Smokin'* revealingly documents the foundations that Lang built upon two years later with the release of his international debut.

***(*) Lie To Me
A&M 540 640 *Lang; Art Edmaiston, Dedrick Davis, Larry McCabe (brass, reeds); Pat Hayes (h); Bruce McCabe (kb, o, p, clavinet, v); Tony Black (o, string syn); Jack Holder (o, g); Ricky Peterson (o); Billy Franzee, Ted Larsen, Kevin Bowe, Dennis Morgan (g); David Smith (b); Steve Potts (d, perc); Rob[b] Stupka (d); David Z, Bekka Bramlett, Marcia Langseth, Heidi Jo (v).* 97.

Lie To Me sparked widespread critical and popular acclaim, perhaps most notably for a soulful and immediately characteristic voice that belied Lang's age. The gritty sound suggested a burnt-out Chicago old-timer, yet his wavy blond hair and clean-cut good looks should have placed him in an LA teen show about surfing and burger bars. The combined influence of major label and big-name producer (David Z had worked with Prince) is likely to have informed the commercial style that Lang has followed ever since, with its slick arrangements and a quota of catchy numbers edited with an eye on radio play. This has had some positive effect, particularly in the way Lang creates areas of light and shade, both in his versatile singing and in the space that's unindulgently allocated to his tasteful soloing.

The album opens emphatically with the zippy title track, followed by several slower blues where Lang's warm guitar tones shine but leave ample room for his voice to dominate on the standout songs 'Darker Side' and 'A Quitter Never Wins'. 'Matchbox' recalls the busy guitar style of Freddie King, while in a superb version of Sonny Boy Williamson I's 'Good Morning Little School Girl' Lang's cutting delivery reminds one of a young Mick Jagger throat-wrenching for the devil. Although more than half the songs use tight blues formulas, soul and funk influences are frequently heard and contribute equally to the overall effect. In its later tracks the album runs out of steam a little, and the two songs co-written by Lang are among the least memorable.

***(*) Wander This World
A&M 540 989 *Lang; Eric Leeds (s); Jack Holder (kb, g); Bruce McCabe, Ricky Peterson (kb); Paul Diethelm (Do); Tommy Burroughs (g, v); Steve Cropper, Kevin Bowe (g); David Smith (b); Richie Hayward (d); Bekka Bramlett, William Brown, Jessica Boucher, Jimmy Davis, J. D. Steele, Javeeta Steele, Fred Steele, Billy Steele (v).* 98.

Lang wrote more of the material for *Wander This World*, and his growing maturity is obvious. He still draws from classic soul (smooth, fluid guitar lines, gospellish backing vocals) and now too from West Coast rock (funky, tight grooves), but his desire to be recognized as an artist rather than a bluesman may explain why this album is much less blues-oriented. The 12-bar 'Angel Of Mercy' and 'Cherry Red Wine' are welcome retreats from the more clinical pop-song structures that populate the album. Even so, the outstanding tracks are those which situate Lang between the bluesiness of his debut and the voice he is gradually carving for himself. 'Still Rainin'' creates a gutsy mood that lasts throughout the record, 'Second Guessing' and 'Breakin' Me' are among his most emotive vocal performances to date, and the intoxicating groove and sharp assembling of the title track provide the album's high point.

*(*) Long Time Coming
A&M B0001145 Lang; Gary Grant, Jerry Hey (t); Bill Reichenbach (tb); Dan Higgins, Larry Williams (woodwinds); Steven Tyler (h); Marti Frederiksen (kb, p, g, b, d, perc, v); Robbie Buchanan, Michael Bearden (kb); Jim Cox (o, p); John Beasley (p); Bruce McCabe, Paul Santo (clavinet); various (strings); John Goux, Greg Poree (g); Ron Fair (b, vb); Alex Al (b); Joey Waronker, Abe Laboriel Jr, Gary Novack (d); Lenny Castro (cga); Alex Acuna (perc); Anthony Hamilton, Kayla Parker (v). 03.

Lang's songwriting is foregrounded here, as he collaborated with producer Marti Frederiksen on all but two of the songs. He duly sounds closer to the material than at any time before, and each track is delivered with conviction and control. The downside is that except for the raw, charged power of the acoustic title track – which comes last and seems at odds with its predecessors – there is barely a sign of a blues on the album, and the unfortunate corollary of this redirection is that Lang's own material is shrouded in commercial rock formulas. Lyrically naive, musically straitjacketed and predictable, *Long Time Coming* is a repetitive collection of summery lovesongs with little credibility even as Californian funk rock (which is executed much better already by groups like Superunloader). The vocal in 'Touch' soppily imitates modern R&B, while 'The One I Got' slumps into the insulting laziness of a 'nah nah nah' refrain. Lang's musical maturity has evolved so far that, at 24, he could take any of a number of exciting directions, but after this album one hopes that the blues will soon feature more prominently. RR

Booker T. Laury (1914–95)
VOCAL, PIANO

Laury was a friend of Memphis Slim and Roosevelt Sykes, but unlike them he stayed in Memphis, making occasional forays into Arkansas and Missouri, and didn't record as a young man. In the early '80s, a session produced by Memphis Slim on a trip home led to tours and recording in Europe. A role in the Jerry Lee Lewis biopic Great Balls Of Fire *finally raised Laury's profile at home.*

**** Blues On The Prowl
Wolf 120.929 Laury; Dana Gillespie (sp). 1/87.

Laury's fast right-hand triplets and chordal basses reflect his friendship with Slim and Sykes, but he wasn't an imitator of either man; rather, he was a fellow exponent of the style they took north. Most of Laury's material came from recordings or tradition, but his versions were fresh and incisive. The material on this superbly recorded disc derives from concerts in Austria, and its generous playing time includes most of Laury's repertoire. He seems to have been galvanized by his reception, playing with ferocious strength (his bass figures, hammered out with just three of his four remaining fingers, are a marvel) and hollering his songs in an ursine roar.

(***) Memphis Piano Blues Today
Wolf 120.928 Laury; James Robertson (d). 12/89.

This CD is shared with Mose Vinson. Laury's eight tracks are live, although the rather good drummer was overdubbed. *Great Balls Of Fire* had recently premiered (the 1990 recording date shown by Wolf is incorrect), and the gig may have been promotional. The audience seems to have wanted rowdy histrionics, and to some extent Laury obliges, although it should be noted that the producer dubbed on additional crowd noise. This was apparently suggested by Dennis Quaid, who played Jerry Lee Lewis in the film. If Quaid ever dabbles in post-production again, we urge him to remember Duke Ellington's view that 'too much talk stinks up the place'.

***(*) Nothin' But The Blues
Bullseye Blues CD BB 9542 Laury; Ron Levy (sp). 93.

Nothin' But The Blues is shorter than *Blues On The Prowl*, but covers much of the same ground. The vocals are sometimes rather distant, but Laury's playing is as powerful as ever, and the disc is a well-rounded portrait, which may be easier for American readers to find. One can only admire the producer's courage in opening with Laury's story of how he got the nickname 'Slop Jar'. (A jealous girlfriend brained him with a full one at a party.) CS

Johnny Laws (born 1943)
VOCAL, GUITAR

Laws started performing professionally in the '60s, taking some guitar lessons from Jimmy Reed and Buster Benton. For some time he has maintained a residency at the Cuddle Inn, on Chicago's South Side. His singing is influenced by soul and country music; an admirer of Brook Benton, Laws also does an occasional Marty Robbins number.

**(*) My Little Girl
Wolf 120.881 Laws; Little Mac Simmons (h); John Primer (g); Nick Holt (b); Earl Howell (d). 6–7/94.

*** Blues Burnin' In My Soul
Electro-Fi 3361 Laws; Chris Whitely (t, h, g); John Deehan (ts); Tyler Yarema (o, p); Victor Bateman (b); Bucky Berger (d). 4/99.

My Little Girl mixes Laws's own compositions and Chicago standards, with John Primer taking most of the guitar solos; on four tracks, Mac Simmons's harmonica rings some changes on the Teardrops' rather unvaried lope. Several songs are over-extended, notably a seven-minute 'Hoochie Coochie Man' and an insipid 'Somebody Loan Me A Dime'. However, Laws's warmly soulful tenor suits Howlin' Wolf's 'I Should Have Quit You' surprisingly well, and despite a nondescript start, the disc finishes strongly; Laws is at his best as both composer and vocal gymnast on 'Don't You Lie', and he and The Teardrops romp through Junior Parker's 'Mother In Law Blues'.

Laws ranges more widely on Electro-Fi, including a Marty Robbins song (pleasant, but no more) and a leavening of soul hits; given his preferences, it's odd that the least compelling of these is Brook Benton's 'I'll Take Care Of You'. Most of the CD is blues and soul favourites of the '50s and '60s and, if much is familiar, the over-familiar is usually avoided; when it isn't, Laws's almost perverse capacity for the unexpected ensures that two Jimmy Reed numbers are among the disc's most successful. The piano is too closely miked, but Electro-Fi offer some imaginative instrumental permutations while resisting the temptation to over-egg the pudding. *Blues Burnin' In My Soul* strengthens the impression of a middleweight artist who can sometimes find surprising new insights but can equally be ordinary where one would expect him to shine. CS

Sam Lay (born 1935)
DRUMS, VOCAL

Lay was born in Birmingham, Alabama, and began playing drums in his teens. By his early 20s he was working in Chicago with Little Walter. He then spent several years with Howlin' Wolf before joining the Paul Butterfield Blues Band. Always keen to be recognized as a singer as well as drummer, he first made an album in his own name in 1969 (Sam Lay In Bluesland on Blue Thumb). He has worked with many Chicago figures, and can be heard on record with Muddy Waters, James Cotton, Carey Bell, 'Wild Child' Butler, Rockin' Jimmy and others.

*** Stone Blues//Shuffle Master
Evidence ECD 26081//Appaloosa AP 085 *Lay; Billy C. Farlow (h); Phil Rugh (o); Jay Spell (p); Fred James (g); Bob Kommersmith (b); Mary-Ann Brandon, Clifford Curry, band (v). 1/94.*
**(*) Live
Appaloosa AP 115 *Lay; Billy C. Farlow (h); Jay Spell (p); Chris 'Guitar' James (g); Patrick Rynn (b); band (v). 1/94.*
**(*) Live On Beale Street
Blue Moon CDBM 134 *Lay; Billy C. Farlow (h, v); Mary-Ann Brandon (g, v); Fred James (g); Bob Kommersmith (b); Clifford Curry (v). 10/94.*
*** Rush Hour Blues
Telarc CD-83482 *Lay; Greg 'Fingers' Taylor (h); Celia Ann Price (o, p); Larry Burton, Fred James (g); Bob Kommersmith (b). 7–8/96.*

After his years in the drum chair behind various solid Chicago blues citizens, there isn't much Sam Lay doesn't know about steering a band, and even with the distractions of bandleading and singing he unfailingly constructs a stout rhythmic platform for his fellow musicians. They're no slouches themselves, not innovative stylists but competent players in the Chicago bar-band idiom, with an occasional backtrack to an earlier Memphis sound, as in 'That's Alright Mama' on *Stone Blues*. This studio set is the best of the three 1994 albums, the conciseness of the performances contrasting favourably with the sometimes unduly prolonged workouts on the Nashville and Memphis club dates. As a singer Lay is a burly blue-collar operative, getting the job done without fuss; listeners who crave more variety at the vocal mike might care to investigate *Live On Beale Street*, where the leader hands some of the songs to Nashville's Clifford Curry or to band members Farlow and Brandon, though the recording quality is indifferent. Not so *Rush Hour Blues*, a carefully balanced studio effort that foregrounds Lay's voice better than any of the previous albums while retaining all the feel of an ensemble performance. Producer Fred James relegates himself to rhythm guitar on all but one track, giving Larry Burton the opportunity to hustle on 'I Like Women' and scrawl wriggling lines through 'Second Man' and the title track. Deliberately made to conjure the spirit of the classic Chicago band sound, this unpretentious album does precisely that. TR

Lazy Lester (born 1933)
VOCAL, HARMONICA, GUITAR, PERCUSSION

Leslie Johnson started playing guitar and harmonica as a teenager in south Louisiana. His first records, for Excello, were as an accompanist – he was the customary object of Lightnin' Slim's summons 'Blow your harmonica, son!' – but he made his own name in the late '50s with the hit singles 'I'm A Lover Not A Fighter' and 'Sugar Coated Love' and continued to record until the mid-'60s. Barely visible for the next 20 years, he re-emerged in 1987 and since then has toured and recorded, the latter fitfully but discriminatingly.

*** I'm A Lover Not A Fighter
Ace CDCHD 518 *Lazy Lester; Lionel Torrence (ts); Sylvester Buckley (h); Katie Webster (o, p); U. J. Meaux (o, b); Merton Thibodeaux, Tal Miller, Carol Fran (p); Bobby McBride (g, b); Guitar Gable, 'Blue Charlie' Morris, Al Foreman, Pee Wee Trahan, Tony Perreau, Leroy Washington, Isaiah Chatman, Hank Redlich, unknown (g); Yank Perrodin, Rufus Thibodeaux, Emile Joseph (b); Jockey Etienne, Henry Clement, Warren Storm, Sammy Hogan, Elton Thibodeaux (d); Sammy Drake (cardboard box). 8/56–64.*

Lester's voice, younger and less lived-in than Lightnin' Slim's or Lonesome Sundown's, was perfect for the confections of blues and bayou rock 'n' roll that Excello initially offered him. Their popularity, however, didn't stand in the way of his recording more downhome numbers like 'Patrol Blues' or the Jimmy Reed-styled 'I Told My Little Woman' and 'You're Gonna Ruin Me Baby', though 'Bloodstains On The Wall' and the moody 'Sad City Blues', which could have been a hand-me-down from Lonesome Sundown, were left unissued at the time. (The other tracks described as 'previously unissued' are generally alternative takes of issued singles.) There is no questioning Lester's versatility, but quite a lot of the material is lightweight.

**(*) Harp & Soul
Alligator ALCD 4768 *Lazy Lester; Teo Leyasmeyer, Lucky Peterson (p); Kenny Neal, Robert 'Town Crier' Thomas, Ernie Lancaster, Pete Carr (g); Bob Greenlee (b, prod); Floyd Miles, Denny Best (d); Fred Reif (wb). 88.*

This was Lester's second album after his return to the business. (The first, *Lazy Lester Rides Again* for Blue Horizon, is out of print.) Giving himself a little more space than a two-and-a-half-minute single, he blows long, singing harmonica choruses on pieces from his past like 'Patrol Wagon Blues' and 'Bloodstains On The Wall'. Age has turned his voice rather gnarly, and the soul number 'Take Me In Your Arms' doesn't work at all, but 'Dark End Of The Street' is surprisingly successful, even poignant. The accompaniments are purposeful but unremarkable.

*** All Over You
Antone's ANT 0042 *Lazy Lester; Gene Taylor (p); Sue Foley, Derek O'Brien (g); Sarah Brown (b); Mike Buck (d). 98.*
*** Blues Stop Knockin'
Antone's TMG-ANT 0046 *As above, except add Riley Osbourn (p), Jimmie Vaughan (g), Speedy Sparks (b). 01.*

After another long interval, Lester returned to catalogue with the vivacious *All Over You*. His Texan collaborators are adept at re-creating the spare accompaniments of his Excello days, which is handy, since virtually the entire repertoire is drawn from that period ('I'm A Lover Not A Fighter', 'You're Gonna Ruin Me Baby', etc.), but not exclusively from his own recordings, fish being reeled in from the private ponds of Lightnin' Slim ('Hello Mary Lee', 'Nothing But The Devil') and Lonesome Sundown ('My Home Is A Prison'). The last two are solos by Lester with guitar and footboard. Much of the vitality in this music depends on crisp, economical drumming, which Mike Buck unfailingly provides.

With a few exceptions, *Blues Stop Knockin'* is also stocked from the Excello catalogue. 'Sad City Blues' affords Sue Foley her one appearance on guitar, while Lester himself plays guitar, alone, on 'No Special Rider Blues'. Elsewhere the ensembles are denser than on *All Over You*, and Lester responds to the driving guitars of Vaughan and O'Brien with aggressive harmonica playing and vocals half drawled, half snarled.

About the same time, Lester made one of the quartet of veteran harmonica players on *Superharps II* (Telarc CD-83514). The four numbers where he's the lead player are all old favourites of his (yet another 'Bloodstains On The Wall'), but they're well performed and recorded and the accompaniments are very sympathetic. TR

Leadbelly (1888–1949)
VOCAL, GUITAR, PIANO, ACCORDION, TAP DANCING

Not for nothing is Charles Wolfe and Kip Lornell's biography called The Life And Legend Of Leadbelly. *For too long after his discovery in Angola Penitentiary by John and Alan Lomax, writers and audiences fixated on Huddie Ledbetter's wild young days in Shreveport's red-light district, his convictions for murder and other violent crimes, and his singing his way to a pardon from Governor Pat Neff of Texas. For both racists and romantics, the combination of sexuality, mayhem and musical talent dovetailed with stereotypes of black masculinity; press reports about 'the homicidal harmonizer' helped sell Leadbelly to the public, but it was an image he hated. There's no doubt that he was hot-tempered and impulsive as a young man, but after marrying Martha Promise in 1935 and moving to New York, Leadbelly settled down (eventually; aged 51, he did eight months on Rikers Island for a stabbing). He developed a dignified and charming presentation of himself and his music, and determinedly pursued a career as a professional entertainer, even trying unsuccessfully to pitch himself to Hollywood in 1944. When discovered, Leadbelly already had a huge repertoire, which he sang in a resonant, piercing voice, accompanied by the rolling thunder of his 12-string guitar. The spoken narratives he created to clarify his songs to white audiences were a considerable creative achievement, but otherwise his music scarcely altered, and he recorded many songs many times. He continued to write new numbers, however, often on topical and progressive subjects, and to acquire songs from diverse sources, including commercial blues records, Woody Guthrie, the Irish-American singer Sam Kennedy and the Trinidad calypsonian Lord Invader. Leadbelly was the first black folk musician to become widely known in America and beyond; that his name and music meant virtually nothing to African-Americans doesn't diminish his importance in the history of popular music, or his stature as both bearer of tradition and creative genius.*

In recent years, the spelling 'Lead Belly', favoured by his family, has become more widely used, but except when quoting CD titles we have stuck with the more familiar version.

(*) Midnight Special
Rounder CD 1044 Leadbelly. 7/34–3/35.

(*) Remaining ARC & Library Of Congress Recordings – Vol. 1 (1934–1935)
Document DOCD-5591 Leadbelly; Sloan Wright (dance calls); John Lomax (sp). 7/34–3/35.
(*) The Titanic
Rounder 1097 Leadbelly. 7/34–8/40.
**** Leadbelly
Columbia CK 300035 Leadbelly. 1–3/35.
***(*) King Of The Twelve-String Guitar**
Columbia 467893 Leadbelly. 1–3/35.
(*) Remaining Library Of Congress Recordings – Vol. 2 (1935)
Document DOCD-5592 Leadbelly. 2–3/35.
(*) Gwine Dig A Hole To Put The Devil In
Rounder CD 1045 Leadbelly. 2/35–8/40.
(*) Remaining Library Of Congress Recordings – Vol. 3 (1935)
Document DOCD-5593 Leadbelly. 3/35.
(*) Remaining Library Of Congress Recordings – Vol. 4
Document DOCD-5594 Leadbelly; Jim Garland, Sarah Garland [Sarah Ogan Gunning] (v). 3/35–12/38.
(*) Nobody Knows The Trouble I've Seen
Rounder 1098 Leadbelly; Martha Ledbetter (v). 3/35–12/38.
(**(*)) Go Down Old Hannah
Rounder 1099 Leadbelly. 3/35–8/40.
(*) Remaining Library Of Congress Recordings – Vol. 5
Document DOCD-5595 Leadbelly; Sonny Terry (h, v); Brownie McGhee (g, v). 12/38–5/42.
(**(*)) Let It Shine On Me
Rounder CD 1046 Leadbelly. 8/40–1/42.

The comprehensive recording of a folk singer's repertoire, such as the Lomaxes undertook with Leadbelly, was an unprecedented mode of research in its day, and the eleven and a half Rounder and Document CDs which contain most of his Library of Congress recordings are still an invaluable resource for students of black music: spirituals, worksongs, dance tunes, ballads, blues, children's songs, topical commentary and more are all here, and all performed by a master musician. To discuss the content and significance of Leadbelly's recordings in detail would require far more space than is available, but none of the Library of Congress CDs – and scarcely a CD in this entry – is without at least one track that's historically important, musically thrilling or both.

For all its importance, though, the Library of Congress material can be hard going for casual listeners. Many of the original recordings were of intrinsically low fidelity, and many deteriorated in storage; some of Leadbelly's longer songs could not be recorded complete, so that there are gaps while the disc is flipped as quickly as possible; and at times the microphone is being moved from guitar to mouth and back again. Apart from these intrinsic problems, some of the so-called monologues (really interviews by Alan Lomax about the songs being played) are more valuable as documentation than as entertainment.

Document's CDs derive from a tape made many years ago as the basis for selecting a box set of three LPs; Rounder's six volumes, issued under licence, were newly taped from the original recordings. Some of these had further deteriorated, and the transfers were done without much attention to detail, with the ironic result that Document's bootlegged sound is generally superior to Rounder's. Other presentational failings make Rounder's series something of a botch: *Let It Shine On*

Me includes some songs twice, and some of those are repeated a third time on *Go Down Old Hannah*, while *Midnight Special*'s 'Matchbox Blues' reappears on *The Titanic* as 'Blind Lemon Blues'. The first three CDs carry a useful biographical note, to which is added comment on each disc's content, but the final three have a brief, identical note, which gives an incorrect timespan for the recordings, and mentions five songs 'that appear on this [*sic*] release'; only one of them is actually present on any of the other discs.

Document's many 'remaining recordings' have drawbacks of their own: the 'complete in chronological order' philosophy leads to the inclusion of multiple, not always significantly different versions of some songs; digs, scuffs and skips make some tracks very hard listening; and the notes to all five volumes consist only of the apologia for poor sound that was published with the old LP box. Nevertheless, Document's discs are on balance more recommendable than Rounder's.

The VAC *Field Recordings Vol. 5: Louisiana, Texas, Bahamas (1933–1940)* (Document DOCD-5579) contains Leadbelly's first recordings for the Lomaxes, but the first two tracks (of seven) are the merest fragments of 11 songs whose decayed condition renders them important chiefly to masochistic obsessives. It's worth noting that this disc also includes Leadbelly's uncle, Bob Ledbetter, 80 years old in 1940, quavering affably through 'Irene', accompanied by Lead's nephew, Noah Moore.

In early 1935, ARC recorded no fewer than 40 songs, plus some alternative takes, but to contemporary black audiences Leadbelly's music was oldfashioned, and the three issued 78s sold poorly. We're still very lucky that Leadbelly was recorded in studio-quality sound while revved up by the hope of commercial success; highlights include the cumulative force of a two-part 'Death Letter Blues', the breakneck tribute to Shreveport, 'Mister Tom Hughes' Town', and two versions of 'My Friend Blind Lemon' with exquisite slide guitar. Document's *Remaining ARC & Library Of Congress Recordings – Vol. 1* reissues 13 tracks from *Leadbelly* which are not also on *King Of The Twelve-String Guitar*. It appears from Columbia's website that *Leadbelly* is still in catalogue, however; it's the stronger of the two compilations, although there are many important tracks on *King Of The Twelve-String Guitar*, among them a version of Jimmie Rodgers's 'Daddy And Home'.

(*) Bridging Lead Belly
Rounder CD 1151 Leadbelly. 10/38–12/46.

Bridging Lead Belly combines 12 familiar songs cut for the BBC in New York with five from a party at the home of a Salt Lake City academic. The BBC material is naturally well-recorded, but Leadbelly's singing and playing are atypically listless. The 1946 wire recordings are almost unlistenable, and the late Sean Killeen's tireless boosterism and pedantic exegesis are more than either session deserves.

*** **Leadbelly – Vol. 1 (1939–1940)** [sic]
Document DOCD-5226 Leadbelly; The Golden Gate Quartet (v). 2/35–6/40.
***(*) **Take This Hammer**
Bluebird 50957 As above. 6/40.
***(*) **Leadbelly – Vol. 2 (1940–1943)**
Document DOCD-5227 As above, except add Sonny Terry (h). 6/40–summer 43.

Document's collation of the post-Library of Congress recordings starts with two alternative takes from ARC, followed by ten sides made for the small Musicraft label. They include the first commercial recording of 'The Bourgeois Blues', a brief burst of tap dancing between the hectic reels 'Poor Howard' and 'Green Corn', and perhaps Leadbelly's best (because not over-extended) version of the repetitive 'Gallis Pole'. It's unfortunate that Document have dubbed 'De Kalb Blues' from an LP on which it's faded early. Musicraft's pressings are fairly vivid, but crackly; the sound of the remaining tracks, from Victor and Bluebird, is greatly superior.

On two of the four Victor sessions (which are completed, as far as was then possible, on Document's *Vol. 2*), Leadbelly was joined by The Golden Gate Quartet; six 78s were issued as an album, *The Midnight Special And Other Southern Prison Songs*. Leadbelly and the Gates were suspicious of the concept (dreamed up by Alan Lomax), but the quartet learned the songs quickly, abandoning their usual polished arrangements for rough, improvised unisons and harmonies. (They also sing swear words and sexual lyrics enthusiastically.) Occasionally the Gates' rhythm is slightly stiff but, as Lomax noted, these sessions were 'the nearest thing to [authenticity] that could be achieved away from the prison farms themselves'. *Take This Hammer* includes songs not available to Document, and is the logical way to acquire these sessions.

Vol. 2 sees the start of Leadbelly's association with Moses Asch, a famously disorganized producer who nevertheless seems to have had a plan for documenting aspects of Leadbelly's repertoire: having completed the Victor sessions, the CD presents three albums of 78s: *Play Parties In Song And Dance*, *Work Songs Of The U.S.A.* and *Songs By Lead Belly*. The children's songs are a charming collection, and the worksongs include the shanty 'Haul Away Joe' and 'Cornbread Rough', Leadbelly's first recording on accordion. *Songs* is most notable for Sonny Terry's exciting harmonica, and for the first commercially released version of Leadbelly's theme song, 'Goodnight Irene'. This appears in two versions, the better one being without Terry, who is surprisingly hamfisted on a take which only emerged in 1950, after the Weavers' hit version.

(**(*)) **Good Morning Blues**
Biograph BCD 113 Leadbelly; Woody Guthrie (sp). 6/40.
(*) **Black Folk Singers: Leadbelly & Josh White (1937–1946)
Document DOCD-1018 As above, except add Sonny Terry (h, v), Willie 'The Lion' Smith (p), Brownie McGhee (g, v), Pops Foster (b), Paul Mason Howard (dolceola). 6/37–c. 6/46).

Good Morning Blues is shared with Rev. Gary Davis and the harmonica-playing evangelist Dan Smith; Leadbelly's contribution is part of a radio broadcast, and totals just over 12 minutes, including Guthrie's announcements. The sound is good, but the material holds no surprises, and the other artists are not at their strongest.

Black Folk Singers contains the opening 90 seconds of the radio broadcast, omitted by Biograph, and some tracks which in 1999 were newly issued by Smithsonian Folkways. Three songs from radio broadcasts feature fervid guitar, and a Library of Congress song about the Spanish-American War is historically important, but this is a catch-up operation for completists.

*** **Leadbelly – Vol. 3 (1943–1944)**
Document DOCD-5228 Leadbelly; Sonny Terry (h); Josh White (g, v). c. 10/43–4/44.

Disc, Asch, Stinson and a return visit to Musicraft: the picture begins to get more typically confusing as Moe Asch sets up new labels, and some material goes to Herbert Harris of Stinson after their falling out. *Vol. 3* begins with six fine sides, recorded on 12-inch masters and containing a cross-section of Leadbelly's repertoire: blues, spirituals, cowboy tunes, ballads, worksongs and a four-minute 'John Hardy' with mournful but funky accordion. There's another good version, with guitar, among the Musicraft tracks, which also include vehement accounts of 'Bill Brady' and 'House Of The Rising Sun'. The medleys of children's songs which finish the disc are more dutiful than those on *Vol. 2*, but in the middle of them comes a brief but marvellous version of Blind Lemon Jefferson's ragtime piece 'Hot Dogs'.

(*) Leadbelly – Vol. 4 (1944) [sic]
Document DOCD-5310 Leadbelly; Sonny Terry (h); Woody Guthrie (g, v); Paul Mason Howard (dolceola); audience (v). c. 5/44–c. 6/46.

**** **Huddie Ledbetter's Best**
BGO BGOCD 403 Leadbelly; Paul Mason Howard (dolceola). 10/44.

(*) Leadbelly – Vol. 5 (1944–1946)
Document DOCD-5311 Leadbelly; Mutt Carey (t); Kid Ory (tb); Joe Darensbourg (cl); Sonny Terry (h); Willie 'The Lion' Smith, Buster Wilson (p); Woody Guthrie (md, g, v); Brownie McGhee, Cisco Houston (g, v); Pops Foster (b, v); Ed Garland (b); Alton Redd (d); children (v). 10/44–c. 10/46.

**** **Leadbelly – Vol. 6 (1947)** [sic]
Document DOCD-5568 Leadbelly; Sonny Terry (h); Brownie McGhee (g); Pops Foster (b); Anna Graham, The Oleander Quartet (v). summer 43–9/47.

The versions of 'Corn Bread Rough' on *Vols 2* and *4*, of 'Easy Rider' on *Vols 4* and *5*, and of 'Pigmeat' on *Vols 5* and *6* are identical; 'Goodnight, Irene' on *Vol. 6* is a shortened version of the weaker take on *Vol. 2*. It's a pity that Document didn't sort out these confusions in the rush to reissue. *Vol. 4* is notable for a sequence of topical songs, among them the first and best 'Jim Crow', a strong remake of 'Bourgeois Blues', the doughboy's gripe 'Army Life' and 'National Defense'. It concludes in California, with ten of 12 numbers made for Capitol. The final two open *Vol. 5*, which continues with a schools' radio broadcast, where Leadbelly's charisma and rapport with children are apparent. Unfortunately Kid Ory's band, guesting on two numbers, can't find compatible accompaniments. Five songs with permutations of Sonny & Brownie, Willie 'The Lion' Smith and Pops Foster are delightfully bouncy, but Guthrie and Houston's automatic vocal responses and indifference to key seriously weaken the eight concluding tracks.

The plinking of the dolceola (a zither with keyboard attachment) makes the Capitol sessions unique in Leadbelly's output, and probably in black recorded music. (The '20s gospel singer Washington Phillips, reported to have played the instrument, is now thought to have used a standard zither.) Leadbelly mainly sticks to familiar numbers (although this is his first recording of 'Backwater Blues'), but Howard gives them a zesty lift, playing with formidable swing and a well-developed feel for the emotional nuances of the blues. Four titles by Leadbelly solo include a potent revival of Bumble Bee Slim's 'Bricks In My Pillow' and two frenzied versions of his piano showpiece 'Eagle Rock Rag'.

Document's *Vol. 6* concludes with a poorly recorded live version of 'Eagle Rock Rag' which is its only letdown. Otherwise it contains two Folkways LPs thought to have been recorded in 1947, and a session of unknown origin presumed to be from the same year. Many of the songs are remakes, and many from the LPs are quite brief, but Leadbelly sings and plays with great vigour; among titles new to record are the accordion dance tunes 'Laura' and 'Sukey Jump' and the 'Cotton Song' (a.k.a. 'Cottonfields'), which attracted many covers, all of them cosier than the original, which stresses the catastrophic effects of crop failure. The songs from the unissued session are longer, but just as forceful; they include songs he hadn't recorded since the Library of Congress days, and an explosive variant of 'Good Morning Blues', with verses fervently condemning Jim Crow.

***(*) Leadbelly – Vol. 7 (1947–1949)**
Document DOCD-5640 Leadbelly; Sonny Terry (h, sp); Martha Ledbetter (v). 6/47–6/49.

Vol. 7 is mainly devoted to radio broadcasts. Four titles deposited with the Library of Congress seem to have been recorded by the folklorist Mary Elizabeth Barnicle, an old friend to whom Leadbelly slyly dedicates the risqué 'Noted Rider'. By now he was beginning to suffer from the degenerative disease which killed him, but his playing and singing remain dynamic. 'John Henry' and 'Pick A Bale Of Cotton', both featuring an inspired Sonny Terry, stand out from airshots of the *WNYC Jazz Festival*, which originally formed the splendid LP *Shout On*. Two concluding spirituals from the University of Texas concert (see below) were not available elsewhere in 1999. They exemplify Document's quest for the grail of completeness; it sometimes entails variable sound quality and multiple versions, but these seven CDs contain plenty of great music, and their notes pack much informed comment into a tight word limit.

***(*) Private Party, Minneapolis, Minn., 1948**
Document DOCD-5664 Leadbelly; audience, child (v). 11/48.

There are the usual problems of informal recording – abrupt starts and finishes, jumps as tape reels are changed – but the sound is surprisingly good, and this is an important and enjoyable CD. It captures Leadbelly interacting with a sympathetic audience, relaxed enough to talk about his arrest in Louisiana and sing the bawdy British squib 'Samuel Hall'. As well as performing his standard repertoire, he dredges a 'Hawaiian Song' from his bottomless memory, sings two swinging versions of the blues 'Mississippi River', improvises 'Lake Superior' to the tune of 'La Cucaracha' in honour of his hosts, and coaches a little girl through 'Goodnight Irene'. This is Leadbelly at his most versatile and magnetic.

**** **Bourgeois Blues**
Smithsonian Folkways SF CD 40045 Leadbelly; Sonny Terry (h, v); Willie 'The Lion' Smith (p); Woody Guthrie (md, v); Brownie McGhee, Cisco Houston (g, v); Pops Foster (b). 40–9/48.

**** **Where Did You Sleep Last Night**
Smithsonian Folkways SF CD 40044 Leadbelly; Sonny Terry (h); Brownie McGhee (g, sp); Pops Foster (b); The Oleander Quartet (v). 41–47.

***(*) Shout On**
Smithsonian Folkways SF CD 40105 Leadbelly; Sonny Terry (h, sp); Willie 'The Lion' Smith (p); Woody Guthrie (md, g, v) Cisco

Houston (g, v); Brownie McGhee (g); Pops Foster (b). c. 41–10/48.

Smithsonian Folkways' great advantage when reissuing Leadbelly's Asch recordings is their possession of the original masters. Anyone accustomed to the muffled sound of many previous – and some subsequent – issues will be startled by the rich sonorities revealed on these three CDs. The scholarly annotation is a great advance on all prior documentation; a very few probable errors could be pointed out, but Asch's chaotic filing and record-keeping make such slips virtually inevitable. The upside of his packrat approach is that compiler Jeff Place has found numerous previously unknown performances, some of very high quality: whether it comes from slavery time or was Leadbelly's own creation, the moving ballad-plus-sermon 'Abraham Lincoln' on *Bourgeois Blues* is astonishing; 'If You Want To Do Your Part' on *Shout On* is also striking, although the notes slide past the fact that this World War II rallying cry is based on an anti-immigrant rant from 1915. It seems impossible for Smithsonian Folkways to admit that while Woody Guthrie's mandolin (heard clearly for the first time) has its charms, he and Cisco Houston were poor singers of black music; their presence on five tracks reduces *Shout On*'s value somewhat.

*** Lead Belly Sings For Children
Smithsonian Folkways SFW 45047 *Leadbelly; Kid Ory (tb); Joe Darensbourg (cl); Buster Wilson (p); Ed Garland (b); Alton Redd (d); children, The Oleander Quartet (v).* 5/41–10/48.

*** Leadbelly Sings Folk Songs
Smithsonian Folkways CD SF 40010 *Leadbelly; Sonny Terry (h); Woody Guthrie, Cisco Houston (g, v); Brownie McGhee (g); Pops Foster (b).* summer 43–c. 10/46.

**(*) Folkways: The Original Vision
Smithsonian Folkways CD SF 40001 *As above, except add Anne Graham (v).* 4/44–10/48.

Lead Belly Sings For Children reissues the content of the LP *Negro Folk Songs For Young People*, and interweaves 13 additional tracks. Apart from a previously unreleased 'Take This Hammer', the extra items are available elsewhere on Smithsonian Folkways. *Sings Folk Songs* is a straight reissue of a good LP, but it's superseded by the longer playing time, superior sound and meticulous documentation of *Bourgeois Blues*, *Where Did You Sleep Last Night* and *Shout On*. As its issue number suggests, *The Original Vision*, which is shared with Woody Guthrie, was essentially a publicity and marketing tool for the Smithsonian's acquisition and relaunch of Folkways.

♛ **** Lead Belly's Last Sessions
Smithsonian SF CD 40068/71 4CD *Leadbelly; Martha Ledbetter, Charles Edward Smith (v).* 9–10/48.

Frederic Ramsey Jr's aim (not fulfilled in the event) was to document Leadbelly's complete repertoire. He felt that the Library of Congress recordings were 'highly unfaithful to the original' and hoped to correct this by recording on one of the newfangled magnetic tape recorders. The sound quality is certainly good for its day and acceptable in ours, but the original tapes had already begun to deteriorate when the material was released on LPs, and this reissue uses the production masters, except for two titles which were omitted in 1953. 'Somebody's Diggin' My Potatoes' includes swearing, but it's not clear why 'Alcoholic Blues' was left out, or why it's listed as 'Winnsboro Cotton Mill Blues'.

'Alcoholic Blues' is a 1919 pop song reacting to Prohibition, and it illustrates one of the reasons the *Last Sessions* are important. At ease with friends (significantly, 'Jail House Blues' mentions his imprisonment in New York), and unconstrained by either a purist agenda or time limits, Leadbelly digs out songs that are new on record, but often very old: among them are 'Blue Tail Fly', 'I'll Be Down On The Last Bread Wagon' (a World War I parody of 'The Darktown Strutters' Ball'), 'How Come You Do Me Like You Do?', 'Bully Of The Town' and the stunning holler, 'I Don't Know You, What Have I Done?' (which Leadbelly liked to sing while doing the dishes!). More recent are Gene Autry's 'Springtime In The Rockies' and a song praising 1940 presidential candidate Wendell Wilkie.

Naturally there are also numbers from the core repertoire that he'd recorded many times before: 'Midnight Special', 'Rock Island Line', 'Irene' and the rest had long reached their definitive versions, but Leadbelly's singing and his churning guitar riffs are as exciting as ever. Alongside these songs and the pop and songster material, there are numerous fine worksongs, spirituals and blues: 'I Ain't Gonna Drink Anymore' (unaccompanied, like all tracks on the first disc of the set) is an outstanding reworking of Big Bill Broonzy's 'Good Liquor Gonna Carry Me Down'.

It's both impossible and misleading to write about Leadbelly without stressing the historical importance of his recordings. It's easy to overstress that aspect, however, and there's no better place than *Lead Belly's Last Sessions* to discover that they're also terrific entertainment.

(****) Live!
Fabulous FABCD 105 *Leadbelly.* 6/49.
**** Absolutely The Best Vol. 2 (Live)
Fuel 2000 302 061 274 *Leadbelly; Martha Ledbetter (v).* 6/49.
**** 'Live' New York 1947 & Austin, Texas 1949
Document DOCD-5676 *As above, except add Bunk Johnson (t), Jimmy Archey (tb), Omer Simeon (cl), Ralph Sutton (p), Cyrus St Clair (bb), Freddie Moore (d).* 9/47–6/49.

These CDs present Leadbelly's last public concert. (Document's three poorly recorded opening tracks with incompatible accompanists can be ignored.) Leadbelly had to be transferred from a wheelchair to a seat on stage before the curtains opened, but there's scarcely a sign of his impaired health in the performance. The pleasure he expresses about performing for 'downhome folks' is plainly sincere, and it spurs him to give of his best. Among captivating renditions of the familiar favourites is probably his last composition, 'C'Est Bon, Les Oeufs', a swinging plea to his hosts on a recent trip to France not to burn his scrambled eggs! All these CDs have good sound, but Fabulous pointlessly omit two concluding spirituals. Fuel 2000's release is made in cooperation with Leadbelly's estate, but Document have the edge, thanks to some fascinating ephemera, and detailed notes by Sean Killeen about the concert and its context.

**(*) The Stinson Collectors Series: Leadbelly Memorial Vols 1 & 2
Collectables COL-CD-5603 *Leadbelly; Sonny Terry (h).* 1/35–summer 47.
**(*) Bourgeois Blues – Golden Classics Part 1
Collectables COL-CD-5183 *Leadbelly.* 4/39–c. 10/43.

*(*) The Stinson Collectors Series: Leadbelly Memorial Vols 3 & 4
Collectables COL-CD-5604 *Leadbelly; Sonny Terry (h); Woody Guthrie, Cisco Houston, Brownie McGhee (g, v); Pops Foster (b, v).* 4/39–c. 10/46.
*** Absolutely The Best
Fuel 2000 302 061 080 *Leadbelly; Sonny Terry (h); Josh White (g, v).* 4/39–10/48.
**(*) The Stinson Collectors Series: Party Songs/Sings & Plays
Collectables COL-CD-5609 *Leadbelly; Woody Guthrie (md, g, v); Josh White, Cisco Houston (g, v).* 5/41–c. 10/46.
**(*) Goodnight Irene
Tradition TCD 1006 *Leadbelly; Sonny Terry (h); Josh White (g, v).* summer 43–4/44.
**(*) Defense Blues – Golden Classics Part 2
Collectables COL-CD-5196 *Leadbelly; Brownie McGhee (g); Pops Foster (b).* poss. c. 5/44–10/48.
**(*) In The Shadows Of The Gallows Pole
Tradition TCD 1018 *Leadbelly.* 4/39–c. 10/43.
***(*) The Tradition Masters
Tradition TCD 1086 *As for above Tradition CDs.* 4/39–4/44.

These reissues derive from Musicraft, Stinson and assorted Asch labels. Collectables draw on the 1939 Musicraft recordings, on Folkways recordings as late as the *Last Sessions*, and on masters apparently retained by Herbert Harris after his break with Moe Asch. Most of the latter seem to be duplicates or alternative takes, but the discographical complexities are formidable: 'See See Rider' on *Leadbelly Memorial Vols. 1 & 2* came – who knows how? – from a then unissued ARC master!

Collectables' sound quality is unspectacular, and the two *Golden Classics* CDs are very short; the notes range from short but adequate (*Bourgeois Blues*), to short and skin-deep, to non-existent (*Defense Blues*). As a general rule, the more carefully contextualized Document CDs represent better value. So does the 23-track *Tradition Masters*, which combines and makes redundant the other two Tradition CDs. Fuel 2000's 15-tracker mainly relies on Musicraft; 'Midnight Special' comes from the *Last Sessions*. It's decently remastered and serviceably annotated, although Josh White's presence on 'Pretty Flower In Your Back Yard' has been missed.

*** Bourgeois Blues 1933–1946 [sic]
Frémeaux FA 269 2CD *As for relevant CDs above.* 7/34–6/46.
**(*) You Don't Know My Mind
Fabulous FABCD 113 *As above.* 7/34–10/44.
**(*) Kings Of The Blues: Leadbelly
Pulse PLSCD 680 *As above.* 7/34–2/45.
(**(*)) Goodnight Irene
Music Digital CD 6404 *As above.* 7/34–c. 6/46.
*** The Very Best Of Leadbelly
Music Club MCCD 106 *As above.* 7/34–10/48.
**(*) Rock Island Line
Naxos 8.120675 *As above.* 1/35–summer 43.
**(*) Masters
Collectors Edition CDBM 119 *As above.* 1/35–c. 10/43.
(**(*)) My Last Go Round
Snapper Recall SMDCD 240 2CD *As above.* 1/35–10/44.
(**(*)) Midnight Special
Prism Leisure PLATCD 290 *As above.* 1/35–2/45.
*** Blues & Folk Singer
Saga Blues 982 076-7 *As above.* 1/35–c. 10/46.
(***) The Essential
Classic Blues CBL 200003 2CD *As above.* 1/35–10/48.
(***) Take This Hammer
Snapper Complete Blues SBLUECD 004 *As above.* 1/35–10/48.
***(*) The Definitive Leadbelly
Catfish KATCD 220 3CD *As above.* 1/35–10/48.
**(*) The Best Of Leadbelly
Blues Forever CD 68006 *As above.* 1/35–6/49.

Finally we come to CDs compiled from hither and yon. *My Last Go Round* begins with 20 ARC titles; its second disc claims to open with two tracks from Musicraft, but the Library of Congress 'Bourgeois Blues' plays. It claims to close with five from Capitol, but 'Irene' is the 1943 version with Sonny Terry and 'Rock Island Line' is from the 2/45 schools' broadcast. The rest of Disc 2 appears to be from RCA, as advertised. *Bourgeois Blues* is also not error-free: its first track is a version of 'The Western Cowboy' from 1934, not 1933 as claimed. The collection draws most of its content from ARC, Victor and Asch, and it draws a distinction between Leadbelly's blues and his 'folk music', concentrating, though not exclusively, on the former; *Blues & Folk Singer* takes a similar view, but presents 12 tracks under each heading. These compilations are entertaining enough, *Blues & Folk Singer* the more so of the two, but it's questionable whether, and if so to what extent, either Leadbelly or his first white audiences categorized his music in this way.

Rock Island Line collates the issued ARC and Musicraft titles, adding 'Good Morning Blues', 'How Long' and the two versions of 'Irene' from summer 1943, and reverting to 1942 for the title track. The dubbing appears to have been done from 78s in all cases, and the booklet has full discographical details and acceptable notes, but noise reduction has been applied with a heavy hand.

Midnight Special and *Goodnight Irene* have variable sound, ungainly, error-prone notes and no logical basis of compilation. *Kings Of The Blues*, which is an unacknowledged reissue of the deleted *Good Morning Blues* (Indigo IGOCD 2007), has more consistent sound and is very cheap, but it, too, feels slung together. Also bargain-priced, *You Don't Know My Mind* is chronologically sequenced and includes a discography, but the sound ranges from nothing special to poor, and the notes over-emphasize Leadbelly's violent side. They also add a brand new error to the heap by making Pat Neff a prison governor (it's 'Warden' in Texas). *Masters* is better annotated, but acoustically enervated.

The Essential is more skilfully engineered; it darts about with chronological abandon, but the sequencing has been done with some care. 'Bull Cow' appears where 'Salty Dog' is listed, however, and notes which smack their lips over the badman image are no compensation for the absence of discographical data. *Take This Hammer* has decent sound, and longer, better balanced notes, but once again there are no recording dates, perhaps because 'Somebody's Diggin' My Potatoes', lifted from the *Last Sessions*, was first issued in 1994. Blues Forever's proclaimed *Best Of* clones an LP which drew on the 1940 sessions with the Golden Gates; an ARC title from 1935 and 'Goodnight Irene' from the University of Texas concert are pointlessly tacked on.

Music Club's title also invites a challenge, but *The Very Best Of* comes closer to justifying itself. The material is licensed from Smithsonian Folkways and Rounder, and the sound is about as good as can be achieved, although in the case of 'C.C. Rider' musical excellence has to fight severe surface noise. The disc has been compiled with some care, as can be seen, among other things, from its inclusion of the long and very angry first recording of 'Bourgeois Blues', in which Leadbelly relates exactly how the song was inspired by the racism he encountered in Washington, DC. That version also appears on *The Definitive Leadbelly*, which is one more hubristic attempt to claim what's probably unachievable with such a protean artist. Whether for sound, selection, sequencing or annotation, however, *The Definitive Leadbelly* is easily the best and most comprehensive of these omnium-gatherums. It draws more extensively than most of them on the *Last Sessions*, and copyright (in)sensitivities may explain the need to complain, one more time, about the lack of a discography. CS

Lafayette Leake (1920–90)
VOCAL, PIANO

Born in Winona, Mississippi, Leake was a desperately shy man, and much of his life remains mysterious. He seems to have had formal training at some point; he was proud of his ability to play Chopin, and would notate his friend Little Brother Montgomery's playing by ear. In the early '50s, Leake replaced Leonard Caston in the Big Three Trio, and although he never recorded with that group, his enduring friendship with Willie Dixon, his reliability and his good taste made him a session mainstay, who recorded with all the major stars of Chicago blues.

*** Easy Blues
Black & Blue BB 434 *Leake; John Littlejohn (g); Nick Holt (b); Fred Below (d). 11/78.*

Easy Blues was cut during a European tour, in Black & Blue's customary one day, but it has no feeling of haste or perfunctoriness, and is very well recorded. It's obvious that the other musicians found Leake a pleasure to accompany: Below's drumming has its habitual, crisply perfect bounce, Holt is unobtrusive but unceasingly propulsive, turning his instrument down to sound like an upright bass, and Littlejohn's echoing solos add a welcome tinge of aggression and emotion. Leake's own playing is unfailingly tasteful and intelligent, not outstaying its welcome even during the more than seven minutes of 'Fast Boogie No. 1'. As a singer, he is dry but not unemotional, working within a narrow range but always securely on pitch. 'Trouble In Mind' and 'Outskirts Of Town' are obviously the choices of an occasional singer, but they are done with a commitment that characterizes the whole album; among Leake's own compositions, 'Feel So Blue' has a well-crafted lyric of some bleakness. It's a pity that he was not recorded as a featured artist more often. CS

Calvin Leavy (born 1941)
VOCAL, GUITAR

Calvin Leavy, born in Scott, Arkansas, joined his older brother Hosea to play in the Little Rock area. In the early '60s they moved to California, but Calvin's 'Cummins Prison Farm' (1968) attracted enough attention to bring them some years of work in the Southwest.

**(*) The Best Of Calvin Leavy
Red Clay RCL 8303 *Leavy; unknown (ts); 'Todd', unknown (o); Robert Tanner, unknown (g); Hosea Leavy, unknown (b); Maurice Haygood, unknown(s) (d). 68, 70s.*

Calvin Leavy's 'Cummins Prison Farm' was one of the most explicit topical blues of the '60s but because of its small-label origins is not as well-known as it should be. Leavy's wholly involved vocal and Robert Tanner's vituperative guitar solo combine with a lyric that pulls few punches: 'I said, "Warden, I'll be a good man, if you only free me from this pen." The warden looked me in the eye, said, "Down here, son, we have a lot of good men ..."' The rest of the album, recorded later and probably with different musicians, is composed of attractive but rather derivative blues and Southern soul songs: imagine Little Johnny Taylor accompanied by The Fieldstones. Readers interested only in Leavy's best recording may prefer to acquire it on the obscure French compilation *My Guitar Wants To Kill Your Mama* (Lenox 1012). TR

Hosea Leavy (born 1927)
VOCAL, GUITAR

An older brother of Calvin Leavy, Hosea Leavy played bass on his hit 'Cummins Prison Farm' and worked with him for some years. He also made a few singles in his own name. When the two separated, Hosea settled in Fresno.

**(*) You Gotta Move
Fedora FCD 5002 *Leavy; Jay Van Horn (h); Jeff Levine (kb); Jeff Henry (b); Chris Millar (d). 9/97.*

Leavy's first recordings for Fedora, made in the early '90s, are sampled on *West Fresno Blues Masters Volume 1* (Fedora CD 0002). With a style rooted in the rough-hewn downhome blues of the '50s and '60s and an acknowledged admiration for Muddy Waters, he comes across like a West Coast cousin of Magic Slim, particularly on one of the two original songs, 'Searchin''. Some five years later, with almost the same band, he remade the other, 'Goin' Back To The Country', for *You Gotta Move*. The song has not changed much, but the superior recording gives a better impression of Leavy's lusty singing and uncomplicated but well-judged guitar lines, features that also distinguish 'Hey Boss!', 'Going Blind', 'Crazy Mary' and most of the other, largely original, songs on the album. Leavy has since recorded with Harmonica Slim (q.v.). TR

Rosie Ledet (born 1971)
VOCAL, ACCORDION

Rosie Ledet learned accordion by watching her husband, Morris, then practising while he was at work. Can a biopic be far behind?

*** Sweet Brown Sugar
Maison de Soul MdS-1052 *Ledet; Pat Breaux (s); Eddie Bodin (kb); Kent August (g); Morris Ledet, Mark Miller (b); Corey Ledet (d); Lanice Ledet (rb). 94?*

*** **Zesty Zydeco**
Maison de Soul MdS-1056 *As above, except Bodin plays d, perc rather than kb; add Jeff Laperous (p), Tony Ardoin (g).* 95?

(*) **Zydeco Sensation
Maison de Soul MdS-1064 *Ledet; Kent August, Bobby Broussard (g); Morris Ledet (b); Corey Ledet (d, rb); Lanice Ledet (rb); Jay Doucet (v).* 96?

*** **I'm A Woman**
Maison de Soul MdS-1071 *As above, except Doucet plays g rather than sings; Ray Johnson (g) replaces Broussard.* 99?

(*) **It's A Groove Thing!
Maison de Soul MdS-1075 *Ledet; Pat Breaux (s); Ed Gore (kb); Kent August, Keith Frank, Kevin Cormier (g); Morris Ledet (b); Corey Ledet (d); Wilfred 'Caveman' Pierre (rb); Annie Joe Cormier (v).* 00?

(*) **Show Me Something
Maison de Soul MdS-1077 *Ledet; Pat Breaux (s); J. J. Caillier (kb); Kent August (g); Chuck Bush (b); Lukey Ledet, Kevin Stelly (d); Lanice Ledet (rb); Charlene Howard (v).* 01?

(*) **Now's The Time
Maison de Soul MdS-1080 *Ledet; Ed Gore (o); Chuck Bush (g, b); Cookie Chavis, Kevin Cormier (g); Lukey Ledet (d, rb); Kevin Stelly (d); Lanice Ledet (rb).* 03?

*** **Pick It Up**
Maison de Soul MdS-1085 *Ledet; Chuck Bush (g, b, v); Kent August, Kevin Cormier (g); Lukey Ledet (d, rb); Lanice Ledet (rb, v).* 05?

The diminutive Rosie Ledet projects herself effectively as a sexy, assertive zydeco sweetheart. She's a soulful singer of mostly self-composed songs; they're all good dance inducers, and although their lyrics never rise to greatness, 'Big Brother' (*It's A Groove Thing!*) is a pretty piece of nostalgia and 'You Can Eat My Poussière' (*I'm A Woman*) definitely isn't. The rhythms are always and increasingly influenced by *nouveau zydeco*, and they always swing mightily, no doubt thanks to the cohesion and stability of the family band that's at the core of the lineups. Ledet's first two releases are more connected to tradition than later CDs: 'The Mardi Gras' on *Sweet Brown Sugar* is an admirable minor-key original with pedigree. *Zydeco Sensation* takes a wrong turning, with Ledet trying to be Belle Jocquette and overdoing rhythm and riffs at the expense of melody. *I'm A Woman* is back on track, and includes a fine revival of 'My Toot Toot' in memory of Rockin' Sidney. The guest stars on *It's A Groove Thing!* and *Show Me Something* don't much improve the music (the great Chuck Bush rampages through *Show Me Something*'s opening track, but thereafter is comparatively restrained), and the occasional capricious application of a vocoder is a definite disimprovement. On *Now's The Time* the vocoder is dumped and Bush is a full-fledged band member, playing bass at his habitual best, and almost compensating for some trite blues-rock guitar solos. *Show Me Something* includes a killer version of 'Lady Marmalade', and all these CDs have their merits, but the early ones, where Rosie and family have something to prove, are the most rewarding. *Pick It Up* features some very soulful singing, and the title track, a funny tribute to Viagra, is one of several that illustrate Ledet's increasing assurance as a songwriter. Pity about the hackneyed guitar solos. CS

Julia Lee (1902–58)
VOCAL, PIANO

Lee grew up in a musical family in Kansas City, learning piano at high school and university and playing it in theatres and clubs. During the '20s she sang with her older brother George's orchestra, and after it broke up found a nightclub residency which she maintained from 1934 to 1950. In the '40s, after a spell with Jay McShann, she signed with Capitol and enjoyed several years' success with suggestive novelties.

*** **Julia Lee 1927–1946**
Classics 5119 *Lee; Albert 'Budd' Johnson (t, cl, ts); Sam Utterback, Harold Knox, Oliver Todd, Clarence Davis, Vernon 'Geechie' Smith, Karl George (t); Thurston 'Sox' Maupins, Jimmy Jones (tb); Tommy Douglas (cl, as); Clarence 'Tweety' Taylor (ss, as); George E. Lee (ss, ts, bs); Herman Walder (as); Claiborne Graves, Harry Ferguson, Freddy Gulliver, Henry Bridges Jr, Dave Cavanaugh (ts); poss. Jesse Stone, Jay McShann (p); Charles Russo (bj, g); unknown (bj); Efferge Ware, Nappy Lamare, Lucky Enois (g); Clint Weaver, Walter Page, Ben Curtis, Billy Hadnott, Red Callender (b); Abe Price, Pete Woods, Sam 'Baby' Lovett (d).* 27–8/46.

*** **Julia Lee 1947**
Classics 5144 *Lee; Red Nichols (c); Ernie Royal, Bobby Sherwood, Geechie Smith (t); Vic Dickenson (tb); Benny Carter (as); Dave Cavanaugh (ts); Jack Marshall (g); Harry Babasin, Red Callender (b); Sam 'Baby' Lovett (d); Red Norvo (x); Joe Alexander (v).* 6–11/47.

**** **Kansas City's First Lady Of The Blues**
JSP JSPCD 3405 2CD *Lee; Red Nichols (c); Oliver Todd, Clarence Davis, Geechie Smith, Karl George, Ernie Royal, Bobby Sherwood (t); Vic Dickenson (tb); Tommy Douglas (cl, as); Dave Cavanaugh (cl, ts); Benny Carter (as); Claiborne Graves, Freddie Gulliver, Harry Ferguson, Henry Bridges (ts); Jay McShann (p); Efferge Ware, Nappy Lamare, Lucky Enois, Jack Marshall (g); Walter Page, Ben Curtis, Billy Hadnott, Red Callender, Harry Babasin, Charles Drayton (b); Sam 'Baby' Lovett (d); Red Norvo (x).* 11/44–11/47.

***(*) **Snatch & Grab It: The Essential Julia Lee Volume 1**
[Indigo IGOCD 2514] *As above, except Douglas also plays ts, and Cavanaugh does not play cl; add Jim 'Daddy' Walker (g), Clint Weaver (b); omit Sherwood, Drayton.* 11/44–4/49.

***(*) **Snatch And Grab It**
EPM Blues Collection 15970 *Similar to above.* 11/44–4/49.

***(*) **A Proper Introduction To Julia Lee: That's What I Like**
Proper INTRO CD 2018 *Similar to above.* 11/44–4/49.

Lee is best known today for sly point numbers like 'King Size Papa', 'My Man Stands Out', 'Snatch And Grab It' and the wonderful 'I Didn't Like It The First Time (The Spinach Song)', all of which she sings with considerable but not overstated relish, accompanied by her own unobtrusively graceful piano playing and small but buoyant swing groups. Those titles, and several others in the same vein such as 'Come On Over To My House' and 'Tonight's The Night', form a core group that can be found on each of the Indigo, EPM and Proper sets. Likeable as they are – the corkscrew of sexual metaphor has seldom been twisted with such panache – they are only one aspect of Lee's music, and it's JSP's 2CD set, which is virtually complete for the period covered, that offers a truly wide-angle view. Lee confidently handles superior pop songs like 'I'll Get Along Somehow' or 'When You're Smiling', the last featuring polished solos by Red Norvo, Red Nichols and Benny Carter, but even better are her blues interpretations, which run all the way from wry to tender to dolorous, often prompting inventive soloing like guitarist Jack Marshall's in 'Blues For Someone'. Classics' first volume prefaces the first 17 tracks on JSP with eight crisply arranged sides by George E. Lee's Orchestra from the late '20s, Julia's contribution to which was three vocals and possibly some of the piano playing. The quality of sound is exceptional on all these CDs.

**** **Kansas City Star: Complete Known Recordings 1927–1957**
Bear Family BCD 15770 5CD *As for Julia Lee 1927–1946 and Kansas City's First Lady Of The Blues, except Douglas also plays ts; add Elmer W. Price (t), Franz Bruce, unknown (as), Gene Carter, Bob Dougherty, unknown (ts), Jim 'Daddy' Walker, James Scott, Ted Williams, unknown (g), Leonard Johnson, Cleophus Berry, Jacky Lewis, unknown (b), William Nolan, Robert Jordan, Corky Jackson, unknown (d), Joe Alexander (v). 27–57.*

The picture of Julia Lee revealed by the albums above is not quite complete: Bear Family, characteristically, cover every inch of the canvas. What's added includes a previously unissued rehearsal session from 1946, her handful of recordings from the '50s, and the customary big book of notes (by Bill Millar), pictures and discography. TR

Leecan & Cooksey
DUET

Harmonica player Robert Cooksey and guitarist/banjoist Bobby Leecan were active in the New York recording studios of the '20s and were documented as living in the city in early 1926, though clues in their music suggest they were also familiar with Philadelphia and Chicago, and, in Leecan's case, with Macon, Georgia. Nothing is heard of either after the early '30s.

*** **Leecan & Cooksey – Vol. 1 (1924–1927)**
Document DOCD-5279 *Cooksey (h, k, v); Leecan (bj, g); Bubber Miley (c); Edgar Dowell, Phil Worde, poss. Mike Jackson (p); Elmer Snowden (bj); Alfred Martin (g); Viola McCoy, Sara Martin, Elizabeth Smith, Sidney Easton, Helen Baxter, Margaret Johnson (v). 4/24–3/27.*

*** **Leecan & Cooksey – Vol. 2 (1927–1928)**
Document DOCD-5280 *Cooksey (h, v, sp); Leecan (bj, g, k, v); Tom Morris (c); El Watson (h, sp); Mike Jackson (p); Alfred Martin (md, g); unknown (vc); Eddie Edinborough (d, wb, v). 4/27–5/28.*

Though both Leecan and Cooksey recorded independently, the bulk of their work was done together, either as a duet or in small groups such as the South Street Trio, with guitarist Alfred Martin, or Leecan's five-piece Need-More Band. The characteristic sound of their harmonica–guitar duets was established by the 1926 coupling 'Black Cat Bone Blues'/'Dirty Guitar Blues'. Leecan, by the standards of the time a sophisticated guitarist, busily dispenses a mixture of chordal and single-string passages while Cooksey pours long, pure draughts of melody. Cooksey's sound is unusual because he often plays in first position, using a harmonica in the key of the tune and chiefly blowing notes, whereas the majority of blues players select a harmonica five semitones higher and utilize mostly drawn notes. The former method makes note-bending much harder to achieve, but assists the execution of clean, high-register melodic lines, Cooksey's forte.

The duo's novel instrumental blend also earned them several sessions accompanying singers. Their date with Margaret Johnson, thanks in part to excellent recording, is delightful. Leecan's double-time playing in 'Second-Handed Blues' energizes what might otherwise have been an ordinary performance, while Cooksey responds to Johnson's doleful singing of 'Dead Drunk Blues' by almost turning into Noah Lewis. Cooksey's earlier encounter with Sara Martin is remarkable for the strange sonic cocktail of harmonica and Bubber Miley's growl cornet.

Vol. 2 opens with 'Washboard Cut Out', 'Shortnin' Bread' and two other tunes by the Need-More Band, happy skiffle not much marred by the ungainly and out-of-tune cellist. Amidst further duet and trio sides are four credited to the Dixie Jazzers Washboard Band, who were Cooksey, Leecan, Eddie Edinborough on washboard and drums, Mike Jackson on piano, and cornettist Tom Morris – prestigious jazz company in which our twosome play with unflustered confidence, helping to create music with both sparkle and depth. The final South Street Trio date is noteworthy for Leecan's bright banjo-mandolin playing on 'Cold Mornin' Shout', 'Suitcase Breakdown' and 'Dallas Blues'. Much of what is on these two CDs is in effect jugless jugband music, and anyone who appreciates the breadth of the repertoire and the variety of the ensembles in the work of the Memphis Jug Band is likely to enjoy Leecan and Cooksey no less. TR

The Legendary Blues Band
GROUP

Jerry Portnoy, Pinetop Perkins, Calvin Jones and Willie Smith were part of the band Muddy Waters discarded in mid-1980. Joined by Louis Myers, they took on a new identity as The Legendary Blues Band, toured and made several albums.

(*) **Life Of Ease
Rounder CD 2029 *Jerry Portnoy (h, v); Pinetop Perkins (p, v); Louis Myers, Duke Robillard (g); Calvin Jones (b, v); Eddie Butler Jr (b); Willie Smith (d). 81?*

The ghost of Muddy Waters may stalk the battlements, but his players put on quite a good show in their own right. Jones and Perkins, who share the vocals more or less evenly, are both competent, and each finds the opportunity in a slow blues – Jones in 'Woke Up With The Blues', Perkins in 'Eye To Eye', both written by Willie Smith – to create something of a Muddy ambience. 'Snakeskin Strut' gives Portnoy the chance to walk like Little Walter. Little Richard's 'Lucille' and Jimmy Reed's 'Hush Hush', dull choices, detract from an otherwise sound set. Their subsequent Rounder album *Red Hot And Blue* (CD 2035) and three for Ichiban are out of print. TR

Kim Lembo (born 1966)
VOCAL

Lembo was born and raised in Syracuse, New York. She formed her first band in her 20s, and signed with Blue Wave in 1993. She now lives in San Francisco.

** **Blue Heat**
Blue Wave CD 125 *Lembo; Pete McMahon, Nick Langan (h); Mark Doyle (kb, g, b, perc); Mike Doyle, Paul Laronde (b); Cathy Lamanna, Mark Tiffault (d). 10/93–3/94.*

** Mama Lion
Blue Wave CD 127 *Lembo; John Kane (s); Mark Doyle (kb, o, p, g, perc, v); Mark Nanni (o, p, clav); Mike Doyle, Paul 'Big Daddy' Laronde (b); Cathy Lamanna (d, perc); Mark Tiffault (d).* 10/93, 1/95.

**(*) Ready To Ride
Blue Wave CD 132 *Lembo; Pete McMahon (h); Mark Nanni (o, p, v); Scott Ebner (o); Kim Simmonds (Do); Terry Mulhauser (g); Joel Kane, Paul 'Big Daddy' Laronde (b); Rob Spagnoletti, Mark Tiffault (d); Julius Williams (perc, v).* 4/97–1/98.

**(*) Paris Burning
Blue Wave CD 140 *Lembo; Mark Nanni (o, p, v); Frank Grace (g); Stephen T. Winston (b); Garnet Grimm (d).* 1/00.

Mark Doyle, who co-produced *Blue Heat* and *Mama Lion* and played most of the keyboards and all the guitars, is clearly a versatile man – but these are Lembo's albums, and he might have acknowledged that by not upstaging her so often. As it is, she is constantly fighting to be heard, and her voice isn't so powerful that she has any natural advantage in the fray. The music itself often sounds as if it's gasping for breath, and the hesitant beauty of Walter Davis's 'My Tears Came Rolling Down' on *Blue Heat* is crushed by an unsubtle arrangement. Both CDs are intrinsically interesting blends of material drawn from writers like Isaac Hayes, Peter Green and Nick Gravenites, which Lembo handles with verve and fair technical resource, her manner sometimes fleetingly reminiscent of Janis Joplin, Bonnie Raitt or Maria Muldaur.

Ready To Ride was produced with more discretion. Picking songs from the repertoires of Otis Rush, Tampa Red, King Biscuit Boy and Lester Butler, it also makes a louder bid for the notice of the blues enthusiast. Rush's 'Keep On Lovin' Me Baby' and Tampa Red's 'Love Crazy' are enhanced by Pete McMahon's pungent harmonica. Butler's hectic 'Goin' To The Church' recurs on *Paris Burning*, as does 'Love To Ride', evidently a favourite with Lembo, since this is its third appearance in her output. New to her recorded repertoire are Jimmy McCracklin's 'Think', Bo Diddley's 'You Don't Love Me', James Harman's 'Kiss Of Fire' (another Bo Diddley groove) and Jimmy Reed's 'Baby What You Want Me To Do'. The album was recorded during three nights at Paris's Chesterfield Café, a setting that encourages Lembo to play down her stylistic resourcefulness and play up the mannerisms. TR

J. B. Lenoir (1929–67)
VOCAL, GUITAR

J. B. Lenoir (pronounced Lenore) grew up in Mississippi and New Orleans, settled in Chicago at the age of 20, and soon made his mark in blues circles, not only for his highly distinctive singing but for writing songs that examined public issues as well as personal. He made a great impact on European audiences in 1965 and '66, and his death in 1967 following a road accident was regarded as one of the severest losses in the blues community. His music has touched many listeners outside the ranks of blues enthusiasts, inspiring film-makers like John Jeremy and Wim Wenders, who made The Soul Of A Man, *partly about Lenoir, for the Martin Scorsese TV series* The Blues *in 2003.*

***(*) J. B. Lenoir 1951–1954
Classics 5128 *Lenoir; J. T. Brown, Lorenzo Smith (ts); Sunnyland Slim, Joe Montgomery (p); Leroy Foster (g); unknown (b); Alfred Wallace, Al Galvin (d).* 51–10/54.

*** His JOB Recordings
Paula PCD-04 *As above.* 10/51–1/53.

*** Mojo Boogie: An Essential Collection
Fuel 2000 302 061 182 *Lenoir; J. T. Brown, Donald Hankins (ts); Jarrett Gibson (bs); Sunnyland Slim, Lafayette Leake (p); Milton Rector, unknown (b); Alfred Wallace, Willie Smith (d); 'Peeples' (bgo); Willie Dixon (v, sp).* 10/51–1/53, 7/63.

*** Blues Guitar Legends
Fuel 2000 302 061 401 2CD *As above.* 10/51–1/53, 7/63.

*** I Feel So Good
Universe UV 102 *As above.* 10/51–1/53, 7/63.

Lenoir had one of the most beautiful voices in postwar blues, and it may be that the men who recorded him deliberately gave it unintrusive, even skeletal accompaniment. Or perhaps it was just a matter of budget. Sometimes the dryness of the setting seems to dehydrate the music, but his best recordings achieve a fine balance between the soaring architecture of his vocals and the stolid buttressing of the accompaniment. Feelings of aspiration or dissatisfaction, always implicit in Lenoir's high, clear singing, were often given specific shape, either in topical compositions about tax or the Korean war or in meditations on (usually) female behaviour such as 'Man Watch Your Woman'.

Much of J. B.'s best early work was done for J.O.B. The primary source for those sides is *Mojo Boogie*, which also includes the later USA single of 'I Feel So Good' and 'I Sing Um The Way I Feel'. The Universe CD is virtually the same, while Paula omit the USA sides but add five 1/53 tracks from a session with Sunnyland Slim. *Mojo Boogie* reappears as the first disc of *Blues Guitar Legends*, the other being by Magic Sam. Tidy-minded readers may prefer to follow Lenoir's work chronologically on Classics. Their first CD has an early Chess session, all the J.O.B. sides and seven from Parrot (for which see below).

*** The Parrot Sessions
Relic 7020 *Lenoir; Alex Atkins (as); Lorenzo Smith, Ernest Cotton (ts); Joe Montgomery (p); Al Galvin (d).* 54–55.

*** The Parrot Sessions
Re 545 450 598 *As above.* 54–55.

Lenoir's Parrot sides include some of his most affecting work, such as 'We Got To Realise (We Can't Go On This Way)', quietly reasonable in the manner of Lonnie Johnson or Bill Gaither, and 'Sittin' Down Thinkin'', a meditation on mortality. These grave songs are balanced, as with the J.O.B.s, by cheerful up-tempo numbers like 'Mama, Talk To Your Daughter' and 'Mojo Boogie'. 'We Got To Realize' also contains one of Lenoir's infrequent guitar solos, gawky as usual but more inventive than the chorus in 'Mama, Talk To Your Daughter', where he plays the same chord 20 times in succession. Parrot also issued three topical compositions: 'I'm In Korea' is a fairly conventional letter-home-from-the-front piece, but it was coupled with 'Eisenhower Blues', and in the repressive political climate of 1954 a black musician naming the President in a blues was decidedly uppity. The record was withdrawn and the song replaced by the virtually identical but more circumspectly titled 'Tax Paying Blues'. The Re issue, described as 'expanded', has the same contents as the Relic, in a different running order, but has been remastered at a higher level.

*** **If You Love Me**
Universe UV 131 *Lenoir; Alex Atkins (as); Lorenzo Smith, Ernest Cotton (ts); Sunnyland Slim, Joe Montgomery (p); Leroy Foster (g); Alfred Wallace, Al Galvin (d).* 51–55?

*** **Martin Scorsese Presents The Blues**
MCA B0000617-02 *Lenoir; Alex Atkins (as); Lorenzo Smith, Ernest Cotton (ts); Leonard Caston (o); Sunnyland Slim, Joe Montgomery (p); Leroy Foster, Robert Lockwood (g); Willie Dixon, unknown (b); Alfred Wallace, Al Galvin (d).* 51–58.

*** **The Topical Bluesman**
[Blues Encore CD 52017] *As above, except add Junior Wells (h); Jesse Fowler (d).* 51–10/65.

With *Natural Man* (MCA/Chess CHD-9323) deleted, the selection of 11 Chess/Checker sides (preceded by four for Parrot) on *Martin Scorsese Presents ...* currently gives the widest access to Lenoir's recordings for the label in 1955–58, which were stiffened by a couple of saxophones. A good selection, well presented. *If You Love Me* has eight of those later Chess sides, plus two early ones and 13 from Parrot, annoyingly omitting 'Tax Paying Blues'. *The Topical Bluesman* has nine of the same tracks in inferior sound, but among its remaining 15 are several important items available nowhere else, such as the 1958 Shad single 'Back Door'/'Lou Ella' and four songs taped by Paul Oliver in 1960, previously issued on the LP *Conversation With The Blues* and a Blue Horizon 45. The CD may not be easy to find, but for a serious Lenoir collector it's essential.

(***) **One Of These Mornings**
JSP JSPCD 2154 *Lenoir; Fred Below (d); Willie Dixon (v, sp).* 62–65.

*** **Alabama Blues**
Snapper Complete Blues SBLUECD 033 *As above.* 62–65.

In 1962 Willie Dixon made a tape of Lenoir singing and playing, probably as a demo for possible bookers in Europe. Seven songs, with surrounding conversation by the two men, are on these CDs, which are boosted to a reasonable album length with nine more numbers, at least some of which are thought to have been recorded in Europe in '65. The demo tape is of interesting songs indifferently recorded; the later material is from Lenoir's European concert repertoire ('Alabama Blues', 'Remove This Rope', etc.) and remarkable, but it's all on *Alabama Blues!* and *Vietnam Blues* (see below) in superior performances and better recorded. The JSP and Snapper are identical in content but the latter arranges it more appealingly, with the best tracks first and the Dixon tapes all together at the end.

*** **J. B. Lenoir, Sunnyland Slim & Friends: Live In '63**
Fuel 2000 302 061 300 *Lenoir; Sunnyland Slim (p, v); Michael Bloomfield (g, v); John Lee Granderson, St Louis Jimmy Oden (v).* 7/63.

An *audio-vérité* recording by Norman Dayron of an evening's music at Nina's Lounge, a small West Side bar. Sunnyland and J. B. are the main acts, but there are guest performances by Bloomfield, who does three numbers, and Granderson and Oden, who have one each. Lenoir does mostly familiar songs – 'Louise', 'I Want To Know', 'Mojo Boogie' – but that's unimportant; what you'll buy this album for is ambience and occasion.

**** **Alabama Blues!**
Bellaphon CDLR 82001 *Lenoir; Fred Below (d); Willie Dixon (v).* 3/65.

♛ **** **Vietnam Blues**
Evidence ECD 26068 *As above.* 3/65, 9/66.

Anyone who was listening attentively to J. B. Lenoir's music in the early '60s knew he had it in him to write songs that transcended blues commonplaces and resonated in both the head and the heart. Even so, the two albums that he left as his last testament were astonishing. Although the agonizing struggles and dashed hopes of the Civil Rights movement shadowed the lives of every African-American, few in the blues community found it possible to speak explicitly about them in their music; for that, black America, and the part of white America that shared its concerns, listened instead to musicians like Charlie Mingus, John Coltrane or Archie Shepp, who found new means of expressing grief and anger in the language of jazz. In a climate that distrusted the blues as an ingenuous legacy of bad old times, it seemed impossible that any blues singer could make a statement as eloquent as Coltrane's 'Alabama Song'. It took Lenoir to disprove that – with a song called 'Alabama'. 'I never will go back to Alabama – that is not the place for me. You know, they killed my sister and my brother, and the whole world let the peoples down there go free.' Those were the opening lines of an album, *Alabama Blues*, that proceeded, in 'Move This Rope' and 'Alabama March', to give a bluesman's passionate response to the horror stories emanating from Birmingham and Oxford. A year later Lenoir issued another communiqué, *Down In Mississippi*, with compositions like 'Shot On James Meredith' and the numbing 'Born Dead': 'Why was I born in Mississippi, when it's so hard to get ahead? Every black child born in Mississippi, you know the poor child was born dead ... He will never speak his language, the poor baby will never speak his mind. The poor child will never know his mind, why in the world he's so far behind.'

If all the songs on these albums had been pitched at that level of intensity they would have been hard to bear, but they are interspersed with playful numbers like 'Round And Round', exuberant ones like 'I Feel So Good' and 'Mojo Boogie', the sinuous dances of 'Voodoo Music' and 'Feelin' Good' – songs of the kind Lenoir's admirers were used to. But, slight and happy though they were, they did not mute the effect of the others; letting a little sunlight in, they made the darkness more visible. No blues singer has ever done anything quite like it; perhaps no blues singer will ever have to again.

Alabama Blues – though not, apparently, *Down In Mississippi* – is still in catalogue, but the two albums are joined on *Vietnam Blues*, and that is the way to hear them. TR

Furry Lewis (1899–1981)
VOCAL, GUITAR

Walter Lewis was born in Greenwood, Mississippi, and nicknamed as a child; his family moved to Memphis when he was seven. Furry gave his birthdate as 1900 when asked by researchers, gradually pushing it back to 1893, but the date given here is supported by official records. He played in the streets and on medicine shows to supplement his income from day labour, and at some point lost a leg trying to hop a freight. In 1959, Lewis resumed recording and began performing for the new white audience; in the '60s he became something of a mascot for the Memphis alternative music scene. He kept working until his death and, although age and alcohol undermined his musicianship, he was venerated as a loveable old geezer from America's past; his cameo as 'Uncle Furry' in the film *W.W. And The Dixie Dancekings* exemplifies the process.

***(*) In His Prime 1927–1928
Yazoo 1050 *Lewis; Charles Johnson (md); Landers Waller (g); unknown (sp).* 4/27–8/28.
**** The Vintage Recordings (1927–1929)
Document DOCD-5004 *As above.* 4/27–9/29.
***(*) Furry Lewis 1927–1929
Wolf WSE-101 *As above.* 4/27–9/29.

The young Furry Lewis was an adventurous guitarist who blended intricate ragtime patterns with the forceful rhythms of Mississippi, sometimes fingerpicking over a drone bass, and deploying a precise, gleaming slide technique on occasion. He recorded valuable versions of the ballads 'Casey Jones', 'John Henry' and 'Stack O'Lee' alongside his blues; the latter feature striking lyrics, whose sober awareness of poverty and injustice is camouflaged and alleviated by macho boasting, cynical humour and extravagant images.

Yazoo's 14-tracker is an LP transferred to CD; the analogue master tape is pretty good, but the package is let down by short playing time, and notes that refer to Furry as still alive. Document's *Vintage Recordings*, distinguishable by its two-colour cover, is a remastered version of *Furry Lewis (1927–1929)*, which had black and white artwork and the same issue number. It has the decisive advantage of offering Furry's adventurous playing and crafty lyrics complete; Wolf, with acceptable sound quality, omit two alternative takes and the important second part of 'Kassie Jones'. Great sound, but not completeness, can be had from the VAC *Memphis Blues Singers Volume 2* (Frog DGF 22), which presents Lewis's ten Victor sides in transfers so good that a crowing rooster is audible on one track.

***(*) Shake 'Em On Down
Fantasy FCD-24703//[Ace CDCH 486] *Lewis.* 4–5/61.

Like many rediscovered blues singers, Lewis worked with a limited songbook, and his guitar skills were also somewhat diminished. There's much repetition of material from session to session, and few CDs without at least moments of aimless clanking as he recovers from a fumble. As might be expected, *Shake 'Em On Down* is among the best of Furry's later recordings; his rhythms are more nimble and more varied than they became later (he uses the 'Big Road Blues' bass figure from time to time), and there are songs included that he soon dropped or forgot, a pleasing 'Frankie And Johnny' among them. The too close recording of his singing is an unfortunate blemish on an otherwise enjoyable disc.

***(*) Good Morning Judge
Fat Possum FP 80374 *Lewis; Will Shade (b).* 62–8/67.

Well recorded, *Good Morning Judge* holds surprises like the banjoistic picking on 'Blues Around My Bed' among the familiar songs; the latter include 'Brownsville Blues', misnamed 'Roll And Tumble Blues', and 'See That My Grave Is Kept Clean', inexplicably listed as 'Furry Lewis's Careless Love'. Shade's oil-can bass features on 'Furry Lewis Rag', which starts as 'Red Wing' before segueing into 'Take Your Time', 'Farewell I'm Growing Old' gallops through a sentimental song, and 'Old Hobo' is one of Furry's best stabs at 'Waiting For A Train'. The long 'Don't You Wish Your Mama' is another of the collages of semi-related verses that Lewis assembled to entertain visitors, but the intense dialogue between voice and slide guitar gives it an imposing unity.

**(*) Party! At Home
Arcola A CD 1001 *Lewis; Bukka [Booker] White, Bob West, Calvin Gill, Little Man, assorted friends and neighbours (sp).* 7/68.
***(*) At Home In Memphis
Autogram ALCD-5805 *Lewis.* 9/68.

The Arcola CD, mostly recorded at the party of its title, is shared with Booker White. Furry performs some of his favourites and 'Mama's Fish', an impromptu lyric in praise of the cooking he'd recently enjoyed on a trip to Seattle. Unfortunately, he's not in good enough form to justify putting up with the extensive, semi-audible and inconsequential chatter between, and sometimes during, the songs.

Neighbours' children and listeners' laughter can be heard on Autogram, but the focus is firmly on Lewis, and he takes his music and lyrics much more seriously; the unexpected but perfectly placed slide harmonics at the end of a long, unusually profound 'Brownsville Blues' are one instance. Lewis the entertainer is present, of course, juggling the guitar and playing it with his elbow, but the emotional depth of 'See That My Grave Is Kept Clean', 'Highway 61' and even parts of 'Furry Lewis Rag' is exceptional and absorbing.

*** When I Lay My Burden Down
Biograph BCD 130 *Lewis.* 11/68.

Another shared disc, this time with Fred McDowell and Robert Wilkins. Lewis's six songs are well recorded, and he sings and plays vigorously, although there are one or two distracting slips. 'Harry Furry Blues', a tribute to his friend Harry Godwin, puts engaging new words to a favourite melody.

*** Fourth And Beale
Universal/Maison de Blues 982 241-7 *Lewis.* 3/69.

Fourth And Beale derives from a session held at Lewis's home. It's one more outing for the usual suspects – 'John Henry', 'Casey Jones', 'Judge Boushe Blues', and so on – but producer Terry Manning seems to have sparked Furry's energy and enthusiasm; he's more emotionally engaged than was sometimes the case, and these are some of the best versions of his autumnal career. He'd recently recovered from pneumonia, and thoughts of mortality make 'When The Saints Go Marchin' Home' unexpectedly moving. As ever, some allowances have to be made; the guitar part on 'John Henry' briefly goes very flat, and he muddles the words when 'Goin' Back To Gary' segues into 'Every Day In The Week'.

This CD is a reissue of the deleted *Fourth & Beale* (Lucky Seven CD 9202), augmented with six tracks from *Blues Magician* (Lucky Seven CD 9206), also deleted. *Blues Magician* had some weak tracks; Barclay have selected the strongest, and although the Lucky Seven discs may still be around, the latest version will suffice for most readers.

*** Take Your Time
Adelphi GCD 9911 *Lewis; Lee Baker Jr (g, v).* 10/69.

Occasionally, Baker and Lewis get in each other's way or diverge harmonically, but Baker provides rhythmic stability and energy, and enables Furry to play guitar as well as possible within his limitations, rather than striving for complexities he can no longer achieve. Not unconnectedly, his singing is very strong and expressive. There are no great surprises in the playlist, although the familiar 'How Long?' is an addition to Lewis's repertoire. (He's reminded of it by Baker's pancake-flat singing of the first verse.) The waltzes heard on *Blues Magician* return, in better versions, and for the first time since *At Home In Memphis* Furry includes 'Bang away, my Lula, don't bang away so strong, What I'm gonna do for bangin', when Lula's dead and gone?' in 'St. Louis Blues'.

**(*) On The Road Again
Adelphi/Genes GCD 9918 *Lewis; Mike Stewart, Willie Morris (g); Dewey Corley (b, k).* 10/69.

Furry leads on five songs, and accompanies Gus Cannon on another; Cannon and Booker White have the balance of the CD. Lewis was still singing and playing strongly, and still doing the same old songs; the producers seem to have felt the need to put them in new settings, and 'On The Road Again', with Stewart and Corley, is a pleasant, if unrevelatory retread of 'Casey Jones'. Willie Morris was an exceptional singer and guitarist in the Delta style, but his seconding of Furry on two tracks is an experiment that doesn't come off; their styles are divergent and their playing poorly coordinated.

*** Heroes Of The Blues: The Very Best Of Furry Lewis
Shout Factory DK 30248 *Lewis; Landers Waller, Lee Baker Jr (g).* 4/27–10/69.

Shout Factory combine three early recordings (vivid but hissy) with four tracks from *Shake 'Em On Down*, two from *When I Lay My Burden Down*, six from *Take Your Time* and one from *On The Road Again*. Within the limits imposed by age, this is a pleasant enough portrait, but it's beyond debate that Lewis's very best recordings are his first, and the CD's subtitle should not be taken seriously. CS

Johnie Lewis (born 1908)
VOCAL, GUITAR, HARMONICA, KAZOO

Born in Alabama, Lewis grew up in Georgia, but headed for Chicago in the '30s after trouble with the law. Music was always a sideline to his self-employment as a house painter, but among his customers were the Cokliss family, whose film director son, Harley, included Lewis in the documentary Chicago Blues. *Arhoolie Records' last contact with him was in 1991.*

*** Alabama Slide Guitar
Arhoolie CD 9007 *Lewis; Charlie Musselwhite (h).* 8/70, 1/71.

Johnie Lewis's solo numbers in *Chicago Blues* are a surprising and enjoyable contrast to the film's expected, and equally enjoyable, amplified bar bands, and it's no wonder that they prompted Chris Strachwitz to record him. His late recording debut and semi-professional status no doubt account for the not unwelcome archaism of his song list: 'Poor Boy' and 'Hobo Blues' are from the earliest days of the music, other songs derive from recordings of the '30s, and the World War II vintage 'Uncle Sam Ain't No Woman' is about as contemporary as he gets. (Two heartfelt tributes to Martin Luther King may seem to be exceptions, but both are adaptations of venerable spirituals.)

Lewis accompanies himself with simple bottleneck lines over chordal rhythms, and it's probably because he never had to prove his versatility to record producers that the texture of both voice and guitar is rather unvaried. Charlie Musselwhite's presence on one track makes for a welcome change, as does 'Lewis' Little Girl Done Stole A Black Cat Bone', on which Johnie plays solo harmonica. He has a handsome tone, similar to DeFord Bailey's, but runs out of ideas well before the song's end. 'Jumpin' Jive', a kazoo and guitar instrumental, also breaks up the pattern, but is predictably lightweight. Had Lewis recorded a couple of 78s, or disappeared after appearing in *Chicago Blues*, his music might have become an obscure object of desire, but the CD documents a pleasant journeyman, content to do competent work within the boundaries of the style he grew up with. CS

Meade Lux Lewis (1905–64)
PIANO, CELESTE, HARPSICHORD, WHISTLING

Inspired by hearing Jimmy Yancey, Lewis learned piano in Chicago alongside his fellow cab driver Albert Ammons. His classic 1927 recording of 'Honky Tonk Train Blues' prompted John Hammond to record him again in the mid-'30s, but Lewis only became widely known after the 1938 From Spirituals To Swing *concert; he joined Ammons and Pete Johnson in the Boogie Woogie Trio, but left in 1940, usually working solo thereafter. Lewis disliked being stereotyped as a boogie player, and responded with faster and more superficial renditions. He died in a car crash.*

***(*) Meade Lux Lewis 1927–1939
Classics 722 *Lewis; Albert Ammons, Pete Johnson (p).* c. 12/27–1/39.

Lewis's cloudy, unorthodox harmonies, big clusters of sound and fondness for the middle of the keyboard make his best music more mellow than febrile, even at speed. He may have come to hate his big hit (there are three versions on this disc, and another on the next), but the composition deserves its reputation as a masterpiece of swing and cross-rhythm, and its early incarnations are graceful and disciplined.

The mastering on this and the next Classics disc is very variable, and some readers may settle for the 1927 'Honky Tonk Train Blues' on *Shake Your Wicked Knees* (Yazoo 2035) or *Piano Blues: The Essential* (Classic Blues CBL 200004 2CD). That would be to miss out on a good deal of very interesting music, including the two-part 'Boogie Woogie Prayer', perhaps the only three-piano collaboration to rise above gimmickry. Two celeste solos aren't gimmicky either, but nor are they persuasive. The disc concludes with Lewis's first Blue Note recordings, which are admirable examples of his introspective blues playing. Their titles alone – 'Melancholy', 'Solitude' and a five-part exploration of 'The Blues' – prove that there was more to Lewis than florid showmanship.

***(*) Hey! Piano Man
JSP JSP 7747 4CD *Lewis.* 11/35–c. 2/39.

This is the best disc in JSP's box, which is shared with the other members of the Boogie Woogie Trio and Jimmy Yancey. It contains all Lewis's commercially recorded piano solos from the 1935 rerecording of 'Honky Tonk Train Blues', through the first Blue Note session, to the first three of five superlative titles recorded for Solo Art. It could have been improved by including the complete Solo Art session at the expense of the two celeste novelties.

***(*) Meade Lux Lewis 1939–1941
Classics 743 *Lewis; J. C. Higginbotham (tb); Albert Ammons (p); Teddy Bunn (g); Johnny Williams (b); Sid Catlett (d). 1/39–4/41.*

Mostly solos, mostly from Blue Note, this volume includes two duets with Ammons and a pleasant quintet version of 'Basin Street Blues'. Blue Note's 12-inch masters let Lewis stretch out, which was not always a good thing; 1941's 'Honky Tonk Train' exceeds safe speeds and runs out of steam. Its fellow train imitation, 'Six Wheel Chaser', and the ingenious 'Bass On Top' are gems of boogie playing, however, and 'Rising Tide Blues' makes telling use of dissonance between the hands. The most valuable tracks, despite mediocre sound quality, are five exquisite blues from Solo Art, none faster than medium tempo and all harmonically and rhythmically adventurous. Two harpsichord solos conclude the disc (and two more open Classics' next volume); they are less bizarre and more idiomatic than might be expected.

**** Ammons & Lewis – The First Day
Blue Note CDP 7 98450 *Lewis; Albert Ammons (p). 1/39.*

Lewis is the minority shareholder in Blue Note's inaugural session, responsible for seven solos, and duetting on 'Twos And Fews' and 'Nagasaki'. Quite apart from the quality of the performances, its organic coherence and superior sound will commend this disc to readers who want to appreciate the greatness of Lewis (and Ammons), but don't need their every note.

*** Boogie Woogie Stomp
Delmark DD-705 *Lewis; Albert Ammons (p, sp); Herbert Marshall (b). 12/38–10/39.*

*** The Boogie Woogie Trio Vol. 1 & 2
Storyville 103 8057 2CD *Lewis; Albert Ammons, Pete Johnson (p); unknown (b); Smokey Stover (d). 9/39–9/54.*

These collections issue airshots from the Boogie Woogie Trio's Hotel Sherman residency. Delmark include four Lewis solos and a duet with Ammons, to which Storyville add the breezy solo 'Whistling Blues', a pair of six-handed crowd-pleasers, and 'Closing Time', a record of drunks with piano accompaniment. This problem also afflicts Lewis's lovely minor-key 'Chapel Blues'. He shines, too, on the introspective 'Dupree Blues' and the vigorous, harmonically daring 'Try Again' (which is some 30 seconds longer on Delmark). Delmark also include an informal four-title studio session, to which Lewis contributes a perky 'Yancey Special' and a brisk, percussive 'Bear Cat Shuffle'.

Lewis's 1954 recordings appear on the first of Storyville's two discs. His eight tracks (of 22) are live recordings from the Club Hangover in San Francisco. Stover lays down a swinging if unvaried shuffle and Lewis responds with enthusiasm but variable artistic success. 'Mr. Freddie Blues' is a lexicon of blues-piano technique, and the first of two versions of 'Six Wheel Chaser' is well-structured, gradually building excitement, but 'Glendale Glide' is speed without meaning, and

'Boogie Tidal' is amorphous by comparison with the earlier version included on Classics' third volume (see below).

**** Boogies And Blues
Topaz TPZ 1069 *Lewis; Frankie Newton (t); J. C. Higginbotham (tb); Sidney Bechet (cl, ss); Edmond Hall (cl); Teddy Bunn, Charlie Christian (g); Johnny Williams, Israel Crosby (b); Sid Catlett (d). 1/36–2/41.*

Most tracks here come from Blue Note, including 'Melancholy', 'Solitude', and the four parts of 'The Blues' that were issued on 78. The remastering is occasionally lacklustre, but generally acceptable; on the 1936 versions of 'Yancey Special' and 'Mr. Freddie Blues', it's markedly better than on Classics. Lewis is present, but not prominent, on the Port Of Harlem Seven's 'Blues For Tommy'; more interesting, and at times very interesting indeed, are four tracks by the Edmond Hall Celeste Quartet, with Christian and Lewis creating some beautiful textures.

***(*) Meade Lux Lewis 1941–1944
Classics 841 *Lewis. 4/41–8/44.*

Classics' third volume offers the balance of the Blue Note recordings, including a superior account of 'Yancey Special' and a hard-driving 'Chicago Flyer'. On the V-Disc 'Doll House Boogie', Lewis plays piano and celeste simultaneously to good effect. Nine tracks from Asch include a 'Honky Tonk Train Blues' played at a dismissively lunatic speed, but the winding, chromatic 'Boogie Tidal' is the work of an artist still striving to create, as are the meditative 'Denapas Parade' and 'Special No. One'.

**(*) Meade 'Lux' Lewis (1939–late 1940s)
Document DOCD-5561 *Lewis; Harry James, Ziggy Elman, Chris Griffin, poss. Johnny Anderson (t); Red Ballard, Vernon Brown, Williams Woodman (tb); Benny Goodman, Edmond Hall (cl, as); Dave Matthews, Noni Bernardi (as); Arthur Rollini, Jerry Jerome, Wild Bill Moore (ts); Jess Stacey, Albert Ammons (p); Ben Heller, Charlie Christian, Irving Ashby (g); Harry Goodman, Israel Crosby, prob. Jesse Simpkins, Red Callender, unknown (b); Buddy Schutz, prob. Shadow Wilson, Chico Hamilton, unknown (d); Joe Turner, Helen Humes (v); Johnny Mercer, Dan Seymour, George Raft, Ernie 'Bubbles' Whitman, James Stewart, Louis Armstrong, unknowns (sp). 1/39–late 40s.*

There are good things here, including spirited Joe Turner renditions of 'Roll 'Em' and 'Low Down Dog', a stirring 'V-Disc Stomp', and a 'Lux's Boogie' in G that's quite different from the similarly titled piece in C on the third Classics disc. However, this CD, summarized on its back cover as *Alternate Takes, Live Performances, Soundies, Etc.*, is for those who must have everything, from tediously frenetic live boogies to 'Untitled Phrases' from a cartoon soundtrack, to Jimmy Stewart in *It's A Wonderful Life*, talking over 32 seconds of distant piano. For preference, we suggest *Boogie Woogie Boys* (Document BDCD-6046), which includes Lewis's 1938 Library of Congress recordings: three versions of 'Honky Tonk Train Blues' (of course), but good ones, with important interview material interspersed.

** Barrel House Piano
Jasmine JASMCD 2536 *Lewis; unknown (g); prob. Red Callender (b). 3/56.*

** Tidal Boogie
Tradition TCD 1029 *As above.* 3/56.

These CDs derive from a 16-track LP on Tops; Jasmine reissue it complete, and Tradition select ten items. Most of the programme consists of jazz and pop standards that Lewis had not recorded before, like 'Tisho Mingo Blues' [*sic*], 'Someday Sweetheart' and 'Basin Street Blues'. Teamed with a fabulously inventive electric guitarist, he attacks the material with gusto and imagination. Unfortunately, the producer saw fit to prepare the piano with thumbtacks, provoking cries of 'What?', 'Why?' and 'Cretin!' in rapid sequence.

(***) Gliding From Glendale To Chicago
Jasmine JASCD 417 2CD *Similar to relevant CDs above, except add Frank Williams (d), George Hannah (v).* c. 10/30–3/56.

Forty-six tracks range from an accompaniment to the obscure George Hannah, lugubriously proclaiming himself a freakish man on an eponymous blues, to a large chunk of the annoying Tops LP already available on Jasmine. *Gliding From Glendale To Chicago* also includes items from Lewis's 1951 Atlantic session, with Israel Crosby (bass) and the heavy-handed Frank 'Sweet' Williams. None of this is discoverable from a remarkably disjointed booklet note, and the CDs' running order seems to have been determined by drawing track names out of a hat. The sound is mostly acceptable – there's occasional overload here and there – and *Gliding From Glendale* works as a cheap, context-free collection: piano blues and boogie as ambient music.

*** The Blues Piano Artistry Of Meade Lux Lewis
Original Jazz Classics OJCCD 1759 *Lewis.* 11/61.

Convention holds that Lewis was bored with his music by the time of this penultimate LP, but that's plainly not the case; nor, *pace* our colleagues at *The Penguin Guide To Jazz Recordings*, is it a 'group of remakes'. The cross-rhythms on 'Hammer Chatter' are as remarkable as any he recorded (yes, including those on his incubus), the chordal basses on 'Frompy Stomp' are fascinatingly unpredictable and, all in all, Lewis seems as engaged as he'd ever been; that he knocked off a session consisting almost entirely of new tunes in two hours is an index of professionalism, not superficiality. The disc is devalued slightly by the silent-movie clichés of 'Fate', and more seriously by three tracks with celeste, which don't go beyond tinkly tweeness, but it's a lot better than it's sometimes been painted. CS

Smiley Lewis (1913–66)
VOCAL, GUITAR

If anyone called Overton Amos Lemons by his real name, he became very unsmiley. Born in rural Louisiana, Lewis was raised by a white family in New Orleans after his mother's death. He was an entertainer by the age of 20, also working at day jobs until 'Tee-Nah-Nah' became a local hit in 1950. Thereafter, Imperial tried everything they knew to break him nationally until 1960, with only occasional success. After Imperial let him go, Lewis made a few more records for OKeh, Dot and Loma, but struggled to make a living from music until his death.

♛ **** Shame, Shame, Shame
Bear Family BCD 15745 4CD *Lewis; Melvin Lastie (c); Dave Bartholomew, unknowns (t); Waldren 'Frog' Joseph, William Myles, unknown (tb); Clarence Hall (as, ts); Joe Harris, Meyer Kennedy, unknowns (as); Lee Allen, Herb Hardesty, Warren Payne, Nat Perrilliat, unknowns (ts); Red Tyler, unknowns (bs); unknown (h); Tuts Washington, Edward Frank, poss. Fats Domino, poss. Joe Robichaux, Huey 'Piano' Smith, poss. Salvador Doucette, James Booker, Harold Battiste, Allen Toussaint (p); Ernest McLean, Justin Adams, Prince La La, Lawrence Nelson, unknowns (g); Papa John Joseph, Frank Fields, Chuck Badie, unknowns (b); Earl Palmer, poss. Charles 'Hungry' Williams (d, perc); Herman Seale, Robert French, Oscar Moore, unknowns (d); unknowns (handclaps); The Toppers, Gerri Hall, unknowns (v).* 9/47–12/65.

**** The Best Of Smiley Lewis, I Hear You Knocking
Collectables COL-CD-5630 *Similar to above.* 3/50–8/56.

**** A Proper Introduction To Smiley Lewis
Proper INTRO CD 2039 *Similar to above.* 3/50–7/53.

Writers, musicians and producers have puzzled over Smiley Lewis's failure to make it as big as his talent deserved. Part of the problem was white singers stealing his thunder; Smiley had R&B hits with 'I Hear You Knocking' and 'One Night', but it was Gale Storm and Elvis Presley respectively who took them into the pop charts. Presley added insult to injury by bowdlerizing 'one night of sin' into 'one night of love', which offers a pointer to Lewis's specific difficulty. His songs and singing were usually too grown-up and realistic to appeal to the teenage market; if Fats Domino was the Crescent City's cuddly, crossover teddy bear, Smiley, also short and stout, was more like Ferdinand the Bull, powerful and aggressively masculine. His singing had the same resonance as Joe Turner's, and like Joe he could dominate a band without a microphone, but his delivery was harder-edged and less outgoing. Turner at 46 could make 'Teenage Letter' convincing; Smiley never sounded less plausible than when pursuing Chuck Berry's audience with 'School Days Are Back Again' – but it's still a very good record, with a notable guitar solo.

Indeed, with Dave Bartholomew putting together the bands, Lewis's Imperial sessions are a masterclass in New Orleans R&B accompaniment, with track after track offering impeccable second-line rhythm, piano work that ripples and rocks by turns, and demonstrations of all the ways to play a tenor chorus. Smiley is always the dominant presence, though, and Bear Family's boxed set of the complete recordings shows just how commanding and versatile he was and remained. (The orthodox verdict is that his voice declined after Imperial, but it's Allen Toussaint's narcissistic piano that screws up the Loma session.)

Those whose budgets will not stretch so far will be well served by the 24 carefully chosen tracks on Collectables; licensed from Capitol, *I Hear You Knocking* emphasizes hits and belters, and has good sound and helpful annotation, although inevitably this falls short of Bear Family's 36 large pages. Proper also have 24 well mastered tracks (a third of them in common with Collectables) and detailed notes. Cutting off at 1953 for copyright reasons does no harm to the selection; indeed Proper commendably avoid some of the obvious hits in favour of slow blues like 'Slide Me Down', 'Don't Jive Me' (a revival of 'I'd Rather Drink Muddy Water') and 'If You Ever Loved A Woman', and bravely include the hilarious calypso novelty 'Little Fernandez'.

Nevertheless *Shame, Shame, Shame* is the one to get if possible, for it offers facets of Smiley Lewis that are missed or under-represented on Collectables and Proper: the balladeer offering velvet versions of 'I Love You For Sentimental Reasons' and 'When Did You Leave Heaven', and the downhome blues singer with a yearning revival of Leroy Carr's 'How Long' and a retitled cover of Howlin' Wolf's 'Forty Four'. Completism inevitably entails a few clunkers; among the 100 tracks are an absurd 'You Are My Sunshine', and a late session where Bartholomew rather desperately imposes fussy big-band charts, but the overall standard is remarkably high. If there was a better male R&B singer than Smiley Lewis living in New Orleans in the '50s, he didn't make records. CS

Jimmy Liggins (1922–83)
VOCAL, GUITAR

The Oklahoma-born Jimmy Liggins entered the music business as his brother Joe's driver, but soon took his own road as a songwriter and bandleader. He was signed by Specialty in 1947, three years before his brother, and had some hits, but overall his career was less successful than Joe's.

*** Jimmy Liggins And His Drops Of Joy
Specialty SPCD-7005//Ace CDCHD 306 *Liggins; Glen Willis, Harry D. Jones, Boppie Parker, poss. Bobby Summers (t); James Dedmon, Don Canway, poss. Toussaint Allen (as); Harold Land, Charles 'Little Jazz' Ferguson, Maxwell Davis, Earl Carter, James 'Doc' Thomas, poss. Red Conner, poss. Willie Johnson (ts); Fred Jackson, Eugene Watson, poss. Clarence 'Bo' Cyphers (p); Jonathan Bagsby, Ralph Hamilton, poss. Thomas Blake (b); Leon Petties, Herman Manzy, unknown (d); John Stevenson, David Monroe (unknown instruments). 9/47–53.*

*** Vol. 2: Rough Weather Blues
Specialty SPCD-7026//[Ace CDCHD 437] *Similar to above.* 11/47–53.

Liggins is a dry, stolid singer, without as much humour or blues feeling as Louis Jordan (an obvious model – check 'Saturday Night Boogie Woogie Man') but capable of delivering infectious, danceable music in the jump-blues idiom popularized by Jordan, Roy Milton and his own brother Joe. His first hit, 'I Can't Stop It', a busy blues replete with horn riffs and refrain singing by the band, was a template for sides like 'Cadillac Boogie' (itself a partial prototype of Jackie Brenston's 'Rocket 88'), 'Move Out Baby' and 'Nite Life Boogie', a programme occasionally interrupted by smoochy slow blues like 'Don't Put Me Down'. The 1947 sides often contain solo and duet choruses by the tenor saxophonists Harold Land and 'Little Jazz' Ferguson; Land, at the beginning of a distinguished career in jazz, is heard at length in 'Come Back Baby'. Later recordings generally feature Maxwell Davis, though he may not be the simmering tenorman on 'Shuffle Shuck', a period-perfect riff tune led by an energetic but unidentified drummer. Other sides often feature one or another boogie pianist, but seldom the leader's guitar playing. By 1951 Liggins was singing with more vim and making efficient proto-rock 'n' roll recordings like 'Train Blues'.

All those tunes are on the first volume. *Rough Weather Blues* is a repeat voyage using the same session logs, and while the musical view is essentially the same, the passenger's attention is drawn to different points of interest: there are more instrumentals, a good many more slow blues and several of Liggins's vinegary guitar solos, notably on 'Goin' Down With The Sun'. Land and Ferguson steer the band towards bebop in a five-minute version of Charlie Parker's blues theme 'Now's The Time' and an 'Unidentified Instrumental', two of a dozen previously unreleased recordings excavated by the reissue producer Billy Vera. This CD is no less interesting than its predecessor; some listeners may prefer it. TR

Joe Liggins (1915–87)
VOCAL, PIANO

In 1932 the Liggins family moved from Oklahoma to San Diego, where the teenaged Joe soon began writing and arranging for local bands. He moved in 1939 to LA, playing with Illinois Jacquet and other leaders before recording in his own name. Following 'The Honeydripper', a huge hit in 1944–45, Liggins had numerous successful records on Exclusive and Specialty, among them 'I Got A Right To Cry' and 'Pink Champagne', the biggest R&B record of 1950. His career lost momentum in the mid-'50s, but he continued to record for other labels for a few years. He had a comeback in the '80s, playing at LA clubs and appearing in TV programmes with his colleague of 40 years' standing, saxophonist Little Willie Jackson.

*** Joe Liggins 1944–1946
Classics 5020 *Liggins; Joe Darensbourg (cl); Little Willie Jackson (ss, as, bs); James Jackson (ts); Frank Pasley (g); Red Callender or Eddie Davis (b); Preston 'Peppy' Prince (d). 11/44–46.*

*** The Honeydripper
Night Train NTI CD 7031 *As above, except Little Willie Jackson also sings. 3/45–49.*

*** Joe Liggins 1946–1948
Classics 5063 *As above, except add Gene Phillips (g), unknown (v); omit Darensbourg, Davis. 46–48.*

*** Joe Liggins 1948–1950
Classics 5108 *Liggins; Little Willie Jackson (as, bs); James Jackson, Maxwell Davis (ts); Frank Pasley (g); Red Callender, Eddie Davis (b); Preston 'Peppy' Prince (d). 48–4/50.*

*** Joe Liggins & His Honeydrippers
Specialty SPCD-7006//Ace CDCHD 307 *Liggins; Lawrence Lofton (tb); Floyd Turnham (cl, s); Little Willie Jackson (as, ts); Jewell Grant (as); Maxwell Davis, James Jackson, William Woodman, 'Bo' Rhambo (ts); Frank Pasley, Harold Grant (g); Eddie Davis, William Cooper, Red Callender, Teddy Shirley (b); Peppy Prince, Nathaniel Jack McFay, Earl Carter (d); Wallace Sanford (unknown instruments); Candy Rivers (v). 1/50–3/54.*

**(*) Volume 2: Dripper's Boogie
Specialty SPCD-7025//[Ace CDCHD 436] *Similar to above.* 1/50–3/54.

*** Joe Liggins 1950–1952
Classics 5155 *Liggins; Floyd Turnham (cl, s); Willie Jackson (as, bs); James Jackson, Wallace Sandford, William Woodman, Maxwell Davis (ts); Frank Pasley, Harold Grant (g); Eddie A. Davis, William Cooper (b); Peppy Prince, Nathaniel 'Monk' McFay (d); Candy Rivers (v). 4/50–3/52.*

*** The Shuffle Boogie King
Proper PVCD 117 2CD *Liggins; unknown (t); Floyd Turnham (cl, s); Joe Darensbourg (cl); Little Willie Jackson (ss, as, bs); James Jackson, Maxwell Davis, William Woodman (ts); Frank Pasley, Johnny Moore, Gene Phillips, Harold Grant (g); Red Callender, William 'Keg' Purnell, Eddie Davis, William Cooper (b); Peppy Prince, Nathaniel McFay (d); Herb Jeffries, Candy Rivers (v). 3/45–10/51.*

With its rocking two-note piano figure and its yes-it-is-no-it-isn't false ending, 'The Honeydripper' could hardly fail with the jukebox trade, but one wonders what Liggins's new fans made of some of its successors like 'Sugar Lump', 'Caravan' or the Ellingtonian 'Harlemesque'. Actually such show music represented Liggins's background and leanings much more accurately. Although the 'Honeydripper' effect could not be resisted – 'I Know My Love Is True' and the faintly oriental-sounding 'Tanya', an alto feature for Little Willie Jackson, contained similar riffs – and another two-part record, 'Dripper's Boogie', foregrounded his piano in a conventional but romping boogie-woogie tune, Liggins continued to record, and score with, pop songs like 'I've Got A Right To Cry'. These dawn choruses of the LA jump-blues scene are faithfully documented on *Joe Liggins 1944–1946*, the first of three Classics CDs covering Liggins's Exclusive output. (It's prefaced by the scratchy first recording of 'The Honeydripper', for Bronze.) The second Classics set is much taken up with pop standards like 'Sweet Georgia Brown', 'The Darktown Strutters' Ball' and 'Siboney', and its appeal for readers may be concentrated in instrumentals like 'Blow Mr. Jackson', 'Down Home Blues' and 'Spooks Holiday', where the Jacksons find a wide range of tone colours on their palette of four horns. The final tranche of Exclusive sides on the third Classics is predominantly instrumentals, ranging from the lushly mock-Oriental 'Fascination' and the Cubanesque 'Hey Mama!' to boogie and jump tunes like 'Key Jam' and the two-part 'Three O'Clock Jump', conventional in form but sometimes enlivened by thoughtful arrangements.

The remaining 11 tracks on *1948–1950* and the whole of *1950–1952* are from Specialty and are all on one or other of the Specialty/Ace CDs discussed below. *The Honeydripper* is a well-judged epitome of this period, embracing most of the titles commended above.

In 1950 Liggins moved to Specialty, where his recordings often followed the formula, based on 'The Honeydripper' and repeated in the hits 'Pink Champagne' and 'Rag Mop', of a catchy melody with refrain or hook phrase chanted by the band. What prevents them becoming rowdy singsongs is Liggins's insinuating vocals, by turns regretful and seductive, and the delicacy of the rhythm playing, even on the fastest numbers. How cleverly Liggins miniaturized the big-band sound for seven- or eight-piece groups comes across well on the clearly recorded sides selected for *Joe Liggins & His Honeydrippers*, especially in the remake of 'Tanya'. 'The Flying Dutchman' is a skidding tenor feature on the model of 'Flying Home'.

Dripper's Boogie is selected from the same sessions, but at times seems almost like the work of another band, especially when Liggins hands the vocal microphone to Candy Rivers. On the mock-hillbilly 'That's The One For Me' she comes on like a yodelling cowgirl, and one might almost be listening to Sue Thompson with Hank Penny, or even Jo Stafford with Red Ingle. It's more fun than her sob-sister treatment of the pop songs 'Bob Is My Guy' and 'Tenderly'; here and occasionally elsewhere, as in 'Cryin' Over You', the Honeydrippers cease to be recognizable as a blues band – or the boppish ensemble that opens 'Little Black Book' with a flourish, or the cornball Dixieland outfit of 'My Heart Cried' – and ooze lounge music.

The Proper set consists of 36 tracks from Exclusive and 14 from Specialty. The latter are all on the first Specialty/Ace CD, while the material from Exclusive duplicates the entire Night Train and much of the three Classics CDs. The long arm of Louis Jordan touches the music in the Caribbean 'Gal With A Whole Lotta Loot', while a Hawaiian guitar creates a different island setting for 'I Cover The Waterfront'.

*** The Essential Recordings
Purple Pyramid CLP-0965 *Liggins; Little Willie Jackson (as, bs); Jack Kelso (ts); Shuggie Otis (g, b); Johnny Otis (d).* c. 72.

Liggins and Little Willie Jackson had been playing together for almost 30 years when they cut this set for Johnny Otis's Blues Spectrum label, and much of the programme is a journey into their shared past, amiably revisiting such key moments as 'The Honeydripper', 'Pink Champagne', 'Tanya' and 'I've Got A Right To Cry'. Among the other four cuts is a long swaggering blues, 'Stinky', which might as well have been labelled 'File Under Music To Strip By'. Shuggie Otis, who is loud to the point of obstreperousness on some other Blues Spectrum sessions, is much better behaved here. TR

Papa Lightfoot (1924–71)
VOCAL, HARMONICA

A forceful, characterful rather than virtuosic musician, Alexander Lightfoot made a handful of records in the early '50s notable for their energy if not their expertise. Rediscovered in 1969 after more than a decade outside music, he was recorded and made a few forays into the concert and festival circuit, including the 1970 Ann Arbor Blues Festival. Plans for a tour of Europe were being contemplated when he died from cardiac arrest.

*** Blues Harmonica Wizards
Official CD 5254 *Lightfoot; Tommy Ridgley, unknown (p); Edgar Blanchard, unknown (g); unknown (b); John Cooks (d).* 49–2/55.

Lightfoot's reputation rests upon the handful of releases gathered here. (The remainder of the CD is by Sammy Myers.) The aggression and rhythmic intensity of his playing on 'Wine, Women & Whiskey' and various versions of 'Mean Old Train' are enhanced by his habit of singing through the harmonica's microphone in a forced manner reminiscent of Louis Armstrong. Hence the inclusion of 'When The Saints Go Marching In'. 'Mean Old Train' and 'P. L. Blues' are based on 'The Honeydripper', with the latter echoing 'Evans Shuffle', Little Walter's version of the same theme. On the negative side, all tracks save 'After-While' are taken at the same tempo and Lightfoot's solos begin to blend into one. Shorn of an amplifier to accompany Edgar Blanchard and John 'Silver' Cooks, his limitations are evident and in stark contrast to the knockabout simplicity of other performances that memory has gilded with an extra slice of gingerbread.

**(*) Goin' Back To The Natchez Trace
Ace CDCHD 548 *Lightfoot; Carson Whitsett (p); Jerry Puckett (g); Ron Johnson (b); Tommy Tate (d).* 8–9/69.

The weight of expectation engendered by the chimeric reputation of his early work isn't wholly met by an ill-prepared session that perpetuates Lightfoot's limitations without reinforcing his strengths. He's at his best on the opening 'My Woman Is Tired Of Me Lyin'' and 'Ah Come On

Honey', the latter a solo feature hinting at more virtuosity than he's called upon to exercise elsewhere. The backing musicians quickly settle for a rhythmic pulse that encourages Lightfoot's tendency to indulge in choruses of vamping chords rather than improvisation. Five previously unissued tracks are added to the eight released on LP in 1969, of which 'Goin' Back To Natchez' is the most notable. The instrumental 'Train Tune' begins as 'Take The "A" Train' before careering off on a looping branch line. There are moments when this music is reminiscent of Buster Brown but the dead weight of the backing band prevents an under-rehearsed Lightfoot from transcending the dimensions of the studio. NS

Lightnin' Slim (1913–74)
VOCAL, GUITAR

Older than his near-contemporaries Muddy Waters and Johnny Shines, Lightnin' Slim (born Otis Hicks) was 41 when he made his first records. Though he was a capable band musician, the production style evolved by his producer Jay Miller relied upon the stark presentation of Slim's voice and guitar, augmented by harmonica and a range of 'found' percussion. This became the basis of the 'swamp blues' style for which Miller and the Excello label became famous. Later attempts to popularize Slim's material were largely unsuccessful and led to his retirement. 'Rediscovery' and a short second career re-established him as an adept at what Miller described as 'low-down gutbucket blues'. Less original than Waters or Shines, Slim was nevertheless a considerable stylist and a major contributor to postwar blues awareness.

**** It's Mighty Crazy
Ace CDCHD 587 *Lightnin' Slim; Wild Bill Phillips, Schoolboy Cleve [White], Lazy Lester (h); Ray 'Diggy Do' Meaders, Sammy Drake, Clarence 'Jockey' Etienne, poss. Roosevelt Semple (d); Monroe Vincent (perc); Carol Fran (v). 54–58.*

Lightnin' Slim's first records were released on Miller's Feature label but tapes of his debut single, 'Bad Luck' and 'Rock Me Mama', were sent to Excello and appear on this first volume of a broadly chronological set of reissues. The rich baritone voice is immediately impressive but is yet to assume its particular distinctive timbre, while his guitar playing is less proscribed and more versatile than was later deemed necessary. The distinctive four-bar harmonica break that came to identify a classic Lightnin' Slim performance had yet to be formulated, so Phillips and Cleve, though hardly virtuosi, get whole choruses to prove it. The iconic 'blow your harmonica, son' is there from the start, as is a rudimentary form of timekeeping only later qualifying as drumming. Miller's newly defined 'swamp' sound required the use of bizarre percussive elements, both real and contrived, alongside or instead of a drumkit. Though novel at the time, these additions now sound factitious and at times infantile.

Copyright information to the contrary, Slim was more often an interpreter than a songwriter, recasting others' material when he wasn't relying on Miller's imagination. Thus 'Feelin' Good', 'Boogie Chillen', 'I'm A Man', 'Still A Fool' and 'Hoodoo Man' are all spectrally present. Six of these 24 tracks are taken from a now deleted US Excello collection, *I'm Evil* (CD 3002), covering a broader time-frame but including alternative takes of four songs included here. Miller recorded Slim prolifically for almost a decade, retaining alternative takes and unheard songs that subsequently appeared on the Flyright CDs *Rolling Stone* (FLYCD 08) and *King Of The Swamp Blues* (FLYCD 47), also deleted. These and the present collection are indispensable for an understanding of the formulation of Lightnin' Slim's unique style and appeal.

*** Rooster Blues
Hip-O HIPD 40134 *Lightnin' Slim; Lazy Lester (h); Katie Webster (p); Guitar Gable (g); unknown (b); Roosevelt Semple, Kenneth Sample (d). 55–59.*

*** Rooster Blues/Lightnin' Slim's Bell Ringer
Ace CDCHD 517 *As above, except Webster also plays o. 55–65.*

Hip-O reissue the original Excello album *Rooster Blues* with three tracks added, while Ace combine it with Slim's next Excello LP, duplicating six tracks on *It's Mighty Crazy*. Neither of the originals was compiled with continuity in mind but *Rooster Blues* is largely taken from 1957–59, whereas *Bell Ringer* concentrates on 1961–63, adding isolated items from as early as 1955. Consequently the second half of the Ace bluntly juxtaposes an early 'Mean Old Lonesome Train' with 'Baby Please Come Back', a jangling, organ-dominated, cheesy trifle. Similarly, an atmospheric re-creation of Wolf's Patton phase, 'Somebody Knockin'', and a complete rewrite of 'Don't Start Me Talking' are trivialized by the swamp pop of 'Have Mercy On Me Baby'. These later productions often betray their lack of purpose by fading out as the singer is in mid-verse. The focus of the earlier album has no such problems, combining such repertoire stalwarts as 'G.I. Slim', 'Hoo-Doo Blues', 'Long Leanie Woman' and 'My Starter Won't Work'.

***(*) Nothin' But The Devil
Ace CDCHD 616 *Lightnin' Slim; Lazy Lester (h); Tal Miller (p); Guitar Gable, Al Foreman (g); Bobby McBride, Rufus Thibodeaux (b); Clarence Etienne, Roosevelt Sample, Warren Storm (d). 58–61.*

This is middle-period Slim, where formulaic arrangements begin to emerge, a slow blues pattern that draws upon Lightnin' Hopkins guitar riffs ('My Starter Won't Work', 'Feelin' Awful Blue', 'My Little Angel Child') and a medium-fast boogie with stop-time verses ('Long Leanie Mama', 'Too Close Blues', 'Cool Down Baby'). The mania for 'box and broom' percussion has subsided but still makes an occasional appearance. Most significant here is the consolidation of the partnership between Slim and Lazy Lester. Direct influences are less apparent; 'Too Close Blues' and 'I Just Don't Know' are little changed from the Sonny Boy Williamson II originals but 'Death Valley Blues' quickly departs from Big Boy Crudup's. The previously unissued 'I Gonna Leave' follows the arrangement of Muddy's 'She's All Right', while 'Driftin' Blues', though credited to Charles Brown, has but a tenuous connection. The 1960/61 sessions see the arrival of a second guitarist, usually Al Foreman, taking solos on 'I'm Tired Waitin' Baby' and 'Hello Mary Lee'. Slim's commitment falters on occasions, reducing the mystique created by his earlier recordings.

**(*) Winter Time Blues
Ace CDCHD 674 *Lightnin' Slim; U. J. Meaux (o); Sonny Martin, unknown (p); Al Foreman (g); Bobby McBride, Rufus Thibodeaux (b); Austin Broussard (d). 62–65.*

These final sessions represent an accelerating dilution of Slim's essential qualities. More often than not, he is no longer playing guitar and his accompanists display more competence than inspiration, thus denying any song a chance of individuality. Slim himself sounds unfocused and uncommitted to songs he's had no hand in writing. His final attempt at 'Lonely Stranger' (adapted from Bill Gaither's 'Rocky Mountain Blues') is one of the few occasions the classic swamp-blues sound is re-created. At the opposite extreme, 'If You Ever Need Me' is pure swamp pop, complete with monotone recitative. Three tracks, including an alternative take of 'Baby Please Come Back To Me', contain an alien organ presence that makes a travesty of the artist's previous repertoire. Other previously unissued songs, 'Sittin' And Thinkin'', 'I Can Hear My Baby Calling' and a 'Lonesome Cabin Blues' that combines elements of Sonny Boy Williamson II and Mercy Dee Walton, drag by at bland tempos, as though everyone present has lost interest but not quite pride. This is what happened when blues began to reach beyond its natural constituency, seeking to snare an eager but younger and thus less discerning audience.

** High And Low Down/Over Easy
Ace CDCHD 578 *Lightnin' Slim; Stacy Goss, Mike Stough, Sonny Royal, Charles Rose (brass, reeds); Tippy Armstrong (h); Clayton Ivy (o, p); Jesse Carr (g); Bob Wary (b); Fred Proudly (d). 71.*

Excello's foray into purpose-built album sessions was short and less than wildly successful. On those terms, Lightnin' Slim's trip to the Quinvy Studio in Sheffield, Alabama, can't be categorized a total failure, but by any other yardstick it's a mess. Producer Jerry (Swamp Dog) Williams laid down ten functional backing tracks and justified his arranger's fee with some panoramically voiced horn charts that flattered his ego while ignoring the source material. They also failed to enhance his artist's limited but distinctive vocal powers. In a programme that includes four of his own compositions and blues standards such as 'Things I Used To Do', 'My Babe' and 'Can't Hold Out Much Longer', Slim struggles to make his presence and his bedrock blues guitar patterns felt. This is his *Brass And The Blues* and *Electric Mud* rolled into one, here combined (because of its brevity) with Whispering Smith's own baptism in brass, the album *Over Easy*. *High And Low Down*, resequenced and grandiosely retitled *King Of The Louisiana Swamp Blues*, was also issued on Aim 2008.

*** Blue Lightning
[Indigo IGOCD 2002] *Lightnin' Slim; Laurie Garman (h); Pete Wingfield (p); Paul Butler, Rick Hayward (g); John Best (b); Kenny Lamb (d). 3/72.*

Slim was already in London to work with producer Mike Vernon on *London Gumbo* (not currently available), so the same team made use of the Marquee Club's studio facilities to cut a live session that then remained unissued for 20 years. The backing band, otherwise working as Jellybread, was led by pianist Wingfield, with Garman and Hayward notable additions. 'Mama, Talk To Your Daughter', 'The Sky Is Crying' and 'Help Me Spend My Gold' (the last actually Jimmy Reed's 'The Sun Is Shining') had already formed part of the *Gumbo* sessions. The first half of the set works well; Slim is generous with allocating solo time and the band plays with something approaching restraint most of the time. 'G.I. Slim' is performed solo, while 'I Want You To Love Me' and 'Bed Bug Blues' strive to emulate the classic swamp-blues sound with qualified success, although Garman sounds less confident. The final selections are likewise less successful, suggesting rehearsal time hadn't stretched this far. Slim is in fine form throughout and his stage persona carries the lapses when they occur, making this a surprisingly enjoyable if undemanding experience. NS

Li'l Brian (born 1972)
VOCAL, ACCORDION

Brian Terry and his band, the Zydeco Travelers, are Houston-based. Terry began playing at 13 and was sending demo tapes to Rounder a year later.

*** Fresh
Rounder CD 2136 *Li'l Brian; Lee Allen Zeno (g, perc); Patrick Terry, Russell 'Sly' Dorion (g, v); Emerson 'E. J.' Jackson (b); Charles 'Red/Cool Daddy' LaMark II (d, v); Anthony 'Peanut' Chenevert (rb, perc); Scott Billington (v). 9/94.*

**(*) Z-Funk
Rounder CD 2146 *Li'l Brian; Scott Billington (h, v); David Torkanowsky (o); Patrick 'Heavy P' Terry (g, v); Lee Allen Zeno (g); Emerson 'E. J.' Jackson (b); Charles 'Red/Cool Daddy' LaMark II (d, perc, v); Kenneth 'Skin' Terry (rb); Darius 'Third Leg' Barnett (rap); Alena Zeno, Chantelle Durall (v). 10/96.*

**(*) Funky Nation
Tomorrow TMR 70003 *Li'l Brian; Stanley 'Buckwheat' Dural (o, clavinet); Patrick 'Heavy P' Terry (g, v); Emerson 'Funky E' Jackson (b, v); Albert 'Tony' Stewart (d); Mandrell 'Green Eyed Bandit' Rideau (rb). 99.*

Li'l Brian blends elements of contemporary R&B and hip-hop with zydeco. It's apparent from tracks like 'Allons Manger' that he and the band on *Fresh* have a good grasp of traditional zydeco's lexicon, and their augmentation of it with pulsating bass and funk drumming is craftily done; this is most obvious on 'Sugar B', an affecting waltz-time song about Terry's daughter which alternates between traditional and double-kick rhythms. The disc's most radical venture is 'FuNkABlUeSa-DeCo', with rap lyrics and chromatic bass breaks; there's another well-integrated rap interlude and some neat voicebox guitar on Paul Kelly's 'Hooked, Hogtied And Collared'.

Subsequent CDs have documented a decreasing engagement with times past. Even those who don't find the hip-hop elements on *Z-Funk* excessive are likely to be disappointed by its title track, which is just a not very good rap with backing that includes an accordion. 'Tang The Hump' is one of the few tracks to repeat *Fresh*'s successful synthesis of old and new; an uncouth revival of James Brown's 'Back Up And Try It Again' (in two mixes) most certainly doesn't, and 'Sunday Walk' is appropriately pedestrian. All compositions on *Funky Nation* are by the Terry brothers. They make an occasional obeisance to tradition, most notably on 'Uncle Cliff', but mainly venture further into hip-hop; the occasional ballads mine a rich vein of banality. ('If we all had the mind of a black butterfly, there would be no crime, no need to cry.' Er, right.) Two tracks feature the paranoid dissing of rivals that's crept into zydeco from gangsta rap. CS

Charley Lincoln (1900–1963)
VOCAL, GUITAR

Charley Hicks was the brother, two and a half years older, of Robert Hicks (Barbecue Bob). He is thought to have learned guitar from Savannah Weaver, mother of the bluesman Curley Weaver. In the '20s, living in Atlanta, he played with his

brother, and in 1927 they both began recording for Columbia, Charley adopting the surname Lincoln, but the younger man proved much the more successful. Robert's early death and other misfortunes drove Lincoln to alcoholism and eventually to jail, where he died.

*** Charlie Lincoln & Willie Baker (1927–1930)
RST Blues Documents BDCD-6027 *Lincoln*. 11/27–4/30.

Although in his approach he is superficially similar to his brother, and to Atlanta-area contemporaries such as Curley Weaver and Willie Baker, Lincoln has a deeper, heavier voice and lacks Bob's speed as a guitarist. 'Chain Gang Trouble' is the old common-stock song 'Ruben's Train'/'900 Miles', sung as if from within penitentiary walls, and the air of the vaudeville stage hangs about 'If It Looks Jelly Shakes Like Jelly It Must Be Gelatine', but the rest of his dozen solo recordings are conventional blues. 'Mama Don't Rush Me' is a number he may have got from Willie Baker (who shares this CD), or vice versa. A couple of Lincoln's early sides are prefaced with bursts of laughter, and he was billed on the labels as 'Laughing Charley'; he repeats the trick on his two two-part comic duets with Bob, which are included on the latter's *Vol. 1* (Document DOCD-5046) and *Vol. 3* (DOCD-5048). TR

Hip Linkchain (1936–89)
VOCAL, GUITAR

Willie Richard's father took the name 'Linkchain' from one of the tools of his work as a logger and passed it on to his son, who also acquired the childhood sobriquet 'Hipstick'. He grew up in Mississippi, moved to Chicago in the early '50s and formed a band with Tyrone Davis. In the '80s, with albums for MCM and JSP behind him, he toured in Europe and North America.

** I Am On My Way
Storyville STCD 8039 *Linkchain*; Jimmy Miller (g); Ernest Gatewood (b); Tyrone Centenary (d). 11/76.

**(*) Airbusters
Evidence ECD 26038 *Linkchain*; Otis White (o, p); 'Barrelhouse' Chuck (p); Rich Kirch, Jon McDonald (g); Frank Bandy, 'Big' John Trice (b); Ted Harvey, Robert 'Huckleberry Hound' Wright (d). 7/84–5/87.

I Am On My Way is the MCM album (credited, as frequently happened to Linkchain, to 'Hip Lankchan'), and like many others on that label (see Jimmy Dawkins, Jimmy Johnson, 'Big Voice' Odom, etc.) is only the roughest of guides to the artist's talent. He and Jimmy Miller get some way down and dirty as they throw the guitar lead back and forth, but the settings are uncompromisingly uniform and the leader's gritty vocals are not recorded with enough presence to rise out of the ensemble. Nor does he seem very engaged by the material, which is hardly surprising since it's mostly club standards like 'Last Night', 'All Your Love', 'Black Night' and 'Somebody Loan Me A Dime'. Linkchain *was* on his way, but this album wasn't the boost he needed. *Airbusters*, though it came too late in his life to be much help, was better. Working with mostly his own songs, not all of which are totally formulaic, he sounds more involved in his performance, and his decision to draw on two sessions with different bands injects a little textural variety into the programme. The majority come from an '85 session which was considerably strengthened by the presence of Barrelhouse Chuck. In the absence of *Change My Blues* (Teardrop 1006), which appears to be no longer available, *Airbusters* is the only album that represents Linkchain's talent fairly, but, to be equally fair to the reader, it's still generic Chicago blues by a second-rank musician. TR

Errol Linton
VOCAL, HARMONICA, GUITAR

Linton was born in Brixton in south London, where his Jamaican parents had settled in the late '50s, and began to play harmonica in his teens. While busking on the Brixton Underground (subway) station he was heard by the BBC radio producer John Walters, an encounter that led to radio spots and a 1991 BBC-TV documentary. During the '90s Linton played regularly with singer/guitarist 'Pigmeat' Pete Smith (1952–99), later forming his own band. He still busks, and London commuters using Oxford Circus Underground station are familiar with the rangy figure who sets up his amp and plays long stream-of-harmoniconsciousness blues.

*** Vibing It!
Ruby RR 01 *Linton*; Dom Pipkin (o, p); Richard Rhoden, Adam Blake (g); Jean-Pierre Lampé (b); Phil Myers and/or Sam Kelly (d); Tyrone Balkisoon (wb, bgo); band (v). 98.

*** Roots Stew
Ruby RR 02 *Linton*; Chris Lee (t); Mike Hobart (as); Dom Pipkin (o, p); Adam Blake (g, b); Jean-Pierre Lampé, Dave Farren (b); Phil Myers (d, perc); Sam Kelly (d); Tyrone Balkisoon (wb, cga); Mark Payne, Susan Payne (v, sp). 00–01.

To get a measure of Linton's stamina you need to catch him busking, when he'll stretch a blues to 20 or 30 minutes, interweaving voice and harmonica with the intricacy, and some of the sound, of Sonny Boy Williamson II. His records, credited to Errol Linton's Blues Vibe, are more relaxed affairs, mostly three- or four-minute songs with accompaniments that switch easily from sedately pretty to bustling. The repertoire on *Vibing It!* is partly original, partly drawn from Howlin' Wolf, J. B. Lenoir, Papa Lightfoot and other reliable sources, but wholly blues, and Linton's only clear reference to his Caribbean heritage seems to be the emphasis on percussion. *Roots Stew* develops the cross-cultural theme, mixing basic blues ingredients with herbs and spices from other musical cuisines. It's a fusion that in other artists' hands has sometimes blown up in their faces, but Linton and his partners succeed in integrating the '50s Chicago style of 'Too Many Cooks', 'Eyes Keep Me In Trouble' or 'She's Gone' and the gentle reggae rhythms of 'Man Shot Down' or 'Skank Easy' and preserving the flavours of both. TR

Mance Lipscomb (1895–1976)
VOCAL, GUITAR

Not until he was 65 did Mance Lipscomb add recording and playing on the folk music circuit to being the finest musician in Navasota, Texas. Until then he'd spent most of his life sharecropping six days a week and playing all night at weekend dances. He was seconding his father's fiddle playing at 12, and estimated his repertoire at 350 songs, including blues, church songs, waltzes, polkas, ballads, children's songs, turn-of-the-century pop songs, rags, boogies and rock 'n' roll. A living almanac of 20th-century black folk music, Lipscomb was also a wise and dignified man; his life, times and personality are vividly presented in I Say Me For A Parable, *an oral autobiography compiled by Glen Alyn.*

**** Texas Songster
Arhoolie CD 306 *Lipscomb. 6/60–11/64.*
**(*) Texas Blues Guitar
Arhoolie CD 001 *Lipscomb. 6/60–11/64.*
**** Captain, Captain!
Arhoolie CD 465 *Lipscomb. 8/60–4/66.*
**(*) Trouble In Mind
Rhino RHM2 7829 *Lipscomb. 7/61.*
**** You Got To Reap What You Sow
Arhoolie CD 398 *Lipscomb. 5/64.*
**** Live! At The Cabale
Arhoolie CD 482 *Lipscomb. 11/64–72.*
** Trouble In Mind
Aim 1306 *Lipscomb. 65.*
*** Live At The 1966 Berkeley Blues Festival
Arhoolie CD 484 *Lipscomb. 4/66.*
***(*) Pure! Texas Country Blues
Arhoolie CD 9026 *Lipscomb; Powell St John (h); Mike Birnbaum, Charlie Pritchard (g); Frank Lipscomb (b); Wayne Davis (d). 12/68–5/73.*

When Chris Strachwitz and Mack McCormick turned up on his porch in 1960, Mance Lipscomb recorded 23 songs in five hours, all perfect on the first take. Consistency was his watchword, and 'constitution of an ox' doesn't begin to describe his stamina. Mastery of ten keys in standard tuning, and of open tuning for slide guitar pieces, kept his hands from tiring; aged 77, he played for 17 hours out of 24 at a Fourth of July picnic.

Those CDs which disappoint do so for presentational reasons. *Trouble In Mind* is a 2,500-copy limited edition which greatly expands an LP issued on Reprise. The separation of voice and guitar into different speakers is distracting, and there is wow on 'Rocks And Gravel Make A Solid Road'. Mance plays 12-string guitar on Aim, which makes for an intriguingly different sound, but the recording was made in an echoing room through one microphone, and the guitar overwhelms his voice. The Berkeley concert is shared with Clifton Chenier and Lightnin' Hopkins; Lipscomb contributes seven songs and modestly describes himself as a fice (a small dog) in comparison to the other two, but doesn't seem to bond with the audience. *Texas Blues Guitar* has no annotation; although available separately, it was issued to supplement the guitar tutor *Mance Lipscomb: Texas Blues Guitar Solos.* Some tracks on the mid-price *Pure! Texas Country Blues* show a slight loss of vigour, and it's not as cohesive as the other Arhoolie releases, but there are many good things here, including two tantalizing songs from a session where Lipscomb played electric guitar, supported by bass and drums.

All the other Arhoolie albums are outstanding. The range of *Texas Songster* is particularly wide, from the unique murder ballad 'Freddie' to 'Big Boss Man'. *Captain, Captain!* concentrates more on blues, as did Mance when playing for his new audience, but it also includes a jolly 'Heel And Toe Polka' and the marvellous 'Mr. Tom's Rag'. It also features a version of 'Tom Moore's Farm', which acidly describes and protests against the brutal paternalism which was the reality of sharecropping in the Brazos Bottoms. Further versions appear on *Live At The Cabale,* where Lipscomb performs with exceptional commitment, and on *You Got To Reap What You Sow.* Any of these discs is a good place to get acquainted with Lipscomb's music in its almost infinite variety. CS

Aynsley Lister (born 1976)
VOCAL, GUITAR

Lister grew up in Manchester, picking up the guitar at the age of eight and quickly revealing a natural talent. He formed his own band at 18 and gained the attention of the public, and of Ruf Records' Thomas Ruf, after successful performances at the Colne blues festival playing support to Walter Trout, who duly offered his patronage.

**(*) Aynsley Lister
Ruf 1031 *Lister; Jonny Dyke (kb); Walter Trout (g, v); Matt Kay (b); Wayne Proctor (d). 10/98.*

Lister has made as impressive a start in his career as any of the younger British bluesmen. Both writing and playing potential are evident in his debut, which, though quite good, sounds like the work of an artist searching for the right route to express his music on record. A string of blues-laced songs have solid substance but lack the sonic gleam that makes for compulsive listening. Through sludgy production, many of the riffs don't punch enough, and they sometimes drop uneasily into sparser sections that struggle to maintain the atmosphere. But 'She's A Woman' has slick blues licks, Eddie Boyd's 'Five Long Years' finds Lister in tasteful ballad mode, and 'Identity Blues' slips from a warm slide introduction into a delicious full-band groove. Perhaps the standout moment is 'Since I Met You Baby', where Lister, soloing fluently, holds his own next to his vastly more experienced guest, Walter Trout, and they trade off with gusto between Lister's wrenching vocals.

***(*) Everything I Need
Ruf 1055 *Lister; Jesse Davey (o, perc); Matt Kay (b); Wayne Proctor (d). 00.*

What was missing from Lister's first outing was the edge, especially in the arrangement and treatment of the sounds, that was needed to boost his promising original compositions. Six reappear here, emboldened, authoritative and propped up with snappy, varied guitar lines. It's not all strictly blues, but the songs never lean too far away, which helps to ground Lister in an intelligible artistic identity. The roaring title track slips from Led Zep riff-rock into an ethereal breakdown where big, sweeping guitar feedback reminds one of fellow Mancunian Johnny Marr. (It is understandably a live favourite.) In the catchy 'Angel O' Mine' Lister reveals a voice that's both clean and commanding, before employing a grittier delivery in a superb, unpredictable cover of Tony Joe White's 'As The Crow Flies'. Meanwhile the funky 'Soundman' and 'I Believe' find Lister in his element. Other tracks include some formulaic poppy numbers that dangerously suggest Bryan Adams, but a credible solo electric version of the Hendrix classic 'Little Wing', all mellow tones and smooth licks, is nicely juxtaposed with the final (hidden) track, a recast, faster version of 'Identity Blues' with furious acoustic slide playing and foot stomping. The best album Lister has made to date, by some distance.

*** **Supakev N Pilchards**
Ruf 1074 *Lister. 7/01.*

A stripped-down solo performance of popular blues and one original. While Lister is on top playing form, the absence of his own repertoire prompts comparison with the plethora of performers who play such classics but with greater range. His guitarmanship is awesome at points, especially during his solos in John Lee Hooker's 'Mad Man Blues' and Lightnin' Hopkins's 'Come Go Home With Me'. Four Robert Johnson numbers, however, are so formularized that they lose all the vigour and subtlety of their originator. Too often Lister is merely trundling along an overcrowded blues highway of 12-bar progressions and competent singing. Even so, if you've liked anything else by him, this is certainly worth a listen.

*(*) **All Or Nothing**
Ruf 1082 *Lister; Geoff Downes (o); James Townend (b); Alex Thomas (d, v); Greg Haver (perc, strange noises); John Payne (v). 02.*

The title suggests steamy conviction, and the cover supports the idea: Lister catching his guitar, seemingly from the heavens, against a fiery sunset sky. All set for an incendiary, epic journey into the unknown? No: a batch of ordinary songs, further marred by lazy arrangements, clichéd lyrics and colourless singing. The feel of the record doesn't change until the (now obligatory) hidden last track reveals a pretty acoustic instrumental. If you want blues, Lister does it far better elsewhere than on the masked occasions where it crops up here.

*** **Aynsley Lister Live!**
Ruf 1100 *Lister; James Townend (b); Sarah Jones (d). 03/04.*

Another concert recording, this time placing the Aynsley Lister Band in the spotlight. The material is almost exclusively Lister's but the trio sound is at times too thin and fails to convey on record what might have been a electrifying experience on the night. Nevertheless, the album crystallizes nuances that have become trademarks, such as the momentary crooning contrasted with a croaky rasp, and blistering blues-rock riffs and stirring solos à la Jimmy Page, full of movement and controlled force. The extended ad-lib instrumentals inevitably become repetitive as the album progresses, but a late change of tone with the pensive 'Sometimes It Gets 2 Me', which is pure Stevie Ray Vaughan, provides breathing space. The version of 'Soundman' is sparkling, too, and the set includes some new songs that hold out the enticing prospect of Lister's next studio venture. RR

Virginia Liston (c. 1890–1932)
VOCAL

Liston was singing blues in Philadelphia by 1912. She settled in New York with her husband, Sam Gray, and they toured in revue until the marriage broke up in 1925. Shortly after her last recording session she moved to St Louis, remarried, and thereafter devoted herself to church work.

** **Virginia Liston – Vol. 1 (1923–1924)**
Document DOCD-5446 *Liston; Louis Armstrong, unknown (c); Charlie Irvis (tb); Ernest Elliott (cl); Sidney Bechet (cl, ss); unknown (as); Clarence Williams, poss. Porter Grainger (p); Buddy Christian (bj); poss. Sylvester Weaver (g); Sam Gray (v). 9/23–10/24.*

** **Virginia Liston – Vol. 2 (1924–1926)/Lavinia Turner (1921–1922)**
Document DOCD-5447 *Liston; unknown (c); Ernest Elliott (cl); Clarence Williams (o, p); poss. Sam Gray, unknown (p); unknown (md); Buddy Christian, unknown (bj). 10/24–5/26.*

Liston's voice on the first of these discs is small and colourless, and her pitch is sometimes insecure. Clarence Williams is nearly ubiquitous, and usually listless. Many of the songs are undistinguished, too; Bessie Smith's 'Jail House Blues', which isn't, is well out of Liston's league. Her husband duets on two numbers, and turns out to be an unctuously syrupy baritone. Two titles accompanied by Clarence Williams' Blue Five are inevitably the best, but even here, Liston manages to make 'You've Got The Right Key But The Wrong Keyhole' – on which Bechet and Armstrong try to solo at the same time, with unfortunate results – unequivocally dull.

Vol. 2 starts with a lively 'Night Latch Key Blues', and while it's never great, Liston's singing on her last 13 recordings is often much improved. Her final, four-song session features a confident, anonymous cornettist; it's by some distance her most expressive and enthusiastic work, and one wonders what she might have done had she not retired. The road to that farewell is unfortunately potholed by three desperately awful numbers on which Clarence Williams plays funereal, inept reed-organ, and Liston's singing matches him for dullness.

It's Lavinia Turner's misfortune that her ten recordings handily complete *Vol. 2*; Turner was another comparatively small-voiced singer, and her material hovers on the border between blues and Tin Pan Alley, but her delivery is invariably bursting with pep and personality, and she's well worth hearing. Her musicians match her for liveliness; their identities are usually conjectural, but James P. Johnson's unmistakable and splendid piano is heard solo on two tracks, and he leads his Harmony Seven on another two. CS

Little Buster & The Soul Brothers
GROUP

Edward 'Little Buster' Forehand (born 1942) left North Carolina in his teens to live with his sister in Long Island. He was already playing guitar, and was soon doing so for a living. In the '60s he recorded a few singles and frequently opened concerts for top soul acts. In later years he played at clubs in Long Island and Manhattan, where he was appreciated for his command of the classic soul/R&B repertoire.

(*) **Work Your Show
Fedora FCD 5020 *Jerry Harshaw, Timothy 'Saxy Rick' Richardson (ts); Robert Schlesinger (kb); Allen Levy (b); Frank Anstiss (d). 12/99.*

Right On Time! (Bullseye Blues CD BB 9562) (1995) put Little Buster before a new audience and won him a lot of notice. Its contents were almost exclusively '60s- and '70s-styled soul and R&B numbers, mostly original, generally well written and performed with conviction, but beyond the reach of this book. *Work Your Show* is another matter. There are none of Buster's songs at all, but a handful of mostly medium-grade soul and R&B numbers and half a dozen blues standards – and we do mean standards: 'Hi Heel Sneakers', 'Ain't That Lovin' You Baby', etc. He deals with most of these straightforwardly but succinctly, taking his time only in B. B. King's 'How Blue Can You Get'. King has stated that Buster is 'the only person who could fill his shoes'; Buster, who is clearly a man with a sense of proportion, finds that hard to believe, and, with the best will towards his work, one can see why he would. However, at the end of the album he holds the floor alone with his electric guitar and delivers Lightnin' Hopkins's 'Mojo Hand' with vim and invention you wouldn't have suspected he possessed. If he has another dozen performances like that in him, there's a fascinating album waiting to be made. TR

Little Charlie & The Nightcats
GROUP

When Charlie Baty (born 1953) and Rick Estrin (born 1949) met in 1976, they were both harmonica players; Baty changed over to guitar and they formed a band. For about a decade they were chiefly known around Sacramento and the San Francisco Bay Area, but after signing with Alligator they moved on to the national stage, and in recent years they have appeared at several European festivals.

*** All The Way Crazy
Alligator ALCD 4753 *Nancy Wright, Mike Amato (s); Rick Estrin (h, v); Charlie Baty (g); Jay Peterson (b, v); Dobie Strange (d); J. J. Malone (v).* 86.

*** Disturbing The Peace
Alligator ALCD 4761 *Rick Estrin (h, v); St James Bryant (o); Little Charlie Baty (g); Jay Peterson (b); Dobie Strange (d).* 88.

**(*) The Big Break
Alligator ALCD 4776 *As above, except Jimmy Pugh (p) replaces Bryant.* 89.

*** Captured Live
Alligator ALCD 4794 *Rick Estrin (h, v); Little Charlie Baty (g); Brad Lee Sexton (b, v); Dobie Strange (d).* 90.

Somewhere on *Captured Live* Rick Estrin introduces Charlie Baty to the audience as 'the most unusual guitar player I've ever met'. It's a fair description of a musician who can play rockabilly, jazz and several kinds of blues, all with equal facility and prodigious inventiveness. On tearaway pieces like 'Eyes Like A Cat' (*All The Way Crazy*, *Captured Live*), 'Run Me Down' (*Disturbing The Peace*, *Captured Live*) and 'Kansas City Woman' (*The Big Break*) he sounds like the product of an unholy union between Charlie Christian and Scotty Moore, but he can also stretch out in a long, slow blues, as he trenchantly proves with a 12-minute version of Buddy Guy's 'Ten Years Ago' (*Captured Live*).

The other USP of this entertaining band is Estrin, a clever harmonica player in the mewing style of Sonny Boy Williamson II and a dispenser of hip narrations; each album contains at least one or two of the latter, such as 'Clothes Line' (*All The Way Crazy*) and 'The Big Break'. Here the paternity might have been Cab Calloway and the guy who did the talking bits for The Coasters. Estrin is not so effective on straight, slow blues, where his delivery is too mannered to let the song speak for itself, but such numbers are a lowish priority for a band whose manifesto, according to Baty, is 'We play for dancing and partying.' With a reliable pulse from bass and drums, the Nightcats are versatile enough to need no outside help, and the saxes and keyboard players who contribute to the first three CDs do so very sparingly.

Incidentally, those three albums also have amusingly set-dressed cover images, though they were even more effective as LP sleeves.

**(*) Night Vision
Alligator ALCD 4812 *Jeff Lewis (t); Tim Devine (ts, bs); Rick Estrin (h, v); Jimmy Pugh (o, p); Joe Louis Walker (g, v, prod); Little Charlie Baty (g); Brad Lee Sexton (b); Dobie Strange (d); Donnie Woodruff (v).* 92.

**(*) Straight Up!
Alligator ALCD 4829 *John Firmin (ts); Rick Estrin (h, v); Jimmy Pugh (kb); Little Charlie Baty, Rusty Zinn (g); Ronnie James Weber (b); Dobie Strange (d).* 94/95.

*** DeLuxe Edition
Alligator ALCD 5603 *As for all above CDs.* 86–94/95.

**(*) Shadow Of The Blues
Alligator ALCD 4862 *Rick Estrin (h, g, v); Jimmy Pugh (o, p); Little Charlie Baty (g); Ronnie James Weber (b); June Core (d, maracas).* 98.

**(*) That's Big!
Alligator ALCD 4883 *John Firmin (ts); Rob Sudduth (bs); Rick Estrin (h, v); Steve Lucky (o, p); Chris Siebert (p); Little Charlie Baty, Rusty Zinn (g); Frankie Randall (b); Joey Ventittelli (d); Icepick James Harman (v).* 01/02.

**(*) Nine Lives
Alligator ALCD 4902 *John Firmin (ts); Scott Peterson (bs); Rick Estrin (h, v); Chris Siebert (p); Little Charlie Baty (g); Lorenzo Farrell (b); J. Hansen (d, perc, v); The Original Faded Boogie Quartet (Rusty Zinn, George Zinn, R. H. Hairless, Ronnie James Weber) (v).* 03/04.

From *Night Vision* onwards, the band's albums have delivered at the efficient but unambitious level of 'business as usual'. A pattern has emerged: a couple of guitar instrumentals, one or two harmonica instrumentals, one or two blues oldies and a high proportion of songs written or co-written by Estrin, which he sings like Percy Mayfield on tranquillizers. By now, listeners will presumably have decided how they feel about Estrin's musical persona, and those for whom it's too style-over-substance will have handed back their fanclub membership cards, unless they're happy to buy the band's albums for Baty's guitar playing. This is unfailingly bright, and, if there's less of the rockabilly stuff, there are always exhilarating jump-blues instrumentals like 'Gerontology' (*Straight Up!*), 'Percolatin'' (*Shadow Of The Blues*), 'Bayview Jump' (*That's Big!*) and 'Tag (You're It)' (*Nine Lives*). The non-original blues, such as 'Cryin' Won't Help You' (*Night Vision*), 'Too Close Together' (*Straight Up!*) or 'Steady Rollin' Man' (*That's Big!*), are very well done by both principals, the last a tour de force of Estrin's voice and harmonica with just a slapped bass for accompaniment. It's probably unrealistic to wish that the band would play a few more of those and take some of the writing responsibility off Estrin's drape-jacketed shoulders, but it might have a refreshing effect. His lyrics are fairly consistently quirky but their tunes have become rather conventional, and assertions like Alligator's 'His songs stand shoulder to shoulder with those of Willie Dixon and Leiber and Stoller' receive only fitful support from these albums. 'Circling The Drain' on *Nine Lives* is weirdly gripping, but when it comes to funny the best thing he's done in a while is the ingeniously suggestive 'Dirty Dealin' Mama' (*Shadow Of The Blues*), which is by other writers.

DeLuxe Edition is a sampler drawn from the first six albums, with a slight bias in favour of the first and last. TR

Little Joe Blue (1934–90)
VOCAL, GUITAR

Joseph Valery was born in Vicksburg, Mississippi, and raised across the river in Louisiana. As a young man he moved to Detroit, where he returned after army service and worked in blues clubs. In the late '50s he settled in Reno, Nevada. Working with the producer and songwriter Fats Washington, he had a minor hit in 1966 with 'Dirty Work Going On', which led to further singles for Checker and Jewel and, in the '70s and '80s, albums for various small labels.

** **The Very Best Of Joe Blue**
Collectables COL-5744 *Little Joe Blue; unknowns (brass, reeds, h, kb, o, p, syn, g, b, d, perc, v).* early '70s.

His friends maintained that Little Joe Blue 'never tried to imitate anybody', which is what friends are for. To the disinterested listener he was nothing less, and only occasionally something more, than a stand-in for B. B. King. On tracks like 'Shopping Instead' (i.e. 'I Got A Mind To Give Up Living') or the two-part 'Give Me An Hour In Your Garden' ('… and I'll show you how to plant a rose') he sounds so like his model that even a seasoned ear could be deceived. What gives the game away is the low-budget production. (The CD was derived from two albums Blue made with producer Mel Alexander, issued on Space and Kris.) But on his own hit, 'Dirty Work Going On', he shows that he could find an independent voice; pity it's so badly recorded. There is some decent guitar playing here and there, but as to whether it's Blue's, there are no clues. TR

Little Mike & The Tornadoes
GROUP

New Yorker Mike Markowitz (born 1955) formed his first band in 1978. He also accompanied Pinetop Perkins and Hubert Sumlin when they played in the NY area, and produced and played on albums by both.

*** (*) **Heart Attack**
Blind Pig BP 73990 *Mike Markowitz (h, p, v); Paul Butterfield (h, v); Pinetop Perkins (p, v); Collin Jr Green, Hubert Sumlin, Ronnie Earl, Big Daddy Kinsey, Tony O (g); Brad Vickers (b); Rob Piazza (d, v); Pete DeCoste (d).* 87–90.

With help like that, the band could hardly go wrong. The only drawback, from the Tornadoes' point of view, is that the guests' contributions might take up too much of the listener's attention. It's certainly hard not to listen closely to the five tracks with Butterfield, both for the quality of his harmonica playing and because this was one of his last sessions. 'Me And The Blues', with its melodic memory of his recording of 'I've Got A Mind To Give Up Living', has a special poignancy. Earl slashes his signature on two numbers, while Perkins plays with casual authority on five, taking the vocal on 'Ida B'. So what's left? Likeably unaffected singing and playing by Markowitz, original songs that are something more than generic, and a consistency of approach that the guests do nothing to obscure.

** (*) **Payday**
Blind Pig BP 74992 *Mike Markowitz (h, p, v); Ray Sabatello (o, v); John Edelmann, Warren Hayes (g); Ken Stearns (b); Dave Sweet (d); Bobby Nigro (v).* 92?

** (*) **Flynn's Place**
Flying Fish FF 70641 *Mike Markowitz (h, p, v); Mitch Margold (o); Kenny Stearns (md, g, v); John Edelmann (g, v); Joe Fontenot (b, v); Bobby 'Boom Boom' Einreinhofer (d, v).* 95?

Another risk element of *Heart Attack* was that it would be a hard act to follow. Although both Markowitz and Edelmann are talented and diligent players, neither *Payday* nor *Flynn's Place* has any moments of brilliance or surprise to lift it out of the crowd of albums by competent Chicago-style bands. Markowitz's insistence on using almost exclusively original material is admirable in principle, but one would applaud it more warmly if most of the songs were not so doggedly orthodox. TR

Little Milton (1934–2005)
VOCAL, GUITAR

Born near Leland, Mississippi, Milton Campbell began playing guitar in his teens and worked in clubs in Leland and Greenville. Moving to Memphis in 1950, he made his first recordings for Sun and Meteor. He then moved to East St Louis, where he recorded several singles for Bobbin, but his career profile took a sharp upward turn in the '60s with hits on Checker like 'Blind Man', 'We're Gonna Make It' (an R&B #1 in spring 1965), 'Who's Cheating Who', 'Feel So Bad' and 'Grits Ain't Groceries', which established him as a leading soul-blues artist, his popularity on the Southern chitlin circuit rivalling B. B. King's. In 1984 he began a 20-year association with the Southern soul label Malaco.

*** **Anthology 1953–1961**
Varèse Sarabande 302 066 359 *Little Milton; Larry Prothe (t); Oliver Sain (as, vb); Lawrence Taylor (as); C. W. Tate, James Carr (ts); Vernon Harrell (bs); Ike Turner, unknown (p); Jesse Knight Jr, Cleophus Robison, Willie Dotson (b); Willie Sims, Lonnie Hayes, Jerry Walker (d); The Rockers (v).* 7/53–61.

Milton's Sun and Bobbin recordings are a heady brew of shameless imitation and lawless bravado. His vocal style was shaped by Roy Brown and Fats Domino, but he was perfectly capable of imitating his Memphis friends like Bobby Bland ('I Found Me A New Love') and, especially, B. B. King: the arrangement of 'Somebody Told Me' in two tempos is lifted from a King record, and his vocals on 'I'm Tryin' and 'That Will Never Do' are so close to King's it's practically actionable. (As if to show off his range of reference, in 'My Baby Pleases Me' he sounds more like Sammy Davis Jr.) But his guitar playing on Sun (he's calmer on Bobbin) is something else, all spiky lines and dirty tone. Unfortunately *Anthology* doesn't include the unissued take 2 of 'Lookin' For My Baby' with its two choruses of spitting instrumental abuse. What it does offer is the three Sun singles and half a dozen outtakes, and all seven of his singles for Bobbin. This material has also been dispersed on *The Sun Masters* (Rounder SS 35), *The Bobbin Blues Masters Volume One* (Collectables COL-CD-5474) and *Volume Two* (COL-CD-5475), and *St. Louis Blues Revue* (Ace CDCHD 633), but the Ace is definitely deleted, and the availability of the others is uncertain.

*** Greatest Hits
MCA/Chess CHD-9386 *Little Milton; Larry Prothe, Joe Campbell, David Hines, Murray Watson, —— Pozzolano, unknowns (t); John Watson (tb); Lawrence Taylor, Oliver Sain (as, bs); James Carr, Ben Branch (ts); Robert 'Sax' Crowder (bs); George Patterson, unknowns (s); Donny Hathaway (kb, poss. p); Leonard Caston (o, p); Fontella Bass, Charles Stepney, Sonny Thompson, Tom Washington, poss. Floyd Morris (p); Gerald Sims, Phil Upchurch, Cash McCall (g); Roosevelt Williams, Louis Satterfield, unknown (b); Jerry Walker, Ira Gates, Maurice White, Morris Jennings, Al Duncan (d); unknown (vb); The Gems, The Radiants (v). 61–11/69.*

***(*) The Complete Checker Hit Singles
Connoisseur VSOP CD 351 *Similar to above. 61–70.*

As noted above, Milton has always listened attentively to the work of his peers, and his first few recordings for Checker, such as 'Losing Hand', 'Blind Man' and the anthemic 'We're Gonna Make It', had much of the ambience of Bobby Bland. But as the listener follows him through the second half of the '60s and such poised displays as 'Grits Ain't Groceries' (a '50s hit for Little Willie John as 'All Around The World'), clear blue water can be seen to separate Milton from his contemporary, as he replaces Bland's emotional style with a dry, wry delivery closer to Lowell Fulson. The album, and the decade, closes with 'If Walls Could Talk', bouncing on Donny Hathaway's organ riff. During these years Little Milton cut loose from his Memphis and St Louis connections to remake himself as a soul-blues spokesman for the entire African-American community.

Greatest Hits appears to be the only survivor (though even its status is uncertain) of an MCA/Chess list that once numbered *If Walls Could Talk* (CHD 9289//(E) MCD 09289) and *Welcome To The Club* (CHD2-9350 2CD). It's worth searching for, but even more so is the Connoisseur collection, which absorbs all the 16 tracks of *Greatest Hits* and adds eight more, among them 'The Dark End Of The Street' and Gene Barge's spacious arrangement of Otis Rush's 'I Can't Quit You Baby', culminating in a grand layer-cake arrangement of horns and strings on 'Somebody's Changin' My Sweet Baby's Mind'.

*** Walkin' The Back Streets
Stax 8514//SCD-24 8514 *Little Milton; Memphis Horns (brass, reeds); Lester Snell (kb); Bobby Manuel, Michael Toles (g); William Murphy, David Weatherspoon (b); Willie Hall (d). 72, 74.*

*** Waiting For Little Milton/Blues 'N' Soul
Stax 8518//(E) CDSXD 052 *Little Milton; Memphis Horns (brass, reeds); Lester Snell, Charles Hodges, Shane Keister, Carl Hampton, Marvell Thomas (o, p); Memphis Symphony Orchestra (strings); Raymond Jackson, Bobby Manuel, Michael Toles (g); William Murphy, Leroy Hodges, Joe Turner, David Weatherspoon (b); Willie Hall, Al Jackson, Calep Emphery (d). 73–74.*

*** The Complete Stax Singles
Stax CDSXD 106 *Similar to above Stax CDs. 71–75.*

Milton's voice and guitar and the Stax house team were a near-perfect match, and his spell on the label produced many sides that were both artistically satisfying and at least moderately successful in the R&B charts. *The Complete Stax Singles* documents these years in the stated terms, and gives the fullest picture of how Milton positioned himself in the soul market while holding on to the blues-loving segment of his audience. *Walkin' The Back Streets* and *Waiting For Little Milton/Blues 'N' Soul* are reissues of LPs, each of which has some of the singles, encircled by album cuts like 'Blue Monday' (*Walkin' The Back Streets*), 'The Thrill Is Gone' (*Waiting For Little Milton*) or 'Worried Dream' (*Blues 'N' Soul*) that give Milton room to stretch out into impassioned blues preaching.

(**) Friend Of Mine
Collectables COL-CD-5434 *Little Milton; Tennyson Stephens (kb); John Bishop, Danny Raye Leak (g); Bernard Reed (b); Joseph Quinton (d); Bobby Christian (vb); The Haywood Singers (v). 76.*

(**) Me For You, You For Me
Collectables COL-CD-5435 *Similar to above. 77.*

These albums were recorded for Henry Stone's TK Records in Florida and originally issued on Glades. Except for a couple of blues on the second, the repertoire is mediocre soul, dolled up with girl groups and enlivened by a chittering monkey chorus of wah-wah guitars: period pieces from a bad period.

**(*) The Blues Is Alright!
Evidence ECD-26026 *Little Milton; Lucky Peterson (o, p); John Primer (g); Nick Holt (b); Nate Applewhite (d); band (v). 12/82.*

*** Live At Westville Prison
Delmark DE-681 *Little Milton; Lucky Peterson (kb); Ricky Earl (g); Frank McClure (b); Tony Brown (d). 1/83.*

Milton always made it plain that he didn't wish to be typed as a blues singer. His range – musically, emotionally, intellectually – was wider than that. But from time to time he agreed to make an all-blues album, and these are two of them. 'The Blues Is Alright' would become an irritating rah-rah chorus for blues fans to chant like a football crowd, but in 1982 it was still fresh, and timely. The Evidence CD, recorded in Paris and first issued on Isabel, also has two B. B. King numbers, 'Bad Luck Is Falling' and 'Chains And Things', but by this stage Milton had exchanged tracing paper for sketch pad and his treatments are fully personal. 'Bad Luck', 'I'd Rather Drink Muddy Water' and 'Walking The Back Streets And Crying' were fixtures in his set at this time and duly recurred at the Westville Prison gig a few weeks later, 'Back Streets' forming part of a seven-song, 16-minute medley along with 'Part Time Love', 'Drowning On Dry Land' and other soul-blues standbys. As the notes explain, the last three numbers were delivered 'when the men file[d] out of the auditorium and the female inmates arrive[d]', and it's fascinating to hear how Milton adapts his act, in both content and delivery, to his new audience.

**(*) Playing For Keeps
Malaco MALCD 7419 *Little Milton; Harrison Calloway, Ben Cauley, Jim Horn, Charles Rose, Harvey Thompson (brass, reeds); Carson Whitsett (kb); Mickey Davis, Bob McNally, Claudette Hampton, Cathy Robinson, Bennett Randman, Janet Dressler, Peggy Plucker, Ann McNally (strings); Jimmy Johnson, Michael Toles, Dino Zimmerman (g); Ray Griffin (b); James Robertson (d); Jewell Bass, Thomisene Anderson, Valerie Williams, The Downtown George Brown Singers (v). 84.*

**(*) Annie Mae's Cafe
Malaco MALCD 7435 *As above, except Ronnie Eades (s) replaces Horn; Catherine Henderson (v) replaces Valerie Williams; add Greg 'Fingers' Taylor (h), Larry Addison (kb); omit Johnson,*

Toles, The Downtown George Brown Singers. 86.

*** Movin' To The Country
Malaco MALCD 7445 *As above, except Jim Horn (s) replaces Eades; omit Taylor.* 87.

(**) Back To Back
Malaco MALCD 7448 *As above, except Clayton Ivey (kb) replaces Addison; add Mike Haynes, Gary Armstrong (brass, reeds), Michael Toles, Jimmy Johnson (g).* 88.

**(*) For Real
Malaco MCD 7494 *Little Milton; Jim Williamson, Steve Patrick (t, flh); Tom Malone (tb, s, fl); Charles Rose (tb, arr); Doug Moffat (s, fl); Harvey Thompson (s); Jim Horn (bs, bss, fl); Clayton Ivey, Chalmers Davis (kb); Will McFarlane, Jimmy Johnson, Eddie Rasberry (g); David Hood, Willie James Hatten (b); James Robertson, Forrest Gordon (d); Thomisene Anderson, Jewell Bass, Quanda Brooks (v).* 98.

*** Welcome To Little Milton
Malaco MCD 7500 *Little Milton; Steve Patrick, Jim Williamson (t); Charles Rose (tb); Harvey Thompson, Doug Moffat (ts); Jim Horn (bs); Clayton Ivey (o, p); Keb' Mo', Dave Alvin, G. Love (g, v); Warren Haynes, Will McFarlane (g); Allen Woody, David Hood, Jim Prescott (b); George Lawrence (d, perc); Matt Abts, Jeff Clemens (d); Susan Tedeschi, Lucinda Williams, Peter Wolf, Delbert McClinton, Jewell Bass, Freddie Young, Jerry Smith, The Children Of Israel (v); John Sinclair (sp).* 99.

** Guitar Man
Malaco MCD 7513 *Little Milton; Vinnie Ciesielski (t, flh); Charles Rose (tb); Harvey Thompson (ts, bs); Clayton Ivey (kb, o, p, syn, vb); Reggie Young, Jimmy Johnson, Larry Byrom (g); David Hood (b); George Lawrence (d); Jewell Bass, Valerie Kashimura, Freddie Young, Karen Brown (v).* 02.

Like his old friend Bobby Bland, another stalwart of the Malaco catalogue, Milton kept his brand identity alive with regular albums, supported by the same team of house musicians and writers. The character of the music is similar to Bland's but with a thicker thread of blues running through it; even though *Playing For Keeps* may let blues-lovers off the hook in 'Misty Blue' and 'Goodnight My Love', it reels them in again with 'I'll Catch You On Your Way Down'. The blues contact points on *Annie Mae's Cafe* are 'Too Hurt To Cry' and the feisty title track about a diner patronized by some of Malaco's staffers, whose proprietress 'keeps a .38 special behind the counter, and the other one in her pocketbook'. Better than either CD is *Movin' To The Country*. Not only is its blues quota significantly higher (six tracks out of ten) but the other numbers are stronger than usual; the slipping-around story of 'Room 244' is narrated over a just-won't-quit rhythm riff. The top cut on *Back To Back* is Forest Jackson's song 'I Don't Believe In Ghosts', which neatly updates the old blues theme of 'who's been here since I've been gone?': 'I got home just a little early, tryin' my best to catch that man – y'see, the cologne that I wear is Lagerfeld, but the air was filled with Pierre Cardin.' 'Penitentiary Blues' is good, too, but most of the rest of the album is over-dramatized soul, culminating in a teeth-grindingly earnest reading of 'The Wind Beneath My Wings'. In *For Real* Milton takes on repertoire like the Bee Gees' 'To Love Somebody' and Tony Joe White's 'Rainy Night In Georgia', and given his talent it's not surprising that he renders a polished performance of each, but most readers are likely to skip impatiently to the run of three blues near the end, 'Blues For Mr. "C"', 'If That's What You Wanna Do' and 'I'd Rather Go Blind'.

Welcome To Little Milton may have been his reaction to albums like B. B. King's *Blues Summit* and *Deuces Wild*, in which an imperial figure receives tributes from his allies and dependants. Whatever the motivation, it's an enjoyable record that sounds as if it was enjoyable to make, too. The guests mostly meet Milton on his own territory, rather than dragging him over to theirs, and on a couple of numbers, 'Right To Sing The Blues' and 'Lump On Your Stump', it's pretty much Milton conducting business as usual. English customers will be gratified by the traycard photograph, which shows the road sign for the Oxfordshire village of Little Milton. With *Guitar Man* Milton returned to his template. Though there are early signs that this will be an untypically bluesy set ('Take Time Out To Hear Me Some Blues', 'Blues Tune-Up'), they are delusive: 'Mr. & Mrs. Untrue' replays the scenario of 'Room 244' without the groove, George Jackson's 'You Were On The Right Street' was written on autopilot, and 'My Way' is … not Milton's way.

These are just a selection from Milton's Malaco catalogue. For most readers, we suspect, two or three of his albums will be enough information about what he was doing, but for the insatiable contingent the others are *I Will Survive* (MALCD 7427), *Too Much Pain* (MALCD 7453), *Reality* (MALCD 7462), *Strugglin' Lady* (MALCD 7465), *I'm A Gambler* (MALCD 7473), *Little Milton's Greatest Hits* (MCD 7477), *Cheatin' Habit* (MCD 7482) and *Feel It* (MCD 7506).

** Think Of Me
Telarc CD-83618 *Little Milton; Jon Tiven (h, g, perc); Bruce Katz (o); Mark Sorrells (p); Peter Shoulder (g); Sally Tiven (b); Chuckie Burke, Billy Block, Per Hanson (d); Ellis Hooks, Scat Springs (v).* 05.

The declared intention of this set of new songs, many of them written by Milton and the Tivens, was to 'capture Milton's traditional Southern soul roots tied into a contemporary vibe'. The album certainly breaks away from the Malaco house sound, but it would have profited from some of the idiomatic skill of the Malaco writers, who would have grounded a theme like 'Second Hand Love' in narrative specificity rather than resorted to reiterated soul clichés. If the Tivens are at less than their best, so too is Milton, whose voice shows signs of strain and is sometimes lost in the surrounding music. TR

Little Sonny [Jones] (1931–89)
VOCAL

Johnny 'Little Sonny' Jones became Fats Domino's warm-up singer at the age of 16. He cut a few 78s under his own name but the big break proved elusive, and he left Domino in 1961 to join the Lastie Brothers Combo, before quitting altogether in 1968. Re-emerging in the mid-'70s, he became a favourite at the New Orleans Jazz & Heritage Festival, making his last appearance in the year of his death.

*** New Orleans Rhythm & Blues
Black Magic 9023 *Jones; Dave Lastie, Clarence Ford (ts); Dave 'Fat Man' Williams (p); Justin Adams (g); Frank Fields (b); Bob French (d).* 3–4/75.

Little Sonny's resonant voice immediately conjures up thoughts of Smiley Lewis but, if he's a lesser artist than Lewis, Jones is no mere imitator, and his singing offers a great deal of pleasure. His brand of R&B was out of fashion in 1975, but

Sonny and the session veterans assembled to back him perform enthusiastically, dishing out the powerful but relaxed, rolling swing of the Crescent City at its best; Justin Adams, in particular, supplies a feast of gleaming, jazzy solos. On two tracks, Little Sonny sits out, and Dave Williams sings. The material was also released as *New Orleans R&B Gems* (Black Top CDBT 1113, deleted). CS

Little Sonny [Willis] (born 1932)
VOCAL, HARMONICA

Aaron Willis grew up in Alabama, moved to Detroit at 21 and first recorded in 1958. A mainstay of the city's blues scene through the '60s, he had his chance at the big time when he signed with Stax Records and cut three albums for their Enterprise label between 1969 and 1973.

Little Sonny recorded about half a dozen singles in the '50s and '60s. The echo-drenched Excello coupling 'Love Shock'/ 'I'll Love You Baby (Until The Day I Die)' is on *Deep Harmonica Blues* (Ace CDCHD 604).

*** **New King Of The Blues Harmonica/Hard Goin' Up**
Stax CDSXD 968 Willis; unknowns (brass); unknowns (reeds); Rudy Robinson (kb, o); Aaron Willis Jr, Sam Witcher, Eddie Willis, unknowns (g); Rod 'Peanut' Chandler, unknown (b); George Davidson, Curtis Sharp (d); unknowns (v). 69, 73.

(*) **Black & Blue
Stax SCD 8575//(E) CDSXE 057 Willis; The Bar-Kays (brass, reeds); Tommy Williams (ts, bs); Ron Gorden (o); Bobby Manuel, Eddie Wallis (g); unknown (b); Willie Hall (d). 70/71.

*** **Hard Goin' Up**
Stax SCD 8599 Willis; unknowns (brass); unknowns (reeds); Rudy Robinson (kb, o); Aaron Willis Jr, Sam Witcher, Eddie Willis (g); Rod 'Peanut' Chandler (b); Curtis Sharp (d); unknowns (v). 73.

Apart from 'Baby, What You Want Me To Do' and 'Don't Ask Me No Questions' (the only track with horns), *New King Of The Blues Harmonica* is all instrumental, a set of repetitive, funky grooves like 'Eli's Pork Chop' in which Willis's harp is constantly urged on by lithe bass playing and drumming. Imagine variations on Sonny Boy Williamson II's 'Help Me', energized by a soul beat conceived in Memphis or Muscle Shoals. The album is coupled on an English issue with the later *Hard Goin' Up* (also available on its own), a set of brisk, purposeful blues-funk, a little dated in its sound but not so much so that it has become an embarrassment to itself or others. That description also fits *Black & Blue*, a blend of soul songs, instrumentals and one or two blues. Little Sonny's subsequent releases *Blues With A Feeling* (Schoolkids SKR 2102//Sequel NEX CD 279), recorded at the 1972 Ann Arbor Blues Festival, and *Sonny Side Up* (Glynn GR-1-1001//Sequel NEX CD 276), a 1995 studio recording, are deleted. IR

Little Walter (1923–68)
VOCAL, HARMONICA, GUITAR

Blues literature, notoriously prone to hyperbole, regularly grants ordinary talents mythical status, creating impossible criteria for others to meet. But as with all rules there are exceptions, and Marion Walter Jacobs is one. Little Walter created his own legend, that of a child prodigy of the harmonica whose genius was self-promoted. The reality was a laborious journey north from Louisiana with stopovers in Helena, Arkansas, Memphis and St Louis, during which he took vicarious instruction from Sonny Boy Williamson II and Walter Horton and listened closely to the records of Sonny Boy Williamson I. A member of Muddy Waters's band before launching an immediately successful solo career, he was one of the first to amplify the harmonica, creating a vocabulary for the instrument that reflected the work of saxophonists like Louis Jordan from whom he also gained inspiration. A volatile temperament and a mercurial character undermined the success he achieved as a recording artist and bandleader but at its height his talent was unequalled by mentors and contemporaries alike.

***(*) **The Blues World Of Little Walter**
Delmark DD-648 Little Walter; Muddy Waters, Jimmy Rogers (g, v); [Baby Face] Leroy Foster (d, v). 1/50.

After two years of being denied studio time as the Muddy Waters band, it was hardly surprising the unit went elsewhere to get on record. A session for the Parkway label dominates this 13-track compilation. Muddy takes a back seat, leaving the vocal chores to Walter and Foster, who split the eight titles between them. Apart from a spirited remake of the Ora Nelle 'I Just Keep Loving Her' (see below), Walter elects to play guitar on his other three sides, 'Muskadine Blues' (his version of 'Take A Little Walk With Me'), 'Bad Acting Woman' and 'Moonshine Blues'. Bravado characterizes the teenager's vocal style rather than technique but he was no slouch on the guitar and he successfully integrates with Muddy's heavy-handed rhythm and Rogers's more delicate touch.

The session was a raucous one with constant exclamations by all present. Any attempt to hide Muddy's presence was thwarted by Walter's frequent references to him and Muddy's own retorts. His most obvious contributions were during Baby Face Leroy's tremendous two-part 'Rollin' And Tumblin'', regarded by many as postwar Chicago blues' greatest achievement. Part group chant, part vocal, the song was propelled by Muddy's slide guitar, his moans and verbal outbursts unmistakable, and the dogged persistence of Foster's bass drum. Walter's acoustic harmonica solos on this, 'Boll Weevil' and 'Red Headed Woman' show him working towards the riff-based technique that would dominate his amplified style. Despite the vague promise of its title, this collection (which also includes material by J. B. Lenoir and Sunnyland Slim) documents an historically important period of transition in both Walter's career and Chicago blues itself.

*** **Little Walter 1947–1953**
Classics 5091 Little Walter; poss. Henry Gray (p); Othum Brown (g, v); Jimmy Rogers, Muddy Waters, Louis Myers, David Myers (g); Ernest 'Big' Crawford, Willie Dixon (b); Elga Edmonds, Fred Below (d). 47–7/53.

*** **A Proper Introduction To Little Walter: Juke**
Proper INTRO CD 2006 As above, except Jimmy Rogers also sings; add Sunnyland Slim, Eddie Ware (p); Leroy Foster (d). 47–7/53.

**** **His Best**
MCA/Chess CHD-9384 Little Walter; unknown (o); Otis Spann (p); Muddy Waters, Jimmy Rogers, Louis Myers, Dave Myers, Robert Lockwood, Luther Tucker, Leonard Caston, Bo Diddley, Jimmie Lee Robinson, Fred Robinson (g); Willie Dixon (b); Elga

Edmonds, Fred Below, George Hunter, Billie Stepney (d); band (v). 5/52–12/60.

***(*) Blues With A Feelin'
[MCA/Chess (A) CHD2–9357]//(E) MCD 09357 2CD *Similar to above, except Fred Robinson also plays b; add Donald Hankins, J. T. Brown (ts), Jarrett Gibson (bs), Henry Gray, Lafayette Leake (p), Buddy Guy, Lee Jackson (g), Jack Myers, Junior Pettis (b), Al Duncan, George Cook (d). 5/52–2/66.*

Walter's 1952 debut single for Chess's Checker label utilized Muddy's band, and their stolid competence on the instrumental 'Juke' can't keep his harmonica under restraint, as he strings together a series of riffs and set pieces that indicates he'd listened to honking saxmen like Big Jay McNeely and Hal Singer. Its B side, 'Can't Hold Out Much Longer', is adapted from Sonny Boy Williamson I's 'Black Gal' and shows how Walter managed to make expressive use of what was no more than an adequate singing voice. Once free of Muddy, and with a band comprising the Myers brothers and Fred Below, Walter gave vent to his brilliantly inventive imagination with 'Boogie' and an atmospheric 'Blue Midnight' while tradition was satisfied by 'Mean Old World', although it was another instrumental, 'Sad Hours', that made his second single an R&B hit.

Thereafter there was chart success with 'Blues With A Feeling', 'You're So Fine', 'You'd Better Watch Yourself' and 'My Babe', and later singles like 'Hate To See You Go' and 'It Ain't Right' maintained a high standard. Equally significant were the instrumentals that accompanied these vocal outings; 'Off The Wall', 'Quarter To Twelve', 'Lights Out' and 'Roller Coaster' revealed his expertise at any tempo. The subtle onset of decline became evident in 1957, with Walter no longer writing his own material and resorting to a series of Willie Dixon originals and stalwarts such as 'Confessin' The Blues' and 'Key To The Highway', the latter his last Top Ten R&B hit in 1958. 'Everything's Gonna Be Alright' and a 1960 session that included 'Just Your Fool' were late rallies but subsequent recordings were often sorry displays. Alcohol and drugs had destroyed a magnificent talent, and his death, resulting from a street brawl, was both tragic and unsurprising. Nevertheless, the ignominy of his end cannot tarnish the music he made at his peak.

The 20 tracks on *His Best* contain most of those singled out above, though with just four instrumentals the album relies a little heavily on Walter's robust but untutored vocal talent. It illustrates the backing he received from an exceptional group of musicians, among whom the Myers brothers, Robert Lockwood, Luther Tucker and Fred Below are outstanding. Their unselfish interplay created the perfect backdrop for Walter's flights of imagination, setting a high standard for those who followed.

Classics and Proper tilt the balance more towards instrumentals, including 'Quarter To Twelve' and 'Lights Out', missing from *His Best*, as well as the unissued-at-the-time 'Last Boogie' and 'Fast Boogie'. They also preface their Checker selections with 'Ora Nelle Blues'/'I Just Keep Loving Her', the former sung by guitarist Othum Brown; this was Walter's debut single on a short-lived (two issues) Maxwell Street label. Proper shares 21 of its 23 tracks with Classics, adding 'Blue Baby', originally credited to Sunnyland Slim, and Jimmy Rogers's 'Chance To Love'. Both sets avoid the material on *The Blues World Of Little Walter* (see above), but copyright restrictions prevent them exploring his Checker work beyond his first two years on the label. The most extensive survey of Walter in his prime, *The Essential Little Walter* (MCA/Chess CHD2–9342 2CD), has been deleted.

The 40-track *Blues With A Feelin'* offers the chance to study Walter's work in depth, being rich in alternative takes, including a staggeringly prolific 'Juke' bearing little resemblance to the issued version; at least a third of the contents either were never meant for issue or present variations on known themes. Previously unissued material like 'Driftin' and 'That's It' illustrates some of the difficulties experienced early on in getting Walter's presentation right. Other finished tracks discarded at the time include 'My Kind Of Baby', 'Come Back Baby', 'I Love You So (Oh Baby)' and 'Mercy Babe', the last an ill-fitting jigsaw-puzzle of 'My Babe'. All have merit but fail to earn the highest recommendation, and the same goes for later instrumentals like 'Flying Saucer', 'Teenage Beat' and 'Shake Dancer'. A final 'Chicken Shack' from 1966, an unacknowledged version of Jimmy Smith's tune, is a brave but desultory exhibition; where once Walter dominated his ensembles, here he's overwhelmed by raucous but rather mundane backing.

* Windy City Blues
Blue Moon CDBM 028 *Little Walter; unknown (g); unknown (b); unknown (d). 67.*

Poorly recorded and short on playing time, this CD contains live performances by Walter and Otis Rush. (They are also on the VAC *The Chicago Blues Festival* [Blue Moon CDBM 125].) Walter's four titles, 'Goin' Down Slow', 'Walter's Blues', 'Lovin' You All The Time' (actually 'You're So Fine') and 'Watermelon Man' (disguised as 'Blue Mood'), show the pitiful state to which he was reduced before his end. He seems aware of his condition during 'Goin' Down Slow', completely loses the plot during 'You're So Fine' and leaves an under-achieving guitarist to play much of 'Watermelon Man', mercifully faded before its conclusion. Such painful listening should never have been marketed. NS/TR

Little Whitt & Big Bo
DUET

Singer/guitarist Jolly 'Little Whitt' Wells (born 1931) was playing guitar at jukes and parties from the age of 12, and in later years drove a dumper for Tuscaloosa County. His fellow Alabamian, singer/harmonica player 'Big Bo' McGee (1928–2002), who learned the harmonica from his grandmother, also played for picnics and parties, but made his living as a truck driver. The two men formed a band together after military service, but waited until retirement before turning to music fulltime. In 1995, they toured Europe to considerable acclaim.

*** Moody Swamp Blues
Vent VR-30009 *Little Whitt; Big Bo; Michael McCracken (g); Tommy Gardner (b); Leif Bondarenko (d, perc). 2/95.*

Moody Swamp Blues starts tediously, with yet another Robert Johnson song (who could have predicted that 'Walking Blues' would become boring by the end of the 20th century?) but thereafter, four monotonous minutes of 'I Got A Woman' apart, it becomes much more interesting and enjoyable. Whitt and Bo's repertoire mostly consists of cover versions of '50s Chicago blues hits, including songs as familiar as 'Mean Old World' and 'Can't Be Satisfied', but this is the music they played for their local African-American audience for many years, and the songs are renewed by their commitment and their obvious pleasure in performance. Big Bo did a little songwriting: 'Overseas Blues' is an uninspired lyric about the prospect of touring Europe, but 'You Go Your Way' is a tense reflection on lost love, and 'The Burning' a sad, angry account of racism in Mississippi. Little Whitt's writing extends only as far as pleasant reworkings of two Jimmy Rogers tunes: 'Chicago Bound' becomes 'Moody Swamp Blues' and the 'Gold-Tailed Bird' has its plumage turned to silver. The backing musicians do a good job, and the spoons on 'Can't Be Satisfied' are a brilliant piece of lateral thinking. *Moody Swamp Blues* is the kind of CD that turns up too seldom, presenting community-based musicians playing with the confidence and the competence of long experience. CS

Little Willie Littlefield (born 1931)
VOCAL, PIANO

Littlefield made a name for himself in Houston in the late '40s as a boogie-woogie boy wonder. After some recording for local labels he was signed to Modern in 1949 and promptly had a hit with 'It's Midnight'. Over the next few years he recorded and toured prolifically. The '60s and '70s were mostly spent in obscurity, but after moving to the Netherlands he became well known in Europe.

*** Boogie, Blues And Bounce
Ace CDCHD 1056 Littlefield; Jake Porter, James Williams, Doug Byars, unknowns (t); Charlie Thomas (as); Don Wilkerson, Earl Jackson, Buddy Floyd (ts); unknowns (bs); unknowns (s); Chuck Norris, unknowns (g); unknowns (b); Ray Martinez, unknowns (d); John Jones (unknown instrument). c. 4–12/49.

*** Kat On The Keys
Ace CDCHD 736 Littlefield; James Williams, Doug Byars, unknowns (t); Charlie Thomas (as); Don Wilkerson, Buddy Floyd, Floyd Turnham, Maxwell Davis, unknown (ts); unknown (bs); unknowns (s); Jesse Ervin, Mitchell 'Tiny' Webb, unknowns (g); Bill Davis, Bill Hadnott, unknowns (b); Ray Martinez, Al 'Cake' Wichard, Peppy Prince, Bill Douglass, unknowns (d); John Jones (unknown instrument); Little Lora Wiggins (v). 6/49–8/51.

Littlefield is most effective at opposite ends of the tempo range, either punching out fast, triplet-laden piano tunes like 'Nakite Stomp', 'Love Me Tonight' and 'Rockin' Chair Mama' on *Kat On The Keys* and 'Drinkin' Hadacol' on *Boogie, Blues And Bounce* or slowly disclosing misery and ill-fortune in a blurred, congested voice in 'Once Was Lucky' (*Boogie*), 'Life Of Trouble', 'Too Late For Me' and the eerie 'Lump In My Throat' (all *Kat*). It's clear that he had listened attentively to contemporaries like Amos Milburn; 'Mello Cats' (*Boogie*) heists the melody of 'Chicken Shack Boogie'. Nevertheless, these are potent performances from a man barely into his 20s. Both albums are divided approximately 50/50 into recordings issued at the time and rejected items brought to light by Ace's vault-searchers. *Boogie* has more of the latter, including seven solo demos. If you don't want exhaustive coverage, choose the *Kat*.

*** Going Back To Kay Cee
Ace CDCHD 503 Littlefield; Jewell Grant (as, bs); Maxwell Davis, Rufus Gore, Wardell Gray (ts); Herman 'Tiny' Mitchell, Charlie Grayson, Jesse Irvin, unknown (g); Ralph Hamilton, Edwyn Conley, Mario Delagarde (b); Jesse Sailes, Bill Douglas, unknown (d); band (v). 8/52–10/53.

Leaving Modern, Littlefield spent a year or so with Federal, where he made better-produced but otherwise broadly similar recordings, among them 'K.C. Lovin'', the earliest version of Leiber & Stoller's 'Kansas City', heard here both in its original version and with a dubbed-on guitar intro. Jazz lovers intrigued by the presence on the last session of Wardell Gray will find little more to reward their enquiry than a solo chorus on 'Goofy Dust Blues'. The album is prefaced by two duets with Little Esther and one with Lil Greenwood.

**(*) Paris Streetlights
EPM Blues Collection 15780 Littlefield. 5/80.

During the '80s and '90s Littlefield recorded numerous albums in Europe, but none of his CDs on Chrisly or Oldie Blues appears to be in print. Unfortunately this leaves as the sole example of his mature work only *Paris Streetlights*. Some of this record is decent blues and boogie material. 'Cours De Vincennes' (announced as 'L.W. Boogie') is a solid six-minute boogie workout, 'Dirty' a long, meandering and very lowdown blues instrumental; these are likely to be most blues-fanciers' favourites. 'Sometimes' and 'Paris', however, are cocktail music, whose dominant flavour is the syrup of Littlefield's francophilia. TR

John(ny) Littlejohn (1931–94)
VOCAL, GUITAR

John Funchess was born in Lake, Mississippi, and grew up in Jackson. In the early '50s he moved to Gary, Indiana, where he played with Jimmy Reed and John Brim. Later he moved to Chicago and worked for some years with Howlin' Wolf and Jimmy Rogers. In the '60s he cut a few singles and a session, unissued at the time, for Chess, but the '70s brought him more opportunities, including overseas tours, though his musical activities were frequently interrupted by ill health.

*** Slidin' Home
Arhoolie CD 9019 Littlejohn; Robert Pulliam, Willie Young (ts); Monroe Jones Jr (g); Alvin Nichols (b); Booker Sidgrave (d). 11/68.

** Dream
Storyville STCD 8034 Littlejohn; Larry Burton (g); Aron Burton (b, v); Andrew 'Blueblood' McMahon (b); Candy Utah (d). 11/76.

**(*) Sweet Little Angel
Black & Blue BB 443 Littlejohn; Lafayette Leake (p); Alabama Pettis Jr (g); Nick Holt (b); Fred Below (d). 11/78.

**(*) John Littlejohn's Blues Party
Wolf 120.859 Littlejohn; Ken Barker, Christian Dozzler (p); John Primer (g); Willie Kent (b); Timothy Taylor (d). 2–6/89.

**(*) When Your Best Friend Turns Their Back On You
JSP JSPCD 809 Littlejohn; Ralph Lapetina (p); Craig Davis (g); Harlan Terson (b); Jody Young (d). 92.

Many people on the Chicago scene, both musicians and journalists, spoke warmly about John Littlejohn during his lifetime, so it is frustrating that his records give so sketchy an account of his talent. Although he was known for his slide guitar playing, which he modelled in part on Elmore James's, his recordings feature it no more, and often less, than his regular lead guitar playing, which is not specially distinctive.

He relied, too, on a small core of songs. '29 Ways', which he first recorded in the '60s, shows up on four of the albums under review and 'Dream' on three, and as late as 1992 he was still working with material he had first used at least 25 years earlier.

Dream and *Sweet Little Angel* are gravid with standards originated by B. B. King, Elmore James and others. *Dream* was recorded for MCM, as usual in an empty club, and sounds as lifeless as many other albums on that label. *Sweet Little Angel* is more vivacious, but his guitar sound would have profited from being beefed up. A decade on, he is no luckier in the balancing of his guitar on his six *Blues Party* pieces (the other three tracks are by Willie Kent and Tail Dragger). The engineering of the JSP album is more sympathetic, but the settings are mundane. By then Littlejohn's strength had been sapped by his poor health, and he plays like a man too tired to think beyond the familiar.

For an idea of how he sounded when he was fitter and more optimistic, it's necessary to go back to his first album. *Slidin' Home* was previously issued as *John Littlejohn's Chicago Blues Stars* (Arhoolie CD 1043), and the new title, though more succinct, is less apt, since he plays slide only on the title tune, 'Shake Your Money Maker' and his own 'Dream'. Those aside, the listener is reminded less of Elmore James than of Littlejohn's sometime employer Jimmy Rogers, particularly in tracks like 'Been Around The World' and the downhome version of 'Catfish Blues'. But what comes across here as on none of the other albums (and it's unlikely that the reissue of his 1985 Rooster Blues LP *So-Called Friends* would modify this opinion) is how involved he seems in his music, and how sharp are the tools he uses to make it.

Readers who pursue Littlejohn into the VAC thicket will find their diligence rewarded. Three cuts on *Chicago Blues At Home* (Testament TCD 5028), recorded in 1970, are placid duets with Jimmy Rogers, while three from 1979 on *Genuine Mississippi Blues . . . Plus* (The Ace (MS.) Blues Masters Volume 4) (Westside WESM 579) are emphatic band blues in the Muddy Waters manner with Sam Myers on harp. Few of these tracks have much of Littlejohn's guitar, but they find him in stronger voice than on most of his albums. TR

Robert (Jr) Lockwood (born 1915)
VOCAL, GUITAR

Lately the billing has been Robert Lockwood Jr; the reference always was to Lockwood's father, not to his mother's famous boyfriend. Lockwood learned a lot from Robert Johnson, and has a high regard for his music, but he long ago became fed up with those who only valued him for his association with Johnson and Sonny Boy Williamson II, and only wanted to hear Johnson's songs. He's a master guitarist in his own right (he was a mainstay of Chess sessions in the '50s), a musical adventurer when allowed to be, and a capable, if rather dry, singer.

***(*) **Mississippi Blues (1935–1951)**
Wolf WBCD-005 *Lockwood; Sunnyland Slim (p, v); Alfred Elkins, Big Crawford (b); Alfred Wallace (d). 7/41–11/51.*
*** **Sweet Home Chicago – The JOB Sessions 1950s**
P-Vine PCD-24051 *Lockwood; Alex Atkins (as); Sunnyland Slim (p); Alfred Elkins (b); Alfred Wallace (d). 3/51–55.*

Lockwood shares *Mississippi Blues* with Otto Virgial and Robert Petway (q.v.); his portion is four titles from 1941 and a Mercury 78. Robert Johnson's influence is obvious on the earlier material, but on 'Take A Little Walk With Me' so is Charlie Christian's. Lockwood's detached singing of the homicidal nursery rhyme 'Little Boy Blue' generates considerable tension. The Mercury 78 includes the first postwar recording of 'Dust My Broom', and attempts, not entirely successfully, to synthesize Delta blues and small-group swing.

Lockwood's J.O.B. sessions bracket the Mercury recordings, and include more attempts at musical fusion (and at 'Dust My Broom'). 'Aw Aw Baby', a version of 'Sweet Home Chicago' with Atkins prominent, is a gem, but 'Sweet Woman From Maine', also with Atkins, tries too hard to be sophisticated. The CD is shared with Johnny Shines; Lockwood's J.O.B. recordings are also on the deleted but possibly still findable VAC *Sunnyland Slim & Friends: Sunnyland Special* (Westside WESA 910).

**** **Steady Rollin' Man**
Delmark DD-630 *Lockwood; Louis Myers (g); Dave Myers (b); Fred Below (d). 8/70.*

Delmark wanted old favourites and Robert Johnson songs; Lockwood's reaction, as given to *Living Blues*, was 'I don't care nothin' about it. It was just the same things. I only got two tunes on there that I respect a little bit and they were new.' Despite his reservations about the material, Lockwood and the Aces perform it with the utmost precision, confidence and grace, and as always, Below's drumming is a masterclass in swing.

**** **The Complete Trix Recordings**
Savoy Jazz SVY 17312 2CD *Lockwood; Maurice Reedus (ts); Marc Hahn (g); Gene Schwartz (b); George Cook, Jimmy Jones (d). 6/73–12/75.*

Two Trix LPs get a CD each; not surprisingly, *Contrasts* mixes old numbers, some of them by Robert Johnson, with original blues and jazz. Maurice Reedus bleats forlornly on 'Come Day, Go Day', but this is not typical; elsewhere his lyricism and grit are a good match for the same qualities in Lockwood's playing. *Does 12*'s title refers to the 12-string guitar the 60-year-old Lockwood had just adopted (and has played ever since); the 11 tracks include a tigerish 'Walking Blues', some highly inventive jazz and a 'King Biscuit Time' that revives the spirit, if not the sound, of Lockwood and Sonny Boy on KFFA. Offered room for self-expression, whether through originals or oldies, Lockwood seizes it eagerly and usually very successfully.

***(*) **Just The Blues**
Bullseye BBB 9623 *Lockwood; Peter Haskin, Bobby Marcus (as); Harold D. Arnold Sr, Paul Combs, Maurice Reedus (ts); Scott Billington (h); Harold D. Arnold Jr, Carl Carter (p); Johnny Shines (g); James C. Garrett (b); Wirtford Core, Jimmy Hoare (d); J. K. Terrell (cga, perc). 1/80–4/81.*

Lockwood and Johnny Shines had been friends since 1927; they were were both exploratory musicians, and both tired of being pigeonholed as Robert Johnson's heirs and disciples. Producing two LPs for Rounder offered a chance to spread their wings. *Just The Blues* (which isn't) pulls together the tracks where Lockwood is leader. Among them are four intricate acoustic duets, performed with almost arrogant ease. Elsewhere, Lockwood (joined by Shines on three tracks) is backed by bands of various sizes. The results are not uniformly successful; 'Here It Is, Brother', flirting with funk, takes the wah-wah too far-far, and an electric piano discolours the title track. Still, 'Rockin' Free' does just that, the sax sections have velvet power, and the two-guitar instrumental 'Razzmadazz' is simply perfect.

*** Ramblin' On My Mind
Black & Blue BB 438 *Lockwood.* 11/82.
*** Plays Robert And Robert
Evidence ECD-26020 *Lockwood.* 11/82.

Given the obviousness of the concept, and Lockwood's comments on his Delmark session, one might expect a work of surpassing dullness. On the contrary: he whips through six songs by you-know-who and six of his own with some passion. Is he a professional, giving the public what it wants, or an unreliable narrator, playing postmodernist games with the critics? Perhaps it's simply that when a musician as good as Lockwood meets a songwriter as good as Johnson, sparks are bound to fly. Black & Blue add five alternative takes to those which Evidence licensed, but they don't add much value; two false starts on 'Little Boy Blue' are a surprise, but hardly buried treasure.

**(*) The Blues Of Robert Lockwood Jr. & Boogie Bill Webb
Storyville STCD 8055 *Lockwood.* 8/84.

Lockwood's nine tracks derive from a video of a New Orleans concert, and a 20-year wait for CD release gives them, perhaps unfairly, the air of being just another Lockwood session. There's some similarity in both material and delivery to the more recent *Legend Live*, but Lockwood seems disengaged here, going through a well-worn routine without much attempt to engage with his audience beyond politely acknowledging their presence.

*** Delta Crossroads
Telarc CD-83509 *Lockwood.* 12/99.

As with the Black & Blue session 17 years earlier, about half of *Delta Crossroads* is Robert Johnson songs. Lockwood's playing and singing continue to be remarkable, but the rider 'for his age' attaches itself at times; 'We're Gonna Ball Tonight', revived from Rounder, is not the only song that starts haltingly, although all of them eventually develop enough momentum to be respectable. There are many worse CDs around, but in Lockwood's catalogue there are better.

*** The Legend Live
M.C. MC-0051 *Lockwood.* early 03.

Leroy Carr and Robert Johnson dominate this set, recorded in Phoenix, Arizona; a jazzy 'Exactly Like You' is perhaps an indication of what Lockwood would rather be playing. Tempos are usually medium or slower, but at 88 he's still an assured guitarist, a strong, laconic singer, and better listening than many a musician half his age. CS

Cripple Clarence Lofton (1897–1957)
VOCAL, PIANO, WHISTLING

Lofton was born in Tennessee; by the '20s he was in Chicago, working as a clerk for the C.B. & Q. Railroad. He played in South Side clubs, and made a few recordings for the 'race' market before being lionized by white jazz fans as one of the forerunners of boogie woogie. The recording and performing opportunities that resulted did not generate much income, nor did the operation of a School of Boogie Woogie. Lofton was ejected from the musicians' union for defaulting on his dues and, with professional engagements effectively debarred, he returned to obscurity. Willie Mabon's 1952 hit recording of 'I Don't Know' generated no royalties for Lofton, who was working in a garage at the time of his death.

*** Cripple Clarence Lofton – Vol. 1 (1935–1939)
RST Blues Documents BDCD-6006 *Lofton; poss. Odell Rand (cl); Al Miller (g, v); Big Bill Broonzy (g); unknown (b); unknown (wb); Red Nelson [Wilborn] (v). 4/35–c. 39.*

The bearer of a nickname conferred in a less sensitive age, Lofton was congenitally lame, but it didn't stop him from being, in William Russell's famous description, 'a three-ring circus' who would enliven a performance with dancing, whistling, finger snaps and drumming on the body of the piano. That extrovert, crowd-pleasing aspect is often strong on his five recordings for the African-American market. 'Strut That Thing', with a powerful bass line and stop-time breaks, is Lofton's first version of 'I Don't Know', matched for *joie de vivre* only by the swaggering 'Brown Skin Girls', with whistling, scat singing and Big Bill's lilting guitar. Slower, grittier, and sporting enigmatic lyrics are 'Monkey Man Blues', 'You Done Tore Your Playhouse Down' ('I drove the nails, mama, and you pulled them out of your bones') and 'Policy Blues', which is peppered with gambling slang.

Four accompaniments to Red Nelson, and two to Al Miller, complete Lofton's 'race' recordings. Miller's hokum numbers are of minimal merit, and further disfigured by a wheezing clarinet, but Red Nelson is another matter. Red was often a dull, inexpressive singer, but Lofton's discipline and drive push him to another level altogether on 'Streamline Train' (a version of 'Cow Cow Blues') and the moving 'Crying Mother'. 'Sweetest Thing Born' and the topical 'When The Soldiers Get Their Bonus' are less compelling, but only by comparison with those two unexpected masterpieces.

Vol. 1 concludes with the first three sides that Lofton recorded for bartender and jazz fan Dan Qualey's Solo Art label. The best, despite a muffled transfer, is 'Had A Dream', an ominous slow blues that seems to evoke the bleakness of Chicago in the Depression; instrumental versions of 'Streamline Train' and 'I Don't Know' foreshadow the rush and indiscipline that often mar Lofton's later recordings. Better are six numbers cut at a party not long before the Solo Art session; these, too, are mostly in three-ring circus mode, but Lofton takes more trouble with both detail and structure.

**(*) Cripple Clarence Lofton – Vol. 2 (1939–1943)
RST Blues Documents BDCD-6007 *Lofton.* c. 39–12/43.

Vol. 2's 20 tracks are split evenly between the balance of the Solo Art material and Lofton's last session, for the Session label, another short-lived, fan-run enterprise. All but two numbers are instrumentals, and the listener gets a full dose of Clarence's characteristics: fast right-hand trills, short, hammered treble figures repeated over climbing basses, hectic tempos and a cavalier attitude to structure. Critics have often reproached Lofton for the last attribute in particular, and they started early; reviewing the original 78, *Down Beat* protested that 'He murders Pinetop's classic.' The real offence, one feels, was failure to replicate what white cognoscenti regarded as the canonical version.

The boogie police have sometimes continued to reproach Lofton for arbitrary chorus lengths and a shortage of ideas; the former attribute need only bother those who think that to bend the rules is *ipso facto* to fail artistically. There is more substance to the latter charge, but it's only fair to note that some performances are similar because, although given different titles, they are actually alternative takes; this is the case with 'More Motion' and 'Sweet Tooth', as it is also with 'Sixes And Sevens' and 'Clarence's Blues'. Nevertheless, it can't be denied that Lofton recycled a limited number of themes; he made two versions of 'Streamline Train' and three of 'I Don't Know' for Session, and 'Early Blues' is 'Brown Skin Girls' without the vocal. On Solo Art especially, he was allowed to get away with a good deal of playing that's showy, pointlessly fast and error-prone. This is probably the combined result of motives that were documentary rather than commercial, and of reluctance to give instruction to a man regarded as a progenitor of the art of boogie.

In truth, Lofton was at his best at slower tempos, as is shown by 'Lofty Blues', a medium-paced reworking of 'Had A Dream', and especially by 'Deep End Boogie' (a.k.a. 'South End Boogie'), named after its clenched, grumbling bass figures. There's a lot of fun to be had from the fast and furious tracks, but heard in bulk they make it clear that Lofton had, and rather too often reached, his technical and artistic limits. Speaking of matters technical, there is slight wow on some tracks, most obviously on 'The Fives'. CS

John 'Juke' Logan (born 1945)
VOCAL, HARMONICA, ORGAN, PIANO, PERCUSSION

Born in LA, John Farrell Logan was drawn to the blues by the records of Ray Charles, Mose Allison and Jimmy Reed, among others. He earned his nickname by continually playing Little Walter's tune 'Juke'. He has worked with Ry Cooder, Los Lobos and Dave Alvin, and between 1992 and 2000 co-hosted KPCC's Friday Nite Blues Revue, but his widest exposure has been playing harmonica on the theme tunes of the TV shows Roseanne *and* Home Improvement.

**(*) The Chill
Razor & Tie R 2818//Sky Ranch 87834 *Logan; David Hidalgo (ac, g); Denny Freeman (kb); Brenda Burns (g, v); Junior Watson (g); Gregory Boaz, Conrad Lozano (b); Jerry Angel (d, tamb); Joe Yuele (d).* 93.

**(*) Juke Rhythm
Sky Ranch 40943//Mocombo M-55001 *Logan; Gary Primich (h); Brenda Burns (g, spoons, v); Rick Vito (g, v); Kid Ramos, David Hidalgo, Glenn Nishida (g); Dan Durran (b, v); Gregory Boaz, Conrad Lozano (b); Joe Yuele (d, v); Richard Innes, Jerry Angel (d); Michael Tempo (perc); Topanga Dick (sp).* 95.

One of Logan's favourite MOs is a hipster narrative over a bubbling dance beat, often with Latin percussion. With its cool beat-poet lyrics and general air of mean-streets knowingness, his music sounds a little like what you'd get if a bunch of minor characters out of Elmore Leonard novels formed a Tom Waits cover band. There are neat ideas at work here, such as the fusion of Bo Diddley and zydeco in 'Bayou Diamond Ring' (get it?) on *The Chill*, but they aren't always clever enough to deserve to go on so long, and the sociopolitical numbers like 'Fan The Flames' (*The Chill*) or 'Life On The Center Divider (Go Figure)' (*Juke Rhythm*) are little more than slogans with a beat. Logan is a lively player on harmonica and keyboards and it's clear from pieces like 'Play Tha' Blues' (*The Chill*) and 'The Blues Hip Hop' (*Juke Rhythm*) that his appreciation of the music is wide, but the ways he demonstrates that in his own work are often roundabout, and listeners who want to follow them will need to be catholic in their tastes. Logan has also recorded a duet album with Doug MacLeod (q.v.). TR

Lonesome Sundown (1928–95)
VOCAL, GUITAR

Born in Louisiana, Cornelius Green moved to Texas in his 20s, taking a job at the Gulf Oil refinery in Port Arthur. In 1955 he joined Clifton Chenier's band for a few months as second guitarist, then married and settled in Opelousas, Louisiana. He began recording for the producer Jay Miller in nearby Crowley and, although his releases never appeared in the charts, Excello Records continued to issue them for a decade, until, in 1965, he deserted music. Over the years, however, enthusiasts elevated him to the top rank of Excello artists, alongside Lightnin' Slim and Slim Harpo, and he was persuaded to return to the business for a few years at the end of the '70s.

**** I'm A Mojo Man
Ace CDCHD 556 *Lonesome Sundown; Lionel Prevost (ts); unknowns (s); Lazy Lester, Sylvester Buckley (h); Talton Miller, Katie Webster (p); Guitar Gable, Al Foreman, prob. Leroy Washington, prob. Isaiah Chatman (g); John 'Fats' Perrodin, Bobby McBride, Rufus Thibodeaux (b); Lloyd Reynaud, Clarence 'Jockey' Etienne, Sammy Hogan, Warren Storm (d).* 56–64.

Lonesome Sundown could rock an up-tempo number like 'I'm A Mojo Man' with élan, or chug along a Jimmy Reed groove in 'Don't Say A Word', but it was on slow blues that he really showed what he could do. As a singer he sounds quite like Lowell Fulson, but what he captures best in the other man's style is his calm in the face of misfortune: whatever falls out of the sky, he ducks, shrugs and carries on. 'I gets cold love in the mornin', and secondhand kisses at night,' he recounts in 'Lonely Lonely Me', 'but I still loves my baby, and I keep on treatin' her right.' The song is prefaced with a guitar figure as sombre as tolling bells; first heard on his debut single 'Lost Without Love', it became a trademark, particularly memorably on 'My Home Is A Prison', where, not for the only time, the desolation of the narrative is magnified by studio echo. This excellent CD includes one or both sides of virtually all his Excello singles and four previously unissued tracks.

**** Been Gone Too Long
Hightone HCD 8031 *Lonesome Sundown; David Ii (reeds); Nat Dove, Ernest Vantrease, Bill Murray (kb); Phillip Walker, Tony Mathews (g); Dennis Walker (b, prod); Franchot Blake (d); Aaron Tucker, Choctaw Slim (perc); The Melody Kings, The Joliettes (v); Bruce Bromberg (prod).* 77.

Been Gone Too Long is among the finest accomplishments of producers Bruce Bromberg and Dennis Walker and one of the most thoroughly satisfying later-life records by any blues artist. Mesmerizing slow blues tracks like 'Dealin' From The Bottom Of The Deck', 'If You Ain't Been To Houston' and 'This Is The Blues', each with Sundown's signature guitar intro, were to be expected, but not, perhaps, his sure handling of the soul numbers 'Midnight Blues Again' and 'You Don't Miss Your Water', with their idiomatically spot-on responses by The Melody Kings. (Matthews, incidentally, plays the lead guitar on 'Midnight', Phillip Walker on 'Water' and 'One More Night'.) Sundown was reportedly unenthusiastic about emerging from retirement to make this album, but the eminently sympathetic playing of the accompanying musicians, Phillip Walker and Nat Dove in particular, seems to have created an ambience that dispelled his doubts and elicited a performance of unwavering conviction. TR

Hamilton Loomis (born 1975)
VOCAL, GUITAR, HARMONICA, BASS

Based in Houston, Loomis began playing music early and by the age of 14 was singing in a vocal group with his parents. He has toured with his own band since his late teens.

(**(*)) Kickin' It
Blind Pig BPCD 5084 *Loomis; Kenny Borak (t); Kevin Needham (ts); Brant Leeper (kb, o, p, v); Mike Cross (b, v); Nico Leophonte, Levi Haddock III (d). 03.*

This is the fifth album Loomis has made since his self-produced 1994 debut, but his first on an internationally distributed label. He describes his music as 'blues outside the box' and asks: 'Where is the music going? Is it gonna stay inside that little twelve-bar box? Or will it progress?' So much for the vast legacy of all those unprogressive artists who have been fulfilled by working in conventional blues formats. Readers who turn with interest to a practical demonstration of Loomis's 'outside' thinking will find ten original songs lightly touched by the wing of the blues eagle, the majority of them rooted in soul or funk forms. Though his voice is blues-lite at best, the general effect is not unappealing. If you have the opportunity to sample a soundbite, try the rhythmically lissome 'Take A Number (Stand In Line)'. But there are a few startling infelicities like the vocoder interpolations on 'Get My Blues On', and surprisingly scant evidence of the 'Texas swagger' or 'blues-god guitar' that reviewers have discerned in his earlier albums. TR

The Lost American Bluesmen
GROUP

The late Jimmie Lee Robinson tracked down various old friends so that Living Blues staffer John Anthony Brisbin could interview them; they turned out to be keen to record as well.

** The Lost American Bluesmen
Midnight Creeper CD 2002 *Sleepy Otis Hunt (h, v); Jimmie Lee Robinson (g, b, v); Frank Scott, Willie Hudson (g, v); Bert Mell (g); Robert Perkins, Maurice Houston, Willie Black (b); Bill Warren (d, v). late 95–early 96.*

Only Jimmie Lee Robinson is well known among these Chicago musicians who got their start in the '50s. Bill Warren once drummed for Buddy Guy and Junior Wells; Frank Scott ran the Great Scott label, which issued an early 45 by Albert Collins; Willie Hudson played guitar for Willie Mabon; and Otis Hunt sat in at South Side clubs. Hunt and Scott each have four tracks as leader, Warren has three, and Hudson and Robinson two apiece. The notes describe them as journeymen (which is severe on Robinson), and acknowledge that years of inactivity have resulted in some rough edges. This is honest; opening the CD with its three weakest tracks is perverse. Thereafter the quality seldom rises higher than adequate, and there's frequent rhythmic and harmonic confusion, some of the latter caused by Robinson's unshared penchant for minor chords. Hunt, who died in 1998, got his chance to record too late, and Scott shows only that he must once have been a convincing J. B. Lenoir imitator. Hudson's 'Fat Meat Is Greasy' has a sly lyric, but lack of practice means that Robinson had to play lead for him. At 78 Warren is still a thrusting drummer and a strong singer; with Robinson playing lead, rhythm and bass on his tracks, the 'band' is at its most coherent. Robinson and Warren are The Lost American Bluesmen's most convincing members, but the CD's value is historical rather than aesthetic. CS

Joe Hill Louis (1921–57)
VOCAL, HARMONICA, GUITAR, BASS DRUM, HI-HAT CYMBAL

At 14, Lester (or Leslie) Hill ran away from an abusive stepmother, fetching up in Memphis, a few miles north. There he met Billy and Drew Canale, teenage sons of a wealthy white family; he was to work for the Canales for the rest of his life. (The boys nicknamed him after Joe Louis when he outfought a local tearaway.) Gradually, Joe perfected his one-man-band act, becoming a popular performer around Memphis, and as 'The Be-Bop Boy' on WDIA. He died of tetanus after a cut became infected.

Louis's discography is exceptionally complicated in terms of labels, pseudonyms, alternative and edited versions, retitlings and mistitlings. At its core, however, are masters recorded by Sam Phillips, and variously issued by him, leased to Modern and Checker, or left unissued until collector interest unearthed them. One each of Louis's recordings for Columbia and House of Sound can be heard on *Stompin', Vol. 19* (Stompin' 319), but they don't add much to the picture. Four sides made for Rockin', issued as by Leslie Louis or Johnny Lewis, are on *Rockin' Blues* (Rockin' HTCD 5502); with the exception of 'Ridin' Home', which features agonizingly bitonal saxophone, they are well worth hearing.

*** Boogie In The Park
Ace CDCHD 803 *Joe Hill Louis; Ford Nelson (p); unknown (d); unknown (clapping). 7/50–2/53.*

Carefully compiled and documented, *Boogie In The Park* includes 'at least one version of each surviving piece recorded by Sam Phillips for release on Modern Records', and another eight recorded by Modern on their own account. It's always easy to hear Joe Hill Louis's influences and borrowings; prominent in the mix are John Lee Hooker, Howlin' Wolf and both Sonny Boy Williamsons, although Joe's rack harp was necessarily simplified. He's always his own man, however, and at his best makes straightforward, entertaining and wonderfully well-integrated music, whether he's chugging cheerfully through medium-fast boogies, laying down doomy slow blues or doing his nut on an unlikely version of 'At The Woodchopper's Ball'. 'Twisting And Turning' and 'Backslide Boogie' (both originally issued on a Howlin' Wolf LP!) are outstanding blues-band, never mind one-man-band, instrumentals.

Looking back, Sam Phillips thought he could have arranged

the mikes better, but the blasting, in-your-face roughness is part of Joe's appeal as a no-frills, kick-ass entertainer. There are some drawbacks, however. Louis was an occasional and successful pioneer of deliberate guitar distortion, but he was also liable to go out of tune, especially on slow blues; he has obvious problems on 'Mistreat Me Woman', and 'Chocolate Blonde' is excruciating. His harp fills could be wayward at times, too; after 28 tracks, Louis's limitations are as apparent as his merits, and *Boogie In The Park* could usefully have been shortened. There's far too much good and occasionally great music here to make the disc of value only to completists, but it would be wrong to recommend it without also recommending judicious use of the skip button.

***(*) The Be-Bop Boy
Bear Family BCD 15524 *Joe Hill Louis; Walter Horton (h); Jack Kelly, Albert Williams, unknown (p); Nolen Hall, Willie Nix, unknown (d). 3/52–c. 5/53.*

As well as Joe Hill Louis the lead artist, this disc features him accompanying Walter Horton and Mose Vinson. On Ace, only 'Eyesight To The Blind', with Ford Nelson and a drummer, escapes the one-man-band format, but his tight, focused performance clarifies Phillips's wish to record him with accompanists. The fruits of that wish are on show here, beginning with 'She Treats Me Mean And Evil', perhaps Louis's finest recording, with its emotional vocals, snarling, overloaded guitar and Nolen Hall's minimalist drumming. Its flipside, 'Dorothy Mae', backs Joe's singing and guitar with an all-star band, but Horton merely comps, while Kelly and Nix are under-recorded. This lineup (with Albert Williams replacing Kelly) recurs, much more successfully, and on one session Joe resumes the full one-man-band rig, with just Williams on piano. Louis and his accompanists romp and stomp to consistently good effect; the high points, both featuring a magisterial Walter Horton, are 'Hydramatic Woman', which revamps 'Rocket 88', and the rampantly boastful 'Tigerman'. CS

Louisiana Red (born 1932)
VOCAL, HARMONICA, GUITAR

Iverson Minter was an orphan by the age of five, and was raised by family members in Pittsburgh, where he began playing guitar in his early teens. In 1949 he joined the blues circle in Detroit, hanging out with John Lee Hooker and Eddie Burns. His first recordings, in 1952, were variously in the style of Hooker, Lightnin' Hopkins or Muddy Waters, his chief models. The 1962 album The Lowdown Back Porch Blues *brought him international exposure, but he did not exploit it until the '70s, when he began touring Europe regularly. He has played and recorded in Germany (where he has lived since 1982), France, England, Greece, Poland and other countries.*

Red's 1953 single 'Gonna Play My Guitar'/'Sugarcane Highway', issued as by Playboy Fuller, is on the VAC *Detroit Blues* (JSP JSP 7736 4CD).

***(*) The Lowdown Back Porch Blues
Collectables COL-CD-5419 *Louisiana Red; Carl Lynch (b); Panama Francis (d). c. 10/62–64.*

The Lowdown Back Porch Blues caused a stir when it was first issued. Here was a youngish black musician wholly committed to the blues, plainly influenced by Muddy Waters and Lightnin' Hopkins yet capable of speaking in a distinctive, modern voice and often in words of his own (though, if the composer credits were trustworthy, he had no hand in the songs with the sharpest edge of social commentary, 'Red's Dream' – an updating of Big Bill Broonzy's 'Just A Dream' – and 'Ride On, Red, Ride On').The contrast of his economical guitar and harmonica playing and the fluency and expressiveness of his singing was enormously attractive, and even 40-odd years later the album makes a convincing bid to be regarded as a minor classic.

*** The Best Of Louisiana Red
Evidence ECD 26059 *Louisiana Red; Bill Dicey (h); Dave 'Baby' Cortez (o); Tommy Tucker (p, d); Robert Banks, Don Cook (p); James Brooks (g, b); Ken Mims, Napoleon Allen, Doug Cook (g); Paul Martinez, Jimmy Lewis, Leonard Gaskin (b); Jim Evans, Chas Otis, Earl Williams, Ralph Jones (d); Herb Abramson (prod). 9/65–9/73.*

Producer Herb Abramson (the least remembered of the founders of Atlantic Records) thought a lot of Red and recorded him repeatedly in the decade or so after the release of *The Lowdown Back Porch Blues*. Apart from a couple of remakes of songs on that album, this selection is split between Red's versions of songs associated with Muddy Waters, Jimmy Reed, Big Boy Crudup, etc., sometimes quite personalized, sometimes not, and several of his own compositions – though, as often as not, they also turn out to be nods to his models. 'Where Is My Friend?', for instance, fits neatly over the template of Elmore James's 'It Hurts Me Too'. Red's verve in repossessing the past, however, makes him more fun to listen to than many more stolidly imitative artists.

*** Walked All Night Long
The Blues Alliance TBA-13011//Corazong 255023 *Louisiana Red; Kyril Bromley (p); Lefty Dizz (g). 1/75.*

But for one detail, this would be a typical Louisiana Red record. The principal does his usual job of putting new lyrics in familiar settings: 'Pinetop' and probably 'Mary' are based on Muddy Waters motifs, 'Going Train Blues' sounds like early Hooker, 'Going Down Georgia' uses the melody of 'One Kind Favor'/'See That My Grave Is Kept Clean'. The untypical detail is the presence of Lefty Dizz, whose sharp, spare playing, learned in a very different school from Red's, gives the album unexpected colour and distinctiveness.

**(*) Blues For Ida B
JSP JSPCD 2106 *Louisiana Red. 5/82.*
*** Sittin Here Wonderin [sic]
Earwig 4932 *Louisiana Red. 5–7/82.*

'Right now I'm not in good spirits,' Red announces at the start of *Blues For Ida B*. 'I just lost the one that I love deeply.' But his depression lifts enough for him to give a genial nod to a girlfriend in 'Chicken Licken' and indulge in some rock-star hollering in 'Nothing But The Blues'. The album's most notable feature is the studio echo: embedded in this huge wobbly jelly of reverberation, 'Nothing But A Gypsy Man' reproduces the sound of early Hooker with an accuracy even more spooky than usual. There are the usual stylistic references to Muddy Waters ('If I Had A Dollar') and Lightnin' Hopkins ('This Little Letter'); 'Love Me True' was inspired by Guitar Slim's 'The Things That I Used To Do'. *Sittin Here*

Wonderin, though more conventionally recorded, is a cocktail mixed to the same recipe: Hooker is again eerily reanimated on 'E Street Bridge' and 'Bumble Bee', Muddy Waters flows through 'I'm Lonesome' (based on 'Still A Fool'), 'Prison Blues #1' and 'Stella Blues', and the title number has a ring of Hopkins. The mood is generally sombre.

**(*) To Blues Sinanta To Rembetiko
Evthomi Diastasi SD-CD-007 *Louisiana Red; Stelios Vamvakaris (bouzouki)*. 9/88.

The title means 'Blues Meets Rebetika'. A collaboration between a bluesman and a musician schooled in a form that can justly be called a kind of Greek blues is a tantalizing idea, but, as is often the way with these cross-cultural encounters, the music produced is compromised, not expanded, by the players' differences. Vamvakaris, son of the famous rebetic singer and bouzouki player Markos Vamvakaris, plays along with four of the structurally conventional blues that occupy most of the programme, lending them some exotic tone colour, but his solos belong to neither idiom. The only track on which he takes the lead is the last, 'Imagination Within Power'; this is music from his tradition, and it's Red's turn to doodle round the edges. 'Korea Blues', 'Hey Now Baby!!' and 'That's All Right', a free interpretation of a theme by Arthur Crudup, are performed by Red on his own.

**(*) Last Mohican Of The Blues
Polton CDPL 047 *Louisiana Red; 'Long' Slawomir Wierzcholski (h, v); Jerry Kossacz (p); Tomasz Kaminski (vn); Marek Dabrowski (g); 'Bruner' Andrzej Gulczynski (b)*. 6/92.

The sides with several musicians tend to be untidy, but there are some very appealing duets, with Wierzcholski on 'You Wreck My Mind Baby' and the Hopkinsian 'All You Texas Women', which starts out as a song and turns into a recitation of his CV, and with Kossacz on 'Memory Of The Blues Experience', where Red recalls days spent on Ashland Avenue, while giving an accurate impression of Robert Nighthawk's slide playing. 'I Wonder Why' warns unfriendly critics on *Living Blues* magazine that he has mojo connections. But at 73.14 the album is way too long, and the genial backslapping with his accompanists on the last three tracks is not worth the almost 20 minutes it occupies.

**(*) The Blues Spectrum Of Louisiana Red
JSP JSPCD 803 *Louisiana Red; Lenni (s); Sugar Blue, Steve Bell (h); Dave Bainbridge (kb); Jon Cleary (p); Norman Beaker, Richard Studholme, Lurrie Bell (g); Chip O'Connor, Marty David, Tyson Bell (b); Tim Franks, Geoff Nichols, James Bell (d)*. 78–92.

Trawling through their catalogue of Louisiana Red recordings, JSP haul up a duet with Sugar Blue, solos from both studio and club dates and band-accompanied tracks from three sessions. The association of Red and JSP has been long and productive – a fact Red gracefully acknowledges in 'The Best Place' by namechecking the label and its proprietor – and JSP could have done better by him: two of the live recordings are of poor technical quality, 'Love Me Mama' is one of the least interesting songs on *Blues For Ida B* (see above) and there was room for three or four more tracks.

** Over My Head
Chrisly CR 20003 *Louisiana Red*. 4–6/97.

**(*) I Hear The Train Coming
Chrisly CR 20004 *Louisiana Red; Detlef Schmidt (b); Holger Mock (d)*. 4–6/97.

Possibly in response to reaching 65, Red appears to have decided to ignore the signposts of other men's styles and go his own way. As an advertisement for this new approach *Over My Head* is not at all persuasive, the songs blunt-edged, the guitar accompaniments dull. *I Hear The Train Coming* has more slide playing, evidently modelled on Tampa Red's, and the backing musicians add an almost rockabilly zip, but Red's own songs are still underdeveloped and several tracks are too long. His other Chrisly CDs, *Sugar Hips* (CD 30004), *Back To The Roots* (CD 60004) and *Ashland Avenue Blues* (CD 70001), all originally on Ornament/CMA, are of uncertain availability.

***(*) Millennium Blues
Earwig CD 4943 *Louisiana Red; Willie 'Big Eyes' Smith (h); Allen Batts (kb); Brian Bisesi (g); Willie Kent (b); Dave Jefferson (d)*. 11/98.
**(*) Driftin'
Earwig CD 4947 *As above, except add Michael Frank (h)*. 11/98, 6/99.

Millennium Blues envelops Red in the thick, murky ambience of the Chicago blues band. Since the clock is being turned back 30-odd years, it's appropriate that the album opens with 'Red's Vision', a retelling of 'Red's Dream', though it's brought up to date with allusions to Clinton, Kosovo and the Oklahoma City bombing. In a solo interlude, a stark reminiscence of childhood abuse leads into 'Orphanage Home Blues' and other songs drawn from deep in his past. The band returns to steer 'Arlene Blues' and 'That Detroit Thing' as if supervised by the spirit of Muddy Waters, but Red is always the driving force, and this is one of his most personal recordings.

Red liked working with the *Millennium Blues* band so much that it was reconvened for several tracks of *Driftin'*. The rest are solos that find Red both refreshing himself from familiar sources – Hopkins in 'Bring Me Some Water', Hooker in 'Leaving Grandma' – and trying something different with the hymns 'In The Garden' and 'He Will See You Through', which add a little more detail to the elaborate self-portrait Red has painted on his many records.

*** No Turn On Red
HMG HMG 1010 *Louisiana Red; Bob Corritore (h, prod); Matt Bishop (p); Johnny Rapp, Buddy Reed (g); Paul Thomas, Mario Moreno (b); Chico Chism, Paul Fasulo, Brian Fahey (d)*. 5/82, 8/99–9/03.

No turn, indeed: once again Red shuffles his pack of impersonations and deals strong-willed performances in the style of Hooker, Hopkins, Muddy and Elmore James, interspersing them among less allusive pieces. The Hopkins effect is used, aptly enough, for a 'September 11th Blues', but such a subject demands a less mundane response than conventional expressions of shock and regret. In other respects, though, this is a strong set that will please Red's admirers. The only track that wasn't made relatively recently is the closing 'Everybody Laughs At Me', an outtake from the 1982 *Sittin Here Wonderin* sessions. TR

Willie Love (1906–53)
VOCAL, PIANO

A popular entertainer in the clubs along Greenville's Nelson Street, Love benefited from a 1942 meeting with Rice Miller, becoming a part-time King Biscuit Boy and eventually backing Miller (as Sonny Boy Williamson) on his first Trumpet sessions in 1951. A limited but boisterous pianist, his own records over the next two years made him the label's second most popular blues artist. Their initial vigour was gradually dissipated by the alcoholism that claimed his life four months after his last session.

*** Greenville Smokin'
Purple Pyramid CLP-0832 *Love; Otis Green, Richard 'Dicky Boy' Lillie (ts); Willie Kyles, Carlton Wells or Bernard Williams (s); Lonnie Holmes, Elmore James, Joe Willie Wilkins, Little Milton Campbell, Lester Williams (g); T. J. Green, Walter 'Buck' Henson (b); Alex Wallace, Junior Blackman, Oneal Hudson, Rusty Alfred (d). 4/51–4/53.*

Unlike his harmonica-playing friend, there's little sense of calculation about Love's recordings. A clamorous energy invests his debut release, 'Take It Easy Baby', redolent of the clubs in which he made his living. It's also apparent in 'Everybody's Fishing' and 'Vanity Dresser Boogie', the first featuring vocal encouragement from Elmore James and Joe Willie Wilkins. The latter comes from an eight-title session marking the recording debut of teenager Little Milton Campbell that also includes 'Nelson Street Blues', in which Love presents a guided tour of his workplace. There's a sense of tradition in Love's repertoire, drawing upon Big Bill Broonzy ('Little Car Blues'), Johnnie Temple ('Seventy Four Blues'), Buddy Moss ('V-8 Ford') and Leroy Carr ('Shady Lane Blues'). An attempt to broaden his appeal into mainstream R&B in his final sessions falters from mundane material and off-centre if spirited performances from Love himself.

The remastering is generally acceptable, but the final handful of tracks are dubbed from noisy acetates. Three of those are better reproduced on *Shout, Brother, Shout!* (Alligator ALCD 2800), while *Delta Blues 1951* (Alligator ALCD 2702, shared with Big Joe Williams and Luther Huff) includes the second single ('Everybody's Fishing'/'My Own Boogie') and half of the 12/51 session with Campbell on guitar. NS

Lovie Lee (1917–97)
VOCAL, PIANO

Eddie 'Lovie' Lee Watson became a musician in Meridian, Mississippi, where he also became unofficial adoptive father to a teenage runaway, Carey Bell. Watson and Bell moved to Chicago in 1957, where Lovie led the Sensationals at evenings and weekends until retiring from his day job in 1979, whereupon he became Muddy Waters's last pianist. After Waters's death he returned to playing around Chicago.

**** Good Candy
Earwig CD 4928 *Lovie Lee; Boney Fields (t); Jimmy Bauma (as); Garrick Patten, Willie Young (ts); Carey Bell, Steve Bell (h); Lurrie Bell, Eddie Taylor, Vance Kelly (g); Douglas Watson, Lee Johnson (b); Odie Payne, Earl Howell, Jesse Lee Clay, Joe Poston (d). 84–9/92.*

Lovie Lee's music sometimes goes way back: 'She's Gone' is a distinctly original reworking of 'Big Road Blues', and 'Naptown', one of four tracks on *Living Chicago Blues – Vol. III* (Alligator ALCD 7703), is well out of the usual run of Leroy Carr revivals. At the same time, most of his playing during a long career was for neighbourhood audiences, who had to be kept entertained with new numbers like 'West Side Woman', a striking tale of life and love in the ghetto. Lovie's connections with the Bell family and other Chicago musicians enabled him to put together a series of effective bands for the *Good Candy* sessions; the drummers are consistently fine, and all three guitarists pull exciting solos out of the air. Carey Bell is sometimes too low in the mix, and on 'Whoopin' Thighs' [*sic*] Fields and Patten are cramped and distant; but these are minor grumbles about a CD that unpretentiously revives some of the power and the glory of Chicago blues in its postwar heyday. CS

Robert Lowery (born 1932)
VOCAL, GUITAR

The Arkansas-born Lowery moved to California in 1956. Living in Santa Cruz, he began playing at parties and on the street. In 1974 he made his first major public appearance at the San Francisco Blues Festival and soon afterwards cut some singles for the Blues Connoisseur label. His high, clear voice, versatility on guitar and propensity for composing original blues made him one of the most attractive younger artists playing oldfashioned blues to emerge in the '70s.

**(*) Earthquake Blues
Orleans OR 1017 *Lowery. 10/89.*
*** A Good Man Is Hard To Find
Orleans OR 1411 *Lowery; Virgil Thrasher (h); Katie Webster (p); Raphael Semmes (b). 7/92.*

Half a dozen of the 11 songs on *Earthquake Blues* are preceded by what are listed as monologues: brief autobiographical reminiscences, which give the listener a sense of Lowery's background and interests. The title song is an original about a recent event, in the style of Lightnin' Hopkins – a favourite model, whom Lowery later turns to for 'One Kind Of Favor' and 'Fan It'. He also sings three Robert Johnson songs, prefacing 'Crossroads' with the words: 'There's many musicians have tried to play his music … but I never saw a one that come closer to doin' it than I am fixin' to do it right now.' He earns higher marks for chutzpah than for achievement, a judgement that can be applied to the album as a whole.

His next outing was more cautious and, perhaps not coincidentally, more successful. Genre standards like John Lee Hooker's 'Hobo Blues' and Muddy Waters's 'Louisiana Blues' are enhanced by his close partnership with Thrasher, an excellent harmonica player, and the two men prolong their winning streak on Lowery's own 'Snake Hippin' Mama' and 'My Baby's Callin' Me'. A couple more Robert Johnson songs, 'If I Had Possession Over Judgement Day' and 'Last Fair Deal Gone Down', are adequately done. Only a cursory 'When The Saints Go Marching In' lets down an enjoyable album.

**(*) Goin' Away Blues
Wolf 120.932 *Lowery; Virgil Thrasher (h). 10/97.*

*** **Rainin' Down Blues**
Wolf 120.933 *As above, except add David Scoll (washtub b).* 2/99.

Both these albums contain several songs whose familiar titles mislead you into expecting familiar lyrics, such as 'Drink Little Woman', 'Chauffeur Blues' and 'Walkin' Your Log' on *Goin' Away Blues* or 'Rock Me Baby', 'Going South', 'Big Hip Woman' and 'Move That Thing' on *Rainin' Down Blues*. In fact non-original pieces – 'Sittin' On Top Of The World' and a couple of Robert Johnson songs on *Goin' Away Blues*; Sleepy John Estes's 'Someday Baby' (one of a few numbers with electric guitar) on *Rainin' Down Blues* – are in the minority. For the most part Lowery's music is an attractive amalgam of generic and individual elements. Thrasher's harmonica, which was heard almost throughout *A Good Man Is Hard To Find*, is restricted to two appearances on the first album but has more space on the second. TR

Robert Lucas (born 1962)
VOCAL, GUITAR, HARMONICA

The burly Lucas (he describes himself in one of his songs as '50 pounds of bone wrapped up in 200 pounds of ham') grew up in Long Beach, California, where he began playing harmonica at 13 and slide guitar at 16. He gained experience as a sideman with Bernie Pearl's band, then formed his own group, Luke And The Locomotives. From 1995 to 2000 he was a member of Canned Heat.

(*) **Usin' Man Blues
AudioQuest AQ-CD 1001 *Lucas; Michael Harrison (vn); Devitt Feeley (md, g); Francis Banich (g); Mark Goldberg (b).* 7/90.
(*) **Luke And The Locomotives
AudioQuest AQ-CD 1004 *Lucas; Steve F'dor (p); Paul 'Pops' Bryant (g); Al 'Bedrock' Bedrosian (b); Bob 'Max' Ebersole (d).* 12/90.
(*) **Built For Comfort
AudioQuest AQ-CD 1011 *Lucas; Steve F'dor (p); John Schneiderman (bj); Dave Melton, Kevin Doherty (g); Denny Croy (b); Freebo (tu); Stephen Hodges (d).* 5/92.
(*) **Layaway
AudioQuest AQ-CD 1021 *Lucas; Harry McKitrick (tb, bs); Spider Mittleman (ts); Benny Yee (o); Steve F'dor (p); Dave Melton, Paul 'Pops' Bryant, Robert Lieberman (g); Mark Goldberg (b); Lee Campbell (d); Max Bangwell (perc, chair).* 5/93.
(*) **Completely Blue
AudioQuest AQ-CD 1045 *Lucas; Fred Kaplan (kb, perc); Alex Schultz, David Melton (g); Tyler Pederson (b); Johnny Morgan (d); Fito de la Parra (perc).* 10/96.

Readers making their first foray into the work of Robert Lucas may soon find themselves facing a decision which could determine how keenly they pursue their journey. For some his rasping, undisciplined voice production may be a technique that convincingly matches the play of emotion in his music; others may find its strangled effortlessness an obstacle.

Like Lucas's deleted first album, *Across The River* (Delta Man DMM 901), *Usin' Man Blues* is predominantly solo. The quiet restraint of 'Me And The Devil' elevates it above the other two Robert Johnson songs he chooses, but Son House's 'Jinx Blues' (titled 'Jinx Around My Bed') is chanted to a jaunty rhythm that subverts the song's meaning. A few tracks are by a stringband of mandolin, guitars and sometimes violin, and these have a lumbering but not graceless swing.

Luke And The Locomotives is by a quartet throughout, with piano added on four tracks, and the band setting goes a little way towards controlling Lucas's vocal unruliness. When he plays slide guitar, the ensemble avoids the raucous manner of Hound Dog Taylor or George Thorogood, instead creating a laidback music full of space and air. On other numbers he leaves the lead role to Bryant, who plays like a Memphis hotshot making plans to move north and justifies Robert Jr Lockwood's approving comment: 'This record has that old sound, that old Chicago sound.' As on *Usin' Man Blues*, the repertoire is about half original pieces and half songs by Wolf, Muddy, Elmore James and Sonny Boy Williamson I.

That description also applies to *Built For Comfort*, which mixes band sides, solos like 'Just A Kid' or a further Johnson song, 'Come On In My Kitchen', and a couple of duets; on one of the latter, 'Sleeping By Myself', F'dor's piano playing recalls Big Maceo. F'dor is also splendid on the ribald 'Chiropractor Blues' on *Layaway*, which differs from its predecessors both in its higher proportion of original songs (eight out of ten) and in Lucas's casting his stylistic net wider to embrace a T-Bone Walkerish 'High Priced Baby', where Bryant is again on form.

Completely Blue breaks farther away, eliminating the voice-and-slide-guitar solos, foregrounding Lucas's pungent harmonica playing and giving most of the guitar solo spots to Melton and Schultz. Lucas's singing is on a tighter rein, and for songs like 'Party Girl' and 'I'm Gonna Whisper' he uses a softer voice, confiding and tremulous in the manner of Sonny Boy Williamson II, that he'd occasionally revealed on his earlier albums. Apart from an easygoing, front-porchy version of Hendrix's 'Voodoo Chile' the material is all original. Lucas is more articulate in the personal realm than the political: 'Pain In Our Cities', like *Built For Comfort*'s 'My Home Is A Burning', confronts the sickness of urban America, but all it offers by way of diagnosis is 'This country got a cancer – that cancer's called poverty.' TR

Connie Lush
VOCAL

Lush has been singing since the '80s and is widely considered Britain's leading blueswoman. She has been voted Best UK Female Vocalist five times by readers of Blues In Britain. *In 1998 she and her band supported B. B. King on his tour of Europe.*

(*) **Blues Shouter
Mystic MYS CD 123 *Lush; Dave Edge (s); Andy Wilson (p); John Lewis, Alistair Crook (g); Terry Harris (b); Carl Woodward (d); Jake Woodward (cymbal); Jennifer John, Saphena Aziz (v).* 00?
(**(*)) **Unfaithfully Yours?**
Blue Rhythm BR 103 *Lush; Tony Peers (t); Alby Donnelly (s); Henry Priestman (ac, o, v); Steve Alun Jones (p); John Lewis (g); Terry Harris (b); Carl Woodward (d); Gary Christian, Carla Russell (v).* 02.

Lush is what another generation might have called a revue artiste, in her element when delivering a varied programme with panache and pzazz. Her range is considerable: *Blues Shouter* encompasses Helen Humes's sexy 'Million Dollar Secret' and Noël Coward's 'Mad About The Boy', with Etta James's 'Out Of The Rain' somewhere between. It's a pity her rendition and arrangement of the last song are so frankly modelled on James's, because elsewhere she shows some independence from her sources: 'Secret' sounds more like Dinah Washington than Humes, and 'One Monkey' nothing like its originator, Big Mama Thornton. The Etta James songbook was at hand again for *Unfaithfully Yours?*, and Lush is equally faithful to her model in 'I'd Rather Go Blind'. The rest of the album, apart from a Randy Newman composition, was collectively written by Lush and some of her bandsmen. The songs are well crafted and Lush delivers them with skill, concentration and versatility, but if you were searching for a word to follow 'File Under', you wouldn't immediately think 'Blues'. TR

Professor Eddie Lusk (1948–92)
VOCAL, KEYBOARDS

Lusk learned organ in his father's Chicago church, and his blues playing retained a gospel influence. A busy sideman and session musician, Lusk killed himself after being diagnosed with AIDS.

** Professor Strut
Delmark DD-650 *Lusk; Paul Mundy (as, ts); Joey Woolfolk (g, b, v); Al Mann (g, b); Donald Coleman (d); Karen Carroll (v).* 1/89.

Lusk's only extended release is credited to 'Professor's Blues Revue featuring Karen Carroll'. The opening 'Come On Down To The Blues Bar' is a generic shuffle with muffled vocals; the sound on subsequent tracks is better without being good. None of the singers is exceptional, and Carroll's attempt at Sarah Vaughan on 'Everything Is You' is very ill-advised indeed. Woolfolk applies rococo vocal mannerisms in an unsuccessful attempt to rejuvenate 'They Call It Stormy Monday'. Credit where it's due, though; Woolfolk's breezy solos are the only interesting aspects of both the meandering title track and 'This Little Light Of Mine', which concludes 38 minutes that seem much longer. CS

Joe Lutcher (born 1919)
ALTO SAXOPHONE, FLUTE, VOCAL

Joseph Lutcher was born in Lake Charles, Louisiana, and had his first musical experience playing in a family band. In the '40s he moved to LA, where he led his Society Cats at Café Society and, in 1947, began recording, first for Specialty but soon for Capitol, where his sister Nellie was beginning her successful career as a novelty singer and pianist. After further label moves but no big hits, the disappointed Lutcher quit the business and joined the Seventh Day Adventist Church. For the last 40 years or so he has owned a gospel record shop.

**(*) Joe Lutcher 1947
Classics 5075 *Lutcher; Karl George (t); Bill Ellis (ts); Leon Beck (bs); Harold Morrow (p); Ulysses Livingstone (g); William Cooper (b, v); Bea Booker (b); Booker T. Hart (d); Cliff Holland, band (v).* 4–11/47.

**(*) Jumpin' At The Mardi Gras
Ace CDCHD 753 *Lutcher; unknown (t); 'Big Bill' [Ellis?], poss. Leon Beck, Bumps Myers (ts); unknown (bs); poss. Harold Morrow (p); poss. Chuck Norris (g); poss. William Cooper (b, v); poss. Booker T. Hart (d); unknown (v).* 49–8/50.

This well-rehearsed group made lively music in the 'little big band' idiom of Louis Jordan or Joe Liggins, mixing blues, boogies and novelty instrumentals like 'Bagdad Bebop' (Classics) and 'Ojai' (Ace). Lutcher's tone is clear and hard, lacking Jordan's warmth or humour but imparting a vigorous swing to tunes like 'Shuffle Woogie', 'Mo-Jo' and 'Joe-Joe Jump' (Classics) and 'Foothill Drive' and 'Rag Mop' (Ace). The two CDs dovetail, Classics covering his Specialty and Capitol recordings and Ace his contract with Modern, which yielded eight issued sides and about a dozen rejected ones. Some of the latter are alternative takes, but there's also a surprise polka, 'Please Be My Honey'. Ace conclude with a blues/ballad coupling by the Lutcher band and guest soloist Bumps Myers, recorded in concert. TR

Lynwood Slim (born 1953)
VOCAL, HARMONICA, FLUTE

Richard Duran grew up in the Lynwood section of LA. Moving to Minneapolis, he established himself on the club scene. Returning to LA, he played with Kid Ramos and Junior Watson, recording with both. In 1995 he moved to Chicago to join Dave Specter & the Bluebirds. He has produced albums by R. J. Mischo and Nick Moss.

*** Soul Feet
Atomic Theory ATM 1121//Cold Wind CWR 9406 *Lynwood Slim; Rick O'Dell, Scott Johnson, Bob Byerson (s); Mark Ashe (o, p); Jimmy Hill (o); Leonard 'Baby Doo' Caston, Cornbread Harris (p); James Smith, Phil Schmid, Dan Schwalbe (g); Larry Hayes, Bill Black (b); Donald Robertson, Robb Stupka, Dwight Dario (d).* 4/84, 5/93.

*** Lost In America
Atomic Theory ATM 1135 *Lynwood Slim; Fred Kaplan (p); Junior Watson, Kid Ramos, Joel Foy, Dave Gonzales (g); Tyler Pederson, Larry Taylor, Tom Yearsley (b); Robb Stupka, Brian Fahey (d).* 8/90.

*** Lost In America
Black Magic BMCD 9017 *As above.* 8/90.

**(*) Back To Back
Crosscut CCD 11059 *Lynwood Slim; Fred Kaplan (p); Junior Watson (g, v); Rick 'L.A. Holmes' Holmstrom (g); Larry Taylor (b); Richard Innes (d).* 10/97.

**(*) World Wide Wood
Pacific Blues PBRC 9903 *Lynwood Slim; Jeff Turmes (ts, bs); Egidio Ingalla (h); Fred Kaplan, unknown (p); Kid Ramos, Kirk Fletcher, Marc Thijs, Jr Valentine, Manny Makis, Andy Carrera (g); Larry Taylor, Rick Reed, Max Pitardi, Peter Sack (b); Richard Innes, Paul Fasulo, Joe Rossi, Art Mack (d); band (v).* late 90s.

Lynwood Slim is a useful man to have in a band: whether vocally or on harmonica, he isn't hugely distinctive but he's very reliable. *Soul Feet* (availability uncertain) contains his earliest recordings, nine tracks with the Hill–Caston–Smith group, recorded in '84; Smith is the artist later known as Jimi 'Prime Time' Smith. These are crisp performances and, so far as Slim is concerned, among the most flattering in his discography. The remaining six tracks are from '93.

There are many moments in *Lost In America* when lovers of '40s/'50s blues are liable to hug themselves with glee, so precisely do Slim and Junior Watson evoke the phrasing and accent of the period. On 'Just Your Fool' Watson's touch has all the dreamy silkiness of Johnny Moore's, but five minutes later, in 'Tell Me What I've Done', he is transformed into the young

Jimmy Rogers, and Slim into one of the Walters. 'Cried Last Night' and 'Atlanta Blues' feature Slim's controlled chromatic harp playing. The variation between the two issues is that the Atomic Theory follows 'Ain't Enough Time' with another, much more rough-cut, take of the same number, on which everyone sounds different. The Black Magic CD omits this.

Back To Back, jointly credited to Slim and Watson, reassembles the principal players from the *Lost In America* sessions, with Rick Holmstrom added on four tracks. Kaplan and Watson lay a gorgeously soft carpet for the Charles Brownish 'Best Wishes', and Watson's tremolissimo reading of Earl Hooker's 'Happy Blues', accompanied only by drums, is delightful, but the brisk vocal blues like 'Much Later For You Baby' or 'Young And Able', which predominate, seem a little inconsequential. The studio sound is discreet and unassertive, as if engineered by librarians.

Much of *World Wide Wood* is shaped by Californian friends like Kirk Fletcher and Fred Kaplan, who are each on six cuts; 'Come Back', on which both play, is the standout track. Other items are with musicians from Belgium, Canada and Italy. The programme, as usually with Slim, is a mixture of originals and received repertoire, all done straightforwardly and without fuss. A little more drama wouldn't have come amiss.

Slim also sings on most of Kid Ramos's first album, *Two Hands One Heart* (Black Magic) and on Dave Specter's 1996 album *Left Turn On Blue* (Delmark). See also Big Rhythm Combo. TR

Willie Mabon (1925–85)
VOCAL, PIANO, HARMONICA

A Memphian by birth, Mabon came to live in Chicago in 1941, where he hung out with Sunnyland Slim and insinuated himself into the club scene. During the '50s he had several hits on Chess, and in the '60s on USA, but thereafter work fell off and in 1972 he moved to France, settling in Paris.

*** Willie Mabon 1949–1954
Classics 5154 Mabon; Paul King, unknown (t); Milt Larkin (tb); Andrew Gardner, unknown (as); Ernest Cotton, Fred Clark, Charles Ferguson, Herbert Robertson, Harold Ashby (ts); unknown (bs); Sam Casimir (g); Andrew Harris, Billy Evans, 'Cool Breeze' [Joseph Bell], Ted Sturgis, Bill Anderson (b); Billie Stepney, Steve Boswell, Oliver Coleman, unknown (d); unknowns (v). 8/49–c. 10/54.

*** Chess Blues Piano Greats
MCA/Chess CHD2–9385 2CD As above, except add unknowns (s, g, b, d), Willie Dixon (v); omit Casimir, Harris. 52–60.

Mabon was one of the few musicians in Chicago to employ the soft-voiced style of Charles Brown, which was probably a factor in the runaway success of his 1952 Chess (originally Parrot) single 'I Don't Know' – a song passed on to him by Cripple Clarence Lofton, who had recorded it a decade and a half earlier – and the good sales of follow-ups like 'I'm Mad', 'Poison Ivy' and 'The Seventh Son'. But there was more to it: Mabon added to the Brown manner a disarmingly confidential slyness that was appealing and distinctive. (One artist who evidently thought so was the English singer Georgie Fame, whose style is imbued with Mabon's.) Another distinguishing feature of Mabon's Chess recordings was the almost invariable absence of a guitar, all the melodic work being carried out by his piano and various groupings of brass and reeds. A good 18-track selection from his Chess sides occupies nearly half of the fitfully available MCA/Chess 2CD, the bulk of the rest being by Eddie Boyd. Classics preface the first couple of years' Chess output, including most of the songs mentioned above, with Mabon's debut single on Apollo.

The four sides from 1957 preserved on *Chicago Blues From Federal Records* (Ace CDCHD 717) are pleasant enough but in subtracting the horns and adding a guitar they rob Mabon of some of the distinctiveness he had been able to develop on Chess.

**(*) I Don't Know – Chicago Rhythm & Blues Piano
Wolf WBJ 020 Mabon; Earl Crosley, John Cameron (s); Billy Emerson (o); Willie Hudson, Eugene Pierson, Lacy Gibson (g); Bob Hudson, Jack Myers, Reggie Boyd (b); Al Duncan, Clifton James, Al Thompson (d). 62–64, 74.

After leaving (or being left by) Chess, Mabon recorded for Formal, source of the first four tracks here, and for USA, whence come the next six. 'Sometime I Wonder' is built on the same frame as 'I Don't Know', and 'I Got To Have Some' and its successor 'Just Got Some' have a similar elbow-in-the-ribs style, but other pieces are more left-field: 'Too Hot To Handle' is a song by the Texas country artist Eddie Noack, while 'I'm Hungry' borrows part of the melody of 'Stormy Weather'. Mabon's USA recordings are more interesting, and better recorded, than this selection suggests. The CD is completed by five solo performances from a club date in Germany in 1974, which are more consistently satisfying. Whether because of age or preference, Mabon's voice is slightly coarser than it was ten years before, and his manner less wheedling. Neither change is detrimental, and his memorials to Clarence Lofton, 'I Don't Know' and a long 'Shake That Thing', are among his best sides.

The five solo pieces on *I Blueskvarter: Chicago 1964, Volume One* (Jefferson SBACD 12653/4 2CD) include another 'I Don't Know', 'I'm The Fixer' and a reading of Charles Brown's 'New Orleans Blues' that makes very clear the kinship of their styles.

*** Cold Chilly Woman
Black & Blue BB 463 Mabon; Emmett Sutton (b); Bill Warren (d). 12/72.

*** Shake That Thing
Black & Blue BB 435 Mabon; Louis Myers, Jimmy Rogers (g); Dave Myers (b); Fred Below (d); Koko Taylor (v). 12/73.

These warm, happy recordings were made in the first year or so after Mabon settled in France. *Cold Chilly Woman* is split almost evenly between trios and solos, where Mabon often plays piano and rack harmonica together. The title track seems to foresee the ritual of televised confession and its priest Jerry Springer: 'I got a cold, chilly woman, just as mean as she could be. All we do is fuss and fight – we should be on TV.' Like almost all the programme, it's his own work; the exceptions are Ray Charles's 'Mary-Ann' and Sam Theard's 'You Rascal You', the latter a startlingly accurate impression of Louis Armstrong. Those two tracks are among six added to the original LP.

On *Shake That Thing* he reprises hits like 'Poison Ivy', 'I'm Mad' and 'I Don't Know', with Louis Myers putting in some agreeable, undemanding lead work. The original LP has been inflated by a rejected take of 'Got To Have Some', two *soi-disant* monologues that are merely brief stage introductions, and two further versions of 'Shake That Thing', Mabon's take on Ray Charles's 'What'd I Say', one a live recording with

Koko Taylor joining in. But even cutting off this fat and putting it on the side of your plate leaves a filling and flavoursome meal.

**(*) Chicago Blues Session
Evidence ECD 26063 *Mabon; Hubert Sumlin, Eddie Taylor (g); Aron Burton (b); Casey Jones (d). 7/79.*

Mabon returned to Chicago for this session. The band was a strong one, but unsuitable for a style as intimate as his, and on 'I'm Mad' he is virtually drowned out. 'Lonely Blues' quite successfully captures the feeling of Big Maceo, Sumlin's slide guitar standing in for Tampa Red's, but most of the time Mabon settles for generic performances of Chicago blues standards like 'Little Red Rooster' and 'Seventh Son' or tributes to bygone artists, including a rather grotesque imitation of Howlin' Wolf in 'Louise'. Only on the last track, 'A Change Is Gonna Come', does the band sit out and leave him the space to sound like himself. TR

Eddie Mack
VOCAL

Eddie Mack, whose real name was Mack Edmundson or Edmondson, was active as a singer on the Brooklyn club scene of the late '40s and early '50s. Producer Lee Magid remembered him as 'a baldheaded, husky guy'. He followed Eddie 'Cleanhead' Vinson into the vocalist's spot with Cootie Williams's band and made a few records with them, as well as others for Apollo and, as 'Pigmeat Peterson', for King, before disappearing without trace.

*** The Complete Recordings 1947–1952
Blue Moon BMCD 6026 *Mack; Cootie Williams, Bob Merrill, prob. Bobby Johnson, prob. Jimmy Harris, prob. Sammy Lowe, Frank Galbraith, Lammar Wright, Abdul Salaam, Jimmy Nottingham, unknown (t); Bob Range, Henderson Chambers, Fred Zito, Tyree Glenn (tb); Rupert Cole (cl, as); Haywood Henry (cl, bs); Bobby Smith, Hilton Jefferson, Rudy Powell (as); Bill 'Weasel' Parker, Willis Jackson, Julian Dash, Count Hastings, Harry Johnson, George Kelly (ts); Norman Thornton, Dave McRae (bs); Arnold Jarvis, Lester Fauntleroy, Duke Anderson, Ace Harris, Danny Small, Kelly Owens, unknown (p); prob. Leroy Kirkland, poss. René Hall, Bill Jennings, Mickey Baker (g); Leonard Swain, Lee Stanfield, Richard Fullbright, Lloyd Trotman, Grachan Moncur (b); Sylvester 'Vess' Payne, Gus Johnson, Joe Murphy, Ed Thigpen, Ed Shaugnessy, Les Erskine, Bobby Donaldson (d); band (v). 47–6/52.*

*** Hoot & Holler Saturday Night!
Delmark DE-754 *Mack; prob. Bobby Johnson, prob. Jimmy Harris, prob. Sammy Lowe, unknown (t); Bob Range (tb); Haywood Henry (cl, bs); Bobby Smith (as); Willis Jackson, Julian Dash (ts); Duke Anderson, Ace Harris, unknown (p); prob. Leroy Kirkland, poss. René Hall (g); Lee Stanfield (b); Joe Murphy (d). 9/49–12/50.*

'He had good diction,' said Lee Magid. 'Not the kind of guy you would think of as a blues shouter.' Shoutophiles shouldn't be perturbed by this judgement. Mack does sing clearly, but with no loss of heft, and, while he may not be as ebullient as Wynonie Harris, he often hits a note with a Roy Brown yell; 'Behind Closed Doors' is a good example. His proficiency suggests that he had a good deal of experience of singing with a band, and on the nine dates represented on the Blue Moon CD he had challengingly good musicians to impress, often from the Cootie Williams, Erskine Hawkins and Lucky Millinder orchestras. Catchy material like 'Hoot And Holler Saturday Night' and 'Everybody Loves A Fat Man' and a couple of hits from the country charts, 'Shotgun Boogie' and 'Divorce Me C.O.D.', contribute to making this set more than averagely entertaining. Ten tracks derived from Apollo recur on the Delmark CD, sounding considerably clearer because they are sourced from masters rather than issued pressings. They are augmented by three previously unissued sides and an alternative take of 'How About That'. The remainder of the CD is by Piney Brown (q.v.), also a moderately rewarding artist, and readers who are fond of this sort of music but not obsessed with collecting everything by its second-rank exponents may find *Hoot & Holler Saturday Night!* the more appealing option. TR

Dave MacKenzie
VOCAL, GUITAR

The only non-musical fact revealed about MacKenzie by his records is that he looks somewhat like the elderly Jerry Lewis (circa The King Of Comedy*). If a reference in one of his songs is to be taken at face value, he is in his early 60s.*

**(*) Old, New, Borrowed & Blue
Black & Tan B&T 004 *MacKenzie; Dave Fleming (b); Paul Griffith (d). 6/99.*

MacKenzie's acoustic guitar has a big, warm sound, whether he's playing slide or finger-style, while his voice has a wry, world-weary tone that's sometimes a little reminiscent of Dave Alvin. Like Alvin, too, his own songs are often built to blues designs, their more or less generic tunes being fitted with original, sometimes very amusing lyrics. 'Loaded And Laid', for instance, uses a raggy melody out of Blind Blake or Blind Boy Fuller as the backdrop for a randy-musician-on-the-road story. His interpretations of formidable repertoire standards like Robert Johnson's 'Me And The Devil' and Skip James's 'I'm So Glad' are low-key, and he's better suited to Furry Lewis's 'Turn Your Money Green'.

MacKenzie also released two albums in the mid-'90s, *Rats In My Bedroom* (Hey Baby! HBCD 1002) and *Slender Man Blues* (Hey Baby! HBCD 1004), possibly still available (Hey Baby! Records, POB 150081, Nashville, TN 37215). They are more diverse collections of his own songs but both are scattered with blues references, and the reader who warms to *Old, New, Borrowed & Blue* should seek them out. TR

Doug MacLeod (born 1946)
VOCAL, GUITAR

MacLeod was born in New York and grew up in St Louis. He began playing bass in his teens, then guitar, and after navy service studied jazz guitar at Berklee. Settling in LA in the '70s, he worked with Ernest Banks, George Smith, Pee Wee Crayton and others. Since the mid-'90s he has devoted himself to acoustic playing and to writing songs, several of which have been taken up by other artists.

**(*) No Road Back Home
Hightone HCD 8002 *MacLeod; Nolan Smith (t, flh); David Ii (s); George 'Harmonica' Smith (h); Marc Ritter (kb); Eric Ajaye,*

Bradley Bobo (b); Lee Spath (d, perc); Patti Joy MacLeod, Barbara Baines, Susan Boyd (v); Bruce Bromberg, Dennis Walker (co-prod). 84.

Is it only the Bromberg–Walker production style that makes this album seem faintly similar to contemporary work by MacLeod's Hightone contemporary Robert Cray? At the time both musicians favoured a springy guitar sound somewhat reminiscent of Mark Knopfler, but they diverged in their songwriting: Cray soon discovered a distinctive voice, but MacLeod would need a little longer to expunge tired thoughts like 'Every baby born, somebody dyin' – every truth that's told, somebody lyin' ('Long Black Train'). The title track is a good composition affectingly presented.

(*) You Can't Take My Blues
AudioQuest AQ-CD 1041 *MacLeod*; Carey Bell (h, v); Heather Hardy (vn); Jeff Turmes, Bill Stuve (b); Jimi Bott (d, perc). 12/95.

*** **Unmarked Road**
AudioQuest AQ-CD 1046 *MacLeod*; Michael Thompson (o); John 'Juke' Logan (p); Jeff Turmes (b); Steve Mugalian (d); Oliver Brown (perc); Clydene Jackson, Monalisa Young, Carmen Twillie (v). 2/97.

(*) 'Live' As It Gets
Mocombo M-55003 *MacLeod*; John 'Juke' Logan (h, v). 99?

*** **Whose Truth, Whose Lies?**
AudioQuest AQ-CD 1054 *MacLeod*; James Harman (h); Rich Del Grosso (md); Denny Croy (b); Dave Kida (d); Janiva Magness, Terry Evans, Ray Williams (v). 3/00.

*** **A Little Sin**
Black & Tan CD B&T 013 *MacLeod*; Denny Croy (ah, b); Dave Kida (d, perc). 7/02.

*** **'Dubb'**
Black & Tan CD B&T 022 *MacLeod*; Carl Sonny Leyland (p); Denny Croy (b); Dave Kida (d, perc). 8/04.

MacLeod's husky singing and spare acoustic guitar playing occasionally suggest common stylistic ground with Dave Alvin, an impression strengthened by a song like 'East Texas Sugar' on *A Little Sin*. There are traces too of the young Bob Dylan, but all in all MacLeod is a musician who can fairly claim to stand on his own. He has little truck with interpreting other people's blues, instead writing virtually everything he records, often in blues forms, though almost always without obvious models. *A Little Sin* and *'Dubb'* are particularly original in that respect, and for readers unfamiliar with his work the best introductions to it, but there is similarly striking material on *Unmarked Road* like 'Lost Like The Wind At Night', inspired by J. B. Lenoir and accompanied by guitar and percussion in a way he would have appreciated, or 'Old Country Road', played with slide in a very oldfashioned manner. *Whose Truth, Whose Lies?* has what might be heard as a combined echo of Lenoir and early John Lee Hooker in 'You Won't Find Me'; this, a couple of slide pieces and the peaceful blues melody of 'Norfolk County Line' more than compensate for the ingenuous political musing of the title track. What sounds like a melodic first draft of 'Norfolk County Line', 'Things'll Be Better, You See' (though they're probably both based on 'Betty And Dupree'), is among the more arresting tracks on *You Can't Take My Blues*, which includes some of MacLeod's last recorded work on electric guitar. Carey Bell is on four tracks. All these albums were recorded with the exemplary clarity that is a trademark of AudioQuest Records. (Label boss Joe Harley also produced *A Little Sin*.)

'Live' As It Gets, a joint venture with John 'Juke' Logan, described as a 'very extremely "live" recording with no "studio-fixes"', captures the two men at B. B. King's club in Universal City, California. They perform mostly songs by MacLeod, some previously recorded (two, 'High Priced Woman' and 'Cold Rain', on the deleted *Ain't The Blues Evil* [Volt VCD-3409]). The interplay of voices, harmonica and guitar is adept, but, as one might expect at a club gig, several numbers are extended by anecdotes and byplay, which could be irritating if heard repeatedly. TR

Magic Sam (1937–69)
VOCAL, GUITAR

From an eldritch perspective, Samuel Gene Maghett's early death, at the age of 32, was a shrewd career move for an artist whose reputation continues to capture the imagination of musicians and fans, despite being based on promise as much as achievement. A contemporary of Buddy Guy and Freddie King, he was one of the first to attempt the move from strictly blues music into the broader commercial sphere of soul, an ambition that would remain unfulfilled. A series of high-profile gigs immediately before his demise, including a tour of Europe, brought an approach from Stax Records. The role he might have played at the label was later taken by Little Milton, while some see him as a forerunner of Robert Cray.

***(*) ... With A Feeling!: The Complete Cobra, Chief And Crash Recordings 1957–1966**
[Westside WESA 890] Magic Sam; Boyd Atkins (ts); Little Brother Montgomery, Harold Burrage, [Little] Johnny Jones (p); Mac Thompson (g); Willie Dixon, Odell Campbell (b); Billie Stepney, Odie Payne Jr, S. P. Leary (d); Ammons Sisters, Four Duchesses (v grp). 57–61.

*** **The Essential Magic Sam: The Complete Cobra, Chief And Crash Recordings 1957–1966**
Fuel 2000 302 061 104 *As above.* 57–61.

*** **Blues Guitar Legends**
Fuel 2000 302 061 401 2CD *As above.* 57–61.

Vocal power and an exuberant performance are the principal attributes of any Magic Sam recording but particularly of his earliest. He developed a guitar technique in Chicago's West Side clubs that combined rhythm and lead playing and drew his inspiration from the wide repertoire required in that milieu. His first and most famous record, 'All Your Love', was fashioned from Lowell Fulson's 'It's My Own Fault' and Ray Charles's 'Lonely Avenue'. Unfortunately, it also became the template for five subsequent releases on Cobra and Chief that progressively diminished the original song's impact, even though all his energy went into each one. His work on the latter label reflected owner Mel London's search for commercial success. 'Mr Charlie' dabbled with Bo Diddley's 'Say Man', while 'Doin' The Camel Walk' and a two-part 'Square Dance Rock' squandered his talent on trivia ... *With A Feeling!* brings together all eight Cobra and Chief singles and four alternative takes, adding 'Out Of Bad Luck' and 'She Belongs To Me' from a subsequent single on Crash. It also features two singles by Shakey Jake Harris backed by Sam's band. *The Essential Magic Sam* omits these latter four titles, thereby sharpening its focus but offering less value for money.

Blues Guitar Legends puts the same material in a 2CD set, the other disc being by J. B. Lenoir.

** The Late, Great Magic Sam
Evidence ECD 26079 *Magic Sam; Johnny 'Big Moose' Walker (o, p); Mac Thompson (b); Bob Richey, Robert St Julien (d).* 10/63–10/69.

This collection cobbles together a pair of sessions that had remained unissued until Sam's death and a pair of titles from his appearance at London's Albert Hall with the 1969 AFBF. The studio tracks are marred by indifferent engineering and Walker's profligate organ technique (he plays piano on just one song). The earliest recording of 'Feeling Good' in particular is ruined by his trenchant chords. Two of the better performances are faded just as Sam's guitar solos commence and only one track, 'Baby, You Torture My Soul' (an 'All Your Love' clone), is allowed to run its complete course. His Albert Hall songs, 'Looking Good' and 'Easy Baby', are belittled by the looming presence of the venue but somewhat ameliorated by an enthusiastic audience. By the time this album first appeared Magic Sam was both late and great but none of the evidence is present here.

***(*) West Side Soul
Delmark DD-615 *Magic Sam; Stockholm Slim [Per Notini] (p); Mighty Joe Young (g); Earnest Johnson, Mac Thompson (b); Odie Payne Jr, Odie Payne III (d).* 7–10/67.

Although it attained iconic status in the decades after Sam's death, this album's importance today is historic rather than artistic. Along with Junior Wells's *Hoodoo Man Blues*, it was one of the first albums directed at the collectors' market. Sam saw it as a showcase for his aspirations, combining warhorses like 'Sweet Home Chicago' and J. B. Lenoir's 'Mama Talk To Your Daughter' with more eclectic material from the repertoires of B. B. King, Bobby Bland, Little Milton and Jimmy McCracklin. Producer Bob Koester, plainly taken with Sam's ebullient artistry, mixes his voice and guitar way above the accompaniment. At times neither piano nor drums can be discerned in the mix and none of the band is allowed to solo. The phenomenal power of Sam's voice sometimes overloads the microphone but it can also sound shrill at times, while fumbled guitar notes and chords occasionally impinge. With its minor flaws, the album remains a significant but qualified achievement.

*** Black Magic
Delmark DD-620 *Magic Sam; Eddie Shaw (ts); Lafayette Leake (p); Mighty Joe Young (g); Mac Thompson (b); Odie Payne Jr (d).* 10–11/68.

Once again, it's necessary to be aware of this album's impact when it was released immediately after Sam's death. Curiously, it's less soul-oriented than its predecessor and very much like one of its song titles, 'I Have The Same Old Blues', which along with 'Stop! You're Hurting Me' is one of the set's high points. The covers include a Freddie King instrumental and songs by Rosco Gordon, Willie Cobbs and Otis Rush. Several songs outstay their welcome, with too many repeat choruses testing the listener's patience. A superior mix means that Sam's voice and guitar are better integrated with the backing band. Even so, there's a lack of direction from the control room that forces him to rely upon his own ingenuity to make each song count. Inevitably, he falls back upon what he knows he can deliver rather than being forced to stretch himself. An enjoyable record, nonetheless.

*** The Magic Sam Legacy
Delmark DD-651 *Magic Sam; Eddie Shaw (ts); Shakey Jake Harris (h); Per Notini, Lafayette Leake (p); Mighty Joe Young (g); Mac Thompson (b); Bob Richey, Odie Payne Jr, Odie Payne III (d).* 2/66–11/68.

Mostly drawn from the sessions that produced *West Side Soul* and *Black Magic*, this album has four alternative takes and a different recording of 'I Feel So Good' among its 13 tracks. 'Legacy' may be coming it a bit high for a record that relies so heavily on recycled material. Sam performs 'Walkin' By Myself', 'Hoochie Coochie Man' and 'Everything's Gonna Be Alright' with his customary gusto but these and others maintain rather than enhance his reputation. The instrumental 'Blues For Odie Payne', with solo space for tenor sax, piano and both guitarists, was originally entitled 'Sam In A Jam', which perhaps better reflects the situation he found himself in at this stage of his career. Although it evinces little of the direction he was trying to pursue, this is nevertheless a worthwhile addition to his discography.

**** Live
Delmark DE-645 *Magic Sam; Eddie Shaw, A. C. Reed (ts); Tyrone Carter (p); Mac Thompson, Bruce Barlow (b); Bob Richey, Robert (Huckleberry Hound) Wright, Sam Lay (d).* 10/63–8/69.

This combines two gigs from Sam's residency at the Club Alex with his triumphant set at the 1969 Ann Arbor Blues Festival. The gig tapes made by Pete Kroehler are of indifferent quality but they can't mask the energy coming from the bandstand. Sam was a talented guitarist but that was merely an adjunct to the forceful personality projected in his vocals. His repertoire was unsurprisingly eclectic, taking songs from Jimmy McCracklin, Freddie King, Junior Wells and others. His accompanists are just that; Eddie Shaw gets to take a solo in 'You Were Wrong' but otherwise rhythm is his and their business. A. C. Reed's tenor is added to the 2/64 session and the sound on these five tracks is fractionally improved.

The Ann Arbor set, taken from the PA by John Fishel, suffers the vagaries of engineers trying to achieve a balance. Sam sweeps all before him, accustomed to leading from the front and grateful if musicians keep up. Material from Freddie and B. B. King, Willie Cobbs, Junior Parker and his own 'All Your Love' is subordinated to his will. Audience approval is sluggish until he whips a feverishly fast 'I Feel So Good' on them and builds to a climax of approbation with an equally hectic 'Looking Good'. The CD omits 'I Got Papers On You Baby' from this sequence but suffers not at all. Despite its technical shortcomings, this is the most comprehensive and satisfying example of Magic Sam's stagecraft.

**(*) Rockin' Wild In Chicago
Delmark DG-765 *Magic Sam; Eddie Shaw (ts, v); A. C. Reed (ts); Tyrone Carter (p); Mac Thompson, unknown (b); Bob Richey, Robert 'Huckleberry Hound' Wright, Odie Payne Jr, unknown (d); Shakey Jake Harris (v).* 11/63–68.

It's a measure of the enduring interest in Magic Sam that yet another album of poorly recorded club gigs can be issued more than 30 years after his death. That said, this is a testing experience for even the most hardened enthusiast. Only the four tracks from Mother Blues are in anything approaching listenable quality. The first eight titles from the Copacabana sound telephonic and four from the Alex Club are little better. Sam is as forceful and energetic as ever, particularly good on 'Dirty Work Going On' and 'How Long Can This Go On', but his vocals are frequently close to inaudible. As previously, the sets are an eclectic mix of material by Albert Collins, Jimmy McCracklin, Lowell Fulson, Otis Rush, Little Milton and Earl Hooker. Backing musicians are virtually inaudible throughout and all are subordinated to their leader. A set for extreme collectors and obsessives.

**(*) Give Me Time
Delmark DD-654 *Magic Sam; Eddie Boyd (v)*. 1/68.

This collection of home recordings would never have been released but for a continued demand for Magic Sam product of any quality. The dozen songs, taped by Bill Lindemann, are neither demos nor rehearsals but find Sam singing for his and his family's pleasure. Children interrupt in their imperative way and Eddie Boyd sings a brief 'Come Into My Arms'. Sam's choices range wide, from Faye Adams's 'Shake A Hand' to the Falcons' 'You're So Fine' via 'Sweet Little Angel', 'I Can't Quit You Baby' and a clutch of soul-inflected covers. He confines his guitar work to chords and riffs but doesn't stint when a song requires his full voice. Sound quality is acceptable but by its nature this is a record supplementary to requirements for all but the dedicated collector. NS

Magic Slim (born 1937)
VOCAL, GUITAR

The piano was Morris Holt's first instrument in Grenada, Mississippi; he switched to guitar after losing a finger in a cotton gin. Moving to Chicago in 1955, he played bass for Magic Sam, who bestowed the nickname in tribute to Holt's height (still 6'6") and leanness (now long gone). An attempt at bandleading brought no success, and Slim returned to Mississippi to woodshed; he reconstituted The Teardrops, with his brothers as a nucleus, and headed north again in 1965. Slim's grainy, phlegmatic singing and hard-edged guitar style with its ringing finger vibrato became fixtures on the South Side, supported by rhythm guitar, lurching bass and a heavy backbeat. In the mid-'70s Slim and The Teardrops gained wider recognition, and have since toured and recorded extensively, presenting a seemingly infinite repertoire. Not always Chicago's most technically accomplished musicians, for many years the different Teardrops lineups have been its most consistent.

(***) Magic Slim Vol. 1: Born On A Bad Sign [sic]
Storyville STCD 8033 *Magic Slim; Alabama Jr Pettis (g, v); Nick Holt (b); Douglas Holt (d)*. 11/76.
(***) Magic Slim Vol. 2: Let Me Love You
Storyville STCD 8040 *As above, except Pettis does not sing*. 11/76.

Slim made a couple of singles for Ja-Wes in the '60s, but his first exposure to a wider audience came via French record companies. These recordings were made for MCM with a small, reserved audience present. Lack of atmosphere and probably difficulty communicating with the producer seem to have thrown The Teardrops back on themselves for ideas, inspiration and encouragement. Many tracks reach high energy levels and generate fine solos, but they often get there from untypically desultory beginnings. The sound is unhelpfully balanced, with the lead guitar and drums too loud, the vocals too low and the bass and second guitars murky.

**** Highway Is My Home
Black & Blue BB 425 *Magic Slim; Alabama Jr Pettis (g, v); Nick Holt (b); Fred Below (d)*. 11/78.
**** Highway Is My Home
Evidence ECD 26012 *As above*. 11/78.

This session took place during a tour of France by a Chicago blues package; the recording quality and balance are excellent, and Below's authoritative, infallibly tasteful swing pushes the regular band members to a higher level. Black & Blue add two non-crucial alternative takes to the material licensed by Evidence; in either version, this remains one of Magic Slim's best CDs, but don't confuse it with the similarly titled volume in Wolf's *Zoo Bar Collection* (see below).

***(*) Raw Magic
Alligator ALCD 4728 *As above, except Nate Applewhite (d) replaces Below; add band (v)*. 3/80.

In 1978 Alligator recorded four good tracks for *Living Chicago Blues – Vol. II* (ALCD 7702), but this release selects titles from two LPs on the French Isabel label. Slim's guitar is thinner than usual, with a neurotic edginess, and unusually for this band some tracks are over-extended.

**** Grand Slam
Rooster Blues R 2618 *Magic Slim; Alabama Jr Pettis (g, v); Pete Allen (g); Nick Holt (b); Steve Cushing, Nate Applewhite (d)*. 5/75, 6/82.

Grand Slam ends with three tracks produced by Cushing in 1975 for issue on his own label; they share a paradoxically disciplined anarchism with the 1982 material, which was recorded 'live-in-studio'; 'Give Me Back My Wig' is only the most obvious example of why The Teardrops inherited Hound Dog Taylor's Sunday afternoon jam sessions at Florence's. After a slow start, the disc is mostly brisk power blues; in contrast, '1823 South Michigan Avenue' is a deliberate instrumental with Pete Allen, only briefly a Teardrop, playing a lead part that employs some unsettling rhythmic displacements.

***(*) Don't Tell Me About Your Troubles: The Zoo Bar Collection Vol. 1
Wolf 120.301 *Magic Slim; Alabama Jr Pettis (g); Nick Holt (b); Joel Poston, Nate Applewhite, 'Lee Baby' Holt (d)*. 3/79.
***(*) See What You're Doin' To Me: The Zoo Bar Collection Vol. 2
Wolf 120.302 *Magic Slim; Alabama Jr Pettis (g, v); Pete Allen (g); Nick Holt (b, v); Joel Poston, Nate Applewhite (d)*. 3/79, 4/82.
*** Teardrop: The Zoo Bar Collection Vol. 3
Wolf 120.303 *Magic Slim; Pete Allen, John Primer (g); Nate Applewhite, Michael Scott (d)*. 4/82, 84?
♛ **** Spider In My Stew: The Zoo Bar Collection Vol. 4
Wolf 120.304 *Magic Slim; John Primer (g, v); Nick Holt (b, v); Michael Scott (d, v); Earlene Owens (v)*. mid-80s.
**(*) Highway Is My Home: The Zoo Bar Collection Vol. 5
Wolf 120.305 *As above, except omit Owens*. late 80s.

The Teardrops were great favourites at the Zoo Bar in Lincoln, Nebraska; eventually, Slim moved to Lincoln, although the band members continued to live in Chicago. The first two volumes benefit (which is by no means always a sure thing) from interaction with enthusiastic audiences. They have their defects: on *Vol. 1*, Slim can't overcome the familiarity of 'Got My Mojo Working' or the inherent dullness of 'Tramp', and a buzzing amplifier irritates on several tracks. (The problem recurs, though less often, on other discs in this series.) On *Vol. 2*, Applewhite's drumming on 'Zoo's Blues' is a triumph of self-assertion over taste, and the audience participation on 'Goin' To New York' is pestiferous. Nevertheless, these are minor blemishes on very good compilations.

A godlike rendition of the title track notwithstanding, *Teardrop* is inferior to its predecessors; the flow is disrupted by a surfeit of set openers and closers, with their concomitant announcements, and there's more community singing, on another version of 'Goin' To New York' and that dreadful anthem, 'The Blues Is All Right'. Most dispiriting is 'Last Night', with Slim bellowing unfunny wisecracks that resonate all too well with the audience's whooping rowdiness.

'The Blues Is All Right' also closes *Vol. 4*, but it's the bearable climax of a CD which, though no doubt selected from various evenings, sounds like a single night of coherent madness and full-tilt majesty. Everyone is in the zone throughout; Primer and Scott are hugely creative and energetic, Nick Holt is habitually steady, and more than with earlier versions of The Teardrops, Slim is *primus inter pares*, even though he's the only lead singer apart from Earlene Owens. Owens' lungpower is exceeded only by her lack of nuance, and it's no hardship that her medley of chestnuts is gone in under three minutes. *Vol. 5* is anticlimactic; it panders to the mob, with too much enquiry after the audience's all-rightness, and too much encouragement to sing (or rather yell) along. Most of the numbers, and many of the solos within them, are aimless and overlong.

*** Alone & Unplugged
Wolf 120.882 *Magic Slim*. 84.

This CD wasn't issued until the '90s, when acoustic sessions were rock music's flavour of the moment and a window of commercial opportunity. Within the limits of a style which is largely derivative of Hooker, Hopkins and Jimmy Reed, Slim is an accomplished acoustic guitarist. The tracklisting is heavy on covers, but then so is Slim's band repertoire; here, as there, they are convincingly appropriated, and *Alone & Unplugged* is more than a discographical curiosity.

**** Magic Slim & The Teardrops
Wolf 120.849 *Magic Slim; Christian Dozzler (p); John Primer (g, v); Nick Holt (b); Nate Applewhite, Michael Scott, Timothy Taylor (d). 9/86–2/89.*

This was a worthy winner of Magic Slim's first (of three) Handys on Wolf. The running order adroitly varies tempos and running times, and the musicians play with their customary power, but also with consistent focus and discipline; 'So Easy To Love You', the longest number at 7.32, is also the best. On 'She Moves Me', John Primer achieves the difficult feat of paying vocal tribute to his old boss, Muddy Waters, while yet making the song his own.

**(*) Teardrops Blues Jam
Wolf 120.855 *Magic Slim; Joachim Palden (p); John Primer (g, v); Nick Holt (b, v); Earl Howell (d, v); Michael Scott, Alex Munkas, Jerry Porter, Nate Applewhite (d). 9/86–6/92.*

A jam this is not, except in the sense of jamming together 12 tracks recorded in Vienna and Chicago over seven years. The aim is to showcase the band members as well as the boss; Slim only sings lead on three songs, and sits out altogether on three more. Nick Holt sings rather stiffly on the opening three numbers before Alex Munkas takes over on drums while Earl Howell sings 'Sweet Papa John'; this doesn't display either Howell or Munkas to advantage. The rest of the CD is better, but it lacks coherence, what with the zigzagging in time and space, and drummers coming and going as if through a revolving door. (Over and above those listed, Tim Taylor backs Alabama Jr on the last two, Slim-less tracks.)

***(*) Magic Slim And Nick Holt & The Teardrops
Wolf 120.856 *Magic Slim; John Primer (g, v); Nick Holt (b, v); Michael Scott, Jerry Porter (d). 2/89–5/91.*

Nick Holt handles four of the ten songs on Wolf's second Handy winner, sombre tales of disappointment in love that are well suited to his declamatory voice and a good contrast to his brother's more upbeat, outgoing delivery. 'Dust My Broom' (one of two titles recorded in Vienna in 1991) is done by rote, and makes a disappointing conclusion to an otherwise routinely well-performed collection.

**(*) Live And On The Road
Wolf 120.864 *Magic Slim; John Primer (g, v); Nick Holt (b, v); Michael Scott (d). 3/90.*

**** Medley Blues
Wolf 120.870 *Magic Slim; John Primer (g, v); Nick Holt (b); Jerry Porter (d). 5/91.*

***(*) 44 Blues
Wolf 120.895 *Magic Slim; John Primer (g, v); Nick Holt (b); Earl Howell (d); Bonnie Lee (v). 6/92.*

These three discs were all recorded in Austria. Proving that you can take the band out of Chicago, but you can't take Chicago out of this band, *Magic Blues*, the only studio set, is much the best. Slim is as commanding as ever, but Porter's slambang drumming and Primer's second lead are important ingredients in a very successful disc; Primer also sings a version of 'Evil' that convinces entirely on its own terms, without evoking comparisons, adverse or otherwise, with Howlin' Wolf.

Live And On The Road completes the hat trick of Handys; it may have deserved to defeat that year's other nominees, but it stacks up less well against Magic Slim's own best efforts. Harmony vocals by Nick Holt and Primer are very effective on 'Honest I Do', much less so (and distantly recorded) on 'Pretty Girls Everywhere'; Holt also takes the extended coda of 'Long Distance Call' to new heights of silliness. Much of the time, Slim is leading a pep rally for the blues and, as so often with live albums, it's more fun being in an over-excited audience than listening to one. *44 Blues* is better, although the title track's shuffle rhythms give the band some problems; otherwise, it's business almost as usual, except when Bonnie Lee tornadoes her way through 'I'm Good'. The 'almost' relates to Earl Howell's penchant for clacking his sticks together, not always with total accuracy; acceptable in a piano trio, in this context it merely irritates.

**(*) Blues Guitar Summit
[Charly CDGR 273] *Magic Slim; Matthew Skoller (h); John Primer (g); Nick Holt (b); Earl Howell (d). c. 91.*

This disc, which also features Son Seals and Lonnie Brooks, derives from a TV series filmed at Buddy Guy's Legends. It's hard to imagine how a harmonica would improve the Teardrops' sound, and these four tracks shed no light; Skoller, though listed, is inaudible. Slim and the band are uninspired, Howell is cowbell-fixated, and the recording quality is unremarkable.

*** **Gravel Road**
Blind Pig BP 73690//Crosscut CCD 11027 *Magic Slim; John Primer (g, v); Steve Freund (g); Nick Holt (b, v); Michael Scott (d, v).* 2/90.
**** **Scufflin'**
Blind Pig BPCD 5036 *Magic Slim; Jake Dawson (g, v); Nick Holt (b, v); Earl Howell (d, v).* 95?

Gravel Road is the 20th CD in this entry, so it seems important to stress that its shortcomings are real, not an artefact of (non-existent) critical fatigue. Though far from bored or boring, The Teardrops seem to be favouring material that's familiar (to them, not necessarily to purchasers) and getting it taped as quickly as possible; the songs are mostly short and musically unadventurous, and delivery and engineering both have a dutiful, buttoned-up quality. Happily, *Scufflin'* is a return to top form. Most of the songs are again comparatively brief, but most of them are also new to record, and done with much more relish; despite the general brevity, there's plenty of gleeful, intuitive soloing. And not least, this is where Howell ditches the gimmicks, instead giving his kit an unremitting thrashing that's an important ingredient in the disc's success.

**** **Black Tornado**
Blind Pig BPCD 5046 *Magic Slim; Shawn Holt (g, v); Michael Dotson (g); Nick Holt (b, v); Allen Kirk (d).* 98.
*** **Snakebite**
Blind Pig BPCD 5060 *As above, except omit Shawn Holt.* 99.

For *Black Tornado*, producer Dick Shurman got Slim's agreement that all the tunes would be new to record. This seems to have released fresh resources of energy; 21 years after the Black & Blue sessions, the result is another of Magic Slim's best CDs, and a monument to longevity and consistency. The title track showcases his affection for country music (albeit with an obvious input from the late Earl Hooker), and 'Still A Fool' is one more track that out-Muddys Muddy. Shawn Holt makes a promising debut with the appropriately titled 'Young Man's Blues'; his voice sounds slightly piping, but only by comparison with his father and uncle; it would be powerful in any other context.

Snakebite is less satisfactory; seven of the 11 tracks are Morris Holt compositions, and another is by brother Nick. They are all respectable songs, played with the usual enthusiasm, but none of them stands out as a classic either of writing or of performance. Two covers (of Muddy and Milton Campbell) also manage to be surprisingly low-impact; the most startling track is 'Lonesome Trouble', composed and sung by Michael Dotson, on which The Teardrops take an unprecedented trip into the minor mode.

(*) **Blue Magic
Blind Pig BPCD 5076//Dixiefrog DFGCD 8540 *Magic Slim; Popa Chubby (g, b, d, sampled loops); Michael Dotson (g); Danny O'Connor (b); Allen Kirk (d).* 4/02.

Blue Magic affirms Magic Slim and the Teardrops' abilities without challenging them; this sort of marking time is not unprecedented in their *oeuvre*, but a dreadful version of Merle Haggard's 'Today I Started Loving You Again' takes the grading down a further notch. Blues-rocker Popa Chubby's main contribution seems to have been to encourage Michael Dotson to be more aggressive, generally to good effect; his own playing on four tracks is not inventive enough to be either praiseworthy or offensive, and if anything 'Chickenheads' would have been improved by a more daring use of sampling than it gets. The final track is presented both in conventional form and in a *vidéo-vérité* version that allegedly 'will operate on most computer CD players'; it crashed the writer's iMac, but worked on a PC.

***(*) **Anything Can Happen**
Blind Pig BPCD 5098 *Magic Slim; Jon McDonald (g, v); Chris Biedron (b); Vernal Taylor (d, v).* 04?

Slim and a completely revised Teardrops, recorded live in California. Not unexpectedly, the recruits are sympathetic to their boss's vision of Chicago blues as clangorous, rough-edged and not played from a setlist, although it's inevitable after so many years that some familiar numbers crop up. This is not a problem when one of them is 'Still A Fool', of which Slim is now owner and sole proprietor. Vernal Taylor is an exceptional drummer, hard-hitting but swinging, and in complete command of timbre; 'Black Tornado', which functions as a showcase for his talent, is only the most obvious proof. The singalong 'Back To Mississippi' panders to a cosy white construction of the blues world, and is intrinsically not a very good song, but otherwise this is one more fine Magic Slim CD; not quite up there with his very best, but still a lot better, and less compromised, than much of what's out there. The gig is also available on DVD (Blind Pig BPDVD 6003), with three songs added and two omitted. CS

Sidney Maiden (born 1923)
VOCAL, HARMONICA

Maiden was born in Louisiana, and migrated to California after World War II; there he worked with K. C. Douglas and Slim Green, and made a few records. He was living in Fresno in the early '60s when Chris Strachwitz recorded him, under his own name and backing Mercy Dee Walton. Thereafter, Maiden drifted back into obscurity.

Maiden's '50s recordings with electric bands have been sporadically reissued, mostly on obscure Japanese LPs; his celebrated 'Eclipse Of The Sun' (credited on its original release to K. C. Douglas) is available on *California Blues 1940–1948* (Frémeaux FA 175 2CD), and 'Hand Me Down Baby', recorded in 1957 with Slim Green's band, is on *Dig These Blues* (Ace CDCHD 334, deleted).

*** **Trouble An' Blues**
Original Blues Classics OBCCD-574 *Maiden; K. C. Douglas (g, sp).* 4/61.

Trouble An' Blues is an acoustic session, mostly of favourites from the '30s and '40s, including songs as well-known as 'Good Morning Little Schoolgirl' (retitled 'Buy Me An Airplane'), 'Me And My Chauffeur' and 'Worried Life Blues'. Tucked in among the cover versions, 'San Quentin Blues' is a moving original lyric about imprisonment, but the general familiarity of the material by no means implies routine or substandard performances.

Maiden was strongly influenced by John Lee 'Sonny Boy' Williamson and, while 'Sidney's Fox Chase' proves that he was no virtuoso, his playing and singing elsewhere have much of the plaintiveness that Williamson brought to his slow and mid-tempo blues. In lighter mood, and at a lively pace, 'Tell Me, Somebody' takes 'Fannie Mae', then a recent #1 for Buster Brown, on a trip downhome. Throughout, K. C. Douglas provides accompaniment that is energetic without being overbearing. *Trouble An' Blues* adds up to a very pleasant CD that should not be overlooked. CS

J. J. Malone (1935–2004)
VOCAL, PIANO, GUITAR

Born in Alabama, Malone began playing guitar in his teens and gained experience in a band while in the USAF. Based in Fresno, California, in the early '60s, he and his service buddies worked with the singer/guitarist Troyce Key. In 1967 he took a job as a mechanic at the Naval Air Station at Alameda, where he worked until his retirement in 1988. Meanwhile he played in the Oakland area, for a while with Sonny Rhodes, and recorded numerous singles and LPs. From 1980 to 1992 he was a member of the resident band at Eli's Mile High Club in West Oakland.

*** Highway 99
Fedora FCD 5003 *Malone; Bobby Logan (ts); Jeff Levine (o, p); Clarence Walker (g); Jeff Henry (b); Chris Millar (d). 6/97.*

**(*) See Me Early In The Morning
Fedora FCD 5012 *As above, except omit Logan, Levine. 7–11/98.*

Lowell Fulson, Jimmy McCracklin, the young Ray Charles: echoes of these and similar figures – and dissimilar ones like Muddy Waters and Howlin' Wolf – resonated in Malone's work, but never loudly enough to drown his individuality. Some of that lay in his trick of scatting in unison with his guitar, but what coloured his music as vividly as the Hawaiian shirts he liked was a youthful zest for making it: listeners unaware of his age would probably have guessed him to be anything from ten to 20 years younger. As a writer (half of the dozen or so songs on each album are his) he worked to formulas in *Highway 99*'s 'Old Fashioned Blues' – not so much a nod as an obeisance to Z. Z. Hill's 'Down Home Blues' – and 'Biscuit Bakin' Woman', but the title track has narrative sinew and 'Long Way From San Antone' an attractive strolling tempo, while 'Sittin' Here Thinkin'' is enhanced by a nicely understated arrangement. 'Leave Here Walkin'' on *See Me Early In The Morning*, unusually for contemporary blues, is concerned with magic beliefs, but the most gripping track on this CD is 'Peace Breakin' People', its only accompaniment a snarling guitar and a bass drum. Had it been recorded for a small label in the '50s, this would be regarded as a downhome classic of its period and have become a pricey collector's item. TR

Woody Mann (born 1954)
VOCAL, GUITAR, GUITARRA PORTUGUESA

Mann studied with Gary Davis, then at the Juilliard School of Music and with the jazz pianist Lennie Tristano. He is the author of an extensive series of instructional books and videos.

**(*) Stories
Greenhays GR 70724 *Mann. 94?*

*** Stairwell Serenade
Acoustic Music 319.1072 *Mann. 95?*

**(*) Heading Uptown
Shanachie 8025 *Mann; Charlie Giordano (ac); Dave Keyes (p); Danny Mallon (perc); Terry Roche (v). 96.*

***(*) Get Together
Acoustic Music 319.1187 *Mann; Bob Brozman (g). 99?*

**(*) Cat Burglar
Lee Haywood Studio [unnumbered] *As for above CDs, except add Poul Ehlers (b), Tim Pleasant (d). 94–00?*

Mann's music takes in much more than blues: Bahamian, Iberian and other influences are prominent, and his studies with Tristano evidently extended his harmonic and rhythmic vocabulary. The all-instrumental *Stairwell Serenade* exemplifies his complete technical command of the guitar, and his sensitive dynamics and phrasing. 'Green River Rising' and 'Buggy Wagon' are the most obviously bluesy tracks; the latter is a Gary Davis medley, while the former draws inspiration from Charley Patton and the Portuguese virtuoso Carlos Paredes. This track and 'Blast Off', described as 'for Lennie Tristano and ... Skip James', exemplify Mann's fusion-based approach which, though usually technically and aesthetically successful, makes much of his music of at best peripheral blues interest.

Stories and *Heading Uptown* both include some stiff, inexpressive vocals; the lyrics, mostly by or adapted by Steve Calt, peddle prosaic clichés about blues singers, love and geopolitics. Only a splendid arrangement of 'Blind Arthur's Breakdown' on *Stories*, and *Heading Uptown*'s 'So Glad' and 'For B. D.', respectively inspired by Skip James and Rev. Davis, offer much to blues fans.

Get Together teams Mann with Bob Brozman, best known as a master of Hawaiian music, but like Mann also in command of many other styles. Theirs is a highly successful partnership of equals, and a welcome aspect is that Mann loses most of his intermittent artiness. *Get Together* is dominated by blues: 'The Abyss' and 'Through The Alley' in the disc's first half are precursors of the final seven tracks. Collectively titled 'An American Suite', they joyfully explore various blues guitar styles until the final 'Moonlight Kisses Over Brooklyn', whose sentimental tweeness is a puzzling but definitive subversion of the whole concept.

It's not clear whether *Cat Burglar*, which samples its predecessors and adds two hitherto unissued tracks, is available more widely than from www.woodymann.com, but in any case the selection is very light on blues. CS

The Mannish Boys
GROUP

This West Coast supergroup consists of guitarists Kirk Fletcher and Frank Goldwasser, pianist Leon Blue, Ronnie James Weber on bass, June Core on drums and the veteran Finis Tasby on vocals.

*** That Represent Man
Delta Groove DGPCD 100 *David 'Woody' Woodford (s); Johnny Dyer, Randy Chortkoff (h, v); Leon Blue (p, v); Roy Gaines (g, v); Frank Goldwasser, Kirk Fletcher, Paul Oscher (g); Ronnie James Weber (b); June Core (d); Finis Tasby, Mickey Champion, Barbara Nivens (v). 04.*

A determinedly retro set of minor classics from the '50s and

'60s like 'Call My Job', 'I'm A Lover Not A Fighter', Jimmy Anderson's 'Going Crazy Over T.V.' and Eddie Taylor's 'I Feel So Bad', retailed with enthusiasm by Finis Tasby, urged on by the indefatigably up-for-it guitarists Kirk Fletcher and Frank Goldwasser. Of the guests, Johnny Dyer makes the most impact with his readings of Little Walter's 'Temperature' and 'You're Sweet'. The band's playing is faultlessly unprogressive throughout. If you count yourself a stick-in-the-mud blues fan, you'll find this to be a glorious hour's wallow. TR

(Steady Rollin') Bob Margolin
(born 1949)
VOCAL, GUITAR, BASS

A Boston residency with Luther 'Georgia Boy'/'Snake' Johnson brought Margolin to Muddy Waters's attention and a place in his band in 1973. Already well versed in vintage Chicago blues, Margolin refined his techniques, especially with the slide, by standing at Waters's side for the next seven years. He has led his own band since 1980, producing himself and other artists, including Muddy's son Big Bill Morganfield.

*** Down In The Alley
Alligator ALCD 4816 *Margolin; Mark 'Kaz' Kazanoff (ts, bs, h); Tom 'Mookie' Brill (h, b); David Maxwell (p); Ronnie Earl (g); Rod Carey, Steve 'Slash' Hunt (b); Per Hanson, Wes Johnson, Jim Brock, Chuck Cotton (d); Mike Avery (perc); John Brim, Nappy Brown, Terry Harris (v).* 93.

Margolin loads his bases with guest appearances by Maxwell, Earl, Brim and Brown. He shares vocals with the composer on a faithful rerun of Brim's 'Tough Times', while Brown sings the title track with gospel-based fervour, accompanied by Margolin's acoustic slide guitar. Their other collaboration, 'Worried Life Blues', closes the album with a larger than necessary dose of histrionics. Earl beefs up four band numbers, including the opening 'Boogie At Midnight', as well as 'Wee Wee Hours', performed as an acoustic duet. Margolin is sparing with his slide technique, using it on just three numbers, favouring his erstwhile leader's later frenetic style. His own songs pass muster alongside material from Elmore James, Roy Brown and Muddy Waters, but after a strong opening sequence the album loses impetus halfway through and ends weakly.

*** My Blues And My Guitar
Alligator ALCD 4835 *Margolin; John M. Thornton (t); Chris Buckholz (tb); Kaz Kazanoff (ts); Les Izmore (bs); Snooky Pryor (h, v); David Maxwell (p); Steve 'Slash' Hunt (b); Chuck Cotton (d); Jim Brock (perc).* 95.

Another exhibition of versatility begins rowdily and strongly with 'Movin' South', one of seven originals along with two more co-written with Kazanoff. Cotton's drumming is highly reminiscent of Fred Below and a major addition to Margolin's drive for authenticity. This works for songs broadly in the Chicago mould, such as 'I Can Get Behind That', helped by Pryor's signature harmonica sound, but less well with a mannered 'Rip It Up' and earnest vocals on 'Going Home' and 'The Same Thing'. Once again, slide is dispensed sparingly and once again with undue fervour. That aside, the instrumental strengths displayed almost compensate for the vocal shortcomings, although that isn't the case with the rockabilly bluster of 'The Door Is Open', from which the album's title is taken.

**(*) Up & In
Alligator ALCD 4851 *Margolin; Gary Slechta (t); Kaz Kazanoff (ts, bs, h); David Maxwell (o, p); Pinetop Perkins (p); Chris Carroll, Tad Walters, Ron Brendle (b); Chuck Cotton, Wes Johnson, Jim Brock (d); Sweet Betty Journey (v).* 97.

With elements of Memphis soul, rockabilly and jazz added to the bedrock Chicago blues that ought to be his forte, Margolin here succumbs to the urge to synthesize and homogenize what ought to remain distinct and separate. In doing so, he devalues what he does best, here displayed in 'Goin' Back Out On The Road' and 'Not What You Said Last Night'. This last is one of the better of his ten compositions, which reveal an irritating penchant for adolescent humour in 'Alien's Blues' and 'Blues For Bartenders'. He tips over into melodrama with 'She And The Devil' and 'Why Are People Like That' before redeeming himself with 'Just Because', a homiletic list worthy of Willie Dixon. Best of all here is Sweet Betty's soulful rendering of 'Coffee Break', supported by Margolin's acoustic guitar and Kazanoff's inspired tenor sax.

*** Hold Me To It
Blind Pig BPCD 5056 *Margolin; Tad Walters (h, g, b, v); Kaz Kazanoff (h); Sherry Margolin (p); Big Bill Morganfield (g, v); Wes Johnson (d).* 99.

A change of label seems to have polarized Margolin as an artist. The same broad spectrum of musical styles is evident but the gulf between what he does well and what might be termed honourable failure has widened. The title track, 'Mean Old Chicago', 'Slam 'Em Down' and 'Lost Again' are extremely well performed, making the best use of Margolin's and Walters's instrumental abilities. But 'meaningful' and experimental elements in 'No Consolation' and Dylan's 'Not Dark Yet' inject a note of cloying sentimentality into his work. Margolin is yet to square the circle with the genres he chooses to work in; advancing on a broad front may not be as rewarding as consolidating the ground he already stands upon. NS

*** All-Star Blues Jam
Telarc CD-83579 *Margolin; Mookie Brill (h, b, v); Carey Bell (h); Pinetop Perkins (p); Hubert Sumlin (g); Willie 'Big Eyes' Smith (d).* 3–12/02.

Reunited with fellow Muddy Waters Band alumni Perkins and Willie Smith, Margolin re-creates Chicago blues sounds of the '50s, focusing on the epic Waters lineup with Jimmy Rogers and delivering 'Sweet Black Angel', 'Juke', 'The Last Time', 'Country Boy' and others with both fidelity and energy. Sumlin's presence is limited to two unplugged performances recorded at Margolin's home. TR

Johnny Mars (born 1942)
VOCAL, HARMONICA

South Carolina born, Mars played harmonica from the age of 13; trivia buffs will wish to know that in the early '60s he recorded in New York with The Train Riders and (on bass) with Burning Bush. Moving to San Francisco in 1967, Mars concentrated on chromatic harmonica, developing a style that

owed much to Little Walter. He came to Britain in 1972 and became popular on the European club and festival circuits; he is now back in the USA.

**(*) Mighty Mars
JSP JSPCD 2144 *Mars; Mel Simpson (o, p); Colin Fletcher (g); Wayne Elliott (b); James Matthews (d, perc); band (v). 12/80.*

** Life On Mars
BGO BGOCD 159 *Mars; Steve Sidwell (t); Bimbo Acock (ts); Nick Magnus (kb); Ray Fenwick (g, v); Terry Pack (b, v); Peter J. Shaw (d); Colin Fox, Annie Kavanagh (v). 3/81.*

Two tracks from LPs recorded in the '70s appear on *Don't Worry 'Bout The Bear* (Indigo IGOXDCD 2502 2CD). By the '80s Mars had moved onward, if not always upward. *Mighty Mars* is a fairly successful medley of blues and blues-rock, although 'Rocket 88' is not the only track done no favours by the 'louder! faster!' approach. The supporting musicians are capable, but only Simpson is in danger of originality; his playing, particularly on organ, is a consistently interesting complement to Mars's harp work and to his pleasantly soulful singing.

Life On Mars is an artistic collaboration with British session veteran Fenwick; of the CD's ten songs, he wrote or co-wrote an outstandingly derivative six. Mars had 'a secret desire to form a really heavy blues-rock band', and the wish to get away from recycling old numbers is understandable, but most of this disc is coarse and bombastic.

*** Stateside
MMK 31001 *Mars; Bill Martin (kb, prog, v); Robert Berry (o); Dan Kennedy (g, b, prog, v); Joe Orlando (b); Dave Lauser (d, d composition); Stephanie Kennedy, Stacey Kennedy (v). 8/93–4/94.*

Stateside continues the attempt to blend blues and rock, and it's apparent that Mars had worked hard at developing his ideas during more than a decade away from the studios. Forget the ritual invocations of Hendrix; there are passing hints of empty flashiness, but usually the right balance is struck between display and emotion. Mars's playing is almost always relevant to the lyrics, and Martin has a real gift for programming big horn sections. It's not perfect: the instrumental 'Move' doesn't much rhythmically or at all emotionally, 'Home Sweet Home' is bathetic eco-nonsense, and Kennedy's share of the conversation on the acoustic 'Remember …?' is whitebread; so are some of the backup vocals. Worth investigating, though, and excellently recorded.

**(*) On My Mind
Springboard Media SMCDPHJM 001 *Mars; John Dart, 'Jinx' Jenkins, Andy Urquhart (t); Steve Hayes, Paul Clark (tb); Dave Burgess (as); Howie Casey (ts); Pete Bettle (bs); Steve Darrel Smith (kb); Glen Frazer, Tim Mycroft (p); Lucy-Ann Allen, Dan Baker, Barbara Hooper (vn); Aiden Fisher (vl); Chaz Dickie (vc); Paul Hart (g); Chris Lonergan, Marion Dolton (b); Alan Edwards, Sam Brown (d); Pete Brown (perc); Sheila McKinley, Victoria Hardy, Helen Hardy (v). 03.*

On My Mind is credited to Johnny Mars & Paul Hart with the Barrelhouse Blues Orchestra, and Mars guests with this British big band on eight tracks of 12. The musicians are professional, and probably fun to see live, but their playing has little of the barrelhouse's freewheeling spirit. Save for Helen Hardy's Etta James imitation, the lead vocals on tracks where Mars is absent are anaemically English, as is the backing trio throughout; it's only the tracks where Mars is in the ascendant that are of much interest. He plays chromatic harp, usually in a busy, jazzy style, which works notably well on an instrumental version of 'Georgia On My Mind'. 'Striking On You Baby' and T-Bone Walker's 'Don't Give Me The Runaround' get jaunty treatments, and Mars makes the most of the expressive possibilities of the pop song 'Evening'; strange, then, that he's dull on 'Please Send Me Someone To Love'. This is not a bad CD, but it scores more marks for competence than for inspiration. CS

Johnnie Marshall (born 1961)
VOCAL, GUITAR

Marshall lives where he was born, in Whigham, Georgia, a small town not far north of Tallahassee, Florida, where he has played regularly at Dave Claytor's Dave's CC Club. He has not been playing blues for very long, but he has a keen sense of its traditions and purposes.

**(*) 98¢ In The Bank
JSP JSPCD 2150 *Marshall; Jamie Finegan (t); Bruce Feiner (ts, arr, prod); Robert Feiner (bs); Brian Charette (o); Johnny Rawls (g, v, prod); Eddie Kirkland, Sonny Rhodes, George Boone, Slam Allen (g, v); Jason Arnold (d). 01.*

Marshall's previous albums, *Live For Today* (1998) and *With All My Might* (1999), both for JSP, having been rather swiftly deleted, he is currently represented only by his third for the label, on which he shares his space with both up-and-comers and veterans. He is gifted with a handsome, soulful voice – which might have been treated with more care by the engineers on some tracks, where it's either occluded by echo or too far down in the mix – and as a guitarist he shows lively ideas; in fact his whole performance is vivacious and enthusiastic, and compares creditably with the workaday contributions of Kirkland and Rhodes. Boone and Allen have more to gain from the exposure, and Boone grabs his opportunity with a snarling solo on 'That Ain't Right'. Co-producer Bruce Feiner wrote most of the songs, shuffling and dealing blues and soul motifs that are as familiar as the titles ('Don't Do Me Wrong', 'Hard Lovin' Man', etc.). It makes for an enjoyable enough album, but it would be interesting to hear Marshall tackle stronger, more individual material. TR

Carl Martin (1906–79)
VOCAL, GUITAR, MANDOLIN, VIOLIN, BASS

Born in Virginia, Martin moved to Knoxville, Tennessee, as a boy. Drafted into his brother Roland's stringband on guitar, he rapidly learned all the other instruments, and acquired a multicultural repertoire. In the late '20s, Martin formed his own band with Howard Armstrong (q.v.) and Ted Bogan (1910–90), and they made their way to Chicago, where Martin settled. After military service in World War II, Martin largely gave up music until found by researchers in the '60s. In the '70s, he was reunited with Bogan and Armstrong.

**(*) Carl Martin (1930–1936)/Willie '61' Blackwell (1941)
Document DOCD-5229 *Martin; unknown (ts); Chuck Segar, unknown (p); Howard Armstrong (vn); Roland Martin, poss. Willie B. James (g); Roland Armstrong (b). 4/30–4/36.*

**(*) Carolina Blues
Wolf WSE 114 *As above.* 4/30–4/36.

Both these discs begin with the Tennessee Chocolate Drops coupling, where Roland and Carl Martin play guitar and bass respectively behind Howard 'Louie Bluie' Armstrong's fiddle; Document also include two cyclonic instrumentals by Louie Bluie and Ted Bogan (one with mandolin lead, one with fiddle), on which Carl isn't present. His 13 Chicago recordings are more mainstream; there's an increasing influence from Big Bill Broonzy, but initially Martin was concerned to show off his particular talents on guitar. Although there's some repetition of ideas between songs, the mandolin-inspired runs on 'Crow Jane Blues' and the speed and precision of 'Old Time Blues' are dazzling. For his last four titles, Carl is saddled with largely uncongenial accompanists. Both reissues use some very noisy originals; Wolf complete their disc with six random tracks by Brownie McGhee, while Document use the Willie '61' Blackwell Bluebirds. Document offer better value, but most listeners will only need the stringband titles, on Old Hat, and the virtuoso guitar pieces, on Yazoo.

**** Crow Jane Blues
Testament TCD 6006 *Martin; Johnny Young (md, g); John Lee Granderson (g); Pete Welding (interviewer).* 5–6/66.

Martin's voice is a little croaky, but still strong, and remakes of 'Crow Jane Blues' and 'Good Morning Judge' show that his guitar skills were intact. The main emphasis is on his mandolin work, however; it's even heard on two tracks where the notes promise violin. That instrument only appears on a disorganized 'Railroad Blues', but more of it, and of Martin's guitar, can be heard with the Chicago String Band. The tracklisting is an enthusiastically attacked blend of familiar songster material ('Corrina', 'Liza Jane', 'John Henry') and blues, with two versions of the startling 'State Street Pimp' standing out. Two tracks by Ted Bogan complete the CD; with Johnny Young on mandolin and John Lee Henley's harmonica, they are lively throwbacks to the sound of the early Sonny Boy Williamson I sessions.

***(*) That Old Gang Of Mine
Flying Fish FF 70003 *Martin; Howard Levy (h, p, vb); Jeff Gutcheon (p); Howard Armstrong (vn, v); Jethro Burns (md); Ted Bogan, Steve Goodman (g, v); Tom Armstrong (b, v); Hugh McDonald, Jim Tulio (b); Sheldon Platkin (d).* 74–77.

Martin, Bogan & The Armstrongs (which is the credit for this CD) were wildly eclectic, both because it widened their customer base and because they liked it that way. Indeed, it's usually their blues numbers which are the more routine, tending towards gloomy vocals, dragging tempos and sobbing fiddle obbligatos. The *double entendre* 'Ice Cream Freezer Blues' is well done, as is an unlikely stringband arrangement of the prison blues 'In The Bottom', but it's the broader-minded listener who will find most to enjoy; successful kitschectomies are undergone by items as improbable as the title track, 'Sweetheart Of Sigma Chi', 'Jamaica Farewell' and the entirely splendid 'You'll Never Find Another Kanaka Like Me'. CS

Eddie Martin
VOCAL, HARMONICA, GUITAR, DRUMS

The London-born Eddie Martin began playing guitar at 15 and formed his first blues band a few years later. Though a formidable guitarist in a group setting, he also works as a one-man-band, playing rack harmonica and a partial drumkit. Since the mid-'90s he has been prominent on the British and European blues scene, though he has also gigged in Texas. He keeps up a schedule of nearly 300 shows a year and has received several awards.

*** Blue To The Bone
Blueblood 003 *Martin; Steve Trigg (t); Andy Gillams (tb); Dick Heckstall-Smith (ss, as, ts); Patsy Gamble (ts); John Baggott (kb, p); Gary Baldwin (o); Tony Caddle (b); Mike Hoddinott (d).* 96?

*** Fires & Floods
Blueblood 004 *Martin; Steve Trigg (t); Andy Gillams (tb); Dick Heckstall-Smith, Patsy Gamble (ts); Paddy Milner (kb, p); Gary Baldwin (o); Tony Caddle (b); Mike Hoddinott (d).* 98.

*** Keep On Working
Blueblood BB BB 006 *Martin; Paddy Milner (p); Dave Griffiths (md, b); Simon Preston (d).* 00?

*** Pillowcase Blues
Blueblood BB 007 *Martin; Steve Trigg (t); Patsy Gamble (ts, bs); Dick Heckstall-Smith (bs); Guthrie Kennard (b); Jimmy Pendleton (d); Mike Hoddinott (cga); Marc T (tamb, claps); Nicky Knowles (claps).* 02.

*** Ice Cream
Blueblood BB 008 *Martin; Andy Sheppard (ss); Gary Baldwin (o); Paddy Milner (kb, p); Marion Dolton (b); Michael Wiedrich (d).* 03.

*** Play The Blues With Feeling
Blueblood BB 009 *Martin; Steve Trigg (t); Andy Gillams (tb); Patsy Gamble (ts); Gary Baldwin (o); Paddy Milner (p); Tony Caddle, Marion Dalton (b); Mike Hoddinott, Michael Wiedrich (d).* 98, 05.

'You've got to play the blues with feeling,' Martin says in one of his songs, 'or don't you play the blues at all.' It's a credo he lives up to, but there is intelligence in his music as well, and originality, as you might guess from song titles like 'You Can't Hold Mercury', 'Prickly As A Porcupine' or 'The Devil's Joker'. While we're keeping score, chalk up versatility, since he is capable of working in every setting from solo with guitar to Chicago-style electric band to a horn-driven little-big-band effect. Although he can play precisely in the style of Elmore James ('I Want To Live With You' on *Fires & Floods*, 'Selfish Guy' on *Play The Blues With Feeling*) or Freddie King ('Cherry Red' on *Ice Cream*), he rarely covers other people's songs, but rather borrows bits of them to weld into his own creations. 'Sad Time' on *Blue To The Bone*, for instance, is driven by the riff from 'Milestones', or something like it, and several other songs find Martin's ear cocked to John Lee Hooker or B. B. King or Barbecue Bob. (His listening has been wide-ranging too.)

His albums are all rewarding, but not quite all alike. *Pillowcase Blues* is billed as by Eddie Martin & The Texas Blues Kings; the latter are Kennard and Pendleton, who play Double Trouble to Martin's SRV. *Keep On Working* is all acoustic. By now the reader will have gathered that Martin is at his best when expressing his own ideas, and sure enough the few pieces of received repertoire on *Keep On Working* like Robert Johnson's '[Little] Queen Of Spades', Tampa Red's 'It Hurts Me Too', 'Bundle Up And Go' and 'Mean Ole Frisco' are less gripping than the original songs that surround them. If you're unfamiliar with Martin's work – which isn't a condition you should allow yourself to remain in – we suggest you try *Ice Cream* or *Fires & Floods*, which give particularly good accounts of his talent, ingenuity and commitment. TR

Sara Martin (1884–1955)
VOCAL

Martin was of the generation of Ma Rainey and Mamie Smith: stage-show and vaudeville performers whose repertoire was not confined to blues but was greatly expanded by them during the blues craze of the '20s. She alternated stage work on the TOBA circuit and, later, recordings with spells of work as a maid or seamstress in Louisville, Kentucky, the city of her birth. After a decade of great popularity she lost her voice during an engagement and, interpreting it as a divine warning, quit blues singing and worked for the church. She became a gospel singer and later ran a nursing home for the aged until her retirement, through ill health, in 1948.

** Sara Martin – Vol. 1 (1922–1923)
Document DOCD-5395 *Martin; Tom Morris, poss. Thomas 'Tick' Gray (c); Sylvester Bevard (tb); unknown (cl); unknown (ts); Clarence Williams (p, v); Shelton Brooks (p, sp); Charlie Hillman, Fats Waller, prob. Clarence Johnson (p); unknown (bj); Archie Walls (bb); unknown (d); Eva Taylor (v).* 10/22–7/23.

**(*) Sara Martin – Vol. 2 (1923–1924)
Document DOCD-5396 *Martin; Tom Morris (c); John Masefield (tb); Sidney Bechet (ss); Clarence Williams, prob. Porter Grainger (p); Sylvester Weaver (bj, g); Buddy Christian (bj).* 7/23–3/24.

**(*) Sara Martin – Vol. 3 (1924–1925)
Document DOCD-5397 *Martin; Tom Morris, June Clark, 'Big Charlie Thomas', unknown (c); Charlie Irvis, prob. Jimmy Harrison, unknown (tb); poss. Ernest Elliott (ss); poss. Buster Bailey, unknown (as); Clarence Williams (p, v); Lemuel Fowler (p); E. L. Coleman (vn); Buddy Christian, Charles Washington (bj); Sylvester Weaver (g).* 3/24–11/25.

**(*) Sara Martin – Vol. 4 (1925–1928)
Document DOCD-5398 *Martin; 'Big Charlie Thomas', Harry Cooper, Louis Metcalf, Bubber Miley, Ed Allen, King Oliver, poss. Shirley Clay, unknowns (c); Charlie Irvis, Ed Cuffee, unknowns (tb); Artie Starks, Arville Harris (cl, as); Ben Waters (cl); unknown (ss); unknown(s) (as); prob. Barney Bigard (ts); Clarence Williams (p, v); Earres Prince, Eddie Heywood, Richard M. Jones (p); Bernard Addison, prob. Buddy Christian, unknowns (bj); Cyrus St Clair (bb); Cliff Jones (d).* 11/25–12/28.

*** The Famous Moanin' Mama 1922–1927
Retrieval RTR 79028 *As for relevant CDs above.* 12/22–4/27.

In her early recordings Martin, like many of her contemporaries, sings blues without quite qualifying as a blues singer: her exaggeratedly correct diction, with its rolled 'r's, does little to distinguish her from contemporary white vaudeville artists, and at first she cannot command either the blue tone of a Sippie Wallace or the colloquial delivery of a Victoria Spivey. About midway through 1923, however, she seems to get the idea, in the sequence of blues on *Vol. 2* beginning with 'Sweet Man Was The Cause Of It All'. Despite Clarence Williams's uninspired accompaniment, she moans the blues with abandon in 'Mistreated Mama Blues'. 'Blind Man Blues', another fervent performance, benefits from its backing by a Williams-organized group prominently featuring the soprano saxophone of Sidney Bechet, as do 'Atlanta Blues' and 'Graveyard Dream Blues'.

Towards the end of *Vol. 2* we hear Martin's first collaborations with her fellow Louisvillean Sylvester Weaver. At the time, a blues singer accompanied on guitar, rather than on piano or by a band, was a tremendous novelty and was so advertised in the African-American press. What is interesting about these records is not so much Weaver's deliberate guitar (and banjo) playing as the power it has to draw Martin still further from her vaudeville background and towards the kind of singing recently introduced on records by Ma Rainey and Bessie Smith. The partnership continues into *Vol. 3*, which opens with a spirited 'Pleading Blues' and more animated playing by Weaver. At a later meeting Weaver plays slide guitar on 'Strange Lovin' Blues'. This and its session-mate 'I Can Always Tell When A Man Is Treating Me Cool', both accompanied by a trio of guitar, banjo and violin, elicit some of Martin's most expressive blues singing to date.

During the period covered by *Vol. 3* Martin recorded ten titles with 'Her Jug Band', namely Clifford Hayes (violin), Curtis Hayes (banjo) and Earl McDonald (jug); these tracks – the first ever recorded by a jugband – are on *Clifford Hayes & The Louisville Jug Bands – Vol. 1 (1924–1926)* (RST Jazz Perspectives JPCD 1501). Her confident handling of the narrative in 'I Ain't Got No Man' ('what I want most is a big stick of peppermint') shows how much she had learned in two years. Now thoroughly habituated to blues in the Southern style, she matches her accompanists in vigour in 'Papa, Papa Blues' and 'I'm Gonna Be A Lovin' Old Soul'.

As the datespan of *Vol. 4* indicates, Martin, in common with many of her female contemporaries, lost ground in the later '20s to the newly popular male blues artists. Pen Bogert explains in his notes, a very fine and well-researched essay spread across the four volumes, that she resumed her career as a versatile vaudeville artist, a move reflected in the variety of her recorded material, which includes standards-to-be like 'Yes, Sir, That's My Baby' and 'Alabammy Bound'. Her hearty readings of 'Late Last Night' and 'Some Sweet Day' are backed with gusto by Richard M. Jones's Jazz Wizards, but most of her studio bookings were with Clarence Williams, hence her vocal version of 'Cushion Foot Stomp' and other Williams compositions. But she did not desert the blues. There were a couple more dates with Sylvester Weaver, found on *Sylvester Weaver – Vol. 1 (1923–1927)* (Document DOCD-5112), and at her final session she produced stately readings of 'Death Sting Me Blues' and 'Mean Tight Mama' with pungent responses by King Oliver and an unidentified trombonist.

Many verses and phrases that passed into blues language are found on Martin's records; that may not have been their point of origin, but her consistently good sales probably played a part in scattering them throughout the black community. (And elsewhere: 'Mistreated Mama Blues' was learned from her record by the white rural singer Dock Boggs.) The bracketing of the third stars on the Document CDs is a reflection not on the quality of the music but on the regrettable condition of many of the source recordings. This is much less of a problem on the Retrieval CD, remastered by John R. T. Davies, but this set cannot be recommended without qualification. The selection is deliberately uneven, emphasizing the recordings with jazz musicians such as Fats Waller and Sidney Bechet (but not King Oliver or the Jazz Wizards) and excluding both the jugband sides and those with

Tony Mathews (born 1941)
VOCAL, GUITAR

An Okie from near Muskogee, Mathews grew up amidst gospel groups. He moved to LA in the early '60s and worked with Ray Charles (1966–67) and Little Richard (1967–70) before taking a break for musical and other studies. He rejoined Charles in 1974 and recorded his first album in 1981, but little has been heard of him in recent years.

**(*) Condition: Blue
HMG HMG 5502 *Mathews; Nolan Smith, John Cross (t); Ken Tussing (tb); David Ii (s, arr); Robert Whitfield, Ernest Vantrease (kb); Michael McKinney, Dennis Walker (b, prod); Buster Jones (d, v); Bruce Bromberg (prod).* 81.

This album has not acquired much of a reputation among blues enthusiasts, and listening to it two decades after it was made one can guess why: the blues tracks like 'White Powder', 'Laid Off' and 'The Changes' not only have a little more of the Bromberg–Walker 'house sound' than is good for them but are weakened by their association with the unmemorable funk of 'Coming Home To You' and 'Let Me Know When You're Comin'. A pity: Mathews is an expressive singer and a guitarist with the slithering speed of a cobra. Perversely, the track that lingers in the memory is the least typical of the album, 'Uncle Joe', an affectionate reminiscence in the talking-blues manner of John Lee Hooker's 'Tupelo', with appropriately lazy guitar. It would have been interesting to hear Mathews at another point in his life, but subsequent recordings have not reached the international blues audience. TR

David Maxwell (born 1950)
PIANO, ORGAN, VOCAL

A Bostonian, Maxwell discovered the blues in the '60s and hung out with Otis Spann, Pinetop Perkins and Sunnyland Slim. He has worked with Freddie King, Bonnie Raitt, James Cotton and Otis Rush, among others, as well as playing in the house bands of various Boston-area clubs and logging recording dates with Cotton, Ronnie Earl, Bob Margolin, Hubert Sumlin, Roy Gaines and many other artists.

*** Maximum Blues Piano
Tone-Cool CD TC 1160 *Maxwell; Scott Aruda (t); Ray Green (tb); [Sax] Gordon Beadle (ts, bs); Mark 'Kaz' Kazanoff (ts); Ronnie Earl, Duke Levine, Kevin Barry (g); Marty Ballou (b); Marty Richards (d, perc); Mickey Bones (rb); Darrell Nulisch (v).* 97?

**(*) Max Attack
Dixiefrog DFGCD 8559 *Maxwell; Kevin Robinson (t, flh); Fayaz Virgi (tb); Patrick Clahar (ts); Kim Wilson (h, v); James Cotton (h); Gary Sanctuary (o); Pinetop Perkins (p); Hubert Sumlin (g, v); Ronnie Earl, Duke Robillard, Richard Studholme (g); Michael 'Mudcat' Ward, Ian Jennings, Marty Ballou, Randy Hope-Taylor (b); Per Hanson, Mike Thorn, Richard Bailey (d); Liane Carroll (v).* 7–11/02.

Maxwell acknowledges Otis Spann, Pinetop Perkins and Sunnyland Slim as important models for his playing, and tracks on *Maximum Blues Piano* like 'Blues Don't Bother Me' and 'Deep Into It' are eloquent testimonies to his absorption in the music of such forerunners, but he is by no means bounded by Chicago city limits. The loose-limbed body-weaving of 'Breakdown On The Bayou', for instance, comes from Professor Longhair, 'Down At P. J.'s Place' nods to Pete Johnson and 'Take Me On Home' has the aspirational tone of a gospel anthem.

In his notes to *Maximum Blues Piano* Dick Shurman attributes the belatedness of Maxwell's debut as a front man to 'the usual Curse Of The Non-Vocalist'. (The only singing to be heard on the album is Darrell Nulisch's on 'Heart Attack'.) By the time he came to make *Max Attack*, Maxwell must have decided that the curse had been lifted, and he sings on about half of the dozen tracks; more accurately, he murmurs the lyrics in a meandering undertone, and many listeners will probably wish he hadn't bothered, since the ensemble playing is plenteous and interesting enough in its own right. Ronnie Earl plays at the top of his game on both albums. TR

John Mayall (born 1933)
VOCAL, HARMONICA, KEYBOARDS, ORGAN, PIANO, GUITAR, VIBRAPHONE

Mayall was born in Macclesfield, Cheshire. As a boy he absorbed his father's jazz collection, which included Leadbelly and Albert Ammons, and in his teens he began to play piano, guitar and harmonica. After study at art college and army service in Korea, he worked as a graphic designer, playing music in The Powerhouse Four and The Blues Syndicate. Encouraged by Alexis Korner, he moved to London and founded the Bluesbreakers, eventually hiring Eric Clapton and recording Blues Breakers. *After Clapton left to join Cream, Mayall hired a series of musicians who went on to join higher-profile bands, such as Peter Green, John McVie and Mick Fleetwood (Fleetwood Mac) and Mick Taylor (The Rolling Stones). He also backed John Lee Hooker, T-Bone Walker and Sonny Boy Williamson II on English club tours. In the late '60s, attracted by the climate and culture of California, he moved to LA's Laurel Canyon and thereafter employed mostly American musicians. In 1982 he re-formed the Bluesbreakers with Mick Taylor and John McVie for tours and a concert video; public reaction encouraged him to maintain the band, for which he successively hired as lead guitarists Coco Montoya, Walter Trout and, in 1993, Buddy Whittington, who at the time of writing still fills that position.*

***(*) Blues Breakers
Deram 800 086//882 967 *Mayall; Dennis Healey (t); Alan Skidmore (ts); John Almond (bs); Eric Clapton (g, v); John McVie (d).* c. 6/66.

***(*) John Mayall & The Bluesbreakers With Eric Clapton
Deram 844 827 As above. c. 6/66.

*** A Hard Road
London 820 474 *Mayall; Ray Warleigh (as); Alan Skidmore (ts); John Almond (bs); Peter Green (g, v); John McVie (b); Aynsley Dunbar (d).* 10–11/66.

**(*) The Blues Alone
Deram 820 535 *Mayall; Keef Hartley (d).* 5/67.

*** Crusade
Deram 820 537 *Mayall; Chris Mercer (ts); Rip Kant (bs); Mick Taylor (g); John McVie (b); Keef Hartley (d).* 7/67.

Blues Breakers is an iconic album in the annals of British blues, chiefly for its revelation of the talent of Eric Clapton. The cheeky expertise of his instrumental display pieces 'Hideaway' and 'Steppin' Out' is matched by the intense slow blues improvisation in 'Have You Heard'. His one vocal, on Robert Johnson's 'Ramblin' On My Mind', is rather undeveloped, but as things fell out he would have many subsequent opportunities to improve on it. Most of the performances are short and to the point, and the nearly six minutes of 'Have You Heard' are justified by Clapton; the only time-waster is 'What'd I Say', which is burdened with an interminable and unimaginative drum solo. *John Mayall & The Bluesbreakers With Eric Clapton* couples both mono and stereo versions of *Blues Breakers. A Hard Road* is also highly regarded for its early report on the playing of Peter Green, another musician of lofty status in the British blues story. It has notable performances like the instrumental 'The Super-Natural' and Elmore James's 'Dust My Blues', but also oddities like 'There's Always Work' and outright failures like 'Living Alone'.

Of the three guitarists who played in the Bluesbreakers in 1966–67 Mick Taylor is regarded with the least awe. On the evidence of *Crusade* there's little doubt that he was less arrestingly gifted than Clapton or Green, or that, though an equally fluent player, he was also the most facile. But as a band recording *Crusade* is unquestionably smoother and more organized than *A Hard Road*, and its excellently chosen material ('I Can't Quit You Baby', My Time After Awhile', etc.) elicits Mayall's most consistent singing so far.

Between *A Hard Road* and *Crusade* Mayall put in a day's work to record a solo set of his own compositions, *The Blues Alone*. (Hartley is on only a few cuts.) Studio echo lends a hollow, desolate ambience to tracks like 'Down The Line', 'Broken Wings' and the piano piece 'Marsha's Mood'. Although the album presents Mayall handling almost all the instruments of a blues band, the listener comes away from it less impressed by the playing than by the personal disclosure of the songs.

*** Bare Wires
Deram 820 538 *Mayall; Henry Lowther (c, vn); Dick Heckstall-Smith (ss, ts); Chris Mercer (ts, bs); Mick Taylor (g); Tony Reeves (b); Jon Hiseman (d, perc). 4/68.*

From the composition and coloration of the opening 'Bare Wires – Suite' and the following 'I'm A Stranger' you might guess that Mayall had been listening to certain recent jazz composers; their pastoral textures glint with light refracted through Mingus or early Ornette Coleman. But if the gently swinging riffs of the horn section there paint a backdrop as sedate as a Constable, the overlaying of harmonica on wah-wah guitar and bongos in 'No Reply' strikes a more modern and urban note: the soundtrack for an Italian erotic horror film, perhaps. The settings of the other pieces are more blues-conventional, as indeed are the songs themselves; it's the first three tracks that give a previously unsuspected view of Mayall's talent as a musical conceptualist.

*** Looking Back
Deram 820 331 *Mayall; Dick Heckstall-Smith (ss, ts); Chris Mercer (ts); Bernie Watson, Roger Dean, Eric Clapton, Peter Green, Mick Taylor (g); John McVie, Jack Bruce, Paul Williams (b); Martin Hart, Hughie Flint, Aynsley Dunbar, Mick Fleetwood, Keef Hartley (d). 2/64–12/67.*

*** The Best Of ... As It All Began 1964–1969 [sic]
Deram 844 785 *Mayall; Henry Lowther (t); Dick Heckstall-Smith (ss, ts); Nick Newell, Chris Mercer (ts); John Almond, Rip Kant (bs); unknowns (s); Paul Butterfield (h); Bernie Watson, Roger Dean, Eric Clapton, Peter Green, Mick Taylor (g); John McVie, Paul Williams, Tony Reeves, Steve Thompson (b); Martin Hart, Hughie Flint, Aynsley Dunbar, Mick Fleetwood, Keef Hartley, Jon Hiseman, Colin Allen (d). 2/64–8/68.*

**(*) Thru The Years
Deram 844 028 *Mayall; Henry Lowther (t); Dick Heckstall-Smith (ss, ts); Chris Mercer (ts); Peter Green (h, g, v); Bernie Watson, Roger Dean, Mick Taylor (g); John McVie, Paul Williams, Tony Reeves (b); Martin Hart, Hughie Flint, Aynsley Dunbar, Keef Hartley, Jon Hiseman (d). 3/64–4/68.*

These compilations swell the documentation of the Bluesbreakers years. *Looking Back* and *Thru The Years* were assembled in 1990 as interlocking collections. The first spins both sides of five singles and adds a previously unissued and poorly recorded 'They Call It Stormy Monday' with Clapton and Jack Bruce. 'So Many Roads' and 'Double Trouble' show how bewitched Mayall was by Otis Rush – and who can blame him? – but are no more than loyal copies. *Thru The Years* also rounds up some singles but then finds eight outtakes from the *Hard Road* date and sessions in spring '67, all featuring Peter Green, often singing as well as playing guitar (and occasionally harmonica). 'Out Of Reach' quite successfully captures an Otis Rush ambience without being an Otis Rush song, and it's puzzling that it wasn't chosen for *A Hard Road*. It may be less of a mystery that 'Alabama Blues' wasn't, since Green delivers the J. B. Lenoir song with an unforced simplicity beyond the reach of his leader. Other cuts come from the *Plays John Mayall* and *Bare Wires* sessions.

The Best Of, issued seven years later, was a frustrating release. Half of it came from singles: most of them had already been recovered for the earlier compilations, but not 'Lonely Years' and 'Bernard Jenkins', duets with Clapton, first issued on a Purdah 45 and much sought after by devotees of the guitarist. There was also a cut from the EP with Paul Butterfield ('Eagle Eye', not the best). The remaining items were from albums, of which a few may not be currently available. If you didn't have either of the others, this would be a well-organized collection. All the Deram CDs have irritating notes by John Tracy, whose efficient research into dates and personnels is retailed in the breezy prose of a long-gone music-trade press: 'on this sceptred isle a 45 was culled to assist in promoting its big brother,' etc., etc.

**(*) Blues From Laurel Canyon
London 820 539 *Mayall; Mick Taylor, Peter Green (g); Steve Thompson (b); Colin Allen (d). 8/68.*

In which Our Hero is Enchanted by the City of Los Angeles – Her Natural Beauties – a Visit with Mr and Mrs Zappa – Mr Hite's Record Collection – a Romantic Encounter – Another of the Same – Return to West Hampstead.

(**(*)) Live: 1969
Eagle EDMCD 163 2CD *Mayall; Johnny Almond (as, ts, fl); Mick Taylor, Jon Mark (g); Steve Thompson (b); Colin Allen (d). 5–6/69.*

***(*) The Turning Point
BGO BGOCD 145 *As above, except omit Taylor, Allen. 7/69.*

***(*) **The Turning Point**
Polydor 314 549 423 *As above.* 7/69.

In the notes to *The Turning Point* Mayall announced, 'The time is right for a new direction in blues music.' Dispensing with drums and replacing an electric lead guitarist with a finger-style acoustic player, he intended 'to explore seldom-used areas within the framework of low volume music.' Specifically, he had been inspired by the playing of the Jimmy Giuffre Trio with guitarist Jim Hall in the movie *Jazz On A Summer's Day*, especially their pastoral blues 'Train And The River', and that effect is replicated by Almond and Mark many times during *The Turning Point*. (Listeners may discern stirrings in the same general direction on *Bare Wires*.) The discreet setting encourages Mayall to sing in a more relaxed voice, though because of the length of the songs (the album was taped in performance at the Fillmore East in New York) there is proportionately less singing than usual. With only the small reservation that it may be a little leisurely for modern taste, this can be recommended as one of Mayall's most successful and accessible recordings. BGO reissue the LP, while Polydor add three previously unreleased items. *Live: 1969*, after a single track from 5/69 by the *Blues From Laurel Canyon* lineup, is devoted to the Almond–Mark–Thompson band, as heard at various dates during the 6/69 British tour that preceded the recording of *The Turning Point*. The tracks on the second disc come from a night at London's Marquee Club and were previously available on *Live At The Marquee 1969* (Eagle EAMCD 070); most of the songs had been recorded at the earlier gigs, and indeed all the repertoire on both discs reappears on the extended version of *The Turning Point*. That and the modest sound quality make *Live: 1969* a luxury for anyone but a Mayall-or-nothing fan.

** **Rock The Blues Tonight**
Sanctuary CAS 36090 2CD *Mayall; Blue Mitchell (t, flh); Fred Clark (ts); Sugarcane Harris (vn); Harvey Mandel, Freddie Robinson (g); Larry Taylor, Victor Gaskin (b); Paul Lagos, Keef Hartley (d).* 9/70–late 71.

(*) **Rockin' The Roadshow
Castle CMDDD 639//Sanctuary CAS 36091 2CD *As above, except add James Quill Smith (g), Kevin McCormick (b), Soko Richardson (d), Maggie Parker (v).* 9/70–late 71, 81.

The 14 performances on *Rock The Blues Tonight* were illicitly taped at three gigs, but their release has been approved by Mayall, with the caveat that his vocals 'are, in most cases, excruciating and erratic to say the least'. So why issue them? Because these generally lengthy pieces often have long passages of what Mayall regards as fine playing by Mandel, Harris and, on the last three tracks, Mitchell. But the conjunction of rough vocals, documentary sound quality and overlong jams – including two versions of 'Possessive Emotions' totalling more than 35 minutes – must limit the appeal of the album to specialists. *Rockin' The Roadshow* contains the same material, minus 'My Pretty Girl' and the shorter 'Possessive Emotions', but bulks up what's left with the 1981 album *Road Show Blues*, discussed below.

** **Back To The Roots**
Polydor 314 549 424 2CD *Mayall; Johnny Almond (as, ts, fl); Sugarcane Harris (vn); Eric Clapton, Harvey Mandel, Mick Taylor, Jerry McGee (g); Larry Taylor, Steve Thompson (b); Paul Lagos, Keef Hartley, Joe Yuele (d).* 11/70, 1/88.

The idea behind *Back To The Roots* was to assemble alumni of Mayall's past bands. Clapton, Mandel and Mick Taylor are each on about a third of the numbers, occasionally all three together, as in 'Accidental Suicide', a slight obituary for Jimi Hendrix. Not for the first or last time, the quality of the playing frequently fails to find a match in Mayall's singing: no impartial judge, for instance, would have okayed the vocal on 'Goodbye December'. Then again, no impartial judge would have passed the lyrics of 'Mr. Censor Man' (' – don't teach us your morality: if it gives offence, stay away from pornography'), or 'No Children', or 'Unanswered Questions', where the sentiments are conveyed by callow sloganizing. Too often, the desired happy marriage of words and music is reduced to an awkward, unsatisfying one-night stand. Displeased with the sound of some of the original tracks, Mayall remixed them in 1988, adding new drums and redoing his vocals; those eight adapted items are provided as bonus tracks.

(*) **New Year, New Band, New Company/Lots Of People
BGO BGOCD 492 *Mayall; Bill Lamb (t, tb); Nolan Smith (t); Ann Patterson (as, fl, oboe); Red Holloway, Jimmy Roberts (ts); David Ii (bs); Jay Spell (kb, clavinet); Don 'Sugarcane' Harris (vn); Rick Vito (g); Larry Taylor (b); Soko Richardson, Frank Wilson (d); Warren Bryant (perc); Dee McKinnie, Pepper Watkins, Patty Smith, Beckie Burns (v).* 75, late 76.

(*) **Notice To Appear/A Banquet In Blues
BGO BGOCD 495 *Mayall; Nick Messina, Blue Mitchell (t); Benny Powell (tb); Red Holloway (as, ts); Lon Price, Johnny Almond (ts, fl); Larry Blouin (bs); Jay Spell (kb, o, p, clavinet); Doug Bare (kb, o, p); Allen Toussaint (kb, p, clavinet, prod); James Booker (o); Ronnie Barron (clavinet, v); Don 'Sugarcane' Harris (vn); Novi Novag (vl); Rick Vito (g, v); Steve Hughes, Mike Cooley, Jon Mark (g); Larry Taylor, Tony Broussard, John McVie, Larry Gales, Lenny McDaniel, Alex Dmochowski (b); Soko Richardson, Herman Ernest, Roy McCurdy, Phil Despommier (d); Kim Joseph (cga); Buck Clarke (perc); Dee McKinnie (v).* fall 75, 5/76.

(*) **A Hard Core Package/The Last Of The British Blues
BGO BGOCD 493 *Mayall; Cliff Ervin, Steve Madio (t); Bradford Henry Thoelke III, Jim Price (tb); Buddy McDaniel, Trevor Laurence (ts); Ann Patterson (fl); James Quill Smith (g, v); Steve Thompson (b); Soko Richardson (d); Jody Linscott (perc); Pepper Watkins, Edna Richardson, Rebecca Burns, Mindy Mickel, Marilyn Scott, Marty Gwynn, Donna Washburn, Judy Brown, Colleen, Maureen (v).* 77.

(*) **The ABC Years 1975 To 1982
MCA MCAD2–11787 2CD *As for above three CDs, except add Mick Taylor (g), Colin Allen (d).* 75–77, 82.

The six albums on the three BGO CDs cover Mayall's spell with ABC. The new band advertised on the first included guitarist Rick Vito and the not-so-new Sugarcane Harris, who is given his head in 'Driving On' and 'Taxman Blues'. Dee McKinnie, the first woman singer to be featured in a Mayall lineup, comes on strong in 'Step In The Sun'. *Notice To Appear* was produced in New Orleans by Allen Toussaint, who, Mayall remembers, 'was totally in charge. I was lucky to get two songs on it!' Toussaint's compositions were neatly tailored to Mayall's voice, though, and brought some rhythmic novelty. Mayall's 'Old Time Blues' is a tribute to blues records heard in his youth. 'Seven Days Too Long' on *A Banquet In Blues* half echoes one of them, Eddie Boyd's '24 Hours', but 'Fantasyland', with its passages for flute and viola and viola and guitars, lies somewhere between contemporary 'east/west' fusions and the Van Morrison of *Astral Weeks*. Here in particular Mayall widens the gap separating him from the Bluesbreakers of the '60s, to develop a music for which the blues was merely one source. *Lots Of People* was recorded at the Roxy in LA with a 14-piece band, Red Holloway taking several substantial solos. Gary Rowles's solo on 'He's A Travelling Man' shows how far Mayall's ideas about lead guitarists had changed since the days of Clapton and Green. If the backing singers and horn-section stabs suggest '60s soul, and 'A Helping Hand', driven by fretless bass, has the sassiness of contemporary TV themes, 'Play The Harp', 'Burning Down' and 'Separate Ways' find Mayall coming home to the blues.

He then cut back to a quartet, with James Quill Smith on guitar. This is the core band on *A Hard Core Package* and *The Last Of The British Blues*, but the albums are quite different. Studio-recorded, *Package* surrounds the quartet with horn sections; 'An Old Sweet Picture' and 'The Last Time' are straight blues, but elsewhere the busy rhythms recall the big-cast sound of *Lots Of People*. *Last Of The British Blues*, however, is hardcore small-group music, including the blues standards 'Parchman Farm', where Mayall juggles voice and harmonica, and 'Another Man [Done Gone]'. The meaning of the album's title is obscure, since the British blues scene was years behind him, and most of his recent playing had been with Americans. Perhaps it implied a fresh paragraph in the story: when Mayall cut a new album for a new company the following year he had made yet another change of direction. *The ABC Years* gathers tracks from the six albums, adding an outtake from *Notice To Appear* and four numbers from a 1982 concert in Washington, DC.

(*) Road Show Blues
Aim 1067 *Mayall; James Quill Smith (g); Kevin McCormick (b); Soko Richardson (d); Maggie Parker (v)*. 81.

Originally the third album of his contract with DJM, *Road Show Blues* is an uncomplicated blues set, mostly studio-recorded but with two live cuts, advancing no new business plan but simply minding the store. There are songs by or about J. B. Lenoir, Jimmy Reed and John Lee Hooker, while 'Lost And Gone' refers to the disastrous 1979 fire that consumed his possessions, including his musical archives. The album is also part of the 2CD *Rockin' The Roadshow* (see above).

(*) Rolling With The Blues
Shakedown SHAKEBX 116 2CD+DVD *Mayall; Blue Mitchell (t, flh); Clifford Solomon, Red Holloway (ts); Freddie Robinson, James Quill Smith, Mick Taylor (g); Victor Gaskin, Kevin McCormick, John McVie, Steve Thompson (b); Keef Hartley, Soko Richardson, Colin Allen (d)*. 5/72–12/82.

Disc 1 contains concert performances in Frankfurt from 1972–73 with Blue Mitchell, one or the other of the saxmen and Freddie Robinson. Other live recordings by these lineups have not been sonically to Robinson's advantage, so these tapes are valuable as a record of his relaxed playing. Disc 2 assembles tracks from a handful of US and Italian gigs in the early '80s, mostly by the reunited Bluesbreakers with Mick Taylor. Disc 3 is a DVD of a 2002 interview.

(*) Return Of The Bluesbreakers
Aim CD 1004 *Mayall; Larry Raspberry (p); Don McMinn, Bobby Manuel, Mick Taylor (g); Jeff Davis, Kevin McCormick (b); Mike Gardner, Colin Allen (d); Don Nix (prod)*. 81–82.

The centrepiece of this CD is five tracks from a 1982 Washington, DC, concert (two of which are also on *The ABC Years*, above), with magisterial slide guitar by Mick Taylor. These are preceded by five from a Memphis session of '81 with studio musicians, produced (as the '82 tapes evidently were) by Don Nix and thus giving the world yet another opportunity to hear 'Same Old Blues', and followed by three studio recordings of unknown provenance.

*** Behind The Iron Curtain**
GNP-Crescendo GNPD 2184 *Mayall; Coco Montoya, Walter Trout (g); Bobby Haynes (b); Joe Yuele (d)*. 6/85.

Mayall's output in the mid- and late '80s is only patchily covered by current CDs, and this extract from a Hungarian concert – if it *is* currently available – is valuable to the serious collector as a record of the Bluesbreakers in their Trout–Montoya formation. Some of the selections come from early pages in the Mayall folio, like 'Parchman Farm' and 'Steppin' Out' from *Blues Breakers* and 'The Laws Must Change' from *The Turning Point*, but Mayall's musical philosophy has radically altered since the latter album and he is once again building with the rock cornerstones of electric guitar and drums. Old or new, the seven tracks are largely vehicles for barnstorming playing. 'Parchman Farm' is dominated by Mayall's harmonica playing, the slow blues 'Have You Heard' is a feature for Montoya and 'Fly Tomorrow' for Trout, while 'Rolling With The Blues' and 'Steppin' Out' have dramatic solos by both guitarists.

*** Wake Up Call**
Silvertone 41518//(E) ORECD 527 *Mayall; Darrell Leonard (t); Joe Sublett (s); Tom Canning (kb, o); Buddy Guy (g, v); Coco Montoya, Mick Taylor, Albert Collins, David Grissom (g); Rick Cortes (b, v); Joe Yuele (d); Dave McNair, Mike Bruno (perc); Mavis Staples, Maggie Mayall (v)*. 93.

*** Spinning Coin**
Silvertone 41541//(E) ORECD 537 *Mayall; Joe Sublett (s); [John] Juke Logan (h); R. S. Field (g, perc); Buddy Whittington (g); Rick Cortes (b); Joe Yuele (d, wb, perc); Dave McNair (perc)*. 5–8/94.

(*) Blues For The Lost Days
Silvertone 41605//(E) ORECD 547 *Mayall; Darrell Leonard (t); George Bohanon (tb); Red Holloway, Clifford Solomon (ts); Tommy Eyre (kb, o); John Porter (mandola, g, prod); Mike Martsolf (bj, Do); John Paulus (g, b); Buddy Whittington (g); Joe Yuele (d); Debra Dobkin, Tony Braunagel (perc)*. 10/96.

*** Silver Tones – The Best Of John Mayall & The Bluesbreakers**
Silvertone 41658//(E) 0591222 As for above three CDs. 93–10/96.

Mayall's Silvertone albums present an artist in no way diminished by 30 years of indefatigable touring. In fact he seems refreshed, and *Wake Up Call* is his strongest album in years. This may be partly due to good repertoire selection – Mayall's own contribution is down to four songs out of 12, the others including worthwhile pieces by Chris Smither and Tony Joe White – but it also helps to have cameos by Buddy Guy and Albert Collins, and a peppery Mavis Staples singing on the title track. *Spinning Coin* introduces Buddy Whittington, a tidy guitarist. The stripped-down combo pours thick, unsluggish rhythmic oil for Mayall to go slipping and sliding on, croaky as ever but with some good riffs. It often sounds like a soundtrack for something ominous and Southern directed by Robert Penn or Walter Hill. *Blues For The Lost Days* increases Mayall's writing credits to seven out of 12, yielding a Loftonesque piece about his wife ('I Don't Mind') and another prosaic song about admired musicians ('All Those Heroes'). *Silver Tones* is a 'best of' only so far as the Silvertone albums are concerned. Four tracks were selected from each of the three, and there are two previously unissued numbers from the *Wake Up Call* and *Spinning Coin* sessions.

*** Padlock On The Blues

Cleopatra 077//Eagle EAGCD 077//EDL EAG 172 *Mayall; Darrell Leonard (t); Joe Sublett (s); Ernie Watts (ts); Tommy Eyre (o); Mike Martsolf (bj, Do); Buddy Whittington, John Lee Hooker, Coco Montoya (g); John Paulus (b); Joe Yuele (d); Steve Leshner (perc). 10/98.*

'People ask,' Mayall sings in the title song, '"Why don't you sing the blues with a voice full of gravel and growl?"' Now you mention it ... but one should be cautious with one's flippancy, because, as he later remarks, 'Sometimes I stop to wonder what some critics out there would have me do', and the fairest answer may be: 'Keep on making records like this.' *Padlock On The Blues* is a beguiling set of bluesy originals with a strong dash of personal nostalgia in numbers like 'The Strip' and 'Always A Brand New Road', enhanced by Whittington's clean, inventive lead guitar lines and a brief cameo by John Lee Hooker.

**(*) Along For The Ride

Eagle EAGCD 150 *Mayall; Dick Heckstall-Smith (as); Red Holloway (ts); Tom Canning (kb, o, p); Billy Preston (kb, melodica, clavinet, v); Reese Wynans (o); Jeff Healey, Shannon Curfman, Andy Fairweather Low (g, v); David Z (g, prod); Buddy Whittington, Steve Cropper, Billy F. Gibbons, Jonny Lang, Peter Green, Steve Miller, Gary Moore, Joe Delgado, Davy Graham, Mick Taylor (g); David Smith, John McVie, Bob Delgado, Greg Rzab (b); Joe Yuele, Mick Fleetwood (d); Lenny Castro (perc); Crystal Taliefero, Wendy Moten, Chris Rea, Otis Rush (v). late 00.*

This is Mayall's '& Friends' album, with guest spots by a dozen or so blues notables and, remarkably, only one original, 'California', written years before with Steve Thompson for *The Turning Point*. It was noticeable on the Silvertone albums that Mayall was employing a mellower instrument than the scrawny, squalling voice of the past, and *Along For The Ride* maintains that improvement, but the material itself is inconsistently interesting and the cameo appearances are dutiful rather than inspired.

**(*) Stories

Eagle EAGCD 223 *Mayall; Tom Canning (kb, o, p, v); Buddy Whittington (g, v); Hank Van Sickle (b); Tom Yuele (d, perc); Lenny Castro (perc); Maggie Mayall (v); David Z (prod). 2–3/02.*

*** 70th Birthday Concert

Eagle EDGCD 246 2CD *Mayall; Henry Lowther (t); Chris Barber (tb); unknowns (reeds); Tom Canning (kb, o, p); Buddy Whittington (g, v); Mick Taylor, Eric Clapton (g); Hank Van Sickle (b); Tom Yuele (d, perc). 7/03.*

These albums ushered in a new lineup of the Bluesbreakers, Canning–Whittington–Van Sickle–Yuele. On *Stories* David Z does his best to keep the music light-footed but has to contend with the leaden writing of 'Kids Got The Blues' and 'Oh, Leadbelly' ('Goodnight Irene. I wonder who she was/Your song reached millions showed 'em who was boss/With your twelve-string guitar you really cut across'). It seems that whenever Mayall writes about the blues or bluesmen his ears immediately turn to tin. Fortunately there are decent songs from other sources, like Julie & Buddy Miller's 'Dirty Water', an object-lesson in writing a distinctive blues with a single strong image. A few songs from *Stories* show up early in the festivities of the *70th Birthday Concert*, held in Liverpool's King's Dock, but the bulk of the programme, naturally enough, refers to music made earlier in Mayall's four-decade career, such as 'Oh, Pretty Woman' from *Crusade*, 'Walking On Sunset' from *Blues From Laurel Canyon* and 'California' from *The Turning Point*. The current Bluesbreakers are joined first by Mick Taylor, then a horn section, Eric Clapton and Chris Barber. Clapton and his one-time boss duet on 'No Big Hurry', then, with the band, revisit 'Hideaway', 'All Your Love' and others, including a long stay (18.04) with 'Have You Heard'. Fittingly, the album ends with a song by one of Mayall's favourite singers and chief inspirations, J. B. Lenoir. TR

Texas Pete Mayes (born 1938)
VOCAL, GUITAR

Born in Double Bayou, Texas, where his uncle operated a dancehall, Mayes was a professional musician at 16 and on the Houston scene by 1957. When not leading his own band he toured with bigger names, and played on sessions for Junior Parker and others. Mayes had a single released in 1969, but didn't record at length until the '80s. He took over the Double Bayou Dance Hall in 1983 when his uncle died, but diabetes has lately curtailed his touring.

***(*) For Pete's Sake

Antone's 10040 *Mayes; Gary Slechta, Kevin Stone (t); Randy Zimmerman, Jon Blondell (tb); John Mills (ts, bs); Kaz Kazanoff, Don 'Big Dog' Rollins (ts); Gene Taylor, Bert Lewis (p); Derek O'Brien (g); Jack Barber, Eugene 'Spare Time' Murray (b); George Rains, Johnny Prejean (d). 97?*

Mayes is (or rather was, see below) a very proficient guitarist and singer who acknowledges that T-Bone Walker was his idol but brings plenty of his own ideas to the table. He is an infrequent composer but his borrowings, from Bobby Bland, Junior Parker and Albert King, among others, demonstrate good taste and an ear for what suits his own voice. He's backed by deft rhythm sections and by horn arrangements that shift easily from punchy to lush. 'Next Time You See Me' is a lumbering exception to the good things on offer, and 'House Party', one of two Mayes copyrights on *For Pete's Sake*, is a feast of clichés, but otherwise this solid set justifies Mayes's considerable reputation in southeast Texas.

**(*) Live! At Double Bayou Dance Hall

Goldrhyme SG 602 *Mayes; Shedrick Cormier, William Green Jr, Ronnie Allen (ts); Bert Lewis (kb, v); John Broussard (g); Charles McCall (b); Johnny Prejean (d). 5/03.*

Health problems mean that Mayes is unable to play guitar, but Broussard substitutes very ably; he's the best thing about a band that otherwise doesn't venture far beyond competence.

(Prejean's pitiless hammering of the offbeat is in startling contrast to his work on *For Pete's Sake*.) Mayes's cousin Bert Lewis sings the warm-up songs, which are 'Kansas City' and 'Blueberry Hill'. His voice, like Mayes's, is sometimes strained; unlike Mayes, he hits some wrong notes. The CD goes from those familiar openers to 'Down Home Blues' and 'Sweet Home Chicago', which – surprise! – turns into 'Hey! Hey! The Blues Is All Right'. With the exception of Dave Bartholomew's 'Pony Tail', the playlist in between is equally predictable. CS

Percy Mayfield (1920–84)
VOCAL, PIANO

Percy Mayfield had scored seven Top Ten hits for Specialty in two years when a 1952 car accident tore apart his matinee-idol good looks, and understandably affected his self-confidence. Mayfield continued to perform and record, but there was no chart action for many years, and his main income came from songwriting. Fortunately, he was one of black music's outstanding lyricists; 'But On The Other Hand, Baby', 'Danger Zone' and 'Hit The Road Jack', composed during five years as a staff writer for Ray Charles, were a small part of a career-long output of great songs.

*** Percy Mayfield 1947–1951
Classics 5114 *Mayfield; Vernon Smith (t); Marshall Royal, unknown (as); Maxwell Davis, Richard Wells, Jack McVea, unknown (ts); Floyd Turnham, Charles Waller, Maurice Simon (bs); John Crawford (s); Willard McDaniel, Eddie Beal, Lee Wesley Jones, unknown (p); Chuck Norris, Gene Phillips, Tiny Webb, Herman Mitchell (g); Roy Hamilton, Red Callender, Billy Hadnott, unknown (b); Henry Williams, Lee Young, unknown (d). 47–7/51.*

**** Poet Of The Blues
Specialty SPCD-7001/Ace CDCHD 283 *As above, except add Jewell Grant (as), James Jackson Jr, Bumps Myers, William Woodman (ts), Richard Wells (s), Fletcher Smith, William Pyles, Gerald Wiggins (p), Ulysses Livingston, Harold Grant (g), Ralph Hamilton, David Bryant, Theodore Shirley (b), Jesse Sailes, William Douglas, Robert Pittman (d), The Maytones [Meadowlarks] (v); omit Smith, Royal, Wells, Hamilton, Williams, unknowns. 8/50–10/54.*

**** Vol. 2 Memory Pain
Specialty SPCD-7027/[Ace CDCHD 438] *As above, except add Jesse Jones, Earl Jackson (ts), William Lundy (bs), Christine Chatman (p), Rene Hall, Clifton White (g), Ted Brinson (b), Earl Palmer (d), Joy Hamilton (v); omit James Jackson Jr. 8/50–c. 60.*

*** Percy Mayfield 1951–1954
Classics 5150 *Mayfield; Jewell Grant (as); Maxwell Davis, James Jackson, Bumps Myers, Earl Jackson, William Woodman (ts); Maurice Simon, Floyd Turnham (bs); John Crawford (s); Willard McDaniel, Fletcher Smith, Gerald Wiggins (p); Herman Mitchell, Mitchell Webb, Chuck Norris, Ulysses Livingston, William Pyles, Harold Grant (g); Billy Hadnott, Ralph Hamilton, David Bryant, Theodore Shirley (b); Lee Young, Jesse Sailes, William Douglas, Robert Pittman (d); Joy Hamilton (v). 7/51–3/54.*

Percy Mayfield sang for listeners who wanted lush sounds and sophisticated lyrics, and was at his best on ballads and slow blues. He favoured downbeat themes, which were treated with disturbing openness; the reaction to lost love was often not merely heartache, but mental turmoil, or even suicide, to which 'River's Invitation' is almost a lovesong. Traditional lines are effortlessly combined with original, and often startling ideas; anyone might write a song called 'Please Send Me Someone To Love', but only Percy Mayfield would make it a prayer for peace, and carry off a line like 'I lay awake nights, and ponder world problems.' He sang in a narrow bass–baritone range, with impeccable taste, moving easily from reedy musing to powerful declamation, and his relaxed swing and perfect timing have justly evoked comparison with Billie Holiday and Frank Sinatra. *Poet Of The Blues* includes Mayfield's finest work for Specialty, and is marred only by a couple of numbers using incongruous shuffle rhythms. He is accompanied by some of the best West Coast session musicians, playing imaginative and well-recorded arrangements. Most of *Memory Pain* is from the same era, and it features a number of alternative takes to songs on *Poet Of The Blues*, and an interesting, unaccompanied demo of 'Hit The Road Jack'. The alternative takes are individually strong, but taken as a whole, *Memory Pain* is very slightly the lesser of these compilations.

Classics' first disc begins with four extremely worn sides from GruVtone, where Mayfield is still finding his distinctive voice as both writer and performer. 'Two Years Of Torture' is a significant harbinger, though; a rapidly maturing Mayfield remade it at a much better recorded session for Supreme, where he was backed by high-calibre musicians, several of whom appear on the early Specialty sessions. Specialty recordings supply the balance of the first Classics CD and the whole of the second. All this material, reorganized into chronological order and with alternative takes omitted, is drawn from *Poet Of The Blues* and *Memory Pain*. The four Supreme tracks are important, but the more consistent quality and superior presentation of the official releases wins out.

Between 1962 and 1967 Mayfield was writing for Ray Charles and recording on Ray's Tangerine label. In 2003 *His Tangerine And Atlantic Sides* (Rhino Handmade RHM2 7828) appeared in a 2,500-copy limited edition, which rapidly sold out. Readers who find a secondhand copy of this wonderful compilation should pay whatever price is asked.

♛ **** Walking On A Tightrope
Acadia ACAM 8021 *Mayfield; unknowns (t); unknown (as); prob. Willie Henderson (ts); unknown (o); unknown (p); poss. Wayne Bennett (g); unknown (b); unknown (d). 68.*

Brunswick teamed Mayfield with a band directed by Willie Henderson, and remembered by the singer only as 'Chicago cats'. Their sound is a (then) up-to-the-minute blend of soul and blues, supplied respectively by punchy brass and reeds, and by a very fine guitarist, who listens intently to what Mayfield is doing and saying and responds imaginatively. Up front, Mayfield carries on doing what he did best; his vocal range had become even narrower by this time, but his phrasing was still the hippest in the business. He was still writing great songs too, and alongside the inevitable remake of 'Please Send Me Someone To Love' are classics like 'Walking On A Tightrope', 'My Mind Is Trying To Leave Me' and 'Danger Zone', another meditation on the tense state of the world. The jaunty 'I Made It Just The Same', as close as Mayfield ever came to rock 'n' roll, provides light relief with its tale of nursing a jalopy across the South, but, as ever, life's challenges, refracted by his exceptional songwriting ('An empty room makes quite a sound, the mirror seems to be upside down'), are at the forefront of Mayfield's concerns.

***(*) **Live//Live In San Francisco**
Winner 445//Acrobat ACMD 4044 *Mayfield; Dr Wild Willie Moore, Julien Vaught, Bobbie Webb (ts); Mark Naftalin (o, p); Pee Wee Crayton, Bobby Murray, Ron Thompson (g); Leonard Gill, Henry Oden, Francis Rocco Prestia, Ted Wysinger (b): Fred Casey, Francis Clay, Kelvin Dixon, Gary Silva (d). 7/81–8/83.*

**** **Hit The Road Again**
Timeless CD SJP 170 *Mayfield; Hollis Gilmore (ts); Lou Mathews (p); Phillip Walker (g); Dennis Walker (b); Ed Ahern (d). 11/82.*

Mayfield came back as a performer in the '80s, encouraged by friends and fellow musicians, and the Winner/Acrobat disc compiles material from *Mark Naftalin's Blue Monday Party*, a Bay Area radio show. Mayfield is obviously enjoying himself as he runs through some of his best-known compositions, assisted by whichever musicians were in town and available for the show. Naftalin's piano is heard on all but the final track, on which he switches to organ, and Mayfield makes his only recorded appearance on piano. Like all the accompanists, Naftalin provides respectful, responsive support; everyone involved is conscious of being in the presence of greatness, and determined to provide an appropriate setting for it. On the debit side, Mayfield had taken to inserting a knowing chuckle, often irrespective of its relevance to the lyrics; the perfect timing with which he does this makes it more, not less, annoying, but it's a small blemish on a fine CD.

Better still is *Hit The Road Again*, a studio session recorded on a visit to the Netherlands. The chuckle is kept to a minimum; this time, it's Mayfield's frequent use of the tag 'I ain't lying' that may generate mild irritation. The disc is another parade of his classics, including 'River's Invitation', 'My Jug And I' and 'The Highway Is Like A Woman' ('soft shoulders and dangerous curves'). The musicians' rhythm is as sinuously cat-footed as Mayfield's, and their sound – smoky tenor, rippling guitar and piano, self-effacingly supportive bass and drums – is an ideal backdrop for his world-weary, night-prowling sophistication. If scotch on the rocks could sing, it would sound the way Percy Mayfield does on this last display of his extraordinary writing and performing skills. cs

'Earring' George Mayweather
(1927–95)
VOCAL, HARMONICA

Mayweather began playing harmonica as a child in Montgomery, Alabama. In his early 20s he moved to Detroit, then to Chicago, where he took a day job in a steelmill and played with his neighbour J. B. Hutto and drummer Porkchop; the trio recorded under Hutto's name for Chance in 1954. Mayweather later worked with Eddie Taylor and depped in Little Walter's and Howlin' Wolf's bands when the leaders were on tour. His nickname was conferred by DJ Big Bill Hill: 'He'd call me "Earring George, the boy from Africa."' Latterly he played in the blues clubs around Boston, and Richard Rosenblatt, executive producer of his sole album, described him as 'the Boston scene's main link to the original Chicago blues scene'.

(*) **Whup It! Whup It!
Tone-Cool CD 1147 *Mayweather; 'Sax' Gordon (ts, bs); Ron Levy (o, p); Chris 'Stovall' Brown (g); Buster Wylie (b); Tuffy Kimble (d). 92.*

You can tell from the composer credits of these dozen songs that this was a voyage of reminiscence for Mayweather, back to Chicago in the '50s and '60s, and, genially blown along by his band, he doesn't make too heavy weather of it. At times his voice is rather rough and his harmonica playing sounds as if it needs a little more breath than he's capable of coming up with, but the slow, prowling tempo of 'In The Evening' (actually Jimmy Rogers's 'Money, Marbles And Chalk'), Muddy Waters's 'Gypsy Woman' and Little Walter's 'Bad Actin' Woman' has an authentic period ring.

Mayweather's recordings with J. B. Hutto are on *Down Home Blues Classics: Chicago 1946–1954* (Boulevard Vintage BVBCD 1014 4CD). TR

Randy McAllister
VOCAL, HARMONICA, DRUMS

McAllister was raised in northeast Texas and exposed to music by his father, a house-party singer and drummer. He began singing and playing drums in his teens, and took up harmonica while serving in the USAF in 1979–80. He has led bands since the late '80s, based from 1992 in the Dallas/Fort Worth area.

** **Diggin' For Sofa Change**
JSP JSPCD 297 *McAllister; Oliver Mowat (kb); Andrew 'Jr Boy' Jones (g, prod); Tommy Tucker (b); Tommy Hill (d). 97.*

(*) **Grease, Grit, Dirt And Spit
JSP JSPCD 2114 *McAllister; Oliver Mowat, Ron Mason (o); Mike Morgan, Robin Sylar, Smokey Logg, Hash Brown (g); John Bradley, Chuck Rainey (b); Kevin Schermerhorn, Bobby Baranowski (d). 98.*

(*) **Double Rectified Bust Head
JSP JSPCD 2130 *McAllister; John Street (o, p); Oliver Mowat (p); Texas Slim (g, v); Robin Sylar, Hash Brown, Smokey Logg, Jim Suhler, Mighty Paul Young (g); Chuck Rainey, Bill Cornish (b); Danny Cochran, Bobby Baranowski (d); Johnny Mack (wb); Robin Banks (v). 2–6/99.*

'I love all the old players,' McAllister says, 'but I believe in trying to make your own statement.' In keeping with that credo, there's not a cover to be found anywhere on these albums. Instead, McAllister displays a talent for writing songs whose titles jump out at you. *Grease, Grit, Dirt And Spit* offers 'Bullets For Breakfast', 'Do The Math Fool', 'Duct Tape And Bailin' Wire' and 'You Ain't Barbie And I Ain't Ken', while *Double Rectified Bust Head* ripostes with 'Nasty Little Day Dreams', ' "S" On My Chest' and '$127.00 Sandwich'. However, the songs are not always as interesting as their titles promise and, since McAllister sings almost everything with a kind of 'you lookin' at me?' pugnacity, some listeners may find a whole album at a sitting indigestible. Harmonica devotees, however, should enjoy his playing on both diatonic and chromatic instruments. All three CDs have rather murky studio sound, and it may be that McAllister would be more effective with another producer. For the time being, *Grease, Grit, Dirt And Spit*, which has the best songs, does him most justice. TR

Lee McBee (born 1951)
VOCAL, HARMONICA

Born in Kansas City, Missouri, McBee began playing harmonica about the age of 18 and was inspired to play blues by hearing a record of George 'Harmonica' Smith. His chief

models, he says, are Smith and Sonny Boy Williamson II. In 1988 he joined Mike Morgan & The Crawl, and after a break in 1993–95 returned to the band; he sings and plays harmonica on most of their albums.

*** 44
Red Hot RHR 5001//Me & My Blues MMBCD 704 *McBee; Kevin McKendree (p); Anson Funderburgh, Kid Ramos, Marvin Hunt (g); Willie Campbell (b); Stephen Hodges (d). 2/95.*

*** Soul Deep
Pacific Blues PBRC-2201//Crosscut CCD 11072 *McBee; Jimmy Shortell (t); Kaz Kazanoff (s); Gene Taylor (o, p); Jon Moeller, Hash Brown (g); Johnny Bradley (b); Wes Starr (d, perc); Cynthia Manley, Jessica Williams (v). 02.*

McBee may not be quite as well known as some other singing harmonica players on the current scene but on record he gives a very good account of himself. You get a fair idea of his tastes from *44*, where he offers his interpretations of songs originated by Howlin' Wolf, Snooky Pryor, Lightnin' Slim and others. Gifted with a strong, meaty voice and wide-ranging harmonica skills, he does good work with this familiar but durable material, supported by tight playing from the band. Funderburgh and Ramos expertly re-create the sound of early-'50s Memphis on tracks like 'Keep What You Got' or Eddie Taylor's 'I'm Gonna Love You', and the woven guitar lines of Muddy Waters and Jimmy Rogers on 'Everybody Loves My Baby'.

The bigger production of *Soul Deep*, while doing nothing to repress McBee's vitality, gives the album more textural variety, an expansion furthered by a setlist that includes not only the archaic 'Country Blues II' and the elderly-sounding 'Gonna Find My Baby' but the title number (from Clarence Carter) and 'Mohair Sam'. 'Your Turn To Cry' is a breath of old New Orleans, with rippling piano by Gene Taylor. This is another estimable and enjoyable set. TR

Jerry McCain (born 1930)
VOCAL, HARMONICA

Beginning his recording career at Trumpet and Excello ensured a certain fame for the Alabamian McCain but his reputation was consolidated by a songwriting talent that combined homespun wisdom with judicious humour. He went on to make solidly entertaining records throughout the '60s for labels both established and obscure. McCain's 1960 song 'She's Tough' became a 1986 Top Ten hit for the Fabulous Thunderbirds and helped to resurrect his own career. Sadly, most of the albums he's recorded since then have fallen victim to the contraction of the blues recording industry.

*** Strange Kind Of Feelin'
Alligator ALCD 2701 *McCain; Bernard Williams (ts); David Campbell (p); Christopher Collins, J. V. Turner (g); Herman Fowlkes, Raz Roseby (b); Walter McCain, Junior Blackman (d). 10/53–11/54.*

McCain made two singles a year apart for Trumpet but the rough-and-ready energy of 'East Of The Sun' and 'Stay Out Of Automobiles' couldn't disguise an uneasy alliance between the Alabama amateurs and the professionals of Jackson, Mississippi. McCain's simple harmonica playing is obliterated by Williams's tenor sax on the first song and overwhelmed by Turner's fluent guitar in the latter, while piano and bass are virtually inaudible throughout. Three previously unissued songs, including 'Crazy 'Bout That Mess', also suffer from poor engineering but none equal 'Love To Make Up', a medium-slow blues on which McCain's confidence as an artist finally emerges. Historical value outweighs musical worth in a compilation aimed at the collector. (Other tracks are by Tiny Kennedy and Clayton Love.)

**(*) The Jig's Up
JMC 2111 *As above, except add unknown (ts), Ed 'Skippy' Brooks, Fred Bush (p), Robert Christian, L. M. Jackson (g), Roosevelt McCain, Jimmy Sheffield (d). 10/53–62.*

**(*) Rockin' Harmonica Blues Men
Wolf WBJ 018 *McCain; Christopher Collins, Robert Christian (g); Roosevelt McCain (d). 56.*

With the disappearance of *That's What They Want* (Excello CD 3009), the only way to hear McCain's six singles for the company is the well-produced but hard-to-find *The Jig's Up*, whose 31 tracks also feature material from Trumpet and OKeh and eight of the 11 home-produced songs featured on *Rockin' Harmonica Blues Men*, which is shared with Kid Thomas. An engaging mixture of blues, rockabilly and rock 'n' roll, the Excello sides include the hilarious 'My Next Door Neighbor' and 'Trying To Please', 'Courtin' In A Cadillac', the Little Richard-inspired 'Run, Uncle John! Run' and 'That's What They Want', sung to the tune of 'I'm A Man'. The home recordings are chaotic, badly recorded and utterly irresistible. Considering the dubious quality of the original tape, the Wolf CD contrives a better sound picture than the noisy vinyl from which JMC's versions are drawn. Once again, history plays its part in rendering these tracks collectable but McCain's irrepressible character is hard to ignore.

**(*) Good Stuff
Varèse Vintage VSD-6022 *McCain; unknown (ts); unknown (o); Fred Bush (p); Christopher Collins, L. M. Jackson, unknown (g); unknown (b); Walter McCain, unknown (d); unknowns (v). 60–86.*

An uninspiring title holds good for roughly half of an album combining material from three decades, all from the same producer. Beginning strongly with 'She's Tough' and 'Steady' and later including 'Welfare Cadillac Blues', the programme falters on poppy nonsense like 'Ting-Tang-Tagalu'. It then gets bogged down in seven album tracks from 1980 and 1986 that show McCain apparently writing to various contemporary formulas rather than pleasing himself. Of these, only 'Blues Singing Man' and '53 Year Old Man' are comfortable vehicles for his humanity and wit. The album ends with 'Pussycat A-Go-Go', a piece of 1965 dance trivia for a long-forgotten label on which McCain takes a lone harmonica chorus. It's claimed that the backing band is Sam The Sham & The Pharoahs but, at this remove, who cares?

*** Somebody's Been Talking//Absolutely The Best
[Westside WESM 626]//Fuel 2000 302 061 098 *McCain; unknown (t); unknown (fl); unknowns (s); unknown (p); unknown (g); unknown (b); unknown (d). 68–72.*

This was absolutely the last sustained effort to set McCain's work before the dwindling blues singles market of the late '60s. 'She's Crazy 'Bout Entertainers' and 'Homogenized Love' showed his humour was undimmed, while '728 Texas (Where The Action Is)' and 'Midnight Beat' verified the efficacy of his harmonica chops. Unfortunately, these didn't totally compensate for soul and pop trivia like 'Sugar Baby', 'Stick 'Em Up' and 'Love Ain't Nothing To Play With'. Best of all is the Westside title track, a long medium-slow blues from 1972, although probably recorded earlier. Its B side, 'Soul Spasm', gorily documents the fatal crash between static funk chord changes and flute-based Shreveport psychedelia, an ignominious end to a halfway decent sequence of records. The Fuel 2000 issue is identical to the Westside in contents and artwork but substitutes the falsely hyperbolic title *Absolutely The Best*.

***(*) This Stuff Just Kills Me
Jericho 9005 *McCain; Johnnie Johnson, Carl Sonny Leyland (p); John Primer, Bob Kirkpatrick, Anson Funderburgh, Jimmie Vaughan, Derek O'Brien (g); Leroy Hodges, Tommy Shannon (b); Steve Potts, Chris Layton (d). 99.*

An impressive roster of musicians subordinate their talents to the service of McCain's most satisfying album for several years. Approaching 70, in songs like 'Viagra Man', 'Slave Master', 'Mama's Gone' and 'Ain't No Use For Drug Abuse' McCain proves he's still capable of perceptive social comment laced with occasional mirth, also present in the final 'Pull Up In My Garage'. It's best not to refer to the castlist, since it distracts (and detracts) from the quality of the artist's singing and harmonica playing, the latter showcased in 'Madison Wood'. A seven-year hiatus between this and his previous release, *I've Got The Blues All Over Me* (Ichiban, deleted), did nothing to diminish McCain's relish for music-making, here displayed very nearly at its best.

**** Unplugged
Music Maker MMCD 21 *McCain; Tim Duffy, Microwave Dave (g); Ardie Dean (d). 01.*

A delightful acoustic session that disguises its preparation in an easy mix of impromptu humour and understated musicianship. Despite the impositions of age, McCain shows that he's lost none of his songwriting and performance skills and his backing band gives him sterling support. Starting strongly with the country rock of 'Olla Mae' and 'Gal Named Mary', a Jimmy Reed pastiche, he erupts into humour in 'Sexual Harassment' and, more mordantly, 'If Love Kills Me'. Thereafter, the project gets a trifle bogged down in a sequence of medium-slow blues, thrown off by 'I Got You' and 'If You Love Me'. The final 'Look At Me' is an unacknowledged second attempt at 'Bad Love Blues'. Goodwill and confidence are exuded by all present, resulting in an album that shames the overproduced banality of many contemporary blues sessions. NS

Tommy McClennan (1908–62)
VOCAL, GUITAR

McClennan was a garrulous and impulsive performer, whose highly personalized style and delivery made a striking contrast with the numbing conformity of some of his Bluebird stablemates. His brief recording career failed to survive World War II and the last years of his life were spent as an incurable alcoholic in the hobo jungles of Chicago. Although he was once disparaged for his discursiveness, critical appreciation of his unique qualities has risen in recent years.

***(*) The Bluebird Recordings 1939–1942
[Bluebird 67430] 2CD *McClennan; Ransom Knowling, unknown (b); Joe McCoy (imb). 11/39–2/42.*

***(*) Big Joe Williams And The Stars Of Mississippi Blues
JSP JSPCD 7719 5CD *As above. 11/39–2/42.*

**(*) Travelin' Highway Man
Travelin' Man TMCD 06 *As above. 11/39–2/42.*

** A Guitar King 1939–1942
[EPM Blues Collection 15870] *As above. 11/39–2/42.*

** I'm A Guitar King
Wolf WBCD-001 *As above. 11/39–2/42.*

** Cotton Pickin' Blues
Acrobat ACRCD 188 *As above. 11/39–2/42.*

Spontaneity is intrinsic to McClennan's work, although he can be inhibited by his periodic accompaniment if it consists of something as unwieldy as an imitation string bass. The wilful resolve of his guitar technique has frequently been mistaken for a lack of one, but few would agree with the self-assessment of 'I'm A Guitar King'. He chose to ignore or was never troubled by the music's formal structures and frequently indulged in lengthy verbal asides to himself or to his guitar, most notably in 'Baby, Please Don't Tell On Me', in which he devotes an entire chorus to an obsessive monologue. His accompaniments were equally erratic, ranging from the purely rhythmic, interspersed with flashily imperfect treble phrasing, to merely playing pedal notes to mark the beat.

McClennan forced his vocals in the manner of Charley Patton and Blind Willie Johnson, and contemporaries like David 'Honeyboy' Edwards were impressed that such a loud voice could emanate from his diminutive frame. His garrulity enhanced the immediacy of his performance, making the overall effect more important than the means of achieving it. He shares this trait with fellow Mississippian Big Joe Williams and it can be traced today in the work of T-Model Ford. There's an undoubted sense of humour at work in his songs, notably 'She's Good Huggin' Size', whereas bursts of laughter elsewhere can be put down to nerves.

Much of his repertoire was imported. There's a 'New Shake 'Em On Down', a 'New Highway 51' and a 'New Sugar Mama', while 'Baby Don't You Want To Go', 'Love With A Feeling', 'Drop Down Mama', 'Bluebird Blues' and 'Deep Blue Sea Blues' hardly stray from their origins. 'Bottle It Up And Go' became his most notorious recording for its inclusion of 'nigger and a white man playing seven-up' verse, self-censored in other artists' versions. As soon as he's sung it, he seems to be distracted by the reaction of the studio staff. The song crops up again later, suitably sanitized as 'Shake It Up And Go'. A lascivious 'Cross Cut Saw Blues' is also associated with his name but this too may have arrived from elsewhere. Other songs of note include 'Whiskey Head Woman', 'Cotton Patch Blues', 'Down To Skin And Bones Blues' and 'Travelin' Highway Man'.

There's a subtle diminution of commitment as the five sessions progress, as though alcohol had begun to erode his skills. At his final session, at which he joined his erstwhile partner (and clone) Robert Petway (q.v.) for 'Boogie Woogie Woman', his voice sounds nasal and congested, his playing at times mechanical.

McClennan's self-destructive lifestyle was a blues variation on *The Rake's Progress* but for one courting death his music was uniquely vibrant and alive. To appreciate it fully, Bluebird's set prepared from original masters (if it can be found) is the recommended choice. This material also occupies most of two CDs in the JSP box. The Wolf and

Charlie McCoy (1909–50)
VOCAL, MANDOLIN, GUITAR

According to all who remember him McCoy was the outstanding instrumentalist around Jackson, Mississippi, in the late '20s. Moving in the early '30s to Chicago he recorded prolifically as an accompanist, and occasionally, though usually pseudonymously, for himself, on both guitar and mandolin. He was also a member of the Harlem Hamfats and other groups formed by his brother Joe.

*** **Charlie McCoy (1928–1932)**
RST Blues Documents BDCD-6018 *McCoy; Georgia Tom Dorsey (p); Bo Carter (vn, v); Walter Vincson (g, v); prob. Joe McCoy (v); Rosie Mae Moore (v).* 2/28–2/32.

McCoy first recorded in February 1928, accompanying Rosie Mae Moore, Tommy Johnson and Ishmon Bracey. All those sides can be heard in excellent transfers on *Memphis Blues Singers Volume 1* (Frog DGF 21). His rippling second parts behind Johnson on 'Bye Bye Blues' and 'Maggie Campbell Blues' are crucial to the ambience of those famous recordings. Over the next three years he worked on record with Bo Carter and Walter Vincson in various instrumental lineups, for various labels and under various names. Sides by the Mississippi Mud Steppers, of which two are here and four on the next album, are mostly features for his mandolin playing, including four waltzes. Other sides of McCoy's talent are shown by 'That Lonesome Train Took My Baby Away', a song written to the skipping tune of 'Cow Cow Blues'; the arresting topical coupling 'The Northern Starvers Are Returning Home'/'Mississippi I'm Longing For You', sung in duet with Bo Carter; and several hokum recordings based on 'It's Tight Like That', such as 'It Ain't No Good' and 'It Is So Good'. Amidst these collaborations he recorded a couple of solo blues with guitar, 'Glad Hand Blues' and the powerful slide-accompanied 'Last Time Blues'.

***(*) **Mississippi String Bands & Associates (1928–1931)**
RST Blues Documents BDCD-6013 *McCoy; unknown (p); Bo Carter (poss. vn, g, v); Walter Vincson (g, v); poss. Joe McCoy (g); Alec Johnson (v).* 11/28–1/31.

Like the previous album, this is a testament to the adaptability of McCoy, Bo Carter and Walter Vincson. Carter and Vincson play on most of the tracks but McCoy is on virtually all of them, accompanying Alec Johnson, playing mandolin waltzes with the Mississippi Mud Steppers and filling various blues roles with the Mississippi Blacksnakes, including singing on 'It's All Over Now', 'It's So Nice And Warm', 'It Still Ain't No Good', 'Easy Going Woman Blues' – which despite its title is an explicit Depression blues – and 'Bye Bye Baby Blues'. Wedged between the blocks of Blacksnakes recordings are two couplings by '"Sam Hill" From Louisville', i.e. Vincson, on which McCoy is one of the guitarists and may be the slide player on 'Things 'Bout Coming My Way'. (This untypically detailed discographical comment is supplied because the CD's own discography is confused.)

In comparison with that briskly professional blues job – all 14 of the Blacksnakes/'Sam Hill' recordings were cut over three days – the session a couple of years earlier with Alec Johnson belongs to another age of entertainment. McCoy and his colleagues (allegedly his brother, Bo Carter and an unidentified pianist) form a lively and expressive pit orchestra to accompany a set of antique minstrel songs and a couple of blues. Johnson is a singer with great presence, but the most attractive feature of his performance is that it is entirely without self-parody, and the listener is much less likely to be discomfited by it than by, say, the blackface routines of Emmett Miller. That said, not everyone will be able to take a song like 'Mysterious Coon' on its own historical terms, but, for those who can, it is among the most vivid performances of African-American vaudeville to survive on record.

*** **The McCoy Brothers – Vol. 1 (1934–1936)**
RST Blues Documents BDCD-6019 *McCoy; Jimmie Gordon, prob. Chuck Segar, prob. Black Bob (p); Joe McCoy (g); unknown (b); unknown (wb).* 8/34–4/36.

*** **The McCoy Brothers – Vol. 2 (1936–1944)**
RST Blues Documents BDCD-6020 *McCoy; prob. Black Bob (p); unknown (b).* 4/36–9/36.

The first CD in this entry ended with McCoy's first recordings outside the South. *The McCoy Brothers – Vol. 1* opens in Chicago in 1934, with both McCoys recording busily for the newly founded Decca label. Charlie's most characteristic work in this period was his vinegary guitar playing on records by Jimmie Gordon and Johnnie Temple, among others, but his own blues features are quite individual, such as his version of the 'Sweet Old Kokomo' theme called 'Baltimore Blues', a rare blues reference to that city. He is not a particularly expressive singer, but effective in moody songs like the slide-accompanied 'Motherless And Fatherless Blues'. After a batch of sides by Joe, the CD ends with half of the 1936 session by Papa Charlie's Boys, a swing trio with piano and bass, fronted by Charlie playing the jazzy mandolin he would bring to many other artists' sessions in the late '30s and early '40s. One of these trio sides is 'Too Long', an original composition in a popular song form which proved to be his moneymaker: as well as being recorded by himself (twice), the Mississippi Sheiks and other black groups, it was adopted by two or three Western Swing bands.

Vol. 2 has the other two Papa Charlie's Boys sides and a coupling issued as by Tampa Kid, in which Charlie approximates the style of Tampa Red. The remaining tracks are nominally Joe's but Charlie plays mandolin on many of them, and in the 1942 session by Big Joe & His Rhythm it is the lead instrument throughout. In 'It Ain't No Lie' he recalls the tune of 'Cow Cow Blues' again.

Readily identifiable backup playing by McCoy on guitar and mandolin can be spotted on innumerable Chicago recordings of the period by all three of the major labels. He is also heard as mandolinist, occasionally guitarist and, once, singer on recordings by the Harlem Hamfats. TR

Joe McCoy (1905–50)
VOCAL, GUITAR

From Jackson, Mississippi, McCoy played Kansas Joe to his wife's Memphis Minnie on their many popular blues recordings made between 1929 and 1932. After they separated in the mid-'30s McCoy occupied himself in Chicago blues circles as a recording artist – solo, with his brother Charlie, leading small bands or singing with the Harlem Hamfats – and increasingly as a songwriter, particularly for Lil Green. He has the curious distinction of having recorded under nine pseudonyms but only once in his own name.

*** **The Story of Kansas Joe 1929/1944**
EPM Blues Collection 15934 *McCoy; Edgar Saucier (as); Robert Lee McCoy (h); Little Brother Montgomery, poss. Chuck Segar (p); unknown (vn); Charlie McCoy (md, g); Memphis Minnie (g, v); Ransom Knowling (b); Amanda Sortier (wb, v); Washboard Sam, unknown (wb); Harmon Ray, unknown (v).* 6/29–12/44.

*** **The McCoy Brothers – Vol. 1 (1934–1936)**
RST Blues Documents BDCD-6019 *McCoy; prob. Jimmie Gordon, poss. Black Bob, unknown (p); unknown (vn); Charlie McCoy, poss. Willie Lofton (g); unknown (b); unknown (tamb); unknowns (v).* 1–11/35.

*** **The McCoy Brothers – Vol. 2 (1936–1944)**
RST Blues Documents BDCD-6020 *McCoy; poss. Herb Morand (t, v); Odell Rand (cl); Edgar Saucier (as); Robert Lee McCoy (h); Horace Malcolm, Little Brother Montgomery (p); Charlie McCoy (md); Ransom Knowling, prob. John Lindsay, unknown (b); prob. Amanda Sortier (wb, v); Washboard Sam, unknown (wb); Harmon Ray (v).* 10/37–12/44.

Joe McCoy had little of his brother Charlie's instrumental versatility, but he had abilities just as useful to a working musician. As *The Story Of Kansas Joe* explains, he managed to keep a toehold in the 'race' record business for a decade and a half. He also had a gift for redeveloping other people's musical properties. 'Evil Devil Woman' is a smoothed-out treatment of Skip James's most famous song, with Charlie playing the melody on guitar with mandolin-like tremolos. 'Going Back Home', from the same session, is pure Tommy Johnson, and here Charlie could replay his own guitar figures of six years earlier. Both recordings are on *The Story Of Kansas Joe*, surrounded by a selection of his collaborations with Memphis Minnie (also discussed in her entry) and pieces in other settings like 'Look Who's Coming Down The Road', another reminiscence of Tommy Johnson, with vigorous shuffle-bowing by an unidentified fiddler.

The Blues Documents CDs, which contain virtually all of Joe's recordings from the stated period, include some material that *The Story Of Kansas Joe* does not touch on, notably the eight sermons issued under the sobriquet Hallelujah Joe. These have several of the characteristic elements of the recorded sermonette: sung intro and coda, congregational responses and moaning, and on some a hot piano. McCoy is not an outstanding preacher – he starts straining too soon and then, in dramatic terms, has nowhere else to go – but he sounds involved in the performances, the sermons make sense and there is no reason, on this evidence, to suppose that he was making comic novelties. Also on *Vol. 1* is 'Something Gonna Happen To You', whose bouncing guitar riff is a startling throwback to the style of Garfield Akers. *Vol. 2* has a session by the Palooka Washboard Band, i.e. the Harlem Hamfats, but is chiefly devoted to the groups billed as Big Joe & His Washboard Band or Big Joe & His Rhythm, early-'40s lineups playing what might be called skiffle blues. The blend of perky harmonica, stolid rhythm guitar and washboard produces an unusual but shallow ensemble sound and, although it is somewhat freshened by the addition of Charlie McCoy's mandolin and, on one session, the vocals of Harmon Ray, a

disciple of Peetie Wheatstraw, the half-dozen examples on *The Story Of Kansas Joe* may for some listeners be all the late Joe McCoy they need. TR

Robert McCoy (1908–77)
VOCAL, PIANO

McCoy spent virtually all his life in Birmingham, Alabama. His older brothers Johnny and Willie learned to play piano from local heroes like Cow Cow Davenport and Jabo Williams, and in his teens Robert followed their example, honing his skill at rent parties. At a Birmingham session in 1937 he recorded accompaniments to Guitar Slim, Charlie Campbell and Peanut The Kidnapper, but to record in his own name he had to wait until the '60s, when a teenaged Birmingham blues fan, Pat Cather, issued two LPs of his work, Barrelhouse Blues And Jook Piano *and* Blues And Boogie Classics, *on Vulcan.*

***(*) **Bye Bye Baby**
Delmark DE-759 *McCoy; Clarence Curry (d).* 12/58–mid-'60s.

McCoy was in his mid-50s when the bulk of these recordings were taped and, unlike some of the musicians who survived from an earlier era of recording, not in the least decrepit. His playing is energetic, full of busy, jingling right-hand figures (hear him rock on 'Church Bell Blues'), and his voice, though not big or strong, has quite enough of the character his songs require. Some of these he drew from recordings by contemporaries like Leroy Carr ('Gone Mother Blues', 'Straight Alky Blues'), but there are numerous echoes of local players he knew at first hand, such as Jabo Williams and Walter Roland; the cadences of the opening title track are very Roland-like. He was not mired in the music of his youth: he had acquired Piano Red's 'Rockin' With Red' and even (though it's one of the album's lesser performances) 'Let's Go Get Stoned'. Nevertheless, his style is essentially of the time when he was in his 20s, preserved as if in aspic, and that gives this CD enormous documentary value. Just as importantly, it has great warmth and spirit. *Bye Bye Baby* incorporates almost all of McCoy's first album (but none of his second), adding other studio and location recordings, the latter of poor technical quality, and, in the notes, a candid reminiscence by Cather. TR

Viola McCoy (c. 1900–1956)
VOCAL, KAZOO

McCoy's name began to show up in the New York theatrical press in 1922. The following year she started recording industriously for Gennett, Columbia (as Amanda Brown) and Vocalion, and thereafter worked for several other companies. She was active in musical comedy and revue until the late '30s, sometimes based in Philadelphia. Her last years were spent in Albany, New York.

(*) **Viola McCoy – Vol. 1 (1923)
Document DOD-5416 *McCoy; poss. Tom Morris (c); poss. Charlie Irvis (tb); poss. Ernest Elliott (cl); unknown (as); Porter Grainger, Bob Ricketts, unknown (p); poss. Buddy Christian or Elmer Snowden (bj); unknown (eff).* 3–9/23.

***(*) **Viola McCoy – Vol. 2 (1924–1926)**
Document DOD-5417 *McCoy; Elmer Chambers, Rex Stewart, Louis Metcalf, poss. Tom Morris, poss. Bubber Miley (c); Teddy Nixon, prob. Jake Frazier (tb); Don Redman, Bob Fuller (cl);*

unknown (h); Fletcher Henderson, Edgar Dowell, Louis Hooper, Cliff Jackson, poss. Arthur Ray, poss. Porter Grainger (p); unknown (vn); Elmer Snowden (bj); Charlie Dixon (bj, g); Billy Higgins (v). 2/24–12/26.

*** **Viola McCoy – Vol. 3 (1926–1929)/Julia Moody (1922–1925)**
Document DOD-5418 *McCoy; Louis Metcalf, Rex Stewart, prob. Horace Holmes, unknown (c); Bob Fuller, unknown (cl); Cliff Jackson, Louis Hooper, unknown (p); poss. unknown (b).* 12/26–1/29.

Like many of her contemporaries, McCoy started out in vaudeville but assimilated the blues techniques which the success of Bessie Smith and Ma Rainey made almost statutory for African-American women singers. Unlike some of them, she learned fast, and as early as 4/23 she was giving assured performances in the new style such as 'Gulf Coast Blues' and 'Chirping The Blues'. She often recorded the same song for two or three labels, and seven of the songs on *Vol. 1* are heard in two versions, but since almost all of them are with Porter Grainger, not the most inventive of accompanists, there is not much in the way of interesting variation. In fact all the sides on this CD are piano-accompanied, except for two with a spirited band led by Bob Ricketts, but McCoy's warm and communicative voice keeps boredom at bay.

Early in *Vol. 2* appear two couplings with Fletcher Henderson's Jazz Five, 'I Ain't Gonna Marry, Ain't Gonna Settle Down'/'If Your Good Man Quits You, Don't Wear No Black' and 'I Don't Want Nobody That Don't Want Me'/'It Makes No Difference Now'. The band is in superb form, going like a rocket through the second number, and McCoy matches them for verve. The act proves a hard one to follow, but there is a pair of songs with guitar accompaniment by Charlie Dixon, 'Mama's Gone, Goodbye' and 'You Don't Know My Mind', that are unusual and attractive, a fine band-accompanied 'Memphis Bound' and four sides from Vocalion that would be exceptional if they were not such gritty transfers. McCoy's singing casts its rare spell throughout. If this selection were to be carefully remastered from good originals, there would be few CDs in this idiom to compete with it.

McCoy may have eschewed some of the blues devices used by contemporaries, such as Bessie Smith's growl, but no one hearing her sliding the notes and dragging behind the beat in 'Fortune Teller Blues', one of her dozen tracks on *Vol. 3*, would be inclined to question her credentials. Similar practices in 'Black Snake Blues' were no doubt dictated by the need to create a plausible cover version of Victoria Spivey's song, but her reading of 'Back Water Blues' is splendidly independent of Bessie Smith's, and the cornettist, thought to be Horace Holmes, responds manfully. After another good coupling, 'Gay-Catin Daddy' and 'Dyin' Crap Shooter's Blues', McCoy made only one more record, a year and a half later. 'I Want A Good Man (And I Want Him Bad)' and 'If You Really Love Your Daddy' are sung with brio, but, disappointingly, they are in the Sophie Tucker manner affected by several of her peers about that time. TR

Jimmy McCracklin (born 1921)
VOCAL, PIANO, HARMONICA

McCracklin (his real name is James David Walker) was born in Helena, Arkansas, and grew up in St Louis and Indianapolis. After serving in the US Navy in World War II he settled in Oakland and began what Colin Escott describes as 'a long, mutually antagonistic relationship' with the producer Bob Geddins. After a decade of recording for various labels he had a hit in both R&B and Pop charts in 1958 with 'The Walk', which led to a brief association with Mercury and a longer one with Imperial, during which he wrote one of his most enduring songs, 'Think'. Though often absent from recording studios for long periods, he has continued to write and perform. In 1991 he received a Pioneer Award from the Rhythm and Blues Foundation.

*** **Jimmy McCracklin 1945–1948**
Classics 5062 *McCracklin; unknown (t); Malcolm Taylor (tb); Lloyd Prince Harrison (ts); David Blunston (p, sp); J. D. Nicholson, Warren Bracken (p); Robert Kelton, unknown (g); Shifty Henry, unknown(s) (b); Alvy 'Jo-Jo' Kid, Little Red (d); unknown, band (v).* 45–48.

*** **Jimmy's Blues 1945–1951**
Acrobat ACRCD 101 *As above, except add Joe Conwright (as), Charles Sutter (ts), prob. Pee Wee Kingsley, Lafayette Thomas (g), Joe Toussaint (b), San Francisco Jeffers (d).* 45–51.

(*) **"The Rockin' Man" Sings His Early Stuff!
Courtney CRCD-5000 *McCracklin; unknown (t); Malcolm Taylor, unknown (tb); Joe Conwright, Johnny Parker, Raymond Bond (as); Lloyd Prince Harrison, Charles Sutter, Wild Willie Moore, Willie Cowart (ts); unknown (bs); unknowns (s); Warren Bracken (p); Robert Kelton, prob. Pee Wee Kingsley, Lafayette Thomas (g); Shifty Henry, Joe Toussaint, Horace Hall, unknowns (b); Alvy 'Jo-Jo' Kid, San Francisco Jeffers, Ray Cotton, unknowns (d); band (v).* 46–c. 4/58.

*** **Jimmy McCracklin 1948–1951**
Classics 5110 *McCracklin; Joe Conwright (as); poss. Maxwell Davis, Charles Sutter, unknown (ts); Robert Kelton, Lafayette Thomas, prob. Pee Wee Kingsley (g); Joe Toussaint, unknowns (b); Little Red, San Francisco Jeffers, unknown (d).* 48–c. 1/51.

*** **The Modern Recordings 1948–1950** [sic]
Ace CDCHD 720 *McCracklin; Jake Porter (t); Maxwell Davis, —— Brown, poss. Charles Sutter (ts); Robert Kelton, Lafayette Thomas (g); Joe Toussaint, unknown(s) (b); Little Red, unknown(s) (d).* 49–50.

*** **Blues Blastin': The Modern Recordings Volume 2**
Ace CDCHD 993 *McCracklin; poss. Jake Porter (t); Johnny Parker (ts, v); poss. Charles Sutter, unknown (ts); unknown (bs); Alvin 'Baby Pee Wee' Parham, Lafayette Thomas (g, v); Robert Kelton (g); unknowns (b); unknowns (d); band (v).* 49–55.

McCracklin's earliest recordings, six sides for Globe accompanied only by J. D. Nicholson, would not have sounded stylistically anachronistic if they had been recorded a decade before; the combination of voice and piano on 'Miss Mattie Left Me' and 'Highway 101' instantly recalls Walter Davis. Of his subsequent sides for other small West Coast labels, where he generally plays his own piano, some are similar throwbacks, like the contemplative 'Bad Luck And Trouble' and 'Jimmy's Blues', a few have a more modern propulsiveness, and 'Bad Condition Blues' is a sly imitation of Lowell Fulson. In the middle of these duets and trios are four sides with a sextet, like the two-part 'Rock & Rye'; they are conventional jump-band settings, but McCracklin is equally comfortable there. This stretch of McCracklin's work is covered by the first Classics and the first quarter of the second, and by rather more than half of the Acrobat. A selection of the Globes and the band sides, nine tracks in all, is on the VAC *Elko Blues Volume 3* (Wolf 120.616).

As McCracklin acquired confidence and bigger bands he unfolded a versatility beyond the scope of many of his better-known contemporaries. Moody blues, reflective blues, shouting blues – he could handle them all, and indeed write them all: virtually all of the 25 numbers on the first Ace CD (14 of which are duplicated on Classics' *1948–1951*) are his, and most of those on the second. His penetrating examinations of bad luck, deception and escape show that he was one of the most literate songwriters of his time and place. It's possible to discern in these artfully varied recordings the foundations of the adept R&B repertoire of later years.

Typically painstaking productions, the Ace CDs augment the previously released sides with unissued masters and demos, all featuring one or both of two remarkable guitarists, Lafayette Thomas and Robert Kelton. The bulk of *Blues Blastin'* is from McCracklin's second stint with Modern, in 1954–55. 'The Panic's On' and 'Please Forgive Me Baby' are enhanced by startling guitar by Thomas, while 'Gonna Tell Your Mother' and 'I Got Eyes For You' bear witness to McCracklin's commercial savvy, being close imitations of J. B. Lenoir's 'Mama, Talk To Your Daughter' and Muddy Waters's 'I Just Want To Make Love To You'. The 1955 session puts McCracklin's harmonica on record for the first time. Six tracks feature sidemen Parker, Parham and Thomas as vocalists; Thomas's 'Lost Mind' and 'Don't Have To Worry' are terrific. The album is completed by outtakes from earlier sessions.

The Courtney CD (reviving a marque on which some of McCracklin's earliest 78s appeared) fits neatly into the time gap between the Aces, the bulk of its contents being early-'50s sides for Swing Time and Peacock, some thoughtful, some roistering. McCracklin specialists will be grateful to obtain 29 tracks, most of which are not available elsewhere, as long as they don't mind amateurish presentation, no notes, and very crackly sound.

*** Oakland Blues: The Irma Recordings
Wolf 120.613 *McCracklin; Raymond Boyd (as); Johnny Parker, Willie Cowart (ts); unknown (bs); Lafayette Thomas (g); Horace Hall (b); Ray Cotton (d). 56.*

This VAC has eight well-recorded sides by McCracklin with band accompaniments that allow breathing-room for his piano and Thomas's guitar. 'Fare-well' and 'I'm The One' are delivered with the patient reasonableness of Lowell Fulson, while 'Savoy Jump', which namechecks the Richmond, California, club where McCracklin then had a residency, is based on Amos Milburn's 'Chicken Shack Boogie'. The same sides are also included in *"The Rockin' Man" Sings His Early Stuff!* (see above).

*** The Walk: Jimmy McCracklin At His Best
Razor & Tie RE 2124 *McCracklin; John Turk (t, p); Thomas Gayters, unknowns (t); poss. Al Jones, George Corley, unknowns (tb); Raymond Boyd, unknown (as); Johnny Parker, Willie Cowart, David 'Bubba' Brooks, Wiley Kizart, Bob K. Smith, unknowns (ts); unknowns (bs); unknowns (s); Bob Geddins Jr (o, p); unknowns (o); unknowns (p); Lafayette Thomas, Johnny Heartsman, Al King, unknowns (g); Horace Hall, Everett Barksdale, Henry Oden, unknowns (b); Ray Cotton, Panama Francis, Victor Leonard, Fred Casey, unknowns (d); unknowns (v). 56–69.*

This collection of singles from Imperial, Mercury and other labels includes the hit versions of 'The Walk' (which reached the Pop Top Ten), 'Just Got To Know' and 'Think', but it also gathers less well-known sides that are sometimes revealing about McCracklin's writing. 'Think', for example, was transformed from a song first issued seven years earlier, 'Later On': whole chunks of the lyrics are the same, but in the redesign McCracklin drops the hackneyed second theme and throws the weight of the song on to the word 'think', thus giving himself a hook, a hit and one of his most enduringly valuable copyrights. A few sides were dubbed from excessively crackly originals.

A complete collection of his Mercury output from 1958–60 was assembled on *The Mercury Recordings* (Bear Family BCD 15558), one of the few CDs on that label to have been deleted.

*** High On The Blues
Stax (A) SCD 8506//[(E) CDSXE 072] *McCracklin; Memphis Horns (brass, reeds); Charles Hodges (o, p); unknowns (strings); Mabon Hodges (g); Leroy Hodges (b); Al Jackson Jr, Howard Grimes (d); Jessica Smith, Venetta Fields, Carolyn Crawford, Donna Rhodes, Charles Chalmers, Sandra Rhodes (v). 5–10/71.*

During the lean years of the '70s a few blues artists managed to keep some grip on the black record market. McCracklin was one of the sturdiest members of that group. *Yesterday Is Gone*, as this set was called when first issued, was an Al Jackson–Willie Mitchell production rich in funky rhythm patterns and sweet-and-sour string arrangements that put colourful backdrops behind McCracklin's wry tales and asides ('Times is as tight as a 'gator's shoes … across the instep'). The contrast is surprising but never incongruous, since McCracklin makes an entirely convincing soul-blues singer, often sounding as if he might have been, say, Otis Redding's uncle. The all-original programme includes crisp updates of 'Just Got To Know' and 'Think', and a couple of previously unissued tracks, 'I Got Somebody' and 'Girl Stealer', the latter accompanied on piano probably by McCracklin himself.

**(*) Rockin' This Joint Tonite
JSP JSPCD 2146 *McCracklin; Wily Coyote (as); Wild Willie Moore (ts); Stuart Borbridge (g); Kenneth Jenkins (b); Raymond Cotton (d). late 70s?*

McCracklin's nine songs make up a substantial slice of this VAC, the rest of which is divided between Kid Thomas, Floyd Dixon and Ace Holder. The group's playing is raucous and untidy, and Borbridge more than once wanders out of the key, but McCracklin's bursts of piano on 'Arkansas' and elsewhere, and his readings of 'Where I Got My Start', 'Copyright On Your Love' and 'You're The One', are enough reasons for his admirers to pay attention.

**(*) My Story
Bullseye Blues CDBB 9508 *McCracklin; Scott Aruda, Oscar Myles, John Turk (t); Lawrence McClellan Jr, 'Tricky Trombone' Lawson (tb); Pee Wee Ellis (as, ts); Tony Hart, Earl 'Good Rockin'' Brown (as); 'Sax' Gordon (ts, bs); Dr Wild 'Willie' Moore, Wiley Coyee (ts); Bobbie Webb (bs); Ron Levy (o, p); Wayne Bennett, John Mooney, Ron Thompson, Warn Cushberry (g); Erving Charles, Bobby Reed (b); Herman Ernest, Chris Daniel (d); Irma Thomas, E.L.S., The McCracklin Girls (v). 90.*

*** **A Taste Of The Blues**
Bullseye Blues CDBB 9535 *McCracklin; Joe Campbell (t); Bernard Baisden (tb); William Zimmerman (ts); Eddie 'Saxman' Synigal (bs); Bobby Forte (s); Ron Levy (o); Larry Davis, Lowell Fulson, Barbara Lynn, Smokey Wilson (g, v); Pee Wee Thomas, Terry 'Big T' DeRouen (g); Darby Hicks Jr [Ron Levy] (p); James B. Wyatt (b); Craig Kimbrough (d); Johnny Otis (vb); The McCracklettes (v).* 94?

My Story, McCracklin's comeback album (though he disowned the description, saying 'I never went away anywhere to come back from'), was carved out of two sessions, one in New Orleans with a biggish band including Wayne Bennett and Ron Levy, Irma Thomas joining in on two numbers, and the other in Oakland with a smaller combo in which McCracklin plays piano; he is featured on 'After Hours', which gets a characteristic arrangement from Pee Wee Ellis. The new material he brought to the sessions carries a recognizable maker's mark without throwing up another 'Think' or 'Tramp'.

The accompaniments on *A Taste Of The Blues* tend to be lighter and airier, which may partly explain why McCracklin's voice sounds a good deal stronger. They are also more varied, since the band has to accommodate itself to a series of guests. Fulson, Wilson and Forte play on several tracks, Larry Davis writes his signature on 'Outside Help' and Barbara Lynn helps McCracklin to improve on the original recording of 'Yesterday Is Gone'. Again the material is mostly original, with 'Put Up Or Shut Up' and the title track standing out.

*** **Tell It To The Judge!**
Gunsmoke SMO-3109 *McCracklin; various accompaniments.* 61–97.

This 1999 release requires some analysis. 'Think' and 'I Just Got To Know' are the original '60s recordings, four tracks are from *High On The Blues* and three each from *My Story* and *A Taste Of The Blues*. 'Same Lovin' In Return' was on a late-'80s album for Evejim. The remaining four numbers, 'Good Old Days', 'Hate Will Destroy The World', 'Bad Situation' and 'Tell It To The Judge', date from sessions in 1997. Maddening for the collector, no doubt, but for someone stumbling across McCracklin for the first time, not at all a bad introduction to his catalogue. The presentation is folksy. TR

Larry McCray (born 1960)
VOCAL, GUITAR

McCray's family left Arkansas for Detroit when he was 12. He learned to play guitar from his sister. A highly touted album, Ambition, *opened Pointblank's blues catalogue in 1990, but subsequent work has attracted less attention. As well as his own albums he has recorded with James Cotton and Larry Garner.*

*(*) **Meet Me At The Lake**
Atomic Theory ATM 1124 *McCray; Charlie Walmsley (o, p); Jim Gilmore (g); Kelly Gilmore (b, v); Rob Clendening (d); Lori Walmsley, Kim Gilmore Stegman (v).* 6/96.

(*) **Believe It//Blues Is My Business
Magnolia 2001//Dixiefrog DFGCD 8522 *McCray; Roosevelt Purifoy (kb); Noel Neal (b); Steve McCray (d).* 01.

With his Pointblank albums *Ambition* and *Delta Hurricane* and the later *Born To Play The Blues* (House Of Blues, 1998) out of print, McCray's catalogue currently stands at two. *Meet Me At The Lake* is a collaboration with Michigan band The Bluegills, whose Charlie Walmsley has played keyboards with McCray for some years. Several of the vocals are handled by the Bluegills' three women singers, whose colourless Andrews Sisters harmonies are utterly at odds with the blues-rock feeling McCray tries to generate. The Walmsleys also wrote almost all the songs, which suggests that McCray urgently needs an artistic adviser. *Believe It*, or *Blues Is My Business* on its European release, is a considerable improvement, though its piledriving blues-rock attack gets to be tiring and in some cases is inimical to the interests of the material. The title tracks and the slow, intense 'Love Gone Bad' suggest that McCray does have a good album in him – somewhere, some time. TR

Floyd McDaniel (1915–95)
VOCAL, GUITAR

McDaniel spent much of his career in vocal groups; joining a novelty washboard band from high school, he went with them to New York, where they became the Cotton Club Tramp Band. Returning to Chicago, he spent 15 years with the Four Blazes from 1941, and after a slack spell he joined a version of the Ink Spots between 1971 and the late '80s. In 1986 he appeared at the Chicago Blues Festival, standing in for the late Ollie Crawford in a revived Big Three Trio, and thereafter got back into the blues with Willie Dixon's encouragement.

(*) **Switchin' In The Kitchen
Delmark DE-768 *McDaniel; Mike McLaughlin (t); Mwata Bowden, Martin 'Van' Kelly (cl, bs); Paul Mundy (as); Dave Clark (ts); Donny Nichilo (p); Bill Yancey (b); Robert 'Hindu' Henderson (d).* 6/91–8/92.

**** **Let Your Hair Down!**
Delmark DE-671 *McDaniel; Mike McLaughlin (t); Martin 'Van' Kelly (cl, bs); Paul Mundy (as); Dave Clark (ts); Donny Nichilo (p); Bill Yancey (b); Robert 'Hindu' Henderson, Kansas Fields (d).* 2–3/94.

***(*) **West Side Baby**
Crosscut CCD 11057//Delmark DE-706 *McDaniel; Tad Robinson (h); Dave Specter (g); Mike McCurdy (b); Mark Fornek (d).* 5/94.

T-Bone Walker was Floyd McDaniel's idol, and 'West Side Baby', his most famous composition, is a spot-on homage; it turns up on all three of these CDs. *Let Your Hair Down!* relies on swing-era classics like 'I Want A Little Girl', 'R. M. Blues' and 'Sent For You Yesterday'. This is ideal material for Dave Clark's Blues Swingsters, who pounce with glee on well-crafted charts by Clark and John Meggs. The Swingsters are always listening and reacting to each other, the solos are full of fire and ingenuity, and Henderson and Fields are admirable both technically and musically. McDaniel shines like a diamond in this setting, spicing his fluent chordal and single-string lines with unorthodox but meticulously selected harmonies, and singing with the vigour of one far younger than his 78 years.

West Side Baby, recorded in Germany, features a lineup that's more attuned to contemporary notions of a blues band. Dave Specter & The Bluebirds do a more than respectable job, and Specter and McDaniel bounce ideas off each other to good effect, notably on 'Red Top', where they convincingly prove McDaniel's assertion that 'this might sound to you like jazz … but the blues was here before jazz.' Nevertheless, this is a marginally less exciting disc, thanks to the inclusion of hack material like 'Everyday I Have The Blues' and 'Sweet Home

Chicago', which are plainly pandering to overseas knowledge – or perhaps ignorance.

Switchin' In The Kitchen, recorded first but issued last, is by 'Dave Clark's Blues Swingers featuring Floyd McDaniel'; he appears on nine tracks cut as audition demos. (The remaining six were recorded in 1999.) McDaniel's share of this CD is altogether less interesting: the arrangements are more generic and less adventurously played, and McDaniel the singer fails to impose himself on a set of too-familiar songs. He's better, though, than the characterless Jasen Schrock, whose vocals on three of the 1999 titles further reduce the CD's appeal.

Let Your Hair Down! and *Switchin' In The Kitchen* both revive 'Mary Jo' (a #1 R&B hit in 1952) from McDaniel's stint with the Four Blazes. Tommy Braden, rather than McDaniel, was the lead vocalist on this and most other Blazes songs, but many readers will enjoy the mix of blues, jazz, ballads and jive on *Mary Jo* (Delmark DE-704). CS

Fred McDowell (1904–72)
VOCAL, GUITAR

McDowell spent most of his life in west Tennessee, where he was born, or in north Mississippi, where he regularly went to find work in the cotton-picking season. Learning to play guitar from older musicians like Raymond Payne and Eli Green, he entertained in juke-joints and at house parties; he also played in church, accompanying small singing groups. He became internationally famous in the '60s, appearing at many festivals, touring overseas, recording a stack of albums for several labels and leaving his mark on the music of many younger players.

♛ ****** The First Recordings**
Rounder CD 1718 McDowell; Miles Pratcher (g); Fanny Davis (comb); Sidney Carter, Rose Hemphill, Annie Mae McDowell, James Shorty (v). 9/59.

**** Mississippi Fred McDowell
Rounder CD 2138 McDowell. 4/62.

***(*) My Home Is In The Delta
Testament TCD 5019 McDowell; Annie Mae McDowell (v). 11/63, 2/64.

**** You Gotta Move
Arhoolie CD 304 McDowell; Eli Green (g, v); Annie Mae McDowell (v). 2/64, 3/65, 7/65.

*** Good Morning Little School Girl
Arhoolie CD 424 McDowell; Annie Mae McDowell, Hunter's Chapel Singers (v). 2/64, 5/65, 7/65.

The first anyone outside Como, Mississippi, heard of Fred McDowell was a handful of songs scattered across volumes of *Southern Folk Heritage* and *Southern Journey*, album series of the early '60s devoted to field-recorded Americana collected in a long sweep through the South by Alan Lomax. Amidst the prison worksongs, straining preachers and banjo-picking balladmongers, McDowell's gentle but firm blues singing and slide guitar playing evinced not only the dignity of tradition but a spark of contemporaneity, an awareness of the blues outside. He seemed to combine the authenticity of a Son House or Booker White with a skill unimpaired by age and an ear for music younger than himself. What a find! He was duly found again, and five years later the Arhoolie LP *Mississippi Delta Blues* catapulted this unassuming and likeable man into the world of folk festivals and international tours. But the Lomax recordings, made on stormy summer evenings in the pinewoods of north Mississippi, with friends and neighbours stopping by to play or sing a little, are like music from Eden.

The First Recordings gathers and adds to those anthologized tracks. The other Rounder CD is a session recorded by the collector Dick Spottswood at McDowell's home in 1962 but not issued until many years later. *My Home Is In The Delta* (recorded by Pete Welding) and *Good Morning Little School Girl* are evenly divided between blues and church songs, some of the latter sung by or with his wife Annie Mae. *You Gotta Move* absorbs Arhoolie's *Mississippi Delta Blues* LP and its parade of songs that are inseparably linked with his name, such as 'Write Me A Few Lines', 'Louise', 'I Heard Somebody Call', 'Kokomo Blues' and 'Shake 'Em On Down', together with more from the same session and a couple of pieces sung by his teacher Eli Green (1897–1968). All these albums are absolutely recommendable, with the small reservation that there is some duplication of material among them, since it took a little while for McDowell to expand, or recall, his repertoire, and in any case he was unaware of how – or whether – these tapes would be released. But there are differences in the performances beyond their different settings.

**** Amazing Grace
Testament TCD 5004 McDowell; Hunter's Chapel Singers (Annie Mae McDowell, Fannie Davis, Grace Bowden, James Collins) (v). 2/66.

On Sundays McDowell often sang and played at Hunter's Chapel in Como, in the company of his wife and three friends. This album, though a studio re-creation rather than a location recording, faithfully documents the undulating polyphony of African-American rural church singing in well-loved themes like 'Jesus Is On The Main Line' and 'This Little Light Of Mine'. Other songs are presented as duets or solos; among the latter, Fannie Davis's 'I Know I've Been Converted' is overwhelming in its quiet certainty. McDowell's steadily pulsating guitar is like another vocal line, echoing the singers' slides and melismas.

*** Long Way From Home
Original Blues Classics OBCCD 535 McDowell. 11/66.

Long Way From Home balances favourite items in McDowell's repertoire like 'The Train I Ride' with pieces dredged from the obscurer reaches of his memory like 'Millionaire's Daughter Blues' and 'You Drove Me From Your Door', or 'Big Fat Mama', which, he asserts elsewhere, was the first tune he learned on guitar. He plays less slide on this album than on any other, but there is nothing denatured or uncharacteristic about his performances.

**** Mama Says I'm Crazy
Fat Possum 80364 McDowell; Johnny Woods (h, v). 8/67.

When this informal session was taped (by the photographer/folklorist George Mitchell), McDowell was an international name and Woods an unknown homeboy from Senatobia, Mississippi. It was McDowell's idea that they combined record together, and his instinct was right. The combined energy of his slide and Woods's harmonica, as they leap into the title track (actually 'Diving Duck Blues') or 'Shake 'Em On Down', could have supplied Senatobia's power needs for a year. Woods sings 'Long Haired Doney' and a few others in a strong countryman's voice. The rest of the vocals are McDowell's – all songs he often played, but seldom with such absorption or recorded with such presence.

*** Levee Camp Blues
Testament TCD 6007 *McDowell*. 2/66, 3/68.

The purpose of the 3/68 recording (the two 1966 tracks are from the *Amazing Grace* session) was to document McDowell's earliest acquired songs. A few tracks bear the traces of specific records: 'Pea Vine Special' came from Charley Patton, 'Won't Be Worried Long' has a strong flavour of Furry Lewis and the blues-ballad 'Jim Steam Killed Lula' may have been learned indirectly from the Memphis Jug Band's version, 'Jim Strainer Blues.' These apart, the programme consists of songs that attracted McDowell in the repertoires of the musicians he learned from, such as Raymond Payne, or ones that he put together himself, some firmly based on common motifs, others, like 'Dankin's Farm', more original. But anyone looking to this record for a revelation of a lost early *style* will be disappointed. McDowell either began very much as he went on or refashioned the pieces he learned as a young man and forgot earlier versions. Although several songs have intriguing titles, they usually prove to be familiar McDowell melodies. 'My Baby Don't Treat Me Like Humankind', for example, has more or less the tune of 'Drop Down Mama'.

*** This Ain't No Rock And Roll
Arhoolie CD 441 *McDowell*; prob. Steve Talbot (h); Mike Russo (g); John Kahn (b); Bob Jones, John Francis (d). 3/68, 8/69.

While filling an engagement in LA in 3/68, McDowell informally recorded some songs for Arhoolie's Chris Strachwitz. The ten issued (for the first time) on this CD include several that are also on *Levee Camp Blues*, but here McDowell is plugged in; in fact these are his first known recordings with an electric guitar. A year and a half later, he presented this new face publicly on a studio-recorded album backed by Russo, Kahn and Jones. Here the amplified sound of the guitar was much fuller, and when he played with a slide, as on 'My Baby', very much spikier. The bass and drums do no more than mark time, but now and then Russo gets a little busy, which in 'Diamond Ring' elicits a good-tempered 'Take it easy!'

**(*) When I Lay My Burden Down
Biograph BCD 130 *McDowell*. 2/69.

McDowell has six blues and three gospel songs on this album shared with Furry Lewis and Robert Wilkins. After decoding a couple of misleading titles ('If You See My Baby' is 'Shake 'Em On Down'; 'See What My Lord Has Done' is 'Keep Your Lamps Trimmed And Burning') the collector will find that none of the nine pieces is an addition to McDowell's known repertoire. The versions are mostly quite short and not particularly well recorded.

*** Steakbone Slide Guitar
Tradition TCD 1012 *McDowell*. 3/69.
**(*) Train I Ride
Aim 0012 *McDowell*. 3/69.
*** Shake 'Em On Down
[Blue Boar CDBB 1003] *McDowell; Jo Ann Kelly (v)*. 3/69.

While in England in the spring of 1969, McDowell cut two studio albums for Transatlantic. The first seems never to have been transferred to CD, but the second has been issued several times, most recently on Tradition. The ten tracks are all staples of McDowell's repertoire ('The Train I Ride', 'You Got To Move', etc.), except the intriguing 'Unknown Blues', learned from Raymond Payne, with a guitar part that might have been conceived by Robert Wilkins. McDowell plays electric guitar throughout, but not at the piercing level of his session for Arhoolie a few months later (see *This Ain't No Rock And Roll* above). *Train I Ride* is four fifths of the same album, omitting 'You Ain't Gonna Worry My Life Anymore (aka Fred's Worried Life Blues)' and 'What's The Matter With Papa's Little Angel Child?', and in inferior sound quality.

Two days later McDowell gave a concert at the Mayfair Theatre in London, an engagement captured on *Shake 'Em On Down*. Again, and in the circumstances understandably, he devoted himself to songs his audience might know from his records, such as 'Kokomo', '61 Highway' and 'Write Me A Few Of Your Lines', but 'I Asked For Whiskey, She Brought Me Gasoline', a patchwork of pieces from 'Big Road Blues' and his own 'Black Minnie', was less familiar. Once again playing electric guitar, McDowell gives a totally amiable performance. Jo Ann Kelly is listed as singing on 'Glory Hallelujah' but actually does so on 'When I Lay My Burden Down', another version of the same song.

*** Mississippi Delta Blues Jam In Memphis, Vol. 1
Arhoolie CD 385 *McDowell; Johnny Woods* (h). 6/69.

Chris Strachwitz, who seems to have made a point of getting together with Fred McDowell and recording equipment every year or two, taped these five sides in Memphis during the 1969 blues festival. Two are solos, one the introspective 'A Dark Cloud Rising', and three duets with Woods, including a thrillingly tight arrangement of 'Shake 'Em On Down'. For the rest of this VAC see COMPILATIONS: MISSISSIPPI.

*** "I Do Not Play No Rock 'N' Roll"
Fuel 2000 302 061 158 *McDowell; Jerry Puckett (b); Dulin Lancaster (d)*. 9/69.

The original *I Do Not Play No Rock 'N' Roll*, a Malaco production for Capitol, was McDowell's best-distributed and best-selling LP. So far as his electric guitar is concerned, it was also his best-recorded album, his playing sounding exceptionally rich and forceful. The songs were a typical haul ('Kokomo', 'Little School Girl', '61 Highway', etc.), but 'Everybody's Down On Me' is differentiated by a long prefatory monologue. This issue augments the original album's nine tracks with five more from the session. An earlier reissue with the same title (Capitol 33919) ran to 20 tracks on two CDs but is currently unavailable.

*** Shake 'Em On Down//You Got To Move
Labor LAB 7004//Charly CPCD 8165//Blues Factory BFY 47020// Corazong 255 019// *McDowell; Tom Pomposello (b)*. 11/71.

McDowell's last issued recordings are a set taped at the Gaslight in New York City with his then regular accompanist Tom Pomposello on bass. This is McDowell as many people will remember him, spinning his long, leisurely stories to an appreciative audience. Some are favourites like 'Shake 'Em On Down' and 'You Got To Move', while others are less familiar assortments of verses and guitar patterns, like 'Mercy' or 'The Lovin' Blues'. The rarest piece is 'White Lightnin'', rooted in a riff resembling that of Howlin' Wolf's 'Smokestack Lightning'. The track timings on the Charly issue are significantly longer, and correctly so; the Labor CD's producers didn't time the talking, tuning and so forth between numbers. This will be an inconvenience only for DJs; a more serious problem is the sound, which is distorted by an electrical fault, but not intolerably so. The Blues Factory and Corazong CDs are titled *You Got To Move*.

***(*) Heroes Of The Blues: The Very Best Of Mississippi Fred McDowell
Shout! Factory DK 30256 McDowell; Johnny Woods (h); Mike Russo (g); John Kahn, Jerry Puckett (b); Bob Jones, Darin Lancaster (d); Annie Mae McDowell, James Collier (v). 9/59–9/69.

*** Heritage Of The Blues
Hightone HCD 8151 McDowell; Hunter's Chapel Singers (Annie Mae McDowell, Fannie Davis, Grace Bowden, James Collier) (v). 11/63–3/68.

*** The Best Of Mississippi Fred McDowell
Arhoolie CD 501 As for Heroes Of The Blues, *except add unknowns (v); omit Puckett, Lancaster, Collier*. 2/64–6/69.

The Hightone and Arhoolie CDs are samplers from McDowell's Testament and Arhoolie catalogues respectively. *Heritage Of The Blues* takes four tracks each from *My Home Is In The Delta*, *Amazing Grace* and *Levee Camp Blues*. The Arhoolie plucks four to six tracks from each of *You Gotta Move*, *Good Morning Little School Girl* and *This Ain't No Rock And Roll*, adding a duet with Johnny Woods, 'Keep Your Lamp Trimmed And Burning', from the Arhoolie VAC *Mississippi Delta Blues Jam in Memphis, Vol. 1* and a previously unissued 6/65 concert recording of 'Shake 'Em On Down'/'Louise'. Either would make a good introduction to McDowell's work, but with 18 tracks the Arhoolie offers better value. Better still is the Shout! Factory: its 16 well-chosen tracks span almost all of McDowell's recording life, from the *al fresco* Lomax tapes to the power-trio music of "I Do Not Play No Rock 'N' Roll", omitting none of his favourite songs. TR

Charlie McFadden (1894–1969)
VOCAL

McFadden was a St Louis singer remembered by Roosevelt Sykes and by Big Joe Williams, who thought him the city's best, and by Henry Townsend, who added that he could also play piano a little, though he seems not to have done so on his records. Because of his poor sight he was nicknamed 'Specks'.

*** Charlie "Specks" McFadden (1929–1937)
Document BDCD-6041 McFadden; Roosevelt Sykes, Eddie Miller, Pine Top (Aaron Sparks), unknown (p); poss. Lonnie Johnson (vn); unknown (b). 6/29–4/37.

McFadden's singing, plaintive in tone but determined in attitude, is particularly aptly accompanied by Eddie Miller, and it is a pity that their collaboration was confined to four sides. The singer's heartfelt delivery of 'Gambler's Blues' suggests that the theme appealed to him, and Mike Rowe reports in his notes, drawing on police files, that McFadden was frequently arrested for gambling offences. 'Harvest Moon', with a very St Louisian chorded bass, bluesifies the pop song 'Shine On Harvest Moon'. At his next session, accompanied by Roosevelt Sykes, he introduced 'People People Blues' and 'Groceries On The Shelf', which must have become his trademark songs, for he recorded both repeatedly. The latter's opening line, 'My name is Piggly Wiggly, I've got groceries on my shelf', alludes to the Piggly Wiggly chain of grocery stores, which pioneered self-service shopping. Sykes continued to accompany him on his recordings, except when ceding the piano stool to 'Pine Top' Sparks, whose sensitive playing lends a different shade of blue to McFadden's singing of 'Friendless Blues' and 'Times Are So Tight'. After a three-year break McFadden returned to the recording studios for the last time in 1937, accompanied by a pianist who sounds not at all like Sykes; though the two songs issued were his personal standards again, he managed, as always, to present them a little differently. TR

Barrelhouse Buck McFarland
(1903–62)
VOCAL, PIANO

Thomas McFarland was a pianist and singer from Alton, Illinois, who spent his working life in the clubs of St Louis.

**(*) Piano Blues – Vol. 2 (1927–1956)
Document DOCD-5220 McFarland; unknown (cl); unknown (vn); Peetie Wheatstraw (g). 11/29–7/35.

**(*) Barrelhouse Piano (1929–1935)
Wolf WSE-116 As above. 11/29–7/35.

The almost martial piano rhythm of 'St. Louis Fire Blues', McFarland's first recording, relaxes into the small-group swing of 1934's 'I Got To Go Blues' and 'Mercy Mercy Blues', made with a raucous band billed as Peetie Wheatstraw's Blue Blowers. Yet the St Louis character of Buck's piano playing is evident throughout, particularly in the chorded bass. His hoarse singing in 'Weeping Willow Blues' is rather in the manner of Wheatstraw, who may accompany him on guitar. Both CDs contain his seven recordings from the period; the Document is a VAC, while the Wolf is otherwise given over to Speckled Red. McFarland's 1961 recordings originally issued on Folkways have not been transferred to CD. TR

Rico McFarland (born 1960)
VOCAL, GUITAR

McFarland began playing bass, guitar and drums before he was in his teens, often accompanying his father at clubs and house parties. In his teens he worked with Artie 'Blues Boy' White and Little Milton, later with Albert King, Syl Johnson, Sugar Blue, Valerie Wellington, Lucky Peterson and James Cotton, to name just some blues jobs in a long and varied CV. In the studio he has collaborated with Carl Weathersby, and arranged and played on some of Big Time Sarah's albums for Delmark.

***(*) Tired Of Being Alone
Evidence ECD 26113 McFarland; Kenny Anderson (t); Bill McFarland (tb); Hank Ford (ts); Billy Branch (h, v); Dan Bellini, Sugar Blue (h); Roosevelt Purifoy (o, p); Sumito Ariyoshi (p); Chico Banks, Melvin Taylor, Carl Weathersby (g); Charlie Hosch, Dave Smith (b); Brady Williams, Steve Potts (d); Otis Clay, Syl Johnson, Teela (v). 11/00.

Many blues albums are composed from a restricted palette. McFarland's remarkable debut is a riotous action painting, aswirl with the colours of blues, funk and soul. The superbly articulated guitar parts of two adjoining and quite different tracks, 'Johnny B' and 'Giving Me The Blues', serve notice that McFarland is a formidable player, and he drives the point home in the straightforward blues 'Made Up My Mind' and the downhome soul of Al Green's 'It Ain't No Fun To Me'. The latter is sung by Syl Johnson, sounding extraordinarily like Lowell Fulson, and there are other guest vocalists, but they were not called in to mask a deficiency in the front man, who is as competent with the summertime soul of 'Rockin' Chair' as with the brassy funk of 'Bad Attitude' or the early-morning blues of the title track. TR

Tom McFarland (1945–2004)
VOCAL, GUITAR

McFarland was born in LA but grew up in rural Oregon, where he learned guitar, influenced by T-Bone Walker, Pee Wee Crayton and B. B. King. From 1966 to 1973 he played in clubs in Portland, Oregon, then moved to Seattle and later the San Francisco Bay Area. He returned to the Pacific Northwest in 1981 and continued to play in clubs there until the mid-'90s.

**(*) Travelin' With The Blues
Arhoolie CD 9055 *McFarland; Steve Ehrmann (b); Bobby Broadhead (d).* 78.

McFarland's best-known song was 'Going Back To Oakland', which was also recorded by Seattle bluesman Isaac Scott (on a long-gone Red Lightnin' LP). A relaxed slow blues, it's typical of this quietly likeable album. McFarland was an unpretentious singer and guitarist, evidently content to express himself in the musical language of his models and uninterested in the brasher rock-influenced blues played by some of his contemporaries. The recording is very simple, documentary rather than dramatic, and the album may be a little too sedate for some tastes, but listeners prepared to accept it on its own terms will be admitted to a performance of honest, seasoned craftsmanship. TR

Cookie McGee
VOCAL, GUITAR

A Dallas resident almost all her life, Carmen McGee began playing as a child, encouraged by her neighbour Freddie King. She has been in bands since her teens, playing with Freddie King Jr, Deacon Jones, Tutu Jones and others.

** Right Place
JSP JSPCD 2113 *McGee; Ron Mason (kb); Benny Booker (g); Tommy Tucker (b); Tommy Hill (d, v).* 4–8/98.

Like chicken-fried steak, Cookie McGee may be impossible to appreciate fully outside Texas. On disc, the musician described by local writers as a 'wonder' and a 'monster talent' is elusive. It's hard to determine how much character her voice has, since it's covered in layers of irrepressibly prolix organ playing and over-loud drums, but her guitar manages to force itself through the sonic mulch and even bloom in 'Everlastin' Tears', 'Bottom's Falling Out' and the instrumental 'Groovin' In Garland'. For McGee it may be a useful calling-card, with possible appeal to clubgoers as a souvenir, but as an album to listen to purely on its own terms it is unsubtle and ultimately tiring. TR

Brownie McGhee (1915–96)
VOCAL, GUITAR, PIANO, JAZZHORN

An attack of polio in childhood left Walter Brown McGhee with one leg shorter than the other, and kept him on crutches until an operation in 1937 enabled him to walk with the aid of a built-up shoe. Understandably, he soon left Knoxville, Tennessee, to wander in the southeastern states, fetching up in Durham, North Carolina. The chance to record came when talent scout J. B. Long saw McGhee as a potential replacement for Blind Boy Fuller. In 1942 he formed a partnership with Sonny Terry, and they moved to New York in pursuit of joint and separate work opportunities. Terry and McGhee took their easygoing, accessible 'folk blues' around the world in a double act that endured for 40 years, although towards the end of that time endurance was the mot juste, *as two bored, mutually hostile musicians feuded onstage and never spoke off it. McGhee made a few recordings after they split up, but spent his last decade in virtual retirement.*

Brownie McGhee and Sonny Terry made many recordings as a team. This entry deals with CDs credited to Brownie McGhee alone. Those credited to 'Brownie McGhee & Sonny Terry' or vice versa have an entry of their own (see Terry), as do CDs credited to Sonny Terry alone.

*** The Complete Brownie McGhee
Columbia/Legacy C2K 52933 2CD *McGhee; Jordan Webb (h, v); Sonny Terry (h); Buddy Moss (g,); Oh Red [Bull City Red], Washboard Slim (wb).* 8/40–10/41.
*** A Black Woman's Man
[Indigo IGOCD 2509] *As above, except Webb does not sing.* 8/40–10/41.
**(*) Not Guilty Blues
Collectors Edition CBCD 004 *As above.* 8/40–10/41.
** Carolina Blues
Wolf WSE 114 CD *As above, except omit Terry.* 8/40–5/41.

Many of McGhee's OKeh records had 'Blind Boy Fuller No. 2' bracketed after his name, and on many of them he was using Fuller's National guitar, but from the first he comes across as an artist with his own ideas. His assured fingerpicking makes some borrowings from Fuller, but his melodic three-finger style had been formed well before they met. There are tradition-based songs among these early recordings, and others adapted from hits of the day, but McGhee was already a writer of original, quite complex lyrics: the autobiographical 'Be Good To Me', about the hardships of life as a lame child, is unlike anything that his contemporaries were writing.

Columbia's 47 tracks include 18 unissued or alternative takes and one of 'studio chatter', and are a splendid resource for the serious collector and researcher. There are some suspect chords on 'Unfair Blues', but it was seldom poor performance that led to material being held back; the downside of this reliability is that the alternative takes are not significantly different, and the chronological programming makes for occasional *longueurs*. It should be added that noise reduction has been applied with a heavy hand; the early sides, played on a wooden guitar, are disappointingly lifeless.

Indigo and Collectors Edition both source from Columbia/Legacy. *Not Guilty Blues*' track details are inaccurate ('Step It Up And Go' is listed, but 'Step It Up And Go No. 2' plays), and there is a pervasive tape hiss. With better annotation and longer playing time than Collectors Edition, and sound that is more vibrant than the source CDs', *A Black Woman's Man* is the best bet for non-completists. Wolf, adding six random McGhee titles to a Carl Martin LP, and mistitling one of them, aren't in the frame.

*** The Same Ol' Diddley Dee (From Blues To R&B)
[Zircon Bleu 518] *McGhee; Hal Singer (ts); Sonny Terry (h); Daddy Merritt, Champion Jack Dupree, Lannie Scott, Big Chief Ellis, George Rhodes (p); prob. Ralph Willis (g); Pops Foster, Count Edmondson, Curley Russell, Franklin Skeete, Gene Ramey, unknown (b); Sticks Evans, Baby Dodds, Arthur Herbert, Heywood Jackson, unknown (d). 12/44–12/48.*

*** New York Blues 1946/1948
EPM Blues Collection 15952 *As above, except Terry also sings; omit Ellis, Willis, unknowns. 46–12/48.*

**(*) Mean Ole Frisco
Arpeggio ARB 008 *As above. 46–12/48.*

McGhee recorded for the white 'folk' audience as soon as he settled in New York, but he was also very active in the African-American market; 'My Fault', with Hal Singer's suave tenor, was a hit that almost made him a star. These CDs draw mainly on the Alert and Savoy labels; many fine recordings for both firms are not yet on CD, which makes it doubly unfortunate that there are six duplicated titles, but between them Zircon Bleu and EPM offer a good portrait of McGhee's R&B years. He was still cutting numbers from the Carolina tradition and reviving the hits of others, but his songwriting was increasingly original and his singing and playing more confident and expressive; his fleet, swinging amplified guitar is a particular treat. Sound quality is acceptable, but allowance must be made for Alert's sometimes crackly pressings.

Mean Ole Frisco is dubbed from *New York Blues*, right down to a tape flutter on Stick McGhee's first version of 'Drinkin' Wine Spo-Dee-O-Dee' (which does not feature brother Brownie). Arpeggio substitute superficial notes and incomplete discographical details for EPM's careful presentation.

**** Circle Blues Session
Southland SCD-9 *McGhee; Stick(s) McGhee (g, v). 6/46.*

At the end of a Dan Burley session, Brownie and his brother knock off six lively titles: two revivals ('Kansas City' and 'Rocks In My Bed'), two fervent gospel songs that were issued on a 78 credited to 'The Tennessee Gabriel'(!), and two from downhome: 'Railroad Bill' (Stick's vocal debut, with some unusual lyrics) and a jumping 'Tennessee Shuffle' that gives their acoustic guitar skills a thorough workout. Pure pleasure.

***(*) The Folkways Years, 1945–1959
Smithsonian Folkways CD SF 40034 *McGhee; Sonny Terry (h, v); poss. Big Chief Ellis (p); Gene Moore (d); Coyal McMahan (maracas, v). prob. late 40s–7/59.*

Moses Asch recorded Brownie McGhee extensively in the '50s in a variety of settings. *The Folkways Years* is a very well chosen selection, featuring Brownie alone (occasionally playing electric guitar, not the anti-commercial Asch's favourite instrument), broadcasting with a virtually inaudible pianist, and of course with Sonny Terry. Among the most enjoyable tracks are those featuring the maracas and resonant *basso* of Coyal McMahan. McGhee plays some formidable guitar, and 'Living With The Blues' demonstrates the easygoing interplay that made Sonny and Brownie the world's favourite blues singers for a while. Once or twice, McGhee hams it up a bit; he continued to do this for white audiences at times, but never as annoyingly as Josh White.

**** Brownie's Blues
Original Blues Classics OBCCD-505 *McGhee; Sonny Terry (h); Bennie Foster (g). 10/60.*

The notes hint that Bennie Foster is a pseudonym for Stick McGhee, who was signed to Herald at the time of recording; the imaginative second-guitar lines are certainly as well-integrated as Terry's harmonica. Most songs are originals, some of them quite lengthy (nine tracks fill 40 minutes of playing time), and *Brownie's Blues* is a superior showcase for his talents as both musician and songwriter. The only letdown is some baroque vocal ornamentation on 'Trouble In Mind'.

**** The Best Of Brownie McGhee
Storyville STCD 8014 *McGhee; Sonny Terry (h); Svend Erik Nørregaard (d). 11/71.*

Recorded in Denmark, *The Best Of Brownie McGhee*, which is mostly solo, pretty well deserves its name. There are virtually no new songs to be heard, but it's certainly the best showcase for McGhee's considerable acoustic guitar skills, and his warm, sensitive singing focuses on the songs rather than the audience; hence it's free of the unctuousness sometimes found elsewhere.

**(*) Going It Alone
Corazong 255 020 *McGhee; Sugar Blue (h); Louisiana Red (g, prob. b); Tom Pomposello (b); Candy McDonald (d). 1/76.*

**(*) But Not Together
Tomato TOM-2106 *As above. 1/76.*

**(*) Blues Is Truth
Corazong 255 017 *McGhee; Louisiana Red (h, g); Sugar Blue (h); Sam Price (p); Bobby Foster (g); Alex Blake (b); Brian Brake (d); Jim Robinson (v). 5/76.*

In 1976 Terry and McGhee were still touring together, and signed to the same label, but there was no question of their recording together; the Blue Labor recordings on *Going It Alone* and *But Not Together* (both scrupulously credited to Sonny Terry/Brownie McGhee) are divided between them. Brownie is in good voice, most of his six songs are at least newish, and he plays a pretty solo during 'Keep On Loving', but neither Red nor Sugar Blue is famous for tactful underplaying, and Pomposello's bass is narcotic. McGhee plays piano on two tracks, but is obviously out of practice.

Blues Is Truth has some repertoire in common with the previous CDs, but it boasts a much better rhythm section; Blake, who has a distinguished jazz CV, is notably creative on the slower numbers. Red and Blue continue to be broadly incompatible with McGhee's style, however, and the former's bottleneck melodramatics reach a tiresome peak on 'Mean And Evil'. The larger band often sounds congested (seven tracks feature three guitarists), and Brownie's voice is sometimes under pressure.

*** Facts Of Life
Blue Rock'It BRCD 104 *McGhee; Mark Hummel, Mark Ford (h); Clay Cotton (p); Robben Ford (g); Steve Ehrman[m] (b); Patrick Ford (d). 2–3/85.*

'Blues Had A Baby', which gained some fame from Muddy Waters's version, turns up for the third time in as many CDs;

the lyric is still sketchy and sycophantic, but the chugging arrangement makes this the preferable version. 'Lo Mo Cra De' proves that Brownie could still write clever songs. 'Sap Sucker', with just guitar and harmonica, is a surprising venture into sexual violence, but elsewhere Robben Ford takes the lion's share of the guitar work, and Brownie is in effect the vocalist (showing his age, but not distractingly) with a proficient Chicago-style band that includes a noteworthy pianist.

*** Omega: The Final Recordings
[Westside WESA 871] *McGhee; London Phillips (h, g, v); Mark Fenichel (h); Elmer Lee Thomas (g, v); Ken Webb (b). 5/95.*

In the mid-'90s McGhee came out of retirement to support the younger West Coast musician Elmer Lee Thomas (born 1946), whose band accompanies here. There are no surprises: the newest song is 'Rainy, Rainy Day', first recorded in 1961, and the rest look back to Brownie's R&B days, and to his friendships with Leadbelly and Big Bill Broonzy. The band give solid if unspectacular support; only Phillips's disjointed harmonica on 'Pick A Bale Of Cotton' disappoints. *Omega* is a judicious remix of the deleted *Brownie's Blues* (Goldstar 001); this disc was to have been sold on a joint Antipodean tour, but by October McGhee's terminal cancer had been diagnosed, and the tour was cancelled. Given that he was already unwell, Brownie displays signal vigour and enthusiasm; *Omega* is a sterling example of music as medicine, but it's also enjoyable on its own merits. CS

Stick(s) McGhee (1917–61)
VOCAL, GUITAR

Granville McGhee was Brownie McGhee's younger brother. He acquired his nickname in childhood, from the stick with which he pushed a cart carrying Brownie, at that time disabled by polio, around Kingsport, Tennessee. In 1949, J. Mayo Williams, owner of the small Harlem label, offloaded his unsold stock of Stick's 1947 recording 'Drinkin' Wine Spo-Dee-O-Dee' to a distributor in New Orleans, where it became a local hit. Atlantic Records saw a gap in the market, and a remade version reached #3 in the charts. For the rest of his recording career, McGhee tried to repeat the success of 'Drinkin' Wine' while putting its lyrics into practice.

**(*) Sticks McGhee 1947–1951
Classics 5012 *McGhee; poss. Joe Morris (t); Al King (ts, prob. v); poss. Johnny Griffin, poss. Wally Williams, unknown (ts); poss. Bill McLemore (bs); Sonny Terry (h); Big Chief Ellis, poss. Elmore Sylvester, Harry Van Walls (p); Brownie McGhee (g, v); Bob Harris (b, v); Gene Ramey, poss. Bobby Burton, Thomas Barney, unknown (b); poss. Sinclair Abbott, Ernest Heyward, prob. Gene Brooks, unknown (d); band (v). 47–1/51.*

Stick McGhee's first recordings, made in duet with his brother, are discussed in Brownie's entry. After 'Drinkin' Wine Spo-Dee-O-Dee', Stick had one more big hit, with 'Tennessee Waltz Blues', a sax-led instrumental version of the Patti Paige smash; both hits are on this CD.

Stick was no virtuoso on guitar, but his springy chords and clear diction were important to the success of 'Drinkin' Wine Spo-Dee-O-Dee'. Its light-hearted rhythmic bounce and clever lyrics remain irresistible, but heard at length McGhee is too often let down by his material. A penchant for sentimental ballads was not matched by a talent for singing them, and too many numbers simply put new words to the tune of 'Drinkin' Wine Spo-Dee-O-Dee'. The various sessions all have their positive points – brother Brownie's lead guitar work, the solid brass and reed riffs, thought to be provided by members of the Joe Morris Orchestra, the piano playing of Big Chief Ellis and Harry Van Walls, Sonny Terry's harmonica – but none of Stick's other songs has the paradoxically enduring status of his novelty hit.

The deleted *Sticks McGhee Vol. 1 (1947–1951)* (RST 91627) was two tracks longer than the Classics CD; with ten tracks by McGhee and 13 by other artists, *Vol. 2 (1951–1960)* (RST 91628) completed the reissuing of his recordings, other than those made for King. Their unavailability is regrettable, but hardly tragic.

*** Stick McGhee & His Spo-Dee-O-Dee Buddies: New York Blues
[Ace CDCHD 502] *McGhee; Ed Vanderveer (t); Charles Rawlins or Maxwell Lucas (as); Charles Rawlins, Maxwell Lucas, James Buchanan, Jimmy Wright (ts); Douglas Blackman, Sir Charles Thompson, Duke Parham (p); Mickey Baker (g); Clifford Bryan, Carl Pruitt, Prince Babb (b); George Ward, Specs Powell, Gene Brooks (d). 1/53–2/55.*

Excellently remastered, McGhee's dozen songs for King feature an assortment of fine session musicians and distinctly variable material. 'The Wiggle Waggle Woo' is as puerile as might be expected, while two blues-ballads are as dispiriting as Stick's other attempts at the form. Inevitably, there are half a dozen odes to joy juice and, equally inevitably, two of them are 'Spo-Dee-O-Dee' clones, but 'Double Crossin' Liquor' is an unprecedented (for this artist) catalogue of the demon drink's adverse effects. 'Dealing From The Bottom' is another strong and serious lyric, but most of the songs are accorded better musicianship than their words deserve. Concentration on sound, rather than sense, is the key to enjoyment here.

Four of the remaining eight tracks are by Ralph Willis (q.v.), accompanied by Sonny Terry, Brownie McGhee and Gary Mapp, a bassist so bouncy he could be on a trampoline. The balance are credited to Big Tom Collins, a contract-jumping pseudonym for both Brownie McGhee and Champion Jack Dupree, taking two enthusiastic vocals apiece on a 1951 session which features some of Brownie's funkiest electric guitar. CS

Big Dave McLean
VOCAL, GUITAR, HARMONICA, MANDOLIN

McLean has been performing in western Canada since the '70s and is based in Winnipeg.

**(*) Blues From The Middle
Stony Plain SPCD 1290 *McLean; Gord Kidder (h); Graham Guest (o, p); Sue Foley (g, v); Chris Carmichael, Jason Nowicki, Duke Robillard (g); Ryan Menard (b); Ken McMahon (d); Lloyd Peterson (jh); Rick Fenton (tamb); John Scoles (clapping). 03?*

McLean has a thick, road-worn voice, roughly in the Tom Waits vein but less subtle, and plays decent slide and regular guitar and harmonica. 'I Got Love If You Want It' captures the feel of Slim Harpo's original without parroting it, and other sound-links with past masters such as Muddy Waters and Bo Diddley are well forged, though Booker White's 'Fixin' To Die' is a challenge too far. 'St. Mary (At Main)', a long, slow blues with a faint air of Otis Rush, has a brave solo by Sue Foley, but the McLean–Foley vocal duets 'Lowdown Dirty Rotten Blues' and 'Johnny Tornado' are respectively slight and incongruous. TR

Andrew 'Blueblood' McMahon
(1926–84)
VOCAL

The Louisiana-born McMahon arrived in Chicago in 1949. After a decade's apprenticeship on the club circuit he joined Howlin' Wolf's band, where he played bass from 1960 to 1973. In the early '70s he recorded as a singer for Bea & Baby, Dharma and the French MCM label, but he was unable to boost his career and returned to Louisiana in 1976.

McMahon's four sides for Bea & Baby are on the VAC *Meat & Gravy From Bea & Baby* (Castle CMDDD 610 2CD). His vocals are a little raw, but the accompaniments, led by Little Mac Simmons, Sunnyland Slim and Hubert Sumlin, have a dishevelled vigour.

*(*) Go Get My Baby
Storyville STCD 8038 McMahon; Johnny Littlejohn, Jimmy Dawkins, Larry Burton, Richard Kirch (g); Aron Burton, Sylvester Boines (b); Candy Utah, Tyrone Centuray (d). 11/76.

This is McMahon's MCM album, with some extra tracks recorded at the same time. Like other MCM recordings it was a no-frills production, heavy with blues standards that would need little rehearsal like 'Got My Mojo Working', 'It Hurts Me Too', 'Little Red Rooster' and 'You Don't Have To Go'. Dawkins, the lead guitarist on the majority of the tracks, does his best to make overlong performances eventful, but he is up against a problem beyond his solving: McMahon's voice is in terrible shape. This probably explains why it is so low in the mix, but a kinder solution would have been not to issue the record at all. TR

Big Jay McNeely (born 1927)
TENOR AND BARITONE SAXOPHONES, VOCAL

Cecil James McNeely, born in Watts, California, inherited his first instruments – initially an alto sax, then a tenor – from his older brother Bob. He made a name for himself in local clubs, hooked up with Johnny Otis and landed a contract with Savoy, scoring a hit in 1949 with his second release, 'The Deacon's Hop'. He subsequently recorded instrumentals for many of the leading R&B labels of the day, but his next significant chart success, in 1959, was with a vocal number, 'There Is Something On Your Mind'. By the late '60s he had quit the business to work as a mailman, and in his spare time as a Jehovah's Witness, but in 1983 he was drawn back to music.

** Big Jay McNeely 1948–1950
Classics 5009 McNeely; John Anderson (t); John 'Streamline' Ewing, Britt Woodman (tb); Bob McNeely (as, bs); Jimmy O'Brien (p); Candy Stanzel (g); Ted Shirley, Cecil Harris (b); William Streetser, Leonard 'Tight' Hardiman, Johnny Walker (d); Charles McNiles (bgo); Clifford Blivens, unknowns (v). 11/48–c. 1/50.

** Big Jay McNeely 1951–1952
Classics 5058 McNeely; John Henderson (t, as); John Ewing, Britt Woodman (tb); Bob McNeely (as, bs); Earl Jewels (bs); Jimmy O'Brien (p); Melvin Glass (g); Ted Shirley, William 'Buddy' Woodson (b); 'Tight' Hardiman, poss. Wayne Robinson (d); Charles McNiles (cga); Mercy Dee Walton, Jesse Belvin, Three Dots & A Dash, Marvin Philipps (v). 1/51–8/52.

** Big 'J' In 3-D
King KCD 650 McNeely; Bob McNeely (bs); Dwight David (o); Jimmy O'Brien, Boyd Dunlop, Edward Moody (p); 'Porkie' (g); Buddy Woodson, Ike Brown, Cecil Harris (b); 'Tight' Hardiman, Darnell Cole (d); prob. Charles McNiles (bgo). 8/52–4/54.

McNeely's tone on tenor is hard, with a buzz somewhat reminiscent of Earl Bostic and almost no vibrato: ideal for the attack he brings to the straightforward blues and jump tunes that compose most of his repertory. On his Savoy and Exclusive sides of 1948–49 it is deployed with vigour but a deal of restraint. Sometimes he is not the lead voice, and in the piano-led 'K&H Boogie' he doesn't even solo. At his single session for Aladdin in 1950, however, he became more impetuous, careering at high speeds through 'Jay's Frantic' and 'Real Crazy Cool' and coarsening his tone for the slower 'Deacon's Blowout'. This cruder approach, discernible with hindsight as a prototype of one kind of rock 'n' roll, would reappear intermittently over the next few years. It's dormant during the first half of the second Classics CD, mostly novelty numbers sung by Jesse Belvin and a trio, but McNeely shakes himself awake on tracks like 'Blow Blow Blow', 'The Goof', 'Jet Fury' and 'Deacon's Express', the last two recorded live before an audience evidently lifted to ecstasy by his high-register squeals. 'The Goof' is from his first date for King's Federal label and recurs on the King CD alongside similar blowouts like '3-D', but 'Whipped Cream' presents him as a cat of a different colour – no pussyfoot, certainly, but with his claws sheathed – while the lissom 'Beachcomber', eschewing the rasps and overblowing, suggests, as some earlier recordings had done, an admiration for Charlie Parker.

**(*) Live At Birdland
Collectables COL-CD-5131 McNeely; Bob McNeely (bs); Wendell Johnson (g); Dillard McNeely (b); 'Tight' Hardiman (d); Little Sonny Warner (v). late 57.

(**) Swingin'
Collectables COL-CD-5133 As above, except add unknowns (v). 58–60.

Live At Birdland was recorded at a club in Seattle. When the tapes were issued 30-odd years later, the event was described by one reviewer as 'tantamount to the unearthing of King Tut's tomb'. Hardly that, but it is a well-recorded document of an R&B horn band in public action during the rock 'n' roll era, and how many of those are extant? Little Sonny Warner tears up a few songs and the McNeely brothers rip through 'Flying Home', 'Honky Tonk' and 'Deacon's Hop', now and then mellowing out for a 'Tenderly' or 'How High The Moon'.

Swingin' gathers a bunch of singles made for DJ Hunter Hancock's Swingin' label, mostly featuring singers. Warner, the best of them, is restrained and Clyde McPhatter-like in the R&B ballad 'There Is Something On Your Mind' but snaps his leash in 'Back … Shack … Track'. These and other numbers also show up in the Birdland set. McNeely has an exhilarating chase with brother Bob on 'Flying Home', one of six previously unissued tracks, but the bulk of this album is beyond our scope. TR

Blind Willie McTell (1903/4–59)
VOCAL, GUITAR

McTell grew up in east central Georgia, some of whose towns and cities, such as Savannah and Statesboro, turn up in his songs. After attending a state school for the blind he became an itinerant musician, but was somehow always in Atlanta when a recording crew came through, and betwen 1927 and 1935 recorded for Victor, Columbia, OKeh, Vocalion and Decca, accompanying himself with vibrant 12-string guitar playing. He was in the city again in 1940, when John A. Lomax recorded him for the Library of Congress, and appears to have spent the remainder of his life there, playing on the street.

♛ ****** The Definitive Blind Willie McTell 1927–1935**
Catfish KATCD 229 3CD *McTell; William Shorter (bj); Curley Weaver (g, v, sp); Ruby Glaze (poss. g, v, sp); Alfoncy Harris, Bethenea Harris, Ruth Willis, Kate McTell (v). 10/27–4/35.*

**** The Best Of Blind Willie McTell
Yazoo 2071 *McTell; Curley Weaver (g, sp); Ruby Glaze (v, sp). 10/27–4/35.*

(****) 1927–1933 The Early Years
Yazoo 1005 *McTell; Curley Weaver (g, v). 10/27–9/33.*

(****) 1927–1935
Yazoo 1037 *McTell; Curley Weaver (g, v); Ruth Willis, Kate McTell (v). 10/27–4/35.*

***(*) Broke Down Engine Blues
Wolf Blues Classics BC 004 *McTell; Curley Weaver (g, sp); Ruby Glaze (v, sp); Kate McTell (v). 10/27–4/35.*

*** Atlanta Strut
Snapper Complete Blues SBLUECD 011 *As above. 10/27–4/35.*

***(*) The Essential
Classic Blues CBL 200007 2CD *As for The Definitive Blind Willie McTell 1927–1935. 10/27–5/49 or 50.*

*** Blind Willie McTell 1927–49
Wolf WSE-102 *McTell; Curley Weaver (g); Ruby Glaze (poss. g, v, sp); Ruth Willis, Kate McTell (v). 10/27–5/49 or 50.*

***(*) The Definitive Blind Willie McTell
Columbia C2K 53234 2CD *McTell; Curley Weaver (g, v, sp); Ruth Willis (v). 10/29–9/33.*

*** Blind Willie McTell – Vol. 1 (1927–31)
Document DOCD 5006 *McTell. 10/27–10/31.*

*** Blind Willie McTell – Vol. 2 (1931–1933)
Document DOCD 5007 *McTell; Curley Weaver (g, v, sp); Ruby Glaze (poss. g, v, sp); Ruth Willis (v). 10/31–9/33.*

*** Blind Willie McTell – Vol. 3 (1933–1935)
Document DOCD 5008 *McTell; Curley Weaver (g); Kate McTell (v). 9/33–4/35.*

'Nobody can sing the blues like Blind Willie McTell,' averred Bob Dylan. It's the kind of thing that could be said about many blues originals, but you can guess what Dylan might mean. McTell's singing carries overtones – of wistfulness, of resignation, of cocky salaciousness – that distance him from a Son House or Blind Lemon Jefferson. One of his recordings was given the title 'Hillbilly Willie's Blues', and he does indeed sound whiter than many of his peers, particularly in humorous narratives such as 'Travelin' Blues', with its medley of old-time songs, or 'Atlanta Strut', where his guitar impersonates a whole band of other instruments. Pieces like those also suggest that he grasped more quickly than many blues artists the dramatic potential of the 3½-minute record, and that impression is reinforced by the way he uses second voices, such as Ruby Glaze's sexy commentary in 'Mama, Let Me Scoop For You'. But if McTell had an unusual talent for lighting his performances, it was not because they had shortcomings that needed masking. Absorbed in the intimacy of his storytelling, we may risk overlooking what a dextrous guitarist he was. The blues machine-tools of guitar and slide adapt to the hands that use them and the places where they are used: if Booker White's riffs are bolts riveting the lines together, McTell's patterns are ornamental ironwork. But when he set his slide aside he could create the hectic ragtime dances of 'Razor Ball' and 'Georgia Rag', or later, working with Curley Weaver as the Sunshine Boys of the blues, conversations for two guitars as intricately scripted as crosstalk routines. With the addition of his wife Kate, the Decca sides of 1935 offer, for the first time in his work, antiphonal gospel duets in the tradition of Blind Willie Johnson and his partners, which replace the diffidence of a 'Writing Paper Blues' or 'Love Changing Blues' with the phlegmatic certainty of Christian belief.

The Catfish is not the only McTell album called *Definitive* but it's the only one that justifies the title, its 74 tracks comprising everything he recorded in the stated period, including alternative takes and eight accompaniments (to Weaver, Ruth Willis and Harris & Harris, a vaudeville duet in the manner of Butterbeans & Susie). Columbia's 2CD, necessarily confined to Columbia, OKeh and Vocalion recordings, is less than definitive, and the remastering is sometimes imperfect. Readers coming fresh to McTell's work may prefer a single CD; the best, beyond question, is Yazoo's *Best Of*, remastered to the highest modern standards and embracing many of the songs mentioned above, as well as 'Statesboro Blues', famously covered by both the Allman Brothers and Taj Mahal, and the shimmeringly lovely 'Mama, Tain't Long Fo' Day'. Yazoo's other sets are converted LPs with only 14 tracks each, wonderful in their time but extensively duplicated by the *Best Of*, and are probably being discontinued. Wolf Blues Classics and Snapper offer good and fairly different selections from eight years' recording, but both share about half their contents with *Best Of*. The other Wolf and the three Documents were made quite a long time ago and don't match the others in sound quality. The 36-track selection on Classic Blues' *The Essential* strays beyond the confines of McTell's first recording spell to cherrypick songs from the Library of Congress session and postwar discs. On the face of it an attractive collection, it has to be marked down a little for preferring secondary material like the Harris & Harris accompaniments to major pieces like 'Travelin' Blues'.

**** Library of Congress Recordings (1940)
RST Blues Documents BDCD-6001 *McTell. 11/40.*

**** Crapshooter's Blues
Collectors Edition CBCD 022 *McTell. 11/40.*

**** The Devil Can't Hide From Me
Fuel 2000 302 061 441 *McTell. 11/40.*

The music McTell chose, or was asked, to perform for John A. Lomax in this hotel room session was mostly gospel songs and blues-ballads. The delicacy of 'Mama Tain't Long Fo' Day' touches 'Murderer's Home Blues' but on the whole the repertoire is narrative – the stories of 'Chainey' and 'Delia', 'Will Fox' and 'The Boll Weevil' – and the introspection of his blues is recalled rather by his meditative versions of 'I Got To Cross The River Jordan' and other sacred songs. Interspersed among these delectable performances are what Lomax called monologues but are actually answers to Lomax's questions. On subjects like changing styles in blues or his own recording history McTell is voluble and fascinating, but when Lomax presses him for songs about the hard times black people have endured, he is politely evasive. To hear McTell suddenly step out of the one-dimensional role of a blues singer on a record and reveal uncertainty and embarrassment like plain folk is curiously moving.

*** **Pig 'N Whistle Red**
Biograph DK 30171 *McTell; Curley Weaver (g, v)*. 5/49.
*** **Blind Willie McTell & The Regal Country Blues**
Acrobat ADMCD 5015 2CD *As above.* 5/49.
*** **The Postwar Recordings Of Blind Willie McTell & Curley Weaver (1949–1950)**
RST Blues Documents BDCD-6014 *As above.* 5/49–50.
*** **Atlanta Twelve String**
Atlantic 82366 *McTell.* c. 10/49.

Twice in 1949 McTell recorded an album's worth of songs for scouting record men; first for Fred Mendelsohn of Regal, then a few months later for Ahmet Ertegun and Herb Abramson of Atlantic. (The Regal session has also been dated to 1950, but it's uncertain on what evidence.) Both sets of recordings find McTell handling a mixed programme of ragtime songs, pop ballads, gospel songs and blues, but with his customary canniness he gives each company a wholly different selection from his repertoire. It's interesting how few of the pieces from the '20s and early '30s that present-day listeners value most reappear in McTell's later years. For Atlantic he sang 'Broke Down Engine' and 'The Razor Ball' (the latter very unlike the 1930 recording), and for Regal 'Love Changin' Blues' and some of the blues from the '33 Vocalion session, no doubt because Curley Weaver was there to remind him of them. But there were no remakes of 'Statesboro Blues' or 'Mama Tain't Long Fo' Day', and one wonders if they ever settled in his repertoire, or were merely created for a record date and discarded. Both the '49 sessions elicited a handful of sacred songs, and 'Pearly Gates' on *Atlanta Twelve String* is a very beautiful slow hymn. From about halfway through the Atlantic session McTell's voice begins to crack, but this doesn't make his music any less moving. Of the three CDs containing the Regal material the Biograph has just that; Acrobat add further Regal sides from the same period by other artists (for which see COMPILATIONS: LABEL HISTORIES & SHOWCASES); Blues Documents bookend the Regals (and another Weaver solo, 'She Don't Treat Me Good No More', available only there) with a pair of singles Weaver cut for Sittin' In With.

***(*) **Last Session**
Original Blues Classics OBCCD-517 *McTell.* c. 10/49, 9/56.
***(*) **Blind Willie McTell**
Warner Blues 36917 *McTell.* c. 10/49, 9/56.

McTell's last recordings were informally taped by an admirer, Ed Rhodes, late one night in 1956 in his record store, with a few friends for an audience. It was not a gathering of blues fans, and McTell naturally gave them a sampling of his street repertoire: ragtime songs like 'Kill It Kid', 'Salty Dog' and 'That Will Never Happen No More', vaudeville pieces like 'A Married Man's A Fool', 'A To Z Blues' and 'The Dyin' Crapshooter's Blues', and a dash of country music in Roy Acuff's 'Wabash Cannonball'. The minute and a half of 'Goodbye Blues' is the only hint that behind the ingratiating grin of the entertainer there once lay a more sardonic smile. But to say that is not to disparage the *Last Session*; for one thing, McTell may have regarded his early blues less fondly than we do; for another, the street songs are excellent demonstrations of his powers as a narrator and humorist. And, if his guitar playing was a shade less swift or delicate, his singing had hardly changed in almost 30 years. How these tapes survived makes a good story, which Sam Charters tells in the notes to the OBC CD; this issue adds the two songs from the 1949 Atlantic session that were released at the time, 'Kill It Kid' and 'Broke Down Engine Blues'. The French Warner Blues CD interleaves almost all of *Last Session* with almost all of *Atlanta Twelve String*, omitting the latter's 'Ain't It Grand To Live A Christian' and 'Soon This Morning'. Of the two songs shared by both source albums, 'Kill It Kid' comes from *Last Session*, 'Dying Crapshooter's Blues' from *Atlanta Twelve String*. It's an economical way to hear both albums, and the alternation of Atlantic's studio recordings and *Last Session*'s more informal performances, which you might think would be unsettling, isn't. TR

Jack McVea (1914–2000)
ALTO, TENOR AND BARITONE SAXOPHONES

McVea learned banjo from his father, an LA bandleader, and played with him in the '20s. Switching to tenor sax he played in various LA bands, sometimes alongside musicians of the calibre of Don Byas and Herschel Evans. Stints with Lionel Hampton and Snub Mosley were followed by a period of popularity in the '40s when he was prominent on the LA nightclub scene and recorded for several local labels, having a hit with the novelty number 'Open The Door, Richard!'. In 1966, after a spell of retirement, he began playing clarinet in a strolling band at Disneyland, a job he held for some 25 years.

*** **Jack McVea/Rabon Tarrant: The Complete Recordings Volume 1 (1944–1945)**
Blue Moon BMCD 6031 *McVea; Cappy Oliver (t, v); Teddy Buckner, Joe 'Red' Kelly (t); Ram Ramirez, Buster Bailey (cl); Bob Mosley (p); Gene Phillips (g); Frank Clarke (b); Rabon Tarrant (d, v); Betty Roché, Arthur Duncan, band (v)*. 44–9/45.
*** **Jack McVea/Rabon Tarrant: The Complete Recordings Volume 2 (1945–1946)**
Blue Moon BMCD 6032 *McVea; Cappy Oliver (t, v); Teddy Buckner, Sammy Yates, Joe 'Red' Kelly, Jesse Perdue, Russell Jacquet (t); Marshall Royal (cl, as); Wild Bill Moore (ts); Bob Mosley, Tommy 'Crow' Kahn, Jimmy Shackleton, John Shackleford, Call Cobbs (p); Gene Phillips (g); Frank Clarke (b); Rabon Tarrant (d, v); Estelle Edson, band (v)*. 9/45–2/46.
*** **Jack McVea/Rabon Tarrant: The Complete Recordings Volume 3 (1946–1947)**
Blue Moon BMCD 6033 *McVea; Joe 'Red' Kelly, Sammy Yates (t); Melba Liston (tb); Marshall Royal (cl, as); Tommy 'Crow' Kahn (p, v); Lloyd Glenn (p); Gene Phillips, Irving Ashby (g); Frank Clarke (b); Rabon Tarrant (d, v); Arthur Duncan, band (v)*. 9/46–2/47.
*** **Jack McVea/Rabon Tarrant: The Complete Recordings Volume 4 (1947–1952)**
Blue Moon BMCD 6034 *McVea; Sammy Yates (t, v); Tommy 'Crow' Kahn (p); Gene Phillips (g); Frank Clarke (b); Rabon Tarrant (d, v); Arthur Duncan, band (v)*. 2–12/47.

*** McVoutie's Central Avenue Blues
Delmark DE-756 *McVea; Teddy Buckner, prob. Jesse Purdue (t); Marshall Royal (as); Bob Mosley, Jimmy Shackleton (p); Gene Phillips (g); Frank Clarke (b); Rabon Tarrant (d, v); Wynonie Harris, Duke Henderson (v). 8–12/45.*

McVea declares his jazz credentials from the very first with businesslike tenor choruses on the up-tempo blues 'Jump Jack' and furry, Hawkinsesque ones on the slow 'Rainy Day Blues' and the ballad 'Silver Symphony'. Soon afterwards he is playing insouciant alto on the boppish 'O-Kay For Baby'. And so it goes through Blue Moon's four carefully researched volumes, as McVea blows with calm versatility on blues, boogies and miscellaneous pop material, the lively vocals mostly coming from drummer Rabon Tarrant (blues), Cappy Oliver or Sammy Yates (novelties) and Arthur Duncan (ballads). Early in *Volume 3* we meet 'Open The Door, Richard!', and for the rest of that CD the programme is peppered with comedy routines of the same kind, like 'The Key's In The Mailbox' and 'Crow's Being Evicted'. This volume is also graced by a six-track session of boogie tunes featuring Lloyd Glenn. By *Volume 4* McVea is paying close attention to the contemporary work of Louis Jordan: he switches from tenor to alto, and the band produces workmanlike covers of 'Don't Let The Sun Catch You Crying' and 'Inflation Blues'. (McVea's portion of this volume ends in 1947 and the disc is completed with two tracks each by Sammy Yates and Rabon Tarrant in different company.) Mild displays of opportunism and his involvement with comedy material shouldn't obscure the fact that McVea was a considerable figure on the Central Avenue scene of the '40s.

McVea's Apollo recordings, distributed over Blue Moon's first two volumes, are also on *McVoutie's Central Avenue Blues*. Five of the 23 tracks are without him: two vocals by Tarrant with a Lucky Thompson band (also on Blue Moon's *Volume 2*) and one by Cee Pee Johnson, and a couple of boogie tunes by pianist Mosley and tenor saxophonist Wild Bill Moore. TR

John McVey
VOCAL, GUITAR

In Little Rock, Arkansas, McVey played with Larry Davis and Fenton Robinson. In 1986 he moved to Austin, Texas, where he worked with Hook Herrera & The Hitchhikers, Paul Orta, Lavelle White and Lewis Cowdrey. He currently lives in Fort Worth.

**(*) Gone To Texas
Doc Blues DB 6803 *McVey; Kim Wilson (h); Joel Guzman (ac, v); Riley Osbourn (kb); Derek O'Brien (g, prod); Larry Fulcher (b); Barry 'Frosty' Smith (d, perc); Mike Buck (d); Erin James, Eve Monsees (v). 02.*

McVey plays guitar with slide effects and a huge tremolo, as if he were trying to sound simultaneously like Earl Hooker, Magic Sam and Sonny Landreth. Blended with strong-minded drumming and percussion, it creates a Texan ambience that should beguile anyone who likes their blues loud, chicken-fried and with a jalapeño pepper. Apart from Albert King's 'Don't Throw Your Love On Me So Strong' and Detroit Jr's 'Call My Job', the songs are virtually all McVey's and range from the weighty slow blues of the title track to shake-a-leg numbers like 'Sweet Little Upsetter'. He's not a gifted singer, but the energy and unconventional character of his guitar playing go some way to make up for that. TR

The Mellow Fellows
GROUP

The band that accompanied Big Twist through the '80s carried on after his death in 1990, Martin Allbritton taking over the vocal role.

*** Street Party
Alligator ALCD 4793 *Don Tenuto (t); Gene Barge (ts, v, arr); Terry Ogolini (ts); Chris Cameron, Matt Rose, Sid Wingfield (kb); Pete Special, David Mick (g); Bob Halaj (b); William 'Kax' Ratliff, Jeff Thomas, Steve Cobb, Morris Jennings, Eric Jensen, Wayne Stewart (d); Martin Allbritton, Johnny Rutledge (v). 90.*

The sound created by Big Twist & The Mellow Fellows is very faithfully re-created on this recording made in the months after his death. In fact, without any slight to Big Twist's memory, this is the band's best album, the eight-piece lineup delivering a huge broadside of sound and Allbritton filling almost every inch of his predecessor's shoes. The hyperactive ensemble playing is an irresistible invitation to listeners to get up and dance round the room; mercifully a few slower numbers like 'Feels Like Rain' and an instrumental 'Since I Fell For You' give them a chance to catch their breath. The band later renamed itself the Chicago Rhythm & Blues Kings; see that entry for an excellent album by most of the same lineup. TR

Memphis Jug Band
GROUP

Singer, guitarist and harmonica player Will Shade (1898–1966) founded the Memphis Jug Band, probably about 1925/26, to play in the city's parks, streets and taverns. They recorded more prolifically than any other jugband, cutting 80-odd sides between 1927 and 1934 and drawing on a large pool of local players: 19 musicians recorded under the MJB name. Their diary expanded to include political rallies, store-openings and other civic affairs. By the late '30s jugband music had lost its appeal and engagements came less easily, but Shade was still finding musical work in the '50s, and in the last decade of his life made a number of documentary recordings, few of them currently available.

**** Memphis Jug Band Volume 1
Frog DGF 15 *Will Shade (h, g, v); Vol Stevens (bj-md, g, v); Will Weldon (g, v); Ben Ramey (k, v); Charlie Polk (j); Jennie Clayton (v). 2/27–2/28.*

**** Memphis Jug Band Volume 2
Frog DGF 16 *Will Shade (h, g, v); Charlie Nickerson (p); Milton Roby (vn); Vol Stevens (bj-md, g); Charlie Burse, Tewee Blackman (g, v); Ben Ramey (k, v); Jab Jones (j, v); Hattie Hart (v). 9/28–10/29.*

**** Memphis Jug Band Volume 3
Frog DGF 18 *Will Shade (h, g, v); Charlie Nickerson (p, v); Milton Roby (vn); Charlie Burse (md, g, v); Vol Stevens (bj-md); unknown (bj); Memphis Minnie, Will Weldon (g, v); Ben Ramey (k, v); Charlie Polk, Jab Jones (j, v); Hambone Lewis, unknown (j); Hattie Hart, unknown (s) (v). 2/27–11/30.*

***(*) **Memphis Jug Band – Vol. 1 (1927–1928)**
Document DOCD-5021 *Will Shade (h, g, v); Vol Stevens (bj-md, g, v); Will Weldon (g, v); Ben Ramey (k, v); Charlie Polk (j); Jennie Clayton (v).* 2/27–2/28.

***(*) **Memphis Jug Band – Vol. 2 (1928–1929)**
Document DOCD-5022 *Will Shade (h, g, v); Jab Jones (p, j, v); Charlie Nickerson (p); Milton Roby (vn); Vol Stevens (bj-md, g); Will Weldon, Charlie Burse, Tewee Blackman (g, v); Ben Ramey (k, v); Charlie Polk (j); Hattie Hart, Minnie Wallace (v).* 2/28–10/29.

***(*) **Memphis Jug Band – Vol. 3 (1930)**
Document DOCD-5023 *Will Shade (h, g, v); Charlie Nickerson (p, v); Milton Roby (vn); Charlie Burse (md, g, v); Vol Stevens (bj-md); unknown (bj); Memphis Minnie (g, v); Ben Ramey (k, v); Hambone Lewis, Jab Jones, unknown (j); Hattie Hart, unknown(s) (v).* 5–11/30.

***(*) **Memphis Jug Band (1932–1934)**
RST Blues Documents BDCD-6002 *Will Shade (h, g, v); Jab Jones (p, j, v); Charlie Pierce (vn); Charlie Burse (md, g, v); Vol Stevens (md, v); Laura Dukes (md, u); Otto Gilmore, Robert Burse (d, wb, perc); unknown (v).* 8/32–11/34.

***(*) **The Best Of The Memphis Jug Band**
Yazoo 2059 *As for relevant CDs above.* 2/27–11/34.

***(*) **Memphis Jug Band**
Yazoo 1067 *As for relevant CDs above.* 2/27–11/34.

***(*) **The Essential**
Classic Blues 2000015 2CD *As for relevant CDs above.* 2/27–11/34.

(**) **He's In The Jailhouse Now**
Acrobat ACRCD 190 *As for relevant CDs above.* 2/27–11/34.

If Will Shade had a business card, he might have put on it an old show-business phrase: 'Memphis Jug Band – Music For Every Occasion'. The group that he founded and led for so long played from a book that included blues, ragtime tunes, comic songs, breakdowns, waltzes, old Southern country songs and glee-club quartet numbers: altogether one of the most varied and fascinating repertoires in the history of African-American music.

Although Shade claimed later that he had been inspired to form the MJB by the sounds coming from Louisville, Kentucky, the first city of jugband music, he neither steered his associates in that somewhat jazzy direction nor deployed the same resources. The Louisville bands mixed their instrumental palette with fiddles, banjos and clarinets. The MJB's primary colours were harmonica, kazoo and a couple of guitars (the jug, of course, was a given) and their first session, in 2/27, was all blues. But before long the band diversified into traditional songs and old pops and, in due course, new numbers of their own composition or recomposition, such as the topical 'Lindberg Hop', the lilting lovesong 'Stealin' Stealin'' and the incomparably wistful 'K.C. Moan'. Their captivating performances of the latter two songs have established them as staples of the jugband repertoire.

So they could do pretty, but they could also do raunchy, proving it on sides like 'Memphis Yo Yo Blues' and 'Bumble Bee Blues'. To be sure, they had notable guest singers, Hattie Hart and Memphis Minnie respectively, but Hart's sexy delivery is framed by beautifully relaxed playing and bridged with a handsome non-blues instrumental midsection. Touches like that – the hummed trio ending of 'K.C. Moan' is another – are found all over the MJB's recordings, revealing Shade as an arranger of rare talent. Although the core of the group's sound remained the harmonica, guitar, kazoo and jug with which they started, Shade frequently tinkered with the prototype, adding Milton Roby's angular violin, Jab Jones's piano or Vol Stevens's mandolin, and experimenting with different lead singers, replacing his own doleful, phlegmy voice or Will Weldon's rather plain one with the more expressive Jones or Charlie Burse, or the effervescent Charlie Nickerson, whose mock-solemn storytelling in 'Move That Thing' marks him out as one of the great comic singers of the blues. The MJB was also exceptional among secular groups in its frequent use of vocal harmony.

'Move That Thing' and 'You Got Me Rollin'', cut near the end of 1930, were the MJB's last recordings for a while, but, luckier than their local rivals like Gus Cannon's Jug Stompers, they returned to the studio, first in the summer of 1932 for Gennett, who marketed their discs so ineffectually that several of them have not yet been found, and then in 1934, when they made their way to Chicago for OKeh Records and a triumphant swansong. It was not the MJB sound of the '20s but a bouncier ensemble coloured by Charlie Pierce's alley fiddling, Jab Jones's romping piano, the mandolin and Callowayesque scat singing of Charlie Burse and the plinking and clattering of his brother Robert's percussion kit. Sides like 'Jazzbo Stomp' and 'Gator Wobble' were some of the most exciting rough-cut music to be heard on record in the mid-'30s, but the session closed on the elegiac note of 'Jug Band Quartette', the MJB paying an affecting tribute to their own special brand of music: 'it sounds so sweet … oh, you know, it's hard to beat … jugband music certainly was a treat to me.'

Reissues have sliced this rich layer-cake several different ways. The Victor period (1927–30) is covered chronologically by the three volumes on Frog, whose scrupulous remastering from clean original pressings elevates them above the three volumes on Document covering more or less the same ground. *Memphis Jug Band (1932–1934)* contains the handful of discovered recordings from the '32 session (sadly just five) and the 16 sides issued by OKeh. This CD is both a major document of the African-American stringband and an hour's worth of exhilarating music, and only the indifferent remastering of a few tracks forbids a four-star rating.

The other compilations mix Victor and OKeh material so as to cover the group's entire recording career. In sonic terms the best are the two Yazoos, but they overlap infuriatingly, having 12 tracks out of 23 in common; *The Best Of* is the better selection, but key tracks are scattered on both. Given that, the easiest set to recommend to the beginner is the inexpensive 2CD on Classic Blues, which embraces all but one of the titles singled out above, as well as many other deserving tracks, and is mostly quite well remastered. The good selection of songs on Acrobat's *He's In The Jailhouse Now* is locked in the dark by its awful sound. The VAC *Memphis Jug Band Associates & Alternate Takes* (Wolf WBCD-004) is chiefly devoted to band members recording in their own names, such as Will Weldon, Vol Stevens and Hattie Hart (the same sides are also on Frog's *Volume 2* and *Volume 3*), and to peripheral figures like the singer Kaiser Clifton. The five genuine MJB items are alternative takes also found on Frog's *Volume 3*. TR

Memphis Minnie (1897–1973)
VOCAL, GUITAR, MANDOLIN

As she sang, Lizzie Douglas was 'born in Louisiana, raised in Algiers', but at seven her family moved to Walls, Mississippi. By

1910 she was playing guitar in nearby Memphis; she soon joined a travelling show, and next turns up in the Delta, where she worked with Willie Brown for five years. Back in Memphis in the mid-'20s, she struck up a relationship with Will Weldon of the Memphis Jug Band, then a more enduring one with Joe McCoy. Christened Memphis Minnie and Kansas Joe by Columbia, they had a big hit with 'Bumble Bee', and recorded together until their marriage foundered in 1934, seemingly because Joe was jealous of his wife's greater fame. By that time they were living in Chicago, where Minnie continued to record and perform, also visiting the South from time to time. In 1939 she married third husband (and again second guitarist) Ernest 'Little Son Joe' Lawlars. Postwar, Minnie's recording career faltered as the music and public tastes changed; with Joe in poor health, they moved back to Memphis in 1958, to be near relatives. By the time Joe died in 1961, Minnie was already in a wheelchair after a stroke, and her last years were spent in poverty.

(*) **Memphis Minnie & Kansas Joe – Vol. 1 (1929–1930)
Document DOCD-5028 *Memphis Minnie; Will Shade (h); Kansas Joe (g, v); Charlie Burse (g); Hambone Lewis (j).* 6/29–5/30.

***(*) **Memphis Minnie & Kansas Joe – Vol. 2 (1930–1931)**
Document DOCD-5029 *Memphis Minnie; prob. Jed Davenport (h); Kansas Joe (g, v); prob. Hambone Lewis (j).* 6/30–1/31.

*** **Memphis Minnie & Kansas Joe – Vol. 3 (1931–1932)**
Document DOCD-5030 *Memphis Minnie; Kansas Joe (g, v).* 1/31–2/32.

***(*) **Memphis Minnie & Kansas Joe – Vol. 4 (1933–1934)**
Document DOCD-5031 *As above.* 11/33–9/34.

Big Bill Broonzy's comment that Memphis Minnie played and sang 'as good as any man' has often been deplored by the politically correct, but the world in which she worked was a tough and sometimes dangerous one, and it took a forceful woman to impose herself on it. These volumes cover the first phase of Minnie's recording career, when she was married to Joe McCoy. The 'Kansas Joe' soubriquet was fanciful, but 'Memphis Minnie' makes stylistic sense as a *nom de disque*; their two-guitar sound is very reminiscent of their fellow Memphians Stokes and Sane: tightly arranged, vibrantly rhythmic and often ragtime-influenced. Minnie's singing is often harshly aggressive and occasionally (but not unattractively) squawky; she can also be knowing and coquettish. In duet, Joe's warmer voice contrasts pleasingly with Minnie's, and their sexual sparring is between equals, with formulaic battleaxe woman/henpecked man skits largely excluded.

These CDs also include records where Kansas Joe is the only singer, with Minnie confined to playing guitar; she's absent altogether from five tracks on *Vol. 4*, where Joe collaborates with his brother Charlie and with a small group including pianist Charlie Segar. On this volume, perhaps because their marriage was unravelling, there are also several tracks where Minnie performs alone, and the likes of 'Too Late' and 'Banana Man Blues' are conclusive proof that she was the star guitarist of the team. This is not to dismiss Kansas Joe's musicianship: tracks like 'When The Levee Breaks' (*Vol. 1*), 'Preachers Blues', 'Shake Mattie' (both *Vol. 2*), the bleak 'Joliet Bound' (*Vol. 3*) and 'Evil Devil Woman' (*Vol. 4*) are the work of a significant lyricist, singer and picker, and his contribution to the outstanding instrumental 'Let's Go To Town' (*Vol. 3*) is as important as Minnie's.

All these discs contain much memorable music; the first two include five versions of the career kick-starter, 'Bumble Bee', one of them a collaboration with the Memphis Jug Band, but the duo's creativity was too rampant to be confined by record-company formulae. *Vol. 1* is unfortunately compiled from some rough originals, and some that have passed through several generations of tape before reaching Document. The second disc includes the grippingly personal 'Memphis Minnie-Jitis [i.e. Meningitis] Blues' and a charming 'Frankie Jean (That Trotting Fool)', where Minnie reminisces about her father's horse as the guitars mimic his gait. Especially notable on *Vol. 3* are 'After While Blues', where Minnie plays mandolin, and 'Outdoor Blues', a striking, possibly autobiographical anecdote of hobo life.

*** **Memphis Minnie Vol. 1 (1935)**
RST Blues Documents BDCD-6008 *Memphis Minnie; Black Bob, unknowns (p); prob. Big Bill Broonzy, Casey Bill Weldon (g); Bill Settles (b); unknown male, unknown female (v).* 1/35–10/35.

*** **Memphis Minnie Vol. 2 (1935–1936)**
RST Blues Documents BDCD-6009 *Memphis Minnie; unknown (t); Black Bob (p); Casey Bill Weldon (g); Bill Settles, unknowns (b); unknowns (perc); Bumble Bee Slim (v).* 12/35–11/36.

(*) **Memphis Minnie Vol. 3 (1937)
RST Blues Documents BDCD-6010 *Memphis Minnie; prob. Alfred Bell (t); Arnett Nelson (cl); prob. Blind John Davis, unknown (p); unknown (b); Fred Williams (d).* 6/37–12/37.

These three CDs on one of Document's associated labels cover a period when most of Minnie's recordings were made with small groups. They have sometimes been disparaged, and it's true that many sides lack the musical adventurousness and the personalized lyrics of her earlier work. This was a time when record companies thought they had a handle on public taste, and set out to satisfy it methodically. Like Big Bill Broonzy and Bumble Bee Slim, Memphis Minnie had the skills needed to create new material on demand and in quantity, and the aesthetics of mass production are sometimes dominant.

That's not to suggest that these CDs are only of documentary value. On *Vol. 1* Decca, Vocalion and Bluebird all seem to be tinkering with Minnie's post-Kansas Joe music, and among the less successful tracks are two unconvincing gospel songs and a comatose 'Down In New Orleans'; offsetting these, however, are a rollicking, piano-driven 'Dirty Mother For You' and the New Deal vignette 'Sylvester And His Mule', about a farmer who secured FDR's intervention in the foreclosure of his farm. Black Bob arrives two thirds of the way through *Vol. 1*, and is the star of the rambunctious 'Joe Louis Strut', celebrating the Brown Bomber's victory over Primo Carnera. Bob's playing, always inventive, euphonious and tough, is perhaps the major selling point of these three discs; it's certainly more valuable than the insecure trumpeters who straddle the second and third of them, and than Arnett Nelson's vaudevillian vulgarities at the end of *Vol. 3*. All these CDs feature some interesting and original lyrics, but their musical settings are undeniably more formulaic, a problem highlighted by a number of alternative, but not significantly different, takes on *Vols 2* and *3*.

*** **Queen Of Country Blues**
JSP JSP 7716 5CD *As for all above CDs, except omit Nelson, Davis.* 6/30–6/37.

Nicely packaged, well annotated and seductively priced, *Queen Of Country Blues* offers 'all the published sides', meaning Minnie's solo vocals and duets with Joe up to the cut-off date, which is determined only by what will fit on five CDs. Among its 124 tracks are a few – mainly alternative takes, but also two 'new' songs – which only appeared on volumes in Document's *"Too Late, Too Late"* sequence of gap-fillers. The sound quality tracks the fluctuation of Document's, and though it has been tweaked a bit during (re)remastering, it's plain that JSP are sourcing from CDs, not 78s. *Queen Of Country Blues* is a handy, if vaguely titled collection, but – like its progenitors – is perhaps too much for the casual listener.

(*) Memphis Minnie Vol. 4 (1938–1939)
RST Blues Documents BDCD-6011 *Memphis Minnie; unknown (p); Charlie McCoy (md); Little Son Joe (g); unknown (b); prob. Fred Williams (d). 6/38–2/39.*

**** Memphis Minnie Vol. 5 (1940–1941)**
RST Blues Documents BDCD-6012 *Memphis Minnie; Little Son Joe (g, v); Alfred Elkins, unknown (b). 6/40–12/41.*

After a session with her ex-brother-in-law on pretty but unadventurous mandolin, Minnie plays second guitar for Son Joe. At this stage, he was a nervous, wooden singer and an unexciting guitarist. He produces some original lyrics (and the first recording of 'Diggin' My Potatoes'), but the desperately out-of-tune guitars on "Key To The World" are the worst moment of a poor session, and when Minnie takes over as vocalist the results are also disappointing. The last five tracks on *Vol. 4* were recorded three days later, and there must have been some frank discussion in the interval; much more dynamic, they foreshadow the good things on *Vol. 5*.

The long interval between sessions was perhaps used for intensive woodshedding; on *Vol. 5* there's a consistently confident interplay between Joe's acoustic rhythm guitar and Minnie's lead, at first steel-bodied, later amplified. Though not as complex as her early sides with Kansas Joe, these guitar duets have great swing and a loose, improvisatory feel. 'Me And My Chauffeur', with its boogie rhythms and double meanings, was the big hit, but it's just one example of a notable songwriting streak (by both artists) that also produced the autobiographical 'Nothing In Rambling' and 'In My Girlish Days', a touching tribute to 'Ma Rainey' and the ingenious 'Don't Turn The Card'. The CD concludes with two songs from Son Joe: 'Black Rat Swing' was *his* big hit, and although it's obvious why some copies were credited to 'Mr. Memphis Minnie', he's altogether more lively and self-assured.

((*)) Memphis Minnie Vol. 1 (1944–1946)**
Wolf WBCD-008 *Memphis Minnie; Little Son Joe (g); Ransom Knowling (b); Fred Williams (d). 12/44–2/46.*
(*) Memphis Minnie Vol. 2 (1946–1947)
Wolf WBCD-009 *As above, except add Blind John Davis (p), Judge Riley (d), band (v); omit Williams. 2/46–12/47.*
(***) Memphis Minnie Vol. 3 (1949–53)
Wolf WBCD-010 *Memphis Minnie; Little Walter (h); Sunnyland Slim, poss. Roosevelt Sykes, Little Brother Montgomery, unknown (p); Little Son Joe (g, v); Jimmy Rogers (g); prob. Ransom Knowling, Big Crawford (b); unknowns (d); band (v). 4/49–10/53.*

When recording resumed after the Petrillo ban, Minnie and Joe carried on much as before, but Wolf's *Vol. 1* is unsatisfactory. It begins with an eight-title session featuring Fred Williams at his noisiest and most disjointed. The remaining 19 tracks of *Vol. 1*, and the first five of *Vol. 2*, are the entirety of a 2/46 session. Despite Ransom Knowling's reliable bass, Minnie and Joe seem purposeless and uninspired. Only one song was issued, and it was the only one captured in a single take; the remaining five songs are represented by between four and seven takes apiece, some of them incomplete. This makes listening to *Vol. 1* for entertainment virtually impossible.

Columbia persisted, although the long gaps between sessions indicate a decreasing commitment to Minnie's music. Once past five takes of 'The Man I Love', there's far more power and enthusiasm about *Vol. 2*, where much of the (sometimes quite intricate) single-string soloing is by Son Joe. Again, though, several numbers feature in multiple takes: there are 23 tracks, but only 12 songs. There are sometimes significant differences between takes, and this disc is not such hard work as *Vol. 1*, but its value, too, is mainly archival.

After a final Columbia session, which begins *Vol. 3*, Minnie and Joe managed to get sessions at Regal, Checker and J.O.B., from each of which a 78 was issued. An additional eight songs were recorded, however (three of them in two versions), and they've appeared piecemeal on LP and CD; *Vol. 3* handily gathers everything together. Minnie and Joe were trying to bring their music into line with contemporary Chicago blues, and much of the time they succeed: 'Night Watchman Blues' (with very different guitar solos on each take) and three titles with Little Walter, one a remake of 'Me And My Chauffeur', are notable fusions of the old and new. J.O.B. issued a romping 'Kissing In The Dark' and a dour 'World Of Trouble', with Montgomery outstanding on piano, but the label's unissued material is also very worthwhile; Son Joe's 'Ethel Bea' is perhaps the high point. However, the Columbia session, with its multiple takes (six songs, 11 tracks) and emphasis on not very good ballads, prevents an unqualified recommendation.

**** Queen Of The Delta Blues Vol. 2 [sic]**
JSP JSP 7741 5CD *As for above five CDs, except add Arnett Nelson (cl); omit Little Walter, unknown (p), one unknown (d). 6/36–10/53.*

JSP's second box is even more vaguely titled than its predecessor (insofar as Minnie was a Delta blues singer, she wasn't one by 1937), but it has the same merits: cheapness, acceptable remastering and good notes, which don't shrink from pointing out musical shortcomings where appropriate. Sensibly, only the complete takes from the postwar Columbia sessions are included; even so, their multiplicity is hard going. JSP's two box sets are the best way for serious collectors whose interest falls short of must-have-everything obsession to acquire most of Memphis Minnie's output (and all of Son Joe's). They should note, however, that JSP, doubtless aware of who has the bigger lawyers, have left out the five Checker recordings.

(***) Me & My Chauffeur Blues
Aim 0018 *As for relevant CDs above. 6/29–5/41.*
***** The Queen Of The Blues 1929–1941**
Frémeaux FA 259 2CD *As for relevant CDs above. 6/29–12/41.*
(***) The Essential
Classic Blues CBL 200001 2CD *As for relevant CDs above. 6/29–12/41.*

*** **Me And My Chauffeur**
Proper PVCD 129 2CD *As for relevant CDs above.* 6/29–12/44.
(***) **In My Girlish Days**
Blues Forever CD 68018 *As for relevant CDs above.* 6/29–7/52.
** **Crazy Crying Blues**
Fabulous FABCD 111 *As for relevant CDs above.* 2/30–5/41.
(*) **Hot Stuff
Collectors Edition CBCD 002 *As for relevant CDs above.* 6/30–5/41.
(**(*)) **Moonshine**
Columbia River CRG 120005 *As above.* 6/30–5/41.
(***) **Hoodoo Lady (1933–1937)** [sic]
Columbia/Legacy CK 46775 *As for relevant CDs above.* 11/33–6/38.
(*) **Me And My Chauffeur 1935/1946
EPM Blues Collection 15882 *As for relevant CDs above.* 1/35–9/46.
*** **American Blues Legend**
Charly CPCD 8234 *As for relevant CDs above.* 1/35–12/47.

There is heavy duplication among the selective surveys; even *Queen Of The Blues*, where an attempt has been made to avoid (what the compiler regards as) over-reissued items, has many tracks in common with the others. Despite no 'Let's Go To Town' and no 'Me And My Chauffeur', the Frémeaux set is a very good selection, with the first CD devoted to Minnie's work with Kansas Joe, and the second split between well-chosen band tracks and collaborations with the other Joe. The notes (in French, with an abridgement in English) are extensive, if occasionally eccentric. *The Essential* covers the ground adequately, in generally good sound, but the notes are skimpy, there's no chronology, and 'Frisco Town' plays where 'That Will Be Alright' is listed. The sound quality is more variable on Proper's *Me And My Chauffeur*, but the annotation is thorough and detailed; only one, not very good, track is from 1944. Aim's 18 tracks have been subjected to aggressive, bass-loving audio processing, and the notes are impressionistic.

In My Girlish Days also has 18 tracks, generally excellent sound, and the widest timespan of any of these cherrypickers but, while chronological order isn't a shibboleth, it's hard to see merit in Blues Forever's reverse chronology; the intention may be to hide the slightly inferior sound of the earliest sides at the end of the disc. Telegraphic notes and the listing of 'Black Bop' and 'Bill Dettles' among the musicians are further demerits. *Crazy Crying Blues* is cheap, but rules itself out by dreadful remastering. Next to it, *Hot Stuff* sounds great, but objectively is no more than adequate. The notes are vague and discursive; *Moonshine* is the same collection, with no notes at all.

Hoodoo Lady features 'Chicago Minnie', performing mainly with small bands in the gap between husbands; Columbia's presentation is superior, but given that the label owns the masters, the sound restoration is no more than adequate, and the choice of material uninspired. EPM and Charly cover similar ground, but both labels also include tracks with Son Joe, and both dip into the postwar Columbia sessions, although EPM only include two tracks from this period. This *Me And My Chauffeur* shares six tracks with *Hoodoo Lady*, and offers generally similar sound quality; it also includes Son Joe's 'Diggin' My Potatoes' and 'My Black Buffalo', seemingly on grounds of rarity rather than quality. *American Blues Legend* offers skilful transfers and, as the only selective CD to include much from post-1944 Columbia, is a useful way to avoid Wolf's alternative-takefest; unfortunately two of these six tracks are dominated by Fred Williams's noisemaking. CS

Memphis Slim (1915–88)
VOCAL, PIANO, ORGAN, CELESTE, HARPSICHORD, CLAVICHORD

John L. Chatman, who later took his father's name, Peter, was born in the city that gave him his recording pseudonym and died in Paris, France, his home since 1962. He'd moved there via Chicago, where he made his first records, and St Louis, his postwar base as a popular R&B artist. Slim was quick to spot changing tastes, and was an early beneficiary of white interest in blues. Making his first European visit in 1960, he found the more relaxed racial atmosphere congenial, swiftly returned and married a Parisienne. For the rest of his life he made a comfortable living from the copyright of 'Every Day I Have The Blues' and as a self-proclaimed 'ambassador of the blues'.

*** **The Complete Recordings 1940/1941**
EPM Blues Collection 15803 *Memphis Slim; unknown (h); Leroy Batchelor (b, prob. v); Alfred Elkins (b); Washboard Sam (wb). 8/40–12/41.*
(***) **This Life I'm Living**
Our World 3309 *As above.* 8/40–12/41.
*** **This Life I'm Living**
History 201948 2CD *As above.* 8/40–12/41.
*** **Grinder Man Blues**
Snapper Complete Blues SBLUECD 021 *As above.* 8/40–12/41.

For OKeh Peter Chatman majored in unexciting imitations of Washboard Sam; moving to Bluebird, he became Memphis Slim and found his own voice, both literally and artistically. He still owed a good deal to Roosevelt Sykes at this stage, although his fingering was neither as complex nor always as accurate as his inspiration's, but his original, often sardonically humorous lyrics were delivered in the sonorous, dark-brown tones that remained his trademark.

EPM present all the early recordings apart from three alternative takes, later issued on the deleted *Bluebird Recordings* (Bluebird 66720); this near-completeness is laudable, although it entails listening to a painfully out-of-tune harmonica on 'Blues At Midnight'. On *This Life I'm Living* (eccentrically credited to Peter Chatman) Our World's aggressive audio processing is more acceptable than usual, but there is a distracting vocal echo on 'Diggin' My Potatoes No. 2'. Snapper's 20 tracks are acceptably remastered, but since 'Blues At Midnight' is included at the expense of better material, one might as well have it on EPM. History's *This Life I'm Living*, which is shared with T-Bone Walker, also has reasonable sound for its low price; it includes all but two of Slim's prewar songs, but 'Blues At Midnight' is not merely among them, it actually opens the CD.

*** **The Complete Recordings Vol. 2 1946/1948**
EPM Blues Collection 15986 *Memphis Slim; Ernest Cotton (as, ts); Alex Atkins (as); Willie Dixon (b, v); Big Crawford, Charles Jenkins (b); unknown (d).* 46–48.
(***) **Blue And Lonesome**
Arpeggio ARB 012 *As above.* 46–48.
*** **The Complete Recordings Vol. 3 1948/1950**
EPM Blues Collection 16014 *Memphis Slim; Alex Atkins (as); Ernest Cotton, Timothy Overton (ts); Floyd Hunt (p); Big Crawford, Betty Overton, Alfred Elkins (b); Leon Hooper,*

unknown (d); Lillie Mae Kirkman, The Vagabonds (v). 48–50.
(***) The Very Best Of Memphis Slim: Messin' Around With The Blues
Collectables COL-CD-2892 *As for above three CDs, except omit Hunt, Elkins, Hooper, Kirkman, The Vagabonds. 46–1/49.*

By the mid-'40s Slim was leading a band that emulated the jump-blues combos of Louis Jordan and Joe Liggins, but differed from them in having neither brass nor guitar. The result, even on up-tempo numbers, was a pungent, penumbral sound, and these recordings make a fascinating alternative to the emerging Chicago guitar bands. EPM's thorough research makes some important recordings generally available for the first time, and careful listening has clarified a long-running confusion over remakes, which impairs the annotation of the selective CDs discussed below. Completeness embraces some below-par compositions, some low-fidelity originals and the presence of the world's worst drummer on four tracks of *Vol. 2*, but these are still valuable compilations.

Blue And Lonesome gets the discographical details right; being cloned from EPM, it should. Cursory notes recycled from *Soul Blues* (see below) replace the source CD's scholarship. Collectables' 27 tracks purport to be nearly all the Hy-Tone and Miracle recordings later purchased by King, but as usual the four titles that Slim remade for King appear in place of the originals. The remakes are the better versions so, like the cover drawing of a guitarist, this may only matter to pedants.

**(*) Every Day I Have The Blues
Prism Leisure PLATCD 497 *As for relevant CDs above. 8/40–48.*
*** Messin' Around With The Blues
[Blue Boar CDBB 1029] *As for relevant CDs above. 8/40–49.*
*** Life Is Like That
King KCD 6006 *As for relevant CDs above. 46–1/49.*
*** Ambassador Of The Blues
[Indigo IGOCD 2505] *As for relevant CDs above. 46–49.*

Most of Prism's selection (in rather brittle sound) is from OKeh and Bluebird, but there's just enough later material included to ensure that non-chronological programming leads to disconcerting stylistic lurches. Blue Boar use three early sides as a disparate prelude to 18 postwar titles; King and Indigo confine themselves to the early postwar years. Sound on all three is as good as can reasonably be expected. *Ambassador Of The Blues* carries a curmudgeonly note, but its 25 tracks (King's plus eight) are adroitly programmed and offer best value to those who don't need everything.

*** The Complete Recordings Vol. 4 1951/1952 [sic]
EPM Blues Collection 16039 *Memphis Slim; Alex Atkins (as); Timothy Overton, Neil Green, Purcell Brockenborough, Nelson Berry, Charles Ferguson (ts); Matt Murphy (g, b); Ike Perkins (g); Alfred Elkins, Ransom Knowling, John Frazier, Henry Taylor (b); Leon Hooper, Oscar Larkin, Otho Allen (d); Terry Timmons, unknown (v); unknown (sp). 50–11/52.*

The House Rockers' sax-dominated sound persists on *Vol. 4*, but there are changes: Dinah Washington soundalike Terry Timmons duets with Slim on four far from vital songs, and in two cases irredeemably soppy ones. Jazz guitarist Ike Perkins sits in on another four titles, among them "Fore Day", a Hawaiian guitar feature that owes everything to 'Floyd's Guitar Blues'. Matt Murphy's appearance on the final two tracks is a harbinger of change, but for the moment it's the second tenor that catches the ear, replacing Atkins's alto and making the harmonies still more plump and dusky.

**(*) The Ultimate Memphis Slim Hits Collection
Blue City BCCD-816 *As for relevant CDs above, except add T-Bone Walker (g); Jump Jackson (d). 47–10/62.*

Twenty-nine tracks in fair sound, the first of them from a 1962 European tour, without notes or discography.

**** The Come Back
Delmark DE-762 *Memphis Slim; Neil Green, Purcell Brockenborough, Jimmy Conley (ts); Matt Murphy (g, b, v); Curtis Mosley, Henry Taylor (b); Otho Allen, Fred Below (d); Terry Timmons, unknowns (v). 11/52–9/54.*
***(*) Memphis Slim U.S.A.
Delmark DE-710 *Memphis Slim; Neil Green, Jimmy Conley (ts); Matt Murphy (g); Henry Taylor (b); Otho Allen (d); unknown (bgo). 3–9/54.*

'I couldn't stand no damn guitar … but Murphy was such a damn genius, man, till I had to use him.' Thus Memphis Slim, saying most of what needs saying about these CDs. Murphy fuses the ideas of West Coast and Memphis guitarists with his own technical and imaginative brilliance; the complexity and energy of his lines, inspired by swing and bop saxophonists, unhinge the jaw. His playing sent a charge through the House Rockers, and United captured the results on recordings whose quality is way ahead of most small labels of the day. Both CDs are splendid, but *Memphis Slim U.S.A.*, filled out with alternative takes and some inconsequential jamming, is a notch below *The Come Back*, where a generous complement of instrumentals spotlights Conley's full-throated tenor as well as Murphy.

**(*) Midnight
WSM 31642 *Similar to above two CDs. 11/51–9/54.*

Ten unannotated tracks, mostly from United.

♛ **** At The Gate Of Horn
Charly SNAP 137 *Memphis Slim; John Calvin (as, ts); Alex Atkins (as); Ernest Cotton (ts); Matt Murphy (g); Sam Chatmon (b); Billie Stepney (d). 1/58–8/59.*
**** At The Gate Of Horn
Collectables COL-CD-7130 *As above, except Calvin plays ts only. 8/59.*

The Gate of Horn was a club which catered to the new, white audience that bought LPs of (what it could consider) folk music, but this is uncompromising R&B, recorded in the Vee-Jay studios with a band who charge full-tilt at the playlist behind Slim at his most brass-lunged and piano-pounding. He'd had already recorded some of these songs more than once, but these are the versions to cherish. Collectables reissue the original LP; Charly usefully append four songs released on singles.

(***) The Come Back & Other Classics
Masters 1129 *As above, except add Benny Waters (ss, ts), Guy Pedersen (b), Kansas Fields (d). 8/59–5/62.*

Vee-Jay material (see above) dovetails well with 1962 Paris recordings (see below), but playing time is short and there are no notes; either source disc offers better value.

*** **Chicago Blues Masters Vol. 1**
Capitol CDP 29375 *Memphis Slim; Muddy Waters (g); Otis Spann (p); Al Hall, unknown (b); Shep Sheppard, poss. Francis Clay (d).* 4/59–c. 2/61.

*** **Broken Soul Blues**
BGO BGOCD 373 *As above, except omit Spann, Hall, Sheppard.* c. 2/61.

Broken Soul Blues, often misreported as a 1959 Carnegie Hall concert, includes two tracks by Muddy Waters without Slim, and two by Slim on which Otis Spann has been wrongly said to play second piano. Some genuine 1959 live material is added on *Chicago Blues Masters*: two more Slim-free numbers by Muddy, and three by Slim; Spann really does contribute to one of these. A slow-burning 'Stackalee' apart, the 1961 session is mainly notable for the chance to hear Waters in an unusual context, although he fluctuates in the mix and sometimes goes out of tune. Muddy plays with more fire on the 1959 tracks, and the duet with Spann boisterously re-creates an aspect of the *From Spirituals To Swing* concerts presented at the same venue 20 years earlier.

** **The Folkways Years 1959–1973**
Smithsonian Folkways SFW CD 40128 *Memphis Slim; Jazz Gillum (h, v); Pete Seeger (bj, v); Arbee Stidham (g, v); Matt Murphy (g); Willie Dixon (b, v); Jump Jackson (d).* 59–73.

The Folkways Years is too keen to touch all bases, hence a concluding organ solo, fittingly titled 'The Gimmick'. A clever vocal arrangement of 'Stewball' stands out among too many collaborations with Willie Dixon. There are also solo numbers, three duets with Murphy which are the CD's best tracks, and accompaniments to Gillum (past it), Stidham (one of two tracks with abominable drumming) and Seeger, in full-strength poseur mode on 'Midnight Special'. Slim's vocals are often convincingly mournful, but he has fingering problems on fast tunes like 'The Dirty Dozens', and when he's alone defective harmony, with right-hand chord changes ignored in the bass, is a frequent problem.

** **Raining The Blues**
Fantasy 24705/[Ace CDCH 485] *Memphis Slim; Buster Brown (h); Lafayette Thomas (g); Wendell Marshall (b).* 4–11/60.

(*) **Blue This Evening
1201 Music 9034 *Memphis Slim; Alexis Korner (g); Stan Greig (d).* 7/60.

(*) **Blues Masters Vol. 9
Storyville STCD 8009 *Memphis Slim; Erik Mølbach (b); Bjørn Elniff (d).* 8/60–6/61.

*** **Travelling With The Blues**
Storyville STCD 8021 *Memphis Slim.* 8/60.

** **Memphis Slim's Tribute To Big Bill Broonzy Etc.**
Candid CCD 79023 *Memphis Slim; Jazz Gillum (h, v); Arbee Stidham (g, v).* 1/61.

** **Memphis Slim, U.S.A.**
Candid CCD 79024 *As above.* 1/61.

** **Blues In The Evening**
Drive CD DRIVE 3208 *As above.* 1/61.

On *Raining The Blues* Memphis Slim plays alone, in duet with Brown and in a trio with Thomas and Marshall. The harp–piano combination works better than might be expected, but elsewhere Slim is usually phoning it in; his ennui spreads to Marshall, and Thomas's potential is largely wasted. An occasional renamed standard has more willpower, but these moments don't compensate for an overdose of jaded instrumentals.

Slim is usually more lively on *Blue This Evening*, recorded in Britain, but the intermittent between-song narration is desultory, and 'Memphis Woman' is not the first or the last bored reunion with his 'Beer Drinking Woman'. Korner's guitar is often underpowered, while Greig errs in the other direction. The title track is the first appearance on disc of 'If You See Kay', done so deadpan that it's easy to miss the joke.

Blues Masters' first 11 tracks, with a rhythm section, are focused and quite well done, unlike most of the unissued and ex-anthology solos which complete the CD. There's a glut of wrong notes on '3 And 1 Boogie' and 'Frankie And Johnny', and the celeste's sugar plum fairy pings are wildly at odds with the sombre lyrics of 'Bertha May'. The harmonies are usually better controlled on the other Storyville CD, where Slim talks a new audience through his version of blues history while playing some favourite numbers. In 1960 this disc was information-rich for Europeans, and although the concept has dated, the music's still pleasant.

There's a similar air of the magic lantern lecture about the parade of other people's greatest hits on Candid's *Tribute* LP, here reissued in indifferent sound. Stidham loses his way during 'I Feel So Good', and elsewhere only confirms his journeyman status, while Gillum's final recordings are a ghost of what he once could do. The transfers are better on the second album, which was recorded at the same session, and the songs are less uniformly hackneyed, but wrong notes are a recurrent problem, even on a song as frequently performed as 'Harlem Bound'. For what it's worth, Drive's selection from these sessions has better sound than either Candid CD.

**** **Ambassador Of The Blues**
Collectors Edition CBCD 020 *Memphis Slim; John Calvin (as); Johnny Board (ts); Matt Murphy (g); Sam Chatmon (b); Billie Stepney (d).* 61.

**** **Soul Blues**
Ember EMBCD 3422 *As above.* 61.

**** **I'll Just Keep On Singing The Blues**
Savoy Jazz SVY 17296 *As above.* 61.

***(*) **Born With The Blues**
Fuel 2000 302 061 410 *As above, except add unknown (ts), Lowell Fulson, unknown (g), Carey Bell, unknown (b), S. P. Leary, unknown (d).* 7/60–10/69.

It seems unlikely that any blues singer recorded more intensively than Memphis Slim did in 1961, probably in order to finance his move to France. Most releases were aimed at the 'folk-blues' market, but he made an outstanding return to his R&B roots for the Strand LP of which these are all reissues; only the fake sobbing on 'Cold Blooded Woman' is regrettable. As at Vee-Jay, Sam Chatmon's band, The Sparks, supply backing; once again Matt Murphy is all over every track, but he never outguns Johnny Board's resourceful, snarling tenor. *Soul Blues* is also available in a slipcase with *John Lee Hooker Sings The Blues*; their collective number is Ember EMBDCD 003 and, superficial notes apart, this is good value. Fuel 2000 tack on two numbers from the identically titled Jewel CD discussed below, and two more from a 1960 London session with a sparky rhythm section and an inventive tenorist.

(**) The Essential Masters
Purple Pyramid CLP 1084 *As for relevant CDs above.* 50–61.

Six tracks from Strand, seven from Candid and four from the early '50s are too heterogeneous; the notes are not improved by the delusion that Memphis Slim and Lightnin' Slim are the same person.

*** Alone With My Friends
Original Blues Classics OBCCD 581 *Memphis Slim; Josh White (sp).* 4/61.

The programme consists of well-known numbers by others, most of them from the '30s and '40s, although 'Goin' To The River' is a startling revival of a Blind Lemon Jefferson song. Slim sings and plays straightforwardly, without histrionics or an excess of tedious narration.

*** All Kinds Of Blues
Original Blues Classics OBCCD 507 *Memphis Slim.* 61.

The ingeniously explicit 'Churnin' Man Blues' is a welcome newcomer, but Slim had recorded most of the tunes here already, some of them several times. These versions are generally better handled, though, as can be heard by comparing 'Three-In-One Boogie' and 'Frankie And Johnny Boogie' with their counterparts on Storyville.

**(*) Steady Rolling Blues
Original Blues Classics OBCCD 523 *Memphis Slim.* 10/61.

Some effective piano blues with an emphasis on *double entendre* are compromised by four tracks with organ; 'Celeste's Boogie' [*sic*] is moderately successful, but elsewhere Slim's pianistic technique doesn't suit the instrument, and he employs an array of nasty, squawking tone colours.

***(*) The Blues Is Everywhere
Collectables COL 5904 *Memphis Slim; Benny Waters (cl, ss, ts); Guy Pedersen (b); Kansas Fields (d).* 5/62.

At his first recording date after settling in Paris, Slim collaborates with a local bassist and two fellow exiles with illustrious jazz backgrounds. Waters, who also had R&B pedigree with Roy Milton, is obviously having a nostalgic blast, Fields's drumming is as tasteful as it's frisky, and Pedersen keeps Slim on the harmonic rails. There are no repertoire surprises, and facetiousness taints 'All By Myself', but this piece of the jigsaw shouldn't be overlooked.

**(*) Memphis Slim And Willie Dixon In Paris: Baby Please Come Home!
Original Blues Classics OBCCD 582 *Memphis Slim; Willie Dixon (b, v); Philippe Combelle (d, v).* 11/62.

**(*) Aux Trois Mailletz
Verve 519 729 *As above.* 11/62.

Despite the order of artists, Dixon is lead singer on eight tracks of 13, and this club set is for those who don't find his writing poppish and his delivery emollient. 'Cool Blooded' ('Cold Blooded' on Verve) achieves a grumbling unease, but most of the time Dixon and Slim make too few demands on themselves, their music and their listeners.

**(*) L'Ambassadeur Du Blues
Warner Blues 25576 *As above, except add Harold Ashby (ts), Wally Richardson, Lafayette Thomas (g), Wendell Marshall (b), Gus Johnson (d).* 4/60–11/62.

Tracks are selected from *Baby Please Come Home!, Raining The Blues, Steady Rolling Blues* (no organ, thankfully), *Alone With My Friends, All Kinds Of Blues* and *Willie's Blues*. Four titles from the first of these is too many; the last-named (for detailed discussion see Willie Dixon's entry) furnishes two neurasthenic instrumentals with Ashby, Richardson and Johnson.

*** Legacy Of The Blues Vol. 7
GNP-Crescendo GNPD 0017 *Memphis Slim; unknown (t); Eddie Chamblee (ts); unknowns (s); Billy Butler (g); Lloyd Trotman (b); Herbie Lovelle (d).* 10/67.

*** The Sonet Blues Story: Memphis Slim
Universal 986 925-3 *As above.* 10/67.

*** I Am The Blues
Prestige CDSGP 080 *As above.* 10/67.

*** Born With The Blues
Jewel JCD-5004 *Memphis Slim; Carey Bell (h, b); Lowell Fulson (g); S. P. Leary (d).* 10/69.

Most of the ten tracks on *Legacy Of The Blues* and its Universal reissue lurk among *I Am The Blues*' 20; the recordings, which have also been dated to 1966 and 1969, were made during a visit home. By this time readers will have detected the view that Slim is usually better with a band, and the New York studio veterans who back him do an expectedly competent job. The trouble is that they and Slim seldom exceed that level, although Chamblee's snorting solo on 'This Little Woman' and Butler's intuitive responses to a soulful vocal on 'Forty Years Or More' (which is 'Plow Hand Blues', Big Bill's plaint against sharecropping) are exceptions. Both songs are only on Prestige.

Born With The Blues is worth hearing, even though Slim plays an unresponsive piano, Bell's harmonica is muffled on its two appearances, and some numbers end abruptly as feedback is hastily chopped off. Recorded in Paris, the session was no doubt just another gig for all concerned, but Slim and the visiting firemen work quickly and professionally; a happy side-effect of sticking to mostly familiar songs is that Slim gets no chance to become either pretentious or portentous.

** Blue Memphis
Wounded Bird WOU 1899 *Memphis Slim; Henry Lowther, Harry Beckett, Kenny Wheeler (t); Nick Evans, John Manfred (tb); Carl Jenkins, Brian Smith, Stan Saltzman [Sulzmann], Jerry Gibbs, Peter King (s); Duster Bennett (h); Pete Wingfield (o, p, cel); John Paul Jones (o); Peter Green, Chris Spedding, Ray Dempsey (g); Larry Steel, Stephen Thompson (b); Conrad Isidore (d); Tristan Fry (perc); Johnny Dean (chimes).* 6/70.

When it was an LP, this disc and its autobiographical first side were called *Blue Memphis Suite*; the threat of a meeting between the blues and prog-rock pretentiousness is largely fulfilled. The horn charts are not bad, but the British session veterans playing them must compete with cluttered, twiddly keyboard sounds and grandstanding guitarists; Peter Green's inarticulate fluency is especially annoying. On Side 2, where the arrangements continue to resemble a musical food fight, Slim's thoughts on Vietnam and the trial of the Chicago Seven have dated, and are conveyed via prosaic, dashed-off lyrics; so is a tribute to the recently deceased 'Otis Spann And Earl Hooker'.

** Memphis Heat
Universal/Maison de Blues 982 274–2 *Memphis Slim; Wayne Jackson (t); Jack Hale (tb); Andrew Love, Ed Logan (ts); James Mitchell (bs); Terry Manning (h); Joel Scott Hill (g, v); Henry Vestine, James Shane (g); Richard Hite, Antonio de la Barreda (b); Fito de la Parra (d).* 9/70–11/73.

***(*) Southside Reunion
Universal/Maison de Blues 982 274–3 *Memphis Slim; Jimmy Conley (as, ts); A. C. Reed (ts); Junior Wells (h); Buddy Guy (g, v); Phil Guy (g); Earnest Johnson (b); Roosevelt Shaw (d).* 9/70.

On *Memphis Heat* Slim does assorted familiar songs (and 'Paris', a trivial suck-up) in incompatible association with two incarnations of Canned Heat, whose guitarists spin a web of blues-rock cliché atop morose, self-absorbed bass and drums. The Memphis Horns are overdubbed on several tracks, but minimalist charts offer them few opportunities to shine.

What a difference a week makes. Guy, Wells and (crucially) their Chicago club band were touring with The Rolling Stones; on *Southside Reunion* they're joined by Jimmy Conley, who'd followed his former boss to Paris. This isn't quite a return to the glories of Slim's days with Matt Murphy and the House Rockers, but it's the next-best thing, for in 1970 Guy was still playing logical fills and solos, rather than clowning in Eric Clapton's shadow. Wells also plays with concise good taste, but he's often under-recorded and struggles to compete with the saxes. He excels on 'Help Me Some', but elsewhere could have been omitted without much harm.

***(*) Double Barreled Boogie
Universal/Maison de Blues 982 242–2 *Memphis Slim; Roosevelt Sykes (p, g, v).* 12/70.

When he sings 'Mr Sykes Blues' it's obvious why Slim once said, 'They used to call me the carbon copy Roosevelt Sykes.' In 1931 he'd replaced the Honeydripper as pianist at the Midway Café in Memphis, and their between-song reminiscing is not the least entertaining aspect of this session. The playlist is similarly retrospective: sticking to familiar numbers from the '30s and '40s makes it easy to generate two-piano accompaniments that give the material unexpected freshness. The stereo separation shows off the pianists' easy interaction very clearly, though it also reveals that Sykes is unexpectedly tentative on 'Going Down Slow'. The pleasure the two men take in their reunion is evident, and it spills over into their music-making. *Double Barreled Boogie* is very worthwhile, despite Sykes's rudimentary guitar on 'Roosevelt's Daddy's Blues'.

**(*) Paris Mississippi Blues
Universal 981 961//Sunnyside SSC 3025 2CD *Memphis Slim; Wayne Jackson, Bobby Haughey, John Mitchell, unknown (t); Jack Hale, unknown (tb); Jimmy Conley (as, ts); Sonny Criss (as); A. C. Reed, Andrew Love, Ed Logan, Eddie Mordue, Keith Bird (ts); James Mitchell (bs); Charlie McCoy (h); Jacques Denjean (o, p); Roosevelt Sykes (p, v); David Briggs (p); Steve Davis (clavinet); Buddy Guy (g, v); Mickey Baker, Phil Guy, Russ Hicks, Dale Saliero, Reggie Young, Henry Vestine, Peter Green, Freddie King, Chris Ray, Chris Spedding (g); Henri Tischlitz, Willie Dixon, Earnest Johnson, Guy Pedersen, Henry 'South Pole' Strzelecki, Antonio de la Barreda, Stephen Thompson, Benny Turner, Andy Brown, Dave Wintour, unknown (b); Michel Denis, Philippe Combelle, Roosevelt Shaw, André Arpino, Kenneth Buttrey, Fito de la Parra, Conrad Isidore, Melvin Jones, Barry de Souza, unknown (d); Peter Ahern,* Tristan Fry (perc); *Sister Gerry, Doris Dawson, Dolores Powell. (v).* 11/62–3/75.

Paris Mississippi Blues tries to rehabilitate Slim's later output. It samples a swarm of LPs that have not been transferred to CD, and also includes three tracks from *Aux Trois Maillets*, five from *Double Barreled Boogie*, three from *Southside Reunion* and one apiece from *Blue Memphis (Suite)* and *Memphis Heat*. The accompanists range from jazz-oriented acoustic rhythm sections to electric blues and blues-rock bands. There are also the massive forces assembled for *Going Back To Tennessee*'s incoherent attempts to fuse blues with C&W, and for *Memphis Slim Plays Classical American Music – The Blues*, which on the evidence of 'Prodigal Son' was as classical as Victor Silvester, and about as bluesy. The package features extensive, thoughtful notes and some striking photographs, but too often the music defeats itself. The fifth columnists are offhand performance, slapdash compositions and the staleness induced by repetition; if there was a way to revitalize 'Everyday I Have The Blues', it wasn't Freddie King's flirtation with rock.

** Live At The Caveau De La Huchette, Paris 1977
Laserlight 17 151 *Memphis Slim; Michel Denis (d).* 2/77.

** Live At The Hot Club
Milan 72557 *As above.* 12/80.

** HCF Boogie
Milan 198 522 *As above.* 12/80.

**(*) Boogie For 2 Pianos
Jazztrade SL-CD-1501 *Memphis Slim; Jean-Paul Amouroux (p); Gilles Chevaucherie (b); Michel Denis (d).* 11/81.

Years of performing a largely static repertoire to an audience that venerated him for living in France did Slim's art no favours. By this time 'All By Myself' is played *prestissimo*, lasts about a minute and includes a yodelling chorus; like Slim's indulgence in deliberate wrong-note breaks and codas, it's emblematic of boredom. The frequently vulgar drumming is made more off-putting by the twin suspicions that Denis doesn't know it's vulgar and Slim does. The Milan CDs are from the same concert; *HCF Boogie* is shorter and reprogrammed, but its sound is no better.

Ammons and Johnson they're not, but on *Boogie For 2 Pianos* Slim and Amouroux bounce off each other fairly entertainingly, and Denis is much more involved and attentive to detail than on the live CDs. Chevaucherie knows how to slap that bass, and proves it during two solos, but otherwise he's almost entirely redundant. There are moments of dislocation between the pianos, but more seriously detrimental are the bleating organ on 'Blues In The Afternoon' and the ridiculous textures produced when an allegedly 'Low Down Harpsichord' squeaks and clanks feebly over piano bass figures.

**(*) Boogie For My Friends
Black & Blue BB 454 *Memphis Slim; Bob Stroger (b); Odie Payne (d).* 11/83–4/86.

This is nominally a concept album: most tracks are instrumentals, titled using the formula 'Blues/Boogie For X', but there's no attempt to replicate the styles of the dedicatees. The involuntary wrong-note problem recurs, especially when Slim plays solo (there are some horrible discords on 'Blues For Jimmy'), and he does better when assisted by his visitors, two of Chicago's most reliable session musicians. The occasional singing is more reflective than usual, perhaps as a result of age and recent illness; 'Roll And Tumble' is unexpectedly fine.

** **Americans** [sic] **Swinging In Paris**
EMI 539666 Memphis Slim; Jean-Paul Amouroux (o, p, cel); Michel Denis (d). 8/84.

Most of this live set is two-piano boogie; there are three brief, under-recorded vocals, two tracks with Amouroux's organ (even more dispensable than Slim's) and a decent stab at 'Yancey Special', marred by unnecessary celeste decorations. There's also some unintentional rhythmic and harmonic slippage and a shortage of emotional depth, save on the atypically contemplative 'Huchette Blues'; more like it would have made for more satisfying listening. CS

Bob Merrill (born 1918)
VOCAL, TRUMPET

The Oklahoma-born Merrill played trumpet in various territory bands in the late '30s and early '40s, then both played and sang with Jay McShann (1942–44) and Cootie Williams (1945–49). He subsequently made a few vocal recordings under his own name. He was last heard of in the early '60s.

(*) The Complete Recordings 1943–1961
Blue Moon BMCD 6041 Merrill; Dave Mitchell, Jesse Jones, Willie Cook, Cootie Williams, E. V. Perry, George Treadwell, Billy Ford, Gene Redd, Otis Gamble (t); Alonzo Pettiford, Alfonso Fook, Rudy Morrison, Ed Burke, Edward Johnson, Bob Horton, Julius Watson, Al Outcalt (tb); Chuck Clarke (as, ts); John Jackson, Rudolph Dennis, Rupert Cole, Daniel Williams, unknown (as); Paul Quinichette, Bill Goodson, Sam 'The Man' Taylor, Everett Gaines, Edwin Johnson, Count Hastings, Ike Quebec, Willis Jackson, unknowns (ts); Rae Brodely, Bob Ashton, Eddie De Verteuil (bs); Jay McShann, Arnold Jarvis, Lester Fauntleroy, unknowns (p); Sam Allen, Pee Wee Tinney, unknown (g); Gene Ramey, Dallas Bartley, Norman Keenan, Leonard Swain, unknowns (b); Dan Graves, George 'Butch' Ballard, Sylvester Payne, Gus Johnson, William Parker, unknowns (d); band, unknown female group (v). 12/43–60/61.

Merrill is an enthusiastic and technically well-equipped vocalist whose '40s recordings, mostly with Cootie Williams's orchestra, are creditable examples of blues singing in a big-band swing setting. He seems to have modelled his style on Eddie Vinson's, borrowing the hoarse whooping effect, as in 'You Took My Woman' and 'Blues Without Booze' (both written by Leonard Feather and Wesley Wilson); there's also a hint of Wynonie Harris in 'I Shoulda Been Thinkin' Instead Of Drinkin'' and of Roy Brown in 'The Blues Is Here T'Nite'. Apart from a couple of standards and one or two leaves from the Louis Jordan book like 'Save The Bones For Henry Jones', he chiefly recorded blues and boogie numbers. While he usually gave them something better than routine readings, no one is likely to conclude from this CD that his obscurity is a monstrous injustice. TR

Hazel Meyers
VOCAL, POSS. BANJO

Meyers was a 'feature star' in the revue Steppin' High *in 1924, and can be traced in a couple of other shows, but disappears from the African-American press after 1928.*

(*) Hazel Meyers – Vol. 1 (1923–1924)
Document DOCD-5430 Meyers; Joe Smith, Howard Scott, Elmer Chambers, Bubber Miley (c); Don Redman, Bob Fuller (cl); Porter Grainger, Leslie A. Hutchinson ('Hutch'), Fletcher Henderson, Louis Hooper, unknown (p); unknown (bj). c. 9/23–c. 6/24.

*** **Edna Hicks – Hazel Meyers – Laura Smith – Vol. 2 (1923–1927)**
Document DOCD-5431 Meyers; Bubber Miley, Louis Metcalf, Shirley Clay or Bernie Young (c); Preston Jackson (tb); Bob Fuller (cl); Artie Starks (as); Louis Hooper, Fats Waller, Richard M. Jones or George Reynolds, unknown (p); Johnny St Cyr (bj); unknown (eff). c. 7/24–6/26.

At her best, Hazel Meyers could be very good indeed, but her recording career started with limp renditions of vaudeville songs, limply accompanied by Porter Grainger. She doesn't have what it takes to cover Ida Cox's 'Graveyard Dream Blues' either, but things look up with the arrival of Joe Smith and Fletcher Henderson. Although Smith's bizarre hiccuping on 'Awful Moanin' Blues' is awful indeed, he encourages Meyers to deliver 'Chicago Bound Blues', another Ida Cox number, with much more authority. The return of Porter Grainger on two songs recorded early in 1924 confirms that the quality of Meyers's performances was heavily dependent on the quality of both her material and her accompanists. On *Vol. 1*'s last nine tracks, she's backed by the likes of Bubber Miley, Don Redman and Louis Hooper, and seems a different singer, enthusiastic, hot and swinging where before she had been staid, cautious and short on blues feeling. As so often with the women singers of the early '20s, it appears that she has taken a lesson from Bessie Smith. The change is not irrevocable, unfortunately; 'Black Star Line', which satirizes Marcus Garvey and West Indians, is sung with commendable lack of conviction (and incompetently engineered to boot), and 'You Better Build Love's Fire' is over-enunciated pop music, with minimalist banjo, possibly played by Meyers herself.

Two songs which were unavailable for *Vol. 1* are included on *Female Blues (1921–1928) – The Remaining Titles* (Document DOCD-1005). Of the 11 tracks by Meyers on *Vol. 2*, 'You'll Never Have No Luck By Quittin' Me' is an awful song, awfully done. Fortunately, it's not typical, and her interactions with Miley, Hooper, Bob Fuller and Louis Metcalf are variously lively, majestic and impassioned, although the wind machine on 'Cold Weather Papa' makes for hard listening. On a couple of jazz songs, euphoniously accompanied by Fats Waller, Meyers successfully uses a lighter vocal tone. After a two-year break from recording, she bows out with two sides accompanied by Starks' Hot Five, a small Chicago band whose cheerful, unbuttoned playing encourages her to give of her best one last time. CS

Amos Milburn (1926–80)
VOCAL, PIANO

Born into a large Houston family, Amos Milburn discovered a natural talent for the piano when he was five years old. After service in the US Navy he took up music professionally, playing in Houston clubs and, from 1946 onwards, recording regularly for Aladdin. He stayed with the label until the late '50s, cutting some 150 sides, including two R&B #1s in 'Chicken Shack Boogie' (1949), which brought him awards that year from both Billboard *and* Down Beat, *and 'Bad Bad Whiskey' (1950). By the end of the '50s, however, his career had been wrecked by alcoholism and rock 'n' roll. He spent a couple of years with Motown in the early '60s, but little came of that, and his last years were racked with illness.*

*** **Amos Milburn 1946–1947**
Classics 5018 *Milburn; Maxwell Davis, unknown (ts); unknowns (g); unknowns (b); unknowns (d); unknown (v).* 9/46–10/47.
(***) **Chicken Shack Boogie**
[Blue Boar CDBB 1013] *As above.* 9/46–12/47.
*** **Amos Milburn 1948–1949**
Classics 5077 *Milburn; Maxwell Davis, Don Wilkerson, Willie Smith, unknown (ts); Willie Simpson Jr (bs); Gene Phillips, Chuck Norris, Johnny Brown, unknown (g); Ralph Hamilton, Harper Cosby, unknown (b); Jesse Sailes, Lee Young, Calvin Vaughan, unknown (d).* 10/48–12/49.
*** **Amos Milburn 1950–1951**
Classics 5117 *As above, except add Lawrence Norman, poss. Lawrence Marable, Oscar Lee Bradley, Eldeen McIntosh (d), unknown (v); omit Sailes, Young, Vaughan.* 1/50–4/51.
*** **Bad Bad Whiskey 1946–1950**
EPM Blues Collection 16002 *As for* Amos Milburn 1948–1949, *except add poss. Frank Haywood (g), Oscar Lee Bradley, Eldeen McIntosh (d), unknown (v); omit unknown (ts).* 9/46–9/50.
*** **Booze, Babes, Blues & Boogie: The Essential Amos Milburn**
[Indigo IGODCD 2506 2CD] *Similar to above.* 9/46–4/51.
*** **The Chicken Shack Boogie Man**
Proper PVCD 102 2CD *Similar to above.* 9/46–4/51.
(*) **The Best Of Amos Milburn: Down The Road Apiece
EMI America 27229 *Similar to above.* 11/47–9/56.

The Amos Milburn of the Aladdin recordings is clearly a man on the same musical track as his West Coast contemporaries Charles Brown, Ivory Joe Hunter and Floyd Dixon. Like them he specializes in slow blues and peppy piano boogies, diverging occasionally into pop balladry. He sings as if suffering from a chronic, if mild, head cold, the slightly blurred delivery creating a believable ambience of confidentiality or, on blues like 'After Midnite' or 'Train Time Blues' (which he borrowed from another contemporary, Cecil Gant), quiet reflection. His most popular numbers, though, tended to be more extrovert, such as 'Chicken Shack Boogie', which became so closely identified with him that he re-created its format of humorous narrative and boogie piano several times, as in 'Roomin' House Boogie' and 'Sax Shack Boogie'. A prolific poet of the liquor cabinet, he reblended 'Bad Bad Whiskey' – another catchy hit – as 'Good, Good Whiskey' and 'Vicious Vicious Vodka', following them with 'One Scotch, One Bourbon, One Beer'. The setting for many of these sides was piano trio or quartet plus tenor sax, the latter commonly played by Maxwell Davis; later recordings might add another horn or two.

The Indigo and Proper sets both work through the first five years of Milburn's Aladdin output, session by session, selecting somewhat differently but winding up in the same place with 'Just One More Drink'. Indigo's 48 tracks are not chronologically sequenced, while Proper's 52 are. There's a vast amount of overlap between them, as well as with the other, single, CDs: anyone plumping for the Proper will have everything on the Blue Boar set, and almost everything on the EPM. But the remastering is a shade sharper, and the notes better, on Indigo than on Proper. The reader who is serious about collecting Milburn's work should opt for the Classics series, which presents it in recording order. The first three volumes contain several tracks not found on any of the other CDs, and their successors will no doubt do the same. The rather restricted diet of blues and boogies is spiced on 1948–1949 by a couple of sessions with the Texas tenorist Don Wilkerson, zestfully abrasive on 'Bow-Wow!' and 'Don's Idea'. *The Best Of Amos Milburn* has only ten tracks, but they include the later Aladdin sides 'Let Me Go Home Whiskey', 'One Scotch, One Bourbon, One Beer' and the '56 remake of 'Chicken Shack Boogie' with New Orleans sidemen – none of which can be found on other Milburn CDs.

** **The Essential Recordings**
Purple Pyramid CLP 0961 *Milburn; Johnny Otis (p, d); Shuggie Otis (g, b); Edgar Willis (b); Melvin Wonder (d).* 77.

Milburn's Motown material is not currently available, but *The Essential Recordings* gives us his last session, originally made for Johnny Otis's Blues Spectrum label. In common with others for this label, the album recycled some of the artist's hits, in this instance 'Chicken Shack Boogie', 'Bad, Bad Whiskey' and 'One Scotch, One Bourbon, One Beer', but the sentimental journey is not an entirely happy one. Having suffered a stroke, Milburn could play only with his right hand; that much he manages adequately, but his voice is timeworn, and slow numbers like 'Bewildered' are wraiths of their originals rather than reincarnations. TR

Josie Miles
VOCAL

Miles was born in Summerville, South Carolina, perhaps around 1900, but was in New York by 1922, when she toured briefly in Shuffle Along. *The following year she appeared in* Runnin' Wild *and broadcast on WDT. Her career as a blues recording artist ended in 1925, and she reportedly moved to Kansas City, dying in a motoring accident 'c. 1953–1965', but even this vague information may apply to another singer of the same name.*

** **Josie Miles – Vol. 1 (1922–1924)**
Document DOCD-5466 *Miles; Joe Smith, Louis Metcalf, Bubber Miley, unknown (c); unknown (t); prob. George Brashear, unknowns (tb); poss. Clarence Robinson, prob. Bob Fuller, unknowns (cl); Q. Roscoe Snowden, Fletcher Henderson, Stanley Miller, Cliff Jackson, Arthur Ray, unknowns (p); poss. Ralph Escudero (bb).* c. 8/22–9/24.
(*) **Josie Miles – Vol. 2 (1924–1925)
Document DOCD-5467 *Miles; poss. Johnny Dunn, Louis Metcalf, Bubber Miley, Rex Stewart, unknown (c); Jake Frazier (tb); Bob Fuller (cl, as, ts); unknown (cl); unknowns (as); unknown (ts); poss. Charlie Pryme, Louis Hooper, unknowns (p); Elmer Snowden, unknowns (bj); Joe Davis, unknown (eff); Billy Higgins (v).* 10/24–c. 3/25.

Josie Miles began her recording career performing light-weight pop songs with an azure tinge. Her repertoire became bluesier, and she became a better blues singer, as A&R directors bowed to musical fashion, but for most of *Vol. 1* she is ill at ease, and not helped by her accompanists; even Joe Smith quacks feebly on 'War Horse Mamma'. Miles's pitch is quite often wobbly on these early sides, especially when she has to sing an unaccompanied break or hold an extended note. Only towards the end of the disc does she begin to sound secure; 'Pipe Dream Blues' is a confidently sung hophead's fantasy, and 'Freight Train Blues' is acceptable, if unable to stand comparison with Trixie Smith's definitive version. The lively 'Lovin' Henry Blues', on which Louis Metcalf and Cliff Jackson play a scurrying double-time chorus, is a harbinger of better things to come.

Vol. 2 finds Miles continuing to employ the more resonant, declamatory style she apparently developed during 1924. On most tracks she is accompanied by various permutations of Ajax house musicians, collectively dubbed the Choo Choo Jazzers; some of the same musicians constitute the Kansas City Five on Edison. The combination of a more outgoing Miles with a coterie of distinguished jazz musicians makes for a great improvement in the quality of most performances, although Bob Fuller occasionally resorts to sabotage by laughing clarinet. Despite Billy Higgins's narrow vocal range, half a dozen duets with him are lively and amusing, a version of the razor-relishing 'A to Z Blues' excepted as always. It's not all good news, unfortunately; on 'Mad Mama's Blues', Miles pays minimal attention to the song's extraordinary violence, and it marks the limits of her interpretive skills. 'De Clouds Are Gwine To Roll Away' and 'It Ain't Gonna Rain No Mo'' are sung in 'darkie' dialect with banjo accompaniment, presumably because producer Joe Davis saw a potential market; one can hardly blame Miles for two understandably dreadful performances.

Josie Miles was a minor figure, sometimes forceful and interesting, especially on her later recordings, but also artistically limited and inconsistent. It's often said that she re-emerged as the fiery Missionary Josephine Miles, from Kansas City, who made gospel recordings in 1928, but this seems most improbable; readers wishing to hear the evidence will find it on *Gospel Classics – Vol. 3* (Document DOCD-5350). CS

Lizzie Miles (1895–1963)
VOCAL, KAZOO

Elizabeth Mary Landreaux was half-sister to Edna Hicks. By 1914, she was married to J. C. Miles, and working with him in a travelling circus. He died of the Spanish flu in 1918, but Lizzie was soon back on stage, and established on the New York cabaret scene by the time she began recording. In 1924, Miles went to France, performing in Montmartre in both English and Creole French. (During this time, Edna Hicks suffered a horrific death by fire.) Returning to the USA in 1927, Miles went back to the Harlem clubs, but her career flagged in the Depression, and in 1935 she moved to Chicago, where she combined singing with work as a maid. She returned to her native New Orleans in 1942 to care for her mother, and remarried, becoming Lizzie Pajaud. Back in show business in 1950, still using Miles as her stage name, she became very active in revivalist jazz. In 1959 she retired from music to devote herself to prayer and penance, but she kept up an extensive correspondence with fans.

** Lizzie Miles – Vol. 1 (1922–1923)
Document DOCD-5458 *Miles; unknown (c); unknowns (t); unknowns (tb); unknowns (cl); unknown (ss); unknowns (as); Bob Ricketts, Clarence Johnson, unknowns (p); unknowns (vn); unknowns (bb); unknowns (d); unknowns (eff).* c. 2/22–4/23.

Lizzie Miles admired Sophie Tucker's bellowing approximation of African-American singing, and her forcefulness on these early recordings is startling; she bursts through the shroud of acoustic recording far more vividly than her accompanists. Unfortunately, the songs are often undistinguished Tin Pan Alley material, reaching a nadir early with 'Virginia Blues' and its vision of piccaninnies and 'darkies singing round the cabin doors'. The only identifiable musician on the first 19 tracks is Bob Ricketts, presumably responsible for arranging the coarse clichés played by Ricketts' Stars. The utterly swing-free white musicians of the OKeh house band are in even greater need of the cloak of anonymity. Only the last three tracks, with just Clarence Johnson's sparky stride piano, augmented on 'Haitian Blues' by Miles's unexpectedly hot kazoo, have much to recommend them.

**(*) Lizzie Miles – Vol. 2 (1923–1928)
Document DOCD-5459 *Miles; Louis Metcalf (c); Bob Fuller, unknown (cl); Clarence Johnson, Spencer Williams, Louis Hooper, Porter Grainger, unknown (p).* 4/23–2/28.

For much of *Vol. 2*, solo pianists provide the accompaniment; Louis Metcalf swaggers agreeably on two tracks, Miles kazoos it with a feeling on one, and a clarinet is heard on six. The reduction of forces is beneficial, for Miles, if not exactly subtle on the CD's opening tracks – she delivers the pop song 'My Pillow And Me' with an oomph that's utterly alien to its sad lyrics – at least doesn't feel obliged to blow out the windows. A four-year gap between tracks 8 and 9 coincides with Miles's stay in Paris, during which she presumably developed the more intimate delivery heard on the balance of the disc. She even uses it, very effectively, on 'A Good Man Is Hard To Find', but regrettably most of this later material is derived from worn 78s. As a result, it's often an effort to enjoy either the new Lizzie Miles or incidental pleasures like the chalumeau-register playing on 'Mean Old Bedbug Blues' and the hoodoo lyrics of 'Shootin' Star Blues'.

**** Lizzie Miles – Vol. 3 (1928–1939)
Document DOCD-5460 *Miles; King Oliver, Louis Metcalf, unknown (c); unknown (t); Henry Hicks (tb); Charlie Holmes, unknown (cl, as); Bob Fuller (cl); Albert Socarras (as, fl); Charlie Grimes (as); unknown (ts); Louis Hooper, Clarence Williams, poss. Cliff Jackson, Jelly Roll Morton, Harry Brooks, Porter Grainger, unknown (p); Elmer Snowden, unknown (bj); Teddy Bunn (g); Pops Foster (b); Bass Moore (bb); unknown (d).* 5/28–10/39.

This is the one to get; the sound quality is better, sometimes verging on superior, she's figured out how to balance her voice against a band, and the musicians are distinctly classy. The calisthenic briskness of 'Shake It Down', which opens the disc, makes an enjoyable alternative to Lillian Glinn's sultriness, and the blend of Afro-Cuban Albert Socarras's skylark flute with King Oliver's stateliness on 'You're Such A Cruel Papa To Me' is so unexpectedly lovely that it's easy to overlook Miles's warm and subtle singing. The same danger arises when she works with 'Jasper Davis and His Orchestra', as Louis Metcalf and Henry Hicks shoot the breeze over Bass Moore's acrobatic grunting. Speaking of which, 'My Man O'War', which Miles recalled as 'my biggest tip getter', is one of porno-blues' more blatant and ingeniously enjoyable efforts. *Vol. 3* concludes with eight tracks featuring the Melrose Stompers ('Mellow Rhythm' is an instrumental); they are wonderful examples of small-group swing, with Miles giving it everything she's got, supported by a terrific and, despite much informed speculation, anonymous session band.

**(*) Lizzie Miles
American Music AMCD-73 *Miles; Johnny Wiggs (c); Avery Howard (t); Jack Delaney, Jim Robinson (tb); Raymond Burke, George Lewis (cl); Fred Neumann, Lester Santiago, Jeff Riddick, Alton Purnell (p); Lawrence Marrero (bj); Frank Federico, Ernest McLean (g); Joe Loyacano, Richard McLean, Sherwood Mangiapanne, Alcide Pavageau (b); Abbie Brunies, Joe Watkins (d). 12/51–mid-50s.*

Lynn Abbott has neatly characterized the latterday Lizzie Miles as 'the matron saint of the 1950s New Orleans "jazz revival"'. She recorded for Verve with Bob Scobey's band and for Capitol with Sharkey Bonano, and made four LPs for Cook. A raucously vivacious six-title set with Sharkey is included on *Jazzin' The Blues (1943–1952)* (Document DOCD-1019), and the Cook material can be ordered from Smithsonian Folkways on custom-made CDs, but American Music's compilation from four sessions is the only extended portrait that's generally available.

The material consists entirely of standards of the revival like 'Bill Bailey', 'Pallet On The Floor', 'Someday Sweetheart' and 'Basin Street Blues' (in three versions!). The chance to hear Miles singing in fractured French on a couple of tracks is not a compelling reason for purchase; more important is a passionate reading of 'Careless Love', underpinned by the bubbling single-string work of Frank Federico. She's in good form with a Johnny Wiggs group, and in rowdy form with George Lewis, recorded live in San Francisco. Unfortunately, seven out of eight tracks made informally at the home of Richard McLean feature a grossly out-of-tune piano. When this awful noisemaker drops out, Miles sings a fine version of 'After You've Gone', responding to Ernest McLean's guitar with husky playfulness, but it's not enough to undo the damage. CS

Al Miller [A]
VOCAL, MANDOLIN, BANJO, GUITAR

Chicago references such as the song 'Thirty First And State' and the group name of the Market Street Boys suggest Miller's sphere of operations in the late '20s, but he does not figure in the recollections of other Chicago musicians, and it may be that outside the recording studio he played in contexts different from theirs.

**(*) Al Miller (1927–1936)
Document DOCD-5306 *Miller; poss. Odell Rand (cl); Cripple Clarence Lofton, prob. Frank Melrose, unknowns (p); –– Rodgers (g, v); unknowns (g); unknowns (v). 7/27–2/36.*

When the history of African-American mandolin playing is written, a page will have to be reserved for Al Miller. From that instrumental angle his earliest recordings are his most interesting: the popular songs 'I Found A Four-Leaf Clover' and 'Someday Sweetheart', sung and played with brio and a sure touch, and a slow blues, issued with the ironic title 'Saturday Night Hymn'. When he next recorded, a year and a half later, partnered by a certain Rodgers, he had been bitten by the hokum bug, a condition he would seldom shake off during the following busy year's record-making, as 'I Would If I Could' was succeeded by 'Somebody's Been Using That Thing', and both by further versions. It seems likely that

through the hokum craze of 1928–30 he served his record labels, chiefly Brunswick, as their in-house competition to The Hokum Boys and Tampa Red & Georgia Tom. Miller's tales of sexual double-dealing were now and then interspersed with pieces such as 'Mister Mary Blues', 'On An Island All By Myself' and 'No Fish For Me' which gave him an opportunity for rippling playing in the 12-bar blues form. On his last '20s side, 'Bone Blues', he took an accompanist's seat behind a tantalizingly unidentified singer/guitarist. At a comeback session in 1936 he switched to guitar but remained faithful to the sort of material he had purveyed before, with the unsurprising result that he was not recalled to the studio again. TR

Al Miller [B]
VOCAL, HARMONICA, GUITAR

Miller began playing harmonica and guitar in his teens. He worked with Michael Bloomfield in 1969–71, then left music to concentrate on his business and family, occasionally returning for a gig or a recording.

** Wild Cards
Delmark DE-675 *Miller; Rob Mazurek (t); Dez Desormeaux (ts, bs); John Brumbach (ts); Ken Saydak (o, p); Phil Baron (o); Donny Nichilo (p); Don Stiernberg (md); Steve Freund (g, v); Dave Specter (g, prod); Willie Kent (b, v); Harlan Terson, Mike McCurdy (b); Mark Fornek (d); Tad Robinson (v). 2/94.*

As a presentation of a new signing this is oddly timid. Having played leading actor on the first track, Miller is absent from the next three. He appears, in fact, on only eight of the 14, and sings on just three of them – a contribution exactly matched by the other vocalists on the date, Freund, Kent and Robinson. If Delmark were the sort of company to make such things, you would take this to be a vanity record by someone who isn't very vain.

The explanation seems to be that Miller doesn't have it in him to dominate so strong a company. As a harmonica player, rooted in the idiom of Chicago musicians of the '40s and '50s such as Snooky Pryor, he is perfectly capable of handling material like 'Red Top Boogie' or Johnny Young's 'Deal The Cards', but as a guitarist he is barely heard and as a singer he barely counts. It was always likely that he would be edged out of the spotlight by his collaborators. Of these Kent stands out for his old hand's singing on 'Seventy-Four', 'Deal The Cards' and 'Jockey Blues', but Saydak, Specter, Freund and Fornek are all in good form. TR

Luella Miller
VOCAL

Miller and her husband, the pianist Eddie Miller, lived in the Compton Hills section of St Louis. After a recording career that lasted for little more than two years she disappears from blues history.

**(*) Luella Miller (1926–1928)
Document DOCD-5183 *Miller; unknown (c); prob. James Johnson, unknowns (p); Lonnie Johnson (vn, poss. bj, g); unknown(s) (vn); poss. Al Miller (md); unknown (bj); poss. Edward Hill, unknown(s) (g). 7/26–8/28.*

The nasal snarl that opens 'Pretty Man Blues', one side of

Miller's first record, signals the arrival of a singer with a pungent, unpretty blues voice and not the slightest trace of vaudeville in her manner. Her two dozen recordings are consistent in style, tempo and attitude, accurately epitomized in song titles like 'Rattle Snake Groan' and 'Tombstone Blues'. Death and bad news permeate her repertoire: the lines of hearses in 'Peeping At The Rising Sun Blues', the climatic disasters of the coupled 'Muddy Stream Blues' and 'Tornado Groan', and heartbreaking men everywhere. A feature of her 1926–27 sessions is the string music of Lonnie Johnson and another musician, who between them share guitar, violin and banjo parts; it may be different musicians who furnish the stringband accompaniment on 1928's 'Chicago Blues'. Her cadences, for instance in 'East St. Louis Blues', and occasional lines such as the 'jelly' verse of 'Brick House Blues' were sometimes echoed in her husband's recordings. The Document CD is complete; five sides are also included in the revised (2004) version of the VAC *The Best Of Country Blues Women Vol. 1 (1923–1930)* (Wolf WSE-117). TR

Roy Milton (1907–83)
VOCAL, DRUMS

One of the architects of small-group R&B in postwar California, Milton used his previous big-band experience to refine the essentials he required. Like his contemporaries Johnny Otis and Joe Liggins, he opted for a three-man trumpet and saxophone section and had the good fortune to engage an outstanding pianist, Camille Howard, who became a successful recording artist in her own right. An undemonstrative drummer, Milton tried to resist the onset of the backbeat as long as he could, ultimately losing out to his record company's success with rock'n'roller Little Richard. He enjoyed something of a renaissance during the '70s as a member of Johnny Otis's shifting troupe of veteran R&B stars.

*** Roy Milton 1945–1946
Classics 5041 *Milton; Hosea Sapp (t); Earl Simms, Caughey Roberts (as); Lorenzo 'Buddy' Floyd (ts); Camille Howard (p, v); Dave Robinson (b). 9/45–46.*

Milton and his Solid Senders began as they meant to carry on, in the sense that many of these 26 songs, recorded for Hamp-Tone, Juke Box and his own Roy Milton label, were rerecorded or rereleased when the band signed with Specialty in 1947. The intriguing two-part 'Burma Road Blues' was probably too topical to be repeated but the extended 'Rainy Day Confession' underwent liposuction for its Specialty release. Milton is the principal vocalist, his drumwork minimal but apposite, while Howard gets to sing two versions of 'Groovy Blues', 'Mr Fine' and 'Pack Your Sack, Jack'. A smattering of standards is a small price to pay for over 70 minutes of solidly sending music.

*** Roy Milton & His Solid Senders
Specialty SPCD-7004//[Ace CDCHD 308] *Milton; Hosea Sapp, Arthur Walker, Charles Gillum (t); Earl Simms, Clifton Noel, Jackie Kelso [John J. Kelson] (as); Lorenzo 'Buddy' Floyd, William Gaither, Benjamin A. Waters, Eddie Taylor (ts); Camille Howard, Willard McDaniel (p); Johnny Rogers (g); David Robinson, Clarence Jones, Dallas Bartley, Lawrence Cato, William Day, Billy Hadnott (b). 12/45–6/52 or 7/52.*

It's obvious from 'Milton's Boogie' and 'R. M. Blues' how fundamental Howard was to the success of the Solid Senders' formula. The pianist's firm left-hand patterns are the music's rhythmic centre and the horns' syncopated riffs apply a light and airy ambience to each song's handbag of unconnected verses. Eighteen of these 25 tracks reached the R&B Top Ten, a feat unequalled by Milton's contemporaries. With two writers in their ranks, the band had little need of outside material but their record company required hits like 'Oh Babe' and 'The Hucklebuck' to be covered. Guitarist Rogers made his presence felt in 'Junior Jives', a rather pregnant guitar feature, and the sturdier (and more successful) 'T-Town Twist'. Milton's predilection for supper-club repertoire accounts for the presence of 'Porter's Love Song' and 'Blue Turning Grey Over You'. The deceptive simplicity of the elements here combined formed the necessary bridge between the big bands of the '40s and the mid-'50s onset of rock 'n' roll, making this a lesson in both music and history.

**(*) Groovy Blues
Specialty SPCD-7024//[Ace CDCHD 435] *As above, except add James Jackson Jr (ts), Harold Grant (g). 12/45–4/53.*

**(*) Roy Milton & His Solid Senders 1945–1949
EPM Blues Collection 15973 *Similar to above CDs. 45–49.*

With all the hits consigned to the previous album, *Groovy Blues* broadens its perspective on Milton's career. A fuller picture of the band's repertoire is culturally informative but makes for less rewarding listening. A hustling 'Rhythm Cocktail' is the first of several cuts to slip into the jazz room, along with 'Roy Rides' and a raucous, unfocused 'One O'Clock Jump', and there's more mainstream fare with 'On The Sunny Side Of The Street', 'My Blue Heaven' and Irving Berlin's 'Marie'. Altogether this is an entertaining collection that has the merit of one of its titles, being for the most part 'Short, Sweet And Snappy'. The EPM set draws together 18 tracks, a mixture of hits and near-misses, from the above compilations and adds 'X-Temporaneous Boogie' and 'Ferocious Boogie' by the Camille Howard Trio. Little apparent logic went into the track selections, making this a less than ideal overview of Milton's recording career, except for those with less to spend.

** Blowin' With Roy
Specialty SPCD-7060//[Ace CDCHD 575] *As for Groovy Blues, except add Roy Montrell (g), Donald Hines (b). 3/47–10/53.*

These are not scrapings from the Milton barrel, but a 25-track album of which half is previously unissued should indicate some diminution of quality and focus. The previous volumes made it obvious that the bandleader had half an eye on the double-knit and paste jewellery crowd and his label indulged the hoary clinkers that crept on to the occasional B side. He was allowed 'Them There Eyes', 'Old Man River' and 'When I Grow Too Old To Dream' but a line was drawn through 'Coquette', 'The Song Is Ended', 'Along The Navajo Trail' and a hip-scat canter through 'Blue Skies'. On the other hand, 'L.A. Hop' and 'Blowin' With Roy', though also previously unissued, are eminently fit to join the Milton canon. Even so, the arbitrary nature of much of its contents makes this one for collectors and obsessives only. One 1947 track announces 'I've Had My Moments' but sadly there aren't enough here to loose the tracker dogs. NS

** Instant Groove
Black & Blue BB 459 *Milton; George Kelly (ts); Ram Ramirez (p); Billy Butler, Roy Gaines (g); Al Hall (b); Eddie Locke (d). 4/77.*

This French studio date produced a programme of Milton's compositions, all blues except 'Hush!', which the band execute with quiet competence. Milton was three months short of his 70th birthday; not only were his drumming days behind him but his voice was rather frail, so he left abundant room for solos. Gaines, Butler and Ramirez are unfailingly elegant, but the length of the title track and 'Information Blues' overtaxes Kelly's imagination as a blues soloist. The original LP has been swelled by two takes of 'Cryin' Won't Help You' and alternatives of three others to achieve almost an hour of sedate, bloodless music. TR

R. J. Mischo (born 1960)
VOCAL, HARMONICA

Born in Wisconsin, Mischo moved in his early teens to Minneapolis, where he took up harmonica, mainly listening to '50s blues masters but also getting help from Lynwood Slim. He worked with the locally based Percy Strother and Mojo Buford, and in 1992 formed a band with guitarist Teddy 'Kid' Morgan. By the mid-'90s Mischo was in demand throughout the Midwest and at European blues festivals.

** Ready To Go!
Atomic Theory ATM 1126 *Mischo; Bruce McCabe (p); Teddy 'Kid' Morgan (g); Bill Black (b); Robb Stupka (d); Percy Strother (v). 12/91.*

Ready To Go!, first issued on Blue Loon, documents the short-lived Mischo–Morgan band of the early '90s. Mischo and Strother split the vocals, Mischo taking the more West Coast or rock 'n' roll-styled numbers like 'Baby, I Don't Care', while Strother does a Muddy on 'Forty Days' and a Wolf on 'Evil'. The recording is rather fuzzy, especially of the vocals, and the musician who comes out best is Morgan.

**(*) Rough 'N' Tough
Crosscut CCD 11049 *Mischo; Jeremy Johnson (g); John Schroder (b); Dave Larson (d). 6/95.*

**(*) Cool Disposition
Crosscut CCD 11055 *Mischo; Barrelhouse Chuck (p); Jeremy Johnson, Nick Moss (g); Billy Black (b); Richard Innes (d). 2/97.*

*** West Wind Blowin'
Mountain Top 3//Crosscut CCD 11062 *Mischo; Bob Welsh (p, b); Rusty Zinn, Steve Freund (g, v); Justin MacCarthy (g); Randy Bermudes, Johnny Ace (b); Walter Shufflesworth, Jimmy Mulleniux (d). 8–10/98.*

*** Meet Me On The Coast
Crosscut CCD 11075 *Mischo; John 'Juke' Logan (o, tamb); Bob Welsh (p); Frank Goldwasser, Jeremy Johnson, Marc Thijs, Junior Watson, Fillmore Slim (g); Marc Carino, Ronnie James, Johnny P. Weckworth (b); Eddie Clark, Robi Bean (d). 1–2/01.*

The Crosscut albums are technically several steps ahead of *Ready To Go!*, but Mischo himself remains immovably positioned in the '50s Chicago bar-band style that first inspired him. That's particularly obvious on *Rough 'N' Tough* and *Cool Disposition*, where he finds a natural partner in the attacking and versatile Jeremy Johnson, whether investigating the portfolios of Sonny Boy Williamson II, Howlin' Wolf, Little Walter and Junior Parker or writing his own songs and tunes in their spirit. (Johnson went on to do good work with Big George Jackson.) Mischo's singing is robust and fairly unmannered, and his playing, within the stylistic boundaries he has drawn for himself, is very idiomatic. The concert sound of *Rough 'N' Tough*, recorded at the Breminale blues festival, is rather boxy; *Cool Disposition* has a more open ambience and the asset of Barrelhouse Chuck at the piano. Its only fault is a lack of textural variety, a problem that Mischo's subsequent albums might be expected to have solved with their expanded castlists. The talented guitar team hired for *West Wind Blowin'*, however, responds a little too dutifully to Mischo's period agenda. For readers who approve of that policy, of course, this will be a recommendation. *Meet Me On The Coast* is somewhat less conventional, especially on the four tracks where the guitarists are Watson and Goldwasser, and Mischo's singing and playing reach new levels of strength and confidence. This would be the album to choose to introduce yourself to his work. Mischo and Goldwasser subsequently recorded in the Down Home Super Trio (q.v.). TR

Miss Angel
VOCAL

Born in Mississippi, Miss Angel has been singing blues professionally since 1992. She has recorded as a backing singer with Mel Brown. Her main models are Odetta, Dinah Washington and Koko Taylor.

** That's The Way I Tumble
Electro-Fi 3389 *Miss Angel; unknown (ts); Mel Brown (o, p, g); John Lee (o, p); Al Richardson, Leo Valvassori (b); Jim Boudreau (d). 05?*

'I need a man with a whole lot of energy,' sings Miss Angel in 'Country Man', with all the animation of Blanche Dubois asking for a little more iced tea. What this *record* needs is more energy. While you want to welcome a singer whose style isn't all growl and big-mama strut, you do wish she would show some spirit and pep, and not sing so strictly on the beat. The most out-of-the-rut tracks are 'Just Your Fool', accompanied only by Brown's acoustic guitar, 'My Baby Bought A Ticket', which uses the airy melody of Howlin' Wolf's 'Who's Been Talkin'', and a live recording of 'Hipshake' (augmented by an unidentified sax player), which is more animated. Unfortunately they come at the end of the CD, and the impatiently sampling listener may not stay so long. TR

Mississippi Heat
GROUP

Despite the name, Mississippi Heat is a Chicago blues band; it was founded in 1992 by Belgian harmonica player Pierre Lacocque, who has been resident in Chicago since 1969. The band has gone through a series of personnel changes during its existence; that, and the presence on CD of numerous guest musicians, means that Mississippi Heat sometimes seems more like a blues revue than a conventional band. This doesn't make Lacocque the Johnny Otis of the Midwest, but there's no doubting his energetic promotional and organizational skills, his songwriting talent or his mastery of his instrument.

***(*) Handyman
Crosscut CCD 11064 *Phillip Perkins (t); Bill McFarland (tb);*

Sonny Seals (ts); Pierre Lacocque (h, finger snaps, hand claps); Billy Boy Arnold (h, v); Barrelhouse Chuck Goering (o, p, finger snaps, hand claps, v); Jasper Buchanan (o, p, v); George Baze (g, v); Carl Weathersby, Wilbert Crosby, Chris Winters, Greg Guliuzza (g); Ike Anderson, Bernard Reed, Steve Howard (b); Kenneth Smith (d); Michael Freeman (tamb); Michel Lacocque (finger snaps, hand claps); Katherine Davis, Lonie Rucker, Caleb Dude, Chester McSwain, Mthiyane, Audrey Qween Roy, Vivian Hampton, Paris R. Walker (v, hand claps); Zora Young (v). 4/98–2/00.

*** **Footprints On The Ceiling**
Crosscut CCD 11071 *Burgess Gardner (t); Willie Woods (tb); Kenneth Clark (ts, bs); Billy Boy Arnold (h, v); Pierre Lacocque, Peter 'Madcat' Ruth (h); Roger Weaver (kb); Pat Brennan (o, p); Phil Baron (p); Chris Winter, Carl Weathersby (g, v); Michael Thomas (g); Stephen Howard (b); Kenneth Smith (d); Michael Freeman (tamb); Inetta Visor, Theresa Davis, Byron Woods (v).* 6/01.

Originally issued on Van der Linden, *Handyman* is here expanded with two tracks recorded in 2000. (The band's three Van der Linden CDs are deleted, but residual copies are available from their website.) The core band in 1998 was Lacocque, Davis, Goering, Baze, Anderson and Smith; everyone else is described as 'special guests', which encompasses as little as one vocal (Young), and as much as playing guitar on all the 1998 tracks (Weathersby). There seem to be three or four guitars on most tracks, plus various combinations of keyboards, horns, rhythm instruments and rather stodgy backing vocals. Not surprisingly the textures that result are sometimes excessively dense, but it's possible to hear that Kenneth 'son of Willie' Smith does fine work throughout. Katherine Davis is that rare and admirable thing in these days, a woman who sings the blues with a concern for meaning rather than the projection of bogus sexual aggression, and Billy Boy Arnold brings depth and nuance to three Lacocque compositions, although the brass quotes from 'La Cucaracha' on 'Ghost Daddy' are disruptive. Lacocque's technical facility is remarkable, the more so when it's considered that he plays diatonic harmonica except on one track; occasionally technique gets the upper hand, and Lacocque tumbles into pointless jazzy warbling, but most of the time he plays with sensitivity and admirable tonal command, striking a sure balance between supportiveness and virtuosity.

The core band for *Footprints On The Ceiling* is Lacocque, Visor, Winters, Thomas, Weaver, Howard and Smith, although once again Carl Weathersby is a ubiquitous 'guest', playing on all tracks and singing on three. This time, Chris Winters is the only white band member to get a vocal; he's a polished and tasteful guitarist, but a much less convincing singer than Chuck Goering was on the previous CD's 'Farewell To S. P. Leary'. Visor has a smaller and less flexible voice than Katherine Davis, but a similarly serious, committed delivery. There's rather more musical flashiness from Lacocque this time out; his duet with Peter Ruth is meant to astonish, and does, but, more often here than on *Handyman*, there are times when the urge to show off gets the better of blues feeling. This is an intermittent problem, not a defining drawback, and as a writer Lacocque again provides opportunities for Billy Boy Arnold, and especially Carl Weathersby, to show what they're capable of; Weathersby finds unexpected depths in the light-hearted Latin rhythms of 'Caribbean Queen'. The CD carries notes by Lacocque's manager and brother, Michel; their pretentious sentimentality would make Pollyanna go out and mug a pensioner for crack money. CS

Mississippi Sheiks
GROUP

The core members of the Mississippi Sheiks on record were fiddler Lonnie Chatmon and guitarist/singer Walter Vincson, augmented on occasion by the voices and guitars of Chatmon's brothers Bo and Sam (see entries for Bo Carter and Sam Chatmon). (Bo also played fiddle but it is debatable whether he can be heard doing so on any of the Sheiks' records.) The considerable sales of 'Sitting On Top Of The World', their second release in 1930, guaranteed them regular visits to the studio for several years.

*** **Mississippi Sheiks – Vol. 1 (1930)**
Document DOCD-5083 *Lonnie Chatmon (vn); Walter Vincson, Sam Chatmon, Bo Chatmon (g, v).* 2–6/30.
*** **Mississippi Sheiks – Vol. 2 (1930–1931)**
Document DOCD-5084 *As above, except omit Sam Chatmon, Bo Chatmon.* 12/30–10/31.
*** **Mississippi Sheiks – Vol. 3 (1931–1934)**
Document DOCD-5085 *unknown (p); Lonnie Chatmon (vn, v); Walter Vincson, Bo Chatmon (g, v); unknown (g).* 10/31–3/34.
*** **Mississippi Sheiks – Vol. 4 (1934–1936)**
Document DOCD-5086 *Lonnie Chatmon (vn, v); Walter Vincson, Bo Chatmon, Sam Chatmon (g, v); Eugene Powell, unknown (g); Dan Hornsby (sp).* 3/34–10/36.

The 20 tracks on Document's *Vol. 1* are an accurate microcosm of the Sheiks' work. Titles like 'Driving That Thing', 'Grinding Old Fool' and 'Loose Like That' indicate that they were aware of trends in the 'race' record market, but they were able to balance such hokum material with interesting original blues, some topical like the Depression themes 'West Jackson Blues' and 'Times Done Got Hard', or 'Yodeling Fiddling Blues', which alludes to the then hugely popular country singer Jimmie Rodgers. The Sheiks themselves drift into the periphery of country music with the harmonized duetting of 'Jailbird Love Song', and several of their instrumental records were actually issued in OKeh's old-time series rather than the 'race' catalogue – reasonably enough, since Lonnie Chatmon's waltz playing has something in common with that of contemporary white Mississippi fiddlers like Willie Narmour or Will Ray.

Bo Chatmon, alias Bo Carter, sang a few of the pieces on *Vol. 1*, but *Vol. 2* is devoted to the rich, thoughtful singing of Walter Vincson. It's more or less evenly deployed on hokum songs like 'She's A Bad Girl', where he tends to play a simple boom-chang rhythm, and blues, on which his guitar tends to be more interesting: note, for instance, the spirited follow-up to their earlier hit 'Stop And Listen Blues' (a close relative of Tommy Johnson's 'Big Road Blues'), 'The World Is Going Wrong' or the gripping 'Livin' In A Strain', beautifully played by both men.

Vol. 3 tracks the Sheiks as they move from OKeh to Paramount to Bluebird. Paramount's recording engineer balanced the instruments slightly differently, so that Vincson's guitar sounds stronger, but except for 'I'll Be Gone, Long Gone', where the fiddle gives place to an unidentified pianist, the group made no significant changes in its repertoire or approach. Bo Chatmon rejoins them for part of the first

Bluebird session, adding guitar passages that could only be his, but when Vincson takes over again, early on *Vol. 4*, the music is indistinguishable from that of four years earlier. Bo Chatmon returns to participate in 'Sales Tax', an amusing topical song, and most of the Sheiks' final (1935) session. The last eight tracks of *Vol. 4* are by Lonnie and Sam Chatmon and, though not nominally Sheiks recordings, can be treated as part of the Sheiks' *oeuvre*. Sam's gamey singing is a fresh twist, but Lonnie's fiddling and the general tenor of the music are wholly familiar.

*** **Honey Babe Let The Deal Go Down: The Best Of The Mississippi Sheiks**
Columbia/Legacy CK 65709 *Lonnie Chatmon (vn); Walter Vincson (g, v); Bo Chatmon (poss. g, v); unknown (sp).* 2/30–10/31.

***(*) **Stop And Listen**
Yazoo 2006 *Lonnie Chatmon (vn); Walter Vincson, Bo Chatmon (g, v); Dan Hornsby (sp).* 2/30–3/34.

***(*) **The Essential**
Classic Blues CBL 200030 2CD *As for relevant Document CDs.* 2/30–10/36.

With the Sheiks, as with some other artists considered in this book, the listener's pleasure in the music may be cooled by regret that the group was not allowed to make it more diverse. They preferred to play for white audiences and had material appropriate for that context which was significantly different from their blues and hokum repertoire. But of that other side their recordings yield only fleeting, tantalizing glimpses. The ideal album for the inquisitive listener would scatter some of those snapshots among the commoner images, and in that respect there's little to choose between the Yazoo and Classic Blues compilations. Both contain essential tracks like 'Stop And Listen Blues', 'Sitting On Top Of The World', 'Livin' In A Strain', 'Sales Tax' and 'I've Got Blood In My Eyes For You', while the Sheiks' other repertoire is illustrated by 'That's It' on Yazoo and 'The Sheik Waltz' and 'The Jazz Fiddler' on Classic Blues. Readers devoted to value for money are directed to the Classic Blues, an inexpensive double album with few tracks in less than excellent transfers. *Honey Babe Let The Deal Go Down* has most of the key blues and 'The Jazz Fiddler' but, necessarily, none of the Bluebird sides; instead there are three numbers by Texas Alexander, accompanied by Bo and Sam Chatmon. A few tracks are spoiled by distortion. TR

Sam Mitchell
VOCAL, GUITAR

Son of a professional steel guitarist who played with Felix Mendelssohn's Hawaiian Serenaders, Mitchell took up guitar in his teens and after hearing Robert Johnson began to specialize in blues slide guitar techniques. In the early '70s he worked with Rod Stewart, playing on the albums Gasoline Alley *and* Every Picture Tells A Story, *and in bands such as Uncle Dog. He has also worked with Long John Baldry and Dana Gillespie and, while based in Denmark, with The Sandmen. Now back in Liverpool, his hometown, he plays at occasional festivals and workshops.*

*** **The Art of Bottleneck/Slide Guitar**
Shanachie 98007/8 *Mitchell; Charlie Musselwhite (h); Stefan Grossman (g); Steve York (b); George Butler, Jeff Rich (d).* 70s.

On this essentially instructional CD, drawn from *Bottleneck/Slide Guitar* and other Kicking Mule LPs, Mitchell plays blues, gospel songs and original display pieces, in a variety of slide methods, on Dobro, regular six- and 12-string acoustics and electric guitar. The booklet includes notes by Mitchell on the tunes and tunings (open A, E, E6 and G) and playing tips by the producer Stefan Grossman. By remaining within the time limits of a 78, Mitchell manages to squeeze in two dozen performances and his range is impressive, embracing not only Robert Johnson, Blind Willie Johnson and Kokomo Arnold but slow blues in the Earl Hooker style, Hawaiian-flavoured tunes and even, in the opening 'Ambidextrous March', a passage from 'The Teddy Bears' Picnic'. His singing, on the few tracks where he does any, is a little pale. TR

Mobile Strugglers
GROUP

The Mobile Strugglers would travel to New Orleans to play for tips in Jackson Square, where jazz researcher Bill Russell saw them perform and arranged to record them in Montgomery, where, despite their name, most of the band lived. The lineup normally included a washboard, but Tyler Jackson was in jail the week of the session. The Mobile Strugglers had a shifting personnel; when recorded in 1954, they consisted of Jackson (playing one-string bass), guitarist Moochie Reeves, guitarist/kazooist Ollie Crenshaw and a jug player.

*** **Mobile Strugglers & Louis James' String Band**
American Music AMCD-14 *James Fields, Charles Jones (vn, v); Lee Warren (md, bj, 'streamline bass', v); Paul Johnson (g, v); Wesley Williams (b, v).* 7/49.

For many years, all that was available of the 1949 Mobile Strugglers' raucous music was a 78, pressed in an edition of 100, of 'Memphis Blues' and 'Fattening Frogs For Snakes'. This CD raises the score to seven titles; the rest of the disc is by New Orleans fiddler and clarinettist Louis James, whose much smoother music makes a charming contrast (and also includes a version of 'Memphis Blues'), but is outside the scope of this guide. If it comes to that, 'Cornfed Indiana Gal', 'Billboard March' and 'Don't Bring Lulu' stretch the definition of 'blues on CD', but in practice they sit quite happily alongside 'Original Blues'. Irrespective of provenance, every track is unmistakably African-American in sensibility and performance, with the two fiddles carrying on an animated, rough-edged dialogue, and the double bass (replaced on 'Indiana Rag' by a one-string 'streamline bass') generating a booming, bluesy swing. Great fun, and important as one of the few recordings of African-American twin fiddling.

Material from the 1954 session was issued on Folkways and RBF; so far, only 'Raise A Ruckus Tonight' on *Blues Masters Vol. 10: Roots* (Rhino R2 71135) has made it to CD. CS

Little Brother Montgomery (1906–85)
VOCAL, PIANO

By the age of 11, Eurreal Montgomery was ready to leave home and become a professional pianist in barrelhouses like the one his father owned in Kentwood, Louisiana. Little Brother played solo, in New Orleans jazz bands and with guitarists and

singers. In the '30s, he led a swing band based in Jackson, Mississippi. Moving to Chicago in 1942, he kept busy playing in jazz bands, with blues singers from Big Bill Broonzy to Otis Rush, and even at an Irish tavern. From the early '60s he connected with the new blues audience, visiting Europe several times. His excellent memory was a treasure house of information which made him an ideal subject for Karl Gert zur Heide's biography Deep South Piano.

♛ **** **Little Brother Montgomery (1930–1936)**
Document DOCD-5109 *Montgomery; 'Hicks', Walter Vincson (g); prob. Minnie Hicks, Jesse 'Monkey Joe' Coleman (sp).* c. 9/30–10/36.

*** **Little Brother Montgomery (1930–1954)**
Document BDCD-6034 *Montgomery; Lee Collins (t); Oliver Alcorn (cl, ts); Walter Vincson (g); Ernest Crawford (b); Jerome Smith (d); Irene Scruggs, Minnie Hicks, Annie Turner, 'Creole' George Guesnon (v).* c. 9/30–5/54.

Little Brother was adept at blues, jazz, stride, boogie and pop, which he synthesized into a personal style that ranged easily from the bopping earthiness of 'Frisco Hi-Ball Blues' to the pearl-stringing elegance of 'Shreveport Farewell'. His high voice and bleating vibrato are unmistakable, especially on his signature piece, 'Vicksburg Blues', a polyrhythmic showcase for his acute but never pedantic timing. It's also an example of Brother's poetry of geography; many of his songs, and even the titles of his instrumentals, are rich evocations of places he knew and the railroads that carried him between them.

There are several versions of 'Vicksburg Blues' on *1930–1936*, which collates Montgomery's early recordings under his own name, including an epic 1936 session of 18 titles cut in one day. The Tin Pan Alley stereotypes of 'Chinese Man Blues' aside, their quality is extraordinarily high, reaching its lyrical peak with a disquieting incarnation of the blues as persecutor in 'The First Time I Met You', and a musical peak with three concluding piano solos.

The 1936 session also included five accompaniments, which are among 11 on *1930–1954*. The 1930 titles by Minnie Hicks and Irene Scruggs come from ferociously worn discs, and Hicks is simply not very good. George Guesnon's track from 1936 is boring pop. Fifteen-year-old Annie Turner projects a smouldering sensuality, triumphing over her low volume and dicey pitch with help from Montgomery and Vincson's wonderfully attentive accompaniment. The early postwar material includes four lively titles with Lee Collins's jazz band and nine tracks (eight of them piano solos) from Regal and Windin' Ball. There's a preponderance of remakes, but they're good ones, and five exquisite minutes of 'Winding Ball Blues' [*sic*] surmount the sharp tuning of the eponymous company's piano.

**** **Tasty Blues**
Original Blues Classics OBCCD-554 *Montgomery; Lafayette Thomas (g); Julian Euell (b).* 7/60.

*** **Chicago Blues**
Southland SCD-10 *Montgomery; Corky Robertson (b); Jump Jackson (d); Sunnyland Slim (v).* 7/60.

*** **The La Salle Chicago Blues Recordings Vol. 1**
Wolf 120.296 *As above, except add prob. Robert Jr Lockwood (g).* 7/60.

Montgomery was a keen writer of pop tunes and singer of hymns, but he knew what the public wanted, and much of *Tasty Blues* is familiar, although the poetry of travel reaches outer space with the topical 'Satellite Blues'. What separates *Tasty Blues* from the pack is the presence of West Coast master guitarist Lafayette Thomas. 'Deep Fried' and 'Sneaky Pete Blues' are instrumental features for him, but throughout the set Montgomery and Euell, who supplies a steady, swinging undertow, give Thomas plenty of room to twine his elaborate, imaginative musical cats' cradles.

The Southland and Wolf discs have much but not all of their content in common; the recordings were made in Jump Jackson's studio during field research by Paul Oliver. Once again, Brother runs through his favourites, but he does so enthusiastically, whether alone or with effective support. Wolf's selection has the edge, thanks to very good versions of 'Pinetop's Boogie Woogie' and 'Farrish [*sic*] St. Jive', and a 'Cow Cow Blues' on which Montgomery sings up a storm. On two tracks he accompanies Sunnyland Slim, with whom these CDs are shared; they're hesitant collaborators at times, and Slim's voice overwhelms the microphones.

** **Chicago: The Living Legends**
Original Blues Classics OBCCD-525 *Montgomery; Ted Butterman (c); Bob Gordon (cl); Rufus Brown (ts); Mike McKendrick (bj); Elaine McFarland (v).* 9/61.

McKendrick was a workaday veteran, and Rufus Brown a pseudonym. The rest were young enthusiasts; Gordon made a career in jazz, and Butterman continued to gig around Chicago, but his derivative cornet is not noticed by works of reference. McFarland later became Spanky, of Spanky & Our Gang; on the evidence of 'Oh, Daddy', she *must* have been better at folk-rock than blues. Montgomery seems well aware of his associates' shortcomings, playing and singing without much enthusiasm and perpetrating an extended passage of wrong notes during 'Something Keeps Worryin' Me Blues'.

***(*) **I Blueskvarter: Chicago 1964, Volume Two**
Jefferson SBACD 12655/6 2CD *Montgomery; Mike Bloomfield (g); Olle Helander (interviewer).* 5/64.

There are no repertoire surprises in the five tracks here, recorded for Swedish radio; a sixth, on *Volume Three* (Jefferson SBACD 12658/9 2CD) is inevitably 'Vicksburg Blues'. Montgomery is in excellent form, however, and Bloomfield's acoustic guitar obbligatos – tasteful, inventive and wholly idiomatic – are delightful. Olle Helander also conducts a short interview with Montgomery.

(*) **At Home
Earwig CD 4918 *Montgomery; Tollie 'Duke' Montgomery (p); Truck Parham (b); James Herndon, Red Saunders, Roy Slaughter (d); Edith Wilson, Jan Montgomery (v).* 11/67–7/82.

** **No Special Rider**
Genes GCD 9913 *Montgomery; Mike Stewart (g); Jeanne Carroll (v).* 9/69.

***(*) **Blues Masters Vol. 7**
Storyville STCD 8007 *Montgomery.* 9/72.

Though recorded in Montgomery's living room, the tracks on Earwig were intended for release on his FM label and others, and their sound quality is acceptable. Three instrumentals with Parham and Herndon have terrific élan, and 'Mini-Skirt Blues' features Otis Spann-like accompaniment from Little Brother's little brother. In the debit column are some sentimental pop songs, including 'Jan', dedicated to Mrs

Montgomery, and 'Without You Sweetheart', amateurishly sung by her. Brother both remembered and wrote an enormous number of songs, and *At Home* includes several that he seldom played in public, but it's not the best place for casual listeners to meet the man or his music.

Inadvisable for all but the most dedicated is *No Special Rider*, with an out-of-tune piano, Carroll's obstinately average singing and Stewart's under-rehearsed guitar. (To give Carroll her due, she does a lot better with 'Oh Daddy' than Elaine McFarland.) Brother makes a number of rhythmic errors and verbal slips. This session waited 30 years for issue, and it seems unlikely that Montgomery, who rejected a track on *At Home* because he *almost* mispronounced 'oleander', would have been happy to see it released in his lifetime.

There are some wrong notes on *Blues Masters* too, but they emerge from a greatly superior piano, and the errors are not fatal. They're the corollary of Montgomery's being asked to recall tunes he'd learned in his youth, several of them named after the men he heard them from, like Vanado Anderson, Miles Davis (no, not that one) and Cooney Vaughn, whose lovely 'Tremblin' Blues' is only preserved thanks to Brother. Other standouts include a '44 (Vicksburg) Blues' shorn of its usual vocal, and a scintillating revival of 'Shreveport Farewell'. When Montgomery sings he's in excellent voice, and *Blues Masters* makes a good alternative to Document's first volume for those made uneasy by surface noise and/or remastering that's less than top-notch.

***(*) Goodbye Mister Blues
Delmark DE-663 *Montgomery; Leon Scott, Leroi Nabors (t); Preston Jackson (tb, v); Oliver Alcorn, Franz Jackson (cl, ss, ts); Ikey Robinson (bj, g); Truck Parham, Ed Wilkinson (b); Red Saunders (d). 9/73–1/76.*

Most of *Goodbye Mister Blues*, which is credited to Little Brother Montgomery's State Street Swingers, is lively jazz, played by Chicago veterans whose enthusiasm belies their years. Montgomery sings on three tracks, and 'Boy In The Boat' has a prominent, gracious piano part. Readers wishing to investigate Brother's jazz playing will enjoy this disc. CS

Coco Montoya (born 1951)
VOCAL, GUITAR

Montoya began his musical life as a drummer and it was in this capacity that he began a five-year stint with Albert Collins in the mid-'70s. During that time he also became proficient with the guitar under Collins's tuition. A chance encounter with John Mayall led to a ten-year residency in the revived Bluesbreakers, the springboard for his eventual solo career, which he began in 1995.

*** Gotta Mind To Travel
Blind Pig BPCD 5020 *Montoya; Darrell Leonard (t); Joe Sublett (ts); John Mayall (h, v); Benny Yee (o, p); Mike Finnegan, Al Kooper (o); Rob Rio (p); Debbie Davies (g, v); Albert Collins (g); Albert Molinari (b); Mark T. Williams (d, perc); Joe Yuele, Richie Hayward (d); Keillie Rucker (v). 95.*

Both Collins and Mayall appear in support of their ex-band member for his solo debut. As befits someone of his experience, Montoya can really play the guitar, even if what he plays rarely contains anything original. He has a pleasant singing voice that stops short of being distinctive, as do his four songs here, with the possible exception of 'You Don't Love Me'. Other material comes from Albert Collins, Freddie King and John Mayall and the album finishes with a slightly ponderous version of the Cate Brothers' 'Am I Losing You'. The various musicians all do well, particularly Davies, who sings and plays lead guitar in 'Nothin' In The Streets'. The record was deemed good enough to garner Montoya the title of Best New Blues Artist in the following year's Handy Awards.

*** Ya Think I'd Know Better
Blind Pig BPCD 5033 *Montoya; Ernest Williamson (kb); Benny Yee (o, p); Earl Cate (g, v); Michael Toles, Lee Roy Parnell (g); Steve Ehrmann (b, v); Dave Smith (b); Marty Binder (d, perc); Steve Potts (d); William Brown, Bertrand Brown, Ernie Cate, Lee Roy Parnell (v). 96.*

The number from which this album takes its name is Montoya's only contribution as composer to this 11-song sequence and its least blues-oriented item, the slide-dominated arrangement sounding more like Lowell George's work with Jackson Browne. He makes a good fist of Ike Turner's 'Fool In Love' and 'Big Boy Pete' but 'Seven Desires' and 'The Heart Of Soul' are less felicitous choices. 'Hiding Place' and 'Can't Get My Ass In Gear' and 'Too Much Of A Good Thing' are this album's successes, and Albert Collins's 'Dying Flu' would have joined the list if Montoya hadn't made it an over-emotional dirge. Once again, the musicianship is striking and fulfils all the criteria of modern rock-blues.

**(*) Just Let Go
Blind Pig BPCD 5043 *Montoya; Benny Yee, Ernest Williamson (kb); Earl Cate, Chuck 'Sonny Boy' Kirkpatrick (g, v); Steve Ehrmann, Dave Smith (b); Marty Binder, Steve Potts (d); Ernie Cate, Shaun Murphy, William Brown, Bertrand Brown (v). 97.*

After Robert Ward's 'Fear No Evil' has been given the full rock treatment, things go markedly off the boil, as Montoya and his producer strive to illustrate his versatility. He's responsible wholly or in part for writing five of the 13 selections, including the title track, the only one of note being 'My Side Of The Fence'. Otherwise, there's the obligatory Albert Collins piece, 'Do What You Want To Do', three David Steen songs and two by Frankie Miller. What becomes an immaculate ramble through country, soul and rock balladry is all very well but the traycard refers to 'a modern blues master' and Montoya provides precious little evidence of it here to support the assertion.

**(*) Suspicion
Alligator ALCD 4871 *Montoya; Steve Howard (t); Jon Smith (ts); Jeff Robbins (bs); Benny Yee, Tommy Eyre (kb); Chuck Kirkpatrick (g, v); David Steen (g); Boyd Lafan, Bob Laub, Armando Compeon (b); Joey Pafume, Tony Braunagel, Randy Hayes, Willie Ornelas (d); Scott Kirkpatrick (v). 99.*

A change of label sees no alteration in the Montoya project, which continues to present blues as merely one colour in a broadening musical palette. Even Albert Collins's 'Get Your Business Straight' is heavily disguised in rock and funk clichés. A number of songs, among them 'Don't Take It Personally' and 'Good Days, Bad Days', would not sound out of place on a Foreigner album. Montoya continues his collaboration with David Steen on three songs, with a further three by Steen also present, of which 'You Didn't Think About That' has some merit. The musical quality is consistent, Montoya sings and plays well enough, but it's an album that is more concerned with Californian values than those of Chicago or any other blues town.

*** Can't Look Back
Alligator ALCD 4885 *Montoya; Darrell Leonard (t); Joe Sublett (ts); Benny Yee, Tommy Eyre (kb); Chuck Kirkpatrick (g); Steve Evans, Bob Glaub (b); Randy Hayes, Scott Kirkpatrick, Tony Braunagel (d).* 02.

Very much a facsimile of *Suspicion*, using many of the same musicians and relying on the Montoya/Steen partnership, accounting for five songs, with a further two by Steen alone. Some, like 'Can't See The Streets For My Tears' and 'Back In A Cadillac', approach a blues context, although their arrangements lean more towards rock. The requisite Albert Collins feature is 'Same Old Thing' but more time was obviously spent on a spirited version of the Four Tops' 'Something About You'. The eclecticism of the material is a little less pronounced this time around but still Montoya has come a long way from his formative years and even from his debut album. Whether that journey has value in a blues context is another question to be decided by the taste and inclination of the listener. NS

Julia Moody
VOCAL

Possibly from Baltimore, Moody began her stage career at the age of 16 and over the next decade or so appeared in several successful New York productions. She quit show business in the mid-'30s.

**(*) Viola McCoy – Vol. 3 (1926–1929)/Julia Moody (1922–1925)
Document DOD-5418 *Moody; Joe Smith, Bubber Miley, Robert Starr, unknown (c); Jake Frazier, Ted Nixon, prob. George Brashear, unknown (tb); Bob Fuller, Percy Glascoe, poss. Clarence Robinson, unknown (cl); Fletcher Henderson, Louis Hooper, Edgar Dowell, unknown (p); Elmer Snowden, James Thomas (bj); poss. Ralph Escudero, unknown (bb).* c. 8/22–9/25.

Moody had a similar stage career to Viola McCoy, with whom she shares this CD, but may have been a few years older. If she does not display McCoy's swift apprehension of blues technique it may be because it was a lesson she did not need to learn, being gifted with a big, resonant voice that is more obviously suited to the blues, though this becomes more apparent on the later and better-recorded of these 13 sides, in particular the closing 'He'll Do You Wrong'. When partnered by musicians who took their role seriously she was capable of producing very good records. 'Broken Busted, Can't Be Trusted Blues' has excellent cornet playing by Bubber Miley, as does the remarkable 'Mad Mama's Blues', which Howard Rye well describes as 'a surreal terrorist's manifesto', while 'Midnight Dan' and 'He'll Do You Wrong' house thoughtful muted solos by Robert Starr. Such passages help one to forget clarinettist Percy Glascoe filling the air of 'Strivin' Blues' with monkey noises. Four of Moody's better sides are on *Tight Women And Loose Bands 1921–1931* (Timeless CBC 1–068). TR

John Mooney (born 1955)
VOCAL, GUITAR, MANDOLIN

Who expects a Mississippi blues legend to be living on their block? That good fortune happened to Rochester, New York, native Mooney, who got to learn slide technique from Son House and accompanied him during his last performing years. Mooney moved to New Orleans in the '70s and formed Bluesiana in 1983, intending to combine Delta blues and New Orleans rhythms. Despite slide guitar having become the garni du jour *among younger guitarists, his distinctive style has made Mooney one of its best and most lyrical exponents.*

*** Comin' Your Way
Blind Pig BP 70779 *Mooney; Rich Lataille (as); Greg Piccolo (ts); Doug James (bs); Nick Langan (h, ac, p); Steve Nardella (h); Bob Cooper (p); Brian Williams (b); Tom McDermott (d).* 77.

Cut in his new hometown, Mooney's debut finds him in an acoustic setting reminiscent of Steve James or Catfish Keith. His vocal mannerisms are already in place, though somewhat muted by inexperience. He's also more of an ensemble player here than he would later become, happy to share solo space with harmonica players and pianists. A three-piece saxophone section is used sparingly, with one tenor solo during 'Ain't Gonna Get Drunk No More'. With just one song, 'Reap What You Sow', taken at a medium-slow tempo, matters frequently get frantic without adversely affecting a high standard of musicianship, particularly in Mooney's deft slide guitar playing. While significantly different from his subsequent work, it's an album of promises that he would come to fulfil.

*** Travelin' On
Blue Rock'It BRCD 123//Crosscut CCD 11032 *Mooney; Glenn Fukunaga (b); Kerry Brown (d).* 6/91.

This is by Bluesiana, recorded live at the '91 Breminale in Germany. The group seems more closely aligned with funk than New Orleans. Brown's snare and Fukunaga's bass chop their rhythms into finger-poppin' portions, over which Mooney capers with finger and slide. Slow blues by Robert Johnson and Muddy Waters are performed in a ländler-like slow-swing tempo, while 'Junco Partner' and the title track get up a head of steam as the guitarist indulges in long strummed solos that send the audience increasingly wild. Mooney's vocals are yet to attain their fully stylized nasal twang and his slide playing makes a late but effective entry halfway through the almost hour-long set. As the only representation of Mooney's initial concept, this provides the context for the records that follow.

*** Testimony
Domino DOMCD 001 *Mooney; Ivan Neville (o, p, clav); Dr John [Mack Rebennack], Jon Cleary (p); Tommy Malone (g); George Porter Jr (b); John Vidacovich (d); Daryl Johnson, Tommy Malone (v).* 92.

Disparities between Delta blues and New Orleans second line are displayed in an album of solid musicianship that attempts with qualified success to cover its bases. 'Lil' Queen Of Spades' is a superior Robert Johnson adaptation and 'Married Woman Blues' hints at the Tommy Johnson axis but a Latinate treatment of Son House's 'Levee Camp Moan' trivializes its origin. A delicate interpretation of Percy Sledge's 'Take Time To Know Her', on which Mooney's vocal evokes the

Band's Richard Manuel, provides the album's still centre. A pair of Longhair romps are pleasant but standard New Orleans fare, whereas Mooney's own 'I Plead Guilty' and 'Maybe Baby' successfully blend the two strands of his inspiration. He's well served by an elite guestlist but their contributions play their part in dissipating the music's focus.

** Sideways In Paradise
Blind Pig BPCD 5006 *Mooney; Jimmy Thackery (md, mandocello, g); John Nagy (g, v).* 93.

To achieve this pleasant little extravagance, the musicians put themselves to the intolerable inconvenience of recording at a private villa in Jamaica. Mooney takes the lion's share of the vocals and has written four of the ten tracks, while Thackery seems content to harmonize and supplement the rhythmic pulse. Their programme is eclectic, ranging from Bukka White to Sam Cooke, via another version of 'Take Time To Know Her' and Robert Johnson's 'Travelin' Riverside Blues'. Engineer Nagy adds the occasional vocal and instrumental part to a set that reminds the listener of a more indulgent time and struggles to justify its existence.

*** Dealing With The Devil
Tradition & Moderne T&M 007//Ruf 1057 *Mooney.* 8/95.

Mooney returned to Bremen for a solo gig that combined warm audience rapport with accomplished musicianship. The lack of rhythmic emphasis allows the guitarist to add unaccustomed nuances to a programme that successfully integrates the expected blues covers with original songs like 'Sacred Ground' and 'It Don't Mean A Doggone Thing'. Instrumentally, the transitions from finger patterns to slide are equally adept and spontaneous. His singing style, with its eccentrically enunciated vowels, has by now reached maturity, although he's careful to save its excesses for his own material. Even so, despite its surprising effectiveness, this CD is by no means essential to an understanding of Mooney's talent.

***(*) Against The Wall
Ruf 1019 *Mooney; Bob Andrews (o, p); Tony Hall, Jeff Sarli, David Lee Watson (b); George G. Recile (d, perc); Carlo Nuccio (d); Michael Ward (cga).* 96.

Mooney comes into his constituency here, subordinating an assortment of accompanists to his musical will. With the exception of Michelle Shocked's 'The Bitter Pill', all the songs are his own and, although his principal influences are present, they're contributory elements rather than determining factors. 'Late In The Evening' is the sole overtly blues-oriented song, 'Sacred Ground' and 'Broken Mould' pulsate to a second-line heartbeat, while 'Doggone Thing' and 'Pill' are ideal vehicles for Mooney's laconic vocal style. Once or twice his penchant for elaborate riff-based rhythms lets him down but the confidence and skill of his performance carry the day. (Previously on House Of Blues 70010 87006.)

**** Gone To Hell
Blind Pig BPCD 5063 *Mooney; Dr John [Mack Rebennack] (p); Jeff Sarli (b); Kerry Brown (d); Alfred 'Uganda' Roberts (cga, perc).* 00.

***(*) All I Want
Blind Pig BPCD 5074 *Mooney; Jeff Sarli (b); Bernard 'Bunche' Johnson (d); Alfred 'Uganda' Roberts (perc).* 02.

A return to first principles makes *Gone To Hell* the most rewarding display of Mooney's talent. Trenchant deconstructions of Son House's 'Dry Spell Blues' and 'Down South Blues' (originally 'County Farm') and Skip James's 'Cypress Grove' burnish his blues credentials while a quartet of songs aided by the presence of Dr John's piano top up the album's New Orleans quotient. Mooney's slide work dominates proceedings, frantic but deft in 'Down South' and the other solo performance, 'I Wonder Blues'. Mordant humour flavours 'Glass House', 'Funky Arkansas', 'No' and 'Gone To Hell', transcending the conventionality encountered elsewhere. His rhythm team give sterling support, although Roberts's congas are at times superfluous. Co-producer Cindy Lea gets an additional credit as 'photo assistant/stylist'. Is there nothing she can't put her hand to?

All I Want, another rewarding set, finds Mooney relying even more upon his own resources, with six out of 11 songs performed solo on National steel and other guitars. His slide playing has a pearlescent tone, here decorating 'Baby Please', 'You Got To Move' and others, that sets him apart from other steel-flourishers. Visits to the repertoires of Son House and Willie Brown are more than mere pastiches, while the crazed mambo of Professor Longhair's 'Hey Little Girl' also drives 'She Ain't No Good' and 'Feel Like Hollerin'', and this time Roberts's congas are perfectly integrated. Mooney's laconic humour is confined to 'Buried Treasure', a slacker's anthem on what might have been achieved with the application of a little energy, a surfeit of which went into the production of this album. NS

Aaron Moore (born 1928)
VOCAL, PIANO

Moore left Greenwood, Mississippi, for Chicago in 1951. His skills immediately impressed his peers, but with a family to raise Moore joined the Department of Sanitation, eventually rising to deputy commissioner, and only gigging at weekends. He'd been retired from the day job for some years when he made his recording debut, backing Brewer Phillips on Delmark.

*** Hello World
Delmark DE-695 *Moore; James Wheeler (g); Willie Black (b); 'Huckleberry Hound' [Robert Wright] (d).* 7/95.

*** Boot 'Em Up!
Delmark DE-731 *Moore; James Wheeler (g); Bob Stroger (b); Willie 'Big Eyes' Smith (d).* 10/98.

Aaron Moore's wife thinks he may be knocking ten years off his date of birth; if so, he sounds 30 years younger than his true age, rather than a mere 20. Moore sat in with Muddy, Wolf and B. B. King, and turned down requests to tour with all of them, so it's no surprise that he attacks the keyboard with vigour and élan. What is surprising is that his playing and singing are closely modelled on the hollering swing-blues that Roosevelt Sykes expounded in the '40s, and owe little to the Chicago band pianists of later decades; Moore dallies with Otis Spann's smoky introversion on *Hello World*'s 'Lonely Blues', and does so very effectively, but the change of gear is a jolting one. If anything, though, one could wish it happened more often; Moore's energy is admirable, but a certain stylistic sameness keeps these discs out of the first division. Nevertheless, they both have considerable merits, not least James Wheeler's polished guitar work; *Boot 'Em Up!* is the better of the two, thanks largely to Bob Stroger's superior bass playing. CS

Whistling Alex Moore (1899–1989)
VOCAL, PIANO

Moore began playing about the age of 12, and by the time he was 20 was performing at house parties and in clubs around Dallas. Rarely able to make a living from music alone, he worked as a mule-driver, hotel porter or janitor. He recorded in every decade from the 1920s to the '80s.

*** Whistlin' Alex Moore (1929–1951)
Document DOCD-5178 Moore; Blind Norris (poss. g, v); poss. Coley Jones, unknown (g); unknown (d); Nick Nichols, Perry Dixon, unknown (v). 12/29–51.

You'll go a long way before you find a more unusual opening to a blues lyric than the first on this CD: 'They may not be my toes …'. But out-of-the-rut ideas and a distinctive way with words were Alex Moore's stock-in-trade. 'The wolves howled till midnight, wild ox moaned till day,' he sings in 'West Texas Woman'. 'The man in the moon looked down on us, but had nothing to say.' Or again, in 'Blue Bloomer Blues': 'While standing at the car line, reckon what that old woman done? She hugged and kissed me, then bit me on my tongue. I asked her to give me what mama did, when I was three months old: she said, "I'll make you a sugar teat, daddy" – I can't stand that to save my soul.' The song culminates in: 'Next morning, she said, "Daddy, I hope you'll be in good humour" – I said, "Providing, baby, I tie the string in them blue bloomers."'

Moore delivers his tales of erotic encounter and domestic reproof in a throaty, wavering, exhausted voice to steady, undramatic piano accompaniments. The bulk of the CD is drawn from two sessions in 1929 and 1937, with a few later tracks that show no change in his vocal manner, but reveal a more forthright pianist in the stomping 'Neglected Woman' and the virtually instrumental 'Lillie Mae Boogie'. Five tracks from the '29 and '37 sessions are also on the VAC *Texas Blues (1927–1937)* (Wolf WSE 112).

*** From North Dallas To The East Side
Arhoolie CD 408 Moore. 47, 7/60, 10/69.

A large part of this CD is Moore's 1960 comeback album, supplemented with a couple of songs recorded on a 1969 visit to Europe. Since none of those performances was designed for issue on a 78 or 45, it might be supposed that a man of Moore's restless and prolific imagination would have exploited these opportunities – as, say, Booker White did – to record unrestricted by the usual time-limits, but only four numbers go much beyond three and a half minutes. Several songs are remakes of earlier recordings, a fact sometimes masked by retitling: 'Going Back To Froggy Bottom', for example, is 'Bull Corn Blues'. 'Boogie In The Barrel', 'July Boogie' and 'Boogiein' In Strassburg' release sprightly right-hand figures. Among a further eight tracks recorded at a radio station in 1947 and surviving on rather bass-heavy acetates are a couple of rag tunes, 'Alex's Rag' and 'Alex's Wild Blues'.

**(*) Wiggle Tail
Rounder CD 11559 Moore. 2/88.

As if making up for his brevity on earlier albums, Moore allowed himself in these club recordings to be expansive: 'Chasin' Rainbows' runs to 11.34 and 'Elephant Brain Man' to 13.34. The former is not the old pop song but a blues, while 'Elephant Brain' is a memoir of Dallas in the early 20th century, with vignettes like the story of two policemen who were so fat that when one got in the front of the squad car, the other had to sit in the back to restore its balance. Age has sapped his voice, and stiffened his fingers so that faster tunes like 'Knockin' On My Door' and 'Lonesome' are not always coherent, but the years have signally failed to diminish his appetite for cackling anecdote. TR

Alice Moore (c. 1903–50)
VOCAL

On record, at least, Alice Moore was one of the most popular of the St Louis bluesmen of the '20s and '30s. Henry Townsend remembered her as 'a nice mixer with the public' and 'devoted to her blues singing'.

*** St. Louis Women – Vol. 1 (1927–1929)
Document DOCD-5290 Moore; Ike Rodgers (tb); Henry Brown (p). 8–c. 11/29.

*** St. Louis Women – Vol. 2 (1934–1941)
Document DOCD-5291 Moore; Ike Rodgers (tb); Peetie Wheatstraw (p, g); Henry Brown, Jimmie Gordon, unknown (p); unknown (vn); unknown (g); unknown (b). 8/34–11/37.

Moore's pinched, nasal tone and her preference for funereal tempos seem appropriate tools for a woman much given to accounts of discouraging relationships with disappointing men. Such blues span her career, from 'My Man Blues' in 1929 to 'Too Many Men' in 1937. Her most popular theme, however, appears to have been the more thoroughly dissatisfied '(Blue) Black And Evil Blues', a disturbingly bitter song of which she recorded four versions. The first two were with Rodgers and Brown, who accompanied her in a sombre, stately fashion throughout her 1929 and 1934 sessions. Thereafter her most frequent recording partner was Peetie Wheatstraw, whose typical piano figures accent the gravity of her blues. In 'Hand In Hand Women' (1937) she was warmer towards men and sang less aggressively than was her wont, but in the same session's 'Midnight Creepers', about violence against women on the streets, and 'Tired Of Me Blues' she returns to more familiar topics. 'Push Cart Pusher' and 'Unlucky Play Blues', her last recordings, are sung with a little of the style of Roosevelt Sykes, who may play the piano. Both CDs are shared with St Louis Bessie.

Moore's six 1936 recordings were with Wheatstraw and guitarist Kokomo Arnold and are found on the latter's *Vol. 3* (Document DOCD-5039). The combination was a good one, Arnold's lush slide guitar moistening the dryness of singer and pianist. TR

Wild Bill Moore (born 1918)
TENOR SAXOPHONE, VOCAL

The Houston-born Moore was an amateur boxer in his teens and almost took it up professionally, but decided instead to go into music as a tenor saxophonist. In the '40s he played on both coasts and in Detroit, and made numerous records both as an

accompanist (to Helen Humes, Big Joe Turner and others) and in his own name. He continued to be active in the '60s and '70s.

**(*) The Complete Recordings: Volume 1 1945–1948
Blue Moon BMCD 6042 *Moore; Teddy Buckner, Phil Guilbeaux, unknown (t); George 'Happy' Johnson (tb); Gene Montgomery, unknowns (ts); Paul Williams, unknown (bs); Wilbert Baranco, Russ Freeman, Floyd Taylor, T. J. Fowler, Milt Buckner (p); John 'Shifty' Henry, Leroy Gray, Herman Hopkins, unknown (b); prob. Rabon Tarrant, Ken Kennedy, Reetham Mallett, unknown (d); band (v). 12/45–48.*

**(*) The Complete Recordings: Volume 2 1948–1955
Blue Moon BMCD 6043 *Moore; Jonah Jones, Russell Green, Willie Wells, unknown (t); James Buxton (tb); Joe Gayles, Paul Quinichette, Louis Barnett, unknown (ts); Bill Graham, Tate Houston, unknown (bs); Milt Buckner (o, p); Walter Bishop, Ted Sheely, Barry Harris, unknowns (p); Emmitt Slay, poss. Jimmy Spruill (g); Ivan Rolle, Franklin Skeete, Lewis Martin, poss. Doug Watkins, unknowns (b); Eddie Grant, Joe Harris, Leonard Christian, Bob Atcheson, unknowns (d); band (v). c. 48–c. 55.*

The period covered by these albums was the heyday of the tenor sax soloist. Jukeboxes gobbled up hundreds of sax-led instrumentals of blues, boogies and ballads, while in concert tenor-men bent over backwards – literally – to present their music more and more outrageously. It's in that context that we should listen to Wild Bill Moore, as to contemporaries like Big Jay McNeely. He had some ability as a conventional jazz player, as he occasionally shows in a 13-minute version of 'What Is This Thing Called Love?' (*Volume 1*) and in the warm ballad playing of 'Blue Journey' (*Volume 2*), but his records, reflecting market forces, are mostly blues ('Boulevard Boogie', 'Harlem Parade', 'We're Gonna Rock', etc.) and pop tunes like 'Bubbles', played with the ritual gestures of honk and squeal, repetition and overblowing. They're exciting for a few minutes, but after a while you need to throw open a window and let the heat out before your brain boils. As usual, Blue Moon's compilation and research are irreproachable. TR

Deacon John Moore (born 1941)
VOCAL, GUITAR

John Moore's mother favoured classical music, but he was playing R&B professionally in high school, and dropped out of college to form the Ivories. Moore made a few R&B singles which went nowhere, but he was a key session musician, making vital contributions to the biggest hits of Ernie K-Doe, Lee Dorsey, Aaron Neville, Chris Kenner and Irma Thomas. He led The Ivories for many years, doing what he had to, including playing pop hits for white dances and psychedelia in the late '60s, and continues to adorn the New Orleans scene.

** Singer Of Song [sic]
JoGeo JG-2001 *Moore; prob. George Davis (syn, g, b, d prog); Doug Shaw, Treva L. Burke, Wendy M. Pederson (v). 90?*

**(*) Live At The 1994 New Orleans Jazz Fest
Redbone RBR-L 1994 *Moore; Brian E. Murray (t); Bruce Hammond (tb); Fred Kemp (ts); J. D. Hill (h); Robert J. Dabon (p); Charles Moore (b); Oliver Alcorn III (v). 4/94.*

♛ **** Deacon John's Jump Blues: Music From The Film
VCC VET 0557 *Moore; Bernard E. Floyd, Brian E. Murray (t); Jeffery V. Albert, Jerome S. Verges Jr (tb); Julius J. Handy (as);* Amadee Castenell, Joseph H. Saulsbury (ts); Carl A. Blouin Sr (bs); Henry Butler, Davell Crawford, Dr John [Mack Rebennack], Allen Toussaint (p); Chris Severin, Charles Moore (b); Herlin Riley, Shannon Powell (d); Realove, Teedy Boutté, Pamela Landrum, Danon Smith (v). 4/01.

Deacon John is probably tired of being New Orleans's best-kept secret, but the CDs before *Jump Blues* don't do him justice. *Singer Of Song* is a co-production with George Davis, who wrote or co-wrote all the songs, including 'Tell It Like It Is'. The rest of the material is mostly soul ballads, with input from funk, reggae and disco; *Singer Of Song* is marginal, and made more so by the insensitive handling of synthesizers and drum programs. The live CD consists of covers of well-known Chicago blues, with the songs and sound of Elmore James prominent. This is giving the public what they want, and it's professionally done, but the material is excessively familiar and the horns muffled.

Jump Blues is also retrospective, but it's the CD where Deacon shows what he can do with the music of his native city, and why he's so respected there. These are studio recordings of some of the songs on the unreservedly recommended DVD *Deacon John's Jump Blues: A Concert Of Music From The Film* (VCC VET 0558). (*The Film* itself is a documentary which doesn't seem to have been released yet.) On some numbers, Deacon only plays guitar as a band member, and there are tracks by Dr John, Davell Crawford and the Zion Harmonizers where he's absent; but when he sings he's magnificent, whether doing belters like 'Jumpin' In The Morning' and a Smiley Lewis medley, or blues-ballads like 'Someday' and 'Losing Battle'. A re-creation of Shirley & Lee with Teedy Boutté is sexy fun (and sexier and funnier on DVD). The accompaniments are shared between an excellent small combo and a big band that's devastatingly swinging, thanks to Herlin Riley's drumming and Wardell Quezergue's brilliant charts. CS

Gary Moore (born 1952)
VOCAL, GUITAR

In his teens Moore played in Skid Row before forming his own Gary Moore Band. During the '70s he served three spells in Thin Lizzy, played in Colosseum II and formed his own G-Force. After only moderate success in the '80s he set a new direction for his music with Still Got The Blues *(1990), which would become one of the best-selling blues albums of the period. Although he has continued to work in rock and blues-rock contexts, he regularly touches base with the blues.*

*** Still Got The Blues
EMI MOORECD 8 *Moore; unknowns (brass, reeds, h, kb, strings); Albert King (g, v); unknowns (g, b, d, v). 90.*

*** After Hours
EMI MOORECD 9//Virgin CDV 2684 *Moore; unknowns (brass, reeds, kb, strings); B. B. King, Albert Collins (g, v); unknowns (g, b, d, v). 91.*

**(*) Blues Alive
Virgin CDV 2784 *Moore; unknowns (brass, reeds, kb, strings, g, b, d, v). 92.*

*** Blues For Greeny
EMI MOORECD 10//Virgin CDV 2784 *Moore; unknowns (brass, reeds, kb, strings, g, b, d, v). 95.*

*** **Parisienne Walkways: The Blues Collection**
EMI 91100 *Moore; unknowns (brass, reeds, kb, strings); Albert King (g, v); unknowns (g, b, d, v).* 90–95.

*** **The Best Of The Blues**
Virgin CDVX 2943 2CD *Moore; unknowns (brass, reeds, kb, strings); Albert King, B. B. King (g, v); unknowns (g, b, d, v).* 90–95.

Moore has an extensive catalogue: EMI's MOORECD series alone runs to a dozen albums, of which *Still Got The Blues*, *After Hours* and *Blues For Greeny* are the most relevant to this book. On *Still Got The Blues* the in-your-face guitar of 'Oh Pretty Woman' (a duet with Albert King) and 'Walking By Myself' is balanced by more restrained performances, and the same careful control of dynamics benefits *After Hours*. The best of the three is *Blues For Greeny*, dedicated to Moore's old friend Peter Green, with such impressive tracks as the slow, ominous 'Love That Burns', the B. B. King-flavoured 'Merry Go Round' and the admirably sung 'Need Your Love So Bad', which deserves the attention of anyone who thinks that Moore's vocal ability is limited to a conventional blues-rock bellow. Here, too, even more than on his other blues albums, Moore reveals a sensitivity to the material, and to the guitar's role in re-enacting it, that decisively separates him from the blues-rock herd. *Blues Alive* has a tribute song to B. B. King, 'King Of The Blues', and a rerecording of Moore's 1979 hit 'Parisienne Walkways', a handful of tourists' photographs artlessly reconstituted as a song with a vaguely bluesy guitar line.

The Best Of The Blues contains a well-made selection from those albums, with the second disc devoted to live recordings (including five numbers heard on Disc 1 in studio versions). But its 31 tracks don't invalidate other compilations. *Parisienne Walkways* duplicates only 'Oh Pretty Woman' and 'Walking By Myself'; it also shares the title track and 'Need Your Love So Bad', but the former is longer than the cut on *Best Of*, while the *Best Of* version of 'Need Your Love So Bad' is a four-minute edit of the original, which *Parisienne Walkways* offers at full length.

(*) **Back To The Blues
Sanctuary SANCD 072 *Moore; Martin Drover (t); Frank Mead, Nick Pentelow (ts); Nick Payn (bs); Vic Martin (kb); Pete Rees (b); Darrin Mooney (d).* 00.

The dynamic subtlety commended in some of the albums above is less in evidence here. Listeners who like their performances to rev up gradually rather than start with the throttle wide open will flinch a little at the volume and penetration of the introduction to 'Ain't Got You' or 'Stormy Monday', and may welcome with relief the more dulcet opening passages of 'Picture of The Moon', 'Drowning In Tears' or 'The Prophet'. The first is rather a wet song but 'The Prophet' redeploys the long, humming lines of 'Parisienne Walkways' in the less irritating context of an anthemic instrumental, while 'Drowning In Tears' is an effective chill-out after the earlier heat. TR

Gatemouth Moore (1913–2004)
VOCAL

Born in Topeka, Kansas, Dwight Moore was winning talent contests by the age of nine with renditions of 'When Irish Eyes Are Smiling' and 'My Yiddishe Mama'. Until he left home with a carnival in 1930 he was managed by the wealthy white family for whom his mother worked, and it was with commercial motives that he switched to blues. Moore's first recordings, on the Gilmore's Chez Paree label, included his best-known compositions, 'Did You Ever Love A Woman' (for many years a feature of B. B. King's show) and 'I Ain't Mad At You', both of which he remade more than once. In 1949, Moore experienced an onstage revelation, renounced the blues and entered the ministry. He became a gospel recording artist and DJ, although in 1977 Johnny Otis persuaded him to make a secular LP. He became pastor of a church in Yazoo City, Mississippi, but until nearly the end of his life he made occasional appearances at festivals, performing his hits both sinful and sacred.

(*) **Cryin' & Singin' The Blues
Savoy Jazz SVY 17327 *Moore; Bill Martin, Dick Vance, Russell Royster (t); Jimmy Hamilton (cl, ts); Harry Carney (as, bs); Flaps Dungee, Herman Flintall (as); John Jackson, Budd Johnson, John Hardee (ts); Sam Benskin (p, cel); poss. Pete Johnson (p); Tiny Grimes, unknown (g); Dallas Bartley, Al Hall, Al 'Junior' Raglin (b); prob. Hillard Brown, J. C. Heard, Eddie Nicholson (d); band (v).* 5/45–10/46.

(*) **Hey Mr. Gatemouth
[Westside WESF 100] *Moore; Bill Martin, unknown (t); Bert Patrick, unknown (as); Moses Gant, unknown (ts); Allen Smith, Nat Walker, Simeon Hatch (p); Willie Gaddy (g); Dolphus Dean, Monty Morrison, James Adams (d); band (v).* 8–12/47.

Gatemouth Moore didn't care for some kinds of blues, nor for audiences who did: 'I am not accustomed and don't know nothing about that gut-belly stuff in the joints.' These two packages, which between them wrap up his National and King recordings, bear out his self-description as one who 'put on tuxedoes, dressed up [and] sang intelligent.'

Critical shorthand classifies Moore as a blues shouter, which is a fair account of songs like 'Let's Go Back And Try One More Time' and 'Love Doctor Blues', but elsewhere on National his singing is often lighter and more open, as much reminiscent of Louis Jordan as of Wynonie Harris; 'They Can't Do This To You', with its hilarious lyrics about infidelity, is particularly Jordan-like. The backing comes from small combos led by Tiny Grimes, Dallas Bartley or Budd Johnson (who fronts a stellar lineup including Vance, Hamilton, Carney and Heard), and the arrangements strengthen the sense that Moore and National were chasing Jordan's audience.

The first session for King was backed by piano, guitar and drums, probably in emulation of Charles Brown, and its first song was a version of country singer Ted Daffan's 'I'm A Fool To Care'. Moore's vocalizing is very lush on this number, and still more so on the syrup-smooth 'East Of The Sun'. 'Christmas Blues' and 'Highway 61 Blues' are a touch rougher, but this, artistically Moore's most successful session for King, is the least likely to appeal to present-day blues fans.

Elsewhere on both CDs, Moore embraces full-blooded stentorianism and gives subtlety the elbow. The bellowing is less pronounced, and less problematic, on *Cryin' & Singin' The Blues*, but 'Bum Dee Dah Rah Dee' on that disc is made tedious as much by Moore's delivery as by its novelty lyric. There are some neat lines and some chili-hot trumpet solos by Bill Martin on *Hey Mr. Gatemouth*'s later tracks, but in the end Moore has a bigger claim to fame as the composer of 'I

Ain't Mad At You Pretty Baby' and 'Did You Ever Love A Woman' (which both appear on both CDs) than as a singer. CS

Johnny B. Moore (born 1950)
VOCAL, GUITAR

Moore was born in Clarksdale, Mississippi, and moved to Chicago at the age of 14. He hit the blues club scene in the early '70s, a protégé of Letha Jones, widow of pianist Johnny Jones and Moore's godmother. He was hired by Koko Taylor in 1975 and played on her album The Earthshaker *(1978), and subsequently worked with Willie Dixon's Chicago Blues All Stars, but it was not until 1987 that he made his own debut album,* Hard Times. *In addition to his own output, he has played on Delmark albums by Willie Kent, Bonnie Lee, Karen Carroll, Shirley Johnson and Tail Dragger. He had a stroke in 2003, from which, at the time of writing, he was making a steady recovery.*

*** Lonesome Blues
Wolf 120.851 *Moore; Lester Davenport (h); Willie Davis, Eddie Taylor (g); Willie Kent (b); Tim Taylor (d). 8/84, 2–8/87.*

*** 911 Blues (Chicago Blues Session – Vol. 27)
Wolf 120.873 *Moore; Eddie Shaw (s); Billy Branch (h); Detroit Jr (p); Willie Davis, John Primer, Minoru Marayama (g); Willie Kent, Peter 'Lobo' Nemec (b); Tim Taylor, Cleo Williams, Larry Taylor (d). 2/87, 10/92–1/95.*

Hard Times, made for the B.L.U.E.S. R&B label, has not been transferred to CD, but most of *Lonesome Blues* was made about the same time. Moore had been an admirer of Magic Sam since his teens, and 20 years later he still sounds like him on 'Knocking At Your Door'. He has other models; indeed, in 'Blues Medley' he parades them in a series of impersonations (Muddy Waters, Howlin' Wolf, Jimmy Reed) or tributes (Junior Parker, Elmore James, Lightnin' Hopkins). But there are more distinctive pieces like 'Mean Mistreater', with jabbing West Side guitar playing, and a track perplexingly titled 'Up Side The Wall' with downhome acoustic slide guitar.

911 Blues also kicks off with a Magic Sam groove, 'Lookin' Good', but the next four tracks are originals. This is the electric, band-accompanied portion of the entertainment, and it's an interestingly varied set. For the rest of the programme Moore plays acoustic guitar on original and acquired material, often duetting with Branch, and sounds, on tracks such as Hopkins's 'Candy Kitchen Blues', as if he has time-machined himself back 40 years – or, in Robert Wilkins's 'That's No Way To Get Along', still farther.

*** Live at Blue Chicago
Delmark DE-688 *Moore; Ken Saydak (kb); Bob Levis, Minoru Maruyama (g); Johnny B. Gayden, Mike 'Sleepy' Riley (b); 'Baldhead Pete' [Cleo Williams] (d); Karen Carroll, Willie Kent, Melvina Allen (v). 7/95.*

With three numbers derived from Muddy Waters and two from Magic Sam, Moore seems determined to carry on testifying to his chief models. Perhaps the club setting dictated a familiar setlist; the other songs include 'Sweet Little Angel', 'Boogie Chillen', a Hopkins medley ('Back Door Friend') and a couple from Bobby Bland, and the only original is a second, and excellent, version of 'Mean Mistreater'. But Moore's treatments are integrated into a personal style, characterized by declamatory singing and agile guitar playing which, while it still bears the marks of the Magic Sam mould, he has reworked into an individual and expressive idiom.

**(*) Troubled World
Delmark DE 701 *Moore; Kenny Anderson (t); Hank Ford (ts); Willie Henderson (bs); Ken Saydak, Roosevelt Purifoy (p); Minoru Maruyama (g); Mike 'Sleepy' Riley (b); 'Baldhead Pete' [Cleo Williams] (d). 96/97.*

**(*) Born In Clarksdale, Mississippi (Chicago Blues Session Vol. 57)
Wolf 120.804 *Moore; Chicago Playboy Horns (s); Sugar Blue (h); Ken Barker (p); Willie Kent (b); Larry Taylor (d). 3/98.*

**(*) Acoustic Blue Chicago
Blue Chicago BC 5004 *Moore; Lester 'Mad Dog' Davenport (h); Willie Kent, Bonnie Lee (v). 11/98.*

These are by no means poor records, but in terms of career development they have Moore running on the spot. *Troubled World* blends blues standards – though for once there is nothing by Magic Sam – and soul numbers. His congested voice occasionally makes him sound like someone hauled off the farm to record for, say, Fat Possum, particularly in the hoary old smutty song 'Stoop Down Baby'. His guitar is penetrating but sonically unvarying, and one could wish that piano or horns had been added on more tracks. *Born In Clarksdale, Mississippi* doesn't merely mark time but calls back its hands: an 'Elmore James Medley' and 'Legends Of The Blues', less a song than a dull list of names, bracket tributes to Howlin' Wolf, Sonny Boy Williamson II and Magic Sam, reminding us of the younger man who tried to make an impression with impressions. The one wholly successful track is Bobby Rush's 'Dangerous', a one-chord song which Moore handles with verve and ingenuity.

Having played electric guitar for most of those albums, Moore unplugged for the Blue Chicago date, playing, either solo or with Davenport, a typical selection of Chicago standbys like Jimmy Rogers's 'Ludella' and 'Going Away Baby' and Wolf's 'Baby How Long' and revisiting 'That's No Way To Get Along'. Moore is better able than most of his contemporaries to fashion an acoustic set out of such material, but his guitar accompaniments are often not much more than repeated rhythm patterns, and in that respect he is no Garfield Akers.

**** Rockin' In The Same Old Boat
Delmark DG-769 *Moore; Hirotaka Konishi (g); Robert 'Bass Playin' Pete' Peterson (b); Cordell Teague (d). 2/03.*

Guitarist Justin O'Brien in his notes describes *Rockin' In The Same Old Boat* as Moore's 'most soulful' and 'most personal' album, and is right on both counts. As often with Moore, 'personal' refers less to compositional input (only one song is his) than to his creative appropriation of other people's material: his second recording of 'Lookin' Good' is exuberantly developed from Magic Sam's version, 'Cut You A Loose' cuts loose from Junior Wells and the title number is another bravura exploration of a one-chord tune. It must have helped that he was backed by a superbly pushy bass player. This is Moore at his recorded best, and one hopes that he can recover the power to equal it. TR

Kid Prince Moore
VOCAL, GUITAR

Not a thing is known about this artist. The sites of his recordings, New York and Charlotte, North Carolina, imply that he was active in one or more of the East Coast states.

**(*) Kid Prince Moore (1936–1938)
Document DOCD-5180 Moore; Shorty Bob Parker (p, v). 4/36–6/38.

Moore's tuneful singing and guitar playing are difficult to locate on a stylistic map of the blues, if you're seeking to pin him down to something more precise than 'East Coast'. A couple of his performances show a fleeting resemblance to Josh White, others like 'Honey Dripping Papa' a stronger one to Blind Blake, and 'Market Street Rag' is cut from the same cloth as Blind Boy Fuller's 'Rag, Mama, Rag'. Certain vowel sounds (e.g. 'house' in 'Market Street Rag' or ''bout' in 'Talkin' 'Bout The Snuff') suggest he may have been from east Virginia. The more evidentially useful recordings in this respect, and also the more rewarding for the listener, are the 1936 solos, which occupy the first 11 tracks of this CD; seven of these had not been issued before. The 1938 duets with Parker have less character and more repetition. Of those dozen sides Moore sings the first six and Parker the rest. After nearly an hour of Moore's voice, Parker's comes as some relief, especially when he launches into the boisterous 'Ridin' Dirty Motorsickle'. More than a few of the tracks on this CD sound as if they came from second- or third-generation tapes. TR

Monette Moore (1902–62)
VOCAL, KAZOO

Monette Moore was born in rural Texas, but show business and the big city soon beckoned. By the early '20s she was in Kansas City, playing the piano for silent movies, in 1923 she made her first records, and by 1925 she was appearing on the New York stage. The '30s were a busy cycle of club and theatre engagements, and for a time she owned and ran Monette's Place. When Moore moved to Los Angeles in 1942, the club appearances continued, and she also featured with touring trad bands and secured small movie roles. In the '50s Moore gave up music for domestic service, but in 1961 she secured an engagement at Disneyland with the Young Men From New Orleans, and was working there when she suffered a fatal emphysema attack.

**(*) Monette Moore – Vol. 1 (1923–1924)
Document DOCD-5338 Moore; Tommy Ladnier, Rex Stewart, Bubber Miley (c); Jake Frazier (tb); Jimmy O'Bryant, Bob Fuller, unknown (cl); Clarence Johnson, Clarence Jones, Naomia Carew, James Cassino [poss. Cassino Simpson], Jimmy Blythe, John Montagu, Louis Hooper (p); Wyatt Houston (vn); Joe Davis (eff). c. 1/23–c. 11/24.

**(*) Monette Moore – Vol. 2 (1924–1932)
Document DOCD-5339 Moore; Bubber Miley, Rex Stewart (c); Jake Frazier (tb); Ernest Elliott (cl); Bob Fuller (cl, as, h); unknown (bcl); unknown (fl); Elmer Snowden (ts); Louis Hooper (p, u); poss. Phil Worde, Fats Waller (p); Elmer Snowden (bj); Billy Higgins (v); prob. Joe Davis (eff). c. 11/24–9/32.

Monette Moore's earliest recordings have a light-hearted chirpiness, but she soon becomes darker-voiced, and a surprising number of her songs are concerned with death, albeit sometimes in a facetious vein. (Her one appearance on kazoo is on 'Graveyard Bound Blues', quoting 'The Death March'.) On the first two thirds of *Vol. 1* she is usually accompanied by a solo pianist, often the excellent and underrated Clarence Jones, but when she moved on from Paramount small jazz ensembles became the norm. There are some famous names on both volumes, and they play consistently well, but there are no classic solos to be heard. Moore herself is workwomanlike, and sprightly or doleful as the lyrics require, but there's seldom a sense of personal involvement or creative fire, although it's worth singling out her versions of 'Gulf Coast Blues' and 'Down Hearted Blues', which were recorded just before Bessie Smith's, and don't deserve to be obliterated by the Empress's fame.

Twenty-one of Moore's 22 Ajax recordings were credited to Susie Smith on release, and one senses that she was content with anonymity. (In any case, no singer with a yearning for credibility would want to be associated with 'Memphis Blues' and 'Texas Special Blues', with their bizarrely awful accompaniment on harmonica, ukulele and banjo.) Her revue and cabaret material was probably heavier on jazz and pop, and she may have found these styles more congenial. Certainly her finest recording, 'Shine On Your Shoes/Louisiana Hayride', is some distance from the blues; the last song on *Vol. 2*, it's a jivey medley with sparkling accompaniment by Fats Waller, and Moore gives it all she's got, singing with radiant, bouncy swing and throwing in a gravelly Louis Armstrong imitation.

Scattered titles appear on VACs; Document omit her featured vocals with Charlie Johnson's important band (see *The Penguin Guide To Jazz Recordings*), which are on *The Complete Charlie Johnson Sessions* (Hot 'N Sweet FCD 5110). There's great fun to be had from 'Rhythm For Sale' and 'Two Old Maids In A Folding Bed', on *Jazzin' The Blues 1936–1946* (RST Jazz Perspectives JPCD-1515), but they supply further confirmation that Moore was happiest when getting hip to the jive. CS

Jimmy Morello (born 1955)
VOCAL

Growing up in Pittsburgh, Pennsylvania, Morello learned drums and formed his first band in his teens. A concert in 1971 directed his energies towards blues, and he worked for a few years with Louisiana Red. He spent most of the '80s in Sacramento, California, where he began singing, then, based in Phoenix, Arizona, worked with Pat Boyack & The Prowlers (1994–96), singing on their first two albums, and with Bob Margolin. Since the late '90s he has produced several artists for JSP.

*** Can't Be Denied
JSP JSPCD 287 Morello; Tom Mahon (p); Jeff Ross, Paul Bryant (g); Rick Reed (b); Paul Fasulo (d). 8/96.
** The Road I Travel
JSP JSPCD 2115 Morello; Johnny Viau (ts); Troy Jennings (bs); Mitch Kashmar (h); Tom Mahon (p); John Marx (g, v); Alex Schultz (g); Rick Reed (b); Paul Fasulo (d); Leroy 'Tons Of Fun' Carter (v). 8/98.
*** West Coast Redemption
JSP JSPCD 2151 As for above CDs. 8/96, 8/98.

Can't Be Denied reveals Morello's vocal models: Roy Brown

in 'I Read Your Letter' and 'Where Have You Gone', Big Joe Turner in 'Mercy Miss Percy'. These skilful *hommages* are lent weight by the energy and versatility of the accompanying musicians. The bigger budget that was evidently available for *The Road I Travel* produced a glossier sound, but too often it was at the expense of character. The horn riffs are conventional and the studio sound is cold: not so much a roomful of blues as a freezer cabinet. But Kashmar's harmonica solo in 'I Got To Know' is excellent.

West Coast Redemption, released in 2001, served as a calling-card for Morello in both his roles, selecting four tracks from each of the above albums and adding nine that he produced for other JSP acts such as Kirk Fletcher, Roy Gaines, Sweet Betty Journey and Kris Wiley. TR

Mike Morgan (born 1959)
GUITAR, BASS, VOCAL

The Dallas-born Morgan was drawn to the blues by hearing Stevie Ray Vaughan; he also studied the work of the Fabulous Thunderbirds, Anson Funderburgh and Ronnie Earl. In the mid-'80s he formed The Crawl with Darrell Nulisch, who was later replaced by Lee McBee. The band worked extensively in the Southwest and Europe, and during the '90s recorded for Black Top; Morgan also recorded with singer/guitarist Jim Suhler.

*** Lowdown & Evil
Me & My Blues MMBCD 703 *Morgan; Steve Howard (t); John Osborne (tb); Chris Whynaught (ts, v); Ernest Youngblood Jr (ts); Mark 'Kaz' Kazanoff (s); Lee McBee (h, v); Nick Connelly (o, p); Riley Osbourn, Ron Levy (p); Jim Suhler (g, v); Tater Britches (g); Rhandy Simmons, Richard 'Grady' Grigsby, Frankie J. Meyer, John L. Bradley, Carlton Powell (b); Marc Wilson (d, perc); Uncle John Turner (d).* 90–94.

Morgan's eight Black Top albums having been deleted, it's handy to have this compilation drawn from the first five, with a couple of additional tracks from a Black Top VAC. The album opens with two choruses of McBee's harmonica and three of his singing before we hear Morgan at any length, and this proves to have been an accurate trailer for the main feature, since McBee fronts 12 of the 15 tracks. Fair enough: Morgan was doing no singing at this point and McBee, his longtime partner in The Crawl, is always worth listening to, whether singing or blowing harmonica, but it leaves the top-billed artist oddly located in the background for much of the playing time. What one does hear of him is varied and ingenious, whether he is retracing the blurred line of Frankie Lee Sims's 'Frankie's Blues' or wailing high up the neck in 'Blue Cat Blues' or 'Kiss Me Baby'. If you admire Stevie Ray Vaughan or Anson Funderburgh and haven't yet come across Mike Morgan, his acquaintance is worth making.

**(*) Three Shades Of Blues
Charly CDGR 275 *Morgan; Chris Whynaught (s, v); Grady Grigsby (b); Marc Wilson (d).* c. 91.

These eight tracks (the rest of the CD is by Keb' Mo' and Maria Muldaur) are by the lineup of The Crawl that had saxophonist Chris Whynaught as vocalist. The recordings were made in concert, the sound is basic and there are several irritating fades. The general effect is closer to SRV and Double Trouble than to the more carefully made performances on *Lowdown & Evil*.

**(*) Texas Man
Me & My Blues MMBCD 7 *Morgan; Gary Primich (h); Riley Osbourn (o, p); Anson Funderburgh, Jon Moeller (g); Rhandy Simmons (b); Wes Starr (d, cowbell); Kevin Schermerhorn (d).* 00?

Up to this point Morgan had seldom let his voice be heard on record, but on *Texas Man*, apart from three instrumentals, he sings throughout. Technically speaking there's nothing wrong with his voice, but by comparison with McBee's or Whynaught's it doesn't have a great deal of weight or blues character. On the other hand, the absence on most tracks of any competing lead instrument means that Morgan's guitar is more prominently featured than on the foregoing CDs, and he achieves a splendidly bleary slide sound on Elmore James's 'Wild About You' and three Hound Dog Taylor numbers, 'Gimmie Back My Wig', 'Taylor's Rock' and 'See Me In The Evening'. Primich is excellent on two tracks, helping to give 'I Had To Put You Down' the antique patina of an early Howlin' Wolf recording. TR

Big Bill Morganfield (born 1956)
VOCAL, GUITAR, BASS

The son of Muddy Waters and Mary Brown, Morganfield was raised by his grandmother in Fort Lauderdale, Florida. He began playing guitar a few years after his father's death in 1983, but did not make a serious move towards playing music professionally until the '90s. Holding degrees in English and Communications, he made his living for a time as a teacher. Currently resident in the Atlanta area, he was voted Best New Blues Artist in the 2000 W. C. Handy Awards.

**(*) Nineteen Years Old: A Tribute To Muddy Waters
Taxim TX 1047 *Morganfield; 'Robert Nighthawk II' [Robert Tooms] (h, p); Blind Mississippi Morris (h); Al Gamble (o); Bob Margolin (g, b); Billy Earl McClelland (g); Aram Doroff (b); Darin James (d).* 97.

*** Rising Son
Blind Pig BPCD 5053 *Morganfield; Paul Oscher (h); Pinetop Perkins (p); Bob Margolin (g, prod); Robert Stroger (b); Willie Smith (d).* 99.

*** Ramblin' Mind
Blind Pig BPCD 5068 *Morganfield; Bill Lupkin, Billy Branch, Paul Oscher (h); Mr B, Pinetop Perkins (p); Taj Mahal (g, v); Billy Flynn, Bob Margolin (g); Nick Moss, Robert Stroger (b); Kenny Smith, Willie Smith (d); Theresa Davis, Robin Robinson (v).* 99, 01.

Although *Nineteen Years Old* was recorded two years earlier, it was not issued until 1999, the year when the sun also rose on *Rising Son*, and for many listeners the better distributed Blind Pig album (which indeed was billed as 'his recording debut') was their introduction to Big Bill Morganfield. *Rising Son* demonstrated that he had a lot of his father's big, proud tone, his growl and his holler, while his slide guitar playing in the title track and 'Left Hand Blues' had an authentic brooding vibrato. It was advantageous, of course, that he was surrounded by such alumni of Waters's band as Perkins, Smith, Margolin and Oscher, and that they performed several of Waters's songs like 'The Same Thing', 'Screamin' & Cryin' and

'Champagne & Reefer'. Margolin also contributed mightily to the Taxim CD, which, despite its title, has only three numbers directly connected with Waters. Unfortunately he was not also its producer; had he been, perhaps he could have encouraged Morganfield to project himself as a singer rather than chew and mumble the lyrics. He might also have vetoed the inapt 'Caldonia'. As it is, his trenchant slide guitar parts on 'She's Nineteen Years Old' and 'Rollin' And Tumblin'' are among the best things on a disc whose chief fault is that its subject was not quite ready to make it. At the time, then, it was fairer to regard *Rising Son* as Morganfield's real debut, though it was still possible to wonder if, in the long term, it would prove to have been more of a featherbed than a launching-pad. The mantle of respect lay so heavily on the musicians' shoulders that it was unclear if Morganfield's talent extended beyond an eerie capacity to conjure up the dead.

Ramblin' Mind provided an answer, if not quite an unequivocal one. A path substantially of Morganfield's own making, nine of the albums 14 songs being credited to him, it still bears the imprint of a Muddy shoe. Morganfield makes his way with perceptibly growing confidence, but the record remains a deeply filial exercise, with its oscillating slide guitar, the slow prowl of 'Dirty Dealin' Mama' and the tight collaborations with Lupkin that raise the ghosts of Muddy and Little Walter. That said, sounding like Muddy was a favoured *modus operandi* for plenty of artists before Bill Morganfield. A generous-hearted listener might prefer to eschew comparisons and simply taste this album as a tangy cocktail skilfully made to a classic Chicago bar recipe, straight up with a couple of olives in the duets with Taj Mahal.

*** **Blues In The Blood**
Blind Pig BPCD 5086 *Morganfield; Tad Walters (h, g, b, v); Jimmy Vivino (o, p, md, g); Brian Bisesi (g); Kenny Smith (d). 03?*

Morganfield's concern not to take predictable paths leads him here into interesting diversions: he drives backwards into blues history to catch, on 'Evil', something of the Sonny Boy Williamson–Yank Rachell sound of the '30s, Walters and Vivino playing the harmonica and mandolin roles, while in 'Whiskey' he and Walters weave a guitar duet that could be heard as a Mississippi translation of the Alec Seward–Louis Hayes manner. 'Feel Like Dyin'' also explores that older way of making music, somewhat in the manner of Jimmy Burns's recent Delmark albums. Elsewhere the musicians faultlessly echo Chicago blues styles of the '50s and '60s, Walters's harmonica on 'Anything Just For You' sounding so period-accurate that the track could almost be mistaken for a lost Muddy Waters recording. The song's lyrics, however, would give the game away, for here, as in the arrangement of 'Left Alone' and elsewhere, Morganfield plainly uses his own ideas. Hearing him develop those ideas, album by album, is an uncommon and valuable opportunity. TR

Joe Morris (1922–58)
TRUMPET, VOCAL

Morris, from Montgomery, Alabama, played first with the Alabama State Collegians, then with Lionel Hampton, for whom he wrote several tunes. In 1946 he organized his own band with another former Hampton musician, Johnny Griffin. His recordings for Atlantic at first had only regional success, but 'Anytime, Any Place, Anywhere' was an R&B #1 in 1950. Subsequent sides for Herald like 'Shake A Hand' were equally good sellers, but a promising career was terminated by Morris's death from a cerebral haemorrhage.

(*) **Joe Morris 1946–1949
Classics 5057 *Morris; Matthew Gee, Alfonso King (tb); Johnny Griffin, Wally Williams (ts); Bill McLemore (bs); Wilmus Reeves, Elmore 'Sylvester' (Elmo) Hope (p); George Freeman, unknown (g); Embra Daylie, Percy Heath, Bobby Burton, unknown (b); Leroy Jackson, Philly Joe Jones, Sinclair Abbott, Al Jones, unknown (d); band (v). 46–11/49.*

(*) **Anytime, Anyplace, Anywhere
Acrobat ACMCD 4008 *As above, except add unknowns (tb, s, p, g, b, d), Laurie Tate, Billy Mitchell (v). 46–2/51.*

** **Joe Morris 1950–1953**
Classics 5125 *Morris; unknowns (tb, s, p, g, b, d); Laurie Tate, Jimmy Lewis, Billy Mitchell, Teddy Smith (v). c. 7/50–53.*

Though capable of more diverse music-making, Joe Morris's bands of the '40s were constrained by popular taste, or record companies' forecasts of it, to devote most of their time in the studio to blues and boogie tunes featuring their leader and the tenor player Johnny Griffin. The latter would go on to a distinguished career in jazz, from which he might have looked back at this apprentice work with some embarrassment, but the obligatory honk-and-screech effects are often tempered by more disciplined playing, especially in the 1948–49 lineup with Gee and Hope, another jazz notable in the making, who plays some stout boogie woogie in 'The Applejack'. Morris himself is a stylish trumpeter and a competent vocalist; both facets are on view in 'Lowdown Baby' and 'Wig Head Mama Blues'. Although these recordings were contemporaneous with the first flowering of bebop, even performances that have some claim to be considered jazz, such as 'Wilma's Idea' and 'Tia Juana', are barely touched by the new music.

1950–1953 opens with 'Anytime, Any Place, Anywhere', a slow pop ballad piercingly sung by Laurie Tate. Its success broadened the band's repertoire beyond blues and boogies, and a good deal of this CD is pop songs by the high-voiced crooner Billy Mitchell. Acrobat draw about two thirds of their tracks from the first Classics, omitting some of the abovementioned tracks, and the remaining eight from the second. TR

Buddy Moss (1914–84)
VOCAL, GUITAR, HARMONICA

Eugene Moss was born in Jewell, Georgia, and taught himself harmonica as a child. Arriving in Atlanta in 1928, he fell in with the circle of musicians around Curley Weaver and took up the guitar. A successful recording career was interrupted in 1935, when Moss killed his wife and went to prison. That it was only five years before he was paroled into the custody of J. B. Long, who wanted to add Moss to his roster of recording artists, suggests that there were extenuating circumstances. Moss's resumption of his recording career was aborted by America's entry into World War II, which led to shellac rationing, and by the AFM ban on recording. Moss re-emerged in 1966 and played occasional festivals into the '70s, but became embittered when a session for Columbia was not issued, and thereafter refused to record.

***(*) **Buddy Moss – Vol. 1 (1933)**
Document DOCD-5123 *Moss; prob. Fred McMullen, Curley*

Weaver (g); Ruth Willis, Blind Willie McTell (sp). 1/33–9/33.

Moss made his recording debut at 17, playing harmonica in the Georgia Cotton Pickers alongside Curley Weaver and Barbecue Bob. Their recordings are included on *Barbecue Bob – Vol. 3* (Document DOCD-5048); the similar-sounding Georgia Browns, with Fred McMullen replacing Bob, can be heard on *Curley Weaver (1933–1935)* (Document DOCD-5111). Moss's guitar on early sides like 'Daddy Don't Care' shows a strong debt to the ragtime blues of Blind Blake. This song and others also prefigure the music of Blind Boy Fuller, and it's generally accepted that Moss was a strong influence on Fuller.

Moss's guitar playing synthesizes his own creativity, Blake's complex, freewheeling ragtime and the equally complex but more sombre style of Curley Weaver. The songs on *Vol. 1* are all accompanied by splendid guitar duets, usually with Weaver; he's occasionally replaced by Fred McMullen's citric slide work. As a singer and songwriter, Moss was a serious, not to say dour, artist, preoccupied with jealousy, infidelity, hard luck and hard times; 'T.B.'s Killing Me' with its mix of unblinking realism and cynical misanthropy is the work of a man who was not much interested in being liked. A number of tracks in *Vol. 1*'s second half are taken from noisy discs, but the quality of the music makes penetrating the susurrations worthwhile.

***(*) **Buddy Moss – Vol. 2 (1933–1934)**
Document DOCD-5124 *Moss; Curley Weaver (g).* 9/33–8/34.

Vol. 2 starts with five tracks that wrap up Moss's collaborations with Curley Weaver; thereafter he is heard solo. 'New Lovin' Blues', his first side in this vein, is a version of a song that McTell and Weaver called 'Ticket Agent Blues' and sang as a jaunty paean to their love-making abilities; Moss, playing brilliant guitar flourishes, sounds Eeyoreishly fed up that, as a result of his prowess, 'these Georgia womens just won't let poor Buddy Moss rest.' For most of this disc, Moss's slogan is 'I don't do cheerful.' His voice is deeper and more sullen, and he continues to be preoccupied with death, misery and relationships going or gone wrong. Even *double entendre* numbers like 'Dough Rolling Papa' and the clever 'Stinging Bull Nettle' come across as combative assertions of sexual superiority, not tantalizing promises of a good time. Throughout, the guitar playing is magnificent; polished and carefully crafted, it nevertheless sounds like a spontaneous response to the lyrics. Some of the source discs have again been well played.

***(*) **Buddy Moss – Vol. 3 (1935—1941)**
Document DOCD-5125 *Moss; Sonny Terry (h); Brownie McGhee (p, sp); Josh White (g, v); Oh Red [Bull City Red], Robert Young (wb).* 8/35–10/41.

Document's final volume begins with three solo numbers, one of them the savagely funny 'Going To Your Funeral In A Vee Eight Ford'. For the next 12 songs, Moss is joined by Josh White. The pairing works perfectly most of the time, with Josh playing ringing treble decorations or supplying strolling bass patterns as Moss takes off and flies. Only two spirituals let the side down; Joshua White (The Singing Christian) is habitually earnest, but Moss's bored vocal responses and poorly worked out guitar figures make him sound like Eugene Moss (The Singing Agnostic). More successful, and a harbinger of White's move to folk blues and protest, is their vocal duet on the prison song 'Talking About My Time'; it's taken from a decidedly rough 78, though.

As it turned out, the song was also a harbinger of jail time for Moss, hence a six-year gap before the CD's last tracks. Of a dozen titles recorded, only five were issued, although a test pressing of a sixth survives. Even within this small sample, there are solos, a piano–guitar duet with Brownie McGhee and small band numbers. Columbia's Art Satherley was evidently keen to explore his new signing's potential; in doing so, he documented a more light-hearted side of Moss's music.

**** **The Essential**
Classic Blues CBL 200029 2CD *Similar to above CDs.* 1/33–10/41.

The Essential includes two sides by the Georgia Browns and accompaniments to the singing of Ruth Willis and Curley Weaver. Its 36 tracks are well chosen and well programmed. Otherwise careful remastering, mostly from pristine 78s, makes a brief but very loud electronic anomaly at the end of track 1 all the more irritating. Classic Blues' habitual skimping on information beyond a tracklisting is also an annoyance, but musically and technically this is the set for non-completists.

***(*) **Atlanta Blues Legend**
Biograph BCD 139 *Moss; Jeff Espina (h, g); John Jackson (g).* 5–6/66.

In the mid-'60s Moss fell in with the Atlanta Folk Music Society and made a number of appearances around town. One of them was attended by Columbia producer John Hammond, who remembered Moss from 1941 and decided to record him; the first seven tracks of this CD are from that session. Moss was still a skilful guitarist and a forceful harp player, but he veers between trying to emulate the refined elegance of his old associate, Josh White, and settling for rough-edged first drafts. Especially when playing harmonica, Espina doesn't listen to Moss, and the results sound like a demo tape. It's no great surprise that Columbia shelved the session.

Things were very different a month later when Moss played a concert in Washington, DC, with assistance from John Jackson on seven of 11 numbers. Moss began on harmonica with 'I'm Sitting On Top Of The World' and 'Kansas City', before switching to guitar. Much of the concert consists of similarly well-known songs, like 'Step It Up And Go', 'Betty And Dupree' and 'I've Got To Keep [sic] To The Highway', but Moss was committed, energetic and spurred on by Jackson's supportive, competitive second guitar. This was a night when everything came right, and the resulting LP was one of the most undervalued successes of the '60s 'blues revival', the more so because Moss declined to record again. Its reissue on CD is made slightly less treasurable by the inferior material used to extend the playing time. cs

Nick Moss (born 1969)
VOCAL, GUITAR, BASS, HARMONICA

Moss represents the next generation of Chicago guitarists after players like Dave Specter and Steve Freund. He began playing in clubs while still in his teens, initially on bass; in his 20s he worked for Jimmy Dawkins, for Willie 'Big Eyes' Smith in The Legendary Blues Band, and, now playing guitar, for Jimmy Rogers. He founded his band, The Flip Tops, in the late '90s.

(*) **First Offense
Blue Bella BBCD 1001 *Moss; The 'Big Dez' Baby Orchestra [Dez Desormeaux] (reeds); Lynwood Slim (h); Eric Michaels (o); Donny Nichilo (p); Sho Komiya (b); Kenny Smith, Mark Fornek (d).* 01?

*** **Got A New Plan**
Blue Bella BBCD 1002 *Moss; Dez Desormeaux (s); Bill Lupkin, Lynwood Slim (h); John Kattke (o); Harunobu (Hal) Tsushida (p); Gareth Best, Joe Moss (g); Andy Lester, James DiGerolomo (b); Greg (Smokey) Campbell (d, perc). 7/01.*

***(*) **Count Your Blessings**
Blue Bella BBCD 1003 *Moss; Sam Myers, Curtis Salgado, Lynwood Slim (h, v); Barrelhouse Chuck (o, p, v); Kate Moss, Anson Funderburgh (g); Andy Lester, Bob Stroger, Johnny Bradley (b); Greg Campbell, Willie 'Big Eyes' Smith (d). 12/02–1/03.*

***(*) **Sadie Mae**
Blue Bella BBCD 1004 *Moss; Gerry Hundt (h, g); Bob Welsh (o, p); Dave Wood (b); Victor Spann (d). 2/05.*

Bill Dahl, in the notes to *Got A New Plan*, calls Moss's music 'resolutely traditional', a fair description. Whether discoursing in the musical accent of Chicago, New Orleans or LA, Moss is well-read and fluent. Although primarily a guitarist, he is not lost in admiration of his ability, which is considerable, but has the self-control to play slowly and uncomplicatedly when the song calls for it, as in 'She Keeps Me Worried' on *First Offense* or 'My Daddy Was Right' on *New Plan*. But when the emotional temperature is higher, as in 'Let's Try This Plan Again' (*New Plan*), he matches it with intense, wrenched playing. He wrote all but one of the numbers on *Offense* and most of those on *New Plan*, but it's not always easy to assess them, partly because his articulation tends to be unclear and partly because the vocal tracks often fail to stand out in the mix, so that his voice is entangled with sounds in the same frequency range like the harmonica or even his own guitar playing. ('Ain't Got That Time' on *New Plan* is a particularly impenetrable example.) Fortunately this peculiarity of engineering is only intermittent on *New Plan* and doesn't affect tracks like 'Katie Ann', a slow blues in an early Muddy or Jimmy Rogers manner with apt harmonica by Lynwood Slim.

The promise of the preceding albums is more fully realized in *Count Your Blessings*, which also benefits from superior studio sound and the practised accompanying work of Barrelhouse Chuck, Curtis Salgado and Lynwood Slim. Swinging into the zestful tempos of 'Do You Know', 'Porchlight' or 'Panic Attack', Moss conjures up ghosts like Magic Sam, only to return to the deep blues groove of 'Break Bad'. These and other original songs come first in the programme; the second half, a varied handful of other people's compositions, is mostly an opportunity for cameos by his collaborators.

Sadie Mae, made with his regular band The Flip Tops, is less eventful but more even-textured. Moss's singing improves all the time, and his guitar rings and swings in the open-weave quintet setting. All but three of the 16 numbers are his, and while they sometimes allude to professed models like Muddy Waters ('One-Eyed Jack') or Jimmy Rogers ('Just Like That'), their themes and lines are new-cut. TR

Mr B
PIANO, VOCAL

Mark 'Mr B' Braun is a Detroit-based pianist who has made a number of albums in his own right and has accompanied Steve Freund and Big Bill Morganfield, among others, on theirs.

*** **Shining The Pearls**
Blind Pig BP 71886 *Mr B; Marcus Belgrave (t); Johnny 'T Bone' Paxton (tb); Louis Barnett (ts); Rick Steiger (bs); George Bedard (g); Curt [Kurt] Krahnke (b); J. C. Heard (d, v); Jeanne Carroll (v). 86–88?*

Braun's only currently available album expands the original *Shining The Pearls* LP with tracks from the later *Partners In Time*. Most of the listed musicians appear on only a few numbers, the bulk of the pieces being duets for piano and drums, drawn chiefly from the blues and boogie-woogie library (Cow Cow Davenport's 'Cow Cow Blues', Big Maceo's 'Chicago Breakdown', etc.) but including an evocation of Little Brother Montgomery ('Little Brother') and a couple of original boogies. Braun is obviously steeped in his source material and his playing is never less than sturdy and often exhilarating. Jeanne Carroll sings on three numbers, Heard on one and Braun himself, pleasantly, on five. The recording of the piano is close, but the mixing deprives Heard's drumming of much of its tone. TR

Muddy Waters (1913/15–83)
VOCAL, GUITAR

McKinley Morganfield was born in Rolling Fork, Mississippi, and worked as a young man on the Stovall plantation near Clarksdale, where he was fortuitously recorded by Alan Lomax for the Library of Congress in 1941, and again in 1942. Not long afterwards he migrated to Chicago and, with the encouragement of senior members of the blues clique like Big Bill Broonzy, began to play in clubs. His records for Aristocrat (later Chess) first made his name as a singer and slide guitarist, then, from the mid-'50s onwards, charted his refinement of the Chicago bar-band sound. When in Chicago he held court at Pepper's Lounge or Smitty's Corner, but he was often on the road touring, and after visiting Europe with the 1963 AFBF he made regular trips overseas. During the '70s, with a new manager (and, after 1975, a new record label), Muddy moved on to the growing college-town circuit, where he enjoyed his status as a founding father of modern blues. He was also one of the most influential bandleaders in the music's history, schooling innumerable players, many of whom embody his legacy to this day.

**** **The Complete Plantation Recordings**
MCA/Chess (A) CHD 9344//(E) MCD 09344 *Muddy Waters; Son Simms [Henry Sims] (vn, g); Louis Ford (md, v); Percy Thomas (g, v); Charles Berry (g). 8/41–7/42.*
*** **The Field Recordings 1941/42**
[Zircon Bleu 501] *As above. 8/41–7/42.*

In some of these remarkable recordings a group of musicians from rural Mississippi give Alan Lomax a fleeting image of the stringband music that had once been heard all over the South. Either because of the collector's interests or the musicians', the repertoire is all blues, and thus an acknowledgement of the tidal wave that is drowning the old sounds. By a superb irony, one of the players in the Son Simms Four will be a leading figure in the next stage of the blues' history. Lomax was evidently taken with the young Muddy Waters, for he devoted most of his discs to performances by him, either solos like 'Country Blues' and 'I Be's Troubled', which have the stamp of Robert Johnson, or gentler blues with a second guitarist like 'Burr Clover Blues'. These serendipitous recordings also include conversations between Waters and Lomax that are almost as absorbing. The scrupulously presented MCA

CD is the definitive source; Zircon juxtapose ten of the items with a dozen by Son House, also recorded for the Library of Congress in 1941–42.

*** The Chronological Muddy Waters 1941–1947
Classics 5008 *As above, except add unknown (ss), Alex Atkins (as), poss. Lee Brown, James Clark, Sunnyland Slim (p); Homer Harris (g), Ernest 'Big' Crawford, unknown (b), Judge Riley, unknown (d). 8/41–47.*

(***) The Muddy Waters Story
Chrome Talk ABCD 041 4CD *As above, except add [Little] Johnny Jones (p), Leroy Foster (g, d), Jimmy Rogers (g). 8/41–49.*

*** Muddy Waters (1941–1950)
Document DOCD-5146 *As above. 8/41–1/50.*

*** Greatest Hits
Going For A Song GFS 246 *Muddy Waters; Sunnyland Slim (p); Son Simms, Charles Berry, Leroy Foster (g); Ernest 'Big' Crawford (b); unknown (d). 8/41–2/50.*

*** The Blues/Rolling Stone 1941–1950
Frémeaux FA 266 2CD *Muddy Waters; Alex Atkins (as); Little Walter (h, sp); James Clark, Sunnyland Slim, [Little] Johnny Jones (p); Son Simms (vn); Louis Ford (md); Leroy Foster (g, d); Percy Thomas, Homer Harris, Jimmy Rogers (g); Ernest 'Big' Crawford (b); Judge Riley, Elga Edmonds (d). 8/41–10/50.*

(***) Martin Scorsese Presents The Blues: Muddy Waters
Universal B 0000482 *Muddy Waters; A. C. Reed (ts); Little Walter (h, sp); Junior Wells, James Cotton (h); Johnny 'Big Moose' Walker (o); James Clark, Otis Spann, Lafayette Leake, Pinetop Perkins (p); Homer Harris, Jimmy Rogers, poss. Pat Hare, poss. Hubert Sumlin, Earl Hooker, Buddy Guy, Johnny Winter, Bob Margolin (g); Ernest 'Big' Crawford, Willie Dixon, Earnest Johnson, Charles Calmese (b); Judge Riley, Elga Edmonds, poss. Fred Below, Francis Clay, S. P. Leary, Bobby Little, Willie 'Big Eyes' Smith (d). 8/41–10/76.*

(***) Feel Like Going Home
Snapper Complete Blues SBLUECD 0003 *As for The Blues/Rolling Stone 1941–1950, except add Charles Berry (g); omit Atkins, Clark, Ford, Thomas, Harris, Riley. 7/42–10/50.*

(***) Ol' Man Mud
Arpeggio ARB 001 *Muddy Waters; unknown (ss); Alex Atkins (as); poss. Lee Brown, James Clark, Sunnyland Slim (p); Homer Harris, Leroy Foster (g); Ernest 'Big' Crawford, unknown (b); Judge Riley, unknown (d). 46–11/48.*

(***) Aristocrat Of The Blues 1946/48
[Zircon Bleu 506] *As above. 46–11/48.*

***(*) Baby Please Don't Go
[Indigo IGODCD 2552 2CD] *Muddy Waters; unknown (ss); Alex Atkins (as); Little Walter (h, g, v, sp); Junior Wells, Walter Horton (h); poss. Lee Brown, James Clark, Sunnyland Slim, [Little] Johnny Jones, Otis Spann (p); Leroy Foster (g, d); Jimmy Rogers (g, v); Homer Harris (g); Ernest 'Big' Crawford, unknown (b); Judge Riley, Elga Edmonds, Leonard Chess, unknown (d). 46–9/53.*

In 1946 Columbia had a chance to announce the new dawn of Chicago blues, and missed it: having recorded Muddy Waters, albeit in an unsympathetic piano trio setting, they left the masters on the shelf. Muddy had already cut an odd, obscure single, 'Mean Red Spider', under the name of James 'Sweet Lucy' Carter. Those four sides are on several of these CDs. Classics sandwich them between 16 Library of Congress recordings and the first Aristocrat coupling; Document put them between 12 LC numbers, the rest of the day's work at Columbia, when pianist James Clark and guitarist Homer Harris took over the vocal mike, and the Parkway record of 'Rollin' And Tumblin'' by Muddy and Leroy Foster. Arpeggio, Zircon and Indigo use the '46 four to preface selections of Aristocrat/Chess recordings, which are discussed below. Going For A Song's absurdly titled (but absurdly cheap) *Greatest Hits* ducks the 1946 session and simply glues together a dozen LC recordings and a dozen from Aristocrat/Chess. The Scorsese selection sandwiches 13 of the better-known Aristocrat/Chess sides between two earlier cuts and one from *Hard Again* (see below): not a bad collection by any means, but too short and arbitrary to appeal to anyone but a beginner. The Zircon has the same contents as the Arpeggio but adds six sides by Sunnyland Slim and St Louis Jimmy on which Muddy played guitar. The musical 2CD in *The Muddy Waters Story* contains the LC session (without the interviews), the entire 1946 material, including Muddy's accompaniments to Clark and Harris, further accompaniments to St Louis Jimmy and Sunnyland and a few early Aristocrats. The other 2CD is a spoken biography. It's reasonably accurate and informative but was produced with the utmost economy – no actuality or interview material, scarcely any music. The Indigo and the somewhat shorter Frémeaux, being 2CDs, march a good deal further into the Chess catalogue and in doing so are almost complete for the periods they cover; their better value makes most of the single-CD selections, especially the untidy *Feel Like Going Home*, seem rather unsatisfactory.

♛ **** Rollin' Stone: The Golden Anniversary Collection
MCA/Chess 088 112 301 2CD *Muddy Waters; Alex Atkins (as); Little Walter (h, g, v, sp); poss. Junior Wells (h); Sunnyland Slim, [Little] Johnny Jones (p); Leroy Foster (g, d); Jimmy Rogers (g, v); Ernest 'Big' Crawford (b); Elga Edmonds, Len Chess, unknown (d). 47–9/52.*

♛ **** Hoochie Coochie Man: The Complete Chess Masters Volume 2, 1952–1958
Hip-O Select/Chess B 0002758 2CD *Muddy Waters; Marcus Johnson, unknown (ts); Little Walter, poss. Junior Wells, Walter Horton, James Cotton (h); Otis Spann (p); Jimmy Rogers, Pat Hare, prob. Robert Jr Lockwood, poss. Luther Tucker, poss. Fred Robinson (g); Ernest 'Big' Crawford, Willie Dixon (b); Elgin Evans [Elga Edmonds], Fred Below, Francis Clay (d); band (v). 9/52–11/58.*

This is the work of Muddy's prime for the Aristocrat and Chess labels: momentous recordings. As well as all the other things they are, they are key documents of the great blues project of the '40s: transporting the music of Southern small towns to urban streets and bars; matching the geographical shifts of black Americans with stylistic changes in the music some of them listened to; resetting country time to a city clock. As Lowell Fulson moved from Oklahoma to California, so, almost simultaneously, Muddy Waters rode the train from Clarksdale to Chicago, and within a few years both men had contributed prodigally, each in his new state, to the altered state of the blues. But whereas Fulson's changes would be incorporated into the development of a West Coast blues and become invisible, Muddy's would both dramatically transform the sounds coming out of Chicago clubs and seed a new blues that had no Southern roots at all, in places where a Southern sun had never shone.

But in the period when these recordings were cut, Muddy was simply concerned with erecting a flag in the Windy City that could not be blown down. He made his mark with records that were louder and sexier than anybody else's. 'I'm a man – "M" ... "A", child ... "N" – that represent man.' Though they contain nothing but a voice, an amplified guitar and a stand-up bass, sides like 'I Can't Be Satisfied' or 'Train Fare Home' are as thrusting, as resonant, as *big* as a full band. At least, they are on record: in a club it would be otherwise, and Muddy eventually acquired a full band of his own, which Chess, still taken with the success of the Muddy–Big Crawford duets and the gorgeous trio sides with Little Walter like 'Sad Letter', 'Long Distance Call' and 'She Moves Me', only cautiously allowed him to introduce, in 1953, on 'Blow Wind Blow' and 'Mad Love'. But the following year the triumphant success of Muddy's band recordings of 'I'm Your Hoochie Coochie Man' and 'I Just Want To Make Love To You' made it plain that there could now be no turning back. For the rest of the '50s Muddy would preside over the rigorously controlled mayhem of performances like 'I'm Ready', 'Manish Boy', 'Just To Be With You', 'Got My Mojo Working' ... the mere titles are so well known that one needn't labour the point. For about a dozen years 'Muddy Waters' and 'Chicago blues' were phrases so close in meaning that you couldn't separate them with a cheesewire.

These two collections are, as Joe E. Brown would have said, the berries, but picking them is not as straightforward as it appears. You wouldn't know from looking at them that they were complementary: not only are they on different labels, but *Rollin' Stone*, which isn't billed as *Volume 1*, comes in a normal 2CD jewelcase, whereas *Hoochie Coochie Man* is a small card-bound book. Much more annoyingly, for non-American readers, MCA permit neither set to be distributed in any territory outside the United States. But a dumb marketing decision isn't a good enough reason to deny these sets our highest rating.

*** **The Real Folk Blues/More Real Folk Blues**
MCA/Chess 088 112 822//BGO BGOCD 436 *Muddy Waters; Little Walter (h, g); prob. Walter Horton, Junior Wells (h); Sunnyland Slim, [Little] Johnny Jones, Otis Spann (p); Jimmy Rogers, Pat Hare, Luther Tucker, Buddy Guy (g); Ernest 'Big' Crawford, Willie Dixon (b); Leroy Foster, Elga Edmonds, Francis Clay, Odie Payne, S. P. Leary (d). 47–4/64.*

**** **His Best 1947 To 1955** [sic]
MCA/Chess (A) CHD 9370//(E) MCD 09370 *Muddy Waters; Little Walter (h, g, sp); Junior Wells, Walter Horton (h); Otis Spann (p); Jimmy Rogers (g); Ernest 'Big' Crawford, Willie Dixon (b); Elga Edmonds, Leonard Chess, Fred Below, Francis Clay (d); band (v). 4/48–11/55.*

*** **One More Mile**
MCA/Chess CHD2–9348//(E) MCD 09348 2CD *Muddy Waters; Marcus Johnson, Boyd Atkins (s); Louis Myers (h, g); Little Walter, James Cotton, Mojo Buford (h); Charles Stepney (o); Otis Spann (p); Leroy Foster, Jimmy Rogers, Pat Hare, Luther Tucker, Lafayette Thomas, Matt Murphy, Sammy Lawhorn, Pee Wee Madison (g); Ernest 'Big' Crawford, Willie Dixon, Andrew Stephens, Milton Rector, Jerome Arnold, Calvin Jones (b); Leonard Chess, Fred Below, Francis Clay, Willie 'Big Eyes' Smith, Al Duncan (d). 11/48–6/72.*

***(*) **The Essential Collection**
Spectrum 544 349 *Similar to above, except add Pinetop Perkins (p). 2/50–3/72.*

**** **The Anthology**
MCA/Chess 088 112 649 2CD *Similar to above. 47–72.*

If you don't want Muddy complete, just compacted into one collection of the famous sides, *His Best 1947 To 1955* might have been made for you. Virtually all the songs highlighted in the foregoing discussion are on it – except, curiously, 'Mojo' – plus colossal early performances like 'Louisiana Blues' and 'Rollin' Stone'. *The Essential Collection*, also a 20-tracker, is about half the same, and it *does* have 'Mojo', but it tails off with a few secondary sides. *The Anthology* covers much the same '40s/'50s ground as those two CDs but in greater detail, presses on (by way of a few album tracks) to 1964 and the remarkable coupling 'The Same Thing'/'You Can't Lose What You Ain't Never Had', and adds just two later items. If you can't get hold of our top recommendations above, or don't need Muddy complete, this is the next best thing. The 24-track twofer *The Real Folk Blues/More Real Folk Blues* recycles two '60s LPs that largely avoided the well-known material, so it's strong in the early sides with Little Walter like 'Early Morning Blues' and 'Too Young To Know', though it also reaches forward to the mid-'60s. *One More Mile* was carefully compiled to jibe with what was then (1994) MCA's Muddy catalogue. Its programme of late singles, alternative takes and originally unissued tracks, including a batch from 6/63 with James Cotton, Otis Spann and Luther Tucker, leaves a few gaps still unfilled but is clearly one for the collector's shelf – the more so as the last 11 tracks on Disc 2 are an unreleased 6/72 session in Switzerland with just Louis Myers and Mojo Buford. Apart from remembering an old Bo Carter song, 'My Pencil Won't Write No More', Muddy keeps to repertoire from his Chicago heyday like 'Standin' Around Cryin'' and 'Feel Like Goin' Home', some of which goes well with a trio setting, though others are sketchy and sound like demos.

**** **Rollin' Stone**
Proper PVCD 104 2CD *Muddy Waters; Little Walter (h, g, v, sp); Sunnyland Slim, [Little] Johnny Jones (p); Leroy Foster (g, d); Jimmy Rogers (g, v); Ernest 'Big' Crawford (b); Elga Edmonds, Leonard Chess (d). 47–12/51.*

***(*) **Screamin' And Cryin'**
Saga Blues 982 093–2 *Muddy Waters; Little Walter (h, g, sp); prob. Junior Wells, Walter Horton (h); Sunnyland Slim, [Little] Johnny Jones, Otis Spann (p); Leroy Foster (g, d); Jimmy Rogers (g); Ernest 'Big' Crawford (b); Elga Edmonds (d). 47–9/53.*

*** **The Chronological Muddy Waters 1948–1950**
Classics 5029 *Muddy Waters; Alex Atkins (as); Sunnyland Slim, [Little] Johnny Jones (p); Leroy Foster (g, d); Jimmy Rogers (g); Ernest 'Big' Crawford (b). 4/48–2/50.*

***(*) **A Proper Introduction To Muddy Waters: Mad Love**
Proper INTRO CD 2066 *Muddy Waters; Little Walter (h, g, sp); prob. Junior Wells, Walter Horton (h); Otis Spann (p); Leroy Foster, Jimmy Rogers (g); Ernest 'Big' Crawford (b); Elga Edmonds, Leonard Chess (d). 4/48–9/53.*

(***) **Mississippi Mud**
Arpeggio ARB 014 *Muddy Waters; Little Walter (h, g, v, sp); [Little] Johnny Jones (p); Jimmy Rogers (g, v); Ernest 'Big' Crawford (b); Leroy Foster, Elga Edmonds, Leonard Chess (d). 7/49–12/51.*

*** **Muddy Waters 1950–1952**
Classics 5109 *As above, except add Junior Wells (h); omit Jones, Foster. 6/50–9/52.*

All these are unofficial maps of the Aristocrat/Chess terrain. The most detailed, Proper's 44-track *Rollin' Stone*, is complete for its five-year span (except for a single recording that has never been issued) and competitively priced. The same label's *Introduction* is shorter (24 tracks) but goes a little further into Muddy's catalogue; Saga's selection is about three fifths the same; if all you want is an inexpensive sampling of early Muddy, either will do very well. The Classics sets conduct their usual miss-nothing scour of the catalogue. Arpeggio, as usual, spoil the effect of a decent 20-track selection with brief, unhelpful notes and shoddy artwork.

**(*) Sings "Big Bill"/Folk Singer
BGO BGOCD 397 *Muddy Waters; James Cotton (h); Otis Spann (p); Pat Hare, Buddy Guy (g); Andrew Stephens, Willie Dixon (b); Willie Smith or Francis Clay, Clifton James (d). 6/59, 9/63.*

Muddy Waters Sings "Big Bill", released in 1959, must be one of the first blues albums to be dedicated to a past master. Although Muddy probably did it because he felt he owed Bill one, rather than because it was a natural career move, the two men's singing styles are not so different that the concept is peculiar, and, if the accompaniments furnished by Cotton and Spann are less rhythmically insistent than Bill's backing groups were, that merely reflects the two decades of blues history that separated them. For all that, this is not an inviting album, chiefly because the stereo separation and balance make the musicians sound like partitioned-off soloists rather than a band. For *Folk Singer*, which used the Guy–Dixon–James lineup, see below.

*** At Newport 1960
MCA/Chess 088 112 515 *Muddy Waters; James Cotton (h); Otis Spann (p, v); Pat Hare, Lafayette Thomas (g); Andrew Stephens (b); Francis Clay (d). 7/60.*

*** Muddy Waters At Newport/Muddy Waters Live
BGO BGOCD 314 *As above, except add Paul Oscher (h), Pinetop Perkins (p), Sammy Lawhorn, Pee Wee Madison (g), Calvin Jones (b), Willie Smith (d). 7/60, 6/71.*

The original *At Newport* LP is an item of iconic importance in Britain, since it introduced blues fans – the few there were in 1960 – to 'Got My Mojo Working', which would become a staple of the British R&B repertoire. Muddy is plainly in strutting, sexy form, and there are some very strong vocals, not least the measured reading of Jimmy Oden's 'Soon Forgotten', but the sound balance is hopeless. Lafayette Thomas, reportedly present only on the concluding 'Goodbye Newport Blues' (affectingly sung by Otis Spann), is described in *BR* as 'very faint'. Oh, and Pat Hare isn't? On most of the tracks it's almost impossible to detect any guitar playing at all. Cotton isn't very audible either, and the burden of the accompaniment is carried largely by Spann. Still, history alone prompts a three-star rating. *Muddy Waters Live*, coupled with the Newport concert on BGO, is *Live At Mr Kelly's* (see below).

**(*) Folk Singer
MCA/Chess CHD 12027 *Muddy Waters; Buddy Guy (g); Willie Dixon (b); Clifton James (d). 9/63.*

Even Muddy himself wasn't sure if this was the way for him to go in 1963, and some of the album's first reviewers declared it a wrong turning, though probably for different reasons: whereas Muddy might have seen no point, at that stage in his career, in returning to the acoustic setting of his early records, a lot of blues fans would have been all for it – so long as it really did sound like 1948 or thereabouts. But of course it didn't: there was no Big Crawford to press the beat, no Little Walter to fire Muddy's imagination, just Buddy Guy quietly chording and Dixon and James taking their cue from the boss, who was in a deeply ruminative mood, fingering old songsheets like 'Country Boy' and 'Feel Like Going Home' as if lost in a nostalgic reverie. Had he been listening to John Lee Hooker's similarly pensive 'folk blues' albums?

*** Goin' Way Back
Just A Memory JAM 9130 *Muddy Waters; Mojo Buford (h, v); Otis Spann, Luther 'Georgia Boy/Snake' Johnson (g, v); Sam Langhorn [Sammy Lawhorn] (g). 10/67.*

Way back indeed. In the informal setting of the Montreal rooming house where the band was staying, Muddy got to thinking about some of his earliest recordings and recalled songs long absent from his repertoire like 'Gypsy Woman' and 'Little Anna Mae', his first Aristocrat single. After five numbers by Muddy partnered by Lawhorn, Johnson sings three, Spann two (playing guitar, for the only time on record) and Buford one. This unplugged, unbuttoned, reminiscent session was a quiet morning off from the noise and hurry of touring. The listener can replicate the effect somewhat by playing it between two no-holds-barred albums and enjoying it as a tranquil intermission.

** Electric Mud
MCA/Chess MCD 09364 *Muddy Waters; Gene Barge (ss, ts, fl); Charles Stepney (o); Pete Cosey, Phil Upchurch, Roland Faulkner (g); Louis Satterfield (b); Morris Jennings (d). 5/68.*

Probably no album in the blues library has generated as much debate as *Electric Mud*. Blues pundits at the time excoriated its blues-meets-psychedelia agenda as a travesty of everything Muddy's music stood for. Guitarist Pete Cosey, getting his chance to respond in a documentary 35 years later, dismissed them as ridiculous. Meanwhile, the album had become a collectable in British dance-music circles, where it seems to have been regarded as a kind of blues equivalent of acid jazz. Mark Humphrey, in his notes to the CD issue, carefully contextualizes it: 1968 was the year of Hendrix's *Electric Ladyland*, of student riots in Paris and race riots in the US. His point is that *Electric Mud* is a document of its time, as frozen in its *Zeitgeist* as a Stanley Mouse poster or Terry Southern's *Candy*. This commends the album to the historian, but listeners without a taste for cultural landmark-spotting will simply want to know if the setup works, if anything musically worthwhile came from this improbable encounter. On a few of his standby numbers – 'She's Alright', 'The Same Thing', 'Mannish Boy' – Muddy wears the fancy dress of fuzz guitars and flutes without obvious discomfort, even perhaps with some amusement, but 'Let's Spend The Night Together' is simply embarrassing. In short, time is not on the side of *Electric Mud*: whatever patchouli fragrance it gave off in 1968 has long since turned stale. All the same, anyone with a serious interest in Muddy's life and work should try to hear it.

**(*) Fathers And Sons
MCA/Chess 088 112 648 *Muddy Waters; Paul Butterfield, Jeff Carp (h); Otis Spann (p); Michael Bloomfield, Paul Asbell (g); Donald 'Duck' Dunn, Phil Upchurch (b); Sam Lay, Buddy Miles (d). 4/69.*

'Who put out this stiff?' asks a Chess staffer, unpacking yet another carton of returned copies of *Fathers And Sons*. 'Told that it is Marshall [Chess],' Peter Guralnick continues in his essay on the label in *Feel Like Going Home*, 'the man nods understandingly.' But after the message of 'things are going to change around here' that was implicit in *Electric Mud*, which Marshall also produced, *Fathers And Sons* keeps to the script; okay, there are a few white guys in the band, but they play by Muddy's rules. The musicians spent three days in a studio producing ten of the album's tracks, trenchant performances of familiar '50s repertoire like 'All Aboard', 'Forty Days And Forty Nights' and 'Sugar Sweet' which throw a flattering light on Butterfield. On the fourth day (the phrase gains resonance if you've seen the cover artwork) they repaired to Chicago's Auditorium Theater for the Super Cosmic Joy-Scout Jamboree, 'presented by The Phoenix Fellowship – an Academy of open enquiry designed to explore all cultural concepts, with the idea of creating new approaches to ethics, religion, philosophy, art and science': in other words, a bunch of hippies. The concert generated six tracks, which, if not exactly cosmic, are not earthbound. There's nothing musically amiss with *Fathers And Sons*, but nearly everything on it had been done as well, or better, before.

**(*) Live At Mister Kelly's
Chess CHD-9338 Muddy Waters; Paul Oscher, Joe Denim [James Cotton] (h); Pinetop Perkins (p); Sammy Lawhorn, Pee Wee Madison (g); Calvin Jones (b); Willie Smith (d). 6/71.

Playing with his regular band at a smart Chicago niterie, Muddy introduces a few new or newish numbers such as 'What Is That She Got' and 'Strange Woman', plays shrill slide on several tracks and sings with majestic calm. A unhurried set and, by the end, a rather unexciting one. This issue adds two tracks to the original album, 'She's Nineteen Years Old' and 'Long Distance Call', which are not on the BGO *At Newport/Live* CD (see above).

*** Take A Walk With Me
Snapper SMDCD 249 2CD Muddy Waters; Paul Oscher, Carey Bell, George 'Harmonica' Smith, Jerry Portnoy (h); Pinetop Perkins (p); Luther 'Guitar Jr' Johnson (g, v); Buddy Guy, Sammy Lawhorn, Pee Wee Madison, Bob Margolin (g); Sonny Wimberley, Calvin Jones (b); Willie 'Big Eyes' Smith (d). 70–4/76.

**(*) The Lost Tapes
Blind Pig BPCD 5054 Muddy Waters; George 'Harmonica' Smith (h); Pinetop Perkins (p); Sammy Lawhorn, Pee Wee Madison, Bee Houston (g); Calvin Jones (b); Willie 'Big Eyes' Smith (d). 10/71.

**(*) The Lost Tapes
Blue Moon CDBM 131 As above. 10/71.

**(*) Mojo: The Live Collection
Music Club MCCD 425 As above, except add Jerry Portnoy (h), Luther 'Guitar Jr' Johnson, Bob Margolin (g). 10/71, 4/76.

The Lost Tapes and the second half of *Mojo: The Live Collection* originate in two Northwestern concerts in 1971, at the universities of Washington and Oregon. The Blind Pig CD differs from the Blue Moon only in adding video material (an interview and a band version of 'Long Distance Call'), not accessible to Mac users. The first half of *Mojo* catches a different lineup of the band at a Swiss gig in 1976; these seven numbers, with five more from the same occasion, make up Disc 1 of *Take A Walk With Me*, the rest of which is derived from other '70s gigs and broadcasts and from the soundtrack of the documentary *Chicago Blues*. There isn't so much studio material from this period that one can brush these CDs away as superfluous, and the performances are seldom less than solid, but only devotees need feel they should investigate them in depth; for the casual collector *Take A Walk With Me* will be plenty.

**(*) The London Muddy Waters Sessions
MCA CHLD 19105 Muddy Waters; Ernie Royal, Joe Newman (t); Garnett Brown (tb); Seldon Powell (ts); Carey Bell (h); Steve Winwood, Georgie Fortune [Fame] (o, p); Sammy Lawhorn, Rory Gallagher (g); Rick Grech (b); Mitch Mitchell, Herbie Lovelle (d); Rosetta Hightower (v). 12/71.

The London album is not highly regarded by Muddy's more conservative admirers; perhaps they should listen again, not just for the old-time two-guitar setting of 'Walkin' Blues', which is easy to like, but for the uncompromised power of 'Sad Sad Day' and 'Who's Gonna Be Your Sweet Man When I'm Gone'. Admittedly the New York horn section adds little to most of the tracks on which it was dubbed, but it lends something to 'I'm Gonna Move To The Outskirts Of Town'; Hightower's vocal responses, however, were a pointless decoration on 'Blind Man Blues' (not, as stated, 'Walkin' Blues').

*** Paris, 1972
Pablo PACD-5302 Muddy Waters; Mojo Buford (h); Pinetop Perkins (p); Louis Myers (g); Calvin Jones (b); Willie 'Big Eyes' Smith (d). 72.

Unlike some of his concert recordings, this has Muddy on stage from the start. He delivers 'Honey Bee', 'Rollin' 'N' Tumblin'' and 'Walkin' Blues' with massive, brooding authority. Also on the programme is a succinct version of 'Hoochie Coochie Man' and what would have been another of 'Got My Mojo Workin'', had the audience not kept him there chanting for a further five minutes. Buford and Myers enact the routines with quiet competence, while Perkins makes a more pungent contribution, but Muddy's voice and guitar constantly swirl to the top of the brew.

**(*) The Muddy Waters Woodstock Album
[MCA/Chess CHD 9359] Muddy Waters; Garth Hudson (s, ac, o); Howard Johnson (s); Paul Butterfield (h); Pinetop Perkins (p, v); Fred Carter (g, b); Bob Margolin (g); Levon Helm (b, d); Henry Glover (prod). 2/75.

Muddy appears to enjoy his couple of days at the Bearsville studio, but the mix of musicians, on paper rather intriguing, doesn't quite suit him. In particular, Garth Hudson's floating lines on organ and accordion, perfect in the context of The Band, let too much cool air into the sweltering engine-room where Muddy's bandsmen are accustomed to work. Once you've subtracted 'Caldonia', 'Let The Good Times Roll' and 'Kansas City', overdone songs that we certainly didn't need to hear Muddy doing over, all that's left is some ostensibly new but familiar-sounding Watertoons and Bobby Charles's 'Why Are People Like That', which, perversely, may be the best track.

***(*) **Hard Again**
Epic/Legacy EPC 515161 *Muddy Waters; James Cotton (h); Pinetop Perkins (p); Johnny Winter (g, prod); Bob Margolin (g); Charles Calmese (b); Willie 'Big Eyes' Smith (d). 10/76.*

Late in 1975 Muddy ended his almost 30-year association with Chess Records. In the following year he signed with Blue Sky, a subsidiary of Epic, and, working with Johnny Winter, made his best album in ages. From the controlled riot of the opening 'Mannish Boy' to the warm geniality of 'Deep Down In Florida', a song inspired by his new girlfriend, Marva Jean Brooks, whom he'd first met in the Sunshine State, Muddy is in great voice, high spirits and good hands. Most of the musicians had played with him before, and Winter was so in tune with Muddy's music that his playing on the album deceived many of its listeners into thinking they were hearing the older man. (Margolin reveals that Muddy didn't pick up his guitar during the entire session.) This reissue adds a previously unissued 'Walking Through The Park'.

(*) **Screamin' And Cryin': Live In Warsaw 1976
Acrobat ACMCD 4045 *Muddy Waters; Jerry Portnoy (h); Pinetop Perkins (p, v); Bob Margolin, Luther 'Guitar Jr' Johnson (g); Calvin Jones (b); Willie 'Big Eyes' Smith (d). 10/76.*

(*) **Hoochie Coochie Man
Just A Memory JAM 9142 *As above, except Johnson also sings. 1/77.*

From Muddy's set or sets at the Warsaw Jazz Jamboree come 16 tracks, including four instrumentals by the band, presumably played before Muddy came on stage but here scattered through the programme. Muddy chose a mixture of staples like 'Mojo', 'Hoochie Coochie Man' and 'Baby Please Don't Go' and more left-field numbers like 'Howlin' Wolf' and 'Garbage Man', singing them quite heartily but without a great deal of engagement, and playing slide guitar on only a few of them. Three months later Muddy and Co. were in Montreal, using quite a lot of the same setlist – the two CDs share 'Baby Please Don't Go', 'Howling Wolf', 'Hoochie Coochie Man' and 'Can't Get No Grindin'' (a.k.a. 'What's The Matter With The Mill') – and putting it over with rather more vim, though that quality ebbs away during the 11.07 of 'Kansas City'.

*** **I'm Ready**
Epic/Legacy EPC 515162 *Muddy Waters; Walter Horton, Jerry Portnoy (h); Pinetop Perkins (p); Jimmy Rogers (g, v); Johnny Winter (g); Bob Margolin (b); Willie 'Big Eyes' Smith (d). 10/77.*

Muddy's second Blue Sky album was in a similar vein to *Hard Again* but with rather more songs from the old band book, such as 'I'm Ready', 'I'm Your Hoochie Coochie Man' and 'Screamin' And Cryin' – probably because two of the old band were playing them, Muddy and Jimmy Rogers, reunited on record for the first time in years. (You could count Horton as a third, since he played on several of Muddy's '50s recordings.) Rogers even gets to sing 'That's All Right' again – or at least he does now, since the reissue producers have added three previously unheard tracks, and this rather special performance is among them.

*** **Muddy "Mississippi" Waters Live**
Epic/Legacy 512888 2CD *Muddy Waters; James Cotton, Jerry Portnoy (h); Pinetop Perkins (p); Johnny Winter, Bob Margolin, Luther 'Guitar Jr' Johnson (g); Charles Calmese, Calvin Jones (b); Willie 'Big Eyes' Smith (d). 3/77, 8/78.*
*** **King Bee**
Epic/Legacy 515163 *As above. 10/76, 5/80.*

*** **Muddy "Mississippi" Waters Live/King Bee**
BGO BGOCD 584 *As above. 10/76–5/80.*
*** **King Of The Electric Blues**
Epic/Legacy (A) ZK 65215//(E) 487847 *As for all Epic/Legacy CDs. 10/76–5/80.*

The original *Muddy "Mississippi" Waters Live* was derived from a 1978 club gig by the lineup Muddy had taken overseas with him in 1976–77, except for three tracks ('Nine Below Zero', 'Howling Wolf' and 'Deep Down In Florida') from the 1977 tour promoting *Hard Again*. That's what you get as half of BGO's twofer, but Epic's reissue adds an entire CD of unheard material from the '78 engagement, vividly recorded but with no surprises in either the repertoire or the treatment (and another nine and a half minutes of 'Kansas City').

The band reconvened in 5/80 to record what would be their last album for Blue Sky. Margolin, whose notes are one of the hidden pleasures of the Epic/Legacy reissues, explains that the album was made by a band splitting apart (a couple of months later everyone quit) and says he can hear it in the music, but listeners not so close to the action may not catch the undertone of revolt. Muddy sings as commandingly as ever, mostly on tested repertoire like 'Too Young To Know' and 'Sad Sad Day' but throwing in a new song, 'Forever Lonely', jointly written with his partner Marva, to which either Johnson or Margolin contributes a small but imaginative detail. Threaded through the song are phrases from the exquisite guitar line of William Brown's 'Mississippi Blues', which Alan Lomax, collecting for the Library of Congress's Archive of American Folk-Song, recorded on an Arkansas plantation in 1942. Just a few days later Lomax hauled that same recording machine to Stovall, Mississippi, for a session with Muddy Waters.

Since the session wasn't judged to have produced enough satisfactory material, the original *King Bee* (as heard on BGO) was augmented with two outtakes from *Hard Again*, 'I Feel Like Going Home' with Winter and Margolin playing acoustic guitars, and a ragged version of '(My Eyes) Keep Me In Trouble'. Epic's reissue, however, contests that 'unsatisfactory' verdict by finding two further tracks from 1980, of which 'Clouds In My Heart' is superb. *King Of The Electric Blues* is a précis of the Epics, with three to six tracks from each. TR

Geoff Muldaur (born 1945)
VOCAL, MULTI-INSTRUMENTALIST

Muldaur grew up in New York state listening to jazz and blues. In the '60s he and his then wife Maria were members of Jim Kweskin's Jug Band and recorded a couple of albums together. He spent part of the '70s in Paul Butterfield's Better Days, recorded some solo albums and saw out the decade in a duo with the guitarist Amos Garrett. After almost two decades of virtual retirement from professional music-making, he caught a lot of ears with 1998's The Secret Handshake.

*** **Blues Boy**
Bullseye Blues & Jazz BBB 9635 *Muldaur (cl, as, p, bj, g, wb, v, arr); Peter Ecklund (t, flh, arr); Amos Garrett (tb, g, v); Nicholas ten Broek (tb); Chris Cioe (as, ts, bs, arr); Len Nitmar (ts, bs); Scott Matthews (ts, d, perc); Dave Burgin (h, v); Pierre Beauregard (h); Mike Utley (p); Michael Melford (md, v); Stephen Bruton (g); Bill Rich (b); Fritz Richmond (j, v): Sammy Creason, Rich Dishman, Dennis Whitted (d); Barbara*

Mendelsohn (hdu); Steve Burdett, Whit Griswold, George Leh, Jenny Muldaur (v). 78–79.

The success of *The Secret Handshake* prompted this 2001 reissue of songs from Muldaur's late-'70s Flying Fish LPs *Geoff Muldaur And Amos Garrett* and *Blues Boy*. With hindsight one can see in some of these recordings early notice of the taste and ingenuity he was to display more prodigally on *Handshake*, such as the Walter Davis songs 'Tears Came Rolling Down' and 'Feelin' Good', Sleepy John Estes's 'Sloppy Drunk Blues' and 'Meanest Woman', based on a theme by Ishmon Bracey.

*** The Secret Handshake
Hightone HCD 8097 *Muldaur* (bj, g, pennywhistle, tamb, v, arr, prod); Gary Slechta (t); Randy Zimmerman, Dave Bargeron (tb); Jon Clark, Larry Ragent (frh); Lenny Pickett (cl, ts); Dan Block (as); Kaz Kazanoff, George Young (ts); Howard Johnson (bs, tu); Rufus Olivier (bsn); John Magnie (ac, p, v); Riley Osbourn (o); John Nicholas (p); Eric Levine, Richard Greene (vn); David Grisman (md); Stephen Bruton (mandola, g); Mayne Smith (Do); Amos Garrett (g, v); Bruce Forman (g); Bill Rich, Sean Hopper (b); Kester Smith (d, cga, cowbell); Larry Thompson (d); Hal Ketchum, Malford Milligan, Tim Cook, Jenni Muldaur (v). 98.

**(*) Beautiful Isle Of Somewhere
Tradition & Moderne T&M 025 *Muldaur*. 5/99.

**(*) Password
Hightone HCD 8125 *Muldaur* (cl, p, bj, g, v, arr, prod); Roswell Rudd (tb); Larry Ragent (frh); Tony Strickland (cl); Rufus Olivier (bsn); John Sebastian (h); Van Dyke Parks (ac, o); John Herron (o, p); Mike Finnigan (o, v); Richard Greene, Margaret Wooten (vn); Jimbo Ross (vl); Bob Siggins (bj, v); David Lindley, Dave Alvin, Greg Leisz, Billy Watts, Stephen Bruton (g); Tim Emmons, Bill Rich, Sean Hopper (b); Fritz Richmond (j, v); Wally Ingram, Don Heffington (d); James Cruce (perc); Clare Muldaur, Kate McGarrigle, Anna McGarrigle, Bill Lynch, Bob Neuwirth (v). 00.

The Secret Handshake, Password ... the titles imply membership of an inner circle of illuminati, and certainly some of Muldaur's references are arcane enough to tickle even specialists in Americana. *Handshake*'s opening track 'The Wild Ox Moan', for example, is derived from a field recording by the Alabamian singer Vera Hall, and 'I Can't See Your Face' from a '30s disc by the generally underregarded Walter Davis, while 'Mistreated Mama' is Muldaur's rearrangement of the old-time singer Dock Boggs's rearrangement of a blues by Sara Martin. But it is not only by his sources that Muldaur proves he has an enquiring mind: his settings are often refreshingly novel, too, as when he thickens the 'Bo Diddley' riff of 'Chevrolet' with a New Orleans horn section.

Password too has texturally attractive passages: Muldaur and Lindley's interlocked guitars in 'Kitchen Door Blues', Clare Muldaur's *ingénue* vocal paced by Richard Greene's antique vaudeville fiddling on Bessie Smith's 'At The Christmas Ball', the woodwinds on Jimmie Rodgers's 'Prairie Lullaby'. Muldaur does not shun more radical transformations, recasting Charley Patton's 'Some Of These Days (I'll Be Gone)' as a Victorian parlour ballad – or, should one say, taking it back to something like its source? Like *Handshake, Password* is nothing if not eclectic, but its orientation is slightly less African-American, and the bracketing of the third star reflects that, not the quality of the music or the thought behind it.

The rating of *Beautiful Isle Of Somewhere*, on the other hand, has nothing to do with its repertoire, since the programme is tilted towards blues and gospel; the problem is that many of the songs are on *Blues Boy, Handshake* or *Password*, in elaborate arrangements which leave these solo versions sounding like preliminary sketches. Muldaur sings them prettily, but his guitar playing is not varied enough to to be entirely satisfactory as the only accompaniment. TR

Maria Muldaur (born 1942)
VOCAL

Maria D'Amato discovered American vernacular music as a teenager in New York. In the '60s she sang saucy numbers, and occasionally played fiddle, with Jim Kweskin's Jug Band, and in the '70s, after a couple of albums with her then husband Geoff, made a striking solo debut with Maria Muldaur, *which contained the original, ineffably sultry recording of 'Midnight At The Oasis'. She has worked and recorded steadily ever since, dealing only intermittently with blues material but always using first-rate musicians and making a point of featuring songs by a small group of favourite writers.*

Muldaur is an extraordinary singer, an improbable amalgam of Memphis Minnie and Betty Boop: now feistily, now languorously sexy, flamboyantly mannered – and far too eclectic to be filed under any one category. The majority of her albums in the last couple of decades have mingled blues, jazz songs, Broadway standards and more recent material composed in what could perhaps be called a sophisticated rock idiom. *Sweet And Slow*, originally released in 1983 and reissued ten years later (Stony Plain SPCD 1183), is a jazz/vaudeville blend with fine accompaniment by two small bands, Dr John and Kenny Barron successively occupying the piano stool to good purpose. *Jazzabelle* (Stony Plain SPCD 1188) (1993) finds her in a piano trio setting, singing two songs associated with Bessie Smith, 'Weeping Willow Blues' and 'Do Your Duty' and Mose Allison's 'Everybody Cryin' Mercy'. She also does her personal barnburner, 'Don't You Feel My Leg', which she learned from Blue Lu Barker only to triumphantly upstage her with it, but this reading is less animated than the one on 1992's *Louisiana Love Call* (Black Top, deleted). A second Black Top CD, *Meet Me At Midnite* (1994), is also deleted.

Muldaur has always had a love of Louisiana music. *Fanning The Flames* (Telarc CD-83394) (1996) was recorded there with the help of locals like keyboards player David Torkanowsky and slide guitarist Sonny Landreth, several songs by Jon Cleary and a couple of duets with Johnny Adams. Neither this nor 1998's *Southland Of The Heart* (Telarc CD-83423) is in any useful sense a blues record, but the next one edged in that direction. *Meet Me Where They Play The Blues* (Telarc CD-83460) (1999) was conceived to commemorate the 'rich melted chocolate' voice of Charles Brown, with the intention of Brown himself contributing substantially to it, both singing and playing piano. Fate, however, was having none of it, and all that was possible was taping Brown in a nursing home, singing his duet part in 'Gee Baby, Ain't I Good To You': it was his last recording. What's left is an oblique tribute to Brown's late-hours style, evoked not in his own repertoire (except for 'The Promised Land') but in standards and newer near-blues songs like John Hiatt's 'It Feels Like Rain'.

***(*) Richland Woman Blues
Stony Plain SPCD 1270 *Muldaur; Dave Mathews (p); David*

Wilkie (mandocello); Bonnie Raitt, Alvin Youngblood Hart, Taj Mahal (g, v); John Sebastian, Amos Garrett, Roy Rogers, Ernie Hawkins (g); Roly Salley (b); Angela Strehli, Tracy Nelson (v). 01.

*** Sweet Lovin' Ol' Soul
Stony Plain SPCD 1304 Muldaur; Kevin Porter (tb); Dave Mathews, Pinetop Perkins (p); Suzy Thompson (vn); Steve James (md, g); Dave Earl (md); Taj Mahal (bj, g, v); Alvin Youngblood Hart (g, v); Del Rey, Steve Freund (g); Rowland [Roly] Salley, Vance Ehlers (b); Fritz Richmond (j); Paul Revelli (d); Tracy Nelson (v). 04/05.

The listener who comes to *Richland Woman Blues* remembering Muldaur's erotic recording of the title song with Jim Kweskin's Jug Band may be surprised by the change in her voice. She can still negotiate the leaps and slides that so seductively adorned the earlier 'Richland Woman Blues' or 'Midnight At The Oasis', but now she sings deeper, often with a rasping growl – characteristics eminently suitable for the blues and gospel songs assembled here. The album's inspiration was a visit to the grave of Memphis Minnie, and Muldaur selects four of her songs, 'Me And My Chauffeur Blues' and 'In My Girlish Days' with adroit guitar by Roy Rogers, and two conversational duets with Alvin Youngblood Hart, faithful to Minnie's exchanges with Joe McCoy. Almost all her collaborators are well chosen: pianist Dave Mathews, who accompanies her on three Bessie Smith numbers; John Sebastian, playing Mississippi John Hurt's lilting guitar part on the title song; guitarist Ernie Hawkins on the rousing 'I Belong To That Band'; and Bonnie Raitt on the magnificent 'It's A Blessing'. Only 'Far Away Blues', a ponderous duet with Tracy Nelson, risks breaking the listener's connection to a record made with ingenuity and love.

After that Muldaur recorded *A Woman Alone With The Blues* (Telarc CD-83568) (2003), an elegantly sung and decorously played remembrance of Peggy Lee, and *Love Wants To Dance* (Telarc CD-83609) (2004), which has no blues content. The record many blues enthusiasts would have preferred would have been a near-facsimile of *Richland Woman Blues*, and their patience was rewarded in 2005 when that was exactly what they got.

Sweet Lovin' Ol' Soul was a second serving of Memphis Minnie songs (five this time, one of them sung with Hart, another with Nelson), more Bessie Smith ('Empty Bed Blues') and more duets with Taj Mahal, the Holiness chant 'Take A Stand' and the Butterbeans & Susie-styled vaudeville routine 'Ain't What You Used To Have'. The Del Rey–Steve James guitar duets on some of the Memphis Minnie numbers are utterly delightful. But, while the performances have no less brio than those on *Richland Woman Blues*, the material is slightly less captivating, and the acute sense of *déjà entendu* may disappoint owners of the previous album. TR

Frank Muschalle (born 1969)
PIANO

From Münster, Germany, Muschalle played piano from the age of seven. He became attracted to boogie woogie in his late teens and learned from Axel Zwingenberger, recordings of the great originals and contemporary Viennese boogie pianists.

**(*) Live
Styx CD 1003 Muschalle; Daniel Gugolz (b, whistling); Peter Müller (d). 1–2/00.

***(*) Frank Muschalle Trio Featuring Rusty Zinn
Styx CD 1010 Muschalle; Rusty Zinn (g, v); Daniel Gugolz (b, v); Peter Müller (d). 01–02.

Muschalle's playing sometimes has a mildly academic air, but his stylistic versatility and technical command are notable; his hands are very independent, and his articulation of the inner parts of chords very clear. Despite these advantages, *Live* is often paradoxically dispassionate and clinical, and some of the slow numbers are too long and rather directionless; 'Bad Excuse Blues' and the concluding 'Whistling Ourselves The Blues' are splendid exceptions, but too often the attention wanders until fast exhibition pieces jerk it back.

The successor CD, some of which is also live, is altogether better. Fast numbers like 'Bottle Rocket' and 'Stormin'' well deserve their auditors' enthusiasm, which for once is not elicited by empty showiness; these and other Muschalle originals are characterized by tremendous swing and disciplined, inventive exploration of interesting ideas. Slower tunes like 'Movin' In With Katie' are equally successful blends of creativity and control, and 'Rhumba Bounce' generates deep blues feeling over an oft-abused rhythm. Gugolz and Zinn take two unidiomatic vocals each, and once or twice Zinn's playing wanders into self-absorbed doodling, but for the most part this collection manages to be both ambitious and unpretentiously enjoyable. CS

Charlie Musselwhite (born 1944)
VOCAL, HARMONICA, GUITAR

Musselwhite was born in Kosciusko, Mississippi, but grew up in Memphis, where he was attracted to country and rockabilly music and later blues. He took up guitar and harmonica and in his teens hung out with Memphis's senior blues citizens like Will Shade and Furry Lewis. At 18 he moved to Chicago, where he developed his harp playing in the blues joints and played with older musicians like Johnny Young and Big Joe Williams. Since the late '60s he has toured the world, often with his own band, which at different times has included Robben Ford, Freddie Roulette and Andrew 'Jr Boy' Jones. He has recorded with Elvin Bishop, John Hammond, John Lee Hooker, Big Joe Williams and many others.

**(*) Stand Back! Here Comes Charley Musselwhite's South Side Band
Vanguard VMD 79232 Musselwhite; Barry Goldberg (o, p); Harvey Mandel (g); Bob Anderson (b); Fred Below Jr (d). 67.

**(*) Stone Blues
Vanguard VMD 79287 Musselwhite; Clay Cotton (o, p, v); Tim Kaihatsu, Larry Welker (g); Karl Sevareid (b); Eddie Ho (d). 68.

*** Tennessee Woman
Vanguard VMD 6528 Musselwhite; Rod Piazza (h); Skip Rose (p); Fred Roulette (sg); Tim Kaihatsu (g, v); Larry Welker (g); Karl Sevareid (b); Lance Dickerson (d). 69.

**(*) Best Of The Vanguard Years
Vanguard VCD 79556 As for above CDs, except add Walter Horton (h), Garth Hudson (o), Michael Bloomfield (p), John Hammond (g, v), Magic Sam, Robbie Robertson, Johnny Shines (g), Jimmy Lewis, Floyd Jones (b), Lester Dorsey, Levon Helm, Frank Kirkland (d), Shakey Jake (h). early 60s–93.

Musselwhite's Vanguard albums show how quickly he became comfortable with the business of making one. *Stand Back!* isn't bad, but *Tennessee Woman* is streets, or at least a city block, ahead in assurance. The first album's several slow numbers prompted droning guitar and organ lines which now seem to carry a joss-stick whiff of their time, and Sam Charters's ears must still have been on a lunchbreak during 'Chicken Shack', because the guitar is horribly out of tune. *Stone Blues* is more of a Chicago-oriented set, with four numbers by Little Walter and others by Elmore James, Magic Sam and A. C. Reed. The guitarists get to play a long game in the nearly 11-minute 'Bag Gloom Brews'.

On *Stand Back!* Musselwhite had played 'Christo Redemptor' (correctly 'Cristo Redentor', written by jazz pianist Duke Pearson and made famous in a recording by Donald Byrd) as a three-minute tune. On *Tennessee Woman* he got serious about the piece and explored it for almost 12 minutes – or rather one should say 'he and the band', since he is the most unselfish of musicians and invariably gives his accompanists abundant solo space. Skip Rose, for example, has long, jazzy solos both there and in his own blues tune 'A Nice Day For Something', and the two guitarists don't go short. Songs from Little Walter, Junior Wells and Fenton Robinson are matched by soulful originals like 'I'm A Stranger'. *Best Of* is composed of tracks from the three albums plus a harp duet with Walter Horton from the *Chicago/The Blues/Today!* project, two cuts from John Hammond's *So Many Roads*, two '60s recordings with Shakey Jake, made in his basement with Magic Sam, and 'Too Hot To Touch' from 1993. Space considerations probably led the compiler to prefer the shorter and inferior 'Christo Redemptor' to the longer, but it was tactless to open with 'Chicken Shack'.

*** **Memphis Charlie**
Arhoolie CD 303 *Musselwhite; Skip Rose, Lafayette Leake (p); Robben Ford, Tim Kaihatsu (g); Gerald Pedersen, Karl Sevareid (b); Patrick Ford, Larry Martin (d). 71, 8/74.*

Musselwhite was a guitarist first, and nowadays he likes to remind himself and his admirers of that by slipping a guitar track or two on to his albums. *Memphis Charlie* marks the first time he did so, on 'Blue Steel' and the very old-time-north-Mississippi 'Taylor's, Arkansas'. But the harmonica quotient is still high, especially in the slow blues 'Takin' My Time' – where he takes it for ten minutes – and 'If Trouble Was Money', played on chromatic harp.

*** **The Harmonica According To Charlie Musselwhite**
Blind Pig BPCD 5016 *Musselwhite; Bob Hall (p); Sam Mitchell (md, g); Stefan Grossman (g); Steve York (b); Jeff Rich (d, perc). 78.*

A charming session, originally done for the Kicking Mule label. Hearing Musselwhite in an acoustic setting with sympathetic accompaniment, you feel as if you are sharing his memories of growing up in Memphis when the echoes of jugband music had not quite died away. A particular memory inspired 'Fast Life Blues', and Musselwhite tells the story with self-effacing calm, showing that personal tribulation doesn't have to be mediated through bombast. 'Azul Para Amparo' is a Brazilian tune, the first of several he will record.

*** **Where Have All The Good Times Gone**
Blue Rock'It 103 *Musselwhite; Clay Cotton (p); Robben Ford (g); Steve Ehrman[n] (b); Patrick Ford (d). 11/83–2/84.*

(*) **Mellow-Dee
Crosscut CCD 11013 *Musselwhite; Rudi Schmuecker (p); Jim Kahr (g); Anselm Zueghart (b); Andy Steil (d). 7–8/85.*
(*) **Live 1986: Up And Down The Highway
Sanctuary 81260 *Musselwhite; Bob Hall (p); Dave Peabody (g). 86.*

Reunited with the Ford brothers on *Where Have All The Good Times Gone*, Musselwhite leaps in with Baby Boy Warren's 'Hello Stranger' and out with Jimmy Rogers's 'Going Away Baby' (forget the minute and a half of the theme from *Exodus*), between times mourning the death of Muddy Waters in 'Seemed Like The Whole World Was Crying' and of love in 'Where Have All The Good Times Gone'. 'Baby-O' and 'I'll Get A Break Someday' are solos with acoustic guitar and would be peaceful interludes, were the ensemble tracks not played with such restraint and taste that they don't need them to be. 'I'll Get A Break' turns up again on *Mellow-Dee*, with three other acoustic solos, surrounded by band numbers that are competently played by the mostly German musicians, and a third version of 'Christo Redemptor'. *Live 1986* was taped during a European tour, and has the common disadvantage of club recordings, excessively long songs: Lightnin' Hopkins's 'Candy Kitchen' runs to 10.59 and almost all the other numbers to six or seven minutes. Since Musselwhite hasn't the most winsome of voices, and his English partners' playing, though tight, is at times rather formulaic, listeners may find their attention wandering now and then.

*** **Ace Of Harps**
Alligator ALCD 4781 *Musselwhite; Andrew Jones Jr (g); Artis Joyce (b); Tommy Hill (d). 90.*
*** **Signature**
Alligator ALCD 4801 *Musselwhite; Lou Soloff (t); Art Baron (tb); Lenny Pickett (ts, bs); John Lee Hooker (g, v); Andrew Jones Jr (g); Artis Joyce (b); Tommy Hill (d). 91.*
***(*) **In My Time**
Alligator ALCD 4818 *Musselwhite; Gene Taylor (p); Junior Watson, Andrew 'Junior Boy' Jones (g); Larry Taylor, Felton Crews (b); Stephen Hodges, Tommy Hill (d); The Blind Boys Of Alabama (v). 94.*

Musselwhite is a consistent artist, but Alligator seem to have pushed him to a particularly high level of performance. No doubt it helped that he was working with a more or less settled lineup and the versatile Andrew Jones, but the confidently curling harmonica line of 'The Blues Overtook Me' on *Ace Of Harps* and the huge sound he gets on *Signature*'s '.38 Special', Walter Horton-like in its fatness, suggest that Musselwhite, a modest man, had finally decided to trust with his fans had long been telling him about his skill. *Ace Of Harps* and *Signature* are essentially quartet records – the horns on the latter are used on only two tracks – and the only performances from a different mould are 'My Road Lies In Darkness' on *Ace Of Harps*, another of Musselwhite's acoustic guitar songs, with a back-country feel like early Lightnin' Hopkins or John Lee Hooker, and *Signature*'s 'Cheatin' On Me', which *is* Hooker, in his late stream-of-consciousness manner – not easy to accompany, but Musselwhite, who has been there before, has no trouble. *In My Time* is rather different. Musselwhite evidently thought of it as a summary of how he'd got to *here* starting from *there*, so it opens with three solo guitar numbers, two played with slide, 'Brownsville Blues' in the manner of Furry Lewis, and the third eerily backgrounded by The Blind Boys Of Alabama. Then there are five cuts with the Watson–Taylor group and six with his road band, to represent his Chicago-and-onward period – the ensemble playing superb on both – before he and the Blind Boys gather again to sing 'Bedside Of A Neighbor'. Undoubtedly his best album so far.

*** DeLuxe Edition
Alligator ALCD 5612 *As for above Alligator CDs, except add Will Shade (v). early 60s, 90–94.*
*** Harpin' On A Riff: The Best Of Charlie Musselwhite
Music Club MCCD 400 *As for* Memphis Charlie, The Harmonica According To Charlie Musselwhite, Ace Of Harps, Signature *and* In My Time. 71–94.

DeLuxe Edition is an astute selection from the Alligator albums with two previously unissued tracks, one an ancient tape of Charlie playing guitar for Memphis jugband alumnus Will Shade. The Music Club cornucopia holds five songs from *Memphis Charlie*, including 'Taylor's, Arkansas', six from *The Harmonica According To Charlie Musselwhite*, including 'Fast Life Blues', and three each from the Alligator CDs, only three of which are also on *DeLuxe Edition*. Unassuming vocals, bravura harmonica playing, a few touches of downhome guitar: it isn't the best of Musselwhite – the Alligators in particular could have been better represented – but it's thoroughly typical and, with 20 tracks and a low price, good value.

**(*) Rough News
Pointblank 42856//(E) VPBCD 42 *Musselwhite; Stu Blank (kb, v); John Lawrence (g, churrango); Junior Watson (g, v); Kid Ramos, Cesar Rosas, Fenton Robinson (g); Felton Crews (b, v); Larry Taylor, A. G. Hardesty, Rene Coman (b); Stephen Hodges (d, v); Victor Bisetti, Jeffrey 'House' Clemens (d); Dick Shurman (v). 96.*

Hard to say why, but this doesn't feel like a happy record. It was made in a piecemeal fashion, seven tracks coming from a 4/96 Chicago date with Junior Watson, produced by Dick Shurman, the other five from undated sessions in California and New Orleans with different musicians, but it isn't stylistic discontinuity that's the problem: Musselwhite just sounds as if his heart isn't quite in it. It's revealing that his only solo acoustic number, 'Clarksdale Boogie', is his dullest so far.

** One Night In America
Telarc CD-83547 *Musselwhite; Peter Re (o); Marty Stuart (md, g); Robben Ford, G. E. Smith (g); T-Bone Wolk (b); Per Hanson, Michael Jerome (d); Kelly Willis, Christine Ohlman (v). 6/01.*
***(*) Sanctuary
Real World 597379//(E) CDRW 117 *Musselwhite; Charlie Sexton (g, v); Jared Michael Nickerson (b); Michael Jerome (d); Ben Harper, The Blind Boys Of Alabama (v); John Chelew (prod). 04.*

Both these albums engage with the South. The broad palette of *One Night In America* implies the musical colours of Memphis in the '50s, so alongside the blues are country songs old (Johnny Cash's 'Big River') and new (Kieran Kane's 'In A Town This Size') and the bluegrass gospel classic 'Rank Stranger[s] To Me'. 'From time to time,' he says in the notes, 'I have been criticized for some of my forays outside a strict blues structure'; he'll get no grief from us on that score, but what *is* troubling is how drab he makes some of these songs.

'Rank Stranger' may not demand a Ralph Stanley, but it does call for a certain kind of voice, with edge and penetration, and Musselwhite's lazy, tonally wavering drawl is not it. His style is far better suited to the bluesy back-country meditations of *Sanctuary* like 'My Road Lies In Darkness', Sonny Landreth's 'Shootin' For The Moon' (though the arrangement is too derivative) and Randy Newman's 'Burn Down The Cornfield'. The landscape is full of shadows and storm-clouds, and sometimes Musselwhite refuses to turn on the clear beam of his harmonica and dispel them, preferring to trudge through the murk to the steady beat of a guitar. So cumulative is the effect that you could legitimately call this a concept album; at any rate, it's an extraordinary performance. TR

Louis Myers (1929–94)
VOCAL, HARMONICA, GUITAR

Myers left Mississippi for Chicago in 1941. By 1946 he was playing in a band, and in 1950 he was a founder member of The Aces. He worked with many of Chicago's leading artists and enjoyed a high reputation for his skills as an ensemble player.

**** I'm A Southern Man
Testament TCD 5026 *Myers; Chuck Garnett (t); David Ii (ts); Nathaniel Dove (p); Freddy Robinson, Tony Mathews (g); Dennis Walker, Larry Taylor (b); Buster Jones (d). 3/78.*

When Myers was invited to make this album, he had spent some 30 years in music yet amassed a discography under his own name that ran to little more than a pair of harmonica instrumentals, 'Just Whaling' and 'Bluesy', which are on *Goin' Down To Eli's: The Cobra & Abco Rhythm & Blues Anthology 1956–1958* (Westside WESA 868) and *Abco Records* (Wolf 120.298), and a couple of tracks backed by Magic Sam, found on *Sweet Home Chicago* (Delmark DD-618). *I'm A Southern Man* shows that this skimpy coverage was no reflection of Myers's abilities. As might have been anticipated from an artist with his CV, it's a swatch of good, hard-wearing blues in attractive patterns, inspired by but not copied from predecessors like Robert Johnson ('Kind Hearted Woman'), Lightnin' Hopkins ('Short Haired Woman') or Sonny Boy Williamson II ('All My Love In Vain'). Myers takes his songs calmly, trusting his voice and his accompanists to make the performances interesting, and he is justified on both counts. He plays slide on 'Southbound Blues' and harmonica on 'Just Woke Up', a perfectly paced instrumental, and a couple of others; elsewhere the traditional role of the Chicago harp is rather cleverly usurped by Ii's tenor sax. There is nothing flashy about any of this music; rather, it radiates the quiet confidence of a seasoned musician who knows what he does best and sees no point in doing anything else.

**(*) Tell My Story Movin'
Earwig 4919 *Myers; 'Barrelhouse' Chuck Goering (p); Steve Freund, John Primer (g); Robert Stroger (b); Sam Burton (d). 91.*

Despite the artistic success of *I'm A Southern Man*, Myers went another dozen years without finding a label interested in recording him. By the time Earwig remedied that, he had suffered a minor stroke and hadn't regained full fitness. Consequently his singing is somewhat strained and he plays guitar on only one track, but he compensates by playing lots of harmonica, rooted in the style of 40-years-earlier buddies like Little Walter. Freund, Primer and Goering use their space effectively, and altogether this is a pleasing recital of oldfashioned Chicago band music. TR

Sam Myers (born 1936)
VOCAL, HARMONICA

Myers, who has very limited sight, was educated at the Piney Woods School for the Blind, and played a number of instruments before settling for harmonica at 12. Despite joining the Elmore James band for a time, and recording under his own name and, in the '70s, as a member of the Mississippi Delta Blues Band, Myers's fame was largely confined to the Jackson, Mississippi, area until 1984, when he joined Anson Funderburgh's band as a featured artist.

**(*) Blues Harmonica Wizards
Official CD 5254 *Myers; Walter Berry, Dave Campbell 'Big Moose' Walker (p); Tommy Lee Thompson, James Russell, Elmore James (g); Walter Crowley, Leon Dixon, Sammy Lee Bully (b); King Mose Taylor (d). 57–61.*

Most of this CD is devoted to Papa Lightfoot; the seven tracks credited to Myers include one that's actually by Jerry McCain and Myers's celebrated contribution to Elmore James's 'Look On Yonder Wall'. 'Sleepin' In The Ground', with its menacing vocal, horn-like harmonica and Thompson's ominous guitar, is a classic of postwar downhome blues, and nothing else here is less than good, although a tranquillizer would have improved the drumming on 'You Don't Have To Go'.

This material is lifted from legitimate issues, and Official's annotation is plagiarized, minimal and out of date. Myers's Ace recordings are better heard, if the CDs can be found, on the deleted Westside VACs *Tuff Enuff* (WESM 570), which has the original versions of 'Sleepin' In The Ground' and 'My Love Is Here To Stay', and *Shuckin' Stuff* (WESD 240 2CD), with the same songs, each in two excellent alternative takes.

** Change In My Pocket
Bullseye Blues & Jazz 9573 *Myers; John Street (o, p); Anson Funderburgh (g); J. P. Whitefield (b); Danny Cochran (d). 8/98.*

With the collapse of Black Top, this CD is one of only two examples in catalogue of Myers and Funderburgh's synthesis of Texas guitar and Mississippi harp. (For the other see Funderburgh's entry.) Credited to 'Anson Funderburgh & The Rockets featuring Sam Myers', it's not recommended; Myers's singing is stiffly megaphonic, and although Funderburgh's guitar work is tasteful, only the drumming is more predictable. Even so, Myers is out of sync with the (prerecorded?) band on the title track. 'Highway Man' and an unlisted 'Key To The Highway' rise a little way above the plateau.

**(*) Coming From The Old School
Electro-Fi 3383 *Myers; Pat Carey (ts); Mel Brown (o, p, g); Michael Fonfara (o, p); Jack de Keyzer (g); Alec Fraser (b); Jim Boudreau (d). 1/04.*

Myers and the band – and especially Myers and Mel Brown – are much more together on *Coming From The Old School*, and the rhythm section is looser and less humdrum. There are some unequivocally good tracks here, notably 'My Daily Wish', on which Brown plays both organ and guitar. On balance, though, this is a disappointing CD; most tracks are at least one solo too long, and while Myers's harp retains its big, bold tone, his stock of ideas is relatively small. As a singer, he seldom escapes a hoarsely inflexible holler. CS

Nathan & The Zydeco Cha Chas
GROUP

Nathan Williams (born 1963) plays piano accordion (and lately also triple-row), and is a gifted songwriter; his music descends from Clifton Chenier, and more directly from Stanley 'Buckwheat' Dural, and stresses melody and harmony, rather than the riff-based minimalism of recent times.

**(*) Zydeco Live!
Rounder CD 2069 *Fred Charles (ts); Nathan Williams (ac, v); Paul Daigle (g); Adam Harrison (b); Kevin Menard (d); Mark Williams (rb). 3/88.*

**** Steady Rock
Rounder CD 2092 *As above, except Eugene Alfred (g) replaces Daigle. 11/88.*

**** Your Mama Don't Know
Rounder CD 2107 *'Doctor' John Wilson (ts, v); Bill Samuel (bs); Scott Billington (h); Nathan Williams (ac, v); James Benoit, Dennis Paul Williams (g); Russell Benoit (b, v); Johnny Batiste (d); Mark Williams (rb, v). 10/90.*

**** Follow Me Chicken
Rounder CD 2122 *Allen 'Cat Roy' Broussard (as, v); Bill Samuel (ts, bs); Scott Billington (h, v); Nathan Williams (ac, v); Dennis Paul Williams (g, tri, v); James Benoit (g); Bobby Matthews (b); Johnny Batiste (d); Mark Williams (rb, v); Kenyatta Simon (djembe). 2/93.*

The Zydeco Cha Chas make music for dancers, needless to say, but on these early CDs their energy is tempered by a lilting warmth. Indeed, their contribution to *Zydeco Live!* (shared with Boozoo Chavis) is relatively restrained, and unfortunately the audience responds in kind. The three studio albums that followed are much more successful, establishing Williams as a musician and songwriter with an individual voice; the band sways gracefully around and across the beat behind his swirling harmonies, its rhythms coloured by the music of Jamaica, the Spanish-speaking West Indies and the R&B of New Orleans, always as much a northern Caribbean city as a southern American one. The textures, particularly the interplay of accordion and sax, also have a flavour of the islands, recalling Dominican merengue and the scratch bands of St Croix, and the djembe's two appearances on *Follow Me Chicken* add a remarkable polyrhythmic richness.

*** Creole Crossroads
Rounder CD 2137 *Allen 'Cat Roy' Broussard (as, ts, v); Nathan Williams, Sid Williams (ac, v); Michael Doucet (vn); Dennis Paul Williams (g); Clinton 'Yank' Perrodin (b); Gerard St Julien Jr (d); Mark Williams (rb); Scott Billington (v). 3/95.*

The notes make much of the way this CD explores the common roots of zydeco and Cajun music, and there are some fine things included, especially the two purposefully archaic fiddle–accordion duets and 'Jolie Noir', on which Nathan's brother Sid takes vocal and accordion duties. Too often, though, the music is not a seamless robe, but a zydeco suit with Cajun patches; the full band overpowers Doucet's fiddling, and has to throttle back abruptly to let his (excellent) solos be heard. Doucet drops out altogether on a few tracks, among them a notable version of Z. Z. Hill's 'Everybody Got To Cry'. *Creole Crossroads* is good, but to rate it more highly would be to let goodwill trump objectivity.

**** I'm A Zydeco Hog
Rounder CD 2143 *Allen 'Cat Roy' Broussard (as, perc, v); Nathan Williams (ac, v); Dennis Paul Williams (g, perc, v); Wayne Burns (b); Gerard St Julien Jr (d); Mark Williams (rb, v). 1/97.*

Recorded live at the Rock 'n' Bowl in New Orleans, *I'm A Zydeco Hog* has none of the tentativeness of the earlier live session; Williams and the band burn up the dancefloor from the outset. It's obvious that the Cha Chas have taken notice of trends in the music; St Julien uses modern zydeco's double-kick rhythms, and the new bass player's work is loud, nimble and slinky. However, Nathan is still using both sides of the piano accordion to generate catchy melodies and rich harmonies, the sax and guitar still dart and dance around him, and the resulting synthesis of new and old is very successful.

*** Let's Go!
Rounder CD 2159 *Allen 'Cat Roy' Broussard (as, ts, v); Derek Houston (ts); Scott Billington (h); Nathan Williams (ac, v); Dennis Paul Williams (g); Wayne Burns (b); Gerard St Julien Jr (d); Mark Williams (rb, v). 6–7/99.*

There are plenty of excellent moments here, like the soulful singing and the biting guitar solo on 'Put A Hump In Your Back', but there's seldom the almost telepathic togetherness of the earlier discs. Sometimes the accordion lines are fussy, or the harmonies mushy, and some tracks go on that little bit too long. On its own terms, *Let's Go!* is a fine CD, and the extended, autobiographical 'Hard Times' is splendid; but too often there's a sense that the objective is to stay in the public eye while awaiting a renewal of inspiration. CS

Kenny Neal (born 1957)
VOCAL, GUITAR, HARMONICA

Throughout the '90s, Kenny Neal seemed groomed for blues stardom. The oldest son of Raful Neal, he joined his father's band at 13 and five years later was playing bass for Buddy Guy. In 1980, he took his brothers to Canada, where they impressed Toronto as the Neal Brothers Blues Band. A return to Louisiana and an appearance on his father's album brought him a contract of his own, since when he's built a career as a dependable entertainer.

***(*) Big News From Baton Rouge
Alligator ALCD 4764 *Neal; Bruce Staelens (t); Bill Samuel, Buzz Montsinger (ts); Bob Greenlee (bs); Lucky Peterson, Kenny Burch (o, p); Ernie Lancaster (g); Noel Neal, Darnell Neal, Anthony Hardesty (b); Gralin Hoffman, Jim Payne (d). 88.*

Initially released as *Bio On The Bayou*, this album has been remixed and re-edited, with two tracks replaced. It's not difficult to understand the fervour of its initial reception, since as an unproven talent Neal shows himself to be an impressive singer and instrumentalist. The songs mix up the genres, 'Baby Bee' tipping a nod to Slim Harpo, 'Evalina' strutting its funky stuff and 'Bio On The Bayou' warmly evoking his youth spent listening to his father play the harmonica. With this last song as an exception, hindsight can identify the beginning of Neal's fundamental problem, the lack of depth and credibility in his lyrics. For all that, this was a notable debut.

*** Devil Child
Alligator ALCD 4774 *Neal; Sylvester Polk (t); Edgar Winter (as); Bill Samuel, Buzz Montsinger (ts); Bob Greenlee (bs, b); Lucky Peterson (kb); Noel Neal (b); Jim Payne (d). 89.*

As a virtual facsimile of *Big News*, this needed to be better than in fact it is. Apart from Raful Neal's 'Change My Way Of Livin'', the songs are written by various combinations of Neal, Payne and producer Greenlee. 'The Son I Never Knew' by the latter pair is the best of a series of formulaic songs that have a surface gloss but no depth. Production values of a mix laden with reverb are similarly disappointing. Neal's vocals, their timbre aged beyond his years, are muffled and undynamic, the brass audible but with little presence. His harmonica playing is serviceable but lacking the easy fluency of his guitar solos, which again do their job without being impressive. The results reveal an artist with ability who has yet to be distinctive.

*** Walking On Fire
Alligator ALCD 4795 *Neal; Bruce Staelens, Danny 'Boney' Fields (t); Fred Wesley (tb); Maceo Parker (as); Bill Samuel (ts); Bob Greenlee (bs, b); Leroy Cooper (bs); Lucky Peterson (kb); Ernie Lancaster (g); Russell Jackson (b); Tony Coleman, Jim Payne (d). 91.*

A different blend of the same ingredients produces a slightly better recipe, although the songs remain cliché-ridden, at their worst in 'Blues Stew'. A few more dynamics in the production bring more clarity to Neal's vocals but Peterson's keyboards remain for the most part hidden. The hyperventilating title track is a brief tribute to James Brown, allowing Neal to shout 'Maceo!' when Parker takes a solo. Since *Devil Child*, Neal had appeared on Broadway in *Mule Bone*, a play by Langston Hughes, and 'Morning After' and 'Bad Luck Card' are Hughes poems set to music. These acoustic recordings with Neal playing guitars and harmonica project the character missing from the band tracks.

**(*) Bayou Blood
Alligator ALCD 4809 *Neal; Lucky Peterson (kb, o); Noel Neal, Darnell Neal (b); Kennard Johnson (d). 92.*

A stripped-down production gives undue prominence to the rhythm section, and the drummer's snare overshadows Neal's vocals on most tracks. Peterson's keyboards are still buried in the mix, apart from the instrumental 'Neal And Prey', in which he takes an organ solo. Neal's progressively more fluent guitar takes a firm lead on this and solos copiously elsewhere, particularly well on 'Right Train, Wrong Track'. His harmonica playing on the opening 'Howling At The Moon' and four other songs is competent rather than commanding. Once again, the combination of facile songs and Neal's inability to work a lyric make this a pleasant but less than memorable experience.

*** Hoodoo Moon
Alligator ALCD 4825 *Neal; Bruce Staelens (t); Bill Samuel (ts); Bob Greenlee (bs); Lucky Peterson, Dwight Champagne (kb); Noel Neal (b); Kennard Johnson (d). 94.*

This is perhaps Neal's most satisfying album thus far, in terms of both production and performance. There's more diversity in the arrangements and a better balance in the mix. The lyrics of some of the songs, including the opening 'I'm A Blues Man', remain trite and predictable but there's good wordplay in 'If Heartaches Were Nickels' and 'Money Don't Make The Man'. Best of all is 'Carrying The Torch', in which Neal acknowledges his musical antecedents and the responsibility they place upon him. One of those is Slim Harpo and there are subtle references to 'Tip On In' during the title track. Neal has always been a capable performer but here the listener senses a greater depth in what he sings and plays.

***(*) DeLuxe Edition
Alligator ALCD 5604 *As for above CDs.* 88–94.

This is a 'Best Of' in all but name and the ideal way to become acquainted with Neal's skills as a singer, guitarist and occasional harmonicist. Four tracks each from *Big News From Baton Rouge* and *Bayou Blood* and three from *Devil Child* reveal Alligator's opinion of his five albums for the company. Most of the 16 songs are collaborations between Neal and producer/arranger Bob Greenlee and efficiency is their watchword, although much of what's played is formulaic and lacks an adventurous spirit. These performances seemed to have great promise when they first appeared. The necessary growth in artistic stature hasn't shown itself yet but the groundwork is undoubtedly here.

*** Blues Fallin' Down Like Rain
Telarc CD 83435 *Neal; Fredrick Neal (o, p); Doug Bare, Richard Bell (o); Warren King (g); Darnell Neal (b); Kennard Johnson, Gralin Hoffman (d); Christine Ohlman, Anne Donahue (v).* 10–12/97.

A change of label makes little difference, and the presence of 'Big Boss Man', 'My Babe' and 'I'm Ready' might indicate a failure of nerve, yet despite their familiarity Neal's relaxed approach makes these and the other eight tracks eminently listenable. Four of the latter are written by Neal and his erstwhile producer Bob Greenlee and like their previous efforts they're competent without being striking. Neal's voice isn't particularly well recorded but his guitar playing, some on a lap steel, bites where necessary. Overall, this album makes a virtue of brevity, although one or two songs are reluctant to fade. This is an enhanced CD, containing photographs, biography and live footage of Neal onstage with his brothers.

*** Easy Meeting//Double Take
Isabel IS 649801//Alligator ALCD 4894 *Neal; Billy Branch (h, v).* 5/98.

Though this is billed as an acoustic session, Neal and the jointly credited Branch power up for five of the 12 tracks. They share the vocals and while Neal sings his own compositions, 'The Son I Never Knew' and 'Baby Bee' among them, Branch goes for the tried and tested, including 'Don't Start Me Talking', 'My Babe' and 'Mannish Boy'. Branch is the principal soloist, particularly on the unflagging 'Billy And Kenny's Stomp', while Neal takes one brief solo in 'My Babe', which also features some subtle additional guitar tracks. Both perform well and the results are solidly entertaining. NS

**(*) Homesick For The Road
Telarc CD-83454 *Neal; Raful Neal (h, v); Debbie Davies, Tab Benoit (g, v); Bruce Katz (o); Rod Carey (b); Per Hanson (d).* 9/98.

Neal has a hand in nearly all the tracks on this three-header with Tab Benoit and Debbie Davies, taking the lead part on 'I've Been Mistreated', 'Bop 'Til I Drop' and 'Still Called The Blues' and an even share of 'Luberta'. It isn't distinctive material and Neal's handling of it is restrained at best, at worst sluggish. TR

**(*) What You Got
Telarc CD 83467 *Neal; Marshall DeMott (ts, bs); Anthony Geraci (o, p); Noel Neal (b); Kennard Johnson (d).* 7/99.

Perhaps now is the time to admit it: Kenny Neal makes *nice* records. Trouble is, there's very little to choose between them. One of the 12 tracks here is 'Deja Vu' and it must be said, it's all been heard before. Neal had a hand in the writing of all but three songs, one of them the title track. There's another successful go at 'Neal And Prey', the instrumental from *Bayou Blood*, but this time he dominates all 16 choruses. Titles such as 'Two Wrongs Don't Make A Right', 'Never Thought About Growing Old' and 'Blues Ain't Nothing But A Good Man Feeling Bad' promise more than they deliver as Neal consistently refuses to sound committed. Apart from a tendency towards over-extended codas, all present perform well but the result of their labours is better suited to a branch of Starbucks than to the home.

** One Step Closer
Telarc CD 83523 *Neal; Jason Ward (bs); T-Bone Wolk (ac, md, b); unknown (o); Mary Jo Carlsen (vn); Denny Breau (g); Darren Thiboutot (d); Andrea Re (perc, v).* 1/01.

A glance at the instruments should raise the odd eyebrow. Whatever Neal is approaching, it certainly isn't the blues. Composer credits include Bob Dylan, John Hiatt and Nick Lowe, alongside two each from Fred James and Colin Linden. Neal himself makes a late attempt to improve the blues quota with a pair of literate but lame titles. He seems to have opted for his own version of Dylan's Rolling Thunder Revue, with a miscellany of combinations of mandolin, violin, baritone sax, accordion and organ. Add to that Re's dispirited vocals in harmony or response. Much of the time, usually for at least the last minute of a song, nothing happens until everyone meanders into the fade. As far as being regarded as a blues musician, Neal seems to be shuffling in the same direction. NS

Raful Neal (1936–2004)
VOCAL, HARMONICA

Neal performed on the Baton Rouge scene from the '50s, and recorded a few singles; he was the father of Kenny Neal and several other musical children.

**(*) Louisiana Legend
Alligator ALCD-4783 *Neal; Bruce Staelens (t); Jon Paltishall (tb); Noble Watts (ts); Bob Greenlee (bs, b); Barry Rupp, Red Simpson (kb); Kenny Neal, Bryan Bassett, Ernie Lancaster (g); Jim Payne, Scott Corwin, Denny Best (d).* 87?

Raful Neal was an adequate, no-frills harmonica player and a forceful vocalist, but here he barks out the songs, heedless of whether his subject is murder ('Luberta'), love ('Honest I Do') or ethics (a dreadful revival of 'Let's Work Together'). A lot of production was invested in this CD, which places Neal in settings from revived swamp pop to repro Muscle Shoals soul; all the musicians work hard, and Kenny Neal's guitar lines are consistently well-conceived, but the case for legendary status is not made. Neal went on to record for the defunct Ichiban; 1998's *Old Friends* (Club Louisianne 1111) seems to be unavailable too. He also recorded with the Hoodoo Kings (q.v.). CS

Chicago Bob Nelson (born 1944)
VOCAL, HARMONICA

As a boy in Bogalusa, Louisiana, Robert Lee Nelson picked up some tuition on harmonica from Lazy Lester and Slim Harpo. He moved to Chicago in his late teens and became an avid sitter-in at blues sessions. In 1965 he formed a band in Boston with Luther 'Georgia Boy' Johnson, which toured widely in the US and visited France. After Johnson died in 1976 Nelson moved to Atlanta, where he worked and recorded with the Heartfixers and with what became the Shadows.

*** Just Your Fool
High Water HMG 6506 Nelson; Bob Page (o, p); J. T. Speed (g); El Rog (b); Bob Rice (d). 2/87.

Unwaveringly dedicated to the '50s downhome idiom of his native south Louisiana and to its Chicago blues models, Nelson fell in with a group of like-thinkers, the Shadows, and made this very satisfying album. His book is thick with songs from Jimmy Rogers, Little Walter, Jimmy Reed, Slim Harpo, J. B. Lenoir and J. B. Hutto, and the few numbers that are credited to him are built out of very similar material. Gruff-voiced and forthright, his style may remind some listeners of 'Wild Child' Butler. The versatile Speed plays with an acute understanding of what's called for in each song: in 'Your Time To Choose', for instance, he is busy and loquacious but never so much so as to stand in Nelson's way. Studio echo is used unsubtly and the mix is somewhat bass-heavy. Nelson's subsequent albums *Hit & Run Lover* (Ichiban) and *Back To Bogalusa* (King Snake) are out of print. TR

Jimmy 'T99' Nelson (born 1928)
VOCAL

Nelson left his home in Philadelphia in his teens to find work on the West Coast. Hearing Joe Turner, he discovered that he too had a talent for blues singing and began working in clubs and bars in the San Francisco Bay Area. He had a sizeable hit with 'T-99 Blues' (RPM, 1951), but could not repeat it. In 1955 he settled in Houston, Texas, where he recorded occasional singles over the next decade or so, but he was unable to make a living from music and worked for a construction company. In the '80s and '90s he appeared at festivals in the US and Europe, and at the time of writing he was continuing to perform at clubs and festivals in the Southwest.

*** Cry Hard Luck: The RPM And Kent Recordings 1951–61 [sic]
Ace CDCHD 976 Nelson; Big Windy Morgan, unknown (t); Charles Waller, Bumps Myers (ts, bs); Maxwell Davis, unknowns (ts); unknown (bs); Peter Rabbit (p, vb); Eddie Beal, Willard McDaniel, unknowns (p); Junior Simmons, Chuck Norris, poss. Irving Ashby (g); Robert Jackson, Red Callender, Ted Brinson, unknowns (b); Lee Young, Charles Blackwell, unknowns (d); band (v). 51–60.

Nelson is an oldfashioned stand-out-front vocalist in the Joe Turner mould but with enough character of his own to have deserved better luck than he has enjoyed for most of his career. This meticulous reissue collects his early work and makes a convincing case for Nelson being not only a weighty singer but a songwriter of considerable ingenuity, developing an idea in 'Big Mouth Blues' or conjuring up lines like 'I can't afford to lay my last good head on a dusty railroad line'.

** Hot Tamale Baby
Collectables CO-CD-5259 Nelson; Ralph Hamilton, Calvin Owens, unknown(s) (t); Arnett Cobb, Conrad Johnson, Jimmy Ford, unknowns (s); Charles Dancye, unknowns (kb); Clarence Hollimon, Pete Mayes, Chris Holzhaus, unknown (g); Larry Lambert, unknown (b); Carl Lott, Ronny Wynne, unknown (d); unknowns (v). 63–70.

About half of this CD was recorded in 1963 and possibly '65 with unknown musicians and partly issued on singles on small Houston labels; the other half is from a couple of 1970 sessions produced by Roy C. Ames for his Home Cooking label but mostly never issued. The majority of these sides are poorly engineered or remastered, and Nelson is seldom heard in really sympathetic conditions.

** Rockin' And Shoutin' The Blues
Bullseye Blues & Jazz BB 9593 Nelson; Carl Querfurth (tb); Rich Lataille (as); [Sax] Gordon Beadle (ts); Doug James (bs); Matt McCabe (p); Clarence Hollimon (g); Marty Ballou (b); Neil Gouvin (d); The Pink Spots (v). 9/98.

Sadly, this isn't up to much. Nelson's voice sounds tired and old, but the problems go deeper. Few of his core audience will care to witness him corralling warhorses like 'When You're Smiling' and 'Don't Let The Sun Catch You Crying'. Nor can he bring anything fresh to 'How Long Blues' or 'Boogie Woogie Country Girl'. A couple of tracks remind us that he is a pithy songwriter, 'House Of The Blues' and the boisterous 'New Shack Lover' ('I was shackin' up with a no-account, good-condition, don't want to work, lyin' girl …'), and the backing band, which includes a couple of the horns from Roomful Of Blues and a Houston acquaintance of Nelson's in guitarist Clarence Hollimon, cushions his voice sympathetically. But if Nelson can still rock and shout, this album is a poor advertisement. TR

Hambone Willie Newbern
VOCAL, GUITAR

An obscure singer and guitarist, possibly from eastern Arkansas or western Tennessee, Newbern was known to Sleepy John Estes, who thought he was born around 1899 and died in prison in 1947.

**** The Greatest Songsters (1927–1929)
Document DOCD-5003 Newbern. 3/29.

Three of Newbern's six recordings are rag tunes: 'She Could Toodle-Oo', which uses a similar chord progression to 'Take Your Fingers Off It', 'Way Down In Arkansas', akin to 'Alabama Jubilee', and 'Nobody Knows (What The Good Deacon Does)', all with rich, flowing guitar accompaniments. The others are blues. 'Shelby County Workhouse Blues' is an apparently autobiographical piece that finds Newbern travelling back and forth between Memphis and Marked Tree, Arkansas, and running foul of the law. 'Roll And Tumble Blues' is the song more often called 'Rollin' And Tumblin''; many singers of Newbern's time knew it, and it was a lucky accident that he was the first to record it. The remainder of the CD is given over to Richard 'Rabbit' Brown and Mississippi John Hurt. TR

Robert Nighthawk (1909–67)
VOCAL, GUITAR

Romance and mystery are natural constituents of the blues but few bluesmen embodied restless melancholia better than Robert Lee McCoy (born McCollum). Taught guitar by his cousin Houston Stackhouse, McCoy already played harmonica and would do so on records by Sleepy John Estes and others but not his own. He and Sonny Boy Williamson I made their recording debuts on the same day in May 1937 and accompanied one another at two further sessions. He adopted and refined Tampa Red's slide guitar style to complement his doleful vocal timbre and it's for this that he has been remembered. Because of his rootless and enigmatic nature, his postwar sessions, under the name of Robert Nighthawk, were rare, but they were of a consistently high standard. He passed on his slide technique to a teenaged Earl Hooker.

*** The Bluebird Recordings 1937–1938
[RCA Bluebird 67416] McCoy; John Lee 'Sonny Boy' Williamson (h); poss. Walter Davis, prob. Speckled Red (p); [Big] Joe Williams, Henry Townsend (g). 5/37–12/38.
*** Robert Lee McCoy (Robert Nighthawk) (1937–1940)
Wolf WBCD-002 As above, except add Ann Sortier (wb, v), unknown (v). 5/37–6/40.

These early sessions are serviceable rather than distinguished, the first most notable for the erratic interplay of the two guitars, McCoy playing single-note bass patterns over the splenetic chords and percussive string-snaps of Joe Williams. The voice is already devoid of humour, and the closest he gets to being light-hearted is 'Take It Easy, Baby'. 'Prowling Nighthawk', from which he took his resonant stage name, is a precursor of Tony Hollins's 'Crawling King Snake'. Other songs of note include 'I Have Spent My Bonus', 'Mamie Lee' (with an elaborate seasonal metaphor, 'she let me hang my little stocking in her Christmas tree') and 'Every Day And Night', which later became known as 'When My Heart Beats Like A Hammer' and 'Hard Pill To Swallow'.

Both compilations contain the first three sessions, but the Wolf also includes McCoy's 1940 session as 'Peetie's Boy', which he shared with the singer and washboard player Ann Sortier. Her raggy 'Gonna Keep It For My Daddy', with McCoy and another chanting the choruses, contrasts starkly with 'Never Leave Me' (the collection's one noisy transfer), for which she adopts a striking imitation of Billie Holiday. McCoy sings a curiously stilted 'Mama Don't Allow Me' to the tune of 'Shake 'Em On Down' and 'Friar's Point Blues', about the Mississippi riverside town he nonetheless locates in 'dear old Dixieland' and on which his slide technique, inspired by Tampa Red, makes its recording debut.

*** Bricks In My Pillow
Delmark DE-711 Nighthawk; Bob Call or Roosevelt Sykes, prob. Curtis Jones (p); unknown (g); Ransom Knowling (b); Jump Jackson, unknown (d). 7/51–10/52.

Nighthawk played at Muddy Waters's wedding to Mabel Berry in 1932 and it was through Muddy that he cut three sessions for Aristocrat between 1948 and 1950. Thirteen songs were recorded, of which four were sung by his companion Ethel Mae Brown and a fifth remains unissued. The remaining eight form part of the VAC *The Aristocrat Of The Blues* (MCA/Chess CHD2–9387 2CD [deleted]), a summary of the label's acts largely devoted to Muddy. On 'My Sweet Lovin' Woman' Nighthawk was supported by Sunnyland Slim; Ernest Lane and Pinetop Perkins took over the piano chair for the other sessions. His reinvigorations of two Tampa Red songs, 'Sweet Black Angel' and 'Anna Lee', with their pellucid slide accompaniment, became the definitive Nighthawk recordings. 'Return Mail Blues', 'Six Three 0' and 'Jackson Town Gal' receive the same treatment but are lesser songs. 'She Knows How To Love A Man' and Leroy Carr's 'Prison Bound' are played conventionally with a light vibrato on the guitar amp. While his voice and guitar playing were a perfect marriage, Nighthawk's dignified and reticent style already sounded oldfashioned in 1950.

Eighteen months after his last Aristocrat recordings, Nighthawk was in at the beginning of the United and States labels. Apart from the uncertain identity of the pianist, there is confusion within the band itself, typified by curiously disjointed but martial drum patterns and tentative piano chording on 'Crying Won't Help You' and 'Feel So Bad', although Nighthawk and bassist Knowling seem to be at one. Coordination improves with a revived 'Take It Easy Baby' and 'Kansas City', although the thrusting rhythm section, with Knowling's slapped and syncopated patterns prominent, pressurizes Nighthawk's normally laidback delivery. Knowling was the only identified participant in a later session at which versions of Tommy Johnson's 'Maggie Campbell' and Bumble Bee Slim's 'Bricks In My Pillow' were cut. The former adopts a busy split rhythm that masks Nighthawk's adaptation of Johnson's original guitar part. A fleet-fingered second guitarist embellishes the first of the two takes featured and 'U/S Boogie', one of two time-filling instrumentals. Second takes of 'The Moon Is Rising' and 'Seventy Four' have no fresh revelations beyond the band's inability to provide effective accompaniment. NS

*** Ramblin' Bob
Saga Blues 982 076–9 Nighthawk; Sonny Boy Williamson I (h, sp); poss. Walter Davis, prob. Speckled Red, Sunnyland Slim, Ernest Lane, Pinetop Perkins, Roosevelt Sykes or Bob Call, prob. Curtis Jones (p); [Big] Joe Williams, unknown (g); Willie Dixon, Ransom Knowling (b); prob. Jump Jackson, unknown (d). 5/37–10/52.
(***) Prowling With The Nighthawk
Document DOCD-32-20-6 As above. 5/37–10/52.

These are sound selections from Nighthawk's first 15 years of record-making, divided more or less evenly between the Bluebird sessions and the Aristocrat–United–States period. Saga Blues follow the chronology, but Document prefer randomness. They are well-filled baskets, Saga Blues having 22 items and Document 26, but 19 were on both shopping lists. Thanks to the high quality of Chess and Delmark mastering, the sound of the later material is irreproachable, but on Document the Bluebirds have been subjected to aggressive sonic treatment which replaces the authentic sound of a period recording with the improbable sheen of a facsimile. TR

**** **And This Is Maxwell Street**
Rooster Blues R 2641 3CD *Nighthawk; Johnny Young or John Lee Granderson, Michael Bloomfield (g); Robert Whitehead or Jimmy Collins (d)*. 9/64.

***(*) **Live On Maxwell Street 1964**
Bullseye Blues & Jazz 9624 *As above*. 9/64.

The LP of *Live On Maxwell Street 1964* won a Handy Award for the Best Vintage Reissue of 1980. That and its latest incarnation bear a production credit to Norman Dayron. *And This Is Maxwell Street*, a double CD of music performed by Nighthawk, Young, Big John Wrencher, Carey Bell, Arvella Gray and others and a supplementary CD of interviews with Nighthawk by Michael Bloomfield, emerged two decades later. Its title refers to a documentary film shot in Chicago's Maxwell Street area during the late summer of 1964 by Mike Shea. Booklet writer Colin Talcroft insists that Dayron was employed by Shea on a 'work for hire' basis as a sound engineer and that the collection bearing Dayron's name was 'unauthorised', mastered from 'low-quality second-generation' copy tapes and issued without Shea's knowledge.

Contention aside, Nighthawk's performance, captured 'at the corner of 14th and Peoria', is magnificent. The gusto with which he sings and plays and the broad spectrum of music he covers are a revelation. Equally adept with finger and slide, he frequently indulges both in the course of a song. The second guitarist is playing through a distorted amplifier and is an inadequate presence on tape but nevertheless effective. Jimmy Collins was Nighthawk's drummer at the time and is the likelier candidate for a percussionist who accelerates at any tempo. The repertoire includes Doctor Clayton's 'Cheating And Lying Blues', Big Joe Turner's 'Honey Hush' and Junior Parker's 'I Need Love So Bad' as well as a medley of Nighthawk's own 'Anna Lee' and 'Sweet Black Angel', a revamped 'Take It Easy, Baby', 'The Time Have Come' and two improvisations, 'Peter Gunn Jam' and 'Back Off Jam'. It seems likely that some guitar solos, including one during 'The Time Have Come', are played by Michael Bloomfield.

The Bullseye compilation (an expansion of the earlier Rounder CD 2022) concentrates on Nighthawk's set(s) but also includes two songs by Johnny Young, 'Juke Medley' by Carey Bell, a version of 'Mama Talk To Your Daughter' probably sung by Andrew 'Big Voice' Odom and a previously unissued 'I Got News For You', attributed to Bell but more likely to be by Big John Wrencher. The final track consists of extracts from the Bloomfield interview. Nighthawk is a reticent interviewee and, as the booklet notes, Bloomfield proves to be a less than probing questioner. But for those who indulged in the process at the time, the mixture of incomprehension and misinformation feels entirely authentic.

*** **Masters Of Modern Blues**
Testament TCD 5010 *Nighthawk; John Wrencher, Little Walter (h); Johnny Young (g)*. 5–10/64.

With the exception of 'Kansas City', recorded live with Little Walter in May, Nighthawk's portion of this album (the rest is by Houston Stackhouse) was recorded in 10/64. Both Wrencher and Young had worked with him throughout the summer and their empathy is striking. However, though confidently played and sung, these performances, which include 'Crying Won't Help You', 'Black Angel Blues' and 'Maggie Campbell', lack the unpredictability and tension of the live versions. Nighthawk's vocals are almost conversational and, while his performance is faultless, one senses power held in check. 'Bricks In My Pillow' and 'Crowing Rooster Blues' emphasize his reliance upon traditional repertoire, contrasted with Charles Brown's 'Merry Christmas Baby' and his own 'I'm Getting Tired'.

Three years later and within two months of his death, he and drummer Peck Curtis supported Stackhouse at a session in Dundee, Mississippi. Four previously unissued titles have been added to the four on the original LP but Nighthawk was in no condition to make a positive contribution. Nevertheless, these titles bring symmetry to the collection as a whole. NS

The Nighthawks
GROUP

The band was founded in Washington, DC, in 1972 by Jimmy Thackery and Mark Wenner. Jan Zukowski and Pete Ragusa joined in 1974. After Thackery's departure in 1986 the remaining members worked for several years backing other artists, such as Elvin Bishop, or on tours organized by the Rosebud Agency. An indefatigable road band, they have played more than 7,000 gigs.

** **Rock 'N' Roll**
Varrick VRCD 007 *Mark Wenner (h, v); Jim Thackery (g, v); Jan Zukowski (b, v); Pete Ragusa (d, v)*. 74/75.

(*) **Open All Nite
Genes GCD 4105 *As above, except add Pinetop Perkins (p)*. 75/76.

(*) **Live
Genes GCD 4110 *As above, except omit Perkins*. 76–77.

(*) **Side Pocket Shot
Genes GCD 4115 *As above, except add The Rhythm Kings Horns (Ed Jonnet, Chris Patarini, Van Crozier, John Hogue) (brass, reeds), Tommy Hannum (psg), Rick Anderson (perc), Lucille Schoettle, Judy Coughlin (v)*. 77?

(*) **Times Four
Genes GCD 4130 *Mark Wenner (h, v); Dave Maxwell (o, p); Jim Thackery (g, v); Jan Zukowski (b, v); Pete Ragusa (d, v)*. 77.

*** **Jacks & Kings Volume I & II**
Genes GCD 4120 *The Rhythm Kings Horns (Ed Jonnet, Chris Patarini, Van Crozier, John Hogue), The Phantom Horns (George McWhirter, Jamie McKinnon) (brass, reeds), Mark Wenner (h, v); Dave Maxwell (o, p); Pinetop Perkins (p, v); Jim Thackery, Luther 'Guitar Jr' Johnson (g, v); Bob Margolin (g); Jan Zukowski (b); Pete Ragusa (d)*. 77/78.

*** **Best Of The Nighthawks**
Genes GCD 4140/45 *As for source CDs above*. 75/76–78/79.

(*) **Ten Years Live
Varrick VRCD 001 *Mark Wenner (h, v); Jim Thackery (g, v); Jan Zukowski (b, v); Pete Ragusa (d, perc, v)*. 12/81.

(*) **Hard Living
Varrick VRCD 022 *As above, except add Greg Wetzel (kb, v), Steuart Smith (syn, g, perc, v)*. winter 85.

(*) **Live In Europe
Varrick VRCD 033//Crosscut CCD 11014 *As for Ten Years Live, except Zukowski does not sing*. 7/86.

(*) **Backtrack
Varrick VRCD 036 *Similar to above*. 86.

'Blues' is not to be found in any of The Nighthawks' album titles, and almost never in their contents. That isn't to say that tracks like 'Nine Below Zero' on *Open All Nite* or 'Black Night' on *Live In Europe* aren't blues, but the rarity of the word itself is suggestive, implying that the 'hawks don't want to be seen merely as the Washington, DC, chapter of the American Federation of Blues Bands. On their first album, *Rock 'N' Roll* (you see?), they implied that their stock-in-trade would be R&B, as the term was then understood – a blend of blues, Southern soul and Motown – with a measure of rockabilly and a dash of contemporary rock. Most of their albums have, in fact, taken that sort of direction, Wenner or Thackery usually handling the blues material and Ragusa the soul. In that respect, *Open All Nite*, with its set of received blues repertoire from Sonny Boy Williamson II, Jimmy Reed, Elmore James and Muddy Waters, and the guest-stacked *Jacks & Kings Volume I & II* (which comprises the LPs *Jacks & Kings* and *Full House*), look almost like aberrations, though blues-lovers will be glad of them.

It was an ambitious project, and it took a while for the band to bring it off; in their early work they sound not all that different from contemporaries like the J. Geils Band or George Thorogood & The Destroyers, only less fired up. Repertoire choices like 'Memo From Turner' or the Presleyan 'Little Sister' seal the fate of *Rock 'N' Roll* as a period piece, but even the blend of blues and rock 'n' roll epitomized by *The Best Of The Nighthawks*, whick draws from the five preceding Genes CDs, seems a little dated. By the time they made *Hard Living*, however, the band had built a wall of sound that could be imposing on soul numbers like 'Lot Of Love' or Wenner's instrumental features such as 'Inaugural Freeze'.

**(*) Trouble
Ruf 1064 Mark Wenner (h, v); Mitch Collins (o); Mike Cowan (p); Danny Morris (g, v); Bob Margolin (g); Jan Zukowski (b); Pete Ragusa (d, v); Ratso, Juanita Deshagior (v). 1/91.

**(*) Rock This House
Big Mo 1023 Mark Wenner (h, v); Danny Morris (g, v); Jan Zukowski (b); Pete Ragusa (d, v). 93.

*** Still Wild
Ruf 1037//(A) 51416–1448 Mark Wenner (h, v); Darryl Davis (kb); James Solberg (g, v); Pete Kanaras, Jimmy Nalls (g); Jan Zukowski (b, v); Pete Ragusa (d, v). 98.

*** Pain And Paradise
Big Mo 1030//Ruf 1080 Mark Wenner (h, v); Steuart Smith (kb); Pete Kanaras (g); Jan Zukowski (b, v); Pete Ragusa (d, v); The Orioles (Reese Palmer, Diz Russell, Larry Jordan), Tommy Lepson, John Brittain (v). 00?

*** Live Tonite!
Ruf 1079 Mark Wenner (h, v); Pete Kanaras (g); Jan Zukowski (b, v); Pete Ragusa (d, v). late 01.

Live In Europe and *Backtrack* were recorded shortly before Thackery left to make a career in his own name, and it would be more than four years before the band recorded again as The Nighthawks. With Morris as a competent, unshowy replacement for Thackery, and Cowan filling out the ensemble, *Trouble* gives pleasure in uncomplicated blues numbers like 'Hard Hearted Woman' and the hip 'The Chicken And The Hawk'. Lending a Chicago blues accent to Bob Dylan's 'Most Likely You Go Your Way (And I'll Go Mine)' is less successful.

After *Rock This House* Morris left, to be succeeded in 1995 by Pete Kanaras, first heard on *Still Wild*. He's a more incendiary guitarist than his predecessor, and louder, though that's probably because of the well-managed studio sound, something of a first for this band. But from the opening bars of the first track, 'Tiger In Your Tank', it's clear that the dominant strain in the ensemble, as usual, will be Wenner's forceful and versatile harmonica playing, and appropriately the album signs off with a slow harmonica blues that Little Walter would have approved of. Walter and Muddy Waters are specifically remembered, in three numbers each, on the two following albums. *Pain And Paradise* comes from the standard Nighthawks mould, polished by exemplary studio sound. *Live Tonite!*, culled from tapes of half a dozen gigs in the Greater Washington area, is an extended letter of thanks to some of the band's models, the others including Howlin' Wolf and Jimmy Reed. For readers of strict blues tastes, this is one of their most obviously appealing albums. TR

Nine Below Zero
GROUP

Dennis Greaves formed his first blues combo in 1977, inspired by the J. Geils Band; some commentators saw them as a South London riposte to the challenge of the Essex R&B band Dr Feelgood. After a busy few years playing in Britain, Europe and the United States, Nine Below Zero broke up in 1982, but Greaves re-formed the band in 1990 with new players and they have been active ever since.

**(*) Doing Their Homework
Castle CMDDD 899 2CD Mark Feltham (h, v); Alan Glen, Billy Miskimmin (h); Dennis Greaves (g, v); Hubert Sumlin (g); Mickey Burkey, Gerry McAvoy (b); Dennis Ratcliffe, Brendan O'Neill (d). 79–97.

The snarling face of this music recalls the early Rolling Stones. Imagine a young R&B band from back then, preserved in ice like the mammoths and defrosted decades later. It's the attitude of Nine Below Zero that recalls the past more than their raw, bare-bones quartet sound or their material, which is partly original, partly covers, often of Otis Rush ('Homework', 'I Can't Quit You Baby') and Sonny Boy Williamson II ('Nine Below Zero', naturally). *Doing Their Homework* compacts almost all of the 1979 album *Live At The Venue*, most of 1982's *Live In London* (including three studio demos) and all of 1997's *Don't Give Me No Lip Child*, which had two tracks with Hubert Sumlin. The high-octane energy of the Venue gig, pumped up by the aggressive playing of Feltham and Greaves, comes at the cost of out-of-tune singing on the early tracks, but the balance is good for a concert recording, whereas on *Live In London* the vocals are more boxed-in. They are too on the studio-recorded *Lip Child* but Miskimmin is a fit successor to Feltham and the smell that comes off the music is authentically pungent.

*** Hat's Off
Zed ZCD 1008 Mark Feltham (h, tamb, v); Ben Waters (o, p); Dennis Greaves (g, v); Gerry McAvoy (b); Brendan O'Neill (d). 04.

NBZ also have a string of albums on their own label, Zed, which are of more limited availability. We particularly recommend *Hat's Off*, an all-covers set of mostly classic Chicago repertoire from Muddy Waters, Elmore James, John Brim and other usual suspects, performed with spirit and knowhow and better recorded than any of the material on *Doing Their Homework*. But this is not a typical NBZ album, and readers who'd like to hear them on a wider range of material, including their own, should investigate CDs like 2002's *Chilled* (ZCD 1006). TR

Hammie Nixon (c. 1908–84)
VOCAL, HARMONICA, KAZOO, JUG

The AFM files say that Nixon was born in 1913 but, whatever the date, he was raised by a white family near Brownsville, Tennessee. He first played harmonica with Sleepy John Estes as an 11-year-old, and their partnership lasted until Estes's death in 1977. Nixon's other main partner through the '30s was Son Bonds; he accompanied both men on record, and also Lee Green and Charlie Pickett. He was less active in music from the '40s, but Estes's rediscovery in 1962 led to Nixon's, and the two men, at first joined by Yank Rachell, played concerts worldwide.

***(*) Tappin' That Thing
High Water HMG 6509 Nixon; William 'Boogie Man' Hubbard (p, b); Richard Hite (g, b, j); David Evans, Big Lucky Carter (g, v); John Hunninen (g); Tom 'Jazzbo' Janzen (d); Bob Vinisky (j). 6/82–1/84.

Hammie Nixon was an extrovert showman, and much more dynamic than his chief partner, but during his second career he was always booked as Sleepy John Estes's sideman. It's no wonder he thought about retiring when Estes died, but fortunately he was encouraged by David Evans to perform in the jugband setting heard on *Tappin' That Thing*. This was good thinking on a number of counts, not least because Nixon was still a vigorous musician with no traditional audience for his music. Equally important, Nixon solo was apt to meander aimlessly and, as may be heard on the VAC *Living Country Blues* (Evidence ECD 26105 3CD), to indulge in fluttertonguing and Bronx cheers regardless of context. The band curbed these tendencies by adding rhythmic and contextual discipline to his still abundant energy. Nixon's forcefulness is very striking on three tracks backed by electric guitar, piano, bass and drums; elsewhere, a variety of acoustic lineups is heard, from solo guitar to full band. The musicians play sympathetically but without compromise, never carrying, always pushing. Nixon's sensitive accompaniments to Sleepy John Estes remain his greatest achievement, and make his boisterousness as a featured artist the more surprising, but the notes' pre-emptive description of the kazoo as 'much maligned' is unduly apprehensive. Everybody on these sessions had fun, and it comes over loud and clear. CS

James Nixon (born 1941)
VOCAL, GUITAR

A lifelong resident of Nashville, Tennessee, Nixon has played on the local scene for over 40 years with NTS Limited, Past, Present & Future and The Imperial 7. He has also recorded and produced albums in the gospel field and taught in the Blues In The Schools programme.

**(*) No End To The Blues
Black Magic CD 9045 Nixon; Dennis Taylor (ts, bs); Shannon Williford (h); Billy Earheart (o, p); Fred James (g, cga, prod); Jeff Davis (b); Bryan Owings (d); Mary-Ann Brandon (v). 5–6/01.

This well-made album reveals a singer whose apprenticeship has been in the borderlands where blues converge with Southern soul. About half the numbers are straightforward blues, and if 'The Best In Town' is no more than a weary slog over the melodic terrain of 'Baby What You Want Me To Do', the title track and 'Please Come Back To Me' are handsome performances, very roughly in the idiom of Little Milton and Junior Parker, with heartfelt singing and effectively economical guitar. In contrast to those polished tracks, the harmonica-and-acoustic-guitar settings of 'Sweet Thing', 'You're The One' and 'I'm Your Handy Man' use the conventions of Southern movie scores (*In The Heat Of The Night*, *The Chase*, etc.) to evoke an ambience of rural back roads. TR

The Johnny Nocturne Band
GROUP

The band came to life in the Bay Area in 1989. Its founder, tenor saxophonist John Firmin (born 1947), grew up in Alaska, moved in his 20s to New York and thence to San Francisco, where he led pianist Mitch Woods's band The Rocket 88s. Brenda Boykin was the band's vocalist from 1991 to 1997, then left to sing with Home Cookin' and was succeeded by Kim Nalley.

*** Wailin' Daddy
Bullseye Blues CDBB 9526 Dan Buegeleisen, Glen Appell (t); Marty Wehner (tb); John Firmin (ts, ldr); Danny Bittker (bs); Henry Salvia (p); Anthony Paule (g); Alex Baum (b); Terry Baker (d); Brenda Boykin (v). 11/91–5/92.

*** Shake 'Em Up
Bullseye Blues CDBB 9553 As above, except Bill Ortiz (t) replaces Buegeleisen; omit Appell. 3/94.

*** Wild & Cool
Bullseye Blues CDBB 9586 As above, except Rob Sudduth (bs) and Kent Bryson (d) replace Bittker and Baker. 6/97.

Firmin, alias Nocturne, is dedicated to commemorating the 'Little Big Band Era' and, as he puts it, 'the whole film noir sax thing'. He certainly plays in period, whether with the coarse tone of 'Howling At Midnight' or the creamy one of 'I'm A Fool To Want You' (both on *Wailin' Daddy*), but he eschews the overblowing and freak effects to which some of his models occasionally resorted. He seems to have exercised the same taste in hiring: Paule and Salvia are both accomplished and versatile, and Wehner is a particularly fine player. It's not only an adept band but seemingly a happy one, retaining its personnel almost intact through most of a decade. Not surprisingly, its albums are consistently well-made and enjoyable. *Shake 'Em Up* stands out a little because it leans more towards the blues than the albums either side of it; the reading of Phineas Newborn's 'New Blues' is particularly suave. But all three CDs advance Firmin's evident belief that he and his comrades are better occupied playing good old tunes than trying to create pastiches of them, an abstemiousness more bands might adopt.

*** Million Dollar Secret
Bullseye Blues & Jazz BB 9626 Bill Ortiz, Pete Sembler (t); Marty Wehner (tb); John Firmin (cl, ts, ldr); Rob Sudduth (bs); Henry Salvia (p); Anthony Paule (g); Alex Baum (b); Kent Bryson (d); Tommy Kesecker (vb, perc); Kim Nalley (v). 8/98–3/99.

Million Dollar Secret is cut to much the same pattern as its predecessors, but lent a distinct style by the new singer. Brenda Boykin's manner tended to the rhetorical, in a grand old jazz and vaudeville tradition; Nalley's is slinkier, à la Dinah Washington. The band continues to look backwards for its tunes, celebrating songs written by or associated with Duke Ellington, Nellie Lutcher and Helen Humes. It was always on the cards that the band would record 'Harlem Nocturne' and here it is, in a serpentine rendition by the ever-reliable Firmin.

*** Blues Volume
Blue Bucket BBR 001 *Pete Sembler (t); Derek James (tb); John Firmin (ts, bs, bss, ldr); Rob Sudduth (bs); Henry Salvia (ac, p); Dick Fegy (md); Anthony Paule (g); Alex Baum (b); Kent Bryson, Sly Randolph (d); Miss Dee (v).* 01–02.

Three years on, Kim Nalley's place is taken by a former vocalist with Johnny Otis and the music changes again. Except on smoochy numbers like 'Person To Person' and 'Since I Fell For You', Miss Dee uses a rasping tone that gives the songs a more conventional blues character, which is appropriate enough to Willie Dixon's '29 Ways', B. B. King's 'It's My Own Fault' and Bessie Smith's 'Young Woman's Blues'. In sharp contrast, Firmin and Paule duet prettily on Big Jay McNeely's 'Is There Something On Your Mind?' to open an instrumental medley that continues with 'Lee Allen', featuring accordion and mandolin, and circles back to McNeelyville in 'Wild Wig'. Not the band's most striking album, but it maintains its reputation for accomplished versatility. TR

Sugar Ray Norcia (born 1955/56)
VOCAL, HARMONICA, ACCORDION

Raymond Alan Norcia has been a stalwart of the blues scene in the Northeastern US since the '70s. He founded the original Sugar Ray & The Bluetones in 1979 with Ronnie Earl, and led the band for 12 years. From 1991 to 1997 he was the primary singer for Roomful Of Blues. He then re-formed the Bluetones. Among many guest vocal spots, he has appeared on albums by Walter Horton (one of his models), Pinetop Perkins and Otis Grand.

**(*) Knockout
Varrick VRCD 037 *Norcia; Greg Mazel (ts, bs); Tom 'La Bumba' Mahfood (bs); Anthony 'B. B.' Geraci (o, p); Kid Bangham (g); Michael 'Mudcat' Ward (b); Neil Gouvin (d); Monica Lauderdale, Gail Parker (v).* 89?

*** Don't Stand In My Way
Bullseye Blues CDBB 9507 *Norcia; Joe Cravinho (t); Joseph Raia (ts); David Sholl (bs); Anthony Geraci (o, p); Kid Bangham (g); Michael 'Mudcat' Ward (b); Neil Gouvin (d).* 90.

The debut album of Sugar Ray & The Bluetones (most of Norcia's work has appeared under that byline) seems to have been designed as a revolving showcase for its leader. Here he sings a '50s downhome blues (Elmore James's 'I Can't Hold Out', a.k.a. 'Talk To Me'), there something more modern in style like 'Bite The Dust', meanwhile throwing in a cajun chant ('Hope Valley', evidently located in Johnnie Allan's promised land), a ballad, a harp instrumental and a few original songs. The record's far from dull, the playing is vigorous and unabashed, yet there's a sense of being conducted round the blues by a tour guide who isn't quite as authoritative as he wants you to think he is. That impression fades during *Don't Stand In My Way*, where the material is similarly varied but Norcia's confidence is matched by his command. Most of the songs were generated within the band; particularly striking are Michael Ward's 'F. Lee Bailey Blues', referring to the controversial defence attorney, and 'The Arsonist'.

*** Sweet & Swingin'
Bullseye Blues & Jazz CDBB 9607 *Norcia; Greg Mazel (ts); Doug James (bs); Matt McCabe (p); Kid Bangham, Rob Nelson (g); Marty Ballou (b); Neil Gouvin (d); The Jordanaires (Neal Matthews, Duane West, Louis Nunley, Michael Black) (v).* 1/98.

Norcia was fresh out of Roomful Of Blues when he made this, and the album is to a great extent an acknowledgement of the experience he'd gained in the previous six years, with its assured readings of cool repertoire like 'Jack She's On The Ball', Percy Mayfield's 'Lost Mind' and a Joe Turnerish 'It's A Low Down Dirty Shame'. At the same time he reclaims the harp-led Chicago blues-band style with Walter Horton's 'Need My Baby' and Jimmy Rogers's 'Money, Marbles And Chalk'. Whatever the material, he sings with warmth and enthusiasm.

Because of the nature of the material on *Sweet & Swingin'*, Norcia didn't play as much harmonica as usual. The following year he made up for that with his contribution to the VAC *Superharps* (Telarc CD-83472), where, accompanied by most of the Bluetones, he is featured on three of his own compositions. The lazy Louisiana groove of 'I'm Gonna Steal Your Baby' is one of his most appealing performances. He also contributes to tracks by fellow harpists Charlie Musselwhite, Billy Branch and James Cotton.

**(*) Rockin' Sugar Daddy
Severn CD-0012 *Norcia; Kid Bangham (g); Michael 'Mudcat' Ward (b); Neil Gouvin (d).* 01?

*** Sugar Ray And The Bluetones Featuring Monster Mike Welch
Severn CD-0019 *Norcia; Anthony Geraci (o, p); Monster Mike Welch (g, v); Michael 'Mudcat' Ward (b); Neil Gouvin (d).* 02?

Norcia and The Bluetones give sterling performances on *Rockin' Sugar Daddy*, and the stories of Ward's 'She's Blued And Broken' and Bangham's 'Room 531' are arresting, but the quartet setting is just a little too simple and unvarying to hold the listener's attention throughout. The next Severn CD replaced Bangham with Welch, who not only plays admirably throughout but brings five well-made dishes to the table. 'I Believe' and 'Get Over Me' open the menu attractively, then, after Norcia has dipped into the '30s swing repertoire and turned 'And The Angels Sing' into a pleasing harmonica tune, the Welch-composed slow blues 'Love And Trouble' elicits the fiercest guitar playing of the session. 'I Asked My Baby', also by Welch, finds him sauntering down a T-Bone Walker groove, while 'Funk-Shun' proves that he can build an Albert memorial, and 'Feeling Blue' that both he and Norcia can play with assurance when unplugged. Norcia's warm, confiding singing is particularly well recorded on the last of these. At the heart of the album are two songs prompted by tragedy on the world stage, 'Burial Season' and the concluding 'From Now On This Morning (11 September)', a wordless anthem evoking both grief and hope. TR

North Mississippi Allstars
GROUP

The North Mississippi Allstars are Luther Dickinson (guitar et al.), Cody Dickinson (drums et al.) and African-American

bassist Chris Chew; Dwayne 'son of R. L.' Burnside (guitar) joins them from Polaris onward. The Dickinsons are the sons of veteran Memphis musician, producer and agent provocateur Jim Dickinson; Chew is a friend from high school in Hernando, Mississippi, who was playing bass with gospel groups when asked to complete the Allstars. The Dickinsons made music from an early age, and have been exposed to punk, rock and other influences, but as their name denotes, it's the blues of north Mississippi that – at least initially – inspired the Allstars.

***(*) Tate County Hill Country Blues
Delta Experimental Projects 1447 *Othar Turner (fife); Jim Dickinson (o, snare d, v); Luther Dickinson (md, g, sitar, v); Chris Chew (b, v); Paul 'Snowflake' Taylor (b); Cody Dickinson (d, wb, v); Rising Star Fife & Drum Band (d); Jimmy Crosthwait (wb); Tate County Singers (v).* late 90s.

**** Shake Hands With Shorty
Tone-Cool/Blanco Y Negro 471177//(E) 83418 *Othar Turner (fife); 'East Memphis Slim' [Jim Dickinson] (p); Luther Dickinson (md, g, v); Cody Dickinson (g, sampler, d, v); Alvin Youngblood Hart, Steve Selvidge, Jimbo Mathus (g); Chris Chew (b, v); Garry Burnside, Richard 'Hombre' Price (b); Cedric Burnside (d); Jimmy Crosthwait (wb); Tate County Singers, Harmony Four (v).* 99.

All the songs on *Shake Hands With Shorty* are versions of African-American originals; 'K. C. Jones (On The Road Again)' comes from Furry Lewis, and is done in a gentle, pixilated jugband style (without the jug), but otherwise the Allstars rework the music of R. L. Burnside, Junior Kimbrough, Fred McDowell and Otha Turner. 'K. C. Jones' apart, *Shake Hands With Shorty* is high-volume, high-energy music, inspired by the heat, noise and sweat of Kimbrough's juke-joint and the earth-trembling fife and drum music of the Turner family's annual goat barbecue. For once, there's no sense that white musicians are flirting with black music to acquire an unearned aura of outlawry; the Dickinsons bring some rock baggage to the local blues tradition, but on *Shake Hands With Shorty* they and Chew work with and within that tradition. This is the blues-rock CD for people who don't like blues-rock.

Tate County Hill Country Blues appears to predate *Shake Hands With Shorty*, although it only became easily obtainable in 2005. Jim Dickinson says that it was 'produced as my sons learned the music', and it shows; there are some extended cliché workouts, some songs, notably a seven-minute 'Shimmy She Wobble', go on too long, and the occasional wah-wah guitar and Farfisa organ are intrusively irritating. On the other hand, the sitar on Jessie Mae Hemphill's 'Used To Be' is a terrific notion, the fusion of Captain Beefheart with T-Model Ford on 'Let Me In' is entirely successful and the whole disc is, to quote the senior Dickinson again, 'recorded with due respect'.

**** Shimmy She Wobble
Tone-Cool/Blanco Y Negro (E) 85807 *Carwyn Ellis (o); Cody Dickinson (g, sampler, d, wb, v); Luther Dickinson (g, v); Chris Chew (b, v).* 8/00.

There are only five tracks on this CD, two of them versions of the Otha Turner number after which it is named. The rest are from Fred McDowell ('I'm In Jail'), Junior Kimbrough ('All Night Long', also the closing song on *Shake Hands With Shorty*) and Roebuck Staples ('Freedom Highway', which also appears on *51 Phantom*). The disc is priced in accordance with its short playing time, thus offering sceptical readers a cheap way to test the water.

**(*) 51 Phantom
Tone-Cool/Blanco Y Negro 471182 //(E) 41199 *Othar Turner (fife); 'East Memphis Slim' [Jim Dickinson] (p, omnichord, dolceola); Luther Dickinson (808, g, v); Cody Dickinson (g, d, tamb, wb, v); Chris Chew (b, v); John C. Stubblefield (b); Paul Taylor (perc); Brenda Patterson, Susan Marshall, Jackie Johnson, Ben Nichols, Jesse 'Chip' Davis (v).* 01.

51 Phantom consists of originals, except for an obligatory Junior Kimbrough song, 'Freedom Highway' and 'Mud', which is semi-original, a frenzied collage concocted from the Allstars' own imaginings plus fragments by local drummer R. L. Boyce, George Hamilton IV and James Cavanaugh & Harry Barris, whose 'Mississippi Mud' is turned from patronizing nonsense to voodoo chant. 'Mud' is a bacchanalian finale to an uneven CD; the Allstars seem to be suffering from Jagger–Richards Syndrome, in which admiration for tradition mutates into a lust for originality and songwriting royalties. Sometimes, the results are satisfactory – the venomous 'Snakes In My Bushes', 'Up Over Yonder' with its pretty flashes of dolceola coloration, the elegiac 'Leavin' – but the title track is novelettish, 'Storm' sounds like the Byrds, and despite Otha Turner's fife, 'Circle In The Sky' just sounds like any old rock band.

*** The Word
Ropeadope 93046 *John Medeski (kb); Robert Randolph (sg); Luther Dickinson (g); Chris Chew (b); Cody Dickinson (d, wb).* 10/01.

This collaboration springs from the Allstars and jazz-rock organist John Medeski's shared admiration for the steel guitar music of the House of God, an African-American sanctified sect. Robert Randolph is one of the church's leading musicians, and his recorded playing was influencing Luther Dickinson by the time of *Shake Hands With Shorty*. Everyone involved in making *The Word* clearly had a good time, and the results are lively, although it's best to skip Medeski's twittery attempts to parallel north Mississippi fife sounds in 'Blood On That Rock'. The relentless chromaticism of 'I Shall Not Be Moved' is arty and calculated, too, but overall *The Word* is an enjoyable and successful project. However, readers should first investigate the less self-conscious and far more astonishing music which inspired it, on Arhoolie's series of *Sacred Steel* CDs.

** Polaris
Tone-Cool ATO 0012//Cooking Vinyl COOKCD 294 *'Tower Of Sour' (t, s); Virginia Cupples (flh); Patrick Plunk (cl): Robyn Oakes (oboe); Michael Scott (bsn); Jim Spake (bs); Othar Turner (fife, v); Cody Dickinson (o, p, G4, 808, g, d, v); Carwyn Ellis (o); Jim Dickinson (omnichord, mellotron, fuzzwahclav, p); Heather Trussell (vn); Diden Somel (vl); B. Gokham Somel, Jonathan Kirksey (vc); Luther Dickinson (g, d, v); Dwayne Burnside, Steve Selvidge (g, v); Shawn Lane (g); Chris Chew (b, v); John C. Stubblefield (b); Noel Gallagher, Jim Crosthwait, Susan Marshall, Reba Russell (v); Cody Burnside (rap).* 02.

**(*) Instores & Outtakes
Tone-Cool ATOEP 21524 *Jim Dickinson (p, omnichord); Luther Dickinson, Dwayne Burnside (g, v); Chris Chew (b, v); John C.*

Stubblefield (b); Cody Dickinson (d, v); Susan Marshall, Reba Russell (v). 03.

Polaris is unlikely to interest blues fans. Despite the addition of Dwayne Burnside, the Allstars reduce the blues to a minor component in tunes that seem to seek a synthesis between Southern rock and the more vapid aspects of Britpop: 'Time For The Sun To Rise' is 'Imagine' without the hardnosed realism. To make Junior Kimbrough's 'Meet Me In The City' sound pretty is an achievement of some kind, but that track and the worksong-based 'Be So Glad' are as prominent as the blues gets. Dedicated to the incarcerated David Malone Kimbrough, 'Be So Glad' samples Otha Turner and features Cody Burnside's no-talent rapping.

There's a better, acoustic version of 'Meet Me In The City' on the six-track *Instores & Outtakes*, whose leaner forces make a less clotted sound altogether. The instrumental 'Goin' Home' is an attractive flamenco-tinged blues, but these tracks sit among unconvincing covers of The Rolling Stones ('Stray Cat Blues') and The Band ('The Weight'), a remake of 'Eyes' from *Polaris* and the AOR of 'Skyway'.

*** Hill Country Revue
ATO 21529//Cooking Vinyl COOKCD 334 *Jim Dickinson (kb, o, v); JoJo Hermann (kb, o); Cody Dickinson (g, d, wb, v); Dwayne Burnside (g, d, v); Luther Dickinson (g, v); Garry Burnside (g); Chris Chew (b, v); R. L. Boyce (snare d, v); Rodney Evans, Aubrey Turner (snare d); Andre Evans (bass d); R. L. Burnside, Chris Robinson (v); Cody Burnside (rap).* 6/04.

Live at the Bonnaroo festival, the Allstars stir up a brew of north Mississippi blues, punk, Southern rock and rap, assisted by members of the Burnside family, the drummers of the Rising Star Fife & Drum Band and others. In other words, *Hill Country Revue* returns to the spirit of *Shake Hands With Shorty*, and is all the better for it; there's more rock in the blues-rock mix this time, though. This being a festival gig, some time is inevitably spent working the crowd into a frenzy, and it doesn't translate well to CD; 'Psychedelic Sex Machine' (with electric washboard and cigar box guitar) must also have been more fun to see than it is to hear. Enthroned centre stage, R. L. Burnside presides, but does little more than holler benevolent approval. Everyone involved in *Hill Country Revue* obviously had a great time, and much of the fun comes across on disc; Cody Dickinson's hellfire drumming alone is a good reason to listen. CS

Darrell Nulisch (born 1952)
VOCAL, HARMONICA

Nulisch comes from Dallas, where he joined Anson Funderburgh in 1981. He later worked with Ronnie Earl and in an early version of The Crawl with Mike Morgan, and formed his own band, Texas Heat, in 1991. He has made guest vocal appearances on albums by Kenny Parker, David Maxwell, James Cotton and others.

** Bluesoul
Higher Plane HPR 511 *Nulisch; Rayse Biggs (t); David McMurray (ts); Arnold Clarington (bs); Bruce Elsensohn (o, p); Jon Moeller (g); Steve Gomes (b); Steve Ramsay, Robb Stupka (d); Lorenzo Brown, Kenny Barker (perc).* 96.

**(*) The Whole Truth
Severn CD-0003 *Nulisch; Michael Fitzhugh, Eric MacMillan (t); Douglas Gilchrist, Jacques Johnson (ts); Benjie Porecki (kb); Jon Moeller, David Earl (g); Steve Gomes (b); Robb Stupka (d); Ricardo Monzon (perc); Marjorie Clark, Deirdre Wright, Natalie Jackson (v).* 99?

*** I Like It That Way
Severn CD-0007 *Nulisch; Tommy Williams, Chris Walker (t); John Jensen (tb); Scott Young (as, ts); Benjie Porecki (kb); David Maxwell (p); Jon Moeller (g); Steve Gomes (b); Robb Stupka (d); Alejandro Lucini (perc); Joe Maher, Jessie Yawn (v).* 00.

*** Times Like These
Severn CD-0020 *Nulisch; Tommy Williams, Kenny Rittenhouse (t, flh); John Jensen (tb); Scott Silbert (bs); Bruce Swain, Jeff Antoniuk, Scott Young (s, fl); Benjie Porecki (kb); Jon Moeller (g); Steve Gomes (b); Robb Stupka (d, perc); Steve Cyphers (perc).* 03.

It's clear, both from his own compositions and from his choice of material by other people, that Nulisch leans towards soul-blues, with the accent – despite the title of his first album – on the first half of the term. But an artist making entire albums in that vein while depending chiefly on his own writing needs to be able to produce a few songs with the timeless virtues of universal themes and strong hooks, and *Bluesoul*, though well performed, just doesn't have that kind of soul muscle. *The Whole Truth* applies a somewhat stronger grip on the listener's attention, inasmuch as the writing is more diverse, but it still lacks a song you could take to the bank and draw on. A couple of straight-down-the-line blues are included, 'Like Reed' and George Smith's 'Telephone Blues', and that policy is maintained on *I Like It That Way* with 'Mean Old World' and B. B. King's 'Worried Dream'. The strength of this album is partly in the production: thanks to clearer separation of the voice, Nulisch comes over as a better singer than one might have thought, and when that clarity is combined with a strong lyric, biting guitar and a calculatedly resonant ambience, as in 'After All', the listener is prompted to serious revaluation. None of the other songs is quite that good, but for variety and high production values this is easily Nulisch's best album so far.

When he came to make *Times Like These*, he had had the same production team for three or four years and the same core sidemen, Moeller, Gomes and Stupka, for a good deal longer; that settled regime surely accounts for the smooth, stylish execution of the album. The programme is evenly divided between Nulisch–Gomes compositions and songs from Otis Redding, Little Milton and other classy suppliers, and, for the first time, the original material can stand comparison with the imported: 'Good Thing' and 'Times Like These' chase the elusive butterfly of anthemic power and catch it by the wing. With several sturdy blues tracks too, the album has what it takes to please enquiring blues fans as well as regular patrons. TR

St Louis Jimmy Oden (1903–77)
VOCAL, PIANO

Born in Nashville, Tennessee, James Burke Oden began singing, playing piano and writing songs in his 20s in St Louis. He recorded frequently in the '30s, '40s and '50s, usually accompanied by Roosevelt Sykes, and introduced several songs that would become blues standards, notably 'Going Down

Slow'. In Chicago in the late '40s and '50s he kept busy both as a songwriter and as co-owner, with Joe Brown, of J.O.B. Records, but after a car accident in 1957 he concentrated on writing, providing songs for Muddy Waters, in whose basement he lived, and other artists. He made guest appearances as a singer on several other artists' sessions in the '60s, and, had he not withdrawn from the tour, would have been seen by European enthusiasts on the 1968 AFBF.

*** St. Louis Jimmy Oden – Vol. 1 (1932–1944)
Document DOCD-5234 Oden; Odell Rand (cl); Roosevelt Sykes (p, sp); Artie Mosby, unknown (vn); Big Bill Broonzy, Ted Summitt, poss. Charlie Jordan (g); unknown(s) (b); Alfred Elkins (imb); Jump Jackson (d). 9/32–12/44.

*** St. Louis Jimmy Oden – Vol. 2 (1944–1955)
Document DOCD-5235 Oden; Johnny Morton, unknown (t); Oett 'Sax' Mallard, Alex Atkins (as); J. T. Brown, Bill Casimir, Eddie Chamblee, Oliver Alcorn (ts); unknowns (s); Roosevelt Sykes, Bill Owens, Henry Brown, Sunnyland Slim, unknown (p); Ted Summitt, Muddy Waters, Robert Lockwood Jr, Sam Casimir, unknowns (g); Willie Dixon, Ransom Knowling, Big Crawford, Andrew Harris, unknowns (b); Jump Jackson, Red Saunders, unknowns (d). 12/44–55.

Oden could never be called an exciting artist, but his lyrics always had both head and heart in their making and he sang them with a craftsman's pride in his own good work. One of his themes, developed in 'The Road To Ruin', 'Come Day Go Day' and 'One More Break', is the woman who is too fond of whiskey, a disposition that eventually compels him to break with her, as he reports in 'Soon Forget You' and 'Can't Stand Your Evil Ways'. But he did not restrict himself to criticizing others' failings: he addresses his own in 'My Dream Blues', while in 'Back On My Feet Again' he turns from the personal to the political, exhorting his listeners to welcome wartime curbs on their amusements: 'We all like Uncle Sam, let us all stick together – give up our pleasure car and get right back on leather.' His most lasting composition has been 'Going Down Slow', in which a dying man bleakly settles the account of a misspent life. All those songs are on *Vol. 1*, an absorbing collection whose rating might have been higher if it were not for the inconsistent quality of the transfers.

In the period covered by *Vol. 2* Oden sold his wares widely: the two dozen songs were scattered on ten labels. Apart from an 8/49 Apollo session with Sunnyland Slim (see below), this CD has almost everything he recorded in those years. There are two more versions of 'Going Down Slow' but otherwise Oden seldom repeats himself. His typical performance is a ruminative lyric delivered at a slow tempo, which can make him tiring to listen to at length, but *Vol. 2* has a few examples that buck this trend, such as 'Jack L. Cooper', a plug for a disc jockey, and 'Hard Luck Boogie', and the settings go beyond the piano trios of *Vol. 1* to the small swing orchestras accompanying him on 'Yancey's Blues' or 'Why Work'. An Aristocrat coupling of 'Florida Hurricane' and 'So Nice And Kind' is individualized by glistening slide guitar solos immediately recognizable as by Muddy Waters.

At the Apollo date with Sunnyland Slim, Oden sang five numbers, only two of which, 'Sad Old Sunday' ('Mother's Day') and 'Chicago Woman', were issued at the time. The five are on Slim's *House Rent Party* (Delmark DD-655). 'Hard Luck Boogie' and 'Good Book Blues' are also on Roosevelt Sykes's *West Helena Blues* (Wolf WBJ 005).

** Goin' Down Slow
Original Blues Classics OBCCD 584 Oden; Robert Banks (p); Jimmie Lee Robinson (g); Leonard Gaskin (b); Belton Evans (d). 11/60.

In 1960, Oden made something of a return. Otis Spann, commissioned to record an album for the new Candid label, took the older man with him to New York, where he sang several of his favourite pieces, though none would be issued until years later. Spann was evidently an admirer of Oden's writing, for he recorded 'Evil Ways' at that session and 'Goin' Down Slow' and others on later albums.

Three months later Oden returned to New York to make his own debut album, for Bluesville. *Goin' Down Slow* is a good set of songs, including both seasoned compositions like the title track, 'Poor Boy' and 'Monkey Faced Woman' and what seems to be more recent work, but as a recorded recital it leaves a good deal to be desired. It was to be expected that all the numbers would have much the same melody and tempo, but Oden delivers them without much animation and Banks, the only soloist (Robinson is inaudible, if indeed he was there at all), soon uses up his small stock of blues ideas.

'Monkey Face Blues' reappears on the Roosevelt Sykes CD *Chicago Boogie* (Delmark DD-773) with three other Sykes–Oden duets, all from a 5/63 date and all previously unissued. The most striking is 'Complete This Order', in which Oden sets his lover a series of tasks drawn from the Old Testament: 'Bring me the ashes of the Hebrew children that was cast in the furnace of fire; bring me the stone David throwed that killed the giant Goliath ... when you complete this order, I'll know that it's me that you really do love.' He recorded it again a year later, together with remakes of 'Can't Stand Your Evil Ways' and 'Poor Boy Blues' and the newer 'The Girl I Love', for Swedish radio (*I Blueskvarter: Chicago 1964, Volume Two* [Jefferson SBACD 12655/6 2CD]). Those were his last recordings, but he continued to write for several years. TR

Andrew 'Big Voice' Odom (1936–91)
VOCAL

By day a Chicago taxi-driver, by night Odom was known in the clubs as a singer with a leaning towards the styles of B. B. King and Bobby 'Blue' Bland. He grew up in Louisiana, moving with his family in 1955 to St Louis, where he fell in with Earl Hooker. Resettling in Chicago in 1960, he sang regularly with Hooker and Jimmy Dawkins; he recorded with Hooker and in his own name on Bluesway, and with Dawkins on his Delmark album All For Business. *He also made albums, and toured, in France. He died of a heart attack while driving between gigs.*

**(*) Going To California
Storyville STCD 8037 Odom; Carey Bell (h); Jimmy Dawkins, Jimmy Johnson (g); Sylvester Boines (b); Tyrone Centuray (d). 10/76.

Apart from Bell, who guests on one track, the lineup is the same as on Jimmy Dawkins's *"I Want To Know"*, recorded for the same label (the French MCM) exactly a year before. Odom's one song on that set was spoiled by a faulty mike, but here everything goes smoothly, resulting in one of the better of MCM's location-recorded albums, though with the series' recurrent faults of over-reliance on standard repertoire and programming too many slow numbers together. Odom's characteristic vocal manner is what old-time preachers used to call 'straining', sometimes, as in 'I Don't Know' and 'Stormy Monday Blues', with a Bobby Bland tone. Dawkins plays in his recently developed economical style but with an almost explosive attack; his opening chorus on 'Sitting Here Wondering' sounds like gunshots ricocheting round the room.

*** Goin' To California
Flying Fish 70587 *Odom; Michael Fonfara (o); Gene Taylor (p); Steve Freund, Steve Katz (g); Doran Katz; Jerome Fitzpatrick (d). 12/91.*

The title song is much more inventively arranged than it was on the previous album, Freund scrawling complex guitar figures over solemn organ chords, and Odom gives it a more relaxed reading. The alternation of fast and slow numbers makes for an untaxing programme, though Odom is usually more interesting, because less generic, on slow blues ('Don't Ever Leave Me All Alone' is another good one) than he is on songs like Jimmy Reed's 'You Don't Have To Go'. Freund is worth hearing at any tempo. TR

Erskine Oglesby (1937–2004)
VOCAL, TENOR SAXOPHONE

A native St Louisian, Oglesby began playing in his teens and worked with most of the city's well-known acts, such as Albert King, Little Milton and Ike Turner's Kings of Rhythm.

**(*) Blues Dancin'
Black & Tan CD B&T 006 *Oglesby; Bob Lohr (p); Brian Melching (g); Charles 'Nephew' Davis (b); Kenny Lawrence (d). 5/00.*
*** Honkin' & Shoutin'
Black & Tan CD B&T 010 *Oglesby; Michael Arlt (h); Roel Spanjers (o, p); Andreas Arlt, Jan Mittendorp (g); Henning Hauerken (b); Andreas Bock (d). 4/01.*

Oglesby belonged to the small band of saxophonists who are also blues singers. *Blues Dancin'*, which the record company describes as an accurate sample of his club repertoire, is a well-played selection of blues – a couple by Jimmy Reed, Junior Parker's 'Next Time You See Me', the St Louis favourite 'Tore Up' – with instrumental interludes like 'Jack And Coke', 'Two Franc Blues' and 'Back At B. B.'s' that recall saxophone tunes of the honking '50s such as Tiny Bradshaw's 'Soft'. *Honkin' & Shoutin'*, recorded in the Netherlands with local musicians, was intended to range more widely, include more new material and throw more of the spotlight on his saxophone playing, and succeeds in all three aims. Oglesby holds the listener well enough with stories like 'Let Me Go Judge', 'Fair Skin Woman', 'Mind Games' and 'I Don't Want To Be No Fat Man', the last uncharacteristically accompanied by harmonica and two guitars; it's just a pity that the vocal track wasn't given a little more prominence in the mix. The songs are again interspersed with bright saxophone episodes such as the welcoming first track 'Cold Duck', with its twinned saxophone–guitar line, 'Backstreet' and 'Jam Bang', which borrows the riff from Miles Davis's 'Milestones'. This is unsurprising music, but very approachable. TR

Omar & The Howlers
GROUP

Led by singer/guitarist/songwriter Omar Dykes, the Howlers are the essence of a Texas roadhouse band, hot on rhythm, cool on melody. Dykes's distinctive vocal timbre resembles Howlin' Wolf heard through a cheap transistor radio with a touch of Wolfman Jack on a tranquillizer or two. The blunt impact of his singing is complemented by the blue-collar imagery in his lyrics and the bedrock simplicity of the music. The band has been constantly on the road since the '80s, warmly welcomed by audiences throughout the USA and Europe, spurred on by regular record releases.

** Live At The Opera House
Provogue PRD 7122 *Eric Scortia (kb); Omar Dykes (g, v); Bruce Jones (b); Gene Brandon (d). 8/87.*

Released 13 years later, this live appearance coincided with the release of the band's third Columbia album, *Hard Times In The Land Of Plenty*, and featured nine of that set's ten songs, including its title track. Despite titles like 'Mississippi Hoodoo Man' and Jerry McCain's 'Rock And Roll Ball' as an encore, there's little blues content here, although the music's general orientation is in that direction. Dykes occasionally emphasizes a lyric with a deliberate Wolfian growl and there's a distant aroma of Magic Sam's signature guitar style in his chorded rhythms. Despite occasional *longueurs*, the audience's enthusiasm for a local hero is conveyed to the listener.

**(*) Monkey Land
Provogue PRD 7013//Antone's 74209 *Omar Dykes, John Inmon (g, v); Bruce Jones (b, v); Gene Brandon (d). 90.*

Omar's assertion that he's 'just another monkey in Monkey Land' is ripe for misunderstanding in some quarters, although he refers to what he does as 'monkey music' in interviews. For all that, blues only rears its head with 'Loud Mouth Woman', whereas 'Modern Man' and 'Ding Dong Clock' invade rockabilly territory. Questionable forays into Lennon & McCartney's 'She's A Woman' and the Bob Segerish 'Night Shadows' broaden the album's scope but diminish its interest.

*** Blues Bag
Provogue PRD 7028//Bullseye Blues CDBB 9519 *Fingers Taylor (h); Omar Dykes (g, v); Bruce Jones (b); Gene Brandon (d). 91.*

Allegedly not originally intended for issue, this album finds Dykes playing acoustic guitar on nine of its 15 tracks, with only the last four, including the traditional 'Blues In The Bottle', featuring the full band. Apart from this and songs by Hound Dog Taylor, Sam Myers and Robert Johnson, the balance consists of blues-oriented originals, with overt references to Jimmy Reed, Lightnin' Slim, Magic Sam and Elmore James. Once again, entertainment values are high but the thought persists that Dykes has done this to show that he can rather than because he needed to.

**(*) Live At Paradiso
Provogue PRD 7035//Bullseye Blues CDBB 9529 *Omar Dykes (g, v); Bruce Jones (b); Gene Brandon (d). 9/91.*

Four years on from the Opera House gig, The Howlers are still relying on much the same repertoire, with a handful of numbers from Omar's *Blues Bag* and Dykes's tribute to Bo Diddley, 'Magic Man'. The absence of a keyboard player has tightened the band, although under-recorded bass and drums leave the sound rather thin at times. Dykes's guitaristics are better balanced between exhibitionism and practicality, although his favourite tricks are soon learned. There's a streamlined inevitability to it all that inflames his Dutch audience but flattens out in the living room.

*** Courts Of Lulu
Provogue PRD 7045//Bullseye Blues CDBB 9541 *John Mills (ts); Ponty Bone (ac); Danny Levin (o, p, vn); Reese Wynans (o); Omar Dykes (g, v); Bruce Jones, Spencer Starnes (b); Gene Brandon, Greg 'Frosty' Smith (d); Kris McKay (v).* 92.

A fairly relentlessly paced set of 13 original songs benefits from increased attention to production values. While the focus remains on the basic trio, augmentations by tenor sax, organ, violin and accordion inject a welcome variety into the arrangements. Only the swamp-obsessed 'Pushin' Fire' and a final instrumental, 'South Congress Blues', slacken the onrush of satisfyingly metallic guitar riffs and guttural howls. 'I've Tried' evens out the strut of 'Smokestack Lightning', while 'Do It For Daddy' dirties up the Bo Diddley beat. With few exceptions, each song is short, splenetic and entertaining.

** Muddy Springs Road
Provogue PRD 7060 *Gary Primich (h); Nick Connolly (o, p); Omar Dykes (g, v); Bradley Kopp (g); Gerry 'Phareaux' Felton (b); George Rains (d); Mark Hallman (perc).* 94.

** World Wide Open
Provogue PRD 7080 *Gary Primich (h); Nick Connolly (o); Robert McEntee, Bradley Kopp, Mark Hallman (g, perc); Omar Dykes (g, v); Paul Junior (b); Steve Kilmer (d); Chris Searles (perc).* 95.

**(*) Southern Style
Provogue PRD 7095 *Nick Connolly (o); Omar Dykes (g, v); Stephen Bruton (g); Paul Junior (b); Steve Kilmer (d); Mark Hallman (perc).* 96.

With its frequent nods to Creedence Clearwater, Bo Diddley and Magic Sam, *Muddy Springs Road* finds Dykes in a holding pattern, circling around his significant influences without adding greatly to what he can do with them. A trustworthy wordsmith, with the occasional assistance of others, he nevertheless rarely comes up with a set of lyrics that transcends its function within individual rhythm schemes. *World Wide Open*, with its similar castlist and dependable musicianship, has nothing to add by way of innovation or experiment. Notable tracks include a hectic 'Hey Joe' and 'Low Down Dirty Blues', acknowledging the links that run from Robert Johnson to Howlin' Wolf and Muddy Waters. Remakes of 'Bessie Mae' and 'Angel Child' (as 'Angel Blues') from *Blues Bag* alongside 'Burn It To The Ground' make *Southern Style* marginally more interesting blueswise. Bruton's slide guitar and Connolly's ubiquitous but subdued presence fill out what has become a signature sound.

*** Swingland
Provogue PRD 7115 *Gary Slechta (t); Mark 'Kaz' Kazanoff (ts, bs); David 'Fathead' Newman (ts); Gary Primich (h); Nick Connolly (o, p); Cindy Cashdollar (sg); Omar Dykes (g, v); Derek O'Brien (g); Paul Junior (b); George Rains (d).* 98.

Perhaps aware that the Howlers were in something of a rut, Dykes comes up with a homage to pioneers like Louis Jordan, Wynonie Harris and Percy Mayfield, along with more recent heroes such as Albert Collins and Taj Mahal. Somewhere in between are Elmore James, Mercy Dee Walton and Nat Adderley's 'Work Song'. An augmented band features frequent solos by Newman and Kazanoff and excellent work by Connolly, whose organ bass propels 'Just Like A Woman'. Dykes takes his foot off the Wolf pedal to deliver some more naturalistic vocals, although he can't match the insanity of Screamin' Jay Hawkins's 'Yellow Coat'. An oddity, but an entertaining one.

*(*) The Screamin' Cat
Provogue PRD 7126 *B. E. 'Frosty' Smith (o, d, perc); Omar Dykes (g, v); Malcolm (Papa Mali) Welbourne (g); Paul Junior (b); Rich Chilleri (d).* 00.

In a regrettable lapse of control, Dykes cedes production to Welbourne and Smith and aural mayhem results. Superfluous noises and childish effects on instruments and voices swamp most of these 12 tracks. When he isn't auditioning for The Residents, Welbourne displays a slide technique reminiscent of Sonny Landreth, while Smith's organ playing strives for atmosphere rather than melody. Relief is palpable as Dykes finishes the set with a conventional performance of Willie Love's 'Automatic', with just Junior and Chilleri in tow.

**(*) Big Delta
Provogue PRD 7132 *Malcolm (Papa Mali) Welbourne (g, sitar); Omar Dykes (g, v); Roscoe Beck (b); B. E. 'Frosty' Smith, Terry Bozzio (d).* 01.

A curious album that revisits songs from *Monkey Land*, *Muddy Springs Road*, *World Wide Open* and *Wall Of Pride* (their deleted second Columbia album), along with an underpowered stab at Mountain's 'Mississippi Queen' and one or two new numbers. With the exception of 'Muddy Springs Road', there's little attempt to radically rethink arrangements, so performance and sound are the only criteria for judgement. On that basis, Dykes had little new to say. The inclusion of jazz bassist Beck and ex-Zappa sideman Bozzio does put him on his mettle, suggesting that a better record could have been made with their total involvement. NS

Anders Osborne (born 1966)
VOCAL, GUITAR, BANJO, HARMONICA, ORGAN, PIANO, PERCUSSION, SITAR, BASS, MANDOLIN, DRUMS

Osborne was born in Sweden, the son of a professional drummer, and grew up listening to American R&B and rock 'n' roll, and later to singer/songwriters like Dylan and Neil Young. His first instrument was drums but in his mid-teens he took up guitar. At 18 he began travelling the world and while doing so decided to make a career in music. He has been based since 1988 in New Orleans, where he made his first album, Doin Fine *(Rabadash, deleted), in 1990. His major-label debut,* Which Way To Here *(OKeh/550 Music, deleted), followed in 1995.*

(**) Break The Chain
Shanachie 5746 *Osborne; Brian Graber (t, ts); Randy Carstater (t); Thaddeus Richard (ss); John G. Autin (kb, o, p, v); Theresa Andersson (vn, perc, v); Marvin Williams (b, perc, v); Michael Messer (d, perc); Gregory Boyd (perc); Darlene Raven (didgeridoo); Gary Hirstius, Mari Serpas-Vigueira (v).* 94?

** **Living Room**
Shanachie 5735 *Osborne; Fred Bogert (t, ac, kb, p); James Andrews (t); Mark McGrain (tb, fl); Tim Green (s); John Magnie (kb); Tommy Malone, Keb' Mo', Kostas (g, v); Frederic Koella (g); Leon Medica (b); Kirk Joseph (sousaphone); Johnny Vidacovich, Steve Brewster, John Gardner (d, perc); Carlo Nuccio (d); Theresa Anderson, Jonell Mosser, Vickie Cannico, Tareva Henderson (v).* 99.

(*) **Ash Wednesday Blues
Shanachie SH 5744 *Osborne; Charles Joseph (tb); David Grillier (cl); Tim Green (ts); Davell Crawford (o, p, v); Keb' Mo' (bj, g, perc, v); Jonny Lang (g, v); Leon Medica (b); Kirk Joseph (sousaphone); Kevin O'Day (d); Cyril Neville (perc); Charlene Howard (v).* 01.

(*) **Bury The Hatchet
Shanachie SH 5747 *Osborne; Raymond Williams Sr (t); Charles Joseph (tb); Tim Green (s); David Torkanowsky (p); Dave Easley (psg); Brian Stoltz (g, v); unknown (b); Kirk Joseph (sousaphone); Doug Belote, Herman Ernest (d); Big Chief Monk Boudreaux (tamb, v); Reuben Williams, Chris Boone (v).* 02.

Osborne is a clear-cut example of a kind of artist some blues enthusiasts find problematic. While he frequently uses blues structures, devices, coloration and so forth, both his material and his presentation come from places beyond the broad highway of the blues' lineage. It isn't just that he doesn't sound like any blues antecedent – that in itself scarcely matters – but that the creative sensibility behind his music, most of which he writes himself, has been shaped by more influences than would have touched earlier blues artists. A typical Osborne album will contain a few performances that would fit most people's definition of blues, perhaps a song or two with more kinship to country music, some examples of New Orleans funk, and other pieces that bear witness to Osborne's early interest in the singer/songwriters of the '60s and '70s. 'Every Bit Of Love' on *Ash Wednesday Blues*, for instance, is an almost comically accurate pastiche of Van Morrison; all it lacks is the poetry (which is a lot to lack). But it's characteristic of Osborne that it should be sandwiched between the New Orleans strut of 'Ho-Di-Ko-Di-Ya-La-Ma-Ma' and the lilting ditty 'Stuck On My Baby' with Keb' Mo' on banjo.

Idiomatically varied, sprinkled with catchy melodies like 'Me & Lola' and recorded with the ambience of the sitting-room rather than the studio, *Ash Wednesday Blues* is the most immediately attractive of Osborne's Shanachie albums. *Living Room* starts promisingly with the blues-based 'Boxes, Bills And Pain' and 'Greasy Money' (another collaboration with Keb' Mo') but the rest is diverse without being distinctive. *Break The Chain* (a reissue of his second album for Rabadash) lives up to its title, being not at all like the typical Osborne album described above. The sultry slide guitar of 'Real World' and other tracks and certain similarities in the songs ally Osborne with Sonny Landreth, but the blues content has diminished to invisibility. *Bury The Hatchet* is jointly credited to the leader of the Mardi Gras 'tribe' The Golden Eagles, Monk Boudreaux, who wrote five of the numbers and sings on most. As befits a homage to New Orleans, the music is dominated by marching and dancing rhythms, chanted refrains and horn figures from the brass-band vocabulary, and Osborne frequently exchanges guitar for banjo. The groove is very different from that of *Ash Wednesday* and, except in 'Junko Partner', seldom intersects the blues, but it's an accomplished album which should appeal to amateurs of New Orleans music. TR

Paul Oscher (born 1949)
VOCAL, HARMONICA, GUITAR, PIANO, MELODICA, ACCORDION

Brooklyn-born, Oscher made his name when he joined Muddy Waters's band in November 1967, a position he held for exactly four years. After leaving Muddy he played around Brooklyn for a few years, recorded with Johnny Copeland and toured Europe with Louisiana Red. Then, depressed by changes in the music, he took a long rest from the business between 1980 and 1992. Since then has recorded both in his own right and with several other artists.

*** **Knockin' On The Devil's Door**
Viceroots VCR 8028 *Oscher; Steve Guyger (h); Dave Maxwell (p); 'Mudcat' Ward (b); Willie 'Big Eyes' Smith (d).* 12/95.
*** **Living Legends – Deep In The Blues**
Blues Leaf BL 9811 *Oscher; Steve Guyger (h, v); Mike Lampe (b).* 8/99.

For a highly talented exponent of the instrument, Oscher is surprisingly chary about getting his harmonica out on these albums. On *Devil's Door* he spends much more time playing guitar, while on *Living Legends* he divides his contributions three ways by adding piano. On all three instruments he plays as if time had stood still in, say, 1970 – in other words, about the time he left Muddy Waters. 'Our aim,' says producer Dave Peverett of *Devil's Door*, 'was to capture the feel of those classic Chess recordings', meaning the Chicago sound of the '50s and '60s as moulded by Muddy and Jimmy Rogers. Since Oscher's unshowy but period-perfect guitar playing is rooted in the styles of those men, and Guyger's idiomatic accuracy on harmonica is equally precise, the album fulfils its brief. 'Kind Hearted Woman', where Oscher sings Muddy singing Robert Johnson, is spot on, likewise another acoustic piece, 'Mean Disposition'. More of Oscher's own personality comes across in 'Blues In The Alley', a slow chromatic instrumental where his playing, as always, is beautifully articulate. His singing is understated – no bad thing in itself – but at times too self-effacing.

Oscher describes *Living Legends* as 'really Steve's project'; Guyger replies, 'It's really Paul's'. It is a genuinely shared album, not Oscher with a little help from his friend, but Oscher takes more of the vocals and does the greater part of the instrumental work. His guitar skills have developed since the previous album, and his piano playing is fine on 'Sometimes I Wonder'; Guyger responds by playing at the top of his game, for example on the instrumental 'Thunder', and singing better than on his own records. Though the material and treatments continue to echo the two men's resolutely oldfashioned tastes, there are unexpected moments: 'The Things I Used To Do' is remade on the model of Sonny Boy Williamson II's 'Mighty Long Time', played by Oscher on bass harmonica with a veiled vocal and only a bass for backing.

(*) **Alone With The Blues
Electro-Fi 3384 *Oscher; Jim McKaba, David Maxwell (p); Ted 'Little T' Attorino (g); Kurt Strange, Calvin Jones (b); Cam Robb, Willie 'Big Eyes' Smith (d).* c. 93–2/01.

For reasons not made clear, Oscher's 2001 solo session for Electro-Fi furnished only eight tracks for this album, and it was completed with material, mostly with other musicians, from as much as eight years earlier. One wonders if Electro-Fi felt, as some listeners will surely do, that the solo recordings were too quiet and contemplative to stand alone. Of the other cuts 'Louis Collins', John Hurt's song rather pleasingly done with an accordion, comes from the deleted *Rough Stuff* (Lollipop CD 1243), while two produced by Jimmy Vivino may be from around the time of *The Deep Blues Of Paul Oscher* (Blues Planet BPCD 1427, deleted). Four others are from an undated session for Kingsnake Records; 'Standing At The Crossroads' is modelled not, as one might expect, on Muddy but on the latterday John Lee Hooker, right down to the stamping foot. TR

Johnny Otis (born 1921)
VOCAL, PIANO, DRUMS, VIBRAPHONE, CONGAS

John Veliotes's parents ran a store in a mainly black area of Berkeley; they were Greek-Americans, but their son decided (before becoming a musician or meeting his wife, as he has emphasized) that Negro culture held more attraction for him than the white world, and became Johnny Otis, genetically white but culturally black. By the age of 18, Otis was drumming professionally; since then, he's been bandleader, session musician, composer, club owner, talent scout, label owner, producer, disc jockey, TV host, painter, sculptor, cartoonist, author, political aide, unsuccessful candidate for office, pastor of a non-denominational church, chicken farmer and apple juice manufacturer. Despite some excitable writers, this doesn't make Otis a renaissance man, except in the sense of his rebirth as an African-American, but his energy, talent and versatility are certainly beyond the common run.

When Johnny Otis was inducted into the Rock 'n' Roll Hall of Fame, it was in the non-performing section. Odd though this may seem, it's true that his activities as facilitator, instigator and entrepreneur have been as important as his playing and singing. By our usual criteria, many of the CDs below are VACs, but we have taken the view that discs credited to 'Johnny Otis' or 'The Johnny Otis Show' are what they are because Otis presided, for better and sometimes for worse, over their creation.

**** Johnny Otis 1945–1947
Classics 5027 Otis; Teddy Buckner, Billy Jones, Loyal Walker, Harry Parr Jones, Lester Current, Eddie Preston, Walter Williams, John Anderson (t); George Washington (tb, v); Henry Coker, Eli Robinson, John Pettigrew, Jap Jones, Sonny Durham, Herb Mullins (tb); René Bloch, Bob Harris, Kenneth Pope, Preston Love, Buddy Collette (as); Paul Quinichette, James Von Streeter, Big Jay McNeely (ts, v); Lem Tally (bs, v); Leon Beck (bs); Bill Doggett, Gene Gilbeaux, Henry Owens, Lee Wesley Jones, Devonia Williams (p); Bernie Cobbs, Pete Lewis (g); Curtis Counce, Joe Comfort, Mario Delagarde (b); Jimmy Rushing, 'Darby Hicks', The Four Bluebirds, Cathy Cooper, Bardu Ali, band (v). 9/45–47.

Classics present all Otis's Excelsior recordings, on which he plays drums throughout, in generally excellent sound. His 17-piece swing band was short-lived, but produced 12 outstanding sides; Basie's 'Jeff-Hi Stomp' and two Jimmy Rushing vocals are highlights. On the rest of the disc, economics reduce the lineup to seven pieces, and the arrival of Big Jay McNeely, Pete Lewis and Devonia Williams results in rougher, bluesier music, with titles like 'Midnight In The Barrelhouse', 'Hog Jaws' and 'The Jelly Roll'.

*** Be Bop Baby Blues
Night Train NTI CD 7003 Otis; unknown (t); unknown (as); Maxwell Davis (ts); unknown (bs); poss. Devonia Williams (p); Joe Swift (g, v); unknown (b); Emmanuel 'Gaucho' Vaharandes (bgo); unknown (claves); unknown (maracas). 48.

(***) Too Late To Holler
Night Train NTI 7006 As above. 48.

Credited to Otis, these CDs contain Excelsior recordings by Joe Swift, some of them previously unissued, and tracks from Swing Time, Down Beat and Supreme by Clifford Blivens, Earl Jackson and Johnny Crawford. There's no evidence that the Otis band accompanies these artists, and two of Swift's tracks on *Too Late To Holler* are backed by the Red Callender Quintet. *Be Bop Baby Blues* is a nicely varied selection of jump blues, in good sound. The arrangements acknowledge the jazzy sounds of Joe Liggins, Louis Jordan and Roy Milton, but even the title track stays on the downhome side of Central Avenue. *Too Late To Holler* maintains the high musical quality, but distant transfers make it much less desirable.

**(*) Blues, Bounce, Beat, Boogie, Bebop & Ballads
[Blue Boar CDBB 1017] Similar to above. 9/45–48.

Blue Boar reissue material from Exclusive and Excelsior, but the remastering on the first 16 tracks is inferior to Classics'. The balance of the disc collates various Joe Swift vocals; their sound quality is acceptable (less good than *Be Bop Baby Blues*, markedly better than *Too Late To Holler*), but Swift's limitations are apparent when he's heard at length.

**(*) The Johnny Otis Rhythm & Blues Caravan
Savoy Jazz SVY 17059 3CD Otis; Teddy Buckner, Billy Jones, Loyal Walker, Harry Parr Jones, Eddie Preston, Walter Williams, Don Johnson, Lee Graves, John Anderson, Hosea Sapp (t); George Washington (tb, v); Henry Coker, Eli Robinson, John Pettigrew, Jap Jones, Herb Mullins (tb); Walter Henry (as, bs); René Bloch, Bob Harris, Preston Love, Buddy Collette, Floyd Turnham (as); Paul Quinichette, James Von Streeter, Lorenzo Holden, Big Jay McNeely (ts); Leon Beck, Lem Tally, Bobby McNeely (bs); Devonia Williams (p, v); Bill Doggett, Lee Wesley Jones (p); Marylin Scott (g, v); Bernie Cobbs, Pete Lewis, Gene Phillips, unknowns (g); Curtis Counce, Joe Comfort (b); Leard Bell (d); Emanuel 'Gaucho' Vaharandes (perc); Jimmy Rushing, Little Esther [Phillips], Redd Lyte, Junior Ryder, The Robins, Mel Walker, Lee Graves, Linda Hopkins, band (v). 9/45–3/51.

The complete Savoy recordings – 77 handsomely packaged tracks – begin with five titles licensed from Excelsior, but most tracks thereafter feature Otis the vibraphonist. He and Mel Walker spend a lot of time working on a tenor-voice-plus-vibes sound that's sometimes shimmeringly sensuous, but often treacly. (The perfection of this sound, and the hits, came when Otis played behind Johnny Ace on Duke.) Redd Lyte does Roy Brown imitations, and Little Esther marches on Dinah Washington. Esther was an exceptional singer – 'Double Crossing Blues' has chart-topper written all over it – but at 14 she was a stylistically limited one. Add that The Robins had some improving to do before morphing into The Coasters, and it may seem that there's little to recommend this collection.

That's not the case, of course; there are fine tracks throughout, among them a rare Devonia Williams vocal, Linda Hopkins's high-powered debut sides and the obscure Marylin Scott's alley specials. There are also adventuresome solos aplenty, with Pete Lewis's aggression noteworthy on the earlier tracks. Otis and his musicians were recording for jukebox and radio play, not to create works of art or to be heard at this length; they hit the bull's-eye commendably often, but the sentimental and second-rank material reduces the set's overall value.

**** **Johnny Otis & The R&B Caravan Vol. 1 1945/1950**
[EPM Blues Collection 16006] *Similar to above.* 9/45–2/50.

EPM make a very good selection from the early sides. The first six tracks, from Excelsior and Exclusive, are separated from the Savoy material by Little Esther's debut recording on Modern; apart from 13-year-old Esther's offer of good loving, this track has venturesome contributions by Pete Lewis and Devonia Williams. EPM include 'Double Crossing Blues', inevitably but rightly, among the Little Esther tracks, favour toughness when selecting items by The Robins and the other Savoy vocalists, and wisely include Devonia Williams's heartfelt 'I'm Not Falling In Love With You'. The CD is admirably remastered and thoroughly annotated.

(*) **Johnny Otis 1949–1950
Classics 5067 *Otis; Don Johnson, Lee Graves, John Anderson (t); George Washington (tb); Floyd Turnham (as); James Von Streeter, Lorenzo Holden, Big Jay McNeely (ts); Walter Henry, Bobby McNeely (bs); Devonia Williams (p, v); Pete Lewis, Gene Phillips, unknown (g); Mario Delagarde (b); Leard Bell (d); Little Esther, Junior Ryder, Redd Lyte, The Robins, Mel Walker, band (v).* 8/49–1/50.

(*) **Johnny Otis 1950
Classics 5102 *As above, except Williams does not sing; add Hosea Sapp (t), Walter Henry (as), Lee Graves (v); omit Anderson, Turnham, Big Jay McNeely, Bobby McNeely, Phillips, unknown (g), Ryder.* 2/50–9/50.

1949–1950 begins with Otis's last Modern session; the laidback 'Thursday Night Blues' and the rocking 'Good Ole Blues' both have lovely guitar, and the former makes imaginative use of muted trumpets. Thereafter, these CDs replicate the first two thirds of Savoy's *Rhythm & Blues Caravan* (see above).

***(*) **Johnny Otis & The R&B Caravan Vol. 2 1950/1952**
EPM Blues Collection 16041 *As above, except add Gerald Wilson (t), John Pettigrew (tb), Earle Warren, Floyd Turnham (as), Ben Webster, Paul Quinichette (ts), Curtis Lowe, Fred Ford (bs), Marylin Scott (g, v), Albert Winston (b), Emmanuel 'Gaucho' Vaharandes (perc), Linda Hopkins, The Dominoes, George Washington, Big Mama Thornton (v); omit The Robins.* 6/50–12/52.

EPM's second volume is another good selection, from Savoy, Federal, Mercury and Peacock. The band sounds much the same whatever the label (why tamper with a hitmaking formula?), but Big Mama's 'Hound Dog' is a tiresomely obvious inclusion. Better value comes from Esther Phillips on Federal, and notably from the lubricious 'Deacon Moves In', where the other Dominoes voyeuristically enjoy her spat with Clyde McPhatter. Ben Webster's brief spell with Otis is ignored by most jazz reference books; more fool them, on the evidence of 'Goomp Blues'.

(*) **Midnight At The Barrelhouse
JSP JSP 7713 5CD *As for all above CDs, except add Alfred Cobbs (tb), Corky Corcoran, Willie Smith, Eli Wolinsky (ts), Pete Lewis (h, v), Cal Jackson, Hampton Hawes (p), Oscar Pettiford, Billy Hadnott (b), Miguelito Valdez (perc), Ivie Anderson, Joe Turner, Gene Phillips, Bobby Nunn (v); omit Thornton.* 9/45–8/52.

This 120-track box comes with discographical details and compact but informative notes. The first disc includes an AFRS broadcast that's not on the CDs above, with Joe Turner in great form and a genteel Ivie Anderson; the final disc usefully restores four tracks by Pete Lewis to circulation, and extends the availability of Little Esther and Mel Walker. The latter two artists' tracks aren't revelatory, though, and Classics will presumably catch up with them in due course. The obvious comment would be that *Midnight At The Barrelhouse* is for completists, but it's not complete: the final Modern session has been omitted, and odd tracks here and there are also passed over. Still, it's a cheap and convenient way to acquire-and-file 'the most of Johnny Otis to 8/52', although both packaging and notes avoid admitting that's what's on offer.

*** **Juke Box Hits 1946–1954**
Acrobat ACMCD 4199 *As for relevant CDs above, except add Charles Brown (p, v), Johnny Moore (g), Eddie Williams (b), Johnny Ace (v).* 9/45–53.

The CD title's dates relate to when the hits were hits, not when they were recorded. Otis plays drums on Charles Brown's 'Drifting Blues', and Joe Swift gets his 15 minutes of fame with 'That's Your Last Boogie' on Exclusive; at the other end of the disc, Otis scores a solitary hit for Mercury before moving to Duke/Peacock, where his band backs the unavoidable 'Hound Dog' and Johnny Ace's 'Please Forgive Me'. The tracks between come from Savoy; no fewer than ten of them charted in 1950, beginning with 'Double Crossing Blues' and 'Mistrustin' Blues', #1 hits that made Little Esther and Mel Walker the year's hottest stars. By using contemporary African-American taste as its organizing principle, *Juke Box Hits* gains a useful historical perspective, and avoids the bloat afflicting Savoy Jazz and JSP.

***(*) **Creepin' With The Cats**
Ace CDCHD 325 *Otis; Paul Lopez, Don Johnson (t); George Washington (tb); Jackie Kelso (prob. fl, as); James Von Streeter (ts); Fred Harman (bs); Devonia Williams (p); unknowns (strings); Jimmy Nolen (g); Johnny Parker (b); Leard Bell (d).* 56–57.

*** **Rock 'N' Roll Hit Parade**
Ace CDCHD 774 *Similar to above, except add The Jayos, Jeannie Barnes, Arthur Lee Maye, Mel Williams, Harold Lewis, Prince Moreland (v).* 57.

These CDs explore the archives of Otis's short-lived Dig label. *Creepin' With The Cats* blends gutbucket instrumentals with Otis's first extended foray into singing, usually imitating crossover artists like Fats Domino and Little Richard. The mixture is enjoyable, if slightly schizoid. *Rock 'N' Roll Hit Parade* expands an LP that consisted of covers of hits. Jeannie Barnes sings flat on 'Shake A Hand', but this is uncharacteristic; the Jayos were Maye, Williams, Richard Berry and Jesse Belvin, and their counterfeits of The Chords, The Penguins, The Clovers and others are top-quality, but much of this disc is at the limit of our range.

*** The Greatest Johnny Otis Show
Ace CDCHD 673 *Otis; Don Johnson, Paul Lopez (t); George Washington (tb); Jackie Kelso (as, ts, bs); Fred Harman (ts, bs); Plas Johnson (ts); Ernie Freeman (p); unknowns (strings); Jimmy Nolen (g); Curtis Counce (b); Earl Palmer (d); unknowns (perc); Marie Adams & The Three Tons Of Joy, Mel Williams, Jeannie Sterling & The Moonbeams, Marci Lee (v). 8/57–10/59.*

**(*) The Capitol Years
Collectables COL-CD-2773 *Similar to above, except omit Jeannie Sterling & The Moonbeams. 8/57–10/59.*

Otis led a rock 'n' roll revue on Capitol, topping the British charts with Marie Adams's ebullient 'Ma (He's Making Eyes At Me)', and scoring his most enduring American hit, 'Willie And The Hand Jive'. Otis has sometimes disparaged this material, and commercial compromise did generate dross like 'Three Girls Named Molly, Doin' The Hully Gully', but these sessions are the work of black musicians (apart from Jeannie Sterling *et al.*, shedding Doris Daylight on an old Orioles hit), and they apply solid R&B experience to the material. 'Willie And The Hand Jive' deserves its paradoxical status as a novelty classic, and the rocked-up 'Ma' retains its charm; its flipside, only included on Ace, was a rootsy 'Romance In The Dark' with some fiery guitar.

There's extensive duplication between these collections. They both contain enough blues and bluesy rockers to make for entertaining if seldom deep listening, and Collectables add some interesting unissued items, including an Afro-Cuban arrangement of 'Why Don't You Do Right?' and a lengthy, Basie-to-bop 'Vine Street Swing'. Concentrating on Otis's singing makes *The Capitol Years* less varied than the Ace CD, however, and Collectables' remastering is decidedly inferior.

*** Vintage 1950s Broadcasts From Los Angeles
Ace CDCHD 981 *Otis; 1953 and 1958 versions of The Johnny Otis Band [similar to contemporary lineups above, and including: Don Johnson (t, sp); Fred Harman (ts); Ed Rice, Jimmy Nolen (g)]; Marie Adams & The Three Tons Of Joy, The Penguins, Little Arthur Matthews, The Jayos (v); Slim Gaillard, Tim 'Kingfish' Moore, announcers (sp). c. 53–58.*

Despite the title, there's also an ad from Otis's early-'60s run for state assembly; the rest of the disc comprises two disc-jockey shows, a 1958 TV programme and a remote broadcast from the 5/4 Ballroom. This, the earliest material on the CD, is a fascinating sample of Otis's band in transition from swing ('One O'Clock Jump', 'Flyin' Home') to R&B ('I Don't Know', 'Mama He Treats Your Daughter Mean'). On the other radio shows Otis spins current platters, which are enjoyable enough; The Penguins guest on the TV programme, which otherwise features Otis's rock 'n' roll revue, and an inevitable 'Willie And The Hand Jive'. The commercials and announcements add a good deal to the CD's charm. ('Charles Ltd, men's clothiers at 725, South Broadway [where] all fitting and measuring is done on the amazing new Charles-scope, a new tailoring innovation so novel it defies description.')

** Let's Live It Up
King KCD 6015 *Otis; unknowns (t); unknown (tb); unknown (ts); unknown (bs); Robert Gross (o); Johnny 'Guitar' Watson (prob. p, g, v); Ernie Freeman (p); Johnny Rogers (g); Chuck Norris (b); Gaynel Hodge (d); 'Betty', The Interludes, unknowns (v). 10/61–12/62.*

Otis seems directionless and uninspired; the material includes attempts to rekindle past glories (a tired 'Hand Jive One More Time'), and to board the dance-craze gravy train. 'Queen Of The Twist' goes for the double by using the hand jive riff. There's some stinging guitar work, and Otis delivers one of his most soulful vocals on 'She's All Right', but Gross's eructations often spoil potentially good tracks, and the memorable numbers are often memorable for the wrong reasons, like the Interludes' extremely 'Wilted Rose Bud' and Watson's callow vocal on 'Cold Cold Heart'.

***(*) Cold Shot!
J&T JT 107 *Otis; Shuggie Otis (h, g, b); Sugarcane Harris (vn, v); Al Rivera, Broadway Thomas (b); Hootie Galvan, Buddy Redd (d); Delmar Evans (v). 68.*

***(*) Cold Shot/Snatch And The Poontangs
Ace CDCHD 855 *As above, except Shuggie Otis also plays o; add unknown women (heavy breathing). 68.*

Otis kept busy in the '60s as a disc jockey, artist, writer and activist; he also produced X-rated comedy albums, so *Snatch And The Poontangs* isn't unprecedented, either in his output or in black culture. Most of it consists of musical settings of toasts, the ultra-obscene, often violent oral poetry that celebrates bad men, tricksters and male sexual potency while relentlessly denigrating women. There's no point in skating around this; many women and not a few men will greatly dislike these songs. On the other hand, while there's no room here to discuss the complex functions and meanings of toasts, it's worth noting that, for all their power to offend, most of the songs on *Snatch And The Poontangs* are ingenious, witty and (important, this) preposterously exaggerated. They're also delivered with great gusto by Delmar Evans. For those who find such material unendurable, *Cold Shot!* by itself (and with the exclamation mark) offers similar musical pleasures, notable among them the fiercely logical guitar solos of the teenaged Shuggie Otis.

**(*) Live In Los Angeles 1970 [sic]
Wolf 120.612 *Otis; unknown (t); unknown (tb); Eddie 'Cleanhead' Vinson (as, v); unknown (as); unknown (ts); unknown (bs); Charles Brown (p, v); T-Bone Walker, Lowell Fulson (g, v); Shuggie Otis (g); Wilton Felder (b); Paul Lagos (d); Joe Turner, Roy Milton, Little Esther Phillips (v). 69.*

♛ **** Live At Monterey!
Epic/Legacy EK 53628 *Otis; Melvin Moore (t); Gene 'Mighty Flea' Connors (tb); Richard Aplanalp (ss, ts); Preston Love (as, bs); Eddie 'Cleanhead' Vinson (as, v); Clifford Solomon (ts); Big Jim Wynn (bs); Jim 'Supe' Bradshaw (h, g); Ivory Joe Hunter (p, v); Roger Spotts, Leonard Feather (p); Shuggie Otis (g, b); Pee Wee Crayton (g, v); Lawrence 'Slim' Dickens (b); Paul Lagos (d); Little Esther Phillips, Joe Turner, Roy Milton, Roy Brown, Margie Evans, Delmar 'Mighty Mouth' Evans (v). 9/70.*

At this time, Otis was leading a rhythm & blues revue, and trying to obtain belated recognition and some paydays for the greats who were still on the LA scene. Wolf's CD is the soundtrack of a TV programme broadcast in 1970; Otis and the other singers do two greatest hits each, except for T-Bone Walker, whose one track is a duet with Shuggie Otis. The recording is adequate and the band alert, but the tinder never ignites.

As edited for disc, the Monterey Jazz Festival show follows much the same format, but this was a miraculous afternoon. Spurred on by an enthusiastic audience and a punchy band,

and doubtless by the wish to outdo each other, the veterans perform as well as they did at any time during their careers. The younger, unrelated Margie and Delmar Evans come close to their forerunners' standards, and the Mighty Flea does impossible things with his tongue and a trombone. The disc isn't perfect – 'The Time Machine' is slide guitar noodling – but overall it's a wonderful summation of West Coast R&B.

**(*) The Essential Recordings
Purple Pyramid CLP 0963 *Otis; Melvin Moore (t); Gene Connors, John 'Streamline' Ewing (tb); René Bloch (as); Jackie Kelso, Clifford Solomon (ts); Big Jim Wynn (bs); Shuggie Otis (p, g, b); Willie 'Jitterbug' Webb (g); Al Rivera (b); Hootie Galvan (d); Delmar Evans (v). 68–74.*

Two tracks from *Cold Shot!*, and seven from an LP on Otis's own Blues Spectrum label, including yet another 'Hand Jive'. (The personnel given here attempts to reconcile conflicting Blues Spectrum album notes.) Otis's modest opinion of his singing abilities often seems harsh, but here he appears to see yelling as the key to excitement, and Shuggie Otis is over-indulged on guitar. The CD is lovingly remastered and budget-priced, but not essential. In passing, we counsel avoidance of *Willie And The Hand Jive* (Going For A Song GFS 577), from the same era. It's ultra-low-priced, but all tracks have been speeded up, turning Otis and Evans into Chipmunks.

Otis continued to produce records through the '70s, often with very limited distribution. They kept up with trends; *Watts Funky* (BGP CDBGPD 144) includes a smidgen of blues, most of them available elsewhere, but the majority is funk, soul, disco and outside our scope.

** The New Johnny Otis Show
Alligator ALCD 4726 *Otis; Plas Johnson (ts); Zaven Jambazian (h); David Pridgen (p, v); Shuggie Otis (g); Edgar L. Willis (b); Earl Palmer (d); Nicky Otis, Talmadge Baker (perc); Linda Dorsey, Delmar Evans, Vera Hamilton, Wendell D. Perry, Charles Williams (v). 4/81.*

The playing of Plas Johnson and Earl Palmer is a perfect treat, but they bestow it on mostly unexceptional material and some indifferent singers. Charles Williams and Linda Dorsey, plucked from the choir at Otis's Landmark Community Church, are run-of-the-mill, and Vera Hamilton is stridency incarnate. The other vocalists are better, but the general shortage of inspiration is summed up by the tired notion of setting 'Drinkin' Wine Spo-Dee-O-Dee' to (yes) the hand jive riff.

** Otisology
Magnum Force CDMF 095 *Otis; Harry Kim (t); John 'Streamline' Ewing (tb); Fred Clark, Michael Turre (s); Shuggie Otis, Gary Bell (g); Jerry Abrams (b); unknown (d); Barbara Morrison, Charles Williams, Bob Frazier, Opal Jones, Paula Denson, Delmar Evans (v). 85.*

'Hand Jive '85' starts surprisingly well, with new, ghetto-smart lyrics and a blaring brass arrangement, but it goes on too long. Elsewhere, there's a revival of 'Roll With Me Henry', a Chuck Berry pastiche, and soul tunes that range from generic originals to covers of Holland–Dozier–Holland hits. 'Fonkitup' and 'Nut Pony' are *ersatz* Sly Stone, and beyond tedious.

*** Good Lovin' Blues
Ace CDCHM 299 *Otis; Larry Douglas, Mack Johnson (t); John 'Streamline' Ewing, Charlie Schofner (tb); Clifford Solomon (as, ts); Ronald Wilson (bs); Shuggie Otis (o, g, b); Brad Pie (g); Nicky Otis (d, v); 'Ramona', Jackie Payne, La Dee Streeter (v). 89.*

Good Lovin' Blues is the epitome of middleweight, a pleasant but almost never inspired collection of blues and bluesy soul; the horn charts are well-crafted, and Shuggie Otis's lead guitar always businesslike, but only 'Pop And Sons Boogie', a throwback to late-'40s jump blues, stands out.

** R&B Dance Party Vol. 1
J&T JT 101 *Otis; George Spencer, Larry Douglas (t); Danny Armstrong (tb, cga); Jules Broussard, Ronald Wilson (s); Shuggie Otis (o, g); Gail 'Little Bit' Muldrow, Larry James (g, v); Levi Lloyd (g); Lucky Otis (b, v); Nicky Otis (d, v); Jackie Payne, Charles Williams, Dianne Swann, Ms D, Christine Lawrence (v). 74–97?*

Willie does that hand jive one more time, then the concept behind *Rock 'N' Roll Hit Parade* is revived, 40 years on and much less successfully. There are some overworked blues standards here, but most of it is soul hits of the '50s and '60s, done by singers who don't have the talent to compete with the original artists.

**(*) Blues And Swing Party Vol. 1
J&T JT 102 *As for relevant CDs above, except add Bob Mitchell (t), Little Willie Jackson (as, bs), Louis Jordan (as, v), Irv Cox (ts), Joe Liggins (p, v), Ron Selico (d), Richard Berry, Barbara Morrison (v). 57–98.*

Otis raids the vaults for a 40-year survey of his recording activities from Dig on down. Many tracks are on CDs discussed above, but there's also Al Simmons's 1957 classic 'Old Folks Boogie', on which Otis is not present, and jazz from the '90s with Barbara Morrison. Alongside eight tracks from Otis's Blues Spectrum session, there are samples of other Blues Spectrum productions: Richard Berry is listless on 'Louie Louie', but Jordan, Liggins, Joe Turner and Eddie Vinson each do a greatest hit with gusto.

The jazz tracks are the best, and it should be mentioned that Otis's continued engagement with jazz has produced 1990's *Spirit Of The Black Territory Bands* (Arhoolie CD 384) and 2002's *Food For Life* (J&T JT 108). They are both off this book's patch, but it's unlikely that swing fans will be disappointed. CS

Shuggie Otis (born 1953)
VOCAL, GUITAR, HARMONICA, ORGAN, PIANO, CELESTE, HARPSICHORD, BASS, DRUMS, PERCUSSION

Johnny Otis Jr recorded in his father's band at 14, was signed by Epic at 15 and in his early 20s turned down The Rolling Stones, who were looking to replace Mick Taylor. By that time, Shuggie's music encompassed much more than blues, and he was exploring orchestration and electronics; 1975's Inspiration Information *took so long and cost so much that Epic dropped him. Since then, health problems and his own preferences have confined him to live and session work on the West Coast.*

**(*) Here Comes Shuggie Otis/Freedom Flight
Raven RVCD-141 *Otis; Melvin Moore, Bob Mitchell (t); Willie Ruff, Richard Mackey (flh); Gene 'Mighty Flea' Connors (tb); Richard Aplanalp (fl, oboe, ts); Preston Love, Hank Jernigan, Jack Kelso (fl, s); Plas Johnson, Jim Horn (s); Jim 'Supe'*

Bradshaw (h, v); Leon Haywood, George Duke (o, p, cel); Al Kooper (o, p); Johnny Otis (p, cel, harpsichord, timp, perc, v); Ray Johnson (p); Wilton Felder (cel, harpsichord, b); Ginger Smock, Joe Lichter, Isadore Roman, Eunice Wennermark (vn); Rollice Dale, Marilyn Baker (vl); Hyman Gold, Irving Lipschitz (vc); Al McKibbon, Stu Woods (b); Stix Hooper, Abe Mills, Paul Lagos, Mike Kowalski, Aynsley Dunbar, Wells Kelly (d); Clydie King, Shirley Matthews, Venetta Fields, The Harris Robinson Singers (v). 6/69–4/71.

*** **Shuggie Otis Plays The Blues**
Epic/Legacy EK 57903 *Similar to above, except add Mark Klingman (p), Sugarcane Harris (vn, v), Ron Selico (d); omit Aplanalp, strings, backing vocalists.* 6/69–4/71.

The young Shuggie Otis was a musical prodigy, but his blues were seldom musically prodigious, unlike the psychedelic soul of *Inspiration Information* (Luaka Bop 50473), which, however, is way outside our compass. *Plays The Blues* selects from *Kooper Session – Al Kooper Introduces Shuggie Otis*, the LPs reissued by Raven and the Johnny Otis Show's *Cuttin' Up*. Shuggie has a real feel for the blues on his many instruments, but it's no surprise that the guitar features most prominently; it was a time when record companies, critics and the public were even keener than usual to deify guitarists. In the circumstances, the most striking aspects of Shuggie's blues playing are his good taste and his reluctance to showboat; only briefly and very occasionally does speed take over. The rueful realism of 'Me And My Woman', his only vocal here, is too much for a teenager, and the extended workouts sometimes lapse into formula. Brisk dance tunes like his Freddie King knock-off 'The Hawks' and the blues-funk of 'Bootie Cooler' stand the test of time better than the more self-conscious explorations.

That goes double for the two LPs reissued complete on Raven, with a non-bonus bonus track in the shape of a dreadfully twee 'One Room Country Shack' from *Kooper Session*. There are some enjoyable blues here, like the instrumental 'Funky Thithee', probably omitted from *Plays The Blues* for political incorrectneth; but there are also Otis *père*'s bubblegum composition 'Knowing (That You Want Him)', some tiresome hippy-dippy ballads, including 'Strawberry Letter 23' (later an inexplicable million-seller for the Brothers Johnson), and the Sergeant-Pepper-meets-the-blues pretensions of 'Oxford Gray'.

(*) In Session Information
RPM 509 *Otis; Kurt Sletten, Melvin Moore (t); Doug Wintz, Gene Connors, John 'Streamline' Ewing (tb); Little Willie Jackson (as, bs); Eddie Vinson (as, v); René Bloch (as); Jack Kelso, Preston Love (ts); Freddy Clark (s); Richard Berry (kb, v); Charles Brown (o, p, v); Johnny Otis (p, d, vb, v); Joe Liggins (p, v); Larry Reed (p); Melvin Wonder (g); Edgar Willis, Al Lopez (b); Hootie Galvan (d); Delmar Evans, Roy Milton (v).* 73–77.

In Session Information (!) is credited to Shuggie Otis; it compiles tracks recorded by R&B veterans for his father's Blues Spectrum label, selected to showcase Otis Jr's contributions on guitar and bass. None of it's poor, but none of it's great either; the featured artists were mostly past their peak, and there's too much of the dull Richard Berry. cs

Jack Owens (1904–97)
VOCAL, GUITAR

Opinion still varies as to whether there was a Bentonia school of minor-key guitar playing, rather than it being the preserve of its most famous exponent, Skip James. Owens, James's contemporary and like him a native of the Mississippi town, was found there in 1966 by folklorist David Evans. Christened L. F. Nelson, he was renamed when raised by his mother's family. His father and uncle formed part of a group of musicians in the area, including Henry Stuckey, Adam Slader and Rich Griffin, and both young men were taught by its members. Although he could play in seven tunings, Owens favoured the E minor mode predominantly used by James. After Evans discovered him, many amateur and professional recordists beat a path to his front porch but he is still sparsely represented on CD, apart from individual tracks fleshing out a number of VACs.

***(*) It Must Have Been The Devil**
Testament TCD 5016 *Owens; Bud Spires (h).* 9/70.

Comparisons with James may be unavoidable but this record identifies a number of striking differences between the two. Though using the same tuning, Owens is a less fastidious player, content to set a rhythm from which, once established, he rarely deviates. Where James creates rigid melodic patterns in his playing and continuity in his verses, Owens remains fluid and adaptable, his songs lasting as long as his inspiration, a case in point here being a near-ten-minute 'It Must Have Been The Devil', his version of 'Devil Got My Woman'. He has an astonishing voice at odds with his diminutive stature, although his solo performance of 'Jack Ain't Had No Water' is unusually subdued. Spires is present on five selections, providing quiet chorded support. On several songs, including the opening 'Can't See, Baby', Owens plays with a thumb-pick while feathering the treble strings with his fingers, creating a noticeable imbalance within the guitar, which isn't present when he plays slide on another solo piece, 'I Won't Be Bad No More'. Owens was less of a conscious artist than James, and his work reflects his almost lifelong status as a neighbourhood juke-joint entertainer.

*** **The Last Giants Of Mississippi Blues**
Wolf 120.931 *As above.* 6/80–9/91.

Owens was 75 and 87 when these 11 tracks were cut. (The balance of the CD is by Eugene Powell.) His guitar playing was inevitably more deliberate and he used a 12-string's wider fretboard to ensure precision. His voice had lost some of its power, most notably on the 1981 solo tracks. 'Cherry Ball', 'Hard Times' and 'Devil' are less dramatic than of yore but have acquired a stately demeanour. Unfortunately all six songs suffer from a creaking chair and 'Please Give Me Your Money' is over-recorded for its first verses. Bud Spires's presence on the 1991 recordings draws a stronger performance from Owens on further essays at 'Hard Times', 'Devil' and 'Jack Ain't Had No Water' (here as 'Cool Water'). 'Keep On Rumblin'' is a 1980 duet on which Owens seems to be using a rather tinny amplifier. Despite their overt shortcomings, these tracks retain an aura of what Jim O'Neal characterized as 'an almost extinct and quite revered historical style of blues'. NS

Junior Parker (1927/32–71)
VOCAL, HARMONICA

Herman Parker grew up in West Memphis, Arkansas, listening to Sonny Boy Williamson II on local radio and absorbing his harmonica playing. In the late '40s he worked with him and

Howlin' Wolf. He had an R&B chart hit with 'Feelin' Good' (Sun) in 1953 and for the next dozen or so years recorded for Duke, having chart success with 'Driving Wheel' and other numbers. He had a considerable following on the black club circuit, but in working and recording almost exclusively for that constituency he was virtually invisible to the new blues audience of the '60s – an obscurity that was only deepened by his early death, during an operation for a brain tumour.

**** Mystery Train
Rounder CD SS 38 *Parker; James Wheeler, unknowns (s); William Johnson, unknown (p); prob. Floyd Murphy, Pat Hare (g); poss. Kenneth Banks, unknowns (b); John Bowers, unknowns (d). 53–54.*

'Feelin' Good' and its slightly revised version, 'Feelin' Bad', are based in part on John Lee Hooker's 'Boogie Chillen', but the chuntering guitar and Parker's extraordinary vocal – husky, slightly breathless, but abruptly arching into a glorious full-throated cry – transform them into a loose-limbed country dance. If this brings us close to rockabilly, the swinging guitar and springy rhythm of 'Love My Baby' and 'Mystery Train' push us the rest of the way. But then, displaying the adaptability that would both steer and, perhaps, divert his later career, Parker turns from that cheeky, upbeat music and, in 'Fussin' And Fightin' or 'Sittin' Drinkin' And Thinkin'', croons the blues like a Memphis cousin of Charles Brown. Contemporary Sun sides by James Cotton (three) and guitarist Pat Hare (two) follow Parker's nine in this set of historically momentous recordings.

**** Junior Parker
Universal/Gitanes Blues 112 343 *Parker; Joe Scott, Tommy Nevue, John Brownie, unknowns (t); Pluma Davis, unknown (tb); Joe Fritz (as); Jimmy Johnson, Bill Harvey, Theodore Arthur, Gilbert Caple, 'Foot', unknowns (ts); Rayfield Devers, Charles Crawford, unknown (bs); unknowns (s); unknown (o); Bill Johnson, Donnie McGowan, Connie Mack Booker, unknowns (p); Pat Hare, Wayne Bennett, Johnny Brown, unknowns (g); Hamp Simmons, Otis Jackson, Vernon Heard, unknowns (b); Sonny Freeman, John 'Jabo' Parks, Randolph Odom, unknowns (d). 12/53–8/66.*

*** Driving Wheel
MCA MCD 32643 *Similar to above. 56–65.*

Not a few seasoned commentators have recorded their perplexity at Junior Parker's low standing, even among blues aficionados. The last sentence of the biographical sketch above provides a couple of explanations, yet it remains odd that his work tends to be erratically documented and, even when it is made available, to disappear again. At the time of writing, it was impossible to feel confident that any of the albums discussed from here onwards would enjoy a long catalogue life.

MCA's two volumes of Duke recordings, *Junior's Blues* (MCAD 10669) and *Backtracking* (MCAD 11786), having been deleted, the only access to Parker's work in his most productive period is the French Universal CD, a careful selection spanning the entire Duke era, from the Sun-alike 'I Wanna Ramble' to the thrusting big-band arrangement of 'These Kind Of Blues' with its mariachi trumpet intro. The MCA CD is the Duke album *Driving Wheel*, recorded in 1961–62, supplemented with eight mostly earlier recordings; it duplicates seven of *Junior Parker*'s tracks, but includes several important pieces in his repertoire like the title number, 'Sweet Home Chicago' and the Percy Mayfield song 'Strange Things Happening'.

Either album quickly makes the essential point about Junior Parker: he was one of the premier singers of his time. Had he confined himself to soul music he might now be rated alongside contemporaries like Little Willie John or even Sam Cooke. Even considered purely as a blues singer he was in the same league as B. B. King. Listen to the way his warm, intimate, infinitely flexible voice caresses the lyrics of Mayfield's 'I Need Love So Bad' (*Driving Wheel*) or swoops and glides through 'Man Or Mouse' (*Junior Parker*). On *Driving Wheel* his singing is sometimes obscured by poor recording balance; *Junior Parker* not only solves that problem on the shared tracks but ignores rock 'n' roll novelties like 'Annie Get Your Yo-Yo'.

*** I'm So Satisfied: The Complete Mercury & Blue Rock Recordings
Mercury 314 558 549 *Parker; Gene 'Bowlegs' Miller, Willie Mitchell, unknown(s) (t); Fred Ford (ts); Jimmy Mitchell (bs); unknowns (s); Bobby Emmons, unknown (o); Joe Hall, unknown (p); Reggie Young, Tommy Cogbill, Doug Sahm, unknown (g); Mike Leech, unknown (b); Sam Creason, unknown (d); unknowns (v). 8/66–69.*

*** The Mercury Recordings
Collectables COL-CD-5624 *As above, except omit Sahm. 8/66–8/68.*

I'm So Satisfied puts together two Mercury-group albums, *Like It Is* and *Honey Drippin' Blues*, and a handful of singles and unissued items: 31 tracks in all, and an astounding playing time of 79.07. Among the earlier material are a version of Percy Mayfield's 'Baby Please', superbly sung and arranged, and a reading of Walter Davis's 'Come Back Baby' with a guitarist who stings like a hornet. The *Honey Drippin' Blues* sessions yield fewer blues and generally noisier arrangements, but whatever the song, Parker takes charge of it. The Collectables CD, which contains the 11 tracks of *Like It Is* and three that appeared on singles, has most of the best Mercury material and should satisfy anyone but a completist.

*** The Collection
Spectrum 068 910 *As for* Driving Wheel *and* The Mercury Recordings. *c. 6/56–9/67.*

A useful epitome of the Duke/Mercury period: ten tracks from the former label, including 'Driving Wheel', 'Sweet Home Chicago', 'These Kind Of Blues' and other first-class sides (all of them also on *Driving Wheel*), then seven good selections from Mercury. At Spectrum's budget price, an admirable introduction.

***(*) Way Back Home: The Groove Merchant Years
Connoisseur VSOP CD 291 *Parker; unknowns (brass); Fats Theus (ts); unknowns (reeds); Jimmy McGriff, unknown (o); Horace Ott (p); unknowns (strings); O'Donel Levy, unknowns (g); unknowns (b); unknowns (d). 70–71.*

Scattered through this 23-track selection from Parker's last few albums are the ten tracks originally grouped as *You Don't Have To Be Black To Love The Blues*, later as *Blue Shadows Falling*: either way, his finest album. Given small-group settings that left room for his harmonica, these quiet, pastoral performances of genre standards like 'Sweet Home Chicago' and 'That's All Right' could be used as a manual of blues singing; 'Five Long Years', in particular, is exquisite. The half-dozen tracks from *The Outside Man* and the seven from a pair of albums with the organist Jimmy McGriff are generally busier and occasionally date-stamped by funk clichés, but Parker's own performance is consistently rewarding. TR

Kenny Parker (born 1952)
GUITAR

Parker, from Albion, Michigan, began playing guitar in his teens. After graduating he moved to Detroit, where he worked on the Cadillac assembly line. In the '90s he played with local musicians Mr Bo and the Butler Twins, becoming the Twins' lead guitarist and producing their second JSP album.

**(*) Raise The Dead
JSP JSPCD 2109 *Parker; Darrell Nulisch, Clarence Butler, Sommerville Slim (h, v); Tim Sparling (o, p); Bill Heid (p); Curtis Butler (g); Mick Marshall (b); Martin Gross (d). 96.*

Parker is no singer, at least publicly, and the vocals on this album are mostly taken care of by Nulisch, who is in good form on both voice and harmonica. 'Shake Hands With The Devil' and 'You're So Sharp' feature the Butler Twins and would have sat equally well on one of their CDs, being blues solidly in the idiom of '50s Muddy Waters, with Spannesque piano by Bill Heid. Four of the dozen tracks are instrumentals, and the slow 'Blues For Mr. Bo', in memory of one of Parker's mentors, and 'Afterglow' have an attractive B. B. Kingish sound. So far as content goes, it has nearly all been said before, but Parker does say it again. TR

Sonny Parker (1925–57)
VOCAL, DRUMS

Parker began singing and dancing as a protégé of Butterbeans & Susie. He joined Lionel Hampton's band in 1949, and was touring France with Hampton in 1955 when he suffered an onstage stroke. He never recovered, and a further stroke two years later was fatal.

***(*) Sonny Parker 1948–1953
Blue Moon BMCD 6003 *Parker; King Kolax, Jesse Perry, Walter Williams, Benny Bailey, Eddie Mullens, Duke Garrette, Leo Shepard, Quincy Jones (t); Al Grey, Benny Powell, Jimmy Wormick, Paul Higaki, Jimmy Cleveland (tb); Johnny Board (as, ts); Archie Washington, Bobby Plater, Jerome Richardson (as); Lonnie Shaw, Curtis Lowe (ts, bs); Paul Renfro, Gene Morris, Billy Williams, Gil Bernal, unknown (ts); Ben Kynard (bs); Milt Buckner (o, p); Pick Gordon, Floyd Dixon, Douglas Duke, Jesse Stone, Sam Price (p); Wes Montgomery, Billy Mackel, Chuck Norris, unknown (g); Monty Morrison, Roy Johnson, unknown (b); Ellis Bartee, Curley Hamner, Earl Walker, unknown (d); Lionel Hampton (vb). 12/48–12/53.*

***(*) Sonny Parker With Lionel Hampton 1949/1951 [sic]
EPM Blues Collection 16028 *As above, except add Gus Domerette (p), Rudolph Mason (g); omit Kolax, Perry, Mullens, Jones, Washington, Renfro, Gordon, Stone, Morrison, unknowns. 4/49–52.*

Parker's hero was Joe Turner, but his recordings are in thrall to the soulful, and at that time all-conquering, sound of Roy Brown. Equally effective on slow blues and up-tempo material, Parker could whip his accompanists into a frenzy by the force and swing of his vocals. He's less well known to blues fans than he should be; premature death deprived him of the chance to establish an extensive catalogue under his own name, and blues discographers have left the recordings with Hampton to their jazz counterparts.

Blue Moon present six tracks with Hampton's big band, 14 with small groups drawn from it, and six without Hamptonian associations. Among the latter are Parker's debut recordings, which are marred by unimaginative tenor, but the rest of the disc is much better, and 'She Sets My Soul On Fire', with ecstatic solos by Al Grey and Johnny Board, is one of the greatest moments of blues shouting on disc. The small-group sides are generally preferable; not having to coalesce into a musical juggernaut, the musicians have more opportunities to stretch out. Part of Parker's job with Hampton was evidently to cover contemporary hits; one outcome is a grindingly dull 'Drinking Wine Spo-Dee-O-Dee', but Parker and the big band take 'Merry Christmas Baby' to places Charles Brown never imagined. Seventeen of EPM's tracks are also on Blue Moon, but 'Merry Christmas Baby' is not among them, and Blue Moon's claim to have selected the best recordings with Hampton is generally accurate; of EPM's five 'new' items, 'Jumpin' With G. H.' is a classic rocker, but the rest are natural B-sides with contrived lyrics. CS

Jordan Patterson (born 1969)
VOCAL, HARMONICA

Patterson grew up in an academic family in Ontario and was musically educated by an older brother. He began playing guitar, then switched to harmonica. In his 20s he moved to western Canada, where he began to play in public and became involved in artist management, particularly with Bobby Parker, whom he acknowledges as a great influence on his music. Since 1994 he has lived in Washington, DC.

**(*) Give Me A Chance
JSP JSPCD 263 *Patterson; Josh Brown Jr (as); James Evans (ts); Bobby Rush (h, v); James 'Hot Dog' Lewis (o, p); Shawn Kellerman, Bobby Parker (g); Anthony Gonsalves (b); El Torro Gamble (d). 95.*

Busy, enthusiastic, ambitious – there's much to commend in Patterson's debut. Quite good writing, too, in the eight songs (out of ten) that are his, among them a 'Blue Hotel' set to a Bo Diddley rhythm and a slow blues, 'The Thing I Do For You'. The other two are 'Those Pretty Eyes' by, and featuring, Bobby Parker, whose hand may also be felt in some of the funkier arrangements, and Guitar Shorty's 'No Educated Woman', a confident reading with Bobby Rush contributing a harmonica accompaniment and some jive exchanges. Patterson's own harmonica is bold and unclichéd. However, nothing has been heard of him on record since this CD, and, given his age and associations, it's possible that he has moved on from the blues stage documented by *Give Me A Chance*, and into other kinds of music. TR

Neal 'Big Daddy' Pattman (1926–2005)
VOCAL, HARMONICA

Pattman learned harmonica from his father as a child on the farm. He lost his right arm at the age of nine in an accident, and in adulthood followed a variety of day jobs in Athens, Georgia, devoting himself to music more fully from the late '70s.

****(*) Live In London**
Erwin Music EM-9701 *Pattman; 'Shrimp City Slim' [Gary Erwin] (p, wb); Dave Peabody (g); Matt Radford (b); Brian Nevill (d).* 4/95.

***** Prison Blues**
Music Maker 91003 *Pattman; Lee Konitz (as); Taj Mahal (p, bj, g, b); Cootie Stark (g, v); Jimmy Rip, 'Mudcat', Timothy Duffy (g); Mark Levinson (b).* 98.

Live In London is adequately recorded, although Pattman recedes into the mix at times, but it's little more than a pleasant souvenir of an enjoyable evening. Pattman is vigorous and the band are competent, but their playing is generic (from a different genre, in the case of the Chicago-inspired piano), and on longer numbers it outstays its welcome. There is considerable overlap of repertoire between the two CDs, but *Prison Blues* is clearly the better; its lineups are smaller (ranging from no accompanists to two) and much more varied, and the intention is always to supply a setting in which Pattman can shine. He does so on a wide-ranging programme of display pieces, gospel and blues, both original and well known, although there are no new insights on 'Catfish Blues', and Lee Konitz's alto on 'Talkin' 'Bout You Baby' contrasts strangely with the downhome sound of the rest. CS

Charley Patton (1891–1934)
VOCAL, GUITAR

Charley (or Charlie) Patton grew up on plantations in Bolton and Edwards, Mississippi, but spent his teens and 20s at Dockery Farms, by the Sunflower River. His local reputation attracted the interest of H. C. Speir, a Jackson, Mississippi, music-store owner who acted as a talent agent for several labels, and he recorded quite prolifically for Paramount in 1929–30. Not long after a final session for Vocalion in 1934 he died of a heart attack, but his records and personal appearances had stamped a deep impression on fellow musicians such as Booker White, Big Joe Williams and Howlin' Wolf, and some of his songs are embedded in the standard repertoire.

♛ **** Screamin' And Hollerin' The Blues
Revenant 212 7CD *Patton; Henry Sims (vn, v); Willie Brown (g); Bertha Lee (v).* 6/29–2/34.

**** Complete Recordings 1929–1934
JSP JSPCD 7702 5CD *As above.* 6/29–2/34.

**** The Definitive Charley Patton
Catfish KATCD 180 3CD *As above, except Sims does not sing.* 6/29–2/34.

**** The Voice Of The Delta: The Charley Patton Legacy
Indigo IGOTCD 2560 3CD *As for* Screamin' And Hollerin' The Blues. 6/29–2/34.

** Screamin' & Hollerin' The Blues
Snapper SMDCD 473 2CD *As above.* 6/29–2/34.

***(*) The Voice Of The Delta
Black Swan HCD 21/22 2CD *As above, except omit Bertha Lee.* 6/29–5/30.

In the best-known photograph of Charley Patton a youngish man faces posterity with a straight but somewhat apprehensive gaze. Some of what lay ahead he might have predicted: a hard life, early death, obscurity. What was not on the cards was that some 30 years later he would begin to be described as one of the most singular musicians of the 20th century, a voice of the blues like no other, a teller of stories from a time and place that for his new listeners were as unimaginable as the dark side of the moon. His sometimes strangled utterances, already half choked by the surface noise of old discs, gradually revealed themselves to be passages from an oral history of black Mississippi in the 1910s and '20s: its dirt roads and rivers, drinking places and jails, the pest-ravaged cottonfields of 'Mississippi Bo Weavil Blues', the drought of 'Dry Well Blues', the flooded bottomlands of 'High Water Everywhere' and, turning from natural disasters to man-made ones, the layoff of railroad workers in 'Mean Black Moan'. These reports, and the many other types of songs he recorded, from blues-ballads like 'Frankie And Albert' and rags like 'Shake It And Break It' to hymns and transformed popular songs, are delivered in a voice as tough as steel, to guitar melodies as densely springy as ryegrass. It is extraordinary music, not always easy to understand, but so full of incident that it quickly becomes totally absorbing.

In the mountaineering circles of the reissue business, where the talk is ever of scaling this or that peak of rarity, the Everest of achievement is the conquest of Mt Patton. *The Definitive Charley Patton*, Catfish's boxed set containing all the issued recordings in generally very good transfers, came close, but it was conclusively beaten to the summit by the extraordinary Revenant set, undoubtedly the most lavish, exhaustive and abundantly documented production ever devoted to a blues artist of any style or period. Within an elaborate reconstruction of the kind of album used in bygone days to house a handful of 78s are seven CDs containing all Patton's issued sides, some alternative takes, the recordings of associates like Son House, Willie Brown, Buddy Boy Hawkins and the Delta Big Four, later versions of Patton's songs by Howlin' Wolf and others and a disc of interviews. The notes and appendices, by several hands, are of book length, and a further book is included, a facsimile reprint of John Fahey's 1970 monograph *Charley Patton*. The remastering quality is all that one would expect from so careful a production. The only criticisms that can be levelled against the set are that some of the commentary is tendentious and parts of the text have been designed more for the art director's satisfaction than for the reader's convenience.

The JSP set includes all Patton's issued sides, plus his four accompaniments to fiddler Henry Sims (who also accompanies him on many of his) and two with his partner Bertha Lee, as well as four alternative takes and 30 tracks by associated figures. All this is also on the Revenant, and the sonic evidence suggests that the material was sourced from that set but re-equalized to yield a slightly different sound. Like other boxed sets on this label it is very attractively priced. Indigo's *The Voice Of The Delta* has the same Patton–Sims–Lee contents but the tracks by associated figures are reduced to 14 (seven by Son House, five by Louise Johnson, two by Willie Brown).

Snapper's 2CD set contains all but four of Patton's issued sides, randomly sequenced. Even by present standards of etiquette in the PD reissue business this is a startlingly opportunistic release, filching not only its material from the Revenant box but its title and parts of its artwork. The job was

Black Swan's *The Voice Of The Delta* contains all Patton's issued Paramounts (42 sides), sequenced as they were issued, but stops there, ignoring his later recordings. It would be an unusual Patton enthusiast who had no regard at all for the 1934 sides, so this set is more likely to frustrate than to please. But it's quite well presented and annotated, and, although the sound quality falls short of Revenant's, it doesn't do so by much.

♛ **** **Founder Of The Delta Blues**
Yazoo 2010 *Patton; Henry Sims (vn); Willie Brown (g).* 6/29–2/34.

***(*) **Founder Of The Delta Blues**
Yazoo 1020 *As above.* 6/29–2/34.

**** **King Of The Delta Blues**
Yazoo 2001 *Patton; Henry Sims (vn); Bertha Lee (v).* 6/29–2/34.

**** **The Best Of Charlie Patton**
Yazoo 2069 *Patton; Henry Sims (vn); Willie Brown (g).* 6/29–1/34.

***(*) **Pony Blues**
Wolf Blues Classics BC 002 *As above.* 6/29–2/34.

***(*) **A Proper Introduction To Charley Patton: Pony Blues**
Proper INTRO CD 2040 *As above.* 6/29–2/34.

*** **Hang It On The Wall**
Snapper Complete Blues SBLUECD 005 *Patton.* 6/29–2/34.

If you want only one Patton CD, *Founder Of The Delta Blues* on Yazoo 2010 is it. (But see the next paragraph.) 'Mississippi Bo Weavil Blues', 'High Water Everywhere', 'A Spoonful Blues', 'Pony Blues' and 'Moon Going Down', the last from a small group of recordings on which Patton's guitar is entrancingly meshed with his friend Willie Brown's, head a 26-track selection unrivalled by any of the other single CDs, either for selection or for overall sound quality. The identically titled Yazoo 1020 appears to be the same collection minus 'Magnolia Blues' and 'Devil Sent The Rain', but it's likely that Yazoo 2010 profited from access to superior remastering technology. *King Of The Delta Blues* was compiled to work in tandem with *Founder*, and thus includes a good deal of relatively less astonishing work, as well as a few alternative takes and some pieces that had to be sourced from worn originals.

The reservation expressed above stems from Yazoo's later issue of *The Best Of Charlie Patton*, which combines 15 tracks from Yazoo 2010 and seven from 2001, plus 'Elder Green[e] Blues', which is on both (in different takes). Yazoo claim that the remastering quality of 2069 is superior, and careful comparative listening confirms it, but the difference is a matter of very fine tuning, and for some listeners it may not compensate for the loss of 'High Water Everywhere – Part 2'.

The Wolf and Proper CDs are acoustically a little cruder than the Yazoos but otherwise estimable selections. Wolf shut out Bertha Lee and drop the second parts of 'High Water Everywhere' and 'Prayer Of Death', both of which Proper restore. *Hang It On The Wall*, uniquely among Patton CDs, presents him only as a solo artist. All these collections duplicate each other, and Yazoo 2010 and 2069, so heavily that it only makes sense to buy one of the seven: see the foregoing, to which it should be added that the Yazoos have far better notes.

(****) **Charley Patton – Vol. 1 (1929)**
Document DOCD-5009 *Patton; Henry Sims (vn).* 6–c. 10/29.
(****) **Charley Patton – Vol. 2 (1929)**
Document DOCD-5010 *Patton; Henry Sims (vn, v).* c. 10/29.
(****) **Charley Patton – Vol. 3 (1929–1934)**
Document DOCD-5011 *Patton; Henry Sims (vn, v); Willie Brown (g); Bertha Lee (v).* c. 10/29–2/34.
(***) **1929–1934 The Remaining Titles**
Wolf WSE-103 *Patton; Henry Sims (vn).* 6/29–2/34.

The Documents were compiled a long time ago and in terms of sound quality are inferior to the Yazoos and others described above. The Wolf was designed to complement early LP reissues and has been marginalized by subsequent collections. TR

Jackie Payne (born 1945)
VOCAL

Payne is the nephew of the harmonica player Neal Pattman. He first sang with his father's gospel choir, and at 13 with a band in Atlanta. At 17 he moved to south Texas and worked in clubs in Port Arthur, Galveston and Houston, warming the audience up for the night's attraction. He also sang with Albert Collins and made some singles. In 1968 he resettled in California, and since 1986 has often worked with Johnny Otis.

** **Day In The Life (Of A Bluesman)**
JSP JSPCD 296 *Payne; Noel Catura (ts, bs); Ken Baker (ts, arr); Austin [Audie] deLone (o, p); Kenny 'Blue' Ray (o, g, prod); Frank DeRose (b); Kevin Coggins, Gene Pardue (d).* 7/97.

The title track, opened by Ray's soaring guitar, reveals Payne's thoughts about his profession ('a bluesman is treated like an outlaw, Lord, about the same as Jesse James') and introduces the Bobby Bland-like voice that got him into it. But what this performance promises, the album as a whole fails to deliver. There are no other slow numbers like 'Day In The Life (Of A Bluesman)', too many bright medium-tempo songs that flow together in the memory, too little in the lyrics that rises above the ordinary.

Payne also sings on three tracks of Ray's contemporaneous album for JSP, *In All Of My Life* (JSPCD 289), and on most of Ray's 2001 release *Soulful Blues* (Tone King TKCD 1066).

*** **Partners In The Blues**
Burnside 49 *Payne; John Middleton, Mike Rose (t); Carl Green; Terry Hanck (ts); Rik Munson (bs, v); Bernard Anderson (bs); John (Johnny P) Peterson (h); Austin DeLone [Audie deLone] (kb, o, p); Jim Pugh (o, vb); Franco Corsetti (o); Steve Edmonson, Rusty Zinn (g); Tim Wagar, Bill Singletary (b); June Core, Walter Shufflesworth (d).* 03?

A great improvement. Payne sings better than on *Day In The Life*, and the band slips expertly into his soul-blues idiom, but the important difference is the material, carefully selected from people like Albert King and Little Milton. 'I Need Your Love So Bad' is no more than competent, but Payne finds something to get a grip on in 'That's How Strong My Love Is' and Johnny Copeland's 'The Devil's Hand'. The only tracks that don't work, because they don't really suit his manner, are the Chicago-style 'Close To You' and 'Cryin' For My Baby'. Edmonson does most of the lead guitar work, which is fair enough, since he's joint leader of the band, and is both fast and fluent; Zinn chiefly plays rhythm but takes his few solo opportunities with panache. TR

Asie Payton (1937?–97)
VOCAL, GUITAR

A plain working man indifferent to the blandishments of fame, Asie Payton resisted all his record company's cajolery to come to a studio and make a proper record. Songs cut at the two sessions that did take place were regarded as demos until his sudden death forced a radical rethink.

***(*) Worried
Fat Possum 80326 *Payton; poss. Justin Berry (bs); poss. Howe Gleb (o); poss. Leo Schwamm (g); Sam Carr (d). 96.*

A tantalizingly brief showcase for one of Fat Possum's most charismatic artists, these ten tracks are essentially duets between Payton and drummer Sam Carr. Some, like the rocking 'Worried Life', 'All I Need Is You' and 'Come Home With Me', remain unaugmented, while 'Please Tell Me You Love Me' and the final 'I Love You' are solo performances. All else has varying degrees of overdubbing, notably the opening version of 'I Love You', a mesmeric tape montage eventually used in the film *Big Bad Love*. Appearances are deceptive: 'Worried Life' isn't the well-known blues, 'Please Tell Me' is Jimmy Reed's 'Honest I Do', 'All I Need Is You' is 'Since I Met You Baby' and Joe Tex's 'Skinny Legs & All' isn't even disguised. Little wonder the house publishing company is called Big Legal Mess. Payton was a true amateur with talent beyond the rough but compelling evidence provided here.

**(*) Just Do Me Right
Fat Possum 80353 *Payton; Justin Berry, Jeff ——— (s); Tom Malbank, Saylor Breckenridge (h); Jimmy Carr, Howe Gleb (o); John Hermann (p); Christian Quermalet, Leo Schwamm, Kenny Brown (g); Daniel Worley (b); Ted Gainey, John Convertino, Sam Carr (d). 80–94.*

You've had the best, now here's the rest. A small army of supplementary musicians mostly fail to add anything meaningful to another 13 songs ('Back To The Bridge' appears twice). A handful – '1000 Years', 'Livin' In So Much Pain', 'Why'd You Do It' and a romp through Little Walter's 'You Better Watch Yourself' with slide guitar from Kenny Brown – would have been worthy additions to *Worried*. The rest are haphazard at best, more often scrappy bordering on inept. Instead of complementing whatever Payton is doing, the players impose themselves at his expense, underlining the fragility of his talent. Where previously failings were conquered with sheer charm, inadequacy is the focus here. Nevertheless, Asie Payton remains an intriguing curiosity. NS

Dave Peabody (born 1948)
VOCAL, GUITAR, HARMONICA

Peabody is a seasoned performer with a long track record on the British and Continental club scenes. He has promoted the music of numerous older musicians both by playing and recording with them and through his work as a journalist and photographer.

**(*) Dream Of Mississippi
Appaloosa AP-079 *Peabody; Charlie Musselwhite (h); Bob Hall (p); Top Topham (g). 90.*

**(*) Hands Across The Sea
Appaloosa AP 096 *Peabody; Chicago Bob Nelson, Little George Sueref, Rob Mason (h); Gary Erwin (kb, p, wb); Robert Lucas, Big Joe Louis (g); Ted Donlon, Matt Radford (b); Jay Niver, Brian Nevill (d); Big Boy Henry, Sandra Hall (v). 11/92–5/93.*

**(*) Down In Carolina
Appaloosa AP 127 *Peabody; John E. Cobb (as); Dan 'King Tone' O'Reilly (bs); Neal Pattman (h, v); Juke Joint Johnny (h); Gary Erwin (p, wb); Steve James (md, g); Jerome J. Griffin (b); Dudley Birch (d); Cora Mae Bryant (v). 2/96.*

An album that draws its repertoire not only from Robert Johnson and Charley Patton but from Sonny Boy Nelson and Barrelhouse Buck McFarland is plainly the work of a man with an extensive and well-absorbed record collection. But *Dream Of Mississippi* is not an exercise in reproduction: Peabody often alters the settings, and makes no attempt to mimic the vocal character or accent, of the original recordings. That personal showcase filled, he made his next two projects patchworks of collaborations with musicians with whom he feels an affinity. *Hands Across The Sea* contains duets with Robert Lucas, trios and quartets with Big Boy Henry, Gary Erwin and Rob Mason, and band tracks with Big Joe Louis & His Blues Kings and an American group, while *Down In Carolina* is a get-together with mostly South Carolinian musicians, arising out of the 1996 Low Country Blues Bash in Charleston. The material on both CDs is largely original, and although Peabody's feeling for idiom is seldom in doubt, the writing is sometimes awkward. The outstanding cuts on *Hands* are the back-country music of the Peabody–Henry–Erwin–Mason group, enhanced by Mason's lovely antique harmonica playing, and on *Carolina* the not dissimilar tracks by Peabody, Pattman and James such as 'Kansas City Blues' (an unexpectedly lively roasting of that chestnut) and 'Blues Bash Breakdown'. The electric combo performances are less striking on both sets, partly because Peabody's unaggressive singing tends to submerge itself in the ensemble rather than crest the wave.

Two Trains Running (Indigo IGOXCD 519, deleted), a 1999 duet session with harmonica player Brendan Power, played to all Peabody's strengths and is worth looking for.

*** Side By Slide
Appaloosa AP 156 *Peabody; Steve James (md, g); Mary Flower (g, v); Gypsy Dave Smith, Michael Messer (g). 03?*

Peabody here performs four songs each with four slide guitarists, also using a slide himself on numerous tracks. Those with Flower are the prettiest, especially the Memphis Minnie–Kansas Joe song 'You Got To Move Pt. 1', and those with Messer the most muscular; there's also an exhilarating, fast-fingered four-hander with James on Sylvester Weaver's 'Guitar Rag'. As usual, Peabody intersperses his own songs with some *recherché* selections from the blues library like Bobby Grant's 'Lonesome Atlanta Blues' and Lonnie Coleman's 'Old Rock Island Blues.' TR

Peg Leg Sam (1911–77)
VOCAL, HARMONICA

The wooden leg, a scar that dragged his mouth and eye towards what was left of his right ear and his ability to play two harps at once made Peg Leg Sam a striking figure. Born Arthur Jackson, he was already playing when he ran away from home aged 10; thereafter he hoboed compulsively even after losing his leg to a train in 1930, played in the streets and worked on medicine shows. As late as 1972, Sam was draw man for the last show still operating; it closed only when pitchman Chief Thundercloud died. Located by researchers in 1970, Sam mainly played blues festivals during his last years.

**** Kickin' It
[32 Jazz 32211] *Sam; Baby Tate (g, v); Henry Johnson (g, v).* 8/70–11/72.

His medicine-show background made Peg Leg Sam a dancer and raconteur as well as a musician. *Kickin' It* includes an 'Ode to Bad Bill' and the monologue 'Born In Hard Luck', but, amusing as they are, it's the music which makes one glad that Baby Tate held Sam in town until the folklorists Bruce Bastin and Pete Lowry got back. Peg Pete (as he was also known) was a gruff, gleefully extrovert singer, and one of the Carolinas' finest harmonica players, with a big, rich tone and total command of his instrument. Alongside the Blind Boy Fuller tunes and the expected but very fine display pieces, he marshalled material as venerable as 'Reuben' and 'Greasy Greens', and as surprising as Bo Diddley's 'Who Do You Love' and 'Nasty Old Trail', an instrumental version of 'Along The Navaho Trail'. Tate and Johnson, both longtime playing partners of Sam's, give excellent support.

***(*) Early In The Morning
Labor LAB 7009//Corazong 255029 *Sam; Louisiana Red (g, v).* 2/75.

'Navaho Trail' appears again, this time with a serious, surprisingly affecting vocal, and 'Fox Chase' is lightly disguised as 'Dog Chase', but elsewhere *Early In The Morning* valuably extends Sam's range. 'John Henry' and 'Poor Boy' are not unexpected, but both are forcefully done, as are two spirituals. There's some variability, however; Sam makes verbal slips on 'Mr. Ditty Wa Ditty' which another take would have corrected, and his accompaniment to Louisiana Red's 'Going Train Blues' is merely dutiful. When Red accompanies Sam, it's sometimes obvious that he's having trouble restraining his fondness for the dramatic, but he usually manages it. On 'Strollin'' his discreet, steady rhythm is crucial, giving Sam space to make a minor masterpiece of this meditation on crime and punishment. CS

Morris Pejoe (1924–82)
VOCAL, GUITAR

A singer and guitarist of the second rank, Morris Pejoe (originally Pejas) arrived in Chicago from Louisiana in 1951 and teamed up with pianist Henry Gray soon thereafter. He made two singles for Checker and others for Vee-Jay, Abco and Atomic-H over the next decade; other sessions with Gray remained unissued until the LP and CD eras. A final single was released in 1969 before Pejoe moved to Detroit, where he continued to work until his death from heart failure.

Contemporaries like Jimmy Dawkins maintained that Pejoe was a better live performer than his records indicated, which from the evidence could well be true.

Pejoe's 1952 debut recording, 'Tired Of Crying Over You', found on *Chess Blues Guitar 1949–1969* (MCA/Chess CHD2-9393), is a medium-paced, rather deliberate boogie with a simple, repetitive guitar riff serving as introduction, solo and coda. Pejoe's voice is plain and untutored, his lyrics familiar since this was a theme first recorded by Fats Domino the year before.

*** Wrapped In My Baby
Delmark DD-716 *Pejoe; Stanley Grim, unknown (as); unknown, unknown (ts); Henry Gray, unknown (p); Milton Rector, Andrew McMahon (b); Earl Phillips, unknown (d); band, unknown (v).* 12/54, 59/60.

Though mastered for release, the seven songs and one alternative take recorded in producer Al Smith's basement in 1954 have all the informality and rough sound quality of demo recordings. Pejoe's voice has improved a little but his guitar solos remain earthbound. The two takes of 'Let's Get High' (first recorded in 1951 by Grant 'Mr Blues' Jones) lurch alarmingly, the first so ramshackle that a voice intones 'ooooh shit!' at its end. 'May Bea' is an effective slow blues, already recorded for Checker and cut in 1956 for Abco as 'Maybe Blues'. Another vocalist, possibly Gray, tackles 'Move It On Out And Go', his piano on this and the other titles under-recorded, a fate not granted to drummer Phillips, who has some difficulty locating the offbeat. Both voice and guitar are stronger on 'You Gone Away' and 'She Walked Right In', an Atomic-H single that perhaps deserved better distribution. (The remainder of the CD is by Arthur 'Big Boy' Spires.)

The Abco single is on *Goin' Down To Eli's – The Cobra & Abco Rhythm & Blues Anthology 1956–1958* (Westside WESA 868) and *Abco Records* (Wolf 120.298). A more confident Pejoe lays down his instrument in favour of an unidentified guitarist, who makes significant contributions to both an up-tempo 'Screaming And Crying' and the medium-slow 'Maybe Blues'. The singer's voice has coarsened and, while he still lacks technique, there's a brash commercial edge to his performance. Two sides recorded in 1957/58 were not released at the time but issued on *Chicago Ain't Nothin' But A Blues Band* (Delmark DE-624): a nondescript rendition of 'Let's Get High' and a 'Baby I'm Lonely' that was a half-hearted (and half-tempoed) attempt to corral Little Richard to a Chicago backbeat. The musicians make their changes on time and provide lusty ensemble vocals on both tunes but neither is more than a pleasant curiosity. NS

Pinetop Perkins (born 1913)
VOCAL, PIANO

Born in Belzoni, Mississippi, Joe Willie Perkins played both piano and guitar, but had to give up the latter instrument in 1944, after his arm was slashed at a party. By then he'd worked on King Biscuit Time with Sonny Boy Williamson, and with Robert Nighthawk. Heading for Chicago in 1950, Perkins accompanied Nighthawk on Chess before joining Earl Hooker's band, who backed him at Sun in 1953 on the signature tune he'd borrowed from Pine Top Smith. Perkins went on to play in bands around East St Louis; in the late '60s he emerged from retirement, rejoining Earl Hooker before replacing Otis Spann in the Muddy Waters band. In 1980 he was among the musicians who left to form The Legendary Blues Band; since the late '80s he's been a solo act.

*** Pinetop Is Just Top
Black & Blue BB 424 *Perkins; Luther 'Guitar Jr' Johnson (g); Calvin Jones (b); Willie 'Big Eyes' Smith (d). 11/76.*
*** Boogie Woogie King
Evidence ECD 26011 *As above. 11/76.*

Record companies seem to be entranced by Perkins's longevity and his association with various greats. He can't be blamed for recording at the drop of a contract, and he didn't get to be Muddy's pianist without being good, but his playing is relatively simple and his singing seldom offers new insights into mostly familiar material.

These recordings were made during one of Muddy's European tours; Black & Blue's reissue is longer by two titles and an alternative take. Production is minimal, most of the songs are familiar and Jones and Smith are no more than efficient. Nevertheless, this is one of Perkins's better releases, thanks mainly to Luther Johnson's inventive guitar.

*(*) After Hours
Blind Pig BP 73088 *Perkins; Little Mike [Markowitz] (h); Tony O, Ronnie Earl (g); Brad Vickers (b); Pete DeCoste (d); band (v). 88.*

Tired material is a problem here, as it will continue to be; *After Hours* goes from 'Got My Mojo Working' to 'Pinetop's Boogie Woogie' via 'Hoochie Coochie Man' and 'Every Day I Have The Blues'. Bigger drawbacks, though, are muffled, bass-heavy sound and the band's utter lack of imagination, only emphasized by Ronnie Earl's guest spot on 'You Don't Have To Go'.

*** Chicago Blues Session Vol. 12
Wolf 120.858 *Perkins; Tim Taylor, Michael Strasser (d). 2/90.*

Perkins shares this CD with John Brim; accompanied only by good drummers (Taylor on four songs, Strasser on one), he plays and sings forcefully and with attention to detail.

*(*) Pinetop Perkins With The Blue Ice Band
Earwig CD 4934 *Perkins; Chicago Beau (h, v); Halldór Bragason (g, v); Guthmundur Pétursson (g); Haroldyr Thorsteinsson (b); Ásgeir Óskarsson (d). 11/91.*
*(*) Blues Legend
Prestige CDSGP 0292 *As above. 11/91.*
*(*) Got My Mojo Working
Blues Legends BLS 12242 *As above. 11/91.*

November nights in Reykjavik are very long; the Blue Ice Band's tasteless blues-rock must make them seem eternal. They're utterly inappropriate accompanists for Perkins. Earwig's tracklisting is slightly different from the other two, not that it matters.

** On Top
Deluge DELD 3002//Sky Ranch SR 652330 *Perkins; Jerry Portnoy (h); Ron Levy (o); David Maxwell (p); Peter Parcek, T. J. Wheeler, Charlie Baum, Paul Rishell (g); Michael 'Mudcat' Ward (b); Steve Ramsay (d); band (v). 1/92.*
*** Pinetop's Boogie Woogie
Antone's 74210 *Perkins; James Cotton, Kim Wilson (h); Matt Murphy, Derek O'Brien, Duke Robillard, Jimmy Rogers, Hubert Sumlin, Luther Tucker (g); Preston Hubbard, Calvin Jones, Bob Stroger (b); Fran Christina, Ted Harvey, Willie 'Big Eyes' Smith (d). 92?*

On Top's brief closing solo, 'Just A Gigolo', certainly escapes over-familiarity, but most of the time Perkins bumbles along, unable or unconcerned to show much enthusiasm. Ward and Ramsey are effective, and Portnoy is excellent on six tracks, but the guitarists are prone to grandstanding, egregiously so on 'Yancey Special', which starts a badly sagging central section; it's followed by a slapdash 'Four Hand Strut', the funereal ballad 'Since I Fell For You' and a tedious organ–piano duet.

Though not listed on the Antone's website, *Pinetop's Boogie Woogie* seems to be still available. It's the product of several sessions, featuring stellar bands who often goad Perkins into the enthusiasm that *On Top* lacks; his singing, in particular, has a lot more grit than usual. The budget for guitarists alone must have been considerable; Sumlin's contribution to 'High Heel Sneakers' (his only appearance) is nugatory, but Robillard is excellent and Jimmy Rogers is fired up by Kim Wilson's re-creations of Little Walter. James Cotton has an equally good time sparring with Murphy, whose bop-influenced solo on the title track is eye-poppingly inventive.

**(*) Portrait Of A Delta Bluesman
Omega OCD 3017 *Perkins. 93?*

This CD is conceived as a musical autobiography, with the songs broken up by brief anecdotes. Alone, Perkins naturally has to work a bit harder, especially with his left hand, and although several tunes are recycled, not for the first or last time, he digs out some new ones, including a pleasant 'Chains Of Love' and a good 'Come Back Baby'. There are drawbacks, though; 'Forty Four' is beyond his technique, and the first chorus of 'Chicago Stomp' is in two keys at once.

** Live Top
Deluge DELD 3010 *Perkins; David Gill (h, v); Dan Lacasse (h); Jake Isaacson (p, sp); Doug Wainoris (g); Jack Tukey (b); 'Bongo' Bob Noyes (d). 10/94.*
**(*) Live At Antone's Vol. 1
Antone's TMG-ANT 0045 *Perkins; Kaz Kazanoff (ts); Kim Wilson (h); Rusty Zinn (g); Calvin Jones (b); Willie 'Big Eyes' Smith (d). 7/95.*
***(*) Sweet Black Angel
Verve 537 187 *Perkins; Kaz Kazanoff (ts, h, v); [Sax] Gordon Beadle (bs, v); Bob Margolin (g, v); Duke Robillard (g); Calvin Jones (b); Willie 'Big Eyes' Smith (d); Jay Newland (v). 6–7/96.*

On *Live Top* the Blue Flames, and Gill in particular, are competent and tactful, but once again the material is too familiar; the CD preserves one more spark-free payday. *Live At Antone's Vol. 1* (there doesn't seem to be a Vol. 2) is a bit better; the band are more than competent, even managing to enliven 'Got My Mojo Working', and their affection for Perkins is obvious. Kazanoff's solos are a treat, but the songs are the same old same old, and Perkins's singing is constricted.

There are sparks aplenty on *Sweet Black Angel*, with Perkins invigorated by a fat-toned sax section and his former colleagues in the Waters band. The producer's apparent insistence on new material also pays off, although 'Five Long Years' sneaks in and 'Down The Road I'll Go' is 'You Don't Have To Go'. The notes say that Perkins 'plays a little guitar,' presumably referring to 'Look On Yonder Wall', where it's the only instrument, clearly played by Margolin. Perkins's playing and singing owe some of their strength to Vince Caro's peerless engineering skills, but this is unquestionably his best CD.

In the mid-'90s Perkins also recorded *Solitaire* (Lunacy 77732), which only seems to be available direct from the company, and *Eye To Eye* with Ronnie Earl (q.v.).

(*) Down In Mississippi
HMG HMG 1004 Perkins. 10/96–10/97.
(*) Heritage Of The Blues
Hightone HCD 8159 Perkins. 10/96–10/97.

Recorded at home, Perkins takes a relaxed stroll around his musical domain. Once again, the performances are mostly acceptable (although 'Pinetop's Piano Shuffle' is a very rusty reprise of 'Just A Gigolo'), but seldom exciting. It's obvious that Pinetop can keep doing the same old songs in his sleep; in ours too. Hightone issue the complete sessions, adding laidback and not entirely error-free versions of 'Kansas City' and 'Everyday I Have The Blues'.

(*) Born In The Delta
Telarc CD-83418 Perkins; Jerry Portnoy (h); Tony O (g); Brad Vickers (b); Willie 'Big Eyes' Smith (d). 11/96.

This is an enhanced CD; the computer-equipped gain videos of an interview and the title track. 'Born In The Delta' is a rather good solo blues; if only Pinetop didn't sign off with 'Jingle Bells'. He does the same at the end of seven brain-destroying minutes of 'Baby, What You Want Me To Do?' That penultimate track is where *Born In The Delta* starts to run out of steam; until then Perkins is unwontedly lively, thanks to determined pushing by the musicians. (Credit where it's due: Tony O is greatly improved since the Blind Pig days.)

** **Legends**
Telarc CD-83446 Perkins; Annie Rishell (h, v); Hubert Sumlin, Doug Wainoris (g, v); Rod Carey (b); Per Hanson (d, perc). 5/98.

The other legend is Sumlin, another ex-sideman on whom the mantle of leader has often sat uneasily. Of Perkins's numbers, only 'Come Back Baby' is worth hearing; 'Got My Mojo Working', sung in duet with Sumlin, is excruciating, and the umpteenth recording of 'Sunnyland Slim' (an adaptation of Memphis Slim's 'Grinder Man') is extruded to interminable length.

(*) Live At 85!
Shanachie 9022 Perkins; Tim Clark (ts); 'Donnie C.' Castellow (bs); George Kilby Jr (g, v); Lee Marvin (b); Eric Halvorson (d); band (v). 7/98.

Quite often the band are carrying Perkins, but it only becomes obvious when 'Look On Yonder's Wall' gets a very shaky solo intro. Of all things, 'Hoochie Coochie Man' is compelling, with the saxes making the stop time riffs darkly ominous, and Perkins singing as if the lyrics were new to him, but the CD is patchy; the horns add beef, but the rest of the band seem reluctant to cut loose, Pinetop rambles on a couple of slow blues, and the backing vocals on 'Down In Mississippi' are comically robotic.

*** **Back On Top**
Telarc CD-83489 Perkins; Sugar Ray Norcia (h); Corey Harris (g, perc); Denny Breau (g); Michael 'Mudcat' Ward (b); Per Hanson (d). 7/99.

The accompanists' polished musicianship can't save 'Down In Mississippi' from intrinsic dullness, and the woodblock on 'Just A Little Bit' doesn't work. Still, this semi-acoustic set is exceptionally well recorded, and Perkins's singing and playing have great presence. 'Pinetop's Blues' is a fine, reflective closer, and Harris and Hanson's drive makes 'Pinetop's Boogie' the best version, if not since Sun in 1953, then at least since 1992 and Antone's.

One Heart (Geographic GR 9901), a set of instrumental duets with Michael Parrish, recorded c. 1999, had very limited distribution.

(*) Ladies Man [sic]
M.C. MC-0053 Perkins; Jerry Vivino (ts); Willie 'Big Eyes' Smith (h, d, v); Lisa Otey, Marcia Ball, Ann Rabson (p); Deborah Coleman, Susan Tedeschi, 'Ms. Carmen Getit', Madeleine Peyroux (g, v); Jimmy Vivino, Elvin Bishop (g); Bob Stroger (b, v); Ron Perry, Brad Vickers (b); Mark Carpentieri, Kenny Smith (d); Ruth Brown, Odetta (v). 5/03–3/04.

Ladies Man contains 11 collaborations with female musicians, plus Angela Strehli's 'Hey Mr. Pinetop Perkins', which peddles the nonsense that he wrote 'Pine Top's Boogie Woogie'. Perkins broke an arm part-way through the project, and consequently either plays piano or (on four live tracks) sings. His voice is small and scratchy, but pretty good for a nonagenarian. Within its no-frills limits, his playing is also pretty good; at times the bands have to slow down to stay with him, and he's hesitant when duetting with Ann Rabson on 'Careless Love'. On the other hand, his playing on 'Pinetop's New Boogie Woogie', though somewhat slapdash, quite overwhelms Marcia Ball. Susan Tedeschi sings sharp, Odetta hams it up on 'Trouble In Mind', and Ruth Brown is self-regardingly raucous on an interminable 'Chains Of Love'. Deborah Coleman's sulky 'Meanest Woman' and Madeleine Peyroux's jazzy 'He's Got Me Going' are the best tracks on a CD which has its disappointments, but at least (Strehli apart) confines the sentimental sycophancy to its notes. CS

Bill Perry
VOCAL, GUITAR

Like Charlie Parker and Jimi Hendrix, Perry's heritage is half Afro-American and half Native American, and he grew up listening to blues and gospel. Born and raised in New York, he was an early starter on the guitar, following his influences of Cream, Hendrix, Freddie King and Curtis Mayfield. As a teenager he sneaked into blues clubs to jam with local musicians, later starting his own band and eventually joining Richie Havens, with whom he spent four years on the road before releasing his first album in 1994. Perry is currently regarded as one of America's most exhilarating new bluesmen.

** **High Octane**
Car Wash CWR 1001 Perry; Jeremy Baum (o); Dean Scala (g); Johnny B. Gayden (b); Papa John Mole (d); Paul Orofino (co-prod). 11/98.

*** Fire It Up
Blind Pig BPCD 5069 Perry; Jimmy Vivino (o, md, g, v, co-prod); David Bennett Cohen (p); Johnny B. Gayden, Jerry Vasilatos (b); Rob Curtis (d); Frank Pagano (perc); Paul Orofino (co-prod). 01.

High Octane, credited to The Bill Perry Band, was recorded at Manny's Car Wash, a renowned New York blues club. It's everything you'd expect from a run-of-the-mill blues-rock outfit – extended instrumentals with an energy that struggles to recover exhausted cover versions ('Johnny B. Goode', 'Little Wing', 'Watchtower'); so much so that the artist's own, weaker compositions fit into the set unnoticeably. Perry's voice bites less here than on later releases, and his fuzzy guitar tone supports a style overshadowed by countless other axemen in the genre, so that although always sounding assured it fails to emboss, as do the innocuous sonic contours set by his accompanists. His Blind Pig debut is immediately better: more tight blues, less loose rock. 'Itchin' For It' kick-starts the proceedings with a suitably nagging Slim Harpo groove, and Perry's voice is now identified clearly. His low growl is complemented by the sparkling addition of Jimmy Vivino, whose sweeping guitar flashes and writing and production contributions are crucial. At times the songs' nuclei don't present a blues stemming outwards, but those chordal and structural diversions are often given the familiar coating of pentatonic scales and beckoning solos. A climax is arguably reached in the latter half, with Perry's forceful numbers 'Thinkin' Of You' and 'G & L Jump', and later the chiming boogie woogie of 'Heaven In A Pontiac' and the acoustic slide closer 'Cheatin' Blues', all of which are as bluesy as they come.

*** Crazy Kind Of Life
Blind Pig BPCD 5078 Perry; Chris O'Leary (h); Jimmy Vivino (o, p, g, v, co-prod); Jeremy Baum (o); David Bennett Cohen (p); Richie Havens (g, v); Tim Tindall, Johnny B. Gayden (b); Rob Curtis (d); Frank Pagano (perc); Paul Orofino (co-prod). 02.

***(*) Raw Deal
Blind Pig BPCD 5093 Perry; Dave Keyes (o); Popa Chubby (g, v, prod); John Redden (g); Tim Tindall (b); Rob Curtis (d); Galea (v). 04.

In *Crazy Kind Of Life* the songwriting is again split between Perry and Vivino and, although it gets off to a subdued start, 'Too Hot' is just that, followed by B. B. Kingesque fills in the croakily delivered 'Honey Pie'. Beside sweet piano, Perry's dextrous soloing makes 'Morning Spiritual' a marvellous instrumental, and the ghostly voice of old pal Richie Havens guesting on the Rolling Stones' 'No Expectations' contributes to a standout final track. This album and its successor are marked by a blues-funk-rock blend, but you can choose between the pleasantly restrained, medium-throttle excursions here or turn to *Raw Deal* to hear more gas being added to the engine.

New York legend Popa Chubby produced Perry's latest and the vibe throughout is most definitely 'in house', its sound redolent of an inner-city music factory. Perry's guitar runs are at their zippiest, his gruff vocal timbre hinting at barroom excess and Tom Waits (whose 'Til The Money Runs Out' he covers), his songs as expressive as the gritty energy with which they are presented. One of several highlights, 'Harlem Child', blows out in your face with a Led Zeppish thunder riff and bruised funk overdubs as Perry confesses with a conscience, 'There's no one else to ask for living on these Harlem streets.' Shades of Hendrix, Perry's furry Gibson Les Paul tone, and snappy drums and a Hammond organ layering a velvety background call to mind a similar and excellent New York outfit, Michael Hill's Blues Mob. As *Raw Deal* burns on, some might find the seesawing structures of vocal/solo/vocal/solo a little tiring, but towards the end 'Man On The Side' has a neat trick up its sleeve. RR

King Perry (born 1920)
VOCAL, ALTO AND TENOR SAXOPHONES, CLARINET

Oliver King Perry, from Gary, Indiana, learned several instruments as a boy but in his teens settled on the reed family. By his early 20s he was leading his own band in Detroit and Chicago. Stranded in LA after a tour in 1945, the band quickly found a following there and began recording. By 1950 Perry was popular enough to have his own TV show, but by the end of the decade he had quit the music business to go into real estate. He retired in the '80s and is reported to be playing again.

**(*) King Perry 1945–1949
Classics 5081 Perry; Maxie Ward, Norman Bowden, unknown (t); George 'Happy' Johnson, Ralph Bowden, unknown (tb); unknowns (ts); Jeep Underwood, Walter Fleming, Earl Payton, unknown (p); Ike Brown, Wes Prince, unknowns (b); Dan Graves, Joe Harris, Al Wichard, unknowns (d); unknowns (v). 7/45–4/49.

**(*) King Perry 1950–1954
Classics 5129 Perry; Maxie Ward, unknown (t); Ralph Bowman, unknown (tb); unknown(s) (ts); Joe Dietrichson (bs); Fletcher Smith, poss. Earl Payton, Jimmy Beasly, unknown (p); Chuck Norris, unknown (g); Ike Brown, Vic Greenwood, unknown (b); Daviel Graves, Al Wichard, unknown(s) (d); The Riders, band (v). 2/50–c. 54.

Perry never had any hits, which seems explicable when you listen to his first couple of years' recordings, which are littered with slightly dated arrangements of standards like 'The Man I Love' and 'Laughing At Life' – but then he hit form in a sequence of 1948 sides for Excelsior, such as 'Keep A Dollar In Your Pocket' and 'Hold Your Gold', homilies in the Louis Jordan style, and 'The Ice Man', a recasting of an old joke. The general approach may have been based on Roy Milton's but, thanks to Perry's exuberant singing and pungent blowing on alto and tenor, and the strong bass playing, the band always sounds cheerful and involved. This is equally true of the 1950 Specialty and 1953 RPM recordings on the second Classics, and the listener begins to wonder why these buoyant and well-executed sides are not more highly rated. Perhaps part of the answer is that Perry liked to diversify his blues vocals with performances in the florid style of Cab Calloway, like 'I Ain't Got A Dime To My Name' (1950–1954) or his jive reinterpretation of 'Stardust' (1945–1949). Both albums contain quite a few three-star tracks but the rating is reduced on the first by the corn and on the second by novelties like 'The Animal Song' and 'I Must Have Been An Ugly Baby', which opens with a minute of rather terrible standup. TR

Lucky Peterson (born 1963)
VOCAL, GUITAR, ORGAN, PIANO, KEYBOARDS

Peterson was playing drums at three, and by five was featuring on organ at his musician father's club in Buffalo. This brought

him to Willie Dixon's attention, and a single and LP led to appearances on national television. The 'five year old genius' was a nine days' wonder, but Lucky was Little Milton's musical director at 17, and at 20 was featured keyboardist with Bobby Bland. He went solo in 1988.

*** **Ridin'**
Evidence ECD 26033 *Peterson; Melvin Taylor (g); Titus Williams (b); Ray Allison (d). 3/84.*

(*) **Lucky Strikes!
Alligator ALCD 4770 *Peterson; Sylvester Polk (t); Bill Samuel (ts, bs); Ernie Lancaster, Bryan Bassett (g); Bob Greenlee (b); Scott Corwin, Denny Best (d); Vycki Walls, Nadine Brown, Donna Staples (v). 88.*

*** **Triple Play**
Alligator ALCD 4789 *Peterson; Sylvester Polk, Bruce Staelens (t); Ray Anderson (tb); Bill Samuel (ts); Bob Greenlee (bs, b); Ernie Lancaster, Bryan Bassett, George Taylor (g); Dale Harton (b); William Pell Pinner III, Jim Payne (d); Lester Chambers (v). 89.*

Given Lucky's early start, 'juvenilia' isn't quite the word for these three CDs, but they are the work of an artist still finding a voice of his own. On *Ridin'*, cut on tour in France, Peterson plays organ and piano, leaving the flamboyant guitar work to Taylor, who also recorded an LP that day. Despite the haste, and an almost total reliance on overworked standards copped from Jimmy Reed, Booker T. & The MGs, Willie Dixon, B. B. King and Bobby Bland, this is a pleasant CD: there's a jazzy ambience to the arrangements ('Baby What You Want Me To Do' gets a notably fresh treatment), the rhythm section is solid, Lucky sings without the strain sometimes apparent on later releases, and his organ work is fiery, if obviously indebted to Jimmy Smith and Jack McDuff.

The best thing about *Lucky Strikes* is its obviously titled title track, another jazz-tinged organ workout. Elsewhere the guitarist owes a lot to Albert Collins and Little Milton, and something to Jimi Hendrix. He also cranks up the vocal power, presumably intending, usually without much success, to convey emotional intensity. 'Louder and rockier' are the watchwords here, a process exemplified by the two obnoxious drummers, one of whom aspires to sound like a rivet-gun orchestra. All tracks are written or co-written by producer and bassist Bob Greenlee, whose lyrics sometimes deserve better treatment than they get.

Triple Play is cut from similar cloth, but is more successful, thanks in part to somewhat more subtle drummers (who are also mixed a bit lower). 'Six O'Clock Blues' and 'Locked Out Of Love' have clever lyrics, and Wilson Pickett's vocal delivery and Robert Ward's guitar obbligatos are stirringly revived on 'I Found A Love', but too many songs are generic vehicles for guitar gymnastics, vanishing without trace as soon as they're over. 'Funky Ray' is a vehicle for Anderson's tiresome trombone gymnastics.

***(*) **Double Dealin'**
Blue Thumb 314 549 475 *Peterson; Darrell Leonard (t, trombonium); Joe Sublett (ts); Jon Cleary (kb); Johnny Lee Schell, John Porter (g); Reggie McBride (b); Tony Braunagel (d); Tamara Peterson (v). 7/00.*

Between 1992 and 2000 Peterson released six CDs on Universal's Verve, EmArcy and Blue Thumb imprints, of which *Double Dealin'* appears to be the only survivor. The difference a decade makes is noticeable. Voice and guitar are more comfortable with each other, although the priority accorded to loudness means that at times they both aim for ardour and arrive at anonymity, and the songs are selected for quality rather than publishing income. The soul and rock influences are considerable – some may think them excessive – and it's a pity that Peterson's organ playing is usually ancillary to his guitar; but it must be conceded that he's his own man, putting his stamp on all the songs (hear, for instance, the reinvigoration of his old boss Bobby Bland's 'Ain't Doin' Too Bad') and hiring musicians who can articulate his musical visions.

** **Black Midnight Sun**
Birdology FDM 36623 *Peterson; Graham Haynes (c); Henry Threadgill (fl); Alex J. Harding (bs); Bill Laswell (b); Jesse Dulman (tu); Jerome 'Bigfoot' Brailey (d). 3–4/02.*

With a former P-Funk drummer, jazz flautist Henry Threadgill's horn arrangements and Bill Laswell producing, this is certainly different. Despite its origins on the notorious *Electric Mud*, 'Herbert Harper's Free Press News' turns out to be a strong song, and Syl Johnson's gloomy 'Is It Because I'm Black?' gets a churchy makeover; but the presence between them of Mick Jagger's smirking pastiche 'Lucky In Love' bodes ill. Much of *Black Midnight Sun* is too far up itself for words, as indeed is 'Black Midnight Sun', doubtless the only cover of David Sylvian in this book. The nadir is 'Smokestack Lightning' with wah-wah bass and flute. It didn't work in 1968; somewhere the Wolf's shade is growling, 'Still dogshit!' It's hard to believe that Jerry Ragovoy wrote the numbingly repetitious 'She's A Burglar', and covers of James Brown and Sly Stone shamble flabbily after their progenitors. Lucky's spiritual 'Truly Your Friend' is moving, and his 'Change Your Ways' is gutsy, but they aren't enough.

*** **If You Can't Fix It**
JSP JSP 5100 *Peterson; James Finegan (t); Robert Feiner (ts); unknown (h); Bruce Feiner (p); James Peterson (g, v); Jennie Feiner, Clarence Spady (g); Mike Nunno (b); Trevor Somerville, Jason Arnold (d); Mary Taylor (v). 04.*

The artist credit here is to James & Lucky Peterson, and it's dad who snarls his gravelly way through the vocals, huskily assisted by Mary Taylor on the soulful 'Time To Go'. No one could call James one of the blues' great singers, but he's more expressive than Lucky, with more power in reserve. Both from this angle and, more positively, from listening to the terse but torrid playing on *If You Can't Fix It*, it's hard not to conclude that Lucky's ability on his various instruments is his longer suit. James is a songwriter of some originality, with a cynical cast of mind and no time for conventional wisdom: 'Cripple Man' wastes no pity on crack addicts, and 'Never Take Sand To The Beach' eulogizes separate vacations, improbably lifting the tune of 'Killing Floor' to do so. CS

Alabama Jr Pettis (1932–88)
VOCAL, GUITAR

Also known as Daddy Rabbit, Coleman Pettis was born in Alabama, and learned guitar at the age of eight. Moving to Chicago in 1959, he played bass with Little Walter and guitar for Lee Jackson, J. B. Hutto and others. In 1973 he began a

ten-year stint with Magic Slim, his precise but imaginative rhythm guitar an essential ingredient in the sound of The Teardrops.

***(*) **Nora Lee**
Wolf 120.850 *Pettis; Christian Dozzler, Daniel Gugolz (p); John Primer (g, v); Magic Slim (g); Nick Holt (b); Timothy Taylor (d). 2/87.*

Like his old boss, Lee Jackson, Pettis was reliable, original and usually to be found hard at work behind better-known musicians. On his only CD, he's backed by permutations of The Teardrops, with occasional assistance from visiting European pianists. On two tracks, Pettis reverts to his customary role of second guitarist as his successor, John Primer, leads the band; the CD is completed by 'Bad Luck', with Magic Slim on vocals and no contribution at all by Pettis. The lurching power of *Nora Lee* will be familiar from many a Magic Slim CD, but Wolf do well to spotlight a musician whose stylish web of harmonies tied the Teardrops' sound together, but was not always as highly regarded as it should have been. Pettis's singing is occasionally a little strident as he tries to match up to the instrumental earth tremors going on around him. CS

Robert Petway
VOCAL, GUITAR

Like his playing partner Tommy McClennan, Petway was born near Yazoo City, Mississippi, perhaps around 1908. Honeyboy Edwards remembers meeting the pair in Greenwood, Mississippi, about 1930. Petway probably followed his friend to Chicago, where he recorded, but after that his trail disappears.

*** **Mississippi Blues Vol. 3 (1936–1942)**
Document DOCD-5671 *Petway; Alfred Elkins (b); Tommy McClennan (v, sp). 3/41–2/42.*
*** **Mississippi Blues (1935–1951)**
Wolf WBCD-005 *As above. 3/41–2/42.*
** **Cotton Pickin' Blues**
Acrobat ACRCD 188 *As above. 3/41–2/42.*

In his gruff, unpolished singing, stomping guitar playing and fondness for asides like 'Play 'em, man, play 'em a long time', Petway greatly resembles Tommy McClennan. His 'Catfish Blues', perhaps the finest of all recordings of this popular theme, and 'Ride 'Em On Down' have close relatives in McClennan's 'Deep Blue Sea Blues' and 'New "Shake 'Em On Down"'. Altogether their combined work is one of the most striking examples of musical kinship in the blues. The blood-brother pact is sealed, you might say, in the vivacious 'Boogie Woogie Woman', where they divide the vocal between them. The Document and Wolf CDs both contain all Petway's 14 sides. (So does the VAC *Big Joe Williams And The Stars Of Mississippi Blues* [JSP JSP 7719 5CD].) The Document, which has fractionally better transfer quality (though several tracks are from poor 78s), is rounded off with the complete recordings of Sonny Boy Nelson (Eugene Powell) and Mississippi Matilda, the Wolf with six early tracks by Robert Lockwood and four by the obscure Mississippi singer/guitarist Otto Virgial, whose untidy but strongly individual blues are full of echoes of J. D. Short or, in the case of 'Bad Notion Blues', Charley Patton. The Acrobat CD scatters seven of Petway's recordings, variably remastered, amidst 18 of McClennan's. TR

Kelly Joe Phelps (born 1959)
VOCAL, GUITAR

Phelps's interest in the blues was kindled by hearing records of Fred McDowell and Robert Pete Williams. Before that the Washington-born musician had played jazz and taught guitar, banjo and mandolin in schools. His album Roll Away The Stone *attracted attention far beyond the Northwest, particularly among admirers of the contemplative guitar music of John Fahey and Leo Kottke.*

*** **Lead Me On**
Burnside BCD-0015 *Phelps. 94?*
*** **Roll Away The Stone**
Rykodisc RCD-10393 *Phelps. winter 96.*

Now sullenly introverted, now sunlit with religious faith, Phelps's songs evoke by turns the pathology of Skip James and the theology of Blind Willie Johnson. Both men are among the models for his brooding guitar, sometimes finger-fretted, sometimes played with a shimmering slide. Unlike *Lead Me On*, *Roll Away The Stone* is weighted with as much gospel as blues, offering a lovely reading of 'When The Roll Is Called Up Yonder' and an eerie 'See That My Grave Is Kept Clean'. Both albums have an air of monkish contemplation, intensified on *Roll Away The Stone* by the intimate recording. This is hard music to find a term for, but it is easy to be gripped in its sinuous coils and tranquil mystery.

(***) **Shine Eyed Mister Zen**
Rykodisc RCD 10476 *Phelps; unknown (h). 99?*
(**) **Sky Like A Broken Clock**
Rykodisc RCD 10612 *Phelps; Jim Fitting (h); Dinty Childs (ac, o); Tom West (o); David Henry (vc); Larry Taylor (b); Billy Conway (d, perc). 2/01.*

Two songs on *Shine Eyed Mister Zen* are derived from recordings by old-time musicians with a leaning towards the blues, 'Dock Boggs Country Blues' and Frank Hutchison's 'Train Carried My Girl From Town'. These and the traditional ballad 'House Carpenter' interleave a programme of original songs, with a bluesy harmonica part on 'Piece By Piece'. The set finishes with a 'Goodnight Irene' as peaceful as an evening raga. Phelps's drift away from received repertoire is much more pronounced on *Sky Like A Broken Clock*, where he exchanges the plain-speaking of blues and gospel for enigmatic tales from a private world of the imagination. The total effect – maintained on his subsequent recordings *Slingshot Professionals* (Rykodisc RCD 10633) and *Tap The Real Cane Whirlwind* (Rykodisc RCD 10801) – is still singular but may hold less appeal for listeners who prefer a more palpable connection with familiar traditions. TR

Brewer Phillips (1924/25–99)
VOCAL, GUITAR

Phillips was best known as the rhythm guitarist in Hound Dog Taylor's Houserockers. Born in north Mississippi, he played in that region before moving to Chicago in his mid-30s. He soon joined Taylor and played with him and drummer Ted Harvey for some 15 years, developing his own career, such as it was, with occasional recordings for small labels.

** **Well Alright**
Black Rose 1017 *Phillips; Hound Dog Taylor, J. B. Hutto, Cub*

Koda, Louis Myers (g); Mark Harris (b); Ted Harvey, Leroy Pina (d). 72–80s.
(*) Good Houserockin'
Wolf 120.608 Phillips; Mike Allen (p); J. B. Hutto, Cub Koda, Steve Plair (g); Mark Harris, Right Hand Frank (b); Ted Harvey (d). 3/77–6/82.

Phillips's presence in the Houserockers, whether behind Hound Dog Taylor or later stand-ins like J. B. Hutto or Cub Koda, was exuberant, gnarly and unmistakable. It's most faithfully documented on Taylor's recordings; his own albums are less satisfactory, since they necessarily highlight his rasping vocals and run-of-the-mill material. The better of these two is *Good Houserockin'*, though with other players grabbing their share of the action you hear less of Phillips's rugged guitar than you might expect. The original studio-recorded LP, *Ingleside Blues*, has been expanded with half a dozen live tracks with Hutto; Phillips sings better on these, but the sound is poor. *Well Alright* is a ragbag of tracks, several of which can be found on Wolf CDs by Taylor, Hutto and Koda. The sound is generally mediocre. If you're anxious to know what Phillips sounded like when fronting a band, these CDs will give you some idea, but neither can be conscientiously described as entertaining.

*** Homebrew
Delmark DE-686 Phillips; Aaron Moore (p, v); Willie Black (b); 'Huckleberry Hound' [Robert Wright] (d). 6/95.

When Phillips finally had the chance to record under favourable conditions he was perhaps too old or rusty to take full advantage of it. He plays well enough, and with sturdy support from Black and Wright generates a driving rhythm, but he manages to sing on only three numbers. The rest are handled by pianist Moore, here gaining his first exposure to an international audience and revealing a nice oldfashioned touch and taste, sometimes reminiscent of early Memphis Slim. The third star of the rating is at least half his. (A month later he returned to the studio to cut a Delmark album of his own.) TR

Little Esther Phillips (1935–84)
VOCAL

Esther May Jones was born in Houston but in 1949 moved with her mother to LA. 'Man,' Johnny Otis murmured when he first heard the 14-year-old singer, 'that little girl's got a great feeling.' He hired her to sing with his band and from 1949 to 1953 wrote and produced her records, which included several hits like 'Double Crossing Blues'. Dissatisfied with her royalties, 'Little Esther' left Otis and LA and relocated in New York, where her career was shackled by heroin addiction. In the '60s, now billed as Esther Phillips, she had numerous hits for Atlantic, pre-eminently 'Release Me', and in the following decade she achieved some success in the disco arena with 'What A Diff'rence A Day Makes'.

(*) Little Esther 1951–1952
Classics 5066 Phillips; Don Johnson, Gerald Wilson (t); George Washington, Alfred Cobbs, John Pettigrew (tb); Floyd Turnham, Curtis Lowe (as, bs); Earle Warren, Preston Love (as); Lorenzo Holden, Ben Webster (ts); Walter Henry (bs); Devonia Williams (p); Pete Lewis (g); Mario Delagarde (b); Leard Bell (d); The Dominoes (Clyde McPhatter, Charlie White, Joe Lamont, Bill Brown), Mel Walker (v). 1/51–1/52.

(*) Little Esther 1952–1953
Classics 5147 Phillips; Don Johnson (t); George Washington (tb); Eli Wolinsky (as, ts); James Von Streeter, Rufus Gore, unknowns (ts); Fred Ford, unknown (bs); Little Willie Littlefield (p, v); Devonia Williams, Hank Marr, unknown (p); Pete Lewis, John Faire, Mickey Baker (g); Mario Delagarde, Albert Winston, Clarence Mack, unknown (b); Leard Bell, Calvin Shields, unknown (d); Johnny Otis (vb); Bobby Nunn, unknowns (v). 7/52–9/53.

As a teenager Little Esther sounded a little like Dinah Washington's kid sister, her voice narrow in range, thin-textured, sulky but sexy. Her earliest recordings like 'Double Crossing Blues' are most accessible on Johnny Otis CDs (q.v.); Classics' first disc picks up a year or so later, when she had earned primary billing. Ballads like 'Don't Make A Fool Out Of Me' sometimes expose her inexperience, but in come-hither blues like 'Aged And Mellow' or 'I'm A Bad, Bad Girl' she's on home ground, as tangy and distinctive as the anchovy on a pizza. A mixed topping of blues and ballads is served again on 1952–1953, which completes her Federal output and makes a start on the Deccas. She duets feistily with Little Willie Littlefield on 'Last Laugh Blues' and 'Turn The Lamps Down Low' and covers 'Hound Dog', a terrier to Big Mama Thornton's mastiff, but after these vigorous performances the Decca sides seem lightweight. Her later recordings are beyond our scope. TR

Gene Phillips (1915–90)
VOCAL, GUITAR

Phillips played in bands in his hometown of St Louis and elsewhere in the '30s, both on electric guitar and on lap steel, which he was taught by Floyd Smith. Arriving in LA in 1942 as the guitarist with the Mills Brothers, he remained there to work with Lorenzo Flennoy's trio and later led his own group, recording prolifically for Modern. Personal problems forced his career into decline in the '50s.

(*) Drinkin' And Stinkin'
Ace CDCHM 894 Phillips; Jake Porter, Sammy Yates, unknown(s) (t); Marshall Royal, unknown(s) (as); Maxwell Davis, Jack McVea, unknown(s) (ts); unknowns (bs); Lloyd Glenn, Lee Jones, unknown(s) (p); Arthur Edwards, Bill Davis, Clarence Jones, unknown(s) (b); William Streets, Al Wichard, Charles Thompson, unknown(s) (d); band (v). 9/46–50.
*** Swinging The Blues
Ace CDCHD 746 As above. 47–50.

'Snuff dippin' mama, your bottom lip hangs too low …' You don't find too many songs that begin like that these days, but once you enter the '40s West Coast world of Gene Phillips you hear a lot of feisty jive. The obvious model for his good-humoured taunts ('Punkin' Headed Woman') and street-corner philosophy ('To Each His Own, Brother') is Louis Jordan, and the similarity is accentuated by the crisp horn settings and solos from Porter, Royal, Davis and McVea. At least some of these, and McVea for sure, solo forcefully on 'Gene Jumps The Blues', which employs the bop riff from 'Salt Peanuts'. As a guitarist Phillips is less advanced than his contemporary T-Bone Walker, but note the agile playing on 'Jumpin' With Lloyd', the mellow blues picking in 'My Baby's Mistreatin' Me' and the electric steel of 'Gene's Guitar Blues', his version of Floyd Smith's 'Floyd's Guitar Blues'. 'Honky Tonk Train' is a feature for pianist Lloyd Glenn.

All the specified tracks are on *Swinging The Blues*. *Drinkin' And Stinkin'* is drawn from the same period and has a similar blend of material, including a spirited version of Big Bill Broonzy's 'Just A Dream', but some of the source discs or tapes are quite noisy, whereas the recording quality of *Swinging The Blues* is, for the period, outstanding, making the latter definitely the first CD to get. TR

Piano Red (1911–85)
VOCAL, PIANO

William Lee Perryman was born in Hampton, Georgia, a much younger brother of pianist Rufus Perryman, alias Speckled Red. He made a living from music in the '30s, but was less successful in the wartime and early postwar years. His career was reenergized by the hit single 'Rockin' With Red' (1950) and over the next 15 years he had further chart entries like 'Jump Man Jump' (1955) and the novelty song 'Dr Feel-Good' (1961), after which he changed his billing to 'Dr Feelgood & The Interns'. He had his own radio show on Atlanta's WAOK, and was in great demand for college fraternity parties. In 1969 he began playing on week-nights at Muhlenbrink's Saloon in the Underground Atlanta tourist complex, an engagement he filled for ten years. He also made several visits to Europe in the '70s and '80s.

*** The Doctor's In!
Bear Family BCD 15685 4CD *Piano Red; Willie Mays, John Peek, George Tidwell II (t); L. Johnson (as); Budd Johnson, Buddy Lucas, Clyde 'Blow Top' Lynn (ts); Ben Smith (bs); D. Hudson Jr, F. Taylor, 'Big Al' Sears, Charlie O'Kane, Horace Prayor, Boots Randolph, Andrew Goodrich, Johnny Williams, Alfred Wilson (s); Grady Martin (o); Elliot Lawrence (p); Curtis Smith, Roy Lee Johnson Jr (g, v); Wesley Jackson, René Hall, Mary Osborne, Skeeter Best, Kenny Burrell, Leroy Kirkland, Carl Lynch, Eddie Thomas, George Adams, Beverly Watkins, Leroy Tukes, Rudolph Moore, Albert White, unknowns (g); William Jones, George 'Kid' Miller, Charles Holloway Jr, Doles Dickens, Edward Small, Russ Saunders, Milt Hinton, Willie Dixon, Tommy LeGon, Howard 'Long John' Hobbs, Bobby McCrary (b); William Green, Willie Harper, J. Williams, F. M. Hawkins, L. Lawson, Charlie Smith, James C. Jackson, Marty Wilson, James Osie Johnson, Gus Johnson, Marion Booker, Bobby Lee Tuggle, March Maxey Jr, unknown (d); The Four Students, Bertha Colbert, Daniel Andrews Jr, William Glover, Christine Spencer, Samuel Williams (v). 7/50–3/66.*

This boxed set of 122 tracks will please devotees of Piano Red, or of completeness for its own sake, but anyone else would probably be content with a well-selected single CD. Unfortunately there isn't one, so access to this period of Red's work can only be got on these lavish terms. The first CD, from the early '50s, epitomizes much of what follows in the second and third: romping if technically undemanding boogies, novelty songs like 'Right String But The Wrong Yo Yo', a few country standards of the stripe of 'It Makes No Difference Now' and a *very* occasional slow blues. Red performs everything with the heightened enthusiasm of a group-leader at summer camp, shouting the lyrics with gruff bonhomie and banging away at the piano in a relentless two-beat.

From time to time in the next two chapters Red heads for the wild country of rock 'n' roll, though his efforts, thanks partly to bright and unatmospheric studios, prove to be rather tame. The Dixieland corn of 'South' is at least as high as an elephant's eye, and he briefly loses his way in it, but he recovers his sense of direction to arrive at Atlanta's Magnolia Ballroom, where he tapes what may be the first-ever blues concert recording. The ambience is buzzing and Red's extrovert performing style, irrepressible even in the studio, here becomes almost dementedly cheerful.

In 1961 Red unexpectedly had a small hit with the novelty blues 'Dr Feel-Good'. The title later provided a name for a British R&B band, while the flipside, 'Mister Moonlight', was picked up by The Beatles. This gives Red some cachet as a blender in the distillery of British R&B, and, listening to more of his work from that time, as you can on the fourth CD, you feel that its convivial mixture of pop, basic jazz and rock 'n' roll was a cocktail rather well suited to the European taste of that period. But it is uncomplicated music for a simpler time, and new listeners may find it merely trivial.

*** Atlanta Bounce
Arhoolie CD 379 *Piano Red; John Peek (t); Clyde 'Blow Top' Lynn (s); Wesley Jackson (g); George 'Kid' Miller (b); James C. 'Put' Jackson (d). 7/50–3/56, 5/72.*

**(*) The Flaming Hurricane
[Westside WESB 701] *Piano Red; unknown (g); unknown (b); unknown (d).* prob. early 70s.

*** Blues, Blues, Blues
Black Lion BLCD 760181 *Piano Red. 6–7/74.*

*(*) Dr. Feelgood
Delmark DD-740 *Piano Red. 7/76.*

Apart from five tracks on *Atlanta Bounce*, mostly from the 1956 Magnolia Ballroom gig (see above), the music on these albums was all recorded in a four- or five-year period. There is an extensive overlap of repertoire, but the four CDs are not indistinguishable. *The Flaming Hurricane* is a smallish chunk (11 tracks) of Red's core repertoire with efficient but colourless band accompaniment. *Atlanta Bounce* is a longer but broadly similar recital; having the microphone entirely to himself makes Red sound even more of a jolly pub player than usual. The songs are amusing and his pleasure in performing them makes them doubly so. *Blues, Blues, Blues* (which, like *The Flaming Hurricane*, is of questionable availability) was recorded at the Montreux Jazz Festival, a performance carefully tailored for a jazz audience, consisting almost entirely of boogies, popular standards and, exceptionally, several slow blues. Red is, for him, a little subdued, but for some listeners that will be a recommendation. Two years on, however, he sounds old and tired, and the Delmark album would have been more truthfully titled *Dr. Don't-Feel-Good*. TR

Piano Slim (born 1928)
VOCAL, PIANO

Robert T. Smith was born in Texas; by the time he was 21, he had taken up alto sax, switched to drums after losing part of a lung to a bullet, switched again to piano, and cut a 78 on Independent. Ten years later he recorded another for Bobbin, and stayed on in St Louis. Smith quit music for 13 years after getting married, but returned as Piano Slim.

** Sneaky People
Swingmaster CD 2206 *Piano Slim; Lee Mallory, Charles Hill (t); James Boyd (ts); Tom Ray (h); Tom Shay (g); Farlan Reed (b); Melvin Billups (d). 01.*

'Freeway Boogie', from Independent, and 'Workin' Again', from Bobbin, were respectively on *Uptown Boogie* (Catfish KATCD 132) and *Mo' Betta: St Louis R&B 1956–66* (Sequel NEMCD 946), but both are deleted. Piano Slim also has three tracks on the Henry Townsend CD *St. Louis Blues* (Wolf 120.945) and two on the VAC *St. Louis Blues Today* (Wolf 120.941). *Sneaky People* is his third release and first CD on Swingmaster. He is responsible for both the weak songwriting and the chaotic arrangements, which combine to make a recommendation impossible. CS

Rod Piazza (born 1947)
VOCAL, HARMONICA

Piazza learned blues harmonica in part from George 'Harmonica' Smith, whom he worked with from the mid-'60s until 1980 and partnered in the group Bacon Fat. He then founded his own band, the Mighty Flyers, with his wife Honey Alexander, and they have been active on the blues circuit ever since.

**(*) Vintage Live 1975
Tone-Cool CDTC 1170 *Piazza; Hollywood Fats, George Phelps (g); Larry Taylor (b); Richard Innes (d). 75.*

Playing in a club but, judging from the meagre audience reaction, outside normal hours, Piazza and his associates give an enthusiastic performance of Chicago-style blues with an emphasis on Little Walter material ('Mellow Down Easy', 'My Babe', etc.) and a close copy of Muddy Waters's recording of 'Standing Around Crying'. The technically unsophisticated recording doesn't favour Piazza's singing but his harp comes through well enough. The star of the night, however, is Hollywood Fats, whose guitar playing is agile, appropriate and energizing.

*** Blues Harp Summit
Charly CDGR 272 *Piazza; Honey Piazza (p); Alex Schultz (g); Bill Stuve (b); Jimi Bott (d). c. 91.*

Piazza's output in the '80s, such as *Harpburn*, originally made for Murray Brothers and reissued on Black Top, is currently unavailable, as are his early-'90s albums for Black Top, *Blues In The Dark* and *Alphabet Blues*. The five tracks on *Blues Harp Summit*, a CD shared with James Harman and Studebaker John, were recorded at Buddy Guy's club Legends. Piazza's long, almost unaccompanied solo in 'Buzzing' deserves its delighted reception for its sheer stamina. Schultz doesn't get much of a look-in but Honey Piazza's piano lays a firm foundation.

*** Tough And Tender
Tone-Cool CDTC 1165 *Piazza; Jonny Viau, Allen Ortiz (ts); Honey Piazza (p); Rick 'L.A. Holmes' Holmstrom (g); Bill Stuve (b); Steve Mugalian (d). 11/96.*

**(*) Here And Now
Tone-Cool TC 1172 *As above, except Mugalian also plays cga. 98.*

*** Beyond The Source
Tone-Cool TC 1181//Cooking Vinyl BLEUCD 004 *As above, except Scott Thompson (t), Jim Spake (ts) replace Viau, Ortiz; add Kal David, Laurie Bono (v). 01?*

*** Keepin' It Real
Blind Pig BPCD 5088 *Piazza; Honey Piazza (p, v); Henry Carvajal (g, v); Bill Stuve (b, v); Paul Vincent Fasulo (d, perc). 04?*

Little survives of Piazza's early dedication to the Chicago sound – and why should it after 20 years? This is music in its own style, the songs owing little to earlier models, the playing driven not by remembering old ways but by inventing new ones. At the same time, *Tough And Tender* is clearly recognizable as a blues record. Piazza's harmonica swirls about the listener's ears like a wind from some cold blue region, and Holmstrom blows a hailstorm. *Here And Now* has a generally sunnier mood, and some of the songs pass by without leaving much of an impression, but in the slow blues 'I Do Believe' Piazza returns to the rhetorical Chicago style. *Beyond The Source* has a much punchier sound and many of its tracks are rhythmically more insistent, especially Billy 'The Kid' Emerson's 'Shim Sham Shimmy' (a rare non-original number). Even when the band slows down there's a muscularity to the music, and 'Lovin' Daddy Blues' reaffirms Piazza's roots in a Chicago idiom. 'Ghosting', a slow instrumental blues, shimmers like Walter Horton's famous 'Easy'. All three albums are essentially by a quintet, the horns being added on only one or two tracks of each.

Keepin' It Real is a studio recording which Piazza designed, he says, to be 'as close to a good night of the blues as it gets', an objective that's realized with considerable success. Untypically, it includes a string of blues standards like 'Baby Please Don't Go' and 'Just Like A Woman', sometimes, as in 'Good Morning Little School Girl', done in non-standard ways, but it winds to its close with four originals. Honey Piazza has more room to move than on previous records and grabs the opportunity with both hands. TR

Charlie Pickett
VOCAL, GUITAR

Like Son Bonds, Pickett was from Brownsville, Tennessee, and an associate of Sleepy John Estes, whom he accompanied at his 1937 sessions.

*** Son Bonds – Charlie Pickett (1934–1941)
Wolf WBCD 003 *Pickett; Hammie Nixon (h); Lee Brown (p). 8/37.*

Pickett's four recordings in his own name place him in the same stylistic sector as his fellow townsmen Estes and Bonds. 'Trembling Blues' – an apt title for a singer with so pronounced a shake in his voice – and 'Crazy 'Bout My Black Gal', both with pianist Lee Brown, have the jaunty syncopation of Estes's early recordings with Jab Jones. On his other coupling, 'Let Me Squeeze Your Lemon' and 'Down The Highway', Pickett plays alone, and the twisting contours of the vocal and guitar melodies in 'Down The Highway' create a performance as hypnotic as it is unexpected. TR

Dan Pickett (1907–67)
VOCAL, GUITAR

Pickett's real name was James Founty, and he was born and died in Alabama. A number of relatives were located in the '90s, but none of them knew much about Pickett's life; he was

the archetypal rambling blues singer, given to disappearing for months and years at a time, and silent about where he'd been.

**** 1949 Country Blues
Collectables COL-CD-5311 *Pickett.* 8/49.

Dan Pickett is a paradox. His songs derive almost entirely from '30s commercial recordings (his one original, 'Laughing Rag', is a ghastly exception), and repertoire and playing alike make his admiration for Tampa Red obvious. Among others, Pickett also borrowed from Kokomo Arnold, Sonny Boy Williamson I, Bumble Bee Slim, Buddy Moss and Robert Johnson (whose 'Terraplane Blues' he incorporates into Moss's 'Ride To A Funeral In A V-8'!); and yet his recordings are some of the most original downhome blues of their time or any other. Pickett's guitar is unpredictable, fluid and perfectly integrated with his singing, which is passionate, declamatory, and as exuberant as his playing, often cramming a remarkable number of syllables into a line. Pickett takes other people's songs apart and rebuilds them, and although the originals are still recognizable, they are radically transformed, becoming the unmistakable, astonishing music of Dan Pickett. There are three alternative takes (one, alas, is of 'Laughing Rag') and an additional song on the VAC *East Coast Blues* (Collectables COL-CD-5324). CS

Lonnie Pitchford (1955–98)
VOCAL, MONOCHORD, GUITAR, BASS, IMITATION HARMONICA, PIANO, CLAVES

Pitchford began in the usual way of Mississippi kids, stringing baling wire upside the wall with nails; by his teens he was playing guitar in both clubs and churches. Meeting the folklorist Worth Long in 1971, Pitchford mentioned that he made one-stringed instruments, and this led to appearances at folk festivals and overseas. Long also introduced Pitchford to Eugene Powell and Robert Lockwood, from both of whom he learned a great deal. His art was still developing and deepening when AIDS took him.

**** All Around Man
Rooster Blues R 2629 *Pitchford; Terry Williams, Nathaniel Mitchell (b); Norman Clark (d, maracas); 'Bones' Johnson (tamb).* 3/92–3/94.

Pitchford's party piece in live performance was to build a diddley bow on stage before playing it; there are four tracks featuring the instrument (plus two with guitar) on *National Downhome Blues Festival Vol. 1* (Southland SCD-21), and another two on *Living Country Blues* (Evidence ECD 26105 3CD). Without downplaying the folkloric importance of such recordings, the instrument, even in Pitchford's virtuoso hands, doesn't take long to outstay its welcome, and Rooster were wise to emphasize versatility; there are two diddley bow features on *All Around Man*, but they're alongside solo acoustic guitar songs, electric band blues and a gospelly piano version of Bobby Hebb's 'Sunny'. It being the '90s, there's the usual sprinkling of songs by, and influenced by, Robert Johnson, but Pitchford's interpretations owe much to his time with Lockwood, the motivation isn't as coldly commercial as usual, and a band version of 'If I Had Possession Over Judgement Day' is a genuine work of renewal. Pitchford was sometimes pigeonholed as a neo-primitive on account of the diddley bow, but the leisurely pace at which *All Around Man*

was recorded allowed a fuller exploration of his range. The acoustic solo 'Drinkin' Antiseptic' is a stark confrontation with his personal demons, and one of several songs attesting that Pitchford was a creator within tradition, not a mere replicator of it. CS

Sampson Pittman
VOCAL, GUITAR

Apart from his association with Calvin Frazier, virtually nothing is known about Pittman beyond his residence in Blytheville, Arkansas, and his eventual arrival in Detroit. Nevertheless, the handful of recordings he made for the Library of Congress give valuable insight into levee work and life in the labour camps on the river bottoms of Arkansas.

***(*) The Devil Is Busy
Laurie LCD 7002 *Pittman; Calvin Frazier (g, v).* 10–11/38.

Older than Frazier, Pittman drew on personal experience for his songs. 'I Been Down In The Circle Before' refers to the camps and contractors in the Laconia Circle, near the confluence of the White and Mississippi rivers. There's greater and more ironic detail in 'Levee Camp Story', a monologue accompanied by Frazier's guitar, describing an encounter between Pickhandle Slim and 'Mr' Lawrence Lowrence, one of seven brothers who ruled the Arkansas camps. Pittman abandons his vocal in the second verse of 'Highway 61 Blues', which thereafter becomes an exhibition of slide guitar playing. 'Brother Low-Down And Sister Doo-Dad' is an extraordinary extended performance (present in two versions) that combines religious parody and the gospel songs 'I'll Be So Glad' and 'Wouldn't Mind Dying If Dying Was All', his slide guitar closely following both sung and spoken sections. Brief interviews with Alan Lomax after four songs provide further rather sketchy context. As with the Frazier compilation, a generous booklet is compromised by very poor lyric transcriptions. The contents of this CD have also been absorbed into the VAC *Detroit Blues* (JSP JSP 7736 4CD). NS

Doc Pomus (1925–91)
VOCAL

Born in Brooklyn, Jerome Felder suffered in his early life from infantile paralysis and spent much of his time absorbed in music. Initially a jazz fan, he took up singing the blues and recorded for several labels in the late '40s. He also began writing songs in or close to the blues idiom, such as 'Boogie Woogie Country Girl' for Joe Turner and 'Lonely Avenue' for Ray Charles. In the '50s and '60s he collaborated with Mort Shuman on many hits for the Drifters, the Coasters, Elvis Presley and other acts in both R&B and pop fields. One of his last projects was collaborating with Dr John on Jimmy Witherspoon's Midnight Lady Called The Blues.

** Blues Around The Clock
Delmark DE-685 *Pomus; Taft Jordan (t); Tab Smith (as); Johnny Hicks (ts); Leonard Feather, Reggie Ashby (p); Chuck Wayne, Ralph Williams (g); Ben Brown, John Levy (b); Walter Johnson (d).* 10/45–47/48.

Although credited to Willie Bryant, this CD embraces several minor personalities on the late-'40s New York music scene who recorded for Apollo, hence its four tracks by

Pomus. 'Blues In The Red' and 'Blues Without Booze' are accompanied with elegance by a Tab Smith group, while 'Naggin' Wife Blues' and 'Alley Alley Blues' are backed by piano, guitar and bass. Pomus's confident handling of the slow 'Blues In The Red' suggests that the otherwise slightly mannered coarseness of his delivery should be attributed to inexperience rather than poor judgement: he was, after all, in his very early 20s. Unfortunately a more generous survey of Pomus's blues recordings, *It's Great To Be Young And In Love* (Whiskey, Women And … RBD 713), is no longer in print. TR

Popa Chubby (born 1948)
VOCAL, GUITAR, BASS, DRUMS, DRUM PROGRAMMING, PERCUSSION, HARMONICA, KEYBOARDS

Ted Horowitz grew up in Queens, New York, and began playing drums and guitar while in junior high school. In his teens and 20s he played blues, punk and new wave. After winning an award in a radio talent search, he secured the opening spot at the 1992 Long Beach Blues Festival, and thereafter became a busy touring attraction. His major-label debut was Booty And The Beast *(OKeh/550 Music) in 1995.*

*** **How'd A White Boy Get The Blues?**
Blind Pig BPCD 5071//Dixiefrog DFGCD 8500 Popa Chubby; Craig Dryer (ts); Mike Lattrell (o, p, md); Kris Jefferson (b); Steve Holley (d, bgo, perc); Galea (v). 00.

*** **Old School: Popa Chubby & Friends Play Muddy, Willie And More**
Dixiefrog DFGCD 8565 Popa Chubby; Jean-Jacques Milteau, Mason Casey (h); Mike Lattrell (kb, p); Dave Keyes (p, v); Matt Smith (md, bj, Do, v); Bill Perry (g, v); Paul Personne (g); Nicholas D'Amato, Eddie Camiolo (b); Steve Holley (d); Dimitri Archip (v). 11/02–6/03.

*** **Ten Years With Popa Chubby**
Dixiefrog DFGCD 8595 2CD Popa Chubby; various accompaniments. 90s–03.

'I got my chops in the '70s,' Popa Chubby has said, 'but my perceptions were coloured by the '60s – Sly, Jimi, that whole gang.' He is obviously fond of older forms of blues, often refers to its practitioners in his lyrics and occasionally picks blues standards to record. He also writes well-turned songs about the music and his role in it, such as 'Daddy Played The Guitar And Mama Was A Disco Queen' on *How'd A White Boy Get The Blues?*, or 'What's So Great About Rock And Roll' on *Hit The High Hard One*. Nevertheless his aesthetic was moulded by rock, and some blues enthusiasts' response to his music may be conditioned by their feelings about rock practices in volume, dynamics, vocal manner and so forth. For them, *Old School* may be a useful litmus test. The repertoire is unimpeachable: four of the songs are associated with Muddy Waters, three were written by Willie Dixon for Howlin' Wolf and one for Otis Rush, and the others come from 'Big Boy' Crudup and Floyd Dixon. The renditions are sometimes refreshingly independent of the original recordings – 'Got My Mojo Working' is plausibly translated into bluegrass, and 'Little Red Rooster' sheds the swooping slide guitar arrangement – while more conventionally delivered pieces such as 'I Can't Be Satisfied' or 'Low Down Ways', both of which Chubby plays on Dobro, have nothing in them to frighten the horses. The only aspect that may dissatisfy the listener is the singing, which typically reduces the subtle conversational contour of the blues vocal to a raucous flatline.

Another avenue of approach for the inquisitive reader might be *Ten Years With Popa Chubby*, a retrospective that draws 17 tracks from nine studio albums for Disc 1, and ten from four live ones to make Disc 2. It's a pity the single track chosen from *Old School* is 'I Can't Quit You Baby', which Chubby and Paul Personne reduce to a seven-minute guitar duel, but other selections are more acute, and the live disc, despite a few passages of 'Do you feel all right? Say yeah!' exhortation, has more light and shade than you commonly find in concert blues-rock.

It shouldn't be interpreted as a slight on an intelligent and talented musician that we focus on just a few of his albums. Readers who feel that for them Popa really has a brand new bag can dig into it for some or all of the following: *The First Cuts* (Dixiefrog DFGCD 8454), *Hit The High Hard One* (DFGCD 8459), *One Million Broken Guitars* (DFGCD 8466), *Brooklyn Basement Blues* (DFGCD 8485), *One Night Live In New York City* (DFGCD 8496), *Flashed Back* (DFGCD 8520), *The Good, The Bad And The Chubby* (DFGCD 8530), *Black Coffee Blues Band* (DFGCD 8538), *Live at FIP* (DFGCD 8550) and *Peace, Love & Respect* (DFGCD 8570). TR

Ana Popovic (born 1976)
VOCAL, GUITAR

From the former Yugoslavia, Popovic formed her first band, Hush, in 1996. Moving to the Netherlands, she studied guitar at the Utrecht Academy of Music, assembled a band and made a name for herself in the Netherlands and Germany.

** **Hush!**
Ruf 1063 Popovic; Scott Thompson (t); Jim Spake (s); Ernest Williamson, Rob Geboers (o, p); Bernard Allison (g, v); Jack Holder, William Lee Ellis (g); Dave Smith, Sam Shoup, Bart Kamp (b); Steve Potts, Steve Mergen, Ronald Oor (d); Susan Marshal, Jacqueline Johnson (v). 10/00.

*(*) **Comfort To The Soul**
Ruf 1081 Popovic; Lyn Jones (h); Al Gamble (kb, o); Reese Wynans (o); Jack Holder (g); Dave Smith (b); Steve Potts (d); Susan Marshal, Becky Russell (v). 2–4/03.

The rather thin recording of Popovic's vocals on *Hush!* makes it hard to appraise them, but she doesn't yet seem to have developed a distinctive voice. Her slide playing has power on Johnny Copeland's 'Bring Your Fine Self Home' and it's a pity she doesn't do much more in that style, since her other playing is fairly conventional. Also from the blues book are T-Bone Walker's 'The Hustle Is On' and a gender-shifted Buddy Guy song, 'Girl Of Many Words', to which Jim Gaines's wide-screen production gives mass but no subtlety. Most of the remaining songs are originals in a somewhat formulaic blues-rock manner, varied now and then with a cooler, jazzier number like 'Minute 'Till Dawn'. The tracklisting gives only sporadic clues to the running order.

On *Comfort To The Soul* Popovic's singing has more confidence and variety, but these gains must be weighed against fuzzy lyrics like the title number's ('Inspire senses, unfocus your mind/Forget the explanations to the world/Accept your will as primal route,' etc.) and a continued drift into blues-rock waters. Her lack of interest in more generic blues, implicit in a tuneless caricature of 'Sittin' On Top Of

The World', seems to be confirmed by a couple of lines from 'Fool Proof': 'You think that you can … make this rock & roll girl sing the blues – forget about it.' TR

Jerry Portnoy (born 1943)
HARMONICA, VOCAL

Portnoy had been playing harmonica around Chicago for some years when Muddy Waters hired him for his band, a position he held from 1974 to 1980. He then created The Legendary Blues Band with other former Waters sidemen and played with them for another six years. More recently he has toured and recorded with Eric Clapton. He has also recorded with Joe Beard, John Brim, John Campbell, Luther 'Guitar Jr' Johnson, Pinetop Perkins and Duke Robillard. His tutorial package Blues Harmonica Masterclass *is highly regarded.*

*** **Home Run Hitter**
Sanctuary CAS 36112 *Portnoy; Rick Harris (kb); Tommy Lepson (o); Charlie Baum, Duke Robillard (g, v); Mike Dinallo (g); Bobby Del Gizzo (b, v); Michael 'Mudcat' Ward (b); David Roy Kulik, Jordan Steele Lash (d); Brian Templeton, The Hoodoo Kings (v).* 90s.
*** **Down In The Mood Room**
Tiny Town TTCD 2011 *Portnoy; Doug James (bcl, bs); [Sax] Gordon Beadle (ts); Mark Davis (vn, md, mandocello); Duke Robillard (g, v, prod); Troy Gonyea (g); Marty Ballou (b); Steve Ramsay (d); Bob Malone (v).* 01.

Although Portnoy's reputation was made in the hard-blues school of the Muddy Waters band, his tastes, as exhibited by *Home Run Hitter*, extend far beyond the Chicago-style blues of 'She Makes Me' to encompass received repertoire like 'Misty' and the Sonny Terryish 'Runnin' With The Blues' and his own well-wrought compositions both in and outside blues forms, like 'Poison Kisses', 'Shoulda Coulda Woulda' and 'Black Tear Drops'. He sings only a couple of numbers himself, leaving most of the others to the competent but unremarkable Baum. The album is an expanded version of *Poison Kisses* (Modern Blues MBCD 1202, deleted), the three extra tracks involving Templeton and Dinallo of The Radio Kings.

Down In The Mood Room is a closer collaboration with Duke Robillard and, not surprisingly, prompts Portnoy, a jazz buff, to try out tunes like 'Doodlin'' and 'Lullaby Of Birdland', though when he moves to pop standards such as 'Stormy Weather' and 'Sentimental Journey' he does little more than play the melodies straight, albeit with relaxed timing and lovely tone. 'Mood Room Boogie' and the Will Shade tune 'Jug Band Waltz' haul the listener back across the tracks. This one may be more attuned to the interests of harmonica aficionados. TR

Eugene Powell (1908–98)
VOCAL, GUITAR

As a child, Eugene Powell lost an eye to a bow and arrow attack; it wasn't easy being the offspring of a mixed-race relationship in Mississippi. He became known as Sonny Boy Nelson after his mother remarried, and played guitar with his step-brother for dances. By 1936, when he recorded, Powell was living with Matilda Witherspoon and his guitar partner was Willie Harris. Eugene and Matilda broke up in 1952, and he gradually abandoned music, but from the '70s he began performing at festivals and recorded for visitors, remaining active until not long before his death.

*** **Louisiana Blues**
Wolf WSE 109 *Powell; Robert Hill (h, k, v); Willie Harris Jr (g); Mississippi Matilda (v).* 10/36.
*** **Mississippi Blues Vol. 3**
Document DOCD-5671 *As above, except omit Hill.* 10/36.

Powell's relaxed, free-flowing music shows how influential Bo Carter was around Hollandale. The inaccurately titled *Louisiana Blues* (the sessions took place in New Orleans) comprises Matilda's three issued sides, Robert Hill's ten, and six songs credited to Sonny Boy Nelson, among them the charming 'Low Down', sung by Willie Harris. It's thought that the guitarists on 'Low Down' are Harris and Bo Carter, but on all other titles the quirkily dissonant accompaniment is by Powell and Harris. 'Hard Working Woman', sung in a breathless falsetto, is Matilda's masterpiece; her 'A & V Blues' gets a very rough transfer from the only known copy. Powell's numbers are all likeable, and 'Pony Blues', with its bell-like treble flurries and cantering rhythm, is outstanding. Robert Hill was an accomplished harmonica player in a jazzy style that recalls Robert Cooksey; his tunes, which include pop, vaudeville and hokum alongside blues, have a certain faded charm. Document's sound quality is superior, but Hill is omitted in favour of the very different music of Robert Petway.

*(*) **The Last Giants Of Mississippi Blues**
Wolf 120.931 *Powell.* 8/76, 6/81–9/82.

The other 'giant' (i.e. survivor) is Jack Owens. Powell's skills had declined somewhat by this time, but he could still impress on a good day; 'Police In Mississippi', a 1976 remake of 'Pony Blues', is evidence of that. (This track is bootlegged from an Italian LP whose producers misunderstood 'polices and the snitchers done tore my playhouse down'.) Powell performs doggedly on his other nine tracks, but they are laid waste by extraneous noise, from traffic, wind, birds, a baby and what sounds like a suitcase full of cutlery being dropped. CS

Michael Powers (born 1952)
VOCAL, GUITAR

Powers grew up in Bayonne, New Jersey, but as a boy frequently spent summers in the South, where he absorbed blues and gospel music. He took up guitar, started a band in high school and played music fulltime in the '60s and '70s, though it was not until much later, when he had gone solo, that he developed his blues skills.

*** **Onyx Root**
Baryon BYN 002 *Powers; Jimi Zhivago (kb, g); Glen Patascha (p); Neil Jason (b); Steve Jordan (d); Amy Hel, Fiona McBain (v).* 05.

Years of playing in obscure R&B support bands might not seem much of a preparation for a career in later life as a moderately old-school bluesman. Maybe they weren't; perhaps, as his measured renditions of 'Can't Quit You Baby', Muddy Waters's 'Country Boy' and Howlin' Wolf's 'Baby's Got A Train' suggest, Powers is inspired by his boyhood encounters with the blues: memories of his mother's record collection, or hearing

Jimmy Reed at a local club. Whatever the genealogy of his music, he is a wholly convincing blues interpreter, gifted with a wonderfully distressed voice and a pungent guitar style which lay their tints even on the songs that are not formally blues. For readers seeking a signpost or two, there are moments when Powers sounds a little like Taj Mahal, and the carefully engineered intimacy of the session occasionally recalls the albums of James Blood Ulmer, but to say that is not to imply that Powers' powers come from anywhere but inside. TR

Preacher Boy (born 1968)
VOCAL, VARIOUS INSTRUMENTS

Multi-instrumentalist Chris 'Preacher Boy' Watkins became a blues fan at 16 and founded his first band in 1992. He made a considerable impression in 1995 with his debut album and a notable appearance at the San Francisco Blues Festival. Born in Iowa, he now lives in San Francisco.

** Preacher Boy And The Natural Blues
Blind Pig BPCD 5017 *Preacher Boy (t, h, p, md, bj, g, b, wb, tamb, v); Ralph Carney (tb, cl, s, h, k, spoons, cowbell); Jim Campilongo (g); Tom Giesler, Bill MacBeath (b); Steve Escobar (d). 95.*

** Gutters And Pews
Blind Pig BPCD 5034 *Preacher Boy (t, h, ac, o, p, mellotron, melodica, md, bj, g, b, j, wb, tamb, v); Ralph Carney (cl, as, bs, v); Big Bones (h); Jimbo Trout (bj); Hans Raag, Jim Campilongo (g); Danny Uzilevsky, Tom Giesler (b); Steve Escobar (d); Harpo (perc); Miboy Sherman (handclapping, v). 96.*

Recorded at a time when alt.country was establishing itself as a viable idiom, these albums could be seen as pioneer work in alt.blues. A decade later, their project of redesigning skiffle according to the aesthetics of grunge rock doesn't seem to have caught on, at any rate in blues circles. In the plus column are passages of attractive guitar by Watkins, particularly when playing a National, and some quirky compositions, mostly in blues forms on the first album, more diverse on the better-produced *Gutters And Pews*. The big minus is Watkins's singing, a guttural, lyric-mangling Waits/Beefheart growl with a range of about half an octave. *Crow* (Wah Tup WAHTCD 002) (1998) is indubitably alt.something, but not blues. TR

Sam(my) Price (1908–92)
VOCAL, PIANO

Price got his professional start as a dancer, aged 15. By the time he left Texas in 1927, he'd been a talent scout (recommending Blind Lemon Jefferson to Paramount) and led his own big band. In 1937 he arrived in New York via Kansas City (an important influence on his playing), Detroit and Chicago. Price became a staff pianist at Decca, accompanying on many blues and gospel sessions. He first visited France in 1948 and made many return trips, usually with jazz bands. Back in the States he was active in business, local politics and the NAACP, but still found time to write an autobiography and to be an active musician almost to the end of his life. Price was a jazz musician who also played blues and boogie; this discussion is selective, but almost all the CDs included straddle the genres.

**(*) Sam Price 1929–1941
Classics 696 *Price; Doug Finnell, Joe Brown, Ed Mullens, Shad Collins, Bill Johnson, Chester Boone, Chu Berry (t); Bert Johnson, Floyd Brady, Ray Hogan (tb); Fess Williams (cl, as); Lem Johnson (cl, ts); Don Stovall (as); Ray Hill, Lester Young, Skippy Williams (ts); Percy Darensbourg (bj); unknown (g); Duke Jones, Ernest 'Bass' Hill, Billy Taylor, unknown (b); Wilbert Kirk, Doc West, Herb Cowans, J. C. Heard, unknown (d); Yack Taylor, Spo-De-O-Dee Sam [Theard], Ruby Smith, Jack Meredith, band (v); Effie Scott (sp). 9/29–12/41.*

**(*) Sam Price 1942–1945
Classics 1083 *Price; Herman Autrey, Freddie Webster, Bill Coleman (t); Don Stovall, Joe Eldridge (as); David Young, Ike Quebec, unknown (ts); William Lewis (g); Vernon King, Oscar Pettiford, unknown (b); O'Neill Spencer, Doc West, Sid Catlett, unknown (d); Mabel Robinson (v). 1/42–7/45.*

**(*) Sammy Price & The Blues Singers – Vol. 1 (1938–1941)
Document DOCD-5667 *Price; Charlie Shavers, unknown (t); J. C. Higginbotham (tb); Buster Bailey (cl); poss. Leonard Ware, prob. Ham Jackson, unknowns (g); Richard Fullbright, unknowns (b); O'Neill Spencer, unknowns (d); Ebony Three, Bea Foote, Hester Lancaster, Yack Taylor, Sweet Georgia Brown, Ruby Smith (v). 5/38–10/41.*

**(*) Sammy Price & The Blues Singers – Vol. 2 (1939–1949)
Document DOCD-5668 *Price; Charlie Shavers, Dizzy Gillespie (t); Buster Bailey, Jimmy Hamilton (cl); Pete Brown (as); J. T. Brown (ts); Wee Bea Booze (g, v); Ham Jackson, Lonnie Johnson, unknown (g); poss. Wellman Braud, Charlie Drayton, Abe Bolar, unknowns (b); poss. O'Neill Spencer, Roy Nathan, Hal West, unknowns (d); Lether McGraw, James Carter, Nora Lee King, Wee Bea Booze, Harmon Ray (v). 3/39–5/49.*

Jazz predominates on Classics' first disc, but there's a fair-sized helping of vocal blues and a little boogie. 'Jumpin' The Boogie' and 'Just Jivin' Around' are effective, but contemporary hits like 'Cow Cow Blues', 'Oh Red' and 'The Dirty Dozens' are done mechanically, and diabetics should avoid Price's ballad singing. Yack Taylor shines on a warm 'Things 'Bout Coming My Way', and Ruby Smith is better than usual on 'Harlem Gin Blues', but Jack Meredith's crooning of 'Match Box Blues' must be heard to be disbelieved.

Mabel Robinson gets *1942–1945* off to a jovial start; she's succeeded by four instrumental tracks that prophesy R&B, and feature some notable electric guitar. The next eight titles are good jazz, recorded for broadcast syndication, and ten of the remaining 11 are solos made for King Jazz. Sid Catlett joins in on the last of them. They're of no great value, for Price's stock of ideas is limited and his playing coldly cerebral; this damages the boogies less than the blues.

Where Classics focus on Price the bandleader and soloist, Document present the accompanist: reliable, supportive, and sometimes capable of rising to higher things. There's nothing dire on either disc, and a few minor gems, but the object is to reinstate otherwise unavailable titles from the deleted *Sammy Price & The Blues Singers* (Wolf WBJCD-007 4CD), and none of the singers is more than middleweight. On *Vol. 1* Sweet Georgia Brown's alley anecdotes provoke some tough barrelhouse piano, and on *Vol. 2* Wee Bea Booze revives 'See See Rider Blues' and

'Mr. Freddie Blues' in grand style, but much of the rest consists of novelties and imitations: Lil Green, Bessie Smith and Peetie Wheatstraw are all mimicked, with variable success.

***(*) Paris Blues
EmArcy 013 038 *Price; Lucky Thompson (ts); Jean-Pierre Sasson (g); Pierre Michelot (b); Gérard Pochonet (d).* 7/57.
(***) Blues For The Bluesicians
Jazz Colours 874775 *Price; Keith Smith (t); Roy Williams (tb); Sandy Brown (cl); Ruan O'Lochlainn (g); Harvey Weston (b); Lennie Hastings (d).* 12/69.
**(*) Rockin' Boogie
Black & Blue BB 921 *Price; Doc Cheatham (t, v); Gene 'Mighty Flea' Connors (tb); Ted Buckner (as); Carl Pruitt (b); J. C. Heard (d); Marie Buggs (v).* 5/75.
*** Fire
Black & Blue BB 962 *As above, except Cheatham does not sing; omit Buggs.* 5/75.
**(*) Boogie And Jazz Classics
Black & Blue BB 980 *Price; J. C. Heard (d).* 5/75.
**(*) King Of Boogie Woogie
Storyville STCD 5011 *Price; Arvell Shaw (b); Panama Francis (d).* 7/75.

Apart from *Blues For The Bluesicians* and *Boogie And Jazz Classics*, cut in England and Switzerland respectively, these recordings were made in France. *Paris Blues* is credited to Sammy Price and Lucky Thompson; 'Sweet Georgia Brown' apart, the repertoire is boogie, blues (both vocal and instrumental) and the gospel song 'Up Above My Head'. Price leaves most of the soloing to Thompson and Sasson (terrific), but their adventurousness and an unflagging rhythm section goad him into singing and playing with unaccustomed, sweaty vigour.

Blues For The Bluesicians (formerly on Black Lion) features good sound, generous playing time and an unusually thoughtful, introspective Price on the solos 'Honey Grove Blues' and 'Jelly On My Mind'. On *Rockin' Boogie* the sublime J. C. Heard makes the blues instrumentals sound better than they are, but Marie Buggs's yelling of three Bessie Smith songs is execrable. Despite their titles, both CDs are mostly jazz.

Fire is all instrumentals, most of them blues or boogie; a starry band makes for pleasant listening, but an opening sequence of six tunes with just the rhythm section exposes Price's lack of depth. *Boogie And Jazz Classics* has the same problem writ large; despite Heard's attempts to gee him up, Price's playing on nine jazz instrumentals and six boogies is very conservative. Only 'Goin' Back Home Boogie' and Heard's feature 'J. C. Speaks' (which almost disproves the rule that all drum solos are too long) engender much excitement.

King Of Boogie Woogie is scheduled for deletion when stocks run out, which seems unlikely to be soon. Again the rhythm section is terrific, and again the title promises more than it delivers, both in its estimate of Price's status and because half the tracks are lightly jazzed '20s pop standards. Like much of Price's work, it's polished, professional and glib. CS

Big Walter Price (born 1914/17)
VOCAL, PIANO, ORGAN

Price grew up in Gonzales and San Antonio, Texas. He didn't begin singing and playing in public until his late 30s, but after having some regional success in 1955 with 'Shirley Jean' he performed round Houston and cut singles for several Southwestern labels.

** Rockin' With The Blues: G. L. Crockett Meets Big Walter Price
Official OF-CD 5679 *Price; Floyd Arceneaux, unknown (t); Grady Gaines, Clifford Burks, unknowns (ts); Odie Turner, unknown (p); unknown (sg); Nat Douglas, Classie Ballou, unknowns (g); Carl Lott, Sid Lawrence, unknowns (b); Johnny Perry, unknowns (d); unknowns (v grp).* 55–61.

The 'Meets' of the album title just means that Official didn't have enough material for an entire CD by Crockett or Price, so they shoved them together. Price's 18 tracks are almost all his singles from the period, a very mixed bag. 'Pack Fair And Square', a brisk adaptation of 'No More Doggin'' memorably revived by the J. Geils Band on their 1972 debut album, is followed by the mock-Chicano 'Hello, Maria' ('Pasquale missa you so much, baby'), and the switchback ride continues through soul ballads ('I'll Cry For You'), teen pop ('Crazy Dream', 'Shirley Jean') and pleasant but generic Texas shuffles ('San Antonio'). There are some crisp guitar solos but Price's piano playing, on the eight tracks where he does play it, is largely buried by the horns and the sound quality, the latter mediocre at best and sometimes terrible. Price's '70s recordings for producer Huey Meaux, collected on *Git To Gittin'* (Edsel DIAB 8018), are out of print. TR

John Primer (born 1945)
VOCAL, GUITAR

House guitarist at Theresa's Lounge before becoming a sideman for Willie Dixon, Muddy Waters and Magic Slim, John Primer has an eminent pedigree for his role as a principal custodian of the Chicago blues tradition. Years spent as one of Magic Slim's Teardrops gave him a profuse and diverse repertoire encompassing most blues and soul classics, to which he has added his own increasingly accomplished compositions.

**(*) Easy Baby (The Zoo Bar Collection Vol. 6)
Wolf 120.306 *Primer; Nick Holt (b, v); Michael Scott (d, v).* late 80s.

Released a decade later, this live set cut in Lincoln, Nebraska, finds Primer fronting The Teardrops as a warm-up for Magic Slim. As eclectic as his leader, he combines songs from old employers Dixon and Waters, as well as Jimmy Reed, Howlin' Wolf and Magic Sam, with a pair of B. B. King warhorses, Little Milton's 'That What Love Will Make You Do' and two songs associated with Bobby Bland. The trio format places undue pressure on Primer, evident in his sometimes indifferent pitching and in scattershot solos. He begins fairly strongly with Reed's 'A String To Your Heart' but by the time he gets to 'Woke Up This Morning' and 'Get Your Money Where You Spend Your Time', his vocal stamina has begun to desert him. The results are solidly entertaining but not particularly memorable.

**(*) Poor Man Blues (Chicago Blues Session Vol. 6)
Wolf 120.852 *Primer; Billy Branch (h); Leo Davis (p); Michael Coleman, Magic Slim, Junior Pettis (g); Johnny B. Gayden, Nick Holt (b); Ray 'Killer' Allison, James Harrington, Tim Taylor, Jerry Porter (d).* 2/87–4/91.

The spirit of The Teardrops invests several of these 11 tracks, not least because of various members' presence, but whilst being entertaining the set ultimately lacks distinction. All the musicians play their parts well but nowhere is there a feeling that a particular effort is being made. The listener must perforce while away the minutes just as the players do, waiting in vain to be presented with anything memorable. Just two tracks break out of the format of two guitars, bass and drums and one of those is a less than comfortable stab at 'Corinna'. There's competence in abundance here but not enough inspiration to command attention.

*** Stuff You Gotta Watch
Earwig 4924 *Primer; Mervyn 'Harmonica' Hinds (h); Carl Snyder (o, p); Eddie Butler (g); Nick Holt (b); Michael Scott (d). 92.*

The opening title track gets this off to a stirring start, establishing a standard from which it rarely falters. That's if you deny the existence of 'Rhinestone Cowboy', an indescribably dire choice, stolidly performed. An otherwise typically eclectic programme combines covers of songs by Freddie King, Otis Rush, Magic Sam and J. B. Lenoir with six Primer originals, one an instrumental tribute to his mentor Sammy Lawhorn. Best of the rest are 'Inflation Blues' and 'Travelin' Blues'. Primer sings and plays confidently and gets reliable support from his musicians, although Hinds's harmonica is persistently low in the mix and Snyder's keyboard solos sit uncomfortably in the 12-bar scheme.

*** Blues Behind Closed Doors
Wolf 120.875 *Primer; Mike Barber (t); Big James Montgomery (tb); Charles Kimble (ts); Billy Branch (h); Stanley Banks (kb); Magic Slim, Johnny B. Moore (g); Nick Holt (b); Earl Howell (d). 7/92–2/93.*

All but one of these 12 tracks feature The Teardrops, recorded on tour in Vienna, with most tracks augmented by Branch, Banks or the Chicago Playboys Horns. The different personnels add some needed variation to the customary pot pourri of five Primer originals and songs from Elmore James, Lightnin' Slim, Little Walter, Muddy Waters and Freddie King. Sam Cooke's 'Somebody Have Mercy' is an unlikely success, the horns ragged but right and Primer's vocal not too reliant upon Cooke's example. Apart from the leader's guitar, Branch is the only other soloist in four songs, including 'Just Your Fool' and Primer's 'Yes, I'm Crazy 'Bout My Baby'. Primer's performance is well up to par, at his best probably on Slim's 'Good Morning Heartache'.

*** Cold Blooded Blues Man
Wolf 120.885 *Primer; Michael Jackson, Eddie Shaw (ts); Little Mack Simmons, Billy Branch, Chris Sandera (h); Detroit Jr, Oliver Humer (p); George Baze, Magic Slim (g); Nick Holt (b); Earl Howell, Michael Strasser (d). 91–94.*

A game of two halves, with all the goals achieved in the first, amplified, period. These six songs, one recorded in Vienna, the rest in Chicago with elements of The Teardrops, find Primer at his best, singing four of his own compositions, Luther Allison's 'What Love Will Do' and Muddy's 'Sad Sad Day'. Thereafter, he switches to acoustic guitar for a clutch of oddly chosen covers. Spirited duets with Branch on 'Mojo Hand' and Sandera on 'I'm Worried' work well compared to a pair of inappropriate Robert Johnson songs and a brief tilt at Hendrix's 'Red House' that ends in embarrassed laughter. While offering a contrast in performance, Primer's effectiveness without amplification doesn't compensate for the fact that a whole album of the artist in his natural milieu would have been more satisfactory.

**(*) It's A Blues Life
Wolf 120.899 *Primer; Steve Bell (h); Ken Barker (p); Tom Holland (g); Nick Holt (b); Bert Robinson (d). 8/98.*

This bears all the hallmarks of being recorded in one day. All but two of its ten band tracks are taken at an aggressive tempo, with generous solo choruses for harmonica, piano and guitar following a preset formula. Songs from Howlin' Wolf, Muddy, J. B. Lenoir, Albert King, Stevie Ray Vaughan and T-Bone Walker are presented with undifferentiated jangling gusto. It's all good if predictable fun but it short-changes Primer's abilities as a musician and bandleader. Three of his own songs, of which the best is 'Lonesome For Your Love', would have benefited from a little more thought in their arrangement. A sepulchral 'Give Me Back My Wig' and 'Rock Me' are acoustic duets between Bell and Primer that end the album on a quieter note.

***(*) Knocking At Your Door
Telarc CD-83456 *Primer; Matthew Skoller (h); Ken Saydak (o, p); Larry McCray (g); Al Brown (b); Steve McCray (d); Mike Vernon (perc, prod). 1/99.*

This was the third collaboration between Primer and producer Vernon (*The Real Deal* and *Keep On Loving The Blues*, both on Code Blue, are deleted) and the most satisfying. A better balance of covers and originals underlines Primer's growing skill as a writer, although 'Lonely Days And Nights' clearly reveals its origin. The covers, from the work of Jimmy Reed, Johnny Shines and Jerry McCain, merge seamlessly with the more equality-conscious stance of Primer's 'Hard Working Woman' and 'A Woman Was Made To Be Loved'. The standard of musicianship is predictably high, Primer and Skoller the principal soloists, and the backing tracks are taut and economical, with just an occasional over-indulgence in solo space. This album illustrates why Primer remains one of the best exponents of the Chicago blues tradition.

**(*) Blue Steel: A Tribute To Elmore James
Wolf 120.808 *Primer; Little Bobby Neely (ts); Steve Bell (h); Stanley Banks (kb); Detroit Jr (p); Bo Trisko (sg, g); Magic Slim (g); Johnny B. Gayden, Nick Holt, Michael Morrison (b); James Harrington, Earl Howell, Mark Diffenderfer (d). 8/87–02.*

One of the debilitating consequences of the commercialization of the blues has been the short-sighted mania for themed albums, as if history rather than commerce is being served. As many have learned before Primer, imitating Elmore James is a pointless exercise, except in so far as songs like 'Shake Your Moneymaker' and 'It Hurts Me Too' weren't his in the first place and don't need to be slavishly copied. Unfortunately, Primer doesn't take the opportunity as often as he might to impose himself on the material, and a return to his 'I'm A Blues Man' finds him reverting to the slide technique of his old boss, Muddy Waters. For the rest, these are competent if rather sterile reruns of a repertoire that will always remain fundamentally inimitable. NS

Gary Primich (born 1958)
VOCAL, HARMONICA

Primich grew up in Gary, Indiana, and learned harmonica playing round Chicago in his teens. In 1984 he moved to Austin, Texas, where he worked at the University of Texas and began to play in the city's clubs. In 1987 he formed The Mannish Boys with drummer Jimmy Carl Black, and in the early '90s made three now deleted albums for Amazing, Gary Primich, My Pleasure and Hot Harp Blues. He has also recorded with Steve James, Mike Morgan, Omar & The Howlers and numerous other acts.

*** Travelin' Mood
Flying Fish FF 70635 *Primich; Riley Osbourn (o); Floyd Domino (p); Steve James (md, g); Shorty Lenoir, Mark Korpi (g); Mark Rubin (b, d); Dave Wesselowski (b); Robb Stupka (d, perc); Arkadelphia (cowbell); Marvin Dykhuis (v); Jerry McCain (sp); Maryann Price (kiss). 94?*

*** Mr. Freeze
Flying Fish FF 70649 *Primich; Gene Taylor (p); Steve James (bj, g); Shorty Lenoir, Mark Korpi (g); Sarah Brown, Mark Rubin, Dave Wesselowski (b); Robb Stupka, Jeff Minnick (d). 95?*

**(*) Dog House Music
Antone's TMG-ANT 0057//Me & My Blues MMBCD 9 *Primich; John Mills (ts); Mark Kazanoff (bs); Nick Connolly (o, p); Gene Taylor (p); Chris Masterson, John Moeller (g); Randy Glines (b); Jim Starboard (d, v); Barry 'Frosty' Smith (perc). 02?*

On the Flying Fish albums Primich keeps a pleasant balance between aggressive blues-band music, where the lead guitar role passes back and forth between Lenoir and Korpi, and more skiffleish acoustic performances with Steve James like *Mr. Freeze*'s 'Dallas Texas' (a 'Catfish' variant) and 'Easy Ridin' Mama'. Compared with other harmonica players of his generation Primich can often seem like a traditionalist, playing Sonny Boy Williamson I (or II) lines with perfect accuracy, but his repertoire choices are more diverse than that might imply: witness 'Caravan' and 'Knock Me A Kiss' on *Travelin' Mood*, Gene Ammons's 'Red Top' and Clarence Garlow's Chuck Berryish 'Route 90' on *Mr. Freeze*. Each album has several original songs, the best of which are *Travelin' Mood*'s 'Triple Trouble', evidently inspired by Otis Rush's 'Double Trouble' and 'Three Times A Fool', and 'School Of Hard Knocks'.

Primich made a couple of albums with some of the same musicians for Black Top, *Company Man* (CD BT-1136) in 1997 and *Botheration* (CD BT-1153) in 1999, but both went down with the Black Top ship. In his notes to the former Cub Koda listed 'My Top 10 Reasons to Dig Gary Primich': none of them mentions his singing, which is admittedly nothing special but adequate for his purposes. He does more with it than usual on *Dog House Music* and even sounds a little like Omar Dykes on 'Elizabeth Lee', but there's less of his harmonica playing, and the material, though all new, is rather stereotyped. TR

Professor Longhair (1918–80)
VOCAL, PIANO, WHISTLING

When not making music, Henry Roeland Byrd got by as a boxer, a gambler and an odd job man. Some of his records were quite successful – a 1959 recording of 'Go To The Mardi Gras' was reissued every year – but a ban on playing in New Orleans (variously blamed on the police or the Musicians' Union) prevented his capitalizing on this. By 1970, when he was tracked down by British and local enthusiasts, Longhair was sick and poor, but after a triumphant performance at the 1971 New Orleans Jazz & Heritage Festival he never looked back, touring widely and becoming a local hero and part-owner of Tipitina's, the club named after one of his songs. Allen Toussaint probably meant little more than 'Hurray!' when he called Professor Longhair 'the Bach of rock', but as the Cantor of Leipzig synthesized French, German and Italian baroque styles, so Longhair combined blues, boogie, second-line and Caribbean rhythms into his own unmistakable sound. Lately, this has been seen as archetypal of New Orleans R&B, and it certainly influenced many who came after Longhair, but when he sat in with Dave Bartholomew in 1949 his audience acclaimed it as new and sensational.

***(*) Professor Longhair 1949
Classics 5004 *Professor Longhair; unknown (t); Robert Parker (as); Lee Allen, Leroy 'Batman' Rankins, Charles Burbank, unknown (ts); Jack Scott, Walter 'Papoose' Nelson (g); George Miller, unknown (b); Al Miller, Lester 'Duke' Alexis, Louis Joseph, John Boudreaux (d); unknown (claves); band (v). 8–c. 12/49.*

***(*) Byrd's Blues
Collectors Edition CBCD 027 *As above. 8–c. 12/49.*

(***(*)) A Proper Introduction To Professor Longhair
Proper INTRO CD 2024 *Professor Longhair; Robert Parker (as); Lee Allen, Leroy 'Batman' Rankin, Charles Burbank (ts); Red Tyler (bs); Jack Scott, Walter 'Papoose' Nelson (g); George Miller, Edgar Blanchard, unknown (b); Lester 'Duke' Alexis, Louis Joseph, John Boudreaux, Earl Palmer (d); unknown (claves); band (v). 8/49–11/53.*

***(*) Mardi Gras In New Orleans
Nighthawk NHCD-108 *As above, except add unknown (t), unknown (ts), Justin Adams (g), Norman Sinegal, Frank Fields (b), Al Miller, Charles Otis, Charles Williams (d); omit unknown (b), unknown (claves). 8/49–4/57.*

(****) New Orleans Piano
Atlantic 7225 *Professor Longhair; Robert Parker (as); Charles Burbank, Lee Allen (ts); Red Tyler (bs); Walter Nelson (g); Edgar Blanchard, unknown (b); John Boudreaux, Earl Palmer (d); unknown (claves). c. 12/49–11/53.*

Only *New Orleans Piano* includes all the Atlantic recordings, but their musical magnificence is sabotaged by a lamentably foggy transfer from the LP master tape. Nighthawk present 'Tipitina' from Atlantic, the four debut recordings on Star Talent (with wonderful brass call-and-response on 'Professor Longhair's Boogie'), the rough-as-a-bear's-backside Wasco 78 and three sides apiece from Mercury, Federal and Ebb. This is the only Longhair CD with anything from Federal, and most tracks are licensed, which is to be applauded, but the sound quality is only adequate.

Classics and Collectors Edition have the same 24 tracks (from Star Talent, Mercury and the 1949 Atlantic session) in the same order. The material derives from Nighthawk, the Atlantic LP and *The Mercury New Orleans Sessions 1950*, a VAC LP on Bear Family which included nine fine tracks, four of them not issued on 78. Despite using second-generation sources, these discs (one of them plainly a clone of the other) have the best sound; compare the crisp clack of the claves, barely audible on *New Orleans Piano*.

Proper's *Introduction* has the Mercury and Atlantic sides,

minus the latter company's alternative takes of 'Tipitina' and 'Mardi Gras In New Orleans'. Contrary to the booklet discography, the superior take of 'Mardi Gras In New Orleans', with claves, has been used. Less pleasing is that the 1953 Atlantic titles are evidently dubbed from *New Orleans Piano*, and share its murkiness; the rest of the CD has more presence, and presumably derives from Classics.

♛ **** House Party New Orleans Style: The Lost Sessions 1971-1972
Rounder CD 2057 *Professor Longhair; Snooks Eaglin (g); Will Harvey Jr, George Davis (b); 'Shiba' (Edward Kimbrough), Joseph 'Zigaboo' Modeliste (d); prob. Alfred 'Uganda' Roberts (cga). 9/71–6/72.*

**** Mardi Gras In Baton Rouge
Rhino/Bearsville R2 70736 *As above, except add Willie Singleton, Clyde Kerr (t), Alvin Batiste (ts), Edward 'Kidd' Jordan (bs). 9/71–6/72.*

After he re-emerged, recording Longhair (usually live) became a cottage industry. He wasn't concerned to develop new repertoire – after all, the old one was stuffed with classics – but although there's much duplication of songs between discs, there are often very significant differences of interpretation. One real surprise was a penchant for crooning soulful blues-ballads. There are several such numbers on these CDs, which are Longhair's first recordings on the comeback trail; they sit comfortably alongside the expected old favourites and the much less expected likes of 'Cabbagehead' and 'Jambalaya', the latter given a dazzling rumba treatment.

Longhair was revved up and ready to rock on these sessions, as were the musicians assembled to back him. The rhythm sections are outstandingly funky, and Snooks Eaglin, then also making his return to the limelight, plays at the height of his inventiveness; witness, among many other moments, his response to Longhair's Monkish harmonies on – of all things – 'Since I Met You Baby'. It's a crime that this music languished on the shelf, and was only issued *post mortem*.

*** Rock 'N' Roll Gumbo
Dancing Cat DD-3006 *Professor Longhair; Steve Madaio (t); Jerry Jumonville (ts, bs); Gatemouth Brown (vn, g); Julius Farmer (b); Shiba' (g); 'Uganda' [Alfred Roberts] (cga). 4/74–2/85.*

*** Rock 'N' Roll Gumbo
Universal/Maison de Blues 982 246-8 *As above. 4/74–2/85.*

Two previously unissued tracks are added to a French LP that was the Professor's first latterday release; one is 'Go The Mardi Gras', which benefits from an aggressive, posthumous horn overdub. Gatemouth Brown is more predictable than Eaglin, but acquits himself well, although it may be in deference to him that 'Jambalaya' (on which he plays fiddle) is by far Longhair's most rhythmically conventional version. No longer the event it was on its first appearance, *Rock 'N' Roll Gumbo* is notable for a hurtling 'Stag-O-Lee', but the bass is too busy and the percussionists sometimes come adrift, notably on 'Rum And Coke', the other unissued title. The running order of these two versions differs inconsequentially; there is nothing to choose between them for sound quality.

***(*) Go To The Mardi Gras
Wolf 120.609 *Professor Longhair; Andrew Kessler [Andy Kaslow?], George Portebus (ts); Will Harvey (b); unknown (d). poss. c. late 75.*

*** Big Easy Strut: The Essential Professor Longhair
Fuel 2000 302 061 174 *Professor Longhair; prob. Andy Kaslow, Tony Dagradi (ts); Big Will Harvey (g); prob. George Davis (b); prob. David Lee (d); prob. 'Uganda' [Alfred Roberts] (cga). 4/76.*

Go To The Mardi Gras, recorded live in Europe, features a tight, well-rehearsed and well-recorded band. 'Stompin' With Fess', an eight-minute 'Every Day I Have The Blues' and 'Whole Lotta Lovin'' are highlights, but Longhair seems short of breath when whistling on 'Big Chief'. *Big Easy Strut* comes from the New Orleans Jazz & Heritage Festival. Fess is in lively form, singing an outstanding 'Junko Partner' (*sic*), and romping through '501 Boogie', which features an accomplished guitar solo. Unfortunately the mix favours the rhythm section: the horns often sound as if they're playing through a letterbox, and some numbers ride the riff that bit too long.

* The Big Easy
Blue Moon CDBM 094 *Professor Longhair; unknown (t); unknown (ss); Robert Parker (as); unknown (ts); unknown (o); poss. Big Will Harvey (g); unknowns (b); Al Miller, unknown (d); unknown (perc); band (v). 8/49–77.*

* Way Down Yonder In New Orleans
M.I.L. Multimedia MIL 3030 *As above. 8/49–77.*

*(*) Mardi Gras In New Orleans
Aim 0018 *As above. 8/49–77.*

These discs use Star Talent sides to make up the playing time, but most tracks were recorded live in New Orleans, or Santa Cruz, or San Francisco, depending who you believe. The guitarist is good when audible, but the rest seem to be pickup musicians; the soprano sax and organ are appalling, and the sound is dreadful, with tape hiss, sudden, panicky level changes and extreme compression. Aim try to rectify these failings, and are the only label to list the right number of tracks in the right order, but their version still isn't worth hearing.

***(*) Big Chief
Tomato TOM-2040 *Professor Longhair; Tony Dagradi (ss, ts); Andy Kaslow (ts); Big Will Harvey (g); George Davis (b); David Lee (d); 'Uganda' [Alfred Roberts] (cga). 2/78.*

***(*) Rum And Coke
Tomato TOM-2041 *As above. 2/78.*

***(*) The Complete London Concert
JSP JSPCD 202 *Professor Longhair; 'Uganda' [Alfred Roberts] (cga). 3/78.*

Two nights of recording at Tipitina's resulted in a double LP, *The Last Mardi Gras* (Atlantic SD2–4001), which was only issued in 1982; these discs contain overmatter from those sessions, but are decidedly not barrel-scrapings. The usual songs appear, some of them more than once, but Longhair and his band were in fiery form. Some well-loved items get sparky new horn arrangements, and Fess pushes himself to – and occasionally beyond – his limits: the flashy playing of *Rum And Coke*'s title tune seems intended to cut James Booker's head, and the vocal on the same disc's 'Go To The Mardi Gras' takes the song to a whole different level. *Big Chief* includes one of Longhair's rare performances of 'After Hours' (as 'Little Blues') and a 'Stagger Lee' that's – well – staggering. The engineering often collapses bass, drums and congas into a funky fog, but the consistent musical vehemence outweighs this.

There's no problem balancing the instruments in London,

of course, and despite brief feedback on one track the sound is of high quality. So is most of Longhair's performance: there are bum notes in the intro to a brief 'Rockin' Pneumonia', courteously played in response to a request, but overall *The Complete London Concert* is a valuable record of Longhair working almost solo, and almost as well as he ever did with a band; as such, it's more than just a souvenir.

(*) Byrd Lives!
Night Train NTI CD 2002 2CD *Professor Longhair; Andy Kaslow, Tony Dagradi (ts); Jim Moore (bs); Ronald Johnson, Big Will Harvey, 'Billy' (g); David Lee Watson (b); John Vidacovich (d); 'Uganda' [Alfred Roberts] (cga, perc); Stanley John (steel d); band (v).* 78.

**** Ball The Wall!**
Night Train NTI CD *Similar to above, except omit Dagradi, Moore.* prob. 3/78.

These CDs are live recordings from Tipitina's; *Byrd Lives!* is the less well recorded, but it's fascinating to hear the band constructing new arrangements and solos in tribute to their leader's continuing creativity. However, the booklet's suggestion that Longhair was better when unaware that he was being recorded doesn't stand up; there are some very doubtful moments among the gems, and although the only known Longhair version of 'Lucille' starts promisingly, it ends in chaos. Only the unimaginative Ronald Johnson is listed as a guitarist, but Will Harvey (first-rate as ever) and a dire blues-rocker are both called on to solo, the latter mercifully only once.

Steel drummer Stanley John makes under-recorded contributions to the last few tracks of *Byrd Lives!* He's more prominent on *Ball The Wall*, which confirms that what on the face of it should have been a great idea was a very bad one. On riff-based numbers like 'Whole Lotta Lovin'' and 'Hey Little Girl', John adds exotic tone colours quite successfully, but when he plays melody lines they're usually superfluous doublings of the piano, and often out of tune and/or time. Three solo numbers feature a piano that's overdue for tuning.

**** Crawfish Fiesta**
Alligator ALCD-4718 *Professor Longhair; Andy Kaslow, Tony Dagradi (ts); Jim Moore (bs); Dr John [Mack Rebennack] (g); David Lee Watson (b); Walter Payton (tu); John Vidacovich (d); 'Uganda' [Alfred Roberts] (cga).* 11/79.

(*) Fess' Gumbo
Stony Plain SPCD 1214 *Professor Longhair; Andy Kaslow (interviewer).* 11/79.

And we're back in the studio for the Professor's last albums. *Crawfish Fiesta* was also one of his best. The engineering is superb, with the instruments perfectly balanced for clarity and audibility. Dr John joins the working band, and is discreet except when guitar solos are needed, whereupon he comes close to Snooks Eaglin for fluid originality. His 'invaluable production assistance' (and several days of rehearsal) did much to enthuse everyone, above all Longhair; the speed at which 'Baldhead' is taken, and the fact that the chorus is both in tune and properly miked for almost the first time since 1949, can stand for the excellence of the rest of the project. It still seems impossible that Longhair died two months later, just as the LP was shipping, and doubly unlikely that among the illnesses which killed this magnificent singer and whistler were emphysema and chronic bronchitis.

Fess' Gumbo is a curious concept; he played (and occasionally sang) with a band, but only the piano was miked. The notes say that 'only his piano playing was recorded', but tenor sax, vocals and ambient noise leak irritatingly through from time to time. Interview material is interspersed; Longhair was a good storyteller, and these accounts of his life in music are the more revealing and useful aspect of the enterprise. It's a CD for the specialist, though.

***(*) 'Fess: The Professor Longhair Anthology**
Rhino R2 71502 2CD *Similar to relevant CDs above, except add Eddie Nash, Emery Thompson, unknowns (t), Eddie Hines, Warren Bokes, Wendell Eugene, Waldron 'Frog' Joseph (tb), Warren Bell, Clarence Ford (as), Morris Bechamin, Manuel Crusto, Nat Perrilliat (ts), Carl Blouin (bs), unknowns (s), Art Neville (o), Dr John [Mack Rebennack] (p, v), Tuts Washington, Allen Toussaint (p), Alvin 'Shine' Robinson, unknown (g), George Porter Jr. (b, tamb), Richard Payne, Curtis Mitchell, unknowns (b), Smokey Johnson, poss. Freddie Stahli, unknown (d), Sidney Quezergue (shaker), Earl King (v, whistling), Jessie Smith, Rozalin Woods (v).* c. 12/49–2/85 [sic].

Handsomely presented and well annotated, this survey of Longhair's career unfortunately falls short of perfection. It draws on vintage material from Mercury, Atlantic and Ebb, and latterday recordings on Rounder, Rhino/Bearsville, Dancing Cat, Tomato, JSP and Alligator. Also included are two fine tracks from Atlantic's *Last Mardi Gras*, and singles recorded in the late '50s and early '60s for Ron and Watch. (The out-of-print *Collectors' Choice Featuring Professor Longhair* [Rounder CD 2082], which includes ten tracks from Ron, Watch and Rip, is worth looking out for.) Almost as celebrated as Ron's 'Go The Mardi Gras' is Watch's 'Big Chief Part 2'; Wardell Quezergue's pompous big-band arrangement makes this very puzzling. Three video soundtrack items really let the side down, though: 'Tipitina' with the Meters is surprisingly unfunky, and an all-star jam on 'Big Chief' is fatally disorganized even before the robots-on-helium backing vocals start. A concluding 'Boogie Woogie' by Longhair, Washington and Toussaint comes from the documentary *Piano Players Rarely Ever Play Together*, and messily proves it. cs

Willis Prudhomme (born 1932)
VOCAL, ACCORDION

Willis Prudhomme's first brush with music came at the age of 45, when he tried a harmonica. Six weeks after picking up an accordion, he was playing a dance; his initial inspirations came from Cajun greats Iry LeJeune and Nathan Abshire rather than Clifton Chenier. Prudhomme is a prolific composer, whose 'Cornbread Two-Step' was the inspiration for Beau Jocque's 'Give Him Cornbread'.

(*) Zydeco Live!
Rounder CD 2070 *Prudhomme; Cornelius Guidry (g); Herman Guidry (b); James Bill, Lee Andres Thomas (d); James Nicholas (rb); band (v).* 3/88.

(*) Willis Prudhomme & The Zydeco Express
Goldband 7820 *Prudhomme; Cornelius Guidry (g); unknown (b); unknown (d); unknown (rb); band (v).* 90s.

***) You'r [sic] Bad Bad Girl**
Goldband GRC 7826 *Prudhomme; D'Ryan Green (h, g, v); Gus Ardoin (b, v); Dexter Ardoin (d); Derrick Green (rb).* 96?.

** **Call Me Jack Hammer**
Goldband GR-7836 *Prudhomme; unknown (g); unknown (b); unknown (d); unknown (rb); band (v).* 99?

(*) Fais Do Do
Louisiana Red Hot LRHR 1131 *Prudhomme; Kirk Ledee (g); Keith Simon (b); Jocquelle Frank (d); Derek Green (rb); Mark Davis, band (v).* 00?

Prudhomme's one-row button accordion playing is light and bouncy, and his set on *Zydeco Live!* (which is shared with John Delafose) is pleasantly danceable, without the relentlessness of some of his younger competitors. *Zydeco Live!* is always enjoyable, but never more; it's obvious why Prudhomme has a local reputation, and no surprise that, despite his 1992 cameo in *Passion Fish* (soundtrack on Rounder DARI 3008), it hasn't spread.

The eponymous disc is pleasant enough, but the musicians burble happily to themselves, rather than coalescing into a focused, single-minded unit. *You'r Bad Bad Girl* has just such a band: they're tight, driving and together, and in purely musical terms this is Prudhomme's best CD, but it's disastrously under-recorded, with the musicians sounding as if they're wrapped in burlap.

Call Me Jack Hammer is an disastrous capitulation to *nouveau zydeco*, featuring a leaden funk bassist who applies his limited ideas with little regard for what Prudhomme and the other musicians are doing. *Fais Do Do* also applies modernist touches, but with more restraint and a much better band. Ledee's zingy playing is under-exposed, however, and there's overuse of familiar tunes and riffs, given new lyrics. CS

Snooky Pryor (born 1921)
VOCAL, HARMONICA

James Edward Pryor is both the first man (by his own account) to play amplified harmonica in Chicago and, as of this writing, the last practitioner from that era. He's made extravagant claims for his originality but Rice Miller was an acknowledged early influence. Pryor was certainly one of the few harmonica players in postwar Chicago who wasn't totally in thrall to Sonny Boy Williamson I. His recording career began in 1948 and lasted for some ten years. He then gave up music for about a decade, returning in 1972 and continuing until the present day, making records that still epitomize the golden age of Chicago blues.

**** **Pitch A Boogie Woogie If It Takes Me All Night Long**
[Westside WESA 869] *Pryor; Sunnyland Slim, Lazy Bill Lucas (p); Moody Jones, Leroy Foster, Eddie Taylor, Homesick James, Johnny Young, Sylvester Plunkett, unknown (g); Moody Jones, J. C. Hurds, unknown (b); Alfred Wallace, Earl Phillips, Little Joe Harris, unknown (d).* 48–c. 59.

*** **Snooky Pryor**
Paula PCD 11 *Similar to above.* 48–c. 59.

Despite his professed pioneer status, Pryor didn't play amplified harmonica on record until 1953's 'Cryin' Shame'. Not that the extra dimension was missed on the previous three. 'Snooky And Moody's Boogie' from 1948 was a seminal effort, pointing directly towards Little Walter's 'Juke' of four years later. Early vocal sides 'Boogy Fool' and 'I'm Getting Tired' revealed a vocal impediment similar to Williamson's that, unlike Leroy Foster and others, he didn't have to imitate.

Pryor's deserved status rests on a surprisingly small number of records made for a number of independent labels, principally J.O.B. The Paula CD contains 20 tracks; *Pitch A Boogie Woogie* adds a further eight, including some late-'40s tracks by Floyd and Moody Jones and Johnny Young on which Pryor appeared, and the whole collection benefits from superior mastering technology. For once rarity and musical excellence are synonymous, making this indispensable for anyone exploring postwar Chicago blues.

*** **The Big Bear Sessions**
Castle CMDDD 712//Sanctuary 81298 2CD *Pryor; Boogie Woogie Red, Bob Hall (p); Homesick James, Sam Mitchell (g); Roger 'Trigger' Hill, Bob Brunning (b); Uncle Tom Farnell, John Hunt (d).* 73.

Pryor's contributions to this set bring together his LP *Shake Your Boogie* and the relevant tracks from *Homesick James & Snooky Pryor* and *American Blues Legends '73*, all on the Big Bear label. He and Homesick James blend well with each other and with their British rhythm sections. Pryor's vocal and instrumental authority impresses, given his recent emergence from retirement. Apart from 'Cross Town', 'She Knows How To Love Me', three Sonny Boy Williamson I covers, 'Sloppy Drunk' and Tommy McClennan's 'Bottle Up And Go', his remaining ten titles are all new and original. There was to be a considerable hiatus in his recording career but these early offerings are the equal of his subsequent efforts.

*** **Sad & Lonesome**
Wolf 120.409 *Pryor; Homesick James (g).* 10/79.

An impromptu session in Vienna, this came about because one of the duo's concerts had been cancelled. Both men are relaxed and at ease with one another. Pryor leads six of the 14 titles, including a brief 'Harp Boogie'. 'It Seem Like A Dream' betrays its origins in the work of John Lee Williamson and the repetitive 'Rock Me' is simplistic but enjoyable. Best of all are three slow blues, 'It's All Over Now', 'Push Me Well' (Pryor actually sings 'Wish Me Well') and an update of his 'Telephone Blues', during all of which he takes typically striking and fluent solos. Though by no means essential, this catches both musicians at very nearly their best.

*** **Snooky**
Blind Pig BP 72387 *Pryor; Steve Freund (g); Bob Stroger (b); Willie Smith (d).* 87.

This is basically the template for everything that follows. Supported by a selfless backing band, in which Freund takes a handful of demonstrative but controlled solos, Pryor hollers his verses and contributes any number of near-identical but stirring solos. Almost every song begins with a couple of bars of rhythmic harmonica before the band joins in. 'Judgement Day' sets the pattern for 'Why You Want To Do Me Like That', 'Look What You Do To Me' and 'That's The Way To Do It' and the other eight tracks aren't much different. But no matter how similar the melodies and arrangements, Pryor seems to have locked into a magic formula that allows him to be endlessly repetitive and yet continuously entertaining. In a world of fads and transient fame, Snooky Pryor is one of the certainties that sustain the rest.

*** Mind Your Own Business
Antone's 74708 Pryor; Gene Taylor (p); Derek O'Brien, Richard Pryor (g); Earl Pryor (b); Ted Harvey, James Barnes (d). 96.

The third of Pryor's albums for Antone's (regrettably, *Too Cool To Move* [ANT 0017] and *In This Mess Up To My Chest* [ANT 0028] are deleted), this maintains the high standard of its predecessors by letting the music speak for itself. Pryor is on as good form as a 75-year-old is entitled to purvey, playing harmonica with spirit and invention and singing with age-defying strength. His accompanists observe the punctilios of their responsibilities without drawing undue attention to themselves, with the exception of O'Brien's solo duties, with finger and slide, which remain succinct and appropriate. Although all 12 songs are attributed to the artist, including 'Diggin' My Potatoes', the origins of many are fairly transparent and none causes offence. Tempos vary little throughout the set, which comfortably expounds the principles of the Chicago tradition without being trapped in the sterility of other efforts in the genre.

**(*) Can't Stop Blowin'
Electro-Fi 3359 Pryor; Michael Fonfara (o, p); Tyler Yarema (p); Morgan Davis, Teddy Leonard, Mel Brown (g); Curtis Thibodeau (b); Mike Fitzpatrick (d). 8–9/98.

By now Pryor is incapable of making a bad record but he can make an ordinary one. None of the musicians is at fault and their leader works as hard as ever but the result is a warm, cuddly mitten rather than a taut leather glove. Just two tracks, 'Someone To Love Me' and 'I Heard The News' (a lightly disguised 'Good Rockin' Tonight'), dig in with that extra commitment that makes a memorable performance. Guitarist Brown guests on five tracks and solos languidly on all, as do the pianists, who share 12 tracks between them. All save three, by Doctor Clayton, St Louis Jimmy and Tampa Red, are Pryor originals; he also claims the faintly bizarre solo 'Boots 'N' Saddle', closing an album that has too few rewarding moments.

*** Shake My Hand
Blind Pig BPCD 5050 Pryor; Billy Flynn (g); Robert Stroger (b); Jimmy Tillman (d). 99.

Three years have elapsed since *Mind Your Own Business* and this one, with fresh musicians, picks up very much where that left off. Like O'Brien, Flynn stays fairly close to the Robert Lockwood handbook of chorded and phrased accompaniment, remaining unobtrusive until required and never exceeding his brief. Some of the song choices are surprising or, in the case of 'Pistol Packin' Mama', bizarre. A solo rendition of Faye Adams's 'Shake My Hand' is followed by Hank Ballard's 'Work With Me Annie' and John Estes's 'Someday Baby'. The remaining seven songs are Pryor's, with a revisit to 'In This Mess' among them. 'My Babe' turns out to be a reinterpretation of Otis Rush's 'She's A Good Un'. The backings throughout are less ambitious than before, taking the competitive edge away from Pryor, who works as hard as ever.

**(*) Double Shot!
Electro-Fi 3367 Pryor; John Lee, Michael Fonfara (p); Mel Brown (g, v); Al Richardson (b); Jim Boudreau (d). 10/99.

This very much dogs the footsteps of its Electro-Fi predecessor: no inherent faults but precious little to applaud. This time Mel Brown gets equal billing, singing (rather poorly) a pair of his own compositions and Jimmy Rogers's 'That's All Right' and 'Rock This House'. He takes frequent guitar solos but rarely does more than fill the available space. Pryor seems less inclined to write his own material, preferring the talents of Memphis Minnie, Johnny Temple and Louis Jordan. A pedestrian attempt at Johnny Otis's 'So Fine' feels like an imposition from the production team, who coax workmanlike performances from those present without inspiring any real commitment.

**** And His Mississippi Wrecking Crew
Electro-Fi 3373 Pryor; Pinetop Perkins (p, v); Mel Brown, Jeff Healey (g); Bob Stroger (b); Willie Smith (d). 10/01.

In both performance and sound, this is the ultimate showcase for Pryor's undiminished talent. The warm, ambient studio sound emphasizes the power of his singing and harmonica playing, the latter less adventurous than before but still urgent. Six of the ten songs are his own, the others coming from Sonny Boy Williamson ('Decoration Day' and 'Sugar Mama Blues'), Memphis Slim ('Grinder Man Blues', sung by Perkins) and the traditional 'Corinna'. Guest guitarist Healey is a little hyperactive during the three songs on which he's present, whereas Brown's empathy with Pryor's music is now well established. Perkins is a reluctant soloist but takes excessive care not to screw up, while the rhythm team provides a taut cushion for some cracking ensemble playing.

*** Mojo Ramble
Electro-Fi 3381 Pryor; John Lee (o, p); Mel Brown (g); Leo Valvassori (b); Jim Boudreau (d). 11/01.

Pryor is in roaring vocal form on this set from the Li'l Big Horn Saloon in Cambridge, Ontario. Many of the songs have appeared on earlier CDs, but the versions here are accompanied with enormous skill and authority, and although, thanks to Pryor's generosity in the matter of solo space, they are nearly all extended to seven, eight or nine minutes, not a moment is wasted. NS

Joe Pullum (1905–64)
VOCAL

Though born in Alabama, Pullum was ensconced on the Houston music scene by the mid-'30s, when he had a hit with his recording of 'Black Gal What Makes Your Head So Hard?', which was widely copied. He left Houston in 1936 to settle in LA and work for the next 25 years as a presser for a clothing manufacturer. In the early '50s he made a few recordings for local labels but did not repeat his earlier success.

**** Joe Pullum – Vol. 1 (1934–1935)
Document DOCD-5393 Pullum; Robert Cooper (p, sp); Andy Boy (p). 4/34–8/35.

*** Joe Pullum – Vol. 2 (1935–1951)
Document DOCD-5394 Pullum; Chester Boone (t); Andy Boy, Robert Cooper, Lloyd Glenn (p); Melvin Martin, Tiny Webb (g); Billy Hadnott (b); Bob Harvey (b). 8/35–51.

Pullum possesses one of the most singular voices in the blues. Pitched very high, it glides through his songs with subtlety and grace, its purity of tone sometimes harmonious with sentiments of affection or regret, at other times piquantly dissonant with expressions of anger and violence. The contrast is vividly present in his best-known song, 'Black Gal What Makes Your Head So Hard', where a story of an elusive woman climaxes in the sour promise: 'I'm goin' to haunt her with my smokin' .44, and when I find that black gal, her nappy, knotty head won't be hard no more.' At his first two sessions he was accompanied by a notably fine Houston pianist, Robert Cooper. 'Cows, See That Train Comin'' is predominantly a vehicle for Cooper's playing of a favourite Texan barrelhouse tune, and 'West Dallas Drag' and 'West Dallas Drag – No. 2' are piano solos with a hint of ragtime.

Such is Pullum's ease with varieties of blues that one feels he could do equal justice to different kinds of material, and in the 32-bar song 'Dixie My Home' he duly proves it. This is with the Galveston pianist Andy Boy, who accompanies him throughout a session spread over the two CDs. For his last '30s date, however, Cooper returns with a trumpeter and guitarist who make merry on the Fats Walleresque 'Come On If You're Comin'' and 'Swing Them Blues'. *Vol. 2* then provides an intermission programme by Andy Boy (q.v.) before a last act which finds Pullum in LA, a decade and a half later, accompanied by sidekicks of Lowell Fulson and re-creating his trademark song in a voice only slightly tarnished by time. TR

Henry Qualls (1934–2003)
VOCAL, GUITAR

Qualls lived all his life in the hamlet of Elmo, east of Dallas, which he seems to have visited only to hear music. He took up the guitar early in life, and made his living as a labourer in farming and construction, and by hunting, fishing and running house parties. Lionized on his discovery by folklorists, he played engagements in Dallas, but showed no wish to repeat a fleeting 1994 visit to Europe.

**(*) Blues From Elmo, Texas
Dallas Blues Society DBS 8901 *Qualls; Hash Brown (g); Ron Green (b); Marc Wilson (d).* 94.

Henry Qualls led a hard life, which may be why his singing, like his slide playing on gospel songs, is sometimes quavering and insecurely pitched. *Blues From Elmo, Texas* is predominantly reflective and introverted, with only 'Long Gone' and the instrumental 'Elmo Stomp' having the slambang energy that might be expected from a house-party musician. Qualls's music is firmly connected to the postwar Texas tradition, owing much to Lightnin' Hopkins, Frankie Lee Sims and Lil' Son Jackson, but he veers off from it at eccentric angles. This is most obvious when the Newbeats' bubblegum hit 'Bread And Butter' becomes leering, funky dance music, but Qualls's unorthodox, weakly tonal harmony is more fundamental to his status as an original and interesting, albeit minor, musician. CS

Doug Quattlebaum (1927–96)
VOCAL, GUITAR

Originally from Florence, South Carolina, Quattlebaum moved with his mother to Philadelphia at the age of 14. He was given his first guitar by his stepfather, a brother of Arthur 'Big Boy' Crudup. Recordings for the local Gotham label in 1953 did nothing to launch a musical career, and he returned to occasionally accompanying gospel quartets. He was recorded at length by the folklorist Pete Welding in 1961, and cut an obscure 45 in the late '60s, but little is known of his subsequent life except that he became a minister.

*** If You've Ever Been Mistreated
Testament TCD 6003 *Quattlebaum.* 7/61.

The Gotham 78 of 'Don't Be Funny, Baby' and 'Lizzie Lou' may not have done much for the artist, but at least it acquainted the world of record-collecting with his name, and who could forget a blues singer called Quattlebaum? Pete Welding certainly hadn't, and when someone told him about a Mister Softee ice-cream seller of that name in South Philadelphia who drummed up custom by singing and playing guitar, he felt hopeful that it was the same man. It was, and the result of their meeting was a remarkable album, *Softee Man Blues* (Prestige/Bluesville BVLP 1065). This has not been reissued, but recordings Welding made a few months earlier eventually appeared on this Testament CD.

Few singers have staged their performances with such dramatic lighting. Gifted with a voice of singular power and flexibility, and a delivery rich in contrast and ornament, Quattlebaum dresses his songs, often well-known blues from the '40s and '50s, with a theatricality reminiscent of the church. If his presentation, with a bullishly strummed steel-bodied guitar, tends to drub into conformity even such disparate material as Roy Brown's 'Hard Luck Blues', Charles Brown's 'Drifting Blues' and Jimmy Reed's 'Baby, What You Want Me To Do', the pulpit fervour of his performance is as formidable there as it is on the half-dozen of the 19 tracks that are gospel songs. Some of these, like 'Touch The Hem Of His Garment', recall Sam Cooke with The Soul Stirrers.

A few of the Testament tracks are fragments, and the session sounds at times like a rehearsal; it is still very striking, but the Bluesville date would elicit more considered performances. The '53 Gotham sides 'Lizzie Lou', the unissued 'Foolin' Me' and a long version of 'Don't Be Funny, Baby' are on *East Coast Blues* (Collectables COL-CD-5324). TR

Queen Ida (born 1929)
VOCAL, ACCORDION

After moving from Louisiana to California as a child, Ida Lewis married Raymond Guillory, raised a family and drove a school bus. Taking up the accordion in the early '70s, she was soon working with her brother, Al Lewis (a.k.a. Rapone), and became Queen Ida, the first woman to record leading a zydeco band.

**(*) On Tour
GNP-Crescendo GNPD 2147 *Queen Ida; Al Rapone (g, v); Don Nick (b); Gregory DePew (d); Wilbert Lewis (rb, perc).* c. 82.
** In San Francisco
GNP-Crescendo GNPD 2158 *Queen Ida; Pierre Allen (vn, g, v); Douglas Dayson (g, v); Dennis Calloway (b, v); Gregory DePew (d, cga); Wilbert Lewis (rb, perc).* c. 83.
** Caught In The Act
GNP-Crescendo GNPD 2181 *Queen Ida; Myrick Guillory (ac, claves); Douglas Dayson (syn, g, v); Peter Allen (vn, g); Denny Geyer (g, v); Dennis Calloway (b); Jimmy Sanchez (d); Wilbert Lewis (rb, perc).* c. 85.

** Cookin' with Queen Ida
GNP-Crescendo GNPD 2197 *Queen Ida; Steve Madaio (t); Slide Hyde (tb); Bernard Anderson (ts); Robert Martin (s, kb, v); Myrick Guillory (ac, rb, v); James Hurley (vn); Dennis Geyer, Gary Myrick, Neil Norman (g); Terrence Buddingh (b); Ben Holmes (d); Wilbert Lewis (rb); Sylvia St James, Nicole Sill, Cheryl Hawthorne, Larry Hawthorne, Dennis Sims, Brant Biles (v).* c. 89.

**(*) Mardi Gras!
GNP-Crescendo GNPD 2227 *Queen Ida; Mike Gallsatus (t); Mike Birch (tb); Bernard Anderson (s, v); Tom Devine (s); Myrick Guillory (ac, rb, v); Tom Rigney (vn); Doug Dayson (g, v); Terry Buddingh (b); Jimmy Sanchez (d).* c. 94.

** Back On The Bayou
GNP-Crescendo GNPD 2265 *Queen Ida; Bernard Anderson (fl, s); Martin Fierro (s); Al Rapone (ac, v); Gus Garelick (vn); Richard Rowley, James Santiago (g); John Lindberg (b); Paul Disibio (d, perc, v); Ron Guillory (rb, v).* 97.

Marketed as zydeco, Queen Ida's music (and her family's; *Back On The Bayou* is credited to Queen Ida and Al Rapone) often sounds more Cajun than rhythm & blues. She also uses Tex-Mex and Caribbean elements, with limited success; *Back On The Bayou*'s 'Raisin' Cane' and *In San Francisco*'s 'Zydeco Taco' are toe-curlers. Much of the Guillory–Lewis clan's music offers bland, vicarious nostalgia via well-worn signifiers of bayou life (gumbo, crawfish, alligators et cetera); it's a zydeco analogue of the Nashvillized Cajun sound of musicians like Doug Kershaw and Jimmy C. Newman. Also part of the mass-market package are songs by outsiders – John Fogerty and Chas & Dave (!) among them – that either pastiche Louisiana styles or can be crowbarred in, like Nick Lowe's 'Half A Boy And Half A Man', with its not excessively bayou-relevant reference to the SPG.

It doesn't help that as singers Ida, her son Myrick and Al Rapone are respectively scratchy, plummy and stodgy. The best CD is *On Tour*, with dynamic bass, drums and percussion on mainly traditional material. Elsewhere, the pudding is often over-egged, but the lean brass and reed arrangements on *Mardi Gras!* are reasonably effective. In 'Since You Been Gone', *Mardi Gras!* includes an unequivocally excellent blues, but Queen Ida is usually the John Denver of Louisiana music.

** Cookin' Zydeco!
Edsel DIAB 8042 *Similar to above CDs.* 80s–90s.

Compiled from the above CDs, *Cookin' Zydeco!* also includes a track from Myrick Guillory's *Nouveau Zydeco* (GNP-Crescendo GNPD 2203). Edsel select for cliché and pastiche with remarkable consistency. CS

Ann Rabson (born 1945)
VOCAL, PIANO, GUITAR, KAZOO, WHISTLING

Rabson took up guitar at 17, and was playing professionally a year later. She added piano around 1980, and in 1988 co-founded Saffire – The Uppity Bluesswomen, of which she remains a member.

***(*) Music Makin' Mama
Alligator ALCD 4848 *Rabson; Greg Piccolo (ts); Phil Wiggins (h); Mimi Rabson (vn); John Cephas, Bob Margolin (g); Jeff Sarli (b); Big Joe Maher (d).* 96.

Equally proficient on guitar and piano, Ann Rabson is also blessed with a tuneful and flexible voice that she never goads into stridency. As a pianist, she's rhythmically strong, but resists flashiness just as firmly; even 'Blue Boogie' is a gentle homage to Jimmy Yancey, not a rabble-rouser. Alongside some pleasant originals, Rabson covers a wide range of styles and artists, from Cow Cow Davenport to Z. Z. Hill, although 'Hallelujah, I Just Love Him So' was an unwise choice; her voice can't compete with the drummer, and lacks the requisite gospel tone. Elsewhere, Margolin's playing is occasionally boorish, but the accompanists generally acquit themselves well, and are intelligently deployed for variety.

***(*) Struttin' My Stuff
M.C. MC 0041 *Rabson; Marty Ballou (b); Richard Crooks (d, perc).* 4/00.

The piano playing is more exposed here; Rabson only plays guitar on three tracks, and the accompanists appear on less than half the disc. This is no bad thing, for her percussive right hand, deployed rather conservatively on Alligator, gets to frisk and gambol to good effect. Some of the slow songs are rather drippy, and Rabson doesn't manage to substantiate her opinion that 'Let Me Go Home Whiskey' is 'deeply haunting'; on the other hand, Brownie McGhee's 'Sportin' Life Blues' gets a much more moving reading than ever it received from the composer. 'Hassle Attack' and 'Beggin' For You Baby' are very clever lyrics, pulling off the difficult trick of inserting modern images (email, fax) and bourgeois lifestyle preoccupations into the blues without trivializing the idiom.

*** In A Family Way
Emit Doog Music EDM 0008 *Rabson; Dave Harris (tb, o); Mimi Rabson (vn); Liz Rabson Schnore (g); Steve Rabson (p); Kenji Rabson (b).* 05?

No kidding: in the order listed, the musicians are Rabson's brother-in-law, sister, daughter, brother and nephew. We wouldn't want to cause a spat at the Thanksgiving table, so it's a relief, while singling out Harris's guttural trombone playing for special mention, to report that they all acquit themselves entirely adequately. Rabson continues to produce some good originals, among them 'Blindsided', about betrayal, and 'Hopin' It'll Be All Right', about abusive relationships. 'I Want To Hop On Your Harley' is terribly slight, although Rabson might respond that it's meant to be, and 'Three Hundred Pounds Of Joy' confirms the eccentricity of her view that it's a masterpiece. Still, 'Midnight Hour Blues', 'Do Your Duty' and 'See See Rider' are finely interpreted, and it's good to hear the latter song's affecting introductory verse. CS

Yank Rachell (1908–97)
VOCAL, MANDOLIN, GUITAR

James Rachell (sometimes misspelled Rachel) was born near Brownsville, Tennessee. As a child he learned mandolin, obtaining his first instrument in a trade for a pig, and guitar. With fellow Brownsvillean Sleepy John Estes he played on the streets of Memphis and made his first recordings there in 1929. In the '30s he teamed up with Sonny Boy Williamson I and recorded with him and a number of other blues artists.

Re-emerging in the mid-'60s, he was reunited with Estes and appeared alongside him at blues festivals and on overseas tours. He spent his last years in Indianapolis.

*** Yank Rachel – Vol. 1 (1934–1938)
Wolf WBCD-006 *Rachell; Sonny Boy Williamson I (h); Elijah Jones (g, v); Dan Smith, prob. 'Jackson' Joe Williams (g). 2/34–6/38.*

*** Yank Rachel – Vol 2 (1938–1941)
Wolf WBCD-007 *Rachell; Sonny Boy Williamson I (h, v, sp); 'Jackson' Joe Williams (g, v); William Mitchell, Alfred Elkins (imb); Washboard Sam (wb). 6/38–12/41.*

Among the recordings made by Estes and Rachell in 1929–30 are four on which Rachell was the vocalist. These can most conveniently be found *on Sleepy John Estes – Vol. 1 (1929–1937)* (Document DOCD-5015). *Yank Rachel – Vol. 1* opens on half a dozen 1934 recordings, with loose guitar duet accompaniments by Rachell and Dan Smith. The remaining tracks are mostly by trios of Rachell, Sonny Boy Williamson and Elijah Jones or another guitarist, Rachell sharing the vocals with Jones and generally playing mandolin rather than guitar, most vivaciously on 'Texas Tommy', a sparkling dance tune, unfortunately in a poor transfer, and 'Stuff Stomp'. Despite the attractively careworn tone of Rachell's voice and Williamson's ever-eloquent playing, these sides are somehow not quite as gripping as one expects.

Vol. 2 begins with four sides by 'Jackson' Joe Williams, an enigmatic figure whose mournful cadences are not unlike Rachell's own, or indeed Estes's, especially in 'Haven't Seen No Whiskey', a lively variant of Estes's 'Milk Cow Blues'. Rachell's mandolin cascades through these, but for the rest of the album he plays guitar, accompanied by Williamson and a bass and washboard. He sings with more confidence and projection, Williamson is often at his best, the beat is firm and altogether these are successful recordings which appear to have sold quite well and, to judge from later appearances of songs like '38 Pistol Blues', 'Biscuit Baking Woman' and 'Loudella Blues', stuck in the heads of other artists. 'Insurance Man Blues' is an advert for personal accident cover, Rachell recommending a company which even paid out on an electrocuted criminal. The transfer quality is often indifferent.

*** Mandolin Blues
Delmark DE-606 *Rachell; Hammie Nixon (h, j, sp); Sleepy John Estes, Big Joe Williams (g, v); Mike Bloomfield (g). 3/63.*

Rachell, Estes and Nixon, and Williams and Bloomfield when they join them, have no trouble at all re-creating the sound of the leader's '30s recordings, though here it is fuller, remarkably so for home recordings. Despite the presence of other men not notable for their unobtrusiveness, Rachell dominates the session, singing and playing as well as he ever did. He uses mandolin throughout, except on 'Lonesome Blues', a solo with guitar.

The four 1964 recordings included in *I Blueskvarter: Chicago 1964, Volume One* (Jefferson SBACD 12653/4 2CD) find Rachell on mandolin, with Mike Bloomfield on piano. Four more mandolin recordings, from 1967, are on *Mandolin Blues* (Testament TCD 6004).

*** Yank Rachell
Random Chance RCD 2 *Rachell; Backwards Sam Firk (Mike Stewart) (g). 73.*

Commissioned to remember and reproduce songs he had recorded in the '20s and '30s, such as the guitar pieces 'Skinny Woman Blues' and 'Sugar Farm Blues', Rachell eventually overcame his reluctance (a process candidly described in the notes) and delivered a set that his surprised and delighted clients judged 'terrific'. Listeners unaware of the agenda behind both the commission and the judgement may be a little puzzled. While it's true that Rachell succeeded in leapfrogging the decades and landing in his past, he could not become the young man who lived there. Instead of the zest of invention the album offers the quiet satisfaction of rediscovering resources thought to be lost.

**(*) Chicago Style
Delmark DD-649 *Rachell; Pete Crawford (g); Floyd Jones (b); Odie Payne (d). 8/79.*

*** Blues Mandolin Man
Random Chance RCD 1 *Rachell; Peter 'Mudcat' Ruth (h); Peter Roller (g); Sheena Rachell (b); Leonard Marsh Jr (d). 83, 86.*

In sharp distinction to the previous CD, *Chicago Style* and *Blues Mandolin Man* represent the kind of music Rachell thought he ought to be making, music with at least some elements of the here-and-now. So he plays amplified mandolin, backed by electric guitar and rhythm, both on his own old material like 'Sugar Mama' (*Chicago Style*) or 'Des Moines, Iowa' (*Blues Mandolin Man*) and on pieces that evoke Chicago blues of the late '40s like 'Going To St. Louis' (*Chicago Style*) or 'My Baby's Gone' ('Big Boy' Spires's 'Murmur Low') (*Blues Mandolin Man*). Apart from an occasional waver, his voice is strong and true, and he sounds quite comfortable in the band settings. The amplification of the mandolin on *Chicago Style* is fuzzy. A final album, *Too Hot For The Devil* (Flat Rock [unnumbered]), had only local circulation. TR

The Radio Kings
GROUP

The Radio Kings were founded in 1991 by singer and harmonica player Brian Templeton and guitarist Michael Dinallo, and achieved some success in the Boston area. They then worked for a couple of years with Jerry Portnoy. They made a good impression at the 1995 Rhythm & Blues Festival in Peer, Belgium

*** Money Road
Bullseye Blues & Jazz CD BB 9601 *Scott Aruda (t, flh); Scott Shetler (ts, bs); Brian Templeton (h, ac, v); Anthony Geraci (o, p); Michael Dinallo (g); Dean Cassell (b); Bob Christina (d, cardboard box); Fran Christina (d); Gail Nickse, Nola Rose Shepherd, Freddie G (v). 98?*

Dinallo's guitar riff on the opening track, 'I Can't Win', has the ring of Magic Sam playing rockabilly, a touch of ambiguity that neatly characterizes the music of this inventive young band, one of several that juggle blues, soul, rock 'n' roll and honkytonk country music and keep all the balls in the air. Though their methods are quite different, The Radio Kings conduct their musical business with a swagger, and an originality within the parameters of genre, that may remind some listeners of the early J. Geils Band. 'The Shelf', a slow creeper, 'Disturb Me Baby', discernible beneath the arrangement as a Jimmy Reed line, and the acoustic title track are the only examples of the band working with standard blues forms, but listeners sympathetic to their approach will appreciate the ways in which blues ideas are diffused in other songs. The band's earlier CDs for Icehouse, *It Ain't Easy* (1994) and *Live At B. B. King's* (1995), are deleted. TR

Ma Rainey (1886–1939)
VOCAL

Gertrude Pridgett made her professional debut about 1900 in the Bunch Of Blackberries revue; in 1904 she married William 'Pa' Rainey, and they formed a song-and-dance act, but 'Rainey and Rainey, Assassinators of the Blues' had separated by the time she recorded. Rainey didn't conform to the norms of show-business glamour; short, stout and wiry-haired, with a mouthful of gold teeth, she became a star singer, dancer and comedienne on the strength of personality and talent. Her career slowed during the Depression, and she retired to her native Georgia in 1935. Rainey operated two theatres during her last years, but her death certificate listed her occupation as 'housekeeping'.

***(*) **Ma Rainey – Vol. 1 (1923–1924)**
Document DOCD-5581 *Rainey; Tommy Ladnier (c); Jimmy O'Bryant (cl); Charles Harris (as); Lovie Austin (p); Miles Pruitt (bj); Milas Pruitt, unknowns (g).* 12/23–c. 8/24.

(***(*)) **The Paramounts Chronologically 1924 Vol. 1**
Black Swan HCD-1002 *As above, except omit unknowns (g).* 12/23–c. 5/24.

***(*) **Ma Rainey – Vol. 2 (1924–1925)**
Document DOCD-5582 *Rainey; Howard Scott, Louis Armstrong, Tommy Ladnier, prob. Kid Henderson (c); Charlie Green (tb); prob. Lucien Brown (cl, as); Don Redman, Buster Bailey, Jimmy O'Bryant (cl); Hooks Tilford (as); Fletcher Henderson, Lovie Austin, Lil Henderson (p); Charlie Dixon, prob. George Williams (bj); prob. Happy Bolton (d, chimes); unknown (perc); unknown (k, slide-wh).* c. 10/24–c. 8/25.

(***(*)) **The Paramounts Chronologically 1924–1925 Vol. 2**
Black Swan HCD-1002 *As above, except add unknowns (g).* c. 8/24–c. 8/25.

***(*) **Ma Rainey – Vol. 3 (1925–1926)**
Document DOCD-5583 *Rainey; Joe Smith, prob. Bernie Young or Dave C. Nelson (c); Charlie Green, Albert Wynn (tb); Tom Brown (cl, as); Buster Bailey (cl); Doc Cheatham (ss); Coleman Hawkins (bss); Fletcher Henderson, Lil Henderson (p); Charlie Dixon, Rip Bassett (bj); Ben Thigpen (d); unknown (saw).* c. 12/25–c. 6/26.

***(*) **Ma Rainey – Vol. 4 (1926–1927)**
Document DOCD-5584 *Rainey; prob. B. T. Wingfield, Shirley Clay (c); Kid Ory, Al Wynn (tb); poss. Johnny Dodds, poss. Artie Starks (cl); Jimmy Blythe, poss. Tiny Parham, Hop Hopkins, unknown (p); poss. Leroy Pickett (vn); unknowns (bj); Blind Blake (g); unknowns (bb); unknown (d); Jimmy Bertrand (x); unknown males (sp).* c. 11/26–c. 12/27.

***(*) **Ma Rainey (1928)**
Document DOCD-5156 *Rainey; Georgia Tom Dorsey, poss. Eddie Miller (p); Papa Charlie Jackson (bj, v); Martell Pettiford (bj); Tampa Red (g); Herman Brown (wb, tub d, k); Carl Reid (jazzhorn, j); band (moaning).* c. 9/28–c. 12/28.

(***(*)) **The Paramounts Chronologically 1928 Vol. 5**
Black Swan HCD-12005 *As above.* c. 9/28–c. 12/28.

Ma Rainey said that she added the blues to her act in 1902, and it certainly dominated her material by 1923; a novelty like 'Ya-Da-Do' stands out both stylistically and for her unconvincing handling of it. Recorded blues in the early '20s often had a vaudevillian archness; Ma gave the public a distinctively Southern, folk-based music, with lyrics that address life's joys and problems in poetic but simple and direct language. Her voice was heavy, indigo-dark and often sombre, but she had a profound sense of swing, and could impart a roguish air to songs like 'Ma Rainey's Black Bottom' and the lesbian manifesto 'Prove It On Me'. Her artistry has to fight its way past Paramount's notoriously poor sound, but on many sessions A&R man J. Mayo Williams used good, often great jazz accompanists, who relish the challenge of responding to her deep soulfulness. Consistent with her downhome ethos, Rainey was also at ease when backed by guitarists, pianists and the 'Tub Jug Washboard Band' heard on some of her 1928 sides.

Ma Rainey's consistency over her five-year recording career and the high quality of her accompanists make her complete works far more worthwhile than those of many blues singers. Black Swan's project appears to have been abandoned (an announced *Vol. 3* has not appeared), leaving the field to Document. Subject to the inherent defects of the originals, the mastering is adequate; in line with the company's completist mission, all Document's discs except the fourth contain alternative takes, which are not significantly different.

*** **Madam Gertrude 'Ma' Rainey**
Giants Of Jazz CD 53281 *Similar to relevant CDs above.* 12/23–c. 9/28.

(*) **Mother Of The Blues
Blues Forever CD 68802 *As above.* 12/23–c. 9/28.

*** **The Mother Of The Blues 1923/1928**
EPM Blues Collection 15923 *As above.* 12/23–c. 10/28.

(****) **The Essential**
Classic Blues CBL 200020 2CD *As above.* 12/23–c. 12/28.

***(*) **Heroes [sic] Of The Blues: The Very Best Of Ma Rainey**
Shout Factory DK 30252 *As above.* 12/23–c. 12/28.

*** **Don't Fish In My Sea**
Snapper Complete Blues SBLUECD 015 *As above.* 12/23–c. 12/28.

***(*) **Ma Rainey's Black Bottom**
Yazoo 1071 *As above.* c. 3/24–c. 9/28.

*** **Ma Rainey**
Milestone MCD-47021 *As above.* c. 10/24–c. 9/28.

(*) **Countin' The Blues
Collectors Edition CBCD 023 *As above.* c. 10/24–c. 12/28.

Any selective survey of Ma Rainey's output will be musically satisfactory; ranking these discs is a matter of assessing their annotation and remastering. The sound on *Mother Of The Blues* is passable, but its 18 tracks are evidently an abbreviation of the 24 on Giants Of Jazz. Both CDs have a brief timeline in lieu of notes; it asserts that in 1935 she became 'superintendent of the theatres of Georgia'. Yazoo and Shout Factory have good sound and useful commentary, but programmes of 14 and 16 tracks respectively are not over-generous. *Countin' The Blues* is the inverse: adequate playing time, but inferior sound and skimpy notes. Milestone's 24 tracks, supported by extensive and perceptive notes, are transferred from tapes originally used for a double LP. NoNoise technology has been applied with some deftness, and the sound is tolerable; it's rather better on the 20-trackers from EPM and Snapper, but not sufficiently to lift either of them to the next level of evaluation.

Classic Blues' 36 well-mastered mid-price tracks are the easy winners, despite brief notes and the absence of discographical data, which does a disservice to musicians and listeners alike, and is particularly unhelpful when the running order is not chronological. CS

Kid Ramos (born 1960)
GUITAR, VOCAL

David Ramos grew up in Anaheim, California, and began playing guitar at 14, learning from blues records like B. B. King's Live At The Regal. He played with the James Harman Band for most of the '80s, then worked outside music for a few years, except for brief spells with Roomful Of Blues and other bands. He then began playing with Lynwood Slim, Fred Kaplan and Richard Innes as Big Rhythm Combo (q.v.). In the late '90s he was with the Fabulous Thunderbirds.

*** **Two Hands One Heart**
Black Magic BMCD 9031 *Ramos; Scott Steen (t); Spyder Mittleman (ts, bs); Johnny Viau (s); Lynwood Slim (h, v); Johnny 'Juke' Logan (o); Fred Kaplan (p); Tyler Pederson, Johnny Bazz (b); Richard Innes (d); Janiva Magness (v). 1/95.*

By present-day standards Ramos waited a long time before venturing to make an album in his own name, but the benefits of the years of apprenticeship are obvious. There's no grandstanding: Ramos remarks elsewhere that he doesn't 'get too excited about albums where it's just a bunch of guitar. I like it when the guitar's there doing something for the song', and all the tracks are groupwork, the guitar colouring, crosshatching or adding detail rather than dominating the composition. While Ramos plays mostly in the West Coast line of Hollywood Fats, Junior Watson and so forth, he is no less adept at other styles, like the Nighthawkish slide of 'If You Don't Think I'm Sinking' or the back-country acoustic playing of the title number.

*** **Kid Ramos**
Evidence ECD 26104 *Ramos; Anne King (t); Steve Marsh (ts); Jeff Turmes (bs, b); James Harman (h, v); Dave Mathews (o); Rob Rio, Gene Taylor (p); Willie J. Campbell (b); Stephen Hodges (d, cga); Richard Innes (d); Kim Wilson, Cesar Rosas, Willie Chambers, Lynwood Slim, Janiva Magness (v). 5/99.*

***(*) **West Coast House Party**
Evidence ECD 26110 *Ramos; Mike Turner (t); Steve Marsh, Jonny Viau (ts); Jeff Turmes (bs); Kim Wilson (h, v); Joe Krown (o); Fred Kaplan (p); Duke Robillard, Junior Watson, Rusty Zinn (g, v); 'Little' Charlie Baty, Clarence 'Gatemouth' Brown, Rick Holmstrom (g); Larry Taylor (b); Stephen Hodges (d); James Harman, James Intveld, Janiva Magness, Lynwood Slim, Robert 'Big Sandy' Williams (v). 2/00.*

*** **Greasy Kid Stuff**
Evidence ECD 26117 *Ramos; Jeff Turmes (as, ts, bs, g, b); Paul deLay, Johnny Dyer, Rick Estrin, James Harman, Lynwood Slim, Charlie Musselwhite, Rod Piazza (h, v); Tom Mann (p); Richard Innes (d); Stephen Hodges (perc); James Intveld (v). 3–6/01.*

Kid Ramos finds the guitarist playing with a collection of vintage guitars and amps, accompanying a procession of generally on-form singers through a programme of material from, among others, Little Milton, Pee Wee Crayton, Ray Agee and Otis Rush, the last's 'It Takes Time' giving him the chance to capture Rush's dark, dirty guitar tone. Especially fine are two peaceful downhome quintet sides with Harman, 'Walk-Around Telephone Blues' and 'Helsinki Laundromat Blues'. 'I Would Be A Sinner' is a rare Ramos vocal, in a vintage rock 'n' roll manner.

For *West Coast House Party* Ramos wrote an even longer guestlist, not only of vocalists but of guitarists. His choice of Junior Watson to sing Amos Milburn's 'House Party' was inspired, but unfortunately it's Watson's only appearance. Holmstrom is on only one track, too, but most of the other guests are on at least two, and Gatemouth Brown on four. Unflustered by the VIPs, Ramos storms through the programme; in fact the fiercest performance, 'Real Gone Lover', is by the smallest group, just Ramos, Hodges and Wilson, sounding like three guys who stumbled into the Sun studio *circa* 1953. That and another track aside, the three saxes play throughout, creating tidal swells on which the singers and guitarists swoop and skim.

Having given ample blowing room to his guitar-playing friends, Ramos dedicated the next album to the spirit of '50s Memphis and Chicago, assigning all the lead guitar work to himself but inviting a septet of harmonica players. Now and then the volatility of the guests subverts the back-to-basics plan that Ramos began with, but many of the tracks have an admirable simplicity, like Rick Estrin's slow blues for Little Walter, 'Marion's Mood'. In 'Rich Man's Woman' Ramos's slide guitar combines with Charlie Musselwhite's vocal and harp to re-create the ambience of Muddy Waters's original, while Johnny Dyer's version of 'Mean Ol' Lonesome Train' gets a setting faithful to Lightnin' Slim's. By now it's clear that, in the styles that interest him, blues guitar playing holds no secrets for Kid Ramos. TR

Al Rapone (born 1937)
VOCAL, ACCORDION, GUITAR

Rapone (real name Al Lewis) is the brother of Queen Ida. Before becoming her guitarist and producer, he had played in blues bands on the West Coast. On forming the Zydeco Express, he reverted to accordion, his first instrument.

** **Troubled Woman**
Traditional Line 1306 *Rapone; Lady Lisa Haley (vn, v); Patty LaRue Harrison (g, perc, v); Ben Bording (g); Michael O. (b); Ben Holmes (d). 4/84.*

(*) **Live At Dingwall's Dancehall
JSP JSPCD 813 *As above, except Michael O. also sings; omit Haley. 85.*

Troubled Woman was recorded at a concert in East Germany and *Live At Dingwall's* in London, where 'Dresden Zydeco' becomes 'Camden Zydeco' (and remains 'Chère Catin' with new lyrics.) JSP's recording and mixing are superior, there's less of Rapone working the crowd between numbers and, best of all, Harrison sings lead on only one track. Losing the fiddle is also an improvement; on *Troubled Woman* it's just a poorly integrated marker of Louisianadom. Rapone is a competent accordionist in the Clifton Chenier vein, but an unremarkable singer. Bording produces some inventive solos, and on JSP the bass can be heard throbbing effectively from time to time, but what makes the enjoyable elements of *Live At Dingwall's* obvious is the averageness of the music that frames them.

** **Zydeco To Go**
Blind Pig BP 73790 *Rapone; Bobbie Webb (ts); Bob Skye (h); Joe Young, Mitchell Cormier, Orwell Rapone (ac); Mark Naftalin (o); Nick Milo (p, syn); Michael Goods (p); James Hurley, Allen Fontenot, Bob Lieberman, Tom Rigney (vn); Tom Stern (bj); Leonard Gill (g, b); David Nelson (g, v); Richard Rowley (g); Mark Metoyer (b, rb); Bob Emery, Terry Buddingh (b); Darrel Brasseaux (d, perc); Jamie Lease (d, v); Harvey Johnson (d); Gator 'Smith' [sic] (rb); Roy L. Chantier (v).* 90.

Attempting to display his versatility, Rapone adds swamp pop, country and Cajun to zydeco, but does none of them very well; most tracks are overproduced, many are clichéd, and 'Good Ole Cajun Music' may be the worst bayou 'n' boondocks synthesis ever recorded. As with *Live At Dingwall's*, there are moments to like – Naftalin's chunky fills on 'Our Hearts Will Dance In Love Again', the *conjunto*-flavoured accordion on 'Mazuka', a couple of classy solos from Cajun veteran Allen Fontenot – but they are far from enough to elicit a recommendation.

*** **Al Rapone Plays Tribute**
Atomic Theory ATM 1133 *Rapone; Jim Greenwell (ts, bs); Virgil Nelson (prob. h, ac, o, p); Curtis Obeda (g); John Lindberg (b, v); Dan Hostetler (d, perc); Jim Callen (rb); Beve Kirby, Micheale Roberts (v).* 97.

The subject of the tribute is Clifton Chenier, and most of the songs are by or associated with him. This is Al Rapone's best CD because perforce it's straight zydeco, not the tannoy music for Bayouworld. Rapone's working band, the Butanes, have a surprisingly good grasp of zydeco idioms, given that they're from Minneapolis. Despite its merits, though, *Plays Tribute* can't stand the unavoidable comparison with Chenier's originals. CS

Moses Rascoe (1917–94)
VOCAL, GUITAR

Born in North Carolina, Rascoe began playing guitar in 1930 and left home at 14, leading a nomadic existence before settling in York, Pennsylvania, in 1938. He drove a truck for many years; taking up music professionally only after retiring from his day job, Rascoe performed initially at local coffeehouses, later graduating to the festival circuit.

(*) **Blues
Flying Fish FF 70454 *Rascoe; Ken Werner (h).* 5/87.

The repertoire holds no surprises: 'Step It Up And Go', 'Blood Red River' and 'John Henry' are all there, as are a token gospel number and two Jimmy Reed chestnuts, but Rascoe approaches all his songs enthusiastically, giving them interesting arrangements. His voice shows no trace of his 70 years, and his guitar work is always lively; on 'Twelve String Rag', descended from Blind Blake, it's very adroit indeed. *Blues* was recorded at a coffeehouse before a politely enthusiastic audience, most of them evidently hearing the *doubles entendres* of 'Deep Sea Diver' and 'Let Me Play With Your Yo Yo' for the first time. Their pleasure in Rascoe's music was justified, which is more than can be said for the unnecessary and intrusive harmonica, which mars the tracks where it appears, and devalues an otherwise very pleasant disc. CS

Eomot RaSun (born 1945)
VOCAL, HARMONICA

Ezra Lee Blakely Jr was born in Clarksdale, Mississippi, but grew up in South Side Chicago. After serving in the US Navy (1962–66), including three tours in Vietnam, he opened a jeweller's shop in Chicago and changed his name. In the '80s, with the help of Jimmy Rogers and Jimmy D. Lane, he worked on his harmonica playing – he had been singing since long before – and began to secure engagements in Chicago clubs.

(*) **Three Days Walkin'
APO APO 2008 *RaSun; Jimmy D. Lane (g); Bob Stroger (b); Sam Lay (d).* 4/98.

The sound of this record is redolent of Chicago blues in the '50s. RaSun's prime model for harmonica playing was Little Walter, and his versions of 'Last Night' and 'Blues With A Feeling' are very like the originals. But with those obeisances made, he stakes his own claim for respect with original material, much of it written jointly with Jimmy Lane, and with singing and blowing whose energy is matched by his accompanists, especially Lane. The album is impressive a track or two at a time, less so when heard at length, perhaps because the ensemble sound is rather thin. In particular, the closing track, 'Try Your Best', a Sam Cookeish soul number, would have been enhanced by a horn or two. TR

Destini Rawls (born 1976)
VOCAL

The Milwaukee-born daughter of Johnny Rawls has experience of singing in her high-school choir and in church. Called in for some backing vocals on her father's album *Put Your Trust In Me*, she impressed producer Bruce Feiner enough to earn the chance of making her own album.

** **I'm Movin' In**
JSP JSPCD 2149 *Rawls; Jamie Finegan (t); Bruce Feiner (ts, p, syn, prod); Robert Feiner (bs); 'Junior' Badowski (h); Bruce Bears (o); Johnny Rawls (g, v); Phil Guy, Johnnie Marshall (g); Mike Nunno (b); Jason Arnold (d).* 00.

There are three tracks on this album that might interest a blues enthusiast, 'What's Wrong With You?', the title track and 'Just Call Me Junior'. The last is a feature for harmonica player 'Junior' Badowski but Rawls sings the others competently, if rather impassively, and Guy and Marshall are lively on all three. A fourth number, 'I'm Goin' Stonecrazy', also has contributions by Guy and Badowski. Elsewhere the arrangements are dominated by organ and synthesizer, the songs, all written by Johnny Rawls and Bruce Feiner, or by Feiner alone, are more or less in the pop idiom, and the claim in the notes that 'Destini is bound to secure her own reputation as a world class vocalist' seems a little premature. TR

Johnny Rawls (born 1951)
VOCAL, GUITAR

Rawls was born in southern Mississippi and much of his early playing was along the Gulf Coast, accompanying visiting soul and blues acts. In the late '70s he was guitarist and bandleader for O. V. Wright, and after the singer's death he and guitarist L. C. Luckett led an O. V. Wright Band for 13 years. In 1996 his album *Here We Go* initiated a five-year relationship with JSP Records, during which he cut four albums of his own and produced several for other artists, usually in collaboration with the tenor saxophonist, songwriter and arranger Bruce Feiner. Since 1969 he has been based in Milwaukee.

**(*) My Turn To Win
JSP JSPCD 2116 Rawls; Jim Hunt (t); Bruce Feiner (ts, p, syn); Robert Feiner (bs); Roosevelt Purifoy (kb); Kevin Bibbs (b); Allen Kirk (d); 'Fazz' Eddie Gillespie, Greg 'Salt Dog' Allen (v). 99.

**(*) Put Your Trust In Me
JSP JSPCD 2145 Rawls; Jamie Finegan (t); Robert Feiner (ts, bs); Bruce Feiner (ts, p, syn); 'Junior' Badowski (h); Bruce Bears (o, p); Eddie Kirkland, Phil Guy (g, v); Burt Teague (g); Mike Nunno (b); Jason Arnold (d, cowbell); Destini Rawls (v, sp). 00.

*** Get Up And Go: The Best Of The JSP Years
JSP JSP 1101 2CD As for above CDs, except add Peter Bartels (t), Will Redding (tb), Anthony Johnson, Samuel Ross (as), Rodney 'Hot Rod' Brown (s), David Taylor (o), Bernard Watts (g), Daryl Johnson, Calvin Beale (b), Eddie Gillespie (d). 3/96–00.

Stylistically Rawls's home is built on the state line between blues and Southern soul. His voice is a smooth amalgam of Little Johnny Taylor, Sam Cooke, Z. Z. Hill and his former employer O. V. Wright, and his compositions, though often blues in form, are full of allusions to their work. On both *My Turn To Win*, the first of his albums made with Bruce Feiner, and its successor, *Put Your Trust In Me*, he gives warm and appealing performances, but the uplifting effect of his singing and elegant guitar playing is dampened by the ordinariness of the material. For the sympathetic listener either album will yield a mild and continuous pleasure, but probably no jolts of excitement or surprise.

Get Up And Go, which marked Rawls's departure from JSP to start his own label, combines ten tracks by himself, fairly evenly selected from the above CDs and their deleted forerunners *Here We Go* (1996) and *Louisiana Woman* (1997), and ten by JSP artists he has produced or worked with in some other capacity, such as Deitra Farr, George Stancell, Mary Taylor and his daughter Destini Rawls. TR

Kenny 'Blue' Ray (born 1950)
GUITAR, ORGAN, VOCAL

Among Ray's earliest inspirations were his father, an amateur musician who bought him his first guitar, and the night-time broadcasts of DJ Wolfman Jack. In 1975–76 he played guitar with Little Charlie & The Nightcats, then moved to LA to join the house band at Smokey Wilson's Pioneer Club and record with William Clarke. In the '80s, based in Austin, Texas, he played for several years with Marcia Ball. Since the early '90s he has lived in southern California, fronting his own band, building guitars and issuing numerous CDs and instructional videos.

*** In All Of My Life
JSP JSPCD 289 Ray; Rob Sudduth (ts, bs); John Firmin (ts); Charlie Chavez (h, v); Austin DeLeon [Audie deLone] (o); Frank DeRose (b); Jimmy Morello (d, v); Kevin Coggins (d); Jackie Payne (v). 1/97.

*** Soulful Blues
Tone King TKCD 1066 Ray; John Middleton (t); Rob Sudduth (ts, bs); Carl Green (ts); Audie deLone (o, p); Steve Edmonson (g); Burton Winn, Treena Foster, Mike Phillips, Liz Peel (b); Shad Harris, Gene Pardue (d); Jackie Payne (v). 1–10/00.

**(*) Got Blues!
Blue Kat BKCD 052 Ray; Rock Hendricks (ts); Ronnie Boy Edwards (h, p, v); Charlie Chavez (h, v); Stan Powell, Screamin' Iain (h); Duke Jethro (o); Chip Roland, Audie deLone (p); Liz Peel, Bob Mistretta, David Brown, Treena Foster, Burton Winn (b); Gene Pardue, Kenny Gross, Eric Mossbarger, Jim Overton, June Core (d); Little Danny (v). 1/91–1/02.

No singer, Ray makes guitar-based albums with guest vocalists, one of his favourites being Jackie Payne, who helps to give *In All Of My Life* a good start by singing on three early tracks. Interleaving the vocal numbers – others are by co-producer Jimmy Morello and Charlie Chavez – are original instrumentals like ''56 Eldorado', 'Bayou Boogie' and 'Bailin' On The Gator' featuring Ray's fat Strat playing. The listener who enjoys tracing the lineage of guitar riffs and effects will detect echoes of Albert Collins, Stevie Ray Vaughan, John Lee Hooker and many other players, but Ray's synthesis of all that he has heard and thought up for himself is respectably personal.

The Tone King and Blue Kat CDs are the most recent of a sequence of 12 albums that Ray has released on these personal labels since 1994. Most of the others are out of print, but *Keep The Mojo Workin'* (Tone King TKCD 1064) and *Blues Obsession* (TKCD 1065) may still be available. *Soulful Blues* stands out, having a resident vocalist – Payne again – and an exclusively non-original programme that embraces T-Bone Walker's 'Mean Old World', Hendrix's 'Voodoo Chile' and Howlin' Wolf's 'Who's Been Talkin''. *Got Blues!* is a selection from out-of-print predecessors with one previously unissued cut, 'Stop Breakin' Down', for which Ray breaks his rule and sings, though off-mike. The other vocal numbers, handled without much subtlety by Chavez and Edwards, are mostly standard repertoire like Buster Brown's 'Fannie Mae' and Magic Sam's 'Everything's Gonna Be Alright', but four instrumentals are Ray originals in a variety of styles. TR

Paul Reddick
VOCAL, HARMONICA

His producer Colin Linden calls Reddick 'one of the most original and inventive singer-songwriters in blues today'. Reddick acknowledges the influence on his work of Sleepy John Estes, Fred McDowell and Alan Lomax's field recordings – as well as William Blake and William Carlos Williams. In 2002 *Rattlebag* was voted Blues Album Of The Year by the Toronto Blues Society and nominated for a W. C. Handy Award.

*** Rattlebag
NorthernBlues NBM 0005 Reddick; Richard Bell (o, p); Colin Linden (md, Do, g, v, prod); Kyle Ferguson (g); Greg Marshak (b); Vince Maccarone (d). 01.

*** Villanelle
NorthernBlues NBM 0025 Reddick; Richard Bell (o, p); Kathleen Edwards (vn); Colin Linden (md, g, b, v, prod); Larry Taylor, John Dymond (b); Stephen Hodges, Gary Craig (d, perc); Bryan Owings (d). 04.

Reddick obviously knows the blues, but he seldom does anything as obvious as drop a direct musical quote. Nevertheless, his work is so suffused with blues effects that it resonates continuously on a blues frequency. Some of that is due to Colin Linden, who is plainly on Reddick's wavelength, creating a rich, deep background hum of overlaid guitar parts – electric, acoustic; 12-string, six-string; finger-style, slide – as a surface upon which Reddick can scrawl his verses. These, thanks to his silted voice, are not always easy to decipher, and even when they are they can be rather shapeless, but, especially when they are more neatly boxed by the blues form, as in 'Blind River Bound' on Rattlebag or 'Hooks In The Water' and 'Dogcatcher' on Villanelle, they have a strange, almost ominous power, accentuated by Reddick's tart harmonica and, on some numbers, by a dim undertrack of chanting and moaning on vocal loops. Rattlebag (credited to Paul Reddick & The Sidemen) is a fractionally less baroque production and, for the reader whose curiosity is tempered with caution, perhaps a better starting-point, but both albums are ingenious and impressive. TR

A. C. Reed (1926–2004)
VOCAL, TENOR SAXOPHONE

Aaron Corthen moved from Missouri to Chicago in his teens. He changed his name and became a fulltime musician in the early '50s, recording a number of singles from 1960 onwards. Reed was a sideman with Earl Hooker, Buddy Guy, Albert Collins, Son Seals and others as well as leading his own band and operating the Ice Cube label.

*** I Got Money
Black & Blue BB 464 Reed; Maurice John Vaughn (g); Douglas Watson (b); Julian Vaughn (d). 11/85.
** I'm In The Wrong Business!
Alligator ALCD 4757 Reed; Jimmy Markham (h); Allen Batts (o, p); 'George' (p); Bonnie Raitt, Maurice John Vaughn (g, v); Larry Burton, Phil Guy, Stevie Ray Vaughan, Marvin Jackson, 'Tripple Horn', Steve Diztell (g); Aron Burton, Freddie Dixon, Douglas Watson, Johnny B. Gayden, Nate Applewhite (b); Casey Jones (d); Miranda Louise, Vicki Hardy (v). late 79–early 87.
***(*) A. C. Reed/Big Wheeler
Wolf 120.860 Reed; Luther Adams, John Primer (g); Willie Kent (b); Timothy Taylor (d). 11/89.
**** Junk Food
Delmark DE-726 Reed; Ed 'Fishman' Madden, Michael Barber, Jeffery Evans (t); Joe Burton, Dharamdas Harkes Duke (tb); Eric Lawrence (as, ts, bs); Kelly Connors (as); Steve Koerner (ts, bs); Douglas Fagan (ts); Paul Simeone, Roosevelt Purifoy (o); Albert Collins, Maurice John Vaughn, Sammy Fender (g, v); Jerry DeMink, Marvin Jackson, Ed Wooten, Essex 'Grownman' Johns (g); Doug Watson, Mike Morrison, Johnny B. Gayden, Avery 'Abe' Brady (b); Casey Jones, Arthur 'Sambo' Irby (d, v); Jeff Taylor (d); Amy Cochrane, Stan Jones (v). 80–c. 98.

Whether or not they were half-brothers, as A. C. sometimes claimed, he was a longtime occasional borrower of Jimmy Reed's drawl and his loping rhythms. The other distinguishing features of A. C.'s music are the skinny rasp of his sax and the singing of blues about how the singing of blues doesn't pay. The joke wears thin with repetition, but it's symptomatic of a talent for original, often witty lyrics that get away from the standard topics.

The band is tight on *I Got Money*, but from 'Boogie Chillen' to 'Big Boss Man', Reed's five tracks (Maurice John Vaughn does the other five) are over-extended versions of over-familiar songs; it's only fair to note, though, that 'Big Boss Man' is revitalized by a choppy funk beat. A. C. also gets five of the nine tracks on Wolf; they're an excellent set of uncomplicated Chicago blues, with Primer in coruscating form and the whole band chivvied along by Tim Taylor's clipped rhythms.

Alligator's three tracks from the *Living Chicago Blues* sessions are enjoyably sardonic, but with or without big-name guests, the mid-'80s recordings seldom escape predictability. Vaughan's solos are empty energy, Raitt superimposes predictable slide figures regardless of their relevance and Reed's songwriting seems to have hit a dry spell: the restaurant trope on 'Fast Food Annie' is a convoluted, lo-cal substitute for humour, and 'These Blues Is Killing Me' sticks doggedly with the obvious. 'Don't Drive Drunk' is good advice expressed through musical and verbal clichés (Maurice John Vaughn's rap included).

Arthur Irby's stentorian delivery of the Doors' 'Roadhouse Blues' must be heard to be believed, and on two live tracks from 1980 Albert Collins's guitar both matches and goads Reed's assertive singing; but *Junk Food* is chiefly notable for the very assured handling of large brass and reed sections. 'Florine', melodically and vocally indebted to Howlin' Wolf's 'Killing Floor', gets one of the finest horn arrangements in the whole corpus of recorded blues, and while nothing else is quite up to that standard, nothing is far below it either; despite a swarm of guitarists, *Junk Food* is a splendid riposte to the dominance of guitar bands. CS

Jimmy Reed (1925–76)
VOCAL, HARMONICA, GUITAR

Mathis James Reed was born in Leland, Mississippi, where he did farm work before leaving for the Chicago area in the mid-'40s. There he worked in a steel mill and played in clubs with Eddie Taylor (a childhood friend) and John Brim. In 1953 he signed with the new Vee-Jay label and between 1955 and 1961 racked up more R&B – and Pop – chart hits than any other Chicago blues artist. His career outside the studio, however, was disrupted by erratic health, drink problems and unreliable management, and despite his unique approach to the blues he never attained the status of contemporaries like B. B. King or Muddy Waters.

**** The Very Best Of Jimmy Reed
[Rhino 79802] Reed; Henry Gray (p); Remo Biondi (vn, g); John Brim, Eddie Taylor, John Littlejohn, W. C. Dalton, Lefty Bates, Philip Upchurch, Lee Baker, unknown (g); Milton Rector, Marcus Johnson, Willie Dixon, prob. Jimmy Reed Jr, unknowns (b); Albert King, Earl Phillips, Vernell Fournier, Al Duncan (d); Mary 'Mama' Reed (v). 6/53–63.
** The Best Of Jimmy Reed
GNP-Crescendo GNP 10006 Similar to above. 6/53–64.
♛ **** Boss Man
Snapper Recall SMDCD 232 2CD Similar to above. 6/53–65.
***(*) The Legend – The Man
[Collectables COL-CD-7115] Similar to above. 6/53–64.
*** The EP Collection
See For Miles SEECD 708 Similar to above. 6/53–64.
***(*) The Sun Is Shining
Snapper Complete Blues SBLUECD 018 Similar to above. 6/53–9/57.

*** His Greatest Recordings
Aim 9001 *Similar to above.* 12/53–63.

Even by the standards of the Blues Club, where lifelong membership can be assured by the careful deployment of one decent idea, Reed had a very good run. Many pages of his recorded folio are in effect fuzzy photocopies of others, and at the level of the average performance he was usually repetitious, often insubstantial and sometimes downright lazy. Admittedly, a kind of laziness was what he was going for. As you listen you imagine him with his hat over his eyes and his chair tilted back against a porch wall, drawling his songs out of the side of his mouth to a sleepily strummed guitar. The absent-mindedness, you might almost say the aimlessness, of the music is part of its charm. At his best he was, in his way, incomparable, and that best is succinctly defined by his best-known recordings, 'Ain't That Lovin' You Baby', 'Baby What You Want Me To Do', 'Big Boss Man', 'Bright Lights, Big City', 'Honest I Do', 'Shame Shame Shame' and 'You Don't Have To Go'. A CD including those seven key tracks, and perhaps augmented with 'You Got Me Dizzy', 'Take Out Some Insurance' and 'Going To New York', would figure in any sensible list of albums desirable in a representative blues collection.

Rhino's 17-track *Very Best Of* has them all, nicely presented. Enough said. So does GNP-Crescendo's 20-track *Best Of*. Not enough said: the transfer quality is poor. *Boss Man*, *The Legend – The Man*, *The Sun Is Shining* and *His Greatest Recordings* each fall short of the golden ten by one track ('Shame Shame Shame', 'Take Out Some Insurance', 'You Got Me Dizzy' and 'Going To New York' respectively), and *The EP Collection* by two. The rest of *The EP Collection*'s 27 tracks are mostly lateish work and unremarkable, but *Boss Man* and *The Sun Is Shining* match the Rhino as a best-of, or indeed, for the casual listener, as an all-I-need-of. *Boss Man*, with 36 tracks, is the longer, and that generous selection from a dozen years of Reed's recording life provides all the evidence a reader might need for verifying – or disputing – the judgement given above.

*** I'm Jimmy Reed
[Collectables COL-CD-7108]//Charly SNAP 131 *Reed; John Brim, Eddie Taylor, John Littlejohn, W. C. Dalton, Remo Biondi, unknown (g); unknown (b); Albert King, Ray Scott, Earl Phillips, Vernell Fournier (d).* 6/53–3/58.

*** Rockin' With Reed
Charly SNAP 146 *Reed; Henry Gray (p); Remo Biondi (vn, g); Eddie Taylor, John Littlejohn, W. C. Dalton, Lefty Bates, unknown (g); Milton Rector (b); Albert King, Earl Phillips (d).* 12/53–3/59.

**(*) Blues Is My Business
[Collectables COL-CD-7114] *As above, except add Mary 'Mama' Reed, band (v); omit Biondi.* 12/53–12/60.

***(*) At Carnegie Hall
[Collectables COL-CD-7210] *Reed; Eddie Taylor, John Littlejohn, Remo Biondi, Lefty Bates, Phil Upchurch, Lee Baker, unknown (g); Marcus Johnson, Curtis Mayfield, Willie Dixon, unknown (b); Albert King, Vernell Fournier, Earl Phillips (d); Mary 'Mama' Reed (v).* 12/53–61.

I'm Jimmy Reed and *Rockin' With Reed* are reissues of Vee-Jay LPs that were primarily random collections of singles, though both contained a few tracks that had not been previously issued. Each of the Charly issues adds four items not readily available on other CDs. Previously unissued tracks predominate on *Blues Is My Business*, but they are unremarkable. *At Carnegie Hall* is partly 'a celebratory re-creation' of a 1961 concert there but mostly a collection of tracks from earlier sessions with different groups. Since those include nine of the ten 'key tracks' identified earlier, this too can be recommended for both coverage and value.

**(*) Found Love
[Collectables COL-CD-7110]//Charly SNAP 080 *Reed; Henry Gray (p); W. C. Dalton, Eddie Taylor, Lefty Bates, Phil Upchurch, Lee Baker (g); Milton Rector, Marcus Johnson, Willie Dixon (b); Earl Phillips (d); Mary 'Mama' Reed (v).* 7/55, 3/59–3/60.

**(*) Now Appearing
[Collectables COL-CD-7111] *Reed; Lefty Bates, Phil Upchurch, Eddie Taylor (g); Earl Phillips (d); Mary 'Mama' Reed, unknowns (v).* 6–12/60.

**(*) Just Jimmy Reed
[Collectables COL-CD-7116] *Reed; Jimmy Reed Jr (g, b); Lefty Bates (g); Phil Upchurch (b); Al Duncan (d); Mary 'Mama' Reed (v).* 62.

**(*) 'Tain't No Big Thing But He Is … Jimmy Reed
[Collectables COL-CD-7117] *Reed; Eddie Taylor, prob. Lefty Bates, unknown (g); prob. Jimmy Reed Jr (b); prob. Al Duncan, unknown (d).* 63.

When these sets first appeared as Vee-Jay LPs, *Found Love* contained four sides that had not been issued elsewhere, *Now Appearing* nine, *Just Jimmy Reed* five and *'Tain't No Big Thing* eight. A few of these have found their way on to other CDs, but many have not. Serious Reed collectors will therefore need to investigate all four, but less devoted readers should note that Reed's work in the early '60s obeys the law of diminishing returns. In particular, his voice, once fetchingly distressed, is sometimes simply distressing. The second half of *Just Jimmy Reed* has some interest beyond the usual in that finished performances have not been neatly excised from the session tapes but rough-edited to include some surrounding chitchat.

** Jimmy Reed Sings The Best Of The Blues
[Collectables COL-CD-7118] *Reed; Eddie Taylor, unknown (g); unknown (b); unknown (d).* 63.

** Jimmy Reed Plays 12-String Guitar Blues
[Collectables COL-CD-7127] *Reed; unknown (12-string g); others (see below).* 63.

** Jimmy Reed At Soul City
[Collectables COL-CD-7112] *Reed; Eddie Taylor, poss. Hubert Sumlin, unknowns (g); unknowns (b); unknowns (d).* 64.

These come from a period when Vee-Jay was ready to try anything to exploit their once hot but now slightly cooling property. *The Best Of The Blues* was a set of standards like 'See See Rider', 'Trouble In Mind' and 'St. Louis Blues', some not unsuited to Reed's style, some, like 'Roll 'Em Pete', laughably inapt. *12-String Guitar Blues* wiped Reed's vocals from existing tracks and substituted an anonymous 12-string guitarist. *At Soul City* was a batch of studio recordings made fake-live by dubbing on an audience.

**(*) Jimmy Reed Is Back
[Collectables COL-CD-5436] *Reed; Jimmy Reed Jr (g, b); Eddie Taylor, Lefty Bates, Wayne Bennett (g); Phil Upchurch, Jimmy Gresham (b); Al Duncan, Jimmy Tillman (d).* 66–67, 71?

His contract with Vee-Jay over, Reed made four albums in 1966–68 for Bluesway, *The New Jimmy Reed Album*, *Soulin'*, *Big*

Boss Man and *Down In Virginia*. His reputation gained little from these recordings. They were guitar-heavy – in addition to Reed himself there were always two other guitarists, sometimes three – and even when Reed wasn't singing his back catalogue he was still mostly repeating himself. *Jimmy Reed Is Back* takes six tracks from *Soulin'*, four from *Big Boss Man* and two, 'Keep The Faith' and 'Turn Me On Like A TV', from an early-'70s session, which is as much of Reed's later work as anyone but a devotee would want. TR

Lula Reed (born poss. 1927)
VOCAL

Born in Port Clinton, Ohio, Lula Reed began singing in church. She was married to Sonny Thompson, whose band accompanies her on King/Federal; she also recorded on Argo and Tangerine. Now back in the bosom of the church, Reed declines to be interviewed about her show-business career.

*** Lula Reed 1951–1954
Classics 5126 Reed; Dennis Brooks, Fred Clark (as); David Brooks (ts); Walter Hiles, Tommy Purkson (bs); Sonny Thompson (p); Lord Westbrook, Bill Johnson, Clarence Kenner (g); Clifford McGray, Oscar Crummie, Joe Williams, Clarence Mack, James Royal (b); Norman F. Johnson, Bill English, Isaac Cole, Philip Thomas, Robert Boswell (d); Paul Tate, unknowns (v). 12/51–2/54.
*** I'll Drown In My Tears
Ace CDCHD 984 As above, except add Tommy Purkson, Jewell Grant (as), Rufus Gore (ts), Albert Bartee (d); omit Mack, Thomas, Tate. 12/51–3/55.
(***) Blue And Moody
King KCD-604 As above, except add Ray Felder (ts), Alexander Nelson (bs), Thomas Palmer (g), Albert Winston (b); omit Grant, Crummie, unknowns. 12/51–8/56.

Nasal and penetrating without being shrill or affected, girlish but sexy and sophisticated, Lula Reed's voice is a very recognizable instrument, whether she's singing blues-ballads that presage '60s soul, swinging up-tempo, sometimes Latin-inflected numbers, or collaborating with gospel quartets with an enthusiasm that foreshadows her later withdrawal from the world. Much of Reed's fame rests on the original version of 'I'll Drown In My (Own) Tears', later appropriated by Ray Charles, but her records are more than a footnote to the fame of others, thanks to the impeccable pitch and timing she brings to quality songs, often composed by Henry Glover. Sonny Thompson's piano (which sometimes heads into Thelonious Monk territory) is also a vital ingredient, as are his superior arrangements; the deployment of acoustic guitar on some titles is admirably imaginative. Ace's 24 tracks and detailed notes inevitably get the nod over *Blue And Moody*'s unannotated dozen, but the latter disc includes three tracks from a 1956 session on which Thomas Palmer's fierce electric guitar is not the only challenge to Ace's claim that *I'll Drown In My Tears* includes 'every important recording' for King. Classics' disc is the first of a projected three that will issue Reed's complete output; it includes nine songs and one alternative take that are not on Ace. Of these, 'The Wild Stage Of Life' is a soppy rejection of its subject, but four gospel songs are projected with just as much soul and conviction as her secular numbers, and the tremendous King 4630 ('My Poor Heart'/'I'm Losing You') is a pairing whose omission by Ace is inexplicable.

Sonny Thompson's *Complete Recordings Vol. 4* (Blue Moon BMCD 6044) also includes King material, and *The E.P. Collection* (See For Miles SEECD 702) has four of Reed's early-'60s Federal sides. These discs are discussed in Thompson's entry. CS

Irene Reid (born 1934)
VOCAL

Reid left Savannah, Georgia, in her teens to go to New York, where she won amateur talent contests at the Apollo and graduated to singing with jazz bands. In 1961–62 she was the vocalist with Count Basie's orchestra. For the next 30-odd years she worked in clubs in Harlem and elsewhere, but in the late '90s her Savant CDs exposed her to a larger audience, and she has appeared in Britain and South Africa.

** Million Dollar Secret
Savant SCD 2007 Reid; James Rotondi (t); Eric Alexander (ts); Charles Earland (o, prod); Bob De Vos (g); Greg Rockingham (d). 2/97.
** I Ain't Doing Too Bad
Savant SCR 2012 As above. 3/98.
** The Uptown Lowdown
Savant SCD 2022 As above, except add Mike Karn (ts); Bill Boris (g) replaces De Vos. 99.

Like Helen Humes, whose 'Million Dollar Secret' she tells on her first album, Reid is a singer acquainted with several shelves of the jazz vocal library. One she knows particularly well is labelled 'blues'. 'Big Fat Daddy' and 'One Eyed Man' on *Million Dollar Secret* are salty tales recounted in the pugnacious tone of Dinah Washington (an admitted model but, Reid is careful to point out, only one of many), while *I Ain't Doing Too Bad* contains Mose Allison's 'Your Mind Is On Vacation', the title song and Percy Mayfield's 'Walking On A Tightrope' (misnamed 'Tightrope' and wrongly attributed), and *The Uptown Lowdown* has 'Long John Blues' and Fats Domino's 'I'm Walkin''. Her band responds expertly, and these are all likeable performances. The bulk of each album, however, is nightclub material, sometimes with jazz pedigree, like 'Sweet Lotus Blossom' on *I Ain't Doing Too Bad*, more often show tunes like 'What I Did For Love'. TR

Jean Paul Rena (born 1957)
VOCAL, GUITAR, MANDOLIN

Rena was born in Holland and grew up in a domestic environment of jazz, rock 'n' roll and African chants. To his father's chagrin, he was drawn towards the electric guitar and the blues. After spending several years in various local bands, Rena elected to front his own outfit, Terrawheel.

* Introducing …
Corazong 255067 Rena; Bas Kleine (h); Marco De Waal (o, p); Rolf Caron (p, d); Ruben Byther (b); Sjin-Ki Vie, Henk Koorn (v). 04.

Introducing … opens with a bar's snare roll from Caron, and then swiftly veers downhill. Cluttered production, crushingly unimaginative songwriting, questionable vocals, absurdly dirty harmonica tones and relentlessly fixed dynamics make this introduction a grim experience. The tracks are almost exclusively up-tempo electrified Chicago foot-stompers, which may work in a live setting but suffer here from spectacularly poor execution. On the positive side, Rena's guitar work is strong, the band can lay down something resembling a groove, and if you can bear to listen as far as track 11, the inclusion of De Waal's piano and a touch of breathing space on 'Remember Me' is refreshing. JF

Sonny Rhodes (born 1940)
VOCAL, GUITAR

Rhodes was born Clarence Edward Smith in Smithville, Texas, and began playing guitar in his teens. Prompted, he says, by a line in a B. B. King record, he served in the US Navy, after which he moved to Fresno, California, and then in 1965 to Oakland. In the late '60s he recorded several singles for Galaxy and in the '70s he worked for Albert Collins and Jimmy McCracklin as well as touring and recording in his own name, both in the US and overseas. In the late '80s he moved to New Jersey. He is one of the few blues guitarists to have made a point of playing lap steel as well as conventional guitars.

***(*) I Don't Want My Blues Colored Bright
Black Magic CD 9024 Rhodes; Harold Attyberry (t); Brad Johnson (as); Ken Baker (ts); Gary Smith (h); J. J. Malone (p, v); Junior Watson (g); Steve Gomes, Charles Banks (b); Harold Banks, Richard Milton (d). 8/76, 3/77.

Some of the time he sounds like Junior Parker – there are three Parker numbers here, including a very fine reading of 'Sitting & Thinking' – and some of the time like Muddy Waters, but to say this is not to classify Rhodes as a chameleon. He admires excellent models and some of their style has rubbed off on him without in turn erasing his own, which may be discerned in his intense, absorbed renditions of his own songs like 'Country Boy' and 'All Night Long They Play The Blues'. This is deep blue music, tinted with some humour but no hilarity. The listener who agrees with the proposition in the title will like this album very much indeed.

Rhodes's '60s recordings of 'All Night Long They Play The Blues' and 'Country Boy' are on *All Night Long They Play The Blues* (Specialty SPCD-7029//Ace CDCHD 440).

** In Europe
Appaloosa AP 023 Rhodes; Little Willie Littlefield (p); Ron Thompson, Mississippi Johnny Waters, Luther Tucker (g); Mike Lewis (b); Harold Banks (d). 5/80.

*(*) Won't Rain In California
EPM Blues Collection 15778 Rhodes; Sonny Grey, Longineu Parsons (t); Marc Steckar (btb, tu); Michel Crocquenoy (oboe); Sulaiman Hakim (as); Johnny Griffin, Richard Raux (ts); Michel Carras (kb, vb); Nile (kb); Larry Martin (p, g, arr, prod); various (strings); Paul Pechenaert (g); Zox (b); Dennis Lescoeur (d, perc). 7–9/80, 12/82.

These are Continental recordings, the first cut in Italy, the second in France. *In Europe* suffers from a common failing of records made in Europe, production that's simultaneously indulgent and uncritical. All the tracks are overlong, yet once the ear gets past the front man, there is little happening, except on the two songs involving Littlefield. The problems of the French recording are slightly different. Eight tracks are with a small band, eight with a larger group including brass, reeds and sometimes a string section from the Paris National Symphony Orchestra. Whether the more elaborate setting was devised specifically for the artist or was just a producer's fantasy awaiting a chance to be realized, the results are inconsistent. A couple of tracks capture something of the piquant blend of blues band and strings that was attained on B. B. King's *Indianola Mississippi Seeds*, one of the albums that set the agenda for this sort of thing, but in general the combination of Rhodes's elemental blues and the French orchestra's ormolu decoration degrades the virtues of both. Even in the small-group performances Rhodes's singing (he plays guitar on only four tracks) is submerged beneath layers of synthetic music.

*** Just Blues
Evidence ECD 26060 Rhodes; Jonathan Paul (tb); Bernard Anderson (as, ts, bs); J. J. Malone (p); Steve Gannon, Troyce Key (g); Jerry 'Cowboy' Haynes (b); Chris Daniels (d). 3/85.

After the European experiment, Rhodes came back home in both senses with this uncomplicated and accurately titled set. Songs from the folios of Jimmy McCracklin, Percy Mayfield, B. B. King, Guitar Slim and Elmore James, and a few from Rhodes's own notebook like 'Cigarette Blues', elicit hearty performances with characteristically acrid solos on conventional and lap steel guitars.

*** Out Of Control
King Snake KS-031 Rhodes; Danny Fields (t); Bill Samuel (ts, bs); Dwight Champagne (o, p); Frederic Neal (o); Warren King, Ace Moreland, Kenny Neal (g); Bob Greenlee (b, prod); Gerald 'Cowboy' Haynes, Darnell Neal (b); Ronnie 'Byrd' Foster, Andre Wright, Ken Johnson (d). 96.

**(*) Blue Diamond
Stony Plain SPCD 1257 Rhodes; Bobby Pickwood (t); Rich 'Hurricane' Johnson (ts, bs); Noble 'Thin Man' Watts (ts); Anthony 'Pack Rat' Thompson, Mark Hodgson (h); Doug Bare (kb); Bob Greenlee (g, b, prod); Ace Moreland, Warren King (g); Ronnie 'Byrd' Foster, Theo Brown, Jim Payne (d); Jimitre Smith, Yvonne Saddler (v). 11/98–1/99.

**(*) A Good Day To Play The Blues
Stony Plain SPCD 1273 Rhodes; David Weaver (t); Charlie DeChant (ts, bs); Doug Bare (o, p); Steve Leigh (o); Bob Greenlee (g, b, prod); Ace Moreland (g); Anthony Mitchell (b); Ronnie 'Bird' Foster, Theo Brown (d); Juan Perez (perc); Bill Samuel (arr). 01?

After *Just Blues* Rhodes recorded several albums for Ichiban and King Snake, of which *Out Of Control* may still be available. This and the Stony Plain CDs were supervised by King Snake's Bob Greenlee, who collaborated in much of the writing and gave the records the big, brash sound that's his trademark. With a few pacy exceptions, *Out Of Control* and *Blue Diamond* follow Rhodes's familiar format of blues stories told at unruffled tempos, though on the former the soul ballad 'Another You', with impassioned guitar playing by Warren King, breaks the sequence to good effect. The Neal family appears only on 'Drink Muddy Water'. Rhodes's voice on *Blue Diamond* is less pliant than it used to be, and less foregrounded in the mix than it might have been, but admirers of his lap steel playing will find more of it on these two albums than on any of their forerunners. *Blue Diamond* concludes with a 20-minute interview. *A Good Day To Play*

The Blues was entirely written by Rhodes and Greenlee, jointly or individually. Some ingenious arrangements fail to conceal the fact that the material, though quite varied, is consistently humdrum, and Rhodes's voice, even when one can hear it plainly above the high noise-level of the accompaniments, is not the well-conditioned instrument of his middle years. TR

Walter 'Lightnin' Bug' Rhodes
(1939–90)
VOCAL, GUITAR

Rhodes spent his early years in North Carolina, where he learned to play guitar. Moving with his mother to Brooklyn, he played in gospel groups, with Kenny & Moe (The Blues Boys), in a duo with his cousin Arthur Little and with Wilson Pickett. He also made singles as The Blonde Bomber and Little Red Walters, and a solo album, *The Blues Goes On*, as Lightnin' Bug, in 1983. Returning to North Carolina to look after his mother, he made contact with Gary Erwin of the Low Country Blues Society, which led to appearances in Europe and further recordings.

*** Now Hear This!
Swingmaster CD 2207 *Rhodes; Fred Reining (g).* 10/88–3/89.

Rhodes introduces himself in 'The Life Of Lightnin' Bug Rhodes', calmly describing life as an albino child with poor sight, then proceeds to a recital of blues, delivered in an attractively husky voice. Interspersed with received repertoire like Blind Boy Fuller's 'Step It Up And Go' and 'You Got To Do Better' and Brownie McGhee's 'Auto Mechanic Blues' are original pieces, often with moral messages, as in 'It's Not What You Do' and 'Blues Star Blues'. The Dutch player Fred Reining adds elegant Fulleresque guitar to eight of the dozen songs, but not because Rhodes stands in need of support, as he proves in a trenchant solo version of Lightnin' Hopkins's 'Give Me Back My Wig'. A low-key recording, perhaps, but estimable and enjoyable. TR

'Philadelphia' Jerry Ricks (born 1940)
VOCAL, GUITAR

In the '60s, Ricks booked traditional musicians for Philadelphia's Second Fret coffeehouse, and took the opportunity to work with and learn from the acoustic big names of the 'blues revival'; Brownie McGhee, John Hurt, Gary Davis and Mance Lipscomb were major influences. From 1969, Ricks led a nomadic life, much of it spent in Europe, and only returned to the USA in 1990.

**(*) Deep In The Well
Rooster Blues R 2636 *Ricks.* 12/96.

Ricks made a number of LPs in Europe, but this is his American recording debut. It's disappointing, for his voice is colourless, narrow-ranged and not always securely pitched. His guitar playing is very pleasant on a reworking of John Hurt's 'Avalon Blues' and a brief, instrumental 'Gary Davis Medley'; but elsewhere the bass lines are metronomic, inflexible and tedious, especially on the several tracks that extend to six or more minutes. Some of the shorter pieces are enjoyable: 'Down In Luck' has a Blind Boy Fullerish bounce and there's fine slide on 'Ain't Afraid Of These Blues', but they don't rescue the project from its shortcomings.

***(*) Many Miles Of Blues
Rooster Blues RBLU 2639 *Ricks.* 1/00.

Ricks lived in Clarksdale for some time after returning to the States, and he writes in the notes about how exploring 'between West Tennessee and the Delta and just jumping across into Arkansas' has affected his writing and playing. So have vintage recordings from the same terrain; Ricks now incorporates elements from Robert Johnson and Charley Patton among others, not by straight copying but by creative use of their sounds and ideas. 'No More Ramblin'', for instance, is much more interesting and enjoyable than one more cover of 'Ramblin' On My Mind' would have been. His narrow vocal range is still something of a problem, but Ricks is considerably more expressive and emotionally involved. *Many Miles Of Blues* is a very successful artistic and musical reinvention; the recording quality is better, too, the guitar in particular having far more presence. CS

Lesley Riddle (1905–80)
VOCAL, GUITAR, PIANO

Born in Burnsville, North Carolina, Riddle went to work in the local cement plant as a teenager, and lost a leg in an accident. He turned to music, and played in stringbands in the tri-cities area (Kingsport, Johnson City and Bristol) on the Virginia/Tennessee border, collaborating with Brownie McGhee among others. In the late '20s, Riddle met A. P. Carter, and for several years joined him on trips to find new songs for the Carter Family, also teaching the family some of his own songs and elements of his guitar style. In 1942, Riddle moved to Rochester, New York, and gave up making music in 1945. In the '60s, Mike Seeger learned from Maybelle Carter that Riddle had been the source for 'Red River Blues' and 'The Cannon Ball', sought him out, and persuaded him to resume playing.

*** Step By Step
Rounder CD 0299 *Riddle; Mike Seeger (ah).* 65–78.

Step By Step's cover carries the slogan 'Lesley Riddle Meets The Carter Family', which is understandable as marketing, but disingenuous as musical history. It's fascinating to hear 'The Cannon Ball' and 'I Know What It Means To Be Lonesome' from their source, and important to acknowledge Riddle's indirect influence on generations of old-time and revivalist musicians, but he's also very much worth hearing on his own merits. A gentle singer, he plays guitar with considerable rhythmic subtlety, integrating it with his singing very skilfully, especially on the occasional knifestyle numbers. About half of *Step By Step* consists of spirituals, played soberly but by no means dully. Mike Seeger's autoharp is added on the title track, and on 'Hilltop Blues' Riddle ventures some tentative piano. CS

Dave Riley (born 1949)
VOCAL, GUITAR

Retiring from a career as a Joliet State Penitentiary guard, Riley has taken up the musical career he always coveted. A late apprenticeship with Frank Frost and Sam Carr in Helena,

Arkansas, has led to the formation of his own trio and appearances at festivals in the USA and Europe.

*** Whiskey, Money & Women
Fedora FCD 5028 *Riley; John Weston (h); Dave Riley Jr (b); Sam Carr (d).* 01.

The presence of Sam Carr guarantees that a juke-joint ambience pervades most of these 11 songs. Riley's guitar playing rarely rises above the functional but is sufficient for the material's needs. 'Smokestack Lightning' suffers from Carr's indecision and the singer's inability to combine vocal and instrumental precision. This, 'Call My Job' and Homer Banks's 'Angel Of Mercy', although enthusiastically played, are the album's subtle failures. Riley's own songs, including the title track, inhabit familiar territory without aspiring to the memorable. That quality is reserved for two solo performances, 'Tribute' and 'Imagine', the first a catalogue of blues and soul artists whom Riley regards as inspirational, the second a surprisingly successful treatment of John Lennon's song prefaced by an autobiographical monologue. It makes a brave ending to an entertaining album that hints at further development. NS

Paul Rishell (born 1950)
VOCAL, GUITAR

A New Yorker by birth, Rishell's first venture into music was playing drums in a surf-rock band, but he discovered blues guitar and dedicated himself to learning it. In the early '70s he moved to Cambridge, Massachusetts. In the late '80s he began playing with Annie Raines (born 1969), a local girl who had dropped out of college to play blues harmonica, and they have been a team ever since.

*** Swear To Tell The Truth
Tone-Cool CDTC 1148 *Rishell; Richard Rosenblatt, Little Annie Raines (h); David Maxwell (p); Ronnie Earl (g); Rod Carey, Albey Balgochian (b); Per Hanson, Forrest Padgett (d).* 93.

What makes Rishell a particular pleasure to listen to – and somewhat exceptional – is his ability to perform blues that were first done by great singers and not leave the listener uncomfortably conscious of that fact. When taking on challenging pieces like Son House's 'Depot Blues' and Tommy Johnson's 'Canned Heat Blues', as well as more approachable ones like 'Mamie' by Blind Boy Fuller, he produces attractive, individual and convincing interpretations; his version of Skip James's 'Devil Got My Woman', a song to approach with wariness and respect, is second only to the original. Even in that context, 'Some Of These Days' is something else. 'I heard this quiet wistful song inside Charl[ey] Patton's muscular, syncopated version,' Rishell writes in the notes, an accurate but too modest description of his fascinating transformation of the song. Earl and his Broadcasters sit in on three tracks, particularly effectively on Howlin' Wolf's 'Somebody In My Home'. Rishell's 1990 release *Blues On A Holiday* (Tone-Cool CDTC 1144) is of uncertain availability.

*** I Want You To Know
Tone-Cool CDTC 1156 *Rishell; Annie Raines (h, p, v); Jay Ungar (md); Ronnie Earl, John Sebastian (g); Damian Purro (b); Chuck Purro (d); E. Duato Scheer (wb).* 95?

**(*) Moving To The Country
Tone-Cool TC 1174 *Rishell; [Sax] Gordon Beadle (ts); Scott Shetler (bs); Annie Raines (h, kb, md, v); Chris Rival, Troy Gonyea (g); Jesse Williams, Damian Purro (b); Marty Richards (d).* 99.

*** Goin' Home
Tone-Cool/Artemis/Rykodisc RCD 17306 *Rishell; Scott Aruda (t); [Sax] Gordon Beadle (ts); Scott Shetler (bs); Annie Raines (h, o, p, md, Hawaiian mandolin harp, perc, v); Damian Purro (b, perc); Jesse Williams, Reed Butler (b); Marty Richards (d, perc); Vanessa Rishell, Cam Geraci (v).* 04.

Annie Raines, who played on a few tracks of *Swear To Tell The Truth*, is a full partner throughout these albums and jointly billed. Though on the face of it a programme with such old favourites as 'Key To The Highway' and 'Step It Up And Go' (*I Want You To Know*) does not promise much in the way of novelty, Rishell and Raines demonstrate the uncommon skill of playing such songs as if discovering them for the first time. They are versatile, too: Rishell flawlessly segues from the impetuous slide guitar of Barbecue Bob's 'Yo Yo Blues' to a brooding Muddy Waters/Lightnin' Slim riff on 'Nothin' But The Devil'. Raines, for her part, is simply one of the most capable and tuneful harmonica players around. *Moving To The Country* is a similar blend of received and original material in acoustic and electric settings. The Bo Carter songs 'I Get The Blues' and 'Twist It Babe' and Joe Callicott's 'Fare Thee Well' are particularly apt choices for a fingerpicker as scrupulous as Rishell. The acoustic performances generally have more individuality than the band sides, and on *Goin' Home* they are clearly in the ascendant, as Rishell plays songs associated with Blind Lemon Jefferson, William Moore ('Ragtime Millionaire' with Noah Lewis-like harmonica by Raines) and Charley Jordan and revisits the repertoire of Charley Patton to pick 'I'm Goin' Home' and renew his acquaintance with 'Some Of These Days'. Amidst these and some good-humoured originals lies a crystalline performance of Washington Phillips's 'I Had A Good Mother And Father', with Raines re-creating the bell-like sound of Phillips's zither on Hawaiian mandolin harp. TR

Michael Roach (born 1955)
VOCAL, GUITAR

Born in Washington, DC, Roach took up guitar in his late 20s and learned from recordings and local musicians, among them John Jackson, Archie Edwards and John Cephas. He was president of the DC Blues Society between 1988 and 1992, and now lives in Britain, where he is president of the European Blues Association.

*** Ain't Got Me No Home
Stella STCD 001 *Roach; Mike Baytop (h); Richard 'Mr Bones' Thomas (bones).* 6–7/93.

*** The Blinds Of Life
Stella STCD 003 *Roach; Ian Briggs, Mike Baytop (h); Richard 'Mr Bones' Thomas, Len 'The Bonesman' Davies (bones).* 90s.

Roach's debut CD mixes originals, some of them dealing with topical social issues, and covers of vintage recordings. He doesn't manage to make Son House's 'My Black Mama' his own, and here, as elsewhere on *Ain't Got Me No Home*, his changes of vocal dynamics can sound arbitrary. Throughout, however, it's evident that Roach is concerned to develop a personal but tradition-based music through his own compositions and the songs of others; he succeeds in doing so more often than not, even managing to find new perspectives on Jesse Fuller's 'San Francisco Bay Blues'.

Recorded in the US and England, The Blinds Of Life is in many respects an improvement on its predecessor; 'Shotgun Stalker', for instance, revisits Son House's aggressive style to much better effect, applying it to lyrics about a personally experienced fear of random violence. Alongside creative borrowings and adaptations from Leadbelly, John Hurt and others, there are a number of well-constructed originals, although Roach's lyrics are occasionally prosaic, and there's some acquiescence in false quantity, rhyming 'me' with 'loneLY' and the like.

***(*) **Good News Blues**
Stella STCD 005 Roach; Ian Briggs (h); Neil Smith (kb, string prog); Gary Hunt (perc); Helen Roach, Michelle Roach (v); Otis Williams (sp). 00.

The improvement continues as Roach digs deeper into personal and traditional resources. As a writer, he seems set to become the new millennium's Brownie McGhee, offering philosophy and commentary alongside songs about relationships and the occasional gospel number. 'The Ole Folks Song' and 'The Acorn' are pleasing settings of proverbial wisdom; of the older material, 'Bricks In My Pillow' and 'Keep Your Hands Off' are authoritatively played and sung, and setting 'Trouble In Mind' to the tune of 'When I Lay My Burden Down' brilliantly revitalizes a hackneyed number. A couple of experiments don't pay off; 'Vote For The Wino' is clever, but let down by crudely overdubbed backing vocals, and 'Good News Blues' is not improved by the use of a poor recording of its lyricist reading three poems. Nevertheless, this is Roach's most consistent and assured CD to date.

*** **Cypress Grove**
Stella STCD 007 Roach; Ian Briggs (h); Andrew Butler (o, kb, b, d, tamb); John Vickers (vn, bj, b); Bernie Marsden (g); Richard Dennery (spoons); Helen Roach, Michelle Roach (v). 00–02.

Most of Cypress Grove, which is dedicated to the memory of John Jackson, was recorded in 2002; two tracks from 2000 are its least rewarding listening, being 'prentice work written in 1983 and sentimental agitprop composed by Marsden. The rest of the disc is a lot better: Roach writes in the notes that 'I experimented with instrumental ideas and combinations of songs intent upon giving the listener a sense of continuity, tension, grief, humour, love and praise', but the CD comes across simply as a nicely varied, slightly uneven collection of traditional blues and spirituals that are not linked by any obvious rationale beyond Roach's affection for them. The added instruments are adroitly used, notably the pleasantly corny banjo on 'What Month Was Jesus Born In' and the sweet but not sickly fiddle on 'Lonesome Valley'. By setting 'C C Rider' to a tumbling north Mississippi riff, Roach repeats the trick he pulled off with 'Trouble In Mind'. He fails to do it a third time with 'Special Rider', transposed to a new key and given a fussy rhythm, but despite occasional shortcomings Cypress Grove's good moments clearly outweigh the less good. CS

Terry Robb
VOCAL, GUITAR

Growing up in the Pacific Northwest, Robb was inspired to play by an uncle who was a professional guitarist, acquiring a wide knowledge of blues, jazz and country music. He has worked with Curtis Salgado and the Acoustic Guitar Summit, and runs his own guitar school. His CV as a producer includes several albums by John Fahey, and albums by fellow Burnside acts Sheila Wilcoxson and Paul Brasch.

** **Acoustic Blues Trio**
Burnside BCD-0019 Robb; Curtis Salgado (h, v); Bill Rhoades (h); Alan Hager (g, v); Albert Reda (b); Greg Fisher (d). 94?

** **Stop This World**
Burnside BCD 0025 Robb; Curtis Salgado (h); Skip Parente (vn); Brad Price (bouzouki); Eddy Clearwater, Paul Chasman (g); Albert Reda (b); Jeff Minniewether (d); Maria Muldaur (v). 96?

** **Heart Made Of Steel**
Burnside BCD 0040 Robb; Steve Cannon (t); Tom 'Bone[s]' Malone (tb); Jeff Homan (ss, as); Warren Rand (as); Tim Bryson (ts, bs); Garry Harris (ts); Peter Boe, Janice Scroggins (p); Steve James (md); Albert Reda (b, v); John Mazzocco (b); Carlton Jackson, Jeff Minniewether (d). 00?

The songs and tunes on Acoustic Blues Trio are drawn from Son House, Elizabeth Cotten, Muddy Waters, Mississippi John Hurt and other highly respectable sources, and in general demonstrate that Robb, though clearly not aiming for close replication, has a good guitarist's grasp of their styles. Most of the album fits its title; the other three musicians make only guest appearances. Stop This World is a mixture of solo and trio tracks with occasional additional coloration, the most vivid being Maria Muldaur's singing of John Hurt's 'Louis Collins'; the bouzouki on Charlie Rich's 'Lonely Weekends' is the faintest of tints. The original songs that occupy about half of Stop This World and virtually all of Heart Made Of Steel are more often than not blues, but uninspired in their lyrics and settings. While each of these CDs has tracks a curious listener might want to return to, like the sprightly guitar–mandolin duet with Steve James on Heart Made Of Steel, Robb's singing is seldom up to the demands of the material. TR

Sherman Robertson (born 1948)
VOCAL, GUITAR

Robertson grew up in Houston, Texas, and began playing guitar professionally in his teens. In the '80s he worked with Clifton Chenier and Rockin' Dopsie, the latter connection giving him a place in the castlist of Paul Simon's album Graceland. In 1993 he was one of the first signings to an ambitious new label, Code Blue, but a few years later the company dropped its blues roster.

*** **Going Back Home**
AudioQuest AQ-CD 1050 Robertson; Joe Sublett (ts); Bill Payne (kb); Bob Glaub (b); Richie Hayward (d). 3/98.

Robertson's albums for Code Blue, I'm The Man and Here And Now, are no longer in print. It's a loss that the artist, at least, may find easy to bear, since he has said that he disliked their production, and that he much prefers Going Back Home for its accurate portrayal of how he sounds in person. Lovers of straight-down-the-line blues are likely to share his good opinion of the album. Encouraged by backseat drivers such as Little Feat's Bill Payne and Richie Hayward, Robertson takes to the road with an old guitar, a high-octane blend of fuel – songs from Albert King and Johnny Copeland among his own – and a new clarity of direction. The recording is clear but a little cold, suggesting that the next album might profitably be a live one. TR

Duke Robillard (born 1948)
VOCAL, GUITAR, MANDOLIN, CUMBUS, BASS

From Providence, Rhode Island, Robillard was drawn to jazz and blues in his teens by the festivals at nearby Newport. In 1967 he was a founder member of Roomful Of Blues, which he left in 1979 to form a trio, The Pleasure Kings, though he also worked briefly with The Legendary Blues Band and for two or three years with the Fabulous Thunderbirds. Since the '90s he has assembled a formidable list of accompanying and producing credits. As well as his extensive command of blues guitar styles he is a skilled jazz player, especially in the swing idiom.

**(*) Rockin' Blues
Rounder CD 11548 *Robillard; Doug James (bs); Anthony Geraci (p); Thomas Enright (g, b, v); Tom DeQuattro (d); Scott Billington (perc, 'space piano'). 2/83–12/84.*

(***) Swing
Rounder CD 3103 *Robillard; Scott Hamilton (ts); Mike LeDonne (o, p); Chris Flory, Jim Kelly (g); Phil Flanigan (b); Chuck Riggs (d). 9/86.*

**(*) You Got Me
Rounder CD 3100 *Robillard; Matthew Quinn (kb); Dr John [Mack Rebennack], Ron Levy (o, p); Jimmie Vaughan (g); Thomas Enright (b); Tom DeQuattro (d); Scott Billington (perc, v). 5/87.*

** Turn It Around
Rounder CD 3116 *Robillard; Malcolm Walsh (o); Scott Appelrouth (b); Doug Hinman (d); Susann Forrest, The Pink Tuxedos, John Paul Gauthier (v). 4/89–4/90.*

(***) After Hours Swing Session
Rounder CD 3114 *Robillard; Al Basile (c); Rich Lataille (cl, as); Greg Mazel (ts, vb); Doug James (bs); Al Copley (p); Preston Hubbard (b); Chuck Laire (d). 5/90.*

(***) Plays Jazz: The Rounder Years
Bullseye Blues CDBB 9597 *As for* Swing *and* After Hours Swing Session. *9/86, 5/90.*

**(*) Plays Blues: The Rounder Years
Bullseye Blues CDBB 9598 *As for* Rockin' Blues, You Got Me *and* Turn It Around *except omit Quinn, The Pink Tuxedos, Gauthier. 2/83–4/90.*

Rockin' Blues contains virtually all of Robillard's first two Rounder albums, *Duke Robillard & The Pleasure Kings* (CD 3079) and *Too Hot To Handle* (CD 3082). It's basically a guitar trio CD – the additional musicians are on only a few tracks – but the texture is thickened by Robillard overdubbing extra guitar parts, so that, for example, the Chuck Berry song 'It's My Own Business' has typical Chuck Berry rhythm and lead parts at the same time. Robillard shows off his dexterity in many styles, but at this stage his singing still needed work, and too many numbers are delivered in an undifferentiated generic shout. The best track is 'Duke's Mood', a laidback *hommage* to T-Bone Walker.

Swing is an out-and-out jazz set, done with relaxed skill in a mainstream-to-early-modern idiom, but it's worth mentioning because *The Penguin Guide To Jazz Recordings* has not dealt with it and the standards and jazz compositions are interspersed with several instrumentals in blues form, culminating in an exhilarating duet with Kelly.

You Got Me finds our man in Southwestern gear, easing along New Orleans grooves with Dr John and playing rockabilly bad boys with Jimmie Vaughan. Robillard's singing shows less exertion and is the better for it, but his material is rather humdrum. *Turn It Around* is something of a one-man guitarfest, Robillard using at least ten models, sometimes as many as four on a single number. Apart from 'Sweets For My Sweet' and an obscure Buddy Holly song, the songs are mostly original and inconspicuous. Except on the concluding blues, 'I Think You Know', the vocals are too often lost beneath the welter of guitars, which is no great loss, since they aren't up to much.

Having shown on *Turn It Around* that he could do the power-trio thing, Robillard used his next project to retreat into the past again – this time a little farther back than on *Swing*, to the late-'30s idiom of the Benny Goodman–Charlie Christian small groups and the like. Again, *After Hours Swing Session* is an album that merits inclusion in the *Guide To Jazz*, and its appeal to readers of the present book may be confined to those who also enjoy this kind of jazz or are interested in anything Robillard does – though, given the personnel, it also counts as a Roomful Of Blues spin-off. Incidentally, Robillard has also made a couple of albums with the jazz guitarist Herb Ellis, *Conversations In Swing Guitar* (Stony Plain SPCD 1260) and *More Conversations In Swing Guitar* (SPCD 1292).

In 1997 Rounder took a look at their Robillard back catalogue and compiled a pair of selections from his six albums for the label. *Plays Jazz* is necessarily drawn from just two of them but adds a previously unissued 'Time's A Wastin' from the *Swing* date. *Plays Blues* takes three or four tracks from each of the other four sets, making it a useful CD for the listener who wants a compact account of Robillard's development in the '80s.

***(*) Duke's Blues
Stony Plain SPCD 1195 *Robillard; Al Basile (c); Greg Mazel (ts, bs, vb); 'Sax' Gordon Beadle (ts, bs); Matt McCabe (p); Paul Murphy (g); Marty Ballou (b); Jeffery McAllister (d). 9/93.*

***(*) Stretchin' Out – Live
Stony Plain SPCD 1250 *Robillard; 'Sax' Gordon Beadle (ts, bs); Marty Ballou (b); Marty Richards (d). 11/95.*

In *Duke's Blues* Robillard finally produced the first-rate all-blues album he had always had in him. Multiskilled isn't the half of it. The album reveals a confident voice, sidemen who know every move to make, and a display of guitar versatility that could cast rivals into terminal depression. Whether sliding into the warm embrace of T-Bone Walker's 'Glamour Girl', walking the high-tension wire in Guitar Slim's 'Something To Remember You By', stretching out on a long Albert Collins-styled 'Dyin' Flu' or magically reviving Magic Sam's huge tremolo in 'Never Let You Go', Robillard seems to have every guitar style in the blues primer down cold.

Stretchin' Out – Live is virtually a live performance of *Duke's Blues*, seven of the nine tracks being shared by both albums, but Robillard is so unstintingly inventive that every moment is worthwhile.

(*) New Blues For Modern Man//La Palette Bleue
Shanachie 9017//Stony Plain SPCD 1259//Dixiefrog DFGCD 8486 *Robillard; Al Basile (c); Doug James (bcl, ts, bs); Dennis Taylor (ts); Marilynn Mair (ac, md, mandola); Tom West (kb, o, p); Mark Davis (mandola, mandocello); John Packer (b); Marty Richards (d, maracas).* 6/98.

(*) Explorer
Shanachie 9025//Stony Plain SPCD 1265 *Robillard; Doug James (bcl, ts, bs); 'Sax' Gordon Beadle (ts); Jerry Portnoy (h); Marilynn Mair (ac, md); Tom West (o, p); Mark Davis (vn, mandocello); John Packer (g, b, v); Jeff McAllister (d, perc, laugh box).* 99/00.

As their titles and instrumentation imply, Robillard used these albums to investigate fresh settings for blues-based original material. On *New Blues For Modern Man* (retitled for the European issue on Dixiefrog) the combination of blasting horns, thumping rhythm and snarling guitar on tracks like 'Addiction', 'Fishnet' and Charley Patton's 'Pony Blues' has a distinct flavour of late Howlin' Wolf, an effect that also characterizes some of the arrangements on *Explorer*. In his songwriting Robillard employs blues forms to a greater extent than many of his contemporaries, which will please conservative listeners and frustrate forward-looking ones. He is sometimes less sure-footed when he steps out of that comfort zone.

*** Living With The Blues
Stony Plain SPCD 1277//Dixiefrog DFGCD 8527 *Robillard; Carl Querfurth (tb); Doug James (ts, bs); Sax Gordon Beadle (ts); Bruce Katz (o, p); John Packer, Jesse Williams (b); Mark Teixeira (d, perc).* 02.

*** Exalted Lover
Stony Plain SPCD 1293//Dixiefrog DFGCD 8562 *Robillard; Scott Aruda (t); Carl Querfurth (tb); Doug James (ts, bs); Sax Gordon [Beadle] (ts); Steve Burk (o, p); Matt McCabe (p); Debbie Davies (g, v); Jesse Williams, Marty Ballou (b); Mark Teixeira (d, perc); Pam Tillis (v); Aimée Hill (sp).* 03.

As on *Duke's Blues*, Robillard devotes most of his time in *Living With The Blues* to received repertoire, which again prompts him to first-class playing. As well as songs from the B. B. King, Guitar Slim and Freddie King books, he ventures upon his first unplugged solo recording, Tampa Red's 'Hard Road', which is so attractive that you can't help wondering what an all-acoustic set would be like. But, not for the first time, the listener may be puzzled that a musician who is so sharp as a guitarist should so often use his voice as a blunt instrument. 'I Live The Life I Love' is a good example: for the quiet authority that Muddy Waters brought to the lyric Robillard substitutes rasping over-emphasis, turning it from manifesto to melodrama.

In *Exalted Lover* he returns (with a couple of exceptions) to his own material, which continues to be rooted in blues idioms, as in the New Orleans strut 'Tore Up' and the Texas shuffle 'How Long Has It Been', the latter a duet with Debbie Davies. The title song is made distinctive by Robillard using a guitar synth to create a ghostly muted trumpet, and throughout the record instrumental colour is applied with deftness and originality.

**** Blue Mood
Stony Plain SPCD 1300//Dixiefrog DFGCD 8580 2CD *Robillard; Al Basile (c); John Abrahamsen (t); Carl Querfurth (tb); Billy Novick (cl, as); Doug James (ts, bs, h); Sax Gordon Beadle (ts); Jerry Portnoy (h); Matt McCabe (p); Jesse Williams, Marty Ballou (b); Mark Teixeira (d); unknowns (perc).* 04.

Of all the guitarists Robillard has listened to, he has perhaps learned most from T-Bone Walker. The first disc in this set is a frank tribute to the Daddy Cool of amplified blues guitar, and a glowing one. Robillard almost completely controls his tendency to exaggerated vocal gesture, and the period sound of the guitar playing and horn arrangements is so accurate that you feel at any moment Easy Rawlins may stroll into the studio.

We speculated above about an all-acoustic set. Evidently Robillard did so, too, because the second disc is just that. Some tracks are very old-time, like Sleepy John Estes's 'Someday Baby', with Robillard on guitar and mandolin and Doug James on harmonica, 'Big Bill's Blues' with McCabe playing the Black Bob role, and a thoroughly in-the-spirit rendition of Jimmie Rodgers's 'Jimmie's Texas Blues' with standard and Dobro-style guitar parts. This disc is billed as a bonus and doesn't push the CD's price up, so its brevity (28.29) is no reason for complaint, but, when the music is so understandingly and entertainingly done, it could well be grounds for disappointment.

***(*) The Duke Meets The Earl
Stony Plain SPCD 1303//Dixiefrog DFGCD 8589 *Robillard; Jimmy McGriff, Dave Limina (o); Matt McCabe (p); Ronnie Earl (g); Jesse Williams, Rod Carey (b); Mark Teixeira (d); Mighty Sam McClain (v).* 04/05.

With those names, it was inevitable that Ron and Rob would make an album together and call it this – the only surprise is that it took so long to happen. Tracks like 'Two Bones & A Pick', 'What Have I Done Wrong' and 'I Need You So Bad', reminders of their shared admiration for T-Bone Walker, Magic Sam and B. B. King respectively, are exhilarating vehicles for the swapping of fours, while Earl's 'Zeb's Thing' is a tribute to Earl Hooker and 'A Soul That's Been Abused' a lingering lament sung by McClain. Elsewhere the vocals are by Robillard, and the effort that goes into them is somewhat at odds with the easy flow of the guitar dialogue. TR

Elzadie Robinson
VOCAL

Elzadie Robinson sounds like a Texan singer come north, but nothing definite is known about her.

(*) Elzadie Robinson Vol. 1 (1926–1928)
Document DOCD-5248 *Robinson; poss. B. T. Wingfield or Shirley Clay (c); poss. Albert Wynn (tb); Artie Starks, Johnny Dodds (cl): Will Ezell, Richard M. Jones, Bob Call, prob. Jimmy Blythe, poss. Tiny Parham (p); prob. Leslie Corley (bj); Blind Blake (g, wh); Johnny St Cyr (g); Jimmy Bertrand (x).* c. 9/26–c. 5/28.

(*) Elzadie Robinson Vol. 2 (1928–1929)
Document DOCD-5249 *Robinson; Will Ezell, poss. Tiny Parham (p).* c. 6/28–c. 3/29.

Elzadie Robinson began her recording career projecting unsubtly and ended it as a rather more nuanced singer, probably because of the change from acoustic to electrical technology. On the majority of her recordings she was backed by Paramount staffer Will Ezell. His accompaniments often sound semi-improvised, but heard at length it becomes obvious that Ezell achieves his effects by recycling a limited number of ideas. He plays excellent walking basses on '2.16 Blues' and 'Galveston Blues', but elsewhere often sounds febrile and disorganized. Robinson herself is variably interesting; her passionate singing and Bob Call's doomy playing make 'The Santa Claus Crave' and 'St. Louis Cyclone Blues' important for more than their topical and sociological content, but her collaborations with Blind Blake and Johnny Dodds are marred by mutual uneasiness. Robinson is good at conveying weariness with the ways of men, but her *oeuvre* is short on memorable songs, and many of them have been transferred to CD from beaten-up 78s. Six alternative takes by Lottie Kimbrough complete *Vol. 2*. CS

Fenton Robinson (1935–97)
VOCAL, GUITAR

At the age of 18 Robinson left Mississippi for Memphis, where he made his first record. By 1962 he had moved to Chicago, where he made several singles, including the original recording of his composition 'Somebody Loan Me A Dime', and, eventually, some admirable albums, none of which brought him the status he deserved. His sometime producer Bruce Iglauer wrote in 1984 that 'his reserved personality and musical subtlety may keep him from ever becoming a major star', and his guess was accurate. Robinson left Chicago soon afterwards and thereafter his appearances on the blues circuit were sporadic.

**** Somebody Loan Me A Dime
Alligator ALCD 4705 Robinson; Norval D. Hodges, Elmer Brown Jr (t); Bill McFarland (tb); Dave Baldwin (ts, arr); Bill Heid (kb); Mighty Joe Young (g); Cornelius Boyson (b); Tony Gooden (d). 7/74.

Robinson's voice is a thing of beauty, uniting the wistfulness of Bobby Bland and the forthrightness of Lowell Fulson. As a guitarist he belongs to the B. B. King school but asserts his individuality with darting breaks and inventive solos. The outstanding performances on this utterly assured album are of his own songs 'Somebody Loan Me A Dime' and 'You Don't Know What Love Is', but none of the tracks is a makeweight, and the set ends spectacularly with the storming guitar of 'Texas Flood'. (He had played the lead guitar on the song's first recording, 16 years earlier, by its writer, Larry Davis.) To call this a no-frills production is not to depreciate it: the plainness and naturalness of the sound draw the listener inexorably to the man at the centre of it.

**** I Hear Some Blues Downstairs
Alligator ALCD 4710 Robinson; Bill Brimfield (t); Bill McFarland (tb); Earl Crossley (ts); Bill Heid (kb); Steve Ditzell (g); Larry Exum (b); Ashward Gates Jr (d). 7/77.

There are fewer of Robinson's own songs here than on the previous album, and none quite as memorable as 'Somebody Loan Me A Dime', but the title number is a vivid evocation of the call of the blues, with a steady beat reminiscent of Lowell Fulson, and the minor-key 'I'm So Tired' is wafted on the breeze of an exhilarating arrangement. 'Just A Little Bit' and 'West Side Baby' offer extensive views of his intricately ravelled guitar playing at fast and slow tempos respectively, while 'Tell Me What's The Reason' is Walker to the T-bone. A good part of the album's excellence is owed to the vitality of the band: the rhythm patterns woven by Ditzell, Exum and Gates on 'I Wish For You' and 'Going West' are as exciting as Robinson's

lead parts, and on 'Killing Floor' perhaps more so. The album rises to a peak with the closing track, a perfectly poised reading of 'As The Years Go Passing By'.

*** Blues In Progress//Nightflight
Black Magic CD 9005//Alligator ALCD 4736 Robinson; Paul Howard, Sonny Covington (t); Leon Randall (ts); Jimmy Martin (bs); Junior Wells (h); Leo Davis (kb); Larry Burton (g); Aron Burton (b); Roy Robertson (d). 2–3/84.

The mellow studio acoustics of this album have a mollifying effect on Robinson's singing and playing. Perhaps, since he was its co-producer, that was what he intended, but some listeners may regret that he does not stand out against his accompaniment as starkly as he did on his previous albums. He sings 'The Feeling Is Gone' with the entranced melancholy he could always bring off so well, and his guitar lines travel in unexpected directions on 'I Lost My True Love' and 'Nightflight'. A horn section is employed on four tracks, rather uninterestingly; Junior Wells is present only on Little Walter's 'Can't Hold Out Much Longer'. Made for the Dutch label Black Magic and issued as *Blues In Progress*, the album was retitled *Nightflight* when licensed to Alligator.

**(*) Special Road
Black Magic BMCD 9012//Evidence ECD 26025 Robinson; Johan de Roos (as, ts, h); Luther Taylor (ts); Leon Ragsdale Jr (kb); Willem van Dullemen (g); Anthony Hardesty (b); Robert Covington (d). 4/89.

Recorded in the Netherlands while the artist was on tour, this album, like its predecessor, displays a more laidback performer than the Robinson of the '70s. Indeed, the man who made 'Texas Flood' and the meandering guitarist of 'Too Many Drivers' are scarcely recognizable as the same player. What may be on display here is the result of Robinson's long immersion in formal music study: the playing is considered, detailed and substantial – probably the cleverest he put on record. But it's also quiet, and when the band is desultory, as it sometimes is, the overall effect can be rather monochrome. 'Blue Monday', especially as Robinson sings it here, is a song with some dramatic potential, all of which is dissipated by the sedate accompaniment. TR

Frank Robinson (born 1932)
VOCAL, GUITAR

Robinson learned most of his style from Lightnin' Hopkins, who was his uncle, and Frankie Lee Sims. Born in Crockett, Texas, he has lived there all his life, apart from occasional forays into West Texas, New Mexico and Arizona to find work picking cotton.

***(*) Deep East Texas Blues
Black Magic CD 9028 Robinson; Mark 'Kaz' Kazanoff (ts); Powell St John, Mel Davis (h); Mike Buck, Ernie Durawa, Maryann Price (d). 94–95.

Stylistically, Robinson owes almost everything to his more famous mentors, and he also relies on them heavily for songs; there are no original compositions among his 11 tracks (six by Guitar Curtis complete the disc, and are discussed separately), but originality is not the issue. The key point is that Robinson is a notably fine interpreter, especially of his Uncle Lightnin's songs, although he also produces two surprising, emotive reworkings of 'See That My Grave Is Kept Clean'. 'Tom Moore

Blues' is a notch below Hopkins's definitive account of the Moore Brothers' brutal paternalism, but it's of a piece with the rest of Frank Robinson's music – oldfashioned, even anachronistic, but always deeply rooted in local traditions and experience. It's a drawback, but not a major one, that neither harmonica player is very effective. CS

Freddy Robinson (born 1939)
VOCAL, GUITAR, HARMONICA

Raised near West Memphis, Arkansas, Robinson began playing guitar at the age of nine and was inspired to take up music seriously by hearing Joe Willie Wilkins. In 1956, now in Chicago, he played with Birmingham Jones, Jimmy Dawkins, Little Walter and Howlin' Wolf, participating in important recordings by the last two. His range extended by guitar lessons, he worked with Jerry Butler, Syl Johnson, Ray Charles and John Mayall. Following a small hit with the instrumental 'Black Fox' (1970) he cut two albums for the Stax subsidiary Enterprise. Soon afterwards he joined the Islamic faith and changed his name to Abu Talib.

*** Bluesology
Ace CDCHD 728 Robinson; Oscar Brashear (t); George Bohanon (tb); Red Holloway (ts); Delbert Hill (bs); Joe Sample (kb, o, p); Lester Snell (kb); Monk Higgins (o, p); Sidney Sharp (strings); Al Vescovo (g); Wilton Felder, 'Sugar Bear' (b); Paul Humphrey (d, perc); Harold Mason, Willie Hall (d); Bobbie Hall (cga, perc); Alex Brown, Clydie King, Venetta Fields, Darlene Love, Deborah Lindsey, unknowns (v); Memphis Symphony Orchestra, unknowns (various instruments). 72–73/74.

In 'Bluesology' Robinson reminisces fondly about Theresa's Lounge, one of the Chicago blues clubs he knew in his youth, and in 'At The Drive-In' he plays the sort of slow, late-night blues that would have gone down well there. These and 'I Found My Soul Last Night' are the only survivors of *At The Drive-In*, Robinson's first album, but its successor, *Off The Cuff*, is more generously sampled, its eight tracks ranging from the blues of 'Changing Dreams' and Percy Mayfield's 'River's Invitation' to the funk of 'Medicine Man'. The combination of Robinson's guitar, Sample's keyboards and Felder's bass produces deliciously relaxed grooves. The remaining nine tracks include much of what would have been Robinson's third album, recorded in Memphis with the Isaac Hayes band but never issued. A good deal of this is funk and soul, but the instrumental 'After Hours' shows how Robinson's blues guitar playing has been refined by his work in jazz and funk contexts, and there are more blues lines in 'House Hunting,' 'The Creeper' and 'Good Feeling'. For a man who made his name as a guitarist Robinson is a convincing and versatile singer, telling his blues stories with a dry, good-humoured resignation that recalls Lowell Fulson or Jimmy McCracklin. TR

Iceman Robinson (born 1934)
VOCAL, GUITAR

Mississippi-born Robinson has been a part-time musician in Chicago since the early '70s, playing with, among others, John and Sylvia Embry and L. V. Banks.

**(*) I've Never Been Loved
Fedora FCD 5026 Robinson; Frank Goldwasser (g); Willie Kent (b); Chris Millar (d). 9/00.

The torrential slide guitar playing on the opening 'My Baby's Comin' Home' and 'Workin' Man' places Robinson in the line of musicians like Elmore James and Hound Dog Taylor. Tracks without slide are not quite so dramatic but no less intense, and the direct presentation and firm beat of 'Baby How Long' (Howlin' Wolf's 'How Many More Years') and others suggest that he shares the no-frills philosophy of artists like Willie Kent – his bassist on this date – and Magic Slim. TR

'Banjo' Ikey Robinson (1904–90)
VOCAL, BANJO, TENOR GUITAR, GUITAR, CLARINET

Born into a musical family in Virginia, Robinson was on the road with his banjo by the age of 14. In 1926 he moved to Chicago, where he played with Jelly Roll Morton and Jabbo Smith. He spent 1930–34 in New York, hitching his wagon to the Clarence Williams train, then returned to Chicago, where he spent the rest of his life, latterly working as a lounge pianist. Hugely versatile, Robinson was an indefatigable stoker in the engine-room of Chicago jazz and blues for some 60 years.

*** 'Banjo' Ikey Robinson (1929–1937)
RST Jazz Perspectives JPCD-1508 Robinson; Jabbo Smith (c, v); Omer Simeon (cl, as); unknown (cl, bs); Cecil Scott (cl); Willie Rendall (as); Ralph Anderson (k); Alex Hill (p, v); Jimmy Flowers, Ralph Tervalon, poss. William Barbee, unknowns (p); Robert Waugh (vn); Count Turner (bj); Mike McKendrick, unknown (g); Lawson Buford (bb); Bill Johnson, Leonard Bibbs, John Lindsay (b); Walter Bishop, unknown (d); Tressie Mitchell, Charlie Slocum, unknown (v). 1/29–5/37.

Discographies and album notes tend to be indecisive, or plain wrong, about whether Robinson is playing guitar or banjo on a given recording. As often as not it is a tenor guitar, probably a steel-bodied model; this is what he uses on the exquisite Clarence Williams Jug Band session of August 1933 (not here but on *Clarence Williams And His Orchestra Vol. 1 1933–1934* [Timeless CBC 1–056]), and the same ringing, cleanly executed playing can be heard immediately on his eponymous CD, first in crystalline jazz performances with Jabbo Smith, then on the vocal blues 'Pizen Tea Blues' and 'Rock Pile Blues'. He switched to banjo, on which he was something of a virtuoso, when playing with Cecil Scott and Alex Hill in the Hokum Trio, a group assembled by Columbia to cash in on the success of other labels' hokum bands (some of which he played in as well), but he used both instruments with the Pods Of Pepper, a skiffle quartet featuring the squalling kazoo tooter Ralph Anderson, while with his own Windy City Five he doubled tenor guitar and very fair clarinet. After all that small-group jollity, the CD concludes with Robinson twirling guitar lines around four vocal blues by the stolid Charlie Slocum. TR

Jimmie Lee Robinson (1931–2002)
VOCAL, GUITAR, BASS, WHISTLING, SPURS

Robinson grew up near Maxwell Street and became one of the open-air market's musicians. He worked with Elmore James, Little Walter, Freddie King and Magic Sam among others, was a busy session player in the '50s and '60s and recorded for Bandera. Robinson visited Europe in 1965 with the AFBF; he

returned a decade later, but was already withdrawing from music, and was largely inactive until the late '80s. He was prominent in the unsuccessful campaign to save Maxwell Street from redevelopment by the University of Chicago, contributing songs and written reminiscences and staging an 81-day hunger strike. In the '90s Robinson issued the self-produced Guns, Gangs And Drugs and Maxwell Street Blues (Amina Records CD-1001 and 1002 respectively) but the label died with its owner, who took his own life while suffering from cancer.

** Lonely Traveller
Delmark DE-665 *Robinson; Scott Dirks (h); Johnny Burgin (g); Steve Cushing (d).* 8/92–9/93.

***(*) Chicago Jump
Random Chance RCD 14 *As above, except Twist Turner (d) replaces Cushing; add Sho Komiya (b).* 11/95–2/96.

Robinson's Bandera sides are on *Blues And Gospel From The Bandera, Laredo And Jerico Road* [sic] *Labels Of Chicago* (Ace CDCHD 808); see COMPILATIONS: LABEL HISTORIES & SHOWCASES.

There are some characteristically quirky solos on *Lonely Traveller*, notably on the title track, but this is a disappointing comeback, as comparison of the remade 'All My Life' with its predecessor confirms. Robinson often sings with an aimless aggression that neither derives from nor illuminates the lyrics, and many songs are too long. His spiky rhythms are difficult to accompany, and although Dirks and Burgin are adequate, Cushing is frequently reduced to minimalist pounding.

Chicago Jump is much better. Robinson's angular guitar lines are still the CD's focus, but this time Komiya and Turner set the rhythmic framework, and Robinson collaborates with the band rather than heading for the horizon, leaving them to follow as best they can. Apart from two instrumentals, the content is covers of Robinson's favourite songs: Little Walter and Willie Mabon feature prominently among his sources, and 'Drifting Blues' pays devoted homage to Charles Brown. Jimmy Reed and B. B. King are less well served, for Robinson indulges in some pointless bawling, but this is much the best of his comeback CDs; a pity, then, that it was issued posthumously.

**(*) Remember Me
APO APO 2006 *Robinson; Jimmy D. Lane (g).* 2/98.

*** … All My Life
APO APO 2011 *As above, except add Madison Slim (h).* 2/99.

Robinson's Amina productions were marred by excessive amounts of artiness, sentimentality and whistling, and by a general tendency to go on a bit; on APO's acoustic sessions those weaknesses are kept in bounds, if not quite eliminated. The material is mostly familiar, even when Robinson gets the composer credit. ('I Will Be Your Dog' is 'Baby Please Don't Go'; 'Wagon Wheels' is 'Rock Me Baby'.) Broadly speaking, *Remember Me* relies on older, traditional material, while *… All My Life* takes Chicago blues of the '50s and unplugs them, often generating new shadings and insights by doing so. 'Easy Baby' was mishandled on Delmark, but the reading here is sensuously understated, and J. B. Lenoir's anti-lynching 'If I Get Lucky' is a tightly controlled blend of accusation and anger. Robinson had a penchant for recitations, and *Remember Me* includes a couple, among them a 'Boll Weevil' which makes the racial subtext clearer than usual, but is overextended. Despite signing off with 'What A Wonderful World', *… All My Life* is the better disc, not least because the harmonica adds textural variety. CS

L. C. Robinson (1915–76)
VOCAL, STEEL GUITAR, GUITAR, VIOLIN

'Good Rockin'' Robinson, as he was dubbed by the Oakland DJ Jumpin' George Oxford, was born in Texas. In his teens he worked the carnival circuit, playing guitar and fiddle, with his brother A. C. He was introduced to the steel guitar by Leon McAuliffe, who played it in Bob Wills's Texas Playboys. After World War II the brothers moved to the San Francisco Bay Area, where they made a few obscure singles; A. C. gave up music for the church in 1959, but L. C. carried on. In 1975 he appeared at the Berkeley Blues Festival and toured Scandinavia.

*** Mojo In My Hand
Arhoolie CD 453 *Robinson; A. C. Robinson (h, v); Charlie Musselwhite (h); Ren Hawkins (p, v); Pinetop Perkins, Dave Alexander [Omar Sharriff] (p); Pee Wee Madison (g, v); Sammy Lawhorn (g); Calvin Jones, William Hyatt (b); Willie Smith, Teddy Winston (d).* 9–12/71, 11/75.

The LP on which this CD is based placed Robinson first with the Muddy Waters band, then with a trio headed by pianist Dave Alexander. At both sessions he used all three of his instruments. Not surprisingly, the latter setting gives him more room to operate, as well as to avoid occasional dissonances between his steel and the larger group's guitars, and he stretches out with violin on 'She Got It From The Start', with steel in 'I've Got To Go' and with guitar on 'Things So Bad In California'. The CD adds a further number from the Waters band session, 'Can't Be A Winner' sung by Pee Wee Madison, and two with the trio, 'I'm Just A Country Boy' and the steel guitar instrumental 'L. C.'s Theme'. It also includes half a dozen performances with his brother, in which permutations of violin, harmonica, piano, drums and two voices tackle four gospel songs, and L. C. fiddles the old-time breakdown 'Ida Red' and a blues. *Mojo In My Hand* is a persuasive advertisement for Robinson's skills as a bluesman, with several highly satisfactory performances, but he was a musician with an unusual and interesting background, and it's a pity he was not recorded in more depth. TR

Matthew Robinson (born 1948)
VOCAL, GUITAR

Robinson's father was a preacher and a multi-instrumentalist; his son soon discovered the Austin blues clubs, taught himself guitar and joined the Mustangs in 1964. The group graduated from the campus circuit to touring as a support act, but in 1971 Robinson returned to Austin. He formed the Texas Blues Band in 1996.

** Bad Habits
Fedora FCD 5008 *Robinson; Donald 'Duck' Jennings (t); Larry D. C. Williams (s); Mickey 'Tickey' Bennett (kb); Eddie James Stout (b); William Norman Fagen (d).* 5/98.

** **Matthew Robinson And The Texas Blues Band**
Dialtone DT 0006 *Robinson; Donald 'Duck' Jennings, Ephraim Owens (t); J. W. Davis (ts); Mickey Bennett (o); Johnny Moeller (g); Eddie Stout (b); Charles Shaw (d); Glenda Sue Hargis (v).* 01?

Robinson sings soul-blues in a small, inflexible voice, and attempts to convey emotion by haphazard and unconvincing straining; Hargis, who sings two songs on Dialtone, is derivative and one-dimensional. Robinson is a competent but uninventive guitarist; Johnny Moeller has more technique, but uses it to generate arbitrary and vulgar blues-rock solos. These discs present a neighbourhood bar band with delusions of grandeur. CS

Tad Robinson (born 1956)
VOCAL, HARMONICA

Robinson grew up in New York City, where he absorbed the sounds of '60s soul from radio and records. He moved to Chicago in the mid-'80s and for a couple of years played regularly at Rosa's Lounge on the West Side. He made his recording debut on Delmark as vocalist on Dave Specter's 1994 album Blueplicity. *Currently he lives in Indiana and plays part-time.*

**(*) One To Infinity
Delmark DE-673 *Robinson; Kenny Anderson, Rob Mazurek (t); Bill McFarland (tb); Hank Ford, John Brumbach (ts); Willie Henderson (bs, arr); Dez Desormeaux (bs); Ken Saydak (o, p); Chris Cameron (o); Jon Weber (p); Alex Schultz, Robert Ward, Richie Davis, Dave Specter (g); Harlan Terson, Rob Amster (b); Jon Hiller (d); Kay C. Reed, Theresa Davis, Rita Warford (v); Gene Barge (arr).* 1–2/94.

*** Last Go Round
Delmark DE-722 *Robinson; Kenny Anderson (t); Hank Ford, Sonny Seals (ts); Willie Henderson (bs, arr); Kevin McKendree (o, p); Alex Schultz (g); Harlan Terson (b); Jon Hiller (d).* 5/98.

Robinson is a versatile songwriter, his thinking untrammelled by fealty to the blues form, and a singer with a medium-weight, muscular voice. On *One To Infinity*, as on *Blueplicity*, his impressive debut with Dave Specter & The Bluebirds, the songs that come off best in performance are those closest in kind to the '60s soul that shaped him, such as the title track, 'Raining In New York' and 'At The End Of The Tunnel' – one of two tracks featuring Robert Ward, whose oscillating guitar is even more oriental on the other, 'Give Love A Chance'.

Last Go Round has more blues tunes, such as 'If I Had It To Do Again', 'No Exit Blues' and Little Walter's 'I've Got To Go', and they come off much better than their equivalents on the previous album; the soul compositions, like 'Since You've Been Gone' and 'Another Song, Another Day', are a shade less effectively realized. In 'Some Of My Best Friends Are The Blues' singer and musicians expertly mix a disenchanted late-night cocktail reminiscent of Sinatra's 'One For My Baby' with a dash of Ray Charles. Blues enthusiasts will probably find this album more to their taste than its forerunner.

Robinson recorded with Dave Specter again on his 1995 album *Live In Europe*, and with Floyd McDaniel on *West Side Baby*.

***(*) Did You Ever Wonder?
Severn CD-0025 *Robinson; Kenny Rittenhouse, Tom Williams (t, flh); John Jensen (tb); Scott Young (as, ts, fl); Jeff Antoniuk, Rick Humphreys, Bruce Swain (ts); Don Lerman, Scott Silbert (bs); Benjie Porecki, Kevin McKendree (kb, o, p); Alex Schultz (g); Harlan Terson, Tony Brown (b); Marty Binder (d); Winston 'Stone' Damon (perc); Otis Clay, Denise Davis (v).* 04.

With this sophisticated, adult album of blues and soul songs Robinson firmly stakes his claim to be considered one of the premier singers in his field, a man who can employ Otis Clay as a backing singer yet not leave the listener feeling that the roles should have been reversed. Perfectly fitting horn parts and polished guitar by Schultz adorn a sequence of well-written songs by Robinson and his lyricist John P. Bean and well-chosen ones by other people. TR

Rockin' Dopsie (1932–93)
VOCAL, ACCORDION

Alton Rubin had been playing button accordion, left-handed and upside down, for 20 years before he recorded, and had been working in Louisiana clubs since 1955. His big break came when he was spotted by Sam Charters and signed to the Swedish Sonet label. Having become popular in Europe, Dopsie (sometimes spelled differently, but always pronounced Doopsie) began to build a wider reputation at home; he appeared on Paul Simon's Graceland *because Clifton Chenier was unwell, and on CDs by Bob Dylan and Cindi Lauper – and turned down* Saturday Night Live *because he was committed to a church dance in Houston. As if to confirm his lack of career skills, Dopsie also managed to alienate much of his downhome audience by having himself crowned 'King of Zydeco' only three weeks after Chenier's death.*

*** Clifton Chenier & Rockin' Dupsee
Paula PCD 17 *Dopsie; unknown (ts); unknown (o); unknowns (g); unknowns (b); unknown (d); Chester Zeno (rb).* c. 69–c. 74.

***(*) In New Orleans
Storyville STCD 8052 *Dopsie; John Hart (ts); prob. Paul 'Lil Buck' Senegal [Sinegal] (g); prob. Alonzo Johnson (b); Alton Rubin Jr (d); David Rubin (rb).* 3/84.

*** Saturday Night Zydeco
Maison de Soul MdS-104 *Dopsie; John Hart (ts); Sherman Robertson, Russell 'Sly' Dorion, Paul Senegal [Sinegal], poss. others (g); Alonzo Johnson, poss. others (b); Alton Rubin Jr, poss. others (d); David Rubin, poss. others (rb).* 80s.

**(*) Louisiana Music
Atlantic 82307 *Dopsie; John Hart (ts); Selwyn Cooper (g); Alonzo Johnson (b); Alton Rubin Jr (d); David Rubin (rb).* 91?

None of the six LPs Dopsie recorded for Sonet in the '70s is currently available on CD. His 12 tracks (of 20) on Paula were originally recorded for release on singles, but they coalesce into a good portrait of an artist whose mainstream style owes a lot – allowing for the different possibilities of their instruments – to Clifton Chenier, without being merely derivative. The Maison de Soul disc is notable mainly for the presence of the blind saxophonist John Hart, a former Chenier sideman who fused Texas and New Orleans influences into a style that was simultaneously angular and lyrical. His driving solos are a highlight, and Dopsie continues to make good use of inventive guitarists. The CD is let down by recording quality that's adequate at best, and by covers of Joe Turner and

Professor Longhair that are too obviously aimed at the musical tourist.

In New Orleans was recorded live, and catches a band in exceptional form working up a considerable sweat; Dopsie's sons supply percussion that's as insistent as their father's singing and playing. He also encourages Hart and the guitarist to play solos that often go down unexpected avenues, yet always remain concise, logical and exciting. With all this in the CD's favour, it's the more regrettable that Hart is out of tune for the first half of 'Allons A Lafayette', and that the concluding 'I Got A Woman' is comparatively desultory. *Louisiana Music*, recorded in the wake of the fuss over *Graceland*, has a number of tunes in common with *In New Orleans*, and it feels as though the Zydeco Twisters are running through a fixed and familiar setlist on cruise control. Ahmet Ertegun can't find a way to shake things up, and Atlantic's studio sound crosses the line between pristine and sterile. cs

Rockin' Dopsie Jr (born 1962)
VOCAL, RUBBOARD, PERCUSSION

Rockin' Dopsie Sr's real name was Alton Rubin, but Rockin' Dopsie Jr, who took over the leadership of the Zydeco Twisters after Alton's death, is his son, David; Alton Jr is the band's drummer.

*** Feet Don't Fail Me Now
Aim A 1 *Dopsie Jr; Li'l Rascals Brass Band, New Birth Brass Band, The Quezergue Players (Ronald Jones, Charles Moore, Erving Charles, Fred Kemp, Stacy Cole, Brian Murray) (brass, reeds, other instruments); Kermit Ruffins, Wardell Quezergue (t); Jerry Jumonville (ts); Anthony Dopsie [Anthony Rubin] (ac, v); Dwayne Dopsie [Dwayne Rubin] (ac); Waylon Thibodeaux (vn); Paul 'Little Buck' Senegal [Sinegal], Shelton Sonnier (g); Alonzo Johnson (b); Tiger Dopsie [Alton Rubin Jr] (d, v); Willie 'The Whip' Edmond (tamb); Wanda Rouzan, Michelle Shocked (v).* c. 9/93.

*** Everybody Scream
Aim A 6 *Dopsie Jr; Jerry Jumonville (ts); Patrick Williams (h); Anthony Dopsie (ac, v); Dwayne Dopsie [Rubin] (ac); Kim Phillips (kb); Paul Senegal [Sinegal], Joseph Veasie (g); Alonzo Johnson (b); Tiger Dopsie [Alton Rubin Jr] (d, v); Nathaniel Jolivette (d); Willie 'T. J.' Bruno (perc); Terry De Gruy, Troy Netters, Lisa Netters, Ronald Jones (v).* 97?

*** Turn Up The Zydeco!
Mardi Gras MG 1040 *Dopsie Jr; Chuck Arnold (t); Joe Raines (tb); Milton Lewis (as); Jerry Jumonville, Tim Green (ts); Jerry Embree (bs); Patrick Williams (h); Anthony Dopsie [Rubin] (ac, v); Kim Phillips (kb, p); Paul Senegal [Sinegal], Melvin Veazie (g); Alonzo Johnson (b); Tiger Dopsie [Alton Rubin Jr] (d, v); Terry De Gruy, Marva Wright, Lisa Amos (v).* 98?

*** Zydeco Man
Mardi Gras MG 1048 *Dopsie Jr; Milton Lewis (as); Patrick Williams (h); Anthony Dopsie [Rubin] (ac); Kim Phillips (kb, o); Paul Senegal [Sinegal], Derwin 'Big D' Perkins (g); Alonzo Johnson (b); Tiger Dopsie [Alton Rubin Jr], Cyril Neville (d, v); Michelle Ploue, Scherri Horaist (v).* 3/00.

**(*) Rockin' Zydeco Party!
Mardi Gras MG 1061 *Dopsie Jr; Charles Hudson (t); Milton Lewis (as); Jerry Jumonville (ts); Jerry Embree (bs, kb); Patrick Williams (h, v); Anthony Dopsie [Rubin] (ac, kb); Kim Phillips (kb); Davell Crawford (o); Jon Cleary (p); Russell 'Sly' Dorion (g, voicebox); David Jaurequi (g); Parker Shy (b, v); Tiger Dopsie [Alton Rubin Jr] (d); Elaine Foster, Elizabeth Foster, Erica Falls, Rachael Cook, Robyn Rechard (v).* 02?

*(*) I Got My Mojo Working
SONO 1067 *Dopsie Jr; Charles Hudson (t); Milton Lewis (as); Tom Saunders (bss); Patrick Williams (h): Anthony Dopsie [Rubin] (ac); Ricky McQuills, Raymond Fletcher (kb); Nick Farkas, Keith Vinet (p); Les Getrex (g, v); David Jaurequi (g); Taylor Murphy, Alonzo Johnson, Gary Edwards (b); Dwayne Nelson, Oliver 'Lee Lee' Alcorn (d); Zondra W. Jones, Fadra White, Larry Hebert (v).* 04?

The Zydeco Twisters are New Orleans-based, and their music is shaped in large measure by the requirements of the local tourist industry. The Twisters' synthesis of zydeco, New Orleans R&B, soul and rock is distinctive, but it's a manifestation of mass culture, no longer umbilically connected to the folkways of French-speaking black Louisiana. That doesn't mean that it's *ipso facto* artificial or valueless; Rockin' Dopsie's sons and their accomplices are skilful and dynamic performers, and their first three CDs convey much of their vigour and showmanship, offering consistently peppy and enjoyable music, and some exceptionally good tracks: *Feet Don't Fail Me Now* has a six-minute 'Baby What You Want Me To Do?' that swings mightily, and a 'Jambalaya' with phenomenally fierce and ingenious percussion; 'Bad Luck And Trouble' on *Zydeco Man* is a very fine piece of oldfashioned blues composition and performance (and compensation for another, inferior 'Jambalaya'); and the house remix of 'Hot Tamale Baby' on *Turn Up The Zydeco!* invigorates one of Clifton Chenier's least interesting numbers. However, despite fine revivals of 'Key To The Highway' and 'Night Time Is The Right Time', *Rockin' Zydeco Party*, with the inevitable 'Mustang Sally', and covers of Stevie Wonder, the Pointer Sisters and the Beatles' 'Come Together'(!) is a soundtrack for getting tanked on Bourbon Street, as – in an even more thoroughly pop vein – is *I Got My Mojo Working*. The accordion appears only on 'I Can See Clearly Now' and Bob Dylan's 'On A Night Like This', and all tracks are covers, most of them soul numbers featuring bad imitations of Solomon Burke, Otis Redding, James Brown and Wilson Pickett among others. The rhythmically repulsive title track and 'House Of The Rising Sun' are as close to blues as it gets, and the wrong notes in the latter's vocal are by no means unique. cs

The Rockin' Johnny Band
GROUP

Rockin' Johnny Burgin (born 1969) grew up in the South and began playing guitar at 16. Two years later he moved to Chicago, where he began playing with Tail Dragger in 1990. He has recorded with Tail Dragger for St George and Delmark, and with Jimmy Burns, Jimmie Lee Robinson and Big Wheeler for the latter label.

**(*) Straight Out Of Chicago
Delmark DE-720 *Jesse Scinto, Willie Young (ts); Martin Lang (h); Rockin' Johnny Burgin (g, v); Rick Kreher, Illinois Slim (g); Sho Komiya (b); Sam Lay (d, v); Kenny Smith (d); Tail Dragger, Robert Plunkett (v).* 11/97.

**(*) Man's Temptation
Delmark DE-732 *Martin Lang (h); Donny Nichilo (p); Rockin' Johnny Burgin (g, v); Rick Kreher (g); Sho Komiya (b); Kenny Smith (d).* 10/98, 4/99.

'My own playing is mostly early '60s Chicago blues,' says Burgin. 'That whole era sounds modern to me, with room for further development ... I like a piercing, clear sound.' And he gets it. It's fitting that he should record for Delmark, since he's obviously acquainted with some of the label's albums of the '60s and '70s, such as those by Jimmy Dawkins. The Delmark recording aesthetic of those days – dry, the instrumental lines discrete, the total effect somewhat undramatic – also finds an echo on *Straight Out Of Chicago*, though the tracks by a larger ensemble including sax(es) have more heft. *Man's Temptation*, which is almost entirely by a quintet, has a more vivid sound, and both Lang and Komiya make an excellent impression. It will be Burgin's singing that's a problem for some listeners, since it's markedly unaggressive. On the first album he divided the vocals with guests like the ghostly Plunkett and the earthy Tail Dragger, but on *Man's Temptation* he enlists no help, and while Jimmy Reed's 'Little Rain' and the Lonnie Johnson hit 'Tomorrow Night' take no harm from gentle handling, some may feel that other songs would have benefited from a more rugged approach. A later album, *More Real Folk Blues* (Marquis [unnumbered]), has had limited circulation. TR

Rockin' Sidney (1932–98)
VOCAL, HARMONICA, ACCORDION, KEYBOARDS, GUITAR, BASS, DRUM MACHINE

Sidney Semien's fame rests on writing 'My Toot Toot', zydeco's only crossover hit. That was in 1985, but he'd been recording R&B, pop and soul since 1957, adding zydeco in the wake of Clifton Chenier's regional success. The many versions of 'My Toot Toot', including hits by Jean Knight in the States, Denise LaSalle in Europe and its composer (in the Country Top 40!), generated publishing income that enabled Sidney to buy two radio stations, and spend much of his time recording material in his home studio, for release on his own ZBC label or under licence.

** My Toot Toot
Ace CDCH 160 *Rockin' Sidney*; Willie Trahan, unknown (ts); unknown (bs); George Lewis (h); Katie Webster, unknown (p); Sherman Thomas, Thomas Shreve (g); Francis Semien, Sherman Webster, Mark Miller, unknown (b); Roger Semien, Warren Storm (d). 59–84.

'My Toot Toot' was a hit on the strength of its ambiguous title and undeniable (which is not the same as irresistible) catchiness. It's among ten songs (of 25) that feature Sidney multitracking, and when the booklet refers to a 'lamentable drum machine', it's advisable to take note. The percussion does indeed clack robotically, and the sound is aseptically unreal, but poor songwriting is a more fundamental fault: songs like 'Jalapeno Lena' and 'Twist To The Zydeco' are no better than their titles, and the latter is not the only highly derivative number included. Compare 'Let Me Take You To The Zydeco' with the Staple Singers' 'I'll Take You There', for instance, and 'It's Good For The Gander' with anything by Johnnie Taylor; but note also that the latter is Sidney's one great composition.

The first 12 tracks derive from '60s singles; they're inoffensive but lightweight, and the cover versions further emphasize the weaknesses in Sidney's own writing. 'My Little Girl', the earliest recording here, has a punchy tenor chorus. The last three tracks, also with a band, are well worth hearing; more of the same – for which see the other *My Toot Toot*, below – would have made for a better CD.

*(*) The Goldband Years
Goldband GR-7839 *Rockin' Sidney*; unknown (ts); Katie Webster (kb, v); unknown (g); unknown (b); unknown (d); unknown female (v). prob. 60s.

Three of Sidney's four tracks (Webster has the other 12) are poorly recorded, musically second-rate d-i-y. 'Cajun Pogo' is probably the feeblest song covered by this book.

**(*) My Toot Toot
Maison de Soul MdS 1009 *Rockin' Sidney*; Willie Trahan (ts); Katie Webster (p); Thomas Shreve, John Garr (g); Mark Miller, Burton Garr (b); Warren Storm, Dwight Landry (d). 82–90.

The first nine songs on this *Toot Toot* are multitracked. At first glance they duplicate those on Ace, but five of them are 1990 remakes. By that time drum programs offered more realistic sounds, and these versions, though not masterworks, are far more listenable than those on Ace; so are the four which are not remakes, thanks to added reverb, which makes for a more natural sound. The rest of the disc comprises early-'80s recordings with bands that include some of Louisiana's most reliable sessioneers; thanks especially to Webster and Trahan, these are comfortably Sidney's best and bluesiest recordings.

* A Holiday Celebration With Rockin' Sidney
Maison de Soul ValueDisc VMS-7001 *Rockin' Sidney*. 83.

Six tracks that plumb the depths of kitsch, cheap but still wildly overpriced. The bluesy guitar on 'Christmas Without You' is worthy of a better cause.

** I'm Your Man
JSP JSPCD 814 *Rockin' Sidney*; 'Lenni' (ts); Dave Bainbridge (kb); Katie Webster (p); Thomas Shreve, Richard Studholme, Norman Beaker (g); Mark Miller, Bernard Wallace, Kevin Hill (b); Anthony Charles, Stuart Langridge, Tim Franks (d). c. 84–85.

The not very good opening track was cut in Louisiana, and the rest during a British tour. The band on three live numbers includes a gutsy sax, but the keyboardist has a penchant for cheesy electric piano sounds. The concluding 'Oo Poo Pa Doo' is a medley of that song and two by Little Richard, sung with a mind-blowing absence of fervour. The studio material is nondescript and the band too cautious: 'Blues In June' and 'Just Jammin'' are pleasant accordion features, but the percussion would have been equally lively if Sidney's drum machine had replaced Langridge.

** King Zydeco
Mardi Gras MG 1070 *Rockin' Sidney*; Judy Ann Peters, Janice Peters (v). mid–late 80s.

*(*) Mais Yeah Chère!
Maison de Soul MdS-1046 *Rockin' Sidney*; Agnes 'Creola' Semien (v). mid 80s–early 90s.

** Zydeco Is Fun
Maison de Soul 1061 *Rockin' Sidney*; unknowns (v). mid 80s–early 90s.

After the hit, Sidney's recording career was mostly vanity publishing. *Mais Yeah Chère!* is fatally wounded by the drum machine, once again pedestrian and too loud, and by poor songwriting; choosing between 'Funky Attitude' and 'Moo Cow-A-Sockee' is like revisiting Dr Johnson's dispute over precedence between a louse and a flea. *King Zydeco* and *Zydeco Is Fun* are more listenable but far from necessary, despite some good guitar solos. 'Harlem Shuffle' and 'Squeeze That Thang' appear on both discs; less forgivable is the former's unadmitted second appearance on Mardi Gras, masquerading as 'Zydeco Shuffle'. CS

Mighty Mo Rodgers (born 1945)
VOCAL, KEYBOARDS, ORGAN, PIANO, SYNTHESIZERS, ACCORDION, KALIMBA, PERCUSSION, TAMBOURINE, KAZOO

Maurice Rodgers was born and raised in East Chicago, Indiana, where he heard blues at his father's nightclub. He learned piano and while at Indiana State University led a soul/R&B band. Moving in the late '60s to the West Coast, he did session work as a keyboards player and produced an album by Sonny Terry & Brownie McGhee, which included three of his compositions. Returning to college he took a degree in philosophy. Then, in his early 50s, he devoted himself to music fulltime.

**** Blues Is My Wailin' Wall
Blue Thumb 547 781 *Rodgers; Ray Smith (t); Kenny Walker, Harold Bennett (ts); David L. Woodford (s); Darrell Dunmore (h, Do, g); Vic Shoemaker (h); Michael Murphy (o); Steve F'dor (p); Chris Walsh, Tim Pierce, Jim Gibson (g); Albie Burks (b, v); Burleigh Drummond, Clarence Harris (d); Rasheed Ali, George James (perc); Sounds Of Africa, Mary Harris-Drummond, Brie Darling, Breta Troyer (v); Fruity Moon, Bill Nesbitt (sp).* 3–9/98.

The memorable image embodied in the title and the opening track is merely the first sign of the original thought and clever writing that abound here. Among other engaging moments are a blues that begins 'I know what was on the 18 minutes of the Nixon Tapes', the tranquil kalimba patterns of 'Took Away The Drum', and 'Tuskegee Blues', a sober *in memoriam* for the African-Americans victimized by the medical profession in a notorious experiment. As well as being a striking composer and, as the extremely diverse settings prove, an inventive arranger, Rodgers has a very fine voice, whether for a tough-minded blues like 'No Regrets' or for the loving anthem '(Bring Back) Sweet Soul Music'. Fascinating, provocative and repeatedly listenable, this is an exceptional album.

***(*) Red, White And Blues
Verve 589 847 *Rodgers; Lee Thornburg (t); Bruce Paulson (tb); Tom Peterson (cl, ts, bs); Ernie Watts (s); Darrell Dunmore, Steve Guillory (h, g); John 'Juke' Logan (h); Michael Thompson (ac, o); Rev. Bradford Comer (o, v); Tim Pierce (md, g); Audley 'Chissy' Chisholme, Terence Thomas, Anthony Wilson, Billy Watts, Chris Walsh, Gary Myrick (g); Albie Burks (b, perc, v, sp); Fabian Cooke, Pablo Stennett, Smiley Lang, Christoff Luty, 'Hutch' Hutchinson, Mick Mahan (b); Burleigh Drummond (d, perc); Carlton 'Santa' Davis, Alvino Bennett, Clarence Harris (d); Iao (cga, ajimbe, perc); Richard Martinez (cga, perc); Joyce Lawson (v, handclaps); Mary Love Comer, Iman Burks (v); John Lee Hooker (sampled g, sp).* 8/00–1/02.

One of the strongest preoccupations in Rodgers's work is the inheritance of African-American music. As he says in one of these songs, 'I don't do this for the living – I do this for the dead.' Or again, in 'The Holy Howl': 'This is the music that is the markers to buried bones.' And in 'The Boy Who Stole The Blues' he engages with one of the touchiest subjects in musical history, passing a familiar judgement on Elvis Presley – 'Some say Jim Crow made him the King of Rock and Roll' – only to overturn it by comparing him to the black baseball player Jackie Robinson: 'Just like Jackie broke the color line too – freein' America to love the blues.' Elsewhere he celebrates the legacy of John Lee Hooker ('The Boogie Man') and remembers a lesson taught him by 'an old blues man' when he first arrived in LA ('Welcome To The Faultline').

Other songs take other routes into history. 'Have You Seen The American Dream?' addresses a nation at a crossroads – and who knows more than a bluesman about crossroads? In abrupt contrast, 'Happy As a Runaway Slave' jubilantly blends history, politics and the blues into an exhilarating cocktail topped with jokes and puns: 'When I get my Forty Acres and a Mule, I'm gonna make sure it's up in Malibu – I'm gonna Man Tan Moreland and Surf the Blues …'

The musical settings are not as consistently captivating as those of *Blues Is My Wailin' Wall*, but 'Prisoners Of War' and 'American Dream' (both co-produced by Dennis Walker) offset their themes of uncertainty with tranquil melodies, while harmonica and slide guitar gambol merrily alongside 'Runaway Slave' on the unending journey up the blues highway.

**(*) Black Paris Blues
Isabel IS 640302 *Rodgers; Steve Guillory (h, g, v); Chizzy Chisholm (g, v); Pablo Stennett (b, v); Clarence Harris (d).* 7–8/03.

This is Rodgers on the road, with his regular band, giving a Parisian club audience a selection of published work – 'Sweet Soul Music' and the title song from *Blues Is My Wailin' Wall*, 'Prisoners Of War' and 'The Boy Who Stole The Blues' from *Red, White And Blues* – but also essaying a standard, 'Goin' Down Slow', and premiering seven new compositions. These are, on the whole, either unambitious or incompletely realized. 'The Art Of Smoking' and 'I Believe In Evolution (She Made A Monkey Out Of Me)' merely raise a smile, while the title number amounts to little more than 'Hello, Paris! Great to be here!' courteously extended to six minutes. The band is good but, after the richness and detail of the studio albums, it inevitably seems rather meagre and monochrome. Don't start your Rodgers listening here. TR

Jimmy Rogers (1924–97)
VOCAL, GUITAR

Jimmy Rogers (James A. Lane) was the fulcrum around which the Muddy Waters band turned. His rhythmically acute guitar progressions lent direction and diversity to Muddy's more emotive singing and playing. An obvious traditionalist, he nonetheless had a flair for recasting established themes in a contemporary guise, which he sang in an attractive light baritone voice. His own records were more experimental, resulting in a style that initially had merit but suffered when public taste moved away from the blues. However, by then he'd created a body of work that would sustain him throughout his subsequent career.

***(*) The Complete Chess Recordings
[MCA/Chess CHD2–9372]/[(E) MCD 09372] 2CD *Rogers; Ernest*

Cotton, J. T. Brown (ts); Little Walter, Walter Horton (h); Eddie Ware, Henry Gray, Otis Spann (p); Muddy Waters, Little Walter, Po' Bob Woodfork, Robert Lockwood, Jody Williams, Mighty Joe Young, Reggie Boyd, Fred Robinson, Luther Tucker (g); Ernest 'Big' Crawford, Willie Dixon (b); Elga Edmonds, A. J. Gladney, S. P. Leary, Odie Payne, Francis Clay, George Hunter (d); Margaret Whitfield, Little Walter, unknowns (v). 8/50–11/59.

**** Chicago Bound
MCA/Chess CHD 93000 As above. 8/50–11/59.

Rogers's first Chess recordings, such as 'That's All Right', 'Goin' Away Baby' and 'Today, Today Blues', were small masterpieces that demonstrated the continuity in Chicago blues. But while his themes continued to contain traditional elements, he quickly moved into a more confrontational style with 'The World's In A Tangle' and 'Money, Marbles And Chalk'. A sequence of excellent releases, 'The Last Time', 'Chicago Bound', 'Sloppy Drunk' and 'You're The One', came to a climax with 'Walking By Myself' and its overpowering harmonica solo from Walter Horton. Thereafter, his sessions diminished and his songs became less blues-oriented; his last release, 'My Last Meal', was a cover of a three-year-old single by Hurricane Harry. The 51 titles on *The Complete Chess Recordings* comprise every extant master, along with one previously unissued song and 12 alternatives that vary little from the originals. Though light in content, just 14 titles, *Chicago Bound* concentrates on the best of Rogers's output, making it preferable for those who wish to sample rather than collect.

*** Chicago Blues Masters Volume 2
Capitol 33916 Rogers; Bill Lupkin (h); Bob Riedy (p); Louis Myers, Freddie King, Jim Kahr, Frank Capek (g); David Myers, Jim Wydra (b); Fred Below, Richard 'Hubcap' Robinson (d). 1/72–73.

This was Rogers's first album after spending most of the previous decade away from music. Cut at three sessions, one co-produced by Freddie King, it combined rerecordings of 'That's All Right' and others with newer material like 'Information Please', 'Gold-Tailed Bird' and 'Dorcie Belle'. Much of it was played with gusto, although the opening 'Act Like You Love Me' sounds rushed. The session with King provided eight titles but invention flags during the instrumental 'Live At Ma Bee's' and an unnecessarily cluttered 'You're The One'. The last four titles were never issued and not surprisingly are the least successful. Nevertheless, the vigour that Rogers exhibits helps to make this one of the better comeback records.

**(*) That's All Right//Sloppy Drunk
Black & Blue BB 452//Evidence ECD 26036 Rogers; Willie Mabon (p); Louis Myers (g); David Myers (b); Fred Below (d). 12/73.

Recorded while the Aces and Rogers were on tour in France, this is a mixture of live and studio recordings, none of which fulfil the promise of the musicians involved. Once again, the repertoire consists of reworkings of Rogers's best-known compositions, with only 'Shelby County' making a debut appearance. Least impressive is Mabon, who plays well enough in the ensembles but becomes entirely reticent when called upon to solo. Solos taken by Louis Myers are low in the mix and confined to one side of the stereo, and the normally ebullient Below starts well but then goes missing for several songs. Rogers himself is dependable but distinctly lacking in passion and commitment. All these factors are less noticeable in the five live numbers but nonetheless present.

*** Feelin' Good
Blind Pig BPCD 5018 Rogers; Rod Piazza (h, v); Honey Piazza (p); Junior Watson, Steve Killman (g); Bill Stuve, Alex Schultz (b); Bill Swartz, Jimi Bott (d). 83–84.

An engaging album with Piazza's Mighty Flyers, one of the leading bands playing West Coast Chicago-style blues. Rogers sounds comfortable throughout his nine songs, combining his standbys 'Rock This House' and 'Chicago Bound' with new material, including 'Blue And Lonesome' (on which he takes his solitary solo), 'Tricky Woman' and 'St. Louis'. Both Piazzas and Watson take frequent idiomatic solos and everyone plays with the sort of enthusiasm and precision that ultimately become ever so slightly taxing. This is most obvious in three tracks (not on the original album) by the band without Rogers, made at a later date. The traycard calls the result 'intoxicating' but we're talking alcopops rather than Armagnac.

***(*) Chicago Bound (Chicago Blues Session Vol. 15)
Wolf 120.861 Rogers; Billy Branch (h); John Primer, Jimmy Rogers Jr (g); Willie Kent (b); Timothy Taylor (d). 10/89.

All this excellent session lacks is a Chess studio and engineer. In six tracks, Rogers and his band breathe new life into a handful of his best songs, including 'Goin' Away Baby', 'Sloppy Drunk' and 'The Last Time', adding another version of 'St. Louis' and 'Lemon Squeezer' to the honour roll. Primer's solos may be a little modern for the ensemble sound but that's more than compensated for by Branch's amplified harmonica, evoking the sound and energy of Little Walter and Walter Horton on the original records without descending into imitation. Instrumentally, Rogers takes a back seat but his voice remains tireless and timeless. The balance of the CD is by Big Moose Walker.

*** With Ronnie Earl & The Broadcasters
Crosscut CCD 11033//Bullseye Blues CDBB 9544 Rogers; Sugar Ray Norcia (h, v); Dave Maxwell (p); Ronnie Earl (g); Michael 'Mudcat' Ward (b); Per Hanson (d). 6/91.

Recorded live in Bremen, this is an entirely satisfactory set that nevertheless winds up like another *Feelin' Good*. Everyone performs well, in Earl's case sometimes too well, and the audience is wildly grateful but at the end of 77 minutes the listener feels satiated with perfection. The admirable control that each musician exhibits leaves no room for the music to flex and to live, and when most songs exceed six minutes a degree of aural stamina becomes necessary. Rogers performs to his usual high standard and takes more guitar solos than later became customary at his live appearances. Indeed, their exploratory nature forms a marked contrast to the occasional profligacy of Earl's contributions. Ingratitude it may be but less is sometimes more.

***(*) Blue Bird
APO APO 2001 Rogers; Carey Bell (h); Johnnie Johnson (p); Jimmy D. Lane (g); Dave Myers (b); Ted Harvey (d). 11/93.

An excellent illustration of the last point and of the fact that technical ability is worth little if you don't have the touch. This set has 14 tracks, the last of which is an eight-minute jam, and yet it packs more entertainment into its 58 minutes than the album above. Starting with 'I'm Tired Of Crying Over You',

Rogers and his band of veterans blend into a tight but malleable unit that typifies the Chicago sound. Most of the songs are his, apart from a couple of Howlin' Wolf staples and Jimmy Reed's 'Big Boss Man'. Bell, Johnson and Lane (the youngest man present) are the principal soloists and none outstays his welcome. The measure of their achievement is the impromptu jam session that segues from a piano-led boogie into two versions of 'St. Louis Blues', an uncontrived exhibition of each musician's relaxed expertise.

**(*) Blues Blues Blues
Atlantic 83148 *Rogers; Taj Mahal (h, v); Kim Wilson, Carey Bell (h); Johnnie Johnson (p); Jeff Healey, Eric Clapton, Lowell Fulson, Stephen Stills (g, v); Jimmy D. Lane, Keith Richards, John Koenig, Jimmy Page (g); Freddie Crawford (b); Ted Harvey (d); Mick Jagger, Robert Plant (v). 97.*

Some disappointment was inevitable when Rogers died before the sessions for what was projected as a double CD were finished. (The final single CD was issued as by the Jimmy Rogers All-Stars.) It would be charitable to suppose that some of the less felicitous performances enshrined here, with Stills, Plant and Page the obvious candidates, would have been improved. So too Jagger and Richards, leaving Clapton and Healey as the only successes from the white fraternity. Fulson duets with Rogers in 'Ev'ry Day I Have The Blues', Taj Mahal in 'Ludella' and 'Bright Lights Big City'. What saves the project from ignominy is the quality of the backing tracks, for which Bell, Johnson, Lane and Harvey were retained from the *Blue Bird* sessions. The integrity of their performance and Rogers's good-natured vocals ensure that the failings of the rock figures are to some extent assuaged. NS

Roy Rogers (born 1950)
VOCAL, GUITAR, PIANO, MANDOLIN, VARIOUS PERCUSSION

In the '70s Rogers played with Luther Tucker, and in the '80s and '90s with John Lee Hooker, producing his comeback album The Healer *and its successors* Mr. Lucky, Boom Boom *and* Chill Out. *Meanwhile, based in San Francisco, he has maintained his own playing and recording career, often working in a duo with the harmonica player and singer Norton Buffalo.*

** Slidewinder
Blind Pig BP 72687 *Rogers; Scott Mathews (h, p, g, d, perc, v); Allen Toussaint (p); Rich Girard, Steve Ehrmann (b); Terry Baker (d); Keta Bill, Charlie Owens, John Lee Hooker, Dave Terry, Ned Claflin, Tom Nelson (v). 88?*

**(*) Blues On The Range
Blind Pig BP 73589//Crosscut CCD 11026 *Rogers; Mark Naftalin (ac, p); Steve Evans (b); Scott Mathews (d, bgo, perc); Ed Michaels (d). 6–8/89.*

The chief problem with these albums is Rogers's singing, which has no blues inflections at all. Consequently the most successful pieces are the instrumentals 'Blues On The Range' and 'Spanish Blues' (from *Blues On The Range*), examples of a Cooderesque mood music that suggest Rogers could write for movies. His slide playing, whether in the acoustic 'Down In Mississippi' on *Slidewinder* or the electric 'Baby, Please Don't Go' on *Range*, is often ingenious and lively, but the original songs that predominate on both albums tend to be either callow or clichéd. *Slidewinder*'s best parts are two romping duets for acoustic slide guitar and piano with Allen Toussaint, 'Tip-Walk' and 'Red Hot', and a guest appearance by John Lee Hooker in what may have been his only recording of a Robert Johnson song, 'Terraplane Blues'. Rogers's own versions of Johnson songs – 'Walkin' Blues' on *Slidewinder*, 'Hellhound On My Trail' and 'Ramblin' Blues' on *Range* – are well enough played, but so far as the vocals are concerned it's like watching Hamlet played by Chevy Chase.

**(*) R&B
Blind Pig BP 74491 *Rogers; Norton Buffalo (h, v); Phil Richardson (vn); Doug Harman (vc); Scott Mathews (perc). 91.*

*** Travellin' Tracks
Blind Pig BPCD 5003 *Rogers; Norton Buffalo (h, perc, v); Doug Harman (vc); Robin Sylvester (b); Scott Mathews (d). 92.*

These are jointly credited to Rogers and Norton Buffalo, whom old hippies may remember from Commander Cody's Lost Planet Airmen. *R&B*'s opening track, 'So Much To Say And So Few Words', with its close-harmony singing and free-ranging harmonica, predicts the mood of the album, one of easy-swinging Southern music, more country than blues. All the tracks except for Rev. Robert Wilkins's 'Heaven Sittin' Down' are originals by one or the other, with 'Song For Jessica' a further example of Rogers in soundtrack mode. After that mostly acoustic duet set the two men plugged in for some of *Travellin' Tracks* and on two numbers added a rhythm section, but even when these energy sources are not connected sparks fly, especially from live recordings like Elmore James's 'Shake Your Moneymaker', K. C. Douglas's 'Mercury Blues' and a remake of 'Down In Mississippi'. Up to this point this is unequivocally Rogers's best record. His subsequent '90s albums, *Slide Of Hand* and *Slide Zone* for Liberty and *Rhythm & Groove* and *Pleasure And Pain* for Pointblank, have left the catalogue building.

**(*) Slideways
Singular 2001//Evidence ECD 26121 *Rogers; Norton Buffalo (h); Phil Aaberg (kb, harmonium, p); Freddie Roulette (lap steel); Steve Evans (b); Scott Mathews, Francis Clay (d, perc); Jim Sanchez, Zigaboo Modeliste (d). 1/01.*

Slideways finds Rogers greeting a new decade without a vocal mike, playing unflagging slide guitar in the company, except on the solos 'Swamp Dream' and 'For The Children', of equally zestful rhythm sections. But despite plenty of changes of mood and tempo and astute work in both studio and control room, it all feels oddly impersonal.

** Roots Of Our Nature
Blind Pig BP 5077 *Rogers; Norton Buffalo (h, v); Jeremy Cohen (vn); Doug Harman (vc); Rich Girard, Scoop McGuire (b); Jim Sanchez (d); James Henry (cga, shaker, chimes). 02.*

Another collaboration with Buffalo, this reprises the country ambience of *R&B* rather than the bluesy vitality of *Travellin' Tracks*. The interplay of harmonica and acoustic guitar is attractive in a jogalong cowboy-movie style, but not buoyant enough to save the lyrics from sinking beneath their load of platitudes. TR

Walter Roland (1903–72)
VOCAL, PIANO, GUITAR

Recording at a time when few blues artists were, between 1933 and '35, Roland made over a hundred sides, either in his own

name or accompanying the singer Lucille Bogan. He was active, like her, in and around Birmingham, Alabama, but little else is known of his life.

**** Walter Roland – Vol. 1 (1933)
Document DOCD-5144 *Roland; Sonny Scott (g, v, sp); Lucille Bogan (sp). 7/33.*

*** Walter Roland – Vol. 2 (1934–1935)
Document DOCD-5145 *Roland; Josh White (g); Lucille Bogan (sp). 7/34–3/35.*

*** Lucille Bogan & Walter Roland (1927–1935)
Yazoo 1017 *Roland; Sonny Scott (g, sp); Josh White (g); Lucille Bogan (sp). 7/33–3/35.*

*** Lucille Bogan & Walter Roland: The Essential
Classic Blues CBL 200032 2CD *Roland; Josh White (g); Sonny Scott (perc, dancing, sp, v); Lucille Bogan (sp). 7/33–3/35.*

Roland's first recording, and probably the song he was signed for, was a composition tuned to the grim music of the Great Depression, 'Red Cross Blues'. Describing the food relief provided to poor families by the Red Cross, and the discomfort some of them felt at having to rely on welfare, it sold well and was copied or adapted by several other artists. Roland himself, perhaps anticipating its success, immediately afterwards cut a 'Red Cross Blues No. 2' with different lyrics, accompanying himself not, as before, on piano but on guitar, an instrument he used on about ten of his 50-odd recordings. When playing piano he liked to create the illusion of disorienting the beat by heaping right-hand note-clusters on skeletal left-hand figures, a practice first observed in 'Last Year Blues'. Whatever the accompaniment, he favoured slow, slouching tempos and a quiet, often reflective vocal manner, though there are numerous exceptions: the hokum number 'Whatcha Gonna Do?', the effervescent piano solos 'Jookit Jookit', 'Piano Stomp' and the rag-blues 'Hungry Man's Scuffle' – with buck dancing by Sonny Scott and backchat by Lucille Bogan – and a wonderful trio of guitar duets with Scott, 'Guitar Stomp', 'Railroad Stomp' and 'Frisco Blues'.

Those and other excellent performances, the astonishing yield of a four-day session, make up Document's *Vol. 1*, a totally absorbing collection. The Roland of *Vol. 2* is a less startling musician. He plays no more guitar, and his material is largely confined to slow blues, though he shifts gear for 'Early In The Morning No. 2', which, like the two versions on *Vol. 1*, is based on Charlie Spand's 'Soon This Morning', and for 'Big Mama', a version of Jabo Williams's 'Fat Mama Blues'. The sexually explicit 'I'm Gonna Shave You Dry' – constructed on the musical framework of 'Red Cross Blues' – responds to the version by Lucille Bogan cut at the same time. The 1935 recordings that occupy the second half of the album find Roland playing at being Leroy Carr, who had cut his last recordings only days earlier. Since Roland had always had a taste for blues expressing melancholy or introspection, he slides easily into the role, supported by Josh White, who had taken a practical course in Carr maintenance as his accompanist the year before. The sudden right-hand bursts disappear, the more even piano playing is matched by the suave guitar, and pieces like 'Cold Blooded Murder' and '45 Pistol Blues' may have been close enough to Carr's manner to deceive the unwary listener.

The Yazoo contains three vocal blues by Roland with piano, one with guitar, two guitar duets and a piano solo; he also accompanies Bogan on three of her seven songs. Considered as a plate of *amuse-gueules* it serves well enough, but there is a lot more in Roland's work, as in Bogan's, to get one's teeth into. The serving provided by the Classic Blues set is more generous, Roland claiming about a third of the 36 tracks, but the odd sonic effects caused by the sound processing leave a slightly sour taste. TR

Roomful Of Blues
GROUP

Founded in Providence, Rhode Island, in 1967, Roomful Of Blues broke away from prevailing models of the blues band to work in a style derived from jump-blues bands of the '40s. The band was fronted until 1979 by Duke Robillard. In the '80s, with saxophonist Greg Piccolo as main singer and Ronnie Earl on guitar, they collaborated on albums with Eddie Vinson and Big Joe Turner and accompanied Earl King on Glazed*; the horns also joined Stevie Ray Vaughan at his '84 Carnegie Hall concert. In the '90s the band recorded with Pat Benatar, made a big-selling album and toured with the Canadian singer Colin James, went through a couple of significant personnel changes and continued the nationwide touring which, together with its albums, has earned it a wide following and numerous awards and nominations.*

*** The 1st Album
Hyena TMF 9307 *Richard Lataille (as); Greg Piccolo, Scott Hamilton (ts); Doug James (bs); Al Copley (p); Duke Robillard (g, v); Preston Hubbard (b); John Rossi (d). 77?*

**(*) Hot Little Mama
Varrick VRCD 021//Ace CDCHM 39 *Danny Motta (t); Porky Cohen (tb); Rich Lataille (as, ts); Greg Piccolo (ts, v); Mr Low (bs); Al Copley (o, p); Ronnie Earl (g); Jimmy Wimpfheimer (b); John Rossi (d). 9–10/80.*

**(*) Dressed Up To Get Messed Up
Varrick VRCD 018 *Bob Enos (t, v); Porky Cohen (tb); Rich Lataille (as, ts); Greg Piccolo (ts, v); Doug James (bs); Al Copley (o, p); Ronnie Earl (g, v); Preston Hubbard, Rory McLeod (b); John Rossi (d, perc, v); John Lamoia (perc); 14 Karat Soul (Glenny T., David Thurmond, Russell Fox II, Brian Simpson, Reginald Brisbon), Kim Wilson, band (v). early 84.*

*** Live At Lupo's Heartbreak Hotel
Varrick VRCD 024 *Bob Enos (t, v); Porky Cohen (tb); Rich Lataille (as, ts); Greg Piccolo (ts, v); Doug James, Steve Berlin (bs); Ron Levy (o, p, v); Cesar Rosas (g, v); Ronnie Earl, David Hidalgo (g); Rory McLeod (b); John Rossi (d); Curtis Salgado (v). 4/86.*

Precisely what kind of band this crew intends to be has always been a difficult question to answer. Simultaneously manly and mercurial, they might, you sometimes feel, have been better named Changing-Roomful Of Blues. The late-'70s edition on *The 1st Album*, the only one in catalogue from the Robillard era (and now on its fourth time around on CD), had no brass and a largely generic 12-bar repertoire – not exactly the format most of the band's fans consider typical – but, considered on its own terms, it's an attractive album. Like a lovingly waxed and carefully maintained car, it still provides a smooth, comfortable ride.

The early-'80s ROB mixed a different drink, spritzing the jump-blues repertoire with shots of rock 'n' roll and generally coming on like a Little League Johnny Otis Revue. *Dressed Up To Get Messed Up* was the first album to feature what became the best lineup of the ROB horns, which makes it odd that it's so dominated by a Piccolo: the tenor player wrote seven of the ten numbers, did all the lead singing and found breath for at least his share of sax solos. Oh, and produced the album as well. The word the reader may be expecting, and rightly, is 'overstretched'.

Live At Lupo's is considerably better, and goes some way to solving two of ROB's perennial problems. The live recording gets what studios almost never do, a big, brash, wall-to-wall sound from the horns, while the choice of mostly other people's songs, and good ones like 'Pink Champagne' and 'Three Hours Past Midnight', gives the band more space to strut its stuff than the merely workmanlike material they often prefer.

(*) Dance All Night
Bullseye Blues CDBB 9555 *Bob Enos (t); Carl Querfurth (tb, prod); Rich Lataille (as); Greg Piccolo (ts); Doug James (bs); Sugar Ray Norcia (h, v); Matt McCabe (p); Chris Vachon (g); Ken 'Doc' Grace (b); John Rossi (d).* 9/93.

*** Turn It On! Turn It Up!
Bullseye Blues CDBB 9566 *As above, except Lataille also plays ts; omit Piccolo.* 12/94–5/95.

*** Under One Roof
Bullseye Blues CDBB 9569 *As above.* 12/95–8/96.

(***) Roomful Of Christmas
Bullseye Blues CDBB 9591 *As above, except Norcia does not play h.* 97.

There were a couple of significant changes in the ROB lineup between *Live At Lupo's* and *Dance All Night*: Ronnie Earl had left in 1988, to be succeeded in 1990 by Chris Vachon, while Sugar Ray Norcia had been singing with the band since 1991. He had clearly settled in, handling the wideish range of material in the band's book confidently and competently. After one more personnel shift, the departure of charter member Greg Piccolo, a settled lineup made the next three albums. *Turn It On! Turn It Up!* and *Under One Roof*, recorded with greater clarity than *Dance All Night*, give a more detailed picture of the band's musical landscape, flooding voice, guitar and horns with dramatic lighting. *Under One Roof* also foregrounds band compositions, with three pieces written or co-written by Norcia and four by Vachon. Norcia gets to play a shade more harmonica this time, which draws one's attention to a problem never entirely absent during his stay with the band: his essentially Chicagoan approach, for example on the Muddyesque 'Still Livin' In Prison', is at odds with the ROB aesthetic, derived as it is from jump blues and, since the arrival of Carl Querfurth, swing-era jazz – idioms in which the harmonica had no role. That small issue aside, *Turn It On!* and *Under One Roof* are nicely varied and enjoyable programmes. Thematic variety is less of a concern with the Christmas album, for which the band reached into the folios of Lowell Fulson and Fats Domino but spent more time investigating the 'Seasonal' shelf of the standards library ('Have Yourself A Merry Little Christmas', 'The Christmas Song', etc.). Norcia negotiates lines like 'Tiny tots with their eyes all aglow will find it hard to sleep tonight' with aplomb, and Vachon doesn't find it hard at all to winkle a blues guitar solo out of 'White Christmas'. As such things go this is well done, but its appeal will be chiefly to committed fans of the band, or of Christmas.

*** There Goes The Neighborhood
Bullseye Blues & Jazz 9609 *Bob Enos (t); John Wolf (tb); Rich Lataille (as, ts); Kevin May (bs); Albert Weisman (o, p); Chris Vachon (g, co-prod); Marty Ballou (b); John Rossi (d); Mac Odom (v).* 1–2/98.

Another personnel shakeup at the end of 1997 saw the departure of Querfurth, James, McCabe and Norcia. It was probably not a coincidence that there was also a change in the Roomful decor, the warm colours of Basie-styled swing being largely replaced by a design of mixed blues: Percy Mayfield's 'Lost Mind', Memphis Slim's 'The Comeback', Larry Davis's 'I Tried', Duke Ellington's 'Rocks In My Bed'. The horns are still loquacious but play a diminished role in the dialogue. McKinley 'Mac' Odom, stepping up to the plate in Norcia's place, demonstrates as much versatility as the narrower-range programme permits. The album probably satisfied the casual fan, but those who'd been riding the ROB bus for longer may have felt that it had taken a new and less scenic route.

*** The Blues'll Make You Happy, Too!
Rounder Heritage Series RRCD 11589 *As for relevant CDs above, except add Big Joe Turner (v).* 9/80–2/98.

A retrospective of ROB's first two decades, drawing one to three tracks from each of the albums above except *The 1st Album* and *Roomful Of Christmas* and adding a couple of previously unissued items, one a live track from 7/82 with Big Joe Turner. The detailed notes by the band's long-stay manager Bob Bell are almost worth a star in themselves.

**(*) Watch You When You Go
Bullseye Blues & Jazz 9638 *Bob Enos (t); Ray Gennari (tb); Rich Lataille (ts); Hank Walther (kb); Chris Vachon (g, prod); Thom Enright (b); Chris Lemp, Tom Petteruti (d); Mac Odom (v).* 01.

Vachon's 'The Salt Of My Tears' and 'Over My Head' aren't bad songs but the rest of the programme, whether original or received material, is undistinguished and the instrumental 'Backlash' positively dull.

*** That's Right!
Alligator ALCD 4889 *Bob Enos (t); Rich Lataille (as, ts); Mark Earley (ts, bs); Mark DuFresne (h, v); Mark Stevens (o, p); Chris Vachon (g, prod); Brad Hallen (b); Jason Corbiere (d).* 02?

**(*) Standing Room Only
Alligator ALCD 4900 *As above, except Vachon also sings; Travis Colby (o, p) replaces Stevens.* 03?

These albums represent the lineup that came together between late 2001 and spring 2002. DuFresne maintains the ROB tradition of virile, versatile vocalists, and his harp playing, when there is any, fits in reasonably well. What's immediately noticeable on *That's Right!*, though, is the quality of the material, which hasn't always been a strong point with this band. For the first time since *Hot Little Mama* there's no original input, just solid repertoire like T-Bone Walker's 'I Know Your Wig Is Gone', Fenton Robinson's 'Tennessee Woman', Jimmy McCracklin's 'Just Got To Know' and Smiley Lewis's 'Shame, Shame, Shame'. In contrast, *Standing Room Only* makes plenty of space for bandwork (four songs by Vachon, four more by other members) and is the less enticing for it. It would be hard to dislike amiable, lightweight pieces such as Vachon's 'Just Keep On Rockin'', Colby's 'Jona Lee' and Earley's 'Flip Flap Jack', but equally hard to remember any of them half an hour later. TR

Dr Ross (1925–93)
VOCAL, HARMONICA, GUITAR, DRUMS

Isaiah Ross was born on a farm in Tunica, Mississippi, to parents of Native American origin. He began playing harmonica as a boy, and entertained at house parties with guitarist Wiley Galatin. After two spells in the army he took a job with General Motors, first in Illinois and then, in 1954, in Flint, Michigan, where he spent the rest of his life, working at the Chevrolet plant. He recorded for Sun in the early '50s but it was through later singles for Fortune and associated labels that he earned a reputation in the '60s which led to him being booked for the 1965 AFBF. After that he was frequently invited back to Europe.

**** Boogie Disease
Arhoolie CD 371 *Ross; Henry Hill (p); Wiley Galatin (or Gatlin) (g, v); Reuben Martin (wb); Barber Parker (d).* 11/51–54.

Between leaving the army and moving north Ross spent some time as a semi-professional musician in Mississippi and neighbouring states. He made numerous recordings at the Sun studio in Memphis; only six were issued, but many more survived on tapes which Ross kept and, years later, licensed to Arhoolie. Though at this stage he was playing only rack harmonica and guitar – the reduced drumkit of bass drum and hi-hat was added later – his music was not unlike that of the contemporary Memphis-based one-man-band Joe Hill Louis, but its texture was clearer and he was a better singer. He had an interestingly mixed bag of songs, many from Sonny Boy Williamson I but also including Lil' Son Jackson's 'Bad Whiskey, Bad Women' and Blind Lemon Jefferson's 'Wartime Blues'. His up-tempo pieces like 'Chicago Breakdown' are effervescent juke-joint dance tunes, but even at slower tempos the music has tremendous impetus.

*** I'd Rather Be An Old Woman's Baby Than A Young Woman's Slave
Fortune FS 3011 *Ross; unknown (o, p); unknowns (g); unknowns (b); unknowns (d); unknowns (v).* 58–73.

Scattered through this collection are the recordings that introduced European enthusiasts to Ross in the '60s, among them 'The Sunnyland', 'Cat Squirrel', 'Thirty-Two-Twenty' (Yank Rachell's '38 Pistol Blues') and 'Industrial Boogie', his personalized version of John Lee Hooker's 'Boogie Chillen'. The combination of steady, Hooker-like guitar rhythms, downhome singing and harmonica phrases apparently floated, like transfers, from old Sonny Boy Williamson I records was extremely attractive, and one could easily excuse them for being crudely recorded. So are most of the other tracks here, which come from a session in the late '60s made with – or in some cases despite – the accompaniment of musicians imperfectly acquainted with his music. The closing track, 'Boogie Disease', is from the 1973 Ann Arbor Blues Festival. Much of this is too untidy to be wholly satisfying, but the singles tracks are splendidly jaunty. Several of the items on this CD are anthologized on *A Fortune Of Blues Vol. 1* (Regency RR 119) and *Vol. 2* (RR 120).

**(*) One Man Band
Takoma CDTAK 7087 *Ross.* 1/65.
***(*) Call The Doctor
Testament TCD 5009 *Ross.* 1/65 or 2/65.

*** Blues And Boogie From Detroit
Chrisly CD 30006 *Ross.* 6/72.
*** I Want All My Friends To Know – Live At The Burnley Blues Festival
JSP JSPCD 810 *Ross.* 3/91.

A busy year for Dr Ross, 1965. He played a gig at the University of Chicago, which furnished the tracks on *One Man Band*, and either the next day or a week later cut an album for Testament. In the fall he joined the AFBF, playing his way round Europe and impressing the many people who had never before seen a one-man blues band. Despite its title, *One Man Band* is not a typical performance, since Ross plays only harmonica and guitar. On *Call The Doctor*, however, he adds his percussion kit, and that factor, the longer programme (17 tracks, including eight of the ten songs on *One Man Band*) and the more intimate recording make this much the better buy. The notes are enhanced by a delightful autobiographical memoir.

While Ross was in London, an impromptu hotel bedroom session was taped which became *The Flying Eagle*, the first LP on the Blue Horizon label and later something of a collector's item. Readers are warned that the reissue of that album (augmented with other material of the period) as Blue Horizon CD-1 is neither a genuine Blue Horizon release nor authorized by its owner. *The Flying Eagle*'s only legitimate CD issue was in 1997 as number 89 of the UK partwork *The Blues Collection* (BLU NC 089).

The repertoire that he carried round with him in 1965 would serve Ross for the rest of his life. 'Cat Squirrel', 'Hobo Blues', '32-20', 'Good Morning, Little Schoolgirl', 'China Blues', 'Chicago Breakdown' – these and other songs from *Call The Doctor* recur on most or all of his subsequent albums, hardly augmented at all by newly acquired material. *Blues And Boogie From Detroit*, recorded in performance in Germany, has a slide number in the Tampa Red or Robert Nighthawk idiom, 'Sweet Black Angel', while at Burnley in 1991 he recalled one of the Fortune recordings, 'G.M. [i.e. General Motors] Blues'. Both these CDs are reasonably faithful portraits of the Doctor in operation, but with only 11 tracks each they cannot quite do him justice. TR

Freddie Roulette (born 1939)
VOCAL, LAP STEEL GUITAR

Roulette was playing pop, country and Hawaiian tunes on steel guitar at the age of six, but only added blues when he started jamming with Earl Hooker as a teenager. After military service he joined Hooker's band for three years, appearing on some of Hooker's recordings, and on singles by Big Moose Walker and others. In 1969 he went on the road with Charlie Musselwhite's band, eventually settling in California, where he joined Harvey Mandel's group Pure Food And Drug Act; he has since continued to work with Mandel and others on the West Coast, and has recently sought wider exposure on the blues circuit.

**(*) Back In Chicago
Hi Horse 4044 *Roulette; Ken Barker (o, p); Vernon 'Chico' Banks (g, b); Willie Kent (b); Cleo Williams (d).* 9/96.
*** Spirit Of Steel
Tradition & Moderne T&M 014 *Roulette; Rudy Costa (ss, as, ts, kalimba, zither); Wendell Holmes (g); Sherman Holmes (b); Popsy Dixon (d).* 10/98.

Roulette has accurately characterized his blues playing as jazz over basic blues changes, which can lead him to ignore his accompanists; on *Back In Chicago* Willie Kent's Gents do their stolid thing while Roulette goes his own untrammelled way. This shines a bright light on Roulette's exceptional technique and imaginative sonorities, but it doesn't make for very satisfactory listening; nor does it help that Roulette isn't much of a singer. The Holmes Brothers are more in touch on *Spirit Of Steel*, and the only drawback to Rudy Costa's saxophone obbligatos is that there aren't enough of them, but the results are uneven; the instrumental 'Dis Tang' strikes a perfect balance between blues feeling and multitracked steel guitar adventures, but it's followed by a 'Lucille' that exposes all the limitations of Roulette's singing. One doesn't want to say that Roulette is too good for the blues, but often he seems chafed by its confines; the best things on *Spirit Of Steel* are Horace Silver's 'Song For My Father' and a fantastically unkitsch 'Cherry Pink and Appleblossom White'. Explorers beyond our hinterland may wish to try *The Psychedelic Guitar Circus* (Rykodisc RCD 10347//Sky Ranch 394322), a collaboration with Harvey Mandel, David Kaiser and Steve Kimock. cs

Otis Rush (born 1934)
VOCAL, GUITAR

Rush left Mississippi in his teens and by 1955 was entrenched in the Chicago blues scene, developing with contemporaries like Magic Sam and Buddy Guy what came to be called the West Side sound. The effect of his startling debut recordings for Cobra was dissipated by unlucky associations with other labels and by personal problems, and for periods in the '70s and '80s the quality of his personal appearances and recordings was erratic. During the '90s he seemed to surmount his problems, but in 2004 he was reported to have suffered a stroke.

**** Good 'Uns – The Classic Cobra Recordings 1956–1958
[Westside WESA 858]//Fuel 2000 302 061 077 Rush; Harold Ashby (ts, bs); Red Holloway, Lucius Washington (ts); Jackie Brenston (bs); Walter Horton, Little Walter (h); Lafayette Leake, Little Brother Montgomery (p); Wayne Bennett, Jody Williams, Louis Myers, Reggie Boyd, Ike Turner (g); Willie Dixon (b); Al Duncan, Odie Payne, Fred Below (d). 56–58.

***(*) His Cobra Recordings 1956–58
[Paula PCD-01] As above. 56–58.

Rush's early sides possess a screaming intensity that seems to burst out of a suddenly freed energy. The effect is exaggerated by the technical limitations of the recordings: the drums are mixed back, the bass sometimes hardly audible, guitars and saxophones tangled in a mass. 'I Can't Quit You Baby' was an astonishing debut recording, full of the suspense of a tough band held in check, beautifully sung, with a brief but petrifying guitar solo. 'Double Trouble' is a masterpiece of its period, a blues about social dissatisfaction whose mood is precisely mirrored in its arrangement. 'Love That Woman', 'Checking On My Baby', 'Groaning The Blues' and 'All Your Love' are all excellent. But there are failures, too, chiefly the faster numbers like 'Jump Sister Bessie' and 'She's A Good 'Un'; some would add the ballads like 'Violent Love', but 'My Love Will Never Die' isn't half bad. The Westside/Fuel 2000 version is the better produced.

*** Door To Door
MCA/Chess CHD-9322//[(E) MCD 09322] Rush; Bob Neely (ts); unknown (bs); Lafayette Leake (p); Matt Murphy, Willie Dixon (b); Odie Payne (d). 1–9/60.

This CD shared with Albert King has six of Rush's sides for Chess, the best of which, 'So Many Roads, So Many Trains' and 'I Can't Stop Baby', have the fervour of his Cobra work.

**(*) Chicago/The Blues/Today! Vol. 2
Vanguard VMD 79217 Rush; Robert 'Sax' Crowder (ts); Luther Tucker (g); Ernest Gatewood (b); Jesse Green (d). 12/65.

The recordings made for the *Chicago/The Blues/Today!* project were uneven, but Rush was luckier than most. The studio ambience is cold, and there's an abrupt jump in the level during Crowder's solo on 'It's My Own Fault', but Rush gives a very good account of 'I Can't Quit You Baby' and skips through an instrumental 'Rock'. He has five cuts on the album; the rest are by James Cotton and Homesick James. The contents of the CD are also on *Chicago/The Blues/Today!* (Vanguard 172/74 3CD).

Mourning In The Morning, the interesting but not entirely satisfactory album Rush recorded for Atlantic in 1968/69, last on CD as Atlantic 82367, is currently out of print.

***(*) Right Place, Wrong Time
Hightone HCD 8007 Rush; John Wilmeth (t); Hart McNee (as); Ron Stallings (ts); Ira Kamin (o); Mark Naftalin (p); Fred Burton (g); Doug Kilmer, John Kahn (b); Bob Jones (d). 2/71.

Capitol recorded this album, decided not to issue it but seven years later licensed it to a small blues label. On the whole it's a hard-blues album, only 'Rainy Night In Georgia' approaching the blues-pop synthesis that was then in vogue, and even that is soberly arranged and sung. The heart of the album is the churning slow blues 'Your Turn To Cry', 'Take A Look Behind' and the title song, which have much of the trembling intensity of the best Cobra sides and seem, indeed, to have been arranged to give that impression. There is only one of the old songs themselves, 'Three Times A Fool', in a smooth-rolling arrangement quite different from the lurching original. Jumpier numbers come less eloquently from Rush, but 'Tore Up' is stirringly done. 'I Wonder Why' is an expressive slow blues instrumental similar to Earl Hooker's 'Cotton Pickin' Blues'.

**(*) Screamin' And Cryin'
Evidence ECD 26014 Rush; Jerome Van Jones (o, p); Sunnyland Slim, Willie Mabon (p); Jimmy Dawkins (g); James Green (b); Bob Plunkett (d). 11/74.

The outstanding track on this French studio recording is the opening 'Looking Back', in which the singer reviews his life with candour and no self-pity. The low point is a version of 'Every Day I Have The Blues' which Rush seeks to individualize by wordless shrieking. Between these poles can be found overlong readings of songs by Hubert Sumlin and B. B. King and his own 'I Can't Quit You Baby' (in two takes). The accompaniments are colourlessly efficient. This is an album that screams (or cries) for more direction from the control room.

*** Cold Day In Hell
Delmark DE-638 *Rush; Abb Locke (ts); Chuck Smith (bs); Big Moose Walker (o, p); Mighty Joe Young, Bob Levis (g); James Green, Bob Stroger (b); Jesse Green (d). 4–5/75.*

The brisk and brief opening track, 'Cut You A Loose', promises a more focused set than the previous album. It's certainly more attentively produced, and several of the performances, such as the title track and the two takes of 'You're Breaking My Heart', find Rush approaching the top of his form. It's frustrating, then, when he again replaces words with screams; and the two numbers in the style of T-Bone Walker, 'Society Woman' and 'Mean Old World', would have made more effect if they had not been placed next to each other. For all that, this is one of Rush's better albums.

**(*) So Many Roads
Delmark DE-643 *Rush; Jimmy Johnson (g); Sylvester Boines (b); Tyrone Centurary (d). 7/75.*

Unsupported by horns or keyboards, and with Johnson playing rhythm as if in a sulk, Rush is forced to fill a great deal of this album with his guitar, wrenching long notes from the instrument that sound like the sighs or gasps of a man racked with pain. It's a compelling performance, but necessarily one that hasn't much light and shade.

** Live In Europe
Evidence ECD 26034 *Rush; Bob Levis (g); Bob Stroger (b); Jesse Green (d). 10/77.*

**(*) Lost In The Blues
Alligator ALCD 4797 *As above, except add Lucky Peterson, Allen Batts (o, p). 10/77.*

These sets were both made during a European tour, *Live In Europe* in concert in France, the Alligator a week later in a studio in Sweden. Most of the songs on *Live In Europe* had been featured on the three previous albums, Rush's guitar is under-recorded, and, as on *So Many Roads*, the backing trio is too skimpy to provide the sort of orchestrations his music requires. When *Lost In The Blues* (originally titled *Troubles, Troubles*) was reissued on CD in 1991, it was remixed with added keyboards by Peterson (Batts is only on 'Little Red Rooster'). That, and a fresher setlist, makes it the better of the two albums, though not by much; Rush's guitar is still a little less penetrating than one would wish.

*** Tops
Blind Pig BP 73188 *Rush; Larry Jones (t); Julien Vaught (s); Jimmy Pugh (kb); Bobby Murray (g); Leonard Gill (b); Kelvin Dixon (d). 9/85.*

Another concert recording, this time from the San Francisco Blues Festival. While it's good to hear Rush with a bigger band, it would have been even better if the band had had time to work out more interesting arrangements, especially for long numbers like 'Gambler's Blues' and 'I Wonder Why'. But the rhythm section chugs efficiently, Rush sings and plays with energy and, all in all, this is one of his best live albums.

*** Live & Awesome
Genes GCD 4131 *Rush; Ken Vangel (p); Duke Levine (g); Tim Green (b); Julian Vaughn (d). early 90s.*

'A recent tour of Europe' is all the notes tell you about the provenance of this collection of concert recordings. (The CD was issued in 1996.) After an awkward start, Rush delivers long versions of 'Gambler's Blues', 'Feel So Bad', 'Right Place, Wrong Time', 'Cold Day In Hell' and other favourite pieces. Since he has recorded all these before, some of them repeatedly, readers who already have a few Rush albums may want to think twice about adding this one. If they decide against it, they will miss a set of good, sometimes above-average performances, skilfully accompanied and recorded with presence.

***(*) Ain't Enough Comin' In
This Way Up/Mercury 518 769 *Rush; The Texacali Horns [Darrell Leonard (t); Joe Sublett (ts); Marty Grebb (bs)]; Jimmy Powers (h); Ian McLagan (o, p); Mick Weaver (o); Bill Payne (p, clavinet); Johnny Lee Schell, John Porter (g); Greg Rzab (b); Tony Braunagel (d, perc). 93.*

This finds Rush flicking through the songbooks of Albert King ('Don't Burn Down The Bridge'), B. B. King ('It's My Own Fault'), Sam Cooke ('Somebody Have Mercy'), Ray Charles ('A Fool For You') and Little Milton ('That Will Never Do') and reworking only a couple of his old hits, one of them the long-neglected 'Homework', which he first recorded in 1962 during a brief and unhappy connection with Duke Records. The combination of excellent performances, appropriate accompaniments (listen for Ian McLagan's Booker T. organ licks) and understanding production makes this his best record since *Right Place, Wrong Time*, and one that was intelligently conceived to introduce him to a new generation of fans.

Any Place I'm Going (House of Blues 51416 1343) (1998), recorded in Memphis and co-produced by Willie Mitchell, continued the restoration of Rush's stature with a well-chosen set of blues and soul numbers; unfortunately the album is no longer in circulation. TR

Saffire – The Uppity Blues Women
GROUP

The core members of Saffire are Gaye Adegbalola and Ann Rabson (who also have individual entries). They had been working with Earlene Lewis, whose background was in bluegrass, for a few years before the group went fulltime in 1988; Lewis was replaced by Andra Faye McIntosh in 1992. Saffire's brand of blues privileges a feisty feminism which consciousness-raising makes rather different from the female feistiness of Bessie Smith and Lucille Bogan. They offer confirmation that the middle-aged can have fun and be sexy, and a radicalism that's often more comforting than challenging.

**(*) Saffire – The Uppity Blues Women
Alligator ALCD 4780 *Mark Wenner (h); Ann Rabson (p, v); Gaye Adegbalola (g, v); Earlene Lewis (b, v). 89.*

*** Hot Flash
Alligator ALCD 4796 *As above, except Rabson also plays g, k; Billy Branch (h) replaces Wenner. 90.*

As it has continued to be, Saffire's playing on the debut disc is consistently good, with Rabson's piano particularly telling. Adegbalola dominates the vocals, taking eight to Rabson's two and Lewis's one, which is 'Even Yuppies Get The Blues'; it's a typical Saffire updating of old themes, but not a very good one, and is sung most unidiomatically. Adegbalola favours the bellow-and-rasp that Etta James and Koko Taylor have made dominant, which is expressively limited, and wearing in large doses. She's a convincing balladeer, as 'Silent Thunder In My Heart' proves; more in this vein would have been welcome.

Hot Flash is better balanced, giving more space to Rabson's huskily euphonious voice and her alert matching of delivery to meaning; as a result, Adegbalola's aggression becomes a proportionate part of the mixture. Lewis's blues singing is more secure, too. Generally, the group seem less convinced that liberation is the freedom to be as childishly vulgar as men; this is beneficial, and even '(No Need) Pissin' On A Skunk' is a neat and witty lyric.

***(*) BroadCasting
Alligator ALCD 4811 *Gaye Adegbalola (h, g, v); Tony Zamagni (o); Ann Rabson (p, g, v); Andra Faye McIntosh (vn, md, v); Steve Freund (g); Larry Gray (b).* 92.

McIntosh soon joined the band, but here she's one of the guest musicians, and Saffire is a duo. *BroadCasting* is a well-judged, well-performed mix of covers and originals, a comment that's been made on many a CD; this one stands out for the quality of the songwriting on the originals. Adegbalola's 'Ragtime Rag' is a clever double-take inducer about male insensitivity to the side-effects of menstruation, and 'If It Had Been A Dog' is a powerfully angry response to racial violence. Rabson advises 'Don't Treat Your Man Like A Dog' because men don't have dogs' virtues, after which half of Saffire's audience may agree that 'It's All Right For A Man To Cry'.

**(*) Old, New, Borrowed & Blue
Alligator ALCD 4826 *Clark Dean (ss); Gaye Adegbalola (h, g, v); Ann Rabson (p, g, v); Andra Faye McIntosh (vn, md, g, b, v).* 94.

'Bitch With A Bad Attitude', written as a riposte to Dolly Parton's 'I Will Always Love You', is perhaps the quintessential Saffire song, and there are other fine performances here, but there's a shortage of classic ones, and the uppitiness seems more of a *schtick* than a creative impetus. McIntosh's fiddle and mandolin are rather sweet-toned for blues (though not as aptly saccharine as Clark Dean on 'Sweet Substitute'); her C&W-influenced singing works well on a Lonnie Mack song, pretty well on a Sippie Wallace song, and not well at all on Ma Rainey's 'Yonder Come The Blues'.

**** Cleaning House
Alligator ALCD 4840 *As above, except Adegbalola also plays perc; add Steve Freund (g); omit Dean.* 96.

Cleaning House is more like it; *How Saffire Got Their Groove Back* might be an alternative title. Adegbalola plays her first significant harmonica solos; Rabson is excellent throughout (as she is on all Saffire's CDs); McIntosh's mandolin now has the necessary sour edge, and her singing is adequately bluesy. It may help male listeners that this time round the battle-of-the-sexes songs are amusing, rather than hectoring or patronizing.

**(*) Live & Uppity
Alligator ALCD 4856 *Gaye Adegbalola (h, g, v); Ann Rabson (p, g, k, v); Andra Faye [McIntosh] (vn, md, g, b, v).* 10/97.

As with many live albums, much of whatever magic there was at the venue doesn't transfer to disc; what chiefly survives is clumsiness in the crosstalk between songs, and mutual admiration between Saffire and their audience. This arises out of smugly shared political assumptions and unambitious notions of what constitutes nasty talk; if 'Silver Beaver' were half as outrageous as all concerned believe, it would be very outrageous indeed. It's right to note, however, that '1-800-799-7233' (the number of the National Domestic Violence Hot Line) is thoughtfully written and movingly performed.

**(*) Ain't Gonna Hush!
Alligator ALCD 4880 *As above, except Rabson omits k; add Juno Pitchford, Chris Murphy, Bruce Iglauer (v).* 01.

There seems to be a process of countrification taking place here; Patsy Cline's influence dominates Andra Faye's vocals, and many of the up-tempo numbers tend to the rockabilly side. The band members are in the minority as composers, and too many tracks are epigrams ('It takes a good man to be better than no man at all'), padded out to song length and equipped with catchy hooks. 'If I Should Die Tonight' is a splendid lovesong, and 'Happy Birthday To Me', about spending the anniversary alone with your vibrator, is clever, funny, erotic and dirty. It's a shoo-in for the eventual *Best Of* CD, but little else here demands attention. CS

Curtis Salgado (born 1954)
VOCAL, HARMONICA

Born in Everett, Washington, Salgado made his name in the Pacific Northwest in the late '70s, often working with Robert Cray, then based in Eugene, Oregon. It was through that association that he crossed paths with the actor John Belushi and gave him some ideas for the character of Jake Blues in the movie The Blues Brothers. *In the '80s he fronted Roomful Of Blues for a couple of years, then formed his own band, the Stilettos. He has recorded with Cray, Otis Grand, Ronnie Earl, Too Slim & The Tail Draggers, Nick Moss and numerous other artists.*

*** Hit It 'N Quit It
Lucky LRS-040 *Salgado; Tim Bryson (reeds); Dave Stewart, Peter Boe (p); Terry Robb (g, v); John Mazzocco (b); Butch Cousins, Jeff Minnieweather (d).* 96.

**(*) Wiggle Outta This
Shanachie 9014 *Salgado; Peter Boe (kb, v); Louis Payne, Christopher Turner (o); Marlon McClain (g, v); John Wedemeyer, Duke Robillard, Terry Robb (g); Victor Little, Nathaniel Phillips (b); Reinhardt Melz, Mark Lomax (d); Sean Holmes, Ericka Warren, Mary Linn, Margaret Linn (v).* 99?

** Soul Activated
Shanachie 9028 *Salgado; Wayne Jackson (t); Andrew Love (ts); Nate Phillips (kb, g, b); D. K. Stewart (kb); Al Gamble (o); Janice Scroggins (p); Jesse Young, John Wedemeyer, Jimmie Vaughan, Lloyd Jones, Marlon McClain (g); Tracy Arrington, Willie Barber (b); Reinhardt Melz, Bruce Carter (d); Lou Ann Barton, Ericka Warren, Margaret Linn, Sean Holmes (v).* 01.

Hit It 'N Quit It, jointly credited to Salgado and Terry Robb and recorded partly in the studio and partly live, is a set of blues mostly from the repertoires of Muddy Waters, Little Walter, Elmore James and the like, very competently played in a '40s/'50s Chicago idiom, sometimes, as in 'Still A Fool' or 'Too Young To Know', closely following the original recording. In this company, the original composition 'Bitter Tears' and the instrumentals 'Hit It 'N Quit It' and 'El Gado Rumba Azúl' stand up well. Both artists give good accounts of themselves, Salgado singing with confidence and Robb sounding more at ease than he often does on his own albums.

The Shanachie CDs give us another Salgado, an aficionado of soul; actually two new Salgados, since he also had a hand in writing seven of the ten songs on *Wiggle Outta This* and four of the 11 on *Soul Activated*. Compared with *Hit It 'N Quit It*, both sets are highly produced (by Marlon McClain), but seldom so as to dampen the spirit of Salgado's singing, whether in assertive or plaintive mood. Standard blues repertoire is virtually invisible – J. B. Lenoir's 'I Feel So Good' on *Wiggle* is the only exception – and Salgado plays less than harmonica fans would wish, but the general character of quite a lot of the music on both CDs should not seem unduly exotic to anyone who has listened widely to contemporary blues. That said, coming to terms with material like 'Summertime Life', 'The Harder They Come' and 'Everytime You Go Away' on *Soul Activated* may be farther than some listeners want to go. TR

Sam Brothers 5
GROUP

Chris Strachwitz recorded one song by accordionist Herbert 'Good Rockin" Sam in 1961; they next met in 1979 at the New Orleans Jazz & Heritage Festival, where Sam was managing his five sons, then aged between 11 and 18. The brothers also recorded for Maison de Soul before marriage and work scattered them. In 1997 Leon's Boogie Is Back! (MTE 5054) appeared, credited to Leon Sam & The Sam Brothers, but it seems to be currently unavailable.

*** Sam (Get Down!)
Arhoolie CD 9044 *Leon Sam (ac, o, v); Herbert Sam (ac, v); Carl Sam (g); Glen Sam (b); Rodney Sam (d); Calvin Sam (rb).* 7/79.

The cover shot of five young brothers with Afros is a reminder that the Jackson Five were big in those days; so were Chic, whose disco floor-filler 'Le Freak' is, er, important to the title track, on which Leon Sam plays organ. The big man on the bayou was Clifton Chenier, though, and even before one hears the CD, 15-year-old Leon's headband gives away his primary musical inspiration. As he recalled to Michael Tisserand, '[In San Francisco] we did some shows with Queen Ida. ... The next morning it came out in the paper that Clifton Chenier had shrunk.' Setlist and styles are both derivative, but all the brothers' musical skills were fully formed; this was not a novelty act, but a mainstream zydeco band that happened to consist of teenagers. Their father (who died in May 2004) straps on the box for two tracks that make one wish he had a more extensive discography.

*** Tribute To Clif
T. Potter 8187 *Leon Sam (ac, kb, v); Tom Potter (g); Thurman Hurst (b, v); Joe Rossyion (d, perc, v); Mike Vee (rb, perc); Nicole Hurst (v).* 00?

Credited to Leon Sam & The Zydeco Dots, *Tribute To Clif* is naturally heavy on the Chenier covers; at 36, Leon Sam is still an unabashed admirer of the great man, and for much of the CD just as proficient an imitator. He goes down some other alleys, though, most successfully with a hoarsely soulful cover of Johnnie Taylor's 'Stop Doggin' Me'. The 'Prelude' in 'Prelude/Sam Shuffle' is a mighty entertaining version of 'In The Mood'! The same cannot be said of the mariachi clichés on 'LA in Mexico', but on the concluding 'Rock And Rollish' Potter's slide guitar makes an unusual and effective replacement for the accordion. CS

Bill Samuels (1911–64)
VOCAL, PIANO

Samuels was born in Mississippi and grew up in Chicago. A child piano prodigy, he had his own band in his teens. By the '40s he was leading the Cat's N Jammer Three (named after the comic-strip Katzenjammer Kids), appearing on radio and TV and playing major venues like the Apollo, where the columnist Walter Winchell saw him and described him as 'incomparable'. The trio's 'I Cover The Waterfront' was an R&B #3 but by the end of the decade Samuels had lost both his band and his recording contract. He spent his later years in Minneapolis.

** Bill Samuels 1945–1947
Classics 5112 *Samuels; Bill Coleman (t); Ram Ramirez (p); Adam Lambert, Mundell Lowe (g); Sylvester Hickman (b, v); Billy Taylor (b); Hillard Brown, Morey Feld (d).* 9/45–late 47.

A crooner with the exaggeratedly precise diction of Al Hibbler, Samuels applied his velvet-fog voice to standards like 'Ghost Of A Chance', 'I Surrender Dear' and 'Moonglow' and less memorable pop material, occasionally diversifying into Louis Jordan jive numbers like 'That Chick's Too Young To Fry' and 'I Know What You're Puttin' Down' and an infrequent blues. His best-selling coupling of 'I Cover The Waterfront' and 'Jockey Blues' (heard here in two versions) seems likely to have been known to John Lee Hooker, who covered both songs, and 'One For The Money' (1947) may have sowed the idea of Little Richard's 'Rip It Up'. Those historical footnotes aside, Samuels's svelte lounge music is unlikely to find a large present-day audience, especially with its liberal dusting of surface noise. TR

Will Roy Sanders (born 1934)
VOCAL, GUITAR

Originally from Byhalia, Mississippi, Sanders began playing guitar after his family moved to the outskirts of Memphis in the mid-'40s. Since the mid-'50s he has played in local bands like the Binghampton Blues Boys, Hodges' Funky Four, the Fieldstones and his own Memphis Soul Blues Band. He has paid occasional visits to Europe, but the big time seems destined to remain elusive.

(**) The Last Living Bluesman
Shangri-La Projects 029 *Sanders; unknown (tb); Slim Moss (p); James Boner, unknown (g); Fred Ingram, Harold Boner (b); George Walker, Jerry Parnell (d).* 64, 2/97–2/99.

The CD's absurd title is best ignored, as is its annotator's spluttering indignation that Sanders isn't exempt from the law on drunk driving. *The Last Living Bluesman* is the soundtrack of a video of the same name, and alternates interview snippets (with a good deal of ambient noise) and studio recordings. On these, Sanders is mostly heard solo, although an uncredited second guitar is present on some tracks. His guitar playing has minimal harmonic movement, and fits uneasily with a melismatic singing style, which is itself handicapped by dynamics and ornaments that often seem imposed on the lyrics, rather than suggested by them. 'Old Man & Whiskey' and 'Saddle Up My Pony' are successful exceptions to a generally unimpressive studio set. 'Green's Lounge Shuffle', recorded live with a band that includes a raucous trombonist, is rough, but authentically funky. The CD concludes with both sides of the Binghampton Blues Boys' very rare 1964 single. 'Cross Cut Saw' and 'Slim's Twist' both have their merits, but the 45 used for dubbing appears to have been marinading in a pool of beer for 30 years. CS

(Jumpin') Johnny Sansone
VOCAL, HARMONICA, ACCORDION, GUITAR

Sansone has been based in New Orleans since 1989; before that he had spent time playing in Austin, Kansas City and elsewhere and filled the harmonica post for several years in Ronnie Earl's Broadcasters.

*** **Crescent City Moon**
Bullseye Blues CD BB 9585 *Sansone; Larry Carter (t); Joe Cabral (ts, perc, v); Derek Huston (ts); Doug James (bs); Ron Hodges (ac, v); Jon Cleary (p); Waylon Thibodeaux (vn); Rick Olivarez, Sonny Landreth (g); Steve Riggs (b); Jim Starboard (d). 3/94.*

*** **Watermelon Patch**
Bullseye Blues & Jazz BB 9615 *Sansone; Duke Heitger (t); Joe Cabral (ts, bs); Derek Huston (ts); Joe Krown (o, p); Jon Cleary (p, perc); Rick Olivarez (g); Dave Ranson (b); Kenneth Blevins (d); Eric Lucero (rb). 12/98.*

Even without the clue in the title, the bubbling stew flavoured with strutting drums and Cajun accordion would declare the provenance of *Crescent City Moon*, and spicy cameos by Landreth and Cleary hang out the South Louisiana flag for all to see. Sansone's 'musical hybrid of Mississippi and Chicago blues, zydeco, and New Orleans R&B is a stone original', Greg 'Fingers' Taylor notes approvingly. This is the sort of thing notewriters are supposed to say, but here it's accurate, and while the R&B ingredients are more dominant than the blues, the blend is colourful, the tunes fresh, the arrangements imaginative and Sansone's pugnacious singing and harmonica and accordion playing as flamboyant as a leader's should be.

A blues flavour is stronger in *Watermelon Patch*, explicitly in 'Civilized City' and the instrumentals 'Pig's Feet & Tailmeat' and 'Stink Bait', where Sansone's chromatic harp howls and gurgles like some nameless creature of the night. But the zydeco merriment of 'Mon Fleur' and 'Think Of Me' promises a less ominous after-dark scenario, while 'Loveline' sweeps the listener up into a parade band, swaying to Blevins's and Ranson's effervescent rhythm. TR

Eric Sardinas (born 1970)
VOCAL, GUITAR

Initially picking up a guitar at the age of six, the left-handed Sardinas developed his skills as a right-handed player would, contributing towards an unorthodox technique. During the '90s he gained recognition in the clubs around LA. His playing often betrays a two-sided array of influences – the raw style of early Delta blues and the more recent rock leanings of Hendrix, Led Zeppelin, and Cream. Sardinas's slide technique on electric resonator guitars is highly acclaimed, earning him a place on the Favored Nations label alongside such rock virtuosos as Steve Vai, Rob Balducci and Mattias Eklundh.

(*) Devil's Train
Evidence ECD 26116 *Sardinas; David 'Honeyboy' Edwards (g, v); Paul Loranger (b); Scott Palacios (d). 01.*

Sardinas showcases high-powered slide guitar. Most of the tracks follow a basic power-trio blues-rock template, with few surprises musically or lyrically. Relief from this monotony is provided by Sardinas's slick and quick-fire guitar soloing, which is most impressive. It is a shame that vocally he cannot match his instrumental talent: the singing is sometimes strained, shallow and off-the-mark. The outstanding tracks are those where Sardinas deviates from formulaic songwriting. The instrumentals 'Texola' and 'Sidewinder' allow guitar performance to occupy the limelight, Honeyboy Edwards's guest appearance on the impromptu 'Gambling Man Blues' is a treat, and Sardinas's acoustic work and relaxed vocals on '8 Goin' South' contribute to a particularly pleasing final track.

*** **Black Pearls**
Favored Nations FN 2300 *Sardinas; Paul Loranger (b); Mike Dupke, Chris Frazier (d). 03.*

Although the resonator guitar and brass slide are still foregrounded, ensuring that a blues aesthetic remains in place, *Black Pearls* acts as a vehicle for Sardinas to explore his rock sensibilities and influences further than on previous releases. This is particularly evident on the opening track, 'Flames Of Love'. Once again his own songs unleash few surprises, but the album is altogether superior to its predecessor, Eddie Kramer's production seeming to coax strong performances from the trio, who were recorded live and without digital editing. The guitar work throughout is once more top-grade, particularly on 'Ain't No Crime', 'Liar's Dice Blues' and the bluegrass-tinted 'Old Smyrna Road'. *Black Pearls* also reveals some improvement in the singing, although it seems fair to suggest that Sardinas will not be remembered for his vocal contributions to the genre. JF

Satan & Adam
DUET

Singer, guitarist and percussionist Mr Satan is Sterling Magee (born 1936), who made some records under his real name in the '60s for Tangerine and Sylvia, and worked in the bands of Noble Watts, Etta James and others. When he and the fortuitously named Adam Gussow (born 1958), who sings and plays harmonica, formed their salt-and-pepper duo in the mid '80s, Satan was working in Harlem as a one-man-band and maker of cabbalistic artwork. Gussow, then a graduate student, is now an assistant professor at the University of Mississippi. His book Mister Satan's Apprentice tells the story of their partnership; more recently he has published Seems Like Murder Here: Southern Violence And The Blues Tradition.

(*) Harlem Blues
Flying Fish FF 70567 *Satan; Adam. 2/90–2/91.*

(*) Mother Mojo
Flying Fish FF 70623 *As above, except add Gammy Figueroa (perc). 1/93.*

(*) Living On The River
Flying Fish 666 Satan; Adam; Larry Etkin (t); Bob Funk (tb); Crispin Cioe (as, bs); Arno Hecht (ts); Ernie Colon (perc); Yasmin Alers, Karmine Alers (v). 12/96.

Adam Gussow has said that he'd rather people focused on the duo's unified sound than their diverse origins, and it's true that his beefy harmonica playing follows Satan very closely, and accordingly is characterized by rhythmic force rather than melodic or tonal variety. Satan's music is capable of more subtlety than is often apparent; the cross-rhythms on 'I Want You', which opens *Harlem Blues*, are emphasized by his use of a different dynamic level on each hi-hat-with-tambourine-atop. The thoughtful guitar playing on the same disc's 'Don't Get Around Much Any More' and *Mother Mojo*'s 'Mr Cantrell' suggests that recording Satan with, rather than as, a band might have been fruitful. However, the results would probably have been less commercial than a one-man-band with a white partner. That's not to say that Satan & Adam's music is gimmickry; far from it. What it seldom is, unfortunately, is interesting; usually, the two musicians set up a riff and thrash it to death as Satan bellows the lyrics. 'Sanctified Blues' on *Living On The River* is one of several songs that are evidence of an original songwriting talent, but more typical is its predecessor, a mannered account of 'Ode To Billy Joe' that drains the enigmatic specificity out of it. CS

Sax Gordon (born 1965)
TENOR SAXOPHONE, VOCAL

The Detroit-born Gordon Beadle grew up in Davis, California, discovering his destiny as a musician while still in high school. He has worked on the road with Johnny Heartsman, Luther 'Guitar Jr' Johnson, Matt 'Guitar' Murphy, Roomful Of Blues and Duke Robillard, and has recorded with several of them and with Jack Dupree, Jay McShann and many other blues artists.

*** **Have Horn Will Travel**
Bullseye Blues & Jazz CD BB 9589 Sax Gordon; Bob Enos (t); Porky Cohen, Carl Querfurth (tb); Rich Lataille (as, ts); Doug James (bs); Tom West (o, p); Duke Robillard (g, prod); Marty Ballou (b); Marty Richards (d); band (v); Eric 'Two Scoops' Moore (sp). 3/97.

*** **You Knock Me Out**
Bullseye Blues & Jazz CD BB 9604 Sax Gordon; Scott Aruda (t); Tino Barker (ts); Doug James (bs); Tom West (o); Matt McCabe (p); Duke Robillard (g, v, prod); Marty Ballou (b); Marty Richards (d); Sugar Ray Norcia (v). 2/99.

The notes to *Have Horn Will Travel* drop names like Junior Walker and Gene Ammons, but the bristly tone and hog-squeals of the opening title track point more towards someone like Big Jay McNeely. By the end of the album, however, Gordon has had room to air his versatility in a shimmy tune ('Waterbed Lou'), a blues from the Bill Doggett folio ('Squashy'), the florid tenor-and-organ sound of 'Melancholy Serenade' and a tenderly fuzzy reading of the traditional 'Deep River'. *You Knock Me Out* follows a similar programme, with 'Tino's Dream' for smoochy and 'Lonely For You' or 'Big Mouth' for hoochie-coo, but Robillard is more involved, playing Elmore James to Gordon's J. T. Brown on 'Speed Rack' and contributing considerably to several other tunes. Collectors of saxophone chase sequences will enjoy the tenor–baritone duel 'Lorenzo Leaps In'. Robillard and engineer Jack Gauthier give both productions a big echoing soundstage reminiscent of many of the old recordings Gordon must have absorbed. TR

Ken Saydak (born 1951)
PIANO, ORGAN, ACCORDION, VOCAL

Raised in Chicago, Saydak has played in the city's blues bands since the mid-'70s. He has worked with Mighty Joe Young, Lonnie Brooks and Johnny Winter, and as a sideman has appeared on a score or more Delmark albums by Dave Specter, Lurrie Bell and others.

*** **Foolish Man**
Delmark DE-725 Saydak; Ron Sorin (h); Rob Amster, Roland Miller (b); Jon Hiller, Kenny Smith (d). 6–8/98.

** **Love Without Trust**
Delmark DE-751 Saydak; John Brumbach (ts); Ron Sorin (h); Mark Wydra, James Wheeler, Bob Levis (g); Roland 'Stumpy' Miller, Bob Stroger, Harlan Terson, Rob Amster (b); Greg Bigger (d); Roberta Thomas (v). 1/01.

Foolish Man introduces the spectacle of Saydak's big brown bear of a voice tussling amicably with his own quizzical lyrics in songs like 'Where Is My Life?' and 'Shoppin' And Snackin''. His piano playing comes into focus most sharply on the solo pieces 'Time I Spend Alone', somewhat in the style of Memphis Slim, and the title track, while his ability as an ensemble player is attested by Eddie Boyd's 'Save Her Doctor' and Amos Milburn's 'Thinking And Drinking'. The original compositions on *Love Without Trust* tend to be less witty and more wordy, though Saydak's delivery is still predominantly jovial. Despite the larger roster of musicians, the group sound is not very different from *Foolish Man*'s, and by the end of this longish album the listener may be wishing for a little variety. TR

Charlie Sayles (born 1948)
VOCAL, HARMONICA

Raised by foster parents and in a boys' home, Sayles first heard the blues in Vietnam; on leaving the army he led a restless, wandering existence, often playing harmonica in the streets. In the mid-'70s he recorded a well-received LP, The Raw Harmonica Blues of Charlie Sayles (Dusty Road LP 701), made some appearances at folk festivals and settled in Washington, DC, where he has mainly but intermittently been active since.

*** **Night Ain't Right**
JSP JSPCD 241 Sayles; Larry Wise (h); Robert Palinic (g); Kerry Sayles (b); Chip Oswald (d). 90.

(*) **I Got Something To Say
JSP JSPCD 261 Sayles; Shawn Kellerman, Deborah Coleman (g); Anthony Gonsalves (b, v); 'Slam' (d); Jordan Patterson (v). 95.

(*) **Hip Guy: The Best Of The JSP Sessions
JSP JSPCD 2141 As for above CDs. 90, 95.

Sayles is a skilled and exciting harp player, but his songwriting is very variable. 'Night Ain't Right' and other songs are evocative despatches from life's insecure, dangerous edge, but he's also prone to wooden-tongued doggerel: 'Bill Monroe' (on *Night Ain't Right* and *Hip Guy*) celebrates the bluegrass maestro with jubilant harmonica and utterly flat words. (In the '70s, Sayles and Monroe shared a manager.)

'Zydeco', on *I Got Something To Say*, is an even duller tribute, this time to a genre but not in its style.

Much of *I Got Something To Say* features blues-rock guitar and a very loud bass, the latter perhaps influenced by go-go, black Washington's funk-based dance music. The unremitting throb gets wearing, and a couple of tracks in straight 4/4 are welcome; so are six 'alternate mixes', with quieter bass. The rhythms on *Night Ain't Right* are rather busy, too, but both band and music are more idiomatically bluesy, and Sayles the singer does some enjoyable, jazzy syllable-stretching.

Hip Guy is a strangely conceived 'best of', since five of its 12 tracks are previously unissued, among them 'Woodie' (Sayles's best instrumental), 'Drifting Blues' (his best vocal) and the unbelievably sketchy 'Hendrix'. It's difficult to recommend this level of variability. cs

Matt Schofield (born 1977)
VOCAL, GUITAR

Growing up in Gloucestershire on a musical diet of his father's blues records, Schofield was inspired to develop his guitar ability by live footage of B. B. King, Albert Collins and Stevie Ray Vaughan. He played his first gig at 13, and by 19 had decided to follow a professional playing career. After enjoying spells with acts including the Lee Sankey Group, Corrina Greyson and the Lester Butler Tribute Band, Schofield commenced performing with his own trio in 2003.

**** The Trio, Live
Nugene NUG CD 401 Schofield; Jonny Henderson (o); Evan Jenkins (d). 04.

The eight tracks demonstrate a wealth of individual ability wonderfully combined with brilliantly slick and spontaneous interaction. Repertoire is split between blues and funky jazz covers, the latter notable for a superb rendition of the Meters' 'Cissy Strut'. Performances throughout this debut are exemplary, with Henderson's Hammond organ work particularly striking. Schofield's stunning Robben Ford-tinted guitar outings maintain blues phrasing and tonality even where harmonic content deviates from tried and tested formats, while his voice is pleasantly mature and complements the dynamic perfectly. It is hard to imagine a smoother version of Memphis Slim's 'Everyday I Have The Blues', while the trio makes Albert Collins's 'Travellin' South' its own. A truly exciting debut. JF

**** Siftin' Thru Ashes
Nugene NUG 501 As above, except add Jeff Walker (b). 05.
***(*) Live At The Jazz Cafe!
Nugene NUG 503 As for The Trio, Live. 04/05.

Siftin' Thru Ashes is as accomplished a recording as its predecessor. The programme is much the same: some blues, mostly original but including an independent-minded reading of Albert Collins's 'Lights Are On, But Nobody's Home', another terrific version of a Meters number, 'People Say', and organ–guitar jazz jamming in fine '60s Blue Note style. Though done in a studio, it has almost all the presence of a live recording. *Live At The Jazz Cafe!* is available only from the label's web site <www.nugenerecords.com>, presumably because nearly all the tunes the trio played at the gig are on the other CDs. Some, like 'Lights Are On' and 'Cissy Strut', are longer or more exploratory than their previous versions. TR

Son Seals (1942–2004)
VOCAL, GUITAR

Frank Seals was raised in Osceola, Arkansas, where his father owned the Dipsy Doodle Club, and began playing music in his teens, much influenced by the local hero Albert King. He moved to Chicago in 1971, took over Hound Dog Taylor's gig at the Expressway Lounge when Taylor went on tour, and was heard there by Bruce Iglauer of Alligator Records, who promptly signed him. He spent over 30 years on the Chicago scene without being fully recognized as one of its most intense communicators of the blues experience.

*** The Son Seals Blues Band
Alligator ALCD 4703 Seals; Johnny 'Big Moose' Walker (o); John Riley (b); Charles L. Caldwell (d). winter 72.
***(*) Midnight Son
Alligator ALCD 4708 Seals; Kenneth Cooper (t); Bill McFarland (tb); Reggie Allmon (ts); Alberto Gianquinto (kb, o, p); Steve Plair (g); Harry 'Snapper' Mitchum (b); Bert 'Top Hat' Robinson (d). 7/76.
**(*) Live And Burning
Alligator ALCD 4712 Seals; A. C. Reed (ts); Alberto Gianquinto (p); Lacy Gibson (g); Snapper Mitchum (b); Tony Gooden (d). 1/78.
*** Chicago Fire
Alligator ALCD 4720 Seals; Paul Howard, Ken Cooper (t); Bill McFarland (tb); Henri Ford (as, bs); Jerry Wilson (ts); King Solomon (kb); Mark Weaver (g); Snapper Mitchum (b); David D. Anderson (d). 79.
**(*) Bad Axe
Alligator ALCD 4738 Seals; Billy Branch (h); Sid Wingfield, Carl Snyder Jr (kb); Carlos Johnson (g); Johnny B. Gayden, Nick Charles (b); Willie Hayes, Rick Howard (d). 84.

'How can he sing so clean and play so dirty?' someone once said of Albert King. No such question could be asked about Son Seals: he plays *and* sings dirty. His guitar sound is rooted in King's, and he has the same fondness for riding a riff, wringing infinitesimal variations out of it to build tension. His tone is sour and wailing and in a small-group setting like that of his debut album it dominates the music, even, at times, drawing one's attention from his singing. The album begins unpromisingly with dull readings of Junior Parker's 'Mother-In-Law Blues' and 'Sitting At My Window', but original songs such as 'Your Love Is Like A Cancer', 'Cotton Picking' and 'Now That I'm Down' make Seals sound much better. *Midnight Son* adds three horns, a move described in the notes as 'an integral part of Son's concept for this album, not an overdubbed afterthought'. Their role is, indeed, organic, and they enormously enhance Seals's performance, though there is much else to listen to in intense slow numbers like 'Telephone Angel' or the minor-key, and faintly Otis Rush-like, 'Going Back Home'.

It could be guessed from those albums that Seals was a formidable live act, but that doesn't fully come across in *Live And Burning*. It may be the club-friendly repertoire of standards like 'I Can't Hold Out' and 'Last Night', or the rather stifled sound, but something puts a damper on the proceedings. It doesn't help that Gibson is felt rather than heard, and that Gianquinto is on only one cut. Fortunately A. C. Reed interjects a pithy secondary voice.

Chicago Fire lets Seals use his own material and restores the horns that lend colour to his music. The value of both factors is clear in pieces like 'Leaving Home', and it's surprising that when Seals and Alligator Records next collaborated, on *Bad Axe*, neither party insisted on the same terms. Seals's decreased input (he wrote four of the ten numbers) is not a drawback, since other people's songs like 'I Can Count On My Blues' or 'Goin' Home (Where Women Got Meat On Their Bones)' are well suited to him, but the smaller group prompts him to play long, inflammatory solos and restore the Albert King effect that had diminished over the previous three albums.

**(*) Blues Guitar Summit
[Charly CDGR 273] *Seals; 'Big Dan' Rabinovitz (t); Red Groetzinger (s); Red John Randolph (g); Jerry Barr (b); David Russell (d). c. 91.*

Recording for a TV show at Buddy Guy's Legends, Seals relies mostly on comfortable genre classics like Jimmy Reed's 'The Sun Is Shining', Tampa Red's 'Don't Lie To Me' and Memphis Slim's 'Every Day I Have The Blues', the last barely recognizable disguised as a hearty stomp. At 2.59 it's also the longest of the five tracks. Such fast-food service is unflattering to Seals's music, but he does dish up 'I Can't Hold Out' with a memorable guitar solo *flambé*. The remainder of the CD is by Lonnie Brooks and Magic Slim.

**(*) Living In The Danger Zone
Alligator ALCD 4798 *Seals; Red Groetzinger (ts, fl); Sugar Blue (h); Sid Wingfield (o, p); Kevin Tremblay (g); Ray Williams, Johnny B. Gayden (b); Kerman Frazier, Ray 'Killer' Allison (d). 91.*

***(*) Nothing But The Truth
Alligator ALCD 4822 *Seals; Dan Rabinovitz (t, flh); Red Groetzinger (ts, bs, fl); Tony Zamagni (o, p); John Randolph (g); Noel Neal, Johnny B. Gayden (b); David Russell (d). 94.*

*** Live – Spontaneous Combustion
Alligator ALCD 4846 *Seals; Dan Rabinovitz (t); Red Groetzinger (as, ts, fl); Sidney James Wingfield (kb); Justin Smith (g); Johnny B. Gayden (b); David Russell (d). 6/96.*

*** DeLuxe Edition
Alligator ALCD 5611 *As for all Alligator CDs. 72–6/96.*

Seals's seven-year spell away from the studio didn't seem, judging by *Living In The Danger Zone*, to have wrought any changes in his music. In fact the whining guitar tone and the obsessive circling round a small group of notes continued the stylistic retreat of *Bad Axe*. But *Nothing But The Truth* found him energized by well-chosen material and hand-chosen musicians, and the sequence of 'Before The Bullets Fly', 'I'm Gonna Take It All Back', 'Life Is Hard' and 'Tough As Nails' is the most exciting stretch of music on any of his albums, the declamatory vocals accompanied by a firework display of inventive guitar.

Seals's second live set, from Buddy Guy's Legends, not unreasonably embraces some favourite pieces like 'Don't Pick Me For Your Fool' and a dynamically renovated 'Your Love Is Like A Cancer', but also introduces good fresh ones like 'Mother Blues'. The recording is more spacious than *Live And Burning*'s, but since the setlist is dotted with the same sort of recognizable repertoire as on *Blues Guitar Summit*, and the horns play a more conventional antiphonal role than some of their forerunners, this is an exercise in consolidation rather than innovation.

DeLuxe Edition is a selection from all eight Alligators, and a discriminating one: for example, only one track was taken from the disappointing *Living In The Danger Zone*, and it's the untypically lively 'Bad Axe'. 'Life All By Myself', left over from his first session, is superior to several of the tracks chosen for *The Son Seals Blues Band*.

**(*) Lettin' Go
Telarc CD-83501 *Seals; Mark Pender, Dan Rabinovitz (t); Jerry Vivino (ts); Richard Rosenberg (bs); Scott Healy (kb); Al Kooper, Tim Wire (o); Jimmy Vivino, Trey Anastasio, Jeff 'Jabo' Bihlman (g); Mike Merritt, Jason Kott (b); James Wormworth, Scott 'Little' Bihlman (d); Fred Walcott (perc). 8–11/99.*

Leaving Alligator, Seals gained, according to the notes, 'the freedom he had never been given in the past to record the material he wanted to play.' It's probably true that his former label, offered 'Rockin' And Rollin' Tonight' (a secular makeover of a gospel song) or 'Osceola Rock' ('Jailhouse Rock' with new words), would have rejected them, but it wouldn't have harmed the album if Telarc had done so too. Other songs are better matched to his skills, such as 'Bad Blood' and 'Doc's Blues', co-written with the crime writer Andrew Vachss, or 'Bad Luck Child', but the settings, except for a vigorous remake of his 'Funky Bitch' with different musicians, abandon the fervour of his previous work for a more temperate and contemplative mood. TR

Alec Seward (1901/02–72)
VOCAL, GUITAR

In his early 20s Seward moved from Newport News, Virginia, to New York, where he became an admirer of Lonnie Johnson; he had been playing guitar since his teens. In the mid-'40s he met Louis Hayes, a singer and guitarist from North Carolina 11 years his junior, and under the soubriquet of Guitar Slim & Jelly Belly they played at house parties and made a number of records for their own Tru-Blue label, Apollo and other companies. Seward also fell in with Brownie McGhee, who helped him to develop his guitar playing, and with Sonny Terry, who came to live nearby and was a close friend and musical partner for many years. Seward earned his living as a longshoreman; music was never more than a spare-time occupation.

**** Carolina Blues: New York City 1944
Arhoolie CD 460 *Seward; Louis Hayes (g, v). c. 44?*
***(*) The Back Porch Boys
Delmark DE-755 *Seward; Louis Hayes (g, v). autumn 47.*

The migration of black Southerners into New York City during World War II created an audience for downhome blues that the city's longer-settled musicians didn't play. Seward and Hayes provided those new arrivals from Virginia, the Carolinas and Georgia with music such as many of them had grown up with, placid blues accompanied on two close-meshed guitars in the manner of, say, Buddy Moss and Curley Weaver. ('Bad Acting Woman' and 'You're My Honey', rare shifts into a higher gear, have a ring of Weaver and Willie McTell.) Both men sing, either solo or back-and-forthing like Memphis Minnie and Kansas Joe, sometimes swapping experiences and anecdotes, as in 'Travelin' Boy's Blues'. The Arhoolie CD identifies Seward as the 'smooth' singer and Hayes as the 'rough' one; it may be helpful to add that Hayes sounds younger and sings in a higher register. Although many of their songs are on generic topics like misbehaving women, their lyrics are very often fresh-made and sometimes themed, like 'Jail And Buddy Blues', 'Cooking Big Woman' or 'South Carolina Blues', which remembers the days of rural self-subsistence. Hayes's 'Humming Bird Blues' introduces a novel sexual metaphor: 'I belong to the fowl family – all the roosters and me is friends. Says I can sample three or four flowers, while he's sampling just one hen.'

The Arhoolie CD contains 29 tracks, taken from superb acetate masters which bely their age. According to Hayes they were recorded about 1944; discographers incline to date them a few years later, after the 11 Apollo sides gathered on the Delmark, which are somewhat surfacey but in exactly the same vein, the two guitars moving in an unhurried couple dance. The Delmark also contains Apollo sides by Champion Jack Dupree and Regals by McTell (including a couple available nowhere else) and Dennis McMillon.

*** Late One Saturday Evening
[The Blues Alliance TBA-13007] *Seward; Sonny Terry (h, v); Brownie McGhee (g, v); Washboard Doc (wb); Julia Carr (v).* autumn 66.

In 1950 Seward recorded with Sonny Terry for Elektra (*Sonny Terry & His Mouth Harp* [Original Blues Classics OBCCD-689]), and in 1965 he made an admirable but unreissued album for Bluesville, *Creepin' Blues*. *Late One Saturday Evening* (availability uncertain) was recorded at a party where he sang some of the Bluesville repertoire and other songs, often accompanied by Terry and with a guest appearance by McGhee on 'Her Ways Are So Sweet'. The tape was no doubt made simply as a memento of friends playing for and with friends, and there are passages when Seward is off-mike or someone bumps the mike cable, but there are not so many documents of this kind that we can afford to be picky about them, and the recording is certainly good enough to give us an accurate picture of the man: a guitarist playing now like Brownie's rusty rural cousin, and a singer whose hoarse countryman's voice addresses us with a compelling intimacy. TR

Harmonica Shah (born 1946)
VOCAL, HARMONICA

Formerly Thaddeus Hall, Seward Shah (which is now his legal name) was raised in his native California and Texas. Moving to Detroit after leaving school, he worked at Ford for 15 years. Shah was initially exposed to blues by his grandfather, who played guitar and harmonica, but only became a musician himself in 1976, after being fired by Ford.

*** Motor City Mojo
Blue Suit BS-114D *Shah; Bill Heid, Detroit Piano Fats, Uncle Jessie White (p); Little Junior Cannaday, Joe Mitchell, Eddie Kirkland, Doug Deming, Emmanuel Young, Jesse Blades (g); Leon Horner, Pat Prouty (b); R. J. Spangler, Duke Dawson (d).* 00?

The backing on *Motor City Mojo* is usually supplied by two guitars plus rhythm section, and whichever permutation of musicians is employed, the sound is dark and aggressive. Only on 'My Old Time Used To Be', recorded live, does rough-edged spontaneity become under-rehearsed confusion. Shah's playing is limited, but commitment and enthusiasm overcome this, except on 'The Sky Is Crying', where Heid is the only accompanist and Shah is over-exposed. Shah presents himself (not, it seems, altogether untruthfully) as a street hustler who works only if he must, and a 'Dirty Old Bastard' who 'don't mean no woman no damn good.' This may not be attractive but, like *Motor City Mojo* as a whole, it's honest and uncompromising.

*** Deep Detroit
South Side SSR 004 *Shah; Howard Glazer (g); Gary Rasmussen, Scott Gatteno, Lou Wilson (b); Matt Stahl (d).* 00?

Deep Detroit is less deep than its predecessor, but just as rough, and enjoyable. Shah is accompanied by a blues-rock band, and Glazer borrows freely from the flamboyant, post-Clapton Buddy Guy, and to a lesser extent from Albert Collins and Stevie Ray Vaughan. Occasionally, the rock overpowers the blues, but this is a successful instance of recording 'as live', and the band's raw power pushes Shah into singing and playing more strongly than on *Motor City Mojo*. It's an advantage that he admires Junior Wells, and no disadvantage that he can't match Junior's strutting flamboyance. A version of Frank Patt's 'Bloodstains On The Wall' finds new levels of ferocity in that terrifying song.

** Tell It To Your Landlord
Electro-Fi 3377 *Shah; Howard Glazer (g); Bob Godwin (b); Art 'Thunder' Vaughn, Charles Stuart (d).* 1–7/02.

Shah's third CD is disappointing; graceless bass and solipsistic drumming fail to corral Glazer's aggression, and as a result there's too much rock-guitar carpet bombing. The Hookerish 'Mean And Evil', with good acoustic guitar, makes a welcome contrast but highlights the problem. Shah's lyrics are often sketchy, short-winded first drafts, and the combination of weak material and undisciplined accompaniment makes the limitations of his playing and singing more apparent. The honesty and enthusiasm that appealed on previous releases are largely replaced by posturing. CS

Shakey Jake (1921–90)
VOCAL, HARMONICA

James D. Harris was a professional gambler and hustler (he preferred the term 'street lawyer') who had some talent as a blues singer and harmonica player. Resident in Chicago since he was a child, he formed a band in the '50s in which he gave exposure to his nephew Magic Sam. After a remarkable single for Artistic, two unsatisfactory albums for Bluesville and an appearance on the first AFBF in 1962, he devoted himself to managing Sam's career. Living Blues reported in 1973 that he had retired from music to run his trucking business and devote his spare time to The Institute of Devine [sic] Metaphysical Research, Inc., but he was intermittently involved in music-related activities in LA until shortly before his death.

The 1958 Artistic single 'Roll Your Moneymaker'/'Call Me (If You Need Me)', with Magic Sam and Freddie King on guitars, is a typical Willie Dixon production of its time, brash and memorable. Magic Sam is all over 'Call Me'. He also accompanied his uncle, alongside Otis Spann and Louis Myers (harmonica), on the 1966 coupling 'Respect Me Baby/'A Hard Road'; the single was billed as by 'Shakey Joke' but the music is wholly serious and extremely powerful. The four sides are on the Magic Sam CD ... *With a Feeling! – The Complete Cobra, Chief and Crash Recordings 1957–1966* (Westside WESA 890//Fuel 2000 302 061 104).

** Mouth Harp Blues
Original Blues Classics OBCCD 559 *Shakey Jake; Robert Banks (p); Jimmie Lee [Robinson] (g); Leonard Gaskin (b); Junior Blackmon (d).* 11/60.

Bluesville, who originated this album, spectacularly missed the boat here. Had they recorded Jake with the band he had used two years earlier, or at least with Magic Sam, they might have produced the first album of Chicago's new West Side style. Their policy, however, was not to record working blues bands; instead they hired jazz sidemen who were on the books of their parent company, Prestige. Jake sings and blows with determination, but his accompanists, though competent players at their own game, are simply the wrong team. The only Chicagoan present was Jimmie Lee Robinson, and he was a guitarist of the second rank at best. It's unfortunate that this is Jake's only in-print CD, for he made at least eight albums, most of which were more representative and some rather good. One of the latter, the World Pacific LP *Further On Up The Road*, was reissued on Sequel NEX CD 211 (deleted) and also included in *Chicago Blues Masters Vol. 3* (Capitol 36288 2CD, deleted). TR

Mem Shannon (born 1959)
VOCAL, GUITAR, HARMONICA, BASS

Shannon turned to blues after discovering B. B. King in his father's record collection, and played in bands from high school onwards. After his father died in 1981, Shannon drove a cab in his native New Orleans to pay his family's bills, but continued to hone his performing and writing skills, and went fulltime as a musician in 1996 after the success of his first CD.

**** A Cab Driver's Blues
Hannibal HNCD 21387 *Shannon; Lance Ellis, Tim Green (ts); Jackie Banks (kb); Peter Carter (b); Barry Thomas, Wilbert 'Junk Yard Dog' Arnold (d).* 95?

**** Mem Shannon's 2nd Blues Album
Hannibal HNCD 1409 *As above, except Jeffrey 'Jelly Bean' Alexander, James Varnardo (d) replace Thomas, Arnold; add Chuck Chaplin (p), Mark Bingham (b), Carlos 'Du Du' Martinez (perc).* 96?

*** Spend Some Time With Me
Shanachie 9013 *Shannon; Tracy Griffin (t, flh); Mark Mullins (tb); Jason Mingledorff (cl, s, v); Chuck Chaplin (kb); Jackie Banks (o, clavinet); Dave Easley (sg); Jimmy Ives (b); Tony Seruntine (d); Pupi Menes (cga).* 99?

***(*) Memphis In The Morning
Shanachie 9031 *Shannon; Wayne Jackson (t, tb); Andrew Love (ts); Robert 'Rhock' Dabon (kb, p); Joe Sherman (b); Doug Belote (d); Dennis Walker (shaker, tri).* 01?

A Cab Driver's Blues announced the arrival of an original songwriter, singer and guitarist; it also gained media attention by including surreptitiously recorded snippets of conversation with passengers, but it's no loss that most of them have vanished from later pressings. Shannon plays clean, agile guitar lines over busy rhythms and sings in a dark, flexible baritone that recalls Percy Mayfield. Mayfield also comes to mind when considering Shannon's songwriting, which ponders the follies of the world with wry amusement, grumpy cynicism and an admirable lack of cliché. He's particularly good on the older generation's wisdom, and the influence it should have on the young; his responses to violence, addiction and the plight of the homeless are equally powerful. 'Old Men' and 'Charity' on the *2nd Blues Album* are the most forceful examples of these sides of Shannon's writing, but social justice and the family are concerns that recur from disc to disc. So do songs about the centrality of funk to his music, which are considerably less inventive, and correspondingly less compelling.

By comparison with its predecessors, *Spend Some Time With Me* is disapppointing; 'The Last Time I Was Here' is a remarkable reflection on slavery and its after-effects, but elsewhere Shannon can sound crabby and self-absorbed. The production fusses and fiddles with the music, replacing the Hannibal CDs' interlocutory tenor with a large horn section whose responses are too often semi-automatic. *Memphis In The Morning* is better, not least because its smaller forces include the vastly experienced Memphis Horns. The downside is that when Jackson and Love sit out, the arrangements sound sketchy, and the CD sags in the middle. Shannon's writing is as accomplished as ever, though: 'S.U.V.' is hilariously cantankerous, and 'Tired Arms', describing the relationship between a boy and his grandfather through the motif of fishing, is masterly.

***(*) I'm From Phunkville
NorthernBlues NBM 00029 *Shannon; Barney Floyd (t); Troy 'Trombone Shorty' Andrews (tb); Jason Mingledorff (cl, s); Frederick 'Shep' Sheppard (s); Robert 'Rhock' Dabon (kb); A. C. Gayden Jr (g); Ian Michael (b); Doug Belote, Josh 'The Little Kid' Milligan (d); Billy Martin (perc); Tyrone Pollard (v).* 04?

Produced by Shannon, *I'm From Phunkville* starts unpromisingly, with four songs that are less sharply witty and musically more generic. Once past the overstretched title track, things come right, though, beginning with the gross-out humour of 'I'll Kiss A Pitbull', which is prefaced by an acerbic rap about the absurdity of addressing the men and women in the audience 'as if the ladies just gonna go deaf and not listen to what he's saying long enough for him to say his piece to the guys.' A version of 'Eleanor Rigby' makes that song as good as critics think it is, but otherwise the songs are Shannon originals. Once again, he pays serious attention to his subjects, even the light-hearted ones; standing out are 'Battle Ground', a Southern soul epic of troubled love, and 'No Religion', the Muddy-meets-Philip-Larkin musings of a man 'way past twenty-one' and troubled by his lack of a faith. Shannon's guitar work is as clean and clever as ever, and it's supported by a phalanx of fine musicians, among whom the drummers deserve special mention. CS

Preston Shannon
VOCAL, GUITAR

Shannon was born in Olive Branch, Mississippi, but grew up in Memphis. He has been playing in bands since he was 18 and has experience of many kinds of music. In 1987 he began touring with the singer Shirley Brown, and in 1991 formed his own band.

**(*) Break The Ice
Bullseye Blues CD BB 9545 *Shannon; Wayne Jackson (t, tb); Andrew Love (s); Billy Ross (o); Archie Turner (p); Steve Hines*

(b, perc, v); Claude Franklin (d); Rusty 'Mopar' McFarland, Lynn Hines, Darby Hicks Jr [Ron Levy] (v). 94.

*** Midnight In Memphis
Bullseye Blues CD BB 9575 *Shannon; Ben Cauley (t); Jack Hale (tb); Lannie McMillan (ts); James Mitchell (bs); Ron Levy (o); Lester Snell (p); Thomas Bingham (g); Milton Price (b); Steve Potts (d); William Brown, Bertram Brown, Mashaa (v); Willie Mitchell (co-prod). 96.*

**(*) All In Time
Bullseye Blues BB CD 9595 *Shannon; Scott Thompson (t); Jack Hall Sr (tb); Jim Spake (ts); James Mitchell (bs); Lester Snell (kb); Thomas Bingham (g); Leroy Hodges (b); Steve Potts (d); William Brown, Bertram Brown, Mashaa (v); Willie Mitchell (prod). 99.*

Shannon's guitar style comes out of the foundry built by B. B. and Albert King, and his rasping vocals are cast in a purely Albertian mould. These are tools well suited to straightforward blues, so it's surprising that the two on *Break The Ice*, 'Forty Days And Forty Nights' and 'Crosscut Saw', are among the album's less compelling tracks. More satisfying are 'Have Your Woman Ever Loved You So Good', with its perky little guitar figure, and 'I Got Everything I Need', sung in the style of one of his models, Otis Redding.

The one downhome blues on *Midnight In Memphis*, Muddy Waters's 'Can't Lose What You Never Had', is okay, but more typical are 'Handee Man', trampolining on a rubbery bass line, and 'Round Midnight', two of several Willie Mitchell–William Brown compositions on the album. Another is 'The Clock', based on the old Wynonie Harris–Roy Brown favourite – 'I looked at the clock, the clock struck one, I said, "Turn over, baby, let's have some fun"', etc. – but taken at a slow, dreamy tempo that transforms it from a laddish chant into a fervent celebration of physicality and simply being alive. The closing title track, similarly paced, is an inventive and beautifully executed guitar blues.

The blues tracks 'Jail Of Love' and 'Welfare Woman' on *All In Time*, though not outstanding, will be more to most readers' taste than 'Are You In The Mood?' or 'Be With Me Tonight', tiresome songs of erotic solicitation that dress Shannon in a Barry White robe. This CD also delivers Shannon's version of 'Purple Rain', forecast in the notes to *Break The Ice*; listeners unmoved by its inconsequential prettiness will be able to skip to the closing track, 'Cold Beer Good Time', and breathe a fervent 'That's more like it!' TR

Ray Sharpe (born 1938)
VOCAL, GUITAR

Sharpe grew up in Fort Worth, equally fond of country music and blues. 'Linda Lu' made the lower reaches of the Hot 100 in 1959, but follow-up success eluded him. Sharpe has continued to perform, making his first visit to Europe in 1992.

** Linda Lu
Bear Family BCD 15888 *Sharpe; Melvin Lastie (t); unknowns (brass); Jim Horn (fl, ts); Plas Johnson, Harold Battiste (ts); 'Easy Deal' Wilson, Larry Knechtel, Connie Crunk, Marcel Richards (p); Duane Eddy, Don Cole, Buddy Long, Donnie Owens, Al Casey, Roy Montrell (g); Buddy Wheeler, Alvin Simmons, Chuck Badie (b); Robert C. Taylor Jr, Jimmie Troxel, John Boudreaux (d); The Evelyn Freeman Singers (v). 4/58–62.*

Ray Sharpe's hit has been much covered by both blues singers and rock 'n' rollers; irresistibly catchy and satisfyingly obscure, it's by far his biggest claim to fame. Its two flipsides are enjoyable ('Monkey's Uncle', a spot-on Chuck Berry pastiche, was substituted for 'Red Sails In The Sunset'), and his debut recording, 'Oh My Baby's Gone', has some tough guitar, but most of Sharpe's output is second-rate rock 'n' roll, often compromised by puerile lyrics or crass vocal group overdubs. The best-sung, best-arranged track here is 'On The Street Where You Live', but a Sammy Davis Jr imitation won't sell *Linda Lu* (the CD) to blues fans. 'Linda Lu' (the song) is worth having, though; it's on *The Golden Age Of American Rock 'N' Roll Vol. 4* (Ace CDCHD 500) in better company, most of it admittedly outside our scope. CS

Omar Sharriff (born 1938)
VOCAL, PIANO

Born in Louisiana, Sharriff was inspired to play around 1945 by hearing Albert Ammons on the radio. He moved to the West Coast in 1958, where he converted to Islam in 1960, and played benefits for the Black Panthers. Sharriff made his recording debut in the late '60s, using his birth name, David Alexander. Subsequently, a series of personal tragedies and career difficulties kept him away from recording for nearly two decades.

*** The Raven
Arhoolie CD 365 *Sharriff; Frank Sipes, Larry Murdo (b); Skip Dysart, Mickey Durio (d). 7–12/72, 91.*

Sharriff has a commanding technique and an acute awareness of his musical heritage, from the boogie pianists of the '40s to Tatum and Monk; he also admires Gershwin, Jerry Lee Lewis and Hoagy Carmichael, and his playing blends jazz, blues, pop and classical elements. (The title track, an anguished response to his brother's murder, turns the slow movement of the 'Moonlight Sonata' into convincing blues.) When singing, Sharriff often crams many syllables into a single line, perhaps influenced by jazz vocalists like King Pleasure and Jon Hendricks. Credited to 'Omar Shariff' with one 'r', this CD contains his best (and best-recorded) sides to date, combining material from the days before he changed his name with his first comeback recordings.

**(*) Black Widow Spider
Have Mercy HMCD-08 *Sharriff; Steve Ghundi (s); James Winnegan (h); Richard Golde, Bobby G. (g); Al Arnett, Geno, Darryl Hutchins (b); Jerry Banks, 'Rat-a-Tat' Pat Balcom (d). 93.*

**(*) Baddass
Have Mercy HMCD-11 *Sharriff; Steve Ghundi (s); Richard Golde, Lewe Fratis, Jimmy Pailer, Ron Hull (g); Geno, Dave Garrity, Erik Kleven (b); Steve Pitts (d, cga); 'Rat-a-Tat' Pat Balcom (d). 95.*

Black Widow Spider is an eclectic mix of originals and covers, including songs by Ray Charles, Bob Dylan ('All Along The Watchtower', via Hendrix) and Rodgers & Hammerstein ('My Favorite Things', via Coltrane). Sharriff's mumbling, rapid-fire delivery makes him hard to understand. This is not always a disadvantage; what sounds at first like extreme misogyny turns out to be mostly self-pity resulting from failure to pull, but that doesn't make it any more attractive. Sharriff's political and racial militancy is integral to his songwriting, and 'Burn Baby Burn' is an acid comment on the Rodney King case, but his lyrics too often seem like first drafts rather than finished songs.

Baddass continues in similar vein, with more complaints about rejection by women, including the homophobic 'Is There A Real Woman In The House?', and topical commentary. 'Blame It On The Nigger' is Sharriff's understandably outraged response to the Susan Smith murder case, although one might have expected an African-American to pause before recommending a lynching. The piano work is energetic, notably on a fine version of Coltrane's 'Blue Train', but again the lyrics, for all their originality and passion, are often unpolished, prosaic streams of consciousness, and too many numbers go on too long and nowhere in particular. A 'Mystery Bonus Track' is the slow movement of the 'Moonlight Sonata', this time played straight, but not well.

** **Anatomy Of A Woman**
Have Mercy HMCD-13 *Sharriff; John Mullick (t); Steve Ghundi (s); Little Aaron King (g); Erik Kleven (b); Keeno Burns (d). 98.*

This concept album expounds Sharriff's mostly dysphoric views on the war between men and women, ranging from the general ('It's The Booty Not The Beauty') to the specific ('Ms Julie is the devil, and Sacramento, California's a living hell') and glancing at politico-sexual scandal ('The President And The Tramp') en route. Some will undoubtedly find his opinions offensive, but that's probably to dignify them with more attention than they deserve; more problematic is a shortage of variety in both tunes and delivery, and a fondness for pointless displays with the right hand. CS

Eddie Shaw (born 1937)
VOCAL, ALTO AND TENOR SAXOPHONES, HARMONICA

Shaw left Greenville, Mississippi, in 1957, hired by Muddy Waters after sitting in at a gig. In Chicago he worked with Magic Sam, Earl Hooker, Freddie King and many others. From 1972 to 1976 he led Howlin' Wolf's band, pacing the show so that its star was presented as favourably as his chronic health problems would allow. After Wolf's death, Shaw kept the Wolf Gang going and launched himself as a name artist; he also operated the 1815 Club for several years.

(*) Movin' And Groovin' Man
Isabel IS 269298//Evidence ECD 26028 *Shaw; Eddie 'Cleanhead' Vinson (as); Ken Sajdak [Saydak] (p); Melvin Taylor (g); Harlan Terson (b); Merle Perkins (d). 5/82.*

***(*) The Blues Is Good News!**
Wolf 120.866 *Shaw; Detroit Junior (o); Leo Davies, Joachim Palden (p); Eddie 'Vaan' Shaw Jr, John Primer, Hubert Sumlin (g); Lafayette 'Shorty' Gilbert, Willie Kent (b); Robert Plunkett, Tim Taylor, Chico Chism (d). 77–1/92.*

*** **In The Land Of The Crossroads**
Rooster Blues R 2624 *Shaw; Vaan Shaw (g); Shorty Gilbert (b); Robert Plunkett (d). 92.*

***(*) Home Alone**
Wolf 120.879 *Shaw; Detroit Junior, Ken Barker (p); Vaan Shaw, Johnny B. Moore, Jake Dawson (g); Shorty Gilbert, Willie Kent (b); Tim Taylor, Cleo Williams (d). 7/93–3/94.*

*** **Too Many Highways**
Wolf 120.892 *Shaw; Michael Pevey (s); Vaan Shaw, Johnny B. Moore (g); Shorty Gilbert (b, v); Tim Taylor (d). 11/96.*

**** **Can't Stop Now**
Delmark DE-698 *As above, except Gilbert does not sing; add Detroit Junior (p); omit Pevey, Moore. 12/96.*

Shaw's singing has some of the rheumy contemplativeness of Willie Dixon, and rather more of the uncomplicated directness of Howlin' Wolf, but he wisely avoids imitation, even on numbers associated with his former boss. His gutsy sax is an unusual lead instrument in Chicago blues, but its sound is unmistakably transplanted from the Delta; more predictably, so is his occasional, straightforward harmonica.

Movin' And Groovin' Man was recorded in Europe with a band of good musicians who never quite coalesce into a team. Shaw sings unenthusiastically and his sax often seems to be competing, not always successfully, with Taylor's ostentatiously aggressive playing. The problem is compounded by the engineering, which uses abrupt changes of level to bring forward the soloists.

Any of the subsequent CDs is preferable, and on all of them Shaw works with more sympathetic and familiar musicians. (Vaan Shaw is his son; Plunkett, Gilbert and Detroit Junior were with him in the Howlin' Wolf days.) Some distinctions need to be drawn, though. *In The Land Of The Crossroads* has the best of several versions of 'Highway Bound', and a gritty, uncompromising 'Wine Head Hole', loosely based on Dr Clayton's 'The Woman I Love', but the sound is muzzy and the arrangements insufficiently varied.

Of the three Wolf CDs, *The Blues Is Good News* comes from the early '90s, except for 'Blues Men Of Yesterday', dubbed from a staticky copy of the Simmons LP *Have Blues Will Travel*. This is an acoustically and (thanks to Detroit Junior) musically unsatisfactory conclusion to an otherwise excellent CD of aggressive, oldfashioned Chicago blues; most of the songs are Shaw originals, but there's also what may be the only necessary version of 'Red Rooster' apart from Wolf's and Sam Cooke's. *Home Alone*, also mostly excellent, is similarly marred by its final track, a live 'One Room Country Shack' where Shaw seems to be trying to traverse the 'thousand miles from nowhere' by unassisted lung power. *Too Many Highways* includes two splendid Shaw compositions in 'Going Back To Greenville' and the title track, but too many numbers are either drawn from or in the manner of the brightly poppish repertoire that Willie Dixon pressed on Howlin' Wolf at Chess. Shorty Gilbert should not have been allowed to sing 'Rainy Night In Georgia'.

On *Can't Stop Now*, the Shaws and Detroit Junior are energized and inventive throughout, with Gilbert and Taylor building a firm platform from which they can strut their stuff. 'Casino Blues' and 'Chicago Man' are fine examples of Shaw's songwriting, and his singing and playing are at their strongest, whether he's careering through 'Howlin' For My Darling' or tackling Little Milton's optimistic anthem 'We're Gonna Make It'. CS

Eddie Vaan Shaw (born 1955)
VOCAL, GUITAR

Shaw was born in Chicago and began playing guitar at 11. In his teens he played in his father Eddie Shaw's band at the 1815 Club, backing Howlin' Wolf, Eddie Taylor and other artists. After Wolf's death he toured and recorded with his father's Wolf Gang.

(*) Morning Rain (Chicago Blues Session Vol. 26)
Wolf 120.872 *Shaw; Vince Salerno (s); Eddie Shaw (h); Sidney*

James Wingfield (p); John Primer (g); Willie Kent, Lafayette 'Shorty' Gilbert (b); Robert Plunkett, Cleo Williams, Thomas Dutko (d). 1–4/92.

**(*) The Trail Of Tears
Wolf 120.878 Shaw; Michael Pevey (as); Eddie Shaw (h, v); Chris Sandera (h); Roosevelt 'Mad Hatter' [Purifoy] (kb); Bobby Dixon (p, v); Sid Wingfield (p); John Primer (g); Lafayette 'Shorty' Gilbert, Nick Holt, Eddie Galchick (b); Robert Plunkett, Earl Howell, Tim Taylor, Thomas Dutko (d). 1/92–2/94.

*** Ass Whoopin'
[unnamed label, unnumbered] Shaw; Michael Pevey (as); Vince Salerno (s); Chris Sandera, Eddie Shaw (h); Roosevelt 'Mad Hatter' [Purifoy] (kb); Sid Wingfield (p); John Primer (g); Lafayette 'Shorty' Gilbert (b); Robert Plunkett, Tim Taylor, Thomas Dutko, 'Baldhead Pete' [Cleo Williams] (d). 90s.

Soon after Vaan Shaw was given his first guitar, he was shown his way round it by Magic Sam. Each of these albums' notes mentions that, but since none of them reveals his birthdate, some listeners may not be aware that the anecdote makes him a good deal older than he looks and sounds – though they may guess, from his command of the blues guitar vocabulary, that he must have put a good few years into acquiring it. In fact he was fortunate enough to be able to learn his trade by hanging out at his father's club and playing behind many of Chicago's senior bluesmen.

Morning Rain acknowledges that older generation with several songs by, or associated with, Elmore James and Freddie King. *The Trail Of Tears* makes a similar gesture with versions of 'I'm Ready' and James's 'The Sky Is Crying', the latter a long, dramatic performance, staged in the manner of Buddy Guy. 'Oh, How They Can Love' and 'I'm Crazy Now' are done with acoustic guitar and Sandera's harmonica; these have a ring of Guy working unplugged with Junior Wells. The biting guitar on the plugged-in tracks, sharpened by Shaw's use of compression and sustain effects, goes beyond anything on *Morning Rain*, but it may be the earlier album, with its more homogeneous material, that will gather more admirers. At any rate, when Shaw put together *Ass Whoopin'* in 2001, he ignored *The Trail Of Tears* but reissued six tracks from *Morning Rain*, choosing most of the best ones – 'TV Preacher', with its wordy, witty lyric, suits his light voice particularly well – and taking the opportunity to master them at a higher level. ('Never Used Blues' is a retitled 'Drop Down Baby'.) The notes state that the other eight tracks were recorded in Mississippi, Austria and Germany, but don't say when or with what combinations of musicians. Several are, or have their nucleus in, unplugged duets with Sandera or a second guitarist; 'I've Heard' is a well-turned blues composition, while the accumulating images of 'I Heard Voices Cryin Inside My Head' seem to echo Bob Dylan's 'It's Alright Ma (I'm Only Bleeding)'. The acoustic interlude over, Shaw gives us long live versions of 'Same Old Blues', 'Mornin' Rain' and his best composition, 'I'm Crazy Now', all laced with serpentine guitar playing. This, if it can be found, is the one of Shaw's albums to get first.

** Give Me Time
Wolf 120.894 Shaw; Christian Sandera (h); Oliver Humer (p); Siggi Fassl, Al Cook (g). 10/94.

Released more than a decade after it was recorded, *Give Me Time* contains four of the undocumented tracks that had appeared on *Ass Whoopin'*: 'Give Me Time', 'I Need Your Love' (previously titled 'I've Heard'), 'Bull Shit Blues' (previously 'B.S. Makes The World Go Around') and 'Ain't No Next Time' (previously 'I Heard Voices Cryin Inside My Head'). Shaw also offers third readings of 'Mornin' Rain' and 'I'm Crazy Now' and second ones of 'Ugly Woman' and 'It Hurts Me Too', but the all-acoustic setting doesn't do justice to the range of his talent. TR

Robert Shaw (1908–85)
VOCAL, PIANO

Born in what's now a suburb of Houston, Texas, Shaw joined an informal set of Southwestern pianists who played both in city clubs and in the camps set up for seasonal workers. Retiring from this circuit, he went into the grocery trade in Austin, running a food market and barbecue stand. A well-known member of the city's business community, he often played at private and civic functions, but as his recordings made their way into the world beyond he was invited to festivals all over the US, as well as to Canada and, in 1974, Europe.

**** The Ma Grinder
Arhoolie CD 377 Shaw. 3–8/63, 4/73, 5/77.

*** The 1971 Party Tape
Document DOCD-1014 Shaw. 1/71.

**(*) Giants Of Texas Country Blues Piano
Wolf 120.629 Shaw. 10/81.

A singular form of piano blues was developed in the '30s by a number of itinerant players native to or based in Texas. One can't fully understand the context and appreciate the core repertoire of that music from the recordings made at the time, which were mostly vocal blues, thus excluding important instrumental pieces, and obeyed the record companies' notions of propriety, thus excluding a good deal of sexually explicit verse that was intrinsic to the idiom. Fortunately a couple of musicians avoided the early death that awaited most of their contemporaries, and thanks to the later-life recordings of Buster Pickens and, particularly, Robert Shaw we know much more than we might have about this fascinating regional substyle.

The 11 tracks from 1963 on *The Ma Grinder* are Shaw's definitive testament. Two years later he suffered a stroke, and he never quite recovered the facility and brio that spill out of 'The Ma Grinder' and 'The Cows' – key pieces of the genre, as are 'Here I Come With My Dirty, Dirty Duckings On', a vocal blues based on one of the themes of 'The Ma Grinder'; 'The Fives' and its companion song 'Whores Is Funky'; and 'Hattie Green', an eight-bar blues named for – but not, in this version, very much about – a Houston madam. Also in this 1963 lode are versions of the Texas song 'Black Gal' and a blues that could hardly fail to appeal to a man in Shaw's business, Charlie McFadden's 'Groceries On My Shelf'.

The later recordings that complete *The Ma Grinder* show no loss of power in his husky singing, and not much in his playing; the piano sound improves dramatically between 1973 and '77 because he had bought a new instrument. There's nothing wrong with the piano heard on *The 1971 Party Tape*, which belonged to the party-giver, fellow pianist and Austin resident Ben Conroy, and although at least a third of the tunes are also on *The Ma Grinder*, the versions are often different in detail. The background chatter is less annoying than the persistent tape hiss, but Konrad Nowakowski's long musicological essay on Shaw's entire recorded repertoire is essential reading.

The reader familiar with either of those albums will find nothing wholly new among Shaw's 11 tracks on *Giants Of Texas Country Blues Piano* (the remainder are by Lavada Durst and Whistlin' Alex Moore). Recorded, as he almost always was, at home, he sounds in good spirits as well as good form, and the chief reasons for hedging the third star are tape hiss (again, though not so bad) and a few tracks that are too short to be properly developed. TR

Thomas Shaw (1908–77)
VOCAL, GUITAR, HARMONICA

The Texas-born Shaw was drawn to music by family tradition and by hearing Blind Lemon Jefferson. In his 20s he travelled and played for some months with J. T. 'Funny Papa' Smith. In 1934 he moved to San Diego, California, and sang for a while on a border radio station. After some decades of playing only at home or for friends he appeared at the 1970 San Diego Folk & Blues Festival. In his last years he recorded for Advent and Blue Goose and visited Europe.

*** **Born In Texas**
Testament TCD 5027 *Shaw; Bob Jefferey (p, v).* 5/71–11/72.

Captivated in his teens by the playing of Blind Lemon Jefferson, Shaw spent many hours mastering some of his lines. The outcome of his labours is most obvious in 'All Out And Down' and 'Stocking Feet Blues', though echoes of Jefferson's playing ring out at several points on this album, an augmented reissue of his Advent LP. He worked on a more equal footing with J. T. Smith, absorbing the carefully constructed guitar parts he recalls in 'Hungry Wolf' and 'Born In Texas'. He also encountered Blind Willie Johnson, whom he remembers in 'Motherless Children', and listened to recordings by Texas Alexander and Lowell Fulson, the probable sources of 'Working Man Blues' and 'Sinners Prayer' respectively. 'Mocking The Trains' is an exercise on his first instrument, the harmonica. Shaw also has a couple of tracks on the VAC *San Diego Blues Jam* (Testament TCD 5029), one a 'Jack Of Diamonds' with slide guitar that is very redolent of Jefferson.

Like many recordings by elderly musicians, these are as frustrating as they are rewarding. Shaw sings with the thick, phlegmy voice of a man in his 60s and his guitar playing, mostly on an electric instrument, is not always as deft as he wants it to be. Through this streaked glass one can discern the outlines of a younger, quicker musician who unfortunately never recorded. TR

Ollie Shepard
VOCAL, PIANO

Despite a moderately productive recording career spread over more than 20 years, Shepard has resisted any attempt at biographical research – though, since he is held in generally low regard, the attempts have probably not been persistent – and is remembered, if at all, only for originating a couple of neatly turned blues that other artists have enjoyed using.

(*) **Ollie Shepard – Vol. 1 (1937–1939)
Document DOCD-5434 *Shepard; unknown (t); unknown (cl, ts);* unknown (cl); Edgar Saucier (as); Chu Berry, unknown (ts); Sammy Price (p); Lonnie Johnson, unknown (g); unknown(s) (b); unknown(s) (d). 10/37–4/39.

(*) **Ollie Shepard – Vol. 2 (1939–1941)
Document DOCD-5435 *Shepard; Theodore McCord (cl, ts); Chu Berry, Walter Wheeler, Stafford 'Pazzuza' Simon (ts); Sammy Price, unknown(s) (p); Lonnie Johnson, George Francis (g); Wellman Braud, unknown (b); Johnny Wells, unknown(s) (d); Ollie Potter, unknowns (v); unknown (sp).* 4/39–5/41.

For almost four years, from 1937 to 1941, Shepard supplied the jukebox trade with efficiently made production-line blues, sung in a highish voice without much pep and accompanied by small bands featuring his own piano, a reeds player or two and from time to time Lonnie Johnson on guitar. Absorbing the products of that diligence at album length does Shepard no favours. For every out-of-the-ordinary lyric like 'Frankenstein Blues' (*Vol. 1*) or the 'Shepard Blues' delivered in Pig Latin (*Vol. 2*), and for every jump number like 'This Place Is Leaping' and 'Solid Jack' on *Vol. 1* or 'Jitterbugs Done Broke It Down' on *Vol. 2*, there is a stack of similar medium-tempo blues on common subjects. 'Jitterbugs' has a dash of Louis Jordan's manner but Shepard cannot command his contemporary's breeziness or his verbal skills, and besides he is shackled, as Jordan was not, to blues tunes – a fact that also reduces the impact of the various reeds players, known and unknown. The sound quality is what should be expected of '30s Decca pressings in generally less than fine condition: drab. TR

Kenny Wayne Shepherd (born 1977)
VOCAL, GUITAR

Shepherd began playing guitar as a boy in Shreveport, Louisiana, and by the age of 13 was good enough to play on stage with Bryan Lee. He formed his own band in 1993 and two years later had a huge success with his debut album, Ledbetter Heights.

*** **Ledbetter Heights**
Giant 28829 *Shepherd; unknown (h); Jimmy Wallace (kb, perc); Al Gamble (kb); Joe Nadeau, Bryan Lee (g); Will Ainsworth, Dave Smith (b); Kevin Smith, Chris Layton, Steve Potts (d); Corey Sterling, Jessica Boucher (v); Buddy Flett, Bruce McCabe (unspecified instruments).* 93–95.

** **Trouble Is …**
Revolution 46270 *Shepherd; James Cotton (h); Jimmy Wallace, Reese Wynans (kb); Joe Nadeau (g); Robby Emerson, Tommy Shannon (b); Sam Bryant, Chris Layton (d); Noah Hunt, Stephanie Spruill, Patricia Hodges (v).* 97.

** **Live On**
Giant 67072 *Shepherd; James Cotton, Michey Raphael (h); Reese Wynans (kb); Bryan Lee, Warren Haynes (g); Keith Christopher, Tommy Shannon, Arion Salazar, Les Claypool (b); Sam Bryant, Chris Layton (d); Noah Hunt, Stephanie Spruill, Patricia Hodges (v).* 99.

Ledbetter Heights is a remarkable debut album for an 18-year-old, though just what went into making it so is irritatingly unclear; it's only in the small print that the listener hears about several 'special guest musicians' whose roles aren't specified. But 'While We Cry', a live recording made earlier than the rest of the album, usefully demonstrates Shepherd's skill as a lyrical guitarist, if one rather obviously modelled on Stevie Ray Vaughan, and a good deal else on the album indicates a talented and versatile player who stands out from the blues-rock pack. There's not much standard blues repertoire but Howlin' Wolf's 'I'm Leaving You (Commit A Crime)' is given an appropriately trenchant reading; Booker White's 'Aberdeen' is quirkier.

Trouble Is … has a more diversified repertoire, embracing Jimi Hendrix's 'I Don't Live Today', Bob Dylan's 'Everything Is Broken' (an over-literal reading) and the more straight-ahead blues of '(Long) Gone' with James Cotton on harmonica. But those shifts of the scenery do little to change the action centre-stage, where it's all melodrama and shouting, and similarly on *Live On* the cast deliver their lines at the top of their voices. Coming after the engaging, and quite individual, *Ledbetter Heights*, these are disappointingly routine trips to blues-rock Babel. TR

Lonnie Shields (born 1956)
VOCAL, GUITAR

Born in West Helena, Arkansas, and now resident in Philadelphia, Shields began in gospel music, then performed Al Green tunes with a high-school funk band, the Shades Of Black. An encounter with Sam Carr and the other members of the Jelly Roll Kings steered his music in a more bluesy direction.

**(*) Portrait
Rooster Blues R 2626 Shields; Anthony Royal (t); Dennis Bates (tb); Lorenzo Smith (as, ts, fl); Eddie Shaw (ts); Jason Seth Roach, Frank Frost (o); Kenneth Lackey (p); Eddie Vaan Shaw, Big Jack Johnson, Lucky Peterson (g); Lafayette 'Shorty' Gilbert, David Porter, Loui Villeri, Jimmy Fickle (b); Robert Plunkett, Sam Carr, Earnest Roy Jr, Russ McCanless (d); Brent Endres (shaker, snare d); Arthneice 'Gas Man' Jones (maracas); 'Bones' Johnson (tamb, claves). late 80s–early 90s.

**(*) Tired Of Waiting
JSP JSPCD 270 Shields; prob. Robert Feiner (bs); David Taylor (o); unknown (p); Johnny Rawls (g); Daryl Johnson (b); Eddie Gillespie (d). 96?

*** Blues Is On Fire
JSP JSPCD 298 Shields; Mike Jones (t); Bruce Feiner (ts); Robert Feiner (bs); Brian Charette (kb, o); Johnny Rawls (g, v); Randy Lippincott (b); Barry Harrison (d); Shemekia Copeland (v). 97?

*** Midnight Delight
Rooster Blues RBLU 2633 Shields; Anthony Royal (t); Dennis Bates (tb); Sidney Ford, John Sangster (ts); L. C. Luckett (kb, p, g, b); Johnny Rawls (o, p, g); Charles Hodges (o); James 'Super Chikan' Johnson (g); Eric Thomas (b); Fast Eddie Gillespie (d). 90s.

Shields's music synthesizes elements from gospel, soul, funk and blues; his singing owes much to Al Green, Z. Z. Hill and other Southern soul heroes. He's a competent guitarist, and a fecund songwriter, but these CDs do not suggest that he's the new hope of the blues. Too often, Shields's songs and solos simply go on until they stop; rather than developing and exploring his songs, or exploiting soul music's accumulation and release of tension, Shields putters repetitiously around the idea that was the germ of each song. Production that tries to supply the missing ingredient with busy horn sections usually fails to hit the mark; what does work, on the evidence of *Portrait*'s three tracks with the Jelly Roll Kings, is combining Shields with a small band whose drummer goads the rhythm rather than guiding it. The best and most fervent track on *Midnight Delight*, 'Arkansas Is My Home (No.2)', is a tribute to Frank Frost and Sam Carr. The other catalyst that's usually missing is personal involvement. *Blues Is On Fire*'s 'Doin' Time' reacts to the toils of a paternity suit with genuine anger, and a guitar solo that's a passionate, logical outgrowth from the lyrics. These songs are exceptional in Shields's *oeuvre*; that they both owe a good deal to 'Cummins Prison Farm' perhaps indicates the limits of his creativity. CS

Johnny Shines (1915–92)
VOCAL, GUITAR

Like David 'Honeyboy' Edwards, John Ned Lee Shines had to spend much of his adult life talking about his brief association with Robert Johnson, as if this in some way defined or illuminated his own musical talent. This he did with the characteristic patience of an alert observer of human nature. The combination of Shines's vocal power, his perceptive and sensitive songwriting and his dynamic guitar playing, with finger or slide, made him a singularly gifted individual whose true worth was never sufficiently acknowledged or rewarded during his lifetime.

***(*) Chicago Blues – Vol. 1 (1939–1951)
Document DOCD-5270 Shines; Little Walter (h); Jimmy Rogers (g); Ernest 'Big' Crawford, unknown (b); unknown (d). 2/46–10/50.

Shines's uncompromising vocal power and an overcombative drummer helped to consign his debut session, for Columbia, to the vault. An early harbinger of the revitalized country blues that swept through postwar Chicago, this four-song date was at marked odds with the sophistication of the label's roster. For all his commanding presence, there's melancholia discernible in 'Delta Pine Blues' and 'Evil Hearted Woman Blues', the latter performed to the template of Johnson's 'Kind Hearted Woman'. Almost five years later, Shines's Chess single 'Joliet Blues'/'So Glad I Found You', with Walter and Rogers providing idiomatic support, suffered from the label's perception of a challenge to Muddy Waters's supremacy, an early instance of the perverse circumstances that would dog Shines's later career. For the other tracks on this VAC, by Alfred Fields and Tony Hollins, see COMPILATIONS: CHICAGO I (PREWAR).

**** Evening Shuffle – The Complete J.O.B. Recordings 1952–53
[Westside WESM 635] Shines; J. T. Brown (ts); Walter Horton (h); Sunnyland Slim (p); J. B. Lenoir (g); Moody Jones (b); Alfred Wallace (d). 4/52–1/53.

Despite its damaged state, 'Ramblin'', Shines's adaptation of Johnson's 'Walking Blues', is rightly regarded as a milestone in '50s Chicago blues. The blend of tremulous slide guitar and his full-throated vocal roar creates an atmosphere like no other. 'Fish Tail' is likewise a rebranding of 'Terraplane Blues', its *double entendres* more transparent. A second J.O.B. session brought forth another masterpiece of a different kind. 'Brutal Hearted Woman' is essentially a lopsided duet with Horton, the latter playing three blistering choruses of harmonica either side of Shines's two verses. Two further takes show how this was brought about. Shines also recorded two songs as part of Sunnyland Slim And His Boys. 'Please Don't' is fairly ordinary but 'Livin' In The White House' updates Broonzy's 'Just A

Dream' with perceptive satire. A short but essential sampling of Shines's formative work.

**(*) Chicago/The Blues/Today! Volume 3
Vanguard VMD 79218 *Shines; Walter Horton (h); Floyd Jones (b); Frank Kirkland (d). 12/65.*

This bears all the hallmarks of a rushed, ill-prepared session. Shines's strutting slide guitar obliterates his rhythm team in 'Dynaflow' (another 'Terraplane') but neither Jones nor Kirkland sounds entirely at ease during the whole sequence of six songs. Horton is absent on this and 'Mr Boweevil' and plays within himself except on 'Black Spider Blues'. Coaxed out of retirement for this session, Shines powers on his way regardless, one of a rare breed that tries never to put on a bad performance, although a final 'Hey, Hey', based on the 'My Babe' changes, staggers into a welcome fade. The other contributors to the album are Horton (as leader) and Johnny Young.

*** Masters Of Modern Blues
Testament TCD 5002 *Shines; Walter Horton (h); Otis Spann (p); Lee Jackson (b); Fred Below (d). 6/66.*

An album that caused consternation when it was first released, for its portrayal of Shines as a band musician rather than an acoustic revivalist. The ten tracks are evenly divided between slide and finger-playing, with Horton and Spann absent from the slide pieces. In fact, Horton is present on only three titles and virtually inaudible on all of them. Best of the slide features is 'Walkin' Blues', with just Below's drums to provide the impetus, although the metallic tone of Shines's amplifier is always jarring. The ensemble songs include 'Trouble Is All I See' and 'What Kind Of Little Girl Are You' but Spann's solos are indecisive, as is the whole band on other instrumental choruses. Once again, Shines's vocal power carries the day but a residual impression of disappointment is impossible to avoid.

***(*) With Big Walter Horton
Testament TCD 5015 *As above, except Horton also sings; add Luther Allison (g), Prince Candy (b), Bill Brown (d). 6/66, 1/69.*

Five further tracks from the previous session are combined to much better effect with a 1969 California date. 'Till I Made My Tonsils Sore' and 'I Want To Warn You' would have beefed up the earlier album and a raucous brawl through 'You Don't Have To Go' was only excluded for its indecisive end. Horton is on much better form at the later session, playing a typically robust solo on the opening 'Hello Central' and taking the lead on two takes of an instrumental, 'Sneakin' And Hidin'. He also sings uncredited on 'If It Ain't Me'. Allison is busy but tasteful in a Buddy Guy manner. Despite the rough-and-ready mix, Shines really does sound like a band singer and his lyrics, particularly in 'Tonsils' and two takes of 'I Cry, I Cry', are incisive and literate. No disappointment here.

**(*) Johnny Shines 1915–1992
Wolf 120.914 *Shines; Walter Horton (h); Sunnyland Slim (p); Willie Dixon (b); Clifton James (d). 70–4/74.*

An arbitrary combination of live gigs in Boston and St Louis is hardly the tribute this set's title implies. Four titles by Dixon's Chicago All Stars are ragged and poorly recorded, Shines's vocals are buried in the mix and the ensembles fail to gell. Four years later in St Louis and better recorded, Shines charms a small but enthusiastic audience with self-deprecating introductions and an overlong, homiletic 'Just A Little Tenderness'. Earlier performances of 'Bumble Bee Blues', 'Workin' On The Station' and 'Moanin' The Blues' are more impressive but overall this is an album for completists rather than casual enquirers.

♛ **** Standing At The Crossroads
Testament TCD 5022 *Shines. 11/70.*

Few blues albums in recent decades have been as consistently good as this. As adept a band musician as Shines may be, he is at his best performing solo. Much of what he plays here is in the spirit but not the image of Robert Johnson, with echoes of Charley Patton, Son House and Tommy McClennan. His guitar playing, with finger and slide, is near-faultless, solidly rhythmic but precisely nuanced, his vocal power contained but perfectly balanced with its accompaniment. Shines's songwriting at its best is of a quality seldom encountered in his contemporaries, his narrative ability and humanity always on display, interspersed with startling imagery as encountered in the previously unissued 'Crying Black Angel', 'Death Hearse Blues' (in two versions, one with slide) and 'Your Troubles Can't Be Like Mine'. Essentially a chamber work, and an achievement that Shines rarely surpassed.

*** Johnny Shines
Hightone HCD 8028 *Shines; David Ii (bs); Nat Dove (p); Phillip Walker (g); Charles Jones (b); Murl Downy (d). 11/70, 6/74.*

With the exception of 'Ramblin'', a solo piece from 1974, this album was recorded on one of the days between the two taken for *Standing At The Crossroads*. Five tracks are accompanied by Phillip Walker's band, who really gell only on 'Have To Pay The Cost' and 'My Love Can't Hide', an acknowledged adaptation of 'I Can't Quit You Baby'. Elsewhere, the musicians fail to accomodate Shines's staccato amplified slide work. Slide, both acoustic and electric, dominates the other six titles, including 'Skull & Crossbones Blues', 'Vallie Lee' and 'Can't Get Along With You'. These are more satisfying than the band tracks but not as masterful as those on the Testament session, making this an enjoyable but inessential collection. NS

*** Heritage Of The Blues: Skull & Crossbones Blues
Hightone HCD 8153 *As for Testament and Hightone CDs above. 6/66–11/70.*

Dave Alvin's selection from Shines's Testament and Hightone albums concentrates on the 6/66 session that produced *Masters Of Modern Blues*, drawing seven tracks from it, which leaves room only for 'Fat Mama' from *With Big Walter Horton* and a couple each from *Standing At The Crossroads* and *Johnny Shines*. This would not have been every admirer's pick, but it makes a very listenable if short (37.09) sampling. TR

*** Hey Ba-Ba-Re-Bop!
Rounder CD 2020 *Shines. 71.*

There are times here where Shines's cruise control seems to have been engaged; his performances are worthy but generally lack the spark that ignites 'When Your Troubles Get Like Mine'. Both this and the 'Milk Cow Blues' that follows draw spontaneous reactions from his audience – but then they also hail a perfunctory (make that obligatory) 'Kind Hearted Woman' and the curiously free-form 'I Will Be Kind'. 'Saddle

My Pony', 'Mean Mistreater' and 'Going To The River' have their moments but stop short of real involvement. Nevertheless, a competent live set by a superlative artist who can be forgiven for not rising completely to the challenge.

***(*) Takin' The Blues Back South
Black & Blue BB 437 *Shines; Luther Johnson (g).* 11–12/72.

Shines's adherence to decades-old techniques might be seen as anachronistic but he performs with enough authority to obviate the thought. He seems here to be yielding to the expectation of Robert Johnson-related material, with stylistic phrases and verses interspersed in 'The Devil's Daughter', 'Back To The Steel Mill' and a hectic 'Freight Train'. This is one of four tracks with additional guitar from Luther Johnson, including two recordings of 'Mean Black Gobbler'. The superiority of Shines's writing, articulate and imaginative, is evident in the previously unissued 'Blood Ran Like Wine' and 'Abide My Wish'. Apart from a couple of rushed tempos, Shines's guitar playing is rhythmically sound and consistently appropriate to the text of each song, lacking only the poise evident in his best work.

***(*) Traditional Delta Blues
Biograph BCD 121 *Shines.* 72–74.

Apart from another version of 'Ramblin' Blues', 'Arguing And Noodling' and a 'Dynaflow Blues' that's almost word-perfect with 'Terraplane Blues', Shines eschews the Johnson influence and includes songs from the Mississippi Sheiks, Memphis Minnie and Charley Patton in a programme whose familiarity is its only drawback. Shines sings and plays as well as ever, using the slide less often and relying more on the churning rhythms of north Mississippi blues. 'Glad Rags' is an imaginative adaptation of 'Vicksburg Blues' and 'Jim String' is an extended narrative about a Binghamton pimp and his whore. He also pays tribute to a then still living Howlin' Wolf in 'Little Wolf', the name Shines was given early in his musical career.

**(*) Mr Cover Shaker
Biograph BCD 125 *Shines; Peter Ecklund (c, t); John Payne (s); Lou Terricciano (p); Richard Tiven, Jay Ungar (vn); David Bromberg (md, g); Tony Markellis (b); Mark Bell (d); Jean Leiberman, Beverly Rohlehr, Jane Simms (v).* 72–74.

A curious hybrid, this album combines all but three tracks (two were added to *Traditional Delta Blues*) from the Biograph LP *Johnny Shines And Company*, with six previously unreleased solo recordings from the *Traditional Delta Blues* session. The latter are the equal of their session-mates, including rerecordings of 'The Devil's Daughter' and 'Blood Ran Like Wine'. Another version of the second song is part of the band session in which artist and musicians battle in vain to find common cause. Different combinations of instruments are tried, with only 'I'm Getting Old' and 'Lost Love Letter Blues' enjoying limited success. Shines sounds resigned on most of the songs, although he responds fitfully to the choir accompanying him on 'Stand By Me'. A failed experiment, insufficiently sweetened by the solo material. NS

*** Worried Blues Ain't Bad
Labor LAB 7011 *Shines; Don Audet (h); Richard Baker (g); Bob Derkach (b).* 2/74.

The accompanists contribute to only four tracks; in some of the other nine Shines explores music he seldom performed, tracing in 'Country Blues' the tune of 'Guitar Rag' and in 'Deep Freeze' a theme of Blind Lemon Jefferson's. The Robert Johnson connection is evoked only in the melody and last stanza of 'About My Wish', derived from 'Hell Hound On My Trail'. The album is bookended by two pieces, 'Slavery Time Breakdown' and 'Goodbye', that are imagined memories of slavery in the form of field holler and hymn respectively. Though not essential to an appreciation of Shines's art, the album has rewards for its devotees. TR

*** 'Live' In Europe 1975
Document DOCD-32-20-7 *Shines.* 2/75.

Recorded over three nights at Jazzland, Vienna, Shines mixes originals with well-known songs, among them his only known recording of 'Got My Mojo Working', which is disfigured by idiot clapping on all four beats, but features a strange, fascinating one-chord accompaniment. On some of the songs in standard tuning Shines's chords are minimalist and desultory; some numbers go on too long; and some of the changes of vocal dynamics are so abrupt as to seem mannered. Nevertheless, for much of the time Shines seems to sense and respond to his audience's respect for him and the blues; especially when he plays slide guitar accompaniments, the controlled ferocity and the unity of voice and instrument that he was capable of at his best are manifest. CS

***(*) Too Wet To Plow
Labor LAB 7003//Corazong 255024 *Shines; Louisiana Red (h, g, v); Sugar Blue (h); Ron Rault (b).* 9/75.

There's an air of 'best behaviour' about this set, which nevertheless contains some very fine music. Shines and Red both wield their bottlenecks to stirring effect, with Red clinging to his early Muddy Waters fetish. The full group plays on just two selections, 'Too Wet To Plow' and Red's 'Red Sun', sung to the tune of 'Roll And Tumble'. Blue's harmonica is present on six songs, including 'Pay Day Woman', a duet made more dramatic by his use of the bass notes of the chromatic instrument. Red and Blue both play harmonica on 'Winding Mind' and the former duets with Shines on 'The Wind Is Blowin''. Best of Shines's four solo performances is '30 Days In Jail', where the precision of his slide technique triumphs over an accelerating tempo. 'Hot Tamale' is an unwelcome token nod to Robert Johnson that prevents this from being a wholly excellent album.

*** Back To The Country
Blind Pig BP 74391 *Shines; Snooky Pryor (h); John Nicholas (p, g); Kent Duchaine (g).* 91.

There's pleasure and pain in this late session. Shines, who had suffered a stroke, plays no guitar but Nicholas substitutes ably with slide and finger. Despite the partnership implied by a joint credit, Shines and Pryor play together only on reworkings of 'Cool Driver' and 'Evening Sun' and an original, 'Moon Is Rising', while Pryor has just four songs to himself, the best 'Send Your Man To War'. It was a mistake to open with Shines's strained vocal in 'Trouble In Mind' and to follow it with Pryor's 'Corrine Corrina'. Shines's voice gets stronger and reaches its peak in Nicholas's 'Peace In Hell' and yet another 'Terraplane'. But conflicting emotional responses to the quality and nature of the recordings make this a hard record to quantify. NS

J. D. Short (1902–62)
VOCAL, GUITAR, HARMONICA, BASS DRUM

Born in Port Gibson, Mississippi, and raised in Clarksdale, Short was cousin to Big Joe Williams and Honeyboy Edwards. He'd mastered harmonica, piano and guitar by the time he moved to St Louis in 1923. There he added clarinet, saxophone and drums, and in the '30s played clarinet in Douglas Williams's swing band. Sam Charters, who recorded Short in 1962, remembered him as a gentle character, but it was not always so; in 1932 he stabbed Henry Townsend, who in due course removed Short's testicles with a bullet. This didn't prevent Short being drafted in World War II, but he was injured in training and discharged. Thereafter he made a precarious living as a junk man until his death.

***(*) St. Louis Country Blues (1929–1937)
Document DOCD-5147 *Short*. c. 6/30–8/33.
**** St. Louis Blues
Wolf WSE 115 *Short; James 'Stump' Johnson (p, v), Georgia Boyd (v)*. c. 6/30–8/33.

Only two songs of the six that Short recorded for Paramount have been found, and only three of the four cut for Vocalion; it's generally agreed that a disc credited to Joe Stone is also by Short. These seven sides are made exceptional by Short's insistent guitar rhythms, his heavy vocal vibrato and some highly original lyrics, dealing *inter alia* with riverboats, phallic rattlesnakes and the hoodoo powers of both craneflies and Short himself. 'Hard Time Blues' blends realism with optimism, and ranks with *The Grapes Of Wrath* as an artistic response to the Depression.

Document present the magnificent seven alongside Henry Townsend's early recordings, somewhat ironically in view of their passage of arms. Document's sound is outclassed by Wolf, who add two accompaniments and eight tracks of apocrypha to the canon. Tidy-minded listeners have suggested a number of other singers as pseudonymous Shorts: 'Neckbones' is now known to have been Willie Fields; 'Spider' Carter and Ell-Zee Floyd don't convince. R. T. Hanen is a more plausible candidate, but the verdict remains 'not proven'. Even if none of them is Short, all these artists are worth hearing; so are four instrumentals and two accompaniments by Henry Brown, but they are ill-assorted additions, plainly included to extend a former LP's playing time.

Short recorded again in later years, playing rack harp and occasional bass drum with his guitar, which perhaps as a result became less complex. His lyrics remained very interesting, and his heavy rhythms and accelerating tempos could generate great excitement. In 1958 Short accompanied Joe Williams on *Stavin' Chain Blues* (Delmark DD-609), and sang on three tracks, two of them important versions of the badman ballad that gives the disc its title. Sam Charters's recordings generated one and a half LPs of very worthwhile material: *Blues From The Mississippi Delta*, shared with Son House, can be ordered from Smithsonian Folkways as a custom CD (Folkways F-2467). At presstime Universal were planning to reissue the deleted Sonet CD *Legacy Of The Blues Vol. 8*; look for *The Sonet Blues Story: J. D. Short*. CS

Ian Siegal (born 1974)
VOCAL, GUITAR

Siegal began singing and playing guitar in his teens, busked around Europe and returned to England determined to make his way in music. He has built up a following on the British club circuit, opening for Bill Wyman's Rhythm Kings and touring in a duo with Big Bill Morganfield, but is presently better known in Europe.

**** Meat & Potatoes
Nugene NUG 502 *Siegal; Giles King (h); Jonny Henderson (kb, o); Matt Schofield (g); Andy Graham (b); Nikolaj Bjerre (d, perc)*. 2–3/05.

Imagine a liaison between Howlin' Wolf and Big Mama Thornton. Imagine a son. What sort of singer might he be? One very like Ian Siegal, perhaps. He certainly affirms this hypothetical ancestry in his references to Wolf, which are scattered prodigally through *Meat & Potatoes* in vocals, lyrics and tunes alike, notably on the title number, redolent of 'Back Door Man'. But these are not Wolf covers, nor generic blues of any kind: Siegal writes with a blues sensibility but seldom in blues commonplaces, and pieces like 'Sugar Rush', 'Butter-Side Up' and 'Drowned My Sorrows (But They Sure Learned How To Swim)' hold the listener as much with their wit or verbal resourcefulness as with the vigour and shrewd dynamics of their music. Schofield and Henderson lend occasional support, as skilfully as you would expect from the former's albums, but the core trio of Siegal, Graham and Bjerre is highly listenable on its own, Siegal having a particularly idiomatic touch on acoustic slide guitar. Grounded in tradition, airborne by imagination, this album is a rare combination of cleverness and craft. TR

Corky Siegel (born 1943)
VOCAL, HARMONICA, PIANO

Siegel met guitarist/singer Jim Schwall (born 1942) in 1964, when they were studying at Roosevelt University in Chicago; they began playing together and soon dropped out of college (or, as Siegel puts it, 'just stopped going'). As well as working in Chicago clubs like Pepper's Lounge they recorded numerous albums as the Siegel–Schwall Band for Vanguard and Wooden Nickel. After the band broke up in 1974 Siegel worked in his own name, both in blues contexts and as a guest soloist with various symphony orchestras. The latter encounters led him to focus on composing material that fused Western classical music and blues, and he has played this 'chamber blues' with his own group since 1983. Meanwhile the Siegel–Schwall band, having reunited for a concert in 1987, has continued to regroup for a few performances a year ever since.

** The Complete Vanguard Recordings & More!
Vanguard 190/92 3CD *Siegel; Jim Schwall (md, g, v); Jo Davidson (b, v); Jack Dawson, Rollo Bradford (b); Russ Chadwick, Shelly Plotkin (d)*. 65–70.
**(*) The Reunion Concert
Alligator ALCD 4760 *Siegel; Jim Schwall (g, v); Rollo Radford (b, v); Sam Lay (d)*. 87.
**(*) Flash Forward
Alligator ALCD 4906 *Siegel; Jim Schwall (ac, md, g, v); Sam Lay (g, d, v); Rollo Radford (b, v); Marcy Levy, Holly Siegel (v)*. 05.

These albums are all by, and credited to, the Siegel–Schwall Band. The Vanguard 3CD gathers the contents of their four LPs for the company, together with outtakes from the first and last and a couple of earlier demo tracks. The best one can say of these albums is that the band's versions of received material often show some originality of choice and approach, and that the insubstantiality of the ensemble playing seems to be largely the fault of Sam Charters, who produced the first three. Neither Siegel nor Schwall was at this point a compelling singer, and anyone expecting music with the power or focus of, say, the Butterfield Blues Band will be disappointed. The final LP, from 1970, had a different producer and a beefier sound that foregrounded Schwall's snarling guitar, but the verdict of today's listener will probably be 'too little, too late'. The band's subsequent albums have been digested in *The Very Best – The Wooden Nickel Years (1971–1974)* (Varèse Vintage 6006), and Siegel's work thereafter on *Solo Flight 1975–1980* (Gadfly 254), but the availability of both collections is uncertain.

A couple of decades on, the group's basic sound has changed very little. If they come over better on *The Reunion Concert*, it may be because they have a superior bass player (Radford didn't join them until the last Vanguard album), or because the Vic Theatre has more presence than a studio, or simply because they are more seasoned musicians. At any rate, the spacious, open-weave ensemble sounds more natural, especially in the slow pieces 'Devil' and 'When I've Been Drinkin'. Reassembling again, most of another 20 years later, they get down and dirty on 'The Underqualified Blues', an amusing Schwall lyric to a standard slow-blues melody, but the combination of Siegel's light voice and Levy and Radford's backing vocals on 'Deja Vous' and other numbers has an odd whiff of Dan Hicks & The Hot Licks. The appeal of this band may always be somewhat indeterminate to listeners who know them only from their records.

*** **Corky Siegel's Chamber Blues**
Alligator ALCD 4824 *Siegel; Katherine Hughes, Lisa Wurman, Corinne Stillwell (vn); Richard Halajian (vl); Felix Wurman, Jill Kaeding (vc); Frank Donaldson (tabla, perc); band (v).* 94.

*** **Corky Siegel's Travelling Chamber Blues Show**
Alligator ALCD 4901 *Siegel; Mark Agnor, Jeff Yang, Randy Sabien (vn); Nell Flanders, Richard Halajian (vl); Jill Kaeding (vc); Rollo Radford (b, v); Frank Donaldson (tabla, perc).* 05.

Even readers who instinctively bristle at the idea of fusing blues and 'classical music' – in this instance chamber music in the European tradition – should try to find the patience to listen to Siegel's 'chamber blues'; they may be pleasantly surprised. His fellow musicians are of his generation or younger and able, as many orchestral players are not, to participate vigorously and even spontaneously in unconventional music. Siegel, for his part, is technically and expressively gifted not only on his primary instrument but also on piano, as he demonstrates in 'Concerto For Alberti Blues Piano (Opus 6)' on *Chamber Blues*, while Donaldson's tabla and percussion parts tauten lines that might sometimes meander a little. This is music that has prompted a wide range of reactions, and many readers will not share our cautious approval. Siegel appears to be alone among blues musicians in this experiment, and it's too early to know if he will be seen as brave pioneer or mad scientist. TR

Maynard Silva
VOCAL, GUITAR

Silva, who is based in Martha's Vineyard, Massachusetts, has worked both as a solo acoustic performer and in an electric band setting. His slide guitar playing is partly modelled on that of J. B. Hutto, whom he sometimes accompanied in Boston in the late '70s.

(*) **Howl At The Moon
Wolf 120.288 *Silva; Tom Waicunas (h); Silvertone Steve [Coveney] (g); Charmaine Tam, Steve Morawiec, Norman McCloud (b); Steve Gallagher, Leroy Pina (d).* mid-90s?

Although only one of his songs is included, this set is obviously intended to evoke the spirit of J. B. Hutto: the band is billed as The New Hawks, and includes in Coveney a musician who was close to Hutto in his last years. Silva's playing is not as raw as Hutto's, still less his singing, which is throaty but restrained, but in numbers like 'Somebody Knocked On My Door', 'Hard Luck Alley Cat' and the title track the angular guitar lines compose a recognizable sketch of Hutto's manner. 'Hip Shakin'' gets even closer, since Silva is not only playing a Hutto composition but has (for this cut only) the backing of three former Hawks, Coveney, McCloud and Pina. 'Black Bottom' is done in the style of its composer, Booker White, another of Silva's models. TR

Terrance Simien (born 1966)
VOCAL, ACCORDION

Simien was raised in Mallet, Louisiana, and began playing accordion in 1981, inspired by seeing Clifton Chenier at Slim's Y-Ki-Ki in Opelousas. He was also influenced by Sam Cooke, Bob Marley and Bob Dylan, and has incorporated elements of their music into his own. An active proponent of Creole culture, he has given musical history lessons in schools.

** **There's Room For Us All**
Aim 1049 *Simien; Renard Poche (tb); Tim Green (ts); Reggie Dallas (bs); Daryl Johnson (o, p, string syn, b, v); Danny Williams, Art Neville (o, p); Bill Dillon (p, md, electric sitar, psg, guitorgan, g, b); Jeffrey Greenberg (g, maracas, v); Russell Dorion, Leo Nocentelli (g); John 'Popp' Esprite, George Porter Jr (b); Willie Green (d, perc); Mitch Marine, Ronald Jones, Russell Batiste (d); Ralph Fontenot (rb, perc); Donald Ray Charles, Michael Ward (perc); Sean Tauzier, Teresita Alsador, Suzanne Bonseigneur (v).* 5/92, 1–2/93.

(**) **Positively Beadhead**
Tone-Cool 1173 *Simien; Danny Williams (kb, v); Nicole 'Nicky' Yarling (vn); Wayne Dalcourt (g); Nick Lewis, Harold Scott (b); Dowell Davis (d, v); Ralph Fontenot (rb).* 99.

** **The Tribute Sessions**
Aim 5009 *Simien; Danny Williams (kb, v); Djalma Garnier (vn); Glenn LeBlanc (g); Nick Lewis (b); Danny Devillier (d, perc); Ralph Fontenot (rb).* 01.

(**) **Creole For Kidz And The History Of Zydeco**
Terrance Simien Music 1891 *Simien; Danny Williams (kb, v); Glenn LeBlanc (vn, g); Nick Lewis (b); Danny Devillier (d, perc); Ralph Fontenot (rb); Grandpa Matthew Simien, Marcella Simien (v); Senator Donald Cravins (narration).* 02?

Simien's music has sporadic connections with the older zydeco styles of Boozoo Chavis and Clifton Chenier, but almost none with the *nouveau zydeco* of Beau Jocque or Chris Ardoin. Its points of reference seem rather to be in New Orleans R&B, and its open, airy textures indicate an admiration for the Neville Brothers, which becomes outright imitation in the title track of *There's Room For Us All*. This CD (formerly on Black Top CDBT 1096) does have some old zydeco material like Chavis's 'Dog Hill' and tunes from John Delafose and Fernest Arceneaux, but Simien's accordion playing is too unassertive to give them much character. 'Jolie Blonde', one of the few examples of old repertoire on *Positively Beadhead*, is similarly bleached by anaemic fiddling. This is not to argue that Simien should be valued only for his fidelity to the past, but on present evidence his own music seems stylistically unsettled.

The Tribute Sessions looks set to contradict the opening words of this review. Simien pays his respects to past masters of Creole (and other) music, first with spoken introductions that put them in historical context, then with well-known examples of their work. While there is nothing to take exception with in what he says (though the repeated dreamy backing track is annoying), his performances of John Delafose's 'Joe Pete Got Two Women' and pieces by Clifton Chenier and Rockin' Dopsie give little sense of the originating artists, and 'Les Barres De La Prison' none at all of Canray Fontenot.

Nevertheless, it was clear from that album that Simien had some ability to make Creole tradition accessible to people unfamiliar with it, and his next project, a patchwork of music and narrative designed for entertainment and edification, was hailed as 'address[ing] a long standing need in Louisiana's educational system'. How successfully it fulfils that purpose will be for others to judge. Adult readers from other backgrounds will probably teach themselves about Creole music more efficaciously with *Zydeco: The Early Years* (Arhoolie CD 307) and other CDs described in COMPILATIONS: ZYDECO. TR

Little Mack Simmons (1933–2000)
VOCAL, HARMONICA

As a boy in Arkansas Malcolm Simmons used to play harmonica with his neighbour James Cotton; years later, in Chicago, they often played on each other's records. He formed his first band in Chicago in 1955, and over the next decade and a half was active among the clubs and small record labels. In the '70s he bought his own club and installed a recording studio above it, moves financed by drug dealing that eventually led to his arrest. Although he received a suspended sentence, he lost most of his assets and later, in a fire, the studio, setbacks which sidelined him for much of the '80s, but he returned to the music business in the mid-'90s with a series of estimable CDs.

**(*) Chicago Blues Harmonica Wizard
Famous Groove FG 971051 Simmons; unknowns (t); unknown (tb); John Jackson, Butterscotch (ts); Willie Henderson, unknown (bs); unknowns (s); unknown (fl); James Cotton (h); Detroit Jr (o, p); Lafayette Leake (o); unknown (p); Eddie King, T. Jones, William McDonald, Nat Charles, Lonnie Brooks, William 'Dead Eye' Norris, unknowns (g); Bob Anderson, Kinner Scott, Paul Myers, Robert Covington, Danny Ray Simmons, unknowns (b); Robert Whitehead, Richard Robinson, Billy Davenport, unknowns (d); unknowns (v). 59–70s.

*** The PM/Simmons Collection
Electro-Fi 3360 Simmons; Butterscotch (ts); Willie Henderson (bs); Detroit Jr (o, p); Lonnie Brooks, William 'Dead Eye' Norris (g); Robert Covington, Danny Ray Simmons (b); Billy Davenport (d). 71–82.

The best of Simmons's singles show that he had the knack of delivering conventional blues with unusual energy and flair. 'Times Are Getting Tougher' and 'Don't Come Back' are urgently sung with biting guitar by Eddie King, while 'Mother-In-Law' and 'Woman, Help Me', covers of Junior Parker and Sonny Boy Williamson II respectively, have expressive harp. These and four others from the same label are on the VAC *Meat & Gravy from Bea & Baby* (Castle CMDDD 610 2CD), but all eight are also on *Chicago Blues Harmonica Wizard*, together with 21 other tracks from the '60s and '70s. This is a good-value collection with two drawbacks, poor sound (which is intrinsic to the source material) and no notes.

The PM/Simmons Collection is drawn from a decade or so of self-produced recordings for his own labels. (A few of those also crept into the foregoing CD.) The repertoire encompasses straight-ahead blues like 'Messing With The Kid' and 'Key To The Highway', a mostly instrumental version of 'Rainy Night In Georgia' in an ambitious arrangement with strings, and a sprinkling of soul numbers like the Ohio Players' 'Skin Tight' that he handles with great assurance. Also included are Fenton Robinson's 'Cryin' The Blues', which Simmons produced in 1970, and the amusing 'I'm A Streaker Baby' by the excellent and under-appreciated singer and songwriter Arelean Brown (1924–81), one of three tracks from her 1977 Simmons album *Sings The Blues In The Loop*.

**(*) Blue Lights
Black & Blue BB 450 Simmons; Willie Mabon (p); Lonnie Brooks, Hubert Sumlin (g); Dave Myers (b); Fred Below (d). 12/75.

Blue Lights was recorded on the same day as Hubert Sumlin's *My Guitar And Me*, which employed the same musicians except Simmons, and is equally lacklustre. Of the several songs credited to Simmons, 'Mother-In-Law Blues' actually belonged to Junior Parker, 'Freight Train Arrives' is a mishearing of 'Train I Ride', i.e. 'Mystery Train' (Parker again), and 'I Sure Quit You' is Howlin' Wolf's 'Killin' Floor' (which begins 'I should have quit you'). Sumlin, who played so fiercely on the original 'Killin' Floor', fails to ignite this version. Simmons sings and plays well enough, but everyone else goes about his business as if his thoughts are elsewhere.

*** Come Back To Me Baby (Chicago Blues Session Volume 38)
Wolf 120.884 Simmons; Detroit Jr (p); John Primer, George Baze, Jake Dawson (g); Nick Holt, Willie Kent (b); Earl Howell, Tim Taylor (d); Georgia Hinton Simmons (v). 6–12/94.

**** High & Lonesome
St George STG 7704 Simmons; Tuxedo Ron De War (ts); Mark Brumbach, Erwin Helfer (p); Jr Kreher, Studebaker John (g); Big Mojo Elem, Mike McCurdy (b); Twist Turner (d); George Paulus (prod). 94–95.

Though recorded within a year or so of each other, these are very different albums. If they were cars, the Wolf's bodywork would have the gleam of regular care, while the St George would look like a mud-spattered farm truck. *Come Back To Me Baby* has mainly original songs and polished accompaniment, chiefly by the Primer–Baze–Holt–Howell quartet, in the modern Chicago style. *High & Lonesome* is almost all other people's songs, by such as Elmore James, Little Walter, Howlin' Wolf and Sonny Boy Williamsons I and II, given skilfully reconstructed '40s and '50s settings and then sequenced to emphasize their variety of style and tempo. Simmons is in fine voice and plays very well on both, but he seems to enjoy the St George session a lot more, and, unless you have no taste for the retro sound that the producer and musicians dedicated themselves to creating, so, probably, will you.

**** Little Mack Is Back
Electro-Fi 3355 *Simmons; Tyler Yarema (o, p); Teddy Leonard, Morgan Davis (g); Omar Tunnoch (b, v); Ed White (d, v).* 10/96.

*** Somewhere On Down The Line
Electro-Fi 3356 *As above, except Yarema also sings; add Al Lerman (ts, h, g, v), Joe Yanuziello (g), Nik Tjelios (md); omit Davis.* 71, 7/97.

*** The Best Of Little Mack Simmons: The Electro-Fi Years
Electro-Fi 3368 *As for all Electro-Fi CDs. 70s, 96–97.*

On his debut album for Electro-Fi, the label that would promote him for the remainder of his life, Little Mack was not just back but better than ever. He approached his mid-60s in good voice and with his harmonica skill untarnished, but the enthusiasm that had radiated from his previous recordings seemed even warmer. He had lost none of his ability to pick an unexpected song and handle it with panache – witness the country song 'Lie To Me' – or to prod a sleeping dog of an old standard into alertness, as he does with 'My Babe' or the boogaloosened version of 'Five Long Years'. *Little Mack Is Back* seemed likely to be the harbinger of an unusually sunny Indian summer, and its successor put no more than a cloud or two in the sky. Versions of 'The Things I Used To Do' and 'All Around The World' are, by his standards, ordinary, but he strolls easily down a Muddy road on 'Trouble No More' and 'I'm Ready', takes his own 'Hooked On Your Love' at a cracking pace and lopes through 'Snap Your Fingers' as if born within the sound of the Grand Ole Opry. The bonus track, 'Next Time You See Me' from 1971, was a trailer for *The PM/Simmons Collection* (above).

The Best Of contains seven tracks from *Little Mack Is Back*, five from *Somewhere On Down The Line*, the chromatic harp instrumental 'Blue Lite' from *The PM/Simmons Collection* and previously unissued 1/97 recordings of 'Five Long Years' and 'Mystery Train'. It ends with the social homily 'Revelation Blues', an appropriate *envoi* to an open-hearted man. TR

Frankie Lee Sims (1917–70)
VOCAL, GUITAR

Born in New Orleans, Sims spent his adult years in Texas. Like Smokey Hogg and Ernest Lewis, both of whom he resembles at times, he came from an older musical tradition that initially paid scant attention to metre, although his later records managed to conform. His rough-and-ready songs, which occasionally dipped into traditional themes, were precursors of what became designated 'juke-joint music', as purveyed by Frank Frost, Junior Kimbrough and T-Model Ford.

**** Lucy Mae Blues
Specialty SPCD-7022//Ace CDCHD 423 *Sims; unknown (h);* *unknown (p); unknown (b); Herbert Washington, unknown (d).* 3/53–2/54.

The title track was Sims's first and only hit, sung with a vocal timbre that resembles Sonny Terry. Both his vocals and his guitar playing ramble across the beat that lurches along behind him. The band members, for the most part unknown, were similarly unchallenged by musical expertise but that only increases the music's fascination. His own songs tend to draw from the ever-present pool of floating verses but he launches an assault on Lonnie Johnson's 'Jelly Roll Baker' and two instrumentals from his final session provide evidence of his acquaintance with T-Bone Walker. 'I'm So Glad' and 'I Done Talked And I Done Talked' find him using guitar patterns from the repertoire of Lightnin' Hopkins, whom he claimed as a cousin. Sims's instinctive musicianship and unstoppable brio make this set a delight. NS

Paul 'Lil' Buck' Sinegal (born 1944)
VOCAL, GUITAR

Sinegal was born in Lafayette, Louisiana. As a teenage guitarist he led his own group, Lil' Buck & The Topcats; after it broke up at the end of the '60s he joined Clifton Chenier, playing in his band for most of the '70s. He later worked with Buckwheat Zydeco and both Rockin' Dopsies.

** The Buck Starts Here
NYNO 9612 *Sinegal; Allen Toussaint (kb, o, p, syn, perc, prod); Stephan Clement (o, p); Keith Vinet (o); Joseph Veasie (g); Alonzo Johnson Jr (b, v); Jude 'Curley' Taylor (d); Wallace Johnson (v).* 12/97–6/98.

*** Bad Situation
Lucky Cat LC 1003 *Sinegal; Andy Cornett (h, v); Keith Clements (ac, kb, v); Lee Allen Zeno (b, v); Nathaniel Jolivette (d, v); Mike Chaisson (rb, v); Gloria Williams Wilkes, Chardell Mouton, Mugsie, Donald Senegal [Sinegal] (v).* 02.

'Run Down Cadillac', the opening track of *The Buck Starts Here*, has the flavour of south Louisiana swamp blues in the '60s; at the other end of the album, the explosive playing of bassist and drummer hints at the rhythmic energy of contemporary zydeco. Unfortunately much of what comes between these reference points is music with no particular place to go, or to come from: 'Don't Tell Me About Town' and 'Every Man Needs A Home' are familiar exercises in the B. B. King style, and 'Sleepwalk' and 'Buckin' For Your Love' are dull instrumentals. Sinegal's guitar playing is sharp and rhythmically sure but without much range of expression, and as a singer he sounds older than his years. *Bad Situation* is an altogether more focused production that concentrates on presenting Sinegal as a bluesman. Not a strikingly original one, to be sure; choosing 'Why I Sing The Blues' inevitably makes the listener think of B. B. King again, while the medley of 'I'll Play The Blues For You' and 'Cold, Cold Feeling' gives him the opportunity to sound quite like Albert King and very like Albert Collins. But in his own 'The Blues Is Killing Me' his wasted voice almost makes you believe him. There are other good, if commonplace, blues performances, and in 'Shakin' The Zydeco' an insistent riff tune with Clements on accordion, and altogether it's a likeable album, with fewer *longueurs* than its predecessor. TR

Charlie Singleton (born c. 1930)
ALTO AND TENOR SAXOPHONES, VOCAL

Singleton grew up in Kansas City, where he studied music at Lincoln High, but moved to New York when he was scarcely out of his teens. He led his own band there for several years, recording both in his own name and accompanying H-Bomb Ferguson. Nothing definite has been heard of him since the late '50s.

**(*) Charlie Singleton 1949–1953
Classics 5121 *Singleton; Irving Stokes, Lowell Lewis, Ray Copeland, Jesse Drakes (t); Earl Alexander, Ted Kelly, Buster Cooper (tb); Lou Donaldson (as, bs); Stafford Simon, 'Chan', Moe Jarman, Lucky Thompson, Big John Greer, Morris Lane (ts); Jackie McLean, Eddie Barefield, Numa 'Pee Wee' Moore, Charlie Rouse (bs); Lawrence Keyes, Ram Ramirez (o); Reginald Ashby, Gildo Mahones, Herbie Nichols, Kelly Owens, Jimmy Neely (p); John Saunders, unknowns (g); Martin Rivera, Peck Morrison, Al King, Teddy Cromwell, Steve Cooper, Al Cotton, unknown (b); John Godfrey, 'Sticks' Evans, Lester Jenkins, Kalil Mahdi, Jimmy Cobb, unknown (d); Linwood Sutton, Jake Vaughn, Freddie Jackson (v). 49–summer 53.*

The sides collected here, evidently for the first time in any format, were made to meet the insatiable demand from jukebox operators, in the years just before rock 'n' roll, for saxophone instrumentals, typically issued in couplings of a slow blues or ballad with a hectic boogie or jump tune. What Singleton brought to that idiom was a big, penetrating tone with little vibrato, and a gift for hiring high-quality sidemen: Jackie McLean, Charlie Rouse, Lucky Thompson and Herbie Nichols are just some of the musicians heard here who would go on to distinguished careers in jazz. At least one track, 'Broadway Beat', is already pretty good jazz, with an inventive intro by pianist Gildo Mahones and four sinewy blues choruses by altoist Lou Donaldson. Most of the other tracks are blues, too, and generally rather formulaic, whether fast ('S.O.S.', 'Blow Mr. Singleton') or slow, like 'The Late Creeper' or 'Lonely Lover Blues', which has Singleton's only vocal. TR

T-Bone Singleton (born 1952)
VOCAL, GUITAR

A lifelong resident of Baton Rouge, Terry Singleton listened as a boy to south Louisiana bluesmen such as Silas Hogan and, on record, Lightnin' Slim and Slim Harpo, though the first song he learned to play was Otis Redding's 'Sitting On The Dock Of The Bay'. In his teens he played soul and gospel music, and in the '70s he worked with a show band, but by the '90s he had acquired a local reputation as a blues singer and writer.

**(*) Louisiana Swamp Blues – Vol. 3
Wolf 120.924 *Singleton; Mille Bonereaux, Harmonica Red (h); Andrea Curbelo, Rudi Richard (g); Steve Coleridge (b, perc); 'Lester', James Johnson, A. G. Hardesty (b); Ronnie Houston (d, perc); Pick Delmore (d); Steve Wildman, Harold Washington, Roosevelt Boudreaux (perc). 5/90.*

**(*) Walkin' The Floor
JSP JSPCD 267 *Singleton; Oscar Davis (h); Nelson Blanchard (kb); Denise Brumfield (g); Joe Hunter (b); Lester 'Pick' Delmore, Floyd Saizon (d); Larry Garner (prod). 96.*

Singleton emerged from the same Baton Rouge club scene, and about the same time, as Larry Garner, so it's not surprising, and no slight upon Singleton's talent, that one is sometimes reminded of the better-known man, almost irresistibly so on *Walkin' The Floor* in 'Boogie Train'. The presence of Garner as producer, and of musicians who have worked with him like Hunter, Delmore, Saizon and Davis, obviously accentuates the similarity. Though Singleton doesn't display Garner's quiddity or his wit, he writes, and delivers with energy, thoughtful songs in quite a wide range of melodic types, thus creating interesting lighting effects on what might otherwise – since all but one of the tracks are by the same four-piece group – have been a rather monochromatic stage set. The Wolf CD, which focuses on Singleton, Garner and singer/guitarist Battlerack Scatter (described in the notes as 'unquestionably the most enigmatic figure on the Baton Rouge blues scene'), has four tracks featuring Singleton as front man. The Garner effect is detectable in 'Let Me Be Your Man' and 'Hello, Hello'. The quality of Singleton's singing, playing and writing suggested that he had more than one and a third albums in him, but no successors have appeared. TR

Sista Monica (born 1956)
VOCAL

Born in Indiana, Monica Parker began singing in the choir as a child. In 1987 she moved from Chicago to California, and since 1992 has combined her day job as owner of a recruitment agency with singing professionally and running Mo Muscle.

*** Get Out My Way
Thunderbird TBE 5005 *Sista Monica; Doug Rowan (as, ts, bs); Noel Catura (as, ts, v); Bruce 'Sunpie' Barnes, Johnny Mars (h); David Torkanowsky, Danny Beconcini (o, p); Dale Ockerman, John Turk (o); Michael Osborn (g, v); Vasti Jackson (g); Skylark (b, v); Alonzo Johnson, Paul Jones (b); Ron E. Beck (d, v); Herman Ernest III (d); Tony Lindsay (perc, v); Jim Greiner (perc); Shiela Truso (v). late 94.*

***(*) Sista Monica
Mo Muscle MOR 042756 *Sista Monica; Louis Fastman (t); Fred Wesley (tb); Noel Catura (as); Ken 'Big Papa' Baker (ts, v); Doug Rowan (bs); Rick Hatfield, Andy Santana (h); Jackie Gainey (o, v); Don E. Beck (o); Danny Beconcini (p, v); Steve Kostakes, Steve Lucky (p); Michael Osborn (g, v); Chris Cain, Terry DeRouen, John Morris, Chris Penmentel, Mike Schermer, Guitar Shorty, Chris Smith, Rene Solis, Sam Varela, John Wedemeyer (g); Leonard Gill (b, v); Howard Deere, Paul 'Polo' Jones, Artis Joyce, Mark Karina (b); Ron E. Beck (d, v); James Bott, Kelvin Dixon, Mike Lopez (d); Larry Batiste, Lissa Byrd, Charlotte Parker, Brenda Roy, Leonore Truso, Shiela Truso (v). 97?*

**(*) Give Me That Old Time Religion
Mo Muscle MMRE-704 *Sista Monica; Eddie Ramirez (t); Dayan Kai (cl); Noel Catura (as); Kate Alm (o, p); Jackie Gainey (o); John Turk III (p); Tim Landis (g); Bill Bosch (b); Art Alm (tu); Ron E. Beck (d, v); Adult Choir, Calvary Episcopal Children's Choir, Shiela Truso, Leslie Mixon (v). 98–99.*

***(*) People Love The Blues
Mo' Muscle MMRE-688 *Sista Monica; Tom Barteta, Bill Theurer, Eddie Ramirez, Louis Fastman (t); Ross Wilson (tb); Noel Catura (as, ts); Doug Rowan (as, bs); Frank Ramos, Ken 'Big Papa' Baker (ts); Gary Smith, Andy Just (h); Danny B. (o, p); John Turk (o); Larry McCray, Larry Antonasio, Jimmy Thackery, Tim Landis, Sam Varela Jr, Dan Caron, Michael Osborn (g);*

Skylark, Dewayne Pate, Ruth Davies, Steve Ehrmann, Joe Thomas, Don E. Beck (b); Ron E. Beck (d, v); Paul Revelli, Butch Cousins (d); Brenda Roy, Shiela Truso, D'Layna Dixon, Louise Locki (v). 00?

Sista Monica sings gospel-inflected soul-blues. Her debut disc establishes her as a dynamic performer, but at this stage one more at ease with soul than blues; the strongest tracks are covers of Ted Taylor, James Brown and Al Green (a superb reading of 'Love And Happiness'). *Get Out My Way*'s more strictly blues numbers are run-of-the-mill, and her intermittently wayward harmony at the cadences suggests inexperience with the form. Mainly self-composed, *Sista Monica* is a much better effort, which the artist's website characterizes as 'the foundation of her signature sound'. The many guitarists are in a blues-rock bag and prone to stating the obvious, but the rhythm sections are as tight as the horn arrangements of James Brown alumnus Fred Wesley, whose extended solo on 'Where Is My Teddy' is a gem.

People Love The Blues continues in much the same vein; McCray and Caron's more idiomatic guitar work is a welcome addition, and Ken Baker's absence through death a regrettable loss. The disc offers more evidence of the Sista's songwriting skills, notably with 'The Walking Wounded', a well-crafted response to homelessness and domestic violence. Given the many permutations of musicians employed on these two discs, their consistency testifies to Parker's vision and creativity as composer, performer and producer.

Both playlist and arrangements are predictable on *Give Me That Old Time Religion*'s run-through of gospel favourites, which is credited to Sista Monica Parker; only the Staples Singers' 'Don't Knock' and a fine revival of Dorothy Love Coates's 'Strange Man' are moderately unexpected.

*** Live In Europe

Mo Muscle MMRE-716 *Sista Monica; Noel Catura (ts, g); Danny Beconcini (o, p); Sam Varela (g, v); Kevin Stancil (b); Ron E. Beck (d, v).* 7/00.

Recorded at the Peer Rhythm 'n' Blues Festival, this set starts depressingly with 'Belgium, we need you to make some noise!', 'How y'all doin' out there? Do you feel all right?' and suchlike mob oratory, which cues similarly populist music; by track 3 the crowd is singing along to 'Hey! Hey! The Blues Is All Right'. Thankfully, things become more considered and inventive thereafter, and 'Put It In The Crockpot' and 'The Sista Don't Play' groove along with gusto. Varela continues to present well-worn blues-rock ideas as if he'd just invented them, but Catura and Beconcini, riding loosely over Stancil and Beck's dark, funky rhythms, are more imaginative. By the time Sista Monica does Little Richard on 'Get Out My Way!' she's pretty well atoned for the boorish start; a segue into 'Proud Mary' is accordingly the more regrettable. CS

Matthew Skoller (born 1962)
VOCAL, HARMONICA

Skoller played in Milwaukee before moving to Chicago in 1987. There he worked with the Chi-Town Hustlers and Big Daddy Kinsey before forming his own band in 1992. He has recorded with Kinsey, Larry Garner, H-Bomb Ferguson, Bernard Allison, Michael Coleman, Koko Taylor, Big Time Sarah and Deitra Farr, has appeared at festivals in both the USA and Europe, and plays regularly in the Chicago area.

*** Shoulder To The Wind

Tongue 'N Groove [unnumbered] *Skoller; Sidney James Wingfield (o, p, v); Johnny 'Fingers' Iguana (p); Larry Skoller, Wil Crosby, Vincent Bucher, Carlos Johnson (g); Al 'Get Down' Brown (b); Tim 'Awesome' Austin (d); Heitor Garcia (cga, perc); Stokes, Mike Avery, Deitra Farr, John Primer, Odion 'Boobie' Parker (v).* 99.

**(*) Taproot

Tongue 'N Groove [unnumbered] *Skoller; Johnny Iguana (p); Larry Skoller (g).* 03.

***(*) These Kind Of Blues

Tongue 'N Groove [unnumbered] *Skoller; Willie Henderson (bs); Brian Ritchie (shakuhachi); Sidney James Wingfield (kb, o, p); Johnny Iguana (p); Lurrie Bell, Larry Skoller (g); Willie 'Vamp' Samuels (b, v); Kenny Smith (d); Peaches Stanton (wb); Heitor Garcia (cga); J.A.Q. (v, remix); Mike Avery, Cynthia Butts, James F. Teague, Marro-Di'Jon Murry, Bob Friedman (v).* 04.

The best of the current generation of Chicago blues musicians combine an esteem for their vast inheritance with a healthy disinclination to be weighed down by it. No one, listening to the veiled intensity of Skoller's singing or his true-blue harmonica playing, could be in much doubt about the musicians he has listened to, but in *These Kind Of Blues* and most of *Shoulder To The Wind* he pays his respects obliquely, not dealing in retreads but writing original compositions which he colours with allusions and echoes. 'Down At Your Buryin'' (*These Kind Of Blues*) stems from 'Ride To Your Funeral In A V-8 Ford', a song that several artists have used, but its arrangement, hollow and echoing as a crypt, owes little to any version you will have heard. The same album's 'Handful Of People' has an airborne melody that might have pleased Magic Sam, but when we hear it again at the end of the CD it's in a remix that gently waves ghosts from the past aside and fills their place with a rap track. On some numbers Skoller and his crew are content to row in the mainstream of '50s/'60s Chicago blues – 'Where Can You Be', with its squealing harmonica and chugging rhythm, is obviously waving to the spirit of Jimmy Reed – but a conventional setting should not distract the listener from the sharp lyric of 'Ghosts In Your Closet' or *Shoulder To The Wind*'s 'Delta Combat Zone', a bitter commentary on the casino strip that now edges Highway 61. *Shoulder* ends on a duet with pianist Johnny Iguana, a pointer to the stripped-down traditionalism of *Taproot*, credited to Matthew Skoller's Lost Trio and largely devoted to received repertoire such as Sonny Boy Williamson II's 'Mighty Long Time' and 'Lonesome Cabin', Otis Spann's 'It Must Have Been The Devil' and Big Maceo's 'Worried Life Blues'. This is an unexceptionable set, with some very idiomatic playing by Iguana, but it's on the short side (nine songs, 33.43) and lacks the character of the other albums.

Throughout these CDs Larry Skoller is an excellent all-purpose guitarist, and on *These Kind Of Blues* he and Lurrie Bell make a guitar team anyone would be pleased to lead. Tongue 'N Groove is a vanity label, in that it deals only in Matthew Skoller's music (the first album, *Bone To Pick With You* [1996], is currently out of print), but unlike many such its production values are impeccable, and the care that went into making the admirable music is reflected in the engineering and presentation. TR

Will Slayden (1878–1965)
VOCAL, BANJO

When Charles McNutt recorded him, Slayden was farming near Memphis. He hadn't played for 20 years, since joining the church, but was willing to borrow McNutt's banjo. Research by this writer and David Evans has verified his lifespan and his wife's name, which McNutt noted as Emma.

**** African-American Banjo Songs From West Tennessee
Tennessee Folklore Society TFS-123 *Slayden; Emma [India] Slayden (v).* summer 52.

Most of Will Slayden's songs are familiar ('John Henry', 'When The Train Comes Along', 'Spoonful' and the like), but his versions, accompanied by thrumming banjo, preserve the sound of black music from the early 20th century, before blues became dominant. Slayden's playing is highly percussive and harmonically restricted, his songs are usually built by the varied repetition of a single line, and accelerating tempos and call-and-response are basic. This may sound like a recipe for monotony, but what results is concentrated, gripping rhythmic excitement. Eight songs of 20 are Pentecostal hymns; on three of them India Slayden, who disapproved of her husband's secular material, adds a powerful voice that's sternly confident of God's approval. The recordings were made in one day, and on a few tracks Slayden is still reintegrating his vocal and banjo rhythms after long silence, but even these warm-ups are very important. This celebration of poor people's pleasures – food, dancing, sex and salvation – is just the thing for people who think the blues is a lifestyle accessory. CS

Slim Harpo (1924–70)
VOCAL, HARMONICA, GUITAR

James Isaac Moore was an unlikely candidate for popular success. He came to it late from a tradition of Louisiana blues and R&B that relied heavily on recasting other artists' successes. His 1957 recording debut, the suggestive 'I'm A King Bee', was later covered by The Rolling Stones but by then he'd had a 1961 American Top 40 hit with 'Rainin' In My Heart', a dramatically simple swamp-pop ballad that made him Excello's top-selling artist. Despite a prolific recording schedule, it wasn't until 1966 that he had his second and biggest hit, 'Baby Scratch My Back', another would-be salacious monologue that yet retained a measure of innocence. Four years later, on the verge of an international career and in apparent good health, he died from the consequences of a punctured lung.

**** I'm A King Bee
Ace CDCHD 510 *Harpo; Willie 'Tomcat' Parker (ts); Lazy Lester (h, perc); prob. Sonny Martin (p); Gabriel 'Guitar Gable' Perrodin, Rudolph Richard, James Johnson (g); Clinton 'Fats' Perrodin, T. J. Kitchen (b); Clarence 'Jockey' Etienne, Sammy K. Brown (d).* 3/57–1/64.

It shouldn't have worked. The voice was impossibly nasal and tentative, the backings were minimal and monotonous. But something unfettered and unrefined made Slim Harpo's first records irresistible. It was all there in 'I'm A King Bee' and 'Strange Love', 'You'll Be Sorry One Day', 'Don't Start Cryin' Now' and others that followed. The songs and the instrumentation may have become formulaic but the addition of saxophones and producer Jay Miller's mania for amateur percussion made little difference. Unlike others in Miller's stable, Harpo wrote original material, although he covered Lonesome Sundown's 'My Home Is A Prison' and 'Buzzin'' is a transparent lift of Junior Wells's 'Cha Cha Cha In Blue'. The first of three volumes covering his entire recording career, this contains nine previously unissued songs and alternative takes from his formative (and best) years.

***(*) Sting It Then!
Ace CDCHD 658 *Harpo; Willie 'Tomcat' Parker (ts); Rudolph Richard, James Johnson (g); Sammy K. Brown (d).* 7/61.

The discovery of a tape of Slim's band performing at a 7/61 graduation party in Mobile, Alabama, was unprecedented, a unique snapshot of a working R&B band in action, recorded by a group of enterprising graduates. The mono recording was decidedly amateur and yet all the instruments save Parker's wandering tenor sax are audible, despite Harpo's vocals, sung through his harmonica amp, being rather impaired. The repertoire is satisfyingly broad, encompassing Lee Dorsey, Jimmy Reed, Little Walter and John Lee Hooker. A brave but ill-advised cover of Brook Benton's 'I'll Take Care Of You' fails through Harpo's lack of true vocal power. Richard's lead guitar is particularly notable, especially on extended versions of 'Moody Blues' and 'Sugar Coated Love'. Audience reaction is hard to discern until they join in raucously on 'Little Liza Jane' and 'When The Saints Go Marching In'. Booklet notes by David Kearns, one of the recordists, are an added attraction.

*** Shake Your Hips
[Ace CDCHD 558] *As above, except add unknowns (s), Katie Webster (o), Lazy Lester (perc).* 6/61–9/66.

The middle period of Harpo's recording career found him being drawn into the mainstream of popular black music and in need of a versatility he didn't really possess. Producer Jay Miller phased out his band, replacing them with competent but unsympathetic unknowns, and the material went from reliable fare such as 'What's Goin' On Baby' and 'Harpo's Blues' to trite conventionalities like 'Lovin' You (The Way I Do)' and 'I'm Waiting On You Baby'. Nine previously unissued songs, including a disastrous 'Little Sally Walker' and 'Blueberry Hill', indicate a high failure-rate in releasable material and there's a weaker alternative take of Slim's biggest hit, 'Baby Scratch My Back'. The compilation closes with the four tracks Harpo recorded for Imperial in 1961, including a first attempt at 'Still Rainin' In My Heart', repeated for Excello two years later.

**(*) Tip On In
Ace CDCHD 606 *As above, except add unknowns (brass, reeds), Charles Hodges (o), unknown (p), Mabon 'Teenie' Hodges, Jimmy Johnson (g), Leroy Hodges, unknown (b), Howard Grimes, Roger Hawkins (d), unknown (tamb), unknown (v).* 67–11/69.

No longer directed by Jay Miller, Harpo's sessions took place in Memphis, Nashville and Baton Rouge. Excello's new owners plainly wished their supposed star to fit in with current musical trends. Elements of soul and country music are thrown into the mix, although Harpo, despite writing songs in the manner demanded, remains most comfortable with what he knows. Thus 'Rock Me Baby', 'Jody Man', 'I Just Can't Leave You' and 'The Hippy Song' are sung with more confidence than 'I've Got My Finger On Your Trigger' and 'The Price Is Too High', and he manages to survive the kitchen-sink production of 'Folsom Prison Blues'. The arrangement of the two-part title track turns up several times more, including the bizarre 'Stick Your Chest Out Baby', though never as successfully. Whether European acclaim would have turned Harpo back towards blues remains an intriguing but unanswerable speculation.

**** The Best Of Slim Harpo
Ace CDCHM 410//Rhino R2 70169 *Harpo; Willie 'Tomcat' Parker (ts); Lazy Lester (h, perc); Katie Webster (o); prob. Sonny Martin (p); Gabriel 'Guitar Gable' Perrodin, Rudolph Richard, James Johnson (g); Clinton 'Fats' Perrodin, T. J. Kitchen (b); Clarence 'Jockey' Etienne, Sammy K. Brown (d). 3/57–68.*

There's a tacit acknowledgement in these 18 selections that Harpo's best years were in the first half of his recording career. 'Rock Me Baby' and 'Tip On In, Part 1' are the only inclusions from his final years. Otherwise, the tempo is mostly upbeat, with 'Baby Scratch My Back', 'I'm A King Bee', 'Shake Your Hips' and 'Buzz Me Babe' making early appearances, as well as the inevitable 'Rainin' In My Heart'. Answer records like 'Little Queen Bee', 'Still Rainin' In My Heart' and 'Buzzin'' reflect the simplicity of the times in which they were recorded. Once again, the singularity of Jay Miller's productions and their concentration on the core elements of each song impress the ear and inspire a regret that commercial pressures weakened and stultified a vital partnership. NS

(***) Raining In My Heart
Hip-O HIPD 40135 *As above. 3/57–67.*
**** The Excello Singles Anthology
Hip-O B0000583 2CD *As for all above CDs. 3/57–c. 11/69.*

Excello's current owners commenced their dealings with Harpo's back catalogue by simply reissuing his first album with three extra tracks. Since that entailed duplicating half of *The Best Of Slim Harpo*, it was not, perhaps, the strongest bid for sales, but Hip-O's next move was much better calculated: all 22 of Harpo's singles, 'A' and 'B' sides, in release order, with good sound and notes by John Broven. Obviously it's the ideal way to follow the contours of his career, and the addict will welcome this supersize serving; those who prefer to keep their Slim profile slim should go for the healthy-meal (and, on Ace, pocket-friendly) *Best Of*. TR

Al Smith (born 1936)
VOCAL

Born in Ohio, Albert Alan Smith spent part of his youth in New Orleans, where he learned to sing and play the piano. In 1955 he moved to New York and sang with gospel choirs. During an informal session in a Newark club he came to the attention of Eddie 'Lockjaw' Davis, who set up a recording date with Prestige-Bluesville.

** Hear My Blues
Original Blues Classics OBCCD 514 *Smith; Eddie ['Lockjaw'] Davis (ts); Shirley Scott (o); Wendell Marshall (b); Arthur Edgehill (d). 9/59.*

** Midnight Special
Original Blues Classics OBCCD 583 *Smith; King Curtis (ts); Robert Banks (o); Jimmie Lee Robinson (g); Leonard Gaskin (b); Bobby Donaldson (d). 8/60.*

In the early '60s Prestige's Bluesville label gave album-length exposure not only to bankable figures like Sonny Terry & Brownie McGhee, Memphis Slim and Lightnin' Hopkins but also to field-recordists' discoveries like K. C. Douglas and Memphis Willie Borum (and several others, like Shirley Griffith, Wade Walton and Robert Curtis Smith, whose albums have yet to be transferred to CD). It was a remarkable, if ill-timed, experiment – but even its admirers may not remember that the first name in the Bluesville catalogue, alongside the number 1001, was Al Smith, with *Hear My Blues*. 'He had a really fresh and exciting talent,' Lockjaw Davis said of his find, and Prestige evidently thought they were on to a winner, too, because within the year they had recorded him again. But after *Midnight Special* had shone its light on Smith, he vanished into obscurity.

At this remove it's difficult to understand Prestige's interest. Gospel training had moulded Smith's voice somewhat as it had, say, Clyde McPhatter's, to sound youthful and yearning. With suitable R&B or soul material he might have got somewhere, and Nat Hentoff's notes to *Midnight Special* tentatively predict as much, but the mixture of standard blues and colourless originals on these albums seems to have been the wrong calling-card, left on the wrong desk. TR

Bennie Smith (born 1933)
VOCAL, GUITAR

As a sideman in various St Louis bands since the '50s Smith played with many visiting blues names. In the '90s he toured and recorded with Big Bad Smitty.

** Shook Up
Fedora FCD 5018 *Smith; Harry Simon (s); Eric McFadden (h); Rory Johnson (p); Tom Maloney (g); Sharon Foehner (b); Chuck Walters (d). 9/00.*

If you heard this music in a club you would probably consider yourself to have had a good blues night out, but on record you may find your attention drawn too often to the cracks in the leader's voice, particularly noticeable on vocal showcases like 'Drown In My Own Tears' or his own 'I'm Wondering'. As a guitarist Smith is competent enough to make routine choices like 'Okie Dokie Stomp' or 'Mystery Train' routinely enjoyable, and the band finds an attractive groove in 'Good Morning Little Schoolgirl'. TR

Bessie Smith (1894–1937)
VOCAL, KAZOO

Bessie Smith's was a short life, and her recording career was a short part of it – 1923 to 1931, plus a final four titles in 1933; the preceding two years of silence has been a combined result of the Depression and changing African-American tastes. In her heyday, though, Bessie had been the highest-paid black entertainer in America, with a fame that extended beyond her community, and even beyond her country; hers were among the first jazz records to be marketed to collectors and to overseas audiences. Was she 'the Empress of the Blues'? Pretty much; it was a marketing slogan, but if ever a singer dominated her fellow artists, Bessie Smith did. As Louis Armstrong defined the role of the jazz soloist, or as in later years B. B. King defined the electric blues guitar, so Bessie Smith showed female blues singers how it was supposed to be done: her natural vocal endowment was prodigious, and to it she added commitment to the material (however trivial it might sometimes be), innate swing, and an instinctive grasp of the ways that phrasing, dynamics and decoration (melisma, glissando, microtonal shading and so on) could be used to serve the meaning of the words. The facts of her life are well-known and are related in Chris Albertson's biography Bessie, whose detailed coverage is marred by proprietorial chippiness, and by the revised edition's failure to accommodate research by Lynn Abbott and Doug Seroff into her early years in vaudeville. Albertson's most significant contributions are the debunking of the story (already a rumour in the black community before John Hammond gave it wings) that she was refused admission to a white hospital after her fatal car crash in Mississippi, and the transmission of her niece Ruby Smith's portrait of Bessie as a pan-sexual freebooter. Other contemporaries painted a less lurid picture to Sara Grimes, whose research has unfortunately had only very limited circulation. Even in her lifetime, white intellectuals like Hammond and Carl Van Vechten were using Bessie Smith to channel their conceptions of gender and negritude, and she seems destined to remain contested territory; for a more recent and very different African-American take, see Angela Y. Davis's Blues Legacies And Black Feminism. The reason for all the controversy and adulation is a body of work that at its best is unsurpassed.

In this entry it has seemed more helpful to abandon strict chronology, and to discuss successively 'complete recordings' sets, selective series, extended overviews (double and longer CDs) and single discs.

*** **The Complete Recordings Vol. 1**
Columbia C2K 47091 2CD *Smith; prob. Ernest Elliott, poss. George Baquet, Don Redman (cl); Clarence Williams, Fletcher Henderson, Irving Johns, Jimmy Jones (p); Robert Robbins (vn); Buddy Christian (bj); Harry Reser, John Griffin (g); Clara Smith (v). 2/23–4/24.*

*** **The Complete Recordings Vol. 2**
Columbia/Legacy C2K 47471 2CD *Smith; Joe Smith, Louis Armstrong (c); Charlie Green (tb); Don Redman, Bob Fuller (cl, as); Buster Bailey (cl); Coleman Hawkins (ts); Fred Longshaw (o, p); Stanley Miller (p, prob. sp); Irving Johns, Fletcher Henderson, Isadore Myers, Clarence Williams (p); Robert Robbins (vn); Charlie Dixon, Elmer Snowden (bj); unknown (train eff); Clara Smith (v). 4/24–11/25.*

*** **The Complete Recordings Vol. 3**
Columbia/Legacy C2K 47474 2CD *Smith; Shelton Hemphill, Joe Smith, Tommy Ladnier, Demas Dean (c); Jimmy Harrison, Charlie Green (tb); Don Redman, Ernest Elliott (cl, as); Buster Bailey, Coleman Hawkins, Bob Fuller (cl); Fletcher Henderson, Fred Longshaw, Clarence Williams, James P. Johnson, Porter Grainger (p); Charlie Dixon (bj); Lincoln M. Conaway (g); June Cole (bb). 11/25–2/28.*

*** **The Complete Recordings Vol. 4**
Columbia/Legacy C2K 52838 2CD *Smith; Demas Dean, Ed Allen, Louis Metcalf (c); Louis Bacon (t); Charlie Green, Joe Williams (tb); Abraham Wheat (cl, ss); Ernest Elliott (cl, as, ts); Bob Fuller, Garvin Bushell (cl, as); Greely Walton (ts); Fred Longshaw, Porter Grainger, Clarence Williams, James P. Johnson, Steve Stevens (p); Eddie Lang (g); Cyrus St Clair (bb); Floyd Casey (d); The Bessemer Singers (v). 2/28–6/31.*

(*) The Final Chapter: The Complete Recordings Vol. 5
Columbia/Legacy C2K 57546 2CD *Smith; Joe Smith, Louis Armstrong (c); Russell Smith, poss. Sidney DeParis, Frankie Newton (t); Charlie Green, Jimmy Harrison, Jack Teagarden (tb); Coleman Hawkins (cl, ts); Buster Bailey, Benny Goodman, unknown (cl); Chu Berry, unknown (ts); unknown (h); Fletcher Henderson, Fred Longshaw, James P. Johnson, Clarence Williams, Buck Washington (p); Charlie Dixon (bj); poss. Bernard Addison, Bobby Johnson, unknown (g); Harry Hull, Billy Taylor (b); Kaiser Marshall (d); The Hall Johnson Choir (v); Jimmy Mordecai, Isabel Washington, unknowns (sp). 5/25–11/33.*

**** **Bessie Smith – Vol. 1**
Frog DGF 40 *Smith; prob. Ernest Elliott (cl); Clarence Williams, Fletcher Henderson, Irving Johns, Jimmy Jones (p); Buddy Christian (bj). 2/23–9/23.*

(***) **Bessie Smith 1923**
Classics 761 *As above, except add Clara Smith (v). 2/23–10/23.*

**** **Bessie Smith – Vol. 2**
Frog DGF 41 *Smith; Ernest Elliott or George Baquet, Don Redman (cl); Jimmy Jones, Fletcher Henderson, Irving Johns (p); Robert Robbins (vn); Harry Reser, John Griffin (g); Clara Smith (v). 9/23–4/24.*

(***) **Bessie Smith 1923–1924**
Classics 787 *As above, except add Don Redman (as), Charlie Green (tb); omit Clara Smith. 10/23–8/24.*

♛ **** **Bessie Smith – Vol. 3**
Frog DGF 42 *Smith; Joe Smith, Louis Armstrong (c); Charlie Green (tb); Don Redman (cl, as); Buster Bailey (cl); Coleman Hawkins (ts); Fred Longshaw (o, p); Fletcher Henderson (p); Charlie Dixon (bj). 7/24–5/25.*

(***) **Bessie Smith 1924–1925**
Classics 812 *As above, except Redman does not play as; add Bob Fuller (cl, as), Isadore Myers (p), Elmer Snowden (bj). 9/24–8/25.*

♛ **** **Bessie Smith – Vol. 4**
Frog DGF 43 *Smith; Louis Armstrong, Joe Smith, Shelton Hemphill (c); Charlie Green (tb); Don Redman, Bob Fuller (cl, as); Buster Bailey (cl); Stanley Miller (p, prob. sp); Fred Longshaw, Isadore Myers, Clarence Williams, Fletcher Henderson (p); Elmer Snowden (bj); unknown (train eff); Clara Smith (v). 4/25–3/26.*

(***) **Bessie Smith 1925–1927**
Classics 843 *As above, except add James P. Johnson (p); omit Armstrong, Fuller, Myers, Snowden. 9/25–2/27.*

♛ **** **Bessie Smith – Vol. 5**
Frog DGF 44 *Smith; Joe Smith (c); Jimmy Harrison, Charlie Green (tb); Buster Bailey, Coleman Hawkins (cl); Clarence Williams, Fletcher Henderson, James P. Johnson (p); Charlie Dixon (bj). 3/26–3/27.*

(***) **Bessie Smith 1927–1928**
Classics 870 *As above, except add Tommy Ladnier, Demas Dean (c), Abraham Wheat (cl, ss), Ernest Elliott (cl, as), Bob Fuller (cl), Porter Grainger, Fred Longshaw (p), Lincoln M. Conaway (g), June Cole (bb); omit Williams, Dixon. 3/27–3/28.*

**** **Bessie Smith – Vol. 6**
Frog DGF 45 *Smith; Tommy Ladnier, Demas Dean (c); Charlie Green (tb); Abraham Wheat (cl, ss); Ernest Elliott (cl, as, ts); Bob*

Fuller (cl, as); James P. Johnson, Porter Grainger, Fletcher Henderson, Fred Longshaw (p); Lincoln M. Conaway (g); June Cole (bb). 4/27–8/28.

(***) Bessie Smith 1928–1929
Classics 897 *Smith; Ed Allen, Joe Smith (c); Russell Smith, poss. Sidney DeParis (t); Charlie Green, Joe Williams (tb); Ernest Elliott (cl, as, ts); Bob Fuller (cl, as); unknown (cl); Garvin Bushell (as); Greely Walton, unknown (ts); Porter Grainger, Clarence Williams, James P. Johnson (p); Charles Dixon (bj); Eddie Lang, poss. Bernard Addison (g); Harry Hull (b); Cyrus St Clair (bb); Kaiser Marshall (d); The Hall Johnson Choir (v).* 3/28–8/29.

**** Bessie Smith – Vol. 7
Frog DGF 46 *As above, except add unknown (h), unknown (g), Jimmy Mordecai, Isabel Washington, unknowns (sp).* 8/28–10/29.

(***) Bessie Smith 1929–1933
Classics 977 *Smith; Ed Allen, Louis Metcalf (c); Louis Bacon, Frankie Newton (t); Charlie Green, Jack Teagarden (tb); Garvin Bushell (cl, as); Benny Goodman (cl); Chu Berry (ts); Clarence Williams, James P. Johnson, Steve Stevens, Buck Washington (p); Bobby Johnson (g); Billy Taylor (b); Floyd Casey (d); The Bessemer Singers (v).* 10/29–11/33.

♛ **** Bessie Smith – Vol. 8
Frog DGF 47 *As above.* 3/30–11/33.

The CDs listed above are all 'complete recordings' sets and in view of Bessie Smith's reputation it may seem odd to remark that none of them lacks at least one track with aspects to regret, and sometimes to wince at. Even the collaborations with Louis Armstrong, which at their best scale the summit of jazz and blues artistry, include 'You've Been A Good Ole Wagon', on which Armstrong utterly misjudges the mood. (Joe Smith was Bessie's favourite cornettist, and his lustrously beautiful tone is one of the major pleasures of listening to her records.) The piano accompaniments by Clarence Williams and Fletcher Henderson on Smith's first recordings leave much to be desired, although they both improved later. Seldom, before Chu Berry on her last session, does she encounter a saxophonist who escapes clichéd dreariness, and Ernest Elliott and Bob Fuller's occasional twin clarinets are even worse. The train effects on 'Dixie Flyer Blues' are beyond tedious. Even James P. Johnson, her finest pianist (although Fred Longshaw's talent should not be overlooked), descends into silent-movie clichés on 'Blue Spirit Blues'.

All of that needs to be said (and for a stimulating title-by-title musical analysis, which doesn't flinch from identifying shortcomings, see Edward Brooks's *The Bessie Smith Companion*); but when there are deficiencies in the accompaniments or the material, most of the time Bessie Smith overcomes them by the force of her talents as a singer and interpreter, even in the later years when her voice had coarsened (though not as much as is often claimed). And, of course, in among the occasional tracks that are poor and the many more that are merely excellent, there are songs and performances of the calibre of 'Backwater Blues' (with Johnson), 'Nobody Knows You When You're Down And Out', 'Empty Bed Blues', 'Careless Love' (with Armstrong), 'Downhearted Blues' (her commercially and artistically sensational debut) and 'Gimme A Pigfoot' from her last session. More than for most blues singers who recorded extensively, Bessie Smith's complete works make their own case.

Classics disregard alternative takes, and offer only adequate sound quality. A more serious drawback is that three volumes (761, 897 and 977) seem to be unobtainable. They have not, so far as we know, been formally deleted, and we list them for information, but anyone wanting all Bessie Smith's recordings needs to look elsewhere.

Columbia's is the only complete works series to include illustrations beyond cover photos, and it carries by far the best and most extensive notes. The final volume, which was released (reluctantly, one senses) three years after *Vol. 4*, contains Smith's last Columbia 78, the 1933 OKeh session, five alternative takes and the complete soundtrack of the film *St. Louis Blues*; its second CD consists of interviews by Chris Albertson with Ruby Smith. Particularly since the appearance of Frog's series, it's become accepted wisdom to badmouth the sound quality of the Columbia CDs; in fact it's adequate (and was presumably the source of Classics' similar adequacy), despite the successive application of notch filtering for LP release in the '70s, and of NoNoise compression to the LP master tapes.

'Adequate' is not what one expects from the owners of the masters, though, and in this respect Columbia are blown away by Frog, who canvassed collectors for the best available originals and commissioned John R. T. Davies to remaster them; the resulting sound, particularly on the early, acoustic recordings, has unprecedented warmth, fullness, resonance and transparency. Frog also include all the alternative takes, including several that were not available to Columbia, and one never previously issued test. These items are generally inferior to the issued takes, but no less precious as documentation. The notes are adequate, but rightly refer readers to Albertson and Brooks for further enlightenment. Given the pitfalls that completeness digs for itself, none of these eight CDs is unmixed musical perfection, but the ones with crowns do more than enough to earn them, and if the project had appeared as a box set, we'd have given that a crown. Unquestionably the set for anyone wanting the complete works, Frog's series is both a triumph for and a memorial to John R. T. Davies and label owner Dave French, neither of whom long survived its completion.

**** Downhearted Blues
Naxos Jazz Legends 8.120660 *As for relevant CDs above.* 2/23–4/24.

**** Vol. 2 St. Louis Blues
Naxos Blues Legends 8.120691 *As for relevant CDs above.* 1/24–5/25.

**** Vol. 3 Preachin' The Blues
Naxos Blues Legends 8.120702 *As for relevant CDs above.* 6/25–2/27.

**** Vol. 4 Empty Bed Blues
Naxos Blues Legends 8.120725 *As for relevant CDs above.* 3/27–8/28.

Naxos's presumably ongoing series is virtually chronological, but not complete; as with Frog, the transfers are from 78s rather than by copying previous LP or CD releases. The engineering has been done, if not with Frog's wizardry, then at least with conscientious attention to detail. It should be noted, however, that especially on the first two volumes, Naxos are working with the best 78s they can get hold of, rather than the best 78s; this may explain the inclusion of 'Dixie Flyer Blues' on *Vol. 2*, at the expense of (among other possibilities) 'J. C.

Holmes Blues', one of the finest of the Armstrong collaborations. The series doesn't quite add up to a 'best of Bessie Smith', but it's a good alternative for those who want more than an exemplar CD but don't feel the need for every note and syllable.

***(*) **The Quintessence**
Frémeaux FA 223 2CD *As for relevant CDs above.* 2/23–11/33.

(***) **The Gold Collection**
Proper Retro R2CD 70–09 2CD *As for relevant CDs above.* 2/23–11/33.

(***) **Bessie Smith**
Masters Of Jazz R2CD 8034 2CD *As for relevant CDs above.* 2/23–11/33.

**** **Chattanooga Gal**
Proper PROPERBOX 78 4CD *As for relevant CDs above.* 2/23–11/33.

** **Greatest Hits**
Fabulous FABCD 2004 2CD *As for relevant CDs above.* 2/23–11/33.

*** **The Essential Bessie Smith**
Columbia/Legacy 487398 2CD *As for relevant CDs above.* 4/23–11/33.

*** **Woman's Trouble Blues**
Snapper Recall SMDCD 242 2CD *As for relevant CDs above.* 4/23–11/33.

The Quintessence has outstanding sound quality and a very good selection of material, but unaccountably chooses to include eight minutes (the musical elements) of the *St. Louis Blues* film soundtrack at the expense of (say) 'Nobody Knows You When You're Down And Out' and one of the collaborations with Eddie Lang. The non-chronological *Gold Collection* is well chosen, but the reproduction of the early, acoustic recordings is comparatively indifferent, and there are no notes. The Masters Of Jazz collection has a short, pretentious note, some dubious artwork and enough distortion to prevent a recommendation. Columbia's précis, issued after the *Complete Recordings*, continues the label's trademarks: good notes, evocative illustrations and sound that's no more than acceptable. *Woman's Trouble Blues* is listenable but spends too much time in the early years and consequently short-changes the listener of James P. Johnson, Joe Smith and Charlie 'Trombone Cholly' Green. It gets a cheer for carrying the only notes to use Abbott and Seroff's research into Bessie's vaudeville days, and a Bronx cheer for not including dates and personnels.

Chattanooga Gal is extensively and knowledgeably annotated, and makes a scarcely improvable selection from the Bessie Smith corpus. We don't make a habit of fussing over ethical issues, figuring that our readers are grown-ups and can make their own decisions, but the suspicion that this is a box of cloned Frogs makes us reluctant to award *Chattanooga Gal* a crown. It would be wrong, therefore, to reproach Fabulous for not even bothering to rip off Frog; let's just leave it that ruthless top-slicing of the treble frequencies to achieve noise reduction makes *Greatest Hits* one to avoid.

*** **Careless Love Blues**
Snapper Complete Blues SBLUECD 024 *As for relevant CDs above.* 2/23–5/29.

(**(*)) **Black Mountain Blues**
Chrisly 60016 *As for relevant CDs above.* 2/23–6/31.

*** **The Empress & The Pianist 1923/1931**
[EPM Blues Collection 15952] *As for relevant CDs above.* 2/23–11/31.

(***) **The Ultimate Collection**
Prism Leisure PLATCD 123 *As for relevant CDs above.* 2/23–11/31.

(**(*)) **Empress Of The Blues**
Collectors Edition CBCD 001 *As for relevant CDs above.* 2/23–11/31.

***(*) **Bessie Smith 1923–1933**
L'Art Vocal 3 *As for relevant CDs above.* 2/23–11/33.

(***) **Down Hearted Blues**
Golden Options GO 3811 *As for relevant CDs above.* 2/23–11/33.

***(*) **Bessie Smith Sings The Jazz** [sic]
[EPM Jazz Archives 15790] *As for relevant CDs above.* 4/23–11/33.

**** **Mama's Got The Blues**
Topaz TPZ 1002 *As for relevant CDs above.* 4/23–11/33.

***(*) **Martin Scorsese Presents The Blues: Bessie Smith**
Columbia/Legacy CK 90493 *As for relevant CDs above.* 4/23–11/33.

(***) **The Best Of Bessie Smith**
Blues Forever CD 68001 *As for relevant CDs above.* 10/23–11/33.

*** **Original Jazz Recordings**
Hermes HRM 6003 *As for relevant CDs above.* 5/25–11/33.

(***) **Gin House Blues**
Music Digital CD 6403 *As for relevant CDs above.* 11/25–10/26.

(***) **Young Woman's Blues**
Delta Exclusive CD 4174 *As for relevant CDs above.* 10/26–2/28.

(***) **Bessie Smith**
Members Edition UAE 30502 *As for relevant CDs above.* 9/27–11/33.

Inevitably, there's a lot of duplication among these single CDs. Let's get the ones evaluated at (***) or less out of the way. The mastering on *Black Mountain Blues* is very poor and its notes are limited to discographical details. *The Ultimate Collection* is so incompetently mastered as to make criticism of its inaccurate annotation redundant. *Empress Of The Blues* was mastered by the engineers responsible for the Naxos series discussed above, and probably from the same 78s, but the results are not comparable; the vague and undiscriminating notes make a treasurable reference to 'Fletcher Henderson's Not Six'. *Down Hearted Blues* uses most of its booklet to advertise other releases; the cavernous reverb on 'Kitchen Man Blues' and elsewhere suggests that its source may be the four *Bessie Smith Story* LPs issued in the '50s. Blues Forever's *Best Of* isn't; it features lifeless transfers in the label's eccentric backwards chronology. *Gin House Blues* and *Young Woman's Blues* share an epidermal note and frequent overload distortion. Members Edition achieve good sound by careful application of CEDAR, but the selection is confined to Bessie's later records; this partial picture of her art is not improved by a note that seems to apply to a different compilation, and gets the year of her death wrong.

EPM's two collections (whose availability is uncertain) are to be applauded for addressing her music thematically, rather than throwing together yet another bundle of the well-known and/or available. *The Empress And The Pianist* seeks to throw the spotlight on her singing by confining itself to songs where she's accompanied only by pianists. The notes are unjustifiably keen on the playing of Fletcher Henderson and Clarence Williams, journeymen both; conversely, or perhaps consequently, they underestimate Irving Johns, a better pianist than either, and Fred Longshaw, apart from James P. Johnson her best keyboard partner. *Sings The Jazz* concentrates on Bessie's recordings of popular songs, among which 'Careless Love' and 'T'Ain't Nobody's Bizness If I Do', both with deep folk roots, are included. It's arguable that this CD sets up a false antithesis: the blues aesthetic is about a lot more than structure and chord sequence; inflection, rhythm and tonality are crucial, and they're what Bessie Smith used in order to imbue virtually everything she sang with a blues sensibility. Still, this is one more highly enjoyable collection of the work of a great singer, accompanied by a congeries of jazz greats – and not so greats; 'Yes Indeed He Do' is a classic, but only because her exuberance steamrollers the inadequacies of Bob Fuller and Ernest Elliott.

The remaining discs are general surveys. *Careless Love* is not the only CD where trying to equalize acoustic and electrical recordings induces peak-level distortions in the former. A somewhat sensationalist note suggests that the legend of her being turned away from a white hospital 'has never been properly substantiated'. On the contrary: it's been comprehensively refuted more than once. Hermes evade the problems posed by acoustic recordings by not using any; unfortunately, their engineering is no more than passable. Topaz's skills are altogether better, and their chosen acoustic sides sit happily in among the electrical ones, making this one of the best single CD collections. L'Art Vocal's chronological selection is a sleeper – another disc where CEDAR has been discriminatingly applied to good quality originals. The brief notes are too keen on the rags-to-riches-and-back cliché, and the English version is shakily translated. Columbia, giving the Bessie Smith catalogue one more outing, on the back of the already-seems-like-it-never-happened 'Year of the Blues', seem at last to have abandoned the recycling of old LP tapes in favour of compilation *de novo*; a comparison of 'A Good Man Is Hard To Find' with the same track on Snapper is very instructive in this regard. This is Columbia's best effort to date, but even at mid-price 15 tracks is not an over-generous allowance. CS

Bessie Mae Smith
VOCAL

OKeh listed this singer in the files as Bessie Martin and credited her recordings to Blue Belle; she also recorded for Vocalion, as Bessie Mae Smith, and for Paramount, certainly as St Louis Bessie and probably as May Belle Miller. She is also thought to have been Streamline Mae, whose records carry composer credits to Mary Belle Smith. Big Joe Williams, who said that Bessie Mae Smith had been his old lady, is presumably the authority for that having been her real name.

**** St. Louis Women – Vol. 1 (1927–1929)
Document DOCD-5290 *Smith; prob. DeLoise Searcy, unknown (p); Lonnie Johnson (vn, g, v). 5/27–12/28.*
**(*) St. Louis Women – Vol. 2 (1934–1941)
Document DOCD-5291 *Smith; unknown (p); unknown (g); unknown (b). 1/41.*

These discs are shared with Alice Moore; *Vol. 1* contains the 12 Blue Belle recordings, and *Vol. 2* the four by Streamline Mae. Document distribute her other recordings among Charlie Jordan's *Vol. 1* (DOCD-5097), the VAC *St. Louis Barrelhouse Piano* (DOCD-5104) and Roosevelt Sykes's *Vol. 1* (DOCD-5116) and *Vol. 2* (DOCD-5117).

Blue Belle is a confident singer, ably supported on most titles by Johnson and Searcy. Her songs often feature striking images, with death, dreams and phallic animals (snakes, lizards, eels) recurrent. These beasties are not servants of jocular double meaning; the lyrics of 'Creepin' Eel Blues' seem to be aiming that way, but Smith's pinched, breathless delivery simmers with sexual unease. These blues tap into the id, and are among the few that deserve to be called surreal; equally unsettling, in different ways, are 'High Water Blues', recorded in the immediate aftermath of the 1927 Mississippi flood, and the confrontational 'Sweet Black Woman'. Streamline Mae's songs are pastiches of Memphis Minnie and Lil Green, pleasant but vastly more conventional. CS

Barkin' Bill Smith (born 1928)
VOCAL

Originally from Cleveland, Mississippi, Smith left as a young man and made his way to East St Louis, thence to Detroit and finally Chicago. He has been singing blues in the clubs there since the '50s, in the company of musicians like Homesick James, who gave him his nickname. Around 1974 he had an all-female band, Unisex. Since the mid-'80s he has been a staple of the North Side club scene. He joined Dave Specter & The Bluebirds on their formation in 1989 and sang with them for several years.

**(*) Gotcha!
Delmark DE-672 *Smith; Kenny Anderson (t); Bill McFarland (tb); Hank Ford (ts); Sonny Seals (bs); Tad Robinson (h); Ken Saydak (o, p); Vince Willis (p); Steve Freund, Herb Walker, Craig Davis, Steve Dawson (g); Hank Terson, Vince Oglesby, Nick Charles (b); Jon Hiller, John Felker (d); Diane Christiansen (v). 94.*

Smith's collaboration with Dave Specter, *Bluebird Blues* (Delmark DD-652), is discussed in Specter's entry. *Gotcha!*, billed as by Barkin' Bill, exchanges Specter for one of his Chicago mentors, Steve Freund, but is less of a guitar-based recording than its predecessor. It is also more revealing about Smith's vocal models. 'Someday After Awhile' and, of course, 'No Rollin'' Blues' are in thrall to Jimmy Witherspoon, 'Sufferin' Mind' nods to Percy Mayfield, and the genial spirit of Joe Williams hovers over several of the other numbers. The repertoire net is thrown wide, scooping up songs by Eddie Boyd, Little Johnny Taylor and Brook Benton, whose 'I Got What I Wanted' is handled, appropriately, with velvet gloves. As intermissions there are a couple of instrumentals for Freund to play with, 'Blue Guitar' and 'Hot Tomato'. A well-made record, but one likely to mean most to Smith's circle of friends and admirers. Smith also has two good performances on *Chicago's Best West & South Side Blues Singers Vol. 1* (Wolf 120.862), recorded in 1989 with a band headed by Johnny B. Moore and John Primer. TR

Byther Smith (born 1933)
VOCAL, GUITAR

Encouraged by his kinsman J. B. Lenoir, Smith came to Chicago in the late '50s. His first gigs were playing bass in a jazz trio, but within a few years he was concentrating on guitar, which he played in bands led by Junior Wells, George 'Harmonica' Smith and Big Mama Thornton. He had a long residence in the

'70s at Theresa's Lounge. His 1983 debut album Tell Me How You Like It won him some notice, and since then he has recorded and toured regularly.

***(*) Hold That Train
Delmark DE-774 *Smith; Mike Baietto (g); Bruce Felgen (b); Joe Pusateri (d). 7/81.*

Smith's debut album, originally released on the Grits label in 1983, finally made the transition to CD in 2004, retitled, losing one track ('Cut You Loose') but adding six outtakes. Reinstating it in catalogue was not merely filling a gap in Smith's CD discography, for it was a forceful recording that proves to be a match for much of his later work. Its low-budget simplicity has not been transformed by remixing: it still has the penetrating intensity of, to take one obviously comparable example, the early Otis Rush recordings. Smith's lines, on both guitar and voice, are hard, sharp and probing, and they grip the listener so firmly that one hardly notices the functional trio backing. The tracks new to record include a creditable reading of '[The] Thrill Is Gone', with diamantine guitar and several tempo changes, and satisfactory versions of Little Milton's 'So Mean To Me', Willie Dixon's 'Close To You' and Detroit Jr's 'So Unhappy', but the highlights are still the riveting slow blues 'Walked All Night Long' and 'I Don't Like To Travel'.

*** Housefire
Bullseye Blues CDBB 9503 *Smith; Ernest Potts (as, ts); Carl Alfred (ts); Bert Lewis, Lafayette Leake (kb); Mike Baietto, Leon Skibinski (g); Bruce Felgen (b); Joe Pusateri (d). 6/84.*

This is scary music. Smith's guitar sound is as cold as a tax inspector's heart: listening to 'The Man Wants Me Dead', you feel your ears freezing. The studio ambience gives the rhythm an echoing metallic ring that only accentuates the sounds of anger and alienation that come out of the music. The welter of industrial noise is more than a match for a merely human voice, and at times the lyrics are lost – a disservice in particular to 'Money Tree' and 'Live On And Sing The Blues'. A verse in the latter gives the album its title: 'Lost my mother at the age of one, lost my father at the age of two, lost my sister in a housefire – tell me what more can I lose?' Smith's admiration for Otis Rush, often implied, is explicit in 'Love Me Like I Love You'.

** Blues Knights
Evidence ECD 26042 *Smith; A. C. Reed (ts); Maurice John Vaughn (g); Douglas Watson (b); Julian Vaughn (d). 11/85.*

*** Addressing The Nation With The Blues
JSP JSP 5106 *Smith; Manwell Burr (s); Tim McKinley (kb, p); Charles Fisher (g); Bruce Felgen (b); George Hawkins (d). 89.*

Blues Knights was cut in France while Smith was part of the way through a European tour with Larry Davis and A. C. Reed's Spark Plugs. Smith sings and plays on six tracks, Davis on four, and the Reed band backs them both. The production has none of the edge of *Housefire*, and reduces Smith to a generic Chicago bluesman. The only track with anything distinctive about it is 'Addressing The Nation With The Blues', a rewriting of Otis Rush's 'Double Trouble'. Perhaps feeling he had not been able to do the song justice, Smith recorded it again, and to more arresting effect, on his JSP album, which took it for its title. The murky ambience of Rush's Cobra recordings also touches 'What Have I Done' and permeates 'I Was Coming Home', and these three numbers, with the B. B. Kingish 'I Wish My Mother Was Here' and the curiously patriotic 'Play The Blues On The Moon', form the backbone of a sturdy performance, only slightly marred by inappropriately busy drumming on a couple of tracks. (This remixed SACD issue replaces JSPCD 2105.)

**(*) I'm A Mad Man
Bullseye Blues CD BB 9527 *Smith; Wayne Jackson (t, tb); Jim Spake (ts, bs); Andrew Love (ts); Ron Levy (o, p, prod); James P. Anderson (g); Mike Boyle (b); Lloyd Anderson (d). 7/92.*

*** Mississippi Kid
Delmark DE-691 *Smith; Malachi Thompson (t, arr); Steve Berry (tb); Sonny Seals (ts); Bob Hecht (o, p); Jesse Lockridge (o); Jeff Jozwiak (g); Malvin Smith (b); James E. Knowles (d). 12/95.*

*** All Night Long
Delmark DE-708 *Smith; Malachi Thompson (t, arr); Steve Berry (tb); Sonny Seals (ts); Pat Hall (kb); Jeff Jozwiak (g); Greg McDaniel (b); Tino Cortez (d). 4/97.*

Smith's songwriting grew in individuality with each of these albums. *I'm A Mad Man* bristles with allusions to the work of others: 'Mad Man' is a recomposition of Muddy Waters's 'Manish Boy', 'Funky Man' takes off from Lou Donaldson's 'Everything I Do Gonh Be Funky From Now On' and '35 Years' is yet another oblique withdrawal from the Otis Rush account. The songs on *Mississippi Kid* are less referential and more quirky ('President's Daughter', 'Cora, You Made A Man Out Of Me'), though the strongest is a remake of an early single, 'Give Me My White Robe'. In *All Night Long* he confidently jokes about other blues singers in 'I'm Your New Lover', takes a strong line on disc jockeys in 'Hey Mr. Dee Jay' and patrols a country beat in 'Mother You Say You Don't Like The Black Colors' and 'Is He White Or Is He Black?' On all three sets his choked voice, trenchant guitar and measured pacing of mostly slow and medium-tempo blues give him a strong claim to be carrying Albert King's good work on. His emphatic performance is slightly undermined on *I'm A Mad Man* by dull production and a mix that doesn't always give his voice and guitar due prominence. The Delmarks place both where they should be, front and centre.

*** Smitty's Blues
Black & Tan CD B&T 008 *Smith; Matthijs Willemsen (t); Jon Spijker (ts); Roel Spanjers (o, p); Richard van Bergen (g); Nico Heilijgers (b); Arthur Bont (d). 11/00.*

*** Throw Away The Book
Black & Tan CD B&T 017 *Smith; Roel Spanjers (o, p); Richard van Bergen (g); Nico Heilijgers (b); J. J. Goossens (d). 10/03.*

The notes claim that *Smitty's Blues* is 'as rough and tough as they come these days'. 'Tough' will be interpreted by experienced listeners, correctly, to mean that this is the work of a firm-minded artist who is very happy to work in the Chicago idiom of 30 to 40 years ago. 'Rough' is a mild slur on a well-produced and, by and large, quite smooth performance by both artist and band: this is not the jagged Smith of *Housefire*, but neither is it the jetlagged one of *Blues Knights*. What the notes don't state, but titles like 'Five Long Years', 'She's A Good 'Un' and 'Tramp' indicate, is that this Dutch recording is something new in Smith's output: an album in which his own songs are subordinated to genre standards. He claims only four of the dozen titles as his, and one of those, 'Your Daughter Don't Want Me No More', first heard on

Mississippi Kid, is four fifths J. B. Lenoir's. To this unaccustomed task he brings some independence of interpretation and a good deal of vitality, and the album, though uneventful when compared with his early work, is seldom less than inviting. *Throw Away The Book* is a more emphatic performance, perhaps because Smith is working almost entirely with his own material. A new version of 'The Man Wants Me Dead' loses little of its icy menace, and the abiding influence of Otis Rush permeates 'Love Me Like I Love You' and another remake, 'I Don't Like To Travel'. TR

Carrie Smith (born 1941)
VOCAL

Carrie Smith was born in Georgia, but made her singing debut in church after her family moved to Newark. She appeared at the Newport Jazz Festival in 1957 as a member of a gospel choir, but her secular breakthrough didn't come until 1975, when she sang Bessie Smith's songs with the New York Jazz Repertory Company at Carnegie Hall. Since then she has toured worldwide singing blues, jazz and gospel.

**** When You're Down And Out
Black & Blue BB 904 *Smith; George Kelly (ts); Ram Ramirez (p); Billy Butler (g); Al Hall (b); Eddie Locke (d). 4/77.*

**** Confessin' The Blues
Evidence ECD 26021 *As above, except add Doc Cheatham, Dick Vance (t), Vic Dickenson (tb), Budd Johnson (ss, ts), Eddie Barefield (as), Hank Jones, Sir Charles Thompson (p), George Duvivier (b), Oliver Johnson, Panama Francis (d). 7/76–7/77.*

Carrie Smith takes inspiration from Bessie Smith, Dinah Washington, Billie Holiday and Ella Fitzgerald among others, but she never imitates anyone directly; rather, she takes what she needs from her forerunners' approaches to timing, timbre and note-bending, and incorporates them into her own subtle but always swinging style. Anyone who can find her own interpretation of Bessie's 'Nobody Knows You When You're Down And Out' and 'Do Your Duty', or sing 'Mama (He Treats Your Daughter Mean)' without making the listener think of Ruth Brown, is an artist to be reckoned with. The Black & Blue disc is a slightly expanded LP, which also supplies most of the Evidence CD. Smith gets superb collaboration (accompaniment is quite the wrong word) from a small, sax-led group; Evidence add six songs from other Black & Blue sessions, made with larger but equally distinguished bands.

**(*) Gospel Time
Black & Blue BB 949 *Smith; Andre Franklin (p, v); Oliver Jackson (d); Constance Speed, Clifford Jamerson (v). 4/82.*

It's seldom defensible to condemn a CD on the basis of one track, but 'I Believe' makes the temptation almost irresistible. Nothing else on *Gospel Time* is anywhere near as bad, but despite Smith's church roots, it's a disappointing disc. There's much better gospel singing readily available, some of it on *The Gospel Truth* (Criss Cross 1192) by the Wycliffe Gordon Sextet, where Ms Smith guests on four tracks.

Carrie Smith's secular jazz singing is outside our remit, but we draw the attention of interested readers to *Fine And Mellow* (Audiophile ACD-164) and *Every Now And Then* (Silver Streak SS 203). CS

Clara Smith (c. 1894–1935)
VOCAL

A native of South Carolina, Clara Smith was on the TOBA circuit at an early age, and topping the bill by 1918. In 1923 she arrived in New York, where she operated a club while continuing to appear in revue both locally and out of town. In the '30s the Depression, and perhaps the heart disease from which she died, slowed down her activities.

**(*) Clara Smith Vol. 1 (1923–1924)
Document DOCD-5364 *Smith; Elmer Chambers (c); unknown (t); unknown (tb); Ernest Elliott (cl, as); unknown (cl); Porter Grainger (k); Fletcher Henderson, prob. Stanley Miller, Charles A. Matson (p); Clarence Conaway (md); unknown (bj); Lincoln M. Conaway (g); Bessie Smith (v). 6/23–1/24.*

*** Clara Smith Vol. 2 (1924)
Document DOCD-5365 *Smith; Elmer Chambers (c); Charlie Green (tb); Ernest Elliott (cl, as); Don Redman (cl, goofus); Cecil Scott (cl); Herbert Leonard (h); Porter Grainger (k, p); Fletcher Henderson (p, u); Charles A. Matson (p); Charlie Dixon (bj, g); Clarence Conaway (g, u); Lincoln M. Conaway (g); prob. Kaiser Marshall (d); unknown (woodblocks). 1/24–12/24.*

*** Clara Smith Vol. 3 (1925)
Document DOCD-5366 *Smith; Louis Armstrong, Harry Cooper (c); unknown (t); Charlie Green, Ted Nixon, unknown (tb); Bob Fuller, Ernest Elliott (cl, as); Prince Robinson, unknown (cl); unknown (as); Harry Stevens (bss); Herbert Leonard (h); Stanley Miller (p, prob. sp); Fletcher Henderson, Porter Grainger, Lemuel Fowler, Mike Jackson, unknowns (p); Leon Abbey (vn); Buddy Christian, unknowns (bj); Harry Meyers (g); unknown (wh); Bessie Smith (v). 1/25–11/25.*

***(*) Clara Smith Vol. 4 (1926–1927)
Document DOCD-5367 *Smith; Joe Smith (c); Tom Edwards (tb); Ernest Elliott (cl, as); Clarence Adams (cl); Bob Fuller (as); unknown (ts); Stanley Miller, Lemuel Fowler, Fletcher Henderson, Clarence Parson, Porter Grainger (p); Herman Gibson, unknown (bj); Ethel Grainger, Odette Jackson (v). 5/26–6/27.*

***(*) Clara Smith Vol. 5 (1927–1929)
Document DOCD-5368 *Smith; Gus Aiken, Joe Smith, Ed Allen (c); Freddie Jenkins (t); John Anderson, Charlie Green, unknown (tb); Bob Fuller, poss. George Baquet, poss. Ben Whittet, unknowns (cl); unknown (as); unknown (k); Stanley Miller (o, p); Porter Grainger, Lemuel Fowler, James P. Johnson, unknowns (p); Marion Cumbo (vc); unknown (g); unknown (eff). 7/27–12/29.*

*** Clara Smith Vol. 6 (1930–1932)
Document DOCD-5369 *Smith; Ed Allen (c); Asbestos Burns (p, v); Porter Grainger, J. C. Johnson, Alex Hill, Clarence Williams, Fred Longshaw (p); Lonnie Johnson (g, v). 7/30–3/32.*

***(*) The Queen Of The Moaners 1923/1932
EPM Blues Collection 16004 *Similar to relevant CDs above. 8/23–3/32.*

***(*) The Essential
Classic Blues CBL 200027 2CD *Similar to relevant CDs above. 10/23–8/31.*

***(*) The Essential Clara Smith 1924–1929
Retrieval RTR 79030 *Similar to relevant CDs above. 1/24–12/29.*

If she'd been born Clara Jones, her work would probably be more celebrated, and it wouldn't be necessary for all considerations of Clara Smith to start with variants of 'Despite being overshadowed by Bessie Smith ...' Clara Smith's voice was smaller than the Empress's, as can be heard on the three disappointing duets they recorded, undoubtedly at Columbia's behest, but this is not the point. What matters is that her voice was flexible, melodious and true, with an appealingly husky edge to it; her slides, slurs and blue notes are pinpoint accurate, and used to telling artistic effect, not as gimmicks. A very good all-round blues singer, and a notably sensuous interpreter of songs like 'Whip It To A Jelly' and 'It's Tight Like That' (the finest version on record), she also gives a wholly authentic reading to the spiritual 'Living Humble', and makes a good fist of popular tunes like 'When My Sugar Walks Down The Street'.

Naturally, not every one of Smith's 124 songs is a gem of both composition and performance, and Document's lifelessly remastered *Vol. 1* is further diminished by Fletcher Henderson's drab piano, the only accompaniment on most tracks. Even at this stage, though, Smith's voice, while it had some maturing to do, was a formidable instrument. Henderson is also present on about half of *Vol. 2*, but he usually yields the spotlight to members of his orchestra, and this is a superior, if still an uneven, instalment in the story. Louis Armstrong, appearing on five titles and an alternative take, is the star sideman on *Vol. 3*, but most of the other accompanists, from less famous to totally anonymous, also do good work, although the batsqueaking Herbert Leonard is an egregious exception. *Vols. 4* and *5* are the best of the 'complete works', with consistently good accompaniments (the percussive pianos of Lem Fowler and James P. Johnson are especially noteworthy) and Smith's voice at its strong, smooth, lyric-caressing best. *Vol. 5* includes the extraordinary and brilliant 'Wanna Go Home', a dead-slow lament accompanied by reed-organ and cello. There's a slight falling-off on *Vol. 6*; Clara sometimes sounds tired, perhaps because of ill health, but there are still plenty of fine performances, including four duets with Lonnie Johnson (worth hearing in the context of her *oeuvre* as well as his) and a couple of hilarious point numbers: 'Ol' Sam Tages' chronicles a lecher's downfall to the tune of 'Old Man River', and 'For Sale (Hannah Johnson's Jack Ass)' has fun with a pun. This disc is completed with four 1927 recordings by a different Clara Smith, accompanied by Harold Lewis on very good but sadly muffled cornet.

The three selective sets are all well done, though none of them is perfect. EPM seek to cover Smith's whole career, which means enduring three Henderson accompaniments before getting to the good part; this is, however, the only one of the chrestomathies to include 'Whip It To A Jelly' and 'Living Humble'. Retrieval is primarily a jazz label, and the selection is famous-accompanist-driven: all the songs with Armstrong (but not the alternative take) are included, and all those with James P. Johnson and Coleman Hawkins. Sound restoration is good, but not up to John R. T. Davies's usual standard. The Classic Blues 2CD, with 36 tracks in the best sound and at mid-price, is the pick of the bunch, despite including all the duets with Bessie Smith and only one Armstrong accompaniment. CS

Effie Smith (1914–77)
VOCAL

Effie Bly was born in Oklahoma. In the '30s she worked as a band singer on the West Coast, and by the '40s she was sufficiently well known to contribute some numbers to AFRS Jubilee radio transcriptions, sing with Benny Carter's orchestra and record for several LA labels, some owned by her second husband, the singer/songwriter John L. Criner, who composed much of her material. She had some minor hits in the '60s with comedy numbers, and later worked in promotion at Stax Records.

*** **Effie Smith 1945–1953**
Classics 5116 Smith; Karl George, John 'Teddy' Buckner, Maynard Ferguson, Pete Candoli, Gerald Wilson, unknown (t); Dick Noel, Tom Pederson (tb); Jackie Kelso, Caughey Roberts, Les Robinson, Dave Harris (as); Maxwell Davis, Buddy Floyd, unknowns (ts); Charles Waller, Joe Cook (bs); Clara Lewis, Wilbert Baranco, T. B. Watson, Ike Carpenter, prob. Fletcher Smith, unknown (p); Lucky Enois, Buddy Harper, unknown (g); Red Callender, Dave Robinson, unknowns (b); Johnny Otis, Oscar Lee Bradley, Roy Milton, Jesse Sailes, unknowns (d); Jimmie Grissom, Henry Criner, unknown children, unknowns (v). 45–8/53.

Second-rank singers in '40s California tended to mirror the stars of the day like Charles Brown or Dinah Washington, or at any rate were encouraged to do so on their records. Effie Smith, however, comes over as a refreshingly original vocalist as well as a gifted and intelligent one, and when she has well-chosen accompanists she makes very attractive records. Her half-dozen Aladdin sides with Buddy Harper's All Stars are exceptional, her singing, now tough, now tender, prompting admirable solos from Maxwell Davis, Jackie Kelso and Karl George. Her early work, which also included sessions with Johnny Otis and Roy Milton lineups, was predominantly bluesy, but later recordings had more novelty elements: 'Crazy Crazy' with the Ike Carpenter Orchestra edges towards big-band rock 'n' roll, and 'Dial That Telephone' is a humorous talking item. TR

(Little) George 'Harmonica' Smith (1924–83)
VOCAL, HARMONICA

George Smith was born in Arkansas and raised in Cairo, Illinois, where he took up the harmonica. He began working in Chicago in 1949, moving in 1954 to Kansas City, where he was spotted and signed by Modern Records. His first single, 'Telephone Blues'/'Blues In The Dark', had some regional success. The following year he settled in LA, where he remained for the rest of his life, playing and recording in various settings, including a spell with the Muddy Waters band, and helping to mould the styles of younger harmonica players such as William Clarke, Kim Wilson, James Harman and, in particular, Rod Piazza, with whom he played for several years in the band Bacon Fat.

**** **Harmonica Ace**
Ace CDCHD 337 Smith; Maxwell Davis, unknown (s); unknowns (p, g, b, d). 55–56.
(*) **Blowing The Blues
El Segundo 98001 Smith; Eldee Williams, Paul Madison, Willie Randell, unknown (s); William Clarke (h); J. D. Nicholson (o, p); Ernest Lane, Jim Borden, unknown (p); Pete Lewis, Jimmy Nolen, Marshall Hooks, Craig Printup, unknown (g); Curtis

Tillman, Bob Tate, Al Bedrosian, unknowns (b); Chuck Thomas, Matt Goodwine, unknowns (d); unknown (vb); unknowns (v). 56–78.

*** Now You Can Talk About Me
Blind Pig BP-5049 *Smith*; Rod Piazza (h); J. D. Nicholson (o, p); Honey Piazza (p); Pete Lewis, Marshall Hooks, Jimmy Nolen, Junior Watson, Doug MacLeod, unknown (g); Curtis Tillman, Bill Stuve, unknown (b); Chuck Thomas, Bill Swartz, unknown (d). 60, 66, 4/82.

The big, plushy sound of Smith's harmonica on 'Blues In The Dark' declares him to be one of the most gifted contemporaries of Little and Big Walter, and since he was a better singer than either of them, it may be wondered why he is not held in higher regard. Probably it was because he chose to work in LA, not the most nourishing place for a musician with his roots, and a location that lay beyond the sights of many blues harmonica fans in the '60s. *Harmonica Ace* catches him just before he went West, singing and playing superbly on 'Telephone Blues' and 'Early One Monday Morning', and just after he got there, adapting confidently to a Maxwell Davis arrangement on 'Love Life' and yodelling enthusiastically on 'Hey Mr Porter'. (Note that 'Blues In The Dark' and 'Blues Stay Away' are programmed as a single track, which throws out the numbering of the rest of the CD.)

Blowing The Blues collects virtually all the other singles Smith made on the West Coast, chiefly for the Sotoplay label. They are quite varied, sometimes straightforward downhome blues like 'Good Things', a refit of 'Hi Heel Sneakers', and 'Brown Mule', sometimes bigger productions with horns and a showy guitarist, such as 'Times Won't Be Hard Always' or 'You Can't Undo What's Been Done', which are a little like Bobby 'Blue' Bland's contemporary work for Duke. Much of the music is exciting but the sound is sometimes awful, thanks to the original recordings, which were often ill-balanced to start with, having been issued on villainous pressings. A couple of items from this period not included on this CD are 'Go Ahead On' on *Elko Blues Volume 2* (Wolf 120.615) and 'Just Bluesin'' on *Elko Blues Volume 3* (Wolf 120.616).

Now You Can Talk About Me, after an *hors d'oeuvre* of five '60s singles (all on the El Segundo CD, but Blind Pig's sound is better), serves as its main dish most of Smith's 1982 Murray Brothers album *Boogie'n With George*. This was his last session, but nothing in his performance betrays the fact. True, there is a preponderance of unhurried numbers. Despite its title, 'Astatic Stomp', a duet with Piazza, is no more than a gentle jog. But it was at slow tempos that Smith's playing was most impressive, both for its control and for the limpid tone he always strove to achieve.

These albums give a just account of Smith's abilities, but not by any means a complete one. Regrettably, other worthwhile recordings, such as *Blues With A Feeling: A Tribute To Little Walter* (originally on World Pacific, reissued as part of *Chicago Blues Masters Vol. 3* [Capitol 36288 2CD]) and the albums with Bacon Fat for Blue Horizon and Deram, are not presently available. TR

the '70s he worked with Kevin Coyne, appearing on five of his albums, but since then he has been in semi-retirement.

*** Out Of The Bottleneck
Master Mix CHECD 00120 *Smith*; Bernie Pallo (ac). 99.

On this virtually solo album (an accordionist dropped in to play on Leadbelly's 'Goodnight Irene') Smith displays a casual mastery of blues guitar styles from Mance Lipscomb to Fred McDowell and Blind Blake to Robert Johnson. He sings powerfully and without affectation on Big Bill Broonzy's 'In The Evening', and plays a luxuriant improvisation on Lonnie Johnson's guitar solo 'Blues For [The] West End'. TR

J. T. 'Funny Papa' Smith
VOCAL, GUITAR

Thomas Shaw, who played with him in Oklahoma, remembered Smith as a plantation overseer and a convicted murderer, though it is unclear how he fitted a 25-year sentence around recording dates in 1930–31 and '35. Nothing of Smith's was released from the last session, and his life thereafter is entirely unknown. No photograph of him has been discovered.

*** J. T. 'Funny Paper' Smith (1930–1931)
RST Blues Documents BDCD-6016 *Smith*; Magnolia Harris, Dessa Foster (v). 9/30–7/31.
*** Funny Papa Smith 1930–1931 The Original Howling Wolf
Yazoo 1031 As above. 9/30–7/31.

The original 78s gave his nickname as 'Funny Paper', apparently a mistake. Certainly there is nothing comic about Smith's thoughtfully worded narratives and carefully organized guitar lines. Including his duets with a pair of quintessentially Texan hard-voices, Magnolia Harris and Dessa Foster, his issued work amounts to just 24 sides made in less than a year, and two of those have never been discovered. That he recorded even that much is owing to the success of his debut single, the two-part 'Howling Wolf Blues'. Whether because of its catchy vocal melody or its bragging opening line, 'I'm that wolf that everybody been trying to find out where in the world I prowl', the disc, according to a June 1931 letter to dealers from Brunswick's Dallas office, was 'the biggest selling record on the market today … It is true that this is a Race Record and you might think therefore that its sales would be confined to your colored trade. Not so. You will be surprised how many white folk will buy it.' Smith duly supplied parts 3 and 4 and a two-part 'Seven Sisters Blues', similarly constructed and in the same key of A. His distinctive and deftly executed guitar patterns have appealed to two generations of Texan singer/guitarists, and he is commemorated in the work of, among others, Thomas Shaw and Willie Lane. If it were not for a certain coolness of view, an elegant detachment, he would perhaps be more widely recognized as an artist of the first rank. The Blues Documents CD gathers his complete solo and duet work; the Yazoo (whose cover picture is of Black Ace) is a more selective account, better remastered. TR

Gordon Smith (born 1949)
VOCAL, GUITAR

A Tynesider, Smith is a veteran of the British blues scene, having made his first album, for Blue Horizon, in 1968. During

Jimi 'Prime Time' Smith (born 1960)
VOCAL, GUITAR

Smith is the son of Johnnie Mae Smith (née Dunson), who played drums with Jimmy Reed and other Chicago artists in

the '50s and '60s. He began playing guitar about the age of 12, tutored by Reed, Floyd Jones and Eddie Taylor, and in Reed's last years occasionally accompanied him on stage.

**(*) Give Me Wings
Atomic Theory ATM 1142 *Smith; Tom Burns (h); Michael Pendergast, Brother Jack McDuff (o); Mick Massof (b, v); Donald 'Hye Pockets' Robertson (d, v).* 5/98.

Smith's club act, if it's accurately depicted by this set from Blues Alley in Minneapolis, is an attractive mixture of blues with an occasional instrumental foray into what used to be called soul-jazz, spearheaded by guitar and Hammond organ: here, 'Walkin' The Dog', a tune by, and featuring, McDuff, and 'Killer Joe'. The funky energy of 'Tipping' or Luther Allison's 'Soul Fixin' Man' is contrasted with 'When You're Doin' Alright' or 'U For Me', both Jimmy Reed grooves, Burns playing apt harmonica on the latter, and with poised readings of slow blues such as Albert Collins's 'If Trouble Was Money' and Albert King's 'I'll Play The Blues For You'. Smith has a strong, meaty voice – rather like King's, as it happens – and is a decisive guitarist whose only foible is that in a long solo he sometimes loses himself in rock-guitar hyperspace. Without making great claims for him, you could say he deserves to be a little better known. TR

Laura Smith
VOCAL

Smith is said to have been from Indianapolis, She was appearing in revue by 1920, and toured widely. In 1929 she signed with Paramount Pictures and moved to Los Angeles. The Chicago Defender *reported the completion of her first film the following year, but no copy has been traced. She died in 1932.*

*** Laura Smith – Vol. 1 (1924–27)
Document DOCD-5429 *Smith; Tom Morris, unknown (c); unknown (t); Charlie Irvis, unknown (tb); Ernest Elliott, prob. Bob Fuller, unknown (cl); unknown (as); unknown (h); Clarence Williams, prob. Perry Bradford, prob. Mike Jackson, Lukie Johnson, unknowns (p); unknowns (vn); Buddy Christian (bj); unknowns (g).* c. 8/24–c. 3/27.

*** Edna Hicks – Hazel Meyers – Laura Smith – Vol. 2 (1923–1927)
Document DOCD-5431 *Smith; Clarence M. Jones (p).* 6/27.

Even today, writers on the female blues singers of the '20s usually find it necessary to mention in passing that Clara, Bessie, Mamie and Trixie Smith were unrelated. There was a widespread belief among their contemporary audience that they were sisters, and the record industry doesn't seem to have discouraged it. OKeh saw it as a way to market Laura Smith's records, advertising her as 'the first of that famous blues-singin' Smith family', and the company evidently encouraged her to sing as forcefully as she knew how. She does so successfully, but by 5/26 her voice was sounding strained, and it may be that her absence from records until the following January was enforced.

With two exceptions, the first 16 titles on *Vol. 1* are of high quality. Smith is usually accompanied by Clarence Williams, sometimes alone, sometimes leading bands drawn from his circle of musicians, but on half a dozen titles she's backed by Perry Bradford's Mean Four. On two of these the Mean Four are an orthodox line-up but on the other four they're an eccentric, surprisingly swinging assembly of harmonica, one or two violins, guitar and piano. The two songs that don't work are religious in content. It's scarcely appropriate to call them 'spirituals'; despite Smith's vibrant singing, the whining, foot-dragging backing she receives from two violins and a guitar is as devoid of swing as it is of enthusiasm.

Evidently released from her OKeh contract, Smith spent 1927 label-hopping, returning to OKeh for one more disc. She progressively moderated the force of her singing, but it remains very likeable, and her accompaniments continue to be usually of high calibre; on her return to OKeh, she was joined by an anonymous cornettist who evidently admired King Oliver. Once again, there is an exception to this rule, a solitary side featuring the strange combination of alto sax, violin and piano. *Vol. 1* closes with a charming, husky rendition of the traditional 'Don't You Leave Me Here'. An alternative take of this song is one of two titles on *"Too Late, Too Late"* – *Vol. 6* (Document DOCD-5461), and two OKeh titles unavailable when *Vol. 1* was compiled are on *Female Blues (1921–1928)* – *The Remaining Titles* (Document DOCD-1005).

Vol. 2 contains Smith's last four titles, made for Victor, on which she is accompanied by the excellent and underrated Clarence M. Jones. These songs are given an intimate, quietly sophisticated delivery that's radically different from the vibrato-laden belting of her earlier sides. Two of them deal empathetically with the 1927 Mississippi flood, employing a tone of world-weary resignation that's both an unusual and a successful approach to this theme. CS

Mamie Smith (1883–1946)
VOCAL

Mamie Smith was ten years old when she left Cincinnati for a showbiz career. By 1920 she was a star in Harlem; her OKeh records, and especially 'Crazy Blues', made her a nationwide phenomenon among African-Americans. Smith was not the first black artist to record, and she was by no means one of the greatest, but her records were the first aimed specifically at black purchasers. Their success revealed the existence of a lucrative market and opened doors for other singers. After her recording career faltered, Smith kept busy with live appearances until her long final illness began in 1944.

**(*) Mamie Smith – Vol. 1 (1920–1921)
Document DOCD-5357 *Smith; Ed Cox, Johnny Dunn (c); Jules Levy, Julius Berkin (t); Dope Andrews, poss. Herb Flemming, Eph Hannaford, unknown (tb); Nathan Glantz, unknown (cl, as); Joseph Samuels (cl, vn); Ernest Elliott, Buster Bailey (cl); unknown (bss); unknown (bsn); Willie 'The Lion' Smith, prob. Perry Bradford, Porter Grainger, Phil Worde, Larry Briers (p); Leroy Parker (vn); unknown (bj); Harry Hall or Chink Johnson (bb); Mort Perry, unknown (d).* 2/20–c. 8/21.

**(*) Mamie Smith – Vol. 2 (1921–1922)
Document DOCD-5358 *Smith; Jules Levy, Julius Berkin, Bubber Miley, prob. George Mullen, unknowns (t); Eph Hannaford, Jake Green, prob. Cecil Carpenter, unknowns (tb); Bob Fuller (cl, ss); Nathan Glantz, unknown (cl, as); Joseph Samuels (cl, vn); unknown (cl); prob. Coleman Hawkins, unknown (as); unknown (bsn); Larry Briers, Gilliam, Charles Matson, unknowns (p); Herman Berkin (cel, d); George Bell, unknown (vn); unknowns (bb); Curtis Moseley, poss. Cutie Perkins, unknowns (d).* c. 8/21–c. 5/22.

*** **Mamie Smith – Vol. 3 (1922–1923)**
Document DOCD-5359 *Smith; prob. George Mullen, prob. Bubber Miley, Joe Smith, unknown (t); prob. Cecil Carpenter, unknowns (tb); Ernest Elliott (cl, poss. as); poss. Garvin Bushell (cl, as); Bob Fuller (cl); Sidney Bechet (ss); Herschel Brassfield (as); Coleman Hawkins (prob. as, ts); unknowns (ts); Charles Matson, poss. Harvey Brooks, Clarence Williams, Porter Grainger, unknowns (p); George Bell, poss. Leroy Parker (vn); Samuel Speed, Buddy Christian, unknown (bj); prob. Curtis Moseley or Cutie Perkins, unknowns (d).* c. 5/22–c. 8/23.

(*) **Mamie Smith – Vol. 4 (1923–1942)
Document DOCD-5360 *Smith; prob. Louis Metcalf, Gus Aiken, Horace Holmes, Tom Morris (c); unknowns (t); Jake Frazier, Charlie Irvis, unknowns (tb); Percy Glascoe, Ernie Bullock (cl, s); unknown (ss); Bob Fuller, unknowns (as); unknowns (ts); unknown (bs); Alex Jackson (bss); Porter Grainger, Louis Hooper Leslie A. Hutchinson ['Hutch'], prob. Mike Jackson or J. C. Johnson, unknowns (p); unknown (one-string fiddle); Elmer Snowden, Buddy Christian, unknown (bj); unknowns (g); unknowns (b); unknown (bb); Norman Buster, unknowns (d); The Alphabetical Four, unknowns (v).* c. 8/23–c. 3/40 or 4/40.

(*) **The Best Of Mamie Smith
Columbia/Legacy CK 65712 *Similar to above CDs.* 8/20–2/31.

(*) **The Essential
Classic Blues CBL 200036 2CD *Similar to above CDs.* 8/20–c. 3/40 or 4/40.

Mamie Smith's contemporaries admired her lavish lifestyle, and experienced her success as a vicarious triumph for 'the race'. She was unquestionably a star, but it's evident that she benefited from being first on the scene; her expressive range was limited, and this became apparent as singers emerged who had more emotional commitment and sang more instinctively. By 1923, when OKeh let her go, it was essentially all over. Smith's material was not always of the highest quality; she recorded some deeply shallow novelties, and from time to time was handed eulogies to an imaginary Southern paradise, and tributes to mammy that make Al Jolson sound hard-boiled. She sings these horrors with apparent sincerity, but 80 years on they don't appeal even as camp.

Document's first two volumes are the least likely to attract present-day listeners; apart from Smith's own shortcomings, the accompaniments, even by musicians who elsewhere made important jazz recordings, are undistinguished, declining into pap when a white studio band takes over on the last three tracks of *Vol. 1* and the first 11 of *Vol. 2*. Best of the bunch is *Vol. 3*; Smith sings with more vigour (the appalling 'Sighin' Around With The Blues' excepted), and the accompaniments are more consistent. When Joe Smith and Sidney Bechet lead the band – unfortunately for just one and two songs respectively – they are very good indeed.

Vol. 4 opens with the last side from Smith's original OKeh contract, followed by occasional sessions which she managed to garner between 1924 and 1942. The sound quality is better, and 'Golf Course Papa' and 'Jenny's Ball' are amusing; 'The Lure Of The South' and 'Wonderful Mammy' are not. There's good jazz from a Tom Morris group on Victor, but this disc is essentially a mopping-up operation. Two film soundtracks with Lucky Millinder's band show that Smith was still a strong vocalist at nearly 60, and still an artistically limited one.

It will be evident that *The Essential* Mamie Smith is an oxymoron, notwithstanding its superior remastering. Columbia's claim to issue *The Best Of Mamie Smith* is more defensible, and naturally the sound is excellent. What's not defensible is the claim that two tracks are previously unissued when they've been previously released on Columbia. Completely indefensible is the statement (repeated in the notes, on the back cover and on a sticker) that Mamie Smith was 'the first black vocalist to sing on a commercial American record'. This from the company that had Bert Williams under contract from 1906 to 1922! All that aside, this selection is in any case the best of a second-rank artist. CS

Pine Top Smith (1904–29)
VOCAL, PIANO

Clarence Smith, from Alabama, began performing professionally as a teenager, appearing in vaudeville as a dancer, comedian and musician. He was based in Pittsburgh from about 1920, but moved to Chicago in 1928 to take advantage of recording opportunities. He was killed by a stray bullet in a dancehall in March 1929, two days after making his last, unissued recording.

***(*) **Boogie Woogie & Barrelhouse Piano Vol. 1 (1928–1932)**
Document DOCD-5102 *Smith; poss. Mayo Williams, unknown (sp).* 12/28–1/29.

'Pine Top's Boogie Woogie' got the term on record and generated a multitude of subsequent versions, but it was Smith, instructing the dancers as his playing rolls elegantly towards the famous stop-time breaks, who made the theme irresistible in the first place. Just as authoritative are 'Pine Top Blues' and 'Jump Steady Blues'; each of these three compositions was issued in two versions, and all are worth hearing, although the B take of 'Jump Steady' comes from a rough original. Smith's other five recordings are cynical comic routines with piano; the comedy is savage on 'Big Boy They Can't Do That', an outspoken attack on the police, courts and prisons. One could wish for more of the laconic singing heard on 'Pine Top Blues', but this material is not just valuable for the piano playing. The CD also features Charles Avery and 'Jabo' Williams. Avery plays a masterly 'Dearborn Street Breakdown', and four inventive accompaniments to Freddie 'Redd' Nicholson. ('Tee Roller's Rub', with J. H. Shayne on piano, completes Nicholson's issued recordings.) Williams's eight-title session is one of the finest and most aggressive sets of barrelhouse piano in existence. Some of the 78s it derives from are very battered, and two titles come from the only known copy. Given the limitations of some of the source discs, Document's remastering is generally acceptable; the finest performances here are also on Yazoo VACs in better sound, but Smith's complete works are never less than high-quality music. CS

Spark Plug Smith
VOCAL, GUITAR

Faintly reminiscent of Luke Jordan, this single-session figure may, like him, have been from Virginia. His nickname may have been derived from the famous racehorse, from his hypothetical day job as an auto mechanic or from neither of the above.

** **Spark Plug Smith & Tallahassee Tight (1933–1934)**
Document DOCD-5387 *Smith.* 1/33.

The ordinariness of Smith's 'Motherless Boy' and 'Deserted Man Blues' suggests that the blues form was not particularly to his taste, and indeed these are the only 12-bar pieces in his issued repertoire, his eight other recordings being vaudeville numbers or popular songs, either elderly ones like 'A Shanty In Old Shanty Town' and 'Sweet Evening Breeze' or the more recent 'My Blue Heaven'. Smith delivers them all with a light touch somewhat reminiscent of Cliff Edwards, interspersing verses with scat choruses and accompanying himself on guitar with pallid fluency. His distance from any conventional definition of a blues singer makes him interesting to the student of vernacular recording practice, but the less committed listener will probably find his performances too lightweight to settle in the memory, especially in these transfers from mostly poor originals. The balance of the CD is by Tallahassee Tight. TR

Trixie Smith (1895–1943)
VOCAL

Born in Atlanta, Smith moved when she was about 20 to New York, where she won an important blues-singing contest in 1922. Initially popular on the TOBA circuit, she also appeared in New York revues and musical comedies during the '20s and '30s.

**(*) Trixie Smith – Vol. 1 (1922–1924)
Document DOCD-5332 Smith; Elmer Chambers, prob. Howard Scott, unknown (c); poss. Russell Smith, unknowns (t); Charlie Green, prob. George Brashear, poss. Ted Nixon, unknowns (tb); unknown (cl, as); Don Redman, Buster Bailey, prob. Edgar Campbell, unknowns (cl); unknown (as); prob. Walter Watkins (ts); James P. Johnson, Fletcher Henderson, unknowns (p); unknowns (vn); Charlie Dixon, unknowns (bj); unknowns (bb). 1/22–12/24.

*** Trixie Smith – Vol. 2 (1925–1939)
Document DOCD-5333 Smith; Louis Armstrong, Joe Smith, unknown (c); Charlie Shavers, Henry Allen, prob. Phil Napoleon (t); Charlie Green, prob. Miff Mole, unknown (tb); Johnny Dodds (cl, as); Buster Bailey, Sidney Bechet, Barney Bigard, prob. Jimmy Lytell (cl); Fletcher Henderson, Jimmy Blythe, Sam Price, prob. Frank Signorelli, unknown (p); Charlie Dixon (bj); Teddy Bunn, unknown (g); Richard Fullbright, unknown (b); Ralph Escudero (bb); O'Neill Spencer, prob. Jack Roth, poss. Sidney Catlett (d); Jasper Taylor (perc). c. 1/25–6/39.

Rather more than half of the recordings on *Vol. 1* were made for Black Swan, one of the very few companies of the period under African-American ownership. Paradoxically, however, the orchestras with which Smith was furnished sound antiquated and stiff, more like the military bands of the previous decade. That, coupled with dim recording quality and often undistinguished vaudeville material, reduces her to a less striking performer than she proved to be once her contract was taken over by Paramount. Her sessions were now supervised by Fletcher Henderson, and her accompanists had a sharper apprehension of the blues, which now took up more of her repertoire. 'Freight Train Blues', with its celebrated adage 'when a woman gets the blues, she goes to her room and hides, but when a man gets the blues, he catches a freight train and rides', was one of the most popular records of its day. Although her voice lacked the breadth or grandeur of a Bessie Smith, she was a singer of strength and poise, adept at moaning the blues.

Early in *Vol. 2* she is accompanied on a couple of dates by Louis Armstrong, whose participation in 'Mining Camp Blues', 'The World's Jazz Crazy And So Am I' and 'Railroad Blues' (each heard in two takes) has its usual elevating effect. A later 'Messin'Around', with a Jimmy Blythe washboard band featuring Johnny Dodds, is untypically lively (though not unprecedented: see 'Ride Jockey Ride' on *Vol. 1*). After that she disappeared from record for 12 years, returning to cut several of her old hits with a superb sextet featuring Sidney Bechet, prolific everywhere but swarming over the two-part 'My Daddy Rocks Me' like Russian vine. Her voice had altered little, and the remakes of 'Trixie['s] Blues' and, especially, 'Freight Train Blues' are thoroughly convincing alliances of oldfashioned blues singing and small-group swing, while in 'Jack I'm Mellow' she tackled modern material with no sign of discomfort. Superior transfers of most of this session are on *Charlie Shavers And The Blues Singers* (Timeless CBC 1–025). Six further alternative takes from the Black Swan/Paramount period are on *Classic Blues & Vaudeville Singers (1921–1930) The Alternate Takes* (Document DOCD-5573). TR

Whispering Smith (1932–84)
VOCAL, HARMONICA

Moses Smith moved to Baton Rouge from his native Mississippi in 1957. Jay Miller, who nicknamed Smith in joking tribute to his hoarse, microphone-threatening bellow, recorded him for Excello in the early '60s, just as the local blues record market was about to collapse, and just as 'swamp blues' was becoming a minor cult in Europe. Found by researchers in 1970, Smith recorded again and visited Europe with Lightnin' Slim, but after Slim's death he returned to obscurity. A strong 45 appeared in 1983, but years of excessive drinking killed him soon afterwards.

*** High And Low Down/Over Easy
Ace CDCHD 578 Smith; Leroy Pero, Willie Singleton, Johnnie Cage, Napoleon Martin, Reggie Morrison (brass/reeds); Trombone Obry (tb); Bobby Powell (kb, v); Melvin Hill, Harvey Lexing (g); Alfred Lucas (b); Greg 'Dog' Johnson, Nolan Smith (perc). 71.

Excello issued eight songs on singles in the '60s, which have never been conveniently anthologized; they (and some unissued sides) can be found in ones and twos on Ace VACs. Recordings from 1970 are on *Swamp Blues* (Ace CDCHD 661); three unaccompanied numbers are delightful examples of Smith's uncomplicated singing and playing, but they highlight the deficiencies of the four band tracks.

High And Low Down/Over Easy packages two Excello LPs, respectively by Lightnin' Slim and Smith. The contexts of *Over Easy* range from solo acoustic guitar to bands with a horn section; in the '70s, aficionados of Jay Miller's production values were anorakishly irked, but the project is quite successful on its own terms, although the various accompaniments succeed one another somewhat schematically. The overuse of familiar Lightnin' Hopkins songs is regrettable, but the wheezy instrumental 'I've Got A Sure Thing' is very winning, as is a surprising version of the Staples Singers' 'Why Am I Treated So Bad'. CS

Willie 'Big Eyes' Smith (born 1936)
VOCAL, DRUMS

Smith grew up on his grandparents' farm near West Helena, Arkansas. At 17, on a visit to Chicago, he heard the Muddy Waters band and was inspired to take up the harmonica. Over the next few years he recorded with Arthur 'Big Boy' Spires and Bo Diddley. He then began playing drums and was in Muddy's band from 1961 to 1964 and again from 1968 to 1980, when he left with other members to form The Legendary Blues Band. In recent years he has worked with Bob Margolin and Nick Moss, recorded on drums with Big Bill Morganfield, Snooky Pryor, Aaron Moore and Arthur Williams and on harmonica with Louisiana Red, and headed his own band.

*** Bag Full Of Blues
Blind Pig BPCD 5027 *Smith; Kim Wilson, Ross Bon (h); Pinetop Perkins (p); Gareth Best, James Wheeler, Nick Moss (g); Jimmy Sutton (b).* 95.

*** Nothin' But The Blues Y'All
Juke Joint 001 *Smith; Al Lerman (h); Tyler Yarema (p); Kevin Higgins, Jack DeKeyzer, Morgan Davis (g); Alec Fraser (b).* 11/98–2/99.

**(*) Blues From The Heart
Juke Joint 002 *Smith; Al Lerman (h); Michael Fonfara (p); Jack DeKeyzer (g); Alec Fraser (b).* 5/00.

*** Bluesin' It
Electro-Fi 3385 *Smith; Al Lerman (s, h); Michael Fonfara (o, p); Kenny 'Blues Boss' Wayne (p, v); Jack DeKeyzer (g, v); Frank Krakowski (g); Bob Stroger (b, v); John Mays (v).* 3/03–1/04.

As the prime exponent of the Chicago shuffle, Smith is an asset to any band, but he has ideas above the timekeeping station, as he shows on these albums by leading from the rear as drummer and singer, and very often songwriter too. Though not a singer to make one's pulse race, he handles conventional Chicago-style repertoire perfectly competently. His compositions are sometimes adaptations, or distant memories, of older pieces: on *Bag Full Of Blues*, 'Here I Am' is based on Peetie Wheatstraw's 'Doin' The Best I Can', while 'Hard Times' alludes to Washboard Sam's 'Life Is Just A Book'. *Bag Full Of Blues* is a very relaxed session, as one might expect with a lead guitarist as tranquil as James Wheeler. Moss takes his place on four tracks, including a 'Tired Of Crying' that sharply evokes Howlin' Wolf. The Juke Joint albums are fractionally more excitable. *Nothin' But The Blues Y'All* has a batch of Windy City classics like Muddy's 'Honey Bee' and 'Mannish Boy', Little Walter's 'Mellow Down Easy' and Memphis Slim's 'Rock This House'; the latter two tracks exemplify Smith's ability to drive a band with only a light touch on the wheel. *Blues From The Heart*, by contrast, is almost all original material but it's so solidly in the Chicago idiom that composer credits hardly signify, and the ensemble playing is equally generic.

That description holds for *Bluesin' It*, but the execution and recording quality are distinctly superior. Having five band members share the vocals is advantageous, and if Mays puts a little too much obvious effort into his four, Stroger balances it with the discretion of his two. One of them is 'Blind Man', a sleek performance but belonging to a different time-zone from 'Don't Think I'm Crazy' or Jimmy Rogers's 'Going Away Baby', which are both sung by Smith himself in impeccably early-'50s settings. Wayne's rippling piano part on 'Hard Times' makes you wish he were on more than four numbers. Altogether, Smith's best album. TR

Smoky Babe (1927–76)
VOCAL, GUITAR

Born in Itta Bena, Mississippi, Robert Brown had found his way by the age of 20 to Scotlandville, Louisiana. The folklorist Harry Oster recorded him on numerous occasions in 1959–61 for his own Folk-Lyric label and for Storyville and Prestige-Bluesville. His subsequent life is obscure.

*** The Blues Of Smoky Babe
Original Blues Classics OBCCD-595 *Smoky Babe; Clyde Causey (h, v); 'Henry Thomas' [Lazy Lester] (h).* 2/59–6/61.

*** Louisiana Country Blues
Arhoolie CD 440 *Smoky Babe; 'Henry Thomas' [Lazy Lester], Clyde Causey (h); Sally Dotson, William Dotson (v).* 2/60.

In 'Hottest Brand Goin', a song that provided the title for the original LP issue of *The Blues Of Smoky Babe*, Smoky cheerfully promotes the Conoco gas station where he was employed. As Harry Oster remarks in his notes, 'his lyrics follow the natural flow of talk … he shifts smoothly back and forth between speaking and singing.' Autobiography is also the impulse behind 'Long Way From Home' and 'I'm Goin' Back To Mississippi', and even blues with less specific resonance like 'Cold, Cold Snow' or 'Insect Blues' blend the commonplace and the personal to striking effect, emphasized by guitar playing that is unfailingly muscular, confident and rhythmically sure. There is less autobiography, direct or oblique, in Smoky's 13 tracks on *Louisiana Country Blues* (the other half of the CD is by Herman E. Johnson) and there are a couple more participants, but otherwise the performances are similar in character and quality to those on the OBC album, with a single bottleneck guitar piece, 'Bad Whiskey', to match the other's 'Ocean Blues'. Why this impressive musician never recorded again – indeed, seems never to have been heard of again – is a mystery. TR

Little Smokey Smothers (born 1939)
VOCAL, GUITAR

Like his brother Otis (see next entry), Albert Smothers was already a guitarist when he arrived in Chicago. Ten years younger than Big Smokey, and making the move ten years later, Little Smokey plays in a more modern style, indebted to the aggressive West Side guitarists and to Albert King. He led his own bands, and worked with Howlin' Wolf, Earl Hooker and Paul Butterfield among many others before temporarily quitting music in the '70s.

***(*) Bossman: The Chicago Blues Of Little Smokey Smothers
Black Magic CD 9022 *Smothers; Tony Zamagni (kb); Elvin Bishop (g, v); Billy Flynn (g); Willie Black (b); Pete Williams (d); Lee Shot Williams (v).* 92.

Smothers and Bishop, who was his guitar student in the early '60s, have an obvious mutual affection, but their conversations on 'Remembering' and 'Talking Blues' are more fun for them than for the listener. Bishop's buzzsaw tone obtrudes on the four tracks where he appears, among them an overlong 'Tribute To Earl Hooker', on which Flynn's and

Smothers's solos are equally undernourished. Smokey shines as both singer and guitarist on the rest of the CD, and cousin Lee Shot produces some of his best, bluesiest vocals, but its drawbacks keep *Bossman* out of the top rank.

**** Second Time Around
Crosscut CCD 11051 *Smothers; Bridget Lockett, Kenny Anderson (t); Hank Ford (ts); Willie Henderson (bs); Tony Zamagni (kb); Randall Boykins (g); Johnny B. Gayden (b); Dave Jefferson (d); Theresa Davis, Joi Fité (v). 3–5/96.*

Second Time Around stumbles off the blocks; 'Bluesman' features chirpily mechanical background vocals, and the title track is oddly aloof for a reflection on open-heart surgery. Benny Goodman's 'Soft Winds' is the gateway to a higher plane, however, and the rest of the disc is first-class, its general indebtedness to Albert King never descending to mere imitation. Smothers inspires the band and in turn is inspired by them; Zamagni is especially attentive and inventive, and Jefferson, a veteran of Albert King's band, is outstanding. Smothers is the undoubted star, though, and after those initial glitches he's a consistently energized, imaginative guitarist (the instrumental 'In The Zone' is well named) and an impassioned singer.

** That's My Partner!
Alligator ALCD 4874 *Smothers; Ed Earley (tb, perc, v); Terry Hanck (ts); Steve Gurr (h); S. E. Willis (ac, o, p, v); Elvin Bishop (g, v); Ian Lamson (g); Evan Palmerston (b); Bobby Cochran (d, v). 1/00.*

Bishop takes half the vocals on the jointly credited *That's My Partner!*, recorded live in San Francisco. Most of it is music for white kids to drink beer by and whoop mindlessly at. Smothers's 'Hello, Baby' and 'Annie Mae' are furthest from this aesthetic, and the best tracks, but his 'Little Red Rooster' is dire. CS

Smokey Smothers (1929–93)
VOCAL, GUITAR

Sometimes known as 'Big Smokey' to distinguish him from his brother (see previous entry), Otis Smothers was playing professionally in Mississippi before he moved to Chicago at 17. He played in numerous bands, including that of Muddy Waters, but by the end of the '60s had quit music. His comeback in the '80s was a notable victory over depression and alcoholism.

*** Smokey Smothers Sings The Backporch Blues
Ace CDCHD 858 *Smothers; Louis 'Little' Boyd (h); Freddie King, Fred Jordan (g); prob. Joe Carter (b); Phillip Paul, Jimmy Malender (d). 8/60–2/62.*

**(*) Smokey Smothers Sings The Backporch Blues
Official 779 *As above, except add Dave Waldman, unknown (h), Barrelhouse Chuck (p), Illinois Slim (g), Rich Yescalis, Steve Arvey, unknowns (b), Steve Cushing, unknown (d). 8/60–68, 12/80–12/85.*

King hoped that Smothers would be a rival to Jimmy Reed, but the LP *Sings The Backporch Blues* sold pitifully. It became much sought after by collectors, and Ace's reissue is aimed at that market, with edits and bass overdubs removed, and the disc expanded with singles and alternative takes. Smothers's Jimmy Reed pastiches are least compelling when most accurate; he's more creative when on Muddy Waters's trail, which is decidedly not to say that he's a Waters imitator. Freddie King plays on the six best titles; their high point is 'You're Gonna Be Sorry', a tigerish re-creation of the two-guitar sound fashioned by Waters and Jimmy Rogers. Four 1962 tunes are honest work, slightly blemished by Little Boyd's scattershot harmonica blasts.

Official bootleg the material that King issued on LP and singles, adding a Gamma 45 and just over half a Red Beans LP. The sound is acceptable, but Ace's treatment of the King recordings is clearly preferable. The Gamma record is a pleasing, rough-edged time traveller from the '50s; the '80s tracks also take no account of changes in musical fashion, but they're uneven, ranging from an excellent 'Everybody's Talking' to a 'Hello Little School Girl' which always seems about to fall apart.

*** Chicago Blues Session Vol. 1
Wolf 120.847 *Smothers; Billy Branch (h); Eddie Taylor, John Primer (g); Willie Kent (b); Tim Taylor (d). 8/84–4/91.*

This CD is shared with Boston Blackie (1943–93), a minor but enjoyable Magic Sam acolyte. Four of Smothers's seven tracks are remakes of King material, with 'Hello Little Schoolgirl' getting its third and best outing. There's no sense of going through the motions, though; Smothers attacks the songs with gusto, abetted by enthusiastic sidemen. John Primer shows off occasionally, but these are Smothers's best recordings; among them, 'Sad Sad Day' is a classic by any standard. CS

James Solberg (born 1951)
VOCAL, GUITAR

Solberg grew up in Wisconsin, where he quit school at 15 and headed for Chicago to absorb the blues firsthand. In the '70s, based in Milwaukee, he played for several years with Luther Allison. In 1981, under the pressure of drug dependency, he retired from music and became a motorcycle machinist, but in 1985 he resumed playing and worked with The Legendary Blues Band and The Nighthawks as well as forming his own band. Rejoining Allison in 1993, he collaborated closely with him on Soul Fixin' Man, Blue Streak *and* Reckless *and shared a Handy Award for their composition 'Cherry Red Wine'. He also won Handy Awards for Band Of The Year in 1997 and 1998, and has worked on albums by Sandy Carroll and Deborah Coleman.*

**(*) See That My Grave Is Kept Clean
Dixiefrog DFGCD 8442 *Solberg; H-Bomb Vegas (o); Charlie Bingham (g); Ken Faltinson (b); Robb Stupka (d). 95.*

*** One Of These Days
Atomic Theory ATM 1120//Dixiefrog DFGCD 8453//Ruf 1076 *Solberg; Wayne Jackson (t, tb); Andrew Love (s); Mike Vlahakis (o, p, v); Jon Paris (psg, v); Charlie Bingham (g); Ken Faltinsen (b, v); Bill Black, Dave Smith (b); Robb Stupka (d); Jaquelyn Johnson, Jacquelyn Reddick (v); Jim Gaines (co-prod). 96.*

*** L.A. Blues
Ruf 1026 *Solberg; Mike Vlahakis (o, p); John Lindberg (b); Rob Stupka (d); Jeffrey Reed (sp); Wally Adamski (grinder, laughing). 10/97.*

*** **The Hand You're Dealt**
Ruf 1043 *Solberg; Mike Vlahakis, Ernest Williamson (kb); Luther Allison (g, v); Charlie Bingham (g); Ken Faltinson, Dave Smith (b); Robb Stupka, Lloyd Anderson (d); Jacqueline Johnson, Jacquelyn Reddick, William Brown, Bertram Brown (v); Jim Gaines (prod).* 12/94, 8/98.

Solberg has the whiskey-riddled voice of a rocker who's seen better days, and it's effective in surprising places: on *One Of These Days*, for example, the soul number 'Litehouse Keeper' and Louis Jordan's 'Do You Call That A Buddy?', as well as more obvious blues vehicles like the title track. Meanwhile his guitar playing twists and bites like a rattlesnake with a bad attitude. *L.A. Blues* was named not for the city but for Solberg's former employer and friend Luther Allison, for whom the title song is a memorial. Guitar and organ front 'Robb's Soufflé' (which, if it's a misprint for 'Robb's Scuffle', is a happy one) and there and in 'Bubba's Boogie' Solberg burns rubber, but he slows, and cools, down for 'Say Goodbye' and 'Happy Snails'. Only pedestrian readings of 'Just A Closer Walk With Thee' and 'Ballad Of A Thin Man' mar an interestingly textured and well-executed album.

Solberg's remembrances of Luther Allison have not been confined to *L.A. Blues*: *See That My Grave Is Kept Clean* includes their joint composition 'Bad Love', and *The Hand You're Dealt* reaches back for 'Still Called The Blues', an outtake – but an excellent one – from one of the sessions for Allison's *Blue Streak*. Otherwise *The Hand You're Dealt* is another judicious blend of received repertoire, including two from the Malaco catalogue, 'Members Only' and 'Still Called The Blues', and original songs like the title track or 'Ain't It Hard', a soul lament that's steered away from self-pity by Solberg's moving vocal. TR

Sonny Boy & Lonnie
GROUP

The credit 'Sonny Boy & Lonnie', or variants of it, was used on a handful of intriguing recordings made in New York at the end of World War II. From detective work by Chris Smith it emerges that the three musicians involved were from Cleveland, Ohio, but little more is known of them.

*** **Carolina Blues & Gospel (1945–51)**
Document DOCD-5588 *prob. Lonnie Johnson (p, sp); 'Sonny Boy' Smith, Sam Bradley (g, v, sp).* 45.

Although this Lonnie Johnson is not *the* Lonnie Johnson, the music does have some points of similarity to contemporary recordings by Johnson and Blind John Davis, and the lead singer and guitarist, thought to be 'Sonny Boy' Smith, plainly attempts to sound like Johnson on 'Wiggle Round Me Baby' and 'Big Moose Blues'. The likeness is even more striking on the ballads 'I'll Water You Every Day' and 'I Wonder Who's Holding You', though the latter also suggests some prompting by the then recent Cecil Gant hit 'I Wonder'. 'Big Moose Blues' is a detailed autobiographical composition about wartime service in the Pacific.

Coupled with these remarkable sides are the recordings of Mary Deloatch, a spirited gospel singer in the mould of Sister Rosetta Tharpe, who also cut half a dozen secular pieces under the alias Marylyn Scott. Four of these are conventional blues and boogies with a small band, but the guitar songs 'I Got What My Daddy Likes' and 'Let's Do The Boogie Woogie' sound like serendipitously recorded party music. TR

Sonny Boy Williamson II (c. 1912–65)
VOCAL, HARMONICA

Or pick a date from 1894, 1897, 1899, 1901, 1908 and 1909, variously given by the man himself, his passport and his tombstone. The 1920 census records imply a 1912 birthdate, however. He was probably calling himself Sonny Boy Williamson before 1941, when he began broadcasting on KFFA's King Biscuit Time *with Robert Lockwood, but despite his dogged insistence to interviewers that he was 'the original', the name was purloined from the Bluebird recording star (see under W). The second Sonny Boy's real name was Aleck Ford; he later took his stepfather's name, becoming Aleck Miller, also known as Willie Miller, punningly nicknamed 'Rice'. Until his radio breakthrough, Williamson had led a wandering life, and after landing the KFFA job he soon took off again, working in jukes and plugging patent medicine on other radio stations. Marriage to Mattie Gordon in 1949 steadied Sonny Boy a little, and with John Lee Williamson now dead, the chance to record finally came in 1951. After Lillian McMurry's Trumpet label folded, Sonny Boy was traded to Chess in Chicago. In 1963 he visited Europe with the AFBF and was the hit of the show. He only returned briefly to the States before the 1964 Festival, and but for work-permit problems would probably have stayed in Europe permanently, but he died back in Arkansas, and back on* King Biscuit Time.

**** **Sonny Boy Williamson 1951–1953**
Classics 5094 *Williamson; Bernard Williams, Richard Lillie (ts); Willie Kyle, Carlton Wells (s); Willie Love, Dave Campbell, J. W. Walker (p); Elmore James, Joe Willie Wilkins, Lester Williams, unknown (g); Henry Reed, Leonard Ware, Rusty Alfred, unknown (b); Cliff Givens (sung b, broom); Joe Dyson, O'Neil Hudson, Buck Hinson, unknown (d).* 3/51–4/53.

**** **Nine Below Zero**
Indigo IGOCD 2545 *As above, except James also sings; add Arthur Crudup, Bobo Thomas (g, v), James Williams (g), Herman Fowlkes, 'Sam' (b), Frock O'Dell (d), Frank Crawley (maracas).* 3/51–10/53.

***(*) **King Biscuit Time**
Arhoolie CD 310 *As above, except add Houston Stackhouse (g), Peck Curtis (d); omit Bernard Williams, Lillie, Kyle, Wells, Walker, Crudup, Thomas, Lester Williams, James Williams, Alfred, Fowlkes, 'Sam', unknown (b), Hudson, Hinson, Crawley.* 3/51–5/65.

The Classics and Indigo CDs appeared as soon as Europe's 50-year copyright limit permitted; both have excellent sound, derived from earlier issues of Trumpet material. *Nine Below Zero* substitutes 'Keep It To Yourself' for 'She Brought Life Back To The Dead', and adds Elmore James's celebrated first recording of 'Dust My Broom', two fine Arthur Crudup tracks (issued as by Elmer James), and one by journeyman Bobo Thomas (issued as by Elmo James), on all of which Williamson accompanies. Longer playing time and notes that capture Sonny Boy's blend of orneriness and charisma make Indigo's the preferable collection. Arhoolie offer 16 of Williamson's best Trumpet sides, adding 'Dust My Broom' and one of his last KFFA broadcasts (taped off the artists' microphones, which means that the commercials and announcements are muffled); this is important documentation, but musically routine.

That cannot be said of these early Trumpet recordings, however. They're sometimes parsed as throwbacks to the '40s, but that's to read them through the prism of the Chess recordings; while it's true that the rhythm sections are sometimes rather four-square, the thrusting guitars and pianos take much of their inspiration from contemporary jazz. Above all, there's Sonny Boy himself, his voice and harp – and the gaps he leaves in exactly the right places – making a continuous, relentlessly swinging line. He sometimes has to chivvy his accompanists with cries of encouragement and whiplash finger snaps, but his playing, resonant, inventive and economical, with total control of tone and timbre, announces the arrival of a great talent.

From the first, Williamson was also one of the blues' finest songwriters, whether ruminating on the ways of women, telling how his house burned down, giving out Mrs McMurry's home phone number in an attempt to get bookings (that song stayed unissued!) or grieving for lost love on the miraculously beautiful 'Mighty Long Time', with only Bill Givens's vocal bass in support.

***(*) Boppin' With Sonny
Blue Moon CDBM 088 *Williamson; Bernard Williams, Richard Lillie (ts); J. W. Walker, Willie Love, Dave Campbell (p); Joe Willie Wilkins, Lester Williams, James Williams, J. V. Turner, B. B. King, Carl Jones (g); Rusty Alfred, Herman Fowlkes, Johnny Morgan, Raz Roseby, unknown (b); Oneal Hudson, Buck Hinson, Junior Blackman (d); Frank Crawley (maracas). 3/53–11/54.*

(***(*)) From The Bottom
Collectables COL-CD-5244 *As above. 3/53–11/54.*

Mrs McMurry tinkered with Williamson's sound on some later sessions, and her intermittent experiments with Latin rhythms and saxes, though never disastrous, are sometimes fussy and distracting. 'No Nights By Myself' revives the 'Mighty Long Time' formula, with piano instead of vocal bass, and is very nearly as fine, but by Sonny Boy's standards 'From The Bottom' is banal, although B. B. King, sitting in for this one tune, concocts an ingenious solo. Even so, there's plenty of splendid music on the later Trumpet sides: J. V. Turner and Junior Blackman are keeping up with developments in Chicago, and Williamson continues to buttonhole the listener with inimitable lyrics. Otherwise identical with *From The Bottom*, *Boppin' With Sonny* is longer by two good tracks and has appreciably better sound. There's modest overlap with the Classics and Indigo CDs already discussed.

**** Down And Out Blues/In Memorium [sic]
BGO BGOCD 603 *Williamson; Lafayette Leake (poss. o, p); Billy Emerson (poss. o); Otis Spann (p); Muddy Waters, Jimmy Rogers, Robert Lockwood, Luther Tucker, Eugene Pearson, Eddie King, Matt Murphy (g); Willie Dixon, Milton Rector, unknown (b); Fred Below, Al Duncan (d). 8/55–1/63.*

**** His Best
MCA/Chess CHD-9377 *As above, except add Jarrett Gibson (ts), Donald Hankins (bs), Buddy Guy (g), Jack Meyers (b), Clifton James (d). 8/55–4/64.*

***(*) The Best Of Sonny Boy Williamson
Spectrum 544 277 *Similar to above two CDs. 8/55–4/64.*

***(*) The Real Folk Blues/More Real Folk Blues
MCA/Chess 088 112 823 *As above, except Dixon also sings; add Odie Payne (d); omit Waters, Rogers, Pearson. 9/57–4/64.*

At Chess/Checker, with Fred Below usually on drums, flatfooted rhythms were seldom an issue. Willie Dixon was in charge of most sessions, but until the last of them, when sales and inspiration were flagging, there was little imposition of his ideas about material and arrangements. Given Sonny Boy's world-class mulishness, this is perhaps not surprising; and it's proper to note that alongside some disappointments the later sessions produced classics like 'Bring It On Home To Me' and 'Help Me'. Most of the Chess recordings were Williamson compositions (some by his namesake, honoured with an occasional cover), and his voice and harmonica are always dominant. That doesn't mean that the pianists and guitarists (usually Lockwood, with his acolyte Luther Tucker on rhythm) are unimportant. Lockwood's imaginative runs and riffs are often prominent and structurally vital, but if there's soloing to be done, it's Williamson who does it. His lyrics are as imaginative – sometimes as surreal – as ever, and, until the last days, when there's a noticeable slowing down, his singing and playing are still vigorous, swinging and salty.

Sonny Boy's Chess recordings are not well served by reissues at present. There's heavy duplication, most glaringly (because 1965's *In Memorium* is *The Real Folk Blues*, cynically retitled) between the CDs which combine two LPs. The *In Memorium/Down And Out Blues* coupling is preferable; *More Real Folk Blues* is overweight with lesser material from 1963 and 1964. (Needless to say, there's not much folksiness about either 'folk blues' LP; on 'The Hunt' Dixon and Williamson pursue Sonny Terry & Brownie McGhee's audience, but soon lose the scent.) The 'best ofs' both have 20 tracks; the Spectrum release is mid-priced, but *His Best* is preferable. Its notes are longer, deeper and more accurate (Spectrum swallow Williamson's tall tale of making records in the '30s), and it's also marginally the better selection: of eight songs not common to both discs, 'Like Wolf' on Spectrum is a surprising but scarcely essential imitation of Sonny Boy's quondam brother-in-law.

*** In Europe
Evidence ECD 26071 *Williamson; Otis Spann (p, v); Sunnyland Slim (p); Matt Murphy, Hubert Sumlin, Eric Clapton, Chris Dreja (g); Willie Dixon, Paul Samwell-Smith (b); Billie Stepney, Clifton James, Jim McCarty (d). 10/63–10/64.*

*** Keep It To Ourselves
Storyville STCD 4176 *Williamson; Memphis Slim (p, v); Matt Murphy (g); Billie Stepney (d). 11/63.*

*** Portrait Of A Bluesman
Analogue Productions CAPR 3107 *As above. 11/63.*

**(*) Blues Masters Vol. 12
Storyville STCD 8012 *As above, except add Lennart Nylen (g), Sture Nordin (b). 11/63.*

(**) Pontiac Blues
Midnite Jazz & Blues Collection MJB 092 *Williamson; Alan Price (o, p); Hilton Valentine (g); Chas Chandler (b); John Steel (d); Eric Burdon (v). 12/63.*

(**) Rock Generation Vol. 3
Spalax CD 14552 *As above. 12/63.*

(***) The Complete Crawdaddy Recordings
Sunspots SPOT 545 *Williamson; Eric Clapton, Chris Dreja (g); Paul Samwell-Smith (b); Jim McCarty (d). 12/63–2/64.*

(**(*)) U.K. Blues
Fuel 2000 302 061 130 *As for above three CDs.* 12/63–2/64.

Williamson's available European recordings on CD draw on sessions for Storyville, AFBF concerts and gigs with British 'beat groups'. Fans of The Animals and The Yardbirds (or, more accurately, of Eric Clapton) are the primary target of the latter material's frequent recycling, but if for nothing else these recordings would be worth hearing for Williamson's increased and very effective use of low-register playing.

Happily, there are more reasons to recommend his collaborations with The Yardbirds; they took the blues seriously, and Clapton's spare, clear-headed playing is a new and often very successful response to Williamson. McCarty's drumming, too, is restrained, creative and swinging. Sunspots and Fuel 2000 claim to issue the complete recordings with the Yardbirds, and don't: *U.K. Blues* has 11 tracks to *The Complete Crawdaddy Recordings'* 14, but both lack the solo 'Baby Don't Worry'. *U.K. Blues* also leaves out the better of two versions of 'Take It Easy Baby', yet includes the lightweight instrumental 'A Lost Care' and 'The River Rhine', where the band are at rhythmic loggerheads with Williamson.

The key to choosing among reissues of the Yardbirds collaborations is the company they keep. The Sunspots CD begins with six tracks by the band alone, which are not bad. This is not litotes for 'very good', but they are certainly far better than the nine tracks on *U.K. Blues* with backing from The Animals. Fuel 2000 have lavished considerable engineering skills on poor master tapes, but Sonny Boy was having an off night, thanks to toothache. It also seems likely that he had The Animals in mind when he told Levon Helm that British groups 'want to play the blues so bad, and they play it so *bad*'.

The choice for all but Yardbirds completists must be *In Europe*, which prefaces nine Crawdaddy tracks (the inferior version of 'Take It Easy Baby' is again substituted for 'Baby Don't Worry') with five items from AFBF concerts which convey much of the star quality that conquered European audiences. The semi-improvised 'I'm Trying To Make London My Home' is a masterpiece of hopeful autobiography, and Hubert Sumlin plays splendid guitar on 'Had My Fun' (sung by Otis Spann) and 'Dissatisfied'. Poor sound rules out both *Pontiac Blues*, which adds six risible tracks by The Animals, and *Rock Generation*, which is shared with the Graham Bond Organisation.

The recordings Williamson made in Scandinavia have been praised for allowing him to extemporize, often at greater length than when he was recording for release on singles. (It can also be argued that this material gives some idea of the Sonny Boy who played on street corners before radio and records.) There are some successful numbers in this vein, like 'Movin' Down The River Rhine' (on *Portrait Of A Bluesman* and *Blues Masters*), where he muses about his wife back home while harmonica and finger snaps convey the onrush of the train; but on *Blues Masters* there's also – without impugning their sincerity – a glut of rather queasily host-flattering songs about the excellence of Europe.

It must also be said that the Storyville recordings do not support the received opinion that Williamson was an outstanding improviser of lyrics; many of them are prosaic near-doggerel. (This is not incompatible with the view that he had earlier been a great songwriter; considered craftsmanship usually produces better results than stream-of-consciousness.) At the time of writing, *Keep It To Ourselves* is also available in an audiophile limited edition (Analogue Productions CAPB 036). *Portrait Of A Bluesman* does not seem to be a limited edition; eight of its ten tracks are also on *Blues Masters*, but the latter CD's greater length is not an advantage, and *Portrait* has most of the most successful Storyville tracks, where Williamson is propelled and kept on track by a trio featuring Stepney's in-the-pocket drumming. CS

Charlie Spand
VOCAL, PIANO

Spand's playing has stylistic links to the Birmingham pianists; he was living in Detroit in 1929, and was photographed in Chicago in 1940. This is all that's known for certain; rumour has him moving to Los Angeles. Georgia Tom recalled a 'Charlie Spann' in Atlanta, but the suggestion that Spand sings of being 'born in Ellijay' (Georgia) on 'Evil Woman Spell' rests on the mishearing of a reference (authenticating, not autobiographical) to Algiers, Louisiana, famous for the hoodoo which is the song's subject.

***(*) Charlie Spand (1929–1931)
Document DOCD-5108 *Spand; Blind Blake (g, sp); unknown (g).* 6/29–c. 9/31.

**** Dreaming The Blues: The Best Of Charlie Spand
Yazoo 2062 *As above, except add prob. Alex Hill (sp).* 6/29–c. 9/31.

Yazoo begin with a six-second introduction of Spand excerpted from 'Hometown Skiffle', a sampler 78 of Paramount's leading artists. Spand's popularity was well-deserved; he was an inspired pianist with a strong but subtle touch, whether playing rolling walking basses or deliberate, stately stride, and like Leroy Carr he wrote polished, often poetic lyrics and sang them in a clear, intimate voice. 'Soon This Morning' became popular with other pianists, but it's just one example of his consistently fine songwriting and delivery. Blind Blake, who joins him on a number of titles (and who may also be the 'unknown' listed by cautious discographers), plays at the peak of his considerable form; the romping 'Hastings St.' is among the greatest of all piano–guitar duets.

Document offer all Spand's Paramounts except two alternative takes, which are on *"Too Late, Too Late Blues" – Vol. 1* (Document DOCD-5150), but their sound is inferior to the exemplary remastering on *Dreaming The Blues*. Yazoo forfeit the crown that Spand deserves for omitting 'Tired Woman Blues', for notes which, though otherwise excellent, don't follow the running order, and for timorously grouping the hissier tracks at the end of the disc.

In 1940, Spand cut eight sides for OKeh, with unexciting guitar accompaniment. His piano was still admirable, if slightly less adventurous, and his lyrics imaginative. At present this material is unavailable on CD unless a copy of the deleted *Charlie Spand (1940)/Big Maceo (1941–1952)* (Old Tramp OTCD-04) can be found. CS

Otis Spann (1930–70)
VOCAL, PIANO, ORGAN

There may have been better pianists than Otis Spann in '50s Chicago but history is loth, if not unable, to identify them. Born in Jackson, Mississippi, and schooled in the piano by a local musician, Friday Ford, Spann arrived in Chicago in 1947.

Five years later he joined the Muddy Waters Band, where he remained until shortly before his death. His forceful but balanced technique made him the natural successor to Big Maceo Merriweather, from whom he took tuition, while his smoky, masticated vocals combined reticence and passion. He made his solo recording debut in 1960 but band and session work limited his own album sessions until he left Waters in 1968. A brief flurry of recording was brought to a too swift end by his death from liver cancer.

Despite being an almost daily presence in the Chess studios, Spann made only two sessions as a leader for the label, the first a poorly distributed single, the second unissued for four decades. All four titles pursue a sprightly tempo and the first pair involve a long-disputed set of musicians, including the unmistakable presence of B. B. King playing the opening solo on the instrumental 'Five Spot'. Spann's forthright but distorted vocal on 'It Must Have Been The Devil' led to suggestions that it might have been a bootleg recording. Superior engineering enhances 'I'm Leaving You' and 'I'm In Love With You Baby', both featuring harmonica solos by Walter Horton. Spann's piano stays in the ensemble apart from a brief solo in 'Five Spot' and it must be supposed his vocals failed to impress the Chess hierarchy. Hindsight regards them more favourably. They can be heard on the VAC *Chess Blues Piano Greats* (MCA/Chess CHD2–9385).

**** Otis Spann Is The Blues
Candid CCD 79001 Spann; Robert Lockwood (g, v). 8/60.

The natural ebullience of Spann's two-fisted technique is perfectly captured at this session, although the famously ill-tempered Lockwood initially does all he can by way of indifferent tuning and a digital variation of St Vitus's Dance to inhibit the listener's enjoyment of it. The onward rush of Spann's improvisations in 'Great Northern Stomp' is hampered by a recording balance that favours the guitarist's inept but insistent contributions. By 'Worried Life Blues' he's in tune but still distracting and it's not until 'The Hard Way' that he properly fulfils his role as accompanist. None of this inhibits Spann, whose 'Otis In The Dark', performed solo, is the most comprehensive exhibition of his pianistic power, with rolling bass figures and unstoppable treble inventions. Humour and fatalism invest 'Country Boy', 'Beat-Up Team' and 'The Hard Way', each a form of idealized autobiography. He then becomes the perfect accompanist to Lockwood's four songs, including two by Robert Johnson and his own 'Little Boy Blue'.

**** Good Morning Mr Blues
Storyville STCD 8010 Spann; Lonnie Johnson (g). 10/63.

Recorded during the 1963 AFBF tour, this finds Spann in a richly inventive but reflective mood, applying his unique skills to a judicious mix of original songs and blues standards such as 'Trouble In Mind', 'Going Down Slow' and 'Worried Life Blues'. In fact, some of his own compositions are lightly veiled copies of better-known songs, but all are performed with absolute authority. His hands are finely balanced, melodic lines travel smoothly from hand to hand, firm bass lines echo and contrast with treble inventions, and sudden flashes of brilliance can occur in any register. His singing ranges from forthright to wistful, at all times calibrated with its accompaniment. Spann sings 'Jelly Roll Baker' but composer Lonnie Johnson appears on 'Trouble In Mind', tastefully underpinning the vocal line. To the original LP's 11 tracks this set adds three songs that appeared on Storyville compilations. In terms of its artistic integrity, this album surpasses the Candid session. NS

***(*) The Blues Of Otis Spann/Cracked Spanner Head
BGO BGOCD 668 Spann; Rod M. Lee (t); Steve Gregory (ts); Bud Beadle (bs); 'Brother' [Muddy Waters], Spit James, Eric Clapton (g); Ransom Knowling (b); Little Willie Smith (d). 5/64, 68.

The Blues Of Otis Spann, recorded in London while Spann was in town with Muddy Waters, was immediately hailed as one of the best blues albums ever made in Britain, and even discounting nostalgia that judgement holds up four decades later. No doubt Spann was reassured by the presence of regular playing companions. The 'Brother' credited as guitarist on the original LP was Muddy, but anyone hoping to catch the gleam of his guitar in the ensemble will be disappointed; probably for contractual reasons, Decca Records provided him with a bushel to hide his light under. It hardly matters, because in numbers like 'I Came From Clarksdale' and 'The Blues Don't Like Nobody' Spann speaks directly to the listener's heart. After that, *Cracked Spanner Head* is superfluous – literally, because it consists of the same dozen tracks, resequenced, sometimes edited or remixed, and tricked out with overdubbed guitar or horns. It was costume jewellery, to give an honest-to-goodness blues album the glitz of late-'60s Carnaby Street, and it has worn about as well as you'd expect. BGO have added four fine tracks first issued on a 1964 compilation, *Raw Blues*. On three of them Muddy throws off his disguise, while the fourth, 'Pretty Girls Everywhere' (which was also issued as a single), has a dubbed lead by Eric Clapton. TR

** The Blues Never Die!
Original Blues Classics OBCCD 530 Spann; James Cotton (h, v); James Madison, 'Dirty Rivers' [Muddy Waters] (g); Milton Rector (b); S. P. Leary (d). 10/64.

This is a mundane session from a well-oiled machine, manufacturing souvenirs rather than making masterpieces and fatally flawed by shoddy production. Despite the artist credit, vocals are shared between Spann and Cotton and bizarrely located in the left channel of the stereo. If anything, Cotton expends more energy on his five songs, 'One More Mile', 'Feelin' Good' and 'I'm Ready' among them. His acoustic harmonica rarely dominates the mix, while Spann's piano drifts from left to centre on the odd occasion he takes a solo. His five songs include the title track, 'After Awhile' and a desultory 'It Must Have Been The Devil'. Muddy is inaudible throughout and the bass guitar and elements of the drumkit are distorted. Brevity is this album's only asset.

***(*) Otis Spann's Chicago Blues
Testament TCD 5005 Spann; James Cotton, Big Walter Horton (h); Johnny Young, Johnny Shines (g); Jimmy Lee Morris, Lee Jackson (b); S. P. Leary, Robert Whitehead, Fred Below (d). 65–66.

Spann proved to be a willing collaborator with Testament's owner Pete Welding, appearing on albums by Johnny Shines, Johnny Young, Floyd Jones and Eddie Taylor. This album comes from four sessions, one solo, the others with various accompanists. He's at his best performing alone, although he resorts to a number of classic blues, including 'Vicksburg Blues', 'See See Rider' and 'One Room Country Shack'. Best of all is an impressively faithful version of Big Maceo's 'Worried Life Blues'. Five of the six band titles find him hoarse but still effective. Luckily, Cotton is in blinding form, raising the temperature of the opening 'Get Your Hands Out Of My Pocket' and 'Sarah Street'. Horton plays on the instrumental 'G. B. Blues', alongside Shines and Below. Spann plays organ on two songs, blasting his fellow musicians out of the aural picture. The sometimes indifferent sound quality is this album's sole imperfection.

**(*) Live The Life
Testament TCD 6001 *Spann; Slim Willis, unknown (h); Muddy Waters (g, v); poss. Sammy Lawhorn, James 'Pee Wee' Madison, Johnny Young (g); poss. Calvin Jones, prob. Willie Dixon (b); Francis Clay or [Little] Willie Smith, Robert Whitehead (d). 65–69.*

Compiled from material discovered after Welding's death, this consists of two live sessions, one by the full Muddy Waters band, a pair of Spann solo efforts, and outtakes from Johnny Young and Slim Willis sessions. Both live sessions suffer from variable sound but retain sufficient interest to obviate strong criticism. Spann's 'Tribute To Martin Luther King', with Waters on acoustic guitar, and an intense rendition of 'Tin Pan Alley' with the Waters band are particularly impressive, as is Waters's performance of a sepulchral 'Five Long Years'. But the rest of the band performances are as scrappy as the sound balance. Spann's solo excursions contain his sturdiest piano playing and his accompaniments to Young and Willis are as reliable as ever. A record for completists.

*** I Wanna Go Home
Hightone HCD 8155 *As for above two CDs. 65–69.*

A mid-price compilation from *Otis Spann's Chicago Blues* and *Live The Life*. The six tracks from each are quite well chosen, including 'One Room Country Shack', 'Get Your Hands Out Of My Pocket' and 'Tin Pan Alley', but 'Worried Life Blues' is the inferior later version.

*** Chicago/The Blues/Today! Vol. 1
Vanguard VMD 79216 *Spann; S. P. Leary (d). 12/65.*

These five duets, with just two vocals, fall a degree or two short of the standard Spann has previously set for himself. His voice on 'Burning Fire' and 'Sometime I Wonder' is congested and hoarse, his piano playing sturdy but repetitive. 'Marie' and 'S. P. Blues', the latter based on 'Vicksburg Blues', find him playing within himself, unwilling or unable to add those flourishes that make a Spann performance memorable. These he injects into 'Spann's Stomp', urged on by Leary's light but urgent drumming. Elsewhere, the drummer manages to be ponderous and over-busy in succeeding choruses, often using Spann's solos as target practice. The other artists featured on this album are J. B. Hutto and Junior Wells.

***(*) Down To Earth: The Bluesway Recordings
MCA MCAD-11202 *Spann; George Smith, Mojo Buford (h); Muddy Waters, Luther Johnson, Sammy Lawhorn (g); Mac Arnold, Sonny Wimberley (b); Francis Clay, S. P. Leary (d); Lucille Spann (v). 8/66–11/67.*

This CD (availability uncertain) brings together two albums, *The Blues Is Where It's At* and *The Bottom Of The Blues*, recorded 15 months apart, the first before a small studio audience, the second featuring the debut of Spann's wife, Lucille. The first session sticks fairly close to the Waters band's regular repertoire: 'My Home Is In The Delta', 'T'Ain't Nobody's Bizness', even 'Steel Mill Blues' turns out to be 'Five Long Years'. 'Popcorn Man', despite its 'Morganfield' credit, is a busy boogaloo indicative of its time. Everyone solos with gusto, even Muddy on a couple of occasions, but with little focus. The lack of an audience concentrates the players' minds on the second session and Spann's solos are more frequent and rewarding. Lucille duets with her husband on three songs and has one slow blues feature, 'My Man'. The bands are dependable throughout but neither harmonica player manages to make his mark.

**(*) Cryin' Time
Vanguard VMD 6514 *Spann; Barry Melton, Luther Johnson (g); Jos Davidson (b); Lonnie Taylor (d); Lucille Spann (v). 3/68.*

**(*) Best Of The Vanguard Years
Vanguard VCD 79537 *As above, except add S. P. Leary (d). 12/65–3/68.*

A bizarre lineup spoils whatever pretensions *Cryin' Time* may have had to be a viable Spann release. He plays and sings well enough without managing anything memorable but his producer allows (or requires) him to assault an organ on the instrumental title tune, 'Blind Man' and 'The New Boogaloo', neglecting to discover whether Spann had a technique for it – which he doesn't. Lucille adds her histrionic vocals to 'Blind Man' and 'Some Day'. Worst of all is the inclusion of Melton (a refugee from Country Joe & The Fish) as lead guitarist. His arhythmic noodlings drown Johnson's worthier efforts and neither man pays attention to what the other is playing. They enhance the piano feature 'Twisted Snake' by their absence. *Best Of The Vanguard Years*, a title to challenge the Trades Descriptions Act, combines this with the Spann titles from *Chicago/The Blues/Today!*, a flag of convenience that can't save it from beaching itself.

***(*) The Biggest Thing Since Colossus
[Columbia COL 475972] *Spann; Peter Green, Danny Kirwan (g); John McVie (b); S. P. Leary (d). 1/69.*

This would have been an unqualified success but for the separation problems in the studio. Leary's rowdy drumkit bleeds into Spann's vocal mike resulting in both voice and piano appearing lower in the stereo than Green's strident reverb-laden guitar. Despite that, Spann is in excellent form, hollering his lyrics and playing sturdy, two-handed solos. Green too plays well but is guilty of overplaying his role as an accompanist. That, combined with the volume of his guitar, makes this less of a collaboration than a personality contest, albeit a good-natured one, that Spann has to win. This he does and perhaps the competition draws an extra level of commitment from him. Some experiments, like the instrumental 'Walkin'', fail but these are offset by two slow blues, 'Temperature Is Rising' and 'Ain't Nobody's Business'. Spann made one further session as a leader but this is effectively his last great performance.

*(*) Last Call
Mr Cat MCAT 1014 *Spann; Luther 'Snake' Johnson (g, v); Peter Malick (g); Ted Parkins (b); Richard Ponte (d); Lucille Spann (v). 4/70.*

Recorded live in Boston just three weeks before Spann's death, this is a protracted and increasingly painful listening experience, a record that might have better served his memory by not being released. His wife attributes his non-singing role to laryngitis but he's barely able to sustain the solos he's called upon to perform in each of the nine songs included. She over-compensates by screaming her vocals à la Koko Taylor, making each painfully executed piano solo an anticlimax. Johnson sings three songs, among them 'Long Distance Call' and an inevitable 'Mojo', and contributes an indifferently tuned solo to 'My Baby'. Bandleader Malick's 'Blues For Otis' is a bonus track but his evident sincerity here and in his booklet notes cannot diminish the discomfort this record engenders. NS

Sparks Brothers
DUET

Sullie and Ruth Gant's twins, Aaron (c. 1908; date of death unknown) and Marion (c. 1908–63), changed their surname when Ruth remarried, and Marion changed his given name to Milton in 1929. They moved from Tupelo to St Louis about 1920; by 1928 they were probably making music professionally, both of them singing and Aaron playing piano, and were certainly known to the police. Milton was arrested some 50 times for fighting, gambling and other minor offences, and the less aggressive Aaron, who probably died shortly after their last recording session, was picked up 18 times. Milton drew six months for manslaughter in 1936, and afterwards was arrested less often; in the '50s he rejoined the church and renounced the blues. Their nicknames, 'Pinetop' and 'Lindberg', allude to Aaron's mastery of 'Pine Top's Boogie Woogie' and Milton's abilities as a lindyhopper.

***(*) The Sparks Brothers (1932–1935)
Document DOCD-5315 *Sparks Brothers; unknown (cl); Walter Davis, unknown (p); unknown (vn); prob. Peetie Wheatstraw, Henry Townsend (g); Elizabeth Washington, Tecumseh McDowell, Doretha Trowbridge (v). 2/32–7/35.*

Even without the biographical details, one could infer from their songs that the Sparks Brothers led disorderly lives; gambling, jail, alcohol, women and hoboing are their staple topics, railroads and the St Louis ghetto their context. Despite the street-corner machismo of its subjects, the Sparks Brothers' music often sounds surprisingly tender, even romantic, whether we hear Milton's strong, nasal voice or, on four tracks, Aaron's mellow warmth, sometimes shading into a relaxed falsetto. Aaron's playing features the steady chordal basses typical of St Louis, and a very inventive right hand, endowed with melodic grace and propulsive energy. He was also a capable boogie player, with a singing line and a fondness for medium tempos. When other pianists and other instruments appear, the combinations are usually successful, and Henry Townsend's clinking guitar blends especially well; but the raucous clarinet and violin on two songs are in jarring contrast to the lyricism prevalent elsewhere. The three women whom Aaron accompanies on seven songs aspire to Alice Moore's hard-bitten style, but none of them has much distinction. This makes for a slightly uneven CD, but the Sparks Brothers were important artists. It's historically interesting that their recordings of 'Every Day I Have The Blues' and '61 Highway' are the first on disc; more significant is that they are among the best. CS

Speckled Red (1892–1973)
VOCAL, PIANO

Rufus Perryman was born in Monroe, Louisiana, but grew up in Hampton, Georgia, and Detroit. Like his younger brother William, a.k.a. Piano Red, he suffered from albinism and derived his professional name from its effects. In the late '20s he worked with the Red Rose Minstrels. His meeting with Jim Jackson led to his recording for Brunswick in 1929–30. He spent the second half of his life in St Louis.

*** Speckled Red (1929–1938)
Document DOCD-5205 *Speckled Red; Sonny Boy Williamson I (h); Willie Hatcher (md); Robert Lee McCoy (g). 9/29–12/38, 9/56.*
**(*) Barrelhouse Piano (1929–1935)
Wolf WSE-116 *As above. 9/29–12/38.*

Red was surely not the first person to fashion a song out of the verbal contest routine known to African-Americans as 'The Dirty Dozens', but he was the first to make a record of it, and it gave his career a vigorous push, which was repeated a few months later by the rag song 'The Right String – But The Wrong Yo Yo'. Fortunately the success of a couple of novelty songs did not prevent him from exhibiting his swiftness at the keyboard in 'Wilkins Street Stomp' and 'Speckled Red's Blues'. Unaccountably, after this good start in 1929–30, he did not record again until 1938, in a trio with Hatcher and McCoy. Songs like 'Welfare Blues', 'Down On The Levee' and 'Early In The Morning' find Red holding cards dealt him by Walter Roland, Leroy Carr and Charlie Spand, and he plays them confidently enough, but it's in bouncing pieces like 'Do The Georgia', 'Take It Easy' and the instrumental 'St. Louis Stomp' that he shows his own hand. Sonny Boy Williamson joins in on the last number of the day, 'You Got To Fix It'. This is where the Wolf stops, augmenting its 18 Speckled Red tracks with seven by Barrelhouse Buck McFarland, but the Document carries on with two more recordings by Red, Hatcher and McCoy on which Hatcher takes the vocals, both nicely integrated blues performances, and concludes with three solo pieces from 1956.

*** The Dirty Dozens
Delmark DE-601 *Speckled Red. 5/55–6/57.*
*** Blues Masters Vol. 11
Storyville STCD 8011 *Speckled Red. 7/60.*

Seven tracks from 1955, recorded by jazz fan Paul Affeldt for his Euphonic label, are on the VAC *Biddle Street Barrelhousin'* (Delmark DE-739), but the piano is horribly out of tune. The instrument available at the sessions from which most of *The Dirty Dozens* was selected was far better, and Red was also in good form, whether charging through favourites like 'The Dirty Dozens', 'The Right String But The Wrong Yo Yo' and 'Wilkins Street Stomp' or slowing down for 'Highway 61 Blues' or 'Early In The Morning'. The opening title track is Red's suitable-for-record version, much as he did it in 1929, but the closing 'The Dirtier Dozens' and 'The Dirtiest Dozens' are as raunchy as any scatophile could wish. A little of the Delmark repertoire crops up again on the Storyville album, but not enough to deter the reader with a serious interest in Red's work, and in any case he also redoes some of the Euphonic titles like 'Dad's Piece' on a respectable instrument. Both CDs are accurate accounts of Red's boisterous music in his far from decrepit later life. TR

Dave Specter (born 1963)
GUITAR

Chicago-born, Specter modelled his guitar playing on Magic Sam, B. B. King, T-Bone Walker and Otis Rush. He started playing professionally in the early '80s and worked with Sam Lay, Johnny Littlejohn, Hubert Sumlin, Son Seals and The Legendary Blues Band before forming his band the Bluebirds in 1989. Since then he has worked with the singers Barkin' Bill Smith, Tad Robinson, Lynwood Slim and Lenny Lynn, while he and the Bluebirds have accompanied Jesse Fortune and Floyd McDaniel on Delmark albums.

*** Bluebird Blues
Delmark DD-652 *Specter; Dez Desormeaux (ts); Red Groetzinger (bs); Ken Saydak (o, p); Ronnie Earl (g); Bob Stroger, Michael McCurdy (b); John Hiller (d); Barkin' Bill Smith, Deitra Farr (v).* 11/90.

Jointly credited to Specter and vocalist Barkin' Bill Smith, this was each man's debut album for Delmark. If Specter was the more immediately impressive, it's because at 27 he clearly commanded a wide range of blues guitar styles. The listener has only to follow him through the Earl Hookerish 'Bluebird Blues' and into the jazzy instrumental 'Wind Chill' to get a measure of his versatility. He holds his own valiantly against the more experienced Ronnie Earl, who shares the lead work evenly throughout and plays Nighthawkish slide on the title track. Smith, who has 30-odd years on his collaborator, is a sturdy singer in the mould of Jimmy Witherspoon or a less sleek Joe Williams, perhaps most at home on uppish numbers like 'Buzz Me' and 'Tell Me What's The Reason', where the guitars and saxes provide a fat, bouncy rhythm.

*** Blueplicity
Delmark DD-664 *Specter; Rob Mazurek (t); John Brumbach (ts); Tad Robinson (h, v); Ken Saydak (o, p); Bob Dogan (p); Mike McCurdy (b); Mark Fornek (d).* 5/93.

*** Live In Europe
Delmark DD-677//Crosscut CCD 11047 *Specter; Tad Robinson (h, v); Mike McCurdy (b); Mark Fornek (d).* 5/94.

Blueplicity unequivocally presents Specter as a Chicago picker who plays outside the beefy stereotypes, more T-Bone Walker than T-bone steak. Indeed, the title track could almost be an outtake from Kenny Burrell's *Midnight Blue*, and the closing number, Mal Waldron's 'Cattin', evokes a similar mood of nocturnal prowling. Tad Robinson sings on eight of the 12 tracks, and the minor-key blues 'On The Outside Looking In' (one of several songs he wrote) and his Sam Cookeish reading of 'That's How Strong My Love Is' are sensitive soul singing of high quality. The spacious auditorium sound of *Live In Europe* unmasks a more biting tone on Specter's Stratocaster, clarifying his affection for the playing of Magic Sam and Otis Rush in 'West Side Stroll'. The setting and the absence of horns and keyboards require Robinson to play more harmonica than was heard on previous albums, which he does with panache on 'Little By Little', 'Bluebird Blues' and others. He also revisits three of his compositions premiered on the previous year's studio album and with the help of Specter's shuddering Rush-like guitar stretches 'On The Outside Looking In' to an eight-minute showstopper.

*** Left Turn On Blue
Delmark DE-693 *Specter; Rob Mazurek (c); John Brumbach (ts); Lynwood Slim (h, v); Jack McDuff, Ken Saydak (o); Barrelhouse Chuck, Randy Tressler (p); Michael Scharf (b); Mark Fornek (d).* 10/95.

Blues club punters, Specter says, sometimes tell him, 'We like you, but you gotta stop playing all that jazz stuff.' With a disregard for audience opinion that might have been approved by Miles Davis, Specter responds by driving to the jazz side of town and finding a long-stay parking spot. Explicitly in 'Stop! Hold It', 'Killer Jack', 'Left Turn On Blue' and 'Unleavened Soul', obliquely on almost all the other tracks, Specter, Mazurek and Brumbach play as if dreaming that they're at a '60s Blue Note or Prestige session, an illusion made all the more believable when they're joined, on the four titles cited above, by a veteran of the period, Brother Jack McDuff. Singer Lynwood Slim matches the mood with sleepy readings such as Eddie Vinson's 'Juice Head Baby'. Readers who side with the 'we like you, but –' party may be happier with others of Specter's records, but those prepared to trust his instincts will find imaginatively conceived music energized in equal parts by blues and jazz ideas.

*** Blues Spoken Here
Delmark DE-721 *Specter; Dez Desormeaux (ts, bs); Eric Alexander, John Brumbach (ts); Rob Waters (o, p); Ken Saydak (p); Harlan Terson (b); Mike Schlick (d, perc); Lenny Lynn (v).* 1/98.

Lenny Lynn, who shares the credit on this album, appeals to Specter with what the guitarist calls his 'Joe Williams/Jimmy Witherspoon blues shouter style ... it's rare today to find a singer that sings in that style authentically.' That seems a careless remark, given how Specter's recording career started – and an odd one, since the ambience of *Blues Spoken Here* can hardly help reminding the listener of that first collaboration. But the records are not interchangeable: *Blues Spoken Here* speaks plainly of the progress of Specter's taste and ability over seven years. Like the jazzier parts on *Left Turn On Blue*, Horace Silver's 'Señor Blues', Bobby Timmons's 'Moanin'' and the original instrumental 'Boss Funk' resound with echoes of tracks on Blue Note albums made about the time Specter was born. Also, Lynn is more versatile than Barkin' Bill Smith, cheerfully taking on both Eddie Harris's 'Listen Here' and Big Bill Broonzy's 'Just A Dream'. Now reread the last sentence of the previous review.

**(*) Speculatin'
Delmark DE-744 *Specter; Rich Parenti (ts); Rob Waters (o); Ken Saydak (p); Harlan Terson (b); Mike Schlick (d); José Rendón (perc).* 1/00.

As if he hadn't made it obvious on *Left Turn On Blue* that he will play what he likes, not what some of his fans would like him to like, Specter drives the point home with *Speculatin'*, an all-instrumental set of mostly original blues and jazz tunes. As on the last two albums, the settings often recall organ–guitar sounds popular in the '60s and '70s, as in 'The Mighty Burner', 'Jade's Dance' and the Meters' 'Look-Ka Py Py', but these beret-and-dark-glasses passages are contrasted with more dressed-down blues like 'Texas Top' and 'Blues For Magic

Sam'. Specter plays with subtlety, slowly raising the temperature of the tunes until they simmer, but the album would have been improved if he'd occasionally let them boil.

*** Is What It Is
Delmark DE-779 Specter; Mark Hummel (h); Rob Waters (o); Barrelhouse Chuck [Goering] (p); Steve Freund (g, v); Harlan Terson (b); Marty Binder (d). 6/04.

This is a joint project with Steve Freund, Specter's sometime guitar teacher. The notes claim that 'although they may be coming from different directions as musicians, their styles mesh perfectly,' and on the genuine duets, like the straightforward blues 'My Little Playhouse' or 'Rollin' Man', this is true. Most of the tracks, however, have a distinct stamp of one player or the other, Specter focusing on atmospheric instrumentals like 'People Get Ready', 'While My Guitar Gently Weeps' and 'Albatross' (these two following each other, which mightn't have been every producer's decision) while Freund prefers mainstream blues like 'Hoverin' Hawk' and 'Too Hot At Home', on which his singing sounds considerably improved. TR

Arthur 'Big Boy' Spires (1912–90)
VOCAL, GUITAR

Arthur Spires inhabited the periphery of the Chicago club and rent-party scene after his arrival in 1943. Louis and David Myers worked with him before they formed The Aces with Junior Wells. He took guitar lessons from Eddie El, who then became a member of his band, the Rocket Four. After 'Murmur Low', his memorable 1952 recording debut, he recorded six titles for Chance (included in the VAC Chicago Blues – The Chance Era *[Charly CDGR 146]) from which a single was released. Apart from the session included here, Spires cut a number of songs for Testament in 1965. Thereafter, the onset of arthritis forced him to withdraw from music.*

*** Wrapped In My Baby
Delmark DD-716 Spires; Willie 'Big Eyes' Smith (h); Willie 'Long Time' Smith (p, v); Eddie El (g); unknown (b); Ted Porter (d). 54–55.

'Dark And Stormy Night' and 'Moody This Morning', cut in producer Al Smith's basement, may never have been intended for release. The first utilizes a distinctly rural reinterpretation of Elmore James' signature riff, over which Spires shouts, while the second slows the tempo for a song that more nearly suits his rich, nasal baritone. The crudity of the recording is matched by the deliberate on-beat drumming that almost overwhelms the constant rippling vibrato of harmonica and piano. Pianist Smith sings 'You Can't Tell' and the title track with a shade more sophistication, aided by El's idiosyncratic guitar. The rest of the CD is by Morris Pejoe. NS

Victoria Spivey (1906–76)
VOCAL, PIANO

Victoria Regina Spivey was born in Houston, Texas, where she began her musical career as a theatre pianist before she was in her teens. Moving to St Louis at 19, she made a splash with her first record, 'Black Snake Blues', followed it a year later with the compelling 'T-B Blues', and went on to make dozens of recordings, meanwhile filling engagements all over the country in revue, as a band singer and in the '40s and early '50s as a club act. After a few years out of show business she was encouraged, in 1960, to come back, whereupon she cut several albums, went overseas with the 1963 AFBF, wrote sections of autobiography for the magazine Record Research *and founded her own record label to give exposure both to old friends and to young talent that attracted her.*

**(*) Victoria Spivey – Vol. 1 (1926–1927)
Document DOCD-5316 Spivey; Pierce Gist (c); unknown (t); unknown (tb); unknown (cl); De Lloyd Barnes, John Erby, Porter Grainger (p); Lonnie Johnson (vn, g); unknown (d). 5/26–10/27.

*** Victoria Spivey – Vol. 2 (1927–1929)
Document DOCD-5317 Spivey; King Oliver (c); Louis Armstrong, Henry Allen (t); Eddie Durham, Fred Robinson, J. C. Higginbotham (tb); Omer Simeon, Albert Nicholas (cl); Charlie Holmes (as); Jimmy Strong, Teddy Hill (ts); Porter Grainger, Clarence Williams, Gene Anderson, Luis Russell (p); Mancy Carr (bj); Lonnie Johnson (g, perc, v); Eddie Lang, Will Johnson (g); Pops Foster (b); Zutty Singleton, Paul Barbarin (d). 10/27–9/29.

*** Victoria Spivey – Vol. 3 (1929–1936)
Document DOCD-5318 Spivey; Henry Allen, Lloyd Hunter, Reuben Floyd, George Lott, prob. Randolph Scott (t); J. C. Higginbotham, Joe Edwards or Elmer Crumbley (tb); Charlie Holmes (ss); Noble Floyd, Archie Watts, Chick Gordon (as); Teddy Hill, Harold Arnold, Leon Washington (ts); Porter Grainger (p, v); Luis Russell, poss. Charles Avery, Georgia Tom Dorsey, Burton Brewer, Dorothy Scott, poss. Addie 'Sweet Pease' Spivey (p); Herbert Hannas (bj); Will Johnson, Teddy Bunn, Tampa Red (g); Pops Foster (b, bb); unknown (b); Wallace Wright (bb); Jo Jones, Bud Washington (d). 10/29–7/36.

**(*) Victoria Spivey – Vol. 4 (1936–1937)
Document DOCD-5319 Spivey; Lee Collins, Henry Allen, unknown (t); poss. Bill Owsley (cl, ts); Arnett Nelson, Albert Nicholas (cl); Charlie Holmes (as); unknown (ts); Dorothy Scott, Addie 'Sweet Pease' Spivey, J. H. Shayne, Luis Russell, prob. Aletha Robinson (p); unknown (g); John Lindsay, Pops Foster, unknown (b); Bud Washington, prob. Fred Williams, unknown (d); unknown (v). 8/36–7/37.

*** The Essential
Classic Blues CBL 200014 2CD Similar to above CDs. 8/26–7/37.

***(*) Queen Victoria 1927–1937
EPM Blues Collection 16036 Similar to above CDs. 4/27–7/37.

She may have had little of the grandeur of Ma Rainey or Bessie Smith, yet Victoria Spivey is one of the most distinctive of blues singers and for present-day listeners perhaps one of the most communicative, while her songs contain some of the music's most vivid images. At least two of her compositions, 'Black Snake Blues' and 'T-B Blues', a death-rattle of a song punctuated by long, sliding moans, went on to become blues standards, but others like 'The Alligator Pond Went Dry' and 'Dope Head Blues', though less widely known, are ingenious and sometimes startlingly lurid.

Since she arrived relatively late on the blues scene, almost all her recordings were electrical and so do justice to a voice that might otherwise have sounded scrawny and limited in range. Moreover, the labels she worked for took care to vary the settings of her records, from Lonnie Johnson's guitar to small bands with King Oliver or Louis Armstrong, or the pungent septet from Luis Russell's orchestra who accompany her on the astonishing 10/29 Victor session that produced 'Blood Hound Blues', 'Dirty T.B. Blues', 'Telephoning The Blues' and the monumental 'Moaning The Blues'. After a five-year break in the early '30s she returned to recording, singing with small swing groups in an up-to-date style that most of her grander-voiced contemporaries were unable to learn. Typically peppy examples are 'Hollywood Stomp', 'Harlem Susie-Kue' and 'Give It To Him'.

Spivey's work is full of surprises and it's rewarding to follow it through Document's four volumes, though the remastering quality is uneven. The best in that respect are *Vol. 2*, which has the lascivious 'My Handy Man' and 'Organ Grinder Blues' and several versions each of the amusing vaudeville numbers 'Funny Feathers' and 'How Do They Do It That Way', and *Vol. 3*, which opens with the abovementioned Victor session. Classic Blues and EPM both skip the original 'Black Snake Blues' in favour of the 1928 remake, a two-part duet with Lonnie Johnson, and the latter CD doesn't include the original 'T-B Blues' either, but these are otherwise representative selections, embracing most of the songs mentioned above and largely avoiding the dull 7/37 sessions that concluded her pre-World War II output. Although shorter (22 tracks against 36, and three of the 22 are by her sister Addie 'Sweet Pease' Spivey), *Queen Victoria* is sonically more reliable and the better buy.

(*) Songs We Taught Your Mother
Original Blues Classics OBCCD-520 *Spivey; J. C. Higginbotham (tb); Buster Bailey (cl); Cliff Jackson (p); Sidney De Paris (tu); Zutty Singleton (d). 8/61.*
*** **Woman! Blues!**
Original Blues Classics OBCCD-566 *Spivey; Lonnie Johnson (g, v). 9/61.*
*** **The Bluesville Years Vol. 8: Roll Over, Ms. Beethoven**
Prestige PRCD-9916 *As for above CDs. 8–9/61.*

Spivey was busy for Prestige's Bluesville label in the summer of 1961. *Idle Hours* (Original Blues Classics OBCCD-518) was mostly Lonnie Johnson's album, her portion being limited to two vocal duets with him, 'Long Time Blues' and the title track, and a solo, piano-accompanied version of 'I Got The Blues So Bad'. Then she divided the dozen *Songs We Taught Your Mother* three ways with two other veterans of the '20s blues world, Lucille Hegamin and Alberta Hunter. Spivey's tracks include 'Got The Blues So Bad' again and a feisty 'Black Snake Blues' encoiled by Buster Bailey's clarinet. *Woman! Blues!* was another collaboration with Johnson but tilted in Spivey's favour: she sings and plays characteristically jerky piano throughout, while Johnson sometimes joins in on guitar and twice on voice. The salacious crosstalk of 'Let's Ride Tonight' naturally reminds one of their earlier duets like 'Furniture Man Blues', but 30 years on they sound less rehearsed and more gleeful. Though not quite the blues moaner she once was, Spivey recaptures much of her bittersweet tone in 'Thursday Girl' and 'Christmas Without Santa Claus'. Both those tracks, 'Let's Ride Tonight' and two others, plus 'Idle Hours' from *Idle Hours*, are added to the contents of *Songs We Taught Your Mother* to produce the Prestige CD. TR

Freddie Spruell (1893–1956)
VOCAL, GUITAR

Born in Lake Providence, Louisiana, Spruell moved in his youth to Chicago, where he recorded on four occasions over nine years, but he seems to have left little impression on his contemporaries. He quit music to become a Baptist preacher in the mid-'40s.

*** **Mississippi Blues – Vol. 2 (1926–1935)**
Document DOCD-5158 *Spruell; Carl Martin (g, v); unknown (sp). 6/26–4/35.*

Freddie Spruell is an anomaly. Although one of the earliest male artists to record what are conventionally called country blues, he spent his entire adult life in Chicago. Indeed, his debut recording, 'Milk Cow Blues', is littered with Chicago references. (The first recording with that title, it has no musical or textual associations with similarly named songs by Sleepy John Estes or Kokomo Arnold.) He is not known to have spent time in Mississippi, yet his 'Low-Down Mississippi Bottom Man' seems to be related to songs recorded later by Charley Patton and Kid Bailey. His guitar playing, however, has no overt stylistic connections with those players, or indeed with any contemporary. His 1935 recordings show no modernization of his approach, though this is somewhat masked, and the stolidity of his rhythm somewhat relieved, by the lead guitar playing of Carl Martin, who is particularly adept on the rag song 'Let's Go Riding'. Spruell's share of this album is ten tracks; for the other contributors, Willie 'Poor Boy' Lofton and Arthur Petties, see its entry in COMPILATIONS: MISSISSIPPI. TR

Houston Stackhouse (1910–80)
VOCAL, GUITAR, HARMONICA

Like David 'Honeyboy' Edwards, Houston Garth Stackhouse is as valuable for his memories as for his music. A friend of Tommy Johnson and his brothers, a cousin to Robert Nighthawk, an acquaintance of Muddy Waters, Robert Johnson, Rice Miller and Elmore James – there weren't many musicians between Memphis and Jackson, Mississippi, with whom Stack didn't play. A gentle soul, he was content to add his skills to others' work rather than develop a style of his own. Consequently, opportunities to record rarely came his way and he was almost 60 before the world turned its attention towards him. Although few of the songs he played were his own, each was imbued with the warm personality that endeared him to all who witnessed his performances.

**** **Masters Of Modern Blues**
Testament TCD 5010 *Stackhouse; Robert Nighthawk (g); Peck Curtis (d, v). 8/67.*

On these recordings made by the musicologist George Mitchell, Stackhouse is accompanied by an ailing Nighthawk, who died three months later; he supplies a rather stolid rhythm for his older cousin, who favoured the repertoire of Tommy Johnson, exemplified by 'Cool Water Blues' and 'Big Road Blues'. Other tracks include Walter Vincson's 'The Wrong Man', 'Take A Little Walk With Me' and 'Mean Old World'. Stackhouse is an engaging singer with a perfect falsetto, and an accomplished soloist with a surprisingly modern touch. The session is graced by the exuberance of Curtis's drumming, his busy hands constantly implying doubled tempos, with random and cavalier assaults on a cowbell. Though distracting, his industry adds to the charm of these recordings. The remainder of the CD is by Nighthawk. *Mississippi Delta Blues Vol. 2* (Arhoolie CD 402), which contained some of the same titles and others, augmented with material by Joe Callicott and R. L. Burnside, has been deleted.

*** **Big Road Blues**
Wolf 120.915 *Stackhouse; Carey 'Ditty' Mason (g); Small Blues Charlie (b); Hans Rabitsch (d). 9/67–10/76.*

Six days after the Mitchell recordings, Stackhouse was visited by David Evans, who taped him and Carey 'Ditty' Mason as a duo. On the VAC *Catfish Blues* (Collectables COL-CD-5269//Blue Moon CDBM 090) each man is represented singing four songs and playing a brief instrumental 'Boogie'. Stackhouse elected to sing numbers by Tommy Johnson, Robert Johnson and Charley Patton and his own 'Talkin' 'Bout You', on which he played harmonica with Willis Kinnebrew on second guitar. Mason (who would die in a car crash two years later) was a less versatile player, so the level of musicianship doesn't quite match the earlier session. Nevertheless, this is still an effective snapshot of the Mississippi blues in transition.

Big Road Blues presents a larger selection from Evans's tapes, the additions being 'Bye Bye Blues', 'Mean Black Spider', 'Dust My Broom' and 'Sweet Home Chicago', along with titles by Mason and Mager Johnson that are also on *Catfish Blues*. Stackhouse and Mason's guitars are perfectly integrated throughout, particularly on the Tommy Johnson piece. Unfortunately, the programme is completed by three live performances from two 1976 Austrian gigs and a solo piece recorded the year before in Crystal Springs, Mississippi. The Austrian accompanists are inept, totally unaware of what to play, and Stackhouse's skills are faltering, most notably in his inability to hold a falsetto. Despite this disincentive, the quality of the Evans tapes demands a recommendation.

*** **Cryin' Won't Help You**
Genes GCD 9904 *Stackhouse; unknown (g). 72.*

This predominantly solo session, unissued until 22 years after its recording, has its *longueurs*. It also marks a subtle deterioration in Stackhouse's skills: his guitar playing has its halting moments, and his falsettos at times are querulous. Various songs from Johnsons Tommy and Robert get another airing, as does 'The Wrong Man', here entitled 'I Got Something', alongside the more recent 'My Babe'. More interesting are a pair of Bumble Bee Slim titles, 'Bricks In My Pillow' and 'Cry On! Cry On!', and an extended performance of 'Sweet Black Angel Blues'. This, 'Crying Won't Help You' and his own 'I'm Gettin' Tired' employ the slide style associated with Robert Nighthawk, derived from Tampa Red. An unidentified second guitarist appears on the latter item, as well as on 'Pony Blues' and 'Maggie Campbell Blues'. As his one studio session, this falls somewhat short of being the memorial he deserved but its singularity enforces a recommendation. NS

George Stancell (born 1939)
VOCAL, GUITAR

Though born in Greenwood, Mississippi, Stancell grew up in Buffalo, New York, where he began playing guitar in 1959. Four years later he settled in Milwaukee, where he has lived ever since, working as a welder by day and playing in clubs at weekends. As a clubowner himself he often booked Johnny Rawls, who, years later, assisted the making of his only album.

(*) Gorgeous George
JSP JSPCD 2133 *Stancell; Jamie Finegan (t); Bruce Feiner (ts); Robert Feiner (bs); Kenny Harris (o); Johnny Rawls (g, prod); Mike Nunno (b); Jason Arnold (d); Mary Taylor (v). 99.*

Stancell belies his age in this stylish and varied set. 'A Bluesman' and 'Standin' In The Rain' have cadences reminiscent of Robert Cray, while 'Mississippi Woman' moves with the purposeful tread of an Albert King and 'Gonna Keep On' swings to a Stax soul beat. It's an original and accomplished debut, slightly undermined by Stancell's voice not always being allowed to rise to the top of the mix. TR

Cootie Stark (1927–2005)
VOCAL, GUITAR

Stark's real name was Johnny Miller; John Henry Stark was his stepfather and Cootie a childhood nickname. He learned guitar from his Uncle Chump and from Baby Tate, a neighbour in Greenville, South Carolina. Becoming a street musician, Stark travelled widely despite his blindness, meeting and working with Peg Leg Howell, Peg Leg Sam and Pink Anderson among others. He returned to Greenville after living in Boston for many years.

*** **Sugar Man**
Cello 91002//Music Maker MMKCD 702 *Stark; Lee Konitz (as); Abraham Reid (h); Michael Parrish (p); Taj Mahal (md); Timothy Duffy (g, b); 'Mudcat', Jimmy Rip, Mick Gaffney (g); Mark Torstenson (b); Ardie Dean (d). 1–9/97.*

*** **Raw Sugar**
Music Maker MMCD 30 *Stark; Taj Mahal (h, p, bj, b, hambone); Abraham Reid (h, foot-cymbals); Cool John Ferguson (p, g); Michael Parrish (p); Sam Duffy (vn); Paul Duffy (md); Lightnin' Wells (bj-u); Timothy Duffy, 'Sol' (g); 'Bill' (b); Ardie Dean (d). 03?*

The hoarse power of Stark's singing somewhat recalls Gary Davis, and his debut disc concludes with a deeply felt 'Were You There When They Crucified My Lord?', but *Sugar Man* features insistently rhythmic guitar rather than the raggy, melodic style more typical of the Piedmont. This would be monotonous if heard unaccompanied at length, and it was sensible to add other musicians throughout *Sugar Man*. They do not invariably shine; Reid's harmonica is often tentative, Lee Konitz is astonishingly feeble on 'Someday Baby' and Taj Mahal can't save 'Cut Down The Old Pine Tree' from the fact that Stark only remembers one verse. Elsewhere, though, Stark offers some very interesting material, in particular the hypnotic dance rhythms of 'Sandyland', 'Metal Bottoms' and 'Jigroo' (a version of 'Hambone'). His blues are less unusual, but he performs them with great strength and conviction; his Uncle Chump's 'Padlock Blues' and 'Blue Smokey Mountain', which he learned from Peg Leg Howell, are outstanding.

Raw Sugar is more narrowly blues-oriented, and its sound is more in the Piedmont mainstream. It also owes more to records: Blind Boy Fuller and his associates are strongly represented – an unlisted tribute to Baby Tate adapts Brownie McGhee's 'Death Of Blind Boy Fuller' – and Johnny Temple's 'Big Leg Women' is no surprise, unlike 'Set A Date', which comes from Memphis Minnie. Stark and his supporting cast do enough to personalize most of the borrowings, and 'Shuckin' Corn' and 'Cootie's Testimony', which revisit the past without false nostalgia, are reminders that Stark has a viewpoint and a voice of his own. The Mighty Wonders' 1997 recording 'Never Seen A Hearse Pulling A U-Haul' makes his composer credit for 'U-Haul' dubious, though. CS

Priscilla Stewart
VOCAL

All Stewart's recordings were made in Chicago, and most of them have piano by Jimmy Blythe. She co-wrote 'Delta Bottom Blues' with him, but it's not known whether 'I was born in Arkansas, raised in Memphis, Tennessee' is autobiography.

**(*) Priscilla Stewart (1924–1928)
Document DOCD-5476 *Stewart; Tommy Ladnier, Shirley Clay (c); Jimmy O'Bryant (cl); Stump Evans (Cms); Jimmy Blythe, J. H. Shayne, Lovie Austin, Clarence 'Jelly' Johnson, prob. Myrtle Jenkins, prob. Tiny Parham (p); W. E. Burton (d).* c. 5/24–c. 12/28.

Stewart starts off well, her voice nasally sulky, her attitude hard-boiled and cynical. Blythe is splendid throughout, playing grumbling, propulsive bass figures and right-hand ornaments that are both tough and pretty. Most of the pianists who occasionally take his place maintain the standard, although Tiny Parham (if it is him on the last two tracks) is disconnected from the vocal line. The trouble is that Stewart doesn't maintain the consistently high quality of her earlier recordings. Sometimes the material is to blame, most obviously when she tries to sing sweet on the pop songs 'Someday, Sweetheart' and 'A Little Bit Closer'. 'Charleston Mad' and 'Charleston, South Carolina' are uninspired, too, mostly because of Ladnier and O'Bryant's evident boredom. There are strong, swinging performances all through the disc, like 'Switch It Miss Mitchell' (another dance tune, with the Charleston mentioned in passing), 'Biscuit Roller', with Shirley Clay's imperious cornet, and two fine readings of J. H. Shayne's 'Mr. Freddie Blues'; but they shine an unforgiving light on the weaker efforts. CS

Arbee Stidham (1917–88)
VOCAL, GUITAR

The son of a professional musician, Stidham began playing as a boy in northern Arkansas, first on harmonica, then saxophone. Moving to Chicago, he fell in with the circle of musicians patronized by Lester Melrose and in 1947 recorded for RCA Victor 'My Heart Belongs To You', a surprise hit that gave him a couple of years' touring and further sessions. He never repeated that success either for Victor or for the several, mostly Chicago-based, labels that signed him in the '50s, but he remained active for many years, latterly based in Cleveland. In the '60s and '70s he recorded albums for Prestige-Bluesville, Folkways and Mainstream.

**(*) The Complete Recordings Volume 1: 1947–1951
Blue Moon BMCD 6038 *Stidham; Frank Galbraith, Ellis 'Stumpy' Whitlock, Calvin Ladner, John Peek (t); Oett 'Sax' Mallard, Tab Smith, Nat Jones (as); Bill Casimir, Harold Clark, Hal Singer, Sugarman Penigar, Cozy Eggleston, J. J. Jones (ts); Bob Call, Sir Charles Thompson, Calvin Jones (p); Tampa Red, Mundell Lowe,* *Willie Lacey (g); Ransom Knowling, H. H. Holmes, unknown (b); Judge Riley, G. Stanton, unknown (d).* 9/47–c. 3/51.

**(*) The Complete Recordings Volume 2: 1951–1957
Blue Moon BMCD 6039 *Stidham; John Peek (t); Andrew 'Goon' Gardner (as); J. J. Jones, 'Mad Man' Jones, J. T. Brown, unknowns (ts); unknown (bs); unknown (s); Walter Horton (h); Calvin Jones, Eddie Ware, Art Sims, Horace Palm, unknown (p); Willie Lacey, Wayne Bennett, Lefty Bates, Earl Hooker (g); Ransom Knowling, Willie Dixon, Quinn Wilson, unknowns (b); Judge Riley, Odie Payne, unknowns (d); unknowns (v).* c. 3/51–7/57.

Stidham's robust voice and his predilection for writing bluesy pop songs have not found favour with the blues' latterday taste-makers, and large tracts of his work, including his singles for Victor (1947–50) and Sittin' In With (1951), were inaccessible on CD until Blue Moon's exploration team opened up the territory. The Victor sides that virtually fill Volume 1 are almost entirely Stidham's own compositions, delivered in a strikingly mature voice for a fairly young man, but both their style and his were five to ten years out of date, and present-day listeners will soon find themselves paying more attention to the bandsmen, who get blowing room on 'Stidham Jumps' and 'Barbecue Lounge'. Volume 2 follows Stidham through briefer stints with other labels, which often teamed him with admirable musicians but failed to update his style. 'Meet Me Halfway' and 'When I Find My Baby', done for Abco, are strong performances, 'Halfway' having fiery guitar by Wayne Bennett and 'Find My Baby' two-tiered harmonica playing by Walter Horton, while 'I Stayed Away Too Long' and 'Look Me Straight In The Eye' on States, his last single, have solos by Earl Hooker. Blue Moon's production is, as usual, admirable, but it's unlikely to improve Stidham's standing very much.

** Tired Of Wandering: The Blues Of Arbee Stidham
Original Blues Classics OBCCD 593 *Stidham; King Curtis (ts); John Wright (p); Leonard Gaskin (b); Armand 'Jump' Jackson (d).* 11/60.

Stidham's relaxed singing seems here to reflect the manner of Lonnie Johnson. So too does his songwriting, which at the time of the recording was motivated by his belief that 'the blues have kind of taken a ballad trend. You've got to make a sweet blues, and it's got to tell a story.' As an instrumentalist, though, he had neither Johnson's ability nor even, as is all too often embarrassingly evident, his ear, and the ten songs, which include 'My Heart Belongs To You' and several other originals and are nearly all at soporific tempos, are generously sprinkled with clinkers. On the subject of wrong notes, a paragraph written for the CD reissue of this Bluesville LP not only misidentifies the pianist as John Young but despatches the principal to the next world 20 years early. TR

Frank Stokes (1887–1955)
VOCAL, GUITAR

Born in the community of Whitehaven, between Memphis and the Tennessee–Mississippi state line, Stokes was playing on the streets of Memphis before he was out of his teens (unless, as recent research suggests, he was actually born in 1877). It may have been in the early '20s that he teamed up with the guitarist Dan Sane, from Hernando, Mississippi, and the violinist Will Batts, who were both younger by 15 years or so. Playing chiefly round Memphis and seldom travelling far outside it, they worked together on and off for some 20 years. Stokes also had a day job as a blacksmith. He retired from music about 1951.

***(*) **Stokes And Sane – The Beale Street Sheiks (1927–1929)**
Document DOCD-5012 *Stokes; Dan Sane (g, sp).* c. 8/27–c. 3/29.

***(*) **Frank Stokes (1928–1929)**
Document DOCD-5013 *Stokes; Will Batts (vn); Dan Sane (g).* 2/28–9/29.

**** **The Best of Frank Stokes**
Yazoo 2072 *Stokes; Will Batts (vn); Dan Sane (g, sp).* c. 8/27–9/29.

**** **Memphis Blues Singers Volume 1**
Frog DGF 21 *Stokes; Dan Sane (g).* 2–8/28.

The first two recordings by Stokes and Sane, 'You Shall' and 'It's A Good Thing', are archaic rag songs with sedate accompaniments, but thereafter the two men's guitar playing and Stokes's singing become more animated. The duetting on the blues 'Half Cup Of Tea' and 'Beale Town Bound' is an almost operatic display, Sane's flatpicked lead guitar chiming like a bell against the background thunder of Stokes' rhythm, Stokes urging the beat with punchy double-time phrases. Remakes of 'You Shall' and 'It's A Good Thing', and other pre-blues songs like 'Mr Crump Don't Like It' and 'Chicken You Can Roost Behind The Moon', share that vigour, but the showiest guitar playing tends to be reserved for the blues tunes. All these 1927 sides are on Document's first volume, which is dedicated to the Sheiks' Paramount recordings; the 1929 session, though exclusively blues, is less vivacious, except for the unissued-on-78 'Jumpin' On The Hill'.

On many of the Paramounts the playing occupies as much space as the vocal, a most unusual practice in blues recording at the time. This is true too of the Victor recordings made between the Paramount sessions in 1928, at least when both Stokes and Sane are present. On some of them, however, Stokes plays alone, and while the effect on blues themes like 'Mistreatin' Blues' and 'Nehi Mamma Blues' is somewhat like listening to a more proficient Jim Jackson, the rag song 'I Got Mine' is delivered with great gusto. The other rags, 'Take Me Back', 'How Long' and the two-part "Tain't Nobody's Business If I Do', are all duets and exemplify the two men's unique blend of vigour and delicacy.

After those 1928 recordings, the second Document leapfrogs over the '29 Paramount session to arrive at Stokes's final recordings, made for Victor in the late summer of '29. The four sides with Will Batts are slow blues without a great deal of variation, but Stokes's corrugated singing and Batts's unhurried fiddling combine to enclose the listener in a tiny soundworld of exquisite melancholy. Two further Stokes–Batts recordings remained undiscovered when this CD was first released; its remastered reissue in 2000 omitted them too, though in the interim they had turned up, and are to be found on *"Too Late, Too Late" – Vol. 5 (1927–1964)* (Document DOCD-5411), as well as on Yazoo.

Both Documents have their share of noisy transfers, and the listener who is more of an audiophile than a completist should investigate the VAC *Memphis Blues Singers Volume 1*, which includes all 12 of the 1928 Victors in fine transfers from mint originals (and similarly clean recordings by Tommy Johnson, Ishman Bracey and Rosie Mae Moore). But fidelity is no substitute for energy, and to hear Stokes and Sane at their best one must own at least a few of the Paramount recordings. Yazoo's 21-track selection has six of them, as well as good notes, and so is our prime recommendation. TR

Babe Stovall (1907–74)
VOCAL, GUITAR

Jewell Stovall was born in Tylertown, Mississippi, where he briefly knew Tommy Johnson, but was living in New Orleans and playing for tourists, hippies and jazz fans by the time he recorded.

*** **The Old Ace**
Arcola A CD 1005 *Stovall; Bob West (interviewer).* 7/68.

In the LP era there were a couple of albums, and tracks on VACs, but this is the only full CD of Stovall's work; four tracks on *I Blueskvarter 1964, Volume Three* (Jefferson SBACD 12658/9 2CD) are worth hearing. He was a lively guitarist who kept up a steady bass rhythm on his National behind ringing, raggy melodies. Many of Stovall's songs came from records ('Baby Let Me Follow You Down' was learned from some hippie friends' Bob Dylan LP!) but he sings everything from 'Candy Man' to 'Will The Circle Be Unbroken' with hoarse-voiced verve. His versions of Tommy Johnson songs have considerable vigour and drive, albeit his attempts at the famous falsettos are token. *The Old Ace* is a pleasant, well-recorded portrait of an entertaining musician who was of the second rank but decidedly not second-rate. CS

Stovepipe No. 1
VOCAL, HARMONICA, GUITAR, STOVEPIPE

Born perhaps in the 1880s, Sam Jones spent the known part of his life in Cincinnati, where he was last seen in the 1960s. Although he made some of his recordings as a one-man-band, he was remembered by younger musicians like Pigmeat Jarrett and James Mays as working with a small group, chiefly in the streets and taverns of the black West End. He is assumed to have taken his name from the length of stovepipe that he played in jug fashion; the 'No. 1' may have been added to assert priority over the artist known as Daddy Stovepipe, who narrowly beat him to the recording studio.

*** **Stovepipe No. 1 & David Crockett (1924–1930)**
Document DOCD-5269 *Stovepipe No. 1; David Crockett (h, g, v); unknown (md, v).* 8/24–12/30.

Jones's earliest recordings were made in 5/24. The only one of them to have been recovered, 'Six Street Blues'/'Spanish Rag' credited to Stove Pipe Jazz Band, is in such poor condition that although the listener can identify the performances as instrumentals, he or she would be hard put to it to determine their tunes. Anyone keen to test this assertion will find the sides on *"Too Late, Too Late" – Vol. 12 (1917–1948)* (Document DOCD-5659). Recordings from 8/24 survive in much better shape and are an intriguing mixture of gospel songs and common-stock breakdowns like 'Cripple Creek' and 'Fisher's Hornpipe', the tunes played by turns on harmonica and a length of stovepipe, which is pitched midway between a kazoo and a jug. Three years on, Jones and the excellent guitarist David Crockett delivered themselves of a 'Court Street Blues' and some more lightweight material; another three years later, joined by an unknown mandolinist, they recorded six titles as King David's Jug Band, including the ebullient 'Tear It Down' (previously recorded by Jones and Crockett as 'Bed Slats'), the raggy 'Georgia Bo Bo' and some fluent blues. (The Document finishes with four tracks by the unconnected Tub Jug Washboard Band.)

If Jones is also the harmonica player on the Cincinnati Jug Band's 'Newport Blues' and 'George St. Stomp', as seems practically certain, those effervescent performances are his finest work on record. The tunes are respectively on *Ruckus Juice & Chittlins, Vol. 1* (Yazoo 2032) and *Vol. 2* (Yazoo 2033), each of which also has two of the King David's Jug Band sides, and both are on *Rare Country Blues – Vol. 3 (1928–1936)* (Document DOCD-5642) and *Cincinnati Blues* (Catfish KATCD 186, deleted). The last included most of Jones's other recordings, too, though unfortunately with no improvement on the variable sound quality of the Document. TR

Angela Strehli (born 1945)
VOCAL

Growing up in Lubbock, Texas, Strehli absorbed blues and gospel from radio and records. She has been active on the Austin blues scene since the '70s, performing regularly at Antone's and recording for the club's label.

**(*) Soul Shake
Antone's 74219 *Strehli; Mark 'Kaz' Kazanoff (s, h, v); Danny Levin (kb); Mel Brown (o, p); Denny Freeman (p, g); Pat Whitefield (b); George Rains (d, perc); John Tranor (perc); Cleveland Chenier (rb).* 87?

**(*) Blonde And Blue
Rounder CD 3127 *Strehli; Keith Winking (t); Kent Winking (tb); Mark Kazanoff (ts, bs, h); The Uptown Horns; unknown (h); Reese Wynans, Paul Griffin (kb); Billy Payne (p); Derek O'Brien, Steve James, Steve Cropper (g); Sarah Brown, John Pierce, Jonathan Sanborn (b); George Rains, Jim Keltner, Will Calhoun (d); Bonnie Hayes, Annie Stocking, Don Covay (v).* 2/92.

Strehli exercises her versatility and a powerful voice in sets of blues, soul numbers and her own compositions. *Soul Shake* is stronger in blues, with selections from Dr Ross, Elmore James, J. B. Hutto, John Brim and Eddie Taylor, but the accompaniments are run-of-the-mill. *Blonde And Blue* has only three blues standards: 'You Don't Love Me', 'Just Your Fool', with rather weedy harmonica by Kazanoff, and 'The Sun Is Shining', to which O'Brien contributes a plausible Elmore James slide part. He also plays excellent twirling guitar on 'Say It's Not So', an original, as is 'Two Bit Texas Town', which is about growing up in one and catching the blues from the airwaves. *Blonde And Blue* closes with a version of Sister Terrell's 'Going To That City', accompanied only by Steve James – a fine performance by both. Strehli also participated, with Marcia Ball and Lou Ann Barton, in the R&B collection *Dreams Come True* (Antone's ANTCD 0014), and made a now deleted set in the late '90s for House Of Blues, *Deja Blue*. TR

Bob Stroger (born 1930)
BASS, VOCAL

Stroger has lived in Chicago since 1955 and has worked with innumerable blues artists there.

**(*) In The House
Crosscut CCD 11065 *Stroger; Ron Sorin (h); Ken Saydak (p, v); James Wheeler, Billy Flynn (g, v); Marty Binder (d).* 11/98.

No one who's listened to much Chicago blues of the past 30 years will be unfamiliar with Stroger's bass playing, but his first CD in his own name reveals quite a personable singer on tracks like 'Stranded In St. Louis' and 'Loan Me Train Fare'. Five of the vocal tracks are his; others are by Flynn, who echoes Muddy Waters in 'Lovin' Man', Wheeler, who occupies a long stretch of the disc with his own 'Extension 309' and 'Gonna Make Some Changes', and Saydak, who does Amos Milburn's 'Thinking And Drinking'. The playing's all good, but the length of the performances, recorded at the Lucerne Blues Festival, and the familiar texture of the material make this a creditable album rather than an exciting one. TR

Percy Strother (1946–2005)
VOCAL, GUITAR, HARMONICA

Born in Vicksburg, Mississippi, Strother led a restless, substance-abusing existence after his father's violent death, soon followed by his mother's after she descended into alcoholism. Eventually settling in Minneapolis, Strother straightened himself out and built a reputation on the local scene, and later more widely.

***(*) The Highway Is My Home
Black Magic 9030 *Strother; Todd Matheson, Tom Johnson (t); Mike Larson (tb); Paul Strickland, Brian Simons (s); Curtis Blake, Pat Hayes (h); Shawn 'Ez-Keez' Lewis, Tony Henderson, Bruce McCabe, Brad Martin, Strings Waleed (kb); Vas-Tie [Vasti] Jackson, Walter Scott, Don Breelove, Larry Burton, James Smith, Jimmy Dawkins, Dan Schwalbe (g); Lee Cain, Dave 'Biscuit' Miller, Johnny Willis, John Derrick 'J. D.' Sykes (b); Dannie Hickman, Robb Stupka, Moe Stevenson (d).* 2/91–1/95.

*** It's My Time
JSP JSPCD 295 *Strother; Mike Jones (t); Bruce Feiner (ts); Robert Feiner (bs); Brian Charette (kb, o); Johnny Rawls (g); Mike Nunno (b); Dwayne 'Cook' Broadnax (d).* 97.

*** Home At Last
Black & Tan CD B&T 002 *Strother; Arend Bouwmeester (ts); Tom Scheep (h); Roel Spanjers (o, p); Jan Mittendorp (g); Ellio Martina (b); Frank Bolder (d).* 98.

Like the deleted *A Good Woman Is Hard To Find* (Blue Moon 012), *The Highway Is My Home* was recorded in Minneapolis. Strother is confident and ambitious; most tracks are his own compositions, and he also handles the arrangements, production and mixing. A large and varied cast is deployed with considerable flair, making for variety within a well defined and consistent soundworld: Jackson's light, lyrical playing on six tracks is exceptionally imaginative, and only Dawkins, guesting on 'You Are So Sweet', fails to make much impression. Fifties Chicago is revisited on 'Easy Baby' and 'Forty Days And Forty Nights' but Strother's writing and singing are mostly in a soul-blues mode. A version of 'I'm Tore Up' is merely dutiful, but Strother's own compositions have both the originality and the conviction to compensate: any blues singer can write a song about a departed lover called 'I've Got The Blues', but few can make the tale and its telling such gripping listening.

Subsequent releases show some retreat from *The Highway Is My Home*'s adventurousness. On JSP, 'Tonight Is My Night, Baby' and 'Ain't Nobody Take Your Place' are as strongly written and sung as anything on the earlier disc, but more often Johnny Rawls's insipid production and too similar arrangements suck the juice out of Strother's vocals, and having him play all the guitar solos exposes his limitations. *It's My Time* is adequate, but anyone hearing it as a first meeting with Strother would wonder what the fuss is about.

Home At Last consists of covers of Chess recordings, with Muddy, Wolf and Little Walter originals unsurprisingly dominant. Black & Tan's house band is one of Europe's most reliable and idiomatic outfits, and the only thing wrong with Bouwmeester's guest appearances is that there are only two of them. Nevertheless, this is not exactly an enthralling CD; much of the material is of extreme familiarity, and Strother isn't able to make it fresh, perhaps because of lack of enthusiasm, more certainly because of decreased vocal strength. CS

Alice Stuart (born 1942)
VOCAL, GUITAR

Stuart became part of the Northwestern folk scene in the early '60s, and was briefly a Mother Of Invention. As well as performing solo, she was one of the first white women to lead a blues band. She left the music business in the '80s to raise a family and attend college.

**(*) Crazy With The Blues
Country Con Fusion CCF 102 *Stuart; Terry Hanck (ts); Jim Bobisuthi (h); Laurie Lewis (vn); Bobby Black (sg); Charlie Wallace (g); Prune Rooney (b, v); Karl Sevareid (b); Allen Boxall (d).* 99.

*** Can't Find No Heaven
Burnside 0044 *Stuart; Paul deLay (h); Louis Pain (o); Janice Scroggins (p); Terry Robb (g, b); Fred Chalenor (b); Kevin Cook(d); Duffy Bishop (v).* 02.

All The Good Times (Arhoolie CD 9034), recorded in 1964, is a folk album with some blues included, and outside our range. *Crazy With The Blues* is a blues album with a folk-rock midsection. The arrangements have been done with some care, the musicians are assured and Stuart's own compositions show a good grasp of blues idioms, but her singing often has a measured elegance that's more likely to appeal to fans of Emmylou Harris than of Memphis Minnie. On *Can't Find No Heaven* a couple of folky navel-gazers interrupt the bluesiness, but overall it's a much tougher proposition, with Stuart's voice riding roughshod over an electric band on a majority of songs, and a more edgy feel to the acoustic numbers, even 'Sugar Babe' and 'Turn Your Money Green'. CS

Studebaker John (born 1952)
VOCAL, HARMONICA, GUITAR

Chicago-born John Grimaldi learned his trade on harmonica by listening to Big John Wrencher, Big Walter Horton and others of the city's bluesmen. In the early '70s he formed a band to work North Side clubs, settling at Kingston Mines, where he conducted a Monday-night blues session. Listening to Hound Dog Taylor and Brewer Phillips inspired him to devote more time to his guitar playing. He has worked extensively on the Midwestern blues club circuit and appeared at festivals in Europe, where he made his first recordings for the Dutch label Double Trouble. He plays on the St George albums by Big Mojo Elem, Little Mack Simmons and Tail Dragger.

**(*) Outside Lookin' In
Blind Pig BPCD 5022 *Studebaker John; Rick Kreher (g); Ron Regnas (b); Bob Carter (d).* 3–11/89.

*** Too Tough
Blind Pig BPCD 5010 *Studebaker John; Mark Brumbach (kb); Rick Kreher (g); Ron Regnas (b, v); Joe Fink (d).* 94.

**(*) Tremoluxe
Blind Pig BPCD 5031 *Studebaker John; Mike Garrett (g, v); Ron Regnas (b, v); Kelly Littleton (d).* 96.

**(*) Time Will Tell
Blind Pig BPCD 5042 *Studebaker John; Wes Cichosz (bs); Pat Brennan (kb); Gerald Berry, Mimi Betinis, John Cosgrove, Gary Heller, The Guitar Suspect (g); John Sefner (b); Earl Howell, Linard Stroud (d).* 97.

**(*) Howl With The Wolf
Evidence ECD 26112 *Studebaker John; Pat Brennan (o, p); Joe Zaklan (g); Felton Crews, Richard Hite (b); Earl Howell (d).* 11–12/00.

Driven by the leader's slide guitar, Studebaker John & The Hawks are a no-messing, back-to-basics blues band. They occasionally sound a little like George Thorogood & The Destroyers. But there are differences: Grimaldi not only plays slashing slide guitar but is a more than competent executant on both diatonic and chromatic harmonica. He also writes his own, strongly blues-based, material, which he delivers with tough, the-hell-witcha brusquerie.

The three albums the band made in the '80s have been deleted, but parts of the second, *Nothin' But Fun*, can be found on *Outside Lookin' In*. Blind Pig issued this as a successor to the band's imposing US debut *Too Tough*, a decision that may have slightly disconcerted the band's new friends, since the earlier ensemble was a touch less subtle; the band had not quite achieved the control to make slow, airy music like *Too Tough*'s 'Somebody Forgot To Tell My Heart' or 'Flame Of Desire'. *Tremoluxe* was produced by Jim Gaines; that and the promise of 'slippery buzz-saw' slide guitar in the Hound Dog Taylor manner may lead the listener to expect a weightier sound, but this is only fitfully evident. *Tremoluxe* prompted the speculation that Grimaldi might have taken his music as far as he knew how, a suspicion that has not been dispelled by subsequent albums. Despite the careful production and involved performance of *Time Will Tell*, and the possibly refreshing effect of a new label on *Howl With The Wolf*, anyone who has followed Grimaldi this far will know exactly what to expect in terms of themes, melodies and overall presentation. Nevertheless, Chicago blues fans who are impatient with received repertoire may appreciate his combination of a hard-blues sound and a rigorous no-covers policy. TR

Little George Sueref (born 1965)
VOCAL, HARMONICA, GUITAR

Sueref began playing harmonica at 21 and immediately discovered downhome blues and Southern soul. About a year later he met the singer/guitarist Big Joe Louis and soon joined his band, The Blues Kings, with whom he played for ten years. In 1999 he decided to concentrate on his own band, The Blue Stars. Following their acclaimed first album they were invited to tour California in 2002. Sueref was voted Blues Harp Player Of The Year four times by readers of the British magazine Blueprint.

*** Little George Sueref & The Blue Stars
Pussycat PCD 001 *Sueref; Lazy Lester (h, g, rhythm board); David Purdy (g); Matt Radford (b); Mike Watts (d); Jimmy Thomas (v). 11/99–6/00.*

Despite familiar titles like 'Treat Your Daddy Right' and '3-6-9', most of Sueref's songs are his own compositions, but their shapes and sounds were moulded by downhome blues of the '50s and '60s, in particular by the sort of music found on Excello, early Sun and Chess, and obscure Chicago labels. 'Feel So Lonesome', for instance, runs on the rails of Junior Parker's 'Mystery Train', while 'Living In The City' uses a Magic Sam figure. 'Tell Your Mother' oozes the flavour of Lightnin' Slim and Lazy Lester, so it's appropriate that Lester contributes to five tracks. There is nothing remarkable about Sueref drawing on sources like those; where he stands apart is in rejecting the standard vocal models like Muddy Waters or Jimmy Reed for the keening high voice of a J. B. Lenoir or Ted Taylor, or, in the limpid reading of his ballad 'The Clock', Johnny Ace. The unpolished small-studio acoustics perfectly suit the deliberately, lovingly backward-looking music on this ingenious and impressive album. TR

Sugar Blue (born 1955)
VOCAL, HARMONICA

Sugar Blue (real name James Whiting) made his first recordings in 1975 as a sideman on Blue Labor and Spivey, then relocated to France, where he guested (sometimes uninvited) with visiting blues musicians and made some records as a leader. Blue also appeared on three Rolling Stones CDs before returning to the USA in 1981.

** Blue Blazes
Alligator ALCD 4819//Ruf RRCD 9.0131 *Sugar Blue; Ken Anderson (t); Bill McFarland (tb); Henri Ford (ts); Roosevelt Purifoy (kb); Motoaki Makino, Rico McFarland, Lurrie Bell (g); Charles Hosch (b); James Knowles (d). 94?*

** In Your Eyes
Alligator ALCD 4831//Trip 7711 *Sugar Blue; Ed St Peter, Carey Deadman (t); Jim Massoth (tb); Dan Johnson (s, fl); Motoaki Makino (kb, g, v); Ken Hale, Roosevelt Purifoy (kb); Pinetop Perkins (p); Herb Walker (g, v); Rob Amster, Charles Hosch (b); Nick Kitzos, James Knowles (d); Alejo Poveva (perc); Shawn Christopher, Leveeta 'Squeaky' Mohannon, Darnell Rush, Joyce 'Peaches' Faison, Elbur Stepney Manuel, Jeff Morrow, Oscar Brown III (v). 95.*

With eight covers and two originals on the first of them, and nine originals and one cover on the second, these CDs are a handy diptych of Sugar Blue's music. He's an exceptional harmonica technician, using the instrument's full range, and the full range of instruments, down to occasional solos on bass harmonica. *Blue Blazes* showcases his mastery of the mouth harp, and the ornate solos and lightning-fast high-register runs cannot but impress. Unfortunately, Blue has little to offer on this disc except technique; his playing is very short on emotional expression, and he sings in an unvaried bellow that similarly ignores meaning and nuance. *In Your Eyes* is less heavy on the harmonica razzle-dazzle and the songs get a more personalized delivery, but they're over-arranged, and mostly pompous, platitudinous or both. 'Gucci Gucci Man' is a great title, but that's as good as it gets. CS

Hubert Sumlin (born 1931)
VOCAL, GUITAR

In his 20s the Mississippi-born Sumlin played with James Cotton; at 23 he moved to Chicago to work with Howlin' Wolf. In the late '50s and early '60s he played outstandingly on many of Wolf's records, such as 'Goin' Down Slow', 'Tail Dragger' and 'Killing Floor'. After Wolf's death in 1975 he played for several years with Eddie Shaw & The Wolf Gang. His work with Wolf gave him an almost iconic status among younger musicians and there have been several attempts to establish him as a frontline artist.

**(*) Blues Anytime!
Evidence ECD 26052 *Sumlin; Sunnyland Slim (p, v); Willie Dixon (g, b, v); Clifton James (d). 11/64.*

Sumlin's primary contribution to this collective enterprise (the album is credited to him, Sunnyland Slim and Willie Dixon) is four solo tracks with acoustic guitar, two vocal and two instrumental. On the former he sounds fleetingly like Lightnin' Hopkins, but his guitar playing, though clever, is unassertive. Most of the rest of the album is by the quartet, with vocals by Slim or Dixon. Sumlin plays electric guitar but still sounds rather tame.

** My Guitar And Me
Evidence ECD 26045 *Sumlin; Willie Mabon (p); Lonnie Brooks (g); Dave Myers (b); Fred Below (d). 12/75.*

** My Guitar And Me
Black & Blue BB 458 *As above. 12/75.*

**(*) Heart & Soul
Blind Pig BP 73389 *Sumlin; James Cotton (h); Little Mike [Markowitz] (p); Tony O (g); Brad Vickers (b); Pete DeCoste (d). c. 89.*

**(*) Blues Guitar Boss
JSP JSP 5110 *Sumlin; unknown (h); Jack Hill (o, p); Richard Studholme (g, b, v); Steve Thorneycroft (d). 6–7/90.*

*** Chicago Blues Session Vol. 22
Wolf 120.868 *Sumlin; Billy Branch (h); John Primer (g); Willie Kent (b); Tim Taylor (d). 4/91.*

**(*) I Know You
APO APO 2004 *Sumlin; Carey Bell (h); David Krull (o, p); Jimmy D. Lane (g); Freddie Crawford (b); Sam Lay (d). 10/97.*

***(*) Wake Up Call
Blues Planet BPCD-1116 *Sumlin; Jerry Vivino (s); Jimmy Vivino (o, g); Scott Healy (kb); Mike Merritt (b); James Wormworth (d). 11/97.*

** Legends
Telarc CD-83446 *Sumlin; Pinetop Perkins (p, v); Annie Raines (h, v); Doug Wainoris (Do, g, v); Rod Carey (b); Per Hanson (d, perc). 5/98.*

Seven of these CDs document their labels' failure to recognize the difference between a valuable sideman and a natural leader. Sumlin's conversational singing is not strong enough, nor his material striking enough, to grip the listener for the length of an album. Perhaps acknowledging this, some producers encouraged instrumental pieces, on both electric and acoustic guitar, only to encounter another problem: the original shapes and vividly vocalized tone of his playing on Howlin' Wolf's records were things Sumlin could bring off only with amplification. Unplugged, he tended to be rather uninteresting; witness the four acoustic tracks on *My Guitar And Me*. Indeed, even on electric guitar he could slip into mere groove-setting; witness, again, several tracks on *My Guitar And Me*. The Black & Blue extends the playing time of the Evidence with alternative takes of 'I'll Be Home On Tuesday' and 'Groove'.

Heart & Soul copes with the intrinsic difficulties better than most, discouraging solo flights and enlisting an old friend, James Cotton – particularly good on a duet called, as it happens, 'Old Friends'. *Blues Guitar Boss*, too, was produced with care. The minimal arrangement of 'You Got To Help Me' elicits some of Sumlin's best singing, while handing over the vocal mike to Studholme on three songs allows the leader to concentrate on producing sharp-edged guitar lines. But neither those nor the instrumental features 'Spanish Greens' and 'Pickin'' are the work of a musician at full stretch.

The two quintet tracks that open the Wolf CD are dull, and the next five belong to Billy Branch, but the last four are Sumlin's most appealing work from this period. He sings, again with a Hopkins-like confidentiality, over a loosely woven duet of two acoustic guitars, his own and John Primer's, and although they trip over each other now and then, their quiet back-porch music is entirely engrossing.

I Know You acknowledges Wolf with versions of 'Howlin' For My Darling' and 'How Many More Years', a '"Smokestack"' that puts new words to the classic riff and a 'Mind Is Rambling' based on a staccato guitar figure somewhat like that of 'Killin' Floor'. At those busy tempos it doesn't matter so much that Sumlin's voice has been reduced to a mumble interspersed with hoarse cries, but on slower numbers like 'That's Why I'm Gonna Leave You' the gulf between what's needed and what's offered is uncomfortably wide. On *Legends*, an unsparkling collaboration with Pinetop Perkins where the singing is split evenly between them, it sometimes yawns even wider. It would be some recompense if Sumlin played with the scorching heat of his youth, but that fire seems to have gone out long ago …

… or so one might have thought, were it not for *Wake Up Call*. Consideringly but trenchantly accompanied by Jimmy Vivino's band, Sumlin puts in a performance in a different league from virtually everything else he's recorded in the last 35 years. His songs are still rather shapeless, often just raps over riffs, but in his guitar playing he rediscovers much of the attack that made his work with Wolf so exciting. The title track, over nine minutes long and none of it wasted, has him spitting his angular phrases as if from a nail-gun. Regrettably, this impressive and, so far as Sumlin's reputation is concerned, important album may be hard to find.

*** About Them Shoes
Artemis/Tone-Cool 51609//Tone-Cool/Artemis/Rykodisc RCD 17307
Sumlin; Paul Oscher (h, v); James Cotton (h); David Maxwell (p); Eric Clapton, Keith Richards (g, v); Bob Margolin (g); Blondie Chaplin (b, perc, v); Mudcat Ward, Paul Nowinski (b); George Receli (d, perc, v); Levon Helm (d); Nathaniel Peterson, David Johansen (v). 05.

The producers of this CD found another way to record Sumlin: purely as a guitarist, while others took on the vocal role. (The one exception is the closing track, an acoustic trio piece on which Sumlin does sing.) The addition of a solid band and a judicious selection of Muddy Waters and Howlin' Wolf songs practically ensured that little could go wrong, and the results are, in fact, very good. Strong vocals by Peterson, Oscher and Johansen compensate for some rather prosaic work elsewhere, and Sumlin's playing is, at its best, uncommonly strong, but what chiefly comes across is a collective determination to play this music in the spirit of its originators, which these musicians are well qualified to do. TR

Amar Sundy
VOCAL, GUITAR

Amar Sundy is a Tuareg from the Sahara region of Algeria, but his birthdate is uncertain. He grew up in France but returned to Algeria in his late teens for four years, searching for his roots and learning guitar. Back in Paris he discovered blues, and he later spent a period in Chicago playing with the likes of Otis Rush and James Cotton. Returning to Europe, he toured with B. B. and Albert King.

*** Najma
Dixiefrog DFGCD 8579 Sundy; David Johnson (s); Johan Delgard (kb); Thierry Jasmin-Banaré (b, v); Latabi Diouani (d); Jeff Grimont (prod). 04.

What's immediately on show is an exquisite guitarist, gliding and guiding us through a sensual record of warmth and patience, his guitar always dominant, never overbearing. Sundy's composite style adds no new rules to the book, however. Diet funk, dreamy grooves and Sundy's Fender Strat narratives recall Dire Straits moments, while tonally, with tinges of delay and the sense of epic journeying, this could be a student of Joe Satriani. Stricter bluesmen are in the blender too: Albert Collins, to whom he dedicates 'Say Hey', and a clutch of other classic figures. Sundy's smooth voice can be compared with Robert Cray's and may be even better, with the odd crackle; some of the vocal arrangements with horn passages are pointed and catchy. It's often 12-bar, always with a blues overtone, on occasion a keyboard-led jazzy departure. 'Rahala', after an exemplary draw-you-in riff, falls into an Ali Farka Touré groove with a French pop slant and improves with each listen. The title track parallels the contemporary North African amalgam of Tinariwen and could attract the uncomfortable tag of world music. Sundy's far-reaching scope is explained: he is 'talking about the blues *all around the world*', so he alternates effortlessly from song to song between English and French lyrics. An ideal CD for driving, cleaning or cooking to, but these are long songs – be prepared for instrumental passages twice or three times as long as the vocals. RR

Sunnyland Slim (1907–95)
VOCAL, PIANO

Born Albert Luandrew in Vance, Mississippi, Slim earned his professional name from singing about the 'Sunnyland' train that ran between Memphis and St Louis. It was in Memphis that he passed the '30s, becoming acquainted with many artists he would work with later in Chicago, where he moved in the early '40s. When the local recording industry took off in 1947 he was regularly in demand, both as an accompanist and as a sonorous blues singer. Constant practice and a deep repertoire eased the transition to album-making in the '60s and '70s, while his network of connections kept him involved in promoting and playing with younger artists, a contribution that was acknowledged by a City of Chicago Medal of Merit and a National Heritage Fellowship.

**** Sunnyland Slim 1947–1948
Classics 5013 *Sunnyland Slim; Alex Atkins (as); unknown (ts); Little Walter (h, v); Blind John Davis (p); Leroy Foster (g, d); Floyd Jones (g, v); Muddy Waters, Big Bill Broonzy, Lonnie Johnson, unknown (g); Ernest 'Big' Crawford, Ransom Knowling, Andrew Harris, unknown (b); Judge Riley, unknown (d). 47–48.*

*** Jivin' Boogie
Collectors Edition CBCD 024 *As above, except Foster does not play d; omit unknowns (ts, g, b), Little Walter, Floyd Jones. 47–48.*

***(*) The Walking Cycloon
[Zircon Bleu 516] *As for Sunnyland Slim 1947–1948, except add Robert Jr Lockwood (g); omit unknowns (ts, g, b) . 47–49.*

*** Sunnyland Slim 1949–1951
Classics 5035 *Sunnyland Slim; Billy Howell (t); Alex Atkins (as); Oliver Alcorn (ts); Snooky Pryor (h); Robert Jr Lockwood, Sam Casimir, Leroy Foster (g); Ernest 'Big' Crawford, Andrew Harris, Moody Jones (b); Alfred Wallace (d, v). 4/49–12/51.*

*** House Rent Party
Delmark DD 655 *Sunnyland Slim; Jimmy Rogers (g, v); Sam Casimir (g); prob. Andrew Harris (b); St Louis Jimmy Oden (v). 8/49.*

*** Sunnyland Special – The Cobra & J.O.B. Recordings 1949–56
[Westside WESA 910] *Sunnyland Slim; Billy Howell (t); J. T. Brown, Ernest Cotton (ts); Walter Horton (h); Robert Jr Lockwood, Pete Franklin, J. B. Lenoir, Prince Candy, Jimmy Rogers (g); Ernest 'Big' Crawford (b, maracas); Moody Jones, Poor Bob Woodfork, Willie Dixon (b); Alfred Wallace, S. P. Leary (d); unknown (v). 2/51–56.*

Slim was a reliable character actor on the blues stage. His work may not exactly sparkle, but it nearly always carries a strong, steady charge. Forthright without being overbearing, on the early postwar Chicago scene he was valued as an accompanist by Muddy Waters, Leroy Foster, Floyd Jones, J. B. Lenoir and many others. Collections of their work and VACs covering the same period are often also warm testimonies to his skill as a supporting player. His own recordings, which he began making in middle age, reveal an artist with a settled style, loud and declamatory in his singing, copious rather than delicate as a pianist.

Sunnyland Slim 1947–1948, Jivin' Boogie and *The Walking Cycloon* all include his 1947 Victor recordings, which were deliberately patterned on those of the recently deceased Dr Clayton, with whom he had worked. These eight sides are supplemented with a sheaf of work for Chicago labels such as Aristocrat, Hytone, Tempo-Tone and Opera, some of which show Deep Southern blues on their way to becoming classic Chicago bar-band music. One untidy but fascinating session (not on *Jivin' Boogie*) puts Slim amidst Floyd Jones, Little Walter, Muddy Waters and Leroy Foster. All of *Jivin' Boogie*'s 18 tracks, and 22 of *The Walking Cycloon*'s 24, are on *1947–1948*. *Sunnyland Slim 1949–1951* dips into Mercury, J.O.B. and Apollo sessions.

House Rent Party gathers the fruits of an Apollo date. Slim sounds very Dr Claytonish indeed on 'I'm Just A Lonesome Man', more himself on 'Brown Skin Woman' and others. Casimir solos urbanely on discreetly amplified guitar. (These are also on *Sunnyland Slim 1949–1951*.) 'I'm In Love' and 'That's All Right' are fronted by Jimmy Rogers; they are among his earliest recordings, and are beautiful.

Sunnyland Special gathers Slim's own-name recordings for J.O.B. and Cobra: 17 in all, though four are attempts at 'Highway 61' – a rough stretch of road, to judge from the disorganization of the music. The J.O.B.s are generally better recorded than much of his early work and show some evidence of arrangement and rehearsal, as well as brilliant flashes of guitar playing by the puckish Robert Jr Lockwood. The remainder of the CD is by Lockwood and Floyd Jones, both sometimes accompanied by Slim.

**(*) The La Salle Chicago Blues Recordings Vol. 1
Wolf 120.296 *Sunnyland Slim; Little Brother Montgomery (p); Corky Robertson (b); Jump Jackson (d). 7/60.*

Seven pieces on this album are by Slim and 18 by Little Brother Montgomery. Slim contributes several of the songs featured on *Slim's Shout*, as well as an 'Everytime I Get To Drinkin'' accompanied, like 'Prison Bound', by Montgomery's piano rather than his own. They are strong performances, but there are superior versions of them all elsewhere in his discography, and the album as a whole is more valuable to admirers of Montgomery.

*** Slim's Shout
Original Blues Classics OBCCD 558 *Sunnyland Slim; King Curtis (ts); Robert Banks (o); Leonard Gaskin (b); Belton Evans (d). 9/60.*

'Shout' is right: Slim's stentorian voice has seldom sounded so strong. On his first album in his own name he sets out the stall he will keep for the rest of his life, presenting personal favourites like 'I'm Prison Bound', 'The Devil Is A Busy Man', 'Brownskin Woman' and 'It's You Baby'. The accompanying groups on early Bluesville LPs were often unsympathetic to the name artist, but this time the damage is limited: Banks takes up too much solo space that might have been Slim's, but Curtis fits in snugly and his intro to 'Decoration Day' is exquisite.

In 1964 Slim performed five songs for a recordist from the Swedish Radio Corporation, Mike Bloomfield joining him on acoustic guitar (*I Blueskvarter: Chicago 1964, Volume One* [Jefferson SBACD 12653/4 2CD]). 'One Room Country Shack' (which he also cut for La Salle) is done in a vividly close imitation of its writer, Mercy Dee Walton.

**** Blues Masters Vol. 8
Storyville STCD 8008 *Sunnyland Slim. 10/64.*

*** Blues Anytime!
Evidence ECD 26052 *Sunnyland Slim; Hubert Sumlin (g); Willie Dixon (g, b, v); Clifton James (d). 11/64.*

The Storyville is Slim's first solo album, recorded while he was on tour in Europe with the AFBF, and a splendid showcase for the gleaming trumpet of his voice. To songs that had already settled in his recording repertoire, like 'Prison Bound', 'Brown Skin Woman' and 'One Room Country Shack', he adds some more that would become long-term residents, among them Curtis Jones's 'Tin Pan Alley' and Jimmy Oden's 'Goin' Down Slow'. Though the spoken introductions and some of the selections suggest a little career guidance from Memphis Slim, our man had not yet metamorphosed into a European concert artist: he was still plain old taters beside the other Slim's *pommes dauphinoises*. *Blues Anytime!*, made on the same trip, was jointly credited to Slim, Hubert Sumlin and Willie Dixon. Slim is the chief contributor, playing on seven tracks, singing on five. 'Levee Camp Moan', with just piano and bass, is a believable evocation of a field holler.

**(*) Midnight Jump

BGO CD 460 *Sunnyland Slim; Walter Horton (h); Johnny Shines (g); Willie Dixon (b); Clifton James (d).* 5/68.

Slim gives his customary wholehearted performance and is riveting on Willie Dixon's song 'I Am The Blues', but the band, impressive though it looks on paper, sounds rather feeble. It would have helped if Horton had had more presence in the mix, but Shines was not the right guitarist for such a setting.

*** Sad And Lonesome

Jewel JCD-5010 *Sunnyland Slim; Eddie Shaw, unknown (ts); Walter Horton (h); Hubert Sumlin, unknown (g); unknown (b); unknown (d); band (v).* c. 72.

If there were ever any doubt that Slim was a bluesman through and through, this would be the album to prove it. The dozen tracks are all unfancified 12-bar numbers, mostly original and including his standbys 'Brown Skin Woman' and 'It's You Baby'. The band fires like a well-tuned engine. Slim, playing electric piano, directs the proceedings but seldom solos; Horton, Sumlin and Shaw do, but always succinctly. The sound could have been sharper.

***(*) Travelin'

Black & Blue BB 433 *Sunnyland Slim.* 12/74.

A well-recorded recital of 15 tunes, many from Slim's personal folio, interspersed with ten 'monologues' – some only a few seconds long, some running to a minute or more and including engrossing reminiscences of his early life and of other artists. If you want just one album of Slim solo, it should be this or the Storyville (above): his playing is a shade better on the Storyville, but *Travelin'* gives a more vivid impression of the man.

**(*) Smile On My Face

Delmark DD-735 *Sunnyland Slim; Lacy Gibson, Lee Jackson (g, v); Willie Black (b); Fred Below (d).* 3/77.

Recorded with unceremonious briskness by the veteran producer Ralph Bass, these are, not surprisingly, routine performances, but even when he wasn't pressed to excel himself Slim gave good value. Among the CD's highlights are measured readings of 'Bessie Mae' and 'Depression Blues' and bursts of enthusiastic, unhackneyed guitar playing by Gibson. The chief reason for trimming the star rating is the inclusion of three vocals by Lee Jackson, one of the duller blues singers.

*** Decoration Day

Evidence ECD 26053 *Sunnyland Slim; Carey Bell (h); Hubert Sumlin, Jeff Swan, Louisiana Red, Eddie Taylor, Lurrie Bell (g); Bob Stroger (b); Odie Payne (d); Eunice Davis (v).* 1/80–3/81.

Decoration Day is a Chicago studio date augmented with recordings made on German tours. Alongside 'Depression Blues' and 'Everytime I Get To Drinking' from the Bass-session repertoire are similar slow blues like 'Tired Of Traveling' and 'Patience Like Jobe [sic]', which is Jimmy Oden's 'Trying To Change My Ways'. 'One Room Country Shack' is given some home improvement by Lurrie Bell's spraying guitar.

*** She Got A Thing Goin' On

Earwig CD 4942 *Sunnyland Slim; Beau Bailey (tb); Sam Burckhardt (s); Mack Simmons, Mark Brumbach (h); Byther Smith (g, v); Eddie Taylor, Hubert Sumlin, Alan Hightman, Magic Slim, Lurrie Bell, Honeyboy Edwards (g); Floyd Jones (b, v); Odell Campbell, Tom Patterson, Nick Holt, John Riley, Bob Stroger (b); Kansas City Red (d, v); Willie Williams, Sam Lay, Mickey Martin, Hasson Miah, Fred Grady (d); Bonnie Lee, Big Time Sarah, Zora Young (v).* 12/71–1/83.

*** Be Careful How You Vote

Earwig CD 4915 *Sunnyland Slim; Beau Riley (tb); Sam Burckhardt (ts); unknown (h); 'Professor' Eddie Lusk (o); Hubert Sumlin, Eddie Taylor, Lurrie Bell, Magic Slim (g); Robert Stroger, John Riley, Nick Holt (b); Chico Chism, Fred Grady, Hasson Miah, Mickey Martin (d).* 77–83.

These CDs are drawn from recordings produced by Slim for his Airway label. True to the values of the man behind it, this was music of a defiantly oldfashioned cast and so beneath the notice of many of the labels recording Chicago acts at that time. *She Got A Thing* generously features its three women singers, Bonnie Lee and Big Time Sarah having four numbers each, Sarah being particularly good on 'Long Tall Daddy'. Zora Young's two include a startlingly aggressive 'Bus Station Blues'. A few tracks seem to have been taped from gritty singles, but generally the sound is adequate. *Be Careful*, evidently derived from some of the same sessions, focuses much more tightly on the proprietor, as he presents new compositions like the title track and 'You Can't Have It All' and looks back at a few older ones such as 'Johnson Machine Gun', 'Past Life' and 'Chicago Jump'. The five (of ten) pieces that have Sumlin on guitar contain some of his better post-Wolf playing.

*** Sunnyland Train

Evidence ECD 26066 *Sunnyland Slim.* 1/83.

Almost 20 years on from his Storyville album, Slim again essays a solo recital, and while there are occasional signs of his age – a little stiffness in his execution, some erosion of his hearty and confident vocal attack – it's a sterling performance that begs no indulgence of the listener. A few songs are repeated from the Storyville, and others like 'Decoration Day', 'Highway 61' and 'Patience Like Job' are of similarly long standing in his repertoire.

*** Chicago Jump

Evidence ECD 26067 *Sunnyland Slim; Sam Burckhardt (ts, prod); Steve Freund (g, v); Bob Stroger (b); Robert Covington (d, v).* 4/85.

Though Slim's voice is in good shape, this session allows him to rest it somewhat: Covington and Freund take over on three numbers, and five are instrumentals featuring Freund's businesslike guitar and lively tenor sax by Burckhardt. Not so much a Sunnyland Slim album, then, as a set by a seasoned working band, but none the worse for that.

**(*) Live at the D.C. Blues Society

Mapleshade 5630 *Sunnyland Slim.* 10/87.

Despite his confession that he's rather hoarse, Slim gets through this set without any vocal crack-ups, meanwhile playing with his usual gusto and much of his usual command, though the boogie-woogie left-hand patterns of two 'Blues

Improvisation's demand a little more technique than he can find. The audience claps the rhythm now and then, and even sings along on the opening 'Got A Thing Going On', but neither participation lasts long enough to be annoying. All in all, though, the CD's appeal is as much memorial as musical, and only Slim's most ardent fans need to investigate it. TR

Super Chikan (born 1951)
VOCAL, GUITAR, HARMONICA, PIANO, KEYBOARDS, BASS

Super Chikan's real name is James Johnson. At 19 he began playing bass and guitar part-time with his uncle, Big Jack Johnson, and other Delta musicians. When not working as a land leveller, or driving trucks, taxis and tractors, Super Chikan writes wide-ranging, quirkily observational songs, and makes hand-painted diddley bows and 'chikantars' from gasoline cans.

***(*) **Blues Come Home To Roost**
Rooster Blues R 2634 *Super Chikan; Jerry Williams (ts); Johnny Rawls (kb, g, b); L. C. Luckett (kb, g, d); Brent Endres, Selina O'Neal (finger snapping).* 96?

*** **What You See**
Fat Possum 80329 *Super Chikan; Harvell Thomas (b); Dion Thomas (d); Cary Hudson, Bryan Barry, Bob Egan, Miro Faracci (two ts, perc, clapping in unknown order).* 99?

***(*) **Shoot That Thang**
Rooster Blues ROB-CD-2645 *As above, except omit Hudson, Barry, Egan, Faracci.* 7–9/00.

It's no surprise that Super Chikan makes poultry noises with both voice and guitar, but it's gratifying that he does so occasionally and briefly. He's a deliberate explorer of himself and his world through words and music; he's not quite a Sleepy John Estes for our time, but a comparison with Alex Moore's eccentric poetics isn't out of place, given lines like 'Them Mennonites don't smoke, but that John Deere sure will' or 'Listen to the raindrops fallin' on my tin top shack, While I'm layin' on the floor pickin' pimples offa Bertha's back.' Chikan's best instrument is the guitar, on which he makes discriminating use of distortion and wah-wah, adding piquancy to a style that's usually warm and mellow; his harmonica is technically limited but richly expressive, and his bass and piano playing never less than serviceable.

None of these CDs is totally successful: *Blues Come Home To Roost* has the strongest and most oddball songs, and the largest helping of mouth harp, but Rawls and Luckett are sometimes rather bland and fussy. The other discs feature Johnson's regular band, the Fighting Cocks. On Fat Possum, they strive to fit the label's 'loud and rough' brand identity, which doesn't always suit Chikan's highly wrought lyrics. *Shoot That Thang* gets a better balance between energy and imagination, ranging comfortably between the title track's eight minutes of humorous, raunchy boogaloo and 'Tin Top Shack', which is gently nostalgic for older days and ways, but never sentimental about them. It's a pity there's only one track with harmonica, though. CS

Sweet Betty (born 1949)
VOCAL

Atlanta's Betty Echols Journey grew up singing in church and listening to records by Jimmy Reed, Big Maybelle and others.
She turned professional in the mid-'80s as featured vocalist with the veteran tenorist Grady 'Fats' Jackson, who died in 1994.

***(*) **They Call Me Sweet Betty**
JSP JSPCD 2101 *Sweet Betty; Johnny Viau (ts); Troy Jennings (bs); Tom Mahon (p); Alex Schultz, John Marx, Marco Fiume (g); Rick Reed (b); Paul Fasulo (d).* 9/97.

Tenor and baritone often dominate the arrangements, and Sweet Betty is at her best when relaxing on their plump cushion of sound, delivering salty renditions of recent compositions that hark back effectively to '50s jump blues. She's slightly more generic, but still enjoyable, on harder-edged soul-blues hybrids; the only serious disappointment is a bellowing cover of Sam Cooke's 'A Change Is Gonna Come'. A less robotic drummer would have made a very good CD better. CS

Roosevelt Sykes (1906–83)
VOCAL, PIANO

Born in Helena, Arkansas, Sykes was brought up by his grandfather, a minister and schoolteacher. At 15 he began travelling, riding freight trains to Memphis, Chicago and St Louis, where his talent as a bar pianist and singer was spotted by the record-store owner Jesse Johnson. His first record, '"44" Blues', was a considerable hit in 1929 and for the next 20-odd years he recorded prolifically on many labels and under several names, originating several blues standards and becoming one of the most bankable names in the 'race' record business. He also played piano behind numerous other artists. At ease with the changes in audience and recording format in the '60s, he continued to make a living from albums, international tours, festivals and nightclub appearances, particularly in his new home of New Orleans.

*** **Roosevelt Sykes – Vol. 1 (1929–1930)**
Document DOCD-5116 *Sykes; prob. Oliver Cobb (c); Oscar Carter [Clifford Gibson] (g, v); Harry Johnson (g); May Belle Miller, Bee Turner (v); prob. Edith Johnson (sp).* 6/29–6/30.

*** **Roosevelt Sykes – Vol. 2 (1930–1931)**
Document DOCD-5117 *Sykes; Henry Townsend, Clifford Gibson (g); St Louis Bessie [Bessie Mae Smith] (v).* 6/30–6/31.

(*) **Roosevelt Sykes – Vol. 3 (1931–1933)
Document DOCD-5118 *Sykes; Arty Mosby (vn); Emerson Houston, James 'Stump' Johnson, Matthew McClure, Eithel Smith, Isabel Sykes, Clarence Harris, Frank Pluitt, Carl Rafferty, Napoleon Fletcher (v).* 9/31–12/33.

***(*) **Roosevelt Sykes – Vol. 4 (1934–1936)**
Document DOCD-5119 *Sykes; unknown (vn); Kokomo Arnold, unknown (g); unknown (b); Johnnie Strauss, Arthur McKay, Dorothy Baker (v).* 8/34–5/36.

*** **Roosevelt Sykes – Vol. 5 (1937–1939)**
Document DOCD-5120 *Sykes; Odell Rand (cl); unknown (b); unknown (imb); unknown (d); unknown (vb); Art McKay (v).* 4/37–4/39.

(*) **Roosevelt Sykes – Vol. 6 (1939–1941)
Document DOCD-5121 *Sykes; Sidney Catlett, unknown (d).* 4/39–2/41.

(*) **Roosevelt Sykes – Vol. 7 (1941–1944)
Document DOCD-5122 *Sykes; Ted Summit, unknown (g); poss. Alfred Elkins (b); Sidney Catlett, Jump Jackson, unknown (d); unknown woman (sp).* 2/41–12/44.

The first item Sykes recorded, '"44" Blues', is both a virtuoso piano piece and a song of strangely shifting images: the '44' is first a pistol, then a train, then the number on the door of his lover's cabin. Sykes performs it with brio, but other songs from his first session on *Vol. 1*, such as as 'The Way I Feel Blues', often follow the mournful cadences associated with the St Louis blues singers of both sexes. 'Oscar Carter''s precise picking and ringing tone sound extremely like those of Clifford Gibson, who was associated with Sykes at the time, and the moment he opens his mouth to sing, on the duet 'I'm Tired Of Being Mistreated', the mask of the pseudonym slips off. 'Boot That Thing' is a version of 'Pine Top's Boogie Woogie', calculatedly played faster than the original. At Sykes's next OKeh session, the piano is less vividly recorded, the songs are mostly slow blues and the mood is generally downbeat, except on the point number 'Bury That Thing'. The transfers are reasonably good, as they continue to be throughout Document's ten volumes.

Vol. 2 finds Sykes using his success on OKeh as an entrée to other companies, recording for Victor as Willie Kelly, Paramount as Dobby Bragg and Melotone as Easy Papa Johnson, but never sounding like anybody but himself. 'Kelly's 44 Blues' sets new lyrics to the template of the previous year's hit, but at this stage in his career Sykes spent little of his time revisiting his own songs and none at all remaking other artists'; instead he issued an unfaltering stream of original compositions like 'Papa Sweetback Blues', about a devil-may-care character who laces his shoes with guitar strings. The effect of such songs was to script the part of a streetwise figure, successful at the gambling table and irresistible to women. It was a role Sykes would play with panache for the rest of his life. (St Louis Bessie's two titles on this CD are probably accompanied by Henry Brown rather than Sykes.)

Vol. 3 presents Sykes in another role, that of a record-company fixer: on 14 of the 23 titles he plays piano for other singers, most of them probably St Louis acquaintances, almost all of them otherwise unknown. (Isabel Sykes was his sister.) Sensitive to their amateur status, Sykes restricts himself to steady accompaniment with few flourishes. The best of the bunch is Carl Rafferty, who imparts a sleepy eroticism to 'Dresser With The Drawers': 'The end of your tongue, mama, just as sweet as a plum, And the way you use your business will make any man … go wrong.'

Vol. 4 opens, tidily, with the first products of Sykes's contract with Decca. The association would last for six and a half years and yield about 70 issued sides; these, with a few accompaniments, fill *Vol. 5*, *Vol. 6* and the first quarter of *Vol. 7*. From 1936 onwards his records were billed as by 'The Honey Dripper'. He immediately lays claim to the brand-name by using it in his first recording of the year, 'D-B-A Blues No. 2', and three days later backs it up with a song *called* 'The Honey Dripper'. During these 2/36 sessions he also recorded a racing adaptation of the 'Cow Cow Blues' tune, 'The Cannon Ball', and the first versions of three of his most enduring compositions, 'Driving Wheel Blues', 'Soft And Mellow' and the ribald 'Dirty Mother For You'. Two further valuable copyrights are premiered on *Vol. 5*, 'Mistake In Life' and the evergreen 'Night Time Is The Right Time', among less hard-wearing but arrestingly titled pieces like 'Hospital, Heaven Or Hell', 'The Dog In A Man' and 'Journey From The Germs'. That kind of inventiveness is no less likely to occur in routine-sounding songs: 'Night Gown Blues', for instance, opens with a typical Sykes trope, 'If you can't love me correctly, mama, it's best that we don't start, Because love is a abscess of the brain and it works right on the heart.' He also begins to exchange blues for popular song structures, as in 'Love Lease Blues' or 'Sad Yas Yas Yas (You Fade Away Like The Morning Dew)'.

Sykes's Decca recordings, and the 1941–42 sides for OKeh which follow them on *Vol. 7*, find him concentrating more of his energy on writing and delivering songs than on finding new ways to accompany them; his piano parts are largely formulaic, though the formulas are at least his own, and lack the bold gestures of his early work. His lyrics are consistently imaginative, and 'Concentration Blues' on *Vol. 6* reveals a vocabulary none of his contemporaries could match, but such attributes will seduce only his most ardent admirers; for other listeners the long sequence of blues with piano and drums that extends through *Vol. 6* and well into *Vol. 7* may be a taxing journey, though *Vol. 6* ends in high spirits with the dance number 'Doin' The Sally Long' and the hip-talking boogie woogie of '47th Street Jive'. *Vol. 7* signs off with a 1944 trio date for Bluebird that's more swing than blues, ending with a cover version of Cecil Gant's current hit 'I Wonder'.

*** **The Essential**
Classic Blues CBL 200010 2CD *Sykes; Artie Mosby (vn); Oscar Carter [Clifford Gibson] (g, v); Kokomo Arnold, unknown (g); unknown (b); Sidney Catlett, unknowns (d); James 'Stump' Johnson, Carl Rafferty, Napoleon Fletcher, St Louis Bessie [Bessie Mae Smith], Emerson Houston (v). 6/29–4/41.*

*** **The Honey Dripper**
Fabulous FABCD 130 *Sykes; Kokomo Arnold, Ted Summitt (g); Sid Catlett, Jump Jackson, unknown (d). 6/29–12/44.*

*** **The Honeydripper**
Aim 21 *As above. 6/29–12/44.*

*** **The Way I Feel: The Best Of Roosevelt Sykes And Lee Green**
Yazoo 2066 *Sykes; Clifford Gibson, Harry Johnson (g). 6/29–6/31.*

** **Roosevelt Sykes (1929–1942)**
Best Of Blues BOB 15 *Sykes; Kokomo Arnold, unknowns (g); poss. Alfred Elkins, unknown (b); Sidney Catlett, unknowns (d). 6/29–4/42.*

** **Roosevelt Sykes (1931–1941)**
Best Of Blues BOB 16 *Sykes; unknowns (b); Sidney Catlett, unknowns (d); Charlie McFadden (v). c. 4/31–4/41.*

*** **The Honey Dripper Vol. 1 1934–1942**
EPM Blues Collection 15956 *Sykes; Kokomo Arnold, unknowns (g); poss. Alfred Elkins (b); Sidney Catlett, unknowns (d); St Louis Jimmy [Oden] (v); unknown woman (sp). 8/34–4/42.*

All these are selective compilations, most of them covering Sykes's work from his debut until the early '40s. With its variety and broad timespan, *The Essential* is representative of everything but Sykes's ability to compose long-lived songs, for it includes none of his mid-'30s hits. It's still good value, though trumped in that respect by the very inexpensive Fabulous CD, which also steers clear of his best-known songs. The Aim is the same, with a different running order. *The Way I Feel* unites Sykes with his sometime travelling companion Lee Green, who probably taught him the ' "44" Blues'; the selection allows the listener to compare the men's versions of that tune and of 'The Way I Feel' and 'All My Money Gone'. Sykes's 15 tracks (Green has eight) are all chosen from his first two years' recording and scrupulously remastered.

The Best Of Blues CDs are somewhat deceptively dated, since the first has only one track earlier than 1936 and the second only four. The second also devotes six tracks to Sykes accompanying the St Louis singer Charlie McFadden, though the remaining tracks include a good selection of his Deccas. Both CDs have a high level of surface noise. EPM choose intelligently from his work in the '30s and early '40s, including two accompaniments to Jimmy Oden, 'Road To Ruin' and 'St Louis Woman Blues'.

*** The Honey Dripper Vol. 2 1944–1950
EPM Blues Collection 15604 *Sykes; Johnny Morton, Lucius Henderson (t); Johnny Walker (cl); J. T. Brown (as, ts, v); Oett 'Sax' Mallard (as); Leon Washington, Bill Casimir, Walker Broadus (ts); Martin Rough, Calmes Julian (s); Ted Summitt, Willie Lacey, Leonard Caston, Sam Casimir, Emmanuel Sayles, unknown (g); John Frazier, Alfred Elkins, Big Crawford, Curtis Ferguson, Ransom Knowling, J. C. Bell, unknowns (b); Jump Jackson, Charles Saunders, Heywood Cowan, W. B. Nelson, Judge Riley, P. F. Thomas, unknown (d); St Louis Jimmy [Oden], unknown (v). 12/44–2/50.*

*** Roosevelt Sykes – Vol. 8 (1945–1947)
Document BDCD-6048 *As above, except omit Broadus, Summitt, Sayles, Knowling, Bell, Riley, Thomas, St Louis Jimmy, unknown (v). 45–10/47.*

**(*) West Helena Blues: The Postwar Years – Vol. 2 (1945–57)
Wolf CD-WBJ 005 *Sykes; Johnny Morton (t); Johnny Walker (cl); Oett 'Sax' Mallard (as); J. T. Brown (ts, v); Bill Casimir, Sugarman Penigar, Walker Broadus, poss. Herb Hardesty, unknown (ts); Sam Casimir, Leonard Caston, Emmanuel Sayles, poss. Walter Nelson, Joe Willie Wilkins, Robert Jr Lockwood, unknowns (g); John Frazier, Big Crawford, Bob Carter, Ransom Knowling, poss. Frank Fields, prob. Willie Dixon, unknowns (b); Charles Saunders, Jump Jackson, W. B. Nelson, Judge Riley, Fred Below, poss. Cornelius Coleman, unknowns (d); St Louis Jimmy [Oden], band (v). 45–57.*

**(*) Rock It
Wolf CD-WBJ 004 *Sykes; Johnny Morton, unknown (t); Oett 'Sax' Mallard, unknown (as); J. T. Brown, Leon Washington, Walker Broadus, Bill Casimir, poss. Herb Hardesty, unknown (ts); Willie Lacey, Leonard Caston, Emmanuel Sayles, Henry Townsend, poss. Walter Nelson (g); Alfred Elkins, Ransom Knowling, J. C. Bell, poss. Frank Fields, unknowns (b); Jump Jackson, Judge Riley, P. F. Thomas, poss. Cornelius Coleman (d); unknowns (v). 7/45–1/55.*

*** Roosevelt Sykes – Vol. 9 (1947–1951)
Document BDCD-6049 *Sykes; Johnny Morton, unknown (t); Oett 'Sax' Mallard, unknown (as); Walker Broadus, Bill Casimir, unknowns (ts); John Brim (g, v); Emmanuel Sayles, Henry Townsend, Willie Lacey, unknown (g); Ransom Knowling, J. C. Bell, unknowns (b); Judge Riley, Jump Jackson, P. F. Thomas, unknowns (d); Grace Brim, unknowns (v). 47–51.*

*** Chicago Boogie
Delmark DD-773 *Sykes; J. T. Brown (ts); Ransom Knowling (b); Jump Jackson (d); St Louis Jimmy [Oden] (v). 3/50–4/51, 5/63.*

*** Raining In My Heart
Delmark DE-642 *Sykes; unknown (t); Oett 'Sax' Mallard (as); Robert 'Sax' Crowder, J. T. Brown (ts); Remo Biondi (vn); John 'Schoolboy' Porter, unknowns (g); Ransom Knowling, Big Crawford (b); Jump Jackson, Fred Below (d); band (v). 7/51–3/53.*

*** Roosevelt Sykes – Vol. 10 (1951–1957)
Document BDCD-6050 *Sykes; unknown (t); Oett 'Sax' Mallard, unknown (as); Robert 'Sax' Crowder, J. T. Brown, poss. Herb Hardesty, unknowns (ts); Remo Biondi (vn); John 'Schoolboy' Porter, poss. Walter Nelson, Joe Willie Wilkins, unknowns (g); Ransom Knowling, Big Crawford, poss. Frank Fields, unknowns (b); Jump Jackson, Fred Below, poss. Cornelius Coleman, unknowns (d); band (v). 7/51–57.*

Sykes continued to record quite busily between 1945 and 1955, initially for Victor (1945–49), then for Bullet, Regal, United and Imperial. Document's *Vol. 8*, *Vol. 9* and *Vol. 10* cover this period with the label's usual thoroughness, *Vol. 9* adding the four sides for Random (a tiny Detroit label) by John and Grace Brim, on which Sykes played. EPM's *Vol. 2* covers approximately the same period as Document's *Vol. 8* and *Vol. 9*, selectively and well.

Many of the late-'40s sides prove that Sykes could meet the jump-blues men on equal terms; indeed, remaking Joe Liggins's 'The Honeydripper', he implies that, as The Artist Currently Known As The Honeydripper, he has a prior claim to the tune. The 1946–47 dates with six- or seven-piece bands throw up several swing numbers arranged in the style of Liggins or Roy Milton, as well as a cover of Charles Brown's 'Sunny Road'. At the same time Sykes continued to pay his dues to the South-to-Chicago teamsters union with sides like 'Tender Hearted Woman Blues' (a possible model for Johnny Jones's 'Big Town Playboy'), 'Southern Blues' and the 1950 Regal session (*Vol. 9*), where he and Jump Jackson turned the clock back ten or 15 years. The two Regal sessions of 1950–51 were subsequently given official issue on Delmark's *Chicago Boogie*, with a couple of previously unissued sides from the second date and half a dozen from a later session done for Delmark itself. Four of the last have vocals by their writer, St Louis Jimmy, and are further discussed in his entry. All the performances are very sturdy, but what leaps out at the listener is the crystalline sound quality of the Regal material.

The United sessions on Document's *Vol. 10* have also had an official issue by Delmark, with four extra items, on *Raining In My Heart*. These vibrant recordings with old friends like 'Sax' Mallard, J. T. Brown and, again, Jump Jackson find Sykes in great spirits – listen to the jam with Biondi and Porter on 'Too Hot To Handle (Hot Boogie)'. *Vol. 10* is completed by a couple of New Orleans sessions for Imperial and, just to show that Sykes could do rock 'n' roll, 'Sputnik', from a 1957 single for the Memphis label House Of Sound. The Wolf CDs are distillations of the three Documents, reasonably good as such but shorter (18 tracks as against two dozen) and without notes. *West Helena Blues* adds a coupling by St Louis Jimmy Oden with Sykes on piano.

* The Return Of Roosevelt Sykes
Original Blues Classics OBCCD 546 *Sykes; Clarence Perry Jr (ts); Frank Ingalls, Floyd Ball (g, b); Jump Jackson (d). 3/60.*

** The Honeydripper
Original Blues Classics OBCCD 557 *Sykes; King Curtis (ts); Robert Banks (o); Leonard Gaskin (b); Belton Evans (d). 9/60.*

The Return Of Roosevelt Sykes is, to put it politely, not one of Rudy Van Gelder's engineering triumphs. The mix is dominated by Ingalls and Ball, especially by whichever of them plays the witless bass guitar parts, and the piano is miked as if it were backing them – a particularly odd balance on instrumental tracks like 'Stompin' The Boogie' which ought to place the pianist at the top of the sonic heap. The major problem, though, is that Sykes's voice is, by his high standards, in terrible shape.

Six months on, lessons have been learned. Inapt guitarists have been dismissed, the balance is sensible and, most importantly, Sykes's voice is back in condition. Banks's Hammond organ, a frequent presence on early Bluesville sessions, is not unwelcome on the long slow blues 'Yes Lawd', and elsewhere keeps its distance; Curtis fills a more necessary role with panache. The repertoire, as on *Return*, mixes pieces from Sykes's back catalogue like 'Miss Ida B' and 'Satellite Baby', a remake of 'Sputnik', with new compositions. But although a significant improvement on its predecessor, this is one of Sykes's lesser albums.

*** Blues By Roosevelt "The Honeydripper" Sykes
Smithsonian Folkways SF CD 40051 *Sykes*. 1/61.
*** Hard Drivin' Blues
Delmark DD-607 *Sykes; Homesick James (g, b)*. 1/62, 5/63.

This, rather than the ill-managed OBC albums, is how Sykes deserved to be presented to the new blues audience of the '60s: on form, with little or no accompaniment (Homesick James is on only a few tracks, and barely audible there), and in the company of people who understood who he was and where he came from. Memphis Slim produced the Folkways album, Sunnyland Slim and Jimmy Oden were present at the Delmark sessions, and Delmark's Bob Koester knew Sykes's music both from records and at first hand. The thrusting boogie of 'Ho! Ho! Ho!' and 'North Gulfport Boogie' (Delmark) or 'R. S. Stomp' (Folkways), the ingeniously disguised smut of 'Kickin' Motor Scooter' (Delmark), the brisk canter round the course of 'Vicksburg Blues' that is 'Ran The Blues Out Of My Window' (Folkways), the cries of 'mercy!' – this was Sykes as anyone who caught his act would experience him, and the albums capture that boisterousness without losing the discipline of the studio.

*** The Honeydripper
Storyville STCD 8027 *Sykes*. 10/66.
*** Gold Mine
Delmark DD 616 *Sykes*. 10/66.

Passing through Copenhagen with the 1966 AFBF, Sykes naturally recorded for the local Storyville label. The music is surprisingly different from that of *Hard Drivin' Blues*. Though Sykes's voice lacks nothing of robustness or projection, the occasion doesn't evoke the earlier album's jollity or its air of bygone barrelhouse days recalled. Slow, reflective blues predominate, many of them new to record and some very striking, like the minor-key 'The Last Laugh'. Even '44 Blues' is steeped in melancholy. *Gold Mine* reissues the original 12-song Storyville LP; *The Honeydripper* expands it with seven tracks that were originally scattered on Storyville compilations.

*** Feel Like Blowing My Horn
Delmark DE-632 *Sykes; King Kolax (t); Oett 'Sax' Mallard (cl, ts); Robert Jr Lockwood (g); Dave Myers (b); Fred Below (d)*. 8/70.

The setting – horns, electric guitar and rhythm – is meant to evoke Sykes's small-group recordings of the late '40s, and does. Sykes is in good humour on tracks like 'I'm A Nut' and 'Sykes' Gumboogie', but turns into a positive-thought guru in

'All Days Are Good Days' and 'Love The One You're With'. Lockwood gives a very characteristic performance, his phrasing inventive, his tone either clanky or cranky.

**(*) The Honeydripper's Duke's Mixture
Universal/Maison de Blues 982 249-9 *Sykes; Memphis Slim (p, v)*. 12/70.

The original ten-track album was a typical cabaret set of standards like 'Sweet Georgia Brown', 'St. James Infirmary' and 'Honeysuckle Rose', spiced with the exuberantly smutty 'Ice Cream Freezer' and 'Dirty Mother For You', two guitar songs and a piano duet with Memphis Slim. Universal have dug up another seven numbers from the session, good-humoured but mostly quite brief performances of things like 'Misty', 'Flat Foot Floogie' and a couple more of Fats Waller's compositions.

**(*) Chicago Blues Festival '70
Black & Blue BB 447 *Sykes; Louis Myers, Homesick James, Eddie Taylor (g); Dave Myers (b); Fred Below (d)*. 12/70.

Sykes shares this French-recorded set with Homesick James and Eddie Taylor, who, with Louis Myers, take turns to accompany him (unevenly balanced by the engineer) on his handful of songs. All three guitarists play on the long instrumental blues 'Mighty Men'. Deeply inessential.

**(*) Dirty Mother For You
Southland 2 *Sykes*. 71.

Sykes got a great deal of mileage, in his club act, out of saucy material like the title track ('There's a cute little secretary, and her name is Terry; all she needs is a big DIC... tionary'), 'Ice Cream Freezer', 'E.Z. Cherry' and 'It Hurts So Good'. Those and others like them are a large part of this set, originally and accurately titled *Roosevelt Sykes Is... Blue And Ribald*. On a couple of tracks he plays guitar, as he liked to do in later life.

*** Music Is My Business
Corazong 255 022 *Sykes; Sugar Blue (h); Johnny Shines, Louisiana Red (g, v)*. 9/75.

It was a curious set of musicians to ask Sykes to collaborate with, and, as Kent Cooper's entertaining notes reveal, Sykes thought so too, but the couple of tracks where all four play are smoothly enough done, and Red's acid guitar blends well with Sykes's piano on two others. Most of the rest of the album is by Sykes on his own, mixing old tunes and new, cheery songs and didactic ones. An excellently recorded set (previously on The Blues Alliance TBA-13010).

**(*) Blue Ivory
Blind Pig BP 74591 *Sykes*. 77.

Sykes has a fourth share of this VAC; the tracks come from his deleted Blind Pig LP *The Original Honeydripper*, recorded in performance at the Blind Pig Café in Ann Arbor, Michigan. He sings and plays two slow blues, a boogie and 'Viper Song', a brisk, brief caper through 'If You're A Viper': nothing to get excited about, but worth mentioning as probably his last in-print recordings. TR

T.V. Slim (1916–69)
VOCAL, GUITAR

Born in Texas, Oscar Wills was a Louisiana resident and a television repairman by the time he recorded 'Flat Foot Sam' for Clif. It was his only hit, although not until Slim acquired the master after Clif went broke, and leased it to Checker. Wills moved to Los Angeles in 1959 and continued to tour, and to run the Speed label, when not fixing TVs. He died in a car crash in Arizona on his way back from an engagement in Chicago.

*** Flat Foot Sam
Official 5660 *T.V. Slim; Robert Parker, unknowns (ts); Red Tyler (bs); unknowns (s); Eddie Williams (p, v); Paul Gayten, unknowns (p); prob. Sugarcane Harris (vn); Justin Adams, Mighty Joe Young, unknowns (g); Frank Field, unknowns (b); Jimmy White, Charles Williams, unknowns (d); unknown (vb). 57–68.*

From time to time, Wills resurrected 'Flat Foot Sam, always in a jam', hoping that the loveable loser would work his chart magic again. He never did, and although 'Flat Foot Sam Is Back', with New Orleans musicians, surpasses the original, 'Flat Foot Sam Meets Jim Dandy' and 'Flat Foot Sam #2' just make one glad that 'Flat Foot Sam Made A Bet' is absent. Slim favoured short songs, and this CD collects no fewer than 31 tracks. 'My Ship Is Sinking', with its out-of-tune vocal, and the 'Johnny B. Goode' ripoff 'Dancing Señorita' are regrettable, but Slim's music was usually better than that – better, indeed, than his hit; there are a number of very pleasing performances here. Whether recorded in LA (the state) or LA (the city), they are part of the Texas–Chicago synthesis inaccurately but evocatively called 'swamp blues'. Slim's borrowings from Elmore James, Jimmy Reed and Muddy Waters are obvious, but he incorporates them into his own style. The Jamesian 'Gravy Round Your Steak' and 'You Can't Love Me' make good use of meaty sax riffs and a jangling second guitar, but Slim is at his best when inspired by John Lee Hooker, on the hoarse, moody 'My Baby Is Gone' and 'Bad Understanding Blues'. Also outstanding are 'The Fight' and 'Going To California', with only Eddie Williams's aggressive piano in support, and worthy of particular mention is 'Don't Knock The Blues'. With unexpected violin and vibes, it's a gently persuasive monologue, speaking up for a music that many African-Americans saw as passé in 1968. CS

Tail Dragger (born 1940)
VOCAL

Tail Dragger's given name is James Yancey Jones and he was born in Arkansas. His schtick is that he virtually reincarnates Howlin' Wolf. He met him soon after he moved to Chicago in 1966 and within a few years he was loosely affiliated to the Wolf pack. After Wolf's death he carried on singing in the clubs, with a break of a year and a half while he was serving time for involvement in an affray in which another bluesman, Boston Blackie, was fatally shot.

*** Crawlin' Kingsnake
St George STC 7706 *Tail Dragger; Studebaker John (h); Rockin' Johnny Burgin, Jr Kreher (g); Sho Komiya, Dan Simon (b); Twist Turner (d). 96.*

*** American People
Delmark DE-728 *Tail Dragger; Eddie Shaw (ts); Billy Branch, Martin Lang (h); Rockin' Johnny Burgin, Johnny B. Moore, Jimmy Dawkins (g); Aron Burton, Willie 'Vamp' Samuels, Karl Meyer (b); 'Baldhead Pete' [Cleo Williams], Rob Lorenz (d). 10–11/98.*

Tail Dragger doesn't just do a Wolf act. 'Country Boy' is Muddy Waters to the letter, 'Cold Outdoors' is a pretty good impersonation of Jimmy Reed, and other numbers ('Monkey Blues', possibly 'I'm In The Mood') are in what may be the singer's natural voice. But the bulk of *Crawlin' Kingsnake* is an extended tribute to the man who gave Tail Dragger his stage name (from one of his own songs), in straightforward covers like 'Do The Do', the title number, adaptations like 'Root Doctor', a new lyric to the tune of 'Smokestack Lightnin'', and other songs that have no connection with Wolf except that TD sings them as Wolf might have done.

American People is similarly composed: a Wolf cover in 'Ooh Baby (Hold Me)', a redevelopment in 'My Woman Is Gone', which uses the riff from 'Somebody In My Home', and several Wolf-styled vocals on TD's own compositions. The most interesting of these is the title track, addressing the nation on the subject of the Clinton/Lewinsky affair and asking it, as one cigar lover (see the photographs on both his CDs) on behalf of another, to go easy on the then President. As before, there's a sense that time has been frozen somewhere in the late '50s or thereabouts; surprisingly, perhaps, the Delmark's superior recording quality emphasizes that effect, recapturing the sound of the Chess studios in their glory days.

Rabid collectors of TD's work should add *Chicago's Best West & South Side Blues Singers Vol. 1* (Wolf 120.862), with its versions of Wolf's 'Highway Bound' and his own 'My Head Is Bald' and 'My Woman's Gone', accompanied by a rock-solid band including harmonica player Billy Branch. TR

Taj Mahal (born 1942)
VOCAL, GUITAR, BANJO, MANDOLIN, HARMONICA, KEYBOARDS, FIFE, WHISTLE, PERCUSSION

Henry Sainte Claire Fredricks grew up in Springfield, Massachusetts, learning guitar as a teenager, and by his early 20s was playing in Boston-area clubs. Moving to LA, he formed the Rising Sons with Ry Cooder, then introduced his idiosyncratic approach to the blues on the albums Taj Mahal *and* The Natch'l Blues. *Never content to do the same thing for long, in the '70s he began to write and play in styles of the Caribbean, where his family originated, and since the '90s has also had fruitful collaborations with Indian, Hawaiian and African musicians. With his range and ear he is a natural composer of film music, and his soundtrack credits include* Sounder, Sounder II, Brothers, Blues Brothers *and* The Hot Spot. *He has worked with a wide variety of musicians, from The Rolling Stones to the Malian kora player Toumani Diabate, and is a popular concert and festival act, but out of the spotlight he has also quietly helped less-publicized 'roots music' projects like the Music Maker Foundation.*

**(*) Rising Sons
Columbia/Legacy CK 52828//(E) 472865 *Taj Mahal; Ry Cooder (md, Do, g, v); Jesse Lee Kincaid (g, v); Gary Marker (b); Kevin Kelley (d, perc). 9/65–5/66, 6/92.*

Taj's earliest recordings were with the Rising Sons, an LA

group of blues- and folk-loving musicians who were supposed, around 1965/66, to be the next big thing, but whose first and only album was buried unheard for almost 30 years. The very differently derived styles of the three guitarists create attractive string textures, and Marker's muscular bass playing contributes considerably to the youthful rock 'n' roll impetus of the music, but the singing is uneven. Chroniclers of Taj's music will find here his earliest recordings of pieces that settled in his repertoire like 'Statesboro Blues' and 'Take A Giant Step'.

***(*) Taj Mahal
Columbia/Legacy 498173//Columbia Rewind 480968 *Taj Mahal*; Jesse Edwin Davis (p, g); Ry Cooder (md, g); Bill Boatman (g); James Thomas, Gary Gilmore (b); Sanford Konikoff, Charles Blackwell (d). 8/67.

***(*) The Natch'l Blues
Columbia/Legacy 498172//Columbia Rewind 483679 *Taj Mahal*; Jesse Edwin Davis (p, g); Al Kooper (p); Gary Gilmore (b); Chuck Blackwell, Earl Palmer (d). 5/68.

*** Giant Step/De Ole Folks At Home
Columbia CGK 18//(E) 491692 *Taj Mahal*; Jesse Edwin Davis (o, p, g); Gary Gilmore (b); Chuck Blackwell (d). 6/69, 69?

These are exhilarating albums, brimming with an energy derived from rock 'n' roll, sheer youth and tireless imagination. What's being done to tracks on *Taj Mahal* like 'Leaving Trunk' and 'Everybody's Got To Change Sometime' (both Sleepy John Estes songs, the latter set to the riff from Howlin' Wolf's 'Tail Dragger') or to 'Corrina' and 'She Caught The Katy And Left Me A Mule To Ride' on *The Natch'l Blues*, or 'Six Days On The Road' on *Giant Step*, is not mere rocking-up but transformation. Such adrenalin shots into the arm of blues revivalism quickened the pulses of listeners across the world. Most of those tracks would become staples of Taj's repertoire – 'Leaving Trunk', 'Corrina' and 'Going Up To The Country And Paint My Mailbox Blue' (*The Natch'l Blues*) have continued to turn up on albums made until the present – but time has done nothing to leach the vitality from the original versions.

The former double album *Giant Step/De Ole Folks At Home* juxtaposed the third chapter in Taj's rewrite of the blues with a set of solo pieces. While there was nothing very surprising about guitar-accompanied songs like 'Stagger Lee' or Henry Thomas's 'Fishin' Blues', it was a daring step in 1969 for a young black musician to ignore its associations and play the banjo, let alone use it for minstrel-era compositions like 'Colored Aristocracy'. *De Ole Folks At Home* proved that, while some of Taj's contemporaries might be technically better exponents of old-time blues, few could slip so naturally into the role of playing them.

*** The Real Thing
Columbia/Legacy 498174 *Taj Mahal*; Bob Stewart (t, flh, tu); Howard Johnson (flh, bs, tu); Joseph Daley (vtb, tu); Earle McIntyre (btb, tu); John Simon (kb, p); John Hall (g); Bill Rich (b); Greg Thomas (d); Kwasi 'Rocky' DziDzournu (cga). 2/71.

There were not too many repertoire surprises for the first listeners to *The Real Thing*, since six of its 11 tracks had appeared on previous albums, but they were reshaped in the concert setting (the album was taped at the Fillmore West) and by the winning combination of Taj and a four-man brass team. 'Ain't Gwine To Whistle Dixie (Any Mo')', on its first outing (*Giant Step*) a minute-long *hors d'oeuvre*, is extended to 9.11, a three-course meal. 'Big Kneed Gal' and 'You're Going To Need Somebody On Your Bond' find Taj treating the crowd to one of his pet devices, compacting a lot of words into a bar or two. The only flaw is that the closing track, 'You Ain't No Street Walker Mama, Honey But I Do Love The Way You Strut Your Stuff', already long, drifts into an interminable fade. Taj's recorded work over the next couple of years, *Happy Just To Be Like I Am* (1971), *Recycling The Blues & Other Related Stuff* (1972) and *Oooh So Good 'N Blues* (1973), is not currently in print. His soundtrack music for *Sounder*, last issued on Pendulum PEG 010, appears also to be unavailable.

**(*) Mo' Roots
Columbia CK 33051 *Taj Mahal*; Rudy Costa (ss, alto fl); Merle Saunders (o); Aston 'Familyman' Barrett (p, remix); Hoshal Wright (g); Bill Rich (b); Kester 'Smitty' Smith (d, timb, perc); Kwasi 'Rocki' Dzidzornu (cga, tamb, perc); Carole Fredericks, Tommy Henderson, Claudia Lennear, Merry Clayton (v); Bob Marley (remix). 74.

Mo' Roots was a letter of musical fellowship to the brothers in the Caribbean, and for listeners of more or less Taj's age its resonances may be moving. Others may feel that at times the message takes over from the messenger, when the highly individual voice of Taj Mahal gives way to the assumed accents of characters retailing Caribbean history, as in Bob Marley's song 'Slave Driver'. Given his family background, Taj can argue that those voices are part of him anyway, leaving the listener to decide whether that justifies 'Slave Driver' sounding so much like an imitation of its composer. Very typically Taj, however, is the reggae setting of 'Blackjack Davey', while 'Cajun Waltz' is the old Creole waltz song 'Ma Negresse', attractively arranged for piano, harmonica guitar and alto flute. The following year's *Music Keeps Me Together* is out of print.

*** Taj's Blues
Columbia CK 52465//(E) 471660 As for relevant CDs above. 8/67–6/73.

*** The Best Of Taj Mahal
Columbia/Legacy 498171 As for relevant CDs above. 8/67–74.

*** World Music
Columbia CK 52755 As for *Mo'* Roots, plus unidentified musicians. 71–75.

These are compilations from Taj's Columbia years. *Taj's Blues* takes most of its dozen tracks from his first three LPs in his own name; there's also a medley from the *Sounder* soundtrack and a long 'East Bay Woman', previously unissued. *The Best Of*, which draws on all Taj's Columbia albums, is better value, with 17 tracks. 'Sweet Mama Janisse', one of his many songs about girlfriends and wives, is a previously unissued version. *World Music*, evidently compiled to balance *Taj's Blues* with a set of songs derived from or influenced by other traditions, reissues three quarters of *Mo' Roots* and fills up with other, mostly Caribbean-flavoured songs like 'When I Feel The Sea Beneath My Soul' and 'West Indian Revelation' from deleted albums.

**(*) Live And Direct
Thunderbolt CDTB 121 *Taj Mahal*; Rudy Costa (s, fl, panpipe, kalimba); Bill Rich (b); Kester Smith (d); Robert Greenidge (steel d); Jumo Santos (cga, timb, perc); Ella Jamerson, Geri Johnson, Blanca Oden, Verlin Sandles, Ola Marie Tyler, Carey Williams (v). 5/79.

*** The Rising Sun Collection
Just A Memory RSCD 0003 Taj Mahal; Rudy Costa (s); Bill Rich (b); Kester Smith (d); Robert Greenwich [Greenidge] (steel d); Jumo Santos (perc). 7/80.

The '80s were not the best of times for Taj, either musically or personally. The few albums of the period are either documents of performances with his International Rhythm Band, like *The Rising Sun Collection*, from an engagement in Montreal, and *Live And Direct*, recorded in a studio direct-to-disc, or more elaborate productions like *Taj* (Gramavision R2 79433, deleted), which generated no strong new repertoire. The dominant flavours of the music were percussion, with Robert Greenidge's steel drums to the fore, and the reeds and woodwinds of Rudy Costa – essentially an Afro-Caribbean aroma, which caused some of Taj's admirers to wrinkle their noses, not so much disappointed as bewildered. *The Rising Sun Collection* is the only set that repeatedly reminds one of Taj's blues past, with tracks like Sonny Boy Williamson I's 'Sugar Mama Blues' and 'Good Morning Little Schoolgirl' – the former preceded, incidentally, by an unlisted version of 'Queen Bee', another of Taj's wife-songs.

*** Like Never Before
Private Music 261 679 Taj Mahal; Howard Johnson (c, bs, tu); Gary McKeen, Ed Kalney (t); Jeff Lego, Art Baron (tb); Haywood Henry (cl, as); Ron Kerber (as); Jammin' Jay Davidson (ts, bs); Claire Daley (ts); Rob Hyman (ac, o, v); Mark Goodman (kb, o, syn); Donald Robinson (kb); Mark Jordan (o, p, syn); Jerry Cohen (o); Dr John [Mack Rebennack] (p); Jim Salamone (syn); Eric Bazilian (md, sg, g); David Lindley (sg, g); Sonny Rhodes (sg); Jerry Williams (g, v); Hiram Bullock, Mike Tyler, Paul Barrere (g); Doug Grigsby, Tony Jones (b); Andy Kravitz (d, perc, tamb); Bill Summers (cga, tri, perc); Myrick 'Freeze' Guillory (rb); David Johnson (perc, bell); Phil Nicolo (cymbal); D.J. Jazzy Jeff (turntables); Andy Bauer, Geri Gates (g technicians); Daryl Hall, John Oates, Sheryl Crow, Flawless, Porter Carroll, Pointer Sisters (v). 91.

*** Dancing The Blues
Private Music 82112 Taj Mahal; Darrell Leonard (t, trombonium); Joe Sublett (ss, ts); Marty Grebb (as, ts, bs, v); Ian McLagan, Mick Weaver, Bill Payne (o, p); Johnny Lee Schell (g, v); John Porter (g, prod); Bob Glaub, Chuck Domanico (b); Tony Braunagel (d, perc); Richie Hayward (d); Michito Sanchez (cga, perc); Joe McGrath (perc); Etta James, Sir Harry Bowens (v). 93.

If the '80s were Taj's wilderness years, the '90s brought him cakewalking back into town, mightily refreshed. The light, airy islands music of the International Rhythm Band made way for the funky blues of 'Blues With A Feeling' and 'Big Legged Mamas Are Back In Style' on *Like Never Before* and 'Blues Ain't Nothin'' and 'Sittin' On Top Of The World' on *Dancing The Blues*. But whereas the surrounding tracks on *Like Never Before* were ingenious and varied orchestrations of new, non-blues material like 'Don't Call Us' and 'Every Wind (In The River)', *Dancing The Blues* was focused on R&B songs Taj grew up to, such as Fats Domino's 'Going To The River' and Inez & Charlie Foxx's 'Mockingbird', accompanied by virtually the same group throughout.

*** An Evening Of Acoustic Music
Tradition & Moderne T&M 004 Taj Mahal; Howard Johnson (pennywhistle, tu). 10/93.

Between the planned studio productions, Taj continued to perform solo gigs like this one in Germany. He plays piano on 'Blues With A Feeling' and 'Big Legged Mamas', as he did on *Like Never Before*, but otherwise mostly guitar, with liberal use of effects pedals. 'Crossing', with lyrics by Langston Hughes, was recalled from 1991's *Mule Bone* (Gramavision GV 79.432, deleted), but numbers like 'Satisfied 'N' Tickled Too', 'Ain't Gwine To Whistle Dixie Anymo" and 'Big Kneed Gal' had been embedded in his repertoire much longer. Howard Johnson sat in on the last five numbers, re-creating with Taj the tuba–banjo duet 'Tom & Sally Drake' they first played on *The Real Thing* more than 20 years before.

**(*) Mumtaz Mahal
Water Lily Acoustics WLA-CS-46 Taj Mahal; N. Ravikiran (chitra vina); V. M. Bhatt (Mohan vina). 4/94.

Narasimhan Ravikiran is a distinguished exponent in Carnatic music of the chitra vina, a large lute-like instrument played flat and fretted with a cylinder of ebony. V. M. Bhatt, from the Hindustani tradition, plays a related instrument of his own devising, which uses the same structure of melody strings and sympathetic strings but on a body similar to that of a vintage arch-top guitar; he frets with a metal rod. In other words, Taj has surrounded himself with the Indian equivalent of two slide guitarists, though it's only Bhatt's instrument that has much likeness to the sound of a blues player. Against this shimmering backdrop Taj, who plays only guitar, performs half a dozen songs: blues, soul, gospel, reggae and original. (The concluding 'Curry And Quartertones' is just talk and doodling.) As a musical conversation it sounds elegant, but one senses, for instance during the long 11 minutes of Robert Johnson's 'Come On In My Kitchen', that it doesn't present the Indian musicians with much of an intellectual challenge, and that the result is a civilized and courteous exchange of small talk.

*** Phantom Blues
Private Music 82139 Taj Mahal; Darrell Leonard (t, trombonium); Joe Sublett, Bernard 'Dr B.' Anderson (ts); David Hidalgo (ac); Mick Weaver (o); Jon Cleary (p, clavinet, g, v); John Brion (g, chamberlin); Johnny Lee Schell (g, v); John Porter (g, prod); Mike Campbell, Eric Clapton, John Parks, Dean Parks, Joe McGrath (g); Larry Fulcher (b, v); James 'Hutch' Hutchinson (b); Tony Braunagel (d, perc, tamb); Myrick 'Freeze' Guillory (rb); Sir Harry Bowens, 'Sweet Pea Atkinson', Terrence Foresythe, Bonnie Raitt, Regina Taylor, Alphanette Durio, Billy Barnum (v). 5/95.

Like *Dancing The Blues*, *Phantom Blues* finds Taj wandering through the blue remembered hills of his youth, the R&B anthems of the '50s that diverted him from a career in animal husbandry towards marrying blues, country and Caribbean music. But while he delivers oldies like 'Let The Four Winds Blow', 'Lonely Avenue' and 'Ooh Poo Pah Doo' with his usual buoyancy, the lilting country feel of his one original number, 'Lovin' In My Baby's Eyes', leaves you a little wistful for more of that inventive, exuberant individuality.

*** Señor Blues
Private Music 82151 Taj Mahal; Darrell Leonard (t, tb, frh); Joe Sublett (ts); Mick Weaver (o); Jon Cleary (p); Johnny Lee Schell (g); Larry Fulcher (b); Tony Braunagel (d, perc, tamb); Sir Harry Bowens, Donna Taylor, Terrence Foresythe (v); John Porter (prod). 97.

On *Señor Blues* Taj continues his field trip around the archaeological sites of black music, but visits new terrain – Horace Silver's title track, Hank Williams's blues 'Mind Your Own Business', the old vaudeville ditty '(I'll Be Glad When You're Dead) You Rascal You' – as well as blues and R&B locations like Otis Redding's 'Mr Pitiful' and Washboard Sam's 'Sophisticated Mama'. As for his own pieces, he revisits 'Queen Bee' and adds a new one to his folio of songs for significant others, '21st Century Gypsy Singin' Lover Man', though this one is really about him: 'When I kiss you goodnight/in the dark hours of the morning/and pack a guitar bag/and head on out the door/I know that you know that I really hate to leave you/but it's that time again and I simply got to go …' *That* old excuse.

***(*) In Progress And In Motion 1965–1998
Columbia/Legacy C3K 64919 3CD *Taj Mahal; various accompaniments.* 65–98.

***(*) The Essential Taj Mahal
Columbia/Legacy 74500 2CD *Taj Mahal; various accompaniments.*
65–99/00.

*** Martin Scorsese Presents The Blues: Taj Mahal
Columbia/Legacy 512575 *Taj Mahal; various accompaniments.* 8/67–97.

*** The Very Best Of Taj Mahal
Global RADCD 100 2CD *Taj Mahal; various accompaniments.* 69–97.

*** Blues With A Feeling – The Very Best Of Taj Mahal
Private Music/BMG Heritage 55610 *As for relevant Private Music CDs above.* 91–98.

** Best Of The Private Years
Private Music 82189 *As above.* 93–97.

More retrospectives. *In Progress And In Motion 1965–1998* is fascinating and, given the present incomplete state of Taj's back catalogue, valuable as well, sampling deleted albums like *Ooh So Good 'N Blues, Recycling The Blues & Other Related Stuff, Happy Just To Be Like I Am* and *Music Keeps Me Together*. Better still, for serious collectors, there are three previously unreleased 1968 songs from the Rolling Stones' *Rock And Roll Circus*, three 1990 dittos from *Austin City Limits*, and a bunch more from sessions in 1971 and 1973, plus further outtakes – altogether 15 numbers making their first appearance. The autobiographical notes are absorbing too. *The Essential* is in effect a reduced version of the 3CD set, having 21 of its 26 Columbia-derived tracks in common with it. The remaining ten items are mostly from the later Private Music albums, with tasters from *Kulanjan* and *Shoutin' In Key*. If, as we suspect, this is intended to take the place of *In Progress And In Motion*, it will fit the bill well. The Scorsese selection concentrates on the Columbia period and has a fair amount of overlap with the earlier compilations *Taj's Blues* and *The Best Of Taj Mahal* (see above). In contrast, Global's inexpensive 2CD gives only token attention to the Columbia albums (three items), the rest of its 32 tracks being evenly selected from the Private Music sets *Like Never Before, Dancing The Blues, Phantom Blues* and *Señor Blues. Best Of The Private Years* is an evenhanded but short (13 tracks) and dull selection from *Dancing, Phantom* and *Señor*, other albums being excluded evidently because they were not produced by John Porter. The later compilation *Blues With A Feeling* was not so hamstrung, its 20 tracks (six also on *Best Of*) spanning the five Private Music CDs from *Like Never Before* to *Sacred Island* (for which see below) and it's a better set. Note, though, that 14 of its tracks are on the Global 2CD.

**(*) Sacred Island//Taj Mahal And The Hula Blues
Private Music 82165//Tradition & Moderne T&M 009 *Taj Mahal; Rudy Costa (cl, ss, as, Cms, fl, panpipe, zither, kalimba, v); Fred Lunt (sg); Wayne Jacintho, Carlos Andrade (g, u, v); Pat Cockett, Michael Barretto (u, v); Pancho Graham (b, v); Kester Smith (d, cowbell); Carey Williams (v).* 5/97.

'This "Hula Blues Project",' Taj explains, 'is the beginning of a lifelong wish to learn the music of and interface … with Hawaiian music and musicians.' Unlike similar ventures by Ry Cooder, Taj's concept of Hawaiian music does not focus on slide or slack-key guitar but gives a leading role to Costa's reeds, thus drawing it closer to his earlier experiments with Caribbean sounds with the International Rhythm Band. It would be going too far to call this inconsequential music, but it does tend to trickle prettily and inconclusively.

(***) Kulanjan
Hannibal HNCD 1444 *Taj Mahal; Bassekou Kouyate (ngoni, bass ngoni); Ugouye Koulibaly (kamalengoni, bolon); Toumani Diabate, Ballaké Sissoko (kora); Kassé-Mady Diabaté (g, v); Banning (g); Lasana Diabate (balafon); Ramata Diakaté (v).* 98/99.

*** Shoutin' In Key
Hannibal HNCD 1452 *Taj Mahal; Darrell Leonard (t, flh); Joe Sublett (s); Mick Weaver (p); Larry Fulcher (b); Tony Braunagel (d).* 99/00.

**(*) Hanapepe Dream
Tradition & Moderne T&M 017 *Taj Mahal; Rudy Costa (cl, ss, as, ts, fl, kalimba, v); Fred Lunt (sg); Carlos Andrade (g, v); Wayne Jacintho, Pat Cockett, Michael Barretto (u, v); Pancho Graham (b, v); Kester Smith (d); Carey Williams (v).* 2–8/00.

*** Live Catch
Tradition & Moderne T&M 026 *Taj Mahal; Bill Rich (b); Kester Smith (d).* 12/02.

(***) Mkutano
Tradition & Moderne T&M 031 *Taj Mahal; Haj Juma Wadi (nai); Rajab Sulieman (ac, qanun, v); Taimur Rukun (ac, v); Said Mwinyi (ac); Kesi Juma (vn, v); Juma Shadhili, Juma Abdallah (vn); Said Nassor (udi); Mahmoud Juma (b, v); Bill Rich (b); Amour Haj (sunduku); Kester Smith (d); Foum Faki, Saleh Yussuf (dumbak, bgo); Bikidude, Rukia Ramadhani, Makame Faki, Nihifadhi Abdallah, Subira Ali, Mtumwa Mbaruk, Fatma Juma, Fatma Abdisalami, Ali Hassan (v).* 9/03.

If any blues artist was prepared for 'world music' it was Taj Mahal. Long before the phenomenon had any significance in the Western music industry, his background and interests had steered him towards cross-cultural collaborations. With pacts already signed with the Caribbean, the Asian subcontinent and Hawaii, it was practically foreseeable that he would find his next allies among African musicians, as he did in *Kulanjan* with the Malian kora player Toumani Diabate and in *Mkutano* with the Culture Music Club of Zanzibar. The albums are mixtures of pieces from Taj's songbook like 'Queen Bee' (*Kulanjan*) or 'Catfish Blues' (both), lent fresh colour by the African musicians, and material from the other tradition, in which Taj's presence is more subtly felt, if at all. Cross-cultural events like these tend to prompt journalists to expound on shared traditions and common roots, wild talk with no anchorage in ethnomusicologically safe water. If there's an occasional performance that seems to straddle the two traditions, like 'Mississippi–Mali Blues' (*Kulanjan*), it does so because it draws on principles of music-making, such as modal improvisation, that are common to both, and indeed to many other vernacular idioms. That isn't to say, of course, that these convergences are valueless, or that border-jumping and jamming doesn't often produce luscious and surprising music. Our bracketing of the ratings merely acknowledges that, so far as the blues is concerned, Taj is playing an away game.

The intervening albums, all recorded live, find him back on home ground, reworking his back catalogue in a variety of settings. And we do mean reworking. *Shoutin' In Key* has charts as old as 'Leaving Trunk', 'Corrina' and 'Mail Box Blues' (i.e. 'Going Up To The Country And Paint My Mailbox Blue'), while *Live Catch* reopens 'Mailbox' and revisits 'Corinna' [sic] as well as dusting off 'Creole Belle', 'Stagger Lee' and 'Black Jack Davey', all of which are also on *Hanapepe Dream*. This is not miserliness on Taj's part, though one can't help noticing that he doesn't write, or recompose, that kind of material so often these days. While his vocal arrangements don't alter much from version to version, the settings are very different: *Shoutin' In Key* is with the Phantom Blues Band, *Live Catch* with just his rhythm section and *Hanapepe Dream* with the Hula Blues Band, in other words the cast of *Sacred Island*. *Shoutin' In Key* has the most musical merriment, but each of the albums gives a vivid impression of the fun dispensed at a Taj Mahal gig, as always the best place to find him. TR

Tallahassee Tight
VOCAL, GUITAR

Louis Washington, as he was called on his sacred recordings, seems likely, from references in his blues, to have been from northwestern Florida.

** Spark Plug Smith & Tallahassee Tight (1933–1934)
Document DOCD-5387 *Tallahassee Tight*. 1/34.

'We can not [sic] tell if Washington was a street singer with a repertoire to suit all needs, a bluesman who happened to know a few spirituals, a gospel performer who had formerly been a blues singer and saw an opportunity to make extra money recording blues in the studio, or simply someone who led a double life.' Thus David Evans in his notes, carefully listing all the options. It may take a tolerant listener to care very much, since Washington's 14 issued recordings, four sacred numbers and ten blues, stretch a modest talent thin. His voice, a rich and resonant baritone, is attractive and his lyrics harbour some quirky phrases – 'Worked till I got a tail like a oxen and got feet like a buffalo,' he sings in 'Ramblin' Mind Blues' – but his range of melodies is narrow and his guitar fingering fallible. (Evans heard a second guitar on 'most, if not all, of his recordings', but no one else appears to have done so.) 'Black Gal' is adapted from 'Red Cross Store Blues' and 'Tallahassee Women', his best piece, from 'Deep Elm Blues'. The sound quality is consistently gritty. The rest of the CD is by Spark Plug Smith. TR

Tampa Red (1903–81)
VOCAL, GUITAR, PIANO, KAZOO

Other dates of birth, ranging from 1900 to 1908, are also given. Hudson Woodbridge was orphaned at a young age, and brought up as Hudson Whittaker by his maternal grandmother. He learned guitar as a child, and played in Florida jukes before moving to Chicago around 1925. There he married Frances ('Mrs Tampa' as she was known to other musicians), who managed his career. He found steady work in local clubs, ran a boarding house-cum-rehearsal room for other Bluebird artists in the late '30s, and recorded almost constantly for 25 years, except when the Depression and the Petrillo ban enforced interruptions. His wife's death sent Tampa into alcoholism, and a nervous collapse so severe that he was institutionalized for a time; he recorded again in 1960, but spent the rest of his life on welfare, ending his days in a home after his companion, Effie Tolbert, died in 1974.

**(*) Tampa Red – Vol. 1 (1928–1929)
Document DOCD-5073 *Tampa Red; Junie Cobb (ss, ts, v); Georgia Tom [Dorsey] (p, v); Alex Hill (p); Martell Pettiford (g); unknown (bb); Jimmie Bertrand (d, swanee wh); Herman Brown (wb, k); Carl Reid (jazzhorn, j); Foster & Harris, Madlyn Davis, Frankie Jaxon, Papa Too Sweet, Harry Jones (v). c. 5/28–1/29.*

**(*) Tampa Red – Vol. 2 (1929)
Document DOCD-5074 *Tampa Red; Georgia Tom [Dorsey] (p, v); Charles Avery, unknown (p); prob. Bill Johnson (b); Herman Brown (wb); Frankie Jaxon (scraper, v); Carl Reid (jazzhorn, j); Gospel Camp Meeting Singers, Lil Johnson (v). 1/29–6/29.*

**(*) Tampa Red – Vol. 3 (1929–1930)
Document DOCD-5075 *Tampa Red; Georgia Tom [Dorsey] (p, v); prob. Cow Cow Davenport, Bill O'Bryant (p); Bill Johnson, unknown (b); Jasper Taylor (wb); Frankie Jaxon (scraper, v); unknown (k, j); Jenny Pope (v). 7/29–c. 6/30.*

**(*) Tampa Red – Vol. 4 (1930–1931)
Document DOCD-5076 *Tampa Red; Georgia Tom [Dorsey] (p, v); unknown (p); Carl Reid (jazzhorn, j); Sweet Papa Tadpole, Frankie Jaxon (v). 7/30–10/31.*

**(*) Tampa Red – Vol. 5 (1931–1934)
Document DOCD-5077 *Tampa Red; Georgia Tom [Dorsey] (p, v); Black Bob (p). 10/31–3/34.*

**(*) Tampa Red – Vol. 6 (1934–1935)
Document DOCD-5206 *Tampa Red; Henry '45' Scott (p, v); poss. Black Bob (p, sp); Carl Martin (g, v); prob. Mississippi Sarah, unknown (j); unknown (sp). 4/34–5/35.*

**(*) Tampa Red – Vol. 7 (1935–1936)
Document DOCD-5207 *Tampa Red; Arnett Nelson (cl); Myrtle Jenkins, Black Bob (p); Willie B. James, unknown (g); poss. Bill Gaither, unknowns (b). 7/35–8/36.*

** Tampa Red – Vol. 8 (1936–1937)
Document DOCD-5208 *Tampa Red; unknown (t); Arnett Nelson, unknown (cl); unknown (ts); Black Bob, prob. Blind John Davis (p); Willie B. James (g); unknowns (b); unknown (d). 8/36–10/37.*

**(*) Tampa Red – Vol. 9 (1937–1938)
Document DOCD-5209 *Tampa Red; unknowns (t); unknowns (ts); Blind John Davis, prob. Black Bob (p); Willie B. James (g); unknowns (b). 10/37–6/38.*

**(*) Tampa Red – Vol. 10 (1938–1939)
Document DOCD-5210 *Tampa Red; Charlie Idsen (t); Bill Owsley (ts); prob. Black Bob, Blind John Davis, unknown (p); Bill Settles, Ransom Knowling, unknowns (b). 6/38–11/39.*

**(*) Tampa Red – Vol. 11 (1939–1940)
Document DOCD-5211 *Tampa Red; Blind John Davis, unknown (p); unknowns (b). 11/39–11/40.*

*** **Tampa Red – Vol. 12 (1941–1945)**
Document DOCD-5212 *Tampa Red; Big Maceo (p, v); Blind John Davis (p); Ransom Knowling (b); Clifford 'Snags' Jones, Tyrell Dixon (d). 6/41–7/45.*

(*) Tampa Red – Vol. 13 (1945–1947)
Document DOCD-5213 *Tampa Red; Walter Williams (t); Oett 'Sax' Mallard (cl, as); John Gardner (as); Bill Casimir (ts); Big Maceo (p, v); Blind John Davis, Bob Call (p); Alfred Elkins, Big Crawford, Ransom Knowling (b); Tyrell Dixon, Chick Sanders, Jump Jackson, Judge Riley (d). 7/45–10/47.*

(*) Tampa Red – Vol. 14 (1949–1951)
Document DOCD-5214 *Tampa Red; Eddie 'Sugarman' Penigar (ts); [Little] Johnny Jones (h, p, v); Pete Franklin (g, v); Ransom Knowling (b, v); Odie Payne (d). 1/49–3/51.*

(*) Tampa Red – Vol. 15 (1951–1953)
Document DOCD-5215 *Tampa Red; Bill Casimir (ts); Sonny Boy Williamson II, Walter Horton (h); [Little] Johnny Jones (p, v); unknown (p); L. C. McKinley (g, v); Willie Lacey (g); Ransom Knowling (b, v); Odie Payne, unknown (d). 7/51–12/53.*

Tampa Red was always in touch with trends in the blues; quite often, he set those trends, beginning with his and Georgia Tom's first recording together. 'It's Tight Like That', the archetypal hokum song, was a huge hit, spawning innumerable covers and imitations, not a few of them by Tom and Tampa. It speaks for itself that Tampa's complete works on 78 (excluding a few discs of which no copy has been found, and including some accompaniments to others) occupy 15 CDs. The usual caveats relating to prolific artists on Document apply: the sound quality, especially on the earlier volumes, is uneven; there's inevitable repetitiveness; not every track is a classic; and these recordings were never intended to be heard at CD length.

Nevertheless, Document provide a valuable resource to historians, and there are superior, and sometimes very important, performances sprinkled all through these discs. Tampa's slide technique, with its rich, liquid tone and very accurate fretting, was widely admired, and influential on the likes of Robert Nighthawk, Elmore James and Earl Hooker; the agility and inventiveness of his playing are often far more than the songs, especially the more formulaic hokum pieces, deserve. Tampa was also a prolific composer, and although many of his songs are ephemeral, and were never intended to be anything else, not a few became canonical, including 'Sweet Black (or Little) Angel', 'Stranger Blues', 'It Hurts Me Too', 'Don't You Lie To Me' and 'Love (Her) With A Feeling'.

Document's *Vol. 1* includes four sides by Madlyn Davis where Tampa's playing is at its most agile, and three State Street Stompers tracks with Junie Cobb's imposing tenor sax. Scattered through the first four volumes are all the recordings by 'Tampa Red's Hokum Jug Band', a studio group fronted by Frankie Jaxon, as fizzy as champagne spiked with sherbet and as camp as a row of pink tents. These send-ups of current hits are among the few humorous blues records that stay that way on repeated playing; it's a pity that their lunatic and often remarkably filthy wit isn't available on a single disc. Downsides of these early volumes include accompaniments to dullards like Papa Too Sweet, Jenny Pope and Sweet Papa Tadpole, and the hokum becomes predictable; but against these drawbacks must be set some elegant guitar instrumentals and, as the hokum gives way to 12-bar blues, numerous thoughtful and well-crafted lyrics.

Vol. 5 sees the end of Tampa's collaboration with Georgia Tom, who made his final break with secular music in 1932; it also finds Tampa moving from Vocalion to Bluebird, beginning a rewarding studio partnership with Black Bob, and introducing his kazoo. Tampa's fondness for this instrument has been much regretted by critics, and it's undeniably hard going when heard in quantity; but it's only fair to note that he plays it with brio, and as much expressiveness as can be got out of amplified humming. Many of his kazoo solos would be perfectly acceptable hot dance music if they were played on brass or reeds; unfortunately, they're played on kazoo.

Another aspect of Tampa's music that's often censured is his penchant for 32-bar pop songs, often sentimental in character. It used to be thought that these, and especially the 1936–38 Chicago Five recordings, were aimed at white purchasers, the unspoken assumption being that black audiences in the '30s (and white ones in the '60s!) had better taste. It seems doubtful, though, that either Tampa or those who bought his 78s made fine distinctions between blues, hokum and pop, or ranked them in a musical hierarchy. None of this means that contemporary listeners will or should prefer 'Worthy Of You' to 'Stockyard Fire', or 'You Stole My Heart' to 'Nutty And Buggy Blues', which make gratingly adjacent pairings on *Vol. 6* and *Vol. 7* respectively. It would take a heart of stone and an ear of tin to reject the panache of 'When I Take My Vacation In Harlem', or the rumba rhythms on 'When You Were A Girl Of Seven' (both on *Vol. 7*), and even 'I Do' (*Vol. 9*), Tampa's most mediocre pop composition, provokes a decent trumpet solo; but judged on their merits rather than condemned for not being blues, most of these tunes, which comprise most tracks from the end of *Vol. 7* to the start of *Vol. 10*, are unappealing.

'Nutty And Buggy Blues' is one of the first tracks to feature Tampa playing piano, with Willie B. James on guitar. Tampa was an excellent pianist, heavily indebted to Leroy Carr, and Bluebird seem to have had a policy of cutting a couple of these duets at each session; they afford some relief from the Chicago Five sides. Other such pleasures include the twin-guitar workouts 'Travel On' and 'Seminole Blues' (*Vol. 9*). On *Vol. 10* and *Vol. 11*, Tampa starts to play electric guitar, and establishes an effective partnership with Blind John Davis, but the songs often seem to be stamped out with a cookie cutter. On *Vol. 11*, jaunty original versions of 'Anna Lou' and 'It Hurts Me Too' make strange listening for those habituated to Elmore James's impassioned revivals; this disc concludes with a solo session that includes some fine non-slide playing.

All but four tracks of *Vol. 12* and about half of *Vol. 13* celebrate the meeting of Tampa Red and Big Maceo, one of the blues' truly great piano–guitar partnerships. The thundering majesty of Maceo's piano and the intuitive sensitivity of his responses to Tampa's singing and playing are a wonder to hear – and Tampa's kazoo is not. If he'd swatted the amplified wasp, *Vol. 12* would be a four-star disc; instead, listeners must try to tune it out. The duo was cruelly broken up by Maceo's stroke, and on the balance of *Vol. 13* Tampa performs mostly lightweight jump blues with brass and reeds in support. These tracks are variably successful: Sax Mallard's alto and clarinet are aimless on four titles where he's the only wind player, but he's more effective when joined by Bill Casimir's tenor and Bob Call's hefty piano.

Vol. 14 begins with Tampa's last recordings on piano, accompanying Pete Franklin on three splendid revivals of the Leroy Carr–Scrapper Blackwell sound; Franklin sings like Carr, plays like Blackwell, and delivers three well-crafted lyrics of his own. On the balance of this disc, and half of *Vol. 15*, Tampa works with Big Maceo's pupil Little Johnny Jones, soon to join Elmore James along with Ransom Knowling and Odie Payne. These are odd recordings: several are remakes of Tampa's hits (they even include 'It's Good [i.e. Tight] Like That'), and the intention is clearly to bring his music up to date, but there are too many ingredients in the recipe. Some powerful electric guitar and Jones's lively piano are opposed by the unstoppable kazoo and frequent ensemble vocals. The latter are probably an attempt to emulate the Big Three Trio, but their laddish coarseness becomes wearing. Tampa's career on 78 sputters to a close with further attempts to update his sound: L. C. McKinley and Willie Lacey play some progressive single-string guitar, but neither they nor the harmonica players sound comfortable with the material.

(***) Bottleneck Guitar 1928–1937
Yazoo 1039 *As for relevant CDs above, except add Ma Rainey (v).* c. 5/28–10/37.

*** The Story Of The Guitar Wizard
[EPM Blues Collection 15789] *As for relevant CDs above.* 10/28–11/40.

(***) The Guitar Wizard
Columbia/Legacy CK 53235 *As above.* 12/28–5/34.

Yazoo's 14-tracker is the shortest of the selective CDs; in its original LP format, it usefully challenged contemporary opinions of Tampa Red. It's still a good and varied selection, mostly from his earlier recordings. Two titles with lead vocals by Georgia Tom are polished but sedate (and one comes from a crackly 78); playing time is short by present-day standards. *The Story Of The Guitar Wizard* is a well thought-out selection with acceptable sound; it includes two Chicago Five sides, which is about right, and more important, 'Black Hearted Blues', with magnificent piano by the mysterious Bill O'Bryant. Columbia offer thorough annotation and careful transfers, which, however, are not always from masters: Yazoo's crackly copy of 'If You Want Me To Love You' has been used again, and even some titles from 1934 are distractingly swishy. Coverage necessarily stops in that year, when Tampa left Vocalion, but it would have been possible to include less hokum, and beginning a 17-track CD with both Papa Too Sweet sides is not consumer-friendly.

***(*) The Essential
Classic Blues CBL 200006 2CD *As for relevant CDs above, except add Lucille Bogan (v).* 1/29–11/50.

*** Slide Guitar Wizard, Chicago 1931–1946
Frémeaux FA 257 2CD *As for relevant CDs above.* 10/31–9/46.

Both these double sets have 36 tracks, and both steer a wide path round the Chicago Five. Classic Blues cover most of Tampa's career on 78 (the 1950 end date is imposed by copyright law); his work as an accompanist is under-represented, although Lucille Bogan's 'Coffee Grindin' Blues' is a fine example. The sound restoration is mostly first-class, and non-chronological programming makes for varied and entertaining listening. As usual with Classic Blues, the drawback is brief, superficial commentary without discographical details; the casual purchasers at whom the set is aimed will enjoy it, but will not learn that Tampa plays piano on some tracks, get much idea of how his music developed or find out who any (!) of his pianists were after Georgia Tom.

Slide Guitar Wizard was released in 1997, so copyright is again the stop-light. At the other end of the set, a solitary track with Georgia Tom is one of only three from Vocalion: in effect, this is a 'best of' Tampa's Bluebird recordings as a blues guitarist (no pop, no piano). One or two originals are scuffed, but there are no serious problems with sound quality; the chronological programming highlights the formulaic aspects of some of Tampa's Bluebird output, however. The notes in French are extensive and detailed, but the English version of them is ineptly translated and clumsily abridged.

*** Tampa Red & Big Maceo
EPM Blues Collection 15907 *As for relevant CDs above.* 6/41–2/46.

This CD concentrates on the partnership with Big Maceo, and is discussed in his entry. This is perhaps the place to repeat that Maceo's piano playing is the most compelling aspect of their collaboration, and Tampa's kazoo decidedly the least.

***(*) Keep Jumping 1944–52 [sic]
Wolf CD-WBJ 001 *As for relevant CDs above.* 12/44–12/53.

Keep Jumping surveys Tampa's last recordings for black audiences, when he was finding ways to engage with contemporary changes in Chicago blues. The tracks are carefully programmed for variety, and the selection usefully avoids most of the rugger-club singalongs. The notes are confined to discography, but *Keep Jumping* makes a useful appendix to *The Essential*.

** Don't Tampa With The Blues
Original Blues Classics OBCCD 516 *Tampa Red.* 60.
** Don't Jive Me
Original Blues Classics OBCCD 549 *Tampa Red.* 60.

In 1960 Tampa Red was tired and rusty; even his kazoo had lost its ooh, and on these sessions he confines himself to reprising greatest hits (mostly his own, but also the obvious songs by Leroy Carr, Jim Jackson and Johnnie Temple). Tampa's guitar skills had declined to the point where he no longer used a slide, and he takes every piece at a cautious tempo; even so, his chording is often inaccurate, and a weakness in his fingers lets the strings buzz annoyingly on *Don't Tampa With The Blues*. (Was that the best title Bluesville could think of?) His singing has some wistful charm, but these discs are a sad contrast to the vibrant personality he once projected. *Don't Jive Me* features somewhat more secure playing, but neither CD is recommendable. CS

Finis Tasby (born 1940)
VOCAL

Finis (pronounced Fynis) Tasby grew up in the Dallas–Fort Worth area, hanging out with bluesmen like Mercy Baby, Frankie Lee Sims and Zuzu Bollin. Having learned to play drums and bass, he formed a band in the '60s which was a launch-pad for the singers Z. Z. Hill and Joe Simon and backed touring stars like Lowell Fulson and Jimmy McCracklin. After the band broke up Tasby served for a time as Freddie King's driver, then in 1973 moved to LA, where he worked as an auto mechanic and took occasional gigs playing bass and singing.

** People Don't Care
Shanachie 9007 *Tasby; Darrell Lenard (t); Ken Tussing (tb);*

Robert Martin (s, o, p, v); Joe Sublett (s); Jay 'Hurricane Jake' Fitzgerald (h); Robert Lieberman, Elvin Bishop, Mick Taylor, Vernon Reid (g); Taras Prodaniuk, Mark Goldberg, Bob Babbitt (b); Charles E. Collins (d, v, prod); Brian Kilgore (perc); Cynthia Manley, Jessica Williams, Patricia Hodges, George Merrill, Lowell Fulson, Ricky Collins (v). 95.

*** Jump, Children!
Evidence ECD 26097 *Tasby; David 'Woody' Woodford (ts, bs); Lester Butler, Randy Chortkoff (h); Rob Rio (p); Rick Holmstrom, Kid Ramos, Coco Montoya (g); Larry Taylor (b); Richard Innes (d); Cynthia Manley, Jessica Williams (v). 7/97–5/98.*

*** What My Blues Are All About
Electro-Fi 3390 *Tasby; David Rotundo (h); Mel Brown (o, p, g); Julian Fauth (p); Enrico Crivellaro (g); Alec Fraser, Shane Scott (b); Jim Boudreau (d). 8/04.*

Tasby is a superior singer with an obvious affiliation to the style of Lowell Fulson. His attractive debut album, recorded in 1976 for Big Town (and issued almost a decade later in the UK as *Blues Mechanic* [Ace, 1984]), has yet to be transferred to CD, so the first item in his current catalogue is a set which, he said afterwards, didn't represent him accurately. The title song, one of four written by Tasby and an old collaborator, Deacon Jones, opens the album with verve, but even this early there are signs of an aesthetic at work that's likely to clash with the singer's natural idiom, and when the clichéd vocal-group refrains and competent but characterless ensemble playing are augmented with inappropriate producer-generated material like 'Gonna Miss Your Love', the best result you can hope for is that Tasby should emerge with some dignity. He does, but it's not an experience you would want him, or yourself, to go through again.

Jump, Children!, by contrast, is a downright blues set. The choice of songs acknowledges several figures in Tasby's background, 'It's Your Fault, Baby' coming from Fulson, 'Georgia Slop' and 'I Just Got To Know' from Jimmy McCracklin, and 'Mercy's Blues' from Mercy Baby. The lead guitar work is shared chiefly between Holmstrom and Ramos, who can both play this sort of material in their sleep but never give the impression that they're doing so. The backing singers are still largely unnecessary but there are fewer of them and they're less obtrusive. Tasby sounds thoroughly at home with these songs and in this company, and the album ought to please any listener who's content to take him and them on their own terms. After that Tasby contributed to albums by guitarists Kirk Fletcher and Enrico Crivellaro, made *Blues: A Tribute To John Lee Hooker* (KonKord KON-6617), which had only limited circulation, and was primary vocalist on a CD by The Mannish Boys. His own next album was even more solidly in the blues groove than *Jump, Children!*, with no backing singers at all, thoroughly appropriate playing by Crivellaro, Rotundo and the excellent Fauth and a sheaf of good original compositions, conventional in form but pithily worded and delivered in the dry, unsentimental manner of Percy Mayfield. TR

Baby Tate (1916–72)
VOCAL, GUITAR

Charles Henry Tate was born in Georgia, but moved as a child to Greenville, South Carolina, where he knew Blind Boy Fuller. After serving in the Army in World War II, he moved to Spartanburg, and was active in that city's blues scene when not pursuing his trade as a bricklayer. Tate recorded in the '60s through his association with Pink Anderson, and again in 1970, although few titles from the later sessions have been issued, and none on CD.

*** The Blues Of Baby Tate – See What You Done Done
Original Blues Classics OBCCD 567 *Tate. 8/61.*

Blind Boy Fuller's influence on Baby Tate was very strong, but not all-pervading: a sleek and slippery version of 'Catfish Blues' probably comes from Robert Petway's recording, and 'My Baby Don't Treat Me Kind' acknowledges Lightnin' Hopkins. Tate wasn't an originator, and he'd learned most of his songs two or three decades before he recorded them, but his versions are lively, meaningful and personalized; even at his most Fullerish he wasn't a mindless imitator. It's easy to identify the bricks that Baby Tate used to build his music, but the mortar which binds them together is his considerable talent as singer and picker alike. Seven of these songs are included in the VAC *The Bluesville Years Vol. 6: Blues Sweet Carolina Blues* (Prestige PRCD 9914). CS

Eddie Taylor (1923–85)
VOCAL, GUITAR

Born in Benoit, near Greenville, Mississippi, Taylor grew up listening to local blues guitarists and began playing himself at 13. In 1943 he moved to Memphis, where he had a job as a truck driver and played with Joe Hill Louis, among others. Moving on to Chicago in 1949, he renewed his acquaintance with Jimmy Reed, a childhood friend, and played with him in person and on records for years.

The handful of singles Taylor cut for Vee-Jay and other labels between 1955 and 1964, such as 'Bad Boy', 'Ride 'Em On Down' and his version of Johnny Jones's 'Big Town Playboy', are among the best of their time and place – succinct, lively and almost always memorable. Absurdly, though odd tracks are on VACs, the full set of 15 songs cannot be found on any current US or European CD, and must be procured from Japan as *Big Town Playboy* (P-Vine PCD-5259).

**(*) Masters Of Modern Blues
Testament TCD 5001 *Taylor; Big Walter Horton (h); Otis Spann (p); Floyd Jones (b); Fred Below (d). 6/66.*

This session was split with Floyd Jones, the band accompanying both singers. Taylor made lighter work than Jones did of his eight tracks (one an alternative take), sounding, for him, quite involved, but his guitar and Spann's piano are not sufficiently separated in the mix, and there are occasional tuning problems.

*** I Feel So Bad: The Blues Of Eddie Taylor
Hightone HCD 8037 *Taylor; David Ii (s, perc); George Smith (h); Jimmy Sones; Phillip Walker (g); Charles Jones (b); Johnny Tucker (d); Little H. Williams (perc). 6/72.*

Much of the programme comes from downhome: 'Stroll Out West', played solo, is a version of 'Catfish Blues' that sounds terribly like Robert Petway's, 'Bullcow Blues', also a solo, is a throwback to Charley Patton, and 'Jackson Town' is from Robert Nighthawk, whose stolid delivery and thoughtful slide playing Taylor is naturally qualified to imitate. He also waves his hat to Elmore James ('Twelve Year Old Boy') and

Jimmy Reed ('Going Upside Your Head'), but despite these references this is Taylor's most individual as well as his most varied and satisfying album.

(*) Ready For Eddie Plus
Castle CMRCD 629//Sanctuary CAS 36152 *Taylor; Bob Hall (p); Roger Hill (g); Graham Gallery, Bob Brunning (b); Peter York (d). 2–4/74.*

**** Long Way From Home**
Blind Pig BPCD 5025 *Taylor; Louis Myers (h, g, v); Dave Myers (b); Odie Payne Jr (d, v). 12/77.*

(*) My Heart Is Bleeding
Evidence ECD 26054 *Taylor; Carey Bell (h); Sunnyland Slim (p); Hubert Sumlin (g, v); Steve Beal (g); George Kitta, Robert Stroger (b); Odie Payne (d). 1–5/80.*

***** Bad Boy**
Wolf 120.711 *Taylor; Johnny B. Moore (g); Willie Kent (b); Larry Taylor, Tim Taylor (d); Vera Taylor (v). 7/83, 8/84.*

The 'Plus' of the Castle CD's title means that this is the 1975 Big Bear album *Ready For Eddie* with two additional tracks from the same sessions, which were held in London, since Taylor was in Britain with the American Blues Legends '74 tour. At the time this was a revealing album, since the recordings by which Taylor was known to enthusiasts hadn't fully shown what a dextrous and driving lead guitarist he could be. The programme is divided into his own songs and mostly unsurprising choices from other people's like Albert King's 'Cross Cut Saw', Bo Diddley's 'You Don't Love Me' and Jimmy Rogers's 'Sloppy Drunk'. The English musicians groove energetically behind him. A touch self-effacing, but a thoroughly professional job.

Long Way From Home was recorded in concert (in Japan) but not particularly well, so at times it feels as if one's listening backstage. Taylor and Louis Myers start some brisk two-guitar action on 'Hoy Hoy' but elsewhere the tempos tend to be sluggish and there are several moments when the band drifts apart. The ensemble sound on *My Heart Is Bleeding*, thanks to Sunnyland Slim and Carey Bell, is full and busy, though Bell overdoes his imitation of a police siren on 'Blow Wind Blow' and 'Wreck On 83 Highway'. Taylor plays Nighthawkish slide on the title track and the instrumental 'Lawndale Blues', but proves he has absorbed more recent ideas by laying 'Soul Brother' over the riff from Lowell Fulson's 'Tramp'. To the nine Chicago-recorded tracks of the original L+R album have been added five from concerts in Germany, two with vocals by Sumlin, all of them ordinary.

Bad Boy somewhat resembles the Hightone album of a dozen years earlier by including several old blues played on acoustic guitar, like 'Long Home Blues', 'I Do Know Right From Wrong' (related to 'Drop Down Mama') and 'I Got Long To Stay', but these are more than counterweighted by the quartet tracks, on which he swaps rhythm and lead parts with Johnny B. Moore while working efficiently through standards both personal ('Bad Boy') and general. His wife Vera brings a light, youthful style to her four vocal numbers. TR

Edward Taylor (born 1972)
VOCAL, GUITAR

Taylor is the sixth of Eddie and Vera Taylor's eight children.

***** Lookin' For Trouble**
Wolf 120.890 *Taylor; Eddie Shaw (ts); Martin Lane (h); Ken Barker (p); Johnny B. Moore (g); Willie Kent (b); Larry Taylor (d, v); Tim Taylor (d); Vera Taylor (v). 11/97.*

***(*) Worried About My Baby**
Wolf 120.811 *As above, except add Rockin' Johnny Burgin (g), Sho Kamiya (b); omit Shaw, Lane, Vera Taylor. 5/00.*

Lookin' For Trouble proclaims itself 'a tribute to Eddie Taylor', and half the songs come from the senior man or his longtime associate Jimmy Reed. The younger Taylor's singing and playing owe a lot to his father, which is no bad thing. His voice is too light to rescue 'Dust My Broom' from charges of predictability and kowtowing to fashion, but otherwise this stylish debut disc achieves retrospection without solemnity, and respect for the family heritage without sentimentality. Vera Taylor's guest appearance on 'Ain't Gonna Cry' confirms that she was a gifted, undervalued singer.

Edward Taylor claims composer credits on *Lookin' For Trouble*'s last two tracks. In the case of 'Tell Me Mama', that's pure cheek, but the unpretentious, tradition-grounded rhythms and lyrics of 'Greyhound Blues' suggest a promise largely fulfilled by the follow-up volume. Although credited to Eddie Taylor Jr, *Worried About My Baby* features only one of his father's compositions, and is the work of a musician who developed considerably between sessions, as both songwriter and guitarist. The record slumps midway, with Tim Taylor unaccountably hamfisted on 'Stop Breakin' Down', and Edward Jr not measuring up to Muddy Waters on 'Clouds In My Heart'; but his playful duelling with Johnny B. Moore on 'Groovin' With Eddie' gets things back on course, and Larry Taylor's version of Syl Johnson's 'Sock It To Me' provides grainy contrast to his brother's smoother vocals. CS

Gene Taylor (born 1952)
PIANO, ORGAN, VOCAL

Eugene Davis Taylor Jr grew up in Fort Worth, Texas. He has worked with James Harman, Ronnie Hawkins, Canned Heat and the Fabulous Thunderbirds, and played on albums by The JW-Jones Blues Band, Lee McBee, Gary Primich and Kid Ramos.

***** Gene Taylor**
Pacific Blues PBCD 2303 *Taylor; James Harman (h, v); Bill Bateman (d); Dave Carroll (perc). 03?*

Taylor unostentatiously parades his knowledge of piano blues history in tunes by Pine Top Smith, Meade Lux Lewis and, less predictably, Peetie Wheatstraw. His touch is very firm and his range of expression considerable, from the show-off boogies like 'Pete's Thing', a homage to Pete Johnson, to the slow 'Blues For Jerry West'. He's also an unobtrusively good singer. Most of the tracks are duets with Bateman, but Taylor's old friend and sometime employer James Harman drops in occasionally with his harmonica and sings on their jointly composed blues 'The Loser And The Wheel', one of the stronger performances on a well-thought-out album. TR

Hound Dog Taylor (1915–75)
VOCAL, GUITAR

Theodore Roosevelt Taylor grew up around Greenwood, Mississippi, and hung out with Elmore James and the King Biscuit circle of musicians. He moved to Chicago in 1942 and

went into music fulltime in 1957. Seeing him play at Florence's, one of his regular spots, Bruce Iglauer was motivated first to record him and then to create a label to issue the album on: thus was Alligator Records born. In the four years left to him Taylor, with his HouseRockers, became hugely popular on the campus and festival circuit.

***(*) **Hound Dog Taylor & The HouseRockers**
Alligator ALCD 4701 *Taylor; Brewer Phillips (g); Ted Harvey (d).* 5–6/71.

To listeners encountering Taylor's slide guitar playing for the first time, he seemed to be cast in a similar mould to J. B. Hutto, as a rough-cut but intense disciple of Elmore James. As well as an abrasive tone – his guitar was regularly compared to a chainsaw – his playing had a wild unpredictability that enlivened what might otherwise have been merely energetic performances. The trio format in which he preferred to work throws a lot of weight on his shoulders, which he bears easily in numbers like 'I Just Can't Make It', where the thickness of his sound virtually stands in for a horn section. Phillips, too, has a fat tone, while Harvey works exceedingly hard. The studio sound conveys a club-like atmosphere, loud, harsh, boxy and exciting. 'Give Me Back My Wig' and the instrumental boogies 'Walking The Ceiling' and '55th Street Boogie' really move.

(*) **Have Some Fun
Wolf 120.300 *As above.* 11/72.
(*) **Freddie's Blues
Wolf 120.600 *As above.* 11/72.
*** **Live In Boston**
Charly CDGR 218 *As above, except Phillips also sings; add unknown (g).* 11/72.

The Wolf CDs were taped in performance at Joe's Place in Cambridge, Massachusetts. The recordings have presence and a reasonable balance, but they include a good deal of stage chatter and are heavy on instrumentals, each album having six (out of 11 tracks). This may be a fair picture of the HouseRockers' act, but at times it's rather a boring one. *Live In Boston* picks six cuts each from the two Wolf CDs and adds three others: a brisk 'Give Me Back My Wig', 'Mama, Talk To Your Daughter' sung by Phillips and 'The Sky Is Crying', sabotaged by an unidentified guitarist who plays one note, off key, for over five minutes. That aside, the CD's low total of instrumentals makes it a good buy, if it can still be found.

*** **Natural Boogie**
Alligator ALCD 4704 *As for* Hound Dog Taylor & The HouseRockers. 9/73.
(*) **Genuine Houserocking Music
Alligator ALCD 4727 *As above, except Phillips also sings.* 6/71, 9/73.
*** **Beware Of The Dog!**
Alligator ALCD 4707 *As for* Hound Dog Taylor & The HouseRockers. 1–11/74.
*** **DeLuxe Edition**
Alligator ALCD 5605 *As above.* 71–11/74.
***(*) **Release The Hound**
Alligator ALCD 4896 *As above, except add Levi Warren (d).* 71–3/75.

Natural Boogie is a less incendiary performance than the first Alligator album but by no means lacking in bonhomie. Again Taylor makes explicit his fundamental debt to Elmore James, here in 'Hawaiian Boogie', 'Roll Your Moneymaker' and 'Talk To My Baby'. This was the last album to be issued in Taylor's lifetime, but before his death he had approved the programme for *Beware Of The Dog!*, a lively selection from taped gigs, mostly from three nights at the Smiling Dog Saloon in Cleveland, Ohio. The band's repertoire evidently hadn't changed greatly in the two years since the Joe's Place engagement, but the Cleveland recordings are somewhat superior, and the version of 'The Sun Is Shining' is Taylor's best. 'Comin' Around The Mountain' is a medley of that tune and 'Steel Guitar Rag', after the manner of Earl Hooker.

For *Genuine Houserocking Music* Alligator returned to Taylor's three studio sessions. While there's nothing wrong with the performances, it's usually clear why they failed to make the cut for ... *& The HouseRockers* or *Natural Boogie*. 'My Baby's Coming Home', 'The Sun Is Shining' and 'Crossroads' maintain the Elmore James quota. *DeLuxe Edition* is composed of four tracks from the first album, three each from *Natural*, *Genuine* and *Beware* and two previously unissued live numbers: a good introduction.

Twenty-nine years after Taylor's death, Alligator dug into their unissued tapes to produce *Release The Hound*. Apart from three tracks left over from the studio sessions, most of the numbers were recorded at gigs, mainly the Cleveland ones that were the primary source of *Beware Of The Dog!*, hence extended performances like 'Sadie' (7.08) and 'Things Don't Work Out Right' (10.40). A few pieces are a little out of the ordinary – 'The Dog Meets The Wolf' is an instrumental based on the riff from 'Howlin' For My Darling', while 'Walking The Ceiling', another instrumental, features Harvey in a two-minute drum solo – but on the whole this is Taylor as anyone who has the earlier records will know him, though that isn't to say that the album is superfluous or even secondary: actually its blend of raucous and relaxed is unexpectedly revealing and totally absorbing. TR

Koko Taylor (born 1935)
VOCAL

Growing up in Memphis, Tennessee, Cora Walton was drawn to the blues by hearing it on local radio stations. At the age of 18 she moved to Chicago, where she sang in clubs. Her recording career began ten years later and was encouraged by Willie Dixon, who got her on to Chess. In 1965 she had a hit with 'Wang Dang Doodle', a Dixon song previously recorded by Howlin' Wolf. Since the '70s she has been one of the most popular artists on the US and international blues circuits and has won several awards. She appears in David Lynch's 1990 film Wild At Heart.

(*) **The Chess Years
MCA/Chess CHD 9328/[(E) MCD 09328] *Taylor; unknown (t); Gene Barge (ts); prob. Donald Hankins (bs); unknowns (s); Walter 'Shakey' Horton (h); Lafayette Leake (o, p); Robert Nighthawk, Buddy Guy, Matt Murphy, Johnny 'Twist' Williams, Rufus Crume, poss. Johnny Shines (g); Willie Dixon (b, v); Jack Meyers, Dillard Crume, unknowns (b); Clifton James, Fred Below, Al Duncan, unknowns (d); unknowns (v grps).* 6/64–72.
(*) **Koko Taylor
MCA/Chess 088 112 519 *Similar to above.* 1/65–4/69.

Taylor's first single for Checker, 'I Got What It Takes'/'What

Kind Of Man Is This', exhibited a promisingly strong, if undisciplined, singer. A year and a half later, her pugnacious reading of Willie Dixon's 'Wang Dang Doodle' confirmed her as one of Chicago's most exciting new talents. Much of that promise was betrayed by her subsequent Checker sides, as Dixon led her through a series of peculiar compositions like 'Fire', 'Insane Asylum' and 'Egg Or The Hen', while the striking lineups on some of those sessions were often subverted by bizarre sound-balancing and effects. Taylor's star would only shine clearly when she got away from Dixon and the Chess studios. *The Chess Years* has 18 examples while *Koko Taylor* has 14, eight in common with the former.

** South Side Lady
Black & Blue BB 426//Evidence ECD 26007 *Taylor; unknown (h); Willie Mabon (p); Jimmy Rogers, Louis Myers (g); Dave Myers (b); Fred Below (d). 12/73.*

Taylor might have left Chess but she still relied on the repertoire she had developed there: she sings four Dixon songs, including two versions each (one studio-recorded, one live) of 'Twenty Nine Ways' and 'I Got What I Takes', and others she'd previously recorded like 'I'm A Little Mixed Up' and 'What Kind Of Man Is This'. But even such character as Dixon imparted to those numbers when he produced them as singles is lost in these undifferentiated and spiritless recordings.

*** I Got What It Takes
Alligator ALCD 4706 *Taylor; Abb Locke (ts); Bill Heid (kb); Mighty Joe Young, Sammy Lawhorn (g); Cornelius Boyson (b); Vince Chappelle (d). 1/75.*

*** The Earthshaker
Alligator ALCD 4711 *As above, except Pinetop Perkins (p), Johnny B. Moore (g) replace Heid, Young; add Mervyn 'Harmonica' Hinds (h). 1/78.*

*** From The Heart Of A Woman
Alligator ALCD 4724 *Taylor; A. C. Reed (ts); Billy Branch (h); Bill Heid (kb); Criss Johnson, Sammy Lawhorn, Emmett 'Maestro' Sanders (g); Cornelius Boyson (b); Vince Chappelle (d). 81.*

*** Queen Of The Blues
Alligator ALCD 4740 *Taylor; Abb Locke (ts); James Cotton (h); 'Professor' Eddie Lusk (kb); Criss Johnson, Lonnie Brooks, Albert Collins, Son Seals (g); Johnny B. Gayden (b); Ray 'Killer' Allison (d). 85.*

**(*) Live From Chicago – An Audience With The Queen
Alligator ALCD 4754 *Taylor; Michael 'Mr Dynamite' Robinson, Eddie King (g); Jerry Murphy (b); Clyde 'Youngblood' Tyler Jr (d). 1/87.*

I Got What It Takes is a simple menu of oldfashioned, home-cooked blues such as 'Blues Never Die' and the Elmore James-derived 'Happy Home', with a couple of side-orders of Southern soul like 'That's Why I'm Crying' and a surprise dessert of the country song 'Honky Tonk'. Production values are basic – you can hear an amp buzzing on 'That's Why I'm Crying' – but Young and Locke play sturdily throughout and Taylor sings with the gravelly ferocity that would soon be recognizable as her trademark.

The next two albums were made to a similar recipe of blues with a dash of soul. *The Earthshaker* has a good moody reading of Little Milton's 'Walking The Back Streets', but most of the other pieces are uppish in tempo, with nods to Dixon in 'Spoonful' and a remade 'Wang Dang Doodle'. *From The Heart Of A Woman* has a stronger flavour of Southern soul in the Ann Peebles or Irma Thomas manner. Criss Johnson is a forceful addition to the band and remains so on *Queen Of The Blues*, unfazed by the star guests whom Alligator brought in to spice the dish. (Brooks and Collins play on one track each, Cotton on two.) This album marked a shift away from soul repertoire towards swaggering blues like 'Queen Bee' and 'I Cried Like A Baby'. That and the album's title suggested that Taylor and her people were focusing on establishing her as the reigning blues diva.

If that was the strategy, it probably dictated the next move and its billing. *Live From Chicago – An Audience With The Queen* was undeniably something fresh in Taylor's output, as it captured some of the flavour of a club gig (at Fitzgerald's in the Chicago suburb of Berwyn), but the price of this novelty, for fans who had invested in her previous records, was a great deal of familiar material: she had recorded six of the ten tracks on Alligator albums alone. That might not have mattered if this set had been a satisfactory epitome of its predecessors, but, although it's a decent record, it can't take the place of four. Also, Taylor had begun to use a strained growl effect ('I'd Rather Go Blind' is littered with it) that one could foresee becoming an irritating mannerism.

*** Jump For Joy
Alligator ALCD 4784 *Taylor; Elmer Brown II (t); Edwin Williams, Orville McFarland (tb); Henri Ford, Gene Barge (ts); Willie Henderson (bs); Billy Branch (h); Jim Dortch (kb); Lonnie Brooks (g, v); Criss Johnson (g); Jerry Murphy (b); Ray 'Killer' Allison (d). 89–90.*

** Force Of Nature
Alligator ALCD 4817 *Taylor; Byron Bowie, Burgess Gardner (t); Edwin Williams (tb); Gene Barge (as); Henri Ford (ts); Willie Henderson (bs); Carey Bell (h); Jeremiah Africa (kb); Buddy Guy (g, v); Criss Johnson, Calvin 'Vino' Louden (g); Jerry Murphy (b); Ray 'Killer' Allison, Brady Williams (d). 93.*

** Royal Blue
Alligator ALCD 4873 *Taylor; Larry Bowen (t); Steve Berry (tb); Jerry DiMuzio (as); Mark Colby (ts); Willie Henderson (bs); Keb' Mo' (h, g, v); Matthew Skoller (h); Dolpha Fowler Jr (o); Johnnie Johnson, Ken Saydak (p); B. B. King (g, v); Criss Johnson, Kenny Wayne Shepherd (g); Kenny Hampton (b); Kriss T. Johnson Jr (d). 98–99.*

Jump For Joy was made soon after the death of Robert 'Pops' Taylor, Koko's husband and road manager and a popular figure on the blues circuit. No doubt it was coincidental that her first album of the '90s felt like something of a new start. She or her co-producers eliminated old blues and soul standbys, matching the fresh material with less conventional settings, including horn arrangements by Gene Barge and inventive interventions by Criss Johnson, back as sole guitarist except on 'It's A Dirty Job', a duet by Taylor and Lonnie Brooks. A similar team was behind *Force Of Nature*, but by now the strained growl referred to above had indeed become an overused device, and the album suffers from too much untempered intensity. '63 Year Old Mama' is a puzzling song: either Taylor is anticipating the unbridled lustfulness of five years ahead or all the reference books have her age wrong.

Carey Bell had joined her on that album for 'Mother Nature' and Buddy Guy for an overlong 'Born Under A Bad Sign'. Such guest appearances were becoming a routine feature of her records, and *Royal Blue* was stuffed with them: pianists

Johnnie Johnson and Ken Saydak, Kenny Wayne Shepherd on 'Bring Me Some Water' and B. B. King on 'Blues Hotel'. In a quieter collaboration, Taylor sings her own 'The Man Next Door' partnered only by Keb' Mo' on harmonica and National guitar. But it's increasingly evident, despite the efforts of her accompanists and visitors to buttress it, that the once robust edifice of Taylor's voice is in sad repair.

*** DeLuxe Edition
Alligator ALCD 5610 *As for relevant CDs above.* 75–98/99.

DeLuxe Edition draws from all eight of Taylor's previous Alligator albums, adding 'Man Size Job', a previously unissued and unremarkable track from the *Royal Blue* sessions. The hour-long programme naturally embraces crowd-pleasers like 'I'm A Woman' (Koko's answer to Bo Diddley's 'I'm A Man') and 'Wang Dang Doodle', the latter the studio version from *The Earthshaker* in improved sound but with half a minute of Abb Locke's closing tenor solo knocked off. 'Born Under A Bad Sign' from *Force Of Nature* is also docked, by about a minute and a half, to its advantage. TR

Melvin Taylor (born 1959)
VOCAL, GUITAR

A fleet-fingered guitarist with a technique that encompasses elements of blues, R&B and jazz, Melvin Taylor led his own group, the Transistors, at the age of 15. A stint with The Legendary Blues Band brought him to Europe in 1981 and he made his recording debut in the following year. This and another French-recorded album were issued in the US a decade later, forming the basis of a recording career notable for its eclecticism and the speed and clarity of his guitar playing

*** Blues On The Run
Evidence ECD 26041 *Taylor; Johnny 'Big Moose' Walker (p); Johnny Dollar (g); Willie Love (b); Casey Jones (d).* 4/82.

With this album, recorded in Chicago originally for the French label Isabel, Taylor sprang fully formed from his shell. His effortless extended improvisations confine a 43-minute programme to just six tracks, the longest a ten-minute exploration of Kenny Burrell's 'Chitlins Con Carne'. Other sources are Albert King, T-Bone Walker and Louis Jordan, with the artist's sole contribution a seven-minute instrumental, 'Escape'. Although his musicians are given little to do except keep up, they do so willingly, with an occasional solo from Walker. Taylor is a weak vocalist here but verses are merely bookends for his guitar solos, in which he displays unflagging invention. But for all their dexterity, these profligate solos lack character and dynamic contrast, numbing the ear to whatever fleeting emotion may be present.

*** Plays The Blues For You
Evidence ECD 26029 *Taylor; Lucky Peterson (kb); Titus Williams (b); Ray Allison (d).* 84.

Recorded in Paris, this nine-song set combines instrumental originals with covers that include 'T.V. Mama', 'I'll Play The Blues For You' and 'Cadillac Assembly Line'. Apart from 'Tribute To Wes' and 'Groovin' In Paris', instrumental speed is still the watchword and even these titles aren't completely free of it. Peterson is an appropriate accompanist, being a more than adequate soloist himself. Taylor's vocals remain unsatisfactory, although curiously apt as a contrast to the relentless musicianship. Lack of vocal power does affect his penchant for Albert King and the listener longs for some of the restraint that was the hallmark of King's own recordings. Otherwise, the menu is much as before.

**(*) Melvin Taylor & The Slack Band
Evidence ECD 26073 *Taylor; Will Smith (b); Steve Potts (d).* 95.

The inclusion of Hendrix's 'Voodoo Chile (Slight Return)' telegraphs this album's intention of re-exploring the possibilities of the guitar trio in a blues context. But as good as his technique may be, Taylor cannot hope to improve upon that particular original. That he then applies varying degrees of the same bludgeoning approach to songs by Larry Davis, Otis Rush, Albert King and T-Bone Walker negates the inherent differences in the material, reducing each song to a vehicle for his unstoppable guitar trips, with Smith and Potts clinging to his coat-tails. The fact that he can be endlessly inventive shouldn't be his entire *raison d'être*, when what he dispenses is so overtly lacking in pace and taste. Only the final 'Tequila' shows he's capable of the latter, but by then it's too late.

**(*) Dirty Pool
Evidence ECD 26088 *Taylor; Ethan Farmer (b); James Knowles (d).* 97.

Same trip, different passengers. And that regrettably is what Farmer and Knowles become. They have sufficient stamina to keep up with their leader but are restricted to the function of metronomes. Once again, each of the nine songs must contain at least one extended solo (and often two), meted out with little concern for tune or tempo. Each one extends like a string of DNA or a paragraph of prose with no punctuation. His singing has improved but not enough to be more than a brief interlude before the main guitar event begins. Wolf's 'I Ain't Superstitious' lacks stature and menace, while Albert King's 'Born Under A Bad Sign' and 'Floodin' In California', played consecutively, could have come off the same Cadillac assembly line he sang about before. Taylor may well believe that the blues needs to go to new places but this is like a mystery tour where the driver wins the prize.

**(*) Bang That Bell
Evidence ECD 26107 *Taylor; Sugar Blue (h); Norris Johnson (kb); Matt Tutot, Eric Gales (g); Dave Smith (b); Steve Potts (d).* 7–10/99.

Producer John Snyder manages to inject some variety of pace and tone into these ten selections but with few exceptions Taylor's dedication to profligacy remains true. 'My Life' and Larry Garner's 'Another Bad Day' find him switching his allegiance to George Benson's post-Wes Montgomery style but the latter is spoiled by the seven choruses of wah-wah guitar that conclude it. But at least it comes to an end. Eight songs do not, each fading out during yet another grandstanding solo. 'Don't Cloud Up On Me' and 'Even Trolls Love Rock & Roll' up the ante by having dual solos assaulting one another. Sugar Blue's equally virtuosic harmonica is heard on two songs, providing a welcome contrast to the effect-laden backing tracks. This is probably rock-blues of a high order but sensory overload baffles the judgement.

**(*) Rendezvous With The Blues
Evidence ECD 26123 *Taylor; Marshall Cyr, Scott Thompson (t); Jerry Mallet (ts); Sidney Janise (bs); Lucky Peterson (kb, o, g);*

Mato Nanji (g); Dave Smith (b); Steve Potts (d, cga); Brian Brignac (perc). 9/01.

Two thoughts present themselves: yet another set of ten cover songs suggests that Taylor's songwriting skill has atrophied, and after five albums of hyperfast finger-twitching, the elastic band of his improvisatory thrust is becoming slack. While the speed of his playing continues unabated, there are moments here when his flow is brought up short and he resorts to mere noisemaking. The song choices are eclectic, from Stephen Stills to Herbie Mann, from Prince to ZZ Top, with B. B. King, Jimmy Reed, Sonny Boy Williamson II and a tribute to John Lee Hooker stiffening the blues sinews. Moments of respite in 'Comin' Home Baby', 'Help Me' and 'Eclipse' come courtesy of the George Benson variations but even here there's a lack of originality. As a product rather than a blues album, this succeeds, but until Taylor becomes a true creator rather than a cover merchant, he will remain just a spectacle. NS

Montana Taylor (1903–60s?)
PIANO, VOCAL

Arthur Taylor was that rare thing, a blues artist born in Montana – in Butte, where his father owned the Silver City cabaret and gambling club. He grew up, however, in Indianapolis, where he began playing piano at the age of 20 and performed at rent parties and in clubs. He made a few records for Vocalion but was discouraged by their meagre reward and left town for Cleveland, Ohio, where he 'just knocked about doing nothing'. Introduced by Cow Cow Davenport to the historian Rudi Blesh, he recorded about a dozen sides for Circle in 1946, but afterwards disappeared.

***(*) Montana Taylor/"Freddie" Shayne (1929–1946)
Document DOCD-5053 Taylor; Almond Leonard (k, wb); Marcel Pettiford, Herman Brown (v, v eff); Bertha 'Chippie' Hill (v). 4/29–46.

Taylor's reputation among blues-lovers was decisively established with his 1929 sides 'Indiana Avenue Stomp' and 'Detroit Rocks'. The former is played at a bustling march tempo, the latter with a driving boogie-woogie pattern in the basses over which the right hand pours cascades of sparkling notes. These are among the most famous of blues piano solos and can be found on many VACs, unlike his other two 1929 sides, 'Whoop And Holler Stomp' and 'Hayride Stomp', which are interfered with by a couple of jokers chattering, scatting and, worst of all, singing. Some of the 1946 sides similarly obscure the piano playing with washboard and kazoo, and others are accompaniments to the singing of 'Chippie' Hill, but what remains is often exquisite. On 'Rotten Break Blues', 'I Can't Sleep' and 'Montana's Blues' Taylor reveals a poignantly doleful voice, and the accompaniment to 'I Can't Sleep', with its shifts into the minor key, is perfectly conceived. The piano solos include another journey down Indiana Avenue and a very slow blues, 'In The Bottom', to which Taylor adds whistling and humming choruses.

The CD is completed by six pieces from J. H. 'Freddie' Shayne, a contemporary of Taylor who spent his life in Chicago and took his nickname from his best-known number, 'Mr Freddie Blues'. Two vocal blues cut in 1936 are followed by four Circle recordings: two accompaniments to 'Chippie' Hill and two piano pieces, a rag and a slow boogie, both featuring passages of expert stickwork by Baby Dodds. TR

Otis Taylor (born 1948)
VOCAL, GUITAR, BANJO, MANDOLIN, HARMONICA

Taylor has been a musician since his teens; he claims to have signed for Blue Horizon in 1969, but no records were released, and he spent the 20 years from 1977 as an antiques appraiser. Taylor characterizes himself as a singer/songwriter working in the medium of blues.

**(*) When Negroes Walked The Earth
Shoelace OT 333 Taylor; Kenny Passarelli (kb, b); Lionel Young (vn); Eddie Turner (g). 99.

**(*) White African
NorthernBlues NBM 0002 As above, except add Cassie Taylor (v); omit Young. 00.

**(*) Respect The Dead
NorthernBlues NBM 0009 As above, except Passarelli also plays o, p. 01.

** Truth Is Not Fiction
Telarc CD-83587 As above, except Passarelli does not play o; add Ben Sollee (vc), Donna Concha, Nicholas Concha (perc, v). 03.

**(*) Double V
Telarc CD-83601 Taylor; Ron Miles (t); Ben Sollee, Shaun Diaz, Lara Turner, Marcelo Sanches (vc); Cassie Taylor (b, v). 04.

*** Below The Fold
Telarc CD-83627 As above, except add Brian Juan (o), Rayna Gellert (vn), Fushio Morioka (g), Greg Anton (d); omit Diaz, Turner, Sanches. 05.

As well as writing about emotions and relationships, Otis Taylor explores the past and present meanings and consequences of being black in America. His most successful songs offer imaginative responses to history's violence and oppression, sometimes inspired by the stories of family and friends. Taylor's music – described on *Below The Fold* as 'certified trance blues' – is melodically and harmonically restricted, with a heavy rhythmic pulse; it owes much to John Lee Hooker, although the influence of old-time banjo players is also palpable. On the first four CDs, Eddie Turner overlays a more fluid, Hendrix-influenced lead guitar and Passarelli augments the dark and doomy ambience. Unfortunately, colour and texture are frequently used to conceal a dearth of melodic ideas; similarly, rhetorical gestures – notably abrupt dynamic changes and semi-spoken delivery – camouflage songwriting that raises important issues of social justice but often gives a jejune and sketchy response.

There's little change to either the musical forces or the quality of the writing on Taylor's first Telarc CD. Far too often he simply plonks an idea in front of the listener and repeats it with slight variations until the song peters out. Often, these inflated songlets need a booklet note to clarify what they're about. They're also mostly very gloomy, which wouldn't matter if Taylor brought a mature artistic vision to his dysphoric worldview. Bald statements that slavery and segregation were cruel, death is certain and Native Americans have had it hard are all true, but they're not enough. The songs on *Double V* continue to be melancholy and underwritten, but Taylor makes more varied and interesting use of textures and tone colours, deploying from one to four cellists on seven tracks; 'Buy Myself Some Freedom' effectively pairs Miles's trumpet with Cassie Taylor's ethereal voice. On *Below The Fold* Taylor's skills as an arranger increasingly look like his most considerable talent. Fiddle and cello are used to achieve some intense and dramatic effects, and the harmonica, trumpet and side drum combination on 'Right Side Of Heaven' is a creative variant of the fife and drum sound. More generally, *Below The Fold* has more swing and drive than its immediate predecessors. These positives don't solve the problem of meagre lyrics, but much of the time they distract attention from it fairly successfully. CS

Vera Taylor (1943–99)
VOCAL

Vera Taylor moved from Mississippi to Chicago in 1952, and fell pregnant at 12. She met Eddie Taylor when she was 15, and they were together from 1961 to his death in 1985; of their large family, Edward, Tim and Larry also became musicians,. Vera sang with her husband's bands and recorded a few numbers, but retired from music when he died; she came back when Edward cut his first CD, but died soon after her first full recording session.

***(*) You Better Be Careful
Wolf 120.802 Taylor; Eddie Shaw (ts); Ken Barker (p); Eddie Taylor, Edward Taylor, Johnny B. Moore (g); Willie Kent (b); Tim Taylor, Larry Taylor (d). 7/83–8/99.

Vera Taylor was a skilful songwriter – or rather lyricist: more than once she fits her words to the 'Rollin' And Tumblin'' riff. As that choice implies, her music was the Chicago blues she'd grown up with, and it's a real pleasure to hear a woman just singing about her life and relationships without the clichéd raunchiness often demanded by contemporary fashion. So much of a pleasure, in fact, that it's important not to over-estimate Vera Taylor's only CD. Eddie Shaw's tenor does little more than clutter the texture, and unfortunately two tracks from 1983 with Eddie Sr on guitar define his son, who plays on the other tracks, as just a competent follower in father's footsteps. It's also obvious that, perhaps because of illness, Vera Taylor's voice became both weaker and harsher by the late '90s. It cannot be emphasized too strongly, therefore, that her introspective, often downbeat singing always carries conviction, and can be very moving; '14 Years Before My Time' is a truly remarkable song, simultaneously recounting the mistake that was her first sexual encounter, the good luck of marrying Eddie Taylor, and the pain of his death. CS

Walter Taylor
VOCAL, WASHBOARD, KAZOO

Taylor, from western Kentucky, was associated with the 12-string guitarist John Byrd, who was probably based in or around Huntington, West Virginia.

**** Rare Country Blues – Vol. 2 (1929–1943)
Document DOCD-5641 Taylor; unknown (md); C. J. Anderson (bj, v); unknown (bj); John Byrd, George Davis (g, v). 2/30–6/31.

Seven tracks on this CD are definitely by a trio of Taylor, Anderson and Byrd, while five others are duets by Byrd and a Washboard Walter who seems likely (in this writer's opinion; *B&GR* disagrees) to be Taylor. The trio sides are exuberant performances of the common-stock pieces 'Don't Let The Deal Go Down' (as 'Deal Rag') and 'You Rascal You' and several blues, some, like 'Thirty-Eight And Plus', with a hokum flavour. With their jaunty banjo and kazoo playing, harmony singing and, on 'Deal Rag', yodelling, these recordings have some kinship with the work of contemporary hillbilly acts like the Allen Brothers. Some of the same effect is conjured up by the duet sides 'Disconnected Mama' and 'Wasn't It Sad About Lemon', an obituary song to the recently deceased Blind Lemon Jefferson, both of which are sung in harmony, but the remaining Byrd–Taylor numbers are slow blues sung by the latter. On a further coupling, issued as by Taylor's Weatherbirds, Taylor sings 'Coal Camp Blues', a lugubrious commentary on unemployment in the mines.

Also included is Byrd's only record issued in his own name. 'Billy Goat Blues', allowing for some discontinuity in the telling, is a comic song about a goat; 'Old Timbrook Blues', on the other hand, is a narrative song about a horse – the same racehorse as the one commemorated in the bluegrass song 'Mollie And Tenbrooks'. A pair of sermons issued as by 'Rev. George Jones' has Byrd acting as preacher and incidental singing by 'Sister Jones', almost certainly the blues singer Mae Glover, who recorded with Byrd on the same day.

The CD is filled up with four compelling blues by Bob Campbell, a singer/guitarist from Alabama, and four very choice duets by Skoodle Dum Doo & Sheffield, a duet probably from Virginia, recorded in 1943, whose harmonica–guitar interplay rivals the best work of Sonny Terry & Brownie McGhee. The addition of these artists to the disconnected Taylor and Byrd may be entirely arbitrary, but it makes an already valuable album triply desirable. TR

Susan Tedeschi (born 1970)
VOCAL, GUITAR, PIANO

Whether tearing her vocal cords or sweetening the ears with delicate falsettos, Tedeschi is a singer with grace and optimum control, and a fine guitarsmith. Her journey began with the blues band she fronted in her home state of Massachusetts, and in 2000 she earned a Grammy nomination for Best New Artist. Comparisons with Bonnie Raitt, Janis Joplin and similarly soulful female performers have worked to position her accurately both inside and outside the contemporary blues milieu.

**(*) Better Days
Susan Tedeschi Band CD 950215 Tedeschi; Little Annie Raines (h); Adrienne Hayes (g); Jim Lamond (b); Mike Aiello (d). 95.

Better Days is a set of 12-bar ambles marked out by Tedeschi's singing, which is rich in volume, consistency and natural ease, with a use of melisma that hints at classic soul. Unfortunately the lyrics, lacking the knowing poetry which can turn an average blues into a meaningful one, undermine the authority that Tedeschi establishes with her voice. Her dominance is rarely contested by the minimal instrumental backing, although Annie Raines's guest harmonica slots are pleasant; the best guitar moment is the one occasion when Tedeschi plays lead, on 'You're On My Hair'. She doesn't yet sound like a comfortably moulded player, but this would change by the time of her first official release three years later.

***(*) **Just Won't Burn**
Tone-Cool CDTC 1164 *Tedeschi; [Sax] Gordon Beadle (ts); Tino Barker (bs); Annie Raines (h); Tom West (o, p); Ian Kennedy (vn); Sean Costello, Adrienne Hayes, Tim Gearan (g); Jim Lamond, Norm 'The Screaming Bird of Truth' DeMoura (b); Tom Hambridge (d, timbales, tamb, perc, v); Mike Levesque (d); Buck Taylor, Bird Taylor (v).* 98.

The punchy opener 'Rock Me Right' gets Tedeschi's fine Tone-Cool debut off to a flying start: a thumping rhythm section and effective pauses emphasize her full-throttled projection and more honed guitar licks, based on a classic Texan, bitty, Fender Tele sound. In most of the remaining songs Tedeschi concentrates less on developing that blistering tone than on working in a mellower style with patient tempos, soft funk grooves and smooth, gospellish backing vocals. The songwriting is both more stylish – helped by textured arrangements and production – and, in the case of the half that's written by her, markedly more personal. This produces the singalong highlight 'You Need To Be With Me' and a title track that demonstrates Tedeschi's admirable soloing as well as a soul voice that couldn't be more suited to the slow-burning material, which only occasionally begins to drag. The interest is maintained towards the end with a beautiful cover of John Prine's ballad 'Angel From Montgomery', although this pinpoints the fact that Tedeschi's interests lie as much in American roots music as in blues.

** **Wait For Me**
Artemis/Tone-Cool 51146//Tone-Cool/Artemis/Rykodisc RCD 17003 *Tedeschi; Scott Aruda (t); Paul Ahlstrand, Tino Barker (ts); [Sax] Gordon Beadle (bs); Annie Raines (h); Noah Simon (mellotron); Jason Crosby (kb, o, p, vn); Kofi Burbridge (o, p); Tom West (o); Johnnie Johnson (p); Dave McNair (g, b); Milt Reder, Kevin Barry, Derek Trucks, Colonel Bruce Hampton, Paul Rishell (g); Dean Cassell, Todd Smallie, Ron Perry, Drew Glackin (b); Yonrico Scott (d, perc); Dave Mattacks, Jeff Sipe, Joe Bonadio (d); Eguie Castrillo (perc).* 02.

Wait For Me represents maturity but lacks zest and surprise. Its mostly tiresome songs are awash with clichés that suppress individuality – as in the torrid lines 'He took me to a dance/I knew that this was gonna be one hell of a romance' – and are produced with a sentimentality as saccharine as a melting peardrop. As ever, Tedeschi's voice is flexible and soaring, and she slips effortlessly into jazzy bar-room mode for 'Blues On A Holiday' and 'Wait For Me'. But the blues is more of a background effect than a prevailing force, and although there are refreshing guitar solos by Tedeschi and her guests, blues fans may be put off by diluted funk, seven minutes of feel-good drivel ('The Feeling Music Brings') and sickly Celine Dion balladeering.

(*) **Live From Austin TX
New West NW 6065 *Tedeschi; Jason Crosby (kb, vn, v); William Green (o, v); Ron Perry (b, v); Jeff Sipe (d, v).* 6/03.

This live release arrives long overdue for such a seasoned performer. It is disappointing that only two numbers are featured from *Just Won't Burn* against nine from the weaker follow-up. However, the stage generates more panache, particularly in Bob Dylan's 'Don't Think Twice, It's All Right', which Tedeschi claims as her own with an intimate rendition. The discrepancy between her stake in blues and other genres is attested by Stevie Wonder and Sly Stone covers, a repeat of 'Angel From Montgomery' and Tedeschi's continuing dedication to soul. She is the first to acknowledge this diversity and, while the later tracks 'Lost Lover Blues' and 'I Fell In Love' restore the balance somewhat, the album's demure relationship with heavy-duty blues material shadows its relevance in the context of this book. RR

Johnnie Temple (1906–68)
VOCAL, GUITAR

Temple was born in Canton, Mississippi, but grew up in Jackson, the stepson of guitarist 'Slim' Duckett and an acquaintance of Tommy Johnson, Ishmon Bracey, the McCoy brothers and Skip James, who resided with him for some time in about 1930. A year or two later he moved to Chicago, where he worked with guitarist Willie B. James and, playing mandolin, in a string trio with the McCoys. Though he periodically returned to Jackson, he was part of the Chicago blues community until the mid-'50s, playing with, but gradually sidelined by, younger musicians like Baby Face Leroy Foster and Walter Horton. He then returned to Jackson, where he died.

*** **Johnnie Temple – Vol. 1 (1935–1938)**
Document DOCD-5238 *Temple; Odell Rand (cl); Joshua Altheimer, Horace Malcolm (p); Charlie McCoy, Joe McCoy (g); John Lindsay, Ransom Knowling, unknown (b); Fred Flynn, T. C. Williams (d).* 5/35–4/38.

At his first session in 5/35 Temple sang blues with numerous references to Jackson, the city he had lived in since he was 14. He was accompanied by two guitars, his own and Charlie McCoy's, McCoy playing not much differently from the way he had with Tommy Johnson seven years earlier. At a second session in 11/36, accompanied by piano and guitar, Temple revised a blues standard and created a new one. At first glance, the contrast between these sessions seems like a graphic illustration of the blues in swift transition: in just 18 months a Southern rural idiom has been transformed into music fit for city clubgoers and jukeboxes. In fact music of the kind Temple adopted in 1936 had been around at least since Leroy Carr and Scrapper Blackwell started recording it in 1928. Conversely, the guitar duet performances were old hat by 1935 and Temple was lucky to find a company willing to record them. The timing is deceptive, a consequence of the record industry's telescoping of musical history.

But this is not to say that Temple does not sing blues in, so to speak, two different time-zones. A clash of Southern and Northern references, both musical and textual, recurs throughout his work. David Evans describes him in his notes as 'someone who gave further life to a highly idiosyncratic and regional music and exposed elements of it to larger audiences that could never have been reached by its original creators'. That role of a mediator of tradition is less effectively realized in, say, 'The Evil Devil Blues', his curbed, tidied version of Skip James's 'Devil Got My Woman', or 'Jacksonville Blues', a delocalization of the Jackson theme 'Doodleville Blues', since the audience they reached appears to have been minuscule, than in more widely distributed pieces such as 'East St. Louis Blues' or 'Louise Louise Blues'. The latter, a huge hit, couples a universal theme – the lover doubtful about where his loved one's affections really lie – with a catchy tune to which the words are perfectly fitted.

The success of 'Louise Louise Blues' made it a template for much of Temple's subsequent work – the next session's 'Snapping Cat' is virtually a facsimile – but the piano–guitar setting, which at the time was practically statutory, was shortly replaced by the Harlem Hamfats, whose sound, at once swingy and redolent of old New Orleans, echoes the South/North, old/new dissensions inherent in Temple's work. It may have been no accident that his first two recordings with the band, coupled on the session's first release, were an athletic fun song, 'Gimme Some Of That Yum Yum Yum', and a sober narrative about magic, 'Hoodoo Women', decorated with interjections of 'ooh, Lord', a device he varied with the 'ooh, well, well' associated with Peetie Wheatstraw.

*** **Johnnie Temple – Vol. 2 (1938–1940)**
DOCD-5239 *Temple; Odell Rand, John Robinson, Buster Bailey (cl); Sam Price, poss. Joshua Altheimer (p); Lonnie Johnson, prob. Teddy Bunn, prob. Al Casey (g); John Lindsay, unknown(s) (b); Herb Cowans (d).* 10/38–4/40.
*** **Johnnie Temple – Vol. 3 (1940–1949)**
Document DOCD-5240 *Temple; Henry 'Red' Allen, unknown (t); Buster Bailey (cl); unknown (ts); Sam Price, Lil Armstrong, Horace Malcolm, poss. Jimmie Gordon (p); prob. Al Casey, unknown (g); unknowns (b); Herb Cowans, unknowns (d).* 4/40–49.

At the point where *Vol. 2* begins, Temple was a significant player in the 'race' record business. In yet another stylistic antithesis, his delivery, with its Southern accent, pronounced vibrato and momentary octave leaps at word-endings, was set against urbane small-group settings, giving his records a character that distinguished them from much contemporary blues. He continued to recycle the format of 'Louise Louise' in songs like 'Good Suzie (Rusty Knees)' and 'Mississippi Woman's Blues', which has verbal reminiscences of Ishmon Bracey's 'Saturday Blues', a Jackson reference he also consulted for 'Better Not Let My Good Gal Catch You Here'. 'Big Leg Woman', however, which would be his next-biggest hit, borrows the melody of 'Shake 'Em On Down'. He reached back, too, for 'If I Could Holler', which alludes to his 1935 recording 'Big Boat Whistle', and 'Cherry Ball', a distant descendant of a Skip James theme.

Interesting though the origins of his material might be, and piquant the themes he sometimes treated in his newly written numbers, Temple's performance had become firmly formularized. Variety of tune and tempo has a low priority in these volumes, and the listener looking for a little relief must be content with the cool spirals that rise from Buster Bailey's clarinet and the pithy trumpet of Red Allen. Exceptions are 'Corrine Corrina' and a buoyant 'Fix It Up And Go', based on Blind Boy Fuller's 'Step It Up And Go', which spurs Allen and Bailey to energetic riffing. Temple's final pre-World War II session reverted to the piano–guitar format of five years before, Horace Malcolm playing the former and Temple himself, rather boringly, the latter.

Five years on, Temple still had the cachet to win a recording date at King, and on his boisterous revision of 'Yum Yum Yum' showed that he understood the vigorous approach the times required. A later coupling for Miracle found him still gamely trying to adapt to a changing market, though the material, a remake of the 11-year-old 'Between Midnight And Dawn' and a fragment of chant-along nonsense, 'Sit Right On It', may have worked against him. Between the two sessions he cut an 'Olds

"98" Blues', with just guitar, for the Maxwell Street label Ora Nelle. An unexpected gracenote, it has some of the rockabilly drive of an early Sun recording.

Some time after the Documents came out, five more sides from the King session, previously unissued, turned up on the VAC *Broke, Black & Blue* (Proper PROPERBOX 7 4CD). Like the issued coupling, which is also included, they are trenchantly accompanied by a small band with trumpet, tenor and piano, the solo space mostly occupied, to good effect, by the tenor. As 'Dixie Flyer' reveals, even this far into his career Temple had not forgotten the impact of Skip James's 'Devil Got My Woman'. The Devil also has a walk-on part in 'Believe My Sins Have Found Me Out', the last in Temple's decade-long sequence of songs of mild moral reproof.

*** **The Blues/From Mississippi To Chicago 1935–1940**
Frémeaux FA 256 2CD *As for relevant CDs above.* 5/35–4/40.
*** **The Essential**
Classic Blues CBL 200038 2CD *As above.* 5/35–49.

Readers interested in following the path of Temple's work but not spending quite so long over it can choose between these 2CDs, both representative surveys including the majority of the tracks singled out above, but with 20 (of 36) tracks in common. The Classic Blues is cheaper but, as usual, has briefer notes and no recording information. TR

Sonny Terry (1911–86)
VOCAL, HARMONICA, JEW'S HARP

Sanders Terrell (other spellings are given, but this is from census records) was born in Greensboro, Georgia (not North Carolina as often reported), and raised on a farm. He took up the harmonica in emulation of his father, and the instrument became his livelihood after two accidents left him blind in one eye and with very limited sight in the other. Terry was living in North Carolina when he met Blind Boy Fuller in 1937, and soon recorded with him. The next year Fuller was in jail when John Hammond came recruiting for the From Spirituals To Swing *concert, and Terry took his place, thereby connecting with the white jazz and blues audience. In 1942 he and Brownie McGhee formed a partnership which took their music to New York and later the world. The duo lasted for 40 years, latterly with increasing acrimony and decreasing creativity.*

Sonny Terry and Brownie McGhee made many recordings as a team. This entry deals with CDs credited to Sonny Terry alone. Those credited to Brownie McGhee alone are discussed under his name, while CDs credited to 'Sonny Terry & Brownie McGhee' or vice versa are dealt with in the entry following this one.

*** **Blowin' The Blues**
Fabulous FABCD 109 *Terry; Jordan Webb (h); Blind Boy Fuller, Brownie McGhee (g, v); Woody Guthrie (g); Bull City Red, Washboard Slim (wb).* 4/38–4/44.
*** **American Blues Legend**
Charly SNAP 126 *Terry; Daddy Merritt (p); Brownie McGhee, Woody Guthrie, Stick(s) McGhee (g); Baby Dodds (d); Oh Red [Bull City Red] (wb).* 12/38–11/47.
*** **Worried Man Blues**
Past Perfect 204393-203 *Similar to above two CDs; omit Webb, Washboard Slim; McGhee does not sing.* 12/38–11/47.

**** **Sonny Terry (1938–1945) Plus Alonzo Scales (1955)**
Document DOCD-5230 Terry; Jordan Webb (h); Bob Gaddy (p); Woody Guthrie (md, g, v); Blind Boy Fuller, Brownie McGhee, Cisco Houston, Alec Seward, Alonzo Scales (g, v); unknown (b); Oh Red [Bull City Red], Washboard Slim (wb); George Wood (d). 12/38–c. 8/55.

The Carnegie Hall audience's astonishment at Sonny Terry's spectacular blend of falsetto voice and virtuoso harmonica is audible on John Hammond's acetates of the concerts. Two titles that were issued on LP are on Fabulous and Document; they and a 'Fox Chase' appear legitimately on *From Spirituals To Swing* (Vanguard 169/71 3CD). Not surprisingly, producers and folklorists encouraged Terry to emphasize display music, and Document's collection includes multiple fox chases and train imitations. This does not mean monotony or boredom, however; Terry seems both the complete master of his humble instrument and completely possessed by it, and his rhythmic freedom and unpredictable tonal variations create edge-of-the-seat excitement. *Blowin' The Blues* includes commercially recorded accompaniments to Fuller and Brownie McGhee, which makes for a more rounded but less breathtaking portrait; it's cheap, but the sound is variable.

Charly and Past Perfect both append early recordings to Capitol sides (see below). The combination of display pieces with band blues doesn't work well, especially on Charly, where the early music comes after the Capitol sides. Document's three bonus tracks by Alonzo Scales with Terry in the band are also incongruous, but less jarringly; more annoying is that they purport to be 'the complete Alonzo Scales' and aren't. The three missing titles are on *"Too Late, Too Late"* – Vol. 7 (Document DOCD-5525).

** **Sonny Terry – Vol. 2 (1944–1949)**
Document DOCD-5657 Terry; Woody Guthrie (h, vn, md, u, g, v); Alec Seward (g, v); Brownie McGhee (g); orchestra; Alan Gilbert, The Lyn Murray Singers (v). 4/44–10/49.

(*) **Sonny Terry & His Mouth Harp/Blind Gary Davis The Singing Reverend
Collectables COL-CD-5607 Terry; Woody Guthrie (g, sp); prob. Gary Davis (g). prob. 44–prob. 4/54.

** **Chain Gang Blues**
Collectables COL-CD-5195 Terry; Woody Guthrie (vn, u, g, v); Alec Seward (g, v). prob. 44.

Document's second volume includes *Chain Gang Blues* and most of *Sonny Terry & His Mouth Harp*; the track with Davis (probably) was recorded in 1954 (probably), and Document omit it for copyright reasons. This material is topped by two collaborations with Woody Guthrie; it's tailed with the opening number from *Finian's Rainbow*, which begins with a brief Terry solo before warpdriving away from the blues, and a track from the Folkways collection discussed below.

Chain Gang Blues was originally issued on two ten-inch LPs which are among the blues' first concept albums; poor sound suggests that they may derive from airshots. Southern prisons were segregated in the '40s, and Guthrie's participation is an unrealistic act of solidarity that was doubtless sincerely motivated, but often comes over as wannabe intrusiveness: his timing is often at odds with Terry and Seward, his comments sound smug and his singing, which is frequently out of tune, is minstrelsy. More worthwhile by far are Terry's many accompaniments to Guthrie's folk singing, some of which are on Smithsonian Folkways' four volumes of *Asch Recordings*.

On most of *Sonny Terry & His Mouth Harp* Guthrie shuts up and plays, which is a help; the recording quality is not great, but Terry is in good form, notably on the solo 'You Don't Want Me Blues'. The rest of the Collectables CD is another ten-inch LP, on which Terry accompanies Davis; see the latter's entry for discussion of its considerable merits.

***(*) **The Folkways Years 1944–1963** [sic]
Smithsonian Folkways CD SF 40033 Terry; J. C. Burris (h, bones, body perc, v); Pete Seeger (bj, v); Brownie McGhee (g, v); Alec Seward (b, prob. v); Frank Robertson (b); Coyal McMahan (sung b, maracas, v); Gene Moore (d); Washboard Doc, William Edward Cooke (wb). c. 4/44–12/57.

Often in partnership with Brownie McGhee, Sonny Terry pursued a twin-track strategy in New York, performing downhome, usually acoustic blues for whites and small-band R&B for African-Americans. Moses Asch documented Terry's more archaic music intensively, and *The Folkways Years* makes a good, varied selection, although its discographical notes are all over the place and the limits of Asch's engineering skills are sometimes apparent. Alongside the expected collaborations with McGhee, the disc is notable for 'Skip To My Lou', with a stringband including Seeger's charming banjo, a 'Shortnin' Bread' which is the only currently available sample of Terry on jew's harp, and Burris's bones, body slaps and second harp. Terry had virtually abandoned falsetto singing by this time, and his pitch in his normal register could be insecure; 'Poor Man' is a severe example of this problem.

***(*) **Froggy Went A Courtin'**
Blue City BCD-813 Terry; unknown (ts); J. C. Burris (h, v); Fletcher Smith (p); Brownie McGhee (g, v); Mickey Baker, Stick(s) McGhee, unknown (g); Johnny Williams, Milt Hinton, unknown (b); Coyal McMahan (sung b); Marty Wilson, Gene Brooks, unknown (d); Bobby Donaldson (bgo); unknown (train wh). 12/44–58.

Froggy Went A Courtin' is shared with Cousin Leroy (q.v.), on whose recordings Terry plays. The rest of the CD is a useful roundup of Terry's R&B recordings for a number of labels, including Gramercy, for whom he scored his biggest hit, 'Hootin' Blues', here mistitled 'Hootin' The Blues'. Inaccurate titling and the absence of notes and discography are an irritant, but musically this release is a gem. Playing through an amplifier with an electric band, Terry can be amazingly rowdy, and his tendency to yell, detrimental in other settings, becomes an asset; his accompanists match his high spirits note for clanging note and downbeat for thrashed downbeat.

***(*) **Whoopin' The Blues: The Capitol Recordings, 1947–1950**
Capitol 29372 Terry; Daddy Merritt (p, d); Big Chief Ellis (p, v); Stick(s) McGhee, Brownie McGhee (g); Baby Dodds (d). 3/47–2/50.

From here onwards, it should be taken as read that Sonny Terry's singing is sometimes troublesomely sharp; it's obvious, for instance, why 'Mad Man Blues' stayed unissued until this CD. Capitol signed Terry in the wake of his stint in *Finian's Rainbow*, which made him by far the blues harmonica player best known to white audiences. It's gratifying, therefore, that the company recorded him playing gritty blues and harp exhibition pieces with solid little bands. The lineups, whether guitar and drums, guitar and piano, or guitar, piano and drums, always sound larger and more vibrant than their size would suggest. 'Custard Pie' and 'Crow Jane', with Brownie McGhee and Merritt's piano, stand out as sparkling versions of much-recorded numbers.

**(*) Sonny Terry And His Mouth-Harp
Original Blues Classics OBCCD-589 *Terry; Alec Seward (g). 50.*

This session for the nascent Elektra label has also been assigned to 1953, but whatever the recording date, it's devalued by Alec Seward's cheap and under-recorded guitar. On 'John Henry' and one or two other songs some imaginative picking strives to be heard, and 'Old Woman Blues' is amusingly grumpy about mutton dressed as lamb, but sonic deficiencies and the familiarity of many songs make this an inessential segment of Terry's *oeuvre*.

*** Sonny Terry
Collectables COL-CD-5307 *Terry; Doc Bagby (o, prob. maracas); Daddy Merritt (p, d); Brownie McGhee (g, v); James Harris (b); poss. Billy Bagby (d). 8–10/52.*

This CD derives from two sessions for Gotham, who were probably hoping for R&B coin in the wake of Gramercy's surprise hit with 'Hootin' Blues'. There are 14 tracks here but only eight songs; nevertheless, skilful programming makes this an enjoyable collection, with enough differences between takes to prevent tedium. McGhee's electric guitar work is a particular pleasure.

**** Sonny's Story
Original Blues Classics OBCCD 503 *Terry; J. C. Burris (h); Stick(s) McGhee (g); Belton Evans (d). 10/60.*

**(*) Sonny Is King
Original Blues Classics OBCCD 521 *Terry; Lightnin' Hopkins, Brownie McGhee (g); Leonard Gaskin (b); Belton Evans (d). 10/60–9/62.*

There's much repetition of material (and consequent retitling) in Sonny Terry's output, whether as name artist or as half of 'sonnyandbrownie'; neither of these sets is an exception, although 'Pepperheaded Woman' on *Sonny's Story* is one of the wittiest 'short-haired woman' blues, and one which Terry didn't record again. *Sonny's Story* also benefits from the exceptional engineering of Rudy Van Gelder, and the texture is enriched by Burris's punchy second harmonica. Stick McGhee deps ably for his more famous brother, and Belton Evans is subtly effective, as indeed he is on the half of *Sonny Is King* where he, Hopkins and Gaskin accompany. Hopkins's playing is cautious, however, and when Brownie McGhee takes over as accompanist he can't be bothered to push himself or Terry; this is an altogether more routine affair than *Sonny's Story*.

**** Wizard Of The Harmonica
Storyville STCD 8018 *Terry; Brownie McGhee (g, v); Svend Erik Nørregaard (d); Leif Johansson (wb). 11/71.*

There are no unexpected songs; like its companion Storyville CDs, credited to McGhee and to the duo, *Wizard Of The Harmonica* is a recapitulation of Terry's 'folk-blues' repertoire, cut over two days in Denmark. The salient point is that the numbers are uniformly well recorded and enthusiastically performed, making the disc as a whole quite the best summation of Sonny's rasping, back-country singing and inflammatory harmonica. Perhaps it was the Carlsberg.

**(*) Going It Alone
Corazong 255 020 *Terry; Michael Rura (p); Bob Malenky (g, v). 4/74.*

**(*) But Not Together
Tomato TOM-2106 As above. *4/74.*

By 1974 Terry and McGhee were only meeting onstage, and in either version this CD of material recorded by Blue Labor is accurately titled, and accurately credited to Brownie McGhee/Sonny Terry. There's an attempted makeover using new songs, several written by Malenky and/or label owner Kent Cooper, but they're pastiche and don't stick in the mind. ('Cut Off From My Baby', composed by Terry, is far more rooted and memorable.) Malenky's occasional singing is unidiomatic, and Rura's playing is skilful but academic.

*** Whoopin'
Alligator ALCD 4734 *Terry; Johnny Winter (p, g, v); Willie Dixon (b); Styve Homnick (d). 7/81.*

More makeover: 'I tried to make a record with a lot of Delta feel to it, like we'd cut the record in Mississippi,' says Winter, who produced as well as playing. Lee Dorsey's 'Ya Ya' apart, most of the songs are familiar, and the experiment is not as radical as Winter supposes: the end result is pretty much an accidental revival of the sounds heard on *Froggy Went A Courtin'*, with some bearable blues-rock flourishes added here and there. *Whoopin'* lacks the casual authenticity of those earlier sides, but with that reservation it's an enjoyable leave-taking. CS

Sonny Terry & Brownie McGhee
DUET

For biographical details, see the artists' individual entries.

This entry deals with CDs credited to 'Sonny Terry & Brownie McGhee' or vice versa. CDs credited to either McGhee only or Terry only will be found in their individual artist entries.

***(*) Sonny Terry & Brownie McGhee 1938–1948
JSP JSP 7721 5CD *Terry; McGhee; Hal Singer (ts); Jordan Webb (h, v); Daddy Merritt, Champion Jack Dupree, Lannie Scott, Big Chief Ellis (p); Blind Boy Fuller, Stick(s) McGhee (g, v); Buddy Moss, prob. Ralph Willis (g); Pops Foster, Count Edmondson, Franklin Skeete, Gene Ramey, unknown (b); Sticks Evans, Baby Dodds, Arthur Herbert, Heywood Jackson (d); Bull City Red, Washboard Slim (wb). 12/38–9/48 or 10/48.*

(**(*)) Back Home Blues
Prism Leisure PLATCD 603 *Terry; McGhee; Hal Singer (ts); Jordan Webb (h); Daddy Merritt, Lannie Scott (p); Woody Guthrie (g, sp); Stick(s) McGhee (g); Franklin Skeete, Pops Foster, unknown (b); Heywood Jackson, Arthur Herbert (d); Washboard Slim, Oh Red [Bull City Red] (wb). 12/38–52.*

(**(*)) Pawnshop Blues
Snapper Complete Blues SBLUECD 025 *Terry; McGhee; Daddy Merritt, Big Chief Ellis (p); Ralph Willis (g, v); Blind Boy Fuller, Stick(s) McGhee (g); Pops Foster, Gene Ramey, unknown (b); Baby Dodds (d); Oh Red [Bull City Red] (wb). 12/38–10/49.*

(***) My Skin Is Black, My Soul Is Blue
Trilogie 205890-349 3CD *Terry; McGhee; Jordan Webb (h, v); Daddy Merritt (p); Blind Boy Fuller, (g, v); Buddy Moss, Woody Guthrie, Stick(s) McGhee (g); Baby Dodds (d); Bull City Red, Washboard Slim (wb). 12/38–2/50.*

***(*) Sportin' Life Blues
Proper PVCD 125 2CD Terry; McGhee; Hal Singer (ts); Jordan Webb (h); Daddy Merritt (p, d); Big Chief Ellis (p, v); Lannie Scott, Champion Jack Dupree (p); Woody Guthrie (md, u, g, v); Blind Boy Fuller, Cisco Houston, Alec Stewart (g, v); prob. Ralph Willis, Stick(s) McGhee (g): Pops Foster, Franklin Skeete, Gene Ramey, Bob Harris (b); Baby Dodds, Arthur Herbert, Heywood Jackson, Willie Jones (d); Oh Red [Bull City Red], Washboard Slim (wb). 3/40–52.

*** Harlem Troubadours
Saga Blues 982 991-7 Terry; McGhee; Daddy Merritt (p, d): Big Chief Ellis, Bob Gaddy (p); Blind Boy Fuller (g, sp); Buddy Moss, Stick(s) McGhee (g); Curley Russell, Pops Foster, Bob Harris (b); Baby Dodds, Arthur Herbert, unknown, George Wood (d); Oh Red [Bull City Red], Washboard Slim (wb). 3/40–52.

A joint credit doesn't always signify folk-blues recordings by the duo who eventually came to regard each other the way the Ancient Mariner did the albatross; sometimes it's just a brand name. *My Skin Is Black, My Soul Is Blue* (pretentious, *nous*?) opportunistically collates some early solos by Terry, most of McGhee's OKeh recordings, and 15 of Terry's 16 Capitol sides. The transfers are middling, and there are no notes. JSP's bargain-priced box set is equally opportunistic, trawling through previously released LPs and CDs rather than seeking out reissued recordings; but generous playing time, superior engineering and extensive notes give it a substantial edge. JSP's cut-off date entails the omission of Terry's last Capitol session, but there are more harp solos as compensation, as well as all McGhee's OKeh sides, and sizeable chunks of his work, both with and without Terry, for Alert, Savoy, Circle, Disc and Sittin' In With.

Sportin' Life Blues also has thorough annotation; for the most part, its 51 tracks are a well-chosen sampler of harp showpieces, of both men making the transition from acoustic to amplified blues, and of the first auguries of folk blues. Sound quality is generally excellent, even on four songs from *Chain Gang Blues* (which is three too many; Alec Seward's fine 'Rock Me Momma' would have been enough). *Sportin' Life Blues* is a well-balanced and varied collection, which would have been improved by giving more space to McGhee's Savoy material at the expense of Terry's Capitol recordings. (As on Trilogie, all but one of the latter are included.)

On *Pawnshop Blues* 'Goin' Down Slow', supposedly a 1946 McGhee vocal, is sung by Terry and dates from 1952; the lively 'I'm Gonna Rock' features McGhee accompanying Ralph Willis, but is omitted from the discographical data; and 'Rum Cola Papa' plays where the title track should be. These lapses prevent a recommendation of what is in any case a rather random compilation. The budget-priced *Back Home Blues* is also a scattershot collection and also has its problems: 'No Love Blues', which Terry recorded with a band in 1952, is listed, but the 1938 solo 'New Careless Love' plays; more generally, many tracks come from 78s in poor shape, and those which don't lack sparkle.

It's not unimportant, therefore, that *Harlem Troubadours* delivers the tracks listed, and in decent transfers. Its division into three parts ('Sonny Terry', 'Brownie McGhee' and one which may be inferred) is somewhat arbitrary, since McGhee plays on four of Terry's six tracks, and Terry on one of McGhee's. Most of the material derives from Capitol, Savoy and Jax; the three early recordings included aren't very informative about how Terry and McGhee developed the music they offered African-American listeners after World War II, but *Harlem Troubadours* is pleasant enough listening.

** The Giants Of The Blues
Legacy International CD 368//Madacy SD-2-4964 Terry; McGhee; Woody Guthrie (vn, u, g, v); Alec Seward, Lightnin' Hopkins, Big Joe Williams (g, v); Jimmy Bond (b). prob. 44–8/61.

** Wine Headed Woman
Collectables COL-CD-6381 As above, except add Doc Bagby (o, prob. maracas), Daddy Merritt (p, d), James Harris (b), poss. Billy Bagby (d). prob. 44–8/61.

** Blowin' The Fuses
Tradition TCD 1043 Terry; McGhee; Woody Guthrie (u, g, v); Alec Seward (g, v). prob. 44–8/61.

The Giants Of The Blues (identical on both labels) begins with five duo numbers from 8/61 and two from a 1960 session with Hopkins and Williams; these are discussed below. They then lurch back to 1944 and *Chain Gang Blues*. These 12 tracks are performed by Terry, Guthrie and Seward, and their shortcomings are discussed under Sonny Terry's entry.

Wine Headed Woman's stylistic mix and mismatch is an even more jarring jumble of four lively R&B tracks made for Gotham (see Terry's entry), five from *Chain Gang Blues*, six from 8/61 and one from the encounter with Hopkins and Williams.

Blowin' The Fuses begins with all eight titles from 8/61; the CD is extended to 47 minutes by four 'archival bonus tracks' from *Chain Gang Blues*. It helps that these are tacked on at the end, but inferior sound, short playing time and the inherent deficiencies of the 'bonus' material obstruct a recommendation.

(****) Sonny Terry and Brownie McGhee Sing The Blues
Sony Music Special Products A 26430 Terry; McGhee; Bob Gaddy (p); Bob Harris (b); George Wood (d). 51–52.

**** Key To The Highway
Universe UV 117 As above, except add 'Marie' (v). 51–52.

*** Harmonica Train
Past Perfect 220357 As above, except add Doc Bagby (o), Daddy Merritt (p, d), Champion Jack Dupree, Fletcher Smith (p), Stick(s) McGhee or Benny Foster, Mickey Baker (g), James Harris, Johnny Williams (b), Coyal McMahan (sung b), poss. Billy Bagby, Gene Brooks, Willie Jones, Marty Wilson (d), Bobby Donaldson (bgo); omit Gaddy, 'Marie' (v). 51–8/53.

Whether as an acoustic twosome or with a rocking little band, Terry and McGhee made some of their best recordings aimed at black purchasers for Bob and Morty Shad. It's therefore disappointing that the only product to result from Sony's purchase of Bob Shad's back catalogue is a ten-track, 28-minute CD without notes. Universe repeat some venerable discographical errors and indulge in some pointless retitling, but their 19 tracks, which include two where Terry and McGhee back Bob Gaddy, easily eclipse Sony's half-hearted effort.

Despite a joint credit, *Harmonica Train* is a compilation of Sonny Terry numbers, on most of which McGhee is present. Seven tracks from the Shad brothers' labels are splendid, as are Terry's Red Robin single and two titles from a manic Victor session where Baker, Smith and Wilson thrash their instruments unmercifully. The CD is completed by seven much more restrained titles from Terry's Gotham sessions, and 'Dangerous Woman' from Gramercy. This last title is in startlingly poor sound, and the diverse sources and moods give *Harmonica Train* a somewhat thrown-together feel, but its budget price is mitigation.

(*) California Blues
Fantasy 24723//[Ace CDCH 398] *Terry; McGhee*. 3–11/57.
(*) Just A Closer Walk With Thee
Original Blues Classics OBCCD-541 *Terry; McGhee*. 11/57.

Although they'd worked together off and on since 1942, it was a three-year stint in *Cat On A Hot Tin Roof* that cemented the partnership into a long-term way to make a living. The material on these CDs was recorded while they were appearing in the San Francisco production.

California Blues unites two LPs on a CD as the team work out how to be a folk-blues act; there are acoustic versions of songs they'd previously done with bands, new compositions, mainly by McGhee, and more arrangements of worksongs than featured in later years. Given that many of the songs here were recorded many times, lifeless remastering makes *California Blues* superfluous for most listeners. The sound is better on the all-gospel *Just A Closer Walk With Thee*, but McGhee's penchant for unctuousness and Terry's for bellowing are both given free rein.

(*) Brownie McGhee And Sonny Terry Sing
Smithsonian Folkways CD SF 40011 *Terry; McGhee; Gene Moore (d)*. 11/57.

It was an obvious idea to make a session with the emphasis on vocal duets, but given Terry's tendency to sing sharp, it wasn't a good one. Moore's drumming veers alarmingly from subtle brushwork to crassly clouted rimshots. An angry 'John Henry' and an ingenious reworking of 'Key To The Highway' into 'Guitar Highway' stand out on a generally disappointing disc.

***(*) Pye Blues Legends In London**
Castle CMETD 562//Sanctuary CAS 36167 3CD *Terry; McGhee; Pat Halcox (t); Chris Barber (tb, b); Monty Sunshine (cl); Eddie Smith (bj); Dave Lee (p, humming); Dick Smith (b); Graham Burbidge (d)*. 5/58.
** **Great Bluesmen In Britain**
Avid AMSC 736 *Terry; McGhee*. prob. 5–6/58.
*** **Nothin' But The Blues**
Southland SCD-15 *Terry; McGhee*. c. 10/59.

These sets were all recorded in Britain. Both *Pye Blues Legends* and *Great Bluesmen* were made on Sonny & Brownie's first tour, and both are shared with Bill Broonzy and Josh White. Terry and McGhee's third of *Blues Legends* conjoins three sessions: one with Chris Barber's band, one with Dave Lee added on piano, and as the usual double act. The warm welcome the two men received in Britain probably explains their dynamism during these sessions. Lee's piano augments the texture effectively, reviving some of the muscular high spirits of the amplified band recordings. Chris Barber promoted this and other early visits by American blues artists, but six tracks with his trad band are less successful, both because of the clash of idioms and because Terry is often overwhelmed by the other wind players.

The relevant portion of *Great Bluesmen* was taped at a party in Glasgow, and suffers from hiss and occasional fluctuations in recording speed. A bigger drawback is the effect of liquid hospitality on an increasingly somnolent, random and tuneless Sonny Terry. Brownie's conscientious singing for his supper can't offset these defects.

Nothin' But The Blues catches Terry and McGhee in concert, performing with great enthusiasm, and while there's nothing here that wasn't recorded many times, their vigour, the humour and mutual respect that disappeared later, and good recording quality combine to give it the edge over many similar exercises.

*** **Rediscovered Blues**
Capitol 29376 2CD *Terry; McGhee; Lightnin' Hopkins, Big Joe Williams (g, v); Jimmy Bond (b)*. c. 11/59–c. 6/60.
(*) Best Of Country Blues: Southern Camptown Blues
Wolf 120.101 *As above, except add unknown (interviewer)*. c. 6/60–c. late 70s.

By 1960, Terry and McGhee had stopped making records for the R&B market, but the early days of 'the blues revival' brought intensive studio activity as a folk-blues duo. It's often been said, with some justification, that they were over-recorded, and it's at this time that the charge carries most weight, but they can scarcely be blamed for being popular, reliable and available. The combination of reliability and productivity does sometimes make their output hard to differentiate, though.

Part of *Rediscovered Blues* (which also reissues a Big Joe Williams LP) is a 12-track McGhee and Terry LP cut in 1959 and less than two hours. It's a model of their *modus operandi*: an assortment of familiar blues, some of them rejigged a bit – 'Baby Please Don't Go' takes some unexpected turnings – and a couple of harmonica showpieces, all smoothly performed and accessible to fans and casual listeners alike. Five opening tracks with Hopkins, Williams and the excellent Jimmy Bond feature communal ribbing and competitive verse-swapping in an atmosphere of authentic, sometimes edgy machismo. (A sixth track from this session is a solo by Hopkins.) The three guitarists sometimes have trouble collaborating, though; in particular, McGhee's ideas about harmony are not always compatible with those of Hopkins.

Wolf issue the session with Hopkins and Williams, adding two songs and an interview from a broadcast made some time close to the final rupture. The extra material is as automatic as might be expected.

*** **Back To New Orleans**
Fantasy 24708//[Ace CDCH 372] *Terry; McGhee; Roy Haynes (d)*. 12/59–9/60.

McGhee dominates the two LPs reissued here; Terry sings on only six of 21 tracks, and four of those are duets. The first half of the CD features over-familiar songs, done with habitual professionalism but lacking the zest that would encourage shortlisting. The second LP is more adventurous, including some strong compositions that weren't recorded again, and covers of Ray Charles, Fats Domino and Lonnie Johnson ('She's Making Whoopee In Hell Tonight', of all things); the great Roy Haynes gives five titles the lift that's sometimes missing elsewhere.

*** **The Original**
MagMid MM 084 *Terry; McGhee; J. C. Burris (h); Champion Jack Dupree (p); Lightnin' Hopkins, Big Joe Williams (g, v);*

Stick(s) McGhee or Bennie Foster (g); Bob Harris, Jimmy Bond (b); Willie Jones (d). 52–8/61.
*** Absolutely The Best
Fuel 2000 302 061 071 *As above, except omit Dupree, Stick(s) McGhee or Foster, Harris, Jones.* 52–11/71.
** Blowin' The Fuses
Collectables COL-CD-5198 *Terry; McGhee; Lightnin' Hopkins, Big Joe Williams (g, v); Jimmy Bond (b).* c. 6/60–8/61.
(***) Blowing The Fuses
Hallmark 702032 *As above.* c. 6/60–8/61.
*** Po' Boy
IMP 306 *As above.* c. 6/60–8/61.
*** The Real Folk Blues
Prestige CDSGP 0395 *As above.* c. 6/60–8/61.
*** Sun's Gonna Shine
Tomato TOM-2016 *As above.* c. 6/60–8/61.
(***) Trouble In Mind
Chrisly CR 60010 *Terry; McGhee.* 6/60–8/61.

These eight CDs have their origins in an LP which contained eight songs from a 1961 duo session, and two from a second 1960 get-together with Lightnin' and Big Joe. The LP was nevertheless 13 tracks long, because three songs were included twice, with different titles. Hallmark, IMP, Prestige and Tomato drop the duplicated tracks, but Collectables perpetuate the solecism and are downgraded accordingly. Chrisly go further, dropping two more of the 1961 titles and ending up with an eight-tracker; playing time of just over half an hour makes this hard to recommend. Hallmark's lack of notes also prompts a caveat.

The 1960 material is filler, and the critical burden rests on the later titles. They are typically efficient performances, combining and contrasting Sonny's rasping voice and high-spirited harp with Brownie's suave delivery and dextrous guitar work. Three tracks are lengthy instrumental workouts, allowing both men to show what they can do.

The MagMid and Fuel 2000 go further in expanding the original LP. Both discs include two titles cut by Terry for Folkways, and MagMid add four R&B numbers from Red Robin, with the lead artist role shared equally. Fuel 2000 omit the Red Robins in favour of a third title with Hopkins and Williams, and 'In The Evening', cut for Storyville in 1971. If these CDs' content seems arbitrary, the impression is not unjust, but simply in terms of playing time they are ahead of the pack, and *The Original*, conveniently making the fine Red Robin sides available in one place, is the better of them.

***(*) Midnight Special
Fantasy 24721//Ace CDCH 951 *Terry; McGhee; prob. Roy Haynes (d).* 8/60.

This is another reissue of two LPs, both beautifully engineered by Rudy Van Gelder. Versions of 'Midnight Special' and 'Take This Hammer' stand out, and a comparison with earlier attempts on *California Blues* makes this CD's musical and technical superiority plain. Five tracks are enlivened by a spirited, tasteful drummer who sounds uncannily like Roy Haynes. There are some good McGhee originals, but, as ever, many familiar songs are disguised by retitling. The quality of their rendition compensates for this, however – provided Brownie's Bing Crosbyish scatting on 'Muddy Water' is overlooked.

**(*) At Sugar Hill
Original Blues Classics OBCCD-536 *Terry; McGhee.* 12/61.

**(*) Backwater Blues
Fantasy FCD-24750 *As above.* 12/61.
*** At The 2nd Fret
Original Blues Classics OBCCD-561 *As above.* 4/62.

Two of these live CDs are reissued LPs; *Backwater Blues*, which contains more material from Sugar Hill (a San Francisco club), was released in 1999! Fantasy's recording expertise hadn't improved much since the duo's 1957 West Coast sessions; McGhee's guitar is especially ill-served on *At Sugar Hill*. *Backwater Blues* is more skilfully mastered and achieves a more lively sound, although the guitar is still muffled. Since most of the songs are among their most-recorded, and since the majority get routine renditions, *Backwater Blues* is by no means an essential addition to a very large catalogue.

McGhee and Terry alternate as lead singers on *At The 2nd Fret*; clumsy editing makes it obvious that the disc does not present one night's performance, but it's well recorded, and a good way to hear the blend of empathy and contrast that made them such a successful team. On the encore, sung in response to a request, Terry is badly off key and McGhee obviously winging it on guitar; spontaneity can be overrated.

*** Un Duo Magique Et Légendaire
Warner Blues 25577 *Terry; McGhee; J. C. Burris (h); Bennie Foster, Lightnin' Hopkins, Stick(s) McGhee (g); Leonard Gaskin (b); Belton Evans, Roy Haynes (d).* 3/57–4/62.
*** The Bluesville Years Volume Five: Mr. Brownie & Mr. Sonny
Prestige PRCD 9913 *As above, except omit Haynes.* 10/60–4/62.

Five tracks from *Brownie's Blues*, for which see McGhee's entry, and seven from *At The 2nd Fret* start and finish *The Bluesville Years*; between are three titles from *Sonny's Story* and two from *Sonny Is King*, for which see Terry's entry. Warner Blues cast the net more widely, drawing their sampler of the magic and legendary duo's Fantasy and Bluesville recordings from nine CDs (and 11 LPs); it's a measure of the team's consistency that the chosen 16 tracks assemble into an album that's perfectly adequate in its own right. Preferable to either of these collections, though, is a bulk buy of *Midnight Special*, *Sonny's Story* and *Brownie's Blues*.

*** Live At The Bunkhouse
BGO BGOCD 443 *Terry; McGhee.* c. 1/65.
*** Live At The New Penelope Café
Just A Memory JAM 9131 *Terry; McGhee.* 2/67.

Between late 1962 and early 1969 *Live At The Bunkhouse* was the only full LP the 'over-recorded' duo made for contemporary issue. Sonny's singing during their Vancouver residency was accurate and ebullient; Brownie is ingratiating, but prone to sententiousness in his announcements and his new songs. He also shows some irritation with Sonny's between-song clowning, but at this stage boredom with each other and their material wasn't infecting their performances.

Live At The New Penelope Café was recorded in Montreal, but the tapes waited 30 years for issue. It includes a couple of samples of McGhee's jazzhorn, a kazoo fitted with a trombone bell. More important is that they were in fine fettle, playing sparky versions of standbys – the guitar on 'Hootin' The Blues' is outstanding, let alone the harp and the hooting – and revisiting songs they'd not recorded for some time, like 'Pack It Up And Go' and a convincingly emotional 'Cornbread, Peas

And Black Molasses'. The progressively *pianissimo* outro on 'Walking My Blues Away' is deeply irritating, though.

(*) A Long Way From Home
MCA MCAD-11756 *Terry; McGhee; Ray Johnson (p, tamb); Earl Hooker (g); Jimmy Bond (b); Panama Francis (d); Marsha Smith, George McGhee, Clark Kidder (v). 3–9/69.*

(*) I Couldn't Believe My Eyes
BGO BGOCD 407 *As above, except Johnson does not play tamb. 9/69.*

BGO reissue the second of two Bluesway LPs; MCA add six of its ten tracks and an unissued title to the first LP. Sonny & Brownie move forward – or back – into an amplified band setting, but on the first session much of the piano (and especially electric piano) work is ill-fitting, and the percussion is overbearing. There are aspects to like – some neat line-swapping in the vocal duets, an exultant piano solo on 'Hole In The Wall', Terry's pervasive enthusiasm, some adept electric guitar by McGhee – but they don't redeem the enterprise as a whole.

I Couldn't Believe My Eyes has some notoriety as Earl Hooker's last session, but it's understandable that it wasn't issued until 1973; everybody plays conscientiously, and Hooker and McGhee take care not to compete, but the musicians seldom seem to have a more ambitious goal than completing the song without mistakes. The one outstanding track is 'I'm In Love With You Baby', with classy solos by both guitarists and a Muddy Waters pastiche that's one of Terry's finest recorded vocals. This number is also on MCA, whose remastering is immensely superior to BGO's cramped lifelessness.

♛ **** **Blues Masters Vol. 5**
Storyville STCD 8005 *Terry; McGhee; Leif Johansson (wb). 11/71.*

Relations were pretty strained by 1971, and it's a mystery that two days of intensive recording (which also generated CDs credited to each of them alone) produced quite the best renditions of the folk-blues material Terry and McGhee had been wheeling out for years. Maybe Denmark was a particularly agreeable stopover; maybe these sessions were one last try at saving their musical marriage. Extensive retitling tries to disguise the virtual absence of new songs, but the renditions are as spirited as they are skilful. *Blues Masters* is an eloquent summation of their duo repertoire; only the clumsy programming of two successive tracks with contrived *diminuendo* endings vexes.

*** Sonny & Brownie
A&M CD 0829//(E) 397 200 *Terry; McGhee; John Mayall (h, p, g, v); Maurice Rogers [Mighty Mo Rodgers] (p, thumb p, syn); Arlo Guthrie (p, g, v); Sugarcane Harris (vn); Michael Franks, Jerry Cole (bj, g); Al McKay, Jerry McGhee, John Hammond Jr (g); Harry Holt (b); Eddie Green (d); Jim Gilstrap, Marti McCall, Maxine Willard, Clydie King, Venetta Fields, Jackie Ward (v). 72.*

** The Rising Sun Collection
Just A Memory RSCD 0011 *Terry; McGhee; Styve Homnick (d). 7/80.*

*(*) Conversation With The River
World Network WDR 52.989 *As above. 8/80.*

Despite an incomparably uninventive title, *Sonny & Brownie* was a radical attempt at reinvention, with accompaniments that sometimes veer towards country-rock, and compositions by Curtis Mayfield, Sam Cooke and Randy Newman ('Sail Away', where Brownie handles the racial ironies with assurance). Thirty years on, the project still wears well; the arrangements are artfully varied, and only the occasional vocal groups descend into fussiness. The biggest drawback is some pretentious songwriting, and above all the preening sycophancy of Michael Franks's 'White Boy Lost In The Blues'. Nevertheless, *Sonny & Brownie* is worth investigating.

A&M set up a tour to promote the album but, by McGhee's account, Terry refused to learn new songs or hire a band. This provoked the final souring of their relationship, and thereafter they never spoke to each other and met only on stage until the act broke up in 1982.

Inevitably, therefore, the last two CDs in their joint saga are live and depressing. *The Rising Sun Collection* finds them supplying six tracks to a CD shared with Louisiana Red and Lightnin' Hopkins. It would almost be more accurate to say 'three tracks each': McGhee plays as little guitar as he can behind Terry's very coarse singing, and when it's his turn to feature, battling intermittent feedback and vocal dropouts, he jettisons much of his own vocal and instrumental subtlety.

Conversation With The River also has technical defects, with the guitar and harmonica fading and blasting unpredictably. Fatally, though, much of the arbitrariness is also imposed by the artists, whether trying to make life difficult for each other or following their own whimsy. The low point is reached on 'Going to Cansas City' and 'Freigth Train' (both *sic*), where Terry deliberately careers across McGhee's singing, loudly and out of rhythm. Just enough of the quality that used to be dominant fights its way through the musical bickering to make this musical car crash even more harrowing. CS

Texas Eastside Kings
GROUP

The TEKs are a group of veteran musicians who have worked on the East Austin R&B scene since the '60s.

**(*) Texas Eastside Kings
Dialtone DT 0005 *Donald 'Duck' Jennings (t, v); Ephraim Owens (t); Mickey Bennett (o); Nick Connolly (p); George Underwood, Clarence Pierce (g, v); Motoyasu Utsunomiya (g); James Kuykendall (b, v); Willie Sampson (d, v); Charles Shaw (d). 01.*

Most of the TEKs do some singing; the best in that department is Underwood, who has a strong blues voice, but Kuykendall and Sampson are no slouches, Jennings gives a confident reading of 'Stranded' and Pierce is okay, if a little frazzled. Their repertoire consists of a few covers and rather more that are best called adaptations: Sampson's 'Been A Long Time' could have been triggered by 'Walking The Back Streets And Crying' and Underwood's 'Beard Is White' by 'Paying The Cost To Be The Boss', while the latter's 'You Hurt Me More' has a faint air of 'It Hurts Me Too' and the riff running through 'Kuyk's Back' could have been absorbed from Lowell Fulson's 'Tramp'. The two trumpets are heard only on a couple of tracks, one, 'Mrs. Dee', an instrumental out of the soul-jazz bag. This is assured music by experienced players, unlikely to set the listener's pulse racing but varied enough to give quiet pleasure. TR

Jimmy Thackery (born 1953)
VOCAL, GUITAR

Thackery was born in Pittsburgh, Pennsylvania, and raised in Washington, DC, where as a teenager he witnessed performances by Buddy Guy and Jimi Hendrix that changed his life. A founder member of The Nighthawks, he played with them from 1974 to 1987. He then led The Assassins for five years and in 1991 created a trio, Jimmy Thackery & The Drivers.

** Empty Arms Motel
Blind Pig BPCD 5001 *Thackery; Wayne Burdette (b, v); Mark Stutso (d, v).* 92.

** Trouble Man
Blind Pig BPCD 5011 *As above, except Burdette does not sing; add Peter Bonta (o), Jim Gaines (prod).* 94.

** Wild Night Out!
Blind Pig BPCD 5021 *As for* Empty Arms Motel, *except add Zack Patterson (g), Jim Gaines (prod).* 11/94.

** Drive To Survive
Blind Pig BPCD 5035 *Thackery; Michael Patrick (b); Mark Stutso (d, v); Jim Gaines (prod).* 96.

*** Switching Gears
Blind Pig BPCD 5045 *Thackery; Joe McGlohon (s); Chubby Carrier (ac); Al Gamble (o, p); Lonnie Brooks, Joe Louis Walker (g, v); Michael Patrick (b); Mark Stutso (d, rb, tamb); Reba Russell (v); Jim Gaines (prod).* 98.

*** Sinner Street
Blind Pig BPCD 5065 *Thackery; Jimmy Carpenter (s, v); Ken Faltinson (kb, b, v); Mark Stutso (d, v); Reba Russell (v); Jim Gaines (prod).* 00.

*** Guitar
Blind Pig BPCD 5083 *Thackery; Jimmy Carpenter (s); Ken Faltinson (kb, b); Al Gamble (o); Duke Robillard (g); Wayne Burdette, Michael Patrick (b); Mark Stutso (d).* 92–00.

Thackery's music has simple but strong virtues: his guitar playing has bite, and when he sings he strikes no attitudes. It's not music that will root you to the spot in amazement, but it's honest workmanlike stuff. That estimate, however, is based on his best work, and it took a while for him to achieve it. At the beginning of his solo career he was evidently devoted to the trio format (extra musicians make only guest appearances), and it's questionable whether it best served his interests: his first four albums have many stretches of dullness which might have been relieved by the use of horns or keyboards. He's a fierce guitarist but he's no Stevie Ray Vaughan, and most of his original songs are undistinguished, while received ones like Bo Diddley's 'I Can Tell' (*Empty Arms Motel*), William Harris's 'Bullfrog [Blues]' or Albert Collins's 'Don't Lose Your Cool' (both on *Trouble Man*) undergo a drab rebuilding that turns them from eye-catching Modernist structures into Estonian office blocks.

For *Switching Gears*, Thackery reveals, 'the Piggies said this time maybe we should throw a party and invite some of your friends.' This was exactly the right move. Al Gamble's keyboards add valuable texture to the ensemble on most of the tracks, while the guests, though they appear on only one or two cuts each, are very effective; indeed, Brooks's reading of 'It's My Own Fault' and Walker's of his own 'If This Is Love' ('… I'd rather have the blues') are among the best tracks. Thackery himself sings and plays with a clarity that had often eluded him before, at least on record, and that improvement is maintained on *Sinner Street*, which also shows some sharpening of his pen as a songwriter.

Guitar is an instrumental showcase stocked from all the Blind Pig albums, with three previously unissued extras: 'Jump For Jerry' has a guest appearance by Duke Robillard, while Stevie Ray Vaughan's 'Rude Mood' (a longer version than the one on *Empty Arms Motel*) and 'Jimmy's Detroit Boogie' (à la Hooker) enclose 'Edward's Blues' in a bravura 20-minute sequence of Strat-picking from the gig where *Wild Night Out!* was recorded. ('Jerry' and 'Edward' are presumably Blind Pig honchos Jerry Del Giudice and Ed Chmelewski.) Ranging from sprightly jump tunes to the deep blues of 'Roy's Bluz' and 'Blues 'Fore Dawn', this selection shows very clearly where Thackery's guitar strengths lie.

*** We Got It
Telarc CD-83540 *Thackery; Jimmy Carpenter (s); Ernie Cate (kb, v); Ken Faltinson (o, p, b); Earl Cate (g, v); Mark Stutso (d, v); Reba Russell (v).* 10/01.

**(*) True Stories
Telarc CD-83572 *Thackery; Jimmy Carpenter (s); Ken Faltinson (o, b); Mark Stutso (d, v); Reba Russell (v).* 12/02.

** Healin' Ground
Telarc CD-83624 *Thackery; Jimmy Hall (h, v); Gary Nicholson (kb pad, prod); Kevin McKendree (o, p); Kenny Greenberg (g); Steve Mackey, Michael Rhodes (b); Lynn Williams, Tom Hambridge (d); Mark Stutso (v).* 11/04.

We Got It is a tribute to the guitarist Eddie Hinton (1944–95), celebrated member of the Muscle Shoals studio cadre, using eight of his compositions and three originals. Hinton's voice was once described as having more gravel than an Alabama back road, and Thackery roughs up his own accordingly, until on 'It's All Wrong But It's All Right' he almost sounds like the young Otis Redding. Curiously, in paying his respects to another musician he has made an album with more individuality than usual, and while some listeners may not respond to Hinton's material as warmly as Thackery does, those who do will be impressed by how he has immersed himself in the other man's music without drowning his own instincts.

Nine of the 11 titles on *True Stories* are originals by Thackery and, in some cases, his wife Sally. They arrange the building-blocks of blues and blues-like songs with seasoned competence and elicit assured performances from the four-piece band. The most explicitly bluesy numbers are 'Snakes In My Mailbox', a Robert Johnsonish line played on acoustic guitar with soothing tenor sax, and 'Too Tired' in the style of Albert King. The true stories told, Thackery gives Carpenter a run on Buddy Johnson's 'Crazy 'Bout A Saxophone', then reclaims the spotlight to play Roy Buchanan's 'The Messiah Will Come', a nine-minute guitar meditation, powerful in its way but an odd coda to an unpretentiously earthbound album.

The sophisticated production of *Healin' Ground* makes the simple settings of his early albums sound almost primitive, but Thackery has not advanced to this point without loss. Ignoring the lessons of *Switching Gears*, *Sinner Street* and *We Got It*, the album merely exchanges the clichés of the '90s for a different but equally vapid set of formulas, exemplified by the instrumental 'Kickin' Chicken', which has as much kickin' power as a football boot made of jelly. Thackery has also recorded with Tab Benoit (q.v.). TR

Sam Theard (1905–82)
VOCAL

Variously billed as 'The Mad Comic', 'Spo-De-O-Dee' and 'Lovin' Sam From Down In 'Bam', Theard was actually a New Orleanian. He recorded quite extensively, but was chiefly active as a comedian and actor; in the '30s and '40s he was a regular comic at the Apollo, and as late as 1976 he moved to Hollywood, where he found occasional TV and film work. Theard was also a songwriter of some note, composing 'You Rascal You' and co-authoring 'Let The Good Times Roll' with Louis Jordan.

**(*) Lovin' Sam Theard (1929–1936)
Document DOCD-5479 *Theard; poss. Walker Collins (t); unknowns (as); prob. Cow Cow Davenport, H. Benton Overstreet, John Oscar, Albert Ammons, unknowns (p); unknown (bj); Tampa Red (g); unknowns (b); Louis P. Banks, unknown (d). 4/29–5/36.*

** Jazzin' The Blues – Vol. 3 (1937–1941)
Document DOCD-5536 *Theard; unknown (t, hand-clapping, bird-wh, v); unknown (t); unknown (cl, ts); Darnell Howard (cl); Eustis Moore (as); unknown (ts); Tiny Parham (o); unknowns (p); John Henley, unknown (g); unknown (b); Bob Slaughter, unknowns (d); unknown (sp). 8/37–6/40.*

Some of Theard's recordings, including the first version of his hit, 'You Rascal You', are on Document CDs by Cow Cow Davenport and two sides are on *Kokomo Arnold – Vol. 3* (Document DOCD-5039). The eponymous CD mainly features hokum, and although Davenport, Overstreet and Tampa Red all supply quality accompaniment, the disc suffers from hokum's twin curses of repetition and juvenility. There are moments that stand out, among them Overstreet's fiery playing on 'Get It In Front', the occasional falsetto scatting and 'Three Sixes', an enigmatic dirty dozens variant, but Theard's singing lacks the verve of a Frankie Jaxon, or even of an Al Miller. The disc's last four titles are small-group swing, and on the final two Theard is supported by classy piano and trumpet. Theard's very best hokum numbers, 'I'm Crazy Bout My Bozo' and 'That New Kinda Stuff', with John Oscar and Joe McCoy both scintillating, are on the otherwise uninteresting VAC *Black And White Piano Vol. 1* (Document DOCD-5596).

Jazzin' The Blues – Vol. 3 offers 11 more tracks by Theard; neither his singing nor the small-group accompaniments have any great merit. The disc is completed by pleasant minor artists: Nora And Delle offer swingy harmony duets, Jean Brady covers Yack Taylor's cover of Lil Green, Jewell Paige is tunefully forgettable, and the Black Cats And The Kitten are notable mainly for a bubbly electric guitarist. CS

Little Al Thomas (born 1930)
VOCAL

Thomas grew up in the Maxwell Street area of Chicago, and in the '60s and '70s worked in the city's clubs as an opening act. Since the mid-'80s he has worked with 'Mot' Dutko's Crazy House Band.

**(*) South Side Story
AudioQuest AQ CD 1059 *Thomas; Paul Mundy (as); Dave Clark (ts); Van Kelly (bs); Bob Jacobs (o); Sidney James Wingfield (p); John Edelmann (g); T. Ed Galchick (b); Thomas 'Mot' Dutko (d). 99.*

*** In The House
Crosscut CCD 11068 *Thomas; Myron Harvey (as); Bill Voltz (ts); John Edelmann (g); T. Edward Galchick (b); Thomas 'Mot' Dutko (d). 11/00.*

Thomas was unnoticed outside Chicago until his debut album, *South Side Story*, and it didn't help much when the label, Cannonball, folded a year or two later. He greatly improved his standing in the blues world with *In The House*, a set of songs recorded at the Lucerne Blues Festival, and a couple of years later AudioQuest reissued the Cannonball. It's immediately clear from either album, but especially from *In The House*, where his voice seems to be in slightly better condition, that his model is B. B. King. He sings two of his numbers on *South Side Story* and three on *In The House*, including a long 'Sweet Sixteen', but many of the other songs are animated by the same inspiration, and the Crazy House musicians respond very much like the small bands on King's '50s records. A familiar ride, then, but Thomas chauffeurs with such skill and fervour that the journey is always pleasant, and when Edelmann solos it's like rolling the top down and feeling the wind in your hair. TR

Henry Thomas
VOCAL, GUITAR, PANPIPES

Born in Upshur County, Texas, in 1874, Thomas is thought to have spent his life as an itinerant musician. He is barely remembered as a person, but his songs have been refashioned by Bob Dylan and Canned Heat.

♛ **** Texas Worried Blues
Yazoo 1080/81 *Thomas. 10/27–10/29.*

**** Henry Thomas ('Ragtime Texas') (1927–1929)
Document DOCD-5665 *Thomas. 10/27–10/29.*

Flailing his guitar in now forgotten country dance rhythms, whistling delicate melodies on his panpipes, gruffly chanting rag songs and blues, Thomas is a figure almost of legend. Yet there exist almost two dozen recordings of him doing all that, making the legend flesh and blood and providing a wholly absorbing picture of back-country music before it was submerged beneath the tidal wave of the blues. There are blues here, such as 'Bull-Doze Blues', which inspired Canned Heat's 'Going Up The Country', and the intricate 'Texas Easy Street Blues', but Thomas's métier, about a third of his recorded repertoire, was up-tempo square-dance songs like 'Fishing Blues', 'The Fox And The Hounds' (a rare instance of this tune not played on harmonica) and 'Old Country Stomp'. Even more suggestive, to the listener interested in pre-blues Americana, are his patchwork pieces 'Bob McKinney' and 'Arkansas', free-form medleys of old-time songs and reels which memorialize a less racially fissured landscape of Southern music.

The two albums are identical in content, the Document arranging it in recording order and the Yazoo not, and there is little audible difference in transfer quality. The Yazoo, however, is enhanced by Stephen Calt's detailed notes. TR

Hociel Thomas (1904–52)
VOCAL, PIANO

Born in Houston, Hociel Thomas was singing in New Orleans by the age of 12, often alongside her aunt, Sippie Wallace. In 1924, Hociel moved to Chicago to be with her father, pianist, composer and publisher George W. Thomas. He supplied almost all the songs for her '20s recording sessions, and the piano on them was played by her uncle, Hersal Thomas, who was two years her junior. After Hersal's premature death in 1926, a grieving Hociel quit the music business. She recorded again 20 years later, and in 1948 sang with Kid Ory's band in San Francisco. In the late '40s, a fight with a sister left the sister dead and Hociel blind; acquitted of manslaughter, she died of heart disease not long afterwards.

(*) Texas Piano – Vol. 1 (1923–1935)
Document DOCD-5224 *Thomas; unknown (cl); Hersal Thomas, poss. unknown (p); unknown (vn).* 4–6/25.

Hociel Thomas is responsible for five tracks on *Texas Piano – Vol. 1*; for discussion of the rest, see Bernice Edwards. A singer with power but a limited range, Hociel is at her best on 'Worried Down With The Blues' and the swinging 'Fish Tail Dance', with characteristically inventive accompaniments from Hersal Thomas. Elsewhere she struggles to be heard over insensitive clarinet and violin, and a pianist whose generic playing suggests that he may not be Hersal.

** **Hociel Thomas/Lillie Delk Christian (1925–1928)**
Document DOCD-5448 *Thomas; Louis Armstrong (c); Johnny Dodds (cl); Hersal Thomas (p); Johnny St Cyr (bj).* 11/25–2/26.

This disc assembles the ten recordings by Hociel Thomas where Louis Armstrong is among the accompanists; on the first six of them all the musicians listed appear. The problem of Hociel's limited range is immediately apparent on 'Gambler's Dream' and 'Sunshine Baby', where she performs undistinguished songs in, and sometimes out of, an uncomfortable key. These ditties are both pop-blues and pop's blues, and duty to George W., rather than enthusiasm for the material, seems to be her motivation. Even Louis Armstrong can't do much with this sorry stuff, nor with the likes of 'Adam And Eve Had The Blues', where Hociel, being in a higher register, does a bit better. The remaining four songs benefit from being accompanied only by Louis and Hersal, and there is a beautiful low-register solo by the former on 'Listen To Ma'; it's a pity, therefore, that the lyric is sentimental doggerel, and that Hociel's singing is once more wooden and uncertainly pitched. She's similarly uninspired for the rest of this session, on which Armstrong and Hersal lavish more creativity than either the singing or the songs deserve.

The balance – indeed, with 15 songs, the bulk – of the disc is allocated to Lillie Delk Christian, described by *B&GR* as 'not really a blues singer, but … her records were apparently aimed at the blues market'. That's about the size of it; the selling point for latterday jazz and blues fans is the presence on most of her records of Louis Armstrong, Jimmy Noone and Earl Hines. Feminists rightly decry critical perspectives that belittle female singers in favour of their (usually) male accompanists – compare the title of the next CD in this entry – but it's hard to make that argument for the anaemically melodious Delk Christian.

***(*) Mutt Carey & Lee Collins**
American Music AMCD-72 *Thomas; Mutt Carey (t).* 8/46.

This CD is credited to its trumpeters, but the singers are Hociel Thomas and Bertha 'Chippie' Hill. Whatever the drawbacks of Thomas's early recordings, they motivated researchers to find her two decades later, living in Oakland and married to Arthur Tebo. Hociel Thomas at 44 was a very different proposition, most obviously because she played her own piano accompaniment, in a style similar to that of her friend from the Houston days, Bernice Edwards. She'd kept in practice as both singer and pianist, and for this session was able to pick her own material, and comfortable keys for it. The difference is astonishing, and most easily heard on the remake of 'Gambler's Dream', where both singer and song are transformed. Most of the playlist is deeply downhome, only 'Nobody Knows You When You Are Down And Out' being selected – but not performed – on autopilot. Hociel's singing now has both force and subtlety, with an occasional growling tone that gains impact from the restraint with which she unleashes it. On the instrumental 'Tebo's Texas Boogie', her left hand is muffled, probably by poor microphone placement, but this is an important recording of a theme from the Houston barrelhouses. It's also the only track on which Papa Mutt Carey's acidic trumpet is absent. Apart from an unfortunate moment when he plays across Thomas's vocal on 'Go Down Sunshine', Carey rightly confines himself to listening to what she's doing, and playing tactful responses. In truth, his presence is unnecessary, but it does no damage to a remarkable session that's both comeback and valediction. CS

James 'Son' Thomas (1926–93)
VOCAL, GUITAR

When not making music, Thomas lived a hard life in the Mississippi Delta, working as a sharecropper, and later a gravedigger. Discovered by folklorist William Ferris Jr in 1968, he toured extensively, even playing at the Reagan White House, but never managed to escape from poverty. Thomas was also a folk sculptor, specializing in clay heads and skulls of some power.

(*) Mississippi Delta Blues Man
Swingmaster CD 2204 *Thomas.* 5/81.
***(*) Beefsteak Blues**
Evidence ECD 26095 *Thomas; J. W. Williams (b); Cleveland 'Broom Man' Jones (broom b); Moses Rutues Jr (d).* 10/80–10/85.
***(*) James "Son" Thomas**
Bellaphon CDLR 82006 *As above.* 11/82–10/85.
***(*) Hard Times**
Black & Blue BB 440 *Thomas.* 3/86.

'Hard Times', included on both Swingmaster and Black & Blue, is a powerful song, strongly influenced by the minor-key blues of Bentonia. (Thomas's uncle, Joe Cooper, who taught him to play, had worked with Bentonia's Henry Stuckey.) As an original composition, it's very untypical of Thomas; most of his repertoire came from other musicians, and much of it via recordings. His steady guitar rhythms and dark voice, varied with occasional cutting falsettos, made him a popular musician at Leland jukes and house parties.

Mississippi Delta Blues Man, recorded during Thomas's first European visit, finds him in lacklustre form. The unamplified wooden guitar used throughout gives his music an incongruously refined air, making it more suitable for passive listening than participatory bopping. Swingmaster seem unable to generate much enthusiasm in Thomas, who sounds anxious to complete his quota of songs and be on his way.

Two tracks on *Beefsteak Blues* were recorded in Leland; the rest come from German concerts. Working in front of audiences, even ones culturally very distant from the Delta, results in engaged, hardworking performances, and switching between acoustic and electric instruments adds a welcome variety, but some tracks are cursed with clapping on (or sometimes nearly on) all four beats. Williams and Rutues feature on a 'Stormy Monday Blues' that holds no surprises; more compelling by far is Broom Man Jones, scraping out a growling rhythm on 'Rock Me Mama'. The Bellaphon CD is a reordered version of *Beefsteak Blues*, minus one track.

By 1986, Thomas had worked out how to invigorate his music when far from home and without an audience, and he sings with force and conviction throughout *Hard Times*; it helps, too, that his guitar is lightly amplified. He doesn't have the technique to play a convincing 'Steel Guitar Rag', which was rightly left off the original LP, but one must admire a musician who takes the trouble to work out a choppy new riff for 'Rollin' And Tumblin''. The airy serenity of 'Ethel Mae' owes a lot to Arthur Crudup's original, but Thomas makes this, and very much more familiar songs, his own. CS

Jesse Thomas (1911–95)
VOCAL, GUITAR

Born in Logansport, Louisiana, Thomas was the younger brother of Willard 'Ramblin'' Thomas. He became a musician early, recording for Victor when only 18. In 1937, Thomas relocated from Dallas to the West Coast, where he studied theory and sight reading, and worked as a pickup jazz and R&B guitarist. He had an intermittent but fairly extensive recording career postwar, briefly operating his own Club label until distribution problems sank it. In 1957, Thomas returned to Louisiana, and spent many years playing lounge music in Shreveport before hitting the festival circuit in the '80s; he also issued occasional singles, cassettes and CDs on Red River, again with limited distribution. (The Jesse Thomas on Easy In The Apple [Fedora FCD 5021] is a New Orleans R&B singer.)

*** **Ramblin' Thomas & The Dallas Blues Singers (1928–1932)**
Document DOCD-5107 Thomas. 8/29.

At 18, Jesse 'Babyface' Thomas was appropriately nicknamed, but he played with a command well beyond his years. Three of his four songs are indebted to Lonnie Johnson, alike for guitar style and for lyrics which effectively imitate both the acerbic and the sentimental Johnson. The Blind Blake-inspired 'Blue Goose Blues' is the session's undoubted high point, however. The CD is chiefly devoted to Ramblin' Thomas; Troy Ferguson's abominable 'Good Night' is accompanied by a different Jesse Thomas.

⚜ **** **Jesse Thomas (1948–1958)** [sic]
Document BDCD-6044 Thomas; prob. Sam Williams, Maxwell Davis, unknown (ts); Conrad Johnson (bs); unknowns (h); Lonnie Lyons, Lloyd Glenn, Willard McDaniel, unknowns (p); Louis 'Nunu' Pitts, Billy Hadnott, unknowns (b); Allison Tucker, Bob Harvey, Oscar Lee Bradley, unknowns (d); unknown (tamb); band (v). 48–57.

These 28 tracks were recorded for nine companies, with accompaniments ranging from solo guitar to a rocking R&B band to smoky tenor sax and rippling piano. The common denominators are Thomas's ringing guitar, his imaginative,

often optimistic lyrics, and his strong, almost strident voice. His playing is indebted to earlier Texan styles, but Thomas developed an unpredictable, energetic and harmonically advanced sound, in part by transferring saxophone solos and his own piano playing to electric guitar. The 11 solo items feature wonderfully well-integrated playing and singing, and the sides with tenor and a rhythm section are a generally successful blend of West Coast sophistication and downhome directness. Two songs recorded back in Shreveport are let down by an underpowered harmonica player.

*** **Blue Goose Blues**
IMP 704 Thomas; Paul Harrington (h); Dennis Cavalier (p); Steve James, Dan Garner (g); Chris Clark (b); Tyrone Starks (d). 8/29, 90s.

(*) **Blues Is A Feeling
Delmark DD-749 Thomas; Jodie Christian (p); John Primer (g). 6/92.

The Delmark session seems to have taken place without much preparation, but the musicians blend pretty well. There's not much adventurousness, though; 'Jesse, John & Jodie Jam' sticks to well-trodden paths, and some neat lyrics are offset by plonking commonplaces. At 81, and after several minor strokes, Thomas was a weaker singer, and his guitar work, although still tonally and rhythmically impeccable, was a good deal simpler. Slow-to-medium tempos predominate, and the initial impression of faded elegance is overridden by a lack of variety in the songs and their execution.

Blue Goose Blues got more production, and as a result is a better portrait of Thomas in old age. A new version of the title track is the first of nine band numbers; it's followed by four duets with Garner and three solos, the last of which is the original 'Blue Goose Blues'. In keeping with the eclecticism of Thomas's postwar recordings, the band is a polished piano trio – Cavalier has obviously listened closely to Lloyd Glenn's work with Thomas – successfully augmented with more earthy harmonica and slide guitar. As the musicians drop out, Thomas is more exposed and more obviously elderly, but experience and a gentle confidence carry him through a programme of remakes and newer compositions. CS

Kid Thomas (1934–70)
VOCAL, HARMONICA

Louis Thomas Watts was born in Sturgis, Mississippi, and grew up in Chicago, where he talked himself into recording for Federal in 1957. Two years later he moved to LA, and over the next decade recorded for several small labels there, usually as Tommy Louis or Lewis, having a little success with 'Rockin' This Joint Tonite'. He was shot by a man whose son he had killed in a road accident.

(*) **Chicago Blues From Federal Records
Ace CDCHD 717 Thomas; unknown (p); 'James', unknown (g); Little Willie Smith (d). 4/57.

(*) **Here's My Story
Wolf WBJCD 012 As above. 4/57.

Thomas's first recordings are a little cautious – note how he clings to the beat – and derivative – 'Here Is My Story' is told to the tune of Bo Diddley's 'I'm Grown' – but they have plenty of energy, and both singing and harmonica playing have a strong blues character. A couple of songs have whooping choruses, inspired by Howlin' Wolf. There are only minor differences between *Here's My Story* and Thomas's eight-track portion of the Ace VAC (which includes recordings by four other artists) but the latter was mastered from better source material.

**(*) Rockin' Harmonica Blues Men
Wolf WBJCD 018 *Thomas; unknown (ts); Marshall Hooks, unknowns (g); unknown (b); unknowns (d). 60–65.*

This CD, split more or less evenly between Thomas and Jerry McCain, contains ten sides cut by Thomas for small LA labels, most of them not issued at the time. 'Rockin' This Joint Tonite' is a frenetic rock 'n' roll number in the style of Little Richard, and 'Wail Baby Wail' somewhat similar, while other tracks are laidback blues performances such as 'You Are An Angel' (heard in two quite different versions) and a couple of convincing exercises in the Buddy Guy manner, 'Five Long Years' and 'The Hurt Is On'. With its variable recording quality and ugly presentation, this is a less than adequate memorial to an artist whose potential, though perhaps limited, was genuine and unfulfilled.

Six of Thomas's tracks can also be found on *Rockin' This Joint Tonite* (JSP JSPCD 2146), alongside recordings by Floyd Dixon, Ace Holder and Jimmy McCracklin. TR

Ramblin' Thomas (c. 1902–40s)
VOCAL, GUITAR

Little is known about Willard Thomas beyond his birth in Logansport, Louisiana, around 1902, his associations with Oscar 'Buddy' Woods in Shreveport and Blind Lemon Jefferson in Dallas, and their influences on his guitar style. A propensity for melancholia in his writing is occasionally leavened with mordant asides that suggest a dry sense of humour. Nothing is known of his subsequent life beyond an unconfirmed rumour that he died from TB in Memphis during the '40s.

***(*) Ramblin' Thomas & The Dallas Blues Singers (1928–1932)
Document DOCD-5107 *Thomas. c. 2/28–2/32.*

Thomas's entire repertoire came from three sessions, two for Paramount in 1928 and one for Victor four years later. Though limited in scope, his performances are impressively consistent, whether played with slide or fingers. The character of an itinerant man is maintained through song titles like 'Ramblin' Man', 'Poor Boy Blues' and 'Ramblin' Mind Blues', with the first containing the line 'one day and one night [is] the longest I stay in one place'. The other two titles, 'So Lonesome' and seven others have slide accompaniment played in a *rubato* manner that dances attendance on the vocal line. His other playing proceeds in a similarly elastic style, apart from 'Jig Head Blues' and 'Hard Dallas Blues', which appear to emulate Lonnie Johnson (unless it is Johnson himself), and 'No Baby Blues', where the overt influence is Jefferson. The man and his music are enigmatic and compelling.

The other Dallas blues singers of the CD's title are Jesse 'Babyface' Thomas, Sammy Hill and Otis Harris. Ramblin' Thomas's second Victor coupling, 'Ground Hog Blues No. 2'/'Little Old Mamma Blues', unavailable when the CD was compiled, was subsequently issued on *"Too Late, Too Late" – Vol. 2* (Document DOCD-5216) and on *Hard Dallas* (Catfish KATCD 173, deleted), which added an alternative take of the title song. NS

Rockin' Tabby Thomas (born 1929)
VOCAL, GUITAR, PIANO, KEYBOARDS

Ernest 'Tabby' Thomas, who is Chris Thomas King's father, made his first record in Mississippi in 1953 before joining J. D. Miller's roster in Crowley. 'Hoodoo Party' was a regional hit for Excello, and remains Thomas's best-known song. After Miller gave up on blues, Thomas started his own Blue Beat label and became a regular at the New Orleans Jazz & Heritage Festival. Since 1981, he has operated Tabby's Blues Box in Baton Rouge, moving to new premises in 2000 when the original club was demolished to make way for an overpass.

***(*) Greatest Hits Vol. 1
Blue Beat B 1801A *Thomas; unknown (tb); unknowns (ts); Lionel Torrence, unknown (bs); Lazy Lester, unknown (h); unknown (o); Katie Webster, unknowns (p); Rudolph Richard, unknowns (g); Sherman Webster, unknowns (b); unknowns (d); unknowns (v). 54–66.*

As the packaging fails to mention, this disc compiles recordings made for J. D. Miller (some not issued at the time) and a single issued on Thomas's own label. 'Hoodoo Party' is the most memorable track, but it's far from the only one; 'Ball Head Lena' and 'Glass Jar Blues', from Blue Beat, well deserve their wider exposure. This is a consistently good CD, once some slack is cut for 'He's Got The Whole World In His Hand'. Thomas's Excello material carries an obvious influence from New Orleans in the rhythms and the horn arrangements, and more specifically when he imitates Guitar Slim, or jumps on the 'Popeye' dance bandwagon. The tension between the Crescent City's comparative sophistication and the more earthy sounds of Baton Rouge makes for enjoyable listening.

(***) Swamp Man
Blue Beat BBR-2440 *Thomas; Whispering Smith (h); Stanley 'Buckwheat' Dural (p); Wilfred Moore (g); Wilbert Moore (b); Hebert Moore (d). 79.*

This comeback album successfully re-creates the sound of Thomas's Excello recordings, opening, inevitably, with a remade 'Hoodoo Party'. The musicians are grounded in the Louisiana blues idiom, Thomas has retained his energy and ability, and Buckwheat's piano is powerful and inventive. However, telltale clicks and crackles reveal that *Swamp Man* is dubbed from the LP *25 Years With The Blues*, originally released on Blues Unlimited; even disregarding the surface noise, the resulting CD sounds muffled and cramped.

**(*) Swamp Blues Man
B 5331 *Thomas; Milton Batiste (t); Elliot Callier, Greg Tardy (ts); Rickie Monie (kb, o); Mike Johnson (kb); Joseph Payton, (g, b); Wayne Bennett, Eugene Sinegal, Harry Sterling (g); Michael Vernable (b); Kenneth 'Afro' Williams, Alvin Jacques (d, perc). 11/93–2/94.*

**(*) Swamp Man Blues
Aim 1203 *As above. 11/93–2/94.*

Aim's almost unnoticeably retitled reissue is also a few tracks shorter. Some distinguished musicians play on these sessions, and Milton Batiste co-produced, but the results are usually disappointing. Rather than offering a balance of continuity and contrast, the instrumentation varies arbitrarily from track to track, the keyboardists produce odd and inappropriate sonorities, and the drummers often please themselves at the expense of the ensemble.

**** Louisiana Woman
Blue Beat BBR-1421 *Thomas; unknown (h); Henry Gray (o, p); unknown (g); unknown (b); unknown (d).* 90s.

**(*) Long Live The King Of The Swamp Blues
Blue Beat BBR-7208 *Thomas; Mississippi Slim (h); Tom Coerver (o, d); Bob Harbour (p, b); Henry Gray (p); John Lisi, Tab Benoit (g); Brian Evans (b); Carroll Thibodeaux (d).* 1/99.

Louisiana Woman was released after, but seems to have been recorded before, *Long Live The King Of The Swamp Blues*. Only nine tracks on the latter are by Tabby, the balance being a strong modern blues by Chris Thomas King, two good efforts by Tab Benoit and an embarrassment by John Lisi. Thomas's voice is showing its age, but the big drawback is Lisi's unidiomatic and intrusive second guitar, which converts Louisiana blues into generic nonentity. However, *Louisiana Woman* is an excellent set of old favourites from the '50s and '60s done the old way, with Henry Gray in electrifying form and an unremittingly swinging drummer. Thomas's solo piano accompaniment on 'Luberta' is tentative, and the astute reader will guess what 'Zulu Party' is, but overall this is a remarkably fine disc.

**(*) Blues From The Swamp
Blue Beat BBR-2450 *Thomas; Jay Gilmore (h); Randy Arlet (p); Rudolph Richard (g); unknown (b); Sam Hogan (d).* 03?

** Along The Blues Highway
Animated Music 302 066 510 *Thomas; Jay Gilmore (h); Sam Hogan (g, b); Rudolph Richard (g); Chuckie Cross (d).* 03.

Mostly recorded live at the Blues Box, *Blues From The Swamp* starts with an atonally mumbled version of Lightnin' Slim's 'Rooster Blues'. Even here, though, Thomas is supported by a classy band; Richard and Hogan are reliable veterans of the Baton Rouge scene, and the bassist doesn't deserve anonymity. Thomas's singing is much stronger on the rest of the disc, but the songs are not very memorable, and the monologue 'Blues Singers Prayer' [*sic*] truckles to white Deltamania with its references to Son House.

Along The Blues Highway (which presumably passes through the swamp) has nine live tracks from the Blues Box and a studio-recorded 'Little Old Juke Joint', which is also on *Blues From The Swamp*. That track is markedly superior to the live material, which suffers from Chuckie Cross being a lesser drummer than Hogan, and from Hogan being an unexceptional guitarist and bassist. The band have tuning problems on some tracks (the lead guitar intro to 'Nose Wide Open' is painful), and Thomas's vocal pitch is not always secure. The CD is rounded off with five lengthy, generic songs from Michigan singer and harmonicist Annette Taborn. CS

Butch Thompson (born 1943)
PIANO

Thompson, who is also a clarinettist, played in jazz bands in the Minneapolis–St Paul area from 1962; between 1974 and 1986 he appeared on Garrison Keillor's radio show A Prairie Home Companion. *He has toured extensively solo, with his trio and as a member of jazz and ragtime ensembles.*

**(*) Lincoln Avenue Blues
Daring CD 3019 *Thompson.* 5–7/95.
*** Lincoln Avenue Express
Daring CD 3027 *Thompson.* 7/96.

Thompson has made a number of solo CDs, often regionally themed; they include some blues alongside the jazz, stride and ragtime, but these two are almost entirely blues. You have to like a man who credits his piano tuners, and whose notes are entirely about his admiration for the discs' dedicatees (Jimmy Yancey on *Blues*, W. C. Handy for *Express*). Thompson's knowledge of his material, singing line and subtle dynamics are also admirable, and the recording quality matches the classy instruments he's playing. For all their charm and skill, though, these recitals have an air of the salon and the academy; that's not a problem with the elegance of Jelly Roll Morton and Fats Waller, but it does Pine Top Smith's 'Jump Steady Blues' and 'Boogie Woogie' (on *Blues*) no favours. *Express*, which is mostly vaudeville blues by Handy and others, is the more successful set, but its title track epitomizes the problem; it uses the unaccented 6/4 bass from Wesley Wallace's 'No. 29', but next to that evocation of hoboing on a swaying, hurtling freight train, it's just a display of technique. CS

Lil' Dave Thompson (born 1970)
VOCAL, GUITAR

The Mississippi-born Thompson began playing guitar as a boy, listening to records by Albert King and Little Milton. In his late teens he played with Roosevelt 'Booba' Barnes, and in 1996 received a W. C. Handy Award as Best New Talent.

**(*) C'mon Down To The Delta
JSP JSPCD 3701 *Thompson; Jamie Finegan (t); Bruce Feiner (ts, arr, prod); Robert Feiner (bs); Brian Charette (o, p); Mike Nunno (b); Jason Arnold (d); Mary Taylor (v).* 01.

Thompson's first album, *Little Dave And Big Love* (now deleted), was for Fat Possum, but he differed from the rest of that label's roster in coming from a more contemporary, and more conventional, musical background. In turn, *C'mon Down To The Delta* was, by his own admission, 'totally different from that old CD'. It's certainly more professional. Thompson has a light tenor voice and clear enunciation, and his guitar playing, of which there's almost a surfeit, is fluid and inventive. In the title song he remembers the clubs and musicians that helped to form him. Apart from the soulful 'We Can Make It' and 'My Baby Won't Change' and the George Bensonish instrumental 'Cuttin' Loose', the tracks are orthodox blues, their differences blurred by the similarity of their tempos and the proficiency of the musicians. That there's little innovation is beside the point: it's an accomplished exercise in brand packaging. NS

Joe Thompson (born 1918)
VOCAL, VIOLIN

Joe Thompson, his brother Nate (1916–97) and cousin Odell (1911–94) played for frolics around Mebane, North Carolina, from childhood until after World War II, when musical tastes

changed. Joe and Odell were encouraged to resume playing by folklorist Kip Lornell in the early '70s, and Joe has remained active since Odell's tragic death in a road accident.

**** Family Tradition
Rounder CD 2161 *Thompson; Bob Carlin (bj, g); Odell Thompson, Nate Thompson (bj, v); Clyde Davis, Scott Ainslie (g); Pam Davis (b). 3/88–2/98.*

Joe Thompson is one of the last African-American old-time fiddlers, and the last surviving musician of a family whose traditions stretch back to the mid 19th century. He has a strong, firm voice, and plays with the vigour and enthusiasm of a veteran dance musician. He fiddles with no little inventiveness, too, threading original paths through tunes as familiar as 'Soldier's Joy' and 'Old Joe Clark'. On most tracks he is accompanied by younger white musicians, usually playing guitar, banjo and bass. Historically, Southern stringband musicians of both races shared many techniques and tunes, and the accompanists are idiomatic and sympathetic, but the resulting music is often rather different from that made by Joe and Odell, with a smoother, more rolling rhythm. Still, on its own terms this is a very fine collection; if there's a downside, it's that Odell's exciting, choppy banjo only appears on three tracks, and only 'Ain't Gonna Rain No More' features his extraordinary, piercing voice, buzzing like a wasp against a window. (Nate Thompson also sings and plays on this track.) Odell (and Joe) can be heard at length on *Old Time Music From The North Carolina Piedmont* (Global Village C217), which is regrettably only available on cassette. CS

Sonny Thompson (1916–89)
VOCAL, PIANO

Thompson studied at the Chicago Conservatory of Music, but was diverted from the classical path by the music of Earl Hines and Art Tatum. As well as composing prolifically and recording under his own name and as a session musician, Thompson did A&R work for Miracle and later King, where he became A&R director in 1959. In later years he continued to do session work and occasionally appeared at festivals. Thompson was married to Lula Reed.

**(*) Volume 1 1946–1948 [sic]
Blue Moon BMCD 6024 *Thompson; Dick Davis (ts, sp); Eddie Chamblee (ts); Lefty Bates, Arvin Garrett (g); Eddie Calhoun, Leroy Morrison (b); Buddy Smith, Herman 'Red' Cooper (d); prob. Floyd Hunt (vb); Gladys Palmer, Browley Guy, Piney Brown (v). 46–47.*

*** Volume 2 1949–1951 [sic]
Blue Moon BMCD 6030 *Thompson; Floyd Jones, John Hunt, Henry Glover, Lee Z. Harper, unknown (t); Numa Moore (as, bs); Ernest Tanner, unknown (as); prob. Dick Davis, Eddie Chamblee, David Brooks, Gene Phipps, Frank Henderson, Harold Brooks, Robert Hadley, unknown (ts); Walter Hiles (bs); Leo Blevins, Abdood Majeed, Charles Edwins, Bill Shingler, Hurley Ramey, unknown (g); Curtis Ferguson, Walter Buchanan, Zain El Hussaini, Carl Pruitt, unknowns (b); Sonny Cole, Lloyd Cooper, Bill English, Harold Austin, unknowns (d); Jesse Edwards, Royal Brent, unknowns (v). 48–4/51.*

*** Volume 3 1951–1952
Blue Moon BMCD 6037 *Thompson; Dennis Brooks (as, ts); Robert Hadley, David Brooks (ts); Walter Hiles (bs); Hurley Ramey, Jimmy Shirley, Lord Westbrook, Bill Johnson (g); Carl Pruitt, Clifford McGray, Lloyd Trotman, Oscar Crummie (b); Harold Austin, Kelly Martin, Norman F. Johnson, Les Erskine, Bill English, Isaac Cole (d); Brother John Sellers, Lula Reed, unknowns (v). 4/51–10/52.*

***(*) Volume 4 1952–1954
Blue Moon BMCD 6044 *Thompson; Dennis Brooks (as, ts); Fred Clark (as); David Brooks (ts); Walter Hiles, Tommy Purkson (bs); Bill Johnson, Clarence Kenner (g); Oscar Crummie, Clarence Mack, Joe Williams, James Royal (b); Philip Thomas, Isaac Cole, Robert Boswell (d); Lula Reed, Rufus Jr [Rufus Beacham], Paul Tate (v); unknown woman (sp). 8/52–2/54.*

*** Mellow Blues 1947/1952
EPM Jazz Archives 16057 *Similar to above CDs. 47–10/52.*

***(*) The E.P. Collection
See For Miles SEECD 702 *Similar to above CDs, except Tommy Purkson also plays as; add King Curtis, Osborne Whitfield (ts), Thomas Palmer, Freddie Jordan, Lawrence Frazier (g), Albert Winston, Bill Willis (b), Philip Paul (d). 47–3/61.*

Two debutant piano solos on Blue Moon's first volume are homages to Art Tatum, let down by poor recording and some undisciplined execution. Thereafter Thompson settles into leading small jazz-blues groups. Eddie Chamblee's foggily sensual tenor sax and Arvin Garrett's stylish guitar are heavily featured on *Vol. 1*, but Thompson's intelligent, tightly integrated playing shouldn't be overlooked – unlike Browley Guy, drearily crooning 'Tears Follow My Dreams'. *Vol. 1* includes the hits 'Late Freight' and 'Long Gone', which prompted the recording of several more laidback two-part instrumentals.

Bigger horn sections and improved recording quality, which brings Thompson's right-hand cascades into much clearer focus, characterize *Vol. 2*. It's obvious that Thompson is working within a successful formula (mostly medium tempo and moody), but his arranging skills, the eloquent musicians at his disposal and the intermittent jump numbers are effective barriers against monotony. *Vol. 3* sees a reversion to smaller forces, with just one or two saxes. 'Down In The Dumps' and the two-part 'Mellow Blues' are perhaps Thompson's finest excursions in his trademark after-hours mode, and a four-minute 'Flying Home' supplies jet-propelled contrast. It's one of several tracks on the Blue Moon discs resurrected from the deleted *Jam Sonny Jam!* (Sequel NEM CD 900); the sultry guitar feature 'Kenner Cuts One' on *Vol. 4* is another.

Kenner's amplified and acoustic flatpicking is one of the highlights of *Vol. 4*, which is credited to 'Sonny Thompson/Lula Reed'. Half its tracks feature her vocals; four more are fronted by Rufus Beacham, a Charles Brownish smoothie. The heavy overlap with Reed's own CDs (see her entry) might be thought to confine *Vol. 4*'s appeal to completists, but ignore the duplications and it's highly enjoyable; Reed's vocals break up the instrumentals and vice versa, and Thompson the arranger continues to deploy his forces with great aplomb.

Nevertheless, Blue Moon's chronological completism has its drawbacks, exemplified on *Vol. 3* by two genteel gospel songs by Lula Reed and a saccharine male chorus. The selective *Mellow Blues* is worth seeking out as an alternative approach. EPM's 22 tracks conclude with Lula's greatest hits, 'Let's Call It A Day' and 'I'll Drown In My Tears', to the disquiet of the notewriter. One may disagree politely with that assessment and still observe that the notes are knowledgeable and authoritative. The music has the merits that have already been outlined, and the mastering is well done.

See For Miles's arbitrary selection process does no harm to an artist as consistent (and as apparently unconcerned to develop) as Thompson. Most of his and Lula's hits are included, but three two-parters are only represented by their second halves, and the 'Late Freight' has been cancelled. The E.P. Collection's last ten tracks are not on EPM; they include a notably bluesy reading of Mercer Ellington's 'Things Ain't What They Used To Be' (also on Blue Moon's fourth volume), and four Lula Reed vocals from 1961, which range from sensuous blues-balladry to soulful signifying. CS

Big Mama Thornton (1926–84)
VOCAL, HARMONICA, DRUMS

Born in Alabama, Willie Mae Thornton headed for Atlanta and show business at 14. She toured with revues until 1948, when she settled in Houston, joining Don Robey's Peacock roster; in 1957 she moved to California, where some of her Peacock recordings had been made. The #1 success of 'Hound Dog' was not repeated, but the Elvis Presley connection, and in later years 'Ball And Chain' and the Janis Joplin connection, ensured that she kept working, although she cut a sad figure in her last years, when poor health and alcoholism had reduced her from 300lb to 95.

(*) Big Mama Thornton 1950–1953
Classics 5088 *Thornton; Joe Scott, Don Johnson (t); George Washington (tb); unknowns (as); Bill Harvey, James Von Streeter, unknowns (ts); Fred Ford, unknowns (bs); Johnny Ace (p, v); Devonia Williams, unknowns (p); Pete Lewis, unknown (g); Albert Winston, unknowns (b); Leard Bell, unknowns (d); Johnny Otis (vb); unknowns (v). 50–53.*
*** A Proper Introduction To Big Mama Thornton**
Proper INTRO CD 2078 *As above, except add Burt Kendricks (g). 50–54.*
*** Hound Dog/The Peacock Recordings**
MCA MCAD-10668 *As above, except add unknowns (t), Pluma Davis (tb), Roy Gaines (g), Johnny Otis (d), unknown (claves), unknown (maracas). 51–57.*
*** The Original Hound Dog**
Ace CDCHD 940 *As above, except omit Johnny Ace. 51–57.*

First doesn't automatically mean best, but Big Mama's 'Hound Dog' is a pretty good record, not least for Pete Lewis's guitar part. Thornton was initially reluctant to use the growling delivery Leiber & Stoller wanted, and although it's not unique on her Peacock recordings, neither is it typical. She's at her best on slow blues, especially when taking her cue from Roy Brown's anguished psychodramas; her up-tempo numbers are seldom outstanding, but there's usually a decent, and sometimes a memorable, sax, piano or guitar solo.

Duplication among these compilations is very heavy. The Proper CD has the same content as the Classics disc, with the addition of 'Stop Hoppin' On Me' from 1954. A Proper Introduction has the more detailed annotation, and is thus the preferred choice for completists, but Ace and Peacock have better production values than either of the PD releases. Ace's 22 tracks, including the gritty 'Cotton Picking Blues', give it the edge over MCA's 18. Six tracks on Classics and Proper are not on (meaning not copied from) either of the legitimate discs; they include her debut 78, credited to the Harlem Stars.

After leaving Peacock, Thornton made singles for a number of small West Coast labels; they have not been much reissued, but 'Mercy', her finest recorded performance, is among five titles on *Don't Freeze On Me* (El Cerrito ECR 01005).

**** Big Mama Thornton – In Europe**
Arhoolie CD 9056 *Thornton; Walter Horton (h); Eddie Boyd (o, p); Buddy Guy, Fred McDowell (g); Jimmie Lee Robinson (b); Fred Below (d). 10/65.*
(*) Big Mama Thornton With The Muddy Waters Blues Band – 1966
Arhoolie CD 9043 *Thornton; James Cotton (h); Otis Spann (p); Muddy Waters, Samuel Lawhorn (g); Luther Johnson (b); Francis Clay (d). 4/66.*
***(*) Ball N' Chain**
Arhoolie CD 305 *As for above two CDs, except add Everett Minor (ts), Nathaniel Dove (p), Bee Houston (g), Curtis Tillman (b), Gus Wright (d). 10/65–1/68.*

Ball N' Chain, Big Mama's first digital release on Arhoolie, contains eight tracks from the session recorded during the 1965 AFBF tour, six with the Muddy Waters band and two 1968 tracks with her working band. One of the latter is Thornton's first issued recording of 'Ball N' Chain'; Janis Joplin learned the song from live performances and got there first, which once again didn't automatically mean best. Ball N' Chain evidently did well; it was followed, at intervals, by the other two CDs listed above.

The London material was quickly recorded, but the musicians had been backing Thornton on tour, everyone has fun and the results are excellent; the introspective 'My Heavy Load' and 'Chauffeur Blues', accompanied only by Fred McDowell, are much more than that. (McDowell also backs 'School Boy', which has its moments, but Thornton's extended riff on food is definitely not one of them.) 'Chauffeur Blues' is one of three previously unissued tracks (there are also two alternative takes and an interesting interview by Chris Strachwitz); happily, the new material is well worth having, and Thornton's first recording session aimed at white audiences remains her best.

There's obvious synergy between Big Mama and the Muddy Waters band: her vocals are potent and euphonious, and the musicians support her enthusiastically, but there are also shortcomings. Too many songs are in the same key, the engineering gives the band a bright, brittle sound (Otis Spann, of all people, often sounds tinkly), and Luther Johnson's bass is too busy. The band (and particularly Muddy) get carried away on 'Everything Gonna Be Alright', which turns into uncouth thrashing. This results from lack of rehearsal, whose effects are apparent elsewhere: glaringly so on an alternative take of 'Black Rat' and the chaotic two-harp instrumental 'Big Mama's Shuffle', which are among seven cuts passed over when the original LP appeared.

(***) The Way It Is
Mercury 558 550 *Thornton; Jay Hodges (ts); George Smith (h); J. D. Nicholson (p); Bee Houston (g); Flip Graham (b); unknown (d). 10/69.*

Thornton and (inevitably) the Hound Dogs, recorded live on Sunset Boulevard with a programme of competently performed blues standards, plus 'Wade In The Water' and 'Watermelon Man'. You-know-what was doubtless played on the night, but Mercury wisely leave it out. This would be a good account of a good night out but for the recording quality, which makes the band sound as if they're playing behind a safety curtain.

**(*) The Complete Vanguard Recordings
Vanguard 3VCD 175/77 3CD *Thornton; Bill Potter, Buddy Lucas (ts); George Smith (h); Paul Griffin (kb); J. D. Nicholson, Ernie Heyes (p); Bee Houston, Steve Wachsman, Cornell Dupree, Ronnie Miller (g); Bruce Sieverson, Wilbur Bascomb (b); Todd Nelson, Jimmy Johnson (d). 75.*

This set comprises the LPs *Jail*, *Sassy Mama* and *Big Mama Swings*, the last of which was unissued and forgotten until Vanguard set out to compile what had been intended to be a double CD.

Jail, recorded at a Washington prison and an Oregon reformatory, was following in the footsteps of Johnny Cash and B. B. King, and although it didn't emulate their sales it's worthwhile in musical as well as humanitarian terms. Big Mama and her band perform the usual songs with real enthusiasm, although 'Little Red Rooster' mistifies an exuberant version of 'Early One Morning'. Bill Potter's tough tenor is very noteworthy, not least because he finds new things to say on 'Hound Dog'. There's an abrupt decline, however, on the last two tracks: 'Sheriff O.E. & Me' is tentative country & western, and 'Oh Happy Day' is perfunctory.

The other discs feature an impressive lineup of New York session veterans, but they suffer from a lack of distinctive material, the overworked 'Catfish Blues' (mistitled 'Rolling Stone') aside. *Big Mama Swings* is the better of the two, with Lucas and Dupree stepping out in style over the funky grooves set up by the other musicians, but before long the monotonously medium tempos wear down both the musicians' and the listener's enthusiasm. On *Sassy Mama* there's very little brio in Thornton's singing, and none whatever in the accompaniments to a dull, and again uniformly medium-paced, set of songs.

*** Jail
Vanguard VCD 79351 *Thornton; Bill Potter (ts); George Smith (h); J. D. Nicholson (p); Bee Houston, Steve Wachsman (g); Bruce Sieverson (b); Todd Nelson (d). 75.*

** Sassy Mama
Vanguard VCD 79354 *Thornton; Buddy Lucas (ts); Paul Griffin (kb); Cornell Dupree, Ronnie Miller (g); Wilbur Bascomb (b); Jimmy Johnson (d). 75.*

The Complete Vanguard Recordings contains both these albums, and costs only a little more than either one of them; it's a better bargain, therefore, and also the only way to acquire *Big Mama Swings*. On the other hand, *Jail* is the only one of her Vanguard recordings that makes a claim on non-completists; were it available separately, *Big Mama Swings* would have been awarded **(*).

** The Rising Sun Collection: Big Mama Thornton
Just A Memory RSCD 0002 *Thornton; Big Moose Walker (p); Phil Guy, John Primer (g); J. W. Williams (b); Burt Robertson (d). 4/77.*

The band acquit themselves fairly honourably during these 45 minutes from a Montreal club, but they seem nervous of Big Mama, and play with quiet caution for much of the time. Thornton herself is doing the job one more time, dutifully but unenthusiastically. She tries to liven up the material with arbitrary dynamic changes, gospel-influenced codas and would-be salty comments to the audience, but her chief ambition seems to be to get back to the dressing room. cs

George Thorogood (born 1952)
VOCAL, GUITAR

Born in Wilmington, Delaware, Thorogood decided at the age of 18 to become a fulltime musician. Joined by drummer Jeff Simon he played his first gig as George Thorogood & The Destroyers at the University of Delaware in December 1973. Engagements in the Boston area brought them to the attention of Rounder Records, who issued their first album in 1976; it and its two successors met with a response far beyond the expectations of either band or label. In 1981 the band played 50 dates in 50 states in 50 consecutive nights. They subsequently played support to The Rolling Stones, signed with a major label, appeared at the 1985 LiveAid concert (with Albert Collins as a guest) and have continued to tour and record, with a virtually unchanged lineup, ever since.

*** George Thorogood & The Destroyers
Rounder CD 3013 *Thorogood; Ron Smith (g); Billy Blough (b); Jeff Simon (d). 76.*

*** Move It On Over
Rounder CD 3024 *As above, except add Uncle Meat Pennington (tamb, maracas); omit Smith. 78.*

*** I'm Wanted
Rounder CD 3045 *Thorogood; Hank Carter (s); Billy Blough (b); Jeff Simon (d). 80.*

*** Who Do You Love?
Rounder Heritage Series 11614 *As for above three CDs. 76–80.*

Even 30 years on you can hear why George Thorogood & The Destroyers — originally The *Delaware* Destroyers, a bar blues band with a small circle of admirers – caught the imagination of 20something America. Sure, the boy George was good-looking, vivacious and magnetic, but what really mattered was that the band played music that was the stuff of a hundred thousand fantasies: kick-ass blues with rock 'n' roll attitude, the familiar outlines of 12-bar stomps rippling with unexpected musculature – blues with the boring bits removed. Who wouldn't make music like this if they could?

There was no mystery about the origins of Thorogood's music: it was the rattling, slide-guitar-fronted sound of Elmore James ('Madison Blues', 'The Sky Is Crying', 'Baby Please Set A Date'), welded to the rhythm patterns of John Lee Hooker ('One Bourbon, One Scotch, One Beer', presented on the first album, preceded, as it would be in every subsequent recording, by the Hook's 'House Rent Boogie') and the tom-tom beats of Bo Diddley, whose 'Who Do You Love?', premiered on *Move It On Over*, became one of the band's signature numbers. Both that and another, previously unissued, live version from 1979 are heard, along with the other titles just mentioned, on the Rounder Heritage CD, a fair selection from the three original albums.

*** Bad To The Bone
EMI America 46083 *Thorogood; Hank Carter (s, v); Ian Stewart (kb); Billy Blough (b); Jeff Simon (d). 82.*

*** **Maverick**
EMI America 46084//BGO BGOCD 223 *Thorogood; Hank Carter (s, v); Billy Blough (b); Jeff Simon (d). 7/84.*

*** **Live**
EMI America 46329 *Thorogood; Hank Carter (s, perc); 'Sleeveless' Steve Chrismar (g); Billy Blough (b, v); Jeff Simon (d); H-Bomb Ferguson (maracas). 5/86.*

*** **Born To Be Bad**
EMI 46973//BGO BGOCD 224 *Thorogood; Hank Carter (s, v); Steve Chrismar (g); Billy Blough (b); Jeff Simon (d). 88.*

*** **Boogie People**
EMI 92514//BGO BGOCD 250 *As above. 11/90.*

*** **Haircut**
EMI 89529 *As above. 93.*

*** **Live: Let's Work Together**
EMI 31948//BGO BGOCD 508 *Thorogood; Hank Carter (s, kb, v); Johnny Johnson (p); Elvin Bishop (g); Billy Blough (b); Jeff Simon (d). 12/94.*

In 1982 Thorogood signed with EMI America. His departure from Rounder was amicable, and in musical terms hardly a departure at all. His first album under the new contract, *Bad To The Bone*, had songs by John Lee Hooker and Chuck Berry. Its studio successor, *Maverick*, added two more Berry songs and Hooker's 'Crawling King Snake' and rewired the Bo Diddley connection with a thumping 'Willie And The Hand Jive'. *Born To Be Bad* made further withdrawals from the accounts of Chuck Berry and Elmore James ('You Can't Catch Me' and 'Shake Your Money Maker' respectively) and opened a new one with Howlin' Wolf ('Highway 49', 'Smokestack Lightning'). Wolf, Hooker and Berry all recurred on *Boogie People*, which also added Muddy Waters ('Can't Be Satisfied') to the band's portfolio, and there was more Wolf on *Haircut*. The live albums, the first taped in Cincinnati, the second over three nights in St Louis and Atlanta, naturally repeat many of these gestures, magnified by the concert setting and by Thorogood's enthusiastic application of timeworn presentational hoopla: 'We're gonna do some funny things [*guitar snort*] … some dirty things [*guitar squeal*] … and some very *bad* things [*general guitar weirdness*] … and then we're gonna start to party.'

Additions to the original trio made little difference. Hank Carter's tenor sax playing is so rhythmic that it merges into the guitar lines; Chrismar's rhythm guitar thickens the texture, but it wasn't exactly lightweight before. Johnny Johnson and Elvin Bishop join the '94 live set for just the last couple of numbers.

All these are vibrant and exciting albums. In terms of stylistic development the Thorogood of, say, *Boogie People* is almost molecularly identical to the 14-years-younger man of *George Thorogood & The Destroyers*, but no one who'd spent much time listening to him would have expected anything else. In his own corner of the blues business, Thorogood had forged a distinctive and popular brand identity, and so far he'd seen no reason to tinker with it.

(*) **Half A Boy/Half A Man**
CMC 86270//SPV 085-2955 *Thorogood; Hank Carter (s, kb, g, v); Waddy Wachtel (g); Billy Blough (b); Jeff Simon (d, perc). 99.*

With songs from Willie Dixon, Chuck Berry and Fats Domino, *Half A Boy/Half A Man* seemed hardly likely to break the Thorogood mould. There are in fact a few features that set it apart from previous work, but they are not all to the album's advantage; there are too many unremarkable new songs, and the title track, with its fairground organ figure, was an awful choice.

*** **Live In '99**
CMC 86280//SPV 085-2973 *As above, except Carter does not play g; add Jim Suhler (g). 6/99.*

Thorogood has always been at his best on record when caught in performance, and there are passages of this concert from the Fox Theater in St Louis that are as exciting as anything he has done. The recording mix throws everything at the listener in an avalanche of sound, sometimes half burying Thorogood's glinting slide guitar under Carter's hoarse tenor sax solos, but this only enhances the relentless drive of 'Who Do You Love' or Hank Williams's 'Move It On Over', another repertoire item that goes all the way back to the '70s. It's a cocky, testosterone-drenched show that frequently teeters on the edge of Spinal Tap self-parody ('Is everybody haaappy?' Roar. 'Mission accomplished!'), and the rollercoastering 'Be Bop Grandma' and 'You Talk Too Much' are as guyish as week-old socks, but perhaps this macho strut is just George toying with us.

**** **Anthology**
EMI/Capitol 27573 2CD *Thorogood; Hank Carter (s, kb, v); Johnny Johnson (p); Steve Chrismar, Elvin Bishop, Waddy Wachtel (g); Ron Smith (g); Billy Blough (b); Jeff Simon (d). 76–99.*

The story so far: 30 tracks from across the years, starting with half a dozen from Rounder, then two, three or four cuts from each of the EMI albums, ending with 'I Don't Trust Nobody' From *Half A Boy/Half A Man*. Many of the songs singled out above make the pick (if sometimes in different versions), and a swatch of repertoire from Chuck, Bo, Elmore, Hooker and Wolf ensures that the blues content in Thorogood's recorded work is kept front and centre. Hound Dog Taylor's 'Christine' is taken from a promotional disc and hasn't been generally available before. A first-rate introduction to the Peter Pan of the blues.

(***) **The Baddest Of**
Capitol 97718 *Similar to above. 76–93.*

(*(*))** **Greatest Hits: 30 Years Of Rock**
Capitol 74889 *Similar to above. 76–97.*

Baddest is a meagre selection from the Rounder and EMI albums and nine of its dozen tracks are on *Anthology*. *Greatest Hits* is a little more generous to the punter, but 11 of its 16 tracks are on *Anthology* too (and eight of *those* on *Baddest*) and the only noteworthy extras are an alternative take of 'Rockin' My Life Away' and a remix of 'Who Do You Love?' With the admirable *Anthology* still in catalogue, you might wonder what appeal *Greatest Hits* could possibly have to any but the most thoroughgoing of Thorogood fans, but it went to the top of the *Billboard* blues chart just the same. TR

Andrew Tibbs (1929–91)
VOCAL

Melvin Grayson was born in Columbus, Ohio, and moved to Chicago with his family in the late '30s. After attending DuSable High School he began singing in local clubs, using the

professional name 'Andrew Tibbs'. Spotted at the Macombo by its owners, the Chess brothers, he was signed to their new Aristocrat label in 1947 and recorded one of its first releases, 'Bilbo Is Dead'/'Union Man Blues'. Though little was heard of him after the '50s, he continued to sing at private functions for many years.

**(*) Andrew Tibbs 1947–1951
Classics 5028 *Tibbs; Pee Wee Jackson (t); unknowns (brass); Andrew 'Goon' Gardner (as); Dave Young, Tom Archia, Oett 'Sax' Mallard, prob. David Van Dyke (ts); Teddy Conyers (bs); unknowns (reeds); Rudy Martin, Christine Chapman, Buddy Johnson, unknowns (p); Leo Blevins, poss. Jimmy Jackson (g); Bill Settles, Leroy Jackson, unknowns (b); Curtis Walker, Wes Landers, unknowns (d); The Dozier Boys (v). c. 8/47–51.*

Tibbs has a small but secure place in blues history for his straight-faced obituary of Theodore Bilbo, segregationist Governor of Mississippi, and its differently topical flipside. If the records he made later were never quite so interesting, they were always competently written and sung and often left room for big, bold tenor sax solos. One feels like saying that Tibbs was an outrageous Roy Brown imitator, but Brown's first significant recordings were made only a few weeks before Tibbs's, so it might be more circumspect to conclude that the Chicago artist arrived at his florid delivery independently. On the other hand, it isn't by chance that the coda of 'You Can't Win' echoes Brown's 'Hard Luck Blues'. However he came by his style, Tibbs had it well under control and, if it wasn't for his big score of more or less similar slow blues, both he and this record might be more highly rated. TR

Eddie Tigner (born 1926)
VOCAL, ORGAN, PIANO

Eddie Tigner from Atlanta learned piano in the Army in 1945. He played vibraphone in the Maroon Notes, and worked with Elmore James in the early '50s, but he also spent 30 years with a version of the Ink Spots. Lately, he has performed in Atlanta clubs and at festivals.

*** Route 66
Music Maker MMCD 16 *Tigner; Paul Linden (h, p); Felix Reyes, Doug 'Little Brother' Jones (g); Matt Sickles, John Weyland (b); Ron Logsdon, Steve Hawkins (d); Larry Bowie (perc, v); Donnie McCormick, Chris Light (v). 00?*

Tigner's bag is undemanding entertainment rather than personal expression. Evenly split between piano and organ, the 12 tracks on *Route 66* are (save for a generic 'Stompin' With Eddie') standards of the blues and jazz-blues repertoire. Influenced both vocally and pianistically by Nat 'King' Cole, Tigner usually handles his material with assurance, although 'Help Me Make It Through The Night' is terribly mannered, and he flirts with vocal atonality on 'Straighten Up And Fly Right'. Sympathetic electric guitar support does a good deal to boost the bluesiness, and Paul Linden plays fine, jazzy harmonica; only occasionally is it obvious that he's there in lieu of a brass section. This is a pleasant album, which never aspires to be anything more; 'Stormy Monday' and 'Goin' Down Slow', both taken at cheerful medium tempos with punchy organ backing, epitomize the lack of any impetus towards emotion or introspection. CS

Terry Timmons (1927–70)
VOCAL

Timmons grew up in Cleveland, where she was spotted at the Café Tia Juana by Paul Gayten, who briefly hired her. Moving to Chicago, she was taken to Premium by her boyfriend, Memphis Slim, with whose band she was featuring. Premium sold her contract to RCA Victor, who let her go after two years. Timmons fades from view after a final, unissued session for United, allegedly ruined by the bass playing of new love Al Smith.

*** Terry Timmons 1950–1953
Classics 5092 *Timmons; Dick Vance, Taft Jordan, Nat Gusasak, unknowns (t); Claude Jones, Henderson Chambers, Theodore Kelly, George Matthews (tb); unknowns (as); Neil Green, Charles Ferguson, Purcell Brockenborough, unknowns (ts); unknowns (bs); Reuben Phillips, Joe Thomas, Budd Johnson, Willard Brown, Eddie Barefield, Buddy Tate, Stanley Webb, George Berg, Artie Drellinger, (s); Memphis Slim (p, v); Bob Call, George Rhodes, Howard Biggs, Bill Doggett unknown (p); René Hall, James Shirley, Matt Murphy, unknown (g); Henry Taylor, Ransom Knowling, Abie Baker, unknowns (b); Otho Allen, Oscar Larkin, Jimmy Crawford, Charlie Smith, unknowns (d); unknown (harp); band (v). 50–1/53.*

Although she didn't go in for covers of her records, Timmons was a faithful imitator of Dinah Washington, usually at the popular end of Washington's range; it's a reminder of the arbitrariness of definitions that Timmons, familiar mainly by association with Memphis Slim, gets pigeonholed as a blues singer. Listen to her duetting with Slim on one of his CDs, and she sounds out of place; listen to their five duets on Classics' not quite complete Timmons collection, and it's Slim who seems not to belong. However mutually enjoyable their affair, their voices were not very compatible, and these are the disc's least successful tracks. Timmons solo concentrates on lush, azure-tinted ballads, but from time to time she diversifies into lowdown blues, among which the salty 'Mr. Low Love' and the hoodoo-themed 'Evil Eyed Woman' are standouts. There are some distinguished musicians in the studio bands, and numerous good solos emerge, sometimes from unpromising material; hear, for instance, the anonymous tenorist on 'What You Bet'. Notwithstanding their derivativeness, most of Timmons's records are expertly arranged, played and sung, and worth the attention of listeners who forage in the borderlands where jazz, blues and pop meet. CS

Too Slim & The Taildraggers
GROUP

Tim 'Too Slim' Langford, Tom 'The Stomp' Brimm and John 'Midnight' Cage are one of the most popular blues bands in the Pacific Northwest. Based in Spokane, Washington, the band was formed in 1986, made its first album in 1988 and joined the Burnside roster in 1990.

** Rock Em Dead
Burnside BCD-0003 *Tim 'Too Slim' Langford (g, v); Tom 'The Stomp' Brimm (b); John 'Midnight' Cage (d). 90.*
** El Rauncho Grundgé
Burnside BCD-0011 *As above, except add Ron Thompson (p), Little Charlie Baty (g). 92.*

(*) Wanted … Live!
Burnside BCD-0016 *As for Rock Em Dead.* 7/93, 1/94.
(*) Swamp Opera
Burnside BCD-0021 *As above, except add Charlie Musselwhite, Little Charlie (h), Frank Ruffolo (ac), Jimmy Pugh (o).* 5/94.
(*) Blues For EB
Burnside BCD-0028 *Chris Mercer (s); Tim 'Too Slim' Langford (h, g, v); Curtis Salgado (h, v); John Hodgekins (h); Frank Ruffolo (ac); Peter Boe (o, p); D. K. Stewart (p); Tom 'The Stomp' Brimm (b); John 'Midnight' Cage (d, cga, v); Alex Sierra, Terry Currier (v).* 97?
** **King Size Troublemakers**
Burnside BCD 0041 *As for Rock Em Dead, except Cage also plays perc; add Mark Hummel (h), Dave Cebert (p), Sam 'Lightnin'' Hopkins (g).* 00?

This noisy, unrefined power trio works mainly in the Chicago blues idiom, with now and then a burst of rockabilly. Their own material, which predominates on all their CDs, is mostly unmemorable and tends to be shown up by better-class repertoire like Otis Rush's 'Double Trouble' (*Rock Em Dead*) and 'So Many Roads, So Many Trains' (*Wanted … Live!*), Eddie Taylor's 'Bad Boy' (*Blues For EB*, sung by Curtis Salgado) or the two Howlin' Wolf numbers on *Wanted … Live!* El Rauncho Grundgé stands a little apart from the others with its higher proportion of rockabilly tunes, such as the twangy instrumentals 'Sonic Boom' and the title track. *Wanted … Live!* offers new versions of seven of the ten tracks on *El Rauncho Grundgé* and of 'Rumble' from *Rock Em Dead*. Eschewing such good-ol'-boy jollity, *Swamp Opera* gives Langford a chance to shake his guitar credentials in the listener's face, as he echoes Hound Dog Taylor ('Carryin' On') and Chuck Berry ('Girl Trouble') and finds a groove somewhat resembling Stevie Ray Vaughan's 'Lenny' in 'Drinkin' Rye'. The larger castlist on *Blues For EB* gives it diversity, which for some readers may make it an attractive entry-point. Those who want a more typical set should start with *Swamp Opera* or *Wanted … Live!* TR

Henry Townsend (born 1909)
VOCAL, GUITAR, PIANO, HARPSICHORD

Though born in Mississippi, Townsend grew up near Cairo, Illinois, and in St Louis, where he began playing guitar in his teens for parties and on the streets. He recorded for several labels in the '20s and '30s, both in his own name and accompanying artists such as Big Joe Williams, Sonny Boy Williamson I and his friend Walter Davis, with whom he was still working into the '50s. He is the only blues musician to have recorded in every decade from the '20s to the '90s. In recent years he has been a member of the Delta Blues Cartel.

**** St. Louis Country Blues (1929–1937)
Document DOCD-5147 *Townsend; Sonny Boy Williamson I (h); Roosevelt Sykes, unknown (p); Robert Lee McCoy (g).* 11/29–11/37.
*** St. Louis Blues
Wolf WSE 110 *As above.* 11/29–11/37.

When he made his first recordings Townsend was barely 20, yet he had created a highly personal approach which, as it proved, would serve most of his creative needs for the rest of his life. The melancholic burden of themes like 'Mistreated Blues' and 'Poor Man Blues' was carried by insistent guitar strumming, punctuated with string-snapping and a variety of left-hand techniques. It was not a style that fell into his hands out of a clear blue sky: there are connections with Charley Jordan, and even more with the obscure Henry Spaulding, whose 'Cairo Blues' and 'Biddle Street Blues', his only recordings, were made just a few months earlier. What stamped Townsend's work in youth was his unfeigned pessimism. 'You're havin' a good time now, you're like the flower that comes in May,' he observes in 'She Got A Mean Disposition'. 'You havin' your time now, but you got to die some day.' And later, 'Why can't I be happy, people, like everybody else? I just sit around and I worry, I worry my fool self to death.' In later years he would look at the world less bleakly and find some comfort in a phlegmatic reasonableness.

In the '30s, prohibited by changing fashions in blues accompaniment from recording with just his guitar, Townsend made several sides with Roosevelt Sykes, including the uncharacteristically upbeat 'She's Got What I Want' and 'My Sweet Candy', and some in a quartet with Sonny Boy Williamson I, a setting that robbed his music of its rhythmic vitality and cut him down to the sort of generic bluesman that on his own he would never have resembled.

This frustrating legacy is assembled on the Document CD, lacking, since it hadn't then been discovered, the Paramount coupling 'Doctor, Oh Doctor'/'Jack Of Diamonds Georgia Rub' (later included on *"Too Late, Too Late"* – Vol. 5 [Document DOCD-5411]) but augmented by Henry Spaulding's two recordings. The Wolf omits the Paramounts and a Victor coupling, adding Spaulding and eight early sides by Charley Jordan. The remastering is mediocre on both CDs.

*** Cairo Blues
Genes GCD 9916 *Townsend; Andrew Cauthen (h); Henry Brown (p); Mike Stewart (g); Vernell Townsend (v).* 9/69–4/74.

Though Townsend in his early 60s was still an exceptional singer and guitarist, capable of making a perfectly sound album on his own, we are lucky that he made this one in collaboration with Mike Stewart, whose second-guitar parts are unfailingly appropriate and give the proceedings a great lift. The songs are mostly Townsend's – all, according to the notes, but 'Buzz, Buzz, Buzz' is Memphis Minnie's 'Bumble Bee', and 'Cairo Blues' and 'Biddle Street Blues' we have already met – and mostly at slow tempos, though the vitality of the guitar duetting prevents them becoming sedate. On 'Deep Morgan Stomp' Townsend and Henry Brown remember old days in St Louis; Townsend himself plays two piano numbers, but the poor quality of the instrument prevents one wishing for more.

**** Mule
Nighthawk NHCD-202 *Townsend; Yank Rachell (md, g); Norman Merritt (g); Vernell Townsend (v).* c. 79.

Mule offers the exceptional sight of a musician well advanced in his career making a decisive change in the presentation of his music. He had played piano for years before this, originally as a second instrument; here he uses it on ten of the 13 tracks. The album is true to its provenance, the work of a St Louis man who listened carefully to his contemporaries and fellow townsmen Roosevelt Sykes and Walter Davis. On slow blues Townsend's playing resembles Davis's quite strikingly, though the songs do not meander as Davis's sometimes do. Nor do they strut with Sykes's wide-boy confidence, for Townsend adopts neither the stride tendencies of Sykes's left hand nor the audacious flourishes of his right. In short, Townsend's style is a judicious compromise of the clipped and the effusive, and an apt shadow of his sturdy, contemplative lyric stance. Vernell Townsend sings on two tracks, and Yank Rachell plays mandolin or guitar on three – appropriate and decorative contributions, yet they leave little impression on a record firmly stamped with its maker's personality.

*** The Real St. Louis Blues
Arcola A CD 1002 *Townsend; Bob West (g).* 8/79.
*** Harmonica Blues
Arcola A CD 1003 *Townsend; Big Al Calhoun (h); Vernell Townsend (v).* 8/79.
*** St. Louis Blues
Wolf 120.495 *Townsend; Vernell Townsend (v).* 11/80.
**(*) St. Louis Blues Ace
Swingmaster CD 2202 *Townsend.* 8/81, 3/83, 11/87.

It's worth stressing, because the phenomenon is rare, that the music of Townsend's later life is virtually all his own: for almost every album he produces a dozen or more new compositions – and they are genuinely that, not reshufflings of commonplaces. If he borrows an image, it's usually to reframe it, as when he sings 'Get my mojo working – gonna wave it up in your face' ('What Tomorrow Brings' on *St. Louis Blues*). Blues standards scarcely figure in his work at all. Fleeting echoes of Clifford Gibson or Roosevelt Sykes are merely cordial nods to figures from a past which he is happy to recall but has no wish to live in.

On *The Real St. Louis Blues* he divides his attention evenly between guitar (both acoustic and electric) and piano, the latter a fine concert grand made available by a local piano store. On guitar he no longer plays with the urgency of his youth, but tracks like 'Pleasin' Myself' and 'I've Got To Go' ring with his distinctive timbre. West, who organized and recorded the sessions, plays second guitar on two tracks. The piano songs frequently prompt recollections of Walter Davis ('Sad Story', 'Let Her Go'), while in 'My Babe' he dredged from his memory an old 'Stump' Johnson piece. Before leaving the piano store he sat down on another stool and recorded 'Going Back Home' on harpsichord.

Harmonica Blues is nominally by the harmonica player Big Al Calhoun, who plays throughout it (see his entry), but half the vocals are by the Townsends, three each by Henry and Vernell and one duet. The ghost of Walter Davis, seldom absent from Townsend's later-life sessions, would have smiled to hear the cadences of Henry's 'Love Was In Our Hearts', and more broadly as Vernell delivered 'Tears Come Rollin' Down'.

The Wolf and Swingmaster CDs reverse the trend of *Mule* and *The Real St. Louis Blues* by focusing on Townsend as guitarist; the Wolf further separates itself by including other artists' songs, 'Cairo Blues' and Big Joe Williams's 'Baby Please Don't Go', as well as versions of pieces that Townsend did not originate, though he may have contributed to their forming, like 'Sloppy Drunk' and 'M&O'. The latter is one of three piano pieces; the others are 'Going Back Home' again and 'Going Down Slow', sung by Vernell. Townsend is in good form on these recordings, made in Austria partly in a studio and partly in concert.

Although there are passages on *St. Louis Blues Ace* that could have been played by no one but Townsend, there are signs that the distinctiveness of his approach is beginning to fade, and one regrets that the piano segment consists of only four tracks, particularly since 'Night Is Falling' and 'The Cut Back Blues' are among the album's highlights.

*** My Story
APO APO 2014 *Townsend; Ron Edwards, Jimmy D. Lane (g); Sho Komiya (b).* 10/99.

It is a dozen years since the latest recordings on *St. Louis Blues Ace*, yet Townsend seems hardly to have aged. When playing guitar his fingers move less decisively than they used to, which probably explains why his friend Ron Edwards is on hand on most of the tracks, but he still has plenty of facility on piano, which he uses on eight of the dozen pieces. His singing is quiet and confiding, but it has always had those qualities, and it retains its power to grip the listener when he muses, compassionately but unsentimentally, on the passage of his life. 'My baby asks me, "Honey, why do you sing these songs?" I say, "Darling, I've been asked to take these pills all my whole life long."' TR

Tré (born c. 1958)
VOCAL, GUITAR

Tré Hardiman declines to reveal his date of birth; the estimate here is based on internal evidence in CD notes. Hardiman is the son of L. V. Banks; born in Mississippi, he was raised in Chicago by his maternal grandparents, only encountering his father again in the mid-'70s. He was Banks's rhythm guitarist from 1981 to 1987.

**(*) Blues Knock'n Baby
Wolf 120.888 *Tré; unknown (kb); Wayne Zokal (g); 'Stu' (b); Briant Taylor (d); band (v).* mid-90s.

Acknowledging that playing mainly familiar tunes for mainly white audiences at Kingston Mines is a living and a way to gain exposure, Tré also insists that blues is the core music of black culture, and is determined to 'to bring the blues back to the people and make them realize this is what we got'. He's also firm about the need not to 'take it like Buddy Guy, too far into rock', and his clean, shiny lead guitar lines are *Blues Knock'n Baby*'s most attractive aspect – more appealing, certainly, than the often crashingly unsubtle drumming. The disc opens strongly with the ballad 'Heart And Soul' and a clever migration blues, 'From The Country To The City', but their standard is not maintained on the songs (all originals) which follow. Ironically in view of Tré's self-imposed mission, three lyrics about the power of the blues are the disc's most vapid and clichéd. Tré's deleted debut CD (JSP JSPCD 265) was called *Delivered For Glory – Reclaiming The Blues*; the evidence so far suggests that while glory is probably out of reach, the potential for significant achievement is there. CS

Dan Treanor & Frankie Lee
DUET

As well as fronting his own bands, the Texan Frankie Lee (born 1941) has sung with Ike Turner, Albert Collins and Johnny 'Guitar' Watson; he made three highly collectable 45s in the '60s. The main instrument of Dan Treanor (born 1947) is harmonica, which he began playing while serving in Vietnam;

he makes diddley bows and African instruments, and has worked as a sideman in numerous bands, and in music education.

*** African Wind
NorthernBlues NBM 0023 *Treanor (h, kb, g, b, diddley bow, ngoni, khalam, cane flute, prog); Lee (v); Tony Arceneaux (fl); Sammy Mayfield (g, v); David Henderson (g); R. D. Jones (b); Gary Flori (d, snare d, cga, djembe, tablas, surdo, shakers); Tom Quinn (d); Ruben Flores (perc); Erica Brown, Peggy Brown, David Booker (v).* c. 1/04.

Frankie Lee's own CDs are on the soul side of the soul–blues line, but interested readers should investigate *The Ladies And The Babies* (Hightone HMG 5501) and *Going Back Home* (Blind Pig BPCD 5013). On *African Wind*, singing 14 lyrics by Treanor and one adaptation of a Tommy Johnson song, he's definitely on the blues side. His voice, a hoarsely fierce but flexible instrument, is reminiscent of Otis Redding at times. Despite the project's title and underlying ideas, the music seldom has much of an African coloration; percussion apart, the exotic (in blues terms) instruments are usually submerged in a relatively conventional electric blues band. Predictably, the African sonorities are most prominent on the title track and 'The Groit [*sic* 'Griot] Man'; they recall similar romantic efforts by Taj Mahal, not least in being airy-fairy and platitudinous. This is not typical of Treanor's songwriting, it should be said; he's an idiomatic and original lyricist, who usually gives Lee plenty to get his teeth into. CS

Walter Trout (born 1951)
VOCAL, GUITAR, HARMONICA, MANDOLIN

Trout was born in Atlantic City, New Jersey, and began playing in public at 16. In the mid-'70s he moved to the West Coast and formed a band to play his own songs, but was repeatedly invited to join other bands as lead guitarist and had spells in Canned Heat (1979–84) and John Mayall's Bluesbreakers (1984–89). Leaving Mayall, he formed the Walter Trout Band, which first gained recognition in Denmark. During the '90s he built up a formidable reputation in Europe, which he has since extended to his home country.

**(*) Life In The Jungle
Provogue PRD 7020 *Trout; Dan Abrams (o, p); Jim Trapp (b); Leroy Larson (d).* 6–7/89.

** Prisoner Of A Dream
Provogue PRD 7026 *Trout; Ole Hansen (t); Kjeld Ipsen (tb); Bob Ricketts, Jens Haack Olesen (s); Daniel 'Mongo' Abrams (o, p); Jimmy Trapp (b); Klass Anderhell (d); Jacob Andersen (perc); Michael Elo, Lise Dandernell, Big Ed Bar (v).* 90.

** Live (No More Fish Jokes)
Provogue PRD 7051 *Trout; Mungo [Daniel Abrams] (kb); Jimmy Trapp (b); Frank Cotinola, Bernard Pershey (d).* 91–92.

** Transition
Provogue PRD 7044 *Trout; Daniel 'Mongo' Abrams (kb); Jimmy Trapp (b); Bernard Pershey (d).* 92.

*(*) Breaking The Rules
Provogue PRD 7076 *Trout; Martin Gerschwitz (kb, vn); Jimmy Trapp (b); Bernard Pershey (d, perc).* 1–2/95.

** Positively Beale Street//Walter Trout
Provogue PRD 7104//Ruf 1058//(A) 1349 *Trout; Martin Gerschwitz (kb); Jimmy Trapp (b); Charles 'Rick' Elliott (d); William Brown, Bertram Brown, Tricia Freeman, Wally Bass (v); Jim Gaines (prod).* 2–3/97.

** Livin' Every Day
Ruf 1035 *Trout; Scott Thompson (t); Jim Spake (s); Paul Kallestad (o); Ernest Williamson (p); James Trapp (b); Bernard Pershey (d, perc); Jackie Johnson, William Brown, Bertram Brown, Wally Bass (v); Jim Gaines (prod).* 2/99.

*** Face The Music (Live On Tour)
Provogue PRD 7121 *Trout; Paul Kallestad (o); James Trapp (b); Bernard Pershey (d, perc).* 99.

*** Live Trout
Ruf 1051 2CD *Trout; Paul Kallestad (o); James Trapp (b); Bernard Pershey (d); Jim Gaines (prod).* 3/00.

** Go The Distance
Ruf 1067 *Trout; Scott Thompson (t); Pat Register (s); Rick Steff (ac); Bill Mason (kb, o); Jim Trapp (b); Bernard Pershey (d); William Brown, Bertram Brown, James Nelson, Wally Bass, Reba Russell, Jackie Johnson, Trisha Freeman (v); Jim Gaines (prod).* 2–3/01.

Trout's dextrous lead guitar playing is the vital fuse in the circuitry of his many releases. Quick fretboard runs and a classic thick Fender Strat tone are the order of the day, and his eager delivery compensates for the modest levels of colour and surprise in his voice. The combination works well enough on the partly live, partly studio-recorded *Life In The Jungle*, Trout declaring his intent with pummelling force, contorting his strings to the heavens and dinking his vocals into raw falsetto ranges. The mainly studio albums that follow (*Live (No More Fish Jokes)* was recorded at festivals in Denmark and Holland) mix rock 'n' roll shuffles, blues at various tempos and cheesy major-key ballads whose sincerity only adds to their guilelessness. (For a Trout devotee, this would perhaps read as 'more mature songwriting'.) Funk and gospel elements crop up regularly, but the central factor in almost every song is the guitar solo. Here Trout's preference is certainly for more rather than less: crowded bundles of notes whiz by, in the vein of blues-rock peers like Gary Moore, often with a disregard for economy that undermines the skill that laid them bare in the first place. The singing too often arrives as an afterthought, leaving one's hope for refreshment to the arrangements' occasional dalliances with violin and acoustic guitars, which make 'Watch Her Dance' a bright, aromatic closer to *Breaking The Rules*. The need for conciseness is equally apparent in Trout's compositions, which, as well as being lyrically paltry, would often profit from editing. *Positively Beale Street* (retitled *Walter Trout* when reissued by Ruf) trudges through 16 tracks which, though possessing a more thoroughly bluesy sound than much of his earlier work, struggle to grab the ear, and the album stumbles into a high point in the Pink Floydesque pointless meandering of 'Marie's Mood'. There's little discernible progression in the ordinary *Livin' Every Day* (credited, like all subsequent releases, to Walter Trout & The Free Radicals), though it's worth a listen if you liked other Trout records, but the next two releases capture live performances of a higher standing, showcasing Trout and his powerhouse band at their scorching best. The attention to brevity is as scarce as before, but the lion-out-of-its-cage effect of Trout in full crowd-swinging mode, coupled with a throttling group sound, gives the sense of an artist in his prime. Trout pulls off Mozart licks, covers his early hero Bob Dylan's 'I Shall Be Released' and only slightly overbakes John Lee Hooker's 'Serve Me Right To Suffer'. His returns to the studio since have included more of the same riff-rocking, blues-howling and ballad drivel. RR

Bessie Tucker
VOCAL

The photograph of Bessie Tucker in Victor's 'Race Records' catalogue showed a young woman of light complexion and delicate features. Anyone supposing, from that image, that this singer from Dallas, Texas, might be a vaudeville soubrette after the style of Lillie Delk Christian would have been vastly surprised by the strong, hollering voice that rises from her records. Thirty years later Whistlin' Alex Moore recalled her as a 'tough cookie – don't mess with her'. Whether or not that dissuaded researchers, nothing has been uncovered about the life that surrounded her three recording sessions.

***(*) Bessie Tucker (1928–1929)
Document DOCD-5070 *Tucker; K. D. Johnson (p, v); Jesse Thomas, prob. Carl Davis (g); unknown (bb)*. 8/28–10/29.

With her wordless moaning, her long, sliding phrases and her leaning towards subjects like prisons, trains and turbulent relationships, Tucker may remind listeners of her local contemporaries Texas Alexander and Victoria Spivey. 'The man that I'm a-lovin', he's gon' get me killed,' she sings in 'Penitentiary', 'because love is a proposition has got many a poor girl killed.' The juxtaposition of direct statement and aphorism is uncharacteristic: with a few exceptions like 'Black Name Moan' and 'Key To The Bushes Blues', which are related to Texan prison songs recorded by others, most of her songs are stories told with little recourse to blues commonplaces, and some listeners may be tempted to think of them as personally revealing. Though she delivers the hokum number 'Better Boot That Thing' with gusto, her métier is the slow blues, to which K. D. Johnson supplies unobtrusive yet finely decorated piano accompaniment, which is lent a slightly eerie tone by the acoustics of the recording room. Jesse Thomas joins them on the first 1929 session, at first chording sedately but venturing upon single-string lines in 'Mean Old Jack Stropper' and 'Old Black Mary'. The guitarist on the last session sounds quite different, phrasing in the manner of Carl Davis with Texas Alexander. Except for another take of 'My Man Has Quit Me' on *"Too Late, Too Late Blues" (1926–1944)* (Document DOCD-5150), this CD contains all her known recordings, seven with alternative takes. Only the grittiness of some of the transfers compromises a four-star rating: Tucker is a magnificent, affecting and unique singer. TR

Luther Tucker (1933–93)
VOCAL, GUITAR

Tucker was a wild adolescent in Chicago until his mother encouraged his interest in music. He recorded with Sonny Boy Williamson II, James Cotton, Jimmy Rogers, Muddy Waters and many others, but his fame rests on a seven-year stint with Little Walter. In the late '60s, Tucker moved to California, where he worked with John Lee Hooker and led his own band. He lived in Europe for a while, but was back in California when he died.

**(*) Sad Hours
Antone's ANT 0026 *Tucker; Keith Winking (t); Jon Blondell (tb); Mark Kazanoff (as, ts); Red Rails (bs); Kim Wilson (h); Reese Wynans (kb, o); Mel Brown (kb, p); Derek O'Brien (g); Russell Jackson (b); George Rains, Tony Coleman (d); James Fenner (perc)*. 89–90.

*** Luther Tucker & The Ford Blues Band
Blue Rock'It BRCD 122//Crosscut CCD 11040 *Tucker; Andy Just (h, v); John R. Burr (p); John Wedemeyer (g); Willie Riser, Stan Poplin (b); Patrick Ford (d); Holger Petersen (interviewer)*. 9/88–5/93.

Tucker learned guitar from the man he referred to respectfully as 'Mr. Robert Lockwood, Jr.', and his playing is imbued with Lockwood's jazzy sensibility, but his fast, fluttering flatpicking is distinctive and unmistakable. Unfortunately, Tucker was a small-voiced singer, who often sounded strained when trying for passionate. There are plenty of beautiful, imaginative guitar solos on *Sad Hours*, but on the majority of its tracks Tucker is teamed with inappropriate horns and a too loud bass guitar, all mixed into a dense, unpleasant lump of sound.

The 1988 segment of *Luther Tucker & The Ford Blues Band* is an amiable radio interview, used to bulk out studio and concert material. The studio tracks were to be completed with vocal and guitar overdubs; Tucker's sudden death intervened, but the solos he laid down for future reference are very satisfying, as is his singing of 'Little Bitty Man', a slowed-down 'La Cucaracha' with oddball lyrics. The laboured vocals on live versions of 'Mean Old World' and 'Worried Life Blues' are disappointing, as are the raucous overdubs, perforce supplied by Andy Just, on 'Playboy' and 'Sad And Lonely'. Nevertheless, this CD is the better showcase for Tucker's playing, not least because his fondness for Latin rhythms is indulged, to marvellous effect. CS

Tommy Tucker (1933–82)
VOCAL, (ORGAN,) PIANO

Tucker, whose real name was Robert Higginbotham, was working in Newark, New Jersey when he encountered Herb Abramson, who produced sessions on him from 1961. 'Hi-Heel Sneakers', on which Tucker played organ, became a #11 pop hit when leased to Checker in 1964; it has generated innumerable covers. There were no more hits, and Tucker retreated into obscurity. He made some European visits in the '70s, but his comeback was aborted by his sudden death.

** Hi Heel Sneakers
Chrisly CM 30011 *Tucker; Louisiana Red (g, v)*. 11/77.

Chrisly's CD was recorded in a Berlin club which provided Tucker with a substandard piano. The inevitable title track and the amusing 'Alimony' are Tucker compositions, but most of the set consists of R&B standards, including the greatest hits of Roy Brown, Lloyd Price, Hank Ballard and Ray Charles. The only surprises are a brief, delightful 'Married Man's A Fool' (which Tucker punctiliously credits to Butterbeans & Susie) and 'Sweet Little Angel', with Louisiana Red guesting; this turns into a droll, evidently spontaneous mutual jive about drink, drugs and women. Unfortunately, too many songs are marred by wrong notes, rhythmic slips and a fondness for staying on the tonic chord through a whole chorus. CS

Tucker & Thomas
DUET

Singer/drummer Johnny Tucker and singer/bassist James Thomas were long-serving members of Phillip Walker's band before forming a duo. Since Stranded *was recorded, Johnny Tucker has gone solo and been replaced by his brother, Aaron.*

*** Stranded
HMG 1001 Tucker; Thomas; Dino Spells (as, g); Hollis Gilmore (ts); Leon Blue, Leon Haywood, Willie Egans (p); James Armstrong, Tutty Gadson, Johnny Turner (g); Horace Richardson (b); Aaron Tucker (d). 97?

Tucker & Thomas sing a soulful, post-Sam & Dave variant of the blues, accompanied by proficient lineups in which their own funky rhythms and James Armstrong's clean guitar lines stand out. The duo share the vocal leads, and try to vary an inherently self-limiting format as much as possible, but inevitably a degree of similarity percolates from track to track. Some unimaginative song choices also reduce the disc's appeal; if there's a case for more recordings of 'Lawdy Miss Clawdy', 'No More Doggin'' and 'Mustang Sally', these versions don't advance it. That said, revivals of Junior Parker's 'Stranded' and Albert King's 'Don't Throw Your Love On Me So Strong' are notable for their passion and spirit. CS

Charlie Turner & Winston Holmes
DUET

Hardly anything is known of Turner, but Holmes (1879–1946) was a Kansas City music-store owner, founder of the Meritt label and a promoter of KC jazz and blues.

**** Kansas City Blues (1924–1929)
Document DOCD-5152 Turner (h, g, v, sp); Holmes (v, sp, wh). 6/29.

Almost a year after assisting Lottie Kimbrough in making her finest recordings (included on this CD), Holmes returned to the Gennett studios with the 12-string guitarist Charlie Turner. In one of the most musically diverse sessions of African-American music on record, Turner plays the rag tune 'Kansas City Dog Walk', a slide guitar blues behind Holmes's narration 'Rounders Lament', and harmonica and guitar together on the jaunty blues 'The Kansas City Call', named after the city's black newspaper. The two men duet on a comic song, 'Skinner', and in 'The Death Of Holmes' Mule' deliver a two-part comedy routine set in a graveyard, with sound effects and guitar interludes. TR

Eddie Turner (born 1952)
VOCAL, GUITAR

Eddie 'Devilboy' Turner was born in Cuba but raised in Chicago, where he turned to the guitar at the age of 12. Turner's musical growth somewhat overshadowed his academic interests during the years he spent at the University of Colorado, where he enjoyed stints performing with acts including The Immortal Nightflames, Tracy Nelson and Zephyr before taking a break from pursuing a music career. After a decade employed as a real estate agent, Turner rejoined the music industry, working with the Ron Miles group, and from 1995 onwards acting as an essential component in the acclaimed Otis Taylor band.

*** Rise
NorthernBlues NBM 0027 Turner; Kenny Passarelli (pocket t, kb, b); Alex Maryol, David Givens (g); Mark Clark (d, perc); Anna Givens (v). 05.

The immediately striking feature of Turner's first solo body of work is the diversity of material on offer, where the soulful proclamations of the opening title track are presented alongside the rock lead guitar workout of 'It's Me'. Though the variation in styles is broad, the overriding aesthetic of *Rise* is a raw earthiness, which permeates the album and its blues-based approach to the material. Passarelli's production is adventurous, incorporating loops to great effect in parts, particularly on the closing number, 'Secret', while the multilayered gospel vocals of 'Sin' are novel and effective. Turner's guitar work is tasteful and lends the release an open and ethereal quality, although the vocals are less consistently strong. *Rise* is certainly worthy of investigation, and is commendable as an alternative take on modern blues and a departure from convention – a trait exemplified to great effect in Turner's treatment of Hendrix's 'The Wind Cries Mary'. JF

Ike Turner (born 1931)
GUITAR, PIANO, BASS, DRUMS, VOCAL

Turner was born in Clarksdale, Mississippi. Before he was 20 he was leading his Kings Of Rhythm, playing piano and guitar, and recording for Sun; his first release, 'Rocket 88', sung by the band's tenor saxophonist, Jackie Brenston, is sometimes described as the first rock 'n' roll record. Between further Memphis recordings for Sun and Modern he acted as a talent scout for the latter, producing and playing on records by Howlin' Wolf, Bobby Bland and others. Relocated in St Louis, he conducted sessions under the name of the Kings Of Rhythm featuring a variety of singers but had no great success until he hired Annie Mae Bullock (born 1938), who married him and became Tina Turner. The couple fronted one of the most dynamic R&B revue bands of their period and made the iconic 'River Deep, Mountain High' (1966), produced by Phil Spector. Ten years on, they acrimoniously separated, and Ike's career was for a time better documented in court records and tabloid newspapers than in the music press, but in the '90s he began to put himself and his music back together, publishing an autobiography and recording anew.

*** A Proper Introduction To Ike Turner/Jackie Brenston: "Rocket 88"
Proper INTRO CD 2048 Turner; unknowns (t); Jackie Brenston (ts, v); Raymond Hill, unknowns (ts); unknowns (s); Bonnie Turner (p, v); Phineas Newborn Jr (p); Willie Kizart, Calvin Newborn (g); Ben Burton (b); Willie Sims, Phineas Newborn Sr, unknown (d); others [see below]. 3/51–4/52.

*** Rhythm Rockin' Blues
Ace CDCHD 553 Turner; Jackie Brenston (ts, v); Raymond Hill, Eugene Fox, Bobby Fields, Eddie Jones, unknowns (ts); Dennis Binder, J. W. [Johnny 'Big Moose'] Walker (p, v); Bobby Hines, Annie Mae [Tina] Turner (p); Willie Kizart (g); Jesse Knight Jr, unknown (b); Willie Sims, Bob Prindell, Eugene Washington, unknown (d); Lonnie 'The Cat', Billy Gayles, Little Johnny Burton, Johnny Wright, band (v). 3/51–11/55.

*** The Sun Sessions
Varèse Sarabande 302 066 232 *Turner; Oliver Sain (as); Jackie Brenston, Carlson Oliver, Raymond Hill, Bobby Fields, Eugene Fox (ts); James Wheeler, Thomas Reed (s); Bonnie Turner, Dennis Binder, Fred Sample (p); Willie Kizart (g); Jesse Knight Jr (b); Willie Sims, Robert Prindell, unknown (d); Johnny O'Neal, Tommy Hodge (v). 3/51–58.*

*** Blues Kingpins
Virgin 82714 *Turner; unknown (t); Eugene Fox, Bobby Fields (ts); Eddie Jones, Raymond Hill, unknowns (s); Bonnie Turner, Dennis Binder, Clayton Love, J. W. [Johnny 'Big Moose'] Walker (p, v); Annie Mae [Tina] Turner, Fred Sample, unknown (p); poss. Calvin Newborn, unknown (g); Ben Burton, Jesse Knight Jr, unknown (b); poss. Phineas Newborn Sr, Willie Sims, Bob Prindell, Eugene Washington, John Wings, unknowns (d); Billy Gayles, Johnny Wright (v). 4/52–8/59.*

Ike Turner's recording activities in the '50s were multifarious; discographers, meticulously documenting every pie he had a finger in, have re-created a production line rivalling Sara Lee's. Many of the recordings on these collections were issued under the names of the vocalists he put in front of his band, such as Jackie Brenston, Dennis Binder, Billy Gayles or Johnny O'Neal. Everyone was young, and Turner, displaying prodigious creativity for his age, was trying every trick he knew to make commercial discs. Inevitably, some of what was produced was derivative stuff by unformed or second-rank talent, but the off-the-cuff enthusiasm of sides like Brenston's 'Rocket 88' or Binder's rollicking 'I Miss You So' makes up for not-quite-there performances and not-quite-in-tune pianos. *Rhythm Rockin' Blues* and *The Sun Sessions* are discrete collections but *Blues Kingpins* has some overlap with the former, while the Proper CD has only eight items by Turner's band (and four of those credited to Brenston), the rest being by artists whom Turner scouted or accompanied, or both, from B. B. King and Howlin' Wolf to interesting secondary figures from north Mississippi or Arkansas like Sunny Blair, Houston Boines, Charley Booker or Baby Face Turner. These are covered in greater depth on Ace's VACs *The Travelling Record Man: Historic Down South Recording Trips of Joe Bihari & Ike Turner* and *The Modern Downhome Blues Sessions Volume 1* and *Volume 2* (see COMPILATIONS: DOWNHOME).

*** Ike's Instrumentals
Ace CDCHD 782 *Turner; prob. McKinley Johnson (t); Eugene Fox, Bobby Fields, Eddie Silvers, Rasheed Ishmael (ts); Marvin Warwick (bs); unknowns (brass, reeds); Billy Preston (o); Dennis Binder, Fred Sample, unknown (p); Jesse Knight Jr, unknowns (b); Willie Sims, poss. John Wings, TNT Tribble, unknowns (d). 54–65.*

Between his sessions with other artists for Modern, Turner took time out to cut a bunch of guitar instrumentals, including a remarkable extended pastiche called 'All The Blues All The Time', in which he fluently plays the lead guitar lines of eight current hits by B. B. King, Elmore James and others. (Most of these instrumentals are also on *Blues Kingpins*, and 'All The Blues' is additionally on *Rhythm Rockin' Blues*.) Several years later he did a whole album of instrumentals for Sue, catering to almost every rock 'n' roll niche market with titles like 'Potato Mash', 'Twistaroo' and 'The Gulley', and these too are roped into the corral of *Ike's Instrumentals*.

**(*) Call Back Lost Time: The Cobra And Artistic Recordings Of Ike Turner, Betty Everett And Buddy Guy
[Westside WESA 843] *Turner; Carlson Oliver (ts, v); Eddie Jones (ts); Jackie Brenston (bs, v); Fred Sample (p); Willie Dixon (b); Billy Gayles (d, v); Odie Payne (d); Tommy Hodge (v). 58.*

By 1958 it was clear that the prize Ike Turner's eyes were on was not going to be won by making blues records. A date that year with vocalist Tommy Hodge (found on *The Sun Sessions*, though not a Sun session) pointed in the direction of R&B with songs like 'How Long Will It Last', and not long afterwards Turner and Hodge reproduced the number, and other teen-oriented pieces like 'Walking Down The Aisle' and 'Box Top', at a session in Chicago for Cobra. As reproduced by Westside this is somewhat taxing listening – there are five versions of 'Matchbox'/'I'm Gonna Forget About You' and two each of several others – but contemporary Cobra sides by Betty Everett and Buddy Guy, and the four USA sides by Jesse Fortune (q.v.) sweeten the pill of documentation.

*** Ike & Tina Turner Sing The Blues
Acrobat ACMCD 4017 *Turner; unknowns (brass, reeds, h, kb); Albert Collins (g); unknowns (b, d); Tina Turner (v). 69.*

Most of Ike & Tina Turner's work is beyond the scope of this book, but not this. Culled from two albums that Turner recorded under his own auspices and leased to Blue Thumb, who issued them as *The Hunter* and *Outta Season*, it's a set of blues standards like 'Five Long Years', 'Reconsider Baby' and 'Honest I Do', topped and tailed with a few old soul songs like 'I've Been Loving You Too Long' and 'I Know'. Four cuts with horns aside, the songs, which are all sung by Tina alone, are very simply accompanied by murkily recorded keyboards, bass and drums, with Ike's guitar as the responding second voice. Tina's style is a little too melodramatic for simple blues like 'Rock Me Baby' or 'You Got Me Running' (i.e. 'Baby, What You Want Me To Do'), but she makes a sturdy reply to B. B. King in her reading of 'Three O'Clock Blues'. Some of the same material may still be available on *Bold Soul Sister: The Best Of The Blue Thumb Recordings* (Hip-O HIPD 40051).

*(*) My Bluescountry
Mystic MYS CD 115 *Turner; Stefan Brandl (as, bs); Olaf Kübler (ts); Michael 'Mufty' Ruff (kb); Patrick Gammon (o, v); Manuel Lopez (g); Andy Fuchs (b); Harald Kümpfel (d); Jeannette Turner, Isa Sabani, Anita Davies, The Ikettes (Barbra Cole, Audrey Madison, Paulette Williams) (v). 96.*

*** Here And Now
Ikon IKO-CD 8850//CBHCD 2005 *Turner; Lannie McMillan, Andrew Love, James Mitchell, Scott Thompson, Mac Johnson, Evan Pigford, Ernid Field, Louis Taylor, Dan Bell, Jim Spake (brass, reeds); Kenny Krizzelle (h); Ernest Lane (p); James Lewis (g); Dell Akins (b); Preston (Bugsy) Wilcox, Tony Coleman, Steve Potts (d); Little Milton, Joe Kelly, Fuzzy (v). 01.*

'Your enemies cannot harm you,' says the old gospel song, 'but watch your close friends.' *My Bluescountry*, evidently produced by Turner fans who love him not wisely but too well, is so grim a warning against over-indulgence that it should have had a cover design by Hieronymus Bosch. Sedate versions of 'Five Long Years', 'Sweet Black Angel' and 'Early One Morning' somehow found their way to the final cut, but their voices can barely be heard amid the welter of soul clichés. *Here And Now*, fortunately, is another kettle of catfish. Turner is in control, the musicians are both appropriate and disciplined, and the result is an album that balances here-and-now production values with timeless blues content. Turner was no spring chicken when he made it, but from the limber piano of 'Baby's Got It', the lean, mean guitar of 'Ike's Theme' or 'Cold Day In Hell' and the Fulsonesque delivery of 'Gave You What You Wanted' it's obvious that he can still cut a figure in the barnyard. TR

(Big) Joe Turner (1911–85)
VOCAL

Joe Turner was born in Kansas City, and began to make his name there during the '30s as a singing bartender, working with the pianist Pete Johnson. John Hammond heard them and booked them for the From Spirituals To Swing concerts. The boogie-woogie craze of the time carried both men to further work in New York, and they also made many recordings, first under Hammond for Columbia, later for several other labels. Turner also did sessions with other pianists, among them Art Tatum, Sammy Price and Freddie Slack. Signed to Atlantic in 1951 by its jazz-loving directors, he surprised them, and possibly himself, by sending several records up the Pop charts, though not as high up as some of the imitations of them by rock 'n' roll figures like Bill Haley, who bowdlerized his 'Shake, Rattle & Roll'. After a few years entertaining teenagers he was reclaimed by jazz fans and his work in the '60s and '70s was chiefly in jazz clubs and at jazz festivals, just as his recording was mostly for jazz labels like Norman Granz's Pablo. Towards the end he rounded the circle of his musical life by forming a partnership with another boogie-woogie specialist, the German pianist Axel Zwingenberger.

*** **Complete Edition, Vol. 1: 1938–1940**
Masters Of Jazz 134 Turner; Benny Carter (t, as); Hot Lips Page, Eddie Anderson, Bill Coleman (t); Benny Morton (tb); Danny Polo (cl, ts); Ed Hall (cl); Buster Smith (as); Coleman Hawkins (ts); Pete Johnson, Meade Lux Lewis, Albert Ammons, Joe Sullivan, Sonny White (p); Lawrence Lucie, Ulysses Livingston, Freddie Green (g); Abe Bolar, Art Shapiro, Henry Turner, Wilson Myers (b); Eddie Dougherty, George Wettling, Johnny Wells, Yank Porter, unknown (d). 12/38–10/40.

*** **Complete Edition, Vol. 2: 1940–1941**
Masters Of Jazz 146 Turner; Hot Lips Page, Joe Thomas (t); Edmond Hall (cl); Pete Johnson, Willie 'The Lion' Smith, Art Tatum, Sam Price, Freddie Slack (p); John Collins, Oscar Moore, Leonard Ware, prob. Al Hendrickson (g); Abe Bolar, Billy Taylor, prob. Jud De Naut (b); A. G. Godley, Ed Dougherty, Yank Porter (d). 11/40–9/41.

*** **Big Joe Turner 1941–1946**
Classics 940 Turner; Frankie Newton, Warren Brocken (t); Don Byas, Bill Moore, Lloyd Harrison (ts); Sam Price, Freddie Slack, Fred Skinner, Pete Johnson, Al Williams (p); Leonard Ware, prob. Al Hendrickson, Clifford McTyner, Ernest Ashley, Teddy Bunn (g); Billy Taylor, prob. Jud De Naut, Johnny Miller, Dallas Bartley, Al Hall, John 'Shifty' Henry (b); Harold West, Alray Kidd (d). 7/41–1/46.

*** **Big Joe Turner 1946–1947**
Classics 1034 Turner; Warren Brocken, Russell Jacquet, Sammy Yates, unknown (t); poss. Tab Smith, Jack McVea (as); Bill Moore, Lloyd Harrison, Lou 'Freddie' Simon, unknown (ts); Al Williams, Camille Howard, Albert Ammons, Pete Johnson (p); Teddy Bunn, poss. Ike Perkins, Pee Wee Crayton (g); John 'Shifty' Henry, Frank Clarke, unknown (b); Alray Kidd, Walter Murden, Red Saunders, Rabon Tarrant (d). 1/46–11/47.

*** **Big Joe Turner 1947–1948**
Classics 1094 Turner; Charles Grey, James Ross, Art Farmer (t); Riley Hampton, Frank Sleet (as); Otis Finch, Pete Peterson (ts); Milburn Newman (bs); unknown (p, harpsichord); Pete Johnson, unknown (p); Ike Perkins, prob. Barney Kessel (g); poss. Robert Moore, poss. Ellsworth Liggett, Harry Babasin, Addison Farmer (b); James Adams, Don Lamond, Robert Brady (d). 11/47–6/48.

*** **Big Joe Turner 1949–1950**
Classics 1180 Turner; Walter 'Dootsie' Williams, Russell 'Fats' Emory, Dave Bartholomew, unknown (t); Waldron 'Frog' Joseph (tb); Kirtland Bradford, Joe Harris (as); Maxwell Davis, Joe Houston, Clarence Hall, Herb Hardesty, unknown (ts); Jewell Grant (bs); unknowns (s); Pete Johnson, Fats Domino, unknowns (p); Herman Mitchell, Goree Carter, Ernest McLean (g); Ralph Hamilton, Peter Badie, unknowns (b); Jesse Sailes, Thomas Moore, unknowns (d). 49–c. 4/50.

**** **All The Classic Hits 1938–1952**
JSP JSP 7709 5CD Similar to all above CDs. 12/38–9/52.

The standard description of Joe Turner is 'blues shouter', which should encourage a lively distrust of standard descriptions. True, his voice is strong rather than diffident; he doesn't solicit the listener's attention but commands it. But if there's any suggestion that he is a crude or unsubtle singer, it's unjust: he doesn't simply stand up and bawl the blues. In the period covered by these CDs he seldom had to, for, unlike his contemporary Wynonie Harris, he wasn't vying with a big band: quite a lot of these sides are with a piano trio, and some are with just a piano, usually played by his buddy Pete Johnson, as on his debut disc 'Goin' Away Blues'/'Roll 'Em Pete', but on one session by Willie 'The Lion' Smith, with whom he made reflective music of quiet beauty.

Turner wasn't much given to melodic experiment. He had three basic blues formats – very slow ('Piney Brown Blues', 'Wee Baby Blues'), medium-slow ('Cherry Red') and fast boogie ('Rebecca', 'Low Down Dog', 'Sally-Zu-Zazz') – and he deviated from them only when taking on a more individual tune like 'Corrine Corrina', 'Rocks In My Bed', 'Blues In The Night' or 'Morning Glory'. The texture of his voice is so fine, and his control at any tempo so exemplary, that one can listen to him with unimpaired enjoyment for quite a long time, but the listener coming fresh to his work should be prepared for a certain amount of repeated repertoire – 'Low Down Dog' and 'I'm Still In The Dark' were favourite charts – and for a great deal of competent but conventional accompaniment by a series of six- or seven-piece jump-blues bands, though that's sometimes brightened by exceptional contributions such as Camille Howard's piano on 'Sunday Morning Blues'. Readers undeterred by these remarks who plan to collect Turner in a serious way have a choice of three routes: the ongoing complete-and-chronological series on Masters Of Jazz and Classics and the near-complete (for its period) 5CD box on JSP, which wins for value. For selective compilations, read on.

*** **Big Joe's Blues**
Topaz TPZ 1070 Similar to Complete Edition, Vol. 1 and Vol. 2, except add Frankie Newton, Warren Brocken, Russell Jacquet, unknown (t), poss. Tab Smith (as), Don Byas, Bill Moore, Lloyd Harrison, Lou 'Freddie' Simon, unknown (ts), Al Williams,

Camille Howard (p), Ernest Ashley, Teddy Bunn, poss. Ike Perkins (g), Dallas Bartley, Al Hall, John 'Shifty' Henry, unknown (b), Harold West, Alray Kidd, Walter Murden, Red Saunders (d). 12/38–10/46.

*** The Forties: Volume 1 (1940–1946)
Fabulous FABCD 149 *Similar to* Complete Edition, Vol. 1 *and* Vol. 2, *except add* Frankie Newton, Warren Brocken (t), Don Byas, Bill Moore, Lloyd Harrison (ts), Fred Skinner, Al Williams (p), Clifford McTyner, Ernest Ashley, Teddy Bunn (g), Johnny Miller, Dallas Bartley, Al Hall, John 'Shifty' Henry (b), Harold 'Doc' West, Alray Kidd (d). 1/40–1/46.

(***) Blues In The Night
Arpeggio ARB 011 *Similar to* Big Joe Turner 1947–1948, *except add* Russell 'Fats' Emory, Walter 'Dootsie' Williams (t), Kirtland Bradford (as), Joe Houston, Maxwell Davis, unknown (ts), Jewell Grant (bs), Lorenzo Flennoy, unknown (p), Herman 'Tiny' Mitchell, Lucky Enois (g), Winston Williams, Ralph Hamilton, unknown (b), Jesse Sailes, unknown (d). 2/40–c. 49.

*** Blues On Central Avenue
Our World 3305 Turner; Frankie Newton, poss. Bill Martin, Warren Brocken (t); John 'Flaps' Dungee (as); Don Byas, Josh Jackson, Bill Moore, Lloyd Harrison (ts); Sam Price, Freddie Slack, Fred Skinner, Pete Johnson, Al Williams (p); Leonard Ware, prob. Al Hendrickson, Clifford McTyner, Ernest Ashley, Teddy Bunn, unknown (g); Billy Taylor, prob. Jud De Naut, Johnny Miller, Dallas Bartley, Al Hall, John 'Shifty' Henry (b); Harold West, Alray Kidd, unknown (d). 7/41–1/46.

*** Every Day In The Week
Decca Jazz GRD 621 Turner; unknown (t); Buddy Lucas (ts, h); unknowns (s); unknown (o); Fred Skinner (p, v); Freddie Slack, Pete Johnson, Patti Bown, unknown (p); Clifford McTyner (g, v); prob. Al Hendrickson, Ernest Ashley, Wally Richardson, Thornel Schwarz, unknown (g); Johnny Miller (b, v); prob. Jud De Naut, Dallas Bartley, Bob Bushnell, unknown (b); Panama Francis (d); unknowns (v). 9/41–10/44, 11/63–4/67.

*** Around The Clock Blues
[Blue Boar CDBB 1014] Turner; Frankie Newton, Warren Brocken, prob. Charles Grey, unknown (t); prob. Tab Smith, Riley Hampton (as); Don Byas, Bill Moore, Lloyd Harrison, Otis Finch, unknown (ts); Freddie Slack, Pete Johnson, Al Williams, Albert Ammons, Ellsworth Liggett (p); Al Hendrickson, Ernest Ashley, Leonard Ware, Teddy Bunn, Ike Perkins (g); Jud De Naut, Dallas Bartley, Al Hall, John 'Shifty' Henry, Robert Moore, unknown (b); Harold 'Doc' West, Alray Kidd, Red Saunders, James Adams (d). 9/41–12/47.

*** Have No Fear, Big Joe Turner Is Here
Savoy Jazz SV-0265 Turner; Frankie Newton, poss. Bill Martin, Warren Brocken, Russell Jacquet, Charles Grey, unknown (t); John 'Flaps' Dungee, poss. Tab Smith, Riley Hampton (as); Don Byas, Josh Jackson, Wild Bill Moore, Lloyd Harrison, Lou 'Freddie' Simon, Otis Finch, unknown (ts); unknown (harpsichord); Pete Johnson, Al Williams, Camille Howard, Albert Ammons, unknown (p); Leonard Ware, Teddy Bunn, Ike Perkins, unknown (g); Al Hall, Dallas Bartley, John 'Shifty' Henry, Robert Moore or Ellsworth Liggett, unknown (b); Harold West, Alray Kidd, Walter Murden, Red Saunders, James Adams (d). 2/45–11/47.

*** Atomic Boogie
Savoy SC-909 2CD *As above, except add* Benny Carter (t, as), Danny Polo (cl), Coleman Hawkins (ts), Joe Sullivan (p), Ulysses Livingston (g), Artie Shapiro (b), George Wettling (d). 1/40, 2/45–11/47.

*** Jumpin' With Joe: The Complete Aladdin & Imperial Recordings
EMI (A) E2 99293//(E) CZ 527 Turner; Sammy Yates, Dave Bartholomew, unknown (t); Waldron 'Frog' Joseph (tb); Jack McVea, Joe Harris (as); Clarence Hall, Herb Hardesty (ts); Pete Johnson, Fats Domino (p); Pee Wee Crayton, Ernest McLean (g); Frank Clarke, Peter Badie (b); Rabon Tarrant, Thomas Moore (d). 7/47–4/50.

*** Tell Me Pretty Baby
Arhoolie CD-333 Turner; James Ross, Art Farmer (t); Jewell Grant (as, bs); Frank Sleet, Kirtland Bradford (as); Pete Peterson, Maxwell Davis (ts); Milburn Newman (bs); Pete Johnson (p); Herman Mitchell (g); Addison Farmer, Ralph Hamilton (b); Robert Brady, Jesse Sailes (d). c. 11/47–49.

*** The Forties: Volume 2 (1947–1949)
Fabulous FABCD 185 Turner; Charles Grey, James Ross, Art Farmer, Walter 'Dootsie' Williams, Russell 'Fats' Emory (t); Riley Hampton, Frank Sleet, Kirtland Bradford (as); Otis Finch, Pete Peterson, Maxwell Davis, Joe Houston, unknown (ts); Milburn Newman, Jewell Grant (bs); Pete Johnson, unknowns (p); Ike Perkins, Herman Mitchell (g), poss. Robert Moore, poss. Ellsworth Liggett, Addison Farmer, Ralph Hamilton, unknown (b); James Adams, Robert Brady, Jesse Sailes, unknown (d). c. 11/47–c. 49.

**(*) The Big Three
Blue Moon CDBM 095 Turner; Joe Bridgewater, unknown (t); Pluma Davis (tb); Vernon Bates, unknowns (s); Jimmy Toliver, unknown (p); Goree Carter, unknown (g); unknowns (b); unknowns (d). 12/49–c. 12/50.

If all you want is one or two CDs of Turner in his formative years, you won't go far wrong with most of these. The widest-ranging are the Topaz and Blue Boar sets, which have 25 well-chosen tracks, and the ultra-cheap pair on Fabulous. Arpeggio offer only 16 tracks, seemingly picked at random and poorly presented. The rest are more or less label-specific. *Have No Fear, Big Joe Turner Is Here* is a near-complete set of the National recordings, well packaged, while the 2CD *Atomic Boogie* gathers his entire output for National and adds 11 Pete Johnson cuts from the same period, plus Turner's 1940 coupling with the Varsity Seven. *Jumpin' With Joe* looks after his Aladdin and Imperial sides but may no longer be around. *Blues On Central Avenue* is chiefly devoted to the 1941–44 Deccas, an area also covered by *Every Day In The Week*, though that goes on to sample a couple of '60s sessions. *Tell Me Pretty Baby* breaks fresh ground by concentrating on the lesser-known Down Beat and MGM sessions, while Turner's six tracks on *The Big Three* come from Freedom; the rest of that CD is by Joe Houston and L. C. Williams.

**** Joe Turner/Rockin' The Blues
Collectables COL-CD-6419 Turner; Taft Jordan, Joe Morris, Sonny Cohn, Dick Vance, Jimmy Nottingham, Phil Guilbeau, unknowns (t); Salvatore Davis, Pluma Davis, Wilbur De Paris, Melvin Juanzo, unknown (tb); Arlem Kareem (Ernest 'Pinky' Williams) (as, bs); William Burchett, Earle Warren, Jerome Richardson, Hilton Jefferson (as); Budd Johnson, Freddie Mitchell, Lee Allen, J. T. Brown, Boyd Atkins, Grady Jackson, Sam 'The Man' Taylor, Choker Campbell, King Curtis, unknowns (ts); Dave McRae, Haywood Henry, McKinley Easton, unknown (bs); unknowns (s); Mike Chimes (h); Harry Van Walls, Fats Domino, [Little] Johnny Jones, Ernie Hayes, poss. Mike Stoller, poss. Ray Charles, unknown (p); Rector Bailey, poss. Shebs Hobbs, Elmore James,

Billy Mure, George Barnes, Allen Hanlon, Mundell Lowe, unknowns (g); Leonard Gaskin, Jimmy Richardson, Lloyd Trotman, unknowns (b); Connie Kay, Odie Payne, Red Saunders, Panama Francis, poss. Chick Booth, unknowns (d); The Cookies, band, unknowns (v). 4/51–1/58.

**** The Very Best Of Big Joe Turner
Rhino 72968 *Similar to above*. 4/51–9/59.

Turner is often, and rightly, credited with making rock 'n' roll before the term came into wide currency: what should be emphasized is how long before. The chuntering saxes and Teddy Bunn's athletic guitar make the point clearly on 'My Gal's A Jockey', recorded in 1946. But it wasn't until he joined Atlantic that Turner found his groove as a fully contemporary R&B artist, cutting songs like 'Shake, Rattle & Roll', 'Honey Hush' and 'Chains Of Love' that combined the authority of the blues with the catchy hooks and crisp arrangements of pop. Their frequent appearance in nostalgic movies about the '50s confirms that these wonderful, and remarkably consistent, recordings are firmly pasted into the aural scrapbook of the period. Every collection should have some of them, and Rhino's *Very Best* is the way to go. *Joe Turner*, the first disc of a twofer reissuing two Atlantic LPs, is almost identical, while *Rockin' The Blues* adds further material from the same era, most of it less successful in the charts but still highly listenable. 'TV Mama' ('the one with the big wide screen') and a couple of other titles were cut in Chicago with Elmore James and his band, an odd-seeming combination that works quite well.

♛ **** The Boss Of The Blues
Collectables COL-CD-6327 *Turner; Joe Newman, Jimmy Nottingham (t); Lawrence Brown (tb); Pete Brown (as); Frank Wess, Seldon Powell (ts); Pete Johnson (p); Freddie Green (g); Walter Page (b); Cliff Leeman (d).* 3/56.

If you wanted to show a Martian what was meant by the term 'jazz-blues', you couldn't do better than pull out this album. In the company of a medium-sized band of Kansas City players, men like Pete Johnson and Pete Brown who were as steeped in the blues form as he was, Turner presents ten songs – seven blues and three pop standards – with the absolute authority of a man who knows he knows his craft, but also the economy of one who realizes that in this setting he doesn't need to labour the point. True, he was taking no risks with the material – here's 'Cherry Red' again, and 'Low Down Dog', and 'Roll 'Em Pete' – but there's a clarity and definition to these readings that most of his other renditions never matched. This issue appears to have replaced Atlantic's own (last spotted as Atlantic 81459) but, whatever form you find it in, it's an album to cherish for its affirmation of timeless musical values.

**** Big, Bad & Blue – The Big Joe Turner Anthology
Rhino R2 71550 3CD *Turner; various accompaniments.* 12/38–1/83.

If you want to keep your Joe Turner collection compact, just get this and one of the early-days compilations. There are some early recordings on *Big, Bad & Blue*, but it focuses long and hard on the Atlantic period, gathering 28 tracks from singles and four each from the albums *The Boss Of The Blues* and *Big Joe Rides Again*. Three tracks from the '70s and '80s wrap it up. There are some gaps in the story, admittedly, but they don't make the telling of it any less absorbing. James Austin's selection and Pete Grendysa's notes are entirely admirable. We just hope you can still find it.

*** Texas Style
Black & Blue BB 903 *Turner; Milt Buckner (p); Slam Stewart (b); Jo Jones (d).* 4/71.

*** Texas Style
Evidence ECD 26013 *As above.* 4/71.

If the programme is Turner Classic – 'Cherry Red', 'Hide And Seek', 'T.V. Mama', 'I've Got A Pocket Full Of Pencils' – so is his delivery of it, in a voice overflowing with the warring emotions of sexual pride and financial despair. A French recording, well engineered. Black & Blue's reissue of their original LP has an extra cut.

** Honey Hush
Magnum Force CDMF 064 *Turner; Marek Johnson (t); Gene 'Mighty Flea' Connors (tb); Clifford Solomon (ts, bs); Big Jim Wynn (bs); Johnny Otis (kb, p, d, vb); Shuggie Otis (p, g, b); Teresa Butler, Alesia Butler (v).* early 70s.

** The Essential Recordings
Purple Pyramid CLP 0964 *As above.* early 70s.

This set originated on Johnny Otis's Blues Spectrum label and typically concentrates on the artist's past hits: so, 'Shake, Rattle And Roll', 'Cherry Red', 'Honey Hush', 'Wee Baby Blues', etc. Songs that were distinctively arranged on their original recordings, like 'Chains Of Love' and 'Corrine Corrine', are given similar settings, and Shuggie Otis plays the statutory slide on 'T.V. Mama'. It's not badly done, but was it worth doing? The sound quality implies an analog transfer from a less than audiophile LP pressing. The two issues are identical except that *The Essential Recordings* adds a version of 'Roll 'Em Pete'.

*(*) The Midnight Special
Pablo OJCCD-1077 *Turner; Jake Porter (t); Curtis Peagler (as, ts); Roy Brewster (baritone horn); Curtis Kirk (h); Sylvester Scott (p); Cal Green (g); Bobby Haynes (b); Washington Rucker (d).* 5/76.

This is not quite as odd a programme as it looks, for the song listed as Woody Guthrie's 'So Long (It's Been Good To Know Yuh)' isn't, but the mixture of vintage pop standards, Leadbelly's title number, two blues and 'I Left My Heart In San Francisco' is not reassuring, and the otherwise inoffensive ensemble playing is disfigured by an inappropriate and weedy harmonica. Even completists could not add this to their shelves without a groan.

Other Pablo albums made around this time have disappeared. It's not a tremendous loss, since they were uneven, but it is to be regretted that the sterling set Turner made with Roomful Of Blues (originally on Muse, last seen on CD as 32 Blues 32015) is currently off the market.

**(*) Boogie Woogie Jubilee
Vagabond VRCD-8.81010 *Turner; Axel Zwingenberger (p); Roy Milton (d, v); Eddie 'Cleanhead' Vinson, Margie Evans (v).* 5/81.

A gathering of friends at Turner's home, five days after his 70th birthday, elicits cheerful versions of several personal standards and some Turner–Zwingenberger compositions that were probably created on the spot. Time has coarsened Turner's voice, but he still has formidable reserves of power and projection, and humour besides; the light may be dimmed, but the star is far from going down. No doubt he was buoyed up by Zwingenberger's rock-steady playing. The title track is a quarter of an hour of partying with guest appearances by Vinson, Evans and, laying aside his sticks to hold a vocal mike, Milton. TR

Johnny Turner (born 1934)
VOCAL, GUITAR

Turner was born in Altheimer, Arkansas, and spent his teens in North Little Rock, where he played bass and guitar with Fenton Robinson. Moving in 1965 to LA, he worked with the tenor saxophonist Joe Houston, then in the mid-'70s formed Blues With A Feeling with the harmonica player Zaven Jambazian. Nothing has been heard of him in recent years.

**(*) Blues With A Feeling
Testament TCD 5025 Turner; Zaven Jambazian (h); Tony Manriquez (b); Stu Perry (d). 5/76.

The location recording (at The Raven & The Rose, a club in Sierra Madre, California) is technically modest, and although some listeners may enjoy its rough-and-ready fidelity to the ambience of a small blues club, it probably doesn't provide a full index to Turner's skills. On the right kind of song, such as 'Last Night', he sings with the thoughtfulness of his former employer Fenton Robinson. As a guitarist he is fluent enough to play a lead that needs no buttressing by a rhythm player, and from to time he comes up with an inventive line or phrase. Jambazian, Manriquez and Perry all work hard. One can see why Pete Welding was drawn to record the group. But in a studio, with better equipment and perhaps with more original material, Turner might have been able to tell a different story. TR

Nate Turner (born 1937)
VOCAL, BASS

Raised in Miami, Turner moved to Chicago in 1965, by which time he'd already tried out on harmonica, saxophone, drums and guitar before settling on bass guitar. As a freelance bassist he worked for Jimmy Dawkins, Koko Taylor and Lovie Lee among others before forming the Windy City Blues Band in 1992, and eventually assuming the lead guitarist's role.

** Hard Times
Wolf 120.810 Turner; Steve Bell (h); Eddie Lusk, Melvin Robertson (kb); Charles Crane, Lurrie Bell, George Brown (g); James Bell, Bearnard Whitaker [sic] (d); Gladys Cooks (v). 92.

Produced by Mae Stokes and Gladys Cooks, *Hard Times* was originally issued in 1996 as *Yo! Mama* (Planet Blue 7912). It made little impact at the time, and didn't prompt other record companies to take an interest in Turner. The explanation for their indifference is to be found in his jejune and clichéd lyrics, which are accorded predictable arrangements that generate unimaginative solos. Wolf's 2004 reissue is *Volume 52* in the label's *Chicago Blues Sessions* series, and the sound of barrels being scraped is audible. CS

Othar Turner (1907–2003)
VOCAL, FIFE

Until near the end of his long life, Othar Turner (sometimes Otha or Other – long 'O', anyway) still worked his land near Senatobia with mules and horses, ran his annual picnic and goat barbecue (latterly an integrated tourist attraction as well as an African-American celebration), and trained musicians, many of them his descendants, for the Rising Star Fife & Drum Band. The north Mississippi tradition, once on the brink of extinction, seems set to outlive its patriarch, who took up the fife in 1923.

In his 60s, Turner also played drums and guitar; his drumming can be heard on *Traveling Through The Jungle* (Testament TCD 5017) and *Mississippi Delta Blues Jam In Memphis Vol. 1* (Arhoolie CD 385). Two versions of 'Black Gal', one with guitar, one unaccompanied, both hewn from the bedrock, are on *Afro-American Music From Tate And Panola Counties, Mississippi* (Rounder CD 1515).

**** Everybody Hollerin' Goat
Birdman BMR 018 Turner; Luther Dickinson (g); R. L. Boyce (snare d, bass d, v); Rodney Evans, Andre Evans, Aubrey 'Li'l Mix' Turner (snare d, bass d); Bernice T. Evans (snare d, v); K. K. Freeman (snare d). 92–97.

Most of this disc was recorded at Turner's farm, in ambiences ranging from quiet to small but noisy parties to the riotous middle of a picnic; one of the three versions of 'Shimmy She Wobble' was recorded at a Memphis club. In the '40s, fife and drum bands also played popular songs and marches, but for a long time the music's polyrhythms, call-and-response and bluesy dance tunes have stressed the first half of 'African-American'. Turner works from a restricted playlist (fair enough, at his age), but his brief, repetitive licks flicker like a serpent's tempting tongue as the drums shake the earth, compelling body, blood and brain to dance, and critics to reach for the purple ink. On CD and out of context the music inevitably loses some of its power, but *Everybody Hollerin' Goat* comes closer than most recordings to its bacchanalian essence. About a third of the disc is guitar blues by R. L. Boyce, with Luther Dickinson on second guitar; they do a rip-roaring version of the local anthem 'Shake 'Em On Down'.

*** Otha Turner And The Afrosippi Allstars
Birdman BMR 025 As above, except add Sharde Evans [Thomas] (fife), Morikeba Kouyate (kora), Musa Sutton, Manu Walton, Abe Young (djembe, djun djun, sangban, kenkeni, bells, shakers), Matthew Rappaport (perc from instruments listed), musicians among those listed (tamb). 2/99.

Recently, there's been much windbaggery to the effect that 'the blues came from Africa,' so it's cheering that no grandiose theories lurk behind this CD; it simply brings two soundworlds together to see what happens. (It's possible to go too far, though; the injunction to 'forget the categorized, preconceived notions of folklore and musicology' is magnificently categorical and preconceived.)

The fife and drum musicians play their core repertoire: in eight tracks, four songs from *Everybody Hollerin' Goat* recur; 'Shimmy She Wobble' does so twice. The African musicians add what they can; the kora player's short sprays of notes hang out with the fife and drum music rather than blending in, but the percussionists are much more comfortable and relevant, successfully adding rhythmic and textural complexity. 'Senegal To Senatobia', by the African musicians and Luther Dickinson, is trivial Afropop, but much of the rest, and especially the ten-minute 'Stripes', is the outcome of a fruitful cross-cultural collaboration. CS

James Blood Ulmer (born 1942)
VOCAL, GUITAR

Ulmer was born in St Matthews, South Carolina, moved at the age of 19 to Pittsburgh, thence to Detroit and finally to New York City, where he has lived ever since. His track record has mostly been in jazz, but in widely differing contexts: as a young man he played with organists like Big John Patton, but since the late '70s he has been associated with Ornette Coleman and other musicians in Coleman's 'harmolodic' circle. In the '80s, in albums like Odyssey, he developed his interest in idioms closer to the roots of African-American music, and his recent work has been focused on the blues.

*** Memphis Blood: The Sun Sessions
Hyena TMF 9310 *Ulmer; David Barnes (h); Rick Steff (kb, o, p, ac); Charles Burnham (vn, md); Vernon Reid (g, prod); Mark Peterson (b); Aubrey Dayle (d). 4/01.*

There was evidence in his previous work that Ulmer could do interesting things in the blues form. As the authors of *The Penguin Guide To Jazz Recordings* remark, 'most of [his] characteristic distortions of pitch and loud riffing are part of a long-established electric blues idiom.' All the same, *Memphis Blood* probably surprised many with its impressive display of respect and knowledge. The songs are almost exclusively blues standards, chiefly from the '50s/'60s repertoire of Muddy Waters, Sonny Boy Williamson II, John Lee Hooker and, above all, Howlin' Wolf, the point of origin of five of the selections. The Ulmerizing process is not invariable: the bursts of noise guitar in 'I Just Want To Make Love To You' and 'I Asked For Water (She Gave Me Gasoline)' are outnumbered by the less dramatic and (relatively) more conventional Chicago-style arrangements of 'Little Red Rooster', 'Evil' and Otis Rush's 'Double Trouble', and a long, compelling reading of Son House's 'Death Letter'. Barnes's harmonica and Reid's guitar are stylistically accurate too, but the album's chief revelation is that Ulmer is a natural old-school blues singer.

*** No Escape From The Blues: The Electric Lady Sessions
Hyena TMF 9212 *Ulmer; Olu Dara (pocket t); David Barnes (h, v); Leon Gruenbaum (kb, o, p, melodica, v); Charles Burnham (vn, md, v); Vernon Reid (sitar, bj, g, v, prod); John Kruth (tamboura); Mark Peterson (b); Aubrey Dayle (d); Maya Smullyan Jenkins (tap dancing); Queen Esther (v). 4/03.*

With its infusion of songs derived from Waters, Hooker, Wolf, T-Bone Walker and Jimmy Reed, *No Escape From The Blues* is in both senses a blood relative of the previous album, but Ulmer's guitar playing, so responsive there to idiom and period, is here sometimes more abstract: Reed's 'Goin' To New York' comes across like *The Hay Wain* painted by Jackson Pollock. Several tracks inventively coalesce the band's loose polyphony and elements of the original arrangements, and 'Trouble In Mind', steeped in the unusual sonorities of tamboura and melodica, undergoes a potent transformation.

Ulmer's singing, whether of the blues standbys or his own 'Are You Glad To Be In America?', remains deep in a traditional groove.

*** Birthright
Hyena TMF 9335 *Ulmer. 05.*

Ulmer always sounds as if he is immersed in the past, both his own and the blues', and playing solo only accentuates that sense of a man communing with old friends, confronting old devils, exorcizing old ghosts. 'White Man's Jail', 'Take My Music Back To The Church' and 'I Ain't Superstitious' (the last written by Willie Dixon for Howlin' Wolf, and one of only two non-original pieces): each of these in its different way records an aspect of black history, and each finds an echo in the small-scale story of 'Geechee Joe', a memoir of Ulmer's grandfather set to a lilting guitar melody that might have been approved by Mississippi John Hurt. TR

Dave Van Ronk (1936–2002)
VOCAL, GUITAR, DULCIMER, AUTOHARP

Van Ronk started out playing banjo and singing with traditional jazz groups before realizing that a fingerpicking guitarist didn't need a band. He became a guru of the folk revival (although he described himself as 'a jazz singer manqué'), a conduit for the musical ideas of Gary Davis, an influence on the young Bob Dylan and a Greenwich Village institution. This selective entry omits CDs where music other than blues dominates.

**(*) The Folkways Years 1959–61
Smithsonian Folkways CD SF 40041 *Van Ronk; Dick Rosmini (g, v); Bob Yellin, Bob Brill, Roger Abrahams (v). 59–61.*
** Inside Dave Van Ronk
Fantasy FCD-24710 *Van Ronk. 4/62.*
** Two Sides Of Dave Van Ronk
Fantasy FCD-24772 *Van Ronk; John Bucher (c); Dick Dreiwitz (tb); Denis Brady (cl, ss); Hank Ross (p); Eric Hassell (bj); Steve Knight (tu); Robert L. Thompson (d, wb). 7/63–3/81.*
*** Live At Sir George Williams University
Just A Memory JAM 9132 *Van Ronk. 1/67.*
**(*) Sunday Street
Philo CD PH 1036 *Van Ronk. 76.*
**(*) Somebody Else, Not Me
Philo CD 1065 *Van Ronk. 78.*
** Statesboro Blues
[EPM Blues Collection 15784] *Van Ronk. 4/83.*

In the late '50s and early '60s the folk revivalists who recorded were transmitting what they'd heard, on the Harry Smith anthology and other Folkways LPs, at the Library of Congress and from surviving musicians, to a wider audience often ignorant of and uninterested in origins and sociohistorical contexts. It's understandable that Van Ronk's very dramatic presentations of African-American music made a considerable impact; what's odd is that 40 years later, he was still being venerated for them (and, no doubt, for his original compositions and other musical ventures, but they are not part of our remit).

Van Ronk was a very able and enjoyable guitarist; hear, for instance, his transcriptions on Philo of Joplin rags and Morton's 'The Pearls', or his playing, on various CDs, of Gary Davis's 'Candy Man' and 'Cocaine'. His mediation of black vocal music is at its most effective on display pieces like the Davis songs, and humorous numbers like 'Willie The Weeper' (*The Folkways Years*) and 'That Will Never Happen No More' (*Live At Sir George Williams University, Sunday Street*). When he chooses, Van Ronk can also be a pleasant, gentle interpreter of material like John Hurt's 'Spike Driver Blues' (*The Folkways Years, Two Sides Of*).

Usually, however, his singing is characterized by a fervid, straining delivery with much use of growls, rasps and abrupt changes from a bellow to a murmur. The notes to one CD assert that 'none of this chopping and changing is there for show; it all serves the lyrics.' Too often, it would be more accurate to transpose 'none' and 'all', particularly on songs that are highly embedded in black culture, and most notably the prison worksongs 'Poor Lazarus' (*Inside*), 'Rocks And Gravel' (*Two Sides Of*) and 'Old Hannah' (*Somebody Else, Not Me*); of the latter, Van Ronk says ,'I know I can't do it justice, but no one else seems to be singing it just now.' He doesn't seem to have thought about the reasons for either half of that observation.

The Folkways Years will appeal to those for whom the foregoing considerations are not a problem; Van Ronk's comments and reminiscences are often hilarious. *Inside* combines two LPs, the second of which is of white Southern music. *Two Sides* also combines two LPs, and includes tracks with the Red Onion Jazz Band; Van Ronk says elsewhere that he was 'tolerated [by jazz bands] mainly because I didn't mind doing vocals and I sang real loud', which is a fair assessment of his talents in this field. The Philo discs contain some of his finest guitar playing, but are not free of the drawbacks which affect the other CDs under consideration. *Statesboro Blues* is half live, half studio recordings; on the live tracks Van Ronk's spoken introductions are largely inaudible, and virtually all the playlist is available elsewhere. The best of these discs is the other live set, which locates Van Ronk and his music in the lineage of wisecracking observational humorists descended from Mark Twain, Will Rogers and W. C. Fields. On this CD he usually decides on an interpretive approach to a song and sticks to it. 'Gambler's Blues' (a.k.a. 'St. James Infirmary') is as irritating as any of his other versions, but the reinvention of 'Statesboro Blues' as a volcanic eruption is amazingly successful. CS

Jimmie Vaughan (born 1951)
VOCAL, GUITAR

Vaughan was born in Dallas, Texas, three years before his more celebrated younger brother Stevie Ray. He was playing in bands from his early teens, and in the mid-'70s founded the Fabulous Thunderbirds with Kim Wilson, where he remained for over 15 years. In 1993 he set up his own group, and has since toured Europe, won Grammy awards and recorded with the likes of B. B. King, Eric Clapton, Carlos Santana and Bob Dylan.

*** **Strange Pleasure**
Epic (E) 474268 *Vaughan; Bill Willis (o); Dr John [Mack Rebennack] (p); George Rains (d); Lou Ann Barton, Uren Waters, Terry Young, Kevin Dorsey (v).* 94.

** **Out There**
Epic 491220 *Vaughan; Greg Piccolo (ts); Bill Willis, Denny Freeman (o); Dr John [Mack Rebennack] (p, vb); Junior Brantley (p); Nile Rodgers (g, tamb); Larry Lerma (b); George Rains (d); Dave McNair (tamb); Larry Bunker (vb); Dennis Collins, Darryl Tookes, Harry Bowens Jr, Vincent Bonham, Darryl Phinnessee, Michael Newell, Kevin Baker, Donald Bryant (v).* 98.

*(*) **Do You Get The Blues?**
Artemis ARTCD-92//Artemis/Epic 504533 *Vaughan; Greg Piccolo (ts); Herman Green (fl); James Cotton (h); Bill Willis (o); Tyrone Vaughan (g); Roscoe Beck, Billy Horton, Tommy Shannon (b); George Rains, Chris Layton (d); Jose Galeano (perc); Lou Ann Barton, Greg Sain, James Edward Sain, Rayvon Foster, Charlie Whittington (v).* 01.

Vaughan's experience in the Fabulous Thunderbirds clearly informed his solo debut: every instrumental phrase is well measured, guided with reassuring expertise and couched in an early-electric blues guitar sound with a plain, dry tone. Blues fans might welcome *Strange Pleasure* with its retro arrangements, light-hitting songwriting (all Vaughan's own or co-written) and comfortable lack of urgency. At its best, as in the acoustic-on-a-porch slumber of 'Six Strings Down' and the cocktails-by-the-beach conversation between Vaughan's guitar and Dr John's tinkering piano in the title track, it's delightful. The only, but continuous, flaw is Vaughan's singing, which doesn't soar above the backing on bluesy wings, or have any distinguishing features.

Nile Rodgers helps to funk up 'Like A King' as *Out There* provides more uncluttered guitar work, reminiscent of Jimmy Rogers and also employing B. B. King's on-off method of filling gaps. Vaughan prefers to stick to blues roots, but his rigidly consistent approach also prevents the songs from building in intensity; they're more like jogs round an athletics track than sprints down canyons or dives into lagoons. Factor in a voice limited in range, volume and timbre, and there's little to keep 'Can't Say No', 'Astral Projection Blues' and several others from being tiring. His slinky soloing in 'Kinky Woman' hits a spot, but the album needs more in the vein of the solo acoustic closer 'Little Son, Big Son' to maintain the listener's attention.

On *Do You Get The Blues?* James Cotton's harmonica and Vaughan's acoustic slide combine on 'The Deep End' and Lou Ann Barton lends lead vocals to 'Power Of Love' and Johnny Watson's 'In The Middle Of The Night'. The latter also features brother Stevie Ray's bandmates Double Trouble, and Jimmie's son Tyrone plays second guitar on 'Without You'. Nevertheless, the guests barely spruce up the selection of tame, ineffectual material, or cure the syndromes of sameyness and lyrical cliché. Soft, mushy arrangements with funereally dull organ padding, and at one stage flute, make for a trite, artless affair. It may be a good thing, if only for refreshment's sake, that on 'Don't Let The Sun Set' Vaughan sounds vaguely like Sting. RR

Stevie Ray Vaughan (1954–90)
VOCAL, GUITAR

Few guitarists have approached Stevie Ray Vaughan's stature; no bluesman has played harder or with more determination; probably no individual's influence stretches further in the modern era of blues. His combination of musical tone and candour as a performer, his ability to apply dumbfounding force, to exact sentiment from every note he fretted, define him as a legend of his instrument. Born in Dallas, Texas, SRV was handed his first electric guitar at the age of nine by his older brother Jimmie. His connection with the blues was instant as he became addicted to his first record, Lonnie Mack's 'Wham'. He played in numerous groups through his teens and early 20s before forming Double Trouble in 1978 with drummer Chris Layton and Jackie Newhouse on bass, the latter being replaced by Tommy Shannon in 1981. Hype grew after Vaughan played on David Bowie's 1983 smash 'Let's Dance' but on the eve of a tour with Bowie Vaughan pulled out to focus on his own band. He and Double Trouble became the hottest blues act of the decade, despite substance abuse taking its toll and forcing Vaughan into rehab in 1986. One night after a sell-out concert in Alpine Valley, Wisconsin, where Vaughan had jammed on stage with Eric Clapton, Buddy Guy, Jimmie Vaughan and Robert Cray, he boarded a helicopter to return to Chicago; it crashed shortly after takeoff and tragically cut short the life of one of the blues' brightest torch-bearers.

*** **In The Beginning**
Epic 53168//(E) 472624 *Vaughan; Jackie Newhouse (b); Chris Layton (d). 4/80.*

A live broadcast from Austin, Texas, interesting in that it captures SRV before he peaked. He and Double Trouble, with Newhouse still on bass, plough through a vibrant, hopeful set like pistons in a well-oiled machine. Vaughan's playing isn't quite as crisp nor his sparse vocal presence as rousing as they would be when he became a major force in '80s rock 'n' roll. Inklings of trademark SRV guitar seep through occasionally; Guitar Slim's 'They Call Me Guitar Hurricane' is an appropriate cover, 'Love Struck Baby' is distinctly Chuck Berryish, there's a nice wailing slide thing in, er, 'Slide Thing' and 'Live Another Day' forms the template of his 1983 breakthrough hit 'Pride And Joy'.

**** **Live At Montreux 1982 & 1985**
Epic/Legacy 505161 2CD *Vaughan; Reese Wynans (o); Johnny Copeland (g, v); Tommy Shannon (b); Chris Layton (d). 7/82, 7/85.*

It would be the most important show they ever played. Searching for their big break, SRV and Double Trouble launched into a blistering set of raging 12-bars at the 1982 Montreux festival. Only slightly detectable on this recording are the boos and hisses of an increasingly dissatisfied audience, despite Vaughan, as always, playing all out as if his life depended on it. He was understandably crushed, and his dismay would soon be vindicated by the hundreds of thousands who bought five of the eight songs in this set on *Texas Flood*. It nevertheless startled David Bowie, who became instrumental in Vaughan's eventual rise to the top, and so it was a triumphant return in 1985 when classics from *Texas Flood* and *Couldn't Stand The Weather* and numbers from the soon-to-be-released *Soul To Soul* invited roars and hoots. The '85 disc demonstrates the three-year development from the group's primitive form to the more mature writing of 'Life Without You' or, with Johnny Copeland singing, 'Tin Pan Alley', plus a missionary's journey into the land of Hendrix with 'Voodoo Child (Slight Return)'. This 2CD inflates the original album with 11 previously unreleased tracks.

**** **Texas Flood**
Epic 460951//Epic/Legacy 494129 *Vaughan; Tommy Shannon (b); Chris Layton (d). 11/82, 83.*

Over three days in Jackson Browne's studio during Thanksgiving 1982, SRV and Double Trouble recorded a demo which was picked up by the veteran producer and A&R man John Hammond, who secured them a deal with Epic. The same recordings were used for most of the final cut, more a raw, untamed quality – above all in the flagship single 'Pride And Joy', which opens with a pulsating Texas shuffle guitar passage and rests on an axis of radio-friendly vocal hooks. Shannon, Layton and Vaughan create impossibly tight, head-tilting grooves such as 'Testify' and 'Rude Mood', which were among the fastest-sounding blues around. Soon after the album's release, SRV was awarded two Grammys and awards in three categories in *Guitar Player* magazine, one of which, 'Best Electric Blues Guitarist', he continued to win every year until his death. His singing was still developing, and ranges from the promising title track and 'Dirty Pool' to the less assertive 'Mary Had A Little Lamb', which eventually grew into a mammoth live favourite. But while his composing would continue to develop, he never surpassed *Texas Flood*'s majestic closing track, 'Lenny', a fluid, pensive, searching instrumental dedicated to his wife, steered by pleading lead flurries dispersed by dreamy whammy bar swooshes. Sublime. The Epic/Legacy issue has two bonus tracks.

**** **Couldn't Stand The Weather**
Epic 465571//Epic/Legacy 494130 *Vaughan; Stan Harrison (ts); Jimmie Vaughan (g); Tommy Shannon (b); Chris Layton (d); Fran Christina (d). 1/84.*

The follow-up to *Texas Flood* came with a hard-hitting title-track single laced with a sumptuous funk guitar break and catchy bass line. It aired regularly on MTV and completed SRV's ascent into the big league. At a time when spellbinding solos were being excised from popular music, as it explored digital technology and artificial synthesis, Vaughan was busy reinstating them. In doing so, sticking to a no-frills, minimal-effects sound, he represented the authentic craftsman, engineering solos of seemingly infinite directions, fast strums like screeching racing car wheels, multiple gears for switching tempo. His is one of the finer covers of 'Voodoo Chile', but check *SRV*, below, for an arguably better live version. 'Cold Shot's repressed riff creates a sleazy feel with controlled, quivery singing by a man trying to stretch himself in all departments. His unique sound – the ping-pong ball element of attack from his Fender Stratocaster with chunky strings – is especially effective in softer numbers like 'Tin Pan Alley' and the jazzy 'Stang's Swang'. The Epic/Legacy edition comes with four bonus tracks and a short extract of interview footage, all previously unreleased. The CD is also available in a Mastersound version (Epic EK 64425).

**** **Live At Carnegie Hall**
Epic EK 68163//(E) 488206 *Vaughan; Bob Enos (t); Porky Cohen (tb); Rich Lataille (as); Greg Piccolo (ts); Doug James (bs); Dr John [Mack Rebennack] (kb); Jimmie Vaughan (g); Tommy Shannon (b); Chris Layton, George Rains (d); Angela Strehli (v). 10/84.*

With horn sections merely trimmings on their meaty sound, Double Trouble are in their element and live up to the crowd's eruptions for 'Love Struck Baby' and 'Cold Shot'. Angela Strehli lays a gutsy guest vocal on 'C.O.D.', while Vaughan, right from the finger-loosening opener 'Scuttle Buttin'', plays as if he's never been heard before and still has to convince us all. Some may find the heavyweight instrumental feel of the record excessive, but get them on their own and

Vaughan and a guitar are captivating as they close the show with 'Rude Mood' and an extra-long 'Lenny', handled with an enviable guile.

*** Soul To Soul
Epic 466330//Epic/Legacy 494131 *Vaughan; Joe Sublett (s); Reese Wynans (kb); Tommy Shannon (b); Chris Layton (d). 85.*

There's more than a nod to SRV's idol Hendrix in the screaming wah-led opener 'Say What!'. The squeezed notes and unusually lush vocals recall Albert King in 'Ain't Gone 'N' Give Up On Love' and reflect SRV's growing maturity as a composer (five of the original ten tracks). However, the material often requires the injection of something more to achieve magical elevation. It's a painless wave in the face of soul, often with slower tempos than Vaughan had previously averaged, and the newly added Wynans's less serrated keyboard throbs add density to the background. 'Life Without You' has the movement and soothing hand-on-your-shoulder quality of an Otis Redding performance, foregrounding Vaughan's vocals for a change. Elsewhere his Catherine-wheel guitar sparks retain their authoritative glory to improve indifferently treated covers like Willie Dixon's 'You'll Be Mine', which becomes reminiscent of surf guitar king Dick Dale. The Epic/Legacy issue has three previously unreleased bonus tracks: SRV speaking about Hendrix's skill and vision, the superb studio cover of 'Little Wing'/'Third Stone From The Sun', and finally 'Slip Slidin' Slim', 100 seconds of bottleneck narrative set to a frantic Texan rhythm.

*** Live Alive
Epic 466839 *Vaughan; Reese Wynans (kb); Jimmie Vaughan (g, b); Tommy Shannon (b); Chris Layton (d). 7/85, 7/86.*

Live Alive was the first official live release, but since then others, which capture entire shows, have improved on it by conveying the ripples of a band bringing its audience to the boil in a concentrated burst. Compiled from three events – the 1985 Montreux festival, since released separately (see above), and 1986 shows in Austin and Dallas – it doesn't feature SRV at his best but is worth hearing for him and Jimmie teeing off on four tracks, and a decent Hubert Sumlin steal in a version of Howlin' Wolf's 'I'm Leaving You (Commit A Crime)'. Perhaps the most interesting track is a heartfelt cover of Stevie Wonder's 'Superstition', performed the year after *Soul To Soul* was released, which consummates Vaughan's contribution to merging blues and soul.

*** In Step
Epic 463395//Epic/Legacy 494132 *Vaughan; Reese Wynans (kb); Tommy Shannon (b); Chris Layton (d, perc). 1–2/89.*

There may be fewer killer tracks on SRV's final studio outing with Double Trouble, but it's the same focused ambition, conviction and drive to bare all with his instrument. Indeed in Howlin' Wolf's 'Love Me Darlin'' he may as well have forgotten how far he's come, and there are two of his best-ever performances: the soaring version of Buddy Guy's 'Leave My Girl Alone', in which Vaughan's broken 'done me wrong' vocal crystallizes in an idyllic space next to jaw-dropping guitar intensity that echoes Freddie King, and the experimental original composition 'Riviera Paradise', for many listeners an instrumental to rival 'Lenny'. The blues-soul torch of 'Crossfire', a song that became an adored SRV memory, would be grabbed by the teenaged Jonny Lang in his 1997 debut *Lie To Me*. The Epic/Legacy issue has four bonus tracks and an interview excerpt.

***(*) The Sky Is Crying
Epic 47390//468640 *Vaughan; Reese Wynans (kb); Tommy Shannon (b); Chris Layton (d). 1/84–2/89.*

A ten-cut compilation of finished studio tracks which, for one reason or another, were not included on previous albums, except the closing 'Life By The Drop' from *Soul To Soul*. This is no bottom-of-the-barrel collection, and many were staples of the group's live repertoire. 'Boot Hill' is the first of the rare occasions when Vaughan recorded in the studio with slide, and, while it's not often that he switches to acoustic, he does so here when he dons a 12-string for 'Life By The Drop', with a lyric by Doyle Bramhall and Barbara Logan partly alluding to his drug addiction. The title track is a tasty homage to Vaughan's heroes Lonnie Mack and Muddy Waters. 'Wham' does exactly that, in a thundering 12-bar. In 'May I Have A Talk With You' Vaughan borrows Howlin' Wolf's trick of incorporating lyrics from different compositions, his pleading, shade-of-growl voice effectively wrapping up the package. Jazz guitarist Kenny Burrell's influence resonates in 'Chitlins Con Carne', notable for Vaughan's attempt to play in a jazz form he loved listening to but doubted his abilities in; it shares the mellow ballad style of the earlier 'Lenny' and the later 'Riviera Paradise'. Among numerous high points, a now renowned cover of 'Little Wing' takes an instrumental journey from tender to tenacious, rooted in Vaughan's tough tone and a floating sense of departure and resolution. (Hendrix would have been wowed, if a little threatened.) It's gripping, intoxicating, a knotted trial of technique and emotion, and the aural testament of one of the greatest exponents of electric guitar music.

** Family Style
Epic 46225//467014 *Vaughan; Stan Harrison (as, ts); Steve Elson (ts, bs); Rockin' Sidney (ac); Richard Hilton (kb, o, p); Jimmie Vaughan (o, sg, g, v); Nile Rodgers (g); Al Berry, Preston Hubbard (b); Larry Aberman, Doyle Bramhall (d); David Spinner, Tawatha Agee, Brenda White-King, Curtis King Jr, George Sims (v). 3/90.*

Produced by ex-Chic guitarist Nile Rodgers, with writing contributions by the Vaughans, Rodgers and drummer Doyle Bramhall, *Family Style*, credited to The Vaughan Brothers, was released shortly after SRV's untimely death, adding a pathos to the album which would otherwise have been undetectable. Stevie and Jimmie share singing and guitar duties, but Jimmie's vocals are under-confident while Stevie rarely sounds as if he's trying hard. Indeed, little is asked of him, hence limp results with gnawing drums too high in the mixes – probably a sign of the snappy sound developed through '80s pop. 'Hard To Be' begins things well: it is one Stevie had a hand in writing, and his songs invariably have an edge. But the instrumental 'D/FW' sums up an album destined to travel nowhere far. It's as meaningless as 'Good Texan''s arbitrary line 'I dig your chili, you know it's true', and the album slumps furthest in the saccharine soul parade 'Tick Tock', the pre-release litmus test of taste somehow letting through 'Now in this dream universal love was the theme of the day – peace and understanding and it happened this way'. 'Telephone Song' hopes that, since *Family Style* is mainly blues in structure, it can be blues in feel as well. On the penultimate track,

'Baboom'/'Mama Said', a hasty attempt to insert a ripping Stevie solo between Rodgers's watery funk licks confirms that SRV is better when he's in full control.

♛ **** SRV
Epic/Legacy EPC 500930 3CD+DVD *Vaughan; A. C. Reed (s, v); Joe Sublett (s); Reese Wynans, Tony Hymas (kb); Stan Szelest (o, p); Ken Vangel, Tony Llorens, Richard Hilton (p); Johnny Copeland, Albert King, Lonnie Mack (g, v); Denny Freeman, Joel Perry, Marvin Jackson, Jeff Beck, Jimmie Vaughan (g); Alex Napier, Jackie Newhouse, Tommy Shannon, Brian Miller, Guy Thornton, Tim Drummond, Freddie Dixon, Al Berry (b); Rodney Craig, Casey Jones (d, v); Chris Layton, Jimmy Wormworth, Michael Llorens, Dennis O'Neal, Terry Bozzio, Larry Aberman (d); Paul Ray, Angela Strehli, Miranda Louise, Vicki Hardy (v). 77–8/90.*

This lavish compilation covers some of SRV's best work in studio cuts, live tracks and guest appearances with other vocalists. Many of these selections are previously unissued, and there is a live version of 'Hug You, Squeeze You' never before available on CD. Aside from album classics discussed elsewhere in this entry, most relishable are the powerhouse stage performances, alight with energy and purpose. In one intro Vaughan's restless guitar slithers between Layton's relentless drums like a snake being chased by its mat-banging master. 'Crosscut Saw' should have '(Not As Effective As My Electric One)' completing its title, such is the jagged electricity of Vaughan's buzzing tone and the surging rhythmic accompaniment. And while his voice hasn't the dreamy hypnotic quality of Hendrix's, 'Manic Depression' demonstrates how in his guitar interpretations he reaches higher levels than others treading Jimi's path, who make their salutes more as disciples than as peers. 'Little Wing'/'Third Stone From The Sun' and 'Voodoo Chile' take this further, each 11-plus minutes of exquisite noise jams that collapse into the virtual sound of an exploding car lot. Albert King, connoisseur of confessional blues, is recalled in the marvellous 'The Sky is Crying', and 'Leave My Girl Alone' is bellowed with ferocity, so different from the intimate beauty of Vaughan's warm melismas in 'Dirty Pool', which remind us that we're hearing an excellent blues vocalist too, something for which he never received enough praise. There's also room to breathe in three 12-string acoustic numbers from a 1990 MTV *Unplugged*. Of the collaborations, 'Don't Stop By The Creek, Son' has Johnny Copeland's throaty vocal with SRV's guitar further back in the mix to stir up a fizzy refreshment. The first CD closes with an extract from Albert King and Vaughan's juicy jam on *In Session With Albert King* (discussed in King's entry). RR

(***) Greatest Hits
Epic 481025 *As for relevant CDs above.* 11/82–2/89.

(***) The Real Deal: Greatest Hits Volume 2
Epic/Legacy 494133 *As for relevant CDs above.* 4/80–2/89.

*** Martin Scorsese Presents The Blues
Epic/Legacy 512576 *As for relevant CDs above.* 4/80–2/89.

♛ **** The Essential Stevie Ray Vaughan And Double Trouble
Epic/Legacy 510019 2CD *As for relevant CDs above.* 4/80–3/90.

*** Blues At Sunrise
Epic/Legacy 497858 *Vaughan; Reese Wynans, Tony Llorens (kb); Johnny Copeland, Albert King (g, v); Jimmie Vaughan (g);* Tommy Shannon, Gus Thornton (b); Chris Layton, Michael Llorens (d). 11/82–2/89.

Greatest Hits is fairly evenly picked from *Texas Flood, Couldn't Stand The Weather, Soul To Soul, In Step* and *The Sky Is Crying*, the only rogue item being a previously unissued version of George Harrison's 'Taxman'. Among the signature pieces are 'Texas Flood', 'Pride And Joy' and the 'Little Wing' from *The Sky Is Crying*. *The Real Deal* is a more generous selection (16 tracks as against 11), with two more tracks from each of the previously visited albums, a few from others, mostly live, and two collectables, 'Pipeline' from a movie soundtrack and a live 'Leave My Girl Alone' from a promo disc. Important cuts include 'Love Struck Baby', 'Lenny' and 'Riviera Paradise'. The Scorsese selection carves an independent passage through SRV's backlist, foregrounding his versions of repertoire received from Buddy Guy, Elmore James, Otis Rush and other sources. 'Mary Had A Little Lamb', from a 6/87 Philadelphia gig, is previously unissued. *Blues At Sunrise*, billed as 'the slow blues album', is made up of seven album tracks, the long version of the title cut with Albert King from their *In Session* CD and previously unissued versions of 'The Sky Is Crying' and 'Texas Flood'.

All these compilations pale beside *The Essential*, which, indeed, renders two of them superfluous: its 33 tracks swallow up all bar one (the forgettable 'Taxman') from *Greatest Hits* and all bar three from *The Real Deal*, replacing the latter's 'Voodoo Chile (Slight Return)' (from *Couldn't Stand The Weather*), with the superior version from Carnegie Hall (from *SRV*). Readers who have heard a lot about this hugely gifted musician and have always meant to check him out need dawdle no more: this is both a faultless introduction and, with a better than two-for-the-price-of-one tag, a bargain. TR

Maurice John Vaughn (born 1949)
VOCAL, GUITAR, SAXOPHONE

A native Chicagoan, Vaughn played drums and saxophone in his teens, adding the guitar some years later. He worked for spells with Professor Eddie Lusk, Phil Guy, Son Seals and A. C. Reed, whom he has accompanied on several albums; he has also recorded with Zora Young and Detroit Jr, and produced albums by several artists for the Italian Appaloosa label.

**(*) Generic Blues Album
Alligator ALCD 4763 *Vaughn; Leo Davis, Allen Batts (kb); Kenny Pickens (b); Bill Leathers, Casey Jones (d); Zora Young (v).* 84, 87.

** I Got Money
Black & Blue BB 464 *Vaughn; A. C. Reed (ts); Douglas Watson (b); Julian Vaughan (d).* 11/85.

**(*) In The Shadow Of The City
Alligator ALCD 4813 *Vaughn; Nathaniel 'B. J.' Emery (tb, v); Allen Batts (o, p); Kenny Barker, Jimmy Walker (p); Freddie Dixon (b); Michael McGee, Bill Leathers, Robert Covington (d); Jacques LaCava (sp).* 92?

The artist who introduced himself to blues record-buyers in 1984 with the playfully titled *Generic Blues Album* was an odd mixture: a singer with a penchant for sub-Wolfian yodels, a somewhat inconsistent guitarist and a writer capable of devising the amusing 'Generic Blues' and the catchy 'Computer Took My Job', one of the first blues on the subject. In reissuing the original Reecy LP Alligator added a couple of later recordings, 'Wolf Bite', which is nothing out of the ordinary, and 'Nothing Left To Believe In', whose cold mean-streets ambience merited a stronger lyric.

I Got Money, made in France while Vaughn was touring with A. C. Reed, who sings on five of the album's ten tracks, offers another 'Computer Took My Job' and a solo piece, 'Mojo On Me', but since the recording puts a damper on Vaughn's guitar playing and, Reed apart, there isn't much else happening, this is no more than a pencil sketch. The next album captures the artist in colour, and the qualities that notewriter David Whiteis perceives in Vaughn's music, 'the cadences of the city – harsh and unrelenting, yet buoyed by an undercurrent of dreams and optimism', begin to emerge on tracks like 'Can't Nobody', 'Game Over' and 'Eager Beaver'. Nevertheless, Vaughn's determination to display versatility that he can't quite command, which is reflected in the erratic quality of the mostly original material, is likely to leave some listeners unsatisfied.

*** **Dangerous Road**
Blue Suit BS-116D *Vaughn; B. J. Emery (tb, v); Fred Brousse (h, g); Khouki Pontelero (o, p); Allen Batts (o); Detroit Jr (p); Ilaria Lantieri (b, v); Massimo Bertagna, Jerome Moho (d); Velvet McNair (v). 01?*

As might be expected, this is another ungeneric blues album, but the ratio of aspiration to achievement is more even than on *In The Shadow Of The City*. Except for a bouncing 'In The Midnight Hour' the material is all Vaughn's, and this time its variety is supported by better writing and often attractively textured arrangements, as in the title number or the excellent 'Love Abuse'. Having had his say about computers, Vaughn identifies a new technological target in 'The Telephone's Running My Life'. TR

Walter Vincson (1911–75)
VOCAL, GUITAR

His real name, Walter Vinson, never appeared on a 78, although Walter Vincent, Walter Jacobs (his mother's birth name) and a contract-dodging 'Sam Hill from Louisville' all did; he's believed to have been 'Leroy Carter' as well. Most extensively, though, Vinson recorded as a member of the Mississippi Sheiks. He left Mississippi in 1933 for Chicago; in 1961, and again in 1972, he recorded with new versions of the Sheiks.

(*) **Walter Vincson (1928–1941) [sic]
RST Blues Documents BDCD-6017 *Vincson; Robert Lee McCoy (h); Harry Chatmon, Little Brother Montgomery or Ernest Johnson (p); Bo Chatmon [Carter] (prob. vn, g, v); Lonnie Chatmon, unknown (vn); Charlie McCoy (md, g); unknown (g); Alfred Elkins (b); unknown (v). 9/29–8/41.*

This disc begins with a Mary Butler song on which the guitarist is almost certainly Charlie McCoy. Eight of the next nine tracks are by Sheiks-like stringbands, among them four deft instrumentals issued in OKeh's hillbilly series. The exception is Vinson's masterpiece, 'Overtime Blues', on which he reproaches his woman with tetchy dignity and unleashes his considerable guitar skills. (Especially when working with a fiddler, Vinson was often content with respectful chording.) On most subsequent tracks he's joined by a succession of pianists; the final six titles, made in Chicago in 1941, try to come up to date with one-string bass and ill-assorted harmonica. Vinson was a clever lyricist ('Rats Been On My Cheese' is quite a metaphor for adultery), and he composed some distinctive tunes, but the transfers from 78 are often poorly done and/or from worn originals. Four excellent sides by 'Sam Hill' are on *Mississippi String Bands & Associates* (RST Blues Documents BDCD-6013), and *South Side Blues* (Original Blues Classics OBCCD 508) includes three tracks by the 1961 Mississippi Sheiks. CS

Eddie 'Cleanhead' Vinson (1917–88)
VOCAL, ALTO SAXOPHONE

Growing up in Houston, Vinson studied saxophone in school and had his first professional experience with the local bandleader Chester Boone, going on to work on the road with Lil Green and Big Bill Broonzy before landing a job with Cootie Williams's orchestra, where he first recorded his abrasive singing. Forming his own group in 1945, he was popular for a decade thanks to records like 'Kidney Stew' and 'Cherry Red'. He spent much of the '50s and '60s out of music, but thereafter regained a following in both the US and Europe.

*** **Old Maid Boogie**
[Blue Boar CDBB 1008] *Vinson; Cootie Williams, Ermit V. Perry, George Treadwell, Harold 'Money' Johnson, Lammar Wright, Tommy Stevenson, Billy Ford, Gene Redd, Stumpy Whitlock, John Hunt, Joe Bridgewater, Volley Bastine, Clark Terry (t); Ed Burke, George Stevenson, Robert H. Horton, Ed Glover, Dan Logan, Leon Comegys, Rip Tarrant, Arnett 'Nick' Sparrow (tb); Charlie Holmes, Frank Powell, Rupert Cole, Frank Dominguez, Ernest Tanner (as); Eddie 'Lockjaw' Davis, Lee Pope, Sam 'The Man' Taylor, Red Carman (ts); Eddie De Verteuil, George Favors, Greely Walton (bs); Bud Powell, Arnold Jarvis, Earl Van Riper (p); Leroy Kirkland (g); Norman Keenan, Carl Pruitt, Jimmy Glover, Leonard 'Heavy' Swain (b); Vess Payne, Gus Johnson, George 'Butch' Ballard (d). 1/44–12/47.*

*** **A Proper Introduction To Eddie "Cleanhead" Vinson: Kidney Stew Blues**
Proper INTRO CD 2056 *As above, except add Henderson Williams, Calvin Hughes, Rostelle Reese, Cornelius Tate, Joe Wilder, Charles F. Lee (t), James Buxton, Tyree Glenn, Slide Hampton (tb), Harry Porter, Rudy Williams, Buddy Tate, Charlie Rouse (ts), Al Townsend, Orrington Hall, Bill Graham, Walter Hiles (bs), Wynton Kelly, Milt Larkin, Milt Buckner, prob. Joseph Lawson (p), John Faire (g), Franklin Skeete, Dave Richmond, Gene Ramey, prob. Carl Lee (b), Leon Abrams, Rudy Nichols, Percy Brice, Wilbert Hogan (d). 1/44–7/52.*

*** **Eddie Vinson 1945–1947**
Classics 5017 *Vinson; Elmer 'Stumpy' Whitlock, John Hunt, Joe Bridgewater, Volley Bastine, Clark Terry (t); Leon Comegys, Jesse 'Rip' Tarrant, Arnett 'Nick' Sparrow (tb); Frank Dominguez, Ernest 'Lee' Tanner (as); Lee Pope, Red Carman (ts); Greely Walton (bs); Earl Van Riper (p); Leonard 'Heavy' Swain (b); Gus Johnson, George 'Butch' Ballard (d). c. 12/45–4/47.*

*** **Cleanhead Blues 1945–1947**
[EPM Blues Collection 15946] *As above. c. 12/45–12/47.*

*** **Mr Cleanhead Steps Out**
[Zircon Bleu 503] *As above, except add Cootie Williams, Ermit V. Perry, George Treadwell, Billy Ford, Gene Redd, Henderson Williams, Calvin Hughes (t), Dan Logan, Ed Burke, Robert Horton, James Buxton (tb), Rupert Cole (as), Sam 'The Man'*

Taylor, Eddie 'Lockjaw' Davis, Harry Porter (ts), George Favors, Al Townsend (bs), Arnold Jarvis, Wynton Kelly (p), Jimmy Glover, Frank Skeete (b), Vess Payne, Leon Abrams (d). 45–8/49.

*** Eddie Vinson 1947–1949
Classics 5042 Vinson; John Hunt, Henderson Williams, Calvin Hughes (t); James Buxton (tb); Lee Pope, Eddie 'Lockjaw' Davis, Harry Porter (ts); Greely Walton, Al Townsend (bs); Earl Van Riper, Wynton Kelly (p); Leonard Swain, Franklin Skeete (b); George Ballard, Leon Abrams (d). 6/47–8/49.

*** Bald Headed Blues
Ace CDCHD 877 Vinson; Henderson Williams, Calvin Hughes, Rostelle Reese, Cornelius Tate, Joe Wilder, Charles F. Lee (t); Milt Larkin (tb, p); James Buxton, Tyree Glenn, Slide Hampton (tb); Eddie 'Lockjaw' Davis, Harry Porter, Rudy Williams, Buddy Tate, Lee Pope, Charlie Rouse (ts); Al Townsend, Orrington Hall, Bill Graham, Walter Hiles (bs); Wynton Kelly, Milt Buckner, Freddie Washington, prob. Joseph Lawson (p); John Faire (g); Franklin Skeete, Dave Richmond, Gene Ramey, Billy Taylor, prob. Carl Lee (b); Leon Abrams, Rudy Nichols, Percy Brice, Wilbert Hogan. (d). 8/49–7/52.

Singing or blowing alto, Vinson had a hard, penetrating tone that cut through the most boisterous ensemble, and his recordings of the '40s and early '50s, whether with a big band on Hit, Capitol and Mercury or with smaller groups on King, are consistently good examples of the tough, unsentimental idiom conventionally, though not really adequately, described as 'blues shouting'.

The Classics CDs provide a complete and chronological survey of the '40s Mercury sessions (he returned to the label briefly in 1954), the second volume carrying on into the Kings. The Blue Boar, Proper and Zircon sets are selections from the same lode; Blue Boar add six earlier sides with Cootie Williams's orchestra, and Zircon one, while Proper add four but also march farther into King's realm, making it the best buy of the three as well as the most readily available. The EPM Blues Collection confines itself to Mercury and the Ace to the King sides in their entirety. All of these albums are well stocked with the sexual point numbers for which Vinson is best known and which he recorded repeatedly, such as 'Cherry Red (Blues)' and 'Kidney Stew (Blues)'. On such material he habitually used his trademark effect of a hoarse falsetto squeal, but on more reflective slow blues, such as 'If You Don't Think I'm Sinking' or 'Person To Person' on Ace, he tended to drop that device and simply sing straight, in a style close to Big Joe Turner's. Amidst the noisy swagger of the accompaniments, soloists other than Vinson occasionally push forward to blow; the King instrumentals 'Eddie's Bounce' (also on Proper, Zircon and the second Classics) and 'Jump And Grunt', for instance, make room for tenorists Lockjaw Davis and Buddy Tate respectively.

*** Cleanhead's Back In Town
Bethlehem 20-4003//[Charly CDGR 166] Vinson; Joe Newman (t); Henry Coker (tb); Bill Graham (as); Charlie Rouse, Paul Quinichette, Frank Foster (ts); Charlie Fowlkes (bs); Nat Pierce (p); Turk Van Lake, Freddie Green (g); Ed Jones (b); Ed Thigpen, Gus Johnson (d). 9/57.

As he contemplated making this album with a bunch of Basie alumni, one wonders if it occurred to Vinson that Big Joe Turner had done something roughly similar 18 months before. Cleanhead's Back In Town and Boss Of The Blues even shared a song, 'Cherry Red'. Whether it was strategy behind the move or serendipity, Vinson was proud of the album it produced – as well he might be, for it puts a bright morning face even on such oldies as 'Kidney Stew' and 'Trouble In Mind'. The shade of Louis Jordan watches benignly as Vinson enquires 'Is You Is Or Is You Ain't My Baby' and asks Caldonia why her big head's so hard, and Cab Calloway blows a cloud of weedie-wo smoke around 'It Ain't Necessarily So', but much of what's left is standard Vinson material, presented with at least his normal quota of heartiness and gift-wrapped by the glossy orchestra.

*** Cleanhead & Cannonball
Milestone MCD-9324 Vinson; Nat Adderley (c); Cannonball Adderley (as); Joe Zawinul (p); Sam Jones (b); Louis Hayes (d). 9/61, 2/62.

'When Julian Adderley ran into Eddie Vinson in Kansas City late in the summer of 1961,' Orrin Keepnews explains in the notes, '[Cleanhead] wasn't doing too well ... [and] hadn't made a record in several years.' But since Adderley's deal with Riverside Records 'allowed him a pretty free hand in recording anyone who aroused his enthusiasm,' that state of affairs was quickly corrected. The Adderley band of that period was very well suited to accompanying a blues singer like Vinson, and its approach is an elegant alternative to the jump-blues setting of his earlier recordings. Zawinul reads the blues road map with particular skill. As well as the vocal numbers Vinson recorded four instrumentals, 'Arriving Soon', 'Vinsonology', 'Cannonizing' and 'Bernice's Bounce', on which he isn't in the least abashed by the contiguity (Cannonball sat them out, but in the control room) of a rather more famous altoist.

*** Jumpin' The Blues
Black & Blue BB 959 Vinson; Jay McShann (p, v); Gene Ramey (b); Paul Gunther (d). 3/69.

*** Kidney Stew Is Fine
Delmark DD-631 Vinson; Hal Singer (ts); Al Grey (tb); Jay McShann (p); T-Bone Walker (g); Roland Lobligeois (b); Paul Gunther (d). 3/69.

*** Kidney Stew
Black & Blue BB 878 As above, except add Al Grey (tb), Eddie 'Lockjaw' Davis (ts), Wild Bill Davis, Bill Doggett (o), Floyd Smith (g), Milt Hinton (b), J. C. Heard (d). 3/69, 7/72, 7/78.

** Jamming The Blues
Black Lion BLCD 760188 Vinson; Hal Singer (ts); Peter Wingfield (p); Joe Wright (g); Jerome Rimson (b); Peter Van Hook (d). 7/74.

Jumpin' The Blues, recorded live in Paris, opens with five tracks by Jay McShann and his trio, then Vinson joins them to recall the old McShann–Charlie Parker days in the title tune and sing a selection of his specialities ('Kidney Stew', 'Cherry Red', etc.). McShann plays with huge authority and verve throughout, and Vinson responds with some of his most sinewy alto playing.

Kidney Stew Is Fine was also recorded in Paris, about three weeks later, and originally issued by Black & Blue. Vinson takes a fresh look at several of his '40s sides like 'Old Maid Boogie', 'Juice Head Baby' and 'Somebody's Got To Go', with an instrumental interlude of 'Things Ain't What They Used To Be'. Singer and McShann play with the ease of experience, but Walker is both subdued and mixed too low. Black & Blue's own reissue of the album, simply called Kidney Stew, adds four '70s tracks with other accompanists. The best is 'Hey Little

Doggey', a Bill Doggett tune that sends Vinson, Lockjaw Davis and the composer off on a slow blues prowl.

In *Jamming The Blues* Vinson gives a Montreux Jazz Festival audience some of what they probably came for in a curlicued but brief reading of 'Laura' and easy rides through Charlie Parker's 'Now's The Time' and 'C Jam Blues', interspersing them with a few vocal numbers. Wingfield plays bravely but the rest of the rhythm section is unimpressive, and what with the rather too open-air feel of the recording and the crowd's tendency to clap along, this is the least rewarding of Vinson's albums.

**(*) Redux – Live At The Keystone Korner
Savant SCD 2052 *Vinson; Larry Vuckovich (p); James Leary (b); Eddie Marshall (d).* 1/79.

Until it came out in 2003 this set from the San Francisco club had never been issued, but therein lies no cause for excitement: it adds little to Vinson's discography but bulk. The six vocal numbers are all Vinson standbys ('Cherry Red', 'Kidney Stew', 'They Call Me Mr. Cleanhead', etc.), while the four instrumentals are extended by the backing trio being given plenty of time on their own: no hardship when Vuckovich is having his unhackneyed way with a tune, but painful during the bass solos, particularly the five choruses in 'Back At The Chicken Shack'.

*** Blues, Boogie & Bebop – "Meat's Too High"
JSP JSPCD 804 *Vinson; Stan Greig, John Burch (p); Les Davidson (g); Paul Sealy, Lennie Bush (b); Martin Guy, Bobby Orr (d).* 5/80, 3/82.

*** I Want A Little Girl
Original Jazz Classics OJCCD-868 *Vinson; Martin Banks (t); Rashid Jamal Ali (ts); Art Hillery (o, p); Cal Green (g); John Heard (b); Roy McCurdy (d).* 2/81.

The squeaky rasp in Vinson's voice became more jagged with age, but there was nothing rough-edged about his alto playing – of which the JSP album, one of few that he recorded with no other horn player, is a prime showcase, whether in long solos on vocal numbers or in instrumentals at both up and down tempos. The sessions were recorded in London with British musicians; the earlier one, which accounts for nine of the 15 tracks, has somewhat more punch, both Greig and Davidson playing idiomatically and well. Between the two dates Vinson recorded back home with a larger group, which produced a similarly satisfying set of blues, including a long, very slow 'Stormy Monday', and a couple of bop anthems. TR

Mose Vinson (1917–2002)
VOCAL, PIANO

Vinson came to Memphis from Holly Springs, having played music from the age of five. A janitor's job at Sun Records led to a few appearances as a sideman, and a session that remained unissued until much later. Vinson continued to play in Memphis clubs, was recorded again by researchers, and in the '90s became pianist-in-residence at the Center for Southern Folklore.

**(*) Joe Hill Louis – The Be-Bop Boy With Walter Horton And Mose Vinson
Bear Family BCD 15524 *Vinson; Walter Horton (h); Joe Hill Louis (g, hi-hat, sp); poss. Joe Willie Wilkins (g); Kenneth Banks (b); Israel Franklin (d, hand claps); Thomas 'Beale Street' Coleman (d); unknown (rag-popping, sp).* 9/53.

Despite the above, there are unresolved discographical debates around Mose Vinson's Sun recordings. There may have been more than one session, for Joe Willie Wilkins identified himself on some numbers, and Vinson agreed. Contrariwise, Vinson didn't remember accompanying the anonymous rag-popper on 'Shine Boy', although session notes confirm his presence. These minutiae will be incidental for most people, as will the alternative takes in the deleted, but possibly still obtainable, box set *Sun Records: The Blues Years* (Charly CD SUNBOX 7).

Vinson sings in a fierce, tangle-tongued holler, hammering the piano with corresponding force. '44 Blues' hints at the harmonic and rhythmic eccentricities that were to become more prominent in later years, but the drummer's confusion on 'Mistreatin' Boogie' is his own responsibility; this version of 'Pine Top's Boogie Woogie' is Vinson's demonstration piece, and he makes the most of it. There are a number of splendidly grungy guitar solos, although the one on 'Reap What You Sow' wanders away from the key. These seven tracks all have their moments, but few of them are fully achieved, and it's not really surprising that they weren't issued at the time.

(**) Memphis Piano Blues Today
Wolf 120.928 *Vinson.* 10/90.

This CD is shared with Booker T. Laury. The session was recorded at Vinson's home; he's enthusiastic, but the piano is badly out of tune.

*** Piano Man
Center For Southern Folklore CSF 1997-1 *Vinson; Jim Dickinson (p, sp); Judy Peiser (sp).* 94.

At 77, Vinson's still very forceful, and this time he's playing a much better piano. He sometimes treats it disconcertingly, thumping out chords that are virtually tone clusters, abruptly shifting the rhythm, and sometimes making undeniable mistakes: 'Darktown Strutter's Ball' and 'Just Because' are particularly error-prone. *Piano Man* tries to document all aspects of Vinson's music, and he's at his most assured on three instrumental versions of well-known spirituals; their ragtime treatment must have raised some eyebrows in church. On three tracks, Jim Dickinson plays treble parts, which are of little musical importance but contribute to the relaxed atmosphere; along with sympathetic interviewing, this encourages Vinson to produce his most committed blues performances. Occasionally he crosses the line between eccentric and slipshod, but *Piano Man* is a well-rounded portrait of an engaging, idiosyncratic musician. CS

Jimmy Vivino (born 1954)
VOCAL, GUITAR

Based in New York, Vivino has worked with a variety of blues and pop artists, and for a long spell with Al Kooper. He has recorded with Hubert Sumlin, and co-produced and wrote material for Shemekia Copeland's first two albums.

**(*) Do What, Now?
MusicMasters 65157 *Vivino; John Sebastian (h); Al Kooper (kb,*

md, prod); Paul Harris, Reese Wynans (p); Sam Bush (md); Harvey Brooks (b); Anton Fig (d). 5/96.

Though he has recently been involved in the writing of some good songs, Vivino confines himself on this CD to other people's, selecting from Percy Mayfield, Elmore James and others. Except on Blind Willie Johnson's 'God Don't Never Change' and Muddy Waters's 'Little Geneva', which are played on a National steel guitar, and Elmore's 'Stranger Blues', essentially a duet for acoustic guitar and Sam Bush's mandolin, Vivino plays electric, in a style absorbed in part from Mike Bloomfield. This is respectable blues playing, but it's let down by colourless vocals. TR

Jimmy Walker (1905–97)
VOCAL, PIANO

Born in Memphis, Walker moved to Chicago aged three, and began playing piano at 19. He played at clubs and parties, but went unrecorded until white interest in blues burgeoned in the '60s. From 1975, Walker held down residencies at North Side clubs, and remained active to an advanced age.

**(*) Rough And Ready
Testament TCD 5011 Walker; Erwin Helfer (p); Lillian Walker (v). 64.

Six tracks by Helfer with Willie Dixon on bass are discussed in his entry. Eight of the balance are two-piano instrumentals, Walker performs alone on two instrumentals and two vocal blues, and he and Mrs Walker each sing a blues with two-piano accompaniment. On the duets, Helfer usually takes the right-hand part while Walker sets the rhythm; they work together well, and it's evident that both men are enjoying themselves, but Ammons and Lewis they're not. *Rough And Ready* is often an honest description, and there are a number of harmonic collisions, skilfully disguised as near-misses. Meeting Helfer reinvigorated Walker to the point that he bought a second piano soon after they met, but the most valuable tracks, because their success is on his shoulders, are Walker's solos and dry, self-possessed vocals. The recording quality is rather cloudy.

*** Small Town Baby
Wolf 120.712 Walker; Steve Cushing (d). 7/83.

The sound is much better here, and Walker's singing and playing both show the benefit of regular work at Elsewhere and B.L.U.E.S. His staccato humming, which probably serves to keep him on track harmonically, can be disconcerting, 'Sweet Home Chicago' is the downside of playing for tourists, and Cushing's drumming is sometimes pedantic. These snags are more than compensated for, however, by 'Come On, Get Your Morning Exercise' and 'Kansas City Baby' (both, given their titles, unexpectedly introspective), by 'South Side Impressions', which explores Jimmy Yancey's habañera bass, and by a radically revamped 'King Bee', somewhat in the manner of Walter Davis. CS

Joe Louis Walker (born 1949)
VOCAL, GUITAR, HARMONICA

Walker grew up in San Francisco with blues-loving parents and a churchgoing grandmother. He began playing guitar in his teens, and later lived in the same house as Michael Bloomfield, but his musical career lacked direction until he joined The Spiritual Corinthians, a gospel group, in 1975. Ten years later he formed his own blues band, The Boss Talkers, and made his first album. Since then he has risen steadily in the regard of blues audiences, and he has toured and played at festivals in many countries.

*** Cold Is The Night
Hightone HCD 8006 Walker; John Phillips (ts); Kevin Zuffi, Patrick Moten (kb); Henry Oden, Eric Ajaye (b); Steve Griffith (d); Bruce Bromberg, Dennis Walker (prod). 86.

*** The Gift
Hightone HCD 8012 Walker; Wayne Jackson (t, tb); Andrew Love, Steve Berlin (ts); Jimi Stewart (kb); Henry Oden (b); Kelvin Dixon (d); Bruce Bromberg (co-prod). 87/88.

Joe Louis Walker is a high-maintenance bluesman. He demands attention. People don't go to his gigs for the chance to shout 'Yeah, boogie!', and they don't listen to his records for the comfort of blues platitudes and sleek arrangements. All this was immediately apparent on the albums that got his career up and running. The songs, mostly original and only occasionally using standard blues forms, are ingenious and intelligent, the lyrics skewered by the spiky, jabbing guitar, the delivery dry as a bone. At times the effect is a little *too* dry: the studio seems airless, unresonant, and even the Memphis Horns, imported for *The Gift*, don't colour the music very much. Walker would go on to make more textured recordings, but these early albums are still very listenable, besides offering the pleasure-in-hindsight of a promise that would be abundantly fulfilled.

♛ **** Blue Soul
Hightone HCD 8019 Walker; Wayne Wallace (tb); Nancy Wright (ts, bs); David Hidalgo (ac); Jimi Stewart (kb); Kevin Zuffi (p); Henry Oden, Eric Ajaye (b); Terry Baker (d); Dennis Broughton (perc, timbales); Melvin Booker, Donnie Boone (v). 89.

Walker has sharp eyes and ears for good songs, and the ability to make them sound blue whether they are formally blues or not. It is this fidelity to the inner character of the blues rather than its structural exterior that makes him so exciting and, even for the most hardline of blues fans, so rewarding. Nowhere has he demonstrated this more trenchantly than in these nine superb performances. Blues clichés find no resting-place in Walker's lyrics: he uses freshly made images, drawing on the cultural currency of the world he lives in. 'I swore I was gonna stay single. When I leave out and come back is up to me,' he declares in 'Personal Baby'. 'But I gotta take a real good look at that *Playboy* philosophy.' The parched acoustic of his previous albums is watered and greened by larger and more eloquent arrangements, yet *Blue Soul*'s dramatic finale, following the devastating 'City Of Angels', is by Walker alone, playing slide guitar on 'I'll Get To Heaven On My Own', a sceptical Blind Willie Johnson.

*** Live At Slim's Volume 1
Hightone HCD 8025 Walker; Jeff Lewis (t, perc, v); Tim Devine (as, ts, perc, v); Huey Lewis (h); Carl Schumacher (o, p, v); Henry Oden (b); Paul Revelli (d, v); Angela Strehli (v). 11/90.

*** Live At Slim's Volume 2
Hightone HCD 8036 As above, except Lewis, Devine and Schumacher do not sing; omit Strehli. 11/90.

These performances, recorded over two nights at a San Francisco club, have most of the strengths Walker displays in the studio and few of the weaknesses often found in live recordings. Songs are long only when they need to be; 'Don't Know Why', the only number on *Volume 1* to go much beyond five and a half minutes, justifies itself with a rewarding guitar solo, while the longest track on *Volume 2*, 'Thin Line', in which a cheating man faces up to the consequences of his actions, is wholly absorbing for all of its 6.04. The only strike against these otherwise satisfying albums is that five songs are reprised from *Cold Is The Night* and four from *The Gift*.

Between 1993 and 1999 Walker released six albums on Universal-group labels: *Blues Survivor* (Verve 519 063), *JLW* (Verve 523 118), *Blues Of The Month Club* (Verve 527 993), *Great Guitars* (Verve 537 141), *Preacher And The President* (Verve 533 476) and *Silvertone Blues* (Blue Thumb 547 721), all now deleted in most if not all territories. The best of a strong list were *Great Guitars* and *Silvertone Blues*. The former was an hour-long audioconference by CEOs of Blues Guitar, Inc., including Clarence 'Gatemouth' Brown, Little Charlie Baty, Steve Cropper, Robert Jr Lockwood, Gary Moore and Otis Rush. *Silvertone Blues* lifted a curtain on a new Walker, one absorbed in messages from the blues' past. Eight of the dozen tracks were duets, with James Cotton, Kenny Wayne or Alvin Youngblood Hart, and in these thoughtful collaborations Walker turned his gaze backwards and drew inspiration from famous duets like Big Maceo and Tampa Red or Muddy Waters and Little Walter, not to re-create but to reshape them.

(*) Pasa Tiempo
Evidence ECD 26126 *Walker; Wallace Roney (t); Ernie Watts (ts); Barry Goldberg (o); David Arnay (p); Phil Upchurch, Carla Olson (g); Bob Hurst (b); Leon Ndugu Chancler (d); Master Henry Gibson (perc); Wally Snow (vb); Julia Waters, Maxine Waters (v).* 4/01.

Since he left Universal Walker has been a freelancing butterfly, alighting now on this label, now on that, but never, stylistically speaking, staying in one place long. *Pasa Tiempo* is impossible to categorize: there are songs from Van Morrison, Otis Redding, Boz Scaggs and John Hiatt, and of Walker's three original pieces two are Latin-tinged jazz instrumentals featuring the airborne and very Milesian muted trumpet of Wallace Roney. It's clever music, but at times rather impersonal. If you hadn't heard Walker's work before 2001, and someone played you this and the next record in succession, you might not immediately realize they were by the same artist.

*** **Guitar Brothers**
JSP JSPCD 2153 *Walker; Steve Long (t); Cash Farrar, Barrie Martin (ts); George Bisharat (h); Chris Burns (o, p); Otis Grand (g); Robert Watson (b); Clarence 'Starr' James Jr, Steve Griffith (d).* 8/01.

The tension in Walker's music can be so tight that it hurts, and at times it's probably meant to, as in 'Better Off Alone', where he stares bleakly at the collapse of a relationship: 'Our bodies, they live together, but our hearts, they live apart.' Nothing else on the album matches this chilling performance; Walker aims instead for wry humour ('Rude Women', 'I'm Getting Drunk') or for the characteristically quirky observation of 'Snake Bit'. 'I'm Gonna Love You' struts in Jimmy Reed threads, and 'Regal Blues' is an oblique thank-you note to B. B. King. Otis Grand, who brought 'Better Off Alone' to the session (and contributed the vituperative guitar solo), plays second or shared-lead guitar throughout, an impeccable Jeeves to Walker's Wooster.

*** **In The Morning**
Telarc CD-83541 *Walker; unknown (o); G. E. Smith (g); T-Bone Wolk (b); Steve Holley (d); Andrea Re (perc, v).* 1/02.

After some jazz 'n' soul (*Pasa Tiempo*) and a hard-blues session (*Guitar Brothers*), Walker uses a couple of tracks of *In The Morning*, the title song and 'Where Jesus Leads', to reconnect with the gospel music he played as a young man. But for much of the album his hand is steady on the blues tiller, whether it directs him back to the past for 'Joe's Jump' or into Funkytown for the organ–guitar strut '2120 South Michigan Avenue'. The outstanding performance is the long 'Strangers In Our House', another song about a relationship that the ice is forming over, accompanied only by the grim, purposeful stomp of two acoustic guitars and bass.

*** **She's My Money Maker**
JSP JSPCD 2157 *Walker; Geno [Ellis] Blacknell Jr (kb); Robert Watson (b); Willy Jordan (d).* 10–11/02.

*** **New Direction**
Blues Bureau BB 20482//Provogue PRD 7148 *As above, except Carl Carter (d) replaces Jordan.* 03.

Among the musicians Walker heard or played with in his youth, he particularly admired Earl Hooker and Fred McDowell, and memories of both men are implicit in tracks on *She's My Money Maker*. This is Walker's first album exclusively featuring slide guitar, an interesting move. His previous recordings with slide have always been powerful but their effect has often been deliberately wintry, and the seasoned Walkerwatcher's first question will be: will he sustain that tone through an entire album or discover new shades of steel-blue? The former, as it proves: the stark subject-matter of 'Poor Man Blues', 'Ghetto Life', 'Borrowed Time' and 'My Judgement Day' demands and gets glacial soundscapes where the guitar bites and howls in the studio's bleak echo. After that profoundly comfortless experience, *New Direction*, though no funfest, is not so relentlessly harrowing. 'Ain't That Cold', yet another failing-relationship song, is resigned rather than bitter, 'Tempting Me', about women who pass him notes while he's playing, is almost light-hearted, and Walker's multiple guitar lines weave colour and rhythmic diversity into the fabric of the music. TR

Johnny 'Big Moose' Walker (1929–99)
VOCAL, PIANO

Big Moose sometimes attributed his nickname to his long hair, sometimes to being 'the biggest, strongest and wildest of 'em all'. His reputation for eccentricity was not unmerited; he once won $500 by jumping from a third-floor window. (The hospital bill was $495.) Born in Greenville, Mississippi, Walker worked with Ike Turner, Elmore James, Sonny Boy Williamson II, Lowell Fulson, Earl Hooker, Howlin' Wolf and others. He recorded sporadically under various pseudonyms from 1955, and worked steadily as a sideman after settling in Chicago in 1959. A series of strokes halted Walker's musical activities from 1992.

** The Rising Sun Collection: Big Moose Walker
Just A Memory RSCD 0008 *Walker; Andrew Cowan, Jörn Reissner (g); Stephen Barry (b); Paul Paquette (d). 7/73.*

***(*) Mellow Down Easy
Chrisly CM 30010 *Walker. 6/82.*

On the first of these live recordings Walker is teamed with a Canadian pickup band; mutual wariness and an evident lack of rehearsal stifle the enterprise. 'I Don't Want Your Money' starts promisingly, but like several other tracks it crumbles into aimless doodling as everyone tries to find a way to stop. Recording quality is adequate at best.

Mellow Down Easy, from a German tour, is much better recorded, and Walker plays a superior instrument. Equally strong in both hands, Walker's clean articulation and rhythmic drive recall Otis Spann; his music seldom has Spann's emotional depth, but 'One-Eyed Woman' comes close, and he's spectacularly exuberant on up-tempo tunes like 'I'm Tore Up' and 'Talk To Your Daughter'. 'Sixteen Tons' done as a cocktail lounge ballad will try many listeners' patience, and some of the boogie on 'Somebody's Got To Go' is tangle-fingered, but this CD catches both the discipline and the volatility of Big Moose live and revved up.

**(*) Blue Love
Evidence ECD 26082 *Walker. 1/84.*

*** Chicago Bound
Wolf 120.861 *Walker; John Primer, Luther Adams (g); Willie Kent (b); Timothy Taylor (d). 10/89.*

Walker's admiration for Ray Charles expresses itself four times on *Blue Love*, but on these tracks and elsewhere he seems content to sing and play the tunes right, and is not prodded by the producers either to put more of himself into the performances or to dig out material of a less familiar order than 'One Room Country Shack' and 'Mean Old Frisco'. 'Lone Wolf' stands out as an exception, not least because it's one of the few tracks where Walker exerts his right hand much.

Two of Walker's four numbers on *Chicago Bound* (shared with Jimmy Rogers) are also on *Blue Love*, but the band versions are superior, chiefly thanks to John Primer, who re-creates Earl Hooker's style with flair. Even so, these tracks mainly arouse regret for the unavailability on CD of 1969's Bluesway album *Rambling Woman* with the real Hooker. CS

Phillip Walker (born 1937)
VOCAL, GUITAR

Though born in Louisiana, Walker spent his teenage years in Port Arthur, Texas, where he learned to play guitar. He first played professionally with Lonesome Sundown, then with Clifton Chenier and Long John Hunter, before moving in 1958 to LA. After a decade of gigging round southern California and cutting a few locally distributed singles, he fell in with the producer Bruce Bromberg, with whom he would work repeatedly over the next 20 years.

*** Bottom Of The Top
Hightone HCD 8020 *Walker; Ike Williams, Chops Anthony, Sammy Coleman (t); Joel Peskin (as); David Ii (ts, o); Freeman Lacy (ts); Samuel Cross (bs); Teddy Reynolds, Jimmy Vaughn, Nat Dove, Arthur Woods (kb); Dennis Brown (sg); Curtis Johnson, Charles Jones, Dennis Walker (b); Glen McTeer, Johnny Tucker (d); Ina 'Bea Bopp' Walker (v); Bruce Bromberg (prod). 9/69–8/72.*

Though many of the songs on this album were first issued as singles, they have none of the distinguishing marks of their period that sometimes, later, become embarrassments. One or two are cast in a Southern soul mould, but the majority are blues like 'Tin Pan Alley', 'Laughing And Clowning' or the powerful title track, which are delivered with a dry, unsentimental toughness reminiscent of Walker's friend Lowell Fulson. Horns and rhythm provide colour and impetus, leaving space for Walker's twitchy, serpentine guitar solos.

**** Someday You'll Have These Blues
Hightone HCD 8032 *Walker; Al Deville (t); David Ii (s, fl, arr); Bill Murray (kb); Johnny Banks (o); Al Bruno (g); Dennis Walker (b, prod); Freddie Lewis, Archie Francis, Victor Hill, Aaron Tucker (d); Milton Thomas (perc); The Melody Kings (v); Bruce Bromberg (prod). 75–76.*

Unlike its predecessor this was recorded to be an album, with fewer personnel changes, and the sound is a little more homogeneous – not that continuity of sound is ever much of a problem when the production style is as definite as Bruce Bromberg and Dennis Walker's. Whether tackling the soul standards 'Breakin' Up Somebody's Home' and 'Part Time Love', Dennis Walker's compositions 'Mama's Gone' and 'Don't Tell Me' or the down-in-the-alley 'Beaumont Blues' and 'El Paso Blues', Phillip Walker invests every performance with character, and this is a thoroughly satisfying album. Not long afterwards, he contributed valuably to Lonesome Sundown's superb *Been Gone Too Long*, also produced by Bromberg and Walker. His own work over the next dozen years, such as *Tough As I Want To Be* (Rounder, 1983) is largely out of print (but see below).

*** Blues
Hightone HCD 8013 *Walker; Wayne Jackson (t, tb); Andrew Love (ts); Jimi Stewart (kb); James 'Broadway' Thomas, Antoine Salley (b); Johnny Tucker (d); Karen Kraft (v); Bruce Bromberg, Dennis Walker (prod). 88.*

Calling a blues album simply *Blues* (assuming it isn't out of blank desperation) implies a certain confidence in the artist's ability to carry it off. Walker does so with a matter-of-fact adroitness that will surprise no one familiar with his previous work. A good deal of the material is indeed blues, nearly all written for the occasion, like Bromberg's '90 Proof', Dennis Walker's 'Big Rear Window' or the Antoine Salley–Phillip Walker composition 'Her Own Keys'. Dennis Walker also contributed 'Don't Be Afraid Of The Dark', which was later recorded, under the same producers, by Robert Cray.

*** The Best Of Phillip Walker
Hightone HCD 8157 *As for Hightone CDs above, except add Steve Smith (t), Art Hillery (p). 9/69–88.*

As well as choosing discriminatingly from *Bottom Of The Top*, *Someday You'll Have These Blues* and *Blues*, this admirable if short (45.31) collection reinstates three tracks from the deleted Rounder album *Tough As I Want To Be*, including the Lowell Fulson compositions 'I'm Tough (Tough As I Want To Be)' and 'The Blues And My Guitar', Walker singing the latter beautifully over an accompaniment as discreet as a butler's cough.

**(*) Big Blues From Texas
JSP JSPCD 2122 Walker; Noel Norris (t); Peter Beck (as, ts); Mike Hobart (bs); Buzz Brown (h); Steve Diamond (o, p); Otis Grand (g, arr); Dan Quinton (b); Alan Premier (d, perc). 4–5/92.

Recorded in England, away from Walker's usual production team and accompanists, *Big Blues From Texas* nevertheless has much of the flavour of his other work, particularly when he eases into a long slow blues like 'She's Gone' or 'She Torture Me'. The chief difference is the lower score of striking material. Walker's own songs, which predominate, are okay at best, and neither Little Walter's 'You're So Fine' nor Cleo Page's 'Goodie Train' was a well-judged choice. Grand plays lead on two or three numbers, well enough but without Walker's quiddity. The harmonica playing on three tracks is otiose and on 'Beatrice, Beatrice' out-of-tune as well.

*** Lone Star Shootout
Alligator ALCD 4866 Walker; Gary Slechta, Frank Vert (t); Randy Zimmerman (tb); Mark 'Kaz' Kazanoff (as, ts, bs, h, arr); Les Izmore (ts); Red Rails, John Mills, Dr Ernest Youngblood Jr (bs); Riley Osbourn (o, p); Marcia Ball (p); Lonnie Brooks, Long John Hunter (g, v); Derek O'Brien (g); Larry Fulcher (b); Frosty Smith (d, perc); John 'Mambo' Tranor (rb). 99.

Walker's Black Top albums *Working Girl Blues* (1995) and *I Got A Sweet Tooth* (1998) having been deleted, the only example of his work in the later '90s is this six-hander with two fellow Texans, one of them, Hunter, a buddy from way back. Walker's features are 'Boogie Rambler', 'Street Walking Woman', where he trades fours with Hunter in a guitar duel, 'I Can't Stand It No More' and 'I Got The Blues In Person', which is cushioned by a big, soft horn arrangement. He also shares the vocal, or plays rhythm or joint lead guitar, on several other tracks, contributing a particularly feisty solo to 'You're Playing Hooky', a song written by his old employer Lonesome Sundown.

*** Live At Biscuits & Blues
M.C. MC 0047 Walker; Carl Vickers (t, as, ts); Joe Campbell (t); Bobby Lester (ts); Earl Mallory (bs); Charlie Musselwhite, Rick Estrin (h); Alvee Ventura (kb); James Thomas (b, v); Aaron Tucker (d, v); Angela Strehli (v). 6/02.

Recorded at the San Francisco club and billed as by the Phillip Walker Big Band, this set naturally contains a good deal of Walker's core repertoire, such as 'Hello My Darling', 'Don't Be Afraid Of The Dark', '90 Proof' and 'I've Got A Problem', but adds pieces he has not recorded like 'Respirator Blues' and Little Willie Littlefield's slow blues 'Along About Midnight', an eight-minute standout. There are cameos by Musselwhite and Strehli on 'Think' and Estrin on 'Reconsider Baby', but essentially this is Walker and a bustling, noisy, sometimes slightly ragged seven-piece band giving their audience a most enjoyable hour, which a good recording passes on, with undiminished zest, to everyone else. TR

Robert 'Bilbo' Walker (born 1937)
VOCAL, GUITAR

Walker's music combines deep blues feeling with rock 'n' roll showmanship. His eclectic repertoire includes country music and flamboyant Chuck Berry imitations, and his command of the whammy bar recalls the young Ike Turner. Walker lived in Chicago at times from the '50s to the '70s, but now migrates between his native Mississippi and Bakersfield, California, where he has a cotton farm.

**** Promised Land
Rooster Blues R 2632 Walker; Frank Frost (o); David 'Pecan' Porter (b); Sam Carr (d); Eugine Stafford (v). summer 96.

**(*) Rompin' & Stompin'
Fedora FCD 5005 Walker; Clarence Walker (g); Jeff Henry (b); Chris Millar (d). 10/97.

***(*) Rock The Night
Rooster Blues RBLU 2643 Walker; David 'Pecan' Porter (b); Sam Carr (d). 2/00.

Robert Walker has scarcely any original material, but his music sucks in a welter of influences – adding B. B. King, Jimmy Reed and Sam Cooke to those mentioned doesn't end the list – and purees them into an unmistakable sound and style. Not on Fedora, however, where congested, unimaginative accompaniments give him no room to cut up and go crazy. *Rompin' & Stompin'* sounds like any old cover band.

No such problem affects the Rooster CDs, where the musicians are fellow veterans of the Sam Carr Blues Revue. (Stafford, a Californian multi-instrumentalist brought along on one of Walker's trips home, adds graceful harmonies to a Sam Cooke song.) Carr and Porter are as wild as Walker, but less wayward; they tether him to terra firma by a long but strong cable, and the results are emotional, funny and compulsively danceable, sometimes all at once.

Promised Land is studio-recorded, but has the sweaty vigour of a juke-joint Saturday night. The title track makes garbling an art form, a medley of 'The Wild Side Of Life' and 'It Wasn't God Who Made Honky Tonk Angels' must be heard to be believed, and even 'Got My Mojo Working' comes up shiny and new when worked on by Walker's mojo. *Rock The Night* really is a live recording, as the occasional hoarseness and wandering off-mike prove, but paradoxically it has less immediacy, because the interplay with his Chicago audience gets between Walker and the listener. The intro to 'Hideaway' has so many wrong notes that it's almost a new composition, but then it takes off into an exhilarating whammy-bar workout over louche, throbbing bass and a percussion barrage. On the way to that set-closer, Walker, Carr and Porter give Lightnin' Slim, Lloyd Price, Arthur Crudup and many others a thorough mauling. Of the two discs, *Promised Land* has the edge, but only just. CS

T-Bone Walker (1910–75)
VOCAL, GUITAR, PIANO

Aaron Tebow (hence 'T-Bone') Walker grew up in Dallas, entering show business in his teens as a banjo and ukulele player. By the mid-'30s he was working in the clubs of LA's Central Avenue, for a time with Les Hite's orchestra. Though he had made a few earlier recordings, his career on disc began in earnest after World War II, and between 1946 and 1954 he made many popular sides for Black & White, Capitol and Imperial, both his singing and his guitar playing exercising enormous influence over his contemporaries. At the same time he maintained a strong position on the black theatre and club circuit. Sidelined by rock 'n' roll and disregarded in the early years of the blues revival, he made something of a comeback in the late '60s, but in his last years his guitar playing was reduced by a stroke.

**** T-Bone Walker 1929–1946
Classics 5007 *Walker; Paul Campbell, Walter Williams, Forrest Powell, Melvin Moore, Nick Cooper, Joe 'Red' Kelly, Al Killian, unknown (t); Britt Woodman, Allen Durham (tb); Les Hite, Floyd Turnham, Nathan Joseph, Frank Derrick, unknown (as); Quedillas [Quedellis] Martyn, Rodger Hurd, Moses Gant, Jack McVea, unknown (ts); Sol Moore (bs); Douglas Fernell, Nat Walker, Freddie Slack, Marl Young, Tommy 'Crow' Kahn (p); Frank Pasley (g); Al Morgan, Jud De Naut, Mickey Sims, Frank Clarke, unknown (b); Oscar Bradley, Dave Coleman, Red Saunders, Rabon Tarrant, unknown (d). 12/29–12/46.*

♛ ****** The Complete Capitol/Black & White Recordings**
Capitol 29379 3CD *Walker; Joe 'Red' Kelly, Al Killian, Teddy Buckner, George Orendorff (t); Jack McVea, Bumps Myers (ts); Tommy 'Crow' Kahn, Lloyd Glenn, Willard McDaniel (p); Frank Clarke, Arthur Edwards, Billy Hadnott, John Davis (b); Rabon Tarrant, Oscar Lee Bradley (d). c. 6/40–12/47.*

**** T-Bone Walker 1947
Classics 5033 *Walker; Teddy Buckner, George Orendorff (t); Bumps Myers (ts); Lloyd Glenn, Willard McDaniel (p); Arthur Edwards, Billy Hadnott, John Davis (b); Oscar Lee Bradley (d). 9–11/47.*

**** T-Bone Walker 1947–1950
Classics 5074 *Walker; Jack Trainor, George Orendorff, Eddie Hutcherson (t); Edward Hale (as); Jim Wynn (ts, bs); Bumps Myers, Eddie Davis (ts); Willard McDaniel, Zell Kindred (p); Billy Hadnott, Buddy Woodson (b); Oscar Lee Bradley, Robert 'Snake' Sims (d). 12/47–4/50.*

**** The Complete Imperial Recordings, 1950–1954
EMI 96737 2CD *Walker; Eddie Hutcherson, Dave Bartholomew, John Lawton, unknowns (t); Edward Hale, Wendell Duconge, Lee Gross, unknown (as); Jim Wynn (ts, bs); Eddie ['Lockjaw'] Davis, Maxwell Davis, Lee Allen, Walter Cox (ts); Herb Hardesty (bs); unknowns (s); Zell Kindred, Marl Young, Willard McDaniel, poss. Salvador Doucette, T. J. Fowler, unknown (p); R. S. Rankin, Walter Nelson (g); Buddy Woodson, Billy Hadnott, Frank Fields, Henry Ivory, unknown (b); Robert 'Snake' Sims, Oscar Lee Bradley, Cornelius Coleman, Clarence Stamps, unknown (d); Bobby Davis or Tiny Brown (v). 4/50–6/54.*

**** Complete 1950–1954 Recordings
Definitive DRCD 11259 2CD *As above. 4/50–6/54.*

**** Sings The Blues/Singing The Blues
BGO BGOCD 461 *Similar to above. 4/50–6/54.*

**** T-Bone Walker 1950–1952
Classics 5118 *Walker; unknowns (t); Edward Hale (as); Maxwell Davis (ts); Jim Wynn (bs); unknowns (s); Marl Young, Willard McDaniel, poss. Zell Kindred (p); R. S. Rankin (g); Billy Hadnott, Buddy Woods (b); Oscar Lee Bradley, poss. Robert Sims (d). c. 9/50–3/52.*

**** T-Bone Walker 1952–1954
Classics 5152 *As for The Complete Imperial Recordings, 1950–1954, except omit Hutcherson, Eddie Davis, Young, Hadnott, Bradley. 3/52–6/54.*

Walker's 1946–47 recordings for Black & White and Capitol created a new way of putting over the blues. Songs like 'No Worry Blues' or 'I Know Your Wig Is Gone', wry and worldly in tone, coolly conversational in their delivery, articulated attitudes to life and love that were not quite those of his Chicago contemporaries. His guitar playing, too, was otherwise conceived, built not upon the keys and chord progressions of Mississippi and Chicago blues but on a more musically educated knowledge of the instrument and a harmonic sensibility that owed something to jazz. His timing was relaxed yet unfailingly swinging. And in men like trumpeter Teddy Buckner, tenor saxophonist Bumps Myers and pianists Lloyd Glenn and Willard McDaniel he had a stable crew of accompanists who never put a foot, hand or lip wrong. All that, and excellent studio recordings too.

The original cuts of 'Call It Stormy Monday', 'T-Bone Shuffle' and 'T-Bone Jumps Again', with the rest of the 50-odd sides and a couple of dozen alternative takes, are carefully assembled on *The Complete Capitol/Black & White Recordings*, a key document of postwar blues. The set also catches a crucial early moment, his 1942 Capitol single 'I Got A Break Baby'/'Mean Old World', the first exposure of his developed style on electric guitar and a disc with some claim to be called the first modern blues record.

The diligent listener can then proceed to the next stage of Walker's recording career, chronicled on *The Complete Imperial Recordings, 1950–1954*. These too are very fine, lacking a little of the bubbling creativity of the earlier sides but similar in mood and setting and embracing songs that would become staples of the blues repertoire, such as 'Glamour Girl', 'The Hustle Is On' and 'Cold Cold Feeling'. If this, or its carbon-copy on Definitive, is too exhaustive, BGO's *Sings The Blues/Singing The Blues*, a reissue of two Imperial albums, will take its place pretty well, since the 24 tracks miss none of the important songs.

The first three Classics sets cover the Black & White/Capitol period (without the alternative takes); part of the third volume and all of the fourth and fifth are concerned with Imperial. The first Classics also collects Walker's pre-Black & White sides, from his rather tentative debut as a 19-year-old to sessions in 1945 for Rhumboogie and Mercury that reveal much of the artist-in-the-making.

*** The Beginning 1929/1946
EPM Blues Collection 15885 *Similar to T-Bone Walker 1929–1946. 12/29–9/46.*

*** Mean Old World
Our World 3302 *As above. 12/29–9/46.*

*** This Life I'm Living
TIM/History 201948 2CD *As above. 12/29–9/46.*

**** The Blues/Father Of The Modern Blues Guitar 1929–1950
Frémeaux FA 267 2CD *As for relevant CDs above. 12/29–50.*

**** The Original Source
Proper PROPERBOX 38 4CD *As for relevant CDs above. 12/29–12/51.*

*** Midnight Blues
Snapper Complete Blues SBLUECD 009 *As for relevant CDs above. 6/40–12/47.*

*** T-Bone Shuffle
[Blue Boar CDBB 1007] *Walker; Melvin Moore, Nick Cooper, Joe 'Red' Kelly, Teddy Buckner, George Orendorff (t); Nathan Joseph, Frank Derrick (as); Moses Gant, Jack McVea, Bumps Myers (ts); Freddie Slack, Marl Young, Tommy 'Crow' Kahn, Lloyd Glenn, Willard McDaniel (p); Jud De Naut, Mickey Sims, Frank Clarke, Arthur Edwards, Billy Hadnott, John Davis (b); Dave Coleman,*

Red Saunders, Rabon Tarrant, Oscar Lee Bradley (d). 7/42–12/47.

*** **The Best Of T-Bone Walker**
Blues Factory BFY 47019 As above, except add Al Killian, Jack Trainor (t); omit Moore, Cooper, Joseph, Derrick, Gant, Young, Mickey Sims, Coleman, Saunders. 7/42–12/47.

*** **No Worry Blues**
Past Perfect 220387 As above, except omit Trainor, Davis. 7/42–11/47.

*** **Born To Be No Good**
Snapper Recall SMDCD 432 2CD As for T-Bone Shuffle, except add Al Killian, Jack Trainor, Eddie Hutcherson, unknowns (t); Eddie Hale, unknown (as); Jim Wynn (ts, bs), Eddie ['Lockjaw'] Davis, Maxwell Davis (ts), unknowns (s); Zell Kindred (p); Buddy Woodson (b), Robert 'Snake' Sims (d). 7/42–8/51.

*** **A Proper Introduction To T-Bone Walker: Everytime**
Proper INTRO CD 2020 Walker; Joe 'Red' Kelly, Teddy Buckner, George Orendorff, Al Killian, Jack Trainor, Eddie Hutcherson, John Lawton, unknowns (t); Eddie Hale, Wendell Duconge, Lee Gross, unknown (as); Jim Wynn (ts, bs); Jack McVea, Bumps Myers, Eddie ['Lockjaw'] Davis, Maxwell Davis, Lee Allen, Herb Hardesty, Walter Cox (ts); unknowns (s); Freddie Slack, Marl Young, Tommy 'Crow' Kahn, Lloyd Glenn, Willard McDaniel, Zell Kindred, T. J. Fowler, unknown (p); R. S. Rankin, Walter Nelson (g); Jud De Naut, Mickey Sims, Frank Clarke, Arthur Edwards, Billy Hadnott, John Davis, Buddy Woodson, Frank Fields, Hank Ivory, unknown (b); Dave Coleman, Rabon Tarrant, Oscar Lee Bradley, Cornelius Coleman, Clarence Stamps, unknown (d); Tiny Brown (v). 7/42–11/53.

*** **Swinging The Blues**
Saga Blues 982 139–1 Similar to Born To Be No Good. c. 5/45–3/52.

*** **T-Bone Jumps Again**
Ocium OCM 0024 Walker; Joe 'Red' Kelly, Teddy Buckner, Al Killian, Eddie Hutcherson, Dave Bartholomew, unknowns (t); Eddie Hale, Wendell Duconge, unknown (as); Jim Wynn (ts, bs); Jack McVea, Bumps Myers, Eddie ['Lockjaw'] Davis, Maxwell Davis, Lee Allen, Herb Hardesty (ts); unknowns (s); Marl Young, Tommy 'Crow' Kahn, Lloyd Glenn, Zell Kindred, poss. Salvador Doucette, unknown (p); R. S. Rankin, Walter Nelson (g); Mickey Sims, Frank Clarke, Arthur Edwards, Buddy Woodson, Frank Fields, unknown (b); Rabon Tarrant, Oscar Lee Bradley, Cornelius Coleman, unknown (d). 12/45–11/53.

(***) **The Alternate T-Bone**
[Zircon BLEU 512] As for The Complete Capitol/Black & White Recordings. 9/46–12/47.

*** **LA Days**
Arpeggio ARB 002 As for relevant CDs above. 9/46–12/51.

*** **The Best Of T-Bone Walker**
Blues Forever CD 68009 As for relevant CDs above and below. 9/46–12/57.

*** **Blues Masters: The Very Best Of T-Bone Walker**
Rhino R2 79894 As above. c. 5/45–12/57.

Walker's work in this period was so consistent that it would be impossible to make a poor selection from it. Readers with no itch for completeness will get a fair-to-good deal from any of the single CDs on EPM Blues Collection, Our World (similar to the EPM), Snapper Complete Blues, Blue Boar, Blues Factory, Past Perfect, Proper and Saga, and a better (because larger) one from the 2CD sets on Frémeaux and Snapper Recall. This Life I'm Living is also a 2CD, but only the first disc is by Walker (and similar to Our World's), the other being by Memphis Slim. The Ocium CD forges a couple of years further ahead but lacks the important 1942 Capitol coupling. The sets on Arpeggio and Blues Forever offer hors d'oeuvres from Black & White/Capitol and more substantial main dishes from Imperial; the Blues Forever also scoops some marrow (four tracks) from the Atlantic album T-Bone Blues (see below). Comparison shoppers will quickly discover that all these compilations overlap each other to some extent, often considerably. The Alternate T-Bone lifts the 25 unissued takes from The Complete Capitol/Black & White Recordings, which might make it useful to unsated buyers of the Proper box, which omits them (and a couple of earlier items) but is otherwise complete for the stated period and so offers this label's usual value for money. Rhino's Very Best cherrypicks from four labels without quite justifying its title, but it does include a 'How Long Blues' from Atlantic that is not on their T-Bone Blues, and Billy Vera's notes are as sharp an analysis of Walker's strengths as you will find anywhere.

*** **T-Bone Blues**
Atlantic Jazz 8020//Atlantic 81954 Walker; Andrew 'Goon' Gardner (as); Eddie Chamblee, Plas Johnson (ts); McKinley Easton (bs); Junior Wells (h); John Young, Lloyd Glenn, Ray Johnson (p); R. S. Rankin (g, v); Jimmy Rogers, Barney Kessel (g); Ransom Knowling, poss. Willie Dixon, Billy Hadnott, Joe Comfort (b); LeRoy Jackson, poss. Francey [Francis] Clay, Oscar Bradley, Earl Palmer (d). 4/55–12/57.

Atlantic spent more than two and a half years on this album, recording Walker in LA and Chicago. The first LA date, with Glenn, Hadnott and Bradley, shows Walker at his most comfortable, remaking personal standards like 'Call It Stormy Monday' and 'Mean Old World', the latter superbly. The other session on the Coast finds him swapping the lead with Kessel and Rankin on 'Blues Rock' and 'Two Bones And A Pick'; Rankin takes over the vocal mike for 'You Don't Know What You're Doing', one of four tracks that the CD issue added to the contents of the original LP. The Chicago recordings are either with what may have been Eddie Chamblee's combo at the time or with Muddy Waters's men Junior Wells and Jimmy Rogers, the latter a setting that Walker probably found a little too rhythmically constricting. Incidentally, 'Why Not', though accompanied by Chamblee's unit, seems to have given Rogers the idea for 'Walking By Myself'.

*(*) **Back On The Scene**
Sanctuary 81262 Walker; Jimmy Ford (t); unknown (tb); prob. Arnett Cobb (ts); Harmonica Fats (h); Willard 'Piano Slim' Burton (o, p); Joey Long (g); Jimmy Jones (b); unknown (d). 66.

*(*) **The Legendary T-Bone Walker**
Brunswick BRU 81016 As above. 66.

*(*) **Back On The Scene**
Aim 0017 As above. 66.

*(*) **Blue On Blues**
Fuel 2000 302 061 192 As above, except add Johnny Copeland (g). 66, 70.

These albums are derived from dates supervised by the Houston music-business personality Huey P. Meaux, a.k.a. 'The Crazy Cajun'. Meaux is held in some respect as a producer but it can hardly be for these sessions, which imposed unsuitable backing musicians and dreadful studio acoustics on a Walker who was, in any case, in no shape to make a record worthy of him. A little of the old mastery oozes from the track titled 'Afraid To Close My Eyes' on Sanctuary or 'It Ain't No Right In You' on Brunswick and Aim. *The Legendary T-Bone Walker* reissues the LP *The Truth* on which some of this material first appeared, while the Sanctuary and Aim CDs are all different from it and each other, a confusing state of affairs made worse by the arbitrary renaming of many of the songs. The Aim has three tracks that seem to be of unknown provenance, though in the din of retitling it's hard to be sure. *Blue On Blues* is split with Lowell Fulson, Walker's half being three tracks from the above sessions and three from a 1970 Wet Soul album, also produced by Meaux.

(*) Stormy Monday Blues
BGO BGOCD 425 *Walker; McKinley Johnson, Melvin Moore (t); John 'Streamline' Ewing (tb); John Williams (as, bs); Preston Love (as); Mel Jernigan (ts); Lloyd Glenn (p); Mel Brown (g, v); Ron Brown (b); Paul Humphrey (d). 67.*

(*) Funky Town
BGO BGOCD 116 *Similar to above, except add unknown (h), unknown (o). 68.*

*** Stormy Monday Blues: The Essential Collection
Half Moon HMNCD 038 *As for above two CDs. 67–68.*

The BGO sets were originally on Bluesway and, somewhat unusually for that label, the musicians hired for the sessions were entirely compatible with the front man. Lloyd Glenn in particular underscores his fitness for the job by engaging in what amounts to a duet of equals in the laidback 'Going To Funky Town'. Though a number of Walker's personal standards turn up during these sets, such as 'Stormy Monday', 'Cold Hearted Woman' and 'I Gotta Break Baby' on the first and 'Long Skirt Baby Blues' and 'I'm In An Awful Mood' on the second, they come in arrangements that belong to the late '60s rather than 20 years earlier. You get some funk, but it's old guys' funk, and Walker seems at ease with it. Like John Lee Hooker in a similar setting, he gives his collaborators space that once he would have claimed firmly for himself, but he keeps enough of a hold on the proceedings to ensure that the songs have their due variety of shape and weight. He also plays immeasurably better than on the Meaux recordings. These albums are not crucial to an appreciation of Walker, but they usefully extend it by demonstrating how he adapted to rhythmic change. The Half Moon CD is a budget-priced combination of the two.

(*) I Want A Little Girl
Delmark DD 633 *Walker; Hal Singer (ts); George Arvanitas (p); Jackie Samson (b); S. P. Leary (d). 11/68.*

(*) Feeling The Blues
Black & Blue BB 432 *As above. 11/68.*

Walker's guitar is a shadow of its past self on this French session, and his singing sometimes shows his age too, but Singer and Arvanitas are as close and supportive as a couple of goodfellas protecting their *capo*, and the feel of the date is warm, easy and likeable. Walker moves to the piano for 'Ain't This Cold, Baby'. It wasn't the first time he had done so on record – he plays neatly behind John Lee Hooker on the 1962 AFBF album – but this is his longest excursion and its simplicity is touching. The two issues have the same eight tracks but different running orders. *Feeling The Blues* is extended with four numbers by Roy Gaines, also recorded in France (in 1975) but with other musicians.

Walker cut another album while in Paris that month, a busy affair with Manu Dibango and other French-based musicians, last available as *Good Feelin'* (Verve 519 723) but deleted in most if not all territories.

*** Very Rare
Reprise 936 247 758//Wounded Bird 6483 *Walker; Marvin Stamm, Danny Stiles (t, flh); Dizzy Gillespie, Jon Faddis (t); Garnett Brown, Mike Gibson (tb); Tony Studd, Paul Faulise (btb); Jerry Dodgion (as, fl); Seldon Powell (ts, bs, fl); Joe Farrell, Frank Vicari (ts, fl); David 'Fathead' Newman, Al Cohn, Zoot Sims (ts); Gerry Mulligan (bs); Herbie Mann (fl); Ben Benay (h, bj, g); Jerry La Croix (h); Michael Omartian, Charles Brown (o, p); James Booker, Mike Stoller (p); Warren Bernhardt (clavinet); various (vn, vl, vc); John Tropea (electric sitar); Richard Bennett, Dean Parks, Louie Shelton, Larry Carlton, David T. Walker (g); Max Bennett, Joe Osborne, Wilton Felder (b); Paul Humphrey, Jim Gordon (d); King Errisson (cga, tamb); The Sweet Inspirations (Myrna Smith, Sylvia Shemwell, Estelle Brown) (v); David Matthews (arr.). 73?*

This guest-bestrewn and doubtless extremely expensive project was instigated and produced by the songwriters Jerry Leiber and Mike Stoller as a gesture of honour to an artist whom they held in high regard. By this point Walker's performing days were almost all behind him, and he plays on only five of the 20 tracks, but his singing still has authority and, on slow, nocturnal numbers like 'I'm Still In Love With You', 'Evening' and 'Please Send Me Someone To Love', warmth. The arrangements, though elaborate, are seldom fussy and often striking. Country Paul's 'Your Picture Done Faded' combines downhome singing with banjo, sitar and strings in an almost Middle Eastern orchestration, while the contrast of Gerry Mulligan's baritone and the string section makes 'Stormy Monday' a moving as well as an apt closing track. TR

Sippie Wallace (1898–1986)
VOCAL, PIANO

Beulah Thomas, who married Matt Wallace, was nicknamed 'Sippie' as a child. Born in Houston, she was early fascinated by showbiz. She began recording in Chicago with the help of her older brother George, who was a musician and composer, but lost heart when her younger brother and accompanist Hersal died in 1926. When Matt Wallace and George Thomas both died in 1937, Sippie gave up blues for the church, backsliding briefly in 1945. She returned again in 1965 to great acclaim, was felled by a stroke in the '70s, and recovered to make a third comeback in the '80s; her last concert was in Germany, eight months before her death.

*** Sippie Wallace – Vol. 1 (1923–1925)
Document DOCD-5399 *Wallace; Louis Armstrong, Joe Oliver, unknown (c); Tom Morris (t); Charlie Irvis, Aaron Thompson, unknown (tb); Sidney Bechet, poss. Buster Bailey (cl, ss); poss. Ernest Elliott (cl); Rudolph Jackson (ss); Eddie Heywood, Clarence Williams, Hersal Thomas, prob. Perry Bradford (p); Buddy Christian (bj). c. 10/23–8/25.*

***(*) Sippie Wallace – Vol. 2 (1925–1945)
Document DOCD-5400 *Wallace; Louis Armstrong (c, train wh, sp); unknown (c); Natty Dominique (t); Hense Grundy, Honore Dutrey (tb); Artie Starks (cl, as); Johnny Dodds, unknown (cl); Rudolph Jackson (ss); Hersal Thomas, Clarence Williams, Cleo Grainger, Albert Ammons, unknown (p); Buddy Christian (bj);*

Bud Scott, Cal Smith, Lonnie Johnson (g); John Lindsay (b); Tommy Taylor (d). 8/25–9/45.

Vol. 1 starts in fine style with 'Up The Country Blues', but the standard is not always maintained; Clarence Williams plays on two thirds of the tracks, often ploughing doggedly through the sheet music, unresponsive to Wallace's strength and expressiveness. 'Caldonia Blues' is one of several potentially great performances thus rendered ordinary; conversely neither Wallace nor Williams can elevate saccharine stuff like 'Mama's Gone, Goodbye'. Nevertheless, there's much to admire, notably two titles with a band including Armstrong and Bechet, and one accompanied by Hersal Thomas and an elegiac 'King' Oliver. Many tracks come from disconcertingly battered originals.

Wear and tear also affects *Vol. 2*, though less pervasively, and Wallace's singing gains lustre from generally superior accompaniments. Hersal's restrained, dramatic playing adorns nine tracks, on six of which he's joined by Louis Armstrong, playing some of his most authoritative blues solos. Cleo Grainger and an anonymous cornettist are also very good on Wallace's swaggering composition 'I'm A Mighty Tight Woman', but they are outshone by a 1929 remake with Wallace on piano, and Dominique, Dutrey and Dodds in splendid support.

♛ **** Women Be Wise
Storyville STCD 8024 Wallace; Roosevelt Sykes, Little Brother Montgomery (p). 10/66.

Sippie Wallace had sung in church since retiring in 1937, and was initially reluctant to return to blues; when she did, it was ironically plain that gospel singing had preserved and strengthened her range, power and dramatic flair. At 68, she was better than she'd been at 28. This CD, recorded on tour in Denmark, features confident revivals of her early successes, sensitively accompanied by Montgomery, an unexpectedly tactful Roosevelt Sykes and, on one track, Wallace herself.

***(*) Mighty Tight Woman
Drive Archive DE2-41043 Wallace; Geoff Muldaur (cl, md, g, wb, k, v); Otis Spann (p); Richard Greene (vn); Bill Keith (bj); Jim Kweskin (g, comb); Fritz Richmond (b, j, v); Maria Muldaur (v). 11/67.

This encounter between blues matriarch and revivalist jugband is surprisingly successful; everyone's out to have a good time, and Kweskin's musicians are respectful without being reticent (bluegrass genius Bill Keith excepted; he's out of his element and knows it). Wallace adds a couple of '20s pop tunes to her playlist, and a not unpleasant flavour of doo-wacka-doo puts a new spin on some familiar blues. Four tracks accompanied by Otis Spann are undeniably in a different league, though, and while far from being the only reason to hear this CD, they're certainly the main one.

*** Axel Zwingenberger And The Friends Of Boogie Woogie – Vol. 1 Sippie Wallace
Vagabond VRCD 8.84002 Wallace; Axel Zwingenberger (p). 8/83.

**(*) Axel Zwingenberger And The Friends Of Boogie Woogie – Vol. 3 An Evening With Sippie Wallace
Vagabond VRCD 8.86006 Wallace; Axel Zwingenberger (p). 10/84.

The first of these discs is a studio recording, the second live. In her mid-80s, Sippie Wallace was still full of beans, and still recording hitherto unheard songs: both volumes include 'Electric Light', a frank, affecting song about her unhappy first marriage, and gleeful readings of 'Shake It To A Jelly' and 'Fan It', startling from a staunch churchgoer. By this time, however, Wallace had gone from 'wonderful' to 'wonderful for her age'; her range was narrower and her interpretations, especially on *Vol. 3*, less subtle. On this disc there's also some undignified mugging to the audience, and her catchphrase, 'Play it, maestro!' becomes tedious. Axel Zwingenberger is an attentive, affectionate accompanist, better recorded in the studio than on stage, where his bass figures are murky. CS

Mercy Dee Walton (1915–62)
VOCAL, PIANO

Born in Waco, Texas, Walton joined the state's A-team of itinerant piano players in his teens. In the late '30s he moved to Fresno, California, where he recorded for the local Spire label and then for Specialty, having a national hit with 'One Room Country Shack'.

*** One Room Country Shack
Specialty SPCD-7036/[Ace CDCHD 475] Walton; unknown (ts); unknown (b); unknown (d); 'Thelma', 'Lady Fox' (v). 52–54.

*** Mercy's Troubles/Troublesome Mind
Arhoolie CD 369 Walton; Sidney Maiden (h); K. C. Douglas (g); Otis Cherry (d). 2–4/61.

*** Pity And A Shame
Original Blues Classics OBCCD-552 As above, except omit Douglas. 4/61.

Walton's chief gift was to compose pointed blues narratives in precise and highly individual language. 'Before mankind knew what love was, everything was so lovely and gay' is the typically left-field opening of 'The Great Mistake'. Not content merely to devise fresh and often witty images, he would build them into themed songs like the hobo narrative 'The Drifter' or the Chandleresque 'Fall Guy': 'I'm so tired of playin' detective, trailin' you everywhere you go. My heart's in so much misery, and my feet are so doggone sore.' Though he spent much of his working life in southern California, the distinctive cadences and sonorities of his piano playing stem from his Texan background rather than from contemporary West Coast models like Charles Brown, and their back-home references are sardonic subtexts to his songs about the discomforts of rural life, such as 'Lonesome Cabin Blues' and his best-remembered composition, 'One Room Country Shack', which has become a standard.

All the songs mentioned above are included in the Specialty album, which has many entertaining and sometimes surprising sides never issued at the time. The 1961 sets find him sounding exactly the same (and most of his tunes too) and he continues his campaign against the agricultural life in such numbers as 'Walked Down So Many Turnrows' (Arhoolie) and 'Have You Ever Been Out In The Country' (both): 'If I ever get from around this harvest, I don't even want to see a rosebush grow. And if anybody ask me about the country – Lord have mercy on his soul.' TR

Robert Ward (born 1938)
VOCAL, GUITAR

Robert Ward eased into the blues circuit as a late second career after his 1990 rediscovery. Thirty years previously, he'd formed what many regard as the ultimate garage R&B band, The Ohio

Untouchables, its most distinctive feature the rippling vibrato of his Magnatone amp. The group's greatest moment came in providing the accompaniment to the Falcons' 'I Found A Love', while their own records made little impact outside their Dayton, Ohio, base. More soul-oriented than blues-suffused, Ward's songs nevertheless retain the quirky originality that first drew collectors to his music.

**** Hot Stuff

Relic CD 7094 *Ward; Gordon Kemp (t); Ralph 'Pee Wee' Middlebrook, Eli Fountain (as); Clarence 'Satch' Satchell, Al Watson (ts); Andrew 'Mike' Terry, Thomas 'Beans' Bowles (bs); Joe Hunter, Johnny Griffith (p); Don Davis, Eddie Willis, Dennis Coffey (g); Lyvord Fredrick, James Jamerson, Robert 'Bob' Babbit (b); Cornelius Johnson, Uriel Jones, Richard 'Pistol' Allen (d); Jack Ashford (vb); Bennie McCain, The Falcons (Wilson Pickett, Eddie Floyd, Mack Rice, Willie Schofield, Ben Knight) (v). 61–67.*

Although the credit is to Ward, this is essentially a collection of Ohio Untouchables singles, with four Falcons titles and a handful of solo Ward recordings. Pickett's gospel-charged vocals on the Falcons' tracks, especially 'I Found A Love', contrast markedly with the naive but inspired enthusiasm of Ward and his men. 'Forgive Me Darling', the Untouchables' finest achievement, is essentially a backing track masquerading as a guitar solo, with the group chanting the title as a chorus. McCain shares the band's lead vocals, including 'She's My Heart's Desire', 'I'm Tired' and 'Your Love Is Amazing', with commendable fervour. But it's Ward's love affair with his Magnatone amp that provides this album's highspots, particularly 'Workout' and 'Hot Stuff' (in reality 'You Can't Sit Down' and Bo Diddley's 'Diddlin'') and his explosive solo during the Falcons' 'Let's Kiss And Make Up'. Once heard, it's a sound that begets idolatry or indifference.

**** Fear No Evil

[Silvertone ORECD 520] *Ward; Keith Winking (t); Kaz Kazanoff (ts, bs); Saxy Boy (ts); Sammy Berfect, Bruce Elsensohn (o, p); George Porter Jr (b); George Rains (d). 10/90.*

It's rare that a comeback record turns out to be as good as this one. Ward's guitar playing is as anachronistic as ever (note the oriental flavour of the opening arpeggios to 'Your Love Is Amazing'), his fingers almost as deft. The voice has lost some power but his songwriting, on the evidence of 'Born To Entertain', 'Newborn Music' and 'Lord Have Mercy On Me', remains thoughtful and on occasions quirky. No fewer than seven songs are repeated from the above album, including a spot-on re-creation of 'Forgive Me Darling' with Kazanoff emulating Clarence Satchell's blowsy riffing. 'Blessings', 'K-Po-Kee' and 'Dry Spell' are guitar features that move from tranquillity via a raunchy shuffle to a tight up-tempo soul strut, exploiting the virtues of the Magnatone amplifier. A record to savour.

*** New Role Soul

Delmark DE-741 *Ward; Kenny Anderson (t); Hank Ford, Sonny Seals (ts); Willie Henderson (bs); Kevin McKendree (o, p); Bruce Thompson Sr (o); Willie 'Vamp' Samuels (b); Wayne Stewart (d); Roberta Thomas (tamb, v); Roberta Ward, Kay Reed, Theresa Davis (v). 8/99.*

A decade on and the dimensions of Ward's talent are more closely defined. The Magnatone amp is used more sparingly here but two tracks in which it's featured, 'I'm So Proud To Have You For My Love' and the ten-minute 'Whatever I Receive', are the highlights of an album that ultimately sounds more familiar than it should. Ward's guitar playing is highly individual, but devoid of effects its limitations are glaringly obvious. His voice, something of a cracked vessel but at ease on his own material, is put under strain by Eddie Floyd's 'Never Found A Girl', whereas the quasi-religious content of songs like 'Receive' and 'Peace Of Mind' make his humorous treatment of Jimmy Liggins's 'I Ain't Drunk' seem unnatural. His wife Roberta sings her own 'Ark Of Safety' but is less vocally gifted than her husband. Ward's talent remains unique but on this evidence requires a refresher course. NS

Baby Boy Warren (1919–77)
VOCAL, GUITAR

Born in Lake Providence, Louisiana, Warren grew up in Memphis, learning to play guitar from a couple of his brothers. Throughout the '30s he played in the Memphis/West Memphis area, where he met, among others, Little Buddy Doyle and Willie '61' Blackwell, both of whom influenced his songwriting. In 1942 he moved to Detroit, and later recorded for various Detroit and Chicago labels. He retired from music in the '60s but reappeared in the early '70s, visiting Europe and performing at the 1972 Ann Arbor Blues Festival.

*** Stop Breakin' Down

Official OFCD-5901 *Warren; Johnny Hooks (ts); Sonny Boy Williamson II (h); Charley Mills, Boogie Woogie Red, unknown (p); Calvin Frazier, Little George Jackson, unknown (g); Milt Hinton, unknown (b); Curtis Foster, Jimmy Tarrant, unknown (d); Washboard Willie (wb). 49–54, 73.*

Like his models Little Buddy Doyle and Willie Blackwell, Warren brought a hip, literate humour to the blues lyric: 'I asked the lady was she married – "No, but I have a special friend." "Lady, I don't mean to be embarrassin', but is it possible you might cut me in?"' He sang with warmth and excellent diction over muscular guitar lines that sometimes suggest an idea of how Robert Johnson might have sounded if he had lived ten years longer and played pieces like 'Sweet Home Chicago' or 'Stop Breakin' Down' (which Warren recorded) on electric guitar. An astute ensemble player, he slotted into combos with men like Boogie Woogie Red, Calvin Frazier and Sonny Boy Williamson II to make some of the most vivid band music to come out of Detroit in the '50s. All his singles are here, rounded off with a couple of over-busy band performances from Ann Arbor '73. Virtually all these tracks can also be found in the VAC *Detroit Blues* (JSP JSP 7736 4CD). TR

J. W. Warren (1921–2003)
VOCAL, GUITAR

Apart from a 14-year hitch in the military, Warren spent his life farming and entertaining his neighbours in southeastern Alabama.

**** Life Ain't Worth Livin'

Fat Possum FP 1024 *Warren. 9/81–3/82.*

Warren's long story-song 'The Escape Of Corinna' is a remarkable original creation (another version is on *Came So Far* [Music Maker MMCD 129]; see COMPILATIONS: EAST

COAST), and a few tunes come from oral tradition ('Rabbit On A Log' is 'Georgia Buck'), but most of his repertoire is from recordings made in the '30s and '40s. It's easy to identify precursors, notably Blind Boy Fuller and Tommy McClennan, but Warren always makes the songs his own; more than just rescuing 'Louise Louise Blues' from excessive familiarity, his slide guitar accompaniment and ardent singing make 'Little Louise' seem newly created. His arrangements eschew routine picking or strumming, and as a result his songs become intimate, involving conversations between voice and guitar. Warren was a major talent, and these field recordings provoked some interest when they appeared on a Dutch LP, but he was reluctant to travel to festivals. CS

Washboard Sam (1910–66)
VOCAL, WASHBOARD

Robert Brown was born in Walnut Ridge, Arkansas. His birth certificate says 'father: unknown', but Big Bill Broonzy was sure that the man who became Washboard Sam was his half-brother. They were certainly close; from 1935 to 1953 Bill appeared on all but four of Sam's many recordings. Sam was also a busy session percussionist, and popular in Chicago clubs during the '30s and '40s. Broonzy said that he became a policeman after quitting music, but nightwatchman, as Memphis Slim asserted, seems more likely. Towards the end of his life, Sam played some club dates and made a few recordings for the new, white audience.

*** **Washboard Sam – Vol. 1 (1935–1936)**
Document DOCD-5171 *Washboard Sam; Arnett Nelson (cl): Black Bob (p); Big Bill Broonzy (g, v); Louis Lasky (g); John Lindsay, unknowns (b). 6/35–12/36.*

(*) **Washboard Sam – Vol. 2 (1937–1938)
Document DOCD-5172 *As above, except add unknown (p); omit Lasky, Lindsay. 5/37–3/38.*

*** **Washboard Sam – Vol. 3 (1938)**
Document DOCD-5173 *Washboard Sam; Punch Miller, Herb Morand (t); Arnett Nelson (cl); poss. Bill Owsley (ts); Black Bob, prob. Joshua Altheimer (p); George Barnes, Big Bill Broonzy (g); prob. Bill Settles, unknown (b). 3–12/38.*

*** **Washboard Sam – Vol. 4 (1939–1940)**
Document DOCD-5174 *Washboard Sam; Buster Bennett (ss, as, p, v); Joshua Altheimer, prob. Horace Malcolm (p); Big Bill Broonzy (g); Ransom Knowling (b). 5/39–3/40.*

*** **Washboard Sam – Vol. 5 (1940–1941)**
Document DOCD-5175 *Washboard Sam; prob. Buster Bennett (as); prob. Joshua Altheimer, prob. Blind John Davis, Horace Malcolm, Simeon Henry (p); Big Bill Broonzy (g); Leroy Bachelor, William Mitchell, unknowns (b); Josephine Kyles (sp). 7/40–1/41.*

**** **Washboard Sam – Vol. 6 (1941–1942)**
Document DOCD-5176 *Washboard Sam; Frank Owens (as); Memphis Slim, Roosevelt Sykes (p); Big Bill Broonzy (g); William Mitchell, Alfred Elkins, Ransom Knowling (b). 6/41–7/42.*

(*) **Washboard Sam – Vol. 7 (1942–1949)
Document DOCD-5177 *Washboard Sam; Sax Mallard (cl, as); J. T. Brown, Sugarman Penigar (ts); Memphis Slim, Roosevelt Sykes, Bob Call (p); Big Bill Broonzy, Willie Lacey (g); Ransom Knowling, Willie Dixon, Big Crawford (b); Judge Riley. 7/42–10/49.*

Washboard Sam was the only player of his eponymous instrument to become a blues recording star, and much of his success lies in the use he made of it. Although he added a phonograph turntable and a couple of cowbells, they were there for tonal variety, not as tools in a novelty act. What Sam wanted, and infallibly got from his instrument, was a driving swing that spurs his accompanists to respond in kind. He was recorded frequently and at length, and inevitably there are repeated ideas and effects, but he was a prolific and highly original songwriter, who employed striking, often humorous images, clever topical allusions and references to black folkways. Add in a powerful yet lively singing voice, and listening to seven volumes is much more fun than might be expected.

Even so, it's the dedicated collector who will want all Document's discs, and *Big Bill Broonzy Vol. 7* (Masters of Jazz MJCD 172), which includes Sam's first two recordings. (A 1953 session for Chess seems to be unavailable on CD at present.) Document's sound is usually acceptable, although one or two tracks come from seriously sub-standard tape dubs. *Vol. 1* is notable for some swinging guitar duets by Broonzy and Louis Lasky, and for the elegant inventions of Black Bob. Bill and Bob also adorn the next volume, but Arnett Nelson's slaptonguing, rasps and other gimmicks distract from some very good lyrics. Nelson drops out after one track on *Vol. 3*, which is ornamented by Herb Morand's glowing New Orleans trumpet. Buster Bennett is prominent on the next disc and the first half of *Vol. 5*; he has a better feel for the blues than Nelson, but his tone and ideas become predictable when heard at a length that was never intended. There are many excellent lyrics on these discs, though, and *Vol. 4* has Sam's greatest hit, 'Diggin' My Potatoes'. Best of the bunch is *Vol. 6*, with Big Bill playing amplified guitar solos of the utmost grace and inventiveness, and Memphis Slim hammering out ringing obbligatos; on a few sides where Roosevelt Sykes plays piano, the workmanlike Frank Owens joins in. Most of *Vol. 7* is postwar recordings for Victor, with saxes and clarinets the dominant, usually undistinguished accompanying voices. It's worth getting past them to the fine piano work of Bob Call, but Sam's voice is sometimes tired. His writing skills are as finely honed as ever, though: note among others the roistering 'No. 1 Drunkard' and 'Soap And Water Blues', a hilarious ode to odour.

*** **Washboard Blues 1935/1941**
EPM Blues Collection 15866 *Similar to relevant CDs above, except add unknown (t), Casey Bill Weldon (g). 6/35–11/41.*

***(*) **Swinging The Blues 1935–1947**
Frémeaux FA 263 2CD *Similar to relevant CDs above. 7/35–11/47.*

*** **Washboard Sam 1936–1947**
Best Of Blues BOB 1 *Similar to relevant CDs above. 6/36–2/47.*

These selective surveys cover much the same territory; Wolf and Frémeaux dip into the postwar years, but only with one and three tracks respectively. EPM include two sides by the State Street Swingers, a studio group with Sam as vocalist. Wolf's CD has lively sound, but there are no notes, only discographical details. EPM offer thoughtful commentary (with some minor errors of fact) and remastering that's conscientious but a notch below Wolf's. Frémeaux have more extensive coverage, good sound and insightful, if occasionally contestable, annotation. Arnett Nelson appears on 25 per cent of the 36 tracks, which means a corresponding deficit of both

Herb Morand and Memphis Slim, but *Swinging The Blues* is the best overview of Washboard Sam's music.

*** **Get Down Brother**
BMG/Camden 535832 *Similar to relevant CDs above.* 6/41–2/47.

Get Down Brother comes mainly from the same time period as Document's *Vol. 6*, but the transfers are little better than Document's, and certainly less good than could be expected from the owners of the masters. The notes are perfunctory and occasionally inaccurate, and several songs are pointlessly retitled.

*** **I Blueskvarter: Chicago 1964, Volume Two**
Jefferson SBACD 12655/6 2CD *Washboard Sam; Blind John Davis (p); Betty Dupree (b).* 5/64.

The five tracks on this volume are Sam's last recordings, made for the Swedish Broadcasting Corporation. He runs through favourites from his recording career (perhaps he'd got tired of 'Diggin' My Potatoes'). His style is quite unchanged, and his singing and playing little affected by the passing years; Davis and Dupree give solid support. A sixth title, 'Mama Don't Allow', is on *Volume Three* (Jefferson SBACD 12658/9 2CD). CS

Dinah Washington (1924–63)
VOCAL

Rutha Lee Jones was born in Tuscaloosa, Alabama, but grew up in Chicago, where she sang and played piano in her local Baptist church. At 14 she won a talent contest at the Regal Theater, and at 18 she was hired by Lionel Hampton, who gave her her stage name. In the late '40s and early '50s she was regularly in the R&B charts, but by the end of the '50s, following a pop hit with 'What A Diff'rence A Day Made', she had escaped the confines of R&B for the larger stage of mainstream popular music. What could have been a long and distinguished career in that arena was cut short by her early death, from an apparently accidental overdose of prescription drugs.

*** **How To Do It**
Flapper PAST CD 7818 *Washington; Joe Morris, Wendell Culley, Karl George (t); Gene Porter (cl, as, bs); Rudy Rutherford (cl); Herbie Fields, Jewel Grant (as); Arnett Cobb, Lucky Thompson (ts); Lionel Hampton (p, d, vb); Milt Buckner, John Mehegan, Wilbert Baranco (p); Billy Mackel (g); Vernon King, Charles Harris, Charles Mingus (b); Fred Radcliffe, George Jones, Lee Young (d); Milt Jackson (vb); Gus Chappell's Orchestra, Gerald Wilson's Orchestra, Tab Smith's Orchestra.* 12/43–8/46.

*** **I Know How To Do It**
Fabulous FABCD 104 *As above, except Teddy Stewart's Orchestra replaces Gerald Wilson's Orchestra.* 12/43–49.

*** **The Queen Sings**
Proper PROPERBOX 43 4CD *As above, except add Gerald Wilson's Orchestra, Chubby Jackson's Orchestra, Dave Young's Orchestra, Rudy Martin's Trio, Teddy Brannon's Trio, Cootie Williams & His Orchestra, Mitch Miller & His Orchestra, Jimmy Carroll's Orchestra, Walter Buchanan's Orchestra, Nook Shrier's Orchestra, Ike Carpenter's Orchestra, unknown musicians, The Ravens (v).* 12/43–10/51.

*** **Queen Of The Blues**
Living Era CD AJA 5534 *As above, except add Jimmy Cobb's Orchestra, Walter Rodell's Orchestra; omit George, Porter, Grant, Thompson, Baranco, Mingus, Lee Young, Milt Jackson.* 12/43–3/52.

*** **Greatest Hits 1946–1953** [sic]
Fabulous FADCD 2000 2CD *As for* The Queen Sings, *except add Jimmy Cobb's Orchestra.* 12/43–5/52.

*** **Mellow Mama**
Delmark DD-451 *Washington; Karl George (t); Gene Porter (cl, as, bs); Jewel Grant (as); Lucky Thompson (ts); Wilbert Baranco (p); Charles Mingus (b); Lee Young (d); Milt Jackson (vb).* 12/45.

Washington was launched on the disc world with four blues written by the jazz journalist and producer Leonard Feather and accompanied by a small group from the Lionel Hampton orchestra, with whom she had been working for several months. Feather's immediate sense that 'something of lasting value was happening' was ratified over the next few years, initially in a 1945 blues session for Apollo, then in a series of Mercury dates at which she gradually expanded her repertoire beyond the blues with standards like 'Embraceable You' and 'I Can't Get Started'. Whatever the material, the sinuous line, sharp clarity and rhythmic flexibility of her singing marked her as a vocalist of rare ability and character. Although for a time she was known as 'the Queen of the Blues', it was plain that she could conquer larger worlds, and by the mid-'50s she was well on her way to doing so.

Three of the six collections discussed here are chiefly concerned with reaffirming her blues credentials. *The Flapper* – almost identical to the deleted *A Slick Chick (On The Mellow Side)* (Indigo IGOCD 2073) – is good; most of the shorter but cheaper *I Know How To Do It* draws on the same material. *Mellow Mama* is the official reissue of the Apollo session, also included in its entirety on *Flapper*; if the material is sometimes formulaic, the arrangements are less so, and Lucky Thompson's downy tenor solos are unfailingly delectable. *The Queen Sings*, *Queen Of The Blues* and *Greatest Hits 1946–1953* acknowledge the blues hits like 'Blow Top Blues' and the orthodontic 'Long John Blues' but open their doors to much else, from standards, some with very saccharine settings, to Hank Williams's 'Cold, Cold Heart'. A virtuoso reading of Noël Coward's 'Mad About The Boy' (on *Queen Of The Blues*) is one of several performances that seem, with hindsight, to prepare the ground for successors like Esther Phillips and Aretha Franklin. *The Queen Sings* is complete for the period covered and, as usual with Proper's boxed sets, very good value.

*** **Dinah Sings Bessie Smith**
Verve 538 635 *Washington; Fortunatus 'Fip' Ricard, Clark Terry, Blue Mitchell (t); Quentin Jackson, Julian Priester, Melba Liston (tb); Eddie Chamblee, Harold Ousley (ts); McKinley Easton, Charles Davis, Sahib Shihab (bs); James Craig, Jack Wilson, Wynton Kelly (p); Robare Edmonson (b, arr); 'Rail' Wilson, Paul West (b); James Slaughter, Max Roach (d); Ernie Wilkins (arr).* 12/57–7/58.

Not all commentators on this album have judged it an unqualified success; see, for example, the discussion in *The Penguin Guide To Jazz Recordings*. At times, some of the musicians, notably Chamblee and Slaughter, appear to be guying the material, though it might be argued that they are deliberately – if ill-advisedly – re-creating vaudeville styles current in Smith's day. Washington herself seems to be trying to strike a balance between paying due respect to a formidable predecessor and asserting her own way with a song, and for the most part brings it off. The original *Dinah Sings Bessie Smith* LP (plus a couple of alternative takes) is augmented with three numbers recorded at the 1958 Newport Jazz Festival, accompanied by a different lineup that handles the music with more discretion.

*** **Finest Hour**
Verve 543 596 *Washington; various accompaniments.* 12/43–12/61.

The Universal group has made several selections from Washington's first two decades' work; this has slightly more than the others of her early blues sides, while not forgetting well-known recordings like 'What A Diff'rence A Day Made', 'This Bitter Earth' and 'Mad About The Boy'. Regrettably, though, it replaced *First Issue: The Dinah Washington Story (The Original Recordings)* (Mercury 514 841 2CD), which covered the same period in much greater detail (46 tracks against 18) but has been deleted. Among the other collections are *The Definitive* (Verve 589 839), *Ultimate* (Verve 539 053) and *Jazz Masters 19* (Verve 518 200). Of Washington's numerous albums of standard material, *Dinah Jams* (EmArcy 814 639) is a thoroughly satisfying 1954 encounter with a starry jazz lineup including Clifford Brown, Clark Terry, Harold Land and Junior Mance. Some of these albums, and other later work, are dealt with in Washington's entry in *The Penguin Guide To Jazz Recordings*. TR

Tuts Washington (1907–84)
VOCAL, PIANO

Isidore Washington left school after the sixth grade, and was soon working in New Orleans bands and solo. An influence on Professor Longhair, James Booker, Archibald and others, Washington played on some of Smiley Lewis's records, but was reluctant to record commercially under his own name. He had just finished a live set at a festival when he suffered a fatal heart attack.

***(*) **New Orleans Piano**
504 CD 32 *Washington; 'Little Red' Lajoie (bj, v).* 57–60.
** **Live At Tipitina's '78**
Night Train NTI CD 7101 *Washington.* 78.
(*) **New Orleans Piano Professor
Rounder CD 11051 *Washington.* 3/83.

In later years, Washington's only vocal was the scurrilous 'Papa Yellow Blues' ('Tuts Washington's Blues' on *Live At Tipitina's*), and his repertoire was as strong on jazz and standards as on blues. Along with a tuft of hair at the back of the head, versatility was one of the credentials of a piano professor, and 504's notes accurately describe Washington as 'a New Orleans stride player who absorbed blues and boogie-woogie.' An admiration for Art Tatum and Oscar Peterson colours his playing as well, and to the end his technical command was excellent.

Night Train's source is a cassette off the soundboard, which entails intrusive tape hiss, and high ambient noise from a disengaged audience; add that the club's piano needed tuning, and this CD can't be recommended. Rounder's sound quality is impeccable, but this time it's Washington who seems disengaged, setting down the material he played for tourists at the expensive Fairmont Hotel without effort, but also without much fire. Despite some sonic shortcomings, 504's compilation of private recordings is much the best showcase for Washington's virtuosity, and even on the pop tunes his interpretation is at its most consistently bluesy. CS

Crown Prince Waterford (born 1919)
VOCAL

The Arkansas-born Charles Waterford sang in the '30s with bands in Chicago and Kansas City. In 1945 he replaced Walter Brown in Jay McShann's orchestra but did not stay long, and for the rest of the decade he freelanced with various bands and recorded for five labels. He hung on in the business until the early '60s, when he put his expressive voice in the service of the Lord.

*** **Crown Prince Waterford 1946–1950**
Classics 5024 *Waterford; Gerald Wilson, Vernon 'Geechie' Smith, Dave Froebel Brigham, Johnny Grimes, unknown (t); Dickie Harris (tb); Donald Hill, William Doty, unknowns (as); Maxwell Davis, Harold Land, Joe Thomas, unknowns (ts); Orrington Hall (bs); Pete Johnson, Jesse Price (p, d); Jay McShann, John L. Jackson, George Rhodes, unknowns (p); Tiny Webb, unknowns (g); Shifty Henry, Ralph Hamilton, Stanley Joyce, George Duvivier, unknowns (b); Jesse Sailes, Leon Petties, Alphonso Bright, unknowns (d); band (v).* 46–3/50.
(*) **Blues Everywhere
[Westside WESF 110] *Waterford; Dave Froebel Brigham, Johnny Grimes (t); Dickie Harris (tb); William Doty (as); Harold Land, Joe Thomas (ts); Orrington Hall (bs); John L. Jackson, George Rhodes (p); unknown (g); Stanley Joyce, George Duvivier (b); Leon Petties, Alphonso Bright (d).* 6/49–3/50.

The voice production on his earliest sides hints that Waterford might have done some listening to Dr Clayton, but he gradually submerged that eccentricity in a vigorous narrative style, less stentorian than Joe Turner's and less operatic than Roy Brown's but well suited to telling ingenious and often humorous blues tales like 'L.A. Blues' and 'P.I. Blues', nearly all of which he wrote himself. His most entertaining sides are eight with a quintet including Pete Johnson and Maxwell Davis, made for Capitol in 1947. The eight King sides that conclude the Classics CD – also on *Blues Everywhere*, following 16 by Walter Brown – are well recorded but the material is uneven. After several decades' absence from the studio, Waterford reappeared in 2003 with *All Over But The Shoutin'* (Springing The Blues [unnumbered]), which had only limited distribution. TR

Ethel Waters (1896–1977)
VOCAL

Born in Philadelphia, 'Sweet Mama Stringbean' entered vaudeville in 1917, and was a star as singer, actress, comedienne and dancer by the time she recorded. She introduced many hit songs, and was reportedly the first black singer to appear on both radio and television. Always an all-round entertainer, by the '30s Waters had effectively ceased to be a blues singer. She appeared frequently on stage, on television and in films, was the first African-American actress to star in a straight play on Broadway, and was an Oscar nominee (as best supporting actress) for her role in Pinky. In her later years, Waters mainly sang for Billy Graham's revivals.

(*) Ethel Waters 1921–1923
Classics 796 Waters; Joe Smith, prob. Elmer Chambers (c); Wesley Johnson, unknowns (t); Jim Reevy, poss. Chink Johnson, George Brashear, unknowns (tb); poss. Herschel Brassfield (cl, as); Edgar Campbell, Garvin Bushell, poss. Clarence Robinson, unknowns (cl); Clarence Harris, unknown (as); Wilson Kyser, Fletcher Henderson (p); Cordy Williams, poss. Charlie Jackson (vn); Johnny Mitchell (bj); Ralph Escudero, unknown (bb); Kaiser Marshall (d). 3/21–3/23.

(*) Ethel Waters 1923–1925
Classics 775 Waters; prob. Elmer Chambers, Joe Smith, Tommy Ladnier, Horace Holmes (c); George Brashear (tb); Don Redman (cl, ss); Edgar Campbell, Jimmy O'Bryant (cl); unknown (oboe, ss); unknown (bsn); Charles Harris (as); Fletcher Henderson, J. C. Johnson, Pearl Wright, Lovie Austin, unknown (p); Johnny Mitchell (bj); Bill Benford (bb). 3/23–7/25.

About halfway through 1923–1925, Waters switches labels from Black Swan to Paramount, and the sound improves markedly. This cannot often be said of Paramount, and the first volume, in particular, makes heavy demands on the listener. Behind the noise, Waters has a clear, melodious voice, and is much more emotionally, aesthetically and structurally at ease with the blues than were many of her fellow recording pioneers. Her accompanists are usually rather stiff on 1921–1923, but they improve markedly on the second disc, with Ladnier and Horace Holmes especially commanding. Fletcher Henderson is in good form, too, and Waters's regular pianist, Pearl Wright, supplies the first of many sympathetic and well-integrated accompaniments.

*** Ethel Waters 1925–1926**
Classics 672 Waters; Horace Holmes, Harry Tate, Joe Smith, Thornton Brown (c); Joe King, Edward Carr (tb); three unknowns (reeds); Alex S. Jackson, Coleman Hawkins (bss); Pearl Wright, Lester Armstead, Fletcher Henderson, Louis Hooper, Sammy Fain, Maceo Pinkard, Nathaniel Reed, Lorene Faulkner (p); Ralph 'Shrimp' Jones (vn); Maceo Jefferson (bj); Virgil Van Cleave (u); Bill Benford (bb); Jesse Baltimore (d, chimes); unknown (d); 'Slow Kid' Thompson (v); unknown (sp). 8/25–7/26.

All the material here is from Columbia, and henceforth there are no problems with sound quality. Most sides were issued in the 'race' series; among the exceptions issued in the popular series is the vomitous 'Pickaninny Blues', but happily it's also exceptional in terms of its awfulness. The material ranges beyond blues – 'Dinah' and 'Sweet Man' are pop with a jazz tinge, and 'Heebie Jeebies', with Thornton Brown's flamboyant trumpet, is jazz *tout court* – but bluesiness predominates; highlights of an almost uniformly appealing CD include a slow, sensuous 'Shake That Thing' with splendid support from Pearl Wright, and 'Maybe Not At All', where Waters amusingly imitates Clara and Bessie Smith.

(*) Ethel Waters 1926–1929
Classics 688 Waters; Joe Smith, unknown (c); Manny Klein (t); Tommy Dorsey (tb); Jimmy Dorsey (cl, as); Alex S. Jackson (as, bss); Pearl Wright, J. C. Johnson, James P. Johnson, Clarence Williams, Frank Signorelli (p); William A. Tyler, Ben Selvin,

unknown (vn); H. Leonard Jeter, unknown (vc); Joe Tarto (b); male quartet, choir (v). 9/26–5/29.

(*) Ethel Waters 1929–1931
Classics 721 Waters; Manny Klein or Bob Effros, unknown (t); Tommy Dorsey (tb); Jimmy Dorsey (cl, as); Pearl Wright, Frank Signorelli (p); unknowns (vn); unknown (vc); Carl Kress, unknown (g); Joe Tarto (b); Stan King (d). 6/29–31.

These discs present Ethel Waters reinventing herself as a jazz and pop stylist looking for crossover. 1926–1929 includes some classics: Waters's timing is wonderful on 'Jersey Walk', an attempt to follow in the footsteps of 'Charleston', with Pearl Wright turning in a very creditable pastiche of James P. Johnson. Johnson himself is typically splendid on four titles, and Clarence Williams does very well on another four. The drawback is an overdose of sentimental songs with titles like 'Weary Feet', 'Home (Cradle Of Happiness)' and 'Lonesome Swallow'.

Only the first ten tracks of 1929–1931 make it into B&GR, the reader being referred thereafter to *Jazz Records 1897–1942*, and some of those ten are marginal in terms of both style and accompaniment. Which is definitely not to say that they are poor; Waters was usually a better pop and jazz interpreter than she was a blues singer. With that in mind, broadminded readers may care to investigate *Am I Blue?* (Living Era CD AJA 5290) or *An Introduction To Ethel Waters* (Best Of Jazz 4013), which include, but go beyond, some of the blues discussed above, or the fine jazz singing and playing on *Takin' A Chance On Love: The Complete Bluebird Sessions And More* (Definitive DRCD 11114).

(*) Ethel Waters 1946–1947
Classics 1249 Waters; George Treadwell (t); Dickie Harris (tb); Ray Perry (as, vn); Reggie Beane, Herman Chittison (p); Mary Osborne, Everett Barksdale (g); Al McKibbon, Carl Powell (b); J. C. Heard (d). 4/46–47.

Most of this is lightly jazzed pop, and less interesting than the personnel might suggest, but worth noting are a 'St. Louis Blues' with specially written verses, four Leonard Feather point numbers where Waters pinch-hits for Dinah Washington with genteel enthusiasm, and 'Throw The Dirt', which revisits 1926's 'Throw Dirt In Your Face' to exceedingly droll effect. 'Careless Love' and 'Blues In My Heart' are also present, but not exactly essential. cs

Beverly 'Guitar' Watkins (born 1939)
VOCAL, GUITAR

Watkins learned to play in high school in Atlanta. She was Piano Red's guitarist from 1959 to 1966, and wore the nurse's uniform when they became Dr. Feelgood & The Interns. She went on to join Eddie Tigner's Ink Spots for a time, and has continued to play in and around Atlanta.

*** Back In Business**
Music Maker MMCD 91007 Watkins; Eddie Boyd, Sam Anderson (ts); Carl Sonny Leyland (p); Curtis Smith, Albert White (g, v); Danny 'Mudcat' Dudeck, Sammy Blue, Doug Jones (g); Jon Schwenke (b); Ardie Dean, Jason Reichert (d); Chris Uhler (cga, perc); Mike Vernon (tamb, shaker). 98?

** The Feelings Of ... Beverly 'Guitar' Watkins**
Music Maker MMCD 46 Watkins; unknowns (s); Jerry McCain (h); unknown (o); unknown (syn); unknown (b); prob. Ardie Dean (d); unknown (perc); unknowns (v). 04?

Back In Business includes a couple of greatest hits from Piano Red's catalogue of good-natured *Bierkeller* blues stomps, but there's a lot more to Watkins than past glories; she's a skilled and versatile electric guitarist, although some of the solos are presumably played by others. (If the booklet is to be believed, there are four guitars alongside hers on the concluding title track.) Piano Red missed a trick by not featuring Watkins as a singer; she ranges easily from strutting rockers to yearning blues-ballads like 'Blue [sic] In The Night', and gives unaffected readings of straightforward 12-bar blues like 'Red Mama Blues' (about her guitar) and 'Too Many Times'. Arlean Brown's 'Impeach Me Baby', perfunctorily updated from Nixon to Clinton, is unconvincing, but otherwise this is a pleasing disc by a hardworking professional who clearly enjoys her work.

So what happened between *Back In Business* and *The Feelings Of …*? The second CD features banal and prosaic lyrics, one of which is set to a tune that doesn't fit the words, and more than one of which is sung in a key that forces Watkins to strain for the high notes. The band don't give Watkins much room to solo, and the mixing favours the organ and saxes, burying most of what soloing she does. Producer Ardie Dean seems to have lacked the courage either to keep the arrangements simple or to say, 'These songs just won't do.' Music Maker's presentation is substandard, too; how much can it cost to list the musicians? CS

Ollie Watkins (1895–1955)
VOCAL, GUITAR, HARMONICA

Watkins was born in Arkansas and grew up in Oklahoma; his music indicates that he passed through Texas on his way to California, where he worked as a cook and migrant farm labourer.

** Used To Keep Me Worried
Fedora FCD 5025 Watkins; 'Mr Jerry' (d, sp); 'Mr Louis' (sp). early 50s?

A tip-driven repertoire suggests that Watkins was a street musician; he applies his hoarse voice to blues, spirituals, a Jimmie Rodgers blue yodel and an unaccompanied doo-wop ballad. The recordings turned up in a collection bought by Fedora's owner, but it's not known how Watkins met the white men he addresses as 'Mr Lou' and 'Mr Jerry'; nor is it known whether their motives in recording him were documentary or commercial. If the latter, they were optimists indeed, for Watkins's guitar playing is disfigured by abundant wrong notes and stumbles, whether he's playing shuffle rhythms or finger-picking. His occasional harmonica is very limited and painfully dissonant. *Used To Keep Me Worried* has its moments, notably a couple of tracks where Mr Jerry's steady drumming mitigates Watkins's rhythmic insecurity, but moments are what they are. CS

Johnny 'Guitar' Watson (1935–96)
VOCAL, GUITAR, PIANO

Amos Milburn was an early influence after John Watson Jr learned to play piano from his father, but when it came to guitar it was Houston regular Clarence 'Gatemouth' Brown who pointed Watson towards the attacking style that became the hallmark of his most famous records from the mid-'50s. His career went on hold for almost a decade but a partnership with Larry Williams and a British tour resuscitated both their careers. Another makeover as a soul/funk man took him through the '70s but personal problems put paid to that, too. Hanging out with Frank Zappa brought him the odd vocal credit and he was in the process of renewing himself once more when he died on stage during a Japanese tour.

*** Gangster Of Love
King KCD 6004 Watson; Joe Bridgewater, Robert Taylor (t); Edward Hale (as); Billy Smith, Sammy Parker, Milt Bradford, Bill Gaither, Chauncey Lockie (ts); Clyde Dunn, Jim Wynn (bs); Devonia Williams, Ernie Freeman, Robert Gross (p); Sydney Sharp, Leonard Malarsky, Israel Baker, Harry Hyams, Elliott Fisher (vn); Wayne Bennett, Harold Grant, Howard Roberts, Charles Norris (g); Mario Delagarde, Ted Brinson, James Benson (b); Bill English, Robert 'Snake' Sims, Charles Pendergraph, Ed 'Sharkey' Hall, Gaynel Hodge (d). 1/53–5/63.

A spell as pianist with Chuck Higgins's Mellomoods brought Watson a contract with Federal and three sessions in just over 12 months. A remake of 'Motorhead Baby' (first cut with Higgins), 'Highway 60', with an arrangement courtesy of Amos Milburn and Willie Mabon, and 'Space Guitar', a manic instrumental utilizing the latest reverb technology, are the best results from the dozen tracks recorded. Watson had a good piano style but seemed reluctant to use it, while his vocals lacked the personality of his later RPM sides. After his stint with that label he returned to King in 1961, by which time his singing hovered on the edge of self-caricature. He sings 'Cuttin' In' and 'Broke And Lonely' with a false fervour unreflected by the bland accompaniment. 'Gangster Of Love' from two years later was a better song and a more balanced performance, made into a pop hit decades later by Steve Miller.

*** Hot Just Like TNT
Ace CDCHD 621 Watson; James Parr (t); Maxwell Davis, Plas Johnson (ts); Jim Wynn, Jewell Grant (bs); Willard McDaniel (p); Rene Hall (g); Billy Hadnott, Ralph Hamilton (b); Jesse Price, Jesse Sailes (d); Cordelia de Milo, Devonia Williams, Jeanie Barnes (v). 1/55–c. 60.

***(*) Three Hours Past Midnight
[Ace CDCH 909]//Flair 2–91696 As above, except add Chuck Higgins (ts), Googie Rene (p), Barney Kessel (g), Joe Ursery (b), Eli Toney (d), unknowns (v). 52–59.

Watson's string-snapping guitar solos are what make his RPM recordings, a curious and unpredictable combination of speed and sloth at its best in two versions of 'Hot Little Mama', 'Don't Touch Me' and 'Three Hours Past Midnight'. Elsewhere, in 'Give A Little', for instance, it's more sound than content. His vocals, with interjections of 'yeah, yeah' and 'I declare', become annoyingly mannered but his energy and Maxwell Davis's punchy arrangements carry the day. *Hot Just Like TNT* also includes his Keen recording of 'Gangster Of Love' (first heard as the demo 'Love Bandit') and a Rosco Gordon-flavoured 'One Room Country Shack'. Watson is also heard accompanying Cordelia de Milo and Devonia Williams. Sadly, quality dissipates during the final sequence of this 28-track compilation, with previously unissued material (including a very poor imitation of 'What'd I Say') that ought perhaps to have stayed that way. *Three Hours Past Midnight* includes 'Motor Head Baby', his 1952 recording debut with Chuck Higgins, and 'The Bear' and 'One More Kiss', recorded for Class in 1959, as well as a number of alternative takes. Unfortunately some of the latter, including the title track, are decidedly inferior to the issued versions, taking some of the impact from an otherwise attractive package.

***(*) Blues Masters: The Best Of Johnny "Guitar" Watson
Rhino R2 75702 *As above, except add Floyd Dixon (p), unknown (b), unknown (d). 52–5/63.*

In this case, 'the best' means the broadest sampling, encompassing both the original 'Motor Head Baby', its rerecording as 'Motorhead Baby', some others of his Federal recordings, a handful of RPM and later King sides and a couple of recordings for obscure LA labels. One of the latter, the instrumental 'The Late Freight Twist', was issued under Floyd Dixon's name, even though Watson's guitar is featured throughout; the other, 'The Eagle Is Back', was a by then untypical slow blues that leaves the listener wanting more. Also notable are his unlikely but successful treatment of Hank Williams's 'Cold Cold Heart' and a version of 'Gangster Of Love' from 5/63. Something of a grab-bag, the CD adequately reflects the concept of the series. NS

Junior Watson (born 1950)
VOCAL, GUITAR

Based in California, Mike Watson has played for long spells with Rod Piazza and Canned Heat and for shorter ones with many other bands, cumulatively building a reputation as one of the most variously talented and influential guitarists of his time and place.

*** If I Had A Genie
Heart & Soul 10799//Ruf 9861 *Watson; Barron Shul (ts, bs); Gene Taylor (p); Nick Curran (g); Kedar Roy (b); Jimmy Mulleniux (d). 02.*

Thanks to the vagaries of the record business, this is currently the only album in print on which Watson has the leading role. Fortunately it's a good one. An enterprising setlist of tunes ranging from Pee Wee Crayton's 'Blues After Hours' to Amos Milburn's 'House Party' by way of Bumble Bee Slim, Snooks Eaglin and Peppermint Harris proves that Watson has not only rummaged through many shelves of the blues library but commands half a century of guitar styles, a range of skills he demonstrates not by reproduction but by witty adaptation. His singing, though a secondary talent, is genial and well suited to humorous numbers like 'Something's Wrong' or Johnny Otis's title number.

For *Back To Back* (Crosscut CCD 11059), jointly credited to Watson and Lynwood Slim, see the latter's entry, which also describes Watson's very fine playing on *Lost In America* (Atomic Theory//Black Magic). His work as a sideman is touched upon in the entries for Big Al Blake, William Clarke, Mark Hummel, Kid Ramos and others. *Long Overdue* (Black Magic BMCD 9021) is, regrettably, deleted. TR

Kenny Wayne (born 1944)
VOCAL, PIANO, ORGAN

Born in Spokane, Washington, to parents who'd migrated from Louisiana, Wayne (real name Kenny Wayne Spruell) grew up in Compton, California. He played blues, soul, rock and Latin jazz in LA and San Francisco, and now lives in Vancouver.

**(*) Alive & Loose
Blues Roots BR-95101 *Wayne; David 'Hurricane' Hoerl (h); Andreas Schuld (g); Brian Newcombe (b); Chris 'The Wrist' Norquist (d). 7/95.*

*** 88th & Jump Street
Electro-Fi 3371 *Wayne; Chris Whitely (t); William Carn (tb); Richard Underhill, Chris Gale (s); David 'Hurricane' Hoerl (h); Jeff Healey, Mel Brown, Mitchell Lewis (g); Bob Stroger, Russell Jackson (b); Maureen Brown (d, perc); Willie 'Big Eyes' Smith (d); Karen Krystal, Pamela Patmon (v). 6–9/01.*

***(*) Blues Carry Me Home
Isabel IS 640201 *Wayne; Wil [sic] Crosby (g); Russell Jackson (b); Henry Avery (d). 5/02.*

*** Let It Loose
Electro-Fi 3388 *Wayne; Pat Carey, Steve Hilliam (s); Dave 'Hurricane' Hoerl (h); Brandon Isaak, Clifford Dunn, Dave 'Double D' Dykhuizen (g); Russell Jackson (b); Darrell Mayes, Henry Avery, Theo Brown (d); band (v). 05?*

Wayne's blues and boogie mix is chiefly reminiscent of Amos Milburn, but he also ventures into New Orleans R&B from time to time; on Electro-Fi 'Whiskey Heaven' and 'With These Hands' reveal his liking for country music. Wayne is a fertile composer, and a forceful singer and pianist. On *Alive & Loose*, he's supported by an electric band who are competent but, except on two tracks with unsuitably jazzy harmonica, too predictable.

Hoerl switches to a Chicago-based style on *88th & Jump Street*, which is just as well, since on three tracks he's in the company of Mel Brown, Stroger and Smith. They're predictably good, as is Jeff Healey on another three tunes, but the guest stars' main function is to be named on the cover; they by no means outshine Lewis, Jackson and Maureen Brown, who accompany on most tracks, and are augmented by horns for two New Orleans numbers. Self-produced, *88th & Jump Street* is enjoyable, self-confident music that's both personal and grounded in tradition; it would have been better, though, if Wayne had allowed the guitarists less solo space and himself more.

Blues Carry Me Home was recorded in France. Wayne's touring band are all first-class musicians, and like their leader are comfortable playing blues, boogie, the Nat 'King' Cole-style jazz of 'Blues Love Theme' and the funk which throbs at the heart of 'Wine, Beer And Whiskey'. Despite its killer riff, that track is over-extended, as is the trite closer, 'Amazing Boogie/Down By The Riverside', but 'How Long' sustains its interest despite being very familiar and over ten minutes long. The title track is a startling revival of minor-key blues harmony singing in the manner of the Big Three Trio; its success epitomizes Wayne's ability to make confident, original, swinging music in a variety of unapologetically oldfashioned styles.

Most of the the songs of *Let It Loose* are by Wayne; the three which aren't are associated with Amos Milburn. There are a number of good compositions here: 'Joogie To The Boogie', 'Wishing Well' and 'Be A Man' respectively verify Wayne's ability to write celebratory music with a subtle twist, ballads and personal musings; and 'Don't Rush To Judge Me' is wonderfully reminiscent of Central Avenue in the '40s, when it was the headquarters of hipness. Wayne's writing talent is let down by his self-production, though; he rings the personnel changes, but the accompaniments usually emerge as generic, with the musicians constricted into an undifferentiated, over-busy mass of sound. Russell Jackson is present on most tracks, and Henry Avery on five, but where they were Wayne's co-stars on *Blues Carry Me Home*, here they're usually just members of the supporting cast. CS

Carl Weathersby (born 1955)
VOCAL, GUITAR

Weathersby grew up in East Chicago, Indiana, spending the summers in his native Meadville, Mississippi. Family friend Albert King hired him as rhythm guitarist for three tours before he joined the Sons Of Blues in 1982, leaving after the release of his first album.

**(*) Don't Lay Your Blues On Me
Evidence ECD 26075 *Weathersby; David Torkanowsky (o, p); Levy Wash (g); Lee Zeno, J. W. Williams (b); Herman Ernest (d); Tracy C'Vello (perc); Charlene Howard (v). 11–12/95.*

**(*) Looking Out My Window
Evidence ECD 26089 *As above, except add Herman Ernest (perc); omit Williams, C'Vello, Howard. 12/96–3/97.*

*** Restless Feeling
Evidence ECD 26099 *Weathersby; David Torkanowsky (kb, o, p); Rico McFarland (g, v); Dave Smith (b); Steve Potts (d); Juanita Brooks (v). 5/98.*

**** Come To Papa
Evidence ECD 26108 *Weathersby; Wayne Jackson (t, tb); Andrew Love (ts); Lucky Peterson (o, p, clavinet); Rico McFarland (g); Willie Weeks (b); Steve Potts (d); Ann Peebles, John Carlyle, Harold Chandler (v). 12/99.*

Weathersby's debut album was well received, and his songwriting talent is evident, but it's an unsatisfactory production: the inexorable bass and drums are brain-curdlingly loud, and Torkanowsky splashes soupy B-3 chords around indiscriminately. Weathersby left the Sons Of Blues partly because of tensions between his soul and rock influences and Billy Branch's '50s timewarpery; he sounds unhappy on mannered revivals of 'Same Thing' and 'Fanny Mae', and the Wolf imitation on 'Killing Floor' is more Mini-Me than Evil. The best thing about *Don't Lay Your Blues On Me* is Weathersby's guitar, especially when he's channelling Albert King and Little Milton, but too often meaning is sacrificed to capricious blues-rock aggression. *Looking Out My Window* shares its predecessor's faults of relentless rhythm and pointless high-energy guitar solos, with some dislikeable wah-wah second guitar stirred in. A version of John Hiatt's 'Feels Like Rain' chases after Buddy Guy's success with the song, but is vitiated by Weathersby's admitted reluctance to record it, and a lumbering 'Standing At The Crossroads' panders to the archivally minded.

Only Torkanowsky survives on to *Restless Feeling*, and his playing is better integrated into a much better band: Smith, Potts and McFarland have the brawn needed to support Weathersby, but they bring far more attention and invention to the ensemble than their predecessors. Weathersby now seems to be doing the songs he wants in the way he wants – which is not always a good thing: Allen Toussaint's 'We All Wanna Boogie' and Al Green's 'Rhymes' are respectively affected and twee, but they're blemishes on a CD that's an otherwise successful exposition of Weathersby's soul-blues-rock synthesis. An acoustic guitar revival of Lightnin' Hopkins's 'Glory Be' is calculated but effective.

Come To Papa uses the same core band, and Weathersby's music continues to grow. The guest musicians are an important part of the process: Ann Peebles's sexy rasp glorifies the revival-and-reversal of her hit 'Come To Mama', and the seasoned, intuitive soulfulness of the Memphis Horns and Lucky Peterson inducts Weathersby to a higher league. *Come To Papa* is the CD where he claims creative control and proclaims artistic maturity. Only two tracks are Weathersby compositions, and yet throughout one hears his personal voice, synthesizing the soul of Hi and Stax with the gruff authority of Albert King and Little Milton, and tying everything together with guitar work whose jolting turbulence grows organically out of the songs. Only 'Drifting Blues', overlong and – well – drifting, disappoints; perhaps intended as a nod to heritage, it comes over as token.

**(*) Best Of Carl Weathersby
Evidence ECD 26127 *Similar to above CDs. 11/95–12/99.*

Best Of Carl Weathersby draws on the previous four CDs, and adds a solo, acoustic 'Stop Breaking Down Blues', which stumbles along, but stops short of breaking down. So far, *Come To Papa* is the real best of Carl Weathersby.

*** In The House
Crosscut CCD 11078 *Weathersby; Billy Branch (h); Paul Hendricks (g); Calvin 'Skip' Gaskin (b); Leon Smith (d); Otis Clay (v). 11/02.*

Recorded live in Switzerland, Weathersby brings a bluesy touch to covers of Delbert McClinton and Marvin Gaye, is reunited with Billy Branch on two numbers (Otis Clay joining in on 'Hobo Blues'), and pays extended tribute to Stax-era Albert King before closing with a Hendrix-influenced slow blues. Second guitarist Paul Hendricks gets plenty of well-deserved solo space and, perhaps relieved at no longer working together regularly, Weathersby and Branch have fun trading licks. This was obviously a good night out, but as so often some of the crowd-pleasing – gimmicky high-end playing on guitar and harp, mutual admiration pacts, dynamic extremism both *ppp* and *fff* – doesn't translate well to disc.

*** Hold On
Carl Weathersby [unnumbered]//P-Vine PCD-24168 *Weathersby; Michael McDaniel (ts); Johnny Neel (o, p); Richard Waters (g); Chris Kent (b); Leon Smith (d, v); T. C. Davis (tamb, rain stick); Carl Weathersby Jr, Dennis Gulley, Christine Thompson, Eddie Tucker (v). 04?*

The self-produced *Hold On* is a generally successful comeback after health problems. Important to the process are Leon Smith's attentive drumming and the well-constructed organ fills and solos of ex-Allman Brothers keyboardist Neel. 'My Baby' and 'Feels Like Rain' are revived, in better versions than on Evidence, and Homer Banks's 'Angel Of Mercy', which got a good interpretation on *In The House*, gets a better one here. Weathersby's singing is more consistently attuned to the moods of the songs than on previous CDs, but some of his guitar solos sabotage the good work by going into unmotivated overdrive. *Hold On* doesn't reach the level of *Come To Papa*, but it does suggest that there are better things on the way, health permitting. CS

Curley Weaver (1906–62)
VOCAL, GUITAR

As well as teaching her son Curley James Weaver to play the guitar, Savannah Shepard also gave tuition to the Hicks brothers, later known as Barbecue Bob and Charley Lincoln.

The teenaged Weaver teamed up with harmonica player Eddie Mapp and went to Atlanta, where they joined a circle that also included the Hickses, Blind Willie McTell, Fred McMullen and Buddy Moss. Though amassing a significant number of records of his own, gaining the unofficial title of 'Georgia Guitar Wizard', Weaver was also a prolific accompanist, usually with the musicians cited. Apart from a 1949 session with McTell and a four-title set of his own, he retreated into obscurity, a victim of failing eyesight.

**(*) Georgia Blues (1928–1933)
Document DOCD-5110 *Weaver; Eddie Mapp (h); Clarence Moore (g, v). 10/28–11/31.*

Weaver's debut recordings of 'Sweet Petunia' and 'No No Blues' display a marked vocal similarity to the Hicks brothers that may have stalled his career with Columbia. The following year he recut the latter tune with Mapp on one of two singles for QRS. These titles, though hard to discern through the surface noise, indicate the beginning of a distinctive style and a robust bottleneck technique, heard to good effect on the otherwise trite 'Baby Boogie', a 1931 duet with Clarence Moore. He's also heard accompanying Fred McMullen, and duetting on 'Poor Stranger Blues', during sessions featured in greater detail on the next item. (Other tracks on this album are by Mapp, McMullen and 'Slim Barton'.)

***(*) Curley Weaver (1933–1935)
Document DOCD-5111 *Weaver; Buddy Moss (h, g, v); Fred McMullen, Blind Willie McTell (g, v); Ruth Willis (v). 1/33–4/35.*

Further outings of 'No No Blues', one an alternative take and others masquerading as 'Tippin' Tom' and 'Birmingham Gambler', open this album. (Poor copies of the issued 'No No Blues' and 'Early Morning Blues' appear on *"Too Late Too Late" – Vol. 3* [Document DOCD-5276].) More impressive are the six songs by the Georgia Browns (Weaver, McMullen and Moss), scintillating country dance music ranging from stateliness to rollick that indicates Weaver's value as an ensemble musician. Later sessions with Blind Willie McTell find him dispensing with the bottleneck. These tracks, while exhibiting an equivalent standard of musicianship, cast a more sombre light, with the exception of 'Tricks Ain't Walking No More' and 'Oh Lawdy Mama'. All Weaver's recordings on this and the surrounding CDs, and those by the Georgia Browns, are also on *Atlanta Blues* (JSP JSP 7754 4CD).

***(*) Blind Willie McTell & Curley Weaver (1949–1950)
RST Blues Documents BDCD-6014 *Weaver; Blind Willie McTell (g). 5/49–50.*

McTell and Weaver came forward after producer Fred Mendelsohn advertised for artists on Atlanta radio in August 1949. Twenty-one titles were recorded, all but four remaining unissued for decades, most featuring Weaver as an accompanist and harmony vocalist. He cut just four songs of his own and one of those, 'Wee Midnight Hours', was a duet with McTell. The results were no different from the sessions the two men had recorded 14 years earlier, perfectly performed but out of sync with the times. This was also true of four songs cut for Bob Shad's Sittin' In With, the first pair probably recorded in Atlanta, going by McTell's presence on 'Ticket Agent'. The other single, 'Some Rainy Day' and 'Trixie', recalled Weaver's earliest recordings, the latter concealing the identity of 'Tricks Ain't Walking No More'. NS

Sylvester Weaver (1897–1960)
VOCAL, GUITAR, BANJO

This Louisville, Kentucky, musician recorded the first solo guitar accompaniment to an African-American vocal blues when he partnered Sara Martin at a session in October 1923. The following month he opened his own recording account with the instrumentals 'Guitar Blues' and 'Guitar Rag'. Over the next four years he recorded again with Martin and with the young Helen Humes, as well as on his own and with guitarist Walter Beasley. He later left the music business and worked as a chauffeur.

*** Sylvester Weaver – Vol. 1 (1923–1927)
Document DOCD-5112 *Weaver; E. L. Coleman (vn); Charles Washington (bj); Sara Martin, Hayes B. Withers (v). 11/23–8/27.*

*** Sylvester Weaver – Vol. 2 (1927)
Document DOCD-5113 *Weaver; Walter Beasley (g); Helen Humes (v). 8–11/27.*

'Guitar Blues' and 'Guitar Rag' are both played with a slide. Eighty years on, when we have heard so much in this style, 'Guitar Blues' may sound somewhat stilted or sedate, but 'Guitar Rag' has drive and an appealing shape, and one can see why this side (or its electrical rerecording of three and a half years later) attracted old-time and Western Swing musicians as well as later blues guitarists like Earl Hooker. Weaver continued to mingle ragtime tunes like 'Smoketown Strut' with ponderous blues like 'Mixing Them Up In C' or 'Steel String Blues', a trio with violin and banjo. He was first heard singing in a gospel trio, but soon afterwards essayed a blues vocal in 'True Love Blues', revealing a rich baritone but not then, and almost never afterwards, shifting out of the extremely slow gear of his blues instrumentals.

All but two of the tracks on *Vol. 2* are guitar duets with Beasley, mostly with singing by one or the other or Humes. The tempos may be soporific but Beasley plucks the listener's sleeve with lyrics like 'If a toad frog had wings, he would be flyin' all around – he would not have his bottom bumpin', thumpin' on the ground' ('Toad Frog Blues') and Humes does likewise with her 'Garlic Blues'. Weaver, always an idiosyncratic songwriter, upstages them both with 'Me And My Tapeworm'. These delicacies aside, the tastiest performances are the instrumental duets 'St. Louis Blues' and 'Bottleneck Blues'. Weaver also recorded (on *Vol. 1*) a couple of banjo tunes, 'Six-String Banjo Piece' and 'Damfino Stump'. TR

Boogie Bill Webb (1924–90)
VOCAL, GUITAR

Born in Jackson, Mississippi, Webb grew up in New Orleans, where his mother ran parties and fish fries, often bringing Tommy Johnson from Jackson to play. Johnson was a major influence, both then and in the '40s, when Webb moved back to Mississippi for a time. Back in New Orleans, he occasionally sat in with Fats Domino's band, and had one record released by Imperial in 1953. Webb was recorded again from the mid-'60s by researchers who were often chiefly interested in the Tommy

Johnson connection; he obtained some festival work as a result. His nickname came from his guitar arrangement of 'Pine Top's Boogie Woogie'.

Four Imperial masters are split between *Rural Blues – Volumes 1 & 2* (BGO BGOCD 384) and *Rural Blues – Vol. III: Down Home Stomp* (BGO BGOCD 464). Most of Webb's later recordings are not on CD, but *Living Country Blues* (Evidence ECD 26105 3CD) includes two Tommy Johnson songs.

**(*) The Blues Of Snooks Eaglin & Boogie Bill Webb
Storyville STCD 8054 Webb; 'Harmonica Slim' [Robert Gates] (h, v). c. 85.

*** The Blues Of Robert Lockwood Jr. & Boogie Bill Webb
Storyville STCD 8055 As above. c. 85.

Webb's tracks (four on the Eaglin CD, six on the Lockwood) are placed last, and evidently there as filler; stylistically, they're in marked contrast to the erudite and urbane musicianship of the main artists, but their blend of entertainment and broody introversion is worth hearing. Despite the credit to Webb, Harmonica Slim takes two and four vocals respectively. The duo are not over-rehearsed, and occasionally they come adrift, but these are likeable, unpretentious performances, mostly of mainstream blues repertoire.

*** Drinkin' And Stinkin'
Flying Fish FF 70506 Webb; Reggie Scanlan (b); Ben Sandmel (d, wb). 2–9/86.

Much of *Drinkin' And Stinkin'* consists of cover versions, but only one is from Tommy Johnson, which makes room for a repertoire that stretches from Alberta Hunter ('You Can't Tell My Business After Dark') to King Curtis by way of Professor Longhair and Lowell Fulson. Also included are a hokum tune, an ingenious toast, the venerable 'Red Cross Store' and Webb's own compositions, the witty 'Drinkin' And Stinkin'' and an improbably suave 'Love Me 'Cause I Love My Baby So'. As he did on Imperial, Webb plays light, open-textured electric guitar, and even at this late date his music is as confident, relaxed and individual as ever; once or twice, the accompanists' timekeeping descends from steady to stolid, but usually it's a helpful discipline. CS

Garth Webber
VOCAL, GUITAR

An admirer of Robben Ford, Webber succeeded him as Miles Davis's guitarist, but after a few tours quit to concentrate on studio work. He is based in Berkeley, California.

** Get A Grip On The Blues
Blue Rock'It BRCD 112//Crosscut CCD 11034 Webber; Mark Ford (h); Tony Lufrano (kb, o); Frank Martin, John R. Burr (kb); Lizz Fischer (o, p); James Page (o); Myron Dove, Ron Gurewitz, Gary Brown (b); Jimmy Sanchez (d, perc); Bowen Brown, Brent Rampone, Hilary Jones, David Garibaldi (d). 91.

** On The Edge
Blue Rock'It BRCD 119//Crosscut CCD 11045 Webber; Mark Ford (h, v); Frank Martin (kb, o); Tony Lufrano (o); Myron Dove (b); John Mader (d). 93?

If your ideal of a blues singer is John Lee Hooker or Muddy Waters, Webber will probably not appeal to you. It isn't just that his voice lacks any of the colorations associated with blues singing, it's simply not a very interesting voice in itself: thin, pinched, dramatically unconvincing. As a guitarist he is smoothly proficient but seldom surprising. *Get A Grip On The Blues* is the more interesting album of the two, though not for its few examples of received repertoire, since his way of transforming a standard involves discarding its melody. Thus 'Little Red Rooster' is reduced to the lyrics of 'Little Red Rooster' set to a generic fast blues tune, and what could be more pointless than that? *On The Edge* is shared with Mark Ford and so billed. Ford is an articulate harmonica player, for instance on 'Let It Go', but as a singer he was at this point little more persuasive than Webber, and the ensemble vocals on 'It's A Feeling' and 'Hot & Cold Eh' sound like the work of boy scouts. TR

Katie Webster (1939–99)
VOCAL, PIANO, ORGAN

Katie Webster was a busy session pianist for Jay Miller and Eddie Shuler in the '50s and '60s, and made a few recordings of her own; 'Baby Baby' (Kry), a duet with her then boyfriend, Ashton Savoy, is a classic. In 1964 Webster joined Otis Redding's band. She quit music for two years after his death, but in the '70s a British LP of her early recordings generated new interest in her; thereafter she toured extensively at home and abroad. A stroke in 1993 severely affected her sight and her left hand, but she continued to appear occasionally at festivals.

** The Goldband Years
Goldband GR-7839 Webster; unknowns (t, tb, ts, kb, g, b, d, perc). prob. 60s–80s.

Issued posthumously, this disc also includes four tracks by Rockin' Sidney. Webster displays the versatility one would expect of a session player, proving herself a respectable country singer on 'Sick And Tired Of All These Scars' among others; at the blues end of the stall there are fine revivals of Lonnie Brooks's 'Family Rules' and Juke Boy Bonner's 'Going Crazy About You'. Not all the material is at that level, however, and not all the blame attaches to Eddie Shuler's muffled sound and penchant for busy arrangements; Webster wrote 'Trade Winds', the four minutes of Hawaiian cheese-and-pineapple that open the CD.

**(*) I Know That's Right
Arhoolie CD 393 Webster; Bruce Unsworth, Nancy Wright (ts); Jim Peterson (s); Clay Cotton (o); John Lumsdaine, Danny Caron (g); Steve Ehrmann (b); Steve Griffith (d). 11/84–11/85.

Webster was an exceptional boogie pianist, as she demonstrates on the title track and a solo 'Katie's Boogie Woogie'; it's a pity that this aspect of her playing remained only an occasional feature of her shows and CDs. 'Katie's Boogie Woogie' also has the merit of brevity; most of the songs on *I Know That's Right* are far too long for their own good. This is largely the fault of Hot Links, who are polished, unoriginal and determined to squeeze every cliché to the last drop.

**(*) The Many Faces Of Katie Webster
Chrisly CR 60005 Webster. 11/87.

Recorded on one of her many European visits, Webster once again demonstrates both her range and her variability. The opening medley, a boogie treatment of 'Real Gone Guy' plus an unacknowledged 'Honeydripper', is very treasurable, but there's a preponderance of pop – 'Basin Street Blues', 'I Can't Give You Anything But Love' and Dobie Gray's 'Drift Away' are all poorly handled – and undemanding, poppish R&B from Lee Dorsey, Fats Domino and Webster herself.

***(*) **The Swamp Boogie Queen**
Alligator ALCD 4766 *Webster; Wayne Jackson (t, tb); Andrew Love (ts); Joe Sublett (s); Kim Wilson (h, v); Bonnie Raitt (g, v); Andrew [Jr Boy] Jones, Robert Cray, Anson Funderburgh, Dave Gonzales (g); Russell Jackson, Thomas Yearsley (b); Tony Coleman, Scott Campbell (d).* 88.

*** **Two-Fisted Mama!**
Alligator ALCD 4777 *Webster; Wayne Jackson (t, tb); Andrew Love (ts); Vasti Jackson (g, v); Gus Thornton (b); Gerald Warren (d).* 89.

*** **No Foolin'!**
Alligator ALCD 4803 *Webster; Burgess Gardner (t); Edwin Williams (tb); Gene Barge, Henri Ford (ts); C. J. Chenier (ac); Lonnie Brooks, Vasti Jackson (g, v); Raphael Semmes (b); Morris Jennings (d); Peaches Staten (rb); Kathirine [sic] Lee, Donell Rush (v).* 91.

*** **DeLuxe Edition**
Alligator ALCD 5606 *Similar to above three CDs.* 88–91.

The core accompaniment on Webster's Alligator CDs is supplied by her working bands of the time; *DeLuxe Edition* is compiled from the first three, with the addition of two previously unissued titles. All these discs have their moments: on *Two-Fisted Mama!* impeccably sly timing sustains the monologue 'Red Negligee' over nine and a half minutes, and 'C.Q. Boogie' is one more reason to regret that she never recorded at length in the genre. 'Zydeco Shoes And California Blues' on *No Foolin'!* is not without opportunistic elements, but Chenier's participation is an unexpected success, and Webster makes the song a poignant reflection on migration and identity. Her best CD is *Swamp Boogie Queen*, however, thanks to the attentive playing of Silent Partners (Jones, Russell Jackson and Coleman); unlike Hot Links, they respond to what Webster does, rather than just supplying a context to do it in. A surfeit of guest stars is usually a bad omen, but although Raitt's slide guitar and voice don't fit with Webster's music, Cray, Wilson and (predictably) the Memphis Horns excel. CS

Weepin' Willie (born 1926)
VOCAL

Born in Atlanta, the only son of migrant farmworkers, Willie Robinson lost his mother when he was nine or ten and last saw his father when he sent him to a farm in New Jersey at the age of 13. After serving in the Army in World War II he tried to break into the music business as a singer, eventually winning a place in a band and discovering the club scene in Boston, where in the '60s he sang at Louie's Lounge and Basin Street South. He later became friends, and performed, with the singer Mighty Sam McClain, who sponsored the album Weepin' Willie had long wanted to make.

(*) **At Last, On Time
APO APO 2009 *Weepin' Willie; Chuck Langford (ts); George PapaGeorge (kb); Susan Tedeschi (g, v); Jimmy D. Lane, Kevin Belz (g); Tim Ingles (b); Jim Arnold (d); Mighty Sam McClain (v).* 12/98.

The track 'They Call Me Weepin' Willie/Mighty Mighty', in which Robinson sings a personalized version of McClain's song and the composer follows him with the original lyric, shows why Mighty Sam has a name and Weepin' Willie doesn't: one is a star of some magnitude in the night sky of the blues, while the other is a pinpoint of light. Nonetheless, this is an attractive album. Robinson sings with the care of a man who knows he has one shot at fame and is determined to score. His voice is sometimes reminiscent of Lowell Fulson's, particularly on the slow blues 'Dirty Old Man', 'Love Me If You Want To' and 'Can't Go Wrong Woman', which has an aggressive guitar part by Jimmy D. Lane, his only appearance. Tedeschi, a friend since the early '90s, joins him on 'Fever', 'Glory Train' and 'Let The Good Times Roll'; it is not her fault but the material's that they are the least gripping tracks. TR

(Monster) Mike Welch (born 1979)
VOCAL, GUITAR

Mike Welch is something of a child prodigy. At the age of seven he was inspired to learn guitar by the Beatles' recordings, but it was the discovery of Albert King's music two years later that triggered his self-disciplined immersion in the blues. From the age of 11 he knocked his chops into shape on Boston's live circuit. In 1992, at the Cambridge House of Blues, comedian Dan Aykroyd heard Welch's performance and endowed him with the moniker 'Monster'. The Monster has also recorded with Shemekia Copeland, Johnny Winter and Sugar Ray & The Bluetones.

***(*) **These Blues Are Mine**
Tone Cool TC 1154 *Welch; George Leroy Lewis (g); Jon Ross (b); Warren David Grant (d).* 9/95.

** **Axe To Grind**
Tone Cool TC 1159 *As above.* 97.

** **Catch Me**
Tone Cool TC 1167 *Welch; Walter Platt (t); Paul Ahlstrand (ts); Marc Phaneuf (bs); Richard Rosenblatt (h); Bruce Katz, David Maxwell (p); George Leroy Lewis (g); David Hull (b); Warren Grant (d, perc); Amyl Justin (perc, v); G. M. Perriwinkle, 'Sweetie' Lee Pittsfield (perc).* 98.

These Blues Are Mine was a sound debut. The opening instrumental 'Freezer Burn', a tribute to Albert Collins, swiftly asserts an authority on the guitar that is hard to balance against Welch's age (and appearance). Welch's fluid, glassy lead breaks contribute to an impressive individuality that is at times absent among other performers, and Lewis's imaginative accompaniment (through a Leslie speaker), highlighted on 'Leroy's Mood', enlarges the outfit's tonal vocabulary. Unfortunately, flaws surface in Welch's monotonous vocal performances, which fall short of the standards established instrumentally. Despite that, the album offers a host of well-crafted numbers, and particularly high-quality instrumentals, including the superlative 'Jessie's Blues'.

These Blues Are Mine did a lot to establish Welch as a whizzkid, and the follow-up faced the challenge of cementing his reputation as something more than a hot player. Unfortunately, *Axe To Grind* shows little of the development that might be hoped for from a songwriter traversing adolescence. Welch's soloing prowess retains the character that shone through in his debut, but the songs are plagued by mediocrity. His vocal shortcomings are repeatedly compounded by an apparent determination to prevent his accompanists deviating from stiflingly familiar shuffles and dynamics. Thankfully, towards the end a glimmer of passion shines through on the slow-burning 'My Emptiness', but on the whole the album is summed up rather aptly by the closing title, 'Cruise Control'.

If *Axe To Grind* was plagued by a 'writing-by-numbers' approach, *Catch Me* represents a major change of tack for Mike Welch (no longer Monster). The album is largely made up of unchallenging R&B-styled pop-rock, and much of the blues quotient is fulfilled in Welch's distinct soloing, which often appears misplaced against the light-hearted musical backdrop, and perhaps should not be the focus here. *Catch Me* suffers from the same dispassionate content as its predecessor, but there are several highlights, particularly the blues-based numbers. 'Mole's Blues' boasts tasty phrasing by Welch, two duets with pianist David Maxwell are quite stimulating, and 'Blues For Cara' seems to come directly from the heart. JF

Casey Bill Weldon
VOCAL, STEEL GUITAR

Despite several busy years in the recording studio and a couple of medium-sized hits, very little is known about Casey Bill Weldon. A birthdate of c. 1909 was supplied by Big Bill Broonzy, not always a reliable source. Broonzy also said he came from Arkansas, which could well be right, since there appears to have been some kind of connection with a more famous Arkansawyer, Louis Jordan. It has always been assumed that he was the Will Weldon who played with the Memphis Jug Band in its early days, but even that has recently been questioned. There is no evidence that he remained in music after World War II, and the last reported sighting of him was in 1968.

*** **Casey Bill Weldon – Vol. 1 (1935–1936)**
Document DOCD-5217 *Weldon; Arnett Nelson (cl); Peetie Wheatstraw, Black Bob, unknown (p); poss. Tampa Red (g, k); unknowns (g); prob. Bill Settles, unknowns (b); Washboard Sam (wb); unknown (v). 3/35–4/36.*

*** **Casey Bill Weldon – Vol. 2 (1936–1937)**
Document DOCD-5218 *Weldon; Arnett Nelson, unknowns (cl); Black Bob, unknown (p); Charlie McCoy (md); prob. Big Bill Broonzy, unknown (g); Bill Settles, unknowns (b); unknown (woodblocks). 4/36–3/37.*

*** **Casey Bill Weldon – Vol. 3 (1937–1938)**
Document DOCD-5219 *Weldon; unknown (cl, ts); unknowns (cl); unknowns (p); unknowns (g); Ransom Knowling, unknowns (b); unknown (d); Clifford Medlock, Henry Singleton, Calvin Dillard, unknowns (v). 3/37–12/38.*

*** **The Hawaiian Guitar Wizard 1935–1938**
[EPM Blues Collection 15829] *Similar to Document CDs. 10/35–12/38.*

*** **The Blues/Slide Guitar Swing 1927–1938**
Frémeaux FA 268 2CD *Similar to Document CDs, except add Vol Stevens (g, sp). 10/27–12/38.*

*** **Bottleneck Guitar Trendsetters Of The 1930s**
Yazoo 1049 *Weldon; prob. Black Bob (p); Charlie McCoy (md); Vol Stevens (g, sp); prob. Big Bill Broonzy, unknowns (g); poss. Bill Settles, unknown (b); unknowns (v). 10/27–10/37.*

The first recordings incontrovertibly by Casey Bill Weldon were with Peetie Wheatstraw, each accompanying the other. The encounter marked him for life, for his singing style was modelled on Wheatstraw's, but he needed a more reticent pianist if he was to communicate fully his tone and technique on slide guitar. At his next session he had one, and he promptly made the first version of one of his most influential recordings, 'Somebody Changed The Lock On My Door'. The flurry of notes in bars 3 and 4 was the first indication of a blues slide guitarist who had listened to Hawaiian players, and a session the following day by the Washboard Rhythm Kings elicited further passages of playing that was as close to Sol Hoopii as to Tampa Red. Subsequent sessions were chiefly devoted to blues like his other hit, 'We Gonna Move (To The Outskirts Of Town)', which kept Weldon's playing on a leash, but now and then he would find an opening for more adventurous work, as in 'Has My Gal Been Here', 'The Big Boat', the pop song 'Can't You Remember?' – his playing on the last two prettily offset by Charlie McCoy's mandolin – and 'Back Door', which he introduced several months before Washboard Sam's better-known version. More impressive still is his work on 'Guitar Swing', where he may be responding to the bravura playing of an unknown guitarist who may be Ikey Robinson. 'Walkin' In My Sleep' from the same session is a country tune, and at this point the gap between the group and contemporary Western Swing bands narrows dramatically. Not for the last time: 'I Believe You're Cheatin' On Me' opens with a figure from 'Steel Guitar Rag' as recorded by Bob Wills. (The unidentified pianist on this date has the instinct of a Western Swing player, too.) The mystery picker on 'Guitar Swing' seems to reappear on recordings made a couple of months later like 'You Shouldn't Do That', 'Go Ahead, Buddy' and 'Red Hot Blues', much to their advantage.

Virtually all the titles singled out above are to be found on the EPM and Frémeaux CDs, the former an inexpensive single CD, the latter a pricier but well-chosen double. The Yazoo, which is shared with Kokomo Arnold, has a good selection but only seven tracks.

Weldon also participated in half a dozen 1935–36 sides by the Hokum Boys (q.v.). The Will Weldon coupling of 1927, both sides of which are on Frémeaux and one on *Bottleneck Guitar Trendsetters*, has an accompaniment by two guitarists, Weldon and Vol Stevens, very much in the style of the early Memphis Jug Band sides to which both men contributed. It is hard to discern in this artist the makings of the Casey Bill of the '30s. TR

Valerie Wellington (1959–93)
VOCAL, PIANO

Classically trained, Wellington had done some soul singing around Chicago before playing Ma Rainey on stage in 1982. She recorded her debut CD soon after, and also made Life In The Big City *(GBW 002) for a now defunct Japanese label, but mainly worked on TV and radio commercials before her sudden death.*

**** **Million Dollar $ecret**
Rooster Blues R 2619 *Wellington; Billy Branch (h); Sunnyland Slim (p); Magic Slim, John Primer (g, v); Johnny Littlejohn (g); Aron Burton (b, v); Nick Holt (b); Casey Jones (d, v); Nate Applewhite (d). 9–10/83.*

Only 23 when she recorded *Million Dollar $ecret*, Valerie Wellington had a voice that was mature, flexible, melodious and strong enough to ride easily over various augmented versions of The Teardrops. She was also a talented songwriter; her compositions hold their own against well-known songs associated with Bessie Smith (Wellington plays piano on 'Down In The Dumps'), Helen Humes, Elmore James and Howlin' Wolf. 'Smokestack Lightning' is a gallant failure, admittedly, but, as with the CD's other revivals, Wellington applies her own insights, building on the original artists' work without settling for pastiche or imitation. Introspective or rocking, she always quarries the songs for meaning. The musicians are evidently delighted by her, and respond with consistent assurance and inventiveness; Burton's gurgling bass ostinatos are perhaps the greatest of the accompaniments' many pleasures. This was a spectacular debut disc, which a brain aneurysm abruptly turned into a memorial. cs

Junior Wells (1934–98)
VOCAL, HARMONICA

In a long and singular career Amos Wells Blakemore made a series of singles and albums that exemplified the eras in which they were recorded, but the impression remains that he somehow failed to live up to the promise of his early talent. A long informal partnership with Buddy Guy brought recognition outside the blues fraternity and diverted Wells into a soul/R&B performance style that had some initial success but thereafter descended into self-caricature. His own career remained stalled for several years while Guy's stature rose exponentially but a series of albums made during the '90s restored much of the esteem in which he'd once been held. Sadly, his progress was curtailed by cancer of the lymph nodes and a coma induced by a massive heart attack from which he never fully recovered.

**** Blues Hit Big Town
Delmark DD-640 *Wells; [Little] Johnny Jones, Otis Spann (p); Muddy Waters, Louis Myers (g); Dave Myers, Willie Dixon (b); Odie Payne Jr (d). 6/53–4/54.*

The 19-year-old Wells struggles to sound older on 'Hoodoo Man' and 'Ways Like An Angel', chewing his words as if unsure of the lyrics, but his harmonica work on these and the instrumentals 'Junior's Wail' and 'Eagle Rock' challenges the confidence and inventiveness of his mentor Little Walter. A second session with Otis Spann's notable presence provides the album's title track, ''Bout The Break Of Day', a retitling of a Sonny Boy Williamson I song, the all-but instrumental 'Lord Lord' and 'So All Alone', later revisited as 'Prison Bars All Around Me'. This CD reissue adds three alternative takes and 'Can't Find My Baby', a second song from an audition tape with Louis Myers's acoustic guitar backing. With first-class accompaniment throughout, these are the performances that cemented Wells's reputation and set a standard that he rarely equalled thereafter.

***(*) Calling All Blues – The Chief, Profile & USA Recordings 1957–1963
Fuel 2000 302 061 087 *Wells; Julian Beasley (as); Jarrett Gibson, A. C. Reed (ts); Donald Hankins (bs); Johnny Walker (o, p); Billy Emerson (o); Lafayette Leake, Otis Spann (p); Syl Johnson, David Myers, Earl Hooker, Lacy Gibson (g); Willie Dixon (b, v); Jack Myers, Ernest Johnson (b); Eugene Lounge, Fred Below,* *Bobby Little, Gill Day (d); Mel London (v). 9/57–2/63.*

This collection documents Wells's association with songwriter/label owner Mel London, during which the pair tried all the ways they knew to achieve commercal success. In the process, Wells metamorphosed from a talented blues musician to a run-of-the-mill R&B/soul singer burdened with indifferent material such as 'The Things I Do For You', 'Love Me' and 'I Need Me A Car'. To dispel his blues image, he plays harmonica on just a quarter of these 24 tracks, including two instrumentals led by Earl Hooker. Beginning with 'Two Headed Woman' and the minor hit 'Messin' With The Kid', Wells adopted the forced vocal timbre of Muddy Waters and it was this and other such threadbare formulas that hamstrung the material's commercial prospects. Nevertheless, there's much to enjoy on an energetic but trivial level: the instrumental 'Cha-Cha-Cha In Blue', the first version of 'I Could Cry', 'Prison Bars All Around Me' and 'She's A Sweet One', adapted from a Willie Dixon original for Otis Rush.

***(*) Hoodoo Man Blues
Delmark DD-612 *Wells; Buddy Guy (g); Jack Myers (b); Billy Warren (d). 9/65.*

This was one of the first times a working Chicago blues band entered the studio to cut an album that accurately reflected the music to be heard in the city's clubs at the time. The backing musicians are obviously well-rehearsed and provide Wells with a supple springboard from which to launch his idiosyncratic vocals and harmonica solos. One or two mannerisms were already becoming unwelcome tics but here they're subsumed into the sheer ebullience of the group's playing. The programme combines songs from Big Mama Thornton, Willie Cobbs and Sonny Boy Williamson I with a handful of originals and two interesting takes of the title track, on which Guy plays his guitar through a Leslie speaker. Most songs err on the side of brevity, adding sharpness and a dramatic shape to a thoroughly successful session now regarded as a classic of its kind.

*** Chicago/The Blues/Today! Vol. 1
Vanguard VMD 79216 *As above, except Fred Below (d) replaces Warren. 12/65.*

The replacement of Warren by Fred Below gives this brief set (the CD is shared with J. B. Hutto and Otis Spann) a tighter rhythmic focus but Wells's over-indulgent vocal mannerisms undermine the Sonny Boy Williamson II tribute 'Help Me', 'All Night Long' (alias 'Rock Me Mama') and his own 'Messin' With The Kid'. His harmonica playing remains forceful but fragmented and at times similarly trivialized. Guy is for the most part restrained until a typically frenetic and disjointed solo during the only original present, the anti-war 'Vietcong Blues', an example of the potential that Wells stifled in his search for popular acceptance.

*** It's My Life Baby
Vanguard VMD 73120 *Wells; Buddy Guy, Walter Beasley (g); Leroy Stewart (b); Fred Below, Little Al (d). 66.*

*** Best Of The Vanguard Years
Vanguard VCD 79508 *As above. 12/65–66.*

Two thirds studio and one third live recordings, *It's My Life Baby* was a popular record in its time but now seems very much trapped in it. These are further examples of Wells's largely unsuccessful bid to mix the techniques of blues and soul, abetted by Guy's own restless and profligate muse. The skeletal nature of the music, bereft of a piano or a horn section, isn't helped by an adventurous bass player who makes little attempt to coordinate with either drummer. Wells's overweening personality makes short work of trivialities like '(I Got A) Stomach Ache', an assortment of songs from both Sonny Boys and the perennial 'Stormy Monday'. Other standards are disguised, including Muddy's 'Standing Around Crying', here titled 'Look How Baby'. On its release the album was touted as the face of contemporary blues, but with the passage of time it feels as fashionable as a paisley-print kaftan. *Best Of The Vanguard Years* combines both the preceding sessions, dispensing with two tracks and adding two further live performances, and adds 'Hoochie Coochie Man' from a third Vanguard release, *Coming At You*, otherwise unavailable.

**(*) You're Tuff Enough
Mercury 558 551 *Wells; unknowns (s, p, g, b, d)*. 8/66–69.

A composite of five pictures of putative soul star Wells, with a gold medallion the size of a sommelier's cup round his neck, dominates the booklet cover. He was having the time of his life but the music he made now sounds hopelessly redundant; over-loud drums are always busy and the brass gets that way whenever it can. Clichés abound in the arrangements and the grunting soul vocabulary that Wells indulges at will. Often his vocal is buried in the mix but then the banality of the lyrics he's delivering doesn't warrant much attention. Twenty-two songs in less than an hour indicate the assembly-line approach his producers adopted. Ironically, Wells takes frequent harmonica solos but even they are merely variations on a mundane theme. 'Where Did I Go Wrong', 'The Hippies Are Trying', 'You're The One' and 'Leave My Woman Alone' are this album's saving graces and that only by comparison. History can sometimes be very cruel.

***(*) Live At The Golden Bear
Mercury 558 552 *Wells; Douglas Fagan (ts); unknown (bs); Kenneth Britt (g); Willie Monroe (b); Bill Warren (d)*. 68.

A short but stimulating set that captures Wells in his natural constituency, in this case a club in Huntington Beach, California. Apart from his own 'So Tired (I Could Cry)', the set includes material from both Sonny Boys, Willie Dixon, Roosevelt Sykes and Howlin' Wolf, with 'Fever' and James Brown's 'Please, Please Please' as a sop to his 'other' career. Apart from Britt's frenetic guitar work, the band is competent but unexciting, with Fagan and an uncredited baritone player providing conventional horn harmonies and no solos. Wells solos on all but the Brown piece, at length on 'How Many More Years'. A small audience doesn't exert itself when called upon to applaud. Suspiciously faded bursts of clapping punctuate 'Please, Please, Please', although Wells does nothing to justify it. The same ruse is used during his solo on the closing 'Elevate Me Mama', but it can't reduce the favourable impression that he and his band have already made.

**** Southside Blues Jam
Delmark DD-628 *Wells; Otis Spann (p); Buddy Guy (g, v); Louis Myers (g); Earnest Johnson (b); Fred Below (d)*. 12/69–1/70.

His career as a soul singer having run its course, Wells returned to the music to which he was best suited. Recorded over the course of two days, these informal sessions were also the last studio recordings by Otis Spann, to whom the record is dedicated. His is the strongest presence, his rumbling two-handed chords and metronomic trills invigorating each of the eight tracks. Wells is on ebullient vocal form and plays frequent and confident harmonica solos, emulating Sonny Boy Williamson II's keynote riffs during 'I Wish I Knew What I Know Now', better known as 'In My Younger Days'. Muddy Waters also remains a prominent influence, both acknowledged ('I Just Want To Make Love To You') and otherwise ('I Could Have Had Religion', 'You Say You Love Me'). Myers replaces Guy on two tracks and both play on the opener, 'Stop Breaking Down'. Guy adds his vocal to the final 'Trouble Don't Last Always' which rather degenerates into a mutual grooming session. Even so, this is one of Wells's best recording dates from this era.

*** Junior Wells
Warner Blues 36944 *Wells; Clark Terry, Wallace Davenport, Jimmy Owens (t); A. C. Reed, Douglas Fagan (ts); Mike Utley (p); Buddy Guy, Walter Beasley, Eric Clapton, Walter Williams (g); Leroy Stewart, Jack Meyers, Tom Crawford (b); Little Al, Fred Below, Roosevelt Shaw, Levi Warren (d)*. 65–10/70.

This is a mixed bag of Vanguard and Atco recordings that unwittingly documents the beginning of Wells's slide into self-caricature. The 16 tracks are reasonably well chosen, including 'Vietcong Blues', perhaps the last serious blues he wrote, and some of the ebullient live recordings from *It's My Life Baby*. More importantly for completists, there are four tracks from the otherwise unavailable *Coming At You*. There are no great surprises in any of this material and the compilers have neglected to notice that in sampling these albums they've included three versions of the same song, 'My Baby Left Me'. The result is a superficially entertaining set that discourages deep analysis.

*** Drinkin' TNT 'N' Smokin' Dynamite//Messin' With The Kids
Blind Pig BP 71182//Castle CMRCD 1270 *Wells; Pinetop Perkins (p); Buddy Guy (g, v); Terry Taylor (g); Bill Wyman (b); Dallas Taylor (d)*. 74.

Though Guy's name appears first on this recording from the Montreux Jazz Festival, this is Wells's gig, as he sings six of the eight songs, running through plums of his repertoire such as 'Hoodoo Man Blues', 'Messing With The Kid' and 'Checking On My Baby'. Guy confines himself to two slow blues, 'When You See The Tears From My Eyes' and the nearly nine-minute 'Ten Years Ago', both showcases for his guitar technique, though he's by no means reticent behind Wells. The accompanying band fulfil their role with modest efficiency, although the frequent disappearance of Perkins's piano from the mix is regrettable.

*** On Tap
Delmark DD-635 *Wells; Charles Miles (as); A. C. Reed (ts); Johnny 'Big Moose' Walker (o, p); Sammy Lawhorn, Phillip Guy (g); Herman Applewhite (b); Roosevelt 'Snake' Shaw (d)*. 74.

Wells's third outing for Delmark dispenses with Buddy Guy in favour of his younger brother Phil, and the absence of his playmate puts a brake on Wells's excesses except for a tedious 'Watch Me Move' and an interminable 'Junior's Thing' (actually 'Baby Scratch My Back'). The material may be over-familiar, with 'Key To The Highway', 'Goin' Down Slow' and 'Love Her With A Feeling', but Wells makes little effort to modernize these and retitled versions of 'Reconsider Baby' and 'Mystery Train'. Lawhorn is a less gifted guitarist than Buddy Guy but his conventional talent is more consistently satisfying than his predecessor's flickering brilliance. The horn section is well integrated into the arrangements and Reed takes a number of succinct solos. The result presents no challenge to its label-mates but remains solidly entertaining.

***(*) Pleading The Blues
Evidence ECD 26035 *Wells; Buddy Guy, Phil Guy (g); J. W. Williams (b); Ray 'Killer' Allison (d).* 79.

A surprisingly satisfying set recorded in France during a concert tour. Restraint seems to have been the keyword for the day and even Buddy Guy keeps his considerable powers under an abnormally tight rein, while the rhythm section is a model of conciseness. Wells himself keeps his usual excesses to a minimum but indulges his hipness in 'Cut Out The Lights' and 'I Smell Something'. 'Take Your Time Baby' is a recasting of 'So All Alone' and 'Just For My Baby' has something of 'Mystery Train' about it. Most songs manage to extend themselves to between six and eight minutes (the title track even fades in) but, while *longueurs* occur, the participants remain fairly focused on what must be deemed a worthwhile session.

** Better Off With The Blues
Telarc CD 83354 *Wells; Jack Cassidy (t); David Stahlberg (tb); Steven Finckle (ts); Lucky Peterson (o, p, g); Rico McFarland, Buddy Guy (g); Johnny B. Gayden, Noel Neal (b); Brian Jones, Steve McCray (d); Paul Cotton (perc); Jacqueline Johnson, Jacquelyn Reddick (v).* 4–6/93.

The castlist is solidly impressive but sadly Wells's performance too readily descends into caricature for this to be a career-reviving album. Despite songs from Elmore James, Albert King and Jimmy Reed and his own 'Messin' With The Kid', not enough of this interminable ego-fest concerns itself with blues. Even the title song is little more than a chance for Lucky Peterson to indulge his profligate but passionless invention on organ and guitar. Too many songs, including this and the opening 'Cry For Me', wander on aimlessly as Wells's vocal mannerisms, sundry howls and eructations get the better of him. His constant barracking of soloists quickly becomes intensely annoying, indicating poor production control. Wells's sole restraint is in the amount of harmonica he plays and that's easily overwhelmed by the frequently grandiose arrangements.

** Everybody's Gettin' Some
Telarc CD 83360 *Wells; Legendary White Trash Horns (brass, reeds); David Torkanowsky (kb); Rico McFarland, Sonny Landreth, Carlos Santana (g); Willie Weeks (b); Brian Jones (d); Bonnie Raitt (v).* 95.

Ignoring the widespread criticism of their first effort, the same production team repeats its formula of blues-less bluster, while adding a pair of superstars to little effect. Raitt contributes her elegantly wasted vocal to the title track, while Santana commandeers 'Get Down' for his own use. Landreth adds succinct slide guitar to the title track and plays National steel guitar on two acoustic duets, 'Keep On Steppin' and 'Don't You Lie To Me'. These and the infectious 'Trying To Get Over You' represent this album's overt blues quota, markedly less flamboyant than the soul-funk predictability of 'Shaky Ground', 'Use Me' and a remake of 'You're Tough Enough'. Wells plays a little more harmonica than previously but his vocals are still mired in exaggerated mannerisms and barnyard imitations.

♛ **** Come On In This House
Telarc CD 83395 *Wells; Jon Cleary (p); Derek Trucks, Sonny Landreth, Corey Harris, Alvin Youngblood Hart, Tab Benoit, John Mooney, Bob Margolin (g); Bob Sunda (b); Herman Ernest III (d).* 4–5/96.

A radical return to his roots draws an unprecedented performance from Wells, energized by the involvement of an honour roll of slide guitarists, both acoustic and electric. Most impressive are Trucks on 'That's All Right', Landreth on 'Why Are People Like That' and Mooney on 'King Fish Blues'. In fact, only Harris fails to impress, despite appearing on three titles. A particularly strong rhythm section is enhanced every time Cleary's piano joins it. Wells isn't entirely free of his vocal eccentricities but these are restricted to overlong versions of 'Mystery Train' and the title track. Otherwise, his singing and harmonica playing, despite decreased lung power, are exemplary, thoroughly justifying this album's Grammy nomination.

*** Live At Buddy Guy's Legends
Telarc CD 83412 *Wells; Mike Barber (t); Joseph Burton (tb); Douglas Fagan (ts); Johnny 'Fingers' Iguana (o, p); Stevie Lizard, Andy Wahllof (g); Johnny Benny (b); Vernal Taylor (d); Ruben P. Alvarez (perc).* 11/96.

Backed by a well-integrated nine-piece band, Wells, identified as the 'Godfather Of The Blues', gets to perform the funk-based blues that have been his cherished ambition for some decades. He soon dispenses with admonitions to 'git on down' but his presentation is locked into such outmoded techniques. However, this is very much to the taste of the audience, who applaud updated arrangements of 'Messin' With The Kid', 'Little By Little' and 'Hoodoo Man', as well as a narcoleptic 'Got My Mojo Working'. There's little to draw the attention away from Wells beyond the odd feature for his reptilian pianist and guitarist. He works hard to disguise his diminishing breath control, frequently wielding his harmonica even if very little ensues. Although what they play is often predictable, his serviceable musicians carry their leader through to a triumphant conclusion.

*** Keep On Steppin': The Best Of Junior Wells
Telarc CD 83444 *As for preceding Telarc CDs.* 93–96.

A posthumous collection that draws from all four Telarc albums. *Come On In This House* yields up 'Why Are People Like That' and 'Give Me One Good Reason' alongside 'Mystery Train' and 'King Fish Blues', thus condemning the eight remaining tracks to the status of also-rans and underlining the woefully indulgent production values that hamstrung much of the material on the earlier compilations. Nevertheless, this has some value as a sampler if it directs prospective customers to the one worthwhile album from the quartet.

*(*) Live Around The World: The Best Of Junior Wells
Columbia/Legacy 507711 *Wells; Michael Barber (t); Joe Burton (tb); Douglas Fagan (ts); Steve Utting, Johnny Iguana (o, p); Stevie Lizard, Andy Wahllof (g); Willie (Vamp) Samuels, Johnny Benny (b); Vernal Taylor (d).* 10/96–2/97.

Half of the album's title is accurate, since its venues

encompass Japan, London, Paris, Scandinavia and the US. No fewer than eight of the 11 titles correspond with *Live At Buddy Guy's Legends*, making this set, though released six years later, a largely redundant exercise. The backing band is improved by the presence of Utting and Samuels, both of whom take more aggressive roles on stage. Sadly, none of this is to good purpose for Wells has renounced any attempt to deliver a song properly. 'Little Red Rooster', 'Take Off Your Shoes', 'Little By Little' and a ten-minute 'Help Me' end with extended indulgence in mewling, clucking and grunting nonsense that makes a travesty of a once-proud talent – a view not taken by his audiences, who bay their approval of (and occasionally join in with) his every indulgence. This is in no way a tribute. NS

Arthur Weston
VOCAL, GUITAR

Mississippi-born, Weston spent much of his life in East St Louis, where he played for a long time with the harmonica player George Robertson. He is believed to have died in the early '90s, in his 90s.

*** Pea Vine Whistle
Testament TCD 6005 *Weston; George Robertson, Andrew Cauthen (h, v); Big Joe Williams (g, v).* mid-'60s, 7/67.

Weston was one of several musicians who were introduced to collectors' labels by Big Joe Williams, and he recorded on at least three occasions in the '60s, examples initially appearing in compilations on Testament, Storyville and Adelphi. About half of *Pea Vine Whistle* was recorded under the auspices of Williams, who plays and occasionally sings in the background, or at least as far back as his ebullient personality allowed him to go. These tracks, especially when Robertson joins in, have a buoyant swing reminiscent of older recordings by Williams, Sonny Boy Williamson I and Yank Rachell, not only on songs associated with them like 'Decoration Day Blues' and 'Tom Wilson's Place'. The remaining tracks, recorded a few years later by Pete Welding, are solos. Weston mixes the ancestral sounds of Mississippi blues ('Pea Vine Whistle', 'Cryin' Won't Make Me Stay') with St Louis references ('Stack O' Dollars'), delivering the songs hoarsely but vigorously with something of the manner of J. D. Short. TR

John Weston (1927–2005)
VOCAL, HARMONICA, GUITAR, BASS DRUM, TAMBOURINE

Weston returned to his native Arkansas in 1967 after leading a nomadic life. He ran a juke-joint from 1967 to 1992, occasionally playing the guitar he'd first picked up aged 30. He worked with a white country band for a while from 1970, by which time he was also playing harmonica, adding chromatic harp in the mid-'70s under the guidance of Willie Cobbs. Weston played his first solo blues gigs in 1988.

**(*) So Doggone Blue
Fat Possum FP 1003//Evidence ECD 26092 *Weston; Troy Broussard (g); James 'Famous' Jones (b); Nathaniel 'Herk' Williams (d).* 93.

***(*) I'm Doin' The Best I Can
Appaloosa AP 120 *Weston; Troy Broussard, Fred James (g); John Eddie Burns (b); Silas Eason (d).* 96?

*** Got To Deal With The Blues
Midnight Creeper 1002 *Weston; Fred Nicholson (kb, p); Troy Broussard, Mark Simpson (g); Leo Goff (b); Cecil Parker (d); Carla Robinson (v).* 97?

** I Tried To Hide From The Blues
Fedora FCD 5027 *Weston; Dave Riley (b); Carla Robinson (d, v).* 5/01.

Despite his Arkansas origins, Weston's relaxed singing and lazy rhythms are reminiscent of Louisiana, and specifically of Lonesome Sundown. Fat Possum's credit to John 'So Blue' Weston is appropriate; he does heavy business in failing relationships, with a sideline in the perils of drink. His lyrics are often original and insightful, seldom borrowing from others or tradition. Nevertheless, *So Doggone Blue*, on which Weston only plays harmonica, is disappointing. The harp work is pleasingly free of empty virtuosity, but it's subverted by Broussard and Williams, who manage to be both flaccid and pointlessly busy. The biggest problem, though, is Weston's droning vocals, which fuse the songs into an undifferentiated soundscape.

Appropriately, *I'm Doin' The Best I Can* is Weston's best CD; aggressively accompanied, he sings vigorously, sharing his concerns rather than brooding narcissistically over them. Broussard's playing is noticeably more economical and relevant, but Eason's ass-kicking drumming is central to the improvement. On two tracks, the only instruments are Weston's rack harmonica and his tough but delicate acoustic guitar. *Got To Deal With The Blues* also mixes solos with the band tracks, but it's less successful. There are some clever lyrics, but Weston keeps relapsing into self-absorption, and the accompaniment is sometimes cluttered as the musicians squabble for solo space.

On two tracks of *I Tried To Hide From The Blues* Weston works as a one-man-band, adding basic percussion to his other instruments. Robinson adds ricky-ticky drumming to her narcotic backup singing, which disfigures an abysmal version of 'Key To The Highway'. The recycling of five songs from the Midnight Creeper CD is symptomatic of a general shortage of inspiration.

Blues At Daybreak (Wilco WCD 1005) was released in 2000, but swiftly disappeared, and 2003's *Sugar Daddy Blues* (John So Blue JSB 51340) has had extremely limited distribution, which seems likely to shrink even further after Weston's death. CS

Peetie Wheatstraw (1902–41)
VOCAL, PIANO, GUITAR

One of the most prolific blues recording artists of the '30s, Wheatstraw constructed a macho persona that made him a spiritual ancestor of the rap artist. 'Peetie Wheatstraw' was an assumed name (with provocative resonances in black folklore and literature); he was born William Bunch, grew up in Arkansas and spent much of his adult life in East St Louis, where he impressed other musicians as a guitarist as much as a pianist, though he recorded almost exclusively on the latter instrument. His intonation and vocal tricks were much imitated in his day and several musicians even adopted professional names alluding to his.

**(*) Peetie Wheatstraw – Vol. 1 (1930–1932)
Document DOCD-5241 *Wheatstraw; Charley Jordan, unknowns*

(g); unknowns (b); 'Neckbones' [Willie Fields], Pretty Boy Walker (v). 9/30–3/32.

**(*) Peetie Wheatstraw – Vol. 2 (1934–1935)
Document DOCD-5242 *Wheatstraw; prob. Ike Rodgers (tb); unknown (cl); Henry Brown (p); unknown (vn); Casey Bill Weldon (sg); prob. Charley Jordan, poss. Charlie McCoy, unknown (g). 3/34–7/35.*

**(*) Peetie Wheatstraw – Vol. 3 (1935–1936)
Document DOCD-5243 *Wheatstraw; Kokomo Arnold, poss. Charley Jordan, unknowns (g). 7/35–2/36.*

*** Peetie Wheatstraw – Vol. 4 (1936–1937)
Document DOCD-5244 *Wheatstraw; Kokomo Arnold, unknowns (g); unknown(s) (b). 2/36–3/37.*

*** Peetie Wheatstraw – Vol. 5 (1937–1938)
Document DOCD-5245 *Wheatstraw; Kokomo Arnold, Lonnie Johnson, poss. Charley Jordan, unknown (g); unknowns (b); unknown (d). 3/37–10/38.*

**(*) Peetie Wheatstraw – Vol. 6 (1938–1940)
Document DOCD-5246 *Wheatstraw; Jonah Jones (t); 'Rhythm Willie' Hood (h); Sam Price, Lil Armstrong, unknown (p); Lonnie Johnson, Teddy Bunn (g); O'Neill Spencer, Sid Catlett, unknowns (d). 10/38–4/40.*

**(*) Peetie Wheatstraw – Vol. 7 (1940–1941)
Document DOCD-5247 *Wheatstraw; Jonah Jones (t); unknown (ts); poss. Robert Lee McCoy (h); Lil Armstrong (p); unknown (b); Sid Catlett (d). 4/40–11/41.*

Peetie Wheatstraw is a figure as enigmatic as his professional name. Popular in his day, he had negligible impact on the next generation of blues musicians. American taste-makers in record-collecting and reissuing have had little to do with him. To some, indeed, he was a prime example of what had gone wrong with blues in the '30s. The retrieval of his work on both LP and CD has been left almost entirely to Europeans, who at least valued him for his lyrics. Yet two Americans have written monographs about him, thus providing him with a more substantial bibliography than most of his peers.

Like many of those peers, Wheatstraw frets behind the bars of the complete-and-chronological reissue. As a pianist and tunesmith he had a small number of good ideas and he deployed them assiduously, opening song after song with the same piano figure and at much the same tempo, so that anyone listening to long stretches of his recordings is likely to go stir-crazy. His gruff, clogged singing and trademark interjection 'ooh, well, well' have had their detractors, like the woman his biographer Paul Garon cites who exclaimed, 'Good God, why doesn't that man yodel and be done with it?', but as a medium for his narratives they are effective and appealing. In common with other artists who made scores of discs in the '30s, his ideas sometimes dried up, but his output was irrigated at intervals by other people's compositions, some evidently by his friend and frequent accompanist Charley Jordan. But bragging self-identifiers like 'Devil's Son-In-Law' and the two 'Peetie Wheatstraw Stomp's are surely his, and there's no reason to think differently about his excellent topical pieces 'Working On The Project' and 'Third Street's Going Down', an on-the-spot report on urban renewal in black East St Louis. Most of these are on Document's *Vol. 4* and *Vol. 5*, which bracket his first two years' output for Decca, when he was fortunate both in his material and in his accompanists, especially the unpredictable slide guitarist Kokomo Arnold.

The earlier volumes are duller, thanks in part to mediocre source material and low-level remastering, but have their splashes of colour. On four sides on *Vol. 1* Wheatstraw plays guitar rather than piano, in a kind of rough-hewn adaptation of the style of Henry Townsend, while *Vol. 2* has some astute accompaniment by Casey Bill Weldon and the wonderfully riotous small-band performance 'Throw Me In The Alley'. For most of *Vol. 6* and *Vol. 7* Wheatstraw cedes the piano stool to other players, who avoid his clichés but have nothing so characteristic to replace them with. There are still quirky songs to be found, like 'Love Bug Blues', 'Jaybird Blues' and 'I'm A Little Piece Of Leather', and a surrealist moment during 'Pocket Knife Blues' when trumpeter Jonah Jones responds to Wheatstraw's description of a knife-wielding consort by gaily quoting 'Them There Eyes'. All but the first of these are on *Vol. 7*.

*** The Essential
Classic Blues CBL 200037 2CD *As for relevant CDs above. 9/30–11/41.*

*** The Blues/Saint Louis – Chicago – New York 1931–1941
Frémeaux FA 255 2CD *As above. 31–41.*

** Peetie Wheatstraw 1931–41
Best Of Blues BOB 8 *As above. 31–41.*

Wheatstraw country is best approached, at least on a first visit, by the more landscaped route of an anthology. The Best Of Blues CD is very imbalanced, taking 18 of its 24 tracks from 1939–41, when Wheatstraw's accompaniments were highly formularized. The Classic Blues and Frémeaux 2CDs, on the other hand, are fairly balanced selections, each including several of the tracks mentioned above, and although the remastering is no better than adequate they can both be recommended. TR

Golden 'Big' Wheeler (1929–98)
VOCAL, HARMONICA

Wheeler learned to play harmonica from fellow Georgian Buster Brown. From the early '50s he was based in Chicago. For much of his life he was a part-time musician, with a day job as a mechanic, but once he had retired he devoted most of his time to playing.

** Chicago Blues Session Vol. 14
Wolf 120.860 *Wheeler; Luther Adams, John Primer (g); Willie Kent (b); Timothy Taylor (d). 10/89.*

*** Bone Orchard
Delmark DE-661 *Wheeler; Dave Waldman, Johnny Burgin (g); Steve Cushing (d). 8/92, 2/93.*

*** Jump In
Delmark DE-709 *Wheeler; Allen Batts (p); James Wheeler (g); Bob Stroger (b); 'Baldhead Pete' [Cleo Williams] (d). 8/97.*

One of Wheeler's first experiences when he came to live in Chicago was hearing Little Walter. The stripped-down ensemble of harmonica, guitars and drums made a deep impression on him, and years later he devoted a good deal of his recording time to re-creating it. His four sides on the Wolf CD (the other five are by A. C. Reed) include Walter's 'Last Night' and 'Crazy 'Bout You Baby' and are in his manner, though with touches of Jimmy Reed. The same models lie behind the music on *Bone Orchard*, where Wheeler found himself among fellow thinkers. 'We're trying to get the sound the bands had in the 1950s, more of a tightly knit sound,' said guitarist Dave

Waldman. 'That's the way a harmonica should be backed.' The weave of guitars and harmonica in 'Hell Bound Man' makes the point very clearly. Wheeler sings and plays with simplicity and calm that seem deliberate: one is seldom prompted to wonder if this is just a modestly talented artist doing his modest best.

Three and a half years later, with the same band, Wheeler contributed five numbers, all '50s/'60s standards, to *Blues Before Sunrise Live – Volume One* (Delmark DE-699). The period authenticity of the music is exaggerated by a foggy voice mike. Anyone who has enjoyed *Bone Orchard* should like this set for much the same reasons, but it will tell them nothing about Wheeler's music they didn't already know.

Jump In differs from its predecessors in having a fuller ensemble sound and promoting Wheeler's own compositions (seven of the dozen tracks). Nevertheless, the music is as painstakingly retrospective as ever: Chicago blues, for Wheeler, ossified some time in the '60s, and he likes nothing better than polishing the bones. He makes a long job of it, too: five of the numbers go beyond six and a half minutes and only one is under four. Listeners who share his preference for plain blues stories told without artifice or hurry will gladly accompany him on his measured prowls through 'Just To Be With You', 'Big Wheeler's Christmas Bells', 'Bad Situation Worse' or the minor-key 'Chicago Winter Weather Blues', but the restless may get bored. Brother James's guitar playing is profuse and elegant, though for some tastes rather low in the mix. TR

James Wheeler (born 1937)
VOCAL, GUITAR

Born in Albany, Georgia, Wheeler joined his brother, Golden 'Big' Wheeler, in Chicago at the age of 19. He immediately began playing guitar, inspired by Freddie King, and within a few years was playing fulltime in clubs with Joe Carter, initially on bass, later on guitar. From the early '60s to early '70s he was in an R&B band, The Jaguars, and he later worked with Otis Clay, Buddy Scott, Otis Rush (1986–92), Mississippi Heat (1992–96), Magic Slim (1997–2000) and Willie Kent. He has recorded with Aaron Moore.

**(*) Ready!
Delmark DE-719 *Wheeler; Golden 'Big' Wheeler (h); Ken Saydak (p); Billy Flynn (g); Bob Stroger (b); Vernon Rodgers (d); Gloria Thompson-Rodgers (v)*. 12/97.

*** Can't Take It
Delmark DE-743 *Wheeler; Ron Sorin (h); Ken Saydak (o, p); Billy Flynn (g); Bob Stroger (b); Marty Binder (d)*. 12/99.

'James Wheeler,' begin the notes on *Ready!*, 'is a quiet man.' You might guess as much. Both his singing and his playing are unaggressive, the expressions of a temperate personality. Compared with the strenuous, emphatic music of many of his Chicago colleagues, his has a smooth, unruffled texture that evokes the cool manner of a T-Bone Walker – almost explicitly in numbers like 'Extension 309' or 'Hound Dog', which is not the Leiber–Stoller breed but a hound of a different colour, sleepy and slow-moving. Nonetheless, this is, for the most part, essentially Chicago-style music, as with these accompanists it could hardly fail to be, and if it taps discreetly at the listener's door rather than shout through the keyhole, there are respectable precedents for that.

Wheeler's guitar on *Can't Take It* has a slightly keener edge, though this is sometimes softened by Flynn's even-tempered playing. His songs, fairly conventional on the previous album, are here more artful commentaries on domestic blips: 'The Weaker Sex', 'This Can't Be Happening To Me', 'She's Gonna Pay', 'You Make It Hard Baby', etc. 'I'm so dangerous sometimes, I'm scared to be with myself!' he remarks at one point, but it's impossible to take him seriously: he's the most amiable of companions, and the listener who likes long, slow, placid blues with a dash of humour will have a very good time with him and his equally genial associates. TR

Booker White (1909–77)
VOCAL, GUITAR, PIANO, KAZOO

Booker T. Washington White was born in Houston, in the northern Mississippi hill country, and was taught to play guitar by his father. After playing for some years in the Delta counties he moved to Memphis, where he recorded for Victor in 1930. Later he was in Chicago, where he recorded in 1937 and 1940, the sessions bracketing a two-year spell incarcerated in the Parchman, Mississippi, state penitentiary; following a shooting incident. When located by fans in the early '60s he was living in Memphis, where he spent the rest of his life, but in those last years he appeared at festivals at home and overseas and made numerous albums.

♔ **** The Vintage Recordings (1930–1940)
Document DOCD-5679 *White; Napoleon Hairiston (g, v); unknown (g); Washboard Sam (wb); 'Miss Minnie' (v)*. 5/30–3/40.

**** Fixin' To Die
Snapper Complete Blues SBLUECD 022 *As above*. 5/30–3/40.

**** The Panama Limited
Fabulous FABCD 108 *As above*. 5/30–3/40.

**(*) Tennessee Blues
Wolf Blues Jewels WBJ 015 *As above, except omit 'Miss Minnie'*. 5/30–3/40.

**** The Complete Bukka White
Columbia CK 52782 *White; unknown (g); Washboard Sam (wb)*. 9/37–3/40.

The 14 blues recorded by Booker White (as he preferred his name to be spelled) in 1937 and 1940 are a body of work of great concentration and consistency. Many reveal a preoccupation with illness and death, the shame of imprisonment or the ties of family and friends. Listening to them is like turning the pages of his diary. Remarkable, too, and extremely rare in blues, is his fascination with repetitive rhyme schemes and assonances, exemplified by the clanging 'train'/'pain' rhymes of 'Black Train Blues'. This skill as a poet of verbal sound is matched by the precision of his slide playing on numbers like 'Special Streamline' and 'Bukka's Jitterbug Swing'.

The Columbia CD has that material in its entirety. The Document CD adds White's four 1930 recordings – two train themes and two sanctified songs roughly in the manner of Blind Willie Johnson – and his brilliant 1939 Library of Congress sides 'Sic 'Em Dogs On' and 'Po' Boy'. Excellently remastered, this is the album of choice for White's early recordings. The inexpensive *Fixin' To Die* has the same tracks in a jumbled order, while the even cheaper Fabulous CD lacks only the Library of Congress tracks; both are very good value. The Wolf, shared with Sleepy John Estes, has ten randomly selected songs and is rather pointless.

*** **Mississippi Blues**
Takoma CDTAK 1001//Aim 0007 *White; Jimmy Rainey (d).*
63–64.
*** **1963 Isn't 1962**
Genes GCD 9903 *White.* 11/63.
***(*) **Sky Songs**
Arhoolie CD 323 *White; Big Willie Wayne (wb).* 11/63.

When White made the first recordings of his second career, few of his early sides had been reissued, so the rerecordings of 'Aberdeen Mississippi Blues', 'Shake 'Em On Down', 'Parchman Farm Blues' and so forth on *Mississippi Blues* were all the more welcome. At 54 he was perhaps three quarters of the artist he had been 20-odd years earlier: his voice was strong and his guitar forceful and accurate, and if his slide playing seems less glittering it may have been a fault of microphone placement. On 'Drunk Man Blues' he plays piano, and on three tracks he is joined by a drummer.

1963 Isn't 1962, recorded in performance at the Cabale in Berkeley, reprised a few of his old songs, including the hypnotic 'Fixin' To Die', but introduced new compositions, such as 'Vaseline Head Woman' and the title number, that were not so much songs as stories or what folklorists call *cante-fables*, tethered only loosely, if at all, to conventional song shapes and rhyme schemes. To lighten the effect of the slow numbers he interspersed them with commonplace guitar tunes like 'Jump' and 'Boogie 'Til Dubuque' and a 'Corinna, Corinna' partly sung on kazoo.

Sky Songs marked a development in White's music. Welcoming the freedom of the tape recorder, he extended his songs sometimes to twice or three times the length of a 78 side; this set, running over an hour, contains only seven numbers. (On *Mississippi Blues* and *1963 Isn't 1962* only a few performances go beyond four minutes, though an eight-minute 'Streamline Special' on the latter shows the way his mind was turning.) 'Bald Eagle Train' is a rail narrative in the spirit of his earlier 'Special Stream Line', while the fast gospel number 'Jesus Died on the Cross to Save the World' employs the melody and exciting guitar part of 'Poor Boy'. 'Single Man' and 'Sugar Hill' are further examples of his measured piano playing, while a couple of sides with washboard accompaniment recall the sound of the 1940 session.

(*) **Furry Lewis, Bukka White & Friends: Party! At Home
Arcola A CD 1001 *White; Furry Lewis, others (sp).* 7/68.

These performances, divided about 50/50 between White and Lewis, were mostly recorded at the latter's apartment with an audience of a few friends, and some time is spent in chatter, tuning and warming up. 'Grey-Haired Woman' has bass-string figures reminiscent of Charley Patton (White claimed he got the song from a Patton 78), while 'Hambone Blues', learned from an uncle, is among the most archaic songs he recorded. 'I'm Drifting', by contrast, is Charles Brown's '40s song (which he had also done on *1963 Isn't 1962*). 'Little Woman's Bed' is a characteristic swirl of the erotic and the morbid.

*** **Mississippi Delta Blues Jam in Memphis, Vol. 2**
Arhoolie CD 386 *White.* 11/63, 6/69.
(*) **Baton Rouge Mosby Street
Blues Beacon BLU 1003 *White; Whispering Smith (h).* 10/72.

*** **Big Daddy**
Biograph CK 34010 *White.* 73.

White's five tracks on *Mississippi Delta Blues Jam in Memphis, Vol. 2* were recorded during the week of the 1969 Memphis Blues Festival, except for 'Mixed Water' from the 1963 Arhoolie sessions. 'Sad Day Blues' puts new words to the tune and guitar part of 'Poor Boy', and 'Columbus, Miss. Blues' to those of 'Aberdeen Mississippi Blues'. In 'Mixed Water' White entertains the people in the studio with a 26-minute story about drinking, dancing, making music and generally making whoopee in the company of an evidently liberal-minded preacher. (The rest of this CD is by Nathan Beauregard and Sleepy John Estes.)

Baton Rouge Mosby Street, recorded while in Germany with the AFBF, again has long performances: 'Poor Boy' and 'Sic 'Em Dogs On' are new versions of songs he recorded for the Library of Congress, but the other compositions are unique to this record. Harmonica player Whispering Smith, on that tour to accompany Lightnin' Slim, joins in on the enigmatic 'Stone'.

The Memphis session that produced *Big Daddy* was conducted 'under optimum conditions: [he] was fresh and alert, stone cold sober, well-rehearsed, playing a superb early 1930s steel-bodied National Triolian, and performing everything just right': so, at least, its producer asserts, and even after a percentage of exaggeration has been deducted the music remains strong and, as always, entirely distinctive. TR

Georgia White (1903–c. 80?)
VOCAL, PIANO

Despite an extensive recording career, Georgia White has eluded researchers. She played in Big Bill Broonzy's Laughing Trio around 1950, and he is the source for her birthdate, and for Georgia as her native state. White was photographed (but did not record) with Bumble Bee Slim, led an 'all-girl' band in the late '40s and is last glimpsed appearing in a Chicago club in 1959.

*** **Georgia White – Vol. 1 (1930–1936)**
Document DOCD-5301 *White; Jimmie Noone (cl); Eddie Pollack (as); Zinky Cohn, Richard M. Jones (p); Wilbur Gorham, Les Paul, unknowns (g); Bill Newton (bb); John Lindsay, unknowns (b); Johnny Wells (d); unknown (perc).* 5/30–5/36.
*** **Georgia White – Vol. 2 (1936–1937)**
Document DOCD-5302 *White; Richard M. Jones (p); Les Paul, unknowns (g); John Lindsay (b).* 5/36–5/37.
*** **Georgia White – Vol. 3 (1937–1939)**
Document DOCD-5303 *White; Edgar Saucier (as); Richard M. Jones, Sam Price, unknown (p); Lonnie Johnson, Teddy Bunn, unknown (g); John Lindsay, unknown (b); unknowns (d).* 10/37–5/39.
*** **Georgia White – Vol. 4 (1939–1941)**
Document DOCD-5304 *White; Jonah Jones (t); Fess Williams (cl); Edgar Saucier (as); Sam Price, unknown (p); Teddy Bunn, unknowns (g); John Lindsay, unknowns (b); Walter Martin, unknown (d).* 5/39–3/41.
*** **Trouble In Mind 1935/1941**
EPM Blues Collection 15832 *White; Jonah Jones (t); Fess Williams (cl); Edgar Saucier (as); Richard M. Jones, Sam Price, unknowns (p); Les Paul, Lonnie Johnson, Teddy Bunn, unknowns (g); John Lindsay, unknowns (b); Walter Martin, unknowns (d); unknown (perc).* 3/35–3/41.

Decca's billing of Georgia White as 'the world's greatest blues singer' was over the top, but she was confident and easily recognizable; her strong contralto has a raw edge, which she occasionally drives into a throaty rasp. White was a capable pianist, but when Richard M. Jones joined Decca in 1935 he usually confined her to singing, frequently taking over the piano stool himself. Jones's playing often lacks White's bubbly exuberance, but the sides where he's present are far from valueless, and often enhanced by the great bass work of John Lindsay. Georgia White's recordings are also notable for a succession of splendid guitarists. (Ikey Robinson is probably among the unknowns, but exactly where is uncertain.) White stands out, too, as perhaps the blues' first revivalist, covering recordings as far back as Mamie Smith's 'Crazy Blues'. She didn't just resurrect old hits, either; covers of Bessie Smith, Ma Rainey, Sara Martin and Ethel Waters are not surprising, but Lucille Bogan's 'Alley Boogie' is less predictable, and apparent borrowings from Leadbelly ('Pigmeat Blues') and Joe Dean ('I'm So Glad I'm 21 Today') are startling.

None of these discs is entirely satisfactory; Document perform their usual admirable task of putting it all out there, but although Georgia White was very consistent, her consistency entails a degree of saminess, and not everything among these 93 tracks is a gem. The recommendation, despite some lacklustre transfers from swishy originals, goes to *Trouble In Mind*. Some first-class performances are omitted, but most of her best work is there, including the saucy 'Hot Nuts', three splendid collaborations with Jonah Jones and Fess Williams, the affecting title track and White's masterpiece, 'The Blues Ain't Nothin' But …???', with rip-snorting vocals, exuberant barrelhouse piano and Lonnie Johnson's churning electric guitar. CS

Josh White (1914–69)
VOCAL, GUITAR

Born in Greenville, North Carolina, Joshua White had to grow up early after his father was beaten for standing up to a white man and confined to a mental asylum, leaving his wife with six children to support. Before he was ten, Josh was hired out as lead boy to a blind gospel singer, who took him on the road and hired him out to other blind artists. He was not well treated by these men, but one of them, Joe Taggart, took him to Paramount at the age of 14. In 1930 White returned home to attend school, but two years later was signed by ARC. In 1936 White cut his right hand badly, and had to reconfigure his guitar style to cope with its continuing weakness. His break back into show business came in 1940, when he appeared with Paul Robeson in the play John Henry. *It closed after a week, but got Josh back on to records and an engagement at Café Society. He became a star of the New York nightclub scene, a favourite in left-wing circles and a frequent guest at the Roosevelt White House. Visiting Europe for the first time in 1950, he was accused at home of associating with Communists. White refused to name names to the FBI, but told the House Un-American Activities Committee that he had been duped by Communist front organizations, and was a patriotic American who hated racial discrimination. All this appears to be no more than the truth but, already* persona non grata *with the conservative entertainment industry, Josh – the only person who comes out well from these events – was now ostracized by the left for testifying voluntarily to HUAC. He remained popular in Europe, and in the late '50s his American career revived in the wake of the folk boom spearheaded by The Kingston Trio. White recorded frequently in these later years, but by the mid-'60s was in semi-retirement with health problems. He died while undergoing heart surgery.*

*** Josh White – Vol. 1 (1929–1933)
Document DOCD-5194 *White; Warner Carver (h); unknown (p); Noble 'Uncle Bozo' Carver, Robert V. Carver (g). 9/29–11/33.*

*** Josh White – Vol. 2 (1933–1935)
Document DOCD-5195 *White; Marie Miles, Walter Roland, Leroy Carr, Clarence Williams, unknown (p); prob. Scrapper Blackwell (g). 11/33–3/35.*

*** Josh White – Vol. 3 (1935–1940)
Document DOCD-5196 *White; Sidney Bechet (cl); Walter Roland (p); Buddy Moss (g, v); Wilson Myers (b); Bill White (v). 3/35–3/40.*

The phases of Josh White's career have long aroused controversy; as with Big Bill Broonzy, in the '60s many white blues fans dismissed White's 'folk blues' as inauthentic, and his early blues were assumed to be similarly valueless, an assessment now generally agreed to be inaccurate; more recently White's biographer, Elijah Wald, has mounted a stout defence of the later music's technical, artistic and ideological ambitions, and has characterized White's 'race' recordings as unremarkable. While striving to be fair-minded, this discussion doesn't accompany that analysis all the way.

White made his recording debut providing vocal and guitar accompaniment to Blind Joe Taggart; these, and Taggart's other excellent recordings, are available on *Blind Joe Taggart – Vol. 1* and *Vol. 2* (Document DOCD-5153, DOCD-5154). A year later, White contributed a jazzy guitar solo to the white Carver Boys' 'Wang Wang Harmonica Blues', which opens *Josh White – Vol. 1*. Joshua White the blues singer made his debut in 1932, and it's easy to see why this 18-year-old made an impact on black record-buyers in the depths of the Depression: his guitar playing is a taut but smoothly articulate version of the raggy East Coast style, and his singing is clear, cocky and assured, seasoned with growling scat breaks and piercing falsettos. His blues radiate self-confidence, often about his sexiness, and some of them are distinctly raunchy. 'Little Brother Blues' on *Vol. 1* is a hymn to his knife, sung with almost psychotic relish.

Already, though, there's also awareness of social issues: *Vol. 1* includes 'Bad Depression Blues' and 'Low Cotton', and the last 'race' recordings on *Vol. 3* are the outspoken 'No More Ball And Chain' and 'Silicosis Is Killing Me' (which is not, despite numerous writers, a Josh White composition). It's also on *Vol. 1* that Josh launches himself as a gospel singer; his success in this vein soon led ARC to split him into 'Joshua White (The Singing Christian)' and 'Pinewood Tom'. That way, there was no fear of devout customers asking for 'the new Joshua White record' and going home with 'Bed Springs Blues'.

Sacred or secular, White's 'race' recordings occupy most of Document's first three volumes. His solo material is usually good listening (and most tracks come from good-quality originals), as are his collaborations with Walter Roland, Carr–Blackwell and Buddy Moss; Clarence Williams and the unknown pianist on *Vol. 1* have great difficulty dealing with White's urge to anticipate the beat, though. Likeable as they are, what keeps these early sides from greatness is their calculated air, an attribute which was to persist; White often seems to be admiring himself in an invisible mirror.

The last eight tracks of *Vol. 3* are the first recordings aimed at Josh's newly acquired white audience. They were recorded in 1940, after a four-year break during which Josh was rejigging his guitar style after his accident, and not unnaturally are less fluent. Sidney Bechet appears on the first two sides, but is short of ideas. The balance, with Myers, are more successful, and make fewer compromises with nightclub aesthetics than would later be the case; 'Prison Bound' is a very fine rendition indeed, irrespective of its target market.

(*) Josh White – Vol. 4 (1940–1941)
Document DOCD-5405 White; Edmond Hall (cl); Israel Crosby (b); Jimmy Hoskins (d); The Carolinians (v). 3/40–41.

Vol. 4 opens with eight anti-racist blues, originally issued as an album of 78s called *Chain Gang*. Distributors in the South raised Cain, but Columbia stuck by Josh and producer John Hammond. White is accompanied on these songs by The Carolinians, who included future Civil Rights leader and diplomat Bayard Rustin. Leonard de Paur's dignified, doleful arrangements seem today like cautious compromises with classicism, but in their day were probably seen as authentically sorrowful; it should also be remembered that this was a time when Joe Louis could only win respect from whites by superhuman self-restraint. With that in mind, these songs still have something to say, and often do so with confrontational directness. Even more successful are the final six tracks: pointed, angry lyrics by Harlem poet Waring Cuney, originally issued with the collective title *Southern Exposure*. Here White's new single-string style, with its flashing slides and bends, reaches maturity. In between the CD sags badly: five spirituals with The Carolinians are dull retreads in the style, but without the verve, of The Golden Gate Quartet, and Edmond Hall is no happier on four blues (taken from very worn 78s) than was Bechet.

((*)) Josh White – Vol. 5 (1944) [sic]**
Document DOCD-5571 White. 41–3/46.
((*)) Josh White Sings The Blues And Sings Volume 1&2 [sic]**
Collectables COL-CD-5602 White. 41–3/46.
(*) The Remaining Titles (1941–1947)
Document DOCD-1013 White; Sonny Terry (h, v); Bess Lomax Hawes (md, v); Brownie McGhee (g, v); John Simmons, Al McKibbon (b); J. C. Heard (d); Libby Holman, Tom Glazer, Butch Hawes, Bill White (v). 41–6/47.
(*) Black Folk Singers: Leadbelly & Josh White: The Remaining Titles (1937–1946)
Document DOCD-1018 White; Pete Seeger (bj, v); Leadbelly (g, v); John Simmons (b); unknown (d); The Union Boys (v). 3/44–5/46.
((*)) Josh White – Vol. 6 (1944–1945)**
Document DOCD-5572 White; Irving Randolph (t); Henderson Chambers (tb); Edmond Hall (cl); Eddie Williams (ts); unknown (o); Ellis Larkins (p); Al Casey (g); John Simmons, Johnny Williams (b); J. C. Heard, Arthur Trappier, Bill White, unknown (d). 4/44–12/45.

When issued, Document's *Vol. 5* was thought to contain 1944 recordings, most of them made for Asch and Stinson, but as the notes to the first CD of 'remaining titles' explain, two Stinson LPs compiled in the '50s surreptitiously included material from Keynote and Decca (a 1946 'Strange Fruit'). These LPs are conjoined on Collectables, and all but two of their tracks (which are carried over to *Vol. 6*) appear on Document's *Vol. 5*. The sound on Collectables is no better than Document's, and the notes are extremely brief and unhelpful.

Vol. 5 and still more *Vol. 6* (which is mostly Decca recordings) introduce the Josh White that later blues fans disliked so much: the one who added 'Waltzing Matilda', 'Lord Randall', 'Molly Malone', 'I Gave My Love A Cherry' (a.k.a. 'The Riddle Song') and other folk or folk-like material to his blues and topical songs. It's easy to characterize this as selling out, but fairer to recognize that White had constructed a successful act (very successful – no other blues singer was visiting the White House) that incorporated blues, jazz, pop, gospel and folk elements, and that by all accounts was suffused with charismatic sexuality. In this respect, Josh was the Harry Belafonte of his time, but listening without the in-person glamour suggests that he was also like Belafonte in that his mix-and-matching produced a bland, homogenized purée of folk-like music.

There are some fine blues on both CDs: 'Evil Hearted Man' and 'Mean Mistreatin' Woman' stand out on *Vol. 5*, as do two terrific R&B numbers with Edmond Hall's Orchestra on *Vol. 6*. Patriotic war-winners like 'Blues In Berlin' (a witty parody of 'Blues In The Night') and 'Freedom Road', looking for victory over Nazism abroad and racism at home, can still stir the emotions; not so the mawkish 'Beloved Comrade'. A general drawback of both discs is their sound quality, a result of Asch and Stinson's inherently poor pressings and the use of numerous well-chewed Decca 78s.

The first of Document's collections of 'remaining titles' begins with a well-recorded session for Keynote, which includes the best – or from another perspective, the most tolerable – version of 'The Riddle Song'. The rest of the CD is from Asch and Decca; despite being assembled on autopilot, it's better listening than *Vol. 5* and *Vol. 6*, thanks in no small part to the use of cleaner Deccas, which give a clearer impression of Heard's and Simmons's input. 'Josh and Bill Blues', one of four fraternal duets, is a fine, wholly traditional blues. However, completism entails some duplicated songs, and the inclusion of a glutinous eulogy to FDR and two accompaniments to Libby Holman, a white torch singer with delusions of bluesiness; the disc is downgraded accordingly.

Many of Josh's 17 tracks (of 30) on the other 'remaining titles' set are snaffled from the Smithsonian Folkways CD discussed below, and are better approached in that context. The others add little to the picture; this disc is for people who lie awake worrying that there may be a version of 'One Meat Ball' missing from their collection.

(***) The Essential
Classic Blues CBL 200005 2CD *Similar to relevant CDs above, except add Lucille Bogan, Walter Roland, Leroy Carr (v).* 9/29–2/36.
*** **Blues Singer 1932–1936**
Columbia/Legacy 483587 *Similar to relevant CDs above.* 4/32–2/36.
*** **Blues, Spirituals & Folk Songs 1932–1945**
Frémeaux FA 264 2CD *Similar to relevant CDs above.* 4/32–12/45.

Columbia and Classic Blues select from the 'race' recordings; Classic Blues also include both sides of the Carver Boys 78, which sound very ill-assorted popping up part-way through two discs of black blues. *The Essential* includes some accompaniments to other artists, which usefully broaden the picture (White's picking behind Carr is greatly stimulated by competition with Scrapper Blackwell), but non-chronological programming needs better guidance than the brief, semi-random observations offered here. Columbia's booklet is greatly superior; what's odd, given the label's ownership of the masters, is that the transfers are no better than on Classic Blues or Frémeaux. *Blues, Spirituals & Folk Songs* offers not quite a full CD of 'race' records, and just over a CD of songs aimed at the wider market. Both periods have been judiciously winnowed; the later material includes some of White's strongest and bluesiest protest numbers, and the folkier songs have African-American pedigree: 'St. James Infirmary' and 'Frankie And Johnny', not 'Watercress' or 'Johnny Has Gone For A Soldier'.

(***) **Joshua White 1933–1941**
Best Of Blues BOB 7 *White; Wilson Myers (b); Bill White, The Carolinians (v). 8/33–41.*

This reissues the *Chain Gang* and *Southern Exposure* albums, adding a vocal duet with Bill White, four spirituals with The Carolinians (still dull) and five random ARC titles. The sound is lively, which unfortunately means that surface noise is sometimes invasive, and there are no notes apart from dates and personnels.

(***) **The Legendary ... Josh White**
Collectors Edition CBCD 003 *As above, except omit Bill White. 3/40–45.*

(**(*)) **Hard Time Blues**
Columbia River CRG 120010 *As above. 3/40–45.*

(***) **Blues & Ballads**
Acrobat ARCD 166 *As above. 3/40–45.*

*** **Southern Exposure**
Flapper PAST CD 7810 *White; Irving Randolph (t); Henderson Chambers (tb); Sidney Bechet, Edmond Hall (cl); Eddie Williams (ts); unknown (o); Ellis Larkins (p); Pete Seeger (bj, v); Al Casey (g); Wilson Myers, John Simmons (b); J. C. Heard, Arthur Trappier, Bill White, unknown (d); Millard Lampell, Lee Hays (v). 3/40–12/45.*

The Collectors Edition, Columbia River and Acrobat discs have the same content, which adds up to a well-chosen portrait of Josh the black folk singer, but some tracks are hissy to a degree which may bother casual listeners. *Hard Time Blues* rules itself out by having no notes; *Blues & Ballads* is bargain-priced.

Southern Exposure has acceptable sound and extensive notes; careful programming for variety among blues, topical, folk and pop material makes it a good selection of early '40s material. Students of historical pathology will be interested by the Almanac Singers' 'Billy Boy', which Josh seems to have appeared on as a favour to Pete Seeger; it was recorded three months before Hitler invaded the Soviet Union, at a time when the American left was still campaigning to keep America out of World War II.

(*) **Freedom
Bridge 9114 *White; The Golden Gate Quartet (v). 12/40.*

Freedom presents a concert in celebration of the 75th anniversary of the abolition of slavery, held in the acoustically splendid Coolidge Auditorium of the Library of Congress. White performs solo and with The Golden Gate Quartet, who are also heard unaccompanied. Josh and the Gates offered Washingtonian concertgoers a polished, approachable version of black vernacular music, but if their demeanour is unthreatening, their songs are spirited and enjoyable. Unfortunately, the event was intended to educate as well as entertain (hence the booking of artists with clear diction), and the programme of 'Negro Spirituals', 'Blues and Ballads' and 'Reels and Work Songs' is burdened with didactic commentary from Alain Locke, Sterling Brown and Alan Lomax.

(*) **From New York To London
Jasmine JASMCD 3004 2CD *White; Sonny Terry (h); Steve Race (p, cel, grunts); Brownie McGhee, Fitzroy Coleman, Chick Laval (g); John Simmons, Jack Fallon (b); Bill White (d, v); J. C. Heard, Norman Burns (d); Libby Holman, The Stargazers, Beverly White (v); orchestras. 3/42–10/51.*

***(*) **Free And Equal Blues**
Smithsonian Folkways SF CD 40081 *White; Bill Coleman (t); Mary Lou Williams (p); Pete Seeger (bj, v); Leadbelly (g, v); Jimmy Butts (b); Eddie Dougherty (d); The Union Boys (v). 3/44–5/46.*

Jasmine's 2CD includes a disc apiece of American and British Decca recordings, and two sides made for UK Columbia. Simply in terms of engineering, these are by far the best reissues of American Deccas, and as has already been noted, they include some first-class blues performances. Readers who don't have a problem with the interleaved folkie music will doubtless share Elijah Wald's pleasure in it, and may even agree that White's 'most original work was his reworking of non-black Folk material'. To disagree is not to suggest – again in Wald's words – that 'this mix is a dilution of the "pure" Blues tradition'; rather, it's to feel that highly professional musicianship is often disguising inherent triviality. This comment is equally applicable to those British recordings in the same vein (and sometimes of the same songs). There is little musical merit in two songs by Libby Holman, misdescribed by Jasmine as 'bonus tracks', and none in the tasteless orchestral and choral arrangements of 'On Top Of Old Smokey' and 'Black Girl'. 'I Ain't Got Nothing But The Blues' features White's daughter, Beverly, certainly the best 12-year-old interpreter of Duke Ellington on record.

The Smithsonian's trawl through its archives is also annotated by Elijah Wald at length and in depth, but has the added advantage of being compiled by him. Despite starting with 'One Meat Ball', Josh's biggest hit and the least amusing comic song ever recorded, a largely exemplary programme carefully blends Josh's best blues and gospel recordings for Moses Asch with high-quality pop and political pieces. The selection is biased towards material either previously unissued or not then reissued, which is why so much of it rapidly appeared on Document as 'remaining titles'. The minor key and uncomfortable pitch of 'Jim Crow' don't suit Josh, and Bill Coleman is under-recorded on the jumping patriotic jazz number 'Minute Man', but this is the CD of White's mid-'40s music to have, not least for its remarkable sound quality.

(*) **Great Bluesmen In Britain
Avid AMSC 736 *White; Denis Preston, unknown (sp). 7/50.*

Josh's share of *Great Bluesmen In Britain* (the balance is by Big Bill Broonzy and Sonny Terry & Brownie McGhee) is airshots of two BBC broadcasts made during his first British tour. The inter-song conversations are stilted, and some tracks have an intrusive electronic hum, but these recordings are interesting because White favours the African-American rather than the folkie side of his songbook, even reviving 'Howlin' Wolf Blues' from his first recording session as a name artist. There's also some amusement to be had from his effortless outdoing of interviewer Denis Preston's cultivated British accent.

**(*) The Best Of Josh White
Tradition TCD 1082 *White; Steve Race (p, cel, grunts); Fitzroy Coleman, Chick Laval (g); Jack Fallon (b); Norman Burns (d). 7/50–3/51.*

All ten tracks and 28 minutes of *The Best Of* are included in *From New York To London*, but they make a more consistent sound when heard together. That's not to say that the CD lives up to its title: Peter Pears and Benjamin Britten did a raunchier version of 'Foggy Foggy Dew' than the celeste-afflicted one here, and Steve Race embarrasses himself pretending to be a gandy dancer on 'Like A Natural Man'. The musicians give generally competent support, and Fallon is rather better than that, but the familiarity of the material overpowers the novelty of the trio and quintet settings.

*** Wanderings
Living Era CD AJA 5551 *Similar to relevant CDs above. 3/40–11/51.*

'Foggy Foggy Dew' and 'Natural Man' return on *Wanderings*, among ten tracks from British Decca; fortunately, 'Molly Malone' and 'Barbara Allen' are passed over in favour of 'Free And Equal Blues'. The rest of the disc comes from assorted American labels. The transfers are very good, apart from a distorted 'Trouble', with The Carolinians, and the sequencing of blues, pop and folk is skilfully done, although 'The Lass With The Delicate Air' and the Roosevelt tribute 'The Man Who Couldn't Walk Around' remain impossibly effete and unbearably maudlin respectively. The lilting pseudo-folk songs 'Apples, Peaches And Cherries' and 'Bon-Bons, Chocolates And Chewing Gum', not available elsewhere on CD, actually do have the irresistible, sexy charm that Josh's more fervent admirers make so much of.

(***) The Elektra Years
Rhino Handmade RHM2 7879 2CD *White; Al Hall, Bill Lee, unknowns (b); Sonny Greer, Walter Perkins, unknowns (d); Sam Gary, prob. Bill White, unknowns (v). 11/33–62.*

*** Josh At Midnight/Ballads & Blues
Collectables COL-CD-7463 *As above, except omit Lee, Perkins, unknowns (v). 55–56.*

The Elektra LPs *Josh At Midnight* and *Ballads & Blues* were early steps in the emergence of White's American career from the doldrums. 'The Riddle Song' and its like have been discarded, and the repertoire is dominated by blues and spirituals; only an inevitable 'One Meat Ball' bucks the trend on *Josh At Midnight*, and the exceptions on *Ballads & Blues* are pop – 'Miss Otis Regrets', 'Gloomy Sunday' and a notably unsuccessful 'One For My Baby' – rather than folk songs. But if the playlist is mostly retrospective ('Scandalize My Name' is revived from White's time with Joe Taggart), the music is swinging (how not, with Al Hall and Sonny Greer along for the ride?) and very well recorded. On 'Helleleu' [sic] White overdubs an inventive second-guitar part. The bass voice of former Carolinian Sam Gary is prominent on *Josh At Midnight*, sounding like Paul Robeson crossed with Willie Dixon; he's admirably forceful on 'Timber (Jerry The Mule)' and as lead singer on 'Joshua Fit The Battle Of Jericho'.

The Elektra Years is a 2,500-copy limited edition, but it retails at $50 or so, and hence seems likely to be around for a while; it concludes with 'Lay Some Flowers On My Grave' from 1933, but is otherwise drawn from White's six Elektra albums. The ten-inch LP *Story Of John Henry* is included complete as a 23-minute track, and its tapestry of music and narrative testifies to White's creative and communicative skills. *The Elektra Years* is a deftly done portrait, but 18 of its 29 tracks come from *Josh At Midnight/Ballads & Blues*, which represents better value for money.

*** Pye Blues Legends In London
Castle CMETD 562//Sanctuary CAS 36167 3CD *White; Kenny Baker (t); Bertie King (as); 'Fred Hartz' [Kenny Graham] (ts); Benny Green (bs); Jack Fallon (b); Phil Seamen (d). 1/56.*

Jack Fallon returns, in better company than on *The Best Of Josh White*; the brass and reeds appear on four tracks, and acquit themselves effectively. *Blues And ...*, as the original LP was titled, is no masterpiece, but Josh is having fun, and the tracks are an unexpected mix of standards like 'How Long Blues' and 'St. Louis Blues', witty R&B (Danny Barker's 'I Had To Stoop To Conquer You', the Clovers' 'One Mint Julep') and the archaic 'Oh Lula' and 'Dink's Blues', probably acquired from Zora Neale Hurston and Alan Lomax respectively. Other CDs in this box are by Big Bill Broonzy and Sonny Terry & Brownie McGhee.

**(*) Empty Bed Blues
Sepia Tone STONE 14 *White; unknown (ss); unknown (p); Josh White Jr (g, v); Bill Lee, unknown (b); unknown (d). 62.*

White sounds slightly tired on this, his final LP for Elektra, and his vocals on a retrospective set of blues and gospel lack variety; he can't give 'Bottle Up And Go' the exuberance it needs, for instance, and a lengthy 'His Eye Is On The Sparrow' is politely formal. His picking is as pretty as ever, and Bill 'father of Spike' Lee's bass supplies a lot of the missing energy; he's sorely missed when a rhythm section, including an interestingly modernistic pianist, and an aimless, tasteless saxophonist take over on 'Baby Baby Blues'. Josh Jr's contribution to 'That Suits Me' is better integrated but characterless. CS

Sheila Wilcoxson
VOCAL

Wilcoxson moved from her hometown of Detroit to Portland, Oregon, in the early 1980s. A founder member of Back Porch Blues, she performed with the group until it broke up in 1996, thereafter working in her own name. She was nominated for a Handy award in 1998.

**(*) Backwater Blues
Burnside BCD 0027 *Wilcoxson; Curtis Salgado, Bill Rhoades (h); Ellen Whyte (ac); Janice Scroggins (p); Skip Parente (vn); Terry Robb, Alan Hager (g, v); Albert Reda, Fritz Richmond, Angel Townsend (b). 97.*

A set of blues, traditional songs and originals, with accompaniments varying from solo piano on the title track and 'Revival Day' to the cleanly recorded harmonica-and-guitar combinations of 'Keep Your Eyes Open' or 'John The

Revelator'. Wilcoxson's singing of the a cappella 'Sweet Misery' and 'Looky, Looky Yonder/Black Betty' is powerful, if mannered, but when she is accompanied her style inclines more to the intimacy of the coffeehouse than to the drama of the vaudeville stage, and she's less convincing with the sober narrative of 'Backwater Blues' than with the singalong country song 'Testerone Poisoning'. TR

Wildsang
DUET

New Mexico based, Wildsang are Hillary Kay (vocal, guitar, bass), daughter of a Civil Rights activist and great-niece of Joe 'King' Oliver, and Kate Freeman (harmonica), a Sami-descended San Franciscan environmentalist.

*** **Blues**
WS 4511 *Kate Freeman; Hillary Kay; Alberto Alcozar (b); Mark Clark (d).* 01?
*** **Sky – Dirt – Speak Out Truth**
WS2 307 *Kate Freeman; Hillary Kay.* 03.

The blues in the third millennium is not what it was, and one reason is that America's not what it was, either; consider the reception that an interracial lesbian duo with a penchant for songs about violence would have got in 1920. On the other hand, Ma Rainey's 'Prove It On Me Blues' is a precursor of sorts, and given the amount of casual male violence in the blues, there's room for Wildsang's more elaborate tales of rape, murder and lynching. Most songs on both CDs are by Kay, but the covers – of Koko Taylor on *Blues* and Howlin' Wolf on its successor – are indicative of her vocal influences. At times on *Blues* she struggles to be heard over the instruments, and on both discs she's not always in control of the growls and rasps, but her singing, her belligerent guitar and Freeman's basic but vigorous harmonica project blues grrrl personas effectively. There's some imaginative songwriting, too: bringing Achilles dragging Hector round Troy into a song about James Bird (on *Blues*) is daring, but it comes off. So does the opposite strategy, of moving an image from the rhetorical to the vernacular and personal: 'That ain't no strange fruit, that's my daddy' (on *Sky – Dirt – Speak Out Truth*). Not everything is on that level. The line between drama and melodrama is sometimes crossed, and the enviro-rant 'Look To The Earth', on *Blues*, is not the only track where one feels adolescence has been too long prolonged; but in a world where blues is one option for black musicians (Kay played folk and reggae before discovering blues) rather than the default working-class style, Wildsang's voice is one of the more interesting. CS

Kris Wiley
VOCAL, GUITAR

Wiley spent much of the '90s playing in bars in southern California, and has opened for many well-known artists. She released an album, Old, New, Borrowed And Blue, *on her own label in 1999.*

*** **Breaking The Rules**
JSP JSPCD 2126 *Wiley; Robbie Smith (t); Jonny Viau (ts); Troy Jennings (bs); Arlen Schierbaum (o); Tom Mahon (p); Kirk Fletcher (g); Carl Sealove (b); Paul Fasulo (d); Jimmy Morello (prod).* 99.

Wiley has a muscular vocal manner, some decent songs and a capability on guitar that embraces both the rocking Chuck Berry beat of 'Ain't Nobody's Business' and the swooping Albert Collinsy lines of 'Working Late'. She deserves being brought to the attention of anyone bowled over by Susan Tedeschi, but the recommendation may be too late: she has reportedly retired from the music business. She made a brief reappearance in 2002 on the VAC *Hey Bo Diddley – A Tribute!* (Evidence ECD 25124), singing 'You Don't Love Me'. TR

Robert Wilkins (1896–1987)
VOCAL, GUITAR

From Hernando, Mississippi, Wilkins moved to Memphis in 1915. In the '20s and '30s he performed in taverns, but in the late '30s, shocked by violence at a house party where he was playing, he renounced the blues, entered the ministry of the Church of God in Christ and became a herbalist. In the '60s he appeared at the Memphis Country Blues Festival and resumed the recording career he had terminated in 1935, though he would now perform only religious material.

***(*) **The Original Rolling Stone**
Yazoo 1077 *Wilkins; Son Joe [Ernest Lawlars] (g); 'Kid Spoons' (spoons).* 9/28–10/35.
***(*) **Memphis Blues (1928–1935)**
Document DOCD-5014 *As above.* 9/28–10/35.
*** **Memphis Blues**
Wolf WSE-108 *As above.* 9/28–10/35.

Wilkins's first recording, a two-part 'Rolling Stone', has a four-line verse and a droning one-chord tune, an unusual shape that may imply a form predating the three-line blues. Another of his 1928 Victor sides, 'Jail House Blues', uses a picking pattern in the manner of Jim Jackson. Recording for Brunswick in 1929 and '30, however, he shrugs off such archaisms. The lilting guitar melodies of 'Falling Down Blues', 'I'll Go With Her Blues' and 'Police Sergeant Blues' (which incorporates a passage possibly derived from the ragtime-era tune 'Red Wing') suggest a fellowship with Frank Stokes, while 'Get Away Blues' recalls the steady rhythm of Garfield Akers. The overall effect, however, is quite different. With his light voice and private manner, Wilkins prompts the listener to think not of Stokes or Akers but of Joe Callicott (another man from Hernando, like Akers, Jim Jackson and Wilkins himself), or even, vaguely, of Mississippi John Hurt. And although his playing has points of contact with some of his contemporaries, his notion of melody, unconstrained by blues commonplaces, gives his work unique character and charm.

His 1935 sides, his last for 30-odd years, are a curious *envoi*: some conventional blues, the sprightly and lyrically unusual 'New Stockyard Blues' and the rag tunes 'Old Jim Canan's', about a Memphis nightspot, and 'Losin' Out Blues'. The Yazoo CD omits three of these later sides, a depletion remedied by both the albums called *Memphis Blues*; the Document adds the complete work of singer/guitarists Tom Dickson (four sides) and Allen Shaw (two), while the Wolf fills up with a handful by Gus Cannon. Wilkins's four Victor sides are also on the VAC *Memphis Blues Singers Volume 2* (Frog DGF 22) in excellent transfers.

The recordings of Wilkins's later years are vibrant: his voice had remained sure and his fingering fluent. Although he had put an embargo on the blues, he did not mind if echoes of his past smuggled themselves into his playing. '(Jesus Will Fix It) Alright' uses an accelerated 'Rolling Stone' figure, while 'Streamline 'Frisco Limited' begins as a train instrumental in the Booker White manner, though it segues out of the secular. These and a sheaf of gospel songs, some with slide guitar, are on the absorbing ". . Remember Me" (Genes GCD 9902), mostly recorded in 1971. Performances of similar repertoire and quality from the '60s are on *When I Lay My Burden Down* (Biograph BCD 130), an album largely devoted to Fred McDowell and Furry Lewis, and, despite its title, on *Takoma Blues* (Takoma CDTAK 8907). TR

Alanda Williams (born 1952)
VOCAL

Williams was born in Pace, Mississippi, and began singing at a local Baptist church. In his teens he sang with a gospel group and then, living in Philadelphia, with a soul group, which led to a 20-year spell with The Coasters. Moving to Fort Worth in 1991, he worked with the Coronado brothers and recorded with U. P. Wilson.

** Kid Dynamite
JSP JSPCD 292 Williams; Joe Rios, Steve Coronado (s); Danny Ross (kb, o); Andrew 'Jr Boy' Jones, Tone Sommer, John Coronado, James Moreno (g); Rene Mesritz, Chris Maxwell (b); Ty Grimes, Joe Coronado (d). 96.

Four tracks of this, Williams's only album, are with his friends the Coronado brothers, the other eight with a band headed by guitarists Jones and Sommer. The latter session puts a somewhat more interesting frame round Williams's heartfelt renditions of original blues and soul compositions. Given that the soul numbers are nothing special, it's odd that the blues are mostly pushed down the running order. 'Looking For My Baby', 'Keep It In The Groove' and the Texas shuffle 'I Wanna Tell Ya' are competent, if ordinary, but the title track is sung and played with an air of sexual promise that Muddy Waters might have approved, though perhaps raising an eyebrow at the lyrics: 'They call me Kid Dynamite ... I'm just gonna explode all over the bed.' A tempting offer indeed. TR

Arthur Williams (born 1937)
VOCAL, HARMONICA

Arthur Lee 'Oscar' Williams first recorded in 1966, backing Frank Frost (q.v.). Born in Mississippi, Williams grew up in Chicago but returned home in 1958 and soon joined Frost's Jelly Roll Kings, just in time to be drafted, thus missing a session at the Sun studio. A decade later Williams left Mississippi in a hurry after a dispute with his plantation boss. Settling in St Louis, he continued to play, but wasn't recorded again until 1991, initially as a sideman.

*** Harpin' On It
Fedora FCD 5013 Williams; Bob Lohr (p); Larry Griffin, Jimmy Lee Kennett (g); Charles 'Nephew' Davis (b); Chris Millar (d); James 'Boo Boo' Davis (d, v). 12/98.
*** Ain't Goin' Down
Fedora FCD 5019 Williams; Bob Lohr (p); Jesse Hoggard (g); Charles 'Nephew' Davis (b); Sam Carr (d). 7/99.

***(*) Midnight Blue
Rooster Blues RBLU 2646 Williams; Bob Lohr (p, prog); Jesse Hoggard (g); Charles 'Nephew' Davis (b); Willie 'Big Eyes' Smith (d); Doc Terry (v samples). 6–7/01.
***(*) Must Be Jelly – Live From WROX In Clarksdale, Ms
Severn CD-0029 Williams; Bob Lohr (p); Jesse Hoggard (g, v); Calvin 'Fuzz' Jones (b); Willie 'Big Eyes' Smith (d, tamb, v); Sam Carr (d). 04?

Williams is still a top-class harp player, but his voice is rather small and his range restricted, although he does some unexpectedly good Howlin' Wolf imitations on *Ain't Goin' Down*. Williams splits the vocal duties evenly with Boo Boo Davis on the first Fedora CD, but since Davis is also a limited singer, this doesn't help much. On both Fedoras, Charles Davis is the best of the backing musicians. Lohr is accomplished but glacial, and the guitarists seem to be under orders to lay back; when they do step up, their solos are predictable. *Ain't Goin' Down* is the better of these discs, thanks to the great Sam Carr, like Williams a former Jelly Roll King.

One can only wonder what happened between the Fedora sessions and the Rooster, which Lohr produced. He and Hoggard play with much more fire, 'Nephew' Davis is as steady as ever and Willie Smith is predictably excellent. The instruments are recorded with far more crispness and clarity and, above all, Williams not only continues to play inventively and with beautiful tone but sings with far more aggression and commitment; two Sonny Boy Williamson II numbers with acoustic guitar backing are an especially inspired notion. *Midnight Blue* runs out of steam towards the end, and the self-indulgent use of samples and programming on ''67 Cadillac' doesn't refuel the boiler. Nevertheless, it's clearly Williams's best showcase.

There are another two successful acoustic numbers on *Must Be Jelly*. Though credited to the Jelly Roll All-Stars, it's a Williams-centred project; he plays harp on all but two tracks, which are brief speech by him, and sings on six. Smith takes two vocals and Hoggard three. Hoggard's singing of 'King Motel' falls into one of the traps set for white blues artists by being histrionically unsuited to the lyrics, but he does considerably better with his other vocals and plays clever, idiomatic guitar throughout. The other drawback to a generally rewarding CD is Lohr's piano playing, which continues to be technically fine but emotionally aloof. *Must Be Jelly* was recorded 'live in studio' (no isolation booths, no overdubs), but it has much of the spontaneity of a successful bandstand performance, with Jones and the two exemplary drummers ensuring that things never get sloppy. CS

Lil' Ed Williams (born 1955)
VOCAL, GUITAR

Lil' Ed & The Blues Imperials have been playing the Chicago clubs since 1975, enthusiastically conserving the punchy slide-driven ensemble sound developed by J. B. Hutto – Williams's uncle – and Hound Dog Taylor. After several years of being known only on the West Side, the Blues Imperials played the 1984 Chicago Blues Festival, which brought them bookings at North Side clubs and outside Chicago.

**(*) Roughhousin'
Alligator ALCD 4749 Williams; Dave Weld (g); James 'Pookie' Young (b); Louis Henderson (d). 1/86.

*** **Chicken, Gravy & Biscuits**
Alligator ALCD 4772 *Williams; Mike Garrett (g); James 'Pookie' Young (b); Kelly Littleton (d).* 88.

**** **What You See Is What You Get**
Alligator ALCD 4808 *As above, except add Eddie McKinley (ts).* 92.

How Lil' Ed and his men came to make *Roughhousin'* is almost a fairy story. Booked to cut a few tracks for an anthology, the group so impressed the Alligator staff that after five one-take songs had been taped, Bruce Iglauer suggested the band go ahead and record enough for an album. The Blues Imperials proceeded to play 30 songs in three and a quarter hours.

As you might expect from someone hoping for a partnership in James–Hutto, Inc., Williams's music is triumphantly unrefined. Like his models', too, it's best when it gets up a bit of speed, as in 'Old Oak Tree', 'Midnight Rider', 'Pride And Joy' (not the Stevie Ray Vaughan number) or 'You Don't Exist Any More', though 'Walking The Dog' is messy. Williams delivers the lyrics in a modified shout, as if swapping news with someone on the other side of a busy street.

Two years on, the new lineup on *Chicken, Gravy & Biscuits* sounds a little different: not exactly more polished – no one would ever call Lil' Ed polished – but showing that it had learned a few lessons about presenting itself. There's more light and shade: the group knows how to take its time on 'Blues For Jeanette'. But to check that the music's original inspirations are not forgotten you need only hear the Elmoreish slide on 'Walkin'', 'Can't Let These Blues Go' or 'Got My Mind Made Up'.

A small but recurring problem of Williams's first two albums was that slow numbers tended to reveal open spaces between the four musicians where nothing much was happening. On *What You See Is What You Get* they found a solution, Garrett playing fuller rhythm parts and McKinley's tenor sax thickening the texture. Progress in the light-and-shade department was maintained, too. Altogether the album was a happy marriage of enthusiasm and self-control, and Williams's best work thus far.

(*) **Keep On Walkin'
Earwig 4936 *Williams; Jasper Buchanan (o, p, v); Leo Davis (o, p); Andrew Bird (vn); Dave Weld (g, v); Bernard Reed (b, v); Jeff Taylor, Darryl Mahon (d, v).* 4/94, 1–3/96.

(*) **Who's Been Talking
Earwig CD 4941 *Williams; Allen Batts (o, p); Eddie C. Campbell (g); Willie Kent (b, v); Cleotha 'Baldhead Pete' Williams (d).* 6/98.

Keep On Walkin' exposes Williams, for the first time on record, as an acoustic guitarist. It's essentially a duet album with Dave Weld and so billed, five of the tracks being acoustic and nine electric, the latter supplemented by keyboards, bass and drums, and the two men splitting the vocals more or less evenly. In the barer setting of the acoustic numbers Williams is a more versatile guitarist than was apparent from his earlier work, and a better singer too, and tracks like 'North Carolina Bound', 'New Year's Resolution' and 'I Can't Have Nothin'' have a delightful old-time feel. Weld is good on his own 'Confess Diane' but elsewhere his vocals are overbearing. *Who's Been Talking* is also a duet album, with singer/bassist Willie Kent. Two vocalists with character and a band consisting of deeply experienced musicians should have ensured a three-star album. This didn't quite make it, thanks to some by-the-book playing and a couple of poor repertoire choices in 'As The Years Go Passing By' – a splendid song, but not for a gruff and undramatic singer like Kent – and Williams's mundane 'Your Love Is So Strong'.

*** **Get Wild!**
Alligator ALCD 4868 *Williams; Mike Garrett (g, v); James 'Pookie' Young (b, v); Kelly Littleton (d, perc).* 99.

**** **Heads Up!**
Alligator ALCD 4886 *As above, except add Paul Buschbacher (g).* 02.

Seven years on from *What You See*, Williams returned to the Alligator list. Whatever the problems that had kept him out of the studio, they had not dulled the edge of his music. The Blues Imperials, you might say, were still minty-fresh. The clattering intros of 'Standing On The Corner' or Hutto's 'Pet Cream Man' sound like several storeys of scaffolding collapsing at once. But between the dust-raisers are drifting slow numbers such as 'Too Late' and 'Change My Way Of Living' where the echoing guitar recalls young West Siders of three decades before like Luther Allison. *Heads Up!* is equally self-assertive. The Elmore James slide phrasing on several numbers may tell us nothing new about Williams's sources, but it shows that he can still draw on them to good effect. The calmly powerful reading of 'Black Night', on the other hand, would have been beyond the range of the younger man. Mastered at a higher level than *Get Wild!*, the album fizzes with presence and immediacy. TR

Elmo Williams (born 1933)
VOCAL, GUITAR

Elmo Williams is the archetypal Fat Possum artist: his music is crude, raucous and captivating; his guitar playing is untutored but no stranger to excitement; his songs are formless and fragmentary. His partner, drummer Hezekiah Early (see Hezekiah & The House Rockers), like him a native of Natchez, Mississippi, straddles an ill-defined line between form and chaos with complacent energy, expending what breath remains through a rack-mounted harmonica.

**** **Takes One To Know One**
Fat Possum 0313 *Williams; Hezekiah Early (h, d, v); Bob Manning (g).* 97.

Unlike R. L. Burnside and Junior Kimbrough, Williams has never been invited to duplicate or improve upon this brief, bludgeoning masterpiece, nor is it likely that a second episode would reveal any further hidden dimensions. His repertoire relies upon traditional themes like 'Motherless Children' ('Mother's Dead') and 'Blues Jumped The Rabbit' but these are songs through the looking glass, bizarrely changed. 'Insane Instrumental' is just that, devoid of logic and dangerously addictive. A variety of amplification is used, all of it flirting if not copulating with distortion; 'Hoopin' And Hollerin'', performed solo, is the aural equivalent of being sucked into a jet engine. Often Williams and Early achieve their goal of undifferentiated noise; there's a moment in 'Do Your Thing' where the skirling of bagpipes is achieved. Not an experience for the refined taste, perhaps, but like the young lady from Detroit and her partner Durand, their performance together is grand. NS

George Williams & Bessie Brown
DUET

Williams and Brown were a husband-and-wife team, both originally from Texas and both probably born in the 1890s. When not recording together and solo, they toured the vaudeville circuits. Bessie retired in 1932 and is believed to have died about 1970; George's last known stage performance was in 1937, although he recorded one more 78 in the late '40s.

(*) George Williams And Bessie Brown Vol. 1 (1923–1925)
Document DOCD-5527 Williams; Brown; Howard Scott (c); Charlie Green (tb); Don Redman (as); Coleman Hawkins (ts); Fletcher Henderson, Alexander Brown, Lemuel Fowler (p); 'Alabama Joe' [Roy Smeck] (g); Charles Thomas (eff). 8/23–2/25.

(*) George Williams And Bessie Brown Vol. 2 (1925–1930)
Document DOCD-5528 Williams; Brown; Harry Tate (c); Charlie Green (tb); Don Redman (cl); Lemuel Fowler, Fletcher Henderson, Louis Hooper, Roy Banks, unknown (p). 2/25–5/30.

Evidently well liked by contemporary audiences, Williams and Brown will be hard work for most present-day listeners. On Vol. 1 they are not helped by a combination of acoustic recording and indifferent remastering, but in any case their duets usually lack the verve of Grant & Wilson or Butterbeans & Susie. Fletcher Henderson's playing is admirable, which cannot be said of the other pianists, and the various band members he brings along often make useful contributions, although Don Redman's alto on two Williams solos is an exception. Bessie's 'Hoodoo Blues' has excellent lyrics by Spencer Williams, but is one of two songs with Roy Smeck's lamentable guitar; George's 'Chain Gang Blues' ('All I get is flogging, all I get is rough abuse') is also of more verbal than musical interest. Stovepipe No. 1 and Simmie Dooley both acquired songs from Williams's recordings, but his stodginess compares unfavourably with their élan. This disc's appeal is chiefly antiquarian.

Vol. 2 wraps up their last 13 titles; Brown appears only on five duets, which is a pity, for her delivery is stronger and bluesier. The sound quality is better, too, if not brilliant. Henderson is on only two sides, with Green and a much better Redman in support, but Hooper, Banks and Harry Tate all do good work. Four years separate the distressing yodelling on George's penultimate record from the rest. Eleven duets by six obscure pairings complete the CD. Some famous accompanists are present, including pianist Luckey Roberts, Tom Morris and Bubber Miley on cornet, and the unfortunately underrecorded clarinet of Douglas Williams. However, only Hilda Alexander and Mamie McClure make a serious claim for attention, with an enthusiastic rendition of 'He's Tight Like This', accompanied by the Backa-Town Boys, who include an eloquent cornettist and a rock-steady bassist. CS

Jody Williams (born 1935)
VOCAL, GUITAR

Joseph Leon Williams was born in Mobile, Alabama, but grew up in Chicago. At first a harmonica player, he took up guitar at 16, inspired, and taught, by Bo Diddley. In the '50s he was one of Chicago's cleverest young guitarists, his solos brightening records by Howlin' Wolf, Billy Boy Arnold, Jimmy Rogers and many more, but, hearing his ideas borrowed by other musicians, to their profit rather than his, he gave up the music business and became an electrical repairman. With an irony no press agent could devise, the guitarist everyone copied went to work for the Xerox Corporation. For over 30 years he resisted requests for a comeback, but his friends kept asking and in 2001 he finally yielded.

Identifying and tracing Williams's playing on other people's records is specialized work. The notes to Return Of A Legend (see below) are an excellent guide. His own minor-key instrumental 'Lucky Lou', absorbed and redeployed by Otis Rush in 'All Your Love', was on Chess Blues Guitar 1949–1969 (MCA/Chess CHD2–9393//(E) MCD 09393). The same (deleted) VAC also had his 'What Kind Of Gal Is That?' and one of the sides he cut with Bo Diddley, 'Who Do You Love?'.

*** Return Of A Legend**
Evidence ECD 26120 Williams; Kenny Anderson (t); Hank Ford (ts); Willie Henderson (bs, arr); Billy Boy Arnold (h, v); Allen Batts (o, p); Sean Costello, Tinsley Ellis, Rusty Zinn (g, v); Ronnie Baker Brooks (g); Harlan Terson (b); Kenny Smith (d); Dick Shurman (prod). 9/01.

*** You Left Me In The Dark**
Evidence ECD 26130 Williams; Kenny Anderson (t); Hank Ford (ts); Willie Henderson (bs, arr); Rob Waters (o, p); Robert Jr Lockwood, Lonnie Brooks (g, v); Billy Flynn, Chris James (g); Patrick Rynn (b); Willie Hayes (d, perc); Dick Shurman (prod). 9–10/03.

When he finally took the decision to record again, Williams embraced the idea enthusiastically and wrote several sassy, funny songs like 'Brown Eyes And Big Thighs', 'Henpecked And Happy' and 'She Found A Fool And Bumped His Head', which he puts across in a distinctively wry style. He also revisits his back catalogue in 'Lucky Lou', 'Jive Spot', which he originally cut with Otis Spann as 'Five Spot', and 'You May', a philosophical song aptly fitted to the tune of Memphis Slim's 'Mother Earth'. Despite his long retirement, Williams is still a formidable guitarist, and his guests Costello, Ellis and Zinn, who all learned from his records, respond at the same level.

You Left Me In The Dark has much of the same character. Almost all the songs are Williams's, amusing numbers ('What Kind Of Gal Is That?') and homilies ('Young Men Don't Know') interspersed with slow blues like 'Don't Get Caught Sleeping In My Bed' and 'Someone Else'. Lockwood and Brooks make two guest appearances each, and Henderson's arrangements deploy the horns niftily on four tracks. TR

Big Joe Williams (1903–82)
VOCAL, GUITAR, KAZOO

Big Joe Williams covered ground like kudzu. He was constantly on the move, back and forth between Mississippi and St Louis or Chicago, or out to New York or LA, as if he was hoping to win a Handy Award for Rambling. But he always kept his links with the South, and at the end of his life he returned to his birthplace in Crawford, Mississippi. He first left there in his teens to work on travelling shows, in jugbands and with contemporaries like Honeyboy Edwards. In the '30s and '40s, based in St Louis, he made numerous recordings, including many with Sonny Boy Williamson I. He spent much of the '50s in obscurity, from which he lifted himself by making contact with Delmark Records and finding a fresh audience as a living voice from the dead past of Charley Patton and Robert Johnson. Throughout the '60s and into the '70s he was a stalwart of the campus and club circuits. He recorded indefatigably, but was not too much of an egotist to talk up the talents of friends and relations, many of whom thus gained an opportunity to make recordings of their own.

***(*) **Big Joe Williams – Vol. 1 (1935–1941)**
Blues Document BDCD-6003 Williams; Sonny Boy Williamson I (h); 'Dad' Tracy (one-string vn); Henry Townsend, Robert Lee McCoy (g); William Mitchell, Alfred Elkins (imb); Chasey 'Kokomo' Collins (wb). 2/35–12/41.

(***) **Po' Joe**
Fabulous FABCD 122 As above, except add Jump Jackson (d), Clifford Dinwiddie (wb). 2/35–45.

*** **Baby Please Don't Go**
Wolf WBJ 003 As above, except add Ransom Knowling (b), Judge Riley (d); omit Dinwiddie. 2/35–12/47.

*** **Baby Please Don't Go**
Snapper Complete Blues SBLUECD 029 As above, except add Clifford Dinwiddie (wb); omit Townsend, McCoy. 2/35–12/47.

***(*) **The Blues/Baby Please Don't Go 1935–1951**
Frémeaux FA 270 2CD As for Baby Please Don't Go (Wolf), except add T. J. Green (b). 2/35–12/51.

**** **Big Joe Williams And The Stars Of Mississippi Blues**
JSP JSPCD 7719 5CD As for all above CDs. 2/35–12/51.

***(*) **Big Joe Williams – Vol. 2 (1945–1949)**
Blues Document BDCD-6004 Williams; Sonny Boy Williamson I (h); Ransom Knowling (b); Jump Jackson, Judge Riley (d); Clifford Dinwiddie (wb). 7/45–49.

Honeyboy Edwards, who travelled with Big Joe in the '30s, remembered how he 'used to play in Spanish [i.e. open G tuning], put that clamp [i.e. capo] on there, and it sound mostly betwixt a guitar and a mandolin' – an excellent description of the chittering strum he uses on 'Somebody's Been Borrowing That Stuff' and the other songs from his first, remarkable session in 1935. Percussive twangs of the sixth string recall Patton, but in many respects Williams stands apart from his Mississippi contemporaries: Patton – or Tommy Johnson, or Booker White – keeps the guitar line moving beneath the vocal, whereas Williams almost stops playing, marking time with merely a slap on the strings, waiting to respond to his intensely delivered lyrics with agitated flurries.

Those six pieces are our only evidence of how the young(ish) Big Joe sounded on his own; he would not record that way again for many years. The next date put him with a fiddle-and-washboard band, and the next in a trio with Sonny Boy Williamson I, with whom he would record often; the half-dozen tracks they cut at a session in 12/41, including definitive interpretations of '[Baby] Please Don't Go', 'Highway 49' and 'Someday Baby', confirm them as one of the great blues partnerships. They continued recording together until 1947, the delicate architecture of their duets solidly buttressed by bass and drums. It isn't often said, but it seems likely that driving trio and quartet sides like 'Drop Down Blues' (1945) or 'King Biscuit Stomp' (1947) were listened to attentively by some of the younger musicians then finding their voice in Chicago's clubs or on Maxwell Street.

The Blues Documents are complete for the period so far, but marred by the low-level remastering of Vol. 1. Vol. 2 includes the rare 1949 Bullet coupling, 'Jivin' Woman'/'She's A Married Woman'. Po' Joe has virtually all his prewar sides and three from 1945, including the rare 'His Spirit Lives On', commemorating Franklin D. Roosevelt, but even its low price doesn't compensate for lifeless sound. The Wolf and Snapper Complete Blues CDs are better, though not perfectly, remastered and offer selective surveys. Big Joe's unique way with a blues song and a blues guitar in his middle years is very well illustrated for the non-specialist by the Frémeaux 2CD, an astute selection from all the sessions sampled elsewhere plus five cuts from the 1951 Trumpet dates (see below). But for completeness of coverage and overall sound quality the market leader, by a distance, is the JSP set, the first two CDs of which contain everything mentioned above and everything else Big Joe recorded in the period. (For details of the remaining contents see COMPILATIONS: MISSISSIPPI.)

*** **Big Joe Williams & Friends**
Purple Pyramid CLP 0834 Williams; T. J. Green (b). 9–12/51.

With their animated singing and fuzzy amplified guitar, Big Joe's eight sides for the Trumpet label of Jackson, Mississippi, proclaim that he is entering a new decade in buoyant spirits. This is an excellent way to acquire them, since the 'friends' are the contemporary Trumpet artists Luther Huff, Bobo Thomas and Arthur Crudup. Huff's four guitar duets with his brother Percy testify to the lingering influence of Tommy Johnson and Charlie McCoy, while Thomas's 'Catfish Blues', his only recording, is a nicely controlled duet with Sonny Boy Williamson II. The transfers are accurate, the notes minuscule but excellent.

Always assiduous in courting record companies, Joe also recorded during the '50s for, among others, Specialty and Vee-Jay. There are two good cuts on Bloodstains On The Wall: Country Blues From Specialty (Specialty SPCD-7061) and four untidy ones with a small group on Chicago Blues: The Vee Jay Era (Charly CDGR 145 2CD). Some interesting but barely listenable recordings from 1951–52, derived from wrecked acetates, were gathered on Malvina My Sweet Woman (Oldie Blues OLCD 7004, probably deleted).

*** **Absolutely The Best**
Fuel 2000 302 061 141 Williams; Sonny Terry (h, v eff); Erwin Helfer (p); Lightnin' Hopkins, Brownie McGhee (g, v); Jimmy Bond (b). c. 57–9/65.

A curious sandwich of an album. The thick outer slices are nine tracks recorded about 1957, of which more later, and eight from the 10/63 Storyville album (see below). The thin layer of jam (jelly to US readers) consists of 'Chain Gang Blues' and 'Razor Sharp Blues' from c. 6/60 (see Have Mercy! below) and a 1965 recording (made by Norman Dayron) of 'I Feel So Worried', played on six-string guitar. The most interesting and, for any but seasoned collectors, probably the most elusive material here is the '57 session, done for Cobra but never issued, in which Joe rocks along happily with the young Erwin Helfer on piano.

***(*) **Piney Woods Blues**
Delmark DD-602 Williams; J. D. Short (h, g); Bob Koester, John Hartford (sp). 1–2/58.

***(*) **Stavin' Chain Blues**
Delmark DD-609 Williams; J. D. Short (h, g, v). 2/58.

What is most striking about these albums, made before Big Joe had become accustomed to the folkclub and concert circuit, is their understatedness. It may be an odd word to use of such an outgoing performer, but he does seem to take care to let his songs make their point without exaggeration or flourish. Perhaps it's relevant that he was partnered on four tracks of *Piney Woods Blues* and all of *Stavin' Chain Blues* by J. D. Short, a musician he knew well and respected enough to work with rather than dominate. But none of that should be taken as a discreet way of saying that this is music under wraps: though Joe is restrained in comparison with some later recordings, he never lacks energy or drive, and, thanks to Short's tendency to accelerate, several numbers that start temperately enough end up as intoxicating stomps.

(**(*)) Have Mercy!
Tradition TCD 1014 *Williams; Sonny Terry (h, v); Brownie McGhee, Lightnin' Hopkins (g, v); Jimmy Bond (b). c. 6/60.*

Five of these eight tracks come from one of two 'summit meetings' of Big Joe, Lightnin' Hopkins, Sonny Terry and Brownie McGhee that have been shuffled and redealt on many albums (see the others' entries). Joe is on his own in 'Razor Sharp Blues' and takes part in 'Chain Gang Blues', "Buked And Scorned', 'Brand New Car' and (faintly) 'Great Gospel Blues (Right On That Shore)', but he is absent from 'Blues For Gamblers', and 'Stool Pigeon Blues' and 'Ball Of Twine' are solos by Hopkins. For Joe's admirers this is an item of peripheral interest.

♛ **** Shake Your Boogie
Arhoolie CD 315 *Williams; Charlie Musselwhite (h); Mary Williams (v). 59, 10/60, 12/69.*

The heart of this album is the 10/60 session, first issued as *Tough Times* and unquestionably one of Big Joe's most concentrated and affecting performances. He recorded the autobiographical pieces 'Mean Step Father' and 'Brother James' several times, but never with this combination of conciseness and fervour. Throughout this set he tells his stories as if unearthing them from a forgotten songbook and taking enormous satisfaction in the discovery. The other half of the CD, which originally constituted the LP *Thinking Of What They Did To Me*, was recorded nine years later, when Joe had replaced some of his musical tools: the sound of his guitar is less ringing and he frequently uses a slide, to rather tart effect. Again, there are several tracks that issue from a place Joe seems only to have visited when recording for men he knew and trusted, like Arhoolie's Chris Strachwitz and Delmark's Bob Koester: 'Thinking Of What They Did To Me', 'Remember Way Back' and 'The Death Of Dr. Martin Luther King', the last being one of three exquisite duets with Charlie Musselwhite.

*** I Got Wild
Delmark DE-767 *Williams; Ransom Knowling (b). 2/58, 7/61.*
*** Blues On Highway 49
Delmark DD-604 *As above. 7/61.*
*** Nine String Guitar Blues
Delmark DD-627 *As above. 7/61.*
*** Mississippi's Big Joe Williams And His Nine-String Guitar
Smithsonian Folkways SF CD 40052 *As above. 7/61.*

Except for eight tracks on *I Got Wild*, which come from the 2/58 session, all the material on these four CDs was recorded on two days in 7/61. The quality of the performances is consistently high, so there's little to choose between the albums. The Smithsonian Folkways has the largest number of his better-known pieces, whereas *Nine String Guitar Blues* has the most tracks with Ransom Knowling's driving bass; the stomp-down duet 'Jump, Baby – Jump!', done off-the-cuff in the closing minutes of a session, is exhilarating. *Nine String* also has notes by John Simmons, a Chicagoan who once managed him, which are exceptionally informative about both the musician and the man. But there is no shortfall of good music, or valuable notes, on the other sets. Incidentally, Joe expanded a standard guitar to a nine-string by doubling the first, second and fourth strings, so that in his favourite key of open G it would be tuned DGDDGBBDD.

**(*) At Folk City
Original Blues Classics OBCCD 580 *Williams. 2/62.*

A genial set, taped at Gerde's Folk City in New York before an extremely quiet audience, given some novelty by Joe's decision to play kazoo on several tracks.

** 63 Chicago
Acrobat ACRCD 102 *Williams. 63.*
*** Blues Masters Vol. 2
Storyville STCD 8002 *Williams. 10/63.*
**(*) Ramblin' & Wanderin'
Aim 0011 *Williams; Sonny Terry (h, v); Brownie McGhee, Lightnin' Hopkins (g, v). c. 6/60–10/63.*

63 Chicago appears to derive from three sessions, two of them live. Most of the tracks have a mildly irritating effect owing to either room echo or a faulty microphone. Even at its low price this is strictly for completists.

The opening track of *Blues Masters Vol. 2*, 'So Soon I Will Be Goin' My Way Back Home', was inspired by the air journey that brought Big Joe to Europe, probably his first experience of a long flight. Most of what follows is much older: a 'Jinx Blues' possibly from Son House, 'Ramblin' And Wanderin' Blues' (a version of what John Estes called 'The Girl I Love, She Got Long Curly Hair') and several songs recalled from the late '40s, like 'Juanita Blues', 'Vitamin "A" Blues' and 'Don't You Leave Me Here'. A good set, quite well recorded, but with no surprises.

Ramblin' & Wanderin' contains all of *63 Chicago* and seven tracks from the Storyville session, sandwiching five from the 1960 'summit meeting' (see *Have Mercy!* above).

**(*) Classic Delta Blues
Original Blues Classics OBCCD 545 *Williams; prob. Michael Bloomfield (g). 7–9/64.*
*** Back To The Country
Testament TCD 5013 *Williams; Willie Lee Harris (h, v); Jimmy Brown (vn, g, v); Bill Foster (g). winter 64/65.*

At the suggestion of the producer Pete Welding, Joe recorded *Classic Delta Blues* with a six-string guitar. The title concept was also Welding's idea: what he meant by it can be deduced from the dozen songs he chose, which are all associated with Charley Patton, Robert Johnson, Son House, Tommy Johnson or Skip James. Joe was far too much of an individualist to offer anything but his own interpretations of such repertoire, and he invariably replaces the original artist's guitar figures with his own, so that 'Pea Vine Blues' has little of Patton in it and 'Crossroads Blues' almost nothing of Robert

Johnson. But despite making this plain statement of independence, Joe is not at his liveliest here, and the guitar sounds weak compared with the nine-string.

Back To The Country, too, was produced by Welding, though he states in the notes that it was Big Joe's idea to re-create an old-time stringband, choosing in Harris and Brown two old friends from St Louis. Most of the numbers are by that trio, Harris responding to Joe's singing in the manner of Sonny Boy Williamson I, Brown's violin adding a looser line, swaying and shimmying like an exotic dancer. It was also Joe's plan to record what he called 'old-time songs'; musical archaeologists hoping for a glimpse of pre-blues stringband music will be disappointed – but listeners who know Joe's work well will not be surprised – to find that the repertoire is all blues or stomp tunes like 'Shake Your Boogie'. Even the track titled 'Breakdown', one of three Williams–Brown duets, is a blues. Still, this presents Joe as he had not been heard on disc since 1935, and would not be again.

Further recordings for Welding may be heard on the Testament VACs *Can't Keep From Crying* (TCD 5007), *The Sound Of The Delta* (TCD 5012), *Bottleneck Blues* (TCD 5021) and *Down Home Slide* (TCD 6009).

** These Are My Blues
Testament TCD 6010 Williams. 65?

Amplification and cavernous room sound give this concert recording at Rockford College, Illinois, an ambience unlike that of any other Big Joe Williams album. Another diversion from the norm is a stab at the country song 'You Are My Sunshine', but 'Boogie Chillun', after the briefest of nods to John Lee Hooker, is a minute or so of 'Mama Don't Allow Me To Stay Out All Night Long'. Many of the numbers are short like that, and the performance as a whole is monotonous, making this the least desirable of Joe's albums.

**(*) Rediscovered Blues
Capitol 29376 2CD Williams; Sonny Terry (h, v); Brownie McGhee, Lightnin' Hopkins (g, v); Jimmy Bond, unknown (b); unknown (d). c. 6/60, 10/68.

Joe's part of this collection is half a dozen tracks from one of the 'summit meetings' with Terry, McGhee and Hopkins (see the Terry–McGhee entry) and an album recorded in London in 1968, originally issued on Liberty as *Hand Me Down My Old Walking Stick*. As usual in this period (see *Highway Man* below) Joe played amplified guitar, sometimes with a slide, and the loss of detail in his playing is accentuated by the playing of the unidentified bassist and drummer, which is either martial or galumphing. It's unlikely that listeners who admire his Arhoolie and Delmark albums will find this one as much to their taste.

*** Going Back To Crawford
Arhoolie CD 9015 Williams; Austen Pete, John 'Shortstuff' Macon (g, v); Glover Lee Connor, Amelia Johnson (v). c. 3–5/71.

As several recordists discovered over the years, Big Joe had a wide circle of relatives and friends who were more than passable musicians. This absorbing collection focuses on a few of them, notably 'Shortstuff' Macon (1933–73), whose nine songs are played in a highly rhythmic style rather like that of Junior Kimbrough and the young R. L. Burnside. (In the '60s Joe's promotion of his young friend led to him making two and a half albums, but they remain unreissued.) Austen Pete is another singer/guitarist of limited technical means who nevertheless holds the listener's attention. Joe's own contribution is eight songs, some of them unique in his recorded repertoire, accompanied by himself and one or both of Pete and Macon.

*** The Sonet Blues Story: Big Joe Williams
Universal 98692523 Williams. 71/72.

'Hang It On The Wall' is not 'Shake it and break it and …', as per Charley Patton, but takes its title from a verse shared with Walter Rhodes's 'The Crowing Rooster', while 'Canary Bird' dodges back behind Muddy Waters to remember Sonny Boy Williamson I's 'Blue Bird Blues'. On the other hand, 'This Heavy Stuff Of Mine' is Joe's own 'Somebody's Been Borrowing That Stuff' and 'Jefferson And Franklin Blues' is related to his 'King's Highway'. In short, this is a skilful exercise in retrieval and reconstruction, entirely characteristic of Big Joe, and very well recorded in Sonet's studio.

*** Highway Man
Southland SCD 19 Williams. 2/72.

Amplified, Big Joe's guitar loses some of its polyphonic jangle but nothing in its thrust. Several tracks recall Charley Patton, and with much more fidelity than on *Classic Delta Blues*: compare that album's 'Pea Vine Blues' and this one's 'Pea Vine Whistle'. Otherwise the programme is mostly stock Williams material like 'Highway 61' and 'I'm Gonna Overhaul Your Machine', sometimes disguised by small lyric changes: 'Cherry Tree' comes from the same fruit-basket as 'Don't The Apples Look Mellow' and 'Mellow Peaches'.

**(*) Watergate Blues
Chrisly CD 30001 Williams; 'Pony-Tail Slim' [Axel Küstner] (h); B[ert] L. Logan (v). 3/73, 7–8/78.

*** No More Whiskey
Evidence ECD 26096 Williams; Cooper Terry (h); Lydia Carter (v). 3/73–10/80.

Apart from a few 1973 recordings made in Berlin when Joe was on tour, both these albums consist of material recorded at his home in Crawford. The recordist, Axel Küstner, evidently pressed him to dredge from his memory songs he had seldom performed before a microphone; among them on *Watergate Blues* are Roosevelt Sykes's 'Soft And Mellow' ('Stella Blues') and the title song, both greeted with hilarity by bystanders, and a version of Jim Jackson's 'Kansas City Blues' accompanied on Dobro, while *No More Whiskey* has a thoughtful version of Leroy Carr's 'Prison Bound Blues'. Both sets also embrace numerous gospel songs, some unaccompanied, and a few unaccompanied blues. Many of the tracks on *Watergate Blues* are short and the enterprise is chiefly of interest for its revelation of a 'hidden' repertoire. Inasmuch as it has more performances of normal length, *No More Whiskey* is a more typical Big Joe set, but the informal recording situation invests the proceedings with an attractive air of intimacy, and the three duets with Lydia Carter uncover yet another characterful singer of Joe's acquaintance. TR

L. C. Williams (1924/30–60)
VOCAL

Singer, drummer and dancer L. C. Williams was much influenced by Lightnin' Hopkins, and on his first record, for the

Houston label Gold Star (to which Hopkins introduced him), he was billed as 'Lightnin' Jr'. Based in Houston, he went on to record for Freedom, Sittin' In With and Mercury. According to Chris Strachwitz, he 'suffered from tuberculosis and was addicted to cheap wine.'

**** Texas Blues "The Gold Star Sessions"
Arhoolie CD 352 *Williams; Lightnin' Hopkins (p, g); Leroy Carter, Elmore Nixon (p). 47–48.*

The combination of Williams's resigned singing and Hopkins's mercurial guitar lines, as heard on five tracks, produces an effect almost indistinguishable from that of the young Hopkins, but whatever their inspiration, 'You'll Never Miss The Water' and 'Strike Blues' are performances of arresting gravity. Williams has eight pieces, his entire output for Gold Star, on this superb compilation; for the rest see its entry in COMPILATIONS: TEXAS.

Two similarly mesmerizing sides for Sittin' In With with Hopkins on guitar, 'Baby Child' and 'The Lazy J', are on the Hopkins CD *The Remaining Titles – Vol. 1: 1950–1961* (Document DOCD-5609).

**(*) The Big Three
Blue Moon CDBM 095 *Williams; poss. Nelson Mills (t); Conrad Johnson (as); Sam Williams (ts); Lonnie Lyons, Elmore Nixon (p); poss. Lightnin' Hopkins, unknown (g); Louis 'Nunu' Pitts (b); Allison Tucker (d). 49.*

Williams's Freedom recordings, six of which are gathered here, were mostly made with Conney's Combo, a group led by the altoist Conrad Johnson, and except for the slow eight-bar 'Ethel Mae' are in a jump-blues vein. Johnson is the principal soloist, but 'Shout Baby Shout' has a good boogie-woogie piano chorus. This is not the sort of material most likely to elicit Williams's best work, but 'Mean And Evil Blues', with piano and guitar accompaniment, captures much of the spirit of the Gold Star recordings. The transfers are excessively crackly. The other artists on *The Big Three*, also from the Freedom roster, are Big Joe Turner and the alto saxophonist Joe Houston. 'Mean And Evil Blues' is also on the VAC *Texas Guitar Killers* (Capitol 33915) with its original coupling, 'All Through My Dreams', both in much better sound but credited to Lightnin' Hopkins. TR

Lee Shot Williams (born 1938)
VOCAL

Williams made the usual Mississippi-to-Chicago journey and joined the band of his cousin, Little Smokey Smothers; he also sang with Magic Sam and Earl Hooker, and was Bobby Bland's opening act for a time. After 'I Like Your Style' was a regional hit in 1969, Williams became a fixture on the Southern soul circuit; he returned downhome in 1983.

*** Chicago Blues & Deep Soul Legend
Famous Groove FG-CD 972 063 *Williams; Emery Thompson, Stan Webb, unknowns (t); John Watson, unknown (tb); Gene Barge (as, ts); Sonny Seals (ts, bs); Monk Higgins, John Jackson, Dave Baldwin (ts); unknowns (s); Mack Simmons (h); Vince Willis, unknowns (kb); Detroit Junior, Sonny Thompson, unknown (p); unknowns (strings); Freddy Robinson, Bobby King, poss. U. S. Warren, Little Smokey Smothers, Buddy Scott, Joe Spell, Criss Johnson, unknowns (g); Phil Upchurch, Larry Bull, Nick Charles,* *unknowns (b); Billy Davenport, Donnell Hagan, Ira Gates, unknowns (d); unknown (syn d); unknown (cga); unknowns (v). 62–87.*

This collection brings together sides from singles, plus 'The Love You Saved', a strange blend of Civil Rights and marriage guidance from the LP *Country Disco*, which was inevitably better than its title. His debut 45 on Foxy is as hardcore bluesy as Williams ever got; on Federal, Bobby King's guitar impresses more than Williams, and they're both hindered by a bored, occasionally out-of-tune horn section. Following the success of 'I Like Your Style', Williams's music increasingly became soul with a touch of blues, and towards the end of the CD the amusingly macho 'Drop Your Laundry' and the Barry White pastiche 'On The Love Flight' foreshadow the leering on some of his Ecko output. Some of the source singles are in less than pristine condition, and some songs were clearly intended to be B-sides.

*** Cold Shot
Black Magic CD 9029 *Williams; Mike Barber (t); Big James Montgomery (tb); Charles Kimble (ts); Tony Zamagni (o, p); Little Smokey Smothers, James Wheeler (g); Johnny Gayden (b); Ray 'S. D.' Allison (d). 12/94.*

*** Hot 'Shot'
Ecko ECD 1006 *Williams; John Ward (kb, g, prog, rhythm tracks); Joseph McKinney (kb, v); Derrick Jackson (kb); Mark Lee, Rod Hearst, James Holly (g); Darrel James (d); Milton Price (prog, rhythm tracks); William Brown, Bertram Brown, Jackie Johnson (v). 96.*

**(*) She Made A Freak Out Of Me
Ecko ECD 1027 *Williams; Jim Spake (s); Derrick Jackson (kb); John Ward (g, rhythm tracks); William Brown, Bertram Brown, E. Nelson, Quinn Golden (v). 00?*

**(*) Somebody's After My Freak
Ecko ECD 1034 *As above, except add John Ward (sequencing), Morris J. Williams (v). 01?*

** Let The Good Times Roll
Wilson WIL 35 *Williams; Floyd Hamberlin (kb, d, d prog, v); Greg Miller, Chico Banks (g); Dick Fowler, Keith Stewart (v). 02.*

***(*) Get Down Tonight!
Ecko ECD 1058 *Williams; Jim Spake (ts); John Ward (g, rhythm tracks, sequencing); Morris J. Williams (perc, v). 03.*

*** Nibble Man
Ecko ECD 1067 *Williams; Scott Thompson (t); Jim Spake (ts, bs); James Jackson (kb); John Ward (g, rhythm tracks, sequencing); Bobby Manuel (g); Curtis Steele (d); Morris J. Williams, Brenda Williams (v). 04?*

Williams's Black Magic CD aims for crossover to white audiences. His gospely vocals are ably supported by all concerned; Smothers and Wheeler supply generous doses of the guitar work that signals 'Chicago blues' to many white fans. The outcome is good but not outstanding. Several tracks are overstretched, and on 'Drowning On Dry Land' Williams's conventional doubts about his ability to match up to Albert King turn out to be well-founded. Of the remakes, 'Drop Your Laundry' is musically superior to the original, but 'I Feel An Urge Coming On' and 'I'm Tore Up' are less successful.

Subsequent CDs have been aimed at Williams's core audience. *Hot 'Shot'* is among the most successful; there's extensive reliance (which has continued) on synthesizers and rhythm programming, but here they create some whiplash grooves and full arrangements. A driving 'Boogie Down On The Weekend' eclipses Black Magic's version, and Williams is in commanding form throughout, especially when reviving 'I Like Your Style' in, er, style.

The other Ecko CDs tell more tales of sneaking around, and issue more invitations to party down. 'She Made A Freak Out Of Me' and its follow-up tamper wittily with the lurve-god image so central to soul-blues, but by 'Freakology', on the third Ecko disc, the well has run dry. There's some fine singing on the *Freak* CDs, but they rely too heavily on label owner John Ward's compositions, which shuffle a limited range of melodic and rhythmic ideas. 'Somebody Blew The Whistle On Me' on the first of them is a strong song, though, and the list of possible whistle-blowers is a handy guide to Williams's fellow soul-blues singers.

During 2001, *You Turn Me On* (Diamond Lady 713D8) was reviewed in the blues press, but our best efforts have failed to find a source for it; let us know if you do better. There's little to commend about *Let The Good Times Roll*; producer Floyd Hamberlin wrote all the songs, but none of them is memorable, and the electronic instruments are used with far less flair than on Ecko – as *Get Down Tonight*, Williams's return to Ecko, proves. There's still a shortage of melodic ideas, but Williams's urgently intimate singing and Ward's confident handling of his real and synthesized musicians do a lot to overcome the problem. Being instructed to 'cha cha' in a song called 'Juke Joint Slide' is bemusing, but not as much as the presence of three unlisted remixes of it.

'That's Really What The Blues Is All About' on *Nibble Man* makes the point that blues isn't all sad songs, that it's music for having fun to; one may doubt, however, that it's therefore, in the title of another track, 'Nothing But Party Blues'. There are some good jokes here, told with good timing, and producer John Ward continues to make both the electronic and the real musicians swing; but the relentless emphasis on recreational sex becomes tiresome, and overwhelms the CD's considerable musical merits. It can reasonably be countered that this is music for grooving, not for passive listening, but more songs like the reflective and realistic 'You're Slackin' Up In The Bedroom' would still have made *Nibble Man* more interesting. CS

Leona Williams
VOCAL

All Leona Williams's records were made in New York; since she is described on one of them as a 'comedienne', she was presumably a stage artiste.

** Leona Williams & Edna Winston (1922–1927)
Document DOCD-5523 *Williams; Phil Napoleon (c); Moe Gappell, Miff Mole, Charlie Panelli (tb); Doc Behrendson, Jimmy Lytell (cl); Jimmy Durante, Frank Signorelli (p); Jack Roth (d). c. 1/22–c. 2/23.*

Eight days after Leona Williams's brief recording career ended, Bessie Smith's began, and Williams's bright, polished vaudeville blues started to become yesterday's music. Her accompanists, billed as 'Her Dixie Band', were the white jazz band better known as the Original Memphis Five. Winning favour with record companies as a cut-price version of the Original Dixieland Jass Band, the OMF compiled an enormous discography of semi-arranged music, much of it as rhythmically stiff as their accompaniments to Williams. There's some hot playing by Napoleon on 'Decatur Street Blues', by Signorelli on the last two of her 16 sides and by the whole band on 'Got To Cool My Doggies Now', but it's not characteristic; they simply don't challenge Williams enough. Her complete works are consequently of no more than passing interest, but she probably wouldn't have been much good whoever accompanied her. CS

Lester Williams (1920–90)
VOCAL, GUITAR, PIANO

A Texan, Williams formed his first group after wartime service in the US Army and cut his first record, 'Winter Time Blues', for the Macy's label in Houston in 1949. The producer, Steve Poncio, also supervised his early-'50s sessions for Specialty. He subsequently recorded for Duke and Imperial and worked in Texas and adjoining states.

**(*) Goree Carter Volume 2 (1950–1954)/The Remaining Lester Williams (1949–1956)
Blue Moon BMCD 6036 *Williams; prob. Dave Bartholomew, unknown (t); Ike Smalley, Blakey Broadis, Wendell Duconge, unknown (as); Ferdinand Banks, Johnny Spencer, Clarence Hall, Herb Hardesty, unknown (ts); Johnnie Mae Brown, James Hurdle, Salvador Doucette, unknown (p); Walter Nelson (g); James Moseley, Oscar 'Yogi' Adams, Frank Fields, unknown (b); L. D. Mackintosh, Luther Taylor, Cornelius Coleman, unknown (d); band (v). c. 4/49–6/56.*

** I Cant Lose With The Stuff I Use
Specialty SPCD-7037//[Ace CDCHD 476] *Williams; Frank Mims Jr (t or ts); Verdun Banks, Joseph Calloway, Robert Lacefield (ts); Johnnie Mae Brown (p); Oscar 'Yogi' Adams, unknown (b); Luther B. Taylor Jr, unknown (d). 1/52–1/53.*

While Williams's delivery is clearly inspired by the conversational manner of T-Bone Walker, the brassiness of his voice is distinctive enough to allay charges of mere copying. His earliest and best recordings are his ten for Macy's, gathered by Blue Moon (six are also on *Queen Of Hits: The Macy's Recordings Story* [Acrobat ACRCD 228]); among them are his hit 'Winter Time Blues', 'Dowling Street Hop' and the deliberate pastiche of contemporary New Orleans R&B in 'Texas Town'. Curiously, his last recordings, also on the Blue Moon CD, would unite him with the real thing in Dave Bartholomew's band. The title track of the Specialty CD has a fine bragging optimism, but otherwise his material isn't particularly striking, his singing is sometimes ponderous and more often than not his guitar is tuned a little off-pitch. To the eight recordings that were issued at the time the CD adds six unissued sides from the 1952 dates and a further eleven from a 1953 demo session at which Williams played piano or guitar with just bass and drums. 'Crazy 'Bout A Woman' or 'Balling Blues' might, with band arrangements, have made good slow blues B-sides, and a couple of other blues are listenable enough, but Williams, who never regarded himself as purely a blues singer, also took the opportunity to present several pop songs he'd written. The producer endured a full-length rendition of 'Fooling My Heart' but curtly waved Williams silent after a minute or so of 'Life's A Bed Of Roses' *et al.*, a verdict that present-day listeners will probably applaud. TR

Paul Williams (1915–2002)
ALTO AND BARITONE SAXOPHONES

Paul Williams's family moved from the South to Detroit, where he entered professional music from high school. 'The Hucklebuck' stayed on the charts for 32 weeks in 1949, spawning a dance craze and cover versions by many artists, both white and African-American. Nothing else matched its success, but 'The Hucklebuck' kept Williams and his band in live and recording work for years. He led the house band at Harlem's Apollo Theater in the mid-'50s, and later directed the bands of Lloyd Price and James Brown; after retiring from performance in 1964, he opened a booking agency.

**** **Volume 1 1947–1949**
Blue Moon BMCD 6020 Williams; John Lawton, King Porter [James Pope], Phil Guilbeau (t); Walter Cox (as, ts); Wild Bill Moore, Miller Sam, Billy Mitchell, Louis Barrett (ts); T. J. Fowler, Floyd Taylor (p); Hank Ivory, Herman Hopkins, John Holliday (b); Clarence Stamps, Reetham Mallett, Bill Benjamin (d); 'Muddy Water' [Alex Thomas], Johnny Cox (v). 9/47–1/49 or 7/49.

*** **Volume 2 1949–1952**
Blue Moon BMCD 6021 Williams; Jimmy Earl Brown (t, v); King Porter [James Pope], Phil Guilbeau, Blue Mitchell, Henry Boozier (t); Fred Jackson (as, ts); Ted Buckner (ts, bs); Billy Mitchell, Louis Barrett, Miller Sam, Joe Alexander, Shafi Hadi [Curtis Porter], Lee Pope (ts); Floyd Taylor, Lee Anderson, Richie Powell (p); Bobby Parker (g); John Holliday, Pete Glover, James Murphy, Sam Jones, Herman Hopkins (b); Bill Benjamin, Joe Booker, Reetham Mallett (d); Joan Shaw, Connie Allen, Danny Cobb (v). 1/49 or 7/49–52.

***(*) **Volume 3 1952–1956** [sic]
Blue Moon BMCD 6025 Williams; Danny Moore (t, ts); Jimmy Earl Brown (t, v); Henry Boozier, unknowns (t); Harlan Floyd (tb); Lee Pope, Noble Watts, unknowns (ts); unknowns (o); Richie Powell, Freddie Johnson, Cliff Smalls, unknowns (p); Larry Dale, Bobby Parker (g, v); Mickey Baker, unknowns (g); Sam Jones, Steve Cooper, George Washington, unknowns (b); Joe Booker, Belton Evans, Wilfred Eddleton, unknowns (d); Connie Allen, Little Willie John, Lena Gordon, Ethel Drew, band, unknowns (v). 52–62.

Williams managed to unleash his mellow, flowing alto from time to time, including on the big hit, but as Savoy recognized, it was the lead baritone's barking and lowing that made his records distinctive. 'The Hucklebuck' is on *Vol. 1* and, catchy though it is, it's difficult to fathom why it created such a sensation. It's in good company, however; Savoy's engineers knew all there was to know about reverb and, equally important, they recorded Williams with his working band. The first two discs cover the Savoy era, and *Vol. 1* is the better; even before 'The Hucklebuck', the band was full of enthusiasm and ideas, riding high on its popularity with live audiences. 'Thirty-Five-Thirty' and 'The Twister' are outstanding, but the general level of excitement is very high. It's easy to detect the application of structural formulas, notably in the build-ups to a climactic call-and-response between Williams and the band, but they do it so well. *Vol. 2* is in similar vein and also contains much to like, but it's downgraded by Jimmy Earl Brown's stentorian balladeering and the sub-Roy Brown vocals of Danny Cobb.

The last disc wraps up the post-Savoy output; Williams and his musicians trek from label to label, still trying hard for another hit, and making enjoyable music as they do so. Noble 'Thin Man' Watts's nervy energy adorns most tracks, and several numbers feature aggressive guitar by Larry Dale or Bobby Parker, who are also authoritative singers. (That anyone could make 'Suggie Duggie Boogie Baby' convincing is remarkable; Parker did so just before his 19th birthday.) It should be said, however, that alongside the excellent majority of tracks there's some fairly desperate trend-chasing, with the likes of 'Rock It Davy Crockett' and 'Don't Teach Me (To Mambo)'. CS

Robert Pete Williams (1914–80)
VOCAL, GUITAR, KAZOO

Williams was born in Zachary, near Baton Rouge, Louisiana, into a sharecropping family. In his teens or early 20s he began playing guitar, learning from local musicians and the records of Blind Lemon Jefferson. In the '30s he did some playing at house parties, specializing in the songs of Peetie Wheatstraw. In the late '50s he served three years for murder in the State Penitentiary at Angola, Louisiana, where he was extensively recorded by the folklorist Harry Oster. After being paroled in 1959 he continued to record for Oster, who produced several albums of his work, and in the '60s and '70s appeared at numerous festivals, including the 1966 AFBF, but he was never able to give up manual work.

**** **Volume 1: I'm As Blue As A Man Can Be**
Arhoolie CD 394 Williams. 59–60, 4/70.

**** **Volume 2: When A Man Takes The Blues**
Arhoolie CD 395 Williams; unknown (g); unknown (wb); poss. Sallie Dotson (v). 59–60, 4/70.

**** **Poor Bob's Blues**
Arhoolie CD 511 2CD Williams. 59–60s?

**** **Free Again**
Original Blues Classics OBCCD 553 Williams. 11/60.

**** **Rural Blues**
Ace CDCHD 705 Williams. 11/60.

Some artists use the blues, and we admire them for their ways with it. Some *are* the blues – in it and of it – and the notion of their having ways with it hardly seems applicable. Their music is prompted by other imperatives than giving a performance. Often they make their own rules of structure or harmony. This company is a small one, but if anyone belongs in it, it is Robert Pete Williams.

The typical Williams piece is a reflective blues underpinned by hypnotically repetitive guitar figures, generally in a modal structure. Sometimes his source of inspiration fills him with a tense, nervous excitability, which he acts out in frantic boogie playing. At other times he deserts the conventions of blues or boogie woogie and spins long free-form narratives or soliloquies. Verses from other people's songs appear quite often in his, but whole pieces seldom: some are 'Louise' on the first Arhoolie CD, Peetie Wheatstraw's 'Hot Springs Blues' on the second, Lightnin' Hopkins's 'Sad News From Korea' on *Poor Bob's Blues*, and 'Rolling Stone' and 'One Room Country Shack' (as 'A Thousand Miles From Nowhere') on OBC and Ace. (*Rural Blues* is a twofer containing *Free Again* and virtually all of another Bluesville LP, by Snooks Eaglin [q.v.].) 'Levee Camp Blues' on the first Arhoolie is a traditional Texas prison song, and the first two Arhoolies have several gospel items. But although individual songs sometimes have ostensible themes and leave specific impressions, it's equally possible to hear them as merged into a whole, 'The Robert Pete Williams Blues', of which his albums are different but equally valid excerpts. In that sense one Williams CD is as good as another — there is no such thing as a bad one – but when in the company of Harry Oster, who recorded all the albums we are presently considering, he seems to have felt more comfortable than in some other situations, freer to imagine and to invent.

*** **Long Ol' Way From Home: The Chicago Sessions**
Fuel 2000 302 061 391 *Williams*. 1–2/65.

A few of the tracks on *Poor Bob's Blues* (above) are live recordings (presumably from concerts organized by Oster at the University of Iowa, to which he moved from Louisiana in 1963), but the only full album of Williams in concert is this, taped by Norman Dayron at two campus engagements in Chicago. Responding to the setting, he is less discursive than on the Oster tapes, delivering what feels like a prepared setlist of themed songs: a 'Greyhound Blues' with a strong Tommy McClennanish rhythm, 'Louise' again, 'Freight Train Blues', 'Jessie [*sic*] James' and so on, with an unexpected intermission about halfway through when he does a 'Kazoo Blues'. Williams is no less individual than on his other albums, but public performance did restrain his creativity a little.

**** **Louisiana Blues//It's A Long Old Road**
Takoma CDTAK 1011//Aim 1014 *Williams*. 7/66.
***(*) **Robert Pete Williams**
Fat Possum 80349 *Williams*. 12/70.
*** **The Sonet Blues Story: Robert Pete Williams**
Universal 986 925–5 *Williams*. 71/72.
***(*) **Blues Masters Vol. 1**
Storyville STCD 8001 *Williams; Big Joe Williams (k)*. 3/72.
*** **Santa Fe Blues**
EPM Blues Collection 15783 *Williams; Larry Martin (p)*. 11/79.

The reappearance on *Louisiana Blues* of three songs Williams had previously recorded, 'Freight-Train Blues', 'Motherless Children Have A Hard Time' and 'Ugly', might suggest that his exposure to blues audiences had led him to solidify a working repertoire. He did have some standbys for concert use, as noted above, but they rarely impinged on his studio recordings; the programmes of the Fat Possum, Universal, Storyville and EPM CDs repeat hardly any songs he had recorded earlier. In any case, Williams was not given to simple repetition: the 'Ugly' on *Louisiana Blues* is a somewhat different creation from the 'Ugly Man Blues' on *Long Ol' Way From Home*, and neither is a replica of the earlier 'I've Grown So Ugly' on *Free Again*. Like John Lee Hooker, to whom he is sometimes compared, Williams seems to have been temperamentally incapable of producing final versions of his songs. Everything remained work in progress.

Louisiana Blues is an exceptional set. Williams plays with both intensity and accuracy (a combination he didn't invariably achieve), using a fine instrument. 'This Is A Mean Old World To Me' and 'It's A Long Old Road', archetypal segments of the ongoing musical autobiography, are separated by 'High As I Want To Be', where Williams more or less follows conventional blues harmony, an uncharacteristic move that he repeats in 'Matchbox Blues' on Fat Possum. He was evidently sitting near an open window or door when recording this album, for he is occasionally accompanied by a rooster. Storyville's set was more conventionally recorded, but is untypical in other ways: on four numbers Big Joe Williams blows trumpet-like responses on kazoo, and Williams plays the majority of the songs on 12-string guitar, now and then producing single-string runs that are more than usually baroque. He also plays slide (on six-string) on several numbers, not for the first time but with more facility than before. His voice is a little deeper and huskier now, which takes nothing away from his music and perhaps adds a further tint of blue to 'Talkin' Blues', a 13-minute account of his conviction and imprisonment, and of the 'Prisoner's Talking Blues' that helped to secure his parole, retailed over a slide guitar accompaniment reminiscent of Blind Willie Johnson. ('Prisoner's Talking Blues' is on the VAC *Angola Prisoners' Blues* [Arhoolie CD 419].) A further account of his prison time is retailed in 'Angola Penitentiary Blues' on *The Sonet Blues Story*, but the mood of this absorbing set, played on six-string guitar throughout, is generally more upbeat and sexy, as in 'Come Here, Sit Down On My Knee', 'Late Night Boogie', 'Goin' Out Have Myself A Ball' and 'You're My All Day Steady And My Midnight Dream'.

Williams's last record, *Santa Fe Blues*, was made only months before his death. There's some loss of accuracy in his fingering and he plays in fewer keys, but he pulls off his customary trick of sounding like no one but himself while never doing anything exactly as he had done it before. In fact, there are a few things here that he'd seldom done on record at all: another kazoo tune, a virtually unaccompanied song, 'The Woman I Got', and a rollicking duet with pianist Larry Martin on 'Goin' Thru The Bushes Like A Turkey Again'. Robert Pete Williams's life on record was an extraordinary musical journey, from singing his way out of a Louisiana penitentiary to making party music in Paris. We are fortunate to be able to follow him for so much of it. TR

Sharrie Williams (born 1965)
VOCAL

Williams got her start with a church choir in Saginaw, Michigan. Having survived abusive relationships and addictions, she leads her band, The Wiseguys, on the American and European festival circuits. Real Woman *and* Live At Wiseguys *have appeared on her own Faith 3 label, but are not readily available.*

** **Hard Drivin' Woman**
Crosscut CCD 11080 *Williams; Pat Brennan (kb, p); Pietro Taucher (p); James Owens (g, v); Lars Kutsche (g); Marco Franco (b); Sterling Brooks (d, v)*. 7/03–1/04.

Williams is billed as 'The Princess of the Rockin' Gospel Blues', which in practice means sounding like a poor imitation of Etta James; just how poor can be heard when she rips 'I'd Rather Go Blind' to shreds, eliminating any trace of subtlety, poetry or nuance. The rest of the CD consists of originals, most of them co-written with her musicians, although 'The Glory Train' owes more than is admitted to Curtis Mayfield's 'People Get Ready'. 'Selfish' and 'How Much Can A Woman Take', where Williams calms down and pays some attention to meaning, are not bad, but the rest of the disc is insufficiently differentiated rampaging, accompanied by formulaic blues-rock. CS

Sherman Williams
ALTO SAXOPHONE, VOCAL

A resident of Nashville, Tennessee, Williams began playing there in the '30s and by 1940 had his own group. In the late '40s and early '50s he worked on the West Coast, then returned to Nashville, where his trail goes cold.

** Sherman Williams 1947–1951
Classics 5076 *Williams; Charles Gillum, unknowns (t); unknown (tb); William Jones (ts); unknowns (s); Ed 'Skippy' Brooks (p, v); unknowns (p); unknown (g); James Brown, W. Robert, unknowns (b); Alvin Woods, Diz Small, unknowns (d); Iona Wade, Leonard Anderson, The Four Flames, band (v). 47–51.*

Williams's six- and seven-piece bands, and their repertoire of blues, up-tempo dance tunes and pop ballads, were obviously modelled on the jump-blues combos of Roy Milton, Joe Liggins and their kind. Heard at length, Williams's recordings are unimpressive: the material is formulaic, the intonation of the horns sometimes faulty and the sound quality indifferent. TR

Sonny Boy Williams
VOCAL, PIANO

Enoch Williams grew up in Indianapolis, reportedly studied at the Detroit Conservatory of Music and worked in New York from the late '30s onwards, playing at the Famous Door and other clubs and recording for Decca and Super Disc. He may have later moved to Chicago, where he was last heard of playing at the Regal Theater in 1958.

**(*) Sonny Boy Williams (1940–1947) + Yack Taylor, Nora Lee King
Document DOCD-5521 *Williams; Freddie Webster (t); unknown (as, ts); Chauncey Graham, unknown (ts); unknown (p); Jesse Jackson, unknowns (g); Joe Brown, unknowns (b); Cedric Anderson, unknowns (d); band (v); unknown (sp). 12/40–47.*

Williams is chirpy on a jive number like 'Poppin'' and intimate in 'I Want A Little Girl', but on these and the other two songs cut at his first date he is outmatched by his excellent, and unfortunately unidentified, saxophonist and guitarist. The boogie and blues material commissioned for his next session elicited piano playing with a light touch and, on 'Worried Life Blues', a vocal in a somewhat different style. The third Decca date returned him to hepcat repertoire like 'Savoy Is Jumpin'' and 'Rubber Bounce', with tight small-band arrangements and airy solos by Webster and the unidentified tenor player. His final date is by a piano trio, with more forceful piano playing on 'Jump It But Don't Bump It' and 'The Boogie Man'. On the evidence of his recordings Williams was only incidentally a blues performer, but they are estimable performances that may appeal to admirers of artists like Cecil Gant and the young Nat 'King' Cole. The CD's remaining space is filled with a blues coupling by the rasping Yack Taylor and five swing numbers by Nora Lee King (1909–95), of which 'Big Chump Blues' is notable as one of the few blues recordings with a solo on the sweet potato, or ocarina. TR

Warner Williams (born 1930)
VOCAL, GUITAR

Williams was born into a musical family in Takoma Park, Maryland, and from an early age he played in the streets in Prince George's County and nearby Washington, DC, and at juke-joints and house parties. Music became less central while he raised a family, but since retiring from his day job Williams has kept busy playing at festivals, clubs and schools, usually in a duo (billed as 'Little Bit A Blues') with his younger sidekick, Jay Summerour.

**** Blues Highway
Smithsonian Folkways SFW CD 40120 *Williams; Jay Summerour (h, whistling, v); Eddie Pennington (g). 3/93–4/95.*

Williams is a first-rate guitarist whose strong singing has a little of John Jackson's upper South twang. Also like Jackson, he seems to have learned much of an eclectic repertoire from records and the radio: well-known songs associated with Blind Boy Fuller (a very appealing 'Step It Up And Go'), Washboard Sam, Big Maceo and Big Bill Broonzy are among those on *Blues Highway*, which was recorded live at successive Wolf Trap Folk Festivals. More surprising are confident, jazzy versions of 'I'm Confessing That I Love You' and 'Honeysuckle Rose'. 'Mouse On A Hill', a reworked 'Froggie Went A-Courting', features some very deft picking, and a revival of Merrill Moore's 'Big Bug Boogie', with Travis-picker Eddie Pennington sitting in, also attests to Williams's fondness for country music. Where it appears, Summerour's chugging harp is supportive, and except on the rousing sign-off, 'Little Bit A Blues Theme', pleasingly unostentatious; valuably, he knows when to keep quiet. Summerour is also a witty whistler on a couple of tracks, and a pleasant harmony singer. There are no original songs on *Blues Highway*, but there's plenty of very skilful music-making. CS

Sonny Boy Williamson I (1914–48)
VOCAL, HARMONICA

John Lee Williamson was born in Jackson, Tennessee, from where he moved north as a young man; though usually thought of as a Chicago musician, he seems to have lived in St Louis until about 1940, making frequent visits to both Chicago and downhome. He was remembered affectionately by contemporaries as a generous, warm-hearted man, but liable to become aggressive when drunk. In his short life he defined what blues harmonica was supposed to sound like, and it's intriguing to wonder about the way both his music and the blues in general would have gone if he hadn't been fatally mugged at the age of 34.

**** Sonny Boy Williamson – Vol. 1 (1937–1938)
Document DOCD-5055 *Williamson; Walter Davis (p); Yank Rachell (md, g, sp); Robert Lee McCoy (g, v); Big Joe Williams (g, sp); 'Jackson' Joe Williams, unknowns (g). 5/37–6/38.*

***(*) Sonny Boy Williamson – Vol. 2 (1938–1939)
Document DOCD-5056 *Williamson; Walter Davis, Speckled Red (p); Yank Rachell (md, g, sp); prob. Willie Hatcher (md); 'Jackson' Joe Williams (g, sp); prob. Robert Lee McCoy, Big Bill Broonzy (g). 6/38–7/39.*

SONNY BOY WILLIAMSON I

**** Sonny Boy Williamson – Vol. 3 (1939–1941)
Document DOCD-5057 *Williamson; Walter Davis, Joshua Altheimer, Blind John Davis (p); Big Bill Broonzy (g); prob. William Mitchell (b); Fred Williams (d).* 7/39–4/41.

**** Sonny Boy Williamson – Vol. 4 (1941–1945)
Document DOCD-5058 *Williamson; Blind John Davis, Eddie Boyd (p); Big Bill Broonzy, Charlie McCoy, Ted Summitt, Big Sid Cox (g); prob. William Mitchell, Ransom Knowling, Alfred Elkins (b); Washboard Sam (wb); Jump Jackson, unknown (d).* 4/41–7/45.

**** Sonny Boy Williamson – Vol. 5 (1945–1947)
Document DOCD-5059 *Williamson; Big Maceo, Blind John Davis, Eddie Boyd (p); Tampa Red, Willie Lacey, Big Bill Broonzy (g); Ransom Knowling, Willie Dixon (b); Charles Saunders, Judge Riley (d).* 10/45–11/47.

**** Blue Bird Blues
Collectors Edition CBCD 018 *Similar to relevant CDs above.* 5/37–3/38.

***(*) The Bluebird Blues
BMG/Camden 569622 *As above.* 5/37–12/38.

*** Original Sonny
Blue Moon CDBM 113 *As above.* 5/37–7/39.

**** Sonny Boy Williamson Vol. 1 1937/1939
EPM Blues Collection 15760 *As above.* 5/37–7/39.

*** Nothing But The Blues
Collectors Edition CBCD 011 *As above.* 5/37–7/45.

(***) The Masters
Eagle EAB CD 082 *As above.* 5/37–7/45.

*** Chicago 1937–1945
Frémeaux FA 253 2CD *As above.* 5/37–10/45.

(***(*)) The Essential
Classic Blues CBL 200013 2CD *As above.* 5/37–11/47.

*** Bring Another Half Pint
Snapper Recall SMDCD 241 2CD *As above.* 5/37–11/47.

♔ **** Blue Bird Blues
Bluebird 55156 *As above.* 5/37–11/47.

(***) Good Morning Schoolgirl
[Blues Encore CD 52044] *As above.* 5/37–11/47.

*** American Blues Legend
Charly SNAP 116 *As above.* 5/37–11/47.

(***(*)) Good Morning, Little Schoolgirl
Snapper Complete Blues SBLUECD 027 *As above.* 5/37–11/47.

***(*) The Original Sonny Boy
Saga Blues 982 077-4 *As above.* 5/37–11/47.

*** Sonny Boy Williamson
MM 8420312 *As above.* 6/38–12/41.

**** Sonny Boy Williamson Vol. 2 1940/1942
EPM Blues Collection 15810 *As above.* 5/40–7/42.

**** Sonny Boy Williamson Vol. 3 1944/1947
EPM Blues Collection 15927 *Similar to relevant CDs above, except add Big Joe Williams (g, v).* 12/44–12/47.

**** Sonny Boy's Jump: R&B Began Here!
[Zircon Bleu 505] *Similar to relevant CDs above.* 7/45–11/47.

Famously, Sonny Boy Williamson had his name stolen (see Sonny Boy Williamson II under S). No doubt Aleck Ford's motives for taking John Lee Williamson's name in vain were mainly commercial but, even if unintentionally, by doing so he also paid tribute to the man's artistry. The first Sonny Boy was so influential that even his distinctive tongue-tied vocals were regarded by many harp players as worthy of imitation, but it's his playing that set the standard and defined the aesthetic for blues harmonica from his day to ours. He almost invariably played in second position, which favours note-bending, and he made much use of vocalized tones, hand muting and choked chords opening into melodic runs. His harmonica functions as a second, answering voice, filling the space between the vocal lines and commenting on them, making his music exciting and emotional whether it's a sad, slow blues or a jiving dance tune. Above all, Sonny Boy's music swings, and while he usually had naturally swinging musicians to back him on record, he leads from the front, insisting that his accompanists keep up the momentum, and refusing to let them coast. Only a ten-title session with Speckled Red and Willie Hatcher on Document's *Vol. 2* is an exception; the backing musicians stubbornly decline to get excited, and their microphones are poorly placed to boot.

Williamson's music was always developing: he started out playing the west Tennessee blues that he'd learned around Sleepy John Estes and Hammie Nixon, often plaintive but seasoned with dance tunes like 'I'm Tired Trucking My Blues Away'. By the end of his life, he was fronting hard-driving bands which prefigure the postwar Chicago blues sound with their electric guitars, rocking piano and powerful drumming.

Sonny Boy's very first recording gave definitive form to 'Good Morning, [Little] School Girl', and was one of a remarkable number of songs which became much-recorded standards. He turned out issuable first takes with great efficiency: his only studio date in 1939 produced 18 titles in a single day. Inevitably there are repeated effects and ideas, and some 'New' and 'No. 2' versions of hits, but there's no lazy surrender to uniformity. His music is extraordinarily exciting to hear at length, and not just for the playing; Williamson was also an outstanding songwriter, whether singing about his own life, his family and friends (his wife, Lacey Belle, as beautiful as her name, often features), Joe Louis, the progress of World War II or, in songs like 'Collector Man Blues', aspects of daily life in black America. Sonny Boy Williamson may be said to have kept the personal and passionate alive on Chicago blues records during the 'Bluebird beat' years, until Muddy Waters and Howlin' Wolf (his contemporaries, it should be recalled) came along.

Most of Williamson's recordings were reissued on LPs in at least decent sound, and Document's complete works benefit accordingly. Listening to these 124 tracks for this entry was a real treat, and if they were issued as a boxed set, it would get four stars. Readers who don't want the whole megillah are spoilt for choice and, since it's impossible to compile a musically bad Sonny Boy Williamson anthology, sound quality and presentation are the deciding factors.

Collectors Edition's *Blue Bird Blues* has Sonny Boy's first 24 recordings in phenomenal sound, copied from the deleted *Bluebird Recordings 1937–1938* (Bluebird 66723). The notes are adequate but also lifted, from *Nothing But The Blues* on the same label. This, like Magnum's *Original Sonny*, is markedly inferior listening; *Original Sonny* also advances the absurd and doubly inaccurate proposition that 'Never before had anyone played the instrument as a leading element[,] much less amplified!' (Williamson played live through an amplifier in later years, but never on record.) BMG/Camden's *Bluebird Blues* is a likeable selection from the early years, with brief notes and good but not outstanding mastering. Eagle's 18 tracks have recessive sound, and a note which patiently explains the difference between the two Sonny Boys. The CD is easily recognized by its cover picture of the wrong one. The Snapper Complete Blues collection is also distinguishable by a fine photograph of the wrong Sonny Boy, but its sound is much better, and the non-chronological ordering of its 24 tracks is skilfully done.

Of the other single-volume surveys, Charly have acceptable sound, but the programming is unbalanced: three tracks from Williamson's first session, one from later in 1937, one from 1941, then a jump cut to 1945–47 and the R&B bands. Better conceived, if it can be found, is Zircon Bleu's rocking 25-tracker drawn entirely from the later years; it also has superior transfers. MM's 22 tracks, ordered non-chronologically, are adequately remastered, and carry brief, entry-level notes in French. Saga offer ten tracks showing Williamson's musical transition *From The Country To The Big City*, and ten from the postwar sessions, summarized as *From Blues To Rhythm & Blues*. The 'country' chapter of the story is disposed of pretty quickly, and the notes repeat the incorrect assertion that Williamson played amplified harp on the later recordings, but this is otherwise an enjoyable and enlightening collection. Blues Encore's reproduction varies from good on the later sides to very ordinary on the earlier ones; the notes are largely confined to rehearsing the tracklisting. By some distance, the best single-volume survey of Sonny Boy's career as a whole is the latest to be named after his 'Blue Bird Blues': issued on a revived Bluebird label by the material's owners, it has excellent, warmly present sound and extensive, historically informed notes.

EPM's three discs, which are available separately, collectively constitute a sort of Document-lite set, containing 66 well-chosen, well-remastered tracks, or about half Williamson's output under his own name. *Vol. 3* concludes with two of his magnificent accompaniments to Big Joe Williams. Of the double CDs, Snapper Recall and Frémeaux both have extensive notes (not wholly reliable on Frémeaux, notwithstanding some interesting *aperçus*), and both are let down by relatively lifeless transfers; in Frémeaux's case, these are sometimes from less than pristine 78s. *The Essential* is a lot better in this regard (and incidentally is the only collection using material from Sonny Boy's debut session to omit 'Good Morning, School Girl'); however, Classic Blues' chronological hopscotch means that early tracks sometimes give a false impression of listlessness when heard immediately after later, inherently louder material. Given their brevity, the notes do a heroic job of expounding Sonny Boy's career and his importance, but don't alleviate the absence of discographical information. CS

Ralph Willis (1910–57)
VOCAL, GUITAR

Willis settled in New York in the '30s. He was nicknamed "Bama", which is thought to refer to both his birthplace and his countrified ways. His music is thoroughly Carolinian and, for its time and place, oldfashioned. Willis recorded for a number of labels, but scored no hits, nor, despite his friendship with Brownie McGhee, did he intersect with the folk revival.

*** Ralph Willis – Vol. 1 (1944–1950/51)
Document DOCD-5256 Willis; Brownie McGhee (g, v); unknown (g); unknown (b, v); Dumas Ransom, unknown (b); unknown (d); Pete Sanders (wb); Judson Coleman (v). 44–8/50.

*** Ralph Willis – Vol. 2 (1950/51–1953)/Leroy Dallas (1949–1962)
Document DOCD-5257 Willis; Sonny Terry (h); Brownie McGhee (g, v); Dumas Ransom, Gary Mapp, unknown (b); unknown (d). 8/50–1/53.

Willis was always conscious of his audience and keen to entertain; even when he sings 'Blues, Blues, Blues' the mood is amused resignation, not introverted self-pity, and he signposts his solo with 'Gonna play a little bit for you, now'. His delivery is sometimes almost manically ebullient, as when he revives 'Shake That Thing', or does a solo version of 'Church Bells'. A later 'Church Bells' with a small band is very different in mood, and both versions are different again from Luke Jordan's original; during his label-hopping career Willis rerecorded a number of songs, but the varied accompaniments and enthusiastic delivery mean that there's no sense of stale repetition. Many of Document's tracks come from distressed originals, but Willis is worth the surface noise; he could never be described as a major artist, but he was a versatile, swinging guitarist (not all the good solos are by Brownie McGhee), an expressive singer and an often witty lyricist.

Document's second volume includes eight songs by Leroy Dallas (1909–67); like Willis, Dallas was an Alabamian playing downhome Carolinian blues in New York, often with Brownie McGhee in support. Highlights are a rocking 'Jump Little Children Jump' and a 'Baby Please Don't Go' that owes little to Big Joe Williams.

Willis recorded four songs which Jubilee did not issue; they have all appeared on CD, but at present only two are available, on *"Too Late, Too Late"* – *Vol. 10* (Document DOCD-5601). CS

Willie Willis (born 1932)
VOCAL, GUITAR

Born in Fairfield, Texas, Willis learned guitar while at school. He settled in Dallas after military service in Korea, working in a hotel and making music in local bars at weekends.

** Can't Help But Have The Blues
Fedora FCD 5009 Willis; Wilford Sims (as, ts); Jessie Ray (kb); Hash Brown (g); Bobby Henderson (b); Roach (d). 4/98.

Willis is an adequate guitarist, but in need of the support he gets from Hash Brown. The rest of the band are on the same workmanlike level as Willis; Sims, who generates pithily apposite solos from time to time, is the best of them. Willis's singing is an unsubtle holler, occasionally varied with a rasp, and it doesn't do much to sell the material. He's credited with all the songs except Albert King's 'Laundromat Blues', although 'Deep Ellum Boogie' is a lightly rewritten 'Boogie Chillen'. These two numbers make it obvious that Willis is no great shakes as a songwriter either. CS

Michelle Willson (born 1958)
VOCAL

Based in Boston, Willson began singing blues in the early '90s, having previously sung in a soul band; among her models are Dinah Washington and Ruth Brown. She won a Blues Foundation talent competition in 1993, and has retained a loyal following on the New England blues circuit.

*** Evil Gal Blues
Bullseye Blues CD BB 9550 Willson; 'Porky' Cohen (tb); Scott Shetler (cl, ts); 'Sax' Gordon Beadle (ts); Barry Fleischer (bs); Sugar Ray Norcia (h, v); Ron Levy (o); Ken Cook, Harry Van Walls (p); Joe Craig Jones, Darby Hicks Jr (g); Randy Bramwell (b); Stephen D. Brown (d). 94.

** So Emotional

Bullseye Blues CD BB 9580 Willson; Scott Aruda (t); Russell Jewell (tb); Gordon Beadle (as, ts); Scott Shetler (ts, bs); Greg Piccolo (ts); Barry Fleischer (bs); Ron Levy (o, p, g, vb, wh, v); Chuck Chaplin (p); Mike Williams (g); Randy Bramwell, Jesse Williams (b); Steve Brown (d, perc); Ed Scheer (perc); Sugar Ray Norcia, Buck Taylor, Bird Taylor (v). 96.

It's impossible not to notice Willson's vocal similarity to Dinah Washington when she sings numbers associated with her like 'Evil Gal Blues' and 'Long John Blues', and even more so on 'Big Long Slidin' Thing' (the allusion is to Porky Cohen's instrument), but she has listened to other singers, and has her own tricks besides. She also fronts a very competent jump-blues band that swings enthusiastically through a repertoire partly derived from Buddy Johnson, Floyd Dixon and their contemporaries, partly furnished by Willson herself and her producer Ron Levy. Cameo appearances are made by members of Roomful Of Blues and, for a couple of tracks on *Evil Gal Blues*, the former Atlantic Records house pianist Harry Van Walls.

*** Tryin' To Make A Little Love

Bullseye Blues & Jazz 9610 Willson; Charlie Miller (t); Craig Klein (tb); Scott Shetler (cl, bcl, ts, bs); Scott Billington (h, v); Dave Limina (o, p); Cranston Clements (g); James Singleton (b); Johnny Vidacovich (d); Hunderto 'Pupi' Menes (perc); Charles Elam III, Curtis 'Blo' Watson (v). 98.

** Wake Up Call

Bullseye Blues & Boogaloo BBCD 9639 Willson; Scott Shetler (bcl, ts, bs, v); Barry Fleischer (ts, bs, v); Ken Clark (o, v); Dave Limina (p); Mike Mele (g); Zac Casher (d); Jill Gross, Ellie Marshall, Didi Stewart, Scott Billington (v). 12/00–2/01.

The chief drawback with Willson's first two albums was that she occasionally burdened herself with unexciting songs. For *Tryin' To Make A Little Love* her new producer, Scott Billington, introduced fresh material, some by non-generic writers; 'Half Past The Blues', a late-night narrative with a touch of Tom Waits, elicits a dry Martini vocal that is Willson's best on record. It also has stylish piano by Dave Limina, one of only two musicians from her regular band; the producer sidelined the others in order to use New Orleans session players. On *Wake Up Call*, however, Willson is reunited with old friends, here billed as the Evil Gal Festival Orchestra, an extravagant title for a four-piece group with a couple of extras. The album is let down a little by genre pieces to which Willson finds it hard to bring much new, such as Buddy Johnson's 'They Don't Want Me To Rock No More'. She does smoulder very effectively on the title track, but the album as a whole smokes more than it burns. TR

Edith Wilson (1896–1981)
VOCAL

A 1906 birth date is often quoted, but Mrs Wilson knocked ten years off her true age. She entered show business at 15 in a trio with her husband-to-be, Danny, and his sister Lena. Mrs Wilson spent the '20s and '30s in cabaret and revue, visiting Europe several times. In the '40s she emphasized acting, appearing on radio in Amos 'n' Andy before becoming the living embodiment of 'Aunt Jemima', a pancake mix trademark. In this role, Wilson hosted charity fundraisers until 1965, when Civil Rights groups persuaded Quaker Oats that the character was demeaning. She made occasional appearances at festivals and colleges until not long before her death.

**(*) Johnny Dunn & Edith Wilson – Vol. 1 (1921–1922)

RST Jazz Perspectives JPCD-1522 Wilson; Johnny Dunn (c); poss. Bud Aiken, Herb Flemming, Earl Granstaff (tb); Herschel Brassfield (cl, as); Garvin Bushell, Ernest Elliott (cl); Dan Wilson, Leroy Tibbs, unknown (p); Will Tyler, unknown (vn); Johnny Mitchell (bj); Harry Hull (bb). c. 9/21–c. 9/22.

**(*) Edith & Lena Wilson – Vol. 2 (1924–1931)

Document DOCD-5451 Wilson; Elmer Chambers, unknowns (c); Charlie Gaines, Bubber Miley, unknown (t); prob. Teddy Nixon, Wilbur De Paris, prob. Charlie Irvis, unknown (tb); Hilton Jefferson, unknowns (cl, as); poss. Bob Fuller (cl, ts); prob. Don Redman, Emerson Harper (cl); unknown (as); Happy Caldwell, unknown (ts); Fletcher Henderson, Earres Prince, Harry Brooks, Earl Fraser, unknowns (p); unknown (vn); prob. Charlie Dixon, Sam Speed, unknown (bj); 'Alabama Joe' [Roy Smeck], Bernard Addison, unknowns (g); unknown (bb); unknown (b); unknown (d); 'Doc' Straine (v); unknown (sp). 1/24–10/30.

Edith Wilson was a singer, not just a blues singer, and personal expression is not a priority on her collaborations with Johnny Dunn, the last two of which are on *Vol. 2* (RST Jazz Perspectives JPCD-1523). Dunn's Original Jazz Hounds had a good feel for the blues, but the leader's bugle calls and staccato runs are oldfashioned, and the arrangements permutate a limited stock of ideas. Wilson is melodious, but has to sing loud to impose herself on the band and the recording technology. The results are often interchangeable, but 'Frankie' and 'Rules And Regulations "Signed Razor Jim"' stand out for their gusto and, less happily, 'Mammy, I'm Thinking Of You' is a landmark of sentimentality.

There's more variety and better sound on the later recordings. Two sides with Roy Smeck's limping guitar are not typical of the musical quality, but neither is the fine Fletcher Henderson group on the preceding pair. Even a band led by Bubber Miley leans towards sweet dance music, and there's a preponderance of show tunes and cabaret novelties, sung clearly and rather impersonally.

*** He May Be Your Man ... But He Comes To See Me Sometime!

Delmark DD 637 Wilson; Leon Scott, Leroi Nabors (t); Preston Jackson (tb); Oliver Alcorn, Franz Jackson (cl); Little Brother Montgomery (p, v); Ikey Robinson (bj, g); Truck Parham, Ed Wilkinson (b); Red Saunders (d). 5/73–4/75.

In her late 70s, Edith Wilson retained her strength, elegance and accuracy. Accompanied by a lineup of distinguished veterans, she reprises some of her hits, adds some blues standards, and closes with a disarmingly pretty 'Put A Little Love In Everything You Do'. Wilson and Montgomery are asynchronous on the vaudeville duet 'That Same Dog', and 'My Handy Man Ain't Handy No More' is revived with no conviction whatever, but good sound, the band's comfortable swing and Wilson's charm make this her best recording. CS

Hop Wilson (1921–75)
VOCAL, STEEL GUITAR

Hardy or Harding Wilson grew up in Crockett, Texas, where he began playing guitar about the age of ten or 11, and soon

afterwards obtained his first steel guitar. From the mid-'50s onwards, based in Houston, he played with drummer Ivory Lee Semien, recording for Goldband and later for Semien's Ivory label. In the last couple of years of his life he played regularly at the Hayes Lounge in Houston.

*** **Steel Guitar Flash! Plus**
Ace CDCHD 240 *Wilson; unknown(s) (brass); Henry Hayes (ts); unknowns (s); Willie Jackson (h); Elmore Nixon, unknown (p); Fenton Robinson (g, v); Pete Douglas (g); Ice Water, Clarence Green, Slim Parker, unknowns (b); Ivory Lee Semien (d, v); unknown (d); Larry Davis (v). 58–2/62.*

*** **Houston Ghetto Blues**
Bullseye Blues CDBB 9538 *As above, except omit Hayes, Jackson, Ice Water, Green. 10/60–2/62.*

As a steel guitarist Wilson is not much given to startling manoeuvres with bar and pick; his strong point is his sour, blue intonation. He recorded a few up-tempo instrumental novelties ('Dance To It', 'Why Do You Twist', 'Chicken Stuff') but his most effective performances are slow blues like 'I Met A Strange Woman' (Roosevelt Sykes's 'Mistake In Life') or 'Broke And Hungry', where the forlorn singing finds contorted echoes in the guitar playing. Ivory Lee Semien brings a peppier manner to the vocal mike for the rock 'n' roll numbers 'Rockin' In The Coconut Top' and 'Your Daddy Wants To Rock', and there are unexpected appearances by Larry Davis and Fenton Robinson. 'Toot Toot Tootsie Goo'bye' is not the Al Jolson song (which would have been something in Wilson's hands) but a medium-tempo instrumental blues featuring the horns and borrowing the riff from 'You Can't Sit Down'. *Steel Guitar Flash! Plus* has all these and more, 29 tracks in all; *Houston Ghetto Blues*, with 18, omits all the 1958 Goldband sides but otherwise covers the same ground, adding a further take of 'Merry Christmas Darling' which was left off the Ace, evidently by accident. TR

Jimmy Wilson (1923–65)
VOCAL

Wilson was a gospel singer before he was a bluesman, but fell in with the Oakland record producer Bob Geddins, who wrote several songs for him, most importantly 'Tin Pan Alley'. The guitarists Lafayette Thomas (1932–77) and Johnny Heartsman, who both worked with him, remembered him as an excellent singer, but he was unable to recapture the success of 'Tin Pan Alley' and eventually succumbed to alcoholism.

*** **Jumpin' From Six To Six**
Official 5256 *Wilson; unknown (t); Que Martyn, Wild Willie Moore, unknown (ts); unknowns (bs); King Solomon, unknowns (p); Lafayette Thomas, Clarence Garlow, unknown (g); Johnny Heartsman, unknowns (b); unknowns (d); unknowns (v). 51–61.*

'Tin Pan Alley' was the kind of accident that can unseat a career. A mean-streets lyric, Wilson's yearning vocal and Lafayette Thomas's guitar, distorted as if filtered through water, combine to make one of the most mesmerizing performances of its time. But it was a hard act to follow. Wilson admitted as much by repeatedly reconvening its musicians and re-creating its ominous cadences, as in 'Tell Me', 'I Used To Love A Woman', 'I Found Out' and 'Blues In The Alley'.

His earlier work had echoed current West Coast models.

'Honey Bee' and 'Please Believe In Me', from his first session in 1951, uncovered a balladeer with a handsome baritone, half Charles Brown, half Jimmy Witherspoon, while 'Every Dog Has His Day' (1952) was a flagrant imitation of Lowell Fulson. Through these and later costume changes Wilson retained a crucial accessory, Thomas's guitar, which dances like a dervish in 'A Woman Is To Blame' and 'Oh Red'.

This valuable compilation plunders Wilson's discography, concentrating on the early '50s and acknowledging only cursorily his mostly awful later recordings for Goldband and Duke. The remastering has introduced odd sound effects on several tracks, and 'Tin Pan Alley' sounds even weirder than it really was, but at the time of writing this album offered the only CD access to a representative selection of Wilson's work. TR

Kim Wilson (born 1951)
VOCAL, HARMONICA

The Detroit-born Wilson co-founded the Fabulous Thunderbirds in 1974 and is the only original member still playing in the band. He also had a spell singing with Roomful Of Blues. One of the most prolific guest-appearance suppliers of the last 20 years, he has recorded with Lou Ann Barton, Al Copley, Ronnie Earl, Kirk Fletcher, Sue Foley, Steve Freund, Alfred 'Snuff' Johnson, The JW-Jones Blues Band, David Maxwell, John McVey, Pinetop Perkins, Kid Ramos, Katie Webster and doubtless others.

**** **My Blues**
Blue Collar Music BCM 7107 *Wilson; Scott Steen (t); Tom Fabre (ts); Fred Kaplan (p); Junior Watson, Kid Ramos, Rusty Zinn (g); Larry Taylor (b); Richard Innes (d). 10–12/96.*

With his early-'90s albums for Antone's, *Tigerman* and *That's Life*, deleted, Wilson's own-name catalogue currently starts with *My Blues*. The record itself starts with a Roy Milton song, 'Everything I Do Is Wrong', from which it becomes clear, first, that the musicians have this kind of relaxed small-band music at their fingertips and, second, that Wilson is a thoroughly convincing singer, virile, unmannered and bluesy. As the album proceeds a third characteristic emerges: Wilson picks songs that are both well suited to him and absorbing in their own right, drawing on a thick folio that embraces pieces like Eddie Boyd's 'Five Long Years' (outstanding piano by Kaplan here), Jerry McCain's 'Things Ain't Right', done in the style of an early Muddy Waters–Little Walter–Jimmy Rogers work, three by Little Walter himself and a couple by Roosevelt Sykes. On several of the numbers Wilson leaves his harps aside, giving solo space to one or another of the impeccably period-styled guitarists, but when he does pick one up he plays it with the technical command and fat tone for which he's celebrated. This is an exceptionally fine album, worth any amount of hunting.

*** **Smokin' Joint**
M.C. MC-0043 *Wilson; Mark Stevens (p); Rusty Zinn, Billy Flynn, Kirk Fletcher, Troy Gonyea (g); Larry Taylor (b); Richard Innes (d). 2/99, 12/00.*

*** **Lookin' For Trouble**
M.C. MC-0049 *Wilson; Scott Aruda (t); Sax Gordon Beadle (ts); Doug James (bs); Mark Stevens (kb); Troy Gonyea (g); Jon Ross (b); Steve Ramsay, Richard Innes (d). 02.*

Smokin' Joint was recorded at two gigs almost two years apart, at the Rhythm Room in Phoenix, Arizona, with Zinn and Flynn on guitars, and at the Cafe Boogaloo in Hermosa Beach, California, with the Fletcher–Gonyea team. (Fletcher has since joined Wilson in the Fabulous Thunderbirds.) The listener coming to it after *My Blues* will find it informatively different, its generally longer performances (five are on the far side of six minutes, a couple a little too far) prompting extended harp solos. The title track is an object-lesson in how to maintain interest through five minutes of a standard up-tempo 12-bar instrumental; Wilson plays all the way, ideas flowing in an uninterrupted stream. *Lookin' For Trouble* gives us the more diversified music Wilson probably finds easier to achieve in a studio setting, Chicago-style numbers like 'Money, Marble [*sic*] & Chalk', 'Tried To Ruin Me' and Walter Horton's 'Love My Baby' alternating with more West Coastish arrangements like 'Down With It' and 'Hurt On Me' and the New Orleans styling of 'Hook Line & Sinker'. The title track comes in two guises, Texas shuffle and rock 'n' roll. These M.C. albums give impressive accounts of Wilson's methods in different circumstances, but *My Blues* remains, so far, his masterwork. TR

Lena Wilson (c. 1898–c. 1939)
VOCAL

Born in Charlotte, North Carolina, Wilson moved to New York in 1921 and quickly made a name on the stage and by recording for practically every label in the blues business. She toured Europe with the Blackbirds Of 1926 company, was in Sam Wooding's Creole Revues in 1928 and sang with Cliff Jackson's orchestra at New York's Lenox Club in 1929 and later.

(*) Lena Wilson – Vol. 1 (1922–1924)
Document DOCD-5443 *Wilson; prob. Johnny Dunn, Elmer Chambers, prob. Gus Aiken, unknown (c); unknown (t); Herb Flemming, prob. Teddy Nixon, unknowns (tb); Garvin Bushell, Don Redman, unknowns (cl); Coleman Hawkins (ts); Porter Grainger, Fletcher Henderson, prob. Perry Bradford, poss. George Rickson, unknowns (p); John Mitchell, prob. Charlie Dixon, unknown (bj); Lincoln Conaway, unknown (g); Clarence Conaway, unknown (u); unknown (bb); unknown (d). c. 9/22–c. 3/24.*
(*) Edith And Lena Wilson – Vol. 2 (1924–1931)
Document DOCD-5451 *Wilson; Cliff Jackson (p). 2/30–7/31.*

Wilson's ready availability for recording dates made her a busy woman: in the 18 months spanned by *Vol. 1* she recorded for nine companies, producing the 23 sides heard here, two on *Female Blues – The Remaining Titles (1921–1928)* (Document DOCD-1005) and four that have not been recovered. Her accompanying bands vary enough in composition and style to maintain a keen listener's interest in the two versions of 'Deceitful Blues' and three of 'Memphis Tennessee', but it is not until midway through the CD that one can really begin to gauge the quality of her voice and interpretation, when she sings 'Your Time Now' and 'I Need You To Drive My Blues Away' with Fletcher Henderson on piano. She is not a weighty blues singer in the Ma Rainey or Bessie Smith mould, but an appealing vaudeville stylist who can give a song emotional colour, though, as Howard Rye observes in his notes *à propos* songs like 'Bleeding Hearted Blues', not necessarily the colour that would seem to be suggested by the lyrics. 'Hula Blues' is an early example of a blues accompanied by a Hawaiian-style trio of steel guitar, guitar and ukulele.

After six years away from the recording studios, she returned to cut half a dozen sides with pianist Cliff Jackson. (These are her contribution to the *Vol. 2* she shares with her contemporary Edith Wilson.) Like numerous other singers at this time she chose, or was requested, to concentrate on suggestive material like 'Chiropractor Blues' ('Just lay me on your table, start to work the way you should – 'cause the way you rub me seems to do me so much good') and Andy Razaf's metaphorical tour de force 'My Man O' War'. TR

Smokey Wilson (born 1936)
VOCAL, GUITAR

Robert Lee Wilson is a Mississippian who, after a few years playing with 'Booba' Barnes, Frank Frost and their friends, moved away not to Chicago but to LA, where he settled at the beginning of the '70s. As co-owner of the Pioneer Club he led the house band and accompanied visiting acts, but by the '80s he had become well known in his own right as a staunch upholder of oldfashioned Southern juke-joint blues.

(*) 88th Street Blues
Blind Pig BPCD 5026 *Wilson; Rod Piazza (h); Honey Piazza (p); Hollywood Fats (g); Larry Taylor (b); Richard Innes (d). 83.*
*** Smokey Wilson & the William Clarke Band
Black Magic BMCD 9013 *Wilson; William Clarke (h); Fred Kaplan (p); Junior Watson, Joel Foy, Alex Schultz (g); Willie Brinlee (b); Eddie Clark, John Moore (d). 11–12/86.*

88th Street Blues, originally issued on the Murray Brothers label, is the earliest of Wilson's albums that is readily available. (A couple of Big Town sets from the '70s, reissued in Japan on P-Vine, may still be in print.) Anyone unfamiliar with the artist need only run an eye over the tracklisting to place a safe bet on his background: two songs by Howlin' Wolf, one by Elmore James, others by John Lee Hooker and Jimmy Reed. The recording studio may have been in California, but the wellsprings of Wilson's music rose far away in the Deep South, and his stylistic brothers are gruff blue-collar bluesmen like Byther Smith who have never cut their connection with Chicago blues of the '50s and '60s; '88th Street Blues' itself bears some similarity to Smith's 'I Don't Like To Travel'. The set with the William Clarke Band has similar affiliations – songs by Reed and Hooker (the latter's 'Dimples', again) and a downhome Howlin' Wolf impression, on which Clarke is superb – but also ropes in 'The Things I Used To Do' and Johnny Copeland's 'I Wish I Was Single'. The recording is clearer than *88th Street Blues* and the bandwork superior, but on both albums Wilson proves himself a vigorous, attacking singer and guitarist with a wholehearted involvement in his music.

*** Smoke N' Fire
Bullseye Blues CDBB 9534 *Wilson; Joe Campbell (t); William 'Dr Z' Zimmerman (ts); Ron Levy (o, p); Jimmy McCracklin (p); Terry 'Big T' DeRouen (g); James B. Wyatt, Larry Davis (b); Craig Kimbrough (d). 93?*
*** The Real Deal
Bullseye Blues CDBB 9559 *Wilson; Ron Levy (o); Preston Shannon, Darby Hicks Jr [Ron Levy] (g); Lawrence Baulden (b); James Gadson (d). 95?*

*** The Man From Mars
Bullseye Blues CDBB 9581 *Wilson; Scott Thompson (t); Jim Spake (ts, bs); James 'Icepick' Harman (h); Ron Levy (o, p); Andrew 'Jr Boy' Jones (g); Chris Jones (b); Charles 'Sugar Boy' Jones (d). 97?*

These Ron Levy productions seem at times to be trying to distance Wilson from the Mississippi–Chicago axis of his earlier work – *Smoke N' Fire*, for example, relocates him in a funkier context – but he proves difficult to budge, and with only a few exceptions presents himself as a sort of Californian Magic Slim, delivering throaty blues and twisting, snarling guitar lines. Occasionally he looks farther into the past, as in *The Real Deal*'s 'Son Of A … Blues Player' or the early-Muddy-styled 'Feel Like Going Home', but only to demonstrate his personal development by shifting gear, for the rest of the set, into tough electric blues. The Wolf tracks that were statutory on his earlier albums disappear from *Smoke N' Fire* but reappear in pairs on both the subsequent albums. Any of the three CDs will give pleasure to the listener who appreciates Wilson's approach, but none is much different from the others, and perhaps only admirers will need more than one. TR

U. P. Wilson (1935–2004)
VOCAL, GUITAR

Huary Perry Wilson's given name soon mutated into the easier to pronounce U. P. Born in Louisiana, he began playing around Dallas and Fort Worth as a teenager, in company with Zuzu Bollin, Nappy Chin and Robert Ealey. With the latter he formed a guitar-and-drum duo, the Boogie Chillun Boys. In the '80s Wilson's tough music acquired a new audience in Europe.

*** On My Way
Fedora FCD 5014 *Wilson; Bill Eden, Wilford Sims, 'Worm' (s); Steve 'Hook' Herrera, Paul Orta (h); Matt McCabe, Mike Kinred (kb); Eddie James Stout (b); Freddie Walden (d). 88.*

***(*) Texas Blues Party Vol. 1
Wolf 120.630 *Wilson; Tutu Jones (g); Herb Abbs (b); Tyrone Starks (d). 6/94.*

*** Boogie Boy! The Texas Guitar Tornado Returns!
JSP JSPCD 2158 *Wilson; Jerrold Feigenbaum (t); Curtis Massey (s); Ronnie Wilson (kb); Johnny Coronado, Don Lange (g); Pat Trimble (b); Joe Coronado (d); Alanda Williams (v). 94.*

**(*) This Is U. P. Wilson
JSP JSPCD 266 *Wilson; Carl Smoot (ts); Jim Plummer, Dave Jeffery (h); Gary Hampton, Jeff Denny (kb); Don Lange, Holland K. Smith, Mike Penland, Tone Sommer (g); Doug Zabel, Herb Abbs, Chris Thomas, Chris Brewer (b); Steve Meek (d). 8/95.*

**** Whirlwind
JSP JSPCD 277 *Wilson; Jordan Patterson (h); Big Joe Turner (o, b); Shawn Kellerman (g); Anthony Gonzales (b); El Torro Gamble, Steve Meek (d). mid-96.*

**** Booting
JSP JSPCD 2129 *As above, except Turner does not play o. mid-96.*

*** The Good The Bad The Blues
JSP JSPCD 2103 *Wilson; Bill Eden (s); James Hinkle, Tone Sommer, Satch Wig (g); Phil Friend, Chris Brewer, Doug Zabel (b); Steve Meek (d); Johnny Mack (rb); Robert Ealey, Kenny Taylor, Oklin Bloodworth, Johnny Mack (v). 98.*

*** Best Of – The Texas Guitar Tornado
JSP JSPCD 808 *Similar to above five CDs, except add Danny Ross (kb), Bobby Gilmore (g, v), Chuck Rainey (b), Danny Cochran (d). 94–98.*

U. P. Wilson's music incorporates many elements of Southwestern blues, among them the juke-joint rowdiness of Frankie Lee Sims, high-speed note-spinning which recalls Pee Wee Crayton, and the more sophisticated sounds of Lowell Fulson and T-Bone Walker. Nevertheless, Wilson was an original whose music, songwriting and showmanship had been honed by years of competitive gigging in the rougher parts of town, and he made few concessions to the expectations of white audiences.

Indeed, *On My Way*, originally released for local consumption on the bassist's label, has more covers, and of more obvious songs, than do later releases. It's a respectable effort – U. P. even manages to inject passion into 'Mean Old World' – but it's also the first of several CDs to prove that horns and keyboards do Wilson's music no favours. His aggressive playing and singing are best heard fronting a bare-bones rhythm section, not reclining on a bed of harmonies.

Hear, for instance, *Texas Blues Party*, which presents Wilson live at Schooner's in Dallas; 'One Hand Boogie' and 'One Hand Blues' feature a self-evident gimmick, but even without the visual impact the guitar complexities that Wilson produces are arresting. More important, these tracks and the rest of the disc are hard-edged, no-frills guitar blues that hardly ever become self-indulgent, even on some very long numbers.

In contrast, JSP's first two releases suffer from musician overload, and *This Is U. P. Wilson* is further damaged by the use of assorted Dallas wannabes, perhaps with a view to keeping costs down. Even so, it's worth hearing for Wilson's unexpected deployment of a mellow, high-pitched singing style which sometimes sounds a little like the ghost of Joe Pullum. *The Good The Bad The Blues* is oversupplied with guest guitarists and vocalists, and comes across as a collection of available material rather than a unified presentation.

Pick of the litter are *Whirlwind* and *Booting*, derived from a session held in London during a European tour. Their presiding spirit is the tooth-rattling, bacchanal-kindling sound of Frankie Lee Sims, but it's by no means the only one: 'I Believe', on *Booting*, revives the Crowley swamp-blues sound, and on *Whirlwind* 'Who Will Your Next Fool Be?' takes a very unusual look at John Lee Hooker. On the same disc the jazzy instrumental 'Juicin" makes for laidback contrast, and Turner's discreetly plump Hammond on this track and four others makes a satisfying exception to the rule about horns and keyboards. These, rather than JSP's *Best Of* (which includes two tracks from VACs), are the best of U. P. Wilson. CS

Edna Winston
VOCAL

Nothing is known about Edna Winston beyond her recordings, which were made in New York.

*** Leona Williams & Edna Winston (1922–1927)
Document DOCD-5523 *Winston; Tom Morris (c); Charlie Irvis (tb); Bob Fuller (cl, as); Mike Jackson (p); Buddy Christian (bj). 11/26–2/27.*

Edna Winston's eight songs are the work of seven different composers, but despite the odds they all have strong melodies and interesting lyrics; Winston returns the favour by intelligently matching delivery to content. Her easy, relaxed swing and warm, open tones are supported by a consistently excellent and responsive band. It's a pity that Winston cut so few sides, and a greater pity that she's paired on this disc with the tedious Leona Williams. CS

Johnny Winter (born 1944)
VOCAL, GUITAR, MANDOLIN, HARMONICA

John Dawson Winter III grew up in Beaumont, Texas. He and his younger brother Edgar began playing together before they were in their teens and after winning a talent contest recorded 'School Day Blues', which was a local hit. All through the '60s Johnny played in Texas clubs, often backing older blues singers, and recorded for local labels, often under pseudonyms. After a story in Rolling Stone *about a '130-pound cross-eyed albino bluesman with long fleecy hair playing some of the gutsiest blues guitar you have ever heard', he signed with Columbia and made the acclaimed* Johnny Winter (1969), *but his career in the '70s was hindered by drug dependency. He produced Muddy Waters's last albums for Blue Sky, and made some well-received albums for Alligator in the '80s, but in recent years has been only intermittently active.*

As a Winter's tale this is an abridged version. In common with many of his fans, we believe that his time in the rock arena was less profitably spent than his more blues-oriented periods, and although we touch on the former we are chiefly concerned with his blues work.

** Texas Blues
Snapper Recall SMDCD 185 2CD *Winter; Edgar Winter (s, o, p); unknowns (s); D. Holiday (g); I. P. Sweat, Tommy Shannon (b); N. Samaha, Uncle John Turner (d); unknowns (v).* 8/62–c. 69.
*(*) Suicide Won't Satisfy
Thunderbolt CDTB 192 *Similar to above.* 63–c. 69.
** Black Cat Bone
Thunderbolt CDTB 193 *Similar to above, except add Calvin 'Loudmouth' Johnson (v).* 63–c. 69.
** Birds Can't Row Boats
Relix 2034 *As above.* 63–c. 69.

These CDs were derived from the voluminous archive of the Houston producer Roy C. Ames, a figure most safely described as controversial, who recorded Winter both in studios and informally over a period of about eight years. (Ames's Winter tapes furnished Thunderbolt with at least nine other albums, all of dubious availability.) Much of this material is journeyman studio work by a versatile young musician: covers of popular R&B numbers like 'Parchman Farm' and 'Road Runner', original songs in similar styles, the occasional oldie such as 'Harlem Nocturne', which features Edgar on sax and probably also organ, a faint aroma of flower power in 'Birds Can't Row Boats (Spiders Of The Mind)' and even, in 'Avocado Green', an attempt to write in the style of Bob Dylan. It's fair to say of some of these efforts that if Winter's name weren't involved only historians of kitsch would have any regard for them, but amid the motley are several arresting solo blues like 'Low Down Gal Of Mine', possibly inspired by Blind Lemon Jefferson and played on 12-string, the Robert Johnson songs '32-20 Blues' and 'Kindhearted Woman Blues', and a 'Goin' Down Slow' done in Johnson's manner. All these tracks are on *Texas Blues*, and some also on one or other of the Thunderbolts and Relix. *Suicide Won't Satisfy* opens arrestingly with a brief pastiche of Skip James ('My Baby') but only a few of the subsequent tracks are worthwhile. The somewhat better *Black Cat Bone* has a different version of 'Goin' Down Slow', a Buddy Guyish accompaniment to Calvin 'Loudmouth' Johnson on 'Take My Choice' and wild slide on the title track. Production values throughout the four CDs vary, as on all Ames's recordings, from adequate to abysmal.

***(*) The Progressive Blues Experiment
ITM 960009//EMI Europe 832685//One Way 57340//Razor & Tie 82210//BGO CD 457 *Winter; Tommy Shannon (b); Red [Uncle John] Turner (d).* 67/68.

Recorded at the Vulcan Gas Company, a club in Austin, without an audience, *The Progressive Blues Experiment* originally came out on a small Texas label, Sonobeat, but was reissued (by Imperial) about the same time as his Columbia debut (see below). Although the latter occupied most of the spotlight that was being trained upon Winter, prompting even the strict English magazine *Blues Unlimited* to call him 'the best male, white blues guitarist there ever was', some reviewers preferred the rawer production of *The Progressive Blues Experiment*, and it has continued to find admirers ever since. The influence of Muddy Waters hangs over it like a dark blue cloud, from the opening 'Rollin' And Tumblin'' through 'Tribute To Muddy' (actually 'Still a Fool', Muddy's version of 'Catfish Blues') to the acoustic 'Bad Luck and Trouble', which is modelled on Muddy's early work with Little Walter and has Johnny doubling harmonica, mandolin and National steel guitar. Other songs come from Blind Willie McTell, Slim Harpo, Sonny Boy Williamson II, B. B. King and Howlin' Wolf, while 'Mean Town Blues' deploys the riff of John Lee Hooker's 'Boogie Chillun', but his sources are less the point than the deftness with which he shifts his technical gears, from throbbing slide lines through Hookeresque chords to the single-string picking of 'It's My Own Fault'.

*** Johnny Winter
Columbia 471218 *Winter; Edgar Winter (s, kb); Walter Horton (h); Tommy Shannon, Willie Dixon (b); Uncle John [Red] Turner (d, perc).* early 69.
*** Johnny Winter
Columbia SNY 85734 *As above.* early 69.

Whether Winter's major-label debut still sounds as momentous as it did 30-odd years ago is doubtful, but to check you would need to find someone who remembers the late '60s, and ... well, you know how the joke goes. One's inclined to think not, but it remains a solid blues album, with fine performances of songs associated with Muddy Waters ('Mean Mistreater'), Lightnin' Hopkins ('Back Door Friend') and B. B. King ('Be Careful With A Fool'). Winter plays the last with enormous panache and sings it as if choking on a brownie. A couple of cuts are solos with acoustic slide guitar. The second issue listed has three extra, previously unreleased, tracks: another version of 'Dallas', 'Country Girl' and Bobby Bland's song 'Two Steps From The Blues'.

*** Second Winter
Columbia/Legacy COL 511231 2CD *Winter; Edgar Winter (s, kb, o, p, harpsichord, v); Tommy Shannon, Dennis Collins (b); Uncle John [Red] Turner (d, perc).* 7–8/69, 4/70.

Thanks to tracks like 'I'm Not Sure', where the Winter

brothers engage in an electrifying duet of mandolin and harpsichord, *Second Winter* has become enshrined as a key document of early blues-rock freakoutery, though other tracks like 'Memory Pain' and 'Hustled Down In Texas' are less outré. But while its 2004 reissue (with two previously unissued bonus tracks) in a luxurious package will warm the Winter fan's heart, it's the other disc in the set that may commend itself more to the blues enthusiast, since it offers a previously unissued concert at the Royal Albert Hall, London, in 1970, with colossal 11-to-12-minute versions of 'It's My Own Fault' and 'Mean Town Blues'. The downside is that these are followed by the equally long but less than colossal 'Tobacco Road', featuring Edgar's alto, and 'Frankenstein', featuring Edgar's ego. Still, you can always take it off after track 6.

**(*) Still Alive And Well
Columbia Rewind CK 66421 Winter; Jeremy Steig (fl); Rick Derringer (g); Randy Hobbs (b); Richard Hughes (d). 73.
*** Captured Live!
Columbia CK 33944 Winter; Floyd Radford (g); Randy Hobbs (b); Richard Hughes (d). 74.
(*)/* Still Alive And Well/Captured Live!
BGO CD 478 As for above two CDs. 73–74.

For Winter the early '70s were a highway needing more careful negotiation than fast-moving rock stars can often manage. There were times when, in both senses, he came off the road. A man not yet out of his 20s who calls his new album *Still Alive And Well* may be telling us something about his physical or mental health, although his more attentive fans probably had some idea that neither was in A-1 shape. For blues aficionados the standout tracks will probably be 'Rock Me Baby' and 'Too Much Seconal', based on a song by J. B. Hutto. 'Silver Train' was written for Winter by Mick Jagger and Keith Richards, and both there and in 'Let It Bleed' Winter and Derringer create a Stones-like ambience with spirit and skill. The sardonic country song 'Ain't Nothing To Me' is an unexpected treat, too. The Columbia Rewind issue adds two tracks, 'Lucille' and 'From A Buick 6', to the original album's contents; these are not on BGO's twofer. *Captured Live!*, released in 1976, may have been assembled from concert dates a couple of years earlier; the band is the one he took to Europe in the fall of '74, with guitarist Floyd Radford, who leaps into the action on the opening 'Bony Moronie' with enormous gusto and keeps the heat turned up throughout the album. There are nods to the Stones again ('It's All Over Now'), Bob Dylan ('Highway 61 Revisited') and John Lennon ('Rock & Roll People'). 'Sweet Papa John' is an eloquent self-advertisement aimed at bringing female listeners to their knees. Winter's turbulent out-of-time guitar intro heralds his bluesiest playing on the album, and a storming finale.

*** Nothin' But The Blues
Columbia CK 34813 Winter; James Cotton (h); Pinetop Perkins (p); Bob Margolin, Luther 'Guitar Jr' Johnson (g); Calvin Jones (b); Willie 'Big Eyes' Smith (d); Muddy Waters (v). 3/77.

Made while Winter was producing Muddy Waters's albums for Blue Sky, between *Hard Again* and *I'm Ready*, this set brought heartening news to those of Winter's admirers who hadn't heard much they really liked for some years. 'TV Mama' (not the Big Joe Turner song) is done solo with acoustic slide guitar, Winter's genial singing hinting, perhaps, that he might have primed himself with a small sherry. Others are with the full Waters band, the leader himself making an appearance on the closing 'Walking Thru The Park'.

** Live At The Texas Opry House
Thunderbolt CDTB 185 Winter; unknown (b); unknown (d). 1/78.

A mess of an issue. 'Wipeout', as well as being miscredited to Chuck Berry, occupies not the stated 6.25 but 9.10 (most of it a drum solo), 'Brown Eyed Handsome Man' runs to 6.40 rather than 1.30, and 'Hideaway', declared to be 9.25, lasts less than two minutes before being faded out. 'Last Night' plays in place of 'Mississippi Blue' (which should be 'Mississippi Blues') and vice versa. The sound quality is mediocre and most of Winter's spiels to the audience should have been left on the editing-room floor. Irredeemable? No: there are passages of bravura guitar playing in 'Brown Eyed Handsome Man', 'In The Wee Wee Hours' and 'Come On In My Kitchen'. But most tracks are either too long or too short, and only a devotee need bother with it.

*** White Hot Blues
Columbia/Legacy 487848 Winter; various accompaniments. 69–79.
(***) Scorchin' Blues
Columbia CK 52466 As above. 69–79.

Seven albums are plundered for the 19 tracks on *White Hot Blues*, a useful summary of Winter's Columbia years and, with its strong emphasis on blues material ('Leland Mississippi Blues', 'Too Much Seconal', 'Divin' Duck', etc.), a recommendable starter pack for the blues-loving listener coming to him fresh. *Scorchin' Blues* covers the same period but with only ten tracks hasn't the space to do it justice.

***(*) Guitar Slinger
Alligator ALCD 4735 Winter; Don Tenuto (t); Jim Exum (tb); Terry Ogolini, Gene Barge (ts); Steve Eisen (bs); Billy Branch (h); Ken Saydak (kb); Johnny B. Gayden (b); Casey Jones (d). early 84.
***(*) Serious Business
Alligator ALCD 4742 Winter; Jon Paris (h); Ken Saydak (p); Johnny B. Gayden (b); Casey Jones (d). 85.
*** Third Degree
Alligator ALCD 4748 Winter; Mac 'Dr John' Rebennack, Ken Saydak (p); Johnny B. Gayden, Tommy Shannon (b); Casey Jones, Uncle John 'Red' Turner (d). 86.
*** DeLuxe Edition
Alligator ALCD 5609 As for above three CDs. early 84–86.
*** The Return Of Johnny Guitar (The Best Of Johnny Winter 1984–86)
Music Club MCCD 270 As above. early 84–86.

Pared of excess, stocked with songs that played to his strengths, Winter's Alligator albums gave his music the focus and control that had been missing from some of his earlier and more indulgently produced recordings. Of the 30 songs only half a dozen go beyond five minutes, and the prolix playing of his live albums is condensed into solos that say as much in one or two choruses. Whoever chose the material knew what he was doing: numbers like 'Trick Bag', 'Lights Out' and 'Boot Hill' on *Guitar Slinger*, or 'Murdering Blues' (Dr Clayton's 'Cheating And Lying Blues') on *Serious Business*, are precisely tuned to Winter's combination of vehemence and good humour. *Serious Business* ends with a torrent of Chuck Berryish guitar on 'Route 90' and *Third Degree* opens with a neat fusion of J. B. Lenoir and Elmore James in a viciously slide-accompanied 'Mojo Boogie'. Elsewhere, though, *Third Degree* betrays a slight return to guitar showoffery, somewhat offset by two acoustic duets on which Winter plays both slide and rhythm guitar, a Muddyish 'Evil On My Mind' and a 'Bad Girl Blues' about women who (*snicker*) like women.

DeLuxe Edition and *The Return Of Johnny Guitar* are evenhanded deals from the Alligator pack, with 14 and 12 cards respectively, and seven in common. *DeLuxe* regrettably recycles 'Bad Girl Blues' but two of its tracks, 'Georgianna' from '86 and 'Nothing But The Devil' from '84, are previously unissued and give it the edge.

*** Live In NYC '97
Virgin 45527//(E) VPBCD 43 *Winter; Mark Epstein (b, v); Tom Compton (d).* 97.

A focused, high-energy all-blues set, excellently recorded so as to convey the ambience of the night at the Bottom Line without compromising the clarity of Winter's vocals or the balanced dynamics of the trio. Although it lacks little of the intensity caught on previous concert recordings, Winter's performance is calmer and more controlled than it might once have been, and his guitar playing is always to the point. TR

Jimmy Witherspoon (1923–97)
VOCAL

Witherspoon paid one brief and memorable visit to LA as a teenager but returned to his native Arkansas and didn't settle in California until after World War II. While serving with the US Marines he was stationed in Calcutta, where he sang with Teddy Weatherford's band. In 1945 he took over from Walter Brown as the blues singer for the Jay McShann orchestra. Recordings, first under McShann's aegis and then in his own name, established him in the R&B market until the '50s, when, unlike his model Joe Turner, he found no niche in rock 'n' roll, but after a momentous appearance at the 1959 Monterey Jazz Festival he had a secure residence for the rest of his career on the frontier between jazz and blues.

**** Ain't Nobody's Business
[Blue Boar CDBB 1018] *Witherspoon; Major Evans, Clarence Thornton, Forrest Powell, Vernon Smith (t); Edmund Gregory, Theodore Smalls, Frank Sleets (as); Cleophus Curtis, Seeward Evans, Charlie Thomas, Maxwell Davis, Buddy Floyd (ts); Milburn Newman (bs); Jay McShann, Frankie Whyte (p); Mitchell 'Tiny' Webb, Louis Speiginer (g); Raymond Taylor, Percy Gabriel, Benny Booker, Ralph Hamilton (b); Jesse Price (d, sp); Al 'Cake' Wichard, Edward Smith, Pete McShann, Jesse Sailes (d).* 45–48.
**** Confessin' The Blues
[Zircon Bleu 509] *As above.* 45–48.
**** Gone With The Blues
Jasmine JASMCD 3002 *As above, except add Emmett Berry, unknown(s) (t), Theodore Donnelly (tb), Charles Q. Price, Don Hill, unknown (as), Buddy Tate, Vido Musso (ts), unknowns (s), Bill Doggett, Henry McDade, Gene Gilbeaux (p), Charles Norris, unknown (g), Bill Davis, Herman Washington, unknown (b), Chico Hamilton, Henry Green, unknown (d).* 45–5/49.

**** Spoon Sings The Blues 1946/1950
EPM Blues Collection 16009 *As above, except add Ben Webster (ts), Willard McDaniel (p), Mickey Champion (v); omit Major Evans, Gregory, Curtis, Taylor.* 7/46–50.
*** Call My Baby
Night Train NTI CD 7004 *Witherspoon; Forrest Powell, Vernon Smith (t); Frank Sleet (as); Charles Thomas, Buddy Floyd, Maxwell Davis (ts); Milburn Newman (bs); Frankie Whyte, Jay McShann (p); Louis Speiginer, Tiny Webb (g); Benny Booker, Ralph Hamilton (b); Edward Smith, Pete McShann, Jesse Sailes (d).* 10/47–48.
*** Cold Blooded Boogie
Night Train NTI CD 7008 *As above, except add Emmett Berry (t), Theodore Donnelly (tb), Charles Q. Price (as), Buddy Tate (ts), Bill Doggett (p), Chico Hamilton (d).* 10/47–48.
**** Jimmy Witherspoon 1947–1948
Classics 5051 *Similar to above.* 10/47–48.
*** Nobody's Business
Jazz Colours 874721 *Similar to above.* 10/47–48.
**** Ain't Nobody's Business: The Essential Jimmy Witherspoon Volume One
[Indigo IGOCD 2525] *As for* Cold Blooded Boogie, *except add unknown (t), unknown (as), Ben Webster (ts), Willard McDaniel, unknown (p), unknown (g), Bill Davis, unknown (b), Al 'Cake' Wichard, unknown (d); omit Floyd.* 10/47–50.
*** Jimmy Witherspoon & Jay McShann
Black Lion BLCD 760173 *Witherspoon; Forrest Powell (t); Frank Sleet (as); Charles Thomas (ts); Milburn Newman (bs); Jay McShann (p); Louis Speiginer, Tiny Webb (g); Benny Booker, Ralph Hamilton (b); Pete McShann, Jesse Sailes (d).* 11/47–48.
***(*) Jimmy Witherspoon
Blues Forever CD 68008 *Similar to* Gone With The Blues. ?10/47–49.
**** Jimmy Witherspoon 1948–1949
Classics 5080 *Witherspoon; Vernon Smith (t); Don Hill, unknown (as); Buddy Floyd, Maxwell Davis, Vido Musso (ts); Milburn Newman (bs); Jay McShann, Henry McDade, Gene Gilbeaux (p); Tiny Webb, Charles Norris, unknown (g); Ralph Hamilton, Bill Davis, Herman Washington, unknown (b); Jesse Sailes, Al 'Cake' Wichard, Henry Green, unknown (d).* 48–5/49.

All these CDs slice and dice 'Spoon's recordings for West Coast labels such as Mercury, Supreme, Down Beat and Modern. The 'Spoon of these early years was obviously influenced by Joe Turner but not in thrall to him. Even on boisterous up-tempo sides he sings with less huff and puff, while in an occasional slow piece like 'Long About Dawn' he reveals a tenderness that is beyond Turner's range. Sometimes the songs are fortune cookies containing witty or topical messages, as in 'Skid Row Blues' or 'Hey Mr. Landlord', where 'Spoon comments wrily on the fabric of ghetto life: 'There's plenty ventilation where the wall caved in, natural air-conditioning right where the roof should have been.' The point of 'Shipyard Woman Blues' – roll on peacetime, so that women will quit the workforce and overalls and return to being homemakers in dresses – may have been humorous at the time, but it ushered in a series of misogynistic songs to which 'Spoon put his name. The accompaniments are by small jump bands of consistently high quality.

There is a great deal of overlap between these CDs. The Blue Boar and Zircon are almost identical, and the Jasmine and Blues Forever CDs are not very different either from them or from each other, though the latter has fewer tracks. The two-part 'Ain't Nobody's Business', 'Spoon's first hit and now a blues standard, is on every CD except the last Classics, and 'Skid Row Blues', 'Money's Getting Cheaper', 'Spoon Calls Hootie', 'Hey Mr. Landlord' and others are on most. In value-for-money terms, the Blue Boar, Zircon, Jasmine, Classics and Indigo sets, each with 24–26 tracks, are all highly recommendable, though at the time of writing all but the Classics and Jasmine CDs were of uncertain availability. The EPM, which pushes slightly ahead of the others to reach 1950, is also long, well selected and cheap. Jazz Colours break the pattern slightly by inserting a couple of McShann instrumentals, 'McShann Bounce' and 'Jumpin' With Louis'. The Black Lion is only half a 'Spoon album, the remaining tracks being by McShann groups with other vocalists or none.

**** Jimmy Witherspoon
Ace CDCHM 1062 *Witherspoon; Charles Gillum, unknowns (t); Don Hill, Jewell Grant (as); Jack McVea (ts, bs); Buddy Floyd, Maxwell Davis, Vido Musso, Bumps Myers (ts); unknowns (s); Jay McShann, Henry McDade, Gene Gilbeaux, Willard McDaniel, unknown (p); Charles (Chuck) Norris, Tiny Webb, unknowns (g); Bill Davis, Ralph Hamilton, Herman Washington, Red Callender, unknowns (b); Al 'Cake' Wichard, Jesse Sailes, Henry Green, Ray Martinez, unknowns (d). 48–51.*

**** Blowin' In From Kansas City
Ace CDCHD 279 *Witherspoon; unknowns (t); unknown (as); Buddy Floyd, Maxwell Davis, Vido Musso, Ben Webster (ts); unknowns (s); unknown (o); Jay McShann, Henry McDade, Willard McDaniel, unknown (p); Charles (Chuck) Norris, Tiny Webb, unknowns (g); Bill Davis, Ralph Hamilton, unknowns (b); Al 'Cake' Wichard, Jesse Sailes, unknowns (d); unknown (vb); Mickey Champion (v). 48–52.*

**(*) Jay's Blues
King KCD 6008 *Witherspoon; John Anderson, Harry Parr Jones (t); John Ewing (tb); Floyd Turnham (as, bs); Jewell Grant, unknown (as); Maxwell Davis, Jesse Jones, Jimmy Allen, Cleveland Williams, unknown (ts); Clyde Dunn, Jim Wynn (bs); Earl Jackson, Buster Harding, unknown (p); Tiny Webb, Willie Scott, Harold Grant, unknown (g); Ralph Hamilton, Red Callender, Eurales Jefferson, Mario Delagarde, unknown (b); Robert Sims, Billy Douglas, Mitchell Robinson, Al Bartee, unknown (d); The Lamplighters, band (v). 6/52–12/53.*

**(*) Spoon So Easy: The Chess Years
MCA/Chess MCD 93003//Chess CHLD 19108 *Witherspoon; unknown (t); unknown (tb); Eddie Chamblee, Harold Ashby, unknowns (ts); Lafayette Leake, Floyd Dixon, Jay McShann, unknown (p); Lee Cooper, unknowns (g); Willie Dixon (b, v); unknowns (b); Fred Below, unknowns (d); unknown (perc); unknown (v). 6/54–8/56, 1/59.*

Jimmy Witherspoon and Blowin' In From Kansas City are both excellent selections from 'Spoon's years on Modern. The latter finds him looking both forward and back: 'T.B. Blues' is a surprising revival of Victoria Spivey's composition, and 'The Dr Knows His Business' of Georgia Tom's 'Terrible Operation Blues', but 'Rain, Rain, Rain' and the two-part 'I'm Just Wandering' are harbingers of the more measured vocal style 'Spoon developed in the '60s. 'Goin' Around In Circles' is another report from the sexual battle zone – 'I thought all women knew how to love, honour and obey,' 'Spoon sighs regretfully – but softened by magnificent tenor from Ben Webster. *Jimmy Witherspoon* reissues an ancient Crown LP with eight additional items from around the same time, dovetailing neatly with the other CD. Several of the tracks are atmospheric live recordings in which singer and audience conduct a vivid exchange of punchline and response. *Jay's Blues*, derived from King's Federal label, occasionally peeps round the corner to 'Spoon's '60s style ('The Day Is Dawning') but much of the material and accompaniment is rather ordinary, and the King studio echo is tiresome. The mildew stains of echo also tarnish *Spoon So Easy*, an odd collection: some of the songs suit 'Spoon, others don't, and the backings are for the most part sketchy, as if the producer thought he was making demos.

♕ **** The 'Spoon Concerts
Fantasy 24701 *Witherspoon; Roy Eldridge (t); Urbie Green (tb); Woody Herman (cl); Coleman Hawkins, Ben Webster (ts); Gerry Mulligan (bs); Earl Hines, Jimmy Rowles (p); Vernon Alley, Leroy Vinnegar (b); Mel Lewis (d). 10–12/59.*

***(*) Tougher Than Tough
Blue Moon CDBM 123 *Witherspoon; Ben Webster, Teddy Edwards (ts); Gerry Mulligan (bs); Richard 'Groove' Holmes (o); Jimmy Rowles, Paul Moer (p); Herman Mitchell (g); Leroy Vinnegar, Jimmy Bond (b); Mel Lewis, Frank Butler (d). 12/59, 60.*

The first 'concert' on the Fantasy CD is the Monterey Jazz Festival of 10/59. 'Spoon stepped on to the stage a marginal figure, an R&B singer sidelined by rock 'n' roll, an artist with hardly any viable context. He left it, half an hour or so later, a man remade, cresting a wave of applause for a masterly exhibition of jazz-blues singing. True, he could hardly have had better collaborators. Some of them are not much in evidence, but Ben Webster melts the heart with his solo on 'Ain't Nobody's Business'. Two months later, at the Renaissance Club in LA, 'Spoon recorded ten titles with Webster and the Gerry Mulligan Quartet. His readings of 'C.C. Rider', 'Outskirts Of Town' and 'St. Louis Blues' are among the finest these much-sung pieces have experienced, and Mulligan adorns Leroy Carr's 'How Long' with a solo of quiet fervour. *Tougher Than Tough* contains all the Renaissance gig but exchanges the Monterey set for half a dozen tracks from 'Spoon & Groove (see below).

**(*) 'Spoon & Groove
Tradition TCD 1015 *Witherspoon; Teddy Edwards (ts); Groove Holmes (o); Paul Moer (p); Herman Mitchell (g); Jimmy Bond (b); Frank Butler (d). 60.*

'Spoon had always had a special lachrymose voice that he adopted for his most low-spirited songs. Here he seems to use it more indiscriminately, suffusing 'Key To The Highway' and 'Goin' To Chicago' with a solemnity that is inappropriate to the songs' lyrics or emotional atmosphere, and is also somewhat at odds with the little-club-after-dark ambience conjured from Hammond keyboard and tenor saxophone by Holmes and Edwards. Listeners who aren't troubled by that, or don't hear it that way, should find this a pleasant set of blues and a few other pieces, easy to listen to, quickly over and difficult to remember in detail.

*** Sings The Blues Sessions
Ace CDCHD 896 *Witherspoon; unknowns (brass); unknowns (reeds); poss. Billy Lee Riley (h, g); unknown (o); unknowns (p); unknowns (strings); poss. Roy Gaines, unknown (g); Red Callender, unknowns (b); Jesse Sailes or Jesse Price, unknowns (d). 60, unknown dates.*

'Spoon's 1960 Crown LP *Sings The Blues* appeared in two forms, with somewhat different track selections. Ace meticulously collate all the performances involved, adding several hitherto unissued tracks from undated Modern sessions. The original album session, with a warm tenor player and a T-Bone Walkerish guitarist, finds 'Spoon in excellent voice on an almost all-blues repertoire, administering what an Ace strapline neatly calls 'the aural equivalent of aromatherapy'. This is the important part of the CD; the extras, such as a two-part 'Ain't Nobody's Business' with strings and an 'Endless Sleep' with downhome harmonica, are mildly interesting but inessential.

**(*) Hey Mrs. Jones!
Collectables COL-CD-6198 *Witherspoon; Al Porcino, Gerald Wilson, Martin Banks, Conrad Gozzo, John Anderson (t); Frank Rosolino, Dick Nash, Lew McCreary (tb); Ben Webster, Harold Land, Ted Nash, Charles Kennedy, Jay Migliori, William Green, Maurice Simon (reeds); Bill Miller (p, cel); John Vidor, Darrel Terwilliger, Bob Bruce, Sid Sharpe, John De Voogt, Walter Wiemeyer, Jerry Vinci, Harry Hyams, Al Barr, Stan Harris, Jesse Ehrlich, Walt Rower, Justin DiTullio (strings); Al Viola (g); Jimmy Bond (b); Earl Palmer, Mel Lewis (d). 6–8/61.*

Despite the unpromising title and a large and by no means underused string section, the music, except for the hymn 'Have Faith', is seldom as kitsch as the cover art. The tracks with big band rather than strings are all blues, but mostly not ones 'Spoon was used to singing: this was his first time out with Willie Mabon's 'I Don't Know', and he also does Joe Liggins's 'Pink Champagne' and 'Tanya'. The sound is wide-screen Technicolor, and 'Spoon's voice at its most svelte.

**(*) Baby, Baby, Baby
Original Blues Classics OBCCD 527 *Witherspoon; Bobby Bryant (t, flh); Leo Wright (as, tamb); Jimmy Allen (ts); Arthur Wright (h); Gildo Mahones, Ernie Freeman (p); Kenny Burrell, Herman Mitchell (g); George Tucker, Jimmy Bond (b); Jimmie Smith, Jimmy Miller (d). 5–7/63.*

The May session, eight tracks with a quintet featuring Burrell and Leo Wright, is wall-to-wall blues, but since they range from 'Rocks In My Bed' to 'Bad Bad Whiskey' and 'Sail On Little Girl', 'Spoon has the opportunity to show several different ways of handling the form. The four tracks from the July date, with a seven-piece group, open unpromisingly with 'Endless Sleep' but Bryant and Allen take turns in tying woolly scarves round 'Spoon's compositions 'I'll Go On Living' and 'I Can't Hardly See'. A quiet album.

***(*) Evenin' Blues
Original Blues Classics OBCCD 511 *Witherspoon; Clifford Scott (ts, fl); Bert Kendrix (o); T-Bone Walker (g); Clarence Jones (b); Wayne Robertson (d); band (v). 8/63.*

**(*) Blues Around The Clock
Original Blues Classics OBCCD 576 *Witherspoon; Paul Griffin (o); Lord Westbrook (g); Leonard Gaskin (b); Herbie Lovelle (d). 11/63.*

The title and the combination of tenor, organ and a sleek guitarist imply the ambience of a low-lit nightclub, but *Evenin' Blues* is not so predictable, what with its repertoire embracing songs by Roy Brown, Washboard Sam and Leiber & Stoller. The late-hours atmosphere is duly conjured in an excellent, little-known blues lyric, 'Grab Me A Freight', 'Baby, How Long', where Walker is given his head, and what may be the prettiest of 'Spoon's recordings of 'Evenin'', with an uncredited flute obbligato by Scott. But their mood is dispelled by the insistent riff running through 'I've Been Treated Wrong', the vigorous pop-R&B of Jesse Stone's 'Don't Let Go' and the up-tempo blues 'Cane [*sic* Cain] River', 'Kansas City', 'Good Rockin' Man' and 'Drinking Beer'. A short set by today's standards, but so varied that one hardly notices.

The organ–guitar combination recurs on *Blues Around The Clock*, but Westbrook is self-effacing and Griffin's instrument sounds as if it should be accompanying Vincent Price. A pity, because this is another blues-rich programme, interrupted only by a pop standard and a sickly gospel song, and more assertive arrangements of 'I Had A Dream', 'No Rollin' Blues', 'S. K. Blues' and so on would have been worth having.

(***/*) Blue Spoon/Spoon In London
Original Blues Classics OBCCD-591 *Witherspoon; Gildo Mahones (p); Kenny Burrell (g); Eddie Kahn (b); Roy Haynes (d); unknown orch; Benny Golson (arr, cond). 2/64, 6/65.*

(**) Some Of My Best Friends Are The Blues
Original Blues Classics OBCCD 575 *Witherspoon; unknown orch. 7/64.*

(***) Blues For Easy Livers
Original Blues Classics OBCD 585 *Witherspoon; Bill Watrous (tb); Pepper Adams (bs); Roger Kellaway (p); Richard Davis (b); Mel Lewis (d). 65–66.*

Despite its title, *Blue Spoon* is mostly 'Spoon on a Nat King Cole kick with a piano quartet and songs like 'It's All In The Game'. Perhaps because it lasts less than half an hour, it has been augmented with a set recorded in London, where 'Spoon sings undistinguished new pop material accompanied by an orchestra conducted, surely with gritted teeth, by Benny Golson. *Some Of My Best Friends Are The Blues*, another orchestral session, has superior arrangements and one or two blues-related numbers, but this too is strictly for those who admire 'Spoon in the round, not just, or chiefly, as a blues singer. *Blues For Easy Livers* is another ill-titled set, since it's mostly standards, but 'Spoon puts them over with great skill and Watrous plays sublimely.

*** Jazz Me Blues: The Best Of Jimmy Witherspoon
Prestige 11008 *Witherspoon; various accompaniments. 5/58–66.*

A well-chosen survey of 'Spoon's work in this period, including three tracks from *The 'Spoon Concerts*, four from *Baby, Baby, Baby* and two each from *Evenin' Blues*, *Blues Around The Clock* and *Blues For Easy Livers*. The remaining seven tracks come from albums not currently available, four from a 1958 World Pacific date with a seven-piece jazz group and three from a 1961 Reprise set with big-band accompaniment.

**(*) Live In London
Harkit HRKCD 8065 *Witherspoon; Ronnie Scott (ts); Stan Tracey (p); Freddie Logan (b); Bill Eyden (d). 5/66.*

Appearing at Ronnie Scott's with the house band, 'Spoon runs cheerfully through a standard set. Sometimes it isn't so much running as racing, as he disposes of 'Every Day [I Have The Blues]' and 'Big Fine Girl' in a couple of minutes each, and the closing 'Roll 'Em Pete' is gabbled, but he takes his time over 'Mean Mistreater', 'No Rollin' Blues' and a topically updated 'Just A Dream'. Scott is under-recorded until about halfway through, but otherwise the informal recording has plenty of presence.

**(*) With The Junior Mance Trio
Stony Plain SPCD 1231 Witherspoon; Junior Mance (p); Jimmy Woode (b); Kenny Clarke (d). 69.

Three or four years on from *Blues For Easy Livers*, 'Spoon's voice seems coarser, and his singing at slow tempos has lost its satin sheen. But it was his bluesiest studio recording for some time, and it's odd that it wasn't issued until 28 years later. 'Spoon strolls through the galleries of his personal museum, dusting off 'Times Gettin' Tougher Than Tough', 'Ain't Nobody's Business' and 'No Rollin' Blues', unobtrusively accompanied by the trio.

*** Spoonful
Avenue Jazz R2 71707 Witherspoon; Blue Mitchell, Thad Jones, Ernie Royal, Melvin Moore (t); Garnett Brown, Benny Powell (tb); Seldon Powell, Delbert Hill, Don Menza (ts); Arthur Clark (bs); Buddy Lucas (h, g); Horace Ott (kb, arr); Richard Tee (p); Joe Sample (clavinet); Robben Ford, Cornell Dupree (g); Chuck Rainey (b); Gene Estes (d); King Errisson, Omar Clay, Bernard Purdie (perc); Hilda Harris, Ella Winston, Barbara Massey (v). 75.

***(*) Live
Avenue Jazz R2 71262 Witherspoon; Paul Nagle (kb); Robben Ford (g); Stan Poplin (b); Jim Baum (d). 76.

Spoonful distils a certain kind of '70s music-making, 100 per cent pure. The froggy bass and chittering guitars evoke their period as precisely as a tartan carpet bespeaks Victorian England. But while the efforts of this formidable band to sound right-on may now cue a grin half affectionate and half derisive, there's nothing voguish about 'Spoon's contribution: he simply sings the blues – all the tracks are blues except the closing 'Gloomy Sunday' – with huge unflappability. Robben Ford's solos are delectable, but amateurs of his playing will find yards more of it in the quartet setting of the *Live* CD, recorded at the Ash Grove in LA. This is all blues, embracing old 'Spoon favourites like 'No Rollin' Blues' and 'Times Are Getting Tough' and slightly younger songs like 'Kansas City'. 'Spoon gives a relaxed performance, while Ford swings from the declarative melody line of 'Walkin' By Myself' to the subtler sequences, soft as a murmur, that decorate 'Goin' Down Slow' and others.

** American Blues
Avenue Jazz R2 71953 Witherspoon; Lee Oskar (h); Howard Scott (g). 76.

'Spoon's association with Howard Scott dated from 1971, when they were both members, with Eric Burdon and others, of the group War, a coalition documented on record by the album *Guilty!* (United Artists, 1971, fortunately deleted). 'My idea,' 'Spoon said of *American Blues* later, 'was to get a young guitar player who was out of the blues realm. Howard wasn't known as a blues player, but he definitely had the roots to be one.' Scott's sedate chording and modest runs, played mostly on acoustic guitar, seem to please 'Spoon well enough, but they are the most uneventful accompaniment he ever had on record.

*** Ain't Nothin' New About The Blues
Aim 1050 Witherspoon; Clifford Scott (ts); unknown (h); unknown (p); Robben Ford, Howard Scott (g); unknown (b); unknown (d). 77.

The concluding title track comes from *American Blues* and the hasty shopper might conclude that the rest of the CD, being a club gig with Robben Ford, was the same as *Live* on Avenue Jazz, especially as most of the songs on the latter are also on Aim. Nonetheless, the albums come from different occasions. The versions of songs like 'Outskirts Of Town' or 'Kansas City' are sometimes very similar, but these were, after all, 'Spoon staples. Ford is as hot as he was a year earlier, sometimes more so, but Clifford Scott's solos give him less room to prove it. Admirers of 'Spoon – or Ford – will be well rewarded for tracking down this item.

*** Sings The Blues
Aim 1005 Witherspoon; Peter Gaudion (t); Mal Wilkinson (tb); Richard Miller (reeds); Bob Sedergreen (p); Derek Capewell (b); Allan Browne (d). 4/80.

*** Jimmy Witherspoon & Panama Francis' Savoy Sultans
Black & Blue BB 948 Witherspoon; Francis Williams, Irv Stokes (t); Bill Easley, Bobby Smith (as); George Kelly (ts); Red Richards (p); John Smith (g); Bill Pemberton (b); Panama Francis (d, ldr). 5/80.

During the '80s the handsome patina of 'Spoon's voice would begin to show the *craquelure* of age, but on these recordings from the beginning of the decade his singing shows few signs of decay. The Aim CD, recorded at a Melbourne club during an Australian tour, finds 'Spoon in the company of Peter Gaudion's Blues Express, a talented band that finds an immediate rapport with him and plays a programme of his standards ('Ain't Nobody's Business', 'Sweet Lotus Blossom', 'Kansas City', etc.) with great sensitivity. The Black & Blue set is cut from similar cloth: the tempos are friendly and the settings provided by Panama Francis's Savoy Sultans are perfectly fitted to a programme of songs that 'Spoon had lived in for so long that he knew every inch of them. Apart from the up-tempo chants 'Sent For You Yesterday' and 'I May Be Wrong', where the sense of Count Basie smiling in a corner is almost palpable, the prevailing tempo is slow, allowing him to tell his stories with gently unfolding drama expertly matched by his accompanists. The most striking arrangement is that of 'Sometimes I Feel Like A Motherless Child', where he is partnered only by saxophone and bowed bass.

*** Big Blues
JSP JSP 5101 Witherspoon; Peter King (as, ts); Hal Singer (ts); Mike Carr (kb, o, p); Jim Mullen (g); Harold Smith (d). 6/81.

'Lotus Blossom' blooms on many of 'Spoon's later albums, but nowhere as vigorously as in this London-recorded set. Sustained by a well-chosen group, 'Spoon is in good form. Hal Singer is accorded a 'special guest' billing because five tracks feature him rather than 'Spoon – largely as a tenorist, but also singing a blues, 'The Snow Was Falling'. The CD's mostly long tracks give ample blowing room not only to Singer but to King, Mullen and Carr, probably England's most idiomatic Hammond organist for this kind of music. This SACD issue supersedes JSPCD 285.

** **Rockin' L.A.**
Fantasy FCD-9660 *Witherspoon; Teddy Edwards (ts); Gerald Wiggins (p); John Clayton (b); Paul Humphrey (d).* 10/88.

(*) Spoon Meets Pao
Eureka/Eastside EURCD 804 *Witherspoon; Ric Halstead (ss); Dave Packer (p); Eugene Pao (g); Mariano Lim (b); Johnny Abraham (d).* 4/90.

** **Spoon**
TKO/Magnum/Starburst CDSB 1009/[Blues Encore CD 52052]//TIM 205388 *Witherspoon; Walter Ousley (s); Bros Townsend (p); Dave Jackson (b); Walter Perkins (d).* 5/90.

** **"Live" At The Notodden Blues Festival**
Blue Rock'It BRCD 113//Crosscut CCD 11035 *Witherspoon; Espen Fjelle (o); Robben Ford (g); Stan Poplin (b); Patrick Ford (d).* 8/91.

** **The Blues, The Whole Blues And Nothing But The Blues**
Sanctuary CAS 36181 *Witherspoon; Steve Grainger (ss, as); Dick Heckstall-Smith (ss, ts); Pete Thomas (ts); Bob Ross (kb); John Baggot, Pete Wingfield (p); Gary Shaw (g); Bob Jenkins Jr (d); Mike Vernon (perc, prod).* 1–2/92.

** **Spoon's Blues**
Stony Plain SPCD 1211 *Witherspoon; Scott Hamilton (ts); Bruce Katz (o, p); Duke Robillard (g, prod); Marty Ballou (b); Jeffery McAllister (d).* 12/94.

By the late '80s, the fragility of 'Spoon's voice was beyond concealment, and it is impossible to listen to any of these albums without some discomfort. *Spoon Meets Pao* is perhaps the easiest to take. Until shortly before the session 'Spoon had never heard of Eugene Pao, but after a few nights of playing together at the Hong Kong Jazz Club he was ready to describe the Chinese musician as 'the best blues guitarist I've heard since I discovered Robben Ford'. Enthused by the gig, he suggested that he should record with the band. Pao justifies 'Spoon's approval with his long, sinuous solo on 'Sweet Lotus Blossom' and the band as a whole goes about its work very competently. *Spoon* was taped the following month at the New York club Condon's with a dull piano trio and a strangely off-form Ousley. How settled 'Spoon's repertoire was at that time is evident from the contents of these CDs: seven of the former's eight tracks recur on the latter. *Rockin' L.A.*, also a club date (from the bar of the Biltmore Hotel in LA), has a similar setting but superior musicians. Assured playing by Edwards and Wiggins compensates a little for the weakness of 'Spoon's singing and the oh-so-familiar setlist.

The reunion with Robben Ford at Notodden was evidently a source of satisfaction to both, but 'Spoon sounds terribly weak and when he sings 'write my mother, tell her the shape I'm in' ('Going Down Slow') it's hard not to sense the outline of the skull beneath the skin. Ford plays with potency and variety, and his interaction with Fjelle is lively on the instrumental 'Doodlin''.

With *The Blues, The Whole Blues* producer Mike Vernon avoided the problem of hackneyed material by commissioning mainly new songs, some by himself and members of the band and three by Chris Youlden. In that respect it's the most ear-catching of 'Spoon's last albums and the singer, having recovered a little vocal strength since the Notodden gig, gives it his best shot, though he was past scoring bull's-eyes. *Spoon's Blues* mixes the well-worn ('Lotus Blossom', 'Sad Life'), songs from his early days ('Christmas Blues') and the newly written 'Spoon's Life Blues' and 'Spoon's Testimony'. It was a selection of material well calculated not to put too much strain on the singer, and Robillard and Hamilton cushion his progress with discretion, but vocally 'Spoon was too far gone for these courtesies to have much effect. TR

Jamie Wood
VOCAL, KAZOO

Born in Natchez, Mississippi, Wood has lived in California since she was 14. She became interested in the blues in 1982, thanks to her friend Junior Watson, and in 1988 formed the original Roadhouse Rockets, who are much in demand on the West Coast club and festival circuit.

(*) Flyin' High
Bluestime 22006 *Wood; Johnny Rover (h, v); Tom Mahon (p); Nathan James (g, v); Robby Eason (g); Tyler Pederson (b, v); Johnny Morgan (d, v).* 01.

(*) Ain't No Doubt About It
Pacific Blues PBCD 2302 *As above, except Carl Sonny Leyland (p, v) replaces Mahon; add James Harman (sp); omit Eason.* 7–12/02.

After *Flyin' High*, Wood reveals, 'I came to the conclusion that I'm never going to be a black Chicago blues singer.' So, revising her blonde ambition, she refashioned herself as a jump-blues vocalist in the style of, say, Ella Mae Morse. The resulting album is an amiable trip back to the '40s with Wood as peppy tour-guide, spotting such monuments of the period as Louis Jordan's 'Look Out (Sister, Look Out)', Roosevelt Sykes's '47th Street Jive' and Joe McCoy's 'Why Don't You Do Right' and introducing a few compositions of her own, like 'Hock That Rock' or 'I Got A Crush On You', that slot smoothly into the programme. Her tuneful, unaffected vocals are set off by the assured playing of her band, especially Leyland and Rover. Buyers curious enough to track down the earlier album – released in Brazil but available on Wood's website <www.jamie-wood.com> – will find that she does sound a little more Chicagoan (and black) on tracks like 'Early In The Mornin'' and 'When The Blues Come Around', but closer to her later style in 'As Long As I'm Movin''. TR

Mitch Woods (born 1951)
VOCAL, PIANO, ORGAN

Woods began playing rock 'n' roll in his teens, and picked up boogie woogie and blues piano in college, while studying under Archie Shepp. After settling in San Francisco in 1970, he formed the Rocket 88s, adding jump blues and New Orleans R&B to his range.

*** **Steady Date**
Blind Pig BP 71784//Club 88 8801 *Woods; Curtis Linberg (tb, v); John Firmin (s, v); Steve Gurr (h, v); Rich Welter (g); Dave Schallock (b); Lance Dickerson (d); Maryann Price, Skeeter Lavesque (v).* 84?

*** **Mr. Boogie's Back In Town**
Blind Pig BP 72888 *Woods; Peter Ecklund (t); Curtis Linberg (tb, v); John Firmin (cl, ts, bs, v); Al Rapone (ac, rb, unidentified instrument); Danny Caron (g, v); Dave Schallock, Karl Sevareid (b); Lance Dickerson (d); The Haze Sisters (v).* 88?

*** **Solid Gold Cadillac**
Blind Pig BP 74191 Woods; Curtis Linberg (tb); Rich Lataille (as); Rob Sudduth (ts, bs); Greg Piccolo (ts); Doug James (bs); John Firmin (s); Charlie Musselwhite (h); Kenny Ray, Ronnie Earl (g); Steve Wolf (b); Lance Dickerson (d). 91?

*** **Keeper Of The Flame**
Viceroots 54192 Woods; Lee Allen (ts); James Cotton (h); Johnnie Johnson (p); John Lee Hooker, Earl King (g, v). 8/91–5/92.

(*) **Shakin' The Shack
Blind Pig BPCD 5008 Woods; Johnny Viau (as, ts); Michael Peloquin (ts, bs, h); Myrick Guillory (ac, rb); Derek Irving (g); Steve Wolf (b); Mike Rosas, Ben Holmes (d). 93?

(*) **Jump For Joy!
Blind Pig BPCD 5067 Woods; Mike Whitwell, Tim Hyland (t); Mike Rinta (tb); Jeff Ervin (as, ts); Michael Peloquin, Danny Bittker (ts, bs); Michael 'Downtown' Brown (ts); Danny Caron (g); Joe 'Roll 'Em' Kyle (b); Eric Addeo (d); James Henry (cga, perc); Roberta Donnay (v). 8/98.

Woods calls his music 'rock-a-boogie', and one booklet acknowledges 'the dancers and fans who make up half the equation of this jumpin' music'. The Blind Pig CDs are primarily music for swing dancers, well played, wittily arranged and heavy on inconsequential lyrics about chicks, cars and dancing. Woods also draws effectively on second-line and boogie rhythms, but his ventures into slower and more emotional territory are less successful; between them the slow blues numbers and Myrick Guillory's ill-assorted guest appearance downgrade *Shakin' The Shack*. *Jump For Joy!*, featuring an expanded horn section, is let down by too-similar charts and ill-advised parodies of jive vocal styles. This is not music for passive listening, and few readers will want the complete works: in purely musical terms the best of the Blind Pigs is *Solid Gold Cadillac*, with the Roomful Of Blues horns punching out the riffs on four tracks.

Keeper Of The Flame is a set of duets with the African-American musicians listed. The title is presumptuous, but the collaborations are largely successful, although Earl King's two tracks once more prove that he was a great songwriter and an average singer, and by 1992 Hooker had ceased to care about music except as a source of income. Cotton is full of beans on four numbers, Allen plays with silky assurance on two, and of the duets with Johnson two are perfectly adequate; the third, 'Full Tilt Boogie', is an extraordinary performance, with both men playing as if possessed by the spirits of Albert Ammons and Pete Johnson. CS

Oscar Woods
VOCAL, GUITAR

A self-proclaimed troubadour and street rustler, Woods was an exponent of the Shreveport slide style, its precise runs and rich chords played with the guitar held flat across the lap.

*** **Oscar 'Buddy' Woods & Black Ace (1930–1938)**
'Texas Slide Guitars'
Document DOCD-5143 Woods; unknown (t); Kitty Gray, unknown (p); Ed 'Dizzy Head' Schaffer (g, k, v); poss. Joe Harris (g); unknown (b); unknown (d); Jimmie Davis (v). 5/30–12/38.

Nicknamed both 'Buddy' and 'The Lone Wolf', Woods performed in musical contexts as mutable as his personality seems to have been. He and Ed Schaffer were the Shreveport Home Wreckers, their twin slide guitars plangent behind Schaffer's vocal and grumpy kazoo. (Two titles are on this disc; two more, credited to Eddie And Oscar, are on "Too Late, Too Late" – Vol. 4 [Document DOCD-5321].) Solo on three numbers, Woods lives up to his 'Lone Wolf' tag, tensely complaining about women, and not lightening up much for the dance tune 'Don't Sell It – Don't Give It Away'. He rerecorded this song twice: in more extrovert mood as a member of the Wampus Cats (on this CD), and in 1940 for the Library of Congress, one of five tracks on *I Can Eagle Rock* (Travelin' Man TM CD 09). The Cats' seven tracks are of variable quality; 'Baton Rouge Rag' is admirably nimble, but elsewhere the bassist is sometimes clumsy, and the trumpeter combines fine tone with a remarkable lack of ideas. ('Baton Rouge Rag' appears again, along with other titles by Kitty Gray & Her Wampus Cats, on *Texas Piano – Vol. 2* [Document DOCD-5225].)

On all these sessions, Woods's guitar playing is admirable. The best performances on the CD, however, are those where he and Schaffer back the country singer Jimmie Davis. These six songs, which range from very funny to genuinely erotic, are a manifesto for black-influenced blues and illicit sex, from a man who later became governor of Louisiana on a segregationist and socially conservative ticket. Young roosters can be expected to have different sexual perspectives from their older selves; sadder is that collaborating with black musicians raised no issues of respect or equality. Schaffer is the lead guitarist (Davis's estimate of him as a better player than Woods is hard to contest) and gets ample space to show what he can do with a slide, never more successfully than on the narrative 'Saturday Night Stroll', which traverses gospel and dance music, novelty effects and a plethora of hot playing. It also includes the era's only interracial vocal duet, a Woods–Davis soundbite from 'Preaching On The Old Campground'. Opulent readers interested in country music should note that the Jimmie Davis box *Nobody's Darlin' But Mine* (Bear Family BCD 15943 5CD) includes a few more titles accompanied by Schaffer and Woods, and some backed by Schaffer and the great New Orleans guitarist 'Snoozer' Quinn. Document logically complete their CD with the early recordings of Woods's pupil, Black Ace (q.v.). CS

Noah Wotherspoon (born 1981)
VOCAL, GUITAR

Wotherspoon began playing guitar at 11, initially a rock fan – 'Slash was my first guitar hero' – but was converted to blues playing by the records of Stevie Ray Vaughan. He has played in clubs in his hometown of Dayton, Ohio, and several times at the Chicago Blues Festival, where he met Jimmy D. Lane, who connected him with APO Records.

(*) **Buzz Me
APO APO 2018 Wotherspoon; Celia Price (p); Hubert Sumlin (g, v); Marty Romie (b); Josh Johnson (d). 8/00.

At 19 Wotherspoon could hardly be expected to have entirely outgrown his influences. The sound at the core of this album is the guitar–bass–drums trio, on the pattern of SRV and Double Trouble (Sumlin and Price merely guest on a few tracks), but it's only occasionally, as in 'Cold Hearts' or 'Satori In Chicago', that Wotherspoon sounds explicitly Vaughanish, and even there the authentically incandescent guitar playing is somewhat quenched by a curiously dead studio acoustic. It's hard to tell if that's also what represses Wotherspoon's singing, or if his voice has been deliberately fuzzed to mask some of its immaturity. There's more work to be done on the vocals, then, but as a guitarist Wotherspoon is obviously talented and, since he appears to think of playing the blues as a goal rather than a pass, his next move may be interesting. TR

Big John Wrencher (1923–77)
VOCAL, HARMONICA

Raised on a plantation near Clarksdale, John Thomas Wrencher left Mississippi in 1947 and after several years' rambling settled in Detroit. On a trip home to see his father in 1958 he had an automobile accident and lost his left arm. Up to that point he had been only a part-time harmonica player but now music was his chief source of income. He played in Detroit, East St Louis and Chicago, where he moved in 1962 and became a fixture on the Maxwell Street scene. He was warmly received in Europe on an American Blues Legends tour in 1974.

*** **Big John's Boogie**
Castle CMRCD 849//Sanctuary CAS 36183 *Wrencher; Bob Hall (p); Eddie Taylor (g); Bob Brunning (b); Peter York (d). 2–4/74.*

In person, Wrencher earned descriptions like 'exuberant' or 'charismatic', but on record he comes over as rather a restrained performer. His harmonica playing is economical but to the point, and slow blues like 'Trouble Makin' Woman', 'Telephone Blues' or 'Lonesome In My Cabin' are models of unostentatious, thoughtful blues singing, which Hall and Taylor accompany with perfect understanding. Faster numbers like 'Come On Over' or 'Runnin' Wild' (a version of 'Special Rider Blues') are more run-of-the-mill, but fortunately there aren't many of them.

Wrencher's other album, *Maxwell Street Alley Blues*, made for Barrelhouse in 1969 and reissued on Blue Sting STINGCD 028, is deleted. His most interesting tracks on VACs are 'Honey Bee' and 'Take A Little Walk With Me', cut in 7/76 with singer/guitarist Joe Carter, on *Low Blows* (Rooster R 2610). TR

Billy Wright (1932–91)
VOCAL

After five years with Savoy, and four R&B chart hits, Wright made the occasional record, but mainly worked as a nightclub MC in his native Atlanta. He was largely inactive after suffering a stroke in the mid-'70s.

(*) **Billy Wright 1949–1951
Classics 5046 *Wright; John Peck (t, ts); Howard Callender, Roy Mays (t); Willie Wilson (tb, poss. as); unknown (tb); Neil James, James Hudson (as); Fred Jackson, Artie Clark, unknown (ts); Wim Scott, unknown (bs); unknown (p, cel); Sam Cochran, Julius Wimberley, Tom Patton (p); Wesley Jackson, unknown (g); George Battle, unknowns (b); Melvin Booker, J. W. Simpson, Willie Harper, unknown (d). 9/49–5/51.*

*** **Have Mercy Baby**
Blue City BCCD-810 *As above, except add Mason Johnson, Pat Jenkins, unknowns (t), John Haughton (tb), Ben Richardson, unknown (as), Willie Jackson, Eddie Herster, Buddy Tate, unknowns (ts), unknowns (bs), Skip Hall, unknowns (p), unknowns (g), James Pepper, Carl Wilson, unknowns (b), Bobby Donaldson, unknowns (d), unknowns (v). 49–c. mid-60s.*

Wright's material blends dramatic blues-ballads, rock 'n' roll, unexpected revivals (Big Bill Broonzy, Doctor Clayton and Ida Cox are among those plundered) and rewrites of hits both old and more recent. Classics cover roughly the first half of his recording career; their mastering is usually acceptable, but 'Back Biting Woman' comes from a psoriatic 78, and 'Empty Hand' is several tape generations away from the original. The early sides are attractive, with melismatic singing, imaginative horn charts and Sam Cochran's lively piano, but on the latter half of 1949–1951 John Peck's band use some predictable arrangements, and Wright settles for a one-size-fits-all delivery. Blue City, ignoring chronology and completism, can both cast the net more widely and throw back the smaller fry. There's considerable overlap with Classics, but *Have Mercy Baby* includes only four tracks with Peck's band, and one of them is 'Turn Your Lamps Down Low', a flamboyant and amazingly effective reinvention of 'Baby Please Don't Go' as embryonic soul. Blue City's generous playing time, good sound and effective programming are offset, however, by the absence of any notes or discography. CS

Marva Wright (born 1948)
VOCAL

Wright's mother was the great Mattie Gilbert, lead vocalist of the Jackson Gospel Singers, and Wright did most of her singing in New Orleans churches before turning professional in 1987.

** **Heartbreakin' Woman**
Mardi Gras MG 1038 *Wright; Herman J. Bartholomew Jr (t); Brian Cayolle (s); Malcolm Burn (h, cello sounds); J. D. Hill (h); Sammy Berfect (o, p); Ronald Jones (p, d, v); Bill Dillon (g, guitorgan); Daryl Johnson (b, string sounds, v); David Panneck (b); Juanita Brooks (v). 90?*

** **Glitter Queen**
Isabel IS 649201 *Wright; Tracy Griffin (t, v); Gregory Dawson (s); Marc Adams (o, p); Anthony Brown (g); Benny Turner (b, v); Earl Smith (d, v). 11/92.*

Marva Wright is a powerful singer, but on her earlier discs she's not a very good blues singer. *Heartbreakin' Woman* was originally released on a label operated by the New Orleans club Tipitina's, and *Glitter Queen* was recorded on a European tour; they both feel like concert souvenirs. No doubt Wright puts on a memorably energetic stage show, but these CDs are unsatisfactory. Her gospel lineage is apparent on all Wright's recordings, and not just because religious tunes feature on most of them; to that foundation she adds the dominant rhetoric of raunchy aggression. Far too often, the songs on these CDs are forced into that template without regard to its appropriateness

(*) **My Christmas Song
Mardi Gras MG 5013 *Wright; Tracy Griffin (t); Bruce Hammond, Steve Sutter (tb); Tom Fitzpatrick (s); Michael Robinson (kb, prog); Davell Crawford (o, p, v); Clayton H. Neal, Sammy Berfect, Marc Adams (p); Anthony Brown (g); Cornell Williams, Benny Turner (b); Earl Smith (d, v); Jeffrey 'Jelly Bean' Alexander, Wilbert Arnold, Kevin Wharton (d); Tanya Jarvis, Charles Elam, Tara Darnell (v). 94?*

The budget-priced *My Christmas Song* mixes gospel, blues and chestnuts; a medley of 'White Christmas', 'Santa Claus Is Coming To Town' and 'Jingle Bells' is a recommendation by default for *Phil Spector's Christmas Album*, and Wright's 'Silent Night' is as powerful, but also as cloying, as Mahalia Jackson's. Among the sentimental and the trite, though, are some hard-boiled blues, including the self-composed title track and Gary Coleman's 'Christmas Tears', while a brassy arrangement of Amos Milburn's 'Christmas Comes But Once A Year' livens up the proceedings. Not essential, it's better than many of its kind.

(*) Bluesiana Mama
Aim A 8 *Wright; Joe Krown (kb); Darryl Lacurtis Smith (g); Benny Turner (b); Earl Smith (d, v); Tara Darnell (v). 12/94.*

Originally released on the Swiss Blues House label, *Bluesiana Mama* features Wright's working band, and a setlist that's almost entirely well-known (and sometimes overfamiliar) blues numbers. There are some surprising successes, including 'Boogie' (a version of Junior Parker's 'Feeling Good') and 'Mojo Working', both features for some thunderous Meters-style funk from Turner and Smith, but most of the time Wright relies on whipping up febrile excitement without reference to the lyrics.

***(*) Marvalous**
Mardi Gras MG 1026 *Wright; Lannie McMillan (ts); Lester Snell (o, p); unknowns (strings); Thomas Bingham (g); The Staff [sic] (b, d); William Brown, Betram [sic] Brown, Mashaa (v). 95?*

***(*) I Still Haven't Found What I'm Looking For**
Aim A 2 *Wright; Brian Murray, Stacy Cole (t); Alonzo Barnes, Joseph Saulsbury, Mark Miller (s); Raymond Jones (o); Sam Henry (p); unknowns (strings); Anthony Brown (g); Charles Moore (b); Bernard Johnson (d); Tara Darnell, Tanya Jarvis, Erica Falls (v). 5–7/95.*

Marvalous was recorded at Willie Mitchell's Memphis studio with local musicians, playing arrangements that are mellow, soulful and relaxed, giving Wright no room to bellow and rant; instead she's compelled to sing with restrained power, considering each song on its own terms, and giving it as much or as little oomph as needed. This approach even succeeds on 'Wang Dang Doodle' and 'Built For Comfort', which are blowsily extrovert, not vehicles for vacuous exhibitionism. 'Built For Comfort', which got sorry treatment on *Heartbreakin' Woman*, is one of several rerecordings, nearly all of them immensely better.

I Still Haven't Found What I'm Looking For is mainly soul, and on the periphery of this work's coverage, but it's another very good record; again much of this success is down to intelligent production, in this case by New Orleans veteran Wardell Quezergue. More fundamentally, though, Wright's gospel inflections just transfer better to soul than to blues.

(*) Marva
Aim 5010 *Wright; Brian Murray (t); Charles Elam III (s, h, v); Terrance Simien (ac, v); Sam Henry, Josh Paxton, Marc Adams, Michelle Goods (o, p); unknowns (strings); June Yamagishi (g); Cornell Williams, Nick Daniels (b, v); Earl Smith (d, v); Jeffrey Alexander, Doug Belote, Tony Dillon (d); Norwood 'Geechie' Johnson (perc, v); Charmaine Neville, Bo Dollis (v). 11/99–10/00.*

Marva seems to be chasing the Neville Brothers' crossover success, and it's appropriate that the best tracks are a duet with Simien on Daniel Lanois's 'The Maker' and a ferocious 'Serve Somebody', from Bob Dylan's born-again phase. (Wright can find nothing new in 'The Weight' and 'Knocking On Heaven's Door', though.) An emotive 'Guess Who' features B. B. King-style guitar from June Yamagishi, whose playing is tasteful and idiomatic throughout, but much of the CD – even a Meterized 'Rockin' Pneumonia' – seems coldly calculated.

*** Blues Queen Of New Orleans**
Mardi Gras MG 1086 *Similar to Mardi Gras CDs above. 90s.*

Blues Queen purports to be a 'best of', and comprises three of the better tracks from *Heartbreakin' Woman*, six from *Marvalous* and five hitherto unreleased items: of these, 'At Last' is from the *Heartbreakin' Woman* sessions, and overdoses on the 'string sounds'. The rest seem to be from the *Marvalous* sessions: 'Ghetto Woman' is passable, but insufficiently elegiac; the Staples Singers' 'I'll Take You There' is respectful and respectable; and 'I Will Survive' and 'No Drawers' are why CD players have skip buttons. The new material is insufficient reason to prefer this to *Marvalous*.

Marva Wright Sings Her Favorite Traditional Gospel Songs (no label or number) also appeared in 2004, but it's hard to find outside New Orleans. CS

Jim Wynn (1908–77)
TENOR AND BARITONE SAXOPHONES

James A. Wynn Jr was born in El Paso, Texas, and grew up in LA. He began playing tenor saxophone in his teens, formed his first band in his 20s and made his first records, for 4 Star, in 1945. He was known for his extrovert performing style – 'I was the first sax man in LA to lay on his back and play the horn,' he told an interviewer in the '70s – but when other tenor players copied his routines he distanced himself by switching to baritone, on which he was a prolific session musician in the '50s and '60s. He worked with Johnny Otis until not long before his death.

(*) Jim Wynn 1945–1946
Classics 5043 *Wynn; Stanley Casey, unknown (t); David Graham (as); Freddie Simon, unknown (ts); 'Lord' Luther Luper (p, v); Theodore [Ted] Shirley (b, v); Robert 'Snake' Sims (d); Pee Wee Wiley, Claude Trenier (v). 9/45 or 10/45–46.*

(*) Jim Wynn 1947–1959
Classics 5070 *Wynn; Eddie Preston, Eddie 'Goo Goo' Hutcherson, unknowns (t); Eddie Hale (as, v); poss. David Graham, unknowns (as); Eddie ['Lockjaw'] Davis, poss. Pete Peterson, poss. Freddie Simon, Maurice Simon, unknown (ts); Zell Kindred, unknowns (p); Chuck Norris, unknowns (g); Ted Shirley (b, v); Buddy Woodson, unknowns (b); Robert 'Snake' Sims (d, v); unknowns (d); Bernie Anders, band (v). 10/47–c. 59.*

In common with other jump-blues bandleaders of the period like Joe Liggins and Roy Milton, Wynn with his Bobalibans, as his group was billed on his first four sessions, achieved a bigger sound than might have been expected from seven musicians. His three main vocalists enabled the band to handle a wide range of material, Wiley generally handling the blues, Luper the ballads and Trenier novelty items like 'Ee-Bobaliba', a Wynn composition that would do well for Helen Humes. One of the best vocal numbers on the first CD, however, is sung by bassist Ted Shirley, playing the part of a serviceman back from World War II warning his girlfriend to 'Get Yourself In Line'. On that volume Wynn mostly plays tenor, but within a few tracks of *1947–1959* his hog-snorting baritone is prominent in the mix. Many of Wynn's recordings, particularly on the second CD, are energetic, if formulaic, blues with brisk exchanges of solos among the horns, but the above-average playing on 'Snug As A Bug In A Rug' shows what the band could do when not bound by a blues contract. TR

Jimmy Yancey (1898–1951)
VOCAL, PIANO, HARMONIUM

Jimmy Yancey learned piano from his older brother Alonzo in 1915, after retiring from vaudeville. He'd been a dancer since the age of six; in 1913 he visited Europe, appearing in Vienna and Budapest and before King George V in Britain. Although he did some entertaining at parties and clubs, Jimmy mainly played for his own pleasure when not groundskeeping for the White Sox; when jazz writer Bill Russell tracked him down in 1938, he owned a harmonium, but had to visit his sister when he wanted to play piano. Yancey's discovery came about after Meade Lux Lewis recorded 'Yancey Special' in tribute to his and Albert Ammons's mentor; thereafter, Jimmy, occasionally joined by his wife, was recorded sporadically by both fan-owned and commercial labels until just before his death.

(****) In The Beginning
Solo Art SACD-1 *Yancey.* c. 4/39.

**** Jimmy Yancey – Vol. 1 (1939–1940)
Document DOCD-5041 *Yancey; Faber Smith (v).* c. 4/39–2/40.

*** Hey! Piano Man
JSP JSP 7747 4CD *Yancey.* c. 4/39–2/40.

**** Jimmy Yancey – Vol. 2 (1940–1943)
Document DOCD-5041 *Yancey; Estella 'Mama' Yancey (v).* 2/40–12/43.

*** Jimmy Yancey – Vol. 3 (1943–1950)
Document DOCD-5041 *As above.* 12/43–12/50.

Jimmy Yancey came to wider notice in the wake of the boogie-woogie craze, but only once did he play a walking bass on record. Dotted and suspended rhythms are more characteristic of his playing, and a Spanish coloration is often present; Meade Lux Lewis's 'Yancey Special' features Jimmy's famous habanera bass. Yancey had a limited number of themes which he reworked and recombined; in a lesser musician, this would become tedious, but Yancey's timing and touch make every performance a fresh exploration of the possibilities of piano blues. His faster material is rhythmically and technically very exciting; on slow numbers he has few rivals for beauty and depth of feeling. His occasional singing is very engaging; it's not universally liked by critics, which is mysterious. It's easier to understand reservations about Mama Yancey's voice, which is raw and harsh on first acquaintance, but also has considerable subtlety and blunt emotional directness.

Yancey's first sessions yielded 17 sides, but Solo Art issued only two before the money ran out. All 17 are on Document's *Vol. 1*, together with six solos made for Victor and two accompaniments to Faber Smith's attractively blurred singing. *In The Beginning* has only 12 tracks, and its sound is not noticeably better than Document's.

Vol. 2 is another mixture of recordings for large companies and shoestring enthusiasts; it introduces the singing of both Yanceys, and on its final track, Jimmy's wheezy harmonium, which will not appeal to everyone. (It makes another appearance on *Vol. 3*.) Nevertheless, and despite rather variable sound quality, *Vol. 2* is Yancey at his peak, with Session's 12-inch masters letting him stretch out to over four minutes if he wants to.

Vol. 3 begins with the final nine Session titles, including 'White Sox Stomp', with the one and only walking bass, and a gloriously poignant 'At The Window'. It was seven years before Yancey recorded again; he'd been suffering from diabetes, and six titles made for a revived Paramount label are sad listening, with Jimmy's fingers often failing to articulate his ideas. The CD is completed with four titles by Alonzo Yancey, whose ragtime is mostly as energetic as it's slapdash; the slower 'Ecstatic Rag' gives an inkling of what Jimmy acquired from him.

Hey! Piano Man is shared with Ammons, Lewis and Johnson; Yancey's disc contains the Solo Art sides, the Victor solos and the Vocalion pairing 'Bear Trap Blues'/'Old Quaker Blues'. Otherwise excellent remastering, which brings out the cross-rhythms and the interplay of Jimmy's hands very well, is marred by frequent overloading of the bass notes, with consequent distortion.

** The Unissued 1951 Yancey Wire Recordings
Document DOCD-1007 *Yancey; Warren 'Buzz' Reynolds (cl); Phil Kiely, unknown (p); Dick Mushlitz (bj); Estella Yancey (v).* 6/51.

Mushlitz and Kiely, who recorded this evening of music at the Yanceys' apartment, were semi-pro white jazz musicians. There are historically important things here, including Mama and Jimmy's only vocal duet, Jimmy's only recorded rag and his only piece in G. There are also some atmospheric photographs, extensive annotation, and a chirpy 'Scott Joplin's New Rag', probably by the unrelated Walter Joplin. This is not a CD for the casual listener, however, thanks to ambient noise, Jimmy's poor health, primitive recording technology, narcotic sitting-in by Reynolds and Mushlitz and some physical damage.

The VAC *Piano Discoveries* (Document BDCD-6045) includes seven home recordings from 1943, among them three duets by Yancey and Cripple Clarence Lofton. Their styles are not compatible, the sound is poor, and four tracks are mastered too slowly.

*** Chicago Piano, Vol. 1
Atlantic 82368 *Yancey; Estella Yancey (v); Israel Crosby (b).* 7/51.

This session was made two months before Yancey died, and it's been said that Mama sang with such feeling and sensitivity on her four tracks because she knew he hadn't long to live. These are certainly her best recordings; the same can't be said of Jimmy's playing, but he's better than he was in 1950. This is largely because Israel Crosby keeps time with sensitivity and tact, allowing Jimmy to play within the limitations illness had imposed on him. There's some groping for ideas on 'Salute To Pinetop' and 'Blues For Albert', and a nasty clam on 'Yancey's Bugle Call', but this pared-down version of his art often has a spare, autumnal elegance.

(***) The Best Of Jimmy Yancey
Blues Forever CD 68007 *As above.* c. 4/39–7/51.

Eleven Atlantic titles, two from Session and five from Solo Art in that order are certainly not a 'best of,' and if the reverse chronology is deliberate, it's hard to see what it's supposed to achieve. CS

Mama Yancey (1896–1986)
VOCAL

Estella Harris married Jimmy Yancey in 1919, and sang with him, mostly at parties, until his death in 1951. (See Jimmy's entry for recordings of them together.) Thereafter she was sporadically active at folk clubs and festivals.

**** Axel Zwingenberger And The Friends Of Boogie Woogie Vol. 4: The Blues Of Mama Yancey
Vagabond VRCD 8.88009 Yancey; Axel Zwingenberger (p). 10/82–8/83.

**** Maybe I'll Cry
Evidence ECD 26078 Yancey; Erwin Helfer (p). 11/82–1/83.

Four tracks from 1961, with Little Brother Montgomery and a rhythm section, are on *South Side Blues* (Original Blues Classics OBCCD 508); Mama Yancey's shrill, harsh singing on them may take some getting used to. By her 87th birthday (New Year's Day 1983) she had mellowed a little, and weakened hardly at all; she has no need for time-outs while her accompanists solo, even on Vagabond's 7.48 'Midnight Plea'.

At the time of these recordings, Erwin Helfer had been Mama's accompanist for many years, as well as taking affectionate care of her. His playing is more sparky than Zwingenberger's, with less legato; Zwingenberger also gives more weight to the left hand, perhaps because of his background in boogie. This makes the two discs interestingly different, despite a number of songs in common; Mama seems to respond with more emotion on Evidence, and on Vagabond to be more lyrical, and keener to savour her own artistry. Evidence CDs are better distributed, but it's worth trying to find both. CS

Mighty Joe Young (1927–99)
VOCAL, GUITAR

Joe Young was a boxer as a young man, and had the physique to go with his nickname. He recorded singles for a number of small Chicago labels, and was a busy club and session guitarist before becoming a fixture on the American and overseas touring circuits. In 1986, surgery for a pinched nerve in his neck went wrong; it was a year before he could walk again, and having lost feeling in his fingers he was unable to play guitar. Young kept performing as a singer, and worked on the self-produced CD he'd begun before the disaster. In 1999 he underwent further elective surgery, hoping to play guitar again; this time the post-operative complications killed him.

**(*) Blues With A Touch Of Soul
Delmark DD-629 Young; Jordan Sandke (t); Dennis Lansing (ts); Big Moose Walker (o, p); Jimmy Dawkins (g); Sylvester Boines (b); Hezekiah Roby (d). 8/70.

***(*) Chicago Blues
Grammercy 0187 Young; Charles Beecham (t); Walter Hambrick (ts); Bob Riedy (p); Sylvester Boines (b); Alvino Bennett (d). 3/72.

***(*) The Sonet Blues Story: Mighty Joe Young
Universal 986 925-09 As above. 3/72.

The touch of soul is very light; essentially this is West Side Chicago blues. Young's singing and playing are elegant and logical, but four (out of only seven) tracks are far too long, with the band members queuing up to play tensionless, unimaginative solos. The Sonet recordings are far better. Whether on well-known tunes like 'Rock Me Baby' and 'Drivin' Wheel' or his own compositions, Young's playing is articulate, sparkling and surprising, and his singing committed without being theatrical. The accompanists handle some tricky rhythms confidently, and they absolutely never coast – which makes it a pity that the horns are usually mixed way too low. Grammercy's reissue without notes is eclipsed by Universal's, with updated notes from Sam Charters and sparkling remastering – although the chance to bring the horns forward has regrettably been squandered.

***(*) Mighty Joe Young
Blind Pig BPCD 5073 Young; Ken Saydak (kb); Floyd Morris (o, p, clavinet); Ed Tossing (syn); William Chinnock, Ron Steele (g); Cornelius Boyson, Louis Satterfield (b); Alvino Bennett, Ira Gates (d). 1/74–75.

Young's two LPs for Ovation sold poorly; they were probably too bluesy for the contemporary black audience, and too soulful for a white market that wasn't ready for Bobby Rush's 'Chicken Heads'. Blind Pig have done a good deed by making tracks from them available again. Most are originals, and although Young doesn't achieve the final song's ambition to 'Take Over Chicago', he certainly takes the blues in unusual and, even 30 years later, progressive directions. An influence from Albert King is discernible but not overpowering, the touch of soul is much stronger, and on some tracks the successful use of busy rhythms suggests that some good came out of disco.

*** Bluesy Josephine
Evidence ECD 26023 Young; Ken Saydak (o, p); Willie Mabon (p); Cornelius Boyson (b); Willie Hayes (d). 11/76.

*** Bluesy Josephine
Black & Blue BB 442 As above. 11/76.

Young is backed by a terrific touring band; Willie Mabon, then resident in France, guests on two tracks. *Bluesy Josephine* is worth hearing, if only for Hayes's audacious drumming, but the songs repeatedly lose focus by being extended beyond their natural limits. Black & Blue add three alternative takes to the earlier release licensed by Evidence.

**(*) Live At The Wise Fools Pub
Aim 1052//Quicksilver 1 88967 Young; Tommy Giblin (o); Lafayette Leake (p); Benny Turner (b); Willie Hayes (d, v). 1/80.

Young assembles another distinguished band, and this time Hayes gets to deploy a smooth gospel bass on Tyrone Davis's 'Turning Point'. The playlist leans toward material that the mainly white clientele of the Wise Fools would recognize: 'I Can't Quit You Baby' and 'Stormy Monday' (cue whooping and clapping when the vocal starts) are in there; so is 'That's All Right', which Young embellishes with a very creative guitar solo. The band obviously gave the audience value for money, but it doesn't translate to disc.

♛ **** Mighty Man
Blind Pig BPCD 5040 Young; Kenny Anderson (t); Bill McFarland (tb); John Meggs, Hank Ford, Steele Sonny Seals (ts); Willie Henderson (bs); Billy Branch (h); Professor Eddie Lusk (kb); Joe Young Jr (g, v); Will Crosby (g); Bernard Reed, Benny Turner (b); Brian 'B. J.' Jones, 'Abraham' (d); Royalene Wilson (v). 86–96.

It's some small consolation for Young's death that he completed this project, and that it's his best and most original work. 'Turning Point' recurs, but most songs are Young's own, extending and completing his adventurous attempts to synthesize blues and soul to the benefit of both. Young only plays guitar on two 1986 tracks, but his protégé Will Crosby is an entirely satisfactory stand-in. The horn arrangements are by Gene Barge or co-producer Willie Henderson, and the rhythm arrangements by Young himself; the musicians recognize their quality and attack them with relish. The only reservation is that despite Billy Branch's fiery harmonica, it's hard to take a song called 'Wishy Washy Woman' seriously, but Young obviously had a fondness for it, since it's revived from *Chicago Blues*. CS

Johnny Young (1918–74)
VOCAL, MANDOLIN, GUITAR

Young left Mississippi for Chicago about 1940, by then a capable player of guitar and mandolin. Around 1947 he made a few obscure recordings, some in the company of Snooky Pryor, but for the next 15 years he was heard only in the clubs and on Maxwell Street. In the '60s he made some headway in the new world of documentary labels and blues festivals, and visited Europe with the AFBF in 1972. Never a major player on the Chicago scene, he produced a good deal of music that has worn at least as well as much by more celebrated peers.

Young's untidy but vigorous early recordings 'Money Takin' Woman', 'My Baby Walked Out' and 'Let Me Ride Your Mule' are on *Down Home Blues Classics: Chicago 1946–1954* (Boulevard Vintage BVBCD 1014 4CD).

**** **Modern Chicago Blues**
Testament TCD 5008 *Young; Slim Willis (h); Otis Spann, Jimmy Walker (p); Robert Whitehead (d).* c. 62–c. 66.

Young's presence on this VAC is considerable – he sings on seven tracks and plays on four more – and his performances are, without exception, carefully controlled and integrated. He may never have been famous, but he knew how to lead. The album's title was absurd: when these recordings were made, modern Chicago blues was what Magic Sam or Otis Rush were playing. Young and the other contributors, men like John Wrencher and John Lee Granderson, belonged to the neighbourhood clubs of the immediate postwar years and to weekend sessions on Maxwell Street. Yet there's a quiet straightforwardness about their music that seems timeless, and although the recording quality is modest, this is an album to return to over and over again.

*** **Johnny Young And His Friends**
Testament TCD 5003 *Young; Slim Willis, John Wrencher, Little Walter, Walter Horton (h); Otis Spann, Jimmy Walker (p); John Lee Granderson, Robert Nighthawk (g); Robert Whitehead (d).* c. 62–c. 66.

'I recorded Johnny fairly extensively for … several years,' wrote Pete Welding, 'for I found him a fine, expressive traditional performer.' What he may have meant by 'traditional' is that Young stood, stylistically, on the bridge between the Southern downhome music of the '20s and '30s and the Chicago band idiom into which it was gradually transformed. Pieces like 'Sugar Farm Blues' and 'Kid Man Blues', played on mandolin, guitar and harmonica, recall the Yank Rachell–Sonny Boy Williamson I combinations, while 'I Got It' and 'Humpty Dumpty' are a kind of rural rock 'n' roll. As on the previous CD, Young leads from the front, singing with warmth and strength but no melodrama, rather like Jimmy Rogers. Here and elsewhere, his guitar playing is sturdy but on mandolin he swings like a shake dancer. Further proof of that may be found in 'Mandolin Rock' or 'Jumpin' On Eight', two of seven cuts by Young, derived from the Testament sessions, that appear on the VAC *Mandolin Blues* (Testament TCD 6004). Also from this period are the five tracks with Slim Willis, Otis Spann and Robert Whitehead on *I Blueskvarter: Chicago 1964, Volume One* (Jefferson SBACD 12653/4 2CD).

(***) **Back To Chicago**
Delta DCD 1874 *As above, except Granderson also sings; add Paul Oscher (h), Henry Gray (p), Carl Martin (vn, v), Mighty Joe Young, Sammy Lawhorn (g), Willie Dixon (b), Clifton James, S. P. Leary (d).* c. 62–4/69.

This is a magpie's nest. Despite what is stated or implied in the notes, none of Young's '40s sides are included. The CD takes seven tracks from each of the Testament albums (all those from *And His Friends* running fast), two from Testament's Chicago String Band CD, two from the long-gone Decca compilation *Blues Southside Chicago* and the final six from Young's very good Blue Horizon album *Fat Mandolin*. The notes are excerpted without acknowledgement from Pete Welding's for *And His Friends*. The access to the *Fat Mandolin* session, otherwise unavailable on CD, is tempting, but this is not a production the scrupulous collector can buy without unease.

*** **Chicago Blues**
Arhoolie CD 325 *Young; Walter Horton (h, v); James Cotton (h); Otis Spann, Lafayette Leake (p); Jimmy Dawkins (g); Jimmy Lee Morris, Ernest Gatewood (b); S. P. Leary, Lester Dorsie (d).* 11/65, 11/67.

More unfancy but robust band music by two lineups, the Cotton–Spann group in '65 and the Horton–Leake–Dawkins combo in '67. The latter, with production input by Willie Dixon, provides a more modern setting, which doesn't discompose Young in the least. Whereas the Testaments sound as if they were made in musicians' homes, these were studio recordings, which gave Young's voice more definition. The songs, almost all his, are generic yet never dull.

Shortly after the first Arhoolie date Young recorded six songs for Sam Charters's *Chicago/The Blues/Today!* project, which appeared on *Vol. 3* (Vanguard VMD 79218) alongside tracks by Johnny Shines; they were reissued on the 3CD set *Chicago/The Blues/Today!* (Vanguard 172/74). TR

Zora Young (born 1948)
VOCAL

As a girl Young sang in her local church in West Point, Mississippi, before her family moved to Chicago, where she has sung a wide range of music in clubs and at festivals. Her first exposure to audiences much outside Chicago was on the 1982 'Blues With The Girls' tour of Europe with Big Time Sarah and Bonnie Lee, since when she has revisited several times.

(*) **Blues With The Girls
EPM Blues Collection 15758 *Young; Stéphane Guerault (ts); Michel*

Carras (o, p); Larry Martin, Paul Pechenaert, Hubert Sumlin (g); Zox (b); Vincent Daune (d). 2/82.

Young's five songs come first on this album, and rightly. Like the other participants she chose, or was asked to sing, standards to which it's difficult to bring anything new – in her case 'You Don't Have To Go' and 'Got My Mojo Workin'' – but she makes more impact with her own slow blues 'I Feel So Bad' and the soul song 'Steppin' Stone', delivered with smouldering anger.

*** Travelin' Light
Deluge DELD 3003 *Young; Jerry Portnoy (h); Pinetop Perkins (p); Anthony Geraci (o, p); Colin Linden, Charles Baum (g); Michael 'Mudcat' Ward (b); Willie Smith (d). 9/91.*

Despite the exposure of *Blues With The Girls*, almost another decade passed before Young secured an album date of her own. The band is strong – Pinetop Perkins, one of three ex-Muddy Waters sidemen, rolls out hard-wearing lengths of blues piano, and the Canadian guitarist Colin Linden proves to be both versatile and salty – but Young is not abashed, and her readings of standard blues like 'Queen Bee' and 'Key To The Highway' are neither overbearing nor hackneyed. The other numbers are mostly her own. For collectors of new words and phrases in blues, 'Football Widow' offers a probable first sighting of 'couch potato'.

*** Learned My Lesson
Delmark DE-748 *Young; John Brumbach (ts); Ken Saydak (o, p, prod); James Wheeler, Danny Draher (g); Johnny B. Gayden (b); Tim Austin (d); Roberta Thomas (v). 5/00.*

'Learned My Lesson,' Delmark claim, 'is the celebration of Zora Young's lifelong love affair with the blues', but her heart proves to be bigger than that, as she throws her arms round Tina Turner's 'Nutbush City Limits' and Chuck Berry's 'Living In The U.S.A.' and blows a kiss to her gospel past in 'The Lord Helps Those Who Help Themselves'. There remains a hard core of blues like 'My Man's An Undertaker' and her own witty 'Brain Damage', but whatever the song, she does it justice. The band is businesslike but at times, like business at the end of the day, a bit jaded. TR

Rusty Zinn (born 1970)
VOCAL, GUITAR

Zinn grew up in Santa Cruz, California, became interested in blues at 15 and started playing guitar a couple of years later. He has immersed himself in '50s guitar styles, listening to musicians as diverse as Luther Tucker and Bill Jennings. Among the bandleaders he has worked with are Mark Hummel, Jimmy Rogers and Kim Wilson. His 1996 debut album Sittin' And Waitin' *earned him a Handy award as Best New Blues Artist.*

**(*) The Chill
Alligator ALCD 4876 *Zinn; John Firmin (ts); Jimmy Pugh (o); Bob Welsh (p, g); Elvin Bishop (g); Randy Bermudes (b); Richard Innes, Paul Revelli (d). 00.*

Zinn moves round a guitar quicker than most, executing fast trills with carefree brilliance, and anyone who shares his tastes in periods and styles will have no trouble approving of him. He sings with the same youthful enthusiasm he brings to his playing. ('Youthful' is meant literally: there are teenagers who sound older than he does.) Several of the songs, like the title track and 'Dying On The Vine', are originals co-written with Rick Estrin and, like much of Estrin's work for Little Charlie & The Nightcats, are well-turned without being particularly memorable. The earlier albums for Black Top, *Sittin' And Waitin'* (CDBT 1134) and *Confessin'* (CDBT 1151), are out of print. TR

Compilations

Alabama

(*) Alabama Blues 1927–1931
Yazoo 1006 *Ed 'Barefoot Bill' Bell* (2), *Jaybird Coleman*, *Clifford Gibson* (4), *Marshall Owens* (2), *Edward Thompson* (4), *George 'Bullet' Williams*. 27–31.

(*) Alabama Blues: 1927–1930
Wolf WSE 113 *Jaybird Coleman* (10), *Clifford Gibson* (4), *Ollis Martin*, *Frank Palmes* (2), *Bertha Ross*, *George 'Bullet' Williams* (5). 7/27–4/30.

(*) Alabama: Black Secular & Religious Music (1927–1934)
Document DOCD-5165 *Wiley Barner* (2), *Tom Bradford* (2), *Slim Duckett & Pig Norwood* (4), *Moses Mason* (8), *Marshall Owens* (2), *Edward Thompson* (6). 27–34.

(*) Alabama & The East Coast (1933–1937)
Document DOCD-5450 *Charlie Campbell* (2), *Georgia Slim* (6), *Guitar Slim* (2), *Peanut The Kidnapper* (4), *Sonny Scott* (10). 33–37.

Alabama attracted many folklorists, from John Lomax on down, seeking the oldest styles of black music in a state which long had a reputation for backwardness, poverty and racism. LPs of field recordings by Harold Courlander and Fred Ramsey can be ordered on CD-R from Smithsonian Folkways, and the Alabama Center for Traditional Culture continues to document blues and other music on CDs available from its website; but despite flourishing gospel quartet and blues piano traditions, the state's blues are comparatively under-represented on 'race' records.

All the CDs listed have their drawbacks, not least that some of the source 78s are in ferociously worn condition. Yazoo's playing time is scant, and Clifford Gibson, Kentucky-born and St Louis-based, is included only because he once played second guitar behind Ed Bell. There seems to be no evidence to place Edward Thompson in Alabama, or anywhere else; he's a brooding singer whose playing combines old-style strumming with newly fashionable Jeffersonian fingerpicked runs.

The Wolf CD, originally an LP of harmonica blues, is pointlessly augmented with the Clifford Gibson songs from Yazoo. Paul Oliver's notes on the harmonica tracks are predictably useful, and there are thrills aplenty in Coleman's resolute swing and 'Bullet' Williams's manic imitations of trains and bloodhounds. However, the utility of the Wolf and Yazoo CDs depends on what else the reader owns or plans to buy: four of Williams's numbers are also on *Great Harp Players (1927–1936)* (Document DOCD-5100), and all of Bell's, Coleman's and Gibson's are on Document CDs under their names.

The two Document discs listed here round up a gaggle of artists who didn't record enough to get CDs to themselves; and note also *Alabama: Black Country Dance Bands (1924–1949)* (Document DOCD-5166), discussed in the entries for Ben Covington and Daddy Stovepipe. *Black Secular & Religious Music* adds two Edward Thompson songs from a battered 78 to those on Yazoo, whence oldfashioned strummer Marshall Owens is also lifted. The stentorian Wiley Barner is mainly interesting for Jimmy Allen's piano. Guitarist Tom Bradford's recordings for the Library of Congress suffer from speed fluctuations, but the long train narrative 'Going North' is thrilling. Moses Mason's two street vendor's cries are the sort of thing conventionally, but in this case inaccurately, described as 'fascinating'; his two spirituals are routine, and his four sermons are outside our scope. Mason was probably from Mississippi; the Jackson-based guitarists Duckett and Norwood, who perform four appealingly simple spirituals, certainly were.

On *Alabama & The East Coast*, Sonny Scott has some idiosyncratic lyrics, but limited guitar skills and laconic singing make him hard going. Things only perk up when Walter Roland plays second guitar on 'Hard Luck Man', and Scott's voice suddenly acquires dynamics. Six-string banjoist Charlie Campbell and pianist Robert McCoy make a jovial team; they also accompany Guitar Slim on 'Ain't It A Shame?', where Campbell is seemingly added to provide the rhythmic coherence lacking when Slim and McCoy tackle 'Katie May – Katie May'. McCoy (certainly) and Campbell (probably) back Peanut The Kidnapper, whose pseudonym is better than his Peetie Wheatstraw imitations. Vocally, Georgia Slim (probably George Bedford, from Atlanta) is another admirer of the High Sheriff from Hell. His tangy guitar licks make Slim more interesting than many Wheatstraw acolytes, and on 'Ocean Wide Blues' his own musical personality peeps through the 'ooh well well's. CS

Basic Blues

Introductions, surveys, starter packs.

(***) The Story Of The Blues
Columbia 468992 2CD *Texas Alexander*, *Barbecue Bob & Laughing Charlie*, *Big Bill Broonzy*, *Butterbeans & Susie*, *Leroy Carr*, *Bo Carter*, *Fra Fra Tribesmen*, *Blind Boy Fuller*, *Lillian Glinn*, *Chippie Hill*, *Peg Leg Howell*, *Mississippi John Hurt*, *Elmore James*, *Blind Lemon Jefferson*, *Robert Johnson*, *Leadbelly*, *Brownie McGhee*, *Blind Willie McTell*, *Memphis Jug Band*, *Memphis Minnie*, *Mississippi Jook Band*, *Charley Patton*, *Johnny Shines*, *Bessie Smith*, *Otis Spann*, *Joe Turner & Pete Johnson*, *Casey Bill [Weldon]*, *Peetie Wheatstraw*, *Booker White*, *Henry Williams & Eddie Anthony*, *Big Joe Williams*, *Jimmy Yancey & Faber Smith*. 3/27–5/68.

*** The Story Of The Blues
Columbia/Legacy 510278 2CD As above, except add *Jeff Beck Group*, *Willie Dixon*, *Bob Dylan*, *The Electric Flag*, *Lightnin' Hopkins*, *Janis Joplin*, *Keb' Mo'*, *Little Axe*, *Muddy Waters*, *Santana*, *Taj Mahal*, *Stevie Ray Vaughan*, *Johnny Winter*; omit *James*, *Shines*, *Spann*. 3/27–01.

**** Bill Wyman's Blues Odyssey
Document DOCD-32-20-2 2CD *Big Maceo*, *Black Boy Shine*, *Blind Blake*, *Big Bill Broonzy*, *Bumble Bee Slim*, *Bo Carter*, *Rob Cooper*, *Cow Cow Davenport*, *Sleepy John Estes*, *Blind Boy Fuller*, *John Lee Hooker*, *Mississippi John Hurt*, *Papa Charlie Jackson*, *Lil Son Jackson*, *Elmore James*, *Frankie 'Half-Pint' Jaxon*, *Blind Lemon Jefferson*, *Lonnie Johnson*, *Pete Johnson*, *Robert Johnson*, *Luke Jordan*, *B. B. King*, *Meade Lux Lewis*, *Tommy McClennan*, *Blind Willie McTell*, *Memphis Minnie*, *Memphis Slim*, *Muddy Waters*, *Charley Patton*, *Joe Pullum*, *Bessie Smith*, *Mamie Smith*, *Pine Top Smith*, *Speckled Red*, *Frank Stokes*, *Tampa Red & Georgia Tom [Dorsey]*, *Montana Taylor*, *Sonny Terry & Brownie McGhee*, *Jesse 'Babyface'*

Thomas, Joe Turner, Willie Walker, Walter 'Cowboy' Washington, Casey Bill Weldon, Peetie Wheatstraw, Georgia White, Big Joe Williams. 9/25–8/51.

The Story Of The Blues was compiled by Paul Oliver in 1970 to accompany his book of that name. At the time it was a respectable survey of the blues, from early recording stars like Jefferson, Barbecue Bob and Bessie Smith to recent inheritors of the tradition such as Elmore James and Otis Spann; the latest recording on the album was then only two years old. Thirty-three years later, this well-loved old jalopy was in need of an overhaul. By modern standards the original double LP's 32 tracks were an ungenerous portion, and the quality of the transfers from 78s was somewhat primitive. More seriously, the development of the blues in the past half-century could not be epitomized by three tracks. Although the collection bore the stamp of Oliver's interests in pieces like the opening track, a praise-song from Ghana played on two-string fiddle and gourd rattle, or the song by Butterbeans & Susie, it also reflected his lack of curiosity about many subgenres of postwar blues (West Coast, New Orleans, etc.), though some of those might have been difficult to illustrate using only the resources of what was then Columbia. The material available to Sony in 2003 could stock a far wider-ranging collection, and the album was reissued with 13 new tracks, but the problem was not eliminated: most of the additional material was by rock-era figures, and the hole, into which several decades of modern blues had virtually disappeared, was deepened by the subtraction of Elmore James, Johnny Shines and Otis Spann. It's some recompense to have Lightnin' Hopkins and Muddy Waters added, much of the new material is good for what it is and the sound has been brightened, but the contents still fail to deliver the full consignment of goods invoiced by the title.

Bill Wyman's Blues Odyssey also partnered a book, but much more recently, so it has the advantages of modern sound restoration and generous playing time. Copyright law allowed Wyman to select recordings from all the labels of the '20s, '30s and '40s; the downside is that it also prevented him using material issued after 1951, so his *Odyssey* remains an unfinished journey. But as far as it goes – and it does acknowledge the existence of such figures as Muddy Waters, John Lee Hooker and B. B. King – it covers the ground very efficiently, the inevitable choices (Jefferson, McTell, Broonzy, Terry & McGhee, etc.) sometimes nudging elbows with left-field ones like Frankie 'Half-Pint' Jaxon or Walter 'Cowboy' Washington. Commendable too is the strong representation of piano players. An excellent set.

***(*) **Blues/36 Chefs-d'Oeuvre 1927–1942**
Frémeaux FA 033 2CD *Texas Alexander, Blind Blake, Mississippi Bracy, Big Bill Broonzy, Blind Blues [Teddy] Darby, Walter Davis, [David] Honeyboy Edwards, Sleepy John Estes, Jazz Gillum, Blind Lemon Jefferson, Lonnie Johnson, Leadbelly, Noah Lewis, Charlie McCoy, Fred McMullen, Blind Willie McTell, Memphis Jug Band, The Mississippi Moaner, Charley Patton, Robert Petway, Charlie Pickett, Yank Rachell, Rhythm Willie, Tampa Red, Tarter & Gay, Sonny Terry, Jesse Thomas, Big Joe Turner, T-Bone Walker, Peetie Wheatstraw, Josh White, Big Joe Williams (2), Sonny Boy Williamson I (2), Oscar Woods.* 27–42.
***(*) **Good Mornin' Blues**
Living Era CD AJA 5439 *Kokomo Arnold, Big Bill Broonzy, Leroy Carr & Scrapper Blackwell, Arthur 'Big Boy' Crudup, Sleepy John Estes, Blind Boy Fuller, John Lee Hooker, Lightnin'*

Hopkins, Son House, Mississippi John Hurt, Blind Lemon Jefferson, Lonnie Johnson, Robert Johnson, Tommy Johnson, Leadbelly, Blind Willie McTell, Muddy Waters, Charley Patton, Roosevelt Sykes, Sonny Terry & Brownie McGhee, Big Joe Turner & Pete Johnson, T-Bone Walker, Booker White, Big Joe Williams, Sonny Boy Williamson I, Jimmy Witherspoon. 3/27–52.
*** **Blues: The Essential Album**
Essential ESNDCD 230 2CD *Big Maceo, Big Maybelle, R. L. Burnside, Canned Heat, Albert Collins, Peter Green's Fleetwood Mac, Corey Harris, John Lee Hooker, Lightnin' Hopkins, Son House, Helen Humes, Elmore James, Robert Johnson, B. B. King, Leadbelly, Little Esther & Johnny Otis (2), Willie Love, Fred McDowell, Memphis Minnie, Muddy Waters, Robert Nighthawk, Johnny Otis, Sonny Boy Williamson II, Big Mama Thornton, Big Joe Turner (2), Tom Waits, Doc & Merle Watson, Junior Wells, Big Joe Williams, Robert Pete Williams.* 37–99.

The Frémeaux set was assembled by Gérard Herzhaft as a historical narrative, the first disc dealing with early regional styles, the second reflecting the processes of migration and urbanization. There are some strange omissions (Leroy Carr, hokum, barrelhouse and boogie-woogie piano), and opening the programme with Rhythm Willie's sophisticated harmonica solo 'Breathtaking Blues' (before Leadbelly's 'Lining Track', yet) does indeed take the breath away – but it's an acute compiler who recognizes the worth of Charlie Pickett's 'Down The Highway' or Fred McMullen's 'DeKalb Chain Gang'. Even seasoned listeners might find this compilation enlightening; they could hardly fail to find it entertaining. *Good Mornin' Blues* has the more modest aim of simply heaping up in front of the customer a hefty meal of classic blues performances. (It's amusing, by the bye, to see where 'classic' has hardened into 'indispensable'. Three of the four compilations discussed so far have pinned that rosette on Big Joe Williams's 'Baby Please Don't Go' and Joe Turner & Pete Johnson's 'Roll 'Em Pete'.) Since it too was restricted, like *Blues Odyssey*, to PD material, *Good Mornin'* similarly says goodbye with Hooker and Waters. The remastering is well up to modern standards.

Blues: The Essential Album is a peculiar collection, in that its compiler, John Crosby, had access to some licensed material but not so much of it that he could represent blues in the round. There are more latterday recordings than usual in these sets, though sequencing them among earlier ones can make for a sonically bumpy ride. Sound though many of the selections are, and sometimes likeably quirky, 'essential' doesn't really allow for two tracks by Little Esther, or for Big Maybelle's 'Candy' or Peter Green's 'Lazy Poker Blues'.

*** **Legends Of The Blues: Volume 1**
Columbia CK 46215 *Leroy Carr, Bo Carter, Big Bill Broonzy, Blind Boy Fuller, Son House, Mississippi John Hurt, Blind Lemon Jefferson, Lonnie Johnson, Robert Johnson, Blind Willie Johnson, Leadbelly, Blind Willie McTell, Memphis Minnie, Muddy Waters, Charley Patton, Bessie Smith, Peetie Wheatstraw, Booker White, Josh White, Big Joe Williams.* 1/25–4/65.
*** **Legends Of The Blues Volume II**
Columbia CK 47467 *Texas Alexander, Barbecue Bob, Lucille Bogan, Bumble Bee Slim, Champion Jack Dupree, Jazz Gillum, Lil Johnson, Merline Johnson, Curtis Jones, Brownie McGhee, Buddy Moss, Walter Roland, Charlie Spand, Victoria Spivey, Roosevelt Sykes, Tampa Red, T-Bone Walker, Curley Weaver, Casey Bill [Weldon], Robert Wilkins.* 6/29–11/41.

These are drawn purely from Sony-group labels (Columbia,

OKeh, Vocalion, etc.). That kept a few major figures out of the cast, but Sony's archives are quite rich enough to stock representative compilations. Both volumes are devoted to artists who were popular in their day, but, while most of those on *Volume 1* continue to enjoy the approval of blues enthusiasts, about half of *Volume II*'s are less fashionable figures. Together, the albums make a wide-ranging and moderately priced introduction to blues of the '20s, '30s and '40s. A few tracks on *Volume 1* sound rather lifeless but in general the remastering is good. A note to more seasoned collectors: nine of the tracks on *Volume 1*, and 13 on *Volume II*, were not issued at the time they were made.

*** Worried Life Blues
Bluebird 55611 *Big Maceo, Big Bill Broonzy, Arthur Crudup, Sleepy John Estes, Lil Green, Alberta Hunter, Tommy Johnson, Leadbelly, Memphis Slim, Johnny Moore's Three Blazers, St Louis Jimmy [Oden], Robert Petway, Bessie Smith, Tampa Red, Big Joe Williams, Sonny Boy Williamson I.* 2/23–11/50.

More legends of the blues, but this time with legendary songs too: Big Maceo is represented by 'Worried Life Blues', Sonny Boy Williamson by 'Good Morning, School Girl', Tampa Red by 'Sweet Little Angel' and so on. Given the riches of the Victor/Bluebird larder, from which this selection was prepared (except for Bessie Smith's 'Down Hearted Blues', one that Sony made earlier), 16 tracks are short commons, but as a sampling of the most popular blues dishes of three decades it's undeniably tasty on the tongue and light on the pocket.

*** Blues Masters, Volume 6: Blues Originals
Rhino R2 71127 *Bo Diddley, Ann Cole, G. L. Crockett, Arthur 'Big Boy' Crudup, Larry Davis, Howlin' Wolf (2), Elmore James, Robert Johnson, Little Walter, Muddy Waters, Big Walter [Price], Snooky Pryor, Jimmy Reed, Otis Rush, Slim Harpo, Sonny Boy Williamson II, Henry Thomas.* 6/28–65.

Unusually, this collection prioritizes songs over artists, so you get 'Got My Mojo Working' not by Muddy Waters but by Ann Cole, the little-known singer who first recorded it, while fine but relatively obscure items like Big Walter Price's 'Pack Fair And Square', Larry Davis's 'Texas Flood' and Henry Thomas's 'Bulldoze Blues' (a lone item from the '20s) are in because the songs have been mediated to the rock audience by the J. Geils Band, Stevie Ray Vaughan and Canned Heat. None of which prevents this being an enjoyable hour's music.

**(*) Beyond Mississippi
Manteca MANTCD 209 2CD *Justin Adams, B. B. & Group, Chuck Berry, Bo Diddley, Bonzo Dog Band, George 'Bongo Joe' Coleman, Rev. Gary Davis, Dr Feelgood, Dr John [Mack Rebennack], Bob Dylan, Aretha Franklin, The Golden Gate Quartet, Corey Harris, Jessie Mae Hemphill, Lightnin' Hopkins, Howlin' Wolf, Mahalia Jackson, Skip James, Tommy Johnson, Albert King, Errol Linton's Blues Vibe, Little Axe, Cripple Clarence Lofton, Odea Matthews, Memphis Minnie, Van Morrison, Muddy Waters, Charley Patton, Paul Pena, Nina Simone, Otis Taylor, Sonny Terry, Sister Rosetta Tharpe, Tom Waits, Cassandra Wilson.* 6/29–00.

Looking at some of the stuff on this album, you may feel you're being taken for a ride. Which you are, but on nothing worse than a hobbyhorse belonging to compiler Joe Cushley, a proselytizer for 'nu blues' whose theories about the 'otherness' of the blues lead him on a search for it that sometimes ends up in surprising places: riding the next camel to 'desert blues' exponent Justin Adams, dipping into Dr John's gris-gris satchel, rocking in darkest Essex with Dr Feelgood. Some of the tracks are unarguably terrific (Lightnin' Hopkins's 'Jake Head Boogie', George Coleman's 'Eloise', Cripple Clarence Lofton's 'I Don't Know'), many interesting, some decidedly weak (Bo Diddley's 'Heart-O-Matic Love'), some ridiculous (the Bonzo Dog Band's 'Can Blue Men Sing The Whites?'). There are gifts that even the seasoned listener may be surprised by, like Paul Pena's 'Kargyraa Moan', a collision of John Lee Hooker guitar and Tuvan throat singing. What you won't find is a theme, or connections that make a sequence of, say, Chuck Berry to Cassandra Wilson to Sonny Terry illuminating rather than arbitrary. TR

Boogie Woogie

(***) Boogie Woogie Stomp
Living Era CD AJA 5101 *Albert Ammons, Albert Ammons & Pete Johnson, Albert Ammons, Meade Lux Lewis & Pete Johnson, Count Basie, The Boogie Woogie Trio, Cleo Brown, Jim Clarke, Bob Crosby, Clay Custer, Tommy Dorsey, Blind Leroy Garnett, Benny Goodman, Harry James & The Boogie Woogie Trio, Erskine Hawkins, Woody Herman (2), Earl Hines, Meade Lux Lewis (2), Jay McShann, Little Brother Montgomery, Pine Top Smith, Speckled Red, Joe Turner, Jimmy Yancey (2).* 2/23–6/41.

***(*) Boogie Woogie Blues
Biograph BCD 115 *Jimmy Blythe (3), Cow Cow Davenport (3), Lemuel Fowler, Clarence Johnson (2), James P. Johnson (2), Everett Robbins, Hersal Thomas, Clarence Williams (2).* 4/23–12/28.

(***) As Good As It Gets: Boogie Woogie
Disky DO 250512 2CD *Albert Ammons (5), Albert Ammons & Pete Johnson, Big Maceo (4), Jimmy Blythe (2), Leroy Carr, Cow Cow Davenport (3), Champion Jack Dupree, Blind Leroy Garnett, James P. Johnson (2), Pete Johnson (4), Meade Lux Lewis (4), Cripple Clarence Lofton, Little Brother Montgomery, Romeo Nelson (2), John Oscar, Turner Parrish, Red Nelson [Wilborn], Walter Roland, Pine Top Smith (2), Speckled Red (3), Roosevelt Sykes (2), Tampa Red (2), Montana Taylor (2), Joe Turner & Pete Johnson, Clarence Williams (2), Jimmy Yancey (2).* 1/26–7/45.

(****) Boogie Woogie Special
Topaz TPZ 1025 *Albert Ammons (2), Cow Cow Davenport (2), Earl Hines, Pete Johnson (3), Pete Johnson & Albert Ammons (2), Meade Lux Lewis (3), Romeo Nelson, Pine Top Smith (2), Speckled Red, Montana Taylor, Mary Lou Williams, Jimmy Yancey (3).* 7/28–3/44.

Writers on boogie woogie often spend a lot of time defining it, and then refining their definitions with exceptions and qualifications. That boogie is neither all piano music nor all eight-to-the-bar is well known. It should also be said, before the letter-writers get to work, that some of the music in this entry isn't boogie woogie: record companies often use the term loosely, or mingle boogie with other piano styles; perforce, so have we. We have also chosen to include here some discs where rhythm and good times, rather than emotional exploration, are dominant.

Living Era include most of the obvious titles, as do many of the CDs considered in this entry: there's a relatively small subset of boogie masterpieces that can scarcely be avoided, including 'Pine Top's Boogie Woogie', 'Boogie Woogie Stomp', 'Honky Tonk Train Blues' and 'Roll 'Em Pete'; there's another subset, of hits from the days of the boogie craze (Cleo Brown's and Tommy Dorsey's reworkings of 'Pine Top's Boogie Woogie', Earl Hines's 'Boogie Woogie On St Louis Blues', etc.), that are almost as inevitable if coverage extends that far.

All those titles are on *Boogie Woogie Stomp*, although the title track is the Albert Ammons Rhythm Kings' version, rather than the matchless Blue Note solo; more surprising are obscurities like Jim Clarke's gleeful 'Fat Fanny Stomp' and Clay Custer's 'The Rocks', with its trailblazing but, truth be told, not very exciting walking basses. The compilation darts about among the big three of boogie, lesser-known black pianists and swing-era big and little bands. The stylistic and aesthetic switches are often disconcerting, as when the Crosby band's meretricious 'Yancey Special' precedes Yancey's own 'Slow And Easy Blues', which is followed by two Woody Herman novelties.

Topaz primly proclaim that 'The present collection aims to bypass the more commercial aspects of Boogie ... The sole bandleader to be featured is Earl Hines, purely because his performance is much nearer the true tradition than those by other large groups.' Mary Lou Williams's 'Roll 'Em' is small-group jazz, and 'Boogie Woogie Stomp' is again the Rhythm Kings version, but otherwise the pianists are at most supported by bass and drums. The selection is an excellent one, chock full of great performances, so it's a pity that the sound quality is very ordinary, and that a pedantic, defensive booklet note seems determined to inhibit enjoyment of the music.

Biograph strain the meaning of their CD's title by including a good deal of very fine stride piano, and some pop tunes with 'Blues' appended to their titles. Even so, this is a significant disc. It's sourced from piano rolls, which are digital recordings, so the sound quality is remarkable. Other plus points are the inclusion of tunes that Davenport and Thomas never put on 78, and the opportunity to play at length: Hersal's 'Fives' is over four minutes long.

As Good As It Gets lifts seven items from Biograph, among them the James P. Johnson stride pieces; otherwise, it lines up most of the usual suspects. Their music is often wonderful, but the sequencing of tracks is random, and they are copied from many sources. As a result the sound varies wildly from one number to the next both aesthetically and technically. The notes are sketchy and poorly written.

**** Boogie Woogie Piano
Frémeaux FA 036 2CD *Albert Ammons (4), Albert Ammons & Pete Johnson (2), Charles Avery, Jimmy Blythe, The Boogie Woogie Trio, Cleo Brown, Bob Call, Cow Cow Davenport (2), Will Ezell, Cecil Gant, Blind Leroy Garnett, Lionel Hampton & Nat 'King' Cole, Pete Johnson (3), Meade Lux Lewis (3), Cripple Clarence Lofton, Jay McShann, Little Brother Montgomery, Sammy Price, Dot Rice, Pine Top Smith, Speckled Red, Montana Taylor, Hersal Thomas, Jabo Williams, Jimmy Yancey (3).*
4/24–7/45.

**** Roll 'Em Pete: 25 Years Of Piano Blues & Boogie 1928–1953 [sic]
Indigo IGOTCD 2551 3CD *Mozelle Alderson, Albert Ammons, Charles Avery, Raymond Barrow, Big Maceo, Black Ivory King, Eddie Boyd, Charles Brown, Henry Brown, Lee Brown, Bob Call, Leroy Carr, Jim Clarke, Cow Cow Davenport, Walter Davis, Texas Bill Day, Joe Dean, Floyd Dixon, Herve Duerson, Fats Domino, Champion Jack Dupree, Piano Kid Edwards, Will Ezell,* Cecil Gant, Blind Leroy Garnett, Lloyd Glenn, Rosco Gordon, Lee Green, Roy Hawkins, Hokum Boys & Jane Lucas, Camille Howard, Hattie Hudson, Skip James, Lil Johnson, Lonnie Johnson, Louise Johnson, Pete Johnson, Kid Stormy Weather, Meade Lux Lewis, Joe Liggins, Little Willie Littlefield, Cripple Clarence Lofton, Billy Love, Lonnie Lyons, Jimmy McCracklin, Willard McDaniel, Ida May Mack, Jay McShann, Memphis Slim, Lizzie Miles, Amos Milburn, Mississippi Jook Band, Little Brother Montgomery, Whistlin' Alex Moore, Romeo Nelson, John Oscar, Turner Parrish, Piano Red, Professor Longhair, Walter Roland, St Louis Jimmy [Oden], Pine Top Smith, Charlie Spand, Pinetop & Lindberg [Sparks], Speckled Red, Sunnyland Slim, Roosevelt Sykes (2), Charley Taylor, Montana Taylor, Sonny Thompson, Bessie Tucker, Joe Turner & Pete Johnson, Wesley Wallace, Mercy Dee Walton, Peetie Wheatstraw, Arnold Wiley, Jabo Williams, Jimmy Yancey.* c. 12/27–late 52.

Frémeaux's two CDs are divided into recordings from the days when piano boogie's appeal was, for practical purposes, confined to African-Americans, and others (also by black musicians) made after the crossover that started with Cleo Brown's flamboyant revival of 'Pinetop's [sic] Boogie Woogie', and was accelerated by the *réclame* Ammons, Lewis and Johnson (who dominate the second disc) garnered at the *From Spirituals To Swing* concerts. One flinches at section headings that characterize what happened as a movement 'From The Shadows … To The Light', but this collection is sonically consistent, and its compilation and annotation are historically and aesthetically informed.

Roll 'Em Pete has the same virtues, and additionally sells at a low price. It's decidedly a collection of both blues and boogie, as its subtitle avers, but there's a detectable bias to display music and dance: Bessie Tucker and her pianist K. D. Johnson are represented by 'Better Boot That Thing' rather than 'Got Cut All To Pieces', for instance. This is a pretty comprehensive survey, including obscure but notable artists like Kid Stormy Weather and Lonnie Lyons; the third disc, taking the story into the postwar years, is a valuable account of both the continuity and the variety of African-American piano blues (or more accurately, piano-led blues; soloists were a rare breed on record by this time).

**(*) Boogie Woogie & Barrelhouse Piano – Vol. 2 (1928–1930)
Document DOCD-5103 *Raymond Barrow, Bob Call, Piano Kid Edwards (4), Rudy Foster (2), Blind Leroy Garnett (2), Marie Griffin (2), Romeo Nelson (4), James 'Boodle-It' Wiggins (8).*
c. 2/28–c. 12/30.

Uneven content makes this a CD for those who can endure the dull Marie Griffin for the sake of her anonymous accompanist, or who feel a need to add Romeo Nelson's second, disappointing record to his tumultuous rent-party masterpieces. It's useful to have everything by the deep-voiced 'Boodle-It' Wiggins in one place; he seems to have been a magnet for talented accompanists. However, the best tracks are all available elsewhere (see the next three CDs) in significantly better sound. The same comment applies to *Vol. 1* (DOCD-5102), for which see Pine Top Smith.

♛ **** Juke Joint Saturday Night: Piano Blues, Rags & Stomps
Yazoo 2053 *Piano Kid Edwards, Rudy Foster (2), Skip James (2), Louise Johnson (4), Little Brother Montgomery (2), Roosevelt*

Sykes, Charley Taylor (2), Kingfish Bill Tomlin (2), James 'Boodle-It' Wiggins (3), 'Jabo' Williams (4). c. 2/28–c. 5/32.

♛ **** Shake Your Wicked Knees: Rent Parties And Good Times
Yazoo 2035 *Mozelle Alderson, Charles Avery, Henry Brown, Jim Clarke, Cow Cow Davenport (3), Joe Dean, Will Ezell, Hokum Boys & Jane Lucas (2), Lil Johnson, Meade Lux Lewis, Romeo Nelson (2), Pine Top Smith (4), Montana Taylor (3), Jimmy Yancey.* 7/28–12/43.

**** Mama Don't Allow No Easy Riders Here: Strutting The Dozens
Yazoo 2034 *Raymond Barrow, Oliver Brown, Cow Cow Davenport (6), Herve Duerson (2), Will Ezell (4), Blind Leroy Garnett (2), Turner Parrish (2), Speckled Red (3), Arnold Wiley (2).* c. 8/28–7/35.

These three CDs collectively contain the very greatest piano blues and boogie recordings from the era of 'race records', superlatively remastered and adorned by notes that cover the biographical, sociological and musical bases thoroughly and readably. *Juke Joint Saturday Night* and *Shake Your Wicked Knees* are a procession of masterpieces, Bill Tomlin's lyrically interesting but pianistically basic 'Army Blues' apart. Some of the greatest musicians on these CDs recorded only a few sides, like Louise Johnson, Joe Dean, the anonymous pianist behind Rudy Foster, and Judson Brown (Mozelle Alderson's accompanist); those who recorded more extensively, like Davenport, Sykes and Montgomery, are represented by some of their finest items. *Shake Your Wicked Knees* notably uses the 1929 Paramount version of Lewis's 'Honky Tonk Train Blues'; it's low fidelity, even after Yazoo's best efforts, but far superior to the 1935 remake used by most reissuers.

Mama Don't Allow No Easy Riders Here misses out on a crown because its emphasis on music in transition from ragtime to blues makes for an accumulation of sprightly eccentricity. The technical brilliance of musicians like Davenport, Wiley and Parrish is incontestable (Speckled Red gets by on brio), but the CD as a whole generates an excessive amount of nervous energy; it's the aural equivalent of drinking six espressos.

***(*) Boogie Woogie: Rockin' Roots Tracks
Saga 066 478-2 *Albert Ammons (3), Big Maceo, Cleo Brown, Cow Cow Davenport, Cecil Gant, Camille Howard, Pete Johnson (2), Pete Johnson & Albert Ammons, Meade Lux Lewis, Cripple Clarence Lofton, Memphis Slim, Amos Milburn, Little Brother Montgomery, Piano Red, Sammy Price, Hazel Scott, Pine Top Smith, Speckled Red, Montana Taylor, Jimmy Yancey (2).* 6/28–7/50.

Saga's collection holds few surprises, but it does usefully venture into the postwar years, when the craze was over and boogie had largely reverted to being a thread in the fabric of black music. Hazel Scott, Sam Price and Cleo Brown demonstrate that jazz pianists who dabble in boogie often stress technique at the expense of nuance and expressiveness. Price's inflated reputation among French jazz fans and his readiness to flatter them back probably account for the inclusion of 'Eiffel Tower'. The mastering is conscientious, but the treble is sometimes too bright. A companion volume, *Boogie Woogie: Big Bands Boogie* (Saga 981 063-3), is largely outside the scope of this book.

**(*) Boogie Woogie Vol. 1 – Piano Soloists
Jasmine JASMCD 2538 *Albert Ammons (2), Cow Cow Davenport (2), Art Hodes, Pete Johnson (2), Meade Lux Lewis (2), Cripple Clarence Lofton (2), Romeo Nelson, Pine Top Smith (2), Speckled Red (2), Montana Taylor (2), Jimmy Yancey (2).* 7/28–12/43.

** Boogie Woogie Vol. 2 – The Small Groups
Jasmine JASMCD 2539 *Albert Ammons, Count Basie, Big Maceo (2), Will Bradley (2), Erskine Butterfield, Benny Goodman, Lionel Hampton (2), Harlem Hamfats, Woody Herman, Harry James & The Boogie Woogie Trio (2), Buddy Johnson, Pete Johnson & Joe Turner (3), Wingy Manone, Sam Price (2), Tampa Red (2).* 2/36–7/42.

Jasmine's sound restoration is good enough but no more. Art Hodes's dull, anomalous closer apart, the soloists on *Vol. 1* are the obvious choices, represented by the obvious recordings. Much of *Vol. 2*, and virtually all of *Vol. 3 – The Big Bands* (Jasmine JASMCD 2540), consists of jazz and swing bands servicing the brief nationwide craze for boogie. This stuff often features febrile tempos, gimmicky arrangements and predictable solos, and on *Vol. 3* there's frequent descent into schlock.

*** Juke Joint Jump: A Boogie Woogie Celebration
Columbia/Legacy CK 64988 *Albert Ammons, The Boogie Woogie Boys (2), Champion Jack Dupree, Calvin Frazier, Harry James & the Boogie Woogie Trio, Pete Johnson, Pete Johnson (with Big Joe Turner), Memphis Slim, Adrian Rollini Trio, Red Saunders & His Orchestra, Freddie Slack, Willie 'Long Time' Smith, Charlie Spand, Art Tatum, Sir Charles Thompson, Curley Weaver with Clarence Moore, Jimmy Yancey.* 11/31–7/61.

Juke Joint Jump's title would have offended many of the artists featured; it's the least imaginative thing about a CD that features the usual artists with the usual tracks ('Roll 'Em Pete', 'Boogie Woogie Prayer', 'Shout For Joy', 'Boo Woo') but also includes worthwhile obscurities like Willie 'Long Time' Smith, and Weaver and Frazier's zingy guitar boogies. The CD also embraces jazz and swing flirtations with boogie: some, like Sir Charles Thompson's vivacious organ excursion, 'Mister Boogie', and – of all things – Adrian Rollini's vibraphone version of 'Honky Tonk Train Blues', are very successful; some, like Red Saunders's starchy swing-band arrangement of the same tune and the flashy nullities of 'Tatum Pole Boogie', are not.

**(*) Blue Boogie: Boogie Woogie, Stride & The Piano Blues
Blue Note CDP 799099 *Albert Ammons (4), Albert Ammons & Meade Lux Lewis, Sammy Benskin, Earl Hines, Art Hodes (2), James P. Johnson (3), Pete Johnson (2), Meade Lux Lewis (4), Art Tatum.* 1/39–7/49.

Slightly more than half of *Blue Boogie* is allotted to the big three. Two of the tracks credited to James P. Johnson are by the jazz bands of Edmond Hall and Sidney DeParis; 'Blue Note Boogie', with Hall, shows that boogie wasn't really James P.'s thing. His fellow stride pianists Hines and Tatum are their usual accomplished selves, but Hodes and Benskin are undistinguished, and in the former's band trumpeter Max Kaminsky is endlessly uninventive. The booklet notes are deeply confused about the development of jazz and blues piano. *Ammons & Lewis – The First Day* (Blue Note CDP 7 98450) is vastly preferable.

*** Specialty Legends Of Boogie-Woogie
Ace CDCHD 422 *Nelson Alexander Trio (2), Camille Howard (8), Jo Jo Jackson, Joe Liggins, Joe Lutcher (2), Willard McDaniel (4), Roy Milton (2), Smilin' Smokey Lynn*. 4/47–2/52.

It's pointless to criticize Art Rupe for chasing jukebox coin by applying and reapplying the boogie-piano-plus-shuffle-drumming formula that made Camille Howard's 'X-Temporaneous Boogie' an exciting performance and a Top Ten hit. Equally, it would be wrong not to note that it is a formula, and one that's also applied on titles by McDaniel and Jackson. Howard was a member of Roy Milton's band; his tracks, and others with horn sections, are skilfully sequenced to break up her parade of 'Instantaneous', 'Ferocious', 'Miraculous' et cetera boogies. Nelson Alexander's trio – piano, guitar and bass, with unison vocals in the manner of early Nat 'King' Cole recordings – also adds variety.

**(*) Masters Of The Boogie Piano
Delmark DX-908 *Albert Ammons, Ammons–Lewis–[Pete] Johnson, Steve Behr, Pete Johnson, Curtis Jones, Meade Lux Lewis, Robert McCoy, Little Brother Montgomery, Ken Saydak, Speckled Red, Roosevelt Sykes, Sir Charles Thompson*. 9/39–1/01.

Issued as part of Delmark's 50th Anniversary series, *Masters Of The Boogie Piano* demonstrates that boogie is not the label's strongest suit. The Hotel Sherman airshots are not the Boogie Woogie Trio's best or best recorded sides; Sir Charles Thompson is aimless; Pete Johnson's '66 Stomp' is pointless exhibitionism; and among the African-American veterans, only Curtis Jones's harmonically daring reimagination of 'Pine Top's Boogie Woogie' shows much adventurousness. The liveliest tracks are by the revivalists Saydak and Behr, thanks in no small part to the drumming of Greg Bigger and Barrett Deems respectively.

(***) 15 Piano Blues & Boogie Classics
Arhoolie CD 108 *Big Joe Duskin, Henry Gray, Pete Johnson, Lafayette Leake (with Charlie Musselwhite), Whistling Alex Moore, Elmore Nixon (with Clifton Chenier), Pinetop Perkins (with L. C. 'Good Rockin'' Robinson), Piano Red, Omar Sharriff, Robert Shaw, Otis Spann (with Johnny Young), Thunder Smith, Mercy Dee [Walton], Katie Webster, Bukka [Booker] White*. c. 4/49–91.

Like others in this budget-priced series, this sampler is mainly advertising for full-priced Arhoolie releases; photos of their covers stand in for notes. The CD carries out its mission entertainingly, although the selections are not always typical of the artists or the parent discs; anyone led from here to Katie Webster's Arhoolie album is likely to be disappointed.

** Blues 88's: Boogie-Woogie Instrumentals
Easydisc ED CD 7060 *Honey Alexander, Deanna Bogart, James Booker, Al Copley, Davell Crawford, Jay McShann, David Maxwell, Preacher Jack, Roomful Of Blues, Katie Webster*. 4/82–97.

Drawing on the parent Rounder label's own catalogue and several others, this collection contains little of interest apart from Snooks Eaglin's solo on Copley's 'My Bonnie Rocks'. Most tracks feature extreme tempos and flashy figuration, not always successfully executed. Honey Alexander's interminable 'Buzzin' is a duet with the Mighty Flyers' drummer, who recalls Gene Krupa, but without the restrained good taste. Readers are advised to go direct to the parent CDs by Katie Webster (*Two-Fisted Mama!*) and James Booker (*Classified*).

***(*) Great Boogie Woogie News
Document DOCD-7001 *Tibor Grasser (6), Daniel Gugolz (5), Frank Muschalle (5), Martin Pyrker (4)*. 10/93–6/95.

Who could have predicted that at the end of the 20th century German and Austrian musicians would be the most creative successors of the great boogie pianists, and of early blues players like Henry Brown? The reasons – apart from the tireless proselytizing of Axel Zwingenberger – must be for others to seek; here it's sufficient to note that these four pianists, aged between 25 and 41 when recorded, play with great technical command and a maturity of feeling beyond their years. Pyrker is a disciple of Jimmy Yancey, but no copyist; his singing lines and the fecundity of his ideas command respect, although the six-minute 'O.B. Blues' is too long. Gugolz, also sticking to original compositions, favours slow to medium tempos and polyrhythmic complexities; one can admire these and still regret his successful quest for a slightly out-of-tune piano to play them on. All but one of Grasser's tracks is a cover, and 'Hootie's Old Stuff' is a homage; they're excitingly executed, especially when driven by Gugolz's bass and the drumming of Peter Müller, but there's a slight sense of conscientious revivalism. Muschalle's readings of Ammons, Lewis and Little Brother Montgomery can stand comparison with the originals, and his lyrical 'Good Morning Blues' is admirably conceived and played. cs

Chicago I (Prewar)

(***(*)) Chicago Urban Blues 1923–1945
Acrobat ACRCD 194 *Kokomo Arnold, Big Maceo, Big Bill Broonzy, Bumble Bee Slim, Ida Cox, Georgia Tom [Dorsey] & Hannah May [Mozelle Alderson], Jazz Gillum, Lil Green, Harlem Hamfats, Bertha 'Chippie' Hill, Lil Johnson, Lonnie Johnson, Meade Lux Lewis, Tommy McClennan, Memphis Minnie, Memphis Slim, Bob Robinson, Faber Smith, Pine Top Smith, Roosevelt Sykes, Tampa Red, Hersal Thomas, Sippie Wallace, Washboard Sam, Sonny Boy Williamson I*. c. 7/23–45.

Budget-priced and tautologously titled, *Chicago Urban Blues* is one of the few VACs in this area that doesn't either concentrate on the '30s and Bluebird or define Chicago blues as 'blues recorded in Chicago'. Its chronological programming and excellent notes skilfully illustrate the way the city's blues, and its blues recordings, changed: women singers and rent-party performers give way to the hokum craze; A&R man Lester Melrose develops a production-line system that nevertheless generated many great records; and new sounds foreshadow the postwar revolution in the city's music. The mastering is very ordinary, however, and the evaluated copy had multiple skips on the first six tracks.

**** That's Chicago's South Side
Bluebird 63988 *Big Bill Broonzy, Bumble Bee Slim, Leroy Carr, Walter Davis, Jazz Gillum, Lil Johnson, Lonnie Johnson, Merline Johnson, Richard M. Jones, Meade Lux Lewis, Tommy McClennan, Robert Lee McCoy [Robert Nighthawk], Memphis Minnie, St Louis Jimmy [Oden], Joe Pullum, Yank Rachell, Pine Top [Sparks], Speckled Red, Roosevelt Sykes, Tampa Red, Johnnie*

Temple, Sam Theard, Washboard Sam, Peetie Wheatstraw, Sonny Boy Williamson I. 9/31–2/42.

***(*) Chicago Blues
Camden Deluxe 72709 2CD *Eddie Boyd, Big Bill Broonzy (2), Big Maceo (2), Leroy Carr, Doctor Clayton, Arthur 'Big Boy' Crudup (2), Walter Davis, Pete Franklin, Jazz Gillum (3), Lil Green, Lil Johnson, Lonnie Johnson, Robert Lockwood (2), Joe McCoy, Robert Lee McCoy [Robert Nighthawk], Memphis Minnie, Memphis Slim, St Louis Jimmy [Oden], Yank Rachell, Roosevelt Sykes (2), Tampa Red (4), Washboard Sam (2), Big Joe Williams (2), Sonny Boy Williamson I (5). 3/34–12/53.*

That's Chicago's South Side claims to illustrate the great migration and, more convincingly, to tell the story of the blues on Bluebird, RCA's budget label set up in the teeth of the Depression. (Meade Lux Lewis's remake of 'Honky Tonk Train Blues' was aimed at white jazz fans, and appeared on the full-priced Victor label.) Musicians from Texas, Tennessee, St Louis and Mississippi appear alongside Chicago residents, but the recordings were made there (or, if non-union, at a hotel in nearby Aurora), and *That's Chicago's South Side* demonstrates the considerable diversity in the so-called 'Bluebird beat'. Impeccably remastered, it's an entertaining alternative to Document's multivolume single-artist sets, which are valuable but bear no relationship to the way the 78s' original listeners consumed them.

Chicago Blues is another discriminating raid on RCA's treasury. With 40 tracks to fill, compiler Mike Rowe has room to show both the music's variety and the way it changed in the hands of long-term signings like Williamson, Gillum and Tampa Red. In doing so, Rowe ably disproves his own amusing but excessive dismissal of 'the Melrose mess', quoted in the notes. Some out-of-towners again infiltrate the selection, but that's both inevitable and necessary, for music in clubs and taverns across the country was increasingly shaped by music made in the studios. Transfers are good, but a notch below those on *That's Chicago's South Side*.

*** Chicago Blues – Vol. 1 (1939–1951)
Document DOCD-5270 *Alfred Fields (8), Tony Hollins (11), Johnny Shines (6). 7/39–10/51.*

**(*) Chicago Blues – Vol. 2 (1939–1944)
Document DOCD-5444 *Baby Doo [Leonard Caston] (2), Champion Jack Dupree (10), The Five Breezes (8), Gene Gilmore (4), Ruth Ladson (2). 9/39–c. 8/46.*

These two volumes were compiled by the 'what can we fit on a CD?' method, but *Vol. 1* has some narrative coherence. Alfred Fields's dryly querulous singing is reminiscent of St Louis Jimmy; what his accompanists (Big Bill Broonzy, Washboard Sam and probably Joshua Altheimer) do is usually more interesting than what he does. Tony Hollins, from Clarksdale, was a popular and significant figure: John Lee Hooker and Jimmy Rogers learned his songs and assimilated his tumbling rhythms and his forceful but undeclamatory singing. In 1951, Hollins played electric guitar, accompanied by Sunnyland Slim, a second guitarist and a bassist. Two of the four songs recorded were revived from 1941, when the lineup had been acoustic guitar, one-string bass and washboard. Apart from its intrinsic quality, Hollins's output is thus a good picture of how Delta and Chicago blues changed during the intervening decade. Johnny Shines's first recordings are discussed under his entry, but this is where the writer of the booklet notes gives himself a good kicking for asserting that Shines played bottleneck guitar on his Chess session.

Baby Doo and Gene Gilmore both composed sombre accounts of the Natchez dancehall fire which had recently claimed Walter Barnes' Orchestra and 200 audience members. Gilmore also urbanizes Charlie McCoy and Blind Boy Fuller, and Caston sings an unexpectedly bucolic 'I'm Gonna Walk Your Log', accompanied by his own guitar and Ann Sortier's washboard. Both men were members of the Five Breezes, whose Ink Spots imitations are proof of the versatility of musicians and the arbitrariness of definitions. Ruth Ladson's self-assured sexiness is complemented by Lonnie Johnson's poised picking. In no sense are Jack Dupree's tracks – four alternative takes from OKeh, and five numbers recorded in New York – stylistically Chicagoan. There's some rewarding material on *Vol. 2*, but its randomness works against it; so does the unfashionable nature of the Five Breezes' music.

❦ **** Chicago Blues 1940–1947
Frémeaux FA 150 2CD *Big Maceo, Big Three Trio, Eddie Boyd, Big Bill Broonzy, Othum Brown, Doctor Clayton, Walter Davis, Homer Harris, Tony Hollins, Lonnie Johnson, Curtis Jones, Floyd Jones (2), Little Walter (2), Robert Jr Lockwood, Joe McCoy, Robert Lee McCoy [Robert Nighthawk], Memphis Minnie, Memphis Slim, Muddy Waters (2), St Louis Jimmy [Oden], Snooky Pryor, Yank Rachell, Harmon Ray, Charlie Segar, Johnny Shines, Sunnyland Slim, Roosevelt Sykes, Tampa Red, Washboard Sam, Big Joe Williams, Sonny Boy Williamson I, Johnny Young. 2/40–12/47.*

This *Chicago Blues* (what is it about the Windy City that encourages such bald titles?) focuses on the transition from the relatively sophisticated sounds of Chicago recordings in the early and middle '40s to the transplanted, amplified Southern music that came to signify Chicago blues to the world at large. There was some splendid music being made by small combos with brass and reeds, descended from the Harlem Hamfats and driven by the popularity of Louis Jordan and Roy Milton: notable examples here include tracks by Memphis Slim, Eddie Boyd and Roosevelt Sykes; Big Bill Broonzy's song, though it's without horns, inhabits the same aesthetic world. At the same time, the likes of Floyd Jones, Othum Brown, Johnny Young and Snooky Pryor were making rough, tough music redolent of the street and the tavern. The two strains clashed head-on when Muddy Waters made his commercial debut, singing 'Mean Red Spider' with a jazz-minded sax section. That track is one of many imaginative selections (others are by Charlie Segar, Curtis Jones and Harmon Ray) in a collection that invaluably illustrates the complex, dynamic nature of a change that can fairly be described as revolutionary, but in which continuity was just as important. CS

Chicago II (Postwar)

A large part of the Chicago blues story is the contribution of the city's record companies, among them Chess, J.O.B., Vee-Jay, Cobra and United in the '40s–'60s and Delmark, Alligator and others since the '70s. Many compilations devoted to those and other Chicago labels are discussed in LABEL HISTORIES & SHOWCASES, and what follows should be read in conjunction with those reviews.

COMPILATIONS

*** Sweet Home Chicago: A History Of Chicago Blues
Indigo IGOTCD 2534 3CD *Luther Allison, Carey Bell, Big Maceo (2), Eddie Boyd (2), Big Bill Broonzy (3), Lee Brown, Eddie C. Campbell, Joe Carter, Eddy Clearwater, James Cotton, Big Boy Crudup (2), Cow Cow Davenport, Willie Dixon, David 'Honeyboy' Edwards, Baby Face Leroy [Foster] (2), Bill Gaither, Jazz Gillum (2), Buddy Guy, Rosa Henderson, [Bertha] Chippie Hill, Tony Hollins, Homesick James, Howlin' Wolf, Papa Charlie Jackson, Floyd Jones, J. B. Lenoir, Little Walter, Robert [Jr] Lockwood, Tommy McClennan, Memphis Minnie, Memphis Slim (2), Muddy Waters (2), Robert Nighthawk (2), St Louis Jimmy [Oden], Snooky [Pryor] & Moody [Jones], Jimmy Reed, Fenton Robinson, Jimmy Rogers, Little Mac [Simmons], Bessie Smith, Byther Smith, Sparks Brothers (2), Sunnyland Slim (2), Roosevelt Sykes (2), Tampa Red (2), Hound Dog Taylor, Koko Taylor, [Big] Joe Turner, Washboard Sam, Junior Wells, Peetie Wheatstraw, Big Joe Williams, Sonny Boy Williamson I (3), Man [Johnny] Young.* 24–80s.

***(*) Chicago Blues Electric Guitar 1945–1951
EPM Blues Collection 16023 *John Brim, Big Bill Broonzy, Sam Casimir (with Eddie Boyd), Leonard Caston, Arthur 'Big Boy' Crudup (2), Floyd Jones, Willie Lacey (with Jazz Gillum) (2), J. B. Lenoir (2), Little Walter, Robert Jr Lockwood (2), Memphis Minnie (2), Muddy Waters (2), Robert Nighthawk, Jimmy Rogers (2), Johnny Shines, Tampa Red, Johnny Young & Johnny Williams.* 45–51.

**** Down Home Blues Classics: Chicago 1946–1954
Boulevard Vintage BVBCD 1014 4CD *Grace Brim (2), John Brim (5), Lee Brown (3), [Baby Face] Leroy Foster (2), Little Willie Foster (2), Rocky Fuller [Louisiana Red], Tony Hollins (3), Homesick James (4), J. B. Hutto (6), Floyd Jones (10), Little Johnny Jones (2), Albert King (2), J. B. Lenoir (4), Little Walter (2), Robert [Jr] Lockwood (2), Lazy Bill Lucas (2), Muddy Waters (4), Willie Nix (4), Morris Pejoe (3), Snooky Pryor (2), Jimmy Reed (3), Jimmy Rogers (4), Johnny Shines (2), Big Boy Spires (4), Sunnyland Slim (4), Essie Sykes (2), Tampa Red (7), Junior Wells (5), Johnny Young (4).* 46–54.

*** The Golden Age Of Blue Chicago
Blue Chicago BC 5003 *Luther Allison, Billy Boy Arnold, Earl Hooker, Howlin' Wolf, Elmore James, J. B. Lenoir, Little Walter, Robert Jr Lockwood, Magic Sam, Muddy Waters, Jimmy Reed, Otis Rush, Sonny Boy Williamson II, Otis Spann, Sunnyland Slim, Eddie Taylor, Hound Dog Taylor, Junior Wells.* 8/49–71.

***(*) Blues Masters, Volume 2: Postwar Chicago
Rhino R2 71122 *Bo Diddley, Eddie Boyd, Baby Face Leroy [Foster], Buddy Guy, Earl Hooker, Howlin' Wolf, J. B. Lenoir, Little Walter, Robert Jr Lockwood, Magic Sam, Muddy Waters, Jimmy Reed, Jimmy Rogers, Otis Rush, Johnny Shines, Sonny Boy Williamson II, Junior Wells, Jody Williams.* 50–8/61.

**(*) The Rough Guide To Chicago Blues
Rough Guide RGNET 1118 *Eddy Clearwater, James Cotton, Buddy Guy, John Lee Hooker, Elmore James, Johnny Jones & Billy Boy Arnold, Little Walter, John Littlejohn, Magic Sam, Muddy Waters, Charlie Musselwhite, Robert Nighthawk, Otis Rush, Otis Spann (2), Nolan Struck, Roosevelt Sykes, Hound Dog Taylor, Koko Taylor, Valerie Wellington, Junior Wells.* 50–83.

As has already been remarked, not much originality has gone into titling albums of Chicago blues. Amazingly, nobody has even come up with the obvious (you'd think) *West Side Story*. Not that it would do for any of these half-dozen, because they have a South Side story to tell, too, and other narratives besides. They also have to deal with a recording log that stretches over 60 years, not counting the pre-World War II period covered in the preceding section. A single CD can do little more than form a parade of hits, or of recordings generally agreed to be classics. The Rhino set does that particularly well, interspersing famous records like Howlin' Wolf's 'Smokestack Lightnin', Eddie Boyd's 'Five Long Years' and Otis Rush's and Magic Sam's different 'All Your Love's with choice but not so well known pieces like Robert Lockwood's 'Sweet Woman (From Maine)' and Jody Williams's 'You May'. Blue Chicago field a similar cast but a largely different programme (only four duplications). Either of these will thrust the newcomer into the company of many great artists. The Rough Guide set is quirkier – not everyone, given 21 slots to fill with Chicago blues exponents, would choose Eddy Clearwater, let alone Nolan Struck – and some artists are represented by less than thrilling performances.

But it's to the bigger collections that readers will look for the larger picture, and both are illuminating, though differently. *Sweet Home Chicago* backtracks before World War II, partly to show what records were then being made in Chicago by 'race' stars like Broonzy, Memphis Minnie and Sonny Boy Williamson I, partly to fit in some songs *about* Chicago like Papa Charlie Jackson's 'Maxwell Street Blues'. Towards the end of Disc 2, and intermittently through Disc 3, artists like Sunnyland Slim, Jimmy Rogers and Hound Dog Taylor exemplify the changes of the '40s and '50s, but because of licensing restrictions this is a very random sequence, and what look like key recordings are often inferior remakes. Boulevard's box, though similarly circumscribed, embraces the limitation and focuses hard on the crucial eight-year period in which old-school artists like Tampa Red and Lee Brown were drowned out by the new Southern kids on the block: Muddy Waters, Little Walter, Junior Wells, J. B.s Lenoir and Hutto. How history was made in those years would be easier to follow if the 100 tracks had been arranged chronologically, or at least *more* chronologically, but the fragrances of invention and unpredictable inspiration rise in a rich, aromatic fog, and the box's rollcall of four-star recordings is prodigious.

If you do demand an account that unfolds logically, listen carefully to the intelligently chosen *Chicago Blues Electric Guitar*, which shows how the production-line machinery of the old labels like Bluebird was broken up by the Luddites from Mississippi and Arkansas. It isn't so much the sound of the guitar that changes as its role in the performance. Willie Lacey with Jazz Gillum or Sam Casimir with Eddie Boyd are interior decorators; the songs would exist without them, they just wouldn't be so pretty. Muddy Waters, Jimmy Rogers and Robert Jr Lockwood are builders; for them, the guitar line is the structural skeleton of the song. The most momentous thing the Chicago downhome movement of the late '40s did was take the music back to its origins, a man with a guitar, and even when it developed into a band music it was still, very often, a man with a guitar who steered it.

*** South Side Chicago Blues
Delmark DX-912 *Carey Bell, Lurrie Bell, Big Time Sarah, J. B. Hutto, Little Walter, Robert Jr Lockwood, Jimmy Rogers, Byther Smith, Sunnyland Slim, Junior Wells.* 8/49–2/00.

*** West Side Chicago Blues
Delmark DX-906 *Luther Allison, Jimmy Dawkins, Little Arthur Duncan, Syl Johnson, Willie Kent, Magic Sam, Johnny B. Moore, Otis Rush, Tail Dragger.* 7/67–2/99.

These are from the 'Saver Series' that Delmark produced for its 50th anniversary, and no one would expect them to be extensive surveys of their subjects, but each album uses its playing time of around 40 minutes well. *West Side Chicago Blues* is able to draw on original Delmark albums by Otis Rush, Magic Sam, Luther Allison and Jimmy Dawkins that helped to define the style. *South Side*, made up of recordings spanning more than half a century, is inevitably a jerkier ride. Lurrie Bell is near his formidable best on 'All Over Again'.

**(*) Windy City Blues
Stax SCD 8612 *Billy Boy Arnold (3), Willie Dixon (2), Homesick James (3), Albert King (4), Otis Spann (2), Sunnyland Slim (3). 12/59–3/70.*

Windy City Blues opens with a previously unissued 1970 session by Albert King. Backed by a Chicago band organized by Willie Dixon, with Matt Murphy and a horn section led by Gene Barge, King delivers four above-average numbers (three written by Dixon) which any serious collector of his work will want to own. The rest of the CD is made up of tracks from Prestige album sessions by Chicago acts, all available on Original Blues Classics CDs (Homesick James's three are alternative takes); some are good, some mediocre (see the artists' entries for more detailed comment), but clearly their only purpose here is to fill out an album so that the King session could be released.

*** Rare Chicago Blues, 1962–1968
Bullseye Blues CD BB 9530 *James Cotton (3), John Lee Granderson, Johnny Jones (2), Maxwell Street Jimmy, Little Brother Montgomery (4), Robert Nighthawk (2), Otis Spann (2), Rev. Robert Wilkins, Big Joe Williams (3), Robert Pete Williams. 62–68.*

'Rare Chicago blues', as most enthusiasts would use the term, would be obscure 78s on labels like Old Swingmaster or Hy-Tone, so it's a peculiar description for music taped, often informally, at University of Chicago festivals, in clubs, possibly even in people's houses – and, in the case of Robert Nighthawk's tracks, on the street, for these were recorded for a documentary film about Maxwell Street and have been issued elsewhere (see Nighthawk's entry for more on this). But while the title scores no bull's-eyes for accuracy, the album contains several performances that speed unerringly into the listener's heart. Otis Spann's 'Blues For Martin Luther King' and 'Hotel Lorraine' were recorded on the day Dr King was assassinated and bleed with pain like an open wound. The ever-captivating Johnny Jones remembers Big Maceo in 'Worried Life Blues' and accompanies Billy Boy Arnold remembering Sonny Boy Williamson I in 'I Hear My Black Name Ringing'. James Cotton's 'So Glad You're Mine' may be his best recorded vocal. For music like that, and for the many other tracks that are, at the least, honest and affecting, the listener should be happy to pay the small price of occasionally lo-fi recording.

***(*) Chicago/The Blues/Today!
Vanguard 172/74 3CD *James Cotton (5), Homesick James (4), Walter Horton, J. B. Hutto (5), Otis Rush (5), Johnny Shines (6), Otis Spann (5), Junior Wells (5), Johnny Young (4). 12/65.*

In the winter of 1965 Sam Charters went to Chicago to record some of the city's leading blues artists. The results were issued the following year on three albums titled *Chicago/The Blues/Today!* (Vanguard VMD 79216, 79217 and 79218). In 1999 Vanguard reissued the albums as a very handsome 3CD set, with a booklet containing the original sleevenotes and an essay by Charters recalling how the project was conceived and executed. A sticker on this reissue asserts: '"This series got even better with age. Rating 100." – Robert Cray'. In any gathering of blues aficionados that evaluation would probably be hotly debated. It could be argued, and in several of the entries in this book it is argued, that not all the artists were caught at their best. All of them went on to make several, or many, more recordings, generally in more flattering studios and sometimes with more appropriate accompanists. Age, in fact, has left some of this material looking rather threadbare. But the effect of their exposure on a leading folk/blues label was unarguably beneficial for many of the artists, as it was for the rapidly growing audience for Chicago blues, and the project's historical importance is unassailable.

**(*) Sweet Home Chicago
Delmark DD-618 *Luther Allison (2), Big Mojo [Elem] (2), Lucky Lopez [Leo Evans], Magic Sam (4), Louis Myers (2). 2/66–7/68.*

This was a slightly odd album when it first appeared on LP in the late '60s; reissued without additions, it's still a peculiar-looking collection, and not wonderful value if you go by playing time (33.15), but the wise reader will not discount any album containing unique material by Magic Sam and Luther Allison. That said, only a couple of Magic Sam's numbers are significant additions to his discography, and nearly all the performances seem rather thin, as if they were trial runs for more developed recordings that never took place.

*** Crucial Chicago Blues
Alligator ALCD 116 *Luther Allison, Carey Bell, Lonnie Brooks, James Cotton, Magic Slim & The Teardrops, Pinetop Perkins, Fenton Robinson, Son Seals, Hound Dog Taylor, Koko Taylor, Lil' Ed [Williams] & The Blues Imperials. 74–02.*

A raid of the Alligator stables, releasing a dozen Chicago-trained thoroughbreds. Seals's 'Cotton Picking Blues', Lil' Ed's 'My Mind Is Gone' and Cotton's '23 Hours Too Long' set the pace, but Robinson slides home by a head with 'I Hear Some Blues Downstairs'. An inexpensive and exhilarating day at the races.

*** Living Chicago Blues – Vol. I
Alligator ALCD 7701 *Carey Bell (4), Left Hand Frank [Craig] (4), Jimmy Johnson (4), Eddie Shaw (5). 78.*

*** Living Chicago Blues – Vol. II
Alligator ALCD 7702 *Lonnie Brooks (4), Magic Slim (4), Pinetop Perkins (4), Johnny 'Big Moose' Walker (4). 78.*

*** Living Chicago Blues – Vol. III
Alligator ALCD 7703 *Lacy Gibson (4), Lovie Lee & Carey Bell (4), A. C. Reed (4), Scotty & The Rib Tips (4), The Sons Of Blues (3). 78.*

*** Living Chicago Blues – Vol. IV
Alligator ALCD 7704 *Big Leon Brooks (4), Andrew Brown (3), Detroit Jr (4), Queen Sylvia Embry (4), Luther 'Guitar Jr' Johnson (4). 78.*

*** The New Bluebloods
Alligator ALCD 7707 *Michael Coleman, Donald Kinsey & The Kinsey Report, Dion Payton, The Professor's Blues Review, The Sons Of Blues/Chi-Town Hustlers, Melvin Taylor, Maurice John Vaughn, John Watkins, Valerie Wellington, Lil' Ed [Williams] & The Blues Imperials. c. 86.*

COMPILATIONS

Early in 1978 Alligator Records began recording for a series of albums, titled *Living Chicago Blues*, which would showcase working bands that either hadn't recorded before or had no representative material on the market. Three LPs came out later that year, and three more in 1980; their contents, consisting of four or five (occasionally three) tracks by each act, have been rearranged on four CDs. If selection for the project was a tip-off that the artist would go far, or at least some way farther, most of Alligator's predictions came true. All the 18 acts featured went on to add at least one full-length album to their CV, though a few of them, like Left Hand Frank Craig (1939–92), Buddy (Scotty) Scott (1935–94) and Andrew Brown (1937–85), had to go outside the US to do so. Some of the sessions made promises that proved hard to fulfil. Jimmy Johnson and Lacy Gibson took a while to equal the material they cut for Alligator; as it happens, neither artist has recorded for the label since. Since many of the contributions are discussed in the artists' entries, we'll confine ourselves here to brief notes on some that aren't, but it should be emphasized that all the CDs are rewarding as volumes, not just as collections of chapters.

With hindsight one can guess why Craig (*Vol. I*) and Scott (*Vol. III*) proved hard to develop, because both were sturdy, oldfashioned and somewhat anonymous singers. Andrew Brown (*Vol. IV*) is another matter. A handsome singer and guitarist whose music has somewhat the same emotional impact as Fenton Robinson's, he never got his dues in the US, partly because of recurrent health problems, and his two LPs for Dutch labels remain unreissued. His three tracks on *Vol. IV* serve as a too-brief testament. Luther Johnson (*Vol. IV*) plays a spirited set with other Muddy Waters alumni, then some of the same musicians accompany Pinetop Perkins (*Vol. II*) on one of his better sessions. The predominance of such middle-aged artists makes it clear that Alligator were not looking for their successors, but they did place one bet on the distant future in recording the Sons Of Blues, led by Lurrie Bell and Billy Branch, then in their 20s. It was the one band they rerecorded about eight years later when they constructed another showcase album, *The New Bluebloods*, subtitled 'The Next Generation of Chicago Blues'. Here the agenda was quite different. Most of the musicians were in their 20s or early 30s and had never recorded before, and each act had just one chance to register an impact. Quite a few of them did so to some effect: within a few years the Kinseys, Vaughn and Lil' Ed Williams had recorded albums for Alligator, Wellington for Rooster and Coleman, Taylor and Watkins for European companies. *The New Bluebloods*, then, is a fascinating time capsule, but several of the performances, like Watkins's 'Chained To Your Love' and Vaughn's 'Nothing Left To Believe In', stand up to anything the artists recorded later.

(*) From West Helena To Chicago (Chicago Blues Session Vol. 8)
Wolf 120.854 *Eddie C. Campbell (5), Honeyboy Edwards & Johnny B. Moore (5), Magic Slim, Johnny B. Moore (2), John Primer.* 8/84–7/92.

'Mostly unplugged,' it says on the box, but you'd hardly expect Honeyboy Edwards to be hefting a Strat, and anyone familiar with the work of Moore, Primer and Magic Slim knows that they are fond of playing acoustic. Unfortunately they tend to fall back on deeply familiar repertoire like 'Mojo Hand' (Primer) and 'Rock Me [Baby]' (Campbell). Moore's careful seconding keeps Honeyboy's playing a little tighter than it sometimes is, and his own 'Straighten Up Woman', a plain-speaking reproof to an unreliable partner, is the best track. The album is reviewed in this section because most of the performers are primarily associated with Chicago, but musically it could just as well have been placed under MISSISSIPPI.

(*) Chicago Blues Legends
Wolf 120.863 *Detroit Jr (3), Willie Johnson (3), Floyd Jones (2), Dave Myers (4), Jimmie Lee Robinson (3), Mac Thompson (2).* 6/84–1/96.

(*) Chicago's Best West- And Southside Blues Singers Vol. 2
Wolf 120.807 *George Baze (2), Lefty Dizz (2), Johnny Laws, Hip Linkchain (2), Lovie Lee (2), Foree Superstar Montgomery (2), Eddie Taylor Jr, Larry Taylor (3).* 8/87–1/95.

*** Chicago's Best West & South Side Blues Singers Vol. 1**
Wolf 120.862 *Booba Barnes (4), Jake Dawson, Little Wolf (2), Barkin' Bill [Smith] (2), Tail Dragger (3).* 89–1/95.

For many enthusiasts the draw on *Chicago Blues Legends* will be the three tracks that are among the very few latterday recordings of Willie Johnson, guitarist on the early Howlin' Wolf records. Unfortunately the crawling tempo of 'Anna Lee' and 'Rocky Mountain' gives him no reason to relight the fires of '51, even if he could have found the matches. Dave Myers's stolid tracks also have rarity value, since his one album, *You Can't Do That* (Black Top CD BT 1142), has vanished. Johnny B. Moore plays guitar on these, as well as on two Jimmy Reed retreads by bassist Mac Thompson and, with Vance Kelly, on Detroit Jr's amiable 'You've Been Laid'. The second of Wolf's *Chicago's Best* collections may be the more beckoning, with its selections by under-recorded figures like George Baze (1942–98) and Foree 'Superstar' Montgomery (1943–99), and early work by Eddie Taylor's sons Larry and Eddie Jr, but the performances are built to standard specifications throughout. *Vol. 1* could almost be refiled in TRIBUTES & SONGBOOKS, since two of its performers, Lee 'Little Wolf' Solomon and Tail Dragger, are overt Howlin' Wolf devotees and 'Booba' Barnes follows the same star on 'Louise' and 'How Many More Years', though not on his own 'Heartbroken Man', which he does in short and long versions. Vocally Little Wolf sounds nothing like his model but his sides are enhanced by Billy Branch's harmonica and succinct ensemble work. The same group accompanies Tail Dragger and, reduced, Jake Dawson, a guitarist whose credentials are unquestioned, but no singer.

(*) Chicago Blues Rockin' After Midnight
St George STG 7708 *Joshie Armstrong, Chicago Slim, The El Doradoes, Big Mojo Elem, Jo Ann Garrett, Paul Jones, Prez Kenneth, Pretty Things/Yardbird Blues Band, Little Mack Simmons, Studebaker John, Tail Dragger, Andre Williams.* 91–97.

George Paulus, the collector who owns St George, is a retrophile. If you told him these '90s recordings sounded as though they had been made 30 years earlier, he'd be delighted. If you said 40, he'd probably buy you a drink. Here he put together a house band of fellow-thinkers like Studebaker John Grimaldi, who plays harmonica or guitar on every track, with Rockin' Johnny Burgin playing occasional leads, and wheeled in blues singers who match his aesthetic. Some of these may surprise you: Papa Lightfoot's 'Wine, Women & Whiskey' is sung by Phil May of the English R&B band The Pretty Things, and Floyd Jones's 'Keep What You Got' by Paul Jones of The Blues Band; the second, at least, is excellent. Joshie Armstrong and Jo Ann Garrett are soul singers trying their hand at blues, and they don't make much of a fist of it, but the music behind them is okay; odd, though, to have Garrett's 'Scratch My Back' and Studebaker John's 'Back Scratcher' on the same programme. You could call the whole thing a kind of in-joke, but if you share Paulus's taste you'll enjoy it. If not, not.

**(*) Blues Before Sunrise Live – Volume One

Delmark DE-699 *Billy Boy Arnold (2), John Brim (4), Jimmy Burns (2), Big Wheeler (5). 10/96.*

Blues Before Sunrise is drummer and DJ Steve Cushing's long-running radio show on the Chicago public radio station WBEZ, and the CD presents music from a benefit concert for the programme, held at the club B.L.U.E.S. Accompanied by members of The Rockin' Johnny Band, the principals lay down characteristic sets – Brim, doing personal standards like 'Tough Times' and 'Ice Cream Man', is backed with scrupulous period accuracy – but nobody does anything they haven't done elsewhere at least as well, the balance isn't always ideal and, with the gig's original purpose long served, there isn't much to recommend the CD.

**(*) Clark Street Ramblers

Blue Chicago BC 5002 *George Baze (2), Aron Burton, Eddy Clearwater, Michael Coleman (2), Willie Kent (2), Johnny B. Moore (2), Eddie Shaw, Maurice John Vaughn (2). 6–7/97.*

Unlike its companion album *Red Hot Mamas* (Blue Chicago BC 5001), discussed under WOMEN, *Clark Street Ramblers* is deficient in pep, most of its participants sounding assured but faintly bored – which is a pity for collectors of CD art, since the discs are illustrated to be a complementary pair. Aron Burton's tough treatment of Muddy Waters's 'Nothing' stands apart from that judgement, and Michael Coleman is on good form, but the others have all done better work elsewhere. TR

Concerts & Festivals

***(*) From Spirituals To Swing

Vanguard 169/71 3CD *Albert Ammons, Count Basie Orchestra (6), Count Basie, Walter Page & Jo Jones, Big Bill Broonzy (3), Ida Cox (2), The Golden Gate Quartet (3), Benny Goodman Sextet (5), Helen Humes (3), Jam Session, James P. Johnson (3), Kansas City Five/Six (9), Meade Lux Lewis, Lewis, Ammons & [Pete] Johnson (2), Mitchell's Christian Singers (3), New Orleans Feetwarmers (3), Hot Lips Page, Jimmy Rushing, Sonny Terry (3), Sister Rosetta Tharpe (2), Joe Turner with Pete Johnson (2). 6/38–12/39.*

It would be a pity if John Hammond's trailblazing *From Spirituals To Swing* concerts fell down the gap between this book and the parallel guide to jazz, so we mention them here. It's not just a matter of blues artists narrowly defined, and gospel singers who are unlikely to disappoint our readers: blues devices and aesthetics permeate the playing of the Bechet–Ladnier Feetwarmers and of Basie's stupendously swinging musicians in the big band, in quintets and sextets, and backing Hot Lips Page, Humes, Rushing and Cox. Carnegie Hall's echo does some of the singers no favours, and Vanguard used guesswork (their engineer's word) to date material by artists who appeared in both years. It also seems likely that there's a good deal of material lying unissued. Still, this box, if not the definitive version that had been hoped for, is a good-looking, conscientiously mastered souvenir of two remarkable events, which launched Sonny Terry's career as a featured artist, brought Big Bill Broonzy to wider notice, gained Ida Cox a well-merited comeback session and were crucial to the acceleration of the boogie-woogie craze. CS

***(*) The Best Of Gene Norman's Blues Jubilees

GNP-Crescendo GNPD 2261 *Helen Humes (4), Joe Turner (4), Dinah Washington (5), Jimmy Witherspoon (5). 5/49–12/55.*

Gene Norman (the 'GN' in GNP) promoted blues and jazz concerts on the West Coast, bringing the most popular artists of the day to large and enthusiastic audiences. Dinah Washington's soulful readings of two ballads explain why crossover success was inevitable, and three salty celebrations of good loving justify her billing as 'Queen of the Blues'. Accompanied by Roy Milton's Solid Senders, Helen Humes shows that Dinah had precursors in terms of both style and versatility. 'Million Dollar Secret' cynically recommends old men's love and money; elsewhere, Humes handles proto-rock 'n' roll and yearning ballads with equal assurance. Recorded on New Year's Eve 1955, Joe Turner is also accompanied by Milton's band. He runs through some of his Atlantic hits in extended versions which allow plenty of space for Turner to ad-lib and the band members to solo. Not yet bored with 'Ain't Nobody's Business', Jimmy Witherspoon pays tender attention to its details, but his other tracks are more routine; 'No Rollin' Blues' and 'Big Fine Girl' comprised a hit single on Modern, but the would-be waggish interplay with pianist Gene Gilbeaux comes across as loutish. CS

*** Great Bluesmen/Newport

Vanguard VCD 77/78 *Rev. Gary Davis, Willie Doss (2), Sleepy John Estes (2), John Lee Hooker (2), Lightnin' Hopkins (2), Son House (2), Mississippi John Hurt (2), Skip James (2), Mississippi Fred McDowell (2), Doc Reese, Sonny Terry & Brownie McGhee, Robert Pete Williams (2). 59–65.*

(***) Blues With A Feeling

Vanguard VCD2 77005 2CD *Eddie Boyd, Rev. Pearly Brown & Mrs Christine Brown, Paul Butterfield Blues Band (3), Chambers Brothers, Elizabeth Cotten, Jesse Fuller, John Hammond, John Lee Hooker, Lightnin' Hopkins (3), Son House (3), Mississippi John Hurt (2), Skip James, 'Spider' John Koerner, Lafayette Leake, Mance Lipscomb (3), Mississippi Fred McDowell (2), Muddy Waters (2), Dave Van Ronk, Eric von Schmidt, Bukka [Booker] White, Rev. Robert Wilkins, Robert Pete Williams. 59–68.*

**** Newport Folk Festival: Best Of The Blues 1959–68

Vanguard 3VCD 193/95 3CD *Paul Butterfield Blues Band (2), Chambers Brothers, Rev. Gary Davis (2), Sleepy John Estes, Jesse Fuller (2), John Lee Hooker (6), Lightnin' Hopkins (3), Son House (4), Mississippi John Hurt (6), Skip James (2), Mance Lipscomb (3), Mississippi Fred McDowell (2), Memphis Slim (2), Muddy Waters (4), Sonny Terry & Brownie McGhee (5), Bukka [Booker] White, Robert Pete Williams (3). 59–68.*

Viewed strictly from a blues angle, the Newport Folk Festival was the prime showcase for the 'rediscovered' artists who were urged back into performance in the '60s. An impressive appearance, or even just a kindly received one, might be the fast track to a recording contract. For the majority of the onlookers it would also be their first glimpse of figures previously shrouded in record-collectors' legends, such as Skip James, Son House and Mississippi John Hurt. So some of these recordings from the Newport stage resonate with history. 'Devil Got My Woman', sung by James in 1964, may have been his first rendition of the song in front of an audience for more than 30 years.

As can be seen from the castlists, an extraordinary parade of 'country blues' artists mustered for Newport; others, too, but only the multiple sets find much room for them, and on the whole they are not comfortable in that arena. After the knockabout jollity of a Jesse Fuller, or Robert Pete Williams's pensive diaries of life on a labour gang, seasoned and urbane acts like Memphis Slim and Terry & McGhee came over as disengagingly slick. Hooker was simply dull. The artists who seem least oppressed by the occasion are unpretentious entertainers such as Fuller and John Hurt.

Hurt played Newport at least twice, and his tracks appear to come from both years; 'appear', because Vanguard provide no specific dates. A copy of BR will help, but not completely: numerous tracks are not listed there, because Vanguard hadn't issued them on LP. Furthermore, the 3CD set contains several items previously unissued in any format, but don't get your hopes up – they're mostly by the (in this context) least interesting artists. A more serious problem is overlap. Two thirds of Blues With A Feeling, including virtually all the significant performances, are also on Best Of The Blues. So is about half of Great Bluesmen, but the other half includes things not to be found anywhere else, like James's 'Illinois Blues' and House's 'Pony Blues' with, of all things, Mance Lipscomb on second guitar. If you're serious about collecting artists like this, you'll have to consider buying both the Best Of The Blues and Great Bluesmen. Part of your reward will be the latter's two tracks by Willie Doss, who came to Newport in 1965, sang 'Catfish Blues' as if Robert Petway were whispering it in his ear, and returned to obscurity. TR

***(*) **American Folk Blues Festival '62 To '65**
Evidence ECD 26100 5CD *John Henry Barbee, Eddie Boyd (2), Sugar Pie DeSanto (2), Willie Dixon (5), Sleepy John Estes (2), Buddy Guy (2), John Lee Hooker (7), Lightnin' Hopkins (2), Shakey Horton (2), Howlin' Wolf, Lonnie Johnson (3), J. B. Lenoir (2), Fred McDowell (2), Memphis Slim (7), Muddy Waters (5), Matt 'Guitar' Murphy, Jimmie Lee Robinson, Doctor Ross (2), Shakey Jake (2), Sonny Boy Williamson II (7), Otis Spann (2), Sunnyland Slim, Roosevelt Sykes (2), Sonny Terry & Brownie McGhee (2), Victoria Spivey (2), Hubert Sumlin, Big Mama Thornton (2), T-Bone Walker (2), Big Joe Williams (4).* 10/62–10/65.

(***(*)) **American Folk Blues Festival '62 To '65 Highlights**
Evidence ECD 26087 *Eddie Boyd, Sugar Pie DeSanto, Buddy Guy, John Lee Hooker, Lightnin' Hopkins, Howlin' Wolf, J. B. Lenoir, Fred McDowell, Brownie McGhee, Memphis Slim, Muddy Waters, Shakey Jake, Sonny Boy Williamson II, Otis Spann, Sunnyland Slim, Big Mama Thornton, T-Bone Walker.* 10/62–10/65.

Especially in their earlier years, the American Folk Blues Festivals organized by Horst Lippmann and Fritz Rau were a new departure for the blues, and one that had radical long-term consequences. European fans got to see and hear the musicians in the flesh; *Blues Unlimited* suddenly found itself with more readers; blues and jazz audiences began to fission, and, especially in Britain, a flock of beat groups tried their hand at the blues. As for the musicians, a number of important recordings were made that otherwise wouldn't have happened, among them John Henry Barbee's LP and J. B. Lenoir's racial and social prophecies, and many of the artists found a new audience for music that was going out of style back home.

Sonny & Brownie, Memphis Slim and Willie Dixon were already hip to that audience, but other artists had to adjust from being one component of an African-American night out to presenting the blues in concert halls, to audiences which signalled their approval with rapt silence or by clapping along, sometimes on the wrong beat, sometimes on no beat. The width of the cultural chasm and the nature of the assumptions that lurked at the bottom of it are summed up in Horst Lippmann's stern injunction in 1962: 'You are now here in a different area. You're not back in America anymore, where you have to use gimmicks to entertain the people. What we want to do is just bring your message as a blues singer, as a blues artist.' The positive corollaries, of course, were that the musicians were indeed treated as artists – as cultural heroes, in fact; they were well paid and were accorded the respect often denied their race at home.

In most years, LPs were issued after the tour. Evidence's 5CD box builds on those; the 1962 disc is a straight reissue of that year's album, but subsequent years are extensively augmented from tapes preserved by producer Siegfried Loch. (1963 was so fruitful that it occupies two CDs.) It's easy to understand the excitement caused by the physical presence of musicians like Sonny Boy Williamson – the undoubted star of 1963 and 1964 – Muddy Waters, Sleepy John Estes and Big Joe Williams. Forty years later the frisson is diminished, by familiarity with the artists and their other recordings, and by the distancing effect of listening on CD, but much of the music still makes its own case: mindful of the bad reception his electric repertoire got in 1958, Muddy brought an acoustic guitar, and as a result we hear him getting very deep into Willie Dixon's 'My Home Is In The Delta'; Big Joe and Fred McDowell are as thrilling as always; the young Buddy Guy, poorly received at the time, grits his teeth and imposes a terrific 'First Time I Met The Blues' on his audience; and Lonnie Johnson also radiantly defies audience expectations, this time of primitivism. Walter Horton for once in confident form, Sykes in his almost invariably ebullient form, Lightnin' Hopkins overcoming his fear of flying, Doctor Ross's amazing 'Farewell Baby', on which a one-man-band meets one-string harmonies: there's a lot to like here, and a lot that's outstanding by any standard.

It's not all perfect, of course. Memphis Slim and Dixon are blandly self-regarding, Victoria Spivey's ukulele on 'Grant Spivey' is unfortunate, and for once audiences were right when they didn't think much of Sugar Pie DeSanto. Sonny Terry has terrible vocal pitch problems in 1962, Eddie Boyd plays a wheezy organ in 1965, and by that year John Lee Hooker had already calculated how close he could get to the line between hypnotic and soporific. Nevertheless, this well-annotated collection is of far more than just historical and sociological interest; ignore the *hors d'oeuvres* on Evidence's choice of *Highlights*, and go straight for the *menu gourmand*. CS

(***(*)) Lost Blues Tapes/More American Folk Blues Festival 1963–1965
ACT 6000 2CD *Sugar Pie DeSanto, Willie Dixon (2), Sleepy John Estes & Hammie Nixon, Buddy Guy, John Lee Hooker (2), Shakey Horton, Lonnie Johnson (2), J. B. Lenoir, Fred McDowell, Memphis Slim (2), Memphis Slim & Willie Dixon, Muddy Waters (5), Doctor Ross, Sonny Boy Williamson II (4), Otis Spann, Victoria Spivey, Roosevelt Sykes, Big Mama Thornton, Big Joe Williams (3).* 10/63–10/65.

Issued in 2004, the allegedly *Lost Blues Tapes* are those used by Evidence to compile its box set in 1995, and by ACT in 1992 to compile the deleted *Blues Giants In Concert* (ACT 9205). Only Sonny Boy's 'Your Love For Me Is True' and an alternative take of Muddy's 'Captain Captain' are not on Evidence. The notes are limited to discographical data and, despite its high musical quality, this opportunistic release is not recommended. CS

*** The American Folk Blues Festival 1962–1966
Hip-O B 0001030 *Eddie Boyd, Willie Dixon, Lightnin' Hopkins, Howlin' Wolf (2), Lonnie Johnson, Fred McDowell, Memphis Slim, Muddy Waters, Otis Rush, Sonny Boy Williamson II (2), Victoria Spivey, T-Bone Walker, Sippie Wallace, Junior Wells.* 10/62–10/66.

*** The American Folk Blues Festival 1962–1969 Volume 2 [sic]
Hip-O B 0003224 *Willie Dixon, Finale, Earl Hooker, Howlin' Wolf, Son House, Skip James, Magic Sam, Muddy Waters, Sonny Boy Williamson II, Hound Dog Taylor, Koko Taylor, Sonny Terry & Brownie McGhee, Big Mama Thornton, Joe Turner, Bukka [Booker] White.* 10/62–10/69.

Hip-O's CDs derive from three DVDs, compiled, apart from the Muddy Waters track on *Volume 2*, from television broadcasts of the Festivals. They're more of a mixed bag than the Evidence box, partly because the TV studios were sometimes inhibiting settings, and partly because of the 'anyone can back anyone' theory that was the downside of Lippmann & Rau's attempts to make the packages musically diverse but economically viable. Examples of this include Sonny Boy Williamson, off in a world of his own while supposedly accompanying Victoria Spivey; the mismatching of Hound Dog Taylor with Little Walter; and Otis Rush, Little Brother Montgomery, Jack Myers and Fred Below behind Joe Turner, utterly misreading 'Flip Flop And Fly'. This is not to minimize the numerous memorable performances included, by Sippie Wallace, Koko Taylor, Rush and – once he gets warmed up – Son House among others. It's proper to note, however, that Earl Hooker's instrumental is a real dog. The notes to *Volume 2* say that it allows 'the power of these artists' performances to exist in their native environment … without being eclipsed by the majesty of the visuals.' This is special pleading of a high order, given that the sets ranged from bizarre fever dreams of Americana to sterile soundstages, but our recommendation is still to acquire the DVDs instead; unsurprisingly, they're titled *American Folk Blues Festival Vols 1, 2, and 3* (respectively Hip-O B-0000750, B-0000751 and B-000293709). CS

*** American Folk Blues Festival 1965/1966/1967/1969
Bellaphon CDLR 726222 4CD *Carey Bell, Juke Boy Bonner (2), Eddie Boyd (2), Clifton Chenier (2), Sleepy John Estes & Yank Rachell? Buddy Guy, Earl Hooker (2), John Lee Hooker (2), Shakey Horton, Son House, John Jackson (2), Skip James, J. B. Lenoir, Little Walter, Fred McDowell, Magic Sam (2), Little Brother Montgomery, Whistling Alex Moore, Jimmie Lee Robinson, Doctor Ross, Otis Rush (2), Roosevelt Sykes (2), Hound Dog Taylor, Koko Taylor (2), Sonny Terry & Brownie McGhee (3), Big Mama Thornton, Joe Turner (2), Sippie Wallace, Junior Wells (2), Bukka [Booker] White, Robert Pete Williams.* 10/65–10/69.

Bellaphon's sets repackage and reissue L+R CDs; some of them omit tracks that were on the original LPs or double LPs, but all of 1965 is there, and all duplicated on Evidence, therefore. The 1966 festival had a tremendous lineup – not least Fred Below on drums – and Rush, Montgomery, Sykes and Sippie Wallace do not disappoint. As noted above, though, Joe Turner is poorly served by his accompanists, and Junior Wells is undisciplined and self-important, even when paying 'A Tribute To Sonny Boy Williamson'. 'Louise', though atypical in being a cover version, gets a tense performance from Robert Pete Williams. The over-amplification of Yank Rachell's electric mandolin on 'You Shouldn't Do It' is no bad thing. The LP reissued here is an abridgement of two discs on the East German Amiga label (the concert took place in East Berlin), which were combined on the deleted *Blues Behind The Wall* (Mojo CD-MOJO-309).

Cliché dubs 1967 the year of the living legends, but House, White and James only get one track apiece; it may be suggested without risking charges of sexism that Koko Taylor has a weaker claim to immortality. Sonny & Brownie do their routine, routinely, and the Chicago contingent suffers from incompatibility between Little Walter and Hound Dog Taylor, and more generally from the presence of the Soul Stirrers' bassist Dillard Crume, who can't get his head around blues progressions.

No recordings were made in 1968, but 1969, when Arhoolie Records' artists featured heavily, featured one of the most varied and imaginative lineups in the AFBF's history. Knowing that neither Earl Hooker – much better than on Hip-O – nor Magic Sam had long to live doesn't detract from the pleasure of hearing them. Chenier, Bonner, John Jackson and Carey Bell also give it all they've got. Alex Moore's long 'Across The Atlantic Ocean' is amusing, but his eccentricity stands repeated playing less well. CS

**(*) American Folk Blues Festival 1970/1972/1980/1981
Bellaphon CDLR 726123 4CD *Carey Bell (5), John Cephas & Phil Wiggins (3), Chicago Blues All Stars, Jimmy Dawkins' Chicago Blues Band (2), Willie Dixon (2), Champion Jack Dupree (2), Margie Evans (2), Finale, Shakey Horton, Lee Jackson, Lafayette Leake, Lightnin' Slim, Louisiana Red (6), Willie Mabon (2), Memphis Slim (2), Jimmy Rogers, Hubert Sumlin (3), Sunnyland Slim (5), Roosevelt Sykes (2), Eddie Taylor (2), Sonny Terry & Brownie McGhee (4), Big Mama Thornton (2), T-Bone Walker (2), Washboard Doc, Lucky & Flash (2), Bukka [Booker] White (5), Big Joe Williams (2), Robert Pete Williams, Johnny Young.* 11/70–3/81.

The 1970 lineup was comparatively unadventurous, apart from the inclusion of Sister Rosetta Tharpe; by the time of the recorded concert she'd dropped out after suffering a stroke. The producers lucked into a good night, apart from the presence of a vociferous audience member who thinks he's part of the show. The Chicago Blues All Stars were Horton, Leake, Jackson, Dixon and Clifton James: 'Juanita' is a valuable addition to Jackson's too small recorded corpus, and Dixon turns in a magnificent vocal on 'Sittin' And Cryin' The Blues', compensating for a tedious bass solo on Jack Dupree's otherwise dynamic 'Going To Louisiana'. Booker White is more skittish and less lumbering than he could be, and Brownie McGhee gets uncharacteristically involved with 'When I Was Drinking'.

The 1972 recordings were made – before two exceptionally clueless collections of Continental clappers – in March and October. Booker was again in lively form, and the two Williamses were still major blues forces, but Roosevelt Sykes shows signs of age. Memphis Slim works harder than he sometimes got away with though, and Johnny Young's rocking mandolin makes a welcome appearance. Big Mama's accompanists include a very swinging drummer and guitarist, but Hartley Severns' robotic soprano sax honks scupper an otherwise good 'Tell Me Baby'. An inevitable 'Ball In Chain' (sic!) may be Thornton's best version. The same band accompanies T-Bone Walker, confined, probably by alcoholism, to piano and depressingly raucous vocals. Severns redeems himself with a hotly graceful violin solo on the otherwise clichéd instrumental 'Goin' Back To Church'. Whispering Smith's unsubtle harp suits Lightnin' Slim perfectly, and Jimmy Rogers not at all. Dawkins's band backs Big Voice Odom on an effective B. B. King imitation and an awful 'Got My Mojo Workin''.

When Lippmann & Rau unexpectedly revived the AFBF in 1980, the talent pool was less deep and the budget seems to have been tighter. Louisiana Red, resident in Germany, brought his nagging 'look at me, I'm so blue!' melodramatics to the first two latterday festivals, but 1980's highlight, despite Carey Bell's theremin imitations and Eddie Taylor's flat singing on 'Dust My Broom', was the Chicago band, with Bob Stroger and Odie Payne solidly effective on bass and drums. Sunnyland Slim's voice shows some wear, and his 'New Orleans Boogie' is a paradigm of over-extended tedium, but Hubert Sumlin surprises with a pair of bearable semi-spoken vocals. In this he outshines Willie Mabon, who was well past his prime. Washboard Doc *et al.* and Eunice Davis never had primes to be past, and swiftly returned to obscurity.

In many ways 1981 was a replay of 1980; as well as Louisiana Red in even more self-aggrandizing form, the Chicago band returned, with Lurrie Bell a tigerish replacement for Eddie Taylor. Besides doing long but splendid covers of Magic Sam and Buddy Guy, the junior Bell considerably gees up Sunnyland Slim. Margie Evans emulates Big Mama Thornton, with generic backing from the Chicagoans. Cephas & Wiggins give the disc a good start, but a nine-minute assault on 'Next Time You See Me' by the whole cast finishes it, in all senses. CS

(*) American Folk Blues Festival 1982/1983/1985
Bellaphon CDLR 726024 3CD *Carey Bell (2), Chicago's Young Blues Generation, Blues Harp Meeting (2), John Cephas & Phil Wiggins (3), Archie Edwards (3), Sylvia Embry (2), Margie Evans (3), Margie Evans & Cash McCall, Blind Joe Hill, Larry Johnson (2), Louisiana Red (5), Lovie Lee (3), Cash McCall, Lonnie Pitchford (3), James 'Sparky' Rucker (3), James 'Son' Thomas (5), Eddie 'Cleanhead' Vinson, The Young Blues Thrillers (3).* 11/82–10/85.

Son Thomas's excellent tracks from 1982 and 1985 are also available on Evidence or Bellaphon; see his entry. Cephas & Wiggins don't add much to the picture of their music, and Archie Edwards is plagued by wrong notes. Lurrie Bell was back in 1982, co-leading Chicago's Young Blues Generation, an early version of the Sons Of Blues, with Billy Branch; their cover of Albert King's 'Detroit Michigan' has considerable bite. 'Blues Harp Meeting' is Branch, Wiggins and Carey 'permanent fixture' Bell, who are collectively exciting without descending to rabble-rousing; Margie Evans reverses the formula.

The 1983 festival was designated 'in memoriam Muddy Waters', and the Chicago band includes his old guitarist, Jimmy Rogers. '[Louisiana] Red's Tribute To Muddy Waters' rapidly becomes Red's tribute to Red, but he's uncharacteristically disciplined on 'When I Lay Down To Rest', a retrospective song built on the 'Rock Me Baby' riff, on which Carey Bell also shines. Sparky Rucker does a mannered version of the *echt* 'Rock Me Baby', and an ingenious 12-string slide-accompanied 'Crossroads'. Bell's vocal feature, 'She Is Worse', is one of the few songs from the festival's last years that don't feel like self-conscious crowd-pleasers, which is not to suggest that the clichés of Louisiana Red's 'Reagan Is For The Rich Man' don't convey genuine sentiments.

Playing bass for Lovie Lee, Lonnie Pitchford has trouble staying in touch, but Lovie once again proves – a brief and dreary 'Iko Iko' apart – that he was a far better blues pianist than Pinetop Perkins, his predecessor in Muddy's band. Pitchford solo supplies two exciting one-string pieces, and a 'C.C. Rider' that's fruitfully indebted to Robert Lockwood. Larry Johnson is in good form on songs by Leroy Carr and Washboard Sam, and bassist/vocalist Sylvia Embry's 'I Love You' and 'Baby, What Did I Do' are outstanding revivals of the classic Chicago band style, with Red, Bell, Rogers, Lee and drummer Charles Otis submerging themselves in the music.

The AFBF staggered to a conclusion in 1985; the last CD is only 41 minutes long, with only the Young Blues Thrillers (piano, bass and drums) getting more than one track to themselves. As well as taking up a third of the running time, the Thrillers back McCall, Vinson and Evans. Sparky Rucker does Robert Johnson again, very affectedly. On 'Fanny Mae', one-man-band Blind Joe Hill's enthusiasm triumphs over his metronomic rhythm. Cash McCall's conscientious rendition of 'I Can't Quit You Baby' is destroyed by pianist Rickey Grundy's cocktail-lounge Tchaikovsky. He and the other Young Blues Thrillers are better suited to Vinson's jazz-blues, but on Evans and McCall's duet 'Two Lovers In One', as on their own tracks, they're presumably young, sometimes bluesy and not very thrilling at all. CS

*** The Alligator Records 20th Anniversary Tour
Alligator ALCD 107/108 2CD *All Star Jam, Elvin Bishop (4), Lonnie Brooks (4), Koko Taylor (4), Katie Webster (3), Lil' Ed [Williams] & The Blues Imperials (4).* 2–3/92.

Surprising though it may be to some readers, there's a sizeable constituency of blues fans who really don't care very much about records: for them the one-on-one experience of seeing and hearing Lonnie Brooks, say, or Koko Taylor has a charge that no studio album can convey. They obviously have a point, but those who retort that formal recordings have a character impossible to create in a live setting have a point too, and which party you side with will depend on your taste and temperament. So do recordings made *at* gigs offer a middle ground where both groups can mingle amicably? Not really. There are many ways a recording can misrepresent a concert –

sound balance, choice of material, band/audience dynamic, etc. – and even if you avoid all the pitfalls you end up with a mismatch, a document that wants to format itself two different ways. Take this album. Nearly all the artists are known for loud, intense music; light and shade are not going to be much in evidence. And these are concerts: people pay good money to hear Lonnie do 'Two Headed Man' or Koko shake her stuff in 'Wang Dang Doodle', they don't want the experience to be over in three minutes, they want the songs drawn out like gum. Actually, by live-album standards, most of the 20 numbers aren't unduly prolonged, just the 11 minutes of Brooks's 'I Want All My Money Back' and the ten of 'Sweet Home Chicago', the latter indispensable on the night as an all-star sign-off but ass-numbingly dull for the armchair listener. So the commonest drawback of the live album is largely skirted, but there remains the problem of dynamics, the fact that almost every band works at, so to speak, concert pitch. There are few slow blues, no acoustic cool-downs, and just one solo set, by Katie Webster. If all that sounds like a menu you'll relish, bon appétit, but don't expect it to teleport you to a theatre in Philadelphia or Chicago in 1992. The company of live albums that really do work like time machines is very small, and this is not among them. TR

(*) 1993 Portland Waterfront Blues Festival
Burnside BCD-0014 *Back Porch Blues, Duffy Bishop, The Channel Cats, Linda Hornbuckle & No Delay, Lloyd Jones Struggle, Jim Mesi Band, Kelly Joe Phelps, Pin & The Hornits, Mel Solomon, The Switchmasters, Too Slim & The Taildraggers, Margo Tufo.* 93.

Some of these acts are hardly known outside the Pacific Northwest, but the names of Back Porch Blues, Duffy Bishop, Lloyd Jones, Kelly Joe Phelps and Too Slim & The Taildraggers (qq.v.) have been spread more widely by their albums on Burnside; the chief point of interest in this set for many readers may be this early recording by Phelps of Robert Johnson's 'Crossroads'. Several tough – if rather stereotypically tough – female singers are featured, such as Hornbuckle, Tufo and Lily Wilde with the Jim Mesi Band. The recording quality, for a live event, is very good. TR

(*) Blues Routes
Smithsonian Folkways SFW CD 40118 *Etta Baker, Erbie Bowser & T. D. Bell, John Cephas & Phil Wiggins, Boozoo Chavis, Gandy Dancers, Georgia Sea Island Singers, Abner Jay, Luther 'Guitar Jr' Johnson & Pinetop Perkins, Booker T. Laury, Robert Jr Lockwood, Sammy Price, Rapper Dee & C. J., Don Vappie & The Creole Jazz Serenaders, Joe Louis Walker, White Cloud Hunters Mardi Gras Indians, Claude Williams, Warner Williams.* 11/90–4/95.

*** **Live At The W. C. Handy Blues Awards Vol. 1**
Artemis/Tone-Cool 51163//Rykodisc/Tone-Cool/Artemis RCD 17009 *Luther Allison, Deborah Coleman, Rod Piazza, Bonnie Raitt, Paul Rishell & Annie Raines, Bobby Rush, Taj Mahal & The Phantom Blues Band, Susan Tedeschi, Rufus Thomas, Joe Louis Walker.* 5/96–5/01.

Blues Routes comes from a series of concerts titled *Folk Masters*, mostly at Wolf Trap, Virginia (the venue of the National Folk Festival), a few at Carnegie Hall. The in-joke in the title is that the artistic director of *Folk Masters*, musicologist Nick Spitzer, also presents a weekly show for Public Radio International called *American Routes*. The CD seems to be a fair representation of the range of music played at those concerts, which extends a good way beyond the blues, but its appeal to readers of this book is harder to quantify, since most of the blues artists have done the same songs on their own albums sounding less restrained, while acts like the White Cloud Hunters need to be experienced in person. The most vivacious performance is the last, 'Bluesifyin', Joe Louis Walker's tribute to past masters – which coincidentally also opens Rykodisc's collection of performances from the annual W. C. Handy Awards ceremony in Memphis: an unexpected link between events that could hardly be more different. Again, it's difficult to know what purpose the album is supposed to serve. The notes speak of 'dream-team lineups and one-time-only combos', and if the chance to hear Rufus Thomas with Bonnie Raitt, or Deborah Coleman with Bernard Allison, solves a 'what if?' conundrum that's been bothering you, lucky you. If not, there are still high-wire acts by Walker, Luther Allison and Tedeschi to enjoy, and the inimitable Bobby Rush rapping and rambling through eight minutes of 'Hoochie' – but not 'Coochie' – 'Man', all of which probably amounts to justification enough. TR

Detroit

*** **Detroit Blues: Blues From The Motor City 1938–1954**
JSP JSP 7736 4CD *Big Maceo (6), John Brim Combo [Grace Brim] (2), Eddie Burns (4), Detroit Count (2), Calvin Frazier (13), Playboy Fuller [Louisiana Red] (2), L. C. Green, John Lee Hooker (25), Sam Kelly, Eddie Kirkland (7), Louisiana Red (as Playboy Fuller) (2), Walter Mitchell (2), Sampson Pittman (13), Robert Richard (3), Henry Smith (2), Joe Von Battle, Baby Boy Warren (19).* 38–54.

There is plenty of admirable music here, but it's an annoyingly lazy compilation. The Frazier/Pittman Library of Congress recordings that fill the first disc were already available (see their entries) and the discs devoted to John Lee Hooker and Baby Boy Warren/Eddie Kirkland similarly duplicate accessible material. Only the fourth disc gives an impression of the activities of small local labels like JVB, Fortune and Random, which documented the largely obscure musicians who worked in Detroit's black clubs and bars: singer/guitarists L. C. Green and Robert Smith, harmonica players Walter Mitchell and Sam Kelly, pianist Detroit Count. Students of the Detroit scene who want more than one or two tracks by such intriguing figures must look to the East: read on.

*** **Detroit Blues Rarities 1: Blues Guitar Killers!**
P-Vine PCD-5416 *Eddie Burns (6), Calvin Frazier (2), Rocky Fuller, L. C. Green & Sam Kelly (6), Johnny Howard (2), Bobo Jenkins (2), Henry Smith.* mid-50s–mid-60s.

*** **Detroit Blues Rarities 2: Blues Harp-Suckers!**
P-Vine PCD-5417 *Little Sonny, Walter Mitchell (3), Robert Richard (4), Joe Von Battle, Elder R. Wilson (6).* mid-50s.

(*) **Detroit Blues Rarities 4: Hastings Street Blues Opera
P-Vine PCD-5639 *Tommy Burnette (2), Detroit Count (8), Joe & His Kool Kats (3), Miss Detroit Slim, Janet Oldham (2), One String Sam (2), Piano Bill (3), Gip Roberts (2), Fred Woods & The Kool Kats (2).* mid-50s.

These Japanese releases, largely devoted to the products of Joe Von Battle's JVB label, will not be easy to obtain, but lovers of postwar downhome blues will not regret the inconvenience. *Blues Guitar Killers!* has several cuts that, although made in the '50s, sound ten or 15 years earlier in style, such as the Green–Kelly duets, which might have been made by country cousins of Yank Rachell and Sonny Boy Williamson I, or Henry Smith's 'Kansas City Blues', which is scarcely more modern in style than Jim Jackson's 1927 original. Sonny Boy's legacy is also much in evidence on *Blues Harp-Suckers!* in the Mitchell–Richard sides, all of which feature both harmonica players in ragged but exciting collaboration, steered by pianist Boogie Woogie Red and a sturdy bassist. The Elder Wilson sides are of sacred singing backed by four harmonicas, and exhilarating.

Detroit Blues Rarities 3: Blues Screamers & Gospel Moaners! (P-Vine PCD-5418) is light on the former and heavy on the latter, with some black rockabilly in between, but collectors will want to know that it includes Washboard Willie recorded live in a club with Calvin Frazier on hot guitar, and Brother Will Hairston's remarkable two-part protest song 'The Alabama Bus'. *Hastings Street Blues Opera* is more squarely in our sights, containing as it does an exuberant set by Detroit Count – something of a Motor City Cecil Gant, in his mixing ballads and boogies, but also a Hastings Street Hedda Hopper, gossiping about neighbourhood characters in 'Parrot Lounge Blues' and the two-part 'Opera'. One String Sam's 'Need A $100.00', with its slide monochord accompaniment, is a justly treasured rarity, and most of the other sides, though generally by local copyists of nationally known artists, are worth a hearing. Many of the recordings on these albums were never issued as singles and survive on acetates of variable quality. Some of the performances, too, are of only rehearsal standard, like the two takes of Bobo Jenkins's 'Decoration Day Blues' with a piano that belonged in a dumpster. But for anyone seriously interested in Detroit's blues history the four CDs are essential.

*** **A Fortune Of Blues, Vol. 1**
Regency RR 119 Big Maceo (2), Grace Brim, Big Blues Carson, Earl Chapman, John Lee Hooker (7), Bobo Jenkins (4), Eddie Kirkland, Big Jack Reynolds, Dr Ross (5), Joe Weaver, Harry Willis. 50s.

*** **A Fortune Of Blues, Vol. 2**
Regency RR 120 Big Maceo (2), Big Blues Carson, Earl Chapman, Calvin Frazier, John Lee Hooker (6), Bobo Jenkins (2), Eddie Kirkland, Jimmy Milner, Chet Oliver, Big Jack Reynolds (2), Dr Ross (4), Henry Smith, James Walton (2). 50s.

Fortune was a more savvy enterprise than JVB, signing artists who actually stood a chance in the record market of the '50s, and recording them in conditions rather better than the back of Joe Von Battle's record store. Downhome blues fans will value these CDs for the tracks by Dr Ross, like 'Thirty Two Twenty' and 'Sunnyland' on *Vol. 2*, which are among the best things he did; singer and harmonica player Bobo Jenkins's band wheeling confidently through oldies like 'Ten Below Zero' and 'Baby Don't You Want To Go'; and the obscure James Walton, another harmonica player with a crisp band. Big Maceo's tracks are not typical, since he couldn't play much; nor are some of Hooker's, which are in a jump-blues style with a small group. The other artists are mostly second-rankers but far from uninteresting. The notes are exiguous and provide no recording data. TR

Downhome

**** **Down Home Blues Classics 1943–1953**
Boulevard Vintage BVBCD 1003 4CD Willie Baker, Johnny Beck, Big Maceo, Edgar Blanchard, Blue Smitty, The Blues Boys [Alec Seward & Louis Hayes], Charley Bradix, John Brim, Gabriel Brown, Eddie Burns, Chicago Sunny Boy [Joe Hill Louis], Buddy Chiles, Silver Cooks, Rattlesnake Cooper, Arthur 'Big Boy' Crudup, Leroy Dallas, Little Sam Davis, Jimmy DeBerry, Dr Hepcat, Champion Jack Dupree (2), J. D. Edwards, Big Boy Ellis, Leroy Ervin, Rocky Fuller [Louisiana Red], L. C. Green, Stick Horse Hammond, Robert Henry, Harvey Hill Jr, Tony Hollins, Wright Holmes, Earl Hooker, John Lee Hooker, Lightnin' Hopkins, J. D. Horton, Walter Horton, Soldier Boy Houston, Howlin' Wolf, Luther Huff, Pee Wee Hughes, Lee Hunter, Lost John Hunter, Lil' Son Jackson, Elmore James, Jesse James, Leroy Johnson, Sonny Boy Johnson, Eddie 'Guitar Slim' Jones, Floyd Jones, Hank Kilroy, Willie Lane, Lazy Slim Jim, John Lee, Tommy Lee, J. B. Lenoir, Papa Lightfoot, Little Hudson, Little Walter, Clarence London, Willie Love, Brownie McGhee, Stick McGhee, David Pete McKinley, Dennis McMillon, Blind Willie McTell, Walter Mitchell, Alex Moore, Mr Honey [David Edwards], Muddy Waters, Manny Nichols, Robert Nighthawk, Monister Parker, Morris Pejoe, Dan Pickett, Pinetop Slim, Snooky Pryor, Doug Quattlebaum, Jimmy Reed, Robert Richard, Jimmy Rogers, Marylin Scott, Johnny Shines, Frankie Lee Sims, Skoodle-Dum-Doo [prob. Seth Richard] & Sheffield, Thunder Smith, Sonny Boy Williamson II, Luther Stoneham, Sonny Terry, Nat Terry, Andy Thomas, Bobo Thomas, John Tinsley, Square Walton, Baby Boy Warren, Curley Weaver, Junior Wells, Big Joe Williams, L. C. Williams, Ralph Willis, Little David [Wylie]. 43–53.

The combination of restless creativity among musicians and greater access to the public through independent labels made the first decade or so after World War II the most exciting and innovative period that American vernacular music has ever experienced. These 100 tracks, arranged on four CDs devoted to Texas, Chicago/Detroit, Memphis/Deep South and New York/East Coast scenes, catch everyone from Muddy Waters, Howlin' Wolf, Lightnin' Hopkins and Jimmy Reed to fascinating one-offs like Luther Huff, Blue Smitty, L. C. Green, Pinetop Slim and the colossally weird Wright Holmes, a Texas singer/guitarist with a blues equivalent of Tourette's syndrome. This may be the largest gathering of deserving obscurities since the last International Convention of Ghostwriters, and a ticket to the junket should cost no more than the price of one new CD. The reader would be lucky to get a single one of the source discs for that. TR

*** **Rural Blues – Volumes 1 & 2**
BGO BGOCD 384 Country Jim [Bledsoe] (2), Boozoo Chavis (2), Clifton Chenier (2), Snooks Eaglin (4), J. D. Edwards (2), Lightnin' Hopkins (2), Lil' Son Jackson (2), Papa Lightfoot (2), Manny Nichols (2), Slim Harpo (2), Thunder Smith (2), Nathaniel Terry (2), Boogie Bill Webb (2). 11/46–61.

*** **Rural Blues – Volume III: Down Home Stomp**
BGO BGOCD 464 Country Jim [Bledsoe] (2), J. D. Edwards (2), Lowell Fulson, Lil' Son Jackson (2), Papa Lightfoot (2), Manny Nichols, Roosevelt Sykes (2), Boogie Bill Webb (2). 48–9/55.

With the exception of Boogie Bill Webb and Roosevelt Sykes, everyone featured on these two discs (*Rural Blues –*

Volumes 1 & 2 is a one-disc conversion of two LPs) came from the Southwest, chiefly Texas and Louisiana. Most are singer/guitarists, skilled practitioners like Eaglin and Fulson balancing rougher or more limited, but not unappealing, players like Terry and Nichols, or the mysterious J. D. Edwards, but the texture of the albums is nicely varied with work by pianists (Smith, Sykes) and harmonica players (Lightfoot, Slim Harpo) and early zydeco recordings by Chenier and Chavis, including the latter's original, ineffable 'Paper In My Shoe'. TR

**** **Rural Blues Vol. 1 (1934–56)**
Document DOCD-5223 *Johnny Beck (The Blind Boy) (2), Black Diamond [James Butler] (2), Goldrush, D. A. Hunt (2), Monroe Moe Jackson (2), Julius King (4), Willie Lane (5), John Lee (5), 'Little Brother', One String Sam (2). 4/34–56.*

***(*) **Rural Blues Vol. 2 (1951–1962)**
Document DOCD-5619 *Juke Boy Bonner (2), Arthur Crudup, Clifford Gibson (6), Joel Hopkins (5), Sam 'Suitcase' Johnson (2), Jewell Long (4), Bobo Thomas. 51–62.*

About half of each volume of *Rural Blues* is more or less Texan: D. A. Hunt was from Alabama, but he admired Lightnin' Hopkins, as did Black Diamond, recorded in Oakland by a Mr Jaxyson (pronounced Jackson, as his eponymous record labels note). Jaxyson also cut a solitary title by the splendidly gloomy pianist Goldrush. Willie Lane's nickname was 'Little Brother', but Document's assumption that he's the man who recorded for the Library of Congress in 1934 is just that. Lane was an associate of Funny Papa Smith, and his 1949 session shows Smith's influence, and includes a version of 'Howling Wolf Blues'. Johnny Beck whips up an intriguing blend of Texas blues and Blind Boy Fuller.

Julius King, recorded in Nashville, also admired Fuller; it's been suggested that he was white, but it seems unlikely. Monroe Moe Jackson was certainly white; his singing is patronizingly imitative but, for good or ill, 'Go 'Way From My Door' is bravura fun. Other players of One String Sam's instrument are well documented by folklorists, but its wailing overtones are an eerie experience. So is Alabamian John Lee's 'Baby Please Don't Go', made unique by the presence of a funky panpiper. Lee's other tracks are solo, and feature magnificently integrated guitar and vocals.

On *Vol. 2*, the Bobo Thomas track and a Crudup alternative take were included as (then) gap-fillers for completists. Sam Johnson is another Lightnin' Hopkins acolyte, unlike Lightnin's older brother: Joel's implacable rhythms are compelling on 'Good Times Here, Better Down The Road', but four more songs expose his limitations. Jewell Long was another survivor from older days; he's better on guitar, where he adds some poetic touches to the 'Frankie And Albert', than on an out-of-tune piano. Juke Boy Bonner's first record, cut in California, is one of his best, and not just because of Lafayette Thomas's imaginative guitar work.

Clifford Gibson's postwar recordings – two solo audition demos from 1951, and four sides with a band made for Bobbin in 1960 – are of more than merely collectable value. Gibson was still producing imaginative lyrics and dextrous guitar figures; the solos suggest that his style had frozen in the '30s, but on two of the Bobbin sides he duets happily with a jazzy, modernistic second guitarist. The other Bobbin titles are wryly witty hokum survivals, reminiscent of Jim Jackson and Tampa Red. CS

(****) **The Travelling Record Man: Historic Down South Recording Trips Of Joe Bihari & Ike Turner**
Ace CDCHD 813 *Sunny Blair, Charley Booker, Big Charlie Bradix, Drifting Slim (2), Boyd Gilmore, Smokey Hogg, Howlin' Wolf, Lil' Son Jackson (2), Elmore James (2), Joe Hill Louis (3), [Whistlin'] Alexander Moore, Willie Nix, Pinetop Slim, Arkansas Johnny Todd, Jesse Thomas (2), Baby Face Turner, Washboard Willie & Calvin Frazier, Tiny Webb. 48–c. 55.*

**** **The Modern Downhome Blues Sessions Volume 1: Arkansas & Mississippi 1951–1952**
Ace CDCHD 876 *Sunny Blair (2), Houston Boines (2), Charley Booker (3), Red Boyd, Junior Brooks (2), Drifting Slim (2), Boyd Gilmore (8), Elmore James (2), Ernest Lane (2). late 51–early 52.*

**** **The Modern Downhome Blues Sessions Volume 2: Arkansas & Mississippi 1952**
Ace CDCHD 982 *Sunny Blair (4), Houston Boines (6), Charley Booker, Drifting Slim (5), Boyd Gilmore (2), Elmore James (2), Cleanhead Love, Baby Face Turner (5). 51–3/52.*

***(*) **The Modern Downhome Blues Sessions Volume 3: Memphis On Down**
Ace CDCHD 1003 *Bobby Bland, James 'Peck' Curtis (3), Dixie Blues Boys (5), Alfred Harris (2), Walter Horton, Howlin' Wolf (2), Jim Lockhart (2), Joe Hill Louis (4), Willie Nix (2), Robert 'Dudlow' Taylor (4). 11/50–55.*

**** **The Modern Downhome Blues Sessions Volume 4: Southern Country Blues Guitarists 1948–1952**
Ace CDCHD 1057 *Big Charley Bradix (4), Big Bill Dotson (2), Little Son Jackson (2), [Whistlin'] Alexander Moore (4), Pine Top Slim (8), Leroy Simpson (2), Jesse Thomas (4), Arkansas Johnny Todd [prob. Lane Hardin] (2). 48–52.*

The *Travelling Record Man* shares tracks with the *Modern Downhome Blues Sessions* series, and with other Ace releases. Despite the subtitle, not everything was recorded on field trips, or by Joe Bihari and Ike Turner: Thomas and Webb were recorded in Los Angeles, the Lil' Son Jackson sides were licensed from Gold Star, and Joe Von Battle taped Washboard Willie (playing drums) and Calvin Frazier in a Detroit club. Their 'Rock House' is one of numerous tracks aimed at hardcore collectors on a CD that, as the notes acknowledge, contains 'many ... alternate [sic] recordings that are unlikely ever to appear elsewhere.' The downhome recordings made or acquired by the Biharis include some of the most significant blues of the early postwar years, but they have been overshadowed because the dominant narrative promotes Chess and Sun as the key labels. *The Travelling Record Man* contains a deal of magnificent music, but it sacrifices coherence on the altar of rarity.

Non-specialists may be doubtful about the numerous alternative versions and false starts on *Vols 1* and *2* of the *Downhome Blues Sessions* series, but these are some of the most enjoyable alternative versions and false starts in existence. Elmore James and Wolf are represented by some of their most intense performances, but the greatest music here is made by Boines, Gilmore and Booker in Clarksdale and by Turner, Brooks, Blair and Drifting Slim in Little Rock. Taking turns to front their bands, they play and sing with wild, confident looseness, producing songs that are by turns poetic, rowdy, danceable, deep, aggressive and tender, and sometimes all those things at once.

On *Vol. 2*, three demo sides by Drifting Slim are rough stuff, aimed at completists, but that's a minor issue. *Vol. 3* has more serious problems. There's plenty of great music here, but it's a less coherent listening experience: Bobby Bland's Roy Brown imitation really doesn't fit, and Jim Lockhart's halting solo, 'Empty House Blues', comes from a very battered acetate. The Dixie Blues Boys have their merits, but it's hard not to feel that they're included mainly because the musicians' identities have finally been established. Modern chose not to issue anything by Curtis and Taylor, and the odd sound balance and ill-assorted jazz guitarist make it obvious why; it's some unusual lyrics and the presence of Sonny Boy Williamson II that make a less than successful session into a collector's must-have.

Vol. 4 casts a wide net. Of the several Dallasites, Alex Moore (who is on a CD of guitarists thanks to Smokey Hogg's remarkable support) is at his vigorous, disciplined peak as a pianist, and his lyrics are as wryly unique as usual. Charley Bradix, who also has some very original lyrics, may be the guitarist or the pianist in his rough-and-tumble band. Jesse Thomas, recorded in LA where he'd migrated, presents his spry, confident guitar conceptions. Little Son Jackson's 'Talkin' Boogie' is a starchy attempt to piggyback on 'Boogie Chillen'; the enigmatically gloomy 'Milford Blues' is far better. Dotson, who may have been from Louisville, and Simpson, probably from St Louis, are darkly brooding artists; Simpson is accompanied by Todd, whose risqué and riotous tracks couldn't offer greater contrast. Pine Top Slim was an Atlanta street musician; his limited but exciting slide guitar technique turns familiar songs into something rich and strange. CS

(*) Bloodstains On The Wall: Country Blues From Specialty
Specialty SPCD-7061//[Ace CDCHD 576] *Country Jim Bledsoe (4), Honeyboy [Frank Patt] (3), Little Temple [Gus Jenkins] (4), Clarence London (3), Pete McKinley (7), Pine Bluff Pete (2), Big Joe Williams (2).* 52–53.

This curious assembly comprises three groups of artists: Bledsoe, London, McKinley and Pine Bluff Pete, recorded in, and presumably more or less local to, Shreveport, Louisiana; Patt and Jenkins, Alabamians who had settled in LA; and Big Joe Williams, in a class of his own as always. They are thrown together here because they were recorded by Specialty – somewhat speculatively, for only five of the 25 tracks were issued at the time. Another six came out on LP compilations in the '70s, and the rest sat in the vaults until issued on this CD. Of the Shreveport set, both Bledsoe and London play in a highly rhythmic, droning style reminiscent of early John Lee Hooker, McKinley is more versatile but undisciplined, and Pine Bluff Pete – as he was dubbed by a reissue producer: no one noted his name at the time – is strictly an amateur performer. All this material is less fascinating than it might look, and the CD's best tracks are Patt's 'Bloodstains On The Wall', a brooding Lowell Fulsonish number, and Jenkins's enthusiastic adaptations of the Roosevelt Sykes manner. TR

***(*) No Jive: Authentic Southern Country Blues**
Ace CDCHD 652 *Louis Campbell (2), Dixie Doodlers (2), Chas Dowell with James Stewart (2), Shy Guy Douglas (4), Robert Garrett (2), Good Rockin' Bob (2), Arthur Gunter (3), Little Al [Gunter] (4), Slim Hunt, Leap Frogs (2).* 53–4/63.

The stars of *No Jive*, which is drawn from the Excello catalogue, are the Gunter brothers. As well as appearing under their own names, they're members of the Leap Frogs. Louis Campbell was also a Frog man, but on his tracks the Gunters are replaced by piano and a more modern guitarist. Al and Arthur's playful, tumbling guitar shuffles preserve the spirit of Blind Boy Fuller, and fed through into rockabilly. The Dixie Doodlers were Blind James Campbell's street band (see his entry), and their tracks are even more charmingly anachronistic. Shy Guy Douglas's musicians sometimes have differing opinions about key, but the inventive B. B. King fan on two tracks is worth hearing. There's more fiercely creative electric guitar on Robert Garrett's coupling, surely not played by him, but Slim Hunt seems likely to be his own accompanist, given the amount of Lowell Fulson in both voice and guitar lines. James Stewart's fiery harmonica is not the only reason to note Chas Dowell's tracks, and Good Rockin' Bob fronts a superior Louisiana band that may include Lonesome Sundown. CS

*** **Deep South Blues**
High Water HMG 6513 *Ranie Burnette (2), R. L. Burnside, Jessie Mae Hemphill, Hezekiah & The House Rockers (2), Lillie Hill, Raymond Hill, Waynell Jones (2), Junior Kimbrough (2), Hammie Nixon, Uncle Ben & His Nephews (2).* 10/79–12/84.

Deep South Blues brings together singles and previously unissued material recorded by High Water. Kimbrough, Hemphill, Nixon and Hezekiah Early add little to what can be heard on their own High Water CDs (see their entries), but R. L. Burnside's long, bitter 'Bad Luck City' is a significant story-song. Ranie Burnette, an under-appreciated musician who influenced better-known artists like Burnside, contributes a brooding 'Hungry Spell' and one of the best versions of 'Coal Black Mattie' on record. Raymond Hill, formerly of Ike Turner's Kings of Rhythm, plays guitar and overdubbed tenor sax on his and his wife's tracks; on this evidence, they were both strong songwriters, but Mrs Hill's singing of 'Cotton Fields – Boss Man' doesn't do justice to her mordant lyrics. Waynell Jones's 'Chicken Song' and 'Jaybird Boogie' are pleasantly archaic, and Memphis street musician Uncle Ben Perry, wielding distorted electric guitar and a drum machine, comes closest to the outlaw punk ethos that Fat Possum later detected (or encouraged) in some of these musicians. CS

East Coast

**** **Atlanta Blues**
JSP JSP 7754 4CD *Julius Daniels (11), Georgia Browns (7), 'Sloppy' Henry [Waymon Henry] (4), Peg Leg Howell (28), Lillie Mae (4), Lil McClintock (4), Macon Ed [Eddie Anthony] & Tampa Joe (8), Curley Weaver (33), Henry Williams & Eddie Anthony (2).* 2/27–11/49.

Atlanta was where Victor made the first commercial field recordings of blues and country music outside the northern cities, but 'field' is the wrong word; the city was a paradigm of Southern attempts to urbanize and industrialize, and it sometimes seems as if all roads led to the Athens of the South. That's why the itinerant vaudevillian 'Sloppy' Henry and the Carolinians Julius Daniels and Lil McClintock recorded there. Curley Weaver and Peg Leg Howell were rural Georgians, drawn to the city by its perceived opportunities and the buzz of urban life. Even more than is apparent from the artist list, this collection focuses on their work: Weaver was a member of the Georgia Browns, and is thought to be among the musicians backing Lillie Mae; Howell probably and his fiddler Eddie Anthony certainly accompany Sloppy Henry. They (and Julius Daniels) were artists of great accomplishments and historical significance, as is discussed in their individual entries; *Atlanta Blues* is a convenient way to hear the richness and diversity of black folk music, exemplified in one city and just over two decades.

***(*) East Coast Blues 1926–1935
Yazoo 1013 *Blind Blake, Bo Weavil Jackson, Carl Martin (2), William Moore (2), Bayless Rose (2), Tarter & Gay (2), Willie Walker (2), Chicken Wilson & Skeeter Hinton (2). c. 8/26–7/35.*
*** Guitar Wizards
Yazoo 1016 *Billy Bird, Blind Blake (4), Sam Butler [Bo Weavil Jackson] (3), Carl Martin (3), William Moore, Tampa Red (2). c. 8/26–9/35.*
*** Mama Let Me Lay It On You
Yazoo 1040 *Pink Anderson & Simmie Dooley, Blind Blake (2), Walter Coleman, Blind Boy Fuller, Bobby Leecan & Robert Cooksey, Charlie Manson, Irene Scruggs, Smith & Harper (2), Spark Plug Smith, Willie Walker, Josh White, Leola B. Wilson. 11/26–6/36.*

In blues terms, the East Coast states are mainly Georgia, the Carolinas and Virginia. Sometimes musicians who moved to the New York area but continued to play in downhome styles are also included; Florida and West Virginia were musically lively but comparatively neglected by record companies. There were plenty of harmonica players and pianists in the region, but patterns of recording and blues fans' preferences mean that the picture on CD is dominated by guitarists, often virtuoso fingerpickers playing bright, open-textured, ragtime-influenced music.

East Coast Blues may be hard to find, but it's worth seeking out, since it features many of the greatest guitar showpieces of the prewar era; outstanding among them are 'Blind Arthur's Breakdown', Carl Martin's 'Old Time Blues' and Willie Walker's 'South Carolina Rag'. Bo Weavil Jackson's nervy falsetto is jarring in this generally euphonious company; more recent research has established that he was from Birmingham, Alabama, rather than 'down from the Carolinas', as Paramount advertised. Tarter & Gay are also no longer 'completely obscure', contrary to Yazoo's 30-year-old, heavily musicological notes. Transfers are excellent, and the high quality of the CD's content overrides its short running time.

Guitar Wizards is a mixed bag: three of Blind Blake's pieces are among his most brilliant, but his cautious rack harmonica diminishes 'Panther Squall', and Carl Martin's cocktail of clichés on 'Joe Louis Blues' must be endured for the sake of the guitar work. Bo Weavil Jackson continues to sound out of place (and there's off-putting pre-echo on 'Some Scream High Yellow'), and Billy Bird's doleful vocal is not as good as his accompaniment. Tampa Red's speed and accuracy on two instrumentals are exhilarating, though, and William Moore's 'Ragtime Millionaire' is charming.

When it first appeared, a previously unissued take of 'South Carolina Rag' was the main reason to lust after *Mama Let Me Lay It On You*, and sometimes Yazoo seem to be scratching around for worthy material to surround it: Spark Plug Smith and Charlie Manson are pretty slight, and so are Smith & Harper's prequels to Sonny & Brownie. On the other hand,

Fuller (playing runs learned from Gary Davis) and White are heard at their finest, and Blind Blake, who accompanies Scruggs and Wilson, consolidates his reputation, although 'Sweet Jivin' Mama' comes from a 78 that's uncharacteristically worn for Yazoo.

*** Down Home Blues Classics 1943–1953
Boulevard Vintage BVBCD 1003 4CD *Willie Baker, The Blues Boys [Alec Seward & Louis Hayes], Gabriel Brown, Leroy Dallas, Duke Bayou [prob. Alec Seward] & His Mystic 6, Champion Jack Dupree, Big Chief Ellis, Hank Kilroy, Lazy Slim Jim [Carolina Slim], John Lee, Brownie McGhee, Stick McGhee, Dennis McMillon, Blind Willie McTell, Dan Pickett, Pinetop Slim, Doug Quattlebaum, Marylin Scott, Skoodle-Dum-Doo [prob. Seth Richard] & Sheffield, Sonny Terry, John Tinsley & Fred Holland, Square Walton, Curley Weaver, Ralph Willis, Little David [Wylie]. 43–8/53.*
☠ **** Play My Juke-Box: East Coast Guitar Blues 1943–1954
Flyright FLY CD 45 *Gabriel Brown, Big Chief Ellis, Boy Green (2), Guitar Shorty [John Henry Fortesque], Guitar Slim & Jelly Belly [Alec Seward & Louis Hayes] (2), Sunny Jones (2), Hank Kilroy (2), Julius King, Marylin Scott, Skoodle-Dum-Doo [prob. Seth Richard] & Sheffield (4), Tarheel Slim [Alden Bunn], Curley Weaver, Robert Lee Westmoreland (2), Elder R. Wilson & Family. 43–54.*
*** East Coast Blues
Collectables COL-5324 *Dan Pickett (4), Doug Quattlebaum (3), Tarheel Slim [Alden Bunn] (2), Sonny Terry, Ralph Willis (6). 46–53.*

The pertinent disc in the Boulevard Vintage box is called *New York, & The East Coast States: Rub A Little Boogie*. Doug Quattlebaum, born in South Carolina, was based in Philadelphia but, like the Alabamians John Lee and Dan Pickett, he's a useful reminder that styles don't change at state lines. Nor do musicians always fit tidily into after-the-fact patterns: Alec Seward, playing gentle acoustic guitar duets with Louis Hayes and fronting the raucous Duke Bayou & His Mystic 6, is a particularly good example of the complexities hiding behind blanket descriptions like 'East Coast blues'.

Rub A Little Boogie usefully highlights the variety of the eastern seaboard's blues: illustrating but not defining its range are the sophisticated balladry of Miami's Willie Baker, the amplified bands behind Square Walton and Jack Dupree, Pinetop Slim's slashing bottleneck, Little David's plaintive 'Shackles Round My Body' and the mildly dissonant guitars of John Tinsley & Fred Holland, who tend Blind Boy Fuller's flame. Curley Weaver and Blind Willie McTell are living embodiments of earlier days and ways, and the McGhee brothers, Ralph Willis and Carolina Slim are among those looking to bring older sounds up to date. For all its instructiveness, though, the sequence of styles and sounds on *Rub A Little Boogie* is sometimes disjointed.

There are only three duplications between *Rub A Little Boogie* and *Play My Juke-Box*, which also dips a toe into the world of amplified bands, with tracks by Tarheel Slim and Big Chief Ellis; its general ambience is more downhome, though, and the sequencing more skilful. *Play My Juke-Box* includes some formidably rare and obscure sides, among them the only titles by Boy Green (possibly the finest Blind Boy Fuller disciple on record) and the gravel-voiced Robert

Lee Westmoreland. There are some wrong notes in Julius King's 'One O'Clock Boogie', but rarity doesn't mean lack of quality: Sunny Jones's 78 shows a marked improvement over his '30s recordings as Sonny Jones. Elder Wilson was from Mississippi, and living in Detroit when recorded, but his spiritual accompanied by four harmonicas is thrilling. Guitar Shorty was a fertile fantasist in later life but, although he didn't teach The Beatles guitar, he really did record for Savoy in 1952. His falsetto imitation of a harmonica doubtless explains his listing in company files as 'Hootin' Owl'. Of more enduring importance are sides by Seward & Hayes, Curley Weaver and Gabriel Brown, and the complete session by Skoodle-Dum-Doo and his eldritch harmonica player, who switches to second guitar on the relatively elegant 'Broome Street Blues'.

The Collectables CD was originally an LP on Krazy Kat, wrapping up the label's issuing of East Coast blues recorded by 20th Century and Gotham. The Sonny Terry track and three of those by Pickett are alternative takes, and Willis's titles, which range from driving dance music to delicate guitar duets, are available on Document (probably dubbed from Krazy Kat) as part of his complete works. Doug Quattlebaum's rocking 'Lizzie Lou', sped up on 78, is corrected, and 'Don't Be Funny Baby' appears at its original length of more than five minutes. (Gotham's editing to less than half that for issue was skilful, but the original has far more cumulative power.) The CD's crown jewels are the Tarheel Slim tracks, with Slim and an unknown playing lustrous acoustic guitar accompaniments that blend the spirits of Blind Boy Fuller, Ikey Robinson and Lonnie Johnson.

(*) Came So Far
Music Maker MMCD 1294 *Captain Luke [Luther Mayer] (2), Guitar Gabriel, Macavine Hayes (2), Pernell King & Guitar Gabriel, Lucille Lindsey & Guitar Gabriel, Big Boy Henry, Rufus McKenzie, Bishop Dready Manning (2), Marie Manning, Samuel Turner Stevens (2), J. W. Warren, John Lee Zeigler.* late 80s-mid-90s.

(*) Expressin' The Blues
Music Maker MMCD 701 *Etta Baker, Robert Belfour, Precious Bryant, Willa Mae Buckner, Captain Luke [Luther Mayer], Essie Mae Brooks, Preston Fulp, Guitar Gabriel, Macavine Hayes, Big Boy Henry, Algia Mae Hinton, John Dee Holeman, Rufus McKenzie, Bishop Dready Manning, Marie Manning, Neal Pattman, Carl Rutherford, Albert Smith, Cootie Stark, Samuel Turner Stevens, John Lee Zeigler.* late 80s-late 90s.

The eastern states have never acquired the cachet of Mississippi, but from the late '50s onward there has been much significant field recording, by Sam Charters, Glenn Hinson, Kip Lornell, George Mitchell, Peter B. Lowry, Bruce Bastin and others. Few single-artist LPs have made it to CD, however, and even fewer VACs have resulted. These CDs and *Blues Came To Georgia* (see below) function to some extent as showcases for artists who have CDs of their own in Music Maker's catalogue. Most of the musicians are from Georgia and the Carolinas, but *Came So Far* visits J. W. Warren in Alabama, while *Expressin' The Blues* drops in on Mississippi's 'Wolfman' Belfour and Carl Rutherford, a white coalminer and fingerpicker extraordinaire from West Virginia. The artists are variably talented; the intermittent participation of producer Tim Duffy (guitar) and Michael Parrish (guitar and piano) is sometimes superfluous and sometimes all too necessary. The two discs have five tracks in common, among them Marie Manning's fiery gospel song, which is the best thing on either CD; 'Have You Seen Corrina?', J. W. Warren's long story-song about a jail break, with guitar sound effects, gives *Came So Far* the edge.

Carolinas

*** Carolina Blues (1937–1947)
Document DOCD-5168 *Floyd 'Dipper Boy' Council (6), Eddie Kelly's Washboard Band (8), Rich Trice (8), Welly [sic] Trice (2).* 2/37–9/47.

The long shadow of Blind Boy Fuller looms over Floyd Council and the Trice brothers: Council's steel guitar and gritty singing were long assumed to identify a Fuller imitator, and as late as 1947, when Rich Trice recorded for Savoy, the resulting 78 was credited to 'Little Boy Fuller'. Fuller's success led all three men to incorporate elements of his style, but although they lived very near Durham, they only became aware of Fuller after he began recording. Despite occasional suspect chords, Council was a fine musician, notable for some original lyrics. On the Trices' four 1937 titles, their bouncy playing outweighs Richard's intermittently flat singing of 'Come On Baby'. Ten years later, Richard sang with better pitch control and no stylistic change whatever. Four sides not issued until the LP era are superior to those Savoy chose for release; they're also closer to Fuller's sound, which may explain why they stayed in the can. Tracked down by Bruce Bastin and Peter B. Lowry in 1969, Richard had joined the church, but Willie returned to performing and made a well-received LP, *Blue And Rag'd* (Trix 3305). Eddie Kelly's band, playing harmonica, guitar, washboard and kazoo, exemplify a seldom-recorded sector of the Carolina black music scene. Kelly, who was the washboardist, and his associates crank out dance music that's jaunty and tightly integrated, but rather repetitive.

(***) The Bluesville Years Volume Six: Blues Sweet Carolina Blues
Prestige PRCD 9914 *Pink Anderson (8), Gary Davis (2), Larry Johnson (3), Brownie McGhee, Baby Tate (7), Sonny Terry (2).* 10/60–11/65.

The delightful, and delightfully oldfashioned, numbers by a then 27-year old Larry Johnson and second guitarist Hank Adkins come from the LP *The Blues: A New Generation*; all the other tracks are available on CDs which are discussed under the artists' own entries. Sonny and Brownie are their habitually effective selves, but Gary Davis's instrumentals effortlessly outshine everything else here. To say so is not to disparage the other musicians, simply to recognize that Davis transcended the Carolina guitar traditions which the others ably represent. This is a pleasant enough collection, but Prestige could more usefully, though no doubt less profitably, have reissued the Larry & Hank LP complete.

Georgia

*** The Georgia Blues 1927–1933
Yazoo 1012 *Willie Baker (2), Barbecue Bob, Blind Blake (2), Bumble Bee Slim, George Carter (2), Gitfiddle Jim [Kokomo Arnold] (2), Peg Leg Howell, Charlie Lincoln, Fred McMullen, Sylvester Weaver.* 4/27–1/33.

The Georgia Blues is weighted towards the guitarists of Atlanta; they often favoured 12-string instruments, but Fred McMullen plays a six-string on 'Wait and Listen', a poetic reworking of 'Stop And Listen Blues'. It's worth noting the quality of their singing, too: the soaring resonance of Willie Baker, the knowing nasality of Barbecue Bob and his brother Charlie Lincoln, and the warm, dreamy tones of George Carter. Eddie Anthony's fiddle is a perfect match for Peg Leg Howell's mournful 'Rolling Mill Blues', but the inclusion of the suave Kentuckian Sylvester Weaver is puzzling; Blind Blake may also not have been a Georgian, but his brilliancies on 'Police Dog Blues' and 'That'll Never Happen No More' disable pedantry. Less polished but just as dashing is Kokomo Arnold, whose Mach 2 bluesification of 'Paddlin' Madeline Home' makes a spectacular closer. Bumble Bee Slim's 'No Woman No Nickel', with jagged slide guitar, is very different from the assembly-line sedateness of his later career. An outdated booklet adds some pretentious literary criticism to the usual musical analysis.

For *Georgia Blues (1928–1933)* (Document DOCD-5110), which is notable for the remarkable harmonica player Eddie Mapp, see Curley Weaver; for *Georgia Blues & Gospel (1927–1931)* (Document DOCD-5160) see Julius Daniels.

*** Blues Came To Georgia

Music Maker MMCD 23 *Essie Mae Brooks, Cora Mae Bryant, Precious Bryant (2), Willa Mae Buckner, James Davis, Frank Edwards, Guitar Gabriel (2), Rufus McKenzie, Neal Pattman, Cootie Stark, Eddie Tigner, Beverly 'Guitar' Watkins, John Lee Zeigler.* 90s.

The range here is wide, and includes amplified band blues by Beverly Watkins and Eddie Tigner, the unaccompanied spirituals of Rufus McKenzie and Essie Mae Brooks, and John Lee Zeigler's archaic 'Lose My Money, Let Me Lose'. Successive tracks by Edwards (very old), Cora Mae Bryant (monotonous) and Buckner (trivial) try the listener's patience, and equally good versions of Precious Bryant's songs can be heard on her first Terminus CD; but Guitar Gabriel's 'Let No Woman' is one of his strongest solos, and the seven-minute 'Georgia Drumbeat' by James Davis (electric guitar) and Gilbert Henderson (drumkit) is a thrilling mutation of the extinct Georgia fife and drum tradition, recorded live in a juke-joint. CS

Field Recordings

***(*) Field Recordings – Vol. 1: Virginia (1936–1941)

Document DOCD-5575 *Big Boy, James Henry Diggs, group (Emmons Baptist Church) (2), Lemuel Jones (2), Jimmie Owens, Jimmie Strothers & Joe Lee (18), John Williams, Willie Williams (3), James Wilson.* 5/36–41.

Document's 16-volume (so far) series of *Field Recordings* trawls tapes acquired by collectors and deleted LPs, and rearranges the material (most of it recorded for the Library of Congress) first geographically, then chronologically. Many volumes are very collector-oriented, combining tracks omitted when LPs were transferred to CD with performances that are sometimes of low musical and/or acoustic quality; their chronological compilation sometimes produces arbitrary juxtapositions which make for uncomfortably fragmented listening. We list here those discs that we judge to be of wider interest (another is discussed under TOPICAL & DOCUMENTARY); when other CDs in the series include significant material, they are mentioned where appropriate.

The Virginian volume draws most of its material from then-deleted LPs, whch have since been reissued on Global Village (see below and ROOTS). In general the Global Village discs are to be preferred, but Document do good service in bringing together all but one recording by the important songsters Jimmie Strothers and Joe Lee, including several not issued elsewhere.

**** Field Recordings – Vol. 6: Texas (1933–1958)

Document DOCD-5580 *Arthur 'Brother-in-Law' Armstrong (3), James 'Iron Head' Baker (3), Jesse Bradley & 'Track Horse' Haggerty, Wallace Chains & Sylvester Jones (3), George Coleman (2), Hattie Ellis, Clyde Hill, Ace Johnson (2), Richard L. Lewis & Wilbert Gilliam, Mose 'Clear Rock' Platt (4), Phineas Rockmore, Will Roseborough, Henry Truvvillion (4), Lightnin' Washington (2), Ernest Williams & James 'Iron Head' Baker.* 12/33–6/58.

The 1958 tracks by George Coleman include that great eccentric's only recording on piano, but the balance of the disc is Library of Congress recordings from 1933–40. The first 11 tracks are sensationally powerful worksongs; there's some duplication with the Texan CDs in Rounder's *Deep River Of Song* series (see below), but it's worth having this disc as well, generally for the cumulative force of this material and specifically for Mose Platt's 'Barbara Allen', a Cubist collage of half-remembered verses sung with magnificent indifference to meaning. Thereafter, *Texas* darts about among harmonica displays, guitar blues, hunting songs and more worksongs. The sequencing is inevitably capricious, but all tracks are worth hearing, and Arthur Armstrong's three songs with swinging guitar are issued only here.

**** Field Recordings – Vol. 7: Florida (1935–1936)

Document DOCD-5587 *Gabriel Brown (8), John French, Rochelle French (8), Ozella Jones, Booker T. Sapps & Roger Matthews (8).* 6/35–5/36.

Ozella Jones's transformation of Barefoot Bill's 'Bad Boy' into a wavering field holler makes a beautiful conclusion and a sharp contrast to the rest of the CD. The harmonicas of Sapps and Matthews are supported on most tracks by guitarist Willie Flowers. Ballads, blues, instrumental showpieces, the worksong 'Po' Laz'us' and a gospel song all become driving dance music.

Some of Sapps and Matthews's ballads were also recorded by the guitarists Gabriel Brown and Rochelle French, who share the vocal duties, and second each other's playing on several tracks. (Brown also backs John French's heavily self-censored 'Uncle Bud'.) These are very significant recordings by two gifted musicians who shared a broad repertoire of traditional blues, ballads and spirituals; they also had some modernistic originals, at least one of which the researchers dismissed as 'jazz', but fortunately recorded.

Some tracks derive from damaged acetates, and Document omit four songs included on *Red River Blues* (Travelin' Man TM CD 08).

*** Field Recordings – Vol. 8: Louisiana, Alabama, Mississippi (1934–1947)

Document DOCD-5598 *Annabelle Abraham, Cleveland Benoit & Darby Hicks, Bob & Leroy (2), Betty May Bowman, Elinor*

Boyer, Oakdale Carrière, Josephine Douglas, five women, four girls aged about 16 (2), Hattie Goff (2), group of school children, group of women prisoners, Vera Hall, Mary James (3), Joseph Jones, Paul Junius Malveaux & Ernest Lafitte (2), Susie Miller, Mississippi school children, Elizabeth Moore, Josephine Parker (2), Beatrice Perry, Jimmy Peters (3), Wilbur Shaw, Edna Taylor, Mattie May Thomas (4), three children, three girl prisoners, Beatrice Tisdall, Lucille Walker, Eva White. 7/34–47.

***(*) **Field Recordings – Vol. 9: Georgia, S. & N. Carolina, Virginia, Kentucky (1924–39)**
Document DOCD-5599 *Arthur Anderson, Wheeler Bailey & Preston Fulp, Hannah Bessellion [Besselieu] (3), Angie Clark, Georgia fieldhands, group of tobaco workers, Elder Michaux, Belton Reese (2), Uncle John Scruggs, Eddie Thomas & Carl Scott, unknowns (15), Whistler's Jug Band. '24'–3/39.*

These discs are heffalump traps for whatever singers wander by; the Alabama component of *Vol. 8* is one (admittedly lovely) lullaby from Vera Hall, and Bob and Leroy's cheap guitars are as mood-disrupting here as they were on the LP *Murderers' Home*. The Louisiana tracks are all available elsewhere, but have undeniable impact when heard together. A further six songs are by Mississippi children, but the disc is mainly significant for 24 songs by women prisoners recorded in Parchman Farm in 1939. Many are very brief (this is a 42-track disc!), and some are amateurishly artless, but the mix of blues, pop, jazz and children's songs is fascinating, and the group harmonies on some blues are unusual and attractive. In Mattie Mae Thomas researcher Herbert Halpert found a songmaker to rank with the greatest; her hallucinatory 'Workhouse Blues' tells of hand-to-hand combat with lions, spiders, panthers and the hounds of hell.

Six performers on *Vol. 9*, including fieldhands, jugbands and an evangelist, derive from Fox-Movietone newsreel footage; the elderly banjoist Uncle John Scruggs, hollering 'Little Old Log Cabin In The Lane', is captivating. Some Library of Congress recordings are also thrown in, and Belton Reese's stringband (banjo, guitar and bones) is charming, but the unknown artists are the meat of the CD. They were recorded in Georgia and North Carolina by Lawrence Gellert, whose research was driven by his leftist politics; two Rounder LPs of mainly unaccompanied *Negro Songs Of Protest* cry out for release on CD. Document cannibalize a third album, originally on Heritage, which focused on guitar blues. The curators of the Gellert collection supplied recording dates which range from impossible (there was no electrical recording in 1924) to stylistically improbable; at a guess, most of these tracks are from the mid '30s, but more crucial is that the songs, many of them about imprisonment, are strong, and the guitar playing regularly dazzling.

**** **Texas Field Recordings (1934/1939)**
Document DOCD-5231 *Smith Casey (11), Augustus 'Track Horse' Haggerty (4), Pete Harris (13), Jack Johnson, Jesse Lockett, Tricky Sam (3). 4/34–4/39.*

Texas Field Recordings mines deleted Flyright LPs issued by agreement with the Library of Congress. All the artists except Pete Harris were recorded in prison, and all have their merits. The undoubted stars, though, are Harris and Casey (whose real name was Casey Smith, but the error is sanctified by time). The powerful-voiced Harris is quite strongly influenced by Blind Lemon Jefferson, but his guitar accompaniments on a mix of blues, ballads and dance tunes are a dashing melange of slide, banjoistic techniques, rhythmic chords, fingerpicking and bass string licks. Casey is an even more significant artist, who transcends genre. All his performances are of major importance, but most notable are the daring use of dissonance on 'Santa Fe Blues', the ringing vocals that make 'Shorty George' a defining moment of Texas blues, and the transformation of 'When I Lay My Burden Down' into a series of bluesy variations which Casey called 'East Texas Rag'.

♕ **** **Negro Blues And Hollers**
Rounder CD 1501 *Charley Berry, William Brown (3), Church of God in Christ Congregation, Honeyboy Edwards, Silent Grove Baptist Church Congregation, Son House (4), Willie '61' Blackwell. 8/41–7/42.*

**** **Afro-American Spirituals, Work Songs, and Ballads**
Rounder CD 1510 *James 'Iron Head' Baker, Arthur Bell, Joe Washington Brown & Austin Coleman, Convict Group, Wash Dennis & Charlie Sims, Clyde Hill, Frank Jordan, Kelly Pace, Allen Prothro, Jimmie Strothers, Dock & Henry Reed & Vera Hall (3), Lightnin' Washington, Jeff Webb, Ernest Williams, Willie Williams. c. 7/33–8/42.*

**** **Afro-American Blues And Game Songs**
Rounder CD 1513 *Charlie Butler, Smith Casey (3), Hettie Godfrey (2), Ora Dell Graham (3), group of girls, Vera Hall (2), Jim Henry, 'Little Brother', Irwin Lowry, Harriet McClintock (2), Mr & Mrs Joe McDonald, Molly McDonald, Muddy Waters (2), Moses 'Clear Rock' Platt, Katherine & Christine Shipp, Sonny Terry (2). 12/33–8/41.*

***(*) **Negro Work Songs And Calls**
Rounder 1517 *Jesse Bradley, James 'Iron Head' Baker and others, Samuel Brooks (2), Sam Hazel, Thomas J. Marshall (2), Kelly Pace and others (2), Moses 'Clear Rock' Platt & James 'Iron Head' Baker, Allen Prothro, David Pryor, Joe Shores, Henry Truvillion (4), Lightnin' Washington, Willie Williams. c. 8/33–10/40.*

These four CDs are remastered reissues (including the original notes) of Library of Congress LPs originally released as albums of 78s in the '40s. There's a good deal of duplication with Document (of course) and with Rounder's own *Deep River of Song* series (see below), but these collections were very well selected, and provide overviews of their subject areas that are of very high musical quality.

Where the other three CDs range widely, *Negro Blues And Hollers* concentrates on the Coahoma County project, run jointly by the Library of Congress and Fisk University. Most of its secular content has been widely – in the case of Son House, very widely – reissued, and playing time is only 45 minutes and change, but this disc remains one of the finest in-depth examinations of a region's music ever compiled; not a snapshot of Delta blues and spirituals, more like a Cartier-Bresson.

Spirituals, Work Songs And Ballads may seem an odd combination, but the genres had many musical gestures in common. Vera Hall and her cousins are very deep and soulful, as in their own way are the Texan convicts, singing among other things gripping versions of 'Ain't No More Cane On The Brazos' and 'Long Hot Summer Days'. Even 'Iron Head' can't stop 'The Grey Goose' being monotonous, but there's compensation aplenty, notably 'Rosie', which was the 'big song' of the Parchman Penitentiary, Jimmie Strothers's banjo, and the three-man gospel quartet (*sic*) formed by Wash Dennis, Charlie Sims and the uncredited D. B. Prowell.

Blues And Game Songs allots half its tracks to each type of music; the Library's recordings of Casey, Terry and Muddy Waters are available complete elsewhere, but here they are components in an exceptionally good musical sequence. The marvels of Charlie Butler and Vera Hall are discussed elsewhere in this entry; also worth noting is the Texan 'Little Brother's' churning guitar accompaniment. Some readers may wonder about the entertainment value of the game songs, not all of which are sung by children, but all blues singers were children once. From school pupils chanting 'Ain't Gonna Ring No More' to ex-slave Harriet McClintock singing a lullaby, all the artists on this half of the CD swing ferociously.

Negro Work Songs And Calls opens with Henry Truvillion's rapid-fire spoken instructions to a gang 'Unloading Rails'. The DNA of rap is in there, but it's an uncompromising start. Matters become more musical thereafter, but not less challenging: there's a thread (whether intended by the compilers or not) of complaint and protest running through prison recordings like 'Old Rattler', 'It Makes A Long Time Man Feel Bad' and 'O Lord, Don't 'Low Me To Beat 'Em'. Alongside the usual group songs, there are some high and lonesome solo hollers, while Sam Hazel and the appropriately named Joe Shores re-create the sounding calls ('Mark twain!') that were part of life on the Mississippi.

**** Afro-American Folk Music From Tate And Panola Counties, Mississippi

Rounder 1515 *Ranie Burnette, Sid Hemphill (3), The Hunter Chapel Missionary Baptist Choir, Compton Jones (3), Mary Mabeary, Lucius Smith, Napoleon Strickland, Ada Turner, Mae & Alaneda Turner, Othar Turner. 8/42–7/71.*

Fred McDowell, R. L. Burnside and Junior Kimbrough have made the guitar blues of northeast Mississippi famous, but this disc investigates the depth and variety of the area's black music. Three tracks are by bands led by Sid Hemphill in 1942, among them an epic stringband piece about a local train wreck; the remainder were recorded by David Evans in the late '60s and early '70s. The stress is on homemade, community-based music, including fife and drum bands, children's songs, church music and the improvised polyrhythms of Compton Jones's family, beating on chairs, cans, benches and a washtub. As Evans writes in his comprehensive notes, hearing Othar Turner's 'Black Woman', sung first with guitar accompaniment then as a holler, is like witnessing the birth of the blues.

***(*) Deep River Of Song: Black Texicans

Rounder CD 1821 *Angelina Quartet, Arthur Armstrong, James 'Iron Head' Baker, 'Butter Boy', Smith Casey, Pete Harris (4), Ace Johnson, Uncle Billy McCrea, Moses 'Clear Rock' Platt (5), Leadbelly, Don Mooney, Percy Ridge, Phineas Rockmore (2), Will Roseborough, Henry Truvillion (3), unknown axe-cutting group, unknown harmonica player (2), Lightnin' Washington.* 12/33–10/40.

Most of the music in the *Deep River Of Song* series was recorded by John and/or Alan Lomax in the '30s and '40s. Alan hoped that the series would make younger African-Americans aware of their heritage, but in practice the audience, of whatever race, for these 12 CDs (Rounder 1822 and 1832 are collections of Bahamian music) consists mainly of the scholars and hardcore collectors to whom the extensive annotations are pitched. It would be good to enlarge that circle: these discs contain a great deal of splendid music, made in a world whose distance from ours is often hard to grasp.

Some of *Black Texicans*' content was recorded in prisons (which the Lomaxes rightly thought were good places to find old songs), but its object is to survey the wide variety of music made by frontiersmen at work and leisure. The guitar skills of Pete Harris and Smith Casey are available as part of their complete works on Document (see above), but they're integral to a rich selection which includes cowboy songs, ballads of British descent and African-American invention, play-party songs, dance tunes, worksongs and display music that ranges from harmonica showpieces to mouth music.

***(*) Deep River Of Song: Black Appalachia

Rounder CD 1823 *Blind Pete & George Ryan (2), John 'Black Sampson' Gibson (2), Murphy Gribble and others (3), Sid Hemphill and others (6), Brownie McGhee and others (2), Nashville Washboard Band (2), Allen Prothro, Theopolis Stokes, Jimmie Strothers (2), Sonny Terry.* 8/33–9/46.

The Appalachians run from Quebec to Alabama, but the music comes from Virginia, Tennessee, north Mississippi and Arkansas. It seems that Alan Lomax wanted to illustrate both the interaction of white and black music and the emergence of blues as the dominant African-American style. The disc pivots around a block of dance tunes and blues-ballads performed by Mississippi fiddler and quill player Sid Hemphill's band. Before them come the banjo and guitar of Virginia's Jimmie Strothers, and stringbands playing blues and breakdowns with tremendous verve and skill. The CD concludes with worksongs from Tennessee and well-known blues performed by Brownie McGhee and Sonny Terry, with Leadbelly joining in on 'How Long Blues'. The music on these later tracks is of high quality, but the transition is rather abrupt.

The complete Blind Pete & George Ryan session is on *Mississippi Blues & Gospel (Field Recordings 1934–1942)* (Document DOCD-5320). There are other important performances by Hemphill's band on *Field Recordings – Vol. 3: Mississippi (1936–1942)* (Document DOCD-5577) and *Vol. 5: Mississippi (1941–1942)* (Document DOCD-5672).

***(*) Deep River Of Song: Mississippi – Saints & Sinners

Rounder CD 1824 *Big Charlie Butler (2), Crap Eye, Lucious Curtis (2), Dobie Red (2), Frank Evans, Sid Hemphill and others (2), Jim Henry and others (3), Henry Joiner and others, Thomas 'Jaybird' Jones, Deacon Tom Jones (2), Rev. C. H. Savage (6), Joe Shores, Will Starks.* 8/33–8/42.

The last 30 minutes of *Saints & Sinners* consists of ring shouts and other archaic gospel songs, which the singers had learned from their parents and grandparents. The secular tracks similarly focus on older music: the ballads, worksongs, rags and reels that preceded and evolved into the blues. There are some likeable curiosities here: Joe Shores's riverboat sounding calls, 'Crap Eye' (probably a mishearing of 'Scrap Iron') beating a bucket to rouse the convicts on Parchman Farm, and Will Starks singing an English fox-hunting song. There are also a number of out-and-out masterpieces, above all Charlie Butler's haunting, enigmatic 'Diamond Joe', but also 'Stewball' and 'Rosie'; Dobie Red spurs the eight men singing these worksongs with him to sound like 80.

**** Deep River Of Song: Mississippi – The Blues Lineage

Rounder CD 1825 *William Brown (2), Sam Carter and others, Lucious Curtis (2), Honeyboy Edwards, Frank Evans, Willie Ford*

(2), Son House (4), Muddy Waters (2), Hollis 'FatHead' Washington. 4/36–7/42.

Mississippi – The Blues Lineage is the only CD in the *Deep River* series with an exclusively blues content. Inevitably music recorded during the 1941–42 Coahoma County project features heavily, and just as inevitably Son House and Muddy Waters dominate that subset. Most tracks have been previously available on LP and/or CD, but this collection is excellently compiled and superbly remastered. House and Waters apart, William Brown, playing two and sometimes three guitar lines at once, is perhaps the highlight, but the raw hollering of Hollis Washington and Honeyboy Edwards's astonishingly expressive rack harmonica give him a close run.

♛ **** Deep River Of Song: Big Brazos
Rounder CD 1826 *James 'Iron Head' Baker, Jesse Bradley (3), Augustus 'Track Horse' Haggerty (4), Moses 'Clear Rock' Platt, Dave Tippin (3), Lightnin' Washington (6), Ernest Williams (2).* 12/33–11/34.

Big Brazos surveys the worksongs that enabled black convicts to make it in the hell of the prison system, by keeping their spirits up and pacing the work so that it became harder to single out slow workers for whipping. It includes all the greatest songs of the Texas penitentiaries, among them 'Go Down Old Hannah', 'Old Rattler', 'Lost John' and 'Ain't No More Cane On The Brazos', and considering the conditions – essentially a prolongation of slavery – in which they were created and sung, one can only marvel at the life-affirming power of the singers' passion, rage, humour, sadness and stoicism.

**** Deep River Of Song: Virginia And The Piedmont
Rounder CD 1827 *Blind Joe, The Golden Gate Quartet with Josh White (2), Norman Haskins, Robert Higgins, Rollie Lee Johnson, Lemuel Jones, J. Kirby, Joe Lee (2), Ezra Lewis, Michael Lewis, Jimmie Owens, Jimmie Strothers (6), Sonny Terry & Brownie McGhee (3), Albert Shepherd, unidentified group, Willie Williams (3), James Wilson.* 12/34–5/42.

Notwithstanding Sonny Terry's virtuoso harmonica, Jimmie Strothers's banjo and the Blind Blakeish picking of Blind Joe, *Virginia And The Piedmont* is most notable for a succession of magnificent singers, including the polished Golden Gate Quartet, the rough power of Willie Williams, solo and leading a prison work gang, and 71-year-old Joe Lee, booming out nearly six minutes of 'Going To Richmond' to his own considerable guitar accompaniment. (This is the track omitted from Document's *Field Recordings – Vol 1: Virginia*.) Some extraordinary texts are featured alongside more familiar lyrics: topics include agrarian protest and spontaneous human combustion, while Ezra Lewis's 'Tin Can Alley' features trendy scat singing and Robert Higgins's 'Prison Blues' incorporates sacred elements.

**** Deep River Of Song: Georgia
Rounder CD 1828 *Buster Brown (2), Reese Crenshaw, Robert Davis, Gus Gibson & Sidney Stripling, Blind Willie McTell (4), male convict group (2), Camp Morris (2), The Smith Band, James Sneed, Sidney Stripling (3), Paul Sylvester, John Lee Thomas, Jessie Wadley, Sophie Wing.* 12/34–3/43.

Blind Willie McTell's Library of Congress session is available complete, but this overview would be distorted if his music were excluded. The CD's range is very wide, from guitar breakdowns to Sea Island spirituals, and it includes some intriguing worksongs arranged for performance outside a work context; among them, 'Po' Laz'us' is explicitly hostile to prison guards. The elderly banjoist Sidney Stripling is both historically significant and hugely entertaining, as are the little bands of James Sneed and Clifford Smith, respectively playing versions of 'Candy Man' and 'Hindustan'.

(****) Deep River Of Song: Alabama
Rounder CD 1829 *Richard Amerson (3), Tom Bell, Annie Brewer, Rich Brown, Charley Campbell, Willie Carter and others, eight unidentified girls (2), Vera Hall (7), Blind Jessie Harris (2), Thomas Langston and others, Harriet McClintock (2), Mary McDonald (4), Dock Reed and Vera Hall (3), Sim Tartt, unidentified children, Joe F. & Booker T. Williams.* c. 10/34–11/40.

The star here, whether singing secular or religious songs, is Vera Hall, whose voice, with the grace of a dove and the strength of an eagle, is one of American music's greatest glories. An unintended consequence of her pre-eminence is that singers like Harriet McClintock and Mary McDonald, who are by any objective measure very good indeed, seem diminished by comparison. No such problem arises with Jessie Harris, playing a defective piano-accordion whose curiosity value seems to be the reason for his presence. Masochists can find these and another 12 tracks by Harris on *Field Recordings – Vol. 4: Mississippi & Alabama (1934–1942)* (Document DOCD-5578). Rich Amerson's harmonica and Charley Campbell's caustic 'ain't workin' song' shouldn't be overlooked, but the CD is heavy on lullabies and spirituals, and readers may find it marginal.

**** Deep River Of Song: Louisiana
Rounder CD 1830 *Sam Ballard (2), Cleveland Benoit & Darby Hicks, John Bray, Joe (Washington) Brown (4), Joe Harris, Leadbelly (2), Paul Junius Malveaux & Ernest Lafitte (2), Joe Massie (2), Jelly Roll Morton (2), Anderson Moss (2), Jimmy Peters (2), 'Stavin' Chain' [Wilson Jones], unidentified male section group.* 6/34–c. 80.

Anderson Moss's two zydeco tunes were recorded c. 1980, but could easily have come from the '30s like the rest of the disc. Its range is very wide, from the throat-tearing polyphonic ring shouts (religious) and *jurés* (secular) of Washington Brown and Jimmy Peters, to Jelly Roll Morton, singing the pimp's song 'Wining Boy' and urbanely transforming a quadrille into 'Tiger Rag'. Leadbelly's 'Irene' and 'Mama Did You Bring Me Any Silver' are well known but necessary; they don't outshine John Bray's song about his World War I experiences, Stavin' Chain's stringband or Sam Ballard's worksongs.

One song from this CD is also on *The Louisiana Recordings: Creole & Cajun Music* (Rounder CD 1841), and three are on *Creole & Cajun Music II* (Rounder CD 1842). The former disc includes only three African-American songs, but the latter, also 22 tracks long, has ten samples of 'zydeco, juré and the blues'; its ring shouts and *jurés* are as thrilling as those on the *Deep River* anthology.

(***) Deep River Of Song: South Carolina
Rounder CD 1831 *Hannah Besselieu & Mittie Docter (2), Minnie Floyd, Elsie Jenkins, Lillie Knox (2), Lillie & Thelma Knox (2), Zack Knox (4), Luther Mack and others, Michael Maybank and*

others (3), Owens Family, Tina 'Mom' Russell, Willie James Skinner, unknown group, D. W. White (3), Jim Williams (3), Martha Wright and others (3). 12/34–6/39.

We list this CD for completeness, but it is very heavily weighted towards religious music: even some of the worksongs have religious texts. Most of the recordings were made in the isolated, Gullah-speaking community of Murrell's Inlet, and they have as much stylistic affinity with the Bahamas as with the mainland United States. The compilation includes some beautiful singing, but it's on the periphery of this book's vision.

**** Red River Blues
Travelin' Man TM CD 08 *Blind Joe (2), Buster Brown (2), Gabriel Brown, Sonny Chestain, Reese Crenshaw, Robert Davis, Willy Flowers, Gus Gibson (2), Allison Mathis (2), Jimmie Owens, Booker T. Sapps (3), The Smith Band, James Sneed, Jimmie Strothers, Willie Williams, J. Wilson.* 12/34–3/43.

Red River Blues draws on Library of Congress recordings from the eastern seaboard, focusing on instrumentally accompanied blues. The remastering is excellent, although the Florida recordings of guitar and harmonica bands fronted by Sapps, Flowers and Gabriel Brown were in challenging condition. These raucous juke-joint duos and trios are a valuable slice of the Sunshine State's too-seldom recorded blues. A nicely varied programme also includes Blind Joe's other recording (one of three songs about how their convict composers got 'In Trouble'), and Willie Williams's only guitar-accompanied blues, on which he sounds like a Virginian Charley Patton.

**(*) I Can Eagle Rock
Travelin' Man TM CD 09 *Tom Bell (7), Joe Harris & Kid West (4), Noah Moore (5), Washboard Trio (Mobile Washboard Band), Oscar Woods (5).* 10/40–7/41.

The Washboard Trio and Tom Bell were Alabamians; the other artists, also recorded for the Library of Congress, were found in Shreveport, on the Louisiana–Texas border. Bell adds to our picture of Alabama guitar blues, but his cheap instrument is hard listening. The guitar and mandolin duo of Harris & West play rags and stringband blues. Their younger associate Oscar Woods had recorded commercially (see his entry), and he covers his own and other people's records – even 'Boll Weevil Blues' is from Ma Rainey. Noah Moore is a very competent guitarist who owes little to his famous uncle, Leadbelly. He plays slide on two songs in a similar style to Woods, but more important are 'Oil City Blues' and 'Lowdown Worry Blues', at nine and 11 minutes respectively a rare chance to hear '40s blues unconstrained by the limits of 78s. *I Can Eagle Rock* documents some noteworthy music, but it's more for specialists than for casual listeners.

☙ **** Prison Songs Vol. 1: Murderous Home
Rounder CD 1714 *'22' (4), Alex, B. B. (2), Bama [W. D. Stuart] (4), C. B. [Cook] (2), Jimson [Henry Wallace] (2), Tangle Eye [Walter Jackson] (2).* late 47–early 48.

***(*) Prison Songs Vol. 2: Don'tcha Hear Poor Mother Calling?
Rounder CD 1715 *'22' (4), '88' [C. B. Cook], Bama [W. D. Stuart] (3), Bull, Curry Childress (2), Hollie Dew, Dobie Red (4), George Johnson (2), Tangle Eye [Walter Jackson], Percy Wilson (2).* late 47–early 48.

The recordings were made in Parchman Farm, using one of the first commercially available tape recorders, which afforded higher quality (but still mono) sound than discs and cylinders. Alan Lomax felt that worksongs were beginning to decline by 1947: younger convicts disliked them and the older men's voices were wearing out. Dobie Red is certainly diminished since the '30s, and everyone sounds weary on the version of 'Rosie' led by '88' on *Don'tcha Hear Poor Mother Calling?* Nevertheless, these are probably the finest recordings of worksongs, thanks to the combination of improved technology and a still vigorous tradition. The eight tracks alloted to the younger prisoner '22' are a tribute to his inventiveness and power as a leader: the polyrhthmic ingenuity of 'Early In The Morning', sung by '22' and three other convicts as they fell a tree, is breathtaking. That track is on *Murderous Home*, which is the stronger of the two discs because it contains most of the classic LP *Negro Prison Songs*, of which the CDs are an expansion; but there is much enthralling music on the second volume, and some valuable interviews.

Readers who want to hear how the expansion was done will find that *American Folk-Blues Train* (Castle CMETD 648 3CD) includes a dub of the original LP (under its British title, *Murderers' Home*) alongside *Blues In The Mississippi Night* (see TOPICAL & DOCUMENTARY) and *American Song Train Vol. 1*, by the white folk revivalist Guy Carawan.

**(*) Work & Pray
WVU Press SA-4 *Henry L. Dickason (5), Waldo Dickason (4), Memphis T. Garrison (2), Clarence Harmon, Nelson Harmon (2), P. R. Higginbotham, Charles L. Holland (2), Esther Johnson (3), Albert McCoy (3), Bell Edward Pate, Joe Perkins (2), R. L. Pollard (3), Blanche Simmons, unknowns (3), Frank Wade, John Wade (2), Mrs John Wade, Susan White.* 1/50–4/51.

West Virginia's black music is scantily represented on records, and *Work & Pray*, which draws on the fieldwork of African-American musicologist Dr Cortez D. Reece, is a significant CD; some of its content is not recorded elsewhere, and some of the religious material seems considerably influenced by white sources. Regrettably, however, there were no great singers among Dr Reece's informants. Several of them came from the black bourgeoisie (teachers, a physician, a dance school proprietor), and they either aim for or can't avoid a refined delivery of spirituals and worksongs.

**** Southern Journey Vol. 3: 61 Highway Mississippi
Rounder CD 1703 *A. Burton and congregation, Mrs Sidney Carter, John Dudley (2), Mattie Gardner and others, Leroy Gary, Rose Hemphill, Sid Hemphill & Lucius Smith (2), Viola James & congregation, Ed Lewis & prisoners, Fred McDowell (6), Leroy Miller & prisoners, Miles & Bob Pratcher (2), Henry Ratcliff, Ervin Webb (2), Ed & Lonnie Young.* 9–10/59.

**** Southern Journey Vol. 13: Earliest Times
Rounder CD 1713 *Joe Armstrong (2), Joe Armstrong & John Davis, John Davis (7), Peter Davis, Bessie Jones (6), Henry Morrison, Henry Morrison & John Davis, Willis Proctor, unidentified.* 10/59–4/60.

(****) Sounds Of The South
Atlantic 782496 4CD *Boy Blue and others (2), Rev. R. C. Crenshaw (2), John Davis, John Davis & Bessie Jones, Rev. W. A. Donaldson, John Dudley, Felix Dukes, Forrest City Joe [Pugh] (8), Mattie Gardner and others (2), Vera Hall (4), Rose Hemphill, Sid Hemphill & Lucius Smith, Viola James (2), Bessie*

Jones (4), Mary Lee, Ed Lewis (2), Bernice McClellan, Fred McDowell (6), Johnny Lee Moore (2), Henry Morrison, Miles & Bob Pratcher, James Shorty, James Shorty & Viola James (2), Rev. G. I. Townsel, Madame Mattie Wigley, Ed & Lonnie Young (5), others. 9/59–4/60.

Alan Lomax returned to the South in 1959 carrying a stereo tape recorder, which caught far more of the intricacies of singing by work gangs and congregations; microphone placement that puts a voice in one channel and its accompanying guitar in the other is less appealing. LPs appeared on Atlantic and Prestige; the 13 volumes of Rounder's *Southern Journey* expand the Prestige series. Discs devoted to white music and black gospel are outside our scope, but *Vol. 1: Voices From The South* (Rounder CD 1701) gives an overview of the series' immense range and high quality. We should also mention *Vol. 5: Bad Man Ballads* (Rounder CD 1705), whose 17 tracks include seven (mostly worksongs) by black singers. One of its three versions of 'Po' Lazarus' brought James Carter an unexpected Grammy and a tidy sum in royalties after it was used in *O Brother, Where Art Thou?*

Fred McDowell was the greatest discovery of the 1959 trip, and one can only echo the 'perfect' which Lomax wrote in his notes next to '61 Highway Blues'. McDowell was part of a vigorous local scene, though, and on *61 Highway Mississippi* he doesn't outshine the fife music of Sid Hemphill and Ed Young, or the Pratcher brothers' archaic fiddle and guitar dance tunes. Beyond the north Mississippi hills, John Dudley, recorded in Parchman, brilliantly covers Barbecue Bob on 'Po' Boy Blues' and Charley Patton on 'Clarksdale Mill Blues'. The worksong had continued to decline, but there's still a lot of muscle there, most notably in 'Berta Berta', co-led, as the stereo separation reveals, by Leroy Miller and another singer. The eight African-American tracks (five of them religious) which are half of *Vol. 6: Sheep, Sheep Don'tcha Know The Road* (Rounder CD 1706) add to the picture of McDowell and his circle; this disc also includes a rowdy 'Dimples' by an Arkansas juke-joint band.

Earliest Times contains songs from the Georgia Sea Islands; most of them are secular chanteys, worksongs and ring games, and religious texts like 'Live Humble' and 'Union' were important in defining social norms for a remote community. *Earliest Times* and its religious companion, *Vol. 12: Georgia Sea Islands* (Rounder CD 1712), portray a society that hadn't changed much since long before Lomax first visited in 1935; their superior sound offers a more accessible look at Gullah folkways than the *South Carolina* CD in the *Deep River Of Song* series. Two songs on *Earliest Times* are accompanied by the fife of Mississippi's Ed Young, Bahamian drummer Nat Rahmings and the white Virginia banjoist Hobart Smith. They come from a session set up to re-create the black music of colonial America; more examples are on *Vol. 1* and *Vol. 8: Velvet Voices* (Rounder CD 1708). These tracks may or may not be accurate reconstructions; they are certainly sublimely beautiful.

Atlantic's box set transfers the content of seven LPs to four CDs. There are great riches here, but space limitations mean that nine tracks are annoyingly ripped from their original contexts and tacked on to the fourth CD of *American Folk Songs For Children*. About half the 105 tracks are by white artists not listed above; there's much to enjoy among them, notably the Mountain Ramblers' bluegrass and the veteran J. E. Mainer's stringband, but they make *Sounds Of The South* an expensive proposition for black music specialists.

Many of the artists also appear on Rounder, but Vera Hall, Fred McDowell and Bessie Jones are as commanding here as there; so are less celebrated returnees like John Dudley, this time channeling Tommy Johnson. The major point of difference with Rounder is the space alloted to the amplified bands led by Boy Blue and the harmonica player Forrest City Joe. Joe had recorded commercially, imitating John Lee 'Sonny Boy' Williamson; there's more of that here, and some knockabout piano on 'Red Cross Store', but he also stakes a claim to originality with the long solo improvisations 'Train Time' and 'Levee Camp Reminiscence'. One may doubt that Lomax's plans to make Joe a star on the folk scene would have borne fruit while still recognizing the quality of these pieces and regretting his death in a road accident a few months later.

***(*) **The Land Where The Blues Began**
Rounder CD 1861 '22', Bama [W. D. Stuart], Willie '61' Blackwell (2), Big Bill Broonzy, John Cameron, Congregation Of The Church Of God In Christ, Clarksdale, Dobie Red, David 'Honeyboy' Edwards, Forrest City Joe [Pugh], Charles Haffer Jr, Sid Hemphill (2, one miscredited to Alec Askew), Son House, Turner Junior Johnson, Fred McDowell, Memphis Slim and others, Muddy Waters, M. C. Orr, Sampson Pittman, Rev. Ribbins, Rev. C. H. Savage, Joe Shores, Florence Stamp and others, Will Starks, J. H. Terrell, Ernest Williams, Ed & Lonnie Young. 12/33–10/59.

**** **Alan Lomax: Blues Songbook**
Rounder 1866 2CD Albert Ammons, Cecil Augusta, Boy Blue and others (2), Elinor Boyer, Dock Boggs, Big Bill Broonzy, Gabriel Brown, R. L. Burnside, Smith Casey, Sam Chatmon, Lucious Curtis, David 'Honeyboy' Edwards (2), Hattie Ellis, Canray Fontenot & Bois Sec Ardoin, Vera Hall, Vera Hall & Dock Reed, Rosalie Hill, Son House, Howlin' Wolf, Skip James, Pete Johnson, Bessie Jones, Ozella Jones, Leadbelly, Leadbelly, Sonny Terry & Brownie McGhee, Fred McDowell, Blind Willie McTell, Memphis Jug Band, Memphis Slim, Jelly Roll Morton, Muddy Waters, Jack Owens & Bud Spires (2), Miles & Bob Pratcher, Hobart Smith, Tangle Eye [Walter Jackson], Sonny Terry, Sonny Boy Williamson I, Ed Young & Hobart Smith. 7/34–8/78.

The Land Where The Blues Began is a companion to Alan Lomax's book of the same title, which describes his fieldwork in Mississippi from the '30s to the '70s, and presents his conclusions about how black folkways and music were shaped by the pressures of racism. Most of the music is thrilling, but Turner Junior Johnson's bluesy harmonica is more enticing than his dry gospel singing, and Charles Haffer's monotone makes his ballad about the Great War very hard listening. Many tracks have been frequently reissued before, but Haffer's song is among the 25 per cent that are new to disc: they include preaching, congregational singing, a children's song, a joke about 'The Preacher And The Bear' and a rhyming toast.

The *Blues Songbook* casts its temporal and geographical nets more widely, and its musical net more narrowly: apart from a spiritual by Hall & Reed, the content is blues as advertised. Once again, there's a lot of familiar material included, and seven of the tracks described as previously unissued come from commercially available videos. Determined collectors will be enticed by genuinely new material from the fine guitarist Cecil Augusta, the Memphis Jug Band (1959 vintage, with prominent electric guitar) and the Pratcher Brothers (an exhilarating 'Joe Turner'), but despite all the recycling the *Songbook* is worthwhile for more than completist reasons: the notes and the remastering are both exemplary (this is the first chance to hear the tracks by Ammons and Lewis properly), and the very varied content is skilfully sequenced for continuity, contrast and entertainment value. Eight tracks were recorded by John A. Lomax without his son's assistance, but the extent of Alan's blues archive is astonishing – and it was just part of his musical adventures: blues and related musics dominate *Alan Lomax: Popular Songbook* (Rounder 1863, also available, like *Blues Songbook*, in a SACD version) but its Caribbean, Spanish and white folk tracks give an idea of his manifold explorations, even if the disc's rationale (collating songs covered by rock artists) is opportunistic. More adventurous readers are directed to *The Alan Lomax Collection Sampler* (Rounder CD 1700).

*** **Tangle Eye: Alan Lomax's Southern Journey Remixed**
Zoe 1024 *'88' [C. B. Cook] (2), Bright Light Quartet, Mrs Sidney Carter, Jimson [Henry Wallace], Bessie Jones, Ed Lewis, Fred McDowell with Denise & Mattie Gardner and others, Peerless Four, Almeda Riddle with Ed & Lonnie Young, Ervin Webb.* late 47–4/60, 12/01–3/03.

**** **Presenting The Alan Lomax Collection**
CRS CRSCD 810 *As above, except Almeda Riddle and Ed & Lonnie Young have separate tracks.* late 47–4/60.

The second set of dates against *Tangle Eye* relates to sampling, remixing and the overdubbing of beats and musicians. Alan Lomax had become a brand name well before his death, but primly accusing projects like this of exploitation is naive; purists will only get to hear the originals if record companies make enough money to support their release. Equally, though, there's no case for tamely surrendering to the argument that anything which encourages people to seek out the originals can't be bad.

The useful comparison, perhaps, is with Lomax's own experiments – themselves a kind of sampling and remixing – with bringing together Ed & Lonnie Young, the Sea Island singers, Hobart Smith and Nat Rahmings. As has already been noted, this musical salmagundi may have been utterly inauthentic, but it produced masterpieces. Many of *Tangle Eye*'s original tracks were themselves masterpieces, but there are no new ones created by the remixes: at its worst, *Tangle Eye* turns greatness (Ed Lewis's 'John Henry', Mrs Carter's 'Pharaoh', Ervin Webb's 'I'm Going Home') into blandness. That said, the transformations of C. B. Cook's 'Whoa Buck' and 'Rosie' into wild blues-rock are works of real and considerable creativity, the reggaefication of the Peerless Four's fishing chanteys is enchanting, and a track that amalgamates Almeida Riddle's 'Hangman Tree', the Youngs' 'Jim And John' and a band featuring modal fiddling has some of the syncretic synergy of Lomax's experiments.

Tangle Eye would have been better for more risk-taking, but it shouldn't be dismissed out of hand. *Presenting The Alan Lomax Collection* contains the unaltered originals, omitting one of the two versions of 'I Wished I Was In Heaven' which are combined on *Tangle Eye*. It's an admirable (and low-priced) collection of great music.

*** **20 To Life**
Fuel 2000 302 061 161 *Jesse Butcher, The Cool Cats, John Henry Jackson (2), Hogman Maxey (3), Otis Webster (3), Guitar Welch (3).* 59.

***(*) **Angola Prisoners' Blues**
Arhoolie CD 419 *A capella group* [sic], *'Butterbeans', Roosevelt Charles (2), Thelma Mae Joseph, Odea Mathews, Hogman Maxey (4), vocal group, Otis Webster, Guitar Welch (4), Robert Pete Williams (3), Clara Young.* 59–60.

***(*) **Prison Worksongs**
Arhoolie CD 448 *'Big Louisiana' [Rodney Mason] and others (3), Johnny Butler, Roosevelt Charles and others, Emmanuel Dunn (3), Odea Mathews (2), Murray Macon, Willie Rafus and others (2), Rev. Rogers and others, James Russell, Creola & Ceola Scott, Guitar Welch and others (3).* 59–63.

*** **Wake Up Dead Man**
Rounder CD 2013 *W. D. Alexander, Willie 'Cowboy' Craig, Johnny Jackson, Joseph 'Chinaman' Johnson (2), Houston Page, Benny Richardson, Henry Scott, Ebbie Veasley and others.* 8/65–3/66.

The first three CDs are compiled from recordings made by Harry Oster, mostly in the Louisiana State Penitentiary; Emmanuel Dunn and the Scott sisters on *Prison Worksongs* were recorded on the outside. There's also a collection of *Angola Prison Spirituals* (Arhoolie CD 9036).

The unique Robert Pete Williams was Oster's major discovery in Angola, and there's nobody of his stature on *20 To Life*. Its artists are all worth hearing, though: Guitar Welch deserved his nickname, while Butcher's harmonica and Jackson's groaning vocals appear only on this CD. The Cool Cats, featuring a plaintive alto sax, are jarringly different from the other artists, but imprisonment did not cut musicians off from developments in the free world, as proven by Webster and Maxey, both covering Arthur Crudup effectively.

Maxey, Webster and Welch reappear on *Angola Prisoners' Blues*; Maxey's bitonality (singing in one key and playing in another) is never weirder nor more compelling than on 'Stagolee'. Robert Pete Williams's modal approach is as distinctive, and almost as strange, but perfectly suited to his plaintive stream-of-consciousness lyrics. *Prisoners' Blues* is an expanded LP, and the additions are pleasingly varied: as well as more guitar blues, they include a harmonized worksong, a brief toast, a doo-wop group and three unaccompanied songs by women. Not all the added material is unimpeachable: the doo-woppers are uninspired, the toast is unfunny, and Webster's version of 'Careless Love' is strained, but Welch's version of 'Highway 61' is memorable, as is Roosevelt Charles's vivid narrative of a 'Strike At Camp 1'.

As in Parchman, the worksong was a dying tradition in Angola, rejected as 'that old John Henry stuff' by the younger convicts. This is evident on *Prison Worksongs*: some of the singers sound tired, or take a while to warm up; most of the songs are obviously staged (two were used in railroad maintenance, but Angola's 40 miles of track had been torn up in 1948); and the countermelody sung on 'Take This Hammer' would have disrupted the rhythm of actual work. Despite its title, the Scott sisters' 'Picking Cotton All Day Long' is a play-party song, not a worksong. Still, there are some splendid singers here, among them Emmanuel Dunn, a guitarless Guitar Welch, generating enormous swing on 'John Henry', Odea Matthews, singing while machine-sewing, and the leonine Big Louisiana.

Wake Up Dead Man catches the worksong on its last legs, shortly before mechanization and the integration of work gangs killed it. Some of the singers sound worn out, and take a while to build up momentum, and the harmony on some songs is off. The seven-minute-plus 'Jody' is beautiful by any standard, though, and *Wake up Dead Man* does have its advantages: all tracks but one were recorded at work, the use of tape enabled them to be recorded at their true length, and the disc carries an exceptionally useful set of notes by Bruce Jackson, who made the recordings.

**** Country Negro Jam Session
Arhoolie CD 372 *Butch Cage & Willie Thomas (10), Sally Dotson, Smoky Babe & Hillary Blunt, Ben Douglas, Clarence Edwards, Cornelius Edwards & Butch Cage (4), Rebecca Smith, Tom Miller & Ruth Miller, Smoky Babe (2), Leon Strickland, Lucius Bridges & Leslie Anders, Willie Thomas, Martha Thomas & Butch Cage, Otis Webster (3), Robert Pete Williams & Guitar Welch.* 3/59–8/61.

Three complaints about farming by Otis Webster include a 'Boll Weevil Blues' like no other, and for once Robert Pete Williams does a cover version, of Barbecue Bob's 'Mississippi Heavy Water Blues'. These tracks were recorded in Angola, but most of the material was taped at house parties in the Baton Rouge area, and the emphasis is on the fiddle and guitar duo Butch Cage & Willie Thomas, who played vintage pop and gospel music as well as blues; their sound often recalls Peg Leg Howell's Gang, from whose recording they surely learned 'Jelly Roll'. Cage could play smoothly at need, but was often heavy on the double stops, and sometimes deliberately dissonant. He had an excellent ear, and on some of the Edwards brothers' tracks he swiftly works out accompaniments for songs that are new to him: 'Smokestack Lightnin'' and 'You Don't Love Me' with fiddle and two-guitar accompaniment are wholly convincing. Smoky Babe is the most important of the other artists, his exceptional command of guitar dynamics and tone colours always serving the emotional ends of his lyrics.

***(*) I Have To Paint My Face
Arhoolie CD 432 *Butch Cage & Willie Thomas (3), Sam Chatmon (4), K. C. Douglas (4), Jasper Love (3), Sidney Maiden, R. C. Smith (4), Wade Walton, Wade Walton & R. C. Smith, Big Joe Williams (2).* 60.

Two tracks by K. C. Douglas feature an intrusive washtub bass; also intrusive is the eponymous bird on Wade Walton's 'Rooster Blues', which is amusing, but musically slight. The rest of *I Have To Paint My Face* is important and for the most part entertaining documentation of Mississippi blues; the self-hating racism of Sam Chatmon's title track is important and disturbing. Robert Curtis Smith recorded four highly personal blues in Wade Walton's tonsorial establishment, and played guitar as Wade beat out a 'Barbershop Rhythm' with razor and strop. In 1961 Smith recorded the marvellous *Blues Of Robert Curtis Smith* (Prestige/Bluesville BVLP 1064), then disappeared for over 30 years. Jasper Love's percussive attack overcomes the deficiencies of his piano, and there's nothing new about Big Joe's tracks: in other words, he proves his genius once again. Cage & Thomas's 'Forty Four Blues' is repeated from *Country Negro Jam Session*.

*** The Sound Of The Delta
Testament TCD 5012 *Avery Brady (4), Elijah Brown (3), Andrew Cauthen, Bert Logan, Russ Logan, Ruby McCoy (2), Fred McDowell (2), Arthur Weston (2), Big Joe Williams (3).* 64–65.

Big Joe Williams accompanies several singers, including his uncles, Russ and Bert Logan; the latter sings a largely impenetrable but evidently critical 'Don't You Want To Be A Member (Of The United States Government)?' Ruby McCoy admired Bessie Tucker's records, and uncannily replicates her matter-of-fact rage. Fred McDowell is predictably excellent; so is Big Joe, as both accompanist and name artist, and Jimmy Brown's fiddle on 'Walkin' Ground Hog' is archaically delightful. The other musicians are interesting rather than memorable. Avery Brady is an original lyricist whose guitar style bobs along in Bill Broonzy's wake. Seventy-year-old Elijah Brown's music is historically valuable, but his delivery is timeworn. Arthur Weston and Andrew Cauthen cover John Lee Williamson; a second harmonica enlivens Cauthen's 'Canary Bird'.

***(*) I Blueskvarter: 1964, Volume Three
Jefferson SBACD 12658/9 2CD *Earl Bell (2), Paul Butterfield (2), Champion Jack Dupree (7), Snooks Eaglin (10), Walter Horton (3), Furry Lewis, Willie Mabon, Johnny Moment (2), Little Brother Montgomery, Will Shade (2), Babe Stovall (4), Sunnyland Slim, Washboard Sam, Big Joe Williams (3), Mose Williams, Johnny Young.* 5/61–6/64.

In 1964 Olle Helander visited Chicago to record music and interviews for the Swedish Broadcasting Corporation. The musicians on *I Blueskvarter: Chicago 1964, Volume One* (Jefferson SBACD 12653/4 2CD) and *Volume Two* (Jefferson SBACD 12655/6 2CD) get several tracks apiece and, where possible, these are discussed under their own entries; however, readers should note the presence on *Volume Two* of four tracks by Avery Brady.

Volume Three wraps up the Chicago sessions, and also includes the fruit of Helander's visits to New Orleans (see Snooks Eaglin and Babe Stovall) and Memphis. Booze-fuelled animosity between Shade and Lewis made most of their songs unusable, and those issued here are far from their best work; well worth hearing, though, are Johnny Moment's harmonica, the bumpy guitar of Earl Bell, and Mose Williams's raw fusion of gospel, blues and parlour ballad, 'Mother Keep Your Light Burning High In The Window'. Also included are a 1964 interview–plus-music with Jack Dupree, which is padding, and three 1961 numbers by Big Joe Williams, which aren't.

***(*) On The Road Again: Country Blues 1969–1974
Flyright FLY CD 58 *Othar Broadnax, Dewey Corley (2), William Floyd Davis, Fife & Drum Band Of The United Sons And Daughters Of Zion Chapter Nine, Lum Guffin (5), Lincoln Jackson, Walter Miller (3), Lottie Murrell (4), Ashley Thompson, Perry Tillis (3), Joe Townsend.* 69–74.

Gospel singer Perry Tillis came from Alabama, but Bengt Olsson recorded the rest of *On The Road Again* in Tennessee. Quality old-style blues and gospel were hard to find by this time, and some of the one-track musicians probably didn't have much more in them, but *On The Road Again* is a good selection. The guitarist Lum Guffin still had a large and varied repertoire; on this CD he also plays mandolin and fife. Lottie (here credited as Lattie) Murrell was a moonshine-fuelled musician; he's more together than a decade later on *Living Country Blues*. Gus Cannon's former associate Ashley Thompson plays a gentle spiritual, but Dewey Corley, also a jugband veteran, was still a rowdy secularist on piano, kazoo and washtub bass, and his friend Walter Miller's electric guitar blues have an unsubtle kick.

**** **Traveling Through The Jungle**
Testament TCD 5017 *Alec Askew, Sid Hemphill (4), Compton Jones (2), J. W. Jones (11), Napoleon Strickland (6), Othar Turner (4). 8/42–9/70.*

Traveling Through The Jungle is an invaluable survey of fife and drum band music. The tracks led by Askew and Hemphill were recorded in the '40s, and include music with deep African roots, like 'Emmaline, Take Your Time', played on the panpipes, and a now lost repertoire of unsyncopated popular songs, perhaps played primarily for white audiences. The music persists in north Mississippi, where the Rising Star band is now led by Othar Turner's granddaughter, but the Georgian tradition represented by J. W. Jones's band is probably extinct. It relied quite heavily on old minstrel tunes and was less polyrhythmic than the Mississippi sound, with fife playing that was often more melodic and less riff-based. Wherever and whenever recorded, though, the lark-in-a-thunderstorm sound of these bands is gripping.

***(*) **Virginia Traditions: Western Piedmont Blues**
Global Village CD 1003 *Marvin Foddrell (2), Turner Foddrell, Clayton Horsely (2), Luke Jordan (2), James Lowry (3), Rabbit Muse (2), Herb Richardson, John Tinsley (2), Richard Wright. 11/29–5/78.*

***(*) **Virginia Traditions: Tidewater Blues**
Global Village CD 1006 *The Back Porch Boys [Alec Seward & Louis Hayes] (2), 'Big Boy', John Cephas, John Cephas & John Woolfork, Pernell Charity (2), Henry Harris (2), Carl Hodges (2), Monarch Jazz Quartet, William Moore (2), Corner Morris, The Virginia Four. 1/28–3/79.*

**** **Virginia Traditions: Virginia Work Songs**
Global Village CD 1007 *Crew of the Charles J. Colonna, Rev. Timothy Hayes and others (2), Creola Johnson and others, Walter Kegler and crew of the Barnegat, Joe Lee, John Mantley and others, Lena Thompson and others, William Thompson and others (2), John Williams, Willie Williams (3), James Wilson and others, Lee Wynn, Lee Wynn & John Mantley. 5/36–11/80.*

(*) **Virginia Traditions: Southwest Virginia Blues
Global Village CD 1008 *Dock Boggs, Bobby Buford, 'Cowboy' T. Burks, The Carter Family, Dave Dickerson, James Henry Diggs, Fred Galliher, Earl Gilmore, Malcolm Johnson, Carl Martin, Byrd Moore, King Edward Smith, Tarter & Gay, Josh Thomas, Howard Twine. 6/28–9/84.*

The first CD in the *Virginia Traditions* series, *Non-Blues Secular Black Music* (Global Village CD 1001), is discussed under ROOTS. Virginia was not heavily represented on early commercial recordings, but this series, which combines recent and vintage field recordings with commercial releases, handsomely remedies the deficit. The original LPs, issued by the Blue Ridge Institute, carried extensive and scholarly notes; these are abridged for the CD reissues, but the full versions can be purchased from the BRI.

The *Western Piedmont Blues* are guitar-accompanied, Rabbit Muse's surprisingly successful ukulele apart. The influence of Blind Boy Fuller is strong but doesn't overpower individual creativity, especially in the music of the Foddrell brothers and the poetic Clayton Horsely. Some items seem to be included for rarity's sake: James Lowry's songs, taken from radio transcription discs, are historically important, but some may find his cheap guitar hard listening.

Tidewater Blues surveys the east of the state, and also emphasizes guitar blues; the exceptions are by two vocal quartets, taking time out from serving the Lord. (One is certainly a pseudonymous Norfolk Jubilee Quartet; the other may well be.) Corner Morris's playing was affected by age, but the other musicians are in uniformly fine form. Many perform cover versions, but Cephas & Woolfork's 'Richmond Blues' and Pernell Charity's 'Blind Love' transform songs by Bull City Red and B. B. King respectively. A *cante-fable* about railroading by the obscure slide guitarist 'Big Boy' stands comparison with Blind Willie McTell's similar 'Travelin' Blues'.

Willie Williams's tracks on the *Work Songs* collection have been extensively reissued, but their passion and musicality make them a necessary inclusion. They were recorded in prison, as were several other performances from the '30s. Exceptionally, this CD's coverage extends beyond the familiar domains of prison farming and railroad repair, to include sea fishing (two extraordinary recordings made at sea plus two re-creations) and shipyards (caulking the seams of wooden boats, where one man sings as his partner hammers). Four spirituals were sung to relieve the tedium of shucking oysters and cracking crabs, but by 1980 the victory of the portable radio in the corner was nearly complete.

Within the limits imposed by segregation, there was a good deal of musical crossover in southwest Virginia, and half the tracks on the eponymous disc are by white artists. Fred Galliher and King Edward Smith, who are cousins of the great Hobart Smith, contribute instrumentals on harmonica and guitar respectively. Neither of them is at Hobart's level of artistry, and King Edward is not entirely in control of his material. This fault is disturbingly prevalent among the field recordings used on *Southwest Virginia Blues*. No such problem affects the commercial recordings by Tarter & Gay, Dock Boggs, Carl Martin or the Carter Family, whose 'Bear Creek Blues' came from black guitarist Leslie Riddles, but their tracks are available elsewhere in better company. African-American Bobby Buford's entirely idiomatic cover of Hank Williams's 'Long Gone Lonesome Blues' is a pleasure, but not so much as to justify the CD.

*** **Chicago Blues At Home**
Testament TCD 5028 *Homesick James, John Littlejohn (3), Bob Myers (2), Louis Myers (5), Jimmy Rogers (3), Johnny Shines, Eddie Taylor (3). 8/70–3/78.*

Or perhaps Chicago blues singers at home: Louis Myers's choice of songs shows admiration for Lightnin' Hopkins as well as Muddy Waters. Pedantry aside, these recordings are the fruit of the good idea of recording the musicians, solo or in duos, in informal settings. (Homesick James, joined by Andrew McMahon on guitar and Lou Ella Smith on congas, leads the solitary trio in a hypnotic revival of J. B. Lenoir's African hunch rhythm.) Bob Myers's harp is coarse but listenable, and Johnny Shines's revival of 'Ramblin' is almost as exciting as the original. The most consistent quality comes from Littlejohn and Rogers, who take it turns to supply the vocals while Rogers plays his typical steady rhythm and Littlejohn overlays restless treble decorations. Eddie Taylor has Phillip Walker assisting on guitar, and this is another partnership of equals, although on the previously unissued 'Tell Me Baby' they share responsibility for the chaos. Little stumbles and sour notes make it obvious why some of the other added-for-CD tracks were held back, but none of them sinks to that level of unsuitability.

*** San Diego Blues Jam
Testament TCD 5029 *Sam Chatmon* (2), *Sam Chatmon & Bob Jefferey* (2), *Tom Courtney & Louis Major, Tom Courtney & Henry Ford Thompson* (3), *Bonnie Jefferson* (3), *Bob Jefferey* (3), *Bob Jefferey & Sam Chatmon, Louis Major* (2), *Thomas Shaw* (2). 5/71–1/74.

The San Diego blues scene escaped wider notice until Lou Curtiss met Thomas Shaw, who helped him find most of the other artists on this CD. Mississippi's Sam Chatmon, popular on the local folk scene, is here as an honorary San Diegan.

Shaw's slide version of 'Jack Of Diamonds' is a good one; Chatmon's songs are familiar, but his collaborations with Bob Jefferey put them in a new context. Jefferey played percussive piano with a ragtimey elegance, and was an eccentric lyricist. On 'Handsome Stranger', he plays archaic guitar in unison with the vocal line. Bonnie Jefferson blends ragtime guitar with Arkansas blues; 'Got The Blues So Bad', which recalls Robert Pete Williams, and the beguiling 'Crow Rooster Crow' impress more than an insecurely pitched 'Take Me Back'. Louis Major was born in the Bahamas, and the island song 'Handy Brandy' is better than a mannered 'Shotgun Blues'.

Renamed Tomcat Courtney and working with a band, Tom Courtney released the hard-to-find *Little John* (no label or issue number) in the early '90s. Here, his forceful singing recalls Howlin' Wolf and Elmore James; second guitarist Henry Ford Thompson knew Joe Hill Louis in Memphis, and has much of Louis's energy, but a tighter focus.

** Giants of Country Blues Guitar Vol. 1
Wolf 120.911 *Sam Chatmon* (3), *Jessie Mae Hemphill* (2), *Son House, Mager Johnson, Furry Lewis, Jack Owens* (4), *Eugene Powell* (3), *Mott Willis* (3). 9/67–9/91.

** Giants of Country Blues Guitar Vol. 2
Wolf 120.917 *Cornelius Bright & Jimmy Holmes, R. L. Burnside* (6), *Clyde Maxwell, James 'Son' Thomas* (6), *Boogie Bill Webb* (6), *Joe Willie Wilkins*. 7/75–9/91.

** Giants of Country Blues Vol. 3 [sic]
Wolf 120.918 *Ranie Burnette* (3), *L. V. Conerly, Jessie Mae Hemphill* (5), *Roosevelt Holts, Junior Kimbrough* (4), *Jacob Stuckey, Tommy West* (3). 6/81–9/91.

**** Living Country Blues
Evidence ECD 26105 3CD *Walter Brown* (2), *John Cephas & Phil Wiggins* (2), *Sam Chatmon* (4), *Eddie Cusic, CeDell Davis* (2), *Archie Edwards* (5), *Cora Fluker* (2), *Guitar Frank [Hovington]* (5), *Guitar Slim [James Stephens]* (3), *Stonewall Mays, Memphis Piano Red, Flora Molton* (3), *Lottie Murrell* (4), *Hammie Nixon* (3), *Lonnie Pitchford* (2), *Boyd Rivers* (4), *Charlie Sangster, Joe Savage, Sam Shields, Napoleon Strickland, James 'Son' Thomas* (4), *Boogie Bill Webb* (2), *Othar Turner* (4), *Arzo Youngblood* (2). 10–11/80.

Giants-schmiants: Son House and Furry Lewis were once, but not when the tracks on *Vol. 1* (which won a Handy, God knows how) were recorded. Sam Chatmon and Eugene Powell sound tired; Powell can't get his fingers around the intricacies of 'Pony Blues' any more, and the yapping puppy which disrupts one of Chatmon's songs is far from the only extraneous noise on these CDs. Mott Willis starts off well, but is rambling and Tomming by his third song. Jack Owens is the most consistent and considerable artist on *Vol. 1*; Mager Johnson supplies its best and earliest track, awakening regret for various LPs of David Evans's '60s field recordings that aren't on CD. The Austrian enthusiasts who followed in his wake two decades later didn't have the fieldwork skills (or usually, one suspects, the recording equipment) to get the best out of artists who were often past their best anyway.

On *Vol. 2*, Burnside's 'It's Be Troubled' (sic) and Thomas's 'Dust My Broom' feature out-of-tune guitars; other songs by both artists are better, but they offer nothing new by comparison with other versions. Wilkins's 'Walking Blues' is fiery, but vitiated by a poor harmonica player, and although Boogie Bill recalls some surprising songs, including 'Black Night' and 'Seven Sisters Blues', his performances are rusty. Maxwell and Bright & Holmes are minor artists.

Jessie Mae Hemphill does five of her favourites on *Vol. 3*, including reprises of the songs on *Vol. 1*; again, they're acceptably done, but no better than other versions by her. The other artists on *Vol. 3* are disappointing. Burnette, Holts and Conerly had been important artists, but are long past their primes. Junior Kimbrough is on autopilot, and has tuning problems on 'Please Don't Leave Me'. Henry Stuckey's son is out of practice, and wouldn't be of much interest if he were in it. After Hemphill, the derivative Tommy West, joined on one track by a distant harmonica, is the most effective artist on this disc.

More modestly titled than Wolf's series, *Living Country Blues* shows how it should be done: with reel-to-reel tape, a ten-channel mixer, and the prior intention of making recordings of commercial quality. The results of Axel Küstner and Ziggy Christmann's field trip appeared on a series of L+R LPs that came out at exactly the wrong commercial moment. The East Coast disc in this selection of highlights includes the first commercial recordings of Archie Edwards and Cephas & Wiggins, and the last by Guitar Slim and the great Frank Hovington; they're all of very high artistic and sonic quality. On the Mississippi CD, Son Thomas's recordings are his best; Boyd Rivers's electric guitar spirituals and the field and levee camp hollers by ex-cons Savage and Brown are riveting; so is Brown's story-song 'Mississippi Moan', about the place where 'time done come to civilization, and they still call you a nigger'. The third CD in the set visits Tennessee and Arkansas and revisits some of the artists on the first two discs. It's less consistent; Piano Red's instrument is defective, Hammie Nixon indulges himself in jug farts and fluttertonguing, and Lottie Murrell, evidently impressive in the context of a moonshine party, just comes over as meanderingly drunk. However, the revisited artists, and tracks by CeDell Davis, the obscure but significant Charlie Sangster and harmonica player 'Stretch' Shields, offer more than adequate compensation.

**(*) From Mississippi To Chicago
HMG HMG 1008 *Boogaloo Ames* (2), *R. L. Burnside* (5), *Eddie Cusic, Pinetop Perkins* (2), *Robert Curtis Smith* (5). late 90s.

The selling point is the rediscovery of Robert Curtis Smith, who'd moved to Chicago and joined the church; he sings gospel songs, and talks about his conversion following a horrific mishap with lye which should have cost him his sight. Smith's sacred music is as accomplished and powerfully personal as his blues, but occasionally he ventures into an uncomfortably low register. R. L. Burnside runs through a familiar set of tunes, neither adding nor subtracting anything. Pinetop Perkins's tracks are even more familiar, and blemished by fingering errors; they also appear on his *Heritage Of The Blues* (Hightone HCD 8159). Boogaloo Ames, another Mississippi pianist, turns in sturdy versions of 'After Hours' and 'Tommy Dorsey's Boogie Woogie'. Eddie Cusic's track is one of his few original compositions, and one of his best performances. CS

Guitar

This is a deceptively short section. 'With guitar' is practically a default setting for the blues, and a large number of VACs discussed elsewhere, such as many of the regional collections from the prewar era, might equally well have been placed here. We have restricted ourselves to compilations with an explicit guitar agenda, but see also SLIDE GUITAR for recordings in that style.

*** Hellhounds On Their Trail
Indigo IGOTCD 2564 3CD *Mick Abrahams, Luther Allison, Kokomo Arnold, Jeff Beck, Ritchie Blackmore, Scrapper Blackwell, Blind Blake, Big Bill Broonzy, Clarence 'Gatemouth' Brown, Joe Callicott, Cliff Carlisle, Eric Clapton (2), Albert Collins, Pee Wee Crayton, Arthur 'Big Boy' Crudup, Lowell Fulson, Clarence Garlow, Otis Grand, Peter Green, Tiny Grimes, Guitar Slim, Buddy Guy, Buddy Boy Hawkins, Homesick James, Earl Hooker, John Lee Hooker, Lightnin' Hopkins, Son House, Howlin' Wolf, Luther Huff, Mississippi John Hurt, Frank Hutchison, J. B. Hutto, Elmore James, Skip James, Blind Lemon Jefferson, Robert Johnson, Blind Willie Johnson, Dave Kelly, Robert Kelton (with Jimmy McCracklin), Lottie Kimbrough, B. B. King, Freddie King, Alexis Korner, Leadbelly, John Lee, Pete 'Guitar' Lewis, Jimmy Liggins, Lightnin' Slim, Robert [Jr] Lockwood, Tony McPhee, Blind Willie McTell, Magic Slim, William Moore, Muddy Waters, Robert Nighthawk, Charley Patton, Gene Phillips, Jimmy Reed, Fenton Robinson, Jimmy Rogers, Jeremy Spencer, Tampa Red, Eddie Taylor, T-Bone Walker, Sylvester Weaver, Stan Webb, West Texas Slim, Booker White, Robert Wilkins, Big Joe Williams.* 24–01.

What will the listener learn from a collection that spans three quarters of a century and musicians as different as Sylvester Weaver and Stan Webb, other than that blues guitar playing is a many-splendoured thing? Perhaps just that; after all, such compilations are not meant to be study aids but primarily entertaining tours of a feature-filled landscape. The programme is roughly chronological, and the definition of 'blues guitar' generous enough on Disc 1 to include the white West Virginian Frank Hutchison playing a 'Logan County Blues' that's actually the parlour guitar piece 'Spanish Fandango', Blind Willie Johnson's wordless hymn 'Dark Was The Night – Cold Was The Ground' and varieties of rag picking by Blind Willie McTell and Blind Blake. Disc 2 charts the introduction of amplification in the '40s and '50s, while Disc 3 is evenly divided between players of the Buddy Guy–Freddie King–Albert Collins generation and British exponents like Eric Clapton, Peter Green and Jeff Beck. The selection of the latter was contingent on their availability to Sanctuary Records, which means that some examples, like the Mayall–Clapton 'On Top Of The World', don't fairly represent the players' talents; on the other hand, some, like Alexis Korner's 'Hellhound On My Trail', all too revealingly do.

***(*) Country Blues: The Essential
Classic Blues CBL 200008 2CD *Pink Anderson, DeFord Bailey, Willie Baker, Barefoot Bill [Ed Bell], Scrapper Blackwell, Ishman Bracey, Bob Campbell, George Carter, Pearl Dickson, Tom Dickson, Evans & McClain, Troy Ferguson, Freezone, Blind Boy Fuller, Mae Glover, Lane Hardin, Buddy Boy Hawkins, Blind Lemon Jefferson, Little Hat Jones, Luke Jordan, Lottie Kimbrough, Rube Lacey, Furry Lewis, Noah Lewis, Charlie Lincoln, William Moore, Buddy Moss, Hambone Willie Newbern, Arthur Petties, Shreveport Home Wreckers, Henry Spaulding, Frank Stokes, Tarter & Gay, Henry Thomas, Geeshie Wiley, Robert Wilkins.* 27–37.

Except for two harmonica solos by DeFord Bailey and Noah Lewis, this 36-track 2CD is devoted to blues with guitar accompaniment and includes an impressive number of recordings that blues enthusiasts have generally agreed to be classics of their kind, such as Henry Spaulding's 'Cairo Blues', Lottie Kimbrough's 'Rolling Log Blues', Blind Lemon Jefferson's 'Easy Rider Blues' and William Moore's 'One Way Gal'. Although some notable figures are omitted, among them Barbecue Bob, Blind Blake, Skip James, Tommy Johnson and Charley Patton, the album has examples of musical styles prevalent in St Louis, Memphis, Virginia, Georgia, Alabama, Mississippi, Texas and several other areas, and so is a very varied gazetteer of blues guitar playing – and blues singing – in the '20s and '30s. With decent sound quality and a modest price-tag, this is a good compilation to start a collection with.

***(*) Trouble Hearted Blues: Vintage Guitar Blues (1927–1944)
Document DOCD-32-20-4 *Willie Baker, Pillie Bolling, Ishman Bracey, Gabriel Brown, Julius Daniels (2), Mattie Delaney, Tom Dickson (2), Mae Glover, Blind Lemon Jefferson, Lottie Kimbrough, Robert [Jr] Lockwood (2), Memphis Minnie, Willie Reed, Blind Joe Reynolds (2), Rambling Thomas, George Torey, Otto Virgial, Sylvester Weaver, Booker White, Robert Wilkins.* 2/27–9/44.

When there are so many gifted musicians clamouring for admission into a programme like this, it's a little odd to give several artists two tickets, and some may be surprised to find Pillie Bolling or Gabriel Brown here at all. Those small criticisms aside, it's a grand selection of guitarists from ten or more blues centres, most of them playing at the top of their game and on clean original discs that have been carefully remastered (though George Torey's 'Married Woman Blues' is beset by sonic effects). Blind Joe Reynolds's pair are from a unique copy, and this is the only CD on which they can be found together.

**** Ragtime Blues Guitar (1927–1930)
Document DOCD-5062 *Blind Blake, William Moore (8), Bayless Rose (4), Tarter & Gay (2), Willie Walker (3), Chicken Wilson & Skeeter Hinton (6).* 4/27–12/30.

This absorbing collection opens with the scintillating guitar and bones duet 'Dry Bone Shuffle', an alternative take to the one on Blind Blake's *Vol. 1* (Document DOCD-5024), then delves into the fascinating work of William Moore (1894–1951), a barber from Tappahannock, Virginia. At a session for Paramount in 1928 Moore began by recording a couple of 16-bar blues, 'One Way Gal' and 'Midnight Blues', two turn-of-the-century ragtime songs, 'Ragtime Millionaire' and 'Tillie Lee', and a guitar piece, 'Ragtime Crazy'. The remarks on the last are by Moore himself, but the commentaries that run through his remaining recordings, 'Barbershop Rag', 'Raggin' The Blues' and the flowing 'Old Country Rock' (the guitar part of 'One Way Gal' *sans* vocal), are in a different voice, probably that of the Paramount scout Mayo Williams. Free to concentrate on his fingerwork, Moore produces three of the finest guitar solos in recorded African-American music.

Steve Tarter and Harry Gay, from east Tennessee, play a couple of exquisitely planned guitar duets; both tunes have vocal parts, but one feels the men would have been happier to spend their six minutes of fame revelling in the skill of their interplay. There's not a word of speech or singing on Wilson and Hinton's six titles, but their range of instrumental and percussive effects is so wide that their music never sounds incomplete. Wilson is a competent guitarist who blows an occasional kazoo chorus, while Hinton plays harmonica rather in the manner of Robert Cooksey and executes lively finger-dances on a washboard with metallic accessories. Bayless Rose, on 'Black Dog Blues' and 'Original Blues', shares some guitar vocabulary with the white West Virginian guitarist Frank Hutchison, one of the reasons he has sometimes been supposed to have been white himself. His other sides are superb guitar solos, the rag medley 'Jamestown Exhibition' and a slide tune, 'Frisco Blues', similar in conception to Booker White's train pieces.

Josh White thought Willie Walker of Greenville, South Carolina, the best guitarist he ever heard. A mere three recordings are all the evidence we have to make our own judgement, and two of them are the same tune in different takes, but White's estimate is hard to dispute: there are runs in 'Dupree Blues' and the two versions of 'South Carolina Rag' that for speed, clean execution and élan are without equal on recordings by Walker's contemporaries.

(*) Great Blues Guitarists: String Dazzlers
Columbia CK 47060 *Texas Alexander, Big Bill Broonzy (2), Blind Lemon Jefferson, Lonnie Johnson (2), Lonnie Johnson & Eddie Lang (3), Blind Willie Johnson (2), Blind Willie McTell (2), Tampa Red, Sylvester Weaver (2), Sylvester Weaver & Walter Beasley, Casey Bill Weldon, Josh White (2). 6/24–12/40.*

This is a narrow view of blues guitar playing, not so much because the selection is limited to artists in Sony's archives but because one suspects that producer Larry Cohn took the chance to boost some of his favourites. Lonnie Johnson and Eddie Lang were a wonderful duet, and a glistening copy of 'Hot Fingers' kicks the programme off in terrific style, but four examples (since they also accompany Texas Alexander), and two Johnson solos as well, give the album a considerable tilt. A few tracks, like Josh White's 'Prodigal Son' and Big Bill's 'Getting Older Every Day', though good performances, are unremarkable in guitar terms, and a banjo solo by Sylvester Weaver should have been replaced. The remastering is uneven.

* **Blues Guitar Pioneers**
Boulevard Vintage BVBCD 1010 4CD *Lowell Fulson (25), Lonnie Johnson (25), B. B. King (25), T-Bone Walker (25). 2/28–8/53.*

This is an inexpensive way to obtain CDs by four influential figures in blues guitar, and the selections are generally admirable. Johnson is heard primarily as an instrumentalist, and the first vocal isn't until past the halfway mark. Being restricted to PD material is not a problem with Fulson or Walker, since the changes they wrought upon blues guitar playing had been effected by 1953, but it does scant justice to B. B. King, whose most influential work was still to come.

* **Blues Guitar Greats**
Delmark DE-697 *Luther Allison, Lurrie Bell, Lonnie Brooks, Jimmy Dawkins, Sleepy John Estes, Steve Freund (with Barkin' Bill [Smith]), Buddy Guy (with Junior Wells), J. B. Hutto, Jimmy Johnson, Robert Jr Lockwood, Magic Sam, Floyd McDaniel, Johnny B. Moore, Otis Rush, Dave Specter, Big Joe Williams, Mighty Joe Young. 11/61–7/95.*

* **Crucial Guitar Blues**
Alligator ALCD 114 *Luther Allison, Clarence 'Gatemouth' Brown, Roy Buchanan, Michael Burks, Albert Collins, Tinsley Ellis, Dave Hole, Little Charlie & The Nightcats, Lonnie Mack & Stevie Ray Vaughan, Coco Montoya, Son Seals, Johnny Winter. 84–02.*

*(*) **Blues Guitar Masters**
EasyDisc ED CD 7072 *Johnny Copeland, Lowell Fulson, Anson Funderburgh, Jimmy King, Bobby Radcliff, Byther Smith, Hubert Sumlin & Ronnie Earl, George Thorogood, Robert Ward, Smokey Wilson. 80–97.*

* **Blues Guitar Duels**
EasyDisc ED CD 7049 *Ronnie Earl & Duke Robillard, Roy Gaines & Clarence Hollimon, Guitar Shorty & Otis Grand, Buddy & Phil Guy, Smokin' Joe Kubek Band & Bnois King, Mike Morgan & Jim Suhler, Mark Pollock & Ray Jimenez (with Joe Coronado), Hubert Sumlin & Ronnie Earl, Hubert Sumlin & Richard Studholme, Phillip Walker & Otis Grand. 81–96.*

Blues Guitar Greats vs. *Crucial Guitar Blues*: a face-off between Chicago's premier blues labels? Not really. It's only because of different marketing strategies that the Alligator is shorter (12 tracks against 17) and carries a lower price-tag. Alligator are exclusively concerned with the electric instrument and all the tracks are from albums, whereas Delmark acknowledge the acoustic guitar in tracks by Big Joe Williams and Sleepy John Estes, and Magic Sam's 'I Don't Want No Woman' is previously unissued. Note to Stevie Ray Vaughan fans: 'Double Whammy', his high-energy duet with Lonnie Mack on *Crucial*, is not available on any SRV album. The EasyDiscs, as usual, are the kind of cheap 'n' cheerful CDs that you might take to a party or on a road trip and not mind too much if you lost them. Derived, also as usual, from Rounder, Black Top and JSP, they each contain tracks from Black Top that probably aren't available anywhere else, like Bobby Radcliff's 'Bonehead' on *Masters* or the Gaines–Hollimon 'Full Gain' (*Duels*) from the underrated Grady Gaines album of that title. TR

Harmonica

**** **Blowing The Blues**
Indigo IGOTCD 2536 3CD *Billy Boy Arnold, DeFord Bailey, Slim Barton & Eddie Mapp, Carey Bell, Duster Bennett, Sunny Blair, Sonny Blake, Edgar Blanchard, Blues Birdhead, Grace Brim, Paul Butterfield, Jaybird Coleman, Robert Cooksey, Daddy Stovepipe & Mississippi Sarah, Jed Davenport & His Beale Street Jug Band, Paul deLay, Little Buddy Doyle, Driftin' Slim, Good Rockin' Charles [Edwards], Frank Edwards, Forrest City Joe [Pugh], Blind Boy Fuller, Georgia Browns, Jazz Gillum, Walter Horton (2), Howlin' Wolf, Pee Wee Hughes, Paul Jones, Eddie Kelly's Washboard Band, King Biscuit Boy, Paul Lamb, Alfred Lewis, Noah Lewis, Papa Lightfoot, Little Walter (2), Joe Hill Louis, Ollis Martin, John Mayall, Memphis Jug Band, Memphis Minnie (2), Walter Mitchell, Muddy Waters, Charlie Musselwhite, Snooky Pryor (2), Jimmy Reed, Rhythm Willie, Robert Richard, Dr Ross (2), Little Mac [Simmons], Skoodledum*

Doo [prob. Seth Richard] & Sheffield, Whispering Smith, Sonny Boy Williamson II (2), Freeman Stowers, Sonny Terry (2), James Tisdom, Minnie Wallace, El Watson, Junior Wells, George 'Bullet' Williams, Big Joe Williams, Sonny Boy Williamson I (2), Elder Roma Wilson, Big John Wrencher. 26–02.

***(*) Harmonica Masters
Yazoo 2019 *Ashley & Foster, DeFord Bailey, Dr Humphrey Bate & His Possum Hunter, The Bubbling Over Five, Carver Boys, Dutch Coleman & Red Whitehead, Jaybird Coleman, Crook Brothers, Jed Davenport, Sleepy John Estes, Gwen Foster, Salty Holmes, Bobby Leecan & Robert Cooksey, Alfred Lewis, Noah Lewis, Palmer McAbee, David McCarn, William McCoy, Murphy Brothers Harp Band, Six Cylinder Smith, Freeman Stowers, George 'Bullet' Williams, Kyle Wooten.* 26–39.

(***) Harmonica Blues
Yazoo 1053 *Ashley & Foster, DeFord Bailey, Lee Brown, Carver Boys, Jaybird Coleman, Chuck Darling (2), Jazz Gillum, Robert Hill, Bobby Leecan & Robert Cooksey, Alfred Lewis, State Street Boys, Freeman Stowers, Chicken Wilson & Skeeter Hinton.* 26–39.

*** Great Harp Players (1927–1936)
Document DOCD-5100 *Blues Birdhead (4), William Francis & Richard Sowell (2), Alfred Lewis (2), Palmer McAbee (2), Ollis Martin, Smith & Harper (2), El Watson (6), Ellis Williams (2), George 'Bullet' Williams (4).* 27–36.

**** Harmonica Blues
Frémeaux FA 040 2CD *DeFord Bailey (2), Blues Birdhead, George Clarke, Jaybird Coleman, Robert Cooksey (2), Jed Davenport & His Beale Street Jug Band (2), Little Buddy Doyle (2), Frank Edwards, Jazz Gillum (3), Alfred Lewis, Noah Lewis (2), Eddie Mapp, Robert Lee McCoy (2), Memphis Jug Band, Hammie Nixon & Son Bonds (2), Yank Rachell (2), Rhythm Willie (2), Smith & Harper, Sonny Terry, Minnie Wallace, El Watson, Leroy Williams, Sonny Boy Williamson I (3).* 27–41.

** Harmonica Blues
Acrobat ACRCD 193 *DeFord Bailey, The Bubbling-Over Five, George Clarke, Jaybird Coleman, Jed Davenport (2), Little Buddy Doyle, Sleepy John Estes, Georgia Cotton Pickers, Jazz Gillum (2), Elijah Jones, Alfred Lewis, Noah Lewis (2), Eddie Mapp (2), Ollis Martin, Martin & Robert, Mississippi Sarah & Daddy Stovepipe, Smith & Harper, Sonny Terry (2), Sonny Boy Williamson I, Chicken Wilson & Skeeter Hinton.* 3/27–7/45.

Despite its small size and structural limitations, the diatonic harmonica is one of the most versatile of blues instruments. A crucial development was the discovery of 'cross harp' playing, whereby most of the melody can be played on drawn (sucked) rather than blown reeds, which enables the player to bend and otherwise distort notes. With that and other improvised tools to hand, musicians could produce a wide range of effects, devising musical impressions of hunting dogs and moving trains, imitating the human voice, and creating blues melodies and accompaniments from an extensive tonal palette.

Such variety makes blues harmonica a splendid field for discursive anthologizing. Even the 71-track *Blowing The Blues* doesn't exhaust the possibilities of the instrument, though it spans more than 75 years and ranges from obscure early practitioners like George 'Bullet' Williams, through influential transitional artists like Little Walter and the two Sonny Boy Williamsons, to contemporary players such as Charlie Musselwhite and Paul Lamb. Nevertheless, harmonica anthologies, like boogie-woogie ones, tend to resemble each other a little, because of an unspoken agreement that there are some classic recordings no self-respecting collection can do without. Alfred Lewis's remarkable vocalized 'Mississippi Swamp Moan' is on five of these six VACs, Jaybird Coleman's 'Man Trouble Blues' on four, and the same track or two by Noah Lewis, Jed Davenport, Ollis Martin and Smith & Harper keep recurring. The Yazoos differ from the rest in embracing hillbilly harpists like the bubbling Gwen Foster; *Harmonica Masters* is almost half by white musicians. The beginner is recommended to try *Blowing The Blues*, which, despite its size, is inexpensive, or Frémeaux's *Harmonica Blues*, a knowledgeable survey of its chosen period. Yazoo's *Harmonica Blues*, an LP transferred to CD without expansion, is good but necessarily more sketchy, while Acrobat's is let down by the poor quality of the sound restoration. The Document has a different agenda from the others, assembling the complete works of a small number of players. The same label's *Harp Blowers (1925–1936)* (DOCD-5164) is chiefly concerned with DeFord Bailey (q.v.); its remaining tracks are by George Clarke, an erratic player, and John Henry Howard and 'Bert' Bilbro, both white musicians, neither of them first-class.

In the mid- and late '30s, when blues recording practices were producing a more formularized music, some forms of harmonica playing virtually disappeared from the record catalogues, particularly unaccompanied solos and programmatic music like train imitations. Under the influence of Sonny Boy Williamson I, harpists contented themselves with an accompanying role, though one in which rhythmic impetus and voice-like effects were still valued, as well as – in the case of players who were also singers – rapid movement between voice and instrument. By the late '40s, when recording resumed after World War II, the harmonica had become, for musicians on the Mississippi–Chicago strip, the guitar's commonest front-line companion. Its position was strengthened by amplification and the use of hand-held microphones, which gave musicians like Little Walter Jacobs, Walter 'Shakey' Horton and Sonny Boy Williamson II the freedom to develop the blues harmonica into an instrument of almost saxophone-like range and expressiveness.

***(*) Harmonica Blues: Blowing From Memphis To Chicago
Saga Blues 982 078-3 *James Cotton (with Willie Nix), Little Willie Foster, Jazz Gillum, Big Walter Horton (2), Howlin' Wolf, Noah Lewis (2), Little Walter (3), Joe Hill Louis, Memphis Jug Band, Hammie Nixon (with Sleepy John Estes), Snooky Pryor, City Joe [Pugh], Jimmy Reed, Dr Ross, Sonny Boy Williamson II (2), Junior Wells, Sonny Boy Williamson I (3).* 2/27–10/53.

The stylistic shifts described above are clearly outlined in this sound collection. Like other Saga Blues issues it is constructed in two acts, here 'From Memphis' and 'To Chicago', the narrative unfolding from the jugband music of Lewis and the Memphis Jug Band's Will Shade to the Memphis-area players of the early '50s, whom it then tracks north. Sonny Boy Williamson I is, correctly, found at both ends of the story, first conducting the rural swing of 'Good Morning, School Girl' and then, eight years later, the more urgent tavern dance music of 'Sonny Boy's Jump'. The selection being confined to PD material, the history lesson comes to a halt in 1953, but, since it has embraced primal recordings like the Walter Horton–Johnny Shines duet 'Evening Sun' and Little Walter's 'Off The Wall', the important points have mostly been made.

**** **Harp Blues**
Ace CDCHD 710 *Billy Boy Arnold, Chicago Sunny Boy [Joe Hill Louis], James Cotton, Cousin Leroy, Shy Guy Douglas (2), Little Willie Foster, Frank Frost, Eddie Hope & The Manish Boys, Walter Horton (3), Howlin' Wolf, Papa Lightfoot, Little Walter, Jerry McCain, Sammy Myers, Little Junior Parker, Snooky Pryor, Jimmy Reed, Dr Ross, George Smith, Sonny Boy Williamson II, Junior Wells, Sonny Boy Williamson I.* 12/47–10/68.

***(*) **Blues Masters, Volume 4: Harmonica Classics**
Rhino R2 71124 *Billy Boy Arnold, Paul Butterfield Blues Band, James Cotton, Fabulous Thunderbirds, Walter Horton, Howlin' Wolf, Lazy Lester, Little Walter, Hot Shot Love, Jerry McCain, Charlie Musselwhite, Snooky Pryor, Jimmy Reed, Slim Harpo, George 'Harmonica' Smith, Sonny Boy Williamson II, Junior Wells, Big John Wrencher.* 8/52–81.

Rhino's compilations are seldom anything but fine and, as a roundup of the leading figures in blues harmonica over three decades, this selection by Cub Koda does its job very well indeed. Little Walter's 'Juke', Sonny Boy Williamson II's 'Help Me', Jerry McCain's 'Steady' and Walter Horton's majestic 'Easy' were easy choices to make, but not every compiler would have thought of Hot Shot Love's harp-and-jive 'Wolf Call Boogie' or Big John Wrencher's 'Take A Little Walk With Me', or preferred George Smith's 'Last Night' with the Muddy Waters Band to an earlier recording. *Harp Blues* had a few of the same ideas: 'Juke', 'Steady' and 'Easy' all reappear, as well as James Cotton's 'Rocket 88' and Snooky Pryor's 'Boogie Twist', and several other players from the Rhino castlist show up, albeit with different recordings. What gives this album the edge is its length (25 tracks against Rhino's 18), its remembering Sonny Boy Williamson I and Junior Parker, and its care to include such classics of the genre as Sammy Myers's 'Sleeping In The Ground', Eddie Hope's 'A Fool No More' and Jimmy Rogers's 'Walking By Myself', with Walter Horton's famous solo.

***(*) **Deep Harmonica Blues**
Ace CDCHD 604 *Jimmy Anderson (2), Blues Rockers (2), Jolly George (2), Lazy Lester, Lazy Lester (with Lightnin' Slim) (2), Little Sonny (2), Jerry McCain (4), Ole Sunny Boy [poss. Papa Lightfoot] (2), Slim Harpo, Whispering Smith (2), Sonny Boy Williamson II (with Baby Boy Warren) (4).* 54–63.

Most of these recordings were issued on Excello, one of the leading downhome blues labels in the '50s and '60s. Since harmonica-and-guitar practically defines downhome blues, Excello's catalogue was awash with it, and many fine examples surface on this collection, such as Lightnin' Slim's 'I'm Grown', Slim Harpo's 'Wonderin' And Worryin'', the lively pieces by Jerry McCain and – even in this company the headline act – Baby Boy Warren and Sonny Boy Williamson II, hand-in-glove on 'Hello Stranger', 'Not Welcome Anymore' and two others. Jimmy Anderson provides his usual insidiously rhythmic groove but is curiously preoccupied, in 'Rats And Roaches On Your Mind', with the subject of pesticides.

*** **Down Home Harp**
Testament TCD 6011 *Billy Boy Arnold (3), Andrew Cauthen (2), Willie Lee Harris, John Lee Henley, Big Walter Horton (2), Little Walter (2), Elmon 'Driftin' Slim' Mickle (2), George Robertson, James 'Bat' Robinson (2), Dr Ross, Coot Venson (3), Harmonica Slim Willis, Big John Wrencher.* 9/61–1/67.

Like some other Testament CDs, *Down Home Harp* is concerned as much with private music as with public. Few of the artists were recorded before an audience, and several tracks are of music that would not have been played in a club anyway, but kept for informal settings – pieces like John Lee Henley's 'Medley' and Driftin' Slim's train imitations. Some musicians were part-timers, like Big Joe Williams's friends Coot Venson, George Robertson and Andrew Cauthen, but they give good accounts of themselves and are not diminished by sharing album space with Little Walter (accompanying Johnny Young and Robert Nighthawk) or Walter Horton. Billy Boy Arnold, whose later work for Testament was so disappointing, sparkles on a couple of Sonny Boy Williamson I songs, accompanied, as Sonny Boy often was, by Blind John Davis. Except for a third Arnold tune, none of these recordings had been previously issued.

*** **This Is The Blues Harmonica**
Delmark DE-746 *Billy Boy Arnold, Carey Bell, Billy Branch (with Bonnie Lee), Jimmy Burns, Mad Dog Lester Davenport (with Willie Kent), Little Sammy Davis, Harmonica George [Robinson], Big Walter Horton, Little Walter, Lynwood Slim (with Dave Specter), Louis Myers, Hammie Nixon, Junior Wells, Golden 'Big' Wheeler, Kim Wilson (with Steve Freund).* 1/50–6/99.

*** **This Is The Blues Harmonica Vol. 2**
Delmark DE-780 *Carey Bell, Eddie Burns, Mad Dog Lester Davenport, Little Sammy Davis, Alfred 'Blues King' Harris, Big Walter Horton, Mark Hummel (with Steve Freund), Little Walter, Louis Myers, Hammie Nixon, Walto Pace, Tad Robinson, Shakey Jake (with Magic Sam), Little Mack Simmons (with Eddy Clearwater), Junior Wells, Golden 'Big' Wheeler.* 1/50–6/04.

What these present, of course, is the blues harmonica according to Delmark, but since that catalogue spans more than half a century (including labels other than itself) and represents many of the leading players of the period, no one is likely to accuse the label of selling them short. As usual with such compilations, some tracks are harmonica features, like Louis Myers's 'Top Of The Harp' on the first CD, Little Sammy Davis's chromatic 'Devil's Trail' on the second and Carey Bell's instrumentals on both, while others are merely good tracks that happen to have harmonica on them, such as Willie Kent's 'Ain't It Nice', on which Lester Davenport's harp part is attractive but not integral. But both CDs make excellent listening for harpophiles and regular folks alike. Collectors' note: the tracks on both volumes by Carey Bell, Hammie Nixon and Junior Wells are previously unissued, as are those on Vol. 2 by Mark Hummel, Walto Pace, Shakey Jake and Big Wheeler, the latter two being alternative takes of issued pieces. The Nixons are with Sleepy John Estes, whose admirers should not miss the pretty duet 'Love Grows In Your Heart' on *Vol. 2*. Wells's meditative chromatic tune 'This Is The Blues' is an outtake from *Hoodoo Man Blues* and 'Tomorrow Night' (*Vol. 2*) an alternative take of the 1953 States recording. Pace

(c. 1912–91) does a medley of 'Fox Chase/Lost John' in fine old-time style.

*** Chicago Blues Harmonica
Wolf 120.848 *Billy Branch, Dusty Brown (3), James Cotton, Lester Davenport (3), Birmingham Jones (4), Snooky Pryor (2), Little Mac Simmons, Golden 'Big' Wheeler (2). 60s–94.*

All the tracks are songs with harmonica choruses and fills, rather than instrumentals, and most of the players are of the second rank, so this is not a showcase for virtuosity, but it makes a very listenable hour-and-a-bit of mainstream Chicago blues. Several of the artists are backed by bands including bassist Willie Kent and guitarists John Primer or Johnny B. Moore; the latter contributes significantly to Lester Davenport's numbers, and Primer to Dusty Brown's. These are among the very few available recordings by Brown (born 1929) and the phlegmy, effortful Birmingham Jones (born 1937). Intrinsically the best harp players here are Cotton, who sings and plays 'Decoration Day' without other accompaniment, Pryor, though his numbers with Homesick James (from their 1979 *Sad And Lonesome* session) are unspectacular, and Branch, whose 'Take You Down Town', played with brio, is the most exciting track.

**(*) Low Blows: An Anthology Of Chicago Harmonica Blues
Rooster R 2610 *Big Leon Brooks (3), Mojo Buford, Easy Baby, Good Rockin' Charles [Edwards] (5), Walter Horton & Carey Bell, Golden [Big] Wheeler (2), Big John Wrencher (2). 4/72–9/80.*

From a collector's point of view this is a compilation of some value, presenting a number of interesting second-rank players, some scantily represented on CD. The settings throughout are standard Chicago lineups of guitar(s), bass and drums, but among the guitarists are little-recorded figures like Walter 'Big Guitar Red' Smith with Edwards and Easy Baby, Joe Carter with Wrencher and Bobby King with Wheeler. Good Rockin' Charles Edwards (1933–89) was an easygoing singer and workmanlike harp player; five tracks are probably all that anyone but a specialist needs, but it's good that they are here, since little else by him remains in catalogue. Golden Wheeler's pair predate his own albums by a decade and a half and are excellent, not least for King's elegant guitar. 'Second-rank' does not apply, of course, to Horton and Bell, whose 'Avenue Stomp' is an outtake from their Alligator album. There is no forgotten masterwork here, but it's an entertaining programme.

*** Got Harp If You Want It
Blue Rock'It BRCD 111//Crosscut CCD 11030 *William Clarke, Paul Durkett, Rick Estrin (2), Mark Ford, Mark Hummel, Andy Just, Charlie Musselwhite (3), Ralph Shine (2), Dave Wellhausen. late 80s–early 90s.*

'The best of the West Coast harp players,' it says on the box, though inside it's admitted that 'several of the great West Coast players were not available … the fact that Rod Piazza and Paul deLay are not included is regrettable.' True, but it remains an enjoyable collection, covering a wide range of material from the hip compositions of Rick Estrin to Charlie Musselwhite's timeless 'Sundown Blues', though Mark Ford's 'Summertime', well played though it is, seems like an escapee from another album altogether. Durkett covers Jerry McCain's 'Steady', but Just's 'My Babe' is not the Little Walter number. The last two tracks are by Ralph Shine, a competent rather than outstanding player who cut an early album for Blue Rock'It (*Ralph Shine Blues Band* [BRCD 102]) but died in his early 30s. Most of the recordings are unique to this CD.

*** Crucial Harmonica Blues
Alligator ALCD 115 *Billy Boy Arnold, Carey Bell, [John] Cephas & [Phil] Wiggins, William Clarke, James Cotton, James Cotton–Junior Wells–Carey Bell–Billy Branch, Big Walter Horton, Little Charlie & The Nightcats, Delbert McClinton, Charlie Musselwhite, Sugar Blue, Sonny Terry. 72–02.*

An Alligator sampler, of course, and one that points the newcomer to such worthwhile albums as Billy Boy Arnold's *Back Where I Belong*, by way of 'Shake The Boogie', and Carey Bell's *Deep Down*, via 'Lonesome Stranger'. But at the same time it's a varied and attractive menu of blues harp styles, its main dish show-off instrumentals like Clarke's 'Blowin' Like Hell' and Phil Wiggins's exhilarating 'Burn Your Bridges'.

*** Blues Harp Hotshots
EasyDisc ED CD 7073 *Carey Bell, Butler Twins, James Harman, Randy McAllister, Lee McBee (with The Crawl), Sam Myers (with Snooks Eaglin), Sugar Ray Norcia, Jordan Patterson, Rod Piazza (with Rick Holmstrom), Charlie Sayles. 80–97.*

*** Blues Harp Greats
EasyDisc ED CD 7023 *Carey Bell, Mojo Buford, Butler Twins, James Cotton, Mark Hummel, Magic Dick & Jay Geils, James Montgomery Band, Annie Raines & Paul Rishell, Charlie Sayles, Treat Her Right. 88–97.*

Cheap and cheerful, these ten-track showcases give lovers of modern harp playing excellent value. The source labels are primarily Rounder, Bullseye Blues, Black Top and JSP, and the cuts from Black Top, such as those by James Harman, Lee McBee, Sam Myers and Rod Piazza on *Hotshots*, may not be available elsewhere. As often, individual tracks are enhanced by being withdrawn from their original albums and deposited in a different context: Randy McAllister's 'Babe And Nan's Thing' and Jordan Patterson's 'No Educated Woman' on *Hotshots* are just two examples.

*** Harp Attack!
Alligator ALCD 4790 *James Cotton, Junior Wells, Billy Branch, Carey Bell (h, v); Michael Coleman, George Baze (g); Lucky Peterson (p); Johnny B. Gayden (b); Ray 'Killer' Allison (d). 90.*

*** SuperHarps
Telarc CD-83472 *James Cotton, Billy Branch, Charlie Musselwhite, Sugar Ray Norcia (h, v); Anthony Geraci, David Maxwell (p); Kid Bangham (g); Michael 'Mudcat' Ward (b); Per Hanson (d). 4/99.*

*** SuperHarps II
Telarc CD-83514 *Lazy Lester (h, g, perc, v); Carey Bell, Raful Neal, Snooky Pryor (h, v); Anthony Geraci (p); Kid Bangham (g); Michael 'Mudcat' Ward (b); Per Hanson (d). 01.*

**(*) In The Pocket: A Taste Of Blues Harmonica
Telarc CD-83556 *Carey Bell (with Robert Jr Lockwood), James Cotton (2), James Cotton & Billy Branch, Charlie Musselwhite, Charlie Musselwhite–Sugar Ray Norcia–Billy Branch–James Cotton, Kenny Neal, Raful Neal & Lazy Lester, Jerry Portnoy, Snooky Pryor, Annie Raines (with Hubert Sumlin), Matthew Skoller (with John Primer), Junior Wells, Kim Wilson & James Cotton (with Ronnie Earl). 12/94–6/01.*

The first three CDs are not VACs in our usual sense but collective recordings, each featuring four harmonica players, with a more or less stable backing group throughout each album. On *Harp Attack* Cotton and Wells play the major roles, each contributing something – solo, fills, background or vocal – to seven of the 11 tracks. By this date Cotton had lost some of his voice and Wells's taste had been erratic for years, but the presence of rivals – or talented colleagues – put a damper on eccentricity and grandstanding. Cotton's long 'Black Night' is gripping, and Branch, low man on the totem pole in terms of access to the microphone, brings the album to a close with a cheerful, unobsequious tribute to the senior partners.

Telarc's *SuperHarps* CDs ring plenty of changes, with items by one player (mostly on the second) and numerous different combinations of two, and each finishes with an extended slow blues jam called 'Harp To Harp' (11.37 on the first, 8.07 on the second) that features all four. *SuperHarps II* has the edge for variety, thanks to the distinctively piercing style of Snooky Pryor and the swamp-blues orientation of Lazy Lester and Raful Neal, and listeners interested in the whole song rather than its harmonica quotient may find this set more rewarding. Two cuts from *SuperHarps* and one from *SuperHarps II* find their way on to *In The Pocket*, a selection from Telarc's blues list, alongside items from albums by Cotton, Musselwhite and Wells and harmonica-featuring tracks from CDs by Ronnie Earl and John Primer and some of Telarc's songbook sets. It's okay, but you need baggier pockets than this for a really satisfying harp anthology, and most of the collections discussed earlier were tailored with that in mind. TR

Hillbilly Blues

***(*) White Country Blues
Columbia C2K 47466 2CD *Roy Acuff & His Crazy Tennesseans, Allen Brothers (2), Anglin Brothers, Tom [Clarence] Ashley, Blue Ridge Ramblers, Mr & Mrs Chris Bouchillon, Homer Callahan (2), Callahan Brothers, Bill Carlisle (2), Cliff Carlisle (3), [Cliff] Carlisle & [Wilbur] Ball (2), Carolina Buddies, Cauley Family, Bill Cox (2), Bill Cox & Cliff Hobbs (2), Tom Darby & Jimmie Tarlton (2), Al Dexter, Clarence Green, Roy Harvey & Leonard Copeland, Larry Hensley, Frank Hutchison (4), Ramblin' Red Lowery, Asa Martin & His Kentucky Hillbillies, Clayton McMichen, W. T. Narmour & S. W. Smith, W. Lee O'Daniel & His Hillbilly Boys (3), Charlie Poole & The North Carolina Ramblers (3), Prairie Ramblers, Riley Puckett, The Rhythm Wreckers, Val & Pete (2).* 9/26–11/38.

(***) Drunk & Nutty: Hillbillies Foolin' With The Blues
Indigo IGODCD 2520 2CD *Roy Acuff & His Crazy Tennesseans, Allen Brothers (2), Tom [Clarence] Ashley, Ashley's Melody Men, Gene Autry (3), Dock Boggs, Cliff Bruner, Homer Callahan, Callahan Brothers, Bill Carlisle, Cliff Carlisle, [Cliff] Carlisle & [Wilbur] Ball, Carolina Tar Heels, Carter Family, Bill Cox, Bill Cox & Cliff Hobbs, Ted Daffan, [Tom] Darby & [Jimmie] Tarlton, Delmore Brothers, Al Dexter, Dixon Brothers, Gwen Foster, Georgia Crackers, Lonnie Glosson, Larry Hensley, Prince Albert Hunt, Frank Hutchison (2), Buddy Jones, Dick Justice, Dave [McCarn] & Howard [Long], Sam McGee, Frankie Marvin, Roy Newman & His Boys, W. Lee O'Daniel & His Hillbilly Boys, Narmour & Smith, Nelstone's Hawaiians, Charlie Poole & The North Carolina Ramblers (2), Prairie Ramblers (2), Riley Puckett (2), Rhythm Wreckers, Slim Smith, Lemuel Turner, Bob Wills.* 9/26–46.

***(*) Old-Time Mountain Blues
County CO-CD-3528 *'Dock' Boggs, Burnett & Rutherford, Cliff Carlisle, Gwen Foster, Clarence Green, Larry Hensley, Frank Hutchison, Dick Justice, Leake County Revelers, Lester McFarland, Sam McGee (2), David Miller, Byrd Moore & Jess Johnston, Narmour & Smith, Fiddling Doc Roberts Trio, South Georgia Highballers, Lowe Stokes & His North Georgians, Jimmie Tarlton.* 3/27–2/39.

*** Hillbilly Blues 1928-1946 [sic]
Frémeaux FA 065 2CD *Allen Brothers, Chet Atkins, Milton Brown (2), Spade Cooley, Buster Coward, [Tom] Darby & [Jimmie] Tarlton (2), Jimmie Davis (3), Delmore Brothers (2), Jack Guthrie, Hartman's Heartbreakers (2), Adolph Hofner, Helen Hunt (with the Nite Owls), Buddy Jones, Bill Monroe, Moon Mullican (with the Sunshine Boys), Les Paul Trio, Riley Puckett, Rambling Rangers, Jimmie Rodgers, Shelton Brothers, Sunshine Boys (2), Merle Travis, Ernest Tubb (2), T. Texas Tyler, Wiley Walker & Gene Sullivan, Bob Wills (2), Johnny Lee Wills.* 11/27–9/46.

*** Hillbilly Blues
Living Era CD AJA 5361 *Allen Brothers, [Clarence] Ashley & [Gwen] Foster, Bill Carlisle, Cliff Carlisle, Carter Family, [Tom] Darby & [Jimmie] Tarlton, Jimmie Davis, Delmore Brothers, Hartman's Heartbreakers, Jess Hillard, Buddy Jones, Dick Justice, Lone Star Cowboys, Nations Brothers, Roy Newman & His Boys, Norman Phelps & His Virginia Rounders, Riverside Ramblers, Jimmie Rodgers, Shelton Brothers, The Sons Of The Ozarks, Stripling Brothers, Swift Jewel Cowboys, Three Tobacco Tags, Johnny Lee Wills & His Boys, Smoky Wood & His Wood Chips.* 4/29–47.

The blues form has enormous significance in the recorded history of white country music. The first national star of country music, Jimmie Rodgers, established himself with blues songs in the late '20s and continued to record them throughout his life. Several major figures of '30s country music such as Gene Autry, Jimmie Davis and Ernest Tubb began their careers as Rodgers-imitating blues singers. A thick vein of blues runs through the work of Western Swing and proto-honkytonk bandleaders like Bob Wills, Roy Newman, Al Dexter and Ted Daffan, while several prolific recording acts like the Allen Brothers, Shelton Brothers and Buddy Jones practically lived off the blues. In country music prior to World War II some five per cent of all recordings had 'Blues' in their title and at least as many again were also blues though they didn't call themselves so.

But form is only one aspect of the blues. Many white artists use blues structures and devices yet sound radically different from black contemporaries in voice production, vocal/instrumental interplay, rhythmic sensibility and other technical aspects; on top of that they frequently differ in their conception of what blues are *for*. Abbé Niles, an unusually *au courant* reviewer of the time, regarded Jimmie Rodgers's blues as comedy numbers and criticized him when he failed to come up with good new jokes. It is not an observation that has often been made about, say, Blind Lemon Jefferson. (Perhaps it should be.) Clearly there is a vast field for investigation, conjecture and, one hopes, discovery in the study of white blues, and the work has scarcely begun. The material on these CDs, most of which were intended to promote the concept of hillbilly blues to an audience already acquainted with the

African-American model, is a small but vital contribution to that enquiry. This is not, of course, to imply that the performances are not fascinating and rewarding on their own terms.

All of these collections are valuable, but none is without its drawbacks. Probably the best introduction, for range and variety, is *White Country Blues*, which has excellent examples of blues-focused singer/guitarists like Frank Hutchison and the Carlisle brothers and of stringbands like Charlie Poole's that dipped only occasionally into the blues well but made spectacular catches. It spends little time, however, on the many white fiddlers who used the blues as a remarkably expressive medium – an imbalance somewhat redressed by the shorter but scintillating County collection with its selections by Doc Roberts, Leonard Rutherford and Jess Johnston. Frémeaux cast the net wider, devoting more space to Western Swing bands and to '40s artists like the singer-pianist Moon Mullican, whose blues knowhow was crucial to the development of honkytonk music. This is also part of the agenda of the other *Hillbilly Blues* (Living Era), compiled by this writer, which endeavours to illustrate white blues activity across the entire South.

Drunk & Nutty, unlike the other four collections, was not sourced from original 78s but from LP and CD reissues on other labels. The LPs were long gone, which may justify recycling their contents, but *White Country Blues* was not so hard to find that Indigo should be excused for lifting 21 of their 50 tracks from it. If the other albums have occasional duplications, it's because tracks like Larry Hensley's 'Match Box Blues' and Dick Justice's 'Brown Skin Blues' are particularly dramatic examples of white musicians tapping specific black sources, in those instances Blind Lemon Jefferson.

When The Sun Goes Down Vol. 10: East Virginia Blues (Bluebird 60085), described as 'the Appalachian roots of honky tonk', includes a few excellent blues renditions by Gene Autry, Jimmie Davis and others but is a much wider survey of white Southern music in the period from Vernon Dalhart's 'The Prisoner's Song'/'Wreck Of The Old 97' (1924), the first hillbilly hit, to the Blue Sky Boys and Bill Monroe's Blue Grass Boys 16 years later, embracing Old and New World ballads, Victorian 'heart' songs, fiddle breakdowns, gospel songs and newly composed pieces.

*** **Tennessee Saturday Night: The Rural Route To Rock 'N' Roll**
Jasmine JASMCD 3519 Gene Autry (2), Claude Boone, Homer Callahan, Cliff Carlisle, Zeke Clements, Delmore Brothers, Red Foley, Tennessee Ernie Ford, Billy Hughes, The Jubileers, Lone Star Cowboys, Maddox Bros & Rose (2), Bill Monroe & His Blue Grass Boys (2), Bill Nettles, Roy Newman (2), Shelton Brothers, Arthur Smith, Texas Wanderers, Merle Travis, Bob Wills, Johnny Lee Wills. 8/33–late 40s.

*** **The Black And White Roots Of Rock 'N' Roll**
Indigo IGODCD 2549 2CD Tiny Bradshaw, Jackie Brenston, Billy Briggs, Roy Brown, Ruth Brown, The Carlisles, The Clovers, Pee Wee Crayton, The Crows, Bill Darnell, Larry Darnell, Link Davis, Little Jimmy Dickens, The Dominoes, Tommy Duncan, Lucky Enois Quartet, Tennessee Ernie Ford, Hardrock Gunter (2), Bill Haley (3), Lionel Hampton, Wynonie Harris (3), Hawkshaw Hawkins, Bull Moose Jackson, Eddie Mack, Amos Milburn, Clyde Moody, Merrill Moore, Ella Mae Morse, Moon Mullican (2), Hank Penny, Piano Red, Jimmy Preston, Melvin Price, Louis Prima, Wayne Raney, Fat Man Robinson, Charlie Shavers (with Tommy Dorsey), Arthur Smith, Dickie Thompson & His Orchestra, Big Mama Thornton, James Waynes, Hank Williams, Johnny Lee Wills, York Brothers. 45–53.

As recordings from the period immediately preceding rock 'n' roll fell into the public domain, there were several attempts to epitomize that prehistory; and since rock 'n' roll was to a great extent a product of the blues – white blues as much as black – all those compilations were stacked high with recordings by key white blues artists like Bob Wills, Bill Monroe, the Delmore Brothers and so forth. Perhaps the best single VAC dedicated to this purpose is *Tennessee Saturday Night*, knowledgably compiled and annotated by Dave Penny. Though its timespan and roster are not too different from those of Living Era's *Hillbilly Blues* – and indeed they have several artists and tracks in common – its emphasis is more squarely on the '40s. *The Roots Of Rockabilly 1940–1953* (Indigo IGOTCD 2556 3CD) has somewhat the same agenda (and, typically, swipes a bunch of tracks from the Jasmine) but devotes one CD to black recordings in what could be argued – though not very convincingly – to be a black rockabilly idiom. *The Black & White Roots Of Rock 'N' Roll* is a more coherent project, presenting two dozen songs in both black and white versions: so Jackie Brenston's 'Rocket 88' is followed by Bill Haley's, and Big Mama Thornton's 'Hound Dog' by Tommy Duncan's, standing in for the not yet out-of-copyright Elvis Presley version. But the copying isn't all in one direction: several of the pieces were written and first recorded by white artists. This collection was planned with some thought (again by Dave Penny) and is genuinely informative as well as enjoyable. TR

Humour & Erotica

*** **Rude Dudes**
Document DOCD-32-20-5 2CD Barrelhouse Annie, Butterbeans & Susie, Bo Carter (4), Chicago Black Swans, Napoleon Fletcher, Blind Boy Fuller, Georgia Tom [Dorsey] & Jane Lucas, Mae Glover & John Byrd, George Hannah, Bob Howe & Frankie Griggs, Hunter & Jenkins (2), Jesse James, Lil Johnson (4), Lonnie Johnson, Lonnie Johnson & Victoria Spivey, Lillie Mae Kirkman, Louis Lasky, Blind Willie McTell, Lizzie Miles (2), Al Miller, Whistlin' Alex Moore, Bessie Smith, Speckled Red, Victoria Spivey, Roosevelt Sykes, Tampa Red, Sam Theard, Washboard Sam, Ethel Waters, Margaret Webster, Whistling Rufus, Josh White. 8/28–6/41.

*** **Let Me Squeeze Your Lemon: The Ultimate Rude Blues Collection**
Great Voices Of The Century GVC 2012 2CD Barbecue Bob, Barrelhouse Annie, Big Bill Broonzy (2), Cliff Carlisle, Bo Carter (2), Margaret Carter, Dirty Red, Little Buddy Doyle, Champion Jack Dupree, Blind Boy Fuller (2), Georgia Pine Boy [Joe McCoy], Cleo Gibson, Jimmie Gordon (2), Wynonie Harris, Hattie Hart, John Lee Hooker, Lightnin' Hopkins, Bull Moose Jackson, James 'Stump' Johnson, Lonnie Johnson (2), Robert Johnson, Kansas City Kitty [Mozelle Anderson] & Georgia Tom [Dorsey] (2), Leadbelly, Charlie Lincoln, Memphis Minnie, Lizzie Miles, Mississippi Sheiks, Alex Moore, Buddy Moss, Charlie Pickett, Dan Pickett, Carl Rafferty, Bessie Smith, Clara Smith, Victoria Spivey, The Swallows, Roosevelt Sykes (2),

Tampa Red, Bobo Thomas, Blind Squire Turner [Teddy Darby], Minnie Wallace, Sippie Wallace. 20s–50s.

*** Bed Spring Poker
Indigo IGODCD 2502 2CD Barrelhouse Annie, Lucille Bogan, Big Bill Broonzy, Lee Brown, Cliff Carlisle, Bo Carter, Margaret Carter, Eddie Davis, Walter Davis, Little Buddy Doyle, Champion Jack Dupree, Bernice Edwards, Blind Boy Fuller, Cleo Gibson, Jazz Gillum, Jimmie Gordon, Wynonie Harris, Hattie Hart, Tony Hollins, John Lee Hooker, Lightnin' Hopkins, Bull Moose Jackson, Madelyn James, Edith Johnson, James 'Stump' Johnson, Lil Johnson, Lonnie Johnson, Leadbelly, Memphis Minnie, Al Miller, Mississippi Sheiks, Buddy Moss, Charlie Pickett, Dan Pickett, Walter Roland, Bessie Smith, Clara Smith, Victoria Spivey, The Swallows, Roosevelt Sykes (2), Tampa Red, Johnny Temple, Bobo Thomas, Minnie Wallace, Sippie Wallace, Ethel Waters, Ralph Willis. 26–51.

*** He Got Out His Big Ten Inch
Indigo IGOTCD 2562 3CD Kokomo Arnold, Dorothy Baker, Barbecue Bob, Barrelhouse Annie, Lucille Bogan (2), Tiny Bradshaw, Big Bill Broonzy, Roy Brown, Walter Brown, Bo Carter (2), Cow Cow Davenport, Eunice Davis, Walter Davis (2), Floyd Dixon, Champion Jack Dupree, Dorothy Ellis, Napoleon Fletcher, Blind Boy Fuller, Little Boy Fuller, Georgia Tom [Dorsey] & Jane Lucas [Mozelle Alderson] (2), Mae Glover, Jimmie Gordon (2), R. T. Hanen, George Hannah, Hannah May [Mozelle Alderson], Wynonie Harris, Robert Henry, John Lee Hooker (2), Rosetta Howard, Helen Humes, Fluffy Hunter, Hunter & Jenkins, Bull Moose Jackson, Papa Charlie Jackson, Jesse James, Lil Johnson, Lonnie Johnson (2), Louise Johnson, Stella Johnson, Kansas City Kitty [Mozelle Alderson] & Georgia Tom [Dorsey] (2), Lillie Mae Kirkman, Julia Lee (2), Pete 'Guitar' Lewis, Joe McCoy (2), Brownie McGhee, Art McKay, Memphis Jug Band, Memphis Minnie, Amos Milburn, Mississippi Sheiks, Fats Noel, St Louis Jimmy [Oden], Carl Rafferty, Todd Rhodes, Marylin Scott, The Sharps & Flats, Victoria Spivey, The Sultans, The Swallows, Isabel Sykes, Roosevelt Sykes (2), Tampa Red, Danny Taylor, Billy Ward & The Dominoes, Washboard Sam, Ralph Willis, [Oscar] Buddy Woods. 20s–50s.

**(*) Raunchy Business: Hot Nuts And Lollypops
Columbia CK 46783 Barrel House Annie, Lucille Bogan (2), Bo Carter (2), Bernice Edwards, Hunter & Jenkins (2), Lil Johnson (4), Lonnie Johnson (2), Lonnie Johnson & Victoria Spivey (2), Lillie Mae Kirkman, Mississippi Sheiks (2), Buddy Moss. 10/28–6/39.

No American vernacular idiom recorded during the 20th century can rival the blues in providing its audience with sexual material that in any other context would have been unpublishable. Blues managed to do so, and in vast quantities, partly because the songs were dressed in the language of ambiguity, whereby sexual activity was encoded in metaphors of jelly rolling and meat cutting, squeezed lemons and good cabbage, and partly because the 'race' record belonged to an African-American world that the larger society had little interest in probing, let alone censoring. A good deal of study, linguistic, anthropological and psychological, has been devoted to such records, yet all sorts of basic questions about their origin and use remain unanswered; we have only the foggiest ideas about who bought them, in what settings they were played or to what extent they were spontaneously generated by the artists rather than commissioned by record producers.

Those are not questions that these collections are concerned to investigate; they have been compiled as peepholes into the secret world of black sex, as mediated through the ingenious and often humorous imagination of the blues singer. Naturally the quality of that imagination is variable: some of the more prolific producers of sexually themed blues, like Bo Carter, could ring the changes on that bell rather deftly, while Lonnie Johnson and Lil Johnson will probably seem to the present-day listener to strike the same note too often. Occasionally the combination of a clever script and a boisterous performance produces a playlet that is still beguiling, such as 'Terrible Operation Blues' by Georgia Tom & Jane Lucas (Mozelle Alderson) (*Rude Dudes*) and 'Gas Man Blues' by Mae Glover & John Byrd (*Rude Dudes*, *Big Ten Inch*). The admirer of the well-turned lyric will enjoy the elaborately developed metaphor of Andy Razaf's composition 'My Man O' War', sung with steely composure by Lizzie Miles (*Rude Dudes*, *Let Me Squeeze Your Lemon*), or the same writer's 'My Handy Man', done by Ethel Waters (*Rude Dudes*). And no one should miss the chance to hear Lucille Bogan's startlingly explicit 'Shave 'Em Dry' (*Bed Spring Poker*, *Raunchy Business*).

It may appear from the foregoing that the most rewarding of these collections is *Rude Dudes*, a 40-piece garland of garlic flowers arranged by Bill Wyman. It does have some very enjoyable (and well remastered) performances, but not conspicuously more than the other multidisc sets, *Let Me Squeeze Your Lemon*, *Bed Spring Poker* and *He Got Out His Big Ten Inch*. There's such a lot of this material that you can buy three of the four without incurring a great deal of duplication. (*Lemon* and *Poker* share almost two thirds of their contents.) 'Let Me Play With Your Poodle' is walked round the block four times by either Tampa Red or Lightnin' Hopkins, and perhaps a dozen tracks show up twice, but generally speaking you'll get a lot of bang for your bucks. The single CD *Raunchy Business* seems rather meagre by comparison, and if you owned the others you'd have a good deal of it anyway. Unsatisfied erotomaniacs should scan the cut-out bins for *Banana In Your Fruit Basket* (Zircon Bleu 507, deleted) and *The Copulatin' Collection* (Viper's Nest VN-168, deleted), as well as noting the hokum collections below.

** Hokum Blues (1924–1929)
Document DOCD-5370 Feathers & Frogs (2), Ki Ki Johnson (4), The Pebbles (6), Louise Ross (2), Danny Small & Ukulele Mays (4), Swan & Lee (2), The Two Of Spades (2), Ukulele Bob Williams (2). c. 11/24–9/29.

** Hokum, Blues & Rags (1929–1930s)
Document DOCD-5392 Joe Linthecome (2), Pratt & George (2), Rufus & Ben Quillian (16), Three Stripped Gears (2). 10/29–30s.

**(*) Please Warm My Weiner
Yazoo 1043 Tommie Bradley & James Cole, Buddie Burton, Butterbeans & Susie, Bo Carter, Georgia Tom [Dorsey] & Tampa Red, Robert & Charlie Hicks [Barbecue Bob & Charley Lincoln], Hokum Boys, Whistling Bob Howe & Frankie Griggs, Papa Charlie Jackson, Memphis Minnie, Rufus & Ben Quillian, Leola B. & Kid Wesley Wilson, Yazoo All Stars [Paramount All Stars] (2). 28–35.

Hokum was a genuine subgenre of blues: playful songs about sex and other high jinks, typically in a verse/refrain format, often delivered as vocal duets. See the entries for The Hokum Boys and the Famous Hokum Boys for more on this craze of the late '20s and early '30s. Document use the term rather loosely on the CD they call *Hokum Blues*: most of the performances might be better described as black vaudeville or variety, and in some cases, like the stentorian singer Ki Ki Johnson, from quite far down the bill. It's only at the end, in the work of the duets Feathers & Frogs and Swan & Lee, that we meet the insouciant silliness of true hokum. There is more of it in the second collection, in the work of the Quillian brothers, but their refusal to write songs to any other pattern than that of hokum's archetypal hit, 'It's Tight Like That', renders them hard work after two or three reps. One four-track session, however, is enhanced by ambitious guitar playing from the Atlanta maestro Perry Bechtel. The remaining tracks are so disconnected that they might have been chosen with a blindfold and a pin. It should perhaps be noted, however, that these two CDs offer a substantial proportion of the recordings of African-American ukulele players.

The Yazoo, subtitled 'Old Time Hokum Blues', is an untidy job lot of genuine hokum, spoken comedy routines like 'The Alley Crap Game' and the Hicks brothers' 'Darktown Gambling – The Crap Game' and other oddments. The best of the last is the two-part sampler 'Hometown Skiffle', in which Paramount artists create an all-star party in the studio. TR

Jugbands

♛ **** Rukus Juice & Chittlins: The Great Jug Bands Vol. 1

Yazoo 2032 *Birmingham Jug Band (2), Cannon's Jug Stompers (2), Cincinnati Jug Band, Kaiser Clifton, Jed Davenport & His Beale Street Jug Band, Dixieland Jug Blowers, Ben Ferguson (2), John Harris, Jack Kelly & His South Memphis Jug Band, King David's Jug Band (2), Noah Lewis's Jug Band, Earl McDonald's Original Louisville Jug Band, Memphis Jug Band (4), Walter Family, Whistler's Jug Band (2). 12/26–11/34.*

♛ **** Rukus Juice & Chittlins: The Great Jug Bands Vol. 2

Yazoo 2033 *Birmingham Jug Band, Ezra Buzzington's Rustic Revelers, Cannon's Jug Stompers (2), Cincinnati Jug Band, Daddy Stovepipe & Mississippi Sarah, Jed Davenport & His Beale Street Jug Band, Dixieland Jug Blowers (2), Five Harmaniacs, Jack Kelly & His South Memphis Jug Band, Kentucky Jug Band, King David's Jug Band (2), Noah Lewis's Jug Band, Earl McDonald's Original Louisville Jug Band, Memphis Jug Band (3), Phillips Louisville Jug Band, Prairie Ramblers, Minnie Wallace, Whistler's Jug Band. 12/26–2/35.*

In the few years of their vogue on 'race' records, somewhere between a dozen and 20 jugbands made scores of titles in a dizzying variety of lineups. It's an idiom eminently suited to the multi-artist compilation, yet Yazoo occupy the field alone with these superb collections.

Some groups are fronted by harmonica or fiddle, or both, with guitar and jug 'rhythm sections'; that description covers the Memphis-based lineups of Cannon's Jug Stompers, the groups led by Jed Davenport, Jack Kelly and Noah Lewis, and the Memphis Jug Band. Members of the MJB also accompany Kaiser Clifton and Minnie Wallace. The Louisville bands, in contrast, eschewed the harmonica and were generally led by fiddle or reed instruments; thus the Dixieland Jug Blowers, the Kentucky Jug Band and the Earl McDonald, Phillips and Whistler aggregations, and the associated recordings by Ben Ferguson and John Harris. Of the remaining groups, the Birmingham and Cincinnati teams and Daddy Stovepipe & Mississippi Sarah take the Memphis route of a harmonica lead, King David's Jug Band is Stovepipe No. 1 blowing his eponymous instrument with mandolin and guitar support, and the rest are the few white groups that used a jug.

The dominant repertoire is blues in all but the Louisville bands, which vary the diet with common-stock tunes, rags, 'reels' and exhibition pieces like the Dixieland Jug Blowers' 'Banjoreno' (*Vol. 1*). But a line cannot be firmly drawn, as if between two schools: versions of 'He's In The Jailhouse Now' are offered by both the McDonald crew on *Vol. 1* and the MJB on *Vol. 2*, while 'Tear It Down', done by King David's Jug Band on *Vol. 1*, shows up everywhere. Among the 46 titles on the two CDs are some of the most perfectly integrated small-band blues recordings of their period, such as the Cincinnati Jug Band's instrumentals 'Newport Blues' and 'George Street Stomp', the MJB's 'Stealin' Stealin' and the several titles by Cannon's Jug Stompers. Excellent remastering brings out all the detail of the performances. As a portrait of this enchanting idiom, by turns effervescent and poignant, the two albums are virtually faultless.

*** Harps, Jugs, Washboards & Kazoos

RST Jazz Perspectives JPCD-1505 *Five Harmaniacs (14), The Red Devils (2), Rhythm Willie & His Gang (4), Salty Dog Four (2), Scorpion Washboard Band (2). 6/26–10/40.*

'Yazoo occupy the field alone' for jugband VACs, we said above, and including this item doesn't invalidate the claim (though it does compromise the title of this section), since four of the five groups didn't use a jug, and the one that did, the Five Harmaniacs, didn't invariably do so. Nevertheless, this is a CD with what might be called jugband values. The Harmaniacs were a white vaudeville group and closer in spirit to the skiffle-jazz of the Mound City Blue Blowers, or the collaborations of Joe Venuti, Eddie Lang and Adrian Rollini, than to the blues-based jugbands described above, but anyone who enjoys the swing and gaiety of jugband music should appreciate their joyful, weightless playing of tunes like 'Sadie Green Vamp Of New Orleans' and 'Coney Island Washboard'. The Salty Dog Four and The Red Devils are presented here as two manifestations of the same group but probably weren't; the former is a vehicle for hot – indeed, red-hot – kazoo and banjo, while the Devils were fronted on 'Dinah' and 'Tiger Rag' by the wholly brilliant Hawaiian guitarist Benny 'King' Nawahi. The obscure Scorpion Washboard band are from the same mould as better-known African-American bands of the '30s like the Washboard Rhythm Kings (see *The Penguin Guide To Jazz Recordings*). There are no jugs, kazoos or washboards on Rhythm Willie Hood's four titles, just audaciously skilful, jazzy harmonica playing.

(***) Sanctified Jug Bands (1928–1930)

Document DOCD-5300 *Elder Richard Bryant (13), Holy Ghost Sanctified Singers (4), Rev. E. S. (Shy) Moore (2), Brother Williams Memphis Sanctified Singers (2). 2/28–2/30.*

The same studios that witnessed the secular jollity of the Memphis Jug Band or the Dixieland Jug Blowers also saw a procession of African-American preachers, making records of short sermons with small groups of their congregants providing responses and exhortations. Typically the sermonette would be followed by a 30- or 40-second hymn, sung by all present, and sometimes the hymn would be accompanied, since preachers in the Holiness churches, unlike their Baptist counterparts, had no objection to worldly instruments like harmonica, guitar and jug being put to God's work. Two such ministers were the Revs. Bryant, from the Mississippi Delta area, and Moore, from Malvern, Arkansas, who seem, on the aural evidence, to have been set up with members of the Memphis jugband circle. Four of Bryant's sides and all those by the Holy Ghost and Williams lineups omit the sermonizing and just consist of hymn-singing by small ensembles, the Bryant and Williams groups fronted by the colossal Bessie Johnson. These recordings have musical accompaniment throughout, the harmonica player with Bryant and the Holy Ghosters sounding rather like Will Shade of the MJB (who could also be the 'Brother William[s]' of the third group). This is all stirring music that any lover of jugbands should appreciate. Sitting through the remaining 11 sermons for their brief musical codas may be a more specialized pursuit. This is not to imply that the sermons are of no artistic or religious value, but Bryant and Moore are not in the top class of recorded preachers. TR

Label Histories & Showcases

Most of the albums discussed here are historical surveys of a label's activities, documentaries made after their subjects ceased trading. Compilations issued by existing companies with the purpose of letting consumers sample their wares have generally been overlooked, since they're often part of a specific promotional campaign and when it's over tend to disappear. But there are exceptions, and the reader will find them below, together with a number of anniversary collections.

ABCO

*** **Abco Chicago Blues Recordings**
Wolf 120.298 *Freddy Hall (2), Herby Joe (2), Louis Myers & The Aces (2), Morris Pejoe (2), The Ripchords (2), Zona Sago [Allan Williams] (2), Arbee Stidham (4). 56.*

Founded by Joe Brown, Eli Toscano and Ted Daniels, Abco existed for only four months before Toscano split to form Cobra; these 16 tracks are the label's complete output. It seems likely that Brown had material on hand for release, and the recording date shown is indicative rather than definitive. Myers's 'Just Whaling' (*sic*) and 'Bluesy' are classic harmonica instrumentals, and Pejoe's tracks are thought to feature Magic Sam's recording debut. Stidham's four songs are his best recordings, thanks to Willie Dixon's firm hand as producer and a menacing sax section, replaced on 'When I Find My Baby' by the dogfighting harmonicas of Walter Horton and Sonny Boy Williamson II. Freddie Hall and Herby Joe are evidence of Willie Mabon's contemporary popularity, and mainly valuable for their guitarists. The Ripchords are a good doo-wop group, and Zona Sago's Modern Sounds combine Latin piano, Sago's Caribbean percussion and a fiery jazz tenorist to surprisingly good effect. CS

Ace

***(*) **Mojo Working: The Best Of Ace Blues**
Ace CDCHDK 964 *Pee Wee Crayton, Lowell Fulson, Guitar Slim, Arthur Gunter, Smokey Hogg, John Lee Hooker, Lightnin' Hopkins, Howlin' Wolf, Elmore James, Albert King, B. B. King (2), Lazy Lester, Lightnin' Slim, Little Willie Littlefield, Lonesome Sundown, Slim Harpo, Little Johnny Taylor, Ike Turner, Johnny 'Guitar' Watson. 48–67.*

For serious collectors Ace Records is a primary source of fine postwar blues reissues, invariably well produced. Such customers will have little use for a packet of chestnuts like 'Boogie Chillen', 'Rock Me Baby', 'I'm A King Bee' and 'Part Time Love', but they are not the intended audience; this is a menu for the new and hungry blues fan, and it offers a hearty meal for the price of a burger. The tracks are drawn from the most significant labels in Ace's portfolio, notably Modern, Specialty, Excello and Stax, and almost all of them are first-rate. TR

Alligator

*** **The Alligator Records 20th Anniversary Collection**
Alligator ALCD 105/6 2CD *Carey Bell & Junior Wells, Big Twist & The Mellow Fellows, Elvin Bishop, Lonnie Brooks, Clarence 'Gatemouth' Brown, Roy Buchanan, Clifton Chenier, Albert Collins, Albert Collins & Johnny Copeland, James Cotton, Detroit Jr, Tinsley Ellis, Big Walter Horton, Jimmy Johnson, The Kinsey Report, Little Charlie & The Nightcats, Lonnie Mack, Delbert McClinton, Charley Musselwhite, Kenny Neal, The Paladins, Pinetop Perkins, Lucky Peterson, Professor Longhair, A. C. Reed & Stevie Ray Vaughan, Fenton Robinson, Saffire – The Uppity Blues Women, Son Seals, The Siegel–Schwall Band, Hound Dog Taylor, Koko Taylor, Sonny Terry, Katie Webster, Lil' Ed [Williams] & The Blues Imperials, Johnny Winter. 71–91.*

*** **The Alligator Records 25th Anniversary Collection**
Alligator ALCD 110/11 2CD *Luther Allison, Billy Boy Arnold, Carey Bell, Elvin Bishop, Lonnie Brooks, Clarence 'Gatemouth' Brown, Roy Buchanan, Roy Buchanan & Delbert McClinton, [John] Cephas & [Phil] Wiggins, C. J. Chenier, William Clarke, Albert Collins & Johnny Copeland, James Cotton, Floyd Dixon, Tinsley Ellis, Corey Harris, Dave Hole, Michael Hill's Blues Mob, Long John Hunter, Little Charlie & The Nightcats, Lonnie Mack & Stevie Ray Vaughan, Steady Rollin' Bob Margolin, Charlie Musselwhite, Kenny Neal, Lucky Peterson, Professor Longhair, Fenton Robinson, Saffire – The Uppity Blues Women, Son Seals, Eddie Shaw & The Wolf Gang, Sonny Boy Williamson II, Sugar Blue, Hound Dog Taylor, Koko Taylor, Maurice John Vaughn, Katie Webster, Lil' Ed [Williams] & The Blues Imperials, Johnny Winter. 63, 71–95.*

*** **Alligator Records 30th Anniversary Collection**
Alligator ALCD 112/13 2CD *Luther Allison, Marcia Ball, Carey Bell, Elvin Bishop, Lonnie Brooks, Michael Burks, [John] Cephas & [Phil] Wiggins, C. J. Chenier, William Clarke, Albert Collins, Shemekia Copeland, James Cotton, Robert Cray & Albert Collins, Corey Harris, Corey Harris & Henry Butler, Dave Hole, Holmes Brothers, The Kinsey Report, Little Charlie & The Nightcats, Lonnie Mack, Delbert McClinton, Coco Montoya, Saffire – The Uppity Blues Women, Son Seals, Hound Dog Taylor, Koko Taylor, Phillip Walker & Lonnie Brooks, Junior Wells, Lil' Ed [Williams] & The Blues Imperials, Johnny Winter, Rusty Zinn. 74–00.*

Alligator has been a major force in promoting blues for three and a half decades and, very reasonably, they've taken to celebrating their stamina with quinquennial 30-course dinners; they must be preparing to serve another any time now. It's always been one of their strengths that they don't just put out albums, they work on developing the artist in the round, and it's a tribute to their clear eye on that goal that at least a third of the acts on *The 20th Anniversary Collection* were still associated with the label ten years later. The potency and variety of their roster should be evident from a glance at the rollcalls above; this is not a label whose orientation can be summed up in a phrase. Consequently all these albums make excitingly diverse listening. A few previously unissued tracks are scattered here and there; *30th Anniversary*, which is divided into a studio disc and a live one, has five of them, all in the live section, and also a video of Hound Dog Taylor, the artist who put Alligator in business. The company's *Living Chicago Blues* series and *The New Bluebloods* are discussed in CHICAGO II (POSTWAR), and some of their mid-price *Crucial* samplers in other VAC sections. TR

Arhoolie

**** Arhoolie Records 40th Anniversary Collection 1960–2000: The Journey Of Chris Strachwitz
Arhoolie CD 491 5CD *Boisec [Bois Sec] Ardoin & Canray Fontenot, Lawrence Ardoin, Black Ace, Bongo Joe [George Coleman], Juke Boy Bonner, J. C. Burris, Butch Cage & Willie Thomas, James Campbell, C. J. Chenier, Clifton Chenier (3), Albert Chevalier, John Delafose, K. C. Douglas, Canray Fontenot, Charles Ford Band, Preston Frank, Jesse Fuller, Earl Hooker, Lightnin' Hopkins (2), Bee Houston, John Jackson, Lil' Son Jackson, Mance Lipscomb (2), John Littlejohn, Fred McDowell, Fred McDowell & Johnny Woods, Alex Moore (2), Charlie Musselwhite, Piano Red, L. C. Robinson, Omar Sharriff, Robert Shaw, Robert Curtis Smith, Big Mama Thornton, Mercy Dee [Walton], Wade Walton & Robert Curtis Smith, Katie Webster, Booker White, Big Joe Williams (2), Johnny Young, others.* 54–4/00.

***(*) Blues Roots
Tomato TOM-3001 *Black Ace, Juke Boy Bonner, R. L. Burnside, Joe Callicott, Clifton Chenier, George Coleman, Jesse Fuller, Lowell Fulson, Guitar Slim [Alec Seward & Louis Hayes], Earl Hooker, Lightnin' Hopkins (2), John Jackson, Lil' Son Jackson, Mance Lipscomb, John Littlejohn, Fred McDowell, Alex Moore, Robert Shaw, R. C. Smith, Big Mama Thornton, [Big] Joe Turner, Mercy Dee [Walton], Bukka [Booker] White, [Big] Joe Williams, Johnny Young.* 48–11/68.

The story of Arhoolie Records is the story of its founder Chris Strachwitz, one of those stories people say could only happen in America. Born in Lower Silesia, Strachwitz grew up in Nevada, listening to hillbilly radio and collecting jazz records. In his 20s he recorded and issued an LP by Mance Lipscomb. Four and a half decades later the Arhoolie catalogue contains over 300 CDs. Wherever you look in the landscape of American vernacular music, Strachwitz has been there before, sometimes correcting the maps, sometimes drawing them himself. Without him, what would most of us know about *norteño* music, zydeco or 'sacred steel'? Even from the well-ploughed field of the blues he has harvested innumerable fine things: some of the best albums by Lightnin' Hopkins and Clifton Chenier, unquestionably the best work of Fred McDowell, Mance Lipscomb and Juke Boy Bonner. All these figures and idioms are represented in the 107 tracks on Arhoolie's *40th Anniversary* box, together with brass bands and ragtime orchestras from New Orleans, jazz from George Lewis to Sonny Simmons, Cajun music, gospel, bluegrass, old-timey, honkytonk, Tex-Mex *conjunto* music and more. (It's only for reasons of space that we have restricted the castlist above to artists found in this book.) Considered as a diary of a lifelong obsession with roots music and of 40 years spent recording it, the set is entirely fascinating, and the booklet, written by Elijah Wald and illustrated with Strachwitz's evocative photographs, is terrific. As to whether Chris Strachwitz is a great man, the verdict will be posterity's, but there can be no doubt that he is a great friend to great music.

But if you are less concerned with Strachwitz's journey than with what he found when he got there, and for you 'there' is strictly blues country, you'll want something shorter and more focused. You'll want *Blues Roots*. Apart from a few earlier recordings, by Jesse Fuller ('Got A Date At Half Past Eight', mistakenly credited to R. L. Burnside), Lowell Fulson, Guitar Slim and Joe Turner, to which Arhoolie acquired rights, the tracks come from Arhoolie albums recorded during the '60s, by artists who might be as celebrated as Hopkins, Chenier and Earl Hooker or as obscure as R. C. Smith and George Coleman. Twenty-six tracks are not enough to declare the full range of Strachwitz's taste or the reliability of his ear, but they do give the listener a fair idea of the extent and quality of Arhoolie's blues catalogue; more importantly, they meld into a hugely listenable 85 minutes. TR

Atlantic

**** Messing With The Blues
Ace CDCHD 773 *Ray Charles (3), Frank 'Floorshow' Culley, Larry Dale, Lucky Davis, Champion Jack Dupree (2), Jimmy Earle, Jimmy Griffin, Tiny Grimes, John Lee Hooker (2), Little Johnny Jones (5), Chuck Norris (2), Hal Paige, Joe Turner, Odelle Turner, T-Bone Walker (2).* 12/47–61.

*** Let The Boogie Woogie Rock 'N' Roll
Ace CDCHD 718 *Lavern Baker, Ruth Brown, Ray Charles, The Clovers, Frank 'Floorshow' Culley, Eunice Davis, Ivory Joe Hunter, George 'Mr Blues' Jackson, Willis 'Gator Tail' Jackson, Young Jessie [Obediah Jessie], Clyde McPhatter, Frankie Marshall (2), Joe Morris, Hal Paige, Pretty Boy [Don Covay], The Regals, Tommy Ridgley, Carmen Taylor, Mad Man Taylor, The Tibbs Brothers (2), The Tilters, Joe Turner, Odelle Turner.* 5/49–9/61.

Herb Abramson had a respectable track record as a producer, but Ahmet Ertegun, son of the Turkish ambassador to Washington and co-founder of Atlantic, was motivated by enthusiasm for jazz and black culture. Jerry Wexler, who came on board in 1953, was a writer for *Billboard*, where he coined the term 'rhythm and blues'. They turned out to have the right mix of enthusiasm, taste, awareness of trends and business acumen, and a label that was at least in part a fan enterprise became a very big business indeed. Atlantic has been a major player in jazz, soul and rock, and the label's blues output usually plays a small part when writers discuss its iconic status. As so often, there's an issue of definition here, and *Let The Boogie Woogie Rock 'N' Roll* is useful listening for readers wanting to contemplate the arbitrariness of the lines which this book and others have drawn among blues, R&B, jazz, black vocal groups and rock 'n' roll.

Messing With The Blues begins about as well as it could,

with the complete Little Johnny Jones session, where Elmore James does subtle, Johnny sings like a gravelly angel and J. T. Brown bleats as winningly as only he could. The Broomdusters also back Joe Turner's 'T.V. Mama', and there are superior selections from LPs by T-Bone and Champion Jack, and from Ray Charles's early days with the label. Apart from two intense John Lee Hooker sides purchased from Henry Stone, the second half of the CD contains obscurities and rarities. Most of them are good ones: the tough West Coast singer/guitarist Chuck Norris and the emotional Jimmy Earle (Brown, briefly Ruth Brown's bigamous husband) stand out, and Odelle Turner's 'Draggin' Hours' is a classic slow blues on the venerable theme of mistreatment by her man.

Turner's 'Alarm Clock Boogie' on *Let The Boogie Woogie Rock 'N' Roll* is a much lesser effort, though, and not the only track reflecting the process whereby hits generate imitators, in this case of Ruth Brown; Willis Jackson's 'Wine-O-Wine', though not in the same style as its progenitor, is obviously trying to cash in on Sticks McGhee's hit. The Clovers, The Regals and the Tibbs Brothers, from an area we've mostly excluded, are a hiply humorous pleasure to hear, and LaVern Baker's 'Hey Memphis' is an ingenious answer to Elvis's 'Little Sister', but the mix of famous and little-known artists is pitched at collectors, and the relentless emphasis on fast tempos aims to lure rock 'n' roll buffs. Less narrowly focused listeners may find the pace wearing, and only the most dedicated snapper-up of rarities will value Frankie Marshall and Mad Man Taylor ('the Rasputin of Boogie'). Don Covay's mediocre Little Richard imitation, Joe Morris's lumbering 'Beans And Cornbread' and Joe Turner's 'Bump Miss Susie', with its intrusive vocal chorus, don't represent the artists at their best either. CS

Atlas

**(*) Boogieology: The Atlas Records Story
Acrobat ACRCD 208 *King Cole (2), The Four Vagabonds, Luke Jones (15), Red Mack (2), Johnny Moore's Three Blazers (2), Oscar Moore (3), Red Murrell, Merle Travis.* 11/43–45/46.

A minor LA label of the mid-'40s, Atlas has a small place in black music history as an early patron of Nat 'King' Cole and Charles Brown, whose 'Tell Me You'll Wait For Me' was his first recorded vocal. Its blues catalogue, such as it was, was largely generated by Luke Jones, a saxophonist formerly with Roy Milton, and his mixed repertoire of slow blues, jump blues, boogies and novelty numbers quite faithfully echoes that of Milton and Louis Jordan. Jones's band profited from having several more than adequate vocalists, among them drummer George Vann, who specialized in the powerful delivery of slow blues, trumpeter Red Mack and a Clarence Williams. Apart from the svelte guitar playing of the Moores the music is derivative, but generally well performed. The quality of the source 78s is variable, but Dave Penny's notes are packed with information. TR

Atomic-H

**(*) Chicago Ain't Nothin' But A Blues Band
Delmark DE-624 *Eddy Clearwater (6), George [Corner] & His House Rockers (2), Henry Gray, Morris Pejoe (2), Harmonica George [Robinson] (2), Johnny Rogers, Little Mack Simmons,* *Sunnyland Slim (2), unknown, Jo Jo Williams (5).* c. 59–c. 60.

Atomic H was a small-scale Chicago label owned by Rev. H. H. Harrington, a West Side minister who had an interest in recording. One of his chief acts was his nephew Eddy Clearwater, at this stage a fervent admirer of Chuck Berry. Jo Jo Williams (born 1920), a trenchant singer and guitarist in the South Side style, is more impressive and, since these are his only readily available recordings, quite a good reason for buying the CD. (But note that the instrumental 'Davy Crockett's Jingle Bells' plays no part in that evaluation.) Of the two Georges, Corner is a deliberate guitarist while Robinson (born 1934) blows fierce harmonica on 'Sputnik Music', sings breathily on 'Sad And Blue' and is accompanied on both by the near-legendary Willie Johnson. There's also an intriguing slow blues, 'Why Did We Have To Part?', by unknown musicians, in a setting reminiscent of Cobra-period Magic Sam. TR

Bandera & Associated Labels

**(*) Blues And Gospel From The Bandera, Laredo And Jerico Road [sic] Labels Of Chicago
Ace CDCHD 808 *Dusty Brown (4), Bobby Davis (4), Faithful Wanderers (3), Norfleet Brothers (2), Elder Samuel Patterson (3), Grover Pruitt (2), Jimmie Lee Robinson (7), Space Spiritual Singers (2).* 58–67.

Chicago-based Bandera and its associated labels were operated by mother-and-son team Vi Muszynski and Bernie Harville. There are no masterpieces and some pop dross among Jimmie Lee Robinson's six songs, but the spare playing and tricky vocal intervals identify him as a man already following his own road, sometimes to strange destinations. He's at his most compelling on 'All My Life', with its echoes of Otis Rush. Harp player Dusty Brown's issued single is weaker than two sides that were kept back, which is not untypical; Harville and Muszynski seem to have wanted an unchallenging sound from their artists, and one of Bobby Davis's singles was even advertised as 'pop blues'. The titles are the best thing about Davis's 'Hype You Into Selling Your Head' and Grover Pruitt's 'Mean Train', whose combination of lap steel and Bo Diddley riffs promises far more than it delivers. The CD's strongest tracks are the gospel songs, seven by hard-hitting quartets and three by a thrilling electric guitar evangelist. CS

Bea & Baby

*** Meat & Gravy From Bea & Baby
Castle CMDDD 610 2CD *Eddie Boyd (8), Arelean Brown (2), Jimmy Cotton (2), Detroit Jr (2), Tall Paul Hankins, Homesick James (3), Earl Hooker, Willie Hudson (2), L. C. McKinley (2), Andrew McMahon (4), Bobby Saxton, Little Mac [Simmons] (8), Singin' Sam, Sunnyland Slim (7), Hound Dog Taylor (2), Willie Williams (4).* 60–72.

(***) Best Of Bea & Baby Volume 1
Wolf 120.293 *Eddie Boyd (6), James Cotton (2), Homesick James (3), Earl Hooker, L. C. McKinley, Andrew McMahon, Bobby Saxton, Little Mac [Simmons] (4), Sunnyland Slim (2), Hound Dog Taylor (2), Willie Williams (2).* 60–72.

(***) Best Of Bea & Baby Volume 2
Wolf 120.294 *Eddie Boyd (2), Ar[e]lean Brown (2), Detroit Jr (2), Lee Jackson, Clyde Lasley, L. C. McKinley, Andrew*

McMahon (3), Little Mac [Simmons] (4), Sunnyland Slim (3). 60–72.

(**(*)) **Best Of Bea & Baby Volume 3**
Wolf 120.295 *Eddie Boyd (2), Cadillac Baby, Tall Paul Hankins, Willie Hudson, John Littlejohn (2), Menard Rogers (2), Little Mac [Simmons] (4), Singing Sam (2), Sunnyland Slim (2), Willie Williams (2). 60–72.*

In the '60s Narvel Eatmon, alias Cadillac Baby, was a minor player in the Chicago blues business, running a club and a record label. Though releases on Bea & Baby weren't widely enough distributed to threaten the dominance of Chess and Vee-Jay – the nearest the label came to a hit was Bobby Saxton's 'Trying To Make A Living', an impassioned blues with Earl Hooker on guitar – they did give exposure to Eddie Boyd and Little Mac[k] Simmons, as well as adding to the skimpy discographies of L. C. McKinley, Andrew McMahon and Hound Dog Taylor. Many of those recordings are discussed in the artists' entries, but it's fair to say that a Bea & Baby single is usually worth hearing, and the 50 gathered on Castle amount to something like an hour and a half of good, plain blues. Meat and gravy? Certainly meat and potatoes. The same tracks are also dispersed over the three volumes on Wolf, which add a few items for which Castle presumably didn't have room. The 2CD is the recommended purchase. TR

Blind Pig

*** **Blind Pig Records: 20th Anniversary Collection**
Blind Pig BPCD 2001 2CD *Luther Allison, Carey Bell, Boogie Woogie Red, Sarah Brown, Chris Cain, Eddie C. Campbell, Chubby Carrier, Tommy Castro, Otis Clay, Eddy Clearwater, Commander Cody, Deborah Coleman, Joanna Connor, James Cotton, Debbie Davies, Gospel Hummingbirds, Henry Gray, Buddy Guy & Junior Wells, John Lee Hooker, Walter Horton, Magic Slim & The Teardrops, Coco Montoya, Charlie Musselwhite, Pinetop Perkins, Preacher Boy, Snooky Pryor, Al Rapone, Jimmy Rogers, Roy Rogers, Otis Rush, E. C. Scott, Johnny Shines, Studebaker John & The Hawks, Roosevelt Sykes, Jimmy Thackery & The Drivers, Smokey Wilson. 77–97.*

*** **Blind Pig Records: 25th Anniversary Collection**
Blind Pig BPCD 2002 2CD + CD-ROM *Arthur Adams & B. B. King, Norton Buffalo, Chris Cain, Chubby Carrier, Tommy Castro, Tommy Castro & Delbert McClinton, Chicago Rhythm & Blues Kings, Deborah Coleman, Joanna Connor, James Cotton, Pee Wee Crayton, Debbie Davies & Albert Collins, Johnny Dyer, Gospel Hummingbirds, Lloyd Jones, Chris Thomas King, Magic Slim & The Teardrops, Bob Margolin, Memphis Rockabilly Band, Coco Montoya, John Mooney, Big Bill Morganfield & Taj Mahal, Muddy Waters, Pinetop Perkins, Bill Perry, Popa Chubby, Snooky Pryor, E. C. Scott, Johnny Shines, George 'Harmonica' Smith, Studebaker John & The Hawks, Jimmy Thackery & The Drivers, Jimmy Thackery & Joe Louis Walker, The Vipers, Mitch Woods. 77–02.*

Blind Pig squealed their entrance into the blues arena in 1977, taking their name from a blues club in Ann Arbor, Michigan, the Blind Pig Café. Their catalogue now holds well over a hundred albums of what the *20th Anniversary Collection* describes as 'blues, rhythm, and roots music'. Although their main thrust is into the blues market, with a roster headed by names like Magic Slim, Deborah Coleman, Studebaker John, Tommy Castro, Big Bill Morganfield and (until recently) Jimmy Thackery, they have picked up soul, gospel and zydeco acts as well as a few mavericks. All these idioms are represented on both of the anniversary collections, which are derived almost wholly from issued albums; the earlier set has four previously unissued cuts by Gray, Horton, Perkins and Sykes, while the later one has a CD-ROM containing videos of Castro, Popa Chubby and other acts, and interviews with Snooky Pryor and Muddy Waters (the latter beginning unpromisingly with the interviewer saying 'You're from Chicago, right?'). Like similar collections on Alligator, Delmark and Earwig, these CDs are designed primarily as progress reports and may not have much appeal for serious collectors, but for the starting-out blues fan they could be valuable samplings of a wide-ranging catalogue – rather like those lucky-dip packets of assorted stamps with which dealers woo the budding philatelist. TR

Chess

**** **Chess Blues**
MCA/Chess CHD4–9340 4CD *Alberta Adams, Billy Boy Arnold, The Big Three Trio, Eddie Boyd (2), John Brim, Eddie Burns, Detroit Junior, Floyd Dixon, Willie Dixon (2), Baby Face Leroy [Foster], Rocky Fuller [Louisiana Red], Lowell Fulson (2), Paul Gayten & Myrtle Jones, Lloyd Glenn, Henry Gray, Henry Gray & Morris Pejoe, Buddy Guy (2), John Lee Hooker (2), Walter Horton, Howlin' Wolf (10), Elmore James (2), Etta James (2), Gus Jenkins, Little Johnny Jones, Albert King, Lafayette Leake, J. B. Lenoir (2), Little Joe Blue, Little Milton (2), Little Walter (8), Willie Mabon (2), Memphis Minnie (2), Muddy Waters (12), Robert Nighthawk (2), Willie Nix, St Louis Jimmy [Oden], Forrest City Joe [Pugh], Jimmy Rogers (2), Dr Ross, Laura Rucker, Otis Rush, Clarence Samuels, Johnny Shines, Sonny Boy Williamson II (7), Otis Spann, Arbee Stidham, Sunnyland Slim (3), Forrest Sykes, Hound Dog Taylor, Koko Taylor (2), Andrew Tibbs, Jimmy Witherspoon. 47–9/67.*

**** **Chess Blues Legends 1947 To 1956** [sic]
MCA/Chess CHD-9369 *Bo Diddley, Eddie Boyd, Willie Dixon, Lowell Fulson, John Lee Hooker, Howlin' Wolf, Little Johnny Jones, J. B. Lenoir, Little Walter (2), Muddy Waters (4), Sonny Boy Williamson II, Jimmy Rogers. 4/48–12/56.*

***(*) **Chess Blues Legends 1957 To 1967**
MCA/Chess CHD-9368 *Buddy Guy, John Lee Hooker, Howlin' Wolf (3), Elmore James, Etta James (2), Little Milton, Little Walter, Muddy Waters (2), Otis Rush, Sonny Boy Williamson II (2), Koko Taylor. 2/57–8/67.*

***(*) **The Chess Blues-Rock Songbook**
MCA/Chess MCD 09389 2CD *Bo Diddley (3), Chuck Berry (5), Eddie Boyd, John Brim, Bobby Charles, Sugar Boy Crawford, Willie Dixon, Lowell Fulson, Dale Hawkins, John Lee Hooker, Howlin' Wolf (4), Elmore James, Etta James, J. B. Lenoir, Little Milton, Little Walter, Willie Mabon (2), Memphis Slim, Muddy Waters (4), Jimmy Rogers, Sonny Boy Williamson II (2), Tommy Tucker. 50–8/67.*

(****) **The Chess Story 1947–1956**
MCA/Chess 112 694 5CD *Tom Archia, Chuck Berry (3), Jimmy Binkley, The Blue Jays, Blue Smitty, Bo Diddley (3), Eddie Boyd (2), Jackie Brenston (2), John Brim, Buddy & Claudia, Eddie Burns, Bobby Charles, The Coronets, Sugar Boy Crawford, The Dozier Boys (2), The Five Blazes, The Flamingos, Harmonica Frank [Floyd], Leroy Foster, Lowell Fulson (3), The Hawketts,*

John Lee Hooker (3), Howlin' Wolf (6), Jump Jackson, Elmore James, Duke Jenkins, Jimmy [Lee] & Johnny [Mathis], Floyd Jones, Little Johnny Jones, Jimmy Lee & Wayne Walker, J. B. Lenoir, Larry Liggett, Little Walter (11), Billy Love, Willie Mabon (3), Sax Mallard, Mitzi Mars, Percy Mayfield, Memphis Minnie, Memphis Slim, The Moonglows (3), Muddy Waters (20), Jimmy Nelson, Robert Nighthawk (2), Willie Nix, St Louis Jimmy [Oden], Danny Overbea, Doc Pomus, Forrest City Joe [Pugh], The Rays, Jimmy Rogers (6), Laura Rucker (2), Clarence Samuels, Johnny Shines, Sonny Boy Williamson II (2), Otis Spann, Big Boy Spires, Sunnyland Slim (2), Forrest Sykes, Leon D. Tarver & The Chordones, Rufus Thomas, Andrew Tibbs (2), Bobby Tuggle, Washboard Sam, Charles 'Hungry' Williams, Joe Williams [Joseph Goreed], Jimmy Witherspoon. 47–56.

(****) **The Chess Story 1957–1964**
MCA/Chess 112 695 5CD Lee Andrews & The Hearts, Billy 'Curley' Barrix, Fontella Bass & Bobby McClure, Rod Bernard, Chuck Berry (13), Bo Diddley (10), Jan Bradley, Buster Brown, The Calvaes, Jackie Cannon, Bobby Charles, Clifton Chenier, Bobby Cisco, Tony Clarke, Mitty Collier, L. C. Cooke, Cookie & The Cupcakes, The Corsairs, Dave 'Baby' Cortez, G. L. Crockett, Sugar Pie DeSanto (2), Floyd Dixon, Willie Dixon, Eddie Bo, The Flamingos (2), Eddie Fontaine, Johnny Fuller, Lowell Fulson, Paul Gayten, Buddy Guy (3), Dale Hawkins (3), Clarence 'Frogman' Henry (2), Howlin' Wolf (8), Ty Hunter, Betty James, Elmore James, Etta James (4), Etta James & Harvey Fuqua, The Jaynettes, Lou Josie, The Kendall Sisters, Al Kent, Albert King, The Knight Brothers, J. B. Lenoir, Little Milton, Little Walter (3), Jimmy McCracklin (2), The Marathons, The Miracles, Billy Miranda, Stanley Mitchell & The Tornados, The Moonglows (5), The Monotones, Muddy Waters (6), Myles & Dupont, The Pastels, The Radiants, The Ravens, Lula Reed (2), Mel Robins, Jimmy Rogers, Jackie Ross, Otis Rush, Bobby Saxton, The Sensations, Gene Simmons, The Sonics, Sonny Boy Williamson II (7), Billy Stewart (2), T.V. Slim, Joe Tex, Tommy Tucker, The Tuneweavers, The Vibrations, Rusty York. 57–64.

(***(*)) **The Chess Story 1965–1975**
MCA/Chess 112 696 5CD Kip Anderson, Barbara & The Browns, Fontella Bass, Chuck Berry (2), Big Maybelle, Bo Diddley, Solomon Burke, Terry Callier, Gene Chandler, Tony Clarke, Wayne Cochran, Sam Dees, The Dells (6), Big Al Downing, The Dramatics, Lee Eldred, John Lee Hooker (2), Howlin' Wolf (2), Etta James (3), Etta James & Sugar Pie DeSanto, The Knight Brothers, Laura Lee (2), Ramsey Lewis (2), Little Joe Blue, Little Milton (6), John Littlejohn, Bobby McClure, Pigmeat Markham, Maurice & Mac, Bobby Moore & The Rhythm Aces (2), Muddy Waters (4), James Phelps, The Radiants, Jimmy Ruffin, Johnny Sayles, Marlena Shaw, Billy Stewart (2), Hound Dog Taylor, Koko Taylor (3), Irma Thomas (2), Tommy Tucker, The Valentinos, Willie Walker, Andre Williams. 65–2/75.

It can be argued that Chess is the Robert Johnson of record labels: over-emphasized and sometimes over-hyped, endlessly recycled, barnacled with legends and namechecked by *ignorati* anxious to establish their cred. And yet – also like Robert Johnson – in an active life that was fairly short, Chess produced music of vast artistic and historical importance, whose effects have continued to reverberate in unexpected places ever since. When Phil and Leonard Chess bought into the Aristocrat label, they were aware, from Leonard's nightclub operations, of an market for records that wasn't being served. Aristocrat's founding partners were soon bought out, and the label stopped trying to break acts like polka band Lee Monti & The Tu Tones, but its early years, before the change of name to Chess, were like those of many another small label in the postwar era. Company policy, sensibly enough, seems to have been to record anyone who came through the door and sounded promising; the Chess brothers also purchased material from independent producers in the South, like Paul Gayten, Sam Phillips and Stan Lewis, and bought up the assets of other Chicago labels that failed.

It was Muddy Waters's 'I Can't Be Satisfied' that gave Chess – then still Aristocrat – its first big hit, despite Leonard's initial reluctance to release it. As a result, and subject to all sorts of exceptions and qualifications that there's no room to go into here, the course for Chicago blues recording was set away from the jump blues of Andrew Tibbs and Tom Archia, and towards electric band blues. Members of Muddy's band like Jimmy Rogers and Little Walter also made classic recordings, Walter struck out on his own after 'Juke', and the signing of Howlin' Wolf and Sonny Boy Williamson completed a core blues roster of unparalleled greatness. As popular tastes evolved, Chuck Berry and Bo Diddley were added to the mix, supplying rock 'n' roll to both the African-American and the new, much-coveted white teen market; Berry gave Chess its only #1 pop hit – but that was in 1972, and it was 'My Ding-a-Ling'. Oh well.

In 1954 Willie Dixon joined the company as songwriter, bassist, recording artist, A&R man and – more often than he got credit for – producer. The Chess brothers have taken some stick over the years for allegedly swindling artists out of royalties, but in this regard they were probably no worse than any other company of the time, and better than some. What does reveal the limits of their generosity is that Dixon was kept on salary, rather than being made a company officer and given a stake in the business. That's not to say that Dixon was an unmitigated good; his fluency and his ability to write songs that were tailored to specific artists sometimes resulted in unchallenging sessions, and his fondness for bright sounds, busy rhythms and imagery that was more clever than emotionally committed could also be disadvantageous. Equally, though, to say these things is not to deny that the combination of Chess and Dixon resulted in a multitude of great recordings through the '50s and '60s.

By the end of the '60s Chess was having trouble selling the blues to black audiences, and Phil's son Marshall's attempts to rebrand Muddy and Wolf for the hippies, with *Electric Mud* and the album Wolf famously called 'dogshit', were just the most obvious symptoms of trouble. The company's engagement with soul was far more successful, with Little Milton (making the transition from blues), Etta James and Fontella Bass the headliners, but in 1968 Leonard and Phil decided to concentrate on their radio business, and sold the company to GRT shortly before Leonard's sudden death. Blues usually took a back seat as GRT tried to keep things going before selling out to All Platinum, who turned the company into the reissue-only label it's been ever since. In the '80s Chess passed through the hands of Sugar Hill en route to its present owners, MCA (now Universal).

As has been implied, there was more to Chess and its subsidiary marques than blues; as well as soul music, Chess issued many doo-wop classics, was a significant player in gospel music and sermons, made important jazz recordings, cracked the white rock 'n' roll market with Dale Hawkins's 'Susie Q' and even dabbled (briefly and half-heartedly) in country music. Still, blues is what Chess is famous for, and for novices the two volumes of *Chess Blues Legends*, issued as part of the *50th Anniversary Collection*, make a compact and reasonably priced introduction to the big names, equipped with informed notes. A raucously obvious Etta James interpretation of Jimmy Reed on the second disc is the only unwise inclusion.

The *Blues-Rock Songbook* is a self-compiling collection of 'the classic originals' covered by rock musicians. This entails perhaps too much Chuck Berry for some tastes, and confines Sonny Boy Williamson to the late recordings 'Bring It On Home' and 'Help Me', which are, it needn't be said, fine performances. So are most of the other tracks here, although 'Susie Q' seems increasingly crude and formulaic, and Bobby Charles's 'See You Later Alligator' is famous for being famous. The use of Willie Dixon's version of 'Wang Dang Doodle' at the expense of Koko Taylor's is imaginative, although Howlin' Wolf's would have been preferable to either. This CD was part of a *Chess Legendary Masters* series whose availability is patchy; if it can be found, the deleted *Aristocrat Of The Blues: The Best Of Aristocrat Records* (MCA/Chess MCD 09387) is highly recommended.

These are all good entry-level compilations; at the opposite extreme of coverage are the three volumes of *The Chess Story*, released in Europe in 2001. (In summer 2005, Universal's Hip-O division announced the import of 300 sets to the US.) The sound quality is marvellous and the notes thorough and reliable, though surprisingly brief; the final two discs in 1965–1975 are interviews with Phil and Marshall and a decidedly meagre CD-ROM. These collections are for listeners who want the whole ball of wax – up to a point; there are vocal groups aplenty, and even some examples of Chess's abortive fling with country music, but no gospel music, and, if a place could be found for 'My Ding-a-Ling', the omission of Gene Ammons and Big Bill Broonzy seems cavalier. The merits of *The Chess Story* will be obvious, and it's no denigration of the project to observe that its purchasers will need to have deep pockets, catholic tastes, a certain amount of scholarly interest and at times a penchant for the obscure.

A sensible middle course is traced by *Chess Blues*, and by its companion volume, *Chess Rhythm & Roll* (MCA/Chess CHD 4-9352 4CD), which is deleted but can still be tracked down. *Rhythm & Roll* contains much music that's customarily defined these days as blues, including material by Berry, Bo Diddley, Jackie Brenston and Tommy Tucker; it also features many of the vocal groups included in *The Chess Story*, and should be actively sought out. For an in-depth, authoritatively annotated but accessible account of Chess blues as more narrowly defined, though, readers need look no further than, well, *Chess Blues*. Even here, Big Bill and his old buddy Washboard Sam (who sneaked into *The Chess Story*) seem to be beyond the pale, but these four CDs are a very adroitly compiled mix of the hits that couldn't be missed and the masterpieces that didn't sell so well. CS

Cobra

**(*) Goin' Down To Eli's: The Cobra & Abco Rhythm & Blues Anthology 1956–1958
[Westside WESA 868] *Harold Burrage (3), Charles Clark (2), Willie Dixon, Betty Everett (3), Little Willie Foster (2), Guitar Shorty (2), Freddie Hall, Shakey Horton (2), Lee Jackson (2), Clarence Jolly, Louie Meyers [Louis Myers] & The Aces (2), Memphis Slim (2), Morris Pejoe (2), Sonny Boy Williamson II (2), Arbee Stidham (2), Sunnyland Slim (2).* 56–58.

Eli Toscano's Cobra label briefly threatened to become a force on the Chicago scene after the success of its first release, Otis Rush's 'I Can't Quit You Baby'. Innovative production by Willie Dixon, not too much hampered – sometimes arguably enhanced – by the shoebox acoustic of whatever studio he used, gave the recordings of Rush and Magic Sam, Cobra's other star, tremendous presence. Unfortunately the rest of the roster wasn't so exciting, as becomes clear from this tight-packed (31 tracks!) anthology, since Rush and Sam are excluded, having Westside releases of their own. Charles Clark, though not much of a singer, gets a typical Dixon production and a stellar band including Shakey Horton; Little Willie Foster makes a forceful coupling; Horton himself, Sunnyland and Lee Jackson are up to par; but much of the rest of the output is workaday, and the listener gradually realizes that the label didn't have the stuff of survival. Nor did its owner, who in 1959 was found floating in Lake Michigan. The 'Eli Toscano Blues' that concludes this set isn't by him, but a genially abusive verse about him sung by Dixon. The tracks by Hall, Myers, Pejoe and Stidham were done during Toscano's association with Abco and are discussed above. TR

Delmark

*** Delmark Records: 45 Years Of Jazz And Blues
Delmark DD-903 2CD *Lurrie Bell, Jimmy Burns, Karen Carroll, Little Sammy Davis, Jimmy Dawkins & Big Voice Odom, Magic Sam, Floyd McDaniel, Aaron Moore, Johnny B. Moore, Robert Nighthawk, The Rockin' Johnny Band, Byther Smith, Dave Specter & Lenny Lynn, Junior Wells, James Wheeler, Mighty Joe Young, others.* 47–1/98.

***(*) Delmark Records: 50 Years Of Jazz And Blues
Delmark DD-904/905 4CD *Luther Allison, Albert Ammons, Carey Bell, Lurrie Bell, The Big Doowopper, Big Time Sarah, Eddie Burns, Jimmy Burns, Karen Carroll, Sleepy John Estes, Jesse Fortune, Steve Freund, J. B. Hutto, Syl Johnson, Willie Kent, Little Milton, Little Walter, Magic Sam, Johnny B. Moore, Frank Morey, The Moroccos, Reginald R. Robinson, Otis Rush, Speckled Red, Dave Specter, Sunnyland Slim, Roosevelt Sykes, Tail Dragger, Robert Ward, Junior Wells, Big Joe Williams, Edith Wilson, Zora Young, others.* 39–2/03.

It was originally a jazz label, based in St Louis and called Delmar (after the street), but once its owner Bob Koester moved to Chicago, opening a record store in 1959, it was only a matter of time before it engaged with the blues. The early albums were by old-timers like Big Joe Williams and Sleepy John Estes but by 1965 Delmark (as it was now called) had caught up with Junior Wells, by 1967 Magic Sam, and in due course Jimmy Dawkins, Luther Allison and many others. Koester has maintained both the label and the store ever since, an unbroken commitment to the blues that few men can match. In doing so, he's also raised many of the next generation of Chicago recording men: Bruce Iglauer (Alligator) and Michael Frank (Earwig) are just two of the ex-employees of Koester's Jazz Record Mart who went on to found their own labels.

Delmark has kept faith with its origins by continuing to

record jazz, and only space considerations prevent us listing the jazz content of these collections, which is considerable and wide-ranging. On *45 Years* it occupies the whole of Disc 1, thereby making bedfellows of George Lewis and Sun Ra, while on *50 Years* it fills two CDs, again ranging from New Orleans traditional to Chicago avant-garde. (Delmark was an early supporter of local musicians like Roscoe Mitchell and Muhal Richard Abrams.) The dozen blues tracks on *45 Years* are mainly by then current acts, whereas the more spacious *50 Years* accommodates Big Joe Williams and Sleepy John Estes, both heard in previously unissued performances, as well as some of the older recordings that Delmark has acquired along the way, by Little Walter and Albert Ammons. TR

Dolphin's Of Hollywood Labels

(*) Blues From Dolphin's Of Hollywood
Specialty SPCD 2172 *Little [Harry] Caesar (2), Pee Wee Crayton (9), Floyd Dixon (2), Peppermint Harris (2), Percy Mayfield (3), Memphis Slim (4), Jimmy Witherspoon (4).* 1/53–c. 56.

Dolphin's Of Hollywood was a record store owned by African-American businessman John Dolphin. Among its products were discs on his own labels: Recorded In Hollywood, Cash, Money and Lucky. Dolphin had a few national hits, but was usually a big aquatic mammal in a small pond. His business methods proved that black entrepreneurs could bilk the talent as ruthlessly as white ones; in 1958 he was murdered by an aggrieved songwriter.

Pee Wee Crayton's tracks are mostly laidback, and none the worse for making sparing use of his trademark fast figuration. Little Caesar's tale of murder and suicide, 'Goodbye Baby', was a #5 hit for Recorded In Hollywood, but seems to have been omitted for fear of giving offence; what's here is entertaining, but much more routine. Floyd Dixon imitates Fats Domino, not well, and Peppermint Harris is better on the jump blues 'Cadillac Funeral' than wending lugubriously through his composition 'Treat Me Like I Treat You'. That tune gets a better reading from Memphis Slim, who also contributes notable versions of the much-recorded 'Worried Life Blues' and his own 'My Country Girl', but lets himself down with a chaotic 'Pete's Boogie'. Jimmy Witherspoon does his best with the absurd 'Teenage Party'; his other tracks are proper blues for grown-ups, as, of course, are Percy Mayfield's two songs. (Mayfield's third item is a WDIA station ident.) This collection was also issued as Ace CDCHD 357 (deleted). CS

Downey

**** Downey Blues**
HMG HMG 5504 *Chuck Higgins (2), Jessie Hills (6), Ace Holder (5), Little Johnny Taylor (2), T-Bone Walker Jr [R. S. Rankin] (3).* c. 61–64.

Bill Wenzel's main label was named after the suburb of LA where his record shop was located. There were also subsidiaries like Midnite, where T-Bone Walker's nephew and sometime valet appeared. Naturally influenced by his famous uncle, Rankin also takes note of B. B. King. His tracks are minor but likeable, as are those by Ace Holder, an uncomplicated admirer of Little Walter and Sonny Boy Williamson II. Little Johnny Taylor's unissued session was recorded before he'd acquired the authority that made 'Part Time Love' a hit and Taylor an enduring star. With 'Pachuko Hop' and stardom long past, Chuck Higgins contributes two sax instrumentals, also previously unissued. They're like hundreds of other such, but it's Jessie Hill's silly novelty songs that make *Downey Blues* a CD for masochistic completists. CS

Earwig

**** Earwig Music: 20th Anniversary Collection**
Earwig CD 4946 2CD *Willie Anderson, Jim Brewer, Big Leon Brooks, Aron Burton (2), Mad Dog Lester Davenport, Jimmy Dawkins, Johnny Drummer, David Honeyboy Edwards (2), H-Bomb Ferguson, Frank Frost, Liz Mandville Greeson (2), Homesick James, Jelly Roll Kings, Big Jack Johnson (2), Floyd Jones, Johnny Yard Dog Jones, Willie Kent, Louisiana Red (3), Lovie Lee, Little Brother Montgomery, Louis Myers, John Primer, Sunnyland Slim (2), Lil Ed Williams.* 42, 74–99.

Michael Frank's Earwig label has doggedly promoted many unfashionable figures, a dedication to which this 31-track collection is an eloquent testimony. It might well be asked who would have instigated albums by artists like Johnny Yard Dog Jones, Willie Anderson, Big Leon Brooks, Lovie Lee and H-Bomb Ferguson. At any rate, no one else did, and lovers of undeservedly obscure bluesmen should recognize their debt to this feisty Chicago label. Apart from Jim Brewer's track, from an LP that has not been transferred to CD, all the cuts are from available CDs, but if you're not familiar with the Earwig catalogue this will give you several reasons to start writing a wants list. TR

Elko

(*) Elko Blues Vol. 1
Wolf 120.614 *Clifton Chenier (4), Jesse Fuller (2), Smokey Hogg (2), Elmon Mickle (5), Jimmy Nolen Band, George 'Harmonica' Smith (3), Phillip Walker (4), Jimmy Wilson (2).* 53–c. 60.

(*) Elko Blues Vol. 2
Wolf 120.615 *Clifton Chenier (2), Jesse Belvin, Little Willie Egan (2), Beatrice Hill & J. D. Nicholson (2), James Hill, Hollywood Flames, George 'Harmonica' Smith (3), Jesse Thomas, Big Son Tillis & D. C. Bender (6), Mac Willis (2).* 51–56.

**** Elko Blues Vol. 3**
Wolf 120.616 *Ray Agee (5), James Butler (Black Diamond), Lowell Fulson (2), Goldrush, Slim Green (2), Wilma Gene Hill, John Hogg, Jimmy McCracklin (9), George 'Harmonica' Smith.* 45–c. 53.

J. R. Fullbright (1900–1970), a one-time drummer from Oklahoma, recorded many artists from the Southwestern states for his LA-based labels, the most important of which was Elko. Often these were the artist's first sessions: Clifton Chenier and Phillip Walker open their recording accounts on *Vol. 1*, Mac Willis on *Vol. 2*, Jimmy McCracklin and Slim Green on *Vol. 3*. *Vol. 1* also has previously unissued sides by Jesse Fuller and Smokey Hogg; the latter's 'Blue And Lonesome Blues' has a ring of Joe Pullum, a resonance also to be detected on *Vol. 2* in the sides by Mac Willis. The centrepiece of *Vol. 2* is half a dozen sides by Tillis & Bender, a very downhome couple of singer/guitarists. A number of vocalists on *Vol. 2* and *Vol. 3* are accompanied by the pianist J. D. Nicholson, among them McCracklin and Ray Agee. Nicholson was Fullbright's godson, but his playing on Agee's 'Black Night Is Gone' and

McCracklin's stylistically thrown-back 'Miss Mattie Left Me' dissolves any suspicions of nepotism. *Vol. 3* closes with some of Fullbright's earliest recordings, such as Slim Green's 'Alla Blues', a variant of Jimmy Wilson's 'Tin Pan Alley', and the enigmatic Goldrush, a singer and pianist – are they one man or two? – who hark(s) back to Roosevelt Sykes in 'All My Money Gone'. All the recordings on these three CDs are rare and many of them are interesting, but the quality of the original pressings was usually poor. TR

Excello

***(*) The Real Excello R & B
[Ace CDCHD 562] Jimmy Anderson (2), Leon Austin, Charles Friday, Earl Gaines, Al Garner, Arthur Gunter, Silas Hogan (2), Lazy Lester, Lightnin' Slim (2), Lonesome Sundown (2), Jay Nelson, Charles Sheffield, Roscoe Shelton (2), Slim Harpo (3), Whispering Smith (2), Sweet Clifford [Curry]. 54–66.

**** Ernie's Record Mart
Ace CDCHD 684 Jimmy Birdsong, Larry Birdsong, Chuck Brown [Bernard 'King Karl' Jolivette], Lattimore Brown (3), Earl Gaines, Al Garner (2), Good Rockin' Sam [Beasley], Rudy Green (2), Guitar Red, Arthur Gunter (2), Ralph Harris, Ted Jarrett, Jerry McCain, Lillian Offitt, John R. [Richbourg], The Solotones (2), Sugar & Sweet, Eddie Williams (2). 55–61.

***(*) Located In The Record Center Of The South
[Ace CDCHD 686] Johnny Angel, Classie Ballou, Carol Fran (2), Earl Gaines (2), The Gladiolas, Good Rockin' Sam [Beasley], Rudy Green, Guitar Gable [Perrodin], Guitar Gable [Perrodin] with King Karl [Bernard Jolivette], Lazy Lester (2), Lonesome Sundown (2), Jerry McCain (3), Jay Nelson, Lillian Offitt, Slim Harpo (2), Leroy Washington (2). 55–66.

**** Genuine Excello R & B
Ace CDCHD 678 Jimmy Anderson (2), Blue Charlie [Morris] (2), Silas Hogan, Joe Johnson (2), Lazy Lester (5), Lightnin' Slim, Lonesome Sundown (3), Jay Nelson, Slim Harpo, Whispering Smith (2), Tabby Thomas, Leroy Washington (3). 56–66.

**(*) Blues For Hippies?
Ace CDCHD 504 Willie Baker, Rose Davis, Jimmy Dawkins (6), Charles Friday (4), Marion James, Bobby Powell, Slim Harpo (2), Otis Spann (2), James Stewart, Tabby Thomas (3), Tiny Watkins, Mildred Woodard. 9/65–7/72.

Excello is patchily represented on VACs at the time of writing: Ace's discs, the product of a licensing deal with AVI, are disappearing as they sell out, and a six-volume *Excello Story* on Universal's Hip-O label is deleted; so is the excellent *Blues Hangover: Excello Blues Rarities* (Excello CD 2002 2CD), issued by AVI before the label was sold to Universal. For *No Jive: Authentic Southern Country Blues* (Ace CDCHD 652) see DOWNHOME.

To British fans of a certain age, Excello is virtually synonymous with the swamp blues produced by Jay Miller in Crowley, Louisiana, and licensed to the label (see LOUISIANA for *Louisiana Roots: The Jay Miller R&B Legacy* [Ace CDCHD 682]); but in fact Excello, owned until 1966 by Ernie Young, was based in Nashville, where Young also operated the eponymous Ernie's Record Mart; the store did boffo mail-order business, thanks in part to DJ John Richbourg's energetic plugging via WLAC's 50,000 watts.

The Real Excello R & B takes account of the wider picture, including tracks by Tennesseans Austin, Friday, Gaines, Garner, Gunter, Shelton and Sweet Clifford, but the emphasis is on Miller's artists. In this, the disc echoes its progenitor LP: issued on Stateside in the '60s, *The Real R & B* and its predecessor *Authentic R & B* (basis of the splendid but deleted *Authentic Excello R & B* [Ace CD CHD 492]) were inspirations to the contemporary British blues scene. The Tennessee artists on *The Real* make good music – although Gaines's 1962 remake of 'It's Love Baby (24 Hours A Day)' is a touch less exultant than the original, which is on *Ernie's Record Mart* – but they slightly disrupt the unity of the collection. *Genuine Excello R & B* is exclusively Miller productions; *Located In The Record Center Of The South* is half-and-half, the first half being Nashville and the second Crowley.

What the music on these three CDs has in common is attention to detail. Some tracks are trivial responses to commercial trends (Sugar and Sweet's Shirley & Lee knock-off, Jimmy Anderson's 'Frankie & Johnny' on *Genuine*, Johnny Angel's unconvincing Johnny Ace imitation), but it's still clear that each number is getting considered attention from producers and musicians alike. As a result, the way the finished product sounds is usually the way it ought to sound. Lazy Lester isn't suited to the kitsch self-pity of 'Courtroom Blues' on *Genuine*, and the cheesy organ obbligato is all too appropriate, but this track's failure is uncharacteristic. As evidence of Young's producing talent, there's his use of Louis Brooks's accomplished and versatile Hi-Toppers as his studio band in the early years; at the other extreme, there's the decision to let Jimmie Sheffield's thunderous drumming dominate Jerry McCain's records. It's very seldom that the record-buying public's intelligence is insulted by the material that Excello issued on singles, and the high quality of the many tracks only issued much later on research-driven LPs and CDs is further evidence that Miller and Young saw quality as the route to profitability.

Blues For Hippies? surveys Excello's blues releases after Young sold the label to Crescent. The target audience was still black and Southern, but tracks by Dawkins and Spann were produced by Mike Vernon, whose Blue Horizon had issued LPs of the swamp-blues artists in Britain. This CD is a mixed bag: Otis Spann's 'Bloody Murder', with Horton, Shines, Dixon and Clifton James, is significant work; not so the title track, with members of Fleetwood Mac. Dawkins's tracks, recorded in London, were an attempt to synthesize Hi's rhythms with the Albert King of Stax and Dawkins's own shrill West Side sound, in the hope of appealing to black radio stations; 'The Things I Used To Do', incongruously kitted out with a chugging shuffle beat, got airplay but not sales. Tabby Thomas, overlaying soul on swamp blues, does a better but not outstanding job of reinventing himself. Tiny Watkins's rock-blues is derivative of Hendrix, and has dated badly. Most of the other artists are minor (Slim Harpo is a major artist, here doing minor work), but B. B. King disciple Charles Friday and Rose Davis, fiercely involved with 'Sittin' And Drinkin'', are worth notice. CS

Federal

**(*) Chicago Blues From Federal Records
Ace CDCHD 717 Eddie [Eddy] Clearwater (2), Bobby King (4), Willie Mabon (4), Smokey Smothers (4), Kid Thomas (8). 57–64.

**(*) Welcome To The Club
Ace CDCHD 1009 *Jesse Anderson (2), Eddy Clearwater (2), Syl Johnson (6), Danny Overbea, Lee 'Shot' Williams (4), Willie Wright & The Sparklers (9).* 60–64.

Federal was a King subsidiary and didn't have a great deal to do with Chicago blues artists (with the obvious exception of Freddie King), so the contents of these CDs feel rather shoved together. The chief point of interest on the first is the four cuts by the little-recorded but obviously talented singer/guitarist Bobby King (1938–83), here betraying an admiration for Buddy Guy in 'Two Telephones' and a readiness to borrow from 'Hi Heel Sneakers' to get 'W-A-S-T-E-D'. Eddie (*sic*) Clearwater goes Berry-picking yet again, Smothers hides among the Reeds, and Mabon's and Thomas's tracks are discussed in their entries. *Welcome To The Club* is blurbed as 'tough blues and R&B shuffles from the finest young artists on Chicago's West Side in the early 1960s'; the description is accurate up to a point (see below), but there's no one as fine as the West Siders of a few years earlier like Magic Sam and Jimmy Dawkins. The outstanding blues tracks are by Syl Johnson; 'I Just Gotta Make Her Mine', 'I Wanna Know' and 'I've Got To Find My Baby' may be dull titles but Johnson's singing is fervid and his guitar playing, though numbed by the mix, has the authentic West Side cold steel edge. Drummer Willie Wright's band dispenses some decent slow blues and helter-skelter honking-sax tunes but they had nothing to do with Chicago, being Okies from, indeed, Muskogee. TR

Galaxy

***(*) All Night Long They Play The Blues
Ace CDCHD 440 *Charles Brown (2), Bill Coday, Rodger Collins, K. C. Douglas (2), Clay Hammond, Saunders King (2), J. J. Malone, Sonny Rhodes (2), The Right Kind, Merl Saunders, Clarence Smith [Sonny Rhodes], Little Johnny Taylor (4), Big Mama Thornton (2), Phillip Walker (2).* 62–71.

*** Diggin' Gold: A Galaxy Of West Coast Blues
Ace CDCHD 1017 *Del Cunningham (2), Good Time Charlie [Taylor], Clay Hammond (4), Joe Johnson (2), Billy Keene (2), Saunders King, Bill McAfee (2), Rob Robinson (3), Little Johnny Taylor (8).* 62–66.

Galaxy was a subsidiary of the San Francisco jazz label Fantasy. Around 1962 it switched its policy from jazz to R&B, and the following year it had a smash hit with Little Johnny Taylor's 'Part Time Love'. On *All Night Long They Play The Blues* that soul-blues anthem opens a sequence of well-made and superbly engineered singles, including three further blues-oriented numbers by Taylor, a swansong coupling by Saunders King, the title track and other solid blues by Sonny Rhodes and a fine arrangement of Percy Mayfield's 'Danger Zone' sung by J. J. Malone. The settings, in fact, often made all the difference to these recordings, house arranger Ray Shanklin having a sure touch with horns, and even the merely okay performances are worth listening to for the sheer craft of the production. *Diggin' Gold* is more of a collector's pick, eight of the tracks being previously unissued, and the blues:soul ratio is reversed, but there are impressive soul-blues tracks in the Taylor mould by Del Cunningham, Clay Hammond and Rob Robinson. TR

Goldband

(**(*)) The Goldband Blues Collection Part I
Collectables COL-CD-5087 *Elton Anderson (3), Juke Boy Bonner, Bobby Brown, Big Chenier [Morris Chenier] (2), Cookie & The Cupcakes (2), Shelton Dunaway (2), Clarence Garlow (3), Charles 'Mad Dog' Sheffield, Sticks Herman [Guidry] (3), Katie Webster & Ashton Savoy (2), Katie Webster with Cookie & The Cupcakes.* 57–61.

(**(*)) The Goldband Blues Collection Part II
Collectables COL-CD-5088 *Elton Anderson, Juke Boy Bonner (2), Big Chenier [Morris Chenier], Cookie & The Cupcakes, Thaddus Declouet (2), Clarence Garlow (3), King Charles & Left Handed Charlie [Morris], Left Handed Charlie [Morris] (2), Little Bob, Bill Parker & Ola Vaughn, Charles Perrywell, Charles 'Mad Dog' Sheffield (3), Al Smith (2), Sticks Herman [Guidry].* late 53–early 60s.

(**(*)) The Goldband Blues Collection Part III
Collectables COL-CD-5089 *Big Chenier [Morris Chenier] (2), Cookie & The Cupcakes, Thaddus Declouet, Shelton Dunaway, Nat Eckbert, Ivory Jackson, Little Miss Peggie (3), Scottie Milford (2), Blues Boy Palmer (2), Bill Parker & Ola Vaughn, Charles Perrywell, Rockin' Sidney (2), Hop Wilson (2), The Yellow Jackets.* c. 53–80s.

Eddie Shuler operated Goldband out of Lake Charles in southwest Louisiana, and his most important blues artists, Hop Wilson and Juke Boy Bonner, came from Houston, across the Texas state line. Shuler made significant recordings of musicians in other genres, among them Cajun accordionist Iry Lejune, and he produced Phil Phillips's swamp-pop million-seller 'Sea Of Love' for Khoury's, but, as he admitted, Shuler didn't know much about black music or its market. Some Goldband blues productions are gimmicky, and some of them suffer from out-of-tune instruments and odd sound balances. In addition, Collectables' three volumes are sloppily compiled; the inter-song gaps vary in length, some tracks are distant, and occasionally the stylus can be heard descending on a 45. *Part I* lists a Juke Boy Bonner track that isn't there, and Charles Sheffield's 'One Hour Thirty Minutes Too Long' appears on both *Part I* and *Part II*.

Stretching to three volumes means the inclusion of dross like Sticks Herman's drippy teen ballads. Thaddus Declouet's accompanists are literally and metaphorically out of tune with his archaic zydeco accordion, and Declouet returns the compliment on *Part III* when backing Big Chenier, whose 'Let Me Hold Your Hand' on *Part I* is an inferior remake with tweeting organ. It's not all bad: there's Bonner and Wilson, and on *Part III* Scottie Milford's '80s recordings, with Lonesome Sundown on guitar, sound like '50s classics; this disc also includes Rockin' Sidney's blue-collar soul-blues anthem 'Keep On Pushin'', a world away from his usual novelty zydeco. *Part I* is notable for 'Sunday Morning', one of Clarence Garlow's toughest blues, and for Katie Webster and Cookie (Huey Thierry) tussling over 'You Gonna Need Me'. On *Part II* Left Handed Charlie plays eloquent guitar on the acerbic 'But You Thrill Me' and an accomplished revival of Memphis Minnie's 'Bumble Bee', and Charles Perrywell's blues shouting, supported by a vocal group and a throaty tenor sax, is an unexpected treat. These pleasures must be dug out from the surrounding forgettables, however; most readers will do better with *Goin' Down To Louisiana: The Goldband Downhome Blues Anthology* (Ace CDCHD 821), for which see Juke Boy Bonner.

The deleted *Bayou Blues Blasters: Goldband Blues* (Ace CDCHD 427) is less consistent but worth looking out for. CS

J.O.B.

**** Rough Treatment – The J.O.B. Records Story
[Westside WESD 233] 2CD *Eddie Boyd (2), Grace Brim (2), John Brim (4), Ernest Cotton (2), Leroy Foster (4), John Lee [Henley] (2), Floyd Jones (4), Moody Jones (2), J. B. Lenoir (4), Little Hudson (4), Little Son Joe (2), Robert Jr Lockwood (4), Memphis Minnie (2), Little Brother Montgomery (2), Snooky Pryor (5), Johnny Shines (4), Sunnyland Slim (3), Alfred Wallace (2).* 49–58.

J.O.B. was founded in Chicago in 1949 by Joe Brown (1904–76), a businessman with large patches of fog in his personal history, and James Oden, the singer St Louis Jimmy. Although it had only one significant seller, Eddie Boyd's 'Five Long Years', and its production values were modest, over almost a decade it built a catalogue of blues recordings of enduring value: Johnny Shines's 'Ramblin' and three others hardly less astounding, major work by Leroy Foster, Sunnyland Slim, J. B. Lenoir, Robert Jr Lockwood and Floyd Jones, good things by Snooky Pryor and the Brims – J.O.B. consistently elicited performances from these artists that no other label would match. Most of them are discussed in individual entries, but it's worth adding that even the items by minor and entryless figures like Little Hudson (Showers) and John Lee Henley maintain the standard. Unlike Westside's Cobra anthology (see above) this 54-track set tells the full story of its subject; even artists who have larger shares in other Westside releases, like Pryor, Shines and Sunnyland Slim, are given decent coverage. Go to great lengths to find this – it's a vital part of postwar blues history. TR

King

**(*) 25 Years Of Rhythm And Blues Hits
Ember EMBCD 3359 *Annisteen Allen, LaVern Baker, Earl Bostic, Tiny Bradshaw, Roy Brown, Bill Doggett, Champion Jack Dupree, Wynonie Harris, John Lee Hooker, Ivory Joe Hunter, Lonnie Johnson, Lucky Millinder, Muddy Walters [Alex Thomas], The Platters, Sonny Thompson, Billy Ward & the Dominoes.* 47–57.

Though you will have to shout down a crowd of Chess fanatics and Sun-worshippers to make the point, King almost managed to be the most important American music label of the postwar era. The problem was geography: located in Cincinnati, it hardly heard the beat of Chicago blues or Memphis soul. On the other hand, it far outstripped both Chess and Sun in its coverage of Southern white music, be it bluegrass, Western Swing or hillbilly boogie, and it's the interaction between that half of the King catalogue and the blues list, and the label's practice of translating country songs into blues and vice versa, that gives the King team the right to be considered architects of rock 'n' roll no less important than Sun's Sam Phillips.

Unfortunately its present owners have not handled, or enabled licensees to handle, this remarkable catalogue with the creativity it deserves. In the more than 60 years since the King label first appeared on a 78, no comprehensive reissue has ever appeared that approaches the range of *The Chess Story* or *The Specialty Story*. A few boxed sets have been devoted to the label's leading bluegrass acts, but *The King R&B Box Set* (King KBSCD-7002 4CD), which was admirable as far as it went, seems to have disappeared. The only single CD representing the label's contribution to black music is Ember's erratic collection, which checks several important boxes (Lonnie Johnson's 'Tomorrow Night', Roy Brown's 'Hard Luck Blues', Wynonie Harris's 'Good Rockin' Tonight') and diversifies, as it should, into vocal-group music and sax instrumentals, but the sequencing is odd and some of the selections are poor, and altogether it's an unsatisfactory monument to an extraordinary enterprise. TR

La Salle

** The La Salle Chicago Blues Recordings Volume 2
Wolf 120.297 *Eddie Boyd (2), Eddie [Eddy] Clearwater (4), Jump Jackson, Sy Perry (2), Little Mac Simmons (2), King Solomon, Sunnyland Slim, Wilbur 'Hi-Fi' White.* 59–70.

Volume 1 (Wolf 120.296) is dealt with under Little Brother Montgomery and Sunnyland Slim. La Salle was owned by drummer Jump Jackson, who recorded some of his sessions in professional Chicago studios, and some in his garage. The instruments are often badly balanced, and the musicians sometimes in precarious touch with one another. Both faults affect tracks by the biggest names, Sunnyland Slim and Eddie Boyd. Eddy Clearwater imitates Ray Charles and Chuck Berry; Little Mac also does Berry, on a ridiculous arrangement of 'Driving Wheel'. Sy Perry is a minor West Side guitarist and Wilbur White a plummy ballad singer. 'Midnight Shuffle', credited to Jackson, features Floyd McDaniel, playing some pleasant guitar, and an organist apparently wearing boxing gloves. Only King Solomon, misidentified as his brother Lee Solomon (Little Wolf Jr), sings a good song that's well accompanied and well recorded. There are tape dropouts on a track each by Boyd and Clearwater. CS

Macy's

*** Queen Of Hits: The Macy's Recordings Story
Acrobat ACRCD 228 *Harry Choates, Clarence Garlow (4), Bill Grady, Art Gunn, Smokey Hogg (2), Cab McMillan (2), Curley Rash, Hubert Robinson (6), Tommy Scott (2), Barney Vordeman, Lester Williams (6).* 49–50.

Charles and Macy Henry had a record distributorship in Houston, Texas. In the two or three years of their label's life they issued a good deal of excellent blues and country material, mostly by local artists; country is represented on this set in the tracks by Choates, Grady, Gunn, Rash, Scott and Vordeman, all of them taken from a wider survey of hillbilly music on Macy's Recordings, *Cat'n Around* (Krazy Kat KK CD 07). All the blues sides are worthwhile. Clarence Garlow's are in the T-Bone Walker idiom and Hubert Robinson takes after Wynonie Harris; for Williams see his entry. TR

Modern

***(*) The Modern Records Story
Ace CDCHD 784 *Jesse Belvin, Richard Berry, The Cadets, The Cliques, Pee Wee Crayton, Lowell Fulson, Rosco Gordon, Shirley Gunter, Z. Z. Hill, John Lee Hooker, Lightnin' Hopkins, Joe*

Houston, Howlin' Wolf, The Ikettes, The Jacks, Elmore James (2), Etta James, B. B. King, Ira Mae Littlejohn, Marvin & Johnny, Jimmy McCracklin, The Teen Queens, Junior Thompson, Ike Turner, Ike & Tina Turner, Johnny 'Guitar' Watson, Young Jessie. 47–67.

The Bihari brothers' Modern operation out of LA was one of the most extensive catalogues of black music in the late '40s and '50s, embracing blues, doo-wop, gospel, novelty records and much else. *The Modern Records Story* is 28 vivid soundbites, mostly from the '50s, taken from Modern and four of its subsidiaries. As often with compilations like this, part of the fun of listening is the abrupt segue, from The Jacks to Howlin' Wolf, say, or from Ira Mae Littlejohn's apocalyptic 'Go Devil Go' to John Lee Hooker's 'In The Mood'. Anyone with a wide taste in black music of the period should find it vastly entertaining, especially if they've never heard the Cadets' brilliant 'Stranded In The Jungle'. For the four-volume series *The Modern Downhome Blues Sessions* see DOWNHOME. TR

Music Maker

***(*) Dixiefrog Presents Music Maker
Dixiefrog DFGCD 8597 2CD *Little Pink Anderson, Etta Baker, Branchettes, Essie Mae Brooks, Cora Mae Bryant (2), Captain Luke & Cool John (2), Drink Small, Frank Edwards, Preston Fulp, Guitar Gabriel (2), George Higgs, Algia Mae Hinton (2), John Dee Holeman (2), Marie Manning, Jerry McCain, Mother Pauline & Elder James Goins, Mr Q, Mudcat, Jack Owens, Neal Pattman (3), Pura Fé (3), Carl Rutherford (3), Sol (2), Cootie Stark, Samuel Turner Stevens, Sweet Betty [Journey].* 91?–02?

The Music Maker Relief Foundation, based in Hillsborough, North Carolina, promotes and supports 'aging musicians across the South, many of whom have been living in poverty for decades', but to say that may to be give readers a false impression of this set, which contains 38 pieces by 26 artists (almost all from Georgia or the Carolinas), drawn from Music Maker's back catalogue and previously unissued recordings. Unlike some collections of music by the poor and old, this is not a document of fading powers: octogenarians they may have been, but Neal Pattman's harmonica pieces and Etta Baker's banjo picking on 'Johnson Boys' are fine work by any standard, and many other elderly figures like John Dee Holeman, Cootie Stark and Cora Mae Bryant (qq.v.) are heard in good shape and high spirits. There's more to the set, though, than blues and rags by the amateur and the retired. It offers polished work by professionals like Jerry McCain and Sweet Betty Journey, the hardcore country songs of the former West Virginia miner Carl Rutherford, the gospel harmony of Mother Pauline & Elder James Goins and the Branchettes, and the small-town lounge music of Captain Luke and Mr Q. Nor is the programme confined to elderly men and women remembering old tunes: also present are Pura Fé, a guitar-playing singer who celebrates her Native American roots, and Sol, who remixes a couple of pieces by Guitar Gabriel.

This is a long programme (the total running time is 152.20), admirably varied and handsomely presented, with a booklet containing photographs and brief notes on the artists. Annoyingly, the recording information is confined to locations – no dates and, worse, no identification of the musicians heard backing the featured artists. Some, like the altoist Lee Konitz with Neal Pattman, can be pinned down without much trouble, but who are the harmonica player and guitarist with Sweet Betty on 'Coffee Drinkin' Blues', or the admirable old-time fiddler with Etta Baker? TR

Nashville Labels

*** Across The Tracks: Nashville R&B And Rock 'N' Roll
Ace CDCHD 493 *Gene Allison (3), Leevert Allison, Jimmy Beck & His Orchestra, Larry Birdsong (5), The Chellows, The Consolers, 'Little Shy Guy' Douglas, The Fairfield Four, Earl Gaines (2), Clenest Gant, Rudy Green, Chuck Harrod & The Anteaters, Herbert Hunter, Ted Jarrett, Johnny Keaton, Christine Kittrell, Little Ike, Lucille & The Strangers (2), Roscoe Shelton, Jimmy Tig & The Rounders.* 56–65.

*** Across The Tracks Volume 2: More Nashville R&B And Doo Wop
Ace CDCHD 672 *Arthur K. Adams, Gene Allison (3), Jimmy Beck & His Orchestra, Larry Birdsong (4), Cliff Butler, The Clips (2), Don Q [Pullen] & Clenest Gant, 'Little Shy Guy' Douglas, The Fairfield Four, Earl Gaines (3), Earl Gaines & Lucille Johns, Chuck Harrod & The Anteaters, Ted Jarrett, The Kinglets (2), Christine Kittrell, Murfreesboro [Al Garner] (2), Joyce Paul, Roscoe Shelton, Charles Walker & The Daffodils (2).* 56–68.

African-American producer, songwriter and occasional recording artist Ted Jarrett operated a clutch of labels in Nashville: Champion, Cherokee, Kit, Calvert, Ponticello, Spar, Valdot, Hit and Ref-O-Ree are winnowed on these two collections. He also worked as an independent producer for Excello, Nashville's best-known issuer of blues and related music, and Vee-Jay, to whom Jarrett sold 'You Can Make It If You Try', his composition and Gene Allison's hit. When Vee-Jay signed Allison, they also got Larry Birdsong, a better singer, influenced by Sam Cooke and Clyde McPhatter, versions of whose sounds are much in evidence elsewhere on these discs. There's a good deal of vocal-group R&B and doo-wop included, as well as some outstanding gospel, and Chuck Harrod's dispensable rockabilly. In other words, the *Across The Tracks* CDs are a reminder that defining the blues is always to some extent an arbitrary process. These discs get past that problem to produce excellently done portraits of an over-looked facet of the Nashville music scene. There are no unmissable masterpieces included, and some tracks are decidedly ephemeral (Johnny Keaton's 'Twistin' USA' and Birdsong's 'Scooter Poofin' [!] on *Vol. 2* are prime examples of the early-'60s dance-craze infection), but Jarrett was a disciplined and thoughtful producer, and in Jimmy Beck's Orchestra he had a first-rate house band, whose occasional recordings as name artists are splendid. CS

Paramount

***(*) The Paramount Masters
JSP JSP 7723 4CD *Raymond Barrow, Lottie Beaman [Lottie Kimbrough] (2), Ed Bell (2), Freddie Brown, Henry Brown (2), Bumble Bee Slim, John Byrd (2), Lonnie Clark (2), Ben Covington (or Ben Curry) (3), Teddy Darby (2), Side Wheel Sally Duffie, Moanin' Bernice Edwards, Piano Kid Edwards (2), Famous Hokum Boys, Bobby Grant (2), Blind Roosevelt Graves (2), George Hannah (2), Harum Scarums, Buddy Boy Hawkins, King Solomon Hill (3), Jack O'Diamonds (2), Bo Weavil Jackson (3), Papa Charlie Jackson (2), Mary Johnson (2), Rube Lacy (2),*

Meade Lux Lewis, Little Brother Montgomery (2), Alice Moore (2), William Moore (2), Charlie 'Dad' Nelson (2), Marshall Owens (2), Charley Patton, Ruby Paul (2), Alice Pearson, Robert Peeples (2), Ma Rainey, Blind Joe Reynolds (3), Bob Robinson, J. D. Short (2), Charlie Spand (3), Freddie Spruell (2), Sweet Papa Stovepipe (2), Roosevelt Sykes (3), Elvie Thomas (2), Edward Thompson (2), Henry Townsend (2), Wesley Wallace (2), Washboard Walter (2), Barrelhouse Welch (2), James 'Boodle It' Wiggins (3), Geeshie Wiley (2), George 'Bullet' Williams (2), Jabo Williams (2). c. 3/24–c. 5/32.

That any record label should have been an offshoot of the Wisconsin Chair Company might be regarded as unlikely; that it should have been its era's most assiduous and adventurous sponsor of African-American music seems hardly credible. In fact several of the period's leading labels were owned by companies specializing in furnishings of one kind or another: Victrolas, billiard tables, pianos. All of them operated in all the primary markets of the day – black jazz and blues, white dancebands and popular singers, old-time country music – but Paramount alone prioritized the African-American community, building over 12 years a 'race' catalogue of more than 1150 discs.

The Paramount Masters is not a documentary. It ignores the label's many important jazz artists, and bypasses or marginalizes many of its most successful blues acts. Blind Lemon Jefferson, Blind Blake, Alberta Hunter, Ida Cox and The Hokum Boys are absent; Ma Rainey has a single track, Papa Charlie Jackson two. What the set offers instead is a thick gazetteer of blues artists who made one or two visits to the studio, sold mere handfuls of discs and disappeared, many of them never to record again. It might justly be called a chapter of an almost secret history of the blues. Within that remit, it covers a great deal of regional and stylistic ground, assembling guitarists and pianists, artists who specialized in blues and those who worked in adjoining fields such as hokum. Some, like Roosevelt Sykes, Little Brother Montgomery, Henry Brown and Mary Johnson, would carry on to become 'race' stars of some magnitude, whereas others like Marshall Owens and Elvie Thomas are still shrouded in mystery. But if this makes The Paramount Masters sound like a stiff course in obscurity, we have done it, and the reader, a disservice. The 100 tracks embrace many that are recognized as masterpieces: pianist Wesley Wallace's train theme 'No. 29', Charlie Spand's 'Soon This Morning', Little Brother Montgomery's original 'Vicksburg Blues', all the pieces by Ed Bell and King Solomon Hill. That these are juxtaposed with odder, quirkier recordings by lesser figures is part of the collection's point and value.

**(*) Rare Paramount Blues (1926–1929)
Document DOCD-5277 *Freddie Brown* (2), *Lonnie Clark* (2), *Smoky Harrison* (4), *Jack O'Diamonds* (2), *Charlie 'Dad' Nelson* (8), *Paramount All Stars* (2), *Ruby Paul* (2), *Sweet Papa Stovepipe* (2), *Too Bad Boys* (2). c. 9/26–c. 11/29.

Obscurity (and surface noise) is much in evidence here. Little is known about 'Dad' Nelson and Smoky Harrison, and the placenames they prodigally scatter – Harrison, in 'Iggly Oggly Blues', namechecking Montana, New York and Tupelo, among others – are clearly no help. Nelson accompanies himself on ponderous 12-string guitar and kazoo, while Harrison sounds a little like a heavily sedated Blind Blake. Ruby Paul is a tough Southern singer, not a world away from Lucille Bogan in tone; this is her only record, and the same is true of the couplings by Freddie Brown, the barely competent Sweet Papa Stovepipe, Jack O'Diamonds and Lonnie Clark, the last a deliberate pianist with an arrestingly mournful voice. In the two-part 'Hometown Skiffle' a gaggle of Paramount artists have a studio party and play selections from their hits. Many of these sides are also on *The Paramount Masters*. TR

Ram

**(*) Red River Blues
Ace CDCHD 725 *June 'Bug' Bailey*, *Elgie Brown* (3), *Chico Chism* (2), *Sherman (Blues) Johnson*, *Banny Price*, *L. C. Steel*, *Jesse Thomas* (5), *TV Slim* (6), *Little Melvin Underwood* (2), *Vincent Williams* (2), *Sonny Boy Williamson [Jeff Williamson]* (4). 55–63.

Ram Records was owned by Mira Smith, who operated a recording studio in Shreveport, Louisiana. *Red River Blues* surveys the blues output of Ram and its subsidiaries Clif and Jo. It also includes material issued by musicians on their own labels: four of TV Slim's tracks are from Speed, and were supervised by Smith; those by Jesse Thomas, made for his Red River label, were cut at Dee Marais's Bayou studio. Sonny Boy Williamson is, as they say, 'not to be confused' with the other two. There's little chance of that; Jeff Williamson's harmonica is functional rather than virtuoso, but his tracks are enjoyable examples of early-'60s mainstream Louisiana. June Bailey reproaches a winehead with a maturity beyond her 15 years, and Elgie Brown's tracks have exciting guitar by Banny Price, whose own track is a bland instrumental. A noisy dub of TV Slim's extremely rare first record is collector bait, but 'Flat Foot Sam' was his, and Clif's, big hit. It's eclipsed, however, by two sides where Slim's only accompaniment is Eddie Williams's tempestuous barrelhouse piano. The tracks by Johnson, Underwood and Williams went unissued because of falling demand for blues, but they're forgettable anyway. L. C. Steel isn't as tough as his name, and singing drummer Chico Chism's tracks are poorly balanced cliché-fests. Jesse Thomas's 'Guitar Riff' and 'My Baby' feature accomplished, jazzy picking, but his lyrics are insubstantial. CS

Regal

***(*) Blind Willie McTell & The Regal Country Blues
Acrobat ADMCD 5015 2CD *Pee Wee Hughes & The Delta Duo* (2), *Blind Willie McTell* (19), *Memphis Minnie* (5), *Little Brother Montgomery* (3), *St Louis Jimmy [Oden]* (4), *Jimmy Rogers*, *Sunnyland Slim*, *Curley Weaver* (2). 3–5/49.

Some time in 1948 or early '49, Fred Mendelsohn of Regal Records surveyed the R&B charts and realized that there was a craze for sounds way more downhome than the music of New Orleans bandleader Paul Gayten, whose discs had thus far been the label's biggest earners. So he took himself off to Atlanta to record a couple of veterans of the prewar blues business, Blind Willie McTell and Curley Weaver, and while in New Orleans taped the obscure Pee Wee Hughes, a singer and harmonica player from Shreveport. Then, in Chicago, he caught Memphis Minnie and St Louis Jimmy in fine voice and got some exquisite piano solos from Little Brother Montgomery. It's an odd roster (and no less so when you think of the Regal signings who are *not* included, such as Dennis McMillon and Little David Wylie, for whom see EAST COAST), but Acrobat's programming masks that somewhat by putting McTell – who is, as usual, wonderful – on one CD and all the others on the other. As an illustration of one record company's strategy at a particular time it's fascinating, and enhanced by excellent sound quality and lengthy notes. TR

Rounder
**** Box Of The Blues
Rounder 2171 4CD *Johnny Adams, Etta Baker, Marcia Ball, Carey Bell, Rory Block, Buster Brown, Charles Brown, Clarence 'Gatemouth' Brown, Ruth Brown, Solomon Burke, [John] Cephas & [Phil] Wiggins, Otis Clay, Eddy Clearwater, Willie Cobbs, Johnny Copeland, Larry Davis, Theryl 'Houseman' de'Clouet, Chris Duarte Group, Champion Jack Dupree, David 'Honeyboy' Edwards, Lowell Fulson, Anson Funderburgh & The Rockets, Corey Harris, Ted Hawkins, The Holmes Brothers, Mississippi John Hurt, J. B. Hutto, Luther 'Guitar Junior' Johnson, Andrew Jr Boy Jones, Candye Kane, Paul Kelly, Bobby King & Terry Evans, Little Jimmy King, Smokin' Joe Kubek & Little Milton, Little Buster & The Soul Brothers, Lonesome Sundown, Mississippi Fred McDowell, Blind Willie McTell, Geoff Muldaur, Robert Nighthawk, Ann Peebles, Wilson Pickett, Duke Robillard, Jimmy Rogers, Roomful Of Blues, Johnny Shines & Robert Jr Lockwood, Otis Spann, Babe Stovall & Herb Quinn, Tarbox Ramblers, Sonny Terry & Brownie McGhee, Irma Thomas & Tracy Nelson, George Thorogood, Phillip Walker, Walter 'Wolfman' Washington, Boogie Bill Webb, Big Joe Williams, Sonny Boy Williamson I–Memphis Slim–Big Bill Broonzy, Michelle Wilson, Smokey Wilson, Johnny Young.* 11/40–00.

When the Rounder collective started out in 1970 their plans for roots music were simultaneously archival (recording old guys) and *au courant* (recording young guys who had listened to old guys). That policy was reflected in the old-time and bluegrass albums that chiefly occupied them during their first couple of years' business, but their entry into the blues arena was more cautious, as they put out albums of field recordings by George Mitchell and David Evans. With the runaway success of George Thorogood in the late '70s, however, they were catapulted into the big league, where they attracted, and had the money to pay for, bankable acts like John Hammond, Rory Block and Clarence 'Gatemouth' Brown. Since then they haven't looked back – except in the good sense of issuing material from the past, most valuably Alan Lomax's field recordings – and with the addition of the Bullseye Blues marque in the '80s they were able to produce blues albums on several fronts: successful touring acts like Roomful Of Blues, Marcia Ball and Smokin' Joe Kubek, veterans like Champion Jack Dupree and Charles Brown, talents on the rise like Corey Harris and Andrew Jr Boy Jones, and the old firm of Adams, Burke, Clay, Peebles & Pickett, attorneys of soul.

Box Of The Blues tracks the Rounder group's coverage of the music from Southern roots to present-day soul-blues in a roughly stylistic-historical sweep. Apart from a couple of tracks from subsidiary labels and half a dozen from the Library of Congress and Lomax archives, the material is equally sourced from Rounder and Bullseye Blues and nearly all from currently available CDs, though the tracks by Carey Bell, Jimmy Rogers and Johnny Young come from a long-unavailable Bob Riedy Chicago Blues Band LP of 1973

(not, as Rounder date it here, 1987). If you have been listening to blues for a while you probably know a good deal of this music, but it's refreshed by the different context of a VAC, and if you had a long journey ahead of you this compact and inexpensive collection would give you about three hours of extremely varied entertainment. TR

Specialty
**** In His Own Words: Art Rupe – The Specialty Story
Ace CDCH2 542 2CD *See below.* 44–57, 97?
**** The Specialty Story
Specialty 5SPCD-4412 5CD *Tony Allen & The Champs, The Blues Man [Roosevelt Sykes], The Blues Woman [Marion Abernathy], Jesse Belvin, Big Maceo, Alex Bradford, Jerry Byrne, Wynona Carr, Clifton Chenier, The Chimes, The Chosen Gospel Singers, Eugene Church, Sam Cooke, Daddy Cleanhead, Floyd Dixon, Don & Dewey (5), Amos Easton [Bumble Bee Slim], H-Bomb Ferguson, The Four Flames, Johnny Fuller, Vernon Green & The Phantoms, Lil Greenwood, Guitar Slim, Rene Hall's Orchestra, Smokey Hogg, Honeyboy [Frank Patt], John Lee Hooker, Camille Howard (4), Jump Jackson Band, Roddy Jackson, Jesse & Marvin, Ernest Kador, Clydie King, Earl King, Bob Landers, Jimmy Liggins (5), Joe Liggins (5), Little Richard (19), Little Temple, Joe Lutcher, Marvin & Johnny, Arthur Lee Maye & The Crowns (2), Percy Mayfield (7), Li'l Millet, Roy Milton (19), Roy Montrell, Frank Motley, Big Boy Myles, Art Neville, King Perry & His Pied Pipers, The Pilgrim Travelers, Lloyd Price (5), The Sepia Tones, Frankie Lee Sims, The Soul Stirrers (3), The Swan Silvertones, Mercy Dee Walton, Larry Williams (7), Lester Williams, Jim Wynn.* 44–64.
**(*) Specialty Legends of Jump Blues, Vol. 1
Specialty SPCD-7058//Ace CDCHD 573 *Buddy Banks, Nelson Alexander Trio, Duke Henderson, Jimmy Liggins (3), Joe Liggins (4), Joe Lutcher (2), Herman Manzy, Percy Mayfield (2), Roy Milton (3), Frank Motley & Jimmy Crawford, King Perry (4), Jesse Thomas, Lester Williams, Big Jim Wynn.* 47–52.

In 1944, Art Rupe cleared his desk at the defunct Atlas Records and opened for business in his own right as Juke Box Records. Two years later he started Specialty. In 1947 the label had hits with discs by Roy Milton and Jimmy Liggins, and in 1950 its first R&B #1s with Joe Liggins's 'Pink Champagne' and Percy Mayfield's 'Please Send Me Someone To Love'. For most of the next decade Specialty was a front-rank label in the black music business, with a list that included Little Richard, Larry Williams and Sam Cooke & The Soul Stirrers, and classic records such as Guitar Slim's 'The Things That I Used To Do', Mercy Dee Walton's 'One Room Country Shack' and Lloyd Price's 'Lawdy Miss Clawdy'. It was a heady 15 years or so, a story that could be turned into, say, a fascinating audio documentary – which is exactly what *In His Own Words* is. Rupe tells it like it was, brimming with precise recollections and amusing anecdotes, Paul Jones fills in some of the background, and the narrative is repeatedly suspended for extracts or entire recordings of Milton, Mayfield, the Ligginses, Little Richard and many others. The fabric is so cleverly woven that it would take many listenings to wear it out.

Something that emerges clearly from Rupe's reminiscences is how much attention he gave, and how much skill he brought, to making first-rate recordings. Major act or minor, everyone on the label was given a high-quality studio experience, and even run-of-the-mill performances have some of the swagger of hits. It's the hits that come under the spotlight of *The Specialty Story*, though mixed in with them are numerous records that weren't outstanding sellers but have other claims on our attention, like pianist Little Temple's boisterous 'I Ate The Wrong Part', 'Squeeze Box Boogie' by the young Clifton Chenier, or Honeyboy's horror story 'Bloodstains On The Wall'. Billy Vera's production is exemplary. If only there were similarly meticulous histories of all the great labels – but then blues enthusiasts would never leave home.

Oddly – since Ace tend not to miss tricks – there isn't an abbreviated Specialty story on one CD. *Specialty Legends Of Jump Blues, Vol. 1* seems to shape up as a hits collection, with Joe Liggins's 'The Honeydripper' and 'Pink Champagne' and Roy Milton's 'Rainy Day Confession Blues' and 'The Hucklebuck', but much of the rest is less celebrated, though by no means without interest. King Perry & His Pied Pipers must have been an entertaining crew to watch in a club, especially doing a comedy routine like the (previously unissued) 'Duck's Yas Yas Yas': 'How do you do, ladies and gentlemen? I'd like to do a little ditty for you entitled "She Must Have Been A Fisherman's Daughter, Because When I Showed Her The Rod, She Reeled."' *Specialty Legends Of Boogie-Woogie* (Ace CDCHD 422) is discussed in BOOGIE WOOGIE. TR

Stax

*** We'll Play The Blues For You
Stax SCD 8613 *Gus Cannon, Steve Cropper, Joe Hicks, John Lee Hooker, Mable John, Ruby Johnson, Albert King (3), Little Milton (2), Little Sonny (2), Jimmy McCracklin, Otis Redding, Johnnie Taylor, Rufus Thomas.* 63–73.

There are stacks of Stax compilations in the Fantasy and Ace catalogues, but almost all devoted, quite properly, to charting the label's unchallenged track record in soul, R&B and funk. For a detailed map we recommend *The Stax Story* (Stax 4SCD 4429 4CD). If you're interested chiefly in the blues landmarks, *We'll Play The Blues For You* offers notable performances like Albert King's 'Angel Of Mercy' and Jimmy McCracklin's 'Just Got To Know', as well as the startling juxtaposition of Gus Cannon's 'Walk Right In' and Johnnie Taylor's 'Hello Sundown', and of John Lee Hooker's 'Goin' To Louisiana' and Little Milton's 'That's What Love Will Make You Do'. Unfortunately the equally attractive *Blue Monday* (Stax SCD-8528), with well-chosen tracks by King, Milton, Little Sonny and Freddie Robinson, appears to be out of print. TR

Sue

**(*) The UK Sue Label Story: The World Of Guy Stevens
Ace CDCHD 1001 *Ernestine Anderson, Harold Betters (2), Birdlegs & Pauline, The Daylighters, Donnie Elbert, Inez & Charlie Foxx, Lowell Fulson, Wilbert Harrison, Elmore James, Chris Kenner, J. B. Lenoir, Louisiana Red, Jimmy McGriff, The Manhattans, Derek Martin, The Olympics, Bobby Parker, The Pleasures, Billy Preston, Wild Jimmy Spruill, Joe Tex, Ike & Tina Turner, Phil Upchurch, Baby Washington, O. V. Wright.* 55–65.

**(*) The UK Sue Label Story Volume 2: Sue's Rock 'N' Blues
Ace CDCHD 1008 *Big Bob [Kornegay], Buster Brown, James Brown, Lee Diamond, Big Al Downing, Dr Horse [Al Pittman],* *Gene & Al's Spacemen, Ronnie Hawkins, Bobby Hendricks, Homesick James, John Lee Hooker, Lightnin' Hopkins, Elmore James, Etta James, B. B. King, Freddie King, J. B. Lenoir, Willie Mabon, The Megatons, The Bobby Peterson Quintet, Professor Longhair, Otis Redding, Paul Revere & The Raiders, The Righteous Brothers, Rosie & The Originals, Frankie Lee Sims.* c. 9/48–1/62.

The late Guy Stevens blazed the trail which many British explorers of black music followed in the '60s; apart from running Sue, he also compiled LPs of Chess and Excello product, for Pye and EMI respectively, which were seminal ingredients in the British R&B boom. Ace's series extends to a *Volume 3: The Soul Of Sue* (Kent CDKEND 235), but it's outside our scope, as indeed are some of the tracks on these two volumes; Stevens had very eclectic tastes. The audience for the sounds he was championing was small, but his advocacy had considerable consequences for popular music, and not just because the Stones had the stones to think they could do justice to O. V. Wright's 'That's How Strong My Love Is'. Ace have done a thorough job of documenting Stevens' life, tastes and business methods (the booklets include some captivating ephemera) but, although there are numerous classic blues performances on both discs, there's also a good deal of deservedly obscure dross, in the shape of inconsequential instrumentals, strained Little Richard imitations (Big Bob, Lee Diamond, Joe Tex and Otis Redding all go down that road) and naff vocal groups. These CDs are valuable accounts of a significant moment in popular culture, but they're also variably entertaining, and to say that secondhand copies of the old Sue blues LPs would be more rewarding is not just collector's nostalgia. CS

Sun

**(*) Feelin' Good: The Very Best Of Sun Blues
Castle Select SELCD 594 *Walter Bradford, James Cotton, Jimmy DeBerry, David 'Honeyboy' Edwards, Billy 'The Kid' Emerson, Rosco Gordon, Pat Hare, Earl Hooker, Walter Horton, Howlin' Wolf, Lost John Hunter, Sammy Lewis, Little Milton, Joe Hill Louis, Billy 'Red' Love, Coy 'Hot Shot' Love, Big Memphis Ma Rainey, Johnny O'Neal, Little Junior [Parker]'s Blue Flames, Dr Ross, Scott Jr Blues Rockers, Rufus Thomas, Mose Vinson, Albert Williams.* 50s.

There are several commemorative packages devoted to Sam Phillips's Memphis operation, most of them matching the breadth of the Sun catalogue from blues and gospel to rockabilly, rock 'n' roll and country music. Bear Family, for example, are in the process of boxing the label's entire output on 78 and 45 in a series of 4CD sets, *The Complete Sun Singles*. The less imposing *Sun Records: The 50th Anniversary Collection* (BMG Heritage 99000 2CD), co-produced and annotated by Colin Escott, is an admirable 44-track summary, replete with landmark recordings, but necessarily more than half of it is concerned with Elvis Presley, Carl Perkins, Jerry Lee Lewis, Johnny Cash and the entirely white roster of the later '50s and '60s. Which, if you're interested only in Sun's blues output and haven't been able to hunt down a copy of Charly's long-deleted 8CD boxed set *Sun Records: The Blues Years 1950–1958* (CDSUNBOX 7), leaves the inexpensive *Feelin' Good*, which makes room for classic sides like James Cotton's 'Cotton Crop Blues' and Pat Hare's 'I'm Gonna Murder My Baby' but not, annoyingly, for Junior Parker's 'Mystery Train' or Walter Horton's 'Easy' or Billy 'The Kid' Emerson's 'Red Hot' or much else. In fact, 14 of the 24 tracks were never issued by Phillips but exhumed decades later, and, although they represent both the artists and the Sun studio sound fairly, they are far from 'the very best of Sun blues'. TR

United

*** The United Records Story
Delmark DD-775 *Robert Anderson, Paul Bascomb, Dennis Binder, J. T. Brown, Jimmy Coe, Jimmy Forrest, The Four Blazes, Tiny Grimes, Alfred Harris, Grant Jones, Ray McKinstry, Memphis Slim, Robert Nighthawk, Leo Parker, The Pastels, Morris Pejoe, Della Reese, Tab Smith, Roosevelt Sykes, Junior Wells, Johnny Wicks, Chris Woods.* 7/51–1/57.

Blues fans revere Leonard Allen's United and States labels for recording Junior Wells and Robert Nighthawk, and are at least politely grateful for their sessions with Memphis Slim and Roosevelt Sykes (which were excellent), but like any canny operator in the '50s Allen held a much fatter portfolio, which *The United Records Story* justly acknowledges. The jukebox market was courted with sax instrumentals by Tab Smith, Jimmy Coe, Leo Parker and Jimmy Forrest, while the listener too sophisticated to care for harmonica and slide guitar blues was wheedled with Grant Jones and Della Reese. It's a most interesting collection, revealing Allen as a man who knew something about hi-fi recording and only patronized studios that could provide it. What it doesn't quite do is live up to its title. There were several hits in the United/States story (Forrest's 'Night Train', The Four Blazes' 'Mary Jo', etc.) but here they are consistently rejected in favour of lesser-known tracks by the same artists, sometimes ones that were not even issued at the time. It doesn't diminish the music, but it does obscure the history. TR

USA

*** The USA Records Blues Story
Fuel 2000 302 061 209 *Ricky Allen (2), Lonnie Brooks (2), Andrew Brown (2), Jimmy Burns (2), Eddy Clearwater (2), Detroit Jr (2), Jesse Fortune (2), Homesick James (2), J. B. Lenoir, Willie Mabon (2), A. C. Reed, Fenton Robinson (2), Koko Taylor (2), Junior Wells, Mighty Joe Young.* 63–67.

At the time – the mid-'60s – USA looked like a label that could make a difference. Of the other Chicago companies, Chess and Vee-Jay were backing away from the blues market and many of the rest had vanished. Here came USA with a string of singles that spoke the language of the blues in a contemporary accent – witty songs with brassy, horny arrangements, often coupled with numbers that edged towards soul. Willie Mabon's sly 'Just Got Some', Lonnie Brooks's wry 'Figure Head', the brilliantly realized 'Too Many Cooks' by Jessie Fortune, written and produced by Willie Dixon: records like these gave blues collectors in the '60s reassurance that Chicago blues was still a going concern. Perhaps the music was, but the label wasn't, or not for long: it had no real hits, couldn't hold on to its talent and after four or five productive years went out of business. But in that time it had issued such excellent things as Andrew Brown's Otis Rush-like 'You Better Stop', 'Crossroads'/'My Baby's Sweet' by Homesick James,

probably the best record he ever made, and entertaining pieces by A. C. Reed, Detroit Jr and the very Berryish Eddy Clearwater. When the definitive history of Chicago blues comes to be written there ought to be a chapter about this ingenious if unlucky label. The CD is efficiently annotated but despite 24-bit remastering many of the tracks sound the way they did on the 45s, as if they were recorded down a phone line. TR

Vee-Jay

**** The Story Of Vee-Jay
Metro Doubles METRDCD 509 2CD *Gene Allison, The Argo Singers, Billy Boy Arnold, Hank Ballard & The Midnighters, Priscilla Bowman, Jerry Butler (3), Jerry Butler & Betty Everett, Gene Chandler (2), Dee Clark (3), Pee Wee Crayton, The Dells (2), El Dorados (3), Betty Everett (3), Rosco Gordon (2), The Harmonizing Four, John Lee Hooker (3), Fred Hughes, Elmore James (2), Little Richard (2), The Magnificents, Memphis Slim, Original Blind Boys Of Alabama (2), The Pips, Jimmy Reed (3), Joe Simon, The Spaniels (2), Staple[s] Singers (2), Swan Silvertones (2), Eddie Taylor.* 55–65.

Vee-Jay doesn't excite the same adulation as Chess, but in the '50s and '60s it was the hare to the Chess tortoise, its singles bounding up R&B and pop charts alike. From time to time they were straight-ahead blues like John Lee Hooker's 'Dimples' and Jimmy Reed's 'Honest I Do', but more often they were eye-catching pieces from the mosaic of urban black music such as Betty Everett's 'You're No Good', Gene Allison's aspirational 'You Can Make It If You Try' and Dee Clark's 'Raindrops', classic doo-wop by The Dells and The El Dorados, or the splendid idiocy of Gene Chandler's 'Duke Of Earl'. Add the gospel of the Swan Silvertones and the Staples Singers and you have a label that's a model of diversity, moving with the times yet not deserting the past. The 50 tracks, well chosen by John Crosby, tell the story truthfully if history is what you're after, but, if all you want is a couple of hours of top-quality R&B from the '50s and '60s, do like Jerry Butler, make it easy on yourself and invest in this excellent and pocket-friendly album. TR

Louisiana

** Louisiana Swamp Blues
Capitol Blues Collection 52046 *Boo Breeding (4), Boozoo Chavis (2), Clifton Chenier (6), Clarence Garlow (7), Guitar Slim [Eddie Jones] (4).* 5/51–54.

When the British writer Bill Millar coined the terms 'swamp blues' and 'swamp pop', he was probably thinking of Louisiana as the land of bayous, Spanish moss and alligators, permutations of which adorn the covers of most of these VACs. In fact, Lake Charles and Crowley, the most important blues recording centres outside New Orleans, are in the prairie country of southwest Louisiana, but 'swamp blues' – epitomized on disc by Lightnin' Slim, Lazy Lester, Slim Harpo, Lonesome Sundown, Silas Hogan and Whispering Smith – developed in and around Baton Rouge, which is indeed surrounded by marshes, and 'swamp blues' does somehow evoke the sound of their music on disc, with its dark tone colours, loosely rolling rhythms, and creative use of echo and percussion.

Capitol's collection applies the term too loosely, though: it features zydeco, New Orleans guitar bands, and the pop-blues-zydeco novelties of the nasal-voiced, wobbly-pitched Clarence Garlow. Garlow parlayed his regional hit 'Bon Ton Roula' into numerous sessions, most of which generated equally light-weight variants of that song. Two tracks here are duets with the talentless Emma Dee Lee. Boozoo Chavis's catchy 'Paper In My Shoe' was another regional hit; it became a standard, always played with more discipline than the polytonal but irresistible original. Its flipside is much less memorable. Clifton Chenier's first session also has primitive, almost garage-band production values. That's not a problem, unlike the catastrophic speed fluctuations on 'Country Bred', which is available without them on *Rural Blues – Vols 1 & 2* (BGO BGOCD 384). Guitar Slim's first session is evidence of the promise that was fulfilled by 'Things That I Used To Do', but his obscure admirer Boo Breeding, recording after the big hit, is more rewarding than the man himself, recording before it.

***(*) Louisiana Roots: The Jay Miller R&B Legacy
Ace CDCHD 682 *Marva Allen, Classie Ballou, Carol Fran, Guitar Gable [Perrodin] & King Karl [Bernard Jolivette] (2), Eddie Hudson (2), Joe Hudson & His Rocking Dukes with Lester Robertson (2), Bobby Jay, King Karl [Bernard Jolivette], Chuck Martin, Sonny Martin, Joe Mayfield, Jay Nelson & The Jumpers, Vince Monroe, Charles Sheffield (4), Skinny Dynamo [George 'Slim' Sanders], Tabby Thomas, Lionel Torrence, Katie Webster.* 56–66.

Jay Miller's Crowley studio is most celebrated, and rightly so, for recordings by the swamp-blues singers noted above. Miller had started out with Cajun and country music, but in the '50s he moved increasingly into blues, making a licensing deal with the Nashville-based Excello label. For more of Miller's output, see LABEL HISTORIES & SHOWCASES, where Eddie Shuler's productions for his Lake Charles-based Goldband label are also discussed; and see Juke Boy Bonner's entry for *Goin' Down To Louisiana: The Goldband Downhome Blues Anthology* (Ace CDCHD 821). Shreveport-based Ram and its associated labels are also considered under LABEL HISTORIES & SHOWCASES.

Louisiana Roots brings together various Miller artists who don't (Tabby Thomas excepted) fit into the swamp-blues pigeonhole, although Guitar Gable and King Karl's 'Irene' is classic swamp pop. The same team's 'Cool, Calm And Collected' is a gem of black rockabilly, but most of *Louisiana Roots* is one or more of ephemeral, second-rank and derivative. That defines most records in all genres of popular music, and Miller was aiming for sales, not greatness, but tracks by Vince Monroe, Eddie Hudson and Skinny Dynamo (whose pseudonym is far better than his singing) are far from being the only ones for completists. If nothing else, this CD demonstrates that Fats Domino's sound is much harder to get right than it seems. Numerous pleasing guitar and sax solos testify to Miller's ear for good session musicians, and the CD has good notes, but it's not for casual listeners.

*** Louisiana Blues
Arhoolie CD 9004 *Clarence Edwards (2), Henry Gray (3), Silas Hogan (2), Arthur 'Guitar' Kelley (3), Whispering Smith (2).* 4/70.

**(*) Swamp Blues
Ace CDCHD 661 *Clarence Edwards (4), Henry Gray (4), Silas Hogan (5), Arthur 'Guitar' Kelley (4), Whispering Smith (7).* 8/70.

Local researcher Terry Pattison's enthusiasm led to these recordings, and most of the artists saw revivals in their musical careers as a result. On both CDs the artists back one another, assisted by rhythm sections. *Swamp Blues*, which was originally a double LP, also includes 12 solo tracks; these are enjoyable examples of Baton Rouge's then vigorous traditionally based blues scene, although allowance must be made for Henry Gray's harmonic and rhythmic lapses, and for some sour notes from 'Guitar' Kelley. However, the band tracks on this disc are marred by crass percussion overdubs, which ruin Kelley's 'How Can I Stay When All I Have Is Gone' and do nothing for the other tracks where they appear. Also unwise was the overdubbing of frequently incongruous lead guitar parts by 16-year-old Greg Schaefer of Bacon Fat. (Schaefer and Leon Medica were also employed to replace some of Clarence Prophet's bass work.) Silas Hogan copes best with being messed about and, despite those sour notes, Arthur Kelley arouses regret that he recorded very little after these sessions.

Louisiana Blues was recorded four months earlier and even more swiftly (in one day rather than five), but with more successful results. Gray's harmony is still suspect at times, but Kelley is much more on track than in August, and on three dark and doomy numbers he's a very satisfactory substitute for Lightnin' Slim. Whispering Smith takes Lazy Lester's chair here and elsewhere, and as a name artist he makes simple, direct music that's unchanged from his Excello days (which in 1970 were not long past). Silas Hogan, though unquestionably still a major artist, is vocally less subtle either than he had been or than he would soon be again. Clarence Edwards's gritty version of 'Stack Of Dollars' with only a drummer in support reveals that the addition of Henry Gray to his other track, though not damaging, was not necessary.

*** Louisiana Swamp Blues – Vol. 3
Wolf 120.924 *Larry Garner (5), Battlerack Scatter (3), T-Bone Singleton (4).* 5/90.

***(*) Louisiana Swamp Blues – Vol. 5: 40 Years Of Louisiana Blues
Wolf 120.926 *Larry Garner (3), Silas Hogan (2), Cora Jefferson (2), Rudy Richard, Tabby Thomas (4), 'Tootsie'.* 90–91.

Vol. 1 in this series, *Live At Tabby's Blues Box* (Wolf 120.922), is deleted; for *Vols 2, 4* and *6* see Henry Gray, Clarence Edwards and Silas Hogan respectively. *Vol. 3*, produced by English researcher and musician Steve Coleridge, focuses on three of the younger electric guitarists on the 1990 Baton Rouge scene. Garner's blues are stylistically in the modern mainstream. He's an intelligent lyricist; one would think he'd have realized that singing 'the sky is crying, look at the tears roll down my cheeks' (on the CD's only non-original composition) effortlessly destroys the image. T-Bone Singleton and the remarkably named (by deed poll) Battlerack Scatter are also interesting songwriters, with a sound that's more recognizably descended from the likes of Silas Hogan.

'Kleptomania' and 'PMS' on *Vol. 5* are confirmation of Garner's taste for unusual subjects; 'Shut It Down' is a long, cynical monologue. Cora Jefferson is a raucously unsubtle vocalist, but 'Tootsie' is a fine pianist, not unreasonably compared to Katie Webster, and she must have been a considerable singer when in better health; 'County Jail', a rendition of Blind Boy Fuller's 'Big House Bound', is as courageous as it is unexpected. Of the elder statesmen, Silas Hogan at 80 is as amiably eloquent as when making his recording debut 30 years earlier. Tabby Thomas plays guitar on a resolute cover of Roy Brown's 'Long About Midnight', and piano on his other titles. They include yet another 'Voodoo Party', but Tabby is in top form here; David Hill (bass) and Jess Kenchin (drums) are important to the success of his tracks, and to Tootsie's and Hogan's. Rudi Richard, who plays nimble guitar when Thomas plays piano, switches to accordion for a pleasant version of the Cajun standard 'Big Mamou'. CS

Mandolin

**** Vintage Mandolin Music (1927–1946)
Document DOCD-32-20-3 *Blue Ridge Ramblers, Louie Bluie [Howard Armstrong], Dallas String Band (2), Arizona Dranes, Joe Evans & Arthur McClain (2), Nap Hayes & Matthew Prater (2), King David's Jug Band, Charlie McCoy (with Ishman Bracey), Memphis Jug Band (2), Al Miller, Mississippi Mud Steppers, Nashville Washboard Band (2), Yank Rachell (with Sleepy John Estes) (2), Scottdale String Band, Gid Tanner & His Skillet Lickers (2), Paul Warmack & His Gully Jumpers, Phebel Wright.* 12/27–c. 46.

The six tracks by white artists highlight the way that music made by ensembles including a mandolinist often ignored racial barriers: you couldn't put a stylistic tissue paper between the Skillet Lickers' 'Hawkins' Rag' and Evans & McClain's 'Old Hen Cackle'; Hayes & Prater's 'Easy Winner' (actually 'The Entertainer') was issued in OKeh's hillbilly series; and the Nashville Washboard Band's 'Arkansas Traveler' is a giddy synthesis of Scotch-Irish dance music with black jazz. Yank Rachell and Charlie McCoy prove that it's possible to get heavy blues licks out of a mandolin, and the anonymous picker supporting gospel pianist Arizona Dranes offers another perspective, but light-hearted ragtime and virtuoso display are more typical of black mandolin music in the interwar years. One could wish that the compilers had favoured Willie Hatcher or the Birmingham Jug Band over yet another reissue of 'Dallas Rag', but this is a classy selection, with crystalline sound and detailed notes.

*** Mandolin Blues
Testament TCD 6004 *Ted Bogan, Willie Hatcher (3), Carl Martin (2), Yank Rachell (4), Johnny Young (7).* 5/64–2/67.

Perhaps perceived as a 'white' instrument with the rise of bluegrass, the mandolin, never widespread in blues, fell further out of favour in the '40s and later. There was very little recording until surviving players were sought out by researchers in the '60s. Willie Hatcher's instrument was in pawn, and 'Garbage Man Blues', with quirky Depression-era lyrics, is his only full-length performance, but Martin, Rachell and Young (who accompanies Bogan on a curious arrangement of a worksong) still had all their chops. Rachell revives his old partnership with Estes (Taj Mahal standing in for Hammie Nixon), and ranges from deep blues to proto-rock 'n' roll. Martin can't make 'Everyday I Have The Blues' interesting, but his Italianate lines on 'Gravedigger Blues' are very attractive. Young was quite extensively recorded in the '60s. On this disc the results are uneven: 'Highway 61' and 'Stealin'' surge majestically, and 'Mandolin Rock' does what it says, but Jimmy Walker's piano is out of joint on two tracks, one of them a 'Crawling Kingsnake' where it takes producer Pete Welding a while to get the levels right. CS

Memphis

**** Memphis Masters – Early American Blues Classics 1927–34
Yazoo 2008 *Will Batts (2), Gus Cannon (2), Jed Davenport, Pearl Dickson, Tom Dickson, Hattie Hart (2), Jack Kelly, Furry Lewis, Joe McCoy, Memphis Jug Band, Memphis Minnie, Mooch Richardson, Will Shade, South Memphis Jug Band, Frank Stokes (3).* 27–34.

***(*) Frank Stokes' Dream: The Memphis Blues 1927–1931
Yazoo 1008 *Cannon's Jug Stompers, Pearl Dickson, Tom Dickson, Furry Lewis (4), Noah Lewis, Memphis Minnie (2), Frank Stokes (3), Will Weldon.* 27–31.

***(*) Memphis Jamboree 1927–1936
Yazoo 1021 *Will Batts, Gus Cannon, Hattie Hart, Jim Jackson, Furry Lewis, Joe McCoy (2), Memphis Minnie (4), Yank Rachell, Sam Townsend, The Two Charlies.* 27–36.

*** Memphis Blues (1927–1938)
Document DOCD-5159 *John Henry Barbee (5), Pearl Dickson (2), Hattie Hart (4), Madelyn James (2), Charlie 'Bozo' Nickerson (4), Walter Rhodes (2), Ollie Rupert (2), George Torey (2), Sam Townsend (2).* 2/27–9/38.

***(*) Memphis Country Blues Vol. I
Memphis Archives MA 7001 *Will Batts, Cannon's Jug Stompers, Sleepy John Estes, Hattie Hart, Jim Jackson, Furry Lewis, Noah Lewis, Memphis Jug Band (2), Memphis Minnie, Hambone Willie Newbern, Frank Stokes, Will Weldon, Booker White (2), Robert Wilkins (2).* 27–40.

*** Masters Of Memphis Blues
JSP JSP 7725 4CD *Gus Cannon (6), Little Buddy Doyle (9), Furry Lewis (25), Frank Stokes (42), Allen Shaw (2), Robert Wilkins (17).*

River town, railroad junction, nestled in the triple embrace of Tennessee, Arkansas and Mississippi, Memphis has for more than a century been the bowl where the Deep South mixes its musical salads. So it's fitting that much of the city's blues is collaborative music: jugbands, guitar duets. The Memphis Jug Band and Cannon's Jug Stompers have their own space in the Yazoo catalogue, so *Memphis Masters* spends more time on the picking pairs: Memphis Minnie and Kansas Joe, Jack Kelly and Dan Sane with the South Memphis Jug Band, Kelly with Will Batts on the latter's 'Cadillac Baby' and 'Country Woman', Allen Shaw and Memphis Willie Borum behind Hattie Hart, the Harney brothers with Pearl Dickson. Together these tracks are a masterclass in varieties of blues guitar duet playing.

Since *Memphis Masters* carefully avoids duplicating any of the tracks on *Frank Stokes' Dream* and *Memphis Jamboree*, lovers of Memphis blues can confidently buy all three albums – indeed, they are warmly recommended to do so, because both *Dream* and *Jamboree*, though short (14 tracks each against *Memphis Masters*' 20), contain first-rate sides like Pearl Dickson's 'Twelve Pound Daddy' (*Dream*) and Will Batts's 'Highway No. 61 Blues' (*Jamboree*). The only reservation is that half of *Dream* is material by Frank Stokes and Furry Lewis, which readers may prefer to acquire, or already own, on Stokes and Lewis CDs – or on JSP's *Masters Of Memphis Blues*, a raid on the CD larder which stuffs the listener with the complete works not only of of Lewis and Stokes but of Robert Wilkins and Little Buddy Doyle (misnamed Little Buddy Page on the box), as well as Gus Cannon's pre-jugband recordings. It's an appealing menu if all you're concerned about is how much blues you can eat for your dollar, but actually consuming the music this way will give you indigestion.

A similar roster of artists to that on the three Yazoos is assembled on *Memphis Country Blues Vol. I* (though the grounds for including two tracks by Booker White are dubious) and on *Walk Right In: The Essential Recordings Of Memphis Blues* (Indigo IGOCD 2038), deleted but worth finding for its wide-ranging selection, spanning 1927–39, and for the lone recording of the singer and slide guitarist Jim Thompkins.

The Document CD concerns itself with secondary figures. Charlie Nickerson was more fun when guesting with the Memphis Jug Band and Sam Townsend is a drab strummer in the Jim Jackson manner, but Walter Rhodes's solemn blues are practically unique in being accompanied on button accordion. Hattie Hart's 1934 sides with Shaw and Borum are worth having in their entirety, despite indifferent sound, likewise the coupling by the singer and guitarist George Torey, though what an artist recorded in Birmingham, Alabama, and with no known connection to Memphis is doing here is anybody's guess.

Some of what appears on Memphis blues VACs does so only because it happened to be recorded there, the artists having been despatched to the city from Mississippi or Arkansas so as to catch a visiting location-recording team. For example, *Memphis Blues Singers Volume 1* (Frog DGF 21) and *Volume 2* (Frog DGF 22) document Victor sessions held in the city in 1928. Ishman Bracey, Tommy Johnson and Rosie Mae Moore were out-of-towners; the only Memphis residents were Frank Stokes on *Volume 1* and Furry Lewis and Robert Wilkins on *Volume 2*. Their recordings are discussed in their own entries, but it's worth reiterating that these CDs were excellently remastered from mint discs. For *Memphis Blues Vol. 1 (1928–1935)* (Document DOCD-5014) see Robert Wilkins, and for *Memphis Harp & Jug Blowers (1927–1939)* (RST Blues Documents BDCD-6028) see Jed Davenport and Little Buddy Doyle. TR

Miscellaneous I (Prewar)

**** American Primitive Vol. II
Revenant RVN 214 2CD *Blues Birdhead, Kid Brown, The Bubbling Over Five, Cousins & De Moss, Evans & McClain (Two Poor Boys) (4), John Hammond (4), William Harris (3), Elizabeth Johnson (2), Alfred Lewis (2), Red Hot Old Mose/Moses Mason (3), The Mississippi Moaner, Nugrape Twins (2), Bayless Rose (4), Salty Dog Four, Tommy Settlers (2), Homer Quincy Smith (2), Henry Spaulding, Walter Taylor, Pigmeat Terry (2), Elvie Thomas, Mattie May Thomas (4), Otto Virgial (2), Geeshie Wiley (4), [Geeshie] Wiley & [Elvie] Thomas.* 1897–1939.

In fealty to the spirit of John Fahey, who created the Revenant label, this collection zeroes in on the mysterious: artists of obscure or unknown provenance, often giving performances of challenging oddity – the street cries of Red Hot Old Mose, and the voice-and-harmonica tour de forces of Alfred Lewis; Kid Brown, blue yodeller, and Tommy Settlers, professor of kazoology; one-string fiddle vying with harmonica and soprano sax on the Bubbling Over Five's 'Don't Forget Your Good Boy Friend'; cornet with guitar and woodblocks on Elizabeth Johnson's two blues. Such an agenda explains the inclusion of recordings that have not often been paid so much attention, like those of the Nugrape Twins, Pigmeat Terry and Homer Quincy Smith, an evangelist in the throes of ecstasy; but it also entails gathering the complete works of the magnificent Geeshie Wiley and Elvie Thomas (together and apart) and guitarist Bayless Rose, and almost all of the Kentucky singer and banjoist John Hammond (the only white contributor) and the sulphurous Mattie May Thomas, an exceptional blues singer recorded in the Mississippi State Penitentiary at Parchman in 1939. Organizationally speaking, it's a rabble, but the characters you meet, and their stories, are so interesting that only a Dryasdust would cavil. The similarly conceived *American Primitive I*, issued in 1997, has been withdrawn but at presstime was due for a revamped rerelease.

** Male Blues Of The Twenties – Vol. 1 (1922–1930)
Document DOCD-5482 *Oliver Cobb (4), James Crawford (2), Reese Du Pree (4), Willie Dukes (3), 'Sloppy' Henry (4), Billy Higgins (2), Happy Holmes (2), John P. Vigal, Blind Richard Yates (4).* c. 5/22–10/30.

*** Country Blues Collector's Items (1924–1928)
Document DOCD-5169 *Ed Andrews (2), Lewis Black (4), Kid Brown, Sammy Brown (2), Emery Glen (4), Johnnie Head (2), T. C. Johnson & 'Blue Coat' Tom Nelson (2), Johnson–Nelson–Porkchop (2), 'Mooch' Richardson (6).* 24–28.

These collections bristle with obscure names and ferociously noisy discs, but as documents of early manifestations of the blues they are informative, especially *Country Blues Collector's Items*, which is wholly devoted to blues in the South. Ed Andrews's sides, made in Atlanta in 1924, are the first Southern recordings of a male blues singer/guitarist; Emery Glen, Lewis Black, 'Mooch' Richardson and the Johnson–Nelson group, recorded in Atlanta or Memphis three or four years later, sound hardly less primitive in their handling of the form. As well as two blues with fiddle and guitar, the Johnson–Nelson team engage in a couple of group harmony numbers of a kind seldom preserved on record.

'Sloppy' Henry was active in Atlanta and trumpeter Oliver Cobb in St Louis, but the rest of the cast of *Male Blues Of The Twenties – Vol. 1* seem to be Northern-based artists, some with theatrical connections like the manager/singer Reese Du Pree, whose 'Norfolk Blues' and 'One More Rounder Gone', made in 2/24, are the earliest blues recordings with two-guitar accompaniment. 'Theatrical' also describes the vocal styles of James Crawford and Blind Richard Yates in their blues about meteorology ('Flood And Thunder Blues') and podiatry ('Sore Bunion Blues').

*** When The Sun Goes Down/The Secret History Of Rock & Roll Vol. 1: Walk Right In
Bluebird 63986 *Amédé Ardoin & Dennis McGee, DeFord Bailey, Andrew & Jim Baxter, Big Bill Broonzy, Milton Brown & His Musical Brownies, Trixie Butler, Gus Cannon's Jug Stompers (2), Carter Family, Frank Crumit, Julius Daniels (2), Rev. J. M. Gates, The Hall Johnson Choir, Alberta Hunter, Tommy Johnson, Leadbelly (2), Noah Lewis, Robert Petway, Paul Robeson, Taskiana Four, Bessie Tucker, Washington [Booker] White, Big Joe Williams.* 1/26–3/41.

COMPILATIONS

*** When The Sun Goes Down/The Secret History Of Rock & Roll Vol. 2: The First Time I Met The Blues
Bluebird 63987 *Ishman Bracey, Gus Cannon's Jug Stompers, Bo Carter, Daddy Stovepipe & Mississippi Sarah, Genevieve Davis, Jimmie Davis, Sleepy John Estes, Harris & Harris, Jim Jackson, Tommy Johnson, Furry Lewis, McCoy & Johnson [Memphis Minnie & Kansas Joe], Lizzie Miles, Mississippi Matilda, Mississippi Sheiks, Little Brother Montgomery, Blind Willie Reynolds, Jimmie Rodgers, Victoria Spivey, Frank Stokes, Sippie Wallace, Edna Winston.* 2/27–10/36.

The 'secret history of rock & roll' is glossed as 'the beginnings of R&B, folk, rock and soul', as revealed in pre-World War II recordings of blues and, occasionally, country and gospel music. Old hands suspicious of such marketing ploys will be relieved to see that the compilers include Colin Escott and David Evans, experienced players of the reissue game, and to find that the notes and sound restoration are impeccable. What may puzzle them is the contents of the albums – all first- or upper-second-rate performances, to be sure, but on what conceivable principles were they assembled? Why does *Walk Right In*'s almost uninterrupted sequence of blues twist at the tail with tracks by Frank Crumit, Paul Robeson and a choir? Best to assume that the answer to the first question is 'None, really,' and accept these well-filled but mid-priced collections as astute and rewarding raids on the Victor/Bluebird catalogue. *Vol. 3: That's Chicago's South Side* is discussed in CHICAGO I (PREWAR), while *Vol. 6: Poor Man's Heaven* is mentioned in TOPICAL & DOCUMENTARY and *Vol. 10: East Virginia Blues* in HILLBILLY BLUES. The other volumes are by Arthur 'Big Boy' Crudup, Leadbelly, Blind Willie McTell and Sonny Boy Williamson I and are covered in their entries. At presstime the latest item in the series was *Vol. 11: Sacred Roots Of The Blues*, a wide-ranging anthology of African-American religious music.

**** Backwoods Blues (1926–1935)
Document DOCD-5036 *Bobby Grant (2), Lane Hardin (2), King Solomon Hill (6), Bo Weavil Jackson (13).* c. 8/26–7/35.

The bulk of this CD is by Bo Weavil Jackson (q.v.), but the remainder is very far from filler. The Paramount disc by Bobby Grant presents a full-voiced singer playing slide guitar, with a strong rhythm on the faster 'Nappy Head Blues'. The lighter, clearer vocal on 'Lonesome Atlanta Blues' has prompted some listeners to think that another singer was involved. King Solomon Hill was Joe Holmes (1897–1949), a singer and guitarist active in south Mississippi and Louisiana whose high voice and slide guitar playing somewhat resemble those of Sam Collins. His coupling 'Whoopee Blues'/'Down On My Bended Knee' was recorded, uniquely in blues, in two registers, a 'normal' voice and a falsetto one an octave higher. The four takes are all remarkable performances, as is 'The Gone Dead Train', an account of a railroad disaster. Even more striking is the lone coupling by the obscure Lane Hardin, whose rhythmic guitar playing offsets soft, plaintive vocals on the Depression song 'Hard Time Blues' and the thematically unusual 'California Desert Blues'.

**(*) Going Away Blues 1926–1935
Yazoo 1018 *Lottie Beaman [Lottie Kimbrough] (2), Charley Jordan, Charlie Kyle, William McCoy, George 'Big Boy' Owens, J. D. Short, Frank Stokes, Elvie Thomas & Geeshie Wiley, Henry Thomas, Uncle Bud Walker, Robert Wilkins (2), George 'Bullet' Williams.* 26–35.

*** Uptown Blues: A Decade Of Guitar–Piano Duets 1927–1937
Yazoo 1042 *Big Bill Broonzy, Charlie Campbell, Leroy Carr, Bo Carter, Teddy Darby, Down Home Boys, Willie Harris, Cripple Clarence Lofton, Leola Manning, Rufus Quillian & James McCravy (2), Mack Rhinehart & Brownie Stubblefield, Charlie Spand, Watson's Pullman Porters.* 27–37.

*** Favourite Country Blues Guitar–Piano Duets 1929–1937
Yazoo 1015 *Blind Blake, Bumble Bee Slim, Leroy Carr, Walter Davis, Joe Evans (2), Willie Harris, Springback James, Cripple Clarence Lofton, Leola Manning, Charlie Spand (2), Roosevelt Sykes, [Oscar] Buddy Woods.* 29–37.

These are unexpanded copies of LPs, with fairly short playing times, and may no longer be available, but like all Yazoos they are worth mentioning for their quirky selections, accurate transfers and informative notes. *Going Away Blues* is too motley to be completely satisfying, but the narrower theme of the piano–guitar duet is well served by the other two CDs. *Favourite ... Duets* is more committed to standard blues forms, while *Uptown Blues* occasionally veers off into hokum.

* Southern Blues Volume 1
Acrobat ACRCD 130 *Garfield Akers, Bo Carter, Arthur 'Big Boy' Crudup, Jed Davenport & His Beale Street Jug Band, James DeBerry, Sleepy John Estes, Cecil Gant, Rudy Greene, William Harris, Willie Harris, Hattie Hart, Robert Johnson, Tommy Johnson, Furry Lewis, Tommy McClennan, Charlie McCoy, Robert Lee McCoy, Mississippi Jook Band, The Mississippi Moaner, Charley Patton, Frank Stokes, Walter Vincson, Otto Virgial, Booker White, Geeshie Wiley.* 7/27–49.

*(*) Southern Blues Volume 2
Acrobat ACRCD 131 *Texas Alexander, Pink Anderson & Simmie Dooley, Barbecue Bob, Ed Bell, Blind Norris, Lucille Bogan, Pinetop Burks, Hattie Burleson, Bernice Edwards, Blind Boy Fuller, Georgia Cotton Pickers, Georgia Slim, Bobby Grant, Stick Horse Hammond, Peg Leg Howell, Blind Lemon Jefferson, Luke Jordan, Blind Willie McTell, Hambone Willie Newbern, Cool Papa Smith, Funny Paper Smith, Six Cylinder Smith, Henry Thomas, Willie Walker, Emma Wright.* c. 9/27–50.

These are enterprising selections that cover a lot of ground, but thanks to brutal filtering and low-level mastering the reproduction on *Volume 2* is poor and on *Volume 1* appalling. The notes are incompetent, too. Even at their low price these should be avoided.

(***) Roots Of Rock
Yazoo 1063 *Blind Blake (2), Cannon's Jug Stompers, Bo Carter, Skip James, Tommy Johnson, Kansas Joe & Memphis Minnie, Blind Willie McTell, Hambone Willie Newbern, Charley Patton, Blind Joe Reynolds, Henry Thomas, Booker White, Robert Wilkins.* 27–37.

*(*) Roots Of Rock
Acrobat ACRCD 164 *Kokomo Arnold, Blind Blake (2), Big Bill Broonzy, Cannon's Jug Stompers, Bo Carter, Skip James, Robert Johnson (3), Tommy Johnson, Kansas Joe & Memphis Minnie, Blind Willie McTell, Memphis Minnie, Mississippi Sheiks, Charley Patton, Robert Petway, Blind Joe Reynolds, Bessie Smith, Clara Smith, Henry Thomas, Booker White, Robert Wilkins, Big Joe Williams (2), Sonny Boy Williamson I.* 27–41.

Yazoo's *Roots Of Rock* presents the original recordings of blues that were reinterpreted in the '60s and '70s by rock artists, such as Skip James's 'I'm So Glad' and Blind Joe Reynolds's 'Outside Woman Blues' (Cream), Booker White's 'Shake 'Em On Down' and Kansas Joe & Memphis Minnie's 'When The Levee Breaks' (Led Zeppelin) and Henry Thomas's 'Bull Doze Blues', done by Canned Heat as 'Goin' Up The Country'. Timely when released on LP, the album may not serve much purpose for most present-day buyers, and its contents can easily be found elsewhere – most easily, because only Hambone Willie Newbern's 'Roll And Tumble Blues' is missing, on the Acrobat CD of the same name, though many of them have been stunned into insensibility by atrocious sound engineering. Another dozen blues are added that have been embraced by rock musicians, remastered somewhat better but rarely well.

*** Roots Of Rap
Yazoo 2018 *Allen Brothers, Beale Street Sheiks, Butterbeans & Susie, Leroy Carr, Rev. Edward W. Clayborn, Jimmie Davis, Dilly & His Dill Pickles, Dixieland Jug Blowers, Lonnie Glosson, Red Henderson, Frank Hutchison, Frankie 'Half-Pint' Jaxon, Blind Willie Johnson, Luke Jordan, Kansas City Kitty [Mozelle Alderson] & Georgia Tom [Dorsey], Blind Willie McTell, Memphis Jug Band, Memphis Minnie, Pine Top Smith, Speckled Red, T.C.I. Section Crew, Henry Thomas, Willie Walker.* 4/27–10/36.

The notes attempt to justify the title with remarks about rhythmic chanting, talking blues and the dozens, all of which undoubtedly contributed to rap's DNA. The rhymed couplets deployed by Frankie Jaxon in 'Jive Man Blues' and Frank Stokes in the Beale Street Sheiks' 'It's A Good Thing' do bring us close to rap, while Blind Willie McTell and the white Lonnie Glosson exemplify talking blues, but much of the CD is a hotchpotch of comic songs and stories, varieties of sacred singing and a good deal else. So, not precisely the underpinning of a thesis. Regard it instead as an excuse to gather a disparate bunch of records that can't readily be categorized but are engaging and often amusing. It's an index of the album's range that it embraces both Butterbeans & Susie in the vaudeville dialogue ''Tain't None O' Your Business' and John 'Seven Foot Dilly' Dilleshaw from north Georgia reciting a hillbilly farmer's diary in 'Pickin' Off Peanuts'.

*** Good Time Blues
Columbia CK 46780 *Son Becky, Charlie Burse & His Memphis Mudcats (2), Peter Chatman [Memphis Slim] (2), Bernice Edwards, Georgia Browns, Georgia Cotton Pickers (2), Big Joe [McCoy] & His Washboard Band (4), Memphis Jug Band (2), Mississippi Jook Band (4), Buddy Moss (2), Sonny Terry & Jordan Webb.* 12/30–10/41.

Subtitled 'Harmonicas, Kazoos, Washboards & Cow-Bells', and they could have added 'Jugs', but there are not enough of any of those elements to edge this collection into HARMONICA or JUGBANDS. The supremely vivacious music of the Mississippi Jook Band – the Graves brothers and pianist Cooney Vaughan – makes everything else on the album fight to leave as strong an impression. The Memphis Jug Band and the Georgia Cotton Pickers are equal to the struggle, and Moss and Burse play a good losing game, Burse's sax-fronted group edging Western Swingwards, but Joe McCoy's washboard group would seem pallid even in less robust company. Still, this is that uncommon thing, a programme of recorded high jinks with few low spots.

**(*) Rare Country Blues (1928–1937)
Document DOCD-5170 *Freezone, Willie Harris (4), Charlie Kyle (4), Leola Manning (6), Seth Richard (2), Jazzbo Tommy Settlers (8).* 5/28–3/37.

The selection is as arbitrary as the catchall title implies. All the artists are obscure and, to a specialist, interesting, but the rewards for a casual listener are variable. The most approachable is singer/guitarist Willie Harris, whose 'West Side Blues', a duet with an unidentified pianist, comes a respectable second to Blind Blake and Charlie Spand's 'Hastings St.', while 'Never Drive A Stranger From Your Door' is a stomping two-guitar version of 'Make Me A Pallet On The Floor'. The oddest is Tommy Settlers, whose early sides mix singing with vocalese delivered through something like a kazoo, yielding an effect that may remind British readers of Punch & Judy. That's the way to do it, Settlers evidently decided, because when he recorded again in 1937 with a conventional piano–guitar accompaniment he was still gamely tooting his horn. For the rest, Seth Richard is a lively 12-string guitarist, Charlie Kyle a dull one, and Leola Manning a declamatory singer at her best on two local stories about crime in Knoxville, Tennessee.

***(*) Rare Country Blues – Vol. 3 (1928–1936)
Document DOCD-5642 *Billy Bird (4), Cincinnati Jug Band (2), Kid Cole (4), Bob Coleman (3), Walter Coleman (6), Too Tight Henry [Henry L. Castle] (4).* 5/28–6/36.

Rare Country Blues – Vol. 2 (1929–1943) (Document DOCD-5641) is chiefly taken up with Walter Taylor and John Byrd and is reviewed in the former's entry. *Vol. 3* also has a main theme, the blues in Cincinnati, illustrated by the Cincinnati Jug Band, Kid Cole and Bob and Walter Coleman. (The fuller survey of that city's musicians provided by *Cincinnati Blues* [Catfish KATCD 186 2CD], which combined those recordings with material by Stovepipe No. 1, Jesse James and other Queen City figures, is regrettably deleted.) The Cole/Coleman artists are either all one man or two who are closely related, by music as well as by blood, and his/their liltingly delivered blues evince an attractive local style that has no parallel elsewhere. The jugband coupling brings together Kid Cole/Bob Coleman and Stovepipe No. 1, while Walter Coleman's last two sides have unmistakable piano by Jesse James. There are identity issues surrounding the Billy Bird sides as well, but we can put a real name to Too Tight Henry: Henry L. Castle (1899–1972), who is fascinating on his two-part 'Charleston Contest', where he plays two speaking roles and virtuoso 12-string guitar.

**(*) Rare Country Blues – Vol. 4 (1929–c. 1953)
Document DOCD-5643 *Pere Dickson (2), Troy Ferguson (3), Willie B. James (2), Arthur Lewis, Papa Egg Shell [Lawrence Casey] (4), Frank Tannehill (10), Robert Lee Westmoreland (2).* 5/29–c. 53.

Vol. 4 is as random as the first volume in this series. The outstanding tracks are by Robert Lee Westmoreland, a singer and slide guitarist from Georgia who made a single record in about 1953. Troy Ferguson's 'College Blues' has some unusual dialogue with Columbia's Atlanta A&R man Bill Brown. Frank Tannehill, the leading performer (he also accompanies

Dickson), is a sober Texan singer/pianist, a little like Black Boy Shine but even quieter, though 'Four O'Clock Morning Blues', with its uncommon reference to slavery, has a sharper edge.

** **Rare 1930's Blues – Vol. 1 (1934–1937)**
Document DOCD-5331 *Arkansas Shorty (6), Louisiana Johnny & Kid Beecher (10), John D. Twitty/Little Bill (8).* 10/34–5/37.

(*) **Rare 1930s Blues – Vol. 2 (1936–1940)
Document DOCD-5391 *Dusky Dailey (12), George Davis (4), The Jolly Three (2), Little David (4), Three Fifteen & His Squares (4).* 8/36–4/40.

(*) **Rare 1930s & '40s Blues – Vol. 3 (1937–1948)
Document DOCD-5427 *The Florida Kid (8), Willie (Boodle It) Right (7), Charley West (6), Bob White (4).* 5/37–48.

John D. Twitty, sometimes alias Black Spider Dumplin', is the best singer on *Vol. 1* and, assisted by the assured accompaniment of Big Bill and, probably, Black Bob, creates decent production-line blues. James McComb, alias Arkansas Shorty, is a more run-of-the-mill singer with brisk two-guitar backing. Louisiana Johnny & Kid Beecher try a variety of voices and approaches but seldom gell into an effective act, and it is no surprise that six of their ten sides were shelved.

Whereas *Vol. 1* follows a Deep South-to-Chicago axis, *Vol. 2* deals largely with Southwestern performers. Dusky Dailey's dozen, apart from a few pop songs done roughly in the style of Bob Howard or Fats Waller and a striking solo reading of 'Flying Crow Blues', are fairly standardized blues, mostly with small-band backing. George Davis also toes the blues line, though both voice and piano playing imply that he would have been more successful as a cocktail-hour crooner. Three Fifteen & His Squares and The Jolly Three take the Harlem Hamfats' route. Singer/pianist Little David (Alexander, a given name he shared with Black Ivory King) delivers two versions of the suggestive 'Sweet Petunia' theme previously recorded by Curley Weaver and Lucille Bogan and, in a different vein, 'Standing By A Lamp Post', a reflective and unsentimental eight-bar blues that integrates voice and piano in a beautifully balanced performance. Transfer quality on both CDs is generally poor.

Vol. 3 focuses on four artists who had found their way to Chicago or Detroit. West and Right are musically colourless personalities, their accompaniments doggedly utilitarian. More entertaining is The Florida Kid, who sings original lyrics in a loose style rather like Dr Clayton's. His piano accompanist Bob White, alias Detroit Count, concludes the album with 'Hastings Street Opera', a two-part travelogue about Detroit's black entertainment strip.

** **Jack Newman (1938)**
Document DOCD-5351 *James Hall (6), Frankie Jones (6), Black Bottom McPhail (6), Jack Newman (6).* 5/38.

Issuing this collection under the name of Jack Newman was a shot in the dark. All 24 recordings were made at a one-day session, and it's likely that a single group of musicians did all or most of the accompanying work. Newman seems to be present only as the singer of his own six numbers; the compiler, guessing that he played the guitar (though the notewriter disagrees), proposed that he also did so for the other singers, though when Frankie Jones says, in 'Bring Your Mud And Let's Dob', 'Now play it, Mr Newman! Beat it on out there!' the soloing musician is Charlie McCoy, here on mandolin but almost certainly the guitarist on the other sides. The only one of the four singers in the studio with an attested existence outside it was Black Bottom McPhail, who had recorded some years earlier with Scrapper Blackwell. Judging by his voice and the style of the songwriting, James Hall might have been James Oden. Newman himself is not unlike Monkey Joe Coleman. Other than providing a case for discographical detectives, though, the album is not very interesting. McPhail, the best singer, has an unusual 'Boll Weavil' blues and a swing version of 'John Henry', but, these aside, the music is production-line blues at its most mechanized, and the piano–guitar accompaniments are profoundly anonymous.

(*) **Jazzin' The Blues – Vol. 1 (1929–1937)
Document DOCD-5407 *David Cross (5), Four Southerners (2), Connie McLean's Rhythm Boys (6), Willie 'Scare Crow' Owens & Lena Matlock (9), Ike Smith & His Chicago Boys (2).* 3/29–3/37.

(*) **Jazzin' The Blues – Vol. 2 (1939–1946)
Document DOCD-5468 *Bandanna Girls (4), Wingy Carpenter (5), Four Blackamoors (3), The Grooveneers, Creole George Guesnon (6), Mabel Robinson (6).* 1/39–46.

(*) **Jazzin' The Blues – Vol. 4 (1929–1943)
Document DOCD-5611 *Savannah Churchill (4), Edgewater Crows (2), Corny Allen Grier (2), Billie Hayes (3), Richard Huey (2), Willie Lewis Entertainers, Phil Pavey (4), Jack Sneed (2), Beverly White (4).* 2/29–11/43.

(*) **Jazzin' The Blues (1936–1946)
RST Jazz Perspectives JPCD-1515 *Lee Brown (9), W. C. Handy (4), Tiny Mayberry (6), Monette Moore (2), Helen Proctor (4).* 2/36–9/46.

(*) **Swingin' The Blues (1931–1939)
Document DOCD-5354 *Mattie Hardy (5), Ramona Hicks (6), Justine Lamar (2), Emmet Mathews (2), Jimmy McLain (2), John Oscar (2), Laura Rucker (3), Jimmy Strange (2), Elsie Williams (2).* c. 5/31–5/39.

Jazzin' means that the recordings selected for this series, though customarily listed in blues discographies, have some claim to be thought of as jazz, or jazzy. On *Vol. 1*, for instance, reedsman Connie McLean leads a spirited swing sextet, while the vaudeville singers Cross and Owens are backed by talented trumpeters, and The Four Southerners are a vocal quartet in the Mills Brothers mould. The Bandanna Girls on *Vol. 2*, however, are an almost hillbilly-like duet with a piano trio and no jazz character, and a good deal of the tracks on this and subsequent volumes seem to have found their way there because Document couldn't think of anywhere better to put them. For the reader unbothered by that, these are, intermittently, rather entertaining collections. *Vol. 2* has a run of 11 tracks by Carpenter and Guesnon with the excellent but underregarded electric guitarist Jimmy Shirley, while *Vol. 4* penetrates the wild and woolly borderlands of the 'race' catalogues to find black country music (Grier) and Jamaican songs (Sneed). For *Vol. 3* see Sam Theard, and for *Vol. 5* see WOMEN.

Jazzin' The Blues (1936–1946), though outside the sequence, is similar in character. As well as completing Document's reissue of Lee Brown (q.v.), it contains sessions by small New York groups (Buster Bailey, Lil Armstrong, etc.) accompanying the rasping Tiny Mayberry and the pallid Helen Proctor. In a 1939 session of considerable historical curiosity, W. C. Handy, buoyed by an excellent band, plays cautious cornet on four of his own compositions, also singing on two of them.

A few small-swing-group accompaniments make it reasonable to include *Swingin' The Blues* here, though most of the tracks are typical production-line blues of their day. Jimmy Strange's mildly amusing two-part 'Yas Yas Yas' checks some contemporary names (Joe Louis, John Dillinger), and Mattie Hardy finds an unusual theme in 'Striped Ape Blues'.

*** "Too Late, Too Late Blues" – Vol. 1 (1926–1944)
Document DOCD-5150 *Kokomo Arnold, Willie Baker, Blind Blake, Frank Brasswell, Big Bill Broonzy (2), Bo Carter, Little Buddy Doyle, Blind Lemon Jefferson (2), Lonnie Johnson, Kansas City Kitty [Mozelle Alderson] & Georgia Tom [Dorsey] (2), Joe McCoy (2), Memphis Jug Band, Memphis Minnie (3), Charley Patton, Robert Peeples, Rev. D. C. Rice, Charlie Spand (2), Bessie Tucker, George 'Bullet' Williams. c. 10/26–12/44.*

With *"Too Late, Too Late Blues" – Vol. 1* Document initiated a series of albums, currently standing at 12, which filled gaps in previous (mostly single-artist) collections. Like its successors, the CD was put together from newly discovered alternative takes, items unissued on 78 but retrieved from test pressings, and issued but elusive recordings that had not been found when Document were constructing their logical CD homes. Such compilations are practically defined by the term 'collector-oriented', and readers who do not think of themselves as collectors are generally well advised to ignore them, but a few volumes can be regarded as texts in their own right, so to speak, not just assemblages of footnotes. *Vol. 1* has a long castlist of eminent musicians as well as intriguing minor ones like Frank Brasswell, the sound quality is relatively untroubling and the sheer variety of approaches makes for quite exciting listening.

*** "Too Late, Too Late Blues" – Vol. 2 (1897–1935)
Document DOCD-5216 *Kokomo Arnold, Blind Blake (2), Booker Orchestra, Brantley & Williams, Gene Campbell (2), Bo Carter (2), Cousins & De Moss, Jim Jackson, Lonnie Johnson (2), Male Quartette, Rev. Moses Mason (2), Kansas Joe [McCoy] (2), Charley Patton (2), Ma Rainey, Ramblin' Thomas (2), unknown, Joshua White (2). 7/1897–7/1935.*

Vol. 2 makes important additions to Document's holdings of Gene Campbell, Joe McCoy and Ramblin' Thomas, but its most fascinating tracks are four pre-1910 recordings of artists performing vaudeville material which has intriguing connections with later recordings. The African-American banjoists Cousins & De Moss singing 'Poor Mourner' (a.k.a. 'You Shall Be Free') on a Berliner disc of 1897 take us almost as far back into recording history as we can go.

Subsequent volumes are very specialized, and will not be itemized or rated. Many of them have something of unusual interest, though. *Vol. 3* (DOCD-5276) supplies the missing item, 'Don't Speak To Me', from the momentous Lottie Kimbrough–Winston Holmes session (see the former's entry), but it's no 'Rolling Log Blues' and it's also from a gritty disc. *Vol. 4* (DOCD-5321) reveals what's on the rarest of the discs by the Shreveport slide guitarists Eddie (Schaffer) and Oscar (Woods), while *Vol. 5* (DOCD-5411) uncovers the exquisite pairing of Frank Stokes and fiddler Will Batts on 'I'm Going Away Blues' and 'Old Sometime Blues' and offers the scratchy but unique copy of Henry Townsend's only Paramount disc, 'Doctor, Oh Doctor'/'Jack Of Diamonds Georgia Rub'. *Vol. 6* (DOCD-5461) and *Vol. 7* (DOCD-5525) are unremarkable, but *Vol. 8* (DOCD-5574) circulates another disc of notorious rarity,

the North Carolina singer/guitarist Jack Gowdlock's 1931 Victor of 'Poor Jane Blues' (a version of 'Crow Jane') and 'Rollin' Dough Blues'. *Vol. 9* (DOCD-5590) is replete with early recordings of obscure vaudeville singers. The chief attraction of *Vol. 10* (DOCD-5601) is the 1942 Library of Congress session by the Nashville Washboard Band, and of *Vol. 11* (DOCD-5625) eight alternative takes of Papa Charlie Jackson. By *Vol. 12* (DOCD-5659) Document were hunting in the remotest corners of the phonographic archive, and most of the CD will be on the periphery of even a collector's interest. All but the first of the *"Too Late"* series have learned notes by Guido van Rijn. TR

Miscellaneous II (Postwar)

*** The Road To Rhythm & Blues And Rock 'N' Roll – Volume I
Flapper PAST CD 7811 *Albert Ammons (2), Kokomo Arnold, Blind Blake, Big Bill Broonzy, Pete Brown Quintet, Walter Brown (2), Savannah Churchill, Al Cooper & The Savoy Sultans, Harlem Hamfats (2), Erskine Hawkins, Miss Rhapsody, Ella Mae Morse, Hot Lips Page, The Red Caps, June Richmond, Jimmy Rushing (2), Rosetta Tharpe, Big Joe Turner, Eddie 'Cleanhead' Vinson, Dinah Washington, Georgia White. 8/29–9/44.*

*** Roots Of Rhythm & Blues
Frémeaux FA 050 2CD *Albert Ammons, Tiny Bradshaw, Charles Brown, Walter Brown, Nat 'King' Cole, Arthur 'Big Boy' Crudup, Billy Eckstine, Five Red Caps, Cecil Gant, Lionel Hampton, Wynonie Harris, Erskine Hawkins, Johnny Hodges & His Orchestra, Helen Humes, Ivory Joe Hunter, Ella Johnson, Pete Johnson, Louis Jordan, Julia Lee, Joe Liggins, Jack McVea, Roy Milton, Gatemouth Moore, Ella Mae Morse, Johnny Otis, Hot Lips Page, June Richmond, Jimmy Rushing, The Spirits Of Rhythm, (Sister) Rosetta Tharpe (2), Big Joe Turner, Eddie 'Cleanhead' Vinson, T-Bone Walker, Dinah Washington, Rubberlegs Williams. 39–45.*

*** That's All Right
Bluebird 63989 *Henry 'Red' Allen, Big Maceo, Eddie Boyd, The Cats & A Fiddle, Dr Clayton (2), Arthur 'Big Boy' Crudup (3), The Five Breezes, Jazz Gillum, Lil Green, Pete Johnson & Albert Ammons, Little Richard, Robert Lockwood, Memphis Slim, Johnny Moore's Three Blazers, Piano Red (2), Sunnyland Slim, Roosevelt Sykes, Tampa Red (2), Sonny Terry, Washboard Sam. 6/39–11/55.*

*** Blues Masters, Volume 1: Urban Blues
Rhino R2 71121 *Count Basie & His Orchestra, Bobby 'Blue' Bland, Charles Brown, Pee Wee Crayton, Lowell Fulson, Guitar Slim, Erskine Hawkins, Albert King, Johnny Otis Quintette, Junior Parker, Otis Rush, Little Johnny Taylor, Joe Turner, Eddie Vinson, T-Bone Walker, Dinah Washington, Chuck Willis, Jimmy Witherspoon. 6/40–3/66.*

*** The Road To Rhythm & Blues And Rock 'N' Roll – Volume II
Flapper PAST CD 7812 *Big Maceo, Tiny Bradshaw, Cousin Joe (2), Arthur 'Big Boy' Crudup, Numa Lee Davis, Lionel Hampton (2), Wynonie Harris, Helen Humes, Illinois Jacquet, Ella Johnson (with Buddy Johnson), Luke Jones, Louis Jordan (3), Joe Liggins, Jack McVea, Amos Milburn, Freddie Slack, Sister Rosetta Tharpe, Big Joe Turner, Eddie 'Cleanhead' Vinson, T-Bone Walker, Dinah Washington. 9/44–9/46.*

*** The R&B Years Volume 1
Acrobat ACRCD 136 *Count Basie, Hadda Brooks, Arthur 'Big Boy' Crudup, Ella Fitzgerald, Wynonie Harris (2), John Lee Hooker, Buddy Johnson, Louis Jordan (3), Julia Lee (3), Nellie Lutcher (2), Amos Milburn, Sugar Chile Robinson, Sister Rosetta Tharpe, Eddie Vinson, Dinah Washington (2). 5/45–49.*

*** The R&B Years Volume 2
Acrobat ACRCD 137 *Ruth Brown, Lionel Hampton, John Lee Hooker, Bullmoose Jackson, Louis Jordan (4), Julia Lee (2), Joe Liggins, Nellie Lutcher, Sticks McGhee, Amos Milburn (2), Roy Milton, The Ravens, Sugar Chile Robinson, Mabel Scott, Hal Singer, Dinah Washington (2). 44–49.*

*** Rock N' Roll 1947
Frémeaux FA 353 2CD *Chet Atkins, Big Three Trio, Roy Brown, Delmore Brothers, Al Dexter, Red Foley, Paul Gayten, Jazz Gillum, Wynonie Harris, Smokey Hogg, Lightnin' Hopkins, Paul Howard, Louis Jordan, Pee Wee King, Julia Lee (2), Peggy Lee, Jimmy Liggins, Joe Lutcher, Nellie Lutcher, Sticks McGhee, Amos Milburn, Milo Twins, Roy Milton, Wayne Raney, Jack Rivers, Sons Of The Pioneers, Sister Rosetta Tharpe, Merle Travis, Johnny Tyler, T-Texas Tyler, Jimmy Wakely, Hank Williams, Tex Williams, Sonny Boy Williamson I, Luke Wills. 47.*

Most of these compilations, some more explicitly than others, attempt to provide a historically respectable lineage for the squalling infant rock 'n' roll, though they're divided over whether its ancestors were exclusively, or at least primarily, African-American (jazz, boogie woogie, jump blues, etc.) or contributed white genetic material like hillbilly boogie and Western Swing. Their reliability as genealogies may be inconsistent, but they are all highly informative selections of American vernacular music in one of its most creative periods, the decade after the end of World War II.

From their frequent appearances on these CDs the listener can begin to assemble a list of the iconic recordings of the period, items that would have been worn grey on thousands of jukeboxes, such as Erskine Hawkins's 'After Hours' (actually recorded in 1940 but a lasting hit), Lionel Hampton's 'Hey! Ba-Ba-Re-Bop', Eddie Vinson's 'Kidney Stew Blues', Arthur 'Big Boy' Crudup's 'That's All Right' and other numbers by Joe Turner, Dinah Washington and Louis Jordan. So varied was the music of the time that wide-ranging sets like those on Flapper and Acrobat and Frémeaux's *Roots Of Rhythm & Blues* whirl the listener on an effervescent, intoxicating carousel of snappy lyrics and peppy rhythms. The Acrobats are cheap and reasonably well remastered but their contents are rather predictable, whereas the Flapper and Frémeaux sets are more artfully chosen. Rhino's *Urban Blues* has a wider temporal and stylistic remit, Count Basie to Albert King. *That's All Right*, an entry in Bluebird's series *When The Sun Goes Down: The Secret History Of Rock & Roll*, differs from the rest in being derived from a single major label (Victor) rather than a gaggle of independents, and its roster favours established stars like Dr Clayton, Roosevelt Sykes and Tampa Red over new ones, or ones in the making, like Eddie Boyd or Billy Valentine, heard with Johnny Moore's Three Blazers on the original cut of 'How Blue Can You Get'. In common with the rest of the series, its production standards are impeccable. Frémeaux's *1947* cunningly balances the black and white music of the year, so that, for example, a sequence of boogies switches the listener from Louis Jordan to Red Foley to Joe Lutcher to the Milo Twins.

**** Blowing The Fuse – 1945
Bear Family BCD 16700 *Count Basie, Big Maceo, Hadda Brooks [Pete Johnson], Arthur Crudup, Five Red Caps, The Four Clefs, Pvt. Cecil Gant, The Golden Gate Quartet, Lionel Hampton, Wynonie Harris, Erskine Hawkins, Helen Humes, Ivory Joe Hunter, Herb Jeffries, Buddy Johnson, Louis Jordan, Julia Lee, Joe Liggins, Jay McShann, Lucky Millinder, Gatemouth Moore, Johnny Otis, Sister Rosetta Tharpe, Joe Turner, T-Bone Walker, Cootie Williams. 44–45.*

**** Blowing The Fuse – 1946
Bear Family BCD 16701 *Big Maceo, The Blues Woman [Marion Abernathy], Red Callender Trio, Cats'n Jammer Three, [Nat] King Cole Trio, Arthur Crudup, Delta Rhythm Boys, Lionel Hampton, Wynonie Harris, Erskine Hawkins, The Ink Spots, Bull Moose Jackson, Louis Jordan (2), Andy Kirk, Julia Lee, Joe Liggins, Jay McShann, Roy Milton, Johnny Moore's Three Blazers, Velma Nelson, Bill Samuels, Roosevelt Sykes, Joe Turner, Eddie Vinson, T-Bone Walker, Dinah Washington. 45–46.*

**** Blowing The Fuse – 1947
Bear Family BCD 16702 *Albert Ammons, Big Three Trio, Hadda Brooks Trio, Clarence ['Gatemouth'] Brown, Walter Brown, Savannah Churchill, Arthur Crudup, Five Blazes, Lionel Hampton, Wynonie Harris, Bill Johnson, Louis Jordan (2), Annie Laurie, Julia Lee, Nellie Lutcher, Jack McVea, Amos Milburn, Roy Milton, Johnny Moore's Three Blazers, Gene Phillips, The Ravens, Clarence Samuels, Joe Turner, Eddie Vinson, T-Bone Walker, Paul Williams Sextet, Sonny Boy Williamson [I]. 46–47.*

**** Blowing The Fuse – 1948
Bear Family BCD 16703 *Big Three Trio, Roy Brown, Wynonie Harris, Camille Howard, Ivory Joe Hunter, Bull Moose Jackson, Lonnie Johnson, Louis Jordan (2), Julia Lee, Jimmy Liggins, Nellie Lutcher, Amos Milburn, Roy Milton, Bill Moore, Gatemouth Moore, Muddy Waters, The Orioles, The Ravens, Mabel Scott, Hal Singer Sextette, Arbee Stidham, Joe Swift, Sonny Thompson, T-Bone Walker, Crown Prince Waterford, Paula Watson, Paul Williams Sextette. 47–48.*

**** Blowing The Fuse – 1949
Bear Family BCD 16704 *Charles Brown Trio, Clarence ['Gatemouth'] Brown, Roy Brown, Ruth Brown, Pee Wee Crayton, Larry Darnell, T. J. Fowler, Wynonie Harris, John Lee Hooker, Bull Moose Jackson, Louis Jordan, Annie Laurie, Julia Lee, Stick McGhee, Big Jay McNeely, Amos Milburn, Red Miller, The Orioles, Jimmy Preston, Todd Rhodes, Sugar Chile Robinson, Sister Rosetta Tharpe, T-Bone Walker, Dinah Washington, Paul Williams, Jimmy Witherspoon, Billy Wright. 48–49.*

**** Blowing The Fuse – 1950
Bear Family BCD 16705 *Archibald [Leon T. Gross], Calvin Boze, Tiny Bradshaw, Clarence ['Gatemouth'] Brown, Roy Brown, Ruth Brown, Goree Carter, Doc Sausage, Fats Domino, Lowell Fulson, Lloyd Glenn, Wynonie Harris, Roy Hawkins, Lightnin' Hopkins, Ivory Joe Hunter, Louis Jordan, Jewel King, Joe Liggins, Eddie Mack, Percy Mayfield, Roy Milton, Joe Morris, Johnny Otis, Jimmy Preston, Professor Longhair, The Ravens, Joe Turner, T-Bone Walker. 49–50.*

**** Blowing The Fuse – 1951
Bear Family BCD 16706 *Earl Bostic, Tiny Bradshaw, Jackie Brenston, Charles Brown, The Clovers, Margie Day, Floyd Dixon, The Dominoes, The Five Keys, The Four Buddies, Lloyd Glenn, Peppermint Harris, Wynonie Harris, Johnny Hodges, John Lee Hooker, Howlin' Wolf, Louis Jordan, The Larks, Joe Liggins, Amos Milburn, Lucky Millinder, Muddy Waters, Jimmie*

Nelson & The Peter Rabbit Trio, Johnny Otis, Piano Red, The Treniers, Joe Turner, James Wayne. 50–51.

**** Blowing The Fuse – 1952
Bear Family BCD 16707 *Johnny Ace, Marie Adams, Tiny Bradshaw, Charles Brown, Ruth Brown, The Clovers, Varetta Dillard, Fats Domino, The Dominoes, Jimmy Forrest, The Four Blazes, Rosco Gordon, John Greer, Griffin Brothers' Orchestra, Wynonie Harris, Elmore James, B. B. King, Smiley Lewis, Little Caesar, Little Walter, Willie Mabon, Roy Milton, The Orioles, Lloyd Price, The Ravens, The Swallows, Big Joe Turner, Dinah Washington, Lester Williams.* 51–52.

**** Blowing The Fuse – 1953
Bear Family BCD 16708 *Johnny Ace, Faye Adams, Big Maybelle, Tiny Bradshaw, Ruth Brown, Ray Charles, The Clovers, Fats Domino, The Du Droppers, The '5' Royales, Earl Forest, The Four Tunes, Bull Moose Jackson, Jesse & Marvin, Buddy & Ella Johnson, B. B. King, Jimmy Liggins, Little Walter, Willie Mabon, Clyde McPhatter & The Drifters, Amos Milburn, Joe Morris, The Orioles, Little Junior [Parker], The Royals, Shirley & Lee, Big Mama Thornton, Joe Turner, Dinah Washington.* 52–53.

**** Blowing The Fuse – 1954
Bear Family BCD 16709 *Johnny Ace, Faye Adams, Dave Bartholomew, Ruth Brown, The Cadillacs, Ray Charles, The Charms, The Chords, The Clovers, Sugar Boy Crawford, The Crows, The Drifters, Cozy Eggleston, The '5' Royales, Shirley Gunter, Guitar Slim, The Harptones, Joe Houston, Howlin' Wolf, Buddy & Ella Johnson, B. B. King, Little Walter, The Midnighters, Muddy Waters, The Robins, The Spaniels, The Spiders, Big Joe Turner, Chuck Willis.* 53–54.

**** Blowing The Fuse – 1955
Bear Family BCD 16710 *Johnny Ace, LaVern Baker, Chuck Berry, Bo Diddley, Louis Brooks, Nappy Brown, Ray Charles, Fats Domino, The El Dorados, Lowell Fulson, Gene & Eunice, The Jacks, Etta James, Little Willie John, Smiley Lewis, Little Richard, Little Walter, Clyde McPhatter, Jay McShann & Priscilla Bowman, The Moonglows, The Nutmegs, The Penguins, The Platters, Jimmy Reed, The Robins, Shirley & Lee, Sonny Boy Williamson [II], The Turbans, Big Joe Turner.* 54–55.

Listening to blues in genre-based compilations – blues, blues, and more blues – you risk forgetting that it was just one patch in the musical–cultural quilt of black America. To understand the commercial context of the blues, particularly in those fermenting decades, the '40s and '50s, you need to hear it amidst all the other recorded music that vied for the African-American dollar in the record store and the nickel in the jukebox, especially those recordings that the wind of popularity blew into the *Billboard* and *Cash Box* charts. For every blues single by Muddy Waters or Jimmy Reed, or T-Bone Walker or Charles Brown, that made the Top Ten, there was a big-band boogie by Lionel Hampton, a doo-wop ballad by The Orioles or The Moonglows, or a comic novelty like 'Open The Door Richard!'

Several series of year-by-year reissues have been devoted to restitching that patchwork. Much the best is *Blowing The Fuse*, which at the time of writing stretches from 1945 to 1955, with further volumes promised to bring the story up to 1960. Each year's CD is a selection of singles that made some impact on the R&B charts, from downhome blues by Arthur Crudup or Howlin' Wolf to vocal groups, nightclub acts like Hadda Brooks and saxophone soloists like Hal Singer or Earl Bostic. Such variety leads to wonderfully serendipitous juxtapositions: Big Maceo and Herb Jeffries, John Lee Hooker and The Clovers, Junior Parker segueing to Dinah Washington to The Drifters. The selection is generous (26 to 29 tracks), judicious and wide-ranging (though producer Dave Booth does note that 'pop-slanted R&B … [and] blues and doo wop groups are not featured prominently because of time restraints'), the sound quality is almost invariably excellent and the presentation is gorgeous.

***(*) The R&B Years 1947
Boulevard BVBCD 1013 4CD *Various artists.* 46–47.
***(*) The R&B Years 1948
Boulevard BVBCD 1008 4CD *Various artists.* 47–48.
***(*) The R&B Years 1949
Boulevard BVBCD 1007 4CD *Various artists.* 48–49.
***(*) The R&B Years 1950
Boulevard BVBCD 1006 4CD *Various artists.* 49–50.
***(*) The R&B Years 1951
Boulevard BVBCD 1005 4CD *Various artists.* 50–51.
***(*) The R&B Years 1952
Boulevard BVBCD 1002 4CD *Various artists.* 51–52.
*** The R&B Hits Of 1952
Indigo IGOTCD 2532 3CD *Various artists.* 51–52.
***(*) The R&B Years 1953
Boulevard BVBCD 1001 4CD *Various artists.* 52–53.
*** The R&B Hits Of 1953
Indigo IGOTCD 2540 3CD *Various artists.* 52–53.
*** R&B Jukebox Hits 1953 Volume 1
Acrobat ACMCD 4197 *Johnny Ace, Annisteen Allen, Big Maybelle, Eddie Boyd, Tiny Bradshaw, Ruth Brown, The Clovers, Nat 'King' Cole, Fats Domino, The Du Droppers, The '5' Royales (3), Little Walter (3), Willie Mabon, Amos Milburn, Danny Overbea, Rufus Thomas, Big Mama Thornton, The Vocaleers, Billy Ward & His Dominoes (2), Chuck Willis.* 52–53.
***(*) The R&B Years 1954
Boulevard BVBCD 1011 4CD *Various artists.* 53–54.
*** The R&B Hits Of 1954
Indigo IGOTCD 2565 3CD *Various artists.* 53–54.

Given the excellence of the Bear Family series reviewed above, readers might think they needn't look too closely at the similar projects undertaken by Boulevard and, less expansively, Indigo. They would be wrong. In the first place, these 3CD and 4CD sets are obviously much larger, typically containing 75 and 100 tracks respectively. (Space forbids our providing artist listings, but the reader can safely assume that they have many of the same artists, and the same general character, as the parallel Bear Family volumes.) They therefore have room to investigate more deeply idioms that Bear Family admit they cover only selectively, including blues. They can also acknowledge when an artist had a particularly good year, as in Boulevard's *The R&B Years 1947*, which has six cuts by Louis Jordan. Finally, they are very competitively priced. So if you are seriously interested in teleporting yourself back in time to a tavern or diner with a well-stocked jukebox – which, in effect, is what all these year-by-year compilations offer – you certainly need to consider the boxes as well as the Bears. Naturally all of them overlap, but not as much as you may suppose: that 1947 Boulevard, for example, duplicates barely half the contents of the matching Bear Family CD, while at the other end of the sequence *The R&B Years 1954* has just over half of the equivalent Bear tracks. The Indigos, however, overlap the Bear Family sets rather more (particularly in 1954), and they inevitably also share a good deal of common ground with the Boulevards. The Acrobat, OK as far as it goes, is dwarfed by the heavyweights around it. Our advice to the shopper would be to start with *Blowing The Fuse*, then, if your appetite is unsated, add either (but not both) of the boxed series; for length and depth we recommend Boulevard.

*** **Rockin' With The Rhythm & Blues**
El Toro R&B 100 *Jesse Allen & Jimmy Gilchrist, Mr Google Eyes [Joe August], Max 'Blues' Bailey, Honey Brown, Roy Brown, Gunter Lee Carr [Cecil Gant], Goree Carter, Floyd Dixon, Doc Sausage, H-Bomb Ferguson, Great Gates, Big John Greer, Tiny Grimes, Wynonie Harris, Jimmy McCracklin, Memphis Slim, Wally Mercer, Amos Milburn, Freddie Mitchell, Sonny Parker, Jimmy Preston, La Verne Ray & Arlene Talley, The Robins, Little Jimmy Smith, Laurie Tate, The Treniers.* 47–51.

The USP of this diverting collection is that every track's title contains the word 'Rock' or 'Rockin'', enunciated by singers as different as Wynonie Harris ('Rock Mr Blues') and Cecil Gant ('We're Gonna Rock') or translated into instrumentalese by loquacious saxophonists of the stripe of Big John Greer, Charlie Singleton and Freddie Mitchell. There's rare stuff here, efficiently gathered and annotated by Dave Penny and attractively packaged by the Spanish label.

*** **Honkin' The Boogie**
Acrobat ACRCD 200 *Buddy Banks (2), Eddie Chamblee (2), Dick Davis, Erskine Hawkins, Cee Pee Johnson, Big Jay McNeely (2), Jay McShann, Wild Bill Moore (2), Joe Morris (2), King Porter (2), Hal Singer, Sonny Thompson, Paul Williams, Jim Wynn.* 6/40–4/49.

*** **Riff Ridin'**
El Toro R&B 102 *Gene Ammons, Paul Bascomb, J. T. 'Nature Boy' Brown, Eddie Chamblee, Arnett Cobb, Frank 'Floorshow' Culley, Julian Dash, Maxwell Davis, Big Bob Dougherty, Paul Gayten, Big John Greer, Lynn Hope, Joe Houston, Bullmoose Jackson, Morris Lane, Jack McVea, Freddie Mitchell, James Moody, Wild Bill Moore, Bumps Myers, Red Prysock, Charlie Singleton, Sam 'The Man' Taylor, Joe Thomas, Lucky Thompson, David Van Dyke, Ben Webster.* 47–52.

*** **Jumpin' The Blues**
Ace CDCHD 941 *Johnnie Brown, Waymon Brown, Willie Brown (2), Harold Burrage, Goree Carter (2), Eunice Davis, Tiny Davis (2), Margie Day, Doles Dickens, Big Bob Dougherty, Cecil Gant, John Godfrey Trio, Stomp Gordon (2), Connie Jordan, Zilla Mays, Cecil Payne, Joey Thomas, James Von Streeter.* 49–54.

A large piece of the bright patchwork of black music in the '40s and '50s was the saxophone instrumental. Thousands of discs, typically coupling a rambunctious up-tempo blues (one of Bill Doggett's was actually called 'Ram-Bunk-Shush') and a breathy ballad, lined up in the nation's jukeboxes awaiting the march of dimes. It was brusquely functional music for enlivening a tavern evening, and subtlety and imagination were in short supply. Paradigms of the idiom are insistent riff tunes like Hal Singer's 'Cornbread' (*Honkin' The Boogie*), Big Bob Dougherty's 'Big Bob's Boogie' (*Jumpin' The Blues*) or Joe Houston's 'Houston's Hot House' and Charlie Singleton's 'S.O.S.' (*Riff Ridin'*), the last tune played largely on one note. The ballads, of course, were softer fruits, sometimes luscious ones, but the agendas of these collections prevent the listener from tasting any of them. Each CD is virtually end-to-end blues and boogies, variegated by occasional vocals or a more louche tempo, and if you enjoy a muscular saxophonist flexing his pecs any one of them will give pleasure. *Jumpin' The Blues* is derived entirely from Decca recordings and consequently has the best sound quality.

*** **Gonna Rock The Blues**
Official CD 503 *Jesse Allen, B. Brown & His Rockin' McVouts, Harold Burrage, Gunter Lee Carr [Cecil Gant], Bob Gaddy, Big Boy Groves, Homesick James (2), Eddie Hope (2), Lightnin' Hopkins (2), J. B. Hutto, Bobo Jenkins (2), Joe Hill Louis, Louisiana Red, Magic Sam, Jerry McCain, Big Walter [Price], Snooky Pryor, Mister Ruffin, Otis Rush, The Sly Fox (2), T.V. Slim, Tarheel Slim [Alden Bunn], Hound Dog Taylor, Sonny Terry, Mojo Watson, Jo Jo Williams, Jimmy Wilson.* 50s.

When you're offered an album as well filled as this, it seems ungracious to wave a pedantic forefinger at the anonymous compiler and ask what on earth he thought he was doing. Especially when he could reasonably reply, 'Giving you a lot of great music for your money. Got a problem with that?' As far as any theme can be discerned in these 32 mostly splendid performances, occupying almost 80 minutes' playing time, it's that many of them, originating on labels like Spark, Marlin, Atomic H and Atlas, are prized by collectors for their excellence and rarity. For some collectors rarity would be enough on its own, so we should reassure non-hoarding readers that almost everything here earns its place as music – assuming, that is, that they enjoy craggy downhome practitioners like Joe Hill Louis ('Hydramatic Woman') or T.V. Slim ('Can't Be Satisfied') as well as slicker dudes like Big Boy Groves, whose 'I Gotta New Car' is a shameless ripoff of Ray Charles's 'It Should Have Been Me'. No notes, beyond the barest of recording details.

*** **My Guitar Wants To Kill Your Mama**
Lenox 1012 *Earl Hooker (2), Calvin Leavy, The Masked Marvel's Buddy, Guitar Tommy Moore (2), George Smith, Lafayette Thomas (2), Mojo Watson (3), Sly Williams (2).* c. 55–68.

This French release will commend itself to collectors who are not too blasé to get a frisson from obscure compilations of weird stuff. The contents come from rare and discographically mysterious singles, and the CD leaflet does little to dispel the mystery; indeed, identifying one of the sides as 'Screamin' And Hollerin' The Blues No. 2' by The Masked Marvel's Buddy (a Charley Patton joke) seems to have been a deliberate cloaking of its origins. Evidently the compiler's chief motive was to acquaint listeners with some red-hot guitar work, like that of the anonymous player on Sly Williams's 'Boot Hill' and 'I Believe In A Woman', the aforementioned Mr M. M. Buddy, and the inexperienced but ambitious Mojo Watson. Calvin Leavy's 'Cummins Prison', a justly celebrated recording, is discussed in his entry. Lafayette Thomas is in top form on a T-Bone Walkeresque 'Weekly Blues' and the instrumental 'The Thing', which make up for the dull triviality of Earl Hooker's 'Yea Yea' and 'Do The Chicken'.

*** **15 Down Home Urban Blues Classics**
Arhoolie CD 102 *Juke Boy Bonner, Big Joe Duskin, Charles Ford Band, Earl Hooker, Bee Houston, Johnny Littlejohn, Charlie Musselwhite, Piano Red, L. C. 'Good Rockin'' Robinson, Omar Sharriff, Sonny Boy Williamson [II], Big Mama Thornton, Joe Turner (with Pete Johnson), Katie Webster, Johnny Young.* 6/48–85.

What's in a name, indeed? Here you have two terms usually

thought of as contradictory, 'down home' and 'urban', yoked into a single title. Given the inclusion of artists like the Charles Ford Band or Joe Turner, it seems inappropriate to file this CD under DOWNHOME, but even here it's rather out on a limb, since all but two of its 15 tracks were recorded in the '70s or '80s, first appearing on Arhoolie LPs. Still, it covers a lot of stylistic ground, from the Chicago ensemble sound of Johnny Young or Johnny Littlejohn to the amplified blues fiddling of L. C. Robinson ('Ups & Downs'), and it's an inexpensive way to acquaint yourself with some deserving albums. TR

Mississippi

♛ **** **Masters Of The Delta Blues: The Friends Of Charley Patton**
Yazoo 2002 *Kid Bailey (2), Willie Brown (2), Ishmon Bracey, Son House (7), Louise Johnson (2), Tommy Johnson (5), Bertha Lee (2), Booker White (2). 2/28–1/34.*

**** **Mississippi Masters – Early American Blues Classics 1927–35**
Yazoo 2007 *Garfield Akers (3), Joe Callicott, Mattie Delaney (2), John D. Fox (2), William Harris (3), King Solomon Hill (2), Blind Joe Reynolds (2), Otto Virgial, Geeshie Wiley & Elvie Thomas (4). 12/27–10/35.*

Some of the most powerful and affecting blues ever recorded were made by singers and guitarists from Mississippi in the late '20s and early '30s. The presence of pieces like Willie Brown's 'Future Blues', Garfield Akers's 'Dough Roller Blues', William Harris's 'Bullfrog Blues' and Tommy Johnson's 'Maggie Campbell Blues' – besides the complete early work of Son House and the few but wonderful recordings of Kid Bailey and Mattie Delaney – puts these collections in the premier league of blues albums; the only reason for not owning them is having their contents elsewhere (see, for example, below), though even that excuse is weakened by Yazoo's obviously superior sound quality.

The first CD is staffed by what a previous reissue once called 'Delta blues heavy hitters', and there isn't a weak performance on it, scarcely even a secondary one. *Mississippi Masters* shifts out of the Delta to include players from elsewhere in the state: northerners like the drummingly rhythmic Akers and his friend Joe Callicott, southerners like the ethereal Hill, and the mobile Reynolds. Yazoo could have added the two remaining titles by Akers and Callicott, neither of which would have let the side down, but it would take a determined grouch to feel very strongly about that.

***(*) **Son House And The Great Delta Blues Singers (1928–1930)**
Document DOCD-5002 *Garfield Akers (4), Kid Bailey (2), Willie Brown (2), Joe Callicott (2), Son House (7), Rube Lacy (2), Blind Joe (Willie) Reynolds (4), Jim Thompkins. 3/28–5/30.*

*** **Mississippi Blues – Vol. 1 (1928–1937)**
Document DOCD-5157 *Mose Andrews (2), Mississippi Bracy (4), Mattie Delaney (2), Louise Johnson (4), The Mississippi Moaner (2), 'Big Road' Webster Taylor (2), Uncle Bud Walker (2), Geechie Wiley & Elvie Thomas (6). 7/28–5/37.*

***(*) **Lonesome Road Blues: 15 Years In The Mississippi Delta 1926–1941**
Yazoo 1038 *Mississippi Bracy (2), Sam Collins (2), Skip James, Robert [Jr] Lockwood, The Mississippi Moaner, Sonny Boy Nelson [Eugene Powell], Arthur Petti[e]s, Robert Petway, Freddie Spruell (2), Johnnie Temple, Big Joe Williams. 26–41.*

(***) **Mississippi Moaners**
Yazoo 1009 *Joe Callicott, Mattie Delaney, Mae Glover, Bobby Grant, Son House, Papa Harvey Hull & Long Cleve Reed, Mississippi John Hurt, Skip James, Rube Lacy, The Mississippi Moaner, Charley Patton, Blind Willie Reynolds, Uncle Bud Walker, Booker White. 27–42.*

(****) **Jackson Blues**
Yazoo 1007 *Ishman Bracey (3), Bo Carter, Willie Harris, Tommy Johnson (3), Willie Lofton, Charlie McCoy, Mississippi Mudder [Joe McCoy], Mississippi Sheiks, Arthur Petties, Walter Vincent [Vincson]. 28–38.*

Before the arrival of the Yazoo *Masters* CDs discussed above, *Son House And The Great Delta Blues Singers* filled a similar role very well, and for its time the transfer quality was by no means poor, but now almost half of it is duplicated by *Masters Of The Delta Blues* and a further six tracks by *Mississippi Masters*. For the neatnik, however, it does provide those missing Akers and Callicott sides, plus two more by Reynolds. *Mississippi Blues – Vol. 1*, as well as extending the Yazoos' coverage of Wiley and Thomas and of the exuberant singer/pianist Louise Johnson, and adding some minor figures, offers the calm guitar duet music of Caldwell Bracy and his wife. Two of those handsome performances, 'Cherry Ball' and 'Stered Gal', recur on *Lonesome Road Blues*, alongside The Mississippi Moaner's frantic Blind Lemon Jefferson takeoff, 'It's Cold In China Blues', Robert Petway's first-rate version of 'Catfish Blues' and other delights: a random selection, and at 14 tracks a short one, but musically opulent. Much the same verdict could be passed on *Jackson Blues*, with its two superb Ishman Bracey songs 'The Fore Day Blues' and 'Trouble Hearted Blues' and carefully chosen examples of Walter Vinson and the McCoy brothers at their best, but subsequent releases have organized much of this material more coherently. *Mississippi Moaners*, which also reproduces an LP without addition, is more problematic: several of its tracks are on newer and fuller collections, and Mae Glover's 'Gas Man Blues' and, probably, Bobby Grant's 'Lonesome Atlanta Blues' require relocation.

The reader who runs across the deleted *Dust My Broom: The Essential Recordings Of Mississippi Delta Blues* (Indigo IGOCD 2025) or *Down The Dirt Road: The Essential Recordings Of Mississippi Blues* (Indigo IGOCD 2039) will find them to be rewarding assortments of pre-World War II blues by artists mentioned elsewhere in this section, both containing items by Willie Brown, Son House, Skip James, Tommy Johnson, Robert Lockwood, Tommy McClennan, Charley Patton, Robert Petway, Booker White and Big Joe Williams.

***(*) **Mississippi Blues – Vol. 2 (1926–1935)**
Document DOCD-5158 *Willie 'Poor Boy' Lofton (8), Arthur Petties (6), Freddie Spruell (10). 6/26–11/35.*

This absorbing collection covers three singer/guitarists born in the South – Lofton and Petties in Mississippi, Spruell in Louisiana – who spent much of their adult life in Chicago. Spruell, probably the oldest and certainly the most antique in approach, is discussed in his entry. The listener coming fresh to Petties may be sidetracked by his rather lugubrious singing and fail to notice the ingenuity and precise articulation of his guitar parts. Lofton, on the other hand, is a stomper somewhat in the Tommy McClennan mould, and his performances, though hearty, are rather shapeless unless anchored to catchy guitar figures like the Tommy Johnson patterns of 'Dirty Mistreater' and 'Dark Road Blues'. Undistinguished remastering demotes what would otherwise be a four-star album.

**** Blues Masters, Volume 8: Mississippi Delta Blues
Rhino R2 71130 *Willie Brown, Son House (2), Howlin' Wolf, Elmore James (2), Louise Johnson, Robert Johnson, Tommy Johnson (2), Floyd Jones, Albert King, B. B. King, Rube Lacy, Muddy Waters, Robert Nighthawk, Charley Patton, Robert Petway, Sonny Boy Williamson II.* 27–61.

Another fine entry in Rhino's *Blues Masters* series, this gathers such feted recordings as Tommy Johnson's 'Big Road Blues', Willie Brown's 'Future Blues', Robert Petway's 'Catfish Blues', Floyd Jones's 'Dark Road', Elmore James's 'I Believe' … well, you get the picture, and a vivid and faithful one it is too. One of the James or Tommy Johnson tracks might have yielded place to something by Ishman Bracey or Booker White, but apart from that Robert Palmer's selection is hard to fault, as is the sound quality.

**** Legends Of Country Blues
JSP JSP 7715 5CD *Ishman Bracey (23), Son House (26), Skip James (18), Tommy Johnson (15), Booker White (20).* 2/28–7/42.

**** Big Joe Williams And The Stars Of Mississippi Blues
JSP JSPCD 7719 5CD *David 'Honeyboy' Edwards (12), Willie 'Poor Boy' Lofton (8), Tommy McClennan (43), Robert Petway (13), Big Joe Williams (50).* 8/34–12/51.

These inexpensive boxes contain the entire prewar recordings of all the participants (minus the non-musical part of 'Honeyboy' Edwards's Library of Congress session, but taking Big Joe Williams's story on up to the 1951 Trumpets, though omitting two of them). JSP were generally able to avail themselves of excellently engineered official reissues, and the sound quality of the McClennan, Petway and Williams recordings, in particular, is close to as good as it gets. For more on the content, see the individual artists' entries. On the face of it these are laughably good value but, for listeners coming new to this music, stuffing their shelves with the complete works of an artist who could prove to be hard going may not be such a great idea – 43 tracks is a *lot* of Tommy McClennan, and the last mile of Ishman Bracey is a rocky road – and they may do better to enter this magic kingdom through the portal of *Masters Of The Delta Blues*.

** Mississippi Blues
Putumayo PUT 196 *Luther Allison, Bobby Bland, Arthur 'Big Boy' Crudup, John Lee Hooker, Mississippi John Hurt, Chris Thomas King, Memphis Minnie, Memphis Slim, Ike & Tina Turner, Junior Wells, Artie White.* 41–99.

Mississippi Blues is an odd title for an album on which half the contributing artists aren't Mississippians. Its purpose becomes clearer when you read that it is 'a musical journey down the Mississippi River … from Memphis to New Orleans', though that still leaves the distinctly Chicagoan music of Luther Allison and Junior Wells, whose tracks open the album, on the far side of relevance. Neither artist is at his best, anyway, and what with poor contributions by John Lee Hooker and Chris Thomas King, and Memphis Slim's cabaret turn with Willie Dixon on 'Stewball', more than half the 40.29 playing time is lost to mediocrity.

*** Mississippi Delta Blues Jam In Memphis, Vol. 1
Arhoolie CD 385 *Furry Lewis (3), Fred McDowell (5), Memphis Piano Red (2), Napoleon Strickland & Como Drum Band (2), Othar Turner & Como Drum Band, R. L. Watson & Josiah Jones (3).* 6/69.

*** Mississippi Delta Blues Jam In Memphis, Vol. 2
Arhoolie CD 386 *Nathan Beauregard (2), Sleepy John Estes (4), Bukka [Booker] White (5).* 11/63, 6/69.

These fine recordings were made during the 1969 Memphis Blues Festival, but offstage, so the sound quality is uncompromised and the performances sometimes long: 'Furry Lewis' Blues' on *Volume 1* runs to 8.55, and Nathan Beauregard's 'Nathan's Bumble Bee Blues' on *Volume 2* to 10.30. (Booker White's story 'Mixed Water' on *Volume 2* goes all the way to 26.00, but that piece is a leftover from an earlier Arhoolie album session.) Fred McDowell's tracks on *Volume 1*, described in his entry, are worth the ticket price alone, but it's also a treat to hear John 'Memphis Piano Red' Williams (1905–82) on two of his few extant recordings, and Lewis's blues and the three fife-and-drum-band sides are by no means filler. Watson and Jones, who play pretty guitar duets, were actually John Fahey and Bill Barth.

On *Volume 2* the listener's interest can hardly fail to be piqued by a singer/guitarist who claimed to be over 100. Whether Nathan Beauregard really was that old or a mere stripling of 75 or 80 is unlikely to be resolved, but he certainly had the stamina for a long-haul performance, albeit carefully supported by Mike Stewart on second guitar, and though his voice was worn his pitch was still true. His approach is somewhat reminiscent of Joe Callicott's. The contributions by Estes and White are discussed in their entries.

*** Memphis Blues Caravan Vol I
Memphis Archives MA 7008 *Earl Bell, Sam Chatmon, Big Sam Clark, Sleepy John Estes (2), Harmonica Frank [Floyd], Furry Lewis, Sonny Boy Nelson [Eugene Powell], Houston Stackhouse, Bukka [Booker] White, Joe Willie Wilkins.* 11/72–1/75.

*** Memphis Blues Caravan Vol II
Memphis Archives MA 7009 *Charlie Booker, Boy Blue, Joe Dobbins, Little Red Holmes, Skip James, Furry Lewis, Memphis Piano Red, Big Daddy Rucker, Johnny Shines, Joe Willie Wilkins, Bukka [Booker] White.* 2/66–10/79.

The Memphis Blues Caravan was a road show organized in the early '70s by Stephen C. LaVere, and most of the performances on these albums were recorded at MBC events in college auditoria or clubs. Despite the Memphis connection, all the participants on *Vol I* except Sleepy John Estes, and about half those on *Vol II*, were born in Mississippi, and several others nearby in Tennessee or Arkansas, so it seems not inappropriate to discuss the albums here.

The tracks on *Vol I* by Estes and White are typical, but Furry Lewis's 'Mary Tell – Blues' lies outside his usual repertoire, and is followed by a joke. More ear-catching are 'Travelin' Blues' by singer/guitarist Earl Bell, Eugene Powell's attractively picked 'Pony Blues' and two tracks by a band led by Joe Willie Wilkins and Houston Stackhouse. The most noteworthy pieces on *Vol II* include a forceful voice and harmonica piece by Boy Blue, pianist Joe Dobbins's 'Satchel Blues' and a quiet 'Peach Tree Blues' by the little-known Little Red Holmes, but none of the tracks is without interest. Readers with a taste for exploring the nooks and crannies of blues history should note that the items by Bell, Holmes and Big Sam Clark are their sole available recordings, while those by Dobbins, Boy Blue and Charlie Booker are the only performances currently in catalogue from their later years. TR

New Orleans

This entry, like those for individual Crescent City musicians, was written before Hurricane Katrina made New Orleans the city that care remembered much too well. We have left it unchanged, as a reminder of what was and a harbinger of what we trust will be again.

(***) New Orleans Blues
Acrobat ACRCD 140 *Richard 'Rabbit' Brown (2), Sam Collins, Genevieve Davis, Champion Jack Dupree (2), Blind Leroy Garnett, Kitty Gray, Creole George Guesnon, King Solomon Hill, Hot Rod Happy [Country Jim Bledsoe], New Orleans Willie Jackson, Kid Stormy Weather (2), Lizzie Miles, Little Brother Montgomery (2), Jelly Roll Morton, Blind Joe [Willie] Reynolds, Shreveport Home Wreckers, Charley Taylor, Ramblin' Thomas, Annie Turner, [Oscar] Buddy Woods.* 4/26–49.

The dominance of jazz, which in New Orleans involved less improvising than is often believed, perhaps meant that blues was seen there as one musical form alongside others, rather than a vehicle for self-expression. That can be a tricky aesthetic to work with: Jelly Roll Morton's detachment becomes dullness in the hands of Willie Jackson and George Guesnon. There was no purpose-built recording studio in town until 1945, and by no means all the blues singers recorded on field trips were New Orleans residents. Consequently, Acrobat run up against a shortage of material; about half the tracks are by artists whose connection to New Orleans is tangential – in one case, as little as the word 'Louisiana' in an instrumental's title. There's a fair-sized subset of artists from around Shreveport included, for reasons that can only be guessed at. This is a fairly enjoyable record, but not quite what it purports to be.

**** The Sound Of The City: New Orleans
EMI 539271 2CD *Johnny Adams, The Animals, Archibald [Leon T. Gross], Louis Armstrong, Bobby Bland, Gary 'US' Bonds, Roy Brown, Jerry Byrne, Bobby Charles (2), Coolbone, The Dixie Cups, Dr John [Mack Rebennack], Fats Domino, Lee Dorsey, Snooks Eaglin, King Floyd, Barbara George, Guitar Slim [Eddie Jones], The Hawketts, Jessie Hills (2), Chris Kenner, Earl King, Labelle, Smiley Lewis, Little Richard, G. Love & Special Sauce (featuring Rebirth Brass Band), The Meters, Aaron Neville, The Neville Brothers, Lloyd Price (2), Professor Longhair, Alvin Robinson, Ronnie & The Delinquents, Shirley & Lee, The Showmen, Huey 'Piano' Smith, Snakefarm, The Spiders, Willie Tee, Irma Thomas, Allen Toussaint.* 6/28–98.

**** New Orleans Blues
Frémeaux FA 5086 2CD *Archibald [Leon T. Gross], Dave Bartholomew, Edgar Blanchard, Roy Brown (2), Cousin Joe (2), Fats Domino (2), Champion Jack Dupree (2), Paul Gayten, Lil Willie Gibson, Guitar Slim [Eddie Jones] (2), Pee Wee Hughes, Little Sonny [Jones], Earl King, Eddie Lang [Langlois], Annie Laurie, Papa Lightfoot, Little Bubber, Ray Lewis, Smiley Lewis (2), Bobby Marchan, Fats Matthews, Rose Mitchell, Lloyd Price,* *Professor Longhair (2), George Stevenson, Roosevelt Sykes (2), Billy Tate, Boogie Bill Webb.* 6/40–11/53.

*** Gettin' Funky: The Birth Of New Orleans R & B
Proper PROPERBOX 28 4CD *Archibald [Leon T. Gross] (7), Joe 'Google Eyes' August (2), Dave Bartholomew (9), Roy Brown (13), Hosie Dwine Craven, Larry Darnell (3), Fats Domino (12), Champion Jack Dupree (3), Little Joe Gaines, Paul Gayten (10), Erline Harris (2), Johnson Brothers' Combo, Jewel King (4), Smiley Lewis (7), James 'Blazer Boy' Locks (2), George Miller, Alma Mondy (4), Chubby 'Hip Shakin'' Newsome (6), Professor Longhair (18), Tommy Ridgley.* 1/41–50.

*** New Orleans Rhythm And Blues: Good Rockin' Tonight
Saga Blues 982 077-1 *Archibald [Leon T. Gross] (2), Dave Bartholomew (2), Roy Brown (2), Larry Darnell, Fats Domino (2), Champion Jack Dupree, Little Joe Gaines, Paul Gayten & Annie Laurie, Guitar Slim [Eddie Jones], Jewel King, Smiley Lewis, Chubby 'Hip Shakin'' Newsome, Lloyd Price (2), Professor Longhair (3), Shirley & Lee.* 11/41–10/53.

In seeking to define the postwar black music of New Orleans, words like 'melting pot' and 'gumbo' inevitably come to mind. It's more than usually difficult to impose labels, and they're more than usually liable to obscure rather than illuminate the complex realities. New Orleans R&B (the usual shorthand) contains the 12-bar blues, but it also comprehends rock 'n' roll, soul, vocal-group harmony, funk, Caribbean and Latin musics, voodoo and parade chants, and, of course, jazz.

All these aspects and more are represented on *The Sound Of The City: New Orleans*; so are songs inspired by the idea of New Orleans, whether as a far from stately pleasure dome or a more dangerous place altogether. These days Bourbon Street is a seedy tourist trap, and the Mardi Gras mostly a festival of booze and breast-flashing, but Professor Longhair, the Hawketts ('Mardi Gras Mambo') and the Dixie Cups ('Iko Iko') are on hand to reclaim it for the second-liners, the Social and Pleasure Clubs and the Mardi Gras Indians.

Compiler and sedulous annotator Charlie Gillett inevitably includes the big names, many represented by big hits. Shirley & Lee's 'Let The Good Times Roll', Fats Domino's 'Blue Monday', the Meters' 'Cissy Strut' and Lloyd Price's 'Stagger Lee' are no less classic for being famous, and Gillett also includes many equally fine tracks long venerated by collectors, among them 'Stack O'Lee' (Archibald's earlier take on the murder ballad), Barbara George's feisty 'I Know' and Alvin Robinson's 'Down Home Girl'. Two tracks by Bobby Charles is perhaps overdoing the admiration and, for all its magnificence, Satchmo's 'West End Blues' is too obvious; try 'To-Wa-Bac-A-Wa' by Louis Dumaine's Jazzola Eight, or Sam Morgan's Jazz Band with 'Over In The Gloryland', both on *Jazz The World Forgot Vol. 1* (Yazoo 2024). These minor gripes don't come close to being arguments against purchase.

It's fair to say, however, that readers more narrowly interested in the city's blues output will prefer the Frémeaux compilation. There are some issues of definition: singing a 'New Orleans Boogie' doesn't make one a New Orleans blues singer (Roosevelt Sykes, whose tracks are Chicago jump blues), nor does recording in the city: Pee Wee Hughes came in from Shreveport to play his blasting, rustic harmonica. Nevertheless, this is a well-planned collection: it includes all the famous names (provided they recorded before the copyright cut-off date), it takes some care to avoid their obvious numbers, and it does so without sacrificing musical quality. Rose Mitchell's arty assault on 'Baby Please Don't Go' is unfortunate, and Edgar Blanchard's 'Creole Gal Blues', with Papa Lightfoot on harmonica, is an under-rehearsed mess, but for the most part the lesser-known artists are also carefully chosen; Ray Lewis and Billy Tate are revelatory. The notes give a useful account of the historical background and the beginnings of the local recording industry.

Saga's single disc has similar virtues, although it majors more strongly in familiar names. They're often represented by their most famous numbers, but *Good Rockin' Tonight* is saved from predictability by skilful programming, and the inclusion of such lesser-known but likeable items as Fats Domino's 'Careless Love' and Joe Gaines's 'She Won't Love Me No More'. Informed and informative notes, good sound and a low price also help to make *Good Rockin' Tonight* a useful and entertaining introduction.

With all those big names, and 107 tracks, *Gettin' Funky* looks as though it should be the perfect overview of the New Orleans scene in the early postwar years, and indeed the accompanying booklet is lengthy, detailed and well informed, although one would have thought that an account so reliant on the work of Jeff Hannusch could manage to spell his name correctly. The total package is something of a disappointment, however: it falls between the stools of documentation and entertainment, not quite succeeding in providing either in the quality that could have been achieved. The selection from Fats Domino's early singles, for instance, includes 'Korea Blues', with Dave Bartholomew's tasteless bugle calls, and Paul Gayten's piano obbligatos on 'Backtrackin' (Dr Daddy-O)' are so tuneless it must be deliberate sabotage. The ballads 'You Shouldn't' and 'Confused' don't add much lustre to Gayten's reputation either. Smiley Lewis and Roy Brown are represented by better but not unimprovable selections. All Professor Longhair's tracks here are also on *A Proper Introduction To Professor Longhair* (Proper INTRO CD 2024), but the repetition is not altogether pointless, since *Gettin' Funky*'s nine Atlantic sides are not copied from the sonically awful *New Orleans Piano* (Atlantic 7225). Proper's fourth CD, subtitled *Hip Shakin' Mamas, Crooners And Shouters*, relies very heavily on Delmark's *Jump 'N' Shout* (see below), and indeed the whole collection piggybacks on other labels' licensing and sound restoration.

(*) Urban Blues Volumes I & II
BGO BGOCD 456 *Archibald [Leon T. Gross] (2), Dirty Red [Nelson Wilborn] (2), Fats Domino (5), Little Sonny [Jones], Smiley Lewis (4), Fats Mathews, Amos Milburn, Smilin' Joe [Cousin Joe], Roosevelt Sykes (2), Joe Turner (2), Joe Turner & Wynonie Harris, T-Bone Walker (2), Mercy Dee [Walton] (2), Wee Willie Wayne.* 6/47–5/55.

Urban Blues unites two LPs, subtitled *Blues Uptown* and *New Orleans Bounce*, on a single CD. Mercy Dee and T-Bone Walker were West Coasters, Dirty Red (whose gleeful 'Mother Fuyer' is a treat) was from Chicago, and a rowdy 'Battle Of The Blues' between Joe Turner and Wynonie Harris was recorded in New York. The balance of the CD features New Orleans singers, and visitors backed by New Orleans sidemen. The band behind Roosevelt Sykes includes a ferocious electric guitarist who seems to prophesy the sound of West Side Chicago a decade later. 'Travelin' Mood' is nowadays associated with Snooks Eaglin, but Wee Willie Wayne's laidback version, with whistling choruses, is enchanting. Archibald is described as a Fats Domino imitator in the starchily academic notes, but his rough, violent songs have none of the Fat Man's cuddliness. Several titles were previously unissued, and the compilation sometimes seems to truffle for rarity rather than quality.

(*) Jump 'N' Shout
Delmark DE-715 *Joseph 'Google Eyes' August (2), Dave Bartholomew (3), Sammy Cotton, Larry Darnell (3), Erline Harris (3), Johnson Brothers' Combo, Ernie K-Doe (4), Annie Laurie, James 'Blazer Boy' Locks, Chubby 'Hip Shakin'' Newsome (5).* 4/49–11/53.

Jump 'N' Shout derives from the De Luxe, Regal and United labels. Dave Bartholomew's composing and producing have been far more important than either his singing or his paint-stripping trumpet. Erline Harris is unpolished and unremarkable; so is the Johnson Brothers' Combo, despite the presence of Plas Johnson. Sammy Cotton and James Locks respectively imitate Roy and Charles Brown, and Larry Darnell, Annie Laurie and Joe August are not represented by their best work. The collection's appeal derives from the vivacious Chubby Newsome ('a hard-lovin' mama, healthy, firm and fine') accompanied by New York-based jazzmen, and from Ernie K-Doe's unissued debut session. Recorded in Chicago, it features hard-hitting blues rather than the novelties K-Doe later specialized in, and a band which includes a terrific guitarist.

*** Crescent City ... Whole Lotta Blues**
Eclipse 64416 *Dave Bartholomew, Roy Brown, Sugar Boy Crawford, Pee Wee Crayton, Fats Domino, Snooks Eaglin, Paul Gayten & Annie Laurie, Guitar Slim [Eddie Jones], Clarence 'Frogman' Henry, Smiley Lewis, Roy Montrell, Professor Longhair, Irma Thomas, Allen Toussaint, Joe Turner, Boogie Bill Webb.* 12/49–64.

Crescent City is a pretty good entry-level collection. The famous artists are mostly represented by their greatest hits, but there's a seasoning of enjoyable lesser-knowns, like the transplanted Mississippian Boogie Bill Webb, adapting John Lee Hooker on 'Bad Dog' (which is also on the Frémeaux 2CD), and guitarist Roy Montrell, paying frantic tribute to 'That Mellow Saxophone'. Pee Wee Crayton and Joe Turner are out-of-towners, given a boost by the bottomless well of talent that's the Crescent City's session musicians. Allen Toussaint's breezy 'Java' and Frogman Henry's 'But I Do' are at the more lightweight end of an enjoyable selection, but Sugar Boy Crawford's 'Jock-O-Mo' is one of the best versions of 'Iko Iko'.

****(*) Blue Orleans**
Blue Note 534140 *Dave Bartholomew, Roy Brown, Sam Butera, Dr John [Mack Rebennack], Lou Donaldson, Fats Domino (2), Clarence 'Bon Ton' Garlow, Barbara George, Grant Green, Jessie Hills, Ernie K-Doe, Chris Kenner, Earl King, Smiley Lewis, Amos Milburn, Aaron Neville, Prince La La, Shirley & Lee, The Showmen, Benny Spellman, The Spiders, Irma Thomas, The Wild Magnolias, Baby Face Willette.* 10/52–c. 99.

Blue Orleans comes from EMI, and there's some overlap with *Sound Of The City*, but this is a fine collection in its own right, more tightly focused on the iconic ensemble sound of New Orleans: lyrical but driving saxes (both sectional and soloing), rippling second-line backbeats and insistent piano riffs. Among predictable but wonderful titles by Brown,

Domino, Lewis and others are imaginative choices like Dave Bartholomew's misanthropic 'The Monkey Speaks His Mind', a Shirley & Lee track that isn't 'Let The Good Times Roll', Aaron Neville's coolly homicidal 'Over You' and Prince La La, oddly happy that 'She Put The Hurt On Me'. Saxophonist and singer Lou Donaldson and guitarist Grant Green are members of Blue Note's jazz roster, having successful encounters with Meters-style rhythm sections, but Baby Face Willette's organ jazz is bland, and Ernie K-Doe and Benny Spellman made better records than the weak songs here.

**(*) Creole Kings Of New Orleans Vol. 1
Specialty SPCD-2168 *Edgar Blanchard, Jerry Byrne, Clifton Chenier, Guitar Slim [Eddie Jones], Alberta Hall, Ernie K-Doe, The Kings, Lloyd Lambert, Joe Liggins, Percy Mayfield (2), Li'l Millet, Roy Montrell, Big Boy Myles (2), Art Neville (2), Leo Price, Lloyd Price (3), Professor Longhair (2), The Royal Kings, Larry Williams (2).* 4/50–11/58.

**(*) Creole Kings Of New Orleans Vol. 2
Specialty SPCD-7038 *Bumps Blackwell, Edgar Blanchard, Jerry Byrne, Clifton Chenier, Guitar Slim [Eddie Jones], Willie Johnson (2), Ernie K-Doe, Earl King, Lloyd Lambert, Little Mr Midnight (2), Li'l Millet, The Monitors, Roy Montrell, Big Boy Myles, Art Neville, Lloyd Price (2), Professor Longhair (3), The Royal Kings, Larry Williams.* 9/50–8/58.

These collections include some classics, notably by Longhair, Guitar Slim and Clifton Chenier; the last is perhaps an early victim of ongoing record- and tourist-industry attempts to rebrand zydeco as a New Orleans music. Among the less-celebrated artists, Lloyd Lambert's band features Joe Tillman, a throaty, lyrical tenorist who can almost make a whole chorus of reed squeaks interesting. Longhair's piano and Lee Allen's sax propel Big Boy Myles, if not to greatness, at least to extremes of foot-tapping pleasure on 'Who's Been Fooling You' (*Vol. 1*) and 'That Girl I Married' (*Vol. 2*), but 'Just To Hold Your Hand' on *Vol. 1* is very ordinary. Little Mr Midnight, backed by Paul Gayten's band, is a prepubescent Roy Brown imitator who is – truly – worth hearing. That can't be said of the tuneless Li'l Millet, nor of Bumps Blackwell's demo of 'Good Golly Miss Molly', which is the most, but far from the only, collector-oriented item. Tracks by Ernie K-Doe, Lloyd Price (except 'Lawdy Miss Clawdy' on *Vol. 1*) and the stiffly barking Larry Williams are ephemeral at best; so is the Monitors' trite 'Rock 'n' Roll Fever'. Guitarist Edgar Blanchard's impromptu 'Bop Sit-In Blues' on *Vol. 1* is objectively pretty good, but it's a masterpiece by comparison with 'Stepping High' on *Vol. 2*, which sounds like an alcoholic C&W band. Non-fanatics should approach with caution.

*** New Orleans Popeye Party
Night Train NTI CD 7075 *Joe Barry (2), Blazer Boy [George Stevenson], Eddie Bo, Berna Dean, James Easterling, Frankie Ford, Barbara George, Joe & Ann, Wallace Johnson, Jimmy Jules (2), Ernie K-Doe, The Medallions, Big Boy Myles, Al Reed, Tommy Ridgley, Huey Smith, Alex Spearman, Betty Taylor, Willie Tee [Turbinton], Lee Tillman, Joe Valentine.* early 60s.

(**(*)) New Orleans Twist Party
Night Train NTI CD 7018 *Eddie Bo (6), Reggie Hall (4), Bobby Mitchell, Professor Longhair (4).* 62–63.

Every record company yearned for a dance-craze hit in the early '60s, and New Orleans marques were no exception. Despite opening with Longhair's 'Whole Lotta Twistin'', *Twist Party* is really a sampler of the short-lived Rip label. Most tracks are dubbed from crackly 45s, and Fess's tracks, not readily available elsewhere, are almost the only reason to get excited. Reggie Hall's 'You Can Think What You Want' and Bobby Mitchell's 'You've Got The Nerve' are decent blues, but Eddie Bo's tracks are a fine blend of slush and gimmickry; the only possible response to 'Let's Limbo' is 'Let's not.'

On the other hand, Eddie's 'Check Mr Popeye'/'Now Let's Popeye' (elided by Night Train into a single long track) easily bridges the gap between novelty and quality, thanks to a horn section that's eaten its spinach and John Boudreaux's exemplary drumming. Bo and Huey Smith had the biggest hits of the Popeye craze, and Ernie K-Doe's 'Popeye Joe' hops on the bandwagon, but most of this anthology is simply infectious dance music, to which one could presumably Popeye if one wished. Listeners will find plenty of opportunities to consider what in the spectrum of New Orleans black pop is blues, what bluesy and what blues-inflected (Wallace Johnson's 'Private Eye' has trivial lyrics and a great blues guitar solo), but the main point is to have fun. *Popeye Party* is a good illustration of the strength in depth of the city's music scene; some of the artists are obscure in the extreme, but the performances are never less than good, and some of them – Willie Tee's 'Always Accused', the tracks by Jimmy Jules, the exceptionally soulful Al Reed and Berna Dean – are great.

*** Keys To The Crescent City
Rounder CD 2087 *Eddie Bo [Bocage] (3), Charles Brown (3), Art Neville (4), Willie Tee [Turbinton] (4).* c. 90.

Charles Brown, not a native of New Orleans, was a big influence on local artists, in part through a long residency at the Dew Drop Inn. Like the other pianists here, Brown has excellent technical skills. Unlike them, he doesn't match a fondness for ballads with an aptitude for earthy funk: Eddie Bo and Willie Tee are joint heirs of Jelly Roll Morton's polished urbanity and Professor Longhair's polyrhythmic ingenuity. Unaccustomed to playing solo, Art Neville uses a keyboard to add organ, horn and drum parts to his second-line struts. Versions of 'Hey Pocky Way' and 'Big Chief' are hardly vital reinterpretations; a reflective 'My Children' makes one wish for more tracks without the optional extras.

*** Doctors, Professors, Kings & Queens: The Big Ol' Box Of New Orleans
Shout Factory D4K 37441 4CD *Johnny Adams, James Andrews, Troy Andrews, Louis Armstrong (2), Balfa Toujours, Marcia Ball, Vernel Bagneris, Dave Bartholomew, Beau Jocque, Beausoleil, Sidney Bechet, Eddie Bo, James Booker, Gatemouth Brown, Buckwheat Zydeco, Henry Butler, Boozoo Chavis, Clifton Chenier, Jon Cleary, Coolbone, Bruce Daigrepont, Geno Delafose, The Dirty Dozen Brass Band with Danny Barker & Eddie Bo, Dr John [Mack Rebennack], Fats Domino, Champion Jack Dupree, Snooks Eaglin, Frankie Ford, Pete Fountain, Galactic (2), Leigh 'Lil' Queenie' Harris (2), The Hawketts, Clarence 'Frogman' Henry, The Iguanas, Al Johnson, Ernie K-Doe, Chris Kenner, Earl King, Sonny Landreth, Tim Laughlin, George Lewis, Smiley Lewis, Little Richard, Tom McDermott & Evan Christopher, Ellis Marsalis, The Meters, J. Monque'D, Deacon John Moore, Jelly Roll Morton, Raymond Myles, Aaron Neville, The Neville Brothers, Charmaine Neville, New Birth*

Brass Band, The New Orleans Jazz Vipers, The New Orleans Klezmer All Stars, Freddy Omar, Kid Ory, Anders Osborne, Anders Osborne & 'Big Chief' Monk Boudreaux, Preservation Hall Jazz Band, Lloyd Price, Professor Longhair, The Radiators, Rebirth Brass Band, The Red Stick Ramblers, Zachary Richard, Steve Riley, Kermit Ruffins, Paul Sanchez, The Savoy-Doucet Cajun Band, Mem Shannon, Shirley & Lee, Huey 'Piano' Smith, Benny Spellman, Irma Thomas, Allen Toussaint, Tuba Fats' Chosen Few Brass Band, Don Vappie, Walter 'Wolfman' Washington, Dr Michael White, The Wild Magnolias. 5/27–03.

*** **New Orleans Blues Party**
Easydisc ED CD 7028 *Chuck Carbo, Davell Crawford, Bo Dollis & The Wild Magnolias, Snooks Eaglin, Carol Fran & Clarence Hollimon, Earl King, Mark 'Kaz' Kazanoff & Snooks Eaglin, George Porter Jr, Professor Longhair, Irma Thomas.* 3/78–3/95.

Metaphorical gumbo again; the Neville Brothers' drummer appears with the Klezmer All Stars, but self-evidently there's far more to the handsomely presented *Big Ol' Box* than blues and black music. The accompanying 80-page book – definitely not booklet – includes discographical details, fine photos of the musicians and their milieux, and informed, helpful track-by-track discussion. Useful to anyone planning a visit are sections like 'Six Places To Eat That Will Make Locals Say, "You Know About THAT Place?"' and 'Things That In Any Other City Would Be A Tourist Trap'. The underlying assumption that sex and food were invented in New Orleans gets tedious after a while, though.

So why only three stars? It's not that there's too much variety, although it's unlikely that many readers will enjoy every style on offer. The merits of the Radiators' roots rock, Leigh Harris's scratchy singing and the Red Stick Ramblers' 'Cajun gypsy swing' certainly eluded us. It's equally true that few people will listen to these 85 tracks without finding something to intrigue them – in our case, banjoist Don Vappie, exploring the French Creole roots of jazz, and the swing blues of Deacon John Moore. Cajun and zydeco music are not native to *la grande ville*, but they're a popular part of its live music scene; given how entertaining most of the selected tracks are, it's probably inadvisable to make heavy weather of their over-representation.

There are many gems here, both old and new; among the vintage black music, there's Ernie K-Doe ('Mother-In-Law'), Benny Spellman ('Lipstick Traces'), Aaron Neville ('Tell It Like It Is'), Huey Smith ('Rocking Pneumonia And The Boogie Woogie Flu') and more; but not everything is at their level of excellence, and too many tracks don't live up to the enthusiasm expressed in the notes. In blues and related areas, Gatemouth Brown turns in a surprisingly laborious vocal, outdone for tedium by Henry Butler's grind through 'Tee-Nah-Nah'; the Wild Magnolias' 'Party' is disfigured by June Yamagishi's nasty blues-rock guitar solo; Danny Barker is very tired, both in himself and of 'Don't You Feel My Leg'; and after Charmaine Neville's version of 'The Right Key But The Wrong Keyhole', one wonders if she kisses her mother with that mouth. James Andrews, leader of the New Birth Brass Band, was billed as 'Satchmo Of The Ghetto' on his debut CD; if the sour, uninventive trumpet on a tribute to his grandfather, Jessie Hill, is typical, that's ridiculous. Andrews's brother Troy mangles Hill's hit 'Ooh Poo Pah Doo' unmercifully.

The Big Ol' Box Of New Orleans looks gorgeous, but 'the city that care forgot' sometimes seems a self-satisfied place where reputation trumps reality, and this box too often affects a similar complacency. Readers with limited budgets or less-catholic tastes will enjoy *New Orleans Blues Party*. JSP furnish the compulsory Longhair track, from 1978; the rest come from Black Top and Rounder. Despite the credit, Bo Dollis, accompanied by a Black Top house band which includes Snooks Eaglin, is the only Wild Magnolia on 'Coconut Milk'. George Porter's 'Woogie Boogie' is a characterless instrumental; not so the Kazanoff–Eaglin collaboration, 'Swanee River Rock', with its routinely miraculous guitar solo. The Fran, Eaglin and Earl King tracks are valuable salvage from the wreck of Black Top, but the sampled Rounder CDs by Irma Thomas and Chuck Carbo include stronger numbers than those used here. Nevertheless, this is an enjoyable, bargain-priced dash around the city's blues scene (with blues, as ever, broadly defined). CS

New York

***(*) **Harlem Blues**
Acrobat ACRCD 155 *Bea Booze, Butterbeans & Susie, Christine Chatman, Champion Jack Dupree, Little Boy Fuller [Richard Trice], Helen Humes, Jelly Belly & Guitar Slim [Louis Hayes & Alec Seward], Lem Johnson, Margaret Johnson, Albinia Jones, Maggie Jones, Hank Kilroy, Leecan & Cooksey, Connie McLean, Sara Martin, Hot Lips Page, Mabel Robinson, Bessie Smith, Sonny Boy & Lonnie, Victoria Spivey, Yack Taylor, Joe Turner, Josh White, Rubberlegs Williams.* 2/23–48.

***(*) **New York City Blues**
Frémeaux FA 5008 2CD *Gabriel Brown, Carolina Slim [Ed Harris], Leroy Dallas, Rev. Gary Davis, Champion Jack Dupree, Big Chief Ellis, Blind Boy Fuller (2), Little Boy Fuller [Richard Trice] (2), Boy Green (2), Louis Hayes, Leadbelly, Brownie McGhee (3), Sticks McGhee (2), Dennis McMillon (2), Buddy Moss (2), Marylin Scott, Alec Seward (2), Skoodle Dum Doo [prob. Seth Richard] & Sheffield, Sonny Boy & Lonnie, Tarheel Slim [Alden Bunn], Sonny Terry (2), Sonny Terry & Jordan Webb, Josh White, Ralph Willis (2).* 3/40–7/50.

**** **New York City Blues: The Big Apple Blues Scene 1951–1954**
Saga Blues 982 992-2 *Annisteen Allen, Lavern Baker, Honey Brown, Ruth Brown, Cousin Leroy, Larry Dale, Champion Jack Dupree (2), Les Harris, Lem Johnson, Jimmy 'Baby Face' Lewis, Brownie McGhee (2), Stick(s) McGhee, Jimmy Newsome, Tarheel Slim [Alden Bunn], Danny Taylor, Sonny Terry (2), Square Walton, Ralph Willis.* 51–10/54.

It's no surprise that blues recording began in New York; the city was the entertainment capital of America, and in Harlem it contained the symbolic political and artistic capital of black America. So much was happening on the black New York music scene, then and since, that it's hard to pin down 'New York blues', to have a mental image of it as one can of 'Chicago blues'. In part, this is the result of trying to impose simplicity and category on a complex, overlapping scene, but it does also seem that a lot of New York blues impulses got subsumed into the city's ever-adventurous jazz scene: for a notion of this process, it's worth trying to find the deleted *Blues Masters Vol. 13: New York City Blues* (Rhino R2 71131). There's sometimes been an excessive emphasis on the migration of 'country' blues musicians from the East Coast states to New York, seen as a parallel to the Mississippi-to-Chicago great migration; this was a real phenomenon, but the two processes differed critically in timing, and in the contexts of departure and arrival.

Harlem Blues is a very well-thought-out compilation, which ably considers New York blues as a product of the recording industry, moving from the first recordings by women singers, through the small jazz-blues band sound overseen in the Decca studios by Sam Price, to the early, sometimes uneasy collaborations of blues singers and beboppers. Neatly woven into this story is the migration narrative, featuring artists who made the long-term move to the city, like Josh White, Hayes & Seward, Brownie McGhee and Jack Dupree, and those who were just passing through, like Clevelanders Sonny Boy & Lonnie, or Leecan & Cooksey from Philadelphia.

New York City Blues takes at once a narrower and a wider view. It concentrates on blues singers who performed in East Coast styles and recorded in the greater New York area, whether they lived there long-term or not. Tarheel Slim's track was cut in Raleigh, North Carolina, before he moved north, however, and it's difficult to see how recording in New York makes Blind Boy Fuller and Buddy Moss New York blues singers. *New York City Blues* also considers the interplay between New York blues musicians and the urban folk music scene, which provided a market for Leadbelly, Sonny & Brownie and Josh White. The allure of radical politics, the articulacy of many participants and the existence of Folkways Records mean that this side of New York music is well documented; that can lead, as it does here, to an overestimation of its importance. *New York City Blues* tells an incomplete story, but its musical content is excellent.

The Big Apple Blues Scene both carries the story forward and takes a more balanced view, dividing its content into *New York Down Home Blues* (transplanted East Coast musicians plus Jack Dupree) and *Harlem Uptown Blues*. The first section can't avoid Terry and McGhee but, like the other 'down home' items, their tracks are robust small-group blues, musically enticing (apart from Cousin Leroy's crude 'Catfish'), and often either hitherto unavailable on CD or hard to find. The second half of the disc is described as rhythm and blues. The boundary between blues and R&B is mutable and contested by critics, and it probably wasn't much perceived by the original audience; there's not a huge stylistic gulf between Tarheel Slim (downhome) and Jimmie Newsome (uptown). Still, there's often a jazzier edge to the 'uptown' saxes and guitars, and to the rhythm sections (many of them recruited from moonlighting jazz musicians); of the guitarists, Jimmy Lewis is outstandingly imaginative as both a name artist and backing Lavern Baker, and Sticks McGhee plays above his usual level on 'Things Have Changed'. This part of the CD is also judiciously chosen, presenting unfamiliar tracks by famous names and classy work from obscurities like Honey Brown, a pleasant singer fronting a knockout trombone-over-saxes arrangement.

For other CDs that include New York musicians playing in downhome styles, see EAST COAST.

*** **Harlem Rock 'N' Blues Vol. 1**
Collectables COL-CD-5208 *Johnny Acey, Rockin' Bradley, B. [Daniel] Brown, Champion Jack Dupree (2), Tiny Grimes, Willis Jackson, King Curtis, Hal Paige, Paul Perriman, Red Prysock (2), Riff Ruffin, Jimmy Spruill (2), Tarheel Slim [Alden Bunn], Sonny Terry, Noble Watts & June Bateman. c. 1/52–65.*

*** **Harlem Rock N' Blues Vol. 2**
Collectables COL-CD-5209 *Johnny Acey, B. [Daniel] Brown, Johnny Clef, Dr Horse [Al Pittman], Champion Jack Dupree (2), King Curtis, Brownie McGhee, Hal Paige, Paul Perriman, Red Prysock (2), Riff Ruffin (2), Jimmy Spruill (2), Sonny Terry, Noble Watts & June Bateman. c. 1/52–65.*

*** **Harlem Rock N' Blues Vol. 3**
Collectables COL-CD-5210 *Johnny Acey, Champion Jack Dupree (2), Tiny Grimes, Willis Jackson (2), King Curtis, Charles Lucas, Brownie McGhee, Hal Paige, Paul Perriman, Red Prysock (2), Riff Ruffin, Buddy Skipper, Jimmy Spruill (2), Noble Watts. c. 1/52–c. 63.*

These three volumes derive from labels operated by veteran Harlem producer and record store operator Bobby Robinson, but since there are no notes, it's inappropriate to call them label surveys. They constitute an enjoyable if uneven cross-section of the amplified blues and near-blues that were being marketed to Harlem, with the hope of a wider break-out hit always there. This is tough, uptown music, with even Sonny & Brownie working in amplified R&B mode: 'Harmonica Hop' is as close to Little Walter as Sonny ever got. The dominant instruments are tenor sax and electric guitar: Jimmy Spruill's exciting playing on the latter is sufficiently dispersed that his limitations are obscured, and only fanatics of the genre will not welcome the similar diffusion of the sax instrumentals. Of the more obscure artists, Riff Ruffin and Paul Perriman are derivative of James Brown and Little Richard respectively and Buddy Skipper is a drippy balladeer. Well worth noting, though, are Dr Horse's rocking cover of Louis Jordan's 'Salt Pork, West Virginia', the very soulful Johnny Acey, and tenorists Hal Paige (whose guitarist may be Spruill) and Noble Watts. The gospelly vocals of June Bateman (Mrs Watts) are also a highlight; her 'Possum Belly Overalls' on *Vol. 2* is both an answer to and far better than 'Hi-Heel Sneakers'. CS

Piano

***(*) **Down In Black Bottom: Lowdown Barrelhouse Piano**
Yazoo 2043 *Bat The Humming Bird, Sammy Brown, Bob Call, Lonnie Clark (2), Cow Cow Davenport, Joe Dean, Joe Evans (2), Willie Harris, Bert Mays (2), Little Brother Montgomery (2), Freddie Nicholson (2), John Oscar, Sylvester Palmer, Turner Parrish (2), Speckled Red, Dan Stewart, Tampa Red. 27–33.*

Though billed as containing 'classic blues, rags and stomps', this collection is mostly occupied by pianists playing slow or medium blues, sometimes accompanying vocalists, like Charles Avery with Freddie Nicholson or Bill O'Bryant with Tampa Red, sometimes singing themselves, like St Louis's Joe Dean, or Turner Parrish, possibly an Indianapolis musician, who acknowledges that city's best-known son, Leroy Carr, in his measured approach to 'Graveyard Blues' and 'Ain't Gonna Be Your Dog No More'. The sky is overcast, pierced only by a few shafts of brightness like Cow Cow Davenport's 'Chimes Blues' and Speckled Red's 'The Right String But The Wrong Yo Yo'. Most of Yazoo's other piano compilations are discussed under BOOGIE WOOGIE or TEXAS.

(***) **Barrelhouse Blues 1927–1936**
Yazoo 1028 *Raymond Barrow, Bob Call, Cow Cow Davenport, Joe Dean, Will Ezell, Jesse James, Lonnie Johnson, Louise*

Johnson, Little Brother Montgomery, George Noble, Charley Taylor, Montana Taylor, [Nolan] Barrelhouse Welsh, Jabo Williams. 27–36.

This was a fine LP 30 years ago, but half of its contents have been relocated on later Yazoos (see BOOGIE WOOGIE) and the CD has probably been discontinued.

*** Piano Blues: The Essential
Classic Blues CBL 200004 2CD *Charles Avery, Black Ivory King, Oliver Brown, Bumble Bee Slim, Bob Call, Leroy Carr, Jim Clarke, Cow Cow Davenport, Walter Davis, Joe Dean, Will Ezell, Rudy Foster, Jesse James, Skip James, Louise Johnson, Meade Lux Lewis, Cripple Clarence Lofton, Memphis Minnie, Eddie Miller, Little Brother Montgomery, Romeo Nelson, Sylvester Palmer, Turner Parrish, Joe Pullum, Walter Roland, Pine Top Smith, Charlie Spand, Sparks Brothers, Speckled Red, Roosevelt Sykes, Montana Taylor, Wesley Wallace, Peetie Wheatstraw, James 'Boodle It' Wiggins, Jabo Williams, Jimmy Yancey*. 28–39.

Given that castlist, and the fact that several important pianists made only a few records, it's inevitable that this collection will bump heads with others discussed here and in BOOGIE WOOGIE. In any case, tracks like Cow Cow Davenport's eponymous blues, Pine Top Smith's eponymous boogie, Wesley Wallace's 'No. 29' and Montana Taylor's 'Detroit Rocks' are practically statutory entries in anthologies of blues piano. In favour of this compilation, its 36 tracks have been soundly and not always predictably chosen. Against it, there's a sequencing error on Disc 1 (tracks 11 and 12 are swapped) and, in the absence of discographical details, listeners who want to know which of Little Brother Montgomery's many recordings of 'Vicksburg Blues' they're listening to will have no way of knowing that it's the 1949 Savoy version. The sound is generally reasonable.

Strut That Thing: The Essential Recordings Of Piano Blues And Boogie (Indigo IGOCD 2031, deleted) was a good selection too, but almost half of its tracks are on the Classic Blues set and none of the others is hard to find.

*** Martin Scorsese Presents The Blues: Piano Blues
Columbia/Legacy 512571 *Count Basie, The Boogie Woogie Boys, Charles Brown (with Johnny Moore's Three Blazers), Dave Brubeck, Ray Charles, Fats Domino, Dr John [Mack Rebennack] (2), Dr John [Mack Rebennack]–Pete Jolly–Henry Gray, Duke Ellington, Jay McShann & Big Joe Turner, Jay McShann & Dave Brubeck, Thelonious Monk, Pinetop Perkins & Marcia Ball, Professor Longhair, Otis Spann, Art Tatum, Henry Townsend, Joe Turner, Jimmy Yancey*. 12/38–7/03.

This collection is explicitly tied to Clint Eastwood's film *Piano Blues*, made for the series of blues films shown on US TV in 2003. It was not a conventional history of the form, so one can't object to the absence of major figures like Little Brother Montgomery, Roosevelt Sykes or Big Maceo, or the inclusion of performances that worked better on film than they do on record, like Brubeck's 'Travelin' Blues' or the six-hander on 'How Long Blues'. Reflecting as it did the director's long affection for jazz, blues and boogie woogie, the film embraced piano blues as played by jazz musicians, and the album's diversity is stepped up by tracks like Ellington's 'Backward Country Boy Blues' (from *Money Jungle*) and Monk's 'Blue Monk', though one would have thought a small-group version of the latter more *à propos* than the orchestral one offered. Quibbles aside, it's excellent listening.

The notes don't make it clear, but the Joe Turner who plays 'The Ladder' is the stride pianist, not Big Joe.

***(*) Piano Blues – Vol. 1 (1927–1936) [sic]
Document DOCD-5192 *Judson Brown, Blind Clyde Church (2), Jim Clarke, Joe Dean (2), Jesse James (4), Bert M. Mays (6), James 'Bat' Robinson (5), Dan Stewart, Pigmeat Terry (2)*. c. 11/27–9/56.

*** Piano Blues – Vol. 2 (1927–1956)
Document DOCD-5220 *Jesse Clayton [Dr Clayton] (2), Willie Jones (2), Barrelhouse Buck McFarland (7), L. C. Prigett (3), Charlie Segar (8), Doug Suggs (2), unknown (2)*. 8/27–56.

**(*) Piano Blues – Vol. 3 (1924–1940s)
Document DOCD-5314 *George Hannah (9), Rob Robinson & Meade Lux Lewis (6), Millard G. Thomas (2), unknown (2), Nolan (Barrel House) Welsh (7)*. 10/24–40s.

** Piano Blues – Vol. 4 (1923–1928)
Document DOCD-5336 *Yodeling Kid Brown, Skeet Brown, Jack Erby (4), Tiny Franklin, Lucius Hardy (2), Stovepipe Johnson (3), Keghouse (2), Ray Logan (2), Q. Roscoe Snowden (2), Sugar Underwood (2), Hermes Zimmerman (2)*. 10/23–11/28.

** Piano Blues – Vol. 5 (1929–1936)
Document DOCD-5337 *George Allison & Willie White (2), Andy Chatman (2), Carrie Edwards (4), Sophisticated Jimmy La Rue (3), Bill Pearson (2), George Ramsey [Georgia Tom Dorsey] (8), Guy Smith (2), Monroe Walker (2)*. 1/29–2/36.

**(*) Piano Blues – Vol. 6 (1933–1938)
Document DOCD-5645 *Ben Abney (6), St Louis Red Mike Bailey (6), Curtis Henry (4), Earl Thomas (4), Whistlin' Rufus (4)*. 12/33–6/38.

These CDs are more or less tidying-up operations, gathering the work of little-recorded pianists into neat bundles and stacking them in no particular order. Nonetheless, the first two volumes have some very worthwhile stuff. On *Vol. 1* Jim Clarke's fastidiously executed boogie 'Fat Fanny Stomp', Joe Dean's blues/boogie coupling and 'Bat' Robinson's 'Humming Blues' are all first-rate. The CD also includes the four tracks recorded by Jesse James, a rough-hewn player from Cincinnati whose stoical 'Lonesome Day Blues' is terribly moving. Most of the remaining tracks are good, but often diminished by poor transfers.

Vol. 2 has some curiosities: 'Throw Me Down', once attributed to Skip James but actually by an unknown singer, and two blues by Willie Jones, recorded in Indianapolis three days after the first sides by Leroy Carr and Scrapper Blackwell, who might conceivably have been his accompanists. The volume's longest chapters are by Barrelhouse Buck McFarland (q.v.) and Charlie Segar, a Louisiana-based pianist (and sometime husband of the singer Nellie Lutcher) who gives crisp solo renditions of 'Cow Cow Blues' and '[Pinetop]'s Boogie Woogie' and reveals a small but expressive voice on 'Dissatisfied Blues' and others.

The dominant figure on *Vol. 3* is Meade Lux Lewis, who accompanies not only Robinson's hokum chants but four intriguing blues by George Hannah, a louche singer with a taste for gay themes ('Freakish Man Blues', 'The Boy In The Boat'). The plaintive Nolan Welsh was lucky enough to have Louis Armstrong on hand for 'The Bridwell Blues' and 'St. Peter Blues', but the assertive piano playing on his solo sides stands up to scrutiny. *Vol. 4* can take some pride in Sugar Underwood's romping rags and elegant solos by Jack Erby and Q. Roscoe Snowden, but less in mediocre vaudeville singers like Lucius Hardy or Stovepipe Johnson, whose partly yodelled rendering of the children's song 'The Green Grass Grows All Around' wins some kind of prize for irrelevance. *Vol. 5* is a similar confection, a shell of minor work by nonentities surrounding a hard centre of rare and wrecked Paramounts by a pseudonymous Georgia Tom.

Vol. 6 also has its share of minor artists: Whistlin' Rufus, who sings suggestive novelties; Ben Abney, whose slightly iffy stride playing is the victim of an ill-tuned instrument; and Earl Thomas, who sounds like Bill Gaither sounding like Leroy Carr, an imitator of an imitator. Red Mike Bailey delivers ingenious lyrics, but the most attractive performer is Curtis Henry, a hoarse, husky singer whose frugal piano playing is sometimes reminiscent of Texan contemporaries.

*** Piano Discoveries (1928–1943)
Document BDCD-6045 *Leroy Carr, Walter Davis, Lee Green, Pete Johnson & Albert Ammons, Cripple Clarence Lofton (3), Memphis Slim, Little Brother Montgomery, Charlie 'Bozo' Nickerson (2), Ezra Howlett Shelton, Ivy Smith & Cow Cow Davenport, Tampa Red & Georgia Tom [Dorsey] (2), Alonzo Yancey (3), Jimmy Yancey (7).* 12/28–43.

Virtually all the tracks on this gap-filler are addenda to their players' Document volumes and need little further comment. You wouldn't need to be a Walter Davis or Little Brother Montgomery completist to enjoy their excellent pieces, but many of the others come from lo-fi sources and most of the tunes by Lofton and the Yanceys suffer from either poor performance or inaccurate recording.

**(*) Barrelhouse Piano Blues & Stomps (1929–1933)
Document DOCD-5193 *Herve Duerson (9), Turner Parrish (11), Kingfish Bill Tomlin (4).* 2/29–1/33.

Herve Duerson, from Indianapolis, adds more solos to the two on *Mama Don't Allow No Easy Riders Here* (Yazoo 2034) (see BOOGIE WOOGIE), including an effervescent 'Naptown Special', then backs Teddy Moss, a lugubrious singer. So too, but more sedately, does Turner Parrish, who also adds to his selections on Yazoo. Tomlin is dull on one of his two couplings, livelier on the other, possibly because he yielded the piano stool to a superior player. The best sides here could hold their own in a four-star collection, but weaker material and indifferent sound reduce the rating.

*** Chicago Piano (1929–1936)
Document DOCD-5191 *Eddie Miller (8), Eddie Morgan (2), George Noble (8), John Oscar (6).* 4/29–12/36.

The album's title is inaccurate, since Eddie Miller, its most formidable contributor, lived in St Louis and plays in a style associated with that city. His 1929 sides 'Good Jelly Blues' and 'Freight Train Blues' are magnificently thoughtful performances; beside them his later recordings sound uninvolved. His voice has become coarser, too, which lends some weight to the proposition that he was also responsible for the Eddie Morgan coupling. John Oscar's sides span five years, which probably accounts for the differences in his vocals, though there remains some doubt that he was the singer of the Jelly Roll Morton-like 'Mama Don't Allow No Easy Riders Here'. George Noble is known to have worked with Kokomo Arnold, which explains both the derivation of 'New Milk Cow Blues' and 'Sissy Man Blues' and something of his vocal attack. The weightiest of the pianists in this compilation, he invests his recordings – all more or less explicit covers of other people's numbers – with a broodiness that distances them from their models.

*** Deep South Blues Piano (1935–1937)
Document DOCD-5233 *Blind Mack (2), Harry Chatmon (8), Kid Stormy Weather (2), Mack Rhinehart & Brownie Stubblefield (12).* 1/35–4/37.

David Evans in his notes calls Mack Rhinehart (who was also 'Blind Mack') 'definitely a major artist' with 'an outstanding recorded legacy'. The reader may not go all the way with Evans on this, but will probably agree that Rhinehart stands high in the company of '30s singer/pianists who took their primary inspiration from Leroy Carr. Occasionally he sounds more like Peetie Wheatstraw, but even when he does, as in 'I Can't Take It Anymore', he betrays his major model by borrowing a melodic tag from Carr's 'Baby Don't You Love Me No More'. These 14 thoughtful performances, together with Kid Stormy Weather's peppery pair, justify a three-star rating, but readers are warned that Harry Chatmon's interesting-looking titles are profoundly dull.

**(*) The Bluesville Years Volume Four: In The Key Of Blues
Prestige PRCD 9908 *Curtis Jones (4), Memphis Slim (2), Little Brother Montgomery (4), Sunnyland Slim (2), Roosevelt Sykes (4), Mercy Dee [Walton] (4).* 12/59–61.

*** Blues Piano Orgy
Delmark DE-626 *Curtis Jones (3), Memphis Slim (2), Little Brother Montgomery (4), Otis Spann, Speckled Red, Sunnyland Slim (4), Roosevelt Sykes (4).* 47–12/69.

The Bluesville albums from which the Prestige CD was derived were very unequal in quality, ranging from an excellent set by Walton to a dire one by Roosevelt Sykes. With that reservation, this is a decent compilation by Samuel Charters, several of the artists being heard on signature pieces like 'Vicksburg Blues' (Montgomery), 'One Room Country Shack' (Walton) and 'Lonesome Bedroom Blues' (Jones). Most of the cast reappear on *Blues Piano Orgy*, where they are almost invariably in better form or more sympathetically accompanied, often both. Montgomery's four splendid solos, the quartet by Sunnyland Slim and a few other tracks are unavailable anywhere else.

*** Heavy Timbre: Chicago Boogie Piano
The Sirens SR-5002 *Blind John Davis (4), Erwin Helfer (2), Willie Mabon (4), Sunnyland Slim (6), Jimmy Walker (3).* 6/76.

These recordings were made at what the notes describe as 'a "studio party" … where the challenge of having to play in front of one another clearly brought out the best in each player.' This is most true of Blind John Davis, whose three opening tracks are as good as anything he recorded at this stage in his life, but everyone is in excellent form. Davis's later and less interesting 'Kansas City' belongs to a group of performances that were taped at the session but not issued on the original LP; none of them is outstanding, but they give some impression of the *camaraderie* of the occasion.

**(*) Blue Ivory
Blind Pig BP 74591 *Boogie Woogie Red (3), Henry Gray (3), Mr B (6), Roosevelt Sykes (4).* 77–88.

The tracks by the Detroit-based Boogie Woogie Red

(1925–72) and Henry Gray come from Blind Pig LPs that have not been converted to CD; a couple of Red's are not very well recorded, but there is little of his work in catalogue. Sykes's are discussed in his entry, while those by Mr B are all on his CD *Shining The Pearls* (see his entry), 'When I Lost My Baby' being there correctly titled 'I Almost Lost My Mind'.

***(*) 8 Hands On 88 Keys: Chicago Blues Piano Masters
The Sirens SR-5003 *Barrelhouse Chuck (4), Detroit Junior (4), Erwin Helfer (2), Pinetop Perkins (4)*. 11/01.

The reader unsure of acting on the warm recommendation of Barrelhouse Chuck's *Prescription For The Blues* (The Sirens SR-5004) can sample him here on four equally fine tracks, two, 'It's You Baby' and 'Miss Ida B.', acknowledging his teacher Sunnyland Slim. Detroit Junior sits in to accompany him sturdily on the latter, then performs on his own, fumbling occasionally but generally playing better than on some of his own records. His last number, 'Ain't Nobody's Business', is handsomely accompanied by Erwin Helfer, who goes on to crown the collection with gorgeous readings of Jimmy Yancey's '4 O'Clock Blues' and, backing Pinetop Perkins, 'I Almost Lost My Mind'. Perkins's solos are also of a higher standard than many on his own albums, justifying the notes' claim that the occasion brought out the best in all its participants. TR

Roots

Collections of African-American musics older than the blues, sometimes described as 'pre-blues' or in 'the songster tradition', which survived into the recording era, and others that draw parallels between African-American and African music.

(***) Yonder Come The Blues
Document DOCD 32-20-1 *Big Bill Broonzy, Pinetop Burks, Butch Cage & Willie Thomas, Lonnie Coleman, Tom Darby & Jimmie Tarlton, Rev. J. M. Gates, Georgia Browns, Bertha 'Chippie' Hill, Hokum Boys, Blind Lemon Jefferson, Lil Johnson, Blind Willie Johnson, Kunaal & Sosira, Ladzekpo & Ewe Drum Orchestra, Lil McClintock, Mamprusi Tribesmen, Whistlin' Alex Moore, Charlie Poole, Prairie Ramblers, Thyam Si Griots, Too Tight Henry [Henry L. Castle], Othar Turner, Robert Wilkins, Bob Wills*. 11/25–c. 65.

(****) Africa And The Blues
Neatwork AB 101 *Alexandra Junior Bright Boys, Muhamadu Sarki Banbadawa, Robert Belfour, Ed Bell, Gonga Sarki Birgui & Hamadjam Sarki Siyawa, Samuel Brooks, Chamba People, Dyula-Speaking Urban Musicians, Glen Faulkner, Desiré Basil Fouda, Dija Gambara, Adamou Meigogue Garoua (2), Hausa Trader, Sid Hemphill, Blind Lemon Jefferson, Kachamba Brothers (2), Gombani Lange & Lucas Shishonge, Baba Chale Mafala, Limited Mfundo, Mississippi Matilda, Jack Owens, Napoleon Strickland (2), Tikar man, Tikar woman 1, Tikar woman 2, Ali Farka Touré, two Mpyema boys, Omaru Sanda, Othar Turner, Mose Vinson, Elvis Viyuyu, Big Joe Williams, Zangyani girl*. c. 9/27–1/94.

Yonder Come The Blues illustrates the Cambridge University Press book of the same title, which republishes *Savannah Syncopators: African Retentions In The Blues* by Paul Oliver, *Blacks, Whites And Blues* by Tony Russell and *Recording The Blues* by Robert M. W. Dixon & John Godrich. When originally published in 1970, these volumes were accompanied by 16-track LPs; the CD reissues seven, eight and nine tracks from the respective discs, and carries abridgements of the LP notes.

Savannah Syncopators suffers most from the process of compression: issues like the possible connection of African xylophone playing to blues piano, and of praise-songs to gospel music, are now unillustrated. *Blacks, Whites And Blues* is more successfully redacted and, although the omission of 'Yodeling Fiddling Blues', the Mississippi Sheiks' response to Jimmie Rodgers, is regrettable, there's no denying the emotional depth of Jimmie Tarlton's swooping falsettos on 'Sweet Sarah Blues'. With only seven titles excised, *Recording The Blues* covers most of the necessary bases: the discovery of a market, the recording of women, Southern singers and preachers, the growing dominance of 'urban' styles and the impact of the Depression. All this segment's tracks are readily available elsewhere, however.

Africa And The Blues also illustrates an eponymous book, by Gerhard Kubik, published by University Press of Mississippi. Its concluding tracks illustrate the impact of black American sounds on African popular music, but most of the disc makes connections in the opposite direction, using Kubik's African field recordings and American field and commercial recordings, most of them from Mississippi. There are some fascinating and suggestive comparisons, such as those between fiddler Chasey Collins (accompanying Big Joe Williams) and Adamou Garoua's bowed lute, between the ethereal voices of Mississippi Matilda and a Tikar woman whose 'Grinding Song' generates tremendous swing, and between Sid Hemphill and Baba Mafala, playing panpipes in Mississippi and Mozambique. The notes comment briefly on each track, but the points illustrated are only discussed in depth in the book. Page references are given, but the CD's illustrative value is necessarily lessened for anyone listening without the volume to hand.

**** Before The Blues Vol. 1
Yazoo 2015 *Andrew & Jim Baxter, Cincinnati Jug Band, Sam Collins, Teddy Darby, Denson Quartet, Dick Devall, [Joe] Evans & [Arthur] McClain, Rev. J. M. Gates, Papa Harvey Hull, Mississippi John Hurt, Little Hat Jones, Buell Kazee, Lottie Kimbrough, Rube Lacy, Mississippi Mud Steppers, Bayless Rose, Seventh Day Adventist Choir, B. F. Shelton, Taylor's Kentucky Boys, Henry Thomas, Willie Walker, [Sylvester] Weaver & [Walter] Beasley, Robert Wilkins*. 11/26–10/31.

**** Before The Blues Vol. 2
Yazoo 2016 *Emry Arthur, Dallas String Band, Golden P. Harris, Nap Hayes & Matthew Prater, Peg Leg Howell, Hattie Hudson, Lulu Jackson, Blind Lemon Jefferson, Frank Jenkins, Louise Johnson, Blind Willie Johnson, Charley Jordan, Bobby Leecan & Robert Cooksey, Tommy McClennan, Memphis Jug Band, Charley Patton, Walter Roland & Sonny Scott, Eck Robertson, Frank Stokes, Blind Joe Taggart, Tennessee Chocolate Drops, Minnie Wallace, Geeshie Wiley*. c. 5/26– 9/41.

**** Before The Blues Vol. 3
Yazoo 2017 *Texas Alexander, Clarence Ashley, Barbecue Bob, Biddleville Quintette, Blind Blake, Cannon's Jug Stompers, Buster Carter & Preston Young, Cow Cow Davenport, [Joe] Evans & [Arthur] McClain, Blind Boy Fuller, Bobby Grant, John Hammond, Nap Hayes & Matthew Prater, Mississippi John Hurt, Coley Jones, Luke Jordan, Furry Lewis, Lil McClintock,*

Moses Mason, Memphis Minnie, Frank Stokes, Taylor's Kentucky Boys, Henry Thomas. c. 1/27– 6/40.

As well as commentary on each track, these CDs have a shared note which argues that 'before the Civil War there did not exist in America two distinct bodies of music, one white and one black. Both groups shared a common tradition and repertoire. Indeed, the divergence of white music and black music into two separate genres doesn't really become clear until the turn of [the 20th] century.' The CDs attempt to illustrate this with ballads, minstrelsy, ragtime, breakdowns and a variety of sacred and secular modal songs. There was undoubtedly a complex and dynamic interaction between the music of blacks and (mostly Scotch–Irish) whites, and the common use of gapped, modal scales had a lot to do with it; but the notes downplay both the complexity and the dynamism, ignore black music that doesn't fit, like the polyrhythmic, highly African ring shout, and come close to reducing black music before the blues to white music played by blacks. They also slide past the not unimportant issues of class (there was a free black bourgeoisie even before Emancipation), slavery (if you think you own someone, you can 'share' anything you please) and segregation: Jim Booker and Doc Roberts may 'play together like they were brothers raised in the same house', but the simile collapses the second they put their instruments away. All this may seem dustily academic, so it had better be said that the music is not; it's intrinsically magnificent and superbly remastered, and the juxtapositions are often illuminating. So are the track-by-track comments, although Ma Rainey might dispute that Texas Alexander was 'the only successful blues singer who was not self-accompanied'.

**** The Songsters Tradition: Before The Blues
Saga Blues 982 076-5 *Alabama Sheiks, Pink Anderson & Simmie Dooley, DeFord Bailey, Andrew & Jim Baxter, Richard 'Rabbit' Brown, Gus Cannon, Bo Carter, [Tom] Darby & [Jimmie] Tarlton, Joe Evans & Arthur McClain, Peg Leg Howell, Papa Harvey Hull & Long Cleve Reed (2), Mississippi John Hurt, Frank Hutchison, Luke Jordan, Dick Justice, Jack Kelly, Leadbelly & The Golden Gate Quartet, Furry Lewis, Hobart Smith, Frank Stokes, Freeman Stowers, Taylor's Kentucky Boys, Henry Thomas. 3/27–46.*

Saga's 24 tracks are divided into 'Traveling Troubadours' and 'Vaudeville And Medicine Show Influences'. This is somewhat artificial (John Hurt as a travelling man?), and for all the splendour of their undeniably black-influenced music, the inclusion of white artists (Justice, Hutchison, Smith, Darby & Tarlton) is agenda-driven: to whites, a 'songster' was a songbook; only African-Americans used the term to refer to musicians. Still, this is a highly enjoyable and well remastered collection, which efficiently covers a lot of bases: topical ballads, dance tunes, humour, virtuosity and minstrel-show survivals.

*** The Songster Tradition (1927–1935)
Document DOCD-5045 *Big Boy Cleveland (2), Eli Framer (2), Papa Harvey Hull & Long Cleve Reed (6), Luke Jordan (8), Louis Lasky (3), William & Versey Smith (4). 4/27–4/35.*

The title is a peg on which to hang the artists, but *The Songster Tradition* certainly exemplifies musical variety. Big Boy Cleveland plays fife on the silvery 'Quill Blues' and slide guitar on 'Goin' To Leave You Blues'. He may also have been Long Cleve Reed, who formed a little band with Harvey Hull and guitarist Sunny Wilson; their music charmingly grafts parlour guitar, barbershop harmony and scat singing on to blues, ballads and pop songs. Excitingly percussive and dissonant, William & Versey Smith sing of salvation, shipwreck and war. Alabamian Eli Framer's repetitive, banjoistic guitar harks back to older days; Louie Lasky's forceful flatpicking begins to outstay its welcome by his third track. Luke Jordan's bouncy, Spanish-tinged fingerpicking complements lyrics that paste traditional and original verses into eccentric collages. Two Jordan titles found after this CD was issued are on *"Too Late, Too Late"* – Vol. 8 (Document DOCD-5574).

**** Altamont: Black Stringband Music
Rounder CD 0238 *Nathan Frazier & Frank Patterson (7), Murph Gribble, John Lusk & Albert York (7). 3/42–49.*

The tracks by Frazier (banjo and vocal) and Patterson (fiddle) include 'Corinna', already widely popular with whites by 1942, and the only blues on the disc. The duo often played for white dances with a caller, but Frazier also worked as a street musician in the black section of Nashville. Their music is showy and extrovert, never more so than on the minstrel tune 'Old Dan Tucker', 19th-century in origin but neatly updated with 'You take the phonograph, I'll take the flivver.'

The John Lusk band from south central Tennessee played a repertoire of square-dance instrumentals. Albert York's guitar supplies the steady rhythm needed for dancing, freeing Lusk (fiddle) and Gribble (banjo) to cut some wild melodic and rhythmic capers. There are precedents in country music for Gribble's three-finger banjo, but it still sounds extraordinarily like the playing of Earl Scruggs, then just coming to prominence with Bill Monroe's Blue Grass Boys.

Altamont is a glimpse of a lost world, much of it destined to be for ever unmapped; Charles Wolfe's notes take exploration about as far as it can go. It's a pity that the disc was issued on the cusp of the shift from LP to CD; only 36 minutes long, it omits further recordings by both bands. Fortunately, the balance of the Frazier/Patterson session can be heard on *Black Fiddlers* (Document DOCD-5631), for which see STRINGBANDS.

***(*) Blues Masters, Volume 10: Roots
Rhino R2 71135 *Sister Dora Alexander, Rich Amerson, Daddy Hotcakes, Fula Flutist [sic], Lightnin' Hopkins, Joe Hunter, Eddie 'One-String' Jones, Furry Lewis, Mandingo Griots, Mobile Strugglers, Ethel Perkins, Ethel Perkins & Equila Hall, J. D. Short, Jali Nyama Suso, Texas Prison Camp Work Gang, Robert Pete Williams. early 50–11/76.*

Sam Charters compiled *Roots* from the Folkways catalogue and his own field and studio recordings. His notes are commendably cautious about such uncertainties as the nature and extent of African connections, and whether the free styles of Robert Pete Williams and Daddy Hotcakes are pre-blues, a variant style or simply personal artistic solutions. An imaginative selection includes the haunting unaccompanied singing of Rich Amerson (secular) and Ethel Perkins (sacred); the rollicking dance music of J. D. Short and the Mobile Strugglers; prison worksong, unfiltered on 'Go Down Old Hannah' and inspiring Lightnin' Hopkins's gripping 'Penitentiary Blues'; and street evangelist Dora Alexander, reproving the launching of 'Sputnickels' on 'Russia, Let God's Moon Alone'.

***(*) **Virginia Traditions: Non-Blues Secular Black Music**
Global Village CD 1001 *James Applewhite, Leonard Bowles & Irvin Cook, John Calloway, John Cephas, Sanford L. Collins, Irvin Cook, Isaac Curry, Marvin Foddrell, Turner Foddrell, Lewis Hairston (2), Clayton Horsely, John Jackson, Lemuel Jones, Jimmie Strothers (2), John Lawson Tyree, Clarence Waddy, Uncle Homer Walker, Daniel Womack.* 5/36–11/77.

(For other CDs in this series, see FIELD RECORDINGS.) Marvin Foddrell considered 'Reno Factory' to be 'an old country song', and distinguished it from 'a straight blues'. Arguments over definitions are not exclusive to white listeners, but they can artificially fragment a more holistic reality; Daniel Womack had renounced blues, but the instrumental march which he once played for school closing ceremonies is suffused with bluesy intonations. Still, it's patent that most of the music in this collection predates the rise of blues. Some of it was hanging on by a thread: accordion playing, once widespread in Virginia, had almost died out by the '30s, and Isaac Curry and Clarence Waddy were very old when their chugging music was recorded four decades later. Nothing else here is quite as surprising, and most, it must be said, is more accessible. The collection covers a very diverse range of styles and material, including dance music, ballads, agrarian protest songs and display pieces, and does so in both entertaining and scholarly fashion. Only Sanford Collins' simple harmonica playing seems included to cover a base rather than on merit.

(****) **Roots Of The Blues**
New World NW 802252 *Congregation Of New Brown's Chapel, Rev. Crenshaw, John Dudley, Forrest City Joe [Pugh], Leroy Gary, Rose Hemphill [Rosalie Hill], Sid Hemphill (miscredited as Alec Askew), Jimson [Henry Wallace] (miscredited as Tangle Eye), Bessie Jones, Fred McDowell (3), Leroy Miller, Miles & Bob Pratcher (2), Henry Ratcliff & Bakari-Badji, Percy Wilson (miscredited as Tangle Eye), Ed & Lonnie Young.* 8/42–9/61.

This CD reissues an LP drawn from Alan Lomax's field recordings. The music is wonderful, Lomax's notes are instructive and, as Lomax observes, a track which intercuts hollers by Henry Ratcliff and a Senegalese singer recorded by David Sapir is 'like a conversation between second cousins over a backyard fence'. There are a number of careless misattributions, however, and those noted above are not the full extent of the errors: Rosa Lee Hill, said to be accompanied by Fred McDowell, clearly plays her own guitar. Virtually all the material is now available on CDs in Rounder's *Alan Lomax Collection*. See FIELD RECORDINGS, and in particular *The Land Where The Blues Began*, for which this disc can be seen as a dry run.

***(*) **Black Banjo Songsters Of North Carolina And Virginia**
Smithsonian Folkways SF CD 40079 *Etta Baker & Cora Phillips, Leonard Bowles, Irvin Cook & Leonard Bowles, Lewis Hairston, John Jackson, Rufus Kasey, Dink Roberts (10), James Roberts, John Snipes (8), Joe & Odell Thompson (4), Joe Thompson & Tommy Thompson, John Tyree, Homer Walker.* 1/74–3/97.

The banjo came to America from Africa, but cheap guitars, associations with slavery and minstrel stereotypes meant that its use by black musicians began to decline from about 1900. The notes to *Black Banjo Songsters* make the good point that black banjo music is as unfamiliar to most African-Americans as to anyone else, and these 32 tracks include some remarkable survivals: John Snipes's 'Long Tail Blue' is traceable back to the 1830s. Many tracks are quite brief, but not because the tunes are half-remembered or fragmentary; the pieces are spontaneous creations, not fixed texts, and from the 37 seconds of Dink Roberts's 'High Sheriff' to Rufus Kasey's gripping 4.41 'Coo Coo Bird' they are as long as necessary. A couple of tracks feature the white banjoist Tommy Thompson working with black fiddlers, and usefully highlight the massive influence of black musicians on their white counterparts. The music is joyous, complex and variegated; the booklet notes are extensive, academic and sometimes very technical. CS

Slide Guitar

***(*) **Country Blues Bottleneck Guitar Classics**
Yazoo 1026 *Barbecue Bob, Black Ace, King Solomon Hill, Bo Weavil Jackson, Jim & Bob (The Genial Hawaiians), Robert Johnson, Kansas Joe [McCoy] & Memphis Minnie, Irene Scruggs, Shreveport Home Wreckers, Ramblin' Thomas, Sylvester Weaver, Ruth Willis, Bukka [Booker] White, Oscar Woods.* c. 8/26–6/37.

***(*) **The Voice Of The Blues: Bottleneck Guitar Masterpieces**
Yazoo 1046 *Barbecue Bob, Sam Butler [Bo Weavil Jackson], Jimmie Davis, Blind Willie Davis, Georgia Browns, Georgia Cotton Pickers, Hokum Boys, Irene Scruggs, Roy Smeck, Tampa Kid [Charlie McCoy], Sister O. M. Terrell, Too Bad Boys, Ramblin' Thomas, Buddy [Oscar] Woods.* c. 8/26–2/53.

*** **The Rough Guide To Bottleneck Blues**
World Music Network RGNET 1151 *Kokomo Arnold, Bob Brozman, John Fahey, Stefan Grossman, Pete Harris, Willie Harris, Son House, Jim & Bob (The Genial Hawaiians), Robert Johnson, Blind Willie Johnson, Furry Lewis, Fred McDowell, Blind Willie McTell, Muddy Waters, Hambone Willie Newbern, Charley Patton, Dan Pickett, Allen Shaw, Martin Simpson, Sylvester Weaver, Casey Bill Weldon, Bukka [Booker] White.* 8/26–04.

***(*) **The Slide Guitar: Bottles, Knives & Steel**
Columbia CK 46218 *Barbecue Bob, Blind Boy Fuller, Son House, Robert Johnson, Blind Willie Johnson (2), Leadbelly, Charley Patton, Tampa Red, Sister O. M. Terrell, Sylvester Weaver (3), Casey Bill Weldon, Bukka [Booker] White (2), Ruth Willis, Buddy [Oscar] Woods (2).* 4/27–4/65.

*** **The Slide Guitar: Bottles, Knives & Steel Vol. 2**
Columbia CK 52725 *Walter Beasley, Sam Collins, Nellie Florence, Georgia Browns, Hokum Boys, Helen Humes (2), Sam Montgomery (2), Buddy Moss (3), Papa Too Sweet, Allen Shaw, Tampa Red (3), Tampa Red & Georgia Tom [Dorsey] (3).* 11/27–4/36.

*** **Slide Guitar: The Streamline Special**
Columbia/Legacy 489890 *Michael Bloomfield, Blind Boy Fuller, Georgia Browns, Georgia Cotton Pickers, Son House, Robert Johnson, Blind Willie Johnson, Keb' Mo', Jo-Ann Kelly, Leadbelly, Blind Willie McTell, Buddy Moss, Muddy Waters, Shuggie Otis, Charley Patton, Allen Shaw, Taj Mahal, Tampa Red & Georgia Tom [Dorsey], Sylvester Weaver, Casey Bill Weldon, Bukka [Booker] White, Buddy [Oscar] Woods.* 11/27–6/80.

*** **Slide Guitar: The Streamline Special**
Columbia/Legacy CK 65518 *As above, except omit Michael Bloomfield, Georgia Browns, Son House, Blind Willie Johnson, Keb' Mo', Shuggie Otis.* 11/27–6/80.

The Columbia CDs appeared in the wake of the Robert Johnson box, when executives could be persuaded that blues would be good for the balance sheet. The first volume covers many of the expressive possibilities which slide playing offered to acoustic blues and gospel guitarists: among them are the stylish marquetry of Sylvester Weaver & Walter Beasley's 'Bottleneck Blues'; the emotional intensity of the Mississippians (with Booker White's dance music and train imitation as reminders that it wasn't all darkness on the Delta); and lithe complexities as far apart as Chicago, Texas and Georgia, played by stylists as different as Casey Bill, Oscar Woods and Willie McTell (accompanying Ruth Willis). Barbecue Bob and Sister Terrell are reminders that simplicity can be equally successful. *Vol. 2* has its moments, among them Curley Weaver's seconding of Buddy Moss and Allen Shaw's austere 'Moanin' The Blues', but it's overweight with Tampa Red, who makes a seventh appearance backing the tedious Papa Too Sweet.

Yazoo's collections have several artists in common with Columbia's, but there's minimal duplication of tracks: 'Bottleneck Blues' is on *Bottleneck Guitar Classics* (fair enough; it is one), and the Georgia Browns' bouncy 'Decatur Street 81' is on *Voice Of The Blues*. Yazoo could cherrypick all the 'race' catalogues, and throw in a few white and Hawaiian musicians too, so despite shorter playing time these collections have more stylistic variety. In line with the label's philosophy, there's also more emphasis on virtuosity: Roy Smeck's 'Laughing Rag' and Jim & Bob's 'St. Louis Blues' are both mind-boggling. As well as the predictably fine likes of Booker White, Robert Johnson and Barbecue Bob, Irene Scruggs's able, anonymous accompanist stands out on both discs; so does Bo Weavil Jackson, whose harsh guitar is in hair-raising sympathy with his metallic falsetto.

The Streamline Special shares eight tracks (nine on the longer European version) with the two *Bottles, Knives & Steel* volumes. It's mainly the more recent recordings that are lopped from the shorter version. Taj Mahal's instrumental and Jo-Ann Kelly, interpreting Robert Johnson in her Charley Patton persona, are welcome retentions; otherwise only Muddy Waters (with Johnny Winter playing the slide guitar) survives the cut. One can't regret the loss of Bloomfield or Keb' Mo', who both act out their songs rather than interpreting them, and Son House and Shuggie Otis, with tracks from their '60s Columbia albums, have (very different) age problems. On both versions of the CD, the early material is an excellent selection for variety and quality; the shorter disc, being less keen to prove the continued vitality of the tradition in the face of the evidence, is preferable.

With the exception of Bob 'can't sing, will sing' Brozman, the white musicians on the *Rough Guide*, turning folk sounds into accomplished art music, make a better case for the ongoing relevance – in a different way, and to a different audience – of acoustic slide guitar blues. A cynic might wonder if they – and Robert Johnson – are included to attract the less-informed punter. If so, and if it works, fair enough; the *Rough Guide* is a well-compiled collection, which covers a wide range of moods and styles, and includes important lesser-knowns alongside the obvious but inescapable names. The notes are adequate, but not always up to speed on recent biographical research.

(***) Blues Masters, Volume 15: Slide Guitar Classics
Rhino R2 71126 *Allman Brothers, Chuck Berry, Black Ace, Paul Butterfield, Canned Heat, Joe Carter, Ry Cooder, Homesick James, Earl Hooker, J. B. Hutto, Elmore James, Blind Willie Johnson, Muddy Waters, Robert Nighthawk, Johnny Shines, Hound Dog Taylor, Hop Wilson, Johnny Winter. 12/27–c. 87.*

Acoustic slide is represented by Blind Willie Johnson's unsurpassable 'Dark Was The Night – Cold Was The Ground' and by fellow Texan Black Ace's 1960 version of his theme song, but the emphasis is on electric guitar blues. The selection ably blends necessary classics (Elmore James's 'Dust My Broom', Waters, Nighthawk on Maxwell Street) with imaginative surprises (Joe Carter's larynx-scarring bar-room holler, Homesick James frolicking on the bass strings). Earl Hooker's wah-wah is deeply irritating, though, and Chuck Berry's command of the pedal steel guitar sometimes uncertain. More fundamentally problematic are the white bands, considerately placed last. These early incarnations of the Butterfield band and Canned Heat were trying to find respectful but unfossilized ways to play black music; idiomatic playing wins unconvincing vocals some tolerance, but this cannot be extended to Winter and the Allmans' blustering machismo, or to Cooder's droning monotone.

Blues Masters Vol. 18: More Slide Guitar Classics (Rhino R2 75348) has an attractive roster, but is deleted.

**** Roll And Tumble Blues: A History Of Slide Guitar
Indigo IGOTCD 2548 3CD *The All-Stars featuring Jeff Beck, Kokomo Arnold (2), Willie Baker, Barbecue Bob, Walter Beasley, Black Ace, The Blues Band featuring Dave Kelly, Gabriel Brown, Sam Butler [Bo Weavil Jackson], Cliff Carlisle, Eric Clapton & Jimmy Page, Sam Collins, [Tom] Darby & [Jimmie] Tarlton (2), Jimmie Davis, Dixon Brothers, Fleetwood Mac featuring Jeremy Spencer, Nellie Florence, Blind Boy Fuller, Georgia Browns, Bobby Grant, Peter Green, Willie Harris, Donna Hightower, King Solomon Hill, Homesick James, Lightnin' Hopkins, Son House (2), Frank Hutchison (2), Elmore James, Blind Lemon Jefferson, Robert Johnson, Blind Willie Johnson, Brian Knight & Toni Vines, Leadbelly, John Lee (2), Furry Lewis, Robert Lockwood, Charlie McCoy, Robert Lee McCoy [Robert Nighthawk] (2), Fred McMullen, Blind Willie McTell, Buddy Moss, Muddy Waters (3), Hambone Willie Newbern, St Louis Jimmy [Oden], Charley Patton, Dan Pickett, Pinetop Slim, Riley Puckett, Blind Joe [Willie] Reynolds, Bayless Rose, Allen Shaw, Johnny Shines (2), Frankie Lee Sims, Shreveport Home Wreckers, Tampa Red, Hound Dog Taylor, Sister O. M. Terrell, Ramblin' Thomas, Jim Thompkins, Lemuel Turner, Curley Weaver, Sylvester Weaver, Casey Bill Weldon, Bukka [Booker] White (2), Big Joe Williams, Ruth Willis, Oscar [Buddy] Woods. 11/27–90s.*

Roll And Tumble Blues is cheap, has variable but never less than good sound and includes all the important black slide guitarists up to the copyright cut-off. It also features enjoyable minor artists like Jim Thompkins and Willie Harris, and samples the most important hillbilly musicians who favoured slide guitar blues. The notes are useful (and the only place in the package where Frank Hutchison's surname is spelled correctly), but it's traducing Son House to call him 'a shadow of his former self' in 1941. *Roll And Tumble Blues* is the obvious slide guitar best buy, despite relying on British bands for the final six tracks: only Jeremy Spencer's hero-worshipping homage to Elmore James makes much of a case for itself.

*** Chicago Slide Guitar Masters: From Tampa Red To Elmore James
Saga Blues 982 077-8 *Kokomo Arnold (2), Eddie Duncan, Bob Dunn, Homesick James, Earl Hooker, Elmore James (2), Robert*

Jr Lockwood, Charlie McCoy (2), Robert Nighthawk, Alice Moore, Muddy Waters, St Louis Jimmy [Oden] (2), Johnny Shines, Tampa Kid [Charlie McCoy], Tampa Red (3), Joe Turner (with Elmore James), Casey Bill Weldon (2). 5/28–11/53.

Chicago Slide Guitar Masters makes the important (because true) and often overlooked case that the progenitor and most influential exponent of Chicago slide guitar blues was Tampa Red. The CD's postwar half is an assemblage of masterpieces (although in the case of the St Louis Jimmy tracks it's only Muddy's solos that qualify for the description). The prewar section is less exciting: Casey Bill is formulaic, fake sobbing makes Kokomo Arnold's 'Crying Blues' one of his weaker sides, and Charlie McCoy (whose 'Please Baby' was credited by Decca to brother Joe) mimics Tampa's playing rather than being inspired by it. When they discuss the alleged enthusiasm of African-Americans for Western Swing and the origins of slide guitar, both generally and in blues, the notes should be treated with extreme caution.

***(*) Bottleneck Blues
Testament TCD 5021 *Chicago String Band, David [Honeyboy] Edwards, John Lee Granderson, J. B. Hutto, Robert 'Nighthawk' Johnson (2), Johnny Littlejohn, Fred McDowell (2), Robert Nighthawk, Jack Owens, Herb Quinn, Johnny Shines, Napoleon Strickland (2), Blind Connie Williams (2), Big Joe Williams (3), Mott Willis (2). 5/61–9/70.*

*** Down Home Slide
Testament TCD 6009 *John Henry Barbee, Elijah Brown, George Coleman, David 'Honeyboy' Edwards, John Littlejohn, Fred McDowell, Fred & Annie Mae McDowell, Robert Nighthawk (3), Johnny Shines, Eddie Taylor, Arthur Weston, Blind Connie Williams (2), Big Joe Williams (4). 5/61–5/72.*

Announced as an LP in the '60s, *Bottleneck Blues* appeared 25 years later, expanded into a CD. In effect, it illustrates a lengthy essay by David Evans, which begins with African-American slide guitar's origins in the one-string 'jitterbug' or 'diddley bow' before considering the playing techniques that developed: single string sliding with chordal percussion, barred chords in open tunings, the incorporation of Hawaiian-influenced harmonies, and chording with slider and fingers in open and standard tunings. *Bottleneck Blues* isn't perfect: Honeyboy Edwards is dull, Big Joe and McDowell hold no surprises (thanks in part to other Testament releases) and the amplified bands led by Hutto and Littlejohn seem to have had only a single microphone aimed at them. Nevertheless, the CD is an illuminating blend of analysis and musical pleasure, especially perhaps for anyone who thinks the slide guitar's primary role is to provide high-volume accompaniment to headbanging.

Featuring many of the same artists, *Down Home Slide* functions as an appendix to *Bottleneck Blues*. Nighthawk's tracks, recorded at a University of Chicago concert, feature Little Walter and Johnny Young, but none of the trio is at his best. John Henry Barbee's surging 'I Know She Don't Love Me' is among the finest of his too few recordings, and Honeyboy's scurrying 'Sweet Home Chicago' is far better than his track on *Bottleneck Blues*, but it's one of five that are available elsewhere on Testament.

**(*) Slidin' ... Some Slide
Bullseye Blues CD BB 9533 *Earl Hooker, J. B. Hutto (2), Elmore James, Smokin' Joe Kubek with B'nois King, Sonny Landreth, Ron Levy with Ronnie Earl & Wayne Bennett, John Mooney, Muddy Waters, Robert Nighthawk, Taj Mahal & Ry Cooder, Hound Dog Taylor, George Thorogood, Lil' Ed [Williams] & The Imperials, Hop Wilson (2). 4/48–early 90s.*

*** Crucial Slide Guitar Blues
Alligator ALCD 117 *Luther Allison, Elvin Bishop, Corey Harris, Michael Hill, Dave Hole, Kinsey Report, Sonny Landreth, Bob Margolin, A. C. Reed with Bonnie Raitt, Hound Dog Taylor, Lil' Ed [Williams], Johnny Winter. 70s–90s.*

(***) Slide Guitar
Fab14 50120 *Monti Amundson, Bob Brozman, Ronnie Earl, John Hammond, J. B. Hutto, Imperial Crowns, Luther 'Guitar Junior' Johnson, Bobby King & Terry Evans, Smokin' Joe Kubek with B'nois King, Magic Slim, John Mooney, Mike Morgan, Jim Suhler, George Thorogood. 70s–90s.*

At its best *Slidin' ... Some Slide* is very good, but the tracks by Elmore James, Nighthawk and Muddy Waters are not the norm. Hound Dog Taylor, J. B. Hutto and J. B.'s nephew Lil' Ed proffer raucous good times; George Thorogood takes inspiration from their sound and spirit, but 'Delaware Slide' is let down by callow singing and gross overstretch: it would be twice as effective at a third of the length. John Mooney's cranked-up reimagining of Son House is a deeper, more lived-in response to black music, and Sonny Landreth's proficiency can only be admired. The other white slide-wielders make statements of the obvious, and Earl Hooker's 'Blue Guitar' is also pretty inconsequential. The Hop Wilson tracks feature an astonishing amount of surface noise.

Hound Dog Taylor looms large on Alligator's low-priced sampler. The tracks by Allison (wonderful) and Landreth come from a tribute album, and Dog's exultancy permeates the tracks by Hill and Hole. Lil' Ed is his usual uninhibited self, and 'It's My Life, Baby' is the track for people who only need one Johnny Winter track. Bonnie Raitt is out of place on A. C. Reed's CD (see his entry), but one number from it is bearable. Corey Harris's acoustic solo makes an effective change of pace. On the downside, Bishop's song is fluffy pop, Margolin vulgarizes Muddy, and hammy vocals mar the Kinseys' song, inspired by reports of an outbreak of racist church burning.

Also bargain-priced, the Fab14 CD samples Rounder and its associated labels. Luther Johnson's magnificent 'Walkin' With You Baby' is the ideal start, John Mooney affirms his stature, and Ronnie Earl finds more in 'Blue Guitar' than Earl Hooker could. Elsewhere, there are problems with weak material or unpersuasive vocals. The CD's target audience seems to be white males who occasionally wonder if a tattoo would be cool. It gets the marketing job done, but anyone seeking more depth and less posturing is likely to be disappointed.

***(*) The Best Of Slide Guitar
Wolf 120.103 *Honeyboy Edwards, Homesick James, J. B. Hutto, Cub Koda, John Littlejohn, Johnny B. Moore, Muddy Waters, Louis Myers, John Primer, Maynard Silva, Houston Stackhouse, Eddie Taylor, Hound Dog Taylor, Lil' Ed [Williams] (2). 11/72–96.*

It's a hyperbolic title, of course, but this is the best of the electric slide collections discussed here. There are drawbacks: Hound Dog's voice is distant, Moore's vocal parodies don't make a nine-minute 'Blues Medley' more than fitfully amusing, Silva is in all senses a pale imitation of J. B. Hutto, and Stackhouse is plagued by wrong notes; but these problems are outweighed by the sheer reliability of artists like Hutto, Littlejohn, Primer, Eddie Taylor and Myers, and by songs like 'Dim Lights' and 'Bloody Tears', which are emotionally meaningful, not just launch-pads for slide-slinging. Recorded in concert somewhere in Europe, Muddy gets further into 'Long Distance Call' than usual, and Johnny B. Moore's seconding steadies Honeyboy's erratic time, making this 1987 'Sweet Home Chicago' one of his best. CS

St Louis

(*) St. Louis (1927–1934)
Document DOCD-5181 *Jelly Roll Anderson (4), Red Mike Bailey (2), Georgia Boyd (2), 'Spider' Carter (3), Ell-Zee Floyd, Bert 'Snake Root' Hatton (2), Henry Johnson & His Boys (6), Jesse Johnson (2), Jimmy Strange (2).* 4/27–8/33.

(*) St. Louis Girls (1927–1934)
Document DOCD-5182 *Katherine Baker (8), Johnnie Strauss (2), Elizabeth Washington (2), Lizzie Washington (13).* 4/27–8/34.

St Louis is a node of road, rail and river traffic, and in the prewar years was an important destination for migrant African-Americans, who supported a lively and varied blues scene. The artists on *St. Louis* didn't record enough to get a CD to themselves; in the case of Jesse Johnson, one must be glad. Red Mike Bailey's six titles on *Piano Blues – Vol. 6* (Document DOCD-5645) are duller than these two, which come from a very crackly 78. Hatton and Strange are stiff and stagey, but Hatton's 'Freakish Rider Blues' has some startling lyrics. 'Spider' Carter is more involved with his material, and Ell-Zee Floyd is assisted by a fine pianist. It's been implausibly suggested that both Carter and Floyd are really J. D. Short, who backs one title by the yearning Georgia Boyd; Roosevelt Sykes is on the other.

The most interesting tracks on *St. Louis* are those involving Henry Johnson & His Boys (one of whom is Lonnie Johnson). The group also backs Jelly Roll Anderson, and its four members deploy various combinations of guitars (including a slide guitar played way up the neck), violin, piano, celeste and percussion, plus two instruments identified by B&GR as a hurdy-gurdy and a wind instrument which 'might be a kazoo or a member of the bagpipe family'. These experiments with unusual sonorities and extreme registers are unparalleled in blues, and the results are fascinating, if not always easy listening.

Henry Johnson's men also back Katherine Baker and Lizzie Washington on *St. Louis Girls* (which includes some extremely noisy transfers); on Baker's 'Wild Women Blues', James Johnson's piano is the only instrument, but otherwise the strangeness continues, reaching a peak with the violin and celeste duo on Baker's 'Mistreated Blues'. Baker and Washington often sound detached and unemotional, perhaps in order to distance themselves from the violence, betrayal and prostitution that feature heavily in lyrics that are often strikingly poetic. Elizabeth Washington (a different singer) is accompanied by pianists Aaron Sparks (sensitive) and Jesse Bell (clodhopping), and Johnnie Strauss growls her lyrics in competition with an equally raucous fiddler. There are more titles by Elizabeth Washington on *The Sparks Brothers (1932–1935)* (Document DOCD-5315).

**** St. Louis Town 1929–1933
Yazoo 1003 *'Hi' Henry Brown (2), Teddy Darby (2), Jim Jackson, Charley Jordan (4), Henry Spaulding, Joe Stone and Jelly Jaw Short [J. D. Short] (3), Henry Townsend.* 5/29–8/33.

**** St. Louis Blues 1929–1935
Yazoo 1030 *Georgia Boyd, 'Hi' Henry Brown (2), Charley Jordan (4), Joe Stone [J. D. Short], Henry Townsend (5), Peetie Wheatstraw.* 11/29–12/33.

As former LPs, *St. Louis Town* and *St. Louis Blues* are of short duration, but their content is of the highest quality and very well remastered. The stars are Charley Jordan and Henry Townsend, who both recorded extensively enough to generate CDs under their own names, but whose finest sides are on these discs. Henry Spaulding, 'Hi' Henry Brown and J. D. Short recorded less, but are no less important, and Jim Jackson, from Memphis, infiltrates a musically simple but irresistibly engaging version of W. C. Handy's greatest hit. These collections may be hard to find, but they combine into a masterly portrait of the city's greatest prewar guitarists (Peetie Wheatstraw plays his second instrument), with their dazzling skills, idiosyncratic phrasing and spontaneous yet disciplined approaches to rhythm and sonority. The notes concentrate on the technicalities of their guitar playing, but rightly point out the originality of many lyrics.

St. Louis Country Blues (1929–1937) (Document DOCD-5147) is covered by the entries for J. D. Short and Henry Townsend.

*** St. Louis Barrelhouse Piano (1929–1934)
Document DOCD-5104 *Henry Brown (5), Henry Brown & Ike Rodgers (2), Tee McDonald, Dolly Martin, Sylvester Palmer (4), Robert Peeples (4), Ike Rodgers (3), Bessie Mae Smith (2), Wesley Wallace (2), Peetie Wheatstraw.* 5/29–8/34.

**** Down On The Levee: The Piano Blues Of St. Louis Vol. 2
Yazoo 2065 *Henry Brown (3), Ell-Zee Floyd, James 'Stump' Johnson (2), Lonnie Johnson, Mary Johnson, Eddie Miller, Alice Moore, St Louis Jimmy [Oden], Specks Pertum [Charlie McFadden], Sparks Brothers (5), Roosevelt Sykes, Doretha Trowbridge, Blind Squire Turner [Teddy Darby], Wesley Wallace (2), Peetie Wheatstraw.* 5/29–7/35.

**** Twenty First St. Stomp: The Piano Blues Of St. Louis
Yazoo 2061 *Dorothy Baker, Henry Brown (2), Walter Davis, James Gordon, James 'Stump' Johnson (3), Mary Johnson (3), Tecumseh McDowell, Charlie McFadden (2), Eddie Miller (2), Robert Peeples, Milton Sparks, Sparks Brothers (3), Roosevelt Sykes, Peetie Wheatstraw.* 8/29–5/37.

The piano blues of St Louis in the interwar years are characterized (though not exclusively) by spacious, chorded 4/4 bass patterns, which move the music forward with an easy swagger. The confident, coiled energy of Henry Brown's very varied playing is perhaps the finest achievement of a very competitive scene, although a strong case can be made for Pinetop Sparks, whether accompanying himself, his twin brother Milton or one of the harsh-voiced women who were as ubiquitous as bootleg alcohol and gambling. Several of Yazoo's artists recorded at sufficient length to have CDs of their own, usually on Document, but the selected tracks are among their finest. Equally compelling are less extensively recorded pianists like the wistful singer Eddie Miller, who also accompanies Charlie McFadden, and Wesley Wallace, whose train imitation 'No. 29' is far more imaginative and onomatopoeic than the better known 'Honky Tonk Train Blues'. Dubbed from 78s in superb condition and expertly annotated, the Yazoo CDs are as definitive and enjoyable as the label's parallel guitar collections. (Eddie Miller's complete recordings are gathered on *Chicago Piano (1929–1936)* [Document DOCD-5191], discussed in PIANO.)

St. Louis Barrelhouse Piano is for specialists, and enables them to decide whether Sylvester Palmer and Robert Peeples were pseudonyms for Wesley Wallace (highly unlikely in both cases). Wallace supplies stiffly cautious accompaniment to Peeples on two tracks, and to Bessie Mae Smith on another two, but Sylvester Palmer is an underrated pianist with a darting, semi-improvised right hand. *St. Louis Barrelhouse Piano* is most valuable for including all Ike Rodgers's collaborations with Henry Brown except their accompaniments to Mary Johnson and Alice Moore. Rodgers's trombone playing was economical to the point of parsimony, using a narrow range of notes and an assortment of mutes – the strange, veiled sighing on 'Screening The Blues' was allegedly achieved by playing through the head of a side drum – to create a vocalized and deeply bluesy sound.

*** St. Louis Blues Today
Wolf 120.491 *Tommy Bankhead (4), Doc Terry [Adail] (2), Piano Slim (2), J. R. Reed (4), Oliver Sain.* 10–11/91.

The postwar scenes in St Louis and across the river in East St Louis, Illinois, were vibrant, but currently they're not well served by VACs. Readers should look out for *East St Louis – The Stevens Sessions* (Sequel NEM CD 940) and *Mo' Betta: St Louis R&B 1956–66* (Sequel NEMCD 946), both of which are deleted. The latter includes an early track by Piano Slim, whose tracks on *St. Louis Blues Today* are much better than those on the CD discussed under his name. *St. Louis Blues Today* is an unpretentiously pleasing collection by some of the city's senior musicians, although an egomaniacal drummer afflicts J. R. Reed's tracks. Harp player Doc Terry's band can't be graded higher than 'adequate', but his revival of 'Aunt Caroline Dyer Blues' is a pleasant surprise. Producer Oliver Sain's 'Underground Blues' is a smoky after-hours instrumental on which Sain plays organ and alto, and Eddie Fisher some graceful, jazzy guitar. Tommy Bankhead's voice shows its age, but his guitar work and songwriting are both resourceful. *St. Louis Blues Today – Vol. 2* (Wolf 120.942) is split between Big Bad Smitty and Eugene Fluker, and is discussed in the former's entry. CS

Stringbands

♛ **** Violin, Sing The Blues For Me
Old Hat CD-1002 *Alabama Sheiks, Andrew & Jim Baxter (2), Louie Bluie [Howard Armstrong] & Ted Bogan, Booker Orchestra, Tommie Bradley (2), Bo Carter, Cow Cow Davenport, Johnson Boys [Nap Hayes & Matthew Prater], Peg Leg Howell, Kansas City Blues Strummers, Jack Kelly, Memphis Jug Band, Mississippi Mud Steppers, Mississippi Sheiks, Mobile Strugglers, 'Blue Coat' Tom Nelson, Henry Sims, Frank Stokes, Tennessee Chocolate Drops, Whistler & His Jug Band, Henry Williams & Eddie Anthony, [Big] Joe Williams.* 7/26–7/49.

**** Folks, He Sure Do Pull Some Bow!
Old Hat CD-1003 *Abrew's Portuguese Instrumental Trio, Alabama Rascals, The Bubbling-Over Five, Bo Carter, James Cole, Dixieland Jug Blowers, Georgia Yellow Hammers, Clifford Hayes, The Blue Boys [Nap Hayes & Matthew Prater], Peg Leg Howell, Alec Johnson, Memphis Jug Band, Mississippi Sheiks (2), Banjo Ikey Robinson And His Bull Fiddle Band, [Jack Kelly's] South Memphis Jug Band, State Street Boys (2), Frank Stokes, Tennessee Chocolate Drops, Peetie Wheatstraw & His Blue Blowers, Henry Williams & Eddie Anthony, [Big] Joe Williams (2).* 6/27–10/35.

***(*) String Bands (1926–1929) [sic]
Document DOCD-5167 *Alabama Sheiks (4), Andrew & Jim Baxter (7), Booker Orchestra, Georgia Yellow Hammers, Nap Hayes & Matthew Prater (4), Kansas City Blues Strummers (2), Old Pal Smoke Shop Four (2), Taylor's Kentucky Boys (4).* 7/26–1/31.

Singing or sawing, raucous or polished, virtuosically flashy or jaggedly poignant, there's a great range of possibilities in the too-seldom recorded music of African-American fiddlers, and Old Hat's two surveys illustrate those possibilities with admirable attention to detail. Many tracks are also available on CDs devoted to single artists, but both these discs are necessary acquisitions for even the most dedicated collector. They do all the things that a good anthology should: the notes and illustrations are extensive and comprehensive, and the material is both judiciously chosen and astutely sequenced. Above all, the sound restoration is astonishing: quite apart from the fiddles, the accompanying guitars, jugs *et cetera* are heard with a clarity never before attained by reissuers of this material.

That can be confirmed by listening to *String Bands*, which nevertheless performs a useful service by pulling together the works of artists recorded on spec by companies who neither knew nor cared that future generations would lament the rarity of such material. The Kansas City Blues Strummers and the Old Pal Smoke Shop Four both favour impersonal vocals and firm rhythms, chopped out by cello and bowed bass respectively. African-American fiddler Jim Booker joins the white Taylor's Kentucky Boys to power through four vibrant square-dance tunes. Booker's completely idiomatic collaborations with the brilliant banjoist Marion Underwood are the CD's high point. Booker, two of his sons and kazooist Robert Steele are the Booker Orchestra, whose playing of 'Camp Nelson Blues' is more distinctively black; its flipside is on *Violin, Sing The Blues For Me*. Andrew Baxter sits in with the white Georgia Yellow Hammers before joining his guitarist son to play plaintive blues, vigorous dance tunes (including a cakewalk) and a full-steam-ahead train imitation. Hayes & Prater's mandolin–guitar duets bubble enticingly, and include two rags by Scott Joplin (very passé in 1928). The dully derivative Alabama Sheiks make a disappointing finale.

Mississippi String Bands & Associates (1928–1931) (RST Blues Documents BDCD-6013) is discussed under Charlie McCoy.

**(*) Black Fiddlers (1929–c. 1970)
Document DOCD-5631 *Andrew & Jim Baxter (4), Cuje Bertram (24), Nathan Frazier & Frank Patterson (6).* 11/29–c. 70.

Copies of the Baxters' remaining issued titles were only found after *String Bands* appeared; these are not bad performances, but they add little to the picture already drawn. Frazier & Patterson's tracks complete the Library of Congress session partially issued on *Altamont* (see ROOTS), and are every bit as exciting as the material on that CD; even an 18-second fragment of 'Fisher's Hornpipe' generates enough oomph to tantalize as it fades.

Born in Tennessee in 1894, Cuje Bertram was recorded informally, with children chattering in the background on several tracks. He'd associated with white musicians in the '20s, and 'Careless Love' and 'Goodnight Irene' are as close to blues as he gets. Bertram has imperfect recall of some lyrics, but his playing of 'Billy In The Low Ground', 'Flop-Eared Mule', 'Eighth Of January' and other tunes from the white repertoire is hearty and proficient; 19 tracks are under two minutes long, though, and important as this material is, it's more valuable as documentation than as entertainment. cs

Texas

(*) The Blues Of Texas, Arkansas & Louisiana 1927–1932
Yazoo 1004 *Texas Alexander, Buddy Boy Hawkins, King Solomon Hill (2), Sammy Hill (2), Blind Lemon Jefferson, Little Hat Jones (2), Willie Reed, Six Cylinder Smith (2), Henry Thomas (2). c. 6/27–c. 1/32.*

*** Texas Blues**
JSP JSP 7730 4CD *Black Ace (6), Smith Casey (7), Pete Harris (4), Coley Jones (4), Little Hat Jones (10), Willie Reed (6), Henry Thomas (23), Jesse 'Babyface' Thomas (4), Ramblin' Thomas (19), Oscar Woods (17). 6/27–4/39.*

(**(*)) Texas Blues (1927–1937)
Wolf WSE 112 *Black Ivory King (2), Blind Norris (2), Gene Campbell (12), Whistlin' Alex Moore (5), Henry Thomas (5). 6/27–2/37.*

All the companies involved in the blues business in the '20s and '30s made frequent recording trips to Dallas and San Antonio, and the music they collected and issued is a rich, colourful mixture of theatre and club artists, street singers and pianists circuit-riding the logging camps. It's too varied a subject to be fully taken in by a single CD, and it's regrettable that the well-chosen *Texas Blues* (Catfish KATCD 181 2CD) is out of print.

The Yazoo is an unexpanded transfer from an LP and its Texan contributors account, probably, for only nine of the 14 tracks. The music is irreproachable and the sound quality good, but as a survey of Texas blues it's of limited utility. The 100-track JSP set is similarly circumscribed: Texas had its share of outstanding singer/guitarists, but to concentrate on them alone, excluding all the piano players, stringbands and women artists, is to deny the diversity that makes Texas so singular. But fans of tidiness at a low price should note that it includes the complete (prewar) works of all the Joneses and Thomases involved.

The Wolf has been marginalized by others: anyone interested enough in Gene Campbell to want a lot of him will probably opt for his Document CD, while the other contributors can be sampled elsewhere.

Another deleted item worth keeping an eye out for is *Easin' In: The Essential Recordings Of Texas Blues* (Indigo IGOCD 2043), which, although it spends too long on Henry Thomas and Jefferson (and the sound of some of the Jeffersons is poor), is otherwise a reasonable selection from the '20s and '30s, arriving at the brink of the modern era by closing on T-Bone Walker's 'Got A Break Baby'.

**** Texas: Black Country Dance Music (1927–1935)
Document DOCD-5162 *Dallas String Band (8), Carl Davis & Dallas Jamboree Jug Band (4), Will Day (2), Frenchy's String Band (2), Jake Jones & The Gold Front Boys (2), William McCoy (6). 12/27–9/35.*

The context in which the Dallas String Band operated was probably larger than providing dance music: the group's recordings are among the very few that connect us to the serenading stringbands of the late 19th and early 20th century, which played requests on the streets of cities like Dallas and New Orleans and are intricated in the prehistory of jazz. The best-known DSB recording, because so often reissued, is the sparkling mandolin-led instrumental 'Dallas Rag', but the majority of their sides are popular songs like 'Shine' and 'Sugar Blues', sung by a harmony trio in glee-club style. The group's eight recordings are not only fascinating and valuable historical documents but vivacious and well executed.

The other artists on the album deal in blues. Both Will Day and Jake Jones's group offer blues vocals with clarinet and rhythm accompaniment; floating in Jones's 'Southern Sea Blues' is the joke 'I went down to the ocean to get a permanent wave.' Frenchy's String Band features the cornettist Polite Christian. Carl Davis's band reworks the tune of 'Don't Sell It, Don't Give It Away', a Texas favourite, as 'Dusting The Frets', with guitars, kazoo and washboard; its other numbers are less jittery blues. William McCoy's harmonica pieces stand out amidst these small-band performances, but most of them too are blues, with a guest appearance on 'Out Of Doors Blues' by a rustic clarinettist, possibly the musician heard with Day and/or Jones.

***(*) Texas Blues (1927–1935)
Document DOCD-5161 *'Bo' Jones (2), Coley Jones (4), Little Hat Jones (10), Willie Reed (6), Oak Cliff T-Bone [Walker] (2). 12/27–9/35.*

Prefacing the blues performances of the rest of this album's cast are four archaic pieces by the Dallas singer and guitarist Coley Jones, ponderously delivered but of considerable folkloric interest. 'Drunkard's Special' is a rare African-American recording of the Old World ballad 'Our Goodman'. 'Bo' Jones's exercises in the Texas Alexander–Lonnie Johnson idiom act as an overture to the recordings of Little Hat Jones, who actually worked with Alexander but seems to have been vocally untouched by the experience: his voice is small, high and plaintive and roped to the beat of his highly rhythmic, and quite varied, guitar playing. He is fond of changing tempo in the course of a song, sometimes opening at a brisk medium-fast then braking dramatically when he starts singing, as in 'Little Hat Blues'. 'Bye Bye Baby Blues' is an attractive variant of 'Fare Thee, Baby, Fare Thee Well'.

Willie Reed (also one of Texas Alexander's accompanists) plays his 'Texas Blues' with a busy right thumb, creating a rhythmic bounce rather like Mance Lipscomb's. 'Leavin' Home' and 'Goin' Back To My Baby', made a year later, are strikingly different: the leisurely singing and single-string passages seem further proofs of the Alexander effect, something still detectable in his last (1935) recording 'All Worn Out And Dry Blues'. Oak Cliff T-Bone's 'Trinity River Blues' is neither worn out nor dry: the theme is flooding and the artist is the teenaged T-Bone Walker, on his first record date.

*** Texas Girls (1926–1929)
Document DOCD-5163 *Bobbie Cadillac (5), Hattie Hudson (2), Ida May Mack (10), Lillian Miller (5), Gertrude Perkins (2). 26–29.*

*** Territory Singers – Vol. 2 (1928–1930)
Document DOCD-5471 *Hattie Burleson (7), Cleo Gibson (2), Jewell Nelson (2), Mel Parker (2), David Pearson (2), Ollie Ross (3), Horace Smith (4), Hattie Snow (3). 11/28–c. 11/30.*

Texas – or, it's probably more accurate to say, the entertainment districts of black Dallas and Houston – seems to have swarmed with estimable women singers in the '20s. Besides Bessie Tucker and Victoria Spivey, who have their own entries, there were most of the artists on *Texas Girls* (the provenance of Lillian Miller remains questionable) and Burleson, Nelson and Ross on *Territory Singers – Vol. 2*. Burleson, an *entrepreneuse* who probably secured sessions for several of the other singers, was also an original songwriter: witness, for example, the detail of 'Sadie's Servant Room Blues'. The debate about whether she was also Hattie Hudson remains unsettled but Hudson is certainly a fine singer, with two haunting songs. Ida May Mack has a measured moaning style very similar to that of Bessie Tucker, whose piano accompanist, K. D. Johnson, she shares. Most of these artists wrote or picked songs with vivid and sometimes violent imagery; Bobbie Cadillac's 'Carbolic Acid Blues' is a striking example, and it's unfortunate that her other recordings are hokum duets with Coley Jones and much less interesting.

Apart from the monumental Cleo Gibson, who is discussed elsewhere, the remainder of *Territory Singers – Vol. 2* is of minor interest. There are a couple of good Texan singers on *Territory Singers – Vol. 1 (1922–1928)* (Document DOCD-5470), Ben Norsingle and Emma Wright, but they account for just five of its 23 tracks.

***(*) Dallas Alley Drag
Yazoo 2054 *Bobbie Cadillac, Texas Bill Day (5), Hattie Hudson, Billiken Johnson (4), Ida May Mack (2), Whistlin' Alex Moore (5), Jack Ranger (2), Bessie Tucker (3). 12/27–12/29.*

*** Texas Piano – Vol. 2 (1927–1938)
Document DOCD-5225 *Texas Bill Day (6), Kitty Gray (11), Billiken Johnson (4), Jack Ranger (3). 12/27–12/38.*

Dallas Alley Drag shares 11 tracks with *Texas Piano – Vol. 2*, but its wider-ranging selection and superior remastering make it the sensible choice for anyone but a completist or a Kitty Gray fan. With its small but good selection of blues by women, it also usefully epitomizes the theme of the two albums discussed above. Of the artists spotlit by both CDs, Texas Bill Day sings in a hoarse, wheedling tone a little like Alex Moore's, while Billiken Johnson – evidently a transportation buff, since three of his four songs are about trains or buses – intersperses his vocals with kazoo and whistling choruses. Kitty Gray on the Document CD sings and scats roguish swing numbers like 'Round And Round' and 'Posin'', buoyantly accompanied by her Wampus Cats. This is very close to being black Western Swing.

Texas Piano – Vol. 1 (1923–1935) (Document DOCD-5224) is chiefly concerned with Bernice Edwards and Hersal Thomas (qq.v.).

*** San Antonio Blues (1937)
Document DOCD-5232 *Son Becky (6), Pinetop Burks (6), Big Boy Knox (4), Ted Mays & His Band (6). 3–10/37.*

Son Becky and Pinetop Burks were members of the loose sodality of itinerant pianists who played for the workers in lumber camps and 'turpentine farms'. It seems unlikely that the repertoire they used on that barrelhouse circuit is fairly represented by their recordings (included here in their entirety), which are predominantly blues, but the historical record has been set straight by contemporaries such as Robert Shaw who survived longer and were able to record under fewer constraints. All that aside, both Becky and Burks are emphatic performers, even at times boisterous – as in Becky's 'Black Heart Blues' and 'Midnight Trouble Blues' and Burks's 'Shake The Shack' – and, despite the formulaic material and the dull remastering, the listener can get some impression of the sort of show they might have put on. Knox is an unpolished singer and pianist, a sort of country cousin of Little Brother Montgomery, but the quiet melancholy of 'Poor Man Blues' and 'Blue Man Blues' is gripping. In such company Ted Mays's band, a small swing group with a vigorous female singer, Claytie Polk, strikes a more urbane note.

***(*) Blues Masters, Volume 3: Texas Blues
Rhino R2 71123 *Zuzu Bollin, Charles Brown, Clarence 'Gatemouth' Brown, Albert Collins, Johnny Copeland, Pee Wee Crayton, Fabulous Thunderbirds, Anson Funderburgh & The Rockets, Lillian Glinn, Lightnin' Hopkins, Blind Lemon Jefferson, Freddy King, Mance Lipscomb, Percy Mayfield, Frankie Lee Sims, Big Mama Thornton, Stevie Ray Vaughan, T-Bone Walker. 4/27–2/87.*

After a brief preface set in the '20s (Jefferson, Glinn), this settles down to tell the Texas story from the close of World War II to the near-contemporary sounds of the Fabulous Thunderbirds, SRV and Anson Funderburgh – and tell it well, duly acknowledging major events like Walker's 'Call It Stormy Monday' and 'Gatemouth' Brown's 'Okie Dokie Stomp' but also marking less celebrated but stirring performances like Bollin's 'Why Don't You Eat Where You Slept Last Night'. Within the limits of what can be done in little over an hour, this is an admirable collection.

*** Texas Guitar Killers
Capitol 33915 2CD *Clarence 'Gatemouth' Brown (4), Pee Wee Crayton (2), Lowell Fulson (8), Smokey Hogg (13), L. C. Williams (2), T-Bone Walker (10). 12/45–10/53.*

This 2CD is not the random collection it might seem. The four tracks by Lowell Fulson on the first disc, peacefully accompanied by two guitars, are balanced by four on the second disc in small-band settings; over five years Fulson has exchanged overalls for a city suit. T-Bone Walker's tracks similarly freeze the moving picture of his career at two points five years apart. Even Smokey Hogg, for whom the notion of artistic progress held little meaning, sounds a little more suave in 1953 than in 1950, doubtless because someone took his guitar away. The recordings mostly originated on Aladdin or Imperial (L. C. Williams's, incorrectly attributed to Lightnin' Hopkins, are from Freedom), and have been excellently restored.

**** Down Home Blues Classics: Texas 1946–1954
Boulevard Vintage BVBCD 1012 4CD *Texas Alexander, Johnny Beck, Perry Cain, Buddy Chiles, Rattlesnake Cooper, Sonny Boy Davis (2), Leroy Ervin, Clarence Garlow (2), Stick Horse Hammond (4), John Hogg (2), Smokey Hogg (2), Wright Holmes*

(2), Lightnin' Hopkins (25), Soldier Boy Houston (3), Lil Son Jackson (4), Sunny James (2), Leroy 'Country' Johnson, Willie Lane (3), Ernest Lewis (7), David Pete McKinley (2), Miss Country Slim, Manny Nichols (5), Monister Parker, Bill Simpson, Frankie Lee Sims (3), Thunder Smith (4), Luther Stoneham, The Sugarman (2), Andy Thomas (3), Big Son Tillis (3), James Tisdom (2), Mercy Dee Walton (3), D. C. Washington, L. C. Williams (3). 11/46–53/54.

**** **Texas Blues "The Gold Star Sessions"**
Arhoolie CD 352 *Perry Cain (1), Buddy Chiles (1), Leroy Ervin (2), Lee Hunter (1), Lil' Son Jackson (10), Thunder Smith (3), Andy Thomas (1), L. C. Williams (8). 47–51.*

*** **Texas Country Blues 1948–1951**
Flyright FLYCD 941 *Rattlesnake Cooper (3), Sonny Boy Davis (2), Sunny James, Leroy Johnson (2), Sunny Jones, Cleo Harves, Willie Lane (2), Mr Honey, Monister Parker (2), Frankie Lee Sims, Andrew Thomas (2), James Tisdom (5). 48–51.*

**** **Texas Down Home Blues 1948–1952**
Frémeaux FA 5062 2CD *Texas Alexander, Johnny Beck, Charlie Bradix, Buddy Chiles, Rattlesnake Cooper, Big Bill Dotson, Lavada Durst, Leroy Ervin, Lowell Fulson, Guitar Slim Green, John Hogg, Smokey Hogg, Wright Holmes, Lightnin' Hopkins, Lawyer Houston, Lee Hunter, Lil' Son Jackson, Jesse James, Sam 'Suitcase' Johnson, Willie Lane, Ernest Lewis, Alex Moore, Manny Nichols, Frankie Lee Sims, Thunder Smith, Sonny Boy [Holmes], Luther Stoneham, The Sugarman, Nat Terry, Andy Thomas, Jesse Thomas, James Tisdom, Mercy Dee Walton, Peter Warfield, L. C. Williams, Little Son Willis. 48–52.*

Gold Star was the label for which Lightnin' Hopkins recorded some of his finest early material, but in the same period it also issued notable sides by Lil' Son Jackson and L. C. Williams, which are discussed in their entries, and some lesser-known but equally absorbing pieces by the singer/pianists Thunder Smith, Lee Hunter and Leroy Ervin. Stylistically, any of these three artists might have been recorded ten or 15 years earlier. While Hopkins had moved several steps beyond, say, J. T. Smith or Willie Reed, the Texas pianists seemed to mark time. Also on the Arhoolie CD are rare sides by Andy Thomas, Perry Cain, whose buttered singing recalls Charles Brown, and singer/guitarist Buddy Chiles.

The Flyright compilation is from much the same period but consists of rare singles from smaller labels than Gold Star, like Talent, Freedom and the audaciously named but ephemeral Swing With The Stars. All the artists except pianist Sonny Boy Davis are singer/guitarists, and almost all seem unaffected by the contemporary success of Lightnin' Hopkins. Rattlesnake Cooper and Willie Lane play like disciples of J. T. Smith, Monister Parker has a distinct whiff of Jesse Thomas, and Sunny Jones and James Tisdom are what you might call generic old-timers. (Mr Honey, though recorded in Houston, is the Mississippian 'Honeyboy' Edwards.) There are no stellar performances here, but many curious and interesting ones.

Curious and interesting, too, are many of the sides on *Texas Down Home Blues 1948–1952*, a compilation stuffed with super-rarities like Peter Warfield's 'Morning Train Blues', or John Hogg (brother of the more famous Smokey) with his 'West Texas Blues'. But there is much more to this 2CD set than a high risk of giving collectors the vapours. Smokey Hogg's compelling two-part 'Penitentiary Blues' and Mercy Dee Walton's 'One Room Country Shack' are classics of their era, and there are sterling examples of Fulson, Hopkins, Lil' Son Jackson and others. As for the collectables, though they may be rough-hewn, under-rehearsed or even stumbling, serendipitously documented performances like Wright Holmes's serpentine boogie 'Good Road Blues' are arresting in their singularity. Absorbing this collection, the listener is reminded, time after time, of the limitless mutability of the blues.

Admirably, the set not only duplicates very little of the Arhoolie and Flyright CDs (just four tracks) but amplifies them by providing the missing flipside of the Buddy Chiles Gold Star and a further James Tisdom. Boulevard's box, by contrast, helps itself greedily to the material on the other sets, sharing about a dozen tracks with each of them. As a survey it's imbalanced: the presence of several Louisiana-born figures implies that 'Texas' should be understood (as often) to mean 'Southwest', yet there's nothing by Lowell Fulson or Jesse Thomas and a mere two tracks by the prolific Smokey Hogg. Hopkins, on the other hand, has an entire CD. But if value for money is more important to you than the crossing of historical 't's (for Texas), this is clearly a bargain.

(*) **Texas Blues Volume 1: Houston Hotshots
Acrobat ACMCD 4003 *Edgar Blanchard (2), Clarence 'Gatemouth' Brown (2), Silver Cooks (2), Lavada Durst (2), Joe 'Papoose' Fritz (2), Memphis Slim (2), Paul Monday (2), Elmore Nixon (2), R. B. Thibadeaux (2), Bettye Jean Washington (2). 49–51.*

*** **Texas Blues Volume 2: Rock Awhile**
Acrobat ACMCD 4004 *Carl Campbell (2), Goree Carter (5), Joe 'Papoose' Fritz, Joe Houston, Lonnie Lyons (3), Smilin' Smokey Lynn, Memphis Slim, Elmore Nixon, Peppermint Harris, Clarence Samuels, Fatman Smith, Jesse Thomas, L. C. Williams. 49–52.*

*** **Texas Blues Volume 3: Gonna Play The Honky Tonks**
Acrobat ACMCD 4005 *Marie Adams, Walter Brown (2), Carl Campbell, Goree Carter (2), Joe 'Papoose' Fritz (2), Henry Hayes, Willie Johnson, Lonnie Lyons (2), Jimmy McCracklin, Memphis Slim, Elmore Nixon, Sonny Parker, Peppermint Harris, Fatman Smith, Robert Smith, 'Rocky Thompson' [Goree Carter]. 49–52.*

The busy Houston recording scene in the late '40s and early '50s was a reflection of, if not a match for, LA's, and the musics the two centres documented had considerable stylistic kinship, though Houston's was also subject to emanations from New Orleans. The bands on these CDs, typified by altoist Conrad Johnson's group, Conney's Combo, which accompanies Goree Carter, Lonnie Lyons, Jesse Thomas and L. C. Williams, generally have two or three horns, piano, guitar (sometimes dispensed with), bass and drums; the model was no doubt the jump-blues combo as led by Roy Milton or Joe Liggins. (Pianist Lyons's 'Sneaky Joe' on *Volume 2* sneaks its arrangement from Liggins's 'Honeydripper'.) The vocalists are something of a gazetteer of the period's styles: Joe Houston on 'Jumpin' The Blues' apes Roy Brown, while Carl Campbell, Elmore Nixon and R. B. Thibadeaux incline towards the blocked-nose manner, as do Carter in 'Tell Me Is There Still A Chance' (*Volume 2*) and Lyons in 'Betrayed' (*Volume 3*), both outrageous imitations of Charles Brown. Carter is the most prominent personality on these CDs, playing, in a style sometimes similar to T-Bone Walker's but often with a whimsicality all his own, not only on seven tracks in his name and an instrumental 'Bullcorn Blues' as 'Rocky Thompson' but also on sides by Campbell, Houston, Lyons, Nixon, Henry

Hayes and possibly Peppermint Harris. Memphis Slim – present, though a foreigner, in this company because he happened to be in Houston – is in excellent form. *Volume 1* has some lacklustre material, but the others are fairly consistently interesting. The reproduction of the recordings, which were mostly made for Freedom or Peacock, is at times rather thin.

**(*) "T" For Texas: Texas Blues Masters Volume One
Fuel 2000 302 061 219 *Texas Alexander, Zuzu Bollin, Clarence 'Gatemouth' Brown, Goree Carter, Albert Collins, Johnny Copeland, Clarence Garlow, Clarence Green, Smokey Hogg, Lightnin' Hopkins, Ivory Joe Hunter, Freddie King, Little Willie Littlefield, Frankie Lee Sims, Big Mama Thornton, T-Bone Walker, Lester Williams, Johnny Winter. 48–70.*

Many leading Texas artists are heard here, occasionally in late and unrepresentative recordings like Walker's 'T-Bone's Back' but often on early or obscure sides like Hopkins's thunderously amplified 'Late In The Evening' from TNT, Hogg's 'I Used To Be Rich' from Rays or Thornton's 'All Right Baby' (with the Harlem Stars) from E&W. An entertaining collection, well annotated by Bill Dahl, but the rating reflects the erratic transfer quality; the tracks by Collins and Littlefield are on the borders of the listenable.

** Beware Of The Texas Blues Vol. 2
Blue Moon CDBM 085 *James Bolden (2), Lowdown Brown, Mabel Franklin (2), Clarence Green, Henry Hayes (2), Kilroy King (2), Pete Mayes, Joe Medwick, Big Walter [Price], Albert Rideaux, Johnny Winter. 59–92.*

A ragbag of recordings selected by the Houston producer Roy C. Ames, mostly from his own tape archives. Some were by artists who were new on the Houston scene when the CD was assembled, like Lowdown Brown, or more seasoned but still active, like Pete Mayes, Clarence Green and Henry Hayes. Other participants, like Big Walter or Mabel Franklin, had retired. Johnny Winter enthusiasts should note the presence of his first single, 'School Day Blues'. The production and recording quality are generally dreadful. *Beware Of The Texas Blues Vol. 1* (CDBM 064), which had a more impressive castlist (T-Bone Walker, Albert Collins, Johnny Copeland, etc.), is no longer available.

**(*) From Hell To Gone And Back: Texas Blues
Vanguard VCD 79704 *Pee Wee Crayton (4), Lightnin' Hopkins (4), Mance Lipscomb (3), Lee Roy Parnell (3), Big Mama Thornton (4). 64–01.*

The roster – not an obvious selection of Texan blues artists – was determined by what Vanguard owned: the Hopkins and Lipscomb tracks come from Newport Folk Festivals (two of Hopkins's are previously unissued), while those by Crayton and Thornton are from albums discussed in their entries.

*** Texas Blues Guitar
EasyDisc ED CD 7037 *Clarence 'Gatemouth' Brown, W. C. Clark, Johnny Copeland, Anson Funderburgh & The Rockets, Clarence Hollimon, Joe 'Guitar' Hughes, Smokin' Joe Kubek Band, Mike Morgan & The Crawl, Phillip Walker, U. P. Wilson. 81–96.*

An enjoyable ten-track (but cheap) collection of Texas guitarists, mostly from Rounder, Bullseye Blues and Black Top; some tracks from the last label, like Clarence Hollimon's sleek 'Blues For Carol', are not otherwise available.

*** Texas Blues Party – Vol. 2
Wolf 120.631 *Robert Ealey (5), Joe Hughes, Pete Mayes (4), Curly 'Barefoot' Miller, Robin Sylar. 84–86, 94.*

Robert Ealey (1924–2001) was a popular club artist in Fort Worth with a tough, direct style, a little like a Texan Muddy Waters. Since none of his own CDs are in print, it's good that Wolf have leased these five tracks from Topcat. Their rough vigour is in sharp contrast to the smoothness of Pete Mayes, whose exercises in the T-Bone Walker style are taken from deleted Double Trouble albums. *Texas Blues Party – Vol. 1* is by U. P. Wilson (q.v.). TR

Topical & Documentary

** Voodoo Blues: Hoodoo & Magical Practices
Saga Blues 982 991-3 *Barbecue Bob, Jackie Brenston, Doctor Clayton, Big Boy Crudup, Jimmie Gordon, Sloppy Henry, Lightnin' Hopkins, Blind Lemon Jefferson, Lil Johnson, Louis Jordan, Leecan & Cooksey, Charley Lincoln, Ma Rainey, Memphis Minnie, Memphis Jug Band, J. D. Short, J. T. 'Funny Paper' Smith, Johnnie Temple, James Wayne, Curley Weaver, Casey Bill Weldon, Sonny Boy Williamson I. 5/25–54.*

Voodoo (the syncretic religion of Haiti) and hoodoo (African-American magical, folk medical and divinationary practices) are often confused; even Casey Bill Weldon does so, singing about 'going to the voodoo woman', and Saga Blues may be forgiven their compilation's title. The notes give a useful account of the defining characteristics of magical systems: it's easy to understand the appeal of determinism (spell *x* produces effect *y*) and omnipotence (control over money, people etc.) to a powerless people.

Hoodoo is a comprehensive system of beliefs and operations; Harry Middleton Hyatt's research, carried out in the '30s, fills five volumes and nearly 5,000 pages. The geographical dispersion and stylistic variety of the CD's content, from downhome guitarists and jugbands to city jazz and jump combos, is also indicative of hoodoo's pervasiveness in black culture during the years covered, but a potentially valuable survey is vitiated by carelessness: wrong discographical data are given for the Leecan & Cooksey track, and 'goofer dust' has no etymological connection with imbecility ('goofiness'). More seriously, hoodoo-free tracks by the Memphis Jug Band and Sloppy Henry play instead of those listed, and Jackie Brenston's 'Rocket 88' gets its gazillionth reissue where The Sly Fox's fabulous 'Hoodoo Say' should be. Curley Weaver's 'Two-Faced Woman' and James Wayne's 'Two-Faced Man' play as listed, but neither has any relevant content. This project was evidently hoodooed.

**** News & The Blues – Telling It Like It Is
Columbia CK 46217 *Lucille Bogan, Big Bill Broonzy (2), Doctor Clayton, Alfred Fields, Blind Boy Fuller, Bill Gaither, Homer Harris, Mississippi John Hurt, Blind Willie Johnson (2), Jack Kelly, Charley Patton, Ma Rainey, Bessie Smith, Willie 'Long Time' Smith, Victoria Spivey, Sister O. M. Terrell, Casey Bill Weldon, Bukka [Booker] White. 2/27–12/47.*

News & The Blues covers a wide range of subjects, some of them only loosely news, like Blind Willie Johnson's account of Samson and Delilah and Sister Terrell's enthusiastic disapproval of 'The Gambling Man'. The quality of the musicianship matches the interest of the lyrics throughout, and the compilation artfully balances matters of national importance with the everyday concerns of black Americans: the obvious subjects are all there – war, the Depression and New Deal, natural disasters, the sinking of the *Titanic*, the exploits of Joe Louis – but there are also tributes to deceased blues singers, Charley Patton's story of being run off Dockery's Plantation, Booker White's tirade against Parchman Farm and Blind Boy Fuller's tale of having to pawn his guitar. Victoria Spivey dispassionately notes the way drugs disconnect their users from reality, and Dr Clayton, who sounds as if he's been doing serious research into his subject, celebrates moonshine. The sound quality is excellent, and the notes extensive, if occasionally somewhat laborious.

(*) Jake Leg Blues
Jass J-CD-642 *Allen Brothers, Gene Autry, Black Ace, Ishman Bracey, Maynard Britton (2), Tommy Johnson, Willie Lofton, Dave McCarn & Howard Long, Asa Martin, Mississippi Sheiks, Byrd Moore, Narmour & Smith (2), Ray Brothers (2), Lemuel Turner. 2/28–8/60.*

During Prohibition, a popular drink in the South was 'jake', made by mixing extract of Jamaica ginger and various adulterants with alcohol. In February 1930, bootleggers adulterated a batch with a varnish containing triorthocresyl phosphate; the result, for 50,000 drinkers in the South and Midwest, was paralysis. Those affected walked with a distinctive gait, the jake leg or jake walk. John P. Morgan, MD, tells the story in the notes to a CD which presents five jake-related recordings by black blues singers and 12 by white country musicians. Some songs mention jake only incidentally, and four tracks are instrumentals, among them Lemuel Turner's 'Jake Bottle Blues', which predates the epidemic, and whose title probably refers to his slide. The contrast of attitudes is instructive: the black singers are disinclined to moralize, and prepared to mention impotence ('the limber leg') as a symptom. This enlightening CD may yet be peripheral for casual listeners and those not interested in country music.

*** Field Recordings Vols. 10/11: Texas & Arkansas (1933–1941)
Document DOCD-5600 2CD *John Henry Faulk, John Handcock (5), Lester Powell, Laura Smalley (2), Aunt Harriet Smith, Lightnin' Washington. 12/33–11/41.*

Songs by Washington and Powell (included because they had to be somewhere in Document's reissue programme) precede a 33-minute introduction by Faulk to his conversations with former slaves Laura Smalley (who sings a few spirituals in a clear, wavering alto) and Harriet Smith. Anyone who thinks their memories of violence and defiance, patronizing paternalism and secret worship in brush arbours are irrelevant to the blues should listen and learn. Faulk's account of realizing that his black neighbours wore a mask when dealing with whites, and his gradual understanding that equality was not his to offer but theirs to take, is also salutary listening. Stressing the continuity of oppression and struggle, the CD concludes with some courageous Depression-era recruiting songs by the Southern Tenant Farmers' Union activist John Handcock (correctly Handcox); his complete *oeuvre*, including some 1985 interviews and anti-Reagan songs, has subsequently appeared, in significantly better sound, as *John L. Handcox: Songs, Poems And Stories Of The Southern Tenant Farmers' Union* (WVU Press SA 6).

*** Roosevelt's Blues: African-American Blues And Gospel Songs On FDR
Agram Blues ABCD 2017 *Annie Brewer, Doctor Clayton (2), Buster 'Buz' Ezell, Rev. J. M. Gates (2), Jimmie Gordon, Otis Jackson (2), Louis Jordan, Jack Kelly, Leadbelly, James 'Jack Of All Trades' McCain, Memphis Minnie, Lucky Millinder, Mississippi Sheiks (2), Joe Pullum, Walter Roland, Rev. R. H. Taylor, unidentified man, Casey Bill Weldon, Big Joe Williams. 7/33–9/49.*

*** The Truman And Eisenhower Blues
Agram Blues ABCD 2018 *'Little Maxie' Bailey, Memphis Willie B. [Borum], Cousin Joe, Tommy Dean, Dizzy Dixon, Champion Jack Dupree, The Echoes Of Zion, The Golden Gate Quartet, The Gospel Pilgrims, Brother Will Hairston, Smokey Hogg, Homesick James, Bobo Jenkins, Tommie Jenkins, Louis Jordan, Chris Kenner, J. B. Lenoir, Jack McVea, Memphis Slim, The Pilgrim Travelers, Harmon Ray, The Royal Harmonaires [The Dixieaires], Sister Rosetta Tharpe, Andrew Tibbs, Josh White (2). 4/45–60.*

These CDs illustrate Guido van Rijn's books of the same names, respectively published by the University Press of Mississippi and Continuum, which analyse blues and gospel songs about topical and political issues, with particular reference to African-American attitudes to the presidency. FDR was the first president since Lincoln who seemed to black Americans to make a positive difference, and it's fascinating to follow their responses to the New Deal and World War II in song. Where Roosevelt was usually seen as a benevolent *über*-bossman, by the time of Truman and Eisenhower there's a growing readiness to criticize policies, parties and politicians. In purely musical terms, the Roosevelt disc is marginally stronger (it also includes a rampagingly obscene 'Hitler Toast'), but the diversity of styles and issues (the Cold and Korean Wars, hard times, the space race, Civil Rights) makes the second disc just as interesting and enjoyable.

Hard times in general, and the Depression in particular, hit black Americans worst, but the misery was widespread. There's much stirring music and commentary on *Poor Man's Heaven* (Bluebird 50958) and *Hard Times Come Again No More Vol. 1* and *Vol. 2* (Yazoo 2036 and 2037). Most of the music on Yazoo is by white country artists; *Poor Man's Heaven* is equal parts hillbilly, Tin Pan Alley and black music, and expects a more generalized interest in Americana from its listeners. There are intriguing contrasts and commonalities, and the black music is usefully set in wider social, artistic and historical contexts.

**(*) Joe Louis: An American Hero
Rounder 1106 *Cab Calloway, The Dixieaires, Bill Gaither, Rev. J. M. Gates, Billy Hicks, Lil Johnson, Jack Kelly, The Lion & Atilla [sic], Renee Manning, Carl Martin, Memphis Minnie, Sampson Pittman, Joe Pullum, Paul Robeson, Jack Sneed, Sonny Boy Williamson I. 8/35–2/91.*

The Brown Bomber was idolized by African-Americans well before he won the world championship in 1937. These songs (and a dull sermon) in praise of Joe Louis track his career very closely; some of them were recorded almost immediately after the fights they respond to. Will Batts's fiddle accompanying Jack Kelly, the Dixieaires' catchy gospel singing and the sparring guitars on Carl Martin's track are notable, but the lyrics are often banal; Sonny Boy Williamson's 'Joe Louis And John Henry Blues' is one of the few tracks where words and music are of equally high quality. Lion & Atilla's calypso is another, but the combination of Count Basie, Paul Robeson and Richard Wright's arty lyrics is predictably disastrous. Renee Manning's drab 1991 torch song, mining boxing for sexual metaphors, is an anticlimactic closer.

♛ **** Blues In The Mississippi Night
Rounder CD 1860 *Big Bill Broonzy, Bull & group, Bull, Hollie Dew & group, Vera Hall, Jimson [Henry Wallace] & group, Memphis Slim (5), Sonny Boy Williamson I, unidentified leader & congregation.* 3/47–prob. c. 49.

Blues In The Mississippi Night is a conversation with occasional music among Big Bill Broonzy, Memphis Slim and Sonny Boy Williamson. The other singers listed made field recordings for Lomax, which are interpolated for illustrative purposes. Alan Lomax recorded the conversation in New York, but the reference to Mississippi has a double function. It signifies that the three men talk frankly about their experience of Southern racism, so much so that they feared for family members still living in the South if such outspokenness became known. Accordingly, when an LP was issued in 1957, Lomax fictionalized the circumstances of its recording, and gave the speakers pseudonyms. 'Sib' (Williamson), 'Leroy' (Slim) and 'Natchez' (Broonzy) were easily identified by sympathetic listeners, but only after they were all dead did the material appear under their true names. Given the way things were in 1947, we shouldn't underestimate either their courage or Lomax's achievement in winning their trust.

The original LP of *Blues In The Mississippi Night* is included in *American Folk-Blues Train* (Castle CMETD 648 3CD) alongside *Murderers' Home* (see FIELD RECORDINGS) and *American Song Train Vol. 1*, by the white folk revivalist Guy Carawan. The differences among this original version, the Rounder CD and a deleted version on Rykodisc RCD 90155 are of some scholastic interest, but the heart and soul of the disc is the conversation. Even the driest pedant cannot fail to be both appalled by the content and enthralled by the eloquence of these accounts of racist violence, the squalor of the prisons and levee camps and the absurd but potentially fatal taboos of Jim Crow. ('You didn't say "Gimme a can of Prince Albert [tobacco]." Not with that white man on the can. "Gimme a can of *Mister* Prince Albert."') Singing the blues, they agree, is a consolation for 'women troubles and so forth and so on like that', but it's also a way to cuss out the boss without his knowledge, 'signifying and getting your revenge through songs'. Even when racism no longer routinely sustains segregation by violence, these stories are a salutary reminder that the blues is not just a culturally neutral system of musical sounds.

***(*) Can't Keep From Crying: Topical Blues On The Death Of President Kennedy
Testament TCD 5007 *Avery Brady (2), James & Fannie Brewer (3), Jimmy Brown, John Lee Granderson, Bill Jackson, Mary Ross, Otis Spann, Big Joe Williams, Johnny Young (2).* late 63–early 64.

Anyone old enough to remember, as the cliché has it, where they were when President Kennedy was shot in November 1963 will also recall America's and the world's shock and grief in the days that followed. This LP, reissued with two additional tracks, became a project after several singers told Pete Welding they had written commemorative songs. Forty years on, JFK is no longer the *preux chevalier* sold to the world via compliant mass media, and it's evident that until late in his presidency he regarded the Civil Rights movement as a problem to be managed rather than a cause to be espoused. Despite that, most black Americans felt that Kennedy was on their side and trying to take racial issues in the right direction, a conviction crystallized by the traumatic circumstances of his death.

It's unwise, therefore, to apply too much hindsight to the moving and often poetic expressions of grief that Welding collected. Big Joe Williams reworks the song he wrote when FDR died (and he recycled it again when Martin Luther King was assassinated), but like the other singers he's patently sincere. Given the immediacy of their responses, it's often the controlled artistry with which sorrow is transmuted into music that impresses; only Johnny Young's 'Tribute To J.F.K.', added for CD release, is below par, with prosaic lyrics and Walter Horton unable to develop a harmonica part. Otherwise, *Can't Keep From Crying* is an unforgettable encounter with history by blues bands, gospel singers, solo guitarists, pianist Otis Spann and Jimmy Brown's agonized violin.

**** And This Is Maxwell Street
Rooster Blues R-2641 3CD *Carey Bell (5), Fannie Brewer, James Brewer Group (2), Big Mojo Elem, Arvella Gray (2), Little Arthur King, Robert Nighthawk (11), Carrie Robinson, unknown, Big John Wrencher (3), Johnny Young (2).* 8–10/64.

As well as taking the lion's share of tracks under his own name, Robert Nighthawk is among the musicians accompanying Bell, Elem, Wrencher and Young, who all contribute excellent performances. Nighthawk plays slide guitar of the utmost precision, beauty and originality, and sings with detached ferocity; most of his tracks, and some accompaniments, are available separately on *Live On Maxwell Street* (Bullseye Blues CDBB 9624), which is discussed in his entry. *And This Is Maxwell Street* adds more music recorded during the shooting of the documentary *And This Is Free*, and on the third disc an interview by Mike Bloomfield with an unfortunately somewhat guarded Nighthawk. Alongside the blues bands, steel guitarist Arvella Gray, hollering 'Corinna, Corinna' and 'John Henry', is engagingly oldfashioned, and an anonymous harmonica player's story-song 'Lost John' is even more archaic; guitarist Little Arthur King's medley of 'Red Top' and 'Ornithology' isn't. *And This Is Maxwell Street* very successfully portrays the varied, spirited music that could be heard at the famous open-air market until the University of Chicago 'redeveloped' the area. The musicians might have disputed the film's title; the competition for nickels and dimes contributed to their music's raggedy dynamism, although the gospel singers also had souls to save.

*** The Devil's Music: The Soundtrack To The 1976 BBC TV Documentary Series
Indigo IGOTCD 2537 3CD *The Aces (2), Billy Boy Arnold (2), Sonny Blake (2), Joe Carter, Sam Chatmon (3), James De Shay (6), Laura Dukes, Good Rockin' Charles [Edwards] (2), Memphis Slim (4), Little Brother Montgomery (2), Matt Murphy, Fenton Robinson (2), Sonny Boy Williamson II (5), Victoria Spivey, Houston Stackhouse (2), Henry Townsend (2), Mose Vinson (2), Bukka [Booker] White, Joe Willie Wilkins, Big Joe Williams (5), Edith Wilson.* 10/63–1/76.

Only two thirds of this set is as advertised; the final disc reissues an LP of Sonny Boy and Memphis Slim in concert on the 1963 AFBF tour. The sound is boxy, there's a hum from faulty electronics and Slim is blasé, but Matt Murphy's guitar, heard behind both of them as well as on his own track, is as marvellous as usual, and Sonny Boy sounds as if he was in an exceptionally evil mood, which was always beneficial to his music.

The Devil's Music was a history of the blues, so it's no surprise that most of the artists play their own or other people's greatest hits. It would have been kinder to exclude Victoria Spivey, filmed not long before her death. Little Brother makes some uncharacteristic slips, and Robinson and the Aces only do enough to prove that they're professionals. However, the tracks by Big Joe Williams, Sam Chatmon and various combinations of Blake, Vinson, Wilkins and drummer L. T. Lewis are not the only ones to possess a winning, rough-hewn vigour. The star of the show, despite his lack of renown, is James De Shay. Recorded in his St Louis club, the Santa Fe Lounge, he reaches back to Charley Patton for 'Pony Blues', and only comes forward as far as Howlin' Wolf's 'Evil'. De Shay's tracks are atmospherically redolent of smoke, barbecue, booze and good times. cs

**** Blues With A Message
Arhoolie CD 510 *Juke Boy Bonner (2), Sam Chatman [Chatmon], Brother Willie Eason, Lowell Fulson, Lightnin' Hopkins, Bee Houston, John Jackson, Essie Jenkins, Herman E. Johnson, Johnie Lewis, Mance Lipscomb, Fred McDowell, Dr Ross, Mercy Dee [Walton], Big Joe Williams, Robert Pete Williams, Johnny Young & Big Walter Horton.* 48–7/96.

'The blues, contrary to popular conception, are not always concerned with love, razors, dice, and death.' Thus Richard Wright, almost 50 years ago. The stereotypes have changed somewhat, but some fans still view the blues as if they were wearing blinkers, expecting little more than erotic soliloquy and get-down boogie, and, not too surprisingly, some artists are content to provide them. Wrapped in this cosy conspiracy, it's possible to forget the stark facts that scar the history of the original bluesmakers and their communities: a feudal agricultural system, pitiless penitentiaries, deprivation, marginalization and segregation. Not all blues singers have chosen to bring such subject-matter into their music, and some have done so only circumspectly, but a few have ventured, in favourable circumstances, to record candid material that might have got them into trouble, such as the songs by Lightnin' Hopkins and Mance Lipscomb about the farm boss Tom Moore, or the mordant reportage of Mercy Dee Walton's 'Walked Down So Many Turn Rows'. Not many of the songs in this powerful and affecting collection are that direct, but there are layers of the unspoken, perhaps even the unspeakable, beneath Essie Jenkins's sober account of the 1919 influenza epidemic, or the quiet resignation of Robert Pete Williams's 'Prisoner's Talking Blues' and Juke Boy Bonner's 'That's Enough'. TR

Tributes & Songbooks
(alphabetically by subject)

** Hey Bo Diddley – A Tribute!
Evidence ECD 26124 *Michael Burks, Tommy Castro, Roy Gaines, Guitar Shorty, Corey Harris, Coco Montoya, Charlie Musselwhite, Otis Rush, Eric Sardinas, Son Seals, Sugar Blue, Taj Mahal, Walter Trout, Joe Louis Walker, Kris Wiley.* 01.

Bo Diddley's songs are essentially chants over rhythm tracks, and almost all their charm resides in Bo's execution of them, whoops, growls, effects and all. The hooks are great, and you can easily see what fun it must be for a musician to stomp off and go on 'Mona' or 'Who Do You Love?', but it's an indulgence that should be reserved for gigs and then oblivion; the last thing the world needs is literal-minded rerecordings. Evidence, evidently, think otherwise, and have provided us with 15 of them, all well played, nearly all (Corey Harris makes an effort) thumpingly unoriginal: a backhanded tribute to one of music's true archetypes. TR

**(*) Kent Cooper – The Blues & Other Songs
Labor LAB 7036 *Marc Galbo, George Higgs (2), Jemima James (2), Kristi Johnson, Louisiana Red (6), Deneen McEachern, Willie Murphy, Sonny Terry (2), Lightnin' Wells.* 4/74–12/01.

**(*) Kent Cooper – The Blues & Other Songs Vol. 2
Labor LAB 7044 *Marc Galbo, George Higgs (2), Jemima James (2), Jemima James & George Higgs, Jemima James & Deneen McEachern, Louisiana Red (4), Deneen McEachern (3), Sonny Terry, Lightnin' Wells.* 4/74–3/03.

Stressing failed relationships, poverty, lost opportunities, violence and death, Kent Cooper's lyrics are not a barrel of laughs. In the notes to the first of these CDs, he links his preoccupations to a painful upbringing and a hardscrabble adulthood. Cooper's response to and use of the blues is artistically valid, but the John Lee Hooker LP that was a key moment in his engagement with the music obviously didn't include 'Boogie Chillen' or 'I'm In The Mood'. Unsurprisingly, his songs respond well to the overwrought, self-dramatizing approach of Louisiana Red, the artist most heavily represented here, but George Higgs's grave, measured delivery, tactfully defusing the histrionics, also suits them. Michael Rura's academic piano hinders enjoyment of Sonny Terry's tracks. Marc Galbo does respectable work, and Deneen McEachern's enormous voice is startling, if rather inflexible, but Canadian Kristi Johnson's faux-Southern accent is irritating, and Willie Murphy's interpretation of 'Sweetblood Call' is self-consciously self-important. Cooper describes the violently worded 'Sweetblood Call' as a lovesong, which is either ingenuous or disingenuous. The 'other songs', sung by Jemima James and Lightnin' Wells, are in country & western vein. Wells is listenable, and his archaic banjo on 'If She's Gone Bad' (*Vol. 2*) is charming; but James's nasal drone is the sound that people who don't like country music think epitomizes the genre. cs

***(*) Gary Davis Style
Inside Sounds ISC-0508 *Ellen Britton, Ian Buchanin with the Otis Brothers, John Cephas & Phil Wiggins, Pat Conte, Ari Eisinger, William Lee Ellis, Mary Flower, Blind Boy Fuller, Mitch Greenhill & Mayne Smith, Ernie Hawkins, Penny Lang & Friends, Perry Lederman, Maria Muldaur, Eric Noden, Peter, Paul & Mary, Jerry Ricks, Rick Ruskin, Dave Van Ronk & Friends, Willie Walker, Ken Whiteley & Friends.* 12/30–c. 00.

Walker and Fuller were Davis's contemporaries, but most of the CD is played by his students and 'grandstudents'. Not every track is a display of guitar (and once banjo) virtuosity: Lang's 'God Knows How Much We Can Bear' is a gentle rendition of a song she learned from Davis, Van Ronk's 'Soon My Work Will All Be Done' revives hootenanny singalong, and the only thing to be said for Peter, Paul & Mary's twee 'Samson & Delilah' is that the royalties paid for Reverend Davis's house. The rest of the CD is enjoyable listening, although there are some dubious vocals, and only Greenhill & Smith (the latter playing country Dobro on a second version of 'Samson & Delilah') and the astonishing Perry Lederman do much to take Davis's music in new directions. Most of the musicians are content to replicate his arrangements to the best of their considerable abilities. CS

**(*) The Songs Of Willie Dixon
Telarc CD-83452 *Tab Benoit, Clarence 'Gatemouth' Brown, Deborah Coleman, Ronnie Earl, John Ellison, Luther 'Guitar Junior' Johnson, Eddie Kirkland, Sonny Landreth, David Maxwell, John Mooney, Kenny Neal, Christine Ohlman, Jerry Portnoy, Eddie Shaw, Willie Smith, Doug Wainoris (2). 7–8/98.*

This is a good choice from Dixon's vast *oeuvre*, tracks like 'Wang Dang Doodle', 'I Ain't Superstitious' and 'Spoonful' attesting to his highly profitable exploitation of African-American folklore. Kenny Neal's rumbling vocal on 'Bring It On Home' has an authentic ring of the big man, and Ronnie Earl's guitar is aptly yearning on 'My Love Will Never Die', but some of the renditions are so far under the influence of canonical recordings by Howlin' Wolf or Muddy Waters that they're practically sedated. TR

*(*) Songs Of Bob Dylan – All Blues'd Up!
Compendia 9619 *The Band, R. L. Burnside, John Hammond, Alvin 'Youngblood' Hart, Isaac Hayes, Holmes Brothers, Luther 'Guitar Jr' Johnson, Larry McCray, Leon Russell, James Solberg, Mavis Staples, Taj Mahal.* 02?

** Blues On Blonde On Blonde
Telarc CD-83567 *Eric Bibb, Clarence Bucaro, C. J. Chenier, Deborah Coleman, Sean Costello, Sue Foley, Cyril Neville, Anders Osborne, Duke Robillard, Brian Stoltz, Walter Trout, Joe Louis Walker. 7/02.*

So much of Bob Dylan's music is nourished and quickened by the blues that the would-be interpreter has an enormous range of options – and, to go with them, a trail of pitfalls with signposts such as 'Too Obvious', 'Wilfully Eccentric' and 'Plain Silly'. Most of the participants in these collections slip effortlessly into the first, though some seem to be trying to occupy two at once. TR

*** Blue Haze: Songs Of Jimi Hendrix
Ruf 1053 *Bernard Allison, Eric Bibb, Eric Burdon (2), Friend 'N' Fellow, Eric Gales & Trudy Lynn, Alvin Youngblood Hart, Aynsley Lister, Buddy Miles & Double Trouble, Ana Popovic, Vernon Reid & Michael Hill, Michelle Shocked, Taj Mahal & The Hula Blues Band, Walter Trout & The Free Radicals (2), Walter Trout, Popa Chubby & Jimmy Thackery. 12/99–8/00.*

Compilations of this nature tend to peak when an artist interprets the song using his own zest and individual style, as in the superb piano–vocal rendition of 'Angel' by Eric Bibb. Friend 'N' Fellow transform 'Purple Haze' with acoustic guitar and Constanze Friend's downbeat vocals, and it's given a roll by programmed beats and samples that bring the original up to date. Taj Mahal adds his inimitable croaky pouts to 'All Along The Watchtower', with an interesting arrangement of saxophone, ukuleles and Hawaiian guitar, and Alvin Youngblood Hart puts a honey glaze on 'Remember'. Elsewhere you might ask whether standardizing Hendrix isn't missing the point. Formulaic blues-rock covers by Trout and, worse, Eric Burdon trudge on with numbingly dull singing, and even when Buddy Miles's soul-soaked voice accompanies Double Trouble, the end product flattens out the drama in dynamics with which Hendrix made 'The Wind Cries Mary'. Some of the more faithful handlings are persuasive: Bernard Allison's emotive 'Hear My Train Coming', played on 12-string, a sort of medley of extracts from early Mississippian masters, and Aynley Lister's dutiful chops in 'Little Wing' are respectable. Michael Hill does the standardizing more stylishly, adding his wheezing slide guitar fills to Vernon Reid's soloing in 'Red House', and so does Eric Gales with his scintillating wah-wah lead guitar alongside Trudy Lynn's standout vocal in 'Voodoo Chile'. RR

** From Clarksdale To Heaven – Remembering John Lee Hooker
Eagle EAGCD 228 *Jeff Beck (2), Booker T & Randy California, Gary Brooker & Andy Fairweather-Low (2), Jack Bruce & Gary Moore (2), Peter Green Splinter Group, Greggs Eggs, John Lee Hooker, Zakiya Hooker, LLC, T. S. McPhee & Dick Heckstall-Smith (2), Mick Taylor & Max Middleton. 3/89, 10/01–6/02.*

Many of these renditions are calculatedly distanced from Hooker's recordings, most strikingly McPhee and Heckstall-Smith's duet on 'Ground Hog Blues', where acoustic guitar and tenor saxophone create a back-country ambience reminiscent of the Ornette Coleman of 'Ramblin''. Jeff Beck's 'Hobo Blues' also breaks fresh ground, but most of the other tracks are disadvantaged by mundane vocals. The bonus track is a previously unissued recording of Hooker singing 'Red House' in 1989. TR

*** A Tribute To Howlin' Wolf
Telarc CD-83427 *James Cotton, Debbie Davies, Henry Gray, Ronnie Hawkins, Colin James, Cub Koda, Sam Lay, Colin Linden, Kenny Neal, Christine Ohlman, Eddie Shaw, Hubert Sumlin, Taj Mahal, Lucinda Williams. 7/97.*

The presence of grizzled members of the Wolf pack like Shaw and Sumlin ensures a spirit of reminiscence both fond and unreserved, as they lead younger admirers (Davies, Peterson) and senior blues citizens (Cotton, Hawkins) alike over the rough paths where the Wolf once dragged his tail. The set includes sturdy versions of 'The Red Rooster', 'Built For Comfort', 'Riding In The Moonlight' and, of course, 'Smokestack Lightnin'', fronted by Gray, but to end it with – perhaps even to include – Lucinda Williams's drowsy 'Come To Me Baby' was a peculiar error of judgement. TR

**(*) Avalon Blues; A Tribute To The Music Of Mississippi John Hurt
Vanguard VCD 79582 *Beck, Pete Case & Dave Alvin, Bruce Cockburn, Steve & Justin Earle, Ben Harper, Alvin Youngblood Hart, John Hiatt, Geoff Muldaur, Bill Morrissey, Mark Selby, Chris Smither, Taj Mahal, Gillian Welch, Lucinda Williams, Victoria Williams.* 01.

Hurt's gentle, jogalong songs have an obvious attraction for the guitar-picking folksinger. Here they elicit amiable performances in a more or less Hurtian mould from Chris Smither and Bruce Cockburn, and perhaps a little less predictably, from Beck, Steve Earle and John Hiatt. There's more individuality to Alvin Youngblood Hart's 'Here Am I, Oh Lord,

Send Me' and Taj Mahal's Hawaiian-styled 'My Creole Belle'. Probably because there's so little macho in his manner, women singers are often drawn to Hurt's songs; the dismal cadences of Lucinda Williams make an apt setting for 'Angels Laid Him Away' (i.e. 'Louis Collins') and Gillian Welch gives a characteristically sober reading to 'Beulah Land'. These go some way towards blotting out the posturing of Victoria Williams, the Violet Elizabeth Bott of folk music. TR

*** The Blues Of Robert Johnson
EasyDisc ED CD 7029 *Rory Block (3), Bob Brozman, John Hammond (3), Kristina Olsen, Paul Rishell, Johnny Shines (3).* 71–97.

*** Hellhound On My Trail: The Songs Of Robert Johnson
Telarc CD-83521 *Clarence 'Gatemouth' Brown, Keith Brown, Honeyboy Edwards, Eric Gales, Alvin Youngblood Hart, Chris Thomas King (2), Robert Jr Lockwood, Bob Margolin, Robert Palmer, Pinetop Perkins, Lucky Peterson, Taj Mahal, Susan Tedeschi, Joe Louis Walker, Carl Weathersby.* 2/99–4/00.

There are two main roads out of Johnsonville. The EasyDisc party take the straighter one, remaking Johnson's songs on his principles as much as their own: they all perform solo, accompanying themselves on acoustic guitar. Shines has the authority of having known Johnson as more than a voice on a record, but apart from Brozman's boorish singing on 'Stones In My Passway' all the contributions, most of them derived from Rounder albums, are creditable. Some of the *Hellhound On My Trail* team, however, choose the more winding route of reinterpretation. Eric Gales delivers 'Me And The Devil Blues' in a doleful drone; Margolin and Perkins make a historical point in translating 'Kindhearted Woman Blues' and 'Sweet Home Chicago' into the slide guitar and piano setting of Muddy Waters and Sunnyland Slim; Robert Palmer intensifies the purposeful rhythm of 'Milkcow's Calf Blues' with tuba, drums and multiple guitars. Most of the other participants play it straight, though not always preserving Johnson's format. Taj Mahal takes bass and drums to the crossroads (and a dull journey it is, too), while James Cotton and Carey Bell add occasional harp parts, one of Cotton's being to Alvin Youngblood Hart's haunted singing of the title track. As with the Dylan albums discussed above, the project was threatened by potholes, but this time there were no accidents. TR

**(*) Preachin' The Blues: The Music Of Mississippi Fred McDowell
Telarc CD-83536 *Tab Benoit, Sue Foley, Paul Geremia, Scott Holt, Steve James, David Maxwell, Charlie Musselwhite, Kenny Neal, Anders Osborne, Johnny Sansone, Colleen Sexton, Brian Stoltz.* 01.

Fred McDowell touched many people, both as a musician and as a man, and you wonder how easy it was to keep the cast for this project down to a dozen. On the whole, it's the more senior members who evoke McDowell's music most vividly: Geremia with a beautifully controlled 'Get Right Church', Musselwhite with '61 Highway', James. Maxwell's solo piano rendering of 'I Heard Somebody Call' was an imaginative choice. Osborne and Stoltz, having no access to the warmth at the heart of McDowell's music, settle for replicating the noise it makes. There's at least a point to that, but none at all to Sansone's 'That's Alright', a song that was McDowell's only in the arrangement he gave it, which Sansone discards in favour of a conventional electric blues-band setting. TR

*** Down The Dirt Road: The Songs Of Charley Patton
Telarc CD-83535 *Kid Bangham, Guy Davis, Corey Harris, Steve James(2), Charlie Musselwhite, Graham Parker, Snooky Pryor, Paul Rishell & Annie Raines, Colleen Sexton, Dave Van Ronk, Joe Louis Walker.* 01.

Perhaps because it has great variety of form, the music of Charley Patton prompts widely divergent treatments. Unlike some discussed here, this tribute album is not dulled by obsequious imitations; on the contrary, some are startlingly left-field. Guy Davis and his collaborators turn 'Some Of These Days' into a square-dance tune played by a cowboy band, Steve James growls 'Shake It And Break It' as if from a minstrel stage, with Mark Rubin parping on tuba, and Kid Bangham plays 'Some Summer Day' as an electric guitar hymn. Paul Rishell sings 'I Shall Not Be Moved' with moving simplicity; listeners who enjoy this approach should also hear his version of 'Some Of These Days' (see his entry). Colleen Sexton's treatment of 'Down The Dirt Road Blues'/'When Your Way Gets Dark', perhaps intended to reshape the songs in the manner of Cassandra Wilson, and Graham Parker's reduction of 'Poor Me' to snarl-and-strum are the only failures in an inventive sequence of interpretations. TR

*** Hound Dog Taylor: A Tribute
Alligator ALCD 4855 *Luther Allison, Elvin Bishop, Ronnie Earl, Gov't Mule, Michael Hill's Blues Mob, Dave Hole, Cub Koda & The Houserockers, Sonny Landreth, Magic Slim, Steady Rollin' Bob Margolin, Vernon Reid & Alvin Youngblood Hart, Son Seals, George Thorogood, Lil' Ed [Williams] & The Blues Imperials.* 97.

Hound Dog Taylor didn't do subtle. You listen to his music not for nuance but for a gusty life-force that sweeps into you and leaves you warm and happy. Alligator's first release, in 1971, was Taylor's debut album, so they were the ideal company to circulate his friends and admirers and invite them to celebrate his work, which they did with respect, affection and above all enthusiasm. Outstanding features include Allison's 'Give Me Back My Wig', Earl's intense 'Wayward Angel' and the blue-steel slide of Hole, Landreth and Thorogood. More than a dutiful tip of the (hard) hat, this is an album of industrial-strength Chicago blues by experienced steel-workers. TR

**(*) Master & Disciples
Blue Moon CDBM 092 *T. D. Bell, Clarence 'Gatemouth' Brown, Goree Carter, Johnny Copeland, Freddie King, Texas Pete Mayes (2), Pat O'Bryan (2), Red, Hot & Blue, T-Bone Walker (2), T-Bone Walker Jr [R. S. Rankin] (2).* 51–90s.

*** Blues T-Bone Style
EasyDisc ED CD 7019 *Clarence 'Gatemouth' Brown, Johnny Copeland, Ronnie Earl, Buddy Guy, Joe Houston, Duke Robillard, Roomful Of Blues, Alex Schultz, Phillip Walker, Phillip Walker & Otis Grand.* 81–95.

T-Bone Walker, the 'master' of Blue Moon's title, is not at his best, but then this CD comes from the shelves of Roy Ames, so production values are not at a premium. Discount nearly eight badly recorded minutes of a Freddie King gig, a distorted R. S. Rankin item and a poor dub of a Goree Carter disc, and that's nearly a quarter of the album gone already. Texas Pete Mayes takes good care of 'T-Bone Shuffle' and 'Cold

Cold Feeling'; it's Walker-by-numbers, but he does follow the directions conscientiously. T. D. Bell is also very listenable in 'Bobby Sox Blues', and the two cuts by singer/guitarist Pat O'Bryan suggest that blues tourists heading for Texas might do well to remember his name. *Blues T-Bone Style*, gathered from Rounder, Black Top and JSP albums, presents a variety of approaches to Walker-style guitar playing, from the mellowness of Robillard's 'Duke's Mood' to the biting attack of Johnny Copeland and Phillip Walker. This set aces the Blue Moon in every respect. TR

West Coast

Other VACs relevant to blues on the West Coast are discussed in LABEL HISTORIES & SHOWCASES.

** California Blues
Acrobat ACRCD 156 *Charles Brown (2), Lowell Fulson, Cecil Gant (3), Wynonie Harris (4), Duke Henderson, Helen Humes, Jack McVea, Amos Milburn (3), Roy Milton, Bob Mosley, T-Bone Walker (4), Dinah Washington (2).* 40–46.

***(*) California Blues 1940–1948
Frémeaux FA 175 2CD *Black Diamond [James Butler], Hadda Brooks, Charles Brown (2), Clarence 'Gatemouth' Brown, Nat 'King' Cole, Pee Wee Crayton, Floyd Dixon, Lowell Fulson, Cecil Gant, Lloyd Glenn, Guitar Slim Green, Smokey Hogg, Ivory Joe Hunter, Sonny Boy Johnson, Saunders King, Jimmy Liggins, Little Willie Littlefield, Joe Lutcher, Jimmy McCracklin (2), Sidney Maiden, Percy Mayfield, Amos Milburn (2), Roy Milton, Gene Phillips, Jesse Price, Joe Pullum, Thunder Smith, Jesse Thomas, Big Joe Turner, T-Bone Walker (2), Mercy Dee Walton, Jimmy Witherspoon.* 40–48.

** West Coast Down Home Blues
Acrobat ACRCD 133 *Black Diamond [James Butler](2), Goldrush, R. Green & Turner (2), Slim Green (2), John Hogg, Smokey Hogg, Sonny Boy Johnson (3), Ernest McClay (2), Jimmy McCracklin (2), Beverley Scott (2), Big Son Tillis, James Tisdom (2), Mercy Dee Walton (2), Mac Willis (2).* 45–53.

Throughout the '40s the black entertainment districts of LA and the Bay Area pulsated with music: big-band jazz, jump blues, piano trios in the quiet niteries, ex-Texan singer/guitarists in the neighbourhood bars. Wartime industry meant that there was plenty of work, and even before the conflict was over entrepreneurs were getting discs pressed and put on jukeboxes, thereby grabbing a share of the record business from the clique of long-established labels who had virtually monopolized it in the '30s.

Any properly conceived compilation of California's black music in those mercurial times should give the listener a sense of the try-anything enterprise that animated independent labels like Exclusive, Aladdin, Down Beat, Specialty and their dozens of rivals. Frémeaux's 2CD set succeeds because it has room to stretch and embrace both the back-home harmonica-and-guitar music of Slim Green, Sidney Maiden and Sonny Boy Johnson and the sounds of change: the crooning pianists like Charles Brown, the 'little big bands' of Roy Milton and Jimmy Liggins, the urbane self-confidence of a T-Bone Walker. It's also adequately remastered, whereas the Acrobats, admirable selections on paper, have been so viciously filtered that the music sounds as if it's coming through the wall from next door.

*** West Coast Jive
Delmark DD-657 *Wynonie Harris (3), Frank Haywood (2), Duke Henderson (4), Cee Pee Johnson (6), Al 'Stomp' Russell Trio (3).* 8/45–2/46 or 3/46.

Despite its opaque title – *West Coast Jump* would have been more informative – this is a rewarding collection of R&B novelties like Cee Pee Johnson's 'The "G" Man Caught The "T" Man' and 'Miss Jiveola Brown', which bookend the programme, and polished jump blues. Wynonie Harris's three numbers are also on his *Everybody Boogie* (Delmark DE-683), but many of the remaining tracks were previously unissued. The source label is Apollo, and the sound quality admirable.

**(*) Swing Time Shouters
Night Train NTI CD 7010 *Clifford Blivens, Earl Brown (2), Mickey Cooper (2), Felix Gross (4), Earl Jackson, Jimmy McCracklin (2), Sylvestor Mike (3), Joe Swift, Big Joe Turner, Jimmy Witherspoon.* 47–49.

**(*) Swing Time Shouters Volume 2
Night Train NTI CD 7014 *Clifford Blivens (2), Earl Brown, Mickey Cooper, Felix Gross (6), Earl Jackson, Jimmy McCracklin (2), Percy Mayfield, Sylvestor Mike (2), Jimmy Witherspoon (2).* 47–49.

About halfway through *Swing Time Shouters*, and a little farther into *Volume 2*, there are a couple of tracks by Jimmy McCracklin. By his standards they are nothing special, but the arrival of an original artist after a parade of derivative ones briefly transforms both albums. Turner, 'Spoon and Mayfield are OK, of course, and Clifford Blivens's tracks are blessed with an interestingly jazzy guitarist, evidently Louis Speiginer, but Gross, Cooper, Mike and the others never rise above remorseless ordinariness. It would take a very dedicated collector of jump blues to find these albums exciting. Both are drawn from the Down Beat and Swing Time labels, and several tracks on each are previously unissued alternate takes. The sound quality is quite variable. TR

Women

Despatching blues singers who happen to be female to the isolation ward of a category called WOMEN is obviously unsatisfactory, but that's how recordings by women blues singers are often presented, in compilations by artists who may have nothing in common but their gender, and we have reluctantly gone along with it.

♛ **** I Can't Be Satisfied: Early American Women Blues Singers – Vol. 1 – Country
Yazoo 2026 *Jennie Clayton, Mattie Delaney, Pearl Dickson, Ruby Glaze, Mae Glover (2), Hattie Hart, Bertha Henderson, Hattie Hudson, Elizabeth Johnson, Lottie Kimbrough (2), Bertha Lee (2), Memphis Minnie, Lillian Miller, Rosie Mae Moore, Irene Scruggs (2), Bessie Tucker, Lizzie Washington, Geeshie Wiley (2).* 27–34.

**** I Can't Be Satisfied: Early American Women Blues Singers – Vol. 2 – Town
Yazoo 2027 *Katherine Baker, Lucille Bogan, Alberta Brown, Hattie Burleson (2), Martha Copeland, Madlyn Davis, Bertha 'Chippie' Hill (2), Edith Johnson, Margaret Johnson, Sara Martin (3), Ma Rainey (2), Clara Smith, Ivy Smith, Victoria Spivey (2), Sippie Wallace (3).* 23–29.

Blinded by the aurora of Blind Lemon Jefferson and his fellow bluesmen, it is easy to lose sight of the fact that for much of the '20s blues was almost exclusively women's business, whether on the vaudeville stage or amidst the smoking lights of of the tent show. This is the world of *Vol. 2 – Town*, where Ma Rainey, Sippie Wallace, Victoria Spivey and Chippie Hill, among others, declaim against a backcloth of sumptuous jazz. On *Vol. 1 – Country*, even that artifice is stripped away, revealing the singer stark as a lonesome pine, woman and guitar: Ruby Glaze with Blind Willie McTell, Bertha Lee with Charley Patton, Memphis Minnie with her own sweet self. Brave, bitter, amused, disgusted, these are among the most magnificent of blues recordings. They are also remastered to the very highest standards, and it should be particularly noted that the transfers of Lottie Kimbrough's masterpieces, the Gennett versions of 'Going Away Blues' and 'Rolling Log Blues', are superior to any others.

***(*) Women In Blues: New York–Chicago–Memphis–Dallas 1920–1943
Frémeaux FA 018 2CD *Mildred Bailey, Lucille Bogan, Wea Bea Booze, Martha Copeland, Ida Cox, Mattie Delaney, Pearl Dickson, Lillian Glinn, Lil Green, Lucille Hegamin, Rosa Henderson, Bertha 'Chippie' Hill, Billie Holiday, Rosetta Howard, Helen Humes, Alberta Hunter, Lil Johnson, Merline Johnson, Lottie Beaman [Kimbrough], Ida May Mack, Sara Martin, Tiny Mayberry, Hattie McDaniel, Memphis Minnie, Lizzie Miles, Alice Moore, Ma Rainey, Clara Smith, Mamie Smith, Victoria Spivey, Rosetta Tharpe, Dinah Washington, Ethel Waters, Georgia White, Edith Wilson. 20–43.*

(***) Tight Women And Loose Bands
Timeless CBC 1–068 *Bessie Brown (4), Mary Dixon (2), Maggie Jones (2), Julia Moody (4), Bessie Smith, Clara Smith (2), Mamie Smith (2), Sophie Tucker, Ethel Waters (2), Essie Whitman (4), Edith Wilson (2). 10/21–2/31.*

**(*) The Best Of Country Blues Women Vol. 1 (1923–1930)
Wolf WSE 117 *Lucille Bogan (5), Lottie Kimbrough (5), Luella Miller (5), Victoria Spivey (5), Sippie Wallace (5). 10/23–3/30.*

*** Ladies Sing The Blues
Living Era CD AJA 5092 *Mildred Bailey, Ada Brown (2), Una Mae Carlisle, Ida Cox (2), Lillian Glinn, Adelaide Hall, Billie Holiday (2), Rosetta Howard (2), Lizzie Miles (2), Ma Rainey (2), Bessie Smith (2), Clara Smith, Laura Smith, Mamie Smith, Trixie Smith, Victoria Spivey, Sippie Wallace. 9/23–10/39.*

*** Gin House Blues
Flapper PAST CD 9788 *Rosetta Crawford (2), Babe Hines (2), Rosetta Howard (2), Margaret Johnson (2), Lether McGraw (2), Bessie Smith (5), Mamie Smith (3), Trixie Smith, Edna Winston (2). 3/26–3/39.*

Ladies Sing The Blues and *Gin House Blues* represent a jazz collector's view of women's blues, focusing on stage singers with pianists or bands and ignoring both the guitar-playing blueswomen like Memphis Minnie and the hokum specialists like Lil and Merline Johnson. That still leaves them with plenty of stylistic room to move, and both collections are well stocked with first-rate performances: Ida Cox and Lillian Glinn on *Ladies*, Margaret Johnson on *Gin*, Bessie and Trixie Smith and Rosetta Howard on both. Remastering is good throughout, but the wider reach of *Ladies* gives it the edge. *Tight Women & Loose Bands*, however, seems to have been compiled for the sake of jazz fans who like the sounds of black women's voices but are easily bored by the blues. So you get Bessie Smith, but singing 'Cake Walking Babies From Home'; Mary Dixon, but 'I Can't Give You Anything But Love'; Clara Smith, but 'When My Sugar Walks Down The Street'. And so on. Such a compilation makes perfectly good sense both historically and musically, and the production (by Mark Berresford and John R. T. Davies) is scrupulous, but it can be recommended only to readers who have a taste for the vaudeville repertoire.

Women In Blues offers an altogether wider view of the terrain, and not just because it has more space available. Compiler Jean Buzelin has selected evenhandedly and knowledgably from the sound library of African-American women's music, building a programme of first-rate artists and often summoning their strongest material. Only a few important figures are overlooked, most obviously Bessie Smith, but Frémeaux probably reasoned that they had done her justice with a 2CD of her own. A place might also have been found for Sippie Wallace, who does get her share of attention on the Wolf CD, even if it's under the peculiar description of 'country blues woman'. It isn't the only odd thing about this album: while the songs of Lucille Bogan, Luella Miller and Victoria Spivey have been sensibly chosen, Lottie Kimbrough's are all early sides, no harbingers of the majesty she would later display. The transfers are accurate but noisy.

Another balanced selection was achieved on *Fattenin' Frogs For Snakes: The Essential Recordings Of The Blues Ladies* (Indigo IGOCD 2042), which drew its contents from both the Smith–Rainey axis and the hokum chanteuses. This is deleted, like its label-mate *Little Rock Blues: The Essential Recordings Of Country Girls* (Indigo IGOCD 2124), which concentrated on guitar-accompanied blues by Nellie Florence, Mae Glover, Lottie Kimbrough and so forth, but either CD, if spotted used or remaindered, is worth nabbing.

***(*) Men Are Like Street Cars ... Women Blues Singers 1928–1969
MCA MCAD2–11788 2CD *Alberta Adams, Marie Adams (2), Blue Lu Barker, Margie Day, Mattie Delaney, Donna Hightower, Bertha 'Chippie' Hill, Gladys Hill, Billie Holiday (2), Rosetta Howard (2), Helen Humes, Alberta Hunter (2), Betty James, Etta James (2), Ella Johnson, Gwen Johnson, Mildred Jones, Nora Lee King, Lovey Lewis, Memphis Minnie (2), Lillian Offitt, Rosetta Perry, Esther Phillips, Jenny Pope, Mabel Scott, Trixie Smith, Victoria Spivey, Rosetta Tharpe (2), Koko Taylor (2), Irma Thomas, Big Mama Thornton (2), Ike & Tina Turner, Dinah Washington, Katie Webster, Georgia White (2), Lavelle White. 28–69.*

With its wider timespan than *Women Of The Blues* (above) and its 46 tracks astutely chosen from Decca, Chess, Duke/Peacock and other Universal-owned labels, this is probably the best long-range survey you can buy of blues sung by women. Some titles selected themselves – Memphis Minnie's 'Bumble Bee' and 'Me And My Chauffeur Blues', Rosetta Howard's 'If You're A Viper', Rosetta Tharpe's 'Rock Me' (a surprisingly dull transfer), Big Mama Thornton's 'Hound Dog', Koko Taylor's 'Wang Dang Doodle' – but scattered through the collection are alluring one-offs like Margie Day's 'Take Out Your False Teeth Daddy' or Donna Hightower replying to John Lee Hooker in 'I Ain't In The Mood' with Floyd Smith darting around on lap steel. A little more space might have been given to recordings from the '20s, but the shortfall is cleverly concealed by having artists such as Alberta Hunter, Trixie Smith, Victoria Spivey remake their '20s hits with '30s technology. Mary Katherine Aldin earns a bouquet for her compilation and notes, and MCA another for keeping this 1999 release in catalogue for so long.

***(*) Barrelhouse Mamas
Yazoo 2044 *Mozelle Alderson, Dorothy Baker, Lucille Bogan (3), Freddy Brown (2), Cow Cow Davenport & Ivy Smith, Lil Johnson, Mary Johnson (3), Ida May Mack, Leola Manning, Elzadie Robinson, St Louis Bessie [Mae Smith] (2), Margaret Thornton (2), Doretha Trowbridge, Bessie Tucker, Elizabeth Washington, Margaret Whitmire.* 27–35.

Construe the title to mean 'uncompromising women blues singers with piano accompaniments', the latter by such estimable players as Charles Avery (Bogan), Judson Brown (Alderson, Mary Johnson), Bob Call (Robinson), Aaron 'Pine Top' Sparks (Trowbridge, Washington) and possibly Henry Brown and Roosevelt Sykes. Bogan's 'Alley Boogie', 'Sloppy Drunk Blues' and 'They Ain't Walking No More' are three of her finest recordings, and their early appearance, all in a row, has the unfortunate result of slightly diminishing everything that follows. Listeners are recommended to use the random or shuffle command, which may allow them to appreciate on their own terms the excellent cuts by Lil Johnson, Mary Johnson and Mozelle Alderson and the utterly distinctive husky whine of Elizabeth Washington.

**(*) Barrelhouse Women – Vol. 1 (1925–1930)
Document DOCD-5378 *Katherine Adkins (2), Evelyn Brickey (2), Clara Burston (10), Bertha Ross (4), Frances Wallace (4), Frances Wallace & Clara Burston (2).* 3/25–9/30.

** Barrelhouse Women – Vol. 2 (1924–1928)
Document DOCD-5497 *Mattie Dorsey (4), Sodarisa Miller (15), Star Page (2), Alice Pearson (5).* c. 8/24–c. 8/28.

The heart of *Vol. 1* is 16 tracks by Frances Wallace and Clara Burston, who appear to have had some connection beyond the fact that they may both have worked in Cincinnati. Both are tough but somewhat inexpressive singers, usually accompanied by a pianist. Bertha Ross, so far as she can be heard through a haze of surface noise, is a dead ringer for Lucille Bogan. *Vol. 2* concentrates on Sodarisa Miller, a vaudeville stylist of middling talent. Jimmy Blythe, her usual accompanist, sparkles on 'Sunshine Special' and one or two other tracks. Alice Pearson is a blues specialist but from the grimness of her delivery you would think she was singing at gunpoint. Almost all the recordings on this CD were made for Paramount, and the dimness of the sound is a deterrent to prolonged listening.

** Blue Girls – Vol. 1 (1924–1930)
Document DOCD-5503 *Helen Beasley (2), Sadie James (2), Edna Johnson (2), Julia Johnson (2), Alura Mack (12), Coletha Simpson (4).* 24–30.

**(*) Blue Girls – Vol. 3 (1924–1938)
Document DOCD-5646 *Virginia Childs (2), Anna Lee Chisholm (2), Lulu Jackson (8), Eva Parker (4), Cora Perkins (2), Ruby Smith (6).* c. 4/24–5/38.

**(*) Jazzin' The Blues – Vol. 5 (1930–1953)
Document DOCD-5666 *Blue Lu Barker (2), Ann Cook, Baby Hines (2), Lizzie Miles, Monette Moore (5), 'Momma' Alberta Price, Helen Proctor (2), Yack Taylor (4), Babe Wallace (3).* 2/30–10/53.

As often with compilations like this, listeners to *Blue Girls – Vol. 1* may be more impressed by the sturdy work of the pianists than by the unevenly talented vocalists they accompany. Alura Mack is quite a convincing blueswoman by the time she reaches her last session but, as earlier recordings show, the idiom did not come to her naturally. Coletha Simpson is more of a blues specialist, and well accompanied by pianist James Williams, but her voice is irredeemably ugly, while Helen Beasley is just eccentric. Of the rest, the most surprising track is Edna Johnson's very early version of the 'Red River Blues' theme, accompanied by fiddle and guitar.

That echo of country music, if that's what it is, is more distinctly heard on *Vol. 3* – from two directions. Virginia Childs, a white singer from Atlanta, rather uncertainly covers 'Down Hearted Blues' and 'The St Louis Blues' with the hillbilly guitarist Riley Puckett, whereas Lulu Jackson, black and perhaps from Indianapolis, picks her way delicately through old-timey lovesongs and melodramas like 'Little Rosewood Casket' and 'You're Going To Leave The Old Home, Jim'. Just what market Jackson's recordings were expected to tap is anyone's guess, but the question is not an idle one: her debut disc of '… Old Home, Jim' and 'Careless Love' was a substantial hit, prompting a double cover job a few months later by Victor's Eva Parker, a coupling also included in this tantalizing collection. For *Blue Girls – Vol. 2 (1925–1930)* (Document DOCD-5504) see Mozelle Alderson and Mary Dixon. *Jazzin' The Blues – Vol. 5*, like others in this series (see MISCELLANEOUS I [PREWAR]), is a mixture of gap-fillers (Barker, Miles, Moore) and one-off sessions like the pugnacious Yack Taylor's.

Women singers who recorded blues in the '20s and early '30s were very numerous, but many of them belonged to a tradition of stage singing that has not appealed much to recent generations of blues enthusiasts. Consequently they had been passed over by most reissue compilers until Document began its project to reissue everything in *B&GR*. Having settled most of the more prolific or interesting artists on albums of their own or collections like *Barrelhouse Women* or *Blue Girls*, Document initiated a series called *Female Blues Singers* which ran through the alphabet from Ora Alexander to Billie Young, dispersing 90-odd singers on 14 volumes (DOCD-5505 to DOCD-5518). Some of these artists are impressive, or at least interestingly odd; others, one would guess, were recorded only because the blues disc business was so profitable in the early and middle '20s; most of them are separated from us by the thick curtain of the acoustic recording process, which reduces all but the strongest voices to squeaks, and muffles their accompanists. Obviously, these albums don't offer the uncompromised pleasures of Yazoo's *I Can't Be Satisfied* sets. Their main audience will be historically minded listeners who are curious about early and once sellable figures like Alice Leslie Carter (*Vol. 4*), Fannie May Goosby (*Vol. 7*), Mattie Hite (*Vol. 9*) and Mary Stafford (*Vol. 13*).

One all-but-forgotten singer of this period, however, must be singled out. Tucked unobtrusively in the middle of *Territory Singers – Vol. 2 (1928–1930)* (Document DOCD-5471), which is primarily concerned with Texan singers and dealt with in TEXAS, is the one disc made by an obscure stage singer, Cleo Gibson, in Atlanta in 1929. The playing of trumpeter Henry Mason, passionate yet controlled, is a wonderful thing in itself, but Gibson's triumphant boast 'I've Got Ford Movements In My Hips' ('… ten thousand miles guarantee') puts her among the stars.

*** Blue Ladies (1934–1941)
Document DOCD-5327 *Hattie Bolten (5), Stella Johnson (3), Kansas Katie (4), Minnie Mathes (3), Irene Sanders (3), Lorraine Walton (6).* 10/34–12/41.
**(*) Female Chicago Blues (1936–1947)
Document DOCD-5295 *Trixie Butler (3), Merline Johnson (The Yas Yas Girl) (7), Billie (Willie Mae) McKenzie (10), Clara Morris (4).* 4/36–3/47.

Blue Ladies' Hattie Bolten is Hattie Hart, formerly of Memphis, now residing in Chicago, and her sides, artfully written and vivaciously delivered, are the pick of this CD, despite their poor sound. Kansas Katie is on a Lil Green kick but does it very well. Stella Johnson was a Chicago nightclub singer and evidently the writer of the 'Hot Nuts' song that was taken to success by other singers. The remaining performers, and *Female Chicago Blues*' Trixie Butler, Billie McKenzie and Clara Morris, are unknown figures who were probably active on the Chicago club scene of the time. All of them are provided with house-band accompaniments – Blind John Davis, Black Bob and Big Bill Broonzy were kept quite busy – and all of them manage to make decent second-rate recordings.

*** Charlie Shavers And The Blues Singers
Timeless CBC 1–025 *Grant & Wilson (4), Rosetta Howard (5), Alberta Hunter (6), Lether McGraw (2), Trixie Smith (6).* 5/38–8/39.

Charlie Shavers (1917–71) was a gifted trumpeter, best known to jazz enthusiasts for his work with the John Kirby Sextet. In common with other Kirbyites like clarinettist Buster Bailey and drummer O'Neil Spencer (both heard here), he was frequently summoned to Decca's New York studios to accompany their blues talent. This CD gathers some of those sessions, admirably restored by John R. T. Davies. The veterans Trixie Smith and Alberta Hunter were both on prime form; with Smith (q.v.), Shavers is elbowed into a secondary role by the ever-loquacious Sidney Bechet, but on the dates with Hunter, Rosetta Howard and Lether McGraw (whose only coupling this is, and a likeable one) Bechet is replaced by the more serene Bailey and Shavers has room to insert a few elegant solos.

**(*) Jazzin' The Blues (1943–1952)
Document DOCD-1019 *Ada Brown, Bertha 'Chippie' Hill (8), Lizzie Miles (6), Mama Alberta Price, Ruby Smith (4).* 1/43–12/52.

This CD exists chiefly to extend Document's holdings of Chippie Hill and Lizzie Miles (qq.v.).

*** Wild About That Thing: Ladies Sing The Blues
Delmark DX-913 *Blu Lu Barker, Big Time Sarah, Bonnie Lee, Karen Carroll, Katherine Davis, Mary Johnson (2), Shirley Johnson, Graná Louise, Betty Roché, Dinah Washington, Edith Wilson, Zora Young.* 4/44–7/02.

From Delmark's 50th-anniversary 'Saver Series' this inexpensive 13-tracker is essentially a sampler of the label's current talent, with some '40s tracks from acquired labels like Apollo (Barker, Washington, Roché) and a couple of previously unissued gospel songs recorded in 1955 by the veteran St Louis singer Mary Johnson, which may interest her admirers but don't merit repeated playing. Though the tracks by younger women like Shirley Johnson, Bonnie Lee and Zora Young are well chosen, they pale a little alongside the almost octogenarian Edith Wilson declaring 'He may be your man … but he comes to see me sometimes.' What a trouper.

**(*) Blues Women 1944–1952: He May Be Your Man
Acrobat ACMCD 4006 *Annisteen Allen, Varetta Dillard (4), Albinia Jones (3), Etta Jones, Little Miss Sharecropper [LaVern Baker] (3), Miss Rhapsody (7), Mabel Scott (4).* 11/44–5/52.
** Swing Time Sisters
Night Train NTI CD 7012 *Emanon Trio (2), Dell Graham (2), Mabel Scott (5), Joan Shaw, Frantic Faye Thomas (3), unknown, Paula Watson (6).* 47–51.

By a neat coincidence, another version of 'He May Be Your Man' appears on the Acrobat CD. Viola Wells, a.k.a. Miss Rhapsody, who sings it, commands a stately delivery on old-school numbers like that and 'Downhearted Blues', and she is accompanied, as are most of her companions on this CD, by well-known jazz musicians, but the other women are more in key with their period; LaVern Baker, Varetta Dillard and Mabel Scott nudge the listener towards a synthesis of blues and what would soon be called rock 'n' roll. Scott is sometimes hard to distinguish from, say, Ella Mae Morse, and that's equally true of her earlier recordings on *Swing Time Sisters*. The other major contributor to that CD, Paula Watson, exercises her fingers on the keyboard in 'Paula's Nightmare' but her vocal numbers are mostly trivial. Frantic Faye Thomas is also a piano adept but affects the girly style of Rose Murphy. The sound quality is very erratic, and the CD's main attraction is the tough unidentified singer who asks 'I Wonder Who's Boogeying My Woogie Now'.

**(*) Don't Freeze On Me: Independent Women's Blues
El Cerrito ECR 01005 *Marie Adams, Al & Nettie, Olive Brown, Delilah (3), Sugar Pie DeSanto (3), Dell Graham, Betty James (2), Jessie Mae, Camille La Vah, Mary Ann Miles & Ray Agee, Blanche Thomas, Ella Thomas (4), Big Mama Thornton (5).* 54–67.

Buy this CD and you've got a one-way ticket to Collectorville. Someone has combed the shelves of an enviable collection and shaken out little-known singles on mostly Californian labels like Flag, Shirley, Bay-Tone and Sotoplay. Ella Thomas's answer song 'I'm Your Part Time Love' and her others are accompanied by guitarist Johnny Heartsman, a West Coast Mickey Baker; so are Delilah's 'I'll Rock You Baby' and 'Worried Feeling', idiosyncratic and terrific. Another answer song is Al & Nettie's 'Now You Know', responding to Jimmy McCracklin's 'Just Got To Know' and accompanied by his band. The notes plausibly suggest that the downhome guitarist on Betty James's sides may be Tarheel Slim, but leave the buyer with most of the rest of the discographical work to do.

*** Chicago's Finest Blues Ladies
Wolf 120.874 *Melvina Allen (3), Bonnie Lee (3), Karen Carroll (2), Deitra Farr (2), Mary Lane (3), Zora Young (2).* 8/87–7/93.
*** Women Of Blue Chicago
Delmark DD-690 *Big Time Sarah (2), Bonnie Lee (2), Karen Carroll (2), Katherine Davis, Shirley Johnson (2), Lynne Jordan (2).* 9/92–2/96.

*** Red Hot Mamas
Blue Chicago BC 5001 *Bonnie Lee (2), Karen Carroll (2), Liz Mandville Greeson (2), Shirley Johnson (2), Lynne Jordan (2), Patricia Scott (2), Peaches Staten.* 6–7/97.

**(*) Mojo Mamas
Blue Chicago BC 5005 *Big Time Sarah (2), Maggie Burrell, Shirley Johnson (2), Mary Lane (2), Graná Louise (2), Pat Scott (2), Gloria Shannon (2), Zora Young.* 12/99.

All these CDs present women who are active members of the Chicago blues community. *Chicago's Finest Blues Ladies* was co-produced by Willie Kent and John Primer, who play on most of the tracks, weaving a uniform ensemble sound which, over a long programme (74.17) of mostly slow blues, comes to sound rather drab. Bonnie Lee, Karen Carroll, Deitra Farr and Zora Young (qq.v.) are all at or near their sturdy best, and Young's 'Bad Track Record' is a song that deserves to acquire a good one. Mary Lane is a plain storyteller, while Melvina Allen does herself no favours by recording soul-blues material as well-worn as 'Steppin' In' and 'Breakin' Up Somebody's Home'.

The other CDs are all connected with the North Side club Blue Chicago, though loosely in the case of the Delmark, which is mainly a compilation from the label's backlist, wisely including such standouts as Karen Carroll's 'Goin' Down Slow' and Big Time Sarah's 'The Thrill Is Gone'. The only fresh songs are by Shirley Johnson and Lynne Jordan. Johnson rolls smoothly down the scenic highway of 'As The Years Go Passing By', but it's guitarist Johnny B. Moore who's at the wheel. Jordan has more of a stage manner (she majored in theatre at Northwestern) and brings tremendous brio to Alex Hill and Andy Razaf's point number 'If I Can't Sell It'. Her only other recordings appear to be her two cuts on *Red Hot Mamas*; 'Mama (He Treats Your Daughter Mean)' suggests that she'd be a serious contender in a casting call for a Dinah Washington role. The women on *Red Hot Mamas* are united in having gigged regularly at Blue Chicago; what they don't share is a musical policy. While Shirley Johnson comes on like a low-budget Millie Jackson in 'Hold What You've Got', with its 'I wanna talk to you men/women' homilies, Peaches Staten recalls the young Koko Taylor and Karen Carroll delivers 'Sweet Home Chicago' and 'Blue Chicago Blues' with the gravitas of an elder stateswoman. You might ask for more new material, but the bands are rehearsed to a sheen and there is no shortfall in gusto, remarks equally applicable to *Mojo Mamas*, another well-made studio recording (though there's video of Big Time Sarah on stage at the club). The husky Pat Scott, who was no more than mildly interesting on *Red Hot Mamas*, finds a deeper groove in 'Today I Sing The Blues', and Mary Lane has done some work on her delivery since her Wolf session. Two singers make their recording debuts: Gloria Shannon, described as 'a sweet grandmother', takes the retro route with 'Baby, Won't You Please Come Home' and an Irene Reid song, while Graná (pronounced 'Granay') Louise is feisty in 'Good Woman Go Bad'. The backing bands are drawn from a small pool of musicians, with Maurice John Vaughn and Johnny B. Moore the main guitarists.

***(*) Any Woman's Blues
Rounder Heritage Series 11597 *Marcia Ball, Marcia Ball–Irma Thomas–Tracy Nelson, Rory Block, Ruth Brown, Ruth Brown & Charles Brown, Miki Honeycutt, Candye Kane, Barbara Lynn, Maria Muldaur, Tracy Nelson, Kim Nalley, Ann Peebles, Angela Strehli, Irma Thomas, Irma Thomas & Tracy Nelson, Michelle Willson.* 72–99.

**(*) Every Woman's Blues: The Best Of The New Generation
Shanachie 9009 *Alicia, BB Queen, Rory Block, Deanna Bogart, Sarah Brown, Deborah Coleman, Joanna Connor, Debbie Davies, Sue Foley, Liz Mandville Greeson, Zakiya Hooker, Lady Bianca, Saffire, Lucinda Williams.* 80s–90s.

If you were coming fresh to the music of Shanachie's 'new generation', *Every Woman's Blues* wouldn't be a bad introduction. Rory Block opens with guitar and wordless moaning, energetic workouts by Sue Foley and Lady Bianca step up the momentum, and the programme only sags when presenting lightweight acts like Deanna Bogart and Alicia Levy, or ending with an uncharacteristically dull performance by Saffire and a mannered one by Lucinda Williams. But given the catalogues available – tracks were licensed from Blind Pig, Rounder, Alligator and several other labels – seasoned enthusiasts may feel that Shanachie could have come up with a stronger selection. Rounder, drawing only on their own resources, achieve a much more successful result. Admittedly, the younger artists are supported by a strong team of veteran performers like Irma Thomas and Ann Peebles, and the repertoire embraces a good deal of soul-blues, but sheer variety and well-considered programming combine to produce a compellingly listenable album. TR

Zydeco

♛ **** Zydeco: The Early Years
Arhoolie CD 307 *George Alberts, Sidney Babineaux, Clifton Chenier (2), Albert Chevalier (4), Clarence Garlow, Willie Green (4), Peter King & Lester Hebert, Paul McZiel & Wallace Gernger (3), Herbert Sam.* 49–62.

The Early Years ends with Clifton Chenier's debut recordings and Clarence Garlow's catchy 'Bon Ton Roulet'. The other tracks were recorded in 1961–62, mainly at houseparties and taverns in Louisiana and Houston. (It seems likely that, despite its indelible association with Louisiana, the blend of Creole music, *juré* and the blues that became zydeco evolved in Houston's Frenchtown, and made its way back across the state line.) The accordion was already the music's *sine qua non* (some of the tracks here feature lead and rhythm accordions), and scraped percussion was also virtually universal, although the worn-like-a-vest rubboard had not yet replaced the washboard.

Some of the musicians on *The Early Years* were born in the 19th century, and the music is Janus-faced: forward-looking in its use of blues and rock 'n' roll, it's also very deep-rooted. French Creole music, with its tense, emotional singing and playing (hear Albert Chevalier's keening harmonica on 'Moman Couché') easily assimilated English-language blues like Willie Green's 'Baby Please Don't Go' and George Alberts's 'You Havin' A Good Time'; but most of the songs are sung in French, and waltzes, one-steps and two-steps are the dominant dance rhythms. They're played on single- and triple-row diatonic accordions, on which push and pull give different notes, so that the music chugs rather than flowing smoothly. Sometimes recorded at less than optimum fidelity, *The Early Years* faithfully captures the rowdy, sweaty pleasures of eating, drinking and dancing with friends and neighbours on a hot summer afternoon.

(***(*)) J'Ai Été Au Bal Vol. 1
Arhoolie CD 331 *Nathan Abshire (2), Amédé Ardoin & Dennis McGee, Bois Sec Ardoin, Harry Choates, Michael Doucet (2), Joe Falcon & Cleoma Breaux, Odile Falcon, Solange Falcon, Canray Fontenot (2), The Hackberry Ramblers, Chuck Guillory, Iry Lejune (2), Lionel Leleux, Lionel Leleux & Michael Doucet, Dennis McGee (2), Walter Mouton (2), Queen Ida, Marc Savoy, Marc & Ann Savoy, Leo Soileau*. 4/28–88.

(***) J'Ai Été Au Bal Vol. 2
Arhoolie CD 332 *Johnny Allen, Sidney Babineaux, Balfa Brothers Band, Dewey Balfa, Rodney Balfa, Boozoo Chavis, Clifton Chenier (3), Paul Daigle, John Delafose, Michael Doucet & Beausoleil (2), Joseph Jones, D. L. Menard (2), Jimmy Peters, Belton Richard, Rockin' Sidney, Wayne Toups & Zydecajun*. 8/34–88.

The two volumes of *J'Ai Été Au Bal* are expanded versions of the soundtrack of a scholarly and entertaining documentary (Brazos Films DVD BF-103). They touch all the Creole and zydeco bases, but *Vol. 2*, which is the heavier on zydeco, is diminished by Rockin' Sidney's long, dull version of 'My Toot Toot' and by Wayne Toups's attempt to fuse Cajun music, zydeco and Southern rock on a horrible version of 'Allons A Lafayette'. Cajun music dominates these CDs: much of it is wonderful, and particular mention should be made of Nathan Abshire and Iry Lejune, heavily black-influenced and deeply bluesy, but the discs' value as an introduction to zydeco is limited. It had better be said that neither this comment nor some elsewhere in this entry are intended as strictures on Cajun music and culture in general, but even so we direct readers to the DVD rather than the CDs.

**** Zydeco Champs
Arhoolie CD 328 *Amédé Ardoin, Bois Sec Ardoin & Canray Fontenot (2), Lawrence Ardoin (2), C. J. Chenier (2), Clifton Chenier (5), John Delafose (2), Preston Frank & Leo Thomas (2), Clarence Garlow, Paul McZiel & Wallace Gernger, Ambrose Sam, Sam Brothers 5 (2), Herbert Sam*. 12/34–3/88.

***(*) 15 Louisiana Zydeco Classics
Arhoolie CD 105 *Amédé Ardoin, Bois Sec Ardoin, Lawrence Ardoin, C. J. Chenier (2), Clifton Chenier (3), John Delafose (2), Canray Fontenot, Preston Frank, Peter King & Lester Hebert, Ambrose Sam, Sam Brothers 5*. 12/34–3/88.

Zydeco Champs draws the listener in with zydeco's best-known name, Clifton Chenier, doing two old-style numbers, and ends with his Red Hot Band in red hot form at a California dance. In between, the disc takes an entertaining and educational stroll through the music's history from Amédé Ardoin onwards. It affords generous exposure to the violin, now virtually extinct in zydeco, but here played by Canray Fontenot, Edouard Poullard (accompanying Lawrence Ardoin), and Morris Chenier and Carlton Frank behind their respective nephews. The contrast between deep blues and good-time dance music is very neatly demonstrated, and Amédé Ardoin's soulful 'La Valse De Ballard' is not the only track proving that the two can be combined.

Shorter and without notes, the budget-priced *15 Louisiana Zydeco Classics* covers much the same ground (and the Sam Brothers' 'Lafayette Special' is on both discs). *Zydeco Classics* is more obviously promotional, but C. J. Chenier's rendition of his late father's 'I'm Coming Home' (a staple of zydeco funerals) is very moving, and Preston Frank's scurrying 'Tante Na-Na' is one more reason to regret that the LP he shares with Ambrose Sam, *Zydeco Vol. 2* (Arhoolie 1090), has yet to appear on CD.

**(*) Zydeco Festival
Maison de Soul MdS 101 *Buckwheat Zydeco (2), Carrière Brothers, Boozoo Chavis (2), Wilfred Chevis (2), Clifton Chenier (3), John Delafose, Michael Doucet & Beausoleil, Morris Francis, Chuck Martin, Rockin' Dopsie (2), Rockin' Sidney (2), Terrance Simien, Zydeco Brothers*. mid 70s–mid 80s.

**(*) 101 Proof Zydeco
Maison de Soul MdS-1030 *Lynn August (2), Boozoo Chavis (2), Clifton Chenier, John Delafose, Major Handy (2), Nathan & The Zydeco Cha Chas, Jo Jo Reed, Zachary Richard, Rockin' Dopsie, Rockin' Sidney, Sam Brothers Five (2), Terrance Simien, Zydeco Brothers, Zydeco Force*. mid 70s–late 80s.

Based in Ville Platte, Louisiana, Maison de Soul primarily serves the local market (although its mail-order service at <www.floydsrecordshop.com> is prompt and helpful). Floyd Soileau has recorded many artists who went on to wider fame and some, like Clifton Chenier, who were always happy to make another session. He's also recorded musicians whose fame has remained strictly local, like the rough-edged but excellent Wilfred Chevis and Major Handy. These two CDs are uneven: the big and biggish names are predictably authoritative, and Lynn August's 'Zydeco Groove' thrums with power, but his 'Whatever Boils Your Crawfish' is tiresomely facetious. Rockin' Dopsie is represented by tracks from a good CD that's not his best, and Rockin' Sidney gets away with murder thanks to 'My Toot Toot', which is the basis of Chuck Martin's tedious 'Make It Hot'. The Cajun band Beausoleil went on to better things, and Zachary Richard's Cajun rock is unfettered by issues of taste. Despite such weak moments, these discs' blend of worldwide and local stars is worth hearing: *Zydeco Festival*, ranging from the Carrière Brothers' archaic 'Blues A Bébé' to the Zydeco Brothers' pulsating cover of the Staple Singers' 'Reach Out', is the stronger. The deleted *Zydeco Party!* (Ace CDCHD 430) was a good selection from these two CDs; it may still be around.

*** Rockin' Zydeco Party!
Maison de Soul MdS-1049 *Cory Arceneaux, Lynn August, Beau Jocque, Roy Carrier, Boozoo Chavis, Clifton Chenier, Wilfred Chevis, John Delafose, Keith Frank, Preston Frank, Ann Goodly, Rosie Ledet, Rockin' Dopsie, Rockin' Sidney, T-Lou & L.A. Zydeco Band, Zydeco Force*. 11/75–early 90s.

*** Dat's Zydeco!
Maison de Soul MdS-1079 *Boozoo Chavis (2), Clifton Chenier, John Delafose, Morris Francis, Keith Frank (2), Jean Pierre [Blanchard], Rosie Ledet, Li'l Malcolm [Walker], Willis Prudhomme, Rockin' Sidney, Sam Brothers Five, Zydeco Force (2), Zydeco Joe [Mouton]*. 11/75–late 90s.

Clifton Chenier accounts for the start dates, but these collections are otherwise from the '80s and '90s. *Rockin' Zydeco Party!* is diminished by Sidney Semien's cheesy 'No Good Woman', Lynn August's trivial 'Amazon Annie' and the clichéd guitar and out-of-tune bass behind T-Lou, but this is a worthwhile CD, notably for otherwise unavailable tracks by the veteran Preston Frank and the deep soul diva of zydeco,

Ann Goodly, diverted from stardom by religion and child-rearing. Wilfred Chevis's 'Chère Marie' is a knockabout version of 'Chère Catin' with bustling tenor, organ and guitar solos.

Dat's Zydeco! proclaims itself 'some of the best "old-skool" [*sic*] zydeco ever recorded'; that's an overstatement, but this is the most consistent of the Maison de Soul CDs discussed here. It's heavy on French-language songs, waltzes and two-steps (although Willis Prudhomme's 'Cornbread Two-Step' blazes a trail that Beau Jocque was shortly to follow). 'Josephine C'Est Pas Ma Femme' is a glimpse of the post-adolescent Sam Brothers, still in thrall to *le grand* Clifton, but taking his music drag-racing. Among the lesser-known names, Zydeco Joe, letting the *bon temps rouler*, is the rootsy essence of homemade music, and the saxes on Morris Francis's blend of swamp pop, jump blues and zydeco are delightful.

***(*) Cajun Music And Zydeco
Rounder CD 11572 *Bois Sec Ardoin & Canray Fontenot, Dewey Balfa, Beausoleil, Buckwheat Zydeco, Boozoo Chavis, Clifton Chenier, Bruce Daigrepont, John Delafose, Preston Frank, Dennis McGee, Nathan & The Zydeco Cha-Chas, Felix Richard, Zachary Richard, Steve Riley, Aldus Roger, The Savoy-Doucet Cajun Band, Zydeco Force.* 5/65–early 90s.

*** More Cajun Music And Zydeco
Rounder CD 11573 *Amédé Ardoin & Dennis McGee, Bois Sec Ardoin & Canray Fontenot, Balfa Brothers, Balfa Toujours, Beausoleil, Boozoo Chavis, Clifton Chenier, John Delafose, David Greely, D. L. Menard, Jimmy Peters, Hackberry Ramblers, McCauley, Reed & Vidrine, Nathan & The Zydeco Cha-Chas, Zachary Richard, Steve Riley, Jo-El Sonnier, Jesse Stafford, Wayne Toups, Zydeco Force.* 12/29–2/93.

These CDs were compiled by Phillip Gould and Barry Jean Ancelet to complement their book *Cajun Music And Zydeco* (Louisiana State University Press, 1992). The music and Ancelet's notes combine into an admirable account of the history, development and interaction of the two musics, their sub-regional diversities and the often, but not always, fruitful tension between preservation and innovation. It's an advantage that Rounder range well beyond their own catalogue: the majority – in the case of *More Cajun Music And Zydeco*, the great majority – of tracks are licensed, from labels including Arhoolie, Maison de Soul and Lanor (Preston Frank and his kids, with a phenomenal rerecording of Preston's hit 'Why Do You Want To Make Me Cry?'). The first volume is the stronger, let down only by an abnormally lethargic 'Paper In My Shoe' from Boozoo Chavis, and by Zydeco Force's uncouth 'Zydeco Extravaganza Theme'; *More* delves deeper into the past, with items like Ardoin & McGee's bluesy waltz 'Madam Atchen' and Jimmy Peters's highly African *juré*, but it's handicapped by some of the Cajuns: Balfa Toujours's talent is not at the level of their preservationist zeal, Zachary Richard is militantly morose and Wayne Toups's 'Zydeco Est Pas Salé' is seven minutes of mindless agitation.

**** Music From The Zydeco Kingdom
Rounder CD 11579 *Amédé Ardoin, Chris Ardoin, Beau Jocque, Buckwheat Zydeco, The Carrière Brothers, Boozoo Chavis, C. J. Chenier, Clifton Chenier (2), John Delafose, Canray Fontenot & Bois Sec Ardoin, Keith Frank, Little Latour's Sulphur Playboys, Rosie Ledet, Nathan & The Zydeco Cha Chas, Queen Ida, Rockin' Dopsie, Ambrose Sam, Zydeco Force.* 12/29–95.

This is the CD to play while reading Michael Tisserand's essential *The Kingdom Of Zydeco* (Arcade, 1998) and waiting for Robert Mugge's film of the same name to appear on DVD. Tracing the paths of continuity and change from Amédé's 'Eunice Two-Step' (a.k.a. 'Chère Catin') to Chris and Sean's 'Ardoin Two-Step' via Clifton Chenier's 'Cher Catin' [*sic*], Tisserand achieves his self-imposed challenge of compiling a CD that's both party mix and history. (This seems like the place to mention that readers who just want to get down will find many ten-track zydeco bargains on Rounder's Easydisc imprint.) *Music From The Zydeco Kingdom* casts its net widely: especially important catches are Little Latour's wrenching 'C-Key Blues', Ambrose Sam, from his wonderful Arhoolie half-LP, John Delafose (recorded by the BBC!) and eight minutes of Beau Jocque from Robert Mugge's film; it's 'Give Him Cornbread' again, but it's a hell of a version. This collection is so good (even 'Hot Tamale Baby' is worth hearing at Buckwheat's insane speed) that Queen Ida's presence is excusable; the CD isn't called *Music From The Zydeco Monarchy*, so it can't be a gesture to political correctness.

**(*) Alligator Stomp: Cajun & Zydeco Classics
Rhino R2 70946 *Johnnie Allan, Beausoleil, Boozoo Chavis (2), Clifton Chenier (2), Cleveland Crochet, Bruce Daigrepont, Rusty & Doug [Kershaw], D. L. Menard, Queen Ida (2), Rockin' Dopsie (2), Rockin' Sidney (2), Jo-El Sonnier (2).* 55–84.

**(*) Alligator Stomp Vol. 2: Cajun & Zydeco Classics
Rhino R2 70740 *Nathan Abshire, Balfa Brothers, Beausoleil, Buckwheat Zydeco, Boozoo Chavis, Clifton Chenier (2), Lesa Cormier, John Delafose, Fats Domino & Doug Kershaw, Rusty & Doug [Kershaw], Iry Lejune, D. L. Menard, Queen Ida, Belton Richard, Rockin' Dopsie, Terrance Simien, Jo-El Sonnier.* 48–late 80s.

Rhino's two collections have brief but user-friendly notes. Especially on the Cajun side, they include some classics: on the first disc there's Cleveland Crochet's bluesy 'Sugar Bee' and Johnnie Allan's cover of Chuck Berry's 'Promised Land', while the second has D. L. Menard's 'The Back Door' and Iry Lejune's 'Evangeline Special'. Against this must be set undistinguished remastering and a leaning towards the relatively well-known but (or because?) bland likes of Queen Ida, Rusty & Doug's Nashvillized Cajun pop, and Rockin' Sidney, whose 'My Toot Toot' inevitably opens the first volume, and is unappealingly covered by Fats Domino and Doug Kershaw on the second.

***(*) Stomp Down Zydeco
Rounder CD 11566 *Lynn August (3), Buckwheat Zydeco, Boozoo Chavis, John Delafose (5), Nathan & The Zydeco Cha-Chas (2), Pee Wee & The Zydeco Boll Weevils, Zydeco Force (2).* 4/85–10/90.

*** Zydeco Shootout At El Sid O's
Rounder CD 2108 *Lynn August (3), Warren Ceasar (2), Morris Ledet, Pee Wee & The Zydeco Boll Weevils (2), Jude Taylor (2), Zydeco Force (3).* 10/90.

On *Zydeco Shootout* Lynn August redeems the solecisms on Maison de Soul, Jude Taylor's B. B. King-meets-zydeco 'Move On Down The Line' is pure pleasure and the Zydeco Boll Weevils' 'Don't Mess With My Ya Ya', propelled by a frenzied drummer, is the essence of hedonism; but Morris 'husband of Rosie' Ledet shows why she's a star and he's not, and singing trumpeter Warren Ceasar's songs (C&W and reggae) are a waste of Fernest Arceneaux's band. Like many a live album,

Zydeco Shootout raises expectations that are doomed to disappointment.

The Zydeco Cha-Chas' 'Everything On The Hog' excepted, *Stomp Down Zydeco* uses previously unissued material from studio dates, from the *Zydeco Shootout* sessions and from the Richard's Club dances that produced two CDs called *Zydeco Live!* (see entries for Boozoo Chavis, John Delafose, Willis Prudhomme and Nathan & The Zydeco Cha-Chas). The Zydeco Boll Weevils' track is one more failure to justify the popularity of 'Hot Tamale Baby', and Zydeco Force live up to their name, with a bass guitar doubling the accordion, but John Delafose's tracks are among his finest recordings, and they're in good company. Much of the disc consists of admirable homages to Clifton Chenier, among which Lynn August's 'Hippy Ti Yo', accompanied for its first three minutes by accordion and percussion, is just about perfect; the bass guitar's eventual entry is a *coup de théâtre*.

*** **Zydeco: The Essential Collection**
Rounder Heritage Series 11605 *Chris Ardoin (2), Lynn August, Beau Jocque (2), Buckwheat Zydeco (2), Boozoo Chavis (2), Bruce Daigrepont, Geno Delafose (2), John Delafose, Li'l Brian, Nathan & The Zydeco Cha-Chas (2), Steve Riley. 4/83–4/01.*

Though not essential, it's a handy overview of zydeco at the end of the 20th century as recorded by Rounder, although one wonders how many times they can recycle 'Give Him Cornbread'. The 24-bit remastering makes an audible difference to some tracks, and Scott Billington's notes are a good outline of how modern-day zydeco artists take their inspiration from either Chenier (piano accordion, eclectic and syncretic) or Chavis (button box, local and rootsy). Beau Jocque, singing Clifton's 'I'm On A Wonder', exemplifies the problems involved in synthesizing the two strains; on a more general level, the contrast between the more traditional artists and the young funksters is sometimes jarring. Of the token Cajuns, Steve Riley's band, with C. J. Chenier guesting on sax, make a good job of the blues 'J'Ai Reveillé À Ce Matin', but Bruce Daigrepont's attempt to sing like Amédé Ardoin on a revival of 'Madam Atchen' is cringemaking. cs

Index

'22' 761, 762
'88' [C. B. Cook] 761, 763
——, Jeff 80, 513
——, Kevin 350
——, Mabel 208
——, Sam 364
14 Karat Soul 559
Aaberg, Phil 43, 558
Aarons, Albert 357
Abbey, Leon 592
Abbott, Sinclair 446, 477
Abbott, Susanne 21
Abbs, Herb 721
Abdallah, Juma 625
Abdallah, Nihifadhi 625
Abdisalami, Fatma 625
Aberman, Larry 668, 669
Abernathy, Marion 1, 788, 798
Abernathy, Stanley 359
Abney, Ben 808
Abney, Don 40, 245, 300
Abraham, Annabelle 757
Abraham, Johnny 728
Abraham, Nat 170
Abrahams, Mick 767
Abrahams, Roger 665
Abrahamsen, John 148, 324, 549
Abrams, Daniel 'Mongo' 657
Abrams, Jerry 507
Abrams, Leon 295, 670, 671
Abrams, Ray 140
Abramson, Herb 410
Abramson, Leon 321, 322
Abrew's Portuguese Instrumental Trio 816
Abshire, Nathan 831, 832
Abts, Matt 402
Ace, Johnny 352, 353, 464, 505, 651, 799
Ace Of Cups, The 52
Aces, The 1, 781, 822
Acey, Johnny 306, 307, 807
Achols, Darryl 330
Acock, Bimbo 217, 223, 424
Acock, Peter 223
Acuff, Roy 772
Acuna, Alex 376
Adail, Doc Terry 816
Adair, Scott 81
Adami, Carl 2
Adams, Alberta 201, 779, 827
Adams, Arnold 315
Adams, Arthur K. 1, 209, 358, 779, 786
Adams, Carl 354, 355
Adams, Clarence 134, 592
Adams, Dwight 27, 250
Adams, Eddie 138
Adams, Eugene 300
Adams, Faye 799

Adams, George 133, 521
Adams, Greg 273
Adams, James 473, 661, 662
Adams, Jo-Jo 1
Adams, Johnny 84, 223, 788, 803, 805
Adams, Justin 26, 75, 166, 207, 307, 391, 402, 529, 622, 739
Adams, 'Lil Crip' 176
Adams, Luther 'Slim' 57, 64, 171, 345, 541, 675, 697
Adams, Marc 35, 214, 730, 731
Adams, Marie 506, 799, 819, 827, 829
Adams, Mark 52
Adams, Oscar 'Yogi' 712
Adams, Pepper 726
Adams, Placide 83
Adams, Reginald 39
Adams, Tony 49, 50
Adamski, Wally 599
Adcock, Amy 189
Adcock, C. C. 21
Adcock, Jack 189
Addeo, Eric 729
Adderley, Cannonball 671
Adderley, Nat 53, 671
Addison, Bernard 426, 587, 588, 718
Addison, Larry 401
Adegbalola, Gaye 2, 51, 563, 564
Adkins, Katherine 828
Adler, Murray 210
Adult Choir 583
Africa, Jeremiah 632
Agami, Al 8
Agee, Ray 782, 829
Agee, Tawatha 668
Agnor, Mark 580
Ahern, Ed 433
Ahern, Peter 458
Ahern, Robert James 87
Ahlstrand, Paul 179, 636, 691
Ahrens, Rolf 344
Aiello, Mike 635
Aikels, Rudy 357
Aiken, Bud 718
Aiken, Gus 315, 592, 596, 720
Ainslie, Scott 650
Ainsworth, Will 575
Ajaye, Eric 146, 416, 673
Akers, Garfield 794, 801
Akins, Dell 660
Al, Alex 376
Al & Nettie 829
'Alabama Joe' [J. M. 'Doc' Miller] 336
'Alabama Joe' [Roy Smeck] 707, 718
Alabama Rascals 816
Alabama Sheiks 811, 816
Alaimo, Steve 270
Albert, Jeffery V. 472

Alberts, George 830
Albright, Genovis 156
Albright, Gerald 343
Albritton, Boyd 273
Alcorn, Alvin 219
Alcorn, Oliver 80, 467, 468, 500, 616, 718
Alcorn, Oliver 'Lee Lee' 554
Alcorn III, Oliver 472
Alcott, Red 81
Alderson, Mozelle 2, 69, 167, 191, 740, 741, 742, 774, 795, 797, 828
Aldrich, Jeff 6
Alers, Karmine 567
Alers, Yasmin 567
Alesi, Tommy 196
'Alex' 14, 761
Alex, Quincy 12
Alexander, Clifford 118, 243
Alexander, Curby 245
Alexander, Dan 273
Alexander, Dave [Omar Sharriff] 552
Alexander, Earl 583
Alexander, Elmer 245
Alexander, Eric 543, 606
Alexander, George 77, 233
Alexander, Gregory 'Popeye' 241
Alexander, Herman 2
Alexander, Honey 742
Alexander, James 349, 350
Alexander, Jeffrey 'Jelly Bean' 179, 571, 730, 731
Alexander, Joe 384, 385, 713
Alexander, Nelson 742, 788
Alexander, Scott 81, 185
Alexander, Sister Dora 811
Alexander, Texas 3, 321, 737, 738, 768, 794, 810, 817, 818, 819, 820
Alexander, W. D. 763
Alexander Jr, Clifford 118
Alexandra Junior Bright Boys 810
Alexis, Bobby 130
Alexis, Lester 'Duke' 529
Alfred, Carl 591
Alfred, Eugene 489
Alfred, James Joseph 118
Alfred, Rusty 412, 600, 601
Ali, Bardu 504
Ali, Rasheed 556
Ali, Rashid Jamal 672
Ali, Subira 625
Ali, Wali 374
Alicia 830
All-Stars, The 813
Allair, John 274
Allan, Johnnie 832
Allbritton, Martin 450
Allen, Annisteen 300, 785, 799, 806, 829
Allen, Boogie Woogie 33

Allen, Colin 428, 429, 430
Allen, Connie 713
Allen, Crazy Rick 365
Allen, David 355
Allen, Ed 164, 426, 587, 588, 592
Allen, George 248, 257
Allen, Greg 'Salt Dog' 540
Allen, Henry 'Red' 24, 80, 98, 142, 287, 311, 597, 607, 637, 797
Allen, Jackie 244
Allen, Jesse 800
Allen, Jimmy 725, 726
Allen, Johnny 300, 831
Allen, Lee 26, 58, 75, 140, 166, 167, 207, 307, 358, 391, 529, 662, 677, 678, 729
Allen, Lil 240
Allen, Lucy-Ann 424
Allen, Marva 791
Allen, Melvina 474, 829
Allen, Mike 299, 520
Allen, Napoleon 410
Allen, Otho 455, 654
Allen, Pete 30, 32, 419
Allen, Peter 534
Allen, Pierre 534
Allen, Richard 'Pistol' 681
Allen, Ricky 790
Allen, Ronnie 431
Allen, Sam 459
Allen, Slam 424
Allen, Tony 788
Allen Brothers 772, 795, 821
Alley, Vernon 366, 725
Allgood, Vernon 90
Allison, Bernard 3, 6, 524, 824
Allison, Gene 786, 790
Allison, George 808
Allison, Leevert 786
Allison, Luther 4, 5, 222, 318, 577, 600, 744, 745, 751, 767, 768, 776, 779, 781, 802, 814, 825
Allison, Malcolm 228
Allison, Ray 34, 35, 138, 234, 518, 633
Allison, Ray 'Killer' 4, 31, 234, 235, 260, 527, 569, 632, 695, 771
Allison, Ray 'S. D.' 711
Allison Family, The 4
Allman, Duane 238
Allman Brothers 813
Allmon, Reggie 568
Allsop, Brian 50
Allston, Joe 245
Alm, Art 583
Alm, Kate 583
Almond, Johnny 33, 175, 427, 428, 429
Alonzo 76
Alper, Greg 133
Alphabetical Four, The 596
Alsador, Teresita 580
Alston, Johnnie 244
Altheimer, Joshua 69, 218, 321, 326, 636, 637, 682, 716

Altman, John 81, 210, 217
Altschul, Barry 233
Alvarez, Dino 186, 317
Alvarez, José 180
Alvarez, Ruben P. 695
Alvarez, Rubin 42
Alvin, Dave 139, 342, 402, 485, 824
'Amando' 125
Amaro, Big John 299
Amato, Joe 358
Amato, Mike 399
Ambrose, Steve 170
Amerson, Richard 760, 811
Ames, Boogaloo 766
Ames, Ruth 277, 278
Amis, Danny 126
Ammons, Albert 7, 16, 69, 88, 259, 326, 327, 328, 389, 390, 645, 661, 662, 679, 739, 740, 741, 742, 747, 762, 781, 797, 798, 809
Ammons, Gene 7, 800
Ammons Sisters 417
Amos, Lisa 554
Amouroux, Jean-Paul 458, 459
Amster, Rob 553, 567, 614
Amundson, Monti 814
Anastasio, Trey 569
Anderhell, Klass 657
Anders, Bernie 731
Anders, Leslie 764
Andersen, Jacob 657
Andersen, Mads 'Tiny' 8, 223
Andersen, Mike 8
Anderson, Alfa 358
Anderson, Anthony 365
Anderson, Arthur 758
Anderson, Bernard 'Dr B.' 84, 193, 229, 512, 535, 544, 624
Anderson, Bill 415
Anderson, Bob 138, 141, 486, 581
Anderson, C. J. 635
Anderson, Cat 245
Anderson, Cedric 715
Anderson, Chris 175
Anderson, David 217
Anderson, David D. 568
Anderson, Duke 63, 86, 416
Anderson, Eddie 661
Anderson, Elton 784
Anderson, Ernestine 789
Anderson, Gene 607
Anderson, Harold 295
Anderson, Herbert 340
Anderson, Ike 23, 317, 465
Anderson, Ivie 505
Anderson, James P. 591
Anderson, Jelly Roll 815
Anderson, Jesse 125, 784
Anderson, Jimmy 770, 783
Anderson, John 291, 295, 447, 504, 505, 592, 725, 726
Anderson, Johnny 390

Anderson, Keith 'Wolf' 242
Anderson, Keith 291
Anderson, Kenneth 311
Anderson, Kenny 7, 33, 41, 57, 96, 109, 129, 260, 318, 330, 346, 443, 474, 553, 590, 599, 614, 681, 707, 733
Anderson, Kip 82, 780
Anderson, Lawrence 84
Anderson, Lee 40, 713
Anderson, Leonard 715
Anderson, Little Pink 10, 786
Anderson, Lloyd 6, 84, 591, 600
Anderson, Mildred 7, 8
Anderson, Mozelle 773, 774
Anderson, Osee 68
Anderson, Pink 9, 755, 756, 767, 794, 811
Anderson, Ralph 551
Anderson, Ray 518
Anderson, Robert 357, 790
Anderson, Sam 685
Anderson, Shake 135
Anderson, Theresa 503
Anderson, Thomisene 113, 257, 358, 401, 402
Anderson, Wessell 84
Anderson, Willie 782
Anderson, Little Willie 10
Andersson, Theresa 502
Andino, Dino 52
Andrade, Carlos 625
Andrew, Brad 21
Andrews, Ben 10
Andrews, Bob 470
Andrews, Dope 595
Andrews, Ed 793
Andrews, 'Guitar' Jake 11, 296
Andrews, James 503, 805
Andrews, Lee 780
Andrews, Mose 801
Andrews, Troy 'Trombone Shorty' 571, 805
Andrews, Wilbert 149
Andrews Jr, Daniel 521
AnDrieux, Simon 4
Andrus, Curnis 193
Angel, Eddie 126
Angel, Jerry 408
Angel, Johnny 783
Angel 217
Angelina Quartet 759
Angelou, Maya 355
Angerer, Karl 143
Anglin Brothers 772
Animals, The 803
Annie 36
Another Blessed Creation Choir 6
Anstiss, Frank 398
Anteaters, The 786
Anthony, Chops 675
Anthony, Chuck 37
Anthony, Eddie 287, 737, 754, 816
Anthony, Ray 369

INDEX

Anthony, William 286
Antoine, Fulton 118
Antoine, Nolan 67
Anton, Greg 634
Antonasio, Larry 583
Antoniuk, Jeff 499, 553
Aplanalp, Richard 506, 507
Apostolic Family Chorus, The 155
Appell, Glen 496
Appelrouth, Scott 548
Appleby, Peter 73
Applewhite, Herman 125, 694
Applewhite, James 812
Applewhite, Little 193
Applewhite, Nate 97, 401, 419, 420, 541, 692
Aranoff, Kenny 359
Arceneaux, Cory 831
Arceneaux, Dalton 'Del' 11
Arceneaux, Fernest 11
Arceneaux, Floyd 47, 527
Arceneaux, Tony 657
Archer, Bernard 315
Archey, Jimmy 90, 255, 294, 381
Archia, Tom 1, 39, 245, 292, 321, 654, 779
Archibald [Leon T. Gross] 798, 803, 804
Archip, Dimitri 524
Ardoin, Alphonse 'Bois Sec' 11, 195, 762, 777, 831, 832
Ardoin, Amédé 12, 793, 831, 832
Ardoin, Chris 12, 13, 14, 832, 833
Ardoin, Dexter 13, 531
Ardoin, Erica 12
Ardoin, Gustav 11, 196, 531
Ardoin, Lawrence 'Black' 11, 13, 196, 777, 831
Ardoin, Morris 11, 195
Ardoin, Scott 29, 202
Ardoin, Sean 12, 13
Ardoin, Tony 14, 384
Ardoin, Trey 14
Ardoin, Vanessa 14
Ardoin II, Sean 14
Areas, Chepito 274
Arenas, Jan 66
Argo Singers, The 790
Ariyoshi, Sumito 141, 443
Arkadelphia 529
Arkansas Shorty 796
Arlet, Randy 649
Arlt, Andreas 17, 501
Arlt, Michael 17, 501
Armstead, Jo 185
Armstead, Jos[h?]ie 356
Armstead, Lester 685
Armstrong, Arthur 'Brother-in-Law' 757, 759
Armstrong, Danny 507
Armstrong, Gary 402
Armstrong, Howard 14, 88, 216, 424, 425, 792, 816
Armstrong, James 14, 659

Armstrong, Joe 761
Armstrong, Joshie 746
Armstrong, Lil 24, 80, 98, 287, 294, 311, 321, 637, 697
Armstrong, Louis 98, 223, 224, 255, 294, 321, 325, 336, 338, 390, 398, 537, 587, 592, 597, 607, 646, 679, 803, 805
Armstrong, Nate 368
Armstrong, Richard 169
Armstrong, Roland 424
Armstrong, Tippy 349, 350, 395
Armstrong, Tom 14, 425
Arnay, David 674
Arnett, Al 572
Arno, Victor 75
Arnold, Billy Boy 15, 54, 101, 138, 465, 707, 744, 745, 747, 768, 770, 771, 776, 779, 790, 822
Arnold, Chuck 554
Arnold, Harold 607
Arnold, Jason 424, 518, 539, 540, 609, 649
Arnold, Jeane 351
Arnold, Jerome 15, 52, 99, 164, 289, 481
Arnold, Jim 691
Arnold, Joe 238, 348, 350
Arnold, John 320
Arnold, Kokomo 16, 325, 618, 619, 697, 738, 742, 756, 767, 774, 794, 797, 812, 813
Arnold, Mac 272, 273, 604
Arnold, Pat 364
Arnold, Tom 45
Arnold, Wilbert 'Junk Yard Dog' 571, 730
Arnold Jr, Harold D. 406
Arnold Sr, Harold D. 406
Aronoff, Kenny 34
Arpino, André 458
Arrington, Tracy 564
Arrow, Andy 335
Arter, Bill 84
Arthur, Emry 810
Arthur, Theodore 357, 509
Artlip, Billy 58
Aruda, Scott 427, 536, 546, 549, 567, 636, 718, 719
Arvanitas, George 679
Arvans, James 164
Arvey, Steve 599
Arvizu Jr, Reynaldo 'Daddy Ray' 43
Asalé, Kotti 133
Asbell, Aimes 168
Asbell, Paul 266, 272, 273, 276, 282, 482
Ashby, Doug 195
Ashby, Harold 84, 95, 164, 165, 232, 283, 415, 457, 562, 725
Ashby, Irving 209, 292, 340, 355, 390, 449, 492
Ashby, Reggie 86, 523, 583
Ashe, Mark 414
Asherson, Rick 367

Ashford, Jack 681
Ashley, Clarence [Tom] 769, 772, 810
Ashley, Ernest 328, 661, 662
Ashley's Melody Men 772
Ashton, Bob 459
Ashton, Tony 231
Askew, Alec 762, 765, 812
Askew, Fleming 114
Aspery, Ron 372
Asselin, Brian 341
Atamanuik, Larry 368
Atcheson, Bob 472
Ateba, Sammy 5
Athas, Rocky 17, 65
Atkins, Alex 386, 387, 406, 454, 455, 480, 481, 500, 616
Atkins, Boyd 305, 417, 481, 662
Atkins, Chet 772, 798
Atkins, Poppy 262
Atkins, Stanley 232
Atkinson, Bill 328
Atkinson, Sweet Pea 198, 343, 624
Attenoux, Michel 77
Attle, George 107, 202, 203
Attorino, Ted 'Little T' 503
Attyberry, Harold 544
Audain, Courtney 361
Audel, Jean Pierre 193
Audet, Don 578
Auger, Brian 363
August, Joe 'Google Eyes' 800, 803, 804
August, Kent 202, 203, 383, 384
August, Lynn 831, 832, 833
Augusta, Cecil 762
Augustine, Kent Pierre 29
'Aurelia' 295
Austin, Bill 69
Austin, Charlie 206
Austin, Harold 650
Austin, Leon 783
Austin, Lovie 98, 141, 142, 294, 301, 537, 610, 685
Austin, Reneé 111
Austin, Sil 63
Austin, Tim 'Awesome' 125, 131, 330, 584, 735
Austin, William 338, 340
Autin, John G. 179, 502
Autrey, Herman 526
Autry, Gene 772, 773, 821
Avant, Robert 93
Avery, Charles 55, 320, 607, 626, 740, 741, 808
Avery, Elijah 105
Avery, Henry 687
Avery, Mike 324, 423, 584
Avilla, José 135
Ayers, Earl 'Little Joe' 346
Ayres, Leslie 63, 82, 300
Aziz, Saphena 413
B., Danny 583
B., Memphis Willie [Borum] 821

B. B. 761
B. B. & Group 739
B. B. & The Blues Shacks 17
Babasin, Harry 384, 661
Babb, Prince 446
Babbington, Ray 33
Babbit, Robert 'Bob' 681
Babbitt, Bob 629
Babcock, David 20
Babineaux, Curtis 214
Babineaux, Sidney 830, 831
Babko, Jeff 198
Baby Doo [Leonard Caston] 41, 743
Baby Duke 41
Babylon, Guy 359
Bach, Esben 53
Bachelor, Leroy 682
Back Porch Blues 18, 751
Back Porch Boys, The [Alec Seward & Louis Hayes] 765
Backbone Slip 18
Backman, Joacim 37
Backwards Sam Firk 18, 536
Bacon, Louis 587, 588
Bad Boys, The 81
Badanjek, John (The Bee) 350
Badau, Lee 44, 374
Badie, Peter 'Chuck' 26, 83, 391, 572, 661, 662
Badowski, 'Junior' 539, 540
Baer, Stuart 90
Bagby, Billy 639, 640
Bagby, Chuck 107
Bagby, Doc 639, 640
Bagge, Nigel 74
Baggott, John 97, 425, 728
Bagneris, Vernel 805
Bagsby, Jonathan 392
Bah, Hassan 36
Baietto, Mike 591
Bailey, Andy 4
Bailey, Beau 617
Bailey, Benny 510
Bailey, Buster 24, 80, 224, 237, 240, 287, 294, 311, 336, 426, 449, 526, 537, 587, 595, 597, 608, 637, 679
Bailey, Clarence 169
Bailey, Dave 81
Bailey, DeFord 18, 767, 768, 769, 793, 811
Bailey, June 'Bug' 787
Bailey, Kid 801
Bailey, Max 'Blues' 800
Bailey, 'Little Maxie' 821
Bailey, St Louis Red Mike 808, 815
Bailey, Mildred 827
Bailey, Rector 84, 662
Bailey, Richard 427
Bailey, Steve 34
Bailey, Wheeler 758
Bainbridge, Dave 32, 411, 555
Baines, Barbara 417
Bair-Bey, Vincent 1, 39, 83, 245

Baird, Joe 84
Baisden, Bernard 210, 440
Bak, Peter 8
Bakari-Badji 812
Baker, Abie 40, 81, 654
Baker, Bud 72
Baker, Cy 328
Baker, Dan 424
Baker, Dorothy 618, 774, 815, 828
Baker, Eddie 1
Baker, Etta 19, 751, 756, 786, 788
Baker, Harold 83, 295
Baker, Israel 686
Baker, James 254
Baker, James 'Iron Head' 757, 758, 759, 760
Baker, Katherine 815, 826
Baker, Ken 'Big Papa' 14, 196, 274, 341, 512, 544, 583, 703
Baker, Kevin 666
Baker, LaVern 777, 785, 799, 806, 829
Baker, Lee 541, 542
Baker, Leslie 164
Baker, Marilyn 508
Baker, Mickey 1, 19, 40, 77, 81, 84, 114, 115, 173, 174, 245, 295, 340, 416, 446, 458, 520, 638, 640, 713
Baker, Phil 18
Baker, Richard 578
Baker, Ronnie 356
Baker, Sam 222
Baker, Talmadge 507
Baker, Terry 496, 558, 673
Baker, Tom 143
Baker, Willie 20, 752, 755, 756, 767, 783, 797, 813
Baker Jr, Lee 389
Balakrishnan, David 145
Balcom, 'Rat-a-Tat' Pat 572
'Baldhead Pete' [Cleo Williams] 109, 330, 346, 474, 574, 622, 697
Baldry, Long John 20, 371
Baldwin, Dave 550, 711
Baldwin, Gary 425
Baldwin, John 174
Baldwin, Paul 27
Balfa, Christine 12, 161
Balfa, Dewey 831, 832
Balfa, Rodney 831
Balfa Brothers 831, 832
Balfa Toujours 805, 832
Balgochian, Albey 546
Balkisoon, Tyrone 396
Ball, Floyd 620
Ball, Leroy 14
Ball, Marcia 20, 68, 123, 139, 342, 516, 676, 776, 788, 805, 808, 830
Ball, Tom 21
Ball, Wilbur 772
Ballard, George 'Butch' 459, 670
Ballard, Hank 790
Ballard, Red 8, 328, 390

Ballard, Sam 760
Ballou, Classie 527, 783, 791
Ballou, Marty 239, 427, 492, 497, 525, 535, 548, 549, 560, 567, 728
Ballou Jr, Classie 117
Balls, Danny 153
Baltimore, Jesse 685
Bama [W. D. Stuart] 761, 762
Bamont, Johnny 43
Banbadawa, Muhamadu Sarki 810
Band, The 824
Bandanna Girls 796
Bandy, Frank 25, 396
Bangham, Kid 191, 497, 771, 825
Bangwell, Max 413
Banich, Francis 413
Bankert, Pete 370
Bankhead, Tommy 22, 816
Banks, Buddy 788, 800
Banks, Charles 193, 544
Banks, Chico 22, 443, 711
Banks, Clifton 347
Banks, Earl 'The Pearl' 54, 126
Banks, Ferdinand 712
Banks, Harold 544
Banks, Jackie 571
Banks, Jerry 572
Banks, Johnny 675
Banks, Kenneth 509, 672
Banks, L. V. 23
Banks, Louis P. 645
Banks, Martin 296, 363, 365, 672, 726
Banks, Paul 347
Banks, Robert 9, 40, 81, 334, 410, 500, 571, 586, 616, 620
Banks, Robin 433
Banks, Roy 707
Banks, Stanley 528
Banks, Verdun 712
Banks, Vernon 'Chico' 346, 561
Banning 625
Banzer, Russell 227
Baptiste, Dino 218
Baquet, George 587, 592
Bar, Big Ed 657
Bar-Kays, The 403
Baranco, Wilbert 252, 472, 593, 683
Baranowski, Bobby 17, 65, 433
Barard, David 135
Barbara & The Browns 780
Barbarin, Paul 24, 321, 607
Barbecue Bob 23, 737, 738, 756, 773, 774, 794, 810, 812, 813, 820
Barbee, John Henry 24, 748, 792, 814
Barbee, William 311, 551
Barber, Chris 53, 340, 431, 641
Barber, Eric 275
Barber, George 250
Barber, Jack 431
Barber, Mike 528, 541, 695, 711
Barber, Willie 564
Barber, Willy 43

INDEX

Barbour, Dave 292
Bard, Michael 336
Bare, Doug 429, 491, 544
Barefield, Eddie 326, 583, 592, 654
Barefoot Bill [Ed Bell] 767
Barenberg, Russ 58
Barfield, Bob 366
Barfield, Mike 148
Barge, Gene 42, 121, 233, 260, 450, 482, 553, 631, 632, 691, 711, 723
Barge, James [Gene?] 138
Bargeron, Dave 485
Bari, Choo 139
Barker, Danny 24, 25, 90, 140, 255, 805
Barker, Duke 77
Barker, Guy 53
Barker, Ken 57, 64, 345, 346, 405, 474, 499, 528, 561, 573, 630, 635, 669
Barker, Blue Lu 24, 827, 828, 829
Barker, Tino 66, 176, 324, 372, 567, 636
Barksdale, Everett 81, 295, 439, 685
Barlow, Barriemore 226
Barlow, Bruce 418
Barlow, Port 164
Barnacle, Gary 53
Barner, Wiley 737
Barnes, Alonzo 731
Barnes, Bruce 'Sunpie' 583
Barnes, Danny 310
Barnes, David 256, 665
Barnes, De Lloyd 311, 607
Barnes, Earl 24, 82
Barnes, Fred 160
Barnes, George 69, 157, 218, 326, 663, 682
Barnes, James 533
Barnes, Jeannie 505, 686
Barnes, Jeffrey 153
Barnes, John 343
Barnes, Reggie 236
Barnes, Roddy 2
Barnes, Roosevelt 'Booba' 25, 746
Barnett, Darius 'Third Leg' 395
Barnett, Louis 472, 479
Barney, Thomas 446
Barnicle, Norman 73
Barnum, Billy 624
Barnwell, Ysaye 2
Baron, Art 487, 624
Baron, Joey 314
Baron, Lisa 217
Baron, Phil 131, 462, 465
Baron, Ronnie 133
Barr, Al 726
Barr, Jerry 569
Barranco, Johnny 257
Barreda, Antonio de la 103, 104, 273, 458
Barrelhouse Annie 773, 774
Barrelhouse Chuck 25, 293, 464, 465, 479, 488, 599, 606, 607, 810
Barrelhouse Welch 787
Barrere, Paul 624

Barrero, Eddie 229
Barrett, Aston 'Familyman' 623
Barrett, Don 257
Barrett, Louis 713
Barretto, Michael 625
Barretto, Ray 81
Barri, Steve 48
Barrix, Billy 'Curley' 780
Barron, Ronnie 104, 429
Barrow, George 40
Barrow, Marlene 271
Barrow, Raymond 740, 741, 786, 807
Barry, Bryan 29, 199, 618
Barry, Joe 805
Barry, Kevin 427, 636
Barry, Michael 241
Barry, Stephen 675
Barsby, Jack 253
Bartee, Albert 543, 725
Bartee, Ellis 77, 510
Bartels, Peter 192, 540
Bartelstein, Todd 129
Barteta, Tom 583
Bartholomew, Dave 25, 140, 166, 307, 362, 391, 661, 662, 677, 678, 712, 799, 803, 804, 805
Bartholomew Jr, Herman J. 730
Bartley, Dallas 328, 338, 340, 459, 463, 473, 661, 662
Barton, Lou Ann 21, 26, 168, 564, 666
Barton, Slim 768
Bartz, Gary 233
Bascomb, Dud 81
Bascomb, Paul 1, 790, 800
Bascomb, Wilbur 357, 652
Basie, Count 292, 315, 353, 739, 741, 747, 797, 798, 808
Basile, Al 126, 548, 549
Bass, Fontella 401, 780
Bass, Gary 82
Bass, Jewell 257, 358, 401, 402
Bass, Lester 63, 300
Bass, Wally 657
Bassett, Bryan 491, 518
Bassett, Johnnie 27, 250
Bassett, Rip 537
Bastian, Antonin 4
Bastine, Volley 670
Bat The Humming Bird 807
Batalla, Perla 198
Batchelor, Leroy 454
Bate, Dr Humphrey 769
Bateman, Bill 630
Bateman, June 807
Bateman, Victor 65, 376
Bates, Dennis 576
Bates, Lefty 269, 270, 271, 541, 542, 610, 650
Bates', 'Mr 321
Bates, Vernon 662
Batista, Louis 125
Batiste, Alvin 530

Batiste, Johnny 489
Batiste, Larry 583
Batiste, Milton 173, 232, 648
Batiste, Russell 580
Batiz, Javier 104
Batteau, David 198
Battiste, Earl 83
Battiste, Harold 307, 391, 572
Battle, George 730
Battle, Joe Von 268, 751
Batts, Alan [Allen] 129
Batts, Allen 23, 92, 96, 125, 126, 129, 130, 134, 151, 171, 181, 217, 316, 330, 346, 411, 541, 563, 669, 670, 697, 706, 707
Batts, Will 343, 611, 792
Baty, Little Charlie 239, 399, 538, 654
Bauer, Andy 624
Bauer, Judah 94
Baulden, Lawrence 1, 720
Baum, Alex 496, 497
Baum, Charlie 515, 525, 735
Baum, Jeremy 151, 152, 195, 516, 517
Baum, Jim 197, 727
Bauma, Jimmy 412
Bauser, Gail 257
Bautista, Ronald 357
Baxter, Andrew 793, 810, 811, 816
Baxter, Helen 385
Baxter, Jim 793, 810, 811, 816
Baytop, Mike 546
Baze, George 465, 528, 581, 746, 747, 771
Bazilian, Eric 624
Bazz, Johnny 538
BB Queen 830
Beacham, Rufus 650
Beadle, Bud 363, 364, 603
Beaker, Norman 32, 411, 555
Beal, Eddie 292, 432, 492
Beal, Steve 630
Beale Street Sheiks 795
Beale, Calvin 540
Beaman [Kimbrough], Lottie 786, 794, 827
Bean, Robi 464
Beane, Reggie 685
Beard, Chris 27
Beard, Joe 27, 36
Bearden, Michael 376
Bears, Bruce 539, 540
Beasley, Helen 828
Beasley, John 376
Beasley, Julian 265, 693
Beasley, Good Rockin' Sam 783
Beasley, Walter 291, 292, 689, 693, 694, 768, 810, 812, 813
Beasly, Jimmy 517
Beau Jocque 28, 805, 831, 832, 833
Beauregard, Nathan 802
Beauregard, Pierre 484
Beausoleil 805, 831, 832
Beavers, Dale 153, 347
Beavis, Ray 53

Bechamin, Morris 362, 531
Bechet, Sidney 140, 224, 294, 325, 390, 398, 426, 596, 597, 679, 700, 702, 805
Bechtel, Perry 219
Beck 824
Beck, Don E. 583, 584
Beck, Blind James 2
Beck, Jeff 234, 669, 737, 767, 813, 824
Beck, Jimmy 47, 786
Beck, Johnny 752, 818, 819
Beck, Johnny (The Blind Boy) 753
Beck, Leon 414, 504
Beck, Peter 231, 676
Beck, Ron E. 100, 111, 273, 583, 584
Beck, Roscoe 21, 196, 197, 198, 502, 666
Beckerman, Peter 156
Beckers, Lazy Lew 301
Beckett, Barry 6, 209, 238, 282, 349, 350
Beckett, Harold 371, 372, 457
Becky, Son 795, 818
Beconcini, Danny 100, 583, 584
Bedard, George 479
Bedrosian, Al 'Bedrock' 413, 594
Beecham, Charles 733
Beecher, Kid 796
Behne, Peter 17
Behr, Steve 742
Behrendson, Doc 712
Behrens, Stanley 104, 164
Beighton, Steve 237
Belanger, Michelle 81
Belcher, Charles 69
Belfour, Robert 29, 251, 756, 810
Belgrave, Marcus 114, 115, 116, 359, 479
Bell, Aaron 81, 245, 294
Bell, Alfred 69, 326, 452
Bell, Arthur 758
Bell, Carey 29, 32, 33, 35, 64, 74, 101, 121, 125, 126, 165, 183, 184, 187, 188, 265, 266, 272, 284, 375, 412, 417, 423, 456, 457, 483, 500, 557, 558, 614, 617, 630, 632, 744, 745, 749, 750, 768, 770, 771, 776, 779, 781, 788, 822
Bell, Charles 20
Bell, Dan 660
Bell, Earl 764, 802
Bell, Ed 'Barefoot Bill' 31, 737, 767, 786, 794, 810
Bell, Eddy 125
Bell, Gary 507
Bell, George 102, 595, 596
Bell, Graeme 72
Bell, Herman 84
Bell, J. C. 620
Bell, James 30, 32, 165, 411, 664
Bell, Jimmy 114, 115
Bell, John 86
Bell, Joseph 415
Bell, K. D. 325
Bell, Leard 307, 504, 505, 520, 651
Bell, Lurrie 30, 31, 63, 96, 101, 125, 163, 165, 411, 412, 584, 614, 617, 664, 744, 768, 781
Bell, Mark 578
Bell, Ollan Christopher 275
Bell, Richard 51, 195, 369, 370, 491, 540
Bell, Rick 368
Bell, Roger 72
Bell, Steve 30, 32, 411, 412, 528, 664
Bell, T. D. 33, 296, 751, 825
Bell, Tom 760, 761
Bell, Tyson 30, 32, 165, 411
Bell, Warren 76, 114, 115, 166, 531
Bell Jr, Carey 30
Bellas, Norm 43
Belle, Laval 342, 343
Belleau, Chris 79
Bellini, Dan 443
Belote, Doug 503, 571, 731
Below, Fred 1, 10, 20, 62, 66, 67, 79, 125, 164, 165, 185, 209, 217, 233, 265, 271, 283, 289, 290, 299, 306, 307, 323, 335, 341, 383, 387, 403, 404, 405, 406, 415, 419, 455, 480, 481, 486, 557, 562, 577, 581, 601, 603, 614, 617, 620, 621, 629, 631, 632, 651, 693, 694, 725
Below, Sonny 374
Belton, John 13
Belton, Larry 244
Belvin, Jesse 447, 782, 785, 788
Belz, Kevin 691
Benay, Ben 48, 210, 357, 679
Bender, D. C. 782
Benford, Bill 685
Benjamin, Bill 26, 321, 322, 713
Benjamin, William 'Benny' 245, 269, 271
Benner, Jimmy 84
Bennett, Alvino 1, 231, 556, 733
Bennett, Buster 33, 69, 128, 221, 326, 682
Bennett, Daryl 20
Bennett, Don 21
Bennett, Duster 33, 175, 228, 356, 372, 457, 768
Bennett, Harold 133, 556
Bennett, Jim 216
Bennett, Max 48, 679
Bennett, Mickey 'Tickey' 552, 553, 643
Bennett, Richard 679
Bennett, Stella Sutton 34
Bennett, Wayne 47, 95, 139, 176, 185, 233, 273, 306, 307, 432, 439, 509, 542, 562, 610, 648, 686, 814
Benny, Johnny 695
Benoit, Cleveland 757, 760
Benoit, Felix James 118, 119
Benoit, James 489
Benoit, Johnny 200
Benoit, Russell 489
Benoit, Tab 34, 151, 152, 262, 370, 491, 649, 695, 824, 825
Benskin, Sammy 84, 473, 741
Benson, Gail 275
Benson, James 686

Bentley, Gladys 35
Benton, Buster 35, 64
Benton, Leon 3
Bentsi-Enchill, Kofi 36
Berdoll [Bordeau?], Kenny 5
Berfect, Sammy 179, 362, 681, 730
Berg, George 81, 654
Berg, Kurt 64
Berg, Lee 50
Berg, Peter 273
Bergen, Richard van 591
Berger, Bucky 65, 238, 376
Berger, Dave 273
Berkin, Herman 595
Berkin, Julius 595
Berlin, Jeremy 291
Berlin, Steve 87, 191, 274, 559, 673
Berline, Byron 21, 22
Bermudes, Randy 293, 464, 735
Bermudez, Carlos 164
Bernal, Gil 510
Bernard, Jimmy 38
Bernard, Rod 780
Bernard, Rodney 193
Bernardi, Noni 8, 328, 390
Bernardi, Sonny 169, 170, 368
Bernhardt, Clyde 245, 327, 328
Bernhardt, Warren 2, 50, 51, 679
Bernstein, Artie 142
Berosh, Slim Bob 291
Berry, Al 249, 668, 669
Berry, Brooks 46
Berry, Charles 479, 480, 758
Berry, China 41
Berry, Chu 24, 526, 575, 587, 588
Berry, Chuck 739, 779, 780, 799, 813
Berry, Cleophus 385
Berry, Emmett 328, 724
Berry, Ian 274
Berry, Justin 513
Berry, Nelson 455
Berry, Richard 307, 507, 508, 785
Berry, Robert 424
Berry, Steve 345, 591, 632
Berry, Walter 489
Bertagna, Massimo 670
Bertolucci, Parris 14
Bertram, Cuje 816
Bertrand, Jimmy 48, 69, 537, 549, 626
Besman, Bernie 267, 269
Besselieu, Hannah 758, 760
Bessemer Singers, The 587, 588
Best, Clifton 245
Best, Denny 377, 491, 518
Best, Denzil 227, 291, 292
Best, Gareth 479, 598
Best, John 356, 395
Best, Skeeter 81, 521
Besterman, Little Paul 38
Betters, Harold 789
Bettle, Pete 424
Betts, Dickey 275

INDEX

Betts, Tim 118
'Betty' 506
Bevard, Sylvester 426
Beyer, Ed 77, 104
Bhatt, V. M. 624
Bibb, Eric 36, 824
Bibb, Leonard 292
Bibb, Matilda Mandolina 37
Bibbs, Kevin 41, 540
Bibbs, Leonard 551
Bickham, Pat 79
Biddleville Quintette 810
Bidgood, John E. 182
Bidwell, Dave 34
Biedron, Chris 421
Bierman, Ben 133
Big Bad Smitty 37
Big Bill [Ellis?] 414
Big Bo 404
Big Bones 526
'Big Boy' 757, 765
'Big Chief Drumstick' [Keef Hartley] 175
'Big Dez' Baby Orchestra, The [Dez Desormeaux] 478
Big Doowopper, The 781
Big Guitar Red [Walter Smith] 345
Big Jim 169
Big Joe Louis 38, 513, 538
'Big Louisiana' [Rodney Mason] 763
Big Maceo 38, 66, 69, 218, 627, 716, 737, 738, 739, 740, 741, 742, 743, 744, 751, 752, 788, 797, 798
Big Maybelle 39, 738, 780, 799
Big Rhythm Combo 40
Big Three Trio 41, 743, 779, 798
Big Time Sarah 32, 41, 57, 125, 617, 744, 781, 829, 830
Big Tiny 129
Big Twist 42, 776
Bigard, Barney 287, 311, 322, 328, 426, 597
Bigeou, Esther 42
Bigger, Greg 567
Biggs, Howard 81, 654
Biggs, Rayse 499
Bihlman, Jeff 'Jabo' 569
Bihlman, Scott 'Little' 569
Bikidude 625
Biles, Brant 535
'Bill' 609
Bill, James 531
Bill, Keta 558
Biller, David Leroy 148
Billings, John 135
Billington, Scott 28, 117, 161, 162, 299, 342, 395, 406, 489, 490, 548, 718
Billups, Viola 34
'Billy' 531
Binder, Dennis 659, 660, 790
Binder, Marty 127, 130, 468, 553, 607, 612, 698

Bingham, Bob 374
Bingham, Charlie 6, 599, 600
Bingham, Mark 571
Bingham, Robert 284
Bingham, Thomas 126, 158, 366, 572, 731
Binkley, Jimmy 779
Biondi, Remo 541, 542, 620
Birch, Bob 359
Birch, Dudley 513
Birch, Dyan 53
Birch, Gaylord 76, 274
Birch, Mike 535
Bird, Andrew 706
Bird, Billy 755, 795
Bird, Keith 458
Bird, Tim 194
Birdlegs & Pauline 789
Birdsong, Jimmy 783
Birdsong, Larry 783, 786
Birgui, Gonga Sarki 810
Birmingham Jug Band 42, 775
Birnbaum, Mike 397
Bisesi, Brian 236, 299, 325, 411, 477
Bisetti, Victor 274, 488
Bisharat, George 674
Bishop, Bonnie 21
Bishop, Dave 53
Bishop, Duffy 43, 613, 751
Bishop, Elvin 43, 52, 99, 119, 138, 273, 275, 516, 598, 599, 629, 653, 735, 750, 776, 814, 825
Bishop, Joe 150, 221
Bishop, John 401
Bishop, Matt 411
Bishop, Terrance 80
Bishop, Walter 472, 551
Biskis, Tauras 291
Bitelli, Dave 217
Bittker, Danny 496, 729
Bizor, Billy 279, 281, 282
Bjerre, Nikolaj 579
Black, Bill 374, 414, 464, 599
Black, Billy 464
Black, Bobby 613
Black, Lewis 793
Black, Michael 497
Black, Sonny 44
Black, Tony 375
Black, Willie 10, 32, 217, 409, 470, 520, 598, 617
Black Ace 44, 777, 812, 813, 817, 821
Black Bob 69, 88, 185, 218, 240, 259, 320, 326, 436, 437, 452, 626, 682, 692
Black Boy Shine 45, 181, 737
Black Diamond [James Butler] 753, 782, 826
Black Ivory King 740, 808, 817
Blackburn, Cliff 260
Blackjacks, The 45
Blackman, Douglas 446
Blackman, Junior 165, 289, 412, 434, 601
Blackman, Tewee 450, 451

Blackmon, Junior 571
Blackmore, Ritchie 767
Blacknell Jr, Geno [Ellis] 674
Blackwell, Bumps 805
Blackwell, Charles 363, 365, 492, 623
Blackwell, Chuck 623
Blackwell, Scrapper 45, 88, 106, 107, 167, 220, 255, 700, 738, 767
Blackwell, Willie '61' 46, 758, 762
Blade, Brady 37
Blades, Jesse 570
Blair, Leonard 242
Blair, Sunny 753, 768
Blake, Adam 396
Blake, Al 47, 123, 124, 261
Blake, Alex 445
Blake, Curtis 612
Blake, Eubie 293
Blake, Franchot 408
Blake, Ginger 48
Blake, Sonny 768, 822
Blake, Thomas 392
Blakey, Art 158
Blanchard, Edgar 26, 83, 114, 140, 232, 393, 529, 752, 768, 803, 805, 819
Blanchard, Nelson 583
Blanchard, Jean Pierre 831
Bland, Bobby 'Blue' 47, 221, 360, 753, 797, 802, 803
Bland, Milton 233
Blank, Stu 111, 488
Blazer Boy [George Stevenson] 805
Bledsoe, Country Jim 752, 754, 803
Blevins, Kenneth 566
Blevins, Kenny 76, 179, 362
Blevins, Leo 158, 354, 650, 654
Blind Blake 48, 105, 224, 301, 537, 549, 602, 737, 738, 755, 756, 767, 794, 797, 810
Blind Boys Of Alabama, The 487, 488
Blind Joe 760, 761
Blind Mack 809
Blind Mississippi Morris 49
Blind Pete 759
Blisterstring 50
Blivens, Clifford 447, 826
Bloch, René 504, 507, 508
Block, Billy 402
Block, Dan 485
Block, Rory 2, 50, 139, 788, 825, 830
Blondell, Jon 11, 21, 26, 431, 658
Bloodworth, Oklin 721
Bloom, Micky 336
Bloom, Rube 134
Bloomfield, Michael 52, 99, 188, 237, 238, 387, 467, 482, 486, 494, 536, 709, 812
Blough, Billy 652, 653
Blouin, Carl 359, 362, 531
Blouin, Larry 429
Blouin Sr, Carl A. 472
Blount, Herman 'Sonny' 244

Blovin, Carl 76
Blowers, Johnny 255
Blue, Elisha 101
Blue, Leon 241, 351, 422, 659
Blue, Sammy 685
Blue Boys, The [Nap Hayes & Matthew Prater] 816
Blue Jays, The 779
Blue Junction 53
Blue Ridge Ramblers 772, 792
Blue Smitty 752, 779
Bluebloods, The 252
Bluefish, The 291
Blues Band, The 53, 813
Blues Birdhead 768, 769, 793
Blues Boys, The [Alec Seward & Louis Hayes] 752, 755
Blues Busters, The 54
Blues Harp Meeting 750
Blues Imperials, The 745, 750, 776, 825
Blues Man, The 788
Blues Rockers 770
Blues Swingers, The 25
Blues Woman', 'The [Marion Abernathy] 788, 798
Bluestone, Harry 75, 210
Blumberg, Seth 374
Blunston, David 438
Blunt, Hillary 764
Blythe, Arthur 133
Blythe, Hilary 237
Blythe, Jimmy 45, 48, 224, 259, 320, 347, 475, 537, 549, 597, 610, 739, 740
Bo, Eddie 222, 265, 780, 805
Bo Diddley 54, 136, 403, 739, 744, 779, 780, 799
Bo-Ettes 55
Boals, Richard 55
Board, Johnny 47, 77, 352, 353, 354, 355, 456, 510
Boardman, Billy 369
Boatman, Bill 623
Boaz, Gregory 408
Bob, Joseph 214
Bob & Leroy 757
Bobisuthi, Jim 613
Bobo, Bradley 417
Bocage, Charles 42
Bocage, Eddie 222, 265, 780, 805
Bocage, Peter 42
Bock, Andreas 17, 501
Boddington, Steve 284
Bodin, Eddie 29, 383
Bodner, Larry 170
Bodner, Phil 81
Boe, Peter 143, 547, 564, 655
Bogan, Lucille 55, 559, 628, 701, 738, 774, 794, 820, 826, 827, 828
Bogan, Ted 14, 88, 425, 792, 816
Bogart, Deanna 742, 830
Bogart, Peter 223
Bøgelund, Nikolai 8

Bøgelund, Rasmus 8
Bogert, Fred 503
Boggs, Dock 762, 765, 772
Boghossian, Samuel 210
Bohanon, George 351, 357, 358, 430, 551
Bohman, Jenny 36
Bohn, Mark 16, 293
Boines, Houston 753
Boines, Sylvester 125, 160, 165, 317, 447, 500, 563, 733
Bokes, Warren 531
Bolar, Abe 60, 326, 327, 328, 526, 661
Bolden, James 358, 359, 820
Bolder, Frank 120, 152, 612
Bolds, Ollie 127
Boler, Lemon 140
Bolin, Johnny 17
Boling, Arnold 63
Bollin, Zuzu 818, 820
Bolling, Pillie 31, 767
Bolten, Hattie 829
Bolton, Dupree 315
Bolton, Happy 537
Bon, Ross 598
Bona, Tom 195
Bonadio, Joe 636
Bond, Debbie 367
Bond, Jimmy 266, 278, 281, 282, 640, 641, 642, 643, 708, 709, 710, 725, 726
Bond, Raymond 438
Bond, Robert 237
Bondarenko, Leif 404
Bonds, Gary 'US' 803
Bonds, Son 56, 187, 769
Bondy, Gavin 43
Bone, Ponty 502
Boner, Harold 565
Boner, James 565
Bones, Jimmy 365
Bones, Mickey 291, 427
Bongo Joe 777
Bonham, Vincent 359, 666
Bonner, Floyd 364
Bonner, Juke Boy 56, 749, 753, 777, 784, 800, 823
Bonner, Lee 6
Bonnie Lee 57, 345, 420, 474, 617, 770, 829, 830
Bono, Laurie 522
Bonseigneur, Suzanne 580
Bont, Arthur 591
Bonta, Peter 644
Bonzo Dog Band 739
Boogie Woogie Boys, The 741, 808
Boogie Woogie Red 267, 268, 269, 532, 681, 779, 809
Boogie Woogie Trio, The 739, 740, 741
Book Binder, Roy 57
Booker, Arthur 58
Booker, Bea 414
Booker, Benny 444, 724
Booker, Charley 753

Booker, Charlie 802
Booker, Connie Mack 47, 133, 352, 353, 354, 509
Booker, David 657
Booker, James 58, 178, 362, 363, 391, 429, 679, 742, 805
Booker, Joe 713
Booker, Marion 521
Booker, Melvin 673, 730
Booker Orchestra 797, 816
Boone, Chester 315, 526, 533
Boone, Chris 503
Boone, Claude 773
Boone, Donnie 673
Boone, George 424
Boone, Harvey 249
Boone, Theodore 247
Boorman, Dave 271
Booth, Chick 663
Booze, Wee Bea 60, 526, 806, 827
Boozier, Henry 77, 352, 353, 354, 355, 713
Borak, Kenny 409
Borbridge, Stuart 439
Borden, Jim 593
Bording, Ben 538
Borenius, King Louis 45
Boris, Bill 543
Borowiecki, Teddy 20
Borum, Memphis Willie 60, 821
Bosch, Bill 583
Boscia, Monica 155
Boss, Mickey 15
Boss, Pete 'Guitar' 97, 217
Bostic, Earl 73, 140, 785, 798
Bostrom, Figge 37
Boswell, Robert 543, 650
Boswell, Steve 245, 415
Bott, Jimi 16, 123, 124, 164, 191, 293, 417, 522, 557, 583
Boublitz, Bill 197
Bouchard, Sweet William 231
Boucher, Dominic 85
Boucher, Jessica 235, 375, 575
Bouchillon, Mr & Mrs Chris 772
Boudreau, Jim 80, 464, 489, 533, 629
Boudreaux, Jeff 4
Boudreaux, John 59, 529, 572
Boudreaux, Lynn 118
Boudreaux, 'Big Chief' Monk 35, 503, 806
Boudreaux, Ronnie 107
Boudreaux, Roosevelt 182, 583
Boulware, Will 356
Bourne, Lisa 60
Boutté, Teedy 472
Bouwmeester, Arend 120, 612
Bowden, Grace 441, 443
Bowden, Mwata 440
Bowden, Norman 517
Bowden, Ralph 39, 517
Bowe, Kevin 111, 375
Bowen, Bill 315

Bowen, Larry 632
Bowens, Sir Harry 343, 359, 624
Bowens Jr, Harry 666
Bowers, Jamie 274
Bowers, John 509
Bowie, Byron 318, 632
Bowie, Larry 654
Bowler, Phillip 282
Bowles, Charles 355
Bowles, Leonard 812
Bowles, Thomas 'Beans' 681
Bowman, Betty May 757
Bowman, Ed 374
Bowman, Priscilla 790, 799
Bowman, Ralph 517
Bown, Patti 662
Bowser, Erbie 33, 296
Boxall, Allen 613
Boy, Andy 60, 533
Boy Blue 761, 762, 802
Boyack, Pat 21, 61, 123
Boyce, R. L. 243, 251, 499, 664
Boyd, Eddie 39, 61, 218, 419, 651, 685, 716, 740, 743, 744, 747, 748, 749, 778, 779, 785, 797, 799
Boyd, Georgia 579, 815
Boyd, Gregory 502
Boyd, Louis 'Little' 599
Boyd, Raymond 320, 439
Boyd, Red 753
Boyd, Reggie 146, 233, 265, 415, 557, 562
Boyd, Susan 417
Boyer, Elinor 757, 762
Boyette, Mike 186
Boykin, Brenda 263, 293, 496
Boykins, Randall 599
Boyle, Mike 591
Boyson, Cornelius 550, 632, 733
Boze, Calvin 798
Bozzio, Terry 502, 669
Bracey, Ishman 62, 330, 767, 792, 794, 801, 802, 821
Bracken, Warren 438
Bracy, Mississippi 738, 801
Bradbury, Scott 141
Bradford, Alex 788
Bradford, Frankie 269
Bradford, James 55
Bradford, Kirtland 661, 662
Bradford, Milt 686
Bradford, Perry 294, 595, 679, 720
Bradford, Rollo 579
Bradford, Tom 737
Bradford, Walter 789
Bradfute, George 126, 222
Bradix, Charley 752, 753, 819
Bradley, Herman 245
Bradley, Jan 780
Bradley, Jesse 757, 758, 760
Bradley, John L. 476
Bradley, Johnny 210, 433, 434, 479
Bradley, Keith 200

Bradley, Marie 190
Bradley, Oscar Lee 88, 89, 292, 460, 593, 647, 677, 678
Bradley, Owen 295
Bradley, Rockin' 807
Bradley, Sam 600
Bradley, Tommie 45, 127, 774, 816
Bradley, Will 83, 741
Bradshaw, Jim 'Supe' 506, 507
Bradshaw, Tiny 62, 773, 774, 785, 797, 798, 799
Brady, Avery 'Abe' 541, 764, 822
Brady, Denis 665
Brady, Floyd 526
Brady, Robert 661, 662
Bragason, Halldór 'Blue Ice' 160, 515
Bragg, Billy 242
Brailey, Jerome 'Bigfoot' 518
Brake, Brian 50, 445
Bramhall, Doyle 21, 668
Bramhall II, Doyle 122, 168, 359
Bramhall, Ronnie 332
Bramlett, Bekka 235, 375
Bramlett, Randall 238
Bramwell, Randy 717, 718
Branch, Ben 352, 353, 354, 401
Branch, Billy 30, 32, 36, 57, 63, 66, 67, 91, 96, 107, 126, 164, 260, 318, 344, 345, 368, 443, 474, 476, 491, 527, 528, 557, 563, 568, 599, 614, 622, 632, 688, 692, 723, 733, 770, 771
Branch, J. Plunky 242
Branch, Russell 111, 229
Branchettes 786
Brandl, Stefan 660
Brandon, Gene 501, 502
Brandon, Mary-Ann 335, 377, 496
Brandon, Skeeter 81, 127
Brandye 350
Brannon, Teddy 683
Brantley, Junior 666
Brantley & Williams 797
Brasch, Paul 64
Brashear, George 293, 294, 460, 469, 597, 685
Brashear, Oscar 357, 551
Brasseaux, Darrel 539
Brassfield, Herschel 596, 685, 718
Brasswell, Frank 68, 191, 797
Braud, Wellman 24, 80, 224, 287, 294, 311, 322, 526, 575
Brauer, Adam 342
Braun, Mark [Mr B] 204
Braunagel, Tony 123, 235, 342, 343, 359, 430, 468, 469, 518, 563, 624, 625
Brauner, Morten 53
Bray, John 760
Breau, Denny 265, 491, 516
Breaux, Cleoma 831
Breaux, Leroy 351
Breaux, Pat 21, 118, 383, 384
Brechtlein, Tom 196, 197, 198

Breckenridge, Saylor 513
Brecker, Randy 358
Breeding, Boo 790
Breelove, Don 612
Breezer, Larry 155
Brendle, Ron 423
Brennan, Bill 341
Brennan, Pat 465, 613, 714
Brenston, Jackie 232, 265, 562, 659, 660, 773, 779, 798, 820
Brent, Royal 650
Brethes, Dominic 217
Bretton, Elise 295
Brewer, Annie 760, 821
Brewer, Burton 607
Brewer, Chris 721
Brewer, Clarence 64
Brewer, Fannie 822
Brewer, Blind James 64, 782, 822
Brewer, Jamie 341
Brewer Group, James 822
Brewster, Roy 663
Brewster, Steve 503
Brice, Percy 670, 671
Brickey, Evelyn 828
Bridges, Curley 65
Bridges, Eugene 'Hideaway' 65
Bridges, Henry 292, 384
Bridges, Lucius 178, 764
Bridges, Willie 238, 363, 365
Bridges Jr, Henry 384
Bridgewater, Joe 83, 114, 115, 662, 670, 686
Briers, Larry 595
Briggs, Billy 773
Briggs, David 458
Briggs, Ian 319, 546, 547
Briggs, Leonard 315
Brigham, Dave Froebel 684
Bright, Alphonso 684
Bright, Cornelius 766
Bright, Dalbert 311
Bright, Delbert 7, 8
Bright, Harry James 370
Bright Light Quartet 763
Brignac, Brian 118, 634
Brill, Bob 665
Brill, Tom 'Mookie' 66, 423
Brim, Grace 39, 66, 620, 744, 751, 752, 768, 785
Brim, John 39, 66, 348, 423, 541, 542, 620, 744, 747, 751, 752, 779, 785
Brim Jr, John 66
Brimfield, Bill 550
Brimlee, 'Wild' William 177
Brimm, Tom 'The Stomp' 654, 655
Brinlee, Willie 16, 123, 720
Brinson, Ted 432, 492, 686
Brion, John 624
Brisbois, Bud 210
Brisbon, Reginald 559
Briscoe, Dan 248

Briseno, Modesto 100
Britches, Tater 476
Britt, Bob 135
Britt, Kenneth 694
Brittain, John 495
Britten, Joe 1
Britton, Ellen 823
Britton, Joe 39, 244, 245, 300
Britton, Maynard 821
Broad, Graham 372
Broadhead, Bobby 444
Broadis, Blakey 712
Broadnax, Dwayne 'Cook' 134, 612
Broadnax, Othar 764
Broadus, Walker 620
Brock, Big George 66
Brock, Jim 423
Brocken, Warren 661, 662
Brockenborough, Purcell 61, 455, 654
Brockett, Tim 291
Brodely, Rae 84, 459
Broek, Nicholas ten 342, 484
Bromberg, Bruce 14, 408, 417, 427, 673, 675
Bromberg, David 50, 578
Bromley, Kyril 238, 410
Bronze, Dave 36, 37, 122
Bronze, Kate 36
Brooker, Gary 824
Brookes, Robert C. 217
Brooklyn Slim [Paul Oscher] 133
Brookmeyer, Bob 115
Brooks, Billy 114
Brooks, Bobby 155
Brooks, Christy 1
Brooks, David 245, 344, 543, 650
Brooks, David 'Bubba' 439
Brooks, Dennis 543, 650
Brooks, Ed 'Skippy' 434, 715
Brooks, Essie Mae 756, 757, 786
Brooks, Gene 81, 141, 211, 250, 446, 638, 640
Brooks, George 291
Brooks, Glenn 114, 115
Brooks, Hadda 258, 798, 826
Brooks, Harold 650
Brooks, Harry 461, 718
Brooks, Harvey 52, 191, 596, 673
Brooks, James 410
Brooks, Juanita 688, 730
Brooks, Julius 227
Brooks, Julius 'Billy' 340
Brooks, Junior 753
Brooks, Big Leon 67, 745, 771, 782
Brooks, Lonnie 67, 323, 581, 614, 632, 644, 676, 691, 707, 745, 750, 768, 776, 790
Brooks, Louis 799
Brooks, Michael 'Fly' 43
Brooks, Quanda 402
Brooks, Reg 34
Brooks, Ronnie Baker 68, 707

Brooks, Samuel 758, 810
Brooks, Sarah 51
Brooks, Shelton 426
Brooks, Skippy 47
Brooks, Sterling 714
Brooks, Stuart 175
Brooks, Wesley 245
Broonzy, Big Bill 68, 88, 128, 167, 185, 191, 218, 227, 259, 287, 320, 326, 333, 407, 452, 500, 616, 682, 692, 715, 716, 737, 738, 739, 742, 743, 744, 747, 762, 767, 768, 773, 774, 788, 793, 794, 797, 810, 820, 822
'Brother' [Muddy Waters] 603
Brotherton, Rich 21
Brotman, Stuart 103
Broughton, Dennis 118, 119, 673
Brouse, Roger 272
Broussard, Allen 'Cat Roy' 489, 490
Broussard, Austin 394
Broussard, Bobby 13, 161, 384
Broussard, John 431
Broussard, Jules 246, 507
Broussard, Kevin 107, 108
Broussard, Linton 108
Broussard, Mike 107
Broussard, Shelton 161
Broussard, Tony 429
Broussard, Troy 696
Brousse, Fred 670
Browder, Sally 95
Brown, —— 438
Brown, Ada 827, 829
Brown, Al 528, 584
Brown, Alberta 826
Brown, Alex 343, 351, 551
Brown, Alexander 707
Brown, Andrew 745, 790
Brown, Andy 458
Brown, Angela 73
Brown, Anthony 730, 731
Brown, Arelean 778
Brown, B. [Daniel] 800, 807
Brown, Ben 86, 145, 523
Brown, Benny 344
Brown, Bertram 4, 126, 366, 572, 600, 657, 711, 731
Brown, Bertrand 468
Brown, Bessie 707, 827
Brown, Bill 281, 282, 520, 577
Brown, Bobby 78, 784
Brown, Bowen 274, 275, 369, 690
Brown, Buster 74, 456, 760, 761, 780, 788, 789
Brown, Buzz 231, 676
Brown, Charles 74, 238, 239, 266, 274, 293, 295, 505, 506, 508, 679, 740, 784, 788, 797, 798, 799, 805, 808, 818, 826, 830
Brown, Charlie 81
Brown, Chris 'Stovall' 433
Brown, Mrs Christine 747

Brown, Chuck [Bernard 'King Karl' Jolivette] 783
Brown, Clarence 'Gatemouth' 77, 84, 140, 160, 530, 538, 767, 768, 776, 788, 798, 805, 818, 819, 820, 824, 825, 826
Brown, Cleo 739, 740, 741
Brown, Daniel 48
Brown, Dave 152
Brown, David 540
Brown, Dennis 675
Brown, Donnie 201
Brown, Dusty 323, 771, 778
Brown, Earl 114, 208, 209, 826
Brown, Edgar 245
Brown, Elgie 787
Brown, Elijah 764, 814
Brown, Elmer 316
Brown, Erica 657
Brown, Estelle 679
Brown, Frank 315
Brown, Freddie 786, 787
Brown, Freddy 828
Brown, Gabriel 79, 752, 755, 757, 761, 762, 767, 806, 813
Brown, Garnett 356, 357, 483, 679, 727
Brown, Gary 690
Brown, George 244, 296, 664
Brown, Sweet Georgia 526
Brown, Greg 229
Brown, Hash 25, 172, 433, 434, 534, 717
Brown, Henry 149, 315, 325, 471, 500, 655, 697, 740, 741, 786, 815
Brown, 'Hi' Henry 337, 815
Brown, Herman 537, 626, 634
Brown, Herman 'Rat' 87
Brown, Hillard 41, 473, 565
Brown, Homer 78
Brown, Honey 800, 806
Brown, Ike 447, 517
Brown, Irving 'Skinny' 338
Brown, J. T. 'Nature Boy' 61, 79, 164, 289, 305, 306, 307, 386, 404, 500, 526, 557, 576, 610, 616, 620, 662, 682, 790, 800
Brown, James 715, 789
Brown, Jimmy 709, 822
Brown, Jimmy Earl 713
Brown, Joe 320, 526, 715
Brown, Joe Washington 758, 760
Brown, John 244, 291, 292
Brown, Johnnie 800
Brown, Johnnie Mae 712
Brown, Johnny 460, 509
Brown, Judson 2, 325, 808
Brown, Judy 429
Brown, Karen 402
Brown, Keith 825
Brown, Kenny 78, 80, 94, 95, 153, 251, 337, 347, 513
Brown, Kerry 176, 232, 365, 469, 470
Brown, Kevin 296
Brown, Kid 793

Brown, Kim 81
Brown, Lattimore 783
Brown, Lawrence 663
Brown, Lee 74, 80, 187, 480, 522, 740, 744, 769, 774, 796
Brown, Leroy 125
Brown, Lois 193, 251, 341
Brown, Lorenzo 499
Brown, Lowdown 820
Brown, Lucien 537
Brown, Mark 97
Brown, Maureen 687
Brown, Mel 26, 48, 80, 130, 139, 266, 273, 293, 302, 357, 464, 489, 533, 612, 629, 658, 679, 687
Brown, Michael 'Downtown' 729
Brown, Milton 772, 793
Brown, Myrtle 336
Brown, Nadine 518
Brown, Nappy 81, 136, 423, 799
Brown, Olive 829
Brown, Oliver 417, 741, 808
Brown, Olivia 296
Brown, Ora 190
Brown, Othum 403, 743
Brown, Paulette 358
Brown, Peggy 657
Brown, Pete 140, 173, 174, 176, 221, 291, 292, 424, 526, 663, 797
Brown, Piney 82, 650
Brown, Ray 338, 358
Brown, Reneé [sic] 79
Brown, Rich 760
Brown, Richard 286
Brown, Richard 'Rabbit' 82, 803, 811
Brown, Rodney 'Hot Rod' 41, 192, 540
Brown, Ron 679
Brown, Ronnie 209
Brown, Roosevelt 231
Brown, Roy 82, 506, 773, 774, 785, 798, 800, 803, 804
Brown, Rufus 467
Brown, Russell 74
Brown, Ruth 76, 83, 135, 358, 516, 773, 777, 788, 798, 799, 806, 830
Brown, Sam 424
Brown, Sammy 793, 807
Brown, Sammy K. 585, 586
Brown, Sandy 527
Brown, Sarah 139, 194, 296, 377, 529, 612, 779, 830
Brown, Scoville 291, 292, 315
Brown, Skeet 808
Brown, Stephen D. 717
Brown, Steve 718
Brown, Theo 544, 687
Brown, Thornton 685
Brown, Tiny 677, 678
Brown, Tom 537
Brown, Tommy 229, 283
Brown, Tony 42, 401, 553

Brown, Vernon 8, 291, 328, 390
Brown, Victor 242, 243
Brown, Walter 84, 766, 774, 797, 798, 819
Brown, Waymon 800
Brown, Willard 654
Brown, William 4, 126, 366, 375, 468, 572, 600, 657, 711, 731, 758, 759
Brown, Willie 285, 511, 512, 800, 801, 802
Brown, Yodeling Kid 808
Brown Jr, Elmer 550
Brown Jr, Josh 510
Brown II, Elmer 632
Brown III, Oscar 614
Brown III, William C. 350
Browne, Allan 727
Browne, Jackson 343
Browne, Michael Jerome 37
Brownie, John 509
Browning, John 355, 356
Browning, Misty 364
Browns, Anthony 133
Browns, Georgia 754, 812
Brox, Annette 372
Brox, Victor 175, 371, 372
Broyles, Dorothy 258
Brozman, Bob 310, 422, 812, 814, 825
Brubeck, Chris 357
Brubeck, Dave 808
Bruce, Bob 726
Bruce, Franz 385
Bruce, Harold 84
Bruce, Jack 372, 428, 824
Bruce, John 217
Brumbach, John 92, 141, 200, 251, 462, 553, 567, 606, 735
Brumbach, Mark 185, 581, 613, 617
Brumfield, Denise 583
Bruner, Cliff 772
Brunies, Abbie 462
Brunning, Bob 264, 344, 532, 630, 730
Brunning Sunflower Blues Band 228
Bruno, Al 675
Bruno, Mike 430
Bruno, Willie 'T. J.' 554
Bruton, Stephen 21, 195, 484, 485, 502
Bruton, T. S. 195
Bryan, Clifford 446
Bryan, Raymond 232
Bryans, Bill 170
Bryant, Bob 351
Bryant, Bobby 726
Bryant, Cora Mae 85, 513, 757, 786
Bryant, Danny 85
Bryant, David 75, 432
Bryant, Donald 666
Bryant, Elder Richard 775
Bryant, Frank 91
Bryant, Ken 85
Bryant, Kirk 341
Bryant, N-Nandi 135
Bryant, Paul 475
Bryant, Paul 'Pops' 413

Bryant, Precious 85, 756, 757
Bryant, Sam 575
Bryant, St James 15, 369, 399
Bryant, Tina 275
Bryant, Tony 85
Bryant, Warren 429
Bryant, Willie 86
Bryson, Eric 132
Bryson, Kent 496, 497
Bryson, Tim 547, 564
Bubbling Over Five, The 769, 793, 816
Bucaro, Clarence 824
Buchanan, James 446
Buchanan, Jasper 465, 706
Buchanan, Pat 185
Buchanan, Robbie 359, 376
Buchanan, Roy 768, 776
Buchanan, Walter 650, 683
Buchanin, Ian 823
Bucher, John 665
Bucher, Vincent 584
Buck, Mike 190, 230, 377, 450, 550
Buck, Peter 153, 186
Buckholz, Chris 423
Buckley, Gerard 156
Buckley, Sylvester 258, 377, 408
Buckner, Elbert 299
Buckner, John 'Teddy' 593
Buckner, Milt 77, 211, 244, 245, 472, 510, 663, 670, 671, 683
Buckner, Ted 26, 245, 321, 322, 527, 713
Buckner, Teddy 114, 244, 252, 449, 450, 472, 504, 677, 678
Buckner, Willa Mae 756, 757
Buckwheat Zydeco 86, 805, 831, 832, 833
Buddingh, Terry 229, 535, 539
Buddy & Claudia 779
Buegeleisen, Dan 496
Buehler, Joe 'Mojo' 163
Buffalo, Norton 43, 44, 558, 779
Buford, Bobby 765
Buford, Lawson 551
Buford, Mojo 87, 481, 482, 483, 604, 771
Buggs, Marie 527
Built For Comfort Blues Band 87
Bull, Larry 711
Bull 761, 822
Bull City Red 88, 154, 206, 444, 478, 637, 638, 639, 640
Bullamore, Holly 373
Bullet Bob 98
Bullock, Ernie 596
Bullock, Hiram 624
Bullock, Mike 375
Bully, Sammy Lee 489
Bumble Bee Slim 45, 69, 88, 452, 737, 738, 742, 756, 786, 788, 794, 808
Bunker, Larry 666
Bunn, Alden 755, 800, 806, 807
Bunn, Jimmy 292
Bunn, Teddy 7, 89, 150, 221, 224, 390, 461, 597, 607, 637, 661, 662, 697, 699

Buonadonna, Nick 84
Burbank, Charles 529
Burbidge, Graham 340, 371, 641
Burbridge, Kofi 636
Burch, Jeff 186
Burch, John 672
Burch, Kenny 490
Burch, Mike 87
Burch, Vernon 349, 350
Burchett, William 662
Burckhardt, Sam 204, 617
Burdett, Steve 485
Burdette, Wayne 81, 185, 644
Burdine, Lawrence 352, 353, 354, 355
Burdon, Eric 601, 824
Burgan, Lawrence 84
Burgess, Bob 338
Burgess, Dave 424
Burgess, Tyler 170
Burgin, Dave 484
Burgin, Rockin' Johnny 92, 172, 330, 552, 554, 622, 630, 697
Burk, Steve 549
Burke, Chuckie 165, 402
Burke, Ed 459, 670
Burke, Gary 50, 156
Burke, Raymond 462
Burke, Solomon 780, 788
Burke, Sonny 364
Burke, Treva L. 472
Burkey, Mickey 495
Burks, Albie 556
Burks, Clifford 527
Burks, 'Cowboy' T. 765
Burks, Iman 556
Burks, J. T. 160
Burks, Michael 90, 768, 776, 823
Burks, Pinetop 794, 810, 818
Burleson, Hattie 794, 818, 826
Burley, Dan 90
Burn, Malcolm 730
Burnett & Rutherford 772
Burnette, Jack 232
Burnette, Ranie 754, 759, 766
Burnette, Tommy 751
Burnham, Charles 665
Burns, Adrian Byron 91
Burns, Asbestos 592
Burns, Beckie 429
Burns, Brenda 408
Burns, Chris 674
Burns, Eddie 91, 163, 267, 268, 269, 271, 273, 275, 751, 752, 770, 779, 781
Burns, Hughie 34
Burns, Jethro 425
Burns, Jimmy 91, 747, 770, 781, 790
Burns, John Eddie 696
Burns, Keeno 573
Burns, Kevin 163
Burns, Leon 63
Burns, Norman 702, 703
Burns, Paula 204

Burns, Ralph 115
Burns, Rebecca 429
Burns, Tom 17, 595
Burns, Tracy 17
Burns, Wayne 117, 120, 490
Burnside, Cedric 80, 94, 95, 251, 498
Burnside, Cody 498, 499
Burnside, Daniel 93, 94
Burnside, Dwayne 93, 94, 498, 499
Burnside, Garry 251, 347, 498, 499
Burnside, Joseph 93, 94
Burnside, R. L. 92, 136, 153, 499, 738, 754, 762, 766, 777, 824
Burr, John R. 100, 198, 199, 658, 690
Burr, Manwell 591
Burrage, Harold 95, 232, 417, 781, 800
Burrell, Boz 34, 372
Burrell, Duke 341
Burrell, Kenny 40, 245, 295, 358, 521, 726
Burrell, Maggie 830
Burris, J. C. 95, 279, 638, 639, 641, 642, 777
Burroughs, Alvin 7
Burroughs, Tommy 375
Burrows, Cassell 289, 290
Burse, Charlie 450, 451, 452, 795
Burse, Robert 451
Burston, Clara 828
Burt, Andy 85
Burt, Clarence H. 245
Burton, A. 761
Burton, Aron 30, 96, 97, 125, 129, 138, 183, 316, 405, 416, 447, 541, 550, 622, 692, 747, 782
Burton, Ben 659, 660
Burton, Bobby 446, 477
Burton, Earl 219
Burton, Fred 562
Burton, Little Johnny 659
Burton, Joseph 356, 357, 541, 695
Burton, Larry 96, 129, 130, 316, 317, 318, 351, 377, 405, 447, 541, 550, 612
Burton, Nelson 321, 322
Burton, Sam 488
Burton, W. E. (Buddy) 69, 142, 610, 774
Burtt, Peter Joseph 305
Busby, Frank 212
Buschbacher, Paul 706
Bush, Chuck 14, 28, 29, 384
Bush, Clifford 63, 300
Bush, Fred 434
Bush, Henry 349, 350
Bush, Lennie 672
Bush, Sam 343, 673
Bush, Tony 108
Bushell, Garvin 249, 587, 588, 596, 685, 718, 720
Bushkin, Joe 83
Bushnell, Bob 338, 340, 662
Busse, Henry 253
Buster, Norman 596
Butcher, Jesse 763

Butera, Sam 140, 804
Butler, Alesia 663
Butler, Andrew 65, 547
Butler, Anthony 87
Butler, Billy 76, 140, 237, 238, 245, 294, 332, 355, 363, 369, 457, 464, 592
Butler, Charlie 758, 759
Butler, Clarence 510
Butler, Cliff 786
Butler, Curtis 510
Butler, Ed 81, 127
Butler, Eddie 528
Butler, Frank 725
Butler, George 466
Butler, George 'Wild Child' 97, 282, 316
Butler, Henry 44, 97, 197, 242, 243, 472, 776, 805
Butler, Herman 231
Butler, James (Black Diamond) 753, 782, 826
Butler, Jerry 790
Butler, Joe 362
Butler, Johnny 763
Butler, Lester 16, 94, 629
Butler, Mary 109
Butler, N. 146
Butler, Paul 356, 395
Butler, Reed 546
Butler, Ross 291, 292
Butler, Sam [Bo Weavil Jackson] 755, 812, 813
Butler, Ted 193
Butler, Teresa 663
Butler, Trixie 793, 829
Butler, Victor 366
Butler Jr, Eddie 385
Butler Twins 98, 771
Buttacavoli, Ronnie 307
'Butter Boy' 759
'Butterbeans' 763
Butterbeans & Susie 98, 737, 773, 774, 795, 806
Butterfield, Erskine 741
Butterfield, Paul 52, 99, 138, 400, 428, 482, 483, 747, 764, 768, 770, 813
Butterman, Ted 467
Butterscotch 581
Butterworth, Dean 275
Buttrey, Kenny 238, 458
Butts, Cynthia 584
Butts, Hindai 340
Butts, Jimmy 245, 292, 702
Buwaldi, Allard 6
Buxton, James 472, 670, 671
Buzard, Don 78
Buzzington, Ezra 775
Byam, Roger 256
Byars, Doug 405
Byas, Don 7, 8, 69, 326, 328, 332, 661, 662
Byers, Billy 40
Byers, Hale 253

INDEX   847

Byerson, Bob 414
Byrd, Eddie 338, 340
Byrd, John 220, 635, 773, 786
Byrd, Lissa 583
Byrd, Memphis Joe 150
Byrne, Jerry 788, 803, 805
Byrne, Larry 6
Byrnes, Jim 210
Byrom, Larry 402
Byther, Ruben 543
C., Leon 37
Cabral, Joe 161, 195, 566
Caceres, Ernie 83, 295
Caddle, Tony 425
Cadets, The 785
Cadillac, Bobbie 818
Cadillac Baby 779
Cadillacs, The 799
Caesar, Little [Harry] 782
Cage, Butch 764, 777, 810
Cage, Calvin 231
Cage, John 'Midnight' 64, 654, 655
Cage, Johnnie 597
Cage, Robert 99
Cahoon, Bruce 299
Caillier, J. J. 384
Cain, Chris 99, 199, 583, 779
Cain, Lee 612
Cain, Perry 818, 819
Caiola, Al 295
Caird, Pat 20
Calabrese, Dominic 27
Caldwell, Carl 'EG' 337
Caldwell, Charles 100
Caldwell, Charles L. 568
Caldwell, George 372
Caldwell, Happy 63, 718
Cale, J. J. 239
Calhoun, Big Al 100, 656
Calhoun, Eddie 650
Calhoun, Will 612
California, Randy 824
Calire, Jim 220
Call, Bob 69, 79, 167, 218, 229, 287, 493, 549, 610, 627, 654, 682, 740, 807, 808
Callahan, Homer 772, 773
Callahan Brothers 772
Callen, Jim 539
Callender, Howard 227, 730
Callender, Red 214, 243, 292, 384, 390, 392, 432, 492, 593, 725, 798
Callens, Henry 55
Callicott, Joe 101, 767, 777, 801
Callier, Elliot 648
Callier, Terry 780
Callison, Scott 186
Callow, Simon 74
Calloway, Cab 328, 821
Calloway, Dennis 534
Calloway, Harrison 257, 401
Calloway, John 812
Calloway, Joseph 712

Calmese, Charles 480, 484
Calvaes, The 780
Calvary Episcopal Children's Choir 583
Calvin, John 455, 456
Calypso Boys, The 338
Camarena, Danny 161
Camero, Candido 114
Cameron, Chris 42, 450, 553
Cameron, Clarence 136
Cameron, John 218, 283, 415, 762
Cameron, Rory Coolhand 45
Camille 43
Camiolo, Eddie 524
Camp, Tramp 251
Campagna, Joe 32
Campbell, Arthur 301
Campbell, Barbara Mayson 101
Campbell, Bob 55, 767
Campbell, Carl 819
Campbell, Charles 261
Campbell, Charley 760
Campbell, Charlie 737, 794
Campbell, Choker 209, 662
Campbell, Chuck 296
Campbell, Dave 489, 600, 601
Campbell, David 434
Campbell, Don 336
Campbell, Eddie C. 7, 101, 210, 706, 744, 746, 779
Campbell, Edgar 253, 597, 685
Campbell, Frank 83
Campbell, Gene 101, 797, 817
Campbell, Gordon 53
Campbell, Greg (Smokey) 479
Campbell, James 777
Campbell, Blind James 102
Campbell, Jim 5
Campbell, Joe 164, 210, 401, 440, 676, 720
Campbell, John 102
Campbell, Larry 50, 359
Campbell, Lee 123, 241, 413
Campbell, Louis 754
Campbell, Mike 624
Campbell, Odell 417, 617
Campbell, Paul 677
Campbell, Phil 372
Campbell, Sarah 21
Campbell, Sarah Elizabeth 195
Campbell, Scott 691
Campbell, Sonny 286
Campbell, Wilgur 15
Campbell, Willie 191, 434
Campbell, Willie J. 538
Campilongo, Jim 526
Campo, Bobby 78, 79
Campos, Carla 195
Can, Jimmy 80
Candoli, Pete 291, 593
Candy, Louis 118
Candy, Prince 577
Canfield, Mike 291

Cannaday, Little Junior 570
Cannady, James 39, 40, 245
Canned Heat 103, 748, 813
Cannibal & The Headhunters 104
Cannico, Vickie 503
Canning, Tom 235, 430, 431
Cannon, Gus 48, 105, 789, 792, 793, 794, 811
Cannon, Jack 369
Cannon, Jackie 780
Cannon, Steve 336, 547
Cannon's Jug Stompers 775, 792, 794, 810
Canty, Louis Willie 222
Canway, Don 392
Capek, Frank 557
Capewell, Derek 727
Caple, Gilbert 509
Captain Luke [Luther Mayer] 756, 786
Caranto, Renato 336
Carbo, Chuck 76, 806
Carew, Naomia 475
Carey, Mutt 380, 646
Carey, Pat 65, 169, 170, 489, 687
Carey, Rod 27, 34, 152, 179, 180, 222, 423, 491, 516, 546, 549, 614
Carillo, Frank 239
Carino, Marc 293, 464
Carlin, Bob 650
Carlisle, Bill 772
Carlisle, Cliff 767, 772, 773, 774, 813
Carlisle, Una Mae 827
Carlisles, The 773
Carlock, Keith 314
Carlsen, Mary Jo 491
Carlson, Chris 43
Carlton, Larry 48, 679
Carlyle, John 688
Carman, Red 670
Carmichael, Chris 222, 446
Carmichael, Hoagy 321
Carmon, Tim 359
Carn, William 687
Carnes, Otto 'Bobby' 193, 261, 341
Carney, Harry 140, 322, 473
Carney, Ralph 526
Caro, Jeff 266
Carolina Buddies 772
Carolina Slim 106, 755, 806
Carolina Tar Heels 772
Carolinians, The 701, 702
Caron, Danny 76, 120, 239, 274, 583, 690, 728, 729
Caron, Rolf 543
Caron, Tim 42
Caroompas, Jim 273
Carp, Jeffrey M. 272, 273, 276, 282, 289, 290, 482
Carp-Tones, The 43
Carpender, John 25
Carpenter, Cecil 595, 596
Carpenter, Ike 593, 683

INDEX

Carpenter, Jimmy 35, 644
Carpenter, Randy 118
Carpenter, Wingy 796
Carpentieri, Mark 316, 516
Carr, Barbara 319
Carr, Bruno 116
Carr, Dora 150
Carr, Edward 685
Carr, Gunter Lee 800
Carr, James 400, 401
Carr, Jesse 395
Carr, Jimmy 513
Carr, Julia 570
Carr, Leroy 45, 106, 255, 700, 701, 737, 738, 739, 740, 742, 743, 794, 795, 808, 809
Carr, Mancy 607
Carr, Mike 727
Carr, Pete 377
Carr, Sam 153, 163, 198, 199, 205, 236, 243, 313, 316, 337, 513, 546, 576, 676, 705
Carr, Tony 372
Carr, Wynona 788
Carrack, Paul 359
Carras, Michel 4, 5, 6, 41, 57, 544, 734
Carrera, Andy 414
Carrier, Chubby 34, 107, 644, 779
Carrier, Deran 107
Carrier, Eugene 358
Carrier, Joseph 28
Carrier, Kevin 107, 108
Carrier, Misty 107
Carrier, Phillip 108
Carrier, Ronald 108
Carrier, Roy 107, 831
Carrier, Troy 107, 108
Carrière Brothers, The 108, 831, 832
Carrière, Eraste 108
Carrière, Joseph 'Bébé' 108
Carrière, Oakdale 758
Carriéré [Carrier], Phillip 108
Carrington, Jerome 311
Carroll, Chris 423
Carroll, Dave 630
Carroll, David 21, 258
Carroll, Jeanne 157, 467, 479
Carroll, Jimmy 683
Carroll, Karen 109, 414, 474, 781, 829, 830
Carroll, Liane 427
Carroll, Porter 624
Carson, Asal 'Count' 208, 209
Carson, Big Blues 752
Carson, Nelson 243
Carson, Steve 184
Carstater, Randy 502
Cartelli, Mario 82
Carter, Al 110
Carter, Andre 87
Carter, Benny 24, 384, 661, 662
Carter, Big Lucky 496

Carter, Bo 109, 436, 670, 737, 738, 773, 774, 794, 797, 801, 811, 816
Carter, Bob 204, 613, 620
Carter, Bombay 299
Carter, Bruce 564
Carter, Buster 810
Carter, Carl 406, 674
Carter, Clifford 51
Carter, Dave 58
Carter, Earl 392
Carter, Edward 110
Carter, Fred 483
Carter, Freddie 90
Carter, Gene 385
Carter, George 756, 767
Carter, Geraldine 219
Carter, Gil 112, 113
Carter, Goree 110, 243, 258, 661, 662, 798, 800, 819, 820, 825
Carter, Hank 652, 653
Carter, James 346, 526
Carter, Jerry 110
Carter, Joe 1, 599, 744, 813, 822
Carter, Larry 566
Carter, Leroy 711
Carter, Leroy 'Tons Of Fun' 475
Carter, Lydia 710
Carter, Margaret 773, 774
Carter, Margaret Love 210
Carter, Oscar [Clifford Gibson] 618, 619
Carter, Peter 571
Carter, Roman 110
Carter, Sam 759
Carter, Sidney 441
Carter, Mrs Sidney 761, 763
Carter, 'Spider' 815
Carter, Tyrone 418
Carter, Willie 760
Carter Brothers, The 110
Carter Family 765, 772, 793
Carter Sr, Alvin 236
Carthy, Ron 363, 364
Cartwright, Bernice 87
Carvajal, Henry 262, 522
Carver, Noble 'Uncle Bozo' 700
Carver, Robert V. 700
Carver, Warner 700
Carver Boys 769
Cary, Dick 83, 357
Casady, Jack 275
Casagrande, Andy 176
Case, Bob 299
Case, Pete 824
Casey, Al 140, 294, 572, 637, 701, 702
Casey, Antonio 70
Casey, Floyd 587, 588
Casey, Fred 249, 433, 439
Casey, Howie 34, 424
Casey, Lawrence 795
Casey, Mason 524
Casey, Smith 758, 759, 762, 817
Casey, Stanley 731

Cashdollar, Cindy 310, 311, 502
Casher, Zac 718
Cashman, Glenn 341
Casimir, Bill 61, 69, 70, 72, 287, 500, 610, 620, 627
Casimir, Sam 61, 227, 415, 500, 616, 620, 744
Cassell, Dean 536, 636
Cassidy, Jack 695
Cassino, James [poss. Cassino Simpson] 475
Casson, Jim 170
Cassone, Cyd 37, 251, 311
Castagno, Don 151, 152
Castellana, Mike 369
Castellow, 'Donnie C.' 516
Castenell, Amadee 222, 472
Castillo, Emilio 273
Castle, Dave 371
Castle, Henry L. 151, 795
Castner, Charlie 328
Caston, Leonard 'Baby Doo' 41, 159, 164, 218, 233, 287, 387, 401, 403, 414, 620, 743, 744
Castrillo, Eguie 636
Castro, Lenny 198, 358, 359, 376, 431
Castro, Tommy 110, 779, 823
Catalano, Ron 194
Catania, Brad 199
Cate, Earl 468, 644
Cate, Ernie 468, 644
Catfish Keith 111
Cathey, Tommy 210
Catlett, Sid 7, 8, 80, 83, 140, 221, 287, 311, 390, 526, 597, 618, 619, 697
Cato, Lawrence 366, 463
Cato, Nevada 36, 37
Cats & A Fiddle, The 797
Cats'n Jammer Three 798
Catura, Noel 100, 341, 512, 583, 584
Caudery, Thomas 8
Cauley, Ben 145, 257, 349, 350, 358, 401, 572
Cauley Family 772
Causey, Clyde 598
Cauthen, Andrew 655, 696, 764, 770
Cavalier, Dennis 647
Cavaliere, Felix 135
Cavallo, Jimmy 111
Cavanaugh, Dave 24, 384
Cayolle, Brian 730
Ceasar, Donald Ray 13
Ceasar, Warren 119, 120, 832
Ceaser, Raoul 202
Cebert, Dave 655
Centuray, Tyrone 160, 187, 317, 324, 345, 396, 447, 500, 563
Cephas, John 112, 535, 749, 750, 751, 755, 765, 766, 771, 776, 788, 812, 823
Cerra, Paul 318
Chadwick, Russ 579
Chaffe, Robert 199

Chains, Wallace 757
Chaisson, Mike 107, 582
Chalenor, Fred 613
Chalmers, Charles 439
Chalmers, General 249
Chamba People 810
Chamberlain, W. 32
Chambers, Brad 13
Chambers, Elmer 141, 249, 253, 254, 293, 294, 437, 459, 592, 597, 685, 718, 720
Chambers, Henderson 40, 116, 245, 416, 654, 701, 702
Chambers, Lester 518
Chambers, Roland 356
Chambers, Sean 113
Chambers, Stanislas 161
Chambers, Willie 538
Chambers Brothers 104, 747
Chamblee, Eddie 209, 457, 500, 650, 678, 683, 725, 800
Chambler, Gene 162
Chambon, Xavier 77
Champagne, Dwight 490, 544
Champion, Grady 113
Champion, Mickey 422, 724, 725
Champs, The 788
'Chan' 583
Chancler, Leon Ndugu 274, 674
Chandler, Chas 601
Chandler, Gene 780, 790
Chandler, George 65
Chandler, Harold 688
Chandler, Joe 374
Chandler, Phil 107
Chandler, Rod 'Peanut' 403
Channel Cats, The 751
Channey, Alex 55
Chanter, Irene 372
Chantier, Roy L. 539
Chapel, Joe 229
Chaplet, Jerome 'Nils' 4
Chaplin, Alan 45
Chaplin, Blondie 615
Chaplin, Chuck 222, 571, 718
Chapman, Christine 654
Chapman, Curley 13, 202, 203
Chapman, Earl 752
Chapman, Tracy 359
Chappel, David 257
Chappell, Gus 683
Chappelle, Vince 632
Charette, Brian 27, 424, 576, 612, 649
Charity, Pernell 765
Charles, Anthony 555
Charles, Bobby 779, 780, 803
Charles, Donald Ray 580
Charles, Erving 554
Charles, Frank 363
Charles, Fred 489
Charles, Nat 581
Charles, Nick 91, 92, 234, 568, 590, 711
Charles, Ray 114, 231, 662, 777, 799, 808

Charles, Robert 241
Charles, Roosevelt 763
Charles, Yolander 359
Charles Jr, Erving 179
Charlot, Steve 'Skeeter' 28, 29, 108
Charmella, Jack 213
Charms, The 799
Charters, Marty 192
Charters, Samuel 281
Chasman, Paul 547
Chatman, Andy 808
Chatman, Christine 39, 432, 806
Chatman, Isaiah 258, 377, 408
Chatman, Lonnie 109
Chatman, Peter [Memphis Slim] 795
Chatmon, Bo 3, 465, 466, 670
Chatmon, Harry 109, 670, 809
Chatmon, Lonnie 109, 465, 466, 670
Chatmon, Sam 3, 109, 116, 455, 456, 465, 762, 764, 766, 802, 822, 823
Chatters, Maynard 76
Chautemps, Jean-Louis 5
Chavez, Charlie 540
Chavis, Anthony 117
Chavis, Boozoo 116, 751, 752, 790, 805, 831, 832, 833
Chavis, Charles 117
Chavis, Joe 'Chopper' 202
Chavis, Joseph 28, 87
Chavis, Joseph 'Cookie' 107, 161, 384
Chavis, Poncho 117
Chavis, Rellis 117
Chavis, Retell 28
Chavis Jr, Wilson 117
Cheatham, Doc 237, 294, 527, 537, 592
Cheek, Robert 98
Cheeks, Hayward 295
Chelew, John 488
Chellows, The 786
Chenault, Charlotte 257
Chenevert, Anthony 'Peanut' 395
Cheng, Diane 373
Chenier, C. J. 117, 119, 120, 139, 691, 776, 777, 824, 831, 832
Chenier, Cleveland 117, 118, 119, 120, 612
Chenier, Clifton 118, 742, 749, 752, 776, 777, 780, 782, 788, 790, 805, 830, 831, 832
Chenier, Morris [Big] 118, 784
Chenier, Roscoe 120
Cherry, Michael 240, 241
Cherry, Otis 680
Cheseman, Pritchard 63
Chess, Leonard 480, 481
Chestain, Sonny 761
Chester, Jim 175
Chevalier, Albert 777, 830
Chevalier, Chester 11
Chevalier, Paul 291
Chevaucherie, Gilles 458
Chevis, Wilfred 831
Chew, Chris 251, 498, 499

Chicago All Stars 121
Chicago Beau 515
Chicago Black Swans 773
Chicago Blues All Stars 749
Chicago Blues Reunion 121
Chicago Playboy Horns 474
Chicago Rhythm & Blues Kings 121, 779
Chicago Slim 746
Chicago String Band, The 121, 814
Chicago Sunny Boy [Joe Hill Louis] 752, 770
Chicago's Young Blues Generation 750
Children Of Israel, The 402
Childress, Curry 761
Childs, Dinty 519
Childs, Virginia 828
Chiles, Buddy 752, 818, 819
Chilleri, Rich 200, 502
Chilly Willy 229
Chimes, Mike 662
Chimes, The 788
Chinnock, William 733
Chipmunks, The 103
Chisholm, Anna Lee 828
Chisholme, Audley 'Chissy'/'Chizzy' 556
Chism, Chico 87, 94, 136, 226, 411, 573, 617, 787
Chittison, Herman 685
Chitwood, Bobby 372
Choates, Harry 785, 831
Choctaw Slim 408
Choeny, John 129
Chordones, The 780
Chords, The 799
Chortkoff, Randy 16, 422, 629
Chosen Gospel Singers, The 788
Chrétien, Pierre 341
Chrismar, 'Sleeveless' Steve 653
Christensen, Julie 198
Christensen, Marty 111
Christian, Bobby 401
Christian, Buddy 134, 250, 294, 325, 398, 426, 437, 587, 592, 595, 596, 679, 721
Christian, Charlie 142, 390
Christian, Gary 413
Christian, Jodie 647
Christian, Leonard 472
Christian, Marty 193
Christian, Robert 434
Christiansen, Diane 109, 590
Christiansen, Julie 198
Christiansen, Ole 174
Christie, Ian 72
Christie, Keith 72
Christina, Bob 536
Christina, Fran 21, 26, 61, 135, 190, 191, 515, 536, 667
Christl, Christian 73
Christopher, Evan 805
Christopher, Keith 575
Christopher, Shawn 614
Chromy, Manfred 132

Chruszcz, Bogdan 257
Church, Blind Clyde 808
Church, Eugene 788
Church of God in Christ Congregation 758
Churchill, Savannah 796, 797, 798
Ciesielski, Vinnie 402
Cincinnati Jug Band 775, 795, 810
Cioe, Crispin 130, 134, 325, 484, 567
Cisco, Bobby 780
Claflin, Ned 558
Clahar, Patrick 427
Clair, Michael Great Bear 118
Clanton, Sam 294
Clapton, Eric 87, 122, 174, 234, 236, 275, 289, 290, 359, 364, 372, 427, 428, 429, 431, 558, 601, 603, 615, 624, 694, 767, 813
Clarington, Arnold 499
Clark, Alan 51
Clark, Alden 231
Clark, Allen 77
Clark, Angie 758
Clark, Arthur 727
Clark, Artie 730
Clark, Bill 146
Clark, Buddy 241
Clark, Charles 781
Clark, Chris 647
Clark, Cortelia 122
Clark, Dave 204, 440, 645
Clark, Dee 790
Clark, Don 253
Clark, Eddie 123, 124, 164, 464, 720
Clark, Frank 244
Clark, Frank 'Crying Shame' 265
Clark, Fred 146, 245, 415, 429, 507, 508, 543, 650
Clark, Harold 245, 300, 610
Clark, James 61, 218, 321, 480
Clark, Jon 485
Clark, June 426
Clark, Ken 127, 718
Clark, Kenneth 465
Clark, Lonnie 786, 787, 807
Clark, Marjorie 499
Clark, Mark 305, 659, 704
Clark, Norman 523
Clark, Paul 424
Clark, Reagae 361
Clark, Sam 336
Clark, Big Sam 802
Clark, Tim 516
Clark, W. C. 33, 61, 123, 820
Clarke, Buck 429
Clarke, Chuck 459
Clarke, Frank 252, 315, 449, 450, 661, 662, 677, 678
Clarke, George 769
Clarke, Jim 739, 740, 741, 808
Clarke, Kenny 140, 315, 727
Clarke, Paul 177

Clarke, Pete 295
Clarke, Simon 37, 122
Clarke, Tony 780
Clarke, William 123, 593, 720, 771, 776
Clay, Beauford 102
Clay, Francis 118, 138, 272, 273, 276, 281, 282, 283, 433, 456, 480, 481, 482, 557, 558, 604, 651, 678
Clay, Jesse Lee 412
Clay, Omar 727
Clay, Otis 443, 553, 688, 779, 788
Clay, Shirley 142, 255, 426, 459, 537, 549, 610
Clayborn, Rev. Edward W. 795
Claypool, Les 575
Clayton, Alan 341
Clayton, Buck 291, 292
Clayton, Doctor 124, 743, 797, 820, 821
Clayton, Jeff 358
Clayton, Jennie 450, 451, 826
Clayton, Joe 351
Clayton, John 728
Clayton, Kurt 6
Clayton, Merry 356, 623
Clayton, Nat 84
Clayton, Robin 65
Clayton, Sam 364
Clayton, Steve 223
Clearaires, The 125
Clearwater, Eddy 124, 370, 547, 744, 747, 770, 778, 779, 783, 784, 785, 788, 790
Cleary, Jon 11, 179, 232, 359, 411, 469, 518, 554, 566, 624, 695, 805
Clef, Johnny 807
Clemens, Jeffrey 'House' 402, 488
Clemens, Night Train 143, 144
Clement, Henry 377
Clement, Keith 13
Clement, Stephan 582
Clements, Cranston 718
Clements, Keith 582
Clements, Mark 190
Clements, Zeke 773
Clemson, Clem 359
Clendening, Rob 440
Cleveland, Big Boy 811
Cleveland, Jimmy 81, 340, 510
Click, Danny 305
Clifford, Henry 248
Clifton, Kaiser 775
Climie, Simon 359
Clips, The 786
Cliques, The 785
Cloury, John 33
Cloutier, Andrew 132
Clover, Arthur 184
Clovers, The 773, 777, 798, 799
Cloyd, James 318
Clyman, Larry 68
Coatie, Latasha 67
Coatie, Tekora 67
Coatie Jr, Riley 67

Coatie Sr, Riley 67
Coats, Bret 201
Cobb, Arnett 77, 244, 492, 678, 683, 800
Cobb, Danny 713
Cobb, Jimmy 583, 683
Cobb, John E. 513
Cobb, Junie 626
Cobb, Oliver 618, 793
Cobb, Steve 42, 450
Cobbs, Al 300
Cobbs, Alfred 39, 40, 244, 245, 338, 505, 520
Cobbs, Bernie 504
Cobbs, Call 449
Cobbs, Vera 126
Cobbs, Willie 126, 788
Coccia, Dino 44
Cochran, Bobby 44, 599
Cochran, Dan 49, 50
Cochran, Danny 433, 489, 721
Cochran, Lisa 135
Cochran, Sam 730
Cochran, Wayne 780
Cochrane, Amy 541
Cockburn, Bruce 824
Cocker, Joe 273, 359
Cockett, Pat 625
Coday, Bill 784
Codish, Chris 27
Coe, James 84
Coe, Jimmy 33, 790
Coen, Damian 64
Coen, Davis 251
Coen, Mae 171
Coerver, Tom 649
Coffey, Dennis 681
Coffey, Denny 73
Coffin, Jeff 222
Cogbill, Tommy 238, 509
Coggins, Kevin 204, 512, 540
Cohen, David 48
Cohen, David Bennett 517
Cohen, Jeremy 558
Cohen, Jerry 624
Cohen, Leon 295
Cohen, Porky 324, 362, 559, 567, 667, 717
Cohn, Al 679
Cohn, Sonny 163, 662
Cohn, Zinky 699
Coker, Henry 1, 229, 504, 671
Colaiuta, Vinnie 197, 198
Colbert, Bertha 521
Colby, Mark 632
Colby, Travis 325, 560
Colclessor, Chris 257
Colclough, Tom 20
Cole, Ann 739
Cole, B. J. 37
Cole, Barbra 660
Cole, Darnell 447
Cole, Debbe L. 87
Cole, Don 572

Cole, Donald 315
Cole, Eric 'Ice' 202
Cole, Isaac 543, 650
Cole, James 126, 774, 816
Cole, Jerry 643
Cole, Jimmy 63
Cole, 'Funky' John 54
Cole, June 587, 588
Cole, Kid 795
Cole, Nat 'King' 740, 778, 797, 798, 799, 826
Cole, Reg 175
Cole, Rupert 311, 416, 459, 670
Cole, Sonny 650
Cole, Stacy 76, 222, 554, 731
Cole, Walter 45, 164
Coleman, Austin 758
Coleman, Bill 526, 565, 661, 702
Coleman, Bob 795
Coleman, Cornelius 26, 166, 167, 620, 677, 678, 712
Coleman, Dave 677, 678
Coleman, Deborah 127, 516, 567, 751, 779, 824, 830
Coleman, Donald 129, 414
Coleman, Dutch 769
Coleman, E. L. 426, 689
Coleman, Fitzroy 702, 703
Coleman, George [g] 814
Coleman, George [s] 352, 353, 354, 363, 365
Coleman, George 'Bongo Joe' 128, 739, 757, 777
Coleman, Jaybird 128, 737, 768, 769
Coleman, Jesse 'Monkey Joe' 128, 467
Coleman, Judson 717
Coleman, Lonnie 810
Coleman, Michael 33, 74, 129, 138, 527, 745, 747, 771
Coleman, Oliver 415
Coleman, Pat 20
Coleman, Sammy 675
Coleman, Thomas 'Beale Street' 672
Coleman, Tony 20, 291, 358, 359, 490, 658, 660, 691
Coleman, Walter 755, 795
Coleridge, Steve 182, 214, 226, 370, 583
Coles, Johnny 300
Coley, J. P. 58
Coley, Kid 248
Colleen 429
Collette, Buddy 504
Collier, Frank 129, 318
Collier, James 443
Collier, Joe 300
Collier, Mitty 780
Collins, Al 218
Collins, Albert 129, 134, 144, 151, 274, 358, 430, 468, 472, 541, 632, 660, 738, 767, 768, 776, 779, 818, 820
Collins, Booker 1
Collins, Charles E. 629

Collins, Chasey 'Kokomo' 708
Collins, Christopher 434
Collins, Dennis 343, 666, 722
Collins, Frank 53
Collins, James 441
Collins, Jimmy 494
Collins, John 83, 158, 326, 338, 661
Collins, Lee 320, 326, 467, 607
Collins, Lewis 238, 349
Collins, Mel 217, 372
Collins, Mitch 495
Collins, Ricky 629
Collins, Rodger 784
Collins, Sam 131, 801, 803, 810, 812, 813
Collins, Sanford L. 812
Collins, Shad 24, 62, 140, 142, 315, 526
Collins, Walker 645
Colon, Ernie 567
Colon, Hector 256
Columbo, Chris 77
Columbus, Christopher [Joe Morris] 338, 340
Coman, Rene 232, 488
Combelle, Philippe 165, 457, 458
Combs, Paul 406
Comeaux, Richard 215
Comeaux, Tommy 195
Comegys, Leon 62, 300, 338, 670
Comer, Rev. Bradford 556
Comer, Mary Love 556
Comfort, Joe 145, 504, 678
Commander Cody 111, 779
Como Drum Band 802
Compeon, Armando 468
Compton, Gary 37
Compton, Tim 274
Compton, Tom 724
Conaway, Clarence 592, 720
Conaway, Lincoln M. 253, 587, 588, 592, 720
Conaway, Sterling 249
Concha, Donna 634
Concha, Nicholas 634
Condon, Eddie 83, 321
Conerly, L. V. 262, 766
Congregation Of New Brown's Chapel 812
Congregation Of The Church Of God In Christ, Clarksdale 762
Conley, Edwyn 83, 321, 405
Conley, Jimmy 5, 159, 455, 458
Conn, Steve 126
Conner, Red 392
Connolly, Nick 20, 123, 297, 476, 502, 529, 643
Connor, Charles 173
Connor, Clyde 2
Connor, Glover Lee 710
Connor, Joanna 4, 6, 127, 131, 779, 830
Connors, Gene 'Mighty Flea' 211, 506, 507, 508, 527, 663
Connors, Kelly 541

Consolers, The 786
Conte, Luis 145, 198, 307
Conte, Pat 823
Contrastors, The 292
Convertino, John 80, 513
Convict Group 758
Conway, Billy 519
Conwright, Joe 438
Conyers, Teddy 315, 654
Cooder, Joachim 275
Cooder, Ry 274, 622, 623, 813, 814
Cook, Al 132, 574
Cook, Ann 828
Cook, Anthony 275
Cook, Brad 95
Cook, C. B. 761, 763
Cook, Don 410
Cook, Doug 264, 410
Cook, Frank 103
Cook, George 404, 406
Cook, Gerald 294
Cook, Irvin 812
Cook, James 138
Cook, Joe 593
Cook, Ken 717
Cook, Kevin 613
Cook, Rachael 554
Cook, Tim 485
Cook, Willie 84, 459
Cooke, Donald 351
Cooke, Esten 172, 241
Cooke, Fabian 556
Cooke, L. C. 780
Cooke, Lynwood 'Cookie' 176, 325
Cooke, Roland 351
Cooke, Sam 788
Cooke, William Edward 638
Cookie & The Cupcakes 780, 784
Cookies, The 115, 663
Cooks, Donald 110, 243, 258, 276, 277, 278, 279, 281, 283
Cooks, Gladys 664
Cooks, John 393
Cooks, Silver 752, 819
Cooksey, Ray 210
Cooksey, Robert 325, 385, 768, 769, 806, 810, 820
Cool, Ricky 226
'Cool Breeze' [Joseph Bell] 415
Cool Cats, The 763
Cool John 786
Coolbone 803, 805
Cooley, Jack 7, 8
Cooley, Mike 429
Cooley, Spade 772
Coomer, Ken 195, 222
Cooper, Al 797
Cooper, Bob 469
Cooper, Buster 81, 583
Cooper, Cathy 504
Cooper, Chris 85
Cooper, D. B. 296

Cooper, Dan 'Preacher' 337
Cooper, Fred 286
Cooper, Gene 133
Cooper, Glen 133
Cooper, Harry 336, 426, 592
Cooper, Henry 43, 132
Cooper, Herman 'Red' 650
Cooper, Jeff 291
Cooper, Joey 363
Cooper, Johnnie 366
Cooper, Kenneth 568
Cooper, Lee 61, 79, 283, 289, 725
Cooper, Leroy 116, 209, 490
Cooper, Little 132
Cooper, Lloyd 650
Cooper, Madison 144
Cooper, Mickey 826
Cooper, Nick 677
Cooper, Rattlesnake 752, 818, 819
Cooper, Ray 19, 122
Cooper, Rich 336
Cooper, Robert 533, 737
Cooper, Selwyn 86, 117, 553
Cooper, Steve 583, 713
Cooper, Trenton 133
Cooper, William 392, 414
Copeland, Carl 'CC' 344
Copeland, Johnny 130, 133, 667, 669, 678, 768, 776, 788, 818, 820, 825
Copeland, Keith 76
Copeland, Leonard 772
Copeland, Martha 134, 826, 827
Copeland, Ray 583
Copeland, Shemekia 134, 139, 576, 776
Copley, Al 101, 135, 190, 191, 548, 559, 742
Corbett, Dan 265
Corbett, Robin 367
Corbiere, Jason 560
Corbin, Nathalie 218
Corcoran, Corky 292, 505
Cordes, Dirk 369
Core, June 239, 293, 399, 422, 512, 540
Core, Wirtford 406
Corea, Chick 197
Corley, Dewey 389, 764
Corley, George 439
Corley, Leslie 549
Cormier, Annie Joe 384
Cormier, Kevin 384
Cormier, Lesa 832
Cormier, Mitchell 539
Cormier, Shedrick 431
Corner, George 778
Cornes, Thomas 'Blue' 54, 341
Cornett, Andy 582
Cornish, Bill 433
Coronado, Joe 705, 721, 768
Coronado, John(ny) 705, 721
Coronado, Steve 705
Coronets, The 779
Corritore, Bob 94, 135, 226, 411
Corsairs, The 780

Corsetti, Franco 512
Cortes, Rick 235, 430
Cortez, Dave 'Baby' 410, 780
Cortez, Tino 96, 316, 591
'Cortez' 152, 332
Corwin, Scott 491, 518
Coryell, Randy 80
Cosby, Hank 269, 271, 275
Cosby, Harper 460
Cosey, Pete 16, 482
Cosse, Ike 136
Costa, Rudy 561, 623, 624, 625
Costello, Sean 136, 186, 636, 707, 824
Coteaux, Bert de 351
Cotinola, Frank 657
Cotten, Elizabeth 137, 747
Cotton, Al 583
Cotton, Chuck 16, 423
Cotton, Clay 197, 445, 486, 487, 690
Cotton, Dave 185
Cotton, Dolores 344
Cotton, Ernest 66, 386, 387, 415, 454, 455, 556, 616, 785
Cotton, James 38, 137, 152, 180, 288, 361, 427, 480, 481, 482, 483, 484, 515, 575, 581, 603, 614, 615, 632, 651, 666, 723, 729, 734, 744, 745, 769, 770, 771, 776, 778, 779, 789, 824
Cotton, Johnny 129, 138
Cotton, Lawrence 231, 232
Cotton, Paul 695
Cotton, Ray 438, 439
Cotton, Roger 36, 228
Cotton, Sammy 804
Cotton, Sylvester 139
Cottrell, Louis 42, 219
Coulter, Butch 20
Coulter, Cliff 273
Coulter, Roy 321, 322
Counce, Curtis 504, 506
Council, Floyd 'Dipper Boy' 206, 756
Courance, Edgar 'Spider' 63
Coursey, Farris 213
Courtney, Tom 766
Cousin Joe 140, 160, 797, 803, 804, 821
Cousin Leroy 141, 770, 806
Cousins, Butch 564, 584
Cousins, Richard 103, 113, 143, 144, 274, 358
Cousins & De Moss 793, 797
Covay, Don 612, 777
Coven, Willie 335
Coveney, Silvertone Steve 299, 580
Coverson, Lovejoy 63, 249
Covington, Ben 42, 141, 786
Covington, Robert 138, 141, 151, 217, 550, 581, 617, 669
Covington, Sonny 550
Cowan, Andrew 675
Cowan, Heywood 620
Cowan, Mike 495
Cowans, Herb 526, 637

Coward, Buster 772
Cowart, Willie 438, 439
Cowden, David 229
Cox, Adrian 81
Cox, Big Sid 716
Cox, Bill 772
Cox, Ed 595
Cox, Ida 141, 301, 742, 747, 827
Cox, Irv 341, 507
Cox, Jim 361, 376
Cox, Johnny 713
Cox, Walter 201, 677, 678, 713
Coxe, Bob 14
Coxhill, Lol 372
Coyle, Laurie 20
Coyote, Wily 439
Craig, David 78
Craig, Left Hand Frank 370, 745
Craig, Gary 369, 540
Craig, James 683
Craig, Jay 53
Craig, Rodney 21, 669
Craig, Willie 'Cowboy' 763
Crandall, Kurt 143
Crane, Charles 330, 664
Crap Eye 759
Craven, Hosie Dwine 803
Craven, Joe 22, 305
Cravinho, Joe 497
Cravins, Senator Donald 580
Crawford, Bennie 114, 115
Crawford, Billy 127
Crawford, Bixie 340
Crawford, Carolyn 439
Crawford, Charles 509
Crawford, Davell 84, 472, 503, 554, 730, 742, 806
Crawford, David 356, 358
Crawford, Don 278, 281, 282
Crawford, Ernest 'Big' 39, 66, 70, 72, 79, 80, 201, 403, 406, 453, 454, 467, 480, 481, 500, 557, 576, 616, 620, 627, 682
Crawford, Freddie 375, 558, 614
Crawford, Hank 115, 116, 352, 353, 354, 357, 359
Crawford, James 245, 793
Crawford, Jimmy 40, 81, 237, 654, 788
Crawford, John 219, 432
Crawford, Leslie 233
Crawford, Ollie 41, 164
Crawford, Pete 64, 141, 204, 536
Crawford, Rosetta 827
Crawford, Sugar Boy 779, 799, 804
Crawford, Tom 694
Crawl, The 771, 820
Crawley, Frank 600, 601
Cray, Robert 130, 134, 143, 274, 343, 358, 691, 776
Crayton, Pee Wee 26, 145, 295, 433, 506, 661, 662, 767, 773, 776, 779, 782, 785, 790, 797, 798, 804, 818, 820, 826
Crayton Jr, Marshall 146

Creason, Sammy 484, 509
Creasy, Darrell 166
Creech, Rusty 370
Crenshaw, Rev. R. C. 761, 812
Crenshaw, Reese 760, 761
Creole Jazz Serenaders, The 751
Crews, Felton 171, 487, 488, 613
Cridlin, Maurice 'Mac' 274
Criner, Henry 593
Cripps, Joe 153
Crisci, Lynn-Anne 369
Crisp, Melvin 42
Criss, Sonny 458
Crivellaro, Enrico 146, 241, 629
Crochet, Cleveland 832
Crocker, Richard 82
Crocker, Sal 341
Crockett, David 611
Crockett, G. L. 146, 739, 780
Crockett, Larry 37
Crocquenoy, Michel 544
Croker, Brendan 51
Cromwell, Chad 343
Cromwell, Teddy 583
Cronin, Barry 81, 82
Crook, Alistair 413
Crook Brothers 769
Crooks, Richard 535
Cropper, Steve 135, 210, 235, 348, 349, 350, 358, 375, 431, 612, 789
Crosby, Bob 739
Crosby, Charles 352, 353, 354
Crosby, Israel 7, 8, 33, 390, 701, 732
Crosby, Jason 636
Crosby, Will 4, 31, 125, 318, 369, 465, 584, 687, 733
Crosley, Earl 415
Cross, Chuckie 649
Cross, David 796
Cross, Glenn 296
Cross, John 427
Cross, Mike 21, 123, 409
Cross, Milton 328
Cross, Samuel 675
Crossan, Keith 1, 111
Crossley, Earl 550
Crosthwait, Jim(my) 498
Crow, Sheryl 360, 624
Crowder, Robert 'Sax' 61, 159, 401, 562, 620
Crowley, Walter 489
Crowns, The 788
Crows, The 773, 799
Croy, Denny 413, 417
Crozier, Van 494
Cruce, James 239, 485
Crudup, Arthur 'Big Boy' 146, 600, 738, 739, 743, 744, 752, 753, 767, 794, 797, 798, 802, 820
Crudup, Percy Lee 146
Cruickshank, Pete 271
Crumbley, Elmer 607

Crume, Dillard 631
Crume, Rufus 631
Crumit, Frank 793
Crummie, Oscar 245, 363, 365, 543, 650
Crump, Jesse 141, 142
Crunk, Connie 572
Crusto, Manuel 531
Crutchfield, James 147
Cuber, Ronnie 198, 357, 358
Cudges, Elijah 86, 87
Cues 295
Cuffee, Ed 426
Culley, Frank 'Floorshow' 245, 777, 800
Culley, Wendell 244, 683
Culliver, Freddy 84
Cultural Heritage Choir 37
Culture Fruit 242
Cumbo, Marion 592
Cummings, Albert 147
Cummings, Pete 256
Cunningham, Curtis 262
Cunningham, Del 784
Cunningham, Roy 366
Cunningham, T. David 66
Cupcakes, The 780
Cupples, Virginia 498
Curbelo, Andrea 182, 226, 583
Curbelo, Andrew 226
Curfman, Shannon 343, 431
Curran, Nick 148, 191, 687
Current, Lester 504
Currier, Terry 655
Curry, Ben 786
Curry, Clarence 437
Curry, Clifford 377, 783
Curry, Isaac 812
Curry, Pete 126
Curry, Ted 352, 353, 354
Curtis, Ben 384
Curtis, Brad 366
Curtis, Cleophus 724
Curtis, James 'Peck' 600, 608, 753
Curtis, Jules 77
Curtis, King 81, 175, 176, 363, 369, 586, 610, 616, 620, 650, 662, 807
Curtis, Lucious 759, 762
Curtis, Rob 517
Curtley, Peter 176
Cushing, Steve 32, 419, 552, 599, 673, 697
Cusic, Eddie 148, 766
Custer, Clay 739
C'Vello, Tracy 688
Cyphers, Clarence 'Bo' 392
Cyphers, Steve 499
Cyr, Marshall 118, 633
Cyrus, Gordon 37
Cytron, Samuel 75
Czarnecki, Steve 196
D. [Dickinson], Johnny 374
D.J. Jazzy Jeff 624
Da Costa, Paulinho 357, 359
Daansen, Dave 27

Daawud, Talib 62
Dabbs, Beal 94
Dabon, Robert J. 351, 472, 571
Dabrowski, Marek 411
Daddy Cleanhead 788
Daddy Hotcakes 811
Daddy Stovepipe 148, 768, 769, 775, 794
Daffan, Ted 772
Daffender, Mark 344
Daffodil String Ensemble, The 368
Daffodils, The 786
Dagradi, Tony 179, 530, 531
Daigle, Paul 489, 831
Daigle, Tony 118, 161
Daigrepont, Bruce 805, 832, 833
Dailey, Dusky 796
Dalcourt, Wayne 118, 580
Dale, Larry 141, 173, 174, 176, 713, 777, 806
Dale, Rollice 508
Daley, Claire 624
Daley, John Murry 221, 222
Daley, Joseph 623
Dallas, Leroy 752, 755, 806
Dallas Jamboree Jug Band 817
Dallas String Band 792, 810, 817
Dallas, Reggie 580
Dalton, Marion 425
Dalton, W. C. 541, 542
Daltrey, Roger 360
Dam, Han van 101
D'Amato, Nicholas 524
Dameron, Tadd 300
Damon, Winston 'Stone' 553
Danchin, Sebastian 217
Dancye, Charles 492
Dandernell, Lise 657
Danero, Danny 341
D'Angelo 359
Daniel, Gilmore 261
Daniel, Janet 184
Daniel, Roy 260
Daniels, Cecil A. 136
Daniels, Chris 193, 544
Daniels, David 49
Daniels, Julius 149, 754, 767, 793
Daniels, Nick 215, 731
Daniels, Walter 82
Daniels III, Nick 97, 118
Dara, Olu 156, 243, 665
Darby, Robert 245
Darby, Blind (Blues) Teddy 149, 738, 774, 786, 794, 810, 815
Darby, Tom 772, 810, 811, 813
Darensbourg, Joe 380, 381, 392
Darensbourg, Percy 526
Dario, Dwight 303, 414
Darling, Brie 556
Darling, Chuck 769
Darnell, Bill 773
Darnell, Larry 773, 798, 803, 804
Darnell, Tara 731

Darr, Jerome 173, 315
Dart, John 424
Dash, Julian 416, 800
Daune, Vincent 4, 6, 41, 57, 735
Davenport, Billy 35, 52, 99, 581, 711
Davenport, Chuck 286
Davenport, Cow Cow 55, 149, 626, 645, 737, 739, 740, 741, 744, 774, 807, 808, 809, 810, 816, 828
Davenport, Jed 150, 452, 768, 769, 775, 792, 794
Davenport, Lester 'Mad Dog' 54, 96, 151, 156, 316, 345, 369, 474, 770, 771, 782
Davenport, Wallace 82, 114, 115, 116, 694
Davers, Rayfield 47
Davey, Jesse 397
David, Dwight 447
David, Kal 522
David, Marty 411
Davidson, George 403
Davidson, Jammin' Jay 624
Davidson, Jo 579
Davidson, Jos 604
Davidson, Les 672
Davies, Anita 660
Davies, Cyril 371, 372
Davies, Debbie 34, 130, 151, 468, 491, 549, 779, 824, 830
Davies, Len 'The Bonesman' 546
Davies [Davis], Leo 573
Davies, Roy 363, 364
Davies, Ruth 76, 274, 275, 584
Davies, Theodore 'Dino' 30
Davis, Sister Annie 154, 155
Davis, Bill 145, 163, 219, 258, 327, 338, 340, 405, 520, 724, 725
Davis, Wild Bill 33, 63, 295, 338, 671
Davis, Bobby 5, 677, 778
Davis, Boo Boo 152
Davis, Brian 336
Davis, Carl 3, 658, 817
Davis, Carlton 'Santa' 556
Davis, CeDell 153, 766
Davis, Chalmers 402
Davis, Charles 683
Davis, Charles 'Nephew' 22, 501, 705
Davis, Clarence 384
Davis, Clyde 650
Davis, Craig 405, 590
Davis, Daryl 65, 112, 113, 495
Davis, Dedrick 375
Davis, Denise 553
Davis, Dick 650, 800
Davis, Don 681
Davis, Donna 350
Davis, Dowell 580
Davis, Duke 282
Davis, Eddie A. 24, 392, 677, 774
Davis, Eddie 'Lockjaw' 9, 244, 295, 586, 670, 671, 677, 678, 731
Davis, Eunice 617, 774, 777, 800
Davis, Fannie 441, 443

Davis, Rev. Gary 88, 153, 206, 638, 739, 747, 756, 806
Davis, Genevieve 794, 803
Davis, George 362, 472, 530, 635, 796
Davis, Gregory 87, 274
Davis, Guy 37, 155, 825
Davis, Henry 351, 364
Davis, Honeywoon 244
Davis, Ike 318
Davis, J. W. 553
Davis, Jackie 340
Davis, James 'Boo Boo' 705
Davis, James 757
Davis, Jeff 335, 430, 496
Davis, Jesse 273
Davis, Jesse 'Chip' 498
Davis, Jesse Ed 349, 623
Davis, Jimmie 166, 729, 772, 794, 795, 812, 813
Davis, Jimmy 83, 375
Davis, Maxwell Street Jimmy 156
Davis, Joe 253, 364, 460, 475
Davis, John 677, 678, 761
Davis, Blind John 69, 70, 73, 88, 124, 128, 157, 218, 321, 326, 452, 453, 616, 626, 627, 682, 683, 716, 809
Davis, Katherine 465, 829
Davis, Larry 157, 343, 440, 719, 720, 739, 788
Davis, Leo 125, 166, 236, 527, 550, 573, 669, 706
Davis, Link 773
Davis, Lucky 777
Davis, Madlyn 626, 826
Davis, Mark 126, 525, 532, 549
Davis, Martha 158, 338
Davis, Martial 156
Davis, Maxwell 1, 75, 77, 88, 163, 208, 209, 214, 219, 227, 229, 243, 247, 258, 292, 305, 307, 338, 352, 353, 354, 355, 392, 405, 432, 438, 460, 492, 504, 520, 593, 647, 661, 662, 677, 678, 684, 686, 724, 725, 800
Davis, Mel 33, 550
Davis, Michael 343
Davis, Mickey 257, 401
Davis, Mike 34
Davis, Morgan 533, 582, 598
Davis, Numa Lee 213, 797
Davis, Oscar 182, 214, 258, 583
Davis, Pam 650
Davis, Paulette 'Diva' 43
Davis, Peter 761
Davis, Pluma 47, 77, 352, 353, 354, 355, 509, 651, 662
Davis, Richard 726
Davis, Richie 41, 57, 553
Davis, Rob 51
Davis, Robert 760, 761
Davis, Rose 783
Davis, Salvatore 662

Davis, Little Sammy 158, 265, 752, 770, 781
Davis, Sonny Boy 818, 819
Davis, Steve 307, 458
Davis, T. C. 688
Davis, Theresa 57, 107, 109, 171, 318, 465, 476, 553, 599, 681
Davis, Tiny 800
Davis, Walter 158, 493, 605, 715, 716, 738, 740, 742, 743, 774, 794, 808, 809, 815
Davis, Wayne 397
Davis, William Floyd 764
Davis, Willie 57, 151, 163, 345, 346, 474
Davis, Blind Willie 812
Davis Jr, Stanton 78
Davison, Wild Bill 255
Dawkins, Jeffrey 18
Dawkins, Jimmy 'Fast Fingers' 5, 30, 77, 125, 140, 151, 159, 163, 187, 188, 317, 447, 500, 562, 612, 622, 733, 734, 744, 749, 768, 781, 782, 783
Dawson, Doris 458
Dawson, Duke 370, 570
Dawson, Gregory 730
Dawson, Jack 579
Dawson, Jake [Jacob] 345, 346, 421, 573, 581, 746
Dawson, Steve 590
Day, Bill 'Bassy' 229
Day, Texas Bill 740, 818
Day, Gill 693
Day, Margie 229, 798, 800, 827
Day, Will 817
Day, William 463
Daye, Geoff 341
Dayle, Aubrey 665
Daylie, Embra 477
Daylighters, The 789
Daym, Karin 132
Dayson, Doug 229, 534, 535
De Gruy, Terry 554
De Lange, André 37, 36
De Naut, Jud 661, 662, 677, 678
De Neeve, Carel 301
De Paris, Sidney 40, 89, 294, 587, 588 608
De Paris, Wilbur 662, 718
De Shay, James 822
de Souza, Barry 458
De Verteuil, Eddie 459, 670
De Voogt, John 726
De Vos, Bob 543
De Waal, Marco 543
De War, Tuxedo Ron 185, 581
Deacons, The 36
Deadman, Carey 614
Deamer, Clive 176
Dean, Ardie 230, 435, 609, 685
Dean, Berna 805
Dean, Chris 316
Dean, Clark 204, 564
Dean, Demas 249, 253, 587

Dean, Dolphus 473
Dean, Elton 372
Dean, Joe 740, 741, 807, 808
Dean, Johnny 457
Dean, Roger 428
Dean, Tommy 821
Deane, Dorena 63
Deane, Ed 217, 218, 228
Deane, Sammy 366
D'Earth, John 243
Deaton, Eric 251
DeBerry, James/Jimmy 752, 789, 794
Debij, Louis 157
DeChant, Charlie 544
DeCicco, Jerry 370
Decker, Jeff 243
Declouet, Thaddus 784
de'Clouet, Theryl 'Houseman' 788
DeCoste, Pete 400, 515, 614
Dedmon, James 392
Deegan, Martin 38, 374
Deehan, John 65, 376
Deere, Howard 231, 583
Dees, Robert 146
Dees, Sam 780
DeHart, George 173
Deibert, Kevin 100
Dejan, Ferdinand 219
DeKeyzer, Jack 489, 598
Del Gatto, Lew 235
Del Gizzo, Bobby 525
Del Grosso, Rich 417
Del Nero, Paul 216
Delafose, Geno 161, 162, 805, 833
Delafose, John 161, 777, 831, 832, 833
Delafose, Paul 161, 162
Delafose, Tony 161, 162
Delagarde, Mario 228, 405, 504, 505, 520, 686, 725
Delaney, Jack 462
Delaney, Mattie 767, 801, 826, 827
deLay, Paul 538, 613, 768
DeLeon, Austin [Audie deLone] 540
Delgado, Bob 431
Delgado, Joe 431
Delgard, Johan 615
Delilah 829
Dells, The 780, 790
Delmas, Pascal 223
Delmore, Lester 'Pick' 182, 215, 583
Delmore Brothers 772, 773, 798
deLone/DeLone, Austin [Audie] 111, 204, 512, 540
Delorme, Gaye 20
Delta Duo, The 787
Delta Jukes, The 163
Delta Rhythm Boys, The 83, 798
Delta X [Stephan Michelson] 18
DeMicco, Mike 2, 51
Demick, Rod 374
Deming, Doug 570
DeMink, Jerry 541

Demmer, Eric 78
DeMott, Marshall 491
DeMoura, Norm 'The Screaming Bird of Truth' 636
Demps, Louvain 271
Dempsey, Ray 457
Denham, Vince 197
Denis, Michel 77, 458, 459
Denjean, Jacques 458
Dennard, Quentin 14, 342
Dennery, Richard 547
Dennis, Arthur 244
Dennis, Bernardo 41, 287
Dennis, Emmett 115
Dennis, Rudolph 84, 459
Dennis, Wash 758
Dennis Jr, Harry 'Point Man' M. 242, 243
Dennison, Tom 40
Denny, Jeff 721
Denson Quartet 810
Denson, Paula 507
DePew, Gregory 534
DeQuattro, Tom 548
Derbigny, Leroy 362
Derkach, Bob 578
Derkash, Bob 284
DeRose, Frank 512, 540
DeRouen, Terry 'Big T' 210, 231, 241, 286, 440, 583, 720
Derrick, Frank 677
Derringer, Rick 723
DeSalvo, Pat 112
DeSanto, Sugar Pie 748, 749, 780, 829
Deshagior, Juanita 495
Desormeaux, Chuck 92
Desormeaux, Dez 200, 462, 478, 479, 553, 606
Despommier, Phil 429
Detroit Count 751
Detroit Jr 151, 163, 290, 335, 474, 528, 573, 581, 670, 711, 745, 746, 776, 778, 779, 790, 810
Detroit Piano Fats 570
Devall, Dick 810
Devaux, Christian 77
Devers, Rayfield 47, 509
Deville, Al 675
DeVille, Dallas 13
Devillier, Danny 580
Devine, Tim 358, 399, 673
Devine, Tom 535
DeVito, Harry 245
Devo, Larry 49
Dew, Hollie 761, 822
Dewdrops, The 217
Dewitt, Kristin 21
DeWitt, Wendy 204
Dexter, Al 772, 798
Dey, Tony 249
Di Pietra, Danny 58
Diabaté, Kassé-Mady 625

Diabate, Lasana 625
Diabate, Mamadou 37
Diabate, Toumani 625
Diablo, Elvin 103
Diakaté, Ramata 625
Dial, Harry 338
Diamond, Billy 166, 167
Diamond, Jim 372
Diamond, Lee 789
Diamond, Steve 222, 223, 676
Diaz, Shaun 634
Dicey, Bill 410
Dickason, Henry L. 761
Dickason, Waldo 761
Dickens, Doles 521, 800
Dickens, Little Jimmy 773
Dickens, Lawrence 'Slim' 506
Dickenson, Vic 7, 8, 294, 384, 592
Dickerson (Robinson), Aletha 48, 259
Dickerson, Bryan 43
Dickerson, Dave 765
Dickerson, Lance 293, 486, 728, 729
Dickie, Chaz 424
Dickinson, Cody 498, 499
Dickinson, Jim 246, 498, 499, 672
Dickinson, Johnny 374
Dickinson, Luther 246, 498, 499, 664
Dickson, Hugh 231
Dickson, Pearl 767, 792, 826, 827
Dickson, Pere 795
Dickson, Tom 767, 792
Diethelm, Paul 4, 5, 375
Dietrichson, Joe 517
Diffenderfer, Mark 344, 528
DiGerolomo, James 479
Diggs, James Henry 757, 765
Dillard, Calvin 692
Dillard, Varetta 799, 829
Dillon, Bill 580, 730
Dillon, Tony 731
Dilly & His Dill Pickles 795
Dimmitt, Eddie 45, 127
DiMuzio, Jerry 632
Dinallo, Mike 525, 536
Dinwiddie, Clifford 708
Dinwiddie, Gene 356
Diouani, Latabi 615
Dirks, Scott 32, 552
Dirty Dozen Brass Band, The 805
Dirty Red [Nelson Wilborn] 321, 804
'Dirty Rivers' [Muddy Waters] 138, 603
Dishman, Rich 484
Disibio, Paul 535
Dismukes, Howard 'Holley' 26, 245, 321, 322
Ditcham, Martin 37
Ditta, Carlo 365
DiTullio, Bobby Lewis 365
DiTullio, Justin 726
Ditzell, Steve 541, 550
Dixie Blues Boys 753
Dixie Cups, The 803

Dixie Doodlers 754
Dixie Hummingbirds, The 37
Dixieaires, The 821
Dixieland Jug Blowers 775, 795, 816
Dixon, Arthur 'Butch' 121, 164
Dixon, Bobby 574
Dixon, Charlie 141, 224, 249, 253, 254, 293, 294, 336, 438, 537, 587, 588, 592, 597, 718, 720
Dixon, D. 38
Dixon, Dan 321
Dixon, Dizzy 821
Dixon, D'Layna 584
Dixon, Floyd 163, 510, 687, 725, 740, 774, 776, 779, 780, 782, 788, 798, 800, 826
Dixon, Freddie 32, 35, 67, 121, 163, 164, 541, 669
Dixon, Howard 61
Dixon, Kelvin 433, 563, 583, 673
Dixon, Leon 489
Dixon, Mary 164, 827
Dixon, Ola 284, 325
Dixon, Perry 471
Dixon, Popsy 561
Dixon, R. 207
Dixon, Tyrell 'Little T' 39, 69, 627
Dixon, Vance 311
Dixon, Willie 35, 41, 42, 55, 61, 74, 79, 95, 121, 147, 164, 209, 232, 250, 263, 283, 287, 289, 306, 307, 386, 387, 403, 415, 417, 454, 456, 457, 458, 480, 481, 482, 493, 500, 521, 541, 542, 557, 562, 577, 601, 604, 610, 614, 616, 617, 620, 631, 639, 660, 678, 682, 693, 716, 722, 725, 734, 737, 744, 745, 748, 749, 779, 780, 781
Dixon Brothers 772, 813
Dixon Singers, Jesse 42
Dizz, Lefty 30, 165, 410, 746
DJ Batman 28
DJ Logic 251, 262
DJ Pete B 95
DJ Swamp 95
Dmochowski, Alex 175, 429
Dobbins, Joe 802
Dobie Red 759, 761, 762
Dobkin, Debra/Deborah 21, 430
Dobson, Lorraine 222
Dobson, Martin 53
Doc Sausage 798, 800
Dockery, Terry 214, 215
Docter, Mittie 760
Dodds, Baby 90, 173, 224, 255, 445, 637, 638, 639, 640
Dodds, Johnny 48, 98, 142, 248, 301, 322, 537, 549, 597, 646, 679
Dodgion, Jerry 358, 679
Dods, Dean 22
Dodson, Carlton DeWitt 341
Dodson, Jasper Bernard 341
Dodson, Marty 293
Dodson III, Napoleon 341

Doering, George 361
Dogan, Bob 200, 606
Dogan, Nathaniel 226
Doggett, Bill 86, 244, 291, 292, 300, 338, 340, 504, 654, 671, 724, 785
Doherty, Kevin 413
D'Oliveira, Raul 53
Doll, Robert 38
Doll Jr, Bill 38
Dollar, Johnny 166, 633
Dollis, Big Chief Bo 76, 176, 731, 806
Dolphin, Dwayne 27
Dolton, Marion 424, 425
Domanico, Chuck 235, 624
Dombecki, Lee 374
Domerette, Gus 510
Dominguez, Frank 670
Dominique, Natty 679
Domino, Fats 26, 166, 391, 661, 662, 740, 798, 799, 803, 804, 805, 808, 832
Domino, Floyd 529
Dominoes, The 505, 520, 773, 785, 798, 799
Don & Dewey 788
Donahue, Anne 491
Donaldson, Andrew 193
Donaldson, Bobby 9, 40, 81, 237, 238, 322, 416, 586, 638, 640, 730
Donaldson, Clarence 1, 39, 245, 321
Donaldson, Drew 14
Donaldson, Frank 580
Donaldson, Lou 583, 804
Donaldson, Rev. W. A. 761
Donatto, Poppee 14
Doncaster, Otis 'Big Blues' 325
Donlinger, Tom 52
Donlon, Ted 253, 513
Donnay, Roberta 729
Donnell, Delmar 279
Donnelly, Alby 413
Donnelly, John 34
Donnelly, Steve 37, 344
Donnelly, Theodore 724
Dooley, Simmie 755, 794, 811
Dopsie [Rubin], Anthony 554
Dopsie [Rubin], Dwayne 554
Dopsie, Tiger [Alton Rubin Jr] 554
Dorion, Russell 'Sly' 28, 29, 395, 553, 554, 580
Doroff, Aram 476
'Dorothy' 213
Dorsey, Georgia Tom 2, 68, 88, 167, 191, 255, 303, 311, 436, 537, 607, 626, 737, 742, 773, 774, 795, 797, 808, 809, 812
Dorsey, Jimmy 685
Dorsey, Kevin 666
Dorsey, Lee 803
Dorsey, Lester 486
Dorsey, Linda 507
Dorsey, Mattie 828
Dorsey, Tommy 353, 685, 739, 773
Dorsie, Lester 159, 734

Dortch, Jim 632
Dortin, Daren 49, 246
Doss, Willie 747
Doster, Michael 358, 359
Dotson, Big Bill 753, 819
Dotson, Hobart 355
Dotson, Jimmy 136
Dotson, Michael 92, 96, 316, 421
Dotson, Sallie/Sally 598, 713, 764
Dotson, William 598
Dotson, Willie 400
Doty, William 684
Double Trouble 168, 824
Doubleday, Frank 'Smokey' 38
Doubleday, Marcus 52
Doucet, David 195
Doucet, Jay 13, 384
Doucet, Michael 161, 195, 489, 831
Doucette, Salvador 26, 83, 140, 207, 391, 677, 678, 712
Douezy, Salvador 226
Dougherty, Big Bob 385, 800
Dougherty, Eddie 7, 8, 326, 661, 702
Douglas, Ben 764
Douglas, Bill 366, 405
Douglas, Billy 219, 725
Douglas, Bonnie 210
Douglas, Cynthia 350
Douglas, Freddie 245
Douglas, Jerry 58
Douglas, Josephine 758
Douglas, K. C. 168, 421, 680, 764, 777, 784
Douglas, Larry 507
Douglas, Nat 77, 527
Douglas, Pete 719
Douglas, Shy Guy 169, 754, 770, 786
Douglas, Steve 351
Douglas, Tommy 384
Douglas, William 432
Douglass, Bill 405
Douglass, Rob 200
Dove, Dennis 136
Dove, Myron 78, 100, 136, 690
Dove, Nat 143, 169, 286, 364, 408, 488, 577, 651, 675
Dowell, Chas 754
Dowell, Edgar 253, 385, 438, 469
Down Home Boys 794
Down Home Super Trio 169
Downchild Blues Band 169
Downes, Geoff 398
Downing, Big Al 780, 789
Downing, Billy 55
Downtown George Brown Singers, The 401
Downy, Murl 577
Doxey, Winston 346
Doyle, Little Buddy 170, 768, 769, 773, 774, 792, 797
Doyle, John 148
Doyle, Mark 18, 87, 385, 386

Doyle, Mike 18, 385, 386
Dozier Boys, The 654, 779
Dozzler, Christian 176, 405, 420, 519
Dr Feelgood 739
Dr Hepcat 752
Dr Horse [Al Pittman] 789, 807
Dr John [Mack Rebennack] 43, 76, 103, 111, 135, 168, 356, 357, 359, 368, 469, 470, 472, 531, 548, 624, 666, 667, 739, 803, 804, 805, 808
Draco, Rudy 'Root Doctor' 43, 336
Draheim, Sue 116
Draher, Danny 735
Drain, Ray C. 4
Drake, Max 81, 127, 253
Drake, Fat Richard 6
Drake, Sammy 377, 394
Drakes, Jesse 114, 245, 583
Dramatics, The 780
Dranes, Arizona 792
Draper, Melvin 39, 146
Draper, Whit 18
Drayton, Charlie 1, 198, 291, 292, 338, 384, 526
Dreamers, The 307
Dreares, Alfred 173
Dreiwitz, Dick 665
Dreja, Chris 601
Drellinger, Artie 654
Dressler, Janet 257, 401
Drew, Ethel 713
Drew, Ray 170
Drews, Glen 358
Drifters, The 799
Driftin' Slim 171, 753, 768
Driscoll, Kermit 314
Drivers, The 779
Drover, Martin 473
Drummer, Johnny 1, 171, 344, 782
Drummond, Burleigh 556
Drummond, Tim 239, 669
Dryer, Craig 524
Du Carrier, Dikki 107
Du Droppers, The 799
Du Pree, Reese 793
Duarte, Chris 788
Dubuc, Joe 27
Ducastaign, Charles 311
Duchaine, Kent 578
Duckett, Slim 737
Duconge, Wendell 26, 166, 677, 678, 712
Ducre, Betty 25
Dude, Caleb 465
Dudeck, Danny 'Mudcat' 184, 685
Dudley, John 761, 812
Duerson, Herve 740, 741, 809
Duffie, Side Wheel Sally 786
Duffy, Paul 609
Duffy, Sam 609
Duffy, Timothy 19, 230, 253, 257, 435, 511, 609
Dufrene, Carl 35

DuFresne, Mark 560
Dugas, Dwayne 107
Duke, Dharamdas Harkes 541
Duke, Douglas 510
Duke, George 508
Duke, John 341
Duke Bayou [prob. Alec Seward] 755
Duke Jethro 353, 354, 355, 540
Dukes, Felix 761
Dukes, Laura 451, 822
Dukes, Willie 793
Dullemen, Willem van 40, 101, 228, 550
Dulman, Jesse 518
Dummer, John 210, 344
Dunaway, Shelton 784
Dunbar, Aynsley 62, 175, 427, 428, 508
Dunbar, Frank 22
Dunbar, Scott 171
Duncan, Adolph 'Billy' 221, 222, 289
Duncan, Al 95, 164, 165, 233, 272, 273, 401, 404, 415, 481, 541, 542, 562, 601, 631
Duncan, Arthur 449
Duncan, Little Arthur 172, 744
Duncan, Eddie 813
Duncan, Malcolm 234
Duncan, Stuart 58
Duncan, Tommy 773
Dundee', 'Harris [Aynsley Dunbar] 175
Dungee, John 'Flaps' 473, 662
Dunham, Andrew 267, 268, 269
Dunham, Aubrey 296, 362
Dunlop, Boyd 447
Dunmore, Darrell 556
Dunn, Alan 344
Dunn, Bob 813
Dunn, Clifford 687
Dunn, Clyde 686, 725
Dunn, Donald 'Duck' 186, 348, 349, 350, 363, 365, 482
Dunn, Emmanuel 763
Dunn, Gina 74
Dunn, Johnny 460, 595, 718, 720
Dunn, Keith 228
Dunn, Marshall 38
Dupke, Mike 566
Duplechin, Corey 107
Dupont, Auguste 'Dimes' 114
Dupree, Big Al 172
Dupree, Betty 683
Dupree, Cornell 175, 176, 356, 363, 365, 652, 727
Dupree, Champion Jack 96, 141, 172, 211, 445, 639, 640, 641, 738, 739, 740, 741, 743, 749, 752, 755, 764, 773, 774, 777, 785, 788, 803, 805, 806, 807, 821
Dupree, Robert Lee 145
Dural, Gerald 87
Dural, Sir Reginald Master 87
Dural, Rodney 107
Dural, Stanley 'Buckwheat' 86, 87, 119, 395, 648

Durall, Chantelle 395
Durant, Henry 81
Durante, Jimmy 712
Durawa, Ernie 550
Durham, Allen 677
Durham, Eddie 291, 607
Durham, Sonny 504
Durio, Alphanette 624
Durio, Mickey 572
Durkett, Paul 771
Durran, Dan 408
Durst, Lavada 819
Duskin, Big Joe 53, 177, 742, 800
Dutko, Thomas 'Mot' 204, 574, 645
Dutrey, Honore 679
Duvivier, George 9, 84, 237, 245, 592, 684
Dye, Bill 247
Dyer, Johnny 95, 177, 262, 422, 538, 779
Dyer, Wilbur 229
Dyke, Jon 370
Dyke, Jonny 397
Dykes, Omar 501, 502
Dykhuis, Marvin 529
Dykhuizen, Dave 'Double D' 687
Dylan, Bob 737, 739
Dymond, Jon 369, 540
Dysart, Skip 572
Dyson, Joe 600
Dyula-Speaking Urban Musicians 810
DziDzournu/Dzidzornu, Kwasi 'Rocky'/'Rocki' 623
Dziubla, Ronald 262
E.L.S. 439
Eades, Ronnie 257, 401
Eager, Allen 244
Eagleaires, The 79
Eaglin, Snooks 178, 362, 530, 752, 764, 771, 803, 804, 805, 806
Eaglin Sr, Fird 178
Ealey, Robert 721, 820
Earheart, Billy 335, 496
Earl, Dave 486
Earl, David 499
Earl, Jimmy 198
Earl, Ricky 401
Earl, Ronnie 27, 103, 123, 179, 284, 362, 400, 423, 427, 515, 546, 549, 557, 559, 606, 729, 768, 771, 814, 824, 825
Earland, Charles 543
Earle, Jimmy 777
Earle, John 'Irish' 53
Earle, Justin 824
Earle, Steve 824
Earlettes, The 265
Earley, Ed 43, 44, 599
Earley, Mark 560
Early, Hezekiah 251, 254, 706
Easley, Bill 84, 727
Easley, Dave 503, 571
Easman, Louis 373

Eason, (Robert Charles) Robbie/Robby 240, 241, 728
Eason, Silas 696
Eason, Brother Willie 823
East, Nathan 122, 343, 359
'East Memphis Slim' [Jim Dickinson] 246, 498
Easterling, James 805
Eastman, Ric 260
Easton, Amos [Bumble Bee Slim] 788
Easton, Harold 77
Easton, McKinley 138, 232, 662, 678, 683
Easton, Sidney 134, 385
Easy Baby 180, 771
Ebersole, Bob 'Max' 413
Ebner, Scott 386
Ebony Three 526
Echoes Of Zion, The 821
Eckbert, Nat 784
Eckert, Thomas 125
Ecklund, Peter 484, 578, 728
Eckstine, Billy 797
Eddie Dark & The Eagleaires 79
Eddleton, Wilfred 713
Eddy, Duane 572
Edelblut, Jeannine 18
Edelmann, John 400, 645
Eden, Bill 721
Edge, Dave 413
Edgehill, Arthur 9, 586
Edgewater Crows 796
Edgeworth, Ron 371
Edick, Greg 152
Edinborough, Eddie 385
Edison, Harry 'Sweets' 145, 358
Edmaiston, Art 375
Edmond, Willie 'The Whip' 554
Edmonds, Elga/Elgin 66, 335, 403, 480, 481, 557
Edmondson, Count 173, 445, 639
Edmondson, Derrick B. 374
Edmonson, Robare 683
Edmonson, Steve 512, 540
Edmunds, Dave 191
Edney, Spike 228
Edson, Estelle 449
Edwards, Alan 424
Edwards, Archie 181, 750, 766
Edwards, Art 219
Edwards, Arthur 520, 677, 678
Edwards, Moanin' Bernice 181, 774, 786, 794, 795
Edwards, Bill 136
Edwards, Carrie 808
Edwards, Charles 'Lefty' 26, 245
Edwards, Good Rockin' Charles 768, 771, 822
Edwards, Clarence 136, 182, 764, 791
Edwards, Cornelius 764
Edwards, David 'Honeyboy' 182, 264, 344, 566, 617, 738, 744, 746, 752, 758, 759, 762, 782, 788, 789, 802, 814, 825

Edwards, Frank 184, 757, 768, 769, 786
Edwards, Gary 554
Edwards, J. D. 752
Edwards, Jesse 650
Edwards, Joe 607
Edwards, Joseph 11, 117, 193
Edwards, Kathleen 540
Edwards, Paulo 193
Edwards, Piano Kid 740, 786
Edwards, Richard 53
Edwards, Ron 656
Edwards, Ronnie Boy 540
Edwards, Scott 351
Edwards, Teddy 69, 185, 244, 259, 340, 725, 728
Edwards, Tom 592
Edwins, Charles 650
Efford, Bob 62, 174
Effros, Bob 685
Egan, Bob 618
Egan, Mark 51
Egan, Little Willie 782
Egans, Willie 659
Egea, Claude 318
Eggleston, Cozy 610, 799
Eggleston, Lee 289, 290
Egloff, Goofy 176
Ehlers, Poul 422
Ehlers, Vance 486
Ehrlich, Jesse 726
Ehrmann, Steve 197, 274, 275, 444, 445, 468, 487, 558, 584, 690
Eiland, David 4
Einreinhofer, Bobby 'Boom Boom' 400
Eisen, Steve 42, 118, 260, 723
Eisenberg, Larry 139
Eisinger, Ari 823
El, Eddie 147, 183, 607
El Dorado(e)s, The 746, 790, 799
El Hussaini, Zain 650
El Rog 492
Elam, Charles 730
Elam III, Charles 13, 215, 361, 718, 731
Elbek, Morten 8
Elbert, Donnie 789
Elbol, Jens 6
Eldred, Lee 780
Eldridge, Joe 315, 526
Eldridge, Roy 142, 725
Electric Flag, The 737
Elem, Robert 'Big Mojo' 5, 165, 185, 365, 581, 745, 746, 822
Elferdink, Tom 101
Elhers, Vince 293
Elkins, Alfred 39, 46, 61, 71, 124, 128, 157, 201, 218, 263, 289, 321, 326, 333, 406, 453, 454, 455, 500, 519, 536, 618, 619, 620, 627, 670, 682, 708, 716
Elkins–Payne Jubilee Quartette 294
Ellery, Jesse 172, 173, 212
Ellington, Duke 322, 808
Elliot, Ronny 58

Elliott, Charles 'Rick' 657
Elliott, Ernest 134, 164, 293, 294, 325, 398, 426, 437, 475, 587, 588, 592, 595, 596, 679, 718
Elliott, Wayne 210, 424
Ellis, Big Boy 752
Ellis, Big Chief 445, 446, 638, 639, 640, 755, 806
Ellis, Bill 414
[Ellis?], 'Big Bill' 414
Ellis, Carwyn 498
Ellis, Dorothy 774
Ellis, Hattie 757, 762
Ellis, Lance 107, 571
Ellis, Pee Wee 53, 223, 439
Ellis, Tinsley 81, 185, 707, 768, 776
Ellis, Tony 344
Ellis, William 318
Ellis, William Lee 524, 823
Ellison, John 824
Elman, Ziggy 8, 328, 390
Elniff, Bjørn 456
Elo, Michael 657
Elrod, Tommy 350
Elsensohn, Bruce 6, 222, 499, 681
Elson, Steve 668
Emanon Trio 829
Embree, Jerry 554
Embry, Queen Sylvia 186, 745, 750
Emerick, Mark 369
Emerson, Billy 'The Kid' 365, 415, 601, 693, 789
Emerson, Mike 14
Emerson, Robby 575
Emery, Bob 539
Emery, Nathaniel 'B. J.' 163, 669, 670
Emery, Pete 344
Emma 36
Emmanuel, Leroy 257
Emmons, Bobby 509
Emmons, Tim 485
Emmons Baptist Church 757
Emory, Russell 'Fats' 661, 662
Emphrey, Calep 358, 401
Emphrey Jr, Calep 77, 358, 359, 364
Endres, Brent 576, 618
Enevoldsen, Bob 357
Eng, Tyler 263
English, Bill 543, 650, 686
English, Paul 34
Enois, Lucky 84, 384, 593, 662, 773
Enos, Bob 185, 222, 324, 362, 559, 560, 567, 667
Enright, Ed 204
Enright, Thomas 548, 560
Entress, Lorne 180
Eppley, Mike 358
Epstein, Mark 724
Erby, Jack 808
Erby, John 320, 607
Erickson, David 65
Eriksson, Olle 36, 37

INDEX

Erlanger, Louis X. 153
Ernest, Herman 135, 325, 429, 439, 503, 688
Ernest III, Herman 179, 362, 583, 695
Ernst, Shannon 373
Errisson, King 351, 679, 727
Erskine, Les 63, 245, 300, 416, 650
Ervin, Cliff 429
Ervin, Dee 351
Ervin, Jeff 729
Ervin, Jesse 75, 228, 405
Ervin, Leroy 752, 818, 819
Erwin, Gary 253, 511, 513
Escobar, Steve 526
Escudero, Ralph 249, 253, 460, 469, 597, 685
Eshelman, Dave 100
Esparza, Bill 100
Esparza, Greg 'Lucky' 104
Espina, Jeff 478
Espinosa, Joe 249
Espinoza, Regina 199
Esposito, Charlie 291
Esprite, John 'Popp' 161, 580
Esser, Joe 222
Estefan, Gloria 360
Estes, Gene 727
Estes, Sleepy John 56, 187, 226, 536, 737, 738, 739, 747, 748, 749, 768, 769, 781, 792, 794, 802
Estrin, Rick 239, 293, 399, 538, 676, 771
Etienne, Clarence 'Jockey' 11, 377, 394, 408, 585, 586
Etkin, Larry 134, 179, 567
Eubanks, Robin 358
Euell, Julian 467
Eugene, Wendell (or Homer) 140, 531
Eulitz, Jody 21, 22
Evans, Andre 251, 499, 664
Evans, Belton 229, 279, 281, 283, 334, 500, 616, 620, 639, 642, 713
Evans, Bernice T. 664
Evans, Billy 415
Evans, Brenda 137
Evans, Brian 649
Evans, David 189, 251, 496
Evans, Delmar 'Mighty Mouth' 506, 507, 508
Evans, Elgin [Elga Edmonds] 480
Evans, Frank 759
Evans, Glenn 58
Evans, Herschel 292
Evans, James 74, 510
Evans, Jeffery 541
Evans, Jennie 228
Evans, Jim 410
Evans, Joe 189, 295, 767, 792, 793, 794, 807, 810, 811
Evans, Big John 249
Evans, Lawrence 282
Evans, Leo (Lucky Lopez) 32, 190, 745
Evans, Major 724

Evans, Margie 112, 506, 663, 749, 750
Evans, Nick 175, 372, 457
Evans, Otha Andre 243
Evans, Rodney 243, 251, 499, 664
Evans, Sammie 'Sticks' 245, 445, 583, 639
Evans, Seeward 724
Evans, Steve 44, 469, 558
Evans, Stump 141, 142, 610
Evans, Tania 374
Evans, Terry 20, 198, 274, 336, 417, 788, 814
Evans, Warren 315
Everett, Betty 781, 790
Eves, Mick 363, 364
Evil One, The 186
Ewing, John 'Streamline' 278, 281, 355, 447, 507, 508, 679, 725
Exon, Willie James 348
Exum, Jim 42, 723
Exum, Larry 15, 318, 550
Eyden, Bill 726
Eyre, Tommy 11, 95, 342, 343, 359, 430, 431, 468, 469
Ezell, Buster 'Buz' 821
Ezell, Will 55, 190, 225, 549, 740, 741, 807, 808
Fabre, Tom 719
Fabulous Thunderbirds 190, 770, 818
Faddis, Jon 679
Fagan, Douglas 138, 541, 694, 695
Fagen, William Norman 552
Fahey, Brian 136, 411, 414
Fahey, John 812
Fain, Sammy 685
Fair, Ron 376
Faire, John 26, 83, 300, 520, 670, 671
Fairfield Four, The 786
Fairhurst, Naomi 228
Fairweather Low, Andy 122, 359, 431, 824
Faison, Joyce 'Peaches' 614
Faithful Wanderers 778
Faki, Foum 625
Faki, Makame 625
Falcon, Joe 831
Falcon, Odile 831
Falcon, Solange 831
Falcons, The 681
Falima 36
Fallon, Jack 73, 174, 176, 702, 703
Falls, Erica 554, 731
Faltinson, Ken 6, 7, 35, 599, 600, 644
Fame, Georgie 53, 483
Famous, Kevin 361
Famous Hokum Boys 191, 786
Fanenskov, Mette 242
'Fang' [Tom Hoskins] 18
Faracci, Miro 618
Faragher, Davey 236
Farkas, Nick 554
Farlow, Billy C. 264, 377
Farlow, Tal 112, 113
Farlowe, Chris 372

Farmer, Addison 366, 661, 662
Farmer, Art 661, 662
Farmer, Ethan 633
Farmer, Johnny 192
Farmer, Julius 530
Farnell, Uncle Tom 264, 532
Farr, Deitra 192, 584, 606, 829
Farrar, Cash 674
Farrell, Joe 679
Farrell, Lorenzo 399
Farrell, Matt 148
Farren, Dave 396
Farriss, Carter 296
Fassl, Siggi 132, 346, 574
Fastman, Louis 583
Fasulo, Paul Vincent 55, 60, 194, 202, 211, 220, 241, 342, 411, 414, 475, 522, 618, 704
Fataar, Ricky 343
Fatool, Nick 328
Faulise, Paul 358, 679
Faulk, Chris 16
Faulk, Dave 'Gangsta' 222
Faulk, John Henry 821
Faulk, Kenny 257
Faulkner, Glen 251, 810
Faulkner, Lorene 685
Faulkner, Roland 482
Fauntleroy, Lester 416, 459
Fauth, Julian 629
Favors, George 670, 671
Fazarde, Keith 232
F'dor, Steve 123, 124, 241, 413, 556
Fé, Pura 786
Feather, Leonard 76, 86, 90, 140, 245, 291, 292, 506, 523
Feathers, Charlie 347
Feathers & Frogs 774
Febia, Martin 374
Federico, Frank 462
Feeley, Devitt 413
Feenstra, Wybren 152
Fegy, Dick 497
Feigenbaum, Jerrold 721
Feiner, Bruce 27, 236, 370, 424, 518, 539, 540, 576, 609, 612, 649
Feiner, Jennie 518
Feiner, Robert 27, 236, 370, 424, 518, 539, 540, 576, 609, 612, 649
Feld, Morey 90, 227, 565
Felder, Ray 63, 83, 245, 300, 321, 322, 543
Felder, Wilton 48, 357, 506, 508, 551, 679
Feldman, Lawrence 343
Feldmann, Thomas 74, 220, 312
Felgen, Bruce 591
Felker, John 590
Fellow, Thomas 6
Feltham, Mark 495
Felton, Gerry 'Phareaux' 502
Fender, Billy 351
Fender, David 'Fingers' 78
Fender, Mike 138

Fender, Sammy 541
Fenichel, Mark 446
Fennell, Walter 150
Fenner, James 255, 658
Fenton, Rachel 148
Fenton, Rick 446
Fenwick, Ray 424
Ferguson, Ben 248, 249, 775
Ferguson, Charles 415, 455, 654
Ferguson, Charles 'Little Jazz' 392
Ferguson, Curtis 620, 650
Ferguson, H-Bomb 192, 653, 782, 788, 800
Ferguson, Harry 84, 384
Ferguson, James 186
Ferguson, Cool John 10, 184, 609
Ferguson, Keith 190
Ferguson, Kyle 540
Ferguson, Maynard 593
Ferguson, Troy 767, 795
Ferguson, Walter 264
Fernandez, John 83
Fernell, Douglas 677
Ferrante, Russell 196, 197, 198
Ferreira, Dave 375
Ferreira, Johnny 20
Ferris, Jackie 343
Ferrone, Steve 122, 343, 364
Ferry, Joe 152, 156, 195
Fetzer, Robert 166
Fickle, Jimmy 576
Field, Ernid 660
Fields, Alfred 743, 820
Fields, Bobby 233, 265, 659, 660
Fields, Boney 412
Fields, Brandon 197, 342, 359
Fields', 'Chester [Kim Wilson] 314
Fields, Danny 'Boney' 4, 138, 490, 544
Fields, Ernie 351
Fields, Frank 26, 58, 75, 114, 140, 166, 167, 178, 207, 305, 391, 402, 529, 620, 622, 677, 678, 712
Fields, Geneva 193
Fields, Herbie 244, 291, 292, 683
Fields, Kansas 440, 455, 457
Fields, Ray 'Rainbow' 249
Fields, Thomas 'Big Hat' 193
Fields, Venetta 356, 439, 508, 551, 643
Fields, Willie 697
Fieldstones, The 193
Fierro, Martin 138, 535
Fife & Drum Band Of The United Sons And Daughters Of Zion Chapter Nine 764
Fig, Anton 673
Figueroa, Gammy 566
Filisko, Joe 305
Filleul, Peter 53
Fillman, Tom 21
Fillmore Slim 193, 464
Finch, Otis 267, 269, 661, 662
Finckle, Steven 695

Findley, Charles B. 357
Findley, Chuck 48, 356
Findley, Clark 17
Fine, Jack 63
Finegan, Jamie 236, 370, 424, 518, 539, 540, 609, 649
Finer, Sara 36
Fink, Joe 613
Finlayson, Michael 133
Finnegan/Finnigan, Mike 104, 235, 307, 468, 485
Finnell, Doug 526
Finney, Garland 1
Firmin, John 293, 399, 496, 497, 540, 728, 729, 735
First Priority 364
Fischer, Lizz 100, 690
Fischkal, Freimuth 96
Fish, Alan 15
Fishell, Steve 21
Fisher, Aiden 424
Fisher, Charles 591
Fisher, Elliott 686
Fisher, Greg 547
Fisher, Norm 20
Fisher, Tony 53
Fishkin, Sam 118
Fité, Joi 346, 599
Fitting, Jim 519
Fitzgerald, Ella 338, 798
Fitzgerald, Jay 'Hurricane Jake' 629
Fitzgerald, Nate 350
Fitzhugh, Michael 499
Fitzpatrick, Jerome 501
Fitzpatrick, Mike 533
Fitzpatrick, Tom 730
Fiume, Marco 262, 342, 618
Five Blazes, The 779, 798
Five Breezes, The 743, 797
Five Harmaniacs 775
Five Keys, The 798
Five Red Caps 797, 798
Fjelle, Espen 197, 728
Flaim, Tony 170
Flamingos, The 779, 780
Flanagan, Mike 16
Flanagan, Taylor 219
Flanders, Nell 580
Flanigan, Phil 548
Flawless 624
Flax, Marty 338
Fleetwood, Mick 33, 62, 358, 428, 431
Fleetwood Mac 227, 228, 738, 813
Fleischer, Barry 717, 718
Fleming, Dave 416
Fleming, Gordon 238
Fleming, Rob 78
Fleming, Teagle 114, 115
Fleming, Walter 'King' 244, 517
Flemming, Herb 249, 595, 718, 720
Flemming, Richard 264
Flennoy, Lorenzo 662

Fletcher, Colin 424
Fletcher, Gary 53
Fletcher, Kirk 'Eli' 60, 191, 194, 220, 241, 261, 414, 422, 704, 719
Fletcher, Napoleon 618, 619, 773, 774
Fletcher, Raymond 554
Flett, Buddy 575
Fliegler, Richie 133
Flint, Hughie 53, 176, 428
Flintall, Herman 473
Florence, Nellie 23, 812, 813
Flores, Bill 22
Flores, Ruben 657
Flori, Gary 657
Florida Kid, The 796
Flory, Chris 548
Flower, Mary 513, 823
Flowers, Danny 37
Flowers, Jimmy 311, 551
Flowers, Snooky 52
Flowers, Willy 761
Floyd, Babi 191
Floyd, Barney 78, 84, 571
Floyd, Bernard E. 472
Floyd, Buddy 145, 163, 229, 247, 405, 463, 593, 724, 725
Floyd, Eddie 680
Floyd, Ell-Zee 815
Floyd, Harmonica Frank 779, 802
Floyd, Harlan 713
Floyd, Harold 78, 79
Floyd, King 803
Floyd, Minnie 760
Floyd, Noble 607
Floyd, Reuben 607
Fluker, Cora 766
Flynn, Billy 25, 66, 151, 160, 169, 172, 192, 293, 303, 346, 476, 533, 598, 612, 698, 707, 719
Flynn, Fred 221, 240, 311, 636
Flynt, Shelly 81, 127
Foddrell, Marvin 765, 812
Foddrell, Turner 765, 812
Foehner, Sharon 586
Foley, Red 773, 798
Foley, Sue 194, 293, 377, 446, 824, 825, 830
Folwell, William 233, 272
Fonfara, Michael 52, 169, 170, 489, 501, 533, 598
Fontaine, Eddie 780
Fontenette, Gus 231, 232
Fontenette, Johnny 82, 83
Fontenot, Allen 539
Fontenot, Canray 11, 195, 762, 777, 831, 832
Fontenot, Isom 11
Fontenot, Joe 400
Fontenot, Nathaniel 13, 117, 202
Fontenot, Ralph 580
Fook, Alfonso 84, 459
'Foot' 509

Foote, Bea 526
Foote, Stephen 50
Forbes, Mike 104
Ford, Andrew 'Fats' 245
Ford, Anne Kerry 198
Ford, Barry 356
Ford, Billy 62, 459, 670
Ford, Charles 196, 777, 800
Ford, Clarence 76, 166, 178, 232, 402, 531
Ford, Tennessee Ernie 773
Ford, Frankie 805
Ford, Fred 77, 350, 353, 505, 509, 520, 651
Ford, Gabriel 100, 198, 199
Ford, Henri 'Hank' 33, 41, 57, 67, 96, 109, 129, 316, 318, 330, 346, 368, 443, 474, 553, 568, 590, 599, 614, 632, 681, 691, 707, 733
Ford, James 'T-Model' 25, 198
Ford, Jimmy 492
Ford, Louis 479, 480
Ford, Mark 196, 197, 198, 199, 445, 690, 771
Ford, Patrick 100, 196, 197, 198, 199, 341, 445, 487, 658, 728
Ford, Richard 34, 246
Ford, Robben 196, 197, 199, 343, 445, 487, 488, 727, 728
Ford, Sammy 295
Ford, Sidney 576
Ford, Willie 759
Ford Blues Band, The 199
Fordjour, Jeanana 109
Foreman, Al 258, 377, 394, 408
Foreman, Chris 130
Foreman, Rufus 64
Forest, Earl 221, 799
Foresythe, Terrence 624
Forman, Bruce 485
Forman, Rich 249
Fornek, Mark 200, 204, 440, 462, 478, 606
Fornero, Dan 197, 198
Forrest, Jimmy 790, 799
Forrest, Sonny 116
Forrest, Susann 548
Forrest City Joe [Pugh] 761
Forrester, Bobby 84
Forrester, Randy 43
Forsyth, Gina 182
Forsyth, Guy 200
Forsythe, Terence 359
Forte, Bobby 47, 76, 210, 249, 353, 354, 355, 356, 357, 440
Fortesque, John Henry 755
Fortune [Fame], Georgie 483
Fortune, Jesse 200, 781, 790
Foster, Bennie 445, 640, 642
Foster, Bill 121, 223, 709
Foster, Bobby 445
Foster, Curtis 267, 268, 269, 681
Foster, Desmond 37
Foster, Dessa 594

Foster, Elaine 21, 554
Foster, Elizabeth 554
Foster, Emma Jean 37
Foster, Frank 671
Foster, Gwen 769, 772
Foster, Herman 369
Foster, Jimmy 321
Foster, Leroy 80, 201, 386, 387, 403, 480, 481, 532, 616, 744, 779, 785
Foster, Lisa 21, 361
Foster, Pops 89, 90, 140, 255, 294, 321, 379, 380, 381, 382, 445, 461, 607, 639, 640
Foster, Rayvon 666
Foster, Ronnie 'Bird'/'Byrd' 544
Foster, Rudy 740, 808
Foster, Ruthie 37, 123, 251, 311
Foster, Sharon 21, 361
Foster, Treena 540
Foster, Willie 201
Foster, Little Willie 744, 769, 770, 781
Foster & Harris 167, 626
Foucher, Edmond 25
Fouda, Desiré Basil 810
Fountain, Eli 681
Fountain, Pete 805
Four Blackamoors 796
Four Blazes, The 790, 799
Four Bluebirds, The 504
Four Buddies, The 798
Four Clefs, The 798
Four Duchesses 417
Four Flames, The 715, 788
Four Jacks, The 228
Four Southerners 796
Four Students, The 521
Four Tunes, The 799
Four Vagabonds, The 778
Fournier, Vernell 541, 542
Fowler, David 49
Fowler, Dick 711
Fowler, Jesse 387
Fowler, Lemuel 254, 336, 426, 592, 707, 739
Fowler, T. J. 201, 472, 677, 678, 713, 798
Fowler Jr, Dolpha 632
Fowlkes, Charlie 63, 115, 244, 671
Fowlkes, Herman 434, 600, 601
Fox, Alonzo 227
Fox, Colin 424
Fox, Eugene 659, 660
Fox, John D. 131, 801
Fox, Richard 227
Fox II, Russell 559
Foxx, Charlie 789
Foxx, Inez 789
Foy, Joel 123, 240, 414, 720
Fra Fra Tribesmen 737
Fraga, John 350
Framer, Eli 811
Frampton, Peter 34, 372
Fran, Carol 201, 377, 394, 783, 791, 806

Francis, Archie 675
Francis, David 'Panama' 20, 40, 60, 81, 86, 115, 211, 244, 266, 271, 273, 300, 410, 439, 527, 592, 643, 662, 663, 727
Francis, George 575
Francis, John 442
Francis, Morris 831
Francis, William 769
Franco, Marco 714
Frank, Ani 217, 218
Frank, Arnaud 318
Frank, Brad 202, 203
Frank, Carlton 203
Frank, Edward 26, 77, 305, 391
Frank, Jennifer 202, 203
Frank, Jocquelle 532
Frank, Keith 202, 203, 384, 831, 832
Frank, Michael 96, 411
Frank, Nanette 42, 171
Frank, Preston 203, 777, 831, 832
Franklin, Andre 592
Franklin, Aretha 739
Franklin, Buck 89
Franklin, Claude 572
Franklin, Israel 672
Franklin, James Earl 25
Franklin, Mabel 820
Franklin, Paul 343
Franklin, Pete 66, 203, 218, 616, 627, 743
Franklin, Tiny 808
Franks, Michael 643
Franks, Tim 32, 411, 555
Frantz, John 257
Franzee, Billy 375
Fraser, Alec 80, 302, 489, 598, 629
Fraser, Andy 372
Fraser, Earl 718
Fraser, Elwyn 245
Fraser, Wendy 342
Fratangelo, Larry 350
Fratis, Lewe 572
Frazer, Glen 424
Frazier, Bob 507
Frazier, Calvin 201, 204, 523, 681, 741, 751, 752, 753
Frazier, Chris 566
Frazier, Jake 253, 336, 437, 460, 469, 475, 596
Frazier, John 455, 620
Frazier, Johnny 311
Frazier, Kerman 569
Frazier, Lawrence 650
Frazier, Nathan 811, 816
Fred P G 218
Frederick, John 118
Fredericks, Carole 623
Fredericks, Sonny 315
Frederiksen, Marti 376
Fredman, Dan 146
Fredrick, Lyvord 681
Free Radicals, The 824
Freebo 233, 413

Freed, Audley 222, 246
Freeman, Denny 26, 139, 168, 194, 408, 612, 666, 669
Freeman, Ernie 75, 292, 506, 686, 726
Freeman, George 477
Freeman, K. K. 664
Freeman, Kendrick 305
Freeman, Michael 465
Freeman, Robert 98
Freeman, Russ 472
Freeman, Sonny 47, 352, 353, 354, 355, 356, 357, 509
Freeman, Tricia/Trisha 657
Freeman, Wilbert 356, 357
Freeman Singers, The Evelyn 572
Freezone 767, 795
French, Bob 178, 402
French, George 178, 362
French, John 757
French, Mark 18
French, Robert 178, 362, 391
French, Rochelle 757
Frenchy's String Band 817
Freund, Steve 57, 204, 236, 293, 421, 462, 464, 486, 488, 501, 532, 564, 590, 607, 617, 768, 770, 781
Frey, Glenn 359
Frezek, Dan 201
Friday, Charles 783
Friedkin, Joellen 343
Friedman, Bob 584
Friedman, Brian 52
Friedman, Ron 42
Friel, Randy 81, 127
Friend 'N' Fellow 824
Friend, Constanze 6
Friend, Phil 721
Frigidaires, The 152
Frimer, Ole 53
Frisco Jack [John Stover] 341
Fritz, Joe 'Papoose' 258, 509, 819
Frost, Frank 198, 199, 205, 313, 316, 576, 676, 770, 782
Frost, Steven 126
Frosty [B. E. Smith] 200
Fry, Tristan 457, 458
Fuchs, Andy 660
Fukunaga, Glenn 469
Fula Flutist 811
Fulcher, Larry 21, 68, 123, 195, 246, 255, 450, 624, 625, 676
Fullard, Curtis 111
Fullbright, Richard 150, 221, 416, 526, 597
Fuller, Blind Boy 206, 637, 638, 639, 640, 737, 738, 755, 767, 768, 773, 774, 794, 806, 810, 812, 813, 820, 823
Fuller, Bob 134, 253, 325, 336, 437, 438, 459, 460, 461, 469, 475, 587, 588, 590, 592, 595, 596, 718, 721
Fuller, J. R. 330
Fuller, Jesse 206, 747, 777, 782

Fuller, Johnny 207, 780, 788
Fuller, Little Boy [Richard Trice] 774, 806
Fuller, Playboy [Louisiana Red] 751
Fuller, Rocky [Louisiana Red] 744, 751, 752, 779
Fullerton, Cyril J. 249
Fulp, Preston 207, 756, 758, 786
Fulson, Lowell 199, 208, 219, 272, 350, 358, 440, 456, 457, 506, 558, 629, 752, 767, 768, 776, 777, 779, 780, 782, 785, 788, 789, 797, 798, 799, 818, 819, 823, 826
Fulson, Martin 208, 209
Fulton, Robert 146
Fumando, Jose 373
Funderburgh, Anson 179, 210, 220, 241, 293, 373, 434, 435, 476, 479, 489, 691, 768, 788, 818, 820
Funk, Bob 130, 134, 567
Fuqua, Harvey 307, 780
Furnace, Sam 133
Fussell, Jake 85
Fuster, Ravon 168
Fuzzy 660
G, Freddie 536
G., Bobby 572
Gaardmand, Anders 179
Gabriel, Paul 51
Gabriel, Percy 24, 82, 84, 724
Gadd, Steve 122, 359
Gaddy, Bob 211, 638, 640, 800
Gaddy, Willie 26, 63, 83, 473
Gadson, James 1, 351, 357, 364, 374, 720
Gadson, Tutty 659
Gaffney, Chris 139
Gaffney, Mick 609
Gaillard, Slim 506
Gaines, Charlie 718
Gaines, Earl 169, 335, 783, 786
Gaines, Everett 459
Gaines, Grady 179, 527
Gaines, Jim 68, 130, 131, 148, 151, 599, 600, 644, 657
Gaines, Little Joe 803
Gaines, Roy 47, 211, 351, 422, 464, 651, 725, 768, 823
Gainey, Jackie 583
Gainey, Ted 29, 100, 513
Gaither, Bill 88, 172, 173, 212, 626, 686, 744, 820, 821
Gaither, William 463
Galactic 805
Galasatis, Mike 229
Galatin (or Gatlin), Wiley 561
Galbo, Marc 823
Galbraith, Barry 271, 273
Galbraith, Frank 86, 245, 300, 416, 610
Galchick, T. Edward (Eddie) 574, 645
Gale, Chris 687
Galea 517, 524
Galeano, Jose 666

Gales, Eric 633, 824, 825
Gales, Larry 429
Gallagher, Benny 53
Gallagher, Bernie 176
Gallagher, Noel 498
Gallagher, Rory 350, 483
Gallagher, Steve 580
Gallery, Graham 630
Gallie, John/Jon 349, 363, 365
Galliher, Fred 765
Gallsatus, Mike 535
Galvan, Hootie 506, 507, 508
Galvin, Al 386, 387
Gambara, Dija 810
Gamble, Al 127, 215, 476, 524, 564, 575, 644
Gamble, El Torro 510, 721
Gamble, Otis 459
Gamble, Patsy 65, 425
Gammon, Patrick 660
Gandy Dancers 751
Gannon, Steve 194, 374, 544
Gant, Cecil 213, 740, 741, 794, 797, 798, 800, 826
Gant, Clenest 786
Gant, George 333
Gant, Moses 245, 473, 677
Ganz, Jeffrey 274
Gappell, Moe 712
Garafalo, Jim 1
Garcia, Heitor 584
Garcia, Javier 218
Garcia, Joyce 43
Garcia, Robert 27
Garcia Jr, John 274
Gardner, Albert 'June' 83
Gardner, Andrew 'Goon' 33, 415, 610, 654, 678
Gardner, Burgess 346, 465, 632, 691
Gardner, Debbie 21
Gardner, Denise 763
Gardner, John 252, 503, 627
Gardner, June 351
Gardner, Mattie 761, 763
Gardner, Mike 430
Gardner, Simon 53
Gardner, Steve 251
Gardner, Tommy 404
Garelick, Gus 535
Garibaldi, David 690
Garland, Ed 380, 381
Garland, Jim 378
Garland, Sarah [Sarah Ogan Gunning] 378
Garlow, Clarence 214, 719, 767, 784, 785, 790, 804, 818, 820, 830, 831
Garman, Lawrence 228, 395
Garner, Al 783, 786
Garner, Dan 647
Garner, Larry 214, 583, 791
Garnett, Blind Leroy 739, 740, 741, 803
Garnier, Djalma/D'Jalma 107, 580

Garnier, Tony 236, 291
Garofalo, Bryan 356
Garoua, Adamou Meigogue 810
Garr, Burton 555
Garr, John 107, 555
Garred, Milton 114
Garrett, Al 215
Garrett, Amos 20, 484, 485, 486
Garrett, Arvin 650
Garrett, Greg 43
Garrett, James C. 406
Garrett, Jo Ann 746
Garrett, Mike 613, 706
Garrett, Robert 754
Garrett, Siedah 198
Garrette, Duke 510
Garrison, Memphis T. 761
Garrity, Dave 572
Garry, Tommy 189
Gary, Leroy 761, 812
Gary, Sam 703
Garza, John 61
Gaskin, Calvin 'Skip' 688
Gaskin, Leonard 9, 40, 81, 83, 140, 279, 280, 281, 283, 334, 410, 500, 571, 586, 610, 616, 620, 639, 642, 663, 726
Gaskin, Victor 429, 430
Gaspard, Octave 219
Gates, Ashward 172, 181
Gates, Geri 624
Gates, Great 800
Gates, Ira 401, 711, 733
Gates, Rev. J. M. 793, 810, 821
Gates, Robert 690
Gates Jr, Ashward 550
Gatewood, Ernest 159, 396, 562, 734
Gatewood, Johnny 248
Gatling, Lee 355
Gatteno, Scott 570
Gaudion, Peter 727
Gauld, Sid 234
Gauthier, John Paul 548
Gautreau, Ernie 21, 78, 79
Gayden, Johnny B. 31, 109, 130, 134, 160, 166, 260, 474, 516, 517, 527, 528, 541, 568, 569, 599, 632, 695, 711, 723, 735, 771
Gayden Jr, A. C. 571
Gaydos, Joey 370
Gayles, Billy 157, 659, 660
Gayles, Joe 472
Gayten, Paul 140, 622, 780, 798, 799, 800, 803, 804
Gayters, Thomas 439
Gazell, Phil 58
Gearan, Tim 636
Geboers, Rob 524
Geddins Jr, Bob 439
Gee, Matthew 245, 477
Geechie 76
Geidel, Linda 257
Geils, Jay 152, 771

Geller, Herb 300
Gellert, Rayna 634
Gems, The 401
Gene & Al's Spacemen 789
Gene & Eunice 799
Genn, Antony 95
Gennari, Ray 560
Geno 572
Genome 262
George, Barbara 803, 804, 805
George, Karl 252, 384, 414, 593, 683
'George' 541
Georgia Browns 768, 795, 810, 812, 813
Georgia Cotton Pickers 769, 794, 795, 812
Georgia Crackers 772
Georgia Pine Boy [Joe McCoy] 773
Georgia Sea Island Singers 751
Georgia Slim 737, 794
Georgia Yellow Hammers 816
Geraci, Anthony 'B. B.' 66, 152, 180, 222, 284, 316, 491, 497, 536, 548, 735, 771
Geraci, Cam 546
Gerald, O'Neil 114, 115
Gerard, John 231
Gerass, Danny 231
Gerek, Rick 66
Geremia, Paul 156, 215, 825
Gernger, Wallace 830, 831
Gerrard, Donny 241, 262, 357
Gerschwitz, Martin 657
Getrex, Les 554
Getzoff, James 210
Geyer, Dennis (Denny) 229, 534, 535
Geyer, Rene 235
Ghetto, The 368
Ghundi, Steve 572, 573
Giancarlo, Geraldo 220
Gianquinto, Albert(o) 138, 568
Gibb, Clayton 343
Gibbard, John 'Greyhound' 368
Gibbons, Billy F. 359, 431
Gibbs, Jerry 457
Gibbs, Resa 2
Giblin, Tommy 68, 733
Gibralters, The 81
Gibson, Billy 90, 127
Gibson, Cleo 773, 774, 818
Gibson, Clifford 31, 216, 618, 619, 737, 753
Gibson, Gus 760, 761
Gibson, Herman 592
Gibson, Jarrett 233, 265, 386, 404, 601, 693
Gibson, Jim 556
Gibson, John 'Black Sampson' 759
Gibson, Lacy 217, 233, 265, 415, 568, 617, 693, 745
Gibson, Lee 1
Gibson, Lil Willie 803
Gibson, Master Henry 674
Gibson, Mike 679

Gideonsson, Bjorn 36, 37
Giesler, Tom 526
Gil, Leonard 194
Gilbeaux, Gene 504, 724, 725
Gilbert, Alan 638
Gilbert, Lafayette 'Shorty' 573, 574, 576
Gilbert, Paris 37
Gilchrist, Douglas 499
Gilkey, Randy 82
Gill, Calvin 388
Gill, David 515
Gill, Glover 168
Gill, Leonard 291, 360, 433, 539, 563, 583
Gill, Vince 343
Gillams, Andy 425
Gillespie, Dana 132, 217, 376
Gillespie, Dizzy 90, 291, 292, 332, 526, 679
Gillespie, 'Fast'/'Fazz' Eddie 540, 576
Gillette, Mic 100, 198, 199, 273, 291
Gilliam, Wilbert 757
Gilliam 595
Gilliams, Andy 65
Gillum, Charles 228, 463, 715, 725
Gillum, Jazz 69, 218, 333, 456, 738, 742, 743, 744, 768, 769, 774, 797, 798
Gilmore, Bobby 721
Gilmore, Boyd 753
Gilmore, Earl 765
Gilmore, Gary 623
Gilmore, Gene 743
Gilmore, Hollis 241, 433, 659
Gilmore, Jay 649
Gilmore, Jim 440
Gilmore, John 242, 243
Gilmore, Kelly 440
Gilmore, Otto 451
Gilmore, Randy 256
Gilmour, David 359
Gilstrap, Jim 358, 643
Ginn, Bill 310
Giordano, Charlie 422
Girard, Rich 558
Giraud, Tiye 156
Giron, Peter 6
Gist, Pierce 607
Gitfiddle Jim [Kokomo Arnold] 756
Givens, Anna 659
Givens, Charles 286
Givens, Cliff 600
Givens, David 659
Givenzano', 'Eduardo [Alex Dmochowski] 175
Glackin, Drew 636
Gladiolas, The 783
Gladney, A. J. 557
Glantz, Nathan 595
Glascoe, Percy 469, 596
Glass, Melvin 447
Glaub, Bob 469, 547, 624
Glaze, Ruby 448, 826
Glazer, Howard 570

Glazer, Tom 701
Gleb, Howe 513
Glen, Alan 495
Glen, Emery 793
Glen, Marla 6
Glenn, Lloyd 19, 77, 208, 209, 219, 247, 353, 354, 355, 449, 520, 533, 647, 677, 678, 679, 740, 779, 798, 826
Glenn, Tyree 83, 90, 140, 245, 295, 416, 670, 671
Glines, Randy 529
Glinn, Lillian 219, 737, 818, 827
Glosson, Lonnie 772, 795
Gloud, Vennette 357
Glover, Ed 670
Glover, Henry 62, 86, 315, 483, 650
Glover, Jimmy 670, 671
Glover, Kenny 101
Glover, Mae 220, 767, 773, 774, 801, 826
Glover, Pete 713
Glover, Tony 'Little Sun' 371
Glover, William 521
Gnagey, Caroline 148
Godchaux, Brian 246
Godfrey, Hettie 758
Godfrey, John 583, 800
Godley, A. G. 326, 661
Godwin, Bob 570
Goff, Hattie 758
Goff, Leo 696
Goforth, John 43
Goines, Victor 84
Goins, Elder James 786
Goins, Glen 350
Goins, Herbie 371, 372
Gold, Hyman 508
Gold Front Boys, The 817
Goldberg, Barry 52, 121, 486, 674
Goldberg, Mark 164, 413, 629
Goldberg, Richie 115
Golde, Richard 572
Golden, Jay 4, 6
Golden, Quinn 711
Golden Gate Quartet, The 379, 702, 739, 747, 760, 798, 811, 821
Goldin, Nina 342
Goldmark, Joe 373
Goldrush 753, 782, 826
Goldstein, Robb 50
Goldstein, Steve 342
Goldwasser, Frank 22, 50, 161, 169, 193, 194, 220, 241, 422, 464, 551
Golson, Benny 300, 726
Gomes, Steve 6, 211, 222, 236, 362, 499, 544
Gomez, Al 21
Gonsalves, Anthony 510, 567
Gonsalves, Paul 115
Gonyea, Troy 291, 525, 546, 719
Gonzales, Anthony 721
Gonzales, Babs 173
Gonzales, Dave 241, 341, 414, 691

Gonzales, Mark 'Speedy' 65
Gonzalez, Memo 220
Gonzalez, Sergio 343
Good Rockin' Bob 754
Good, Jack 371
Good, Sam 186
Goode, I. B. 362
Gooden, Tony 550, 568
Goodly, Ann 831
Goodman, Benny 8, 328, 390, 587, 588, 739, 741, 747
Goodman, Harry 8, 328, 390
Goodman, Irving 8
Goodman, Karen 111
Goodman, Mark 624
Goodman, Steve 425
Goodrich, Andrew 295, 521
Goods, Michael 539
Goods, Michelle 731
Goodson, Bill 84, 459
Goodwin, Henry 250
Goodwin, Mark 201
Goodwine, Matt 594
Goossens, J. J. 152, 591
Gorden, Ron 403
Gordon, Bob 467
Gordon, Chick 607
Gordon, Dexter 245, 292
Gordon, Forrest 402
Gordon, Greg 118
Gordon, Jim 273, 343, 356, 363, 364, 679
Gordon, Jimmie 88, 149, 220, 436, 437, 471, 637, 773, 774, 815, 820, 821
Gordon, Lena 713
Gordon, Lloyd 38
Gordon, Pick 510
Gordon, Rosco 221, 740, 785, 789, 790, 799
Gordon, Russell 86, 108
Gordon, Sax 372
Gordon, Stomp 800
Gore, Eddie 135, 384
Gore, Edison 83, 245, 300
Gore, Rufus 63, 245, 300, 405, 520, 543
Goreed, Joseph 780
Gorham, Wilbur 699
Gorman, Ross 253
Gospel Camp Meeting Singers 626
Gospel Hummingbirds 779
Gospel Mets, The 179
Gospel Pilgrims, The 821
Gospel Supremez, The 346
Goss, Stacy 395
Gousset, Claude 77
Gouvin, Neil 6, 222, 239, 492, 497
Goux, John 376
Gov't Mule 825
Gower, Chris 53
Gozzo, Conrad 726
Graber, Brian 502
Grace, Frank 386
Grace, Ken 'Doc' 560

Grace, Tina 217
Gradney, Francis 202
Grady, Bill 785
Grady, Fred 15, 318, 617
Grady Jr, Michael 330
Grady Sr, Michael 330
Graham, Andy 579
Graham, Anna/Anne 380, 381
Graham, Bill 245, 472, 670, 671
Graham, Billy 34
Graham, Chauncey 715
Graham, David 731
Graham, Davy 431
Graham, Dell 829
Graham, Flip 651
Graham, Kenny 73, 703
Graham, Leonard 338, 340
Graham, Lonnie 61
Graham, Ora Dell 758
Graham, Pancho 625
Graham, Richard 189
Grails, Jeff 244
Grainger, Cleo 679
Grainger, Ethel 592
Grainger, Porter 134, 224, 253, 254, 320, 325, 398, 426, 437, 438, 459, 587, 588, 592, 595, 596, 607, 720
Grainger, Steve 728
Grand, Jeff 98
Grand, Otis 6, 222, 231, 674, 676, 767, 768, 825
Grandell, Buddy 31
Granderson, John Lee 121, 223, 387, 425, 494, 734, 745, 814, 822
Granstaff, Earl 718
Grant, Amy 343
Grant, Bob 293
Grant, Bobby 786, 794, 801, 810, 813
Grant, Charles 213
Grant, Eddie 472
Grant, Gary 357, 359, 376
Grant, Harold 392, 432, 463, 686, 725
Grant, Jewel(l) 1, 88, 214, 229, 243, 252, 305, 354, 392, 405, 432, 543, 661, 662, 683, 686, 725
Grant, Robert 194
Grant, Sidney 173
Grant, Warren David 691
Grant, Coot 223, 829
Grasser, Tibor 224, 742
'Grasshopper' 98
Gravenites, Nick 52, 121
Graves, Claiborne 384
Graves, Dan 84, 459, 517
Graves, Daviel 517
Graves, Lee 504, 505
Graves, Blind Roosevelt 190, 225, 786
Graves, Uaroy 190, 225
Gray, Blind Arvella 225, 822
Gray, Charles 33
Gray, Chas. 158
Gray, Cora 248

INDEX 865

Gray, Dobie 135
Gray, Henry 808, 34, 95, 135, 146, 182, 225, 289, 290, 403, 404, 514, 541, 542, 557, 649, 734, 742, 778, 779, 791, 809, 824
Gray, Kitty 729, 803, 818
Gray, Larry 564
Gray, Leroy 472
Gray, Matt 211
Gray, Sam 398
Gray, Thomas 'Tick' 426
Gray, Wardell 295, 405
Graydon, Jay 351
Grayer, Jeff 222
Grayson, Charles 83, 405
Greaves, Dennis 495
Grebb, Marty 235, 358, 563, 624
Grech, Rick 483
Greely, David 117, 832
Green, Benny 73, 703
Green, Boy 755, 806
Green, Cal 663, 672
Green, Carl 44, 193, 512, 540
Green, Charlie 141, 142, 224, 336, 537, 587, 588, 592, 597, 707
Green, Clarence 77, 244, 719, 772, 820
Green, Collin Jr 400
Green, Derek/Derrick 531, 532
Green, D'Ryan 531
Green, Earl 223, 374
Green, Eddie 643
Green, Eli 441
Green, Eugene 62
Green, Freddie 115, 661, 663, 671
Green, Grant 804
Green, Guitar Slim 819, 826
Green, Henry 724, 725
Green, Henry Tucker 292
Green, Herman 666
Green, Jake 595
Green, James 35, 160, 290, 562, 563
Green, Jerome 55
Green, Jesse 562, 563
Green, Jimmy 84
Green, Joe 228
Green, L. C. 751, 752
Green, Larry 209
Green, Lee 226, 740, 809
Green, Lil 227, 739, 742, 743, 797, 827
Green, Mark 170
Green, Marlon 275
Green, Mick 228
Green, Neil 455, 654
Green, Otis 412
Green, Peter 33, 34, 62, 152, 227, 427, 428, 431, 457, 458, 604, 738, 767, 813, 824
Green, Ray 427
Green, Robert 140
Green, Ron 534
Green, Rudy 783, 786
Green, Russell 472

Green, Sam 129
Green, Slim 782, 826
Green, T. J. 412, 708
Green, Tim 503, 554, 563, 571, 580
Green, Tuff 221, 222, 288, 352, 353, 354
Green, Urbie 295, 358, 725
Green, Vernon 788
Green, William 354, 521, 636, 726
Green, Willie 580, 830
Green & Turner, R. 826
Green Jr, William 431
Greenberg, Jeffrey 580
Greenberg, Kenny 644
Greenberg, Mark 180
Greene, Ed 48
Greene, Irving 300
Greene, Jeanne 349
Greene, 'Diamond' Jim 228
Greene, Marlin 238
Greene, Mary Lou 63
Greene, Richard 485, 680
Greene, Rudy 794
Greene, Willie 274
Greenhill, Mitch 823
Greenidge, Robert 623, 624
Greenlee, Bob 377, 490, 491, 518, 544
Greenway, Roly 368
Greenwell, Jim 539
Greenwich, Robert [Greenidge] 624
Greenwood, Derek 'Dee' 12, 13, 14
Greenwood, Lil 228, 788
Greer, Big John 245, 300, 583, 799, 800
Greer, Sonny 90, 295, 322, 703
Greeson, Liz Mandville 96, 171, 782, 830
Greggs Eggs 824
Gregory, Edmund 724
Gregory, Ken 136
Gregory, Mickey 349, 350
Gregory, Steve 363, 364, 603
Gregson, Gray 123
Greig, Stan 456, 672
Greiner, Jim 583
Grennan, Winston 291
Gresham, Jimmy 542
Grey, Al 77, 115, 510, 671
Grey, Charles 661, 662
Grey, Sonny 544
Greyson, Corinna 218
Gribble, Murph(y) 759, 811
Grider, Tom 84
Grier, Cheryl 136
Grier, Corny Allen 796
Grier, Stanford 227
Griffin, Buddy 83, 229
Griffin, Chris 8, 328, 390
Griffin, Glenn 118
Griffin, Haran 81, 257
Griffin, Jerome J. 513
Griffin, Jimmy 82, 229, 777
Griffin, John 587
Griffin, Johnny 83, 245, 446, 477, 544
Griffin, Larry 152, 705

Griffin, Little Brother 56, 116, 214
Griffin, Marie 740
Griffin, Ollie 287
Griffin, Paul 612, 652, 726
Griffin, Ray 257, 358, 401
Griffin, Robert 363
Griffin, Sean 361
Griffin, Tommy 229
Griffin, Tracy 242, 571, 730
Griffin Brothers, The 229, 799
Griffith, Jeff 4
Griffith, John 267
Griffith, Johnny 681
Griffith, Paul 416
Griffith, Steve 673, 674, 690
Griffiths, Dave 425
Griffiths, Malcolm 371, 372
Griffiths, Steve 223
Griggs, Frankie 773, 774
Grigsby, Doug 624
Grigsby, Richard 'Grady' 476
Grillier, David 25, 503
Grillo, Frank 340
Grills, Steve 27
Grim, Stanley 514
Grimes, Charlie 272, 273, 461
Grimes, Chester 227
Grimes, Howard 126, 439, 585
Grimes, Johnny 684
Grimes, Stuart 186
Grimes, Tiny 19, 84, 90, 473, 767, 777, 790, 800, 807
Grimes, Ty 337, 705
Grimm, Garnet 386
Grimm, Mickey 222
Grimont, Jeff 615
Grisman, David 485
Grissom, David 26, 191, 197, 235, 342, 430
Grissom, Jimmie 593
Griswold, Whit 485
Groenveld, Rinus 101
Groetzinger, Red 569, 606
Grofe, Ferdie 253
Groner, Duke 33
Grooveneers, The 796
Groover, Don 'Psycho-Picker' 291
Gros, John 243
Gross, Felix 229, 826
Gross, Jill 718
Gross, Kenny 540
Gross, Lee 201, 677, 678
Gross, Leon T. 798, 803, 804
Gross, Martin (Tino) 100, 365
Gross, Martin 98, 284, 510
Gross, Robert 506, 686
Grossman, Stefan 19, 155, 344, 466, 487, 812
Grosswendt, Martin 216
Groves, Big Boy 800
Groves, Lani 351
Gruenbaum, Leon 665

Gruendler, Donny 262
Grundy, Hense 248, 679
Gryce, Gigi 40
Guadaloupe, Gregorio 318
Gudgeon, Lizzie 218
Gudman, Kenn 372
Guerault, Stéphane 41, 734
Guesnon, Creole George 467, 796, 803
Guess, Bill 182
Guest, Graham 195, 446
Guffin, Lum 764
Gugolz, Daniel 132, 176, 224, 486, 519, 742
Guidry, Cornelius 531
Guidry, Greg 13
Guidry, Sticks Herman 12, 531, 784
Guidry, Madison 118
Guidry, Terrance 296
Guilbeau(x), Phil 116, 472, 662, 713
Guilbeu, Martin 193
Guillory, Chuck 831
Guillory, Harold 13, 14
Guillory, Myrick 'Freeze' 229, 534, 535, 624, 729
Guillory, Ron 535
Guillory, Steve 556
Guinn, Ed 296
Guiraud, Cyril 4
Guitar Curtis 230
Guitar Gable [Perrodin] 377, 394, 408, 783
Guitar Gabriel 230, 253, 756, 757, 786
Guitar Joe 56
Guitar 'Junior' 138
Guitar Nubbit 230
Guitar Red 783
Guitar Shorty 231, 583, 768, 781, 823
Guitar Shorty [John Henry Fortesque] 755
Guitar Slim [Alec Seward & Louis Hayes] 755, 777, 806
Guitar Slim [Eddie Jones] 231, 737, 767, 776, 788, 790, 797, 799, 803, 804, 805
Guitar Slim [James Stephens] 766
Guitar Slim Jr 232
Gulczynski, 'Bruner' Andrzej 411
Guliuzza, Greg 465
Gulley, Dennis 688
Gulley, Lola 186
Gulliver, Freddie 384
Gum, Brian 257
Gunn, Art 785
Gunning, Sarah Ogan 378
Gunter, Little Al 169, 754
Gunter, Arthur 169, 754, 776, 783
Gunter, Hardrock 773
Gunter, Shirley 785, 799
Gunther, Paul 77, 671
Gunther, Tim 136
Gunulfsen, Gene 79
Gurewitz, Ron 199, 690
Gurr, Steve 43, 44, 599, 728

Gusasak, Nat 654
Gutcheon, Jeff 425
Guthorn, Katie 43
Guthrie, Arlo 643
Guthrie, Jack 772
Guthrie, Woody 379, 380, 381, 382, 637, 638, 639, 640
Guy, Browley 650
Guy, Buddy 62, 232, 272, 289, 290, 358, 404, 430, 458, 480, 481, 482, 483, 601, 631, 632, 651, 693, 694, 695, 744, 748, 749, 767, 768, 779, 780, 825
Guy, Fred 322
Guy, Martin 672
Guy, Phil 234, 236, 458, 539, 540, 541, 652, 694, 695, 768
Guyet(t), Jim 274, 369
Guyger, Steve 204, 211, 236, 503
Guyton, Ronnie 157
Guzman, Joel 450
Gwaltney, Joe 116
Gwynn, Marty 429
Gypsey, Guitar 43
'H. B.' 125
Haar, Greg 92
Habenero Horns 113
Hackberry Ramblers, The 831, 832
Hacker, F. G. 132
Hackett, Bobby 83
Haddock III, Levi 409
Haddrell, Bob 44
Haden, Charlie 139
Hadgen, Mary Ellen 27
Hadi, Shafi [Curtis Porter] 713
Hadley, Robert 650
Hadnott, Billy 88, 89, 114, 164, 208, 209, 219, 338, 340, 384, 405, 432, 463, 505, 533, 647, 677, 678, 686
Haffer Jr, Charles 762
Hagan, Andy 81
Hagan, Donnell 350, 711
Hagans, Robert 'Buddy' 166
Hager, Alan 'A. J.' 152
Hager, Alan 547, 703
Haggerty, Augustus 'Track Horse' 757, 758, 760
Hague, Peter 370
Hahn, Fingers 135
Hahn, Marc 406
Haigh, Chris 226
Haines, John 194
Hairiston, Napoleon 698
Hairless, R. H. 399
Hairston, Brother Will 821
Hairston, Lewis 812
Haj, Amour 625
Hakim, Sulaiman 6, 544
Halaj, Bob 42, 121, 450
Halajian, Richard 580
Halbert, Willie Lee 367
Halbreich, Andrew 342
Halby, Mike 104

Halcox, Pat 340, 641
Haldeman, Marguerite 257
Hale, Edward 292, 677, 678, 686, 731
Hale, Jack 144, 145, 191, 349, 458, 572
Hale, Ken 614
Hale, Lisa 179
Hale, Otis 266
Hale, Owen 257
Hale, Stanley 14
Haley, Bill 773
Haley, Lady Lisa 538
Halial 133
Hall, Adelaide 827
Hall, Al 39, 40, 211, 227, 327, 328, 456, 464, 473, 592, 661, 662, 703
Hall, Albert 62, 174
Hall, Alberta 805
Hall, Archie 'Skip' 245
Hall, Bob 53, 217, 236, 264, 344, 487, 513, 532, 630, 730
Hall, Bobbie 210, 551
Hall, Carl 356
Hall, Clarence 26, 58, 140, 166, 178, 391, 661, 662, 712
Hall, Daryl 360, 624
Hall, Ed 'Shark(e)y' 258, 686
Hall, Edmond 142, 291, 332, 390, 661, 701, 702
Hall, Equila 811
Hall, Freddie 776, 781
Hall, George 84
Hall, Gerri 362, 391
Hall, Harry 595
Hall, Herbert 219
Hall, Horace 438, 439
Hall, James 796
Hall, Jerry 40
Hall, Jimmy 111, 644
Hall, Joe 509
Hall, John 51, 623
Hall, Juanita 237
Hall, Kenny 116
Hall, Nolen 410
Hall, Orrington 63, 83, 245, 670, 671, 684
Hall, Pat 96, 591
Hall, Reggie 805
Hall, René 209, 245, 416, 432, 521, 654, 686, 788
Hall, Rick 171
Hall, Sam 369
Hall, Sandra 253, 513
Hall, Sharky 258
Hall, Skip 84, 730
Hall, Solomon 40, 245
Hall, Tony 470
Hall, Tubby 311
Hall, Vera 758, 760, 761, 762, 822
Hall, Willie 349, 350, 401, 403, 551
Hall Sr, Jack 572
Hallen, Brad 560
Hallman, Mark 502

Halperin, Paul 'Texas Red' 136
Halpin, Mike 42
Halstead, Ric 728
Halvorson, Eric 516
Hambelton, Debbie 325
Hamberlin, Floyd 711
Hambrick, Walter 733
Hambridge, Tom 135, 636, 644
Hamilton, Andy 44
Hamilton, Anthony 376
Hamilton, Chico 1, 292, 390, 724
Hamilton, Gino 328
Hamilton, Jimmy 291, 292, 328, 473, 526
Hamilton, Joy 432
Hamilton, Larry 274
Hamilton, Leighton 314
Hamilton, Ralph 1, 114, 209, 229, 305, 307, 353, 354, 392, 405, 432, 460, 492, 661, 662, 684, 686, 724, 725
Hamilton, Roy 432
Hamilton, Scott 548, 559, 728
Hamilton, Vera 507
Hamm, Mark 297
Hammerton, Richard 85
Hammond, Bruce 76, 472, 730
Hammond, Clay 784
Hammond, Jerome 44
Hammond, John 237, 274, 319, 486, 643, 747, 793, 810, 814, 824, 825
Hammond, Stick Horse 752, 794, 818
Hammond, Tosh 98
Hamner, Curley 510
Hampton, Carl 401
Hampton, Claudette 257, 401
Hampton, Colonel Bruce 153, 636
Hampton, Gary 721
Hampton, Ken 22, 632
Hampton, Lionel 90, 142, 328, 510, 683, 740, 741, 773, 797, 798
Hampton, Riley 7, 661, 662
Hampton, Slide 670, 671
Hampton, Vivian 465
Hamric, Todd 186
Hamza 242
Hanck, Terry 43, 44, 204, 293, 336, 512, 599, 613
Hancock, Charles 345
Hancock, Jerry 373
Handcock, John 821
Handy, Julius J. 472
Handy, Major 831
Handy, W. C. 796
Hanen, R. T. 216, 774
Hanes, John 220
Haney, Paul 141
Hankes, Doug 370
Hankins, Donald 233, 263, 265, 266, 289, 386, 404, 601, 631, 693
Hankins, Tall Paul 265, 778, 779
Hanley, John 310
Hanlon, Allen 115, 295, 663
Hanna, Bryan 111

Hannaford, Eph 595
Hannah, George 391, 773, 774, 786, 808
'Hannah May' 1
'Hannah May' [Mozelle Alderson] 69, 191, 742, 774
Hannas, Herbert 607
Hannon, Mark 204
Hansen, Finn Otto 174
Hansen, J. 399
Hansen, Ole 657
Hanson, Dick 53
Hanson, Per 27, 34, 103, 127, 139, 152, 179, 180, 362, 370, 375, 402, 423, 427, 488, 491, 516, 546, 557, 614, 771
Harbert, James 116
Harbour, Bob 649
Hardee, John 84, 90, 140, 245, 292, 473
Harden, Wilbur 82
Hardesty, A. G. 182, 488, 583
Hardesty, Anthony 490, 550
Hardesty, Herb 26, 58, 140, 166, 391, 620, 661, 662, 677, 678, 712
Hardge, Johnny 187
Hardiman, Leonard 'Tight' 447
Hardin, Lane 753, 767, 794
Hardin Jr, Joseph 357
Harding, Alex J. 518
Harding, Buster 725
Harding, Hiram 219
Hardman, Alan 91
Hardman, Bill 63
Hardy, Heather 417
Hardy, Helen 424
Hardy, Lucius 808
Hardy, Mattie 796
Hardy, Solomon 352, 353
Hardy, Vicki 541, 669
Hardy, Victoria 424
Hare, Pat 47, 221, 222, 480, 481, 482, 509, 789
Hargis, Glenda Sue 553
Hargrave, Bill 41
Hargrove, Hosea 239
Harkles, Fernando 146
Harlem Hamfats 239, 741, 742, 797
Harman, Bob 209
Harman, Doug 558
Harman, Fred 505, 506
Harman, James 146, 240, 308, 399, 417, 538, 630, 721, 728, 771
Harmon, Clarence 761
Harmon, Nelson 761
Harmonica Fats 241
Harmonica Red 182, 583
'Harmonica Slim' [Robert Gates] 690
Harmonica Slim 241
Harmonizing Four, The 790
Harmony Four 498
Harms, Jesse 231
Harney, Richard 'Hacksaw' 241
Harper, Ben 275, 488, 824
Harper, Buddy 593

Harper, DeLisle 364
Harper, Emerson 718
Harper, Joe 30, 159, 188, 284
Harper, Lee Z. 650
Harper, Ricky 115
Harper, Willie 521, 730
Harpo 526
Harptones, The 799
Harrell, Vernon 400
Harrington, James 527, 528
Harrington, Janice 242
Harrington, Joe 125
Harrington, Paul 647
Harris, Ace 416
Harris, Alfoncy 448
Harris, Alfred 753, 770, 790
Harris, Andrew 240, 321, 415, 500, 616
Harris, Arville 426
Harris, Barry 472
Harris, Bethenea 448
Harris, Bob 446, 504, 640, 642
Harris, Calvin 112
Harris, Cecil 447
Harris, Charles 90, 141, 142, 291, 292, 537, 683, 685
Harris, Charlie 245
Harris, Clarence 249, 556, 618, 685
Harris, Corey 242, 516, 695, 738, 739, 776, 788, 814, 823, 825
Harris, Cornbread 414
Harris, Cozy 320
Harris, Dave 535, 593
Harris, Dickie 684, 685
Harris, Don 'Sugarcane' 273, 429, 506, 508, 622, 643
Harris, Ed 806
Harris, Erline 803, 804
Harris, Garry 547
Harris, Gene 358
Harris, Golden P. 810
Harris, Henry 765
Harris, Henry 'Sneaky Joe' 307
Harris, Hilda 727
Harris, Homer 480, 743, 820
Harris, James C. 83
Harris, James 639, 640
Harris, Blind Jessie 760
Harris, Jimmy 416
Harris, Joe 26, 58, 140, 166, 391, 472, 517, 661, 662, 729, 760, 761
Harris, John 248, 775
Harris, Kenny 609
Harris, Kevin 87
Harris, Leigh 'Lil' Queenie' 805
Harris, Leroy 63, 86, 245
Harris, Les 806
Harris, Little Joe 532
Harris, Magnolia 594
Harris, Mark 299, 520
Harris, Mary 337
Harris, Norman 356
Harris, Paul 355, 356, 673

INDEX

Harris, Peppermint 243, 782, 798, 819
Harris, Pete 758, 759, 812, 817
Harris, Ralph 783
Harris, Rick 525
Harris, Rolf 217
Harris, Ron 78
Harris, Shad 111, 540
Harris, Stan 726
Harris, Steve 97
Harris, Terry 413, 423
Harris, Thurston 228
Harris, Tom 328
Harris, Tommie 96
Harris, William 244, 793, 794, 801
Harris, Willie 290, 794, 795, 801, 807, 812, 813
Harris, Willie Lee 709, 770
Harris, Woody 52
Harris, Wynonie 244, 450, 773, 774, 785, 797, 798, 799, 800, 804, 826
Harris Jr, Willie 525
Harris-Drummond, Mary 556
Harris & Harris 794
Harrison, Adam 489
Harrison, Barry 27, 135, 576
Harrison, Jimmy 426, 587
Harrison, Lloyd 438, 661, 662
Harrison, Michael 413
Harrison, Patty LaRue 538
Harrison, Paul 73
Harrison, Ray 169
Harrison, Smoky 787
Harrison, Stan 667, 668
Harrison, Wilbert 789
Harrison, William 315
Harrod, Chuck 786
Harry Smiths, The 314
Harsch, Eddie 98, 130, 138
Harshaw, Jerry 398
Hart, Alvin Youngblood 246, 310, 486, 498, 695, 824, 825
Hart, Booker T. 414
Hart, Charlie 217
Hart, Hattie 450, 451, 773, 774, 792, 794, 826
Hart, John 11, 118, 119, 553
Hart, Lisa 336
Hart, Martin 428
Hart, Paul 424
Harter, Bob 296
Hartford, John 708
Hartley, Keef 174, 175, 344, 427, 428, 429, 430
Hartman's Heartbreakers 772
Harton, Dale 518
Hartz', 'Fred [Kenny Graham] 73, 703
Hartzfield, John 245
Harum Scarums 786
Harves, Cleo 819
Harvey, Amos 85
Harvey, Bill 47, 77, 352, 353, 354, 509, 651
Harvey, Bob 208, 209, 219, 533, 647

Harvey, Myron 645
Harvey, Roy 772
Harvey, Ted 140, 160, 299, 370, 396, 515, 520, 533, 557, 558, 631
Harvey, Will 530, 531
Harvey Jr, Will 530
Harwell, Thomas 222
Haskell, Jimmie 356
Haskin, Peter 10, 406
Haskins, Norman 760
Hassan, Ali 625
Hasselbach, Mark 210
Hassell, Eric 665
Hassell, Herman 299
Hastings, Lennie 527
Hastings, Lowell 'Count' 63, 81, 245, 300, 338, 340, 416, 459
Hatch, Little 247
Hatch, Simeon 245, 321, 322, 473
Hatcher, Willie 605, 715, 792
Hatfield, Rick 583
Hathaway, Donny 401
Hatot, Alain 5
Hatten, Willie James 402
Hatter, Harold 249
Hatton, Bert 'Snake Root' 815
Hauerken, Henning 17, 501
Haughey, Bobby 458
Haughton, John 'Shorty' 62, 730
Hausa Trader 810
Havens, Richie 517
Haver, Greg 398
Hawdon, Dicky 72
Hawes, Bess Lomax 701
Hawes, Butch 701
Hawes, Hampton 505
Hawes, Pat 72
Hawkes, Corrine 20
Hawketts, The 779, 803, 805
Hawkins, Buddy Boy 247, 767, 786, 817
Hawkins, Coleman 142, 237, 253, 254, 537, 587, 595, 596, 661, 662, 685, 707, 720, 725
Hawkins, Dale 779, 780
Hawkins, Ernie 486, 823
Hawkins, Erskine 739, 797, 798, 800
Hawkins, F. M. 521
Hawkins, George 591
Hawkins, Hawkshaw 773
Hawkins, Leonard 140
Hawkins, Ren 552
Hawkins, Roger 6, 209, 238, 282, 349, 350, 585
Hawkins, Ronnie 139, 789, 824
Hawkins, Roy 247, 740, 798
Hawkins, Steve 166, 654
Hawkins, Ted 788
Hawks, The 779
Hawley, Ted 296
Hawthorne, Cheryl 535
Hawthorne, Larry 535
Hayden, Fat 89

Hayes, Adrienne 179, 635, 636
Hayes, Billie 796
Hayes, Bonnie 612
Hayes, Chris 231
Hayes, Clifford 247, 816
Hayes, Curtis 248
Hayes, Ernie 40, 81, 83, 272, 340, 662
Hayes, Henry 110, 129, 243, 719, 819, 820
Hayes, Isaac 824
Hayes, Jeff 4, 375
Hayes, Jerome 77
Hayes, Kevin 144, 145, 151, 274, 275, 358, 367
Hayes, Larry 414
Hayes, Lonnie 400
Hayes, Louis 270, 569, 671, 752, 755, 765, 777, 806
Hayes, Macavine 756
Hayes, Nap 320, 792, 810, 816
Hayes, Pat 374, 375, 612
Hayes, Randy 100, 468, 469
Hayes, Ray 38
Hayes, Steve 424
Hayes, Rev. Timothy 765
Hayes, Warren 400
Hayes, Willie 6, 7, 31, 42, 121, 166, 568, 707, 733
Haygood, Maurice 383
Haynes, Billy 211
Haynes, Bobby 430, 663
Haynes, Ernie 118
Haynes, Gerald 'Cowboy' 544
Haynes, Graham 518
Haynes, Mike 186, 402
Haynes, Roy 83, 641, 642, 726
Haynes, Warren 275, 402, 575
Hayney, Burnell 258
Hays, Lee 702
Hays, Mark 372
Hayslett, Eric 14
Hayward, Cedric 282
Hayward, Mike 370
Hayward, Richie 186, 234, 235, 342, 375, 468, 547, 624
Hayward, Rick 395
Haywood, Cedric 366
Haywood, Frank 460, 826
Haywood, Leon 210, 361, 508, 659
Haywood Singers, The 401
Haze Sisters, The 728
Hazel, Sam 758
Head, Johnnie 793
Healey, Dennis 427
Healey, Jeff 431, 558, 687
Healy, Scott 569, 614
Heard, J. C. 8, 77, 140, 292, 326, 327, 328, 473, 479, 526, 527, 671, 685, 701, 702
Heard, John 359, 672
Heard, Vernon 509
Hearst, Rod 711
Hearts, The 780
Heartsman, Johnny 249, 439, 719

Heath, Percy 477
Heatley, Spike 371
Heavy D 359
Hebert, Larry 554
Hebert, Lester 830, 831
Hebrew, Warren 114
Hecht, Arno 130, 134, 567
Hecht, Bob 591
Heckstall-Smith, Dick 371, 372, 425, 428, 431, 728, 824
Hedley, Michael 86
Heffington, Don 485
Hegamin, Bill 249
Hegamin, Lucille 249, 827
Heid, Bill 27, 250, 510, 550, 570, 632
Heidi Jo 375
Heilijgers, Nico 332, 591
Heitger, Duke 566
Hel, Amy 525
Helander, Olle 225, 467
Held, Julius M. 40
Helfer, Erwin 25, 73, 250, 581, 673, 708, 733, 809, 810
Heller, Ben 8, 328, 390
Helm, Amy 137
Helm, Levon 137, 156, 180, 237, 238, 483, 486, 615
Helper, David 156
Hemberger, Al 156
Hemberger, Ted 156
Hembree, Mark 58
Hemphill, Alvin 364
Hemphill, Jessie Mae 251, 739, 754, 766
Hemphill, Rose 441, 761, 812
Hemphill, Shelton 587
Hemphill, Sid 759, 761, 762, 765, 810, 812
Hemsley, Wilbert 'Jiggs' 286
Henderson, Bertha 48, 190, 826
Henderson, Bobby 717
Henderson, Bugs 364
Henderson, Catherine 358, 401
Henderson, David 657
Henderson, Duke 252, 450, 788, 826
Henderson, Fletcher 141, 142, 224, 253, 254, 293, 294, 336, 438, 459, 460, 469, 537, 587, 588, 592, 597, 685, 707, 718, 720
Henderson, Frank 315, 650
Henderson, Harvey 349, 350
Henderson, Herbert 129
Henderson, John 447
Henderson, Jonny 223, 568, 579
Henderson, Kid 537
Henderson, Lil 537
Henderson, Louis 705
Henderson, Lucius 620
Henderson, Luther 227
Henderson, Mike 210, 252
Henderson, Rev. Patrick 363
Henderson, Red 795
Henderson, Robert 'Hindu' 440
Henderson, Rosa 252, 744, 827

Henderson, Steve 'Hoggie Beetle' 140
Henderson, Tareva 503
Henderson, Tommy 623
Henderson, Tony 612
Henderson, William 364
Henderson, Willie 7, 33, 57, 109, 204, 330, 346, 432, 474, 553, 581, 584, 599, 632, 681, 707, 733
Hendley, Fiona 53
Hendricks, Belford 354
Hendricks, Bobby 789
Hendricks, Paul 688
Hendricks, Rock 540
Hendrickson, Al 661, 662
Henley, Darryl 81
Henley, John 645
Henley, John Lee 183, 770, 785
Henn, Ritt 1
Henry, Anthony 'Ant' 337
Henry, Big Boy 253, 513, 756
Henry, Brandon J. 107
Henry, Clarence 'Frogman' 780, 804, 805
Henry, Curtis 808
Henry, David 519
Henry, Haywood 40, 76, 81, 83, 84, 86, 340, 416, 624, 662
Henry, James 558, 729
Henry, Jeff 194, 241, 264, 383, 422, 676
Henry, Jim 758, 759
Henry, John 'Shifty' 252, 438, 472, 661, 662, 684
Henry, Robert 752, 774
Henry, Sam 731
Henry, Simeon 227, 682
Henry, Walter 504, 505, 520
Henry, Waymon 'Sloppy' 287, 754, 793, 820
Hensley, Larry 772
Henson, Purvis 315
Henson, Walter 'Buck' 412
Herbert, Arthur 140, 445, 639, 640
Herbig, Gary 357
Herby Joe 776
Herman, Woody 725, 739, 741
Hermann, John 513
Hermann, Jojo 199, 499
Hernandez, Aurora 370
Hernandez, Ben 308
Hernandez, Jose 370
Herndon, James 467
Herrera, Steve 'Hook' 16, 721
Herrman, Lloyd 78, 79
Herron, John 485
Herster, Eddie 730
Herve, Andre 77
Herve, Michel 77
Heslin, Bob 169, 170
Hewat, Corrina 36, 37
Hewes, Rob 37
Hewgill, James 260
Hey, Jerry 359, 376

Heyes, Ernie 652
Heyward, Ernest 446
Heywood, Eddie 3, 55, 98, 134, 150, 426, 679
Heywood Jr, Eddie 294
Hezekiah & The House Rockers 254, 754
Hiatt, John 824
Hick, Lara 168
Hickman, Dannie 612
Hickman, Sylvester 1, 269, 270, 565
Hickman, William 84
'Hicks' 467
Hicks, Billy 821
Hicks, Bobby Lloyd 64
Hicks, Charles 159
Hicks, Charlie 774
Hicks, Darby 504, 757, 760
Hicks, Edna 254
Hicks, Henry 461
Hicks, Jackie 271
Hicks, Joe 193, 251, 341, 789
Hicks, Johnny 86, 523
Hicks, Minnie 467
Hicks, Ramona 796
Hicks, Robert [Barbecue Bob] 774
Hicks, Ronnie 22
Hicks, Russ 458
Hicks Jr, Darby [Ron Levy] 210, 440, 572, 717, 720
Hidalgo, David 87, 191, 239, 274, 408, 559, 624, 673
Higaki, Paul 510
Higelin, Jacques 5
Higginbotham, J. B. 53
Higginbotham, J. C. 7, 142, 294, 327, 390, 526, 607, 608
Higginbotham, P. R. 761
Higgins, Billy 438, 460, 475, 793
Higgins, Chuck 686, 782
Higgins, Dan 376
Higgins, Kevin 598
Higgins, Monk 551, 711
Higgins, Robert 100, 760
Higgs, 'Doctor' D. M. 343
Higgs, George 254, 786, 823
Higgs, Walter T. 255
Hightman, Alan 617
Hightower, Donna 813, 827
Hightower, Rosetta 483
Hiles, Walter 83, 245, 300, 543, 650, 670, 671
Hill, Aimée 549
Hill, Alex 259, 317, 321, 551, 592, 602, 626
Hill, Beatrice 782
Hill, Bertha 'Chippie' 45, 167, 255, 634, 737, 742, 744, 810, 826, 827, 829
Hill, Blind Joe 750
Hill, Clyde 757, 758
Hill, David 182, 258
Hill, Delbert 138, 551, 727
Hill, Don 63, 208, 209, 684, 724, 725
Hill, Eddie 229

Hill, Edward 462
Hill, Elton 244
Hill, Ernest 'Bass' 526
Hill, Frankie 368
Hill, Gladys 827
Hill, Henri 75
Hill, Henry 561
Hill, Honey 88, 212
Hill, J. D. 472, 730
Hill, Jack 614
Hill, James 782
Hill, Jim 287
Hill, Jimmy 414
Hill, Joel Scott 103, 104, 458
Hill, John 41
Hill, Kathy 255, 256
Hill, Kevin 50, 255, 256, 555
Hill, L. A. 47, 133
Hill, Lillie 754
Hill, Melvin 597
Hill, Michael 134, 255, 776, 814, 824, 825
Hill, Ray 526
Hill, Raymond 305, 659, 660, 754
Hill, Robert 525, 769
Hill, Roger 'Trigger' 264, 532, 630
Hill, Rosalie 762, 812
Hill, Sammy 817
Hill, Teddy 321, 607
Hill, Tommy 332, 433, 444, 487
Hill, Victor 675
Hill, Wilma Gene 782
Hill, Wynette 255, 256
Hill, Z. Z. 256, 785
Hill Jr, Harvey 752
Hill Jr, Luther 232
Hillard, Jess 772
Hiller, Jon 57, 109, 125, 317, 553, 567, 590, 606
Hillery, Art 672, 675
Hilliam, Steve 687
Hillman, Charlie 426
Hills, Jack 32, 87, 190
Hills, Jessie 59, 782, 803, 804
Hilton, Richard 668, 669
Hilton, Tony 38
Himel, Glen 119
Hinds, Jimmy 157
Hinds, Kent 319, 369
Hinds, Mervyn 'Harmonica' 528, 632
Hines, Babe/Baby 827, 828
Hines, Bobby 659
Hines, David 401
Hines, Donald 463
Hines, Earl 248, 725, 739, 741
Hines, Eddie 531
Hines, Lynn 572
Hines, Steve 571
Hinkle, James 21, 721
Hinkley, Tim 372
Hinman, Doug 548
Hinson, Buck 600, 601
Hinton, Algia Mae 257, 756, 786

Hinton, Eddie 209, 238, 282
Hinton, Milt 77, 81, 142, 271, 273, 521, 638, 671, 681
Hinton, Skeeter 755, 767, 769
Hirstius, Gary 502
Hiscox, Steve 341
Hiseman, Jon 428
Hitchcock, Nigel 53
Hitchman, Mansfield 133
Hite, Bob 103, 104
Hite, Les 677
Hite, Richard 77, 103, 104, 458, 496, 613
Hjörleifsson, Jóhann 160
Hluszko, Bohdan 20
Ho, Eddie 486
Hoare, Jimmy 406
Hobart, Mike 222, 223, 231, 396, 676
Hobbs, Cliff 772
Hobbs, Howard 'Long John' 521
Hobbs, John 343
Hobbs, Randy 723
Hobbs, Shebs 662
Hoddinott, Mike 425
Hodes, Art 741
Hodge, Aaron 'Hard Head' 367
Hodge, Dallas 104
Hodge, Gaynel 506, 686
Hodge, Jay 286
Hodge, Tommy 660
Hodge, Travis 367
Hodgekins, John 655
Hodges, Carl 765
Hodges, Charles 126, 130, 401, 439, 576, 585
Hodges, Fred 126
Hodges, Jay 651
Hodges, Johnny 295, 322, 797, 798
Hodges, Leroy 126, 366, 401, 435, 439, 572, 585
Hodges, Mabon 'Teenie' 126, 130, 358, 365, 439, 585
Hodges, Norval D./Norville 350, 550
Hodges, Patricia 575, 629
Hodges, Ron 566
Hodges, Stephen 191, 239, 241, 262, 413, 434, 487, 488, 538, 540
Hodgkinson, Colin 372
Hodgson, Mark 544
Hoe, Simon 347
Hoeflinger, Dan 5
Hoerl, David 'Hurricane' 687
Hoffman, Gralin 490, 491
Hoffman, Ian 14
Hoffnar, Bob 151
Hofner, Adolph 772
Hogan, Alison 274
Hogan, Carl 338, 340
Hogan, Ray 526
Hogan, Sam 258, 649
Hogan, Sammy 377, 408
Hogan, Silas 257, 783, 791
Hogan, Wilbert 670, 671

Hogarth, Nick 217, 218
Hogg, John 782, 818, 819, 826
Hogg, Smokey 44, 258, 753, 776, 782, 785, 788, 798, 818, 819, 820, 821, 826
Hoggard, Jesse 705
Hogue, John 494
Hoh, Eddie 52
Hokum Boys, The 259, 740, 741, 774, 810, 812
Holden, Jeffrey 258
Holden, Lorenzo 504, 505, 520
Holder, Ace 782
Holder, Jack 127, 130, 235, 375, 524
Holder, Joe 366
Hole, Dave 260, 768, 776, 814, 825
Holeman, John Dee 260, 756, 786
Holiday, Billie 827
Holiday, D. 722
Holland, Charles L. 761
Holland, Cliff 414
Holland, Fred 755
Holland, Jools 53, 359
Holland, Matt 218
Holland, Tom 528
Holley, Steve 524, 674
Holliday, John 713
Hollimon, Clarence 21, 47, 201, 244, 492, 768, 806, 820
Hollins, Tony 743, 744, 752, 774
Hollis, Eddie 135
Hollis, Mo 365
Hollon, Kenneth 315, 338
Holloway, Charles 146
Holloway, Fris 260
Holloway, Red 266, 283, 357, 429, 430, 431, 551, 562
Holloway Jr, Charles 521
Holly, James 711
Hollywood All Stars 261
Hollywood Blue Flames 261
Hollywood Fats 123, 261, 273, 522, 720
Hollywood Flames 782
Holman, Libby 701, 702
Holmes, Ben 535, 538, 729
Holmes, Bobby 63
Holmes, Charlie 321, 461, 607, 670
Holmes, Glen 257
Holmes, Groove 725
Holmes, H. H. 610
Holmes, Happy 793
Holmes, Harold 295
Holmes, Horace 438, 596, 685
Holmes, Jimmy 766
Holmes, Lester 22
Holmes, Little Red 802
Holmes, Lonnie 412
Holmes, Michael 78
Holmes, Norvell 291
Holmes, Richard 'Groove' 725
Holmes, Rick 25
Holmes, Salty 769
Holmes, Sean 564

Holmes, Sherman 238, 561
Holmes, Sonny Boy 819
Holmes, Wendell 561
Holmes, Winston 347, 659
Holmes, Wright 752, 818, 819
Holmes III, Ben 229
Holmes Brothers, The 776, 788, 824
Holmon, Kelvin 'Bo' 166
Holmstrom, Rick 'L.A. Holmes' 16, 95, 123, 261, 414, 522, 538, 629, 771
Holstrom, Glen 336
Holt, Douglas 419
Holt, Harry 643
Holt, 'Lee Baby' 419
Holt, Nick 217, 262, 344, 376, 383, 401, 405, 419, 420, 421, 519, 527, 528, 574, 581, 617, 692
Holt, Scott 235, 262, 825
Holt, Shawn 421
Holton, Michael 186
Holts, Herlin 262
Holts, Roosevelt 262, 766
Holy Ghost Sanctified Singers 775
Holzhaus, Chris 492
Homan, Jeff 547
Home Cookin' 263
Homesick James 263, 306, 307, 532, 621, 744, 745, 765, 767, 778, 782, 789, 790, 800, 813, 814, 821
Homnick, Styve 639, 643
Honey, Constance 223
Honeyboy [Frank Patt] 754, 788
Honeycutt, Buddy 27
Honeycutt, Miki 830
Hood, David 6, 209, 238, 282, 349, 350, 402
Hood, 'Rhythm Willie' 80, 697
Hoodoo Kings, The 264, 525
Hooker, Earl 188, 265, 272, 273, 480, 610, 643, 693, 744, 749, 752, 767, 777, 778, 789, 800, 813, 814
Hooker, John Lee 103, 104, 111, 266, 358, 369, 431, 487, 556, 558, 729, 737, 738, 744, 747, 748, 749, 751, 752, 767, 773, 774, 776, 777, 779, 780, 785, 788, 789, 790, 798, 802, 824
Hooker, Robert 273
Hooker, Zakiya 275, 824, 830
Hooks, Charlie 321, 322
Hooks, Ellis 402
Hooks, Johnny 267, 268, 269, 681
Hooks, Marshall 593, 594, 648
Hooper, Barbara 424
Hooper, Leon 454, 455
Hooper, Liz 342
Hooper, Louis 134, 253, 336, 438, 459, 460, 461, 469, 475, 596, 685, 707
Hooper, Nesbert 'Stix' 357, 508
Hoover, Greg 265, 370
Hope, Eddie 770, 800
Hope, Elmore 'Sylvester' (Elmo) 245, 477

Hope, Lynn 800
Hope-Taylor, Randy 427
Hopkins, Claude 237, 322
Hopkins, Donna 186
Hopkins, Herman 472, 713
Hopkins, 'Hop' 537
Hopkins, Joel 276, 277, 280, 753
Hopkins, John Henry 280
Hopkins, Lightnin' 276, 639, 640, 641, 642, 655, 708, 709, 710, 711, 737, 738, 739, 747, 748, 749, 752, 767, 773, 774, 776, 777, 785, 789, 798, 800, 811, 813, 818, 819, 820, 823
Hopkins, Linda 504, 505
Hopkins, Milton 356, 357
Hopkins, Nicky 34, 372
Hopkins, Sammy 300
Hoppen, Larry 50
Hopper, Jeff 112
Hopper, Sean 485
Horaist, Scherri 554
Hormel, Smokey 95
Horn, Jay Van 383
Horn, Jim 135, 144, 191, 257, 401, 402, 507, 572
Hornbuckle, Linda 336, 751
Horne, Lena 8, 326, 328
Horne, Onzie 353
Horne, Steve 204
Horner, Leon 370, 570
Hornsby, Dan 23, 109, 465, 466
Horny Horns, The 350
Horsely, Clayton 765, 812
Horton, Billy 666
Horton, Bob 459
Horton, Bobby 148, 262
Horton, J. D. 752
Horton, Robert H. 670
Horton, (Big) Walter 'Shakey' 35, 121, 165, 170, 183, 283, 299, 335, 410, 480, 481, 484, 486, 557, 562, 576, 577, 603, 610, 616, 617, 627, 629, 631, 651, 672, 722, 734, 745, 748, 749, 752, 753, 764, 768, 769, 770, 771, 776, 779, 781, 789, 823
Hosch, Charles 443, 614
Hoskins, James F. 7, 8, 142, 326, 327, 701
Hoskins, Tom 18
Hostetler, Dan 539
Hot Butter & Soul [i.e. Hot Buttered Soul] 350
Hot Buttered Soul 349, 350
Hot Rod Happy [Country Jim Bledsoe] 803
Hound Head Henry 150
House, Evie 286
House, Rich 170
House, Son 284, 361, 738, 747, 749, 758, 760, 762, 766, 767, 801, 802, 812, 813
Houserockers, The 825
Houston, Bee 286, 483, 651, 652, 777, 800, 823

Houston, Cisco 380, 381, 382, 638, 640
Houston, Derek 490
Houston, Emerson 618, 619
Houston, Joe 661, 662, 785, 799, 800, 819, 825
Houston, John 340
Houston, Lawyer 819
Houston, Maurice 409
Houston, Ronnie 182, 214, 583
Houston, Soldier Boy 752, 819
Houston, Tate 472
Houston, Wyatt 475
Hovington, Frank 286, 766
Hovsepian, Freddy 5
Howard, Avery 462
Howard, Camille 228, 463, 661, 662, 740, 741, 742, 788, 798
Howard, Charlene 215, 384, 503, 688
Howard, Darnell 69, 294, 645
Howard, Joe 164, 229
Howard, John 281, 282
Howard, Johnny 751
Howard, Paul 42, 67, 129, 368, 550, 568, 798
Howard, Paul Mason 379, 380
Howard, Rick 568
Howard, Rosetta 240, 287, 774, 827, 829
Howard, Stephen 465
Howard, Steve 118, 130, 161, 179, 215, 332, 465, 468, 476
Howe, Whistling Bob 773, 774
Howe, Jack 43
Howell, Bert 134
Howell, Billy 335, 616
Howell, Earl 32, 217, 262, 316, 376, 412, 420, 421, 528, 574, 581, 613
Howell, Hammy 210
Howell, Peg Leg 287, 737, 754, 756, 794, 810, 811, 816
Howlin' Wolf 288, 739, 744, 748, 749, 752, 753, 762, 767, 768, 769, 770, 776, 779, 780, 786, 789, 798, 799, 802
Howten, Barry 371
Hoy, Barbara Puciul 291
Hoy, Johnny 291
Hubbard, Neil 234, 359
Hubbard, Preston 135, 148, 191, 342, 515, 548, 559, 668
Hubbard, Roger 10
Hubbard, William 'Boogie Man' 54, 261, 496
Hubert, Barney 352, 353, 354, 355
Hubert, L. C. 288, 289
Hubert, Louis 356, 357
Hubinon, Paul 48
Huby, Barbara 350
Huckbridge, Johnny 34
'Huckleberry Hound' [Robert Wright] 470, 520
Hucknall, Mick 359
Hucko, Peanuts 83
Hudson, Bob 415

Hudson, Cary 618
Hudson, Charles 554
Hudson, Ed 69
Hudson, Eddie 791
Hudson, Garth 237, 238, 483, 486
Hudson, Harry 132
Hudson, Hattie 740, 810, 818, 826
Hudson, James 730
Hudson, Joe 791
Hudson, John 125
Hudson, Keith 101
Hudson, Oliver 69
Hudson, Oneal 412, 600, 601
Hudson, Willie 409, 415, 778, 779
Hudson Jr, D. 521
Huey, Richard 796
Huff, Bill 1
Huff, Luther 752, 767
Hughes, Billy 773
Hughes, Calvin 670, 671
Hughes, Fred 790
Hughes, Joe 'Guitar' 291, 820
Hughes, John 321, 322
Hughes, Katherine 580
Hughes, Pee Wee 752, 768, 787, 803
Hughes, Richard 723
Hughes, Steve 429
Hula Blues Band, The 824
Hulbert, Ted 'Snooky' 63, 300
Hull, Bunny 358
Hull, Harry 587, 588, 718
Hull, Papa Harvey 801, 810, 811
Hull, Ron 572
Humer, Oliver 528, 574
Humes, Helen 291, 320, 390, 689, 738, 747, 774, 797, 798, 806, 812, 826, 827
Hummel, Mark 16, 293, 445, 607, 655, 770, 771
Humphrey, Paul 266, 351, 551, 679, 728
Humphrey, Willie 140
Humphreys, Greg 251
Humphreys, Rick 553
Humphries, Frank 245
Hundt, Gerry 479
Hunninen, John 496
Hunt, Cris/Chris 217, 218
Hunt, D. A. 753
Hunt, Floyd 454, 650
Hunt, Gary 547
Hunt, Helen 772
Hunt, Jim 27, 540
Hunt, John 114, 115, 116, 245, 264, 532, 650, 670, 671
Hunt, Marvin 434
Hunt, Noah 575
Hunt, Prince Albert 772
Hunt, Slim 754
Hunt, Steve 'Slash' 16, 423
Hunter, Alberta 293, 739, 793, 827, 829
Hunter, Chris 21, 262
Hunter, Ellis 61
Hunter, Fluffy 774

Hunter, George 404, 557
Hunter, Herbert 786
Hunter, Joe 91, 214, 215, 269, 271, 275, 361, 583, 681, 811
Hunter, Ivory Joe 295, 506, 777, 785, 797, 798, 820, 826
Hunter, Long John 68, 296, 676, 776
Hunter, Lost John 752, 789
Hunter, Lee 752, 819
Hunter, Lloyd 607
Hunter, Stan 77
Hunter, Tammy 361
Hunter, Tom 4, 158
Hunter, Tom 'Blues Man' 297
Hunter, Ty 780
Hunter & Jenkins 773, 774
Hunter Chapel Missionary Baptist Choir, The 759
Hunter Harmonettes 296
Hunter's Chapel Singers 441, 443
Huntsman, Derek 36
Hurd, Rodger 677
Hurdle, James 712
Hurds, J. C. 532
Hurley, Ed 351
Hurley, James 229, 535, 539
Hurst, Bob 674
Hurst, George 168, 207
Hurst, Nicole 565
Hurst, Thurman 565
Hurt, Mississippi John 297, 737, 738, 747, 767, 788, 801, 802, 810, 811, 820
Hurwitz, Mark 'Lips Lackowitz' 31
Huston, Derek 161, 566
Huston, John 81
Hutchcroft, Kim 357
Hutcherson, Eddie 'Goo Goo' 677, 678, 731
Hutchins, Darryl 572
Hutchinson, James 'Hutch' 342, 343, 359, 556, 624
Hutchinson, Leslie 73
Hutchinson, Leslie A. ('Hutch') 459, 596
Hutchison, Frank 767, 772, 795, 811, 813
Hutto, J. B. 298, 519, 520, 744, 745, 767, 768, 781, 788, 800, 813, 814
Hyacinthe, Jimmy 133
Hyams, Harry 686, 726
Hyatt, William 552
Hyde, David 79
Hyde, Dick 48
Hyde, Earl 219
Hyde, Slide 535
Hyland, Tim 729
Hyman, Dick 295
Hyman, Rob 624
Hymas, Tony 669
Hypolite, Harry 'Big Daddy' 117, 118, 299
Ian, Cass 301
Iao 556
Ice Water 214, 719

Idsen, Charlie 626
Iglauer, Bruce 260, 564
Iguana, Johnny 'Fingers' 31, 584, 695
Iguanas, The 805
Ii, David 143, 408, 416, 427, 429, 488, 577, 629, 675
Ikettes, The 660, 786
Iketts, The 369
Illingworth, Gary 363
Illinois Slim 554, 599
Imhotep 242
Imperial Crowns 814
Imperials, The 814
Imura, Takeeshi 80
Ingalla, Egidio 414
Ingalls, Frank 620
Ingber, Ira 104
Ingen, Ruud van 101
Ingles, Tim 691
Ingram, Billy 273
Ingram, Fred 565
Ingram, Phillip 343
Ingram, Wally 485
Ink Spots, The 798
Inman, Deryll 356
Inmon, John 501
Innes, Mike 53
Innes, Richard 40, 47, 136, 169, 194, 261, 408, 414, 464, 522, 538, 629, 719, 720, 735
Inniss, Roger 91
Interludes, The 506
Intveld, James 113, 538
Ipsen, Kjeld 657
Irby, Arthur 'Sambo' 541
Irvin, Jesse 405
Irvine, Nathan 77
Irving, Derek 729
Irvis, Charlie 249, 294, 325, 398, 426, 437, 595, 596, 679, 718, 721
Isaacs, Byron 137
Isaacs, Ike 83
Isaacson, Jake 515
Isaak, Brandon 687
Isais, Gil 'T' 61, 200
Ishmael, Rasheed 660
Isidore, Conrad 457, 458
Ison, Rahsaana 215
Ives, Jimmy 571
Ivey, Clayton 358, 395, 402
Ivory, Hank 678, 713
Ivory, Henry 201, 677
Ivorytones, The [Cues] 295
Izenhall, Aaron 338, 340
Izmore, Les 21, 61, 68, 123, 255, 297, 373, 423, 676
J.A.Q. 584
Jacintho, Wayne 625
Jack, Germaine 161, 162
Jack, Nathaniel 392
Jack O'Diamonds 786, 787
Jacks, The 786, 799

Jackson, Al 363, 401
Jackson, Alex S. 596, 685
Jackson, Anthony 51
Jackson, Arthur 'Dogman' 266
Jackson, Bill 300, 822
Jackson, Billy 67
Jackson, Bleu 264
Jackson, Bo Weavil 300, 755, 786, 794, 812, 813
Jackson, Bullmoose 300, 773, 774, 798, 799, 800
Jackson, Cal 505
Jackson, Calvin 93, 94, 153, 251, 301, 346
Jackson, Carlton 43, 547
Jackson, Cedric 347
Jackson, Charlie 55, 685
Jackson, Papa Charlie 48, 55, 142, 185, 301, 347, 537, 737, 744, 774, 786
Jackson, Chubby 683
Jackson, Chuck 170
Jackson, Cliff 134, 142, 253, 294, 323, 332, 336, 438, 460, 461, 608, 720
Jackson, Clydene 417
Jackson, Corky 385
Jackson, Dave 728
Jackson, Davina 243
Jackson, Davita 243
Jackson, Derrick 711
Jackson, Dewey 317
Jackson, Earl 405, 432, 725, 826
Jackson, Emerson 'E. J.'/'Funky E' 395
Jackson, Franz 468, 718
Jackson, Fred 392, 713, 730
Jackson, Freddie 583
Jackson, Fruteland 302
Jackson, George 'Mr Blues' 777
Jackson, Big George 303
Jackson, Little George 681
Jackson, Grady 662
Jackson, Greg 121
Jackson, Ham 338, 526
Jackson, Harry 'Pee Wee' 33
Jackson, Heywood 445, 639, 640
Jackson, Ivory 784
Jackson, Jack 294
Jackson, James 304, 340, 392, 432, 711
Jackson, James C. 'Put' 521
Jackson, Jesse 715
Jackson, Jim 303, 792, 794, 797, 815
Jackson, Jimmy 81, 654
Jackson, Jo Jo 742
Jackson, John 84, 304, 459, 473, 478, 581, 711, 749, 777, 812, 823
Jackson, John Henry 763
Jackson, John L. 684
Jackson, Johnny 763
Jackson, Josh 338, 340, 662
Jackson, Joshua 338
Jackson, Jump 7, 79, 146, 147, 159, 455, 456, 457, 493, 500, 610, 616, 618, 619, 620, 627, 708, 716, 780, 785, 788
Jackson, L. M. 434

Jackson, Lee 165, 217, 263, 299, 404, 577, 603, 617, 749, 778, 781
Jackson, Leroy [b] 654
Jackson, Leroy [d] 477, 678
Jackson, Lil' Son 304, 737, 752, 753, 777, 819
Jackson, Lincoln 764
Jackson, Lulu 810, 828
Jackson, Mahalia 739
Jackson, Marvin 42, 125, 130, 141, 541, 669
Jackson, Melvin 47, 357, 358, 359
Jackson, Melvin 'Jack' 277
Jackson, Michael 92, 344, 528
Jackson, Mike 294, 325, 385, 592, 595, 596, 721
Jackson, Milt 683
Jackson, Monroe Moe 753
Jackson, Munyungo 343
Jackson, Natalie 499
Jackson, Odette 592
Jackson, Oliver 175, 176, 351, 592
Jackson, Otis 509, 821
Jackson, Pee Wee 654
Jackson, Preston 255, 311, 459, 468, 718
Jackson, Quentin 115, 683
Jackson, Raymond 401
Jackson, Rob 243
Jackson, Robert 492
Jackson, Roddy 788
Jackson, Rudolph 679
Jackson, Russell 20, 490, 658, 687, 691
Jackson, Shelton 117
Jackson, Terry 314
Jackson, Tony 27
Jackson, Vas-Tie [Vasti] 612
Jackson, Vasti 90, 97, 118, 257, 358, 583, 691
Jackson, Vic 131
Jackson, Viola 357
Jackson, Walter 761, 762
Jackson, Wayne 6, 21, 53, 68, 77, 118, 130, 143, 144, 158, 170, 191, 210, 232, 234, 337, 348, 349, 350, 356, 366, 458, 564, 571, 591, 599, 673, 675, 688, 691
Jackson, Wesley 114, 115, 521, 730
Jackson, Willie 83, 392, 719, 730
Jackson, Little Willie 145, 392, 393, 507, 508
Jackson, New Orleans Willie 803
Jackson, Willis 84, 173, 416, 459, 777, 807
Jackson, Yvonne 368
Jackson Jr, Al 210, 348, 349, 350, 439
Jackson Jr, James 24, 432, 463
Jackson Jr, Paul M. 357
Jackson Strings, The 257
Jacobs, Bob 645
Jacobs, Charlie 33
Jacobs, Randy 21, 359
Jacobs, Ron 170
Jacobs, Steve 31
Jacobs, Little Walter 54

Jacobs-Strain, David 305
Jacobson, Joshua 85
Jacques, Alvin 648
Jacques, Dave 222
Jacquet, Frank 219
Jacquet, Illinois 244, 797
Jacquet, Russell 244, 449, 661, 662
Jägers, Udo 73
Jagger, Mick 359, 558
Jaimoe 370
Jam Session 747
Jambazian, Zaven 507, 664
Jamerson, Clifford 592
Jamerson, Ella 623
Jamerson, James 269, 271, 681
'James' 647
James, Baby 315
James, Betty 780, 827, 829
James, Chris 'Guitar' 377, 707
James, Clifton 15, 35, 55, 101, 121, 165, 233, 263, 289, 415, 482, 577, 601, 614, 616, 617, 631, 734
James, Colin 20, 341, 824
James, Darin 6, 476
James, Darrel 711
James, Degge 370
James, Derek 497
James, Donto 307
James, Doug 16, 126, 148, 152, 185, 190, 222, 264, 299, 324, 362, 469, 492, 497, 525, 548, 549, 559, 560, 566, 567, 667, 719, 729
James, Elmer 89
James, Elmore 305, 412, 489, 600, 662, 737, 738, 739, 744, 752, 753, 767, 776, 779, 780, 786, 789, 790, 799, 802, 813, 814
James, Erin 450
James, Etta 307, 358, 624, 779, 780, 786, 789, 799, 827
James, Frank 'Springback' 308, 794
James, Fred 163, 205, 264, 335, 377, 496, 696
James, George 556
James, Harry 7, 8, 291, 292, 326, 390, 739, 741
James, Ira 282
James, Jemima 823
James, Jesse 752, 773, 774, 807, 808, 819
James, Larry 507
James, Lorenzo Meeks 309
James, Madelyn 774, 792
James, Marcus 186
James, Marion 783
James, Mary 758
James, Nathan 241, 308, 728
James, Neil 730
James, Nick 217
James, Paul 238
James, Ronnie 293, 464
James, Sadie 828
James, Sametto 307

James, Sarah 36
James, Skip 308, 739, 740, 747, 749, 762, 767, 794, 801, 802, 808
James, Spit 603
James, Steve 200, 310, 486, 513, 529, 547, 612, 647, 825
James, Sunny 819
James, T. A. 31
James, Ulysses 247
James, Viola 761, 762
James, Willie B. 88, 128, 226, 308, 326, 333, 424, 626, 795
James Jr, Clarence 'Starr' 674
James Quintet, The 84
Jamison, Debbie 130
Jamison-Harrison, Bobette 343
Jamo 369
Janise, Sidney 633
Janowiak, Johnny 'Showtime' 192
Jans, Rokko 185
Janzen, Tom 'Jazzbo' 189, 496
Jaquelyn, Alyssa 126
Jaramillo, Robert 'Rabbit' 104
Jarette, Johnny 295
Jarman, Moe 583
Jarrett, Ted 169, 783, 786
Jarvis, Arnold 416, 459, 670, 671
Jarvis, John 252
Jarvis, Tanya 730, 731
Jasmin-Banaré, Thierry 615
Jason, Neal/Neil 51, 525
Jaurequi, David 554
Javierre, Vic 370
Jaxon, Frankie 'Half-Pint' 167, 255, 311, 626, 737, 795
Jay, Abner 311, 751
Jay, Baby 149, 190, 225, 317
Jay, Bobby 791
Jay, Doug 312
Jay, Kelly 368
Jay, Thurber 338, 340
Jaynettes, The 780
Jayos, The 505, 506
Jefferey, Bob 575, 766
Jefferson, Blind Lemon 312, 737, 738, 767, 768, 794, 797, 810, 813, 817, 818, 820
Jefferson, Bonnie 766
Jefferson, Cora 791
Jefferson, Darryl 214
Jefferson, Dave 171, 346, 411, 599
Jefferson, Eurales 725
Jefferson, Hilton 81, 245, 416, 662, 718
Jefferson, Kris 524
Jefferson, Leonard 83
Jefferson, Maceo 249, 685
Jefferson, Thomas 140
Jeffery, Dave 721
Jeffrey, Peter 170
Jeffries, Herb 392, 798
Jelly Belly 755, 806
Jelly Roll Kings 313, 782

Jemmott, Gerry 33, 175, 176, 355, 356, 363, 365
Jenkins, Bobo 751, 752, 800, 821
Jenkins, Carl 457
Jenkins, Charles 454
Jenkins, Cliff 84
Jenkins, Duke 780
Jenkins, Elsie 760
Jenkins, Essie 823
Jenkins, Evan 218, 568
Jenkins, Frank 810
Jenkins, Freddie 322, 592
Jenkins, George 83, 90, 245, 315
Jenkins, Gus 754, 779
Jenkins', 'Jeremiah 138
Jenkins, Jerry 291
Jenkins, 'Jinx' 424
Jenkins, Kenneth 439
Jenkins, Lester 583
Jenkins, Marvin 351
Jenkins, Maya Smullyan 665
Jenkins, Myrtle 71, 88, 610, 626
Jenkins, Pat 244, 730
Jenkins, Paul 372, 373
Jenkins, Tommie 821
Jenkins Jr, Bob 728
Jennings, Bill 83, 338, 340, 416
Jennings, Dale 262
Jennings, Donald 'Duck' 552, 553, 643
Jennings, Ian 176, 177, 427
Jennings, Joseph 81
Jennings, Morris 130, 401, 450, 482, 691
Jennings, Troy 55, 60, 123, 124, 194, 202, 211, 342, 475, 618, 704
Jensen, Brian 118
Jensen, Eric 42, 450
Jensen, John 211, 499, 553
Jensen, Steve 141
Jernigan, Hank 507
Jernigan, Mel 679
Jerome, Jerry 8, 24, 328, 390
Jerome, Michael 488
Jerome, O'Neil 82
Jerry, Mike 132
Jesse & Marvin 788, 799
Jessie, Obediah 777
Jessie, Young 786
Jessie Mae 829
Jester, Kyle 342
Jeter, H. Leonard 685
Jett, Sammie 353
Jette, Dave 43
Jewell, Jimmy 67
Jewell, Russell 718
Jewels, Earl 447
Jewkis, Noel 52
Jim & Bob (The Genial Hawaiians) 812
Jimenez, Ray 768
Jimson [Henry Wallace] 761, 763, 812, 822
J'Neen 249
Joan Baby 344

Joe & Ann 805
Joe & His Kool Kats 751
Joe', 'Alabama [J. M. 'Doc' Miller] 336
Joell, Percy 140, 245, 332
Johansen, David 314, 615
Johansson, Leif 639, 643
John, Colin 256
John, Elton 359
John, Jennifer 413
John, Mable 789
John, Stanley 531
John-Douglas, Michele 37
Johnakins, Leslie 40, 245, 315
Johnny Porkchop 163
Johns, Essex 'Grownman' 541
Johns, Irving 587
Johns, Lucille 786
Johnson, A. J. 136
Johnson, Ace 757, 759
Johnson, Al 805
Johnson, Albert 'Budd' 384
Johnson, Alec 436, 816
Johnson, Alfred 'Snuff' 314
Johnson, Alonzo 11, 120, 553, 554, 583
Johnson, Amelia 710
Johnson, Anthony 540
Johnson, Archie 84, 86
Johnson, Barry Sonjohn 156
Johnson, Bernard 731
Johnson, Bernard 'Bunche' 470
Johnson, Bert 526
Johnson, Bill 129, 245, 255, 311, 509, 526, 543, 551, 626, 650, 798
Johnson, Billiken 818
Johnson, Billy 55, 274, 275
Johnson, Bob 'Big Dad' 208, 209
Johnson, Bobby 265, 266, 416, 587, 588
Johnson, 'Bones' 523, 576
Johnson, Brad 544
Johnson, Brian 5
Johnson, Bruce 89
Johnson, Budd 40, 81, 83, 84, 227, 294, 295, 327, 328, 340, 473, 521, 592, 654, 662
Johnson, Buddy 315, 654, 741, 797, 798, 799
Johnson, Bunk 381
Johnson, Buster 127, 150
Johnson, Buzz 158
Johnson, Calvin 81, 127, 253
Johnson, Calvin 'Loudmouth' 722
Johnson, Carlos 64, 568, 584
Johnson, Cee Pee 800, 826
Johnson, Charles 242, 388
Johnson, Charlie 311
Johnson, Chink 293, 595, 685
Johnson, Clarence 63, 254, 338, 426, 461, 475, 739
Johnson, Clarence 'Jelly' 610
Johnson, Conrad 110, 492, 647, 711
Johnson, Cornelius 681
Johnson, Creola 765

Johnson, Criss 318, 632, 711
Johnson, Curtis 675
Johnson, Dan 614
Johnson, Daryl 469, 540, 576, 580, 730
Johnson, David 59, 615, 624
Johnson, David Lee 145
Johnson, Don 307, 504, 505, 506, 520, 651
Johnson, Earl 173
Johnson, Earnest 97, 265, 266, 418, 458, 480, 694
Johnson, Eddie 338, 340
Johnson, Edith 315, 317, 618, 774, 826
Johnson, Edna 828
Johnson, Edward 459
Johnson, Edwin 459
Johnson, Electric Viv 231
Johnson, Elizabeth 793, 826
Johnson, Ella 315, 797, 799, 827
Johnson, Eric 168
Johnson, Ernest 229, 233, 670, 693
Johnson, Erskine 344, 346
Johnson, Esther 761
Johnson, Eugene 157
Johnson, Floyd 368
Johnson, Fred 81
Johnson, Freddie 201, 713
Johnson, George 761
Johnson, George 'Happy' 252, 472, 517
Johnson, Gerald 220
Johnson, Geri 623
Johnson, Gordie 168
Johnson, Greg 'Dog' 597
Johnson, Gus 84, 165, 416, 457, 459, 521, 670, 671
Johnson, Gwen 827
Johnson, Hall 587, 588, 793
Johnson, Harold 'Money' 300, 338, 670
Johnson, Harry 317, 416, 618, 619
Johnson, Harvey 539
Johnson, Henry 322, 514, 815
Johnson, Herman E. 315, 823
Johnson, Hobson 'Hot Box' 333
Johnson, Howard 50, 156, 356, 483, 485, 623, 624
Johnson, J. C. 134, 164, 291, 292, 321, 592, 596, 685
Johnson, Jack 758
Johnson, Big Jack 316, 337, 576, 782
Johnson, Jacqueline (Jackie) 4, 6, 131, 215, 205, 243, 313, 366, 373, 498, 524, 599, 600, 657, 695, 711
Johnson, Jacques 499
Johnson, James 219, 462, 585, 586
Johnson, James Osie 521
Johnson, James P. 89, 134, 142, 253, 321, 587, 588, 592, 597, 685, 739, 741, 747
Johnson, James 'Steady Roll' 320
Johnson, James 'Stump' 317, 579, 618, 619, 773, 774, 815
Johnson, James 'Super Chikan' 576
Johnson, Jellybean 5

Johnson, Jeremy 303, 464
Johnson, Jesse 815
Johnson, Jesse James 55
Johnson, Jimmy 6, 15, 35, 125, 160, 171, 177, 238, 257, 317, 349, 350, 401, 402, 500, 509, 563, 585, 652, 745, 768, 776
Johnson, Joe 783, 784
Johnson, John 209
Johnson, Johnnie 157, 235, 274, 275, 318, 348, 435, 557, 558, 632, 636, 653, 729
Johnson, Joseph 'Chinaman' 763
Johnson, Josh 729
Johnson, Julia 828
Johnson, K. D. 658
Johnson, Keg 116
Johnson, Ken 544
Johnson, Kennard 186, 490, 491
Johnson, Ki Ki 774
Johnson, Kristi 823
Johnson, L. 521
Johnson, Larry 60, 86, 155, 319, 750, 756
Johnson, Lee 344, 412
Johnson, Lem 227, 311, 338, 526, 806
Johnson, Leonard 385
Johnson, Leroy 'Country' 752, 819
Johnson, Lil 71, 319, 626, 738, 740, 741, 742, 743, 773, 774, 810, 820, 821, 827, 828
Johnson, Lonnie 3, 7, 39, 221, 224, 291, 292, 320, 322, 443, 462, 526, 575, 590, 592, 600, 603, 607, 608, 616, 637, 680, 697, 699, 737, 738, 740, 742, 743, 748, 749, 768, 773, 774, 785, 797, 798, 807, 815
Johnson, Louise 740, 774, 801, 802, 807, 808, 810
Johnson, Lukie 595
Johnson, Luther 'Georgia Boy'/'Snake' 272, 273, 323, 482, 578, 604, 651
Johnson, Luther 'Guitar Jr' 67, 180, 324, 345, 483, 484, 494, 515, 723, 745, 751, 788, 814, 824
Johnson, Mac 660
Johnson, Mack 374, 507
Johnson, Mager 766
Johnson, Malcolm 765
Johnson, Manzie 89
Johnson, Marcus 480, 481, 541, 542
Johnson, Marek 663
Johnson, Margaret 325, 385, 806, 826, 827
Johnson, Mary 16, 325, 786, 815, 828, 829
Johnson, Mason 730
Johnson, McKinley 355, 660, 679
Johnson, Merline (The Yas Yas Girl) 326, 738, 742, 827, 829
Johnson, Mike 52, 648
Johnson, Norman F. 543, 650
Johnson, Norris 633
Johnson, Norwood 'Geechie' 731
Johnson, Oliver 592

Johnson, Paul 466
Johnson, Pete 7, 8, 326, 389, 390, 473, 661, 662, 663, 684, 737, 738, 739, 740, 741, 742, 747, 762, 797, 798, 800, 809
Johnson, Plas 53, 164, 358, 506, 507, 572, 678, 686
Johnson, Ray 28, 77, 266, 384, 508, 643, 678
Johnson, Rich 'Hurricane' 544
Johnson, Richard 269, 270, 275
Johnson, Robert 328, 737, 738, 739, 767, 773, 794, 802, 812, 813
Johnson, Robert 'Nighthawk' 814
Johnson, Rollie Lee 760
Johnson, Ron 100, 131, 393
Johnson, Ronald 531
Johnson, Rory 586
Johnson, Roy 510
Johnson, Royal 30
Johnson, Ruby 789
Johnson, Sam 'Suitcase' 753, 819
Johnson, Scott 414
Johnson, Scotty 199
Johnson, Sherman (Blues) 787
Johnson, Shirley 330, 346, 829, 830
Johnson, Smokey 178, 179, 531
Johnson, Sonny Boy 752, 826
Johnson, Stacy 319
Johnson, Stella 774, 829
Johnson, Stovepipe 167, 808
Johnson, Syl 139, 318, 443, 693, 744, 781, 784
Johnson, Syleena 318
Johnson, T. C. 793
Johnson, T. J. 172
Johnson, Tom 612
Johnson, Tommy 330, 738, 739, 793, 794, 801, 802, 821
Johnson, Turner Junior 762
Johnson, Wallace 582, 805
Johnson, Walter 86, 227, 245, 523
Johnson, Wendell 447
Johnson, Wes 66, 186, 423
Johnson, Wesley 249, 685
Johnson, Will 607
Johnson, William 288, 509
Johnson, Willie 110, 243, 258, 288, 289, 307, 392, 746, 805, 819
Johnson, Blind Willie 331, 738, 767, 768, 795, 810, 812, 813, 820
Johnson Boys [Nap Hayes & Matthew Prater] 816
Johnson Brothers' Combo 803, 804
Johnson Jr, Alonzo 11, 119, 120, 582
Johnson Jr, Kriss T. 632
Johnson Jr, Roy Lee 521
Johnson–Nelson–Porkchop 793
Johnston, Jess 772
Johnstone, Davey 359
Joiner, Henry 759
Joliettes, The 408
Jolivette, Bernard 'King Karl' 783, 791

Jolivette, Nathan(iel) 86, 87, 554, 582
Jolly, Clarence 781
Jolly, Pete 808
Jolly George 770
Jolly Three, The 796
Jones, Al 439, 477
Jones, Albinia 332, 806, 829
Jones, Alicia 21
Jones, Allen 349
Jones, Andrew 'Jr Boy' 332, 364, 433, 487, 691, 705, 721, 788
Jones, Arthneice 'Gas Man' 576
Jones, B. J. 131
Jones, Ben 336
Jones, Bessie 761, 762, 763, 812
Jones, Bill 82
Jones, Billy 332, 504
Jones, Birmingham 771
Jones, 'Bo' 817
Jones, Bob 52, 442, 443, 562
Jones, Booker T. 274, 348, 349, 350, 824
Jones, Brad 195, 222
Jones, Brian 'B. J.' 125, 126, 131, 695, 733
Jones, Bruce 501, 502
Jones, Buddy 772
Jones, Buster 143, 427, 488
Jones, Calvin 25, 139, 180, 324, 385, 481, 482, 483, 484, 503, 515, 552, 604, 610, 705, 723
Jones, Carl 321, 601
Jones, Casey 67, 125, 129, 130, 134, 265, 416, 541, 633, 669, 692, 723
Jones, Charles 111, 466, 577, 629, 675
Jones, Charles 'Sugar Boy' 721
Jones, Chris 721
Jones, Christole 332
Jones, Clarence 83, 244, 463, 475, 520, 726
Jones, Clarence M. 595
Jones, Claude 654
Jones, Cleveland 'Broom Man' 646
Jones, Clifford 'Snags' 39, 255, 426, 627
Jones, Coley 471, 810, 817
Jones, Compton 251, 759, 765
Jones, Curtis 333, 493, 738, 742, 743, 809
Jones, Daryll 359
Jones, Dave 58
Jones, David 'Guitar' 264
Jones, Deacon 274
Jones, Deacon Tom 759
Jones, Dill 73
Jones, Doug 'Little Brother' 654, 685
Jones, Duke 526
Jones, Ed 671
Jones, Eddie 'Guitar Slim' 115, 177, 232, 286, 659, 660, 752, 790, 803, 804, 805
Jones, Eddie Lee 334
Jones, Eddie 'One-String' 334, 811
Jones, Elijah 536, 769
Jones, Elsie 140
Jones, Etta 327, 328, 829
Jones, Floyd 183, 334, 352, 353, 354, 486, 536, 577, 616, 617, 629, 650, 743, 744, 746, 752, 780, 782, 785, 802
Jones, Frankie 796
Jones, George 683
Jones, Grant 79, 790
Jones, Guy 171
Jones, Hank 40, 84, 140, 338, 592
Jones, Harold 358
Jones, Harry 626
Jones, Harry D. 392
Jones, Harry Parr 504, 725
Jones, Hilary 690
Jones, J. J. 146, 610
Jones, J. W. 765
Jones, Jab 187, 450, 451
Jones, Jake 817
Jones, James 222
Jones, James 'Famous' 696
Jones, James K. 118
Jones, Jap 504
Jones, Jeff 101
Jones, Jerome Van 160, 562
Jones, Jesse 84, 432, 459, 725
Jones, Jimmy 140, 384, 406, 587, 678
Jones, Jo 142, 292, 300, 607, 663, 747
Jones, Joe Craig 717
Jones, John 405
Jones, John Paul 457
Jones, Johnny 335, 357
Jones, Johnny Yard Dog 335, 782
Jones, Little Johnny 15, 39, 164, 289, 305, 306, 307, 348, 417, 480, 481, 627, 662, 693, 744, 745, 777, 779, 780
Jones, Jonah 311, 472, 697, 699
Jones, Joseph 758, 831
Jones, Josh 246
Jones, Josiah 802
Jones, Kelly 265
Jones, Larry 563
Jones, Lee 228, 520
Jones, Lee Wesley 229, 244, 432, 504
Jones, Lemuel 757, 760, 812
Jones, Leroy 294
Jones, Little Hat 3, 767, 810, 817
Jones, Lloyd 111, 336, 564, 751, 779
Jones, Luke 778, 797
Jones, Lyn 524
Jones, 'Mad Man' 610
Jones, Maggie 336, 806, 827
Jones, Melvin 458
Jones, Mike 576, 612
Jones, Mildred 827
Jones, Moody 66, 335, 532, 576, 616, 744, 785
Jones, Mrs 334
Jones, Myrtle 779
Jones, Nat 1, 610
Jones, Opal 507
Jones, Ozella 757, 762
Jones, Paul 'Polo' 53, 226, 337, 372, 583, 746, 768
Jones, Philly Joe 477
Jones, Prince 315
Jones, Quincy 115, 510
Jones, R. D. 657
Jones, Ralph 410
Jones, Ralph 'Shrimp' 134, 685
Jones, Ray 221
Jones, Raymond 731
Jones, Reunald 81, 295
Jones, Richard 82
Jones, Richard M. 255, 321, 426, 459, 549, 699, 742
Jones, Rick 374
Jones, Rodney 84
Jones, Roger 39, 74
Jones, Ronald 554, 580, 730
Jones, Sam 63, 270, 671, 713
Jones, Sarah 398
Jones, Sheila White 337
Jones, Slick 69, 338, 340
Jones, Sonny 88, 206
Jones, Stan 541
Jones, Steve Alun 413
Jones, Sunny 755, 819
Jones, Sylvester 757
Jones, T. 581
Jones, Thad 727
Jones, Thomas Houston 153
Jones, Thomas 'Jaybird' 320, 759
Jones, Tom 'Mad' 101
Jones, Tony 624
Jones, Tutu 337, 721
Jones, Uriel 681
Jones, Waynell 754
Jones, William 521, 715
Jones, Willie 33, 166, 173, 174, 176, 640, 642, 808
Jones, Wilson 760
Jones, Zondra W. 554
Jones Jr, Monroe 405
Jongen, Jel 6
Jonnet, Ed 494
Joplin, Janis 737
Jordan, Charley 226, 337, 500, 696, 697, 794, 810, 815
Jordan, Connie 800
Jordan, Edward 'Kidd' 362, 530
Jordan, Frank 758
Jordan, Fred 83, 363, 365, 599, 650
Jordan, Joe 244
Jordan, Larry 495
Jordan, Louis 338, 507, 797, 798, 820, 821
Jordan, Ludwig Joe 295
Jordan, Luke 737, 765, 767, 794, 795, 810, 811
Jordan, Lynne 829, 830
Jordan, Mark 233, 624
Jordan, Robert 385
Jordan, Steve 137, 144, 145, 191, 198, 343, 359, 525
Jordan, Taft 40, 84, 86, 295, 523, 654, 662
Jordan, Willie 43
Jordan, Willy 674

Jordanaires, The 497
Joseph, Charles 503
Joseph, Emile 377
Joseph, Harold 'Frenchy' 282, 283
Joseph, Papa John 391
Joseph, Kim 429
Joseph, Kirk 503
Joseph, Louis 529
Joseph, Nathan 677
Joseph, Oneida 232
Joseph, Sylvia 232
Joseph, Thelma Mae 763
Joseph, Waldron/Waldren 'Frog' 362, 391, 531, 661, 662
Josie, Lou 780
Joung, Mike 129
Journey, Sweet Betty 423, 786
Journigan, George 158
Joyce, Artis 249, 487, 583
Joyce, Stanley 684
Joyner, David 341
Jozwiak, Jeff 591
Juan, Brian 634
Juanzo, Melvin 662
Jubileers, The 773
Jubirt Sisters, The 341
Judge, Walter 'Bully' 14
Juhlin, Bo 37
Juju, Allabu (Winston Doxey) 346
Juke Joint Johnny 513
Jules, Jimmy 805
Julian, Calmes 620
Julien, Ricky 203
Juma, Fatma 625
Juma, Kesi 625
Juma, Mahmoud 625
Jumonville, Jerry 11, 79, 118, 364, 530, 554
Jumpers, The 791
Junior, Paul 502
Just, Andy 198, 199, 341, 583, 658, 771
Justice, Dick 772, 811
Justin, Amyl 691
JW-Jones 341
K-Doe, Ernie 804, 805
Ka'apana, Led 37
Kachamba Brothers 810
Kadison, Kad 261
Kador, Ernest [Ernie K-Doe] 788
Kaeding, Jill 580
Kaethner, John 217
Kage, Greg 104
Kahn, Eddie 726
Kahn, John 52, 442, 443, 562
Kahn, Tommy 'Crow' 449, 677, 678
Kahn, Wayne 108
Kahr, Jim 272, 273, 487, 557
Kai, Dayan 583
Kaihatsu, Tim 144, 233, 274, 486, 487
Kalanj, Mike 20
Kallestad, Paul 657
Kalney, Ed 624

Kamalay, Ray 14
Kamin, Ira 52, 562
Kaminski, Keith 27, 250
Kaminski, Tomasz 411
Kamiya, Sho 630
Kamp, Bart 524
Kamp, E. A. 352, 353
Kanaras, Pete 143, 495
Kane, Candye 342, 788, 830
Kane, Joel 386
Kane, John 386
Kane, Shari 51
Kane, Souleyman 243
Kansas City Blues Strummers 816
Kansas City Five/Six 747
Kansas City Kitty [Mozelle Alderson] 773, 774, 795, 797
Kansas City Red 156, 180, 183, 617
Kansas Joe 452, 794
Kansas Katie 829
Kant, Rip 427, 428
Kaphan, Bruce 274
Kaplan, Fred 40, 47, 123, 124, 240, 261, 413, 414, 538, 719, 720
Kappl, Josef 74
Kareem, Arlem (Ernest 'Pinky' Williams) 662
'Karen' 81
Karina, Mark 583
Karl, King 136
Karlok, Andy 325
Karn, Mike 543
Karnes, Pete 274
Karstein, Jim 264
Kasey, Rufus 812
Kashimura, Valerie 402
Kashmar, Mitch 123, 475
Kaslow, Andy 530, 531
Kaspar, Souhail 220
Kast, George 75
Kato, Lawrence 228
Katri 36
Kattke, John 7, 479
Katz, Bruce 27, 34, 146, 152, 179, 180, 222, 402, 491, 549, 691, 728
Katz, Doran 501
Katz, Steve 501
Kaukonen, Jorma 51, 58
Kaulkin, Andy 16, 95, 124, 262
Kavanagh, Annie 424
Kay, Connie 81, 84, 114, 115, 245, 663
Kay, Dave 23
Kay, Matt 397
Kay, Sandy [prob. Sandy Konikoff] 350
Kazanoff, Mark 'Kaz' 20, 21, 26, 33, 61, 68, 123, 139, 168, 179, 210, 230, 255, 284, 296, 297, 342, 362, 373, 423, 427, 431, 434, 476, 485, 502, 515, 529, 550, 612, 658, 676, 681, 806
Kazee, Buell 810
Keane, Brian 51
Kearns, Robert P. 246

Keaton, Johnny 786
Keb' Mo' 51, 342, 402, 503, 632, 737, 812
Kee, Gene 300
Keel, Eugene 207
Keen, Josh 107
Keen, Stan 36
Keenan, Norman 40, 459, 670
Keene, Billy 784
'Keghouse' 320, 808
Kegler Walter 765
Keister, Shane 401
Keith, Bill 680
Kellaway, Roger 726
Keller, Corey 21
Keller, Ricky 185, 186
Kellerman, Shawn 510, 567, 721
Kelley, Arthur 'Guitar' 791
Kelley, Erin 82
Kelley, Jan R. 210
Kelley, Jim 82
Kelley, Joe 230, 296
Kelley, Kevin 622
Kelley, Raymond J. 210
Kellogg, Ricky 104
Kelly, Dave 53, 237, 286, 344, 767, 813
Kelly, Eddie 756, 768
Kelly, George 60, 416, 464, 592, 727
Kelly, Guy 7, 8, 311
Kelly, Jack 170, 343, 410, 775, 792, 811, 816, 820, 821
Kelly, Jamie 118
Kelly, Jim 548
Kelly, Jo Ann 344, 442, 812
Kelly, Joe 97, 660
Kelly, Joe 'Red' 449, 677, 678
Kelly, Martin 'Van' 440
Kelly, Paul 788
Kelly, Robert 344
Kelly, Rodney 358
Kelly, Sam 53, 396, 751
Kelly, Ted 583
Kelly, Terrance 275
Kelly, Theodore 654
Kelly, Van 204, 645
Kelly, Vance 344, 412
Kelly, Vivian Vance 345
Kelly, Vivian 344
Kelly, Wells 508
Kelly, Willie 17
Kelly, Willie [Roosevelt Sykes] 158
Kelly, Wynton 670, 671, 683
Kelso, Jackie 145, 210, 228, 393, 463, 505, 506, 507, 508, 593
Kelson Jr, Jack 48
Keltner, Jim 122, 236, 274, 343, 349, 356, 358, 359, 363, 375, 612
Kelton, Robert 438, 767
Kemp, Fred 76, 176, 179, 472, 554
Kemp, Gordon 681
Kenchin, Jess 182, 225, 258
Kendall, Gary 170
Kendall Sisters, The 780

INDEX

Kendrick, Linda 34
Kendricks, Burt 651
Kendrix, Bert 726
Kenerson, Bernie 82
Kennard, Guthrie 17, 65, 373, 425
Kennard, Hosea Lee 289
Kennedy, Charles 726
Kennedy, Dan 424
Kennedy, Ian 636
Kennedy, Jack 21
Kennedy, Kathy 43
Kennedy, Ken 472
Kennedy, Meyer 26, 178, 391
Kennedy, Mike 364
Kennedy, Stacey 424
Kennedy, Stephanie 424
Kennedy, Steve 367, 368
Kennedy, Tiny 63
Kennedy, Zonder 103
Kenner, Chris 789, 803, 804, 805, 821
Kenner, Clarence 63, 245, 543, 650
Kennett, Jimmy Lee 705
Kent, Al 780
Kent, Chris 688
Kent, Willie 32, 57, 64, 66, 236, 324, 345, 405, 411, 462, 474, 541, 551, 557, 561, 573, 574, 581, 599, 614, 630, 635, 675, 697, 706, 744, 747, 770, 781, 782
Kentucky Jug Band 775
Kenyon, Carol 234
Kenzie [Kinsey], Donald 349
Keown, Dave 296, 297
Keppard, Freddie 301, 311
Kerber, Ron 624
Kern, Katie 132
Kern, Peter 346
Kerr, Clyde 530
Kersey, Ron 356
Kershaw, Doug 832
Kershaw, Rusty 832
Kesecker, Tommy 496
Kessel, Barney 292, 661, 678, 686
Kessler, Andrew 530
Kesterson, Bob 244
Ketchum, Hal 485
Keus, Olaf 101
Key, Troyce 193, 544
Keyes, Cleveland 118, 119
Keyes, Dave 422, 517, 524
Keyes, Lawrence 583
Keys, Ben 85
Keys, Bobby 144, 356
Kibel, Seth 65
Kicks, Marva 343
Kid, Alvy 'Jo-Jo' 438
'Kid Spoons' 704
Kid Stormy Weather 740, 803, 809
Kida, Dave 417
Kidd, Alray 661, 662
Kidder, Clark 643
Kidder, Gord 446
Kielnecker, Timo 369

Kiely, Phil 732
Kilby, Kraig 52
Kilby Jr, George 516
Kilgore, Brian 629
Kilgore, Kenny 186
Killian, Al 677, 678
Killman, Steve 123, 177, 557
Kilmer, Doug 52, 562
Kilmer, Steve 502
Kilpatrick, Spider 279, 280, 281, 282
Kilroy, Hank 752, 755, 806
Kilzer, Jobie 189
Kim, Harry 507
Kimble, Charles 22, 23, 344, 528, 711
Kimble, Tuffy 324, 433
Kimbrough, Craig 210, 440, 720
Kimbrough, Edward 530
Kimbrough, Junior 346, 754, 766
Kimbrough, Kent 251
Kimbrough, Kinney 170
Kimbrough, Lottie 347, 767, 786, 794, 810, 826, 827
Kimbrough, Sylvester 347
Kimbrough Jr, David 170
Kincaid, Jesse Lee 622
Kindred, Mike 26, 139
Kindred, Zell 677, 678, 731
King, Little Aaron 573
King, Al 439, 446, 583
King, Albert 347, 472, 473, 541, 542, 669, 739, 744, 745, 776, 779, 780, 789, 797, 802
King, Alfonso 62, 477
King, Allison 81, 127
King, Anne 538
King, Little Arthur 822
King, B. B. 1, 130, 236, 352, 472, 473, 601, 632, 737, 738, 767, 768, 776, 779, 786, 789, 799, 802
King, Bertie 703
King, Bnois 372, 373, 768, 814
King, Bobby 1, 20, 125, 274, 360, 363, 711, 783, 788, 814
King, Carole 356
King, Chris Thomas 360, 779, 802, 825
King, Clydie 356, 508, 551, 643, 788
King, Earl 362, 531, 729, 788, 803, 804, 805, 806
King, Eddie 581, 601, 632
King, Emmet 133
King, Eric 135
King, Freddie 289, 362, 458, 557, 599, 767, 789, 818, 820, 825
King, Little Freddie 365
King, Gabriel 119, 120
King, Giles 579
King, Haguy F. 346
King, Jewel 798, 803
King, Little Jimmy 365, 768, 788
King, Joe 685
King, John 20
King, Papa John 20

King, Julius 753, 755
King, Kilroy 820
King, Lee 350
King, Lorenzo 333
King, Nora Lee 526, 827
King, Paul 415
King, Pee Wee 798
King, Pernell 756
King, Peter 53, 457, 727, 830, 831
King, Rick 344
King, Robbie 210, 274
King, Sam 350
King, Saunders 366, 784, 826
King, Stan 685
King, Vernon 526, 683
King, Walter 257, 358, 359
King, Warren 491, 544
King, Wayne 81
King, Willie 367
King Jr, Curtis 668
King Biscuit Boy 367, 768
King Charles 784
King Cotton 241
King David's Jug Band 775, 792
King Karl [Bernard Jolivette] 783, 791, 791
King Solomon 208, 209, 217, 568, 719
King Solomon Hill 786, 794, 801, 803, 812, 813, 817
Kinglets, The 786
Kings, The 805
King's Men, The 352, 354
Kingsley, Pee Wee 438
Kinnard, Douglas 366
Kinney, Fern 257
Kinred, Mike 721
Kinsey, Big Daddy 368, 400
Kinsey, Donald 349, 350, 368, 369, 745
Kinsey, Kenneth 368, 369
Kinsey, Ralph 'Woody' 368, 369
Kinsey Report, The 368, 745, 776, 814
Kirby, Beve 539
Kirby, J. 760
Kirch, Richard 25, 160, 161, 274, 396, 447
Kirk, Allen 192, 421, 540
Kirk, Andy 798
Kirk, Curtis 663
Kirk, John 50
Kirk, Sidney 350
Kirk, Wilbert 526
Kirke, Simon 175
Kirkland, Eddie 267, 268, 269, 270, 273, 275, 369, 424, 540, 570, 751, 752, 824
Kirkland, Frank 55, 299, 486, 577
Kirkland, Leroy 86, 416, 521, 670
Kirkland, Toni 27
Kirkman, Lillie Mae 333, 455, 773, 774
Kirkpatrick, Bob 370, 435
Kirkpatrick, Chuck 'Sonny Boy' 468, 469
Kirkpatrick, Scott 468, 469
Kirkscey, Jonathan 498

Kirkwood, John 338, 340
Kirwan, Danny 344, 604
Kissoon, Katie 122, 234
Kitchen, Liz 53
Kitchen, T. J. 585, 586
Kitta, George 630
Kittrell, Christine 786
Kitzos, Nick 614
Kizart, Wiley 439
Kizart, Willie 659, 660
Klass, Lou 210
Klein, Craig 242, 718
Klein, Danny 151
Klein, Harry 62, 174
Klein, Manny 685
Klein, Oskar 176
Kleine, Bas 543
Klemperer, Paul 21, 148
Kleven, Erik 572, 573
Kline, Rex 249
Klingman, Mark 508
Klobas, Mike 336
Knechtel, Larry 572
Knight, Ben 680
Knight, Brian 813
Knight, Jesse 266
Knight, Joe 1, 39, 245, 321, 322
Knight, Steve 665
Knight Jr, Jesse 400, 659, 660
Knight Brothers, The 780
Knopf, Dave 126
Knopfler, Mark 51, 234, 359
Knowles, James 4, 192, 591, 614, 633
Knowles, Nicky 425
Knowling, Ransom 38, 39, 61, 69, 70, 72, 79, 124, 128, 146, 147, 157, 172, 173, 188, 218, 227, 240, 287, 305, 307, 311, 321, 326, 333, 435, 437, 453, 455, 493, 500, 603, 610, 616, 620, 626, 627, 636, 654, 678, 682, 692, 708, 709, 716
Knowling, Willie 263
Knox, Big Boy 818
Knox, Harold 384
Knox, Lillie 760
Knox, Thelma 760
Knox, Zack 760
Koda, Cub 370, 519, 520, 814, 824, 825
Kodyline, Gil 344
Koeckstadt, Dennis 17
Koella, Frederic 503
Koen, Mae 109
Koenig, John 375, 558
Koerner, 'Spider' John 371, 747
Koerner, Ray & Glover 371
Koerner, Steve 541
Koester, Bob 708
Koffman, Moe 367
Kogl, Jim 4
Kohler, Karen 168
Kohlman, Freddie 140
Kokomo Singers, The 53, 344
Kolax, King 510, 621

Kold, Kristian 8
Kold, Sisse 8
Komiya, Sho 32, 92, 151, 172, 181, 478, 552, 554, 622, 656
Kommersmith, Bob 205, 377
Kondor, Robbie 238
Konikoff, Sandy (Sanford) 349, 350, 623
Konishi, Hirotaka 474
Konitz, Lee 511, 609
Kool Kats, The 751
Koonin, Brian 314
Kooper, Al 52, 355, 358, 468, 508, 569, 623, 672
Koorn, Henk 543
Kopp, Bradley 502
Korner, Alexis 174, 176, 356, 371, 456, 767
Kornfeld, Barry 154, 155
Korpi, Mark 529
Kortchmar, Danny 191, 197, 291
Kosek, Ken 50
Kossacz, Jerry 411
Kossoff, Paul 175
Kostakes, Steve 583
Kostas 503
Kott, Jason 569
Koulibaly, Ugouye 625
Kouyate, Bassekou 625
Kouyate, Djimo 113
Kouyate, Morikeba 664
Kowalski, Mike 508
Koziol, Scott 186
Kraft, Karen 675
Krahnke, Kurt/Curt 125, 479
Krakowski, Frank 598
Kramer, Brian 36, 319
Kramer, Chuck 171
Krampf, Craig 236
Kraus, Phil 295
Kravitz, Andy 624
Kreher, Jr 185, 581, 622
Kreher, Rick 554, 613
Kress, Carl 685
Kriss, Eric 52
Krizzelle, Kenny 660
Kroll, Connie 277
Krown, Joe 79, 324, 538, 566, 731
Krull, David 375, 614
Krumbholz, Kenny 299
Kruth, John 665
Krystal, Karen 687
Ktenas, Mike 341
Kubek, Smokin' Joe 372, 768, 788, 814, 820
Kübler, Olaf 660
Kuhfuss, Jörg 73
Kulik, David Roy 525
Kuljit 37
Kummer, Vinzenz 135
Kümpfel, Harald 660
Kunaal & Sosira 810
Kungnon, John Claude 133
Kunkel, Nathaniel 360

Kunkel, Russ 356, 360
Kupka, Steve 273
Kurch, Rick [Richard Kirch] 160
Kurstin, Greg 198
Küstner, Axel 710
Kutsche, Lars 714
Kuykendall, James 643
Kweskin, Jim 680
Kyer, Wilton 'Peaches' 249
Kyle, Billy 140
Kyle, Charlie 794, 795
Kyle, Joe 'Roll 'Em' 729
Kyle, Willie 600
Kyles, Josephine 682
Kyles, Willie 412
Kynard, Ben 510
Kyser, Wilson 685
L.A. Zydeco Band 831
La Croix, Jerry 679
La Rue, Sophisticated Jimmy 808
La Vah, Camille 829
Labelle 803
Laboriel Jr, Abe 376
Lacasse, Dan 515
LaCava, Jacques 669
Lacefield, Robert 712
Lacen, Anthony 'Tuba Fats' 242
Lacey, Willie 61, 218, 227, 610, 620, 627, 682, 716, 744
Lackey, Kenneth 576
Lackey, Shelby 214
Lacocque, Michel 465
Lacocque, Pierre 465
Lacour, Bobby 362
Lacy, Brian 373
Lacy, Frank 318
Lacy, Freeman 675
Lacy, Rube 767, 786, 801, 802, 810
Ladayne, Jason 135
Ladner, Calvin 610
Ladnier, Tommy 89, 141, 142, 294, 475, 537, 587, 610, 685
Ladson, Ruth 743
Lady Bianca 373, 830
'Lady Fox' 680
Ladzekpo & Ewe Drum Orchestra 810
Lafan, Boyd 468
Lafitte, Ernest 758, 760
Lagneaux, Rick 107
Lagos, Paul 429, 506, 508
Laine, Frankie 74, 75
Laire, Chuck 548
Lajoie, 'Little Red' 684
LaMagna, Carl 210
Lamanna, Cathy 18, 385, 386
Lamar, Justine 796
Lamare, Nappy 328, 384
LaMark II, Charles 'Red/Cool Daddy' 395
Lamb, Bill 429
Lamb, Bruce 182, 258
Lamb, Kenny 34, 395

INDEX

Lamb, Paul 237, 373, 768
Lamb, Ryan 374
Lambert, Adam 565
Lambert, Larry 492
Lambert, Lloyd 83, 114, 115, 179, 208, 210, 231, 232, 805
Lamoia, John 559
Lamond, Don 327, 661
Lamond, Jim 635, 636
Lamont, Joe 520
Lamont Cranston Blues Band 374
Lampé, Jean-Pierre 396
Lampe, Mike 503
Lampell, Millard 702
Lamplighters, The 228, 725
Lamson, Ian 44, 599
Lancaster, Byard 133
Lancaster, Darin 443
Lancaster, Dulin 442
Lancaster, Ernie 377, 490, 491, 518
Lancaster, Hester 526
Land, Harold 392, 684, 726
Landau, Michael 358, 359
Landers, Bob 788
Landers, Wes 654
Landis, Tim 583
Landreth, Sonny 21, 79, 117, 195, 370, 566, 695, 805, 814, 824, 825
Landrum, Pamela 472
Landry, Calvin 86, 87
Landry, Carl 107
Landry, Dwight 555
Landry, Geno 280, 282, 283
Landry, Gino 249, 293
Landry, Joseph 13
Landry, Patrick 87
Landry, Terry 191
Landry, Trey 107
Lands, Fred 26
Lane, Chester 338, 340
Lane, Ernest 101, 104, 374, 493, 593, 660, 753
Lane, Jerry 321
Lane, Jimmy D. 97, 184, 299, 374, 539, 552, 557, 558, 614, 656, 691
Lane, Martin 630
Lane, Mary 829, 830
Lane, Morris 583, 800
Lane, Nick 21, 342
Lane, Shawn 498
Lane, Skip 81
Lane, Willie 752, 753, 819
Lang, Eddie 3, 35, 224, 321, 587, 588, 607, 768
Lang [Langlois], Eddie 803
Lang, Jonny 168, 235, 375, 431, 503
Lang, Jorgen 6, 96
Lang, Martin 92, 172, 554, 622
Lang, Penny 823
Lang, Smiley 556
Langan, Nick 385, 469
Lange, Chris 176

Lange, Don 721
Lange, Gombani 810
Lange, Stuff 174
Langereis, Rob 157
Langford, Chuck 691
Langford, Tim 'Too Slim' 654, 655
Langhorn, Sam [Sammy Lawhorn] 482
Langley, Jason 135
Langridge, Luce 190
Langridge, Stuart 555
Langseth, Marcia 375
Langston, Art 230
Langston, Edith 179
Langston, Thomas 760
Lansing, Dennis 290, 733
Lanthier, Rheal 'Ray' 368
Lantieri, Ilaria 670
Lanzara, Reno 273
Laperous, Jeff 384
Lapetina, Ralph 186, 405
Lark, Commodore 295
Larkin, Isaac 84, 315
Larkin, Milt 415, 670, 671
Larkin, Oscar 455, 654
Larkins, Ellis 244, 701, 702
Larks, The 798
Laronde, Paul 'Big Daddy' 18, 87, 368, 370, 385, 386
Laroo, Saskia 101
Larsen, Andrew 132
Larsen, Frank 6, 96, 242
Larsen, Mike 375
Larsen, Neil 1, 198, 358, 359
Larsen, Ted 375
Larson, David 284, 464
Larson, Leroy 657
Larson, Mike 612
Lartigue, David 'Poochie' 291
LaRue, Jack 145
Lash, Jordan Steele 525
Lash, Marjorie 257
Lasken, Ron 92
Lasko, Morwenna 243
Lasky, Louis 69, 682, 773, 811
Lasley, Clyde 778
Laster, Fred 57
Lastie, David 59, 179, 402
Lastie, Melvin 83, 363, 391, 572
Laswell, Bill 518
Lataille, Rich 222, 299, 324, 362, 469, 492, 548, 559, 560, 567, 667, 729
Latimer, Gary 170
Latour, Little 832
LaTowsky, Waldo 78, 205, 264
Latshaw, Jason 373
Lattrell, Mike 524
Laub, Bob 468
Lauchie, Leo 353, 354, 355
Lauderdale, Jim 139
Lauderdale, Monica 497
Laughing Charlie 737
Laughlin, Tim 805

Lauitsen, Kjeld 96
Laurence, Kenny 22
Laurence, Trevor 429
Lauridsen, Lasse 8
Laurie, Annie 798, 803, 804
Lauritsen, Kjelt 6
Laury, Booker T. 376, 751
Lauser, Dave 424
Laval, Chick 702, 703
LaVaughn, Prince 248, 249
Lavern, Robert 108
Lavesque, Skeeter 728
Lavin, Jack 210
Lavin, Tom 20, 210
Lawal, Gaspar 372
Lawhorn, Sammy 10, 97, 138, 272, 273, 481, 482, 483, 552, 604, 632, 651, 694, 734
Lawlars, Ernest 704
Lawrence, Bruce 245
Lawrence, Christine 507
Lawrence, Elliot 521
Lawrence, Eric 541
Lawrence, George 402
Lawrence, John 488
Lawrence, Kenny 501
Lawrence, Quinn 27
Lawrence, Sid 527
Lawrence, Trevor 356, 363, 365
Laws, Aaron 202
Laws, Johnny 376, 746
Laws, Willie J. 374
Lawson, Jacob 222
Lawson, Joseph 670, 671
Lawson, Joyce 556
Lawson, L. 521
Lawson, Lafayette 146
Lawson, Ricky 343
Lawton, John 201, 315, 677, 678, 713
Lay, Sam 25, 30, 97, 99, 121, 125, 138, 181, 289, 290, 375, 377, 418, 482, 539, 554, 579, 614, 617, 824
Layton, Chris 35, 111, 148, 152, 235, 297, 366, 435, 575, 666, 667, 668, 669
Layton, Robert Taylor 67
Lazy Lester 214, 258, 377, 394, 408, 585, 586, 598, 614, 648, 770, 771, 776, 783
Lazy Slim Jim [Carolina Slim] 752, 755
Le Day, Clarence 13
Le Navelan, Stephen 4
Le-Sueur, Artemus 170
Leadbelly 378, 701, 702, 737, 738, 739, 759, 760, 762, 767, 773, 774, 793, 806, 811, 812, 813, 821
Leady, Don 200
Leak, Danny Raye 401
Leake, Lafayette 35, 36, 55, 79, 101, 125, 159, 164, 165, 233, 263, 266, 271, 283, 289, 290, 383, 386, 404, 405, 418, 480, 487, 562, 581, 591, 601, 631, 693, 725, 733, 734, 742, 747, 749, 779
Leake County Revelers 772

Leaon, Joe 240, 241
Leap Frogs 754
Leary, James 672
Leary, S. P. 25, 79, 138, 177, 272, 273, 289, 290, 417, 456, 457, 480, 481, 557, 603, 604, 616, 679, 734
Leary, Washboard Chaz 238, 239
Lease, Jamie 539
Leathers, Bill 669
Leavell, Chuck 122, 135, 186, 191
Leaves, Eddie 86
Leavey, Tom 16
Leavy, Calvin 383, 800
Leavy, Ernest 244
Leavy, Hosea 241, 383
LeBlanc, Glenn 580
Ledbetter, Martha 378, 380, 381
Ledee, Kirk 532
Lederman, Perry 823
Ledet, Corey 203, 383, 384
Ledet, Lanice 383, 384
Ledet, Lukey 384
Ledet, Morris 383, 384, 832
Ledet, Rosie 383, 831, 832
Ledet, Tammy 12, 13
LeDonne, Mike 548
Lee, Anna 79
Lee, Bertha 511, 512, 801, 826
Lee, Bill 37, 269, 270, 271, 703
Lee, Bryan 575
Lee, Carl 670, 671
Lee, Charles 84
Lee, Charles F. 670, 671
Lee, Chris 396
Lee, Curley [Billy Bizor] 281
Lee, Dave 641
Lee, David 179, 530
Lee, Edward 84
Lee, Emma Dell 214
Lee, George 203
Lee, George E. 384
Lee, Jimmy 780
Lee, Joe 757, 760, 765
Lee, John 80, 464, 533, 752, 753, 755, 767, 813
Lee, Julia 384, 774, 797, 798
Lee, Kathirine 691
Lee, Kenny 318
Lee, Kpe 6
Lee, Laura 780
Lee, Lovie 187, 412
Lee, Marci 506
Lee, Mark 711
Lee, Mary 762
Lee, Melvin 365, 366
Lee, Millard 352, 353, 354
Lee, Paul 'Big Foot' 372
Lee, Peggy 798
Lee, Rod M. 603
Lee, Tom 21, 22
Lee, Tommy 752
Lee, Verdi 337

Lee Jr, David 210
Leecan, Bobby 325, 385, 755, 769, 806, 810, 820
Leecan & Cooksey 385, 755, 769, 806, 810, 820
Leech, Mike 509
Leeds, Eric 375
Leeman, Cliff 173, 663
Leeper, Brant 409
Legendary Blues Band, The 385
Legendary White Trash Horns 695
Lego, Jeff 624
LeGon, Tommy 521
Leh, George 485
Lehnberg, Whit 43
Leiberman, Jean 578
Leibman, John 133
Leigh, Steve 544
Leisz, Greg 343, 485
LeJeune, David 107
Lejune, Iry 831, 832
Lelea, Chester 'Tin Man' 229
Leleux, Lionel 831
Lembo, Kim 87, 368, 385
Lemp, Chris 560
Lenard, Darrell 628
Lenchek, Armand 81, 127
Lending, Kenn 6, 96, 176, 242
Lennear, Claudia 363, 623
'Lenni' 411, 555
Lenoir, J. B. 386, 576, 616, 744, 748, 749, 752, 779, 780, 785, 789, 790, 821
Lenoir, Shorty 293, 529
Lent, Mike 20
Lenz, Sara 195
Leon, Rob 51
Leonard, Almond 634
Leonard, Darrell 11, 235, 343, 359, 364, 430, 431, 468, 469, 518, 563, 624, 625
Leonard, Herbert 592
Leonard, Teddy 533, 582
Leonard, Victor 280, 282, 283, 439
Leone, Tony 137
Leophonte, Nico 409
Lepson, Tommy 495, 525
Lerma, Larry 666
Lerman, Al 80, 582, 598
Lerman, Don 553
Lesberg, Jack 83, 90
Lescoeur, Dennis 544
Leshner, Steve 431
Lessey, Bob 63
Lester, Andy 479
Lester, Bobby 676
Lester, Jimmy 126
Lester, Norman 24
Letsch, Glenn 231
Levenson, Barry 124
Levesque, Mike 636
Levi, Donald 348
Levin, Danny 502, 612
Levine, Duke 427, 563

Levine, Eric 485
Levine, Jeff 151, 264, 383, 422
Levine, Sam 186
Levine, Todd 25
Levinson, Mark 230, 511
Levis, Bob 67, 109, 141, 474, 563, 567
Levis, Tony 180
Levy, Allen 398
Levy, Howard 425
Levy, Iki 95, 262
Levy, John 69, 86, 523
Levy, Jules 595
Levy, Marcy 579
Levy, O'Donel 509
Levy, Ron 4, 61, 76, 158, 179, 210, 284, 299, 324, 337, 356, 357, 362, 365, 366, 372, 376, 433, 439, 440, 476, 515, 548, 559, 572, 591, 717, 718, 720, 721, 814
Lewie, Jona 53
Lewis, Alfred 768, 769, 793
Lewis, Art 296
Lewis, Arthur 795
Lewis, Bert 431, 591
Lewis, Billy Lee 111
Lewis, Clara 593
Lewis, Diana 349
Lewis, Earlene 563
Lewis, Ed 761, 762, 763
Lewis, Ernest 819
Lewis, Ezra 760
Lewis, Freddie 675
Lewis, Furry 387, 699, 764, 766, 767, 792, 794, 802, 810, 811, 812, 813
Lewis, George 133, 462, 555, 805
Lewis, George Leroy 691
Lewis, Hambone 450, 451, 452
Lewis, Harold 505
Lewis, Harriet 74
Lewis, Huey 673
Lewis, Jacky 385
Lewis, James 315, 660
Lewis, James 'Hot Dog' 510
Lewis, Jeff 358, 399, 673
Lewis, Jesse 233
Lewis, Jimmy 74, 164, 237, 238, 294, 295, 369, 410, 477, 486
Lewis, Jimmy 'Baby Face' 806
Lewis, John 84, 413
Lewis, Johnie 389, 823
Lewis, Jumbo 9
Lewis, Laurie 613
Lewis, Leroy 222
Lewis, Lockwood 248
Lewis, Lovey 827
Lewis, Lowell 583
Lewis, Maxayne 358
Lewis, Meade Lux 7, 8, 292, 326, 327, 389, 661, 737, 739, 740, 741, 742, 747, 787, 808
Lewis, Mel 725, 726
Lewis, Michael 760
Lewis, Mike 544

Lewis, Milton 554
Lewis, Mitchell 687
Lewis, Nick 580
Lewis, Noah 105, 738, 767, 768, 769, 775, 792, 793
Lewis, Pat 349
Lewis, Pete 'Guitar' 504, 505, 520, 593, 594, 651, 767, 774
Lewis, Ramsey 780
Lewis, Ray 803
Lewis, Richard L. 757
Lewis, Roger 87, 274
Lewis, Sammy 253, 789
Lewis, Shawn 'Ez-Keez' 612
Lewis, Smiley 391, 799, 803, 804, 805
Lewis, Steve 42
Lewis, Terry 229
Lewis, Tony 255, 256
Lewis, Walter 25
Lewis, Wilbert 534, 535
Lewis, William 526
Lewis, Willie 796
Lewiston, Cal 351
Lexing, Harvey 597
Leyasmeyer, Teo 134, 151, 291, 377
Leyden, Jimmy 295, 296
Leyland, Carl 'Sonny' 16, 38, 241, 417, 435, 685, 728
Liban, Jim 68
Liban, Matt 66
Lichter, Joe 508
Lieberman, Bob 539
Lieberman, Robert 413, 629
Liedman, Jon 136
Lige, David 229
Liggett, E. L. 61
Liggett, Ellsworth 661, 662
Liggett, Larry 780
Liggins, Jimmy 392, 767, 788, 798, 799, 826
Liggins, Joe 392, 507, 508, 740, 742, 788, 797, 798, 805
Light, Chris 654
Lightfoot, Papa 173, 393, 752, 768, 770, 803
Lightnin' Slim 394, 749, 767, 770, 776, 783
Lij 222
Li'l Brian 395, 833
Li'l Millet 788, 805
Li'l Rascals Brass Band 554
Lillie, Richard 412, 600, 601
Lillie Mae 754
Lim, Mariano 728
Lima, Steve 217, 218
Limina, Dave 180, 549, 718
Linberg, Curtis 728, 729
Lincoln, Charlie 23, 395, 756, 767, 773, 820
Lindberg, John 535, 539, 599
Lindefeldt, Scott 249

Linden, Colin 37, 195, 343, 369, 540, 735, 824
Linden, Paul 136, 137, 654
Lindholm, Lucas 344
Lindley, David 485, 624
Lindsay, John 7, 42, 185, 220, 221, 240, 311, 320, 437, 551, 607, 636, 637, 680, 682, 699
Lindsay, Tony 583
Lindschouw, Ib 174
Lindsey, Chester 55
Lindsey, Deborah 551
Lindsey, Lucille 756
Linett, Mark 87
Linkchain, Hip 396, 746
Linn, Margaret 564
Linn, Mary 564
Linscott, Jody 429
Linson, Lisa 343
Linthecome, Joe 774
Linton, Errol 396, 739
Lion & Atilla, The 821
Lippincott, Randy 27, 134, 325, 576
Lippitt, Stanley 373
Lipschitz, Irving 508
Lipscomb, Frank 397
Lipscomb, Mance 396, 747, 777, 818, 820, 823
Lisi, John 649
List, Garrett 133
Lister, Aynsley 397, 824
Liston, Melba 115, 449, 683
Liston, Virginia 398
Litteral, Hollywood Paul 130
Little, Bobby 77, 125, 265, 266, 480, 693
Little, Eric 27
Little, Victor 564
Little, Wilbur 229
Little Al 693, 694
Little Axe 737, 739
Little Bill 796
Little Bob 784
'Little Brother' 753, 758
Little Bubber 803
Little Buster & The Soul Brothers 398, 788
Little Caesar 799
Little Charlie & The Nightcats 768, 771, 776, 399
Little Charlie 655
Little Danny 540
Little David 796
Little David [Wylie] 752, 755
Little Esther 505, 738
Little Henry 124
Little Hudson 752, 785
Little Ike 786
Little Joe Blue 400, 779, 780
Little Man 388
Little Mike & The Tornadoes 400
Little Mike 125

Little Milton 373, 400, 412, 660, 779, 780, 781, 788, 789
Little Miss Peggie 784
Little Miss Sharecropper [LaVern Baker] 829
Little Mr Midnight 805
Little Red 438
Little Richard 103, 104, 788, 790, 797, 799, 803, 805
Little Snooks Jr 179
Little Son Joe 343, 453, 785
Little Sonny [Jones] 402, 803, 804
Little Sonny [Willis] 403, 751, 770, 789
Little Temple [Gus Jenkins] 754, 788
Little Tommy 265
Little Walter 66, 201, 335, 403, 453, 480, 481, 494, 557, 562, 576, 616, 734, 739, 743, 744, 749, 752, 768, 769, 770, 779, 780, 781, 799
Little Whitt & Big Bo 404
Little Willie John 173, 713, 799
Little Wolf 746
Littlefield, T. J. 195
Littlefield, Little Willie 110, 228, 229, 405, 520, 544, 740, 776, 820, 826
Littlejohn, Ira Mae 786
Littlejohn, John(ny) 36, 383, 405, 447, 541, 542, 692, 744, 765, 777, 779, 780, 800, 814
Littleton, Ed 116
Littleton, Kelly 92, 330, 613, 706
Lively, Edd 364
Livingston, Ulysses 24, 158, 244, 287, 326, 414, 432, 661, 662
Lizard, Stevie 695
Llanes, Damien 148, 342
LLC 824
Llorens, Michael 41, 351, 669
Llorens, Tony 41, 351, 669
Lloyd, Charles 104
Lloyd, Charlie 132
Lloyd, Levi 507
Loafer 361
Lobligeois, Roland 19, 77, 671
Locke, Abb 68, 95, 125, 130, 217, 233, 289, 563, 632
Locke, Eddie 464, 592
Locke, Guy 185
Lockett, Bridget 599
Lockett, Carl 43, 373
Lockett, James 129
Lockett, Jesse 758
Lockett, Michael 28, 29
Lockhart, Jim 753
Locki, Louise 584
Lockie, Chauncey 686
Lockridge, Jesse 318, 591
Lockridge III, Jesse 318
Locks, James 'Blazer Boy' 803, 804
Lockwood, Robert (Jr) 10, 61, 124, 136, 201, 365, 387, 403, 406, 467, 480, 500, 557, 601, 603, 616, 620, 621, 707, 743,

744, 751, 767, 768, 771, 785, 788, 797, 801, 813, 825
Lodovici, Joe 123
Lofton, Cripple Clarence 69, 407, 462, 739, 740, 741, 794, 808, 809
Lofton, Lawrence 392
Lofton, Willie 'Poor Boy' 437, 801, 802, 821
Logan, B[ert] L. 710, 764
Logan, Bobby 215, 422
Logan, Dan 670
Logan, Ed 77, 238, 350, 458
Logan, Freddie 726
Logan, John 'Juke' 124, 240, 262, 274, 307, 408, 417, 430, 464, 538, 556
Logan, Michael 121
Logan, Ray 808
Logan, Russ 764
Logg, Smokey 433
Logoz, Dinu 176
Logsdon, Ron 654
Logwood, Dejuana 100, 199
Lohr, Bob 22, 152, 501, 705
Lomax, Alan 8, 285, 326
Lomax, Dwayne 350
Lomax, John 378
Lomax, Mark 564
London, Clarence 752, 754
London, Frank 151
London, Mel 693
London Strings Orchestra, The 19, 77
Lone Star Cowboys 772, 773
Lonergan, Chris 424
Lonesome Bob 163
Lonesome Sundown 118, 408, 776, 783, 788
Long, Buddy 572
Long, Del 216
Long, Howard 772, 821
Long, Jewell 753
Long, Joey 133, 678
Long, John 264
Long, Steve 674
Longo, John 136
Longshaw, Fred 321, 587, 588, 592
Lonnie 'The Cat' 659
Loomis, Hamilton 409
Lopes, Chris 185
Lopez, Al 508
Lopez, Bruce 94, 136
Lopez, Chico 223
Lopez, Lucky [Leo Evans] 32, 190, 745
Lopez, Manuel 660
Lopez, Mike 583
Lopez, Paul 505, 506
Lopez, Richard 'Scar' 104
Loranger, Paul 566
Lorenz [Llorens], Michael 351
Lorenz [Llorens], Tony 351
Lorenz, Rob 622
Loria, A. J. 232
Lorimer, Roddy 37, 122

Lorkovic, Radoslav 111
Lost American Bluesmen, The 409
Lott, Carl 77, 296, 492, 527
Lott, George 607
Louden, Calvin 'Vino' 318, 632
Loudermilk, Mike 79
Louie Bluie [Howard Armstrong] 792, 816
Louis, Joe Hill 283, 409, 672, 752, 753, 768, 769, 770, 789, 800
Louise, Graná 829, 830
Louise, Miranda 541, 669
Louisiana Johnny 796
Louisiana Red 30, 187, 350, 410, 445, 514, 578, 617, 621, 658, 744, 749, 750, 751, 752, 779, 782, 789, 800, 823
Lounge, Eugene 693
Louper, J. P. 353
Lourie, Vic 338
Love, Andrew 4, 6, 53, 68, 77, 118, 130, 143, 144, 145, 158, 191, 210, 232, 234, 337, 348, 349, 350, 356, 365, 366, 458, 564, 571, 591, 599, 660, 673, 675, 688, 691
Love, Billy 'Red' 221, 740, 780, 789
Love, Clayton 660
Love, Cleanhead 753
Love, Coy 'Hot Shot' 770, 789
Love, Darlene 551
Love, G. 402, 803
Love, Jasper 764
Love, L. Z. 111
Love, Preston 244, 504, 506, 507, 508, 520, 679
Love, Willie 412, 600, 601, 633, 738, 752
Loveland, Vicki 130
Lovelle, Herbie 34, 40, 280, 281, 355, 356, 457, 483, 726
Lovett, Sam 'Baby' 384
Lovie Lee 412, 745, 746, 750, 782
Lowe, Curtis 366, 505, 510, 520
Lowe, Keith 43
Lowe, Mundell 292, 565, 610, 663
Lowe, Nick 274
Lowe, Sammy 86, 416
Lowenthal, Barry 246
Loweroy, Elsie 14
Lowery, Ramblin' Red 772
Lowery, Robert 412
Lowry, Irwin 758
Lowry, James 765
Lowther, Henry 371, 372, 428, 431, 457
Loyacano, Joe 462
Lozano, Conrad 274, 408
Lozano, Pauline 373
Lucas, Al 40, 173
Lucas, Alfred 597
Lucas, Alonzo 245
Lucas, Buddy 40, 521, 652, 662, 727
Lucas, Charles 807

Lucas, Jane [Mozelle Alderson] 69, 740, 741, 773, 774
Lucas, Maxwell 245, 315, 446
Lucas, Ray 369
Lucas, Robert 104, 413, 513
Lucero, Eric 566
Lucie, Lawrence 244, 326, 661
Lucille & The Strangers 786
Lucini, Alejandro 499
Luckett, L. C. 126, 576, 618
Luck(e)y, Warren 40, 81
Lucky, Steve 44, 239, 293, 399, 583
Lucky & Flash 749
Lufrano, Tony 100, 196, 199, 690
Luis, Jose 101
Lumpkin, Edward 146
Lumsdaine, John 690
Lundberg, John 127
Lundy, William 432
Lunt, Fred 625
Lunt, Nick 374
Luper, 'Lord' Luther 731
Lupkin, Bill 476, 479, 557
Lush, Connie 413
Lusk, Professor Eddie 129, 160, 234, 318, 414, 617, 632, 664, 733
Lusk, John 811
Lutcher, Joe 228, 414, 742, 788, 798, 826
Lutcher, Nellie 798
Lutton, Casey 264
Luty, Christoff 556
Lux, Christina 20
Lux, John 341
Lyle Jr, Lafayette 68
Lynch, Bill 485
Lynch, Carl 81, 327, 410, 521
Lynn, Barbara 440, 830
Lynn, Clyde 'Blow Top' 521
Lynn, Lenny 606, 781
Lynn, Smilin' Smokey 742, 819
Lynn, Trudy 824
Lynwood Slim 40, 95, 414, 478, 479, 538, 606, 770
Lyons, Lonnie 110, 647, 711, 740, 819
Lyons, Willie James 165, 185, 324, 345
Lyras, Nico 130
Lyssarides, Christer 36, 37
Lyte, Redd 504, 505
Lytell, Jimmy 293, 597, 712
Mabane, Bob 84
Mabeary, Mary 759
Mabon, Willie 1, 67, 263, 323, 415, 557, 562, 581, 614, 632, 733, 749, 764, 779, 780, 783, 789, 790, 799, 809
MacBeath, Bill 246, 526
MacCalder, Willie 20, 210
MacCallum, Paul 217
Maccarone, Vince 540
MacCarthy, Justin 464
Macey, Charles 40, 81
Mack, Alura 828
Mack, Art 414

Mack, Bobby 201
Mack, Clarence 63, 83, 245, 300, 321, 322, 520, 543, 650
Mack, Eddie 416, 773, 798
Mack, Ida May 740, 818, 827, 828
Mack, Johnny 433, 721
Mack, Lonnie 363, 669, 768, 776
Mack, Luther 760
Mack, Red 778
Mack, William 223
Mack Sisters, The 315
Mackel, Billy 90, 245, 510, 683
MacKenzie, Dave 416
MacKey, Bernie 300
Mackey, Richard 507
Mackey, Steve 644
Mackie, Craig 217
Mackintosh, L. D. 712
Mackrell, Pat 20
MacLeod, Doug 14, 146, 416, 594
MacLeod, Patti Joy 417
MacMillan, Eric 499
MacMurray, Fred 328
Macon Ed [Eddie Anthony] 754
Macon, John 'Shortstuff' 710
Macon, Murray 763
Madaio, Steve 356, 357, 429, 530, 535
Madden, Ed 'Fishman' 541
Maddox, Lawrence 'Max' 62
Maddox Bros & Rose 773
Mader, John 690
Madison, Audrey 660
Madison, Diane 171
Madison, James 'Pee Wee' 138, 481, 482, 483, 552, 603, 604
Madison, Paul 593
Madison Slim 184, 552
Madrick, Steve 227
Maesto, Christian 336
Maesto, Louis 336
Mafala, Baba Chale 810
Magassa, Ali 243
Magdaluyo, Melecio 373
Magee, Juan 361
Magic Dick 104, 771
Magic Sam 95, 417, 486, 744, 745, 749, 768, 770, 781, 800
Magic Slim 57, 138, 217, 262, 419, 519, 527, 528, 617, 692, 745, 746, 767, 779, 814, 825
Magiera, Jürgen 17
Magness, Janiva 194, 417, 538
Magnie, John 485, 503
Magnificents, The 790
Magnus, Nick 424
Magnuson, Robert 358
Mahan, Mick 556
Mahdi, Kalil 583
Maher, Joe 211, 236, 499, 535
Mahfood, Tom 'La Bumba' 222, 497
Mahlstedt, Jay 81, 82
Mahon, Darryl 706

Mahon, John 360
Mahon, Tom 16, 55, 135, 194, 202, 211, 241, 475, 618, 704, 728
Mahones, Gildo 583, 726
Mahoney, Leigh 168
Maiden, Sidney 421, 680, 764, 826
Mair, Marilynn 126, 549
Majeed, Abdood 650
Major, Louis 766
Major, Mark 118
Makino, Motoaki 614
Makis, Manny 414
Malach, Bob 197, 198
Malachi, John 338
Malarsky, Leonard 210, 686
Malbank, Tom 513
Malcolm, Horace 69, 88, 218, 220, 221, 240, 311, 320, 437, 636, 637, 682
Male Quartette 797
Malender, Jimmy 599
Malenky, Bob 639
Mali, Papa 251
Malick, Peter 138, 604
Malin, David 217, 218
Malina 133
Mallaber, Gary 121
Mallard, Oett 'Sax' 61, 69, 70, 72, 231, 287, 500, 610, 620, 621, 627, 654, 682, 780
Mallet, Jerry 633
Mallett, Reetham 472, 713
Mallett, Terry 296
Mallon, Danny 422
Mallory, Earl 676
Malmestrom, Nick 36
Malone, Bob 525
Malone, Dave 107
Malone, J. J. 194, 220, 399, 422, 544, 784
Malone, Kenny 58, 347
Malone, Russell 359
Malone, Tom 357, 402
Malone, Tom 'Bones' 325, 547
Malone, Tommy 469, 503
Maloney, Lasandra 369
Maloney, Tom 319, 586
Malveaux, Paul Junius 758, 760
Malvin, Arthur 295, 296
Mamprusi Tribesmen 810
Man, Beenie 318
Man, Grown 344
Mance, Junior 233, 727
Mancini, Chris 358
Mandel, Harvey 103, 104, 121, 429, 486
Mandingo Griots 811
Manfred, John 457
Mangiapanne, Sherwood 462
Manhattans, The 789
Manilus, James 63
Manion, Edward 144, 151
Manish Boys, The 770
Manley, Cynthia 220, 434, 629
Mann, Al 414

Mann, Billy 300
Mann, Brian 197
Mann, Charles 356
Mann, Dave 82
Mann, David 343
Mann, Herbie 679
Mann, Tom 538
Mann, Woody 422
Manning, Bishop Dready 756
Manning, Bob 36, 706
Manning, Johnny 133
Manning, Leola 794, 795, 828
Manning, Marie 756, 786
Manning, Renee 821
Manning, Terry 458
Mannish Boys, The 422
Manone, Wingy 213, 741
Manriquez, Tony 664
Manske, Pat 65
Manson, Charlie 755
Mantegari, Frank 4
Mantley, John 765
Manuel, Bobby 349, 350, 401, 403, 430, 711
Manuel, Elbur Stepney 614
Manx, Harry 37
Manz, Charlie 81
Manzy, Herman 392, 788
Mapp, Eddie 689, 768, 769
Mapp, Gary 717
Marable, Lawrence 460
Marathons, The 780
Marayama, Minoru 474
Marchan, Bobby 803
Marcus, Bobby 406
Mardin, Arif 359
Maresh, Chris 21, 195
Margold, Mitch 400
Margolin, Bob 16, 66, 81, 87, 136, 177, 226, 241, 324, 423, 476, 480, 483, 484, 494, 495, 515, 535, 615, 695, 723, 776, 779, 814, 825
Margolin, Sherry 423
Marianne 36
'Marie' 640
Marine, Mitch 580
Marinero, Raul de Pedro 374
Marini, Lou 358
Mark, J. D. 85
Mark, Jon 428, 429
Markellis, Tony 578
Marker, Gary 622
Markham, Jimmy 541
Markham, Pigmeat 780
Markowitz, Little Mike 400, 515, 614
Marks, Gareth 217
Marley, Bob 623
Marogg, Norman 96
Marotta, Jerry 2, 51
Marotti, John 123, 124
Marquart, Curtis 336
Marr, Hank 520

INDEX

Marrero, Lawrence 462
Marriott, Steve 356, 372
Marriner, Southside Steve 341
Marrochello, Paul 180
Mars, Christina 21
Mars, Johnny 101, 423, 583
Mars, Mitzi 780
Marsalis, Branford 130
Marsalis, Delfeayo 84
Marsalis, Ellis 178, 805
Marsden, Bernie 319, 547
Marsh, Audrey 296
Marsh, Carl 135, 257
Marsh, Steve 191, 261, 538
Marsh Jr, Leonard 536
Marshak, Greg 540
Marshal, Susan 524
Marshall, Eddie 672
Marshall, Ellie 718
Marshall, Frankie 777
Marshall, Herbert 8, 390
Marshall, Jack 384
Marshall, Jim 168
Marshall, Joe 81, 84, 295
Marshall, John 372
Marshall, Johnnie 424, 539
Marshall, Johnny 214
Marshall, Kaiser 249, 253, 254, 587, 588, 592, 685
Marshall, Larry 78, 79
Marshall, Leroy 107
Marshall, Mick 510
Marshall, Susan 246, 373, 498, 499
Marshall, Thomas J. 758
Marshall, Wendell 115, 174, 176, 295, 322, 323, 340, 456, 457, 586
Martin, Albert 'Fats' 219
Martin, Alfred 385
Martin, Asa 772, 821
Martin, Barrett 153
Martin, Barrie 223, 674
Martin, Bill 245, 424, 473, 662
Martin, Billy 571
Martin, Boyd 131
Martin, Brad 612
Martin, Carl 14, 69, 88, 89, 121, 218, 220, 223, 424, 608, 626, 734, 755, 765, 792, 821
Martin, Chuck 791, 831
Martin, Derek 789
Martin, Dolly 815
Martin, Eddie 425
Martin, Fiddlin' Joe 285
Martin, Frank 690
Martin, Grady 521
Martin, Jerry 145
Martin, Jimmy 550
Martin, Kelly 245, 295, 300, 650
Martin, Larry 41, 57, 274, 283, 487, 544, 714, 735
Martin, Lee Roy 54
Martin, Lewis Albert 340, 472

Martin, Luci 358
Martin, Melvin 533
Martin, Michael Henry 296
Martin, Mickey 617
Martin, Napoleon 597
Martin, Ollis 128, 737, 768, 769
Martin, Reuben 561
Martin, Robert 535, 629
Martin, Roland 14, 424
Martin, Rudy 654, 683
Martin, Sara 248, 385, 426, 689, 806, 826, 827
Martin, Sonny 394, 585, 586, 791
Martin, Trade 358
Martin, Trudy 296
Martin, Vic 473
Martin, Walter 80, 311, 338, 340, 699
Martin & Robert 769
Martina, Ellio 120, 612
Martinez, Carlos 'Du Du' 571
Martinez, Lorenzo 220
Martinez, Paul 410
Martinez, Ray 405, 725
Martinez, Rene 36
Martinez, Richard 4, 332, 556
Martsolf, Mike 430, 431
Martucci, Vinnie 50, 51
Martyn, Quedellis (Que) 207, 208, 209, 677, 719
Maruyama, Minoru 474
Marvin, Frankie 772
Marvin, Lee 516
Marvin & Johnny 786, 788
Marx, John 55, 60, 123, 194, 202, 211, 475, 618
Maryol, Alex 659
Masefield, John 426
Mashaa 126, 366, 572, 731
Masked Marvel's Buddy, The 800
Mason, Anne 257
Mason, Bill 657
Mason, Carey 'Ditty' 609
Mason, Harold 351, 551
Mason, Moses 737, 793, 797, 811
Mason, Rob 513
Mason, Rod 73
Mason, Rodney 763
Mason, Ron 433, 444
Mason, Rudolph 510
Mason, Rudy 84
Massey, Barbara 727
Massey, Curtis 721
Massie, Joe 760
Massof, Mick 595
Massoth, Jim 614
Masters, Pete 374
Masterson, Chris 529
Mathes, Bob 342
Mathes, Minnie 829
Matheson, Todd 612
Mathew, Eric 172

Mathews, Dave 100, 191, 199, 307, 373, 390, 485, 486, 538
Mathews, Emmet 796
Mathews, Fats 804
Mathews, Lou 433
Mathews, Odea 763
Mathews, Scott 275, 558
Mathews, Tony 143, 408, 427, 488
Mathiasen, Nils 8
Mathis, Allison 761
Mathis, David 98
Mathis, Johnny 780
Mathus, Jimbo 236, 251, 498
Matilda 36
Matle, Rick 250
Matlock, Lena 796
Matrazzo, Dan 78, 79
Matson, Charles A. 254, 592, 595, 596
Mattacks, Dave 636
Mattarochia, Ralph 185
Mattes, Jay 5, 6, 7, 260
Matthews, Al 140, 294
Matthews, Little Arthur 506
Matthews, Bobby 489
Matthews, Dave [arr] 291
Matthews, David [g] 317, 679
Matthews, Fats 803
Matthews, George 62, 291, 292, 654
Matthews, James 424
Matthews, Llew 146
Matthews, Neal 497
Matthews, Odea 739
Matthews, Roger 757
Matthews, Scott 231, 274, 484
Matthews, Sherlie/Shirley 356, 508
Mattson, Randy 2
Maupins, Thurston 'Sox' 384
Maureen 429
Maurice & Mac 780
Maxey, Hogman 763
Maxey Jr, March 521
Maxwell, Chris 705
Maxwell, Clyde 766
Maxwell, David 139, 180, 204, 211, 236, 293, 325, 369, 423, 427, 494, 499, 503, 515, 546, 557, 615, 691, 742, 771, 824, 825
Maxwell Street Jimmy 745
May, Earl 76
May, Kevin 560
May, Mark 291
Mayall, John 62, 174, 198, 235, 350, 427, 468, 643, 768
Mayall, Maggie 430, 431
Maybank, Michael 760
Mayberry, Tiny 796, 827
Maye, Arthur Lee 505, 788
Mayell, Norman 52
Mayer, John 359
Mayer, Luther 'Captain Luke' 230, 756
Mayes, Darrell 687
Mayes, Texas Pete 431, 492, 820, 825

Mayfield, Curtis 542
Mayfield, Joe 791
Mayfield, Percy 432, 780, 782, 788, 798, 805, 818, 826
Mayfield, Sammy 657
Maylor, Steven 4
Maynard, Mark 243
Mayo, Gypie 228
Mays, Bert M. 807, 808
Mays, John 598
Mays, Roy 730
Mays, Stonewall 766
Mays, Ted 818
Mays, Ukulele 774
Mays, Willie 521
Mays, Zilla 800
Maytones, The [Meadowlarks] 432
Mayweather, 'Earring' George 433
Mazel, Greg 497, 548
Mazerick, Phil 81
Mazurek, Rob 462, 553, 606
Mazzocco, John 547, 564
Mbaruk, Mtumwa 625
M'Butu, Count 186
McAbee, Palmer 769
McAfee, Bill 784
McAllister, Jeffery 16, 126, 222, 239, 548, 549, 728
McAllister, Randy 433, 771
McArthur, Glen 76
McAvoy, Gerry 495
McBain, Fiona 137, 525
McBee, Lee 433, 476, 771
McBride, Bobby 258, 377, 394, 408
McBride, Reggie 1, 275, 343, 359, 518
McCabe, Bruce 4, 5, 6, 375, 376, 464, 575, 612
McCabe, Larry 4, 375
McCabe, Matt 16, 126, 179, 222, 492, 497, 548, 549, 560, 567, 721
McCain, Bennie 681
McCain, James 'Jack Of All Trades' 821
McCain, Jerry 434, 529, 685, 770, 783, 786, 800
McCain, Roosevelt 434
McCain, Walter 434
McCall, Cash 164, 401, 750
McCall, Charles 231
McCall, Larry 'Bones' 282
McCall, Louis 350
McCall, Marti 643
McCanless, Russ 576
McCarn, David 769, 772, 821
McCarthy, James 350
McCarty, Eldridge 208, 209
McCarty, Jim 601
McCaughey, Scott 153
McCauley, Michael 81, 185
McCauley, Reed 832
McCauley, Vidrine 832
McCellan, William 256

McClain, Arthur 189, 295, 767, 792, 793, 794, 807, 810, 811
McClain, Jean 343
McClain, Marlon 564
McClain, Mighty Sam 549, 691
McClay, Ernest 826
McCleary, Vince 227
McClellan, Bernice 762
McClellan, Bill 256
McClelland, Billy Earl 476
McClennan, Tommy 435, 519, 737, 742, 744, 794, 802, 810
McClintock, Harriet 758, 760
McClintock, Lil 754, 810
McClinton, Delbert 21, 111, 402, 771, 776, 779
McCloud, Norman 299, 580
McClure, Bobby 780
McClure, Frank 83, 114, 401
McClure, Matthew 618
McCobb, Andy 283
McColgan, John 101
McConnell, John 84
McConnell, Livingstone 84
McCord, Theodore 575
McCormick, Bruce 350
McCormick, Donnie 654
McCormick, Kevin 429, 430
McCory, Cedric 'Cowboy' 365, 366
McCottry, Andre 344
McCoy, Albert 761
McCoy, Austin 258
McCoy, Charlie 62, 69, 88, 109, 128, 151, 220, 221, 240, 311, 326, 330, 333, 436, 437, 453, 458, 636, 670, 692, 697, 716, 738, 792, 794, 801, 813, 814
McCoy, Joe 146, 151, 221, 240, 311, 333, 435, 436, 636, 743, 773, 774, 792, 795, 797, 801, 812
McCoy, Robert 437, 742
McCoy, Robert Lee [Robert Nighthawk] 158, 187, 437, 605, 655, 670, 697, 708, 715, 742, 743, 769, 794, 813
McCoy, Rose Marie 39, 40
McCoy, Ruby 764
McCoy, Viola 385, 437
McCoy, William 769, 794, 817
McCoy & Johnson [Kansas Joe & Memphis Minnie] 794
McCracken, Hugh 135, 355, 356, 357, 359, 363
McCracken, Michael 367, 404
McCracklettes, The 440
McCracklin, Jimmy 77, 209, 210, 353, 438, 720, 740, 767, 780, 782, 786, 789, 800, 819, 826
McCrary, Bobby 521
McCrary, Everett 269, 270, 275
McCravy, James 794
McCray, Larry 215, 440, 528, 583, 824
McCray, Steve 440, 528, 695

McCrea, Uncle Billy 759
McCreary, Lew 210, 726
McCullers, Dezie 201
McCully, Melody 50
McCurdy, Mike 200, 293, 440, 462, 581, 606
McCurdy, Roy 429, 672
McDade, Henry 258, 724, 725
McDaniel, Buddy 429
McDaniel, Floyd 440, 768, 781
McDaniel, Greg 591
McDaniel, Hattie 301, 827
McDaniel, Lenny 151, 429
McDaniel, Michael 688
McDaniel, Willard 88, 145, 214, 243, 247, 258, 305, 307, 432, 463, 492, 647, 677, 678, 686, 724, 725, 740, 742
McDaniels, Harry 224
McDermott, Tom 469, 805
McDonald, Andy 344
McDonald, Candy 133, 445
McDonald, Chris 186
McDonald, Earl 248, 249, 755
McDonald, Huey 50
McDonald, Hugh 425
McDonald, Mr & Mrs Joe 758
McDonald, Jon 141, 396, 421
McDonald, Kathi 20, 363
McDonald, Larry 135
McDonald, Mary 760
McDonald, Michael 198
McDonald, Molly 758
McDonald, Randy 111
McDonald, Stuart 257
McDonald, Tee 815
McDonald, Terry 194
McDonald, William 234, 581
McDowell, Annie Mae 441, 443, 814
McDowell, Mississippi Fred 441, 651, 738, 747, 748, 749, 761, 762, 763, 764, 777, 788, 802, 812, 814, 823
McDowell, Tecumseh 605, 815
McDuff, Brother Jack 595, 606
McEachern, Deneen 823
McElwaine, Jim 151, 152
McEntee, Robert 502
McEwen, John 58
McEwen, Libby 58
McFadden, Charlie 443, 619, 815
McFadden, Eric 586
McFadden, Marvin 291
McFarland, Bill 41, 67, 96, 129, 141, 316, 368, 443, 464, 550, 553, 568, 590, 614, 733
McFarland, Barrelhouse Buck 443, 808
McFarland, Elaine 467
McFarland, Lester 772
McFarland, Orville 632
McFarland, Rico 41, 139, 317, 443, 614, 688, 695
McFarland, Rusty 'Mopar' 572
McFarland, Tom 444

McFarlane, Fred 255, 256
McFarlane, John 'Pops' 136, 226
McFarlane, Will 402
McFay, Nathaniel 'Monk' 392
McGarrigle, Anna 485
McGarrigle, Kate 485
McGee, Cookie 444
McGee, Dennis 12, 793, 831, 832
McGee, Jerry 429
McGee, Michael 163, 669
McGee, Patrick 344
McGee, Sam 772
McGettrick, Kurt 357
McGhee, Brownie 39, 40, 90, 154, 173, 206, 211, 266, 278, 281, 293, 378, 379, 380, 381, 382, 444, 446, 478, 570, 637, 638, 639, 701, 702, 708, 709, 710, 717, 737, 738, 748, 752, 755, 756, 759, 774, 806, 807
McGhee, George 643
McGhee, Howard 244
McGhee, Jerry 643
McGhee, Stick(s) 90, 173, 445, 446, 637, 638, 639, 640, 642, 752, 755, 798, 806
McGlohon, Joe 644
McGowan, Bert 133, 134
McGowan, Donnie 509
McGrain, Mark 503
McGrath, Joe 624
McGraw, Lether 526, 827, 829
McGray, Clifford 543, 650
McGregor, Brian 31
McGriff, Jimmy 130, 180, 509, 549, 789
McGriff, Tom 43
McGuinness, Tom 53, 344
McGuire, Scoop 558
McHugh, Paddy 53
McIntosh, Andra Faye 564
McIntosh, Eldeen 460
McIntosh, Robbie 37
McIntosh Jr, Danny 372
McIntyre, Earle 623
McIntyre, Maurice 299
McKaba, Jim 503
McKay, Al 643
McKay, Art 618, 774
McKay, Bernie 315
McKay, Kris 502
McKee, G. D. 114
McKeen, Gary 624
McKeever, Patrick 126
McKendree, Kevin 31, 186, 434, 553, 644, 681
McKendrick, Mike 467, 551
McKenna, Mike 169, 170
McKenzie, Billie (Willie Mae) 829
McKenzie, Rufus 756, 757
McKenzie, Tommy 76
McKibbon, Al 244, 245, 327, 508, 685, 701
McKinley, David Pete 752, 754, 819
McKinley, Eddie 706

McKinley, L. C. 333, 627, 778
McKinley, Sheila 424
McKinley, Tim 591
McKinney, Joseph 711
McKinney, Michael 427
McKinnie, Dee 429
McKinnon, Jamie 494
McKinnon, Kym 81, 82
McKinstry, Ray 790
McKitrick, Harry 413
McLagan, Ian 53, 235, 563, 624
McLain, Jimmy 796
McLarty, Davis 103
McLaughlin, Mike 440
McLawler, Sarah 245
McLean, Connie 796, 806
McLean, Big Dave 446
McLean, Ernest 26, 140, 166, 391, 462, 661, 662
McLean, Jackie 583
McLean, Richard 462
McLemore, Bill 245, 446, 477
McLeod, Rory 216, 362, 559
McLoughlin, Eamon 148
McMahan, Coyal 445, 638, 640
McMahon, Andrew 'Blueblood' 289, 290, 405, 447, 514, 778
McMahon, Ken 446
McMahon, Pete 385, 386
McMichen, Clayton 772
McMillan, Cab 785
McMillan, Lannie 126, 366, 572, 660, 731
McMillan Jr, Lonnie 68
McMillen, Jim 78
McMillen, Vic 84
McMillon, Dennis 752, 755, 806
McMinn, Don 430
McMullen, Fred 477, 689, 738, 756, 813
McMurray, David 499
McNair, Dave 200, 430, 636, 666
McNair, Velvet 670
McNally, Ann 401
McNally, Bob 257, 401
McNeal, Charles 136, 263
McNee, Hart 52, 562
McNeely, Bob 209, 355, 447, 504, 505
McNeely, Cecil 'Big Jay' 81, 209, 355, 374, 447, 504, 505, 798, 800
McNeely, Dillard 447
McNeely, Rob 186
McNeil, Johnny 74, 75
McNeill, Dean 20
McNeill, Walter 129
McNiles, Charles 447
McNulty, Thomas 365
McPhail, Black Bottom 45, 796
McPhatter, Clyde 520, 777, 799
McPhee, Tony (T.S.) 15, 62, 174, 175, 271, 344, 767, 824
McPherson, Billy 81
McQuills, Ricky 554

McRae, Dave 39, 40, 81, 114, 115, 295, 340, 416, 662
McRae, Teddy 24, 173
McRudy, —— 83
McShann, Jay 77, 84, 145, 208, 209, 384, 459, 671, 684, 724, 725, 739, 740, 742, 798, 799, 800, 808
McShann, Pete 724
McSwain, Chester 465
McTeer, Glenway 233, 675
McTell, Kate 448
McTell, Blind Willie 448, 478, 689, 737, 738, 752, 755, 760, 762, 767, 768, 773, 787, 788, 794, 795, 812, 813
McTyner, Clifford 661, 662
McVay, Floyd 'Bubbles' 201
McVea, Jack 75, 77, 114, 244, 252, 292, 432, 449, 520, 661, 662, 677, 678, 725, 797, 798, 800, 821, 826
McVey, John 450
McVie, John 33, 62, 427, 428, 429, 430, 431, 604
McWhirter, George 494
McZiel, Paul 830, 831
Mead, Andrew 134
Mead, Frank 217, 473
Meaders, Ray 'Diggy Do' 394
Meadowlarks 432
Meaux, U. J. 377, 394
Medallions, The 805
Medeiros, Tony 216
Medeski, John 262, 498
Medica, Leon 78, 119, 503
Medina, Flaco 'Slim' 123
Medlock, Clifford 692
Mednick, Lisa 87
Medwick, Joe 820
Meeder, Scott 186
Meek, Steve 721
Meeks, Philip 187
Megatons, The 789
Meggs, John 57, 733
Mehegan, John 683
Mehrmann, Rene 96
Mejda, Helmut 217
Melching, Brian 501
Melchione, Mike 87
Mele, Mike 718
Melford, Michael 52, 484
Mell, Bert 409
Mellow Fellows, The 450, 776
Melody Kings, The 408, 675
Melrose, Frank 462
Melton, Barry 604
Melton, David 413
Meltzer, Jenny 342
Melville, Bruce 291
Melvoin, Susannah 359
Melvoin, Wendy 359
Melz, Reinhardt 564
Memphis Horns 37, 350, 356, 358, 401, 439

Memphis Jug Band 450, 737, 738, 762, 768, 769, 774, 775, 792, 794, 795, 797, 810, 816, 820
Memphis Minnie 88, 437, 450, 451, 737, 738, 739, 742, 743, 744, 767, 768, 773, 774, 779, 780, 785, 787, 792, 794, 795, 797, 802, 808, 811, 812, 820, 821, 826, 827
Memphis Piano Red 766, 802
Memphis Rockabilly Band 779
Memphis Slim 69, 70, 72, 165, 283, 454, 601, 621, 654, 682, 737, 739, 740, 741, 742, 743, 744, 747, 748, 749, 762, 779, 780, 781, 782, 788, 790, 795, 797, 800, 802, 809, 819, 821, 822
Memphis Symphony Orchestra 349, 401, 551
Menard, D. L. 831, 832
Menard, Kevin 87, 489
Menard, Ryan 446
Mendelsohn, Barbara 484
Mendez, Andres 226
Mendillo, Pete 49
Menes, Hunderto 'Pupi' 571, 718
Menesclou, Thierry 'Juke' 4, 6
Mennecke, Achim 17
Menza, Don 210, 727
Mercer, Chris 363, 364, 427, 428, 655
Mercer, Jim 374
Mercer, Johnny 8, 390
Mercer, Wally 800
Meredith, Jack 526
Mergen, Steve 524
Mero, Gonzalo 295
Merriel, Martha 168
Merrill, Bob 84, 245, 416, 459
Merrill, George 629
Merritt, Daddy 173, 445, 637, 638, 639, 640
Merritt, Jymie 300, 352, 354
Merritt, Michael 133, 134, 135, 569, 614
Merritt, Norman 655
Mesi, Jim 751
Mesquite, Skip 100
Mesritz, Rene 705
Messer, Michael 502, 513
Messina, Nick 429
Metcalf, Louis 98, 134, 164, 253, 336, 426, 437, 438, 459, 460, 461, 587, 588, 596
Meters, The 803, 805
Metoyer, Mark 539
Mewherter, Adam 136, 186
Meyer, Edgar 58
Meyer, Frankie J. 476
Meyer, Helmut 17
Meyer, Karl 172, 181, 622
Meyer, Oscar 293
Meyer, Scott 125, 136
Meyers, Augie 133, 239
Meyers, Charles 'Sugar Boy' 332, 364
Meyers, Harry 592
Meyers, Hazel 459

Meyers, Jack 233, 265, 601, 631, 694
Meyers, Louie [Louis Myers] 781
Meyers, Rick 43
Mezzrow, Mezz 89, 140, 224
Mfundo, Limited 810
Miah, Hasson 617
Michael Hill's Blues Mob 776
Michael, Ian 571
Michaels, Ed 558
Michaels, Edward R. 246
Michaels, Eric 478
Michaux, Elder 758
Michel, Ed 272, 273
Michelot, Pierre 527
Michelson, Jeni 185
Michelson, Stephan 18
Mick, David 121, 450
Mickel, Mindy 429
Mickle, Elmon 'Driftin' Slim' 770, 782
Microwave Dave 435
Middlebrook, Ralph 'Pee Wee' 681
Middleton, John 44, 512, 540
Middleton, Max 824
Midnighters, The 790, 799
Migliori, Jay 726
Mike, Sylvestor 826
Mikell, Francis 1
Milburn, Amos 459, 740, 741, 773, 774, 797, 798, 799, 800, 804, 826
Miles, Buddy 52, 482, 824
Miles, Butch 177
Miles, Charles 694
Miles, Floyd 377
Miles, Josie 460
Miles, Lizzie 461, 740, 773, 794, 803, 827, 828, 829
Miles, Luke 'Long Gone' 278
Miles, Marie 700
Miles, Mary Ann 829
Miles, Pete 344
Miles, Ron 634
Miles, Tommy Lee 100, 198, 199, 236
Miley, Bubber 134, 322, 325, 385, 426, 437, 459, 460, 469, 475, 595, 596, 718
Milford, Scottie 784
Millar, Chris 50, 161, 194, 215, 239, 241, 264, 383, 422, 551, 676, 705
Millard, Bruce 291
Miller, Al 529, 530
Miller, Al [A] 407, 462, 773, 774, 792
Miller, Al [B] 462
Miller, Benny 84
Miller, Bill 726
Miller, Brian 133, 250, 669
Miller, Charlie 84, 357, 718
Miller, Curly 'Barefoot' 820
Miller, Dave 369
Miller, Dave 'Biscuit' 612
Miller, David 772
Miller, Debbie 228
Miller, Dominic 218

Miller, Eddie 326, 328, 357, 443, 537, 808, 809, 815
Miller, Frankie 218
Miller, Gene 'Bowlegs'/'Bo-Legs' 238, 509
Miller, George 529, 803
Miller, George 'Kid' 521
Miller, Greg 711
Miller, J. M. 'Doc' 336
Miller, James 232
Miller, Jimmy 268, 269, 396, 726
Miller, Joe 290
Miller, Johnny 114, 661, 662
Miller, Leroy 761, 812
Miller, Lillian 818, 826
Miller, Luella 462, 827
Miller, Mark 344, 345, 383, 555, 731
Miller, May Belle 618
Miller, Mitch 683
Miller, Norvus G. 112
Miller, Olivette 340
Miller, Punch 69, 311, 326, 333, 682
Miller, Ray 83
Miller, Red 798
Miller, Richard 727
Miller, Robert 295
Miller, Roland 'Stumpy' 567
Miller, Ron 153
Miller, Ronnie 652
Miller, Rurcell 112
Miller, Russ 250
Miller, Ruth 764
Miller, Sammy 58
Miller, Scott 369
Miller, Sodarisa 828
Miller, Stanley 460, 587, 592
Miller, Steve 119, 265, 266, 272, 273, 372, 431
Miller, Susie 758
Miller, Tal 377, 394, 408
Miller, Tom 764
Miller, Walter 764
Miller, Wilbert 87
Miller, Willie 25
Miller Sr, Norvus 112
Millet, Li'l 805
Millian, Baker 295
Milligan, Josh 'The Little Kid' 571
Milligan, Malford 21, 168, 195, 485
Millinder, Lucky 785, 798, 821
Mills, Abraham 209, 508
Mills, Charley 681
Mills, John 11, 21, 68, 123, 210, 297, 342, 431, 502, 529, 676
Mills, Johnny 'V' 368
Mills, Lincoln 62
Mills, Nelson 110, 711
Mills, Paul 123, 361
Mills, Tony 33, 34
Milne, Jim 169, 170, 210
Milner, Jamal 242, 243
Milner, Jimmy 752

Milner, Paddy 65, 425
Milo, Cordelia de 686
Milo, Mick 373
Milo, Nick 539
Milo Twins 798
Milteau, Jean-Jacques 524
Milton, Richard 544
Milton, Roy 228, 463, 506, 508, 593, 663, 742, 788, 797, 798, 799, 826
Milwood, Mike 274
Mims, Ken 410
Mims Jr, Frank 712
Mims III, Nelson 291
Minerve, Harold 'Geezil' 315
Mingledorff, Jason 571
Mingus, Charles 244, 252, 683
Minix, Eric 13, 29
Minnick, Jeff 529
Minnieweather, Jeff 547, 564
Minor, Dan 86, 315
Minor, Everett 286, 651
Minor, Orville 84
Miracles, The 780
Miranda, Billy 780
Miranda, Rafael 340
Miranda, Rudy 260
Mirikitani, Alan 113
Mirikitani, Nikki 113
Miroff, Seymour 40
Mironov, Jeff 51
Mirtsopoulos, Mike 156
Mischo, R. J. 169, 342, 464
Miskimmin, Billy 495
Miss Angel 80, 464
Miss Country Slim 819
Miss Dee 497
Miss Detroit Slim 751
'Miss Minnie' 698
Miss Rhapsody 797, 829
Mississippi Heat 464
Mississippi Jook Band 737, 740, 794, 795
Mississippi Matilda 525, 794, 810
Mississippi Moaner, The 738, 793, 794, 801
Mississippi Mud Steppers 792, 810, 816
Mississippi Mudder [Joe McCoy] 801
Mississippi Sarah 626, 768, 769, 775, 794
Mississippi Sheiks 465, 773, 774, 794, 801, 816, 821
Mississippi Slim 649
Mistretta, Bob 540
Mitchell, Abbye 307
Mitchell, Anthony 544
Mitchell, Bettye 251
Mitchell, Billy 115, 477, 713
Mitchell, Blue 350, 429, 430, 683, 713, 727
Mitchell, Bob 338, 340, 341, 507
Mitchell, Bobby 805
Mitchell, Brian 134, 359
Mitchell, Curtis 83, 133, 531
Mitchell, Dave 84, 459

Mitchell, Frank 114, 115, 129, 214, 231
Mitchell, Freddie 84, 114, 115, 662, 800
Mitchell, George 311
Mitchell, Hal 245
Mitchell, Harold 338
Mitchell, Herman 'Tiny' 1, 75, 88, 90, 228, 244, 405, 432, 661, 662, 725, 726
Mitchell, James 77, 126, 144, 238, 349, 458, 572, 660
Mitchell, Jean 307
Mitchell, Jimmy 509
Mitchell, Joe 570
Mitchell, John [t] 458
Mitchell, John [bi] 685, 718, 720
Mitchell, Kevin 68
Mitchell, Lightnin' 56
Mitchell, Mitch 483
Mitchell, Nathaniel 523
Mitchell, Ollie 356
Mitchell, Razz 338, 340
Mitchell, Rose 803
Mitchell, Sam 217, 344, 466, 487, 532
Mitchell, Stanley 780
Mitchell, Tom 115
Mitchell, Tressie 551
Mitchell, Walter 751, 752, 768
Mitchell, William 536, 682, 708, 716
Mitchell, Willie 352, 353, 354, 509, 572
Mitchell's Christian Singers 747
Mitchum, Harry 'Snapper' 217, 360, 568
Mittendorp, Jan 120, 152, 332, 501, 612
Mittleman, Spyder/Spider 40, 413, 538
Miura, Natsuko 169
Miura, Tad 169
Mixon, Jovaughn 131
Mixon, Leslie 583
Mixon, Stan 6, 131
Mize, Jim 199
Moamed, Souliman 133
Mobile Strugglers 466, 811, 816
Mobile Washboard Band 761
Mock, Holger 411
Modeliste, Joseph 'Zigaboo' 530, 558
Moe, Ross 112
Moeller, Johnny 148, 220, 255, 342, 434, 476, 499, 529, 553
Moen, Tony 374
Moer, Paul 725
Moffat, Doug 144, 402
Mogel, Claudia 291
Mohannon, Leveeta 'Squeaky' 614
Mohead, John 126
Moho, Jerome 670
Moire, Edwin 173
Mølbach, Erik 456
Mole, Miff 597, 712
Mole, Papa John 516
Moleri, Nick 336
Molette, Willie 286
Moliere, 'Kid' Ernest 62, 330
Molinari, Albert 468
Molton, Flora 766

Moment, Johnny 764
Monarch Jazz Quartet 765
Moncur, Grachan 39, 40, 416
Monday, Paul 77, 819
Mondy, Alma 803
Monett, Raymond 119
Money, Zoot 372
Monie, Rickie 648
Monitors, The 805
Monk, Thelonious 808
Monotones, The 780
Monque'D, J. 805
Monroe, Bill 772, 773
Monroe, David 392
Monroe, Jim 293
Monroe, Vince 791
Monroe, Willie 694
Monsbourgh, Adrian 72
Monsees, Eve 450
Montagu, John 475
Montalto, Bob 238
Montana, Vince 356
Monte, Jerry 123
Montgomery, Durious 38
Montgomery, Foree Superstar 746
Montgomery, Gene 472
Montgomery, James 771
Montgomery, 'Big James' 22, 23, 344, 528, 711
Montgomery, Jan 467
Montgomery, Joe 386, 387
Montgomery, Little Brother 79, 233, 417, 437, 453, 466, 562, 616, 670, 680, 718, 739, 740, 741, 742, 745, 749, 764, 782, 785, 787, 794, 803, 807, 808, 809, 822
Montgomery, Robert 227
Montgomery, Rodger 316
Montgomery, Sam 812
Montgomery, Tollie 'Duke' 467
Montgomery, Wes 510
Montoya, Coco 130, 151, 152, 430, 431, 468, 629, 768, 776, 779, 823
Montrell, Roy 167, 463, 572, 788, 804, 805
Montsinger, Buzz 490
Monzon, Ricardo 499
Moody, Clyde 773
Moody, Edward 447
Moody, James 800
Moody, Julia 469, 827
Moon, Fruity 556
Moon', 'Henry 322
Moonbeams, The 506
Mooney, Darrin 473
Mooney, Don 759
Mooney, John 176, 439, 469, 695, 779, 814, 824
Moonglows, The 55, 780, 799
Moore, Aaron 470, 520, 781
Moore, Abra 200
Moore, Whistlin' Alexander 471, 740,

742, 749, 752, 753, 773, 777, 810, 817, 818, 819
Moore, Alfred 291, 292
Moore, Alice 16, 471, 787, 814, 815, 827
Moore, Bass 461
Moore, Bill 211
Moore, Wild Bill 39, 252, 291, 292, 390, 449, 471, 661, 662, 713, 798, 800
Moore, Billy 341
Moore, Bobby 780
Moore, Byrd 765, 772, 821
Moore, Charles 232, 472, 554, 731
Moore, Clarence 689, 741
Moore, Cliff 48
Moore, Danny 306, 307, 713
Moore, Deacon John 472, 805
Moore, Elizabeth 758
Moore, Eric 'Two Scoops' 324, 325, 567
Moore, Rev. E. S. (Shy) 775
Moore, Eustis 645
Moore, Freddie 381
Moore, Gary 130, 431, 472, 824
Moore, Gatemouth 473, 797, 798
Moore, Gene 173, 211, 445, 638, 641
Moore, Hebert 648
Moore, Jim 531
Moore, John 124, 159, 720
Moore, Johnny 74, 75, 247, 295, 392, 505, 739, 778, 797, 798, 808
Moore, Johnny B. 57, 64, 74, 109, 164, 181, 330, 335, 345, 474, 528, 573, 622, 630, 632, 635, 744, 746, 747, 768, 781, 814
Moore, Johnny Lee 762
Moore, Kid Prince 475
Moore, Les Iz [Izmore] 296
Moore, Melvin 1, 209, 355, 506, 507, 508, 677, 679, 727
Moore, Merrill 773
Moore, Monette 475, 796, 828
Moore, Noah 761
Moore, Numa 'Pee Wee' 245, 338, 583, 650
Moore, Oscar 74, 75, 114, 115, 231, 232, 391, 661, 778
Moore, Ralph 358
Moore, Ray 84
Moore, Reggie 73
Moore, Robert 661, 662
Moore, Rosie Mae 436, 826
Moore, Rudolph 521
Moore, Sol 677
Moore, Thomas 26, 661, 662
Moore, Tim 'Kingfish' 506
Moore, Guitar Tommy 800
Moore, Wilbert 648
Moore, Wild Boar 97
Moore, Wild Willie 433, 438, 439, 719
Moore, Wilfred 648
Moore, William 755, 765, 767, 787
Moorland, David B. 232
Moorman, Jimmy 244

Moorshead, John 175
Morales, Armando 111
Morales, Joe 148
Morales, Richie 156
Morales, Rocky 26
Moran, Ed 86
Moran, Tommy 78, 79
Morand, Herb 240, 311, 437, 682
Morawiec, Steve 580
Mordecai, Jimmy 587, 588
Mordue, Eddie 372, 458
Moreland, Ace 544
Moreland, Prince 505
Morello, Jimmy 55, 60, 61, 194, 475, 540, 704
Moreno, James 705
Moreno, Mario 411
Moret, Tony 82
Morey, Frank 781
Morgan, Al 84, 338, 340, 677
Morgan, Big Windy 492
Morgan, Chris 104
Morgan, Dennis 375
Morgan, Eddie 2, 809
Morgan, Johnny 413, 601, 728
Morgan, Les 217
Morgan, Mike 220, 433, 476, 768, 814, 820
Morgan, Stanley 244
Morgan, Teddy 172, 241, 262, 464
Morgan, Theotis 348
Morganfield, Big Bill 423, 476, 779
Morioka, Fushio 634
Moroccos, The 781
Morris, Anthony 318
Morris, Blind Mississippi 476
Morris, Camp 760
Morris, 'Blue Charlie' 377, 783
Morris, Left Handed Charlie 784
Morris, Clara 829
Morris, Corner 765
Morris, Danny 495
Morris, Floyd 401, 733
Morris, Gene 510
Morris, Jimmy Lee 603, 734
Morris, Joe 232, 244, 245, 446, 477, 662, 683, 777, 798, 799, 800
Morris [Brouchet], Joe 118, 119
Morris, John 583
Morris, Nathan 341
Morris, Rex 62, 174
Morris, Rickey L. 291
Morris, Sid 136
Morris, Tom 253, 325, 385, 426, 437, 595, 596, 679, 721
Morris, Willie 389
Morrison, Barbara 507
Morrison, Henry 761, 762
Morrison, James 358
Morrison, Leroy 650
Morrison, Mike 6, 234, 528, 541
Morrison, Monte 321, 322

Morrison, Monty 473, 510
Morrison, Pat 182, 214
Morrison, Peck 583
Morrison, Reggie 597
Morrison, Rudy 84, 459
Morrison, Russell 328
Morrison, Van 273, 274, 275, 359, 739
Morrison Singers, The (Jackie & Donna) 344
Morrissey, Bill 824
Morrissey, Dick 372
Morrow, Greg 'Foots' 365
Morrow, Harold 414
Morrow, Jeff 614
Morse, Ella Mae 773, 797
Mortier, Jasper 152, 312
Morton, Amber July 195
Morton, Benny 328, 661
Morton, Jelly Roll 461, 760, 762, 803, 805
Morton, Johnny 69, 287, 500, 620
Morton, Sylvester 209
Mosby, Artie/Arty 325, 500, 618, 619
Moscato, J. J. 27
Moseley, Curtis 595, 596
Moseley, James 712
Mosley, Bob 244, 252, 449, 450, 826
Mosley, Curtis 455
Mosley, John 84
Moss, Anderson 760
Moss, Buddy 23, 444, 477, 639, 640, 689, 700, 738, 767, 773, 774, 795, 806, 812, 813
Moss, Cecil 34
Moss, Dillard 81
Moss, Joe 32, 479
Moss, Kate 479
Moss, Nick 464, 476, 478, 598
Moss, Slim 565
Moss, Teddy 45
Mossbarger, Eric 540
Mossello, Joe 358
Mosser, Jonell 503
Most, Abe 357
Mostin, John 34
Moten, Patrick 673
Moten, Wendy 431
Mother Pauline 786
Motley, Frank 788
Motta, Danny 559
Motycka, Rev. Murph 148
Mouradian, Jimmy 180
Mouton, Chardell 582
Mouton, Geneva 193
Mouton, Zydeco Joe 831
Mouton, Ray 29, 87
Mouton, Van 21
Mouton, Walter 831
Mowat, Oliver 332, 433
Mr B 239, 476, 479
'Mr Bear' [Teddy McRae] 173
Mr Excello 179, 362

INDEX 891

Mr Google Eyes [Joe August] 800
Mr Greenjeans 242
Mr Honey [David Edwards] 752, 819
'Mr Jerry' 686
'Mr Louis' 686
Mr Low 559
'Mr Percussion' 61
Mr Q 786
'Mr Sheiks' 69, 259, 320
Mr Sunshine 368
'Ms. Carmen Getit' 516
Ms D 507
Ms Rita 100
Mt Zion Singers 349
Mthiyane 465
'Mudcat' 511, 609, 786
Muddy Walters [Alex Thomas] 785
'Muddy Water' [Alex Thomas] 713
Muddy Water Jr 360
Muddy Waters 138, 201, 266, 272, 273, 403, 456, 479, 500, 557, 601, 603, 604, 616, 651, 693, 723, 737, 738, 739, 743, 744, 747, 748, 749, 752, 758, 760, 762, 767, 768, 779, 780, 798, 799, 802, 812, 813, 814
Muddy Waters Jr 265
Mudry, Greg 368
Mugalian, Steve 95, 146, 241, 262, 417, 522
Mugrage, Michael 51
Mugsie 582
Muhammad, W'ali 156
Muhoberac, Larry 210
Muldaur, Clare 485
Muldaur, Geoff 484, 680, 788, 824
Muldaur, Jenny/Jenni 485
Muldaur, Maria 139, 485, 547, 680, 823, 830
Muldrow, Gail 'Little Bit' 507
Mulhauser, Terry 386
Mulherin, Joe 4
Mullen, George 595, 596
Mullen, Jim 727
Mulleniux, Jimmy 464, 687
Mullens, Eddie 510, 526
Müller, Peter 224, 486
Mullican, Moon 772, 773
Mullick, John 573
Mulligan, Gerry 679, 725
Mullins, Herb 504
Mullins, Mark 195, 242, 571
Mumtaz, Effendi 6, 222
Mundy, Paul 414, 440, 645
Mungo [Daniel Abrams] 657
Munier, Bro. 242
Munkas, Alex 420
Munoz, Charlie 'Chaz' 104
Munson, Rik 512
Murden, Walter 75, 661, 662
Murdo, Larry 572
Mure, Billy 295, 663
Murfreesboro [Al Garner] 786

Murphy, Alan 27
Murphy, Chris 564
Murphy, Curtis 244
Murphy, Floyd 509
Murphy, James 713
Murphy, Jerry 632
Murphy, Joe 86, 416
Murphy, Mark 156
Murphy, Matt 'Guitar' 79, 139, 233, 455, 456, 481, 515, 562, 601, 631, 654, 748, 822
Murphy, Michael 556
Murphy, Paul 548
Murphy, Shaun 468
Murphy, Taylor 554
Murphy, Tom 143
Murphy, William 401
Murphy, Willie 823
Murphy Brothers Harp Band 769
Murray, Bill 408, 675
Murray, Bobby 291, 307, 433, 563
Murray, Brian 359, 472, 554, 731
Murray, Dave 228
Murray, David 21
Murray, Elisha 'Eli' 30, 63
Murray, Eugene 'Spare Time' 431
Murray, Lyn 638
Murray, Pat 50
Murray, Robert 358
Murrell, Lottie 764, 766
Murrell, Red 778
Murry, Brian 76
Murry, Marro-Di'Jon 584
Murtagh, Rags 264
Muschalle, Frank 486, 742
Muscle Shoals Horns, The 257, 358
Muse, Rabbit 765
Musgrove, Yoggie 21
Mushlitz, Dick 732
Musselwhite, Charlie/Charley 35, 37, 43, 52, 123, 197, 198, 199, 237, 238, 239, 274, 293, 342, 389, 466, 486, 513, 538, 552, 655, 676, 709, 729, 742, 744, 768, 770, 771, 776, 777, 779, 800, 823, 825
Musso, Vido 724, 725
Mwinyi, Said 625
Myakicheff, Lan 53
Mycroft, Tim 424
Myers, Bob 765
Myers, Bumps 1, 414, 432, 492, 677, 678, 725, 800
Myers, Charles 363, 365
Myers, Dave 1, 19, 66, 67, 147, 266, 290, 293, 299, 323, 341, 403, 406, 415, 557, 581, 614, 621, 630, 632, 693, 746
Myers, Isadore 587
Myers, Jack 404, 415, 693
Myers, Louis 1, 19, 66, 67, 146, 265, 266, 272, 273, 341, 385, 403, 406, 415, 481, 483, 488, 520, 557, 562, 621, 630, 632, 693, 694, 745, 765, 770, 776, 782, 814
Myers, Paul 581

Myers, Phil 396
Myers, Rusty 282
Myers, Sam 210, 306, 307, 479, 489, 770, 771
Myers, Wilson 661, 700, 702
Myhre, Byron 37
Myles & Dupont 780
Myles, Big Boy 788, 805
Myles, Raymond 805
Myles, William 391
Myrick, Gary 229, 535, 556
Mystery Shadow, The 356
Mz Dee [Dejuana Logwood] 100, 199
Nabors, Leroi 468, 718
Nackowitsch, Ralf 220
Nadeau, Joe 575
Naftalin, Mark 52, 99, 193, 198, 273, 433, 539, 558, 562
Nagasaki Slim 169
Nagle, Paul 197, 727
Nagy, John 470
Nagy, Rachel 191
Nalley, Kim 496, 830
Nalls, Jimmy 495
Nance, Brent 337
Nance, Harry 83
Nance, Linny 337
Nance, Ray 295
Nanji, Mato 634
Nanni, Mark 386
Nanton, Tricky Sam 322
Napier, Alex 669
Napoleon, Phil 293, 597, 712
Napoletan, Jill 21
Nardella, Steve 469
Nares, Geordie 374
Narmour, W. T. 772, 821
Nash, Derek 228
Nash, Dick 726
Nash, Eddie 531
Nash, Kenneth 273
Nash, Larry 145
Nash, Nancy 284
Nash, Steve 161
Nash, Ted 726
Nashelles 144
Nashville Washboard Band 759, 792
Nassor, Said 625
Nathan & The Zydeco Cha Chas 489, 831, 832, 833
Nathan, Pete 57
Nathan, Ray 291, 292
Nathan, Roy 526
Nations Brothers 772
Naugahyde, Red 261
Naundorf, Frank 25
Navarro, Sal 215, 239, 241
Navy, Kevin 28
Neal, Clayton H. 730
Neal, Darnell 490, 491, 544
Neal, Dino 317
Neal, Frederic/Fredrick 491, 544

Neal, Kenny 34, 139, 152, 370, 377, 490, 491, 544, 771, 776, 824, 825
Neal, Noel 68, 127, 138, 139, 152, 440, 490, 491, 569, 695
Neal, Raful 34, 152, 265, 491, 771
Neal, Sammy 107
'Neckbones' [Willie Fields] 697
Ned, James 'Chocolate' 202
Neditch, Dave 52
Needham, Kevin 409
Neel, Johnny 688
Neely, Bob 7, 232, 233, 562
Neely, Little Bobby 528
Neely, Frederick 227
Neely, Jerry 87
Neely, Jimmy 583
Neil, Marcia 295
Neilson, Arthur 135, 152
Nelson, Alex 286
Nelson, Alexander 63, 83, 543
Nelson, Arnett 69, 88, 259, 320, 452, 453, 607, 626, 682, 692
Nelson, Chicago Bob 253, 492, 513
Nelson, Charlie 83
Nelson, Charlie 'Dad' 48, 787
Nelson, Clarence 193, 261, 341
Nelson, Dave 142, 190, 537
Nelson, David 539
Nelson, Dwayne 554
Nelson, E. 711
Nelson, Ford 352, 353, 409
Nelson, James 657
Nelson, Jay 783, 791
Nelson, Jewell 818
Nelson, Jimmy 223, 227, 492, 780, 798
Nelson, Juan 275
Nelson, Lawrence 391
Nelson, Oliver 69, 338, 369
Nelson, Red [Wilborn] 321, 407, 739
Nelson, Richard L. 229
Nelson, Ricky 41
Nelson, Rob 497
Nelson, Romeo 739, 740, 741, 808
Nelson, Sara 168
Nelson, Todd 652
Nelson, Tom 558
Nelson, 'Blue Coat' Tom 793, 816
Nelson, Tracy 121, 486, 788, 830
Nelson, Velma 798
Nelson, Virgil 539
Nelson, W. B. 620
Nelson, Walter 26, 166, 529, 620, 677, 678, 712
Nelson, Willie 34, 168, 359
Nelson, Willis 315
Nelstone's Hawaiians 772
Nemec, Peter 'Lobo' 474
Nerenberg, Jon Morris 93, 94
Nesbitt, Bill 556
Netters, Lisa 554
Netters, Troy 554
Nettles, Bill 773

Nettles, Willie 231
Neubauer, Ing. 217
Neuhausser, Eric 192
Neumann, Fred 462
Neuwirth, Bob 485
Nevill, Brian 38, 511, 513
Neville, Aaron 803, 804, 805
Neville, Art 531, 580, 788, 805
Neville, Charmaine 731, 805
Neville, Cyril 35, 503, 554, 824
Neville, Ivan 198, 469
Neville Brothers, The 803, 805
Nevue, Tommy 509
New Birth Brass Band 554, 805
New Directions, The 111
New Orleans Feetwarmers 747
New Orleans Jazz Vipers, The 806
New Orleans Strings 76
New Orleans Klezmer All Stars, The 806
Newbern, Hambone Willie 492, 767, 792, 794, 812, 813
Newborn, Calvin 283, 288, 659, 660
Newborn Jr, Phineas 283, 352, 353, 659
Newborn Sr, Phineas 283, 352, 353, 659, 660
Newcombe, Brian 687
Newell, Michael 666
Newell, Nick 428
Newham, Bob 'The Pacemaker' 124, 177
Newhouse, Jackie 667, 669
Newland, Jay 515
Newman, David 'Fathead' 26, 27, 114, 115, 116, 180, 208, 209, 357, 359, 363, 364, 502, 679
Newman, Floyd 118, 352, 354
Newman, Jack 796
Newman, Joe 1, 115, 244, 363, 483, 663, 671
Newman, Milburn 661, 662, 724
Newman, Paul 107
Newman, Roy 772, 773
Newman, Trevor 4
Newmark, Andy 359
Newsome, Chubby 'Hip Shakin'' 803, 804
Newsome, Jimmy 806
Newton, Bill 81, 699
Newton, Ernie 213
Newton, Frankie 7, 221, 328, 332, 390, 587, 588, 661, 662
Nichilo, Donny 440, 462, 478, 554
Nicholas, Albert 90, 255, 321, 327, 328, 607
Nicholas, George 'Big Nick' 63
Nicholas, James 531
Nicholas, John 284, 296, 485, 578
Nicholas, Johnny 21
Nicholls, Alan 176, 177
Nichols, Alvin 405
Nichols, Ben 498
Nichols, Geoff 30, 32, 81, 87, 411

Nichols, Herbie 583
Nichols, Len 33
Nichols, Manny 752, 819
Nichols, Nick 471
Nichols, Red 384
Nichols, Rudy 670, 671
Nichols, Woodie 24, 140
Nicholson, Eddie 84, 140, 473
Nicholson, Fred 170, 696
Nicholson, Freddie 807
Nicholson, Gary 103, 644
Nicholson, J. D. 438, 593, 594, 651, 652, 782
Nick, Don 534
Nickerson, Charlie 450, 451, 792, 809
Nickerson, Jared Michael 488
Nicks, Stevie 358
Nickse, Gail 536
Nicolo, Phil 624
Nielsen, H. C. 8
Nielsen, Ida 8
Nightcats, The 768, 771, 776
Nighthawk, Robert 233, 283, 493, 608, 631, 734, 738, 742, 743, 744, 745, 752, 767, 779, 780, 781, 788, 790, 802, 813, 814, 822
Nighthawk II', 'Robert [Robert Tooms] 49, 476
Nighthawks, The 494
Nigro, Bobby 400
Nijsen, Lex 101
Nile 544
Niles, Tessa 122, 234
Nine Below Zero 495
Nishida, Glenn 408
Nite Owls 772
Nitmar, Len 484
Nivens, Barbara 422
Niver, Jay 253, 513
Nix, Don 349, 430
Nix, Willie 265, 410, 744, 753, 769, 779, 780
Nixon, Elmore 118, 119, 280, 282, 711, 719, 742, 819
Nixon, Hammie 56, 187, 188, 226, 496, 522, 536, 749, 754, 766, 769, 770
Nixon, James 496
Nixon, Paul 169, 170
Nixon, Teddy 253, 254, 437, 469, 592, 597, 718, 720
No Delay 751
Noble, George 808, 809
Nocentelli, Leo 307, 351, 368, 580
Nocturne, Johnny 496
Noden, Eric 823
Noel, Clifton 463
Noel, Dick 593
Noel, Fats 774
Nolan, William 385
Nolen, Jimmy 505, 506, 593, 594, 782
Noonan, Terry 175
Noone, Jimmie 699

INDEX

Norcia, Sugar Ray 222, 284, 497, 516, 557, 560, 567, 717, 718, 771
Nordin, Sture 601
Norfleet Brothers 778
Norman, Daniel 243
Norman, Lawrence 460
Norman, Neil 535
Norquist, Chris 'The Wrist' 20, 210, 687
Nørregaard, Svend Erik 445, 639
Norris, Blind 471, 794, 817
Norris, Chuck 75, 163, 164, 243, 247, 307, 327, 405, 414, 432, 460, 492, 506, 510, 517, 686, 724, 725, 731, 777
Norris, Noel 676
Norris, Patrick 'Big Bones' 136
Norris, William 'Dead Eye' 581
North Carolina Ramblers 772
North Mississippi Allstars 497
Norton, Jim 373
Norvo, Red 384
Norwood, Pig 737
Notini, Per 418
Nottingham, Jimmy 84, 245, 416, 662, 663
Notto, Sam 58
Novac, Jerry 155
Novack, Gary 376
Novag, Novi 429
Novak, Jim 374
Novick, Billy 549
Nowicki, Jason 446
Nowinski, Paul 615
Noyes, 'Bongo' Bob 515
Nuccio, Carlo 470, 503
Nugent, Charles 172
Nugrape Twins 793
Nulisch, Darrell 103, 139, 222, 427, 499, 510
Nunes, Les 194
Nunley, Louis 497
Nunn, Bobby 505, 520
Nunno, Mike 236, 518, 539, 540, 609, 612, 649
Nutmegs, The 799
Nuttycombe, Gareth 210
Nyland, Ralph 295
Nylen, Lennart 601
O, Tony 400, 515, 516, 614
O., Michael 538
Oakes, Robyn 498
Oakley, Brother Roy 222, 223
Oates, John 624
Obeda, Curtis 539
O'Brien, Charles 315
O'Brien, Derek 21, 26, 34, 68, 123, 139, 168, 194, 230, 255, 296, 297, 377, 431, 435, 450, 502, 515, 533, 612, 658, 676
O'Brien, Eddie 179
O'Brien, Jesse 368
O'Brien, Jimmy 447
O'Brien, Justin 204
O'Brien, Kevin 20

O'Brien, Peter 2
Obry, Trombone 597
O'Bryan, Pat 825
O'Bryant, Bill 626
O'Bryant, Jimmy 141, 142, 294, 475, 537, 610, 685
Ochoa, Billy 58
Ockerman, Dale 583
O'Connor, Chip 32, 411
O'Connor, Danny 421
O'Connor, Kieran 217
O'Connor, Pat 319
O'Connor, Tim 'Juice' 180
O'Daniel, W. Lee 772
O'Day, Kevin 503
O'Dell, Frock 305, 306, 307, 600
O'Dell, Rick 414
Oden, Blanca 623
Oden, Charlie 295
Oden, Henry 52, 161, 358, 433, 439, 673
Oden, St Louis Jimmy 71, 387, 499, 616, 619, 620, 739, 740, 742, 743, 744, 774, 779, 780, 787, 813, 814, 815
Odetta 37, 139, 516
Odom, Andrew 'Big Voice'/'B.B. Jr' 159, 160, 265, 266, 317, 500, 781
Odom, Mac 560
Odom, Randolph 509
Offitt, Lillian 265, 783, 827
Ogden, Robert 82
Oglesby, Erskine 22, 501
Oglesby, Vince 590
Ogolini, Terry 42, 121, 450, 723
Oh Red [Bull City Red] 444, 478, 637, 638, 639, 640
O'Halloran, Shawn 368
Ohashi, Bill 133
Ohlman, Christine 369, 370, 488, 491, 824
Ohlsen, Mark 42
Ohman, Phil 254
O'Kane, Charlie 521
Okon, Jennie 222
O'Laughton, Joe 315
Old Pal Smoke Shop Four 816
Oldaker, Jamie 364
Oldham, Janet 751
Oldham, Spooner 238
Olds, Jerome 185
Ole Sunny Boy [poss. Papa Lightfoot] 770
Oleander Quartet, The 380, 381
O'Leary, Chris 517
O'Leary, Jim 319
Olesen, Jens Haack 657
Olin, Julia 112
Olivarez, Rick 566
Oliver, Cappy 449
Oliver, Carlson 232, 660
Oliver, Chet 752
Oliver, Joe 'King' 3, 98, 321, 426, 461, 607, 679

Oliver, Marvin 340
Olivier, Rufus 485
O'Lochlainn, Ruan 527
Olsen, Fred 52
Olsen, Kristina 37, 825
Olson, Carla 674
Olson, David 143
Olson, Skip 273
Olsson, Nigel 359
Olympics, The 789
O'Malley, Damian 53
O'Malley, Tony 372
Omar & The Howlers 501
Omar, Freddy 806
Omartian, Michael 48, 357, 679
One String Sam 751, 753
O'Neal, Dennis 669
O'Neal, Johnny 660, 789
O'Neal, Leo 244
O'Neal, Rick 341
O'Neal, Selina 618
O'Neil, Charles 220
O'Neill, Brendan 495
O'Neill, Brian 78
O'Neill, Dean 363
O'Neill, Mike 364
O'Neill Twins 363
Oor, Ronald 524
Opalach, Paul 151, 152
Orbon, Jorge 257
O'Reilly, Dan 'King Tone' 513
Orendorff, George 1, 677, 678
Oreshnick, John 94
Original Blind Boys Of Alabama 790
Original Faded Boogie Quartet, The 399
Originals, The 52
Orioles, The 495, 798, 799
Orlando, Joe 424
Orlewitz, Felix 40
Ornelas, Willie 468
Orofino, Paul 516, 517
O'Rourke, Kirsten 81
Orr, Bobby 672
Orr, M. C. 762
Orta, Paul 721
Ortega, Larry 6, 131
Ortiz, Allen 522
Ortiz, Bill 246, 293, 496
Ory, Kid 98, 142, 322, 380, 381, 537, 806
Osborn, Bill 69
Osborn, Michael 196, 274, 583
Osborne, Anders 35, 195, 343, 502, 806, 824, 825
Osborne, Joe 679
Osborne, John 476
Osborne, Mary 245, 521, 685
Osbourn, Riley 11, 17, 21, 61, 68, 123, 148, 168, 194, 195, 255, 342, 377, 450, 476, 485, 529, 676
Oscar, John 79, 645, 739, 740, 796, 807, 809

Oscher, Paul 133, 422, 476, 482, 483, 503, 615, 734
Oshita, Gerald 52
Osiban, Bobby 366
Oskar, Lee 727
Óskarsson, Ásgeir 160, 515
Ossola, Paul 235
O'Sullivan, Jerry 65
Oswald, Chip 567
Otero, O. T. 226
Otey, Lisa 342, 516
Otis, Charles 238, 410, 529
Otis, Charles 'Honeyboy' 187
Otis, Johnny 74, 75, 76, 145, 244, 328, 341, 393, 440, 460, 504, 506, 508, 520, 593, 651, 663, 738, 797, 798, 799
Otis, Lucky 507
Otis, Nicky 507
Otis, Shuggie 76, 145, 341, 393, 460, 506, 507, 663, 812
Otis Brothers 823
Ott, Horace 509, 727
Ottinger, Billy 151
Ousley, Harold 1, 76, 683
Ousley, Walter 728
Outcalt, Al 459
Outten, Karl 101
Overbea, Danny 780, 784, 799
Overhead, Phil 45
Overstreet, H. Benton 645
Overton, Betty 454
Overton, Jim 293, 540
Overton, Richard 227
Overton, Timothy 454, 455
Owens, Bill 500
Owens, Calvin 107, 223, 357, 492
Owens, Carl 77
Owens, Charlie 164, 558
Owens, Donnie 572
Owens, Earlene 419
Owens, Ephraim 553, 643
Owens, Frank 356, 682
Owens, George 'Big Boy' 794
Owens, Henry 504
Owens, Jack 508, 762, 766, 786, 810, 814
Owens, James 714
Owens, Jimmie 757, 760, 761
Owens, Jimmy 694
Owens, Kelly 40, 81, 84, 245, 416, 583
Owens, Marshall 737, 787
Owens, Tary 230
Owens, Willie 'Scare Crow' 796
Owens Family 761
Owings, Bryan 195, 335, 496, 540
Owsley, Bill 69, 326, 607, 626, 682
Oxer, Peter 175
Oxford, Doña 135
Özdemir, Erkan 220
Ozmec, Fritz 299
Pace, Kelly 758
Pace, Mike 78, 79
Pace, Walto 770

Pacheco, Mike 104
Pack, Terry 424
Packer, Dave 728
Packer, John 16, 126, 222, 549
Padgett, Forrest 546
Pafume, Joey 468
Pagano, Frank 517
Page, Bob 492
Page, Hot Lips 1, 7, 39, 90, 140, 142, 245, 321, 326, 327, 328, 661, 747, 797, 806
Page, Houston 763
Page, James 690
Page, Jimmy 558, 813
Page, Sam 44
Page, Star 828
Page, Walter 90, 142, 292, 384, 663, 747
Paice, Mike 53, 217, 218
Paige, Hal 777, 807
Pailer, Jimmy 572
Pain, Louis 613
Pairs, Joe 24
Palacios, Scott 566
Paladins, The 776
Palden, Joachim 129, 217, 420, 573
Paley, Andy 342
Palinic, Robert 567
Palladino, Pino 122, 359
Pallas, Laura 217
Pallo, Bernie 594
Palm, Horace 610
Palmer, Anthony 6, 131, 171
Palmer, Ben 127
Palmer, Blues Boy 784
Palmer, Earl 26, 58, 75, 140, 164, 166, 207, 278, 281, 282, 305, 307, 359, 391, 432, 506, 507, 529, 623, 678, 726
Palmer, Gladys 650
Palmer, Henry 325
Palmer, Reese 495
Palmer, Robert 825
Palmer, Roy 69, 88, 142
Palmer, Sylvester 807, 808, 815
Palmer, Thomas 543, 650
Palmer, Tommy 17
Palmerston, Evan 43, 44, 599
Palmes, Frank 737
Paltishall, Jon 491
Panchezak, Paul 368
Pandis, George 211
Panelli, Charlie 293, 712
Panneck, David 730
Panos, Toss 198
Panosh, Craig 4
Pao, Eugene 728
Papa Egg Shell [Lawrence Casey] 795
Papa Too Sweet 626, 812
PapaGeorge, George 691
Papillion, Jimmy 86
Paquette, Paul 675
Paramount All Stars 774, 787
Parcek, Peter 515
Pardini, Louis 198

Pardue, Gene 512, 540
Parente, Skip 547, 703
Parenti, Rich 606
Parham, Alvin 'Baby Pee Wee' 438
Parham, Duke 245, 446
Parham, Herbert 245
Parham, Tiny 48, 142, 224, 537, 549, 610, 645
Parham, Truck 177, 467, 468, 718
Pariles, Jesse 125
Paris, Jeff 343
Paris, Jon 599, 723
Parker, Barber 561
Parker, Bill 214, 784
Parker, Bill 'Weasel' 416
Parker, Shorty Bob 475
Parker, Bobby 510, 713, 789
Parker, Boppie 392
Parker, Cecil 696
Parker, Charlie 84
Parker, Charlotte 583
Parker, Denise 131
Parker, Eva 828
Parker, Frank 82, 83
Parker, Gail 497
Parker, George 140
Parker, Graham 825
Parker, Ike 171
Parker, J. 344
Parker, Jack 327, 328
Parker, Jacqueline 131
Parker, James 220
Parker, John 'Knocky' 188
Parker, John Lewis 343
Parker, Johnny 77, 372, 438, 439, 505
Parker, Josephine 758
Parker, Little Junior 508, 770, 789, 797, 799
Parker, Kayla 376
Parker, Kenny 98, 510
Parker, Knocky 58
Parker, Leo 790
Parker, Leroy 595, 596
Parker, Maceo 490
Parker, Maggie 429, 430
Parker, Marvin 27
Parker, Mel 818
Parker, Sista Monica 111
Parker, Monister 752, 819
Parker, Odion 'Boobie' 584
Parker, Ray 357
Parker, Robert 58, 529, 530, 622
Parker, Ronnie 'Greystoke' 260
Parker, Roy 227
Parker, Sammy 83, 686
Parker, Sonny 510, 800, 819
Parker, Tad 186
Parker, Tom 31, 271
Parker, William 245, 459
Parker, Willie 'Tomcat' 585, 586
Parkins, Ted 604
Parks, Bud 175

Parks, Dean 48, 357, 359, 624, 679
Parks, James 'Bull' 210
Parks, John 624
Parks, John 'Jabo' 47, 509
Parks, Paul 321, 322
Parks, Van Dyke 485
Parkson, Tommy 245
Parnell, Jerry 565
Parnell, Lee Roy 468, 820
Parr, James 305, 686
Parra, Fito de la 77, 103, 104, 273, 274, 413, 458
Parrish, Michael 230, 253, 609
Parrish, Turner 739, 740, 741, 807, 808, 809
Parry, Dick 34
Parry, Lorenzo 223, 231
Parson, Clarence 592
Parsons, Longineu 544
Partlow, Michael 43
Paryss 127
Pash, Warren 222
Pasley, Frank 392, 677
'Pasquale' 125
Passarelli, Kenny 305, 634, 659
Pastels, The 780, 790
Patarini, Chris 494
Patascha, Glenn 137, 525
Pate, Bell Edward 761
Pate, Dewayne 100, 198, 199, 584
Pate, Jimmy 201
Pate, Johnny 355
Paterson, Buster 324
Patient, Bob 260
Patillo, Val 355
Patmon, Pamela 687
Patric(k), Steve 135, 402
Patrick, Bert 473
Patrick, Michael 644
Patt, Frank 'Honeyboy' 286, 754, 788
Patten, Garrick 412
Patten, Thomas 146
Patterson, Ann 429
Patterson, Brenda 498
Patterson, Elder Samuel 778
Patterson, Frank 811, 816
Patterson, George 401
Patterson, Gus 219
Patterson, John 295
Patterson, Jordan 510, 567, 721, 771
Patterson, Nerak Roth 156
Patterson, Tom 617
Patterson, Vance 128
Patterson, Zack 644
Pattison, Geoff 291
Pattman, Neal 'Big Daddy' 510, 513, 756, 757, 786
Patton, Charley 511, 737, 738, 739, 767, 787, 794, 797, 801, 802, 810, 812, 813, 820
Patton, Garrick 131
Patton, Janis 368

Patton, Tom 730
Paul, Jason 127
Paul, Jonathan 544
Paul, Joyce 786
Paul, Les 699, 772
Paul, Philip 63, 245, 300, 363, 365, 599, 650
Paul, Ruby 787
Paule, Anthony 263, 496, 497
Paulettes, The 53
Paulson, Bruce 556
Paulus, George 581
Paulus, John 104, 430, 431
Pavageau, Alcide 462
Pavey, Phil 796
Paxton, Johnny 'T Bone' 479
Paxton, Josh 731
Payn, Nick 218, 473
Payne, Bert 338, 340
Payne, Bill 197, 235, 275, 359, 547, 563, 612, 624
Payne, Cecil 115, 800
Payne, Frank 321
Payne, Jackie 194, 507, 512, 540
Payne, Jim 490, 491, 518, 544
Payne, Joe W. 222
Payne, John 398, 578
Payne, Louis 564
Payne, Mark 396
Payne (Jr), Odie 30, 36, 39, 67, 95, 165, 188, 232, 305, 306, 307, 412, 417, 418, 458, 481, 536, 557, 562, 601, 610, 617, 627, 630, 660, 663, 693
Payne, Richard 531
Payne, Susan 396
Payne, Sylvester 'Vess' 416, 459, 670, 671
Payne, Warren 178, 391
Payne III, Odie 418
Payne AME Choir, The 51
Payton, Asie 513
Payton, Dion 68, 745
Payton, Earl 365, 517
Payton, Joseph 648
Payton, Walter 531
Payton Jr, Walter 176
Pazdan, John 101
Peabody, Dave 177, 237, 253, 487, 511, 513
Peacock, Burnie 84, 245, 300
Peagler, Curtis 245, 663
Peanut The Kidnapper 737
Pearce, Ernestine 34
Pearl, Bernard 364
Pearl, Bernie 241
Pearl, Donna 195
Pearson, Alice 787, 828
Pearson, Bill 808
Pearson, David 818
Pearson, Eugene 601
Pearson, George 44
Pearson, Ken 195
Peavy, Michael 107, 126
Pebbles, The 774

Pechenaert, Paul 41, 57, 544, 735
Pedersen, Gerald 197, 487
Pedersen, Guy 455, 457, 458
Pederson, P. T. 66
Pederson, Tom 593
Pederson, Tyler 40, 123, 124, 413, 414, 538, 728
Pederson, Wendy M. 472
Peduzzi, Larry 284
Pee Wee & The Zydeco Boll Weevils 832
Peebles, Ann 688, 788, 830
Peebles, Kinny 154
Peek, John 521, 610
Peel, Liz 540
Peeler, Ben 113
Peeples, Robert 787, 797, 815
Peeples, William 114, 115
'Peeples' 386
Peer, Beverley 300
Peerless Four 763
Peers, Tony 413
Peg Leg Sam 514
Peiser, Judy 672
Pejoe, Morris 514, 744, 752, 776, 778, 779, 781, 790
Peliquin, Michael 111
Pellezzi, Pete 336
Peloquin, Michael 729
Pelton, Shawn 51, 235
Pemberton, Bill 295, 727
Pena, Paul 739
Pendarvis, Leon 191, 235, 359
Pender, Mark 137, 144, 151, 569
Pendergast, Michael 595
Pendergraph, Charles 686
Pendleton, Jimmy 17, 65, 373, 425
Penguins, The 506, 799
Penigar, Eddie 'Sugarman' 610, 620, 627, 682
Peniston, Ernie 121
Penland, Mike 721
Penmentel, Chris 583
Penn, Andrew 62, 63, 300
Penn, Leo 357
Pennebaker, James 21
Penner, Jon 194, 195, 293
Pennington, Eddie 113, 715
Pennington, Uncle Meat 652
Penny, Hank 773
Penque, Romeo 295
Pentelow, Nick 36, 473
Peoples, Reugenia 1
Pepper, James 730
Peraza, Armando 274
Perazzo, Karl 274
Perdue, Jesse 252, 449
Perez, Chico 4
Perez, Jerry 273
Perez, Juan 544
Perez, Louie 274
Perez, Pete 125
Perkins, Bill 356

Perkins, Brendan 370
Perkins, Cora 828
Perkins, Cutie 595, 596
Perkins, Derwin 'Big D' 179, 554
Perkins, Ethel 811
Perkins, George 312
Perkins, Gertrude 818
Perkins, Ike 7, 8, 221, 455, 661, 662
Perkins, Joe 761
Perkins, Joe Willie 265
Perkins, Merle 67, 129, 234, 573
Perkins, Pinetop 30, 67, 97, 135, 138, 139, 180, 266, 316, 324, 368, 385, 400, 423, 427, 476, 480, 481, 482, 483, 484, 486, 493, 494, 514, 533, 552, 598, 614, 632, 694, 723, 735, 742, 745, 751, 766, 776, 779, 808, 810, 825
Perkins, Robert 409
Perkins, Walter 153, 282, 703, 728
Perkins, Wayne 349, 350
Perkins, Wordie 193
Perls, Nick 319
Pero, Leroy 597
Perreau, Tony 377
Perri, Dan 227
Perrilliat, Nat 83, 173, 391, 531
Perriman, Paul 807
Perriwinkle, G. M. 691
Perrodin, Clinton 'Fats' 585, 586
Perrodin, Clinton 'Yank' 377, 489
Perrodin, Gabriel 'Guitar Gable' 28, 585, 586
Perrodin, John 'Fats' 408
Perrodin, Pandy 'Guitar Gable Jr' 108
Perrodin Jr, Gabriel 'Pandy' 12
Perry, Beatrice 758
Perry, Bill 516, 524, 779
Perry, Emmett 338
Perry, Ermit V. 459, 670
Perry, Jesse 510
Perry, Joel 133, 134, 669
Perry, Johnny 527
Perry, King 517, 788
Perry, Mort 595
Perry, Ray 685
Perry, Roger 161, 194
Perry, Ron 516, 636
Perry, Rosetta 827
Perry, Stu 664
Perry, Sy 785
Perry, Wendell D. 507
Perry Jr, Clarence 620
Perryman, Tim 101
Perrys, The 236
Perrywell, Charles 784
Pershey, Bernard 657
Persip, Charlie 115, 340
Person, Houston 76
Personne, Paul 524
Persuasions, The 50
Pert, Morris 34
Pertum, Specks [Charlie McFadden] 815

Peskin, Irving 134
Peskin, Joel 675
'Pete' 209
Pete, Alfred 13
Pete, Austen 710
Peter, Robert [St Julian] 119, 120
Peter, Paul & Mary 823
Peterka, Chris 132
Peters, Bernard 'Bunny' 366
Peters, Cyndee 36
Peters, David 78, 79
Peters, Debra 195
Peters, Ellen 263
Peters, Gary 228
Peters, Jamie 80
Peters, Janice 555
Peters, Jerry 351
Peters, Jimmy 758, 760, 831, 832
Peters, Judy Ann 555
Peters, Michael 25
Petersen, Ed 84
Petersen, Holger 20, 658
Petersen, Scott 27
Peterson, Bobby 789
Peterson, James 219, 518
Peterson, Jay 399
Peterson, Jim 690
Peterson, Jimmy 338
Peterson, John (Johnny P) 512
Peterson, Lloyd 446
Peterson, Lucky 20, 31, 139, 318, 368, 377, 401, 490, 517, 563, 576, 633, 688, 695, 771, 776, 825
Peterson, Mark 665
Peterson, Nathaniel 615
Peterson, Pete 661, 662, 731
Peterson, Ricky 4, 197, 198, 375
Peterson, Robert 'Bass Playin' Pete' 474
Peterson, Ronnie 318
Peterson, Scott 399
Peterson, Tamara 518
Peterson, Tom 556
Petersson, Janne 36, 37
Petito, Scott 50, 51
Petteruti, Tom 560
Petties, Arthur 68, 69, 191, 767, 801
Petties, Leon 392, 684
Pettiford, Alonzo 84, 459
Pettiford, Marcel 634
Pettiford, Martell 537, 626
Pettiford, Oscar 244, 291, 292, 295, 505, 526
Pettigrew, John 504, 505, 520
Pettis, Alabama Jr 30, 67, 299, 404, 419, 518, 527
Pettit, Jimmy 103
Pétursson, Gudmundur/Guthmundur 160, 515
Petway, Robert 519, 738, 739, 793, 794, 801, 802
Pevey, Michael 573, 574
Peyer, Ralf-Michael 73

Peyroux, Madeleine 516
Peyton, Darrell 318
Phaneuf, Marc 691
Phantom Blues Band, The 751
Phantom Horns, The 494
Phantoms, The 788
Phares, Shawn 332
Phelps, George 522
Phelps, James 780
Phelps, Kelly Joe 51, 519, 751
Phelps, Norman 772
Philbrick, Skip 'Mississippi Skippy' 325
Philipps, Marvin 447
Philips, Reuben 245
Phillinganes, Greg 343
Phillips, Wild Bill 394
Phillips, Bobby 106
Phillips, Brewer 299, 370, 519, 631
Phillips, Cora 19, 812
Phillips, Earl 1, 269, 270, 271, 275, 289, 514, 532, 541, 542
Phillips, Little Esther 504, 506, 520, 827
Phillips, Gene 219, 244, 252, 392, 432, 449, 450, 460, 504, 505, 520, 767, 798, 826
Phillips, John 673
Phillips, Kim 554
Phillips, London 446
Phillips, Mike 540
Phillips, Nathaniel 564
Phillips, Reuben 338, 340, 654
Phillips Louisville Jug Band 775
Phinnessee, Darryl 666
Phipps, Gene 650
Piano Bill 751
Piano Red 521, 740, 741, 742, 773, 777, 797, 799, 800
Piano Slim 521, 816
Piano Willie 374
Piazza, Honey 146, 177, 262, 522, 557, 594, 720
Piazza, Rob 400
Piazza, Rod 146, 177, 262, 486, 522, 538, 557, 594, 720, 751, 771
Piccolo, Greg 180, 185, 190, 299, 324, 362, 469, 535, 559, 560, 666, 667, 718, 729
Pichon, Walter 89
Pickens, Buster 3, 279, 281
Pickens, Kenny 163, 669
Pickett, Charlie 187, 226, 522, 738, 773, 774
Pickett, Dan 522, 752, 755, 773, 774, 812, 813
Pickett, Jene 234, 318
Pickett, Lenny 235, 273, 485, 487
Pickett, Leroy 150, 537
Pickett, Michael 302
Pickett, Nick 228
Pickett, Wilson 37, 680, 788
'Pickle' 337
Pickwood, Bobby 544
Pie, Brad 507

INDEX

Pierce, Charlie 151, 451
Pierce, Clarence 643
Pierce, John 612
Pierce, Nat 671
Pierce, Tim 556
Pierre, Wilfred 'Caveman' 28, 29, 161, 384
Pierson, Eugene 415
Pietryga, Adrian 344
Pigford, Evan 660
Pigler, Curtis 300
Pigmeat Terry 793, 808
Pilgrim Travelers, The 788, 821
Pilione, Tina 196
Pin & The Hornits 751
Pina, Bob 42
Pina, Leroy 299, 520, 580
Pine, Virginia 328
Pine Bluff Pete 754
Pine Top [Aaron Sparks] 443, 740
Pinetop Slim 752, 753, 755, 813
Pingitore, Mike 253
Pinhorn, Dennis 169, 170
Pink Spots, The 492
Pink Tuxedos, The 548
Pinkard, Maceo 685
Pinkston-Mayo, Valerie 191, 358
Pinner III, William Pell 518
Pino, Ken 133, 134
Pintado, Floyd 370
Piper, Eddie 114
Piper, Julian 258
Pipkin, Dom 396
Pips, The 790
Piron, Armand J. 42
Pisapia, Joe 222
Pitardi, Max 414
Pitchford, Juno 2, 564
Pitchford, Lonnie 523, 750, 766
Pitsch, Shane 65
Pittman, Al 789, 807
Pittman, Herman 238
Pittman, Robert 432
Pittman, Sampson 204, 523, 751, 762, 821
Pitts, Louis 'Nunu' 110, 647, 711
Pitts, Rudy 114, 164, 228
Pitts, Steve 572
Pittsfield, 'Sweetie' Lee 691
Plair, Steve 520, 568
Plaisted, Andy 369
Plant, B. 96
Plant, Robert 372, 558
Platania, John 156
Plater, Bobby 510
Platkin, Sheldon 425
Platt, Mose(s) 'Clear Rock' 757, 758, 759, 760
Platt, Walter 691
Platters, The 785, 799
Plattner, Christian 217
Pleasant, Denice 344
Pleasant, Tim 422

Pleasures, The 789
Plotkin, Shelly 579
Ploue, Michelle 554
Plucker, Peggy 257, 401
Pluitt, Frank 618
Plume, Serge 6
Plummer, Jim 721
Plunk, Patrick 498
Plunkett, Robert 160, 183, 554, 562, 573, 574, 576
Plunkett, Sylvester 532
Poche, Renard 580
Pochonet, Gérard 527
Poindexter, Pony 366
Pointer, Roosevelt 348
Pointer Sisters 624
'Pointman' Dennis, Harry 242
Polk, Charles 357
Polk, Charlie 450, 451
Polk, James 297
Polk, Sylvester 490, 518
Pollack, Eddie 699
Pollak, Mark 364
Pollard, Jeff 78, 119
Pollard, R. L. 761
Pollard, Tyrone 571
Pollock, Mark 768
Polo, Danny 661, 662
Pomposello, Tom 442, 445
Pomus, Doc 86, 523, 780
Ponder, Calvin 158
Ponte, Richard 604
Pontelero, Khouki 670
'Pony-Tail Slim' [Axel Küstner] 710
Pool, Malcolm 174
Poole, Charlie 772, 810
Poole, Tom 1, 111, 199, 307
Popa Chubby 421, 517, 524, 779, 824
'Popcorn' [Arthur Clover] 184
Pope, James 713
Pope, Jenny 626, 827
Pope, Kenneth 504
Pope, Lee 670, 671, 713
Poplin, Stan 196, 197, 199, 658, 727, 728
Popovic, Ana 256, 524, 824
Popwell, Robert 'Pops' 357
Porcaro, Jeff 197
Porcino, Al 726
Porecki, Benjie 211, 499, 553
Poree, Greg 351, 376
'Porkie' 447
Porrsteinsson, Haraldur 160
Portebus, George 530
Porter, Amanda 218
Porter, Curtis 713
Porter, David 576
Porter, David 'Pecan' 676
Porter, Gene 219, 252, 683
Porter, George 35
Porter, Harrell 47
Porter, Harry 83, 295, 300, 670, 671
Porter, Jake 219, 405, 438, 520, 663

Porter, Jerry 126, 420, 527
Porter, John 11, 95, 234, 235, 343, 359, 430, 518, 563, 624
Porter, John 'Schoolboy' 620
Porter, Kevin 199, 486
Porter, King [James Pope] 713, 800
Porter, Larry 112
Porter, Ted 607
Porter, Yank 661
Porter Jr, George 179, 325, 351, 362, 368, 469, 531, 580, 681, 806
Portnoy, Jerry 27, 66, 103, 122, 126, 324, 325, 385, 483, 484, 515, 516, 525, 549, 735, 771, 824
Poston, Joe(l) 412, 419
Potier (Jr), Harold 357
Potter, Bill 652
Potter, Douglas T. 232
Potter, Jerry 300
Potter, Ollie 575
Potter, Tom 565
Potts, Ernest 591
Potts, Steve 6, 68, 90, 127, 135, 151, 198, 215, 366, 375, 435, 443, 468, 524, 572, 575, 633, 634, 660, 688
Potvin, Roxanne 341
Pouliot, Miche 195
Poullard, Danny 195
Poullard, Edward 13, 195
Poveva, Alejo 614
Powell, Austin 340
Powell, Benny 357, 429, 510, 727
Powell, Bobby 597, 783
Powell, Bud 670
Powell, Carl 685
Powell, Carlton 476
Powell, Cozy 228
Powell, Dirk 12, 161
Powell, Dolores 458
Powell, Eugene 465, 525, 766, 801, 802
Powell, Forrest 677, 724
Powell, Frank 670
Powell, Hense 1
Powell, Jesse 40, 173, 295
Powell, Jimmy 86, 245
Powell, Lester 821
Powell, Marion 37
Powell, Richie 713
Powell, Rudy 116, 245, 416
Powell, Seldon 295, 340, 483, 663, 679, 727
Powell, Shannon 25, 232, 472
Powell, Specs 245, 446
Powell, Stan 540
Power, Chris 60
Power, Ralph 372, 373
Powers, Jimmy 235, 563
Powers, Michael 525
Pozo, Francisco 340
Pozzolano, —— 401
Prager, Simon 344
Prairie Ramblers 772, 775, 810

Pratcher, Bob 761, 762, 812
Pratcher, Miles 441, 761, 762, 812
Prater, Matthew 320, 792, 810, 816
Prather, Terrence 136, 137
Pratt, John 133
Pratt & George 774
Prayor, Horace 521
Preacher Boy 526, 779
Preacher Jack 742
Prejean, Johnny 133, 431
Premier, Alan 676
Prescott, Jim 402
Preservation Hall Jazz Band 806
Press, Reinie 210
Prestia, Francis Rocco 433
Preston, Billy 122, 431, 660, 789
Preston, Denis 702
Preston, Don 363, 365
Preston, Eddie 504, 731
Preston, Jimmy 773, 798, 800
Preston, Simon 425
Preston, Wayne 350
Pretty Boy [Don Covay] 777
Pretty Things/Yardbird Blues Band 746
Prevost, Lionel 118, 214, 222, 408
Preyer, Yvette 6
Prez Kenneth 746
Price, Abe 384
Price, Alan 601
Price, 'Momma' Alberta 828, 829
Price, Banny 787
Price, Brad 547
Price, Celia 729
Price, Celia Ann 377
Price, Charles Q. 724
Price, Della Luiese 195
Price, Elmer W. 385
Price, Ernest 300
Price, Evan 145
Price, James 54
Price, Jerome (Jerry) 23
Price, Jesse 84, 327, 684, 686, 724, 725, 826
Price, Jim 343, 356, 429
Price, Leo 805
Price, Lloyd 788, 799, 803, 805, 806
Price, Lon 21, 119, 191, 429
Price, Maryann 529, 550, 728
Price, Melvin 773
Price, Milton 572, 711
Price, Morris 17
Price, Richard 195
Price, Richard 'Hombre' 498
Price, Sam(my) 24, 60, 80, 81, 89, 140, 142, 150, 221, 224, 291, 292, 332, 445, 510, 526, 575, 597, 637, 661, 662, 697, 699, 740, 741, 751
Price, Toni 195
Price, Big Walter 527, 739, 800, 820
Prichard, Charlie 239
Pricpkula, Eric 369
Pride, Norman 363

Pridgen, David 507
Priester, Julian 683
Priestman, Henry 413
Prigett, L. C. 808
Prima, Louis 773
Primer, John 23, 32, 38, 57, 64, 66, 138, 151, 217, 236, 262, 316, 330, 344, 345, 376, 401, 405, 419, 420, 421, 435, 474, 488, 519, 527, 541, 557, 573, 574, 581, 584, 599, 614, 647, 652, 675, 692, 697, 746, 771, 782, 814
Primich, Gary 21, 148, 297, 310, 342, 408, 476, 502, 529
Prince, Earres 426, 718
Prince, Preston 'Peppy' 24, 214, 392, 405
Prince, Ron 368, 369
Prince, Wesley 75, 258, 517
Prince Budda 311
Prince Candy 616
Prince La La 391, 804
Principato, Tom 2
Prindell, Bob 659, 660
Printup, Craig 593
Pritchard, Charlie 397
Procope, Russell 63, 295
Proctor, Helen 796, 828
Proctor, Wayne 397
Proctor, Willis 761
Prodaniuk, Taras 629
Professor Longhair 529, 740, 776, 789, 798, 803, 804, 805, 806, 808
Professor's Blues Review, The 745
Profit, Clarence 89
Prokop, Skip 52
Propp, Carole 342
Prothe, Larry 400, 401
Prothro, Allen 758, 759
Proudly, Fred 395
Prouty, Pat 250, 570
Provis, Skeeter 201
Prudhomme, Charles 161, 162
Prudhomme, Joseph 161
Prudhomme, Willis 531, 831
Pruitt, Carl 245, 300, 446, 527, 650, 670
Pruitt, David 319
Pruitt, Dick 319
Pruitt, Grover 778
Pruitt, Milas 141, 347, 537
Pruitt, Miles 141, 347, 537
Pryme, Charlie 460
Pryor, David 758
Pryor, Earl 533
Pryor, Richard 533
Pryor, Snooky 201, 263, 264, 335, 423, 532, 578, 616, 739, 743, 744, 752, 768, 769, 770, 771, 779, 785, 800, 825
Prysock, Arthur 315
Prysock, Red 63, 82, 245, 300, 321, 322, 800, 807
Przygocki, Eric Mathew 148, 210
Psalm 4 37
Puckett, Jerry 393, 442, 443

Puckett, Riley 772, 813
Pugh, James 358
Pugh, Jim(my) 14, 37, 103, 111, 144, 145, 193, 231, 263, 274, 275, 293, 358, 399, 512, 563, 655, 735
Pugh, Forrest City Joe 762, 768, 769, 779, 780, 812
Pullen, Don Q 786
Pulliam, Robert 405
Pulliam, Steve 86, 315
Pullum, Joe 60, 219, 533, 737, 742, 808, 821, 826
Pumpido, Liliana 358
Punkson, Tommy 357
Purdie, Bernard 'Pretty' 272, 356, 357, 727
Purdue, Jesse 450
Purdy, David 38, 614
Purifoy, Roosevelt 'Mad Hatter' 33, 41, 91, 92, 109, 131, 192, 330, 369, 440, 443, 474, 540, 541, 574, 614
Purkson, Tommy 543, 650
Purnell, Alton 462
Purnell, Patrick 81, 82
Purnell, William 'Keg' 392
Purro, Chuck 546
Purro, Damian 546
Pursley, Roosevelt 127
Pusateri, Joe 591
Pyle, Andy 30, 81
Pyles, William 432
Pyne, Chris 371, 372
Pyrker, Martin 132, 742
Pyrker, Sabine 132
Qualls, Henry 534
Quattlebaum, Doug 534, 752, 755
Quebec, Ike 459, 526
Queen Esther 665
Queen Ida 229, 534, 831, 832
Querfurth, Carl 148, 492, 549, 560, 567
Quermalet, Christian 513
Quezergue, Sidney 531
Quezergue, Wardell 76, 351, 359, 362, 554
Quezergue Players, The 554
Quill Smith, James 429, 430
Quillian, Ben 774
Quillian, Rufus 774
Quinichette, Paul 84, 90, 340, 459, 472, 504, 505, 671
Quinn, Herb 788, 814
Quinn, Matthew 548
Quinn, Tom 657
Quinton, Dan 223, 231, 676
Quinton, Joseph 401
Quitman, Dennis 357
Qwarfordt, Mats 65, 319
R. [Richbourg], John 368, 783
Raag, Hans 526
Rabaste, 'Fast Fran(c)k' 5, 6
Rabbit, Peter 492
Rabbit Trio, Peter 798
Rabinovitz, 'Big Dan' 569

Rabitsch, Hans 609
Rabson, Ann 127, 310, 516, 535, 563, 564
Rabson, Kenji 535
Rabson, Mimi 535
Rabson, Steve 535
Race, Steve 702, 703
Rachell, Sheena 536
Rachell, Yank 14, 159, 187, 188, 535, 655, 715, 738, 742, 743, 749, 769, 792
Radcliff, Bobby 768
Radcliffe, Fred 683
Radford, Floyd 723
Radford, Matt 38, 511, 513, 614
Radford, Rollo 579, 580
Radiants, The 401, 780
Radiators, The 806
Radio Kings, The 536
Radle, Carl 273, 363, 364
Radway, Jerome 185
Raeburn, Dave 237
Raelettes, The 114, 115, 116
Rafael, Mickey 359
Rafferty, Carl 618, 619, 773, 774
Raft, George 390
Rafus, Willie 763
Ragent, Larry 485
Ragin, Melvin 'Wah Wah' 273, 364
Raglin, Al 'Junior' 473
Raglin, Alvin 84
Ragovoy, Jerry 356
Ragsdale Jr, Leon 550
Ragusa, Pete 238, 494, 495
Raia, Joseph 497
Raichelson, Dick 189
Rails, Red 21, 68, 139, 296, 658, 676
Raines, (Little) Annie 51, 516, 546, 614, 635, 636, 751, 771, 825
Raines, Joe 554
Rainey, Big Memphis Ma 789
Rainey, Charles 351
Rainey, Chuck 433, 721, 727
Rainey, Jimmy 699
Rainey, Ma 301, 537, 628, 787, 797, 820, 826, 827
Rains, George 21, 26, 33, 139, 194, 200, 255, 296, 314, 431, 502, 612, 658, 666, 667, 681
Rains, John 81
Raitt, Bonnie 51, 76, 84, 235, 274, 343, 358, 359, 486, 541, 624, 691, 695, 751, 814
Ramadhani, Rukia 625
Rambling Rangers 772
Rameri, Joe 94
Ramerson, Tommy 207
Ramey, Ben 450, 451
Ramey, Gene 84, 245, 445, 446, 459, 639, 640, 670, 671
Ramey, Hurley 227, 650
Ramey, Jimmy 168
Ramirez, Eddie 583
Ramirez, Ivan 156

Ramirez, Ram 292, 449, 464, 565, 583, 592
'Ramona' 507
Ramos, Frank 583
Ramos, Kid 40, 47, 124, 136, 191, 226, 241, 408, 414, 434, 488, 538, 629, 719
Rampley, Dave 100
Rampone, Brent 690
Ramsay, Steve 236, 499, 515, 525, 719
Ramsden, Mark 44
Ramsey, George [Georgia Tom Dorsey] 808
Ramsey, Red 92, 93
Rand, Odell 16, 69, 221, 240, 311, 407, 437, 462, 500, 618, 636, 637
Rand, Warren 143, 336, 547
Randall, Frankie 399
Randall, Keith 34
Randall, Leon 550
Randell, Willie 593
Randle, Raymond 107, 108
Randman, Bennett 257, 401
Randolph, Boots 521
Randolph, Irving 701, 702
Randolph, John 318, 569
Randolph, Marvin 7
Randolph, Orlando 7
Randolph, Percy 178
Randolph, Red John 569
Randolph, Robert 498
Randolph, Sly 497
Raney, Wayne 773, 798
Range, Bob 86, 416
Ranger, Jack 818
Rangno, Rick 341
Rani 35
Rankin, R. S. 677, 678, 782, 825
Rankins, Leroy 'Batman' 82, 83, 529
Rannenberg, Christian 17, 74, 96, 141, 312
Ransom, Dumas 717
Ranson, Dave 566
Raphael, Michey 575
Rapone, Al 222, 534, 535, 538, 728, 779
Rapone, Orwell 539
Rapp, Johnny 87, 136, 226, 411
Rappaport, Matthew 664
Rapper Dee & C. J. 751
Rarey, George 200
Rasberry, Eddie 402
Rascoe, Moses 539
Rash, Curley 785
Rasmussen, Gary 246, 570
Raspberry, Larry 430
Raspovic, Edgar 50
RaSun, Eomot 539
Ratcliff, Henry 761, 812
Ratcliffe, Dennis 495
Ratliff, William 'Kax' 450
Ratso 495
Ratzer, Karl 131
Ratzer, Mette 8

Rault, Philippe 77
Rault, Ron 578
Rausch, Stephan 132
Raux, Richard 544
Raven, Darlene 502
Raven, David 20
Raven', 'The 228
Ravens, The 683, 780, 798, 799
Ravikiran, N. 624
Rawlins, Charles 446
Rawls, Casper 21
Rawls, Destini 539, 540
Rawls, Johnny 27, 126, 192, 236, 424, 539, 576, 609, 612, 618
Ray Brothers 821
Ray, Arthur 438, 460
Ray, Bell 102
Ray, Brian 307
Ray, Chris 458
Ray, Dave 'Snaker' 370, 371
Ray, Diana 26
Ray, Harmon 437, 526, 743, 821
Ray, Jessie 717
Ray, Kenny 'Blue' 21, 512, 540, 729
Ray, La Verne 800
Ray, Paul 26, 669
Rayhoney, Sammy 337
Rays, The 780
Re, Andrea 491, 674
Re, Peter 369, 488
Rea, Chris 431
Realove 472
Reamey, Shelton T. 150
Rebennack, Mack 43, 76, 103, 111, 135, 168, 356, 357, 359, 368, 469, 470, 472, 531, 548, 624, 666, 667, 723, 739, 803, 804, 805, 808
Rebirth Brass Band 803, 806
Recard, Kevin 1
Recchionne, Jimmy 156
Receli, George 615
Rechard, Robyn 554
Recile, George G. 87, 470
Rector, Milton 138, 263, 386, 481, 514, 541, 542, 601, 603
Red Caps, The 797
Red Devils, The 775
Red Hot Old Mose/Moses Mason 793
Red Lane 78
Red Stick Ramblers, The 806
Red, Hot & Blue 825
Reda, Albert 547, 703
Redd, Alton 380, 381
Redd, Buddy 506
Redd, Gene 125, 363, 365, 459, 670
Redden, John 517
Reddick, Jacquelyn (Jackie) 4, 6, 131, 599, 600, 695
Reddick, Paul 540
Redding, Goldman 307
Redding, Greg 49, 131
Redding, Otis 789

Redding, Will 192, 540
Reder, Milt 636
Redlich, Hank 377
Redman, Don 141, 253, 254, 293, 294, 437, 459, 537, 587, 592, 597, 685, 707, 718, 720
Redmond, Donald M. 336
Redmond, Jack 357
Redwing, Clint 'The Chief' 107
Reed, A. C. 67, 129, 130, 158, 233, 265, 266, 418, 458, 480, 541, 568, 591, 632, 669, 693, 694, 745, 776, 790, 814
Reed, Al 207, 805
Reed, Bernard 335, 401, 465, 706, 733
Reed, Bobby 249, 439
Reed, 'Brother Miles' 241
Reed, Dock 758, 760, 762
Reed, Elmo 'Buddy' 136, 241, 411
Reed, Henry 600, 758
Reed, J. R. 816
Reed, Jeffrey 599
Reed, Jimmy 66, 86, 269, 270, 275, 541, 739, 744, 752, 767, 768, 769, 770, 790, 799
Reed, Jo Jo 831
Reed, Johnny 344
Reed, Kay C. 57, 109, 553, 681
Reed, Larry 508
Reed, Long Cleve 801, 811
Reed, Lula 543, 650, 780
Reed, Mary 'Mama' 541, 542
Reed, Mitchell 12
Reed, Nathaniel 685
Reed, Revon 11
Reed, Richard 'Dickie' 362
Reed, Rick 55, 60, 121, 124, 146, 164, 194, 202, 211, 220, 414, 475, 618
Reed, Rusty 20
Reed, Thomas 660
Reed, Waymon 357
Reed, Willie 3, 767, 817
Reed Jr, Jimmy 541, 542
Reedus, Maurice 406
Rees, Pete 473
Reese, Belton 758
Reese, Della 790
Reese, Doc 747
Reese, Rostelle 670, 671
Reeves, Jimmy 229
Reeves, Tony 428
Reeves, Wilmus 477
Reevy, Jim 249, 685
Regals, The 777
Reggell, Chris 240
Register, Pat 657
Regnas, Ron 613
Rehak, Frank 40, 295
Reichenbach, William Frank 359, 376
Reichert, Jason 685
Reid, Abraham 609
Reid, Carl 537, 626
Reid, Irene 543

Reid, Rufus 84
Reid, Vernon 255, 256, 629, 665, 824, 825
Reiersrud, Knut 341
Reif, Fred 377
Reining, Fred 545
Reissner, Jörn 675
Reiter, Christoph 'Jimmy' 312
Rekow, Raul 274
Rena, Jean Paul 543
Renaud, Marco Jean 291
Rendall, Willie 551
Rendón, José 606
Rene, Googie 686
Renfro, Paul 321, 510
Rennie, Bill 350
Renwick, Tim 218
Reser, Harry 587
Reuss, Allen 292
Revelli, Paul 293, 358, 486, 584, 673, 735
Revere, Paul 789
Rey, Del 311, 486
Reyes, Felix 654
Reynaud, Lloyd 408
Reynolds, George 459
Reynolds, Big Jack 752
Reynolds, Joe 170
Reynolds, Blind Joe [Willie] 801, 803, 813, 767, 787, 794, 801
Reynolds, Ted 131
Reynolds, Theodore [Teddy] 47, 244, 357, 675
Reynolds, Warren 'Buzz' 732
Reys, Carlo 101
Rhambo, 'Bo' 392
Rhinehart, Charles 291
Rhinehart, Mack 794, 809
Rhoades, Bill 547, 703
Rhoden, Richard 396
Rhodes, Donna 439
Rhodes, George 445, 654, 684
Rhodes, Michael 644
Rhodes, Orville 52
Rhodes, Randy 133
Rhodes, Sandra 439
Rhodes, Sonny 424, 544, 624, 784
Rhodes, Todd 26, 245, 321, 322, 774, 798
Rhodes, Walter 'Lightnin' Bug' 545
Rhodes, Walter 792
Rhythm Aces, The 780
Rhythm Kings Horns, The 494
Rhythm Willie 738, 768, 769, 775
Rhythm Wreckers, The 772
Ribbins, Rev. 762
Ricard, Fortunatus Paul 'Fip' 33, 683
Ricci, Joe M. 84
Ricci, Paul 40
Rice, Bob 492
Rice, Charlie 338
Rice, Rev. D. C. 797
Rice, Dave 7, 33
Rice, Dot 45, 88, 220, 740
Rice, Ed 506

Rice, Kenneth 363, 365
Rice, Kenny 133, 319, 348
Rice, Mack 680
Rice, Willie 84
Rich, Bill 484, 485, 623, 624, 625
Rich, Herbie 52
Rich, Jeff 466, 487
'Richard' 125
Richard, Belton 831, 832
Richard, Felix 832
Richard, Robert 751, 752, 768
Richard, Rudolph 585, 586, 648, 649, 791
Richard, Seth 752, 755, 768, 795, 806
Richard, Thaddeus 502
Richard, Zachary 78, 806, 831, 832
Richards, Keith 274, 359, 372, 558, 615
Richards, Marcel 572
Richards, Marty 126, 427, 546, 548, 549, 567
Richards, Red 727
Richards, Tim 217, 274
Richardson, Al 80, 464, 533
Richardson, Ben 730
Richardson, Benny 763
Richardson, Edna 429
Richardson, Herb 765
Richardson, Horace 659
Richardson, Jerome 40, 340, 351, 357, 366, 510, 662
Richardson, Jimmy 663
Richardson, Mooch 322, 792, 793
Richardson, Phil 558
Richardson, Rob 255
Richardson, Soko 130, 146, 266, 429, 430
Richardson, Tanya F. 291
Richardson, Timothy 'Saxy Rick' 398
Richardson, Wally 81, 165, 272, 457, 662
Richardson, Willie B. 331
Richey, Bob 5, 418
Richey, Slim 230
Richie [Ringo Starr] 290
Richmond, Barney 173
Richmond, Dave 670, 671
Richmond, Fritz 484, 485, 486, 680, 703
Richmond, June 797
Ricker, Charlie 201
Ricketts, Bob 42, 325, 437, 461, 657
Rickey, Pat 229
Ricks, 'Philadelphia' Jerry 545, 823
Rickson, George 720
Riddick, Jeff 462
Riddle, Almeda 763
Riddle, Lesley 545
Riddle, Nelson 338
Rideau, Mandrell 'Green Eyed Bandit' 395
Rideaux, Albert 820
Riders, The 517
Ridge, Gary 260
Ridge, Percy 759
Ridgley, Tommy 26, 393, 777, 803, 805
Ridley, Greg 356

INDEX

Riedy, Bob 30, 125, 317, 557, 733
Riel, Alex 174
Rietveld, Benny 274
Rigby, Joe 133
Riggins, Richard 168
Riggs, Chuck 548
Riggs, Steve 566
Right, Willie (Boodle It) 796
Right Hand Frank 520
Right Kind, The 784
Righteous Brothers, The 789
Rigney, Tom 535, 539
Riley, Beau 617
Riley, Billy Lee 725
Riley, Dave 163, 545, 696
Riley, Doug 368
Riley, Fred 84
Riley, Herlin 84, 242, 472
Riley, Herman 351
Riley, John 568, 617
Riley, Judge 61, 69, 70, 72, 146, 147, 218, 287, 326, 333, 453, 480, 610, 616, 620, 627, 681, 708, 716
Riley, Mike 'Sleepy' 109, 330, 474
Riley, Steve 12, 161, 806, 832, 833
Riley, Teddy 82, 83, 176
Riley Jr, Dave 546
Rilhac, François 36, 64
Rimson, Jerome 671
Rinta, Mike 729
Rio, Rob 16, 104, 123, 468, 538, 629
Riordan, Paul 374
Rios, Alfred 358
Rios, Joe 705
Rip, Jimmy 511, 609
Ripchords, The 776
Ripp, Brian 260
Riser, Willie 229, 658
Rishell, Annie 516
Rishell, Paul 51, 515, 546, 636, 751, 771, 825
Rishell, Vanessa 546
Rising Star Fife & Drum Band 498
Ritchie, Brian 584
Rittenhouse, Kenny 499, 553
Ritter, Marc 416
Rival, Chris 546
Rivera, Al 506, 507
Rivera, Martin 583
Rivera, Scarlet 343
Rivers, Boyd 766
Rivers, Candy 392
Rivers, Jack 798
Rivers, James 362
Rivers, Sam 273
Riverside Ramblers 772
Rizzo, Anna 52
Rizzo, Bud 50
Rizzo, Tom 52
Roach 717
Roach, Helen 547
Roach, Jason Seth 576

Roach, Max 683
Roach, Michael 319, 546
Roach, Michelle 547
Roady, Tom 135
Roane, Eddie 338, 340
Roane, Kenneth 338
Robb, Cam 503
Robb, Terry 547, 564, 613, 703
Robbins, Dennis 350
Robbins, Everett 739
Robbins, Jeff 130, 468
Robbins, Robert 587
Robert, W. 715
Roberts, Alan 19
Roberts, Alfred 'Uganda' 470, 530, 531
Roberts, Caughey 463, 593
Roberts, Dan 259
Roberts, Dennis 296
Roberts, Dink 812
Roberts, Fiddling Doc 772
Roberts, Gip 751
Roberts, Howard 273, 686
Roberts, James 812
Roberts, Jimmy 429
Roberts, John 351
Roberts, Micheale 539
Roberts, Ozell 282
Roberts, Pixie 72
Roberts, Rob 34
Roberts, Wendy 36
Robertson, Burt 652
Robertson, Corky 467, 616
Robertson, Donald 5, 414
Robertson, Donald 'Hye Pockets' 595
Robertson, Eck 810
Robertson, Frank 638
Robertson, George 696, 770
Robertson, Herbert 415
Robertson, Howard 227
Robertson, James 257, 376, 401, 402
Robertson, Keith 319
Robertson, Lester 791
Robertson, Melvin 664
Robertson, Rob 369
Robertson, Robbie 237, 238, 486
Robertson, Roy 550
Robertson, Sherman 119, 120, 547, 553
Robertson, Wayne 726
Robeson, Paul 793, 821
Robichaux, Joe 391
Robillard, Duke 16, 27, 84, 113, 126, 135, 152, 191, 222, 239, 293, 385, 427, 446, 515, 525, 538, 548, 559, 564, 567, 644, 728, 768, 788, 824, 825
Robin 210
Robinette, Freddie 348
Robins, Mel 780
Robins, The 504, 505, 799, 800
Robinson, A. C. 552
Robinson, Al 315
Robinson, Aletha 69, 326, 607
Robinson, Alex (?) 48

Robinson, Alex 259
Robinson, Allyn 34, 35
Robinson, Alvin 'Shine' 59, 531, 803
Robinson, Arthur 208, 209
Robinson, Bert 'Top Hat' 528, 568
Robinson, Bob 45, 167, 259, 742, 787
Robinson, Carl 193
Robinson, Carla 696
Robinson, Carrie 822
Robinson, Cathy 401
Robinson, Chris 499
Robinson, Clarence 460, 469, 685
Robinson, Cynthia 145
Robinson, Darren 27
Robinson, David 11, 463, 593
Robinson, Donald 624
Robinson, Eli 39, 40, 504
Robinson, Elzadie 48, 549, 828
Robinson, Fat Man 773
Robinson, Fenton 199, 488, 550, 719, 744, 745, 767, 776, 790, 822
Robinson, Frank 550
Robinson, Fred 403, 404, 429, 430, 480, 488, 551, 557, 607, 711
Robinson, Harmonica George 770, 778
Robinson, Harris 508
Robinson, Hubert 785
Robinson, Iceman 551
Robinson, Ikey 14, 167, 255, 259, 311, 468, 551, 718, 816
Robinson, J. Russel 249
Robinson, James 6, 83, 358
Robinson, James 'Bat' 770, 808
Robinson, James 'Geechy' 219
Robinson, Jim 445, 462
Robinson, Jimmie Lee 10, 62, 97, 125, 264, 403, 409, 500, 551, 571, 586, 651, 746, 748, 749, 778
Robinson, Jimmy 63, 300, 321, 322
Robinson, Joe 244
Robinson, John 637
Robinson, Kathy 257
Robinson, Keith 21, 22, 157
Robinson, Kevin 427
Robinson, L. C. 'Good Rockin'' 552, 742, 777, 800
Robinson, Lenjes 369
Robinson, Leonard 194
Robinson, Les 328, 593
Robinson, Mabel 338, 526, 796, 806
Robinson, Matt 82
Robinson, Matthew 552
Robinson, Melvin 345
Robinson, Michael 730
Robinson, Michael 'Mr Dynamite' 632
Robinson, Mike 4
Robinson, Minor 164, 229
Robinson, Mitchell 725
Robinson, Prince 291, 292, 592
Robinson, Ralph 102
Robinson, Reginald R. 781
Robinson, Richard 'Hubcap' 557, 581

Robinson, Rob 156, 784, 808
Robinson, Robby 'Mann' 202
Robinson, Robin 42, 368, 476
Robinson, Rudy 350, 403
Robinson, Sugar Chile 798
Robinson, Tad 440, 462, 553, 590, 606, 770
Robinson, Tiny 154
Robinson, Walter 207
Robinson, Wayne 447
Robison, Cleophus 400
Roby, Hezekiah 733
Roby, Milton 105, 450, 451
Roche, Terry 422
Roché, Betty 449, 829
Rockers, The 400
Rockets, The 788, 818, 820
Rockin' Dopsie 53, 553, 831, 832
Rockin' Dopsie Jr 11, 554
Rockin' Johnny Band, The 554, 781
Rockin' Sidney 555, 668, 784, 831, 832
Rockingham, Greg 543
Rockmore, Phineas 757, 759
Rockwood, John 14
Rockwood, Julia 163
Rockwood, Kevin 163
Rodd, Alcedrik 107
Roddy, Rod 78
Roddy, Ted 230
Roddy, Teddy 195
Rodell, Walter 683
Roden, Bob 'House Wine' 43, 336
Rodgers, —— 462
Rodgers, Charles 38
Rodgers, Ike 149, 315, 325, 471, 697, 815
Rodgers, Jimmie 216, 248, 772, 794
Rodgers, Mighty Mo 556, 643
Rodgers, Nile 666, 668
Rodgers, Paul 235, 372
Rodgers, Vernon 96, 698
Rodriguez, Ernie 104
Rodriguez, Joe 138
Roe, Dave 195
Roger, Aldus 832
Rogers, Arnold 289
Rogers, Glenn 324
Rogers, Jimmy 1, 19, 97, 136, 187, 201, 289, 335, 375, 403, 415, 453, 480, 481, 484, 515, 556, 576, 601, 616, 632, 678, 744, 749, 752, 765, 767, 779, 780, 787, 788
Rogers, Johnny 228, 463, 506, 778
Rogers, Maurice [Mighty Mo Rodgers] 643
Rogers, Menard 779
Rogers, Rev. 763
Rogers, Richard 125
Rogers, Roy 44, 104, 111, 239, 274, 275, 358, 486, 558, 779
Rogers Jr, Jimmy 557
Roggenkamp, Wolfgang 74
Rohlehr, Beverly 578

Rokeach, Dave 37, 373
Rokesch [Rokeach], Dave 373
Roland, Chip 540
Roland, Walter 55, 558, 700, 701, 738, 739, 740, 774, 808, 810, 821
Rolle, Ivan 173, 472
Roller, Peter 536
Rollini, Adrian 741
Rollini, Art 8, 328, 390
Rollins, Don 'Big Dog' 431
Rollins, George 81
Roman, Isadore 508
Romie, Marty 729
Rondo, Eric 217
Rondolone, Tony 170
Roney, Wallace 674
Ronnie & The Delinquents 803
Roomful Of Blues 559, 742, 788, 825
Rooney, Prune 613
Roos, Johan de 550
Roosevelt, Theophilus 267
Rosas, Cesar 191, 274, 488, 538, 559
Rosas, Mike 729
Rosato, Joe 264
Rose, Bayless 755, 767, 793, 810, 813
Rose, Brent 78
Rose, Charles 135, 257, 395, 401, 402
Rose, Curtis 63
Rose, Darrell 242, 243
Rose, Houston 243
Rose, Matt 121, 450
Rose, Mike 512
Rose, Pamela 111
Rose, Skip 197, 486, 487
Roseborough, Will 757, 759
Roseby, Raz 434, 601
Rosenberg, Richard 569
Rosenblatt, Richard 'Rosie' 4, 246, 324, 546, 691
Rosenthal, Hele 272
Rosie & The Originals 789
Rosmini, Dick 665
Rosolino, Frank 726
Ross, Arnold 292
Ross, Bertha 128, 737, 828
Ross, Billy 571
Ross, Bob 217, 728
Ross, Clive 361
Ross, Danny 705, 721
Ross, Dr 561, 748, 749, 752, 768, 769, 770, 779, 789, 823
Ross, Eugene 'High Rise' 210
Ross, Gibbie/Gibby 373
Ross, Hank 665
Ross, Houston 243
Ross, Jackie 780
Ross, James 661, 662
Ross, Jeff 124, 342, 475
Ross, Jimbo 485
Ross, Jon 691, 719
Ross, Louise 774
Ross, Mary 822

Ross, Melissa 257
Ross, Michael 14
Ross, Ollie 818
Ross, Pat A. 136
Ross, Samuel 540
Rossi, Joe 414
Rossi, John 362, 559, 560
Rosso, Alejandro 94
Rossyion, Joe 565
Roth, Dave 136
Roth, Jack 293, 597, 712
Rotondi, James 543
Rotundo, David 629
Rough, Martin 620
Roulette, Freddie 265, 266, 486, 558, 561
Rounders, The 786
Rounds, Chris 112
Rouse, Charlie 300, 583, 670, 671
Rouse, Don 112, 113
Rousseau, Dalton 232
Rouzan, Wanda 554
Rover, Johnny 728
Rowan, Doug 583
Rowan, Jamie 38
Rowan, Paul 176, 344
Rowan, Peter 139
Rowberry, Dave 217
Rowe, Edward 356, 357
Rowe, Lloyd 145
Rower, Walt 726
Rowles, Danny 374
Rowles, Jimmy 725
Rowley, Richard 535, 539
Roy, Audrey Qween 465
Roy, Brenda 583, 584
Roy, Ernest 205, 316
Roy, Kedar 687
Roy, Walter 205, 316
Roy Jr, Earnest 576
Royal, Anthony 576
Royal, Ernie 115, 145, 295, 340, 356, 363, 365, 384, 483, 727
Royal, Frank 315
Royal, James 245, 543, 650
Royal, Marshall 1, 114, 115, 219, 252, 292, 432, 449, 450, 520
Royal, Sonny 395
Royal Harmonaires, The 821
Royal Kings, The 805
Royals, The 245, 799
Royster, Russell 84, 473
Rubin, Alan 358
Rubin, Anthony 554
Rubin, David 553
Rubin, Dwayne 554
Rubin, Mark 310, 529
Rubin Jr, Alton 553, 554
Ruby, Ron 52
Rucker, Big Daddy 802
Rucker, James 'Sparky' 750
Rucker, Keillie 468
Rucker, Laura 48, 779, 780, 796

Rucker, Lonie 465
Rucker, Washington 663
Rudd, Jimmy 292
Rudd, Roswell 485
Rudy, Andy 112
Rudy, James 158
Ruf, Thomas 342
Ruff, Jon 100
Ruff, Michael 'Mufty' 660
Ruff, Willie 507
Ruffin, Jeff 32
Ruffin, Jimmy 780
Ruffin, Joe 211
Ruffin, Mister 800
Ruffin, Riff 74, 306, 307, 807
Ruffins, Kermit 554, 806
Ruffolo, Frank 655
Rufner, Ruf 17, 65
Rufus Jr [Rufus Beacham] 650
Rugh, Phil 335, 377
Rukun, Taimur 625
Rummel, Chris 98
Runge, Bill 20, 210
Rupert, Ollie 792
Rupp, Barry 491
Rupp, Benno 96
Rura, Michael 639
Rush, Bobby 4, 139, 243, 510, 751
Rush, Darnell 614
Rush, Donell 691
Rush, Otis 7, 95, 125, 159, 160, 232, 431, 562, 739, 744, 745, 749, 768, 779, 780, 781, 797, 800, 823
Rush, Pat 170
Rush, Yoshann 307
Rushford, Bob 316
Rushing, Jimmy 504, 747, 797
Ruskin, Rick 823
Russell, Al 'Stomp' 826
Russell, Becky 524
Russell, Carla 413
Russell, Catherine 87, 325
Russell, Curley 63, 445, 640
Russell, David 318, 569
Russell, Diz 495
Russell, Emile 77
Russell, Frank 170
Russell, James 489, 763
Russell, Leon 356, 363, 365, 824
Russell, Luis 321, 607
Russell, Reba 4, 127, 498, 499, 644, 657
Russell, Rebecca 215
Russell, Ron 191
Russell, Rufus J. 208, 209
Russell, Terry 111
Russell, Tina 'Mom' 761
Russo, Charles 384
Russo, Mike 442, 443
Russo, Rich 113
Russo, Tony 5
Ruth, Peter 'Madcat'/'Mudcat' 51, 111, 465, 536

Rutherford, Carl 756, 786
Rutherford, Rudy 683
Rutledge, Johnny 450
Rutues, Moses 36
Rutues Jr, Moses 63, 64, 646
Ryan, George 759
Ryder, Junior 504, 505
Rye, Steve 344
Rynn, Patrick 377, 707
Rzab, Greg 4, 34, 234, 235, 431, 563
Saas, Jon 37
Sabani, Isa 660
Sabatello, Ray 400
Sabien, Randy 111, 580
Sack, Peter 414
Saddler, Yvonne 544
Sadler, Herb 319
Saffire – The Uppity Blues Women 563, 776, 830
Sago, Zona [Allan Williams] 776
Sahm, Doug 11, 509
Sailes, Jesse 75, 208, 209, 219, 229, 243, 247, 305, 307, 353, 354, 355, 405, 432, 460, 593, 661, 662, 684, 686, 724, 725
Sain, Greg 168, 666
Sain, James Edward 666
Sain, Oliver 157, 319, 369, 400, 401, 660, 816
Saizon, Floyd 214, 583
Sajdak [Saydak], Ken 67, 68, 573
Salaam, Abdul 416
Salamone, Jim 624
Salazar, Arion 575
Salerno, Vince 573, 574
Salgado, Curtis 93, 94, 111, 143, 222, 223, 336, 479, 547, 559, 564, 655, 703
Saliero, Dale 458
Salisbury, Joe 76
Salley, Antoine 103, 113, 144, 358, 675
Salley, Earl 'The Pearl Slicker' 107
Salley, Rowland (Roly) 50, 486
Sally, Earl 78, 107
Salty Dog Four 775, 793
Saltzman, Larry 314
Saltzman [Sulzmann], Stan 457
Salvador, Sal 81
Salvia, Henry 496, 497
Salyer, Debra 'Nardi' 127
Salz, Vicki 186
'Sam' 146, 600
Sam, Ambrose 831, 832
Sam, Calvin 108, 565
Sam, Carl 565
Sam, Glen 565
Sam, Herbert 565, 830, 831
Sam, Leon 565
Sam, Miller 232, 713
Sam, Rodney 565
Sam Brothers 5 565, 831
Samaha, N. 722
Samford, Larry 17
Sammon, Marty 129, 236

Sample, Fred 660
Sample, Joe 103, 203, 351, 357, 358, 359, 551, 727
Sample, Kenneth 394
Sample, Roosevelt 394
Sampson, Les 19
Sampson, Willie 643
Samson, Jackie 679
Samuel, Bill 21, 78, 79, 489, 490, 518, 544
Samuel, Hound Dog [Bill Samuel?] 78
Samuels, Bill 332, 565, 798
Samuels, Calvin 'Fuzzy' 370
Samuels, Clarence 779, 780, 798, 819
Samuels, Elen 318
Samuels, Joseph 595
Samuels, Saul 209
Samuels, Willie 'Vamp' 33, 129, 192, 330, 584, 622, 681, 695
Samuels Jr, Willie 'Vamp' 109
Samwell-Smith, Paul 601
San Francisco Jeff(ers) 77, 438
Sanborn, David 143, 356
Sanborn, Jonathan 151, 195, 612
Sanches, Marcelo 634
Sanchez, Jimmy 229, 534, 535, 558, 690
Sanchez, Michito 624
Sanchez, Micky 53
Sanchez, Paul 806
Sanctuary, Gary 427
Sand, Claus 8
Sanda, Omaru 810
Sandbloom, Kevin 198
Sandera, Chris 132, 262, 528, 574
Sandera, Christian 574
Sanders, Chick 627
Sanders, Emmett 'Maestro' 632
Sanders, George 'Slim' 791
Sanders, Irene 69, 829
Sanders, John Lee 20, 100, 198, 199
Sanders, John 274
Sanders, Laura 344
Sanders, Pete 717
Sanders, Richard 221, 222, 262, 352
Sanders, Tim 37, 122
Sanders, Will Roy 193, 341, 565
Sandford, Wallace 392
Sandke, Jordan 290, 733
Sandles, Verlin 623
Sandmel, Ben 177, 690
Sandoval, Chris 111
Sands, Kenny 352, 353, 354, 355
Sane, Dan 343, 611
Sanford, Wallace 392
Sangster, Charlie 766
Sangster, John 576
Sangster, Johnny 72
Sansone, Jumpin' Johnny 34, 566, 825
Santamaria, Mongo 115
Santana 737
Santana, Andy 583
Santana, Carlos 274, 695
Santi, Richard 52

INDEX

Santiago, James 535
Santiago, Lester 462
Santineo, Edward 82, 83
Santo, Paul 376
Santos, David 135
Santos, Jumo 623, 624
Sapp, Hosea 463, 504, 505
Sapps, Booker T. 757, 761
Sara, Kenny 194
Saracco, Frank 295
Sardinas, Eric 566, 823
Sargent, Louis 82
Sarli, Jeff 10, 470, 535
Saslaff, Maury 'Hooter' 316
Sass, John 131
Sasson, Jean-Pierre 527
Satan & Adam 566
Satch Wig 721
Satchell, Clarence 'Satch' 681
Satterfield, Louis 138, 355, 401, 482, 733
Satterfield, Mario 5
Saucier, Edgar 212, 437, 575, 699
Saulsbury, Joseph H. 472, 731
Saulsbury Jr, Joseph 222, 359
Saunders, Charles 39, 41, 146, 159, 287, 620, 716
Saunders, John 583
Saunders, Levi B. 36, 37
Saunders, Merl(e) 623, 784
Saunders, Red 8, 227, 467, 468, 500, 661, 662, 663, 677, 678, 718, 741
Saunders, Richard 221, 353
Saunders, Russ 521
Saunders, Tom 554
Saunders, Tony 275, 373
Savage, Al 97
Savage, Alan 65, 374
Savage, Rev. C. H. 759, 762
Savage, Joe 766
Savakus, Russ 309
Savoy, Ann 831
Savoy, Ashton 784
Savoy, Marc 831
Savoy-Doucet Cajun Band, The 806, 832
Savoy Sultans, The 797
Sawyer, Chris 112
Sawyer, Damon 44
Sawyer, Laura 217
Sax Gordon 16, 66, 148, 152, 176, 222, 312, 325, 427, 492, 515, 525, 546, 548, 549, 567, 636, 717, 718, 719
Saxton, Bobby 778, 780
Saxy Boy 179, 362, 681
Saydak, Ken 32, 57, 109, 346, 462, 474, 528, 553, 567, 573, 590, 606, 612, 632, 698, 723, 733, 735, 742
Sayers, Pete 372
Sayles, Charlie 567, 771
Sayles, Emmanuel 620
Sayles, Johnny 780
Sayles, Kerry 567
Scabs, The 52

Scaggs, Boz 204
Scaggs [Skaggs], Geno 282, 283
Scala, Dean 516
Scales, Alonzo 638
Scales, George 346
Scanga, Frank 341
Scanlan, Reggie 59, 690
Scarlet, Will 116
Scatter, Battlerack 182, 791
Schaffer, Ed 'Dizzy Head' 729
Schallock, Dave 728
Scharf, Michael 606
Schaugaard, Leslie 58
Schedemayer, Julius 83
Scheep, Tom 612
Scheer, E. Duato (Ed) 546, 718
Scheid, Hannsjoerg 194
Schell, Johnny Lee 235, 275, 359, 518, 563, 624
Schenk, Jimmy 81
Schepp, Tom 120
Scher, Paul 374
Schermer, Mike 583
Schermerhorn, Kevin 433, 476
Schertzer, Hymie 8, 328
Schiedt, Duncan (as Bud White) 46
Schierbaum, Arlen 113, 704
Schlesinger, Robert 398
Schlick, Mike 32, 606
Schmachtenberg, Martin 249
Schmid, Phil 303, 414
Schmidt, Danny 5
Schmidt, Detlef 411
Schmidt, Fred 370
Schmuecker, Rudi 487
Schneider, Eric 163
Schneiderman, John 413
Schneller, Tommy 152
Schnirring, Klaus 220
Schnore, Liz Rabson 535
Schofield, Matt 218, 568, 579
Schofield, Willie 680
Schofner, Charlie 507
Scholl, Albey 81, 186
Scholl, Dave 222
Schroder, John 303, 464
Schuld, Andreas 20, 687
Schuler, William 44
Schultz, Alex 17, 123, 124, 146, 169, 194, 220, 413, 475, 522, 553, 557, 618, 720, 825
Schumacher, Carl 673
Schutte, James 160
Schutte, Jimi 5, 68, 151
Schutz, Buddy 8, 328, 390
Schwab, Brian 204
Schwalbe, Dan 414, 612
Schwall, Jim 579
Schwamm, Leo 513
Schwann, Leo 80
Schwartz, Gene 406
Schwarz, Thornel 662

Schwenke, Jon 685
Scinto, Jesse 554
Scoazec, Olivier 87
Scoles, John 446
Scoll, David 413
Sconce, Mike 11
Scorpion Washboard Band 775
Scortia, Eric 501
Scott, Arthur 32
Scott, Beverley 826
Scott, Bud 680
Scott, Buddy 186, 698, 711
Scott, Carl 758
Scott, Cecil 250, 551, 592
Scott, Ceola 763
Scott, Clifford 363, 365, 726, 727
Scott, Creola 763
Scott, 'Curfew' 41
Scott, Delores 344
Scott, Dorothy 607
Scott, E. C. 779
Scott, Effie 526
Scott, Elmer 136
Scott, Frank 409
Scott, Glen 37, 37
Scott, Harold 580
Scott, Hazel 741
Scott, Henry 763
Scott, Henry '45' 626
Scott, Howard 141, 253, 459, 537, 597, 707, 727
Scott, Jack 529
Scott, James 385
Scott, Joe 47, 77, 509, 651
Scott, Keith 371
Scott, Kermit 366
Scott, Kinner 581
Scott, Lannie 445, 639, 640
Scott, Leon 468, 718
Scott, Lulu 128
Scott, Mabel 798, 827, 829
Scott, Marilyn 429
Scott, Marylin 504, 505, 752, 755, 774, 806
Scott, Michael 160, 419, 420, 421, 498, 527, 528
Scott, Patricia 830
Scott, Pete 217
Scott, Philip 83
Scott, Randolph 607
Scott, Ray 160, 542
Scott, Ron 35, 101
Scott, Ronnie 726
Scott, Roosevelt 128
Scott, Shane 629
Scott, Shirley 9, 586
Scott, Sonny 559, 737, 810
Scott, Sylvester 663
Scott, Tom 358
Scott, Tommy 785
Scott, Tony 140
Scott, Walter 109, 612

INDEX

Scott, Willie 725
Scott, Wim 730
Scott, Yonrico 81, 185, 636
Scott Jr Blues Rockers 789
Scottdale String Band 792
Scotty & The Rib Tips 745
Screamin', Iain 540
Scribner, Brad 158
Scribner, Fred 158
Scroggins, Janice 43, 547, 564, 613, 703
Scruggs, Irene 48, 467, 755, 812, 826
Scruggs, Uncle John 758
Scypion, Will 13
Seale, Herman 391
Sealove, Carl 704
Seals, Son 568, 632, 745, 768, 776, 823, 825
Seals, Sonny 109, 345, 465, 553, 590, 591, 681, 711, 733
Sealy, Paul 672
Seamen, Phil 73, 703
Searcy, DeLoise 291, 292, 320, 590
Searles, Chris 502
Searlie, Jimmy 107
Sears, Al 9, 81, 140, 521
Sears, Pete 246
Sebastian, John 50, 51, 180, 485, 486, 546, 672
Sedener, Whit 257
Sedergreen, Bob 727
Sedovic, Mike 143
Seeger, Mike 304, 545
Seeger, Pete 72, 73, 154, 156, 298, 456, 638, 701, 702
Seeger, Toshi 298
Segar, Charlie/Chuck 88, 220, 424, 436, 437, 743, 808
Segebrant, Kjell 37
Seibert, Chris 246
Seidelin, Mogens 174, 175, 176
Seidenberg, Danny 145
Seidler, Alan 50
Selby, Mark 824
Selico, Ron 350, 507, 508
Sellers, Brother John 650
Selvidge, Steve 498
Selvin, Ben 685
Sembler, Pete 496, 497
Semien, Agnes 'Creola' 555
Semien, Francis 555
Semien, Ivory Lee 280, 282, 719
Semien, Roger 555
Semmes, Raphael 412, 691
Semple, Roosevelt 394
Sempra, Betty Anne 374
Sene, Mike 4
Senegal [Sinegal], Donald 582
Senegal [Sinegal], Paul 'Lil' Buck' 11, 87, 119, 553, 554
Sensations, The 780
Sepia Tones, The 788
Serame, Cheryl 111

Serpas-Vigueira, Mari 502
Serrano, Paul 138
Seruntine, Tony 571
Settlers, Jazzbo Tommy 793, 795
Settles, Bill 69, 218, 227, 259, 320, 326, 452, 626, 654, 682, 692
Sevareid, Karl 43, 144, 145, 151, 486, 487, 613, 728
Seventh Day Adventist Choir 810
Severin, Chris 242, 472
Seward, Alec 569, 638, 639, 640, 752, 755, 765, 777, 806
Sexton, Brad Lee 158, 239, 399
Sexton, Charlie 168, 488
Sexton, Colleen 825
Seymour, Dan 390
'Sha-Ba-Ka' 136
Shackleford, John 449
Shackleton, Jimmy 449, 450
Shade, Will 105, 388, 450, 451, 452, 488, 764, 792
Shadhili, Juma 625
Shaffer, Nancy 369
Shah, Harmonica 570
Shakesnider, Wilmer 77, 214
Shakey Jake [Harris] 418, 486, 570, 571, 748, 770
Shanahan, Kevin 92
Shane, James 77, 103, 104, 458
Shank, Buck 291
Shankle, Carl 136
Shanko, Timo 369
Shannon 168
Shannon, Gloria 830
Shannon, Mem 571, 806
Shannon, Preston 571, 720
Shannon, Tommy 26, 35, 111, 148, 152, 235, 297, 366, 435, 575, 666, 667, 668, 669, 722, 723
Shapiro, Artie 661, 662
Sharif, Jamil 359
Sharp, Bill 374
Sharp, Carl 70
Sharp, Curtis 403
Sharp, Sidney 48, 551, 686, 726
Sharpe, E. J. 'The Professor' 256
Sharpe, Ray 572
Sharpe, Rocky 217
Sharps & Flats, The 774
Sharpville, Todd 217, 218
Sharriff, Omar 552, 572, 742, 777, 800
Shaugnessy, Ed 416
Shavers, Charlie 24, 80, 224, 287, 294, 526, 597, 773
Shaw, Allen 792, 812, 813
Shaw, Arvell 527
Shaw, Charles 553, 643
Shaw, Doug 472
Shaw, Eddie 159, 262, 289, 290, 344, 345, 418, 474, 528, 573, 574, 576, 617, 622, 630, 635, 745, 747, 776, 824
Shaw, Eddie Vaan 573, 576

Shaw Jr, Eddie 'Vaan' 573
Shaw, Fred 82
Shaw, Gary 217, 728
Shaw, Geoff 10
Shaw, Joan 713, 829
Shaw, Lonnie 510
Shaw, Marlena 780
Shaw, Martin 53
Shaw, Nate 222
Shaw, Peter J. 424
Shaw, Robert 574, 742, 777
Shaw, Roosevelt 'Snake' 266, 272, 458, 694
Shaw, Thomas 575, 766
Shaw, Wilbur 758
Shayne, J. H. 320, 607, 610
Shea, Frank 369
Sheely, Ted 472
Sheffield 752, 755, 768, 806
Sheffield, Charles 'Mad Dog' 783, 784, 791
Sheffield, J. 146
Sheffield, Jay 136
Sheffield, Jimmy 434
Sheffield, Roosevelt 114, 115
Sheldon, Rev. Herb 51
Shelton, B. F. 810
Shelton, Ezra Howlett 809
Shelton, Louie 679
Shelton, Roscoe 783, 786
Shelton Brothers 772, 773
Shelvin, Tommy 82, 83
Shemwell, Sylvia 679
Shenale, John Philip 235
Shepard, Leo 510
Shepard, Mary 14
Shepard, Ollie 575
Shepard, Thomas 210
Shepherd, Albert 760
Shepherd, Earl 84
Shepherd, Kenny Wayne 168, 575, 632
Shepherd, Mike 182
Shepherd, Nola Rose 536
Shepp, Archie 133
Sheppard, Andy 425
Sheppard, Frederick 'Shep' 40, 81, 456, 571
Sherman, Joe 571
Sherman, Miboy 526
Sherock, Shorty 328
Sherry, Rick 'Cookin'' 184
Sherwood, Bobby 384
Shetler, Scott 536, 546, 717, 718
'Shiba' (Edward Kimbrough) 530
Shields, Calvin 63, 83, 173, 245, 321, 322, 520
Shields, Lonnie 576
Shields, Nab 229
Shields, Sam 766
Shiels, Brian 37
Shihab, Sahib 40, 683
Shilkin, Neil 20

Shine, Ralph 771
Shines, Johnny 121, 165, 183, 263, 283, 323, 406, 486, 576, 603, 617, 621, 631, 737, 743, 744, 745, 752, 765, 779, 780, 785, 788, 802, 813, 814, 825
Shingler, Bill 650
Shipley, Robert 78
Shipman, Scott 182
Shipp, Christine 758
Shipp, Katherine 758
Shirley, Jerry 356
Shirley, Jimmy 140, 245, 327, 328, 650, 654
Shirley, Theodore [Ted] 392, 432, 447, 731
Shirley, Tom 328
Shirley & Lee 799, 803, 804, 806
Shishonge, Lucas 810
Shocked, Michelle 78, 554, 824
Shoemaker, Vic 556
Shoffner, Bob 142, 311, 321
Sholl, David 76, 291, 497
Shores, Joe 758, 759, 762
Shorey, David 52
Short, J. D. 216, 317, 579, 708, 787, 794, 811, 815, 820
Short, Kate 228
Shortell, Jimmy 255, 434
Shorter, William 448
Shortt, Bill 175
Shorty, James 441, 762
Shoulder, Elise 369
Shoulder, Peter 402
Shoup, Sam 524
Showers, Carlos 346
Showmen, The 803, 804
Shreve, Thomas 555
Shreveport Home Wreckers 767, 803, 812, 813
Shrier, Nook 683
'Shrimp City Slim' 511
Shufflesworth, Walter 464, 512
Shul, Barron 687
Shumake, Ron 104
Shumy, Robert 132
Shurik, Jim 59
Shurman, Dick 249, 488, 707
Shy, Parker 554
Siacotos, Steve 199
Sickles, Matt 654
Sida, Rafael 37
Sidgrave, Booker 405
Sidwell, Neil 234
Sidwell, Steve 424
Siebert, Chris 399
Sieberth, Lawrence 78
Siegal, Ian 579
Siegel, Corky 42, 121, 579
Siegel, Holly 579
Siegel–Schwall Band, The 776
Siegrist, Frank 253
Siemen, Wilton 118

Sierra, Alex 655
Sievers, Willie 14
Sieverson, Bruce 652
Siggins, Bob 485
Signorelli, Frank 293, 597, 685, 712
Sihaampai, Ordy Somchai 96
Silbereisen, Lou 72
Silbert, Scott 211, 499, 553
Silent Grove Baptist Church Congregation 758
Sill, Nicole 535
Silva, Gary 43, 433
Silva, Maynard 580, 814
Silva, Michael 77
Silver, Lex 272
Silver Leaf Gospel Singers 180
Silvers, Eddie 660
Silvester, Andy 33, 176, 226
Simeon, Omer 40, 381, 551, 607
Simeone, Paul 541
Simicheck, Craig 195
Simien, Jason 203
Simien, Marcella 580
Simien, Grandpa Matthew 580
Simien, Terrance 78, 580, 731, 831, 832
Simins, Russell 94
Simmonds, Ann 34
Simmonds, Brian 4
Simmonds, Kim 386
Simmons, Alvin 572
Simmons, Blanche 761
Simmons, Danny Ray 581
Simmons, Gene 780
Simmons, Georgia Hinton 581
Simmons, Hamp 47, 509
Simmons, Harvey 222
Simmons, John 701, 702
Simmons, Junior 492
Simmons, Little Mack 67, 125, 266, 323, 376, 528, 581, 617, 711, 744, 746, 768, 770, 771, 778, 779, 785
Simmons, Rhandy 179, 476
Simmons, Richard 65, 97
Simms, Earl 463
Simms, Emmanuel 315
Simms, Jane 578
Simms, Jim 171
Simms, Son [Henry Sims] 479, 480
Simon, Alvin J. 56
Simon, Dan 622
Simon, Gene 244, 300
Simon, Harry 586
Simon, Jeff 652, 653
Simon, Joe 790
Simon, John 290, 623
Simon, Keith 532
Simon, Kenyatta 489
Simon, Lou 'Freddie' 75, 219, 258, 338, 340, 661, 662, 731
Simon, Maurice 1, 40, 81, 88, 114, 292, 340, 432, 726, 731
Simon, Noah 636

Simon, Stafford 245, 338, 575, 583
Simone, Nina 361, 739
Simons, Brian 612
Simpkins, Jesse 'Po' 338, 340, 490
Simpson, Bill 819
Simpson, Brian 559
Simpson, Cassino 475
Simpson, Coletha 828
Simpson, J. W. 730
Simpson, Leroy 753
Simpson, Mark 696
Simpson, Martin 37, 812
Simpson, Mel 424
Simpson, Red 491
Simpson, Steve 36, 37
Simpson, Terry 185
Simpson Jr, Willie 460
Sims, Art 610
Sims, Charlie 758
Sims, David 186
Sims, Dennis 535
Sims, Dick 363
Sims, Frankie Lee 276, 582, 752, 788, 789, 813, 818, 819, 820
Sims, George 668
Sims, Gerald 47, 401
Sims, Henry 479, 511, 512, 816
Sims, Mickey 677, 678
Sims, Robert 'Snake' 83, 209, 677, 678, 686, 725, 731
Sims, Terrance 194
Sims, Wilford 370, 717, 721
Sims, Willie 221, 222, 400, 659, 660
Sims, Zoot 115, 679
Sinclair, John 402
Sinegal, Eugene 648
Sinegal, Norman 529
Sinegal, Paul 'Lil' Buck' 11, 87, 119, 553, 554, 582
Singer, Hal 1, 39, 77, 245, 321, 322, 445, 610, 639, 640, 671, 679, 727, 798, 800
Singin' Sam 778, 779
Singing Angels 163
Singletary, Bill 512
Singleton, Amos 361
Singleton, Charlie 583, 800
Singleton, Henry 692
Singleton, James 59, 84, 718
Singleton, T-Bone 583, 791
Singleton, Wayne 13
Singleton, Willie 530, 597
Singleton, Zutty 89, 221, 294, 607, 608
Siomos, John 34
Sipe, Jeff 636
Sipes, Frank 572
Sissoko, Ballaké 625
Sisson, Dave 87
Sista Monica 583
Sista Teedy 242
Sister Gerry 458
Sivuca 52
Siyawa, Hamadjam Sarki 810

INDEX 907

Sjoblom, Jonas 37
Skaggs, Geno/Gino 265, 266, 272, 273, 276, 282, 283
Skeete, Franklin 245, 295, 300, 321, 322, 445, 472, 639, 640, 670, 671
Skibinski, Leon 591
Skidmore, Alan 53, 175, 427
Skinner, Fred 661, 662
Skinner, James 84, 761
Skinner, Robert 47
Skinny Dynamo [George 'Slim' Sanders] 791
Skipper, Buddy 807
Skipper, Phillip 'Philzone' 186
Sklair, Josh 307
Sklar, Leland 359
Skoller, Larry 584
Skoller, Matthew 4, 41, 129, 192, 368, 420, 528, 584, 632, 771
Skoodle-Dum-Doo 752, 755, 768, 806
Skrimshire, Nevil 72
Sky, Patrick 297, 298
Skye, Bob 539
Skyer, Mark 104
Skylark 583, 584
Slack, Earl 136
Slack, Freddie 661, 662, 677, 678, 741, 797
Slam 127
'Slam' 567
Slater, Chester 244
Slater, Vernon 354, 355
Slattery, Keith 156
Slaughter, Bob 645
Slaughter, James 683
Slaughter, Roy 467
Slay, Emmitt 472
Slayden, Emma [India] 585
Slayden, Will 585
Slaymaker, Thomas 37
Slechta, Gary 11, 21, 61, 68, 123, 210, 296, 297, 342, 373, 423, 431, 485, 502, 676
Sleet, Frank 661, 662, 724
Sletten, Kurt 508
'Slim' 258
Slim Harpo 585, 739, 752, 770, 776, 783
Slim Parker 719
Slocomb Jr, Don 291
Slocum, Charlie 551
Sly Fox, The 800
Small Blues Charlie 299, 609
Small, Danny 416, 774
Small, Diz 715
Small, Drink 786
Small, Edward 521
Small, Randy 65
Smalley, Ike 712
Smalley, Laura 821
Smalley, Scott 113
Smallie, Todd 636
Smalls, Cliff 713
Smalls, Danny 40

Smalls, Theodore 724
Smart, Elandro 114
Smeck, Roy 707, 718, 812
Smilin' Joe [Cousin Joe] 804
Smith, Al 272, 367, 586, 784
Smith, Al Kinnanam 'Kenny' 367
Smith, Albert 756
Smith, Alberta 240
Smith, Allen 366, 473
Smith, Arthur 773
Smith, Aunt Harriet 821
Smith, B. E. 'Frosty' 21, 61, 68, 123, 148, 200, 246, 450, 502, 529, 676
Smith, Barkin' Bill 590, 606, 746, 768
Smith, Ben 86, 521
Smith, Bennie 38, 586
Smith, Bessie 586, 592, 737, 738, 739, 744, 773, 774, 794, 806, 820, 827
Smith, Bessie Mae 337, 590, 618, 619, 815
Smith, Bill 95
Smith, Billy 686
Smith, Bob K. 439
Smith, Bobby 86, 91, 416, 727
Smith, Brian 457
Smith, Buddy 41, 650
Smith, Buster 326, 661
Smith, Byther 590, 617, 744, 768, 781
Smith, Cal 248, 249, 680
Smith, Carrie 592
Smith, Charles Edward 381
Smith, Charlie 39, 40, 338, 521, 654
Smith, Chris 583
Smith, Chuck 125, 129, 563
Smith, Clara 321, 587, 592, 773, 774, 794, 826, 827
Smith, Clarence [Sonny Rhodes] 784
Smith, Cool Papa 794
Smith, Curtis 521, 685
Smith, Dalton 210
Smith, Dan 536
Smith, Danon 472
Smith, Darryl Lacurtis 731
Smith, Dave 4, 6, 68, 90, 127, 151, 215, 235, 375, 431, 443, 468, 513, 524, 575, 599, 600, 633, 634, 688
Smith, Debbie 340
Smith, Dick 340, 641
Smith, Don 157
Smith, Dorothea 'Dottie' 104, 245, 332
Smith, Earl 296, 730, 731
Smith, Eddie 63, 245, 300, 321, 322, 340, 641
Smith, Edward 724
Smith, King Edward 765
Smith, Effie 593
Smith, Eithel 618
Smith, Elizabeth 385
Smith, Faber 732, 737, 742
Smith, Fatman 819
Smith, Fletcher 39, 40, 432, 517, 593, 638, 640
Smith, Floyd 1, 671

Smith, Frank 78
Smith, Freddie 248, 249
Smith, G. E. 139, 235, 370, 488, 674
Smith, Gary 194, 544, 583
'Smith', Gator 539
Smith, Geechie 384
Smith, (Little) George 'Harmonica' 123, 173, 177, 209, 416, 483, 593, 604, 629, 651, 652, 770, 779, 782, 800
Smith, Gordon 594
Smith, Greg 1, 21, 359
Smith, Greg 'Frosty' 502
Smith, Guy 808
Smith, Harold 727
Smith, Harry 253
Smith, Henry 367, 751, 752
Smith, Herman 321, 322
Smith, Hobart 762, 811
Smith, Holland K. 721
Smith, Homer Quincy 793
Smith, Horace 818
Smith, Howling 181
Smith, Huey 'Piano' 231, 391, 803, 805, 806
Smith, Ike 796
Smith, Ivy 150, 809, 826, 828
Smith, J. T. 'Funny Paper'/'Funny Papa' 181, 594, 794, 820
Smith, Jabbo 551
Smith, James 284, 414, 612
Smith, Jerome 467
Smith, Jerry 402
Smith, Jessica 439
Smith, Jessie 531
Smith, Jimi 'Prime Time' 594
Smith, Jimitre 544
Smith, Jimmie 726
Smith, Jimmy 209
Smith, Little Jimmy 800
Smith, Joe 223, 224, 253, 254, 294, 336, 459, 460, 469, 537, 587, 588, 592, 596, 597, 685
Smith, John 133, 192, 727
Smith, Johnnie B. 367
Smith, Jon 33, 118, 130, 161, 215, 468
Smith, Justin 569
Smith, Keith 527
Smith, Keith 'Smitty' 324
Smith, Kenny 25, 32, 92, 96, 163, 172, 204, 316, 325, 335, 465, 476, 477, 478, 516, 554, 567, 584, 707
Smith, Kester 'Smitty' 485, 623, 624, 625
Smith, Kevin 61, 123, 575
Smith, Laura 595, 827
Smith, Lee 16
Smith, Leon 688
Smith, Lorenzo 146, 386, 387, 576
Smith, Lucius 759, 761
Smith, Luke 'The Duke' 359
Smith, Mae 828
Smith, Malvin 591
Smith, Mamie 595, 737, 827

Smith, Marsha 643
Smith, Matt 524
Smith, Mayne 485, 823
Smith, Mildred 214
Smith, Myrna 679
Smith, Neil [sic Bill] 357
Smith, Neil 547
Smith, Nolan 143, 416, 427, 429, 597
Smith, Oscar 332, 341
Smith, Patty 429
Smith, Little Phil 234
Smith, Pine Top 596, 737, 739, 740, 741, 742, 795, 808
Smith, R. C. 764, 777
Smith, Ray 556
Smith, Rebecca 764
Smith, Robbie 342, 704
Smith, Robert 819
Smith, Robert Curtis 766, 777
Smith, Roderick A. 81
Smith, Rollen 249
Smith, Ron 4, 652, 653
Smith, Rosetta 179
Smith, Ruby 526, 828, 829
Smith, Russell 587, 588, 597
Smith, Rusty 81
Smith, S. W. 772, 821
Smith, Sharon 296
Smith, Six Cylinder 769, 794, 817
Smith, Slim 772
Smith, 'Sonny Boy' 600
Smith, Spark Plug 596, 755
Smith, Stan 200
Smith, Steele 68, 69
Smith, Steuart 494, 495
Smith, Steve 675
Smith, Steve Darrel 424
Smith, Tab 8, 86, 244, 523, 610, 661, 662, 683, 790
Smith, Teddy 477
Smith, Thunder 276, 283, 742, 752, 819, 826
Smith, Tommy 84, 321, 322
Smith, Trixie 597, 827, 829
Smith, Vernon 'Geechie' 208, 209, 291, 384, 432, 684, 724
Smith, Versey 811
Smith, Walter 324, 345
Smith, Walter 'Tang' 288
Smith, Ward 179
Smith, Whispering 258, 597, 648, 699, 769, 770, 783, 791
Smith, Wilbert 83
Smith, Will 633
Smith, William 811
Smith, William 'Smitty' 197
Smith, Willie [as] 291, 292
Smith, Willie [ts] 460, 505
Smith, Willie 'Big Eyes' 25, 54, 139, 180, 293, 324, 385, 386, 411, 423, 470, 476, 479, 480, 481, 482, 483, 484, 503, 515,
516, 532, 533, 552, 598, 603, 604, 607, 647, 687, 705, 723, 735, 824
Smith, Willie 'Long Time' 607, 741, 820
Smith, Willie 'The Lion' 250, 379, 380, 595, 661
Smith & Harper 755, 769
Smith Band, The 760, 761
Smith Jr, Earl 361
Smith Jr, Frank Willis 79
Smith Jr, Ulysses 24
Smither, Chris 824
Smock, Ginger 508
Smoky Babe 598, 764
Smoot, Carl 721
Smothers, Abe 289
Smothers, Albert 'Little Smokey' 44, 598, 711
Smothers, Smokey 289, 599, 783
Smulyan, Glen 358
Smythe, Vanita 90
Snakefarm 803
Sneed, Ed 40
Sneed, Jack 796, 821
Sneed, James 760, 761
Snell, George 27
Snell, Lester 349, 350, 366, 401, 551, 572, 731
Snipes, John 812
Snow, Hattie 818
Snow, Wally 674
Snowden, Elmer 253, 323, 336, 385, 437, 438, 460, 461, 469, 475, 587, 596
Snowden, Q. Roscoe 460, 808
Snyder, Carl 317, 318, 528
Snyder, Matt 131
Snyder Jr, Carl 568
Sobb, Matt 341
Socarras, Albert 164, 461
Soejima, Kunitsugu 169
Soileau, Leo 831
'Sol' 609, 786
Solberg, James 5, 6, 7, 127, 495, 599, 824
Solberg, Jim 336
Solis, Rene 583
Sollee, Ben 634
Soloff, Lewis/Lou 343, 487
Solomon, Clifford 76, 104, 145, 350, 430, 506, 507, 663
Solomon, Ellis 'King' 208, 785
Solomon, Mel 751
Solotones, The 783
Solves, Jean-Pierre 5
Somei, Koichi 169
Somel, B. Gokham 498
Somel, Diden 498
Somerville, Trevor 518
Sommer, Ted 115
Sommer, Tone 705, 721
Sommerville Slim 510
Son Joe [Ernest Lawlars] 704
Sones, Jimmy 629
Sonics, The 780

Sonnier, Jo-El 144, 832
Sonnier, Shelton 554
Sonny Boy & Lonnie 806, 600
Sonny Boy Nelson [Eugene Powell] 801, 802
Sonny Boy Williamson [Jeff Williamson] 787
Sonny Boy Williamson II 146, 233, 305, 306, 307, 600, 627, 681, 738, 739, 744, 748, 749, 752, 769, 770, 776, 779, 780, 781, 799, 800, 802, 822
Sonny Guitar 296
Sons Of Blues, The 745
Sons Of Blues/Chi-Town Hustlers, The 745
Sons Of The Ozarks, The 772
Sons Of The Pioneers 798
Sorin, Ron 567, 612, 698
Sorrells, Mark 402
Sortier, Amanda/Ann 218, 437, 493
Sosson, Marshall 75
Soto, Jerry 30, 126, 165
Soul Brothers, The 398, 788
Soul Stirrers, The 788
Sounds Of Africa 556
South Georgia Highballers 772
South Memphis Jug Band 792, 816
Southern Blues Singers 150
Soward, Sam 126
Sowell, Richard 769
Space, Anthony 318, 369
Space Spiritual Singers 778
Spady, Clarence 518
Spagnoletti, Rob 386
Spake, Jim 4, 49, 61, 90, 126, 131, 144, 246, 366, 372, 498, 522, 524, 572, 591, 657, 660, 711, 721
'Spam' [Tommy Lee Miles] 100, 198, 199, 236
Spand, Charlie 48, 602, 738, 740, 741, 787, 794, 797, 808
Spangler, R. J. 27, 250, 570
Spaniels, The 790, 799
Spanjers, Erik 152
Spanjers, Roel 120, 152, 220, 312, 332, 501, 591, 612
Spann, Leo 245
Spann, Leon 315
Spann, Les 232
Spann, Lucille 604
Spann, Otis 54, 138, 233, 272, 273, 289, 323, 335, 403, 456, 480, 481, 482, 557, 577, 601, 602, 629, 651, 680, 693, 694, 734, 737, 742, 744, 745, 748, 749, 779, 780, 783, 788, 808, 809, 822
Spann, Victor 479
Sparklers, The 784
Sparks, Aaron 'Pine Top' 317, 443, 742
Sparks, Milton 'Lindberg' 740, 815
Sparks, Speedy 377
Sparks Brothers 605, 744, 808, 815
Sparling, Tim 510

Sparrow, Arnett 'Nick' 670
Sparrow, Johnny 84
Sparrow, Simon Tex 45
Spath, Lee 103, 113, 143, 146, 417
Spaulding, Henry 767, 793, 815
Spearman, Alex 805
Special, Pete 42, 450
Special Sauce 803
Speckled Red 303, 493, 605, 715, 737, 739, 740, 741, 742, 773, 781, 795, 807, 808, 809
Specter, Dave 30, 32, 96, 200, 204, 440, 462, 553, 606, 768, 770, 781
Spector, John 369
Spedding, Chris 457, 458
Speed, Constance 592
Speed, J. T. 492
Speed, Samuel 596, 718
Speer, Stu 372
Speiginer, Louis 114, 724
Spell, Jay 377, 429
Spell, Joe 711
Spellman, Benny 362, 804, 806
Spells, Dino 130, 136, 659
Spencer, Bobby 193
Spencer, Christine 521
Spencer, Donnell 50
Spencer, Evans 263
Spencer, George 507
Spencer, Jeremy 767, 813
Spencer, Johnny 712
Spencer, Jon 94
Spencer, O'Neill 24, 224, 287, 526, 597, 697
Spencer, Ron 112
Spenner, Alan 372
Spider, Mickey 173
Spiders, The 799, 803, 804
Spijker, Jon 591
Spiller, Norman 233
Spinetti, Henry 37
Spinner, David 668
Spinozza, David 356
Spires, Arthur 'Big Boy' 607, 744, 780
Spires, Bud 508, 762
Spirits Of Rhythm, The 797
Spirn, Steve 111
Spivey, Addie 'Sweet Pease' 607
Spivey, Victoria 321, 323, 607, 738, 748, 749, 773, 774, 794, 806, 820, 822, 826, 827
Spo-De-O-Dee Sam [Theard] 526
Spotts, Roger 506
Spriggs, Michael 358
Springs, Scat 402
Spruell, Freddie 608, 787, 801
Spruell, Leon 98
Spruill, Jimmy 74, 211, 237, 238, 306, 307, 472, 789, 807
Spruill, Stephanie 575
St Anthony 81
St Clair, Cyrus 381, 426, 587, 588

St Cyr, Johnny 98, 255, 322, 459, 549, 646
St James, Sylvia 535
St John, Barry 34, 372
St John, Powell 397, 550
St Judy [St Julian], Robert Peter 118, 119, 120, 418
St Julien, Gerard 87
St Julien Jr, Gerard 107, 489, 490
St Louis Bessie [Bessie Mae Smith] 337, 618, 619, 828
St Peter, Ed 614
St Peter, Mike 369
Stackhouse, Houston 600, 608, 802, 814, 822
Stacy, Jess 292, 328, 390
Staelens, Bruce 490, 491, 518
Staff, The 731
Stafford, Eugine 676
Stafford, Greg 25
Stafford, Jesse 832
Stahl, Matt 570
Stahlberg, David 695
Stahli, Freddie 531
Stahr, Stuart 151, 195
Stainton, Chris 122, 359
Stallings, Ron 52, 373, 562
Stamer, Hans 20
Stamford, Ozzie 166
Stamm, Marvin 679
Stamp, Florence 762
Stamps, Clarence 201, 677, 678, 713
Stancell, George 609
Stancil, Kevin 584
Stanfield, Lee 86, 416
Stanford, Jimmy 315
Stanley, Earl 365
Stanley, Warren 140
Stannard, Terry 34, 372
Stanton, G. 610
Stanton, Peaches 584
Stanzel, Candy 447
Staples, Donna 518
Staples, Mavis 22, 198, 430, 824
Staples, Roebuck 'Pop' 271, 349
Staple[s] Singers 790
Starboard, Jim 529, 566
Stargazers, The 702
Stark, Bobby 291, 292
Stark, Cootie 511, 609, 756, 757, 786
Starks, Artie 7, 255, 426, 459, 537, 549, 679
Starks, John 357
Starks, Tyrone 647, 721
Starks, Will 759, 762
Starnes, Spencer 502
Starr, Ringo 290, 356
Starr, Robert 469
Starr, Wes 21, 210, 434, 476
State Street Boys 769, 816
Staten, Peaches 691, 830
Stauber, Lauren 151
'Stavin' Chain' [Wilson Jones] 760

Stead, Arthur 50
Stearns, Kenny 400
Steckar, Marc 544
Steel, Ben 170
Steel, John 601
Steel, L. C. 787
Steel, Larry 457
Steele, Billy 375
Steele, Curtis 158, 711
Steele, Fred 4, 375
Steele, J. D. 4, 375
Steele, Javeeta 375
Steele, Ron 733
Steele, Willie 288, 289
Steen, David 468
Steen, Scott 146, 538, 719
Steen, Uffe 53
Steff, Rick 6, 657, 665
Stegman, Kim Gilmore 440
Steig, Jeremy 723
Steiger, Rick 479
Steiger, Stix 176
Steil, Andy 487
Stein, Harold 86
Stein, Mindy 191
Stelly, Kevin 384
Stennett, Pablo 556
Stephens, Andrew 481, 482
Stephens, James 766
Stephens, Jas 373
Stephens, Louis 78, 245, 321, 322, 364
Stephens, Stanley 176
Stephens, Tennyson 401
Stepney, Billie 95, 265, 404, 415, 417, 455, 456, 601
Stepney, Charles 233, 401, 481, 482
Sterling, Corey 575
Sterling, Harry 648
Sterling, Jeannie 506
Sterling, Mike 129
Stern, Kenneth 372
Stern, Tom 539
Stevens, Corey 104
Stevens, Dave 8, 223, 374
Stevens, Harry 592
Stevens, John 344
Stevens, Mark 560, 719
Stevens, Samuel Turner 756, 786
Stevens, Steve 587, 588
Stevens, Vol 450, 451, 692
Stevenson, George 670, 803, 805
Stevenson, John 392
Stevenson, Moe 612
Stevenson, Tommy 670
Stewart, Albert 'Tony' 395
Stewart, Alec 640
Stewart, Alonzo 114
Stewart, Billy 780
Stewart, Bob 623
Stewart, D. K. 564, 655
Stewart, Dan 807, 808
Stewart, Dave 143, 336, 564

Stewart, Didi 718
Stewart, Ian 53, 290, 652
Stewart, James 390, 754, 783
Stewart, Jimi 14, 673, 675
Stewart, John 112, 113
Stewart, Keith 711
Stewart, Leroy 233, 693, 694
Stewart, Mike 18, 183, 189, 389, 467, 536, 655
Stewart, Priscilla 610
Stewart, Rex 223, 224, 253, 437, 438, 460, 475
Stewart, Slam 663
Stewart, Teddy 315, 683
Stewart, Wayne 42, 121, 450, 681
Stewart, Winston 126, 349, 350
Stewart-Baxter, Derrick 73
Stick-Em', 'Frank [Terrance Sims] 194
Stidham, Arbee 456, 610, 776, 779, 781, 798
Stiernberg, Don 462
Stiff, Jerry 170
Stiles, Danny 679
Stills, Stephen 558
Stillwell, Corinne 580
Stitt, Sonny 63
Stock, David 'Rip' 233
Stockholm Slim [Per Notini] 418
Stocking, Annie 111, 612
Stokes 584
Stokes, Frank 610, 737, 767, 792, 794, 810, 811, 816
Stokes, Irving 583, 727
Stokes, Lowe 772
Stokes, Theopolis 759
Stoll, Donald 'J. J.' 328
Stoller, Alvin 145
Stoller, Mike 295, 662, 679
Stoltz, Brian 35, 503, 824, 825
Stone, Angie B. 87
Stone, Jesse 384, 510
Stone, Joe C. 317, 815
Stone, Kevin 431
Stone, Martin 264
Stonebridge, Lou 53
Stoneham, Luther 752, 819
[Stoop], Dimestore Fred 125
Storm, Warren 377, 394, 408, 555
Stough, Mike 395
Stout, Adrian 217
Stout, Eddie James 552, 553, 721
Stovall, Babe 611, 764, 788
Stovall, Don 245, 315, 326, 327, 328, 526
Stovepipe No. 1 611
Stover, John 341
Stover, Smokey 390
Stowers, Freeman 769, 811
Straine, 'Doc' 718
Strange, Dobie 239, 399
Strange, Jimmy 248, 796, 815
Strange, Kurt 503
Strasser, Michael 176, 177, 217, 515, 528

Stratham, Henry 227
Stratton, Jeff 199
Strauss, Johnnie 618, 815
Strauss, Kai 220
Strazza, Peter 52
Street, John 210, 433, 489
Streeter, La Dee 507
Streets, William 520
Streetser, William 447
Strehli, Angela 21, 194, 486, 612, 667, 669, 673, 676, 830
Strentz, Chad 374
Strickland, Calvin 315
Strickland, Leon 764
Strickland, Napoleon 251, 759, 765, 766, 802, 810, 814
Strickland, Paul 612
Strickland, Tony 485
Strifler, Volker 198, 199
Strike, Liza 34, 372
Stringer, Larry 87
Stripling, Sidney 760
Stripling Brothers 772
Strittmatter, Daniel 231, 374
Stroger, Bob 30, 36, 67, 97, 101, 125, 151, 163, 204, 293, 458, 470, 476, 479, 488, 515, 516, 532, 533, 539, 563, 567, 598, 606, 612, 617, 630, 687, 697, 698
Stroh, Tim 305
Strong, Jimmy 607
Strother, Percy 464, 612
Strothers, Jimmie 757, 758, 759, 760, 761, 812
Stroud, Ben 227
Stroud, Linard 613
Stroud, Peter 44, 228
Struck, Nolan 35, 744
Strzelecki, Henry 'South Pole' 458
'Stu' 656
Stuart, Alice 613
Stuart, Charles 570
Stuart, Marty 359, 488
Stuart, W. D. 761, 762
Stubblefield, Brownie 794, 809
Stubblefield, John C. 498
Stubbs, George 238, 363, 365, 369
Stuckey, Jacob 766
Studd, Tony 679
Studebaker John 185, 581, 613, 622, 746, 779
Studholme, Richard 10, 30, 32, 37, 81, 87, 190, 411, 427, 555, 614, 768
Studt, Richard 175
Stupka, Robb 4, 6, 7, 127, 211, 222, 375, 414, 464, 499, 529, 599, 600, 612
Sturgis, Rodney 338
Sturgis, Ted 415
Stutso, Mark 35, 644
Stuve, Bill 123, 262, 417, 522, 557, 594
Sublett, Joe 11, 26, 235, 359, 430, 431, 468, 469, 518, 547, 563, 624, 625, 629, 668, 669, 691

Sucher, Herb 335
Sudduth, Rob 293, 399, 496, 497, 540, 729
Sue & Sunny 34
Sueref, Little George 38, 513, 613
Sugar & Sweet 783
'Sugar Bear' 551
Sugar Blue 68, 125, 135, 411, 443, 445, 474, 569, 578, 614, 621, 633, 771, 776, 823
Sugarman, The 819
Suggs, Doug 808
Suhler, Jim 433, 476, 768, 814
Suhr, John 161
Sulieman, Rajab 625
Sullivan, Gene 772
Sullivan, Joe 661, 662
Sullivan, Stuart 200
Sultan, Kenny 21
Sultans, The 774
Sulzmann, Stan 457
Sumlin, Hubert 30, 37, 38, 41, 57, 67, 139, 164, 256, 289, 290, 323, 375, 400, 416, 423, 427, 480, 495, 515, 516, 542, 573, 581, 601, 614, 616, 617, 630, 729, 735, 748, 749, 768, 771, 824
Summer, Mark 145
Summerour, Jay 715
Summers, Bill 624
Summers, Bobby 392
Summers, Joseph 112
Summitt, Ted 500, 618, 619, 620, 716
Sunda, Bob 695
Sundy, Amar 37, 177, 615
Sunnyland Slim 66, 79, 121, 151, 183, 188, 201, 217, 263, 289, 290, 299, 335, 386, 387, 403, 406, 453, 467, 480, 481, 493, 500, 532, 562, 576, 577, 601, 614, 615, 630, 692, 740, 743, 744, 745, 748, 749, 764, 778, 779, 780, 781, 782, 785, 787, 797, 809
Sunseri, Joe 'Champagnski' 78
Sunshine, Monty 641
Sunshine Boys 772
Super Chikan 618
Surman, John 372
Suso, Jali Nyama 811
Sutter, Charles 438
Sutter, Steve 730
Suttle, Dave 344
Sutton, Emmett 125, 323, 415
Sutton, Jimmy 598
Sutton, Linwood 583
Sutton, Musa 664
Sutton, Ralph 255, 381
Sutton, Roger 217
Sutton, Ron 4, 5
Sutton, Stella 34
Sutyak, Gerri 343
'Suzie' 154
Suzuki, Hiromasa 127
Svafnisson, Svenni 96, 242

INDEX

Swain, Bruce 499, 553
Swain, Leonard 63, 416, 459, 670, 671
Swain, Wilson 172, 173
Swallows, The 773, 774, 799
Swan, Frank 266, 284
Swan & Lee 774
Swan Silvertones, The 788, 790
Swancy, Doug 61
Swank, Ken 272, 273, 274
Swann, Dianne 507
Swanstrom, Liska L. 96
Swartz, Bill 557, 594
Swartz, Brian 191
Swartz, Harvie 156
Sweat, I. P. 722
Sweeney, Ted 61
Sweet, Dave 400
Sweet Betty 618
Sweet Inspirations, The 679
Sweet Papa Stovepipe 787
Sweet Papa Tadpole 626
Swift, Joe 504, 798, 826
Swift Jewel Cowboys 772
Swindell, Bill 244
Swinney, Ted 213
Switchmasters, The 751
Sykes, Essie 744
Sykes, Forrest 779, 780
Sykes, Isabel 618, 774
Sykes, John Derrick 'J. D.' 612
Sykes, Roosevelt 16, 66, 71, 79, 158, 216, 218, 226, 315, 317, 321, 325, 443, 453, 458, 493, 500, 618, 655, 680, 682, 738, 739, 740, 742, 743, 744, 748, 749, 752, 773, 774, 779, 781, 787, 788, 790, 794, 797, 798, 803, 804, 808, 809, 815
Sylar, Robin 433, 820
Sylvester, Elmore 446
Sylvester, Paul 760
Sylvester, Robin 558
Sylvestor Mike 826
Synigal, Eddie 'Saxman' 164, 210, 358, 440
Sypher, Jason 365
Szelest, Stan 669
Szymczyk, Bill 273, 355, 356
T., Bryant 131
T., Glenny 559
T, Marc 425
T.C.I. Section Crew 795
T-Lou & L.A. Zydeco Band 831
T.V. Slim 622, 780, 800
Taggart, Blind Joe 810
Tail Dragger 554, 622, 744, 746, 781
Taildraggers, The 751
Taj Mahal 37, 50, 104, 246, 257, 260, 476, 486, 511, 558, 609, 622, 737, 751, 779, 812, 814, 823, 824, 825
Takagi, Yuji 169
Talbert, Wayne 138
Talbot, Steve 442
Taliefero, Crystal 431

Tallahassee Tight 626
Talley, Arlene 800
Tallman, 'Slide' 368
Tally, Lem 504
Tally, Thomas 343
Tam, Charmaine 580
Tamaleir, Jeff 111
'Tampa Joe' 287, 754
Tampa Kid [Charlie McCoy] 812, 814
Tampa Red 2, 38, 39, 55, 150, 167, 255, 303, 311, 317, 320, 325, 537, 607, 609, 610, 626, 645, 692, 716, 737, 738, 739, 741, 742, 743, 744, 755, 767, 768, 773, 774, 797, 807, 809, 812, 813, 814
Tana, Akira 84
Tangle Eye [Walter Jackson] 761, 762
Tangle Eye [Henry Wallace] 812
Tannehill, Frank 795
Tanner, Ernest 'Lee' 650, 670
Tanner, Gid 792
Tanner, Johnny 25
Tanner, Robert 383
Tarbell, Matt 87
Tarbell, Morris 87
Tarbox Ramblers 788
Tarczy, Endre 14
Tardy, Greg 648
Tarheel Slim [Alden Bunn] 755, 800, 806, 807
Tarlton, Jimmie 772, 810, 811, 813
Tarpley, Sam 'Slim' 150, 190
Tarrant, Jesse 'Rip' 670
Tarrant, Jimmy 681
Tarrant, Rabon 244, 252, 449, 450, 472, 661, 662, 677, 678
Tarrant, Rip 670
Tartarsky, Eli 356
Tarter & Gay 738, 755, 765, 767
Tarto, Joe 685
Tartt, Sim 760
Tarver, Leon D. 780
Tasby, Finis 146, 194, 422, 628
Taskiana Four 793
Tate, Baby 514, 629, 756
Tate, Billy 803
Tate, Bob 594
Tate, Buddy 142, 654, 670, 671, 724, 730
Tate, C. W. 400
Tate, Cornelius 245, 670, 671
Tate, Harry 685, 707
Tate, Laurie 477, 800
Tate, Paul 543, 650
Tate, Tommy 257, 393
Tate County Singers 199, 498
Tatterson, Buster Wylie 98
Tatum, Art 661, 741, 808
Taucher, Pietro 714
Tauzier, Sean 580
Taylor, Alfred 315
Taylor, Archie 341
Taylor, Augustus 68
Taylor, Betty 805

Taylor, Billy 83, 84, 86, 142, 526, 565, 587, 588, 661, 662, 671
Taylor, Bird 324, 636, 718
Taylor, Bradbury 84
Taylor, Briant 656
Taylor, Buck 324, 636, 718
Taylor, Carmen 777
Taylor, Cassie 634
Taylor, Charles 222, 288
Taylor, Charley 62, 330, 740, 741, 803, 808
Taylor, Good Time Charlie 784
Taylor, Clarence 'Tweety' 384
Taylor, Dallas 694
Taylor, Danny 774, 806
Taylor, David 540, 576
Taylor, Dennis 78, 79, 87, 126, 335, 496, 549
Taylor, Donna 624
Taylor, Eddie 1, 30, 66, 67, 180, 228, 266, 269, 272, 273, 275, 284, 295, 305, 306, 307, 335, 345, 366, 412, 416, 463, 474, 532, 541, 542, 599, 617, 621, 629, 635, 730, 744, 749, 765, 767, 790, 814
Taylor, Edna 758
Taylor, Edward 630, 635
Taylor, Eva 426
Taylor, F. 521
Taylor, Floyd 472, 713
Taylor, Frank 201
Taylor, Gene 169, 170, 191, 194, 201, 238, 241, 341, 377, 431, 434, 487, 501, 529, 533, 538, 630, 687
Taylor, George 518
Taylor, Greg 'Fingers' 151, 377, 401, 501
Taylor, Harold 'Dink' 219
Taylor, Henry 455, 654
Taylor, Hound Dog 263, 519, 630, 744, 745, 749, 776, 778, 779, 780, 800, 813, 814
Taylor, Jaisson 143
Taylor, James 267
Taylor, Jasper 142, 294, 301, 311, 597, 626
Taylor, Jeff 101, 125, 330, 541, 706
Taylor, Jesse 21
Taylor, John 173
Taylor, Johnnie 789
Taylor, Johnny 90
Taylor, Little Johnny 776, 782, 784, 797
Taylor, Jude 'Curley' 161, 582, 832
Taylor, Julian 32
Taylor, Kenny 721
Taylor, Kevin 296, 297
Taylor, Koko 68, 139, 358, 415, 631, 744, 745, 749, 750, 776, 779, 780, 790, 827
Taylor, Larry 47, 91, 92, 103, 104, 239, 261, 274, 342, 350, 414, 429, 474, 487, 488, 519, 522, 538, 540, 629, 630, 635, 719, 720, 746
Taylor, Lawrence 400, 401
Taylor, Lonnie 233, 604
Taylor, Louis 660

Taylor, Luther 550, 712
Taylor, Mad Man 777
Taylor, Malcolm 438
Taylor, Marcia Ann 52
Taylor, Mary 518, 609, 649
Taylor, Matt 20
Taylor, Melvin 91, 443, 518, 573, 633, 745
Taylor, Michael 366
Taylor, Mick 152, 175, 427, 428, 429, 430, 431, 629, 824
Taylor, Mighty Mick 45
Taylor, Montana 320, 634, 737, 739, 740, 741, 808
Taylor, King Mose 306, 307, 489
Taylor, Otis 634, 739
Taylor, Paul 'Snowflake' 498
Taylor, Peggy 150
Taylor, Phil 344
Taylor, Prince 81
Taylor, Rev. R. H. 821
Taylor, Raymond 724
Taylor, Regina 624
Taylor, Robert 686
Taylor, Robert 'Dudlow' 753
Taylor, Sam 'The Man' 39, 40, 81, 84, 295, 300, 340, 459, 662, 670, 800
Taylor, Samuel 275
Taylor, Terry 25, 694
Taylor, Timothy (Tim) 32, 57, 64, 66, 156, 181, 345, 405, 420, 474, 515, 519, 527, 541, 557, 573, 574, 581, 599, 614, 630, 635, 675, 697
Taylor, Tom 7
Taylor, Tommy 11, 168, 680
Taylor, Vera 630, 635
Taylor, Vernal 421, 695
Taylor, Walter 635, 793
Taylor, 'Big Road' Webster 801
Taylor, Wanderin' Wilf 45
Taylor, Yack 338, 526, 806, 828
Taylor Jr, Eddie 172, 181, 746
Taylor Jr, Luther B. 712
Taylor Jr, Robert C. 572
Taylor's Kentucky Boys 810, 811, 816
Teagarden, Jack 328, 587, 588
Teague, Burt 236, 540
Teague, Cordell 474
Teague, James F. 584
Teardrops, The 745, 779
Teboe, Dana 257
Tedeschi, Susan 168, 402, 516, 635, 691, 751, 825
Tedesco, Chris 342
Tedrow, Lee 161
'Tee' 187
Tee, Richard 727
Teel, Mark 52
Teela 443
Teen Queens, The 786
Teixeira, Mark 549
Temple, Brannen 361
Temple, Johnnie 636, 742, 774, 801, 820

Templeton, Brian 525, 536
Tempo, James Michael 'Bonedaddy' 241
Tempo, Michael 408
Tench, Benmont 198
Tench, Bobby 364
Tennessee Chocolate Drops 810, 816
Tenuto, Don 42, 121, 450, 723
Terkel, Studs 73
Terrell, J. H. 762
Terrell, J. K. 406
Terrell, Sister O. M. 812, 813, 820
Terricciano, Lou 578
Terry & Brownie McGhee, Sonny 639, 737, 738, 747, 748, 749, 760, 762, 788
Terry & Jordan Webb, Sonny 795, 806
Terry, Andrew 'Mike' 269, 271, 681
Terry, Clark 115, 670, 683, 694
Terry, Cooper 710
Terry, Dave 558
Terry, Doc 705
Terry, George 364
Terry, Joe 64
Terry, Kenneth 'Skin' 395
Terry, Nat 752, 819
Terry, Patrick 'Heavy P' 395
Terry, Sonny 88, 141, 154, 173, 206, 266, 278, 279, 281, 283, 378, 379, 380, 381, 382, 444, 445, 446, 478, 570, 637, 701, 702, 708, 709, 710, 717, 738, 739, 747, 752, 755, 756, 758, 759, 762, 769, 771, 776, 797, 800, 806, 807, 823
Terry, Sonny Boy 291
Terry, William 87
Terson, Hank 590
Terson, Harlan 32, 57, 67, 141, 192, 204, 405, 462, 553, 567, 573, 606, 607, 707
Tervalon, Ralph 551
Tervalone, Clement 82, 140, 315
Terwilliger, Darrel 726
Tex, Joe 780, 789
Texacali Horns, The 563
Texas Eastside Kings 643
Texas Prison Camp Work Gang 811
Texas Slim 433
Texas Tonies, The 372
Texas Wanderers 773
Thacker, Jim 370
Thackery, Jimmy 35, 127, 238, 373, 470, 494, 583, 644, 779, 824
Thain, Gary 175
Tharpe, Sister Rosetta 739, 747, 797, 798, 821, 827
Theaker, Guy 228
Theard, Sam 16, 150, 526, 645, 743, 773
Theesink, Hans 37, 132, 217
'Thelma' 680
Themen, Art 371, 372
Theriot, Shane 97
Therrien, Doug 34
Theurer, Bill 583
Theus, Fats 509
Thibadeaux, R. B. 819

Thibodeau, Curtis 533
Thibodeaux, Carroll 649
Thibodeaux, Elton 377
Thibodeaux, Merton 377
Thibodeaux, Rufus 258, 377, 394, 408
Thibodeaux, Waylon 554, 566
Thiboutot, Darren 265, 370, 491
Thiele, Bob 272, 355
Thigpen, Ben 537
Thigpen, Ed 266, 416, 671
Thijs, Marc 17, 414, 464
Thoelke III, Bradford Henry 429
Thoennes, Pete 130
Thom, Jenny 375
Thomas, Little Al 645
Thomas, Alex 398, 713, 785
Thomas, Alfred 357
Thomas, Andy 752, 819
Thomas, Arnold 338, 340
Thomas, Barry 571
Thomas, Blanche 829
Thomas, Bobo 600, 752, 753, 774
Thomas, Broadway 506
Thomas, Carlton 'Guitar' 117
Thomas, Charles 707
Thomas, Charlie 405, 724
Thomas', 'Big Charlie 426
Thomas, Chris 721
Thomas, Chuck 209, 594
Thomas, Cicero 150
Thomas, Cornelius 173
Thomas, Danny 282
Thomas, Demetric 203
Thomas, Dion 618
Thomas, Earl 342, 349, 350, 808
Thomas, Eddie 521, 758
Thomas, Ella 829
Thomas, Elmer Lee 446
Thomas, Elvie 787, 793, 794, 801
Thomas, Eric 576
Thomas, Erroll 350
Thomas, F. T. 226
Thomas, Frantic Faye 829
Thomas', 'George 322
Thomas, Gordon 315
Thomas, Greg 623
Thomas, Harvell 618
Thomas, Henry 190, 645, 739, 767, 794, 795, 810, 811, 817
Thomas', 'Henry [Lazy Lester] 598
Thomas, Hersal 646, 679, 739, 740, 742
Thomas, Hociel 645
Thomas, Ian 360
Thomas, Irma 180, 358, 439, 780, 788, 803, 804, 806, 827, 830
Thomas, James [b] 623
Thomas, James [bj] 469
Thomas, James 'Broadway' 675, 676
Thomas, James 'Doc' 392
Thomas, James H. 83
Thomas, James 'Son' 646, 750, 766
Thomas, Jeff 450

Thomas, Jesse 219, 647, 658, 737, 738, 753, 782, 787, 788, 817, 819, 826
Thomas, Jimmy 614
Thomas, Joe 44, 140, 146, 275, 584, 654, 661, 684, 800
Thomas, Joey 800
Thomas, John 68, 83, 364
Thomas, John Lee 760
Thomas, Jon 63
Thomas, Josh 765
Thomas, K. O. 364
Thomas, Kid 647, 783
Thomas, Lafayette 438, 439, 456, 457, 467, 481, 482, 719, 800
Thomas, Lee Andres 531
Thomas, Leo 831
Thomas, Martha 764
Thomas, Marvell 210, 349, 350, 401
Thomas, Mattie May 758, 793
Thomas, Michael 23, 465
Thomas, Millard G. 808
Thomas, Milt 209
Thomas, Milton 675
Thomas, P. F. 620
Thomas, Paul 87, 136, 226, 411
Thomas, Pee Wee 210, 440
Thomas, Percy 479, 480
Thomas, Pete 217, 218, 236, 728
Thomas, Philip 233, 543, 650
Thomas, Prezs 223
Thomas, Ramblin' 181, 648, 767, 797, 803, 812, 813, 817
Thomas, Raymond 56, 187, 221
Thomas, Richard 'Mr Bones' 181, 546
Thomas, Rob 112, 113
Thomas, Robert 'Town Crier' 377
Thomas, Roberta 41, 109, 330, 567, 681, 735
Thomas, Rufus 262, 751, 780, 789, 799
Thomas, Sharde Evans 243, 664
Thomas, Sherman 119, 555
Thomas, Sidney 30
Thomas, Spencer 61
Thomas, Tabby 34, 265, 361, 648, 783, 791
Thomas, Tasha 356
Thomas, Terence 556
Thomas, Victor 83
Thomas, Willie 764, 777, 810
Thomas 251
Thompkins, Jim 801, 813
Thompson, Aaron 294, 325, 679
Thompson, Al 415
Thompson, Anthony 'Pack Rat' 544
Thompson, Ashley 105, 764
Thompson, Bill 43
Thompson, Bruce 171
Thompson, Butch 649
Thompson, Charles 520
Thompson, Sir Charles 245, 300, 446, 592, 610, 741, 742
Thompson, Chester 135, 274

Thompson, Christine 688
Thompson, D. Clinton 64
Thompson, Danny 371, 372
Thompson, Lil' Dave 649
Thompson, Dickie 773
Thompson, Edward 737, 787
Thompson, Emery 531, 711
Thompson, Ernest 291, 292
Thompson, Harvey 135, 257, 401, 402
Thompson, Henry Ford 766
Thompson, Howard 245
Thompson, Iain 344
Thompson, Joe 649, 812
Thompson, Junior 786
Thompson, Larry 485
Thompson, Lena 765
Thompson, Lucky 252, 527, 583, 683, 800
Thompson, Mac 77, 95, 125, 140, 160, 180, 417, 418, 746
Thompson, Malachi 345, 591
Thompson, Michael 417, 556
Thompson, Michelle 171
Thompson, Nate 650
Thompson, Odell 650, 812
Thompson, Pete 37
Thompson, Robert L. 665
Thompson', 'Rocky [Goree Carter] 819
Thompson, Ron 168, 264, 274, 275, 433, 439, 544, 654
Thompson, Rudolph 248
Thompson, Scott 49, 61, 68, 90, 126, 131, 144, 246, 366, 522, 524, 572, 633, 657, 660, 711, 721
Thompson, 'Slow Kid' 685
Thompson, Sonny 125, 159, 160, 209, 245, 287, 323, 363, 365, 401, 543, 650, 711, 740, 785, 798, 800
Thompson, Stephen 457, 458
Thompson, Steve 428, 429, 430
Thompson, Suzy 486
Thompson, Tommy 812
Thompson, Tommy Lee 489
Thompson, Voneta 1
Thompson, Wilbur 348, 350
Thompson, William 765
Thompson Sr, Bruce 681
Thompson-Rodgers, Gloria 698
Thoms, Peter 53
Thomson, Mike 113
Thorn, Mike 427
Thornburg, Lee 1, 21, 87, 191, 198, 220, 307, 556
Thornbury, James 104
Thorne, Mike 10
Thorne, Spencer 49
Thorneycroft, Steve 614
Thornton, Big Mama 62, 286, 505, 651, 738, 748, 749, 773, 777, 784, 799, 800, 818, 820, 827, 829
Thornton, Clarence 724
Thornton, Gus 351, 669, 691
Thornton, Guy 669

Thornton, John M. 423
Thornton, Margaret 828
Thornton, Norman 416
Thorogood, George 274, 275, 652, 768, 788, 814, 825
Thorpe, Bruce 123
Thorpe, Kevin 370
Thorson, Jim 273
Thorsteinsson, Haroldyr 515
Thorton, Gus [Thornton] 319
Thorup, Peter 372
Thrasher, Sybel 20
Thrasher, Virgil 412
Threadgill, Henry 518
Threats, Willis 219
Three Dots & A Dash 447
Three Fifteen & His Squares 796
Three Stripped Gears 774
Three Tobacco Tags 772
Three Tons Of Joy 506
Thurman, Bob 267, 268, 269
Thurmond, David 559
Thurston, L. C. 234
Thyam Si Griots 810
Tibbs, Andrew 653, 779, 780, 821
Tibbs, Leroy 718
Tibbs Brothers, The 777
Tico, Randy 22
Tidbury, Alan 74
Tidbury, Nick 74
Tidwell, Harold 265
Tidwell II, George 521
Tiffault, Mark 18, 87, 368, 370, 385, 386
Tig, Jimmy 786
Tigner, Eddie 654, 757
Tilbrook, Adrian 372
Tildesley, Bob 20
Tilford, Hooks 537
Tillery, Calvin 263
Tillery, Linda 37
Tillis, Big Son 782, 819, 826
Tillis, Pam 549
Tillis, Perry 764
Tillman, Curtis 209, 286, 364, 593, 594, 651
Tillman, Jimmy 165, 533, 542
Tillman, Joe 114, 115, 231, 232
Tillman, Julia 48, 210, 351, 357
Tillman, Lee 805
Tilters, The 777
Timmons, Terry 455, 654
Tindall, Tim 517
Tingle, Lisa 21
Tini Jr, Ray 350
Tinney, Pee Wee 459
Tinsley, John 752, 755, 765
Tio Jr, Lorenzo 42
Tippin, Dave 760
Tischlitz, Henri 458
Tisdall, Beatrice 758
Tisdom, James 769, 819, 826
Titcomb, Gordon 50

Titré, Mike 249
Titwell, Robert 67
Tiven, Jon 318, 402
Tiven, Richard 578
Tiven, Sally 318, 402
Tjelios, Nik 582
'Todd' 383
Todd, Arkansas Johnny 753
Todd, Oliver 384
Todorovic, Todor 'Toscho' 74, 249
Tolbert, Kai 21
Toles, Michael 130, 210, 349, 350, 358, 401, 402, 468
Tolfree, Larry 228
Toliver, Jimmy 662
Tomassie, Big John E. 364
Tomlin, Kingfish Bill 741, 809
Tomlinson, Beth 21
Toney, Eli 686
Toney, James Sells 357, 358, 359
'Tony' 265
Too Bad Boys 787, 812
Too Slim & The Taildraggers 751, 654
Too Tight Henry [Henry L. Castle] 795, 810
Tookes, Darryl 666
Tooley, Ron 235
Tooms, Robert 'Nighthawk' 49, 476
'Tootsie' 791
Topanga Dick 408
Topham, Anthony 'Top' 33, 34, 237, 513
Topp, Mark 216
Toppers, The 391
Torbenson, Ron 100
Torey, George 767, 792
Torkanowsky, David 215, 325, 362, 395, 503, 583, 688, 695
Tornados, The 780
Torosian, Dan 21
Torrence, Bubba Lee 149
Torrence, Lionel 377, 648, 791
Torres, Bobby 43
Torsch, Don 4
Torstenson, Mark 609
Tortoise Blue 341
Tossing, Ed 733
Touchy, John 78, 84
Tounkara, Djelimady 37
Toups, Wayne 21, 831, 832
Touré, Ali Farka 243, 810
Toussaint, Allen 166, 351, 368, 391, 392, 429, 472, 531, 558, 582, 803, 804, 806
Toussaint, Joe 77, 438
Towel, Jim 150
'Tower Of Sour' 498
Townend, James 398
Townes, Efrem 87
Townes, Willie 171
Townley, John 155
Townsel, Rev. G. I. 762
Townsend, Al 295, 670, 671
Townsend, Angel 703

Townsend, Bros 728
Townsend, Henry 100, 158, 159, 493, 605, 618, 620, 655, 708, 787, 808, 815, 822
Townsend, Joe 764
Townsend, Rob 53
Townsend, Sam 792
Townsend, Vernell 655, 656
Townson, Terry 78
Toyfl, Markus 176
Tracey, Stan 726
Tracy, 'Dad' 708
Tracy, Jeanie 111
Tracy, Steve 177
Trahan, Pee Wee 377
Trahan, Willie 555
Trainor, Jack 291, 677, 678
Tranor, John 'Mambo' 21, 68, 612, 676
Trapp, James 657
Trappier, Arthur 701, 702
Traum, Artie 50
Trauner, Erik 132, 176, 217
Travis, Merle 772, 773, 778, 798
Treadwell, George 459, 670, 685
Treanor, Dan 656
Treat Her Right 771
Trecarten, Steve 341
Tremblay, Kevin 569
Trenier, Claude 731
Treniers, The 799, 800
Trepagnier Jr, Albert 241
Tressler, Randy 606
Tribble, TNT 660
Tribuno, Diane 52
Trice, 'Big' John 396
Trice, Richard 756, 806
Trice, Welly 756
Tricky Sam 758
Trigg, Steve 65, 425
Trimble, Pat 721
Tring', 'Wallace [Gary Thain] 175
'Tripple Horn' 541
Trisko, Bo 528
Tritt, Travis 235
Troiani, William 369
Trolsen, Rick 179, 362
Tropea, John 679
Trotman, Lloyd 40, 81, 84, 114, 115, 140, 173, 295, 300, 416, 457, 650, 663
Trout, Jimbo 526
Trout, Walter 104, 397, 430, 657, 823, 824
Trowbridge, Doretha 317, 605, 815, 828
Troxel, Jimmie 572
Troy, Roger 52
Troyer, Breta 556
Trozell, Mark 229
Trucks, Derek 153, 186, 633, 695
Trumfio, Dave 'Thick Soul' 185
Truso, Leonore 583
Truso, Shiela 583, 584
Trussell, Heather 498
Truvillion, Henry 757, 758, 759

Tschudin, Michael 138
Tsushida, Harunobu (Hal) 479
TT, Rev. Frank 132
Tuba Fats' Chosen Few Brass Band 806
Tubb, Ernest 772
Tucker, Aaron 408, 659, 675, 676
Tucker, Allison 110, 647, 711
Tucker, Alonzo 39, 245
Tucker, Bessie 658, 740, 793, 797, 818, 826, 828
Tucker, Calvin 'Kadakie' 171
Tucker, David 14
Tucker, Eddie 688
Tucker, George 726
Tucker, Johnny 629, 675
Tucker, Luther 43, 138, 139, 199, 272, 273, 403, 480, 481, 515, 544, 557, 562, 601, 658
Tucker, Ricky 133
Tucker, Sophie 827
Tucker, Tommy 332, 410, 433, 444, 658, 779, 780
Tucker & Thomas 659
Tufo, Margo 751
Tuggle, Bobby Lee 521, 780
Tukes, Leroy 521
Tukey, Jack 515
Tulio, Jim 425
Tullos, Terry 21, 78
Tuneweavers, The 780
Tunnoch, Omar 582
Turbans, The 799
Turbinton, Earl 176, 210, 356
Turbinton, Willie Tee 210, 362, 803, 805
Turenne, Mike 195
Turk, John 111, 273, 439, 583
Turk III, John 583
Turmes, Jeff 'Big Dad' 40, 95, 146, 191, 194, 240, 241, 262, 414, 417, 538
Turner, Aaron 318
Turner, Ada 759
Turner, Alaneda 759
Turner, Andrew 'Shine' 163
Turner, Annie 467, 803
Turner, Annie Mae [Tina] 659, 660
Turner, Archie 365, 366, 571
Turner, Aubrey 243, 499, 664
Turner, Baby Face 753
Turner, Bee 618
Turner, Ben 110, 243, 258, 276, 277, 278, 282
Turner, Benny 363, 364, 458, 730, 731, 733
Turner, Bert 315
Turner, Blind Squire [Teddy Darby] 774, 815
Turner, Bobby 363
Turner, Bonnie 659, 660
Turner, Bruce 73
Turner, Charlie 659
Turner, Christopher 175, 564
Turner, Count 551
Turner, Eddie 634, 659

Turner, Henry 338, 661
Turner, Ike 232, 266, 275, 288, 289, 305, 307, 348, 352, 353, 354, 400, 562, 659, 776, 786, 789, 802, 827
Turner, J. V. 434, 601
Turner, Jackie 241
Turner, Jeannette 660
Turner, Jimmy 267, 269, 270
Turner, (Big) Joe 8, 245, 326, 327, 328, 390, 505, 506, 560, 661, 721, 737, 738, 739, 740, 741, 744, 747, 749, 777, 797, 798, 799, 800, 804, 806, 808, 814, 826
Turner, Joe [b] 77, 350, 401
Turner, Uncle John 'Red' 476, 722, 723
Turner, Johnny 15, 659, 664
Turner, Lara 634
Turner, Lemuel 772, 813, 821
Turner, Lonnie 350
Turner, Mae 759
Turner, Merle 219
Turner, Mike 113, 538
Turner, Milton 115
Turner, Nate 664
Turner, Odelle 777
Turner, Odie 527
Turner, Othar 498, 664, 759, 765, 766, 802, 810
Turner, Sharde [Thomas] 251
Turner, Sonny 233, 295
Turner, Tim 341
Turner, Tina 660, 786, 789, 802, 827
Turner, Twist 172, 185, 346, 552, 581, 622
Turnham, Floyd 354, 392, 405, 432, 504, 505, 520, 677, 725
Turre, Michael 507
Turrentine, Stanley 114
Turtle Island String Quartet 145
Tussing, Ken 427, 628
Tutot, Matt 633
TV Slim 787
Twillie, Carmen 357, 417
Twine, Howard 765
Twitty/Little Bill, John D. 796
Two Charlies, The 792
Two Of Spades, The 774
Two Poor Boys [Joe Evans & Arthur McClain] 793
Two Roys, The 255
Tyee Montessori Elementary School Choir 20
Tyler, Alvin 'Red' 21, 26, 58, 59, 75, 78, 166, 176, 207, 210, 232, 391, 529, 622
Tyler, Johnny 798
Tyler, Mike 624
Tyler, Ola Marie 623
Tyler, Roy 111
Tyler, Steven 376
Tyler, T. Texas 772, 798
Tyler, William A. 685, 718
Tyler Jr, Clyde 'Youngblood' 632
Tyree, John Lawson 812
Tyrell, Eric 249

Tyrell, Soozie 239
Tyson, Willie 219
'Uganda' [Alfred Roberts] 530, 531
Ugartechea, Bryan 342
Uhler, Chris 136, 685
Ulander, Pa 319
Uldricks, Chris 22
Ulmer, James Blood 665
'Uncle Ben' 330, 754
Underhill, Richard 687
Underwood, George 643
Underwood, Jeep 517
Underwood, Little Melvin 787
Underwood, Pete 219
Underwood, Sugar 808
Ungar, Jay 546, 578
Union Boys, The 701, 702
Unsworth, Bruce 690
Upchurch, Phil 47, 233, 272, 273, 290, 401, 482, 541, 542, 674, 711, 789
Upchurch, William 351
Uptown Horns, The 612
Uribe, John 356
Urquhart, Andy 424
Ursery, Joe 686
Usher, Frederick A. 334
Utah, Candy 405, 447
Utley, Mike 484, 694
Utstein, Steve 342
Utsunomiya, Motoyasu 643
Utterback, Sam 384
Utting, Steve 695
Uzilevsky, Danny 526
Vachon, Chris 560
Vagabonds, The 455
Vaharandes, Emmanuel 'Gaucho' 504, 505
Val & Pete 772
Valdez, Miguelito 505
Valdina, Eric 50
Valdina, Jordan Block 2, 51
Valdiviez, Lupe 107
Valentine, Cal 43
Valentine, Calvin 261
Valentine, Donald 261
Valentine, Gerald 245
Valentine, Hilton 601
Valentine, Joe 805
Valentine, Jr 414
Valentinos, The 780
Valvassori, Leo 464, 533
Vamvakaris, Stelios 411
Van Cleave, Virgil 685
Van Dyke, David 245, 315, 654, 800
Van Hook, Peter 671
Van Lake, Turk 671
Van Riper, Earl 670, 671
Van Ronk, Dave 665, 747, 823, 825
Van Sickle, Hank 431
Van Walls, Harry 84, 446, 662, 717
Vance, Dick 140, 473, 592, 654, 662
Vance, Terry 344

Vandellas', 'The 271
Vanderveer, Ed 446
Vangel, Ken 133, 134, 563, 669
Vann, Larry 43, 44
Vannice, Mike 143
Vanston, C. J. 359
Vantrease, Ernest 408, 427
Vappie, Don 751, 806
Varco, Vince 57, 109, 129, 346
Varela, Sam 583, 584
Varela Jr, Sam 583
Variames, Andrea/Andrew 131
Varnardo, James 571
Vasey, Jane 169, 170
Vasilatos, Jerry 517
Vaughan, Calvin 460
Vaughan, Jimmie 26, 139, 148, 168, 190, 191, 274, 359, 377, 435, 548, 564, 666, 667, 668, 669
Vaughan, Julian 91, 133
Vaughan, Stevie Ray 21, 133, 351, 541, 666, 737, 768, 776, 818
Vaughan, Tyrone 666
Vaughn, Art 'Thunder' 570
Vaughn, Christie 185
Vaughn, Cooney 225
Vaughn, Jake 583
Vaughn, James 348
Vaughn, Jimmy 675
Vaughn, Julian 158, 541, 563, 591, 669
Vaughn, Maurice John 158, 163, 234, 330, 541, 591, 669, 745, 747, 776
Vaughn, Ola 784
Vaughn, Yashika 168
Vaught, Julien 433, 563
Vdelli, Michael 260
Veasie, Joseph 554, 582
Veasley, Ebbie 763
Veazie, Melvin 87, 554
Vee, Cookie 55
Vee, Joey 342
Vee, Mike 565
Veeder, Larry 269, 271
Vegas, H-Bomb 599
Veley, Alex 153
Velez Jr, Vincent 256
Velzen, Bas van 101
Venson, Coot 770
Ventittelli, Joey 399
Ventura, Alvee 676
Verbeke, Patrick 6
Verdine, Garfield 78, 79
Verges Jr, Jerome S. 472
Verginio, Greg 124
Vermeij, Dirk 152
Vernable, Michael 648
Verner, Henning 242
Vernon, Mike 34, 38, 65, 74, 97, 175, 217, 364, 528, 685, 728
Verplanck, Billy 81
Verploegen, Angelo 101
Verrell, Ronnie 174

Verrett, Harrison 166, 167
Vert, Frank 68, 676
Vescovo, Al 551
Vestine, Henry 77, 103, 104, 273, 274, 458
Viau, Johnny/Jonny 55, 60, 123, 124, 194, 202, 211, 475, 522, 538, 618, 704, 729
Vibrations, The 780
Vic, Frank 201
Vicari, Frank 679
Vick, Shakey 226
Vickers, Brad 400, 515, 516, 614
Vickers, Carl 676
Vickers, John 547
Vickers, Marty 170
Victor, Antoine 119
Vidacovich, John 59, 469, 503, 531, 718
Vidor, John 726
Vie 364
Vie, Sjin-Ki 543
Vig, Steen 242
Vigal, John P. 793
Villeri, Loui 101, 299, 357, 576
Vincent, Eddie 301
Vincent, Monroe 394
Vincent, Pamela 50, 350
Vincent [Vincson], Walter 801
Vinci, Jerry 726
Vincson, Walter 109, 128, 229, 436, 465, 466, 467, 670, 794, 801
Vines, Toni 813
Vinet, Keith 554, 582
Vinisky, Bob 496
Vinnegar, Leroy 21, 725
Vinson, Eddie 'Cleanhead' 506, 508, 573, 663, 670, 750, 797, 798
Vinson, Mose 672, 789, 810, 822
Viola, Al 726
Vipers, The 779
Virgi, Fayaz 427
Virgial, Otto 767, 793, 794, 801
Virginia Four, The 765
Visor, Inetta 465
Visscher, Harry 101
Vitale, Christine 263
Vito, Rick 408, 429
Vivino, Jerry 137, 516, 569, 614
Vivino, Jimmy 134, 477, 516, 517, 569, 614, 672
Viyuyu, Elvis 810
Vlahakis, Mike 4, 5, 6, 7, 127, 599, 600
Vocal Chords, The 353
Vocaleers, The 799
Voeten, Jan 101
Voltz, Bill 645
Von Schmidt, Eric 747
Von Streeter, James 504, 505, 520, 651, 800
Voorman, Klaus 290, 356
Vordeman, Barney 785
Vortis, Jesse 92
Vuckovich, Larry 672
Wachsman, Steve 652

Wachtel, Waddy 653
Waddy, Clarence 812
Wade, Frank 761
Wade, Iona 715
Wade, John 761
Wade, Mrs John 761
Wadi, Haj Juma 625
Wadley, Jessie 760
Wagar, Tim 204, 263, 512
Wagner, R. Zach 121
Wahl, Freddy 78
Wahllof, Andy 695
Waicunas, Tom 580
Wainman, Phil 34
Wainoris, Doug 515, 516, 614, 824
Waits, Tom 239, 738, 739
Wakely, Jimmy 798
Walcott, Fred 135, 569
Walden, Freddie 'Pharaoh' 194, 195, 721
Walder, Herman 384
Waldman, Dave 599, 697
Waldman, Randy 358
Waldman, Steve 319
Waleed, Strings 612
Wali Muhammad, Abdul 156
Walker, Al 20
Walker, Alfred 245
Walker, Alphonse 287
Walker, Arthur 463
Walker, Booker 356
Walker, Cato 356
Walker, Charles 335, 786
Walker, Chris 211, 499
Walker, Chuck 295
Walker, Clarence 215, 422, 676
Walker, Curtis 1, 227, 654
Walker, David T. 679
Walker, Dennis 113, 143, 210, 408, 417, 427, 433, 488, 571, 673, 675
Walker, Derrick 'Big' 36, 37
Walker, Earl 63, 510
Walker, Eddie 366
Walker, George 565
Walker, 'Chicken' George 54
Walker, Herb 166, 590, 614
Walker, Homer 812
Walker, Ina 'Bea Bopp' 675
Walker, J. W. [Johnny 'Big Moose'] 600, 601, 659, 660
Walker, James 352, 353, 354
Walker, Jeff 568
Walker, Jerry 400, 401
Walker, Jim 'Daddy' 384, 385
Walker, Jimmy[g] 84
Walker, Jimmy [p] 64, 223, 250, 669, 673, 734, 809
Walker, Joe Louis 14, 44, 134, 139, 222, 223, 358, 399, 644, 673, 751, 779, 823, 824, 825
Walker, Johnny[cl] 620
Walker, Johnny[d] 447
Walker, Johnny 'Big Moose' 165, 265,

266, 272, 273, 276, 282, 306, 307, 334, 418, 480, 489, 563, 568, 633, 652, 674, 693, 694, 733, 745
Walker, Jonas 315
Walker, Kenny 556
Walker, Lillian 250, 673
Walker, Loyal 504
Walker, Lucille 758
Walker, Li'l Malcolm 831
Walker, Marcus 111
Walker, Mel 504, 505, 520
Walker, Monroe 808
Walker, Moose 67
Walker, Nat 473, 677
Walker, Paris R. 465
Walker, Percy 61
Walker, Phillip 68, 118, 143, 210, 220, 222, 408, 433, 577, 629, 675, 776, 768, 782, 784, 788, 820, 825
Walker, Pretty Boy 697
Walker, Robert 'Bilbo' 215, 676
Walker, T-Bone 455, 506, 671, 676, 726, 738, 748, 749, 767, 768, 777, 797, 798, 804, 817, 818, 820, 825, 826
Walker, Uncle Bud 794, 801
Walker, Uncle Homer 812
Walker, Victor 11
Walker, Wayne 780
Walker, Wes 341
Walker, Wiley 772
Walker, Willie 738, 755, 767, 780, 794, 795, 810, 823
Walker Jr, T-Bone [R. S. Rankin] 782, 825
Wall, Cash 170
Wall, Jack 171
Wallace, Albert 'Birdie' 245
Wallace, Alex 412
Wallace, Alfred 66, 70, 335, 386, 387, 406, 532, 576, 616, 785
Wallace, Babe 828
Wallace, Bernard 555
Wallace, Cedric 173
Wallace, Charlie 613
Wallace, Frances 828
Wallace, Henry 761, 763, 812, 822
Wallace, Ian 34, 372
Wallace, Jimmy 575
Wallace, Minnie 451, 769, 774, 775, 810
Wallace, Nora Jean 160
Wallace, Sam 348
Wallace, Sid 141
Wallace, Sippie 7, 248, 679, 742, 749, 774, 794, 826, 827
Wallace, Wayne 373, 673
Wallace, Wesley 740, 787, 808, 815
Waller, Charles 75, 114, 432, 492, 593
Waller, Fats 253, 294, 426, 459, 475
Waller, Landers 388, 389
Waller, Mickey 177
Waller, Paul 37, 359
Wallis, Eddie 403

INDEX

Walls, Archie 426
Walls, John 344, 345
Walls, Vycki Z. 368, 518
Walmsley, Charlie 440
Walmsley, Lori 440
Walsh, Chris 556
Walsh, Donnie 169, 170
Walsh, Ellis 'Slow' 163
Walsh, Joe 356
Walsh, Malcolm 548
Walsh, Richard 'Hock' 170
Walter Family 775
Walters, Chuck 586
Walters, Glen 263
Walters, Tad 423, 477
Walther, Hank 560
Walton, Blanche Smith 311
Walton, Greely 587, 588, 670, 671
Walton, James 752
Walton, Lorraine 829
Walton, Manu 664
Walton, Mercy Dee 447, 680, 740, 742, 777, 788, 804, 809, 819, 823, 826
Walton, Square 752, 755, 806
Walton, Wade 764, 777
Wamble, Luther 78, 79
Wammo 200
Wamsley, Henry 'Trip' 14
Warburton, James 170
Ward, Billy 360, 774, 785, 799
Ward, Clara 104
Ward, George 446
Ward, Jackie 643
Ward, Jason 491
Ward, John 711
Ward, Ken 18
Ward, Maxie 517
Ward, Michael [perc] 470, 580
Ward, Michael [vn] 182, 242
Ward, Michael 'Mudcat' 66, 180, 222, 284, 370, 427, 497, 503, 515, 516, 525, 557, 615, 735, 771
Ward, Robert 262, 330, 553, 680, 681, 768, 781
Ward, Roberta 681
Ward, Shanon 22
Ware, Billy 196
Ware, Eddie 403, 557, 610
Ware, Efferge 384
Ware, Leon 343
Ware, Leonard 305, 306, 307, 315, 328, 332, 526, 600, 661, 662
Ware, Robert 17
Ware, Wilbur 69
Warfield, Peter 819
Warford, Rita 553
Warleigh, Ray 53, 175, 372, 427
Warmack, Paul 792
Warner, Elmer 291, 292
Warner, Lester 'Duck' 101
Warner, Little Sonny 447
Warner, Sid 52

Warnick, Louis 42
Waronker, Joey 94, 376
Warren, Baby Boy 680, 751, 752, 770
Warren, Bill 245, 323, 360, 409, 415, 693, 694
Warren, Earl(e) 81, 291, 338, 505, 520, 662
Warren, Ericka 564
Warren, Gerald 691
Warren, J. W. 681, 756
Warren, Lee 466
Warren, Leon 358, 359
Warren, Levi 265, 266, 631, 694
Warren, Travis 366
Warren, U. S. 711
Warwick, Dionne 359
Warwick, Marvin 660
Wary, Bob 395
Wash, Levy 688
Washboard Doc 570, 638, 749
Washboard Sam 69, 88, 184, 218, 259, 263, 333, 437, 454, 536, 682, 692, 698, 716, 742, 743, 744, 764, 773, 774, 780, 797
Washboard Slim 444, 637, 638, 639, 640
Washboard Trio (Mobile Washboard Band) 761
Washboard Walter 787
Washboard Willie 681, 753
Washburn, Donna 429
Washington, Bettye Jean 819
Washington, Archie 510
Washington, Baby 789
Washington, Booker T. 61, 159
Washington, Buck 587, 588
Washington, Bud 607
Washington, Charles 426, 689
Washington, D. C. 819
Washington, Dickie 'Little Man' 208, 209
Washington, Dinah 683, 747, 797, 798, 799, 826, 827, 829
Washington, Earl 83
Washington, Elizabeth 248, 249, 605, 815, 828
Washington, Ernie 140
Washington, Eugene 659, 660
Washington, Fats 209
Washington, Floyd 208
Washington, Freddie 671
Washington, 'Ready' Freddie 343, 358
Washington, George 269, 275, 504, 505, 506, 520, 651, 713
Washington, Harold 182, 583
Washington, Herbert 582
Washington, Herman 724, 725
Washington, Hollis 'FatHead' 760
Washington, Horace 39
Washington, Isabel 587, 588
Washington, Jack 291
Washington, James 348, 350
Washington, Kenny 76

Washington, Larry 356
Washington, Leon 607, 620
Washington, Leonard 126
Washington, Leroy 377, 408, 783
Washington, Lightnin' 757, 758, 759, 760, 821
Washington, Lizzie 815, 826
Washington, Lucius 95, 562
Washington, Marvin 332, 337
Washington, O. 144
Washington, Richard 'Didimus' 59
Washington, Rikki P. 217
Washington, Tom 401
Washington, Toni Lynn 222
Washington, Tuts 391, 531, 684
Washington, Walter 'Cowboy' 60, 738
Washington, Walter 'Wolfman' 788, 806
Wasserman, Rob 50, 165
Waterford, Crown Prince 684, 798
Waters, Ben 495
Waters, Benjamin A. 463
Waters, Benny 426, 455, 457
Waters, Ethel 684, 773, 774, 827
Waters, Mississippi Johnny 544
Waters, Julia Tillman 358, 674
Waters, Luther 357
Waters, Maxine 358, 674
Waters, Oren 357
Waters, Richard 688
Waters, Rob 32, 67, 204, 606, 607, 707
Waters, Ronnie 82
Waters, Uren 666
Watkins, Beverly 'Guitar' 521, 685, 757
Watkins, Bill 101
Watkins, Derek 53
Watkins, Doug 472
Watkins, Earl 366
Watkins, Geraint 53, 191, 344
Watkins, James 39, 66, 267, 268
Watkins, Joe 462
Watkins, John 'Mad Dog' 15, 121, 164, 745
Watkins, Ollie 686
Watkins, Pepper 429
Watkins, Tiny 783
Watkins, Walter 597
Watrous, Bill 726
Watson, Al 681
Watson, Bernie 428
Watson, Curtis 'Blo' 718
Watson, Curtis 87
Watson, David Lee 35, 470, 531
Watson, Diane 232
Watson, Doc 139, 738
Watson, Douglas 158, 412, 541, 591, 669
Watson, El 385, 769
Watson, Ernest 232
Watson, Eugene 392
Watson, John 138, 354, 401, 711
Watson, Johnny 'Guitar' 506, 686, 776, 786
Watson, Julius 315, 459

INDEX

Watson, Junior 47, 104, 123, 241, 262, 293, 408, 414, 464, 487, 488, 538, 544, 557, 594, 687, 719, 720
Watson, Kevin 179
Watson, Laurel 86
Watson, Merle 139, 738
Watson, Mike [Junior] 177
Watson, Mojo 800
Watson, Murray 233, 401
Watson, Nigel 228
Watson, Paula 798, 829
Watson, R. L. 802
Watson, Rick 350
Watson, Robert 14, 674
Watson, 'Mississippi Sarah' 148
Watson, T. B. 593
Watson, Wa Wa [Melvin Ragin] 273, 351
Watson, Walter 17
Watson's Pullman Porters 794
Watts, Archie 607
Watts, Bernard 540
Watts, Billy 485, 556
Watts, Charlie 289, 290, 359
Watts, Ernie 48, 350, 431, 556, 674
Watts, Joe 36
Watts, Kenny 69, 140
Watts, Mike 614
Watts, Noble 'Thin Man' 63, 229, 491, 544, 713, 807
Wauchope, Matt 136, 137
Wauchope, Neal 136, 211
Waugh, Robert 311, 551
Wayland, Hank 328
Wayne, Chuck 86, 291, 292, 523
Wayne, George 232
Wayne, James 799, 820
Wayne, Kenny 'Blues Boss' 598, 687
Wayne, Ronald 203
Wayne, Big Willie 699
Wayne, Wee Willie 804
Waynes, James 773
Weathersby, Carl 31, 36, 64, 141, 443, 465, 688, 825
Weathersby, Larry B. J. 4, 346
Weathersby Jr, Carl 688
Weatherspoon, David 401
Weaver, Clint 384
Weaver, Curley 23, 448, 449, 477, 478, 688, 738, 741, 752, 754, 755, 787, 813, 820
Weaver, David 544
Weaver, Joe 752
Weaver, Mark 568
Weaver, Mick 1, 223, 234, 235, 563, 624, 625
Weaver, Roger 465
Weaver, Sylvester 291, 292, 398, 426, 689, 756, 767, 768, 810, 812, 813
Webb, Boogie Bill 689, 752, 766, 788, 803, 804
Webb, Bobbie/Bobby 193, 194, 433, 439, 539

Webb, Brad 49, 50
Webb, Chuck 127
Webb, David 21, 65
Webb, Ervin 761, 763
Webb, Jeff 758
Webb, Jordan 206, 444, 637, 638, 639, 640, 795, 806
Webb, Keith 'The Baron' 226
Webb, Ken 446
Webb, Mitchell 'Tiny' 114, 163, 209, 219, 229, 243, 405, 432, 533, 684, 724, 725, 753
Webb, Riley 114, 115
Webb, 'Spider' 324
Webb, Stan 175, 711, 767
Webb, Stanley 654
Webb, Tom 149
Webb, Willie 'Jitterbug' 507
Webber, Garth 100, 196, 198, 199, 341, 690
Weber, Jon 553
Weber, Raymond 97, 179
Weber, Ronnie James 16, 191, 194, 239, 293, 399, 422
Webster, Al 20
Webster, Ben 84, 145, 327, 328, 505, 520, 724, 725, 726, 800
Webster, Eric 20
Webster, Freddie 244, 338, 526, 715
Webster, John 190
Webster, Katie 53, 56, 73, 214, 258, 358, 377, 394, 408, 412, 555, 585, 586, 648, 690, 742, 750, 776, 777, 784, 791, 800, 827
Webster, Margaret 773
Webster, Otis 763, 764
Webster, Sherman 56, 555, 648
Wechsler, Moe 295
Weckworth, Johnny P. 464
Weddle, Guy 257
Wedemeyer, John 199, 564, 583, 658
Weeks, Willie 137, 145, 215, 343, 688, 695
Weepin' Willie 691
Wehba, Loralei 358
Wehner, Marty 246, 496
Wei, Jon 18
Weinberg, Dover 43
Weinstein, Danny 'Bone' 164
Weisman, Albert 560
Weiss, Anne 305
Welbourne, Malcolm (Papa Mali) 502
Welch, Gillian 824
Welch, Guitar 763, 764
Welch, 'Monster' Mike 134, 293, 497, 691
Weld, Dave 705, 706
Welding, Pete 425
Weldon, Casey Bill 69, 88, 149, 259, 326, 452, 682, 692, 697, 737, 738, 768, 812, 813, 814, 820, 821
Weldon, Will 450, 451, 792
Welker, Larry 486
Wellhausen, Dave 193, 771

Wellington, Valerie 368, 692, 744, 745
Wells, Bob 249
Wells, Carlton 412, 600
Wells, Dickie 116, 140, 142, 271
Wells, Foree 522
Wells, Johnny 575, 661, 699
Wells, Junior 233, 234, 235, 265, 387, 458, 480, 481, 550, 678, 693, 738, 744, 745, 749, 752, 768, 769, 770, 771, 776, 779, 781, 790, 802
Wells, Lightnin' 253, 254, 257, 609, 823
Wells, Mark 78, 79
Wells, Oliver 81, 185, 186
Wells, Richard 432
Wells, Willie 26, 245, 472
Wellstood, Dick 344
Welsh, Bob 464, 479, 735
Welsh, [Nolan] Barrelhouse 787, 808
Welter, Rich 728
Wenger, Bernie 176
Wenner, Mark 10, 181, 238, 494, 495, 563
Wennerbrandt, Goran 36
Wennermark, Eunice 508
Werkmeister, Andre 312
Werner, Ken 539
Wesley, Fred 350, 490, 583
Wesolowski, Mike 253
Wess, Fatz 273
Wess, Frank 115, 300, 363, 365, 663
Wesselowski, Dave 529
West, Alan 241
West, April 342
West, Bob 388, 611, 656
West, Charley 796
West, Duane 497
West, Hal 60, 526
West, Harold 'Doc' 328, 332, 526, 661, 662
West, Kid 761
West, Paul 115, 683
West, Tango 42
West, Tom 126, 519, 549, 567, 636
West, Tommy 766
West, Wally 81
West Texas Slim 767
Westbrook, Lord 9, 543, 650, 726
Westmoreland, Phil 157
Westmoreland, Robert Lee 755, 795
Weston, Arthur 696, 764, 814
Weston, Harvey 264, 527
Weston, John 126, 163, 546, 696
Weston, Steve 374
Weston, West 10
Wettling, George 661, 662
Wetzel, Greg 494
Weyland, John 654
Wharton, Kevin 730
Wheal, Charles 293
Wheat, Abraham 587
Wheatstraw, Peetie 16, 88, 149, 221, 322, 325, 337, 443, 471, 605, 692, 696, 737, 738, 740, 743, 744, 808, 815, 816

Wheeler, Art 232
Wheeler, Buddy 572
Wheeler, Golden 'Big' 236, 697, 698, 747, 770, 771
Wheeler, Ian 340
Wheeler, James 16, 346, 470, 509, 567, 598, 612, 660, 697, 698, 711, 735, 781
Wheeler, Kenny 457
Wheeler, Mike 131
Wheeler, Russell 49, 50
Wheeler, T. J. 515
Wheeler, Walter 575
Whetsol, Artie 322
Whistler & His Jug Band 816
Whistler's Jug Band 758, 775
Whistlin' Pete 148
Whistling Rufus 773, 808
Whitaker, Bearnard 664
Whitcomb, Don 133
White, Albert 521, 685
White, Artie 802
White, Beverly 702, 796
White, Bill 700, 701, 702, 703
White, Bob 796
White, Booker/Bukka 388, 698, 737, 738, 742, 747, 749, 767, 777, 792, 794, 801, 802, 812, 813, 820, 822
White [Duncan Schiedt], 'Bud' 46
White, Charlie 84, 520
White, Schoolboy Cleve 394
White, Clifton 432
White, D. W. 761
White, Darryl 35, 361
White, Ed 582
White, Eva 758
White, Fadra 554
White, Frank 237
White, Georgia 699, 738, 797, 827
White, Harold 348
White, Uncle Jessie 570
White, Jimmy 622
White, Josh 45, 55, 106, 107, 379, 382, 457, 478, 559, 700, 738, 755, 760, 768, 773, 797, 806, 821
White, Kevin 361
White, Lavelle 827
White, Maurice 401
White, Michael 273
White, Dr Michael 806
White, Otis 396
White, P. J. 374
White, Sonny 661
White, Susan 761
White, Washington [Booker] 793
White, Wilbur 'Hi-Fi' 785
White, Willie 808
White Jr, Josh 703
White-King, Brenda 668
White Cloud Hunters Mardi Gras Indians 751
Whitefield, J. P. 489
Whitefield, Pat 612

Whitehead, Red 769
Whitehead, Robert 494, 581, 603, 604, 734
Whitehead, Tom 267, 268, 269, 275
Whitehill, Johnny 374
Whitehouse, Richard 170
Whitely, Chris 65, 302, 376, 687
Whitely, Dan 65
Whitely, Ken 156, 238, 302
Whiteley & Friends, Ken 823
Whitfield, Margaret 557
Whitfield, Mark 13
Whitfield, Osborne 63, 83, 650
Whitfield, Robert 427
Whiting, Joe 18
Whitley, Charles 114, 115
Whitlock, Bobby 236
Whitlock, Ellis 'Stumpy' 610
Whitlock, Elmer 'Stumpy' 670
Whitman, Ernie 'Bubbles' 328, 390
Whitman, Essie 827
Whitmire, Margaret 828
Whitney, James 227
Whitney, Lou 64
Whitney, Mark 341
Whitsett, Carson 257, 358, 393, 401
Whittaker, Leon 'Peewee' 254
Whitted, Dennis 484
Whittet, Ben 592
Whittington, Buddy 430, 431
Whittington, Charlie 666
Whittle, Ric 260
Whitwell, Mike 729
Whynaught, Chris 476
Whyte, Ellen 703
Whyte, Frankie 724
Wichard, Al 'Cake' 145, 163, 219, 228, 244, 258, 405, 517, 520, 724, 725
Wichtl, Martin 217
Wicks, Johnny 790
Wiedrich, Michael 425
Wiemeyer, Walter 726
Wierzcholski, 'Long' Slawomir 411
Wiffin, David 80
Wigfield, Les 175
Wiggins, Gary 73, 141, 249
Wiggins, Gerald 1, 24, 243, 432, 728
Wiggins, James 'Boodle-It' 740, 741, 787, 808
Wiggins, Little Lora 405
Wiggins, Phil 112, 535, 749, 750, 751, 766, 771, 776, 788, 823
Wiggins, Skip 113
Wiggs, Johnny 462
Wigley, Madame Mattie 762
Wilber, Jassen 4, 5
Wilborn, Nelson 321, 804
Wilcher, Darnell 131
Wilcox, Eddie 40
Wilcox, Preston (Bugsy) 660
Wilcox, Steve 342
Wilcoxson, Sheila 18, 703

Wilczewski, David 36
Wild, Martin 53
Wild Magnolias, The 804, 806
Wilde, Barry 175
Wilde, Luscious Lili 43
Wilder, Joe 40, 245, 300, 670, 671
Wildsang 704
Wiley, Arnold 740, 741
Wiley, Ed 110, 243, 258
Wiley, Geeshie 767, 787, 793, 794, 801, 810, 826
Wiley, Kris 704, 823
Wiley, Pee Wee 731
Wilkerson, Don 114, 115, 116, 405, 460
Wilkes, Gloria Williams 582
Wilkes, Willie 221, 222
Wilkie, David 485
Wilkins, Ernie 40, 683
Wilkins, Joe Willie 146, 412, 600, 601, 620, 672, 766, 802, 822
Wilkins, Robert 704, 738, 745, 747, 767, 792, 794, 810
Wilkins, Terry 195, 238
Wilkins, Willie 321, 322
Wilkinson, Ed 188, 468, 718
Wilkinson, Mal 727
Wilkinson, Neil 51
Wilks, Van 168
Willard, Maxine Waters 48, 210, 351, 357, 643
Willemsen, Matthijs 591
Willette, Baby Face 804
Williams, Afro 222
Williams, Al 40, 661, 662
Williams, Alanda 705, 721
Williams, Albert 288, 289, 410, 789
Williams, Allan 776
Williams, Andre 746, 780
Williams, Ardella 192
Williams, Arthur 38, 98, 152, 705
Williams, Arthur Lee 205
Williams, Bernard 412, 434, 600, 601
Williams', 'Bill [Arthur Petties] 69, 191
Williams, Billy 510
Williams, Bob 84
Williams, Ukulele Bob 774
Williams, Bradley 255
Williams, Brady 443, 632
Williams, Brenda 711
Williams, Brian 469
Williams, Carey 623, 625
Williams, Charles 26, 58, 166, 209, 351, 391,. 507, 529, 622, 780
Williams, Cheryl 156
Williams, Clarence 3, 42, 98, 150, 250, 294, 315, 321, 325, 336, 398, 426, 461, 587, 588, 592, 595, 596, 607, 679, 685, 700, 739
Williams, Claude 146, 751
Williams, Cleo ['Baldhead Pete'] 57, 330, 345, 346, 474, 561, 573, 574, 706
Williams, Cleveland 725

Williams, Blind Connie 814
Williams, Cootie 416, 459, 670, 683, 798
Williams, Cordy 685
Williams, Cornell 179, 730, 731
Williams, Courtney 315, 338
Williams, Daniel 459
Williams, Danny 580
Williams, Dave 'Fat Man' 140, 402
Williams, Denise 351
Williams, Dennis Paul 489, 490
Williams, Devonia 307, 504, 505, 520, 651, 686
Williams, Don 180
Williams, Doug 234
Williams, Earl 410
Williams, Earnest 6
Williams, Lil' Ed 135, 705, 745, 750, 776, 782, 814, 825
Williams, Eddie 74, 75, 163, 295, 505, 622, 701, 702, 783
Williams, Edward 345
Williams, Edwin 318, 632, 691
Williams, Eldee 593
Williams, Ellis 769
Williams, Elmer 227, 244, 295
Williams, Elmo 706
Williams, Elsie 796
Williams, Emery 41
Williams, Ernest 757, 758, 760, 762
Williams, Ernest 'Pinky' 662
Williams, Fess 80, 526, 699
Williams, Francis 727
Williams, Frank 391
Williams, Fred 69, 88, 89, 128, 308, 320, 326, 333, 452, 453, 607, 716
Williams, George 537, 707
Williams, George 'Bullet' 737, 769, 787, 794, 797
Williams, Hank 773, 798
Williams, Henderson 295, 670, 671
Williams, Henry 287, 432, 737, 754, 816
Williams, Ike 675
Williams, Irving 250
Williams, Irving 'Punchy' 362
Williams, J. 521
Williams, J. Mayo 48, 68, 596
Williams, J. W. 36, 63, 64, 234, 646, 652, 688, 695
Williams, Jabo 740, 741, 787, 808
Williams, Jackie 294
Williams, James 405, 600, 601
Williams, James 'D-Train' 343
Williams, Jerry 358, 618, 624
Williams, Jesse 546, 549, 718
Williams, Jessica 220, 434, 629
Williams, Jim 761
Williams, Jimmy 83
Williams, Jo Jo 778, 800
Williams, Jody 15, 55, 79, 95, 164, 289, 557, 562, 707, 744
Williams, Joe [b] 26, 173, 245, 321, 322, 543, 650

Williams, Joe [tb] 587, 588
Williams, Joe [Joseph Goreed] 780
Williams, Big Joe 158, 183, 278, 281, 536, 640, 641, 642, 696, 707, 714, 715, 716, 737, 738, 739, 743, 744, 745, 748, 749, 752, 754, 764, 767, 768, 769, 777, 781, 788, 793, 794, 801, 802, 810, 813, 814, 816, 821, 822, 823
Williams, Joe F. 760
Williams, 'Jackson' Joe 536, 715
Williams, John 679, 757, 765
Williams, Johnny [b] 7, 8, 326, 328, 390, 638, 640, 701
Williams, Johnny [d] 306, 307
Williams, Johnny [g,v] 744
Williams, Johnny [s] 521
Williams, Johnny 'Twist' 631
Williams, Julius 386
Williams, Keenath Malachi 192
Williams, Kenneth 351
Williams, Kenneth 'Afro' 648
Williams, Kevin 275
Williams, L. C. 276, 277, 710, 752, 818, 819
Williams, L. V. 290
Williams, Larry 357, 376, 788, 805
Williams, Larry D. C. 552
Williams, Lawmax 203
Williams, Lee 'Shot' 598, 711, 784
Williams, Leo 295
Williams, Leona 712
Williams, Leroy 285, 769
Williams, Lester 412, 600, 601, 712, 785, 788, 799, 820
Williams, Little H. 629
Williams, Louis 209
Williams, Lucinda 195, 402, 824, 830
Williams, Lynn 644
Williams, Mark 135, 489, 490
Williams, Mark T. 468
Williams, Marvin 27, 502
Williams, Mary 709
Williams, Mary Lou 702, 739
Williams, Mel 505, 506
Williams, Mike 139, 718
Williams, Morris J. 711
Williams, Mose 764
Williams, Nathan 489, 490
Williams, Nathaniel 'Herk' 696
Williams, Otis 547
Williams, Otto 65
Williams, Patrick 355, 554
Williams, Paul 84, 306, 307, 428, 472, 713, 798, 800
Williams, Paulette 660
Williams, Pearlis 240, 311
Williams, Pete 598
Williams, Pinky 84, 114, 115
Williams, Pip 34
Williams, Ralph 86, 158, 523
Williams, Ray 198, 417, 569
Williams, Rayburn 125

Williams, Raymond 14
Williams, Reese 148
Williams, Reuben 503
Williams, Robert 'Big Sandy' 538
Williams, Robert Pete 713, 738, 745, 747, 749, 763, 764, 811, 823
Williams, Roosevelt 401
Williams, Rose 349
Williams, Roy 527
Williams, Rubberlegs 797, 806
Williams, Rudy 292, 295, 670, 671
Williams, Sam 110, 647, 711
Williams, Samuel 521
Williams, Sharrie 714
Williams, Sherman 715
Williams, Sid 489
Williams, Skinny 251
Williams, Skippy 526
Williams, Sly 800
Williams, Sonny Boy 715
Williams, Spencer 89, 214, 321, 461
Williams, Steve 21, 112, 113, 211
Williams, T. C. 636
Williams, Ted 385
Williams, Terry 523
Williams, Tex 798
Williams, Titus 518, 633
Williams, Tom 553
Williams, Tommy 349, 350, 403, 499
Williams, Valerie 257, 401
Williams, Victoria 824
Williams, Vince 87
Williams, Vincent 787
Williams, Virgil 136
Williams, Vivian 166
Williams, W. 30
Williams, Wally 446, 477
Williams, Walter 326, 504, 510, 627, 677, 694
Williams, Walter 'Dootsie' 661, 662
Williams, Warner 715, 751
Williams, Wesley 466
Williams, Willie [d] 265, 266, 617, 778, 779
Williams, Willie [v] 295
Williams, Willie [v] 757, 758, 760, 761, 765
Williams, Willie James 367
Williams, Winston 219, 662
Williams Sr, Raymond 503
Williams Memphis Sanctified Singers, Brother 775
Williamson, Ernest 4, 6, 24, 63, 68, 90, 130, 151, 358, 468, 524, 600, 657
Williamson, Jeff 787
Williamson, Jim 402
Williamson I, Sonny Boy 493, 536, 605, 655, 708, 715, 738, 739, 742, 743, 744, 762, 769, 770, 788, 794, 798, 820, 821, 822
Williamson Jr, Ernest 127, 215
Williford, Shannon 496

INDEX

Willingham, Jonathan 81
Willis, Aaron 350
Willis, Anthony 350
Willis, Beatrice 'Toots' 124
Willis, Bill 168, 363, 365, 650, 666
Willis, Carolyn 210
Willis, Chuck 797, 799
Willis, Eddie 350, 403, 681
Willis, Edgar 114, 115, 116, 460, 507, 508
Willis, Glen 392
Willis, Greg 342
Willis, Harry 752
Willis, Johnny 612
Willis, Joshua 115
Willis, Kelly 488
Willis, Larry 10
Willis, Mac [Little Son] 782, 819, 826
Willis, Mott 766, 814
Willis, Ralph 445, 639, 640, 717, 752, 755, 774, 806
Willis, Ruth 448, 478, 689, 812, 813
Willis, S. E. 44, 135, 599
Willis, Slim 604, 734, 770
Willis, Steve 44
Willis, Vince 57, 316, 590, 711
Willis, Wilbert 87
Willis, Willie 146, 717
Willis Jr, Aaron 350, 403
Willison, Christian 96
Wills, Bob 772, 773, 810
Wills, Johnny Lee 772, 773
Wills, Luke 798
Wills, Rick 34, 372
Willson, Michelle 717, 830
Wilmeth, John 52, 562
Wilshire, Teacho 354
'Wilson' 249
Wilson, Abram 84
Wilson, Al 103, 104, 273, 285, 286
Wilson, Alfred 521
Wilson, Andy 413
Wilson, Anthony 556
Wilson, Ben 261
Wilson, Brother 27
Wilson, Buster 380, 381
Wilson, Carl 1, 39, 245, 321, 322, 730
Wilson, Cassandra 739
Wilson, Chicken 755, 767, 769
Wilson, Dale 143
Wilson, Dan 718
Wilson, Dennis 235
Wilson, 'Easy Deal' 572
Wilson, Edith 467, 718, 781, 822, 827, 829
Wilson, Elder Roma 751, 755, 769
Wilson, Frank 429
Wilson, Gerald 505, 520, 593, 683, 684, 726
Wilson, Hop 718, 784, 813, 814
Wilson, J. 761
Wilson, Jack 683
Wilson, James 757, 760, 765
Wilson, Jerry 67, 129, 317, 568

Wilson, Jimmy 719, 782, 800
Wilson, John [b, g] 80
Wilson, John [t] 315
Wilson, John 'Hambone' 260
Wilson, 'Doctor' John 489
Wilson, Johnny 'Da-Doo' 241
Wilson, Joyce 50
Wilson, Kat 4
Wilson, Kim 26, 130, 135, 139, 148, 180, 190, 191, 194, 204, 222, 261, 314, 316, 341, 358, 427, 450, 515, 538, 558, 559, 598, 658, 691, 719, 770, 771
Wilson, Lena 720
Wilson, Leola B. 48, 755, 774
Wilson, Lou 570
Wilson, Marc 179, 223, 476, 534
Wilson, Marty 39, 40, 521, 638, 640
Wilson, Mary 271
Wilson, Michelle 788
Wilson, Percy 761, 812
Wilson, Perdis 68
Wilson, Quinn 269, 270, 271, 275, 610
Wilson, 'Rail' 683
Wilson, Robert 15, 364, 365
Wilson, Ronald 507
Wilson, Ronnie 721
Wilson, Ross 583
Wilson, Royalene 733
Wilson, Russ 127, 253
Wilson, Shadow 245, 292, 338, 340, 390
Wilson, Smokey 440, 720, 768, 779, 788
Wilson, Steve 350
Wilson, Teddy 292, 328
Wilson, U. P. 721, 820
Wilson, Vic 170
Wilson, Virgil 229
Wilson, Kid Wesley 223, 774, 829
Wilson, Willie 730
Wimberley, Julius 730
Wimberley, Sonny 483, 604
Wimmer, Kevin 12
Wimmer, Stutz 185
Wimpfheimer, Jimmy 559
Winch, Matt 223
Winchester, Daisy 338
Winchester, Roosevelt 111
Winfield, Andy 217, 218
Wing, Sophie 760
Wingfield, B. T. 142, 150, 223, 537, 549
Wingfield, Pete 34, 234, 356, 363, 364, 395, 457, 671, 728
Wingfield, Sid 5, 42, 121, 450, 568, 569, 573, 574, 584, 645
Wings, John 660
Winiger, Philipp 176
Winking, Keith 20, 21, 179, 296, 362, 612, 658, 681
Winking, Kent 20, 612
Winn, Burton 540
Winnacker, Frizze 249
Winnegan, James 572
Winning, Martyn C. 97, 217, 218

Winston, Albert 505, 520, 543, 650, 651
Winston, Edna 721, 794, 827
Winston, Ella 727
Winston, Jerry 33
Winston, Stephen T. 386
Winston, Teddy 552
Winter, Chris 465
Winter, Edgar 198, 490, 722
Winter, Johnny 68, 274, 275, 480, 484, 639, 722, 737, 768, 776, 813, 814, 820
Winter, Paul 40
Winters, Chris 465
Wintour, Dave 458
Wintz, Doug 508
Winwood, Stevie 289, 290, 483
Wire, Tim 569
Wirtz, Rev. Billy C. 342
Wise, Dale 316
Wise, Larry 567
Wisham, Bradley 365
Witcher, Sam 403
Witcher, Wolfie 344
Withers, Hayes B. 689
Witherspoon, Jimmy 197, 724, 738, 747, 779, 780, 782, 797, 798, 826
Witmer, John 170
Witt, John 84
Wolf, John 560
Wolf, Peter 402
Wolf, Steve 293, 729
Wolinsky, Eli 505, 520
Wolk, T-Bone 156, 359, 488, 491, 674
Wolke, Thom 156
Womack, Daniel 812
Womack, Diane 346
Womack, Lance 90
Wonder, Melvin 460, 508
Wonder, Stevie 50, 356
Wood, Andrew 315
Wood, Andy 53
Wood, Dave 479
Wood, George 638, 640
Wood, Jamie 728
Wood, Oliver 186
Wood, Ron 359
Wood, Smoky 772
Woodard, Mildred 783
Woode, Jimmy 727
Woodford, David 'Woody' 198, 307, 422, 556, 629
Woodfork, Houston 142
Woodfork, Poor Bob 557, 616
Wooding, Sam 249
Woodman, Britt 291, 447, 677
Woodman, Brother 243
Woodman, William 292, 392, 432
Woodman, Williams 291, 390
Woodrow, Dave 'Woody' 220
Woodruff, Donnie 399
Woods, Alvin 715
Woods, Annie 81
Woods, Arthur 675

Woods, Buddy 677
Woods, Byron 107, 465
Woods, Chris 790
Woods, Fred 751
Woods, Hosea 105
Woods, Joe 268, 269
Woods, Johnny 441, 442, 443, 777
Woods, Mitch 239, 274, 728, 779
Woods, [Oscar] Buddy 729, 738, 761, 774, 794, 803, 812, 813, 817
Woods, Pete 384
Woods, Rozalin 531
Woods, Stu 508
Woods, Willie 465
Woodson, William 'Buddy' 447, 677, 678, 731
Woodward, Carl 413
Woodward, Chet 316
Woodward, David 104, 169, 170, 210
Woodward, Jake 413
Woodward, Nathan 353
Woody, Allen 402
Woolfolk, Joey 414
Woolfork, John 765
Wooten, Ed 541
Wooten, Kyle 769
Wooten, Margaret 485
Wooten, Reggie 135
Worde, Phil 134, 325, 385, 475, 595
Worf, Glenn 252
Workman, Myriam 295
Worley, Daniel 513
'Worm' 721
Wormick, Jimmy 510
Wormworth, James 133, 135, 569, 614, 669
Worrell, Bernie 198
Worst, Rene 20
Worth, Don 336
Worthy, Scooby 14
Wotherspoon, Noah 729
Wrencher, Big John 121, 494, 730, 734, 769, 770, 771, 822
Wright, Andre 370, 544
Wright, Arthur 209, 726
Wright, Billy 730, 798
Wright, Chad 211
Wright, Deirdre 499
Wright, Emma 794
Wright, Gary 356
Wright, Greg 372
Wright, Gus 286, 651
Wright, Hoshal 623
Wright, James 338, 340
Wright, Jimmy 211, 446
Wright, Joe 77, 671
Wright, John 610
Wright, Johnny 659, 660
Wright, Lamar 245, 416, 670
Wright, Larry 201
Wright, Lee Otis 348
Wright, Leo 726

Wright, Martha 761
Wright, Marva 554, 730
Wright, Mel 344
Wright, Miles Kevin 78
Wright, Nancy 43, 358, 399, 673, 690
Wright, O. V. 789
Wright, Pearl 685
Wright, Phebel 792
Wright, Reggie 33
Wright, Richard 765
Wright, Rick 356
Wright, Robert 'Huckleberry Hound' 101, 396, 418, 470, 520
Wright, Ronald 350
Wright, Sloan 378
Wright, Wacko Wade 365
Wright, Wallace 607
Wright, Willie 784
Wright, Zeb 69
Wroten, Craig 21, 78
Wulf, Joe 73
Wulff-Woesten, Prentice 4
Wurman, Felix 580
Wurman, Lisa 580
Wyatt, James B. 210, 440, 720
Wydra, Jim 557
Wydra, Mark 125, 126, 567
Wylie, Buster 324, 433
Wyman, Bill 289, 290, 694
Wynans, Reese 26, 34, 35, 111, 139, 168, 194, 235, 252, 431, 502, 524, 575, 612, 658, 667, 668, 669, 673
Wynn, Albert 142, 537, 549
Wynn, (Big) Jim 83, 145, 209, 243, 307, 506, 507, 663, 677, 678, 686, 725, 731, 788, 800
Wynn, Lee 765
Wynne, Ronny 492
Wysinger, Ted 433
Yamagishi, June 97, 731
Yancey, Alonzo 809
Yancey, Bill 440
Yancey, Estella 'Mama' 732, 733
Yancey, Jimmy 732, 737, 739, 740, 741, 808, 809
Yancey, Yusef 133
Yang, Jeff 580
Yanuziello, Joe 582
Yarbrough, Kim [Keem] 4, 37
Yarema, Tyler 302, 376, 533, 582, 598
Yarling, Nicole 'Nicky' 580
Yas Yas Girl, The 829
Yates, Blind Richard 793
Yates, Sammy 62, 449, 520, 661, 662
Yawn, Jessie 499
Yazoo All Stars 774
Ybarra, Ralph 143
Yearsley, Thomas 414, 691
Yee, Benny 413, 468, 469
Yellin, Bob 665
Yellow Jackets, The 784
Yeoman, Alex 37

Yescalis, Rich 236, 599
Yester, Jerry 37
Yoakam, Dwight 87
York, Albert 811
York, David 'Rock Bottom' 58
York, Marshall 352, 353, 354
York, Peter 264, 630, 730
York, Rusty 780
York, Steve 466, 487
York Brothers 773
Young, Abe 664
Young, Allison 87
Young, Bernie 142, 459, 537
Young, Chip 205
Young, Clara 763
Young, David 1, 227, 311, 526, 654, 683
Young, Earl 356
Young, Ed 761, 762, 763, 812
Young, Emmanuel 370, 570
Young, Freddie 402
Young, George 235, 485
Young, Gus 315
Young, James 'Pookie' 705, 706
Young, Jesse 564
Young, Jody 236, 405
Young, Joe [ac] 539
Young, Joe [d] 250
Young, Mighty Joe 15, 35, 159, 165, 418, 550, 557, 563, 622, 632, 733, 734, 768, 781, 790
Young, Johnny 47, 121, 223, 299, 425, 494, 532, 603, 604, 734, 742, 743, 744, 745, 749, 764, 777, 788, 792, 800, 822, 823
Young, Lee 75, 158, 252, 432, 460, 492, 683
Young, Lester 292, 526
Young, Lionel 634
Young, Lonnie 761, 762, 763, 812
Young, Man [Johnny] 744
Young, Marl 677, 678
Young, Monalisa 417
Young, Mighty Paul 433
Young, Preston 810
Young, Red 21, 194, 220
Young, Reggie 343, 402, 458, 509
Young, Robert 275, 478
Young, Scott 211, 499, 553
Young, Snooky 115, 291, 292, 357
Young, Terry 666
Young, Tommy 332
Young, Willie 405, 412, 554
Young, Zora 57, 163, 465, 617, 669, 734, 781, 829, 830
Young Blues Thrillers, The 750
Young Jessie [Obediah Jessie] 777
Young Jr, Joe 733
Youngblood, Arzo 766
Youngblood Jr, (Dr) Ernest 68, 362, 476, 676
Younger, Richard 194
Ysaguirre, Charles 42

Yuele, Joe 235, 408, 429, 430, 431, 468
Yuele, Tom 431
Yuguchi, Seiji 'Wabi' 215
Yussuf, Saleh 625
Z, David 235, 375, 431
Z., Jimmy [Zavala] 307
Z., Tony 260
Zabel, Doug 721
Zachary, Melvin 136, 137
Zagarino, Joe 356
Zaitz, Tony 58
Zajac, Rodney 112
Zak, Zoe B. 156
Zaklan, Joe 97, 613
Zamagni, Tony 16, 564, 569, 598, 599, 711
Zark, Greg 136
Zawinul, Joe 671
Zdon, John 131
Zeigler, John Lee 756, 757
Zemelman, Dan 275

Zeno, Alena 395
Zeno, Chester 53, 553
Zeno, Lee Allen 86, 87, 395, 582, 688
Zerby, Ted 86
Zhivago, Jimi 137, 525
Ziehl, Bill 58
Zielinski, David 16
Zimmerman, Dino 257, 401
Zimmerman, Hermes 808
Zimmerman, Randy 21, 61, 68, 123, 342, 431, 485, 676
Zimmerman, William 210, 440, 720
Zimmitti, Bob 351
Zinn, George 399
Zinn, Rusty 16, 136, 194, 293, 399, 464, 486, 512, 515, 538, 707, 719, 735, 776
Zippers, The 81
Zito, Fred 245, 416
Zivkovic, Peter 65
Zokal, Wayne 656

Zonn, Andrea 343
Zox 5, 6, 41, 57, 544, 735
Zubot, Jesse 20
Zucchero 359
Zueghart, Anselm 487
Zuffi, Kevin 151, 673
Zukowski, Jan 238, 494, 495
Zunis, Zach 16, 123
Zwerin, Mike 372
Zwingenberger, Axel 132, 176, 663, 680, 733
Zwingenberger, Torsten 176
Zydecajun 831
Zydeco Boll Weevils, The 832
Zydeco Brothers 831
Zydeco Cha-Chas, The 832, 833
Zydeco Force 831, 832
Zydron, Tom 30